D0127061

Presented to

By

On the
occasion of

The Everyday Life Bible

Containing the
Amplified Old Testament
and the
Amplified New Testament

Notes and Commentary
by Joyce Meyer

WARNER
Faith®

New York   Boston   Nashville

Warner Faith
Hachette Book Group USA
1271 Avenue of the Americas, New York, NY 10020

Visit our Web site at www.faithwords.com

Warner Faith and the "W" logo are trademarks of Time
Warner Inc. or an affiliated company. Used under license
by Hachette Book Group USA, which is not affiliated with
Time Warner Inc.

Printed in the United States of America
First Edition: October 2006
10 9 8 7 6 5 4 3 2 1
ISBN-13: 978-0-446-57827-1
ISBN-10: 0-446-57827-4
LCCN: 2006928321

A Personal Word from Joyce Meyer

For thirty years, I have enjoyed and greatly benefited from *The Amplified Bible*. It gives insights that I have not found in other translations I have used. Because God has used *The Amplified Bible* in my life to open up many truths from His Word to me, I wanted to share the insight He has given me and help others. I prayed for many years to get permission from the publishers to produce a specialty Bible using this version and was thrilled when permission was finally granted.

God's Word is very precious to me. I can truly say that I love God's Word. It has changed me and my life. I have also witnessed transformation in the lives of multitudes of people over the years through studying and believing God's Word. God's words are not ordinary words, as the words of other people are. His words are filled with power. The power of God is actually inherent in His Word and it heals, delivers, comforts, saves, corrects, and encourages us.

When people are very discouraged, they can actually take God's Word as medicine for their souls. It encourages the discouraged, lifts up the lowly and downtrodden, heals the sick, saves the lost, fills the empty, and counsels those who need to make a decision.

Jesus is the Word of God Who took on human flesh and dwelt for a while among men (see John 1:14). When we read, study, meditate on, or confess the Word of God, we are fellowshipping with Jesus. We are actually taking Him as nourishment and we find that only He can satisfy our souls. God's Word is our spiritual food and we need it regularly, just as we need natural food. The prophet Jeremiah said, "Your words were found, and I ate them; and your words were to me a joy and the rejoicing of my heart . . . "(Jeremiah 15:16).

God's Word is very important to Him. The Bible says in Psalm 138:2 that He has exalted above all else His name and His word, and He has magnified His word even above His name. We should always respect and honor God's Word and give it a place of priority in our everyday lives. I truly believe that God's Word contains an answer to every problem and situation we encounter in life. It is certainly spiritual, but it is also very practical and has been given for our everyday lives. We are therefore calling this Bible *The Everyday Life Bible*. I believe that many people have made the mistake of only connecting God's Word with church or some other spiritual activity rather than applying it to their lives daily.

I also believe the Bible is largely a book about relationships. It gives in-depth information about our relationships with God, ourselves, and our fellow man. Much of our pain and misery in life is the result of poor relationships. I have learned through God's Word how to receive His love, love myself in a balanced way, and let His love flow through me to others. I pray that this would be your goal because Jesus said that the thing we should concentrate on is loving God and loving others as we love ourselves (see Matthew 22:37–39).

Be a "lifetime learner." Apply God's Word to situations in your life as you would apply medicine to an injury. If you are having a particular problem such as anger, impatience, depression, or fear, go to God's Word and select passages that deal with these subjects (I have provided in the back of this Bible a topical index that makes finding these passages very easy for you). As you read these verses, slowly take them in, and roll them over and over in your mind. You will find a change taking place in your heart and life. I encourage you to love God's Word, for in it you will find resurrection power and contentment far greater than anything the world has to offer.

Now, I want to make sure you are aware of the special features that *The Everyday Life Bible* has to offer because I believe they will help tremendously as you live your life by the Word of God.

Book Introductions: At the beginning of every book of the Bible, you will find basic historical background information on that particular book, along with my thoughts on why each book is important and how it relates to practical living. You will also find "Everyday Life Principles," which summarize the key points and general themes of each book.

Everyday Life Articles: These articles are the longest, most thorough entries in the Bible. They correspond to specific verses or passages, and provide great insight and advice on a variety of topics. I have written many of them especially for this Bible, and I have developed new ones based on my teachings over thirty years of ministry.

Life Points: If you have followed my teaching ministry for long, you may realize that I often use short, catchy, to-the-point phrases or "one-liners" to emphasize certain principles or truths. Life Points include many of these well-known phrases, as well as other nuggets of encouragement and exhortation.

Speak the Word: I believe that confessing God's Word is vital to a successful Christian life. Anywhere you see an entry entitled "Speak the Word," you will find a scripture verse or passage adapted as a first-person confession or prayer. I encourage you to speak and pray these words as you come across them in this Bible and use them to teach you how to pray and confess other verses throughout God's Word.

Putting the Word to Work: We all need to apply the truths of God's Word to our lives. The "Putting the Word to Work" feature takes biblical principles and gives you opportunities to meditate on them, answer questions about them, and think about how you can apply them specifically to the situations in your life.

The Word for Your Everyday Life: In the very back of this Bible, you will find a section called "The Word for Your Everyday Life." There, you will see a list of topics you are likely to face over the course of your life—perhaps many times. Under each topic heading, you will find scripture references pertaining to that topic. Read those verses and passages, and you will discover biblical answers and guidance to help you overcome every challenge and live your everyday life victoriously.

How to Receive Jesus as Your Lord and Savior: The most important relationship of your life is a personal relationship with Jesus Christ. If you would like to receive Him as your Lord and Savior, and enter into the greatest relationship you have ever known, please pray the prayer in the back of this Bible.

Contents

The Books of the Old Testament

Genesis	1	Ecclesiastes	1014
Exodus	88	Song of Solomon	1033
Leviticus	156	Isaiah	1044
Numbers	206	Jeremiah	1145
Deuteronomy	271	Lamentations	1239
Joshua	333	Ezekiel	1250
Judges	373	Daniel	1332
Ruth	411	Hosea	1363
I Samuel	420	Joel	1379
II Samuel	471	Amos	1387
I Kings	514	Obadiah	1399
II Kings	565	Jonah	1403
I Chronicles	611	Micah	1410
II Chronicles	657	Nahum	1421
Ezra	709	Habakkuk	1427
Nehemiah	727	Zephaniah	1435
Esther	752	Haggai	1441
Job	767	Zechariah	1447
Psalms	814	Malachi	1466
Proverbs	957		

The Books of the New Testament

Matthew	1477	I Timothy	1992
Mark	1550	II Timothy	2006
Luke	1599	Titus	2017
John	1673	Philemon	2025
Acts	1732	Hebrews	2029
Romans	1798	James	2059
I Corinthians	1842	I Peter	2073
II Corinthians	1881	II Peter	2087
Galatians	1909	I John	2095
Ephesians	1927	II John	2109
Philippians	1947	III John	2112
Colossians	1961	Jude	2116
I Thessalonians	1974	Revelation	2120
II Thessalonians	1985		

How to Receive Jesus as Your Lord and Savior	2153
Index to Everyday Life Articles	2155
Index to Life Points	2163
Index to Speak the Word Entries	2167
Index to Putting the Word to Work Entries	2171
The Word for Your Everyday Life	2175

Old Testament

Genesis

Author:
Moses

Date:
About 1440 BC

Everyday Life Principles:
Beginnings are important, and thankfully God continually gives us opportunities for a fresh start.

Be watching for the opportunities God brings your way. They will present themselves in the situations of your everyday life, such as your relationships, your workplace, the way you choose to spend your time, and issues of personal integrity.

Only as you take advantage of these opportunities can you move forward in God's plans for your life.

We often hear the book of Genesis described as a "book of beginnings," but I also like to think of it as a book of opportunities. From start to finish, we read stories of people who were presented with opportunities.

First, we see Eve with the opportunity to choose between good and evil—between God's instruction and the serpent's deception. We see Noah with an opportunity to demonstrate his faith when everyone around him thought he was crazy. We see Abraham with an opportunity to believe God's promise when it was naturally impossible and then to obey God when obedience required a willingness to sacrifice the promised son for whom he waited so long. We see Jacob with an opportunity to deceive, which resulted in all kinds of trouble—and later with an opportunity to surrender completely to God, which resulted in great blessing. We see Joseph with opportunities to forgive and to trust God.

Throughout Genesis, people were blessed when they took advantage of opportunities to choose well—to choose truth over deception, faith over fear, peace over strife, forgiveness over bitterness, patience and waiting on God over trying to force something to happen. I hope the stories and principles in this book will help you recognize the opportunities God gives you and make wise choices that will lead to greater blessings than you have ever known.

1 IN THE beginning God (prepared, formed, fashioned, and) created the heavens and the earth. [Heb. 11:3.]

2 The earth was without form and an empty waste, and darkness was upon the face of the very great deep. The Spirit of God was moving (hovering, brooding) over the face of the waters.

3 And God said, Let there be light; and there was light.

4 And God saw that the light was good (suitable, pleasant) *and* He approved it; and God separated the light from the darkness. [II Cor. 4:6.]

5 And God called the light Day, and the darkness He called Night. And there was evening and there was morning, one day.

6 And God said, Let there be a firmament [the expanse of the sky] in the midst of the waters, and let it separate the waters [below] from the waters [above].

7 And God made the firmament [the expanse] and separated the waters which were under the expanse from the waters which were above the expanse. And it was so.

8 And God called the firmament Heavens. And there was evening and there was morning, a second day.

9 And God said, Let the waters under the heavens be collected into one place [of standing], and let the dry land appear. And it was so.

10 God called the dry land Earth, and the accumulated waters He called Seas. And God saw that this was good (fitting, admirable) *and* He approved it.

11 And God said, Let the earth put forth [tender] vegetation: plants yielding seed and fruit trees yielding fruit whose seed is in itself, each according to its kind, upon the earth. And it was so.

12 The earth brought forth vegetation: plants yielding seed according to their own kinds and trees bearing fruit in which was their seed, each according to its kind. And God saw that it was good (suitable, admirable) *and* He approved it.

13 And there was evening and there was morning, a third day.

14 And God said, Let there be lights in the expanse of the heavens to separate the day from the night, and let them be signs *and* tokens [of God's provident care], and [to mark] seasons, days, and years, [Gen. 8:22.]

15 And let them be lights in the expanse of the sky to give light upon the earth. And it was so.

16 And God made the two great lights—the greater light (the sun) to rule the day and the lesser light (the moon) to rule the night. He also made the stars.

17 And God set them in the expanse of the heavens to give light upon the earth,

18 To rule over the day and over the night, and to separate the light from the darkness. And God saw that it was good (fitting, pleasant) *and* He approved it.

19 And there was evening and there was morning, a fourth day.

20 And God said, Let the waters bring forth abundantly *and* swarm with living creatures, and let birds fly over the earth in the open expanse of the heavens.

21 God created the great sea monsters and every living creature that moves, which the waters brought forth abundantly, according to their kinds, and every winged bird according to its kind. And God saw that it was good (suitable, admirable) *and* He approved it.

22 And God blessed them, saying, Be fruitful, multiply, and fill the waters in the seas, and let the fowl multiply in the earth.

23 And there was evening and there was morning, a fifth day.

24 And God said, Let the earth bring

forth living creatures according to their kinds: livestock, creeping things, and [wild] beasts of the earth according to their kinds. And it was so.

25 And God made the [wild] beasts of the earth according to their kinds, and domestic animals according to their kinds, and everything that creeps upon the earth according to its kind. And God saw that it was good (fitting, pleasant) *and* He approved it.

26 God said, Let Us [Father, Son, and Holy Spirit] make mankind in Our image, after Our likeness, and let them have complete authority over the fish of the sea, the birds of the air, the [tame] beasts, and over all of the earth, and over everything that creeps upon the earth. [Ps. 104:30; Heb. 1:2; 11:3.]

27 So God created man in His own image, in the image *and* likeness of God He created him; male and female He created them. [Col. 3:9, 10; James 3:8, 9.]

28 And God blessed them and said to them, Be fruitful, multiply, and fill the earth, and subdue it [using all its vast resources in the service of God and man]; and have dominion over the fish of the sea, the birds of the air, and over every living creature that moves upon the earth.

29 And God said, See, I have given you every plant yielding seed that is on the face of all the land and every tree with seed in its fruit; you shall have them for food.

30 And to all the animals on the earth and to every bird of the air and to everything that creeps on the ground— to everything in which there is the breath of life—I have given every green plant for food. And it was so.

speak the Word

life point

Here in the very first chapter of the Bible, God clearly communicates His desire for our lives to be fruitful. Two things necessary to live fruitful lives are balance and pruning. To stay balanced we need to make sure we get the right amounts of healthy nourishment, rest, work, play, time alone with God, and time to enjoy godly relationships.

Pruning is not always pleasant, but it does ensure that the situations, activities, or relationships that are depleting us will not continue to do so. It means something must be cut off or removed from our lives, but God promises great reward as a result—more fruitfulness than ever!

Stay balanced by letting God, the wise Master Gardener, prune your life as He sees fit, and you will enjoy years of fruitfulness and fulfillment.

31 And God saw everything that He had made, and behold, it was very good (suitable, pleasant) *and* He approved it completely. And there was evening and there was morning, a sixth day.

2 THUS THE heavens and the earth were finished, and all the host of them.

2 And on the seventh day God ended His work which He had done; and He rested on the seventh day from all His work which He had done. [Heb. 4:9, 10.]

Lord, I thank You that You have blessed me and called me to be fruitful in my life. I pray that I will use the resources You have created to serve You and to serve others.
ADAPTED FROM GENESIS 1:28

enjoy your life

When God completed His six days of creation, He took time to look over everything and He saw that "it was very good and He approved it completely" (Genesis 1:31). God took time to enjoy the work of His hands, and we should do the same. In our passion to possess more and more, we often fall into the trap of working, working, working—and we never enjoy the fruit of our labor. Sometimes we should simply take time to relax and enjoy what we have accomplished.

The writer of Ecclesiastes said it is the gift of God for man to find enjoyment in all of his labor (see Ecclesiastes 2:24). I have always been a hard worker. A few years ago, I realized I was working hard but not taking time to enjoy what I was doing. I made a decision to include enjoyment in my life. I no longer just "do" conferences; I enjoy them. When my house is clean and pretty, I take time to look at it and enjoy it. At the end of a year I go over my calendar and remember the various things I have done, and I enjoy the sense of accomplishment. I look at what God has enabled me to do and I say, "It is good."

Many people feel worthless, insecure, and unacceptable, but God looked at *everything* He created, including man, and said, "It is very good." He approved it completely. God knows everything about each of us, and He loves us unconditionally. God approves of us; He may not approve of everything we do, but He does approve of us as His beloved children. I encourage you to make a decision to not only enjoy the labor of your hands, but to approve of and enjoy yourself as well.

Choosing to enjoy and accept myself is one of the best decisions I have ever made. God does not create junk. He is good, and everything He does is good. We cannot believe that God created us and also believe we are worthless. Begin to accept and enjoy yourself where you are, and God will help you get to where you need to be.

3 And God blessed (spoke good of) the seventh day, set it apart as His own, and hallowed it, because on it God rested from all His work which He had created and done. [Exod. 20:11.]
4 This is the history of the heavens and of the earth when they were created. In the day that the Lord God made the earth and the heavens—
5 When no plant of the field was yet in the earth and no herb of the field had yet sprung up, for the Lord God had not [yet] caused it to rain upon the earth and there was no man to till the ground,
6 But there went up a mist (fog, vapor) from the land and watered the whole surface of the ground—
7 Then the Lord God formed man from the ᵃdust of the ground and breathed into his nostrils the breath *or* spirit of life, and man became a living being. [I Cor. 15:45-49.]
8 And the Lord God planted a garden

a The same essential chemical elements are found in man and animal life that are in the soil. This scientific fact was not known to man until recent times, but God was displaying it here.

life point

God created Adam as a living being, in His image (see Genesis 1:26, 27), and gave him authority over everything else He created (see Genesis 1:28). Man was created to rule under God and to be the physical carrier of God's Spirit in the earth. Part of human nature is that we, as living beings like Adam, have a free will. Why? Because God is too loving to force submission from anyone. He wants us to freely choose to love and serve Him. I hope that today you will make a fresh and willful commitment to love and serve God with all your heart.

toward the east, in Eden [delight]; and there He put the man whom He had formed (framed, constituted).

9 And out of the ground the Lord God made to grow every tree that is pleasant to the sight *or* to be desired— good (suitable, pleasant) for food; the tree of life also in the center of the garden, and the tree of the knowledge of [the difference between] good and evil *and* blessing and calamity. [Rev. 2:7; 22:14, 19.]

10 Now a river went out of Eden to water the garden; and from there it divided and became four [river] heads.

11 The first is named Pishon; it is the one flowing around the whole land of Havilah, where there is gold.

12 The gold of that land is of high quality; bdellium (pearl?) and onyx stone are there.

13 The second river is named Gihon; it is the one flowing around the whole land of Cush.

14 The third river is named Hiddekel [the Tigris]; it is the one flowing east of Assyria. And the fourth river is the Euphrates.

15 And the Lord God took the man and put him in the Garden of Eden to tend and guard *and* keep it.

16 And the Lord God commanded the man, saying, You may freely eat of every tree of the garden;

17 But of the tree of the knowledge of good and evil *and* blessing and calamity you shall not eat, for in the day that you eat of it you shall surely die.

18 Now the Lord God said, It is not good (sufficient, satisfactory) that the man should be alone; I will make him a helper meet (suitable, adapted, complementary) for him.

19 And out of the ground the Lord God formed every [wild] beast *and* living creature of the field and every bird of the air and brought them to Adam to see what he would call them; and whatever Adam called every living creature, that was its name.

20 And Adam gave names to all the livestock and to the birds of the air and to every [wild] beast of the field; but for Adam there was not found a helper meet (suitable, adapted, complementary) for him.

21 And the Lord God caused a deep sleep to fall upon Adam; and while he slept, He took one of his ribs *or* a part of his side and closed up the [place with] flesh.

22 And the rib *or* part of his side which the Lord God had taken from the man He built up *and* made into a woman, and He brought her to the man.

23 Then Adam said, This [creature] is now bone of my bones and flesh of my flesh; she shall be called Woman, because she was taken out of a man.

24 Therefore a man shall leave his father and his mother and shall become united *and* cleave to his wife, and they shall become one flesh. [Matt. 19:5; I Cor. 6:16; Eph. 5:31-33.]

25 And the man and his wife were both naked and were not embarrassed *or* ashamed in each other's presence.

3 NOW THE serpent was more subtle *and* crafty than any living creature of the field which the Lord God had made. And he [Satan] said to the woman, Can it really be that God has said, You shall not eat from every tree of the garden? [Rev. 12:9-11.]

a very creative God

I cannot imagine what a job it must have been for Adam to name all the birds and animals. He certainly had to be creative to do that!

I could go on and on about how diverse and imaginative God was in creation, but I am sure, if you think about it, you will agree that our God is awesome not only in His power and His love, but also in His creativity.

Simply take a walk and look around. Watch something about nature on a DVD or on television. Find out what is in the ocean, or learn about how bees and flowers work together. Then realize that the same Holy Spirit present at creation is living inside you if you have truly accepted Jesus Christ as your Lord and Savior.

So much creativity lies within each one of us, and we need to learn to tap into it and express it without fear. Often, instead of exercising creativity, we keep repeating the same things even when we are bored with them, simply because we are afraid to step out and do something different. Even if we like the familiar, we must remember that we all need variety in our lives.

Some people keep the same job or live in the same area all of their lives because they feel those environments and activities are safe. Even if they hate their jobs and feel unfulfilled, at least they know how to do their jobs (they're familiar) and are comfortable with them—and the thought of getting other jobs is terrifying to them! In other cases, people do want to make changes in their lives, but they do not want to fail at something new, so they refuse to try and they stick with the familiar.

I do not encourage people to pursue every whim that crosses their minds or to latch onto every fad that comes their way. But there is a definite time to step out of the ordinary—out of the comfort zone—and into new things.

God has created us to need diversity and variety. We are designed to require freshness and newness in our lives, and there is nothing wrong with feeling that you "just need a change." On the other hand, never being satisfied and always trying the next new thing is another type of problem. Stay within reason, but do not be afraid of the new. Embrace the fresh and different opportunities, experiences, and environments God brings your way. He is a creative God; His creativity did not stop in the Garden of Eden, but is still active today as He continues to shape and refine the wonderful creation He is making in you!

becoming one

The minute two people marry, they are legally joined together. Experientially, though, they do not immediately "become one" when they say, "I do"; they simply begin the *process* of becoming one (see Genesis 2:24). As the process works itself out, each partner should hold marriage in honor and esteem the relationship as worthy and precious. They should treat each other as being very valuable.

Note in Genesis 2:24 a three-step progression that demonstrates how to become one: (1) *Leave*. Sometimes a wife clings excessively to her mother and her mother's opinions about what she ought to do, or a husband runs to his father for advice, when the couple should be trusting and leaning on each other. If two people are married but have not left home (both physically and mentally), they need to do so. (2) *Cleave*. In practical terms, the word *cleave* means to stick to each other like glue. (3) *Become one*. Becoming one means the complete union of body, soul, and spirit—and again, this takes time.

If both people in a marriage relationship are born again, then the spiritual union is in place. The most difficult part of the "becoming one" process is usually the uniting of two souls—the joining of two minds, wills, and sets of emotions. Most marital problems in the arena of the soul result from strife over lack of communication, sexual misunderstanding, money, goals, and the disciplining of children. All of these things need to be worked out in the soulish realm of the marriage union, and in order to become one in that area, a husband and a wife need to give their issues to God and say, "Father, change my mind or my will if I'm wrong." God is the One Who will bring them into agreement with His will and purpose. If each marriage partner is willing to be brought into agreement with the other, they no longer try to force each other to be someone they are not, but realize they need each other to be exactly who God created them to be. They no longer pick on each other's weaknesses. Instead, they partake of their strengths, they enjoy one another, and they enjoy the process of becoming one.

2 And the woman said to the serpent, We may eat the fruit from the trees of the garden,
3 Except the fruit from the tree which is in the middle of the garden. God has said, You shall not eat of it, neither shall you touch it, lest you die.
4 But the serpent said to the woman, You shall not surely die, [II Cor. 11:3.]
5 For God knows that in the day you eat of it your eyes will be opened, and you will be like God, knowing the difference between good and evil *and* blessing and calamity.

6 And when the woman saw that the tree was good (suitable, pleasant)

life point

Adam did what God told him not to do (see Genesis 3:1–6). As a result, Adam became a captive of Satan, who had lured him into going against God's word. By listening to Satan instead of to God, Adam surrendered to Satan the authority to rule the earth that God had originally given to man. Always listen to God and obey His Word.

for food and that it was delightful to look at, and a tree to be desired in order to make one wise, she took of its fruit and ate; and she gave some also to her husband, and he ate.

7 Then the eyes of them both were opened, and they knew that they were naked; and they sewed fig leaves together and made themselves apron-like girdles.

8 And they heard the sound of the Lord God walking in the garden in the cool of the day, and Adam and his wife hid themselves from the presence of the Lord God among the trees of the garden.

9 But the Lord God called to Adam and said to him, Where are you?

10 He said, I heard the sound of You [walking] in the garden, and I was afraid because I was naked; and I hid myself.

11 And He said, Who told you that you were naked? Have you eaten of the tree of which I commanded you that you should not eat?

12 And the man said, The woman whom You gave to be with me—she gave me [fruit] from the tree, and I ate.

13 And the Lord God said to the woman, What is this you have done? And the woman said, The serpent beguiled (cheated, outwitted, and deceived) me, and I ate.

14 And the Lord God said to the serpent, Because you have done this, you are cursed above all [domestic] animals and above every [wild] living thing of the field; upon your belly you shall go, and you shall eat dust [and

the devil's doom

I believe that Adam was clothed with God's glory before he sinned. As soon as Adam and Eve sinned, they realized they were naked. We might say that they lost their "covering." As long as they obeyed God, they were protected from everything the devil wanted to do to them—and, ultimately, through them. Upon seeing what the devil had done, God immediately announced Satan's doom and told him how it would occur.

Satan did not really understand what God was saying; nevertheless, God said it, and it had to come to pass: "And I will put enmity between you and the woman, and between your offspring and her Offspring; He will bruise and tread your head underfoot, and you will lie in wait and bruise His heel" (Genesis 3:15).

To "bruise the head" symbolizes a weakening of authority. God has said that the woman's Offspring (Jesus) will take away Satan's authority. Satan will bruise Jesus' heel (afflict His body—both on the cross and by afflicting mankind).

Through Jesus' death on the cross, God took Satan's authority (which Adam gave him) and gave it first to Jesus and then to every person who will believe—not only that Jesus died for them, but also that Satan has lost authority over them. We need to understand not only that Jesus died for us, but also that He has *redeemed* us!

No matter what the devil tries to do to you, he is doomed to defeat, and you are redeemed and victorious over him through Jesus Christ.

what it contains] all the days of your life.

15 And I will put enmity between you and the woman, and between your offspring and her [b]Offspring; He will bruise *and* tread your head underfoot, and you will lie in wait *and* bruise His heel. [Gal. 4:4.]

16 To the woman He said, I will greatly multiply your grief *and* your suffering in pregnancy *and* the pangs of childbearing; with spasms of distress you will bring forth children. Yet your desire *and* craving will be for your husband, and he will rule over you.

17 And to Adam He said, Because you have listened *and* given heed to the voice of your wife and have eaten of the tree of which I commanded you, saying, You shall not eat of it, the ground is under a curse because of you; in sorrow *and* toil shall you eat [of the fruits] of it all the days of your life.

18 Thorns also and thistles shall it bring forth for you, and you shall eat the plants of the field.

19 In the sweat of your face shall you eat bread until you return to the ground, for out of it you were taken; for dust you are and to dust you shall return.

20 The man called his wife's name Eve [life spring], because she was the mother of all the living.

21 For Adam also and for his wife the Lord God made long coats (tunics) of skins and clothed them.

22 And the Lord God said, Behold, the man has become like one of Us [the Father, Son, and Holy Spirit], to know [how to distinguish between] good and evil *and* blessing and calamity; and now, lest he put forth his hand and take also from the tree of life and eat, and live [c]forever—

23 Therefore the Lord God sent him forth from the Garden of Eden to till the ground from which he was taken.

24 So [God] drove out the man; and He placed at the east of the Garden of Eden the [d]cherubim and a flaming sword which turned every way, to keep *and* guard the way to the tree of life. [Rev. 2:7; 22:2, 14, 19.]

4 AND ADAM knew Eve as his wife, and she became pregnant and bore Cain; and she said, I have gotten *and* gained a man with the help of the Lord.

2 And [next] she gave birth to his brother Abel. Now Abel was a keeper of sheep, but Cain was a tiller of the ground.

3 And in the course of time Cain brought to the Lord an offering of the fruit of the ground.

4 And Abel brought of the firstborn of his flock and of the fat portions. And the Lord had respect *and* regard for Abel and for his offering, [Heb. 11:4.]

5 But for [e]Cain and his offering He had no respect *or* regard. So Cain was exceedingly angry *and* indignant, and he looked sad *and* depressed.

6 And the Lord said to Cain, Why are you angry? And why do you look sad *and* depressed *and* dejected?

7 If you do well, will you not be accepted? And if you do not do well, sin crouches at your door; its desire is for you, but you must master it.

---

b Christ fulfills through his victory over Satan the wonderful promise here spoken. See also Isa. 9:6; Matt. 1:23; Luke 1:31; Rom. 16:20; Gal. 4:4; Rev. 12:17. **c** This sentence is left unfinished, as if to hasten to avert the tragedy suggested of men living on forever in their now fallen state. **d** Cherubim are ministering spirits manifesting God's invisible presence and symbolizing His action (E.F. Harrison et al., eds., *Baker's Dictionary of Theology*). **e** In bringing the offering he did, Cain denied that he was a sinful creature under the sentence of divine condemnation. He insisted on approaching God on the ground of personal worthiness. Instead of accepting God's way, he offered to God the fruits of the ground **which God had cursed.** He presented the product of his own toil, the work of his own hands, and God refused to receive it (Arthur W. Pink, *Gleanings in Genesis*).

putting the Word to work

Cain did not relate well to his brother, Abel. We know that their interests and pursuits were different, because Abel was a shepherd and Cain tilled the ground. We do not know what their other differences were, but Cain's resentment of Abel eventually led to murder (see Genesis 4:8). How do you respond to those who are close to you, yet have different personalities, gifts, or pursuits? Ask God to help you when you are tempted to resent them.

8 And Cain said to his brother, [f]Let us go out to the field. And when they were in the field, Cain rose up against Abel his brother and killed him. [I John 3:12.]

9 And the Lord said to Cain, Where is Abel your brother? And he said, I do not know. Am I my brother's keeper?

10 And [the Lord] said, What have you done? The voice of your brother's blood is crying to Me from the ground.

11 And now you are cursed by reason of the earth, which has opened its mouth to receive your brother's [shed] blood from your hand.

12 When you till the ground, it shall no longer yield to you its strength; you shall be a fugitive and a vagabond on the earth [in perpetual exile, a degraded outcast].

13 Then Cain said to the Lord, My punishment is [g]greater than I can bear.

14 Behold, You have driven me out this day from the face of the land, and from Your face I will be hidden; and I will be a fugitive and a vagabond *and* a wanderer on the earth, and whoever finds me will kill me.

15 And the Lord said to him, [h]Therefore, if anyone kills Cain, vengeance shall be taken on him sevenfold. And the Lord set a [i]mark *or* sign upon Cain, lest anyone finding him should kill him.

16 So Cain went away from the presence of the Lord and dwelt in the land of Nod [wandering], east of Eden.

17 And Cain's wife [one of Adam's offspring] became pregnant and bore Enoch; and Cain built a [j]city and named it after his son Enoch.

18 To Enoch was born Irad, and Irad was the father of Mehujael, and Mehujael the father of Methusael, and Methusael the father of Lamech.

19 And Lamech took two wives; the name of the one was Adah and of the other was Zillah.

20 Adah bore Jabal; he was the father of those who dwell in tents and have cattle *and* purchase possessions.

21 His brother's name was Jubal; he was the father of all those who play the lyre and pipe.

22 Zillah bore Tubal-cain; he was the forger of all [cutting] instruments of bronze and iron. The sister of Tubal-cain was Naamah.

23 Lamech said to his wives, Adah and Zillah, Hear my voice; you wives of Lamech, listen to what I say; for I have slain a man [merely] for wounding me, and a young man [only] for striking *and* bruising me.

24 If Cain is avenged sevenfold, truly Lamech [will be avenged] seventy-sevenfold.

---

f The Hebrew omits this clause, but various other texts show that it was originally included. **g** Some ancient versions read, "too great to be forgiven!" **h** Some versions read, "Not so!" **i** Many commentators believe this sign not to have been like a brand on the forehead, but something awesome about Cain's appearance that made people dread and avoid him. **j** C.H. Dodd (cited by Adam Clarke, *The Holy Bible with A Commentary*) shows that it would have been possible for Adam and Eve, in the more than 100 years he estimates may have elapsed since their union, to have had over 32,000 descendants at the time Cain went to Nod, all of them having sprung from Cain and Abel, who married their sisters.

25 And Adam's wife again became pregnant, and she bore a son and called his name Seth. For God, she said, has appointed for me another child instead of Abel, for Cain slew him.

26 And to Seth also a son was born, whom he named Enosh. At that time men began to call [upon God] by the name of the Lord.

5 THIS IS the book (the written record, the history) of the generations of the offspring of Adam. When God created man, He made him in the likeness of God.

2 He created them male and female and blessed them and named them [both] Adam [Man] at the time they were created.

3 When Adam had lived 130 years, he had a son in his own likeness, after his image; and he named him Seth.

4 After he had Seth, Adam lived 800 years and had other sons and daughters.

5 So altogether Adam lived 930 years, and he died.

6 When Seth was 105 years old, Enosh was born.

7 Seth lived after the birth of Enosh 807 years and had other sons and daughters.

8 So Seth lived 912 years, and he died.

9 When Enosh was 90 years old, Kenan was born to him.

10 Enosh lived after the birth of Kenan 815 years and had other sons and daughters.

11 So Enosh lived 905 years, and he died.

12 When Kenan was 70 years old, Mahalalel was born.

13 Kenan lived after the birth of Mahalalel 840 years and had other sons and daughters.

14 So Kenan lived 910 years, and he died.

15 When Mahalalel was 65 years old, Jared was born.

16 Mahalalel lived after the birth of Jared 830 years and had other sons and daughters.

17 So Mahalalel lived 895 years, and he died.

18 When Jared was 162 years old, Enoch was born.

19 Jared lived after the birth of Enoch 800 years and had other sons and daughters.

20 So Jared lived 962 years, and he died.

21 When Enoch was 65 years old, Methuselah was born.

22 Enoch walked [in habitual fellowship] with God after the birth of Methuselah 300 years and had other sons and daughters.

23 So all the days of Enoch were 365 years.

24 And Enoch walked [in habitual fellowship] with God; and he was not, for God took him [home with Him]. [Heb. 11:5.]

25 When Methuselah was 187 years old, Lamech was born to him.

26 Methuselah lived after the birth of Lamech 782 years and had other sons and daughters.

27 So Methuselah lived 969 years, and he died.

28 When Lamech was 182 years old, a son was born.

29 He named him Noah, saying, This one shall bring us relief *and* comfort from our work and the [grievous] toil of our hands due to the ground being cursed by the Lord.

30 Lamech lived after the birth of Noah 595 years and had other sons and daughters.

31 So all the days of ᵏLamech were 777 years, and he died.

---

k It is now well known that the age of mankind cannot be reckoned in years from the facts listed in genealogies, for there are numerous known intentional gaps in them. For example, as B. B. Warfield

32 After Noah was 500 years old, he became the father of Shem, Ham, and Japheth.

6 WHEN MEN began to multiply on the face of the land and daughters were born to them, **2** The sons of God saw that the daughters of men were fair, and they took wives of all they desired *and* chose. **3** Then the Lord said, My Spirit shall not forever dwell *and* strive with man, for he also is flesh; but his days shall yet be 120 years. **4** There were giants on the earth in those days—and also afterward— when the sons of God lived with the daughters of men, and they bore children to them. These were the mighty men who were of old, men of renown. **5** The Lord saw that the wickedness of man was great in the earth, and that every imagination *and* intention of all human thinking was only evil continually. **6** And the Lord regretted that He had made man on the earth, and He was grieved at heart. **7** So the Lord said, I will destroy, blot out, *and* wipe away mankind, whom I have created from the face of the ground—not only man, [but] the beasts and the creeping things and the birds of the air—for it grieves Me *and* makes Me regretful that I have made them. **8** But Noah found grace (favor) in the eyes of the Lord.

speak the Word

Father, I thank You that I have found grace and favor in Your sight.
ADAPTED FROM GENESIS 6:8

9 This is the history of the generations of Noah. Noah was a just *and* righteous man, blameless *in* his [evil] generation; Noah walked [in habitual fellowship] with God. **10** And Noah became the father of three sons: Shem, Ham, and Japheth. **11** The earth was depraved *and* putrid in God's sight, and the land was filled with violence (desecration, infringement, outrage, assault, and lust for power). **12** And God looked upon the world and saw how degenerate, debased, *and* vicious it was, for all humanity had corrupted their way upon the earth *and* lost their true direction.

putting the Word to work

According to Genesis 6:12, the world around Noah was "degenerate, debased, and vicious." People had "corrupted their way upon the earth and lost their true direction." In the midst of corruption and evil around you today, how can you be like Noah and be righteous before God in your generation?

13 God said to Noah, I intend to make an end of all flesh, for through men the land is filled with violence; and behold, I will ¹destroy them and the land. **14** Make yourself an ark of gopher *or* cypress wood; make in *it* rooms (stalls, pens, coops, nests, cages, and

---

(*Studies in Theology*) points out, the genealogy in Matt. 1:1-17 omits the three kings, Ahaziah, Jehoash, and Amaziah, and indicates that Joram (Matt. 1:8) begat Uzziah, who was his great-great-grandson. The mistaking of compressed genealogies as bases for chronology has been very misleading. So far, the dates in years of very early Old Testament events are altogether speculative and relative, and the tendency is to put them farther and farther back into antiquity. 1 Enoch had warned these people (Jude 14, 15); Noah had preached righteousness to them (II Pet. 2:5); God's Spirit had been striving with them (Gen. 6:3). Yet they had rejected God and were without excuse.

the importance of a right heart

Genesis 6:5–8 reveals two things that displease God: wickedness, and evil imaginations and thinking. Because those things described the condition of people's hearts during Noah's day, God decided to destroy all mankind—everyone, that is, except Noah and his family. God spared Noah's life because Noah found grace and favor in His eyes.

I can only surmise that Noah must have had a right heart; otherwise, he would have been destroyed with all the other people who practiced wickedness, evil imaginations, and evil thinking.

One of the lessons we can learn from Noah's story is that many people today are being destroyed for the simple reason that their hearts are not right before God. In their hearts they regard wickedness, they allow impure imaginations, and they think bad thoughts.

We cannot imagine how many areas of our lives would be straightened out if we would just get our hearts right with God! Our hearts may not be filled with the blatant evil we read about in Noah's time, but bad attitudes and wrong thinking certainly qualify as evil imaginations and evil thinking. We need to have right attitudes toward everything we do, because our attitudes basically determine everything else about our situations. If our hearts are full of bad attitudes and our minds are full of "stinking thinking," we will not make much progress in life.

We need to have pure, tender hearts. We need to hear and heed the voice of conscience so that the moment we realize we have a bad attitude about something or someone, we can make the necessary adjustments. That is why Proverbs 4:23 instructs us: "Keep and guard your heart with all vigilance and above all that you guard, for out of it flow the springs of life."

So often, we fail to guard our hearts as diligently as we should, and we allow too much junk and too many negative thoughts into our minds. We need to remember the familiar phrase "garbage in, garbage out," and realize that we cannot take in garbage and produce good things. We must be attentive not only to our actions, but also to our thoughts, imaginations, motives, and attitudes. God looks at these things because He is a God of hearts. Whatever you do, make sure you have a right heart before the Lord, and you will reap abundant life instead of destruction.

compartments) and cover it inside and out with pitch (bitumen).
15 And this is the way you are to make it: the length of the ark shall be 300 cubits, its breadth 50 cubits, and its height 30 cubits [that is, 450 ft. x 75 ft. x 45 ft.].
16 You shall make a roof or ᵐwindow [a place for light] for the ark and finish it to a cubit [at least 18 inches] above—

m Noah's ark possibly had a window area large enough to admit light and provide ventilation.

and the [n]door of the ark you shall put in the side of it; and you shall make it with lower, second, and third stories.

17 For behold, I, even I, will bring a flood of waters upon the earth to destroy *and* make putrid all flesh under the heavens in which are the breath *and* spirit of life; everything that is on the land shall die.

18 But I will establish My covenant (promise, pledge) with you, and you shall come into the ark—you and your sons and your wife and your sons' wives with you.

19 And of every living thing of all flesh [found on land], you shall bring two of every sort into the ark, to keep them alive with you; they shall be male and female.

20 Of fowls *and* birds according to their kinds, of beasts according to their kinds, of every creeping thing of the ground according to its kind—two of every sort shall come in with you, that they may be kept alive.

21 Also take with you every sort of food that is eaten, and you shall collect *and* store it up, and it shall serve as food for you and for them.

22 Noah did this; he did all that God commanded him.

7 AND THE Lord said to Noah, Come with all your household into the ark, for I have seen you to be righteous (upright and in right standing) before Me in this genera-

tion. [Ps. 27:5; 33:18, 19; II Pet. 2:9.]

2 Of every clean beast you shall receive *and* take with you seven pairs, the male and his mate, and of beasts that are not clean a pair of each kind, the male and his mate, [Lev. 11.]

3 Also of the birds of the air seven pairs, the male and the female, to keep seed [their kind] alive over all the earth *or* land.

4 For in seven days I will cause it to rain upon the earth forty days and forty nights, and every living substance *and* thing that I have made I will destroy, blot out, *and* wipe away from the face of the earth.

5 And Noah did all that the Lord commanded him. [Heb. 11:7.]

6 Noah was 600 years old when the flood of waters came upon the earth *or* land.

7 And Noah and his sons and his wife and his sons' wives with him went into the ark because of the waters of the flood. [Matt. 24:38; Luke 17:27.]

8 Of [o]clean animals and of animals that are not clean, and of birds *and* fowls, and of everything that creeps on the ground,

9 There went in two and two with Noah into the ark, the male and the female, as God had commanded Noah.

10 And after the seven days the floodwaters came upon the earth *or* land.

11 In the year 600 of Noah's life, in the seventeenth day of the second month, that same day all the fountains of the

speak the Word

God, I pray that I will be like Noah and do all that You have commanded me to do.
ADAPTED FROM GENESIS 7:5

n "Here can only be meant an entrance which was afterward closed, and only opened again at the end of the flood. And since there were three stories of the ark, the word is to be understood, perhaps, of three entrances capable of being closed, and to which there would have been constructed a way of access from the outside" (J.P. Lange, *A Commentary on the Holy Scriptures*). **o** Noah had many years in which to interest travelers in securing these animals for him. The five extra pairs of clean animals were for food, and for sacrifice later.

great deep were broken up *and* burst forth, and the windows *and* floodgates of the heavens were opened.

12 And it rained upon the earth forty days and forty nights.

13 On the very same day Noah and Shem, Ham, and Japheth, the sons of Noah, and Noah's wife and the three wives of his sons with them, went into the ark,

14 They and every [wild] beast according to its kind, all the livestock according to their kinds, every moving thing that creeps on the land according to its kind, and every fowl according to its kind, every winged thing of every sort.

15 And they went into the ark with Noah, two and two of all flesh in which there were the breath *and* spirit of life.

16 And they that entered, male and female of all flesh, went in as God had commanded [Noah]; and the Lord shut him in *and* closed [the door] round about him.

17 The flood [that is, the downpour of rain] was forty days upon the earth; and the waters increased and bore up the ark, and it was lifted [high] above the land.

18 And the waters became mighty and increased greatly upon the land, and the ark went [gently floating] upon the surface of the waters.

19 And the waters prevailed so exceedingly *and* were so mighty upon the earth that all the high hills under the whole sky were covered.

20 [In fact] the waters became fifteen cubits higher, as the high hills were covered.

21 And all flesh ceased to breathe that moved upon the earth—fowls *and* birds, [tame] animals, [wild] beasts, all swarming *and* creeping things that swarm *and* creep upon the land, and all mankind.

22 Everything on the dry land in whose nostrils were the breath *and* spirit of life died.

23 God destroyed (blotted out) every living thing that was upon the face of the earth; man and animals and the creeping things and the birds of the heavens were destroyed (blotted out) from the land. Only Noah remained alive, and those who were with him in the ark. [Matt. 24:37-44.]

24 And the waters prevailed [mightily] upon the earth *or* land 150 days (five months).

8 AND GOD [earnestly] remembered Noah and every living thing and all the animals that were with him in the ark; and God made a wind blow over the land, and the waters sank down *and* abated.

2 Also the fountains of the deep and the windows of the heavens were closed, the gushing rain from the sky was checked,

3 And the waters receded from the land continually. At the end of 150 days the waters had diminished.

4 On the seventeenth day of the seventh month the ark came to rest on the mountains of Ararat [in Armenia].

5 And the waters continued to diminish until the tenth month; on the first day of the tenth month the tops of the high hills were seen.

6 At the end of [another] forty days Noah opened *a* window of the ark which he had made

7 And sent forth a raven, which kept going to and fro until the waters were dried up from the land.

8 Then he sent forth a dove to see if the waters had decreased from the surface of the ground.

9 But the dove found no resting-place on which to roost, and she returned to him to the ark, for the waters were [yet] on the face of the whole land. So he put forth his hand and drew her to him into the ark.

10 He waited another seven days and again sent forth the dove out of the ark.

11 And the dove came back to him in

the evening, and behold, in her mouth was a newly sprouted *and* freshly plucked olive leaf! So Noah knew that the waters had subsided from the land.
12 Then he waited another seven days and sent forth the dove, but she did not return to him any more.
13 In the year 601 [of Noah's life], on the first day of the first month, the waters were drying up from the land. And Noah ᵖremoved the covering of the ark and looked, and behold, the surface of the ground was drying.
14 And on the twenty-seventh day of the second month the land was entirely dry.
15 And God spoke to Noah, saying,
16 Go forth from the ark, you and your wife and your sons and their wives with you.
17 Bring forth every living thing that is with you of all flesh—birds and beasts and every creeping thing that creeps on the ground—that they may breed abundantly on the land and be fruitful and multiply upon the earth.
18 And Noah went forth, and his wife and his sons and their wives with him [after being in the ark one year and ten days].
19 Every beast, every creeping thing, every bird—and whatever moves on the land—went forth by families out of the ark.
20 And Noah built an altar to the Lord and took of every clean [four-footed] animal and of every clean fowl *or* bird and offered burnt offerings on the altar.

21 When the Lord smelled the pleasing odor [a scent of satisfaction to His heart], the Lord said to Himself, I will never again curse the ground because of man, for the imagination (the strong desire) of man's heart is evil *and* wicked from his youth; neither will I ever again smite *and* destroy every living thing, as I have done.
22 While the earth remains, seedtime and harvest, cold and heat, summer and winter, and day and night shall not cease.

9 AND GOD pronounced a blessing upon Noah and his sons and said to them, Be fruitful and multiply and fill the earth.
2 And the fear of you and the dread *and* terror of you shall be upon every beast of the land, every bird of the air, all that creeps upon the ground, and upon all the fish of the sea; they are delivered into your hand.
3 Every moving thing that lives shall be food for you; and as I gave you the green vegetables *and* plants, I give you everything.
4 But you shall not eat flesh with the life of it, which is its blood.
5 And surely for your lifeblood I will require an accounting; from every beast I will require it; and from man, from every man [who spills another's lifeblood] I will require a reckoning.
6 Whoever sheds man's blood, by man shall his blood be shed; for in the image of God He made man.

p Possibly overhanging eaves which prevented the rain from coming through the perforated window space had also prevented Noah from seeing the mountaintops. It is well to remember that the Architect of Noah's ark was the omniscient Scientist Whose "ways are past finding out," though men have learned much from them through the centuries. Nothing was lacking in Noah's ark to keep it from being suited for all that was required of it. The comfortable, light, well-ventilated, watertight, perfectly planned boat, large enough to accommodate all the original land animals intelligently and to permit the four human couples to live separately and in peace, needs no apology today. "In 1609 at Hoorn, in Holland, the Netherlandish Mennonite, P. Jansen, produced a vessel after the pattern of the ark, only smaller, whereby he proved it was well adapted for floating, and would carry a cargo greater by one-third than any other form of like cubical content" (J.P. Lange, *A Commentary*). It revolutionized shipbuilding. By 1900 every large vessel on the high seas was definitely inclined toward the proportions of Noah's ark (as verified by "Lloyd's Register of Shipping," *The World Almanac*). Later, ships were built longer for speed, a matter of no concern to Noah.

7 And you, be fruitful and multiply; bring forth abundantly on the earth and multiply on it.
8 Then God spoke to Noah and to his sons with him, saying,
9 Behold, I establish My covenant *or* pledge with you and with your descendants after you
10 And with every living creature that is with you—whether the birds, the livestock, or the wild beasts of the earth along with you, as many as came out of the ark—every animal of the earth.
11 I will establish My covenant *or* pledge with you: Never again shall all flesh be cut off by the waters of a flood; neither shall there ever again be a flood to destroy the earth *and* make it corrupt.
12 And God said, This is the token of the covenant (solemn pledge) which I am making between Me and you and every living creature that is with you, for all future generations:
13 I set My bow [rainbow] in the cloud, and it shall be a token *or* sign of a covenant *or* solemn pledge between Me and the earth.
14 And it shall be that when I bring clouds over the earth and the bow [rainbow] is seen in the clouds,
15 I will [earnestly] remember My covenant *or* solemn pledge which is between Me and you and every living creature of all flesh; and the waters will no more become a flood to destroy *and* make all flesh corrupt.
16 When the bow [rainbow] is in the clouds and I look upon it, I will [earnestly] remember the everlasting covenant *or* pledge between God and every living creature of all flesh that is upon the earth.
17 And God said to Noah, This [rainbow] is the token *or* sign of the covenant *or* solemn pledge which I have established between Me and all flesh upon the earth.
18 The sons of Noah who went forth from the ark were Shem, Ham, and Japheth. Ham was the father of Canaan [born later].
19 These are the three sons of Noah, and from them the whole earth was overspread *and* stocked with inhabitants.
20 And Noah began to cultivate the ground, and he planted a vineyard.
21 And he drank of the wine and became drunk, and he was uncovered *and* lay naked in his tent.
22 And Ham, the father of Canaan, glanced at *and* saw the nakedness of his father and told his two brothers outside.
23 So Shem and Japheth took a garment, laid it upon the shoulders of both, and went backward and covered the nakedness of their father; and their faces were backward, and they did not see their father's nakedness.
24 When Noah awoke from his wine, and knew the thing which his youngest son had done to him,
25 He exclaimed, Cursed be Canaan! He shall be the [q]servant of servants to his brethren! [Deut. 27:16.]
26 He also said, Blessed be the Lord, the God of Shem! *And* blessed by the Lord my God be Shem! And let Canaan be his servant.
27 May God enlarge Japheth; and let

q The language of Noah here is an actual prophecy and not merely an expression of personal feeling. That Noah placed a curse on his youngest grandchild, Canaan, who would naturally be his favorite, can only be explained on the ground that in the prophetic spirit he saw into the future of the Canaanites. God Himself found the delinquency of the Canaanites insufferable and ultimately drove them out or subdued them and put the descendants of Shem in their place. But Noah's foresight did not yet include the extermination of the Canaanite peoples, for then he would have expressed it differently. He would not merely have called them "the servant of servants" if he had foreseen their destruction. The form of the expression, therefore, testifies to the great age of the prophecy (J.P. Lange, *A Commentary*).

18

him dwell in the tents of Shem, and let Canaan be his servant.

28 And Noah lived after the flood 350 years.

29 All the days of Noah were 950 years, and he died.

10 THIS IS the history of the generations (descendants) of the sons of Noah, Shem, Ham, and Japheth. The sons born to them after the flood *were:*

2 The sons of Japheth: Gomer, Magog, Madai, Javan, Tubal, Meshech, and Tiras.

3 The sons of Gomer: Ashkenaz, Riphath, and Togarmah.

4 The sons of Javan: Elishah, Tarshish, Kittim, and Dodanim.

5 From these the coastland peoples spread. [These are the sons of Japheth] in their lands, each with his own language, by their families within their nations.

6 The sons of Ham: Cush, Egypt [Mizraim], Put, and Canaan.

7 The sons of Cush: Seba, Havilah, Sabtah, Raamah, and Sabteca; and the sons of Raamah: Sheba and Dedan.

8 Cush became the father of Nimrod; he was the first to be a mighty man on the earth.

9 He was a mighty hunter before the Lord; therefore it is said, Like Nimrod, a mighty hunter before the Lord.

10 The beginning of his kingdom was Babel, Erech, Accad, and Calneh, in the land of Shinar [in Babylonia].

11 Out of the land he [Nimrod] went forth into Assyria and built Nineveh, Rehoboth-Ir, Calah,

12 And Resen, which is between Nineveh and Calah; all these [suburbs combined to form] the great city.

13 And Egypt [Mizraim] became the father of Ludim, Anamim, Lehabim, Naphtuhim,

14 Pathrusim, Casluhim (from whom came the Philistines), and Caphtorim.

15 Canaan became the father of Sidon his firstborn, Heth [the Hittites],

16 The Jebusites, the Amorites, the Girgashites,

17 The Hivites, the Arkites, the Sinites,

18 The Arvadites, the Zemarites and the Hamathites. Afterward the families of the Canaanites spread abroad

19 And the territory of the Canaanites extended from Sidon as one goes to Gerar as far as Gaza, and as one goes to ʳSodom, Gomorrah, Admah, and Zeboiim, as far as Lasha.

20 These are the sons of Ham by their families, their languages, their lands, and their nations.

21 To Shem also, the younger brother of Japheth and the ancestor of all the children of Eber [including the Hebrews], children were born.

22 The sons of Shem: Elam, Asshur, Arpachshad, Lud, and Aram.

23 The sons of Aram: Uz, Hul, Gether, and Mash.

24 Arpachshad became the father of Shelah; and Shelah became the father of Eber.

25 To Eber were born two sons: the name of one was Peleg [division], because [the inhabitants of] the earth were divided up in his days; and his brother's name was Joktan.

26 Joktan became the father of Almodad, Sheleph, Hazarmaveth, Jerah,

27 Hadoram, Uzal, Diklah,

28 Obal, Abimael, Sheba,

29 Ophir, Havilah, and Jobab; all these were the sons of Joktan.

30 The territory in which they lived extended from Mesha as one goes

---

r Surely no greater proof is needed of the great antiquity of this portion of Genesis than the fact that it mentions as still standing these four cities of the plain, which were utterly destroyed in Abraham's time (Gen. 19:27-29; Deut. 29:23).

toward Sephar to the hill country of the east.

31 These are Shem's descendants by their families, their languages, their lands, and their nations.

32 These are the families of the sons of Noah, according to their generations, within their nations; and from these the nations spread abroad on the earth after the flood. [Acts 17:26.]

11 AND THE whole earth was of one language and of one accent *and* mode of expression.

2 And as they journeyed eastward, they found a plain (valley) in the land of Shinar, and they settled *and* dwelt there.

3 And they said one to another, Come, let us make bricks and burn them thoroughly. So they had brick for stone, and slime (bitumen) for mortar.

4 And they said, Come, let us build us a city and a tower whose top reaches into the sky, and let us make a name for ourselves, lest we be scattered over the whole earth.

5 And the Lord came down to see the city and the tower which the sons of men had built.

6 And the Lord said, Behold, they are one people and they have ˢall one language; and this is only the beginning of what they will do, and now nothing they have imagined they can do will be impossible for them.

7 Come, let Us go down and there confound (mix up, confuse) their language, that they may not understand one another's speech.

8 So the Lord scattered them abroad from that place upon the face of the whole earth, and they gave up building the city.

9 Therefore the name of it was called Babel—because there the Lord confounded the language of all the earth; and from that place the Lord scattered them abroad upon the face of the whole earth.

10 This is the history of the generations of Shem. Shem was 100 years old when he became the father of Arpachshad, two years after the flood.

11 And Shem lived after Arpachshad was born 500 years and had other sons and daughters.

12 When Arpachshad had lived 35 years, he became the father of Shelah.

13 Arpachshad lived after Shelah was born 403 years and had other sons and daughters.

14 When Shelah had lived 30 years, he became the father of Eber.

15 Shelah lived after Eber was born 403 years and had other sons and daughters.

16 When Eber had lived 34 years, he became the father of Peleg.

17 And Eber lived after Peleg was born 430 years and had other sons and daughters.

18 When Peleg had lived 30 years, he became the father of Reu.

19 And Peleg lived after Reu was born 209 years and had other sons and daughters.

20 When Reu had lived 32 years, he became the father of Serug.

21 And Reu lived after Serug was born 207 years and had other sons and daughters.

22 When Serug had lived 30 years, he became the father of Nahor.

23 And Serug lived after Nahor was

s Some noted philologists have declared that a common origin of all languages cannot be denied. One, Max Mueller (*The Science of Language*), said "We have examined all possible forms which language can assume, and now we ask, can we reconcile with these three distinct forms, the radical, the terminational, the inflectional, the admission of one common origin of human speech? I answer decidedly, 'Yes'." *The New Bible Commentary* says, "The original unity of human language, though still far from demonstrable, becomes increasingly probable."

born 200 years and had other sons and daughters.

24 When Nahor had lived 29 years, he became the father of Terah.

25 And Nahor lived after Terah was born 119 years and had other sons and daughters.

26 After Terah had lived 70 years, he became the father of [at different times], ᵗAbram and Nahor and Haran, [his firstborn].

27 Now this is the history of the descendants of Terah. Terah was the father of Abram, Nahor, and Haran; and Haran was the father of Lot.

28 Haran died before his father Terah [died] in the land of his birth, in ᵘUr of the Chaldees.

29 And Abram and Nahor took wives. The name of Abram's wife was Sarai, and the name of Nahor's wife was Milcah, the daughter of Haran the father of Milcah and Iscah.

30 But Sarai was barren; she had no child.

31 And Terah took Abram his son, Lot the son of Haran, his grandson, and Sarai his daughter-in-law, his son Abram's wife, and they went forth together to go from Ur of the Chaldees into the land of Canaan; but when they came to Haran, they settled there.

32 And Terah lived 205 years; and Terah died in Haran.

12 NOW [in Haran] the Lord said to Abram, Go for yourself [for your own advantage] away from your country, from your relatives and your father's house, to the land that I will show you. [Heb. 11:8-10.]

2 And I will make of you a great nation, and I will bless you [with abundant increase of favors] and make your name famous *and* distinguished, and you will be a blessing [dispensing good to others].

3 And I will bless those who bless you [who confer prosperity or happiness upon you] and ᵛcurse him who curses *or* uses insolent language toward you; in you will all the families *and* kindred of the earth be blessed [and by you they will bless themselves]. [Gal. 3:8.]

4 So Abram departed, as the Lord had directed him; and Lot [his nephew] went with him. Abram was seventy-five years old when he left Haran.

5 Abram took Sarai his wife, and Lot his brother's son, and all their possessions that they had gathered, and the persons [servants] that they had acquired in Haran, and they went forth to go to the land of Canaan. When they came to the land of Canaan,

6 Abram passed through the land to the locality of Shechem, to the oak *or* terebinth tree of Moreh. And

t Abram is only mentioned first by way of dignity. Noah's sons also are given as "Shem, Ham, and Japheth" in Gen. 5:32, although Shem was not the oldest, but for dignity is named first, as is Abram here (Adam Clarke, *The Holy Bible with A Commentary*). u Abram's home town was Ur of the Chaldees. As the result of extensive archaeological excavations there by C. Leonard Woolley in 1922-34, a great deal is known about Abram's background. Space will not permit more than a glimpse at excavated Ur, but a few items will show the high state of civilization. The entire house of the average middle-class person had from ten to twenty rooms and measured forty to fifty-two feet; the lower floor was for servants, the upper floor for the family, with five rooms for their use; additionally, there was a guest chamber and a lavatory reserved for visitors, and a private chapel. A school was found and what the students studied was shown by the clay tablets discovered there. In the days of Abram the pupils had reading, writing, and arithmetic as today. They learned the multiplication and division tables and even worked at square and cube root. A bill of lading of about 2040 BC (about the era in which Abram is believed to have lived) showed that the commerce of that time was far-reaching. Even the name "Abraham" has been found on the excavated clay tablets (J.P. Free, *Archaeology and Bible History*). v To look with disfavor on the Jews was to invite God's displeasure; to treat the Jews offensively was to incur His wrath. But to befriend the Jews was to bring down upon one's head the rewards of a promise that could not be broken.

one step at a time

Abraham learned to trust God to lead him one step at a time. God essentially told him, "Trust Me with this first step, because it is best for you to go where I lead you." At that time, Abraham might have wondered whether or not packing up his tent and leaving his family and his country would be to his advantage, but God told him to go to the place that He would show him, and Abraham simply obeyed.

When God gave Abraham this instruction, He gave him only step one, not step two. Abraham would not get to step two until he had accomplished step one. This is so simple, but so profound: God gives us direction *one step at a time.*

You may be like many people who refuse to take step one until they think they understand steps two, three, four, and five. If so, I hope you will be inspired to go forward in God's plan for your life by trusting Him with the first step. Understanding that His will for you is revealed a step at a time should build your confidence to do at least what you already know to do. After the first few steps, your faith will grow because you will realize there is always sure footing beneath each step God instructs you to take.

Know that God has a good plan for your life and that you will be blessed when you obey Him. You can miss out on blessings by not obeying what God clearly tells you to do. He shows you the way to go, and you are to walk in that direction. Sometimes God may be gracious enough to carry you part of the way, but there comes a time when the carrying is over, and He says, "Now walk."

God wants you to obey Him quickly. He does not want you to argue with Him for three or four weeks before you will do a simple little thing. He wants you to trust Him and, like Abraham, take the first step He calls you to take in faith.

the Canaanite was then in the land. **7** Then the Lord appeared to Abram and said, I will give this land to your posterity. So Abram built an altar there to the Lord, Who had appeared to him. **8** From there he pulled up [his tent pegs] *and* departed to the mountain on the east of Bethel and pitched his tent, with Bethel on the west and Ai on the east; and there he built an altar to the Lord and called upon the name of the Lord. **9** Abram journeyed on, still going toward the South (the Negeb). **10** Now there was a famine in the land, and Abram ^wwent down into Egypt to live temporarily, for the famine in the land was oppressive (intense and grievous).

w Some books on archaeology frequently allude to the critical view that strangers could not have come into Egypt in earlier times, quoting Strabo and Diodorus to that effect; but later archaeological discoveries show that people from the region of Palestine and Syria were coming to Egypt in the period of Abraham. This is clearly indicated by a tomb painting at Beni Hassan, dating a little after 2000 bc. It shows Asiatic Semites who had come to Egypt. Furthermore, the archaeological and historical indications of the coming of the Hyksos into Egypt around 1900 bc provided another piece of evidence that strangers could come into that land (J.P. Free, *Abraham in Egypt*).

life point

We can read God's promise to Abraham in Genesis 12:2 and think, *Oh, hallelujah! That applies to me, too!* But we cannot forget that God required a sacrifice of obedience before Abraham could receive the promise. Abraham had to be willing to leave the place where he was comfortable; he had to leave his father and all of his relatives. And he did; he simply moved in faith to the place God said He would show him. If you are willing to have Abraham's kind of obedience, you can have Abraham's kind of blessing.

11 And when he was about to enter into Egypt, he said to Sarai his wife, I know that you are beautiful to behold. **12** So when the Egyptians see you, they will say, This is his wife; and they will kill me, but they will let you live. **13** Say, I beg of you, that you are ˣmy sister, so that it may go well with me for your sake and my life will be spared because of you. **14** And when Abram came into Egypt, the Egyptians saw that the woman was very beautiful. **15** The princes of Pharaoh also saw her and commended her to Pharaoh, and she was taken into Pharaoh's house [harem]. **16** And he treated Abram well for her sake; he acquired sheep, oxen, he-donkeys, menservants, maidservants, she-donkeys, and ʸcamels. **17** But the Lord scourged Pharaoh and his household with serious plagues because of Sarai, Abram's wife. **18** And Pharaoh called Abram and said, What is this that you have done to me? Why did you not tell me that she was your wife? **19** Why did you say, She is my sister, so that I took her to be my wife? Now then, here is your wife; take her and get away [from here]! **20** And Pharaoh commanded his men concerning him, and they brought him on his way with his wife and all that he had.

13 SO ABRAM went up out of Egypt, he and his wife and all that he had, and Lot with him, into the South [country of Judah, the Negeb]. **2** Now Abram was extremely rich in livestock and in silver and in gold. **3** And he journeyed on from the South [country of Judah, the Negeb] as far as Bethel, to the place where his tent had been at the beginning, between Bethel and Ai, **4** Where he had built an altar at first; and there Abram called on the name of the Lord. [Gal. 3:6-9.] **5** But Lot, who went with Abram, also had flocks and herds and tents. **6** Now the land was not able to nourish *and* support them so they could dwell together, for their possessions were too great for them to live together. **7** And there was strife between the herdsmen of Abram's cattle and the herdsmen of Lot's cattle. And the Canaanite and the Perizzite were dwelling then in the land [making fodder more difficult to obtain]. **8** So Abram said to Lot, Let there be no strife, I beg of you, between you and me, or between your herdsmen and my herdsmen, for we are relatives.

x Sarai was Abraham's half sister. They had the same father, but different mothers (Gen. 20:12). **y** Critics have set aside the statement that Abraham had camels in Egypt as an error. But archaeological evidence, including some twenty objects ranging from the seventh century BC to the period before 3000 BC, proves the authenticity of the Bible record concerning Abraham. It includes not only statuettes, plaques, rock carvings, and drawings representing camels, but also "camel bones, a camel skull, and a camel hair rope" (J.P. Free, *Archaeology and Bible History*).

9 Is not the whole land before you? Separate yourself, I beg of you, from me. If you take the left hand, then I will go to the right; or if you choose the right hand, then I will go to the left.

10 And Lot looked and saw that everywhere the Jordan Valley was well watered. Before the Lord destroyed Sodom and Gomorrah, [it was all] like the garden of the Lord, like the land of Egypt, as you go to Zoar.

11 Then Lot chose for himself all the Jordan Valley and [he] traveled east. So they separated.

12 Abram dwelt in the land of Canaan, and Lot dwelt in the cities of the [Jordan] Valley and moved his tent as far as Sodom *and* dwelt there.

13 But the men of Sodom were wicked and exceedingly great sinners against the Lord.

14 The Lord said to Abram after Lot had left him, Lift up now your eyes and look from the place where you are, northward and southward and eastward and westward;

15 For all the land which you see I will give to you and to your posterity forever. [Acts 7:5.]

16 And I will make your descendants like the dust of the earth, so that if a man could count the dust of the earth, then could your descendants also be counted. [Gen. 28:14.]

17 Arise, walk through the land, the length of it and the breadth of it, for I will give it to you.

18 Then Abram moved his tent and came and dwelt among the oaks *or* terebinths of Mamre, which are at Hebron, and built there an altar to the Lord.

14 IN THE days of the kings Amraphel of Shinar, Arioch of Ellasar, Chedorlaomer of Elam, and Tidal of Goiim,

2 They made war on the kings Bera of Sodom, Birsha of Gomorrah, Shinab

lift up your eyes

In Genesis 13, we read that the herdsmen of Abraham and his nephew, Lot, were arguing because there was not enough space for both their flocks and herds to graze. Abraham suggested that Lot go one way and said that he would go the other way so there would be enough room for both their animals and households. Lot chose the best land for himself and left Abraham with an inferior portion (see Genesis 13:10, 11).

At that point, the Lord said to Abraham, "Lift up now your eyes and look from the place where you are, northward and southward and eastward and westward; for all the land which you see I will give to you and to your posterity forever" (Genesis 13:14, 15).

We would do well to remember this story today. Instead of becoming discouraged, depressed, or angry when people disappoint us, God wants us to lift up our eyes, look around, and trust Him to lead us into an even better situation. He wants us to look around and count our blessings instead of focusing on what we *do not* have. He wants us to fix our eyes on Him, not on the work of the enemy, because He has plans to bless us and bring us increase.

of Admah, Shemeber of Zeboiim, and the king of Bela, ᶻthat is, Zoar.

3   The latter kings joined together [as allies] in the Valley of Siddim, which is [now] the [Dead] Sea of Salt.

4   Twelve years they had served Chedorlaomer, but in the thirteenth year they rebelled.

5   And in the fourteenth year, Chedorlaomer and the kings who were with him attacked *and* subdued the Rephaim in Ashteroth-karnaim, the Zuzim in Ham, and the Emim in Shaveh-kiriathaim,

6   And the Horites in their Mount Seir as far as El-paran, which is on the border of the wilderness.

7   Then they turned back and came to En-mishpat, which [now] is Kadesh, and subdued all the country of the Amalekites, and also the Amorites who dwelt in Hazazon-tamar.

8   Then the kings of Sodom, Gomorrah, Admah, Zeboiim, and Bela, that is, Zoar, went out and [together] they joined battle [with those kings] in the Valley of Siddim,

9   With the kings Chedorlaomer of Elam, Tidal of Goiim, Amraphel of Shinar, and Arioch of Ellasar—four kings against five.

10   Now the Valley of Siddim was full of slime *or* bitumen pits, and as the kings of Sodom and Gomorrah fled, they fell (were overthrown) there and the remainder [of the kings] fled to the mountain.

11   [The victors] took all the wealth of Sodom and Gomorrah and all the supply of provisions and departed.

12   And they also took Lot, Abram's brother's son, who dwelt in Sodom, and his goods away with them.

13   Then one who had escaped came and told Abram the Hebrew [one from the other side], who was living by the oaks *or* terebinths of Mamre the Amorite, a brother of Eshcol and of Aner—these were allies of Abram.

14   When Abram heard that [his nephew] had been captured, he armed (led forth) the 318 trained servants born in his own house and pursued the enemy as far as Dan.

15   He divided his forces against them by night, he and his servants, and attacked *and* routed them, and pursued them as far as Hobah, which is north of Damascus.

16   And he brought back all the goods and also brought back his kinsman Lot and his possessions, the women also and the people.

17   After his [Abram's] return from the defeat *and* slaying of Chedorlaomer and the kings who were with him, the king of Sodom went out to meet him at the Valley of Shaveh, that is, the King's Valley.

18   Melchizedek king of Salem [later called Jerusalem] brought out bread and wine [for their nourishment]; he was the priest of God Most High,

19   And he blessed him and said, Blessed (favored with blessings, made blissful, joyful) be Abram by God Most High, Possessor *and* Maker of heaven and earth,

20   And blessed, praised, *and* glorified be God Most High, Who has given your foes into your hand! And [Abram] gave him a tenth of all [he had taken]. [Heb. 7:1-10.]

21   And the king of Sodom said to Abram, Give me the persons and keep the goods for yourself.

22   But Abram said to the king of Sodom, I have lifted up my hand *and* sworn to the Lord, God Most High, the Possessor *and* Maker of heaven and earth,

23   That I would not take a thread or

z One of the notable proofs of the antiquity of the early sections of Genesis is that many of the original names of places about which they speak were so old that Moses, the writer, had to add an explanation in order to identify these ancient names so that the Israelites returning from Egypt might recognize them. Chapter 14 alone contains six such explanatory notes (Gen. 14:2, 3, 7, 8, 15, and 17).

a shoelace or anything that is yours, lest you should say, I have made Abram rich.

24 [Take all] except only what my young men have eaten and the share of the men [allies] who went with me—Aner, Eshcol, and Mamre; let them take their portion.

15 AFTER THESE things, the word of the Lord came to Abram in a vision, saying, Fear not, Abram, I am your ªShield, your abundant compensation, *and* your reward shall be exceedingly great.

life point

If Abraham had bowed his knee to fear, the rest of the story would never have come to pass. He would never have experienced God as his Shield and his great compensation, and he would never have received his exceedingly great reward (see Genesis 15:1).

2 And Abram said, Lord God, what can You give me, since I am going on [from this world] childless and he who shall be the owner *and* heir of my house is this [steward] Eliezer of Damascus?

3 And Abram continued, Look, You have given me no child; and [a ser-vant] born in my house is my heir.

4 And behold, the word of the Lord came to him, saying, This man shall not be your heir, but he who shall come from your own body shall be your heir.

5 And He brought him outside [his tent into the starlight] and said, Look now toward the heavens and count the stars—if you are able to number them. Then He said to him, So shall your descendants be. [Heb. 11:12.]

6 And he [Abram] believed in (trusted in, relied on, remained stead-fast to) the Lord, and He counted it to him as righteousness (right standing with God). [Rom. 4:3, 18-22; Gal. 3:6; James 2:23.]

7 And He said to him, I am the [same] Lord, Who brought you out of Ur of the Chaldees to give you this land as an inheritance.

8 But he [Abram] said, Lord God, by what shall I know that I shall inherit it?

9 And He said to him, Bring to Me a heifer three years old, a she-goat three years old, a ram three years old, a turtledove, and a young pigeon.

10 And he brought Him all these and cut them down the middle [into halves] and laid each half opposite the other; but the birds he did not divide.

11 And when the birds of prey swooped down upon the carcasses, Abram drove them away.

12 When the sun was setting, a deep sleep overcame Abram, and a horror (a terror, a shuddering fear) of great darkness assailed *and* oppressed him.

13 And [God] said to Abram, Know positively that your descendants will be strangers dwelling as temporary residents in a land that is not theirs [Egypt], and they will be slaves there and will be afflicted *and* oppressed

speak the Word

God, I will not fear, because You are my Shield and my abundant compensation. In You my reward shall be exceedingly great.
ADAPTED FROM GENESIS 15:1

a The reference is to the Lord as Abram's King.

give God time

Abraham had a definite word from God about his future. He knew what God had promised, but he had no indication about when the promise would be fulfilled. The same is often true for us. While we are waiting for our manifestation to come forth—waiting for a breakthrough—we may grow frustrated or impatient. Sitting in the waiting room of life is not always easy!

Once God speaks to us or shows us something, we tend to be excited and focus on that revelation. It is as though we are "pregnant" with what God has said. He has planted a seed in us—and then we have to enter a time of preparation before that seed can bear fruit. These seasons of preparation equip us to handle whatever God has promised to give us or do for us.

This process parallels the development and birth of a child. First, a seed is planted in the mother's womb, then a time of preparation (nine months of waiting) is required, and then, finally, the baby is born. During the nine months, so much happens in the mother and in the child. The seed grows to maturity, while the mother's body prepares to give birth, and the family prepares everything necessary for a new baby in the house.

Just as so much development takes place in the hidden place of the mother's womb, there is also much activity taking place in the spiritual realm concerning God's promises in our lives—and we cannot see this, any more than we can watch cells multiply in an unborn baby. The fact that we cannot see or feel any progress does not mean nothing is happening. God does some of His best work in secret; He delights in surprising His children. Whether you know it or not, God is busy bringing good things to pass for you, right this minute! Just give Him time—and you will see.

for 400 years. [Fulfilled in Exod. 12:40.]

14 But I will bring judgment on that nation whom they will serve, and afterward they will come out with great possessions. [Acts 7:6, 7.]

15 And you shall go to your fathers in peace; you shall be buried at a good old (hoary) age.

16 And in the [b]fourth generation they [your descendants] shall come back here [to Canaan] again, for the iniquity of the [c]Amorites is not yet full *and* complete. [Josh. 24:15.]

17 When the sun had gone down and a [thick] darkness had come on, behold, a smoking oven and a flaming torch passed between those pieces.

18 On the same day the Lord made a covenant (promise, pledge) with Abram, saying, To your descendants I

b This prophecy was literally fulfilled. Moses, for example, who led the Israelites back to Canaan after their 400 years in Egypt, was "in the fourth generation" from Jacob—Levi, Kohath, Amram, Moses.　**c** The most important and powerful group of that region. The name "Amorite" later became virtually synonymous with that of the inhabitants of Canaan generally have given this land, from the river of Egypt to the great river Euphrates—the land of

19 The Kenites, the Kenizzites, the Kadmonites,

20 The Hittites, the Perizzites, the Rephaim,

21 The Amorites, the Canaanites, the Girgashites, and the Jebusites.

16 NOW SARAI, Abram's wife, had borne him no children. She had an Egyptian maid whose name was Hagar.

2 And Sarai said to Abram, See here, the Lord has restrained me from bearing [children]. I am asking you to have intercourse with my maid; it may be that I can obtain children by her. And Abram listened to *and* heeded what Sarai said.

3 So Sarai, Abram's wife, took Hagar her Egyptian maid, after Abram had dwelt ten years in the land of Canaan, and gave her to her husband Abram to be his [secondary] wife.

4 And he had intercourse with Hagar, and she became pregnant; and when she saw that she was with child, she looked with contempt upon her mistress *and* despised her.

5 Then Sarai said to Abram, May [the responsibility for] my wrong *and* deprivation of rights be upon you! I gave my maid into your bosom, and when she saw that she was with child,

I was contemptible *and* despised in her eyes. May the Lord be the judge between you and me.

6 But Abram said to Sarai, See here, your maid is in your hands *and* power; do as you please with her. And when Sarai dealt severely with her, humbling *and* afflicting her, she [Hagar] fled from her.

7 But ᵈthe Angel of the Lord found her by a spring of water in the wilderness on the road to Shur.

8 And He said, Hagar, Sarai's maid, where did you come from, and where are you intending to go? And she said, I am running away from my mistress Sarai.

9 The Angel of the Lord said to her, Go back to your mistress and [humbly] submit to her control.

10 Also the Angel of the Lord said to her, I will multiply your descendants exceedingly, so that they shall not be numbered for multitude.

11 And the Angel of the Lord continued, See now, you are with child and shall bear a son, and shall call his name Ishmael [God hears], because the Lord has heard *and* paid attention to your affliction.

12 And he [Ishmael] will be as a ᵉwild ass among men; his hand will be against every man and every man's hand against him, and he will live to the east *and* on the borders of all his kinsmen.

---

d "The Angel of the Lord" or "of God," or "of His presence" is readily identified with the Lord God (Gen. 16:11, 13; 22:11, 12; 31:11, 13; Exod. 3:1-6 and other passages). But it is obvious that the "Angel of the Lord" is a distinct person in Himself from God the Father (Gen. 24:7; Exod. 23:20; Zech. 1:12, 13 and other passages). Nor does the "Angel of the Lord" appear again after Christ came in human form. He must of necessity be One of the "three-in-one" Godhead. The "Angel of the Lord" is the visible Lord God of the Old Testament, as Jesus Christ is of the New Testament. Thus His deity is clearly portrayed in the Old Testament. *The Cambridge Bible* observes, "There is a fascinating forecast of the coming Messiah, breaking through the dimness with amazing consistency, at intervals from Genesis to Malachi. Abraham, Moses, the slave girl Hagar, the impoverished farmer Gideon, even the humble parents of Samson, had seen and talked with Him centuries before the herald angels proclaimed His birth in Bethlehem." **e** "Nothing can be more descriptive of the wandering, lawless, freebooting life of the Arabs than this. From the beginning to the present they have kept their independence, and God preserves them as a lasting monument of His providential care and an incontestable argument of the truth of divine revelation. Had the books of Moses no other proof of their divine origin, the account of Ishmael and the prophecy concerning his descendants during a period of nearly 4,000 years would be sufficient. To attempt to refute it would be a most ridiculous presumption and folly" (Adam Clarke, *The Holy Bible with A Commentary*).

don't have an Ishmael

Abram and Sarai got tired of waiting. They were weary as they watched for God's promise to come to pass, and they wondered if they might do something to help move things along. Sarai decided to see if her handmaid, Hagar, would conceive a child by Abram (see Genesis 16:2). She thought that could be God's way of giving her and Abram the child He promised. God had promised Abram a son *by Sarai* (see Genesis 17:16), but since it appeared God was not doing anything, she must have reasoned, she knew how to help!

Does that sound familiar? Have you ever tried or wanted to "help" God in your life?

In Sarai's case, Abram heeded her advice and Hagar conceived. The child, named Ishmael, was indeed a son, as God had spoken, but he was not the child of the promise. Abram and Sarai waited another fourteen years before Isaac, the true promised son, arrived. I wonder if it took so long because once we give birth to the "Ishmaels" in our lives, we must deal with the consequences. In other words, once an Ishmael is born, we have to change his diapers and take care of him!

We would like to carry out our own plans and then have God bless them, but He taught me years ago that He is not obligated to bless or care for the things I give birth to out of the strength of my flesh. The psalmist affirms this point: "Except the Lord builds the house, they labor in vain who build it" (Psalm 127:1).

God has great things in store for you, and He will bring them to pass in His perfect timing. Let me encourage you to wait on Him. An Ishmael will be a burden in your life, but God's "Isaacs" will bring blessing and delight.

13 So she called the name of the Lord Who spoke to her, You are a God of seeing, for she said, Have I [not] even here [in the wilderness] looked upon Him Who sees me [and lived]? *Or* have I here also seen [the future purposes or designs of] Him Who sees me?
14 Therefore the well was called Beer-lahai-roi [A well to the Living One Who sees me]; it is ᶠbetween Kadesh and Bered.
15 And Hagar bore Abram a son, and Abram called the name of his son whom Hagar bore ᵍIshmael.

16 Abram was eighty-six years old when Hagar bore Ishmael.

17 WHEN ABRAM was ninety-nine years old, the Lord appeared to him and said, I am the Almighty God; walk *and* live habitually before Me and be perfect (blameless, wholehearted, complete).
2 And I will make My covenant (solemn pledge) between Me and you and will multiply you exceedingly.
3 Then Abram fell on his face, and God said to him,

f This, "it is between Kadesh and Bered," is further proof of the antiquity of the original names, since the place had to be identified to the reader in the time of Moses. g Ishmael was the first person whom God named before his birth (Gen. 16:11). Others were: Isaac (Gen. 17:19); Josiah (I Kings 13:2); Solomon (I Chron. 22:9); Jesus (Matt. 1:21); and John the Baptist (Luke 1:13).

4 As for Me, behold, My covenant (solemn pledge) is with you, and you shall be the father of many nations.
5 Nor shall your name any longer be Abram [high, exalted father]; but your name shall be Abraham [father of a multitude], for I have made you the father of many nations.
6 And I will make you exceedingly fruitful and I will make nations of you, and ʰkings will come from you.
7 And I will establish My covenant between Me and you and your descendants after you throughout their generations for an everlasting, solemn pledge, to be a God to you and to your posterity after you. [Gal. 3:16.]
8 And I will give to you and to your posterity after you the land in which you are a stranger [going from place to place], all the land of Canaan, for an everlasting possession; and I will be their God. [Acts 7:5.]
9 And God said to Abraham, As for you, you shall therefore keep My covenant, you and your descendants after you throughout their generations.
10 This is My covenant, which you shall keep, between Me and you and your posterity after you: Every male among you shall be circumcised.
11 And you shall circumcise the flesh of your foreskin, and it shall be a token *or* sign of the covenant (the promise or pledge) between Me and you.
12 He who is eight days old among you shall be circumcised, every male throughout your generations, whether born in [your] house or bought with [your] money from any foreigner not of your offspring.

speak the Word

life point

When God entered into covenant with Abraham, He told him to circumcise himself and all the males eight days old and older (see Genesis 17:10–12). Blood was shed at what we might refer to as "the fountain of life"—the place from which the seed for future generations would come—and circumcision was a sign of the covenant between God and Abraham.

Blood is a powerful element, and that is because life is in the blood (see Leviticus 17:11). When anything is covered by blood, in God's way of looking at it, it is covered with life and thus cleansed. Therefore, when we receive Jesus as our Savior, we are covered by His blood, and God sees us as clean and pure before Him.

13 He that is born in your house and he that is bought with your money must be circumcised; and My covenant shall be in your flesh for an everlasting covenant.
14 And the male who is not circumcised, that soul shall be cut off from his people; he has broken My covenant.
15 And God said to Abraham, As for Sarai your wife, you shall not call her name Sarai; but Sarah [Princess] her name shall be.
16 And I will bless her and give you a son also by her. Yes, I will bless her, and she shall be a mother of nations; kings of peoples shall come from her.

Thank You, God, for making me to walk and live before You and to be blameless, wholehearted, and complete.
ADAPTED FROM GENESIS **17:1**

ʰ This prophecy and promise has been literally fulfilled countless times—for example, by all of the kings of Israel and Judah.

what's in a name?

Names meant so much more to people during Bible times than they do to many of us today. Even here in the early chapters of the Bible, we see that names were tremendously important, for they described a person's character.

In Genesis 17, we read that God gave new names to Abram and Sarai (see Genesis 17:4, 5; 15, 16). He was changing things in their lives, and He wanted to give them new names to declare what He was doing in and through them. Abram and Sarai knew well the importance of names, so they understood the profound significance of God's changing their names. When He gave them new names, He was beginning to speak of "nonexistent things" as though they already existed (see Romans 4:17). The name changes indicated to Abram and Sarai that God was beginning to fulfill His promise when He said to Abram: "Look now toward the heavens and count the stars—if you are able to number them. Then He said to him, So shall your descendants be" (Genesis 15:5).

So what's in a name? A lot more than many of us realize. Think about Sarai, for instance. She was a barren woman, who probably had a poor self-image because, in biblical societies, so much of a woman's worth depended on her ability to bear children. She was an old woman, and, biologically, she had no hope of ever being able to conceive and deliver a baby. But God changed her name.

Sarah means "princess." So when Abraham or anyone else called Sarai by her new name, Sarah, they were helping her change her image of herself. They were calling her beautiful and valuable, a king's daughter—and they were speaking forth the image of the mother God had destined her to be. As a result, she must have begun to see herself differently. She must have felt faith rising in her heart. She must have begun to be sure God would keep His word to her.

Similarly, Abram must have undergone his own transformation and had his own faith bolstered when God changed his name to Abraham, meaning "father of a multitude."

Following this idea through to the New Testament and to our lives today, I encourage you to remember the significance of a name when you speak the name of Jesus. Remember, His is not just a name; it is a word loaded with meaning and filled with life. It declares His character; it proclaims all that He is, all He has done, and all He will do in your life.

---

17 Then Abraham fell on his face and laughed and said in his heart, Shall a child be born to a man who is a hundred years old? And shall Sarah, who is ninety years old, bear a son? **18** And [he] said to God, Oh, that Ishmael might live before You! **19** But God said, Sarah your wife shall bear you a son indeed, and you shall call his name Isaac [laughter]; and I will establish My covenant *or* solemn pledge with him for an everlasting covenant and with his posterity after him. **20** And as for Ishmael, I have heard *and* heeded you: behold, I will bless him and will make him fruitful and will multiply him exceedingly; He will be the father of twelve princes, and I will make him a great nation. [Fulfilled in Gen. 25:12-18.]

21 But My covenant, My promise and pledge, I will establish with Isaac, whom Sarah will bear to you at this season next year.

22 And God stopped talking with him and went up from Abraham.

23 And Abraham took Ishmael his son and all who were born in his house and all who were bought with his money, every male among [those] of Abraham's house, and circumcised [them] the very same day, as God had said to him.

24 And Abraham was ninety-nine years old when he was circumcised.

25 And Ishmael his son was thirteen years old when he was circumcised.

26 On the very same day Abraham was circumcised, and Ishmael his son as well.

27 And all the men of his house, both those born in the house and those bought with money from a foreigner, were circumcised along with him.

18 NOW THE Lord appeared to Abraham by the oaks *or* terebinths of Mamre; as he sat at the door of his tent in the heat of the day,

2 He lifted up his eyes and looked, and behold, three men stood at a little distance from him. He ran from the tent door to meet them and bowed himself to the ground

3 And said, My lord, if now I have found favor in your sight, do not pass by your servant, I beg of you.

4 Let a little water be brought, and you may wash your feet and recline *and* rest yourselves under the tree.

5 And I will bring a morsel (mouthful) of bread to refresh *and* sustain your hearts before you go on further—for that is why you have come to your servant. And they replied, Do as you have said.

6 So Abraham hastened into the tent to Sarah and said, Quickly get ready three measures of fine meal, knead it, and bake cakes.

7 And Abraham ran to the herd and brought a calf tender and good and gave it to the young man [to butcher]; then he [Abraham] hastened to prepare it.

8 And he took curds and milk and the calf which he had made ready, and set it before [the men]; and he stood by them under the tree while they ate.

9 And they said to him, Where is Sarah your wife? And he said, [She is here] in the tent.

10 i[The Lord] said, I will surely return to you when the season comes round, and behold, Sarah your wife will have a son. And Sarah was listening *and* heard it at the tent door which was behind Him. [Rom. 9:9-12.]

11 Now Abraham and Sarah were old, well advanced in years; it had ceased to be with Sarah as with [young] women. [She was past the age of childbearing].

12 Therefore Sarah laughed to herself, saying, After I have become aged shall I have pleasure *and* delight, my lord (husband), being old also? [I Pet. 3:6.]

13 And the Lord asked Abraham, Why did Sarah laugh, saying, Shall I really bear a child when I am so old?

14 Is anything too hard *or* too wonderful ʲfor the Lord? At the appointed

i One of the three guests was the Lord, and since God the Father was never seen in bodily form (John 1:18), only the "Angel of the covenant," Christ Himself, can be meant here; see especially Gen. 18:22 and also the footnote on Gen. 16:7.   j The word "Lord" as applied to God is obviously the most important word in the Bible, for it occurs oftener than any other important word—by actual count more than 5,000 times. **Nothing** is "too hard *or* too wonderful" for Him when He is truly made Lord.

time, when the season [for her delivery] comes around, I will return to you and Sarah shall have borne a son. [Matt. 19:26.]

15 Then Sarah denied it, saying, I did not laugh; for she was afraid. And He said, No, but you did laugh.

16 The men rose up from there and faced toward Sodom, and Abraham went with them to bring them on the way.

17 And the Lord said, Shall I hide from Abraham [My friend and servant] what I am going to do, [Gal. 3:8.]

18 Since Abraham shall surely become a great and mighty nation, and all the nations of the earth shall be blessed through him *and* shall bless themselves by him? [Gen. 12:2-3.]

19 For I have known (chosen, acknowledged) him [as My own], so that he may teach *and* command his children and the sons of his house after him to keep the way of the Lord and to do what is just and righteous, so that the Lord may bring Abraham what He has promised him.

20 And the Lord said, Because the shriek [of the sins] of Sodom and Gomorrah is great and their sin is exceedingly grievous,

21 I will go down now and see whether they have done altogether [as vilely and wickedly] as is the cry of it which has come to Me; and if not, I will know.

22 Now the [two] men turned from there and went toward Sodom, but Abraham still stood before the Lord.

23 And Abraham came close and said, Will You destroy the righteous (those upright and in right standing with God) together with the wicked?

24 Suppose there are in the city fifty righteous; will You destroy the place and not spare it for [the sake of] the fifty righteous in it?

25 Far be it from You to do such a thing—to slay the righteous with the wicked, so that the righteous fare as do the wicked! Far be it from You! Shall not the Judge of all the earth execute judgment *and* do righteously?

26 And the Lord said, If I find in the city of Sodom fifty righteous (upright and in right standing with God), I will spare the whole place for their sake.

27 Abraham answered, Behold now, I who am but dust and ashes have taken upon myself to speak to the Lord.

28 If five of the fifty righteous should be lacking—will You destroy the whole city for lack of five? He said, If I find forty-five, I will not destroy it.

29 And [Abraham] spoke to Him yet again, and said, Suppose [only] forty shall be found there. And He said, I will not do it for forty's sake.

30 Then [Abraham] said to Him, Oh, let not the Lord be angry, and I will speak [again]. Suppose [only] thirty shall be found there. And He answered, I will not do it if I find thirty there.

31 And [Abraham] said, Behold now, I have taken upon myself to speak [again] to the Lord. Suppose [only] twenty shall be found there. And [the Lord] replied, I will not destroy it for twenty's sake.

32 And he said, Oh, let not the Lord be angry, and I will speak again only this once. Suppose ten [righteous people] shall be found there. And [the Lord] said, I will not destroy it for ten's sake.

33 And the Lord went His way when He had finished speaking with Abraham, and Abraham returned to his place.

speak the Word

19

IT WAS evening when the two angels came to Sodom. Lot was sitting at Sodom's [city] gate. Seeing them, Lot rose up to meet them and bowed to the ground.

2   And he said, My lords, turn aside, I beg of you, into your servant's house and spend the night and bathe your feet. Then you can arise early and go on your way. But they said, No, we will spend the night in the square.

3   [Lot] entreated *and* urged them greatly until they yielded and [with him] entered his house. And he made them a dinner [with drinking] and had unleavened bread which he baked, and they ate.

4   But before they lay down, the men of the city of Sodom, both young and old, all the men from every quarter, surrounded the house.

5   And they called to Lot and said, Where are the men who came to you tonight? Bring them out to us, that we may know (be intimate with) them.

6   And Lot went out of the door to the men and shut the door after him

7   And said, I beg of you, my brothers, do not behave so wickedly.

8   Look now, I have two daughters who are virgins; let me, I beg of you, bring them out to you, and you can do as you please with them. But only do nothing to these men, for they have come under the protection of my roof.

9   But they said, Stand back! And they said, This fellow came in to live here temporarily, and now he presumes to be [our] judge! Now we will deal worse with you than with them. So they rushed at *and* pressed violently against Lot and came close to breaking down the door.

10 But the men [the angels] reached out and pulled Lot into the house to them and shut the door after him.

11 And they struck the men who were at the door of the house with blindness [which dazzled them], from the youths to the old men, so that they wearied themselves [groping] to find the door.

12 And the [two] men asked Lot, Have you any others here—sons-in-law or your sons or your daughters? Whomever you have in the city, bring them out of this place,

13 For we will spoil *and* destroy [Sodom]; for the outcry *and* shriek against its people has grown great before the Lord, and He has sent us to destroy it.

14 And Lot went out and spoke to his sons-in-law, who were to marry his daughters, and said, Up, get out of this place, for the Lord will spoil *and* destroy this city! But he seemed to his sons-in-law to be [only] joking.

15 When morning came, the angels urged Lot to hurry, saying, Arise, take your wife and two daughters who are here [and be off], lest you [too] be consumed *and* swept away in the iniquity *and* punishment of the city.

16 But while he lingered, the men seized him and his wife and his two daughters by the hand, for the Lord was merciful to him; and they brought him forth and set him outside the city and left him there.

17 And when they had brought them forth, they said, Escape for your life! Do not look behind you or stop anywhere in ᵏthe whole valley; escape to the mountains [of Moab], lest you be consumed.

18 And Lot said to them, Oh, not that, my lords!

19 Behold now, your servant has found favor in your sight, and you have magnified your kindness and mercy to me in saving my life; but I cannot escape to the mountains, lest the evil overtake me, and I die.

20 See now yonder city; it is near enough to flee to, and it is a little one.

k The valley which Lot had once so much coveted (Gen. 13:10, 11).

Oh, let me escape to it! Is it not a little one? And my life will be saved!

21 And [the angel] said to him, See, I have yielded to your entreaty concerning this thing also; I will not destroy this city of which you have spoken.

22 Make haste and take refuge there, for I cannot do anything until you arrive there. Therefore the name of the city was called Zoar [little].

23 The sun had risen over the earth when Lot entered Zoar.

24 Then the Lord rained on Sodom and on Gomorrah brimstone and fire from the Lord out of the heavens.

25 He overthrew, destroyed, *and* ended those cities, and all the valley and all the inhabitants of the cities, and what grew on the ground.

26 But [Lot's] wife looked back from behind him, and she ˡbecame a pillar of salt.

27 Abraham went up early the next morning to the place where he [only the day before] had stood before the Lord.

28 And he looked toward Sodom and Gomorrah, and toward all the land of the valley, and saw, and behold, the smoke of ᵐthe country went up like the smoke of a furnace.

29 When God ravaged *and* destroyed the cities of the plain [of Siddim], He [earnestly] remembered Abraham [imprinted and fixed him indelibly on His mind], and He sent Lot out of the midst of the overthrow when He overthrew the cities where Lot lived.

30 And Lot went up out of Zoar and dwelt in the mountain, and his two

putting the Word to work

Lot and his wife had to leave the city where they lived in order to escape the destruction God would bring upon that city because of the sin there. They were instructed not to look back as they left the city. In what situations in your life do you need to heed God's instruction not to look back? How can you look ahead instead of behind you in those areas?

daughters with him, for he feared to dwell in Zoar; and he lived in a cave, he and his two daughters.

31 The elder said to the younger, Our father is aging, and there is not a man on earth to live with us in the customary way.

32 Come, let us make our father drunk with wine, and we will lie with him, so that we may preserve offspring (our race) through our father.

33 And they made their father drunk with wine that night, and the older went in and lay with her father; and he was not aware of it when she lay down or when she arose.

34 Then the next day the firstborn said to the younger, See here, I lay last night with my father; let us make him drunk with wine tonight also, and then you go in and lie with him, so that we may preserve offspring (our race) through our father.

35 And they made their father drunk with wine again that night, and the younger arose and lay with him; and he was not aware of it when she lay down or when she arose.

l Lot's wife not only "looked back" to where her heart's interests were, but she lingered behind; and probably overtaken by the fire and brimstone, her dead body became incrusted with salt, which, in that salt-packed area now the Dead Sea, grew larger with more incrustations—a veritable "pillar of salt." In fact, at the southern end of the Dead Sea there is a mountain of table salt called Jebel Usdum, "Mount of Sodom." It is about six miles long, three miles wide, and 1,000 feet high. It is covered with a crust of earth several feet thick, but the rest of the mountain is said to be solid salt (George T. B. Davis, *Rebuilding Palestine According to Prophecy*). Somewhere in this area Lot's wife looked back to where her treasures and her heart were, and "she became a pillar of salt." Jesus said, "Remember Lot's wife" (Luke 17:32).   **m** Not only were Sodom and Gomorrah blazing ruins, but also Admah and Zeboiim (Deut. 29:23; Hos. 11:8), as well as all the towns in the Valley of Siddim; Zoar was the lone exception.

36 Thus both the daughters of Lot were with child by their father.
37 The older bore a son, and named him Moab [of a father]; he is the father of the Moabites to this day.
38 The younger also bore a son and named him Ben-ammi [son of my people]; he is the father of the Ammonites to this day.

20 NOW ABRAHAM journeyed from there toward the ⁿSouth country (the Negeb) and dwelt between Kadesh and Shur; and he lived temporarily in Gerar.
2 And Abraham said of Sarah his wife, She is my sister. And Abimelech king of Gerar sent and took Sarah [into his harem].
3 But God came to Abimelech in a dream by night and said, Behold, you are a dead man because of the woman whom you have taken [as your own], for she is a man's wife.
4 But Abimelech had not come near her, so he said, Lord, will you slay a people who are just *and* innocent?
5 Did not the man tell me, She is my sister? And she herself said, He is my brother. In integrity of heart and innocency of hands I have done this.
6 Then God said to him in the dream, Yes, I know you did this in the integrity of your heart, for it was I Who kept you back *and* spared you from sinning against Me; therefore I did not give you occasion to touch her.
7 So now restore to the man his wife, for he is a prophet, and he will pray for you and you will live. But if you do not restore her [to him], know that you shall surely die, you and all who are yours.
8 So Abimelech rose early in the morning and called all his servants and told them all these things; and the men were exceedingly filled with reverence *and* fear.
9 Then Abimelech called Abraham and said to him, What have you done to us? And how have I offended you that you have brought on me and my kingdom a great sin? You have done to me what ought not to be done [to anyone].
10 And Abimelech said to Abraham, What did you see [in us] that [justified] you in doing such a thing as this?
11 And Abraham said, Because I thought, Surely there is no reverence *or* fear of God at all in this place, and they will slay me because of my wife.
12 But truly, she is my sister; she is the daughter of my father but not of my mother; and she became my wife.
13 When God caused me to wander from my father's house, I said to her, This kindness you can show me: at every place we stop, say of me, He is my brother.
14 Then Abimelech took sheep and oxen and male and female slaves and gave them to Abraham and restored to him Sarah his wife.
15 And Abimelech said, Behold, my land is before you; dwell wherever it pleases you.
16 And to Sarah he said, Behold, I have given this brother of yours a thousand pieces of silver; see, it is to compensate you [for all that has occurred] and to vindicate your honor before all who are with you; before all men you are cleared *and* compensated.
17 So Abraham prayed to God, and God healed Abimelech and his wife and his female slaves, and they bore children,
18 For the Lord had closed fast the

---

n "Primitive geographic expressions such as 'the South country (the Negeb)' (Gen. 12:9; 13:1, 3; 20:1; 24:62) and 'the east country' (Gen. 25:6) are used in the time of Abraham . . . After the time of Genesis they have well-known and well-defined names; I submit that they were written down in early days, and that no writer after Moses could have used such archaic expressions as these" (P. J. Wiseman, *New Discoveries in Babylonia About Genesis*).

wombs of all in Abimelech's household because of Sarah, Abraham's wife.

21 THE LORD visited Sarah as He had said, and the Lord did for her as He had promised.

2 For Sarah became pregnant and bore Abraham a son in his old age, at the set time God had told him.

3 Abraham °named his son whom Sarah bore to him Isaac [laughter].

4 And Abraham circumcised his son Isaac when he was eight days old, as God had commanded him.

5 Abraham was a hundred years old when Isaac was born.

6 And Sarah said, God has made me to laugh; all who hear will laugh with me.

7 And she said, Who would have said to Abraham that Sarah would nurse children at the breast? For I have borne him a son in his old age! [Heb. 11:12.]

8 And the child grew and was ᵖweaned, and Abraham made a great feast the same day that Isaac was weaned.

9 Now Sarah saw the son of Hagar the Egyptian, whom she had borne to Abraham, mocking [Isaac].

10 Therefore she said to Abraham, Cast out this bondwoman and her son, for the son of this bondwoman shall not be an heir with my son Isaac. [Gal. 4:28-31.]

11 And the thing was very grievous (serious, evil) in Abraham's sight on account of his son [Ishmael].

12 God said to Abraham, Do not let it seem grievous *and* evil to you because of the youth and your bondwoman; in

putting the Word to work

Abraham and Sarah had to wait a long time before God's promise came to pass, but it finally did, as we read in Genesis 21:1–3. What promises of God are you waiting to have fulfilled in your life? How can you be like Abraham and wait with a heart full of faith?

all that Sarah has said to you, do what she asks, for in Isaac shall your posterity be called. [Rom. 9:7.]

13 And I will make a nation of the son of the bondwoman also, because he is your offspring.

14 So Abraham rose early in the morning and took bread and a bottle of water and gave them to Hagar, putting them on her shoulders, and he sent her and the �qyouth away. And she wandered on [aimlessly] and lost her way in the wilderness of Beersheba.

15 When the water in the bottle was all gone, Hagar caused the youth to lie down under one of the shrubs.

16 Then she went and sat down opposite him a good way off, about a bowshot, for she said, Let me not see the death of the lad. And as she sat down opposite him, ʳhe lifted up his voice and wept *and* she raised her voice and wept.

17 And God heard the voice of the youth, and the angel of God called to Hagar out of heaven and said to her, What troubles you, Hagar? Fear not, for God has heard the voice of the youth where he is.

18 Arise, raise up the youth and support him with your hand, for I intend to make him a great nation.

19 Then God opened her eyes and

o See footnote on Gen. 16:15.   p This was probably when the child was about three years of age. Samuel served in the sanctuary from the time that he was weaned (I Sam. 1:22-28). A Hebrew mother is quoted in II Maccabees 7:27 as saying to her son that she gave him "suck three years."   q Ishmael was born when Abraham was eighty-six years old (Gen. 16:16), so Ishmael was fourteen when Isaac was born. Isaac was weaned (Gen. 21:8) at least three years later probably (II Chron. 31:16; II Maccabees 7:27).   r The Hebrew says, "she lifted up her voice." *The Septuagint* (Greek translation of the Old Testament) says "he . . ."—which the next verse seems to support. The circumstances allow either.

she saw a well of water; and she went and filled the [empty] bottle with water and caused the youth to drink.

20 And God was with the youth, and he developed; and he dwelt in the wilderness and became an archer.

21 He dwelt in the Wilderness of Paran; and his mother took a wife for him out of the land of Egypt.

22 At that time Abimelech and Phicol the commander of his army said to Abraham, God is with you in everything you do.

23 So now, swear to me here by God that you will not deal falsely with me or with my son or with my posterity; but as I have dealt with you kindly, you will do the same with me and with the land in which you have sojourned.

24 And Abraham said, I will swear.

25 When Abraham complained to *and* reasoned with Abimelech about a well of water [Abimelech's] servants had violently seized,

26 Abimelech said, I know not who did this thing; you did not tell me, and I did not hear of it until today.

27 So Abraham took sheep and oxen and gave them to Abimelech, and the two men made a league *or* covenant.

28 Abraham set apart seven ewe lambs of the flock,

29 And Abimelech said to Abraham, What do these seven ewe lambs which you have set apart mean?

30 He said, You are to accept these seven ewe lambs from me as a witness for me that I dug this well.

31 Therefore that place was called Beersheba [well of the oath], because there both parties swore an oath.

32 Thus they made a covenant at Beersheba; then Abimelech and Phicol the commander of his army returned to the land of the Philistines.

33 Abraham planted a tamarisk tree in Beersheba and called there on the name of the Lord, the Eternal God.

34 And Abraham sojourned in Philistia many days.

22 AFTER THESE events, God tested *and* proved Abraham and said to him, Abraham! And he said, Here I am.

2 [God] said, Take now your son, your only son Isaac, whom you love, and go to the region of Moriah; and offer him there as a burnt offering upon one of the mountains of which I will tell you.

3 So Abraham rose early in the morning, saddled his donkey, and took two of his young men with him and his son Isaac; and he split the wood for the burnt offering, and then began the trip to the place of which God had told him.

4 On the third day Abraham looked up and saw the place in the distance.

5 And Abraham said to his servants, Settle down *and* stay here with the donkey, and I and the young man will go yonder and worship and ˢcome again to you.

6 Then Abraham took the wood for the burnt offering and laid it on [the shoulders of] Isaac his son, and he took the fire (the firepot) in his own hand, and a knife; and the two of them went on together.

7 And Isaac said to Abraham, My father! And he said, Here I am, my son. [Isaac] said, See, here are the fire and the wood, but where is the lamb for the burnt sacrifice?

8 Abraham said, My son, ᵗGod

---

s Abraham was not lying to his servants or trying to deceive them. He believed God, Who had promised him that this young man's posterity was to inherit the promises made to Abraham (Gen. 12:2, 3).
t We must not suppose that this was the language merely of faith and obedience. Abraham spoke prophetically, and referred to that Lamb of God which He had provided for Himself, Who in the fullness of time would take away the sin of the world, and of Whom Isaac was a most expressive type (Adam Clarke, *The Holy Bible with A Commentary*). For Abraham was a prophet (Gen. 20:7). Jesus said Abraham hoped for "My day [My incarnation]; and he did see it and was delighted" (John 8:56).

Himself will provide a lamb for the burnt offering. So the two went on together.

9 When they came to the place of which God had told him, Abraham built an altar there; then he laid the wood in order and ᵘbound Isaac his son and laid him on the altar on the wood. [Matt. 10:37.]

10 And Abraham stretched forth his hand and took hold of the knife to slay his son. [Heb. 11:17-19.]

11 But the ᵛAngel of the Lord called to him from heaven and said, Abraham, Abraham! He answered, Here I am.

12 And He said, Do not lay your hand on the lad or do anything to him; for now I know that you fear *and* revere God, since you have not held back from Me *or* begrudged giving Me your son, your only son.

13 Then Abraham looked up *and* glanced around, and behold, behind him was a ram caught in a thicket by his horns. And Abraham went and took the ram and offered it up for a burnt offering *and* an ascending sacrifice instead of his son!

14 So Abraham called the name of that place The Lord Will Provide. And it is said to this day, On the mount of the Lord it will be provided.

15 The Angel of the Lord called to Abraham from heaven a second time

16 And said, I have sworn by Myself, says the Lord, that since you have done this and have not withheld [from Me] *or* begrudged [giving Me] your son, your only son,

17 In blessing I will bless you and in multiplying I will multiply your descendants like the stars of the heavens and like the sand on the seashore. And your Seed (Heir) will possess the gate of His enemies, [Heb. 6:13, 14; 11:12.]

18 And in your Seed [ʷChrist] shall all the nations of the earth be blessed *and* [by Him] bless themselves, because you have heard *and* obeyed My voice. [Gen. 12:2-3; 13:16; 22:18; 26:4; 28:14; Acts 3:25, 26; Gal. 3:16.]

19 So Abraham returned to his servants, and they rose up and went with him to Beersheba; there Abraham lived.

20 Now after these things, it was told Abraham, Milcah has also borne children to your brother Nahor:

21 Uz the firstborn, Buz his brother, Kemuel the father of Aram,

22 Chesed, Hazo, Pildash, Jidlaph, and Bethuel.

23 Bethuel became the father of Rebekah. These eight Milcah bore to Nahor, Abraham's brother.

24 And his concubine, whose name was Reumah, bore Tebah, Gaham, Tahash, and Maacah.

23 SARAH LIVED 127 years; this was the length of the life of Sarah.

2 And Sarah died in Kiriath-arba, ˣthat is, Hebron, in the land of Ca-

---

u Isaac, who was perhaps twenty-five years old (according to the ancient historian Josephus), shared his father's confidence in God's promise. Was not his very existence the result of God keeping His word? (Gen. 17:15-17.) **v** See footnote on Gen. 16:7. **w** We have the authority of the apostle Paul (Gal. 3:8, 16, 18) to restrict this promise to our blessed Lord, Who was the Seed through Whom alone all God's blessings of providence, mercy, grace, and glory should be conveyed to the nations of the earth (Adam Clarke, *The Holy Bible with A Commentary*). **x** Surely this indicates that this detail was written at a very early date—before Israel had entered the land. No one in later times would need to be told where Hebron was. Not only was it conspicuous in Joshua's and Caleb's day, but it became a "city of refuge." Besides all this, David was king in Hebron for seven years. Obviously the Israelites had not yet entered Canaan and had to be told not only the name of the place where Abraham and Isaac had lived and were buried, but also its location (P. J. Wiseman, *New Discoveries in Babylonia About Genesis*).

naan. And Abraham went to mourn for Sarah and to weep for her.

3 And Abraham stood up from before his dead and said to the sons of Heth,

4 I am a stranger and a sojourner with you; give me property for a burial place among you, that I may bury my dead out of my sight.

5 And the Hittites replied to Abraham,

6 Listen to us, my lord; you are a mighty prince among us. Bury your dead in any tomb *or* grave of ours that you choose; none of us will withhold from you his tomb or hinder you from burying your dead.

7 And Abraham stood up and bowed himself to the people of the land, the Hittites.

8 And he said to them, If you are willing to grant my dead a burial out of my sight, listen to me and ask Ephron son of Zohar for me,

9 That he may give me the cave of Machpelah, which he owns—it is at the end of his field. For the full price let him give it to me here in your presence as a burial place to which I may hold fast among you.

10 Now Ephron was present there among the sons of Heth; so, in the hearing of all who went in at the gate of his city, Ephron the Hittite answered Abraham, saying,

11 No, my lord, hear me; I give you the field, and the cave that is in it I give you. In the presence of the sons of my people I give it to you. Bury your dead.

12 Then Abraham bowed himself down before the people of the land.

13 And he said to Ephron in the presence of the people of the land, But if you will give it, I beg of you, hear me. I will give you the price of the field; accept it from me, and I will bury my dead there.

14 Ephron replied to Abraham, saying,

15 My lord, listen to me. The land is worth 400 shekels of silver; what is that between you and me? So bury your dead.

16 So Abraham listened to what Ephron said *and* acted upon it. He weighed to Ephron the silver which he had named in the hearing of the Hittites: 400 shekels of silver, according to the weights current among the merchants.

17 So the field of Ephron in Machpelah, which was to the east of Mamre [Hebron]—the field and the cave which was in it, and all the trees that were in the field and in all its borders round about—was made over

18 As a possession to Abraham in the presence of the Hittites, before all who went in at his city gate.

19 After this, Abraham buried Sarah his wife in the cave of the field of ʸMachpelah to the east of Mamre, that is, Hebron, in the land of Canaan.

20 The field and the cave in it were conveyed to Abraham for a permanent burial place by the sons of Heth.

24 NOW ABRAHAM was old, well advanced in years, and the Lord had blessed Abraham in all things.

2 And Abraham said to the eldest servant of his house [Eliezer of Damascus], who ruled over all that he had, I beg of you, put your hand under my thigh; [Gen. 15:2.]

3 And you shall swear by the Lord, the God of heaven and earth, that you will not take a wife for my son from the daughters of the Canaanites, among whom I have settled,

---

ʸ Here were buried Abraham and Sarah, Isaac and Rebekah, and Jacob and Leah (Gen. 49:31; 50:13).

4 But you shall go to my country and to my relatives and take ᶻa wife for my son Isaac.

5 The servant said to him, But perhaps the woman will not be willing to come along after me to this country. Must I take your son to the country from which you came?

6 Abraham said to him, See to it that you do not take my son back there.

7 The Lord, the God of heaven, Who took me from my father's house, from the land of my family *and* my birth, Who spoke to me and swore to me, saying, To your offspring I will give this land—He will send His ᵃAngel before you, and you will take a wife from there for my son.

8 And if the woman should ᵇnot be willing to go along after you, then you will be clear from this oath; only you must not take my son back there.

9 So the servant put his hand under the thigh of Abraham his master and swore to him concerning this matter.

10 And the servant took ten of his master's camels and departed, taking some of all his master's treasures with him; thus he journeyed to Mesopotamia [between the Tigris and the Euphrates], to the city of Nahor [Abraham's brother].

11 And he made his camels to kneel down outside the city by a well of water at the time of the evening when women go out to draw water.

12 And he said, O Lord, God of my master Abraham, I pray You, cause me to meet with good success today, and show kindness to my master Abraham.

13 See, I stand here by the well of water, and the daughters of the men of the city are coming to draw water.

14 And let it so be that the girl to whom I say, I pray you, let down your jar that I may drink, and she replies, Drink, and I will give your camels drink also—let her be the one whom You have selected *and* appointed *and* indicated for Your servant Isaac [to be a wife to him]; and by it I shall know that You have shown kindness *and* faithfulness to my master.

15 Before he had finished speaking, behold, out came Rebekah, who was the daughter of Bethuel son of Milcah, who was the wife of Nahor the brother of Abraham, with her water jar on her shoulder.

16 And the girl was very beautiful *and* attractive, chaste *and* modest, and unmarried. And she went down to the well, filled her water jar, and came up.

17 And the servant ran to meet her, and said, I pray you, let me drink a little water from your water jar.

18 And she said, Drink, my lord; and she quickly let down her jar onto her hand and gave him a drink.

19 When she had given him a drink, she said, I will draw water for your camels also, until they finish drinking.

20 So she quickly emptied her jar into the trough and ran again to the well and drew water for all his camels.

21 The man stood gazing at her in silence, waiting to know if the Lord had made his trip prosperous.

22 And when the camels had finished drinking, the man took a gold earring *or* nose ring of half a shekel in weight, and for her hands two bracelets of ten shekels in weight in gold,

23 And said, Whose daughter are you? I pray you, tell me: Is there room

z This chapter is highly illustrative of God the Father, Who sends forth His Holy Spirit to win the consent of the individual soul to become the bride of His Son. Keep these resemblances constantly in mind as you read and see how the story unfolds. First meet the Father and note His concern about His Son's bride. Then get acquainted with the Holy Spirit's great, selfless heart, Whose one purpose is to win the girl for His Master's Son. Then meet the Son and note His tenderness as He claims His bride. The longest chapter in Genesis is devoted to this important story. **a** See footnote on Gen. 16:7. **b** The Holy Spirit does not win unwilling souls, only "whosoever will."

in your father's house for us to lodge there?

24 And she said to him, I am the daughter of Bethuel son of Milcah and [her husband] Nahor.

25 She said also to him, We have both straw and provender (fodder) enough, and also room in which to lodge.

26 The man bowed down his head and worshiped the Lord

27 And said, Blessed be the Lord, the God of my master Abraham, Who has not left my master bereft *and* destitute of His loving-kindness and steadfastness. As for me, going on the way [of obedience and faith] the Lord led me to the house of my master's kinsmen.

28 The girl related to her mother's household what had happened.

29 Now Rebekah had a brother whose name was Laban, and Laban ran out to the man at the well.

30 For when he saw the earring *or* nose ring, and the bracelets on his sister's arms, and when he heard Rebekah his sister saying, The man said this to me, he went to the man and found him standing by the camels at the well.

31 He cried, Come in, you blessed of the Lord! Why do you stand outside? For I have made the house ready *and* have prepared a place for the camels.

32 So the man came into the house; and [Laban] ungirded his camels and gave straw and provender for the camels and water to bathe his feet and

the feet of the men who were with him.

33 A meal was set before him, but he said, ⁿI will not eat until I have told of my errand. And [Laban] said, Speak on.

34 And he said, I am Abraham's servant.

35 And the Lord has blessed my master mightily, and he has become great; and He has given him flocks, herds, silver, gold, menservants, maidservants, camels, and asses.

36 And Sarah my master's wife bore a son to my master when she was old, and to him he has given all that he has.

37 And my master made me swear, saying, You must not take a wife for my son from the daughters of the Canaanites, in whose land I dwell,

38 But you shall go to my father's house and to my family and take a wife for my son.

39 And I said to my master, But suppose the woman will not follow me.

40 And he said to me, The Lord, in Whose presence I walk [habitually], will send His ᵈAngel with you and prosper your way, and you will take a wife for my son from my kindred and from my father's house.

41 Then you shall be clear from my oath, when you come to my kindred; and if they do not give her to you, you shall be free *and* innocent of my oath.

42 I came today to the well and said, O Lord, God of my master Abraham, if

speak the Word

God, I pray that I will walk in Your presence habitually, that You will send Your Angel with me, and that You will prosper me.
ADAPTED FROM GENESIS 24:40

c The characteristics of a model servant of God are pictured here: 1. He is dependable and trustworthy (Gen. 24:2); 2. He is a praying person (Gen. 24:12); 3. He is so in earnest that he refuses to eat before attending to his Master's business (Gen. 24:33); 4. He never speaks his own name but is always speaking about his Master (Gen. 24:35ff.); 5. He gives God all the glory (Gen. 24:48).   **d** See footnote on Gen. 16:7.

You are now causing me to go on my way prosperously—

43 See, I am standing by the well of water; now let it be that when the maiden comes out to draw water and I say to her, I pray you, give me a little water from your [water] jar to drink,

44 And if she says to me, You drink, and I will draw water for your camels also, let that same woman be the one whom the Lord has selected *and* indicated for my master's son.

45 And before I had finished praying in my heart, behold, Rebekah came out with her [water] jar on her shoulder, and she went down to the well and drew water. And I said to her, I pray you, let me have a drink.

46 And she quickly let down her [water] jar from her shoulder and said, Drink, and I will water your camels also. So I drank, and she gave the camels drink also.

47 I asked her, Whose daughter are you? She said, The daughter of Bethuel, Nahor's son, whom Milcah bore to him. And I put the earring *or* nose ring on her face and the bracelets on her arms.

48 And I bowed down my head and worshiped the Lord and blessed the Lord, the God of my master Abraham, Who had led me in the right way to take my master's brother's daughter to his son.

49 And now if you will deal kindly and truly with my master [showing faithfulness to him], tell me; and if not, tell me, that I may turn to the right or to the left.

50 Then Laban and Bethuel answered, The thing comes forth from the Lord; we cannot speak bad or good to you.

51 Rebekah is before you; take her and go, and let her be the wife of your master's son, as the Lord has said.

52 And when Abraham's servant heard their words, he bowed himself to the ground before the Lord.

53 And the servant brought out jewels of silver, jewels of gold, and garments and gave them to Rebekah; he also gave precious things to her brother and her mother.

54 Then they ate and drank, he and the men who were with him, and stayed there all night. And in the morning they arose, and he said. Send me away to my master.

55 But [Rebekah's] brother and mother said, Let the girl stay with us a few days—at least ten; then she may go.

56 But [the servant] said to them, Do not hinder *and* delay me, seeing that the Lord has caused me to go prosperously on my way. Send me away, that I may go to my master.

57 And they said, We will call the girl and ask her [what is] her desire.

58 So they called Rebekah and said to her, Will you go with this man? And she said, I will go.

59 So they sent away Rebekah their sister and her nurse [Deborah] and Abraham's servant and his men.

60 And they blessed Rebekah and said to her, You are our sister; may you become the mother of thousands of ten thousands, and let your posterity possess the gate of their enemies.

61 And Rebekah and her maids arose and followed the man upon their camels. Thus the servant took Rebekah and went on his way.

62 Now Isaac had returned from going to the well Beer-lahai-roi [A well to the Living One Who sees me], for he [now] dwelt in the South country (the Negeb).

63 And Isaac went out to meditate *and* bow down [in prayer] in the open country in the evening; and he looked up and saw that, behold, the camels were coming.

64 And Rebekah looked up, and when she saw Isaac, she dismounted from the camel.

65 For she [had] said to the servant, Who is that man walking across the field to meet us? And the servant [had] said, He is my master. So she took a veil and concealed herself with it.

66 And the servant told Isaac everything that he had done.

67 And Isaac brought her into his mother Sarah's tent, and he took Rebekah and she became his wife, and he loved her; thus Isaac was comforted after his mother's death.

25 ABRAHAM TOOK another wife, and her name was Keturah.

2 And she bore him Zimran, Jokshan, Medan, Midian, Ishbak, and Shuah.

3 Jokshan was the father of Sheba and Dedan. The sons of Dedan were Asshurim, Letushim, and Leummim.

4 The sons of Midian were Ephah, Epher, Hanoch, Abida, and Eldaah. All these were the children of Keturah.

5 And Abraham gave all that he had to Isaac.

6 But to the sons of his concubines [Hagar and Keturah] Abraham gave gifts, and while he was still living he sent them to the east country, away from Isaac his son [of promise].

7 The days of Abraham's life were 175 years.

8 Then Abraham's spirit was released, and he died at a good (ample, full) old age, an old man, satisfied *and* satiated, and ᵉwas gathered to his people. [Gen. 15:15.]

9 And his sons ᶠIsaac and Ishmael buried him in the cave of Machpelah, in the field of Ephron the son of Zohar the Hittite, which is east of Mamre,

10 The field which Abraham purchased from the Hittites. There Abraham was buried with Sarah his wife.

11 After the death of Abraham, God blessed his son Isaac, and Isaac dwelt at Beer-lahai-roi [A well to the Living One Who sees me].

12 Now this is the history of the descendants of Ishmael, Abraham's son, whom Hagar the Egyptian, Sarah's handmaid, bore to Abraham.

13 These are the names of the sons of Ishmael, named in the order of their births: Nebaioth, the firstborn of Ishmael, and Kedar, Adbeel, Mibsam,

14 Mishma, Dumah, Massa,

15 Hadad, Tema, Jetur, Naphish, and Kedemah.

16 These are the sons of Ishmael, and these are their names, by their villages and by their encampments (sheepfolds)—twelve princes according to their tribes. [Foretold in Gen. 17:20.]

17 And Ishmael lived 137 years; then his spirit left him, and he died and was gathered to his kindred.

18 And [Ishmael's sons] dwelt from Havilah to Shur, which is before Egypt in the direction of Assyria. [Ishmael] dwelt close [to the lands] of all his brethren.

19 And this is the history of the descendants of Isaac, Abraham's son: Abraham was the father of Isaac.

20 Isaac was forty years old when he married Rebekah, the daughter of Bethuel the Aramean of Padan-aram, the sister of Laban the Aramean.

21 And Isaac prayed much to the Lord for his wife because she was unable to bear children; and the Lord granted his prayer, and Rebekah his wife became pregnant.

22 [Two] children struggled together within her; and she said, If it is so [that the Lord has heard our prayer], why am I like this? And she went to inquire of the Lord.

23 The Lord said to her, [The

e This often repeated expression forms a remarkable testimony to the Old Testament belief in a life beyond the grave and to our recognition and fellowship with our loved ones there.   f Isaac was seventy-five and Ishmael nearly ninety years of age when their father died. Jacob and Esau were fifteen, and may have been present.

founders of] two nations are in your womb, and the separation of two peoples has begun in your body; the one people shall be stronger than the other, and the elder shall serve the younger.
24 When her days to be delivered were fulfilled, behold, there were twins in her womb.
25 The first came out red all over like a hairy garment, and they named him Esau [hairy].
26 Afterward his brother came forth, and his hand grasped Esau's heel; so he was named Jacob [supplanter]. Isaac was sixty years old when she gave birth to them.
27 When the boys grew up, Esau was a cunning *and* skilled hunter, a man of the outdoors; but Jacob was a plain *and* quiet man, dwelling in tents.
28 And Isaac loved [and was partial to] Esau, because he ate of Esau's game; but Rebekah loved Jacob.
29 Jacob was boiling pottage (lentil stew) one day, when Esau came from the field and was faint [with hunger].
30 And Esau said to Jacob, I beg of you, let me have some of that red lentil stew to eat, for I am faint *and* famished! That is why his name was called Edom [red].
31 Jacob answered, Then sell me today your birthright (the rights of a firstborn).
32 Esau said, See here, I am at the point of death; what good can this birthright do me?
33 Jacob said, Swear to me today [that you are selling it to me]; and he swore to [Jacob] and sold him his birthright.
34 Then Jacob gave Esau bread and stew of lentils, and he ate and drank and rose up and went his way. Thus Esau scorned his birthright as beneath his notice.

26 AND THERE was a famine in the land, other than the former famine that was in the days of Abraham. And Isaac went to Gerar, to Abimelech king of the Philistines.
2 And the Lord appeared to him and said, Do not go down to Egypt; live in the land of which I will tell you.
3 Dwell temporarily in this land, and I will be with you and will favor you with blessings; for to you and to your descendants I will give all these lands, and I will perform the oath which I swore to Abraham your father.
4 And I will make your descendants to multiply as the stars of the heavens, and will give to your posterity all these lands (kingdoms); and by your Offspring shall all the nations of the earth be blessed, *or* by Him bless themselves, [Gen. 22:18; Acts 3:25, 26; Gal. 3:16.]
5 For Abraham listened to *and* obeyed My voice and kept My charge, My commands, My statutes, and My laws.
6 So Isaac stayed in Gerar.
7 And the men of the place asked him about his wife, and he said, She is my sister; for he was afraid to say, She is my wife—[thinking], Lest the men of the place should kill me for Rebekah, because she is attractive *and* is beautiful to look upon.
8 When he had been there a long time, Abimelech king of the Philistines looked out of a window and saw Isaac caressing Rebekah his wife.
9 And Abimelech called Isaac and said, See here, she is certainly your wife! How did you [dare] say to me, She is my sister? And Isaac said to him, Because I thought, Lest I die on account of her.
10 And Abimelech said, What is this you have done to us? One of the men might easily have lain with your wife, and you would have brought guilt *and* sin upon us.
11 Then Abimelech charged all his people, He who touches this man or his wife shall surely be put to death.

life point

One of the things Isaac did when he grew up was to open the wells of his father, Abraham, wells that had been stopped up by their enemies (see Genesis 26:18). The very name Isaac, the one who caused the wells to flow again, means "laughter." I think we may draw from this story the idea that laughter and joy in the Holy Spirit will open the deep wells of life inside us— wells that may have been stopped up by the enemy through depression, discouragement, or disappointment. Go ahead and laugh; and let God's joy bubble up in you right now!

12 Then Isaac sowed seed in that land and received in the same year a hundred times as much as he had planted, and the Lord favored him with blessings.
13 And the man became great and gained more and more until he became very wealthy *and* distinguished;
14 He owned flocks, herds, and a great supply of servants, and the Philistines envied him.
15 Now all the wells which his father's servants had dug in the days of Abraham his father, the Philistines had closed and filled with earth.
16 And Abimelech said to Isaac, Go away from us, for you are much mightier than we are.
17 So Isaac went away from there and pitched his tent in the Valley of Gerar, and dwelt there.
18 And Isaac dug again the wells of water which had been dug in the days of Abraham his father, for the Philistines had stopped them after the death of Abraham; and he gave them the names by which his father had called them.
19 Now Isaac's servants dug in the valley and found there a well of living [spring] water.
20 And the herdsmen of Gerar quarreled with Isaac's herdsmen, saying, The water is ours. And he named the well Esek [contention] because they quarreled with him.
21 Then [his servants] dug another well, and they quarreled over that also; so he named it Sitnah [enmity].
22 And he moved away from there and dug another well, and for that one they did not quarrel. He named it Rehoboth [room], saying, For now the Lord has made room for us, and we shall be fruitful in the land.
23 Now he went up from there to Beersheba.
24 And the Lord appeared to him the same night and said, I am the God of Abraham your father. Fear not, for I am with you and will favor you with blessings and multiply your descendants for the sake of My servant Abraham.
25 And [Isaac] ᵍbuilt an altar there and called on the name of the Lord and pitched his tent there; and there Isaac's servants were digging a well.
26 Then Abimelech went to him from Gerar with Ahuzzah, one of his friends, and Phicol, his army's commander.
27 And Isaac said to them, Why have you come to me, seeing that you hate me and have sent me away from you?
28 They said, We saw that the Lord was certainly with you; so we said, Let there be now an oath between us [carrying a curse with it to befall the one who breaks it], even between you and us, and let us make a covenant with you
29 That you will do us no harm,

---

g With Isaac God came first. Before doing anything else in the new place, he built an altar and then waited there to call upon the Lord. Second came his home; he pitched his tent. Third came his business; his servants dug a well.

inasmuch as we have not touched you and have done to you nothing but good and have sent you away in peace. You are now the blessed *or* favored of the Lord!

30 And he made them a [formal] dinner, and they ate and drank.

31 And they rose up early in the morning and took oaths [with a curse] with one another; and Isaac sent them on their way and they departed from him in peace.

32 That same day Isaac's servants came and told him about the well they had dug, saying, We have found water!

33 And he named [the well] Shibah; therefore the name of the city is Beer-sheba [well of the oath] to this day. [Gen. 21:31.]

34 Now Esau was 40 years old when he took as wife Judith the daughter of Beeri the Hittite, and Basemath the daughter of Elon the Hittite.

35 And they made life bitter *and* a grief of mind *and* spirit for Isaac and Rebekah [their parents-in-law].

27 WHEN ISAAC was old and his eyes were dim so that he could not see, he called Esau his elder son, and said to him, My son! And he answered him, Here I am.

2 He said, See here now; I am old, I do not know when I may die.

3 So now, I pray you, take your weapons, your [arrows in a] quiver and your bow, and go out into the open country and hunt game for me,

4 And prepare me appetizing meat, such as I love, and bring it to me, that I may eat of it, [preparatory] to giving you my blessing [as my firstborn] before I die.

5 But Rebekah heard what Isaac said to Esau his son; and when Esau had gone to the open country to hunt for game that he might bring it,

6 Rebekah said to Jacob her younger son, See here, I heard your father say to Esau your brother,

7 Bring me game and make me appetizing meat, so that I may eat and declare my blessing upon you before the Lord before my death.

8 So now, my son, do exactly as I command you.

9 Go now to the flock, and from it bring me two good *and* suitable kids; and I will make them into appetizing meat for your father, such as he loves.

10 And you shall bring it to your father, that he may eat and declare his blessing upon you before his death.

11 But Jacob said to Rebekah his mother, Listen, Esau my brother is a hairy man and I am a smooth man.

12 Suppose my father feels me; I will seem to him to be a cheat *and* an imposter, and I will bring [his] curse on me and not [his] blessing.

13 But his mother said to him, On me be your curse, my son; only obey my word and go, fetch them to me.

14 So [Jacob] went, got [the kids], and brought them to his mother; and his mother prepared appetizing meat with a delightful odor, such as his father loved.

15 Then Rebekah took her elder son Esau's best clothes which were with her in the house, and put them on Jacob her younger son.

16 And she put the skins of the kids on his hands and on the smooth part of his neck.

17 And she gave the savory meat and the bread which she had prepared into the hand of her son Jacob.

18 So he went to his father and said, My father. And he said, Here am I; who are you, my son?

19 And Jacob said to his father, I am Esau your firstborn; I have done what you told me to do. Now sit up and eat of my game, so that you may proceed to bless me.

20 And Isaac said to his son, How is it that you have found the game so quickly, my son? And he said, Because the Lord your God caused it to come to me.

21 But Isaac said to Jacob, Come close to me, I beg of you, that I may feel you, my son, *and* know whether you really are my son Esau or not.

22 So Jacob went near to Isaac, and his father felt him and said, The voice is Jacob's voice, but the hands are the hands of Esau.

23 He could not identify him, because his hands were hairy like his brother Esau's hands; so he blessed him.

24 But he said, Are you really my son Esau? He answered, I am.

25 Then [Isaac] said, Bring it to me and I will eat of my son's game, that I may bless you. He brought it to him and he ate; and he brought him wine and he drank.

26 Then his father Isaac said, Come near and kiss me, my son.

27 So he came near and kissed him; and [Isaac] smelled his clothing and blessed him and said, The scent of my son is as the odor of a field which the Lord has blessed.

28 And may God give you of the dew of the heavens and of the fatness of the earth and abundance of grain and [new] wine;

29 Let peoples serve you and nations bow down to you; be master over your brothers, and let your mother's sons bow down to you. Let everyone be cursed who curses you and favored with blessings who blesses you.

30 As soon as Isaac had finished blessing Jacob and Jacob was scarcely gone out from the presence of Isaac his father, Esau his brother came in from his hunting.

31 Esau had also prepared savory food and brought it to his father and said to him, Let my father arise and eat of his son's game, that you may bless me.

32 And Isaac his father said to him, Who are you? And he replied, I am your son, your firstborn, Esau.

33 Then Isaac trembled *and* shook violently, and he said, Who? Where is he who has hunted game and brought it to me, and I ate of it all before you came and I have blessed him? Yes, and he shall be blessed.

34 When Esau heard the words of his father, he cried out with a great and bitter cry and said to his father, Bless me, even me also, O my father! [Heb. 12:16, 17.]

35 [Isaac] said, Your brother came with crafty cunning *and* treacherous deceit and has taken your blessing.

putting the Word to work

When Isaac was old and sick, his son Jacob deceived him into thinking that he (Jacob) was his brother Esau (see Genesis 27:30–32). That way, Jacob tricked Isaac into giving him the birthright that should have gone to Esau. Have you, like Isaac, ever been deceived by someone? Have you forgiven that person?

36 [Esau] replied, Is he not rightly named Jacob [the supplanter]? For he has supplanted me these two times: he took away my birthright, and now he has taken away my blessing! Have you not still a blessing reserved for me?

37 And Isaac answered Esau, Behold, I have made [Jacob] your lord and master; I have given all his brethren to him for servants, and with corn and [new] wine have I sustained him. What then can I do for you, my son?

38 Esau said to his father, Have you only one blessing, my father? Bless me, even me also, O my father! And Esau lifted up [could not control] his voice and wept aloud.

39 Then Isaac his father answered, Your [blessing and] dwelling shall all come from the fruitfulness of the earth and from the dew of the heavens above;

40 By your sword you shall live and serve your brother. But [the time shall

come] when you will grow restive *and* break loose, and you shall tear his yoke from off your neck.

41 And Esau hated Jacob because of the blessing with which his father blessed him; and Esau said in his heart, The days of mourning for my father are very near. When [he is gone] I will ʰkill my brother Jacob.

42 These words of Esau her elder son were repeated to Rebekah. She sent for Jacob her younger son and said to him, See here, your brother Esau comforts himself concerning you [by intending] to kill you.

43 So now, my son, do what I tell you; arise, flee to my brother Laban in Haran;

44 Linger and dwell with him for a while until your brother's fury is spent.

45 When your brother's anger is diverted from you, he will forget [the wrong] that you have done him. Then ⁱI will send and bring you back from there. Why should I be deprived of both of you in one day?

46 Then Rebekah said to Isaac, I am weary of my life because of the daughters of Heth [these wives of Esau]! If Jacob takes a wife of the daughters of Heth such as these Hittite girls around here, what good will my life be to me?

28 SO ISAAC called Jacob and blessed him and commanded him, You shall not marry one of the women of Canaan.

2 Arise, go to Padan-aram, to the house of Bethuel your mother's father, and take from there as a wife one of the daughters of Laban your mother's brother.

3 May God Almighty bless you and make you fruitful and multiply you until you become a group of peoples.

4 May He give the blessing [He gave to] Abraham to you and your descendants with you, that you may inherit the land He gave to Abraham, in which you are a sojourner.

5 Thus Isaac sent Jacob away. He went to Padan-aram, to Laban son of Bethuel the Aramean, the brother of Rebekah, Jacob and Esau's mother.

6 Now Esau saw that Isaac had blessed Jacob and sent him to Padan-aram to take him a wife from there, and that as he blessed him, he gave him a charge, saying, You shall not take a wife of the daughters of Canaan;

7 And that Jacob obeyed his father and his mother and had gone to Padan-aram.

8 Also Esau saw that the daughters of Canaan did not please Isaac his father.

9 So Esau went to Ishmael and took to be his wife, [in addition] to the wives he [already] had, Mahalath daughter of Ishmael, Abraham's son, the sister of Nebaioth.

10 And Jacob left Beersheba and went toward Haran.

11 And he came to a certain place and stayed there overnight, because the sun was set. Taking one of the stones of the place, he put it under his head and lay down there to sleep.

12 And he dreamed that there was a ladder set up on the earth, and the top

---

h Here began a feud that was to cost countless lives throughout succeeding centuries. Esau's descendants, the Amalekites, were the first enemies to obstruct the flight of Jacob's descendants from Egypt (Exod. 17:8); and the Edomites even refused to let their uncle Jacob's children pass through their land (Num. 20:17-20). Doeg, an Edomite, all but caused the death of Christ's chosen ancestor David (I Sam. 21, 22). Bloody battles were fought between the two nations in the centuries that followed. It was Herod, of Esau's race (Josephus, *Antiquities of the Jews* 14:1, Section 3), who had the male infants of Bethlehem slain in an effort to destroy the Christ Child (Matt. 2:16). Satan needs no better medium for his evil plans than a family feud, a "mere quarrel" between two brothers. **i** But Rebekah never saw her son Jacob again. He was well over 40 and probably 57 years old when he fled from Esau to Haran, and he stayed there at least 20 years.

of it reached to heaven; and the angels of God were ascending and descending on it!

13 And behold, the Lord stood over *and* beside him and said, I am the Lord, the God of Abraham your father [forefather] and the God of Isaac; I will give to you and to your descendants the land on which you are lying.

14 And your offspring shall be as [countless as] the dust *or* sand of the ground, and you shall spread abroad to the west and the east and the north and the south; and by you and your Offspring shall all the families of the earth be blessed *and* bless themselves. [Gen. 12:2-3; 13:16; 22:18; 26:4; Acts 3:25-26; Gal. 3:8, 16.]

15 And behold, I am with you and will keep (watch over you with care, take notice of) you wherever you may go, and I will bring you back to this land; for I will not leave you until I have done all of which I have told you.

16 And Jacob awoke from his sleep and he said, Surely the Lord is in this place and I did not know it.

17 He was afraid and said, How to be feared *and* reverenced is this place! This is none other than the house of God, and ʲthis is the gateway to heaven!

18 And Jacob rose early in the morning and took the stone he had put under his head, and he set it up for a pillar (a monument to the vision in his dream), and he poured oil on its top [in dedication].

speak the Word

19 And he named that place Bethel [the house of God]; but the name of that city was Luz at first.

20 Then Jacob made a vow, saying, If God will be with me and will keep me in this way that I go and will give me food to eat and clothing to wear,

21 So that I may come again to my father's house in peace, then the Lord shall be my God;

22 And this stone which I have set up as a pillar (monument) shall be God's house [a sacred place to me], and of all [the increase of possessions] that You give me I will give the tenth to You.

29 THEN JACOB went [briskly and cheerfully] on his way [400 miles] and came to the land of the people of the East.

2 As he looked, he saw a well in the field; and behold, there were three flocks of sheep lying by it, for out of that well the flocks were watered. The stone on the well's mouth was a big one,

3 And when all the flocks were gathered there, [the shepherds] would roll the stone from the well's mouth, water the sheep, and replace the stone on the well's mouth.

4 And Jacob said to them, My brothers, where are you from? And they said, We are from Haran.

5 [Jacob] said to them, Do you know Laban the grandson of Nahor? And they said, We know him.

Father, I thank You that You are with me and that You are keeping watch over me wherever I go.
ADAPTED FROM GENESIS 28:15

ʲ "There is an open way between heaven and earth for each of us. The movement of the tide and the circulation of the blood are not more regular than the intercommunication between heaven and earth. Jacob may have thought that God was local; now he found Him to be omnipresent. Every lonely spot was His house, filled with angels" (F. B. Meyer, *Through the Bible Day by Day*). When Jacob found God in his own heart, he found Him everywhere.

6 He said to them, Is it well with him? And they said, He is doing well; and behold, here comes his daughter Rachel with [his] sheep!
7 He said, The sun is still high; it is a long time yet before the flocks need be gathered [in their folds]. [Why not] water the sheep and return them to their pasture?
8 But they said, We cannot until all the flocks are gathered together; then [the shepherds] roll the stone from the well's mouth and we water the sheep.
9 While he was still talking with them, Rachel came with her father's sheep, for she shepherded them.
10 When Jacob saw Rachel daughter of Laban, his mother's brother, and the sheep of Laban his uncle, Jacob went near and rolled the stone from the well's mouth and watered the flock of his uncle Laban.
11 Then Jacob kissed Rachel and he wept aloud.
12 Jacob told Rachel he was her father's relative, Rebekah's son; and she ran and told her father.
13 When Laban heard of the arrival of Jacob his sister's son, he ran to meet him, and embraced and kissed him and brought him to his house. And [Jacob] told Laban all these things.
14 Then Laban said to him, Surely you are my bone and my flesh. And [Jacob] stayed with him a month.
15 Then Laban said to Jacob, Just because you are my relative, should you work for me for nothing? Tell me, what shall your wages be?
16 Now Laban had two daughters; the name of the elder was Leah and the name of the younger was Rachel.
17 Leah's eyes were weak *and* dull looking, but Rachel was beautiful and attractive.
18 And Jacob loved Rachel; so he said, I will work for you for seven years for Rachel your younger daughter.

putting the Word to work

The Bible indicates that Leah was not nearly as beautiful or desirable as Rachel (see Genesis 29:17). Have you ever felt rejected, as she must have? Remember that God loves you; He wants you, and He has an awesome plan for your life!

19 And Laban said, It is better that I give her to you than to another man. Stay *and* live with me.
20 And Jacob served seven years for Rachel; and they seemed to him but a few days because of the love he had for her.
21 Finally, Jacob said to Laban, Give me my wife, for my time is completed, so that I may take her to me.
22 And Laban gathered together all the men of the place and made a feast [with drinking].
23 But when night came, he took Leah his daughter and brought her to [Jacob], who had intercourse with her.
24 And Laban gave Zilpah his maid to his daughter Leah to be her maid.
25 But in the morning [Jacob saw his wife, and] behold, it was Leah! And he said to Laban, What is this you have done to me? Did I not work for you [all those seven years] for Rachel? Why then have you deceived *and* cheated *and* thrown me down [like this]?
26 And Laban said, It is not permitted in our country to give the younger [in marriage] before the elder.
27 Finish the [wedding feast] week [for Leah]; then we will give you [Rachel] also, and you shall work for me yet seven more years in return.
28 So Jacob complied and fulfilled [Leah's] week; then [Laban] gave him Rachel his daughter as his wife.
29 (And Laban gave Bilhah his maid to Rachel his daughter to be her maid.)

30 And Jacob lived with Rachel also as his wife, and he loved Rachel more than Leah and served [Laban] another seven years [for her].
31 And when the Lord saw that Leah was despised, He made her able to bear children, but Rachel was barren.
32 And Leah became pregnant and bore a son and named him Reuben [See, a son!]; for she said, Because the Lord has seen my humiliation *and* affliction; now my husband will love me.
33 [Leah] became pregnant again and bore a son and said, Because the Lord heard that I am despised, He has given me this son also; and she named him Simeon [God hears].
34 And she became pregnant again and bore a son and said, Now this time will my husband be a companion to me, for I have borne him three sons. Therefore he was named Levi [companion].
35 Again she conceived and bore a son, and she said, Now will I praise the Lord! So she called his name Judah [praise]; then [for a time] she ceased bearing.

30 WHEN RACHEL saw that she bore Jacob no children, she envied her sister, and said to Jacob, Give me children, or else I will die!
2 And Jacob became very angry with Rachel and he said, Am I in God's stead, Who has denied you children?
3 And she said, See here, take my maid Bilhah and have intercourse with her; and [when the baby comes] she shall deliver it upon my knees, that I by her may also have children.
4 And she gave him Bilhah her maid as a [secondary] wife, and Jacob had intercourse with her.

5 And Bilhah became pregnant and bore Jacob a son.
6 And Rachel said, God has judged *and* vindicated me, and has heard my plea and has given me a son; so she named him Dan [judged].
7 And Bilhah, Rachel's maid, conceived again and bore Jacob a second son.
8 And Rachel said, With mighty wrestlings [in prayer to God] I have struggled with my sister and have prevailed; so she named him [this second son Bilhah bore] Naphtali [struggled].
9 When Leah saw that she had ceased to bear, she gave Zilpah her maid to Jacob as a [secondary] wife.
10 And Zilpah, Leah's maid, bore Jacob a son.
11 Then Leah said, Victory *and* good fortune have come; and she named him Gad [fortune].
12 Zilpah, Leah's maid, bore Jacob [her] second son.
13 And Leah said, I am happy, for women will call me blessed (happy, fortunate, to be envied); and she named him Asher [happy].
14 Now Reuben went at the time of wheat harvest and found some mandrakes (love apples) in the field and brought them to his mother Leah. Then Rachel said to Leah, Give me, I pray you, some of your son's mandrakes.
15 But [Leah] answered, Is it not enough that you have taken my husband without your taking away my son's ᵏmandrakes also? And Rachel said, Jacob shall sleep with you tonight [in exchange] for your son's mandrakes.
16 And Jacob came out of the field in the evening, and Leah went out to meet him and said, You must sleep with me [tonight], for I have certainly paid your hire with my son's

k Mandrakes were superstitiously supposed to excite and win love.

52

mandrakes. So he slept with her that night.

17 And God heeded Leah's [prayer], and she conceived and bore Jacob [her] fifth son.

18 Leah said, God has given me my hire, because I have given my maid to my husband; and she called his name Issachar [hired].

19 And Leah became pregnant again and bore Jacob [her] sixth son.

20 Then Leah said, God has endowed me with a good marriage gift [for my husband]; now will he dwell with me [and regard me as his wife in reality], because I have borne him six sons; and she named him Zebulun [dwelling].

21 Afterwards she bore a daughter and called her Dinah.

22 Then God remembered Rachel and answered her pleading and made it possible for her to have children.

23 And [now for the first time] she became pregnant and bore a son; and she said, God has taken away my reproach, disgrace, *and* humiliation.

24 And she called his name Joseph [may he add] and said, May the Lord add to me another son.

25 When Rachel had borne Joseph, Jacob said to Laban, Send me away, that I may go to my own place and country.

26 Give me my wives and my children, for whom I have served you, and let me go; for you know the work which I have done for you.

27 And Laban said to him, If I have found favor in your sight, I pray you [do not go]; for I have learned by experience *and* from the omens in divination that the Lord has favored me with blessings on your account.

28 He said, State your salary and I will give it.

29 Jacob answered him, You know how I have served you, and how your possessions, your cattle *and* sheep *and* goats, have fared with me.

30 For you had little before I came, and it has increased *and* multiplied abundantly; and the Lord has favored you with blessings wherever I turned. But now, when shall I provide for my own house also?

31 [Laban] said, What shall I give you? And Jacob said, You shall not give me anything, if you will do this one thing for me [of which I am about to tell you], and I will again feed *and* take care of your flock.

32 Let me pass through all your flock today, removing from it every speckled and spotted animal and every black one among the sheep, and the spotted and speckled among the goats; and such shall be my wages.

33 So later when the matter of my wages is brought before you, my fair dealing will be evident *and* answer for me. Every one that is not speckled and spotted among the goats and black among the sheep, if found with me, shall be counted as stolen.

34 And Laban said, Good; let it be done as you say.

35 But that same day [Laban] removed the he-goats that were streaked and spotted and all the she-goats that were speckled and spotted, every one that had white on it, and every black lamb, and put them in charge of his sons.

36 And he set [a distance of] three days' journey between himself and Jacob; and Jacob was then left in care of the rest of Laban's flock.

37 But Jacob took fresh rods of poplar and almond and plane trees and peeled white streaks in them, exposing the white in the rods.

38 Then he set the rods which he had peeled in front of the flocks in the watering troughs where the flocks came to drink. And since they bred *and* conceived when they came to drink,

39 The flocks bred *and* conceived in

sight of the rods and brought forth lambs *and* kids streaked, speckled, and spotted.

40 Jacob separated the lambs, and [as he had done with the peeled rods] he also set the faces of the flocks toward the streaked and all the dark in the [new] flock of Laban; and he put his own droves by themselves and did not let them breed with Laban's flock.

41 And whenever the stronger animals were breeding, Jacob laid the rods in the watering troughs before the eyes of the flock, that they might breed *and* conceive among the rods.

42 But when the sheep *and* goats were feeble, he omitted putting the rods there; so the feebler animals were Laban's and the stronger Jacob's.

43 Thus the man increased *and* became exceedingly rich, and had many sheep *and* goats, and maidservants, menservants, camels, and donkeys.

31 JACOB HEARD Laban's sons complaining, Jacob has taken away all that was our father's; he has acquired all this wealth *and* honor from what belonged to our father.

2 And Jacob noticed that Laban looked at him less favorably than before.

3 Then the Lord said to Jacob, Return to the land of your fathers and to your people, and I will be with you.

4 So Jacob sent and called Rachel and Leah to the field to his flock,

5 And he said to them, I see how your father looks at me, that he is not [friendly] toward me as before; but the God of my father has been with me.

6 You know that I have served your father with all my might *and* power.

7 But your father has deceived me and changed my wages ten times, but God did not allow him to hurt me.

8 If he said, The speckled shall be your wages, then all the flock bore speckled; and if he said, The streaked shall be your hire, then all the flock bore streaked.

9 Thus God has taken away the flocks of your father and given them to me.

10 And I had a [1]dream at the time the flock conceived. I looked up and saw that the rams which mated with the she-goats were streaked, speckled, and spotted.

11 And the [m]Angel of God said to me in the dream, Jacob. And I said, Here am I.

12 And He said, Look up and see, all the rams which mate with the flock are streaked, speckled, and mottled; for I have seen all that Laban does to you.

13 I am the God of Bethel, where you anointed the pillar and where you vowed a vow to Me. Now arise, get out from this land and return to your native land.

14 And Rachel and Leah answered him, Is there any portion or inheritance for us in our father's house?

15 Are we not counted by him as strangers? For he sold us and has also quite devoured our money [the price you paid for us].

16 For all the riches which God has taken from our father are ours and our children's. Now then, whatever God has said to you, do it.

17 Then Jacob rose up and set his sons and his wives upon the camels;

---

1 We naturally wonder why we have not heard of this dream before and are tempted to question Jacob's truthfulness; but the Samaritan text removes all such doubt by recording the whole dream in the previous chapter (Gen. 30), right after Gen. 30:36 (Adam Clarke, *The Holy Bible with A Commentary*). **m** See footnote on Gen. 16:7. Note especially Gen. 31:13, where the Angel says, "I am the God of Bethel."

18 And he drove away all his livestock and all his gain which he had gotten, the livestock he had obtained *and* accumulated in Padan-aram, to go to Isaac his father in the land of Canaan.

19 Now Laban had gone to shear his sheep [possibly to the feast of sheepshearing], and Rachel stole her father's household gods.

20 And Jacob outwitted Laban the Syrian [Aramean] in that he did not tell him that he [intended] to flee *and* slip away secretly.

21 So he fled with all that he had, and arose and crossed the river [Euphrates] and set his face toward the hill country of Gilead.

22 But on the third day Laban was told that Jacob had fled.

23 So he took his kinsmen with him and pursued after [Jacob] for seven days, and they overtook him in the hill country of Gilead.

24 But God came to Laban the Syrian [Aramean] in a dream by night and said to him, Be careful that you do not speak from good to bad to Jacob [peaceably, then violently].

25 Then Laban overtook Jacob. Now Jacob had pitched his tent on the hill, and Laban coming with his kinsmen pitched [his tents] on the same hill of Gilead.

26 And Laban said to Jacob, What do you mean stealing away *and* leaving like this without my knowing it, and carrying off my daughters as if captives of the sword?

27 Why did you flee secretly and cheat me and did not tell me, so that I might have sent you away with joy *and* gladness and with singing, with tambourine and lyre?

28 And why did you not permit me to kiss my sons [grandchildren] and my daughters good-bye? Now you have done foolishly [in behaving like this].

29 It is in my power to do you harm; but the God of your father spoke to me last night, saying, Be careful that you do not speak from good to bad to Jacob [peaceably, then violently].

30 And now you felt you must go because you were homesick for your father's house, but why did you steal my [household] [n]gods?

31 Jacob answered Laban, Because I was afraid; for I thought, Suppose you would take your daughters from me by force.

32 The one with whom you find those gods of yours, let him not live. Here before our kinsmen [search my possessions and] take whatever you find that belongs to you. For Jacob did not know that Rachel had stolen [the images].

33 So Laban went into Jacob's tent and into Leah's tent and the tent of the two maids, but he did not find them. Then he went from Leah's tent into Rachel's tent.

34 Now Rachel had taken the images (gods) and put them in the camel's saddle and sat on them. Laban searched *and* felt through all the tent, but did not find them.

35 And [Rachel] said to her father,

n Why was Laban making such a great commotion about some small idols? It had never been satisfactorily explained until the answer was found in the excavated Nuzi tablets (J. P. Free, *Archaeology Illuminates the Bible*), which showed that possession of the father's household gods played an important role in inheritance (W. F. Albright, "Recent Discoveries in Bible Lands," in *Young's Analytical Concordance to the Bible*). One of the Nuzi tablets indicated that in the region where Laban lived, a son-in-law who possessed the family images could appear in court and make claim to the estate of his father-in-law (various authors cited by Allan A. MacRae, "The Relation of Archaeology to the Bible," in American Scientific Affiliation, *Modern Science and Christian Faith*). Since Jacob's possession of the images implied the right to inheritance of Laban's wealth, one can understand why Laban organized his hurried expedition to recover the images (J. P. Free, *Archaeology and Bible History*).

Do not be displeased, my lord, that I cannot rise up before you, for the period of women is upon me *and* I am unwell. And he searched, but did not find the gods.

36 Then Jacob became angry and reproached *and* argued with Laban. And Jacob said to Laban, What is my fault? What is my sin, that you so hotly pursued me?

37 Although you have searched *and* felt through all my household possessions, what have you found of all your household goods? Put it here before my brethren and yours, that they may judge *and* decide between us.

38 These twenty years I have been with you; your ewes and your she-goats have not lost their young, and the rams of your flock have not been eaten by me.

39 I did not bring you [the carcasses of the animals] torn by wild beasts; I bore the loss of it; you required of me [to make good] all that was stolen, whether it occurred by day or by night.

40 This was [my lot]; by day the heat consumed me and by night the cold, and I could not sleep.

41 I have been twenty years in your house. I served you fourteen years for your two daughters and six years for your flocks; and you have changed my wages ten times.

42 And if the God of my father, the God of Abraham and the Dread [lest he should fall] *and* Fear [lest he offend] of Isaac, had not been with me, surely you would have sent me away now empty-handed. God has seen my affliction *and* humiliation and the [wearying] labor of my hands and rebuked you last night.

43 Laban answered Jacob, These daughters are my daughters, these children are my children, these flocks are my flocks, and all that you see is mine. But what can I do today to these my daughters or to their children whom they have borne?

44 So come now, let us make a covenant *or* league, you and I, and let it be for a witness between you and me.

45 So Jacob set up a stone for a pillar *or* monument.

46 And Jacob said to his brethren, Gather stones; and they took stones and made a heap, and they ate [together] there upon the heap. [Prov. 16:7.]

47 Laban called it Jegar-sahadutha [witness heap, *in Aramaic*], but Jacob called it Galeed [°witness heap, *in Hebrew.*]

48 Laban said, This heap is a witness today between you and me. Therefore it was named Galeed.

49 And [the pillar or monument was called] Mizpah [watchpost], for he [Laban] said, May the Lord watch between you and me when we are absent *and* hidden one from another.

50 If you should afflict, humiliate, *or* lower [divorce] my daughters, or if you should take other wives beside my daughters, although no man is with us [to witness], see (remember), God is witness between you and me.

51 And Laban said to Jacob, See this heap and this pillar, which I have set up between you and me.

52 This heap is a witness and this pillar is a witness, that I will not pass by this heap to you, and that you will not pass by this heap and this pillar to me, for harm.

53 The God of Abraham and the God of Nahor, and the god [the object of worship] of their father [Terah, an idolator], judge between us. But Jacob swore [only] by [the one true God] the Dread *and* Fear of his father Isaac. [Josh. 24:2.]

---

o *The Latin Vulgate* adds, "Each according to the idiom of his own tongue"—i.e., Laban in Aramaic and Jacob in Hebrew.

54 Then Jacob offered a sacrifice on the mountain and called his brethren to eat food; and they ate food and lingered all night on the mountain.

55 And early in the morning Laban rose up and kissed his grandchildren and his daughters and pronounced a blessing [asking God's favor] on them. Then Laban departed and returned to his home.

32 THEN JACOB went on his way, and God's angels met him.

2 When Jacob saw them, he said, This is God's army! So he named that place Mahanaim [two armies]. [Gen. 32:7, 10.]

3 And Jacob sent messengers before him to Esau his brother in the land of Seir, the country of Edom.

4 And he commanded them, Say this to my lord Esau: Your servant Jacob says this: I have been living temporarily with Laban and have stayed there till now.

5 And I have oxen, donkeys, flocks, menservants, and women servants; and I have sent to tell my lord, that I may find mercy *and* kindness in your sight.

6 And the messengers returned to Jacob, saying, We came to your brother Esau; and now he is [on the way] to meet you, and four hundred men are with him.

7 Then Jacob was greatly afraid and distressed; and he divided the people who were with him, and the flocks and herds and camels, into two groups,

8 Thinking, If Esau comes to the one group and smites it, then the other group which is left will escape.

9 Jacob said, O God of my father Abraham and God of my father Isaac, the Lord Who said to me, Return to your country and to your people and I will do you good,

10 I am not worthy of the least of all the mercy *and* loving-kindness and all the faithfulness which You have shown to Your servant, for with [only] my staff I passed over this Jordan [long ago], and now I have become two companies.

11 Deliver me, I pray You, from the hand of my brother, from the hand of Esau; for I fear him, lest he come and smite [us all], the mothers with the children.

12 And You said, I will surely do you good and make your descendants as the sand of the sea, which cannot be numbered for multitude.

13 And Jacob lodged there that night and took from what he had with him as a present for his brother Esau:

14 Two hundred she-goats, 20 he-goats, 200 ewes, 20 rams,

15 Thirty milk camels with their colts, 40 cows, 10 bulls, 20 she-donkeys, and 10 [donkey] colts.

16 And he put them into the charge of his servants, every drove by itself, and said to his servants, Pass over before me and put a space between drove and drove.

17 And he commanded the first, When Esau my brother meets you and asks to whom you belong, where you are going, and whose are the animals before you,

18 Then you shall say, They are your servant Jacob's; it is a present sent to my lord Esau; and moreover, he is behind us.

speak the Word

Father, thank You for all the mercy and loving-kindness and faithfulness You show to me, even though I am not worthy.
ADAPTED FROM GENESIS 32:10

19 And so he commanded the second and the third and all that followed the droves, saying, This is what you are to say to Esau when you meet him.

20 And say, Moreover, your servant Jacob is behind us. For he said, I will appease him with the present that goes before me, and afterward I will see his face; perhaps he will accept me.

21 So the present went on before him, and he himself lodged that night in the camp.

22 But he rose up that [same] night and took his two wives, his two women servants, and his eleven sons and passed over the ford [of the] Jabbok.

23 And he took them and sent them across the brook; also he sent over all that he had.

24 And Jacob was left alone, and a Man wrestled with him until daybreak.

25 And when [the P Man] saw that He did not prevail against [Jacob], He touched the hollow of his thigh; and Jacob's thigh was put out of joint as he wrestled with Him.

26 Then He said, Let Me go, for day is breaking. But [Jacob] said, I will not let You go unless You declare a blessing upon me.

27 [The Man] asked him, What is your name? And [in shock of realization, whispering] he said, Jacob [supplanter, schemer, trickster, swindler]!

28 And He said, Your name shall be called no more Jacob [supplanter], but Israel [contender with God]; for you have contended *and* have power with God and with men and have prevailed. [Hos. 12:3-4.]

29 Then Jacob asked Him, Tell me, I pray You, what [in contrast] is Your name? But He said, Why is it that you ask My name? And P[the Angel of God declared] a blessing on [Jacob] there.

30 And Jacob called the name of the place Peniel [the face of God], saying, For I have seen God face to face, and my life is spared *and* not snatched away.

31 And as he passed Penuel [Peniel], the sun rose upon him, and he was limping because of his thigh.

32 That is why to this day the Israelites do not eat the sinew of the hip which is on the hollow of the thigh, because [the Angel of the Lord] touched the hollow of Jacob's thigh on the sinew of the hip.

33 AND JACOB raised his eyes and looked, and behold, Esau was coming and with him 400 men. So he divided the children to Leah and to Rachel and to the two maids.

2 And he put the maids and their children in front, Leah and her children after them, and Rachel and Joseph last of all.

3 Then Jacob went over [the stream] before them and bowed himself to the ground seven times, until he came near to his brother.

4 But Esau ran to meet him, and embraced him and fell on his neck and kissed him, and they wept. [Luke 15:20.]

5 [Esau] looked up and saw the women and the children and said, Who are these with you? And [Jacob] replied, They are the children whom God has graciously given your servant.

6 Then the maids came near, they and their children, and they bowed themselves.

7 And Leah also with her children came near, and they bowed themselves. After them Joseph and Rachel came near, and they bowed themselves.

---

p This is God Himself (as Jacob eventually realizes in Gen. 32:30) in the form of an angel. See footnote on Gen. 16:7, as well as Hos. 12:3-4.

everybody limps

Jacob was a man with many weaknesses, yet he pressed on with God and was determined to receive God's blessing. God likes that kind of determination. He actually told Jacob in Genesis 32:28 that he (Jacob) had contended with God and man, and that God would be glorified in him. God can always be glorified through people who will not allow their personal weaknesses to stop Him from flowing through them.

In order for God to flow through us, we must first come face-to-face with the fact that we have weaknesses—and then we must determine not to let them bother us. Our imperfections will not stop God from working through us unless we let them. We need to accept ourselves completely—weaknesses and all—because God does.

I am going to ask you to do something very important. Right now, stop and wrap your arms around yourself. Give yourself a great big hug and say aloud: "I accept myself. I love myself. I know I have weaknesses and imperfections, but I will not let them stop me, and I will not allow them to stop God from working through me." Try doing that several times per day, and you will soon develop a new attitude toward yourself, a new outlook on life, and a greater level of confidence in God.

Jacob wrestled with the Angel of the Lord, who touched the hollow of his thigh. As a result of that encounter, he lived the remainder of his life with a limp (see Genesis 32:24–32). I like to say that Jacob limped away from the fight, but he took his blessing with him! God will bless all of us even though we limp, even though we are not perfect. Remember, God looks at our hearts. If we have faith in Him and hearts that long to obey Him and bring Him glory, then He will work wonders through us in spite of our weaknesses.

8 Esau said, What do you mean by all this company which I met? And he said, These are that I might find favor in the sight of my lord.

9 And Esau said, I have plenty, my brother; keep what you have for yourself.

10 But Jacob replied, No, I beg of you, if now I have found favor in your sight, receive my gift that I am presenting; for truly to see your face is to me as if I had seen the face of God, and you have received me favorably.

11 Accept, I beg of you, my blessing *and* gift that I have brought to you; for God has dealt graciously with me and I have everything. And he kept urging him and he accepted it.

12 Then [Esau] said, Let us get started on our journey, and I will go before you.

13 But Jacob replied, You know, my lord, that the children are tender *and* delicate *and* need gentle care, and the flocks and herds with young are of concern to me; for if the men should overdrive them for a single day, the whole of the flocks would die.

14 Let my lord, I pray you, pass over before his servant; and I will lead on slowly, governed by [consideration for] the livestock that set the pace

before me and the endurance of the children, �۹until I come to my lord in Seir.

15 Then Esau said, Let me now leave with you some of the people who are with me. But [Jacob] said, What need is there for it? Let me find favor in the sight of my lord.

16 So Esau turned back that day on his way to Seir.

17 But Jacob journeyed to Succoth and built himself a house and made booths *or* places of shelter for his livestock; so the name of the place is called Succoth [booths].

18 When Jacob came from Padan-aram, he arrived safely *and* in peace at the town of Shechem, in the land of Canaan, and pitched his tents before the [enclosed] town.

19 Then he bought the piece of land on which he had encamped from the sons of Hamor, Shechem's father, for a hundred pieces of money.

20 There he erected an altar and called it El-Elohe-Israel [God, the God of Israel].

34 NOW DINAH daughter of Leah, whom she bore to Jacob, went out [unattended] to see the girls of the place.

2 And when Shechem son of Hamor the Hivite, prince of the country, saw her, he seized her, lay with her, and humbled, defiled, *and* disgraced her.

3 But his soul longed for *and* clung to Dinah daughter of Jacob, and he

putting the Word to work

Have you, like Dinah, ever been an innocent victim? I can assure you that even in the worst circumstances, God gives us grace to forgive so that we can go on with our lives.

loved the girl and spoke comfortingly to her young heart's wishes.

4 And Shechem said to his father Hamor, Get me this girl to be my wife.

5 Jacob heard that [Shechem] had defiled Dinah his daughter. Now his sons were with his livestock in the field. So Jacob held his peace until they came.

6 But Hamor father of Shechem went out to Jacob to have a talk with him.

7 When Jacob's sons heard it, they came from the field; and they were distressed and grieved and very angry, for [Shechem] had done a vile thing to Israel in lying with Jacob's daughter, which ought not to be done.

8 And Hamor conferred with them, saying, The soul of my son Shechem craves your daughter [and sister]. I beg of you give her to him to be his wife.

9 And make marriages with us and give your daughters to us and take our daughters to you.

10 You shall dwell with us; the country will be open to you; live and trade and get your possessions in it.

11 And Shechem said to [Dinah's] father and to her brothers, Let me find favor in your eyes, and I will give you whatever you ask of me.

12 Ask me ever so much dowry and [marriage] gift, and I will give according to what you tell me; only give me the girl to be my wife.

13 The sons of Jacob answered Shechem and Hamor his father deceitfully, [justifying their intended action by saying, in effect, we are going to do this] because Shechem had defiled *and* disgraced their sister Dinah.

14 They said to them, We cannot do this thing *and* give our sister to one who is not circumcised, for that would be a reproach *and* disgrace to us.

---

q Ever the deceiver, Jacob had no intention of following Esau to Seir. In fact, he heads in the opposite direction.

15 But we do consent to do this: if you will become as we are and every male among you be circumcised,

16 Then we will give our daughters to you and we will take your daughters to us, and we will dwell with you and become one people.

17 But if you will not listen to us and consent to be circumcised, then we will take our daughter and go.

18 Their words pleased Hamor and his son Shechem.

19 And the young man did not delay to do the thing, for he delighted in Jacob's daughter. He was honored above all his family [so, ranking first, he acted first].

20 Then Hamor and Shechem his son came to the gate of their [enclosed] town and discussed the matter with the citizens, saying,

21 These men are peaceable with us; so let them dwell in the land and trade in it; for the land is large enough [for us and] for them; let us take their daughters for wives and let us give them our daughters.

22 But the men will consent to our request that they live among us and be one people only on condition that every male among us be circumcised, as they are.

23 Shall not their cattle and their possessions and all their beasts be ours? Only let us consent to them, and they will dwell here with us.

24 And all the people who went out of the town gate listened *and* heeded what Hamor and Shechem said; and every male was circumcised who was a resident of that town.

25 But on the third day [after the circumcision] when [all the men] were sore, two of the sons of Jacob, Simeon and Levi, Dinah's [full] brothers, took their swords, boldly entered the city [without danger], and slew all the males.

26 And they killed Hamor and Shechem his son with the edge of the sword and took Dinah out of Shechem's house [where she had been all this time] and departed.

27 [Then the rest of] Jacob's [eleven] sons came upon the slain and plundered the town, because there their sister had been defiled *and* disgraced.

28 They took their flocks, their herds, their donkeys, and whatever was in the town and in the field;

29 All their wealth and all their little ones and their wives they took captive, making spoil even of all [they found] in the houses.

30 And Jacob said to Simeon and Levi, You have ruined me, making me infamous *and* embroiling me with the inhabitants of the land, the Canaanites and the Perizzites! And we are few in number, and they will gather together against me and attack me; and I shall be destroyed, I and my household.

31 And they said, Should he [be permitted to] deal with our sister as with a harlot?

35 AND GOD said to Jacob, Arise, go up to Bethel and dwell there. And make there an altar to God Who appeared to you [in a distinct manifestation] when you fled from the presence of Esau your brother. [Gen. 28:11-22.]

2 Then Jacob said to his household and to all who were with him, Put away the [images of] strange gods that are among you, and purify yourselves and change [into fresh] garments;

3 Then let us arise and go up to Bethel, and I will make there an altar to God Who answered me in the day of my distress and was with me wherever I went.

4 So they [both young men and women] gave to Jacob all the strange gods they had and their earrings which were [worn as charms against evil] in their ears; and Jacob buried *and* hid them under the oak near Shechem.

5 And they journeyed and a terror from God fell on the towns round about them, and they did not pursue the sons of Jacob.

6 So Jacob came to Luz, that is, Bethel, which is in the land of Canaan, he and all the people with him.

7 There he built an altar, and called the place El-bethel [God of Bethel], for there God revealed Himself to him when he fled from the presence of his brother.

8 But Deborah, Rebekah's nurse, died and was buried below Bethel under an oak; and the name of it was called Allon-bacuth [oak of weeping].

9 And God [in a distinctly visible manifestation] appeared to Jacob again when he came out of Padan-aram, and declared a blessing on him. [Gen. 32:28.]

10 Again God said to him, Your name is Jacob [supplanter]; you shall not be called Jacob any longer, but Israel shall be your name. So He called him Israel [contender with God].

11 And God said to him, I am God Almighty. Be fruitful and multiply; a nation and a company of nations shall come from you and kings shall be born of your stock;

12 The land which I gave Abraham and Isaac I will give to you, and to your descendants after you I will give the land.

13 Then God ascended from him in the place where He talked with him.

14 And Jacob set up a pillar (monument) in the place where he talked with [God], a pillar of stone; and he poured a drink offering on it and he poured oil on it.

15 And Jacob called the name of the place where God had talked with him Bethel [house of God].

16 And they journeyed from Bethel and had but a little way to go to Ephrath [Bethlehem] when Rachel suffered the pangs of childbirth and had hard labor.

17 When she was in hard labor, the midwife said to her, Do not be afraid; you shall have this son also.

18 And as her soul was departing, for she died, she called his name Ben-oni [son of my sorrow]; but his father called him Benjamin [son of the right hand].

19 So Rachel died and was buried on the way to Ephrath, that is, Bethlehem.

20 And Jacob set a pillar (monument) on her grave; that is the pillar of Rachel's grave to this day.

21 Then Israel journeyed on and spread his tent on the other side of the tower of Edar.

22 When Israel dwelt there, Reuben [his eldest son] went and lay with Bilhah his father's concubine; and Israel heard about it. Now Jacob's sons were twelve.

23 The sons of Leah: Reuben, Jacob's firstborn, Simeon, Levi, Judah, Issachar, and Zebulun.

24 The sons of Rachel: Joseph and Benjamin.

25 The sons of Bilhah, Rachel's maid: Dan and Naphtali.

26 And the sons of Zilpah, Leah's maid: Gad and Asher. These are the sons of Jacob born to him in Padan-aram.

27 And Jacob came to Isaac his father at Mamre or Kiriath-arba, that is, Hebron, where Abraham and Isaac had sojourned.

28 Now the days of Isaac were 180 years.

29 And Isaac's spirit departed; he died and was gathered to his people, being an old man, satisfied *and* satiated with days; his sons Esau and Jacob buried him.

36

NOW THIS is the history of the descendants of Esau, that is, Edom.

2 Esau took his wives from the women of Canaan: Adah daughter of

Elon the Hittite, and Oholibamah daughter of Anah, the son of Zibeon the Hivite,

3 And Basemath, Ishmael's daughter, sister of Nebaioth.

4 Adah bore to Esau, Eliphaz; Basemath bore Reuel;

5 And Oholibamah bore Jeush, Jalam, and Korah. These are the sons of Esau born to him in Canaan.

6 Now Esau took his wives, his sons, his daughters, and all the members of his household, his cattle, all his beasts, and all his possessions which he had obtained in the land of Canaan, and he went into a land away from his brother Jacob.

7 For their great flocks *and* herds *and* possessions [which they had collected] made it impossible for them to dwell together; the land in which they were strangers could not support them because of their livestock.

8 So Esau dwelt in the hill country of Seir; Esau is Edom.

9 And this is the history of the descendants of Esau the father of the Edomites in the hill country of Seir.

10 These are the names of Esau's sons: Eliphaz, the son of Adah, Esau's wife, and Reuel, the son of Basemath, Esau's wife.

11 And the sons of Eliphaz were Teman, Omar, Zepho, Gatam, and Kenaz.

12 And Timna was a concubine of Eliphaz, Esau's son; and she bore Amalek to Eliphaz. These are the sons of Adah, Esau's wife.

13 These are the sons of Reuel: Nahath, Zerah, Shammah, and Mizzah. These are the sons of Basemath, Esau's wife.

14 And these are the sons of Oholibamah daughter of Anah, the son of Zibeon, Esau's wife. She bore to Esau: Jeush, Jalam, and Korah.

15 These are the chiefs of the sons of Esau: The sons of Eliphaz the firstborn of Esau: Chiefs Teman, Omar, Zepho, Kenaz,

16 Korah, Gatam, and Amalek. These are the chiefs of Eliphaz in the land of Edom; they are the sons of Adah.

17 These are the sons of Reuel, Esau's son: Chiefs Nahath, Zerah, Shammah, Mizzah. These are the chiefs of Reuel in the land of Edom; they are the sons of Basemath, Esau's wife.

18 These are the sons of Oholibamah, Esau's wife: Chiefs Jeush, Jalam, and Korah. These are the chiefs born of Oholibamah daughter of Anah, Esau's wife.

19 These are the sons of Esau, that is, Edom, and these are their chiefs.

20 These are the sons of Seir the Horite, the inhabitants of the land: Lotan, Shobal, Zibeon, Anah,

21 Dishon, Ezer, and Dishan. These are the chiefs of the ʳHorites, the sons of Seir in the land of Edom.

22 The sons of Lotan are Hori and Hemam; and Lotan's sister is Timna.

23 The sons of Shobal are these: Alvan, Manahath, Ebal, Shepho, and Onam.

24 These are the sons of Zibeon: Aiah and Anah. This is the Anah who found the hot springs in the wilderness as he pastured the donkeys of Zibeon his father.

25 The children of Anah are these: Dishon and Oholibamah daughter of Anah [Esau's wife].

r Because of the similarity of the word 'Horites' to a Hebrew word for "cave," the term Horite was formerly interpreted as "cave dweller." But later archaeological discoveries have shown that the Horites are not to be explained as cave dwellers, but are to be identified with an important group in the Near East in patriarchal times (J. P. Free, *Archaeology and Bible History*). In fact, neither the Bible nor archaeology has any proof of aboriginal "cavemen." Cities of great antiquity have been unearthed with ever-increasing evidence that "when civilization appears it is already fully grown," and "pre-Semitic culture springs into view ready-made" (Hall, *History of the Near East*).

26 These are the sons of Dishon: Hemdan, Eshban, Ithran, and Cheran.
27 Ezer's sons are these: Bilhan, Zaavan, and Akan.
28 The sons of Dishan are these: Uz and Aran.
29 The Horite chiefs are these: Lotan, Shobal, Zibeon, Anah,
30 Dishon, Ezer, Dishan. These are the Horite chiefs, according to their clans, in the land of Seir.
31 And these are the kings who reigned in Edom before any king reigned over the Israelites:
32 Bela son of Beor reigned in Edom. And the name of his city was Dinhabah.
33 Now Bela died, and Jobab son of Zerah of Bozrah reigned in his stead.
34 Then Jobab died, and Husham of the land of the Temanites reigned in his stead.
35 And Husham died, and Hadad son of Bedad, who defeated Midian in the country of Moab, reigned in his stead. The name of his [enclosed] city was Avith.
36 Hadad died, and Samlah of Masrekah succeeded him.
37 Then Samlah died, and Shaul of Rehoboth on the river [Euphrates] reigned in his stead.

life point

God gave Joseph dreams of greatness, but in his zeal and excitement, Joseph unwisely told his dreams to his brothers, who did not share his enthusiasm (see Genesis 37:5). As a result, they sold him as a slave, and he had to endure some hard years and difficult experiences. During those years, though, God developed wisdom in Joseph and thereby prepared him for his life's call. Just as He did for Joseph, God is able to develop in you whatever you may lack today so that you can fulfill His purpose for your life.

38 And Shaul died, and Baal-hanan son of Achbor reigned in his stead.
39 Baal-hanan son of Achbor died, and then Hadar reigned. His [enclosed] city was Pau; his wife's name was Mehetabel daughter of Matred, the daughter of Mezahab.
40 And these are the names of the chiefs of Esau, according to their families and places of residence, by their names: Chiefs Timna, Alvah, Jetheth,
41 Oholibamah, Elah, Pinon,
42 Kenaz, Teman, Mibzar,
43 Magdiel, and Iram. These are the chiefs of Edom [that is, of Esau the father of the Edomites], according to their dwelling places in their land.

37 SO JACOB dwelt in the land in which his father had been a stranger *and* sojourner, in the land of Canaan.
2 This is the history of the descendants of Jacob *and* this is Jacob's line. Joseph, when he was seventeen years old, was shepherding the flock with his brothers; the lad was with the sons of Bilhah and Zilpah, his father's [secondary] wives; and Joseph brought to his father a bad report of them.
3 Now Israel loved Joseph more than all his children because he was the son of his old age, and he made him a [distinctive] long tunic with sleeves.
4 But when his brothers saw that their father loved [Joseph] more than all of his brothers, they hated him and could not say, Peace [in friendly greeting] to him *or* speak peaceably to him.
5 Now Joseph had a dream and he told it to his brothers, and they hated him still more.
6 And he said to them, Listen now *and* hear, I pray you, this dream that I have dreamed:
7 We [brothers] were binding sheaves in the field, and behold, my sheaf arose and stood upright, and

behold, your sheaves stood round about my sheaf and bowed down!

8 His brothers said to him, Shall you indeed reign over us? Or are you going to have us as your subjects *and* dominate us? And they hated him all the more for his dreams and for what he said.

9 But Joseph dreamed yet another dream and told it to his brothers [also]. He said, See here, I have dreamed again, and behold, [this time not only] eleven stars [but also] the sun and the moon bowed down *and* did reverence to me!

10 And he told it to his father [as well as] his brethren. But his father rebuked him and said to him, What is the meaning of this dream that you have dreamed? Shall I and your mother and your brothers actually come to bow down ourselves to the earth *and* do homage to you?

11 Joseph's brothers envied him *and* were jealous of him, but his father observed the saying *and* pondered over it.

12 Joseph's brothers went to shepherd *and* feed their father's flock near Shechem.

13 [One day] Israel said to Joseph, Do not your brothers shepherd my flock at Shechem? Come, and I will send you to them. And he said, Here I am.

14 And [Jacob] said to him, Go, I pray you, see whether everything is all right with your brothers and with the flock; then come back and bring me word. So he sent him out of the Hebron Valley, and he came to Shechem.

15 And a certain man found him, and behold, he had lost his way *and* was wandering in the open country. The man asked him, What are you trying to find?

16 And he said, I am looking for my brothers. Tell me, I pray you, where they are pasturing our flocks.

17 But the man said, [They were here, but] they have gone. I heard them say, Let us go to Dothan. And Joseph went after his brothers and found them at Dothan.

18 And when they saw him far off, even before he came near to them, they conspired to kill him.

19 And they said one to another, See, here comes this dreamer *and* master of dreams.

20 So come on now, let us kill him and throw his body into some pit; then we will say [to our father], Some wild *and* ferocious animal has devoured him; and we shall see what will become of his dreams!

21 Now Reuben heard it and he delivered him out of their hands by saying, Let us not kill him.

22 And Reuben said to them, Shed no blood, but cast him into this pit *or* well that is out here in the wilderness and lay no hand on him. He was trying to get Joseph out of their hands in order to rescue him *and* deliver him again to his father.

23 When Joseph had come to his brothers, they stripped him of his [distinctive] long garment which he was wearing;

24 Then they took him and cast him into the [well-like] pit which was empty; there was no water in it.

25 Then they sat down to eat their lunch. When they looked up, behold, they saw a caravan of Ishmaelites [mixed Arabians] coming from Gilead, with their camels bearing gum [of the styrax tree], balm (balsam), and myrrh *or* ladanum, going on their way to carry them down to Egypt.

26 And Judah said to his brothers, What do we gain if we slay our brother and conceal his blood?

27 Come, let us sell him to the Ishmaelites [and Midianites, these mixed Arabians who are approaching], and let not our hand be upon him, for he is our brother and our flesh. And his brothers consented.

28 Then as the Midianite [and Ishmaelite] merchants were passing by, the brothers pulled Joseph up and lifted him out of the well. And they sold him for twenty pieces of silver to the Ishmaelites, who took Joseph [captive] into Egypt.

29 Then Reuben [who had not been there when the brothers plotted to sell the lad] returned to the pit; and behold, Joseph was not in the pit, and he rent his clothes.

30 He rejoined his brothers and said, The boy is not there! And I, where shall I go [to hide from my father]?

31 Then they took Joseph's [distinctive] long garment, killed a young goat, and dipped the garment in the blood;

32 And they sent the garment to their father, saying, We have found this! Examine *and* decide whether it is your son's tunic or not.

33 He said, My son's long garment! An evil [wild] beast has devoured him; Joseph is without doubt rent in pieces.

34 And Jacob tore his clothes, put on sackcloth, and mourned many days for his son.

35 And all his sons and daughters attempted to console him, but he refused to be comforted and said, I will go down to Sheol (the place of the dead) to my son mourning. And his father wept for him.

36 And the Midianites [and Ishmaelites] sold [Joseph] in Egypt to Potiphar, an officer of Pharaoh and the captain *and* chief executioner of the [royal] guard.

38 AT THAT time Judah withdrew from his brothers and went to [lodge with] a certain Adullamite named Hirah.

2 There Judah saw *and* met a daughter of Shuah, a Canaanite; he took her as wife and lived with her.

3 And she became pregnant and bore a son, and he called him Er.

4 And she conceived again and bore a son and named him Onan.

5 Again she conceived and bore a son and named him Shelah. [They were living] at Chezib when she bore him.

6 Now Judah took a wife for Er, his firstborn; her name was Tamar.

7 And Er, Judah's firstborn, was wicked in the sight of the Lord, and the Lord slew him.

8 Then Judah told Onan, Marry your brother's widow; live with her and raise offspring for your brother.

9 But Onan knew that the family would not be his, so when he cohabited with his brother's widow, he prevented conception, lest he should raise up a child for his brother.

10 And the thing which he did displeased the Lord; therefore He slew him also.

11 Then Judah said to Tamar, his daughter-in-law, Remain a widow at your father's house till Shelah my [youngest] son is grown; for he thought, Lest perhaps [if Shelah should marry her] he would die also, as his brothers did. So Tamar went and lived in her father's house.

12 But later Judah's wife, the daughter of Shuah, died; and when Judah was comforted, he went up to his sheepshearers at Timnath with his friend Hirah the Adullamite.

13 Then it was told Tamar, Listen, your father-in-law is going up to Timnath to shear his sheep.

14 So she put off her widow's garments and covered herself with a veil, wrapped herself up [in disguise], and sat in the entrance of Enaim, which is by the road to Timnath; for she saw that Shelah was grown and she was not given to him as his wife.

15 When Judah saw her, he thought she was a harlot *or* devoted prostitute [under a vow to her goddess], for she had covered her face [as such women did].

16 He turned to her by the road and

said, Come, let me have intercourse with you; for he did not know that she was his daughter-in-law. And she said, What will you give me that you may have intercourse with me?

17 He answered, I will send you a kid from the flock. And she said, Will you give me a pledge (deposit) until you send it?

18 And he said, What pledge shall I give you? She said, Your signet [seal], your [signet] cord, and your staff that is in your hand. And he gave them to her and came in to her, and she became pregnant by him.

19 And she arose and went away and laid aside her veil and put on the garments of her widowhood.

20 And Judah sent the kid by the hand of his friend the Adullamite, to receive his pledge from the woman's hand; but he was unable to find her.

21 He asked the men of that place, Where is the harlot *or* cult prostitute who was openly by the roadside? They said, There was no harlot *or* temple prostitute here.

22 So he returned to Judah and said, I cannot find her; and also the local men said, There was no harlot *or* temple prostitute around here.

23 And Judah said, Let her keep [the pledge articles] for herself, lest we be made ashamed. I sent this kid, but you have not found her.

24 But about three months later Judah was told, Tamar your daughter-in-law has played the harlot, and also she is with child by her lewdness. And Judah said, Bring her forth and let her be burned!

25 When she was brought forth, she [took the things he had given her in pledge and] sent [them] to her father-in-law, saying, I am with child by the man to whom these articles belong. Then she added, Make out clearly, I pray you, to whom these belong, the signet [seal], [signet] cord, and staff.

26 And Judah acknowledged them and said, She has been more righteous *and* just than I, because I did not give her to Shelah my son. And he did not cohabit with her again.

27 Now when the time came for her to be delivered, behold, there were twins in her womb.

28 And when she was in labor, one baby put out his hand; and the midwife took his hand and bound upon it a scarlet thread, saying, This baby was born first.

29 But he drew back his hand, and behold, his brother was born first. And she said, What a breaking forth you have made for yourself! Therefore his name was called Perez [breaking forth]. [Matt. 1:3.]

30 And afterward his brother who had the scarlet thread on his hand was born and was named Zerah [scarlet].

39 AND JOSEPH was brought down to Egypt; and Potiphar, an officer of Pharaoh, the captain *and* chief executioner of the [royal] guard, an Egyptian, bought him from the Ishmaelites who had brought him down there.

2 But the Lord was with Joseph, and he [though a slave] was a successful *and* prosperous man; and he was in the house of his master the Egyptian.

life point

While we are waiting on God, it is important for us to take our positions and stay faithful. Then, like Joseph, God will raise us up in His timing (see Genesis 39:2–5). Be faithful as you wait on God, do your work well, and people will see that God's hand is upon you for good.

3 And his master saw that the Lord was with him and that the Lord made all that he did to flourish *and* succeed in his hand. [Gen. 21:22; 26:27, 28; 41:38, 39.]

4 So Joseph pleased [Potiphar] *and* found favor in his sight, and he served him. And [his master] made him supervisor over his house and he put all that he had in his charge.
5 From the time that he made him supervisor in his house and over all that he had, the Lord blessed the Egyptian's house for Joseph's sake; and the Lord's blessing was on all that he had in the house and in the field.
6 And [Potiphar] left all that he had in Joseph's charge and paid no attention to anything he had except the food he ate. Now Joseph was an attractive person and fine-looking.
7 Then after a time his master's wife cast her eyes upon Joseph, and she said, Lie with me.
8 But he refused and said to his master's wife, See here, with me in the house my master has concern about nothing; he has put all that he has in my care.
9 He is not greater in this house than I am; nor has he kept anything from me except you, for you are his wife. How then can I do this great evil and sin against God?
10 She spoke to Joseph day after day, but he did not listen to her, to lie with her or to be with her.
11 Then it happened about this time that Joseph went into the house to attend to his duties, and none of the men of the house were indoors.
12 And she caught him by his garment, saying, Lie with me! But he left his garment in her hand and fled and got out [of the house].
13 And when she saw that he had left his garment in her hand and had fled away,
14 She called to the men of her household and said to them, Behold, he [your master] has brought in a Hebrew to us to mock *and* insult us; he came in where I was to lie with me, and I screamed at the top of my voice.

15 And when he heard me screaming and crying, he left his garment with me and fled and got out of the house.
16 And she laid up his garment by her until his master came home.
17 Then she told him the same story, saying, The Hebrew servant whom you brought among us came to me to mock *and* insult me.
18 And when I screamed and cried, he left his garment with me and fled out [of the house].
19 And when [Joseph's] master heard the words of his wife, saying to him, This is the way your servant treated me, his wrath was kindled.
20 And Joseph's master took him and put him in the prison, a place where the state prisoners were confined; so he was there in the prison.
21 But the Lord was with Joseph, and showed him mercy *and* loving-kindness and gave him favor in the sight of the warden of the prison.
22 And the warden of the prison committed to Joseph's care all the prisoners who were in the prison; and whatsoever was done there, he was in charge of it.
23 The prison warden paid no attention to anything that was in [Joseph's] charge, for the Lord was with him and made whatever he did to prosper.

40 NOW SOME time later the butler and the baker of the king of Egypt offended their lord, Egypt's king.
2 And Pharaoh was angry with his officers, the chief of the butlers and the chief of the bakers.
3 He put them in custody in the house of the captain of the guard, in the prison where Joseph was confined.
4 And the captain of the guard put them in Joseph's charge, and he served them; and they continued in custody for some time.
5 And they both dreamed a dream in the same night, each man according to

receive God's favor

Joseph had been unjustly accused and imprisoned, but the Lord was with him and showed him mercy and grace. In Genesis 39:20–23, we see that God gave Joseph favor in the eyes of the prison warden, who basically put him in charge of running the prison. Even in the dismal circumstances of incarceration, the Lord caused Joseph to prosper.

God's favor is also available to us, His children. But like many other good things in life, just because something is available to us does not mean that we will ever partake of it. The Lord offers us many things that we never enjoy because we do not activate our faith to receive what He has provided.

Favor is actually a part of grace. In the English New Testament, the word *grace* and the word *favor* are both translated from the same Greek word *charis*. So the grace of God is the favor of God. And the favor of God is the grace of God—that which causes things to happen in our lives through the channel of our faith. It is the power of God doing something for us that we do not earn or deserve. For example, if you ask someone, "Can you do me a favor?" you are asking that person to do something for you that you have not earned or paid for. You are depending on that individual's goodness to manifest in the form of a blessing, even though there is no natural reason for that person to extend it to you.

God wants to give you favor, just as He did Joseph. But in order to receive that favor, you must follow Joseph's example and believe God for it. Joseph maintained a good attitude in a bad situation, and his "faith attitude" led to God's favor. Expect God's favor and keep your attitude of faith in every situation you face.

[the personal significance of] the interpretation of his dream—the butler and the baker of the king of Egypt, who were confined in the prison.

6 When Joseph came to them in the morning and looked at them, he saw that they were sad *and* depressed.

7 So he asked Pharaoh's officers who were in custody with him in his master's house, Why do you look so dejected *and* sad today?

8 And they said to him, We have dreamed dreams, and there is no one to interpret them. And Joseph said to them, Do not interpretations belong to God? Tell me [your dreams], I pray you.

9 And the chief butler told his dream to Joseph and said to him, In my dream I saw a vine before me,

10 And on the vine were three branches. Then it was as though it budded; its blossoms burst forth and the clusters of them brought forth ripe grapes [almost all at once].

11 And Pharaoh's cup was in my hand, and I took the grapes and pressed them into Pharaoh's cup; then I gave the cup into Pharaoh's hand.

12 And Joseph said to him, This is the interpretation of it: The three branches are three days.

13 Within three days Pharaoh will lift up your head and restore you to your position, and you will again put

Pharaoh's cup into his hand, as when you were his butler.

14 But think of me when it shall be well with you and show kindness, I beg of you, to me, and mention me to Pharaoh and get me out of this house.

15 For truly I was carried away from the land of the Hebrews by unlawful force, and here too I have done nothing for which they should put me into the dungeon.

16 When the chief baker saw that the interpretation was good, he said to Joseph, I also dreamed, and behold, I had three cake baskets on my head.

17 And in the uppermost basket were some of all kinds of baked food for Pharaoh, but the birds [of prey] were eating out of the basket on my head.

18 And Joseph answered, This is the interpretation of it: The three baskets are three days.

19 Within three days Pharaoh will lift up your head but will have you beheaded and hung on a tree, and [you will not so much as be given burial, but] the birds will eat your flesh.

20 And on the third day, Pharaoh's birthday, he made a feast for all his servants; and he lifted up the heads of the chief butler and the chief baker [by inviting them also] among his servants.

21 And he restored the chief butler to his butlership, and the butler gave the cup into Pharaoh's hand;

22 But [Pharaoh] hanged the chief baker, as Joseph had interpreted to them.

23 But [even after all that] the chief butler gave no thought to Joseph, but forgot [all about] him.

41 AFTER TWO full years, Pharaoh dreamed that he stood by the river [Nile].

2 And behold, there came up out of the river [Nile] seven well-favored cows, sleek *and* handsome and fat;

and they grazed in the reed grass [in a marshy pasture].

3 And behold, seven other cows came up after them out of the river [Nile], ill favored and gaunt *and* ugly, and stood by the fat cows on the bank of the river [Nile].

4 And the ill-favored, gaunt, *and* ugly cows ate up the seven well-favored and fat cows. Then Pharaoh awoke.

5 But he slept and dreamed the second time; and behold, seven ears of grain came out on one stalk, plump and good.

6 And behold, after them seven ears [of grain] sprouted, thin *and* blighted by the east wind.

7 And the seven thin ears [of grain] devoured the seven plump and full ears. And Pharaoh awoke, and behold, it was a dream.

8 So when morning came his spirit was troubled, and he sent and called for all the magicians and all the wise men of Egypt. And Pharaoh told them his dreams, but not one could interpret them to [him].

9 Then the chief butler said to Pharaoh, I remember my faults today.

10 When Pharaoh was angry with his servants and put me in custody in the captain of the guard's house, both me and the chief baker,

11 We dreamed a dream in the same night, he and I; we dreamed each of us according to [the significance of] the interpretation of his dream.

12 And there was there with us a young man, a Hebrew, servant to the captain of the guard *and* chief executioner; and we told him our dreams, and he interpreted them to us, to each man according to the significance of his dream.

13 And as he interpreted to us, so it came to pass; I was restored to my office [as chief butler], and the baker was hanged.

14 Then Pharaoh sent and called

Joseph, and they brought him hastily out of the dungeon. But Joseph [first] shaved himself, changed his clothes, *and* made himself presentable; then he came into Pharaoh's presence.

15 And Pharaoh said to Joseph, I have dreamed a dream, and there is no one who can interpret it; and I have heard it said of you that you can understand a dream *and* interpret it.

16 Joseph answered Pharaoh, It is not in me; God [not I] will give Pharaoh a [favorable] answer of peace.

life point

God can speak to us today through dreams, just as He did in Joseph's time (see Genesis 41). But we need to be balanced in our approach because many of our dreams are not spiritual. If God is trying to show you something or speak to you through a dream, I believe He will confirm it in your heart if you ask Him for wisdom, use discernment, and stay in balance with His Word.

17 And Pharaoh said to Joseph, In my dream, behold, I stood on the bank of the river [Nile];

18 And behold, there came up out of the river [Nile] seven fat, sleek, *and* handsome cows, and they grazed in the reed grass [of a marshy pasture].

19 And behold, seven other cows came up after them, undernourished, gaunt, *and* ugly [just skin and bones; such emaciated animals] as I have never seen in all of Egypt.

20 And the lean and ill favored cows ate up the seven fat cows that had come first.

21 And when they had eaten them up, it could not be detected *and* known that they had eaten them, for they were still as thin *and* emaciated as at the beginning. Then I awoke. [But again I fell asleep and dreamed.]

22 And I saw in my dream, and behold, seven ears [of grain] growing on one stalk, plump and good.

23 And behold, seven [other] ears, withered, thin, and blighted by the east wind, sprouted after them.

24 And the thin ears devoured the seven good ears. Now I told this to the magicians, but there was no one who could tell me what it meant.

25 Then Joseph said to Pharaoh, The [two] dreams are one; God has shown Pharaoh what He is about to do.

26 The seven good cows are seven years, and the seven good ears [of grain] are seven years; the [two] dreams are one [in their meaning].

27 And the seven thin and ill favored cows that came up after them are seven years, and also the seven empty ears [of grain], blighted *and* shriveled by the east wind; they are seven years of hunger *and* famine.

28 This is the message just as I have told Pharaoh: God has shown Pharaoh what He is about to do.

29 Take note! Seven years of great plenty throughout all the land of Egypt are coming.

30 Then there will come seven years of hunger *and* famine, and [there will be so much want that] all the great abundance of the previous years will be forgotten in the land of Egypt; and hunger (destitution, starvation) will exhaust (consume, finish) the land.

31 And the plenty will become quite unknown in the land because of that following famine, for it will be very woefully severe.

32 That the dream was sent twice to Pharaoh *and* in two forms indicates that this thing which God will very soon bring to pass is fully prepared *and* established by God.

33 So now let Pharaoh seek out *and* provide a man discreet, understanding, proficient, *and* wise and set him over the land of Egypt [as governor].

34 Let Pharaoh do this; then let him

select and appoint officers over the land, and take one-fifth [of the produce] of the [whole] land of Egypt in the seven plenteous years [year by year].

35 And let them gather all the food of these good years that are coming and lay up grain under the direction *and* authority of Pharaoh, and let them retain food [in fortified granaries] in the cities.

36 And that food shall be put in store for the country against the seven years of hunger *and* famine that are to come upon the land of Egypt, so that the land may not be ruined *and* cut off by the famine.

37 And the plan seemed good in the eyes of Pharaoh and in the eyes of all his servants.

38 And Pharaoh said to his servants, Can we find this man's equal, a man in whom is the spirit of God?

39 And Pharaoh said to Joseph, Forasmuch as [your] God has shown you all this, there is nobody as intelligent *and* discreet *and* understanding and wise as you are.

40 You shall have charge over my house, and all my people shall be governed according to your word [with reverence, submission, and obedience]. Only in matters of the throne will I be greater than you are.

41 Then Pharaoh said to Joseph, See, I have set you over all the land of Egypt.

42 And Pharaoh took off his [signet] ring from his hand and put it on Joseph's hand, and arrayed him in [official] vestments of fine linen and put a gold chain about his neck;

43 He made him to ride in the second chariot which he had, and [officials] cried before him, Bow the knee! And he set him over all the land of Egypt.

44 And Pharaoh said to Joseph, I am Pharaoh, and without you shall no man lift up his hand or foot in all the land of Egypt.

45 And Pharaoh called Joseph's name Zaphenath-paneah and he gave him Asenath daughter of Potiphera, priest of On, to be his wife. And Joseph made an [inspection] tour of all the land of Egypt.

46 Joseph [who had been in Egypt thirteen years] was thirty years old when he stood before Pharaoh king of Egypt. Joseph went out from the presence of Pharaoh and went [about his duties] through all the land of Egypt.

47 In the seven abundant years the earth brought forth by handfuls [for each seed planted].

48 And he gathered up all the [surplus] food of the seven [good] years in the land of Egypt and stored up the food in the cities; he stored away in each city the food from the fields around it.

49 And Joseph gathered grain as the sand of the sea, very much, until he stopped counting, for it could not be measured.

50 Now to Joseph were born two sons before the years of famine came, whom Asenath daughter of Potiphera, the priest of On, bore to him.

51 And Joseph called the firstborn Manasseh [making to forget], For God, said he, has made me forget all my toil *and* hardship and all my father's house.

52 And the second he called Ephraim [to be fruitful], For [he said] God has caused me to be fruitful in the land of my affliction.

speak the Word

from the pit to the palace

Because his brothers hated him, Joseph was thrown into a pit and left there to die (see Genesis 37:23, 24). But God had other plans! As it turned out, Joseph was sold as a slave in Egypt, became a servant to a wealthy ruler, and then was thrown into a pit again for a crime he did not commit (see Genesis 39). Ultimately, Joseph was freed from prison and ended up in the palace, second in command to Pharaoh, the ruler over all Egypt (see Genesis 41:39–46).

How did Joseph get from the pit to the palace? I believe he made that journey by staying positive, refusing to be bitter, being confident in God, and trusting Him. Even though Joseph was labeled a "slave," he refused to have a slave mentality. Even though he appeared to be defeated on many occasions, he kept standing up on the inside. In other words, Joseph had a right attitude. Without a right attitude, we can start in the palace and end up in the pit. This happens to a lot of people. Some people have great opportunities given to them, and they do nothing with their lives. Others may get a very bad start in life, but then overcome all obstacles and succeed.

I also believe Joseph believed in the dreams God had given him. Joseph was a dreamer; he made big plans and refused to give them up (see Genesis 37:5–10). The devil does not want us to have dreams and visions of better things. He wants us to stay in the pit and be "do-nothings."

I challenge you to make up your mind right now to do something great for God. *No matter where you started, you can have a great finish.* If people have mistreated and abused you, do not waste your time trying to get revenge—leave them in God's hands and trust Him to bring justice into your life. Know what you want out of life and what you want to do. Don't be vague; be confident! To be confident means to be bold, open, plain, and straightforward—that does not sound like a vague, sheepish, fearful individual who is uncertain about everything. Decide to leave your mark in this world. When you depart from this earth, people should know that you have been here. Even if you are in a "pit" today, God can still raise you up and do great things in you and through you!

53 When the seven years of plenty were ended in the land of Egypt,
54 The seven years of scarcity *and* famine began to come, as Joseph had said they would; the famine was in all [the surrounding] lands, but in all of Egypt there was food.
55 But when all the land of Egypt was weakened with hunger, the people [there] cried to Pharaoh for food; and Pharaoh said to [them] all, Go to Joseph; what he says to you, do.
56 When the famine was over all the land, Joseph opened all the storehouses and sold to the Egyptians; for the famine grew extremely distressing in the land of Egypt.
57 And all countries came to Egypt to Joseph to buy grain, because the famine was severe over all [the known] earth.

42

NOW WHEN Jacob learned that there was grain in Egypt, he said to his sons, Why do you look at one another?

2 For, he said, I have heard that there is grain in Egypt; get down there and buy [grain] for us, that we may live and not die.

3 So ten of Joseph's brethren went to buy grain in Egypt.

4 But Benjamin, Joseph's [full] brother, Jacob did not send with his brothers; for he said, Lest perhaps some harm *or* injury should befall him.

5 So the sons of Israel came to buy grain among those who came, for there was hunger *and* general lack of food in the land of Canaan.

6 Now Joseph was the governor over the land, and he it was who sold to all the people of the land; and Joseph's [half] brothers came and bowed themselves down before him with their faces to the ground.

7 Joseph saw his brethren and he recognized them, but he treated them as if he were a stranger to them and spoke roughly to them. He said, Where do you come from? And they replied, From the land of Canaan to buy food.

8 Joseph knew his brethren, but they did not know him.

9 And Joseph remembered the dreams he had dreamed about them and said to them, You are spies *and* with unfriendly purpose you have come to observe [secretly] the nakedness of the land.

10 But they said to him, No, my lord, but your servants have come [only] to buy food.

11 We are all one man's sons; we are true men; your servants are not spies.

12 And he said to them, No, but you have come to see the nakedness of the land.

13 But they said, Your servants are twelve brothers, the sons of one man in the land of Canaan; the youngest is today with our father, and one is not.

14 And Joseph said to them, It is as I said to you, You are spies.

15 You shall be proved by this test: by the life of Pharaoh, you shall not go away from here unless your youngest brother comes here.

16 Send one of you and let him bring your brother, and you will be kept in prison, that your words may be proved whether there is any truth in you; or else by the life of Pharaoh you certainly are spies.

17 Then he put them all in custody for three days.

18 And Joseph said to them on the third day, Do this and live! I reverence *and* fear God.

19 If you are true men, let one of your brothers be bound in your prison, but [the rest of] you go and carry grain for those weakened with hunger in your households.

20 But bring your youngest brother to me, so your words will be verified and you shall live. And they did so.

21 And they said one to another, We are truly guilty about our brother, for we saw the distress *and* anguish of his soul when he begged us [to let him go], and we would not hear. So this distress *and* difficulty has come upon us.

22 Reuben answered them, Did I not tell you, Do not sin against the boy, and you would not hear? Therefore, behold, his blood is required [of us].

23 But they did not know that Joseph understood them, for he spoke to them through an interpreter.

24 And he turned away from them and wept; then he returned to them and talked with them, and took from them Simeon and bound him before their eyes.

25 Then [privately] Joseph commanded that their sacks be filled with grain, every man's money be restored

to his sack, and provisions be given to them for the journey. And this was done for them.

26 They loaded their donkeys with grain and left.

27 And as one of them opened his sack to give his donkey fodder at the lodging place, he caught sight of his money; for behold, it was in his sack's mouth.

28 And he said to his brothers, My money is restored! Here it is in my sack! And their hearts failed them and they were afraid *and* turned trembling one to another, saying, What is this that God has done to us?

29 When they came to Jacob their father in Canaan, they told him all that had befallen them, saying,

30 The man who is the lord of the land spoke roughly to us and took us for spies of the country.

31 And we said to him, We are true men, not spies.

32 We are twelve brothers with the same father; one is no more, and the youngest is today with our father in the land of Canaan.

33 And the man, the lord of the country, said to us, By this test I will know whether or not you are honest men: leave one of your brothers here with me and take grain for your famishing households and be gone.

34 Bring your youngest brother to me; then I will know that you are not spies, but that you are honest men. And I will deliver to you your brother [whom I have kept bound in prison], and you may do business in the land.

35 When they emptied their sacks, behold, every man's parcel of money was in his sack! When both they and their father saw the bundles of money, they were afraid.

36 And Jacob their father said to them, You have bereaved me! Joseph is not, and Simeon is not, and you would take Benjamin from me. All these things are against me!

37 And Reuben said to his father, Slay my two sons if I do not bring [Benjamin] back to you. Deliver him into my keeping, and I will bring him back to you.

38 But [Jacob] said, My son shall not go down with you, for his brother is dead and he alone is left [of his mother's children]; if harm *or* accident should befall him on the journey you are to take, you would bring my hoary head down to Sheol (the place of the dead) with grief.

43 BUT THE hunger *and* destitution *and* starvation were very severe *and* extremely distressing in the land [Canaan].

2 And when [the families of Jacob's sons] had eaten up the grain which the men had brought from Egypt, their father said to them, Go again; buy us a little food.

3 But Judah said to him, The man solemnly *and* sternly warned us, saying, You shall not see my face again unless your brother is with you.

4 If you will send our brother with us, we will go down [to Egypt] and buy you food;

5 But if you will not send him, we will not go down; for the man said to us, You shall not see my face unless your brother is with you.

6 And Israel said, Why did you do me such a wrong *and* suffer this evil to come upon me by telling the man that you had another brother?

7 And they said, The man asked us straightforward questions about ourselves and our relatives. He said, Is your father still alive? Have you another brother? And we answered him accordingly. How could we know that he would say, Bring your brother down here?

8 And Judah said to Israel his father, Send the lad with me and we will arise and go, that we may live and not die, both we and you and also our little ones.

9 I will be security for him; you shall require him of me [personally]; if I do not bring him back to you and put him before you, then let me bear the blame forever.

10 For if we had not lingered like this, surely by now we would have returned the second time.

11 And their father Israel said to them, If it must be so, now do this; take of the choicest products in the land in your sacks and carry down a present to the man, a little balm (balsam) and a little honey, aromatic spices and gum (of rock rose) *or* ladanum, pistachio nuts, and almonds.

12 And take double the [grain] money with you; and the money that was put back in the mouth of your sacks, carry it again with you; there is a possibility that [its being in your sacks] was an oversight.

13 Take your brother and arise and return to the man;

14 May God Almighty give you mercy *and* favor before the man, that he may release to you your other brother and Benjamin. If I am bereaved [of my sons], I am bereaved.

15 Then the men took the present, and they took double the [grain] money with them, and Benjamin; and they arose and went down to Egypt and stood before Joseph.

16 And when Joseph saw Benjamin with them, he said to the steward of his house, Bring the men into the house and kill an animal and make ready, for the men will dine with me at noon.

17 And the man did as Joseph ordered and brought the men to Joseph's house.

18 The men were afraid because they were brought to Joseph's house; and they said, We are brought in because of the money that was returned in our sacks the first time we came, so that

he may find occasion to accuse and assail us, take us for slaves, and seize our donkeys.

19 So they came near to the steward of Joseph's house and talked with him at the door of the house,

20 And said, O sir, we came down truly the first time to buy food;

21 And when we came to the inn, we opened our sacks and there was each man's money, full weight, returned in the mouth of his sack. Now we have brought it back again.

22 And we have brought down with us other money to buy food; we do not know who put our money in our sacks.

23 But [the steward] said, Peace be to you, fear not; your God and the God of your father has given you treasure in your sacks. I received your money. And he brought Simeon out to them.

24 And the man brought the men into Joseph's house and gave them water, and they washed their feet; and he gave their donkeys provender.

25 And they made ready the present they had brought for Joseph before his coming at noon, for they heard that they were to dine there.

26 And when Joseph came home, they brought into the house to him the present which they had with them, and bowed themselves to him to the ground.

27 He asked them of their welfare and said, Is your old father well, of whom you spoke? Is he still alive?

28 And they answered, Your servant our father is in good health; he is still alive. And they bowed down their heads and made obeisance.

29 And he looked up and saw his [full] brother Benjamin, his mother's [only other] son, and said, Is this your youngest brother, of whom you spoke to me? And he said, God be gracious to you, my son!

30 And Joseph hurried from the room, for his heart yearned for his brother, and he sought privacy to weep; so he entered his chamber and wept there.

31 And he washed his face and went out, and, restraining himself, said, Let dinner be served.

32 And [the servants] set out [the food] for [Joseph] by himself, and for [his brothers] by themselves, and for those Egyptians who ate with him by themselves, according to the Egyptian custom not to eat food with the Hebrews; for that is an abomination to the Egyptians.

33 And [Joseph's brothers] were given seats before him—the eldest according to his birthright and the youngest according to his youth; and the men looked at one another amazed [that so much was known about them].

34 [Joseph] took and sent helpings to them from before him, but Benjamin's portion was five times as much as any of theirs. And they drank freely and were merry with him.

44 AND HE commanded the steward of his house, saying, Fill the men's sacks with food, as much as they can carry, and put every man's money in his sack's mouth.

2 And put my cup, the silver cup, in the sack's mouth of the youngest, with his grain money. And [the steward] did according to what Joseph had said.

3 As soon as the morning was light, the men were sent away, they and their donkeys.

4 When they had left the city and were not yet far away, Joseph said to his steward, Up, follow after the men; and when you overtake them, say to them, Why have you rewarded evil for good? [Why have you stolen the silver cup?]

5 Is it not my master's drinking cup with which he divines [the future]? You have done wrong in doing this.

6 And the steward overtook them, and he said to them these same words.

7 They said to him, Why does my lord say these things? Far be it from your servants to do such a thing!

8 Note that the money which we found in the mouths of our sacks we brought back to you from the land of Canaan. Is it likely then that we would steal from your master's house silver or gold?

9 With whomever of your servants [your master's cup] is found, not only let that one die, but the rest of us will be my lord's slaves.

10 And the steward said, Now let it be as you say: he with whom [the cup] is found shall be my slave, but [the rest of] you shall be blameless.

11 Then quickly every man lowered his sack to the ground and every man opened his sack.

12 And [the steward] searched, beginning with the eldest and stopping with the youngest; and the cup was found in Benjamin's sack.

13 Then they rent their clothes; and after each man had loaded his donkey again, they returned to the city.

14 Judah and his brethren came to Joseph's house, for he was still there; and they fell prostrate before him.

15 Joseph said to them, What is this thing that you have done? Do you not realize that such a man as I can certainly detect *and* know by divination [everything you do without other knowledge of it]?

16 And Judah said, What shall we say to my lord? What shall we reply? Or how shall we clear ourselves, since God has found out *and* exposed the iniquity of your servants? Behold, we are my lord's slaves, the rest of us as well as he with whom the cup is found.

17 But [Joseph] said, God forbid that I should do that; but the man in whose hand the cup is found, he shall be my servant; and as for [the rest of] you, arise *and* go in peace to your father.

18 Then Judah came close to [Joseph] and said, O my lord, let your servant, I pray you, speak a word to you in private, and let not your anger blaze against your servant, for you are as Pharaoh [so I will speak as if directly to him].

19 My lord asked his servants, saying, Have you a father or a brother?

20 And we said to my lord, We have a father—an old man—and a young [brother, the] child of his old age; and his brother is dead, and he alone is left of his mother's [offspring], and his father loves him.

21 And you said to your servants, Bring him down to me, that I may set my eyes on him.

22 And we said to my lord, The lad cannot leave his father; for if he should do so, his father would die.

23 And you told your servants, Unless your youngest brother comes with you, you shall not see my face again.

24 And when we went back to your servant my father, we told him what my lord had said.

25 And our father said, Go again and buy us a little food.

26 But we said, We cannot go down. If our youngest brother is with us, then we will go down; for we may not see the man's face except our youngest brother is with us.

27 And your servant my father said to us, You know that [Rachel] my wife bore me two sons:

28 And the one went out from me, and I said, Surely he is torn to pieces, and I have never seen him since.

29 And if you take this son also from me, and harm *or* accident should befall him, you will bring down my gray hairs with sorrow *and* evil to Sheol (the place of the dead).

30 Now therefore, when I come to your servant my father and the lad is not with us, since his life is bound up in the lad's life *and* his soul knit with the lad's soul,

31 When he sees that the lad is not with us, he will die; and your servants will be responsible for his death *and* will bring down the gray hairs of your servant our father with sorrow to Sheol.

32 For your servant became security for the lad to my father, saying, If I do not bring him to you, then I will bear the blame to my father forever.

33 Now therefore, I pray you, let your servant remain instead of the youth [to be] a slave to my lord, and let the young man go home with his [half] brothers.

34 For how can I go up to my father if the lad is not with me?—lest I witness the woe *and* the evil that will come upon my father.

45 THEN JOSEPH could not restrain himself [any longer] before all those who stood by him, and he called out, Cause every man to go out from me! So no one stood there with Joseph while he made himself known to his brothers.

2 And he wept *and* sobbed aloud, and the Egyptians [who had just left him] heard it, and the household of Pharaoh heard about it.

3 And Joseph said to his brothers, I am Joseph! Is my father still alive? And his brothers could not reply, for they were distressingly disturbed *and* dismayed at [the startling realization that they were in] his presence.

4 And Joseph said to his brothers, Come near to me, I pray you. And they did so. And he said, I am Joseph your brother, whom you sold into Egypt!

5 But now, do not be distressed *and* disheartened or vexed *and* angry with yourselves because you sold me here, for God sent me ahead of you to preserve life.

6 For these two years the famine has been in the land, and there are still five years more in which there will be neither plowing nor harvest.

7 God sent me before you to preserve for you a posterity *and* to continue a remnant on the earth, to save your lives by a great escape *and* save for you many survivors.

8 So now it was not you who sent me here, but God; and He has made me a father to Pharaoh and lord of all his house and ruler over all the land of Egypt.

9 Hurry and go up to my father and tell him, Your son Joseph says this to you: God has put me in charge of all Egypt. Come down to me; do not delay.

10 You will live in the land of Goshen, and you will be close to me—you and your children and your grandchildren, your flocks, your herds, and all you have.

11 And there I will sustain *and* provide for you, so that you and your household and all that are yours may not come to poverty *and* want, for there are yet five [more] years of [the scarcity, hunger, and starvation of] famine.

12 Now notice! Your own eyes and the eyes of my brother Benjamin can see that I am talking to you personally [in your language and not through an interpreter].

13 And you shall tell my father of all my glory in Egypt and of all that you have seen; and you shall hurry and bring my father down here.

14 And he fell on his brother Benjamin's neck and wept, and Benjamin wept on his neck.

15 Moreover, he kissed all his brothers and wept upon them; and after that his brothers conversed with him.

16 When the report was heard in Pharaoh's house that Joseph's brothers had come, it pleased Pharaoh and his servants well.

17 And Pharaoh said to Joseph, Tell your brothers this: Load your animals and return to the land of Canaan,

18 And get your father and your households and come to me. And I will give you the best in the land of Egypt and you will live on the fat of the land.

19 You therefore command them, saying, You do this: take wagons from the land of Egypt for your little ones and for your wives, and bring your father and come.

20 Also do not look with regret *or* concern upon your goods, for the best of all the land of Egypt is yours.

21 And the sons of Israel did so; and Joseph gave them wagons, as the order of Pharaoh permitted, and gave them provisions for the journey.

22 To each of them he gave changes of raiment, but to Benjamin he gave 300 pieces of silver and five changes of raiment.

23 And to his father he sent as follows: ten donkeys loaded with the good things of Egypt, and ten she-donkeys laden with grain, bread, and nourishing food *and* provision for his father [to supply all who were with him] on the way.

24 So he sent his brothers away, and they departed, and he said to them, See that you do not disagree (get excited, quarrel) along the road.

25 So they went up out of Egypt and came into the land of Canaan to Jacob their father,

26 And they said to him, Joseph is still alive! And he is governor over all the land of Egypt! And Jacob's heart began to stop beating *and* [he almost] fainted, for he did not believe them.

27 But when they told him all the words of Joseph which he had said to them, and when he saw the wagons which Joseph had sent to carry him, the spirit of Jacob their father revived [and warmth and life returned].

28 And Israel said, It is enough! Joseph my son is still alive. I will go and see him before I die.

46

SO ISRAEL made his jour-ney with all that he had and came to Beersheba [a place hallowed by sacred memories] and offered sacrifices to the God of his father Isaac. [Gen. 21:33; 26:23-25.]

2 And God spoke to Israel in visions of the night, and said, Jacob! Jacob! And he said, Here am I.

3 And He said, I am God, the God of your father; do not be afraid to go down to Egypt, for I will there make of you a great nation.

4 I will go down with you to Egypt, and I will also surely bring you [your people Israel] up again; and Joseph will put his hand upon your eyes [when they are about to close in death].

5 So Jacob arose *and* set out from Beersheba, and Israel's sons con-veyed their father, their little ones, and their wives in the wagons that Pharaoh had sent to carry him.

6 And they took their cattle and the gains which they had acquired in the land of Canaan and came into Egypt, Jacob and all his offspring with him:

7 His sons and his sons' sons with him, his daughters and his sons' daughters—all his offspring he brought with him into Egypt.

8 And these are the names of the descendants of Israel who came into Egypt, Jacob and his sons: Reuben, Jacob's firstborn.

9 And the sons of Reuben: Hanoch, Pallu, Hezron, and Carmi.

10 The sons of Simeon: Jemuel, Jamin, Ohad, Jachin, Zohar, and Shaul the son of a Canaanite woman.

11 The sons of Levi: Gershon, Kohath, and Merari.

12 The sons of Judah: Er, Onan, She-lah, Perez, and Zerah; but Er and Onan died in the land of Canaan. And the sons of Perez were Hezron and Hamul.

13 The sons of Issachar: Tola, Puvah, Iob, and Shimron.

14 The sons of Zebulun: Sered, Elon, and Jahleel.

15 These are the sons of Leah, whom she bore to Jacob in Padan-aram, together with his daughter Dinah. All of his sons and his daughters num-bered thirty-three.

16 The sons of Gad: Ziphion, Haggi, Shuni, Ezbon, Eri, Arodi, and Areli.

17 The sons of Asher: Imnah, Ishvah, Ishvi, Beriah, and Serah their sister. And the sons of Beriah: Heber and Malchiel.

18 These are the sons of Zilpah, [the maid] whom Laban gave to Leah his daughter. And these she bore to Jacob—sixteen persons all told.

19 The sons of Rachel, Jacob's wife: Joseph and Benjamin.

20 And to Joseph in the land of Egypt were born Manasseh and Ephraim, whom Asenath daughter of Potiphera, priest of On, bore to him.

21 And the sons of sBenjamin: Bela, Becher, Ashbel, Gera, Naaman, Ehi, Rosh, Muppim, Huppim, and Ard.

22 These are the sons of Rachel, who were born to Jacob—fourteen persons in all.

23 The son of Dan: Hushim.

24 The sons of Naphtali: Jahzeel, Guni, Jezer, and Shillem.

25 These are the sons of Bilhah, [the maid] whom Laban gave to Rachel his daughter. And she bore these to Jacob—seven persons in all.

26 All the persons who came with Jacob into Egypt—who were his own offspring, not counting the wives of Jacob's sons—were sixty-six persons all told.

s Benjamin, whom uninformed artists have frequently pictured as a mere youth when he met Joseph in Egypt, was in fact the father of 10 sons at this time. Joseph was 17 when his brothers sold him; he was in prison 13 years; he had been governor of Egypt during the 7 good years and through 2 years of the famine. So Joseph was 39 years of age at this time, and Benjamin was only a few years younger.

27 And the sons of Joseph, who were born to him in Egypt, were two persons. All the persons of the house of Jacob [including Joseph and Jacob himself], who came into Egypt, were seventy.

28 And he sent Judah before him to Joseph, to direct him to Goshen *and* meet him there; and they came into the land of Goshen.

29 Then Joseph made ready his chariot and went up to meet Israel his father in Goshen; and he presented himself *and* gave distinct evidence of himself to him [that he was Joseph], and [each] fell on the [other's] neck and wept on his neck a good while.

30 And Israel said to Joseph, Now let me die, since I have seen your face [and know] that you are still alive.

31 Joseph said to his brothers and to his father's household, I will go up and tell Pharaoh and say to him, My brothers and my father's household, who were in the land of Canaan, have come to me.

32 And the men are shepherds, for their occupation has been keeping livestock, and they have brought their flocks and their herds and all that they have.

33 When Pharaoh calls you and says, What is your occupation?

34 You shall say, Your servants' occupation has been as keepers of livestock from our youth until now, both we and our fathers before us—in order that you may live in the land of Goshen, for every shepherd is an abomination to the Egyptians.

47 THEN JOSEPH came and told Pharaoh, My father and my brothers, with their flocks and their herds and all that they own, have come from the land of Canaan, and they are in the land of Goshen.

2 And from among his brothers he took five men and presented them to Pharaoh.

3 And Pharaoh said to his brothers, What is your occupation? And they said to Pharaoh, Your servants are shepherds, both we and our fathers before us.

4 Moreover, they said to Pharaoh, We have come to sojourn in the land, for your servants have no pasture for our flocks, for the famine is very severe in Canaan. So now, we pray you, let your servants dwell in the land of Goshen.

5 And Pharaoh spoke to Joseph, saying, Your father and your brothers have come to you.

6 The land of Egypt is before you; make your father and your brothers dwell in the best of the land. Let them live in the land of Goshen. And if you know of any men of ability among them, put them in charge of my cattle.

7 Then Joseph brought in Jacob his father and presented him before Pharaoh; and Jacob blessed Pharaoh.

8 And Pharaoh asked Jacob, How old are you?

9 Jacob said to Pharaoh, The days of the years of my pilgrimage are 130 years; few and evil have the days of the years of my life been, and they have not attained to those of the life of my fathers in their pilgrimage.

10 And Jacob blessed Pharaoh and went out from his presence.

11 Joseph settled his father and brethren and gave them a possession in Egypt in the best of the land, in the land of Rameses (Goshen), as Pharaoh commanded.

12 And Joseph supplied his father and his brethren and all his father's

t Abraham, Jacob's grandfather, had lived to be 175 years old; Isaac, his father, lived to be 180. Jacob lived seventeen years after making this statement to Pharaoh, in which time he had an opportunity to get a much more optimistic view of God's treatment of him. He died at 147, having said, "The redeeming Angel . . . has redeemed me continually from every evil" (Gen. 48:16).

household with food, according to [the needs of] their families.

13 [In the course of time] there was no food in all the land, for the famine was distressingly severe, so that the land of Egypt and all the land of Canaan hung in doubt and wavered by reason of the hunger (destitution, starvation) of the famine.

14 And Joseph gathered up all the money that was found in the land of Egypt and in the land of Canaan [in payment] for the grain which they bought, and Joseph brought the money into Pharaoh's house.

15 And when the money was exhausted in the land of Egypt and in the land of Canaan, all the Egyptians came to Joseph and said, Give us food! Why should we die before your very eyes? For we have no money left.

16 Joseph said, Give up your livestock, and I will give you food in exchange for [them] if your money is gone.

17 So they brought their livestock to Joseph, and [he] gave them food in exchange for the horses, flocks, cattle of the herds, and the donkeys; and he supplied them with food in exchange for all their livestock that year.

18 When that year was ended, they came to [Joseph] the second year and said to him, We will not hide from my lord [the fact] that our money is spent; my lord also has our herds of livestock; there is nothing left in the sight of my lord but our bodies and our lands.

19 Why should we perish before your eyes, both we and our land? Buy us and our land in exchange for food, and we and our land will be servants to Pharaoh. And give us seed [to plant], that we may live and not die, and that the land may not be desolate.

20 And Joseph bought all the land of Egypt for Pharaoh; for the Egyptians sold every man his field because of the overwhelming severity of the famine upon them. The land became Pharaoh's,

21 And as for the people, he removed them to cities *and* practically made slaves of them [at their own request], from one end of the borders of Egypt to the other.

22 Only the priests' land he did not buy, for the priests had a fixed pension from Pharaoh and lived on the amount Pharaoh gave them. So they did not sell their land.

23 Then Joseph said to the people, Behold, I have today bought you and your land for Pharaoh. Now here is seed for you, and you shall sow the land.

24 At [harvest time when you reap] the increase, you shall give one-fifth of it to Pharaoh, and four-fifths shall be your own to use for seed for the field and as food for you and those of your households and for your little ones.

25 And they said, You have saved our lives! Let us find favor in the sight of my lord; and we will be Pharaoh's servants.

26 And Joseph made it a law over the land of Egypt—to this day—that Pharaoh should have the fifth part [of the crops]; it was the priests' land only which did not become Pharaoh's.

27 And Israel dwelt in the land of Egypt, in the country of Goshen; and they gained possessions there and grew and multiplied exceedingly.

28 And Jacob lived in the land of Egypt seventeen years; so Jacob reached the age of 147 years.

29 When the time drew near that Israel must die, he called his son Joseph and said to him, If now I have found favor in your sight, uput your

---

u This was a customary manner of taking a solemn oath. The gesture was a reference to the mark of circumcision, the sign of God's covenant, which is equivalent to our laying our hand upon the Bible. (Adam Clarke, *The Holy Bible with A Commentary*).

hand under my thigh and [promise to] deal loyally and faithfully with me. Do not bury me, I beg of you, in Egypt,
30 But let me lie with my fathers; you shall carry me out of Egypt and bury me in their burying place. And [Joseph] said, I will do as you have directed.
31 Then Jacob said, Swear to me [that you will do it]. And he swore to him. And Israel bowed himself upon the head of the bed.

48 SOME TIME after these things occurred, someone told Joseph, Behold, your father is sick. And he took with him his two sons, Manasseh and Ephraim [and went to Goshen].
2 When Jacob was told, Your son Joseph has come to you, Israel collected his strength and sat up on the bed.
3 And Jacob said to Joseph, God Almighty appeared to me at Luz [Bethel] in the land of Canaan and blessed me
4 And said to me, Behold, I will make you fruitful and multiply you, and I will make you a multitude of people and will give this land to your descendants after you as an everlasting possession. [Gen. 28:13-22; 35:6-15.]
5 And now your two sons, [Ephraim and Manasseh], who were born to you in the land of Egypt before I came to you in Egypt, are mine. [I am adopting them, and now] as Reuben and Simeon, [they] shall be mine.
6 But other sons who may be born after them shall be your own; and they shall be called after the names of these [two] brothers *and* reckoned as belonging to them [when they come] into their inheritance.

7 And as for me, when I came from Padan, Rachel died at my side in the land of Canaan on the way, when yet there was but a little way to come to Ephrath; and I buried her there on the way to Ephrath, that is, Bethlehem.
8 When Israel [almost blind] saw Joseph's sons, he said, Who are these?
9 And Joseph said to his father, They are my sons, whom God has given me in this place. And he said, Bring them to me, I pray you, that I may bless them.
10 Now Israel's eyes were dim from age, so that he could not see. And Joseph brought them near to him, and he kissed and embraced them.
11 Israel said to Joseph, I had not thought that I would see your face, but see, God has shown me your offspring also.
12 Then Joseph took [the boys] from [his father's embrace] and he bowed [before him] with his face to the earth.
13 Then Joseph took both [boys], Ephraim with his right hand toward Israel's left, and Manasseh with his left hand toward Israel's right, and brought them close to him.
14 And Israel reached out his right hand and laid it on the head of Ephraim, who was the younger, and his left hand on Manasseh's head, ᵛcrossing his hands intentionally, for Manasseh was the firstborn.
15 Then [Jacob] blessed Joseph and said, God [Himself], before Whom my fathers Abraham and Isaac lived *and* walked habitually, God [Himself], Who has [been my Shepherd and has led and] fed me from the time I came into being until this day,
16 The ʷredeeming Angel [that is,

v God acts independently of the claims of priority based on time of birth when He chooses men. He too "crossed His hands" in the case of Seth whom He chose over Cain; of Shem over Japheth; of Isaac over Ishmael; of Jacob over Esau; of Judah and Joseph over Reuben; of Moses over Aaron; of David over all his brothers; and of Mary over Martha. **w** The "Angel of the Lord" is here identified as Christ Himself. See also the footnote on Gen. 16:7.

the Angel the Redeemer—not a created being but the Lord Himself] Who
has redeemed me continually from
every evil, bless the lads! And let my
name be perpetuated in them [may
they be worthy of having their names
coupled with mine], and the names of
my fathers Abraham and Isaac; and
let them become a multitude in the
midst of the earth.

17 When Joseph saw that his father
laid his right hand on Ephraim's head,
it displeased him; and he held up his
father's hand to move it to Manasseh's head.

18 And Joseph said, Not so, my
father, for this is the firstborn; put
your right hand upon his head.

19 But his father refused and said,
I know, my son, I know. He also
shall become a people and shall be
great; but his younger brother shall
be ˣgreater than he, and his offspring shall become a multitude of
nations.

20 And he blessed them that day,
saying, By you shall Israel bless [one
another], saying, May God make you
like Ephraim and like Manasseh. And
he set Ephraim before Manasseh.

21 And Israel said to Joseph, Behold,
I [am about to] die, but God will be
with you and bring you again to the
land of your fathers.

22 Moreover, I have given to you
[Joseph] one portion [Shechem, one
mountain slope] more than any of
your brethren, which I took [re-
claiming it] out of the hand of the
Amorites with my sword and with
my bow. [Gen. 33:18, 19; Josh. 24:32,
33; John 4:5.]

49 AND JACOB called for his
sons and said, Gather yourselves together [around
me], that I may tell you what shall
befall you ʸin the latter or last days.

2 Gather yourselves together and
hear, you sons of Jacob; and hearken
to Israel your father.

3 Reuben, you are my ᶻfirstborn, my
might, the beginning (the firstfruits)
of my manly strength and vigor; [your
birthright gave you] the preeminence
in dignity and the preeminence in
power.

4 But unstable and boiling over like
water, you shall ᵃnot excel and have
the preeminence [of the firstborn],
because you went to your father's bed;
you defiled it—he went to my couch!
[Gen. 35:22.]

5 Simeon and Levi are brothers
[equally headstrong, deceitful, vindictive, and cruel]; their swords are
weapons of violence. [Gen. 34:25-29.]

6 O my soul, come not into their
secret council; unto their assembly let
not my honor be united [for I knew

---

x This prophecy begins to be fulfilled "from the days of the judges onward, as the tribe of Ephraim
in power and compass so increased that it became the head of the northern ten tribes, and its name
became of like significance with that of Israel; although, in the time of Moses, Manasseh still out-
numbered Ephraim by 20,000" (Karl F. Keil and F. Delitzsch, *Biblical Commentary on the Old Testament*). Joshua, whom Israel so long regarded as their ruler, was an Ephraimite. The ark of the
covenant was placed in Shiloh in the territory of Ephraim, which increased the tribe's prestige.
How could Jacob have prophesied Ephraim's supremacy so positively except by divine inspiration?   **y** See Deut. 33, where Moses blesses the same tribes in a similar prophetic way.   **z** Reuben
was the eldest of Jacob's twelve sons and therefore entitled to the birthright, which would make him
successor to his father as head of the family or tribe and inheritor of a double portion of his father's
estate. But Reuben forfeited all this by his conduct with Bilhah, his father's concubine (Gen. 35:22).
By adopting Joseph's two sons, Ephraim and Manasseh, and giving each of them a portion of the
inheritance, Jacob virtually gave Joseph Reuben's extra portion of the land. And Judah became the
tribal leader in Reuben's place (Gen. 49:8-10).   **a** The whole fertile territory once occupied by the
tribe of Reuben has long since been deserted by its settled inhabitants and given up to the nomad
tribes of the desert. Reuben did "not excel," and even before Jacob's death he had lost his "preeminence of the firstborn" (John D. Davis, *A Dictionary of the Bible*).

nothing of their plot], because in their anger they slew men [an honored man, Shechem, and the Shechemites], and in their self-will they disabled oxen.

7 Cursed be their anger, for it was fierce, and their wrath, for it was cruel. I will divide them in Jacob and ᵇscatter them in Israel.

8 Judah, you are the one whom your brothers shall praise; your hand shall be on the neck of your enemies; your father's sons shall bow down to you.

9 Judah, a lion's cub! With the prey, my son, you have gone high up [the mountain]. He stooped down, he crouched like a lion, and like a lioness—who dares provoke *and* rouse him? [Rev. 5:5.]

10 The scepter *or* leadership shall not depart from Judah, nor the ruler's staff from between his feet, until Shiloh [the Messiah, the Peaceful One] comes to Whom it belongs, and to Him shall be the obedience of the people. [Num. 24:17; Ps. 60:7.]

11 Binding His foal to the vine and His donkey's colt to the choice vine, He washes His garments in wine and His clothes in the blood of grapes. [Isa. 63:1-3; Zech. 9:9; Rev. 19:11-16.]

12 His eyes are darker *and* more sparkling than wine, and His teeth whiter than milk.

13 Zebulun shall live toward the seashore, and he shall be a haven *and* a landing place for ships; and his border shall be toward Sidon.

14 Issachar is a strong-boned donkey crouching down between the sheepfolds.

15 And he saw that rest was good and that the land was pleasant; and he bowed his shoulder to bear [his burdens] and became a servant to tribute [subjected to forced labor].

16 Dan shall judge his people as one of the tribes of Israel.

17 Dan shall be a serpent by the way, a horned snake in the path, that bites at the horse's heels, so that his rider falls backward.

18 I wait for Your salvation, O Lord.

19 Gad—a raiding troop shall raid him, but he shall raid at their heels *and* assault them [victoriously].

20 Asher's food [supply] shall be rich *and* fat, and he shall yield *and* deliver royal delights.

21 Naphtali is a hind let loose which yields lovely fawns.

22 Joseph is a fruitful bough, a fruitful bough by a well (spring or fountain), whose branches run over the wall.

23 Skilled archers have bitterly attacked *and* sorely worried him; they have shot at him and persecuted him.

24 But his bow remained strong *and* steady *and* rested in the Strength that does not fail him, for the arms of his hands were made strong *and* active by the hands of the Mighty God of Jacob, by the name of the Shepherd, the Rock of Israel, [Gen. 48:15; Deut. 32:4; Isa. 9:6; 49:26.]

25 By the God of your father, Who will help you, and by the Almighty, Who will bless you with blessings of the heavens above, blessings lying in the deep beneath, blessings of the breasts and of the womb.

26 The blessings of your father [on you] are greater than the blessings of my forefathers [Abraham and Isaac on me] *and* are as lasting as the bounties of the eternal hills; they shall be on the head of Joseph, and on the crown of the head of him who was the consecrated one *and* the one separated from his brethren *and* [the one who] is prince among them.

b This was literally fulfilled. Levi got no inheritance except 48 towns scattered throughout different parts of Canaan. As to Simeon, they were originally given only a few towns and villages in Judah's lot (Josh. 19:1). Afterward, needing more room, they formed colonies in districts which they conquered from the Idumeans and the Amalekites [I Chron. 4:39, 40]. (Adam Clarke, *The Holy Bible with A Commentary*).

27 Benjamin is a ᶜravenous wolf, in the morning devouring the prey and at night dividing the spoil.

28 All these are the twelve tribes of Israel, and this is what their father said to them as he blessed them, blessing each one according to the blessing suited to him.

29 He charged them and said to them, I am to be gathered to my [departed] people; bury me with my fathers in the cave that is in the field of Ephron the Hittite,

30 In the cave in the field at Machpelah, east of Mamre in the land of Canaan, that Abraham bought, along with the field of Ephron the Hittite, to possess as a cemetery. [Gen. 23:17-20.]

31 There they buried Abraham and Sarah his wife, there they buried Isaac and Rebekah his wife, and there I buried Leah.

32 The purchase of the field and the cave that is in it was from the sons of Heth.

33 When Jacob had finished commanding his sons, he drew his feet up into the bed and breathed his last and was gathered to his [departed] people.

50 THEN JOSEPH fell upon his father's face and wept over him and kissed him.

2 And Joseph ordered his servants the physicians to embalm his father. So the physicians embalmed Israel.

3 Then forty days were devoted [to this purpose] for him, for that is the customary number of days required for those who are embalmed. And the Egyptians wept and bemoaned him [as they would for royalty] for seventy days.

4 And when the days of his weeping *and* deep grief were past, Joseph said to [the nobles of] the house of Pharaoh, If now I have found grace in your eyes, speak, I pray you, to Pharaoh [for Joseph was dressed in mourning and could not do so himself], saying,

5 My father made me swear, saying, I am about to die; in my tomb which I hewed out for myself in the land of Canaan, there you shall bury me. So now let me go up, I pray you, and bury my father, and I will come again.

6 And Pharaoh said, Go up and bury your father, as he made you swear.

7 And Joseph went up [to Canaan] to bury his father; and with him went all the officials of Pharaoh—the nobles of his court, *and* the elders of his house and all the nobles *and* elders of the land of Egypt—

8 And all the household of Joseph and his brethren and his father's household. Only their little ones and their flocks and herds they left in the land of Goshen.

9 And there went with [Joseph] both chariots and horsemen; and it was a very great company.

10 And they came to the threshing floor of Atad, which is beyond [west of] the Jordan, and there they mourned with a great lamentation and extreme demonstrations of sorrow [according to Egyptian custom]; and [Joseph] made a mourning for his father seven days.

11 When the inhabitants of the land, the Canaanites, saw the mourning at the floor of Atad, they said, This is a grievous mourning for the Egyptians.

---

c The tribe of Benjamin is fitly compared to a ravenous wolf because of the rude courage and ferocity which they invariably displayed, particularly in their war with the other tribes, in which they killed more men than all of their own numbers combined (Adam Clarke, *The Holy Bible with A Commentary*). The tribe was absorbed by the tribe of Judah and is not mentioned after the return from the Babylonian captivity, except in connection with its former land or as the source of some individual person. Ehud, Saul, Jonathan, and the apostle Paul were Benjamites.

Therefore the place was called Abel-mizraim [mourning of Egypt]; it is west of the Jordan.

12 Thus [Jacob's] sons did for him as he had commanded them.

13 For his sons carried him to the land of Canaan and buried him in the cave of the field of Machpelah, east of Mamre, which Abraham bought, along with the field, for a possession as a burying place from Ephron the Hittite.

14 After he had buried his father,

Joseph returned to Egypt, he and his brethren and all who had gone up with him.

15 When Joseph's brethren saw that their father was dead, they said, Perhaps now Joseph will hate us and will pay us back for all the evil we did to him.

16 And they sent a messenger to Joseph, saying, Your father commanded before he died, saying,

17 So shall you say to Joseph: Forgive (take up and away all resentment and

turn your mess into your message

Joseph's brothers were afraid he would never forgive them for wanting him dead and for selling him into slavery. In Genesis 50:20, we see that Joseph had a good and loving attitude as he gave his brothers the assurance that he had forgiven their wrongdoing. They may have meant to do evil against him, but God meant it for good.

It is amazing how many times Satan will set a trap for us, meaning it for our harm and destruction. But when God gets involved, He takes what Satan meant to destroy us and turns it so that it works for our good instead. Nobody else can make things work out that way, but God can. He can take any negative situation, and through His miracle-working power use it to make us stronger and more dangerous to the enemy than we would have been without it.

My own situation bears this out. I was sexually, mentally, and emotionally abused for many years during my childhood. This was certainly a terrible thing to happen to a child, and it was definitely a work of Satan, but God has worked it out for good. My mess has become my message; my misery has become my ministry, and I am using the experience I gained from my pain to help multitudes of others who are hurting.

I encourage you not to waste your pain. God will use it if you give it to Him. He has given me beauty for ashes, just as He promised in Isaiah 61:3, but I had to let go of the ashes. I had to learn to have a good attitude, as Joseph did. I had to learn to let go of the bitterness, resentment, and unforgiveness I felt toward the people who hurt me.

When we have been hurt, it is important not to let the pain go on and on by having a bitter attitude. We hurt only ourselves when we hate people. We would not waste our time hating people if we realized that they are probably enjoying their lives and are not the least concerned with how we feel about them. Remember, God is our Vindicator, and He will bring good out of what the enemy intended for evil.

life point

So often in our lives, Satan thinks he is doing some terrible thing to bring about our destruction, and yet God has another plan entirely (see Genesis 50:20). He intends to take what Satan means for our harm and work it out not only for our good, but for the good of the many to whom we will minister.

all claim to requital concerning), I pray you now, the trespass of your brothers and their sin, for they did evil to you. Now, we pray you, forgive the trespass of the servants of your father's God. And Joseph wept when they spoke thus to him.

18 Then his brothers went and fell down before him, saying, See, we are your servants (your slaves)!

19 And Joseph said to them, Fear not; for am I in the place of God? [Vengeance is His, not mine.]

20 As for you, you thought evil against me, but God meant it for good, to bring about that many people should be kept alive, as they are this day.

21 Now therefore, do not be afraid. I will provide for *and* support you and your little ones. And he comforted them [imparting cheer, hope, strength] and spoke to their hearts [kindly].

22 Joseph dwelt in Egypt, he and his father's household. And Joseph lived 110 years.

23 And Joseph saw Ephraim's children of the third generation; the children also of Machir son of Manasseh were brought up on Joseph's knees.

24 And Joseph said to his brethren, I am going to die. But God will surely visit you and bring you out of this land to the land He swore to Abraham, to Isaac, and to Jacob [to give you].

25 And Joseph took an oath from the sons of Israel, saying, God will surely visit you, and you will carry up my bones from here.

26 So Joseph died, being 110 years old; and they embalmed him, and he was put ᵈin a coffin in Egypt.

speak the Word

Father, I thank You that when others think evil against me, You mean it for good.
ADAPTED FROM GENESIS **50:20**

---

d Joseph's body remained in Egypt until the exodus to the promised land of Canaan about 200 years later. Its final resting-place was Shechem, near Samaria, "in the parcel of ground which Jacob bought from the sons of Hamor, the father of Shechem" (Josh. 24:32). Here each of his brothers was also buried (Acts 7:15, 16).

Exodus

Author:
Moses

Date:
About 1440 BC

Everyday Life Principles:
When God leads us out of a situation, He always takes us into something better.

Deliverance from any kind of bondage is a process, and God takes us through it one step at a time.

Allow God to teach you how to trust Him and how to follow Him as He leads you into a place of fulfilled promises and great blessing.

The entire book of Exodus is a story of deliverance, a story of people who broke free from oppression and began a journey toward the good land that God had promised them. From beginning to end, Exodus teaches us how God brings us out of situations that keep us in bondage in order to take us into something better.

Just as God prepared Moses to deliver Israel, He sent Jesus to be our deliverer. Just as He led the Israelites with a cloud by day and a pillar of fire by night, the Holy Spirit in our hearts leads us today. Just as the Israelites' deliverance was a process, a journey that could be completed only *one step* at a time, God almost always leads us step-by-step instead of moving us instantly from one situation to the next. Just as the Israelites' murmuring and complaining slowed them down, bad attitudes will also impede our progress in God. Just as He gave the Israelites the Ten Commandments as laws to show them how to live a blessed life, He has given us the Bible as a guidebook for our journey through life. Just as He used the Israelites' journey to develop the faith, trust, strength, and character they would need in the Promised Land, He does the same for us in our journey.

As you read Exodus and consider the ways God is leading you out of any area of bondage or oppression in your life right now, determine that you will follow Him faithfully. Keep a good attitude so that you can get where He wants to take you and enjoy the fulfillment of His promises in your life.

1 THESE ARE the names of the sons of Israel who came into Egypt with Jacob, each with his household:

2 Reuben, Simeon, Levi, and Judah,

3 Issachar, Zebulun, and Benjamin,

4 Dan and Naphtali, Gad and Asher.

5 All the offspring of Jacob were seventy persons; Joseph was already in Egypt.

6 Then Joseph died, and all his brothers and all that generation.

7 But the descendants of Israel were fruitful and increased abundantly; they multiplied and grew exceedingly strong, and the land was full of them.

8 Now a new king arose over Egypt who did not know Joseph.

9 He said to his people, Behold, the Israelites are too many and too mighty for us [and they ªoutnumber us both in people and in strength].

10 Come, let us deal shrewdly with them, lest they multiply more and, should war befall us, they join our enemies, fight against us, and escape out of the land.

11 So they set over [the Israelites] taskmasters to afflict *and* oppress them with [increased] burdens. And [the Israelites] built Pithom and Rameses as store cities for Pharaoh.

12 But the more [the Egyptians] oppressed them, the more they multiplied and expanded, so that [the Egyptians] were vexed *and* alarmed because of the Israelites.

13 And the Egyptians reduced the Israelites to severe slavery.

14 They made their lives bitter with hard service in mortar, brick, and all kinds of work in the field. All their service was with harshness *and* severity.

15 Then the king of Egypt said to the Hebrew midwives, of whom one was named Shiprah and the other Puah,

16 When you act as midwives to the Hebrew women and see them on the birthstool, if it is a son, you shall kill him; but if it is a daughter, she shall live.

17 But the midwives feared God and did not do as the king of Egypt commanded, but let the male babies live.

putting the Word to work

When the Hebrew midwives had to choose between fearing God and obeying the orders of the king of Egypt, they chose to fear God (see Exodus 1:15–17). How will you respond when you are faced with a choice between pleasing man and obeying God?

18 So the king of Egypt called for the midwives and said to them, Why have you done this thing and allowed the male children to live?

19 The midwives answered Pharaoh, Because the Hebrew women are not like the Egyptian women; they are vigorous and quickly delivered; their babies are born before the midwife comes to them.

20 So God dealt well with the midwives and the people multiplied and became very strong.

21 And because the midwives revered *and* feared God, He made them households [of their own].

a Is there in all human history a more amazing spectacle than the exodus? A family of 70 immigrants grows into a people of slavery. Suddenly, according to God's detailed and preannounced plan, they are seen flinging away the shackles of generations of slavery and emigrating to a new country and a new life, with miraculous deliverances rescuing them from destruction again and again. The marvel of the exodus grows in wonder when, after more than 3,000 years, we see that same race, often persecuted almost to extinction, carrying out in startling detail God's predictions for their amazing national revitalization and prominence "in the last days" (adapted from many historians).

22 Then Pharaoh charged all his people, saying, Every son born [to the Hebrews] you shall cast into the river [Nile], but every daughter you shall allow to live.

2 NOW [Amram] a man of the house of Levi [the priestly tribe] went and took as his wife [Jochebed] a daughter of Levi. [Exod. 6:18, 20; Num. 26:59.]

2 And the woman became pregnant and bore a son; and when she saw that he was [exceedingly] beautiful, she hid him three months. [Acts 7:20; Heb. 11:23.]

3 And when she could no longer hide him, she took for him an ark *or* basket made of bulrushes *or* papyrus [making it watertight by] daubing it with bitumen and pitch. Then she put the child in it and laid it among the rushes by the brink of the river [Nile].

4 And his sister [Miriam] stood some distance away to [b]learn what would be done to him.

5 Now the daughter of Pharaoh came down to bathe at the river, and her maidens walked along the bank; she saw the ark among the rushes and sent her maid to fetch it.

6 When she opened it, she saw the child; and behold, the baby cried. And she took pity on him and said, This is one of the Hebrews' children!

7 Then his sister said to Pharaoh's daughter, Shall I go and call a nurse of the Hebrew women to nurse the child for you?

8 Pharaoh's daughter said to her, Go. And the girl went and called the child's mother.

9 Then Pharaoh's daughter said to her, Take this child away and nurse it for me, and I will give you your wages. So the woman took the child and nursed it.

10 And the child grew, and she brought him to Pharaoh's daughter and he became her son. And she called him Moses, for she said, Because I drew him out of the water.

11 One day, after Moses was grown, it happened that he went out to his brethren and looked at their burdens; and he saw an Egyptian beating a Hebrew, one of [Moses'] brethren.

12 He looked this way and that way, and when he saw no one, he killed the Egyptian and hid him in the sand.

13 He went out the second day and saw two Hebrew men quarreling *and* fighting; and he said to the unjust aggressor, Why are you striking your comrade?

14 And the man said, Who made you a prince and a judge over us? Do you intend to kill me as you killed the Egyptian? Then Moses was afraid and thought, Surely this thing is known.

15 When Pharaoh heard of it, he sought to slay Moses. But Moses fled from Pharaoh's presence and [c]took refuge in the land of Midian, where he sat down by a well.

16 Now the priest of Midian had seven daughters, and they came and drew water and filled the troughs to water their father's flock.

17 The shepherds came and drove

b They launched the ark not only on the Nile but on God's providence. He would be Captain, Steersman, and Convoy of the tiny ark. Miriam stood to watch. There was no fear of fatal consequences, only the quiet expectancy that God would do something worthy of Himself. They reckoned on God's faithfulness and they were amply rewarded when the daughter of their greatest foe became the babe's patroness (F. B. Meyer, *Through the Bible Day by Day*).   c "There was true heroism in the act, when Moses stepped down from Pharaoh's throne to share the lot of his brethren. But it would take many a long year of lonely waiting and trial before this strong and radiant nature could be broken down, shaped into a vessel meet for the Master's use, and prepared for every good work. . . . One blow struck when God's time is fulfilled is worth a thousand struck in premature eagerness" (F. B. Meyer, *Moses, the Servant of God*).

them away; but Moses stood up and helped them and watered their flock.

18 And when they came to Reuel [Jethro] their father, he said, How is it that you have come so soon today?

19 They said, An Egyptian delivered us from the shepherds; also he drew water for us and watered the flock.

20 He said to his daughters, Where is he? Why have you left the man? Call him, that he may eat bread.

21 And Moses was content to dwell with the man; and he gave Moses Zipporah his daughter.

22 And she bore a son, and he called his name Gershom [expulsion, or a stranger there]; for he said, I have been a stranger *and* a sojourner in a foreign land.

23 However, after a long time [nearly forty years] the king of Egypt died; and the Israelites were sighing *and* groaning because of the bondage. They kept crying, and their cry because of slavery ascended to God.

24 And God heard their sighing *and* groaning and [earnestly] remembered His covenant with Abraham, with Isaac, and with Jacob.

25 God saw the Israelites and took knowledge of them *and* concerned Himself about them [knowing all, understanding, remembering all]. [Ps. 56:8, 9; 139:2.]

3 NOW MOSES kept the flock of Jethro his father-in-law, the priest of Midian; and he led the flock to the back *or* west side of the wilderness and came to Horeb *or* Sinai, the mountain of God.

2 The dAngel of the Lord appeared to him in a flame of fire out of the midst of a bush; and he looked, and behold, the bush burned with fire, yet was not consumed.

3 And Moses said, I will now turn aside and see this great sight, why the bush is not burned.

4 And when the Lord saw that he turned aside to see, God called to him out of the midst of the bush and said, Moses, Moses! And he said, Here am I.

5 God said, Do not come near; put your shoes off your feet, for the place on which you stand is holy ground.

life point

To hear clearly from God, you need to be willing to live on holy ground (a life of purity), and that means keeping your thoughts in line with God's Word. Remember that Jesus said the pure in heart would see God (see Matthew 5:8).

6 Also He said, I am the God of your father, the God of Abraham, the God of Isaac, and the God of Jacob. And Moses hid his face, for he was afraid to look at God.

7 And the Lord said, I have surely seen the affliction of My people who are in Egypt, and have heard their cry because of their taskmasters *and* oppressors; for I know their sorrows *and* sufferings *and* trials.

8 And I have come down to deliver them out of the hand *and* power of the Egyptians and to bring them up out of that land to a land good and large, a land flowing with milk and honey [a land of plenty]—to the place of the Canaanite, the Hittite, the Amorite, the Perizzite, the Hivite, and the Jebusite.

9 Now behold, the cry of the Israelites has come to Me, and I have also seen how the Egyptians oppress them.

10 Come now therefore, and I will

---

d In this report of Moses and the burning bush, "the Angel of the Lord" is identified as the Lord Himself. See especially Exod. 3:4, 6. See also the footnote on Gen. 16:7.

send you to Pharaoh, that you may bring forth My people, the Israelites, out of Egypt.

11 And Moses said to God, eWho am I, that I should go to Pharaoh and bring the Israelites out of Egypt?

12 God said, I will surely be with you; and this shall be the sign to you that I have sent you: when you have brought the people out of Egypt, you shall serve God on this mountain [Horeb, or Sinai].

13 And Moses said to God, Behold, when I come to the Israelites and say to them, The God of your fathers has sent me to you, and they say to me, What is His name? What shall I say to them?

14 And God said to Moses, I AM WHO I AM *and* WHAT I AM, *and* I WILL BE WHAT I WILL BE; and He said, You shall say this to the Israelites: I AM has sent me to you!

15 God said also to Moses, This shall you say to the Israelites: The Lord, the God of your fathers, of Abraham, of Isaac, and of Jacob, has sent me to you! This is My fname forever, and by this name I am to be remembered to all generations.

16 Go, gather the elders of Israel together [the mature teachers and tribal leaders], and say to them, The Lord God of your fathers, the God of Abraham, of Isaac, and of Jacob, appeared to me, saying, I have surely visited you and seen that which is done to you in Egypt;

17 And I have declared that I will bring you up out of the affliction of Egypt to the land of the Canaanite, the Hittite, the Amorite, the Perizzite, the Hivite, and the Jebusite, to a land flowing with milk and honey.

18 And [the elders] shall believe *and* obey your voice; and you shall go, you and the elders of Israel, to the king of Egypt and you shall say to him, The Lord, the God of the Hebrews, has met with us; and now let us go, we beseech you, three days' journey into the wilderness, that we may sacrifice to the Lord our God.

19 And I know that the king of Egypt will not let you go [unless forced to do so], no, not by a mighty hand.

20 So I will stretch out My hand and smite Egypt with all My wonders which I will do in it; and after that he will let you go.

21 And I will give this people favor *and* respect in the sight of the Egyptians; and it shall be that when you go, you shall not go empty-handed.

22 But every woman shall [insistently] solicit of her neighbor and of her that may be residing at her house jewels and articles of silver and gold, and garments, which you shall put on your sons and daughters; and you shall strip the Egyptians [of belongings due to you].

4 AND MOSES answered, gBut behold, they will not believe me or listen to *and* obey my voice;

---

e "There was something more than humility here; there was a tone of self-depreciation which was inconsistent with a true faith in God's selection and appointment. Surely it is God's business to choose His special instruments; and when we are persuaded that we are in the line of His purpose, we have no right to question the wisdom of His appointment. To do so is to depreciate His wisdom or to doubt His power and willingness to become **all that is necessary** to complete our need" (F. B. Meyer, *Moses, the Servant of God*). **f** To know the **name** of God is to witness the manifestation of those attributes and apprehend that character which the name denotes (Exod. 6:3; I Kings 8:33ff.; Ps. 91:14; Isa. 52:6; 64:2; Jer. 16:21) (John D. Davis, *A Dictionary of the Bible*). God's name is His self-revelation (Charles Ellicott, *A Bible Commentary*). The name signifies the active presence of the person in the fullness of the revealed character (J.D. Douglas et al., eds., *The New Bible Dictionary*). **g** There need be no "buts" in our relationship to God's will. Nothing will take the Lord by surprise. The entire field has been surveyed and the preparations are complete. When the Lord says, "I will send thee," every provision has been made for the appointed task. "I will not fail thee." He who gives the command will also give the equipment (John Henry Jowett, *My Daily Meditation*).

"I AM."

If you have ever wondered, "Who am I?" You are not alone. When Moses thought the same thing, God responded with Who He is: "I AM" (Exodus 3:14). I have pondered these awesome words for a long time, and I believe they are much more significant than we realize.

What was God really saying when He referred to Himself as "I AM"? For one thing, He is *so much* that there is no way to explain Him properly. How can we describe Someone Who is *everything* and wrap it up in one name? When Moses asked the question about God's identity in Exodus 3:13, evidently the Lord did not want to get into a long dissertation about Who He was because He simply told Moses, "You shall say . . . I AM has sent me to you" (Exodus 3:14). By way of explanation, He preceded His statement with "I AM WHO I AM and WHAT I AM, and I WILL BE WHAT I WILL BE." God was saying to Moses, "You don't have to worry about Pharaoh or anybody else. I AM able to take care of anything you encounter. Whatever you need, I AM. Either I have it or I can get it. If it does not exist, I will create it. I have everything covered, not just now but for all time. Relax!"

We need not worry about who we are, what we can do, what we cannot do, or anything else. The great "I AM" strengthens us in our weaknesses. As long as He is with us, we can do whatever we need to do. Be more concerned about Who God is than you are about who you are.

To be honest with you, even as I write these words about Who God is, I can sense His presence and anointing. There is power in His name! He can handle what we think is difficult or impossible. God's answer to our "Who am I?" is "I AM WHO I AM." Almighty God is more than sufficient in the face of our lack. He is truly *everything*.

for they will say, The Lord has not appeared to you.

2 And the Lord said to him, What is that in your hand? And he said, A rod.

3 And He said, Cast it on the ground. And he did so and it became a serpent [the symbol of royal and divine power worn on the crown of the Pharaohs]; and Moses fled from before it.

4 And the Lord said to Moses, Put forth your hand and take it by the tail. And he stretched out his hand and caught it, and it became a rod in his hand,

5 [This you shall do, said the Lord] that the elders may believe that the Lord, the God of their fathers, of Abraham, of Isaac, and of Jacob, has indeed appeared to you.

6 The Lord said also to him, Put your hand into your bosom. He put his hand into his bosom, and when he took it out, behold, his hand was leprous, as white as snow.

7 [God] said, Put your hand into your bosom again. So he put his hand back into his bosom, and when he took it out, behold, it was restored as the rest of his flesh.

8 [Then God said] If they will not believe you or heed the voice *or* the testimony of the first sign, they may believe the voice *or* the witness of the second sign.

9 But if they will also not believe

these two signs or heed your voice, you shall take some water of the river [Nile] and pour it upon the dry land; and the water which you take out of the river [Nile] shall become blood on the dry land.

10 And Moses said to the Lord, O Lord, I am not eloquent *or* a man of words, neither before nor since You have spoken to Your servant; for I am slow of speech and have a heavy *and* awkward tongue.

11 And the Lord said to him, Who has made man's mouth? Or who makes the dumb, or the deaf, or the seeing, or the blind? Is it not I, the Lord?

12 Now therefore go, and I will be with your mouth and will teach you what you shall say.

13 And he said, Oh, my Lord, I pray You, send by the hand of [some other] whom You will [send].

14 Then the anger of the Lord blazed against Moses; He said, Is there not Aaron your brother, the Levite? I know he can speak well. Also, he is coming out to meet you, and when he sees you, he will be overjoyed.

15 You must speak to him and put the words in his mouth; and I will be with your mouth and with his mouth and will teach you what you shall do.

16 He shall speak for you to the people, acting as a mouthpiece for you, and you shall be as God to him.

17 And you shall take this rod in your hand with which you shall work the signs [that prove I sent you].

18 And Moses went away and, returning to Jethro his father-in-law, said to him, Let me go back, I pray you, to my relatives in Egypt to see whether they are still alive. And Jethro said to Moses, Go in peace.

19 The Lord said to Moses in Midian, Go back to Egypt; for all the men who were seeking your life [for killing the Egyptian] are dead. [Exod. 2:11, 12.]

20 And Moses took his wife and his sons and set them on donkeys, and he returned to the land of Egypt; and Moses took the rod of God in his hand.

21 And the Lord said to Moses, When you return into Egypt, see that you do before Pharaoh all those miracles *and* wonders which I have put in your hand; but I will make him stubborn *and* harden his heart, so that he will not let the people go.

22 And you shall say to Pharaoh, Thus says the Lord, Israel is My son, even My firstborn.

23 And I say to you, Let My son go, that he may serve Me; and if you refuse to let him go, behold, I will slay your son, your firstborn.

24 Along the way at a [resting-] place, the Lord met [Moses] and sought to kill him [made him acutely and almost fatally ill].

25 [Now apparently he had [h]failed to circumcise one of his sons, his wife being opposed to it; but seeing his life in such danger] Zipporah took a flint knife and cut off the foreskin of her son and cast it to touch [Moses'] feet, and said, Surely a husband of blood you are to me!

26 When He let [Moses] alone [to recover], Zipporah said, A husband of

speak the Word

h He who is on his way to liberate the people of the circumcision has in Midian even neglected to circumcise his second son Eliezer (J.P. Lange, *A Commentary*). It was necessary that at this stage of Moses' experience he should learn that God is in earnest when He speaks, and will assuredly perform all that He has threatened (J.G. Murphy, *A Commentary on the Book of Exodus*).

blood are you because of the circumcision.

27 The Lord said to Aaron, Go into the wilderness to meet Moses. And he went, and met him in the mountain of God [Horeb, or Sinai] and kissed him.

28 Moses told Aaron all the words of the Lord with which He had sent him, and all the signs with which He had charged him.

29 Moses and Aaron went and gathered together [in Egypt] all the elders of the Israelites.

30 Aaron spoke all the words which the Lord had spoken to Moses, and did the signs in the sight of the people.

31 And the people believed; and when they heard that the Lord had visited the Israelites, and that He had looked [in compassion] upon their affliction, they bowed their heads and worshiped.

5 AFTERWARD MOSES and Aaron went in and told Pharaoh, Thus says the Lord, the God of Israel, Let My people go, that they may hold a feast to Me in the wilderness.

2 But Pharaoh said, Who is the Lord, that I should obey His voice to let Israel go? I know not the Lord, neither will I let Israel go.

3 And they said, The God of the Hebrews has met with us; let us go, we pray you, three days' journey into the desert and sacrifice to the Lord our God, lest He fall upon us with pestilence or with the sword.

4 The king of Egypt said to Moses and Aaron, Why do you take the people from their jobs? Get to your burdens!

5 Pharaoh said, Behold, the people of the land now are many, and you make them rest from their burdens!

6 The very same day Pharaoh commanded the taskmasters of the people and their officers,

7 You shall no more give the people straw to make brick; let them go and gather straw for themselves.

8 But the number of the bricks which they made before you shall still require of them; you shall not diminish it in the least. For they are idle; that is why they cry, Let us go and sacrifice to our God.

9 Let heavier work be laid upon the men that they may labor at it and pay no attention to lying words.

10 The taskmasters of the people went out, and their officers, and they said to the people, Thus says Pharaoh, I will not give you straw.

11 Go, get ¹straw where you can find it; but your work shall not be diminished in the least.

12 So the people were scattered through all the land of Egypt to gather the short stubble instead of straw.

13 And the taskmasters were urgent, saying, Finish your work, your daily quotas, as when there was straw.

14 And the Hebrew foremen, whom Pharaoh's taskmasters had set over them, were beaten and were asked, Why have you not fulfilled all your quota of making bricks yesterday and today, as before?

---

i Archaeologists became interested early in examining Egyptian bricks of Moses' time to see if they contained straw. They found that, while many did contain straw, many also did not, leaving the impression that the Bible was wrong. But as usual in such cases, sooner or later it is shown that "the testimony of the Lord is sure, making wise the simple" (Ps. 19:7)—who know no better than to doubt the truth of God's Word. It is now known that oat straw boiled in water, when added to clay, makes the clay much easier to handle. Without the organic material obtained from the straw, the difficulty of making bricks was greatly increased. The fact that brickmakers of Egypt found the use of straw essential, whether visible evidence remains or not, is fully borne out, as various writers have asserted. (See Allan A. MacRae's, "The Relation of Archaeology to the Bible" in *Modern Science and Christian Faith*.)

15 Then the Hebrew foremen came to Pharaoh and cried, Why do you deal like this with your servants?
16 No straw is given to your servants, yet they say to us, Make bricks! And behold, your servants are beaten, but the fault is in your own people.
17 But [Pharaoh] said, You are idle, lazy *and* idle! That is why you say, Let us go and sacrifice to the Lord.
18 Get out now and get to work; for no straw shall be given you, yet you shall deliver the full quota of bricks.
19 And the Hebrew foremen saw that they were in an evil situation when it was said, You shall not diminish in the least your full daily quota of bricks.
20 And the foremen met Moses and Aaron, who were standing in the way as they came forth from Pharaoh.
21 And the foremen said to them, The Lord look upon you and judge, because you have made us a rotten stench to be detested by Pharaoh and his servants and have put a sword in their hand to slay us.
22 Then Moses turned again to the Lord and said, O Lord, why have You dealt evil to this people? Why did You ever send me?
23 For since I came to Pharaoh to speak in Your name, he has done evil to this people, neither have You delivered Your people at all.

6 THEN THE Lord said to Moses, Now you shall see what I will do to Pharaoh; for [compelled] by a strong hand he will [not only] let them go, but he will drive them out of his land with a strong hand.

2 And God said to Moses, I am the Lord.
3 I appeared to Abraham, to Isaac, and to Jacob as God Almighty [El-Shaddai], but by My ʲname the Lord [Yahweh—the redemptive name of God] I did not make Myself known to them [in acts and great miracles]. [Gen. 17:1.]
4 I have also established My covenant with them to give them the land of Canaan, the land of their temporary residence in which they were strangers.
5 I have also heard the groaning of the Israelites whom the Egyptians have enslaved; and I have [earnestly] remembered My covenant [with Abraham, Isaac, and Jacob].
6 Accordingly, say to the Israelites, I am the Lord, and I will bring you out from under the burdens of the Egyptians, and I will free you from their bondage, and I will rescue you with an outstretched arm [with special and vigorous action] and by mighty acts of judgment.
7 And I will take you to Me for a people, and I will be to you a God; and you shall know that it is I, the Lord your God, Who brings you out from under the burdens of the Egyptians.
8 And I will bring you into the land concerning which I lifted up My hand *and* swore that I would give it to Abraham, Isaac, and Jacob; and I will give it to you for a heritage. I am the Lord [you have the pledge of My changeless omnipotence and faithfulness].

speak the Word

Thank You, Lord, for bringing me out from under burdens and out from bondage. Thank You for rescuing me with Your outstretched arm.
ADAPTED FROM EXODUS 6:6

ʲ See footnote on Exod. 3:15.

9 Moses told this to the Israelites, but they refused to listen to Moses because of their impatience *and* anguish of spirit and because of their cruel bondage.
10 The Lord said to Moses,
11 Go in, tell Pharaoh king of Egypt to let the Israelites go out of his land.
12 But Moses said to the Lord, Behold, [my own people] the Israelites have not listened to me; how then shall Pharaoh give heed to me, who am of deficient *and* impeded speech?
13 But the Lord spoke to Moses and Aaron, and gave them a command for the Israelites and for Pharaoh king of Egypt, to bring the Israelites out of the land of Egypt.
14 These are the heads of their clans. The sons of Reuben, Israel's firstborn: Hanoch, Pallu, Hezron, and Carmi; these are the families of Reuben.
15 The sons of Simeon: Jemuel, Jamin, Ohad, Jachin, Zohar, and Shaul the son of a Canaanite woman; these are the families of Simeon.
16 These are the names of the sons of Levi according to their births: Gershon, Kohath, and Merari; and Levi lived 137 years.
17 The sons of Gershon: Libni and Shimi, by their families.
18 The sons of Kohath: Amram, Izhar, Hebron, and Uzziel; and Kohath lived 133 years.
19 The sons of Merari: Mahli and Mushi. These are the families of Levi according to their generations.
20 Amram took Jochebed his father's sister as wife, and she bore him Aaron and Moses; and Amram lived 137 years.
21 The sons of Izhar: Korah, Nepheg, and Zichri.
22 The sons of Uzziel: Mishael, Elzaphan, and Sithri.
23 Aaron took Elisheba, daughter of Amminadab and sister of Nahshon, as wife; she bore him Nadab, Abihu, Eleazar, and Ithamar.

24 The sons of Korah: Assir, Elkanah, and Abiasaph. These are the families of the Korahites.
25 Eleazar, Aaron's son, took one of the daughters of Putiel as wife; and she bore him Phinehas. These are the heads of the fathers' houses of the Levites by their families.
26 These are the [same] Aaron and Moses to whom the Lord said, Bring out the Israelites from the land of Egypt by their hosts,
27 And who spoke to [the] Pharaoh king of Egypt about bringing the Israelites out of Egypt; these are that Moses and Aaron.
28 On the day when the Lord spoke to Moses in Egypt,
29 The Lord said to Moses, I am the Lord; tell Pharaoh king of Egypt all that I say to you.
30 But Moses said to the Lord, Behold, I am of deficient *and* impeded speech; how then shall Pharaoh listen to me?

7 THE LORD said to Moses, Behold, I make you as God to Pharaoh [to declare My will and purpose to him]; and Aaron your brother shall be your prophet.
2 You shall speak all that I command you, and Aaron your brother shall tell Pharaoh to let the Israelites go out of his land.
3 And I will make Pharaoh's heart stubborn *and* hard, and multiply My signs, My wonders, *and* miracles in the land of Egypt.
4 But Pharaoh will not listen to you, and I will lay My hand upon Egypt and bring forth My hosts, My people the Israelites, out of the land of Egypt by great acts of judgment.
5 The Egyptians shall know that I am the Lord when I stretch forth My hand upon Egypt and bring out the Israelites from among them.
6 And Moses and Aaron did so, as the Lord commanded them.

7 Now Moses was 80 years old and Aaron 83 years old when they spoke to Pharaoh.

8 And the Lord said to Moses and Aaron,

9 When Pharaoh says to you, Prove [your authority] by a miracle, then tell Aaron, Throw your rod down before Pharaoh, that it may become a serpent.

10 So Moses and Aaron went to Pharaoh and did as the Lord had commanded; Aaron threw down his rod before Pharaoh and his servants, and it became a serpent.

11 Then Pharaoh called for the wise men [skilled in magic and divination] and the sorcerers (wizards and jugglers). And they also, these magicians of Egypt, did similar things with their enchantments *and* secret arts.

12 For they cast down every man his rod and they became serpents; but Aaron's rod swallowed up their rods.

13 But Pharaoh's heart was hardened *and* stubborn and he would not listen to them, just as the Lord had said.

14 Then the Lord said to Moses, Pharaoh's heart is hard *and* stubborn; he refuses to let the people go.

15 Go to Pharaoh in the morning; he will be going out to the water; wait for him by the river's brink; and the rod which was turned to a serpent you shall take in your hand.

16 And say to him, The Lord, the God of the Hebrews has sent me to you, saying, Let My people go, that they may serve Me in the wilderness; and behold, heretofore you have not listened.

17 Thus says the Lord, In this you shall know, recognize, *and* understand that I am the Lord: behold, I will smite with the rod in my hand the waters in the [Nile] River, and they shall be turned to blood.

18 The fish in the river shall die, the river shall become foul smelling, and the Egyptians shall loathe to drink from it.

19 And the Lord said to Moses, Say to Aaron, Take your rod and stretch out your hand over the waters of Egypt, over their streams, rivers, pools, and ponds of water, that they may become blood; and there shall be blood throughout all the land of Egypt, in containers both of wood and of stone.

20 Moses and Aaron did as the Lord commanded; [Aaron] lifted up the rod and smote the waters in the river in the sight of Pharaoh and his servants, and all the waters in the river were turned to blood.

21 And the fish in the river died; and the river became foul smelling, and the Egyptians could not drink its water, and there was blood throughout all the land of Egypt.

22 But the magicians of Egypt did the same by their enchantments *and* secret arts; and Pharaoh's heart was made hard *and* obstinate, and he did not listen to Moses and Aaron, just as the Lord had said.

23 And Pharaoh turned and went into his house; neither did he take even this to heart.

24 And all the Egyptians dug round about the river for water to drink, for they could not drink the water of the [Nile].

25 Seven days passed after the Lord had smitten the river.

8 THEN THE Lord said to Moses, Go to Pharaoh and say to him, Thus says the Lord, Let My people go, that they may serve Me.

2 And if you refuse to let them go, behold, I will smite your entire land with frogs;

3 And the river shall swarm with frogs which shall go up and come into your house, into your bedchamber and on your bed, and into the houses of your servants and upon

your people, and into your ovens, your kneading bowls, *and* your dough.

4 And the frogs shall come up on you and on your people and all your servants.

5 And the Lord said to Moses, Say to Aaron, Stretch out your hand with your rod over the rivers, the streams *and* canals, and over the pools, and cause frogs to come up on the land of Egypt.

6 So Aaron stretched out his hand over the waters of Egypt, and the frogs came up and covered the land.

7 But the magicians did the same thing with their enchantments *and* secret arts, and brought up [more] frogs upon the land of Egypt.

8 Then Pharaoh called for Moses and Aaron, and said, Entreat the Lord, that He may take away the frogs from me and my people; and I will let the people go that they may sacrifice to the Lord.

9 Moses said to Pharaoh, Glory over me in this: dictate when I shall pray [to the Lord] for you, your servants, and your people, that the frogs may be destroyed from you and your houses and remain only in the river.

10 And [Pharaoh] said, Tomorrow. [Moses] said, Let it be as you say, that you may know that there is no one like the Lord our God.

11 And the frogs shall depart from you and your houses and from your servants and your people; they shall remain in the river only.

12 So Moses and Aaron went out from Pharaoh, and Moses cried to the Lord [as he had agreed with Pharaoh] concerning the frogs which He had brought against him.

13 And the Lord did according to the word of Moses, and the frogs died out of the houses, out of the courtyards *and* villages, and out of the fields.

14 [The people] gathered them together in heaps, and the land was loathsome *and* stank.

15 But when Pharaoh saw that there was temporary relief, he made his heart stubborn *and* hard and would not listen *or* heed them, just as the Lord had said.

16 Then the Lord said to Moses, Say to Aaron, Stretch out your rod and strike the dust of the ground, that it may become biting gnats *or* mosquitoes throughout all the land of Egypt.

17 And they did so; Aaron stretched out his hand with his rod and struck the dust of the earth, and there came biting gnats *or* mosquitoes on man and beast; all the dust of the land became biting gnats *or* mosquitoes throughout all the land of Egypt.

18 The magicians tried by their enchantments *and* secret arts to bring forth gnats *or* mosquitoes, but they could not; and there were gnats *or* mosquitoes on man and beast.

19 Then the magicians said to Pharaoh, This is the finger of God! But Pharaoh's heart was hardened *and* strong and he would not listen to them, just as the Lord had said.

20 Then the Lord said to Moses, Rise up early in the morning and stand before Pharaoh as he comes forth to the water; and say to him, Thus says the Lord, Let My people go, that they may serve Me.

21 Else, if you will not let My people go, behold, I will send swarms [of bloodsucking gadflies] upon you, your servants, and your people, and into your houses; and the houses of the

speak the Word

God, I declare that there is no one like You!
ADAPTED FROM Exodus 8:10

Egyptians shall be full of swarms [of bloodsucking gadflies], and also the ground on which they stand.

22 But on that day I will sever *and* set apart the land of Goshen in which My people dwell, that no swarms [of gadflies] shall be there, so that you may know that I am the Lord in the midst of the earth.

23 And I will put a division *and* a sign of deliverance between My people and your people. By tomorrow shall this sign be in evidence.

24 And the Lord did so; and there came heavy *and* oppressive swarms [of bloodsucking gadflies] into the house of Pharaoh and his servants' houses; and in all of Egypt the land was corrupted *and* ruined by reason of the great invasion [of gadflies].

25 And Pharaoh called for Moses and Aaron, and said, Go, sacrifice to your God [here] in the land [of Egypt].

26 And Moses said, It is not suitable *or* right to do that; for the animals the Egyptians hold sacred and will not permit to be slain are those which we are accustomed to sacrifice to the Lord our God; if we did this before the eyes of the Egyptians, would they not stone us?

27 We will go a three days' journey into the wilderness and sacrifice to the Lord our God, as He will command us.

28 So Pharaoh said, I will let you go, that you may sacrifice to the Lord your God in the wilderness; only you shall not go very far away. Entreat [your God] for me.

29 Moses said, I go out from you, and I will entreat the Lord that the swarms [of bloodsucking gadflies] may depart from Pharaoh, his servants, and his people tomorrow; only let not Pharaoh deal deceitfully any more in not letting the people go to sacrifice to the Lord.

30 So Moses went out from Pharaoh and entreated the Lord.

31 And the Lord did as Moses had spoken: He removed the swarms [of attacking gadflies] from Pharaoh, from his servants, and his people; there remained not one.

32 But Pharaoh hardened his heart *and* made it stubborn this time also, nor would he let the people go.

9 THEN THE Lord said to Moses, Go to Pharaoh and tell him, Thus says the Lord God of the Hebrews: Let My people go, that they may serve Me.

2 If you refuse to let them go and still hold them,

3 Behold, the hand of the Lord [will fall] upon your livestock which are out in the field, upon the horses, the donkeys, the camels, the herds and the flocks; there shall be a very severe plague.

4 But the Lord shall make a distinction between the livestock of Israel and the livestock of Egypt, and nothing shall die of all that belongs to the Israelites.

5 And the Lord set a time, saying, Tomorrow the Lord will do this thing in the land.

6 And the Lord did that the next day, and all [kinds of] the livestock of Egypt died; but of the livestock of the Israelites not one died.

7 Pharaoh sent to find out, and behold, there was not one of the cattle of the Israelites dead. But the heart of Pharaoh was hardened [his mind was set] and he did not let the people go.

8 The Lord said to Moses and Aaron, Take handfuls of ashes *or* soot from the brickkiln and let Moses sprinkle them toward the heavens in the sight of Pharaoh.

9 And it shall become small dust over all the land of Egypt, and become boils breaking out in sores on man and beast in all the land [occupied by the Egyptians].

10 So they took ashes *or* soot of the kiln and stood before Pharaoh; and

Moses threw them toward the sky, and it became boils erupting in sores on man and beast.

11 And the magicians could not stand before Moses because of their boils; for the boils were on the magicians and all the Egyptians.

12 But the Lord hardened the heart of Pharaoh, making it strong *and* obstinate, and he did not listen to them or heed them, just as the Lord had told Moses.

13 Then the Lord said to Moses, Rise up early in the morning and stand before Pharaoh and say to him, Thus says the Lord, the God of the Hebrews, Let My people go, that they may serve Me.

14 For this time I will send all My plagues upon your heart and upon your servants and your people, that you may recognize *and* know that there is none like Me in all the earth.

15 For by now I could have put forth My hand and have struck you and your people with pestilence, and you would have been cut off from the earth.

16 But for this very purpose have I let you live, that I might show you My power, and that My name may be declared throughout all the earth. [Rom. 9:17-24.]

17 Since you are still exalting yourself [in haughty defiance] against My people by not letting them go,

18 Behold, tomorrow about this time I will cause it to rain a very heavy *and* dreadful fall of hail, such as has not been in Egypt from its founding until now.

19 Send therefore now and gather your cattle in hastily, and all that you have in the field; for every man and beast that is in the field and is not brought home shall be struck by the hail and shall die.

20 Then he who feared the word of the Lord among the servants of Pharaoh made his servants and his livestock flee into the houses *and* shelters.

21 And he who ignored the word of the Lord left his servants and his livestock in the field.

22 The Lord said to Moses, Stretch forth your hand toward the heavens, that there may be hail in all the land of Egypt, upon man and beast, and upon all the vegetation of the field, throughout the land of Egypt.

23 Then Moses stretched forth his rod toward the heavens, and the Lord sent thunder and hail, and fire (lightning) ran down to *and* along the ground, and the Lord rained hail upon the land of Egypt.

24 So there was hail and fire flashing continually in the midst of the weighty hail, such as had not been in all the land of Egypt since it became a nation.

25 The hail struck down throughout all the land of Egypt everything that was in the field, both man and beast; and the hail beat down all the vegetation of the field and shattered every tree of the field.

26 Only in the land of Goshen, where the Israelites were, was there no hail.

27 And Pharaoh sent for Moses and Aaron, and said to them, I have sinned this time; the Lord is in the right and I and my people are in the wrong.

28 Entreat the Lord, for there has been enough of these mighty thunderings and hail [these voices of God]; I will let you go; you shall stay here no longer.

29 Moses said to him, As soon as I leave the city, I will stretch out my hands to the Lord; the thunder shall cease, neither shall there be any more hail, that you may know that the earth is the Lord's.

30 But as for you and your servants, I know that you do not yet [reverently] fear the Lord God.

31 The flax and the barley were smitten *and* ruined, for the barley was in the ear and the flax in bloom.

32 But the wheat and spelt [another wheat] were not smitten, for they ripen late and were not grown up yet. **33** So Moses left the city and Pharaoh, and stretched forth his hands to the Lord; and the thunder and hail ceased, and rain was no longer poured upon the earth. **34** But when Pharaoh saw that the rain, the hail, and the thunder had ceased, he sinned yet more, and toughened *and* stiffened his hard heart, he and his servants. **35** So Pharaoh's heart was strong *and* obstinate; he would not let the Israelites go, just as the Lord had said by Moses. [Exod. 4:21.]

10 THE LORD said to Moses, Go to Pharaoh, for I have made his heart hard, and his servants' hearts, that I might show these My signs [of divine power] before him,

2 And that you may recount in the ears of your son and of your grandson what I have done in derision of the Egyptians *and* what things I have [repeatedly] done there—My signs [of divine power] done among them—that you may recognize *and* know that I am the Lord.

3 So Moses and Aaron went to Pharaoh, and said to him, Thus says the Lord, the God of the Hebrews, How long will you refuse to humble yourself before Me? Let My people go, that they may serve Me.

4 For if you refuse to let My people go, behold, tomorrow I will bring locusts into your country.

5 And they shall cover the land so that one cannot see the ground; and they shall eat the remainder of what escaped and is left to you from the hail, and they shall eat every tree of yours that grows in the field;

6 The locusts shall fill your houses and those of all your servants and of all the Egyptians, as neither your fathers nor your fathers' fathers have seen from their birth until this day. Then Moses departed from Pharaoh.

7 And Pharaoh's servants said to him, How long shall this man be a snare to us? Let the men go, that they may serve the Lord their God; do you not yet understand *and* know that Egypt is destroyed?

8 So Moses and Aaron were brought again to Pharaoh; and he said to them, Go, serve the Lord your God; but just who are to go?

9 And Moses said, We will go with our young and our old, with our sons and our daughters, with our flocks and our herds [all of us and all we have], for we must hold a feast to the Lord.

10 Pharaoh said to them, Let the Lord be with you, if I ever let you go with your little ones! See, you have some evil purpose in mind.

11 Not so! You that are men, [without your families] go and serve the Lord, for that is what you want. And [Moses and Aaron] were driven from Pharaoh's presence.

12 Then the Lord said to Moses, Stretch out your hand over the land of Egypt for the locusts, that they may come up on the land of Egypt and eat all the vegetation of the land, all that the hail has left.

13 And Moses stretched forth his rod over the land of Egypt, and the Lord brought an east wind upon the land all that day and all that night; when it was morning, the east wind brought the locusts.

14 And the locusts came up over all the land of Egypt and settled down on the whole country of Egypt, a very dreadful mass of them; never before were there such locusts as these, nor will there ever be again.

15 For they covered the whole land, so that the ground was darkened, and they ate every bit of vegetation of the land and all the fruit of the trees which the hail had left; there remained not a green thing of the trees or the plants of the field in all the land of Egypt.

16 Then Pharaoh sent for Moses and Aaron in haste. He said, I have sinned against the Lord your God and you.

17 Now therefore forgive my sin, I pray you, only this once, and entreat the Lord your God only that He may remove from me this [plague of] death.

18 Then Moses left Pharaoh and entreated the Lord.

19 And the Lord turned a violent west wind, which lifted the locusts and drove them into the Red Sea; not one locust remained in all the country of Egypt.

20 But the Lord made Pharaoh's heart more strong *and* obstinate, and he would not let the Israelites go.

21 And the Lord said to Moses, Stretch out your hand toward the heavens, that there may be darkness over the land of Egypt, a darkness which may be felt.

22 So Moses stretched out his hand toward the sky, and for three days a thick darkness was all over the land of Egypt.

23 The Egyptians could not see one another, nor did anyone rise from his place for three days; but all the Israelites had natural light in their dwellings.

24 And Pharaoh called to Moses, and said, Go, serve the Lord; let your little ones also go with you; it is only your flocks and your herds that must not go.

25 But Moses said, You must give

into our hand also sacrifices and burnt offerings, that we may sacrifice to the Lord our God.

26 Our livestock also shall go with us; there shall not a hoof be left behind; for of them must we take to serve the Lord our God, and we know not with what we must serve the Lord until we arrive there.

27 But the Lord made Pharaoh's heart stronger *and* more stubborn, and he would not let them go.

28 And Pharaoh said to Moses, Get away from me! See that you never enter my presence again, for the day you see my face again you shall die!

29 And Moses said, You have spoken truly; I will never see your face again.

11 THEN THE Lord said to Moses, Yet will I bring one plague more on Pharaoh and on Egypt; afterwards he will let you go. When he lets you go from here, he will thrust you out altogether.

2 Speak now in the hearing of the people, and let every man solicit *and* ask of his neighbor, and every woman of her neighbor, jewels of silver and jewels of gold.

3 And the Lord gave the people favor in the sight of the Egyptians. Moreover, the man Moses was exceedingly great in the land of Egypt, in the sight of Pharaoh's servants and of the people.

4 And Moses said, Thus says the Lord, About midnight I will go out into the midst of Egypt;

5 And all the firstborn in the land [the pride, hope, and joy] of Egypt shall die, from the firstborn of Pharaoh, who sits on his throne, even to the firstborn of the maidservant who is behind the hand mill, and all the firstborn of beasts.

6 There shall be a great cry in all the land of Egypt, such as has never been nor ever shall be again.

7 But against any of the Israelites

putting the Word to work

Do you need favor with the people you work for, as the Israelites did in the sight of the Egyptians? Ask God to give you the favor you need, just as He gave the Israelites favor in the eyes of their taskmasters so long ago (see Exodus 11:3).

shall not so much as a dog move his tongue against man or beast, that you may know that the Lord makes a distinction between the Egyptians and Israel.

8 And all these your servants shall come down to me and bow down to me, saying, Get out, and all the people who follow you! And after that I will go out. And he went out from Pharaoh in great anger.

9 Then the Lord said to Moses, Pharaoh will not listen to you, that My wonders *and* miracles may be multiplied in the land of Egypt.

10 Moses and Aaron did all these wonders *and* miracles before Pharaoh; and the Lord hardened Pharaoh's stubborn heart, and he did not let the Israelites go out of his land.

12 THE LORD said to Moses and Aaron in the land of Egypt,

2 This month shall be to you the beginning of months, the first month of the year to you.

3 Tell all the congregation of Israel, On the tenth day of this month they shall take every man a lamb *or* kid, according to [the size of] the family of which he is the father, a lamb *or* kid for each house.

4 And if the household is too small to consume the lamb, let him and his next door neighbor take it according to the number of persons, every man according to what each can eat shall make your count for the lamb.

5 Your lamb *or* kid shall be without blemish, a male of the first year; you shall take it from the sheep or the goats. [I Pet. 1:19, 20.]

6 And you shall keep it until the fourteenth day of the same month; and the whole assembly of the congregation of Israel shall [each] kill [his] lamb in the evening.

7 They shall take of the blood and put it on the two side posts and on the lintel [above the door space] of the houses in which they shall eat [the Passover lamb]. [Matt. 26:28; John 1:29; Heb. 9:14.]

8 They shall eat the flesh that night roasted; with unleavened bread and bitter herbs they shall eat it.

9 Eat not of it raw nor boiled at all with water, but roasted—its head, its legs, and its inner parts.

10 You shall let nothing of the meat remain until the morning; and the bones *and* unedible bits which remain of it until morning you shall burn with fire.

11 And you shall eat it thus: [as fully prepared for a journey] your loins girded, your shoes on your feet, and your staff in your hand; and you shall eat it in haste. It is the Lord's Passover.

12 For I will pass through the land of Egypt this night and will smite all the firstborn in the land of Egypt, both man and beast; and against all the gods of Egypt I will execute judgment [proving their helplessness]. I am the Lord.

13 The blood shall be for a token *or* sign to you upon [the doorposts of] the houses where you are, [that] when I see the blood, I will pass over you, and no plague shall be upon you to destroy you when I smite the land of Egypt. [I Cor. 5:7; Heb. 11:28.]

14 And this day shall be to you for a memorial. You shall keep it as a feast to the Lord throughout your generations, keep it as an ordinance forever.

15 [In celebration of the Passover in future years] seven days shall you eat unleavened bread; even the first day you shall put away leaven [symbolic of corruption] out of your houses; for whoever eats leavened bread from the first day until the seventh day, that person shall be cut off from Israel.

16 On the first day you shall hold a solemn *and* holy assembly, and on the seventh day there shall be a solemn

apply the blood to your life

God instructed the Israelites to use the blood of a lamb as a token or a sign that they were not to be harmed under the Old Covenant. Notice that the Lord said to them, "When I see the blood, I will pass over you" (Exodus 12:13). In order for the people to be protected from the angel of death, God had to *see* the blood, and He could not *see* it if they did not *put* it on the side posts and tops of their doorframes.

You and I live under the New Covenant, which is far better than the Old Covenant because the applied blood of Jesus is permanent (see Hebrews 9:12–26). How do we "put" the blood on our lives and homes? We do it by believing in Jesus Christ as we simply say in faith, "I believe the blood of Jesus is on my life and my home, cleansing and protecting me." We can apply the blood in any practical situation we face.

Start applying the blood by faith over yourself and that which belongs to you— your children, your car, your home, your body. Are you battling with wounded emotions? Then cover your emotions with the blood of Jesus so you will not continue to be devastated by people who do not seem to know how to give you what you feel you need from them. Are you in financial difficulty? Lay your hands on your tithe checks and on your checkbooks and wallets; pray that they will be protected by the blood of Jesus. Ask God to cause your money to multiply in the work of the Lord and to see to it that Satan does not steal any of it from you. Are you sick? Release your faith for the blood of Jesus to cover and protect your body. The life is in the blood; it cleanses us from all sin and protects us from things that will harm us.

Pray with me: "Father, I come to You in Jesus' name, and I apply the blood of Jesus to my life, to all that belongs to me, and to everything You have given me to steward. I put the blood of Jesus on my mind, my body, my emotions, and my will. I put the blood on my family, my coworkers, and my friends. Thank You for protecting me with Your blood. Amen."

and holy assembly; no kind of work shall be done in them, save [preparation of] that which every person must eat—that only may be done by you.
17 And you shall observe the Feast of Unleavened Bread, for on this very day have I brought your hosts out of the land of Egypt; therefore shall you observe this day throughout your generations as an ordinance forever.
18 In the first month, on the fourteenth day of the month at evening,

you shall eat unleavened bread [and continue] until the twenty-first day of the month at evening.
19 Seven days no leaven [symbolic of corruption] shall be found in your houses; whoever eats what is leavened shall be excluded from the congregation of Israel, whether a stranger or native-born. [I Cor. 5:6-8.]
20 You shall eat nothing leavened; in all your dwellings you shall eat unleavened bread [during that week].

21 Then Moses called for all the elders of Israel, and said to them, Go forth, select and take a lamb according to your families and kill the Passover [lamb].

22 And you shall take a bunch of hyssop, dip it in the blood in the basin, and touch the lintel above the door and the two side posts with the blood; and none of you shall go out of his house until morning.

23 For the Lord will pass through to slay the Egyptians; and when He sees the blood upon the lintel and the two side posts, the Lord will pass over the door and will not allow the destroyer to come into your houses to slay you.

24 You shall observe this rite for an ordinance to you and to your sons forever.

25 When you come to the land which the Lord will give you, as He has promised, you shall keep this service.

26 When your children shall say to you, What do you mean by this service?

27 You shall say, It is the sacrifice of the Lord's Passover, for He passed over the houses of the Israelites in Egypt when He slew the Egyptians but spared our houses. And the people bowed their heads and worshiped.

28 The Israelites went and, as the Lord had commanded Moses and Aaron, so they did.

29 At midnight the Lord slew every firstborn in the land of Egypt, from the firstborn of Pharaoh who sat on his throne to the firstborn of the prisoner in the dungeon, and all the firstborn of the livestock.

30 Pharaoh rose up in the night, he, all his servants, and all the Egyptians; and there was a great cry in Egypt, for there was not a house where there was not one dead.

31 He called for Moses and Aaron by night, and said, Rise up, get out from among my people, both you and the Israelites; and go, serve the Lord, as you said.

32 Also take your flocks and your herds, as you have said, and be gone! And [ask your God to] bless me also.

33 The Egyptians were urgent with the people to depart, that they might send them out of the land in haste; for they said, We are all dead men.

34 The people took their dough before it was leavened, their kneading bowls being bound up in their clothes on their shoulders.

35 The Israelites did according to the word of Moses; and they [urgently] asked of the Egyptians jewels of silver and of gold, and clothing.

36 The Lord gave the people favor in the sight of the Egyptians, so that they gave them what they asked. And they stripped the Egyptians [of those things].

37 The Israelites journeyed from Rameses to Succoth, about 600,000 men on foot, besides women and children.

38 And a mixed multitude went also with them, and very much livestock, both flocks and herds.

39 They baked unleavened cakes of the dough which they brought from Egypt; it was not leavened because they were driven from Egypt and could not delay, nor had they prepared for themselves any food.

40 Now the time the Israelites dwelt in Egypt was 430 years. [Gen. 15:13, 14.]

41 At the end of the 430 years, even that very day, all the hosts of the Lord went out of Egypt.

42 It was a night of watching unto the Lord *and* to be much observed for bringing them out of Egypt; this same night of watching unto the Lord is to be observed by all the Israelites throughout their generations.

43 The Lord said to Moses and Aaron, This is the ordinance of the Passover: No foreigner shall eat of it;

44 But every man's servant who is bought for money, when you have circumcised him, then may he eat of it.

45 A foreigner or hired servant shall not eat of it.

46 In one house shall it be eaten [by one company]; you shall not carry any of the flesh outside the house; neither shall you break a bone of it. [John 19:33, 36.]

47 All the congregation of Israel shall keep it.

48 When a stranger sojourning with you wishes to keep the Passover to the Lord, let all his males be circumcised, and then let him come near and keep it; and he shall be as one that is born in the land. But no uncircumcised person shall eat of it.

49 There shall be one law for the native-born and for the stranger or foreigner who sojourns among you.

50 Thus did all the Israelites; as the Lord commanded Moses and Aaron, so did they.

51 And on that very day the Lord brought the Israelites out of the land of Egypt by their hosts.

13 THE LORD said to Moses, **2** Sanctify (consecrate, set apart) to Me all the firstborn [males]; whatever is first to open the womb among the Israelites, both of man and of beast, is Mine.

3 And Moses said to the people, [Earnestly] remember this day in which you came out from Egypt, out of the house of bondage *and* bondmen, for by strength of hand the Lord brought you out from this place; no leavened bread shall be eaten.

4 This day you go forth in the month Abib.

5 And when the Lord brings you into the land of the Canaanites, Hittites, Amorites, Hivites, and Jebusites, which He promised *and* swore to your fathers to give you, a land flowing with milk and honey [a land of plenty], you shall keep this service in this month.

6 Seven days you shall eat unleavened bread and the seventh day shall be a feast to the Lord.

7 Unleavened bread shall be eaten for seven days; no leavened bread shall be seen with you, neither shall there be leaven in all your territory.

8 You shall explain to your son on that day, This is done because of what the Lord did for me when I came out of Egypt.

9 It shall be as a sign to you upon your hand and as a memorial between your eyes, that the law of the Lord may be in your mouth; for with a strong hand the Lord has brought you out of Egypt.

10 You shall therefore keep this ordinance at this time from year to year.

11 And when the Lord brings you into the land of the Canaanites, as He promised *and* swore to you and your fathers, and shall give it to you,

12 You shall set apart to the Lord all that first opens the womb. All the firstlings of your livestock that are males shall be the Lord's.

13 Every firstborn of a donkey you shall redeem by [substituting for it] a lamb, or if you will not redeem it, then you shall break its neck; and every firstborn among your sons shall you redeem.

14 And when, in time to come, your son asks you, What does this mean? You shall say to him, By strength of hand the Lord brought us out from Egypt, from the house of bondage *and* bondmen.

15 For when Pharaoh stubbornly refused to let us go, the Lord slew all the firstborn in the land of Egypt, both the firstborn of man and of livestock. Therefore I sacrifice to the Lord all the males that first open the womb; but all the firstborn of my sons I redeem.

16 And it shall be as a reminder upon your hand or as frontlets between your eyes, for by a strong hand the Lord brought us out of Egypt.

when life gets difficult

Sometimes God leads us the hard way instead of the easy way because He is doing a special work in us. How will we ever learn to lean on Him if everything in our lives is easy enough for us to handle by ourselves? God led the children of Israel the long, difficult way through the wilderness to prepare them for the battles they would face in possessing the Promised Land. He was concerned that when they saw the enemy they might run back to Egypt and become enslaved again in their former bondage. God wanted to teach them Who He was and that they could depend on Him to fight their battles.

Many of us think that when we enter into our Promised Land we will have no more spiritual battles. Not so! After the Israelites crossed the Jordan River and went in to possess the land of promise, they fought one battle after another. But as they learned to fight in God's strength and under His direction, they won their battles.

If you know God has asked you to do something, do not back down just because it gets hard. When things get tough, spend more time with Him, lean more on Him, and receive more grace from Him. Realize that grace comes at no cost to you; grace is the power of God working in you and through you to do those things you cannot do. As you face challenges in your life, beware of thoughts that say, *I can't do this; it's just too hard*. Do not let your mind give up! Satan knows that if he can defeat you in your mind, he can defeat you in your experience. That is why it is so important not to lose heart and not to grow weary or faint. You can be sure that wherever God leads you, He is able to keep you. He never will allow more to come on you than you can bear (see 1 Corinthians 10:13). You do not have to live in a constant struggle if you learn to continually lean on Him for the strength you need.

17 When Pharaoh let the people go, God led them not by way of the land of the Philistines, although that was nearer; for God said, Lest the people change their purpose when they see war and return to Egypt. **18** But God led the people around by way of the wilderness toward the Red Sea. And the Israelites went up marshaled [in ranks] out of the land of Egypt. **19** And Moses took the bones of Joseph with him, for [Joseph] had strictly sworn the Israelites, saying, Surely God will be with you, and you must carry my bones away from here with you. [Gen. 50:25.]

20 They journeyed from Succoth and encamped at Etham on the edge of the wilderness. **21** The Lord went before them by day in a pillar of cloud to lead them along the way and by night in a pillar of fire to give them light, that they might travel by day and by night. **22** The pillar of cloud by day and the pillar of fire by night did not depart from before the people.

14 AND THE Lord said to Moses, **2** Tell the Israelites to turn back and encamp before Pihahiroth, between Migdol and the

[Red] Sea, before ᵏBaal-zephon. You shall encamp opposite it by the sea.

3 For Pharaoh will say of the Israelites, They are entangled in the land; the wilderness has shut them in.

4 I will harden (make stubborn, strong) Pharaoh's heart, that he will pursue them, and I will gain honor *and* glory over Pharaoh and all his host, and the Egyptians shall know that I am the Lord. And they did so.

5 It was told the king of Egypt that the people had fled; and the heart of Pharaoh and of his servants was changed toward the people, and they said, What is this we have done? We have let Israel go from serving us!

6 And he made ready his chariots and took his army,

7 And took 600 chosen chariots and all the other chariots of Egypt, with officers over all of them.

8 The Lord made hard *and* strong the heart of Pharaoh king of Egypt, and he pursued the Israelites, for [they] left proudly *and* defiantly. [Acts 13:17.]

9 The Egyptians pursued them, all the horses and chariots of Pharaoh and his horsemen and his army, and overtook them encamped at the [Red] Sea by Pi-hahiroth, in front of Baal-zephon.

10 When Pharaoh drew near, the Israelites looked up, and behold, the Egyptians were marching after them; and the Israelites were exceedingly frightened and cried out to the Lord.

11 And they said to Moses, Is it because there are no graves in Egypt that you have taken us away to die in the wilderness? Why have you treated us this way and brought us out of Egypt?

12 Did we not tell you in Egypt, Let us alone; let us serve the Egyptians? For it would have been better for us to serve the Egyptians than to die in the wilderness.

13 Moses told the people, Fear not; stand still (firm, confident, undismayed) and see the salvation of the Lord which He will work for you today. For the Egyptians you have seen today you shall never see again.

14 The Lord will fight for you, and you shall hold your peace *and* remain at rest.

15 The Lord said to Moses, Why do you cry to Me? Tell the people of Israel to go forward!

16 Lift up your rod and stretch out your hand over the sea and divide it, and the Israelites shall go on dry ground through the midst of the sea.

17 And I, behold, I will harden (make stubborn and strong) the hearts of the Egyptians, and they shall go [into the sea] after them; and I will gain honor over Pharaoh and all his host, his chariots, and horsemen.

18 The Egyptians shall know *and* realize that I am the Lord when I have gained honor *and* glory over Pharaoh, his chariots, and his horsemen.

19 And the ¹Angel of God Who went

speak the Word

God, I pray that You will help me not to fear, but to stand still—firm, confident, and undismayed—and see the salvation of the Lord, which You will work for me today.
ADAPTED FROM EXODUS 14:13

k Melvin Grove Kyle has said that travelers who follow the coast of the Red Sea along the line of the exodus need no other guidebook than the Bible. The whole topography corresponds to that mentioned in the Biblical account (Floyd E. Hamilton, *The Basis of Christian Faith*). **l** See footnote on Gen. 16:7; here the "Angel of God" is associated with the cloud (Exod. 13:21).

before the host of Israel moved and went behind them; and the pillar of the cloud went from before them and stood behind them,

20 Coming between the host of Egypt and the host of Israel. It was a cloud and darkness to the Egyptians, but it gave light by night to the Israelites; and the one host did not come near the other all night.

21 Then Moses stretched out his hand over the sea, and the Lord caused the sea to go back by a strong east wind all that night and made the sea dry land; and the waters were divided.

22 And the Israelites went into the midst of the sea on dry ground, the waters being a wall to them on their right hand and on their left.

23 The Egyptians pursued and went in after them into the midst of the sea, even all Pharaoh's horses, his chariots, and his horsemen.

24 And in the morning watch the Lord through the pillar of fire and cloud looked down on the host of the Egyptians and discomfited [them],

25 And bound (clogged, took off) their chariot wheels, making them drive heavily; and the Egyptians said, Let us flee from the face of Israel, for the Lord fights for them against the Egyptians!

26 Then the Lord said to Moses, Stretch out your hand over the sea, that the waters may come again upon the Egyptians, upon their chariots and horsemen.

27 So Moses stretched forth his hand over the sea, and the sea returned to its strength *and* normal flow when the morning appeared; and the Egyptians fled into it [being met by it]; and the Lord overthrew the Egyptians *and* shook them off into the midst of the sea.

28 The waters returned and covered the chariots, the horsemen, and all the host of Pharaoh that pursued them; not even one of them remained.

29 But the Israelites walked on dry ground in the midst of the sea, the waters being a wall to them on their right hand and on their left.

30 Thus the Lord saved Israel that day from the hand of the Egyptians, and Israel saw the Egyptians dead upon the seashore.

31 And Israel saw that great work which the Lord did against the Egyptians, and the people [reverently] feared the Lord and trusted in (relied on, remained steadfast to) the Lord and to His servant Moses.

15 THEN MOSES and the Israelites sang this song to the Lord, saying, I will sing to the Lord, for He has triumphed gloriously; the horse and his rider *or* its chariot has He thrown into the sea.

2 The Lord is my Strength and my Song, and He has become my Salvation; this is my God, and I will praise Him, my father's God, and I will exalt Him.

3 The Lord is a Man of War; the Lord is His name.

4 Pharaoh's chariots and his host has He cast into the sea; his chosen captains also are sunk in the Red Sea.

5 The floods cover them; they sank in the depths [clad in mail] like a stone.

6 Your right hand, O Lord, is glorious in power; Your right hand, O Lord, shatters the enemy.

7 In the greatness of Your majesty You overthrow those rising against You. You send forth Your fury; it consumes them like stubble.

8 With the blast of Your nostrils the waters piled up, the floods stood fixed in a heap, the deeps congealed in the heart of the sea.

9 The enemy said, I will pursue, I will overtake, I will divide the spoil; my desire shall be satisfied upon them; I will draw my sword, my hand shall destroy them.

10 You [Lord] blew with Your wind, the sea covered them; [clad in mail] they sank as lead in the mighty waters.

11 Who is like You, O Lord, among the gods? Who is like You, glorious in holiness, awesome in splendor, doing wonders?

12 You stretched out Your right hand, the earth's [sea] swallowed them.

13 You in Your mercy *and* loving-kindness have led forth the people whom You have redeemed; You have guided them in Your strength to Your holy habitation.

14 The peoples have heard of it; they tremble; pangs have taken hold on the inhabitants of Philistia.

15 Now the chiefs of Edom are dismayed; the mighty men of Moab [renowned for strength], trembling takes hold of them; all the inhabitants of Canaan have melted away—little by little.

16 Terror and dread fall upon them; because of the greatness of Your arm they are as still as a stone—till Your people pass by *and* over [into Canaan], O Lord, till the people pass by whom You have purchased.

17 You will bring them in [to the land] and plant them on Your own mountain, the place, O Lord, You have made for Your dwelling, the sanctuary, O Lord, which Your hands have established.

18 The Lord will reign forever and ever.

19 For the horses of Pharaoh went with his chariots and horsemen into the sea, and the Lord brought back the waters of the sea upon them, but the Israelites walked on dry ground in the midst of the sea.

20 Then Miriam the prophetess, the sister of Aaron, took a timbrel in her hand, and all the women went out after her with timbrels and dancing.

21 And Miriam responded to them, Sing to the Lord, for He has triumphed gloriously *and* is highly exalted; the horse and his rider He has thrown into the sea.

22 Then Moses led Israel onward from the Red Sea and they went into the Wilderness of Shur; they went three days [thirty-three miles] in the wilderness and found no water.

23 When they came to Marah, they could not drink its waters for they were bitter; therefore it was named Marah [bitterness].

24 The people murmured against Moses, saying, What shall we drink?

25 And he cried to the Lord, and the Lord showed him a tree which he cast into the waters, and the waters were made sweet. There [the Lord] made for them a statute and an ordinance, and there He proved them,

26 Saying, If you will diligently hearken to the voice of the Lord your God and will do what is right in His sight, and will listen to *and* obey His commandments and keep all His statutes, I will put none of the diseases upon you which I brought upon the Egyptians, for I am the Lord Who heals you.

27 And they came to Elim, where there were twelve springs of water and seventy palm trees; and they encamped there by the waters.

speak the Word

I declare, God, that You are glorious in holiness, that You are awesome in splendor, that You work wonders, and that in Your mercy and loving-kindness You will lead me.

ADAPTED FROM EXODUS 15:11, 13

16 THEY SET out from Elim, and all the congregation of Israel came to the Wilderness of Sin, which is between Elim and Sinai, on the fifteenth day of the second month after they left the land of Egypt.

2 And the whole congregation of Israel murmured against Moses and Aaron in the wilderness,

3 And said to them, Would that we had died by the hand of the Lord in the land of Egypt, when we sat by the fleshpots and ate bread to the full; for you have brought us out into this wilderness to kill this whole assembly with hunger.

4 Then the Lord said to Moses, Behold, I will rain bread from the heavens for you; and the people shall go out and gather a day's portion every day, that I may prove them, whether they will walk in My law or not.

5 On the sixth day they shall prepare to bring in twice as much as they gather daily.

6 So Moses and Aaron said to all Israel, At evening you shall know that the Lord has brought you out from the land of Egypt,

7 And in the morning you shall see the glory of the Lord, for He hears your murmurings against the Lord. For what are we, that you murmur against us?

8 And Moses said, [This will happen] when the Lord gives you in the evening flesh to eat and in the morning bread to the full, because the Lord has heard your grumblings which you murmur against Him; what are we? Your murmurings are not against us, but against the Lord.

9 And Moses said to Aaron, Say to all the congregation of Israel, Come near before the Lord, for He has heard your murmurings.

10 And as Aaron spoke to the whole congregation of Israel, they looked toward the wilderness, and behold, the glory of the Lord appeared in the cloud!

11 The Lord said to Moses,

12 I have heard the murmurings of the Israelites; speak to them, saying, At twilight you shall eat meat, and between the two evenings you shall be filled with bread; and you shall know that I am the Lord your God.

13 In the evening quails came up and covered the camp; and in the morning the dew lay round about the camp.

14 And when the dew had gone, behold, upon the face of the wilderness there lay a fine, round *and* flake-like thing, as fine as hoarfrost on the ground.

15 When the Israelites saw it, they said one to another, Manna [What is it?]. For they did not know what it was. And Moses said to them, This is the bread which the Lord has given you to eat. [John 6:31, 33.]

16 This is what the Lord has commanded: Let every man gather of it as much as he will need, an omer for each person, according to the number of your persons; take it, every man for those in his tent.

17 The [people] did so, and gathered, some more, some less.

18 When they measured it with an omer, he who gathered much had nothing over, and he who gathered little had no lack; each gathered according to his need.

19 Moses said, Let none of it be left until morning.

20 But they did not listen to Moses; some of them left of it until morning, and it bred worms, became foul, *and* stank; and Moses was angry with them.

21 They gathered it every morning, each as much as he needed, for when the sun became hot it melted.

22 And on the sixth day they gathered twice as much bread, two omers for each person; and all the leaders of the congregation came and told Moses.

grace for today and every day

God miraculously fed the Israelites as they traveled through the wilderness, but He gave them only enough for one day at a time (see Exodus 16:4). Through this, we see one of God's principles at work—that we are to trust Him each day for what we need that day and not worry about tomorrow. Jesus knew this principle when He taught His disciples to pray in Matthew 6:11, saying, "Give us this day our daily bread."

We all like to have what we need for today and plenty set aside for the future. It makes us feel secure to already have all of our provision in hand and not have to trust God for it. We rather enjoy being in control and having everything all neatly planned out, but God does not allow us to do that. Just about the time we think we have everything all figured out and that we have taken good care of ourselves, something happens we did not expect and we have to trust God anyway.

God said the Israelites could gather a day's portion every day so that He might prove them, whether they would walk in His law or not. Giving them what they needed as they needed it was His way of teaching them to trust Him and testing them to see if they would obey His commandments. If they did try to gather more than enough for one day, what they gathered became rotten and started to stink (see Exodus 16:20).

When we worry about tomorrow, we waste today. I believe that we become discouraged and think our lives are worthless because we have never learned to trust God one day at a time.

Trust requires that we have unanswered questions. God's ways are not our ways, but His ways are always best. Trust God and learn to live one day at a time. As you do, you will enjoy life more than ever before.

23 He said to them, The Lord has said, Tomorrow is a solemn rest, a holy Sabbath to the Lord; bake and boil what you will bake and boil today; and all that remains over put aside for you to keep until morning.
24 They laid it aside till morning, as Moses told them; and it did not become foul, neither was it wormy.
25 Moses said, Eat that today, for today is a Sabbath to the Lord. Today you shall find none in the field.
26 Six days you shall gather it, but on the seventh day, the Sabbath, there shall be none.

27 On the seventh day some of the people went out to gather, but they found none.
28 The Lord said to Moses, How long do you [people] refuse to keep My commandments and My laws?
29 See, the Lord has given you the Sabbath; therefore He gives you on the sixth day the bread for two days; let every man remain in his place; let no man leave his place on the seventh day.
30 So the people rested on the seventh day.
31 The house of Israel called the

bread manna; it was like coriander seed, white, and it tasted like wafers made with honey.

32 Moses said, This is what the Lord commands, Take an omer of it to be kept throughout your generations, that they may see the bread with which I fed you in the wilderness when I brought you out of the land of Egypt.

33 And Moses said to Aaron, Take a pot and put an omer of manna in it, and lay it up before the Lord, to be kept throughout your generations.

34 As the Lord commanded Moses, Aaron laid it up before the Testimony to be kept [in the ark]. [Heb. 9:4.]

35 And the Israelites ate manna forty years, until they came to a habitable land; they ate the manna until they came to the border of the land of Canaan.

36 (Now an omer is the tenth of an ephah.)

17 ALL THE congregation of the Israelites moved on from the Wilderness of Sin by stages, according to the commandment of the Lord, and encamped at Rephidim; but there was no water for the people to drink.

2 Therefore, the people contended with Moses, and said, Give us water that we may drink. And Moses said to them, Why do you find fault with me? Why do you tempt the Lord *and* try His patience?

3 But the people thirsted there for water, and the people murmured against Moses, and said, Why did you bring us up out of Egypt to kill us and our children and livestock with thirst?

4 So Moses cried to the Lord, What shall I do with this people? They are almost ready to stone me.

5 And the Lord said to Moses, Pass on before the people, and take with you some of the elders of Israel; and take in your hand the rod with which you smote the river [Nile], and go.

life point

Many of us have real and pressing concerns about the future. We may be dealing with uncertainties in our jobs, our health, our families, or our environment. If you are anxious about what the future holds for you and your loved ones, the first thing you must do is make a decision not to worry. In the same way God provided manna for the Israelites in the wilderness, He will supply what you need today. Believe that He will show you what to do when the time comes. God wants you to know that what you need will be there when you need it. He encourages you to believe and enter His rest—just as the children of Israel rested from the toil of gathering manna on the Sabbath day (see Exodus 16:29, 30).

6 Behold, I will stand before you there on the rock at [Mount] Horeb; and you shall strike the rock, and water shall come out of it, that the people may drink. And Moses did so in the sight of the elders of Israel. [I Cor. 10:4.]

7 He called the place Massah [proof] and Meribah [contention] because of the faultfinding of the Israelites and because they tempted *and* tried the patience of the Lord, saying, Is the Lord among us or not?

8 Then came Amalek [descendants of Esau] and fought with Israel at Rephidim.

9 And Moses said to Joshua, Choose us out men and go out, fight with Amalek. Tomorrow I will stand on the top of the hill with the rod of God in my hand.

10 So Joshua did as Moses said and fought with Amalek; and Moses, Aaron, and Hur went up to the hilltop.

11 When Moses held up his hand,

Israel prevailed; and when he lowered his hand, Amalek prevailed.

12 But Moses' hands were heavy *and* grew weary. So [the other men] took a stone and put it under him and he sat on it. Then Aaron and Hur held up his hands, one on one side and one on the other side; so his hands were steady until the going down of the sun.

13 And Joshua mowed down *and* disabled Amalek and his people with the sword.

14 And the Lord said to Moses, Write this for a memorial in the book and rehearse it in the ears of Joshua, that I will utterly blot out the remembrance of Amalek from under the heavens. [I Sam. 15:2-8.]

15 And Moses built an altar and called the name of it, The Lord is my Banner;

16 And he said, Because [theirs] is a hand against the throne of the Lord, the Lord will have war with Amalek from generation to generation.

18 NOW JETHRO [Reuel], the priest of Midian, Moses' father-in-law, heard of all that God had done for Moses and for Israel His people, and that the Lord had brought Israel out of Egypt.

2 Then Jethro, Moses' father-in-law, took Zipporah, Moses' wife, after Moses had sent her back [to her father],

3 And her two sons, of whom the name of the one was Gershom [expulsion, or a stranger there], for Moses said, I have been an alien in a strange land;

4 And the name of the other was Eliezer [God is help], for the God of my father, said Moses, was my help, and delivered me from the sword of Pharaoh.

5 And Jethro, Moses' father-in-law, came with Moses' sons and his wife to the wilderness where he was encamped at the mount of God [Horeb, or Sinai].

putting the Word to work

If you are in a position of leadership, do you have people who will be as Aaron and Hur to you, strengthening you when you are weary? If not, ask God to give you people like that in your life.

6 And he said [in a message] to Moses, I, your father-in-law Jethro, am come to you and your wife and her two sons with her.

7 And Moses went out to meet his father-in-law and bowed in homage and kissed him; and each asked the other of his welfare and they came into the tent.

8 Moses told his father-in-law all the Lord had done to Pharaoh and the Egyptians for Israel's sake and all the hardships that had come upon them by the way and how the Lord delivered them.

9 Jethro rejoiced for all the goodness the Lord had done to Israel in that He had delivered them out of the hand of the Egyptians.

10 Jethro said, Blessed be the Lord, Who has delivered you out of the hand of the Egyptians and out of the hand of Pharaoh, Who has delivered the people [Israel] from under the hand of the Egyptians.

11 Now I know that the Lord is greater than all gods. Yes, in the [very] thing in which they dealt proudly [He showed Himself infinitely superior to all their gods].

12 And Jethro, Moses' father-in-law, took a burnt offering and sacrifices [to offer] to God, and Aaron came with all the elders of Israel to eat bread with Moses' father-in-law before God.

13 Next day Moses sat to judge the people, and the people stood around Moses from morning till evening.

14 When Moses' father-in-law saw all that he was doing for the people, he said, What is this that you do for

no one can do everything

Moses was a man with many responsibilities. All day, every day, the Israelites came to him for everything. Wanting to please the people, Moses tried to meet all of their needs. When God told Moses through his father-in-law that his task was too heavy for him, the message came through loud and clear: "The thing that you are doing is not good . . . You are not able to perform it all by yourself" (Exodus 18:17, 18).

One of the fastest ways for a person to grow weary in ministry is to be a "people-pleaser" rather than a "God-pleaser." For many years, I did everything in my ministry except lead the worship. I taught in all the sessions, and I prayed for sometimes hundreds of people after the meetings. Between sessions I would greet people at the tape table, sign books, and do just about anything that was asked of me, because I was trying to give people everything I thought they wanted. I finally realized if I kept up that frantic pace, it would physically kill me. I quickly learned that God did not anoint my efforts to be a people-pleaser.

People-pleasers have a hard time setting proper boundaries in ministry. But we need to understand that setting limits is wise and is a sign of strength, not weakness. Like Moses, we need to learn that we cannot do it all. We are on the road to burnout if we try to keep everyone happy and do everything we think they want us to do all of the time. Seek to please God alone, and you will experience peace, freedom, and enjoyment you have never known.

the people? Why do you sit alone, and all the people stand around you from morning till evening?

15 Moses said to his father-in-law, Because the people come to me to inquire of God.

16 When they have a dispute they come to me, and I judge between a man and his neighbor, and I make them know the statutes of God and His laws.

17 Moses' father-in-law said to him, The thing that you are doing is not good.

18 You will surely wear out both yourself and this people with you, for the thing is too heavy for you; you are not able to perform it all by yourself.

19 Listen now to [me]; I will counsel you, and God will be with you. You shall represent the people before God, bringing their cases *and* causes to Him,

20 Teaching them the decrees and laws, showing them the way they must walk and the work they must do.

21 Moreover, you shall choose able men from all the people—God-fearing men of truth who hate unjust gain—and place them over thousands, hundreds, fifties, and tens, to be their rulers.

22 And let them judge the people at all times; every great matter they shall bring to you, but every small matter they shall judge. So it will be easier for you, and they will bear the burden with you.

23 If you will do this, and God so commands you, you will be able to endure [the strain], and all these people also will go to their [tents] in peace.

24 So Moses listened to *and* heeded the voice of his father-in-law and did all that he had said.

25 Moses chose able men out of all Israel and made them heads over the

people, rulers of thousands, of hundreds, of fifties, and of tens.
26 And they judged the people at all times; the hard cases they brought to Moses, but every small matter they decided themselves.
27 Then Moses let his father-in-law depart, and he went his way into his own land.

19 IN THE third month after the Israelites left the land of Egypt, the same day, they came into the Wilderness of Sinai.
2 When they had departed from Rephidim and had come to the Wilderness of Sinai, they encamped there before the mountain.
3 And Moses went up to God, and the Lord called to him out of the mountain, Say this to the house of Jacob and tell the Israelites:
4 You have seen what I did to the Egyptians, and how I bore you on eagles' wings and brought you to Myself.
5 Now therefore, if you will obey My voice in truth and keep My covenant, then you shall be My own peculiar possession *and* treasure from among *and* above all peoples; for all the earth is Mine.
6 And you shall be to Me a kingdom of priests, a holy nation [consecrated, set apart to the worship of God]. These are the words you shall speak to the Israelites.
7 So Moses called for the elders of the people and told them all these words which the Lord commanded him.
8 And all the people answered together, and said, All that the Lord has spoken we will do. And Moses reported the words of the people to the Lord.
9 And the Lord said to Moses, Behold, I come to you in a thick cloud, that the people may hear when I

life point

When God calls a leader, He not only anoints that person to do a certain work, but He also places and anoints people around the leader to do part of that work. That is the great truth Moses discovered when he learned to delegate some of his work to others. Because Moses heeded the wise counsel of his father-in-law (see Exodus 18:18–22), he was better able to endure the stress of his task, and at the same time others were given the opportunity to grow in leadership.

God places certain people in each of our lives to help us. If we do not receive their help, we can become frustrated and overworked. Likewise, they feel unfulfilled because they are not using their gifts and are unable to develop their own sense of accomplishment.

Do you feel overburdened with the enormity of your task? Are you in danger of falling apart emotionally or physically? Learn to delegate. Let as many people help you as possible. If you do, you will last a lot longer and will enjoy yourself a lot more—and others will be blessed as they find purpose in doing their part. God has created us to be interdependent *on* one another, not independent *of* each other. We need each other!

speak with you and believe you *and* remain steadfast forever. Then Moses told the words of the people to the Lord.
10 And the Lord said to Moses, Go and sanctify the people [set them apart for God] today and tomorrow, and let them wash their clothes
11 And be ready by the third day, for the third day the Lord will come down upon Mount Sinai [in the cloud] in the sight of all the people.

dealing with overload

Have you ever told God, "I don't know how much longer I can endure this strain"? I have learned an important truth that has helped me keep in balance and avoid anxiety in ministry: God does not have to anoint anything He does not tell me to do. It is true that Jesus is the Author and the Finisher of my faith (see Hebrews 12:2), but He does not have to finish anything He did not start!

In Exodus 18:23, Moses was told that he would be able to endure the strain if he would do what God commanded him. We need to realize that God does not give us more than we can stand or endure. He will give us the ability to perform the assignments He has given us, and we will not have to drag ourselves around, half-dead with stress. Remember, Jesus said He came that we might "have and enjoy life, and have it in abundance (to the full, till it overflows)" (John 10:10). We are out of balance if we think we can do anything, no matter what it is, without God's direction and anointing. Sooner or later we must hear God say, "No, you cannot do just anything. You can do only the part that I have anointed you to do."

Note also in Exodus 18:23 that Moses was told if he followed wise advice, the people would go home in peace. I believe that when God puts people around us who are anointed to help us, they will be frustrated if we do not let them use their gifts. They will have no peace because they are not able to make progress in their own lives. But if we will allow God to use them as He intended, we will be able to stand the strain and they will be happy and fulfilled.

Everyone in a family needs to contribute to making the home a great place to live. If a mother wears herself out trying to do everything herself, she is in danger of feeling that the other family members are taking advantage of her.

Ask for help and realize that when you allow others to help you, they may not do everything exactly the way you would do it, but you need the help more than you need perfection. Look around you. Do you need to make any adjustments in order to keep yourself in balance? If you will make those adjustments as Moses did, then you will have more joy and peace in your life, you will be releasing others to help and minister, and you will be more effective than ever in ministry and in life.

12 And you shall set bounds for the people round about, saying, Take heed that you go not up into the mountain or touch the border of it. Whoever touches the mountain shall surely be put to death. **13** No hand shall touch it [or the offender], but he shall surely be stoned or shot [with arrows]; whether beast or man, he shall not live. When the trumpet sounds a long blast, they shall come up to the mountain. [Num. 24:8.] **14** So Moses went down from the mountain to the people and sanctified them [set them apart for God], and they washed their clothes. **15** And he said to the people, Be ready by the day after tomorrow; do not go near a woman.

16 The third morning there were thunders and lightnings, and a thick cloud upon the mountain, and a very loud trumpet blast, so that all the people in the camp trembled.

17 Then Moses brought the people from the camp to meet God, and they stood at the foot of the mountain.

18 Mount Sinai was wrapped in smoke, for the Lord descended upon it in fire; its smoke ascended like that of a furnace, and the whole mountain quaked greatly.

19 As the trumpet blast grew louder and louder, Moses spoke and God answered him with a voice. [Deut. 4:12.]

20 The Lord came down upon Mount Sinai to the top of the mountain, and the Lord called Moses to the top of the mountain, and Moses went up.

21 The Lord said to Moses, Go down and warn the people, lest they break through to the Lord to gaze and many of them perish.

22 And also let the priests, who come near to the Lord, sanctify (set apart) themselves [for God], lest the Lord break forth against them.

23 And Moses said to the Lord, The people cannot come up to Mount Sinai, for You Yourself charged us, saying, Set bounds about the mountain and sanctify it [set it apart for God].

24 Then the Lord said to him, Go, get down and you shall come up, you and Aaron with you; but let not the priests

and the people break through to come up to the Lord, lest He break forth against them.

25 So Moses went down to the people and told them.

20 THEN GOD spoke all these words:

2 I am the Lord your God, Who has brought you out of the land of Egypt, out of the house of bondage.

3 You shall have no other gods before *or* besides Me.

4 You shall not make yourself any graven image [to worship it] or any likeness of anything that is in the heavens above, or that is in the earth beneath, or that is in the water under the earth;

5 You shall not bow down yourself to them or serve them; for I the Lord your God am a jealous God, visiting the iniquity of the fathers upon the children to the third and fourth generation of those who hate Me, [Isa. 42:8; 48:11.]

6 But showing mercy *and* steadfast love to a thousand generations of those who love Me and keep My commandments.

7 You shall not use *or* repeat the name of the Lord your God in vain [that is, lightly or frivolously, in false affirmations or profanely]; for the Lord will not hold him guiltless who takes His name in vain.

8 [Earnestly] remember the Sab-

speak the Word

Lord, I know that You are a jealous God, and I declare that I will not worship anyone or anything but You.
ADAPTED FROM EXODUS 20:5

Thank You, God, that You show mercy and steadfast love to me and to a thousand generations of those who love You and keep Your commandments.
ADAPTED FROM EXODUS 20:6

speak God's name with purpose

Do you want to see the power of God released when you speak His name? Then it is important not to take His name lightly or frivolously. I had always thought that to "take the Lord's name in vain" meant to attach a curse word to His name. But it is so much more than that alone. To take the Lord's name in vain means to speak His name in such a way that our words are useless, fruitless, foolish, or irreverent. This sometimes happens when we casually use His name as a verbal exclamation. Let me explain.

The Holy Spirit convicted me early in my walk with the Lord that I had a habit that actually was causing me to break the third commandment (see Exodus 20:7), but I had been deceived and did not even realize I was doing it. I used to say things like "Oh, my God" when I saw something shocking or heard surprising news—even when I dropped something or when one of the children broke something. The Lord revealed to me that His name is more than just a phrase, and when I realized that, I was grieved in my heart and repented thoroughly.

The name of the Lord represents awesome power, and we need to reverently fear it (see Malachi 1:14). I believe the church has lost many things because it has lost reverence for God. It is vital that we return to a reverential fear and awe of God, His name, and His work. We need to have such respect for the Lord and all of His expressive names that we are afraid to speak any of those holy names without purpose. Ask God to reveal to you the power and weight of His name, and when you do use it, honor it and remember how awesome it is.

bath day, to keep it holy (withdrawn from common employment and dedicated to God).

9 Six days you shall labor and do all your work,

10 But the seventh day is a Sabbath to the Lord your God; in it you shall not do any work, you, or your son, your daughter, your manservant, your maidservant, your domestic animals, or the sojourner within your gates.

11 For in six days the Lord made the heavens and the earth, the sea, and all that is in them, and rested the seventh day. That is why the Lord blessed the Sabbath day and hallowed it [set it apart for His purposes].

12 Regard (treat with honor, due obedience, and courtesy) your father and mother, that your days may be long in the land the Lord your God gives you.

13 You shall not commit murder.

14 You shall not commit ᵐadultery. [Prov. 6:25, 26; Matt. 5:28; Rom. 1:24; Eph. 5:3.]

15 You shall not steal. [Prov. 11:1; 16:8; 21:6; 22:16; Jer. 17:11; Mal. 3:8.]

16 You shall not witness falsely against your neighbor. [Exod. 23:1; Prov. 19:9; 24:28.]

m Observe here the expansion of the meaning of the seventh commandment in many catechisms to include whoredom in all its forms, as well as unchastity [premarital relations, sexual impurity, and lustful desire under whatever name] (J.P. Lange, *A Commentary*). Not only is adultery forbidden here, but also fornication and all kinds of mental and sensual uncleanness. All impure books, songs, pictures, etc., which tend to inflame and debauch the mind are against this law (Adam Clarke, *The Holy Bible with A Commentary*).

17 You shall not covet your neighbor's house, your neighbor's wife, or his manservant, or his maidservant, or his ox, or his donkey, or anything that is your neighbor's. [Luke 12:15; Col. 3:5.]

18 Now all the people perceived the thunderings and the lightnings and the noise of the trumpet and the smoking mountain, and as [they] looked they trembled with fear *and* fell back and stood afar off.

19 And they said to Moses, You speak to us and we will listen, but let not God speak to us, lest we die.

20 And Moses said to the people, Fear not; for God has come to prove you, so that the [reverential] fear of Him may be before you, that you may not sin.

21 And the people stood afar off, but Moses drew near to the thick darkness where God was.

22 And the Lord said to Moses, Thus shall you say to the Israelites, You have seen for yourselves that I have talked with you from heaven.

23 You shall not make [gods to share] with Me [My glory and your worship]; gods of silver or gods of gold you shall not make for yourselves.

24 An altar of earth you shall make to Me and sacrifice on it your burnt offerings and your peace offerings, your sheep and your oxen. In every place where I record My name and cause it to be remembered I will come to you and bless you.

25 And if you will make Me an altar of stone, you shall not build it of hewn stone, for if you lift up a tool upon it you have polluted it.

26 Neither shall you go up by steps to My altar, that your nakedness be not exposed upon it.

21 NOW THESE are the ordinances you [Moses] shall set before [the Israelites].

2 If you buy a Hebrew servant [as the result of debt or theft], he shall serve six years, and in the seventh he shall go out free, paying nothing. [Lev. 25:39.]

3 If he came [to you] by himself, he shall go out by himself; if he came married, then his wife shall go out with him.

4 If his master has given him a wife and she has borne him sons or daughters, the wife and her children shall be her master's, and he shall go out [of your service] alone.

5 But if the servant shall plainly say, I love my master, my wife, and my children; I will not go free,

6 Then his master shall bring him to God [the judges as His agents]; he shall bring him to the door or doorpost and shall pierce his ear with an awl; and he shall serve him for life.

7 If a man sells his daughter to be a maidservant *or* bondwoman, she shall not go out [in six years] as menservants do.

8 If she does not please her master who has not espoused her to himself, he shall let her be redeemed. To sell her to a foreign people he shall have no power, for he has dealt faithlessly with her.

9 And if he espouses her to his son, he shall deal with her as with a daughter.

10 If he marries again, her food, clothing, and privilege as a wife shall he not diminish.

11 And if he does not do these three things for her, then shall she go out free, without payment of money.

12 Whoever strikes a man so that he dies shall surely be put to death.

13 But if he did not lie in wait for him, but God allowed him to fall into his hand, then I will appoint you a place to which he may flee [for protection until duly tried]. [Num. 35:22-28.]

14 But if a man comes willfully upon another to slay him craftly, you shall take him from My altar [to which he may have fled for protection], that he may die.

15 Whoever strikes his father or his mother shall surely be put to death.

16 Whoever kidnaps a man, whether he sells him or is found with him in his possession, shall surely be put to death.

17 Whoever curses his father or his mother shall surely be put to death.

18 If men quarrel and one strikes another with a stone or with his fist and he does not die but keeps his bed,

19 If he rises again and walks about leaning upon his staff, then he that struck him shall be clear, except he must pay for the loss of his time and shall cause him to be thoroughly healed.

20 And if a man strikes his servant or his maid with a rod and he [or she] dies under his hand, he shall surely be punished.

21 But if the servant lives on for a day or two, the offender shall not be punished, for he [has injured] his own property.

22 If men contend with each other, and a pregnant woman [interfering] is hurt so that she has a miscarriage, yet no further damage follows, [the one who hurt her] shall surely be punished with a fine [paid] to the woman's husband, as much as the judges determine.

23 But if any damage follows, then you shall give life for life,

24 Eye for eye, tooth for tooth, hand for hand, foot for foot,

25 Burn for burn, wound for wound, and lash for lash.

26 And if a man hits the eye of his servant or the eye of his maid so that it is destroyed, he shall let him go free for his eye's sake.

27 And if he knocks out his manservant's tooth or his maidservant's tooth, he shall let him go free for his tooth's sake.

28 If an ox gores a man or a woman to death, then the ox shall surely be stoned, and its flesh shall not be eaten; but the owner of the ox shall be clear.

29 But if the ox has tried to gore before, and its owner has been warned but has not kept it closed in and it kills a man or a woman, the ox shall be stoned and its owner also put to death.

30 If a ransom is put on [the man's] life, then he shall give for the redemption of his life whatever is laid upon him.

31 If the [man's ox] has gored another's son or daughter, he shall be dealt with according to this same rule.

32 If the ox gores a manservant or a maidservant, the owner shall give to their master thirty shekels of silver, and the ox shall be stoned.

33 If a man leaves a pit open or digs a pit and does not cover it and an ox or a donkey falls into it,

34 The owner of the pit shall make it good; he shall give money to the animal's owner, but the dead beast shall be his.

35 If one man's ox hurts another's so that it dies, they shall sell the live ox and divide the price of it; the dead ox also they shall divide between them.

36 Or if it is known that the ox has gored in the past, and its owner has not kept it closed in, he shall surely pay ox for ox, and the dead beast shall be his.

22 IF A man steals an ox or sheep and kills or sells it, he shall pay five oxen for an ox, or four sheep for a sheep.

2 If a thief is found breaking in and is struck so that he dies, there shall be no blood shed for him.

3 But if the sun has risen [so he can be seen], blood must be shed for slaying him. The thief [if he lives] must make full restitution; if he has nothing, then he shall be sold for his theft.

4 If the beast which he stole is found in his possession alive, whether it is ox or ass or sheep, he shall restore double.

5 If a man causes a field or vineyard to be grazed over or lets his beast loose and it feeds in another man's field, he shall make restitution of the best of his own field or his own vineyard.

6 If fire breaks out and catches so that the stacked grain or standing grain or the field be consumed, he who kindled the fire shall make full restitution.

7 If a man delivers to his neighbor money or goods to keep and it is stolen out of the neighbor's house, then, if the thief is found, he shall pay double.

8 But if the thief is not found, the house owner shall appear before God [the judges as His agents] to find whether he stole his neighbor's goods.

9 For every unlawful deed, whether it concerns ox, donkey, sheep, clothing, or any lost thing at all, which another identifies as his, the cause of both parties shall come before God [the judges]. Whomever [they] shall condemn shall pay his neighbor double.

10 If a man delivers to his neighbor a donkey or an ox or a sheep or any beast to keep and it dies or is hurt or driven away, no man seeing it,

11 Then an oath before the Lord shall be required between the two that the man has not taken his neighbor's property; and the owner of it shall accept his word and not require him to make good the loss.

12 But if it is stolen when in his care, he shall make restitution to its owner.

13 If it be torn in pieces [by some wild beast or by accident], let him bring [the mangled carcass] for witness; he shall not make good what was torn.

14 And if a man borrows anything of his neighbor and it gets hurt or dies without its owner being with it, the borrower shall make full restitution.

15 But if the owner is with it [when the damage is done], the borrower shall not make it good. If it is a hired thing, the damage is included in its hire.

16 If a man seduces a virgin not betrothed and lies with her, he shall surely pay a dowry for her to become his wife.

17 If her father utterly refuses to give her to him, he shall pay money equivalent to the dowry of virgins.

18 You shall not allow a woman to live who practices sorcery.

19 Whoever lies carnally with a beast shall surely be put to death.

20 He who sacrifices to any god but the Lord only shall be utterly destroyed.

21 You shall not wrong a stranger or oppress him; for you were strangers in the land of Egypt.

22 You shall not afflict any widow or fatherless child.

23 If you afflict them in any way and they cry at all to Me, I will surely hear their cry;

24 And My wrath shall burn; I will kill you with the sword, and your wives shall be widows and your children fatherless.

25 If you lend money to any of My people with you who is poor, you shall not be to him as a creditor, neither shall you require interest from him.

26 If you ever take your neighbor's garment in pledge, you shall give it back to him before the sun goes down;

27 For that is his only covering, his clothing for his body. In what shall he sleep? When he cries to Me, I will hear, for I am gracious *and* merciful.

28 You shall not revile God [the judges as His agents] or esteem lightly *or* curse a ruler of your people.

29 You shall not delay to bring to Me from the fullness [of your harvested grain] and the outflow [of your grape juice *and* olive oil]; give Me the first-born of your sons [or redeem them]. [Exod. 34:19, 20.]

30 Likewise shall you do with your oxen *and* your sheep. Seven days the firstborn [beast] shall be with its mother; on the eighth day you shall give it to Me.

31 And you shall be holy men [con-secrated] to Me; therefore you shall not eat any flesh that is torn by beasts in the field; you shall throw it to the dogs.

23 YOU SHALL not repeat *or* raise a false report; you shall not join with the wicked to be an unrighteous witness.

2 You shall not follow a crowd to do evil; nor shall you bear witness at a trial so as to side with a multitude to pervert justice.

3 Neither shall you be partial to a poor man in his trial [just because he is poor].

4 If you meet your enemy's ox or his donkey going astray, you shall surely bring it back to him again.

5 If you see the donkey of one who hates you lying [helpless] under his load, you shall refrain from leaving the man to cope with it alone; you shall help him to release the animal.

6 You shall not pervert the justice due to your poor in his cause.

7 Keep far from a false matter and [be very careful] not to condemn to death the innocent and the righteous, for I will not justify *and* acquit the wicked.

8 You shall take no bribe, for the bribe blinds those who have sight and perverts the testimony *and* the cause of the righteous.

9 Also you shall not oppress a tem-porary resident, for you know the heart of a stranger *and* sojourner, see-ing you were strangers *and* sojourners in Egypt.

10 Six years you shall sow your land and reap its yield.

11 But the seventh year you shall release it *and* let it rest and lie fallow, that the poor of your people may eat [what the land voluntarily yields], and what they leave the wild beasts shall eat. In like manner you shall deal with your vineyard and olive grove.

12 Six days you shall do your work, but the seventh day you shall rest and keep Sabbath, that your ox and your donkey may rest, and the son of your bondwoman, and the alien, may be refreshed.

13 In all I have said to you take heed; do not mention the name of other gods [either in blessing or cursing]; do not let such speech be heard from your mouth.

14 Three times in the year you shall keep a feast to Me.

15 You shall keep the Feast of Unleavened Bread; seven days you shall eat unleavened bread as I com-manded you, at the time appointed in the month of Abib, for in it you came out of Egypt. None shall appear before Me empty-handed.

16 Also you shall keep the Feast of Harvest [Pentecost], [acknowledging] the firstfruits of your toil, of what you sow in the field. And [third] you shall keep the Feast of Ingathering [Booths or Tabernacles] at the end of the year, when you gather in the fruit of your labors from the field.

17 Three times in the year all your males shall appear before the Lord God.

18 You shall not offer the blood of My sacrifice with leavened bread [but keep it unmixed], neither shall the fat of My feast remain all night until morning.

19 The first of the firstfruits of your ground you shall bring into the house of the Lord your God. You shall not boil a kid in its mother's milk.

20 Behold, I send an nAngel before you to keep *and* guard you on the way and to bring you to the place I have prepared.

21 Give heed to Him, listen to *and* obey His voice; be not rebellious before Him *or* provoke Him, for He will not pardon your transgression; for My oName is in Him. [Exod. 32:34; 33:14; Isa. 63:9.]

22 But if you will indeed listen to and obey His voice and all that I speak, then I will be an enemy to your enemies and an adversary to your adversaries.

23 When My Angel goes before you and brings you to the Amorites, the Hittites, the Perizzites, the Canaanites, the Hivites, and the Jebusites, and I reject them *and* blot them out,

24 You shall not bow down to their gods or serve them or do after their works; but you shall utterly overthrow them and break down their pillars *and* images.

25 You shall serve the Lord your God; He shall bless your bread and water, and I will take sickness from your midst.

26 None shall lose her young by miscarriage or be barren in your land; I will fulfill the number of your days.

27 I will send My terror before you and will throw into confusion all the people to whom you shall come, and I will make all your foes turn from you [in flight].

28 And I will send hornets before you which shall drive out the Hivite, Canaanite, and Hittite from before you.

29 I will not drive them out from before you in one year, lest the land become desolate [for lack of attention] and the wild beasts multiply against you.

30 Little by little I will drive them out from before you, until you have increased *and* are numerous enough to take possession of the land.

31 I will set your borders from the Red Sea to the Sea of the Philistines, and from the wilderness to the river [Euphrates]; for I will deliver the inhabitants of the land into your hand and you shall drive them out before you.

32 You shall make no covenant with them or with their gods.

33 They shall not dwell in your land, lest they make you sin against Me; for if you serve their gods, it will surely be a snare to you.

24 GOD SAID to Moses, Come up to the Lord, you and Aaron, Nadab and Abihu [Aaron's sons], and seventy of Israel's elders, and worship at a distance.

2 Moses alone shall come near the

speak the Word

Thank You, God, for sending angels ahead of me to keep me and guard me on my way.
ADAPTED FROM EXODUS 23:20

God, I thank You for driving out my enemies from before me little by little, until I am strong enough to take possession of everything You have for me.
ADAPTED FROM EXODUS 23:30

n See footnote on Gen. 16:7. **o** Representing God's presence.

Lord; the others shall not come near, and neither shall the people come up with him.

3 Moses came and told the people all that the Lord had said and all the ordinances; and all the people answered with one voice, All that the Lord has spoken we will do.

4 Moses ᵖwrote all the words of the Lord. He rose up early in the morning and built an altar at the foot of the mountain and set up twelve pillars representing Israel's twelve tribes.

5 And he sent young Israelite men, who offered burnt offerings and sacrificed peace offerings of oxen to the Lord.

6 And Moses took half of the blood and put it in basins, and half of the blood he dashed against the altar.

7 Then he took the Book of the Covenant and read in the hearing of the people; and they said, All that the Lord has said we will do, and we will be obedient.

8 And Moses took the [remaining half of the] blood and sprinkled it on the people, and said, Behold the blood of the covenant which the Lord has made with you in accordance with all these words. [I Cor. 11:25; Heb. 8:6; 10:28, 29.]

9 Then Moses, Aaron, Nadab, and Abihu, and seventy of the elders of Israel went up [the mountainside].

10 And they saw the God of Israel [that is, a convincing manifestation of His presence], and under His feet it was like pavement of bright sapphire stone, like the very heavens in clearness. [Exod. 33:20-23; Deut. 4:12; Ezek. 28:14]

11 And upon the nobles of the Israelites He laid not His hand [to conceal Himself from them, to rebuke their daring, or to harm them]; but they saw [the manifestation of the presence of] God, and ate and drank. [Exod. 19:21.]

12 And the Lord said to Moses, Come up to Me into the mountain and be there, and I will give you tables of stone, with the law and the commandments which �q I have written that you may teach them. [II Cor. 3:2, 3.]

13 So Moses rose up with Joshua his attendant; and Moses went up into the mountain of God.

14 And he said to the elders, Tarry here for us until we come back to you; remember, Aaron and Hur are with you; whoever has a cause, let him go to them.

15 Then Moses went up into the mountain, and the cloud covered the mountain.

16 The glory of the Lord rested on Mount Sinai, and the cloud covered it for six days. On the seventh day [God] called to Moses out of the midst of the cloud.

speak the Word

God, I declare as the Israelites did: All that You have spoken, I will do.
ADAPTED FROM EXODUS **24:3**

p The contemporary evidence, supplied by archaeology, that writing had long been in common use before the time of Moses now makes conjectures about the contents of the earlier books of the Old Testament being handed down **orally** look absurd. Not only is much of the misleading criticism of the Bible now recognized as unjustified, it is out of harmony with the scientific outlook of the present day (Sir Charles Marston, *New Bible Evidence*). q The two tables were "written with the finger of God" (Exod. 31:18), and "the tables were the work of God" (Exod. 32:16). A man may be said to write what a secretary writes at his dictation; but if he expressly states that certain things are written with his own hand, it is unreasonable to suppose that they were written by the hand of another (J.P. Lange, *A Commentary*).

17 And the glory of the Lord appeared to the Israelites like devouring fire on the top of the mountain. **18** Moses entered into the midst of the cloud and went up the mountain, and Moses was on the mountain forty days and nights.

25

AND THE Lord said to Moses, **2** Speak to the Israelites, that they take for Me an offering. From every man who gives it willingly *and* ungrudgingly with his heart you shall take My offering.

check your "want to"

In Exodus 25:1, 2, we read about giving from a willing heart. Giving to God willingly and ungrudgingly basically boils down to whether or not we desire to give. I call this attitude our "want to," and I believe without it, we will never do anything significant.

Throughout many years of ministry I have had to press through a lot of negative things. Yes, I have a call from God on my life, but I need something in addition to His call. I need to have a lot of "want to." Another word for that is *passion*. It is the thing that motivates us to work hard and make sacrifices with a good attitude.

"Want to" is a powerful thing. With it we can do a job well, lose weight, keep our houses clean, save money, get out of debt, or reach any other goal in life. We do not like to face the fact that our victory or defeat is connected to our "want to." We are often really good at laying the blame for our failures on someone or something else. We like to blame the devil, other people, the past, and on and on, when usually the bottom line is that we do not have enough of the right kind of "want to."

We really need to recognize that we end up doing what we want to do in life. If we have a strong desire to do something, we will somehow find a way to do it. Many of us need to sit down and take a good old-fashioned inventory of our "want to." We should be honest enough to admit, "Lord, I didn't win the victory because I really didn't want to. I didn't pray or read the Bible because I didn't want to. I didn't spend time meditating on the Word and talking with You because I didn't want to. Instead, I sat around all night on the couch watching television because I wanted to." There is nothing wrong with rest and entertainment, but we need to keep our priorities right.

Taking full responsibility for our lives is difficult emotionally, but we should remember that only "the truth" sets us free (see John 8:32).

If you and I are going to serve God and be examples to others, we need to have sanctified "want to." God is not interested in our good works if we are not doing them with a willing heart. Ask God to give you His desires and cause you to want what He wants.

3 This is the offering you shall receive from them: gold, silver, and bronze;

4 Blue, purple, and scarlet [stuff] and fine twined linen and goats' hair,

5 Rams' skins tanned red, goatskins, dolphin *or* porpoise skins, acacia wood,

6 Oil for the light, spices for anointing oil and for sweet incense,

7 Onyx stones, and stones for setting in the ephod and in the breastplate.

8 Let them make Me a sanctuary, that I may dwell among them. [Heb. 8:1, 2; 10:1.]

9 And you shall make it according to all that I show you, the pattern of the tabernacle *or* dwelling and the pattern of all the furniture of it.

10 They shall make an ark of acacia wood: two and a half cubits long, a cubit and a half wide, and a cubit and a half high.

11 You shall overlay the ark with pure gold, inside and out, and make a gold crown, a rim *or* border, around its top.

12 You shall cast four gold rings and attach them to the four lower corners of it, two rings on either side.

13 You shall make poles of acacia wood and overlay them with gold,

14 And put the poles through the rings on the ark's sides, by which to carry it.

15 The poles shall remain in the rings of the ark; they shall not be removed from it [that the ark be not touched].

16 And you shall put inside the ark the Testimony [the Ten Commandments] which I will give you.

17 And you shall make a mercy seat (a covering) of pure gold, two cubits and a half long and a cubit and a half wide.

18 And you shall make two cherubim (winged angelic figures) of [solid] hammered gold on the two ends of the mercy seat.

19 Make one cherub on each end, making the cherubim of one piece with the mercy seat, on the two ends of it.

20 And the cherubim shall spread out their wings above, covering the mercy seat with their wings, facing each other and looking down toward the mercy seat.

21 You shall put the mercy seat on the top of the ark, and in the ark you shall put the Testimony [the Ten Commandments] that I will give you.

22 There I will meet with you and, from above the mercy seat, from between the two cherubim that are upon the ark of the Testimony, I will speak intimately with you of all which I will give you in commandment to the Israelites.

23 Also, make a table of acacia wood, two cubits long, one cubit wide, and a cubit and a half high [for the showbread].

24 You shall overlay it with pure gold and make a crown, a rim *or* molding, of gold around the top of it;

25 And make a frame of a handbreadth around *and* below the top of it and put around it a gold molding as a border.

26 You shall make for it four rings of gold and fasten them at the four corners that are on the table's four legs.

27 Close against the frame shall the rings be as places for the poles to pass to carry the table [of showbread].

28 You shall make the poles of acacia wood and overlay them with gold, that the table may be carried with them.

29 And you shall make its plates [for showbread] and cups [for incense], and its flagons and bowls [for liquids in sacrifice]; make them of pure gold.

30 And you shall set the showbread (the bread of the Presence) on the table before Me always. [John 6:58.]

31 You shall make a lampstand of pure gold. Of beaten *and* turned work shall the lampstand be made, both its base and its shaft; its cups, its knobs, and its flowers shall be of one piece with it.

32 Six branches shall come out of the sides of it; three branches of the lampstand out of the one side and three branches out of its other side;

33 Three cups made like almond blossoms, each with a knob and a flower on one branch, and three cups made like almond blossoms on the other branch with a knob and a flower; so for the six branches coming out of the lampstand;

34 And on the [center shaft] itself you shall [make] four cups like almond blossoms with their knobs and their flowers.

35 Also make a knob [on the shaft] under each pair of the six branches going out from the lampstand and one piece with it;

36 Their knobs and their branches shall be of one piece with it; the whole of it one beaten work of pure gold.

37 And you shall make the lamps of the [lampstand] to include a ʳseventh one [at the top of the shaft]. [The priests] shall set up the [seven] lamps of it so they may give light in front of it.

38 Its snuffers and its ashtrays shall be of pure gold.

39 Use a talent of pure gold for it, including all these utensils.

40 And see to it that you copy [exactly] their pattern which was shown you on the mountain. [Heb. 8:5, 6.]

26 MOREOVER, YOU shall make the tabernacle with ten curtains; of fine twined linen, and blue and purple and scarlet [stuff], with cherubim skillfully embroidered shall you make them.

2 The length of one curtain shall be twenty-eight cubits and the breadth of one curtain four cubits; each of the curtains shall measure the same.

3 The five curtains shall be coupled to one another, and the other five curtains shall be coupled to one another.

4 And you shall make loops of blue on the edge of the last curtain in the first set, and likewise in the second set.

5 Fifty loops you shall make on the one curtain and fifty loops on the edge of the last curtain that is in the second coupling *or* set, so that the loops on one correspond to the loops on the other.

6 And you shall make fifty clasps of gold and fasten the curtains together with the clasps; then the tabernacle shall be one whole.

7 And make curtains of goats' hair to be a [second] covering over the tabernacle; eleven curtains shall you make.

8 One curtain shall be thirty cubits long and four cubits wide; and the eleven curtains shall all measure the same.

9 You shall join together five curtains by themselves and six curtains by themselves, and shall double over the sixth curtain in the front of the tabernacle [to make a closed door].

10 And make fifty loops on the edge of the outmost curtain in the one set and fifty loops on the edge of the outmost curtain in the second set.

11 You shall make fifty clasps of bronze and put the clasps into the loops and couple the tent together, that it may be one whole.

---

r Certain Biblical critics in the past doubted the existence of the tabernacle and asserted that the concept of a sevenfold lamp was unknown until hundreds of years later, in Babylonian times (600 BC). The first objective evidence to the contrary came to light in W. F. Albright's excavation of Tell Beit Mirsim, south of Jerusalem, where he found seven-sprouted lamps from about 1200 BC. The seventh season at Dothan yielded three sevenfold lamps from the period 1200-1400 BC, showing again that this was not a late idea (Joseph P. Free, *Near Eastern Archaeology*).

12 The surplus that remains of the tent curtains, the half curtain that remains, shall hang over the back of the tabernacle.

13 And the cubit on the one side and the cubit on the other side of what remains in the length of the curtains of the tent shall hang over the sides of the tabernacle, on this side and that side, to cover it.

14 You shall make a [third] covering for the tent of rams' skins tanned red, and a [fourth] covering above that of dolphin *or* porpoise skins.

15 And you shall make the upright frame for the tabernacle of boards of acacia wood.

16 Ten cubits shall be the length of a board and a cubit and a half shall be the breadth of one board.

17 Make two tenons in each board for dovetailing *and* fitting together; so shall you do for all the tabernacle boards.

18 And make the boards for the tabernacle: twenty boards for the south side;

19 And you shall make forty silver sockets under the twenty boards, two sockets under each board for its two tenons.

20 And for the north side of the tabernacle there shall be twenty boards

21 And their forty silver sockets, two sockets under each board.

22 For the back or west side of the tabernacle you shall make six boards.

23 Make two boards for the corners of the tabernacle in the rear on both sides.

24 They shall be coupled down below and coupled together on top with one ring. Thus shall it be for both of them; they shall form the two corners.

25 And that will be eight boards and their sockets of silver, sixteen sockets, two sockets under each board.

26 And you shall make bars of acacia wood: five for the boards of one side,

27 And five bars for the boards of the other side of the tabernacle, and five bars for the boards of the rear end of the tabernacle, for the back wall to the west.

28 And the middle bar halfway up the boards shall pass through from end to end.

29 You shall overlay the boards with gold and make their rings of gold to hold the bars and overlay the bars with gold.

30 You shall erect the tabernacle after the plan of it shown you on the mountain.

31 And make a veil of blue, purple, and scarlet [stuff] and fine twined linen, skillfully worked with cherubim on it.

32 You shall hang it on four pillars of acacia wood overlaid with gold, with gold hooks, on four sockets of silver.

33 And you shall hang the veil from the clasps and bring the ark of the Testimony into place within the veil; and the veil shall separate for you the Holy Place from the Most Holy Place.

34 And you shall put the mercy seat on the ark of the Testimony in the Most Holy Place.

35 And you shall set the table [for the showbread] outside the veil [in the Holy Place] on the north side and the lampstand opposite the table on the south side of the tabernacle.

36 You shall make a hanging [to form a screen] for the door of the tent of blue, purple, and scarlet [stuff] and fine twined linen, embroidered. [John 10:9.]

37 You shall make five pillars of acacia wood to support the hanging curtain and overlay them with gold; their hooks shall be of gold, and you shall cast five [base] sockets of bronze for them.

27 AND MAKE the altar of acacia wood, five cubits square and three cubits high [within reach of all].

2 Make horns for it on its four corners; they shall be of one piece with it, and you shall overlay it with bronze.
3 You shall make pots to take away its ashes, and shovels, basins, forks, and firepans; make all its utensils of bronze.
4 Also make for it a grate, a network of bronze; and on the net you shall make four bronze rings at its four corners.
5 And you shall put it under the ledge of the altar, so that the net will extend halfway down the altar.
6 And make poles for the altar, poles of acacia wood overlaid with bronze.
7 The poles shall be put through the rings on the two sides of the altar, with which to carry it. [Num. 4:14, 15.]
8 You shall make [the altar] hollow with slabs *or* planks; as shown you on the mountain, so shall it be made.
9 And you shall make the court of the tabernacle. On the south side the court shall have hangings of fine twined linen, a hundred cubits long for one side;
10 Their pillars shall be twenty and their sockets twenty, of bronze, but the hooks of the pillars and their joinings shall be of silver;
11 Likewise for the north side hangings, a hundred cubits long, and their twenty pillars and their twenty sockets of bronze, but the hooks of the pillars and their joinings shall be of silver.
12 And for the breadth of the court on the west side there shall be hangings of fifty cubits, with ten pillars and ten sockets.
13 The breadth of the court to the front, the east side, shall be fifty cubits.
14 The hangings for one side of the gate shall be fifteen cubits, with three pillars and three sockets.
15 On the other side the hangings shall be fifteen cubits, with three pillars and three sockets.

16 And for the gate of the court there shall be a hanging [for a screen] twenty cubits long, of blue, purple, and scarlet [stuff] and fine twined linen, embroidered. It shall have four pillars and four sockets for them.
17 All the pillars round about the court shall be joined together with silver rods; their hooks shall be of silver and their sockets of bronze.
18 The length of the court shall be a hundred cubits and the breadth fifty and the height five cubits, [with hangings of] fine twined linen and sockets of bronze.
19 All the tabernacle's utensils *and* instruments used in all its service, and all its pegs and all the pegs for the court, shall be of bronze.
20 You shall command the Israelites to provide you with pure oil of crushed olives for the light, to cause it to burn continually [every night].
21 In the Tent of Meeting [of God with His people], outside the veil which sets apart the Testimony, Aaron and his sons shall keep it burning from evening to morning before the Lord. It shall be a statute to be observed on behalf of the Israelites throughout their generations.

28 FROM AMONG the Israelites take your brother Aaron and his sons with him, that he may minister to Me in the priest's office, even Aaron, Nadab and Abihu, Eleazar and Ithamar, Aaron's sons.
2 And you shall make for Aaron your brother sacred garments [appointed official dress set apart for special holy services] for honor and for beauty.
3 Tell all who are expert, whom I have endowed with skill *and* good judgment, that they shall make Aaron's garments to sanctify him for My priesthood.
4 They shall make these garments: a breastplate, an ephod [a distinctive

life point

Skill without good judgment will not take us very far (see Exodus 28:3). In its simplest form, good judgment is just plain old common sense. If you want to succeed in life and in ministry, you need to have spiritual gifts, natural talent, *and* wisdom. Seek God for wisdom to accompany your spiritual gifts and talents, and He will give it to you (see James 1:5).

There are people who have a gift, an ability, or a skill that can help them climb the ladder of success, but once they arrive they do not have enough wisdom to keep them there. Use plenty of wisdom and common sense, and you will succeed in life.

vestment to which the breastplate was to be attached], a robe, long *and* sleeved tunic of checkerwork, a turban, and a sash *or* band. They shall make sacred garments for Aaron your brother and his sons to minister to Me in the priest's office.
5 They shall receive [from the people] *and* use gold, and blue, purple, and scarlet [stuff], and fine linen.
6 And they shall make the ephod of gold, of blue, purple, and scarlet [stuff], and fine twined linen, skillfully woven *and* worked.
7 It shall have two shoulder straps to join the two [back and front] edges, that it may be held together.
8 The skillfully woven girding band which is on the ephod shall be made of the same, of gold, blue, purple, and scarlet [stuff], and fine twined linen.
9 And you shall take two onyx *or* beryl stones and engrave on them the names of the twelve sons of Israel;
10 Six of their names on one stone and the six names of the rest on the other stone, arranged in order of their birth.
11 With the work of a stone engraver, like the engravings of a signet, you shall engrave the two stones according to the names of the sons of Israel. You shall have them set in sockets *or* rosettes of gold.
12 And you shall put the two stones upon the [two] shoulder straps of the ephod [of the high priest] as memorial stones for Israel; and Aaron shall bear their names upon his two shoulders as a memorial before the Lord.
13 And you shall make sockets *or* rosettes of gold for settings,
14 And two chains of pure gold, like cords shall you twist them, and fasten the corded chains to the settings.
15 You shall make a breastplate of judgment, in skilled work; like the workmanship of the ephod shall you make it, of gold, blue, purple, and scarlet [stuff], and of fine twined linen.
16 The breastplate shall be square *and* doubled; a span [nine inches] shall be its length and a span shall be its breadth.
17 You shall set in it four rows of stones: a sardius, a topaz, and a carbuncle shall be the first row;
18 The second row an emerald, a sapphire, and a diamond [so called at that time];
19 The third row a jacinth, an agate, and an amethyst;
20 And the fourth row a beryl, an onyx, and a jasper; they shall be set in gold filigree.
21 And the stones shall be twelve, according to the names of the sons of Israel, like the engravings of a signet, each with its name for the twelve tribes.
22 You shall make for the breastplate chains of pure gold twisted like cords.
23 You shall make on the breastplate two rings of gold and put [them] on the two edges of the breastplate.

24 And you shall put the two twisted, cordlike chains of gold in the two rings which are on the edges of the breastplate.
25 The other two ends of the two twisted, cordlike chains you shall fasten in the two sockets *or* rosettes in front, putting them on the shoulder straps of the ephod;
26 And make two rings of gold and put them at the two ends of the breastplate on its inside edge next to the ephod.
27 Two gold rings you shall make and attach them to the lower part of the two shoulder pieces of the ephod in front, close by where they join, above the skillfully woven girdle *or* band of the ephod.
28 And they shall bind the breastplate by its rings to the rings of the ephod with a lace of blue, that it may be above the skillfully woven girding band of the ephod, and that the breastplate may not become loose from the ephod.
29 So Aaron shall bear the names of the sons of Israel in the breastplate of judgment upon his heart when he goes into the Holy Place, to bring them in continual remembrance before the Lord.
30 In the breastplate of judgment you shall put the Urim and the Thummim [unspecified articles used when the high priest asked God's counsel for all Israel]; they shall be upon Aaron's heart when he goes in before the Lord, and Aaron shall bear the judgment (rights, judicial decisions) of the Israelites upon his heart before the Lord continually.
31 Make the robe [to be worn beneath] the ephod all of blue.
32 There shall be a hole in the center of it [to slip over the head], with a binding of woven work around the hole, like the opening in a coat of mail *or* a garment, that it may not fray *or* tear.

33 And you shall make pomegranates of blue, purple, and scarlet [stuff] around about its skirts, with gold bells between them;
34 A gold bell and a pomegranate, a gold bell and a pomegranate, round about on the skirts of the robe.
35 Aaron shall wear the robe when he ministers, and its sound shall be heard when he goes [alone] into the Holy of Holies before the Lord and when he comes out, lest he die there.
36 And you shall make a plate of pure gold and engrave on it, like the engravings of a signet, HOLY TO THE LORD. [Exod. 39:30.]
37 You shall fasten it on the front of the turban with a blue cord.
38 It shall be upon Aaron's forehead, that Aaron may take upon himself *and* bear [any] iniquity [connected with] the holy things which the Israelites shall give *and* dedicate; and it shall always be upon his forehead, that they may be accepted before the Lord [in the priest's person]. [Luke 24:44; Heb. 8:1, 2.]
39 And you shall weave the long *and* sleeved tunic of checkerwork of fine linen *or* silk and make a turban of fine linen *or* silk; and you shall make a girdle, the work of the embroiderer.
40 For Aaron's sons you shall make long *and* sleeved tunics and belts *or* sashes and caps, for glory *and* honor and beauty.
41 And you shall put them on Aaron your brother and his sons with him, and shall anoint them and ordain and sanctify them [set them apart for God], that they may serve Me as priests.
42 You shall make for them [white] linen trunks to cover their naked flesh, reaching from the waist to the thighs.
43 And they shall be on Aaron and his sons when they go into the Tent of Meeting or when they come near to the altar to minister in the Holy Place,

lest they bring iniquity upon themselves and die; it shall be a statute forever to Aaron and to his descendants after him.

29 THIS IS what you shall do to consecrate (set them apart) that they may serve Me as priests. Take one young bull and two rams, all without blemish,

2 And unleavened bread and unleavened cakes mixed with oil and unleavened wafers spread with oil; of fine flour shall you make them.

3 You shall put them in one basket and bring them in [it], and bring also the bull and the two rams;

4 And bring Aaron and his sons to the door of the Tent of Meeting [out where the laver is] and wash them with water.

5 Then take the garments and put on Aaron the long *and* sleeved tunic and the robe of the ephod and the ephod and the breastplate, and gird him with the skillfully woven girding band of the ephod.

6 And you shall put the turban *or* miter upon his head and put the holy crown upon the turban.

7 Then take the anointing oil and pour it on his head and anoint him.

8 And bring his sons and put long *and* sleeved tunics on them.

9 And you shall gird them with sashes *or* belts, Aaron and his sons, and bind caps on them; and the priest's office shall be theirs by a perpetual statute. Thus you shall ordain *and* consecrate Aaron and his sons.

10 Then bring the bull before the Tent of Meeting, and Aaron and his sons shall lay their hands upon its head.

11 And you shall kill the bull before the Lord by the door of the Tent of Meeting.

12 And you shall take of the blood of the bull and put it on the horns of the altar with your finger, and pour out all the blood at the base of the altar.

13 And take all the fat that covers the entrails, and the appendage that is on the liver, and the two kidneys, and the fat that is on them, and burn them on the altar.

14 But the flesh of the bull, its hide, and the contents of its entrails you shall burn with fire outside the camp; it is a sin offering. [Heb. 13:11-13.]

15 You shall also take one of the rams, and Aaron and his sons shall lay their hands upon the head of the ram.

16 And you shall kill the ram and you shall take its blood and throw it against the altar round about.

17 And you shall cut the ram in pieces and wash its entrails and legs and put them with its pieces and its head,

18 And you shall burn the whole ram upon the altar. It is a burnt offering to the Lord; it is a sweet *and* satisfying fragrance, an offering made by fire to the Lord.

19 And you shall take the other ram, and Aaron and his sons shall lay their hands upon the head of the ram;

20 Then you shall kill the ram and take part of its blood and put it on the tip of the right ears of Aaron and his sons and on the thumb of their right hands and on the great toe of their right feet, and dash the rest of the blood against the altar round about.

21 Then you shall take part of the blood that is on the altar, and of the anointing oil, and sprinkle it upon Aaron and his garments and on his sons and their garments; and he and his garments and his sons and their garments shall be sanctified *and* made holy.

22 Also you shall take the fat of the ram, the fat tail, the fat that covers the entrails, the appendage on the liver, the two kidneys with the fat that is on them, and the right thigh; for it is a ram of consecration *and* ordination.

23 Take also one loaf of bread, and

one cake of oiled bread, and one wafer out of the basket of the unleavened bread that is before the Lord.

24 And put all these in the hands of Aaron and his sons and they shall wave them for a wave offering before the Lord.

25 Then you shall take them from their hands, add them to the burnt offering, and burn them on the altar for a sweet *and* satisfying fragrance before the Lord; it is an offering made by fire to the Lord.

26 And take the breast of the ram of Aaron's consecration *and* ordination and wave it for a wave offering before the Lord; and it shall be your portion [Moses].

27 And you shall sanctify (set apart for God) the waved breast of the ram used in the ordination and the waved thigh of the priests' portion, since it is for Aaron and his sons.

28 It shall be for Aaron and his sons as their due portion from the Israelites perpetually, an offering from the Israelites of their peace *and* thanksgiving sacrifices, their offering to the Lord.

29 The holy garments of Aaron shall pass to his descendants who succeed him, to be anointed in them and to be consecrated *and* ordained in them.

30 And that son who is [high] priest in his stead shall put them on [each day for] seven days when he comes into the Tent of Meeting to minister in the Holy Place.

31 You shall take the ram of the consecration *and* ordination and boil its flesh in a holy *and* set-apart place.

32 Aaron and his sons shall eat the flesh of the ram and the bread in the basket, at the door of the Tent of Meeting.

33 They shall eat those things with which atonement was made, to ordain and consecrate them; but a stranger (layman) shall not eat of them because they are holy (set apart to the worship of God).

34 And if any of the flesh or bread for the ordination remains until morning, you shall burn it with fire; it shall not be eaten, because it is holy (set apart to the worship of God).

35 Thus shall you do to Aaron and to his sons according to all I have commanded you; during seven days shall you ordain them.

36 You shall offer every day a bull as a sin offering for atonement. And you shall cleanse the altar by making atonement for it, and anoint it to consecrate it.

37 Seven days you shall make atonement for the altar and sanctify it [set it apart for God]; and the altar shall be most holy; whoever *or* whatever touches the altar must be holy (set apart for God's service).

38 Now this is what you shall offer on the altar: two lambs a year old shall be offered day by day continually.

39 One lamb you shall offer in the morning and the other lamb in the evening;

40 And with the one lamb a tenth measure of fine flour mixed with a fourth of a hin of beaten oil, and a fourth of a hin of wine for a drink offering [to be poured out].

41 And the other lamb you shall offer at evening, and do with it as with the cereal offering of the morning and with the drink offering, for a sweet *and* satisfying fragrance, an offering made by fire to the Lord.

42 This shall be a continual burnt offering throughout your generations at the door of the Tent of Meeting before the Lord, where I will meet with you to speak there to you.

43 There I will meet with the Israelites, and the Tent of Meeting shall be sanctified by My glory [the Shekinah, God's visible presence].

44 And I will sanctify the Tent of Meeting and the altar; I will sanctify also both Aaron and his sons to minister to Me in the priest's office.

45 And I will dwell among the Israelites and be their God.

46 And they shall know [from personal experience] that I am the Lord their God, Who brought them forth out of the land of Egypt that I might dwell among them; I am the Lord their God.

30 AND YOU shall make an altar to burn incense upon; of acacia wood you shall make it.

2 A cubit shall be its length and a cubit its breadth; its top shall be square and it shall be two cubits high. Its horns shall be of one piece with it.

3 And you shall overlay it with pure gold, its top and its sides round about and its horns, and you shall make a crown (a rim or molding) of gold around it.

4 You shall make two golden rings under the rim of it, on the two ribs on the two opposite sides of it; and they shall be holders for the poles with which to carry it.

5 And you shall make the poles of acacia wood, overlaid with gold.

6 You shall put the altar [of incense] in front *and* outside of the veil that screens the ark of the Testimony, before the mercy seat that is over the Testimony (the Law, the tables of stone), where I will meet with you.

7 And Aaron shall burn on it incense of sweet spices; every morning when he trims *and* fills the lamps he shall burn it. [Ps. 141:2; Rev. 5:8; 8:3, 4.]

8 And when Aaron lights the lamps in the evening, he shall burn it, a perpetual incense before the Lord throughout your generations.

9 You shall offer no unholy incense on the altar nor burnt sacrifice nor cereal offering; and you shall pour no libation (drink offering) on it.

10 Aaron shall make atonement upon the horns of it once a year; with the blood of the sin offering of atonement once in the year shall he make atonement upon *and* for it throughout your generations. It is most holy to the Lord.

11 And the Lord said to Moses,

12 When you take the census of the Israelites, every man shall give a ransom for himself to the Lord when you number them, that no plague may fall upon them when you number them. [Rom. 8:1-4.]

13 This is what everyone shall give as he joins those already numbered: a half shekel, in terms of the sanctuary shekel, a shekel being twenty gerahs; a half shekel as an offering to the Lord.

14 Everyone from twenty years old and upward, as he joins those already numbered, shall give this offering to the Lord. [Matt. 10:24; I Pet. 1:18, 19.]

15 The rich shall not give more and the poor shall not give less than half a shekel when [you] give this offering to the Lord to make atonement for yourselves.

16 And you shall take the atonement money of the Israelites and use it [exclusively] for the service of the Tent of Meeting, that it may bring the Israelites to remembrance before the Lord, to make atonement for yourselves.

17 And the Lord said to Moses,

18 You shall also make a laver *or* large basin of bronze, and its base of bronze, for washing; and you shall put it [outside in the court] between the Tent of Meeting and the altar [of burnt offering], and you shall put water in it;

19 There Aaron and his sons shall wash their hands and their feet. [Tit. 3:5.]

20 When they go into the Tent of Meeting, they shall wash with water, that they die not; or when they come near to the altar to minister, to burn

the blood makes atonement

Exodus 30:10 foreshadows Jesus' crucifixion and the sufficiency of His sacrifice to atone for our sins once and for all. When the high priest went into the Holy of Holies on the Day of Atonement to offer sacrifices for his own sins and the sins of the people, he had to do so with the blood of animals as a substitute. The Bible tells us that the life is in the blood and that the blood has been given on the altar to make atonement for our souls (see Leviticus 17:11). Note that the priest had to go year after year and make the same sacrifices. The priest's sins and the sins of the people were not washed away; they were merely covered over. The blood of animals was placed on their sins to atone for them, but it was not a finished work. It had to be done again and again.

The action by the high priest who repeatedly offered the blood of animals was a type, a mere shadow, of what was to come. The book of Hebrews teaches that when Jesus finished the work of His sacrifice on the cross, He put an end to continual sacrifices (see Hebrews 8:1—10:14). How beautifully Hebrews 9:12 communicates the permanence of Christ's atonement. It says Jesus "went once for all into the [Holy of] Holies [of heaven], not by virtue of the blood of goats and calves [by which to make reconciliation between God and man], but His own blood, having found and secured a complete redemption (an everlasting release for us)."

Jesus offered Himself once as a sacrifice for our sins. He does not have to keep doing it. My husband likes to quip, "If you do the job right, you won't have to keep doing it over and over." That's what Jesus did for us, once and for all. He did it right. His atonement lasts. Forever.

We no longer have to make sacrifices every time we sin. We can now live by faith, trusting God that the sacrifice Jesus made is more than enough to cleanse us and make us whole.

an offering made by fire to the Lord, [John 13:6-8.]

21 So they shall wash their hands and their feet, lest they die; it shall be a perpetual statute for [Aaron] and his descendants throughout their generations.

22 Moreover, the Lord said to Moses,

23 Take the best spices: of liquid myrrh 500 shekels, of sweet-scented cinnamon half as much, 250 shekels, of fragrant calamus 250 shekels,

24 And of cassia 500 shekels, in terms of the sanctuary shekel, and of olive oil a hin.

25 And you shall make of these a holy anointing oil, a perfume compounded after the art of the perfumer; it shall be a sacred anointing oil.

26 And you shall anoint the Tent of Meeting with it, and the ark of the Testimony,

27 And the [showbread] table and all its utensils, and the lampstand and its utensils, and the altar of incense,

28 And the altar of burnt offering with all its utensils, and the laver [for cleansing] and its base.

29 You shall sanctify (separate) them, that they may be most holy;

whoever *and* whatever touches them must be holy (set apart to God).

30 And you shall anoint Aaron and his sons and sanctify (separate) them, that they may minister to Me as priests.

31 And say to the Israelites, This is a holy anointing oil [symbol of the Holy Spirit], sacred to Me alone throughout your generations. [Rom. 8:9; I Cor. 12:3.]

32 It shall not be poured upon a layman's body, nor shall you make any other like it in composition; it is holy, and you shall hold it sacred.

33 Whoever compounds any like it or puts any of it upon an outsider shall be cut off from his people.

34 Then the Lord said to Moses, Take sweet spices—stacte, onycha, and galbanum, sweet spices with pure frankincense, an equal amount of each—

35 And make of them incense, a perfume after the perfumer's art, seasoned with salt *and* mixed, pure and sacred.

36 You shall beat some of it very small and put some of it before the Testimony in the Tent of Meeting, where I will meet with you; it shall be to you most holy.

37 And the incense which you shall make according to its composition you shall not make for yourselves; it shall be to you holy to the Lord.

38 Whoever makes any like it for perfume shall be cut off from his people.

31 AND THE Lord said to Moses,
2 See, I have called by name Bezalel son of Uri, the son of Hur, of the tribe of Judah.

3 And I have filled him with the Spirit of God, in wisdom *and* ability, in understanding *and* intelligence, and in knowledge, and in all kinds of craftsmanship,

4 To devise skillful works, to work in gold, and in silver, and in bronze,

5 And in cutting of stones for setting, and in carving of wood, to work in all kinds of craftsmanship.

6 And behold, I have appointed with him Aholiab son of Ahisamach, of the tribe of Dan; and to all who are wisehearted I have given wisdom *and* ability to make all that I have commanded you:

7 The Tent of Meeting, the ark of the Testimony, the mercy seat that is on it, all the furnishings of the tent—

8 The table [of the showbread] and its utensils, the pure lampstand with all its utensils, the altar of incense,

9 The altar of burnt offering with all its utensils, the laver and its base—

10 The finely worked garments, the holy garments for Aaron the [high] priest and for his sons to minister as priests,

11 And the anointing oil and incense of sweet spices for the Holy Place. According to all that I have commanded you shall they do.

12 And the Lord said to Moses,

13 Say to the Israelites, Truly you shall keep My Sabbaths, for it is a sign between Me and you throughout your generations, that you may know that I, the Lord, sanctify you [set you apart for Myself].

speak the Word

I pray, God, that You will fill me with Your Spirit, with wisdom and ability, with understanding and intelligence, with knowledge and excellence, and help me do what You have called me to do.
ADAPTED FROM Exodus **31:3**

14 You shall keep the Sabbath therefore, for it is holy to you; everyone who profanes it shall surely be put to death; for whoever does work on the Sabbath shall be cut off from among his people.

15 Six days may work be done, but the seventh is the Sabbath of rest, sacred to the Lord; whoever does work on the Sabbath day shall surely be put to death.

16 Wherefore the Israelites shall keep the Sabbath to observe it throughout their generations, a perpetual covenant.

17 It is a sign between Me and the Israelites forever; for in six days the Lord made the heavens and earth, and on the seventh day He ceased and was refreshed.

18 And He gave to Moses, when He had ceased communing with him on Mount Sinai, the two tables of the Testimony, tables of stone, written with the finger of God.

32 WHEN THE people saw that Moses delayed to come down from the mountain, [they] gathered together to Aaron, and said to him, Up, make us gods to go before us; as for this Moses, the man who brought us up out of the land of Egypt, we do not know what has become of him.

2 So Aaron replied, Take the gold rings from the ears of your wives, your sons, and daughters, and bring them to me.

3 So all the people took the gold rings from their ears and brought them to Aaron.

4 And he received the gold at their hand and fashioned it with a graving tool and made it a molten calf; and they said, These are your gods, O Israel, which brought you up out of the land of Egypt!

5 And when Aaron saw the molten calf, he built an altar before it; and

putting the Word to work

We all need regular Sabbaths in our lives (see Exodus 31:14)—times of rest, relaxation, refreshing, and renewal. Do you incorporate such times of refreshing in your life? If so, keep it up! If not, what changes can you make in your schedule so that you can have regular times of rest and renewal?

Aaron made proclamation, and said, Tomorrow shall be a feast to the Lord.

6 And they rose up early the next day and offered burnt offerings and brought peace offerings; and the people sat down to eat and drink and rose up to play.

7 The Lord said to Moses, Go down, for your people, whom you brought out of the land of Egypt, have corrupted themselves;

8 They have turned aside quickly out of the way which I commanded them; they have made them a molten calf and have worshiped it and sacrificed to it, and said, These are your gods, O Israel, that brought you up out of the land of Egypt!

9 And the Lord said to Moses, I have seen this people, and behold, it is a stiff-necked people;

10 Now therefore let Me alone, that My wrath may burn hot against them and that I may destroy them; but I will make of you a great nation.

11 But Moses besought the Lord his God, and said, Lord, why does Your wrath blaze hot against Your people, whom You have brought forth out of the land of Egypt with great power and a mighty hand?

12 Why should the Egyptians say, For evil He brought them forth, to slay them in the mountains and consume them from the face of the earth? Turn from Your fierce wrath, and change Your mind concerning this evil against Your people.

13 [Earnestly] remember Abraham, Isaac, and Israel, Your servants, to whom You swore by Your own self and said to them, I will multiply your seed as the stars of the heavens, and all this land that I have spoken of will I give to your seed, and they shall inherit it forever.

14 Then the Lord turned from the evil which He had thought to do to His people.

15 And Moses turned and went down from the mountain with the two tables of the Testimony in his hand, tables *or* tablets that were written on both sides.

16 The tables were the work of God; the writing was the writing of God, graven upon the tables.

17 And when Joshua heard the noise of the people as they shouted, he said to Moses, There is a noise of war in the camp.

18 But Moses said, It is not the sound of shouting for victory, neither is it the sound of the cry of the defeated, but the sound of singing that I hear.

19 And as soon as he came near to the camp he saw the calf and the dancing. And Moses' anger blazed hot and he cast the tables out of his hands and broke them at the foot of the mountain.

20 And he took the calf they had made and burned it in the fire, and ground it to powder and scattered it on the water and made the Israelites drink it.

21 And Moses said to Aaron, What did this people do to you, that you have brought so great a sin upon them?

22 And Aaron said, Let not the anger of my lord blaze hot; you know the people, that they are set on evil.

23 For they said to me, Make us gods which shall go before us; as for this Moses, the man who brought us up out of the land of Egypt, we do not know what has become of him.

24 I said to them, Those who have any gold, let them take it off. So they gave it to me; then I cast it into the fire, and there came out this calf.

25 And when Moses saw that the people were unruly *and* unrestrained (for Aaron had let them get out of control, so that they were a derision *and* object of shame among their enemies),

26 Then Moses stood in the gate of the camp, and said, Whoever is on the Lord's side, let him come to me. And all the Levites [the priestly tribe] gathered together to him.

27 And he said to them, Thus says the Lord God of Israel, Every man put his sword on his side and go in and out from gate to gate throughout the camp and slay every man his brother, and every man his companion, and every man his neighbor.

28 And the sons of Levi did according to the word of Moses; and there fell of the people that day about 3000 men.

29 And Moses said [to the Levites, By your obedience to God's command] you have consecrated yourselves today [as priests] to the Lord, each man [at the cost of being] against his own son and his own brother, that the Lord may restore *and* bestow His blessing upon *you* this day.

30 The next day Moses said to the people, You have sinned a great sin. And now I will go up to the Lord; perhaps I can make atonement for your sin.

speak the Word

God, I consecrate myself to You and pray that You will restore me and bless me.
ADAPTED FROM Exodus 32:29

time to grow up

The Israelites did not want to take responsibility for their actions. Moses sought God for them, he did their praying for them, and he even tried to do their repenting when they got themselves into trouble (see Exodus 32:30–32). However, this eventually came to an end, and the Israelites had to become responsible.

A baby has no responsibility when he is born. But as the child grows up, he is expected to take on more and more responsibility. One of the most important things parents can do is to teach their children to accept responsibility. God desires that His children learn the same thing.

The Lord has given me the opportunity to be in full-time ministry—to teach His Word on national television and radio and to preach the gospel all over the world. I can assure you that there is a responsibility to that call, a responsibility many people know nothing of. A lot of people say they want to be in ministry. They expect constant excitement and think they will be involved in a continual spiritual event.

The truth is, people in ministry do not float around on a cloud all day singing "The Hallelujah Chorus." We work, and we work hard. We have to get up on time, follow a daily routine, and submit to authority. We walk in integrity and try to do so with excellence. It is a privilege to work in ministry, but it also requires a willingness to take responsibility for our attitudes and actions. Let's not be people who passively let others do for us what we need to do. Let's rise up in faith and be ready to take responsibility for our own lives and ministries.

31 So Moses returned to the Lord, and said, Oh, these people have sinned a great sin and have made themselves gods of gold!
32 Yet now, if You will forgive their sin—and if not, blot me, I pray You, out of Your book which You have written!
33 But the Lord said to Moses, Whoever has sinned against Me, I will blot him [not you] out of My book. [Dan. 12:1; Phil. 4:3; Rev. 3:5.]
34 But now go, lead the people to the place of which I have told you. Behold, My ˢAngel shall go before you. Nevertheless, in the day when I punish I will visit their sin upon them! [Exod. 23:20; 33:2, 3.]
35 And the Lord sent a plague upon the people because they made the calf which Aaron fashioned for them.

33 THE LORD said to Moses, Depart, go up from here, you and the people whom you have brought from the land of Egypt, to the land which I swore to Abraham, Isaac, and Jacob, saying, To your descendants I will give it.
2 I will send an ˢAngel before you, and I will drive out the Canaanite, Amorite, Hittite, Perizzite, Hivite, and Jebusite. [Exod. 23:23; 34:11.]
3 Go up to a land flowing with milk and honey; but I will not go up among you, for you are a stiff-necked people, lest I destroy you on the way.

s See footnote on Gen. 16:7.

4 When the people heard these evil tidings, they mourned and no man put on his ornaments.

5 For the Lord had said to Moses, Say to the Israelites, You are a stiff-necked people! If I should come among you for one moment, I would consume *and* destroy you. Now therefore [penitently] leave off your ornaments, that I may know what to do with you.

6 And the Israelites left off all their ornaments, from Mount Horeb onward.

7 Now Moses used to take [his own] tent and pitch it outside the camp, far off from the camp, and he called it the tent of meeting [of God with His own people]. And everyone who sought the Lord went out to [that temporary] tent of meeting which was outside the camp.

8 When Moses went out to the tent of meeting, all the people rose and stood, every man at his tent door, and looked after Moses until he had gone into the tent.

9 When Moses entered the tent, the pillar of cloud would descend and stand at the door of the tent, and the Lord would talk with Moses.

10 And all the people saw the pillar of cloud stand at the tent door, and all the people rose up and worshiped, every man at his tent door.

11 And the Lord spoke to Moses face to face, as a man speaks to his friend. Moses returned to the camp, but his minister Joshua son of Nun, a young man, did not depart from the [temporary prayer] tent.

12 Moses said to the Lord, See, You say to me, Bring up this people, but You have not let me know whom You will send with me. Yet You said, I know you by name and you have also found favor in My sight.

13 Now therefore, I pray You, if I have found favor in Your sight, show me now Your way, that I may know You [progressively become more deeply and intimately acquainted with You, perceiving and recognizing and understanding more strongly and clearly] and that I may find favor in Your sight. And [Lord, do] consider that this nation is Your people.

14 And the Lord said, My Presence shall go with you, and I will give you rest.

15 And Moses said to the Lord, If Your Presence does not go with me, do not carry us up from here!

16 For by what shall it be known that I and Your people have found favor in Your sight? Is it not in Your going with us so that we are distinguished, I and Your people, from all the other people upon the face of the earth?

17 And the Lord said to Moses, I will do this thing also that you have asked, for you have found favor, loving-kindness, *and* mercy in My sight and I know you personally *and* by name. [Rev. 2:17.]

18 And Moses said, I beseech You, show me Your glory.

19 And God said, I will make all My goodness pass before you, and I will proclaim My name, THE LORD, before you; for I will be gracious to whom I will be gracious, and will show mercy *and* loving-kindness on whom I will show mercy *and* loving-kindness. [Rom. 9:15, 16.]

20 But, He said, You can not see My face, for no man shall see Me and live.

21 And the Lord said, Behold, there

speak the Word

God, I do not ever want to be without You. Do not let me go anywhere that Your presence will not be with me.
ADAPTED FROM EXODUS **33:15**

rest in His presence

Moses had a big job on his hands. He knew he needed God's presence and sought the assurance that God would go with him and help him (see Exodus 33:12–14). That is all we need too—God's presence and His rest. No matter how difficult our circumstance, the knowledge of His presence will strengthen and enable us to do the job at hand. Remember to seek God's presence, not His "presents."

In ministry, sometimes we can get upset and frustrated as we try to bring hope and healing to others, but over the years the Lord has taught me and my ministry team to remain calm, cool, and steady in the face of the challenges. He has shown us the importance of being adaptable, keeping our eyes on Him, and not focusing on our own plans. If things do not work out the way we want them to, we need to stay relaxed and trust Him to show us what to do. I have learned that when I am upset I cannot hear clearly from the Lord; therefore, I pursue peace at all times.

How do you react when your plans fall through and it seems you have no options? Some of us just give up, saying, "Well, that does it! Now my plan is ruined!" We need to think about who did the "ruining." If God ruined our plan, we had the wrong plan to begin with. If the devil ruined our plan, the Lord will give us another plan, one that will be ten times better than the one that failed. Too often we start blaming the devil as a conditioned response when things do not work out just as we want them to. Not everything is the devil's fault. There are times when we are trying to do something that was never God's will. Even though there are things that we want, we must learn to want what God wants even more than we want what we want!

Any time our plans are not working, we must submit it to God and simply rest in His presence. Psalm 91:1 encourages us, "He who dwells in the secret place of the Most High shall remain stable and fixed under the shadow of the Almighty [Whose power no foe can withstand]." We need to realize that God is our Refuge and our Fortress. We can rely and confidently trust in Him. If the devil is resisting you and causing trouble, God will show you that. Then you should take authority over him, reminding him that the greater One lives inside you. As you resist the devil and steadfastly trust God, His plan will always prevail.

Moses asked God to show him His way so he could get to know Him better. The Lord answered by assuring Moses that His presence would be with him and that He would give him rest. What Moses really needed at that difficult time of his life was the presence of God and the rest of God. The same is true for us. As much as we would like to know God's plans for us, what we need most of all is His presence, which will give us rest wherever He sends us and in whatever task He assigns us.

Want God's will more than your own. When things do not work out as you planned, remain peaceful and trust God. Seek His presence at all times. If your trouble and delay are the result of satanic opposition, remember that Satan may come against you one way, but he will have to flee before you seven ways if you keep your eyes on God.

is a place beside Me, and you shall stand upon the rock,

22 And while My glory passes by, I will put you in a cleft of the rock and cover you with My hand until I have passed by.

23 Then I will take away My hand and you shall see My back; but My face shall not be seen.

34 THE LORD said to Moses, Cut two tables of stone like the first, and I will write upon these tables the words that were on the first tables, which you broke.

2 Be ready and come up in the morning to Mount Sinai, and present yourself there to Me on the top of the mountain.

3 And no man shall come up with you, neither let any man be seen throughout all the mountain; neither let flocks or herds feed before that mountain.

4 So Moses cut two tables of stone like the first, and he rose up early in the morning and went up on Mount Sinai, as the Lord had commanded him, and took 'in his hand two tables of stone.

5 And the Lord descended in the cloud and stood with him there and proclaimed the name of the Lord.

6 And the Lord passed by before him, and proclaimed, The Lord! the Lord! a God merciful and gracious, slow to anger, and abundant in loving-kindness and truth,

7 Keeping mercy *and* loving-kindness for thousands, forgiving iniquity and transgression and sin, but Who will by no means clear the guilty, visiting the iniquity of the fathers upon the children and the children's children, to the third and fourth generation.

8 And Moses made haste to bow his head toward the earth and worshiped.

9 And he said, If now I have found favor *and* loving-kindness in Your sight, O Lord, let the Lord, I pray You, go in the midst of us, although it is a stiff-necked people, and pardon our iniquity and our sin, and take us for Your inheritance.

10 And the Lord said, Behold, I lay down [afresh the terms of the mutual agreement between Israel and Me] a covenant. Before all your people I will do marvels (wonders, miracles) such as have not been wrought *or* created in all the earth or in any nation; and all the people among whom you are shall see the work of the Lord; for it is a terrible thing [fearful and full of awe] that I will do with you.

11 Observe what I command you this day. Behold, I drive out before you the Amorite, Canaanite, Hittite, Perizzite, Hivite, and Jebusite.

12 Take heed to yourself, lest you make a covenant *or* mutual agreement with the inhabitants of the land to which you go, lest it become a snare in the midst of you.

13 But you shall destroy their altars, dash in pieces their pillars (obelisks, images), and cut down their Asherim [symbols of the goddess Asherah];

14 For you shall worship no other god; for the Lord, Whose name is Jealous, is a jealous (impassioned) God,

15 Lest you make a covenant with the inhabitants of the land, and when they play the harlot after their gods and sacrifice to their gods and one invites you, you eat of his food sacrificed to idols,

16 And you take of their daughters for your sons, and their daughters play the harlot after their gods and make your sons play the harlot after their gods.

t The two tables of stone are believed to have been pocket-size, easily carried in one hand. The pictures of Moses carrying tombstone-size tables are the result of the misconception of artists, and are not supported by the Bible.

17 You shall make for yourselves no molten gods.

18 The Feast of Unleavened Bread you shall keep. Seven days you shall eat unleavened bread, as I commanded you, in the time of the month of Abib; for in the month of Abib you came out of Egypt.

19 All the males that first open the womb among your livestock are Mine, whether ox or sheep.

20 But the firstling of a donkey [an unclean beast] you shall redeem with a lamb *or* kid, and if you do not redeem it, then you shall break its neck. All the firstborn of your sons you shall redeem. And none of you shall appear before Me empty-handed.

21 Six days you shall work, but on the seventh day you shall rest; even in plowing time and in harvest you shall rest [on the Sabbath].

22 You shall observe the Feast of Weeks, the firstfruits of the wheat harvest, and the Feast of Ingathering at the year's end.

23 Three times in the year shall all your males appear before the Lord God, the God of Israel.

24 For I will cast out the nations before you and enlarge your borders; neither shall any man desire [and molest] your land when you go up to appear before the Lord your God three times in the year.

25 You shall not offer the blood of My sacrifice with leaven; neither shall the sacrifice of the Feast of the Passover be left until morning.

26 The first of the firstfruits of your ground you shall bring to the house of the Lord your God. You shall not boil a kid in his mother's milk.

27 And the Lord said to Moses, Write these words, for after the purpose *and* character of these words I have made a covenant with you and with Israel.

28 Moses was there with the Lord forty days and forty nights; he ate no bread and drank no water. And he wrote upon the tables the words of the covenant, the Ten Commandments.

29 When Moses came down from Mount Sinai with the two tables of the Testimony in his hand, he did not know that the skin of his face shone *and* sent forth beams by reason of his speaking with the Lord.

30 When Aaron and all the Israelites saw Moses, behold, the skin of his face shone, and they feared to come near him.

31 But Moses called to them; and Aaron and all the leaders of the congregation returned to him, and [he] talked with them.

32 Afterward all the Israelites came near, and he gave them in commandment all the Lord had said to him in Mount Sinai.

33 And when Moses had finished speaking with them, he put a veil on his face.

34 But when Moses went in before the Lord to speak with Him, [u]he took the veil off until he came out. And he came out and told the Israelites what he was commanded.

35 The Israelites saw the face of Moses, how the skin of it shone; and Moses put the veil on his face again until he went in to speak with God.

35 MOSES GATHERED all the congregation of the Israelites together and said to them, These are the things which the Lord has commanded that you do:

u The apostle Paul expressly refers to this incident when he says that we all may, with unveiled faces, behold the glory of the Lord, and be transformed (II Cor. 3:13-18). That blessed vision, which of old was given only to the great leader of Israel, is now within reach of each individual believer. The Gospel has no fences to keep the crowd off the mount of vision; the lowliest and most unworthy of its children may pass upward where the shining glory is to be seen. "We **all** . . . are changed" (F. B. Meyer, *Moses, the Servant of God*).

2 Six days shall work be done, but the seventh day shall be to you a holy day, a Sabbath of rest to the Lord; whoever works [on that day] shall be put to death.
3 You shall kindle no fire in all your dwellings on the Sabbath day.
4 And Moses said to all the congregation of the Israelites, This is what the Lord commanded:
5 Take from among you an offering to the Lord. Whoever is of a willing *and* generous heart, let him bring the Lord's offering: gold, silver, and bronze;
6 Blue, purple, and scarlet [stuff], fine linen; goats' hair;
7 And rams' skins tanned red, and skins of dolphins *or* porpoises; and acacia wood;
8 And oil for the light; and spices for anointing oil and for fragrant incense;
9 And onyx stones and other stones to be set for the ephod and the breastplate.
10 And let every able *and* wisehearted man among you come and make all that the Lord has commanded:
11 The tabernacle, its tent and its covering, its hooks, its boards, its bars, its pillars, and its sockets *or* bases;
12 The ark and its poles, with the mercy seat, and the veil of the screen;
13 The table and its poles and all its utensils, and the showbread (the bread of the Presence);
14 The lampstand also for the light, and its utensils and its lamps, and the oil for the light;
15 And the incense altar and its poles, the anointing oil and the fragrant incense, the hanging *or* screen for the door at the entrance of the tabernacle;
16 The altar of burnt offering, with its bronze grating, its poles and all its utensils, the laver and its base;
17 The court's hangings, its pillars and their sockets *or* bases, and the hanging *or* screen for the gate of the court;
18 The pegs of the tabernacle and of the court, and their cords,
19 The finely wrought garments for ministering in the Holy Place, the holy garments for Aaron the [high] priest and for his sons to minister as priests.
20 Then all the congregation of the Israelites left Moses' presence.
21 And they came, each one whose heart stirred him up and whose spirit made him willing, and brought the Lord's offering to be used for the [new] Tent of Meeting, for all its service, and the holy garments.
22 They came, both men and women, all who were willinghearted, and brought brooches, earrings *or* nose rings, signet rings, and armlets *or* necklaces, all jewels of gold, everyone bringing an offering of gold to the Lord.
23 And everyone with whom was found blue or purple or scarlet [stuff], or fine linen, or goats' hair, or rams' skins made red [in tanning], or dolphin *or* porpoise skins brought them.
24 Everyone who could make an offering of silver or bronze brought it as the Lord's offering, and every man with whom was found any acacia wood for any work of the service brought it.
25 All the women who had ability *and* were wisehearted spun with their hands and brought what they had spun of blue and purple and scarlet [stuff] and fine linen;
26 And all the women who had ability *and* whose hearts stirred them up in wisdom spun the goats' hair.
27 The leaders brought onyx stones and stones to be set for the ephod and for the breastplate,
28 And spice, and oil for the light and for the anointing oil and for the fragrant incense.
29 The Israelites brought a freewill

how to get stirred up for God

The people who built the tabernacle of the Lord were stirred up about the things of God, and they gave with willing hearts. You may be thinking, *I wish I could be excited about the Lord's work, but I just don't feel that way. I don't really know how to get myself stirred up.* What can you do to be stirred up for God?

1. Stay around people who are excited about the things of God. Before long, you will be excited and stirred up too. If you associate with a person who is a visionary, you will soon get a vision. But if you stay around lifeless people who want to do nothing but complain, sit on the couch, eat doughnuts, and watch soap operas, then soon you will be doing the same things.

2. Decide to take action about the negative way you feel instead of just wishing things were different. Realize that if you want to have victory over your feelings strongly enough, you will do whatever it takes to get it. If you do not want the victory, no one can motivate you to want it. We need to stop feeling sorry for ourselves. We need to stop whining, "I wish I had this," or "I wish I didn't have that. I wish my parents loved me more. I wish I had more money. I wish my back didn't hurt. I wish . . . I wish . . . I wish . . ." I used to do that. For years I went around "wishing," until the Lord spoke to me and said, "You can be pitiful or you can be powerful, but you cannot be both. So take your pick."

3. Avoid passivity, procrastination, and laziness. A passive person waits to be moved by an outside force before he or she will take action. We are to be motivated and led by the Holy Spirit within us, not by things on the outside. The best way we can guard against the spirit of passivity is to do what we need to do now, and do it with all our might (see Ecclesiastes 9:10).

4. Stay on fire for God. Romans 12:11 encourages us, "Never lag in zeal and in earnest endeavor; be aglow and burning with the Spirit, serving the Lord." In order to always be aglow and burning, we have to stay on fire. I have discovered that the best way to fan the fire is to speak the Word of God in the form of prayer, praise, preaching, or confession. Those disciplines stir up the gift within, keep the fire burning, and prevent my spirit from sinking within me.

Remember, everything we do is to be done unto the Lord and for His glory. We should do it through Him, to Him, for Him, by Him, and with Him. And we should do it willingly, with our whole hearts stirred up within us.

offering to the Lord, all men and women whose hearts made them willing *and* moved them to bring anything for any of the work which the Lord had commanded by Moses to be done. **30** And Moses said to the Israelites, See, the Lord called by name Bezalel son of Uri, the son of Hur, of the tribe of Judah; **31** And He has filled him with the Spirit of God, with ability *and* wisdom, with intelligence *and* understanding, and with knowledge and all craftsmanship,

life point

Sometimes when we see a person as gifted as Bezalel, we try to emulate him instead of exercising our own gifts. We become so busy attempting to do somebody else's ministry that we never get around to doing our own! It is important for us to see that God has given each person different gifts to be used for the benefit of the whole body of Christ (see 1 Corinthians 12:4–30). Often we are not satisfied with what the Lord has given us to do because we are insecure and do not realize who we are in Christ. If God has not given you a ministry of standing in front of people and ministering to them, then do not try to minister that way. You will not be happy or successful if you try to minister with gifts you have not been given. Celebrate and embrace who you are. You will find the most wonderful fulfillment as you do your very best with the gifts God has given you.

32 To devise artistic designs, to work in gold, silver, and bronze,

33 In cutting of stones for setting, and in carving of wood, for work in every skilled craft.

34 And God has put in Bezalel's heart that he may teach, both he and Aholiab son of Ahisamach, of the tribe of Dan.

35 He has filled them with wisdom of heart *and* ability to do all manner of craftsmanship, of the engraver, of the skillful workman, of the embroiderer in blue, purple, and scarlet [stuff] and in fine linen, and of the weaver, even of those who do or design any skilled work.

36 BEZALEL AND Aholiab and every wisehearted man in whom the Lord has put wisdom and understanding to know how to do all the work for the service of the sanctuary shall work according to all that the Lord has commanded.

2 And Moses called Bezalel and Aholiab and every able *and* wise-hearted man in whose mind the Lord had put wisdom *and* ability, everyone whose heart stirred him up to come to do the work;

3 And they received from Moses all the freewill offerings which the Israelites had brought for doing the work of the sanctuary, to prepare it for service. And they continued to bring him freewill offerings every morning.

4 And all the wise *and* able men who were doing the work on the sanctuary came, every man from the work he was doing,

5 And they said to Moses, The people bring much more than enough for doing the work which the Lord commanded to do.

6 So Moses commanded and it was proclaimed in all the camp, Let no man or woman do anything more for the sanctuary offering. So the people were restrained from bringing,

7 For the stuff they had was sufficient to do all the work and more.

8 And all the able *and* wisehearted men among them who did the work on the tabernacle made ten curtains of fine twined linen and blue, purple, and scarlet [stuff], with cherubim skillfully worked on them.

9 The length of each curtain was twenty-eight cubits and its breadth four cubits; all the curtains were one size.

10 [Bezalel] coupled five curtains one to another and the other five curtains he coupled one to another.

11 And he made loops of blue on the outer edge of the last curtain in the first set; this he did also on the inner edge of the first curtain in the second set.

12 Fifty loops he made in the one curtain and fifty loops in the edge of the curtain which was the second set; the loops were opposite one another.
13 And he made fifty clasps of gold and coupled the curtains together with the clasps so that the tabernacle became one unit.
14 And he made eleven curtains of goats' hair for a tent over the tabernacle.
15 The length of one curtain was thirty cubits and four cubits was the breadth; the eleven curtains were of equal size.
16 And he coupled five curtains by themselves and the other six curtains by themselves.
17 And he made fifty loops on the outmost edge of the curtain to be coupled and fifty loops he made on the inner edge of the second curtain to be coupled.
18 He made fifty clasps of bronze to couple the tent together into one whole.
19 He made a covering for the tent of ᵛrams' skins tanned red, and above it a covering of dolphin or porpoise skins.
20 He made boards of acacia wood for the upright framework of the tabernacle.
21 The length of a board was ten cubits and the breadth one cubit and a half.
22 Each board had two tenons (projections) to fit into a mortise to form a clutch; he did this for all the boards of the tabernacle.
23 And he made thus the boards [for frames] for the tabernacle: twenty boards for the south side,

24 And he made under the twenty boards forty sockets or bases of silver, two sockets under one board for its two tenons or hands, and two sockets under another board for its two tenons.
25 For the other side of the tabernacle, the north side, he made twenty boards.
26 And their forty sockets or bases of silver, two sockets under [the end of] each board.
27 And for the rear or west side of the tabernacle he made six [frame] boards.
28 And two boards he made for each corner of the tabernacle in the rear.
29 They were separate below but linked together at the top with one ring; thus he made both of them in both corners.
30 There were eight boards with sixteen sockets or bases of silver, and under [the end of] each board two sockets.
31 He made bars of acacia wood, five for the [frame] boards of the one side of the tabernacle,
32 And five bars for the boards of its other side, and five bars for the boards at the rear or west side.
33 And he made the middle bar pass through halfway up the boards from one end to the other.
34 He overlaid the boards and the bars with gold and made their rings of gold as places for the bars.
35 And he made the veil of blue, purple, and scarlet [stuff] and fine twined linen, with cherubim skillfully worked. [Matt. 27:50, 51; Heb. 10:19-22.]
36 For [the veil] he made four pillars of acacia [wood] and overlaid them

v The final coverings of the tabernacle tent are not to be confused with the second one of goats' hair (Exod. 36:14). There were **four distinct coverings** of the tabernacle tent: 1. A covering of fine twined linen woven with blue, purple, and scarlet, with figures of cherubim upon it. It was made of two long pieces, one running from north to south, the other from east to west [and overlapping for the ceiling] (Exod. 26:1, 6; 36:8ff.). 2. Over this a covering of woven goats' hair was thrown (Exod. 26:7; 36:14). 3. A third covering of rams' skins made red (Exod. 26:14; 36:19). 4. And "above it" another covering of dolphin or porpoise skins, weighing the others down and giving perfect protection from the weather (Exod. 26:14; 36:19).

with gold; their hooks were of gold, and he cast for them four sockets *or* bases of silver.

37 And he made a screen for the tent door of blue, purple, and scarlet [stuff] and fine twined linen, embroidered,

38 And he made the five pillars of it with their hooks, and overlaid their ornamental tops and joinings with gold, but their five sockets were of bronze.

37 BEZALEL MADE the ark of acacia wood—two cubits and a half was the length of it, a cubit and a half the breadth of it, and a cubit and a half the height of it.

2 He overlaid it with pure gold within and without and made a molding *or* crown of gold to go around the top of it.

3 He cast four rings of gold for its four corners, two rings on either side.

4 He made poles of acacia wood and overlaid them with gold.

5 He put the poles through the rings at the sides of the ark to carry it.

6 [Bezalel] made the mercy seat of pure gold, two cubits and a half its length and one cubit and a half its breadth.

7 And he made two cherubim of beaten gold; on the two ends of the mercy seat he made them,

8 One cherub at one end and one at the other end; of one piece with the mercy seat he made the cherubim at its two ends.

9 And the cherubim spread out their wings on high, covering the mercy seat with their wings, with their faces to each other, looking down to the mercy seat. [Heb. 9:23-26.]

10 Bezalel made the [showbread] table of acacia wood; it was two cubits long, a cubit wide, and a cubit and a half high.

11 He overlaid it with pure gold and made a molding of gold around its top.

12 And he made a border around it [just under the top] a handbreadth wide, and a molding of gold around the border.

13 And he cast for it four rings of gold and fastened the rings on the four corners that were at its four legs.

14 Close to the border were the rings, the places for the poles to pass through to carry the [showbread] table.

15 [Bezalel] made the poles of acacia wood to carry the [showbread] table and overlaid them with gold.

16 He made of pure gold the vessels which were to be on the table, its plates and dishes [for bread], its bowls and flagons for pouring [liquid sacrifices].

17 And he made the lampstand of pure gold; its base and shaft were made of hammered work; its cups, its knobs, and its flowers were of one piece with it.

18 There were six branches going out of the sides of the lampstand, three branches out of one side of it and three branches out of the other side of it;

19 Three cups made like almond blossoms in one branch, each with a [calyx] knob and a flower, and three cups made like almond blossoms in the [opposite] branch, each with a [calyx] knob and a flower; and so for the six branches going out of the lampstand.

20 On [the shaft of] the lampstand were four cups made like almond blossoms, with knobs and flowers [one at the top].

21 And a knob under each pair of branches, of one piece with the lamp- stand, for the six branches going out of it.

22 Their knobs and their branches were of one piece with it, all of it ham- mered work of pure gold.

23 And he made of pure gold its seven lamps, its snuffers, and its ash- trays.

24 Of a talent of pure gold he made

the lampstand and all its utensils. [John 1:4, 5, 9; II Cor. 4:6.]

25 And [Bezalel] made the incense altar of acacia wood; its top was a cubit square and it was two cubits high; the horns were one piece with it. **26** He overlaid it with pure gold, its top, its sides round about, and its horns; also he made a rim around it of gold.

27 And he made two rings of gold for it under its rim, on its two opposite sides, as places for the poles [to pass through] to carry it.

28 And he made the poles of acacia wood and overlaid them with gold.

29 He also made the holy anointing oil [symbol of the Holy Spirit] and the pure, fragrant incense, after the perfumer's art.

38 BEZALEL MADE the burnt offering altar of acacia wood; its top was five cubits square and it was three cubits high.

2 He made its horns on the four corners of it; the horns were of one piece with it, and he overlaid it with bronze.

3 He made all the utensils *and* vessels of the altar, the pots, shovels, basins, forks *or* fleshhooks, and firepans; all its utensils *and* vessels he made of bronze.

4 And he made for the altar a bronze grate of network under its ledge, extending halfway down it.

5 He cast four rings for the four corners of the bronze grating to be places for the poles [with which to carry it].

6 And he made the poles of acacia wood and overlaid them with bronze.

7 And he put the poles through the rings on the altar's sides with which to carry it; he made it hollow with planks.

8 He made the laver and its base of bronze from the mirrors of the women who ministered at the door of the Tent of Meeting.

9 And he made the court: for the south side the hangings of the court were of fine twined linen, a hundred cubits;

10 Their pillars and their bronze sockets *or* bases were twenty; the hooks of the pillars and their joinings were silver.

11 And for the north side the hangings were [also] a hundred cubits; their pillars and their sockets *or* bases of bronze were twenty; the hooks of the pillars and their joinings were of silver.

12 But for the west side were hangings of fifty cubits; their pillars and their sockets *or* bases were ten; the hooks of the pillars and their joinings were of silver.

13 And for the front, the east side, fifty cubits.

14 The hangings for one side of the gate were fifteen cubits; their pillars three and their sockets *or* bases three.

15 Also for the other side of the court gate, left and right, were hangings of fifteen cubits; their pillars three and their sockets *or* bases three.

16 All the hangings around the court were of fine twined linen.

17 The sockets for the pillars were of bronze, the hooks of the pillars and their joinings of silver, the overlaying of their tops of silver, and all the pillars of the court were joined with silver.

18 The hanging *or* screen for the gate of the court was embroidered in blue, purple, and scarlet [stuff], and fine twined linen; the length was twenty cubits and the height in the breadth was five cubits, corresponding to the hangings of the court.

19 Their pillars were four and their sockets of bronze four; their hooks were of silver, and the overlaying of their tops and their joinings were of silver.

20 All the pegs for the tabernacle and around the court were of bronze.

21 This is the sum of the things for

the tabernacle of the Testimony, as counted at the command of Moses, for the work of the Levites under the direction of Ithamar son of Aaron, the [high] priest.

22 Bezalel son of Uri, the son of Hur, of the tribe of Judah, made all that the Lord commanded Moses.

23 With him was Aholiab son of Ahisamach, of the tribe of Dan, an engraver, a skillful craftsman, and embroiderer in blue, purple, and scarlet [stuff], and in fine linen.

24 All the gold that was used for the work in all the building *and* furnishing of the sanctuary, the gold from the offering, was 29 talents and 730 shekels, by the shekel of the sanctuary.

25 And the silver from those numbered of the congregation was 100 talents and 1,775 shekels, by sanctuary standards:

26 A beka for each man, that is, half a shekel, by the sanctuary shekel, for everyone who was counted, from twenty years old and upward, for 603,550 men.

27 The 100 talents of silver were for casting the sockets *or* bases of the sanctuary and of the veil; 100 sockets for the 100 talents, a talent for a socket.

28 Of the 1,775 shekels he made hooks for the pillars, and overlaid their tops, and made joinings for them.

29 The bronze of the offering was 70 talents and 2,400 shekels.

30 With it Bezalel made the sockets for the door of the Tent of Meeting, and the bronze altar and the bronze grate for it, and all the utensils of the altar,

31 The sockets of the court round about and of the court gate, and all the pegs of the tabernacle and around the court.

39 AND OF the blue and purple and scarlet [stuff] they made finely wrought garments for serving in the Holy Place; they made the holy garments for Aaron, as the Lord had commanded Moses.

2 And Bezalel made the ephod of gold, blue, purple, and scarlet [stuff], and fine twined linen.

3 And they beat the gold into thin sheets and cut it into wires to work into the blue, purple, and scarlet [stuff] and the fine linen, in skilled design.

4 They made shoulder pieces for the ephod, joined to it at its two edges.

5 And the skillfully woven band on it, to gird it on, was of the same piece and workmanship with it, of gold, blue, purple, and scarlet [stuff], and fine twined linen, as the Lord had commanded Moses.

6 And they prepared the onyx stones enclosed in settings of gold filigree and engraved as signets are engraved with the names of the sons of Israel.

7 And he put them on the shoulder pieces of the ephod to be stones of memorial *or* remembrance for the Israelites, as the Lord had commanded Moses.

8 And [Bezalel] made the breastplate skillfully, like the work of the ephod, of gold, blue, purple, and scarlet [stuff], and fine twined linen.

9 The breastplate was a [hand's] span square when doubled over.

10 And they set in it four rows of stones; a sardius, a topaz, and a carbuncle made the first row;

11 The second row an emerald, a sapphire, and a diamond;

12 The third row a jacinth, an agate, and an amethyst;

13 And the fourth row a beryl, an onyx, and a jasper; they were enclosed in settings of gold filigree.

14 There were twelve stones with their names according to those of the sons of Israel, engraved like a signet, each with its name, according to the twelve tribes.

15 And they made [at the ends] of the breastplate twisted chains like cords, of pure gold.

16 And they made two settings of gold filigree and two gold rings which they put on the two ends of the breastplate.

17 And they put the two twisted cords *or* woven chains of gold in the two rings on the end edges of the breastplate.

18 And the other two ends of the twisted cords *or* chains of gold they put on the two settings and put them on the shoulder pieces of the ephod, in front.

19 They made two rings of gold and put them on the two ends of the breastplate, on the inside edge of it next to the ephod.

20 And they made two [other] gold rings and attached them to the two shoulder pieces of the ephod underneath, in front, at its joining above the skillfully woven band of the ephod.

21 They bound the breastplate by its rings to those of the ephod with a blue lace, that it might lie upon the skillfully woven band of the ephod and that the breastplate might not be loosed from the ephod, as the Lord commanded Moses.

22 And he made the robe of the ephod of woven work all of blue.

23 And there was an opening [for the head] in the middle of the robe like the hole in a coat of mail, with a binding around it, that it should not be torn.

24 On the skirts of the robe they made pomegranates of blue and purple and scarlet [stuff] and twined linen.

25 And they made bells of pure gold and put [them] between the pomegranates around the skirts of the robe;

26 A bell and a pomegranate, a bell and a pomegranate, round about on the skirts of the robe for ministering, as the Lord commanded Moses.

27 And they made the long *and* sleeved tunics woven of fine linen for Aaron and his sons,

28 And the turban, and the ornamental caps of fine linen, and the breeches of fine twined linen,

29 The girdle *or* sash of fine twined linen, and blue, purple, and scarlet embroidery, as the Lord commanded Moses.

30 And they made the plate of the holy crown of pure gold and wrote upon it an inscription, like the engravings of a signet, HOLY TO THE LORD. [Exod. 28:36.]

31 They tied to it a lace of blue to fasten it on the turban above, as the Lord commanded Moses.

32 Thus all the work of the tabernacle of the Tent of Meeting was finished; according to all that the Lord commanded Moses, so the Israelites had done.

33 And they brought the tabernacle to Moses: the tent and all its furnishings, its clasps, its [frame] boards, its bars, its pillars, its sockets *or* bases;

34 And the covering of rams' skins made red, and the covering of dolphin *or* porpoise skins, and the veil of the screen;

35 The ark of the Testimony, its poles, and the mercy seat;

36 The table and all its utensils, and the showbread (bread of the Presence);

37 The pure [gold] lampstand and its lamps, with the lamps set in order, all its utensils, and the oil for the light;

38 The golden altar, the anointing oil, the fragrant incense, and the hanging for the door of the tent;

39 The bronze altar and its grate of bronze, its poles and all its utensils; the laver and its base;

40 The hangings of the court, its pillars and sockets *or* bases, and the screen for the court gate, its cords, and pegs, and all the utensils for the service of the tabernacle, for the Tent of Meeting [of God with His people]; [Exod. 29:42, 43.]

41 The finely worked vestments for ministering in the Holy Place, the holy garments for Aaron the priest, and the garments of his sons to minister as priests.

42 According to all that the Lord had commanded Moses, so the Israelites had done all the work.

43 And Moses inspected all the work, and behold, they had done it; as the Lord had commanded, so had they done it. And Moses blessed them.

40 AND THE Lord said to Moses,

2 On the first day of the first month you shall set up the tabernacle of the Tent of Meeting [of God with you].

3 And you shall put in it the ark of the Testimony and screen the ark [of God's Presence] with the veil. [Heb. 10:19-23.]

4 You shall bring in the [showbread] table and set in order the things that are to be upon it; and you shall bring in the lampstand and set up *and* light its lamps. [Rev. 21:23-25.]

5 You shall set the golden altar for the incense before the ark of the Testimony [outside the veil] and put the hanging *or* screen at the tabernacle door.

6 You shall set the altar of the burnt offering before the door of the tabernacle of the Tent of Meeting.

7 And you shall ᵂset the laver between the Tent of Meeting and the altar and put water in it.

8 And you shall set up the court [curtains] round about and hang up the hanging *or* screen at the court gate.

9 You shall take the anointing oil and anoint the tabernacle and all that is in it, and shall consecrate it and all its furniture, and it shall be holy.

10 You shall anoint the altar of burnt offering and all its utensils; and consecrate (set apart for God) the altar, and the altar shall be most holy.

11 And you shall anoint the laver and its base and consecrate it.

12 You shall bring Aaron and his sons to the door of the Tent of Meeting and wash them with water. [John 17:17-19.]

13 You shall put on Aaron the holy garments, and anoint and consecrate him, so he may serve Me as priest.

14 And you shall bring his sons and put long *and* sleeved tunics on them,

15 And you shall anoint them as you anointed their father, that they may minister to Me as priests; for their anointing shall be to them for an everlasting priesthood throughout their generations.

16 Thus did Moses; according to all that the Lord commanded him, so he did.

17 And on the first day of the first month in the second year the tabernacle was erected.

18 Moses set up the tabernacle, laid its sockets, set up its boards, put in its bars, and erected its pillars.

19 [Moses] spread the tent over the tabernacle and put the covering of the tent over it, as the Lord had commanded him.

w Why was it necessary for one exact position for the laver to be demanded of Moses by God? Those who have published charts of the tabernacle furniture arrangement, with the laver off to one side or the other of the door into the sanctuary, have missed a point here. The laver was to be placed directly "between [the doors of] the Tent of Meeting and the altar [of burnt offering]," thus completing the "cross" made by the arrangement of the furniture, from the ark to the altar. It could have no significance to the Jews of that time, but the One Who planned it had those in mind to whom Christ would one day say, "And these [very Scriptures] testify about Me!" (John 5:39.) How fitting that at the foot of that "cross" there should be the altar, picturing our complete surrender, and then the laver, picturing our cleansing, that we may enter in through Him Who alone is "the Door" to the eternal Holy of Holies (John 10:1-9).

20 He took the Testimony [the Ten Commandments] and put it into the ark, and set the poles [in the rings] on the ark, and put the mercy seat on top of the ark.

21 [Moses] brought the ark into the tabernacle and set up the veil of the screen and screened the ark of the Testimony, as the Lord had commanded him.

22 Moses put the table [of show-bread] in the Tent of Meeting on the north side of the tabernacle outside the veil;

23 He set the bread [of the Presence] in order on it before the Lord, as the Lord had commanded him. [John 6:32-35.]

24 And he put the lampstand in the Tent of Meeting opposite the table on the south side of the tabernacle.

25 Moses set up *and* lighted the lamps before the Lord, as the Lord commanded him.

26 He put the golden altar [of incense] in the Tent of Meeting before the veil;

27 He burned sweet incense [symbol of prayer] upon it, as the Lord commanded him. [Ps. 141:2; Rev. 8:3.]

28 And he set up the hanging *or* screen at the door of the tabernacle.

29 [Moses] put the altar of burnt offering at the door of the tabernacle of the Tent of Meeting and offered on it the burnt offering and the cereal offering, as the Lord commanded him.

30 And Moses set the laver between the Tent of Meeting and the altar and put water in it for washing.

31 And Moses and Aaron and his sons washed their hands and their feet there.

32 When they went into the Tent of Meeting or came near the altar, they washed, as the Lord commanded Moses.

33 And he erected the court round about the tabernacle and the altar and set up the hanging *or* screen at the court gate. So Moses finished the work.

34 Then the cloud [the Shekinah, God's visible presence] covered the Tent of Meeting, and the glory of the Lord filled the tabernacle! [Rev. 15:8.]

35 And Moses was not able to enter the Tent of Meeting because the cloud remained upon it, and the glory of the Lord filled the tabernacle.

36 In all their journeys, whenever the cloud was taken up from over the tabernacle, the Israelites went onward;

37 But if the cloud was not taken up, they did not journey on till the day that it was taken up.

38 For throughout all their journeys the cloud of the Lord was upon the tabernacle by day, and fire was in it by night, in the sight of all the house of Israel.

putting the Word to work

The cloud that led the Israelites on their journey (see Exodus 40:36–38) symbolizes the leading of the Holy Spirit in our lives today. Are you following the "cloud" in your life, patiently waiting on God to lead you on the next phase of your journey and being quick to obey when He does?

Leviticus

Author:
Moses

Date:
About 1440 BC

Everyday Life Principles:

God's laws are in place for our good. He has established them so that we can enjoy His blessings.

Serious consequences result when we do not obey God.

God calls us to live holy lives and to have purity and integrity in every aspect of our everyday lives.

The basic message of Leviticus is: "If you obey God, you will be blessed. If you don't, you won't." The laws and instructions we find in Leviticus, and the commands to obey, all have one purpose: blessing. God knows that sin and disobedience will separate us from Him, so He gives us guidelines for living so we can stay close to Him and live under His blessing. God requires our obedience so we can stay in fellowship with Him and live in His favor.

In addition to showing us the need to obey the laws of God so we can be blessed, Leviticus also calls us to holiness in our everyday lives. The Israelites' idea of holiness was based on laws and rituals; our concept of holiness is much different because of what Jesus did on the cross. While there are certain actions we can take to express holiness, actions alone do not make us holy. Holiness begins in our hearts with faith in Jesus, and He leads us to desire to obey God in everything we do.

I hope you will look beyond the animal sacrifices and elaborate rituals in Leviticus and see the rich symbolism in this book. I hope it will stir you to live a more holy life in the midst of your everyday circumstances and bring about greater obedience in your heart so you can live in greater and greater blessing.

1 THE LORD [a]called to Moses out of the Tent of Meeting, and said to him,

2 Say to the Israelites, When any man of you brings an offering to the Lord, you shall bring your offering of [domestic] animals from the herd or from the flock.

3 If his offering is a burnt offering from the herd, he shall offer a male without blemish; he shall offer it at the door of the Tent of Meeting, that he may be accepted before the Lord. [Rom. 12:1; Phil. 1:20.]

4 And he shall lay [both] his hands upon the head of the burnt offering [transferring symbolically his guilt to the victim], and it shall be [b]an acceptable atonement for him. [Heb. 13:15, 16; I Pet. 1:2.]

5 The man shall kill the young bull before the Lord, and the priests, Aaron's sons, shall present the blood and dash [it] round about upon the altar that is at the door of the Tent of Meeting.

6 And he shall skin the burnt offering and cut it into pieces.

7 And the sons of Aaron the priest shall put fire on the altar and lay wood in order on the fire;

8 And Aaron's sons the priests shall lay the pieces, the head and the fat, in order on the wood on the fire on the altar.

9 But its entrails and its legs he shall wash with water. And the priest shall burn all of it on the altar for a burnt offering, an offering by fire, a sweet *and* satisfying odor to the Lord. [Eph. 5:2; Phil. 4:18; I Pet. 2:5.]

10 And if the man's offering is of the flock, from the sheep or the goats, for a burnt offering, he shall offer a male without blemish.

11 And he shall kill it on the north side of the altar before the Lord, and Aaron's sons the priests shall dash its blood round about against the altar.

12 And [the man] shall cut it into pieces, with its head and its fat, and the priest shall lay them in order on the wood that is on the fire on the altar.

13 But he shall wash the entrails and legs with water. The priest shall offer all of it and burn it on the altar; it is a burnt offering, an offering made by fire, a sweet *and* satisfying fragrance to the Lord.

14 And if the offering to the Lord is a burnt offering of birds, then [the man] shall bring turtledoves or young pigeons.

speak the Word

God, I pray that everything I offer You will be pure and without blemish.
ADAPTED FROM LEVITICUS 1:3

a The first step toward understanding the message of Leviticus is to appreciate its viewpoint indicated here—"The Lord called to Moses out of the Tent of Meeting," and talked to him. Before this a forbidding God had spoken from the burning mountain. But now the tabernacle is erected according to the God-given pattern, and the God Who dwells among His people in fellowship with them talks with His servant Moses "out of the Tent of Meeting." The people, therefore, are not treated as sinners alienated from God, "but as being already brought into a new relationship, even that of fellowship, on the ground of a blood-sealed covenant" (J. Sidlow Baxter, *Explore the Book*). b To render the self-sacrifice perfect, it was necessary that the offerer should spiritually die, sinking it as it were into the death of the sacrifice that had died for him, so that through the mediator of his salvation he should put his soul into a living fellowship with the Lord and bring his bodily members within the operations of the gracious Spirit of God. Thereby he would be renewed and sanctified [separated for holy use], both body and soul, and enter into union with God (Karl Keil and F. Delitzsch, *Biblical Commentary on the Old Testament*).

15 And the priest shall bring it to the altar, and wring off its head, and burn it on the altar; and its blood shall be drained out on the side of the altar.

16 And he shall take away its crop with its feathers and cast it beside the altar on the east side, in the place for ashes.

17 And he shall split it open [holding it] by its wings, but shall not cut it in two. And the priest shall burn it on the altar, on the wood that is on the fire; it is a burnt offering, an offering made by fire, a sweet *and* satisfying odor to the Lord.

2 WHEN ANYONE offers a cereal offering to the Lord, it shall be of fine flour; and he shall pour oil over it and lay frankincense on it.

2 And he shall bring it to Aaron's sons the priests. Out of it he shall take a handful of the fine flour and oil, with all its frankincense, and the priest shall burn this on the altar as the memorial portion of it, an offering made by fire, of a sweet *and* satisfying fragrance to the Lord.

3 What is left of the cereal offering shall be Aaron's and his sons'; it is a most holy part of the offerings made to the Lord by fire.

4 When you bring as an offering cereal baked in the oven, it shall be unleavened cakes of fine flour mixed with oil, or unleavened wafers spread with oil.

5 If your offering is cereal baked on a griddle, it shall be of fine flour unleavened, mixed with oil.

6 You shall break it in pieces and pour oil on it; it is a cereal offering.

7 And if your offering is cereal cooked in the frying pan, it shall be made of fine flour with oil.

8 And you shall bring the cereal offering that is made of these things to the Lord; it shall be presented to the priest, and he shall bring it to the [bronze] altar.

9 The priest shall take from the cereal offering its memorial portion and burn it on the altar, an offering made by fire, a sweet *and* satisfying fragrance to the Lord.

10 What is left of the cereal offering shall be Aaron's and his sons'; it is a most holy part of the offerings made to the Lord by fire.

11 No cereal offering that you bring to the Lord shall be made with leaven, for you shall burn no leaven or honey in any offering made by fire to the Lord. [I Cor. 5:8.]

12 As an offering of firstfruits you may offer leaven and honey to the Lord, but ᶜthey shall not be burned on the altar for a sweet odor [to the Lord, for their aid to fermentation is symbolic of corruption in the human heart].

13 Every cereal offering you shall season with salt [symbol of preservation]; neither shall you allow the salt of the covenant of your God to be lacking from your cereal offering; with all your offerings you shall offer salt. [Mark 9:49, 50.]

14 If you offer a cereal offering of your firstfruits to the Lord, you shall offer for it of your firstfruits grain in the ear parched with fire, bruised *and* crushed grain out of the fresh *and* fruitful ear.

15 And you shall put oil on it and lay frankincense on it; it is a cereal offering.

16 The priest shall burn as its memorial portion part of the bruised *and* crushed grain of it and part of the oil of it, with all its frankincense; it is an offering made by fire to the Lord.

c There is to be no division between one's spiritual life and one's secular life, but the whole of one's life is to be of the nature of a sacrament (Col. 3:23, 24).

3 IF A man's offering is a sacrifice of peace offering, if he offers an animal from the herd, whether male or female, he shall offer it without blemish before the Lord.

2 He shall lay [both] his ^d^hands upon the head of his offering and kill it at the door of the Tent of Meeting; and Aaron's sons the priests shall throw the blood against the altar round about.

3 And from the sacrifice of the peace offering, an offering made by fire to the Lord, he shall offer the fat that covers and is upon the entrails,

4 And the two kidneys with the fat that is on them at the loins, and the appendage of the liver which he shall take away with the kidneys.

5 Aaron's sons shall burn it all on the altar upon the burnt offering which is on the wood on the fire, an offering made by fire, of a sweet *and* satisfying odor to the Lord.

6 If his peace offering to the Lord is an animal from the flock, male or female, he shall offer it without blemish.

7 If he offers a lamb, then he shall offer it before the Lord.

8 He shall lay [both] his hands on the head of his offering and kill it before the Tent of Meeting; and Aaron's sons shall throw its blood around against the altar.

9 And he shall offer from the peace offering as an offering made by fire to the Lord: the fat of it, the fat tail as a whole, taking it off close to the backbone, and the fat that covers and is upon the entrails,

10 And the two kidneys, and the fat on them at the loins, and the appendage of the liver, which he shall take away with the kidneys.

11 The priest shall burn it upon the altar, a food offering made by fire to the Lord.

12 If [a man's] offering is a goat, he shall offer it before the Lord,

13 And lay his hands upon its head, and kill it before the Tent of Meeting; and the sons of Aaron shall throw its blood against the altar round about.

14 Then he shall offer from it as his offering made by fire to the Lord: the fat that covers and is on the entrails,

15 And the two kidneys and the fat that is on them at the loins, and the appendage of the liver which he shall take away with the kidneys.

16 The priest shall burn them on the altar as food, offered by fire, for a sweet *and* satisfying fragrance. All the fat is the Lord's.

17 It shall be a perpetual statute for your generations in all your dwelling places, that you eat neither fat nor blood.

4 AND THE Lord said to Moses,

2 Say to the Israelites, If anyone shall sin through error *or* unwittingly in any of the things which the Lord has commanded not to be done, and shall do any one of them—

3 If it is the anointed priest who sins, thus bringing guilt on the people, then let him offer for his sin which he has committed a young bull without blemish to the Lord as a sin offering. [Heb. 7:27, 28.]

4 He shall bring the bull to the door of the Tent of Meeting before the Lord, and shall lay [both] his hands on the bull's head and kill [it] before the Lord.

5 And the anointed priest shall take some of the bull's blood and bring it into the Tent of Meeting;

6 And the priest shall dip his finger in the blood and sprinkle some of [it] seven times before the Lord before the veil of the sanctuary.

7 And the priest shall put some of

---

d *The Septuagint* (Greek translation of the Old Testament) so reads.

the blood on the horns of the altar of sweet incense before the Lord which is in the Tent of Meeting; and all the rest of the blood of the bull shall he pour out at the base of the altar of the burnt offering at the door of the Tent of Meeting.

8 And all the fat of the bull for the sin offering he shall take off of it—the fat that covers and is on the entrails,

9 And the two kidneys and the fat that is on them at the loins, and the appendage of the liver, which he shall take away with the kidneys—

10 Just as these are taken off of the bull of the sacrifice of the peace offerings; and the priest shall burn them on the altar of burnt offering.

11 But the hide of the bull and all its flesh, its head, its legs, its entrails, and its dung,

12 Even the whole bull shall he carry forth without the camp to a clean place, where the ashes are poured out, and burn it on a fire of wood, there where the ashes are poured out. [Heb. 13:11-13.]

13 If the whole congregation of Israel sins unintentionally, and it be hidden from the eyes of the assembly, and they have done what the Lord has commanded not to be done and are guilty,

14 When the sin which they have committed becomes known, then the congregation shall offer a young bull for a sin offering and bring it before the Tent of Meeting.

15 The elders of the congregation shall lay their hands upon the head of the bull before the Lord, and the bull shall be killed before the Lord.

16 The anointed priest shall bring some of the bull's blood to the Tent of Meeting,

17 And shall dip his finger in the blood, and sprinkle it seven times before the Lord, before the veil [which screens the ark of the covenant].

18 He shall put some of the blood on the horns of the altar [of incense]

which is before the Lord in the Tent of Meeting, and he shall pour out all the blood at the base of the altar of burnt offering near the door of the Tent of Meeting.

19 And he shall take all its fat from the bull and burn it on the altar.

20 Thus shall he do with the bull; as he did with the bull for a sin offering, so shall he do with this; and the priest shall make atonement for [the people], and they shall be forgiven.

21 And he shall carry forth the bull outside the camp and burn it as he burned the first bull; it is the sin offering for the congregation.

22 When a ruler *or* leader sins and unwittingly does any one of the things the Lord his God has forbidden, and is guilty,

23 If his sin which he has committed be known to him, he shall bring as his offering a goat, a male without blemish.

24 He shall lay his hand on the head of the goat and kill it in the place where they kill the burnt offering before the Lord; it is a sin offering.

25 The priest shall take some of the blood of the sin offering with his finger and put it on the horns of the altar of burnt offering and pour the rest of its blood at the base of the altar of burnt offering.

26 And he shall burn all its fat upon the altar like the fat of the sacrifice of peace offerings; so the priest shall make atonement for him for his sin, and it shall be forgiven him.

27 If any one of the common people sins unwittingly in doing anything the Lord has commanded not to be done, and is guilty,

28 When the sin which he has committed is made known to him, he shall bring for his offering a goat, a female without blemish, for his sin which he has committed.

29 The offender shall lay his hand on the head of the sin offering and kill [it] at the place of the burnt offering.

30 And the priest shall take some of its blood with his finger and put it on the horns of the altar of burnt offering and shall pour out the rest of its blood at the base of the altar.

31 And all the fat of it he shall take away, as the fat is taken away from off the sacrifice of peace offerings; and the priest shall burn it on the altar for a sweet *and* satisfying fragrance to the Lord; and the priest shall make atonement for [the man], and he shall be forgiven.

32 If he brings a lamb as his sin offering, he shall bring a female without blemish.

33 He shall lay his hand upon the head of the sin offering and kill it in the place where they kill the burnt offering.

34 And the priest shall take some of the blood of the sin offering with his finger and put it on the horns of the altar of burnt offering and all the rest of the blood of the lamb he shall pour out at the base of the altar.

35 And he shall take away all the fat of it, just as the fat of the lamb is removed from the sacrifice of the peace offerings; and the priest shall burn it on the altar upon the offerings made by fire to the Lord; and the priest shall make atonement for the sin which the man has committed, and he shall be forgiven. [Heb. 9:13, 14.]

5 IF ANYONE sins in that he is sworn to testify and has knowledge of the matter, either by seeing or hearing of it, but fails to report it, then he shall bear his iniquity *and* willfulness.

2 Or if anyone touches an unclean thing, whether the carcass of an unclean wild beast or of an unclean domestic animal or of unclean creeping things that multiply prolifically, even if he is unaware of it, and he has become unclean, he is guilty.

3 Or if he touches human uncleanness, of whatever kind the uncleanness may be with which he becomes defiled, and he is unaware of it, when he does know it, then he shall be guilty.

4 Or if anyone unthinkingly swears he will do something, whether to do evil or good, whatever it may be that a man shall pronounce rashly taking an oath, then, when he becomes aware of it, he shall be guilty in either of these. [Mark 6:23.]

5 When a man is guilty in one of these, he shall confess the sin he has committed.

6 He shall bring his guilt *or* trespass offering to the Lord for the sin which he has committed, a female from the flock, a lamb or a goat, for a sin offering; and the priest shall make atonement for his sin.

7 But if he cannot afford a lamb, then he shall bring for his guilt offering to the Lord two turtledoves or two young pigeons, one for a sin offering and the other for a burnt offering.

8 He shall bring them to the priest, who shall offer the one for the sin offering first, and wring its head from its neck, but shall not sever it;

9 And he shall sprinkle some of the blood of the sin offering on the side of the altar, and the rest of the blood shall be drained out at the base of the altar; it is a sin offering.

10 And he shall prepare the second bird for a burnt offering, according to the ordinance; and the priest shall make atonement for him for his sin which he has committed, and he shall be forgiven.

11 But if the offender cannot afford to bring two turtledoves or two young pigeons, then he shall bring for his offering the tenth part of an ephah of fine flour for a sin offering; he shall put no oil or frankincense on it, for it is a sin offering.

12 He shall bring it to the priest, who shall take a handful of it as a memorial portion and burn it on the altar, on the offerings made by fire to the Lord; it is a sin offering.

13 Thus the priest shall make atonement for him for the sin that he has committed in any of these things, and he shall be forgiven; and the remainder shall be for the priest, as in the cereal offering.

14 And the Lord said to Moses,

15 If anyone commits a breach of faith and sins unwittingly in the holy things of the Lord, he shall bring his trespass *or* guilt offering to the Lord, a ram without blemish out of the flock, valued by you in shekels of silver, that is, the shekel of the sanctuary, for a trespass *or* guilt offering.

16 And he shall make restitution for what he has done amiss in the holy thing, and shall add a fifth to it, and give it to the priest; and the priest shall make atonement for him with the ram of the trespass *or* guilt offering, and he shall be forgiven.

17 If anyone sins and does any of the things the Lord has forbidden, though he was not aware of it, yet he is guilty and shall bear his iniquity. [Luke 12:48.]

18 He shall bring [to the priest] a ram without blemish out of the flock, estimated by you to the amount [of the trespass], for a guilt *or* trespass offering; and the priest shall make atonement for him for the error which he committed unknowingly, and he shall be forgiven.

19 It is a trespass *or* guilt offering; he is certainly guilty before the Lord.

6 AND THE Lord said to Moses,
2 If anyone sins and commits a trespass against the Lord and deals falsely with his neighbor in a matter of deposit given him to keep, or of bargain *or* pledge, or of robbery, or has oppressed his neighbor,

3 Or has found what was lost and lied about it, or swears falsely, in any of all the things which men do and sin in so doing,

4 Then if he has sinned and is guilty, he shall restore what he took by robbery, or what he secured by oppression *or* extortion, or what was delivered him to keep in trust, or the lost thing which he found,

5 Or anything about which he has sworn falsely; he shall not only restore it in full, but shall add to it one fifth more and give it to him to whom it belongs on the day of his trespass *or* guilt offering.

6 And he shall bring to the priest his trespass *or* guilt offering to the Lord, a ram without blemish out of the flock, valued by you to the amount of his trespass;

7 And the priest shall make atonement for him before the Lord, and he shall be forgiven for anything of all that he may have done by which he has become guilty.

8 And the Lord said to Moses,

9 Command Aaron and his sons, saying, This is the law of the burnt offering: The burnt offering shall remain on the altar all night until morning; the fire shall be kept burning on the altar.

10 And the priest shall put on his linen garment and put his linen breeches on his body, and take up the ashes of what the fire has consumed with the burnt offering on the altar and put them beside the altar.

11 And he shall put off his garments and put on other garments, and carry the ashes outside the camp to a clean place.

12 And the fire upon the altar shall be kept burning on it; it shall not be allowed to go out. The priest shall burn wood on it every morning and lay the burnt offering in order upon it and he shall burn on it the fat of the peace offerings.

13 The fire shall be burning continually upon the altar; it shall not go out.
14 And this is the law of the cereal offering: The sons of Aaron shall offer it before the Lord, in front of the altar.
15 One of them shall take his handful of the fine flour of the cereal offering, the oil of it, and all the frankincense which is upon the cereal offering, and burn it on the altar as the memorial of it, a sweet *and* satisfying fragrance to the Lord.
16 And the remainder of it shall Aaron and his sons eat, without leaven in a holy place; in the court of the Tent of Meeting shall they eat it. [I Cor. 9:13, 14.]
17 It shall not be baked with leaven. I have given it as their portion of My offerings made by fire; it is most holy, like the sin offering and the guilt offering.
18 Every male among the children of Aaron may eat of it, as his portion forever throughout your generations, from the Lord's offerings made by fire; whoever touches them shall [first] be holy (consecrated and ceremonially clean).
19 And the Lord said to Moses,
20 This is the offering which Aaron and his sons shall offer to the Lord on the day when one is anointed (and consecrated): the tenth of an ephah of fine flour for a regular cereal offering, half of it in the morning and half of it at night.
21 On a griddle *or* baking pan it shall be made with oil; and when it is fried you shall bring it in; in broken *and* fried pieces shall you offer the cereal offering as a sweet *and* satisfying odor to the Lord.
22 And the priest among Aaron's sons who is consecrated *and* anointed in his stead shall offer it; by a statute forever it shall be entirely burned to the Lord.
23 For every cereal offering of the priest shall be wholly burned, and not be eaten.
24 And the Lord said to Moses,
25 Say to Aaron and his sons: This is the law of the sin offering: In the place where the burnt offering is killed shall the sin offering be killed before the Lord; it is most holy.
26 The priest who offers it for sin shall eat it; in a sacred place shall it be eaten, in the court of the Tent of Meeting.
27 Whoever *or* whatever touches its flesh shall [first] be dedicated and made clean, and when any of its blood is sprinkled on a garment, you shall wash that garment in a place set apart to God's worship.
28 But the earthen vessel in which it is boiled shall be broken, and if it is boiled in a bronze vessel, that vessel shall be scoured and rinsed in water.
29 Every male among the priests may eat of this offering; it is most holy.
30 But no sin offering shall be eaten of which any of the blood is brought into the Tent of Meeting to make atonement in the Holy Place; it shall be [wholly] burned with fire. [Heb. 13:11-13.]

7 THIS IS the law of the guilt *or* trespass offering; it is most holy *or* sacred:
2 In the place where they kill the burnt offering shall they kill the guilt *or* trespass offering; the blood of it shall the priest dash against the altar round about.
3 And he shall offer all its fat, the fat tail and the fat that covers the entrails,
4 And the two kidneys and the fat that is on them at the loins, and the lobe *or* appendage of the liver, which he shall take away with the kidneys.
5 And the priest shall burn them on the altar for an offering made by fire to the Lord; it is a guilt *or* trespass offering.

6 Every male among the priests may eat of it; it shall be eaten in a sacred place; it is most holy.

7 As is the sin offering, so is the guilt *or* trespass offering; there is one law for them: the priest who makes atonement with it shall have it.

8 And the priest who offers any man's burnt offering, that priest shall have for himself the hide of the burnt offering which he has offered.

9 And every cereal offering that is baked in the oven and all that is prepared in a pan or on a griddle shall belong to the priest who offered it.

10 And every cereal offering, mixed with oil or dry, all the sons of Aaron may have, one as well as another.

11 And this is the law of the sacrifice of peace offerings which shall be offered to the Lord:

12 If one offers it for a thanksgiving, then he shall offer with the thank offering unleavened cakes mixed with oil, and unleavened wafers spread with oil, and cakes of fine flour mixed with oil.

13 With cakes of leavened bread he shall offer his sacrifice of thanksgiving with the sacrifice of his peace offerings.

14 And of it he shall offer one cake from each offering as an offering to the Lord; it shall belong to the priest who dashes the blood of the peace offerings.

15 The flesh of the sacrifice of thanksgiving presented as a peace offering shall be eaten on the day that it is offered; none of it shall be left until morning.

16 But if the sacrifice of the worshiper's offering is a vow or a freewill offering, it shall be eaten the same day that he offers his sacrifice, and on the morrow that which remains of it shall be eaten;

17 But the remainder of the flesh of the sacrifice on the third day shall be [wholly] burned with fire.

putting the Word to work

Throughout the book of Leviticus, we read about the sacrifices required to atone for sin. Aren't you thankful that God sent His Son, Jesus, to fulfill all of the laws enumerated in the Old Testament and to be the once-and-for-all, perfect sacrifice for our sins? Tell Him today how grateful you are.

18 If any of the flesh of the sacrifice of his peace offerings be eaten at all on the third day, then the one who brought it shall not be credited with it; it shall not be accepted. It shall be an abomination *and* an abhorred thing; the one who eats of it shall bear his iniquity *and* answer for it.

19 The flesh that comes in contact with anything that is not clean shall not be eaten; it shall be burned with fire. As for the meat, everyone who is clean [ceremonially] may eat of it.

20 But the one who eats of the flesh of the sacrifice of peace offerings that belong to the Lord when he is [ceremonially] unclean, that person shall be cut off from his people [deprived of the privileges of association with them].

21 And if anyone touches any unclean thing—the uncleanness of man or an unclean beast or any unclean abomination—and then eats of the flesh of the sacrifice of the Lord's peace offerings, that person shall be cut off from his people.

22 And the Lord said to Moses,

23 Say to the Israelites, You shall eat no kind of fat, of ox, or sheep, or goat.

24 The fat of the beast that dies of itself and the fat of one that is torn with beasts may be put to any other use, but under no circumstances are you to eat of it.

25 For whoever eats the fat of the beast from which men offer an offering made by fire to the Lord, that person shall be cut off from his people.

26 Moreover, you shall eat no blood of any kind, whether of bird or of beast, in any of your dwellings.
27 Whoever eats any kind of blood, that person shall be cut off from his people.
28 And the Lord said to Moses,
29 Tell the Israelites, He who offers the sacrifice of his peace offerings to the Lord shall bring his offering to the Lord; from the sacrifice of his peace offerings
30 He shall bring with his own hands the offerings made by fire to the Lord; he shall bring the fat with the breast, that the breast may be waved as a wave offering before the Lord.
31 The priest shall burn the fat on the altar, but the breast shall be for Aaron and his sons.
32 And the right thigh you shall give to the priest for an offering from the sacrifices of your peace offerings.
33 The son of Aaron who offers the blood of the peace offerings and the fat shall have the right thigh for his portion.
34 For I have taken the breast that was waved and the thigh that was offered from the Israelites, out of the sacrifices of their peace offerings, and have given them to Aaron the priest and to his sons as their perpetual due from the Israelites.
35 This is the anointing portion of Aaron and his sons out of the offerings to the Lord made by fire on the day when they were presented to minister to the Lord in the priest's office.
36 The Lord commanded this to be given them of the Israelites on the day when they were anointed. It is their portion perpetually throughout their generations.
37 This is the law of the burnt offering, the cereal offering, the sin offering, the guilt or trespass offering, the consecration offering, and the sacrifice of peace offerings,
38 Which the Lord ordered Moses on

Mount Sinai on the day He commanded the Israelites to offer their sacrifices to the Lord, in the Wilderness of Sinai.

8 AND THE Lord said to Moses,
2 Take Aaron and his sons with him, and the garments [symbols of their office], and the anointing oil, and the bull of the sin offering, and the two rams, and the basket of unleavened bread;
3 And assemble all the congregation at the door of the Tent of Meeting.
4 Moses did as the Lord commanded him, and the congregation was assembled at the door of the Tent of Meeting.
5 Moses told the congregation, This is what the Lord has commanded to be done.
6 Moses brought Aaron and his sons and washed them with water.
7 He put on Aaron the long under-tunic, girded him with the long sash, clothed him with the robe, put the ephod (an upper vestment) upon him, and girded him with the skillfully woven cords attached to the ephod, binding it to him.
8 And Moses put upon Aaron the breastplate; also he put in the breastplate the Urim and the Thummim [articles upon which the high priest put his hand when seeking the divine will concerning the nation].
9 And he put the turban or miter on his head; on it, in front, Moses put the shining gold plate, the holy diadem, as the Lord commanded him.
10 And Moses took the anointing oil and anointed the tabernacle and all that was in it, and consecrated them.
11 And he sprinkled some of the oil on the altar seven times and anointed the altar and all its utensils, and the laver and its base, to consecrate them.
12 And he poured some of the anointing oil upon Aaron's head and anointed him to consecrate him.

why the ceremony?

In Leviticus 8:1–30, God detailed to Moses the ritual required to consecrate Aaron and his sons to serve the Lord as priests in His sanctuary, the Tent of Meeting. The meaningful ceremony these priests went through so many centuries ago is filled with significance for us today.

Note in Leviticus 8:23 that Moses put ram's blood on the priests' right ears, the thumbs of their right hands, and the great toes of their right feet. Leviticus 8:30 tells us Moses also sprinkled anointing oil and blood from the altar upon Aaron and his garments and upon his sons and their garments in order to sanctify them and make them holy (see also Exodus 29:20, 21).

The significance of God's instruction to Moses to put the blood on the right side of the body is that in the Bible, the right side represents power. The ear was anointed so the priest would hear clearly and not be deceived, the thumb so that what he laid his hand to do would be right and blessed, and the right toe so everywhere he went would be holy and sanctified.

I believe this ceremony is a physical picture of our spiritual sanctification as priests unto the Lord today (see Revelation 1:5, 6). The shedding of Jesus' blood for our sin sanctifies those it covers; the anointing of the Holy Spirit, represented by the oil, is poured out to empower for service and good works those who are made righteous by the blood of Jesus. We can hear, take action, and go in directions that are safe and divinely led. Just as Aaron and his sons were set apart for God's use, we believers are also set apart for holy use.

Ask God to give you ears that hear what He wants to say, not just what you want to hear. Ask for consecrated ears that are anointed to hear His voice with clear discernment and without the interference of fleshly desires. Ask Him to sanctify your hands to do right and lead your feet to walk in the right path.

13 And Moses brought Aaron's sons and put undertunics on them and girded them with sashes and wound turbans on them, as the Lord commanded Moses.
14 Then he brought the bull of the sin offering, and Aaron and his sons laid their hands on the head of the bull of the sin offering.
15 Moses killed it and took the blood and put it on the horns of the altar round about with his finger and poured the blood at the base of the altar and purified and consecrated the altar to make atonement for it.

16 He took all the fat that was on the entrails, and the lobe of the liver, and the two kidneys with their fat, and Moses burned them on the altar.
17 But the bull [the sin offering] and its hide, its flesh, and its dung he burned with fire outside the camp, as the Lord commanded Moses.
18 He brought the ram for the burnt offering, and Aaron and his sons laid their hands on the head of the ram.
19 And Moses killed it and dashed the blood upon the altar round about.
20 He cut the ram into pieces and

Moses burned the head, the pieces, and the fat.

21 And he washed the entrails and the legs in water; then Moses burned the whole ram on the altar; it was a burnt sacrifice, for a sweet *and* satisfying fragrance, an offering made by fire to the Lord, as the Lord commanded Moses.

22 And he brought the other ram, the ram of consecration *and* ordination, and Aaron and his sons laid their hands upon the head of the ram.

23 And Moses killed it and took some of its blood and put it on the tip of Aaron's right ear, and on the thumb of his right hand, and on the great toe of his right foot.

24 And he brought Aaron's sons and Moses put some of the blood on the tips of their right ears, and the thumbs of their right hands, and the great toes of their right feet; and Moses dashed the blood upon the altar round about.

25 And he took the fat, the fat tail, all the fat that was on the entrails, the lobe of the liver, and the two kidneys and their fat, and the right thigh;

26 And out of the basket of unleavened bread, that was before the Lord, he took one unleavened cake, a cake of oiled bread, and one wafer and put them on the fat and on the right thigh;

27 And he put all these in Aaron's hands and his sons' hands and waved them for a wave offering before the Lord.

28 Then Moses took these things from their hands and burned them on the altar with the burnt offering as an ordination offering, for a sweet *and* satisfying fragrance, an offering made by fire to the Lord.

29 And Moses took the breast and waved it for a wave offering before the Lord; for of the ram of consecration *and* ordination it was Moses' portion, as the Lord commanded Moses.

30 And Moses took some of the anointing oil and some of the blood which was on the altar and sprinkled it on Aaron and his garments, and upon his sons and their garments also; so Moses consecrated Aaron and his garments, and his sons and his sons' garments.

31 And Moses said to Aaron and his sons, Boil the flesh at the door of the Tent of Meeting and there eat it with the bread that is in the basket of consecration *and* ordination, as I commanded, saying, Aaron and his sons shall eat it.

32 And what remains of the flesh and of the bread you shall burn with fire.

33 And you shall not go out of the door of the Tent of Meeting for seven days, until the days of your consecration *and* ordination are ended; for it will take seven days to consecrate *and* ordain you.

34 As has been done this day, so the Lord has commanded to do for your atonement.

35 At the door of the Tent of Meeting you shall remain day and night for seven days, ᵉdoing what the Lord has charged you to do, that you die not; for so I am commanded.

36 So Aaron and his sons did all the things which the Lord commanded through Moses.

---

e We have, every one of us, a charge to keep, an eternal God to glorify, an immortal soul to provide for, needful duty to be done, our generation to serve; and it must be our daily care to keep this charge, for it is the charge of the Lord our Master (Matthew Henry, *Commentary on the Holy Bible*). The laws contained in this book, for the most part ceremonial, had an important spiritual bearing, the study of which is highly instructive (Robert Jamieson, A.R. Fausset and David Brown, *A Commentary*). The Scripture references recorded within the text are intended to be a guide to its spiritual implications.

9 ON THE eighth day Moses called Aaron and his sons and the elders of Israel;

2 And he said to Aaron, Take a young calf for a sin offering and a ram for a burnt offering, [each] without blemish, and offer them before the Lord. [Heb. 10:10-12.]

3 And say to the Israelites, Take a male goat for a sin offering, and a calf and a lamb, both a year old, without blemish, for a burnt offering,

4 Also a bull and a ram for peace offerings to sacrifice before the Lord, and a cereal offering mixed with oil, for today the Lord will appear to you.

5 They brought before the Tent of Meeting what Moses [had] commanded; all the congregation drew near and stood before the Lord.

6 And Moses said, This is the thing which the Lord commanded you to do, and the glory of the Lord will appear to you.

7 And Moses said to Aaron, Draw near to the altar and offer your sin offering and your burnt offering and make atonement for yourself and for the people; and offer the offering of the people and make atonement for them, as the Lord commanded. [Heb. 5:1-5; 7:27.]

8 So Aaron drew near to the altar and killed the calf of the sin offering, which was designated for himself.

9 The sons of Aaron presented the blood to him; he dipped his finger in the blood and put it on the horns of the altar and poured out the blood at the altar's base;

10 But the fat, the kidneys, and the lobe of the liver from the sin offering he burned on the altar, as the Lord had commanded Moses.

11 And the flesh and the hide Aaron burned with fire outside the camp.

12 He killed the burnt offering, and Aaron's sons delivered to him the blood, which he dashed round about upon the altar.

13 And they brought the burnt offering to him piece by piece, and the head, and Aaron burned them upon the altar.

14 And he washed the entrails and the legs and burned them with the burnt offering on the altar.

15 Then Aaron presented the people's offering, and took the goat of the sin offering which was for the people and killed it and offered it for sin as he did the first sin offering. [Heb. 2:16, 17.]

16 And he presented the burnt offering and offered it according to the ordinance.

17 And Aaron presented the cereal offering and took a handful of it and burned it on the altar in addition to the burnt offering of the morning.

18 He also killed the bull and the ram, the sacrifice of peace offerings, for the people; and Aaron's sons presented to him the blood, which he dashed upon the altar round about,

19 And the fat of the bull and of the ram, the fat tail and that which covers the entrails, and the kidneys, and the lobe of the liver.

20 And they put the fat upon the breasts, and Aaron burned the fat upon the altar;

21 But the breasts and the right thigh Aaron waved for a wave offering before the Lord, as Moses commanded.

22 Then Aaron lifted his hands toward the people and blessed them, and came down [from the altar] after offering the sin offering, the burnt offering, and the peace offerings.

23 Moses and Aaron went into the Tent of Meeting, and when they came out they blessed the people, and the glory of the Lord [the Shekinah cloud] appeared to all the people [as promised]. [Lev. 9:6.]

24 Then there came a fire out from before the Lord and consumed the burnt offering and the fat on the altar; and when all the people saw it, they shouted and fell on their faces.

10

AND NADAB and Abihu, the sons of Aaron, each took his censer and put fire in it, and put incense on it, and offered strange *and* unholy fire before the Lord, as He had not commanded them.

2 And there came forth fire from before the Lord and killed them, and they died before the Lord.

3 Then Moses said to Aaron, This is what the Lord meant when He said, I f[and My will, not their own] will be acknowledged as hallowed by those who come near Me, and before all the people I will be honored. And Aaron said nothing.

4 Moses called Mishael and Elzaphan, sons of Uzziel uncle of Aaron, and said to them, Come near, carry your brethren from before the sanctuary out of the camp.

5 So they drew near and carried them in their undertunics [stripped of their priestly vestments] out of the camp, as Moses had said.

6 And Moses said to Aaron and Eleazar and Ithamar, his sons [the father and brothers of the two priests whom God had slain for offering false fire], Do not uncover your heads *or* let your hair go loose or tear your clothes, lest you die [also] and lest God's wrath should come upon all the congregation; but let your brethren, the whole house of Israel, bewail the burning which the Lord has kindled.

7 And you shall not go out from the door of the Tent of Meeting, lest you die, for the Lord's anointing oil is upon you. And they did according to Moses' word.

8 And the Lord said to Aaron,

9 Do not drink wine or strong drink, you or your sons, when you go into the Tent of Meeting, lest you die; it shall be a statute forever in all your generations.

10 You shall make a distinction *and* recognize a difference between the holy and the common *or* unholy, and between the unclean and the clean;

speak the Word

God, I declare that You are holy and that You are honored in my life.
ADAPTED FROM LEVITICUS **10:3**

God, I pray that You will help me distinguish between what is holy and what is unholy, between what is clean and what is unclean, because I want to live a pure, holy life before You.
ADAPTED FROM LEVITICUS **10:10**

f Perhaps few believers have ever identified themselves with Nadab and Abihu, and yet few, if any, of us have not done exactly what they did in principle. Their sin, which God took so seriously and which proved fatal to them, was not a mere matter of failing to obey the letter of God's law for priests. Their inexcusable folly was in trying to please the Lord **their** way instead of **His** way. Who of us cannot recognize himself as the offerer of this prayer, with only the details lacking: "O Lord, make me rich! Then I will make large donations to Your interests!" Yet our very poverty may be the means to the end which He has in love and wisdom planned for us, the ultimate purpose of our creation, perhaps, which substitution of our will for His will would utterly defeat. No wonder God removed Nadab and Abihu from the earth! They, like ourselves, had acted like the child of a great painter who attempted to work on his father's priceless canvas instead of on the tablet assigned to him. They, like the child, were banished from the father's presence. And every believer does well to recognize the importance of being entirely surrendered to "God's will; nothing more; nothing less; nothing else; at any cost." And that does not mean first making an unholy alliance in marriage, or in business, or in thought, and then adjusting it to God's will. Remember Nadab and Abihu, who "offered strange *and* unholy fire before the Lord." It does not pay.

11 And you are to teach the Israelites all the statutes which the Lord has spoken to them by Moses.

12 And Moses said to Aaron and to Eleazar and Ithamar, his sons who were left, Take the cereal offering that remains of the offerings of the Lord made by fire and eat it without leaven beside the altar, for it is most holy.

13 You shall eat it in a sacred place, because it is your due and your sons' due, from the offerings made by fire to the Lord; for so I am commanded.

14 But the breast that is waved and the thigh that is offered you shall eat in a clean place, you and your sons and daughters with you; for they are your due and your sons' due, given out of the sacrifices of the peace offerings of the Israelites.

15 The thigh that is offered and the breast that is waved they shall bring with the offerings made by fire of the fat, to wave for a wave offering before the Lord; and it shall be yours and your sons' with you as a portion *or* due perpetually, as the Lord has commanded.

16 And Moses diligently tried to find [what had become of] the goat [that had been offered] for the sin offering, and behold, it was burned up [as waste]! And he was angry with Eleazar and Ithamar, the sons of Aaron who were left alive, and said,

17 Why have you not eaten the sin offering in the Holy Place? It is most holy; and God has given it to you to bear *and* take away the iniquity of the

congregation, to make atonement for them before the Lord.

18 Behold, the blood of it was not brought within the Holy Place; you should indeed have eaten [the flesh of it] in the Holy Place, as I commanded.

19 But Aaron said to Moses, Behold, this very day in which they have [obediently] offered their sin offering and their burnt offering before the Lord, such [terrible calamities] have befallen me [and them]! If I [and they] had eaten the most holy sin offering today [humbled as we have been by the sin of our kinsmen and God's judgment upon them], would it have been acceptable in the sight of the Lord? [Hos. 9:4.]

20 And when Moses heard that, he was pacified.

11

AND THE Lord said to Moses and Aaron,

2 Say to the Israelites: These are the animals ᵍwhich you may eat among all the beasts that are on the earth. [Mark 7:15-19.]

putting the Word to work

Leviticus contains much instruction on eating. Do you have any eating habits that you know are unwise or displeasing to the Lord? Ask Him to help you eat healthfully!

3 Whatever parts the hoof and is cloven-footed and chews the cud, any of these animals you may eat.

g At first thought the laws given here seem only to have been made obsolete by Jesus. He taught that it is not what goes into the mouth but what comes out of it that defiles a man (Matt. 15:17-20), and Paul said that when the complete and perfect came, the incomplete and imperfect would become void and superseded (I Cor. 13:9, 10), for "there is nothing unclean of itself" (Rom. 14:14 KJV). But while all these specific laws have become void, we must not lose sight of the fact that they are "superseded" by the underlying spiritual principle, which is just as binding. Christ's teaching relates to the whole area of our living, including our eating and drinking, and is dominated by the principle, "Whatever you may do, do all for the honor *and* glory of God" (I Cor. 10:31). We do well to remember that it was Jesus Christ Himself who said, "Do not think that I have come to do away with *or* undo the Law . . .; I have come not to do away with *or* undo but to complete *and* fulfill" it (Matt. 5:17).

please God with your eating

Leviticus 11 sets forth all kinds of guidelines about what the Israelites could and could not eat. Over the years, I have needed God's help in the area of eating, just as the Israelites did. I would like to share ten tips I have learned that have enabled me to eat wisely, healthfully, and in a way that pleases God:

1. Eat when you are truly hungry and not just because someone offers you food or because it is sitting in front of you.

2. If you listen carefully to your body, it will let you know what it needs and wants. Sometimes I actually crave vegetables; at other times I want fish or red meat. That is my body letting me know what it needs. There are times I want something sweet, and it is not wrong to eat sweets if we do so in moderation. Eating a variety of foods is one of the keys to good nutrition.

3. Enjoy what you eat.

4. Eat sitting down. People tend to eat more than they realize when they are standing while they eat.

5. Eat slowly. After about twenty minutes of eating, your brain receives a signal that you are full.

6. Stop eating when you are no longer hungry. Take small portions, planning to have another portion if you want it. Many times, the first small portion will satisfy you.

7. Eat small portions more frequently rather than one or two huge meals a day. Anything your body cannot metabolize and use is stored as fat. Keeping your metabolism working by eating several small meals a day or healthy snacks between meals will actually help you stay fit and trim.

8. Do not make provision for "eating binges" by keeping your refrigerator and pantry full of high-calorie, high-fat, low-quality foods that you know you should not eat.

9. Stay focused on things you need to do and keep your mind off food.

10. Eat necessary food. We all consume many calories that are truly unnecessary every day—a bite of this or that, the piece of bread and butter before the meal, the second helping when in reality we are already getting full. Ask yourself if you really need something before you just mindlessly put it in your mouth.

I think it is amazing that the Bible tells us what to eat. God cares about every area of our lives, not just the spiritual parts. He wants us to be healthy, filled with energy, and looking our best!

4 Nevertheless these you shall not eat of those that chew the cud or divide the hoof: the camel, because it chews the cud but does not divide the hoof; it is unclean to you.

5 And the coney *or* rock badger, because it chews the cud but does not divide the hoof; it is unclean to you.

6 And the hare, because it chews the cud but does not divide the hoof; it is unclean to you.

7 And the swine, because it divides the hoof and is cloven-footed but does not chew the cud; it is unclean to you.

8 Of their flesh you shall not eat, and their carcasses you shall not touch; they are unclean to you.

9 These you may eat of all that are in the waters: whatever has fins and scales in the waters, in the seas, and in the rivers, these you may eat;

10 But all that have not fins and scales in the seas and in the rivers, of all the creeping things in the waters, and of all the living creatures which are in the waters, they are [to be considered] an abomination and abhorrence to you. [I Cor. 8:8-13.]

11 They shall continue to be an abomination to you; you shall not eat of their flesh, but you shall detest their carcasses.

12 Everything in the waters that has not fins or scales shall be abhorrent *and* detestable to you.

13 These you shall have in abomination among the birds; they shall not be eaten, for they are detestable: the eagle, the ossifrage, the ospray,

14 The kite, the whole species of falcon,

15 Every kind of raven,

16 The ostrich, the nighthawk, the sea gull, every species of hawk,

17 The owl, the cormorant, the ibis,

18 The swan, the pelican, the vulture,

19 The stork, all kinds of heron, the hoopoe, and the bat.

20 All winged insects that go upon all fours are to be an abomination to you;

21 Yet of all winged insects that go upon all fours you may eat those which have legs above their feet with which to leap on the ground.

22 Of these you may eat: the whole species of locust, of bald locust, of cricket, and of grasshopper. [Matt. 3:4.]

23 But all other winged insects which have four feet shall be detestable to you.

24 And by [contact with] these you shall become unclean; whoever touches the carcass of them shall be unclean until the evening,

25 And whoever carries any part of their carcass shall wash his clothes and be unclean until the evening.

26 Every beast which parts the hoof but is not cloven-footed or does not chew the cud is unclean to you; everyone who touches them shall be unclean.

27 And all that go on their paws, among all kinds of four-footed beasts, are unclean to you; whoever touches their carcass shall be unclean until the evening,

28 And he who carries their carcass shall wash his clothes and be unclean until the evening; they are unclean to you.

29 These also are unclean to you among the creeping things [that multiply greatly] *and* creep upon the ground: the weasel, the mouse, any kind of great lizard,

30 The gecko, the land crocodile, the lizard, the sand lizard, and the chameleon.

31 These are unclean to you among all that creep; whoever touches them when they are dead shall be unclean until the evening.

32 And upon whatever they may fall when they are dead, it shall be unclean, whether it is an article of wood or clothing or skin (bottle) or sack, any vessel in which work is done; it must be put in water, and it shall be unclean until the evening; so it shall be cleansed.

33 And every earthen vessel into which any of these [creeping things] falls, whatever may be in it shall be unclean, and you shall break the vessel. **34** Of all the food [in one of these unclean vessels] which may be eaten, that on which such water comes shall be unclean, and all drink that may be drunk from every such vessel shall be unclean. **35** And everything upon which any part of their carcass falls shall be unclean; whether an oven, *or* pan with a lid, or hearth for pots, it shall be broken in pieces; they are unclean, and shall be unclean to you. **36** Yet a spring or a cistern *or* reservoir of water shall be clean; but whoever touches their carcass shall be unclean. **37** If a part of their carcass falls on seed which is to be sown, it shall be clean; **38** But if any water be put on the seed and any part of their carcass falls on it, it shall be unclean to you. **39** If any animal of which you may eat dies [unslaughtered], he who touches its carcass shall be unclean until the evening. **40** And he who eats of its carcass [ignorantly] shall wash his clothes, and be unclean until the evening; he also who carries its carcass shall wash his clothes, and be unclean until the evening. **41** And everything that creeps on the ground *and* [multiplies in] swarms shall be an abomination; it shall not be eaten. **42** Whatever goes on its belly, and whatever goes on all fours, or whatever has more [than four] feet among all things that creep on the ground *and* swarm you shall not eat; for they are detestable.

43 You shall not make yourselves loathsome *and* abominable [by eating] any swarming thing that [multiplies by] swarms, neither shall you make yourselves unclean with them, that you should be defiled by them. **44** For I am the Lord your God; so consecrate yourselves and be holy, for I am holy; neither defile yourselves with any manner of thing that multiplies in large numbers *or* swarms. [I Thess. 4:7, 8.] **45** For I am the Lord Who brought you up out of the land of Egypt to be your God; therefore you shall be holy, for I am holy. [I Pet. 1:14-16.] **46** This is the law of the beast, and of the bird, and of every living creature that moves in the waters, and creeps on the earth *and* multiplies in large numbers, **47** To make a difference (a distinction) between the unclean and the clean, and between the animal that may be eaten and the animal that may not be eaten.

12 AND THE Lord said to Moses, **2** Say to the Israelites, If a woman conceives and bears a male child, she shall be unclean seven days, unclean as during her monthly discomfort. **3** And on the eighth day the child shall be circumcised. **4** Then she shall remain [separated] thirty-three days to be purified

speak the Word

[from her loss] of blood; she shall touch no hallowed thing nor come into the [court of the] sanctuary until the days of her purifying are over.

5 But if the child she bears is a girl, then she shall be unclean two weeks, as in her periodic impurity, and she shall remain separated sixty-six days to be purified [from her loss] of blood.

6 When the days of her purifying are completed, whether for a son or for a daughter, she shall bring a lamb a year old for a burnt offering and a young pigeon or a turtledove for a sin offering to the door of the Tent of Meeting to the priest;

7 And he shall offer it before the Lord and make atonement for her, and she shall be cleansed from the flow of her blood. This is the law for her who has borne a male or a female child.

8 If she is unable to bring a lamb [for lack of means] then she shall bring two turtledoves or young pigeons, one for a burnt offering, the other for a sin offering; the priest shall make atonement for her, and she shall be clean. [Luke 2:22, 24.]

13 AND THE Lord said to Moses and Aaron,

2 When a man has a swelling on his skin, a scab, or a bright spot, and it becomes the disease of [h]leprosy in his skin, then he shall be brought to the priest, to Aaron or one of his sons.

3 The priest shall look at the diseased spot on his skin, and if the hair in it has turned white and the disease appears depressed *and* deeper than his skin, it is a leprous disease; and the priest shall examine him, and pronounce him unclean.

4 If the bright spot is white on his skin, not depressed, and the hair on it not turned white, the priest shall quarantine the person *or* bind up the spot for seven days.

5 And the priest shall examine him on the seventh day, and if the disease in his estimation is at a standstill *and* has not spread in the skin, then the priest shall quarantine the person *or* bind up the spot seven more days.

6 And the priest shall examine him again the seventh day, and if the diseased part has a more normal color and the disease has not spread in the skin, the priest shall pronounce him clean; it is only an eruption *or* a scab; and he shall wash his clothes and be clean.

7 But if the eruption *or* scab spreads farther in the skin after he has shown himself to the priest for his cleansing, he shall be seen by the priest again.

8 If the priest sees that the eruption *or* scab is spreading in the skin, then he shall pronounce him unclean; it is leprosy.

9 When the disease of leprosy is in a man, he shall be brought to the priest;

10 And the priest shall examine him, and if there is a white swelling in the skin and the hair on it has turned white and there is quick raw flesh in the swelling,

11 It is a chronic leprosy in the skin of his body, and the priest shall pronounce him unclean; he shall not bind the spot up, for he is unclean.

h Authorities are generally agreed that there certainly was true leprosy as it is known today in the Near East in New Testament times. But from the details of the disease in Lev. 13, it is believed that other very serious skin disorders were also included under the heading of "leprosy" in earlier times. Leprosy in the Old Testament, therefore, is not to be considered as confined to the traits by which it is known today, but rather defined by the symptoms, the treatment, and the history of individual cases as recorded in Leviticus and elsewhere. That it was worse than death is implied by the words of Aaron when his sister Miriam was stricken with it: "Alas, my lord [Moses], . . . Let her not be as one dead, of whom the flesh is half consumed when he cometh out of his mother's womb" (Num. 12:11, 12 KJV).

12 But if [supposed] leprosy breaks out in the skin, and it covers all the skin of him who has the disease from head to foot, wherever the priest looks,
13 The priest shall examine him; if the [supposed] leprosy covers all his body, he shall pronounce him clean of the disease; it is all turned white, and he is clean.
14 But when the raw flesh appears on him, he shall be unclean.
15 And the priest shall examine the raw flesh and pronounce him unclean; for the raw flesh is unclean; it is leprosy.
16 But if the raw flesh turns again and becomes white, he shall come to the priest,
17 And the priest shall examine him, and if the diseased part is turned to white again, then the priest shall pronounce him clean who had the disease; he is clean.
18 And when there is in the skin of the body [the scar of] a boil that is healed,
19 And in the place of the boil there is a white swelling or a bright spot, reddish white, and it is shown to the priest,
20 And if when the priest examines it it looks lower than the skin and the hair on it is turned white, the priest shall pronounce him unclean; it is the disease of leprosy; it has broken out in the boil.
21 But if the priest examines it and finds no white hair in it and it is not lower than the skin but appears darker, then the priest shall bind it up for seven days.
22 If it spreads in the skin, [he] shall pronounce him unclean; it is diseased.
23 But if the bright spot does not spread, it is the scar of the boil, and the priest shall pronounce him clean.
24 Or if there is any flesh in the skin of which there is a burn by fire and the quick flesh of the burn becomes a bright spot, reddish white or white,

25 Then the priest shall examine it, and if the hair in the bright spot is turned white, and it appears deeper than the skin, it is leprosy broken out in the burn. Therefore the priest shall pronounce him unclean; it is the disease of leprosy.
26 But if the priest examines it and there is no white hair in the bright spot and it is not lower than the rest of the skin but is darker, then the priest shall bind it up for seven days.
27 And the priest shall examine him on the seventh day; if it is spreading in the skin, then the priest shall pronounce him unclean; it is leprosy.
28 But if the bright spot has not spread but is darker, it is a swelling from the burn, and the priest shall pronounce him clean; for it is the scar of the burn.
29 When a man or woman has a disease upon the head or in the beard,
30 The priest shall examine the diseased place; if it appears to be deeper than the skin, with yellow, thin hair in it, the priest shall pronounce him unclean; it is a mangelike leprosy of the head or beard.
31 If the priest examines the spot infected by the mangelike disease, and it does not appear deeper than the skin and there is no black hair in it, the priest shall bind up the spot for seven days.
32 On the seventh day the priest shall examine the diseased spot; if the mange has not spread and has no yellow hair in it and does not look deeper than the skin,
33 Then the patient shall be shaved, except the mangelike spot; and the priest shall bind up the spot seven days more.
34 On the seventh day the priest shall look at the mangelike spot; if the mange has not spread and looks no deeper than the skin, he shall pronounce the patient clean; he shall wash his clothes and be clean.

35 But if the mangelike spot spreads in the skin after his cleansing,

36 Then the priest shall examine him, and if the mangelike spot is spread in the skin, the priest need not look for the yellow hair; the patient is unclean.

37 But if in his estimation the mange is at a standstill and has black hair in it, the mangelike disease is healed; he is clean; the priest shall pronounce him clean.

38 When a man or a woman has on the skin bright spots, even white bright spots,

39 Then the priest shall look, and if the bright spots in the skin are a dull white, it is a harmless eruption; he is clean.

40 If a man's hair has fallen from his head, he is bald, but he is clean.

41 And if his hair has fallen out from the front of his head, he has baldness of the forehead, but he is clean.

42 But if there is on the bald head or forehead a reddish white diseased spot, it is leprosy breaking out on his baldness.

43 Then the priest shall examine him, and if the diseased swelling is reddish white on his bald head or forehead like the appearance of leprosy in the skin of the body,

44 He is a leprous man; he is unclean; the priest shall surely pronounce him unclean; his disease is on his head.

45 And the leper's clothes shall be rent, and the hair of his head shall hang loose, and he shall cover his upper lip and cry, Unclean, unclean!

46 He shall remain unclean as long as the disease is in him; he is unclean; he shall live alone [and] his dwelling shall be outside the camp.

47 The garment also that the disease of leprosy [symbolic of sin] is in, whether a wool or a linen garment, [Jude 23; Rev. 3:4.]

48 Whether it be in woven or knitted stuff *or* in the warp or woof of linen or of wool, or in a skin or anything made of skin,

49 If the disease is greenish or reddish in the garment, or in a skin or in the warp or woof or in anything made of skin, it is the plague of leprosy; show it to the priest.

50 The priest shall examine the diseased article and shut it up for seven days.

51 He shall examine the disease on the seventh day; if [it] is spread in the garment, or in the article, whatever service it may be used for, the disease is a rotting *or* corroding leprosy; it is unclean.

52 He shall burn the garment, whether diseased in warp or woof, in wool or linen, or anything made of skin; for it is a rotting *or* corroding leprosy, to be burned in the fire.

53 But if the priest finds the disease has not spread in the garment, in the warp or the woof, or in anything made of skin,

54 Then the priest shall command that they wash the thing in which the plague is, and he shall shut it up seven days more.

55 And the priest shall examine the diseased article after it has been washed, and if the diseased portion has not changed color, though the disease has not spread, it is unclean; you shall burn it in the fire; it is a rotting *or* corroding [disease], whether the leprous spot be inside or outside.

56 If the priest looks and the diseased portion is less noticeable after it is washed, he shall tear it out of the garment, or the skin (leather), or out of the warp or woof.

57 If it appears still in the garment, either in the warp or in the woof, or in anything made of skin, it is spreading; you shall burn the diseased part with fire.

58 But the garment, or the woven or knitted stuff *or* warp or woof, or anything made of skin from which the disease departs when you have washed it, shall then be washed a second time, and be clean.

59 This is the law for a leprous disease in a garment of wool or linen, either in the warp or woof, or in anything made of skin, to pronounce it clean or unclean.

14 AND THE Lord said to Moses, **2** This shall be the law of the leper on the day when he is to be pronounced clean: he shall be brought to the priest [at a meeting place outside the camp];

3 The priest shall go out of the camp [to meet him]; and [he] shall examine him, and if the disease is healed in the leper,

4 Then the priest shall command to take for him who is to be cleansed two living clean birds and cedar wood and scarlet [material] and hyssop. [Heb. 9:19-22.]

5 And the priest shall command to kill one of the birds in an earthen vessel over fresh, running water.

6 As for the living bird, he shall take it, the cedar wood, and the scarlet [material], and the hyssop, and shall dip them and the living bird in the blood of the bird killed over the running water;

7 And he shall sprinkle [the blood] on him who is to be cleansed from the leprosy seven times and shall pronounce him clean, and shall let go the living bird into the open field. [Heb. 9:13-15.]

8 He who is to be cleansed shall wash his clothes, shave off all his hair, and bathe himself in water; and he shall be clean. After that he shall come into the camp, but stay outside his tent seven days.

9 But on the seventh day he shall shave all his hair off his head, his beard, his eyebrows, and his [body]; and he shall wash his clothes and bathe his body in water, and be clean.

10 On the eighth day he shall take two he-lambs without blemish and one ewe lamb a year old without blemish, and three-tenths of an ephah of fine flour for a cereal offering, mixed with oil, and one log of oil.

11 And the priest who cleanses him shall set the man who is to be cleansed and these things before the Lord at the door of the Tent of Meeting;

12 The priest shall take one of the male lambs and offer it for a guilt *or* trespass offering, and the log of oil, and wave them for a wave offering before the Lord.

13 He shall kill the lamb in the place where they kill the sin offering and the burnt offering, in the sacred place [the court of the tabernacle]; for as the sin offering is the priest's, so is the guilt *or* trespass offering; it is most holy;

14 And the priest shall take some of the blood of the guilt *or* trespass offering and put it on the tip of the right ear of him who is to be cleansed, and on the thumb of his right hand, and on the great toe of his right foot.

15 And the priest shall take some of the log of oil and pour it into the palm of his own left hand;

16 And the priest shall dip his right finger in the oil that is in his left hand and shall sprinkle some of the oil with his finger seven times before the Lord;

17 And of the rest of the oil that is in his hand shall the priest put some on the tip of the right ear of him who is to be cleansed, and on the thumb of his right hand, and on the great toe of his right foot, on the blood of the guilt *or* trespass offering [which he has previously placed in each of these places].

18 And the rest of the oil that is in the priest's hand he shall pour upon the head of him who is to be cleansed and make atonement for him before the Lord.

19 And the priest shall offer the sin offering and make atonement for him who is to be cleansed from his uncleanness, and afterward kill the burnt offering [victim].

20 And the priest shall offer the burnt offering and the cereal offering on the altar; and he shall make atonement for him, and he shall be clean.

21 If the cleansed leper is poor and cannot afford so much, he shall take one lamb for a guilt or trespass offering to be waved to make atonement for him, and one tenth of an ephah of fine flour mixed with oil for a cereal offering, and a log of oil,

22 And two turtledoves or two young pigeons, such as he can afford, one for a sin offering, the other for a burnt offering.

23 He shall bring them on the eighth day for his cleansing to the priest at the door of the Tent of Meeting, before the Lord.

24 And the priest shall take the lamb of the guilt or trespass offering, and the log of oil, and shall wave them for a wave offering before the Lord.

25 And he shall kill the lamb of the guilt or trespass offering, and the priest shall take some of the blood of the offering and put it on the tip of the right ear of him who is to be cleansed, and on the thumb of his right hand, and on the great toe of his right foot.

26 And the priest shall pour some of the oil into the palm of his own left hand,

27 And shall sprinkle with his right finger some of the oil that is in his left hand seven times before the Lord.

28 The priest shall put some of the oil in his hand on the tip of the right ear of the one to be cleansed, and on the thumb of his right hand, and on the great toe of his right foot, on the places where he has put the blood of the guilt offering.

29 The rest of the oil that is in the priest's hand he shall put on the head of the one to be cleansed, to make atonement for him before the Lord.

30 And he shall offer one of the turtledoves or of the young pigeons, such as he is able to get,

31 As he can afford, one for a sin offering and the other for a burnt offering, together with the cereal offering; and the priest shall make atonement for him who is to be cleansed before the Lord.

32 This is the law of him in whom is the plague of leprosy, who is not able to get what is required for his cleansing.

33 And the Lord said to Moses and Aaron,

34 When you have come into the land of Canaan, which I give to you for a possession, and I put the disease of leprosy in a house of the land of your possession,

35 Then he who owns the house shall come and tell the priest, It seems to me there is some sort of disease in my house.

36 Then the priest shall command that they empty the house before [he] goes in to examine the disease, so that all that is in the house may not be declared unclean; afterward [he] shall go in to see the house.

37 He shall examine the disease, and if it is in the walls of the house with depressed spots of dark green or dark red appearing beneath [the surface of] the wall,

38 Then the priest shall go out of the door and shut up the house seven days.

39 The priest shall come again on the seventh day and shall look; and if the disease has spread in the walls of the house,

40 He shall command that they take out the diseased stones and cast them into an unclean place outside the city.

41 He shall cause the house to be scraped within round about and the plaster or mortar that is scraped off to be emptied out in an unclean place outside the city.

42 And they shall put other stones in the place of those stones, and he shall plaster the house with fresh mortar.

43 If the disease returns, breaking out in the house after he has removed the stones and has scraped and plastered the house,

44 Then the priest shall come and look, and if the disease is spreading in the house, it is a rotting *or* corroding leprosy in the house; it is unclean.

45 He shall tear down the house—its stones and its timber and all the plaster *or* mortar of the house—and shall carry them forth out of the city to an unclean place.

46 Moreover, he who enters the house during the whole time that it is shut up shall be unclean until the evening.

47 And he who lies down or eats in the house shall wash his clothes.

48 But if the priest inspects it and the disease has not spread after the house was plastered, he shall pronounce the house clean, because the disease is healed.

49 He shall take to cleanse the house two birds, cedar wood, scarlet [material], and hyssop;

50 And he shall kill one of the birds in an earthen vessel over running water,

51 And he shall take the cedar wood, and the hyssop, and the scarlet [material], and the living bird, and dip them in the blood of the slain bird and in the running water, and sprinkle the house seven times.

52 And he shall cleanse the house with the blood of the bird, the running water, the living bird, the cedar wood, the hyssop, and the scarlet [material].

53 But he shall let the living bird go out of the city into the open field; so he shall make atonement for the house, and it shall be clean.

54 This is the law for all kinds of leprous diseases, and mangelike conditions,

55 For the leprosy of a garment or of a house,

56 And for a swelling or an eruption *or* a scab or a bright spot,

57 To teach when it is unclean and when it is clean. This is the law of leprosy.

15 AND THE Lord said to Moses and Aaron,

2 Say to the Israelites, When any man has a running discharge from his body, because of his discharge he is unclean.

3 This shall be [the law concerning] his uncleanness in his discharge: whether his body runs with his discharge or has stopped [running], it is uncleanness in him.

4 Every bed on which the one who has the discharge lies is unclean, and everything on which he sits shall be unclean.

5 Whoever touches that person's bed shall wash his clothes, and bathe himself in water, and be unclean until the evening.

6 And whoever sits on anything on which he who has the discharge has sat shall wash his clothes and bathe himself in water, and be unclean until the evening.

7 And he who touches the flesh of him who has the discharge shall wash his clothes and bathe himself in water, and be unclean until the evening.

8 And if he who has the discharge spits on him who is clean, then he shall wash his clothes and bathe himself in water, and be unclean until the evening.

9 And any saddle on which he who has the discharge rides shall be unclean.

10 Whoever touches anything that has been under him shall be unclean until evening; and he who carries those things shall wash his clothes and bathe himself in water, and be unclean until evening.

11 Whomever he who has the discharge touches without rinsing his hands in water shall wash his clothes and bathe himself in water, and be unclean until evening.

12 The earthen vessel that he with the discharge touches shall be broken, and every vessel of wood shall be rinsed in water.

13 When he who has a discharge is cleansed of it, he shall count seven days for his purification, then wash his clothes, bathe in running water, and be clean.

14 On the eighth day he shall take two turtledoves or two young pigeons and come before the Lord to the door of the Tent of Meeting and give them to the priest;

15 And the priest shall offer them, one for a sin offering and the other for a burnt offering; and [he] shall make atonement for the man before the Lord for his discharge.

16 And if any man has a discharge of semen, he shall wash all his body in water, and be unclean until evening.

17 And every garment and every skin on which the sperm comes shall be washed with water, and be unclean until evening.

18 The woman also with whom a man with emission of semen shall lie, they shall both bathe themselves in water, and be unclean until evening.

19 And if a woman has a discharge, her [regular] discharge of blood of her body, she shall be in her impurity *or* separation for seven days, and whoever touches her shall be unclean until evening.

20 And everything that she lies on in her separation shall be unclean; everything also that she sits on shall be unclean.

21 And whoever touches her bed shall wash his clothes and bathe himself in water, and be unclean until evening.

22 Whoever touches anything she sat on shall wash his clothes and bathe himself in water, and be unclean until evening.

23 And if her flow has stained her bed or anything on which she sat, when he touches it, he shall be unclean until evening.

24 And if any man lie with her and her impurity be upon him, he shall be unclean seven days; and every bed on which he lies shall be unclean.

25 And if a woman has an issue of blood for many days, not during the time of her separation, or if she has a discharge beyond the time of her [regular] impurity, all the days of the issue of her uncleanness she shall be as in the days of her impurity; she shall be unclean. [Matt. 9:20.]

26 Every bed on which she lies all the days of her discharge shall be as the bed of her impurity, and whatever she sits on shall be unclean, as in her impurity.

27 And whoever touches those things shall be unclean, and shall wash his clothes and bathe himself in water, and be unclean until evening.

28 But if she is cleansed of her discharge, then she shall wait seven days, and after that she shall be clean.

29 And on the eighth day she shall take two turtledoves or two young pigeons and bring them to the priest at the door of the Tent of Meeting;

30 He shall offer one for a sin offering and the other for a burnt offering; and he shall make atonement for her before the Lord for her unclean discharge.

31 Thus you shall separate the Israelites from their uncleanness, lest they die in their uncleanness by defiling My tabernacle that is in the midst of them.

32 This is the law for him who has a discharge and for him who has emissions of sperm, being made unclean by it;

33 And for her who is sick with her impurity, and for any person who has a discharge, whether man or woman, and for him who lies with her who is unclean.

16 AFTER THE death of Aaron's two sons, when they drew near before the Lord [offered false fire] and died, [Lev. 10:1, 2.]

2 The Lord said to Moses, Tell Aaron your brother he [i] must not come at all times into the Holy of Holies within the veil before the mercy seat upon the ark, lest he die; for I will appear in the cloud on the mercy seat. [Heb. 9:7-15, 25-28.]

3 But Aaron shall come into the holy enclosure in this way: with a young bull for a sin offering and a ram for a burnt offering.

4 He shall put on the holy linen undergarment, and he shall have the linen breeches upon his body, and be girded with the linen girdle or sash, and with the linen turban or miter shall he be attired; these are the holy garments; he shall bathe his body in water and then put them on.

5 He shall take [at the expense] of the congregation of the Israelites two male goats for a sin offering and one ram for a burnt offering.

6 And Aaron shall present the bull as the sin offering for himself and make atonement for himself and for his house [the other priests].

7 He shall take the two goats and present them before the Lord at the door of the Tent of Meeting.

8 Aaron shall cast lots on the two goats—one lot for the Lord, the other lot for Azazel or removal.

9 And Aaron shall bring the goat on which the Lord's lot fell and offer him as a sin offering.

10 But the goat on which the lot fell for Azazel or removal shall be presented alive before the Lord to make atonement over him, that he may be let go into the wilderness for Azazel (for dismissal).

11 Aaron shall present the bull as the sin offering for his own sins and shall make atonement for himself and for his house [the other priests], and shall kill the bull as the sin offering for himself.

12 He shall take a censer full of burning coals of fire from off the [bronze] altar before the Lord, and his two hands full of sweet incense beaten small, and bring it within the veil [into the Holy of Holies],

13 And put the incense on the fire [in the censer] before the Lord, that the cloud of the incense may cover the mercy seat that is upon [the ark of] the Testimony, lest he die.

14 He shall take of the bull's blood and sprinkle it with his finger on the front [the east side] of the mercy seat, and before the mercy seat he shall sprinkle of the blood with his finger seven times.

15 Then shall he kill the goat of the sin offering that is for [the sins of] the people and bring its blood within the veil [into the Holy of Holies] and do with that blood as he did with the blood of the bull, and sprinkle it on the mercy seat and before the mercy seat. [Heb. 2:17.]

---

i Since the priests have been warned by the death of Nadab and Abihu to approach God with reverence and godly fear, directions are here given how the nearest approach might be made . . . Within the veil none must ever come but the high priest only, and he but one day in the year. But see what a blessed change is made by the Gospel of Christ; all good Christians now have boldness to enter into the Holy of Holies, through the veil, every day (Heb. 10:19, 20); and we come **boldly** (not as Aaron must, with fear and trembling) to the throne of grace, or mercy seat (Heb. 4:16) . . . Now therefore we are welcome to come at all times into the Holy Place "not made with hands." In the past Aaron could not come near "at all times," lest he die; we now must come near "at all times," that we may live. It is [keeping our] distance only that is our death (Matthew Henry, *A Commentary*).

16 Thus he shall make atonement for the Holy Place because of the uncleanness of the Israelites and because of their transgressions, even all their sins; and so shall he do for the Tent of Meeting, that remains among them in the midst of their uncleanness. [Heb. 9:22-24.]

17 There shall be no man in the Tent of Meeting when the high priest goes in to make atonement in the Holy of Holies [within the veil] until he comes out and has made atonement for his own sins and those of his house [the other priests] and of all the congregation of Israel.

18 And he shall go out to the altar [of burnt offering in the court] which is before the Lord and make atonement for it, and shall take some of the blood of the bull and of the goat and put it on the horns of the altar round about.

19 And he shall sprinkle some of the blood on it with his fingers seven times and cleanse it and hallow it from the uncleanness of the Israelites.

20 And when he has finished atoning for the Holy of Holies and the Tent of Meeting and the altar [of burnt offering], he shall present the live goat;

21 And Aaron shall lay both his hands upon the head of the live goat and confess over him all the iniquities of the Israelites and all their transgressions, all their sins; and he shall put them upon the head of the goat [the sin-bearer], and send him away into the wilderness by the hand of a man ʲwho is timely (ready, fit).

22 The goat shall bear upon himself all their iniquities, carrying them to a land cut off (a land of forgetfulness *and* separation, not inhabited)! And the man leading it shall let the goat go in the wilderness. [Ps. 103:12; Isa. 53:11, 12; John 1:29.]

23 Aaron shall come into the Tent of Meeting and put off the linen garments which he put on when he went into the Holy of Holies, and leave them there;

24 And he shall bathe his body with water in a sacred place and put on his garments, and come forth and offer his burnt offering and that of the people, and make atonement for himself and for them.

25 And the fat of the sin offering he shall burn upon the altar.

26 The man who led the sin-bearing goat out and let him go for Azazel *or* removal shall wash his clothes and bathe his body, and afterward he may come into the camp.

27 The bull and the goat for the sin offering, whose blood was brought in to make atonement in the Holy of Holies, shall be carried forth without the camp; their skins, their flesh, and their dung shall be burned with fire. [Heb. 13:11-13.]

28 And he who burns them shall wash his clothes and bathe his body in water, and afterward he may come into the camp.

29 It shall be a statute to you forever that in the seventh month [nearly October] on the tenth day of the month you shall afflict yourselves [by fasting with penitence and humiliation] and do no work at all, either the native-born or the stranger who dwells temporarily among you.

30 For on this day atonement shall be made for you, to cleanse you; from all your sins you shall be clean before the Lord. [Heb. 10:1, 2; I John 1:7, 9.]

31 It is a sabbath of [solemn] rest to you, and you shall afflict yourselves [by fasting with penitence and humiliation]; it is a statute forever.

32 And the priest who shall be

---

j This is suggestive of the part the personal worker has to play in showing the sinner that Christ the great Sin-bearer has made full substitution for him, if he will accept it. Notice the qualifications of this man, sent along to complete the picture of the transaction between the sinner and his only sin-bearer. He is to be a man, says the Hebrew, "timely (ready, fit)" to do such a task.

anointed and consecrated to minister in the priest's office in his father's stead shall make atonement, wearing the holy linen garments;

33 He shall make atonement for the Holy Sanctuary, for the Tent of Meeting, and for the altar [of burnt offering in the court], and shall make atonement for the priests and for all the people of the assembly.

34 This shall be an everlasting statute for you, that atonement may be made for the Israelites for all their sins once a year. And Moses did as the Lord commanded him.

17 AND THE Lord said to Moses,
2 Tell Aaron, his sons, and all the Israelites, This is what the Lord has commanded:

3 If any man of the house of Israel kills an ox or lamb or goat in the camp or kills it outside the camp

4 And does not bring it to the door of the Tent of Meeting to offer it as an offering to the Lord before the Lord's tabernacle, [guilt for shedding] ᵏblood shall be imputed to that man; he has shed blood and shall be cut off from among his people.

5 This is so that the Israelites, rather than offer their sacrifices [to idols] in the open field [where they slew them], may bring them to the Lord at the door of the Tent of Meeting, to the priest, to offer them as peace offerings to the Lord.

6 And the priest shall dash the blood on the altar of the Lord at the door of the Tent of Meeting and burn the fat for a sweet *and* satisfying fragrance to the Lord.

7 So they shall no more offer their sacrifices *or* demons *or* field spirits after which they have played the harlot. This shall be a statute forever to them throughout their generations.

8 And you shall say to them, Whoever of the house of Israel or of the strangers who dwell temporarily among you offers a burnt offering or sacrifice

9 And does not bring it to the door of the Tent of Meeting to offer it to the Lord shall be cut off from among his people.

10 Any one of the house of Israel or of the strangers who dwell temporarily among them who eats any kind of blood, against that person I will set My face and I will cut him off from among his people [that he may not be included in the atonement made for them]. [Ezek. 33:25.]

11 For the life (the animal soul) is in the blood, and I have given it for you upon the altar to make atonement for your souls; for it is the blood that makes atonement, by reason of the life [which it represents]. [Rom. 3:24-26.]

life point

The Bible speaks of blood from Genesis to Revelation. In Leviticus 17:11, we read that there is life in the blood. In Genesis 4:10 we see Abel's blood crying out to God from the ground after Cain murdered him, and in Revelation 19:13 we see Jesus dressed in a robe that was dyed by dipping it in blood. Why does the Word of God speak so much about the blood? Because the life is in the blood, and it is through blood that atonement is made for our souls. In Hebrews 10:18, 19 we learn that Christ's blood was shed for us to permanently atone for our sins. That's good news!

---

k This requirement, that an animal to be killed was to be brought as an offering to the Lord, was no privation for the owner, for after offering it on the altar of burnt offering he received most of it back as a gift from God.

12 Therefore I have said to the Israelites, No person among you shall eat blood, neither shall any stranger who dwells temporarily among you eat blood.
13 And any of the Israelites or of the strangers who sojourn among them who takes in hunting any clean beast or bird shall pour out its blood and cover it with dust.
14 As for the life of all flesh, the blood of it represents the life of it; therefore I said to the Israelites, You shall partake of the blood of no kind of flesh, for the life of all flesh is its blood. Whoever eats of it shall be cut off.
15 And every person who eats what dies of itself or was torn by beasts,

life point

Just as light is the only force that can conquer or overcome darkness, so life is the only force that can conquer death. When God created Adam, He formed him from dust and "breathed into his nostrils the breath or spirit of life, and man became a living being" (Genesis 2:7). Adam's blood was already flowing through his body, but there was no life in it until God breathed His own life into him.

The chemical substance that we call blood carries life. If a person loses his blood, he loses his life. No blood means no life, because the blood carries the life. Life is a spiritual substance, but it must have a physical carrier. As believers in Jesus Christ, our bodies are the temple of the Holy Spirit. The Spirit and the life of God are in us.

speak the Word

whether he is native-born or a temporary resident, shall wash his clothes and bathe himself in water, and be unclean until evening; then shall he be clean. [Acts 15:20.]
16 But if he does not wash his clothes or bathe his body, he shall bear his own iniquity [for it shall not be borne by the sacrifice of atonement].

18 AND THE Lord said to Moses,
2 Say to the Israelites, I am the Lord your God.
3 You shall not do as was done in the land of Egypt in which you dwelt, nor shall you do as is done in the land of Canaan to which I am bringing you; neither shall you walk in their statutes.
4 You shall do My ordinances and keep My statutes and walk in them. I am the Lord your God.
5 You shall therefore keep My statutes and My ordinances which, if a man does, he shall live by them. I am the Lord. [Luke 10:25-28; Rom. 10:4, 5; Gal. 3:12.]
6 None of you shall approach anyone close of kin to him to have sexual relations. I am the Lord.
7 The nakedness of your father, which is the nakedness of your mother, you shall not uncover; she is your mother; you shall not have intercourse with her.
8 The nakedness of your father's wife you shall not uncover; it is your father's nakedness.
9 You shall not have intercourse with or uncover the nakedness of your sister, the daughter of your father or of your mother, whether born at home or born abroad.

Lord, I declare that You are my God. I will obey Your laws and walk in Your statutes and in them, I will find life.
ADAPTED FROM LEVITICUS 18:4, 5

10 You must not have sexual relations with your son's daughter or your daughter's daughter; their nakedness you shall not uncover, for they are your own flesh.

11 You must not have intercourse with your father's wife's daughter; begotten by your father, she is your sister; you shall not uncover her nakedness.

12 You shall not have intercourse with your father's sister; she is your father's near kinswoman.

13 You shall not have sexual relations with your mother's sister, for she is your mother's near kinswoman.

14 You shall not have intercourse with your father's brother's wife; you shall not approach his wife; she is your aunt.

15 You shall not uncover the nakedness of your daughter-in-law; she is your son's wife; you shall not have intercourse with her.

16 You shall not have intercourse with your brother's wife; she belongs to your brother.

17 You shall not marry a woman and her daughter, nor shall you take her son's daughter or her daughter's daughter to have intercourse; they are [her] near kinswomen; it is wickedness *and* an outrageous offense.

18 You must not marry a woman in addition to her sister, to be a rival to her, having sexual relations with the second sister when the first one is alive.

19 Also you shall not have intercourse with a woman during her [menstrual period or similar] uncleanness.

20 Moreover, you shall not lie carnally with your neighbor's wife, to defile yourself with her.

21 You shall not give any of your children to pass through the fire *and* sacrifice them to Molech [the fire god], nor shall you profane the name of your God [by giving it to false gods]. I am the Lord.

22 You shall not lie with a man as with a woman; it is an abomination. [I Cor. 6:9, 10.]

23 Neither shall you lie with any beast and defile yourself with it; neither shall any woman yield herself to a beast to lie with it; it is confusion, perversion, *and* degradedly carnal.

24 Do not defile yourselves in any of these ways, for in all these things the nations are defiled which I am casting out before you.

25 And the land is defiled; therefore I visit the iniquity of it upon it, and the land itself vomits out her inhabitants.

26 So you shall keep My statutes and My ordinances and shall not commit any of these abominations, neither the native-born nor any stranger who sojourns among you,

27 For all these abominations have the men of the land done who were before you, and the land is defiled—

28 [Do none of these things] lest the land spew you out when you defile it as it spewed out the nation that was before you.

29 Whoever commits any of these abominations shall be cut off from among [his] people.

30 So keep My charge: do not practice any of these abominable customs which were practiced before you and defile yourselves by them. I am the Lord your God.

19 AND THE Lord said to Moses,

2 Say to all the assembly of the Israelites, You shall be holy, for I the Lord your God am holy. [I Pet. 1:15.]

3 Each of you shall give due respect to his mother and his father, and keep My Sabbaths holy. I the Lord am your God.

4 Do not turn to idols *and* things of nought or make for yourselves molten gods. I the Lord am your God.

5 And when you offer a sacrifice of

peace offering to the Lord, you shall offer it so that you may be accepted.

6 It shall be eaten the same day you offer it and on the day following; and if anything remains until the third day, it shall be burned in the fire.

7 If it is eaten at all the third day, it is loathsome; it will not be accepted.

8 But everyone who eats it shall bear his iniquity, for he has profaned a holy thing of the Lord; and that soul shall be cut off from his people [and not be included in the atonement made for them].

9 And when you reap the harvest of your land, you shall not reap your field to its very corners, neither shall you gather the fallen ears *or* gleanings of your harvest.

10 And you shall not glean your vineyard bare, neither shall you gather its fallen grapes; you shall leave them for the poor and the stranger. I am the Lord your God.

11 You shall not steal, or deal falsely, or lie one to another. [Col. 3:9, 10.]

12 And you shall not swear by My name falsely, neither shall you profane the name of your God. I am the Lord.

13 You shall not defraud *or* oppress your neighbor or rob him; the wages of a hired servant shall not remain with you all night until morning.

14 You shall not curse the deaf or put a stumbling block before the blind, but you shall [reverently] fear your God. I am the Lord.

15 You shall do no injustice in judging a case; you shall not be partial to the poor or show a preference for the mighty, but in righteousness *and* according to the merits of the case judge your neighbor.

16 You shall not go up and down as a dispenser of gossip *and* scandal among your people, nor shall you [secure yourself by false testimony or by silence and] endanger the life of your neighbor. I am the Lord.

putting the Word to work

The Bible specifically instructs us not to gossip. Let me ask you, how do you handle the things you hear? Remember to always keep confidences, honor other people's "business," and keep their secrets. Do not be what Leviticus 19:16 calls a "dispenser of gossip."

17 You shall not hate your brother in your heart; but you shall surely rebuke your neighbor, lest you incur sin because of him. [Gal. 6:1; I John 2:9, 11; 3:15.]

18 You shall not take revenge or bear any grudge against the sons of your people, but you shall love your neighbor as yourself. I am the Lord. [Matt. 5:43-46; Rom. 12:17, 19.]

putting the Word to work

Do you hold grudges? Remember that the Bible teaches us not to hold grudges (see Leviticus 19:18), but instead to love our neighbors as we love ourselves. Let go of anything that you have against anyone.

19 You shall keep My statutes. You shall not let your domestic animals breed with a different kind [of animal]; you shall not sow your field with mixed seed, neither wear a garment of linen mixed with wool.

20 And if a man lies carnally with a woman who is a slave betrothed to a husband and not yet ransomed or given her freedom, they shall be punished [after investigation]; they shall not be put to death, because she was not free;

21 But he shall bring his guilt *or* trespass offering to the Lord to the door of the Tent of Meeting, a ram for a guilt *or* trespass offering.

22 The priest shall make atonement for him with the ram of the guilt *or* trespass offering before the Lord for his sin, and he shall be forgiven for committing the sin.

23 And when you come into the land and have planted all kinds of trees for food, then you shall count the fruit of them as inedible *and* forbidden to you for three years; it shall not be eaten.

24 In the fourth year all their fruit shall be holy for giving praise to the Lord.

25 But in the fifth year you may eat of the fruit [of the trees], that their produce may enrich you; I am the Lord your God.

26 You shall not eat anything with the blood; neither shall you use magic, omens, *or* witchcraft [or predict events by horoscope or signs and lucky days].

27 You shall not round the corners of the hair of your heads nor trim the corners of your beard [as some idolaters do].

28 You shall not make any cuttings in your flesh for the dead nor print *or* tattoo any marks upon you; I am the Lord.

29 Do not profane your daughter by causing her to be a harlot, lest the land fall into harlotry and become full of wickedness.

30 You shall keep My Sabbaths and reverence My sanctuary. I am the Lord.

31 Turn not to those [mediums] who have familiar spirits or to wizards; do not seek them out to be defiled by them. I am the Lord your God.

32 You shall rise up before the hoary head and honor the face of the old man and [reverently] fear your God. I am the Lord.

33 And if a stranger dwells temporarily with you in your land, you shall not suppress *and* mistreat him.

34 But the stranger who dwells with you shall be to you as one born among you; and you shall love him as yourself, for you were strangers in the land of Egypt. I am the Lord your God.

life point

Many people, including some who consider themselves Christians, participate in practices that God considers vile and evil. They innocently think there is nothing wrong with such things as reading horoscopes and consulting psychics; then they wonder why they do not have peace.

The Bible says that in the latter days many false prophets will rise up and tell people what their itching ears want to hear. People will search for one teacher after another who will tell them something pleasing and gratifying. To suit their own desires, they will turn away from hearing the truth and wander off into listening to myths and man-made fictions (see II Timothy 4:3, 4).

Never before have we seen such an influx of psychics vying for a ready ear. Television programs feature mediums who claim to be connecting with departed loved ones, but the tragic truth is that psychics such as these are taking advantage of grieving people. These mediums are really communicating with familiar spirits who tell half-truths about the past and lies about the future. God's Word clearly says to turn away from mediums and wizards because they will deceive and defile us. This is a serious command! Fortune-telling, physics, horoscopes, mediums, palm readers, tarot card readers, divination, witchcraft, and the like are all forbidden in God's Word (see Leviticus 19:31). We are to be led and guided by the Holy Spirit. We do not need a phony substitute when the real thing is available.

35 You shall do no unrighteousness in judgment, in measures of length or weight or quantity.
36 You shall have accurate *and* just balances, just weights, just ephah and hin measures. I am the Lord your God, Who brought you out of the land of Egypt.
37 You shall observe all My statutes and ordinances and do them. I am the Lord.

20 AND THE Lord said to Moses,
2 Moreover, you shall say to the Israelites, Any one of the Israelites or of the strangers that sojourn in Israel who gives any of his children to Molech [the fire god worshiped with human sacrifices] shall surely be put to death; the people of the land shall stone him with stones.
3 I also will set My face against that man [opposing him, withdrawing My protection from him, and excluding him from My covenant] and will cut him off from among his people, because he has given of his children to Molech, defiling My sanctuary and profaning My holy name.
4 And if the people of the land do at all hide their eyes from the man when he gives one of his children [as a burnt offering] to Molech [the fire god] *and* they overlook it *or* neglect to take legal action to punish him, winking at his sin, and do not kill him [as My law requires],
5 Then I will set My face against that man and against his family and will cut him off from among their people, him and all who follow him to [unfaithfulness to Me, and thus] play the harlot after Molech.

6 The person who turns to those who have familiar spirits and to wizards, [being unfaithful to Israel's Maker Who is her Husband, and thus] playing the harlot after them, I will set My face against that person and will cut him off from among his people [that he may not be included in the atonement made for them]. [Isa. 54:5.]
7 Consecrate yourselves therefore, and be holy; for I am the Lord your God.
8 And you shall keep My statutes and do them. I am the Lord Who sanctifies you.
9 Everyone who curses his father or mother shall surely be put to death; he has cursed his father or mother; his bloodguilt is upon him.
10 The man who commits adultery with another's wife, even his neighbor's wife, the adulterer and the adulteress shall surely be put to death. [John 8:4-11.]
11 And the man who lies carnally with his father's wife has uncovered his father's nakedness; both of the guilty ones shall surely be put to death; their blood shall be upon their own heads.
12 And if a man lies carnally with his daughter-in-law, both of them shall surely be put to death; they have wrought confusion, perversion, *and* defilement; their blood shall be upon their own heads.
13 If a man lies with a male as if he were a woman, both men have committed an offense (something perverse, unnatural, abhorrent, and detestable); they shall surely be put to death; their blood shall be upon them.
14 And if a man takes a wife and her mother, it is wickedness *and* an

speak the Word

Thank You, God, that You are the One Who sanctifies me and makes me holy.
ADAPTED FROM LEVITICUS **20:8**

in God alone

God says that He will set His face against anyone who turns to familiar spirits and wizards to prostitute themselves by following them instead of their Maker (see Leviticus 20:6). Multitudes of people consult the stars before making decisions, even for things as simple as when to cut their hair. However, a study of God's Word shows clearly that these things are an abomination to God. Even wearing and depending on "good-luck charms" is an affront to God. Our faith must be in God alone, not God plus a lot of other things. Those of us who believe in Jesus Christ do not need to depend on luck; we can trust God that He will bless us.

It is wrong to seek guidance for our lives through any means but God Himself, His Word, or a godly friend or counselor that God approves of. He is offended when we look to these other sources, and when we do, we will not have the peaceful, joy-filled, and prosperous lives He intended for us.

If you have been involved in seeking guidance through mediums, spirit guides, horoscopes, or any other occult activity, I strongly encourage you to thoroughly repent, ask God to forgive you, and completely turn away from it. Then I encourage you to keep your heart pure and be careful what you read, watch, and listen to.

Just as you cannot effectively listen to two radio stations at once, neither can you serve two masters (see Luke 16:13). You may have to choose new friends if they are filling you with things contrary to the Word of God. You may have to change television stations at home and choose new radio stations to listen to while you are riding in your car to prevent filling yourself with things not pleasing to God. Do not poison your inner man by being a garbage dump for the devil. Pay attention: if negative, ungodly talk is filling the air around you, change your listening habits. Also, make sure negative, ungodly talk does not come out of your own mouth for yourself and others to hear.

Jesus said, "Blessed . . . are the pure in heart, for they shall see God!" (Matthew 5:8). If you have a pure heart, you will enjoy having clarity of mind. You will perceive clearly God's plan for your life, and you will not feel aimless or confused. To keep your heart pure before the Lord, turn away from the things that defile you. Live a pure, clean life that flows like pure, clean water because God alone is your source.

outrageous offense; all three shall be burned with fire, both he and they [after being stoned to death], that there be no wickedness among you. [Josh. 7:15, 25.]

15 And if a man lies carnally with a beast, he shall surely be [stoned] to death, and you shall slay the beast.

16 If a woman approaches any beast and lies carnally with it, you shall [stone] the woman and the beast; they shall surely be put to death; their blood is upon them.

17 If a man takes his sister, his father's or his mother's daughter, and sees her nakedness and she sees his nakedness, it is a wicked *and* shameful thing; and they shall be cut off in the sight of their people; he has had sexual relations with his sister; he shall bear his iniquity.

18 And if a man shall lie with a woman having her menstrual pains and shall uncover her nakedness, he has made naked her fountain, and she has uncovered the fountain of her blood; and both of them shall be cut off from among their people.

19 You shall not uncover the nakedness of your mother's sister or of your father's sister, for that is to make naked his close kin; they shall bear their iniquity.

20 And if a man shall lie carnally with his uncle's wife, he has uncovered his uncle's nakedness; they shall bear their sin; they shall die childless [not literally, but in a legal sense].

21 And if a man shall take his brother's wife, it is impurity; he has uncovered his brother's nakedness; they shall be childless [not literally, but in a legal sense].

22 You shall therefore keep all My statutes and all My ordinances and do them, that the land where I am bringing you to dwell may not vomit you out [as it did those before you]. [Lev. 18:28.]

23 You shall not walk in the customs of the nation which I am casting out before you; for they did all these things, and therefore I was wearied *and* grieved by them.

24 But I have said to you, You shall inherit their land, and I will give it to you to possess, a land flowing with milk and honey. I am the Lord your God, Who has separated you from the peoples.

25 You shall therefore make a distinction between the clean beast and the unclean, and between the unclean fowl and the clean; and you shall not make yourselves detestable with beast or with bird or with anything with which the ground teems *or* that creeps, which I have set apart from you as unclean.

26 And you shall be holy to Me; for I

the Lord am holy, and have separated you from the peoples, that you should be Mine.

life point

God never speaks words to make us feel bad about ourselves. True godly conviction is a positive thing that moves us into a new level of holiness. The devil's condemnation presses us down under a heavy burden so that we cannot even hear from God. If you sense God speaking to you about something in your behavior, how do you know it is God? You will know because He will not shame you or put you down, but He will motivate you and empower you to change. I could not make progress until I learned to discern the difference between conviction and condemnation, and I do not believe you can either. Remember: conviction makes you aware of a problem and then lifts you up and out of it. Condemnation makes you feel guilty, presses you down, and keeps you "in" the problem.

27 A man or woman who is a medium *and* has a familiar spirit or is a wizard shall surely be put to death, be stoned with stones; their blood shall be upon them.

21 THE LORD said to Moses, Speak to the priests [exclusive of the high priest], the sons of Aaron, and say to them that none of them shall defile himself for the dead among his people [by touching a corpse or assisting in preparing it for burial],

2 Except for his near [blood] kin, for his mother, father, son, daughter, brother,

3 And for his sister, a virgin, who is near to him because she has had no husband; for her he may be defiled.

4 He shall not even defile himself, being a [bereaved] husband [his wife not being his blood kin] *or* being a chief man among his people, and so profane himself.

5 The priests [like the other Israelite men] shall not shave the crown of their heads or clip off the corners of their beard or make any cuttings in their flesh.

6 They shall be holy to their God and not profane the name of their God; for they offer the offerings made by fire to the Lord, the bread of their God; therefore they shall be holy.

7 They shall not take a wife who is a harlot or polluted *or* profane or divorced, for [the priest] is holy to his God.

8 You shall consecrate him therefore, for he offers the bread of your God; he shall be holy to you, for I the Lord Who sanctifies you am holy.

9 The daughter of any priest who profanes herself by playing the harlot profanes her father; she shall be burned with fire [after being stoned]. [Josh. 7:15, 25.]

10 But he who is the high priest among his brethren, upon whose head the anointing oil was poured and who is consecrated to put on the [sacred] garments, shall not let the hair of his head hang loose or rend his clothes [in mourning],

11 Neither shall he go in where any dead body lies nor defile himself [by doing so, even] for his father or for his mother;

12 Neither shall he go out of the sanctuary nor desecrate *or* make ceremonially unclean the sanctuary of his God, for the crown *or* consecration of the anointing oil of his God is upon him. I am the Lord.

13 He shall take a wife in her virginity.

14 A widow or a divorced woman or a woman who is polluted *or* profane or a harlot, these he shall not marry, but he shall take as his wife a virgin of his own people, [I Tim. 3:2-7; Tit. 1:7-9.]

15 That he may not profane *or* dishonor his children among his people; for I the Lord do sanctify the high priest.

16 And the Lord said to Moses,

17 Say to Aaron, Any one of your sons in their successive generations who has any blemish, let him not come near to offer the bread of his God.

18 For no man who has a blemish shall approach [God's altar to serve as priest], a man blind or lame, or he who has a disfigured face or a limb too long,

19 Or who has a fractured foot or hand,

20 Or is a hunchback, or a dwarf, or has a defect in his eye, or has scurvy *or* itch, or scabs *or* skin trouble, or has damaged testicles.

21 No man of the offspring of Aaron the priest who has a blemish *and* is disfigured *or* deformed shall come near [the altar] to offer the offerings of the Lord made by fire. He has a blemish; he shall not come near to offer the bread of his God.

22 He may eat the bread of his God, both of the most holy and of the holy things,

23 But he shall not come within the veil or come near the altar [of incense], because he has a blemish, that he may not desecrate *and* make unclean My sanctuaries *and* hallowed things; for I the Lord do sanctify them. [Heb. 7:28.]

24 And Moses told it to Aaron and to his sons and to all the Israelites.

22 AND THE Lord said to Moses,

2 Say to Aaron and his sons that they shall stay away from the holy things which the Israelites dedicate to Me, that they may not profane My holy name; I am the Lord.

3 Tell them, Any one of your

offspring throughout your generations who goes to the holy things which the Israelites dedicate to the Lord when he is unclean, that [priest] shall be cut off from My presence *and* excluded from the sanctuary; I am the Lord.

4 No man of the offspring of Aaron who is a leper or has a discharge shall eat of the holy things [the offerings and the showbread] until he is clean. And whoever touches any person *or* thing made unclean by contact with a corpse or a man who has had a discharge of semen,

5 Or whoever touches any dead creeping thing by which he may be made unclean, or a man from whom he may acquire uncleanness, whatever it may be, [Lev. 11:24-28.]

6 The priest who has touched any such thing shall be unclean until evening and shall not eat of the holy things unless he has bathed with water. [Heb. 10:22.]

7 When the sun is down, he shall be clean, and afterward may eat of the holy things, for they are his food.

8 That which dies of itself or is torn by beasts he shall not eat, defiling himself with it. I am the Lord.

9 The priests therefore shall observe My ordinance, lest they bear sin for it and die thereby if they profane it. I am the Lord, Who sanctifies them.

10 No outsider [not of the family of Aaron] shall eat of the holy thing [which has been offered to God]; a sojourner with the priest or a hired servant shall not eat of the holy thing.

11 But if a priest buys a slave with his money, the slave may eat of the holy thing, and he also who is born in the priest's house; they may eat of his food.

12 If a priest's daughter is married to an outsider [not of the priestly tribe], she shall not eat of the offering of the holy things.

13 But if a priest's daughter is a widow or divorced, and has no child, and returns to her father's house as in her youth, she shall eat of her father's food; but no stranger shall eat of it.

14 And if a man eats unknowingly of the holy thing [which has been offered to God], then he shall add one-fifth of its value to it and repay that amount to the priest for the holy thing.

15 The priests shall not profane the holy things the Israelites offer to the Lord,

16 And so cause them [by neglect of any essential observance] to bear the iniquity when they eat their holy things; for I the Lord sanctify them.

17 And the Lord said to Moses,

18 Say to Aaron and his sons and to all the Israelites, Whoever of the house of Israel and of the foreigners in Israel brings his offering, whether to pay a vow or as a freewill offering which is offered to the Lord for a burnt offering

19 That you may be accepted, you shall offer a male without blemish of the young bulls, the sheep, or the goats.

20 But you shall not offer anything which has a blemish, for it will not be acceptable for you. [I Pet. 1:19.]

21 And whoever offers a sacrifice of peace offering to the Lord to make a special vow to the Lord or for a freewill offering from the herd or from the flock must bring what is perfect to be accepted; there shall be no blemish in it.

22 Animals blind or made infirm *and* weak or maimed, or having sores *or* a wen or an itch or scabs, you shall not offer to the Lord or make an offering of them by fire upon the altar to the Lord.

23 For a freewill offering you may offer either a bull or a lamb which has some part too long or too short, but for [the payment of] a vow it shall not be accepted.

24 You shall not offer to the Lord any

animal which has its testicles bruised or crushed or broken or cut, neither sacrifice it in your land.

25 Neither shall you offer as the bread of your God any such animals obtained from a foreigner [who may wish to pay respect to the true God], because their defects render them unfit; there is a blemish in them; they will not be accepted for you.

26 And the Lord said to Moses,

27 When a bull or a sheep or a goat is born, it shall remain for seven days with its mother; and from the eighth day on it shall be accepted for an offering made by fire to the Lord.

28 And whether [the mother] is a cow or a ewe, you shall not kill her and her young both in one day.

29 And when you sacrifice an offering of thanksgiving to the Lord, sacrifice it so that you may be accepted.

30 It shall be eaten on the same day; you shall leave none of it until the next day. I am the Lord.

31 So shall you heartily accept My commandments *and* conform your life and conduct to them. I am the Lord.

32 Neither shall you profane My holy name [applying it to an idol, or treating it with irreverence or contempt or as a byword]; but I will be hallowed among the Israelites. I am the Lord, Who consecrates *and* makes you holy,

33 Who brought you out of the land of Egypt to be your God. I am the Lord.

23 THE LORD said to Moses,
2 Say to the Israelites, The set feasts *or* appointed seasons of the Lord which you shall proclaim as holy convocations, even My set feasts, are these:

3 Six days shall work be done, but the seventh day is the Sabbath of rest, a holy convocation *or* assembly by summons. You shall do no work on that day; it is the Sabbath of the Lord in all your dwellings.

life point

I urge you to be a thankful person. The Bible says we are to thank God in everything (see I Thessalonians 5:18). That means we are not to complain, murmur, grumble, or find fault, no matter what is going on in our lives. Whining shows that we have no faith in God's ability to make things better, but thankfulness opens the door to His blessing (see Leviticus 22:29).

4 These are the set feasts *or* appointed seasons of the Lord, holy convocations you shall proclaim at their stated times:

5 On the fourteenth day of the first month at twilight is the Lord's Passover.

6 On the fifteenth day of the same month is the Feast of Unleavened Bread to the Lord; for seven days you shall eat unleavened bread. [I Cor. 5:7, 8.]

7 On the first day you shall have a holy "calling together;" you shall do no servile *or* laborious work on that day.

8 But you shall offer an offering made by fire to the Lord for seven days; on the seventh day is a holy convocation; you shall do no servile *or* laborious work on that day.

9 And the Lord said to Moses,

10 Tell the Israelites, When you have come into the land I give you and reap its harvest, you shall bring the sheaf of the firstfruits of your harvest to the priest.

11 And he shall wave the sheaf before the Lord, that you may be accepted; on the next day after the Sabbath the priest shall wave it [before the Lord].

12 You shall offer on the day when you wave the sheaf a male lamb a year old without blemish for a burnt offering to the Lord.

13 Its cereal offering shall be two-tenths of an ephah of fine flour mixed with oil, an offering made by fire to the Lord for a sweet, pleasing, *and* satisfying fragrance; and the drink offering of it [to be poured out] shall be of wine, a fourth of a hin.

14 And you shall eat neither bread nor parched grain nor green ears, until this same day when you have brought the offering of your God; it is a statute forever throughout your generations in all your houses.

15 And you shall count from the day after the Sabbath, from the day that you brought the sheaf of the wave offering, seven Sabbaths; [seven full weeks] shall they be.

16 Count fifty days to the day after the seventh Sabbath; then you shall present a cereal offering of new grain to the Lord.

17 You shall bring from your dwellings two loaves of bread to be waved, made from two-tenths of an ephah of fine flour; they shall be baked with leaven, for firstfruits to the Lord.

18 And you shall offer with the bread seven lambs, a year old and without blemish, and one young bull and two rams. They shall be a burnt offering to the Lord, with their cereal offering and their drink offerings, an offering made by fire, of a sweet *and* satisfying fragrance to the Lord.

19 Then you shall sacrifice one he-goat for a sin offering and two he-lambs, a year old, for a sacrifice of peace offering.

20 The priest shall wave the two lambs, together with the bread of the firstfruits, for a wave offering before the Lord. They shall be holy to the Lord for the priest.

21 You shall make proclamation the same day, summoning a holy assembly; you shall do no servile work that day. It shall be a statute forever in all your dwellings throughout your generations.

22 And when you reap the harvest of your land, you shall not wholly reap the corners of your field, neither shall you gather the gleanings of your harvest; you shall leave them for the poor and the stranger. I am the Lord your God.

23 And the Lord said to Moses,

24 Say to the Israelites, On the first day of the seventh month [almost October], you shall observe a day of solemn [sabbatical] rest, a memorial day announced by blowing of trumpets, a holy [called] assembly.

25 You shall do no servile work on it, but you shall present an offering made by fire to the Lord.

26 And the Lord said to Moses,

27 Also the tenth day of this seventh month is the Day of Atonement; it shall be a holy [called] assembly, and you shall afflict yourselves [by fasting in penitence and humility] and present an offering made by fire to the Lord.

28 And you shall do no work on this day, for it is the Day of Atonement, to make atonement for you before the Lord your God.

29 For whoever is not afflicted [by fasting in penitence and humility] on this day shall be cut off from among his people [that he may not be included in the atonement made for them].

30 And whoever does any work on that same day I will destroy from among his people.

31 You shall do no kind of work [on that day]. It is a statute forever throughout your generations in all your dwellings.

32 It shall be to you a sabbath of rest, and you shall afflict yourselves [by fasting in penitence and humility]. On the ninth day of the month from evening to evening you shall keep your sabbath.

33 And the Lord said to Moses,

34 Say to the Israelites, The fifteenth day of this seventh month, and for seven days, is the Feast of Taberna-cles *or* Booths to the Lord.

35 On the first day shall be a holy convocation; you shall do no servile work on that day.

36 For seven days you shall offer an offering made by fire to the Lord; on the eighth day shall be a holy convo-cation and you shall present an offer-ing made by fire to the Lord. It is a solemn assembly; you shall do no laborious work on that day.

37 These are the set feasts *or* appointed seasons of the Lord, which you shall proclaim to be holy convoca-tions, to present an offering made by fire to the Lord, a burnt offering and a cereal offering, sacrifices and drink offerings, each on its own day.

38 This is in addition to the Sabbaths of the Lord and besides your gifts and all your vowed offerings and all your freewill offerings which you give to the Lord.

39 Also on the fifteenth day of the seventh month [nearly October], when you have gathered in the fruit of the land, you shall keep the feast of the Lord for seven days, the first day and the eighth day each a Sabbath.

40 And on the first day you shall take the fruit of pleasing trees [and make booths of them], branches of palm trees, and boughs of thick (leafy) trees, and willows of the brook; and you shall rejoice before the Lord your God for seven days.

41 You shall keep it as a feast to the Lord for seven days in the year, a statute forever throughout your gen-erations; you shall keep it in the sev-enth month.

42 You shall dwell in booths (shel-ters) for seven days: All native Israelites shall dwell in booths,

43 That your generations may know that I made the Israelites dwell in booths when I brought them out of the land of Egypt. I am the Lord your God.

44 Thus Moses declared to the Israelites the set *or* appointed feasts of the Lord.

24 AND THE Lord said to Moses,

2 Command the Isra-elites that they bring to you pure oil from beaten olives for the light [of the golden lampstand] to cause a lamp to burn continually.

3 Outside the veil of the Testimony [between the Holy and the Most Holy Places] in the Tent of Meeting, Aaron shall keep it in order from evening to morning before the Lord continually; it shall be a statute forever throughout your generations.

4 He shall keep the lamps in order upon the lampstand of pure gold before the Lord continually. [Rev. 1:12-18.]

5 And you shall take fine flour and bake twelve cakes with it; two-tenths of an ephah shall be in each cake [of the showbread *or* bread of the Pres-ence].

6 And you shall set them in two rows, six in a row, upon the table of pure gold before the Lord.

7 You shall put pure frankincense [in a bowl or spoon] beside each row, that it may be with the bread as a memorial portion, an offering to be made by fire to the Lord.

8 Every Sabbath day Aaron shall set the showbread in order before the Lord continually; it is on behalf of the Israelites, an everlasting covenant.

9 And the bread shall be for Aaron and his sons, and they shall eat it in a sacred place, for it is for [Aaron] a most holy portion of the offerings to the Lord made by fire, a perpetual due [to the high priest].

10 Now the son of an Israelite woman, whose father was an Egyp-tian, went out among the Israelites, and he and a man of Israel quarreled *and* strove together in the camp.

11 The Israelite woman's son

blasphemed the Name [of the Lord] and cursed. They brought him to Moses—his mother was Shelomith, the daughter of Dibri, of the tribe of Dan.
12 And they put him in custody until the will of the Lord might be declared to them.
13 And the Lord said to Moses,
14 Bring him who has cursed out of the camp, and let all who heard him lay their hands upon his head; then let all the congregation stone him.
15 And you shall say to the Israelites, Whoever curses his God shall bear his sin.
16 And he who blasphemes the Name of the Lord, he shall surely be put to death, and all the congregation shall certainly stone him; the stranger as well as he who was born in the land shall be put to death when he blasphemes the Name [of the Lord].

putting the Word to work

Much of our modern society seems to have lost respect for the name of the Lord. Do you honor His name in your speech? Do not use the names God, Lord, or Jesus in a frivolous or disrespectful way. Always remember that His name represents all that He is, and His name is to be honored not only in our hearts but also in our speech.

17 And he who kills any man shall surely be put to death.
18 And he who kills a beast shall make it good, beast for beast.
19 And if a man causes a blemish or disfigurement on his neighbor, it shall be done to him as he has done:
20 Fracture for fracture, eye for eye, tooth for tooth; as he has caused a blemish or disfigurement on a man, so shall it be done to him. [Matt. 5:38-42; 7:2.]
21 He who kills a beast shall replace it; he who kills a man shall be put to death.

22 You shall have the same law for the sojourner among you as for one of your own nationality, for I am the Lord your God.
23 Moses spoke to the Israelites, and they brought him who had cursed out of the camp and stoned him with stones. Thus the Israelites did as the Lord commanded Moses.

25 THE LORD said to Moses on Mount Sinai,
2 Say to the Israelites, When you come into the land which I give you, then shall the land keep a sabbath to the Lord.
3 For six years you shall sow your field, and for six years you shall prune your vineyard and gather in its fruits.
4 But in the seventh year there shall be a sabbath of solemn rest for the land, a sabbath to the Lord; you shall neither sow your field nor prune your vineyard.
5 What grows of itself in your harvest you shall not reap and the grapes on your uncultivated vine you shall not gather, for it is a year of rest to the land.
6 And the sabbath rest of the [untilled] land shall [in its increase] furnish food for you, for your male and female slaves, your hired servant, and the temporary resident who lives with you,
7 For your domestic animals also and for the [wild] beasts in your land; all its yield shall be for food.
8 And you shall number seven sabbaths or weeks of years for you, seven times seven years, so the total time of the seven weeks of years shall be forty-nine years.
9 Then you shall sound abroad the loud trumpet on the tenth day of the seventh month [almost October]; on the Day of Atonement blow the trumpet in all your land.
10 And you shall hallow the fiftieth year and proclaim liberty throughout

all the land to all its inhabitants. It shall be a jubilee for you; and each of you shall return to his ancestral possession [which through poverty he was compelled to sell], and each of you shall return to his family [from whom he was separated in bond service].

11 That fiftieth year shall be a jubilee for you; in it you shall not sow, or reap and store what grows of itself, or gather the grapes of the uncultivated vines.

12 For it is a jubilee; it shall be holy to you; you shall eat the [sufficient] increase of it out of the field.

13 In this Year of Jubilee each of you shall return to his ancestral property.

14 And if you sell anything to your neighbor or buy from your neighbor, you shall not wrong one another.

15 According to the number of years after the Jubilee, you shall buy from your neighbor. And he shall sell to you according to the number of years [remaining in which you may gather] the crops [before you must restore the property to him].

16 If the years [to the next Jubilee] are many, you may increase the price, and if the years remaining are few, you shall diminish the price, for the number of the crops is what he is selling to you.

17 You shall not oppress *and* wrong one another, but you shall [reverently] fear your God. For I am the Lord your God.

18 Therefore you shall do *and* give effect to My statutes and keep My ordinances and perform them, and you will dwell in the land in safety.

19 The land shall yield its fruit; you

life point

We must have reverential fear and awe of God in order to hear from Him and to receive His wisdom and knowledge. Reverential fear is to know that God *is* God and that He means what He says. God has called us His friends, even His sons and daughters, but we are to respect Him and honor Him with reverential obedience (see Leviticus 25:17).

shall eat your fill and dwell there in safety.

20 And if you say, What shall we eat in the seventh year if we are not to sow or gather in our increase?

21 Then [this is My answer:] I will command My [special] blessings on you in the sixth year, so that it shall bring forth [sufficient] fruit for three years.

22 And you shall sow in the eighth year, but eat of the old store of produce; until the crops of the ninth year come in you shall eat of the old supply.

23 The land shall not be sold into perpetual ownership, for the land is Mine; you are [only] strangers and temporary residents with Me. [Heb. 11:13; I Pet. 2:11-17.]

24 And in all the country you possess you shall grant a redemption for the land [in the Year of Jubilee].

25 If your brother has become poor and has sold some of his property, if any of his kin comes to redeem it, he shall [be allowed to] redeem what his brother has sold.

26 And if the man has no one to

speak the Word

I thank You, God, that as I obey You I will dwell safely and eat my fill of the fruit of the land.
ADAPTED FROM LEVITICUS 25:18, 19

redeem his property, and he himself has become more prosperous *and* has enough to redeem it,

27 Then let him count the years since he sold it and restore the overpayment to the man to whom he sold it, and return to his ancestral possession. [I Kings 21:2, 3.]

28 But if he is unable to redeem it, it shall remain in the buyer's possession until the Year of Jubilee, when it shall be set free and he may return to it.

29 If a man sells a dwelling house in a fortified city, he may redeem it within a whole year after it is sold; for a full year he may have the right of redemption.

30 And if it is not redeemed within a full year, then the house that is in the fortified city shall be made sure, permanently *and* without limitations, for him who bought it, throughout his generations. It shall not go free in the Year of Jubilee.

31 But the houses of the unwalled villages shall be counted with the fields of the country. They may be redeemed, and they shall go free in the Year of Jubilee.

32 Nevertheless, the cities of the Levites, the houses in the cities of their possession, the Levites may redeem at any time.

33 But if a house is not redeemed by a Levite, the sold house in the city they possess shall go free in the Year of Jubilee, for the houses in the Levite cities are their ancestral possession among the Israelites.

34 But the field of unenclosed *or* pasture lands of their cities may not be sold; it is their perpetual possession.

35 And if your [Israelite] brother has become poor and his hand wavers [from poverty, sickness, or age and he is unable to support himself], then you shall uphold (strengthen, relieve) him, [treating him with the courtesy and consideration that you would] a stranger or a temporary resident with

you [without property], so that he may live [along] with you. [I John 3:17.]

36 Charge him no interest or [portion of] increase, but fear your God, so your brother may [continue to] live along with you.

37 You shall not give him your money at interest nor lend him food at a profit.

38 I am the Lord your God, Who brought you forth out of the land of Egypt to give you the land of Canaan and to be your God.

39 And if your brother becomes poor beside you and sells himself to you, you shall not compel him to serve as a bondman (a slave not eligible for redemption),

40 But as a hired servant and as a temporary resident he shall be with you; he shall serve you till the Year of Jubilee,

41 And then he shall depart from you, he and his children with him, and shall go back to his own family and return to the possession of his fathers.

42 For the Israelites are My servants; I brought them out of the land of Egypt; they shall not be sold as bondmen. [I Cor. 7:23.]

43 You shall not rule over him with harshness (severity, oppression), but you shall [reverently] fear your God. [Eph. 6:9; Col. 4:1.]

44 As for your bondmen and your bondmaids whom you may have, they shall be from the nations round about you, of whom you may buy bondmen and bondmaids.

45 Moreover, of the children of the strangers who sojourn among you, of them you may buy and of their families that are with you which they have begotten in your land, and they shall be your possession.

46 And you shall make them an inheritance for your children after you, to hold for a possession; of them shall you take your bondmen always,

release your grudges

In Leviticus 25 we read about the Year of Jubilee, in which all debts were forgiven and all debtors were pardoned and set free.

When we are in Christ, every day can be the Year of Jubilee. We can say to those who are in debt to us by their mistreatment of us, "I forgive you and release you from your debt. You are free to go. I leave you in God's hands to let Him deal with you, because as long as I am trying to deal with you, He won't."

According to the Bible, we are not to hold a person in perpetual debt, just as we ourselves are not to be indebted to anyone else. Romans 13:8 instructs us, "Keep out of debt and owe no man anything, except to love one another." We need to learn to forgive people by canceling their debts to us. We also need to realize we can have our own sins forgiven continually through repentance and faith in Jesus Christ. We can enjoy a continual Year of Jubilee.

Can you imagine the joy of a person who learns that he has been pardoned from a ten- or twenty-year prison sentence? That's the good news of the cross. Because Jesus paid our debt for us, God can say to us, "You don't owe Me anything anymore!" Our trouble is either that we are still trying to pay our debt to the Lord, or that we are still trying to collect debts from others. Just as God canceled our debt and forgave us of it, so are we to cancel the debts of others and forgive them what they owe us.

but over your brethren the Israelites you shall not rule one over another with harshness (severity, oppression).

47 And if a sojourner or stranger with you becomes rich and your [Israelite] brother becomes poor beside him and sells himself to the stranger or sojourner with you or to a member of the stranger's family,

48 After he is sold he may be redeemed. One of his brethren may redeem him:

49 Either his uncle or his uncle's son may redeem him, or a near kinsman may redeem him; or if he has enough *and* is able, he may redeem himself.

50 And [the redeemer] shall reckon with the purchaser of the servant from the year when he sold himself to the purchaser to the Year of Jubilee, and the price of his release shall be adjusted according to the number of years. The time he was with his owner shall be counted as that of a hired servant.

51 If there remain many years [before the Year of Jubilee], in proportion to them he must refund [to the purchaser] for his release [the overpayment] for his acquisition.

52 And if little time remains until the Year of Jubilee, he shall count it over with him and he shall refund the proportionate amount for his release.

53 And as a servant hired year by year shall he deal with him; he shall not rule over him with harshness (severity, oppression) in your sight [make sure of that].

54 And if he is not redeemed during these years *and* by these means, then he shall go free in the Year of Jubilee, he and his children with him.

55 For to Me the Israelites are

servants, My servants, whom I brought forth out of the land of Egypt. I am the Lord your God.

26 YOU SHALL make for yourselves no idols nor shall you erect a graven image, pillar, *or* obelisk, nor shall you place any figured stone in your land to which *or* on which to bow down; for I am the Lord your God.

2 You shall keep My Sabbaths and reverence My sanctuary. I am the Lord.

3 If you walk in My statutes and keep My commandments and do them,

4 I will give you rain in due season, and the land shall yield her increase and the trees of the field yield their fruit.

5 And your threshing [time] shall reach to the vintage and the vintage [time] shall reach to the sowing time, and you shall eat your bread to the full and dwell in your land securely.

6 I will give peace in the land; you shall lie down and none shall fill you with dread *or* make you afraid; and I will clear ferocious (wild) beasts out of the land, and no sword shall go through your land.

7 And you shall chase your enemies, and they shall fall before you by the sword.

8 Five of you shall chase a hundred, and a hundred of you shall put ten thousand to flight; your enemies shall fall before you by the sword.

9 For I will be leaning toward you

life point

A continual theme throughout the Bible is that you will be blessed *if* you will keep God's commandments. *The Amplified Bible* explains that "blessed" means you will be happy and spiritually prosperous, with life-joy and satisfaction in God's favor and salvation, regardless of your outward condition. That sounds like a good thing to me! However, you must not miss what you need to do to receive God's blessing. Do you see that little word *if* in Leviticus 26:3? It may be a small word, but it has a big meaning. It means that God has a condition for receiving blessing. He does not require you to be perfect, because no one is perfect, but you do need to be aggressively attempting to do what God instructs you to do—to walk in His statutes and keep and do His commandments.

with favor *and* regard for you, rendering you fruitful, multiplying you, and establishing *and* ratifying My covenant with you. [II Kings 13:23.]

10 And you shall eat the [abundant] old store of produce long kept, and clear out the old [to make room] for the new.

11 I will set My dwelling in *and* among you, and My soul shall not despise *or* reject *or* separate itself from you.

speak the Word

Thank You, God, for leaning toward me with favor and regard, rendering me fruitful and establishing me in all I do.
ADAPTED FROM LEVITICUS 26:9

God, I thank You that You walk with me, that You are my God and that I belong to You.
ADAPTED FROM LEVITICUS 26:12

wait for God's timing

Leviticus 26:4 says, "I will give you rain in due season." When is *due season?* I believe it is when God knows we are ready, when everyone else involved is ready, and when it fits into God's corporate plan. God has an individual plan for our individual lives, but He also has a corporate plan for the entire world.

I remember a time when I was frustrated because nothing was happening in my ministry. I knew I was anointed to teach God's Word, but absolutely no doors opened to me. It seemed I had waited so long. I felt ready. I had been cooperating with God. He had done major work in me, and I just could not understand why something was not happening. I remember asking, "God, what are You waiting for now? Am I not ready?" He responded in my heart, "You are ready, but some of the others who will be involved with you are not yet ready. I am still working some things out in them, and you will need to wait on them now."

God does not push, shove, demand, manipulate, or force people. He leads, guides, prompts, and suggests. Then, each individual is responsible to give his or her will over to Him for His purpose. Sometimes this takes longer for one person than for another. An excellent example of this is the single person who is praying for the right mate. God is, in fact, preparing that mate, but the one praying gets tired of waiting since he or she does not know what is happening behind the scenes. God's good plan does take time, and often more time than we anticipated. Seeing the fulfillment of it requires a willingness to wait for the blessing "in due season."

Our wait is easier to endure when we believe God's timing is perfect, and He is never late, not one single day. Whatever the reason for the delay, Galatians 6:9 encourages us not to "lose heart and grow weary and faint in acting nobly and doing right, for in due time and at the appointed season we shall reap, if we do not loosen and relax our courage and faint." Also, I Peter 5:6 exhorts us to humble ourselves under God's mighty hand so that "in due time He may exalt you."

There is a right time for all things in our lives, and there is safety in being in God's perfect timing. I pray to be in God's perfect will with His perfect timing—not one step ahead of Him, nor one step behind. I hope you will pray that way too.

I also want to remind you to enjoy where you are while you are on the way to where you are going. God's timing is perfect, and being frustrated will not make Him hurry! Enjoy today, because right now it's all you have!

12 And I will walk in *and* with *and* among you and will be your God, and you shall be My people.
13 I am the Lord your God, Who brought you forth out of the land of Egypt, that you should no more be slaves; and I have broken the bars of your yoke and made you walk erect [as free men].
14 But if you will not hearken to Me

and will not do all these commandments,

15 And if you spurn *and* despise My statutes, and if your soul despises *and* rejects My ordinances, so that you will not do all My commandments, but break My covenant,

16 I will do this: I will appoint over you [sudden] terror (trembling, trouble), even consumption and fever that consume *and* waste the eyes and make the [physical] life pine away. You shall sow your seed in vain, for your enemies shall eat it.

17 I [the Lord] will set My face against you and ¹you shall be defeated *and* slain before your enemies; they who hate you shall rule over you; you shall flee when no one pursues you. [I Sam. 4:10; 31:1.]

18 And if in spite of all this you still will not listen *and* be obedient to Me, then I will chastise *and* discipline you seven times more for your sins.

19 And I will break *and* humble your pride in your power, and I will make your heavens as iron [yielding no answer, no blessing, no rain] and your earth [as sterile] as brass. [I Kings 17:1.]

20 And your strength shall be spent in vain, for your land shall not yield its increase, neither shall the trees of the land yield their fruit.

21 If you walk contrary to Me and will not heed Me, I will bring seven times more plagues upon you, according to your sins.

22 I will loose the wild beasts of the field among you, which shall rob you of your children, destroy your livestock, and make you few so that your roads shall be deserted *and* desolate. [II Kings 17:25, 26.]

23 If by these means you are not turned to Me but determine to walk contrary to Me,

24 I also will walk contrary to you, and I will smite you seven times for your sins.

25 And I will bring a sword upon you that shall execute the vengeance [for the breaking] of My covenant; and you shall be gathered together within your cities, and I will send the pestilence among you, and you shall be delivered into the hands of the enemy. [Num. 16:49; II Sam. 24:15.]

26 When I break your staff of bread *and* cut off your supply of food, ten women shall bake your bread in one oven, and they shall ration your bread *and* deliver it again by weight; and you shall eat, and not be satisfied. [Hag. 1:6.]

27 And if in spite of all this you will not listen *and* give heed to Me but walk contrary to Me,

28 Then I will walk contrary to you in wrath, and I also will chastise you seven times for your sins.

29 You shall eat the flesh of your sons *and* of your daughters. [II Kings 6:28, 29.]

30 And I will destroy your high places [devoted to idolatrous worship], and cut down your sun-images, and throw your dead bodies upon the [wrecked] bodies of your idols, and My soul shall abhor you [with deep and unutterable loathing]. [II Kings 23:8, 20.]

31 I will lay your cities waste, bring your sanctuaries to desolation, and I will not smell the fragrance of your sweet *and* soothing odors [of offerings made by fire]. [II Kings 25:4-10; II Chron. 36:19.]

---

1 This chapter abounds in prophecies of what God would do for, or against, His people if they did, or did not, meet His conditions. Each of these prophecies was literally fulfilled in the following centuries. The Scripture references indicate where these fulfillments are recorded; there are at least a dozen of them. Yet some people do not seem to have awakened to the fact that God **keeps His word,** whether for us or against us. It all depends on us.

32 And I will bring the land into desolation, and your enemies who dwell in it shall be astonished at it.

33 I will scatter you among the nations and draw out [your enemies'] sword after you; and your land shall be desolate and your cities a waste. [Ps. 44:11-14.]

34 Then shall the land [of Israel have the opportunity to] enjoy its sabbaths as long as it lies desolate and you are in your enemies' land; then shall the land rest, to enjoy *and* receive payments for its sabbaths [divinely ordained for it].

35 As long as it lies desolate *and* waste, it shall have rest, the rest it did not have in your sabbaths when you dwelt upon it. [II Chron. 36:21.]

36 As for those who are left of you, I will send dejection (lack of courage, a faintness) into their hearts in the lands of their enemies; the sound of a driven leaf shall put them to hasty *and* tumultuous flight, and they shall flee as if from the sword, and fall when no one pursues them.

37 They shall stumble over one another as if to escape a sword when no one pursues them; and you shall have no power to stand before your enemies.

38 You shall perish among the nations; the land of your enemies shall eat you up.

39 And those of you who are left shall pine away in their iniquity in your enemies' lands; also in the iniquities of their fathers shall they pine away like them.

40 But if they confess their own and their fathers' iniquity in their treachery which they committed against Me—and also that because they walked contrary to Me

41 I also walked contrary to them and brought them into the land of their enemies—if then their uncircumcised hearts are humbled and they then accept the punishment for their iniquity, [II Kings 24:10-14; Dan. 9:11-14.]

42 Then will I [earnestly] remember My covenant with Jacob, My covenant with Isaac, and My covenant with Abraham, and [earnestly] remember the land. [Ps. 106:44-46.]

43 But the land shall be left behind them and shall enjoy its sabbaths while it lies desolate without them; and they shall accept the punishment for their sins *and* make amends because they despised *and* rejected My ordinances and their soul scorned *and* rejected My statutes.

44 And [m]yet for all that, when they are in the land of their enemies, I will not spurn *and* cast them away, neither will I despise *and* abhor them to destroy them utterly and to break My covenant with them, for I am the Lord their God. [Deut. 4:31-35; Jer. 33:4, 5, 23-26; Rom. 11:2-5.]

45 But I will for their sake [earnestly] remember the covenant with their forefathers whom I brought forth out of the land of Egypt in the sight of the nations, that I might be their God. I am the Lord.

46 These are the statutes, ordinances, and laws which the Lord made between Him and the Israelites on Mount Sinai through Moses.

---

m No greater evidence that God keeps His word is available than the fact of the existence today of the Jews as a nation. Scattered for twenty-five centuries throughout the world with powerful forces determined to wipe them out, yet they are restored to their homeland because, in spite of all their sins against Him, God refuses to break His covenant with their forefathers and with them. The presence of even a small number of Jews in the world, after all the centuries of diabolical effort to exterminate them, would alone be sufficient assurance that God will keep His promises, whether good or bad, to individuals or to nations.

27 AND THE Lord said to Moses,
2 Say to the Israelites, When a man shall make a special vow of persons to the Lord at your valuation,
3 Then your valuation of a male from twenty years old to sixty years old shall be fifty shekels of silver, according to the shekel of the sanctuary.
4 And if the person is a female, your valuation shall be thirty shekels.
5 And if the person is from five years old up to twenty years old, then your valuation shall be for the male twenty shekels and for the female ten shekels.
6 And if a child is from a month up to five years old, then your valuation shall be for the male five shekels of silver and for the female three shekels.
7 And if the person is from sixty years old and above, if it be a male, then your valuation shall be fifteen shekels and for the female ten shekels.
8 But if the man is too poor to pay your valuation, then he shall be set before the priest, and the priest shall value him; according to the ability of him who vowed shall the priest value him.
9 If it is a beast of which men offer an offering to the Lord, all that any man gives of such to the Lord shall be holy.
10 He shall not replace it or exchange it, a good for a bad, or a bad for a good; and if he makes any exchange of a beast for a beast, then both the original offering and that exchanged for it shall be holy.
11 If it is an unclean animal, such as is not offered as an offering to the Lord, he shall bring the animal before the priest,
12 And the priest shall value it, whether it be good or bad; as you, the priest, value it, so shall it be.

13 But if he wishes to redeem it, he shall add a fifth to your valuation.
14 If a man dedicates his house to be sacred to the Lord, the priest shall appraise it, whether it be good or bad; as the priest appraises it, so shall it stand.
15 If he who dedicates his house wants to redeem it, he shall add a fifth of your valuation to it, and it shall be his.
16 And if a man shall dedicate to the Lord some part of a field of his possession, then your valuation shall be according to the seed [required] for it; [a sowing of] a homer of barley shall be valued at fifty shekels of silver.
17 If he dedicates his field during the Year of Jubilee, it shall stand according to your full valuation.
18 But if he dedicates his field after the Jubilee, then the priest shall count the money value in proportion to the years that remain until the Year of Jubilee, and it shall be deducted from your valuation.
19 If he who dedicates the field wishes to redeem it, then he shall add a fifth of the money of your appraisal to it, and it shall remain his.
20 But if he does not want to redeem the field, or if he has sold it to another man, it shall not be redeemed any more.
21 But the field, when it is released in the Jubilee, shall be holy to the Lord, as a field devoted [to God or destruction]; the priest shall have possession of it.
22 And if a man dedicates to the Lord a field he has bought, which is not of the fields of his [ancestral] possession,
23 The priest shall compute the amount of your valuation for it up to the Year of Jubilee; the man shall give that amount on that day as a holy thing to the Lord.
24 In the Year of Jubilee the field shall return to him of whom it was bought, to him to whom the land belonged [as his ancestral inheritance].

25 And all your valuations shall be according to the sanctuary shekel; twenty gerahs shall make a shekel.

26 But the firstling of the animals, since a firstling belongs to the Lord, no man may dedicate, whether it be ox or sheep. It is the Lord's [already].

27 If it be of an unclean animal, the owner may redeem it according to your valuation, and shall add a fifth to it; or if it is not redeemed, then it shall be sold according to your valuation.

28 But nothing that a man shall devote to the Lord of all that he has, whether of man or beast or of the field of his possession, shall be sold or redeemed; every devoted thing is most holy to the Lord.

29 No one doomed to death [under the claim of divine justice], who is to be completely destroyed from among men, shall be ransomed [from suffering the death penalty]; he shall surely be put to death.

30 And all the tithe of the land, whether of the seed of the land or of the fruit of the tree, is the Lord's; it is holy to the Lord. [I Cor. 9:11; Gal. 6:6.]

31 And if a man wants to redeem any of his tithe, he shall add a fifth to it.

32 And all the tithe of the herd or of the flock, whatever passes under the herdsman's staff [by means of which each tenth animal as it passes through a small door is selected and marked], the tenth shall be holy to the Lord. [II Cor. 9:7-9.]

33 The man shall not examine whether the animal is good or bad nor shall he exchange it. If he does exchange it, then both it and the animal substituted for it shall be holy; it shall not be redeemed.

34 These are the commandments which the Lord commanded Moses on Mount Sinai for the Israelites. [Rom. 10:4; Heb. 4:2; 12:18-29.]

Numbers

Author:
Moses

Date:
About 1440 BC

Everyday Life Principles:
Let God lead you. Move when He says to move, and be still when He says not to move.

When God has brought you out of a place of bondage, do not be tempted to go back. Persevere until you reach the place where He is leading you.

Approach life with a positive attitude and with faith so that obstacles or challenges in life will not intimidate you.

One of the primary themes in Numbers is God's guidance. The Israelites never knew when God was going to ask them to move as they made their journey toward the Promised Land. When He did call them to stop or to resume their travel, He made His leading clear in the appearance of a cloud by day and fire by night.

Even though God's guidance was so evident and the Israelites knew He was leading them into the Promised Land, they grew weary and discouraged along the way. In fact, they became so disheartened that they wanted to go back to Egypt where they had been so miserable!

In order to live victorious lives, we need to be sensitive to God's Spirit and keep making progress without looking back. We need to move when He says to move, and we need to stay where we are when He instructs us to be still. I encourage you to do everything you can to develop an intimate relationship with the Holy Spirit so that you can sense His leading in your life. Do not grow weary or become discouraged if you walk through "wilderness" times, but keep pressing on with a good attitude. Refuse any inclination to go back to an old place, a place of bondage or oppression, and instead follow God into all the great things He has for you.

1 THE LORD spoke to Moses in the Wilderness of Sinai in the Tent of Meeting on the first day of the second month in the second year after they came out of the land of Egypt, saying,

2 Take a census of all the males of the congregation of the Israelites by families, by their fathers' houses, according to the number of names, head by head.

3 From twenty years old and upward, all in Israel who are able to go forth to war you and Aaron shall number, company by company.

4 And with you there shall be a man [to assist you] from each tribe, each being the head of his father's house.

5 And these are the names of the men who shall attend you: Of Reuben, Elizur son of Shedeur;

6 Of Simeon, Shelumiel son of Zurishaddai;

7 Of Judah, Nahshon son of Amminadab;

8 Of Issachar, Nethanel son of Zuar;

9 Of Zebulun, Eliab son of Helon;

10 Of the sons of Joseph: of Ephraim, Elishama son of Ammihud; of Manasseh, Gamaliel son of Pedahzur;

11 Of Benjamin, Abidan son of Gideoni;

12 Of Dan, Ahiezer son of Ammishaddai;

13 Of Asher, Pagiel son of Ochran;

14 Of Gad, Eliasaph son of Deuel;

15 Of Naphtali, Ahira son of Enan.

16 These were those chosen from the congregation, the leaders of their ancestral tribes, heads of thousands [the highest class of officers] in Israel.

17 And Moses and Aaron took these men who have been named,

18 And assembled all the congregation on the first day of the second month, and they declared their ancestry after their families, by their fathers' houses, according to the number of names from twenty years old and upward, head by head,

19 As the Lord commanded Moses. So he numbered them in the Wilderness of Sinai.

20 The sons of Reuben, Israel's firstborn, their generations, by their families, by their fathers' houses, according to the number of names, head by head, every male from twenty years old and upward, all who were able to go to war:

21 Those of the tribe of Reuben numbered 46,500.

22 Of the sons of Simeon, their generations, by their families, by their fathers' houses, those numbered of them according to the number of names, head by head, every male from twenty years old and upward, all who were able to go to war:

23 Those of the tribe of Simeon numbered 59,300.

24 Of the sons of Gad, their generations, by their families, by their fathers' houses, according to the number of names, from twenty years old and upward, all who were able to go to war:

25 Those of the tribe of Gad numbered 45,650.

26 Of the sons of Judah, their generations, by their families, by their fathers' houses, according to the number of names, from twenty years old and upward, all able to go to war:

27 Those of the tribe of Judah numbered 74,600.

28 Of the sons of Issachar, their generations, by their families, by their fathers' houses, according to the number of names, from twenty years old and upward, all able to go to war:

29 Those of the tribe of Issachar numbered 54,400.

30 Of the sons of Zebulun, their generations, by their families, by their fathers' houses, according to the number of names, from twenty years old and upward, all able to go to war:

31 Those of the tribe of Zebulun numbered 57,400.

32 Of the sons of Joseph: the sons of

Ephraim, their generations, by their families, by their fathers' houses, according to the number of names, from twenty years old and upward, all able to go to war:

33 Those of the tribe of Ephraim numbered 40,500.

34 Of the sons of Manasseh, their generations, by their families, by their fathers' houses, according to the number of names, from twenty years old and upward, all able to go to war:

35 Those of the tribe of Manasseh numbered 32,200.

36 Of the sons of Benjamin, their generations, by their families, by their fathers' houses, according to the number of names, from twenty years old and upward, all able to go to war:

37 Those of the tribe of Benjamin numbered 35,400.

38 Of the sons of Dan, their generations, by their families, by their fathers' houses, according to the number of names, from twenty years old and upward, all able to go to war:

39 Those of the tribe of Dan numbered 62,700.

40 Of the sons of Asher, their generations, by their families, by their fathers' houses, according to the number of names, from twenty years old and upward, all able to go to war:

41 Those of the tribe of Asher numbered 41,500.

42 Of the sons of Naphtali, their generations, by their families, by their fathers' houses, according to the number of names, from twenty years old and upward, all able to go to war:

43 Those of the tribe of Naphtali numbered 53,400.

44 These were numbered by Moses and Aaron, and the leaders of Israel, twelve men, each representing his father's house.

45 So all those numbered of the Israelites, by their fathers' houses, from twenty years old and upward, able to go to war in Israel,

46 All who were numbered were 603,550.

47 But the Levites by their fathers' tribe were not numbered with them.

48 For the Lord had said to Moses,

49 Only the tribe of Levi you shall not number in the census of the Israelites.

50 But appoint the Levites over the tabernacle of the Testimony, and over all its vessels and furnishings and all things that belong to it. They shall carry the tabernacle [when journeying] and all its furnishings, and they shall minister to it and encamp around it.

51 When the tabernacle is to go forward, the Levites shall take it down, and when the tabernacle is to be pitched, the Levites shall set it up. And the excluded [any not of the tribe of Levi] who approach the tabernacle shall be put to death.

52 The Israelites shall pitch their tents by their companies, every man by his own camp and every man by his own [tribal] standard.

53 But the Levites shall encamp around the tabernacle of the Testimony, that there may be no wrath upon the congregation of the Israelites; and the Levites shall keep charge of the tabernacle of the Testimony.

54 Thus did the Israelites; according to all that the Lord commanded Moses, so they did.

2 THE LORD said to Moses and Aaron,

2 The Israelites shall encamp, each by his own [tribal] standard or banner with the ensign of his father's house, opposite the Tent of Meeting *and* facing it on every side.

3 On the east side toward the sunrise shall they of the standard of the camp of Judah encamp by their companies; Nahshon son of Amminadab being the leader of the sons of Judah.

4 Judah's host as numbered totaled 74,600.

5 Next to Judah the tribe of Issachar shall encamp, Nethanel son of Zuar being the leader of the sons of Issachar.

6 Issachar's host as numbered totaled 54,400.

7 Then the tribe of Zebulun, Eliab son of Helon being the leader of the sons of Zebulun.

8 Zebulun's host as numbered totaled 57,400.

9 All these [three tribes] numbered in the camp of Judah totaled 186,400. They shall set forth first [on the march].

10 On the south side shall be the standard of the camp of Reuben by their companies, the leader of the sons of Reuben being Elizur son of Shedeur.

11 Reuben's host as numbered totaled 46,500.

12 Those who encamp next to Reuben shall be the tribe of Simeon, the leader of the sons of Simeon being Shelumiel son of Zurishaddai.

13 Simeon's host as numbered totaled 59,300.

14 Then the tribe of Gad, the leader of the sons of Gad being Eliasaph son of Reuel (Deuel).

15 Gad's host as numbered totaled 45,650.

16 The whole number in [the three tribes of] the camp of Reuben was 151,450. They shall take second place [on the march].

17 Then the Tent of Meeting shall set out, with the camp of the Levites in the midst of the camps; as they encamp so shall they set forward, every man in his place, standard after standard.

18 On the west side shall be the standard of the camp of Ephraim by their companies, the leader of the sons of Ephraim being Elishama son of Ammihud.

19 Ephraim's host as numbered totaled 40,500.

20 Beside Ephraim shall be the tribe of Manasseh, the leader of the sons of Manasseh being Gamaliel son of Pedahzur.

21 Manasseh's host as numbered totaled 32,200.

22 Then the tribe of Benjamin, the leader of the sons of Benjamin being Abidan son of Gideoni.

23 Benjamin's host as numbered totaled 35,400.

24 The whole number [of the three tribes] in the camp of Ephraim totaled 108,100. They shall go forward in third place.

25 The standard of the camp of Dan shall be on the north side [of the tabernacle] by their companies, the leader of the sons of Dan being Ahiezer son of Ammishaddai.

26 Dan's host as numbered totaled 62,700.

27 Encamped next to Dan shall be the tribe of Asher, the leader of the sons of Asher being Pagiel son of Ochran.

28 Asher's host as numbered totaled 41,500.

29 Then the tribe of Naphtali, the leader of the sons of Naphtali being Ahira son of Enan.

30 Naphtali's host as numbered totaled 53,400.

31 The whole number [of the three tribes] in the camp of Dan totaled 157,600. They shall set out last, standard after standard.

32 These are the Israelites as numbered by their fathers' houses. All in the camps who were numbered by their companies were 603,550.

33 But the Levites were not numbered with the Israelites, for so the Lord commanded Moses.

34 Thus the Israelites did according to all the Lord commanded Moses; so they encamped by their standards, and so they set forward, everyone with his [tribal] families, according to his father's house.

3 NOW THESE are the generations of Aaron and Moses when the Lord spoke with Moses on Mount Sinai.

2 These are the names of the sons of Aaron: Nadab the firstborn, Abihu, Eleazar, and Ithamar.

3 These are the names of the sons of Aaron, the priests who were anointed, whom Aaron consecrated *and* ordained to minister in the priest's office.

4 But Nadab and Abihu died before the Lord when they offered strange fire before the Lord in the Wilderness of Sinai; and they had no children. So Eleazar and Ithamar ministered in the priest's office in the presence *and* under the supervision of Aaron their father. [Lev. 10:1-4.]

5 And the Lord said to Moses,

6 Bring the tribe of Levi near and set them before Aaron the priest, that they may minister to him.

7 And they shall carry out his instructions and the duties connected with the whole assembly before the Tent of Meeting, doing the service of the tabernacle.

8 And they shall keep all the instruments *and* furnishings of the Tent of Meeting and take charge of [attending] the Israelites, to serve in the tabernacle.

9 And you shall give the Levites [as servants and helpers] to Aaron and his sons; they are wholly given to him from among the Israelites.

10 And you shall appoint Aaron and his sons, and they shall observe *and* attend to their priest's office; but the excluded [anyone daring to assume priestly duties or privileges who is not of the house of Aaron and called of God] who comes near [the holy things] shall be put to death.

11 And the Lord said to Moses,

12 Behold, I have taken the Levites from among the Israelites instead of every firstborn who opens the womb among the Israelites; and the Levites shall be Mine,

13 For all the firstborn are Mine. On the day that I slew all the firstborn in the land of Egypt, I consecrated for Myself all the firstborn in Israel, both man and beast; Mine they shall be. I am the Lord.

14 And the Lord said to Moses in the Wilderness of Sinai,

15 Number the sons of Levi by their fathers' houses and by families. Every male from a month old and upward you shall number.

16 So Moses numbered them as he was commanded by the word of the Lord.

17 These were the sons of Levi by their names: Gershon, Kohath, and Merari.

18 And these are the names of the sons of Gershon by their families: Libni and Shimei.

19 The sons of Kohath by their families: Amram, Izhar, Hebron, and Uzziel.

20 The sons of Merari by their families: Mahli and Mushi. These are the families of the Levites by their fathers' houses.

21 Of Gershon were the families of the Libnites and of the Shimeites. These are the families of the Gershonites.

22 The males who were numbered of them from a month old and upward totaled 7,500.

23 The families of the Gershonites were to encamp behind the tabernacle on the west,

24 The leader of the fathers' houses of the Gershonites being Eliasaph son of Lael.

25 And the responsibility of the sons of Gershon in the Tent of Meeting was to be the tabernacle, the tent, its covering, and the hangings for the door of the Tent of Meeting,

26 And the hangings of the court, the curtain for the door of the court which is around the tabernacle and the altar,

its cords, and all the service pertaining to them.

27 Of Kohath were the families of the Amramites, the Izharites, the Hebronites, and the Uzzielites; these are the families of the Kohathites.

28 The number of all the males from a month old and upward totaled 8,600, attending to the duties of the sanctuary.

29 The families of the sons of Kohath were to encamp on the south side of the tabernacle,

30 The chief of the fathers' houses of the families of the Kohathites being Elizaphan son of Uzziel.

31 Their charge was to be the ark, the table, the lampstand, the altars, and the utensils of the sanctuary with which the priests minister, and the screen, and all the service having to do with these.

32 Eleazar son of Aaron the priest was to be chief over the leaders of the Levites, and have the oversight of those who had charge of the sanctuary.

33 Of Merari were the families of the Mahlites and the Mushites; these are the families of Merari.

34 Their number of all the males from a month old and upward totaled 6,200.

35 And the head of the fathers' houses of the families of Merari was Zuriel son of Abihail; the Merarites were to encamp on the north side of the tabernacle.

36 And the appointed charge of the sons of Merari was the boards *or*

frames of the tabernacle, and its bars, pillars, sockets *or* bases, and all the accessories *or* instruments of it, and all the work connected with them,

37 And the pillars of the surrounding court and their sockets *or* bases, with their pegs and their cords.

38 But those to encamp before the tabernacle toward the east, before the Tent of Meeting, toward the sunrise, were to be Moses and Aaron and his sons, keeping the full charge of the rites of the sanctuary in whatever was required for the Israelites; and the [a]excluded [one not a descendant of Aaron and called of God] who came near [the sanctuary] was to be put to death.

39 All the Levites whom Moses and Aaron numbered at the command of the Lord, by their families, all the males from a month old and upward, were 22,000.

40 And the Lord said to Moses, Number all the firstborn of the males of the Israelites from a month old and upward, and take the number of their names.

41 You shall take the Levites for Me instead of all the firstborn among the Israelites. I am the Lord; and you shall take the cattle of the Levites for Me instead of all the firstlings among the cattle of the Israelites.

42 So Moses numbered, as the Lord commanded him, all the firstborn Israelites.

43 But all the firstborn males from a month old and upward as numbered were 22,273 [273 more than the Levites].

a This ban against "the excluded" from coming near the sanctuary (the sacred tent, the tabernacle proper) is not to be construed as discrimination against people who were not Israelites. It included everyone except the ordained descendants of Levi of the house of Aaron. The tabernacle proper was made up of two small rooms which no one except the priest (or priests) who had the assignment was ever to enter. The congregation entered the outside enclosure only. This was true also of the later temples. Neither Jesus nor any of His disciples or Paul ever entered the sanctuary. When Jesus "taught in the temple" or "entered into the temple," the Greek word invariably indicates that He was in the temple enclosure (*hieron*) and not in the sanctuary (*naos*). (For more information, see Richard Trench, *Synonyms of The New Testament*). For a violation of this ban see II Chron. 26:16-21, which tells of King Uzziah, who attempted to enter the sanctuary to burn incense and while being forcibly put out by eighty priests became a leper—for the rest of his life.

44 And the Lord said to Moses,
45 Take the Levites [for Me] instead of all the firstborn Israelites, and the Levites' cattle instead of their cattle; and the Levites shall be Mine. I am the Lord.
46 And for those 273 who are to be redeemed of the firstborn of the Israelites who outnumber the Levites,
47 You shall take five shekels apiece, reckoning by the sanctuary shekel of twenty gerahs; you shall collect them,
48 And you shall give the ransom silver from the excess number [over the Levites] to be redeemed to Aaron and his sons.
49 So Moses took the redemption money from those who were left over from the number who were redeemed by the Levites.
50 From the firstborn of the Israelites he took the money, 1,365 shekels, after the shekel of the sanctuary.
51 And Moses gave the money from those who were ransomed to Aaron and his sons, as the Lord commanded Moses.

4 AND THE Lord said to Moses and Aaron,
2 Take a census of the Kohathite division among the sons of Levi, by their families, by their fathers' houses,
3 From thirty years old and up to fifty years old, all who can enter the service to do the work in the Tent of Meeting.
4 This shall be the responsibility of the sons of Kohath in the Tent of Meeting: the most holy things.
5 When the camp prepares to set forward, Aaron and his sons shall take down the veil [screening the Holy of Holies] and cover the ark of the Testimony with it,
6 And shall put on it the covering of dolphin *or* porpoise skin, and shall spread over that a cloth wholly of

blue, and shall put in place the poles of the ark.
7 And upon the table of showbread they shall spread a cloth of blue and put on it the plates, the dishes for incense, the bowls, the flagons for the drink offering, and also the continual showbread.
8 And they shall spread over them a cloth of scarlet, and put over that a covering of dolphin *or* porpoise skin, and put in place the poles [for carrying].
9 And they shall take a cloth of blue and cover the lampstand for the light and its lamps, its snuffers, its ashtrays, and all the oil vessels from which it is supplied.
10 And they shall put the lampstand and all its utensils within a covering of dolphin *or* porpoise skin and shall put it upon the frame [for carrying].
11 And upon the golden [incense] altar they shall spread a cloth of blue, and cover it with a covering of dolphin *or* porpoise skin, and shall put in place its poles [for carrying].
12 And they shall take all the utensils of the service with which they minister in the sanctuary, and put them in a cloth of blue, and cover them with a covering of dolphin *or* porpoise skin, and shall put them on the frame [for carrying].
13 And they shall take away the ashes from the altar [of burnt offering] and spread a purple cloth over it.
14 And they shall put upon it all its vessels *and* utensils with which they minister there, the firepans, the fleshhooks *or* forks, the shovels, the basins, and all the vessels *and* utensils of the altar, and they shall spread over it all a covering of dolphin *or* porpoise skin, and shall put in its poles [for carrying].
15 When Aaron and his sons have finished covering the sanctuary and all its furniture, as the camp sets out, after all that [is done but not before],

the sons of Kohath shall come to carry
them. But they shall not touch the
holy things, lest they die. These are
the things of the Tent of Meeting
which the sons of Kohath are to carry.
16 And Eleazar son of Aaron the
priest shall have charge of the oil for
the light, the fragrant incense, the
continual cereal offering, and the
anointing oil, with the oversight of all
the tabernacle and of all that is in it, of
the sanctuary and its utensils.
17 And the Lord said to Moses and
Aaron,
18 [Since] the tribe of the families of
the Kohathites [are only Levites and
not priests], do not [by exposing them
to the sin of touching the most holy
things] cut them off from among the
Levites.
19 But deal thus with them, that they
may live and not die when they
approach the most holy things: Aaron
and his sons shall go in and appoint
them each to his work and to his burden [to be carried on the march].
20 But [the Kohathites] shall not go in
to see the sanctuary [the Holy Place
and the Holy of Holies] or its holy
things, even for an instant, lest they die.
21 And the Lord said to Moses,
22 Take a census of the sons of Gershon, by their fathers' houses, by
their families.
23 From thirty years old and up to
fifty years old you shall number them,
all who enter for service to do the
work in the Tent of Meeting.

24 This is the service of the families
of the Gershonites, in serving and in
bearing burdens [when on the march]:
25 And they shall carry the curtains
of the tabernacle, and the Tent of
Meeting, its covering, and the covering of dolphin or porpoise skin that is
on top of it, and the hanging or screen
for the door of the Tent of Meeting,
26 And the hangings of the court,
and the hanging or screen for the
entrance of the gate of the court
which is around the tabernacle and
the altar [of burnt offering], and their
cords, and all the equipment for their
service; whatever needs to be done
with them, that they shall do.
27 Under the direction of Aaron and
his sons shall be all the service of the
sons of the Gershonites, in all they
have to carry and in all they have to
do; and you shall assign to their
charge all that they are to carry [on
the march].
28 This is the service of the families
of the sons of Gershon in the Tent of
Meeting; and their work shall be
under the direction of Ithamar son of
Aaron, the [high] priest.
29 As for the sons of Merari, you
shall number them by their families
and their fathers' houses;
30 From thirty years old up to fifty
years old you shall number them,
everyone who enters the service to do
the work of the Tent of Meeting.
31 And this is what they are
assigned to carry and to guard [on the
march], according to all their service
in the Tent of Meeting: the boards or
frames of the tabernacle, and its
bars, and its pillars, and its sockets or
bases,
32 And the pillars of the court round
about with their sockets or bases, and
pegs, and cords, with all their equipment and all their accessories for
service; and you shall assign to them
by name the articles which they are to
carry [on the march].

33 This is the work of the families of the sons of Merari, according to all their tasks in the Tent of Meeting, under the direction of Ithamar son of Aaron, the [high] priest.

34 And Moses and Aaron and the leaders of the congregation numbered the sons of the Kohathites by their families and their fathers' houses,

35 From thirty years old up to fifty years old, everyone who enters the service to do the work of the Tent of Meeting;

36 And those who were numbered of them by their families were 2,750.

37 These were numbered of the families of the Kohathites, all who did service in the Tent of Meeting, whom Moses and Aaron numbered according to the command of the Lord through Moses.

38 And those that were numbered of the sons of Gershon, by their families, and by their fathers' houses,

39 From thirty years old up to fifty years old, everyone who entered the service to do the work of the Tent of Meeting,

40 Those who were enrolled of them, by their families, by their fathers' houses, were 2,630.

41 These were numbered of the families of the sons of Gershon, all who served in the Tent of Meeting, whom Moses and Aaron numbered as the Lord commanded.

42 And those numbered of the families of the sons of Merari, by their families, by their fathers' houses,

43 From thirty years old up to fifty years old, everyone who entered into the service for work in the Tent of Meeting,

44 Even those who were numbered of them by their families, were 3,200.

45 These are those who were numbered of the families of the sons of Merari, whom Moses and Aaron numbered according to the command of the Lord by Moses.

46 All those who were numbered of the Levites, whom Moses and Aaron and the leaders of Israel counted by their families and by their fathers' houses,

47 From thirty years old up to fifty years old, everyone who could enter to do the work of service and of burden bearing in the Tent of Meeting,

48 Those that were numbered of them were 8,580.

49 According to the command of the Lord through Moses, they were assigned each to his work of serving and carrying. Thus they were numbered by him, as the Lord had commanded Moses.

5 THE LORD said to Moses, **2** Command the Israelites that they put outside the camp every leper and everyone who has a discharge, and whoever is defiled by [coming in contact with] the dead.

3 Both male and female you shall put out; without the camp you shall put them, that they may not defile their camp, in the midst of which I dwell.

4 The Israelites did so, and put them outside the camp; as the Lord said to Moses, so the Israelites did.

5 And the Lord said to Moses,

6 Say to the Israelites, When a man or woman commits any sin that men commit by breaking faith with the Lord, and that person is guilty,

7 Then he shall confess the sin which he has committed, and he shall make restitution for his wrong in full, and add a fifth to it, and give it to him whom he has wronged.

8 But if the man [wronged] has no kinsman to whom the restitution may be made, let it be given to the Lord for the priest, besides the ram of atonement with which atonement shall be made for the offender.

9 And every offering of all the holy things of the Israelites which they bring to the priest shall be his.

10 And every man's hallowed things shall be the priest's; whatever any man gives the priest shall be his.

11 And the Lord said to Moses,

12 Say to the Israelites, If any man's wife goes astray and commits an offense of guilt against him,

13 And a man lies with her carnally, and it is hidden from the eyes of her husband and it is kept secret though she is defiled, and there is no witness against her nor was she taken in the act,

14 And if the spirit of jealousy comes upon him and he is jealous *and* suspicious of his wife who has defiled herself—or if the spirit of jealousy comes upon him and he is jealous *and* suspicious of his wife though she has not defiled herself—

15 Then shall the man bring his wife to the priest, and he shall bring the offering required of her, a tenth of an ephah of barley meal; but he shall pour no oil upon it nor put frankincense on it [symbols of favor and joy], for it is a cereal offering of jealousy *and* suspicion, a memorial offering bringing iniquity to remembrance.

16 And the priest shall bring her near and set her before the Lord.

17 And the priest shall take holy water [probably from the sacred laver] in an earthen vessel and take some of the dust that is on the floor of the tabernacle and put it in the water.

18 And the priest shall set the woman before the Lord, and let the hair of the woman's head hang loose, and put the meal offering of remembrance in her hands, which is the jealousy *and* suspicion offering. And the priest shall have in his hand the water of bitterness that brings the curse.

19 Then the priest shall make her take an oath, and say to the woman, If no man has lain with you and if you have not gone astray to uncleanness with another instead of your husband, then be free from any effect of this water of bitterness which brings the curse.

20 But if you have gone astray and you are defiled, some man having lain with you beside your husband,

21 Then the priest shall make the woman take the oath of the curse, and say to the woman, The Lord make you a curse and an oath among your people when the Lord makes your thigh fall away and your body swell.

22 May this water that brings the curse go into your bowels and make your body swell and your thigh fall away. And the woman shall say, So let it be, so let it be.

23 The priest shall then write these curses in a book and shall wash them off into the water of bitterness;

24 And he shall cause the woman to drink the water of bitterness that brings the curse, and the water that brings the curse shall enter into her [to try her] bitterly.

25 Then the priest shall take the cereal offering of jealousy *and* suspicion out of the woman's hand and shall wave the offering before the Lord and offer it upon the altar.

26 And the priest shall take a handful of the cereal offering as the memorial portion of it and burn it on the altar, and afterward shall cause the woman to drink the water.

27 And when he has made her drink the water, then if she is defiled and has committed a trespass against her husband, the curse water which she drank shall be bitterness and cause her body to swell and her thigh to fall away, and the woman shall be a curse among her people.

28 But if the woman is not defiled and is clean, then she shall be free [from the curse] and be able to have children.

29 This is the law of jealousy *and* suspicion when a wife goes aside to another instead of her husband and is defiled,

30 Or when the spirit of jealousy *and* suspicion comes upon a man and he is jealous *and* suspicious of his wife; then shall he set the woman before the Lord, and the priest shall execute on her all this law.

31 The [husband] shall be free from iniquity *and* guilt, and that woman [if guilty] shall bear her iniquity.

6 AND THE Lord said to Moses,
2 Say to the Israelites, When either a man or a woman shall make a special vow, the vow of a Nazirite, that is, one separated *and* consecrated to the Lord,

3 He shall separate himself from wine and strong drink; he shall drink no vinegar of wine or of strong drink, and shall drink no grape juice, or eat grapes, fresh or dried. [Luke 1:15.]

4 All the days of his separation he shall eat nothing produced from the grapevine, not even the seeds or the skins.

5 All the days of the vow of his separation *and* abstinence there shall no razor come upon his head. Until the time is completed for which he separates himself to the Lord, he shall be holy, and shall let the locks of the hair of his head grow long.

6 All the days that he separates himself to the Lord he shall not go near a dead body.

7 He shall not make himself unclean for his father, mother, brother, or sister, when they die, because his separation *and* abstinence to his God is upon his head.

8 All the days of his separation *and* abstinence he is holy to the Lord.

9 And if any man dies very suddenly beside him, and he has defiled his consecrated head, then he shall shave his head on the day of his cleansing; on the seventh day shall he shave it.

10 On the eighth day he shall bring two turtledoves or two young pigeons to the priest to the door of the Tent of Meeting,

11 And the priest shall offer the one for a sin offering and the other for a burnt offering and make atonement for him because he sinned by reason of the dead body. He shall consecrate his head the same day,

12 And he shall consecrate *and* separate himself to the Lord for the days of his separation and shall bring a male lamb a year old for a trespass *or* guilt offering; but the previous days shall be void *and* lost, because his separation was defiled.

13 And this is the law of the Nazirite when the days of his separation *and* abstinence are fulfilled. He shall be brought to the door of the Tent of Meeting,

14 And he shall offer his gift to the Lord, one he-lamb a year old without blemish for a burnt offering, and one ewe lamb a year old without blemish for a sin offering, and one ram without blemish for a peace offering,

15 And a basket of unleavened bread, cakes of fine flour mingled with oil, and wafers of unleavened bread spread with oil, and their cereal offering, and their drink offering.

16 And the priest shall present them before the Lord and shall offer the person's sin offering and his burnt offering.

17 And he shall offer the ram for a sacrifice of peace offering to the Lord, with the basket of unleavened bread; the priest shall offer also its cereal offering and its drink offering.

18 And the Nazirite shall shave his consecrated head at the door of the Tent of Meeting, and shall take the hair and put it on the fire which is under the sacrifice of the peace offerings.

19 And the priest shall take the boiled shoulder of the ram, and one unleavened cake out of the basket, and one unleavened wafer and shall

put them upon the hands of the Nazirite, after he has shaven the hair of his separation *and* abstinence.
20 And the priest shall wave them for a wave offering before the Lord; they are a holy portion for the priest, with the breast that is waved and the thigh *or* shoulder that is offered; and after that the Nazirite may drink wine.
21 This is the law for the Nazirite who has made a vow. His offering to the Lord, besides what else he is able to afford, shall be according to the vow which he has vowed; so shall he do according to the law for his separation *and* abstinence [as a Nazirite]. [Acts 21:24, 26.]
22 And the Lord said to Moses,
23 Say to Aaron and his sons, This is the way you shall bless the Israelites. Say to them,
24 The Lord bless you and watch, guard, *and* keep you;
25 The Lord make His face to shine upon *and* enlighten you and be gracious (kind, merciful, and giving favor) to you;
26 The Lord lift up His [approving] countenance upon you and give you peace (tranquility of heart and life continually).
27 And they shall put My name upon the Israelites, and I will bless them.

7 ON THE day that Moses had fully completed setting up the tabernacle and had anointed and consecrated it and all its furniture, and the altar and all its utensils, and had anointed and set them apart for holy use,

2 The princes *or* leaders of Israel, heads of their fathers' houses, made offerings. These were the leaders of the tribes and were over those who were numbered.
3 And they brought their offering before the Lord, six covered wagons and twelve oxen; a wagon for each two of the princes *or* leaders and an ox for each one; and they brought them before the tabernacle.
4 Then the Lord said to Moses,
5 Accept the things from them, that they may be used in doing the service of the Tent of Meeting, and give them to the Levites, to each man according to his service.
6 So Moses took the wagons and the oxen and gave them to the Levites.
7 Two wagons and four oxen he gave to the sons of Gershon, according to their service;
8 And four wagons and eight oxen he gave to the sons of Merari, according to their service, under the supervision of Ithamar son of Aaron, the [high] priest.
9 But to the sons of Kohath he gave none, because they were assigned the care of the sanctuary *and* the holy things which had to be carried on their shoulders.
10 And the princes *or* leaders offered sacrifices for the dedication of the altar [of burnt offering] on the day that it was anointed; and they offered their sacrifice before the altar.
11 And the Lord said to Moses, They shall offer their offerings, each prince *or* leader on his day, for the dedication of the altar.

speak the Word

aglow with God's glory

God pronounced a blessing upon His people, saying that His face would shine upon them and that He would lift up His countenance upon them (see Numbers 6:25, 26).

Our countenance is simply the way we look. When people look at us, we want them to see something about us that is different from what they see about everyone else. They cannot read our minds or see into our hearts, but they can see from the glow on our faces that we have something awesome and wonderful.

Our countenance is important. The look we have on our faces at work and our tone of voice at home are important. It is important that we smile at one another, that we are pleasant and just downright nice to each other. We are supposed to be loving people who reflect God's joy on our faces. But how do we do that?

The Bible talks about Jesus' countenance and how it was "transfigured" when He communed with God the Father on the mountain: "His face shone clear and bright like the sun" (Matthew 17:2). We need that same experience, and it comes to us as it did to Jesus—through worshiping God. We look better when we worship God. Worship puts a smile on our faces. It is almost impossible to scowl while we are praising, worshiping, and thanking God. If we regularly spend time fellowshipping with God and worshipping Him, our countenance will carry His presence. We will look strong, joyful, and peaceful instead of frustrated or stressed.

I remember one time when I was at a conference, a woman looked at my face and said, "I can tell you have been with Jesus." She was right. I had spent a long time that morning in prayer and fellowship with the Lord, preparing for the teaching I would do that day. How could she tell I had been with Jesus? Something about my countenance let her know. Perhaps I looked happy and satisfied, or peaceful. I do not know exactly what she saw, but something about the look on my face let her know Whom I was spending my time with.

It is important that we spend more time talking to God, thanking Him, and worshiping Him; then our faces will carry His glory. We need to ask, "Does my countenance reflect the greatness of my God?"

12 He who offered his offering on the first day was Nahshon son of Amminadab, of the tribe of Judah.
13 And his offering was one silver platter, the weight of which was 130 shekels, one silver basin of seventy shekels, according to the shekel of the sanctuary, both of them full of fine flour mixed with oil for a cereal offering;
14 One golden bowl of ten shekels, full of incense;
15 One young bull, one ram, one male lamb a year old, for a burnt offering;
16 One male goat for a sin offering;
17 And ᵇfor the sacrifice of peace

b Verses 12 to 17 give the detailed description of one tribe leader's offering. Then, instead of saying that the gifts of the other tribe leaders were exactly like this one and naming the leaders, the record goes on for **seventy** verses repeating what has already been said **eleven** more times! Why? These offerings, two oxen, five rams, five male goats, five male lambs a year old. This was the offering of Nahshon son of Amminadab.

18 The second day Nethanel son of Zuar, leader [of the tribe] of Issachar, offered.

19 He gave for his offering one silver platter, the weight of which was 130 shekels, one silver basin of seventy shekels, after the shekel of the sanctuary, both of them full of fine flour mixed with oil for a cereal offering;

20 One golden bowl of ten shekels, full of incense;

21 One young bull, one ram, one male lamb a year old, for a burnt offering;

22 One male goat for a sin offering;

23 And for the sacrifice of peace offerings, two oxen, five rams, five male goats, five male lambs a year old. This was the offering of Nethanel son of Zuar.

24 The third day Eliab son of Helon, leader of the sons of Zebulun, offered.

25 His offering was one silver platter, the weight of which was 130 shekels, one silver basin of seventy shekels, after the shekel of the sanctuary, both of them full of fine flour mixed with oil for a cereal offering;

26 One golden bowl of ten shekels, full of incense;

27 One young bull, one ram, one male lamb a year old, for a burnt offering;

28 One male goat for a sin offering;

29 And for the sacrifice of peace offerings, two oxen, five rams, five male goats, five male lambs a year old. This was the offering of Eliab son of Helon.

30 The fourth day Elizur son of Shedeur, leader of the sons of Reuben, offered.

31 His offering was one silver platter of the weight of 130 shekels, one silver basin of seventy shekels, after the shekel of the sanctuary, both of them full of fine flour mixed with oil for a cereal offering;

32 One golden bowl of ten shekels, full of incense;

33 One young bull, one ram, one male lamb a year old, for a burnt offering;

34 One male goat for a sin offering;

35 And for the sacrifice of peace offerings, two oxen, five rams, five male goats, five male lambs a year old. This was the offering of Elizur son of Shedeur.

36 The fifth day Shelumiel son of Zurishaddai, leader of the sons of Simeon, offered.

37 His offering was one silver platter, the weight of which was 130 shekels, one silver basin of seventy shekels, after the shekel of the sanctuary, both of them full of fine flour mixed with oil for a cereal offering;

38 One golden bowl of ten shekels, full of incense;

39 One young bull, one ram, one male lamb a year old, for a burnt offering;

40 One male goat for a sin offering;

41 And for the sacrifice of peace offerings, two oxen, five rams, five

---

things "were written for our learning" (Rom. 15:4 KJV). Let us seek the answer. Other commentators give Matthew Henry credit for giving the correct view. He says that both in dictating that each tribal leader have a separate day for his gift and in giving the reports equal space, regardless of the contrast in the tribe's strength and rank in the camp, God had a definite purpose: "that an equal honor might thereby be put on each several tribe . . . Thus it was intimated that all the tribes of Israel had an equal share in the altar and an equal share in the sacrifices that were offered upon it. Though one tribe was posted more honorably in the camp than another, yet they and their services were all alike acceptable to God . . . Rich and poor meet together before God . . . He was letting us know that what is given is lent to the Lord, and He carefully records it, with everyone's name prefixed to his gift, because what is so given as a labor of love (Heb. 6:10 KJV) He will repay. Christ took particular notice of what was cast into the treasury (Mark 12:41)" (Matthew Henry, *A Commentary*).

male goats, five male lambs a year old. This was the offering of Shelumiel son of Zurishaddai.

42 The sixth day Eliasaph son of Deuel, leader of the sons of Gad, offered.

43 His offering was one silver platter of the weight of 130 shekels, a silver basin of seventy shekels, after the shekel of the sanctuary, both of them full of fine flour mixed with oil for a cereal offering;

44 One golden bowl of ten shekels, full of incense;

45 One young bull, one ram, one male lamb a year old, for a burnt offering;

46 One male goat for a sin offering;

47 And for the sacrifice of peace offerings, two oxen, five rams, five male goats, [and] five male lambs a year old. This was the offering of Eliasaph son of Deuel.

48 The seventh day Elishama son of Ammihud, leader of the sons of Ephraim, offered.

49 His offering was one silver platter, the weight of which was 130 shekels, one silver basin of seventy shekels, after the shekel of the sanctuary, both of them full of fine flour mixed with oil for a cereal offering;

50 One golden bowl of ten shekels, full of incense;

51 One young bull, one ram, one male lamb a year old, for a burnt offering;

52 One male goat for a sin offering;

53 And for the sacrifice of peace offerings, two oxen, five rams, five male goats, [and] five male lambs a year old. This was the offering of Elishama son of Ammihud.

54 The eighth day Gamaliel son of Pedahzur, leader of the sons of Manasseh, offered.

55 His offering was one silver platter of the weight of 130 shekels, one silver basin of seventy shekels, after the shekel of the sanctuary, both of them full of fine flour mixed with oil for a cereal offering;

56 One golden bowl of ten shekels, full of incense;

57 One young bull, one ram, one male lamb a year old, for a burnt offering;

58 One male goat for a sin offering;

59 And for the sacrifice of peace offerings, two oxen, five rams, five male goats, five male lambs a year old. This was the offering of Gamaliel son of Pedahzur.

60 The ninth day Abidan son of Gideoni, prince *or* leader of the sons of Benjamin, offered.

61 His offering was one silver platter, the weight of which was 130 shekels, one silver basin of seventy shekels, after the shekel of the sanctuary, both of them full of fine flour mixed with oil for a cereal offering;

62 One golden bowl of ten shekels, full of incense;

63 One young bull, one ram, one male lamb a year old, for a burnt offering;

64 One male goat for a sin offering;

65 And for the sacrifice of peace offerings, two oxen, five rams, five male goats, five male lambs a year old. This was the offering of Abidan son of Gideoni.

66 The tenth day Ahiezer son of Ammishaddai, leader of the sons of Dan, offered.

67 His offering was one silver platter, the weight of which was 130 shekels, one silver basin of seventy shekels, after the shekel of the sanctuary, both of them full of fine flour mixed with oil for a cereal offering;

68 One golden bowl of ten shekels, full of incense;

69 One young bull, one ram, one male lamb a year old, for a burnt offering;

70 One male goat for a sin offering;

71 And for the sacrifice of peace offerings, two oxen, five rams, five male goats, five male lambs a year old.

This was the offering of Ahiezer son of Ammishaddai.

72 The eleventh day Pagiel son of Ochran, leader of the sons of Asher, offered.

73 His offering was one silver platter, the weight of which was 130 shekels, one silver basin of seventy shekels, after the shekel of the sanctuary, both of them full of fine flour mixed with oil for a cereal offering;

74 One golden bowl of ten shekels, full of incense;

75 One young bull, one ram, one male lamb a year old, for a burnt offering;

76 One male goat for a sin offering;

77 And for the sacrifice of peace offerings, two oxen, five rams, five male goats, five male lambs a year old. This was the offering of Pagiel son of Ochran.

78 The twelfth day Ahira son of Enan, leader of the sons of Naphtali, offered.

79 His offering was one silver platter, the weight of which was 130 shekels, one silver basin of seventy shekels, after the shekel of the sanctuary, both of them full of fine flour mixed with oil for a cereal offering;

80 One golden bowl of ten shekels, full of incense;

81 One young bull, one ram, one male lamb a year old, for a burnt offering;

82 One male goat for a sin offering;

83 And for the sacrifice of peace offerings, two oxen, five rams, five male goats, five male lambs a year old. This was the offering of Ahira son of Enan.

84 This was the dedication offering for the altar [of burnt offering] from the leaders of Israel on the day when it was anointed: twelve platters of silver, twelve silver basins, twelve golden bowls;

85 Each platter of silver weighing 130 shekels, each basin seventy; all the silver vessels weighed 2,400 shekels, after the shekel of the sanctuary.

86 The twelve golden bowls full of incense, weighing ten shekels apiece, after the shekel of the sanctuary, all the gold of the bowls being 120 shekels.

87 All the oxen for the burnt offering were twelve bulls, the rams twelve, the male lambs a year old twelve, together with their cereal offering; and the male goats for a sin offering twelve.

88 And all the oxen for the sacrifice of the peace offerings were twenty-four bulls, the rams sixty, the male goats sixty, the male lambs a year old sixty. This was the dedication of the altar [of burnt offering] after it was anointed.

89 And when Moses went into the Tent of Meeting to speak with the Lord, he heard the voice speaking to him from above the mercy seat that was upon the ark of the Testimony from between the two cherubim; and He spoke to [Moses].

8 AND THE Lord said to Moses,

2 Say to Aaron, When you set up and light the lamps, the seven lamps shall be made to give light in front of the lampstand.

3 And Aaron did so; he lighted the lamps of the lampstand to give light in front of it, as the Lord commanded Moses.

4 And this was the workmanship of the candlestick: beaten or turned gold, beaten work [of gold] from its base to its flowers; according to the pattern which the Lord had shown Moses, so he made the lampstand.

5 And the Lord said to Moses,

6 Take the ᶜLevites from among the Israelites and cleanse them.

c There are many lessons for the Christian in this section (Num. 8:5-22). He sees here the importance of each member of God's family having his own particular task (I Cor. 12). It is necessary that

7 And thus you shall do to them to cleanse them: sprinkle the water of purification [water to be used in case of sin] upon them, and let them pass a razor over all their flesh and wash their clothes and cleanse themselves. [Num. 19:17, 18.]

8 Then let them take a young bull and its cereal offering of fine flour mixed with oil, and another young bull you shall take for a sin offering.

9 You shall present the Levites before the Tent of Meeting, and you shall assemble the whole Israelite congregation.

10 And you shall present the Levites before the Lord, and the Israelites shall put their hands upon the Levites,

11 And Aaron shall offer the Levites before the Lord as a wave offering from the Israelites *and* on their behalf, that they may do the service of the Lord.

12 Then the Levites shall lay their hands upon the heads of the bulls, and you shall offer the one for a sin offering and the other for a burnt offering to the Lord, to make atonement for the Levites.

13 And you shall present the Levites before Aaron and his sons and offer them as a wave offering to the Lord.

14 Thus you shall separate the Levites from among the Israelites, and the Levites shall be Mine [in a very special sense].

15 And after that the Levites shall go in to do service at the Tent of Meeting, when you have cleansed them and offered them as a wave offering.

16 For they are wholly given to Me from among the Israelites; instead of all who open the womb, the firstborn of all the Israelites, I have taken the Levites for Myself.

17 For all the firstborn of the Israelites are Mine, both of man and beast; on the day that I smote every firstborn in the land of Egypt [not of Israel], I consecrated them *and* set them apart for Myself.

18 And I have taken the Levites instead of all the firstborn of the Israelites.

19 And I have given the Levites as a gift to Aaron and to his sons from among the Israelites to do the service of the Israelites at the Tent of Meeting and to make atonement for them, that there may be no plague among the Israelites if they should come near the sanctuary.

20 So Moses and Aaron and all the congregation of the Israelites did thus to the Levites; according to all that the Lord commanded Moses concerning [them], so did the Israelites to them.

21 The Levites cleansed *and* purified themselves and they washed their clothes; and Aaron offered them as a wave offering before the Lord and Aaron made atonement for them to cleanse them.

22 And after that the Levites went in to do their service in the Tent of Meeting with the attendance of Aaron and his sons; as the Lord had commanded Moses concerning the Levites, so did they to them.

23 And the Lord said to Moses,

24 This is what applies to the Levites: from twenty-five years old and upward they shall go in to perform the work of the service of the Tent of Meeting,

---

special men be designated for particular duties in order that the work of God's kingdom shall be done in orderly fashion. Those who do the work of God must be cleansed from all defilement of flesh and spirit. No one is fit in himself to serve God. It is only as we see ourselves as guilty sinners saved through the sacrifice of the Lord Jesus Christ at Calvary that we can do anything that is worthwhile in God's sight. Apart from Him, "all our righteousnesses *are* as filthy rags" (Isa. 64:6 KJV). (F. Davidson, ed., *The New Bible Commentary*).

25 And at the age of fifty years, they shall retire from the warfare of the service and serve no more,

26 But shall help their brethren in the Tent of Meeting [attend to protecting the sacred things from being profaned], but shall do no regular *or* heavy service. Thus shall you direct the Levites in regard to their duties.

9 THE LORD said to Moses in the Wilderness of Sinai in the first month of the second year after they had come out of the land of Egypt,

2 Let the Israelites keep the Passover at its appointed time.

3 On the fourteenth day of this month in the evening, you shall keep it at its appointed time; according to all its statutes and ordinances you shall keep it.

4 So Moses told the Israelites they should keep the Passover.

5 And they kept the Passover on the fourteenth day of the first month in the evening in the Wilderness of Sinai; according to all that the Lord commanded Moses, so the Israelites did.

6 And there were certain men who were defiled by touching the dead body of a man, so they could not keep the Passover on that day; and they came before Moses and Aaron on that day.

7 Those men said to [Moses], We are defiled by touching the dead body. Why are we prevented from offering the Lord's offering at its appointed time among the Israelites?

8 And Moses said to them, Stand still, and I will hear what the Lord will command concerning you.

9 And the Lord said to Moses,

10 Say to the Israelites, If any man of you or of your posterity shall be unclean by reason of touching a dead body or is far off on a journey, still he shall keep the Passover to the Lord.

11 On the fourteenth day of the second month in the evening they shall keep it, and eat it with unleavened bread and bitter herbs.

12 They shall leave none of it until the morning nor break any bone of it; according to all the statutes for the Passover they shall keep it. [John 19:36.]

13 But the man who is clean and is not on a journey, yet does not keep the Passover, that person shall be cut off from among his people because he did not bring the Lord's offering at its appointed time; that man shall bear [the penalty of] his sin.

14 And if a stranger sojourns among you and will keep the Passover to the Lord, according to [its] statutes and its ordinances, so shall he do; you shall have one statute both for the temporary resident and for him who was born in the land.

15 And on the day that the tabernacle was erected, the cloud [of God's presence] covered the tabernacle, that is, the Tent of the Testimony; and at evening it was over the tabernacle, having the appearance of [a pillar of] fire until the morning. [Exod. 13:21.]

16 So it was constantly; the cloud covered it by day, and the appearance of fire by night.

17 Whenever the cloud was taken up from over the Tent, after that the Israelites journeyed; and in the place where the cloud rested, there the Israelites encamped.

18 At the Lord's command the Israelites journeyed, and at [His] command they encamped. As long as the cloud rested upon the tabernacle they remained encamped.

putting the Word to work

In the midst of your busy life, are you able to be like Moses and "stand still" (see Numbers 9:8) to hear what the Lord wants to say to you? Ask Him to help you hear His voice more clearly.

19 Even when the cloud tarried upon the tabernacle many days, the Israelites kept the Lord's charge and did not set out.

20 And sometimes the cloud was only a few days upon the tabernacle, but according to the command of the Lord they remained encamped, and at His command they journeyed.

21 And sometimes the cloud remained [over the tabernacle] from evening only until morning, but when the cloud was taken up, they journeyed; whether it was taken up by day or by night, they journeyed.

22 Whether it was two days or a month or a longer time that the cloud tarried upon the tabernacle, dwelling on it, the Israelites remained encamped; but when it was taken up, they journeyed.

23 At the command of the Lord they remained encamped, and at [His] command they journeyed; they kept the charge of the Lord, at the command of the Lord through Moses.

10 AND THE Lord said to Moses,

2 Make two trumpets of silver; of hammered *or* turned work you shall make them, that you may use them to call the congregation and for breaking camp.

3 When they both are blown, all the congregation shall assemble before you at the door of the Tent of Meeting.

4 And if one blast on a single trumpet is blown, then the princes *or* leaders, heads of the tribes of Israel, shall gather themselves to you.

5 When you blow an alarm, the camps on the east side [of the tabernacle] shall set out.

6 When you blow an alarm the second time, then the camps on the south side shall set out. An alarm shall be blown whenever they are to set out on their journeys.

7 When the congregation is to be assembled, you shall blow [the trumpets in short, sharp tones], but not the blast of an alarm.

8 And the sons of Aaron, the priests, shall blow the trumpets, and the trumpets shall be to you for a perpetual statute throughout your generations.

9 When you go to war in your land against the enemy that oppresses you, then blow an alarm with the trumpets, that you may be remembered before the Lord your God, and you shall be saved from your enemies.

10 Also in the day of rejoicing, and in your set feasts, and at the beginnings of your months, you shall blow the trumpets over your burnt offerings and your peace offerings; thus they may be a remembrance before your God. I am the Lord your God.

11 On the twentieth day of the second month in the second year [since leaving Egypt], the cloud [of the Lord's presence] was taken up from over the tabernacle of the Testimony,

12 And the Israelites took their journey by stages out of the Wilderness of Sinai, and the [guiding] cloud rested in the Wilderness of Paran.

13 When the journey was to begin, at the command of the Lord through Moses,

14 In the first place went the standard of the camp of the sons of Judah by their companies; and over their host was Nahshon son of Amminadab.

15 And over the host of the tribe of the sons of Issachar was Nethanel son of Zuar.

16 And over the host of the tribe of the sons of Zebulun was Eliab son of Helon.

17 When the tabernacle was taken down, the sons of Gershon and Merari, bearing [it] on their shoulders, set out.

18 The standard of the camp of Reuben set forward by their companies; and over Reuben's host was Elizur son of Shedeur.

19 And over the host of the tribe of

the sons of Simeon was Shelumiel son of Zurishaddai.

20 And over the host of the tribe of the sons of Gad was Eliasaph son of Deuel.

21 Then the Kohathites set forward, bearing the holy things, and the tabernacle was set up before they arrived.

22 And the standard of the camp of the sons of Ephraim set forward according to their companies; and over Ephraim's host was Elishama son of Ammihud.

23 Over the host of the tribe of the sons of Manasseh was Gamaliel son of Pedahzur.

24 And over the host of the tribe of the sons of Benjamin was Abidan son of Gideoni.

25 Then the standard of the camp of the sons of Dan, which was the rear guard of all the camps, set forward according to their companies; and over Dan's host was Ahiezer son of Ammishaddai.

26 And over the host of the tribe of the sons of Asher was Pagiel son of Ochran.

27 And over the host of the tribe of the sons of Naphtali was Ahira son of Enan.

28 This was the Israelites' order of march by their hosts when they set out.

29 And Moses said to Hobab son of Reuel the Midianite, Moses' father-in-law, We are journeying to the place of which the Lord said, I will give it to you. Come with us, and we will do you good, for the Lord has promised good concerning Israel.

30 And Hobab said to him, I will not go; I will depart to my own land and to my family.

31 And Moses said, dDo not leave us, I pray you; for you know how we are to encamp in the wilderness, and you will serve as eyes for us.

32 And if you will go with us, it shall be that whatever good the Lord does to us, the same we will do to you.

33 They departed from the mountain of the Lord [Mount Sinai] three days' journey; and the ark of the covenant of the Lord went before them during the three days' journey to seek out a resting-place for them.

34 The cloud of the Lord was over them by day when they went forward from the camp.

35 Whenever the ark set out, Moses said, Rise up, Lord; let Your enemies be scattered; and let those who hate You flee before You. [Ps. 68:1, 2.]

life point

When the Israelites journeyed from Egypt (the land of bondage) to Canaan (the land of promise), the cloud of the Lord went before them, leading the way. Each time the ark of the covenant was lifted up and carried out before them, Moses cried out to God, "Rise up, Lord; let Your enemies be scattered" (Numbers 10:35). I love that! May we be reminded each day to praise the Lord and expect His power to bring the victory.

speak the Word

Thank You, God, that You have promised good concerning me, just as You did for the Israelites so long ago.
ADAPTED FROM Numbers 10:29

d The record does not say so, but Hobab seems to have remained with the Israelites, for later history shows that his descendants lived in Canaan (Judg. 1:16; I Sam. 15:6).

36 And when it rested, he said, Return, O Lord, to the ten thousand thousands in Israel.

11 AND THE people grumbled *and* deplored their hardships, which was evil in the ears of the Lord, and when the Lord heard it, His anger was kindled; and the fire of the Lord burned among them and devoured those in the outlying parts of the camp.
2 The people cried to Moses, and when Moses prayed to the Lord, the fire subsided.
3 He called the name of the place Taberah [burning], because the fire of the Lord burned among them.
4 And the mixed multitude among them [the rabble who followed Israel from Egypt] began to lust greatly [for familiar and dainty food], and the Israelites wept again and said, Who will give us meat to eat?
5 We remember the fish we ate freely in Egypt *and* without cost, the cucumbers, melons, leeks, onions, and garlic.
6 But now our soul (our strength) is dried up; there is nothing at all [in the way of food] to be seen but this manna.

don't turn back

The Israelites spent a great deal of time grumbling and hating their hardships as they traveled through the wilderness on their way to the Promised Land. The way we behave and the attitudes we display in our own "wilderness experiences" may well be the determining factor in how long we stay there. Some people never stop complaining, and, as a result, they never make any progress in their lives.

Not only did the children of Israel complain, they also frequently wanted to turn around and go back to where they came from. They had made the mistake of bringing unbelieving Egyptians out of Egypt with them. Called in Numbers 11:4 the "mixed multitude" or "rabble," these people did not love God and tempted the Israelites by reminding them of the dubious benefits of Egypt. Similarly, the devil reminds people today of the benefits they had while they were in the world and doing things their own way.

When we decide to live for God, all kinds of things are used by the devil to try to get us to grumble and complain. In 1976, God called me to quit my job and prepare for ministry. In order to do so, we had to trust God for money to pay the bills because my husband's salary alone was not enough. Many times in those days, the devil tried to influence me to go back to work and take care of myself. He reminded me of the days when we had plenty of money, new cars, new clothes, and cash left over. But he failed to remind me of how miserable I was because I was not following God's will for my life.

There are plenty of places in the road where we can park or even turn around and go back the way we came. But if we press on and follow God's plan for our lives, we will be greatly blessed in the end. Being in God's perfect will is the most comfortable place in the world to be. Don't ever turn back. Keep pressing on!

7 The manna was like coriander seed and its appearance was like that of bdellium [perhaps a precious stone]. **8** The people went about and gathered it, and ground it in mills or beat it in mortars, and boiled it in pots, and made cakes of it; and it tasted like cakes baked with fresh oil.

9 And when the dew fell on the camp in the night, the manna fell with it.

10 And Moses heard the people weeping throughout their families, every man at the door of his tent; and the anger of the Lord blazed hotly, and in the eyes of Moses it was evil.

11 And Moses said to the Lord, Why have You dealt ill with Your servants? And why have I not found favor in Your sight, that You lay the burden of all this people on me?

12 Have I conceived all this people? Have I brought them forth, that You should say to me, Carry them in your bosom, as a nursing father carries the sucking child, to the land which You swore to their fathers [to give them]?

13 Where should I get meat to give to all these people? For they weep before me and say, Give us meat, that we may eat.

14 I am not able to carry all these people alone, because the burden is too heavy for me.

putting the Word to work

Do you ever feel, as Moses did, that you are carrying burdens that are too heavy for you? At those times, remember to cast your cares upon God because He cares for you (see I Peter 5:7).

15 And if this is the way You deal with me, kill me, I pray You, at once, and be granting me a favor and let me not see my wretchedness [in the failure of all my efforts].

16 And the Lord said to Moses, Gather for Me eseventy men of the elders of Israel whom you know to be the elders of the people and officers over them; and bring them to the Tent of Meeting and let them stand there with you.

17 And I will come down and talk with you there; and I will take of the Spirit which is upon you and will put It upon them; and they shall bear the burden of the people with you, so that you may not have to bear it yourself alone.

18 And say to the people, Consecrate yourselves for tomorrow, and you shall eat meat; for you have wept in the hearing of the Lord, saying, Who will give us meat to eat? For it was well with us in Egypt. Therefore the Lord will give you meat, and you shall eat.

19 You shall not eat one day, or two, or five, or ten, or twenty days,

20 But a whole month—until [you are satiated and vomit it up violently and] it comes out at your nostrils and is disgusting to you—because you have rejected *and* despised the Lord Who is among you, and have wept before Him, saying, Why did we come out of Egypt? [Ps. 106:13-15.]

21 But Moses said, The people among whom I am are 600,000 footmen [besides all the women and children], and You have said, I will give them meat, that they may eat a whole month!

22 Shall flocks and herds be killed to suffice them? Or shall all the fish of the sea be collected to satisfy them?

23 The Lord said to Moses, Has the Lord's hand (His ability and power) become short (thwarted and

e A council of seventy elders had existed the year before this (Exod. 24:9). It appears to be the source of the Sanhedrin, the highest Jewish assembly for government in the time of our Lord—usually translated "council."

inadequate)? You shall see now whether My word shall come to pass for you or not. [Isa. 50:2.]

24 So Moses went out and told the people the words of the Lord, and he gathered seventy men of the elders of the people and set them round about the Tent.

25 And the Lord came down in the cloud and spoke to him, and took of the Spirit that was upon him and put It upon the seventy elders; and when the Spirit rested upon them, they prophesied [sounding forth the praises of God and declaring His will]. Then they did so no more. [Num. 11:29.]

26 But there remained two men in the camp named Eldad and Medad. The Spirit rested upon them, and they were of those who were selected *and* listed, yet they did not go out to the Tent [as told to do], but they prophesied in the camp.

27 And a young man ran to Moses and said, Eldad and Medad are prophesying [sounding forth the praises of God and declaring His will] in the camp.

28 Joshua son of Nun, the minister of Moses, one of his chosen men, said, My lord Moses, forbid them!

29 But Moses said to him, Are you ᶠenvious *or* jealous for my sake? Would that all the Lord's people were prophets and that the Lord would put His Spirit upon them! [Luke 9:49, 50.]

30 And Moses went back into the camp, he and the elders of Israel.

31 And there went forth a wind from the Lord and brought quails from the sea, and let them fall [so they flew low] beside the camp, about a day's journey on this side and on the other

side, all around the camp, about two cubits above the ground.

32 And the people rose all that day and all night and all the next day and caught *and* gathered the quails. He who gathered least gathered ten homers; and they spread them out for themselves round about the camp [to cure them by drying].

33 While the meat was yet between their teeth, before it was consumed, the anger of the Lord was kindled against the people, and the Lord smote them with a very great plague.

34 That place was called Kibroth-hattaavah [the graves of sensuous desire], because there they buried the people who lusted, whose physical appetite caused them to sin. [I Cor. 10:1-13.]

35 The Israelites journeyed from Kibroth-hattaavah to Hazeroth, where they remained.

12 NOW MIRIAM and Aaron talked against Moses [their brother] because of his ᵍCushite wife, for he had married a Cushite woman.

2 And they said, Has the Lord indeed spoken only by Moses? Has He not spoken also by us? And the Lord heard it.

3 Now the man Moses was very meek (gentle, kind, and humble) *or* above all the men on the face of the earth.

4 Suddenly the Lord said to Moses, Aaron, and Miriam, Come out, you three, to the Tent of Meeting. And the three of them came out.

5 The Lord came down in a pillar of cloud, and stood at the Tent door and called Aaron and Miriam, and they came forward.

---

f "Moses, the minister of God, rebukes our partial love, / Who envy at the gifts bestow'd on those we disapprove. / We do not our own spirit know, who wish to see suppressed, / The men that Jesus' spirit show, the men whom God hath blest" (Charles Wesley). **g** Zipporah, Moses' wife, seems to have died some time before. Marriage with a Canaanite was forbidden, but not with an Egyptian or Cushite. Joseph's wife was an Egyptian (Gen. 41:45).

the meaning of meekness

When you think of a meek person, what image comes to mind? I would like to explain the character trait of meekness to you because we rarely hear much about it. *Meek* does not mean "weak." I believe a good definition of true meekness is *getting angry at the right time in the right measure for the right reason.*

Scripture tells us that Moses was "very meek" (Numbers 12:3). In fact, he was the meekest man on the face of the earth. Said another way, he was able to maintain a careful balance between emotional extremes. What was Moses like? He was patient and long-suffering with the Israelites. When he could have blasted them for their sins and rebellion, he prayed for them instead. As their God-ordained leader and guide, he put up with decades of griping and complaining and insolence from these people who never seemed to tire of testing his patience and endurance. Yet when he came down from meeting with the Lord on the mountaintop and saw the Israelites bowing down and worshipping the golden calf they had made, he became so angry he threw down the tablets with the Ten Commandments written on them!

There is a time to repress anger, and there is a time to express anger—and wisdom knows the difference. A meek person is not someone who never shows anger, but someone who never allows his anger to get out of control. Although Moses was a meek man, he was not a perfect man. There was a time when Moses allowed his anger to get out of control, and God punished him for it. Meekness does not mean being without emotion; it means being in charge of emotion and channeling it in the right direction for the right purpose. Moses was a man to whom God entrusted great power and responsibility. God had given him a great deal, and He expected a great deal from him.

I encourage you to develop true meekness in your life. As you do, remember God's promise in Matthew 5:5: "Blessed . . . are the meek, for they shall inherit the earth!"

---

6   And He said, Hear now My words: If there is a prophet among you, I the Lord make Myself known to him in a vision and speak to him in a dream.
7   But not so with My servant Moses; he is entrusted *and* faithful in all My house. [Heb. 3:2, 5, 6.]
8   With him I speak mouth to mouth [directly], clearly and not in dark speeches; and he beholds the form of the Lord. Why then were you not afraid to speak against My servant Moses?
9   And the anger of the Lord was kindled against them, and He departed.
10 And when the cloud departed from over the Tent, behold, Miriam

speak the Word

God, I pray that I will be like Moses and be trustworthy and faithful before You and that You will speak clearly to me.
ADAPTED FROM NUMBERS 12:7, 8

was leprous, as white as snow. And Aaron looked at Miriam, and, behold, she was leprous!

11 And Aaron said to Moses, Oh, my lord, I plead with you, lay not the sin upon us in which we have done foolishly and in which we have sinned.

12 Let her not be as one dead, already half decomposed when he comes out of his mother's womb.

13 And Moses cried to the Lord, saying, Heal her now, O God, I beseech You!

14 And the Lord said to Moses, If her father had but spit in her face, should she not be ashamed for seven days? Let her be shut up outside the camp for seven days, and after that let her be brought in again.

15 So Miriam was shut up without the camp for seven days, and the people did not journey on until Miriam was brought in again.

16 Afterward [they] removed from Hazeroth and encamped in the Wilderness of Paran.

13 AND THE Lord said to Moses, 2 Send men to explore *and* scout out [for yourselves] the land of Canaan, which I give to the Israelites. From each tribe of their fathers you shall send a man, every one a leader *or* head among them.

3 So Moses by the command of the Lord sent scouts from the Wilderness of Paran, all of them men who were heads of the Israelites.

4 These were their names: of the tribe of Reuben, Shammua son of Zaccur;

5 Of the tribe of Simeon, Shaphat son of Hori;

6 Of the tribe of Judah, Caleb son of Jephunneh;

7 Of the tribe of Issachar, Igal son of Joseph;

8 Of the tribe of Ephraim, Hoshea [that is, Joshua] son of Nun;

9 Of the tribe of Benjamin, Palti son of Raphu;

10 Of the tribe of Zebulun, Gaddiel son of Sodi;

11 Of the tribe of Joseph, that is, of the tribe of Manasseh, Gaddi son of Susi;

12 Of the tribe of Dan, Ammiel son of Gemalli;

13 Of the tribe of Asher, Sethur son of Michael;

14 Of the tribe of Naphtali, Nahbi son of Vophsi;

15 Of the tribe of Gad, Geuel son of Machi.

16 These are the names of the men whom Moses sent to explore *and* scout out the land. And Moses called Hoshea son of Nun, Joshua.

17 Moses sent them to scout out the land of Canaan, and said to them, Get up this way by the South (the Negeb) and go up into the hill country,

18 And see what the land is and whether the people who dwell there are strong or weak, few or many,

19 And whether the land they live in is good or bad, and whether the cities they dwell in are camps or strongholds,

20 And what the land is, whether it is fat or lean, whether there is timber on it or not. And be of good courage and bring some of the fruit of the land. Now the time was the time of the first ripe grapes.

21 So they went up and scouted through the land from the Wilderness of Zin to Rehob, to the entrance of Hamath.

22 And then went up into the South (the Negeb) and came to Hebron; and Ahiman, Sheshai, and Talmai [probably three tribes of] the sons of Anak were there. (Hebron was built seven years before Zoan in Egypt.)

23 And they came to the Valley of Eshcol, and cut down from there a branch with one cluster of grapes, and they carried it on a pole between two [of them]; they brought also some pomegranates and figs.

giant-sized problems

The children of Israel faced giants they feared would stop them from entering their Promised Land. Moses had sent Joshua, Caleb, and ten other men to spy out the land of Canaan and bring back a report (see Numbers 13:17–20). The ten came back and said that the land was full of good fruit, but it was also full of giants who would be difficult to defeat (see Numbers 13:27, 28).

Joshua and Caleb had a different attitude. They too had seen the giants but preferred to keep their eyes on God, Whom they believed was greater than the giants. Caleb urged, "Let us go up at once and possess it; we are well able to conquer it" (Numbers 13:30). How did the negative people respond? They answered, "We are not able . . . they are stronger than we are" (Numbers 13:31).

Isn't this the way it is with life? There are positive people who try to go forward, and there are negative people who try to contaminate everything good and positive with their bad attitudes. Ten of the spies were negative and two were positive. Based on those figures, 80 percent of the people said they were not able to defeat the giants, and only 20 percent believed God was greater than the problem. The same thing is true today. If a higher percentage of people believed in the great power of God, we would see more people succeeding in life. Evil would not be rampant, because the righteous in the land would be aggressively going forth in faith, conquering everything that is not in harmony with God.

Sadly, we often stare at our giant-sized problems instead of at our God. We lose our focus; we become entangled with the problem and lose sight of what God has called us to do. I believe that more time spent worshipping and praising God would help us keep a clear focus and enable us to go forward with a strong, positive attitude, believing we can do anything God tells us to do.

How much time do you spend fellowshipping with your problems compared to the time you spend fellowshipping with God? Sometimes when we supposedly spend time with God, all we do is talk to Him about our problems. We still are not *really* spending time with Him; we have just found another way to talk about all the things we are unhappy about. We can tell God about what concerns us and ask Him to help, but we need to spend more time praising than we do petitioning.

Joshua and Caleb reminded the others that God had promised to give them the land. They encouraged them not to rebel against the Lord and not to fear the giants. They encouraged the people: "The Lord is with us. Fear them not" (Numbers 14:9).

God is not with the enemy; He is with us. And if God is for us, who can be against us? I encourage you to practice maintaining a good attitude. Be content, thankful. Pay attention to what God is doing, and do not simply take note of what you think He is not doing for you. Beware of complaining. Instead, worship God and keep worshipping Him until your breakthrough comes. Having a good attitude will bring your breakthrough faster than being grouchy. However long you have to wait, you might as well be happy while you wait. Enjoy *where* you are—on *the way* to where you are going! Do not fear the giants; slay them with your faith. God is greater than any giant or any giant-sized problem you face.

life point

Possessing the land (see Numbers 13:30) involves dispossessing the current occupants. To the Israelites, the occupants were people; to us, they may be people, situations, or even the devil and his demons. Our spiritual enemy, Satan, seeks to divert the good things that are ours. In order to possess the land and enjoy the many blessings available to God's children, we need to learn how to deal with the devil. We cannot fight him through ordinary means; we must combat him with spiritual warfare (see Ephesians 6:11–18). As we do, we cannot be lazy or irresponsible. We need to be aggressively walking in the righteousness of God. We must wear our shoes of peace and wear our helmets of salvation. We should wield the two-edged sword of the Spirit. To me that means to speak God's Word in every situation. Walk in truth, stay in faith, and pray at all times. We cannot make excuses, because an excuse is just a reason stuffed with a lie.

I think each one of us carries an invisible "excuse bag." When God puts something on our hearts to do what we do not want to do, we just reach into that bag and draw out an excuse, such as "It's too hard" or "I'm afraid"—just as those ten spies did. We think that an excuse relieves us of our responsibility to do what God has said. But God's answer to us is, "Then do it afraid! As you go, I will help you conquer your fear."

Who said that you cannot do what God has told you, even if you have to start off afraid? As you shed your excuses, you will find that God is more than sufficient. Learn from the two men who were confident God would help them possess the land He had given them. Know that God wants you to enter your land of promise, confidently waging spiritual warfare and going forward without excuse.

24 That place was called the Valley of Eshcol [cluster] because of the cluster which the Israelites cut down there.
25 And they returned from scouting out the land after forty days.
26 They came to Moses and Aaron and to all the Israelite congregation in the Wilderness of Paran at Kadesh, and brought them word, and showed them the land's fruit.
27 They told Moses, We came to the land to which you sent us; surely it flows with milk and honey. This is its fruit.
28 But the people who dwell there are strong, and the cities are hfortified *and* very large; moreover, there we saw the sons of Anak [of great stature and courage].
29 Amalek dwells in the land of the South (the Negeb); the Hittite, the Jebusite, and the Amorite dwell in the hill country; and the Canaanite dwells by the sea and along by the side of the Jordan [River].
30 Caleb quieted the people before Moses, and said, Let us go up at once and possess it; we are well able to conquer it.
31 But his fellow scouts said, We are not able to go up against the people

h The scouts probably had not seen walled cities before, having lived their childhood in Goshen in Egypt. Those who forgot God's power to help them naturally found the situation formidable, as happens in the lives of most people. " 'But God' makes all the difference between cowards and Calebs."

slaying the giants in your land

How do you see yourself? How do you look at the obstacles in your way? If we feel we are nothing, it will be hard to accomplish much in life. We will probably shrink back in fear from every challenge, just like the ten men Moses sent into Canaan to spy out the land. They saw it was a good land with abundant fruit, but there was one problem—there were giants in the land. As these men looked at the giants and then at themselves, they fainted in their minds and said, "We were in our own sight as grasshoppers, and so we were in their sight" (Numbers 13:33). The big mistake these men made was that they looked at the giants and they looked at themselves, but *they did not look at God*.

In and of ourselves we are nothing and can do very little, but in Christ we can do all things He asks us to do (see Philippians 4:13). We must keep our eyes on Jesus and not on ourselves or our weaknesses. (We all have weaknesses, but God will show His strength through them if we believe He is greater than they are!) The giants in this world do not have to frighten us if we keep our eyes on God and put our trust in Him. God says we do not have to live in fear, because He is with us at all times. He has promised never to leave us or forsake us. If God is on our side, why should we be afraid of anybody or anything?

Twelve men were sent into the land to see if they could conquer it, but only Joshua and Caleb believed that God is greater than any obstacle. Make a decision today that you will not stand with those who see only their limitations when facing their giants. Decide to stand with those who see God and believe the giants can be slain. Believe that He will take care of the giants and bring you to a place of abundant blessing.

[of Canaan], for they are stronger than we are.

32 So they brought the Israelites an evil report of the land which they had scouted out, saying, The land through which we went to spy it out is a land that devours its inhabitants. And all the people that we saw in it are men of great stature.

33 There we saw the Nephilim [or giants], the sons of Anak, who come from the giants; and we were in our own sight as grasshoppers, and so we were in their sight.

14 AND ALL the congregation cried out with a loud voice, and [they] wept that night.

2 All the Israelites grumbled *and* deplored their situation, accusing Moses and Aaron, to whom the whole congregation said, Would that we had died in Egypt! Or that we had died in this wilderness!

3 Why does the Lord bring us to this land to fall by the sword? Our wives and little ones will be a prey. Is it not better for us to return to Egypt? [Acts 7:37-39.]

4 And they said one to another, Let us choose a captain and return to Egypt.

5 Then Moses and Aaron fell on their faces before all the assembly of Israelites.

6 And Joshua son of Nun and Caleb son of Jephunneh, who were among

life point

Do you see how negative the Israelites were in Numbers 14:1–3? They were complaining, ready to give up too easily, preferring to go back to bondage rather than press through the wilderness into the Promised Land. Actually, they did not *have* a problem; they *were* the problem! These people felt exceedingly sorry for themselves. Every inconvenience became a new excuse to engage in self-pity. I remember when the Lord spoke to me during one of my "pity parties." He said, "Joyce, you can be pitiful or powerful, but you cannot be both." It is vitally important to understand that we cannot entertain self-pity and also walk in the power of God!

the scouts who had searched the land, rent their clothes,

7   And they said to all the company of Israelites, The land through which we passed as scouts is an exceedingly good land.

8   If the Lord delights in us, then He will bring us into this land and give it to us, a land flowing with milk and honey.

9   Only do not rebel against the Lord, neither fear the people of the land, for they are bread for us. Their defense *and* the shadow [of protection] is removed from over them, but the Lord is with us. Fear them not.

10   But all the congregation said to stone [Joshua and Caleb] with stones. But the glory of the Lord appeared at the Tent of Meeting before all the Israelites.

11   And the Lord said to Moses, How long will this people provoke (spurn, despise) Me? And how long will it be before they believe Me [trusting in, relying on, clinging to Me], for all the signs which I have performed among them?

12   I will smite them with the pestilence and disinherit them, and will make of you [Moses] a nation greater and mightier than they.

13   But Moses said to the Lord, Then the Egyptians will hear of it, for You brought up this people in Your might from among them.

14   And they will tell it to the inhabitants of this land. They have heard that You, Lord, are in the midst of this people [of Israel], that You, Lord, are seen face to face, and that Your cloud stands over them, and that You go before them in a pillar of cloud by day and in a pillar of fire by night.

15   Now if You kill all this people as one man, then the nations that have heard Your fame will say,

16   Because the Lord was not able to bring this people into the land which He swore to give to them, therefore He has slain them in the wilderness.

17   And now, I pray You, let the power of my Lord be great, as You have promised, saying,

18   The Lord is long-suffering *and* slow to anger, and abundant in mercy *and* loving-kindness, forgiving iniquity and transgression; but He will by no means clear the guilty, visiting the iniquity of the fathers upon the children, upon the third and fourth generation. [Exod. 34:6, 7.]

19   Pardon, I pray You, the iniquity of

speak the Word

God, let people hear about me what they heard about the Israelites—that You are in the midst of everything I do, that I know You intimately, that Your presence stands over me, and that You go before me in every situation.
ADAPTED FROM NUMBERS 14:14

on your face

Notice in Numbers 14:5 how Moses and Aaron reacted to the Israelites' murmuring and complaining: they fell on their faces. This action of falling on one's face is found throughout the Bible. It was an act of humility and seeking God in prayer. If all the Israelites had been on their faces before God, they would have seen miracle after miracle. But they were too busy getting tripped up by feeling sorry for themselves, talking negatively, finding fault with God and Moses, and wanting to go back to Egypt. I thank God for Moses and Aaron. As they fell on their faces and worshipped God, they demonstrated their reverence for God. I believe they took this action before the whole assembly to show them they needed to do the same.

Joshua and Caleb would not allow negative, unbelieving people to adversely affect them either. These two men remained full of faith and confidence that they could conquer their enemies. Likewise, we need to keep our faith positive by not letting pessimistic people steal our joy. We should not let doubters destroy our confidence; we should believe that God is a good God and has a good plan for our lives. Satan uses people like this to drain us. We must not let their misery and negativism affect or infect our joy.

When you are tempted to complain, shun the negative talk; instead, worship and honor the Lord. Rather than getting sidetracked by all the things in your way, fall on your face before God in humility and prayer. You will see Him work on your behalf.

---

this people according to the greatness of Your mercy *and* loving-kindness, just as You have forgiven [them] from Egypt until now.

20 And the Lord said, I have pardoned according to your word.

21 But truly as I live and as all the earth shall be filled with the glory of the Lord, [Isa. 6:3; 11:9.]

22 Because all those men who have seen My glory and My [miraculous] signs which I performed in Egypt and in the wilderness, yet have tested *and* proved Me these ten times and have not heeded My voice,

23 Surely they shall not see the land which I swore to give to their fathers; nor shall any who provoked (spurned, despised) Me see it. [Heb. 6:4-11.]

24 But My servant Caleb, because he has a different spirit and has followed Me fully, I will bring into the land into

which he went, and his descendants shall possess it.

25 Now because the Amalekites and the Canaanites dwell in the valley, tomorrow turn and go into the wilderness by way of the Red Sea.

26 And the Lord said to Moses and Aaron,

27 How long will this evil congregation murmur against Me? I have heard the complaints the Israelites murmur against Me.

28 Tell them, As I live, says the Lord, what you have said in My hearing I will do to you:

29 Your dead bodies shall fall in this wilderness—of all who were numbered of you, from twenty years old and upward, who have murmured against Me, [Heb. 3:17-19.]

30 Surely none shall come into the land in which I swore to make you

dwell, except Caleb son of Jephunneh and Joshua son of Nun.

31 But your little ones whom you said would be a prey, them will I bring in and they shall know the land which you have despised *and* rejected.

32 But as for you, your dead bodies shall fall in this wilderness.

33 And your children shall be wanderers *and* shepherds in the wilderness for forty years and shall suffer for your whoredoms (your infidelity to your espoused God), until your corpses are consumed in the wilderness.

34 After the number of the days in which you spied out the land [of Canaan], even forty days, for each day a year shall you bear *and* suffer for your iniquities, even for forty years, and you shall know My displeasure [the revoking of My promise and My estrangement].

35 I the Lord have spoken; surely this will I do to all this evil congregation who is gathered together against Me. In this wilderness they shall be consumed [by war, disease, plagues], and here they shall die. [I Cor. 10:10, 11.]

36 And the men whom Moses sent to search the land, who returned and made all the congregation grumble *and* complain against him by bringing back a slanderous report of the land,

37 Even those men who brought the evil report of the land died by a plague before the Lord. [Heb. 3:17-19; Jude 5-7.]

38 But Joshua son of Nun and Caleb son of Jephunneh, who were among the men who went to search the land, lived still.

39 Moses told [the Lord's] words to all the Israelites, and [they] mourned greatly.

40 And they rose early in the morning and went up to the top of the mountain, saying, Behold, we are here, and we intend to go up to the place which the Lord has promised, for we have sinned.

41 But Moses said, Why now do you transgress the command of the Lord [to turn back by way of the Red Sea], since it will not succeed?

42 Go not up, for the Lord is not among you, that you be not struck down before your enemies.

43 For the Amalekites and the Canaanites are there before you, and you shall fall by the sword. Because you have turned away from following after the Lord, therefore the Lord will not be with you.

44 But they presumed to go up to the heights of the hill country; however, neither the ark of the covenant of the Lord nor Moses departed out of the camp.

45 Then the Amalekites came down and the Canaanites who dwelt in that hill country and smote the Israelites and beat them back, even as far as Hormah.

15 AND THE Lord said to Moses,

2 Say to the Israelites, When you come into the land where you are to live, which I am giving you,

3 And will make an offering by fire to the Lord from the herd or from the flock, a burnt offering or a sacrifice to fulfill a special vow or as a freewill offering or in your set feasts, to make a pleasant *and* soothing fragrance to the Lord,

4 Then shall he who brings his offering to the Lord bring a cereal offering of a tenth of an ephah of fine flour mixed with a fourth of a hin of oil.

5 And a fourth of a hin of wine for the drink offering you shall prepare with the burnt offering or for the sacrifice, for each lamb.

6 Or for a ram you shall prepare for a cereal offering two tenths of an ephah of fine flour mixed with a third of a hin of oil.

7 And for the drink offering you shall offer a third of a hin of wine, for a sweet *and* pleasing odor to the Lord. **8** And when you prepare a bull for a burnt offering or for a sacrifice, in fulfilling a special vow or peace offering to the Lord,

9 Then shall one offer with the bull a cereal offering of three tenths of an ephah of fine flour mixed with half a hin of oil.

10 And you shall bring for the drink offering half a hin of wine for an offering made by fire, of a pleasant *and* soothing fragrance to the Lord.

11 Thus shall it be done for each bull or for each ram, or for each of the male lambs or of the kids.

12 According to the number that you shall prepare, so shall you do to everyone according to their number.

13 All who are native-born shall do these things in this way in bringing an offering made by fire of a sweet *and* pleasant odor to the Lord.

14 And if a stranger sojourns with you or whoever may be among you throughout your generations, and he wishes to offer an offering made by fire, of a pleasing *and* soothing fragrance to the Lord, as you do, so shall he do.

15 There shall be one [and the same] statute [both] for you [of the congregation] and for the stranger who is a temporary resident with you, a statute forever throughout your generations: as you are, so shall the stranger be before the Lord.

16 One law and one ordinance shall be for you and for the stranger who sojourns with you.

17 And the Lord said to Moses,

18 Say to the Israelites, When you come into the land to which I am bringing you,

19 Then, when you eat of the food of the land, you shall set apart a portion for a gift to the Lord [called a heave or taken-out offering].

20 You shall set apart a cake made of the first of your coarse meal as a gift [to the Lord]; as an offering set apart from the threshing floor, so shall you lift it out *or* heave it.

21 Of the first of your coarse meal you shall give to the Lord a portion for a gift throughout your generations [your heave or lifted-out offering].

22 When you have erred and have not observed all these commandments which the Lord has spoken to Moses,

23 Even all that the Lord has commanded you through Moses, from the day that the Lord gave commandment and onward throughout your generations,

24 Then it shall be, if it was done unwittingly *or* in error without the knowledge of the congregation, that all the congregation shall offer one young bull for a burnt offering, for a pleasant *and* soothing fragrance to the Lord, with its cereal offering and its drink offering, according to the ordinance, and one male goat for a sin offering.

25 And the priest shall make atonement for all the congregation of the Israelites, and they shall be forgiven, for it was an error and they have brought their offering, an offering made by fire to the Lord, and their sin offering before the Lord for their error.

26 And all the congregation of the Israelites shall be forgiven and the stranger who lives temporarily among them, because all the people were involved in the error.

27 And if any person sins unknowingly *or* unintentionally, he shall offer a female goat a year old for a sin offering.

28 And the priest shall make atonement before the Lord for the person who commits an error when he sins unknowingly *or* unintentionally, to make atonement for him; and he shall be forgiven.

29 You shall have one law for him who sins unknowingly *or* unintentionally, whether he is native born among the Israelites or a stranger who is sojourning among them.

30 But the person who does anything [wrong] willfully *and* openly, whether he is native-born or a stranger, that one reproaches, reviles, *and* blasphemes the Lord, and that person shall be cut off from among his people [that the atonement made for them may not include him].

31 Because he has despised and rejected the word of the Lord, and has broken His commandment, that person shall be utterly cut off; his iniquity shall be upon him.

32 While the Israelites were in the wilderness, they found a man who was gathering sticks on the Sabbath day.

33 Those who found him gathering sticks brought him to Moses and Aaron and to all the congregation.

34 They put him in custody, because it was not certain *or* clear what should be done to him.

35 And the Lord said to Moses, The man shall surely be put to death. All the congregation shall stone him with stones without the camp.

36 And all the congregation brought him without the camp and stoned him to death with stones, as the Lord commanded Moses.

37 And the Lord said to Moses,

38 Speak to the Israelites and bid them make fringes *or* tassels on the corners in the borders of their garments throughout their generations, and put upon the fringe of the borders *or* upon the tassel of each corner a cord of blue.

39 And it shall be to you a fringe *or* tassel that you may look upon and remember all the commandments of the Lord and do them, that you may not spy out *and* follow after [the desires of] your own heart and your own eyes, after which you used to follow *and* play the harlot [spiritually, if not physically],

40 That you may remember and do all My commandments and be holy to your God.

41 I am the Lord your God, Who brought you out of the land of Egypt to be your God. I am the Lord your God.

16 NOW KORAH son of Izhar, the son of Kohath, the son of Levi, with Dathan and Abiram sons of Eliab, and On son of Peleth, sons of Reuben, took men,

2 And they rose up before Moses, with certain of the Israelites, 250 princes *or* leaders of the congregation called to the assembly, men well known *and* of distinction.

3 And they gathered together against Moses and Aaron, and said to them, [Enough of you!] You take too much upon yourselves, seeing that all the congregation is holy, every one of them, and the Lord is among them. Why then do you lift yourselves up above the assembly of the Lord?

4 And when Moses heard it, he fell upon his face.

5 And he said to Korah and all his company, In the morning the Lord will show who are His and who is holy, and will cause him to come near to Him; him whom He has chosen will He cause to come near to Him. [II Tim. 2:19.]

speak the Word

God, I thank You that I belong to You, that You have chosen me, and that through Jesus, I can draw near to You.
ADAPTED FROM NUMBERS 16:5

6 Do this: Take censers, Korah and all your company,

7 And put fire in them and put incense upon them before the Lord tomorrow; and the man whom the Lord chooses shall be holy. You take too much upon yourselves, you sons of Levi.

8 And Moses said to Korah, Hear, I pray you, you sons of Levi:

9 Does it seem but a small thing to you that the God of Israel has separated you from the congregation of Israel, to bring you near to Himself to do the service of the tabernacle of the Lord and to stand before the congregation to minister to them,

10 And that He has brought you near to Him, and all your brethren the sons of Levi with you? Would you seek the priesthood also?

11 Therefore you and all your company are gathered together against the Lord. And Aaron, what is he that you murmur against him?

12 And Moses sent to call Dathan and Abiram, the sons of Eliab, and they said, We will not come up.

13 Is it a small thing that you have brought us up out of a land flowing with milk and honey to kill us in the wilderness, but you must also make yourself a prince over us?

14 Moreover, you have not brought us into a land that flows with milk and honey or given us an inheritance of fields and vineyards. Will you bore out the eyes of these men? We will not come up!

15 And Moses was very angry and said to the Lord, Do not respect their offering! I have not taken one donkey from them, nor have I hurt one of them.

16 And Moses said to Korah, You and all your company be before the Lord tomorrow, you and they and Aaron.

17 And let every man take his censer and put incense upon it and bring before the Lord every man his censer,

250 censers; you also and Aaron, each his censer.

18 So they took every man his censer, and they put fire in them and laid incense upon it, and they stood at the entrance of the Tent of Meeting with Moses and Aaron.

19 Then Korah assembled all the congregation against Moses and Aaron before the entrance of the Tent of Meeting, and the glory of the Lord appeared to all the congregation.

20 And the Lord said to Moses and Aaron,

21 Separate yourselves from among this congregation, that I may consume them in a moment.

22 And they fell upon their faces, and said, O God, the God of the spirits of all flesh, shall one man sin and will You be angry with all the congregation?

23 And the Lord said to Moses,

24 Say to the congregation, Get away from around the tents of Korah, Dathan, and Abiram.

25 Then Moses rose up and went to Dathan and Abiram, and the elders of Israel followed him.

26 And he said to the congregation, Depart, I pray you, from the tents of these wicked men, and touch nothing of theirs, lest you be consumed in all their sins.

27 So they got away from around the tents of Korah, Dathan, and Abiram. And Dathan and Abiram came out and stood in the door of their tents with their wives, and their sons, and their little ones.

28 And Moses said, By this you shall know that the Lord has sent me to do all these works, for I do not act of my own accord:

29 If these men die the common death of all men or if [only] what happens to everyone happens to them, then the Lord has not sent me.

30 But if the Lord causes a new thing [to happen], and the earth opens its mouth and swallows them up, with all that belongs to them, and they go down alive into Sheol (the place of the dead), then you shall understand that these men have provoked (spurned, despised) the Lord!

31 As soon as he stopped speaking, the ground under the offenders split apart

32 And the earth opened its mouth and swallowed them and their households and [Korah and] all [his] men and all their possessions. [Num. 26:10, 11.]

33 They and all that belonged to them went down alive into Sheol (the place of the dead); and the earth closed upon them, and they perished from among the assembly.

34 And all Israel who were round about them fled at their cry, for they said, Lest the earth swallow us up also.

35 And fire came forth from the Lord and devoured the 250 men who offered the incense.

36 And the Lord said to Moses,

37 Speak to Eleazar son of Aaron, the priest, that he take up the censers out of the burning and scatter the fire at a distance. For the censers are hallowed—

38 The censers of these men who have sinned against themselves *and* at the cost of their own lives. Let the censers be made into hammered plates for a covering of the altar [of burnt offering], for they were used in offering before the Lord and therefore they are sacred. They shall be a sign [of warning] to the Israelites.

39 Eleazar the priest took the bronze censers with which the Levites who were burned had offered incense, and they were hammered into broad sheets for a covering of the [brazen] altar [of burnt offering],

40 To be a memorial [a warning forever] to the Israelites, so that no outsider, that is, no one not of the descendants of Aaron, should come near to offer incense before the Lord, lest he become as Korah and as his

company, as the Lord said to Eleazar through Moses.

41 But on the morrow all the congregation of the Israelites murmured against Moses and Aaron, saying, You have killed the people of the Lord.

42 When the congregation was gathered against Moses and Aaron, they looked at the Tent of Meeting, and behold, the cloud covered it and they saw the Lord's glory.

43 And Moses and Aaron came to the front of the Tent of Meeting.

44 And the Lord said to Moses,

45 Get away from among this congregation, that I may consume them in a moment. And Moses and Aaron fell on their faces.

46 And Moses said to Aaron, Take a censer and put fire in it from off the altar and lay incense on it, and carry it quickly to the congregation and make atonement for them. For there is wrath gone out from the Lord; the plague has begun!

47 So Aaron took the burning censer as Moses commanded, and ran into the midst of the congregation; and behold, the plague was begun among the people; and he put on the incense and made atonement for the people.

48 And he stood between the dead and the living, and the plague was stayed.

49 Now those who died in the plague were 14,700, besides those who died in the matter of Korah.

50 And Aaron returned to Moses to the door of the Tent of Meeting, since the plague was stayed.

17 AND THE Lord said to Moses,

2 Speak to the Israelites and get from them rods *or* staves, one for each father's house, from all their leaders according to their father's houses, twelve rods. Write every man's name on his rod.

3 And you shall write Aaron's name on the rod of Levi [his great-grandfather]. For there shall be one rod for the head of each father's house.
4 You shall lay them up in the Tent of Meeting before [the ark of] the Testimony, where I meet with you.
5 And the rod of the man whom I choose shall bud, and I will make to cease from Me the murmurings of the Israelites, which they murmur against you.
6 And Moses spoke to the Israelites, and every one of their leaders gave him a rod *or* staff, one for each leader according to their fathers' houses, twelve rods, and the rod of Aaron was among their rods.
7 And Moses deposited the rods before the Lord in the Tent of the Testimony.
8 And the next day Moses went into the Tent of the Testimony, and behold, the rod of Aaron for the house of Levi had sprouted and brought forth buds and produced blossoms and yielded [ripe] almonds.
9 Moses brought out all the rods from before the Lord to all the Israelites; and they looked, and each man took his rod.
10 And the Lord told Moses, Put Aaron's rod back before the Testimony [in the ark], to be kept as a [warning] sign for the rebels; and you shall make an end of their murmurings against Me, lest they die.
11 And Moses did so; as the Lord commanded him, so he did.
12 The Israelites said to Moses, Behold, we perish, we are undone, all undone!
13 Everyone who comes near, who comes near the tabernacle of the Lord, dies *or* shall die! Are we all to perish?

18 AND THE Lord said to Aaron, You and your sons and your father's house

with you shall bear *and* remove the iniquity of the sanctuary [that is, the guilt for the offenses which the people unknowingly commit when brought into contact with the manifestations of God's presence]. And you and your sons with you shall bear *and* remove the iniquity of your priesthood [your own unintentional offenses].
2 And your brethren also of the tribe of Levi, the tribe of your [fore]father, bring with you, that they may be joined to you and minister to you; but only you and your sons with you shall come before the Tent of the Testimony [into the Holy Place where only priests may go and into the Most Holy Place which only the high priest dares enter].
3 And the Levites shall attend you [as servants] and attend to all the duties of the Tent; only they shall not come near the sacred vessels of the sanctuary or to the brazen altar, that they and also you [Aaron] die not.
4 And they shall be joined to you and attend to the duties of the Tent of Meeting—all the [menial] service of the Tent—and no stranger [no layman, anyone who is not a Levite] shall come near you [Aaron and your sons].
5 And you shall attend to the duties of the sanctuary and attend to the altar [of burnt offering and the altar of incense], that there be no wrath any more upon the Israelites [as in the incident of Korah, Dathan, and Abiram]. [Num. 16:42-50.]
6 And I, behold, I have taken your brethren the Levites from among the Israelites; to you they are a gift, given to the Lord, to do the [menial] service of the Tent of Meeting.
7 Therefore you and your sons with you shall attend to your priesthood for everything of the altar [of burnt offering and the altar of incense] and [of the Holy of Holies] within the veil, and you shall serve. I give you your priesthood

as a service of gift. And the stranger [anyone other than Moses or your sons, Aaron] who comes near shall be put to death. [Exod. 40:18, 20, 26.]

8 And the Lord said to Aaron, And I, behold, I have given you the charge of My heave offerings [whatever is taken out and kept of the offerings made to Me], all the dedicated *and* consecrated things of the Israelites; to you have I given them [as your portion] and to your sons as a continual allowance forever by reason of your anointing as priests. [Lev. 7:35.]

9 This shall be yours of the most holy things, reserved from the fire: every offering of the people, every cereal offering and sin offering and trespass offering of theirs, which they shall render to Me, shall be most holy for you [Aaron] and for your sons.

10 As the most holy thing *and* in a sacred place shall you eat of it; every male [of your house] shall eat of it. It shall be holy to you. [Lev. 22:10-16.]

11 And this also is yours: the heave offering of their gift, with all the wave offerings of the Israelites. I have given them to you and to your sons and to your daughters with you as a continual allowance forever; everyone in your house who is [ceremonially] clean may eat of it.

12 All the best of the oil, and all the best of the [fresh] wine and of the grain, the firstfruits of what they give to the Lord, to you have I given them.

13 Whatever is first ripe in the land, which they bring to the Lord, shall be yours. Everyone who is [ceremonially] clean in your house may eat of it.

14 Every devoted thing in Israel [everything that has been vowed to the Lord] shall be yours.

15 Everything that first opens the womb in all flesh, which they bring to the Lord, whether it be of men or beasts, shall be yours. Nevertheless the firstborn of man you shall surely redeem, and the firstling of unclean beasts you shall redeem.

16 And those that are to be redeemed of them, from a month old shall you redeem, according to your estimate [of their age], for the fixed price of five shekels in silver, according to the shekel of the sanctuary, which is twenty gerahs.

17 But the firstling of a cow or of a sheep or of a goat you shall not redeem. They [as the firstborn of clean beasts belong to God and] are holy. You shall sprinkle their blood upon the altar and shall burn their fat for an offering made by fire, for a sweet *and* soothing odor to the Lord.

18 And the flesh of them shall be yours, as the wave breast and as the right shoulder are yours.

19 All the heave offerings [the lifted-out and kept portions] of the holy things which the Israelites give to the Lord I give to you and to your sons and your daughters with you, as a continual debt forever. It is a covenant of salt [that cannot be dissolved or violated] forever before the Lord for you [Aaron] and for your posterity with you.

20 And the Lord said to Aaron, You shall have no inheritance in the land [of the Israelites], neither shall you have any part among them. I am your portion and your inheritance among the Israelites.

21 And, behold, I have given the Levites all the tithes in Israel for an inheritance in return for their service which they serve, the [menial] service of the Tent of Meeting.

22 Henceforth the Israelites shall not come near the Tent of Meeting [the covered sanctuary, the Holy Place, and the Holy of Holies], lest they incur guilt and die.

23 But the Levites shall do the [menial] service of the Tent of Meeting, and they shall bear and remove the iniquity of the people [that is, be

answerable for the legal pollutions of the holy things and offer the necessary atonements for unintentional offenses in these matters]. It shall be a statute forever in all your generations, that among the Israelites the Levites have no inheritance [of land].

24 But the tithes of the Israelites, which they present as an offering to the Lord, I have given to the Levites to inherit; therefore I have said to them, Among the Israelites they shall have no inheritance. [They have homes and cities and pasturage to use but not to possess as their personal inheritance.]

25 And the Lord said to Moses,

26 Moreover, you shall say to the Levites, When you take from the Israelites the tithe which I have given you from them for your inheritance, then you shall present an offering from it to the Lord, even a tenth of the tithe [paid by the people].

27 And what you lift out and keep [your heave offering] shall be credited to you as though it were the grain of the threshing floor or as the fully ripe produce of the vine.

28 Likewise you shall also present an offering to the Lord of all your tithes which you receive from the Israelites; and therefore you shall give this heave offering [lifted out and kept] for the Lord to Aaron the priest.

29 Out of all the gifts to you, you shall present every offering due to the Lord, of all the best of it, even the hallowed part lifted out *and* held back out of it [for the Levites].

30 Therefore you shall say to them, When you have lifted out *and* held back the best from it [and presented it to the Lord by giving it to yourselves, the Levites], then it shall be counted to [you] the Levites just as if it were the increase of the threshing floor or of the winepress.

31 And you may eat it in every place, you and your households, for it is your reward for your service in the Tent of Meeting.

32 And you shall be guilty of no sin by reason of it when you have lifted out *and* held back the best of it; neither shall you have polluted the holy things of the Israelites, neither shall you die [because of it].

19 AND THE Lord said to Moses and Aaron,

2 This is the ritual of the law which the Lord has commanded: Tell the Israelites to bring you a red heifer without spot, in which is no blemish, upon which a yoke has never come.

3 And you shall give her to Eleazar the priest, and he shall bring her outside the camp, and she shall be slaughtered before him.

4 Eleazar the priest shall take some of her blood with his finger and sprinkle it toward the front of the Tent of Meeting seven times.

5 The heifer shall be burned in his sight, her skin, flesh, blood, and dung.

6 And the priest shall take cedar wood, and hyssop, and scarlet [stuff] and cast them into the midst of the burning heifer.

7 Then the priest shall wash his clothes and bathe his body in water; afterward he shall come into the camp, but he shall be unclean until evening.

8 He who burns the heifer shall wash his clothes and bathe his body in water, and shall be unclean until evening.

9 And a man who is clean shall collect the ashes of the heifer and put them outside the camp in a clean place, and they shall be kept for the congregation of the Israelites for the water for impurity; it is a sin offering.

10 And he who gathers the ashes of the heifer shall wash his clothes, and be unclean until evening. This shall

be to the Israelites and to the stranger who sojourns among them a perpetual statute.

11 He who touches the dead body of any person shall be unclean for seven days.

12 He shall purify himself with the water for impurity [made with the ashes of the burned heifer] on the third day, and on the seventh day he shall be clean. But if he does not purify himself the third day, then the seventh day he shall not be clean.

13 Whoever touches the corpse of any who has died and does not purify himself defiles the tabernacle of the Lord, and that person shall be cut off from Israel. Because the water for impurity was not sprinkled upon him, he shall be unclean; his uncleanness is still upon him.

14 This is the law when a man dies in a tent: all who come into the tent and all who are in the tent shall be unclean for seven days.

15 And every open vessel, which has no covering fastened upon it, is unclean.

16 And whoever in the open field touches one who is slain with a sword, or a dead body, or a bone of a dead man, or a grave, shall be unclean for seven days.

17 And for the unclean, they shall take of the ashes of the burning of the sin offering, and the running water shall be put with it in a vessel.

18 And a clean person shall take hyssop and dip it in the water and sprinkle it upon the tent, and upon all the vessels, and upon the persons who were there, and upon him who touched the bone, or the slain, or the naturally dead, or the grave.

19 And the clean person shall sprinkle [the water for purification] upon the unclean person on the third day and on the seventh day, and on the seventh day the unclean man shall purify himself, and wash his clothes

and bathe himself in water, and shall be clean at evening.

20 But the man who is unclean and does not purify himself, that person shall be cut off from among the congregation, because he has defiled the sanctuary of the Lord. The water for purification has not been sprinkled upon him; he is unclean.

21 And it shall be a perpetual statute to them. He who sprinkles the water for impurity [upon another] shall wash his clothes, and he who touches the water for impurity shall be unclean until evening.

22 And whatever the unclean person touches shall be unclean, and anyone who touches it shall be unclean until evening.

20 AND THE Israelites, the whole congregation, came into the Wilderness of Zin in the first month. And the people dwelt in Kadesh. Miriam died and was buried there.

2 Now there was no water for the congregation, and they assembled together against Moses and Aaron.

3 And the people contended with Moses, and said, Would that we had died when our brethren died [in the plague] before the Lord! [Num. 16:49.]

4 And why have you brought up the congregation of the Lord into this wilderness, that we should die here, we and our livestock?

5 And why have you made us come up out of Egypt to bring us into this evil place? It is no place of grain or of figs or of vines or of pomegranates. And there is no water to drink.

6 Then Moses and Aaron went from the presence of the assembly to the door of the Tent of Meeting and fell on their faces. Then the glory of the Lord appeared to them.

7 And the Lord said to Moses,

8 Take the rod, and assemble the congregation, you and Aaron your

life point

The words the Israelites spoke in Numbers 20:3–5 revealed their total lack of trust in God. They had a negative attitude and had decided they were going to fail before they ever really got started, simply because every circumstance was not perfect. They displayed an attitude that came from a wrong mind-set. Bad attitudes are the fruit of bad thoughts. Ask God to give you thoughts in line with His Word, and watch your attitude change!

brother, and tell the rock before their eyes to give forth its water, and you shall bring forth to them water out of the rock; so you shall give the congregation and their livestock drink.

9 So Moses took the rod from before the Lord, as He commanded him.

10 And Moses and Aaron assembled the congregation before the rock and Moses said to them, Hear now, you rebels; must we bring you water out of this rock?

11 And Moses lifted up his hand and with his rod he smote the rock twice. And the water came out abundantly, and the congregation drank, and their livestock.

12 And the Lord said to Moses and Aaron, Because you did not believe in (rely on, cling to) Me to sanctify Me in the eyes of the Israelites, you therefore [j]shall not bring this congregation into the land which I have given them. [Ps. 106:32, 33.]

13 These are the waters of Meribah [strife], where the Israelites contended with the Lord and He showed Himself holy among them.

14 And Moses sent messengers from Kadesh to the king of Edom, saying, Thus says your kinsman Israel: You know all the adversity and birth pangs that have come upon us [as a nation]:

15 How our fathers went down to Egypt; we dwelt there a long time, and the Egyptians dealt evilly with us and our fathers.

16 But when we cried to the Lord, He heard us and sent an angel and brought us forth out of Egypt. Now behold, we are in Kadesh, a city on your country's edge.

17 Let us pass, I pray you, through your country. We will not pass through field or vineyard, or drink of the water of the wells. We will go along the king's highway; we will not turn aside to the right hand or to the left until we have passed your borders.

18 But Edom said to him, You shall not go through, lest I come out against you with the sword.

19 And the Israelites said to him, We will go by the highway, and if I and my livestock drink of your water, I will pay for it. Only let me pass through on foot, nothing else.

20 But Edom said, You shall not go through. And Edom came out against Israel with many people and a strong hand.

21 Thus Edom refused to give Israel passage through his territory, [k]so Israel turned away from him.

i "And the Rock was Christ," as I Cor. 10:4 explains. Once smitten at Rephidim (Exod. 17:6ff.), He did not need to be smitten, crucified, again. To smite the rock twice was to imply that Christ's death on the cross was not effectual or sufficient for time and eternity. j Possibly Moses was not aware of the significance of what he had been ordered to do, but nevertheless God held him responsible for not obeying Him exactly. Obedience to His will is vitally important, whether we understand His purpose or not. The motto "God's will: nothing more; nothing less; nothing else; at any cost" would have been priceless to Moses and Aaron that day, if they had only followed it. k Israel (Jacob's offspring) did not fight Edom, the offspring of Jacob's brother Esau, because of the Lord's warning, later conveyed in definite instructions (Deut. 23:7). But what had begun as only a quarrel between twin brothers (Gen. 27:41) had now been passed on for generations and was to cost countless lives,

22 They journeyed from Kadesh, and the Israelites, even the whole congregation, came to Mount Hor.

23 And the Lord said to Moses and Aaron at Mount Hor, on the border of the land of Edom,

24 Aaron shall be gathered to his people. For he shall not enter the land which I have given to the Israelites, because you both rebelled against My instructions at the waters of Meribah.

25 Take Aaron and Eleazar his son and bring them up to Mount Hor.

26 Strip Aaron of his vestments and put them on Eleazar his son, and Aaron shall be gathered to his people, and shall die there.

27 And Moses did as the Lord commanded; and they went up Mount Hor in the sight of all the congregation.

28 And Moses stripped Aaron of his [priestly] garments and put them on Eleazar his son. And Aaron died there on the mountain top; and Moses and Eleazar came down from the mountain.

29 When all the congregation saw that Aaron was dead, they wept *and* mourned for him thirty days, all the house of Israel.

21 WHEN THE Canaanite king of Arad, who dwelt in the South (the Negeb), heard that Israel was coming by the way of Atharim [the route traveled by the spies sent out by Moses], he fought against Israel and took some of them captive.

2 And Israel vowed a vow to the Lord, and said, If You will indeed deliver this people into my hand, then I will utterly destroy their cities.

3 And the Lord hearkened to Israel and gave over the Canaanites. And they utterly destroyed them and their cities;

and the name of the place was called Hormah [a banned or devoted thing].

4 And they journeyed from Mount Hor by the way to the Red Sea, to go around the land of Edom, and the people became impatient (depressed, much discouraged), because [of the trials] of the way.

5 And the people spoke against God and against Moses, Why have you brought us out of Egypt to die in the wilderness? For there is no bread, neither is there any water, and we loathe this light (contemptible, unsubstantial) manna.

6 Then the Lord sent fiery (burning) serpents among the people; and they bit the people, and many Israelites died.

7 And the people came to Moses, and said, We have sinned, for we have spoken against the Lord and against you; pray to the Lord, that He may take away the serpents from us. So Moses prayed for the people.

life point

Along with other bad attitudes (see Numbers 21:4, 5), the children of Israel lacked gratitude. They simply could not quit thinking about where they had come from—and where they were—long enough to get where they were going! What could have helped them? They could have considered their forefather, Abraham. He went through some disappointing experiences in his life, but he did not allow them to negatively affect his future. When things get tough, rehearse the good things the Lord has done. That kind of gratitude to God will help you get through any trial with faith and emerge victorious.

extending throughout the Old Testament and into the New, where Herod, remotely related to Esau, tried to take the life of the Babe of Bethlehem, a descendant of Jacob. "See how much wood *or* how great a forest a tiny spark can set ablaze!" (James 3:5).

look and live

The Israelites were dying in large numbers because a plague of snakes had come upon them and were biting them as a result of their sin (see Numbers 21:6). What did Moses do? He prayed. To solve the problem, Moses turned his attention immediately to God, not to himself or anyone else.

I have found that victorious people in the Bible faced their problems with prayer. They did not worry—they prayed. I ask you today: Do you worry or do you take your needs to God in prayer?

Moses sought God about how to handle the snakes. He did not make his own plan and ask God to bless it; he did not try to reason out an answer, nor did he worry. He prayed, and his action brought a response from God. God told Moses to make a bronze serpent, set it on a pole, and put it in front of the people. Every snake-bitten person who looked at it would live. The New Testament tells us this action represented the Cross and Jesus' taking our sin upon Himself: "Just as Moses lifted up the serpent in the desert [on a pole], so must . . . the Son of Man be lifted up [on the cross], in order that everyone who believes in Him . . . may not perish but have eternal life" (John 3:14, 15).

The message is still the same today: "Look and live." Look at Jesus and at what He has done, not at yourself and what you have done or can do. The answer to your problem, whatever it may be, is not worry, but trusting God and praying. Pray and worship God because He is good, and His goodness will be released in your life.

8 And the Lord said to Moses, Make a fiery serpent [of bronze] and set it on a pole; and everyone who is bitten, when he looks at it, shall live. 9 And Moses made a serpent of bronze and put it on a pole, and if a serpent had bitten any man, when he looked to the serpent of bronze [¹attentively, expectantly, with a steady and absorbing gaze], he lived.

10 And the Israelites journeyed on and encamped at Oboth. 11 They journeyed from Oboth and encamped at Iye-abarim, in the wilderness opposite Moab, toward the sunrise. 12 From there they journeyed and encamped in the Valley of Zared. 13 From there they journeyed and encamped on the other side of [the

1 Jesus said that as Moses lifted up the serpent in the wilderness, so must the Son of Man be lifted up, "that everyone who believes in Him [who cleaves to Him, trusts Him and relies on Him] may *not perish, but* have eternal life *and* [actually] live forever!" (John 3:14, 15). Obviously this implies that the look that caused the victim of a fiery serpent to be healed was something far more than a casual glance. A "look" would save, but what kind of a look? The Hebrew text here means "look attentively, expectantly, with a steady and absorbing gaze." Or, as Jesus said in the last verse of the chapter quoted above (John 3:36), "He who believes in (has faith in, clings to, relies on) the Son has (now possesses) eternal life." But whoever does not so believe in, cling to, and rely on the Son "will never see . . . life." The look that saves is not just a fleeting glance; it is a God-honoring, God-answered, fixed, and absorbing gaze!

river] Arnon, which is in the desert *or* wilderness that extends from the frontier of the Amorites; for [the river] Arnon is the boundary of Moab, between Moab and the Amorites.

14 That is why it is said in the Book of the Wars of the Lord: Waheb in Suphah, and the valleys of [the branches of] the Arnon [River],

15 And the slope of the valleys that stretch toward the site of Ar and find support on the border of Moab.

16 From there the Israelites went on to Beer [a well], the well of which the Lord had said to Moses, Assemble the people together and I will give them water. [John 7:37-39.]

17 Then Israel sang this song, Spring up, O well! Let all sing to it, [Rom. 14:17.]

18 The fountain that the princes opened, that the nobles of the people hollowed out from their staves. And from the wilderness *or* desert [Israel journeyed] to Mattanah,

19 And from Mattanah to Nahaliel, and from Nahaliel to Bamoth,

20 And from Bamoth to the valley that is in the field of Moab, to the top of Pisgah which looks down upon Jeshimon *and* the desert.

21 And Israel sent messengers to Sihon king of the Amorites, saying,

22 Let me pass through your land. We will not turn aside into field or vineyard; we will not drink the water of the wells. We will go by the king's highway until we have passed your border.

23 But Sihon would not allow Israel to pass through his border. Instead Sihon gathered all his people together and went out against Israel into the wilderness, and came to Jahaz, and he fought against Israel.

24 And Israel smote the king of the Amorites with the edge of the sword and possessed his land from the river Arnon to the river Jabbok, as far as the Ammonites, for the boundary of the Ammonites was strong.

25 And Israel took all these cities and dwelt in all the cities of the Amorites, in Heshbon and in all its towns.

26 For Heshbon was the city of Sihon king of the Amorites, who had fought against the former king of Moab and taken all his land out of his hand, as far as [the river] Arnon.

27 That is why those who sing ballads say, Come to Heshbon, let the city of Sihon be built and established.

28 For fire has gone out of Heshbon, a flame from the city of Sihon; it has devoured Ar of Moab and the lords of the heights of the Arnon.

29 Woe to you, Moab! You are undone, O people of [the god] Chemosh! Moab has given his sons as fugitives and his daughters into captivity to Sihon king of the Amorites.

30 We have shot them down; Heshbon has perished as far as Dibon, and we have laid them waste as far as Nophah, which reaches to Medeba.

31 Thus Israel dwelt in the land of the Amorites.

32 And Moses sent to spy out Jazer, and they took its villages and dispossessed the Amorites who were there.

33 Then they turned and went up by the way of Bashan; and Og the king of Bashan went out against them, he and all his people, to battle at Edrei.

34 But the Lord said to Moses, Do not fear him, for I have delivered him and all his people and his land into your hand; and you shall do to him as you did to Sihon king of the Amorites, who dwelt at Heshbon.

35 So the Israelites slew Og and his sons and all his people until there was not one left alive. And they possessed his land.

22 THE ISRAELITES journeyed and encamped in the plains of Moab, on the east side of the Jordan [River] at Jericho.

2 And Balak [the king of Moab] son

of Zippor saw all that Israel had done to the Amorites.

3 And Moab was terrified at the people *and* full of dread, because they were many. Moab was distressed *and* overcome with fear because of the Israelites.

4 And Moab said to the elders of Midian, Now will this multitude lick up all that is round about us, as the ox licks up the grass of the field. So Balak son of Zippor, the king of the Moabites at that time,

5 Sent messengers to Balaam [a foreteller of events] son of Beor at Pethor, which is by the [Euphrates] River, even to the land of the children of his people, to say to him, There is a people come out from Egypt; behold, they cover the face of the earth and they have settled down *and* dwell opposite me.

6 Now come, I beg of you, curse this people for me, for they are too powerful for me. Perhaps I may be able to defeat them and drive them out of the land, for I know that he whom you bless is blessed, and he whom you curse is cursed.

7 And the elders of Moab and of Midian departed with the rewards of foretelling in their hands; and they came to Balaam and told him the words of Balak.

8 And he said to them, Lodge here tonight and I will bring you word as the Lord may speak to me. And the princes of Moab abode with Balaam [that night].

9 And God came to Balaam, and said, What men are these with you?

10 And Balaam said to God, Balak son of Zippor, king of Moab, has sent to me, saying,

11 Behold, the people who came out of Egypt cover the face of the earth; come now, curse them for me.

Perhaps I shall be able to fight against them and drive them out.

12 And God said to Balaam, You shall not go with them; you shall not curse the people, for they are blessed.

13 And Balaam rose up in the morning, and said to the princes of Balak, Go back to your own land, for the Lord refuses to permit me to go with you.

14 So the princes of Moab rose up and went to Balak, and said, Balaam refuses to come with us.

15 Then Balak again sent princes, more of them and more honorable than the first ones.

16 And they came to Balaam, and said to him, Thus says Balak son of Zippor, I beg of you, let nothing hinder you from coming to me.

17 For I will promote you to very great honor and I will do whatever you tell me; so come, I beg of you, curse this people for me.

18 And Balaam answered the servants of Balak, If Balak would give me his house full of silver and gold, I cannot go beyond the word of the Lord my God, to do less or more.

19 Now therefore, I pray you, tarry here again tonight that I may know what more the Lord will say to me.

20 And God came to Balaam at night, and said to him, If the men come to call you, rise up and go with them, but still only what I tell you may you do.

21 And Balaam rose up in the morning and saddled his donkey and went with the princes of Moab.

22 And God's anger was kindled because he went, and the ᵐAngel of the Lord stood in the way as an adversary against him. Now he was riding upon his donkey, and his two servants were with him.

23 And the donkey saw the Angel of the Lord standing in the way and His

---

m See footnote on Gen. 16:7.

sword drawn in His hand, and the donkey turned aside out of the way and went into the field. And Balaam struck the donkey to turn her into the way.

24 But the Angel of the Lord stood in a path of the vineyards, a wall on this side and a wall on that side.

25 And when the donkey saw the Angel of the Lord, she thrust herself against the wall and crushed Balaam's foot against it, and he struck her again.

26 And the Angel of the Lord went further and stood in a narrow place where there was no room to turn, either to the right hand or to the left.

27 And when the donkey saw the Angel of the Lord, she fell down under Balaam, and Balaam's anger was kindled and he struck the donkey with his staff.

28 And the Lord opened the mouth of the donkey, and she said to Balaam, What have I done to you that you should strike me these three times?

29 And Balaam said to the donkey, Because you have ridiculed *and* provoked me! I wish there were a sword in my hand, for now I would kill you!

30 And the donkey said to Balaam, Am not I your donkey, upon which you have ridden all your life long until this day? Was I ever accustomed to do so to you? And he said, No.

31 Then the Lord opened Balaam's eyes, and he saw the Angel of the Lord standing in the way with His sword drawn in His hand; and he bowed his head and fell on his face.

32 And the Angel of the Lord said to him, Why have you struck your donkey these three times? See, I came out to stand against *and* resist you, for

speak the Word

your behavior is willfully obstinate *and* contrary before Me.

33 And the ass saw Me and turned from Me these three times. If she had not turned from Me, surely I would have slain you and saved her alive.

34 Balaam said to the Angel of the Lord, I have sinned, for I did not know You stood in the way against me. But now, if my going displeases You, I will return.

35 The Angel of the Lord said to Balaam, Go with the men, but you shall speak only what I tell you. So Balaam went with the princes of Balak.

36 When Balak heard that Balaam had come, he went out to meet him at the city of Moab on the border formed by the Arnon [River], at the farthest end of the boundary.

37 Balak said to Balaam, Did I not [earnestly] send to you to ask you [to come] to me? Why did you not come? Am not I able to promote you to honor?

38 And Balaam said to Balak, Indeed I have come to you, but do I now have any power at all to say anything? The word that God puts in my mouth, that shall I speak.

39 And Balaam went with Balak, and they came to Kiriath-huzoth.

40 And Balak offered oxen and sheep, and sent [portions] to Balaam and to the princes who were with him.

41 And on the following day Balak took Balaam and brought him up into the high places of Bamoth-baal; from there he saw the nearest of the Israelites.

23 AND BALAAM said to Balak, Build me here seven altars, and prepare me here seven oxen and seven rams.

God, I pray that my behavior will never be willfully obstinate or contrary before You, but that You will help me keep my heart and actions pleasing to You.
ADAPTED FROM NUMBERS 22:32

2 And Balak did as Balaam had spoken, and Balak and Balaam offered on each altar a bull and a ram.

3 And Balaam said to Balak, Stand by your burnt offering and I will go. Perhaps the Lord will come to meet me; and whatever He shows me I will tell you. And he went to a bare height.

4 God met Balaam, who said to Him, I have prepared seven altars, and I have offered on each altar a bull and a ram.

5 And the Lord put a speech in Balaam's mouth, and said, Return to Balak and thus shall you speak.

6 Balaam returned to Balak, who was standing by his burnt sacrifice, he and all the princes of Moab.

7 Balaam took up his [figurative] speech and said: Balak, the king of Moab, has brought me from Aram, out of the mountains of the east, saying, Come, curse Jacob for me; and come, violently denounce Israel.

8 How can I curse those God has not cursed? Or how can I [violently] denounce those the Lord has not denounced?

9 For from the top of the rocks I see Israel, and from the hills I behold him. Behold, the people [of Israel] shall ⁿdwell alone and shall not be reckoned *and* esteemed among the nations.

10 Who can count the dust (the descendants) of Jacob and the number of the fourth part of Israel? Let me die the death of the righteous [those who are upright and in right standing

with God], and let my last end be like theirs! [Ps. 37:37; Rev. 14:13.]

11 And Balak said to Balaam, What have you done to me? I brought you to curse my enemies, and here you have [thoroughly] blessed them instead!

12 And Balaam answered, Must I not be obedient *and* speak what the Lord has put in my mouth?

13 Balak said to him, Come with me, I implore you, to another place from which you can see them, though you will see only the nearest and not all of them; and curse them for me from there.

14 So he took Balaam into the field of Zophim to the top of [Mount] Pisgah, and built seven altars, and offered a bull and a ram on each altar.

15 Balaam said to Balak, Stand here by your burnt offering while I go to meet the Lord yonder.

16 And the Lord met Balaam and put a speech in his mouth, and said, Go again to Balak and speak thus.

17 And when he returned to Balak, he was standing beside his burnt offering, and the princes of Moab with him. And Balak said to him, What has the Lord said?

18 Balaam took up his [figurative] discourse and said: Rise up, Balak, and hear; listen [closely] to me, son of Zippor.

19 God is not a man, that He should tell *or* act a lie, neither the son of man, that He should feel repentance *or* compunction [for what He has promised]. Has He said and shall He not do

speak the Word

> *Thank You, God, that You are not a man that You should lie, but that You will make good on everything You have spoken.*
> ADAPTED FROM NUMBERS 23:19

n The literal fulfillment of this prophecy has been obvious during the more than thirty-four centuries since it was spoken. The Jews have always been separate as a nation from other peoples. Though conquered many times, they have never been absorbed by their conquerors or lost their identity. The prophecy had to become true, for "the Lord put [it] . . . in Balaam's mouth" (Num. 23:5).

it? Or has He spoken and shall He not make it good?

20 You see, I have received His command to bless Israel. He has blessed, and I cannot reverse *or* qualify it.

21 [God] has not beheld iniquity in Jacob [for he is forgiven], neither has He seen mischief *or* perverseness in Israel [for the same reason]. The Lord their God is with Israel, and the shout of praise to their King is among the people. [Rom. 4:7, 8; I John 3:1, 2.]

22 God brought them forth out of Egypt; they have as it were the strength of a wild ox.

23 Surely there is no enchantment with *or* against Jacob, neither is there any divination with *or* against Israel. [In due season and even] now it shall be said of Jacob and of Israel, What has God wrought!

24 Behold, a people! They rise up as a lioness and lift themselves up as a lion; he shall not lie down until he devours the prey and drinks the blood of the slain.

25 And Balak said to Balaam, Neither curse them at all nor bless them at all.

26 But Balaam answered Balak, Did I not say to you, All the Lord speaks, that I must do?

27 And Balak said to Balaam, Come, I implore you; I will take you to another place. Perhaps it will please God to let you curse them for me from there.

28 So Balak brought Balaam to the top of [Mount] Peor, that overlooks [the wilderness or desert] Jeshimon.

29 And Balaam said to Balak, Build me here seven altars, and prepare me here seven bulls and seven rams.

30 And Balak did as Balaam had said, and offered a bull and a ram on each altar.

24 WHEN BALAAM saw that it pleased the Lord to bless Israel, he did not go as he had done each time before [superstitiously] to meet with omens *and* signs in the natural world, but he set his face toward the wilderness *or* desert.

2 And Balaam lifted up his eyes and he saw Israel abiding in their tents according to their tribes. And the Spirit of God came upon him

3 And he took up his [figurative] discourse and said: Balaam son of Beor, the man whose eye is opened [at last, to see clearly the purposes and will of God],

4 He [Balaam] who hears the words of God, who sees the vision of the Almighty, falling down, but having his eyes open *and* uncovered, he says:

5 How attractive *and* considerable are your tents, O Jacob, *and* your tabernacles, O Israel!

6 As valleys are they spread forth, as gardens by the riverside, as [rare spice] of lignaloes which the Lord has planted, and as cedar trees beside the waters. [Ps. 1:3.]

7 [Israel] shall pour water out of his own buckets [have his own sources of rich blessing and plenty], and his offspring shall dwell by many waters, and his king shall be higher than °Agag, and his kingdom shall be exalted.

8 God brought [Israel] forth out of Egypt; [Israel] has strength like the wild ox; he shall eat up the nations, his enemies, crushing their bones and piercing them through with his arrows.

9 He couched, he lay down as a lion; and as a lioness, who shall rouse him? Blessed [of God] is he who blesses you [who prays for and contributes to your welfare] and cursed [of God] is

o "Agag" was the title of the Amalekite kings, and it represents here the kingdom of the Gentiles. The Amalekites at that time were the most powerful of all the desert tribes (Num. 24:20).

he who curses you [who in word, thought, or deed would bring harm upon you]. [Matt. 25:40.]

10 Then Balak's anger was kindled against Balaam, and he smote his hands together; and Balak said to Balaam, I called you to curse my enemies, and, behold, you have done nothing but bless them these three times.

11 Therefore now go back where you belong *and* do it in a hurry! I had intended to promote you to great honor, but behold, the Lord has held you back from honor.

12 Balaam said to Balak, Did I not say to your messengers whom you sent to me,

13 If Balak would give me his house full of silver and gold, I cannot go beyond the command of the Lord, to do either good or bad of my own will, but what the Lord says, that will I speak?

14 And now, behold, I am going to my people; come, I will tell you what this people [Israel] will do to your people [Moab] in the latter days.

15 And he took up his [figurative] discourse, and said: Balaam son of Beor speaks, the man whose eye is opened speaks,

16 He speaks, who heard the words of God and knew the knowledge of the Most High, who saw the vision of the Almighty, falling down, but having his eyes open *and* uncovered:

17 I see Him, but not now; I behold Him, but He is not near. A ᵖstar (Star) shall come forth out of Jacob, and a

scepter (Scepter) shall rise out of Israel and shall crush all the corners of Moab and break down all the sons of Sheth [Moab's sons of tumult]. [Matt. 2:2; Rom. 15:12.]

18 And Edom shall be [taken as] a possession, [Mount] Seir also shall be dispossessed, who were Israel's enemies, while Israel does valiantly.

19 Out of Jacob shall one (One) come having dominion and shall destroy the remnant from the city.

20 [Balaam] looked at Amalek and took up his [prophetic] utterance, and said: Amalek is the foremost of the [neighboring] nations, but in his latter end he shall �q come to destruction.

21 And he looked at the Kenites and took up his [prophetic] utterance, and said: Strong is your dwelling place, and you set your nest in the rock.

22 Nevertheless the Kenites shall be wasted. How long shall Asshur (Assyria) take you away captive?

23 And he took up his [prophetic] speech, and said: Alas, who shall live when God does this *and* establishes [Assyria]?

24 But ships shall come from Kittim [Cyprus and the greater part of the Mediterranean's east coast] and shall afflict Assyria and Eber [the Hebrews, certain Arabs, and descendants of Nahor], and he [the victor] also shall come to destruction.

25 And Balaam rose up, returned to his place, and Balak also went his way.

p "This imagery in the hieroglyphic language of the East denotes some eminent ruler—primarily David, but secondarily and preeminently the Messiah" (Robert Jamieson, A.R. Fausett and David Brown, *A Commentary*). Notice that the principal time for these events is set in the prophecy for "the latter days" (Num. 24:14). "The prophecy [concerning Moab] was partially, or typically, fulfilled in the time of David (II Sam. 8:2). Moab and Edom represented symbolically the enemies of Christ and His church, and as such will eventually be subdued by the King of kings (see Ps. 60:8)" (Charles J. Ellicott, *A Bible Commentary*). "The star which the wise men from the East saw, and which led them in the way to the newborn 'King of the Jews,' refers clearly to the prophecy of Balaam (Matt. 2:1, 2)" (J.P. Lange, *A Commentary*).   q After the time of David (who was forced to rescue two of his wives from Amalekite bandits, I Sam. 30:18), the Amalekites are mentioned again only in Hezekiah's time (I Chron. 4:43), before "they disappear from the field of history . . ., So that the word of God here also stood fast; and the first of the surrounding tribes who impiously sought to measure their strength with the cause and people of God were likewise the first to lose their national existence" (Patrick Fairbairn, ed., *The Imperial Bible-dictionary*).

25 ISRAEL SETTLED down *and* remained in Shittim, and the people began to play the harlot with the daughters of Moab,

2 Who invited the [Israelites] to the sacrifices of their gods, and [they] ate and bowed down to Moab's gods.

3 So Israel joined himself to [the god] Baal of Peor. And the anger of the Lord was kindled against Israel.

4 And the Lord said to Moses, Take all the leaders *or* chiefs of the people, and hang them before the Lord in the sun [after killing them], that the fierce anger of the Lord may turn away from Israel.

5 And Moses said to the judges of Israel, Each one of you slay his men who joined themselves to Baal of Peor.

6 And behold, one of the Israelites came and brought to his brethren a Midianite woman in the sight of Moses and of all the congregation of Israel while they were weeping at the door of the Tent of Meeting [over the divine judgment and the punishment].

7 And when Phinehas son of Eleazar, the son of Aaron the priest, saw it, he rose up from the midst of the congregation and took a spear in his hand

8 And went after the man of Israel into the inner room and thrust both of them through, the man of Israel and the woman through her body. Then the [smiting] plague was stayed from the Israelites.

9 Nevertheless those who died in the [smiting] plague were 24,000.

10 And the Lord said to Moses,

11 Phinehas son of Eleazar, the son of Aaron the priest, has turned my wrath away from the Israelites, in that he was jealous with My jealousy among them, so that I did not consume the Israelites in My jealousy.

12 Therefore say, Behold, I give to Phinehas the priest My covenant of peace.

13 And he shall have it, and his descendants after him, the covenant of an everlasting priesthood, because he was jealous for his God and made atonement for the Israelites. [Ps. 106:28-31.]

14 Now the man of Israel who was slain with the Midianite woman was Zimri son of Salu, a head of a father's house among the Simeonites.

15 And the Midianite woman who was slain was Cozbi daughter of Zur; he was head of a father's house in Midian.

16 And the Lord said to Moses,

17 Provoke hostilities with the Midianites and attack them,

18 For they harass you with their wiles with which they have beguiled you in the matter of Peor, and of Cozbi, the daughter of the prince of Midian, their sister, who was slain on the day of the plague in the matter of Peor.

26 AFTER THE plague the Lord said to Moses and Eleazar son of Aaron, the priest,

2 Take a census of all the [male] congregation of the Israelites from twenty years old and upward, by their fathers' houses, all in Israel able to go to war.

3 And Moses and Eleazar the priest told [the people] in the plains of Moab by the Jordan at Jericho,

4 A census of the people shall be taken from twenty years old and upward, as the Lord commanded Moses. And the Israelites who came forth out of the land of Egypt were:

5 Reuben, the firstborn of Israel, the sons of Reuben: of Hanoch, the family of the Hanochites; of Pallu, the family of the Palluites;

6 Of Hezron, the family of the Hezronites; of Carmi, the family of the Carmites.

7 These are the families of the Reubenites; and their number was 43,730.

8 And the son of Pallu: Eliab.

9 The sons of Eliab: Nemuel, Dathan, and Abiram. These are the Dathan and Abiram chosen from the congregation who contended against Moses and Aaron in the company of Korah when they contended against the Lord.

10 And the earth opened its mouth and swallowed them up together with Korah, when that company died and the fire devoured 250 men; and they became a [warning] sign.

11 But Korah's sons did not die.

12 The sons of Simeon according to their families: of Nemuel, the family of the Nemuelites; of Jamin, the family of the Jaminites; of Jachin, the family of the Jachinites;

13 Of Zerah, the family of the Zerahites; of Shaul, the family of the Shaulites.

14 These are the families of the Simeonites, 22,200.

15 The sons of Gad after their families: of Zephon, the family of the Zephonites; of Haggi, the family of the Haggites; of Shuni, the family of the Shunites;

16 Of Ozni, the family of the Oznites; of Eri, the family of the Erites;

17 Of Arod, the family of the Arodites; of Areli, the family of the Arelites.

18 These, the families of the sons of Gad according to their numbering, totaled 40,500.

19 The sons of Judah were Er and Onan, but Er and Onan died in the land of Canaan.

20 And the sons of Judah according to their families were: of Shelah, the family of the Shelanites; of Perez, the family of the Perezites; of Zerah, the family of the Zerahites.

21 And the sons of Perez were: of Hezron, the family of the Hezronites; of Hamul, the family of the Hamulites.

22 These, the families of Judah according to their numbering, totaled 76,500.

23 The sons of Issachar after their families: of Tola, the family of the Tolaites; of Puvah, the family of the Punites;

24 Of Jashub, the family of the Jashubites; of Shimron, the family of the Shimronites.

25 These, the families of Issachar according to their numbering, totaled 64,300.

26 The sons of Zebulun after their families: of Sered, the family of the Seredites; of Elon, the family of the Elonites; of Jahleel, the family of the Jahleelites.

27 These, the families of the Zebulunites according to their numbering, totaled 60,500.

28 The sons of Joseph after their families were Manasseh and Ephraim.

29 The sons of Manasseh: of Machir, the family of the Machirites (and Machir was the father of Gilead); of Gilead, the family of the Gileadites.

30 These are the sons of Gilead: of Iezer, the family of the Iezerites; of Helek, the family of the Helekites;

31 Of Asriel, the family of the Asrielites; of Shechem, the family of the Shechemites;

32 Of Shemida, the family of the Shemidaites; and of Hepher, the family of the Hepherites.

33 Zelophehad son of Hepher had no sons, but only daughters, and their names were Mahlah, Noah, Hoglah, Milcah, and Tirzah.

34 These are the families of Manasseh, and their number was 52,700.

35 These are the sons of Ephraim according to their families: of Shuthelah, the family of the Shuthelahites; of Becher, the family of the Becherites; of Tahan, the family of the Tahanites.

36 And these are the sons of Shuthelah: of Eran, the family of the Eranites.

37 These, the families of the sons of Ephraim according to their number, totaled 32,500. These are the sons of Joseph after their families.

38 The sons of Benjamin according to their families: of Bela, the family of the Belaites; of Ashbel, the family of the Ashbelites; of Ahiram, the family of the Ahiramites;

39 Of Shephupham, the family of the Shuphamites; of Hupham, the family of the Huphamites.

40 And the sons of Bela were Ard and Naaman; of Ard, the family of the Ardites; of Naaman, the family of the Naamites.

41 These are the sons of Benjamin according to their families; and their number was 45,600.

42 These are the sons of Dan according to their families: of Shuham, the family of the Shuhamites. These are the families of Dan according to their families.

43 All the families of the Shuhamites according to their number were 64,400.

44 Of the sons of Asher according to their families: of Imnah, the family of the Imnites; of Ishvi, the family of the Ishvites; of Beriah, the family of the Beriites.

45 Of the sons of Beriah: of Heber, the family of the Heberites; of Malchiel, the family of the Malchielites.

46 And the name of the daughter of Asher was Serah.

47 These, the families of the sons of Asher according to their number, totaled 53,400.

48 Of the sons of Naphtali after their families: of Jahzeel, the family of the Jahzeelites; of Guni, the family of the Gunites;

49 Of Jezer, the family of the Jezerites; of Shillem, the family of the Shillemites.

50 These are the families of Naphtali according to their families; and their number totaled 45,400.

51 This was the number of the Israelites, 601,730.

52 And the Lord said to Moses,

53 To these the land shall be divided for inheritance according to the number of names.

54 To a larger tribe you shall give the greater inheritance, and to a small tribe the less inheritance; to each tribe shall its inheritance be given according to its numbers.

55 But the land shall be divided by lot; according to the names of the tribes of their fathers they shall inherit.

56 According to the lot shall their inheritance be divided between the larger and the smaller.

57 And these were numbered of the Levites according to their families: of Gershon, the family of the Gershonites; of Kohath, the family of the Kohathites; of Merari, the family of the Merarites.

58 These are the families of Levi: the family of the Libnites, the family of the Hebronites, the family of the Mahlites, the family of the Mushites, the family of the Korahites. And Kohath was the father of Amram.

59 Amram's wife was Jochebed daughter of Levi, who was born to Levi in Egypt; and she bore to Amram Aaron, Moses, and Miriam their sister.

60 And to Aaron were born Nadab, Abihu, Eleazar, and Ithamar.

61 But Nadab and Abihu died when they offered strange *and* unholy fire before the Lord.

62 And those numbered of them were 23,000, every male from a month old and upward; for they were not numbered among the Israelites, because there was no inheritance given them among the Israelites.

63 These were those numbered by Moses and Eleazar the priest, who numbered the Israelites in the plains of Moab by the Jordan at Jericho.

64 But among these there was not a

man of those numbered by Moses and Aaron the priest when they numbered the Israelites in the Wilderness of Sinai.

65 For the Lord had said of them, They shall surely die in the wilderness. There was not left a man of them except Caleb son of Jephunneh and Joshua son of Nun.

27 THEN CAME the daughters of Zelophehad son of Hepher, the son of Gilead, the son of Machir, the son of Manasseh, from the families of Manasseh son of Joseph. The names of his daughters: Mahlah, Noah, Hoglah, Milcah, and Tirzah.

2 They stood before Moses, Eleazar the priest, and the leaders, and all the congregation at the door of the Tent of Meeting, saying,

3 Our father died in the wilderness. He was not among those who assembled together against the Lord in the company of Korah, but died for his own sin [as did all those who rebelled at Kadesh], and he had no sons. [Num. 14:26-35.]

4 Why should the name of our father be removed from his family because he had no son? Give to us a possession among our father's brethren.

5 Moses brought their case before the Lord.

6 And the Lord said to Moses,

7 The daughters of Zelophehad are justified *and* speak correctly. You shall surely give them an inheritance among their father's brethren, and you shall cause their father's inheritance to pass to them.

8 And say to the Israelites, If a man dies and has no son, you shall cause his inheritance to pass to his daughter.

9 If he has no daughter, you shall give his inheritance to his brethren.

10 If he has no brethren, give his inheritance to his father's brethren.

11 And if his father has no brethren, then give his inheritance to his next of kin, and he shall possess it. It shall be to the Israelites a statute and ordinance, as the Lord commanded Moses.

12 And the Lord said to Moses, Go up into this mountain of Abarim and behold the land I have given to the Israelites.

13 And when you have seen it, you also shall be gathered to your [departed] people as Aaron your brother was gathered,

14 For you disobeyed My order in the Wilderness of Zin during the strife of the congregation to uphold My sanctity [by strict obedience to My authority] at the waters before their eyes. [These are the waters of Meribah in Kadesh in the Wilderness of Zin]. [Num. 20:10-12.]

15 And Moses said to the Lord,

16 Let the Lord, the God of the spirits of all flesh, set a man over the congregation

17 Who shall go out and come in before them, leading them out and bringing them in, that the congregation of the Lord may not be as sheep which have no shepherd.

18 The Lord said to Moses, Take Joshua son of Nun, a man in whom is the Spirit, and lay your hand upon him;

19 And set him before Eleazar the priest and all the congregation and give him a charge in their sight.

20 And put some of your honor *and* authority upon him, that all the con-

speak the Word

God, I pray that I will never be as a sheep without a shepherd, but that You will always guide me to wise, godly leaders.
ADAPTED FROM NUMBERS 27:16, 17

gregation of the Israelites may obey him.

21 He shall stand before Eleazar the priest, who shall inquire for him before the Lord by the judgment of the Urim [one of two articles in the priest's breastplate worn when asking counsel of the Lord for the people]. At Joshua's word the people shall go out and come in, both he and all the Israelite congregation with him.

22 And Moses did as the Lord commanded him. He took Joshua and set him before Eleazar the priest and all the congregation,

23 And he laid his hands upon him and commissioned him, as the Lord commanded through Moses.

28 AND THE Lord said to Moses,

2 Command the Israelites, saying, My offering, My food for My offerings made by fire, My sweet *and* soothing odor you shall be careful to offer to Me at its proper time.

3 And you shall say to the people, This is the offering made by fire which you shall offer to the Lord: two male lambs a year old without spot *or* blemish, two day by day, for a continual burnt offering.

4 One lamb you shall offer in the morning and the other in the evening,

5 Also a tenth of an ephah of flour for a cereal offering, mixed with a fourth of a hin of beaten oil.

6 It is a continual burnt offering which was ordained in Mount Sinai for a sweet *and* soothing odor, an offering made by fire to the Lord.

7 Its drink offering shall be a fourth of a hin for each lamb; in the Holy Place you shall pour out a fermented drink offering to the Lord.

8 And the other lamb you shall offer in the evening; like the cereal offering of the morning and like its drink offering, you shall offer it, an offering made by fire, a sweet *and* soothing odor to the Lord.

9 And on the Sabbath day two male lambs a year old without spot *or* blemish, and two-tenths of an ephah of flour for a cereal offering, mixed with oil, and its drink offering.

10 This is the burnt offering of every Sabbath, besides the continual burnt offering and its drink offering.

11 And at the beginning of your months you shall offer a burnt offering to the Lord: two young bulls, one ram, seven male lambs a year old without spot *or* blemish;

12 And three-tenths of an ephah of fine flour for a cereal offering, mixed with oil, for each bull; and two-tenths of an ephah of fine flour for a cereal offering, mixed with oil, for the one ram.

13 And a tenth part of fine flour mixed with oil as a cereal offering, for each lamb, for a burnt offering of a sweet *and* pleasant fragrance, an offering made by fire to the Lord.

14 And their drink offerings shall be half a hin of wine for a bull, and a third of a hin for a ram, and a fourth of a hin for a lamb. This is the burnt offering of each month throughout the months of the year.

15 And one male goat for a sin offering to the Lord—it shall be offered in addition to the continual burnt offering and its drink offering.

16 On the fourteenth day of the first month is the Lord's Passover.

17 On the fifteenth day of this month is a feast; for seven days shall unleavened bread be eaten.

speak the Word

18 On the first day there shall be a holy [summoned] assembly; you shall do no servile work that day.

19 But you shall offer an offering made by fire, a burnt offering to the Lord: two young bulls, one ram, and seven male lambs a year old; they shall be without blemish to the best of your knowledge.

20 And their cereal offering shall be of fine flour mixed with oil; three-tenths of an ephah shall you offer for a bull, and two-tenths for a ram;

21 A tenth shall you offer for each of the seven male lambs,

22 Also one male goat for a sin offering to make atonement for you.

23 You shall offer these in addition to the burnt offering of the morning, which is for a continual burnt offering.

24 In this way you shall offer daily for seven days the food of an offering made by fire, a sweet *and* soothing odor to the Lord; it shall be offered in addition to the continual burnt offering and its drink offering.

25 And on the seventh day you shall have a holy [summoned] assembly; you shall do no work befitting a slave *or* a servant.

26 Also in the day of the firstfruits, when you offer a cereal offering of new grain to the Lord at your Feast of Weeks, you shall have a holy [summoned] assembly; you shall do no servile work.

27 But you shall offer the burnt offering for a sweet, pleasing, *and* soothing fragrance to the Lord: two young bulls, one ram, seven male lambs a year old,

28 And their cereal offering of fine flour mixed with oil, three-tenths of an ephah for each bull, two-tenths for one ram,

29 A tenth for each of the seven male lambs,

30 And one male goat to make atonement for you.

31 You shall offer them in addition to the continual burnt offering and its cereal offering and their drink offerings. See that they are without blemish.

29 ON THE first day of the seventh month [on New Year's Day of the civil year], you shall have a holy [summoned] assembly; you shall do no servile work. It is a day of blowing of trumpets for you [everyone blowing who wishes, proclaiming that the glad New Year has come and that the great Day of Atonement and the Feast of Tabernacles are now approaching].

2 And you shall offer a burnt offering for a sweet *and* pleasing odor to the Lord: one young bull, one ram, and seven male lambs a year old without blemish.

3 Their cereal offering shall be of fine flour mixed with oil, three-tenths of an ephah for a bull, two-tenths for a ram,

4 And one-tenth of an ephah for each of the seven lambs,

5 And one male goat for a sin offering to make atonement for you.

6 These are in addition to the burnt offering of the new moon and its cereal offering, and the daily burnt offering and its cereal offering, and their drink offerings, according to the ordinance for them, for a pleasant *and* soothing fragrance, an offering made by fire to the Lord.

7 And you shall have on the tenth day of this seventh month a holy [summoned] assembly; [it is the great Day of Atonement, a day of humiliation] and you shall humble *and* abase yourselves; you shall not do any work in it.

8 But you shall offer a burnt offering to the Lord for a sweet *and* soothing fragrance: one young bull, one ram, and seven male lambs a year old. See that they are without blemish.

9 And their cereal offering shall be of fine flour mixed with oil, three-tenths of an ephah for the bull, two-tenths for the one ram,
10 A tenth for each of the seven male lambs,
11 One male goat for a sin offering, in addition to the sin offering of atonement, and the continual burnt offering and its cereal offering, and their drink offerings.
12 And on the fifteenth day of the seventh month you shall have a holy [summoned] assembly; you shall do no servile work, and you shall keep a feast to the Lord for seven days.
13 And you shall offer a burnt offering, an offering made by fire, of a sweet *and* pleasing fragrance to the Lord: thirteen young bulls, two rams, and fourteen male lambs a year old; they shall be without blemish.
14 And their cereal offering shall be of fine flour mixed with oil, three-tenths of an ephah for each of the thirteen bulls, two-tenths for each of the two rams,
15 And a tenth part for each of the fourteen male lambs,
16 Also one male goat for a sin offering, in addition to the continual burnt offering, its cereal offering, and its drink offering.
17 And on the second day you shall offer twelve young bulls, two rams, fourteen male lambs a year old without spot *or* blemish,
18 With their cereal offering and the drink offerings for the bulls, the rams, and the lambs, by number according to the ordinance,
19 Also one male goat for a sin offering, besides the continual burnt offering, its cereal offering, and their drink offerings.
20 And on the third day eleven bulls, two rams, fourteen male lambs a year old without blemish,
21 With their cereal offering and drink offerings for the bulls, the rams,

and the lambs, by number according to the ordinance,
22 And one male goat for a sin offering, besides the continual burnt offering, its cereal offering, and its drink offerings.
23 On the fourth day ten bulls, two rams, and fourteen male lambs a year old without blemish,
24 Their cereal offering and their drink offerings for the bulls, the rams, and the lambs shall be by number according to the ordinance,
25 And one male goat for a sin offering, besides the continual burnt offering, its cereal offering, and its drink offerings.
26 And on the fifth day nine bulls, two rams, and fourteen male lambs a year old without spot *or* blemish,
27 And their cereal offering and drink offerings for the bulls, the rams, and the lambs, by number according to the ordinance,
28 And one goat for a sin offering, besides the continual burnt offering, and its cereal offering, and its drink offerings.
29 And on the sixth day eight bulls, two rams, and fourteen male lambs a year old without blemish,
30 And their cereal offering and their drink offerings for the bulls, the rams, and the lambs, by number according to the ordinance,
31 And one goat for a sin offering, besides the continual burnt offering, its cereal offering, and its drink offerings.
32 And on the seventh day seven bulls, two rams, and fourteen male lambs a year old without blemish,
33 And their cereal and drink offerings for the bulls, the rams, and the lambs, by number according to the ordinance.
34 And one male goat for a sin offering, besides the continual burnt offering, and its cereal offering, and its drink offerings.

35 On the eighth day you shall have a solemn assembly; you shall do no servile work.

36 You shall offer a burnt offering, an offering made by fire, of a sweet *and* pleasing fragrance to the Lord: one bull, one ram, seven male lambs a year old without blemish,

37 Their cereal offering and drink offerings for the bull, the ram, and the lambs shall be by number according to the ordinance,

38 And one male goat for a sin offering, besides the continual burnt offering, and its cereal offering, and its drink offerings.

39 These you shall offer to the Lord at your appointed feasts, besides the offerings you have vowed and your freewill offerings, for your burnt offerings, cereal offerings, drink offerings, and peace offerings.

40 And Moses told the Israelites all that the Lord commanded him.

30 AND MOSES said to the heads *or* leaders of the tribes of Israel, This is the thing which the Lord has commanded:

2 If a man vows a vow to the Lord or swears an oath to bind himself by a pledge, he shall not break *and* profane his word; he shall do according to all that proceeds out of his mouth.

3 Also when a woman vows a vow to the Lord and binds herself by a pledge, being in her father's house in her youth,

4 And her father hears her vow and her pledge with which she has bound herself and he offers no objection, then all her vows shall stand and every pledge with which she has bound herself shall stand.

5 But if her father refuses to allow her [to carry out her vow] on the day that he hears about it, not any of her vows or of her pledges with which she has bound herself shall stand. And

the Lord will forgive her because her father refused to let her [carry out her purpose].

6 And if she is married to a husband while her vows are upon her or she has bound herself by a rash utterance

7 And her husband hears of it and holds his peace concerning it on the day that he hears it, then her vows shall stand and her pledge with which she bound herself shall stand.

8 But if her husband refuses to allow her [to keep her vow or pledge] on the day that he hears of it, then he shall make void *and* annul her vow which is upon her and the rash utterance of her lips by which she bound herself, and the Lord will forgive her.

9 But the vow of a widow or of a divorced woman, with which she has bound herself, shall stand against her.

10 And if she vowed in her husband's house or bound herself by a pledge with an oath

11 And her husband heard it and did not oppose or prohibit her, then all her vows and every pledge with which she bound herself shall stand.

12 But if her husband positively made them void on the day he heard them, then whatever proceeded out of her lips concerning her vows or concerning her pledge of herself shall not stand. Her husband has annulled them, and the Lord will forgive her.

13 Every vow and every binding oath to humble *or* afflict herself, her husband may establish it or her husband may annul it.

14 But if her husband altogether holds his peace [concerning the matter] with her from day to day, then he establishes *and* confirms all her vows or all her pledges which are upon her. He establishes them because he said nothing to [restrain] her on the day he heard of them.

15 But if he shall nullify them after he hears of them, then he shall be responsible for *and* bear her iniquity.

16 These are the statutes which the Lord commanded Moses, between a man and his wife, and between a father and his daughter while in her youth in her father's house.

3 1 THE LORD said to Moses, **2** Avenge the Israelites on the Midianites; afterward you shall be gathered to your [departed] people.

3 And Moses said to the people, Arm men from among you for the war, that they may go against Midian and execute the Lord's vengeance on Midian [for seducing Israel]. [Num. 25:16-18.]

4 From each of the tribes of Israel you shall send 1,000 to the war.

5 So there were provided out of the thousands of Israel 1,000 from each tribe, 12,000 armed for war.

6 And Moses sent them to the war, 1,000 from each tribe, together with Phinehas son of Eleazar, the priest, with the [sacred] vessels of the sanctuary and the trumpets to blow the alarm in his hand.

7 They fought with Midian, as the Lord commanded Moses, and slew every male,

8 Including the five kings of Midian: Evi, Rekem, Zur, Hur, and Reba; also Balaam son of Beor they slew with the sword. [Num. 22:31-35; Neh. 13:1, 2.]

9 And the Israelites took captive the women of Midian and their little ones, and all their cattle, their flocks, and their goods as booty.

10 They burned all the cities in which they dwelt, and all their encampments.

11 And they took all the spoil and all the prey, both of man and of beast.

12 Then they brought the captives, the prey, and the spoil to Moses and Eleazar the priest and to the congregation of the Israelites at the camp on the plains of Moab by Jordan at Jericho.

13 Moses and Eleazar the priest and all the princes *or* leaders of the congregation went to meet them outside the camp.

14 But Moses was angry with the officers of the army, the commanders of thousands and of hundreds, who served in the war.

15 And Moses said to them, Have you let all the women live?

16 Behold, these caused the Israelites by the counsel of Balaam to trespass *and* act treacherously against the Lord in the matter of Peor, and so a [smiting] plague came among the congregation of the Lord. [Num. 25:1-9; 31:8.]

17 Now therefore, kill every male among the little ones, and kill every woman who is not a virgin.

18 But all the young girls who have not known man by lying with him keep alive for yourselves.

19 Encamp outside the camp seven days; whoever has killed any person and whoever has touched any slain, purify yourselves and your captives on the third day and on the seventh day.

20 You shall purify every garment, all that is made of skins, all work of goats' hair, and every article of wood.

21 And Eleazar the priest said to the men of war who had gone to battle, This is the statute of the law which the Lord has commanded Moses:

22 Only the gold, the silver, the bronze, the iron, the tin, and the lead,

23 Everything that can stand fire, you shall make go through fire, and it shall be clean. Nevertheless it shall also be purified with the water of impurity; and all that cannot stand fire [such as fabrics] you shall pass through water.

24 And you shall wash your clothes on the seventh day and you shall be clean; then you shall come into the camp.

25 And the Lord said to Moses,

26 Take the count of the prey that was taken, both of man and of beast, you and Eleazar the priest and the heads of the fathers' houses of the congregation.
27 Divide the booty into two [equal] parts between the warriors who went out to battle and all the congregation.
28 And levy a tribute to the Lord from the warriors who went to battle, one out of every 500 of the persons, the oxen, the donkeys, and the flocks.
29 Take [this tribute] from the warriors' half and give it to Eleazar the priest as an offering to the Lord.
30 And from the Israelites' half [of the booty] you shall take one out of every fifty of the persons, the oxen, the donkeys, the flocks, and of all livestock, and give them to the Levites who have charge of the tabernacle of the Lord.
31 And Moses and Eleazar the priest did as the Lord commanded Moses.
32 The prey, besides the booty which the men of war took, was 675,000 sheep,
33 And 72,000 cattle,
34 And 61,000 donkeys,
35 And 32,000 persons in all, of the women who were virgins.
36 And the half share, the portion of those who went to war, was: 337,500 sheep,
37 And the Lord's tribute of the sheep was 675;
38 The cattle were 36,000, of which the Lord's tribute was 72;
39 The donkeys were 30,500, of which the Lord's tribute was 61;
40 The persons were 16,000, of whom the Lord's tribute was 32 persons.
41 And Moses gave the tribute which was the Lord's offering to Eleazar the priest, as the Lord commanded Moses.
42 And the Israelites' half Moses separated from that of the warriors'—
43 Now the congregation's half was 337,500 sheep,
44 And 36,000 cattle,
45 And 30,500 donkeys,
46 And 16,000 persons—
47 Even of the Israelites' half, Moses took one of every 50, both of persons and of beasts, and gave them to the Levites, who had charge of the tabernacle of the Lord, as the Lord commanded Moses.
48 And the officers who were over the thousands of the army, the commanders of thousands and hundreds, came to Moses.
49 They told [him], Your servants have counted the warriors under our command, and not one man of us is missing.
50 We have brought as the Lord's offering what each man obtained— articles of gold, armlets, bracelets, signet rings, earrings, neck ornaments—to make atonement for ourselves before the Lord.
51 Moses and Eleazar the priest took the gold from them, all the wrought articles.
52 And all the gold of the offering that they offered to the Lord from the commanders of thousands and of hundreds was 16,750 shekels.
53 For the men of war had taken booty, every man for himself.
54 And Moses and Eleazar the priest received the gold from the commanders of thousands and of hundreds and brought it into the Tent of Meeting as a memorial for the Israelites before the Lord.

32 NOW THE sons of Reuben and of Gad had a very great multitude of cattle, and they saw the land of Jazer and the land of Gilead [on the east side of the Jordan], and behold, the place was suitable for cattle.
2 So the sons of Gad and of Reuben came and said to Moses, Eleazar the priest, and the leaders of the congregation,
3 [The country around] Ataroth,

Dibon, Jazer, Nimrah, Heshbon, Ele-aleh, Sebam, Nebo, and Beon,

4 The land the Lord smote before the congregation of Israel, is a land for cattle, and your servants have cattle.

5 And they said, If we have found favor in your sight, let this land be given to your servants for a posses-sion. Do not take us over the Jordan.

6 And Moses said to the sons of Gad and of Reuben, Shall your brethren go to war while you sit here?

7 Why do you discourage the hearts of the Israelites from going over into the land which the Lord has given them?

8 Thus your fathers did when I sent them from Kadesh-barnea to see the land!

9 For when they went up to the Valley of Eshcol and saw the land, they discouraged the hearts of the Israelites from going into the land the Lord had given them.

10 And the Lord's anger was kindled on that day and He swore, saying,

11 Surely none of the men who came up out of Egypt, from twenty years old and upward, shall see the land which I swore to Abraham, to Isaac, and to Jacob, because they have not wholly followed Me—

12 Except Caleb son of Jephunneh the Kenizzite and Joshua son of Nun, for they have wholly followed the Lord.

13 And the Lord's anger was kindled against Israel and He made them wander in the wilderness for forty years, until all the generation that had done evil in the sight of the Lord was consumed.

14 And behold, you are risen up in your fathers' stead, a brood of sinful men, to increase still more the fierce anger of the Lord against Israel.

15 For if you turn from following Him, He will again abandon them in the wilderness, and you will destroy all this people.

16 But they came near to him and said, We will build sheepfolds here for our flocks and walled settlements for our little ones.

17 But we will be armed and ready to go before the Israelites until we have brought them to their place. Our little ones shall dwell in the fortified settle-ments because of the people of the land.

18 We will not return to our homes until the Israelites have inherited every man his inheritance.

19 For we will not inherit with them on the [west] side of the Jordan and beyond, because our inheritance is fallen to us on this side of the Jordan eastward.

20 Moses replied, If you will do as you say, going armed before the Lord to war,

21 And every armed man of you will pass over the Jordan before the Lord until He has driven out His enemies before Him

22 And the land is subdued before the Lord, then afterward you shall return and be guiltless [in this matter] before the Lord and before Israel, and this land shall be your possession before the Lord.

23 But if you will not do so, behold, you have sinned against the Lord; and be sure your sin will find you out.

24 Build settlements for your little ones, and folds for your sheep, and do that of which you have spoken.

25 And the sons of Gad and of Reuben said to Moses, Your servants will do as my lord commands.

26 Our little ones, our wives, our flocks, and all our cattle shall be there in the cities of Gilead.

27 But your servants will pass over, every man armed for war, before the Lord to battle, as my lord says.

28 So Moses gave command con-cerning them to Eleazar the priest and Joshua son of Nun and the heads of the fathers' houses of the tribes of Israel.

29 And Moses said to them, If the sons of Gad and Reuben will pass with you over the Jordan, every man armed to battle before the Lord, and the land shall be subdued before you, then you shall give them the land of Gilead for a possession.

30 But if they will not pass over with you armed, they shall have possessions among you in the land of Canaan.

31 The sons of Gad and Reuben answered, As the Lord has said to your servants, so will we do.

32 We will pass over armed before the Lord into the land of Canaan, that the possession of our inheritance on this side of the Jordan may be ours.

33 Moses gave to them, to the sons of Gad and of Reuben and to half the tribe of Manasseh son of Joseph, the kingdom of Sihon king of the Amorites and the kingdom of Og king of Bashan—the land with its cities and their territories, even the cities round about the country.

34 And the sons of Gad built Dibon, Ataroth, Aroer,

35 Atroth-shophan, Jazer, Jogbehah,

36 Beth-nimrah, and Beth-haran, fortified cities, and folds for sheep.

37 And the sons of Reuben built Heshbon, Elealeh, Kiriathaim,

38 Nebo, and Baal-meon—their names were to be changed—and Shibmah; and they gave other names to the cities they built.

39 And the sons of Machir son of Manasseh went to Gilead and took it and dispossessed the Amorites who were in it.

40 And Moses gave Gilead to Machir son of Manasseh, and he settled in it.

41 Jair son of Manasseh took their villages and called them Havvoth-jair.

42 And Nobah took Kenath and its villages and called it Nobah after his own name.

33 THESE ARE the stages of the journeys of the Israelites by which they went out of the land of Egypt by their hosts under the leadership of Moses and Aaron.

2 Moses recorded their starting places, as the Lord commanded, stage by stage; and these are their journeying stages from their starting places:

3 They set out from Rameses on the fifteenth day of the first month; on the day after the Passover the Israelites went out [of Egypt] with a high hand *and* triumphantly in the sight of all the Egyptians,

4 While the Egyptians were burying all their firstborn whom the Lord had struck down among them; upon their gods also the Lord executed judgments.

5 The Israelites set out from Rameses and encamped in Succoth.

6 And they departed from Succoth and encamped in Etham, which is at the edge of the wilderness.

7 They set out from Etham and turned back to Pi-hahiroth, east of Baal-zephon, and they encamped before Migdol.

8 And they journeyed from before Pi-hahiroth and passed through the midst of the [Red] Sea into the wilderness; and they went a three days' journey in the Wilderness of Etham and encamped at Marah.

9 They journeyed from Marah and came to Elim; at Elim there were twelve springs of water and seventy palm trees, and they encamped there.

10 They set out from Elim and encamped by the Red Sea.

11 They journeyed from the Red Sea and encamped in the Wilderness of Sin.

12 And they traveled on from the Wilderness of Sin and encamped at Dophkah.

13 And they departed from Dophkah and encamped at Alush.

14 And they set out from Alush and

encamped at Rephidim, where there was no water for the people to drink.

15 And they departed from Rephidim and encamped in the Wilderness of Sinai.

16 And they journeyed from the Wilderness of Sinai and encamped at Kibroth-hattaavah.

17 And they traveled on from Kibroth-hattaavah and encamped at Hazeroth.

18 And they journeyed from Hazeroth and encamped at Rithmah.

19 And they departed from Rithmah and encamped at Rimmon-perez.

20 And they departed from Rimmon-perez and encamped at Libnah.

21 And they removed from Libnah and encamped at Rissah.

22 And they journeyed from Rissah and encamped at Kehelathah.

23 And they went from Kehelathah and encamped at Mount Shepher.

24 And they removed from Mount Shepher and encamped at Haradah.

25 And they set out from Haradah and encamped at Makheloth.

26 And they removed from Makheloth and encamped at Tahath.

27 And they departed from Tahath and encamped at Terah.

28 And they removed from Terah and encamped at Mithkah.

29 And they set out from Mithkah and encamped at Hashmonah.

30 And they traveled on from Hashmonah and encamped at Moseroth.

31 And they journeyed from Moseroth and pitched in Bene-jaakan.

32 And they set out from Bene-jaakan and encamped at Hor-haggidgad.

33 And they set out from Hor-haggidgad and encamped at Jotbathah.

34 And they journeyed from Jotbathah and encamped at Abronah.

35 And they traveled on from Abronah and encamped at Ezion-geber.

36 And they removed from Ezion-geber and encamped in the Wilderness of Zin, which is Kadesh.

37 And they removed from Kadesh and encamped at Mount Hor, on the edge of Edom.

38 Aaron the priest went up on Mount Hor at the command of the Lord, and died there in the fortieth year after the Israelites came out of Egypt, the first day of the fifth month. [Num. 20:23-29.]

39 Aaron was 123 years old when he died on Mount Hor.

40 The Canaanite king of Arad, who lived in the South (the Negeb) in the land of Canaan, heard of the coming of the Israelites.

41 They set out from Mount Hor and encamped at Zalmonah.

42 And they set out from Zalmonah and encamped at Punon.

43 And they set out from Punon and encamped at Oboth.

44 And they traveled on from Oboth and encamped at Iye-abarim, on the border of Moab.

45 And they departed from Iyim and encamped at Dibon-gad.

46 And they set out from Dibon-gad and encamped in Almon-diblathaim.

47 And they traveled on from Almon-diblathaim and encamped in the mountains of Abarim, before Nebo.

48 And they departed from the mountains of Abarim and encamped in the plains of Moab by the Jordan at Jericho.

49 And they encamped by the Jordan from Beth-jeshimoth as far as Abel-shittim in the plains of Moab.

50 And the Lord said to Moses in the plains of Moab by the Jordan at Jericho,

51 Tell the Israelites, When you have passed over the Jordan into the land of Canaan,

52 Then you shall drive out all the inhabitants of the land before you and destroy all their figured stones and all their molten images and completely demolish all their [idolatrous] high places,

53 And you shall take possession of the land and dwell in it, for to you I have given the land to possess it.

54 You shall inherit the land by lot according to your families; to the large tribe you shall give a larger inheritance, and to the small tribe you shall give a smaller inheritance. Wherever the lot falls to any man, that shall be his. According to the tribes of your fathers you shall inherit.

55 But if you will not drive out the inhabitants of the land from before you, then those you let remain of them shall be as pricks in your eyes and as thorns in your sides, and they shall vex you in the land in which you dwell.

56 And as I thought to do to them, so will I do to you.

34 AND THE Lord said to Moses,

2 Command the Israelites, When you come into the land of Canaan (which is the land that shall be yours for an inheritance, the land of Canaan according to its boundaries),

3 Your south side shall be from the Wilderness of Zin along the side of Edom, and your southern boundary from the end of the Salt [Dead] Sea eastward.

4 Your boundary shall turn south of the ascent of Akrabbim, and pass on to Zin, and its end shall be south of Kadesh-barnea. Then it shall go on to Hazar-addar and pass on to Azmon.

5 Then the boundary shall turn from Azmon to the Brook of Egypt, and it shall terminate at the [Mediterranean] Sea.

6 For the western boundary you shall have the Great Sea and its coast.

7 And this shall be your north border: from the Great Sea mark out your boundary line to Mount Hor;

8 From Mount Hor you shall mark out your boundary to the entrance of Hamath, and its end shall be at Zedad;

9 Then the northern boundary shall go on to Ziphron, and the end of it shall be at Hazar-enan.

10 You shall mark out your eastern boundary from Hazar-enan to Shepham;

11 The boundary shall go down from Shepham to Riblah on the east side of Ain and shall descend and reach to the shoulder of the Sea of Chinnereth [the Sea of Galilee] on the east;

12 And the boundary shall go down to the Jordan, and the end shall be at the Salt Sea. This shall be your land with its boundaries all around.

13 Moses commanded the Israelites, This is the land you shall inherit by lot, which the Lord has commanded to give to the nine tribes and the half-tribe [of Manasseh],

14 For the tribes of the sons of Reuben and of Gad by their fathers' houses have received their inheritance, and also the half-tribe of Manasseh.

15 The two and a half tribes have received their inheritance east of the Jordan at Jericho, toward the sunrise.

16 And the Lord said to Moses,

17 These are the men who shall divide the land to you for inheritance: Eleazar the priest and Joshua son of Nun.

18 And [with them] you shall take one head *or* prince of each tribe to divide the land for inheritance.

19 The names of the men are: Of the tribe of Judah, Caleb son of Jephunneh;

20 Of the tribe of the sons of Simeon, Shemuel son of Ammihud;

21 Of the tribe of Benjamin, Elidad son of Chislon;

22 Of the tribe of the sons of Dan a leader, Bukki son of Jogli;

23 Of the sons of Joseph: of the tribe of the sons of Manasseh a leader, Hanniel son of Ephod;

24 And of the tribe of the sons of Ephraim a leader, Kemuel son of Shiphtan;

25 And of the tribe of the sons of Zebulun a leader, Elizaphan son of Parnach;

26 And of the tribe of the sons of Issachar a leader, Paltiel son of Azzan;

27 And of the tribe of the sons of Asher a leader, Ahihud son of Shelomi;

28 And of the tribe of the sons of Naphtali a leader, Pedahel son of Ammihud.

29 These are the men whom the Lord commanded to divide the inheritance to the Israelites in the land of Canaan.

35 AND THE Lord said to Moses in the plains of Moab by the Jordan at Jericho,

2 Command the Israelites that they give to the Levites from the inheritance of their possession cities to dwell in; and [suburb] pasturelands round about the cities' walls you shall give to the Levites also.

3 They shall have the cities to dwell in and their [suburb] pasturelands shall be for their cattle, for their wealth [in flocks], and for all their beasts.

4 And the pasturelands of the cities which you shall give to the Levites shall reach from the wall of the city and outward 1,000 cubits round about.

5 You shall measure from the wall of the city outward on the east, south, west, and north sides 2,000 cubits, the city being in the center. This shall belong to [the Levites] as [suburb] pasturelands for their cities.

6 Of the cities which you shall give to the Levites there shall be the six cities of refuge, which you shall give for the manslayer to flee into; and in addition to them you shall give forty-two cities.

7 So all the cities which you shall give to the Levites shall be forty-eight; you shall give them with their adjacent [suburb] pasturelands.

8 As for the cities, you shall give from the possession of the Israelites, from the larger tribes you shall take many and from the smaller tribes few; each tribe shall give of its cities to the Levites in proportion to its inheritance.

9 And the Lord said to Moses,

10 Say to the Israelites, When you cross the Jordan into the land of Canaan,

11 Then you shall select cities to be cities of refuge for you, that the slayer who kills any person unintentionally and unawares may flee there.

12 And the cities shall be to you for refuge from the avenger, that the manslayer may not die until he has had a fair trial before the congregation.

13 And of the cities which you give there shall be your six cities for refuge.

14 You shall give three cities on this [east] side of the Jordan and three cities in the land of Canaan, to be cities of refuge.

15 These six cities shall be a refuge for the Israelites and for the stranger and the temporary resident among them; that anyone who kills any person unintentionally and unawares may flee there.

16 But if he struck him down with an instrument of iron so that he died, he is a murderer; the murderer shall surely be put to death.

17 And if he struck him down by throwing a stone, by which a person may die, and he died, he is a murderer; the murderer shall surely be put to death.

18 Or if he struck him down with a weapon of wood in his hand, by which one may die, and he died, the offender is a murderer; he shall surely be put to death.

19 The avenger of blood shall himself slay the murderer; when he meets him, he shall slay him.

20 But if he stabbed him through

hatred or hurled at him by lying in wait so that he died

21 Or in enmity struck him down with his hand so that he died, he that smote him shall surely be put to death; he is a murderer. The avenger of blood shall slay the murderer when he meets him.

22 But if he stabbed him suddenly without enmity or threw anything at *or* upon him without lying in wait

23 Or with any stone with which a man may be killed, not seeing him, and threw it at him so that he died, and was not his enemy nor sought to harm him,

24 Then the congregation shall judge between the slayer and the avenger of blood according to these ordinances.

25 And the congregation shall rescue the manslayer from the hand of the avenger of blood and restore him to his city of refuge to which he had fled; and he shall live in it until the high priest dies, who was anointed with the sacred oil.

26 But if the slayer shall at any time come outside the limits of his city of refuge to which he had fled

27 And the avenger of blood finds him outside the limits of his city of refuge and kills the manslayer, he shall not be guilty of blood

28 Because the manslayer should have remained in his city of refuge until the death of the high priest. But after the high priest's death the manslayer shall return to the land of his possession.

29 And these things shall be for a statute *and* ordinance to you throughout your generations in all your dwellings.

30 Whoever kills any person [intentionally], the murderer shall be put to death on the testimony of witnesses; but no one shall be put to death on the testimony of one witness.

31 Moreover, you shall take no ransom for the life of a murderer guilty of death; but he shall surely be put to death.

32 And you shall accept no ransom for him who has fled to his city of refuge, so that he may return to dwell in the land before the death of the high priest.

33 So you shall not pollute the land in which you live; for blood pollutes the land, and no atonement can be made for the land for the blood shed in it, but by the blood of him who shed it.

34 And you shall not defile the land in which you live, in the midst of which I dwell, for I, the Lord, dwell in the midst of the people of Israel.

36 THE HEADS of the fathers' houses of the families of the sons of Gilead son of Machir, the son of Manasseh, of the fathers' houses of the sons of Joseph, came near and spoke before Moses and the leaders, the heads of the fathers' houses of the Israelites.

2 They said, The Lord commanded [you] my lord to give the land for inheritance by lot to the Israelites; and my lord was commanded by the Lord to give the inheritance of Zelophehad our brother to his daughters.

3 But if they are married to any of the sons of the other tribes of the Israelites, then their inheritance will be taken from that of our fathers and added to the inheritance of the tribe to which they are received *and* belong; so it will be taken out of the lot of our inheritance.

4 And when the Jubilee of the Israelites comes, then their inheritance will be added to that of the tribe to which they are received *and* belong; so will their inheritance be taken away from that of the tribe of our fathers.

5 And Moses commanded the Israelites according to the word of the

Lord, saying, The tribe of the sons of Joseph is right.

6 This is what the Lord commands concerning the daughters of Zelophehad: Let them marry whom they think best; only they shall marry within the family of the tribe of their father.

7 So shall no inheritance of the Israelites be transferred from tribe to tribe, for every one of the Israelites shall cling to the inheritance of the tribe of his fathers.

8 And every daughter who possesses an inheritance in any tribe of the Israelites shall be wife to one of the family of the tribe of her father, so that the Israelites may each one possess the inheritance of his fathers.

9 So shall no inheritance be transferred from one tribe to another, but each of the tribes of the Israelites shall cling to its own inheritance.

10 The daughters of Zelophehad did as the Lord commanded Moses.

11 For Mahlah, Tirzah, Hoglah, Milcah, and Noah, the daughters of Zelophehad, were married to sons of their father's brothers.

12 They married into the families of the sons of Manasseh son of Joseph, and their inheritance remained in the tribe of the family of their father.

13 These are the commandments and ordinances which the Lord commanded the Israelites through Moses in the plains of Moab by the Jordan [River] at Jericho.

Deuteronomy

Author:
Moses

Date:
About 1440 BC

Everyday Life Principles:
Blessings and curses are set before us. We need to choose life and continually make good, godly decisions.

We do not live "by bread alone." In other words, real life is not in our possessions, positions, or worldly prestige, but in knowing God, fellowshipping with Him, and trusting Him.

We do not need to strive to be blessed. When we obey God, blessings come as long are we are seeking Him for Who He is and not what He can do for us.

Deuteronomy is a book about our never-ending need for God and His presence in our everyday lives. It is about trusting Him for daily miracles, learning to live in the blessings He gives us, and relying on His guidance in every situation we face.

In Deuteronomy, we see that the Israelites had to learn to worship God in the wilderness, to honor and obey Him while they were *on the way* to the Promised Land, when the journey was difficult. God asks us today, just as He did the Israelites, to worship Him and trust Him when life's journey gets tough. He knows that we will not consistently worship during the good times if we will not worship Him in the hard times. He also knows that our trust in Him is developed and strengthened in difficulty and not when everything is going well for us.

Let Deuteronomy provoke you to trust God and to seek His presence more fervently than ever. Remember that we do not live "by bread alone," but by the Word of God and in the presence of God. Let this book encourage you to live in the blessings of obedience to God and teach you to handle those blessings wisely. Let it inspire you to worship your way through the wilderness times in your own life and to keep choosing life in every situation (see Deuteronomy 30:19).

1 THESE ARE the words which Moses spoke to all Israel [still] on the [east] side of the Jordan [River] in the wilderness, in the Arabah [the deep valley running north and south from the eastern arm of the Red Sea to beyond the Dead Sea], over near Suph, between Paran and Tophel, Laban, Hazeroth, and Dizahab.

2 It is [only] eleven days' journey from Horeb by the way of Mount Seir to Kadesh-barnea [on Canaan's border; yet Israel took forty years to get beyond it].

3 And in the fortieth year, on the first day of the eleventh month, Moses spoke to the Israelites according to all that the Lord had given him in commandment to them,

4 After He had defeated Sihon king of the Amorites, who lived in Heshbon, and Og king of Bashan, who lived in Ashtaroth [and] Edrei.

5 Beyond (east of) the Jordan in the land of Moab, Moses began to explain this law, saying,

6 The Lord our God said to us in Horeb, You have dwelt long enough on this mountain.

7 Turn and take up your journey and go to the hill country of the Amorites, and to all their neighbors in the Arabah, in the hill country, in the lowland, in the South (the Negeb), and on the coast, the land of the Canaanites, and Lebanon, as far as the great river, the river Euphrates.

8 Behold, I have set the land before you; go in and take possession of the land which the Lord swore to your fathers, to Abraham, to Isaac, and to

walk out of your wilderness

Moses pointed out to the Israelites that it was only an *eleven-day* journey to the border of Canaan (the Promised Land); yet it had taken them *forty years* to get there. Then Moses said these great words: "The Lord our God said . . . You have dwelt long enough on this mountain" (Deuteronomy 1:6).

Have you dwelt long enough on the same mountain? Have you spent forty years in the wilderness trying to make an eleven-day trip?

In my own life, there was a time when I finally had to wake up and realize that I was going nowhere. I was a Christian without victory. I had many wrong mind-sets and many mental strongholds that had built up through the years. The devil had lied to me, and I had believed him. I did not even realize I was deceived. I decided I had been on the same mountain long enough. I had spent forty years making what could have been a much shorter journey had I only known the truth of God's Word.

God showed me that the Israelites stayed in the wilderness because they had a "wilderness mentality"—certain types of wrong thinking that kept them in bondage. Let me urge you to make a quality decision to renew your mind and learn to choose your thoughts carefully. Make up your mind that you will not give up until victory is complete and you have taken possession of your rightful inheritance. Do not stay too long in any one place, but keep moving toward everything God has for you.

Jacob, to give to them and to their descendants after them.

9 I said to you at that time, I am not able to bear you alone.

10 The Lord your God has multiplied you, and behold, you are this day as the stars of the heavens for multitude.

11 May the Lord, the God of your fathers, make you a thousand times as many as you are and bless you as He has promised you!

12 How can I bear alone the weariness *and* pressure and burden of you and your strife?

13 Choose wise, understanding, experienced, *and* respected men according to your tribes, and I will make them heads over you.

14 And you answered me, The thing which you have spoken is good for us to do.

15 So I took the heads of your tribes, wise, experienced, *and* respected men, and made them heads over you, commanders of thousands, and hundreds, and fifties, and tens, and officers according to your tribes.

16 And I charged your judges at that time: Hear the cases between your brethren and judge righteously between a man and his brother or the stranger *or* sojourner who is with him.

17 You shall not be partial in judgment; but you shall hear the small as well as the great. You shall not be afraid of the face of man, for the judgment is God's. And the case that is too hard for you, you shall bring to me, and I will hear it.

18 And I commanded you at that time all the things that you should do.

19 And when we departed from Horeb, we went through all that great and terrible wilderness which you saw on the way to the hill country of the Amorites, as the Lord our God commanded us, and we came to Kadesh-barnea.

20 And I said to you, You have come to the hill country of the Amorites, which the Lord our God gives us.

21 Behold, the Lord your God has set the land before you; go up and possess it, as the Lord, the God of your fathers, has said to you. Fear not, neither be dismayed.

22 Then you all came near to me and said, Let us send men before us, that they may search out the land for us and bring us word again by what way we should go up and the cities into which we shall come.

23 The thing pleased me well, and I took twelve men of you, one for each tribe.

24 And they turned and went up into the hill country, and came to the Valley of Eshcol and spied it out.

25 And they took of the fruit of the land in their hands and brought it down to us and brought us word again, and said, It is a good land which the Lord our God gives us.

26 Yet you would not go up, but rebelled against the commandment of the Lord your God.

27 You were peevish *and* discontented in your tents, and said, Because the Lord hated us, He brought us forth out of the land of Egypt to deliver us into the hand of the Amorites to destroy us.

28 To what are we going up? Our brethren have made our hearts melt, saying, The people are bigger and taller than we are; the cities are great and fortified to the heavens. And moreover we have seen the [giantlike] sons of the Anakim there.

29 Then I said to you, Dread not, neither be afraid of them.

30 The Lord your God Who goes before you, He will fight for you just as He did for you in Egypt before your eyes,

31 And in the wilderness, where you have seen how the Lord your God bore you, as a man carries his son, in all the way that you went until you came to this place.

32 Yet in spite of this word you did not believe (trust, rely on, and remain steadfast to) the Lord your God,

33 Who went in the way before you to search out a place to pitch your tents, in fire by night, to show you by what way you should go, and in the cloud by day.

34 And the Lord heard your words, and was angered and He swore,

35 Not one of these men of this evil generation shall see that good land which I swore to give to your fathers,

36 Except [Joshua, of course, and] Caleb son of Jephunneh; he shall see it, and to him and to his children I will give the land upon which he has walked, because he has wholly followed the Lord.

37 The Lord was angry with me also for your sakes, and said, You also shall not enter Canaan.

38 But Joshua son of Nun, who stands before you, he shall enter there. Encourage him, for he shall cause Israel to inherit it.

39 Moreover, your little ones whom you said would become a prey, and your children who at this time cannot discern between good and evil, they shall enter Canaan, and to them I will give it and they shall possess it.

40 But as for you, turn and journey into the wilderness by way of the Red Sea.

41 Then you said to me, We have sinned against the Lord. We will go up and fight, as the Lord our God commanded us. And you girded on every man his battle weapons, and thought it a simple matter to go up into the hill country.

42 And the Lord said to me, Say to them, Do not go up or fight, for I am not among you—lest you be dangerously hurt by your enemies.

43 So I spoke to you, and you would not hear, but rebelled against the commandment of the Lord, and were presumptuous and went up into the hill country.

44 Then the Amorites who lived in that hill country came out against you and chased you as bees do and struck you down in Seir as far as Hormah.

45 And you returned and wept before the Lord, but the Lord would not heed your voice or listen to you.

46 So you remained in Kadesh; many days you remained there.

2 THEN WE turned, and took our journey into the wilderness by the way of the Red Sea, as the Lord directed me; and for many days we journeyed around Mount Seir.

2 And the Lord spoke to me [Moses], saying,

3 You have roamed around this mountain country long enough; turn northward.

4 And command the Israelites, You are to pass through the territory of your kinsmen the sons of Esau, who live in Seir; and they will be afraid of you. So watch yourselves carefully.

5 Do not provoke *or* stir them up, for I will not give you of their land, no, not enough for the sole of your foot to tread on, for I have given Mount Seir to Esau for a possession.

6 You shall buy food from them for money, that you may eat, and you shall also buy water from them for money, that you may drink.

speak the Word

life point

If we choose to serve God and live His way, we can avoid long wrestling matches with Him. Wisdom tells us to let God do with us what He wants, when He wants, so that we do not waste time going around in circles as the Israelites did (see Deuteronomy 2:3). I have met people who have been going around the same obstacles and issues for twenty or thirty years. If they had simply obeyed God in the beginning, they would have moved on with their lives long ago. They would now be enjoying the blessings of God, but instead they are still miserable and very frustrated.

No matter how much we may enjoy where we are, God will not let us stay there and become stagnant. He has new places to take us and new lessons to teach us. He wants to keep us fresh and full of life, full of growth, and full of His great purposes for our lives.

7   For the Lord your God has blessed you in all the work of your hand. He knows your walking through this great wilderness. These forty years the Lord your God has been with you; you have lacked nothing.
8   So we passed on from our brethren the sons of Esau, who dwelt in Seir, away from the Arabah (wilderness), and from Elath and from Ezion-geber. We turned and went by the way of the wilderness of Moab.
9   And the Lord said to me, Do not trouble or assault Moab or contend with them in battle, for I will not give you any of their land for a possession, because I have given Ar to the sons of Lot for a possession.
10   (The Emim dwelt there in times past, a people great and many, and tall as the Anakim.

11   These also are known as Rephaim [of giant stature], as are the Anakim, but the Moabites call them Emim.
12   The Horites also formerly lived in Seir, but the sons of Esau dispossessed them and destroyed them from before them and dwelt in their stead, as Israel did to the land of their possession which the Lord gave to them.)
13   Now rise up and go over the brook Zered. So we went over the brook Zered.
14   And the time from our leaving Kadesh-barnea until we had come over the brook Zered was thirty-eight years, until the whole generation of the men of war had perished from the camp, as the Lord had sworn to them.
15   Moreover the hand of the Lord was against them to exterminate them from the midst of the camp, until they were all gone.
16   So when all the men of war had died from among the people,
17   The Lord spoke to me [Moses], saying,
18   You are this day to pass through Ar, the border of Moab.
19   But when you come near the territory of the sons of Ammon, do not trouble or assault them or provoke or stir them up, for I will not give you any of the land of the Ammonites for a possession, because I have given it to the sons of Lot for a possession.
20   (That also is known as a land of Rephaim [of giant stature]; Rephaim dwelt there formerly, but the Ammonites call them Zamzummim,
21   A people great and many, and tall as the Anakim. But the Lord destroyed them before [Ammon], and they dispossessed them and settled in their stead,
22   As He did for the sons of Esau, who dwell in Seir, when He destroyed the Horites from before them, and they dispossessed them and settled in their stead even to this day.

23 As for the Avvim who dwelt in villages as far as Gaza, the Caphtorim who came from Caphtor destroyed them and dwelt in their stead.)

24 Rise up, take your journey, and pass over the Valley of the Arnon. Behold, I have given into your hand Sihon the Amorite, king of Heshbon, and his land; begin to possess it and contend with him in battle.

25 This day will I begin to put the dread and fear of you upon the peoples who are under the whole heavens, who shall hear the report of you and shall tremble and be in anguish because of you.

26 So I sent messengers from the wilderness of Kedemoth to Sihon king of Heshbon with words of peace, saying,

27 Let me pass through your land. I will go only by the road, turning aside neither to the right nor to the left.

28 You shall sell me food to eat and sell me water to drink; only let me walk through,

29 As the sons of Esau, who dwell in Seir, and the Moabites, who dwell in Ar, [a]did for me, until I go over the Jordan into the land which the Lord our God gives us.

30 But Sihon king of Heshbon would not let us pass by him; for the Lord your God hardened his spirit and made his heart obstinate, that He might give him into your hand, as at this day.

31 And the Lord said to me [Moses], Behold, I have begun to give Sihon and his land over to you. Begin to take possession, that you may succeed him *and* occupy his land.

32 Then Sihon came out against us, he and all his people, to fight at Jahaz.

33 And the Lord our God gave him over to us, and we defeated him and his sons and all his people.

34 At the same time we took all his cities and utterly destroyed every city—men, women, and children. We left none to remain.

35 Only the cattle we took as booty for ourselves and the spoil of the cities which we had captured.

36 From Aroer, which is on the edge of the Arnon Valley, and from the city that is in the valley, as far as Gilead, there was no city too high *and* strong for us; the Lord our God delivered all to us.

37 Only you did not go near the land of the Ammonites, that is, to any bank of the river Jabbok and the cities of the hill country, and wherever the Lord our God had forbidden us.

3 THEN WE turned and went up the road to Bashan, and Og king of Bashan came out against us, he and all his people, to battle at Edrei.

2 And the Lord said to me, Do not fear him, for I have given him and all his people and his land into your hand; and you shall do to him as you did to Sihon king of the Amorites, who lived at Heshbon.

3 So the Lord our God also gave into our hands Og king of Bashan and all his people, and we smote him until not one was left to him.

4 And we took all his cities at that time; there was not a city which we did not take from them, sixty cities, the whole region of Argob, the kingdom of Og in Bashan.

5 All these cities were fortified with high *and* haughty walls, gates, and bars, besides a great many unwalled villages.

6 And we utterly destroyed them, as we did to Sihon king of Heshbon, utterly destroying every city—men, women, and children.

---

a All that is said here is that the Edomites and Moabites sold Israel bread and water. There is no denial, expressed or implied, of their hostility to Israel and their desire for her destruction. The passage is in entire harmony with Num. 20:17, 21, and Deut. 23:3, 4 (J.P. Lange, *A Commentary*).

7 But all the cattle and the spoil of the cities we took for booty for ourselves.

8 So we took the land at that time out of the hand of the two kings of the Amorites who were beyond the Jordan, from the Valley of the Arnon to Mount Hermon

9 (The Sidonians call Hermon, Sirion, and the Amorites call it Senir),

10 All the cities of the plain, and all Gilead, and all Bashan as far as Salecah and Edrei, cities of the kingdom of Og in Bashan.

11 For only Og king of Bashan remained of the remnant of the [gigantic] Rephaim. Behold, his bedstead was of iron; is it not in Rabbah of the Ammonites? Nine cubits was its length and four cubits its breadth, using the cubit of a man [the forearm to the end of the middle finger].

12 When we took possession of this land, I gave to the Reubenites and the Gadites the territory from Aroer, which is on the edge of the Valley of the Arnon, and half the hill country of Gilead and its cities.

13 The rest of Gilead and all of Bashan, the kingdom of Og, that is, all the region of Argob in Bashan, I gave to the half-tribe of Manasseh. It is called the land of Rephaim [of giant stature].

14 Jair son of Manasseh took all the region of Argob, that is, Bashan, as far as the border of the Geshurites and the Maacathites, and called it after his own name, Havvoth-jair, so called to this day.

15 And I gave Gilead to Machir [son of Manasseh].

16 And to the Reubenites and Gadites I gave from Gilead even to the Valley of the Arnon, with the middle of the valley as the boundary of it, as far over as the river Jabbok, the boundary of the Ammonites,

17 The Arabah also, with the Jordan as its boundary, from Chinnereth as far as the Sea of the Arabah, the Salt [Dead] Sea, under the cliffs [of the headlands] of Pisgah on the east.

18 And I commanded you at that time, saying, The Lord your God has given you this land to possess it; you [Reuben, Gad, and the half-tribe of Manasseh] shall go over [the Jordan] armed before your brethren the other Israelites, all that are able for war.

19 But your wives and your little ones and your cattle—I know that you have many cattle—shall remain in your cities which I have given you,

20 Until the Lord has given rest to your brethren as to you, and until they also possess the land which the Lord your God has given them beyond the Jordan. Then shall you return every man to the possession which I have given you.

21 And I commanded Joshua at that time, saying, Your *own* eyes have seen all that the Lord your God has done to these two kings [Sihon and Og]; so shall the Lord do to all the kingdoms into which you are going over [the Jordan].

22 You shall not fear them, for the Lord your God shall fight for you.

23 And I besought the Lord at that time, saying,

24 O Lord God, You have only begun to show Your servant Your greatness and Your mighty hand; for what god is there in heaven or on earth that can do according to Your works and according to Your might?

25 I pray You, [will You not just] let me go over and see the good land that

speak the Word

Thank You, God, that You fight for me. Because You do, I will not fear.
ADAPTED FROM DEUTERONOMY **3:22**

is beyond the Jordan, that goodly mountain country [with Hermon] and Lebanon?

26 But the Lord was angry with me on your account and would not listen to me; and the Lord said to me, That is enough! Say no more to Me about it.

27 Get up to the top of Pisgah and lift up your eyes westward and northward and southward and eastward, and behold it with your eyes, for you shall not go over this Jordan.

28 But charge Joshua, and encourage and strengthen him, for he shall go over before this people and he shall cause them to possess the land which you shall see.

29 So we remained in the valley opposite Beth-peor.

4 NOW LISTEN *and* give heed, O Israel, to the statutes and ordinances which I teach you, and do them, that you may live and go in and possess the land which the Lord, the God of your fathers, gives you.

2 You shall not add to the word which I command you, neither shall you diminish it, that you may keep the commandments of the Lord your God which I command you.

3 Your eyes still see what the Lord did because of Baal-peor; for all the men who followed the Baal of Peor the Lord your God has destroyed from among you, [Num. 25:1-9.]

4 But you who clung fast to the Lord your God are alive, every one of you, this day.

5 Behold, I have taught you statutes and ordinances as the Lord my God commanded me, that you should do them in the land which you are entering to possess.

6 So keep them and do them, for that is your wisdom and your understanding in the sight of the peoples who, when they hear all these statutes, will say, Surely this great nation is a wise and understanding people.

7 For what great nation is there who has a god so near to them as the Lord our God is to us in all things for which we call upon Him?

8 And what large *and* important nation has statutes and ordinances so upright *and* just as all this law which I set before you today?

9 Only take heed, and guard your life diligently, lest you forget the things which your eyes have seen and lest they depart from your [mind and] heart all the days of your life. Teach them to your children and your children's children—

10 Especially how on the day that you stood before the Lord your God in Horeb, the Lord said to me, Gather the people together to Me and I will make them hear My words, that they may learn [reverently] to fear Me all the days they live upon the earth and that they may teach their children.

11 And you came near and stood at the foot of the mountain, and the mountain burned with fire to the heart of heaven, with darkness, cloud, and thick gloom.

12 And the Lord spoke to you out of the midst of the fire. You heard the voice of the words, but saw no form; there was only a voice.

13 And He declared to you His covenant, which He commanded you to perform, the Ten Commandments, and He wrote them on two tables of stone.

14 And the Lord commanded me at that time to teach you the statutes and precepts, that you might do them in the land which you are going over to possess.

15 Therefore take good heed to yourselves, since you saw no form of Him on the day the Lord spoke to you on Horeb out of the midst of the fire,

16 Beware lest you become corrupt by making for yourselves [to worship] a graven image in the form of any figure, the likeness of male or female,

17 The likeness of any beast that is on the earth, or of any winged fowl that flies in the air,

18 The likeness of anything that creeps on the ground, or of any fish that is in the waters beneath the earth.

19 And beware lest you lift up your eyes to the heavens, and when you see the sun, moon, and stars, even all the host of the heavens, you be drawn away and worship them and serve them, things which the Lord your God has allotted to all nations under the whole heaven.

20 But the Lord has taken you and brought you forth out of the iron furnace, out of Egypt, to be to Him a people of His own possession, as you are this day.

21 Furthermore the Lord was angry with me because of you, and He swore that I should not go over the Jordan and that I should not enter the good land which the Lord your God gives you for an inheritance.

22 But I must die in this land; I must not cross the Jordan; but you shall go over and possess that good land.

23 Take heed to yourselves, lest you forget the covenant of the Lord your God which He made with you, and make for yourselves a graven image in the form of anything which the Lord your God has forbidden you.

24 For the Lord your God is a consuming fire, a jealous God.

25 When children shall be born to you, and children's children, and you have grown old in the land, if you corrupt yourselves by making a graven image in the form of anything, and do evil in the sight of the Lord your God, provoking Him to anger,

26 I call heaven and earth to witness against you this day that you shall soon utterly perish from the land which you are going over the Jordan to possess. You will not live long upon it but will be utterly destroyed.

27 And the Lord will scatter you among the peoples, and you will be left few in number among the nations to which the Lord will drive you.

28 There you will serve gods, the work of men's hands, wood and stone, which neither see nor hear nor eat nor smell.

29 But if from there you will seek (inquire for and require as necessity) the Lord your God, you will find Him if you [truly] seek Him with all your heart [and mind] and soul and life.

30 When you are in tribulation and all these things come upon you, in the latter days you will turn to the Lord your God and be obedient to His voice.

31 For the Lord your God is a merciful God; He will not fail you or destroy you or forget the covenant of your fathers, which He swore to them.

32 For ask now of the days that are past, which were before you, since the day that God created man upon the earth, and ask from one end of the

speak the Word

God, You are a requirement, a necessity, in my life. Help me to seek You with all of my heart, mind, soul, and life.
ADAPTED FROM DEUTERONOMY 4:29

Thank You, God, that You are a merciful God. I declare that You will never fail me or forget the covenant You have with me.
ADAPTED FROM DEUTERONOMY 4:31

heavens to the other, whether such a great thing as this has ever occurred or been heard of anywhere.

33 Did ever people hear the voice of God speaking out of the midst of the fire, as you heard, and live?

34 Or has God ever tried to go and take for Himself a nation from the midst of another nation, by trials, by signs, by wonders, by war, by a mighty hand, by an outstretched arm, and by great terrors, as the Lord your God did for you in Egypt before your eyes?

35 To you it was shown, that you might realize *and* have personal knowledge that the Lord is God; there is no other besides Him.

36 Out of heaven He made you hear His voice, that He might correct, discipline, *and* admonish you; and on earth He made you see His great fire, and you heard His words out of the midst of the fire.

37 And because He loved your fathers, He chose their descendants after them, and brought you out from Egypt with His own Presence, by His mighty power,

38 Driving out nations from before you, greater and mightier than yourselves, to bring you in, to give you their land for an inheritance, as it is this day;

39 Know, recognize, *and* understand therefore this day and turn your [mind and] heart to it that the Lord is God in the heavens above and upon the earth beneath; there is no other.

40 Therefore you shall keep His statutes and His commandments, which I command you this day, that it may go well with you and your children after you and that you may prolong your days in the land which the Lord your God gives you forever.

41 Then Moses set apart three cities [of refuge] beyond the Jordan to the east,

42 That the manslayer might flee there, who slew his neighbor uninten-

tionally and had not previously been at enmity with him, that fleeing to one of these cities he might save his life:

43 Bezer in the wilderness on the tableland, for the Reubenites; and Ramoth in Gilead, for the Gadites; and Golan in Bashan, for the Manassites.

44 This is the law which Moses set before the Israelites.

45 These are the testimonies and the laws and the precepts which Moses spoke to the Israelites when they came out of Egypt,

46 Beyond the Jordan in the valley opposite Beth-peor, in the land of Sihon king of the Amorites, who dwelt at Heshbon, whom Moses and the Israelites smote when they came out of Egypt.

47 And they took possession of his land and the land of Og king of Bashan, the two kings of the Amorites, who lived beyond the Jordan to the east,

48 From Aroer, which is on the edge of the Valley of the Arnon, as far as Mount Sirion (that is, Hermon),

49 And all the Arabah (lowlands) beyond the Jordan eastward, as far as the Sea of the Arabah [the Dead Sea], under the slopes *and* springs of Pisgah.

5 AND MOSES called all Israel, and said to them, Hear, O Israel, the statutes and ordinances which I speak in your hearing this day, that you may learn them and take heed and do them.

2 The Lord our God made a covenant with us in Horeb.

3 The Lord made this covenant not with our fathers, but with us, who are all of us here alive this day.

4 The Lord spoke with you face to face at the mount out of the midst of the fire.

5 I stood between the Lord and you at that time to show you the word of the Lord, for you were afraid because of the fire and went not up into the mount. He said,

6 I am the Lord your God, Who brought you out of the land of Egypt, from the house of bondage.

7 You shall have no other gods before Me *or* besides Me.

8 You shall not make for yourself [to worship] a graven image or any likeness of anything that is in the heavens above or that is in the earth beneath or that is in the water under the earth.

9 You shall not bow down to them or serve them; for I, the Lord your God, am a jealous God, visiting the iniquity of the fathers upon the children to the third and fourth generations of those who hate Me,

10 And showing mercy *and* steadfast love to thousands *and* to a thousand generations of those who love Me and keep My commandments.

11 You shall not take the name of the Lord your God in vain, for the Lord will not hold him guiltless who takes His name in falsehood *or* without purpose.

12 Observe the Sabbath day to keep it holy, as the Lord your God commanded you.

13 Six days you shall labor and do all your work,

14 But the seventh day is a Sabbath to the Lord your God; in it you shall not do any work, you or your son or your daughter, or your manservant or your maidservant, or your ox or your donkey or any of your livestock, or the stranger *or* sojourner who is within your gates, that your manservant and your maidservant may rest as well as you.

15 And [earnestly] remember that you were a servant in the land of Egypt and that the Lord your God brought you out from there with a mighty hand and an outstretched arm; therefore the Lord your God commanded you to observe *and* take heed to the Sabbath day.

16 Honor your father and your mother, as the Lord your God commanded you, that your days may be prolonged and that it may go well with you in the land which the Lord your God gives you.

putting the Word to work

Deuteronomy 5:16 tells us that things will go well with us if we honor our parents. How can you better honor your mother and your father?

17 You shall not murder.

18 Neither shall you commit adultery.

19 Neither shall you act slyly *or* steal.

20 Neither shall you witness falsely against your neighbor.

21 Neither shall you covet your neighbor's wife, nor desire your neighbor's house, his field, his manservant or his maidservant, his ox or his donkey, or anything that is your neighbor's.

22 These words the Lord spoke to all your assembly at the mountain out of the midst of the fire, the cloud, and the thick darkness, with a loud voice; and He spoke not again [added no more]. He wrote them on two tables of stone and gave them to me [Moses].

23 And when you heard the voice out of the midst of the darkness, while the mountain was burning with fire, you came near me, all the heads of your tribes and your elders;

24 And you said, Behold, the Lord our God has shown us His glory and His greatness, and we have heard His voice out of the midst of the fire; we have this day seen that God speaks with man and man still lives.

25 Now therefore, why should we die? For this great fire will consume us; if we hear the voice of the Lord our God any longer, we shall die.

26 For who is there of all flesh who has heard the voice of the living God

speaking out of the midst of fire, as we have, and lived?

27 Go near [Moses] and hear all that the Lord our God will say. And speak to us all that the Lord our God will speak to you; and we will hear and do it.

28 And the Lord heard your words when you spoke to me and the Lord said to me, I have heard the words of this people which they have spoken to you. They have said well all that they have spoken.

29 Oh, that they had such a [mind and] heart in them always [reverently] to fear Me and keep all My commandments, that it might go well with them and with their children forever!

30 Go and say to them, Return to your tents.

31 But you [Moses], stand here by Me, and I will tell you all the commandments and the statutes and the precepts which you shall teach them, that they may do them in the land which I give them to possess.

32 Therefore you people shall be watchful to do as the Lord your God has commanded you; you shall not turn aside to the right hand or to the left.

33 You shall walk in all the ways which the Lord your God has commanded you, that you may live and that it may go well with you and that you may live long in the land which you shall possess.

6 NOW THIS is the instruction, the laws, and the precepts which the Lord your God commanded me to teach you, that you might do them in the land to which you go to possess it,

2 That you may [reverently] fear the Lord your God, you and your son and your son's son, and keep all His statutes and His commandments which I command you all the days of your life, and that your days may be prolonged.

3 Hear therefore, O Israel, and be watchful to do them, that it may be well with you and that you may increase exceedingly, as the Lord, the God of your fathers, has promised you, in a land flowing with milk and honey.

4 Hear, O Israel: the Lord our God is one Lord [the only Lord].

5 And you shall love the Lord your God with all your [mind and] heart and with your entire being and with all your might.

6 And these words which I am commanding you this day shall be [first] in your [own] minds *and* hearts; [then]

7 You shall whet *and* sharpen them so as to make them penetrate, *and* teach *and* impress them diligently upon the [minds and] hearts of your children, and shall talk of them when you sit in your house and when you walk by the way, and when you lie down and when you rise up.

speak the Word

Help me, God, to be watchful to do as You have commanded me to do. I declare that I will not turn aside to the right hand or to the left and that I will walk in all Your ways, that it may go well with me.
ADAPTED FROM DEUTERONOMY 5:32, 33

Thank You, God, that as I am watchful to do Your commandments, things will go well for me and I will increase exceedingly.
ADAPTED FROM DEUTERONOMY 6:3

8 And you shall bind them as a sign upon your hand, and they shall be as frontlets (forehead bands) between your eyes.

9 And you shall write them upon the doorposts of your house and on your gates.

10 And when the Lord your God brings you into the land which He swore to your fathers, to Abraham, Isaac, and Jacob, to give you, with great and goodly cities which you did not build,

11 And houses full of all good things which you did not fill, and cisterns hewn out which you did not hew, and vineyards and olive trees which you did not plant, and when you eat and are full,

12 Then beware lest you forget the Lord, Who brought you out of the land of Egypt, out of the house of bondage.

13 You shall [reverently] fear the Lord your God and serve Him and swear by His name [and presence].

14 You shall not go after other gods, any of the gods of the peoples who are round about you;

15 For the Lord your God in the midst of you is a jealous God; lest the anger of the Lord your God be kindled against you, and He destroy you from the face of the earth.

16 You shall not tempt *and* try the Lord your God as you tempted *and* tried Him in Massah. [Exod. 17:7.]

17 You shall diligently keep the commandments of the Lord your God and His exhortations and His statutes which He commanded you.

18 And you shall do what is right and good in the sight of the Lord, that it may go well with you and that you may go in and possess the good land which the Lord swore to give to your fathers,

19 To cast out all your enemies from before you, as the Lord has promised.

20 When your son asks you in time to come, What is the meaning of the testimonies and statutes and precepts which the Lord our God has commanded you?

21 Then you shall say to your son, We were Pharaoh's bondmen in Egypt, and the Lord brought us out of Egypt with a mighty hand.

22 And the Lord showed signs and wonders, great and evil, against Egypt, against Pharaoh, and all his household, before our eyes;

23 And He brought us out from there, that He might bring us in to give us the land which He swore to give our fathers.

putting the Word to work

We know from Deuteronomy 6:23 that God "brings us out to take us in." What has God brought you out of in order to take you into something better? Thank Him today!

24 And the Lord commanded us to do all these statutes, to [reverently] fear the Lord our God for our good always, that He might preserve us alive, as it is this day.

25 And it will be accounted as righteousness (conformity to God's will in word, thought, and action) for us if we are watchful to do all this commandment before the Lord our God, as He has commanded us.

7 WHEN THE Lord your God brings you into the land which you are entering to possess and has plucked away many nations before you, the Hittites, the Girgashites, the Amorites, the Canaanites, the Perizzites, the Hivites, and the Jebusites, seven nations greater and mightier than you,

2 And when the Lord your God gives them over to you and you smite them, then you must utterly destroy them. You shall make no covenant with them, or show mercy to them.

3 You shall not make marriages with them; your daughter you shall not give to his son nor shall you take his daughter for your son,

4 For they will turn away your sons from following Me, that they may serve other gods; so will the anger of the Lord be kindled against you and He will destroy you quickly.

5 But thus shall you deal with them: you shall break down their altars and dash in pieces their pillars and hew down their Asherim [symbols of the goddess Asherah] and burn their graven images with fire.

6 For you are a holy *and* set-apart people to the Lord your God; the Lord your God has chosen you to be a special people to Himself out of all the peoples on the face of the earth.

7 The Lord did not set His love upon you and choose you because you were more in number than any other people, for you were the fewest of all people.

8 But because the Lord loves you and because He would keep the oath which He had sworn to your fathers, the Lord has brought you out with a mighty hand and redeemed you out of the house of bondage, from the hand of Pharaoh king of Egypt.

9 Know, recognize, *and* understand therefore that the Lord your God, He is God, the faithful God, Who keeps covenant and steadfast love *and* mercy with those who love Him and

keep His commandments, to a thousand generations,

10 And repays those who hate Him to their face, by destroying them; He will not be slack to him who hates Him, but will requite him to his face.

11 You shall therefore keep and do the instruction, laws, and precepts which I command you this day.

12 And if you hearken to these precepts and keep and do them, the Lord your God will keep with you the covenant and the steadfast love which He swore to your fathers.

13 And He will love you, bless you, and multiply you; He will also bless the fruit of your body and the fruit of your land, your grain, your new wine, and your oil, the increase of your cattle and the young of your flock in the land which He swore to your fathers to give you.

14 You shall be blessed above all peoples; there shall not be male or female barren among you, or among your cattle.

15 And the Lord will take away from you all sickness, and none of the evil diseases of Egypt which you knew will He put upon you, but will lay them upon all who hate you.

16 And you shall consume all the peoples whom the Lord your God will give over to you; your eye shall not pity them, neither shall you serve their gods, for that would be a snare to you.

17 If you say in your [minds and]

speak the Word

Thank You, God, that You have chosen me to be holy, set apart, and special to You.
ADAPTED FROM DEUTERONOMY 7:6

God, I know and recognize and understand that You are the faithful God Who keeps covenant and steadfast love and mercy with those who fear You and keep Your commandments.
ADAPTED FROM DEUTERONOMY 7:9

hearts, These nations are greater than we are; how can we dispossess them?

18 You shall not be afraid of them, but remember [earnestly] what the Lord your God did to Pharaoh and to all Egypt,

19 The great trials which your eyes saw, the signs, the wonders, the mighty hand and the outstretched arm by which the Lord your God brought you out. So shall the Lord your God do to all the people of whom you are afraid.

20 Moreover, the Lord your God will send the ᵇhornet among them until those who are left and hide themselves from you are destroyed.

21 You shall not dread them, for the Lord your God is among you, a mighty and terrible God.

22 And the Lord your God will clear out those nations before you, little by little; you may not consume them quickly, lest the beasts of the field increase among you.

23 But the Lord your God will give them over to you and will confuse them with a mighty panic until they are destroyed.

24 And He will give their kings into your hand, and you shall make their name perish from under the heavens; there shall no man be able to stand before you, until you have destroyed them.

25 The graven images of their gods you shall burn with fire. You shall not desire the silver or gold that is on them, nor take it for yourselves, lest you be ensnared by it, for it is an abomination to the Lord your God.

26 Neither shall you bring an abomination (an idol) into your house, lest you become an accursed thing like it; but you shall utterly detest and abhor it, for it is an accursed thing.

life point

Just before they entered the Promised Land, the Lord told the Israelites that He would drive out their enemies before them "little by little" (Deuteronomy 7:22), lest the beasts of the field increase among them. I believe pride is one of the "beasts" that will consume us if we receive too much freedom too quickly, and the best way to gain lasting freedom and wholeness is to be liberated one area at a time. That way, we appreciate our freedom more; we realize it is truly a gift from God and not something we can make happen in our own strength. If it seems that freedom is slow in coming to any area of your life, remember that true progress often happens little by little.

8 ALL THE commandments which I command you this day you shall be watchful to do, that you may live and multiply and go in and possess the land which the Lord swore to give to your fathers.

2 And you shall [earnestly] remember all the way which the Lord your God led you these forty years in the wilderness, to humble you and to prove you, to know what was in your [mind and] heart, whether you would keep His commandments or not.

3 And He humbled you and allowed you to hunger and fed you with manna, which you did not know nor did your fathers know, that He might make you recognize *and* personally know that man does not live by bread only, but man lives by every word that proceeds out of the mouth of the Lord.

---

b "... the hornet" with the article, used in a collective sense as a species or kind, is thus evidently to be understood, as in Deut. 2:25, as the terrors of God which should go before Israel, with which also Josh. 24:12 and Ps. 44:2 fully agree (J.P. Lange, *A Commentary*).

life point

I once went through a difficult and upsetting set of circumstances in my ministry. One week I would have a meeting with a large crowd; the next week only half as many would attend. Satan would say to me, "Well, the people didn't like what you said last week, so they didn't come back." When circumstances conveyed to me I was doing well, my emotions were up. When circumstances indicated I was not doing very well, my emotions were down. The devil had me on the run. Every good experience elated me; every bad circumstance deflated me. (I call this "yo-yo" Christianity).

One day I said to God, "Why is this happening?" He impressed upon my heart, "I am teaching you that man does not live by bread alone, but by every word that proceeds out of the mouth of God" (see Deuteronomy 8:3). Bread was the daily sustenance for the children of Israel. Bread kept them going. When the Lord spoke to me about bread, He was saying, "I am trying to teach you that you cannot live by all these other things that seem to keep you going. You must look to Me for your daily strength." The same is true for you. Seek God, not what He can do for you!

4   Your clothing did not become old upon you nor did your feet swell these forty years.
5   Know also in your [minds and] hearts that, as a man disciplines *and* instructs his son, so the Lord your God disciplines *and* instructs you.
6   So you shall keep the commandments of the Lord your God, to walk in His ways and [reverently] fear Him. [Prov. 8:13.]

life point

Often, our first impulse when someone disciplines us is to find fault with him or her. Satan tempts us to do this so we will divert the conversation away from the real issue. God disciplines us too, according to Deuteronomy 8:5. Being corrected by God through people in authority, such as the government, employers, parents, or teachers, is something we all encounter throughout our lives. We may not always like the person or source God chooses to bring correction to us, but we are wise to accept good discipline and instruction in order to make progress in our lives.

7   For the Lord your God is bringing you into a good land, a land of brooks of water, of fountains and springs, flowing forth in valleys and hills;
8   A land of wheat and barley, and vines and fig trees and pomegranates, a land of olive trees and honey;
9   A land in which you shall eat food without shortage and lack nothing in it; a land whose stones are iron and out of whose hills you can dig copper.
10   When you have eaten and are full, then you shall bless the Lord your God for all the good land which He has given you.
11   Beware that you do not forget the Lord your God by not keeping His commandments, His precepts, and His statutes which I command you today,
12   Lest when you have eaten and are full, and have built goodly houses and live in them,
13   And when your herds and flocks multiply and your silver and gold is multiplied and all you have is multiplied,
14   Then your [minds and] hearts be lifted up and you forget the Lord your God, Who brought you out of the land

seek God's presence, not His presents

The Israelites wandered around and around the wilderness, going through the same struggles time and time again. God said He allowed this to teach them the truth of Deuteronomy 8:3: that man does not live by bread alone (worldly things) but by every word that proceeds out of the mouth of God (His promises). God met their basic necessities in the wilderness, but they were a long way from having their desires fulfilled. God wanted them to have abundant life, but first they needed to learn to obey Him and trust Him at all times.

Sooner or later God has to teach us that our true life is in Him, not in anything the world has to offer. It would be great if He could simply tell us that truth and we could believe it, turn our backs on the world, and totally trust Him. It does not happen that way, though. God deals with us and allows us to go through tests and trials so we can learn by experience that doing things His way is the best way. God knows that if we will not serve and worship Him in the hard times of life (the valleys), we will not consistently serve and worship Him in the good times (the mountaintops). He wants to bless us with the desires of our hearts, but He demands first place in our lives at all times.

There is a fine line between serving God because of what He can do for us and serving Him because of Who He is. We can easily be deceived into seeking His hand (His presents) and not seeking His face (His presence) in our lives. We need to seek first the kingdom of God and His righteousness, and then all the other things will be added unto us (see Matthew 6:33).

Are you in a valley? Worship God! Are you on top of the mountain? Worship God! Are all of your needs met? Worship God! Are you in want? Worship God! When all things become the same to you in the light of His glory, He is free to give you all things. Seek His presence, not His presents. Keep God first in your life, and you will be amazed at what He will do for you.

---

of Egypt, out of the house of bondage,

15 Who led you through the great and terrible wilderness, with its fiery serpents and scorpions and thirsty ground where there was no water, but Who brought you forth water out of the flinty rock,

16 Who fed you in the wilderness with manna, which your fathers did not know, that He might humble you and test you, to do you good in the end.

17 And beware lest you say in your [mind and] heart, My power and the might of my hand have gotten me this wealth.

18 But you shall [earnestly] remember the Lord your God, for it is He Who gives you power to get wealth, that He may establish His covenant which He swore to your fathers, as it is this day.

19 And if you forget the Lord your God and walk after other gods and serve them and worship them, I testify against you this day that you shall surely perish.

20 Like the nations which the Lord makes to perish before you, so shall

life point

Many people believe and act upon the biblical principles of tithing and giving offerings, yet they never seem to be able to leave what I call the "land of even." Though their basic needs are met, they are living from paycheck to paycheck. They never get ahead; they just break even. They live "little lives" and miss the joy-filled, fruitful, peaceful, and abundant life that God has for them.

God's Word clearly teaches that He desires for us to live in the "land of plenty" (see Deuteronomy 8:7–9). God brought the Israelites out of the land of *lack*, through the land of *even*, and into the land of *plenty*. He wanted every one of the Israelites to live in abundance, but, sadly, only two of the original Israelites who came out of Egypt actually crossed over the Jordan and lived in the land of promise, the land of plenty.

Precisely the same situation appears in every generation. Only a few people enter into the best God has provided for them through Jesus Christ, while the majority barely get by and have no joy or peace. They struggle and struggle, hearing about a better land but not understanding why they cannot take up residence there.

Be one who makes it all the way to the Promised Land. Remember that God has abundance for you, and determine to live the good life that God prearranged for you to live (see Ephesians 2:10).

you perish, because you would not obey the voice of the Lord your God.

9 HEAR, O Israel. You are to cross the Jordan today to go in to dispossess nations greater and

life point

Apart from God, we really are powerless. Our joy must be in Him, our peace must be in Him, our achievements come through Him, and our abilities are the results of His grace. Take the advice of Deuteronomy 8:17, and do not let your mind and heart try to convince you that your own efforts and the strength of your flesh profit anything. It's all God!

mightier than you are, cities great and fortified up to the heavens,

2   A people great and tall, the sons of the Anakim, whom you know and of whom you have heard it said, Who can stand before the sons of Anak?

3   Know therefore this day that the Lord your God is He Who goes over before you as a devouring fire. He will destroy them and bring them down before you; so you shall dispossess them and make them perish quickly, as the Lord has promised you.

4   Do not say in your [mind and] heart, after the Lord your God has thrust them out from before you, It is because of my righteousness that the Lord has brought me in to possess this land—whereas it is because of the wickedness of these nations that the Lord is dispossessing them before you.

5   Not for your righteousness or for the uprightness of your [minds and] hearts do you go to possess their land; but because of the wickedness of these nations the Lord your God is driving them out before you, and that He may fulfill the promise which the Lord swore to your fathers, Abraham, Isaac, and Jacob.

6   Know therefore that the Lord your God does not give you this good land to possess because of your righteousness, for you are a hard *and* stubborn people.

7 [Earnestly] remember and forget not how you provoked the Lord your God to wrath in the wilderness; from the day you left the land of Egypt until you came to this place, you have been rebellious against the Lord.

8 Even in Horeb you provoked the Lord to wrath, and the Lord was so angry with you that He would have destroyed you.

9 When I went up the mountain to receive the tables of stone, the tables of the covenant which the Lord made with you, I remained on the mountain forty days and forty nights; I neither ate food nor drank water.

10 And the Lord delivered to me the two tables of stone written with the finger of God; and on them were all the words which the Lord spoke with you on the mountain out of the midst of the fire in the day of the assembly.

11 And at the end of forty days and forty nights the Lord gave me the two tables of stone, the tables of the covenant.

12 And the Lord said to me, Arise, go down from here quickly, for your people whom you brought out of Egypt have corrupted themselves. They have quickly turned aside from the way which I commanded them; they have made for themselves a molten image.

13 Furthermore the Lord said to me, I have seen this people, and behold, they are stubborn *and* hard.

14 Let me alone, that I may destroy them and blot out their name from under the heavens; and I will make of you a nation mightier and greater than they.

15 So I turned and came down from the mountain, and the mountain was burning with fire. And the two tables of the covenant were in my two hands.

16 And I looked, and behold, you had sinned against the Lord your God; you had made for yourselves a molten calf. You had turned aside quickly from the way which the Lord had commanded you.

17 I took the two tables, cast them out of my two hands, and broke them before your eyes.

18 Then I fell down before the Lord as before, for forty days and forty nights; I neither ate food nor drank water, because of all the sin you had committed in doing wickedly in the sight of the Lord, to provoke Him to anger.

19 For I was afraid of the anger and hot displeasure which the Lord held against you, enough to destroy you. But the Lord listened to me that time also.

20 And the Lord was very angry with Aaron, angry enough to have destroyed him, and I prayed for Aaron also at the same time.

21 And I took your sin, the calf which you had made, and burned it with fire and crushed it, grinding it very small, until it was as fine as dust; and I cast the dust of it into the brook that came down out of the mountain.

22 At Taberah also and at Massah and at Kibroth-hattaavah you provoked the Lord to wrath.

23 Likewise when the Lord sent you from Kadesh-barnea, saying, Go up and possess the land which I have given you, then you rebelled against the commandment of the Lord your God, and you did not believe Him *or* trust *and* rely on Him or obey His voice.

24 You have been rebellious against the Lord from the day that I knew you.

25 So I fell down *and* lay prostrate before the Lord forty days and nights because the Lord had said He would destroy you.

26 And I prayed to the Lord, O Lord God, do not destroy Your people and Your heritage, whom You have redeemed through Your greatness, whom You have brought out of Egypt with a mighty hand.

27 Remember [earnestly] Your servants, Abraham, Isaac, and Jacob; look not at the stubbornness of this people or at their wickedness or at their sin,

28 Lest the land from which You brought us out say, Because the Lord was not able to bring them into the land which He promised them, and because He hated them, He has brought them out to slay them in the wilderness.

29 Yet they are Your people and Your inheritance, whom You brought out by Your mighty power and by Your outstretched arm.

10 AT THAT time the Lord said to me, Hew two tables of stone like the first and come up to Me on the mountain and make an ark of wood.

2 And I will write on the tables the words that were on the first tables which you broke, and you shall put them in the ark.

3 So I [Moses] made an ark of acacia wood and hewed two tables of stone like the first, and went up the mountain ᶜwith the two tables of stone in my [one] hand.

4 And the Lord wrote on the tables as at the first writing, the Ten Commandments which the Lord had spoken to you on the mountain out of the midst of the fire on the day of the assembly; and the Lord gave them to me.

5 And I turned and came down from the mountain and put the tables in the ark which I had made; and there they are, as the Lord commanded me.

6 (The Israelites journeyed from the wells of the sons of Jaakan to Moserah. There Aaron died, and there he was buried, and Eleazar his son ministered in the priest's office in his stead.

7 From there they journeyed to Gudgodah, and then to Jotbathah, a land of brooks [dividing the valley].

8 At that time the Lord set apart the tribe of Levi to bear the ark of the covenant of the Lord, to stand before the Lord to minister to Him and to bless in His name unto this day.

9 Therefore Levi has no part or inheritance with his brethren; the Lord is his inheritance, as the Lord your God promised him.)

10 And I [Moses] stayed on the mountain, as the first time, forty days and nights, and the Lord listened to me at that time also; the Lord would not destroy you.

11 And the Lord said to me, Arise, journey on before the people, that they may go in and possess the land which I swore to their fathers to give to them.

12 And now, Israel, what does the Lord your God require of you but [reverently] to fear the Lord your God, [that is] to walk in all His ways, and to love Him, and to serve the Lord your God with all your [mind and] heart and with your entire being,

13 To keep the commandments of the Lord and His statutes which I command you today for your good?

14 Behold, the heavens and the heaven of heavens belong to the Lord your God, the earth also, with all that is in it and on it.

15 Yet the Lord had a delight in

---

c One of the many misconceptions of articles and events mentioned in the Bible, innocently perpetuated by artists without adequate knowledge, is that of the size of the two tables of stone on which the Ten Commandments were written. They were not great tombstone-sized slabs, but probably small rectangular plates, two of which could easily be carried in one hand. Dr. George L. Robinson brought from the Sinai area a pair of "tables of stone" believed comparable to those mentioned here, which he put in his coat pocket. Moses says here, "I . . . went up the mountain with the two tables of stone in my [one] hand," and he confirms it in Exod. 34:4.

loving your fathers, and He chose their descendants after them, you above all peoples, as it is this day.

16 So circumcise the foreskin of your [minds and] hearts; be no longer stubborn *and* hardened.

putting the Word to work

Deuteronomy 10:16 instructs us not to be hard-hearted or stubborn. Is there any stubbornness or hardness in your heart or in your mind? Confess your sin in these areas and ask for God's help.

17 For the Lord your God is God of gods and Lord of lords, the great, the mighty, the terrible God, Who is not partial and takes no bribe.

18 He executes justice for the fatherless and the widow, and loves the stranger *or* temporary resident and gives him food and clothing.

19 Therefore love the stranger *and* sojourner, for you were strangers *and* sojourners in the land of Egypt.

20 You shall [reverently] fear the Lord your God; you shall serve Him and cling to Him, and by His name *and* presence you shall swear.

21 He is your praise; He is your God, Who has done for you these great and terrible things which your eyes have seen.

22 Your fathers went down to Egypt seventy persons in all, and now the Lord your God has made you as the stars of the heavens for multitude.

11 THEREFORE YOU shall love the Lord your God and keep His charge, His

statutes, His precepts, and His commandments always.

2 And know this day—for I am not speaking to your children who have not [personally] known and seen it—the instruction *and* discipline of the Lord your God: His greatness, His mighty hand, and His outstretched arm;

3 His signs and His deeds which He did in Egypt to Pharaoh the king of Egypt and to all his land;

4 And what He did to the army of Egypt, to their horses and chariots, how He made the waters of the Red Sea flow over them as they pursued you, and how the Lord has destroyed them to this day;

5 And what He did to you in the wilderness until you came to this place;

6 And what He did to Dathan and Abiram, sons of Eliab, the son of Reuben, how the earth opened its mouth and swallowed up them, their households, their tents, and every living thing that followed them, in the midst of all Israel. [Num. 26:9, 10.]

7 For your eyes have seen all the great work of the Lord which He did.

8 Therefore you shall keep all the commandments which I command you today, that you may be strong and go in and possess the land which you go across [the Jordan] to possess,

9 And that you may live long in the land which the Lord swore to your fathers to give to them and to their descendants, a land flowing with milk and honey.

10 For the land which you go in to possess is not like the land of Egypt, from which you came out, where you sowed your seed and watered it with

speak the Word

Help me, God, to reverently fear You, to walk in all Your ways, to love You, and to serve You with all my mind and heart and entire being.
ADAPTED FROM DEUTERONOMY 10:12

your foot laboriously as in a garden of vegetables.

11 But the land which you enter to possess is a land of hills and valleys which drinks water of the rain of the heavens,

12 A land for which the Lord your God cares; the eyes of the Lord your God are always upon it from the beginning of the year to the end of the year.

13 And if you will diligently heed My commandments which I command you this day—to love the Lord your God and to serve Him with all your [mind and] heart and with your entire being—

14 I will give the rain for your land in its season, the early rain and the latter rain, that you may gather in your grain, your new wine, and your oil.

15 And I will give grass in your fields for your cattle, that you may eat and be full.

16 Take heed to yourselves, lest your [minds and] hearts be deceived and you turn aside and serve other gods and worship them,

17 And the Lord's anger be kindled against you, and He shut up the heavens so that there will be no rain and the land will not yield its fruit, and you perish quickly off the good land which the Lord gives you.

18 Therefore you shall lay up these My words in your [minds and] hearts and in your [entire] being, and bind them for a sign upon your hands and as forehead bands between your eyes.

19 And you shall teach them to your children, speaking of them when you sit in your house and when you walk along the road, when you lie down and when you rise up.

20 And you shall write them upon the doorposts of your house and on your gates,

21 That your days and the days of your children may be multiplied in

life point

There are many things that can become "gods" to us and we are not to turn our hearts toward them (see Deuteronomy 11:16, 17). Even a ministry can become a god if we let it become more important than God Himself. We must never forget that it is the Lord Who places the vision for ministry in our hearts. It is He Who calls us and gives us the desire to minister. He must always have the first and most preeminent place in our lives. Putting the things with which He blesses us before Him is offensive to Him.

We are not going to experience the blessings God desires for us if our hearts are not right before Him. Sometimes we erroneously blame the devil for our lack of blessing; we think everything would be just fine if the devil would just leave us alone. That is not so. We have it backward. If we would live rightly, then the door into our lives would be closed to the devil. He might pester us, but he would have no real power over us, just as he had no real power over Jesus. Let nothing stand between you and God. Put Him first, and you will be blessed.

the land which the Lord swore to your fathers to give them, as long as the heavens are above the earth.

22 For if you diligently keep all this commandment which I command you to do, to love the Lord your God, to walk in all His ways, and to cleave to Him—

23 Then the Lord will drive out all these nations before you, and you shall dispossess nations greater and mightier than you.

24 Every place upon which the sole of your foot shall tread shall be yours: from the wilderness to Lebanon, and from the River, the river Euphrates, to

defeating deception

In Deuteronomy 11:18–21 God told the people to write His words on the doors of their houses, on their gates, on their foreheads, and on their hands. They were to let the Word permeate their entire being, whether they were sitting, lying down, or walking around. Why did God say to do all this? Because He is aware that knowing the Word keeps a person from having a deceived heart. This is what Jesus taught in John 8:31, 32 when He said: "If you abide in My word [hold fast to My teachings and live in accordance with them], you are truly My disciples. And you will know the Truth, and the Truth will set you free."

If we do not really care enough about the Word of God to abide in it, we are going to be in for trouble in these last days in which we live. Religious fluff is not going to be enough to get us through; we have to be deeply serious about learning the Word. When we know the Word, God will protect us and keep us. If we do not, we will be sucked up into deception. Simply stated, deception happens when we believe a lie, and Satan lies to us continually. Without a thorough knowledge of God's Word, we do not even recognize the lies.

Some people deceive themselves by reasoning that is contrary to God's truth. Earlier in my life, before I learned how to really surrender to the will of God, He sometimes impressed me to give something away I wanted to keep, or to do something I did not want to do. I learned from making mistakes that it was very easy to deceive myself when God asked for something I did not want to release.

We make all kinds of excuses to keep us from doing what God asks of us. Sometimes we pretend, "Well, it must not have been God dealing with me about that. It probably was just my imagination or the devil trying to make me miserable by asking for what's precious to me." We can quickly become "spiritually deaf" to the voice of God when He says something we really do not want to hear.

A deceived heart will not do for leaders or for anyone who intends to be victorious in life. We should be diligent to root out any areas of our lives where we are susceptible to deception. We need to live openly and honestly, abiding in the light of God's truth as He reveals it in His Word.

the western sea [the Mediterranean] your territory shall be.

25 There shall no man be able to stand before you; the Lord your God shall lay the fear and the dread of you upon all the land that you shall tread, as He has said to you.

26 Behold, I set before you this day a blessing and a curse—

27 The blessing if you obey the com-mandments of the Lord your God which I command you this day;

28 And the curse if you will not obey the commandments of the Lord your God, but turn aside from the way which I command you this day to go after other gods, which you have not known.

29 And when the Lord your God has brought you into the land which you

life point

God has given us the power of choice. We must choose one way or the other, and whatever pathway we choose will lead to a specific destination (see Deuteronomy 11:26–28). If we choose disobedience, we end up with curses and every kind of misery; but if we choose life, we are blessed. I often wonder why anyone would choose to be miserable when we could be blessed; yet multitudes do just that.

We have an enemy, Satan, who tells us we can do what is wrong and still have good lives, but we have to remember that God's Word tells us he is a liar. Satan told Eve the same lie in the Garden of Eden, and that is where our troubles began. I strongly encourage you to make right choices. Do not procrastinate or delay, because that is one of Satan's favorite ways to deceive us. We intend to do what is right, but say we are not ready just yet. We live as if tomorrow will never come, but it always does. I believe wisdom is choosing to do now what we will be satisfied with later. Remember, we always reap what we have sown. Make a decision to keep God's commands and open the door to the blessed life He wants to give you.

go to possess, you shall set the blessing on Mount Gerizim and the curse on Mount Ebal. [Josh. 8:33.]
30 Are they not beyond the Jordan, west of the road, where the sun goes down, in the land of the Canaanites

living in the Arabah opposite Gilgal, beside the oaks *or* terebinths of Moreh?
31 For you are to cross over the Jordan to go in to possess the land which the Lord your God gives you, and you shall possess it and live in it.
32 And you shall be watchful to do all the statutes and ordinances which I set before you this day.

12 THESE ARE the statutes and ordinances which you shall be watchful to do in the land which the Lord, the God of your fathers, gives you to possess all the days you live on the earth.
2 You shall surely destroy all the places where the nations you dispossess served their gods, upon the high mountains and the hills and under every green tree.
3 You shall break down their altars and dash in pieces their pillars and burn their Asherim with fire; you shall hew down the graven images of their gods and destroy their name out of that place.
4 You shall not behave so toward the Lord your God.
5 But you shall seek the place which the Lord your God shall choose out of all your tribes to put His ᵈName and make His dwelling place, and there shall you come;
6 And there you shall bring your burnt offerings and your sacrifices, your tithes and the offering of your hands, and your vows and your freewill offerings, and the firstlings of your herd and of your flock.
7 And there you shall eat before the Lord your God, and you shall rejoice in all to which you put your hand, you and your households, in which the Lord your God has blessed you.

d The "Name" of God is equivalent to His gracious presence in passages such as this one. The place where God puts His Name is the place where the Lord Himself chooses to dwell. When it stands for God's presence at the sanctuary, "Name" is capitalized.

8 You ^eshall not do according to all we do here [in the camp] this day, every man doing whatever looks right in his own eyes.
9 For you have not yet come to the rest and to the inheritance which the Lord your God gives you.
10 But when you go over the Jordan and dwell in the land which the Lord your God causes you to inherit, and He gives you rest from all your enemies round about so that you dwell in safety,
11 Then there shall be a place which the Lord your God shall choose to cause His Name [and His Presence] to dwell there; to it you shall bring all that I command you: your burnt offerings, your sacrifices, your tithes and what the hand presents [as a first gift from the fruits of the ground], and all your choicest offerings which you vow to the Lord.
12 And you shall rejoice before the Lord your God, you and your sons and your daughters, and your menservants and your maidservants, and the Levite that is within your towns, since he has no part or inheritance with you.
13 Be watchful not to offer your burnt offerings in every place you see.
14 But in the place which the Lord shall choose in one of your tribes, there you shall offer your burnt offerings, and there you shall do all I command you.
15 However, you may kill and eat flesh in any of your towns whenever you desire, according to the provision for the support of life with which the Lord your God has blessed you; those [ceremonially] unclean and the clean may eat of it, as of the gazelle and the hart.

16 Only you shall not eat the blood; you shall pour it upon the ground as water.
17 You may not eat within your towns the tithe of your grain or of your new wine or of your oil, or the firstlings of your herd or flock, or anything you have vowed, or your freewill offerings, or the offerings from your hand [of garden products].
18 But you shall eat them before the Lord your God in the place which the Lord your God shall choose, you and your son and your daughter, your manservant and your maidservant, and the Levite that is within your towns; and you shall rejoice before the Lord your God in all that you undertake.
19 Take heed not to forsake *or* neglect the Levite [God's minister] as long as you live in your land.
20 When the Lord your God enlarges your territory, as He promised you, and you say, I will eat flesh, because you crave flesh, you may eat flesh whenever you desire.
21 If the place where the Lord your God has chosen to put His Name [and Presence] is too far from you, then you shall kill from your herd or flock which the Lord has given you, as I [Moses] have commanded you; eat in your towns as much as you desire.
22 Just as the roebuck and the hart is eaten, so you may eat of it [but not offer it]; the unclean and the clean alike may eat of it.
23 Only be sure that you do not eat the blood, for the blood is the life, and you may not eat the life with the flesh.
24 You shall not eat it; you shall pour it out on the earth like water.
25 You shall not eat it, that all may go

e "It has been too often overlooked that the Law of Moses had a prophetic side. It was given to him and to Israel when they were not in a position to keep it [fully]. It was the law of the land which God would give them. In many ways its observance depended on the completion of the conquest of the land and upon the quietness of the times in which they lived. This prophetic aspect was certainly not unrecognized by the Jews, or they would not (for example) have neglected to dwell in booths at the Feast of Tabernacles from the time of Joshua to Nehemiah (Neh. 8:17)" (Charles J. Ellicott, *A Bible Commentary*).

296

well with you and with your children after you, when you do what is right in the sight of the Lord.

26 Only your holy things which you have [to offer] and what you have vowed you shall take, and go to the place [before the sanctuary] which the Lord shall choose.

27 And offer your burnt offerings, the flesh and the blood, upon the altar of the Lord your God; and the blood of your sacrifices shall be poured out on the altar of the Lord your God, and you may eat the flesh.

28 Be watchful and obey all these words which I command you, that it may go well with you and with your children after you forever, when you do what is good and right in the sight of the Lord your God.

29 When the Lord your God cuts off before you the nations whom you go to dispossess, and you dispossess them and live in their land,

30 Be watchful that you are not ensnared into following them after they have been destroyed before you and that you do not inquire after their gods, saying, How did these nations serve their gods? We will do likewise.

31 You shall not do so to the Lord your God, for every abominable thing which the Lord hates they have done for their gods. For even their sons and their daughters they have burned in the fire to their gods.

32 Whatever I command you, be watchful to do it; you shall not add to it or diminish it.

13 IF A prophet arises among you, or a dreamer of dreams, and gives you a sign or a wonder,

2 And the sign or the wonder he foretells to you comes to pass, and if he says, Let us go after other gods— gods you have not known—and let us serve them,

3 You shall not listen to the words of that prophet or to that dreamer of dreams. For the Lord your God is testing you to know whether you love the Lord your God with all your [mind and] heart and with your entire being.

4 You shall walk after the Lord your God and [reverently] fear Him, and keep His commandments and obey His voice, and you shall serve Him and cling to Him.

life point

Deuteronomy 13:4 commands us to obey God. Obedience keeps us from defiling our consciences and keeps us living for God's glory.

5 But that prophet or that dreamer of dreams shall be put to death, because he has talked rebellion *and* turning away from the Lord your God, Who brought you out of the land of Egypt and redeemed you out of the house of bondage; that man has tried to draw you aside from the way in which the Lord your God commanded you to walk. So shall you put the evil away from your midst.

6 If your brother, the son of your mother, or your son or daughter, or the wife of your bosom, or your friend who is as your own life entices you secretly, saying, Let us go and serve other gods—gods you have not known, you nor your fathers,

7 Of the gods of the peoples who are round about you, near you or far away from you, from one end of the earth to the other—

8 You shall not give consent to him or listen to him; nor shall your eye pity him, nor shall you spare him or conceal him.

9 But you shall surely kill him; your hand shall be first upon him to put him to death, and afterwards the hands of all the people.

10 And you shall stone him to death with stones, because he has tried to draw you away from the Lord your God, Who brought you out of the land of Egypt, from the house of bondage.

11 And all Israel shall hear and [reverently] fear, and shall never again do any such wickedness as this among you.

12 If you hear it said in one of your cities which the Lord your God has given you in which to dwell

13 That certain base fellows have gone out from your midst and have enticed away the inhabitants of their city, saying, Let us go and serve other gods—gods you have not known—

14 Then you shall inquire and make search and ask diligently. And behold, if it is true and certain that such an abominable thing has been done among you,

15 You shall surely smite the inhabitants of that city with the edge of the sword, destroying it utterly and all who are in it and its beasts with the edge of the sword.

16 And you shall collect all its spoil into the midst of its open square and shall burn the city with fire with every bit of its spoil [as a whole burnt offering] to the Lord your God. It shall be a heap [of ruins] forever; it shall not be built again.

17 And nothing of the accursed thing shall cling to your hand, so that the Lord may turn from the fierceness of His anger, and show you mercy and have compassion on you and multiply you, as He swore to your fathers,

18 If you obey the voice of the Lord your God, to keep all His commandments which I command you this day, to do what is right in the eyes of the Lord your God.

14 YOU ARE the sons of the Lord your God; you shall not cut yourselves or make any baldness on your foreheads for the dead,

2 For you are a holy people [set apart] to the Lord your God; and the Lord has chosen you to be a peculiar people to Himself, above all the nations on the earth.

3 You shall not eat anything that is abominable [to the Lord and so forbidden by Him].

4 These are the beasts which you may eat: the ox, the sheep, and the goat,

5 The hart, the gazelle, the roebuck, the wild goat, the ibex, the antelope, and the mountain sheep.

6 And every beast that parts the hoof and has it divided into two and brings up *and* chews the cud among the beasts you may eat.

7 Yet these you shall not eat of those that chew the cud or have the hoof split in two: the camel, the hare, and the coney, because they chew the cud but divide not the hoof; they are unclean for you.

8 And the swine, because it parts the hoof but does not chew the cud; it is unclean to you. You shall not eat of their flesh or touch their dead bodies.

9 These you may eat of all that are in the waters: whatever has fins and scales you may eat,

10 And whatever has not fins and scales you may not eat; it is unclean for you.

11 Of all clean birds you may eat.

12 But these are the ones which you shall not eat: the eagle, the vulture, the ospray,

13 The buzzard, the kite in its several species,

14 The raven in all its species,

15 The ostrich, the nighthawk, the sea gull, the hawk of any variety,

16 The little owl, the great owl, the horned owl,

17 The pelican, the carrion vulture, the cormorant,

18 The stork, the heron of any variety, the hoopoe, and the bat.

19 And all flying insects are unclean for you; they shall not be eaten.

20 But of all clean winged things you may eat.

21 You shall not eat of anything that dies of itself. You may give it to the stranger *or* the foreigner who is within your towns, that he may eat it, or you may sell it to an alien. [They are not under God's law in this matter] but you are a people holy to the Lord your God. You shall not [even] boil a kid in its mother's milk.

22 You shall surely tithe all the yield of your seed produced by your field each year.

23 And you shall eat before the Lord your God in the place in which He will cause His Name [and Presence] to dwell the tithe (tenth) of your grain, your new wine, your oil, and the firstlings of your herd and your flock, that you may learn [reverently] to fear the Lord your God always.

24 And if the distance is too long for you to carry your tithe, or the place where the Lord your God chooses to set His Name [and Presence] is too far away for you, when the Lord your God has blessed you,

25 Then you shall turn it into money, and bind up the money in your hand, and shall go to the place [of worship] which the Lord your God has chosen.

26 And you may spend that money for whatever your appetite craves, for oxen, or sheep, or new wine or strong[er] drink, or whatever you desire; and you shall eat there before the Lord your God and you shall rejoice, you and your household.

27 And you shall not forsake *or* neglect the Levite [God's minister] in your towns, for he has been given no share or inheritance with you.

28 At the end of every three years you shall bring forth all the tithe of your increase the same year and lay it up within your towns.

29 And the Levite [because he has no part or inheritance with you] and the stranger *or* temporary resident, and the fatherless and the widow who are in your towns shall come and eat and be satisfied, so that the Lord your God may bless you in all the work of your hands that you do.

15 AT THE end of every seven years you shall grant a release.

2 And this is the manner of the release: every creditor shall release that which he has lent to his neighbor; he shall not exact it of his neighbor, his brother, for the Lord's release is proclaimed.

3 Of a foreigner you may exact it, but whatever of yours is with your brother [Israelite] your hand shall release.

4 But there will be no poor among you, for the Lord will surely bless you in the land which the Lord your God gives you for an inheritance to possess,

5 If only you carefully listen to the voice of the Lord your God, to do watchfully all these commandments which I command you this day.

6 When the Lord your God blesses you as He promised you, then you shall lend to many nations, but you shall not borrow; and you shall rule over many nations, but they shall not rule over you.

7 If there is among you a poor man, one of your kinsmen in any of the towns of your land which the Lord your God gives you, you shall not harden your [minds and] hearts or close your hands to your poor brother;

8 But you shall open your hands wide to him and shall surely lend him sufficient for his need in whatever he lacks.

9 Beware lest there be a base thought in your [minds and] hearts, and you say, The seventh year, the year of release, is at hand, and your eye be evil against your poor brother and you give him nothing, and he cry to the Lord against you, and it be sin in you.

10 You shall give to him freely without begrudging it; because of this the Lord will bless you in all your work and in all you undertake.

11 For the poor will never cease out of the land; therefore I command you, You shall open wide your hands to your brother, to your needy, and to your poor in your land.

putting the Word to work

God commands us in Deuteronomy 15:11 to "open wide" our hands to those who are less fortunate than we are. In what ways can you be more generous or more attentive to the poor and needy people around you?

12 And if your brother, a Hebrew man or a Hebrew woman, is sold to you and serves you six years, then in the seventh year you shall let him go free from you.

13 And when you send him out free from you, you shall not let him go away empty-handed.

14 You shall furnish him liberally out of your flock, your threshing floor, and your winepress; of what the Lord your God has blessed you, you shall give to him.

15 And you shall [earnestly] remember that you were a bondman in the land of Egypt and the Lord your God redeemed you; therefore I give you this command today.

16 But if the servant says to you, I will not go away from you, because he loves you and your household, since he does well with you,

17 Then take an awl and pierce his ear through to the door, and he shall be your servant always. And also to your bondwoman you shall do likewise.

18 It shall not seem hard to you when you let him go free from you, for at half the cost of a hired servant he has served you six years; and the Lord your God will bless you in all you do.

19 All the firstling males that are born of your herd and flock you shall set apart for the Lord your God; you shall do no work with the firstling of your herd, nor shear the firstling of your flock.

20 You shall eat it before the Lord your God annually in the place [for worship] which the Lord shall choose, you and your household.

21 But if it has any blemish, if it is lame, blind, or has any bad blemish whatsoever, you shall not sacrifice it to the Lord your God.

22 You shall eat it within your towns; the [ceremonially] unclean and the clean alike may eat it, as if it were a gazelle or a hart.

23 Only you shall not eat its blood; you shall pour it on the ground like water.

16 OBSERVE THE month of Abib and keep the Passover to the Lord your God, for in the month of Abib the Lord your God brought you out of Egypt by night.

2 You shall offer the Passover sacrifice to the Lord your God from the flock or the herd in the place where the Lord will choose to make His Name [and His Presence] dwell.

speak the Word

God, help me to always open my hands wide to the poor and give to those in need.
ADAPTED FROM DEUTERONOMY 15:8

3 You shall eat no leavened bread with it; for seven days you shall eat it with unleavened bread, the bread of affliction—for you fled from the land of Egypt in haste—that all the days of your life you may [earnestly] remember the day when you came out of Egypt.
4 No leaven shall be seen with you in all your territory for seven days; nor shall any of the flesh which you sacrificed the first day at evening be left all night until the morning.
5 You may not offer the Passover sacrifice within any of your towns which the Lord your God gives you,
6 But at the place which the Lord your God will choose in which to make His Name [and His Presence] dwell, there you shall offer the Passover sacrifice in the evening at sunset, at the season that you came out of Egypt.
7 And you shall roast or boil and eat it in the place which the Lord your God will choose. And in the morning you shall turn and go to your tents.
8 For six days you shall eat unleavened bread, and on the seventh day there shall be a solemn assembly to the Lord your God; you shall do no work on it.
9 You shall count seven weeks; begin to number the seven weeks from the time you begin to put the sickle to the standing grain.
10 Then you shall keep the Feast of Weeks to the Lord your God with a tribute of a freewill offering from your hand, which you shall give to the Lord your God, as the Lord your God blesses you.
11 And you shall rejoice before the Lord your God, you and your son and daughter, your manservant and maidservant, and the Levite who is within your towns, the stranger or temporary resident, the fatherless, and the widow who are among you, at the place in which the Lord your God

chooses to make His Name [and His Presence] dwell.
12 And you shall [earnestly] remember that you were a slave in Egypt, and you shall be watchful and obey these statutes.
13 You shall observe the Feast of Tabernacles or Booths for seven days after you have gathered in from your threshing floor and wine vat.
14 You shall rejoice in your Feast, you, your son and daughter, your manservant and maidservant, the Levite, the transient and the stranger, the fatherless, and the widow who are within your towns.
15 For seven days you shall keep a solemn Feast to the Lord your God in the place which the Lord chooses; because the Lord your God will bless you in all your produce and in all the works of your hands, so that you will be altogether joyful.
16 Three times a year shall all your males appear before the Lord your God in the place which He chooses: at the Feast of Unleavened Bread, at the Feast of Weeks, and at the Feast of Tabernacles or Booths. They shall not appear before the Lord empty-handed:
17 Every man shall give as he is able, according to the blessing of the Lord your God which He has given you.
18 You shall appoint judges and officers in all your towns which the Lord your God gives you, according to your tribes, and they shall judge the people with righteous judgment.
19 You shall not misinterpret or misapply judgment; you shall not be partial, or take a bribe, for a bribe blinds the eyes of the wise and perverts the words of the righteous.
20 Follow what is altogether just (uncompromisingly righteous), that you may live and inherit the land which your God gives you.
21 You shall not plant for yourselves any kind of tree dedicated to [the goddess] Asherah beside the altar of

the Lord your God which you shall make.

22 Neither shall you set up an idolatrous stone *or* image, which the Lord your God hates.

17 YOU SHALL not sacrifice to the Lord your God an ox or sheep with a blemish or any defect whatsoever, for that is an abomination to the Lord your God.

2 If there is found among you within any of your towns which the Lord your God gives you a man or woman who does what is wicked in the sight of the Lord your God by transgressing His covenant,

3 Who has gone and served other gods and worshiped them, or the sun or moon or any of the host of the heavens, which I have forbidden,

4 And it is told and you hear of it, then inquire diligently. And if it is certainly true that such an abomination has been committed in Israel,

5 Then you shall bring forth to your town's gates that man or woman who has done that wicked thing and you shall stone that man or woman to death.

6 On the evidence of two or three witnesses he who is worthy of death shall be put to death; he shall not be put to death on the evidence of one witness.

7 The hands of the witnesses shall be the first against him to put him to death, and afterward the hands of all the people. So you shall purge the evil from among you.

8 If there arises a matter too hard for you in judgment—between one kind of bloodshed and another, between one legality and another, between one kind of assault and another, matters of controversy within your towns—then arise and go to the place which the Lord your God chooses.

9 And you shall come to the Levitical priests and to the judge who is in office in those days, and you shall consult them and they shall make clear to you the decision.

10 And you shall do according to the decision which they declare to you from that place which the Lord chooses; and you shall be watchful to do according to all that they tell you;

11 According to the decision of the law which they shall teach you and the judgment which they shall announce to you, you shall do; you shall not turn aside from the verdict they give you, [f]either to the right hand or the left.

12 The man who does presumptuously and will not listen to the priest who stands to minister there before the Lord your God or to the judge, that man shall die; so you shall purge the evil from Israel.

13 And all the people shall hear and [reverently] fear, and not act presumptuously again.

14 When you come to the land which the Lord your God gives you and you possess it and live there, and then say, We will set a king over us like all the nations that are about us,

15 You shall surely set as king over you him whom the Lord your God will choose. One from among your brethren you shall set as king over you; you may not set a foreigner, who is not your brother, over you.

16 But he shall not multiply horses to himself or cause the people to return to Egypt in order to multiply horses, since the Lord said to you, You shall never return that way.

17 And he shall not multiply wives to himself, that his [mind and] heart turn not away; neither shall he greatly multiply to himself silver and gold.

18 And when he sits on his royal

f The Hebrew is obscure.

presumption kills

In Old Testament days, God dealt differently with His people than He does now. I am so glad to be living under the dispensation of grace. But if we look at how God dealt with sin under the Old Covenant, we can see how serious it is and be warned not to wink at it or to be passive about eliminating it from our lives. We are being presumptuous if we think that we can purposely sin and get by with it.

In Deuteronomy 17:12, 13, God was telling His people that if one of their leaders acted presumptuously, he was to be killed. This was because leaders communicate through their actions that whatever they do is acceptable for everyone. But God is saying to us, "I will not let a presumptuous leader get by with wrong behavior, because if I do, everyone is going to think it is all right to act the same way." That is exactly why we must keep right heart attitudes if we want God to continue to use us. Leadership carries with it great responsibility. Ministry is more than just standing up in front of people and exercising spiritual gifts. We must live our lives with integrity behind the scenes, and that involves living without presumption. It means we do what is right when nobody can see us but God.

Why is it so important to be on guard against presumption? Presumption causes disrespect and a rebellious attitude toward authority. Presumptuous people think they do not have to listen to those who have been placed in authority over them. Often they are overconfident in their arrogance and unreasonably bold. Presumptuous people talk when they should be quiet. They try to dictate direction to those from whom they should be receiving counsel. They give orders when they should be taking orders. They do things without asking permission. They assume things instead of asking. They think they can make wrong choices and get right results, which never works because it goes against God's principles.

Presumption is a big problem that comes from a wrong heart, as we are told in II Peter 2:10, 11, which tells of "those who walk after the flesh and indulge in the lust of polluting passion and scorn and despise authority. Presumptuous [and] daring [self-willed and self-loving creatures]! They scoff at and revile dignitaries (glorious ones) without trembling, whereas [even] angels, though superior in might and power, do not bring a defaming charge against them before the Lord."

God does not want us to be presumptuous. He wants us to be humble so that others can come to know and honor Him through the way we live our lives.

throne, he shall write for himself a copy of this law in a book, out of what is before the Levitical priests.
19 And he shall keep it with him, and he shall read in it all the days of his life, that he may learn [reverently] to fear the Lord his God, by keeping all the words of this law and these statutes and doing them,
20 That his [mind and] heart may not be lifted up above his brethren and that he may not turn aside from the commandment to the right hand or to the left; so that he may continue long,

he and his sons, in his kingdom in Israel.

18

THE LEVITICAL priests and all the tribe of Levi shall have no part or inheritance with Israel; they shall eat the offerings made by fire to the Lord, and His rightful dues.

2 They shall have no inheritance among their brethren; the Lord is their inheritance, as He promised them.

3 And this shall be the priest's due from the people, from those who offer a sacrifice, whether it be ox or sheep: they shall give to the priest the shoulder and the two cheeks and the stomach.

4 The firstfruits of your grain, of your new wine, and of your oil, and the first or best of the fleece of your sheep you shall give the priest.

5 For the Lord your God has chosen him out of all your tribes to stand to minister in the name [and presence] of the Lord, him and his sons forever.

6 And if a Levite comes from any of your towns out of all Israel where he is a temporary resident, he may come whenever he desires to [the sanctuary] the place the Lord will choose;

7 Then he may minister in the name [and presence of] the Lord his God like all his brethren the Levites who stand to minister there before the Lord.

8 They shall have equal portions to eat, besides what may come of the sale of his patrimony. [Jer. 32:6-15.]

9 When you come into the land which the Lord your God gives you, you shall not learn to follow the abominable practices of these nations.

10 There shall not be found among you anyone who makes his son or daughter pass through the fire, or who uses divination, or is a soothsayer, or an augur, or a sorcerer,

11 Or a charmer, or a medium, or a wizard, or a necromancer.

12 For all who do these things are an abomination to the Lord, and it is because of these abominable practices that the Lord your God is driving them out before you.

13 You shall be blameless [and absolutely true] to the Lord your God.

14 For these nations whom you shall dispossess listen to soothsayers and diviners. But as for you, the Lord your God has not allowed you to do so.

15 The Lord your God will raise up for you [g]a prophet (Prophet) from the midst of your brethren like me [Moses]; to him you shall listen. [Matt. 21:11; John 1:21.]

16 This is what you desired [and asked] of the Lord your God at Horeb on the day of the assembly when you said, Let me not hear again the voice of the Lord my God or see this great fire any more, lest I die.

17 And the Lord said to me, They have well said all that they have spoken.

18 I will raise up for them a prophet (Prophet) from among their brethren like you, and will put My words in his mouth; and he shall speak to them all that I command him.

---

g The insertion of this promise in connection with the preceding prohibition might warrant the application which some make of it to that order of true prophets whom God commissioned in unbroken succession to instruct, to direct, and warn His people; in this view the gist of it is, "there is no need to consult with diviners and soothsayers, for I shall afford you the benefit of divinely appointed prophets, for judging of whose identity a sure clue is given" (Deut. 18:20, 22). But the prophet here promised was preeminently the Messiah, for He alone was "like unto Moses in His mediatorial character; in the peculiar excellence of His ministry; in the number, variety, and magnitude of His miracles; in His close and familiar communion with God; and in His being the author of a new dispensation of religion." This prediction was fulfilled 1,500 years afterwards, and was expressly applied to Christ by Peter (Acts 3:22, 23) and by Stephen (Acts 7:37) (Robert Jamieson, A.R. Fausset and David Brown, A Commentary).

the danger of occult practices

Today many people are going to fortune-tellers and tarot card readers or calling psychics who charge them so much per minute to tell them their futures. There are millions of people who follow horoscopes, making decisions based on the stars. You may be one of them, and if so, I want you to know that there is no need to worship the stars when you can worship the God Who made them.

The Bible has much to say about consulting with mediums and soothsayers and other kinds of activities that God considers an abomination (see also Leviticus 20:6). You may not be familiar with some of the words used in Deuteronomy 18:10–12, but it's talking about such things as horoscopes, tarot cards, psychic readings, mediums, and what we call "New Age" practices.

While the Bible says these occult practices are an abomination to God, I think many people today do not realize that God is opposed to such things. In fact, some churches do not even teach people that those things are wrong. One of the women in a church I attended for a period of time was getting involved in transcendental meditation. Since she did not know whether there was anything wrong with it or not, she asked the pastor. He told her, "I'm not really sure. Let me know whether it works or not; I might even try it myself." I didn't know any better than that either. If God had not intervened in my life, I might have fallen into the dangerous trap of New Age activity. There is no telling how many people are getting sucked into occult practices and the New Age movement simply because they really do not know God's Word well enough to stay away from such dangerous pursuits.

God's Living Word is the only source of truth, and His Spirit is the only One Who can lead us into peace, joy, and victory in our everyday lives. Don't waste your money calling up people who supposedly can tell you about your future. Let God lead your future.

19 And whoever will not hearken to My words which he shall speak in My name, I Myself will require it of him. **20** But the prophet who presumes to speak a word in My name which I have not commanded him to speak, or who speaks in the name of other gods, that same prophet shall die. **21** And if you say in your [minds and] hearts, How shall we know which words the Lord has not spoken? **22** When a prophet speaks in the name of the Lord, if the word does not come to pass or prove true, that is a word which the Lord has not spoken. The prophet has spoken it presumptuously; you shall not be afraid of him.

19 WHEN THE Lord your God has cut off the nations whose land the Lord your God gives you, and you dispossess them and dwell in their cities and in their houses, **2** You shall set apart three cities for yourselves in the land which the Lord your God gives you to possess. **3** You shall prepare the road and divide into three parts the territory of your land which the Lord your God gives you to possess, so that any manslayer can flee to them.

4 And this is the case of the slayer who shall flee there in order that he may live. Whoever kills his neighbor unintentionally, for whom he had no enmity in time past—

5 As when a man goes into the wood with his neighbor to hew wood, and his hand strikes with the ax to cut down the tree, and the head slips off the handle and lights on his neighbor and kills him—he may flee to one of those cities and live;

6 Lest the avenger of the blood pursue the slayer while his [mind and] heart are hot with anger and overtake him, because the way is long, and slay him even though the slayer was not worthy of death, since he had not been at enmity with him previously.

7 Therefore I command you, You shall set apart three [refuge] cities.

8 And if the Lord your God enlarges your territory, as He has sworn to your fathers to do, and gives you all the land which He promised to your fathers to give,

9 If you keep all these commandments to do them, which I command you this day, to love the Lord your God and to walk always in His ways, then you shall add three other cities to these three,

10 Lest innocent blood be shed in your land, which the Lord your God gives you as an inheritance, and so blood guilt be upon you.

11 But if any man hates his neighbor and lies in wait for him, and attacks him and wounds him mortally so that he dies, and the assailant flees into one of these cities,

12 Then the elders of his own city shall send for him and fetch him from there and give him over to the avenger of blood, so that he may die.

13 Your eyes shall not pity him, but you shall clear Israel of the guilt of innocent blood, that it may go well with you.

14 You shall not remove your neighbor's landmark in the land which the Lord your God gives you to possess, which the men of old [the first dividers of the land] set.

15 One witness shall not prevail against a man for any crime or any wrong in connection with any sin he commits; only on the testimony of two or three witnesses shall a charge be established.

16 If a false witness rises up against any man to accuse him of wrongdoing,

17 Then both parties to the controversy shall stand before the Lord, before the priests and the judges who are in office in those days.

18 The judges shall inquire diligently, and if the witness is a false witness and has accused his brother falsely,

19 Then you shall do to him as he had intended to do to his brother. So you shall put away the evil from among you.

20 And those who remain shall hear and [reverently] fear, and shall henceforth commit no such evil among you.

21 Your eyes shall not pity: it shall be life for life, eye for eye, tooth for tooth, hand for hand, foot for foot.

20 WHEN YOU go forth to battle against your enemies and see horses and chariots and an army greater than your own, do not be afraid of them, for the Lord your God, Who brought you out of the land of Egypt, is with you.

2 And when you come near to the battle, the priest shall approach and speak to the men,

3 And shall say to them, Hear, O Israel, you draw near this day to battle against your enemies. Let not your [minds and] hearts faint; fear not, and

gentle as a lamb, bold as a lion

What happens when our hearts faint? In our hearts we say, "I can't do this. It's just too hard." If we are going to be faithful believers in the kingdom of God, we cannot quit when things get tough. We need to be as bold as a lion.

Being bold-hearted does not mean we should be tough and harsh. It is possible to be tender and tough at the same time, and the key is to know when to be tender and when to be tough. We need to be meek, sweet, and gentle toward people, but bold, tough, and aggressive with the devil—because that is the way he is with us.

I used to have a problem understanding how a person could be both tough and tender. When I read the Bible one verse seemed to say that I was to be as gentle as a lamb, while another passage (such as Deuteronomy 20:1–4) seemed to instruct me to be lionhearted. I did not have any trouble with the lion part, but I did have problems with the lamb part. I had a lot of natural lion in me, but I needed to develop the lamb part of me. Gentleness did not come easily to me, partly because I was not raised in a gentle atmosphere, and partly because my personality was not gentle by nature.

Jesus is humble, gentle, meek, and lowly—not harsh, hard, sharp, or pressing. I was not like Jesus, but I wanted to be, so I went to the extreme of collecting little stuffed lambs and placing them all over my house. I had pictures of lambs and paintings of lambs. I had images of Jesus holding lambs, Jesus in the middle of lambs, and Jesus carrying lambs on His shoulders. I had so many lambs in my house that it started to look stupid, so I cleaned a whole bunch of them out and kept only the ones I liked best. But all of the lambs served a purpose: they reminded me to be more gentle. They helped me form new habits in how I dealt with people. We should resist Satan and all of his evil works as agressively and boldly as a lion, but in our dealings with people, we usually should be very gentle unless a situation calls for us to apply some tough love.

The Holy Spirit is also very gentle and sensitive. If we are harsh and hard with people, we can easily offend the Holy Spirit, and we certainly do not want to do that.

Are you more like a lion, or are you more like a lamb? You may be shy and timid, as gentle and meek as a lamb, preferring to avoid hard or controversial issues. So God has to put a bit of lion in you. Or you may have a strong lion in you, as I did, and need to have some lamb qualities developed in you.

No matter what your temperament is, we all face times that call for a lion as well as times that call for a lamb. When we feel fainthearted, we need to dig in our heels and exclaim in lionlike faith, "I am not going to be fainthearted! God will help me! I am not going to give up or quit, no matter how hard it gets or how long it takes!"

do not tremble or be terrified [and in dread] because of them.

4 For the Lord your God is He Who goes with you to fight for you against your enemies to save you. [I Sam. 17:45.]

5 And the officers shall speak to the people, saying, What man is there who has built a new house and has not dedicated it? Let him return to his house, lest he die in the battle and another man dedicate it.

6 And what man has planted a vineyard and has not used the fruit of it? Let him also return to his house, lest he die in the battle and another man use the fruit of it.

7 And what man has betrothed a wife and has not taken her? Let him return to his house, lest he die in the battle and another man take her.

8 And the officers shall speak further to the people, and say, What man is fearful and fainthearted? Let him return to his house, lest [because of him] his brethren's [minds and] hearts faint as does his own.

9 And when the officers finish speaking to the people, they shall appoint commanders at the head of the people.

10 When you draw near to a city to fight against it, then proclaim peace to it.

11 And if that city makes an answer of peace to you and opens to you, then all the people found in it shall be tributary to you and they shall serve you.

12 But if it refuses to make peace with you and fights against you, then you shall besiege it.

13 And when the Lord your God has given it into your hands, you shall smite every male there with the edge of the sword.

14 But the women, the little ones, the beasts, and all that is in the city, all the spoil in it, you shall take for yourselves; and you shall use the spoil of your enemies which the Lord your God has given you.

15 So shall you treat all the cities that are very far off from you, that do not belong to the cities of these nations.

16 But in the cities of these people which the Lord your God gives you for an inheritance, you shall save alive nothing that breathes.

17 But you shall utterly exterminate them, the Hittites, the Amorites, the Canaanites, the Perizzites, the Hivites, and the Jebusites, as the Lord your God has commanded you,

18 So that they may not teach you all the abominable practices they have carried on for their gods, and so cause you to sin against the Lord your God.

19 When you besiege a city for a long time, making war against it to take it, you shall not destroy its trees by using an ax on them, for you can eat their fruit; you must not cut them down, for is the tree of the field a man, that it should be besieged by you?

20 Only the trees which you know are not trees for food you may destroy and cut down, that you may build siege works against the city that makes war with you until it falls.

21 IF ONE is found slain in the land which the Lord your God gives you to possess, lying in the field, and it is not known who has killed him,

2 Then your elders and judges shall come forth and measure the distance to the cities around him who is slain.

3 And the city which is nearest to the slain man, the elders of that city shall take a heifer which has never been worked, never pulled in the yoke,

4 And the elders of that city shall bring the heifer down to a valley with running water which is neither plowed nor sown, and shall break the heifer's neck there in the valley.

5 And the priests, the sons of Levi, shall come near, for the Lord your God has chosen them to minister to

Him and to bless in the name [and presence] of the Lord, and by their word shall every controversy and every assault be settled.

6 And all the elders of that city nearest to the slain man shall wash their hands over the heifer whose neck was broken in the valley,

7 And they shall testify, Our hands have not shed this blood, neither have our eyes seen it.

8 Forgive, O Lord, Your people Israel, whom You have redeemed, and do not allow the shedding of innocent blood to be charged to Your people Israel. And the guilt of blood shall be forgiven them.

9 So shall you purge the guilt of innocent blood from among you, when you do what is right in the sight of the Lord.

10 When you go forth to battle against your enemies and the Lord your God has given them into your hands and you carry them away captive,

11 And you see among the captives a beautiful woman and desire her, that you may have her as your wife,

12 Then you shall bring her home to your house, and she shall shave her head and pare her nails [in purification from heathenism]

13 And put off her prisoner's garb, and shall remain in your house and bewail her father and her mother a full month. After that you may go in to her and be her husband and she shall be your wife.

14 And if you have no delight in her, then you shall let her go absolutely free. You shall not sell her at all for money; you shall not deal with her as a slave *or* a servant, because you have humbled her.

15 If a man has two wives, one loved and the other disliked, and they both have borne him children, and if the firstborn son is the son of the one who is disliked,

16 Then on the day when he wills his possessions to his sons, he shall not put the firstborn of his loved wife in place of the [actual] firstborn of the disliked wife—her firstborn being older.

17 But he shall acknowledge the son of the disliked as the firstborn by giving him a double portion of all that he has, for he was the first issue of his strength; the right of the firstborn is his.

18 If a man has a stubborn and rebellious son who will not obey the voice of his father or his mother and though they chasten him will not listen to them,

19 Then his father and mother shall take hold of him and bring him out to the elders of his city at the gate of the place where he lives,

20 And they shall say to the elders of his city, This son of ours is stubborn and rebellious. He will not obey our voice. He is a glutton and a drunkard. [Prov. 23:20-22.]

21 Then all the men of his city shall stone him to death; so you shall cleanse out the evil from your midst, and all Israel shall hear and [reverently] fear.

22 And if a man has committed a sin worthy of death and he is put to death and [afterward] you hang him on a tree, [Josh. 10:26, 27.]

23 His body shall not remain all night upon the tree, but you shall surely bury him on the same day, for a hanged man is accursed by God. Thus you shall not defile your land which the Lord your God gives you for an inheritance. [Gal. 3:13.]

22 YOU SHALL not see your brother's ox or his sheep being driven away *or* stolen, and hide yourself from [your duty to help] them; you shall surely take them back to your brother. [Prov. 24:12.]

2 And if your brother [the owner] is not near you or if you do not know who he is, you shall bring the animal to your house and it shall be with you until your brother comes looking for it; then you shall restore it to him.

3 And so shall you do with his donkey or his garment or with anything which your brother has lost and you have found. You shall not hide from [your duty concerning] them.

4 You shall not see your brother's donkey or his ox fall down by the way, and hide from [your duty concerning] them; you shall surely help him to lift them up again.

5 The woman shall not wear that which pertains to a man, neither shall a man put on a woman's garment, for all that do so are an abomination to the Lord your God.

6 If a bird's nest should chance to be before you in the way, in any tree or on the ground, with young ones or eggs, and the mother bird is sitting on the young or on the eggs, you shall not take the mother bird with the young.

7 You shall surely let the mother bird go, and take only the young, that it may be well with you and that you may prolong your days.

8 When you build a new house, then you shall put a railing around your [flat] roof, so that no one may fall from there and bring guilt of blood upon your house.

9 You shall not plant your vineyard with two kinds of seed, lest the whole crop be forfeited [under this ban], the seed which you have sown and the yield of the vineyard forfeited to the sanctuary.

10 You shall not plow with an ox [a clean animal] and a donkey [unclean] together. [II Cor. 6:14-16.]

11 You shall not wear a garment of mingled stuff, wool and linen together. [Ezek. 44:18; Rev. 19:8.]

12 You shall make yourself tassels on the four corners of your cloak with which you cover yourself. [Num. 15:37-40.]

13 If any man takes a wife and goes in to her, and then scorns her

14 And charges her with shameful things and gives her an evil reputation, and says, I took this woman, but when I came to her, I did not find in her the tokens of a virgin,

15 Then the father of the young woman, and her mother, shall get and bring out the tokens of her virginity to the elders of the city at the gate.

16 And her father shall say to the elders, I gave my daughter to this man as wife, but he hates *and* spurns her;

17 And behold, he has made shameful charges against her, saying, I found not in your daughter the evidences of her virginity. And yet these are the tokens of my daughter's virginity. And they shall spread the garment before the elders of the city,

18 And the elders of that city shall take the man and rebuke *and* whip him.

19 And they shall fine him 100 shekels of silver and give them to the father of the young woman, because he has brought an evil name upon a virgin of Israel. And she shall be his wife; he may not divorce her all his days.

20 But if it is true that the evidences of virginity were not found in the young woman,

21 Then they shall bring her to the door of her father's house and the men of her city shall stone her to death, because she has wrought [criminal] folly in Israel by playing the harlot in her father's house. So you shall put away the evil from among you.

22 If a man is found lying with another man's wife, they shall both die, the man who lay with the woman and the woman. So you shall purge the evil from Israel.

23 If a maiden who is a virgin is

engaged to be married, and a man finds her in the city and lies with her, **24** Then you shall bring them both out to the gate of that city and shall stone them to death—the young woman because she did not cry for help though she was in the city, and the man because he has violated his neighbor's [promised] wife. So shall you put away evil from among you.

25 But if a man finds the betrothed maiden in the open country and the man seizes her and lies with her, then only the man who lay with her shall die. **26** But you shall do nothing to the young woman; she has committed no sin punishable by death, for this is as when a man attacks and slays his neighbor, **27** For he came upon her in the open country, and the betrothed girl cried out, but there was no one to save her. **28** If a man finds a girl who is a virgin, who is not betrothed, and he seizes her and lies with her and they are found, **29** Then the man who lay with her shall give to the girl's father fifty shekels of silver, and she shall be his wife, because he has violated her; he may not divorce her all his days.

30 A man shall not take his father's former wife, nor shall he uncover her who belongs to his father.

23 HE WHO is wounded in the testicles, or has been made a eunuch, shall not enter into the congregation of the Lord.

2 A person begotten out of wedlock shall not enter into the assembly of the Lord; even to his tenth generation shall his descendants not enter into the congregation of the Lord.

3 An Ammonite or [h]Moabite shall not enter into the congregation of the Lord; even to their tenth generation their descendants shall not enter into the assembly of the Lord forever,

4 Because they did not meet you with food and water on the way when you came forth out of Egypt, and because they hired Balaam son of Beor of Pethor of Mesopotamia against you to curse you.

5 Nevertheless, the Lord your God would not listen to Balaam, but the Lord your God turned the curse into a blessing to you, because the Lord your God loves you.

6 You shall not seek their peace or their prosperity all your days forever.

7 You shall not abhor an Edomite, for he is your brother [Esau's descendant]. You shall not abhor an Egyptian, because you were a stranger *and* temporary resident in his land.

8 Their children may enter into the congregation of the Lord in their third generation.

9 When you go forth against your enemies and are in camp, you shall keep yourselves from every evil thing.

10 If there is among you any man who is not clean by reason of what happens to him at night, then he shall go outside the camp; he shall not come within the camp;

11 But when evening comes he shall

speak the Word

God, thank You for turning curses into blessings in my life because You love me.
ADAPTED FROM DEUTERONOMY 23:5

h It must be remembered that according to the Jewish law the children followed the father, not the mother. [Take the family of Boaz, for example. Although Boaz's wife Ruth was a Moabitess, his family was considered Israelite, including his wife]. The case of Ruth would not, therefore, be touched by this precept (Charles J. Ellicott, *A Bible Commentary*).

bathe himself in water, and when the sun is down he may return to the camp.

12 You shall have a place also outside the camp to which you shall go [as a comfort station];

13 And you shall have a paddle *or* shovel among your weapons, and when you sit down outside [to relieve yourself], you shall dig a hole with it and turn back and cover up what has come from you.

14 For the Lord your God walks in the midst of your camp to deliver you and to give up your enemies before you. Therefore shall your camp be holy, that He may see nothing indecent among you and turn away from you.

15 You shall not give up to his master a servant who has escaped from his master to you.

16 He shall dwell with you in your midst wherever he chooses in one of your towns where it pleases him best. You shall not defraud *or* oppress him.

17 There shall be no cult prostitute among the daughters of Israel, neither shall there be a cult prostitute (a sodomite) among the sons of Israel.

18 You shall not bring the hire of a harlot or the price of a dog (a sodomite) into the house of the Lord your God as payment of a vow, for both of these [the gift and the giver] are an abomination to the Lord your God.

19 You shall not lend on interest to your brother—interest on money, on victuals, on anything that is lent for interest.

20 You may lend on interest to a foreigner, but to your brother you shall not lend on interest, that the Lord your God may bless you in all that you undertake in the land to which you go to possess it.

21 When you make a vow to the Lord your God, you shall not be slack in paying it, for the Lord your God will surely require it of you, and slackness would be sin in you.

22 But if you refrain from vowing, it will not be sin in you.

23 The vow which has passed your lips you shall be watchful to perform, a voluntary offering which you have made to the Lord your God, which you have promised with your mouth.

24 When you come into your neighbor's vineyard, you may eat your fill of grapes, as many as you please, but you shall not put any in your vessel.

25 When you come into the standing grain of your neighbor, you may pluck the ears with your hand, but you shall not put a sickle to your neighbor's standing grain.

24 WHEN A man takes a wife and marries her, if then she finds no favor in his eyes because he has found some indecency in her, and he writes her a bill of divorce, puts it in her hand, and sends her out of his house,

2 And when she departs out of his house she goes and marries another man,

3 And if the latter husband dislikes her and writes her a bill of divorce and puts it in her hand and sends her out of his house, or if the latter husband dies, who took her as his wife,

4 Then her former husband, who sent her away, may not take her again to be his wife after she is defiled. For that is an abomination before the Lord; and you shall not bring guilt upon the land which the Lord your God gives you as an inheritance.

5 When a man is newly married, he shall not go out with the army or be charged with any business; he shall be free at home one year and shall cheer his wife whom he has taken.

6 No man shall take a mill or an upper millstone in pledge, for he would be taking a life in pledge.

7 If a man is found kidnapping any of his brethren of the Israelites and treats him as a slave *or* a servant or sells him, then that thief shall die. So you shall put evil from among you.

8 Take heed in the plague of leprosy, that you watch diligently and do according to all that the Levitical priests shall teach you. As I commanded them, so you shall be watchful and do. [Lev. 13:14, 15.]

9 Remember [earnestly] what the Lord your God did to Miriam on the way after you had come out of Egypt. [Num. 12:10.]

10 When you lend your brother anything, you shall not go into his house to get his pledge.

11 You shall stand outside and the man to whom you lend shall bring the pledge out to you.

12 And if the man is poor, you shall not keep his pledge overnight.

13 You shall surely restore to him the pledge at sunset, that he may sleep in his garment and bless you; and it shall be credited to you as righteousness (rightness and justice) before the Lord your God.

14 You shall not oppress *or* extort from a hired servant who is poor and needy, whether he is of your brethren or of your strangers *and* sojourners who are in your land inside your towns.

15 You shall give him his hire on the day he earns it before the sun goes down, for he is poor, and sets his heart upon it; lest he cry against you to the Lord, and it be sin to you.

16 The fathers shall not be put to death for the children, neither shall the children be put to death for the fathers; only for his own sin shall anyone be put to death.

17 You shall not pervert the justice due the stranger *or* the sojourner or the fatherless, or take a widow's garment in pledge.

18 But you shall [earnestly] remember that you were a slave in Egypt and the Lord your God redeemed you from there; therefore I command you to do this.

19 When you reap your harvest in your field and have forgotten a sheaf in the field, you shall not go back to get it; it shall be for the stranger *and* the sojourner, the fatherless, and the widow, that the Lord your God may bless you in all the work of your hands.

20 When you beat your olive tree, do not go over the boughs again; the leavings shall be for the stranger *and* the sojourner, the fatherless, and the widow.

21 When you gather the grapes of your vineyard, you shall not glean it afterward; it shall be for the stranger *and* the sojourner, the fatherless, and the widow.

22 You shall [earnestly] remember that you were a slave in the land of Egypt; therefore I command you to do this.

25 IF THERE is a controversy between men, and they come into court and the judges decide between them, justifying the innocent and condemning the guilty,

2 Then if the guilty man deserves to be beaten, the judge shall cause him to lie down and be beaten in his presence with a certain number of stripes according to his offense.

3 Forty stripes may be given him but not more, lest, if he should be beaten with many stripes, your brother should [be treated like a beast and] seem low and worthless to you.

4 You shall not muzzle the ox when he treads out the grain. [I Cor. 9:9, 10; I Tim. 5:17, 18.]

5 If brothers live together and one of them dies and has no son, his wife shall not be married outside the family to a stranger [an excluded man]. Her husband's brother shall go in to her and take her as his wife and perform the duty of a husband's brother to her.

6 And the firstborn son shall succeed to the name of the dead brother, that his name may not be blotted out of Israel.

7 And if the man does not want to take his brother's wife, then let his brother's wife go up to the gate to the elders, and say, My husband's brother refuses to continue his brother's name in Israel; he will not perform the duty of my husband's brother.

8 Then the elders of his city shall call him and speak to him. And if he stands firm and says, I do not want to take her,

9 Then shall his brother's wife come to him in the presence of the elders and pull his shoe off his foot and spit in his face and shall answer, So shall it be done to that man who does not build up his brother's house.

10 And his family shall be called in Israel, The House of Him Whose Shoe Was Loosed.

11 When men strive together one with another and the wife of the one draws near to rescue her husband out of the hand of him who is beating him, and puts out her hand and seizes the other man by the private parts,

12 Then you shall cut off her hand; your eyes shall not pity her.

13 You shall not have in your bag true and false weights, a large and a small.

14 You shall not have in your house true and false measures, a large and a small.

15 But you shall have a perfect and just weight and a perfect and just measure, that your days may be prolonged in the land which the Lord your God gives you.

16 For all who do such things, all who do unrighteously, are an abomination to the Lord your God.

17 Remember what Amalek did to you on the way when you had come forth from Egypt,

18 How he did not fear God, but when you were faint and weary he attacked you along the way and cut off all the stragglers at your rear. [Exod. 17:14.]

19 Therefore when the Lord your God has given you rest from all your enemies round about in the land which the Lord your God gives you to possess as an inheritance, you shall blot out the remembrance of Amalek from under the heavens; you must not forget.

26 WHEN YOU have come into the land which the Lord your God gives you as an inheritance and possess it and live in it,

2 You shall take some of the first of all the produce of the soil which you harvest from the land the Lord your God gives you and put it in a basket, and go to the place [the sanctuary] which the Lord your God has chosen as the abiding place for His Name [and His Presence].

3 And you shall go to the priest who is in office in those days, and say to him, I give thanks this day to the Lord your God that I have come to the land which the Lord swore to our fathers to give us.

4 And the priest shall take the basket from your hand and set it down before the altar of the Lord your God.

5 And you shall say before the Lord your God, A wandering *and* lost Aramean ready to perish was my father [Jacob], and he went down into Egypt and sojourned there, few in number, and he became there a nation, great, mighty, and numerous.

6 And the Egyptians treated us very badly and afflicted us and laid upon us hard bondage.

7 And when we cried to the Lord, the God of our fathers, the Lord heard our voice and looked on our affliction

when weariness attacks

Amalek's attack on the Israelites, mentioned in Deuteronomy 25:17, 18, is a type and shadow of Satan and the method he uses to assault, hinder, and stop believers today (see John 10:10). Amalek chose to attack the Israelites when they were faint and weary. Satan tries to wear us down to the point of exhaustion so that once we are in that position, he can intensify his attack to bring us down.

If you, a Christian, are struggling with weariness—if you want to just give up and quit—you are not alone. Satan is bringing this attack of weariness on the body of Christ to keep us from receiving the harvest God has for us. And God is preparing a great spiritual harvest!

When we plant seed in the natural world, a lot happens underground that we cannot see. The root system needs to grow and be established before we notice any harvest. Because God's kingdom is based on the principle of seed planting and harvest (see Mark 4:26–32), God is doing much work "under the ground," out of our sight, to bring our planted seeds to fruition.

This "growing stage" is the point when many of us become weary and want to faint. When we are doing everything we know to do in God—and we are doing it again and again without seeing the results we desire in the natural world—we can become weary in well-doing. We may have planted our seeds of obedience in faithfulness and diligence, but we have lost sight of the manner in which the kingdom of God operates to grow fruit. We need to remember the wonderful promise of Galatians 6:9: "And let us not lose heart and grow weary and faint in acting nobly and doing right, for in due time and at the appointed season we shall reap, if we do not loosen and relax our courage and faint."

When the enemy attacks you in times of weakness or fatigue, stir up your courage, muster your strength, and rise up against him with the truth of God's Word! This is a good time to behave as a bold, aggressive lion.

and our labor and our [cruel] oppression;

8 And the Lord brought us forth out of Egypt with a mighty hand and with an outstretched arm, and with great (awesome) power and with signs and with wonders;

9 And He brought us into this place and gave us this land, a land flowing with milk and honey.

10 And now, behold, I bring the firstfruits of the ground which You, O Lord, have given me. And you shall set it down before the Lord your God and worship before the Lord your God;

11 And you and the Levite and the stranger *and* the sojourner among you shall rejoice in all the good which the Lord your God has given you and your household.

12 When you have finished paying all the tithe of your produce the third year, which is the year of tithing, and have given it to the Levite, the stranger *and* the sojourner, the fatherless, and to the widow, that they may eat within your towns and be filled,

13 Then you shall say before the Lord your God, I have brought the hallowed things (the tithe) out of my house and moreover have given them to the Levite, to the stranger *and* the sojourner, to the fatherless, and to the widow, according to all Your commandments which You have commanded me; I have not transgressed any of Your commandments, neither have I forgotten them.

14 I have not eaten of the tithe in my mourning [making the tithe unclean], nor have I handled any of it when I was unclean, nor given any of it to the dead. I have hearkened to the voice of the Lord my God; I have done according to all that You have commanded me.

15 Look down from Your holy habitation, from heaven, and bless Your people Israel and the land which You have given us as You swore to our fathers, a land flowing with milk and honey.

16 This day the Lord your God has commanded you to do these statutes and ordinances. Therefore you shall keep and do them with all your [mind and] heart and with all your being.

17 You have [openly] declared the Lord this day to be your God, [pledging] to walk in His ways, to keep His statutes and His commandments and His precepts, and to hearken to His voice.

18 And the Lord has declared this day that you are His peculiar people as He promised you, and you are to keep all His commandments;

19 And He will make you high above all nations which He has made, in praise and in fame and in honor, and that you shall be a holy people to the Lord your God, as He has spoken.

27 AND MOSES with the elders of Israel commanded the people, Keep all the commandments with which I charge you today.

2 And on the day when you pass over the Jordan to the land which the Lord your God gives you, you shall set up great stones and cover them with plaster.

3 And you shall write on them all the words of this law when you have passed over, that you may go into the land which the Lord your God is giving you, a land flowing with milk and honey, as the Lord, the God of your fathers, has promised you.

4 And when you have gone over the Jordan, you shall set up these stones, as I command you this day, on Mount Ebal, and coat them with plaster.

5 And there you shall build an altar to the Lord your God, an altar of stones; you shall not lift up any iron tool upon them.

6 You shall build the altar of the Lord your God of whole stones and offer burnt offerings on it to Him;

7 And you shall offer peace offerings, and eat there and rejoice before the Lord your God.

8 And you shall write upon the stones all the words of this law very plainly.

9 And Moses and the Levitical priests said to all Israel, Keep silence and hear, O Israel! This day you have become the people of the Lord your God.

10 So you shall obey the voice of the Lord your God and do His commandments and statutes which I command you today.

11 And Moses charged the people the same day, saying,

12 These [tribes] shall stand on Mount Gerizim to bless the people, when you have passed over the Jordan: Simeon, Levi, Judah, Issachar, Joseph's [sons], and Benjamin.

13 And these [tribes] shall stand on Mount Ebal to pronounce the curse

life point

Obedience is not to be an occasional event; it is to be a way of life. There is a big difference between people who are willing to obey God daily and those who are willing to obey only in order to get out of trouble. God certainly shows people how to get out of trouble, but He showers blessings on those who decide to live wholeheartedly for Him and make obedience to Him their lifestyle.

[for disobedience]: Reuben, Gad, Asher, Zebulun, Dan, and Naphtali.

14 And the Levites shall declare with a loud voice to all the men of Israel:

15 Cursed is the man who makes a graven or molten image, an abomination to the Lord, the work of the hands of the craftsman, and sets it up in secret. All the people shall answer, Amen.

16 Cursed is he who dishonors his father or his mother. All the people shall say, Amen.

17 Cursed is he who moves [back] his neighbor's landmark. All the people shall say, Amen.

18 Cursed is he who misleads a blind man on his way. All the people shall say, Amen.

19 Cursed is he who perverts the justice due to the sojourner *or* the stranger, the fatherless, and the widow. All the people shall say, Amen.

20 Cursed is he who lies with his father's wife, because he uncovers what belongs to his father. All the people shall say, Amen.

21 Cursed is he who lies with any beast. All the people shall say, Amen.

speak the Word

22 Cursed is he who lies with his half sister, whether his father's or his mother's daughter. All the people shall say, Amen.

23 Cursed is he who lies with his mother-in-law. All the people shall say, Amen.

24 Cursed is he who slays his neighbor secretly. All the people shall say, Amen.

25 Cursed is he who takes a bribe to slay an innocent person. All the people shall say, Amen.

26 Cursed is he who does not support *and* give assent to the words of this law to do them [as the rule of his life]. All the people shall say, Amen.

28 IF YOU will listen diligently to the voice of the Lord your God, being watchful to do all His commandments which I command you this day, the Lord your God will set you high above all the nations of the earth.

2 And all these blessings shall come upon you and overtake you if you heed the voice of the Lord your God.

3 Blessed shall you be in the city and blessed shall you be in the field.

4 Blessed shall be the fruit of your body and the fruit of your ground and the fruit of your beasts, the increase of your cattle and the young of your flock.

5 Blessed shall be your basket and your kneading trough.

6 Blessed shall you be when you come in and blessed shall you be when you go out.

7 The Lord shall cause your enemies who rise up against you to be defeated before your face; they shall

God, I will listen diligently to Your voice and be watchful to do all Your commandments, and I am expecting Your favor and blessings in my life.
ADAPTED FROM DEUTERONOMY 28:1, 2

come out against you one way and flee before you seven ways.

8 The Lord shall command the blessing upon you in your storehouse and in all that you undertake. And He will bless you in the land which the Lord your God gives you.

9 The Lord will establish you as a people holy to Himself, as He has sworn to you, if you keep the commandments of the Lord your God and walk in His ways.

10 And all people of the earth shall see that you are called by the name [and in the presence of] the Lord, and they shall be afraid of you.

11 And the Lord shall make you have a surplus of prosperity, through the fruit of your body, of your livestock, and of your ground, in the land which the Lord swore to your fathers to give you.

12 The Lord shall open to you His good treasury, the heavens, to give the rain of your land in its season and to bless all the work of your hands; and you shall lend to many nations, but you shall not borrow.

13 And the Lord shall make you the head, and not the tail; and you shall be above only, and you shall not be beneath, if you heed the commandments of the Lord your God which I command you this day and are watchful to do them.

14 And you shall not turn aside from any of the words which I command you this day, to the right hand or to the left, to go after other gods to serve them.

15 But if you will not obey the voice of the Lord your God, being watchful to do all His commandments and His statutes which I command you this

day, then all these curses shall come upon you and overtake you:

16 Cursed shall you be in the city and cursed shall you be in the field.

17 Cursed shall be your basket and your kneading trough.

18 Cursed shall be the fruit of your body, of your land, of the increase of your cattle and the young of your sheep.

19 Cursed shall you be when you come in and cursed shall you be when you go out.

20 The Lord shall send you curses, confusion, and rebuke in every enterprise to which you set your hand, until you are destroyed, perishing quickly because of the evil of your doings by which you have forsaken me [Moses and God as one].

21 The Lord will make the pestilence cling to you until He has consumed you from the land into which you go to possess.

22 The Lord will smite you with consumption, with fever and inflammation, fiery heat, sword *and* drought, blasting and mildew; they shall pursue you until you perish.

23 The heavens over your head shall be brass and the earth under you shall be iron.

24 The Lord shall make the rain of your land powdered soil and dust; from the heavens it shall come down upon you until you are destroyed.

25 The Lord shall cause you to be struck down before your enemies; you shall go out one way against them and flee seven ways before them, and you shall be tossed to and fro *and* be a terror among all the kingdoms of the earth. [Fulfilled in II Chron. 29:8.]

26 And your dead body shall be food

speak the Word

Thank You, God, that You have made me the head and not the tail, that I am above only and not beneath anything or anyone.
ADAPTED FROM DEUTERONOMY **28:13**

receiving outrageous blessings

God's promises usually come with conditions. He is merciful, and He does certain things for us that we do not deserve. Even when we have not behaved correctly, we can still pray for mercy and ask God to help us. But anybody who wants to live in the radical, outrageous, chase-you-down-the-street-and-overtake-you blessings of God has to do something to receive them.

The blessing package described in Deuteronomy 28:1–14 is conditional. Listen to the condition: "If you will listen diligently to the voice of the Lord your God . . . if you heed the voice of the Lord your God . . . if you keep the commandments of the Lord your God and walk in His ways," *then* "all these blessings shall come upon you and overtake you" (Deuteronomy 28:1, 2, 9). The promised blessings are many: blessings wherever you are or whatever you do; blessings in your family, with your work, and in your possessions; victory over your enemies; blessings of being established as God's holy people.

While we want all these blessings, many times we are not willing to do what it takes to receive them. Radical and outrageous blessings come from radical and outrageous obedience. They come from a willingness to obey God whether He tells us to do something in His Word or by speaking in our hearts. We really do not need to complain about doing what God tells us because He gives us the ability to do the things He calls us to do. Our part is simply to listen to His voice and do what He says without reservation. That's when the blessings come.

for all the birds of the air and the beasts of the earth, and there shall be no one to frighten them away.

27 The Lord will smite you with the boils of Egypt and the tumors, the scurvy and the itch, from which you cannot be healed.

28 The Lord will smite you with madness and blindness and dismay of [mind and] heart.

29 And you shall grope at noonday as the blind grope in darkness. And you shall not prosper in your ways; and you shall be only oppressed and robbed continually, and there shall be no one to save you.

30 You shall betroth a wife, but another man shall lie with her; you shall build a house, but not live in it; you shall plant a vineyard, but not gather its grapes.

31 Your ox shall be slain before your eyes, but you shall not eat of it; your donkey shall be violently taken away before your face and not be restored to you; your sheep shall be given to your enemies, and you shall have no one to help you.

32 Your sons and daughters shall be given to another people, and your eyes shall look and fail with longing for them all the day; and there shall be no power in your hands to prevent it. [Fulfilled in II Chron. 29:9.]

33 A nation which you have not known shall eat up the fruit of your land and of all your labors, and you shall be only oppressed and crushed continually, [Fulfilled in Judg. 6:1-6; 13:1.]

34 So that you shall be driven mad by the sights which your eyes shall see.

35 The Lord will smite you on the knees and on the legs with a sore boil that cannot be healed, from the sole of your foot to the top of your head.

36 The Lord shall bring you and your king whom you have set over you to a nation which neither you nor your fathers have known, and there you shall [be forced to] serve other gods, of wood and stone. [Fulfilled in II Kings 17:4, 6; 24:12, 14; 25:7, 11; Dan. 6:11, 12.]

37 And you shall become an amazement, a proverb, and a byword among all the peoples to which the Lord will lead you.

38 You shall carry much seed out into the field and shall gather little in, for the locust shall consume it. [Fulfilled in Hag. 1:6.]

39 You shall plant vineyards and dress them but shall neither drink of the wine nor gather the grapes, for the worm shall eat them.

40 You shall have olive trees throughout all your territory but you shall not anoint yourselves with the oil, for your olive trees shall drop their fruit.

41 You shall beget sons and daughters but shall not enjoy them, for they shall go into captivity. [Fulfilled in Lam. 1:5.]

42 All your trees and the fruit of your ground shall the locust possess. [Fulfilled in Joel 1:4.]

43 The transient (stranger) among you shall mount up higher and higher above you, and you shall come down lower and lower.

44 He shall lend to you, but you shall not lend to him; he shall be the head, and you shall be the tail.

45 All these curses shall come upon you and shall pursue you and overtake you till you are destroyed, because you do not obey the voice of the Lord your God, to keep His commandments and His statutes which He commanded you.

46 They shall be upon you for a sign [of warning to other nations] and for a wonder, and upon your descendants forever.

47 Because you did not serve the Lord your God with joyfulness of [mind and] heart [in gratitude] for the abundance of all [with which He had blessed you],

48 Therefore you shall serve your enemies whom the Lord shall send against you, in hunger and thirst, in nakedness and in want of all things; and He will put a yoke of iron upon your neck until He has destroyed you.

49 The Lord will bring a nation against you from afar, from the end of the earth, as swift as the eagle flies, a nation whose language you shall not understand,

50 A nation of unyielding countenance who will not regard the person of the old or show favor to the young,

51 And shall eat the fruit of your cattle and the fruit of your ground until you are destroyed, who also shall not leave you grain, new wine, oil, the increase of your cattle or the young of your sheep until they have caused you to perish.

52 They shall besiege you in all your towns until your high and fortified walls in which you trusted come down throughout all your land; and they shall besiege you in all your towns throughout all your land which the Lord your God has given you.

53 And you shall eat the fruit of your own body, the flesh of your sons and daughters whom the Lord your God has given you, in the siege and in the [pressing] misery with which your enemies shall distress you. [Fulfilled in II Kings 6:24-29.]

54 The man who is most tender among you and extremely particular *and* well-bred, his eye shall be cruel *and* grudging of food toward his brother and toward the wife of his bosom and toward those of his children still remaining,

55 So that he will not give to any of them any of the flesh of his children which he is eating, because he has nothing left to him in the siege and in the distress with which your enemies shall distress you in all your towns.

56 The most tender and daintily bred woman among you, who would not venture to set the sole of her foot upon the ground because she is so dainty and kind, will grudge to the husband of her bosom, to her son and to her daughter

57 Her afterbirth that comes out from her body and the children whom she shall bear. For she will eat them secretly for want of anything else in the siege and distress with which your enemies shall distress you in your towns.

58 If you will not be watchful to do all the words of this law that are written in this book, that you may [reverently] fear this glorious and fearful name [and presence]—THE LORD YOUR GOD—

59 Then the Lord will bring upon you and your descendants extraordinary strokes and blows, great plagues of long continuance, and grievous sicknesses of long duration.

60 Moreover, He will bring upon you all the diseases of Egypt of which you were afraid, and they shall cling to you.

61 Also every sickness and every affliction which is not written in this Book of the Law the Lord will bring upon you until you are destroyed.

62 And you shall be ⁱleft few in number, whereas you had been as the stars of the heavens for multitude, because you would not obey the voice of the Lord your God.

63 And as the Lord rejoiced over you to do you good and to multiply you, so the Lord will rejoice to bring ruin upon you and to destroy you; and you shall be ʲplucked from the land into which you go to possess.

64 And the Lord shall scatter you among all peoples from one end of the earth to the other; and there you shall [be forced to] serve other gods, of wood and stone, which neither you nor your fathers have known. [Fulfilled in Dan. 3:6.]

65 And among these nations you shall find no ease and there shall be no rest for the sole of your foot; but the Lord will give you there a trembling heart, failing of eyes [from disappointment of hope], fainting of mind, *and* languishing of spirit.

66 Your life shall hang in doubt before you; day and night you shall be worried, and have no assurance of your life.

67 In the morning you shall say, Would that it were evening! and at evening you shall say, Would that it were morning!—because of the anxiety *and* dread of your [minds and] hearts and the sights which you shall see with your [own] eyes.

68 And the Lord shall ᵏbring you into

---

i The informed reader scarcely needs to be reminded of how literally fulfilled have been many of these predictions of evil made against the chosen people because of their idolatry and rebellion against God. Such verses as Deut. 28:25, 32, 33, 36, 38, 41, 42, and 53 foretell historical facts now recorded in Jewish history, both sacred and secular. Here Deut. 28:62 foretells how the Jewish race has been "thinned and kept down," again and again.   j The Roman emperor Hadrian issued a proclamation forbidding any Jews to reside in Judea, or even to approach its confines (James C. Gray and George M. Adams, *Bible Commentary*).   k "Observe the contrast: you came out from bondage by God's high hand, monuments of His grace and power; you shall be carried back into bondage in men's slave ships. This was literally fulfilled under [the Roman emperor] Titus, and also under Hadrian" (James C. Gray and George M. Adams, *Bible Commentary*). The curses . . . were also fulfilled in a terrible manner during the Middle Ages, and are still in a course of fulfillment, though frequently less sensibly felt (J.P. Lange, *A Commentary*). "Here, then, are prophecies delivered above 3,000 years ago and yet being fulfilled in the world at this very time. . . . I must acknowledge that they not only convince but amaze and astonish me beyond expression; they are truly as Moses foretold (Deut. 28:45, 46) they would be, 'a sign and a wonder forever'" (Bishop Thomas Newton, cited by Robert Jamieson, A.R. Fausset and David Brown, *A Commentary*).

Egypt again with ships by the way about which I said to you, You shall never see it again. And there you shall be sold to your enemies as bondmen and bondwomen, but no man shall buy you. [Hos. 8:13.]

29 THESE ARE the words of the covenant which the Lord commanded Moses to make with the Israelites in the land of Moab, besides the covenant which He made with them in Horeb.

2 Moses called to all Israel and said to them, You have seen all that the Lord did before your eyes in the land of Egypt to Pharaoh, to all his servants, and to all his land;

3 The great trials which your eyes saw, the signs, and those great wonders.

4 Yet the Lord has not given you a [mind and] heart to understand and eyes to see and ears to hear, to this day.

5 I have led you forty years in the wilderness; your clothes have not worn out upon you, and your sandals have not worn off your feet.

6 You have not eaten [grain] bread, nor have you drunk wine or strong drink, that you might recognize *and* know [your dependence on Him Who is saying], I am the Lord your God.

7 And when you came to this place, Sihon king of Heshbon and Og king of Bashan came out against us to battle, but we defeated them.

8 We took their land and gave it as an inheritance to the Reubenites, the Gadites, and the half-tribe of the Manassites.

9 Therefore keep the words of this covenant and do them, that you may deal wisely *and* prosper in all that you do.

10 All of you stand today before the Lord your God—your heads, your tribes, your elders, and your officers, even all the men of Israel,

11 Your little ones, your wives, and the stranger *and* sojourner in your camp, from the hewer of your wood to the drawer of your water—

12 That you may enter into the covenant of the Lord your God, and into His oath which He makes with you today,

13 That He may establish you this day as a people for Himself, and that He may be to you a God as He said to you and as He swore to your fathers, Abraham, Isaac, and Jacob.

14 It is not with you only that I make this sworn covenant

15 But with future Israelites who do not stand here with us today before the Lord our God, as well as with those who are here with us this day.

16 You know how we lived in the land of Egypt and how we came through the midst of the nations you crossed.

17 And you have seen their abominations and their idols of wood and stone, of silver and gold, which were among them.

18 Beware lest there should be among you a man or woman, or family or tribe, whose [mind and] heart turns away this day from the Lord our God to go and serve the gods of these nations; lest there should be among you a [poisonous] root that bears gall and wormwood,

19 And lest, when he hears the words of this curse *and* oath, he flatters *and* congratulates himself in his [mind and] heart, saying, I shall have peace *and* safety, 'though I walk in the stubbornness of my [mind and] heart

1 It is on the strength of the Lord's oath to be Israel's God and so to protect them that this Israelite flatters himself into thinking he is secure, no matter how he may behave. In the history of religion such a delusion has been lamentably frequent, and persons depending upon the unlimited protection of election have presumed on this and recklessly indulged in evil (*The Cambridge Bible*). The Bible emphasizes the "security of the saints," but it is equally emphatic concerning the insecurity of those in conscious and continued indifference to God (Ezek. 3:20; 18:24, 26; Gal. 6:8; James 1:21; II Pet. 1:10, 11; Rev. 22:14).

[bringing down a hurricane of destruction] and sweep away the watered land with the dry.

20 The Lord will not pardon him, but then the anger of the Lord and His jealousy will smoke against that man, and all the curses that are written in this book shall settle on him; the Lord will blot out his very name from under the heavens.

21 And the Lord will single him out for ruin *and* destruction from all the tribes of Israel, according to all the curses of the covenant that are written in this Book of the Law,

22 So that the next generation, your children who rise up after you, and the foreigner who shall come from a distant land, shall say, when they see the plagues of this land and the diseases with which the Lord has made it sick—

23 The whole land is brimstone and salt and a burned waste, not sown or bearing anything, where no grass can take root, like the overthrow of Sodom and Gomorrah with Admah and Zeboiim, which the Lord overthrew in His anger and wrath—

24 Even all the nations shall say, Why has the Lord done thus to this land? What does the heat of this great anger mean?

25 Then men shall say, Because they forsook the covenant of the Lord, the God of their fathers, which He made with them when He brought them forth out of the land of Egypt.

26 For they went and served other gods and worshiped them, gods they knew not and that He had not given to them.

27 So the anger of the Lord was kindled against this land, bringing upon it all the curses that are written in this book.

28 And the Lord rooted them out of their land in anger and in wrath and in great indignation and cast them into another land, as it is this day.

29 The secret things belong unto the Lord our God, but the things which are revealed belong to us and to our children forever, that we may do all of the words of this law.

30 AND WHEN all these things have come upon you, the blessings and the curses which I have set before you, and you shall call them to mind among all the nations where the Lord your God has driven you,

2 And shall return to the Lord your God and obey His voice according to all that I command you today, you and your children, with all your [mind and] heart and with all your being,

life point

Deuteronomy 30:2 encourages us to obey God wholeheartedly. To whatever degree we obey God, that's the measure of our love for Him. Our love for Jesus grows as we obey Him.

3 Then the Lord your God will restore your fortunes and have compassion upon you and will gather you again from all the nations where He has scattered you.

4 Even if any of your dispersed are in the uttermost parts of the heavens, from there the Lord your God will gather you and from there will He bring you.

5 And the Lord your God will bring you into the land which your fathers possessed, and you shall possess it; and He will do you good and multiply you above your fathers.

6 And the Lord your God will circumcise your hearts and the hearts of your descendants, to love the Lord your God with all your [mind and] heart and with all your being, that you may live.

7 And the Lord your God will put all these curses upon your enemies and

on those who hate you, who persecute you.

8 And you shall return and obey the voice of the Lord and do all His commandments which I command you today.

9 And the Lord your God will make you abundantly prosperous in every work of your hand, in the fruit of your body, of your cattle, of your land, for good; for the Lord will again delight in prospering you, as He took delight in your fathers,

10 If you obey the voice of the Lord your God, to keep His commandments and His statutes which are written in this Book of the Law, and if you turn to the Lord your God with all your [mind and] heart and with all your being.

11 For this commandment which I command you this day is not too difficult for you, nor is it far off.

12 It is not [a secret laid up] in heaven, that you should say, Who shall go up for us to heaven and bring it to us, that we may hear and do it?

13 Neither is it beyond the sea, that you should say, Who shall go over the sea for us and bring it to us, that we may hear and do it?

14 But the word is very near you, in your mouth and in your mind *and* in your heart, so that you can do it.

15 See, I have set before you this day life and good, and death and evil.

16 [If you obey the commandments of the Lord your God which] I command you today, to love the Lord your God, to walk in His ways, and to keep His commandments and His statutes and His ordinances, then you shall live and multiply, and the Lord your

God will bless you in the land into which you go to possess.

17 But if your [mind and] heart turn away and you will not hear, but are drawn away to worship other gods and serve them,

18 I declare to you today that you shall surely perish, and you shall not live long in the land which you pass over the Jordan to enter and possess.

19 I call heaven and earth to witness this day against you that I have set before you life and death, the blessings and the curses; therefore choose life, that you and your descendants may live

20 And may love the Lord your God, obey His voice, and cling to Him. For He is your life and the length of your days, that you may dwell in the land which the Lord swore to give to your fathers, to Abraham, Isaac, and Jacob.

31 AND MOSES went on speaking these words to all Israel:

2 And he said to them, I am 120 years old this day; I can no more go out and come in. And the Lord has said to me, You shall not go over this Jordan.

3 The Lord your God will Himself go over before you, and He will destroy these nations from before you, and you shall dispossess them. And Joshua shall go over before you, as the Lord has said.

4 And the Lord will do to them as He did to Sihon and Og, the kings of the Amorites, and to their land, when He destroyed them.

5 And the Lord will give them over to you, and you shall do to them

speak the Word

Thank You, God, that as I live in obedience to You, I will have abundance in all the work of my hands, in my family, and in everything that concerns me.
ADAPTED FROM DEUTERONOMY **30:9**

choose life

Thousands of thoughts are presented to our minds every day, and we must allow our minds to be renewed after the Spirit and not after the flesh. Our carnal (worldly, fleshly) minds have had so much practice operating freely that we can think wrong thoughts without much effort at all. On the other hand, we have to purposely choose to think right thoughts. After we have finally decided to be like-minded with God, then we will need to *choose* and *continue to choose* right thoughts.

When we begin to feel that the battle of the mind is just too difficult and that we are not going to make it, we must cast down that negative kind of thinking. We must choose to think that we are going to make it and decide not to quit. When bombarded with doubts and fears, we need to take a stand and say: "I will never give up! God is on my side. He loves me, and He is helping me!"

You and I will have many choices to make throughout our lives. In Deuteronomy 30:19, the Lord told His people that He had set before them life and death and urged them to choose life. Proverbs 18:21 also tells us we can choose life or death. It says, "Death and life are in the power of the tongue, and they who indulge in it shall eat the fruit of it [for death or life]."

Our thoughts become our words. Therefore, it is vitally important that we *choose* life-giving thoughts.

according to all the commandments which I have commanded you.

6 Be strong, courageous, *and* firm; fear not nor be in terror before them, for it is the Lord your God Who goes with you; He will not fail you or forsake you.

7 And Moses called to Joshua and

life point

Sometimes we think we have to wait until we are no longer afraid before we try to do something. But we probably will not accomplish much for God, for others, or even for ourselves if we wait until all our fear is gone. We need to face our fear with courage and do some things despite our fear. We must learn to "do it afraid." God promises us that He will be with us (see Deuteronomy 31:6).

said to him in the sight of all Israel, Be strong, courageous, *and* firm, for you shall go with this people into the land which the Lord has sworn to their fathers to give them, and you shall cause them to possess it.

8 It is the Lord Who goes before you; He will [march] with you; He will not fail you *or* let you go or forsake you; [let there be no cowardice or flinching, but] fear not, neither become broken [in spirit—depressed, dismayed, and unnerved with alarm].

9 And Moses wrote this law and delivered it to the Levitical priests, who carried the ark of the covenant of the Lord, and to all the elders of Israel.

10 And Moses commanded them, At the end of every seven years, at the set time of the year of release [of debtors from their debts], at the Feast of Booths,

God will go with you

In Deuteronomy 31:6, Moses told the Israelites to be strong, courageous, and firm. Do you know what it means to be firm? It means to stick to what you know is right without letting anything or anyone talk you out of it.

Moses also told Joshua that he was to be strong, courageous, and firm because he was to lead the people into the land that the Lord had given them. He assured him that the Lord would never fail him or forsake him and that *God would go with him* to lead him to victory. God makes that same promise to you and me today.

It is comforting to know that everywhere we go, God has been before us to prepare the way. Our ministry does many conferences, and prior to our conferences in other states or countries, someone always goes ahead of us to get things ready. They make sure all the arrangements are properly made before Dave and I arrive. For example, we once had a conference planned in another part of the world. When our employee arrived ahead of us, he realized that the arena we had planned to use was in an inaccessible part of the city. The traffic would be heavy before and after meetings, there was only one road in and one road out, and it could take as long as four hours for people to get through. We were glad we had sent him months in advance because he was able to change the meeting place and save us a lot of time.

Also, at least two days before we arrive in a city, a team scouts out the arrangements and takes care of details so that when we arrive we can wholly focus on ministering to the people. This makes our ministry much more fruitful. Knowing that someone has gone before me comforts me; it gives me confidence. Likewise, knowing that God has gone before me in every situation of my life gives me great confidence, and I am free to live without fear.

Whatever your situation, know that God promises to go with you. If you have a court case coming up, you need to understand that God has already gone ahead of you into the court before you arrive. Or, if you need to confront your employer about some issue at work, believe what the Word says. Trust God that He will give you favor and give you the right words to speak in loving ways when the time comes.

Whenever you go, whatever your circumstances, ask God to go before you and prepare the way. He will do it—then all you have to do is follow.

11 When all Israel comes to appear before the Lord your God in the place which He chooses [for His sanctuary], you shall read this law before all Israel in their hearing.
12 Assemble the people—men, women, and children, and the stranger *and* the sojourner within your towns—that they may hear and learn [reverently] to fear the Lord your God and be watchful to do all the words of this law,

13 And that their children, who have not known it, may hear and learn [reverently] to fear the Lord your God as long as you live in the land which you go over the Jordan to possess.

14 And the Lord said to Moses, Behold, your days are nearing when you must die. Call Joshua and present yourselves at the Tent of Meeting, that I may give him his charge. And Moses and Joshua went and presented themselves at the Tent of Meeting.

15 And the Lord appeared in the Tent in a pillar of cloud, and the pillar of cloud stood over the door of the Tent.

16 And the Lord said to Moses, Behold, you shall sleep with your fathers, and this people will rise up and play the harlot after the strange gods of the land where they go to be among them; and they will forsake Me and break My covenant which I have made with them.

17 Then My anger will be kindled against them in that day, and I will forsake them and hide My face from them. And they shall be devoured, and many evils and troubles shall befall them, so that they will say in that day, Have not these evils come upon us because our God is not among us?

18 And I will surely hide My face in that day because of all the evil which they have done in turning to other gods.

19 And now write this song for yourselves and teach it to the Israelites; put it in their mouths, that this song may be a witness for Me against the Israelites.

20 For when I have brought them into the land which I swore to their fathers, a land flowing with milk and honey, and they have eaten and filled themselves and become fat, then they will turn to other gods and serve them, and despise *and* scorn Me and break My covenant.

21 And when many evils and troubles have befallen them, this [sacred] song will confront them as a witness, for it will never be forgotten from the mouths of their descendants. For I know their strong desire *and* the purposes which they are forming even now, before I have brought them into the land which I swore to give them.

22 Moses wrote this song the same day and taught it to the Israelites. [Deut. 32:1-43.]

23 And [the Lord] charged Joshua son of Nun, Be strong and courageous *and* firm, for you shall bring the Israelites into the land which I swore to give them, and I will be with you.

24 And when Moses had finished writing the words of this law in a book to the very end,

25 He commanded the Levites who carried the ark of the covenant of the Lord,

26 Take this Book of the Law and put it by the side of the ark of the covenant of the Lord your God, that it may be there for a witness against you.

27 For I know your rebellion and stubbornness; behold, while I am yet alive with you today, you have been rebellious against the Lord; and how much more after my death!

28 Gather to me all the elders of your tribes and your officers, that I may speak these words in their ears and call heaven and earth to witness against them.

29 For I know that after my death you will utterly corrupt yourselves and turn aside from the way which I have commanded you; and evil will befall you in the latter days because you will do what is evil in the sight of the Lord, to provoke Him to anger through the work of your hands.

30 And Moses spoke in the hearing of all the congregation of Israel the words of this song until they were ended:

32

GIVE EAR, O heavens, and I [Moses] will speak; and let the earth hear the words of my mouth.

2 My message shall drop as the rain, my speech shall distil as the dew, as the light rain upon the tender grass, and as the showers upon the herb.

3 For I will proclaim the name [and presence] of the Lord Concede *and* ascribe greatness to our God.

4 He is the Rock, His work is perfect, for all His ways are law *and* justice. A God of faithfulness without breach *or* deviation, just and right is He.

life point

God is our Rock (see Deuteronomy 32:4) and place of refuge. He is solid, stable, steadfast, dependable, always there, always the same, always good and loving, always kind and merciful. He is great and unfailing, faithful and just, perfect and right in all His doings! We may have emotional ups and downs as we encounter the influences of negative circumstances and feelings. But the Lord changes not, and He cannot be moved by circumstances that would flatten us. We can trust our Rock because He does not waver in His faithfulness to us. We can learn to respond to life as He does as we allow ourselves to be molded and transformed into His image. He is our Rock, but He is also our Example. I encourage you to be like He is—faithful and steadfast.

5 They [Israel] have spoiled themselves. They are not sons to Him, and that is their blemish—a perverse and crooked generation!

6 Do you thus repay the Lord, you foolish and senseless people? Is not He your Father Who acquired you for His own, Who made and established you [as a nation]?

7 Remember the days of old; consider the years of many generations. Ask your father and he will show you, your elders, and they will tell you.

8 When the Most High gave to the nations their inheritance, when He separated the children of men, He set the bounds of the peoples according to the number of the Israelites.

9 For the Lord's portion is His people; Jacob (Israel) is the lot of His inheritance.

10 He found him in a desert land, in the howling void of the wilderness; He kept circling around him, He scanned him [penetratingly], He kept him as the pupil of His eye.

11 As an eagle that stirs up her nest, that flutters over her young, He spread abroad His wings and He took them, He bore them on His pinions. [Luke 13:34.]

12 So the Lord alone led him; there was no foreign god with Him.

13 He made Israel ride on the high places of the earth, and he ate the increase of the field; and He made him suck honey out of the rock and oil out of the flinty rock,

14 Butter *and* curds of the herd and milk of the flock, with fat of lambs, and rams of the breed of Bashan, and he-goats, with the finest of the wheat; and you drank wine of the blood of the grape.

15 But Jeshurun (Israel) grew fat and kicked. You became fat, you grew thick, you were gorged *and* sleek! Then he forsook God Who made him and forsook *and* despised the Rock of his salvation.

16 They provoked Him to jealousy with strange gods, with abominations they provoked Him to anger.

17 They sacrificed to demons, not to God—to gods whom they knew not, to new gods lately come up, whom your fathers never knew or feared.

18 Of the Rock Who bore you you were unmindful; you forgot the God Who travailed in your birth.

19 And the Lord saw it and He spurned *and* rejected them, out of indignation with His sons and His daughters.

20 And He said, I will hide My face from them, I will see what their end will be; for they are a perverse generation, children in whom is no faithfulness.

21 They have moved Me to jealousy with what is not God; they have angered Me with their idols. So I will move them to jealousy with those who are not a people; I will anger them with a foolish nation.

22 For a fire is kindled by My anger, and it burns to the depths of Sheol, devours the earth with its increase, and sets on fire the foundations of the mountains.

23 And I will heap evils upon them; I will spend My arrows upon them.

24 They shall be wasted with hunger and devoured with burning heat and poisonous pestilence; and the teeth of beasts will I send against them, with the poison of crawling things of the dust.

25 From without the sword shall bereave, and in the chambers shall be terror, destroying both young man and virgin, the sucking child with the man of gray hairs.

26 I said, I would scatter them afar and I would have made the remembrance of them to cease from among men,

27 Had I not feared the provocation of the foe, lest their enemies misconstrue it and lest they should say, Our own hand has prevailed; all this was not the work of the Lord.

28 For they are a nation void of counsel, and there is no understanding in them.

29 O that they were wise and would see through this [present triumph] to their ultimate fate!

30 How could one have chased a thousand, and two put ten thousand to flight, except their Rock had sold them, and the Lord had delivered them up?

31 For their rock is not like our Rock, even our enemies themselves judge this.

32 For their vine comes from the vine of Sodom and from the fields of Gomorrah; their grapes are grapes of [poisonous] gall, their clusters are bitter.

33 Their wine is the [furious] venom of serpents, and the pitiless poison of vipers.

34 Is not this laid up in store with Me, sealed up in My treasuries?

35 Vengeance is Mine, and recompense, in the time when their foot shall slide; for the day of their disaster is at hand and their doom comes speedily.

36 For the Lord will revoke sentence for His people and relent for His servants' sake when He sees that their power is gone and none remains, whether bond or free.

37 And He will say, Where are their gods, the rock in which they took refuge,

38 Who ate the fat of their sacrifices and drank the wine of their drink offering? Let them rise up and help you, let them be your protection!

39 See now that I, I am He, and there is no god beside Me; I kill and I make alive, I wound and I heal, and there is none who can deliver out of My hand.

40 For I lift up My hand to heaven and swear, As I live forever,

41 If I whet My lightning sword and My hand takes hold on judgment, I will wreak vengeance on My foes and recompense those who hate Me.

42 I will make My arrows drunk with blood, and My sword shall devour flesh, with the blood of the slain and the captives, from the long-haired heads of the foe.

43 Rejoice [with] His people, O you nations, for He avenges the blood of His servants, and vengeance He inflicts on His foes and clears guilt from the land of His people.

44 And Moses came and spoke all the words of this song in the ears of the people, he and Hoshea (Joshua) son of Nun.

45 And when Moses had finished speaking all these words to all Israel,

46 He said to them, Set your [minds and] hearts on all the words which I command you this day, that you may command them to your children, that they may be watchful to do all the words of this law.

47 For it is not an empty *and* worthless trifle for you; it is your [very] life. By it you shall live long in the land which you are going over the Jordan to possess.

48 And the Lord said to Moses that same day,

49 Get up into this mountain of the Abarim, Mount Nebo, which is in the land of Moab, opposite Jericho, and look at the land of Canaan which I give to the Israelites for a possession.

50 And die on the mountain which you ascend and be gathered to your people, as Aaron your brother died on Mount Hor and was gathered to his people,

51 Because you broke faith with Me in the midst of the Israelites at the waters of Meribah-kadesh in the Wilderness of Zin and because you did not set Me apart as holy in the midst of the Israelites.

52 For you shall see the land opposite you at a distance, but you shall not go there, into the land which I give the Israelites.

33 THIS IS the blessing with which Moses the man of God blessed the Israelites before his death.

2 He said, The Lord came from Sinai and beamed upon us from Seir; He flashed forth from Mount Paran, from among ten thousands of holy ones, a flaming fire, a law, at His right hand.

3 Yes, He loves [the tribes] His people; all those consecrated to Him are in Your hand. They followed in Your steps; they [accepted Your word and] received direction from You,

4 When Moses commanded us a law, as a possession for the assembly of Jacob.

5 [The Lord] was King in Jeshurun (Israel) when the heads of the people were gathered, all the tribes of Israel together.

6 Let [the tribe of] Reuben live and not die out, but ᵐlet his men be few.

7 And this he [Moses] said of Judah:

speak the Word

Thank You, God, that You love me, that You are holding me in Your hand, that I can follow You and receive direction for my life from You.
ADAPTED FROM DEUTERONOMY 33:3

m The earlier Bible translators could not believe that Moses meant to say of Reuben, "let his men be few," so they put "not" in italics: "let *not* his men be few." But Reuben had committed a grave offense (Gen. 49:3, 4) which cancelled his birthright, and God meant exactly what He directed Moses to say, as continuous fulfillment of the prophecy proves. "In Judg. 5:16 the tribe [of Reuben] is scorned for its failure to join the others against the Canaanites, and except for I Chron. 5:3-20 it does not again appear in Israel's history. Nor does Misha of Moab, ninth century, BC, name it" (*The Cambridge Bible*). Furthermore, by AD 1951 no Jew was permitted to enter the territory once allotted to the tribe of Reuben. "The whole territory, which is . . . quite capable of cultivation, is now deserted by its settled inhabitants" (John D. Davis, *A Dictionary of the Bible*). It was then being restored not by Israelites but by Arabs.

Hear, O Lord, the voice of Judah, and bring him to his people! With his hands he contended for himself; but may You be a help against his enemies.

8 And of Levi he said: Your Thummim and Your Urim [by which the priest sought God's will for the nation] are for Your pious one [Aaron on behalf of the tribe], whom You tried *and* proved at Massah, with whom You contended at the waters of Meribah; [Num. 20:1-13.]

9 [Aaron] who ⁿsaid of his father and mother, I do not regard them; nor did he acknowledge his brothers or openly recognize his own children. For the priests observed Your word and kept Your covenant [as to their limitations].

10 [The priests] shall teach Jacob Your ordinances and Israel Your law. They shall put incense before You and whole burnt offerings upon Your altar.

11 Bless, O Lord, [Levi's] substance, and accept the work of his hands; crush the loins of his adversaries, and of those who hate him, that they arise no more.

12 Of Benjamin he said: The beloved of the Lord shall ᵒdwell in safety by Him; He covers him all the day long,

and makes His dwelling between his shoulders.

13 And of Joseph he said: Blessed by the Lord be his land, with the precious gifts of heaven from the dew and from the deep that couches beneath,

14 With the precious things of the fruits of the sun and with the precious yield of the months,

15 With the chief products of the ancient mountains and with the precious things of the everlasting hills,

16 With the precious things of the earth and its fullness and the favor *and* goodwill of Him Who dwelt in the bush. Let these blessings come upon the head of Joseph, upon the crown of the head of him who was separate *and* prince among his brothers. [Exod. 3:4.]

17 Like a firstling young bull his majesty is, and his horns like the horns of the wild ox; with them he shall push the peoples, all of them, to the ends of the earth. And they are the ten thousands of Ephraim, and they are the thousands of Manasseh.

18 And of Zebulun he said: ᵖRejoice, Zebulun, in your interests abroad, and you, Issachar, in your tents [at home].

19 They shall call the people unto Mount [Carmel]; there they shall offer sacrifices of righteousness, for �q they

speak the Word

I pray, God, that You will bless everything I have, as You did for Levi, and that You will accept the work of my hands.
ADAPTED FROM DEUTERONOMY 33:11

n The law required that the high priest act just as impartially when one of his immediate family died, as if the departed were no kin to him (Lev. 21:10-12). This throws light on Christ's attitude toward His mother and brothers in Matt. 12:46-50 (see also Heb. 3:1-3; 8:1-6).   **o** The temple in Jerusalem was located almost between the ridges of the territory of Benjamin, suggesting "between his shoulders" (see also Josh. 15:8). Moses sees it as a symbol of the Lord's presence covering Benjamin continually.   **p** Not until 1934 was this prophecy notably in process of fulfillment, when Haifa's bay became one of the great harbors of the Mediterranean Sea, with commerce affecting the whole world.   **q** The great oil pipeline path across Palestine was first opened in 1935. Until then this prophecy fell far short of fulfillment. But 3,400 years before, Moses sent out the inspired headlines, "Zebulun . . . Issachar . . . shall suck the abundance of the seas, and the treasures hid in the sand." Our omnipotent God was "declaring the end *and* the result from the beginning, and from ancient times the things that are not yet done, saying, My counsel shall stand" (Isa. 46:10).

shall suck the abundance of the seas and the treasures hid in the sand.

20 And of Gad he said: Blessed is He Who enlarges Gad! Gad lurks like a lioness, and tears the arm, yes, the crown of the head.

21 He selected the best land for himself, for there was the leader's portion reserved; yet he came with the chiefs of the nation, and the righteous will of the Lord he performed, and His ordinances with Israel. [Num. 32:29-33.]

22 Of Dan he said: Dan is a lion's whelp that leaps forth from Bashan.

23 Of Naphtali he said: O Naphtali, ʳsatisfied with favor and full of the blessing of the Lord, possess the Sea [of Galilee] and [its warm, sunny climate like] the south.

24 Of Asher he said: Blessed above sons is Asher; let him be acceptable to his brothers, and ˢlet him dip his foot in oil.

25 Your castles and strongholds shall have bars of iron and bronze, and as your day, so shall your strength, your rest and security, be.

26 There is none like God, O Jeshurun [Israel], Who rides through the heavens to your help and in His majestic glory through the skies.

27 The eternal God is your refuge and dwelling place, and underneath are the everlasting arms; He drove the enemy before you and thrust them out, saying, Destroy!

28 And Israel dwells in safety, the fountain of Jacob alone in a land of grain and new wine; yes, His heavens drop dew.

29 Happy are you, O Israel, and blessing is yours! Who is like you, a

life point

It is comforting to know that underneath us are God's everlasting arms (see Deuteronomy 33:27). No matter what our circumstances, His loving arms come down to where we are and lift us up. As we make the conscious decision to lean on the arm of the Lord and no longer lean on the arm of the flesh, we will experience the manifest presence of God.

people saved by the Lord, the Shield of your help, the Sword that exalts you! Your enemies shall come fawning *and* cringing, *and* submit feigned obedience to you, and you shall march on their high places.

34 AND MOSES went up from the plains of Moab to Mount Nebo, to the top of Pisgah, that is opposite Jericho. And the Lord showed him all the land—from Gilead to Dan,

2 And all Naphtali, and the land of Ephraim and Manasseh, and all the land of Judah to the western [Mediterranean] sea,

3 And the South (the Negeb) and the plain, that is, the Valley of Jericho, the City of Palm Trees, as far as Zoar.

4 And the Lord said to him, This is the land which I swore to Abraham, Isaac, and Jacob, saying, I will give it to your descendants. I have let you see it with your eyes, but you shall not go over there.

r For many centuries much of the territory of upper Naphtali was little more than a miasmic swamp, unfit for man or beast. But when the Jews returned to Palestine, they drained and redeemed the area, and by 1940 it was dotted over with thriving colonies, as Moses had foretold, "satisfied with favor and full of the blessing of the Lord." s The maps of the territory of Asher sometimes suggest the shape of the sole of a foot, sometimes that of a leg and foot; but in either case the Great International Iraq-Petroleum Enterprise, opened in 1935, crossed the area just at the toe of Asher's "foot." Oil brought nearly 1,000 miles across the sands from Mesopotamia began pouring through pipes into the Haifa harbor, a million gallons of oil a day. Jacob had prophesied about Asher, " . . . his bread *shall be* fat" (Gen. 49:20 KJV), and here Moses says of Asher, "Let him dip his foot in oil"!

5 So Moses the servant of the Lord died there in the land of Moab, according to the word of the Lord,

6 And He buried him in the valley of the land of Moab opposite Beth-peor, but no man knows where his tomb is to this day.

7 Moses was 120 years old when he died; his eye was not dim nor his natural force abated. [Deut. 31:2.]

8 And the Israelites wept for Moses in the plains of Moab thirty days; then the days of weeping and mourning for Moses were ended.

9 And Joshua son of Nun was full of the spirit of wisdom, for Moses had laid his hands upon him; so the Israelites listened to him and did as the Lord commanded Moses.

10 And there arose not a prophet since in Israel like Moses, whom the Lord knew face to face,

11 [None equal to him] in all the signs and wonders which the Lord sent him to do in the land of Egypt—to Pharaoh and to all his servants and to all his land,

12 And in all the mighty power and all the great and terrible deeds which Moses wrought in the sight of all Israel.

speak the Word

Lord, cause me to be like Joshua, full of the spirit of wisdom.
ADAPTED FROM DEUTERONOMY 34:9

Joshua

Author:
Uncertain; attributed to Joshua

Date:
1400 BC–1375 BC

Everyday Life Principles:
We may have to fight for the things God promises us.

Following God requires boldness and brings blessing.

God doesn't tell us *not to feel* fear; He tells us *not to give in* to it.

The book of Joshua teaches us much about the kind of courage we need if we are going to fight for God's promises and enjoy the blessings He has for us. God had already given the Israelites the Promised Land, but they did have to fight for possession of it. They had to believe that God would help them conquer the enemies who stood between them and the Promised Land, and they had to trust that He would miraculously get them across the strong, swift current of the Jordan River when it was so high that it was overflowing its banks. Not only did they have enemies to fight on their way to the Promised Land, they also had enemies to fight once they got there.

As their leader, Joshua not only needed to be courageous himself; he also needed to inspire courage in the people. When God spoke to him to "fear not," He wasn't telling him not to feel fear; He was telling him not to let fear hold him back. In other words, He was saying to Joshua, "Do it afraid." And Joshua did.

I pray that you, like Joshua, will be strong and courageous in your everyday life and that you will inspire others to be bold as well. Do not give in to fear, but take action in spite of it. Press forward with boldness into everything God has for you, and do not allow fear to rob you of any of the blessings God wants to give you.

1 AFTER THE death of Moses the servant of the Lord, the Lord said to Joshua son of Nun, Moses' minister, [Deut. 34:4-8.]

2 Moses My servant is dead. So now arise [take his place], go over this Jordan, you and all this people, into the land which I am giving to them, the Israelites.

3 Every place upon which the sole of your foot shall tread, that have I given to you, as I promised Moses.

life point

"Moses My servant is dead" (Joshua 1:2). With those words plainly said, God opened a new chapter in Joshua's life. God told Joshua that he was to accept a new responsibility—to lead the people across the Jordan into the Promised Land. We also must be willing to take responsibility as we go forward to claim our spiritual inheritance. Every blessing God gives us comes with a measure of responsibility, and we need to take that responsibility seriously.

4 From the wilderness and this Lebanon to the great river Euphrates—all the land of the [a]Hittites [Canaan]—and to the Great [Mediterranean] Sea on the west shall be your territory.

5 No man shall be able to stand before you all the days of your life. As I was with Moses, so I will be with you; I will not fail you or forsake you.

6 Be strong (confident) and of good courage, for you shall cause this people to inherit the land which I swore to their fathers to give them.

7 Only you be strong and very courageous, that you may do according to all the law which Moses My servant commanded you. Turn not from it to the right hand or to the left, that you may prosper wherever you go.

8 This Book of the Law shall not depart out of your mouth, but you shall meditate on it day and night, that you may observe *and* do according to all that is written in it. For then you shall make your way prosperous, and then you shall deal wisely *and* have good [b]success.

life point

How much time do you spend thinking about the Word of God? The Bible says that if you want to find wise answers to your problems and be successful and prosperous in all your dealings, you need to meditate on the Word of God day and night (see Joshua 1:8).

For most of my life, I did not think about what I was thinking about. I simply thought whatever crossed my mind because I did not know that Satan could inject thoughts into my brain. Most of my thoughts were either lies from Satan or just plain nonsense—things that wasted my time because they were not truly important. The devil was controlling my life because he was controlling my thoughts. Meditate on God's Word and you can push back the enemy. When you fill your mind with God's truth, you will find that your thoughts are thoughts of truth, freedom, victory, and peace.

---

a Although the Hittites are mentioned forty-eight times in the Bible, some critics long refused to accept the possibility, or at least the probability, of the importance of such an ancient people. But archaeological discoveries of the twentieth century have confirmed the importance of the Hittites beyond all question. For instance, G. A. Barton in *Archaeology and the Bible* records the existence of an archive of clay tablets containing among other things a military treaty made by the Egyptians and the Hittites nearly thirteen centuries before the birth of Christ. **b** This is the only place in the early English versions where the word "success" is found. The secret of success is given in verses 5 through

leave the past behind

After Moses' death, the law allowed the Israelites thirty days to mourn. After those days were completed, God told Joshua it was time for him to take his new position (see Joshua 1:2). It was time to start moving toward new things. Joshua would miss Moses, but he knew he had to obey God and move on. There is a proper time for mourning those things that we have lost or that have come to an end. But, ultimately, we must make a choice to start living and making progress again. We all have a past, but thank God we all have a future—and a good one, according to His Word (see Jeremiah 29:11).

Because Moses had done many things for Joshua and the Israelites before he died, they needed to learn how to handle new responsibilities after he died. They may not have felt prepared to step out into new things, but God knew they were ready. It is actually a good thing when we do not "feel" ready, because then we are more likely to totally lean on God. If we feel self-sufficient, God can't really use us.

New things always seem frightening, but soon they will become old things, and God will have another "new thing" on the horizon of our lives. We need to grow accustomed to stepping out into new things. The more we do, the more we realize that we don't have to be comfortable to be obedient. In order to take hold of a new thing, we must let go of the old and allow ourselves time to get acquainted with the new. I believe that when God reminded Joshua that Moses was dead, He was encouraging him to let go of the past and press on. I encourage you to do the same.

Remember the good things from your past, but do not get stuck there. God is always doing a new thing! When God called Abraham to a new place, he did not even think about where he was to go. He simply trusted God because he knew God was faithful. Do not be afraid to release and walk away from what God is finished with; He has wonderful new things waiting for you!

9 Have not I commanded you? Be strong, vigorous, and very courageous. Be not afraid, neither be dismayed, for the Lord your God is with you wherever you go.
10 Then Joshua commanded the officers of the people, saying,
11 Pass through the camp and command the people, Prepare your provisions, for within three days you shall pass over this Jordan to go in to take possession of the land which the Lord your God is giving you to possess.
12 And to the Reubenites, the Gadites, and the half-tribe of Manasseh, Joshua said,
13 Remember what Moses the servant of the Lord commanded you, saying, The Lord your God is giving you [of these two and a half tribes a place of] rest and will give you this land [east of the Jordan].
14 Your wives, your little ones, and

9. Joshua accepted Moses' place of leadership without misgivings. God's will for him was his will, and he did not hesitate. To go "all out" for God was already habitual with him; it is the unfailing prerequisite of eternal success (Deut. 6:3-5; Ps. 1:1-3; Luke 10:25-28).

your cattle shall dwell in the land which Moses gave you on this side of the Jordan, but all your mighty men of valor shall pass on before your brethren [of the other tribes] armed, and help them [possess their land]

15 Until the Lord gives your brethren rest, as He has given you, and they also possess the land the Lord your God is giving them. Then you shall return to the land of your possession and possess it, the land Moses the Lord's servant gave you on the sunrise side of the Jordan.

16 They answered Joshua, All you command us we will do, and wherever you send us we will go.

17 As we hearkened to Moses in all things, so will we hearken to you; only may the Lord your God be with you as He was with Moses.

18 Whoever rebels against your commandment and will not hearken to all you command him shall be put to death. Only be strong, vigorous, *and* of good courage.

2 JOSHUA SON of Nun sent two men secretly from Shittim as scouts, saying, Go, view the land, especially Jericho. And they went and came to the house of a harlot named Rahab and lodged there.

2 It was told the king of Jericho,

passing the faithfulness test

Moses was faithful to God's people during the forty years they wandered in the wilderness. Time and time again, he successfully passed the "faithfulness test." But God had spent many years preparing Moses to lead the people out of bondage. On the back side of the desert, God had taught him how to be faithful (see Exodus 2:23—3:1). Likewise, Joshua had learned to be faithful throughout the years and had loyally served under Moses. When God chose Joshua to lead Israel after Moses' death, He knew Joshua would be a faithful leader because he had been trustworthy in the past. Joshua is an excellent example of a faithful person, and his life reminds us that God rewards faithfulness.

God works through and blesses faithful people—people who are faithful in the wilderness (in times of testing) as well as in the Promised Land (in times of blessing). Being faithful means being devoted, supportive, and loyal. Faithful people are worthy of trust or belief; they are reliable, consistent, constant, and steadfast. They will stay wherever God places them and be true to those God has given them to work with.

If we want to exercise authority, we must first learn to come under authority and stay wherever God has placed us until He moves us. Like Joshua, we must respect and be obedient to those in authority over us. We must do the right thing simply because it is right, even though we may never understand the "*why*" of every situation—which is a real test of our faithfulness and obedience. We must be faithful to stay where God has placed us and perhaps under the leadership of an authority figure we do not particularly like.

Do you want to have authority and be respected? Then learn to be reliable and loyal. God loves to reward the faithful.

life point

I love the fact that Rahab was able to get past her past. Before she met the two Israelite spies, she had worked as a prostitute (the Bible uses the word *harlot*) (see Joshua 2:1). But by the end of her life, she too had come to love the God of Israel and is mentioned as an ancestor of Jesus Christ (see Matthew 1:5). No matter how bad your past is, always know that God has a new beginning for you. Like Rahab, you may have a past, but you also have a future. You can get past your past!

Behold, there came men in here tonight of the Israelites to search out the country.

3 And the king of Jericho sent to Rahab, saying, Bring forth the men who have come to you, who entered your house, for they have come to search out the land.

4 But the woman had taken the two men and hidden them. So she said, Yes, two men came to me, but I did not know from where they had come.

5 And at gate closing time, after dark, the men went out. Where they went I do not know. Pursue them quickly, for you will overtake them.

6 But she had brought them up to the roof and hidden them under the stalks of flax which she had laid in order there.

7 So the men pursued them to the Jordan as far as the fords. As soon as the pursuers had gone, the city's gate was shut.

8 Before the two men had lain down, Rahab came up to them on the roof,

9 And she said to the men, I know that the Lord has given you the land and that your terror is fallen upon us and that all the inhabitants of the land faint because of you.

10 For we have heard how the Lord dried up the water of the Red Sea for you when you came out of Egypt, and what you did to the two kings of the Amorites who were on the [east] side of the Jordan, Sihon and Og, whom you utterly destroyed.

11 When we heard it, our hearts melted, neither did spirit *or* courage remain any more in any man because of you, for the Lord your God, He is God in heaven above and on earth beneath. [Heb. 11:31.]

12 Now then, I pray you, swear to me by the Lord, since I have shown you kindness, that you also will show kindness to my father's house, and give me a sure sign,

13 And save alive my father and mother, my brothers and sisters, and all they have, and deliver us from death.

14 And the men said to her, Our lives for yours! If you do not tell this business of ours, then when the Lord gives us the land we will deal kindly and faithfully with you.

15 Then she let them down by a rope through the window, for her house was built into the [town] wall so that she dwelt in the wall.

16 And she said to them, Get to the mountain, lest the pursuers meet you; hide yourselves there three days until the pursuers have returned; and afterward you may go your way.

17 The men said to her, We will be blameless of this oath you have made us swear. [The responsibility is now yours.]

18 Behold, when we come into the land, you shall bind this scarlet cord in the window through which you let us down, and you shall bring your father and mother, your brothers, and all your father's household into your house.

19 And if anyone goes out of the doors of your house into the street, his blood shall be upon his head, and we

will be guiltless; but if a hand is laid upon anyone who is with you in the house, his blood shall be on our head. **20** But if you tell this business of ours, we shall be guiltless of your oath which you made us swear.
21 And she said, According to your words, so it is. Then she sent them away and they departed; and she bound the ᶜscarlet cord in the window. **22** They left and went to the mountain and stayed there three days, until the pursuers returned, who had searched all along the way without finding them.
23 So the two men descended from the mountain, passed over [the Jordan], and came to Joshua son of Nun, and told him all that had befallen them.
24 They said to Joshua, Truly the Lord has given all the land into our hands; for all the inhabitants of the country are faint because of us.

3 JOSHUA ROSE early in the morning and they removed from Shittim and came to the Jordan, he and all the Israelites, and lodged there before passing over.
2 After three days the officers went through the camp,
3 Commanding the people: When you see the ark of the covenant of the Lord your God being borne by the Levitical priests, set out from where you are and follow it.
4 Yet a space must be kept between you and it, about 2,000 cubits by measure; come not near it, that you may [be able to see the ark and] know the way you must go, for you have not passed this way before.
5 And Joshua said to the people, Sanctify yourselves [that is, separate yourselves for a special holy purpose],

for tomorrow the Lord will do wonders among you.
6 Joshua said to the priests, Take up the ark of the covenant and pass over before the people. And they took it up and went on before the people.
7 The Lord said to Joshua, This day I will begin to magnify you in the sight of all Israel, so they may know that as I was with Moses, so I will be with you.
8 You shall command the priests who bear the ark of the covenant, When you come to the brink of the waters of the Jordan, you shall stand still in the Jordan.
9 Joshua said to the Israelites, Come near, hear the words of the Lord your God.
10 Joshua said, Hereby you shall know that the living God is among you and that He will surely drive out from before you the Canaanites, Hittites, Hivites, Perizzites, Girgashites, Amorites, and Jebusites.
11 Behold, the ark of the covenant of the Lord of all the earth is passing over before you into the Jordan!
12 So now take twelve men from the tribes of Israel, one from each tribe.
13 When the soles of the feet of the priests who bear the ark of the Lord of all the earth shall rest in the Jordan, the waters of the Jordan coming down from above shall be cut off and they shall stand in one heap.
14 So when the people set out from their tents to pass over the Jordan, with the priests bearing the ark of the covenant before the people,
15 And when those who bore the ark had come to the Jordan and the feet of the priests bearing the ark were in the brink of the water—for the Jordan overflows all its banks throughout the time of harvest—

c What the blood on the doorposts on the first Passover night in Egypt was to the houses of Israel (Exod. 12:13), the scarlet cord in the window was to the house of Rahab. Her sinful years of ignorance God ignored (Acts 17:30, 31); she became an ancestress, as did Ruth, of David and of Jesus Christ (Matt. 1:1, 5, 6).

common people, uncommon things

Do you want to be used by God as a leader? You can be. God is always looking for people to promote—and you can be one of them. Like Joshua, you have tremendous capabilities and potential; all you need to do is fully develop them. That involves allowing God to change you. The process may hurt at times, but it will benefit you in the long term.

Is a good leader born or made? Some people are born with natural leadership qualities, but they still have to go through a process of development that makes them into all they can be. Do not look at leadership as something attainable only by rare individuals who have great talents. God delights in using common people to accomplish uncommon things. Common people with *uncommon* goals who make an *uncommon* commitment can help an *uncommon* number of other people.

As you develop the leadership qualities God has placed in you, remember that you are investing in the future. You can fulfill the plan God has for you, but you must be determined and refuse to be anything less than all you can be. A major key to moving from where you are to where you want to be is to "keep on keeping on."

Develop your potential to the full, and as you do, encourage others to do the same. Be all you can be, and then help someone else do the same.

16 Then the ^dwaters which came down from above stood and rose up in a heap far off, at Adam, the city that is beside Zarethan; and those flowing down toward the Sea of the Arabah, the Salt [Dead] Sea, were wholly cut off. And the people passed over opposite Jericho. [Ps. 114.]

17 And while all Israel passed over on dry ground, the priests who bore the ark of the covenant of the Lord stood firm on dry ground in the midst of the Jordan, until all the nation finished passing over the Jordan.

putting the Word to work

Have you ever had to believe God for something miraculous in your life, as the Israelites did when they stood at the Jordan ready to cross over (see Joshua 3:15, 16)? Are you in that position right now? As you read about how God led the Israelites across the Jordan on dry ground and about other miracles in the Bible, be encouraged and remember that God is still a God of miracles today!

d The city of Adam has been placed 16 miles up the river from Jericho, and it seems probable that a stretch of 20 or 30 miles of the riverbed was left dry. An interesting parallel of the event here recorded has been found in the pages of an Arabic historian telling how in AD 1266, near a place many experts have identified with Adam, the bed of the [Jordan] river was left dry for ten hours as the result of a landslide. John Garstang (*The Story of Jericho*) cites other parallels. But to accept this "natural" explanation of what happened centuries earlier does not detract in any way from the supernatural intervention which opened the way to Israel just at the moment when they needed to cross. The sight of the priests standing in the dry bed of the river as the whole nation passed over was the sign (Josh. 3:10) that this was the doing of the Lord (F. Davidson, ed., *The New Bible Commentary*).

life point

Joshua 3:17 lets us know that the nation of Israel finally did cross the Jordan to enter the Promised Land. The sad thing is that they could have crossed over much sooner than they did. Why the delay? Wilderness mentalities, patterns of thinking that kept them wandering in the wilderness—and out of the Promised Land—for forty years. One of the Israelites' wilderness mentalities was an impatient attitude. They did not know how to stay calm and to be long-suffering through the hardships of their journey. How could these people possibly be ready to go into the Promised Land and drive off the current occupants so they could possess the land if they could not even remain patient and steadfast during a little inconvenience?

I really encourage you to work with the Holy Spirit as He develops the fruit of patience in you. The more you resist Him, the longer the process will take. Learn to respond patiently in all kinds of trials, and you will find yourself living not in the wilderness, but in the joy of God's promises for your life, your own Promised Land.

4 WHEN ALL the nation had fully passed over the Jordan, the Lord said to Joshua,

2 Take twelve men from among the people, one man out of every tribe,

3 And command them, Take twelve stones out of the midst of the Jordan from the place where the priests' feet stood firm; carry them over with you and leave them at the place where you lodge tonight.

4 Then Joshua called the twelve men of the Israelites whom he had appointed, a man from each tribe.

5 And Joshua said to them, Pass over before the ark of the Lord your God in the midst of the Jordan, and take up every man of you a stone on his shoulder, as is the number of the tribes of the Israelites,

6 That this may be a sign among you when your children ask in time to come, What do these stones mean to you?

7 Then you shall tell them that the waters of the Jordan were cut off before the ark of the covenant of the Lord; when it passed over the Jordan, the waters of Jordan were cut off. So these stones shall be to the Israelites a memorial forever.

8 And the Israelites did as Joshua commanded, and took up twelve stones out of the midst of the Jordan, according to the number of the tribes of the Israelites, as the Lord told Joshua, and carried them over with them to the place where they lodged and laid them down there.

9 And Joshua set up twelve stones in the midst of the Jordan in the place where the feet of the priests bearing the ark of the covenant had stood. And they are there to this day.

10 For the priests who bore the ark stood in the midst of the Jordan until everything was finished that the Lord commanded Joshua to tell the people, according to all that Moses had commanded Joshua. The people passed over in haste.

11 When all the people had passed over, the ark of the Lord and the priests went over in the presence of the people.

12 And the sons of Reuben, Gad, and half the tribe of Manasseh passed over armed before the [other] Israelites, as Moses had bidden them;

13 About 40,000 [of these] prepared for war passed over before the Lord to the plains of Jericho for battle.

14 On that day the Lord magnified Joshua in the sight of all Israel; and

they stood in awe of him, as they stood in awe of Moses, all the days of his life.

15 And the Lord said to Joshua,

16 Order the priests bearing the ark of the Testimony to come up out of the Jordan.

17 So Joshua commanded the priests, Come up out of the Jordan.

18 And when the priests who bore the ark of the covenant of the Lord had come up out of the midst of the Jordan, and the soles of their feet were lifted up to the dry land, the waters of the Jordan returned to their place and flowed over all its banks as they had before.

19 And the people came up out of the Jordan on the tenth day of the first month and encamped in Gilgal on the east border of Jericho.

20 And those twelve stones which they took out of the Jordan Joshua set up in Gilgal.

21 And he said to the Israelites, When your children ask their fathers in time to come, What do these stones mean?

22 You shall let your children know, Israel came over this Jordan on dry ground.

23 For the Lord your God dried up the waters of the Jordan for you until you passed over, as the Lord your God did to the Red Sea, which He dried up for us until we passed over,

24 That all the peoples of the earth may know that the hand of the Lord is mighty and that you may reverence *and* fear the Lord your God forever.

5 WHEN ALL the kings of the Amorites who were beyond the Jordan to the west and all the kings of the Canaanites who were by the sea heard that the Lord had dried up the waters of the Jordan before the Israelites until we had crossed over, their hearts melted and there was no spirit in them any more because of the Israelites.

2 At that time the Lord said to Joshua, Make knives of flint and circumcise the [new generation of] Israelites as before.

3 So Joshua made knives of flint and circumcised the sons of Israel at Gibeath-haaraloth.

4 And this is the reason Joshua circumcised them: all the males of the people who came out of Egypt, all the men of war, had died in the wilderness on the way after they came out of Egypt.

5 Though all the people who came out were circumcised, yet all the people who were born in the wilderness on the way after Israel came out of Egypt had not been circumcised.

6 For the Israelites walked forty years in the wilderness till all who were men of war who came out of Egypt perished, because they did not hearken to the voice of the Lord; to them the Lord swore that He would not let them see the land which the Lord swore to their fathers to give us, a land flowing with milk and honey.

7 So it was their uncircumcised children whom He raised up in their stead whom Joshua circumcised, because the rite had not been performed on the way.

8 When they finished circumcising all the males of the nation, they remained in their places in the camp till they were healed.

9 And the Lord said to Joshua, This day have I rolled away the reproach of

speak the Word

Thank You, God, that Your hand is mighty. May I reverence and fear You forever!
ADAPTED FROM JOSHUA 4:24

Egypt from you. So the name of the place is called Gilgal [rolling] to this day.

10 And the Israelites encamped in Gilgal; and they kept the Passover on the fourteenth day of the month at evening in the plains of Jericho.

11 And on that same day they ate the

roll away the reproach

After Joshua led the Israelites into the Promised Land, they needed to be circumcised before they would be ready to conquer and occupy their first city, Jericho (see Joshua 5:2–7). After the men had been circumcised, the Lord told Joshua that He had "rolled away" the reproach of Egypt from His people. Now they were ready to overcome and capture Jericho (see Joshua 6). Why did reproach have to be lifted off them first? What exactly is a reproach?

The word *reproach* means "blame, disgrace, or shame." When God said that He had "rolled away" the reproach of Egypt from the Israelites, He was making a strong point. Egypt represents the world. After a few years of being in the world and becoming worldly, we all need the world's reproach to be rolled away.

After many years in ministry, I am convinced that about 85 percent of our problems stem from the way we feel about ourselves. In my life, I had a shame-based nature because of things I had done and things that had been done to me. I blamed myself for what had happened to me. This is despite the fact that most of these things happened in my childhood, and there was nothing I could have done to stop them. Disgrace told me that I was no good—not worthy of God's love or help. Shame had poisoned my inner being. I was not only ashamed of what had been done to me, but I was ashamed of myself. Deep down inside, I did not like myself. I needed God to roll away my reproach. He was willing and ready, but I had to believe it was possible. I did believe, and I am a totally different person today. No more shame, blame, or disgrace! I am a new creature in Jesus Christ (see II Corinthians 5:17).

I have said that grace is the power of God coming to us (as a free gift from Him) to help us do with ease what we cannot do ourselves. God wants to give us grace, and Satan wants to give us *dis*grace, which is another word for "reproach." God's action of rolling away our reproach means that we receive the forgiveness He is offering for all our past sins.

Self-hatred, self-rejection, refusal to accept God's forgiveness (by not forgiving yourself), not understanding righteousness through the blood of Jesus, and any related problems will definitely keep you wandering in the wilderness. Your mind must be renewed concerning the right standing you have with God through Jesus—not through your own works. You can never deserve God's blessings or be worthy of them. You can only humbly accept and appreciate them, and be in awe of how good He is and how much He loves you. The Bible says you are a joint-heir with Christ (see Romans 8:17). He earned your blessings by carrying your reproach to the Cross. Let God roll that reproach off you, and experience the freedom from shame that Jesus wants to give you.

produce of the land: unleavened cakes and parched grain.

12 And the manna ceased on the day after they ate of the produce of the land; and the Israelites had manna no more, but they ate of the fruit of the land of Canaan that year.

13 When Joshua was by Jericho, he looked up, and behold, a Man stood near him with His drawn sword in His hand. And Joshua went to Him and said to Him, Are you for us or for our adversaries?

14 And He said, No [neither], but as Prince of the Lord's host have I now come. And Joshua fell on his face to the earth and worshiped, and said to Him, What says my Lord to His servant?

15 And the Prince of the Lord's host said to Joshua, eLoose your shoes from off your feet, for the place where you stand is holy. And Joshua did so. [Exod. 3:5.]

6 NOW JERICHO [a fenced town with high walls] was tightly closed because of the Israelites; no one went out or came in.

2 And the Lord said to Joshua, See, I have given Jericho, its king and mighty men of valor, into your hands.

3 You shall march around the enclosure, all the men of war going around the city once. This you shall do for six days.

4 And seven priests shall bear before the ark seven trumpets of rams' horns; and on the seventh day you shall march around the enclosure seven times, and the priests shall blow the trumpets.

5 When they make a long blast with the ram's horn and you hear the sound of the trumpet, all the people shall shout with a great shout; and the wall of the enclosure shall fall down in its place and the people shall go up [over it], every man straight before him.

6 So Joshua son of Nun called the priests and said to them, Take up the ark of the covenant and let seven priests bear seven trumpets of rams' horns before the ark of the Lord.

7 He said to the people, Go on! March around the enclosure, and let the armed men pass on before the ark of the Lord.

8 When Joshua had spoken to the people, the seven priests bearing the seven trumpets of rams' horns passed on before the Lord and blew the trumpets, and the ark of the covenant of the Lord followed them.

9 The armed men went before the priests who blew the trumpets, and the rear guard came after the ark, the priests blowing the trumpets as they went.

10 But Joshua commanded the people, You shall not shout or let your voice be heard, nor shall any word proceed out of your mouth until the day I tell you to shout. Then you shall shout!

11 So he caused the ark of the Lord

---

e "The real character of this personage was disclosed by His accepting the homage of worship (cf. Acts 10:25, 26; Rev. 19:10), and still further in the command, 'Loose thy shoe from off thy foot' " (KJV) (Robert Jamieson, A.R. Fausset and David Brown, *A Commentary*). *The New Bible Commentary* supports this position (as do J.P. Lange, *The Cambridge Bible,* Charles Ellicott, and many others) when it says, "We believe that this was the Son of God Himself."

to go around the city once; and they came into the camp and lodged in the camp.

12 Joshua rose early in the morning and the priests took up the ark of the Lord.

13 And the seven priests bearing the seven trumpets of rams' horns before the ark of the Lord passed on, blowing the trumpets continually; and the armed men went before them and the rear guard came after the ark of the Lord, the priests blowing the trumpets as they went.

14 On the second day they compassed the city enclosure once and returned to the camp. So they did for six days.

15 On the seventh day they rose early at daybreak and marched around the city as usual, only on that day they compassed the city fseven times.

16 And the seventh time, when the priests had blown the trumpets, Joshua said to the people, Shout! For the Lord has given you the city.

17 And the city and all that is in it shall be devoted to the Lord [for destruction]; only Rahab the harlot and all who are with her in her house shall live, because she hid the messengers whom we sent.

18 But you, keep yourselves from the accursed *and* devoted things, lest when you have devoted it [to destruction], you take of the accursed thing, and so make the camp of Israel accursed and trouble it.

19 But all the silver and gold and vessels of bronze and iron are consecrated to the Lord; they shall come into the treasury of the Lord.

20 So the people shouted, and the trumpets were blown. When the people heard the sound of the trumpet, they raised a great shout, and [Jericho's] wall fell down in its place, so that the [Israelites] went up into the city, every man straight before him, and they took the city.

21 Then they utterly destroyed all that was in the city, both man and woman, young and old, ox, sheep, and donkey, with the edge of the sword.

22 But Joshua said to the two men who had spied out the land, Go into the harlot's house and bring out the woman and all she has, as you swore to her.

23 So the young men, the spies, went in and brought out Rahab, her father and mother, her brethren, and all that she had; and they brought out all her kindred and set them outside the camp of Israel.

24 And they gburned the city with

---

f Any walled town was called a "city" and its headman was called "a king" in ancient times, but the fact that Joshua's army could march around the whole of Jericho seven times in one day shows that it was a very small place. Sir Charles Marston (*New Bible Evidence*) echoes the reports of other archaeologists when he says that the excavations of ancient Jericho do not confirm the conceptions of our youth. Though the walls were so formidable, the area they enclosed only measures seven acres. The whole circumference of the city was about 650 yards. Our disappointment is somewhat modified by the fact that Jebusite Jerusalem, which David captured, was about the same size. Schliemann experienced a similar disillusionment in 1873 when he excavated the city of Troy, which Homer tells us so long withstood the Grecian hosts. Indeed it would almost seem that these ancient cities were more in the nature of places of refuge resorted to when an enemy approached. Under peaceful conditions a large proportion of the inhabitants would dwell outside the city's walls (Sir Charles Marston, *New Bible Evidence*).   **g** Important details of this story are fully substantiated by the findings of Dr. J.B. Garstang in his several excavations of Jericho: 1. The city was thoroughly burned by fire. 2. It had not been thoroughly plundered. Stored grain, for example, was found burned but undisturbed. 3. The "silver, the gold, and the vessels of bronze and of iron" were missing. 4. The walls had fallen, but the one gate had a tower left standing. 5. Well-supported houses had been built on the walls. 6. The gate tower was "an imposing edifice," 54 ft by 24 ft., remarkably well built of gray brick. Its ruins still stand 16 ft high. 7. Only on one side of Jericho is there a mountain, and that is a mountain ridge beginning a mile west of the city (John Garstang, *The Story of Jericho*, Joseph P. Free, *Archaeology and Bible History*, and other sources).

fire and all that was in it; only the silver, the gold, and the vessels of bronze and of iron they put into the treasury of the house of the Lord.

25 So Joshua saved Rahab the harlot, with her father's household and all that she had; and she lives in Israel even to this day, because she hid the messengers whom Joshua sent to spy out Jericho.

26 Then Joshua laid this oath on them, Cursed is the man before the Lord who rises up and rebuilds this city, Jericho. With the loss of his first-born shall he lay its foundation, and with the loss of his youngest son shall he set up its gates. [I Kings 16:34.]

27 So the Lord was with Joshua, and his fame was in all the land.

7 BUT THE Israelites committed a trespass in regard to the devoted things; for Achan son of Carmi, the son of Zabdi, the son of Zerah, of the tribe of Judah, took some of the things devoted [for destruction]. And the anger of the Lord burned against Israel.

2 Joshua sent men from Jericho to Ai, which is near Beth-aven, east of Bethel, and said to them, Go up and spy out the land. So the men went up and spied out Ai.

3 And they returned to Joshua and said to him, Let not all the men go up; but let about two thousand or three thousand go up and attack Ai; do not make the whole army toil up there, for they of Ai are few.

4 So about three thousand Israelites went up there, but they fled before the men of Ai.

5 And the men of Ai killed about thirty-six of them, for they chased them from before the gate as far as Shebarim, and slew them at the descent. And the hearts of the people melted and became as water.

6 Then Joshua rent his clothes and lay on the earth upon his face before the ark of the Lord until evening, he and the elders of Israel; and they put dust on their heads.

7 Joshua said, Alas, O Lord God, why have You brought this people over the Jordan at all only to give us into the hands of the Amorites to destroy us? Would that we had been content to dwell beyond the Jordan!

8 O Lord, what can I say, now that Israel has turned to flee before their enemies!

9 For the Canaanites and all the inhabitants of the land will hear of it and will surround us and cut off our name from the earth. And what will You do for Your great name?

10 The Lord said to Joshua, Get up! Why do you lie thus upon your face?

11 Israel has sinned; they have transgressed My covenant which I commanded them. They have taken some of the things devoted [for destruction]; they have stolen, and lied, and put them among their own baggage.

12 That is why the Israelites could not stand before their enemies, but fled before them; they are accursed *and* have become devoted [for destruction]. I will cease to be with you unless you destroy the accursed [devoted] things among you.

13 Up, sanctify (set apart for a holy purpose) the people, and say, Sanctify yourselves for tomorrow; for thus says the Lord, the God of Israel: There are accursed things in the midst of you, O Israel. You can not stand before your enemies until you take away from among you the things devoted [to destruction].

14 In the morning therefore, you shall present your tribes. And the tribe which the Lord takes shall come by families; and the family which the Lord takes shall come by households; and the household which the Lord takes shall come by persons.

15 And he who is taken with the

devoted things shall be [killed and his body] burned with fire, he and all he has, because he has transgressed the covenant of the Lord and because he has done a shameful *and* wicked thing in Israel. [Josh. 7:25.]

16 So Joshua rose up early in the morning and brought Israel near by their tribes, and the tribe of Judah was taken.

17 He brought near the family of Judah, and the family of the Zerahites was taken; and he brought near the family of the Zerahites man by man, and Zabdi was taken.

18 He brought near his household man by man, and Achan son of Carmi, the son of Zabdi, the son of Zerah, of the tribe of Judah, was taken.

19 And Joshua said to Achan, My son, give glory to the Lord, the God of Israel, and make confession to Him. And tell me now what you have done; do not hide it from me.

20 And Achan answered Joshua, In truth, I have sinned against the Lord, the God of Israel, and this have I done:

21 When I saw among the spoils an attractive mantle from Shinar and two hundred shekels of silver and a bar of gold weighing fifty shekels, I coveted them and took them. Behold, they are hidden in the earth inside my tent, with the silver underneath.

22 So Joshua sent messengers, who ran to the tent, and behold, the spoil was hidden in his tent, with the silver underneath.

23 And they took them from the tent and brought them to Joshua and all the Israelites and laid them out before the Lord.

24 And Joshua and all Israel with him took Achan son of Zerah, and the silver, the garment, the wedge of gold, his sons, his daughters, his oxen, his donkeys, his sheep, his tent, and all that he had; and they brought them to the Valley of Achor.

25 And Joshua said, Why have you brought trouble on us? The Lord will trouble you this day. And all Israel stoned him and those with him with stones, and afterward burned their bodies with fire.

26 And they raised over him a great heap of stones that remains to this day. Then the Lord turned from the fierceness of His anger. Therefore the name of that place has been called the Valley of Achor *or* Troubling to this day.

8 AND THE Lord said to Joshua, Fear not nor be dismayed. Take all the men of war with you, and arise, go up to Ai; see, I have given into your hand the king of Ai, his people, his city, and his land.

life point

No matter what we face in life, Jesus is the Mighty Warrior, the Captain of the Host. He is our Leader, and He is leading His people into victory. I do not believe that we have to live in fear. God has promised to provide for His own. He has assured us, just as He did Joshua, that we will triumph if we listen to Him and obey (see Joshua 8:1). Whatever obstacles are before you today, do not be afraid or dismayed, because God is with you.

2 And you shall do to Ai and its king as you did to Jericho and its king, except that its spoil and its cattle [this time] you shall take as booty for yourselves. Lay an ambush against the city behind it.

3 So Joshua arose, and all the people of war, to go up against Ai; [he] chose thirty thousand mighty men of strength and sent them forth by night.

4 And he commanded them, Behold, you shall lie in wait against the city behind it. Do not go very far from the city, but all of you be ready.

5 And I and all the people who are with me will approach the city. And when they come out against us, as the first time, we will flee before them

6 Till we have drawn them from the city, for they will say, They are fleeing from us as before. So we will flee before them.

7 Then you shall rise up from the ambush and seize the city, for the Lord your God will deliver it into your hand.

8 When you have taken the city, you shall set it afire; as the Lord commanded, you shall do. See, I have commanded you.

9 So Joshua sent them forth, and they went to the place of ambush and remained between Bethel and Ai, on the west side of Ai; but Joshua lodged that night among the people.

10 Joshua rose up early in the morning and mustered the men, and went up with the elders of Israel before the warriors to Ai.

11 And all the fighting men who were with him went up and drew near before the city and encamped on the north side of [it], with a ravine between them and Ai.

12 And he took about five thousand men and set them in ambush between Bethel and Ai, west of the city.

13 So they stationed all the army—the main encampment that was north of the city and their men in ambush behind *and* on the west of the city—and Joshua went that night into the midst of the ravine.

14 When the king [and people] of Ai saw it, they hastily rose early, and the men of the city went out against Israel to battle [at a time and place appointed] before the Arabah [plain]. But he did not know of the ambush against him behind the city.

15 And Joshua and all Israel pretended to be beaten by them, and fled toward the wilderness.

16 So all the people in Ai were called together to pursue them, and they pursued Joshua and were drawn away from the city.

17 Not a man was left in Ai or Bethel who did not go out after Israel. Leaving the city open, they pursued Israel.

18 Then the Lord said to Joshua, Stretch out the javelin that is in your hand toward Ai, for I will give it into your hand. So Joshua stretched out the javelin in his hand toward the city.

19 The men in the ambush arose quickly out of their place and ran when he stretched out his hand; and they entered the city and took it, and then hastened and set it afire.

20 When the men of Ai looked back, behold, the smoke of the city went up to the heavens, and they had no power to flee this way or that way. Then the Israelites who fled to the wilderness turned back upon the pursuers.

21 When Joshua and all Israel saw that the ambush had taken the city and that the smoke of the city went up, they turned again and slew the men of Ai.

22 And the others came forth out of the city against them [of Ai], so that they were in the midst of Israel, some on this side and some on that side. And [the Israelites] smote them, so that they let none of them remain or escape.

23 But they took the king of Ai alive and brought him to Joshua.

24 When Israel had finished slaying all the inhabitants of Ai in the field and in the wilderness into which they pursued them, and they were all fallen by the sword until they were consumed, then all the Israelites returned to Ai and smote it with the sword.

25 And all that fell that day, both men and women, were twelve thousand, including all the men of Ai.

26 For Joshua drew not back his hand with which he stretched out the javelin until he had utterly destroyed all the inhabitants of Ai.

27 Only the livestock and the spoil of that city Israel took as booty for themselves, according to the word of the Lord which He commanded Joshua.

28 So Joshua burned Ai and made it a heap of ruins for ever, even a desolation to this day.

29 And he hanged the king of Ai on a tree until evening; and at sunset, Joshua commanded and they took the body down from the tree and cast it at the entrance of the city gate and raised a great heap of stones over it that is there to this day.

30 Then Joshua built an altar to the Lord, the God of Israel, on Mount Ebal,

31 As Moses the servant of the Lord commanded the Israelites, as it is written in the Book of the Law of Moses, an altar of unhewn stones, upon which no man has lifted up an iron tool; and they offered on it burnt offerings to the Lord and sacrificed peace offerings.

32 And there, in the presence of the Israelites, [Joshua] wrote on the stones a copy of the law of Moses.

33 And all Israel, sojourner as well as he who was born among them, with their elders, officers, and judges, stood on either side of the ark before the Levitical priests who carried the ark of the covenant of the Lord, half of them in front of Mount Gerizim and half of them in front of Mount Ebal, as Moses the servant of the Lord had commanded before that they should bless the Israelites.

34 Afterward, Joshua read all the words of the law, the blessings and cursings, all that is written in the Book of the Law.

35 There was not a word of all that Moses commanded which Joshua did not read before all the assembly of Israel, and the women, and little ones, and the foreigners who were living among them.

9 WHEN ALL the kings beyond the Jordan in the hill country and in the lowland and all along the coast of the Great [Mediterranean] Sea toward Lebanon, the Hittites, Amorites, Canaanites, Perizzites, Hivites, and Jebusites heard this,

2 They gathered together with one accord to fight Joshua and Israel.

3 But when the people of Gibeon heard what Joshua had done to Jericho and Ai,

4 They worked cunningly, and went pretending to be ambassadors and took [provisions and] old sacks on their donkeys and wineskins, old, torn, and mended,

5 And old and patched shoes on their feet and wearing old garments; and all their supply of food was dry and moldy.

6 And they went to Joshua in the camp at Gilgal and said to him and the men of Israel, We have come from a far country; so now, make a covenant with us.

7 But the men of Israel said to the Hivites, Perhaps you live among us; how then can we make a covenant with you?

8 They said to Joshua, We are your servants. And Joshua said to them, Who are you? From where have you come?

9 They said to him, From a very far country your servants have come because of the name of the Lord your God. For we have heard the fame of Him, and all that He did in Egypt,

10 And all that He did to the two kings of the Amorites who were beyond the Jordan, to Sihon king of Heshbon, and to Og king of Bashan, who lived in Ashtaroth.

11 So our elders and all the residents of our country said to us, Take provisions for the journey and go to meet [the Israelites] and say to them, We are your servants; and now make a covenant with us.

12 This our bread we took hot for our

life point

Joshua 9:12 mentions bread that has become dry and moldy. If a loaf of bread is left on a table for very long, a person can touch it and tell it is getting stale. It is on its way to becoming hard and tasteless. The same thing can happen in our lives. If we are not careful, the enemy will deceive us into allowing our lives to become dry and stale. We must resist this by staying fresh—being creative and having different experiences, breaking our routines once in a while, and allowing God to do new things in us, for us, and through us.

provision out of our houses on the day we set out to go to you; but now behold, it is dry and has become moldy.
13 These wineskins (bottles) which we filled were new, and behold, they are torn; and our garments and our shoes have become old because of the very long journey.
14 So the [Israelite] men partook of their food and did not consult the Lord.
15 Joshua made peace with them, covenanting with them to let them live, and the assembly's leaders swore to them.
16 Then three days after they had made a covenant with [the strangers, the Israelites] heard that they were their neighbors and that they dwelt among them.
17 And the Israelites set out and came to their cities on the third day. Now their cities were Gibeon, Chephirah, Beeroth, and Kiriath-jearim.
18 But the Israelites did not slay them, because the leaders of the assembly had sworn to them by the Lord, the God of Israel, [to spare them]. And all the assembly murmured against the leaders.

19 But all the leaders said to all the assembly, We have sworn to them by the Lord, the God of Israel, so now we may not touch them.
20 This we will do to them: we will let them live, lest wrath be upon us because of the oath which we swore to them.
21 And the leaders said to them, Let them live [and be our slaves]. So they became hewers of wood and drawers of water for all the assembly, just as the leaders had said of them.
22 Joshua called the men and said, Why did you deceive us, saying, We live very far from you, when you dwell among us?
23 Now therefore you are cursed, and of you there shall always be slaves, hewers of wood and drawers of water for the house of my God.
24 They answered Joshua, Because it was surely told your servants that the Lord your God commanded His servant Moses to give you all the land and to destroy all the land's inhabitants from before you. So we feared greatly for our lives because of you, and have done this thing.
25 And now, behold, we are in your hand; do as it seems good and right in your sight to do to us.
26 So he did to them, and delivered them out of the hand of the Israelites, so that they did not kill them.
27 But Joshua then made them hewers of wood and drawers of water for the congregation and for the altar of the Lord, to this day, in the place which He should choose.

10 WHEN ADONI-ZEDEK king of Jerusalem heard how Joshua had taken Ai and had utterly destroyed it, doing to Jericho and its king as he had done to Ai and its king, and how the residents of Gibeon had made peace with Israel and were among them,
2 He feared greatly, because Gibeon

was a great city, like one of the royal cities, and because it was greater than Ai, and all its men were mighty.

3 So Adoni-zedek king of Jerusalem sent to Hoham king of Hebron, to Piram king of Jarmuth, to Japhia king of Lachish, and to Debir king of Eglon, saying,

4 Come up to me and help me, and let us smite Gibeon, for it has made peace with Joshua and with the Israelites.

5 Then the five kings of the Amorites—the kings of Jerusalem, Hebron, Jarmuth, Lachish, and Eglon—gathered their forces and went up with all their armies and encamped before Gibeon to fight against it.

6 And the men of Gibeon sent to Joshua at the camp in Gilgal, saying, Do not relax your hand from your servants; come up to us quickly and save us and help us, for all the kings of the Amorites who dwell in the hill country are gathered against us.

7 So Joshua went up from Gilgal, he and all the warriors with him and all the mighty men of valor.

8 And the Lord said to Joshua, Do not fear them, for I have given them into your hand; there shall not a man of them stand before you.

9 So Joshua came upon them suddenly, having gone up from Gilgal all night.

10 And the Lord caused [the enemies] to panic before Israel, who slew them with a great slaughter at Gibeon and chased them along the way that goes up to Beth-horon and smote them as far as Azekah and Makkedah.

11 As they fled before Israel, while they were descending [the pass] to Beth-horon, the Lord cast great stones from the heavens on them as far as Azekah, killing them. More died because of the hailstones than the Israelites slew with the sword.

12 Then Joshua spoke to the Lord on the day when the Lord gave the Amorites over to the Israelites, and he said in the sight of Israel, Sun, be silent *and* stand still at Gibeon, and you, moon, in the Valley of Ajalon!

13 And the sun stood still, and the moon stayed, until the nation took vengeance upon their enemies. Is not this written in the Book of Jasher? So the sun stood still in the midst of the heavens and did not hasten to go down for about a whole day.

14 There was no day like it before or since, when the Lord heeded the voice of a man. For the Lord fought for Israel.

15 Then Joshua returned, and all Israel with him, to the camp at Gilgal.

16 Those five kings fled and hid themselves in the cave of Makkedah.

17 And it was told Joshua, The five kings are hidden in the cave at Makkedah.

18 Joshua said, Roll great stones to the cave's mouth, and set men to guard them.

19 But do not stay. Pursue your enemies and fall upon their rear; do not allow them to enter their cities, for the Lord your God has given them into your hand.

20 When Joshua and the Israelites had ended slaying them until they were wiped out and the remnant remaining of them had entered into fortified cities,

21 All the people returned to the camp to Joshua at Makkedah in peace; none moved his tongue against any of the Israelites.

22 Then said Joshua, Open the mouth of the cave and bring out those five kings to me from the cave.

23 They brought the five kings out of the cave to him—the kings of Jerusalem, Hebron, Jarmuth, Lachish, and Eglon.

24 When they brought out those kings to Joshua, [he] called for all the Israelites and told the commanders of the men of war who went with him,

Come, put your feet on the necks of these kings. And they came and put their feet on the [kings'] necks.

25 Joshua said to them, Fear not nor be dismayed; be strong and of good courage. For thus shall the Lord do to all your enemies against whom you fight.

life point

Fear is not from God. Fear is from Satan. Fear is the spirit Satan uses to try to keep God's people from coming under the leadership of their true Master, Jesus Christ. The only acceptable attitude (and confession) that a Christian can have toward fear is this: "It is not from God, and I will not put up with it or let it control my life! *I will confront fear*, because it is a spirit sent from hell to torment me."

I believe God works powerfully in us to bring us out of bondage, to take us from fear into liberty. The Bible is full of instructions to "fear not." Events in my own life have led me to understand that "Fear not" means "Do not run; face it." I encourage you to press on, and if need be, "Do it afraid"—whatever "it" is in your life. Do not run from fear; instead, "Be strong and of good courage," as Joshua 10:25 exhorts. Confront fear in prayer and take whatever actions God leads you to take.

26 Afterward Joshua smote and slew them and hanged their bodies on five trees, and they hung on the trees until evening.

27 At sunset Joshua ordered and they took the bodies down from the trees and cast them into the cave where the kings had hidden and laid great stones on the cave's mouth, which remain to this very day.

28 Joshua took Makkedah that day and smote it and its king with the sword and utterly destroyed everyone in it. He left none remaining. And he did to the king of Makkedah as he had done to the king of Jericho. [Josh. 6:21.]

29 Then Joshua and all Israel went from Makkedah to Libnah and attacked Libnah.

30 And the Lord gave it also and its king into Israel's hands, and Joshua smote it with the sword, and all the people in it. He left none remaining in it. And he did to its king as he had done to the king of Jericho.

31 And Joshua passed from Libnah, and all Israel with him, to Lachish and encamped against it and attacked it.

32 And the Lord delivered Lachish into the hands of Israel, and Joshua took it on the second day and smote it with the sword, and all the people in it, as he had done to Libnah.

33 Then Horam king of Gezer came up to help Lachish, and Joshua smote him and his people—until he had left none remaining.

34 From Lachish Joshua and all Israel went on to Eglon, laid siege to it, and attacked it.

35 And they took it that day and smote it with the sword and utterly destroyed all who were in it that day, as he had done to Lachish.

36 Then Joshua with all Israel went up from Eglon to Hebron, and they attacked it

37 And took it and smote it with the sword, and its king and all its towns and everyone in it. He left none remaining, as he had done to Eglon, and utterly destroyed it and all its people.

38 And Joshua and all Israel with him returned to Debir and attacked it.

39 And he took it, with its king and all its towns, and they smote them with the sword and utterly destroyed everyone in it. He left none remaining. As he had done to Hebron and to

Libnah and its king, so he did to Debir and its king.

40 So Joshua smote all the land, the hill country, the South, the lowland, and the slopes, and all their kings. He left none remaining, but utterly destroyed all that breathed, as the [h]Lord, the God of Israel, commanded. [Deut. 20:16.]

life point

Joshua fought many battles in order to finally enter the Promised Land. As the Lord gave him direction all along the way, He repeatedly told him to be of good courage. Courage means having a good attitude in the face of dangerous or frightening circumstances.

Have you ever wondered what would have happened if Joshua had not listened to God's encouragement to take courage? When the enemy repeatedly came against him, Joshua could have given up, the children of Israel would never have defeated all their enemies, and they would not have enjoyed living in the Promised Land.

The same is true in our daily walk. Joy and cheer in the Lord give us the strength to pursue the goal that He has given us and to fight the battles we face along the way. When you are tempted to lose courage, remember that the joy of the Lord is your strength (see Nehemiah 8:10). Like Joshua, all of your enemies will be utterly defeated as you stay strong in God.

41 And Joshua smote them from Kadesh-barnea even to Gaza, and all the country of Goshen even to Gibeon.

42 Joshua took all these kings and their land at one time, because the Lord, the God of Israel, fought for Israel.

43 And Joshua returned, and all Israel with him, to the camp at Gilgal.

11 WHEN JABIN king of Hazor heard of this, he sent to Jobab king of Madon, and to the kings of Shimron and Achshaph,

2 And to the kings who were in the north in the hill country and in the Arabah south of Chinneroth and in the lowland and in the heights of Dor on the west;

3 To the Canaanites in the east and west; to the Amorites, the Hittites, the Perizzites, the Jebusites in the hill country; and to the Hivites below [Mount] Hermon in the land of Mizpah.

4 And they went out with all their hosts, much people, like the sand on the seashore in number, with very many horses and chariots.

5 And all these kings met and came and encamped together at the Waters of Merom, to fight against Israel.

6 But the Lord said to Joshua, Do not be afraid because of them, for tomorrow by this time I will give them up all slain to Israel; you shall hamstring their horses and burn their chariots with fire.

7 So Joshua and all the people of

[h] As the presence of "the Prince of the Lord's host" (Josh. 5:13-15) indicates, the Lord will take part in this conflict not as an ally or an adversary but as Commander in Chief. It is not Israel's quarrel, in which they are to ask divine assistance. It is the Lord's own quarrel, and Israel and Joshua are but a division in His host. The wars of Israel in Canaan are always presented by the Old Testament as "the wars of the Lord." The conquest of Canaan is too often treated as an enterprise of the Israelites, carried out with great cruelties, for which they claimed divine sanction. The Old Testament presents the matter in an entirely different light. The Lord fights for His own right hand, and Israel is but a fragment of His army. "The sun stood still"(Josh. 10:13), the stars in their courses fought against His foes (Judg. 5:20) (Charles Ellicott, *A Bible Commentary*).

war with him came against them suddenly by the Waters of Merom and fell
upon them.

8 And the Lord gave them into the
hand of Israel, who smote them and
chased them [toward] populous
Sidon and Misrephoth-maim, and
eastward as far as the Valley of Mizpah; they smote them until none
remained.

9 And Joshua did to them as the
Lord had commanded him: he hamstrung their horses and burned their
chariots with fire.

10 And Joshua at that time turned
back and took Hazor and smote its
king with the sword; for Hazor previously was the head of all those kingdoms.

11 They smote all the people in it
with the sword, utterly destroying
them; none were left alive, and he
burned Hazor with fire.

12 And Joshua took all the cities of
those kings and all the kings and
smote them with the sword, utterly
destroying them, as Moses the servant
of the Lord commanded. [Deut. 20:16.]

13 But Israel burned none of the
cities that stood [fortified] on their
mounds—except Hazor only, which
Joshua burned.

14 And all the spoil of these cities
and the livestock the Israelites took
for their booty; but every man they
smote with the sword until they had
destroyed them, and they left none
who breathed.

15 As the Lord had commanded
Moses His servant, so Moses commanded Joshua, and so Joshua did; he
left nothing undone of all that the
Lord commanded Moses.

16 So Joshua took all that land: the
hill country, all the South, all the land
of Goshen, the lowland, the Arabah
[plain], the hill country of Israel and
its lowland,

17 From Mount Halak, which rises
toward Seir, as far as Baal-gad in the
Valley of Lebanon below Mount Hermon. He captured all their kings and
slew them.

18 Joshua had waged war a long time
[at least five years] with all those kings.

19 Not a city made peace with the
Israelites except the Hivites, the people of Gibeon; all the others they took
in battle.

20 For it was of the Lord to harden
their hearts that they should come
against Israel in battle, that [Israel]
might destroy them utterly, and that
without favor *and* mercy, as the Lord
commanded Moses.

21 Joshua came at that time and cut
off the Anakim [large in stature] from
the hill country: from Hebron, from
Debir, from Anab, and from all the hill
country of Judah and the hill country
of Israel. Joshua destroyed them
utterly with their cities.

22 None of the Anakim were left in
the land of the Israelites; only in
Gaza, Gath, and Ashdod [of Philistia]
did some remain.

23 So Joshua took the whole land,
according to all that the Lord had spoken to Moses, and Joshua gave it for
an inheritance to Israel according to
their allotments by tribes. And the
land had rest from war.

i "Infidels say that it seems wholly inconsistent with what we should suppose to be the merciful
character of God that He should thus command whole nations to be destroyed by the sword . . . [But]
when we see juries in our own country bringing in a verdict of guilty, the judge pronouncing the sentence of death, and that sentence executed, we do not complain that there is anything unjust in the
act. These Canaanites are proved to have polluted and stained the land with [intolerable] crimes; it
was merely the holy Judge [the Lord] pronouncing the sentence on flagrant criminals and [Joshua]
the righteous governor executing that sentence to the letter. It was not an act of arbitrary or private
revenge, but the execution of the sentence of retributive justice, and as such had perhaps as great
mercy to the innocent as justice to the guilty" (John Cumming, cited by James C. Gray and George
M. Adams, *Bible Commentary*).

12

NOW THESE are the kings of the land whom the Israelites defeated and whose land they took possession of east of the Jordan, from the river Arnon to Mount Hermon, and all the Arabah eastward:

2 Sihon king of the Amorites, who dwelt in Heshbon, and ruled from Aroer on the edge of the Valley of the [river] Arnon, and from the middle of the valley as far as the river Jabbok, the boundary of the Ammonites, including half of Gilead;

3 And the Arabah to the Sea of Chinneroth eastward, and in the direction of Beth-jeshimoth, to the Sea of the Arabah, the Salt [or Dead] Sea, southward to the foot of the slopes of Pisgah.

4 And Og king of Bashan, one of the remnant of the Rephaim, who lived at Ashtaroth and at Edrei,

5 And ruled over Mount Hermon and Salecah and all of Bashan to the boundary of the Geshurites and the Maacathites, and over half of Gilead to the boundary of Sihon king of Heshbon.

6 These Moses the servant of the Lord and the Israelites defeated; and Moses the servant of the Lord gave their land for a possession to the Reubenites, the Gadites, and the half-tribe of Manasseh. [Num. 21; 32:33; Deut. 2; 3.]

7 These are the kings of the land whom Joshua and the Israelites defeated on the west side of the Jordan, from Baal-gad in the Valley of Lebanon to Mount Halak, which rises toward Seir. Joshua gave their land to the tribes of Israel for a possession according to their allotments,

8 In the hill country, in the lowland, in the Arabah, on the slopes, in the wilderness, and in the Negeb— the lands of the Hittites, Amorites, Canaanites, Perizzites, Hivites, and Jebusites:

9 The king of Jericho, one; the king of Ai, which is beside Bethel, one;

10 The king of Jerusalem, one; the king of Hebron, one;

11 The king of Jarmuth, one; the king of Lachish, one;

12 The king of Eglon, one; the king of Gezer, one;

13 The king of Debir, one; the king of Geder, one;

14 The king of Hormah, one; the king of Arad, one;

15 The king of Libnah, one; the king of Adullam, one;

16 The king of Makkedah, one; the king of Bethel, one;

17 The king of Tappuah, one; the king of Hepher, one;

18 The king of Aphek, one; the king of Lasharon, one;

19 The king of Madon, one; the king of Hazor, one;

20 The king of Shimron-meron, one; the king of Achshaph, one;

21 The king of Taanach, one; the king of Megiddo, one;

22 The king of Kedesh, one; the king of Jokneam in Carmel, one;

23 The king of Dor in the heights of Dor, one; the king of Goiim in Gilgal, one;

24 The king of Tirzah, one. In all, thirty-one kings.

13

NOW JOSHUA was old and gone far in years [over 100], and the Lord said to him, You have grown old and are gone far in years, and very much of the land still remains to be possessed.

2 This is the land that remains: all the regions of the Philistines and all those of the Geshurites:

3 From the Shihor [River] which is east of Egypt, northward to the boundary of Ekron, all of it counted as Canaanite; there are five rulers of the Philistines, those of Gaza, Ashdod,

Ashkelon, Gath, and Ekron, and those of the Avvites;

4 In the south, all the land of the Canaanites, and Mearah, which belongs to the Sidonians, to Aphek, to the boundary of the Amorites,

5 And the land of the Gebalites; and all Lebanon toward the east, from Baal-gad below Mount Hermon to the gate of Hamath.

6 As for all the inhabitants of the hill country from Lebanon to Misrephoth-maim, even all the Sidonians, I will Myself drive them out from before the Israelites; only allot the land to Israel for an inheritance, as I have commanded you.

7 So now divide this land for an inheritance to the nine tribes and the half-tribe of Manasseh.

8 With the other half-tribe of Manasseh, the Reubenites and the Gadites received their inheritance beyond the Jordan eastward, as Moses the servant of the Lord gave them:

9 From Aroer on the edge of the Valley of the [river] Arnon, and the city in the midst of the valley, and all the tableland of Medeba as far as Dibon;

10 And all the cities of Sihon king of the Amorites, who ruled in Heshbon, as far as the boundary of the Ammonites;

11 And Gilead, and the region of the Geshurites and Maacathites, and all Mount Hermon, and all Bashan to Salecah—

12 All the kingdom of Og in Bashan, who reigned in Ashtaroth and Edrei and alone was left of the Rephaim [giants]; for these Moses had defeated and driven out.

13 Yet the Israelites did not drive out the Geshurites or the Maacathites, but Geshur and Maacath dwell among [them] still.

14 Only to the tribe of Levi Moses gave no inheritance; the sacrifices made by fire to the Lord, the God of Israel, are their inheritance, as He said to him.

15 And Moses gave an inheritance to the tribe of the Reubenites according to their families:

16 Their territory was from Aroer on the edge of the Valley of the [river] Arnon, and the city in the midst of the valley, and all the tableland by Medeba;

17 With Heshbon and all its cities which are on the plain; Dibon, Bamoth-baal, and Beth-baal-meon,

18 Jahaz, Kedemoth, Mephaath,

19 Kiriathaim, Sibmah, and Zereth-shahar on the hill of the valley,

20 Beth-peor, Pisgah's slopes, and Beth-jeshimoth,

21 All the cities of the plain and all the kingdom of Sihon king of the Amorites, who ruled in Heshbon, whom Moses defeated along with the leaders of Midian, Evi, Rekem, Zur, Hur, and Reba, the princes of Sihon who lived in the land.

22 Balaam son of Beor, the soothsayer, the Israelites also killed with the sword among the rest of their slain. [Num. 31:16.]

23 And the border of the Reubenites was the Jordan. This was the inheritance of the Reubenites according to their families, with their cities and villages.

24 Moses gave an inheritance also to the tribe of the Gadites according to their families.

25 Their territory was Jazer, and all the cities of Gilead, and half the land of the Ammonites as far as Aroer east of Rabbah;

26 And from Heshbon to Ramath-mizpeh and Betonim, and from Mahanaim to the territory of Debir;

27 And in the valley, Beth-haram, Beth-nimrah, Succoth, and Zaphon, the rest of the realm of Sihon king of Heshbon, with the Jordan as a boundary, to the lower end of the Sea of Chinnereth east of the Jordan.

28 This is the inheritance of the Gadites according to their families, with their cities and villages.

29 And Moses gave an inheritance to the half-tribe of Manasseh; it was allotted to them according to their families.

30 Their region extended from Mahanaim through all Bashan, the entire kingdom of Og king of Bashan, and all the towns of Jair, which are in Bashan, sixty cities,

31 And half of Gilead, and Ashtaroth and Edrei, cities of the kingdom of Og in Bashan; these were allotted to the people of Machir son of Manasseh for half of the Machirites according to their families.

32 These are the inheritances which Moses distributed in the plains of Moab beyond the Jordan east of Jericho.

33 But to the tribe of Levi, Moses gave no inheritance; the Lord, the God of Israel, is their inheritance, as He told them.

14 THESE ARE the inheritances in the land of Canaan distributed to the Israelites by Eleazar the priest, Joshua son of Nun, and the heads of the fathers' houses of their tribes.

2 Their inheritance was by lot, as the Lord commanded Moses, for the nine and one-half tribes.

3 For Moses had given an inheritance to the two and one-half tribes beyond the Jordan, but to the Levites he gave no inheritance among them,

4 For the people of Joseph were two tribes, Manasseh and Ephraim. And no part was given in the land to the Levites except cities in which to live, with their pasturelands for their livestock and for their possessions.

5 As the Lord commanded Moses, so the Israelites did, and they divided the land.

6 Then the people of Judah came to Joshua in Gilgal, and Caleb son of Jephunneh the Kenizzite said to him, You know what the Lord said to Moses the man of God concerning me and you in Kadesh-barnea.

7 Forty years old was I when Moses the servant of the Lord sent me from Kadesh-barnea to scout out the land. And I brought him a report as it was in my heart.

8 But my brethren who went up with me made the hearts of the people melt; yet I wholly followed the Lord my God.

9 And Moses swore on that day, Surely the land on which your feet have walked shall be an inheritance to you and your children always, because you have wholly followed the Lord my God. [Deut. 1:35, 36.]

10 And now, behold, the Lord has kept me alive, as He said, these forty-five years since the Lord spoke this word to Moses, while the Israelites wandered in the wilderness; and now, behold, I am this day eighty-five years old.

11 Yet I am as strong today as I was the day Moses sent me; as my strength was then, so is my strength now for war and to go out and to come in.

12 So now give me this hill country of which the Lord spoke that day. For you heard then how the [giantlike] Anakim were there and that the cities were great and fortified; if the Lord will be with me, I shall drive them out just as the Lord said.

13 Then Joshua blessed him and gave Hebron to Caleb son of Jephunneh for an inheritance.

14 So Hebron became the inheritance of Caleb son of Jephunneh the Kenizzite to this day, because he wholly followed the Lord, the God of Israel.

15 The name of Hebron before was Kiriath-arba [city of Arba]. This Arba was the greatest of the Anakim. And the land had rest from war.

15 THE LOT for the tribe of Judah according to its families reached southward to the boundary of Edom, to the Wilderness of Zin at its most southern part. 2 And their south boundary was from the end of the Salt [Dead] Sea, from the bay that faces southward; 3 It went out south of the ascent of Akrabbim, passed along to Zin, and went up south of Kadesh-barnea, along by Hezron, up to Addar, and turned about to Karka, 4 Passed along to Azmon, went out by the Brook of Egypt, and ended at the sea. This was their southern frontier. 5 The eastern boundary was the

boundaries are a good thing

After the children of Israel came in and possessed the land, they wisely established clear boundaries (Joshua 15–19 describes this in great detail). Likewise, it is smart for us to draw healthy boundary lines in our lives and relationships.

Just as a person puts up a fence around his property to keep intruders out, so you must establish limits and margins—invisible lines you draw in your life to protect yourself from being used and abused. If you had a privacy fence around your yard, and on a sunny afternoon you looked out into your yard and saw your neighbors sunbathing there while their children played on your swing set without your permission, what would you do? You certainly would not just say, "Oh, my, I do wish those neighbors would leave me alone." You would probably inform them, maybe quite forcefully, that your yard is off-limits to them for their leisure without your permission. You need to be just as lovingly forceful in letting people know you expect them to respect the limits and margins you have established around your personal life.

People-pleasers do not live within limits or margins. In their efforts to please people, they push themselves beyond reasonable boundaries. Let's face it—people often expect us to do things we either should not do or cannot do. People-pleasers will push beyond the bounds of reason, if they think it means everyone will be happy with them.

Some people will take advantage of us if we let them; that is just human nature. And if they *do* take advantage of us, often we become bitter or resentful toward them; we do not realize that we are just as guilty as they are, if not more so. It is impossible for others to keep taking advantage of us unless we allow them to do so. We need to be the ones to take responsibility for ourselves and make sure we do not let people treat us inappropriately.

My responsibility is to manage my life under the direction of the Holy Spirit, and so is yours. Clear-cut boundaries will help keep it that way. If you have a problem setting proper boundaries in your life, ask the Lord to help you set up boundaries with grace and balance. He will do it because He knows that boundaries are a good thing!

Salt [Dead] Sea as far as the mouth of the Jordan. The northern boundary was from the bay of the sea at the mouth of the Jordan;

6 And the boundary went up to Beth-hogla and passed along north of Beth-arabah and [it] went up to the [landmark] Stone of Bohan son of Reuben.

7 And the boundary went up to Debir from the Valley of Achor, and so northward, turning toward Gilgal, which is opposite the ascent to Adummim on the south side of the valley; and it passed on to the waters of En-shemesh and ended at En-rogel.

8 Then the boundary went up by the Valley of Ben-hinnom [son of Hinnom] at the southern shoulder of the Jebusite [city]—that is, Jerusalem; and the boundary went up to the top of the mountain that lies before the Valley of Hinnom on the west, at the northern end of the Valley of Rephaim.

9 Then the boundary extended from the top of the mountain to the spring of the waters of Nephtoah and went on to the cities of Mount Ephron; then it bent round to Baalah, that is, Kiriath-jearim.

10 And the boundary went around west of Baalah to Mount Seir, passed along to the northern side of Mount Jearim, which is Chesalon, went down to Beth-shemesh, and then passed on by Timnah.

11 And the boundary went out to the shoulder of the hill north of Ekron, then bent round to Shikkeron, and passed along to Mount Baalah, and went out to Jabneel. Then the boundary ended at the sea.

12 And the west boundary was the Great Sea with its coastline. This is the boundary round about the people of Judah according to their families.

13 And to Caleb son of Jephunneh, [Joshua] gave a part among the people of Judah, as the Lord commanded [him]; it was Kiriath-arba, which is Hebron, [named for] Arba the father of Anak.

14 And Caleb drove from there the three sons of Anak—Sheshai and Ahiman and Talmai—the descendants of Anak.

15 He went up from there against the people of Debir. Debir was formerly named Kiriath-sepher.

16 Caleb said, He who smites Kiriath-sepher and takes it, to him will I give Achsah my daughter as wife.

17 And Othniel son of Kenaz, Caleb's brother, took it; and he gave him Achsah his daughter as wife.

18 When Achsah came to Othniel, she got his consent to ask her father for a field. Then she returned to Caleb and when she lighted off her donkey, Caleb said, What do you wish?

19 Achsah answered, Give me a present. Since you have set me in the [dry] Negeb, give me also springs of water. And he gave her the [sloping field with] upper and lower springs.

20 This is the inheritance of the tribe of Judah according to their families.

21 The cities of the tribe of Judah in the extreme south toward the boundary of Edom were: Kabzeel, Eder, Jagur,

22 Kinah, Dimonah, Adadah,

23 Kedesh, Hazor, Ithnan,

24 Ziph, Telem, Bealoth,

25 Hazor-hadattah, Kerioth-hezron (Hazor),

26 Amam, Shema, Moladah,

27 Hazar-gaddah, Heshmon, Beth-pelet,

28 Hazar-shual, Beersheba, Biziothiah,

29 Baalah, Iim, Ezem,

30 Eltolad, Chesil, Hormah,

31 Ziklag, Madmannah, Sansannah,

32 Lebaoth, Shilhim, Ain, and Rimmon. All the cities were twenty-nine [later thirty-six] with their villages.

33 In the lowland: Eshtaol, Zorah, Ashnah,

34 Zanoah, En-gannim, Tappuah, Enam,

35 Jarmuth, Adullam, Socoh, Azekah,

36 Shaaraim, Adithaim, and Gederah and Gederothaim; fourteen cities with their villages.

37 Zenan, Hadashah, Migdal-gad,

38 Dilean, Mizpah, Joktheel,

39 Lachish, Bozkath, Eglon,

40 Cabbon, Lahmas, Chitlish,

41 Gederoth, Beth-dagon, Naamah, and Makkedah; sixteen cities with their villages.

42 Libnah, Ether, Ashan,

43 Iphtah, Ashnah, Nezib,

44 Keilah, Achzib, and Mareshah; nine cities with their villages.

45 Ekron, with its towns and villages.

46 From Ekron to the sea, all that lay beside Ashdod, with their villages;

47 Ashdod, with its towns and its villages; Gaza, with its towns and its villages, as far as the Brook of Egypt, and the Great [Mediterranean] Sea with its coastline.

48 In the hill country: Shamir, Jattir, Socoh,

49 Dannah, Kiriath-sannah (that is, Debir),

50 Anab, Eshtemoh, Anim,

51 Goshen, Holon, and Giloh; eleven cities with their villages.

52 Arab, Dumah, Eshan,

53 Janim, Beth-tappuah, Aphekah,

54 Humtah, Kiriath-arba (that is, Hebron), and Zior; nine cities with their villages.

55 Maon, Carmel, Ziph, Juttah,

56 Jezreel, Jokdeam, Zanoah,

57 Kain, Gibeah, and Timnah; ten cities with their villages.

58 Halhul, Beth-zur, Gedor,

59 Maarath, Beth-anoth, and Eltekon; six cities with their villages.

60 Kiriath-baal (that is, Kiriath-jearim) and Rabbah; two cities with their villages.

61 In the wilderness: Beth-arabah, Middin, Secacah,

62 Nibshan, the City of Salt, and En-gedi; six cities with their villages.

63 But the Jebusites, the inhabitants of Jerusalem, the people of Judah could not drive out; so the Jebusites dwell with the people of Judah at Jerusalem to this day.

16

THE ALLOTMENT for the people of Joseph went from the Jordan by Jericho, east of the waters of Jericho, into the wilderness, going up from Jericho into the hill country to Bethel;

2 Then it went from Bethel to Luz and passed on to Ataroth, the border of the Archites.

3 And it went down westward to the territory of the Japhletites as far as the outskirts of Lower Beth-horon, then to Gezer, and ended at the sea.

4 The descendants of Joseph, Manasseh and Ephraim, received their inheritance.

5 The boundary of the Ephraimites according to their families was thus: on the east side their border was Ataroth-addar as far as Upper Beth-horon.

6 Then the boundary went from there to the sea; on the north was Michmethath; then on the east the boundary went out to Taanath-shiloh, and eastward to Janoah,

7 Then it went down from Janoah to Ataroth and to Naarah, touched Jericho, and ended at the Jordan [River].

8 The border went out from Tappuah westward to the brook Kanah and ended at the [Mediterranean] Sea. This is the inheritance of the Ephraimites by their families,

9 With the towns set apart for the Ephraimites within the inheritance of the Manassites, all those towns with their villages.

10 But they did not drive out the Canaanites who dwelt in Gezer; but the Canaanites dwell among the

Ephraimites to this day, and they became slaves required to do forced labor.

17 ALLOTMENT WAS made for the tribe of Manasseh, for he was the firstborn of Joseph. To Machir the firstborn of Manasseh, the father of Gilead, were allotted Gilead and Bashan because he was a man of war.

2 Allotment was also made for the other Manassites by their families— for the sons of Abiezer, of Helek, Asriel, Shechem, Hepher, and Shemida, the male offspring of Manasseh son of Joseph by their families.

3 But Zelophehad son of Hepher, the son of Gilead, the son of Machir, the son of Manasseh, had no sons but only daughters; their names were Mahlah, Noah, Hoglah, Milcah, and Tirzah.

4 They came before Eleazar the priest and Joshua son of Nun and the leaders and said, The Lord commanded Moses to give us an inheritance with our brethren. So according to the Lord's command, Joshua gave them an inheritance among their father's brethren.

5 So there fell ten portions to Manasseh besides the land of Gilead and Bashan, which is on the other side of the Jordan,

6 Because the [five] daughters of Manasseh received an inheritance among his [five] sons. The land of Gilead belonged to the other [half] of the Manassites.

7 The territory of Manasseh reached from Asher to Michmethah east of Shechem; and the border went along southward to the inhabitants of En-tappuah.

8 The land of Tappuah belonged to Manasseh, but the town of Tappuah on the border of Manasseh belonged to the Ephraimites.

9 Then the boundary went down to the brook Kanah. The cities south of the brook lying among the cities of Manasseh belonged to Ephraim. But Manasseh's boundary went on north of the brook and ended at the sea.

life point

We continue to see that once they possessed the land, the Israelites got very involved in setting up their boundary lines. This reminds me that normal Christian life should be lived within the boundaries of balanced living. Once a person has a serious case of burnout, it is not easy to fix. None of us, not even those of us "called by God," can break His natural laws without paying the penalty. Even though we may work for God, we cannot live without limits. I encourage you to take care of yourself. You have only one body, and you need it to live here on the earth. Be sure you rest physically, mentally, and emotionally. Doing some things for yourself while you are also busy doing for others is not wrong. Stay in balance, and you will be able to run your race well and cross the finish line.

10 The land to the south was Ephraim's and that to the north was Manasseh's, and the sea was the boundary; on the north Asher was reached, and on the east Issachar.

11 Also Manasseh had in Issachar and in Asher [these six towns], their inhabitants and their villages: Bethshean, Ibleam, Dor, Endor, Taanach, and Megiddo.

12 Yet the sons of Manasseh could not drive out the inhabitants of those cities, but the Canaanites persisted in dwelling in that land.

13 When the Israelites became strong, they put the Canaanites to

forced labor but did not utterly drive them out.

14 The tribe of Joseph spoke to Joshua, saying, Why have you given [us] but one lot and one portion as an inheritance when [we] are a great [abundant] people, for until now the Lord has blessed [us]?

15 Joshua replied, If you are a great people, get up to the forest and clear ground for yourselves in the land of the Perizzites and the Rephaim, since the Ephraim hill country is too narrow for you.

16 The Josephites said, The hill country is not enough for us, and all the Canaanites who dwell in the valley have iron chariots, both those in Beth-shean and its villages and in the Valley of Jezreel.

17 And Joshua said to the house of Joseph, to Ephraim and to Manasseh, You are a great *and* numerous people and have great power; you shall not have only one lot

18 But the hill country shall be yours; though it is a forest, you shall clear and possess it to its farthest borders; for you shall drive out the Canaanites, though they have iron chariots and are strong.

18 AND THE whole congregation of the Israelites assembled at Shiloh and set up the Tent of Meeting there; and the land was subdued before them.

2 And there remained among the Israelites seven tribes who had not yet divided their inheritance.

3 Joshua asked the Israelites, How long will you be slack to go in and possess the land which the Lord, the God of your fathers, has given you?

4 Provide three men from each tribe, and I will send them to go through the land and write a description of it according to their [tribal] inheritances; then they shall return to me.

5 And they shall divide it into seven

parts. Judah shall remain in its territory on the south and the house of Joseph shall remain in its territory on the north.

6 You shall describe the land in seven divisions, and bring the description here to me, that I may cast lots for you here before the Lord our God.

7 But the Levites have no portion among you, for the priesthood of the Lord is their inheritance. Gad and Reuben and half the tribe of Manasseh have received their inheritance east of the Jordan, which Moses the servant of the Lord gave them.

8 So the men arose and went, and Joshua charged them saying, Go and walk through the land and describe it and come again to me, and I will cast lots for you here before the Lord in Shiloh.

9 And the men went and passed through the land and described it by cities in seven portions in a book; and they came again to Joshua to the camp at Shiloh.

10 Joshua cast lots for them in Shiloh before the Lord, and there [he] divided the land to the Israelites, to each [tribe] his portion.

11 And the lot of the Benjamites came up according to their families; and the territory of their lot fell between the tribes of Judah and Joseph.

12 On the north side their boundary began at the Jordan; then it went up to the shoulder of Jericho on the north and up through the hill country westward and ended at the Beth-aven wilderness.

putting the Word to work

Do you have good boundaries in your life? Ask God to show you where you may need to improve. Are you stressed out all the time? Make some changes so you can enjoy a peaceful life.

13 Then the boundary passed over southward toward Luz, to the shoulder of Luz (that is, Bethel); then it went down to Ataroth-addar by the mountain that lies south of Lower Beth-horon.

14 The boundary extended from there, and turning about on the western side southward from the mountain that lies to the south opposite Beth-horon, it ended at Kiriath-baal (that is, Kiriath-jearim), a city of the tribe of Judah. This formed the western side [of Benjamin's territory].

15 The southern side began at the edge of Kiriath-jearim, and the boundary went on westward to the spring of the waters of Nephtoah.

16 Then the boundary went down to the edge of the mountain overlooking the Valley of Ben-hinnom [son of Hinnom], which is at the north end of the Valley of Rephaim; and it descended to the Valley of Hinnom, south of the shoulder of the Jebusites, and went on down to En-rogel.

17 Then it bent toward the north and went on to En-shemesh and on to Geliloth, which was opposite the ascent of Adummim, and went down to the Stone of Bohan son of Reuben.

18 And it went on to the north of the shoulder [of Beth]-Arabah and down to the Arabah.

19 Then the boundary passed along to the north of the shoulder of Beth-hoglah and ended at the northern bay of the Salt [Dead] Sea, at the south end of the Jordan. This was the southern border.

20 And the Jordan was its boundary on the east side. This was the inheritance of the sons of Benjamin by their boundaries round about, according to their families.

21 Now the cities of the tribe of Benjamin according to [their] families were: Jericho, Beth-hoglah, Emek-keziz,

22 Beth-arabah, Zemaraim, Bethel,

23 Avvim, Parah, Ophrah,

24 Chephar-ammoni, Ophni, and Geba; twelve cities with their villages;

25 Gibeon, Ramah, Beeroth,

26 Mizpah, Chephirah, Mozah,

27 Rekem, Irpeel, Taralah,

28 Zelah, Haeleph, the Jebusite [city]—that is, Jerusalem—Gibeah, and Kiriath-[jearim]; fourteen cities with their villages. This is the inheritance of the tribe of Benjamin according to their families.

19 THE SECOND lot fell to Simeon, to the tribe of the Simeonites according to their families; and their inheritance lay within that of the people of Judah.

2 And they had for their inheritance: Beersheba or Sheba, Moladah,

3 Hazarshual, Balah, Ezem,

4 Eltolad, Bethul, Hormah,

5 Ziklag, Beth-marcaboth, Hazarsusah,

6 Beth-lebaoth, and Sharuhen; [making] thirteen cities and their villages;

7 Ain [with] Rimmon, Ether, and Ashan; [making] four cities and their villages;

8 And all the villages around these cities as far as Baalath-beer, or Ramah of the Negeb. This was the possession of the Simeonites according to their families.

9 Out of the part assigned to the Judahites was the inheritance of the tribe of Simeon, for the portion of the tribe of Judah was too large for them. Therefore the tribe of Simeon had its inheritance in the midst of Judah's inheritance.

10 The third lot came up for the tribe of Zebulun according to their families. The border of its inheritance extended to Sarid.

11 Then its boundary went up westward and on to Maralah and reached to Dabbesheth and to the brook east of Jokneam.

12 And it turned from Sarid eastward to the border of Chisloth-tabor and it went out to Daberath and on up to Japhia,

13 Then passed eastward to Gath-hepher [Jonah's birthplace] and to Eth-kazin, and went on to Rimmon bending toward Neah.

14 The boundary circled on the north to Hannathon, ending at the Valley of Iphtah-el.

15 Included were Kattath, Nahalal, Shimron, Idalah, and Bethlehem; twelve cities with their villages.

16 This is the inheritance of the people of Zebulun according to their families, these cities with their villages.

17 The fourth lot fell to Issachar, to its people according to their families.

18 Their territory included: Jezreel, Chesulloth, Shunem,

19 Hapharaim, Shion, Anaharath,

20 Rabbith, Kishion, Ebez,

21 Remeth, En-gannim, En-haddah, and Beth-pazzez.

22 The boundary reached to Tabor, Shahazumah, and Beth-shemesh, and ended at the Jordan; sixteen cities with their villages.

23 This is the inheritance of the tribe of Issachar according to their families, the cities and their villages.

24 The fifth lot fell to the tribe of Asher according to their families.

25 Their territory included: Helkath, Hali, Beten, Achshaph,

26 Allammelech, Amad, and Mishal; and on the west it touched Carmel and Shihor-libnath.

27 Then it turned eastward to Beth-dagon, touching Zebulun and the Valley of Iphtah-el northward to Beth-emek and Neiel, and continued in the north to Cabul,

28 Ebron, Rehob, Hammon, and Kanah, even to populous Sidon.

29 Then the boundary turned to Ramah, reaching to the fortified city of Tyre; and it turned to Hosah, and ended at the sea—Mahalab, Achzib,

30 Ummah, Aphek, and Rehob; twenty-two cities with their villages.

31 This is the inheritance of the tribe of Asher according to their families, these cities with their villages.

32 The sixth lot fell to the tribe of Naphtali according to their families.

33 Their boundary ran from Heleph, from the oak in Zaanannim and Adami-nekeb and Jabneel as far as Lakkum; and it ended at the Jordan.

34 Then the boundary turned westward to Aznoth-tabor and went from there to Hukkok, touching Zebulun on the south, Asher on the west, and Judah on the east at the Jordan.

35 The fortified cities included Ziddim, Zer, Hammath, Rakkath, Chinnereth,

36 Adamah, Ramah, Hazor,

37 Kedesh, Edrei, En-hazor,

38 Yiron, Migdal-el, Horem, Beth-anath, and Beth-shemesh; nineteen cities and their villages.

39 This is the inheritance of the tribe of Naphtali according to their families, the cities and their villages.

40 And the seventh lot fell to the tribe of Dan according to their families.

41 The territory of their inheritance included: Zorah, Eshtaol, Ir-shemesh,

42 Shaalabbin, Aijalon, Ithlah,

43 Elon, Timnah, Ekron,

44 Eltekeh, Gibbethon, Baalath,

45 Jehud, Bene-berak, Gath-rimmon,

46 Me-jarkon, and Rakkon, with the territory before Joppa.

47 The territory of the tribe of Dan had to be extended [because of the crowding in of the Amorites and Philistines]; so the sons of Dan went up to fight against Leshem (Laish) and took it and smote it with the sword and possessed it and dwelt there, and they called Leshem (Laish) Dan after Dan their [forefather]. [Judg. 1:34; 18:7-10, 27.]

48 This is the inheritance of the tribe of Dan according to their families, these cities with their villages.

49 When they had finished dividing the land for inheritance by their boundaries, the Israelites gave an inheritance among them to Joshua son of Nun.

50 According to the word of the Lord they gave him the city for which he asked—Timnath-serah in the hills of Ephraim. And he built the city and dwelt in it.

51 These are the inheritances which Eleazar the priest, Joshua son of Nun, and the heads of the fathers' houses of the tribes of Israel distributed by lot in Shiloh before the Lord at the door of the Tent of Meeting. So they finished dividing the land.

20 THE LORD said also to Joshua, **2** Say to the Israelites, Appoint among you cities of refuge, of which I spoke to you through Moses,

3 That the slayer who kills anyone accidentally and unintentionally may flee there; and they shall be your refuge from the avenger of blood. [Num. 35:10ff.]

4 He who flees to one of those cities shall stand at the entrance of the gate of the city and explain his case to the elders of that city; they shall receive him to [the protection of] that city and give him a place to dwell among them.

5 If the avenger of blood pursues him, they shall not deliver the slayer into his hand, because he killed his neighbor unintentionally, having had no hatred for him previously.

6 And he shall dwell in that city until he has been tried before the congregation and until the death of him who is the high priest in those days. Then the slayer shall return to his own city from which he fled and to his own house.

7 And they set apart *and* consecrated Kedesh in Galilee in the hill country of Naphtali and Shechem in the hill country of Ephraim and Kiriath-arba (that is, Hebron) in the hill country of Judah.

8 Beyond the Jordan east of Jericho they appointed Bezer in the wilderness tableland from the tribe of Reuben, and Ramoth in Gilead from the tribe of Gad, and Golan in Bashan from the tribe of Manasseh.

9 These cities were for all the Israelites and the stranger sojourning among them, that whoever killed a person unintentionally might flee there and not be slain by the avenger of blood until he had been tried before the congregation.

21 THEN THE heads of the fathers' houses of the Levites came to Eleazar the priest and Joshua son of Nun and the heads of the fathers' houses of the Israelite tribes.

2 They said to them at Shiloh in Canaan, The Lord commanded through Moses that we should be given cities to dwell in, with their pasturelands (suburbs) for our cattle.

3 So the Israelites gave to the Levites out of their own inheritance, at the command of the Lord, these cities and their suburbs.

4 The [first] lot came out for the families of the Kohathites. So those ʲLevites who were descendants of

---

j The Levites were divided into three groups, the descendants of Levi's three sons, Gershon, Kohath, and Merari. But only those Israelites who were descendants of Levi through Kohath's grandson Aaron could be priests. The priesthood was made hereditary in the family of Aaron and restricted to it; however, even some of these were debarred by legal disabilities (Lev. 21:16ff.). The other families of Levi's descendants, the Gershonites and Merarites and those Kohathites who were not descended from Aaron, were charged with the care of the sanctuary. The priests ministered at the altar.

Aaron the priest received by lot from the tribes of Judah, Simeon, and Benjamin thirteen cities.

5 And the rest of the Kohathites received by lot from the families of the tribes of Ephraim, Dan, and the half-tribe of Manasseh ten cities.

6 The Gershonites received by lot from the families of the tribes of Issachar, Asher, Naphtali, and the half-tribe of Manasseh in Bashan thirteen cities.

7 The Merarites received according to their families from the tribes of Reuben, Gad, and Zebulun twelve cities.

8 The Israelites gave by lot to the Levites these cities with their pasturelands (suburbs), as the Lord commanded through Moses.

9 They gave from the tribes of Judah and Simeon the cities here mentioned by name,

10 Which went to the families of the descendants of Aaron, of the Kohathite branch of the Levites, for the lot fell to them first.

11 They gave them [the city of] Kiriath-arba, Arba being the father of Anak, which city is Hebron, in the hill country of Judah, with its pasturelands round about it.

12 But the city's fields and villages they gave to Caleb son of Jephunneh as his own.

13 Thus to the descendants of Aaron the priest they gave Hebron, the city of refuge for the slayer, with its pasturelands (suburbs), and together with their suburbs, Libnah,

14 Jattir, Eshtemoa,

15 Holon, Debir,

16 Ain, Juttah, and Beth-shemesh; nine cities, each with its suburbs, out of those two tribes.

17 Out of the tribe of Benjamin, Gibeon, Geba,

18 Anathoth, and Almon; four cities, each with its suburbs.

19 The cities of the sons of Aaron, the priests, were thirteen, with their suburbs.

20 The rest of the Kohathites belonging to the Levitical families were allotted cities out of the tribe of Ephraim.

21 To them were given, each with its pasturelands (suburbs), Shechem in the hill country of Ephraim, as the city of refuge for the slayer, and Gezer,

22 And Kibzaim, and Beth-horon; four cities, each with its pasturelands (suburbs).

23 And out of the tribe of Dan, each with its pasturelands (suburbs), Eltekeh, Gibbethon,

24 Aijalon, and Gath-rimmon; four cities, each with its pasturelands (suburbs).

25 And out of the half-tribe of Manasseh, Taanach, and [another] Gath-rimmon; two cities, each with its pasturelands (suburbs).

26 All the cities for the families of the remaining Kohathites were ten, with their pasturelands (suburbs).

27 And to the Gershonites of the families of the Levites they gave out of the other half-tribe of Manasseh the city of Golan in Bashan, as the city of refuge for the slayer, and Be-eshterah; two cities, each with its pasturelands.

28 Out of the tribe of Issachar, Kishion, Daberath,

29 Jarmuth, and En-gannim; four cities, each with its suburbs.

30 Out of the tribe of Asher, Mishal, Abdon,

31 Helkath, and Rehob; four cities, each with its pasturelands.

32 And out of the tribe of Naphtali, Kedesh in Galilee, city of refuge for the slayer, and Hammoth-dor, and Kartan; three cities, each with its suburbs.

33 All the cities of the Gershonite families were thirteen, with their pasturelands (suburbs).

34 And to the families of the Merarites, the rest of the Levites, out of the

tribe of Zebulun were given Jokneam, Kartah,

35 Dimnah, and Nahalal; four cities, each with its pasturelands (suburbs).

36 And out of the tribe of Reuben, Bezer, Jahaz,

37 Kedemoth, and Mephaath; four cities, each with its pasturelands (suburbs).

38 And out of the tribe of Gad, Ramoth in Gilead, as the city of refuge for the slayer, and Mahanaim,

39 Heshbon, and Jazer; four cities in all, each with its pasturelands (suburbs).

40 So all the cities allotted to the Merarite families, that is, the remainder of the Levite families, were twelve cities.

41 The cities of the Levites in the midst of the possession of the Israelites were forty-eight cities in all, with their pasturelands (suburbs).

42 These cities all had their pasturelands (suburbs) around them.

43 And the Lord gave to Israel all the land which He had sworn to give to their fathers, and they possessed it and dwelt in it.

44 The Lord gave them rest round about, just as He had sworn to their fathers. Not one of all their enemies withstood them; the Lord delivered all their enemies into their hands.

45 There failed no part of any good thing which the Lord had promised to the house of Israel; all came to pass.

speak the Word

22 THEN JOSHUA called the Reubenites, the Gadites, and the half-tribe of Manasseh,

2 And said to them, You have kept all that Moses the servant of the Lord commanded you, and have obeyed my voice in all that I commanded you.

3 You have not deserted your brethren [the other tribes] these many days to this day but have carefully kept the charge of the Lord your God.

4 But now the Lord your God has given rest to your brethren, as He promised them; so now go, return to your homes in the land of your possession, which Moses the servant of the Lord gave you on the [east] side of the Jordan.

5 But take diligent heed to do the commandment and the law which Moses the servant of the Lord charged you: to love the Lord your God and to walk in all His ways and to keep His commandments and to cling to *and* unite with Him and to serve Him with all your heart and soul [your very life].

6 So Joshua blessed them and sent them away, and they went to their homes.

7 Now to one-half of the tribe of Manasseh Moses had given a possession in Bashan, but to the other half Joshua gave a possession on the west side of the Jordan among their brethren. So when Joshua sent them away to their homes, he blessed them,

Thank You, God, that not one of my enemies can withstand me, but that You deliver them all into my hands.
ADAPTED FROM JOSHUA **21:44**

God, help me to love You, to walk in all Your ways and keep Your commandments. Help me to cling to You and unite with You. Help me to serve You with all my heart and soul, with my very life.
ADAPTED FROM JOSHUA **22:5**

8 And he said to them, Return with much riches to your tents and with very much livestock, with silver, gold, bronze, iron, and very much clothing. Divide the spoil of your enemies with your brethren.

9 So the Reubenites, Gadites, and the half-tribe of Manasseh returned home, parting from the [other] Israelites at Shiloh in the land of Canaan to go to the land of Gilead, their own land of which they had been given possession by the command of the Lord through Moses.

10 And when they came to the region of the Jordan in the land of Canaan, the Reubenites, Gadites, and the half-tribe of Manasseh built there an altar by the Jordan, an altar great to behold.

11 And the [other] Israelites heard it said, Behold, the Reubenites, Gadites, and the half-tribe of Manasseh have built an altar at the edge of the land of Canaan in the region [west] of the Jordan in the passage [belonging to us], the Israelites.

12 When the Israelites heard of it, the whole congregation of the sons of Israel gathered at Shiloh to make war on them.

13 And the [other] Israelites sent to the Reubenites, Gadites, and the half-tribe of Manasseh, in the land of Gilead, Phinehas son of Eleazar, the priest,

14 And with him ten chiefs, one from each of the tribal families of Israel; and each one was a head of a father's house among the clans of Israel.

15 And they came to the Reubenites, Gadites, and the half-tribe of Manasseh, in the land of Gilead, and they said to them,

16 The whole congregation of the Lord says, What trespass is this that you have committed against the God of Israel, to turn away this day from following the Lord, in that you have built yourselves an altar to rebel this day against the Lord?

17 Is the iniquity of Peor too little for us, from which we are not cleansed even now, although there came a plague [in which 24,000 died] in the congregation of the Lord, [Num. 25:1-9.]

18 That you must turn away this day from following the Lord? The result will be, since you rebel today against the Lord, that tomorrow He will be angry with the whole congregation of Israel.

19 But now, if your land is unclean, pass over into the Lord's land, where the Lord's tabernacle resides, and take for yourselves a possession among us. But do not rebel against the Lord or rebel against us by building for yourselves an altar other than the altar of the Lord our God.

20 Did not Achan son of Zerah commit a trespass in the matter of taking accursed things [devoted to destruction] and wrath fall on all the congregation of Israel? And he did not perish alone in his perversity *and* iniquity. [Josh. 7.]

21 Then the Reubenites, Gadites, and the half-tribe of Manasseh said to the heads of the clans of Israel,

22 The Mighty One, God, the Lord! The Mighty One, God, the Lord! He knows, and let Israel itself know! If it was in rebellion or in transgression against the Lord, spare us not today.

23 If we have built us an altar to turn away from following the Lord, or if we did so to offer on it burnt offerings or cereal offerings or peace offerings, may the Lord Himself take vengeance.

24 No! But we did it for fear that in time to come your children might say to our children, What have you to do with the Lord, the God of Israel?

25 For the Lord has made the Jordan a boundary between us and you, you Reubenites and Gadites; you have no part in the Lord. So your children might make our children cease from fearing the Lord.

26 So we said, Let us now prepare to build us an altar, not for burnt offering nor for sacrifice,

27 But to be a witness between us and you and between the generations after us, that we will perform the service of the Lord before Him with our burnt offerings and sacrifices and peace offerings; lest your children say to our children in time to come, You have no portion in the Lord.

28 So we thought, if that should be said to us or to our descendants in time to come, we can reply, Behold the copy of the altar of the Lord, which our fathers made, not for burnt offerings nor for sacrifices, but to be a witness between us and you.

29 Far be it from us that we should rebel against the Lord and turn away this day from following the Lord to build an altar for burnt offerings, for cereal offerings, or for sacrifices, besides the altar of the Lord our God that is before His tabernacle.

30 And when Phinehas the priest and the chiefs of the congregation and heads of the clans of Israel who were with him heard the words that the Reubenites, Gadites, and Manassites spoke, it pleased them.

31 Phinehas son of Eleazar, the priest, said to the Reubenites, Gadites, and Manassites, Today we know the Lord is among us, because you have not committed this trespass *and* treachery against the Lord; now you have saved the Israelites from the Lord's hand.

32 Then Phinehas son of Eleazar, the priest, and the chiefs returned from the Reubenites and Gadites in the land of Gilead to the land of Canaan, to the [other] Israelites, and brought back word to them.

33 The report pleased the Israelites and they blessed God; and they spoke no more of going to war against them to destroy the land in which the Reubenites and Gadites dwelt.

34 The Reubenites and Gadites called the altar Ed [witness], saying, It shall be: A Witness Between Us that the Lord is God.

23 A LONG time after that, when the Lord had given Israel rest from all their enemies round about, and Joshua had grown old and advanced in years,

2 Joshua summoned all Israel, their elders, heads, judges, and officers, and said to them, I am old and advanced in years.

3 And you have seen all that the Lord your God has done to all these nations for your sake; for it is the Lord your God Who has fought for you. [Exod. 14:14.]

4 Behold, I have allotted to you as an inheritance for your tribes those nations that remain, with all the nations I have cut off, from the Jordan to the Great Sea on the west.

5 The Lord your God will thrust them out from before you and drive them out of your sight, and you shall possess their land, as the Lord your God ᵏpromised you.

6 So be very courageous *and* steadfast to keep and do all that is written in the Book of the Law of Moses, turning not aside from it to the right hand or the left,

7 That you may not mix with these nations that remain among you, or make mention of the names of their gods or swear by them or serve them or bow down to them,

k All through the time of Joshua's leadership he kept giving as his warrant of faith the fact that the Lord had spoken, the Lord had promised. The word of God is the guaranty of faith. Genuine faith always advances on the authority expressed in Heb. 13:5, 6, "**He** [God] Himself has said, . . . So **we** take comfort *and* are encouraged *and* confidently *and* boldly say . . ." (emphasis added).

8 But cling to the Lord your God as you have done to this day.
9 For the Lord has driven out from before you great and strong nations; and as for you, no man has been able to withstand you to this day.
10 One man of you shall put to flight a thousand, for it is the Lord your God Who fights for you, as He promised you.
11 Be very watchful of yourselves, therefore, to 'love the Lord your God.
12 For if you turn back and adhere to the remnant of these nations left among you and make marriages with them, you marrying their women and they yours,
13 Know with certainty that the Lord your God will not continue to drive these nations from before you; but they shall be a snare and trap to you, and a scourge in your sides and thorns in your eyes, until you perish from off this good land which the Lord your God has given you.
14 And behold, this day I am going the way of all the earth. Know in all your hearts and in all your souls that not one thing has failed of all the good things which the Lord your God promised concerning you. All have come to pass for you; not one thing of them has failed.
15 But just as all good things which the Lord promised you have come to you, so will the Lord carry out [His] every [warning of] evil upon you, until

He has destroyed you from off this good land which the Lord your God has given you.
16 If you transgress the covenant of the Lord your God, which He commanded you, if you serve other gods and bow down to them, then the anger of the Lord will be kindled against you, and you shall perish quickly from off the good land He has given you.

24 THEN JOSHUA gathered all the tribes of Israel to Shechem, and summoned the elders of Israel and their heads, their judges, and their officers; they presented themselves before God.
2 Joshua said to all the people, Thus says the Lord, the God of Israel, Your fathers dwelt in olden times beyond the Euphrates River, including Terah the father of Abraham and Nahor, and they served other gods.
3 And I took your father Abraham from beyond the Euphrates River and led him through all the land of Canaan and multiplied his offspring. I gave him Isaac,
4 And I gave to Isaac Jacob and Esau. And I gave to Esau the hill country of Seir to possess, but Jacob and his children went down to Egypt.
5 I sent Moses and Aaron, and I plagued Egypt with what I did in the midst of it; and afterward I brought you out.

speak the Word

I know in my heart, God, that not one of all the good things You have promised me will fail, but that all will come to pass for me.
ADAPTED FROM JOSHUA **23:14**

1 Everything depended on whether or not Israel would continue to be faithful to the covenant. Joshua's words do not conceal his apprehension. Seven times he refers to the idolatrous nations still left in Canaan. He knew the snare they would be to Israel, and he therefore prescribed three safeguards. First, there must be brave **adherence to God's word** (Josh. 23:6). Second, there must be a vigilantly continued **separation** from the Canaanite nations (Josh. 23:7). Finally, there must be a cleaving to the Lord with real and fervent **love** (Josh. 23:8-11) (J. Sidlow Baxter, *Explore the Book*).

6 I brought your fathers out of Egypt, and you came to the sea; and the Egyptians pursued your fathers with chariots and horsemen to the Red Sea.

7 When they cried to the Lord, He put darkness between you and the Egyptians, and brought the sea upon them and covered them; and your eyes saw what I did in Egypt. And you lived in the wilderness a long time [forty years]. [Josh. 5:6.]

8 I brought you into the land of the Amorites who lived on the other side of the Jordan; they fought with you, and I gave them into your hand, and you possessed their land, and I destroyed them before you.

9 Then Balak son of Zippor, king of Moab, arose and warred against Israel, and sent and called Balaam son of Beor to curse you.

10 But I would not listen to Balaam; therefore he blessed you; so I delivered you out of Balak's hand. [Deut. 23:5.]

11 You went over the Jordan and came to Jericho; and the men of Jericho fought against you, as did the Amorites, Perizzites, Canaanites, Hittites, Girgashites, Hivites, and Jebusites, and I gave them into your hands.

12 I sent the ᵐhornet [that is, the terror of you] before you, which drove the two kings of the Amorites out before you; but it was not by your sword or by your bow. [Exod. 23:27, 28; Deut. 2:25; 7:20.]

13 I have given you a land for which you did not labor and cities you did not build, and you dwell in them; you eat from vineyards and olive yards you did not plant.

14 Now therefore, [reverently] fear the Lord and serve Him in sincerity and in truth; put away the gods which your fathers served on the other side of the [Euphrates] River and in Egypt, and serve the Lord.

15 And if it seems evil to you to serve the Lord, choose for yourselves this day whom you will serve, whether the gods which your fathers served on the other side of the River, or the gods of the Amorites, in whose land you dwell; but as for me and my house, we will serve the Lord.

16 The people answered, Far be it from us to forsake the Lord to serve other gods;

17 For it is the Lord our God Who brought us and our fathers up out of the land of Egypt, from the house of bondage, Who did those great signs in our sight and preserved us in all the way that we went and among all the peoples through whom we passed.

18 And the Lord drove out before us all the people, the Amorites who dwelt in the land. Therefore we also will serve the Lord, for He is our God.

19 And Joshua said to the people, You cannot serve the Lord, for He is a holy God; He is a jealous God. He will not forgive your transgressions or your sins.

20 If you forsake the Lord and ⁿserve strange gods, then He will turn and do

speak the Word

God, I declare as Joshua did: As for me and my house, we will serve the Lord.
ADAPTED FROM JOSHUA 24:15

---

m See footnote on Deut. 7:20.   **n** Anything which we keep in our hearts in the place which God ought to have is an idol, whether it be an image of wood or stone or gold, or whether it be money, or desire for fame, or love of pleasure, or some secret sin which we will not give up. If God does not really occupy the highest place in our hearts, controlling all, something else does, and that something else is an idol (J.R. Miller, *Devotional Hours with the Bible*).

"i will serve the Lord"

Regardless of what other people may think, serving and following God really is the only way to live a fulfilling, victorious life.

In Jesus' day, many leaders believed in Jesus but would not confess their faith to others. They feared they would be expelled from the synagogue if they went public with their belief in Him (see John 12:42, 43). They were hindered from a relationship with Jesus because they were addicted to approval. Although they wanted a relationship with the Lord, they loved the approval of man more. That is sad, but it happens all the time.

Joshua, on the other hand, was bold about his belief in God, declaring that "as for me and my house, we will serve the Lord" (Joshua 24:15). Be like Joshua, and determine that you and your household will serve the Lord. Follow God, not people!

The leaders of Jesus' day knew that He was real. They believed in Him, but their love of people's approval would not permit them to have a true relationship with Him. I wonder how their lives turned out. What did they miss because they said *yes* to people and *no* to God? I wonder how many of them were never mentioned in the Bible again. I wonder if they faded into oblivion and never fulfilled their destinies because they loved the approval of men more than the approval of God. How many of them spent their lives disrespecting themselves because they were people-pleasers?

We need to realize that not everyone is going to like us. If we live our lives worrying about what other people think, we will never take risks or stretch ourselves into new realms. We will give up our dreams. Satan is a dream thief, and he works through people who are selfish enough to steal our dreams in order to have theirs.

Do not let anyone steal from you what Jesus died to give you—the freedom to follow the leading of the Holy Spirit for you as an individual. As you follow Him, I guarantee that He will lead you into a rewarding life. Like Joshua, make a deliberate, personal decision to serve the Lord and boldly declare: "As for me and my house, we will serve the Lord."

you harm and consume you, after having done you good.

21 And the people said to Joshua, No; but we will serve the Lord.

22 Then Joshua said to the people, You are witnesses against yourselves that you have chosen the Lord, to serve Him. And they said, We are witnesses.

23 Then put away, said he, the for-eign gods that are among you and incline your hearts to the Lord, the God of Israel.

24 The people said to Joshua, The Lord our God we will serve; His voice we will obey.

25 So Joshua made a covenant with the people that day, and made statutes and ordinances for them at She-chem.

26 And Joshua wrote these words in the Book of the Law of God; and he took a great stone and set it up there under an oak that was in [the court of] the sanctuary of the Lord.

27 And Joshua said to all the people, See, this stone shall be a witness against us, for it has heard all the words the Lord spoke to us; so it shall be a witness against you, lest [afterward] you lie (pretend) *and* deny your God.

28 So Joshua sent the people away, every man to his inheritance.

29 After this, Joshua son of Nun, the servant of the Lord, died, being 110 years old.

30 They buried him at the edge of his inheritance in Timnath-serah in the hill country of Ephraim, on the north side of the hill of Gaash.

31 Israel served the Lord all the days of Joshua and of the elders who outlived Joshua and had known all the works the Lord had done for Israel.

32 And the bones of Joseph, which the Israelites brought up out of Egypt, they buried in Shechem in the portion of ground Jacob bought from the sons of Hamor, the father of Shechem, for 100 pieces of money; and it became the inheritance of the Josephites.

33 And Eleazar son of Aaron died; and they buried him at Gibeah [on the hill] of Phinehas his son, which was given him in the hill country of Ephraim.

speak the Word

Lord, I declare with the Israelites of long ago: The Lord my God I will serve; His voice I will obey.
ADAPTED FROM JOSHUA **24:24**

Judges

Author:
Unknown

Date:
About 1050 BC–1000 BC

Everyday Life Principles:
Disobeying and dishonoring God always brings trouble to our lives.

God is merciful, and He sends deliverance when we cry out to Him.

The Spirit of God works through people to do miraculous things.

The book of Judges tells us about a time when the people of Israel departed from God as they settled in the Promised Land. After Joshua had died and they were left with no leader, they stopped honoring and obeying God. They disregarded His laws, forgot their covenant with Him, and began to do whatever they wanted (see Judges 21:25). Because of His mercy, God raised up good leaders such as Deborah, Gideon, and Samson; He also sent His Spirit among the Israelites and upon certain people to lead them, help them, and give them victory over their enemies.

Judges clearly shows us that the Israelites had so much trouble simply because they would not obey God. They found themselves in a continual cycle of turning from God, then becoming oppressed by their enemies, then crying out to God in their misery. When they cried out, God was faithful to answer in His mercy by sending a person empowered by the Holy Spirit to deliver them in miraculous ways. After a period of time they would forget God and, slowly but surely, sink back into being oppressed by their enemies again.

Do not follow the pattern of the Israelites in the book of Judges by departing from God and getting yourself in trouble. Instead, remember how important obedience is, and do everything you can to honor God in every way, keeping your heart loyal and faithful to Him.

1 AFTER THE death of Joshua, the Israelites asked the Lord, Who shall go up first for us against the Canaanites to fight against them?

2 And the Lord said, Judah shall go up; behold, I have delivered the land into his hand.

3 And Judah [the tribe] said to [the tribe of] Simeon his brother, Come up with me into my allotted territory, so that we may fight against the Canaanites; and I likewise will go with you into your territory. So Simeon went with him.

4 Then Judah went up and the Lord delivered the Canaanites and the Perizzites into their hand, and they smote 10,000 of them in Bezek.

5 And they found Adoni-bezek in Bezek and fought against him, and they smote the Canaanites and the Perizzites.

6 Adoni-bezek fled, but they pursued him and caught him and cut off his thumbs and his big toes.

7 Adoni-bezek said, Seventy kings with their thumbs and big toes cut off had to gather their food under my table. As I have done, so God has repaid me. And they brought him to Jerusalem, and there he died.

8 And the men of Judah fought against [Jebusite] Jerusalem and took it, and smote it with the edge of the sword and set the city on fire.

9 Afterward the men of Judah went down to fight against the Canaanites who dwelt in the hill country, in the South (the Negeb), and in the lowland.

10 And Judah went against the Canaanites who dwelt in Hebron. The name of Hebron before was Kiriath-arba. And they defeated Sheshai and Ahiman and Talmai.

11 From there [Judah] went against the inhabitants of Debir. The name of Debir before was Kiriath-sepher [city of books and scribes].

12 And Caleb said, Whoever attacks Kiriath-sepher and takes it, to him will I give Achsah, my daughter, as wife.

13 And Othniel son of Kenaz, Caleb's younger brother, took it; and he gave him Achsah, his daughter, as wife.

14 And when she came to [Othniel], she got his consent to ask her father for a [sloping] field. And she alighted off her donkey, and Caleb said to her, What do you want?

15 And she said to him, Give me a present; since you have set me in the land of the South (the Negeb), give me also springs of water. And Caleb gave her the upper and lower springs.

16 And the descendants of the Kenite, Moses' father-in-law, went up with the Judahites from the City of Palms (Jericho) into the Wilderness of Judah, which lies in the South (the Negeb) near Arad; and they went and dwelt with the people.

17 And [the tribe of] Judah went with Simeon his brother, and they slew the Canaanites who inhabited Zephath and utterly destroyed it. So the city was called Hormah [destruction].

18 Also Judah took Gaza, Askelon, and Ekron—each with its territory.

19 The Lord was with Judah, and [Judah] drove out the inhabitants of the hill country, but he could not drive out those inhabiting the [difficult] valley basin because they had chariots of iron.

20 Hebron was given to Caleb as Moses said, and he expelled from there the three sons of Anak. [Josh. 14:6, 9.]

21 But the Benjamites did not drive out the Jebusites who inhabited Jerusalem; the Jebusites dwell with the Benjamites in Jerusalem to this day.

22 The house of Joseph also went up against Bethel, and the Lord was with them.

23 And the house of Joseph was sent to spy out Bethel. The name of the city formerly had been Luz.

24 And the spies saw a man coming out of the city and they said to him, Show us, we pray you, the way into the city and we will show you mercy.

25 When he showed them the entrance to the city, they smote the city with the sword, but they let the man and all his family go.

26 And the man went into the land of the Hittites and built a city and called it Luz, which is its name to this day.

27 Neither did Manasseh drive out the inhabitants of Beth-shean and its villages, or of Taanach or Dor or Ibleam or Megiddo and their villages, but the Canaanites remained in that land.

28 When Israel became strong, they put the Canaanites to forced labor but did not utterly drive them out.

29 Neither did Ephraim drive out the Canaanites who dwelt in Gezer, but the Canaanites dwelt in Gezer among them.

30 Neither did Zebulun drive out the inhabitants of Kitron or of Nahalol, but the Canaanites dwelt among them and were put to forced labor.

31 Neither did Asher drive out the inhabitants of Acco or of Sidon or of Ahlab or of Achzib or of Helbah or of Aphik or of Rehob;

32 But the Asherites dwelt among the Canaanites, the inhabitants of the land, for they did not drive them out.

33 Neither did Naphtali drive out the inhabitants of Beth-shemesh or of Beth-anath, but dwelt among the Canaanites, the inhabitants of the land; but the inhabitants of Beth-shemesh and of Beth-anath became subject to forced labor for them.

34 The Amorites forced the Danites back into the hill country, for they would not allow them to come down into the plain;

35 The Amorites remained fixed in Mount Heres [mountain of the sun], in Aijalon, and in Shaalbim; yet the hand of the house of Joseph prevailed, so that they became subject to forced labor.

36 And the border of the Amorites was from the ascent of Akrabbim, from the rock Sela and onward.

2 NOW THE ªAngel of the Lord went up from Gilgal to Bochim. And He said, I brought you up from Egypt and have brought you to the land which I swore to give to your fathers, and I said, I will never break My covenant with you; [Exod. 20:2.]

2 And you shall make no covenant with the inhabitants of this land; but you shall break down their altars. But you have not obeyed My voice. Why have you done this?

3 So now I say, I will not drive them out from before you; but they shall be as thorns in your sides, and their gods shall be a snare to you.

4 When the Angel of the Lord spoke these words to all the Israelites, the people lifted up their voice and wept.

5 They named that place Bochim [weepers], and they sacrificed there to the Lord.

6 And when Joshua had let the people go, the Israelites went every man to his inheritance to possess the land.

7 And the people served the Lord all the days of Joshua and all the days

speak the Word

Thank You, God, that You will never break Your covenant with me.
ADAPTED FROM JUDGES 2:1

a See footnote on Gen. 16:7.

of the elders who outlived Joshua, who had seen all the great works of the Lord which He did for Israel.

8 And Joshua son of Nun, the servant of the Lord, died, being 110 years old.

9 And they buried him within the boundary of his inheritance in Timnath-heres in the hill country of Ephraim, north of Mount Gaash.

10 And also all that generation were gathered to their fathers, and there arose another generation after them who did not know (recognize, understand) the Lord, or even the work which He had done for Israel.

11 And the people of Israel did evil in the sight of the Lord and served the Baals.

12 And they forsook the Lord, the God of their fathers, Who brought them out of the land of Egypt. They went after other gods of the peoples round about them and bowed down to them, and provoked the Lord to anger.

13 And they forsook the Lord and served Baal [the god worshiped by the Canaanites] and the Ashtaroth [female deities such as Ashtoreth and Asherah].

14 So the anger of the Lord was kindled against Israel, and He gave them into the power of plunderers who robbed them; and He sold them into the hands of their enemies round about, so that they could no longer stand before their foes.

15 Whenever they went out, the hand of the Lord was against them for evil as the Lord had said, and as the Lord had sworn to them; and they were bitterly distressed. [Lev. 26:14-46.]

16 But the Lord raised up judges, who delivered them out of the hands of those who robbed them.

17 And yet they did not listen to their judges, for they played the harlot after other gods and bowed down to them. They turned quickly out of the way in which their fathers had walked, who had obeyed the commandments of the Lord, and they did not so.

18 When the Lord raised them up judges, then He was with the judge and delivered them out of the hands of their enemies all the days of the judge; for the Lord was moved to relent because of their groanings by reason of those who oppressed and vexed them.

19 But when the judge was dead, they turned back and corrupted themselves more than their fathers, following and serving other gods, and bowing down to them. They did not cease from their practices or their stubborn way.

20 So the anger of the Lord was kindled against Israel; and He said, Because this people have transgressed My covenant which I commanded their fathers and have not listened to My voice,

21 I from now on will also not drive out from before them any of the nations which Joshua left when he died,

22 That through them I may prove Israel, whether they will keep the way of the Lord to walk in it, as their fathers kept it, or not.

23 So the Lord left those nations, without driving them out at once, nor had He delivered them into Joshua's power.

3 NOW THESE are the nations which the Lord left to prove Israel by them, that is, all in Israel who had not previously experienced war in Canaan;

2 It was only that the generations of the Israelites might know and be taught war, at least those who previously knew nothing of it.

3 The remaining nations are: the five lords of the Philistines, all the Canaanites, the Sidonians, and the Hivites who dwelt on Mount Lebanon from

Mount Baal-hermon to the entrance of Hamath.

4 They were for the testing *and* proving of Israel to know whether Israel would listen *and* obey the commandments of the Lord, which He commanded their fathers by Moses.

5 And the Israelites dwelt among the Canaanites, Hittites, Amorites, Perizzites, Hivites, and Jebusites;

6 And they married their daughters and gave their own daughters to their sons, and served their gods. [Exod. 34:12-16.]

7 And the Israelites did evil in the sight of the Lord and forgot the Lord their God and served the Baals and the Ashtaroth. [Judg. 2:13.]

8 So the anger of the Lord was kindled against Israel, and He sold them into the hand of Chushan-rishathaim king of Mesopotamia; and the Israelites served Chushan-rishathaim eight years.

9 But when the Israelites cried to the Lord, the Lord raised up a deliverer for the people of Israel to deliver them, Othniel son of Kenaz, Caleb's younger brother.

10 The Spirit of the Lord came upon him, and he judged Israel. He went out to war, and the Lord delivered Chushan-rishathaim king of Mesopo-

life point

Throughout the Old Testament, as in Judges 3:10, we see that the Spirit of the Lord "came upon" people and gave them power, wisdom, or ability beyond what they naturally had.

Outer power comes from inner purity, and that inner purification (or sanctification) is a work of the Holy Spirit living within us. He wants to fill us with His Spirit and give us the power to live the abundant life that is available through believing in Jesus Christ.

tamia into his hand and his hand prevailed over Chushan-rishathaim.

11 And the land had rest forty years. Then Othniel son of Kenaz died.

12 And the Israelites again did evil in the sight of the Lord, and the Lord strengthened Eglon king of Moab against Israel because they had done what was evil in the sight of the Lord.

13 And [Eglon] gathered to him the men of Ammon and Amalek, and went and smote Israel, and they possessed the City of Palm Trees (Jericho).

14 And the Israelites served Eglon king of Moab eighteen years.

15 But when the Israelites cried to the Lord, the Lord raised them up a deliverer, Ehud son of Gera, a Benjamite, a left-handed man; and by him the Israelites sent tribute to Eglon king of Moab.

16 Ehud made for himself a sword, a cubit long, which had two edges, and he girded it on his right thigh under his clothing.

17 And he brought the tribute to Eglon king of Moab. Now Eglon was a very fat man.

18 And when Ehud had finished presenting the tribute, he sent away the people who had carried it.

19 He himself went [with them] as far as the sculptured [boundary] stones near Gilgal, and then turned back and came to Eglon and said, I have a secret errand to you, O king. Eglon commanded silence, and all who stood by him went out from him.

20 When Ehud had come [near] to him as he was sitting alone in his cool upper apartment, Ehud said, I have a commission from God to execute to you. And the king arose from his seat.

21 Then Ehud put forth his left hand and took the sword from his right thigh and thrust it into Eglon's belly.

22 And the hilt also went in after the blade, and the fat closed upon the blade, for [Ehud] did not draw the sword out of his belly, and the dirt came out.

23 Then Ehud went out into the vestibule and shut the doors of the upper room upon [Eglon] and locked them.

24 When [Ehud] had gone out, [Eglon's] servants came. And when they saw the doors of the upper room were locked, they thought, Surely he [is seeking privacy while he] relieves himself in the closet of the cool chamber.

25 They waited a long time until they became embarrassed *and* uneasy, but when he still did not open the doors of the upper room, they took the key and opened them, and there lay their master fallen to the floor, dead!

26 Ehud escaped while they delayed and passed beyond the sculptured [boundary] stones (images) and escaped to Seirah.

27 When he arrived, he blew a trumpet in the hill country of Ephraim, and the Israelites went down from the hill country, with him at their head.

28 And he said to them, Follow me, for the Lord has delivered your enemies the Moabites into your hand. So they went down after him and seized the fords of the Jordan against the Moabites and permitted not a man to pass over.

29 They slew at that time about 10,000 Moabites, all strong, courageous men; not a man escaped.

30 So Moab was subdued that day under the hand of Israel, and the land had peace *and* rest for eighty years.

31 After [Ehud] was Shamgar son of Anath, who slew 600 Philistine men with an oxgoad. He also delivered Israel.

4 BUT AFTER Ehud died the Israelites again did evil in the sight of the Lord.

2 So the Lord sold them into the hand of Jabin king of Canaan, who reigned in Hazor. The commander of his army was Sisera, who dwelt in Harosheth-hagoiim [fortress or city of the nations].

3 Then the Israelites cried to the Lord, for [Jabin] had 900 chariots of iron and had severely oppressed the Israelites for twenty years.

4 Now Deborah, a bprophetess, the wife of Lappidoth, judged Israel at that time.

5 She sat under the palm tree of Deborah between Ramah and Bethel in the hill country of Ephraim, and the Israelites came up to her for judgment.

6 And she sent and called Barak son of Abinoam from Kedesh in Naphtali and said to him, Has not the Lord, the God of Israel, commanded [you], Go, gather your men at Mount Tabor, taking 10,000 men from the tribes of Naphtali and Zebulun?

7 And I will draw out Sisera, the general of Jabin's army, to meet you at the river Kishon with his chariots and

b According to Num. 11:25, the prophetic gift has its source in the "Spirit of the Lord." The prophet is a spokesman of God and for God. Miriam was the first prophetess who praised God before all the people (Exod. 15:20). Deborah was not like Miriam, the sister of such men as Moses and Aaron. The objective Spirit of her God elevates her above her people, above heroes before and after her. Not only the ecstasy of enthusiasm, but also the calm wisdom of that Spirit Who informs the law dwells in her. Of no judge until Samuel [the last of the major judges] is it expressly said that he was a "prophet." Of none until him can it be said that he was possessed of the popular authority necessary for the office of judge. The position of Deborah in Israel is therefore a twofold testimony: it proves the relaxation of spiritual and manly energy, and, secondly, the undying might of divine truth, as delivered by Moses, comes brilliantly to view. History shows many instances where in times of distress, when men despaired, women arose and saved their nation; but in all such cases there must be an unextinguished spark of the old fire in the people themselves. Israel, formerly encouraged by the great exploit of a left-handed man—Ehud (Judg. 3:15), is now quickened by the glowing word of a noble woman (J.P. Lange, *A Commentary*).

his multitude, and I will deliver him into your hand?

8 And Barak said to her, If you will go with me, then I will go; but if you will not go with me, I will not go.

9 And she said, I will surely go with you; nevertheless, the trip you take will not be for your glory, for the Lord will sell Sisera into the hand of a woman. And Deborah arose and went with Barak to Kedesh. [Fulfilled in Judg. 4:22.]

10 And Barak called Zebulun and Naphtali to Kedesh, and he went up with 10,000 men at his heels, and Deborah went up with him.

11 Now Heber the Kenite, of the descendants of Hobab, the father-in-law of Moses, had separated from the Kenites and encamped as far away as the oak in Zaanannim, which is near Kedesh.

12 When it was told Sisera that Barak son of Abinoam had gone up to Mount Tabor,

13 Sisera gathered together all his chariots, even 900 chariots of iron, and all the men who were with him from Harosheth-hagoiim to the river Kishon.

14 And Deborah said to Barak, Up! For this is the day when the Lord has given Sisera into your hand. Is not the Lord gone out before you? So Barak went down from Mount Tabor with 10,000 men following him.

15 And the Lord confused *and* terrified Sisera and all his chariot drivers and all his army before Barak with the sword. And Sisera alighted from his chariot and fled on foot.

16 But Barak pursued after the chariots and the army to Harosheth-hagoiim, and all the army of Sisera fell by the sword; not a man was left.

17 But Sisera fled on foot to the tent of Jael, the wife of Heber the Kenite, for there was peace between Jabin the king of Hazor and the house of Heber the Kenite.

18 And Jael went out to meet Sisera and said to him, Turn aside, my lord, turn aside to me; have no fear. So he turned aside to her into the tent, and she covered him with a rug.

19 And he said to her, Give me, I pray you, a little water to drink for I am thirsty. And she opened a skin of milk and gave him a drink and covered him.

20 And he said to her, Stand at the door of the tent, and if any man comes and asks you, Is there any man here? Tell him, No.

21 But Jael, Heber's wife, took a tent pin and a hammer in her hand and went softly to him and drove the pin through his temple and into the ground; for he was in a deep sleep from weariness. So he died.

22 And behold, as Barak pursued Sisera, Jael came out to meet him and said to him, Come, and I will show you the man you seek. And when he came into her tent, behold, Sisera lay dead, and the tent pin was in his temples.

23 So God subdued on that day Jabin king of Canaan before the Israelites.

24 And the hand of the Israelites bore more and more upon Jabin king of Canaan until they had destroyed [him].

5 THEN SANG Deborah and Barak son of Abinoam on that day, saying,

2 For the leaders who took the lead in Israel, for the people who offered themselves willingly, bless the Lord!

3 Hear, O kings; give ear, O princes; I will sing to the Lord. I will sing praise to the Lord, the God of Israel.

4 Lord, when You went forth out of Seir, when You marched out of the field of Edom, the earth trembled and the heavens also dropped, yes, the clouds dropped water.

5 The mountains quaked at the presence of the Lord, yes, yonder

Sinai at the presence of the Lord, the God of Israel.

life point

Deborah and Barak gave God glory for their victory over the king of Canaan (see Judges 5:1–5). Let me assure you: God uses people who will give Him the credit and the praise for their accomplishments. According to I Corinthians 1:29, God will not allow a human being to boast in His presence. He will not allow us to steal His glory, which is why He chooses to use and promote those who know they are nothing without Him and who give Him the glory and the credit for all their accomplishments. Every time you have a success in your life, remember to give God the glory.

6 After the days of Shamgar son of Anath, after the days of Jael [meaning here Ehud] the caravans ceased, travelers walked through byways.
7 The villages were unoccupied *and* rulers ceased in Israel until ᶜyou arose—you, Deborah, arose—a mother in Israel.
8 [Formerly] they chose new gods; then war was in the gates. Was there a shield or spear seen among 40,000 in Israel?
9 My heart goes out to the commanders of Israel who offered themselves willingly among the people. Bless the Lord!
10 Tell of it—you who ride on white donkeys, you who sit on rich

carpets, and you who walk by the way.
11 Far from the noise of archers in the places of drawing water, there shall they rehearse the righteous acts of the Lord, even the righteous acts toward His villagers in Israel. Then the people of the Lord went down to the gates.
12 Awake, awake, Deborah! Awake, awake, utter a song! Arise, Barak, and lead away your captives, you son of Abinoam.
13 Then down marched the remnant of the nobles, the people of the Lord marched down for Me against the mighty.
14 Out of Ephraim they came down whose root is in Amalek, after you, Benjamin, with your kinsmen. Out of Machir came down commanders *and* lawgivers, and out of Zebulun those who ᵈhandle the pen *or* stylus of the writer.
15 And the princes of Issachar came with Deborah, and Issachar was faithful to Barak; into the valley they rushed forth at his heels. [But] among the clans of Reuben were great searchings of heart.
16 Why [Reuben] did you linger among the sheepfolds listening to the piping for the flocks? Among the clans of Reuben there were great searchings of heart.
17 Gilead remained beyond the Jordan, and why did Dan stay with the ships? Asher sat still on the seacoast and remained by his creeks. [These came not forth to battle for God's people.]
18 But Zebulun was a people who endangered their lives to the death;

c F. F. Bruce in *The New Bible Dictionary* calls attention to the fact that the repeated Hebrew verb here "may be understood not as the normal first person singular ('I arose') but as an archaic second person singular ('thou didst arise')." **d** Reference at this date (about 1150 BC) to a writer is no more surprising than the mention of "the city of books" in Judg. 1:11. Writing, and alphabetical writing at that, had been practiced for some centuries along the Syrian Coast . . . Quantities of papyrus [the pith of papyrus was used for writing] were exported from Egypt to Phoenicia at around 1100 BC (Judg. 8:14) (F. Davidson, ed., *The New Bible Commentary*). "Zebulun, formerly known only for [its] experts with the ciphering-pencil, had now become a people courageous unto death" (J.P. Lange, *A Commentary*).

Naphtali did also on the heights of the field.

19 The kings came and fought, then fought the kings of Canaan at Taanach by the waters of Megiddo. Gain of booty they did not obtain.

20 From the heavens the stars fought, from their courses they fought against Sisera.

21 The torrent Kishon swept [the foe] away, the onrushing torrent, the torrent Kishon. O my soul, march on with strength!

22 Then the horses' hoofs beat loudly because of the galloping of [fleeing] valiant riders.

23 Curse Meroz, said the messenger of the Lord. Curse bitterly its inhabitants, because they came not to the help of the Lord, to the help of the Lord against the mighty!

24 Blessed above women shall Jael, the wife of Heber the Kenite, be; blessed shall she be above women in the tent.

25 [Sisera] asked for water, and she gave [him] milk; she brought him curds in a lordly dish.

26 She put her [left] hand to the tent pin, and her right hand to the workmen's hammer. And with the wooden hammer she smote Sisera, she smote his head, yes, she struck and pierced his temple.

27 He sank, he fell, he lay still at her feet. At her feet he sank, he fell; where he sank, there he fell—dead!

28 The ᵉmother of Sisera looked out at a window and wailed through the lattice, Why is his chariot so long in coming? Why do the hoofbeats of his chariots tarry?

29 Her wise ladies answered her, yet she repeated her words to herself,

30 Have they not found and been dividing the spoil? A maiden or two for every man, a spoil of dyed garments for Sisera, a spoil of dyed stuffs embroidered, two pieces of dyed work embroidered for my neck as spoil?

31 So let all Your enemies perish, O Lord! But let those who love Him be like the sun when it rises in its might. And the land had peace *and* rest for forty years.

6 BUT THE Israelites did evil in the sight of the Lord, and the Lord gave them into the hand of Midian for seven years.

2 And the hand of Midian prevailed against Israel. Because of Midian the Israelites made themselves the dens which are in the mountains and the caves and the strongholds.

3 For whenever Israel had sown their seed, the Midianites and the Amalekites and the people of the east came up against them.

4 They would encamp against them and destroy the crops as far as Gaza and leave no nourishment for Israel, and no ox or sheep or donkey.

5 For they came up with their cattle and their tents, and they came like locusts for multitude; both they and their camels could not be counted. So they wasted the land as they entered it.

6 And Israel was greatly impoverished because of the Midianites, and the Israelites cried to the Lord.

7 And when they cried to the Lord because of Midian,

8 The Lord sent a prophet to the Israelites, who said to them, Thus says the Lord, the God of Israel, I brought you up from Egypt and brought you forth out of the house of bondage.

9 And I delivered you out of the hand of the Egyptians and out of the

---

e "Who should first suffer anxiety [in the palace of the women] if not the mother? Of a wife, nothing is said; such love thrives not in the harem of a prince. He is his mother's pride, the great hero, who had hitherto been invincible. What she has in him, and what she loses, concerns no other woman" (J.P. Lange, *A Commentary*).

what about prophecy?

Throughout the Bible, we see God sending prophets to speak to an individual or a group for Him, as He did in Judges 6:8. I believe that the prophetic ministry is still operative today and that a true God-inspired prophecy can strengthen, encourage, and comfort the person who receives it (see I Corinthians 14:3).

There is a difference between a person who has a gift of prophecy and someone who is appointed to the office of prophet in the body of Christ. A prophet has a stronger word for the church at large than someone who is operating in the gift of prophecy to simply strengthen and encourage individual believers.

The Word of God encourages us to welcome divinely inspired prophecy (see I Corinthians 14:1, 3, 4). Prophecy must be consistent with the Word of God, and a personal word of prophecy should confirm something that is already in your heart. If a word is truly from God, *He will make it happen* in His own time. Hold the prophecy in your heart and wait to see if God brings it to pass. He does still speak today through prophecy, and He will confirm prophetic words to you when they truly represent His heart.

hand of all who oppressed you, and drove them out from before you and gave you their land.

10 And I said to you, I am the Lord your God; fear not the gods of the Amorites, in whose land you dwell. But you have not obeyed My voice.

11 Now the [f]Angel of the Lord came and sat under the oak (terebinth) at Ophrah, which belonged to Joash the Abiezrite, and his son Gideon was beating wheat in the winepress to hide it from the Midianites.

12 And the Angel of the Lord appeared to him and said to him, The Lord is with you, you mighty man of [fearless] courage.

13 And Gideon said to him, O sir, if the Lord is with us, why is all this befallen us? And where are all His wondrous works of which our fathers told us, saying, Did not the Lord bring us up from Egypt? But now the Lord has forsaken us and given us into the hand of Midian.

14 The Lord turned to him and said, Go in this your might, and you shall save Israel from the hand of Midian. Have I not sent you?

15 Gideon said to Him, Oh Lord, how can I deliver Israel? Behold, my clan is the poorest in Manasseh, and I am the least in my father's house.

16 The Lord said to him, Surely I will be with you, and you shall smite the Midianites as one man.

17 Gideon said to Him, If now I have found favor in Your sight, then show me a sign that it is You Who talks with me.

18 Do not leave here, I pray You, until I return to You and bring my offering and set it before You. And He said, I will wait until you return.

19 Then Gideon went in and prepared a kid and unleavened cakes of an ephah of flour. The meat he put in a basket and the broth in a pot, and brought them to Him under the oak and presented them.

20 And the Angel of God said to him, Take the meat and unleavened cakes

f See footnote on Gen. 16:7.

how to have a healthy self-image

Gideon did not have a very good self-image (see Judges 6:15)! Sometimes, Christians believe that speaking negatively about themselves is an indicator of humility or holiness. It isn't! So, what is a normal, healthy Christian attitude toward "self"? Here are a few thoughts that reflect a wholesome, God-centered self-image:

1. I know God created me, and He loves me.

2. I have faults and weaknesses, and I want to change. I believe God is working in my life. He is changing me bit by bit, day by day. While He is doing so, I can still enjoy myself and my life.

3. Everyone has faults, so I am not a complete failure just because I am not perfect.

4. I am going to work with God to overcome my weaknesses, but I realize that I will always have something to deal with; therefore, I will not become discouraged when God convicts me of areas in my life that need improvement.

5. I want to make people happy and have them like me, but my sense of worth is not dependent on what others think of me. Jesus has already affirmed my value by His willingness to die for me.

6. I will not be controlled by what people think, say, or do. Even if they totally reject me, I will survive. God has promised never to reject me or condemn me as long as I keep believing (see John 6:29).

7. No matter how often I fail, I am not a failure unless I quit trying. Therefore, I will not give up, because God is with me to strengthen and sustain me. He has promised never to leave me or forsake me (see Hebrews 13:5).

8. I like myself. I don't like everything I do, and I want to change—but I refuse to reject myself.

9. I am in right standing with God through Jesus Christ.

10. God has a good plan for my life. I am going to fulfill my destiny and be all I can be for His glory. I have God-given gifts and talents, and I intend to use them to help others.

11. I am nothing, and yet I am everything! In myself I am nothing, and yet in Jesus I am everything I need to be.

12. I can do all the things I need to do, and everything that God calls me to do, through His Son, Jesus Christ (see Philippians 4:13).

and lay them on this rock and pour the broth over them. And he did so.

21 Then the Angel of the Lord reached out the tip of the staff that was in His hand, and touched the meat and the unleavened cakes, and there flared up fire from the rock and consumed the meat and the unleavened cakes. Then the Angel of the Lord vanished from his sight.

22 And when Gideon perceived that He was the Angel of the Lord, Gideon said, Alas, O Lord God! For now I have seen the Angel of the Lord face to face!

23 The Lord said to him, Peace be to you, do not fear; you shall not die.

24 Then Gideon built an altar there to the Lord and called it, The Lord is Peace. To this day it still stands in Ophrah, which belongs to the Abiezrites.

25 That night the Lord said to Gideon, Take your father's bull, the second bull seven years old, and pull down the altar of Baal that your father has and cut down the Asherah [symbol of the goddess Asherah] that is beside it;

26 And build an altar to the Lord your God on top of this stronghold with stones laid in proper order. Then take the second bull and offer a burnt sacrifice with the wood of the Asherah which you shall cut down.

27 Then Gideon took ten men of his servants and did as the Lord had told him, but because he was too afraid of his father's household and the men of the city to do it by day, he did it by night.

28 And when the men of the city arose early in the morning, behold, the altar of Baal was cast down, and the Asherah was cut down that was beside it, and the second bull was offered on the altar which had been built.

29 And they said to one another, Who has done this thing? And when they searched and asked, they were told, Gideon son of Joash has done this thing.

30 Then the men of the city commanded Joash, Bring out your son, that he may die, for he has pulled down the altar of Baal and cut down the Asherah beside it.

31 But Joash said to all who stood against him, Will you contend for Baal? Or will you save him? He who will contend for Baal, let him be put to death while it is still morning. If Baal is a god, let him contend for himself because one has pulled down his altar.

32 Therefore on that day he called Gideon Jerubbaal, meaning, Let Baal contend against him, because he had pulled down his altar.

33 Then all the Midianites and the Amalekites and the people of the east came together and, crossing the Jordan, encamped in the Valley of Jezreel.

34 But the Spirit of the Lord clothed Gideon with Himself *and* took possession of him, and he blew a trumpet, and [the clan of] Abiezer was gathered to him.

life point

As believers we are not to be self-confident but God-confident—and that kind of confidence comes only by the Holy Spirit. The Bible says repeatedly that we are not supposed to have confidence in *ourselves*. Instead, we are to have confidence in God—that He will work mightily *through* us, just as He did through Gideon (see Judges 6:34).

35 And he sent messengers throughout all Manasseh, and the Manassites were called to follow him; and he sent messengers to Asher, to Zebulun, and to Naphtali, and they came up to meet them.

life point

Sometimes people want God to speak to them with a sign, as Gideon did when he laid out a fleece on the threshing floor (see Judges 6:36–40). Even though God did honor Gideon's request, Gideon missed out on God's best. God will sometimes give us a sign, as He did for Gideon, when we are young Christians. However, as we mature in our knowledge of God's leading, He is pleased when we learn to operate in faith, which requires no signs in order to believe and obey.

36 And Gideon said to God, If You will deliver Israel by my hand as You have said,
37 Behold, I will put a fleece of wool on the threshing floor. If there is dew on the fleece only and it is dry on all the ground, then I shall know that You will deliver Israel by my hand, as You have said.
38 And it was so. When he rose early next morning and squeezed the dew out of the fleece, he wrung from it a bowlful of water.
39 And Gideon said to God, Let not your anger be kindled against me, and I will speak but this once. Let me make trial only this once with the fleece, I pray you; let it now be dry only upon the fleece and upon all the ground let there be dew.
40 And God did so that night, for it was dry on the fleece only, and there was dew on all the ground.

7 THEN JERUBBAAL, that is, Gideon, and all the people who were with him rose early and encamped beside the spring of Harod; and the camp of Midian was north of them by the hill of Moreh in the valley.

2 The Lord said to Gideon, The people who are with you are too many for Me to give the Midianites into their hands, lest Israel boast about themselves against Me, saying, My own hand has delivered me.
3 So now proclaim in the ears of the men, saying, Whoever is fearful and trembling, let him turn back and depart from Mount Gilead. And 22,000 of the men returned, but 10,000 remained.

life point

The Lord instructed Gideon to tell the men who were fearful to turn around and go home (see Judges 7:3); twenty-two thousand of them left, leaving ten thousand behind to face the enemy. That tells us there were more men who were afraid than were courageous.

How many times does God put something on our hearts to do, but then we cower when fear comes along, causing us to hesitate and become double-minded? In this circumstance, we may feel fear, but we *can* do things afraid. Remember, God's Word to us is, "Fear not, for I am with you." When fear knocks on your door, let faith answer!

4 And the Lord said to Gideon, The men are still too many; bring them down to the water, and I will test them for you there. And he of whom I say to you, This man shall go with you, shall go with you; and he of whom I say to you, This man shall not go with you, shall not go.
5 So he brought the men down to the water, and the Lord said to Gideon, Everyone who laps up the water with his tongue as a dog laps it, you shall set by himself, likewise everyone who bows down on his knees to drink.

the reward of relying on God

Instead of telling Gideon that He would give him more men, God told him that he had too many men to gain the victory. Interestingly, sometimes God works through our weaknesses better than through our strengths. There are times when we have too much on our side in the natural for God to give the victory. If we depend on ourselves and our own strength too much, God cannot work. Our problem is not big enough for God to give us a miracle if anyone can help us but God. God was telling Gideon that his men were too strong in themselves and that He wanted them in a position where they would have to depend entirely on Him. God cut their army down to a size that made it impossible for them to experience victory without His divine intervention.

Pride and boasting ruin the best of people, so God has to help us stay humble and totally dependent on Him. Israel had repeated the same cycle over and over since their exodus from Egypt. They would lean entirely on God, and He would help them. Then they would become self-sufficient, disobedient, and rebellious, thinking that they did not need God, and their circumstances would once again become bad. When they trusted God, they defeated their enemies; when they did not, their enemies defeated them. Trust God and experience victory in your life.

6 And the number of those who lapped, putting their hand to their mouth, was 300 men, but all the rest of the people bowed down upon their knees to drink water.

7 And the Lord said to Gideon, With the 300 men who lapped I will deliver you, and give the Midianites into your hand. Let all the others return every man to his home.

8 So the people took provisions and their trumpets in their hands, and he sent all the rest of Israel every man to his home and retained those 300 men. And the host of Midian was below him in the valley.

9 That same night the Lord said to Gideon, Arise, go down against their camp, for I have given it into your hand.

10 But if you fear to go down, go with Purah your servant down to the camp

11 And you shall hear what they say, and afterward your hands shall be strengthened to go down against the camp. Then he went down with Purah his servant to the outposts of the camp of the armed men.

12 And the Midianites and the Amalekites and all the sons of the east lay along the valley like locusts for multitude; and their camels were without number, as the sand on the seashore for multitude.

13 When Gideon arrived, behold, a man was telling a dream to his comrade. And he said, Behold, I dreamed a dream, and behold, a cake of ᵍbarley bread tumbled into the camp of Midian and came to the tent and struck it so that it fell, and turned it upside down so that the tent lay flat.

14 And his comrade replied, This is nothing else but the sword of Gideon son of Joash, a man of Israel. Into his

g Alluding to the insignificance of Gideon and his family, or perhaps his whole troop. Barley then, as it is still, was distinguished from "fine flour." "To heare himselfe but a Barly-cake, troubled him not. It matters not how base wee be thought, so wee be victorious" (Bishop Joseph Hall, cited by *The Cambridge Bible*).

praise God preemptively

As soon as Gideon received a personal word from God, he began to talk about the battle before him as though it were already won (see Judges 7:14, 15). He did not wait to see the results of the battle before he proclaimed the triumph of the Lord, but he began to praise and worship God as though he already had the victory.

In the book of Exodus, the Israelites sang the right song after they had passed through the Red Sea and their enemies had been drowned: "For He has triumphed gloriously; the horse and his rider . . . has He thrown into the sea" (Exodus 15:1). However, they sang this song of victory on the wrong side of the river. They were all excited. They had their tambourines out and were singing and dancing. They went into a long dissertation about the greatness of God—*after* they had seen the manifestation of His power. They sang the right song at the wrong time. It would have been so much better if they had sung their victory song before they crossed the river.

We would certainly be remiss if we did not praise and worship God after the victories in our lives, but Gideon did the right thing in worshipping *before* he won his battle. All he needed was to hear from God that he would win—and then he started worshipping. Learning to worship God before the battle gets His attention, demonstrates our faith, and inspires us to boldly enter any challenge we face.

hand God has given Midian and all the host.

15 When Gideon heard the telling of the dream and its interpretation, he worshiped and returned to the camp of Israel and said, Arise, for the Lord has given into your hand the host of Midian.

16 And he divided the 300 men into three companies, and he put into the hands of all of them trumpets and empty pitchers, with torches inside the pitchers.

17 And he said to them, Look at me, then do likewise. When I come to the edge of their camp, do as I do.

18 When I blow the trumpet, I and all who are with me, then you blow the trumpets also on every side of all the camp and shout, For the Lord and for Gideon!

19 So Gideon and the 100 men who were with him came to the outskirts of the camp at the beginning of the middle watch, when the guards had just been changed, and they blew the trumpets and smashed the pitchers that were in their hands.

20 And the three companies blew the trumpets and shattered the pitchers, holding the torches in their left hands, and in their right hands the trumpets to blow [leaving no chance to use swords], and they cried, The sword for the Lord and Gideon!

21 They stood every man in his place round about the camp, and all the [Midianite] army ran—they cried out and fled.

22 When [Gideon's men] blew the 300 trumpets, the Lord set every [Midianite's] sword against his comrade and against all the army, and the army fled as far as Beth-shittah toward Zererah, as far as the border of Abel-meholah by Tabbath.

23 And the men of Israel were called together out of Naphtali and Asher and all Manasseh, and they pursued Midian.

life point

Notice that each man in Gideon's tiny army held a torch in one hand and a trumpet in the other, "leaving no chance to use swords" (Judges 7:20). When God sent them to battle against a vastly superior host of Midianites, He intentionally put these items in their hands so they could not draw their swords to fight on their own. Think about it: God sent out three hundred fearless men who were focused on what they were called to do, and He made sure they had something in each hand so they could not possibly fight their own battle—they had to depend on Him to fight it for them. All they had to do was break a pitcher, hold up a torch, and cry, "The sword for the Lord and Gideon!" (Judges 7:20). We can learn from them to put all of our confidence and trust in God instead of in our ability to help ourselves. What God has asked you to do may be impossible for you, but it is not impossible for Him.

24 And Gideon sent messengers throughout all the hill country of Ephraim, saying, Come down against the Midianites and take all the intervening fords as far as Beth-barah and also the Jordan. So all the men of Ephraim were gathered together and took all the fords as far as Beth-barah and also the Jordan.

25 And [the men of Ephraim] took the two princes of Midian, Oreb and Zeeb, and they slew Oreb at the rock of Oreb, and Zeeb they slew at the winepress of Zeeb, and pursued Midian; and they brought the heads of Oreb and Zeeb to Gideon beyond the Jordan.

8 AND THE men of Ephraim said to Gideon, Why have you treated us like this, not calling us when you went to fight with Midian? And they quarreled with him furiously.

2 And he said to them, What have I done now in comparison with you? Is not the gleaning of the grapes of [your big tribe of] Ephraim better than the vintage of [my little clan of] Abiezer?

3 hGod has given into your hands the princes of Midian, Oreb and Zeeb, and what was I able to do in comparison with you? Then their anger toward him was abated when he had said that.

4 And Gideon came to the Jordan and passed over, he and the 300 men with him, faint yet pursuing.

5 And he said to the men of Succoth, Give, I pray you, loaves of bread to the people who follow me, for they are faint, and I am pursuing Zebah and Zalmunna, kings of Midian.

6 And the princes of Succoth said, Are Zebah and Zalmunna already in your hand, that we should give bread to your army?

7 And Gideon said, For that, when the Lord has delivered Zebah and Zalmunna into my hand, I will thresh your flesh with the thorns and briers of the wilderness!

8 And he went from there up to Penuel and made the same request, and the men of Penuel answered him as the men of Succoth had done.

9 And [Gideon] said to the men of Penuel, When I come again in peace, I will break down this tower.

10 Now Zebah and Zalmunna were

h "Gideon's good words were as victorious as his sword" (Bishop Joseph Hall, cited by Charles Ellicott, *A Bible Commentary*). "He might have said that he could place but little dependence upon his brethren when, through faintheartedness, 22,000 left him at one time (Judg. 7:3), but he passed this by and took a more excellent way" (Adam Clarke, *The Holy Bible with A Commentary*). "The improving of a victory is often more honorable and of greater consequence than the winning of it . . . Humility of deportment is the . . . surest method of ending strife" (Matthew Henry, *Commentary on the Holy Bible*).

in Karkor with their army—about 15,000 men, all who were left of all the army of the sons of the east, for there had fallen 120,000 men who drew the sword.

11 And Gideon went up by the route of those who dwelt in tents east of Nobah and Jogbehah and smote their camp [unexpectedly], for the army thought itself secure.

12 And Zebah and Zalmunna fled, and he pursued them and took the two kings of Midian, Zebah and Zalmunna, and terrified all the army.

13 Then Gideon son of Joash returned from the battle by the ascent of Heres.

14 And he caught a young man of Succoth and inquired of him, and [the youth] wrote down for him [the names of] the officials of Succoth and its elders, seventy-seven men.

15 And he came to the men of Succoth and said, Behold Zebah and Zalmunna, about whom you scoffed at me, saying, Are Zebah and Zalmunna now in your hand, that we should give bread to your men who are faint?

16 And he took the elders of the city and thorns of the wilderness and briers, and with them he taught the men of Succoth [a lesson].

17 And he broke down the tower of Penuel and slew the men of the city.

18 Then [Gideon] said to Zebah and Zalmunna, What kind of men were they whom you slew at Tabor? And they replied, They were like you, each of them resembled the son of a king.

19 And he said, They were my brothers, the sons of my mother. As the Lord lives, if you had saved them alive, I would not slay you.

20 And [Gideon] said to Jether his firstborn [to embarrass them], Up, and slay them. But the youth drew not his sword, for he feared because he was yet a lad.

21 Then Zebah and Zalmunna said, Rise yourself and fall on us; for as the man is, so is his strength. And Gideon arose and slew Zebah and Zalmunna and took the [crescent-shaped] ornaments that were on their camels' necks.

22 Then the men of Israel said to Gideon, Rule over us—you and your son and your son's son also—for you have delivered us from the hand of Midian.

23 And Gideon said to them, I will not rule over you, and my son will not rule over you; the Lord will rule over you.

24 And Gideon said to them, Let me make a request of you—every man of you give me the earrings of his spoil. For [the Midianites] had gold earrings because they were Ishmaelites [general term for all descendants of Keturah].

25 And they answered, We will willingly give them. And they spread a garment, and every man cast on it the earrings of his spoil.

26 And the weight of the golden earrings that he requested was 1,700 shekels of gold, besides the crescents and pendants and the purple garments worn by the kings of Midian, and the chains that were about their camels' necks.

27 And Gideon made an ephod [a sacred, high priest's garment] of it, and put it in his city of Ophrah, and all Israel paid homage to it there, and ¹it became a snare to Gideon and to his family.

28 Thus was Midian subdued before the Israelites so that they lifted up

i The gold and purple of the spoil enabled Gideon to make an ephod, presumably on the pattern of that described in Exod. 28. It was not exactly an idol but a kind of fetish, and it diverted the thoughts of the people from Shiloh and the spiritual worship of the unseen and eternal God. So apt is the human heart to cling to some outward emblem—it may be a crucifix, a wafer, or a church—and miss that worship in spirit and in truth which the Father seeks (John 4:23) (F. B. Meyer, *Devotional Commentary on Joshua—II Kings*).

their heads no more. And the land had peace *and* rest for forty years in the days of Gideon.

29 Jerubbaal (Gideon) son of Joash went and dwelt in his own house.

30 Now Gideon had seventy sons born to him, for he had many wives.

31 And his concubine, who was in Shechem, also bore him a son, whom he named Abimelech.

32 Gideon son of Joash died at a good old age and was buried in the tomb of Joash his father in Ophrah of the Abiezrites.

33 As soon as Gideon was dead, the Israelites turned again and played the harlot after the Baals and made Baal-berith their god.

34 And the Israelites did not remember the Lord their God, Who had delivered them out of the hand of all their enemies on every side;

35 Neither did they show kindness to the family of Jerubbaal, that is, Gideon, in return for all the good which he had done for Israel.

9 NOW ABIMELECH son of Jerubbaal (Gideon) went to Shechem to his mother's kinsmen and said to them and to the whole clan of his mother's family,

2 Say, I pray you, in the hearing of all the men of Shechem, Which is better for you: that all seventy of the sons of Jerubbaal reign over you, or that one man rule over you? Remember also that I am your bone and your flesh.

3 And his mother's kinsmen spoke all these words concerning him in the hearing of all the men of Shechem, and their hearts inclined to follow Abimelech, for they said, He is our brother.

4 And they gave him seventy pieces of silver out of the house of Baal-berith, with which Abimelech hired worthless and foolhardy men who followed him.

5 And he went to his father's house at Ophrah and slew his brothers the sons of Jerubbaal, seventy men, on one stone. But Jotham, the youngest son of Jerubbaal, was left, for he hid himself.

6 And all the men of Shechem gathered together and all of Beth-millo, and they went and made Abimelech king by the oak (terebinth) of the pillar at Shechem.

7 When it was told to Jotham, he went and stood at the top of Mount Gerizim and shouted to them, Hear me, men of Shechem, that God may hear you.

8 One time the trees went forth to anoint a king over them, and they said to the olive tree, Reign over us.

9 But the olive tree said to them, Should I leave my fatness, by which God and man are honored, and go to wave over the trees?

10 Then the trees said to the fig tree, You come and reign over us.

11 But the fig tree said to them, Should I leave my sweetness and my good fruit and go to wave over the trees?

12 Then the trees said to the vine (grapevine), You come and reign over us.

13 And the vine (grapevine) replied, Should I leave my new wine, which rejoices God and man, and go to wave over the trees?

14 Then all the trees said to the bramble, You come and reign over us.

15 And the bramble said to the trees, If in good faith you are anointing me king over you, then come and take refuge in my shade; but if not, let fire come out of the bramble and devour the cedars of Lebanon.

16 Now therefore, if you acted sincerely and honorably when you made Abimelech king, and if you have dealt well with Jerubbaal and his house and have done to him as his deeds deserved—

17 For my father fought for you,

jeopardized his life, and rescued you from the hand of Midian;

18 And you have risen up against my father's house this day and have slain his sons, seventy men, on one stone and have made Abimelech, son of his maidservant, king over the people of Shechem because he is your kinsman—

19 If you then have acted sincerely and honorably with Jerubbaal and his house this day, then rejoice in Abimelech, and let him also rejoice in you;

20 But if not, let fire come out from Abimelech and devour the people of Shechem and Beth-millo, and let fire come out from the people of Shechem and Beth-millo and devour Abimelech.

21 And Jotham ran away and fled, and went to Beer and dwelt there for fear of Abimelech his brother.

22 Abimelech reigned three years over Israel.

23 And God sent an evil spirit between Abimelech and the men of Shechem, and the men of Shechem dealt treacherously with Abimelech,

24 That the violence done to the seventy sons of Jerubbaal might come, and that their blood might be laid upon Abimelech their brother, who slew them, and upon the men of Shechem, who strengthened his hands to slay his brothers.

25 And the men of Shechem set men in ambush against [Abimelech] on the mountaintops, and they robbed all who passed by them along that way; and it was told to Abimelech.

26 And Gaal son of Ebed came with his kinsmen and moved into Shechem, and the men of Shechem put confidence in him.

27 And they went out into the field, gathered their vineyard fruits and trod them, and held a festival; and going into the house of their god, they ate and drank and cursed Abimelech.

28 Gaal son of Ebed said, Who is Abimelech, and who are we of Shechem, that we should serve him? Were not the son of Jerubbaal and Zebul, his officer, servants of the men of Hamor the father *and* founder of Shechem? Then why should we serve him?

29 Would that this people were under my hand! Then would I remove Abimelech and say to him, Increase your army and come out.

30 When Zebul the city's mayor heard the words of Gaal son of Ebed, his anger was kindled.

31 And he sent messengers to Abimelech slyly, saying, Behold, Gaal son of Ebed and his kinsmen have come to Shechem; and behold, they stir up the city to rise against you.

32 Now therefore, rise up by night, you and the men with you, and lie in wait in the field.

33 Then in the morning, as soon as the sun is up, rise early and set upon the city; and when Gaal and the men with him come out against you, do to them as opportunity permits.

34 And Abimelech rose up by night, and all the men with him, and they laid in wait against Shechem in four companies.

35 And Gaal son of Ebed came out and stood in the entrance of the city's gate. Then Abimelech and the men with him rose up from ambush.

36 When Gaal saw the men, he said to Zebul, Look, men are coming down from the mountaintops! Zebul said to him, The shadow of the mountains looks to you like men.

37 And Gaal spoke again and said, See, men are coming down from the center of the land, and one company is coming from the direction of the oak of Meonenim [the sorcerers].

38 Then said Zebul to Gaal, Where is your [big] mouth now, you who said, Who is Abimelech, that we should serve him? Are not these the men whom you have despised? Go out now and fight with them.

39 And Gaal went out ahead of the men of Shechem and fought with Abimelech.

40 And Abimelech chased him, and he fled before him; and many fell wounded—even to the entrance of the gate.

41 And Abimelech lodged at Arumah, and Zebul thrust out Gaal and his kinsmen so that they could not live in Shechem.

42 The next day the men went out into the fields, and Abimelech was told.

43 He took his men and divided them into three companies and laid in wait in the field; and he looked and behold, the people were coming out of the city. And he rose up against them and smote them.

44 And Abimelech and the company with him rushed forward and stood in the entrance of the city's gate, while the two other companies rushed upon all who were in the field and slew them.

45 And Abimelech fought against the city all that day. He took the city and slew the people who were in it. He demolished the city and ʲsowed it with salt.

46 And when all the men of the Tower of Shechem heard of it, they entered the stronghold of the house of El-berith [the god of Berith].

47 Abimelech was told that all the people of the Tower of Shechem were gathered together.

48 And Abimelech went up to Mount Zalmon, he and all the men with him; and Abimelech took an ax in his hand and cut down a bundle of brush, picked it up, and laid it on his shoulder.

And he said to the men with him, What you have seen me do, make haste to do also.

49 So each of the men cut down his bundle and following Abimelech put it against the stronghold and set [the stronghold] on fire over the people in it, so that all the people of the Tower of Shechem also died, about 1,000 men and women.

50 Then Abimelech went to Thebez and encamped against Thebez and took it.

51 But there was a strong tower in the city, and all the people of the city—men and women—fled to it, shut themselves in, and went to the roof of the tower.

52 And Abimelech came to the tower and fought against it and drew near the door of the tower to burn it with fire.

53 But a certain woman cast an upper millstone [down] upon Abimelech's head and broke his skull.

54 Then he called hastily to the young man, his armor-bearer, and said to him, Draw your sword and slay me, so that men may not say of me, A woman slew him. And his young man thrust him through, and he died.

55 And when the men of Israel saw that Abimelech was dead, they departed each man to his home.

56 Thus God repaid the wickedness of Abimelech which he had done to his father [Gideon] by slaying his seventy brothers;

57 And all the wickedness of the men of Shechem God repaid upon their heads and caused to come upon them

---

j This strewing of salt over Shechem was not intended (even if Abimelech had been able to supply enough salt) actually to make the ground unfruitful; but it was a symbol of perpetual desolation, and a sign that Shechem never would be rebuilt. However, such a forecast of a city's fate made by a true prophet of God, or by the Lord Himself, was one thing. This forecast, symbolized by the wicked usurper Abimelech, was quite another thing. For Shechem was later rebuilt (I Kings 12:25), and so was denounced Jericho (I Kings 16:34; see also Josh. 6). But this is not true of Samaria (Mic. 1:6), or Nineveh (Nah. 1:9-12), or Ashkelon (Zeph. 2:4), or the cities of Edom (Ezek. 35:9), or Tyre (Ezek. 26:3, 14), or Chorazin, or Bethsaida, or Capernaum (Matt. 11:20, 21, 23). That these cities, as such, would never be rebuilt permanently was foretold on the authority and by order of God Himself. "Sky and earth will pass away, but My words will not pass away" (Matt. 24:35).

the curse of Jotham son of Jerubbaal. [Judg. 9:19, 20.]

10 AFTER ABIMELECH there arose to rescue Israel, Tola son of Puah, the son of Dodo, a man of Issachar; and he lived at Shamir in the hill country of Ephraim.
2 He judged Israel twenty-three years; then he died and was buried in Shamir.
3 After him arose Jair the Gileadite, and he judged Israel twenty-two years.
4 And he had thirty sons who rode on thirty donkey colts, and they had thirty towns called Havvoth-jair [towns of Jair] which to this day are in the land of Gilead.
5 And Jair died and was buried in Kamon.
6 And the Israelites again did what was evil in the sight of the Lord, served the Baals, the Ashtaroth [female deities], the gods of Syria, the gods of Sidon, the gods of Moab, the gods of the Ammonites, and the gods of the Philistines. They forsook the Lord and did not serve Him.
7 And the anger of the Lord was kindled against Israel, and He sold them into the hands of the Philistines and the Ammonites,
8 And they oppressed and crushed and broke the Israelites that year. For eighteen years they oppressed all the Israelites beyond the Jordan in the land of the Amorites, which is in Gilead.
9 And the Ammonites passed over the Jordan to fight against Judah, Benjamin, and the house of Ephraim, so that Israel was sorely distressed.
10 And the Israelites cried to the

Lord, saying, We have sinned against You, because we have forsaken our God and have served the Baals.
11 And the Lord said to the Israelites, Did I not deliver you from the Egyptians, the Amorites, the Ammonites, and the Philistines?
12 Also when the Sidonians, the Amalekites, and the Maonites oppressed and crushed you, you cried to Me, and I delivered you out of their hands.
13 Yet you have forsaken Me and served other gods; therefore I will deliver you no more.
14 Go, cry to the gods you have chosen; let them deliver you in your time of distress.
15 And the Israelites said to the Lord, We have sinned, do to us whatever seems good to You; only deliver us, we pray You, this day.
16 So they put away the foreign gods from among them and served the Lord, and His heart became impatient over the misery of Israel.
17 Then the Ammonites were gathered together and they encamped in Gilead. And the Israelites assembled and encamped at Mizpah.
18 And the leaders of Gilead [the Israelites] said one to another, Who is the man who will begin to fight against the Ammonites? He shall be head over all the inhabitants of Gilead.

11 NOW JEPHTHAH the Gileadite was a mighty warrior, but he was the son of a harlot. Gilead was Jephthah's father.
2 And Gilead's wife also bore him sons, and when his wife's sons grew up, they thrust Jephthah out and said to him, You shall not have an

speak the Word

inheritance in our father's house, for you are the son of another woman.

3 Then Jephthah fled from his brothers and dwelt in the land of Tob; and worthless men gathered around Jephthah and went on raids with him.

4 And after a time, the Ammonites made war against Israel.

5 And when the Ammonites made war against Israel, the elders of Gilead went to bring Jephthah out of the land of Tob;

6 And they said to Jephthah, Come and be our leader, that we may fight with the Ammonites.

7 But Jephthah said to the elders of Gilead, Did you not hate me and drive me out of my father's house? Why have you come to me now when you are in trouble?

8 And the elders of Gilead said to Jephthah, This is why we have turned to you now, that you may go with us and fight the Ammonites and be our head over all the citizens of Gilead.

9 Jephthah said to the elders of Gilead, If you bring me home again to fight against the Ammonites and the Lord gives them over to me, [understand that] I will be your head.

10 And the elders of Gilead said to Jephthah, The Lord is witness between us, if we do not do as you have said.

11 So Jephthah went with the elders of Gilead, and the people made him head and leader over them. And Jephthah repeated all he had promised before the Lord at Mizpah.

12 And Jephthah sent messengers to the king of the Ammonites, saying, What have you to do with me, that you have come against me to fight in my land?

13 The Ammonites' king replied to the messengers of Jephthah, Because Israel took away my land [which was not true] when they came up out of Egypt [300 years before], from the Arnon even to Jabbok and to the Jordan; now therefore, restore those lands peaceably.

14 And Jephthah sent messengers again to the king of the Ammonites

15 And said to him, Thus says Jephthah, Israel did not take the land of Moab or the land of the Ammonites.

16 But when [Israel] came up from Egypt, [they] walked through the wilderness to the Red Sea and came to Kadesh.

17 Then Israel sent messengers to the king of Edom, saying, Let us, we pray, pass through your land, but the king of Edom would not listen. Also they sent to the king of Moab, but he would not consent. So Israel remained at Kadesh.

18 Then they went through the wilderness and went around the land of Edom and the land of Moab, and came by the east side of the land of Moab and camped on the other side of the Arnon; but they came not within the territory of Moab, for the Arnon was the boundary of Moab.

19 Then Israel sent messengers to Sihon king of the Amorites, king of Heshbon, and Israel said to him, Let us pass, we pray you, through your land to our country.

20 But Sihon did not trust Israel to pass through his territory; so Sihon gathered all his people together and encamped at Jahaz and fought with Israel.

21 And the Lord, the God of Israel, gave Sihon and all his people into the hand of Israel, and they defeated them; so Israel took possession of all the land of the Amorites, the inhabitants of that country.

22 They possessed all the territory of the Amorites, from the Arnon even to the Jabbok, and from the wilderness even to the Jordan.

23 So now the Lord God of Israel has dispossessed the Amorites from before His people Israel, and should you possess them?

24 Will you not possess what Chemosh your god gives you to possess? And all the Lord our God dispossessed before us, we will possess.
25 Now are you any better than Balak son of Zippor, king of Moab? Did he ever strive against Israel or did he ever go to war with them?
26 While Israel dwelt in Heshbon and its villages, and in Aroer and its villages, and in all the cities along the banks of the Arnon for 300 years, why did you not recover [your lost lands] during that time?
27 So I have not sinned against you, but you are doing me wrong to war against me. The Lord, the [righteous] Judge, judge this day between the Israelites and the Ammonites.
28 But the king of the Ammonites did not listen to the message Jephthah sent him.
29 Then the Spirit of the Lord came upon Jephthah, and he passed through Gilead and Manasseh, and Mizpah of Gilead, and from Mizpah of Gilead he passed on to the Ammonites.
30 And Jephthah made a vow to the Lord and said, If You will indeed give the Ammonites into my hand,
31 Then whatever *or* whoever comes forth from the doors of my house to meet me when I return in peace from the Ammonites, it shall be the Lord's, and I will offer it *or* him up as a burnt offering.
32 Then Jephthah crossed over to the Ammonites to fight with them, and the Lord gave them into his hand.
33 And from Aroer to Minnith he smote them, twenty cities, and as far as Abel-cheramim [the meadow of vineyards], with a very great slaughter. So the Ammonites were subdued before the Israelites.
34 Then Jephthah came to Mizpah to his home, and behold, his daughter came out to meet him with timbrels and with dances! And she was his only child; beside her he had neither son nor daughter.
35 And when he saw her, he rent his clothes and said, Alas, my daughter! You have brought me very low, and you are the cause of great trouble to me; for I have opened my mouth [in a vow] to the Lord, and I cannot take it back.
36 And she said to him, My father, if you have opened your mouth to the Lord, do to me according to what you have vowed, since the Lord has taken vengeance for you on your enemies, the Ammonites.
37 And she said to her father, Let this thing be done for me; let me alone two months, that I may go and wander upon the mountains and bewail my virginity, I and my companions.
38 And he said, Go. And he sent her away for two months, and she went with her companions and bewailed her virginity upon the mountains.
39 At the end of two months she returned to her father, who ᵏdid with

k Scholars fail to agree as to what Jephthah really did. For example, "This plain and restrained statement that 'he did with her according to his vow' is best taken as implying her actual sacrifice. Although human sacrifice was strictly forbidden to Israelites, we need not be surprised at a man of Jephthah's half-Canaanite antecedents following Canaanite usage in this matter" (F. Davidson, ed., *The New Bible Commentary*). And, "Although the lapse of two months might be supposed to have afforded time for reflection and a better sense of his duty, there is but too much reason to conclude that he was impelled to the fulfillment by the dictates of a pious but unenlightened conscience" (Robert Jamieson, A.R. Fausset and David Brown, *A Commentary*). And, "The religious system of Israel had fallen into suspension. From the days of Phinehas (Judg. 20:28) to the time of Samuel, we hear nothing of the high priest, the ark or the tabernacle" (*The Cambridge Bible*). On the other hand, J.P. Lange (*A Commentary*) articulates the position of many scholars when he calls attention to stories in Greek mythology in which the virginity of a goddess was celebrated by Greek maidens with song and dance. Summing up, Lange says, "At all events, it does not 'stand there in the text,' as her according to his vow which he had vowed. She never mated with a man. This became a custom in Israel—

40 That the daughters of Israel went yearly to mourn the daughter of Jephthah the Gileadite four days in a year.

12 THE MEN of Ephraim were summoned together and they crossed to Zaphon and said to Jephthah, Why did you cross over to fight with the Ammonites and did not summon us to go with you? We will burn your house over you with fire.

2 And Jephthah said to them, I and my people were in a severe conflict with the Ammonites, and I when I called you, you did not rescue me from their hands.

3 And when I saw that you would not rescue me, I put my life in my hands and crossed over against the Ammonites, and the Lord delivered them into my hand. Why then have you come up to me this day to fight against me?

4 Then Jephthah gathered all the men of Gilead and fought with Ephraim; and the men of Gilead smote Ephraim because they had said, You Gileadites are fugitives of Ephraim in the midst of Ephraim and Manasseh.

5 And the Gileadites took the fords of the Jordan before the Ephraimites; and when any of those Ephraimites who had escaped said, Let me go over, the men of Gilead said to him, Are you an Ephraimite? If he said, No,

6 They said to him, Then say Shibboleth; and he said, Sibboleth, for he could not pronounce it right. Then they seized him and slew him at the fords of the Jordan. And there fell at that time 42,000 of the Ephraimites.

7 Jephthah judged Israel six years. Then Jephthah the Gileadite died and was buried in one of the cities of Gilead.

8 And after him Ibzan of Bethlehem judged Israel.

9 And he had thirty sons and thirty daughters whom he gave [to husbands] outside his tribe, and thirty daughters [daughters-in-law] whom he brought in from outside his tribe for his sons. And he judged Israel seven years.

10 Then Ibzan died and was buried at Bethlehem.

11 After him Elon the Zebulunite judged Israel, and he judged Israel ten years.

12 Then Elon the Zebulunite died and was buried at Aijalon in the land of Zebulun.

13 And after him Abdon son of Hillel the Pirathonite judged Israel.

14 And he had forty sons and thirty grandsons who rode on seventy donkey colts; and he judged Israel eight years.

15 Then Abdon son of Hillel the Pirathonite died, and was buried at Pirathon in the land of Ephraim, in the hill country of the Amalekites.

13 AND THE Israelites again did what was evil in the sight of the Lord, and the Lord gave them into the hands of the Philistines for forty years.

2 And there was a certain man of Zorah, of the tribe of the Danites, whose name was Manoah; and his wife was barren and had no children.

3 And the ¹Angel of the Lord appeared to the woman and said to her, Behold, you are barren and have no children, but you shall become pregnant and bear a son.

Luther wrote, that she was offered in sacrifice." And the fact that the maidens mourned her virginity and not her death seems to prove that she did not die. **1** See footnote on Gen. 16:7. Note that in Judg. 13:22 the Angel of the Lord is identified with God.

4 Therefore beware and drink no wine or strong drink and eat nothing unclean.

5 For behold, you shall become pregnant and bear a son. No razor shall come upon his head, for the child shall be a Nazirite to God from birth, and he shall begin to deliver Israel out of the hands of the Philistines.

6 Then the woman went and told her husband, saying, A ᵐMan of God came to me and his face was like the face of the Angel of God, to be greatly and reverently feared. I did not ask him from where he came, and he did not tell me his name.

7 But he said to me, Behold, you shall become pregnant and bear a son, and now drink no wine or strong drink and eat nothing unclean, for the child shall be a Nazirite to God from birth to the day of his death.

8 Then Manoah entreated the Lord and said, O Lord, let the Man of God whom You sent come again to us and teach us what we shall do with the child that shall be born.

9 And God listened to the voice of Manoah, and the Angel of God came again to the woman as she sat in the field; but Manoah her husband was not with her.

10 And the woman ran in haste and told her husband and said to him, Behold, the Man who came to me the other day has appeared to me.

11 And Manoah arose and went after his wife and came to the Man and said to him, Are you the Man who spoke to this woman? And he said, I am.

12 And Manoah said, Now when your words come true, how shall we manage the child, and what is he to do?

13 And the Angel of the Lord said to Manoah, Let the mother beware of all that I told her.

14 She may not eat of anything that comes from the grapevine, nor drink wine or strong drink nor eat any unclean thing. All that I commanded her let her observe.

15 And Manoah said to the Angel of the Lord, Pray, let us detain you that we may prepare a kid for you.

16 And the Angel of the Lord said to Manoah, Though you detain me, I will not eat of your food, but if you make ready a burnt offering, offer it to the Lord. For Manoah did not know that he was the Angel of the Lord.

17 And Manoah said to the Angel of the Lord, What is your name, so that when your words come true, we may do you honor?

18 And the Angel of the Lord said to him, Why do you ask my name, seeing it is wonderful? [Isa. 9:6.]

19 So Manoah took the kid with the cereal offering and offered it upon a rock to the Lord, the Angel working wonders, while Manoah and his wife looked on.

20 For when the flame went up toward the heavens from the altar, the Angel of the Lord ascended in the altar flame. And Manoah and his wife looked on, and they fell on their faces to the ground.

21 The Angel of the Lord did not appear again to Manoah or to his wife. Then Manoah knew that he was the Angel of the Lord.

22 And Manoah said to his wife, We shall surely die, because we have seen God.

23 But his [sensible] wife said to him, If the Lord were pleased to kill us, He would not have received a burnt offering and a cereal offering from our hands, nor have shown us all these things or now have announced such things as these.

24 And the woman [in due time] bore a son and called his name Samson;

---

m It is clear from Judg. 13:3, 21 that this messenger was the Angel of the Lord.

and the child grew and the Lord blessed him.

25 And the Spirit of the Lord began to move him at times in Mahaneh-dan [the camp of Dan] between Zorah and Eshtaol.

14 SAMSON WENT down to Timnah and at Timnah saw one of the daughters of the Philistines.

2 And he came up and told his father and mother, I saw one of the daughters of the Philistines at Timnah; now get her for me as my wife.

3 But his father and mother said to him, Is there not a woman among the daughters of your kinsmen or among all our people, that you must go to take a wife from the uncircumcised Philistines? And Samson said to his father, Get her for me, for she is all right in my eyes.

4 His father and mother did not know that it was of the Lord, and that He sought an occasion for assailing the Philistines. At that time the Philistines had dominion over Israel.

5 Then Samson and his father and mother went down to Timnah and came to the vineyards of Timnah. And behold, a young lion roared against him.

6 And the Spirit of the Lord came mightily upon him, and he tore the lion as he would have torn a kid, and he had nothing in his hand; but he did not tell his father or mother what he had done.

7 And he went down and talked with the woman, and she pleased Samson well.

8 And after a while he returned to take her, and he turned aside to see the body of the lion, and behold, a swarm of bees and honey were in the body of the lion.

9 And he scraped some of the honey out into his hands and went along eating. And he came to his father and mother and gave them some, and they ate it; but he did not tell them he had taken the honey from the body of the lion.

10 His father went down to the woman, and Samson made a feast there, for that was the customary thing for young men to do.

11 And when the people saw him, they brought thirty companions to be with him.

12 And Samson said to them, I will now put forth a riddle to you; if you can tell me what it is within the seven days of the feast, and find it out, then I will give you thirty linen undergarments and thirty changes of raiment.

13 But if you cannot declare it to me, then shall you give me thirty linen undergarments and thirty changes of festive [costly] raiment. And they said to him, Put forth your riddle, that we may hear it.

14 And he said to them, Out of the eater came forth food, and out of the strong came forth sweetness. And they could not solve the riddle in three days.

15 And on the seventh day they said to Samson's wife, Entice your husband to declare to us the riddle, lest we burn you and your father's household with fire. Have you invited us to make us poor? Is this not true?

16 And Samson's wife wept before him and said, You only hate me, you do not love me; you have put forth a riddle to my countrymen and have not told the answer to me. And he said to her, Behold, I have not told my father or my mother, and shall I tell you?

17 And Samson's wife wept before him the seven days their feast lasted, and on the seventh day he told her because she pressed him with entreaties. Then she told the riddle to her countrymen.

18 And the men of the city said to [Samson] on the seventh day before sundown, What is sweeter than honey? What is stronger than a lion? And he said to them, If you had not plowed with my heifer, you would not have solved my riddle.

19 And the Spirit of the Lord came upon him, and he went down to Ashkelon and slew thirty men of them and took their apparel [as spoil], and gave the changes of garments to those who explained the riddle. And his anger was kindled, and he went up to his father's house.

20 But Samson's wife was [given] to his companion who was his [best] friend.

15 BUT SOME days later, in the time of wheat harvest, Samson went to visit his wife, taking along a kid [as a token of reconciliation]; and he said, I will go unto my wife in the inner chamber. But her father would not allow him to go in.

2 And her father said, I truly thought you utterly hated her, so I gave her to your companion. Is her younger sister not fairer than she? Take her, I pray you, instead.

3 And Samson said of them, This time shall I be blameless as regards the Philistines, though I do them evil.

4 So Samson went and caught 300 foxes or jackals and took torches and turning the foxes tail to tail, he put a torch between each pair of tails.

5 And when he had set the torches ablaze, he let the foxes go into the standing grain of the Philistines, and he burned up the shocks and the standing grain, along with the olive orchards.

6 Then the Philistines said, Who has done this? And they were told, Samson, the son-in-law of the Timnite, because he [the Timnite] has taken his [Samson's] wife and has given her to his companion. And the Philistines came up and burned her and her father with fire.

7 And Samson said to them, If this is the way you act, surely I will take revenge on you, and after that I will quit.

8 And he smote them hip and thigh [unsparingly], a great slaughter; and he went down and dwelt in the cleft of the rock of Etam.

9 Then the Philistines came up and encamped in Judah and spread themselves in Lehi.

10 And the men of Judah said, Why have you come up against us? And they answered, We have come up to bind Samson, to do to him as he has done to us.

11 Then 3,000 men of Judah went down to the cleft of the rock Etam and said to Samson, Have you not known that the Philistines are rulers over us? What is this that you have done to us? He said to them, As they did to me, so have I done to them.

12 And they said to him, We have come down to bind you, that we may deliver you into the hands of the Philistines. And Samson said to them, Swear to me that you will not fall upon me yourselves.

13 And they said to him, No, we will bind you fast and give you into their hand; but surely we will not kill you. So they bound him with two new ropes and brought him up from the rock.

14 And when he came to Lehi, the Philistines came shouting to meet him. And the Spirit of the Lord came mightily upon [Samson], and the ropes on his arms became as flax that had caught fire, and his bonds melted off his hands.

15 And he found a still moist jawbone of a donkey and reached out and took it and slew 1,000 men with it.

16 And Samson said, With the jawbone of a donkey, heaps upon heaps, with the jawbone of a donkey I have slain 1,000 men!

17 And when he stopped speaking, he cast the jawbone from his hand;

and that place was called Ramath-lehi [the hill of the jawbone].

18 Samson was very thirsty, and he prayed to the Lord and said, You have given this great deliverance by the hand of Your servant, and now shall I die of thirst and fall into the hands of the uncircumcised?

19 And God split open the hollow place that was at Lehi, and water came out of it. And when he drank, his spirit returned and he revived. Therefore the name of it was called En-hakkore [the spring of him who prayed], which is at Lehi to this day.

20 And [Samson] judged (defended) Israel in the days of the Philistines twenty years. [Judg. 17:6.]

16 THEN SAMSON went to Gaza and saw a harlot there, and went in to her.

2 The Gazites were told, Samson has come here. So they surrounded the place and lay in wait for him all night at the gate of the city. They were quiet all night, saying, In the morning, when it is light, we will kill him.

3 But Samson lay until midnight, and [then] he arose and took hold of the doors of the city's gate and the two posts, and pulling them up, bar and all, he put them on his shoulders and carried them to the top of the hill that is before Hebron.

4 After this he loved a woman in the Valley of Sorek whose name was Delilah.

5 And the lords of the Philistines came to her and said to her, Entice him and see in what his great strength lies, and by what means we may overpower him that we may bind him to subdue him. And we will each give you 1,100 pieces of silver.

6 And Delilah said to Samson, Tell me, I pray you, wherein your great strength lies, and with what you might be bound to subdue you.

7 And Samson said to her, If they bind me with seven fresh, strong gut-strings, still moist, then shall I be weak and be like any other man.

8 Then the Philistine lords brought to her seven fresh, strong bowstrings, still moist, and she bound him with them.

9 Now she had men lying in wait in an inner room. And she said to him, The Philistines are upon you, Samson! And he broke the bowstrings as a string of tow breaks when it touches the fire. So the secret of his strength was not known.

10 And Delilah said to Samson, Behold, you have mocked me and told me lies; now tell me, I pray you, how you might be bound.

11 And he said to her, If they bind me fast with new ropes that have not been used, then I shall become weak and be like any other man.

12 So Delilah took new ropes and bound him with them and said to him, The Philistines are upon you, Samson! And the men lying in wait were in the inner room. But he snapped the ropes off his arms like [sewing] thread.

13 And Delilah said to Samson, Until now you have mocked me and told me lies; tell me with what you might be bound. And he said to her, If you weave the seven braids of [the hair of] my head with the web.

14 And she did so and fastened it with the pin and said to him, The Philistines are upon you, Samson! And he awoke out of his sleep and went away with the pin of the [weaver's] beam and with the web.

15 And she said to him, How can you say, I love you, when your heart is not with me? You have mocked me these three times and have not told me in what your great strength lies.

16 And when she pressed him day after day with her words and urged him, he was vexed to death.

17 Then he told her all his mind and said to her, A razor has never come

resisting temptation

We can learn a lot from Samson's story (see Judges 13:24—16:30). Samson had extraordinary strength from God, and his might and ability were directly tied to obedience. God had told him not to cut his hair and promised that as long as he obeyed, he would have special strength and be able to do awesome feats. Satan wanted to weaken and destroy Samson, so he sent temptation in the form of a woman named Delilah. Day after day, she pressed him to reveal his secret. Eventually Samson was "vexed," the Bible tells us, so he finally gave in and told Delilah his secret (see Judges 16:15–17). While he was sleeping, she cut his hair and robbed him of his strength.

When Satan comes to tempt us, he is persistent. He keeps up his attack, hoping to eventually wear us out. This is exactly what happened with Samson. He had a weakness for women, and, just as Satan knew Samson's weakness and used it against him, he also knows our weaknesses and tries to take advantage of them.

Let me encourage you to be aware of your weaknesses and to pray regularly for God to strengthen you in the weak spots in your life. Do not wait until you are deep in trouble and then begin to pray. Instead, pray ahead of time. For example, if an overactive appetite is a weakness for you, then pray every time you sit down to eat that God will help you control yourself. Do not wait until you have eaten too much and then spend the rest of the day feeling guilty. Let your new motto be: "I won't delay; I'll pray right away."

Jesus told His disciples to pray that they come not into temptation, and He said the spirit is willing, but the flesh is weak (see Matthew 26:41). He never told them that temptation would not come. He said to pray that they would not give in *when* temptation comes. We will all be tempted, but God will give us the ability to resist if we will be faithful to pray for His strength to recognize and resist whatever attack Satan sends our way, especially when he tries to hit us in our weak spots.

upon my head, for I have been a Nazirite to God from my birth. If I am shaved, then my strength will go from me, and I shall become weak and be like any other man. **18** And when Delilah saw that he had told her all his mind, she went and called for the Philistine lords, saying, Come up this once, for he has told me all he knows. Then the Philistine lords came up to her and brought the money in their hands.

19 And she made Samson sleep upon her knees, and she called a man and caused him to shave off the seven braids of his head. Then she began to torment [Samson], and his strength went from him. **20** She said, The Philistines are upon you, Samson! And he awoke out of his sleep and said, I will go out as I have time after time and shake myself free. For Samson did not know that the Lord had departed from him.

21 But the Philistines laid hold of him, bored out his eyes, and brought him down to Gaza and bound him with [two] bronze fetters; and he ground at the mill in the prison.

22 But the hair of his head began to grow again after it had been shaved.

23 Then the Philistine lords gathered together to offer a great sacrifice to Dagon their god and to rejoice, for they said, Our god has given Samson our enemy into our hands.

24 And when the people saw Samson, they praised their god, for they said, Our god has delivered into our hands our enemy, the ravager of our country, who has slain many of us.

25 And when their hearts were merry, they said, Call for Samson, that he may make sport for us. So they called [blind] Samson out of the prison, and he made sport before them. They made him stand between the pillars.

26 And Samson said to the lad who held him by the hand, Allow me to feel the pillars upon which the house rests, that I may lean against them.

27 Now the house was full of men and women; all the Philistine princes were there, and on the roof were about 3,000 men and women who looked on while Samson made sport.

28 Then Samson called to the Lord and said, O Lord God, [earnestly] remember me, I pray You, and strengthen me, I pray You, only this once, O God, and let me have one vengeance upon the Philistines for both my eyes.

29 And Samson laid hold of the two middle pillars by which the house was borne up, one with his right hand and the other with his left.

30 And Samson cried, Let me die with the Philistines! And he bowed himself mightily, and the house fell upon the princes and upon all the people that were in it. So the dead whom he slew at his death were more than they whom he slew in his life.

31 Then his kinsmen and all the tribal family of his father came down, took his body, and brought it up; and they buried him between Zorah and Eshtaol in the burial place of Manoah his father. He had judged Israel [that is, had defended the Israelites] twenty years. [Judg. 17:6; Heb. 11:32.]

17 THERE WAS a man of the hill country of Ephraim whose name was Micah.

2 And he said to his mother, The 1,100 shekels of silver that were taken from you, about which you cursed and also spoke about in my hearing, behold, I have the silver with me; I took it. And his mother said, Blessed be you by the Lord, my son!

3 He restored the 1,100 shekels of silver to his mother, and she said, I had truly dedicated the silver to the Lord from my hand for my son to make a graven image and a molten image; now therefore, I will restore it to you.

4 So when he restored the money to his mother, she took 200 pieces of silver and gave them to the silversmith, who made of it a graven image and a molten image; and they were in the house of Micah.

5 And the man Micah had a house of gods, and he made an ephod and teraphim and dedicated one of his sons, who became his priest.

6 In those days there was no king in Israel; every man did what was right in his own eyes.

7 And there was a young man in Bethlehem of Judah, of the family of Judah, who was a Levite; and he sojourned there.

8 And the man departed from the town of Bethlehem in Judah to sojourn where he could find a place, and as he journeyed he came to the hill country of Ephraim to the house of Micah.

9 And Micah said to him, From where do you come? And he said to him, I am a Levite of Bethlehem in Judah, and I go to sojourn where I may find a place.

10 And Micah said to him, Dwell with me and be to me a father and a priest, and I will give you ten pieces of silver each year, a suit of clothes, and your living. So the Levite went in.

11 And the Levite was content to dwell with the man, and the young man was to Micah as one of his sons.

12 And Micah consecrated the Levite, and the young man became his priest and was in the house of Micah.

13 Then said Micah, Now I know that the Lord will favor me, since I have a Levite to be my priest.

18 IN THOSE days there was no king in Israel. And in those days the tribe of the Danites sought for itself an inheritance to dwell in, for until then no [sufficient] inheritance had been acquired by them among the tribes of Israel.

2 So the Danites sent from the whole number of their tribe five brave men from Zorah and Eshtaol to spy out the land and to explore it, and they said to them, Go, explore the land. They came to the hill country of Ephraim, to the house of Micah, and lodged there.

3 When they went by the house of Micah, they recognized the voice of the young Levite, and they turned aside there and said to him, Who brought you here? And what do you do in this place? And what have you here?

4 And he said to them, Thus and thus Micah deals with me and has hired me, and I am his priest.

5 And they said to him, Ask counsel, we pray you, of God that we may know whether our journey will be successful.

6 And the priest said to them, Go in peace. The way in which you go is before (under the eye of) the Lord.

7 Then the five men departed and came to Laish and saw the people who were there, how they dwelt securely after the manner of the Sidonians, quiet and feeling safe; and there was no magistrate in the land, who might put them to shame in anything *or* injure them; and they were far from the Sidonians and had no dealings with anyone.

8 The five men came back to their brethren at Zorah and Eshtaol, and their brethren said to them, What do you say?

9 They said, Arise, let us go up against them, for we have seen the land, and behold, it is very fertile. And will you do nothing? Do not be slow to go and enter in and possess the land.

10 When you go, you will come to people [feeling] safe and secure. The land is broad [widely extended on all sides]; and God has given it into your hands—a place where there is no want of anything that is in the earth.

11 And there went from there of the tribe of the Danites, out of Zorah and Eshtaol, 600 men armed with weapons of war.

12 And they went up and encamped at Kiriath-jearim in Judah. Therefore they called that place Mahaneh-dan [camp of Dan] to this day; it is west of Kiriath-jearim.

13 And they passed from there to the hill country of Ephraim and came to Micah's house.

14 Then the five men who had gone to spy out the country of Laish said to their brethren, Do you know that there are in these houses an ephod, teraphim, a graven image, and a molten image? Now therefore, consider what you have to do.

15 And they turned in that direction and came to the house of the young Levite, at the home of Micah, and saluted him.

16 Now the 600 Danites with their weapons of war stood at Micah's gate.

17 And the five men who had gone to spy out the land went up and entered the house and took the graven image, the ephod, the teraphim, and the molten image, while the priest stood by the entrance of the gate with the 600 men armed with weapons of war.

18 And when these went into Micah's house and took the carved image, the ephod, the teraphim, and the molten image, the priest said to them, What are you doing?

19 And they said to him, Be still, put your hand over your mouth, and come with us, and be to us a father and a priest. Is it better for you to be a priest to the house of one man, or that you be a priest to a tribe and family in Israel?

20 And the priest's heart was glad, and he took the ephod, the teraphim, and the graven image, and went in the midst of the people.

21 So they turned and departed and put the little ones, the cattle, and the baggage in front of them.

22 When they were a good way from the house of Micah, the men who were Micah's near neighbors were called out and overtook the Danites.

23 They shouted to the Danites, who turned and said to Micah, What ails you, that you come with such a company?

24 And he said, You take away my gods which I made and the priest, and go away; and what have I left? How can you say to me, What ails you?

25 And the men of Dan said to him, Let not your voice be heard among us, lest angry fellows fall upon you and you lose your life with the lives of your household.

26 And the Danites went their way; and when Micah saw that they were too strong for him, he turned and went back to his house.

27 And they took the things which Micah had made, and his priest, and came to Laish, to a people quiet and feeling secure, and they smote them with the sword and burned the city.

28 And there was no deliverer because it was far from Sidon, and they had no business with anyone. It was in the valley which belongs to Beth-rehob. And they rebuilt the city and dwelt in it.

29 They named the city Dan, after Dan their forefather who was born to Israel; however, the name of the city was Laish at first.

30 And the Danites set up the graven image for themselves; and Jonathan son of Gershom, the son of Moses, and his sons were priests to the tribe of Dan until the day of the captivity of the land.

31 So they set them up Micah's graven image which he made, as long as the house of God was at Shiloh.

19 IN THOSE days, when there was no king in Israel, a certain Levite was living temporarily in the most remote part of the hill district of Ephraim, who took to himself a concubine [of inferior status than a wife] from Bethlehem in Judah.

2 And his concubine was untrue to him and went away from him to her father's house at Bethlehem of Judah and stayed there the space of four months.

3 Then her husband arose and went after her to speak kindly to her [to her heart] and to bring her back, having with him his servant and a couple of donkeys. And she brought him into her father's house, and when her father saw him, he rejoiced to meet him.

4 And his father-in-law, the girl's

father, [insistently] detained him, and he remained with him three days. So they ate and drank, and he lodged there.

5 On the fourth day they arose early in the morning, and the [Levite] prepared to leave, but the girl's father said to his son-in-law, Strengthen your heart with a morsel of bread and afterward go your way.

putting the Word to work

Notice in Judges 19:5 that the Levite's father-in-law encouraged him to "strengthen your heart with a morsel of bread." In today's language, we would call that "emotional eating." Are you an "emotional eater"? If so, ask God to help you learn to find emotional strength in His Word and in no other source.

6 So both men sat down and ate and drank together, and the girl's father said to the man, Consent to stay all night and let your heart be merry.
7 And when the man rose up to depart, his father-in-law urged him; so he lodged there again.
8 And he arose early in the morning on the fifth day to depart, but the girl's father said, Strengthen your heart and tarry until toward evening. So they ate, both of them.
9 And when the man and his concubine and his servant rose up to leave, his father-in-law, the girl's father, said to him, Behold, now the day draws toward evening, I pray you stay all night. Behold, now the day grows to an end, lodge here and let your heart be merry, and tomorrow get early on your way and go home.
10 But the man would not stay that night; so he rose up and departed and came opposite to Jebus, which is Jerusalem. With him were two saddled donkeys [and his servant] and his concubine.
11 When they were near Jebus, it was late, and the servant said to his master, Come I pray, and let us turn into this Jebusite city and lodge in it.
12 His master said to him, We will not turn aside into the city of foreigners where there are no Israelites. We will go on to Gibeah.
13 And he said to his servant, Come and let us go to one of these places and spend the night in Gibeah or in Ramah.
14 So they passed on and went their way, and the sun went down on them near Gibeah, which belongs to Benjamin,
15 And they turned aside there to go in and lodge at Gibeah. And the Levite went in and sat down in the open square of the city, for no man took them into his house to spend the night.
16 And behold, an old man was coming from his work in the field at evening. He was from the hill country of Ephraim but was living temporarily in Gibeah, but the men of the place were Benjamites.
17 And when he looked up, he saw the wayfarer in the city square, and the old man said, Where are you going? And from where did you come?
18 The Levite replied, We are passing from Bethlehem of Judah to the rear side of the hill country of Ephraim; I am from there. I went to Bethlehem of Judah, but I am [now] going [home] to the house of the Lord [where I serve], and there is no man who receives me into his house.
19 Yet we have both straw and provender for our donkeys and bread and wine also for me, your handmaid, and the young man who is with your servants; there is no lack of anything.
20 And the old man said, Peace be to you, but leave all your wants to me; only do not lodge in the street.

21 So he brought him into his house and gave provender to the donkeys. And the guests washed their feet and ate and drank.

22 Now as they were making their hearts merry, behold, the men of the city, certain worthless fellows, beset the house round about, beat on the door, and said to the master of the house, the old man, Bring forth the man who came to your house, that we may have intercourse with him.

23 And the man, the master of the house, went out and said to them, No, my kinsmen, I pray you, do not act so wickedly; seeing that this man is my guest, do not do this [wicked] folly.

24 Behold, here are my virgin daughter and this man's concubine; them I will bring out now; debase them and do with them what seems good to you, but to this man do not so vile a thing.

25 But the men would not listen to him. So the man took his concubine and forced her forth to them, and they had intercourse with her and abused her all the night until morning. And when the dawn began to break, they let her go.

26 At daybreak the woman came and fell down and lay at the door of the man's house where her master was, till it was light.

27 And her master rose up in the morning and opened the doors of the house and went out to go his way; and behold, his concubine had fallen down at the door of the house, and her hands were upon the threshold.

28 And he said to her, Up, and let us be going. But there was no answer [for she was dead]. Then he put her [body] upon the donkey, and the man rose up and went home.

29 And when he came into his house, he took a knife, and took hold of his dead concubine and divided her [body] limb by limb into twelve pieces and sent her [body] throughout all the territory of Israel.

30 And all who saw it said, There was no such deed done or seen from the day that the Israelites came up out of the land of Egypt to this day; consider it, take counsel, and speak [your minds].

20 THEN ALL the Israelites came out, and the congregation assembled as one man to the Lord at Mizpah, from Dan even to Beersheba, including the land of Gilead.

2 And the chiefs of all the people, of all the tribes of Israel, presented themselves in the assembly of the people of God, 400,000 men on foot who drew the sword.

3 (Now the Benjamites [among whom the vile tragedy occurred] heard that the [other] Israelites had gone up to Mizpah.) There the Israelites asked, How did this wickedness happen?

4 And the Levite, the husband of the woman who was murdered, replied, I came to Gibeah which belongs to Benjamin, I and my concubine, to spend the night.

5 And the men of Gibeah rose against me and beset the house round about me by night; they meant to kill me and they raped my concubine, and she is dead.

6 And I took my concubine and cut her in pieces and sent her throughout all the country of the inheritance of Israel, for they have committed abomination and [wicked] folly in Israel.

7 Behold, you Israelites, all of you, give here your advice and counsel.

8 And all the people arose as one man, saying, Not any of us will go to his tent, and none of us will return to his home.

9 But now this we will do to Gibeah: we will go up by lot against it,

10 And we will take ten men of 100

throughout all the tribes of Israel, and 100 of 1,000, and 1,000 out of 10,000, to bring provisions for the men, that when they come to Gibeah of Benjamin they may do to them according to all the [wicked] folly which they have committed in Israel.

11 So all the men of Israel gathered against the city, united as one man.

12 And the tribes of Israel sent men through all the tribe of Benjamin, saying, What wickedness is this that has been done among you?

13 Now therefore, give up the men [involved], the base fellows in Gibeah, that we may put them to death and put away evil from Israel. But the Benjamites would not listen to the voice of their kinsmen the Israelites.

14 But the Benjamites out of the cities assembled at Gibeah to go out to battle against the other Israelites.

15 And the Benjamites mustered out of their cities at that time 26,000 men who drew the sword, besides the inhabitants of Gibeah, who mustered 700 chosen men.

16 Among all these were 700 chosen left-handed men; every one could sling stones at a hair and not miss.

17 And the men of Israel, other than Benjamin, mustered 400,000 men who drew the sword; all these were men of war.

18 The Israelites arose and went up to the house of God [Bethel] and asked counsel of God and said, Which of us shall take the lead to battle against the Benjamites? And the Lord said, Judah shall go up first.

19 Then the Israelites rose in the morning and encamped against Gibeah.

20 And the men of Israel went out to battle against Benjamin and set the battle in array against them at Gibeah.

21 The Benjamites came forth out of Gibeah and felled to the ground that day 22,000 men of the Israelites.

22 But the people, the men of Israel, took courage *and* strengthened themselves and again set their battle line in the same place where they formed it the first day.

23 And the Israelites went up and wept before the Lord until evening and asked of the Lord, Shall we go up again to battle against our brethren the Benjamites? And the Lord said, Go up against them.

24 So the Israelites came near against the Benjamites the second day.

25 And Benjamin went forth out of Gibeah against them the second day and felled to the ground the Israelites again, 18,000 men, all of whom were swordsmen.

26 Then all the Israelites, the whole army, went up and came to the house of God [Bethel] and wept; and they sat there before the Lord and fasted that day until evening and offered burnt offerings and peace offerings before the Lord.

27 And the Israelites inquired of the Lord—for the ark of the covenant of God was there [at Bethel] in those days,

28 And Phinehas son of Eleazar, the son of Aaron, ministered before it in those days—saying, Shall we yet again go out to battle against our brethren the Benjamites or shall we quit? And the Lord said, Go up, for tomorrow I will deliver them into your hand.

29 So Israel set men in ambush round about Gibeah.

30 And the Israelites went up against the Benjamites on the third day and set themselves in array against Gibeah as at other times.

31 And the Benjamites went out against their army and were drawn away from the city; and they began to smite and kill some of the people as at other times, in the highways, one of which goes up to Bethel and the other to Gibeah, and in the open country—about thirty men of Israel.

32 And the Benjamites said, They are routed before us as at first. But the Israelites said, Let us flee and draw them from the city to the highways.

33 And all the men of Israel rose out of their places and set themselves in array at Baal-tamar, and the men of Israel in ambush rushed out of their place in the meadow of Geba.

34 And there came against Gibeah 10,000 chosen men out of all Israel, and the battle was hard; but the Benjamites did not know disaster was close upon them.

35 And the Lord overcame Benjamin before Israel, and the Israelites destroyed of the Benjamites that day 25,100 men, all of whom were swordsmen.

36 So the Benjamites saw that they were defeated. The men of Israel gave ground to the Benjamites, because they trusted in the men in ambush whom they had set against Gibeah.

37 And the men in ambush quickly rushed upon Gibeah, and the liers-in-wait moved out and smote all the city with the sword.

38 Now the appointed signal between the men of Israel and the men in ambush was that when they made a great cloud of smoke arise from the city,

39 The men of Israel should all turn back in battle. Now Benjamin had begun to smite and kill some of the men of Israel, about thirty persons. They said, Surely they are falling before us as in the first battle.

40 But when the [signal] cloud began to rise out of the city in a pillar of smoke, the Benjamites looked behind them, and behold, the whole of the city went up in smoke to the heavens.

41 When the men of Israel turned back again, the men of Benjamin were dismayed, for they saw that disaster had come upon them.

42 Therefore they turned their backs before the men of Israel and fled toward the wilderness, but the battle followed close behind *and* overtook them; and the inhabitants of the cities destroyed those [Benjamites] who came through them in their midst.

43 They surrounded the Benjamites, pursued them, and overtook *and* trod them down at their resting-place as far as opposite Gibeah toward the east.

44 And there fell 18,000 men of Benjamin, all of them men of valor.

45 And [the Benjamites] turned and fled toward the wilderness to the rock of Rimmon, and Israel picked off on the highways 5,000 men of them; they pursued hard after them to Gidom and slew 2,000 more of them.

46 So that all of Benjamin who fell that day were 25,000 men who drew the sword, all of them men of valor.

47 But 600 men turned and fled to the wilderness to the rock Rimmon and remained at the rock Rimmon four months.

48 And the men of Israel turned back against the Benjamites and smote them with the sword, men and beasts and all that they found. Also they set on fire all the towns to which they came.

21 NOW THE men of Israel had sworn at Mizpah, None of us shall give his daughter in marriage to Benjamin.

2 And the Israelites came to the house of God [Bethel] and sat there until evening before God and lifted up their voices and wept bitterly. [Judg. 20:27.]

3 And they said, O Lord, the God of Israel, why has this come to pass in Israel, that there should be today one tribe lacking in Israel?

4 And next morning the people rose early, and built there an altar, and offered burnt offerings and peace offerings.

5 And the Israelites said, Which among all the tribes of Israel did not come up with the assembly to the Lord? For they had taken a great oath concerning him who did not come up to the Lord to Mizpah, saying, He shall surely die.

6 And the Israelites changed their purpose [and had compassion] for the Benjamites their kinsmen and said, There is one tribe cut off from Israel today.

7 What shall we do for wives for those who are left, seeing we have sworn by the Lord that we will not give them our daughters as wives?

8 And they said, Which one is there of the tribes of Israel that did not come up to Mizpah to the Lord? And behold, no one had come to the camp from Jabesh-gilead, to the assembly.

9 For when the people were mustered, behold, not one of the citizens of Jabesh-gilead was there.

10 And the congregation sent there 12,000 of the bravest men, saying, Go and smite the inhabitants of Jabesh-gilead with the sword, also the women and the little ones.

11 And this is what you shall do; utterly destroy every male and every woman who is not a virgin.

12 And they found among the inhabitants of Jabesh-gilead 400 young virgins, who had known no man by lying with him; and they brought them to the camp at Shiloh, which is in the land of Canaan.

13 And the whole congregation sent word to the Benjamites who were at the rock of Rimmon and invited them to be friendly with them.

14 And Benjamin returned at that time, and they gave them the women whom they had saved alive of the women of Jabesh-gilead; and yet there were not enough for them.

15 And the people had compassion on Benjamin, because the Lord had made a breach in the tribes of Israel.

16 Then the elders of the congregation said, What shall we do for wives for those who are left, since the women of Benjamin are destroyed?

17 And they said, There must be an inheritance for the survivors of Benjamin, so that a tribe shall not be wiped out of Israel.

18 But we cannot give them wives of our daughters, for the Israelites have sworn, Cursed be he who gives a wife to Benjamin.

19 So they said, Behold, there is the yearly feast of the Lord at Shiloh, which is north of Bethel, on the east of the highway that goes up from Bethel to Shechem and south of Lebonah.

20 So they commanded the Benjamites, Go and lie in wait in the vineyards,

21 And watch; if the daughters of Shiloh come out to dance in the dances, then come out of the vineyards and catch every man his wife from the daughters of Shiloh and go to the land of Benjamin.

22 And when their fathers or their brothers come to us to complain, we will say to them, Grant them graciously unto us, because we did not reserve a wife for each of them in battle, neither did you give wives to them, for that would have made you guilty [of breaking your oath].

23 And the Benjamites did so and took wives, according to their number, from the dancers whom they carried

speak the Word

off; then they went and returned to their inheritance and repaired the towns and dwelt in them.

24 And the Israelites left there then, every man to his tribe and family, and they went out from there every man to his inheritance.

25 In those days [n]there was no king in Israel; every man did what was right in his own eyes.

---

n This statement is made three times in these latter chapters. All was well while Joshua and those who assisted him lived; then gradually came disorder. "What is the meaning of this? . . . There was no king [or counselor] in Israel because in Israel there was no God. The Lord is King. You cannot have a [true] king if you have not a God. There was no nominal renunciation of God, no public and blatant atheism, no boastful impiety; there was a deadlier heresy—namely, keeping God as a sign but paying no tribute to Him as a King, worshiping Him possibly in outward form but knowing nothing of the subduing and directing power of godliness. That is more to be dreaded than any intellectual difficulty of a theological kind . . . Dead consciences, prayerless prayers, mechanical formalities—these are the impediments which overturn . . . the chariots of progress. This was the case in Israel. Where God is, the king is not [merely] a man with a crown on, but a king in the sense of kingliness, sovereignty, authority, rule—the spirit of obligation and responsibility . . . You find the right monarch where you find the right God" (Joseph Parker, cited by James C. Gray and George M. Adams, *Bible Commentary*).

Ruth

Author:
Unknown; traditionally Samuel

Date:
Between 1050 BC and 500 BC

Everyday Life Principles:
The power of commitment and faithfulness cannot be overemphasized.

Wise, godly choices put us in position for God to bless us.

God rewards faithfulness and sacrifice for others.

The book of Ruth is an awesome story of the power of faithfulness, sacrifice, and wise choices. Ruth made a difficult choice when she decided not to return to her homeland, choosing instead to endure the hardships of going to Bethlehem with her bitter, widowed mother-in-law. Even though Ruth's husband had died and she did not *have* to stay with Naomi, she made the courageous choice to be faithful and merciful to Naomi, to care for her, and to follow Naomi's God. Orpah, on the other hand, made the choice that was easy for her at the moment—and we never hear of her again.

Ruth's difficult choice in the present brought great blessing to her future. It meant that she would have to endure some suffering for a season, but it put her in position for God to reward her faithfulness. God gave Ruth a good, wealthy husband in Boaz, who gave her a child. God caused her to be happy again; and He placed Ruth in the lineage of Jesus Christ.

As you read the book of Ruth, I hope you will commit to be like Ruth—to make wise choices, to be more faithful than ever to the people God has placed in your life, to be merciful, and to have a good attitude when you have to struggle and work hard. When you act on such commitments, God will delight to bless you as powerfully as He did Ruth.

1 IN THE days when the judges ruled, there was a famine in the land. And a certain man of Bethlehem of Judah went to sojourn in the country of Moab, he, his wife, and his two sons.

2 The man's name was Elimelech and his wife's name was Naomi and his two sons were named Mahlon [invalid] and Chilion [pining]; they were Ephrathites from Bethlehem of Judah. They went to the country of Moab and continued there.

3 But Elimelech, who Naomi's husband, died, and she was left with her two sons.

4 And they took wives of the women of Moab; the name of the one was Orpah and the name of the other Ruth. They dwelt there about ten years;

5 And Mahlon and Chilion died also, both of them, so the woman was bereft of her two sons and her husband.

life point

God is a God of purpose. We may not always understand His purpose, but we can be sure He definitely has one. Something may initially look terrible to us, as Ruth's situation must have looked to her and Naomi after the loss of their husbands, and yet all the while God intends to show His glory by working something good from it.

6 Then she arose with her daughters-in-law to return from the country of Moab, for she had heard in Moab how the Lord had visited His people in giving them food.

7 So she left the place where she was, her two daughters-in-law with her, and they started on the way back to Judah.

8 But Naomi said to her two daughters-in-law, Go, return each of you to her mother's house. May the Lord

life point

If you have lost your spouse to death, as Ruth and Naomi did (see Ruth 1:3–5), or to divorce, you will have to make many adjustments as you learn to function alone. You may have to learn to do things you have forgotten how to do or have never done before. You may have to get a job or learn to cook and care for children or make decisions you are not used to making in matters you know nothing about.

While you are doing these new things, you may still hurt, but you can take satisfaction in knowing you are moving forward. Each day you are making progress. God promises to be with you in trouble. While you are waiting for Him to deliver you, you can be comforted by knowing He is with you and working on your behalf even though you cannot always see what He is doing in the natural world. Take comfort in these words that Jesus spoke in Matthew 28:20: "I am with you all the days (perpetually, uniformly, and on every occasion) to the very close . . . of the age."

In the book of Ruth, we see three women who have lost their husbands. One of them, Naomi, not only lost her husband, but her two sons as well. We see Ruth and Naomi recover from their losses and go on to live joy-filled, fruitful lives. When we suffer loss in our lives, we also can recover with God's comfort and help.

deal kindly with you, as you have dealt with the dead and with me.

9 The Lord grant that you may find a home *and* rest, each in the house of her husband! Then she kissed them and they wept aloud.

10 And they said to her, No, we will return with you to your people.

11 But Naomi said, Turn back, my daughters, why will you go with me? Have I yet sons in my womb that may become your husbands?

12 Turn back, my daughters, go; for I am too old to have a husband. If I should say I have hope, even if I should have a husband tonight and should bear sons,

13 Would you therefore wait till they were grown? Would you therefore refrain from marrying? No, my daughters; it is far more bitter for me than for you that the hand of the Lord is gone out against me.

14 Then they wept aloud again; and Orpah [a]kissed her mother-in-law [good-bye], but Ruth clung to her.

15 And Naomi said, See, your sister-in-law has gone back to her people and to her gods; return after your sister-in-law.

16 And Ruth said, Urge me not to leave you or to turn back from following you; for where you go I will go, and where you lodge I will lodge. [b]Your people shall be my people and your God my God.

17 Where you die I will die, and there will I be buried. The Lord do so to me, and more also, if anything but death parts me from you.

18 When Naomi saw that Ruth was determined to go with her, she said no more.

19 So they both went on until they came to Bethlehem. And when they arrived in Bethlehem, the whole town was stirred about them, and said, Is this Naomi?

20 And she said to them, Call me not Naomi [pleasant]; call me Mara [bitter], for the Almighty has dealt very bitterly with me.

21 I went out full, but the Lord has brought me home again empty. Why call me Naomi, since the Lord has testified against me, and the Almighty has afflicted me?

life point

You and I must resist the temptation to speak negatively even when we feel negative, as Naomi did in Ruth 1:21. Blurting out negative statements based on our emotions is extremely unfruitful. Speaking out of our emotions is not the right thing to do. Our emotions usually do not do well in times of testing. But we do have hope, because as we mature in Christ, we learn to control our emotions and our mouths.

22 So Naomi returned, and Ruth the Moabitess, her daughter-in-law, with her, who returned from the country of Moab. And they came to Bethlehem at the beginning of barley harvest.

---

a "How many part with Christ at this crossway! Like Orpah they go a furlong or two with Christ, till He goes to take them off from their worldly hopes and bids them prepare for hardship, and then they fairly kiss and leave Him" (William Gurnall, cited by James C. Gray and George M. Adams, *Bible Commentary*).   b "Ruth is a prophecy, than which none could be more beautiful and engaging, of the entrance of the heathen world into the kingdom of God. She comes forth out of Moab, an idolatrous people full of wantonness and sin, and is herself so tender and pure. In a land where dissolute sensuality formed one of the elements of idol worship, a woman appears, as wife and daughter, chaste as the rose of spring and unsurpassed in these relations by any other [human] character in Holy Writ. . . . Ruth's confession of God and His people originated in the home of her married life. It sprang from the love with which she was permitted to embrace Israelites . . . . The conduct of one Israelitish woman [Naomi] in a foreign land was able to call forth a love and a confession of God like that of Ruth . . . . Ruth loves a woman, and is thereby led to the God Whom that woman confesses" (J.P. Lange, *A Commentary*).

commitment over comfort

Ruth was a woman who experienced loss and tragedy. Her husband, brother-in-law, and father-in-law were all dead. Ruth and her sister-in-law, Orpah, had a decision to make. Would they stay with Naomi, their mother-in-law, or would they return to their own country?

Naomi had nothing to offer them. She had no more sons, she was elderly, and she had no money. She encouraged her daughters-in-law to leave her and go back home where they would be guaranteed a good life. Orpah did leave, but Ruth insisted on staying with Naomi. Ruth knew that without divine intervention her future looked dim, but she insisted on being faithful to Naomi anyway. Ruth swore she would not leave her, saying that she wanted to live in Naomi's homeland and to know and serve Naomi's God (see Ruth 1:16, 17). Many people choose comfort over commitment, but in the end they miss out on the best that God had for them. Ruth did not know what her future held, but she determined to be a woman of godly character, which includes faithfulness. Together Ruth and Naomi went through some lean and difficult times; however, they kept a good attitude, they were thankful for what little they did have, and God kept making special arrangements to bless them. As it turned out, Naomi had a relative named Boaz who was very wealthy and also happened to be single. God gave Ruth favor with him, and they eventually married (see Ruth 4:10).

Faithfulness led Ruth from poverty to abundance. Proverbs 28:20 states that a faithful person will "abound with blessings." Being faithful means we will have to endure some difficulty along the way. We will encounter things that we would rather run away from, but if we wait patiently for the Lord, we will see His salvation in every situation.

2 NOW NAOMI had a kinsman of her husband's, a man of wealth, of the family of Elimelech, whose name was Boaz.

2 And Ruth the Moabitess said to Naomi, Let me go to the field and glean among the ears of grain after him in whose sight I shall find favor. Naomi said to her, Go, my daughter.

3 And [Ruth] went and gleaned in a field after the reapers; and she happened to stop at the part of the field belonging to Boaz, who was of the family of Elimelech.

4 And behold, Boaz came from Bethlehem and said to the reapers, The Lord be with you! And they answered him, The Lord bless you!

5 Then Boaz said to his servant who was set over the reapers, Whose maiden is this?

6 And the servant set over the reapers answered, She is the Moabitish girl who came back with Naomi from the country of Moab.

7 And she said, I pray you, let me glean and gather after the reapers among the sheaves. So she came and has continued from early morning until now, except when she rested a little in the house.

8 Then Boaz said to Ruth, Listen, my daughter, do not go to glean in

better, not bitter

After losing her husband, enduring a famine, and moving back to Judah from Moab, Naomi became bitter (see Ruth 1:20). The word *bitter* refers to something that is pungent or sharp to the taste. Bondage leads to bitterness! Naomi was bitter because she was in bondage to the pain, the disappointments, and the difficulties of her circumstances.

We remember that God instructed the children of Israel to prepare a Passover meal that included bitter herbs when they were about to be led out of Egypt, on the very eve of their departure. Why? God wanted them to eat those bitter herbs as a reminder of the bitterness they had experienced under Egyptian oppression.

It is said that the bitter herbs the Israelites ate were probably akin to horseradish. If you have ever taken a big bite of horseradish, you know it can cause quite a physical reaction. Bitterness causes precisely the same type of reaction in us spiritually.

How does bitterness begin? According to the Bible, it grows from a root. Hebrews 12:15 speaks of bitterness as a "root of resentment (rancor, bitterness, or hatred)" that "shoots forth and causes trouble and bitter torment, and the many become contaminated and defiled by it." Because Naomi was bitter inside, she accused the Lord of dealing "bitterly" with her.

Bitterness can result from the many minor offenses we simply will not let go of, the little things we rehearse over and over inside us until they become monumental. It can also result from significant hurts, offenses, traumas, or losses when we do not deal with them properly.

The longer we allow pain, anger, or disappointment to grow and fester, the more powerful they become, and the more they infect our entire being: our personalities, our attitudes and behaviors, our perspectives, and our relationships.

Just as God turned Naomi's situation around and made it good, we can expect Him to do the same for us if we will release our bitterness, ask Him to help us and heal us, and continue believing that He is good, no matter what we face.

another field or leave this one, but stay here close by my maidens.

9 Watch which field they reap, and follow them. Have I not charged the young men not to molest you? And when you are thirsty, go to the vessels and drink what the young men have drawn.

10 Then she fell on her face, bowing to the ground, and said to him, Why have I found favor in your eyes that you should notice me, when I am a foreigner?

11 And Boaz said to her, I have been made fully aware of all you have done for your mother-in-law since the death of your husband, and how you have left your father and mother and

the land of your birth and have come to a people unknown to you before.

12 The Lord recompense you for what you have done, and a full reward be given you by the Lord, the God of Israel, under Whose wings you have come to take refuge!

13 Then she said, Let me find favor in your sight, my lord. For you have comforted me and have spoken to the heart of your maidservant, though I am not as one of your maidservants.

14 And at mealtime Boaz said to her, Come here and eat of the bread and dip your morsel in the sour wine [mixed with oil]. And she sat beside the reapers; and he passed her some parched grain, and she ate until she was satisfied and she had some left [for Naomi].

15 And when she got up to glean, Boaz ordered his young men, Let her glean even among the sheaves, and do not reproach her.

16 And let fall some handfuls for her on purpose and let them lie there for her to glean, and do not rebuke her.

17 So she gleaned in the field until evening. Then she beat out what she had gleaned. It was about an ephah of barley.

18 And she took it up and went into the town; she showed her mother-in-law what she had gleaned, and she also brought forth and gave her the food she had reserved after she was satisfied.

19 And her mother-in-law said to her, Where have you gleaned today? Where did you work? Blessed be the man who noticed you. So [Ruth] told [her], The name of him with whom I worked today is Boaz.

20 And Naomi said to her daughter-

life point

In response to Ruth's kindness to Naomi, God spoke to Boaz, the owner of the field where Ruth was gleaning and the richest man in the county. God led him to leave handfuls of grain for her "on purpose" (Ruth 2:16).

If you are kind to people everywhere you go, you will find "handfuls" of kindness God has left on purpose, lying around for you. God will return a harvest of kindness to you because you have sown seeds of kindness. His heart is to bless you, so be on the lookout, because His "handfuls" are everywhere.

in-law, Blessed be he of the Lord who has not ceased his kindness to the living and to the dead. And Naomi said to her, The man is a near relative of ours, one who has the right to redeem us. [Lev. 25:25.]

21 And Ruth the Moabitess said, He said to me also, Stay close to my young men until they have harvested my entire crop.

22 And Naomi said to Ruth, It is good, my daughter, for you to go out with his maidens, lest in any other field you be molested.

23 So she kept close to the maidens of Boaz, gleaning until the end of the barley and wheat harvests. And she lived with her mother-in-law.

3 THEN NAOMI her mother-in-law said to Ruth, My daughter, shall I not seek rest or a home for you, that you may prosper?

2 And now is not Boaz, with whose maidens you were, our relative? See,

speak the Word

life point

One of the lessons we learn from Ruth is that loss does not mean everything in your life is over; just that one part of it has ended. One season has passed and another can now begin—if you are willing to believe that you can go forward.

Do not just passively sit around and wait for something to happen or someone to come along. Pray, and then step out in faith. That is what Ruth did, and that was when she stepped into God's plan of restoration in her life (see Ruth 3:1–5).

If you are lonely, do not just sit and wish you would meet others. *Go make new friends!* Find someone else who is lonely too—someone even lonelier than you are—and be a friend to that individual. You will reap what you sow. God will return that friendship to you, multiplied many times over. If you are hurting, go find someone else who is hurting and help him or her. As you sow into the lives of other hurting people, God will heal your wounds.

The Bible teaches us that faith moves us to take God-inspired action (see James 2:17, 18). I am not suggesting works of the flesh, or just fleshly zeal, but I am saying to be bold and step out as God leads. Be like Ruth and put "hands and feet" to your prayers.

he is winnowing barley tonight at the threshing floor.
3   Wash and anoint yourself therefore, and put on your best clothes and go down to the threshing floor, but do not make yourself known to the man until he has finished eating and drinking.
4   But when he lies down, notice the place where he lies; then go and uncover his feet and lie down. And he will tell you what to do.
5   And Ruth said to her, All that you say to me I will do.
6   So she went down to the threshing floor and did just as her mother-in-law had told her.
7   And when Boaz had eaten and drunk and his heart was merry, he went to lie down at the end of the heap of grain. Then [Ruth] came softly and uncovered his feet and lay down.
8   At midnight the man was startled, and he turned over, and behold, a woman lay at his feet!
9   And he said, Who are you? And she answered, I am Ruth your maidservant. Spread your wing [of protection] over your maidservant, for you are a next of kin.
10   And he said, Blessed be you of the Lord, my daughter. For you have made this last loving-kindness greater than the former, for you have not gone after young men, whether poor or rich.
11   And now, my daughter, fear not. I will do for you all you require, for all my people in the city know that you are a woman of strength (worth, bravery, capability).
12   It is true that I am your near kinsman; however, there is a kinsman nearer than I.
13   Remain tonight, and in the morning if he will perform for you the part of a kinsman, good; let him do it. But if he will not do the part of a kinsman for you, then, as the Lord lives, I will do the part of a kinsman for you. Lie down until the morning.
14   And she lay at his feet until the morning, but arose before one could recognize another; for he said, Let it not be known that the woman came to the threshing floor.
15   Also he said, Bring the mantle you are wearing and hold it. So [Ruth] held it, and he measured out six measures of barley and laid it on her. And she went into the town.

16 And when she came home, her mother-in-law said, How have you fared, my daughter? And Ruth told her all that the man had done for her. **17** And she said, He gave me these six measures of barley, for he said to me, Do not go empty-handed to your mother-in-law. **18** Then said she, Sit still, my daughter, until you learn how the matter turns out; for the man will not rest until he finishes the matter today.

4 THEN BOAZ went up to the city's gate and sat down there, and behold, the kinsman of whom Boaz had spoken came by. He said to him, Ho! Turn aside and sit down here. So he turned aside and sat down. **2** And Boaz took ten men of the elders of the city and said, Sit down here. And they sat down. **3** And he said to the kinsman, Naomi, who has returned from the country of Moab, has sold the parcel of land which belonged to our brother Elimelech. **4** And I thought to let you hear of it, saying, Buy it in the presence of those sitting here and before the elders of my people. If you will redeem it, redeem it; but if you will not redeem it, then say so, that I may know; for there is no one besides you to redeem it, and I am [next of kin] after you. And he said, I will redeem it. **5** Then Boaz said, The day you buy the field of Naomi, you must buy also Ruth the Moabitess, the widow of the dead man, to restore the name of the dead to his inheritance. **6** And the kinsman said, I cannot redeem it for myself, lest [by marrying a Moabitess] I endanger my own inheritance. Take my right of redemption yourself, for I cannot redeem it. [Deut. 23:3, 4.] **7** Now formerly in Israel this was the custom concerning redeeming and exchanging. To confirm a transaction, a man pulled off his sandal

life point

Even though Ruth did not believe in the God of Israel when she chose to extend kindness to her widowed mother-in-law, Naomi, she was obeying the biblical principle to be kind and good to others, especially widows (see James 1:27). In fact, Naomi's friends even remarked that Ruth had been better to her than seven sons (see Ruth 4:15).

Being good to someone else helps us overcome the pain, loss, or disappointments we experience; it also releases joy in our lives. Many times people who have been hurt experience depression. I believe this is partially due to the fact that their attention is on their own pain instead of on what they can do to relieve someone else's pain. God has not called us to "in-reach," He has called us to "out-reach." When we reach out to others, God reaches into our souls and heals us. He is the only One Who can heal the brokenhearted and make the wounded better than new. This was certainly true in Ruth's case, as God gave her a kind, godly husband, a baby boy, and a place in the bloodline of Jesus Christ.

and gave it to the other. This was the way of attesting in Israel. **8** Therefore, when the kinsman said to Boaz, Buy it for yourself, he pulled off his sandal. **9** And Boaz said to the elders and to all the people, You are witnesses this day that I have bought all that was Elimelech's and all that was Chilion's and Mahlon's from the hand of Naomi. **10** Also Ruth the Moabitess, the widow of Mahlon, I have bought to be my wife to restore the name of the dead to his inheritance, that the name of the dead may not be cut off from among his

putting the Word to work

The book of Ruth is a wonderful story of restoration and redemption in Ruth's life and in Naomi's. Is there anything you are believing God to restore in your life right now? Begin to thank Him for doing that in His way and in His timing.

brethren and from the gate of his birthplace. You are witnesses this day.

11 And all the people at the gate and the elders said, We are witnesses. May the Lord make the woman who is coming into your house like Rachel and Leah, the two who built the household of Israel. May you do worthily *and* get wealth (power) in Ephrathah and be famous in Bethlehem.

12 And let your house be like the house of Perez, whom Tamar bore to Judah, because of the offspring which the Lord will give you by this young woman.

13 So Boaz took Ruth and she became his wife. And he went in to her, and the Lord caused her to conceive, and she bore a son.

14 And the women said to Naomi, Blessed be the Lord, Who has not left you this day without a close kinsman, and may his name be famous in Israel.

15 And may he be to you a restorer of life and a nourisher *and* supporter in your old age, for your daughter-in-law who loves you, who is better to you than seven sons, has borne him.

16 Then Naomi took the child and laid him in her bosom and became his nurse.

17 And her neighbor women gave him a name, saying, A son is born to Naomi. They named him Obed. He was the father of Jesse, the father of David [the ancestor of Jesus Christ].

18 Now these are the descendants of Perez: Perez was the father of Hezron,

19 Hezron of Ram, Ram of Amminadab,

20 Amminadab of Nahshon, Nahshon of Salmon,

21 Salmon of Boaz, Boaz of Obed,

22 Obed of Jesse, and Jesse of David [the ancestor of Jesus Christ].

First Samuel

Author:
Uncertain

Date:
Between 931 BC and 722 BC

Everyday Life Principles:
God will answer the cries of a pure, desperate heart like Hannah's.

God will expose an evil, rebellious heart like Saul's.

God looks at our hearts. Our actions are important, but He looks beyond them to see the motives and intentions of our hearts.

First Samuel tells the story of Samuel, a priest in Israel, and Saul, Israel's first king. It introduces us to David and gives us extensive background on this man who would later succeed Saul as the ruler of God's people. Among other things and in the midst of some dramatic stories and adventure, this book reveals the importance of the heart.

In the beginning of I Samuel, we see a barren woman with a desperate but pure heart, who prays fervently to God. God answers with a miracle and gives her Samuel as her son. Samuel, in turn, served God with a faithful heart as a prophet and a priest in Israel. He anointed Saul as king, and though God had clearly chosen Saul to rule, we see that his heart was evil, jealous, fearful, and angry. Against the backdrop of Saul's wickedness, we see God raising up the future king, David, who is called "a man after [God's] own heart," (see I Samuel 13:14), so we know that his heart was pure and honorable before the Lord.

First Samuel 16:7 tells us that "man looks on the outward appearance, but the Lord looks on the heart." Determine today that whatever the Lord sees when He looks into your heart will be pleasing to Him.

1 THERE WAS a certain man of Ramathaim-zophim, of the hill country of Ephraim, named Elkanah son of Jeroham, the son of Elihu, the son of Tohu, the son of Zuph, an Ephraimite.

2 He had two wives, one named Hannah and the other named Peninnah. Peninnah had children, but Hannah had none.

3 This man went from his city year by year to worship and sacrifice to the Lord of hosts at Shiloh, where Hophni and Phinehas, the two sons of Eli, were the Lord's priests.

4 When the day came that Elkanah sacrificed, he would give to Peninnah his wife and all her sons and daughters portions [of the sacrificial meat].

5 But to Hannah he gave a double portion, for he loved Hannah, but the Lord had given her no children.

6 [This embarrassed and grieved Hannah] and her rival provoked her greatly to vex her, because the Lord had left her childless.

7 So it was year after year; whenever Hannah went up to the Lord's house, Peninnah provoked her, so she wept and did not eat.

8 Then Elkanah her husband said to her, Hannah, why do you cry? And why do you not eat? And why are you grieving? Am I not more to you than ten sons?

9 So Hannah rose after they had eaten and drunk in Shiloh. Now Eli the priest was sitting on his seat beside a post of the temple (tent) of the Lord.

10 And [Hannah] was in distress of soul, praying to the Lord and weeping bitterly.

11 She vowed, saying, O Lord of hosts, if You will indeed look on the affliction of Your handmaid and [earnestly] remember, and not forget Your handmaid but will give me a son, I will give him to the Lord all his life; no razor shall touch his head.

putting the Word to work

Are you praying fervently for something to happen in your life, as Hannah was praying for a son (see I Samuel 1:1–20)? Remember Hannah and know God hears your desperate cry and He will answer.

12 And as she continued praying before the Lord, Eli noticed her mouth.

13 Hannah was speaking in her heart; only her lips moved but her voice was not heard. So Eli thought she was drunk.

14 Eli said to her, How long will you be intoxicated? Put wine away from you.

15 But Hannah answered, No, my lord, I am a woman of a sorrowful spirit. I have drunk neither wine nor strong drink, but I was pouring out my soul before the Lord. [Gen. 19:34.]

16 Regard not your handmaid as a wicked woman; for out of my great complaint and bitter provocation I have been speaking.

17 Then Eli said, Go in peace, and may the God of Israel grant your petition which you have asked of Him.

18 Hannah said, Let your handmaid find grace in your sight. So [she] went her way and ate, her countenance no longer sad.

19 The family rose early the next morning, worshiped before the Lord, and returned to their home in Ramah. Elkanah knew Hannah his wife, and the Lord remembered her.

20 Hannah became pregnant and in due time bore a son and named him Samuel [heard of God], Because, she said, I have asked him of the Lord.

21 And Elkanah and all his house went up to offer to the Lord the yearly sacrifice and pay his vow.

22 But Hannah did not go, for she said to her husband, I will not go until the child is weaned, and then I will bring him, that he may appear before

the Lord and remain there as long as he lives.

23 Elkanah her husband said to her, Do what seems best to you. Wait until you have weaned him; only may the Lord establish His word. So Hannah remained and nursed her son until she weaned him.

24 When she had ªweaned him, she took him with her, with a three-year-old bull, an ephah of flour, and a skin bottle of wine [to pour over the burnt offering for a sweet odor], and brought Samuel to the Lord's house in Shiloh. The child was growing.

25 Then they slew the bull, and brought the child to Eli.

26 Hannah said, Oh, my lord! As your soul lives, my lord, I am the woman who stood by you here praying to the Lord.

27 For this child I prayed, and the Lord has granted my petition made to Him.

28 Therefore I have given him to the Lord; as long as he lives he is given to the Lord. And they worshiped the Lord there.

2 HANNAH PRAYED, and said, My heart exults *and* triumphs in the Lord; my horn (my strength) is lifted up in the Lord. My mouth is no longer silent, for it is opened wide over my enemies, because I rejoice in Your salvation.

2 There is none holy like the Lord, there is none besides You; there is no Rock like our God.

3 Talk no more so very proudly; let not arrogance go forth from your mouth, for the Lord is a God of knowledge, and by Him actions are weighed.

4 The bows of the mighty are broken, and those who stumbled are girded with strength.

5 Those who were full have hired themselves out for bread, but those who were hungry have ceased to hunger. The barren has borne seven, but she who has many children languishes *and* is forlorn.

6 The Lord slays and makes alive; He brings down to Sheol and raises up.

7 The Lord makes poor and makes rich; He brings low and He lifts up.

8 He raises up the poor out of the dust and lifts up the needy from the ash heap, to make them sit with nobles and inherit the throne of glory. For the pillars of the earth are the Lord's, and He has set the world upon them.

speak the Word

God, my heart exults and triumphs in You. My strength is in You. My mouth is no longer silent; it is opened wide over my enemies because I rejoice in Your salvation.
ADAPTED FROM I SAMUEL 2:1

God, I declare that there is none as holy as You are holy; there is no god besides You; there is no Rock in my life like You.
ADAPTED FROM I SAMUEL 2:2

a He would then be two or three years old. There were women engaged in tabernacle service to whose care he might have been committed. It was important that he should be dedicated as soon as possible. The earliest impressions of his boyhood were to be those of the house of God (*The Cambridge Bible*).

life point

We must remember that what goes up can come down. God lifts up, and God brings down (see I Samuel 2:7). If we are to be leaders in His kingdom, we must develop and maintain strong, godly character and the most intimate communion with God we possibly can so that we will be able to stay in the positions to which He elevates us.

9 He will guard the feet of His godly ones, but the wicked shall be silenced *and* perish in darkness; for by strength shall no man prevail.

10 The adversaries of the Lord shall be broken to pieces; against them will He thunder in heaven. The Lord will judge [all peoples] to the ends of the earth; and He will give strength to ᵇHis king (King) and exalt the power of His anointed (Anointed ᶜHis Christ). [Luke 1:46.]

11 Elkanah and his wife Hannah returned to Ramah to his house. But the child ministered to the Lord before Eli the priest.

12 The sons of Eli were base *and* worthless; they did not know *or* regard the Lord.

13 And the custom of the priests with the people was this: when any man offered sacrifice, the priest's servant came while the flesh was boiling with a fleshhook of three prongs in his hand;

14 And he thrust it into the pan or kettle or caldron or pot; all that the fleshhook brought up the priest took for himself. So they did in Shiloh with all the Israelites who came there.

15 Also, before they burned the fat, the priest's servant came and said to the man who sacrificed, Give the priest meat to roast, for he will not accept boiled meat from you, but raw.

16 And if the man said to him, Let them burn the fat first, and then you may take as much as you want, the priest's servant would say, No! Give it to me now or I will take it by force.

17 So the sin of the [two] young men was very great before the Lord, for they despised the offering of the Lord.

18 But Samuel ministered before the Lord, a child girded with a linen ephod.

19 Moreover, his mother made him a little robe and brought it to him from year to year when she came up with her husband to offer the yearly sacrifice.

20 And Eli would bless Elkanah and his wife and say, May the Lord give you children by this woman for the gift she asked for *and* gave to the Lord. Then they would go to their own home.

21 And the Lord visited Hannah, so that she bore three sons and two daughters. And the child Samuel grew before the Lord.

22 Now Eli was very old, and he heard all that his sons did to all Israel and how they lay with the women who served at the door of the Tent of Meeting.

23 And he said to them, Why do you do such things? For I hear of your evil dealings from all the people.

24 No, my sons; it is no good report which I hear the Lord's people spreading abroad.

25 If one man wrongs another, God will mediate for him; but if a man wrongs the Lord, who shall intercede for him? Yet they did not listen to their father, for it was the Lord's will to slay them.

26 Now the boy Samuel grew and

b Hannah's prophetic prayer was but partially fulfilled in the king soon to be anointed by her son as the deliverer of Israel; it reaches forward to . . . the King Messiah, in Whom alone the lofty anticipations of the prophetess are to be completely realized (*The Cambridge Bible*). **c** Both *The Septuagint* (Greek translation of the Old Testament) and *The Latin Vulgate* read "His Christ" (Luke 2:26).

was in favor both with the Lord and with men.

27 A man of God came to Eli and said to him, Thus has the Lord said: I plainly revealed Myself to the house of your father [forefather Aaron] when they were in Egypt in bondage to Pharaoh's house.

28 Moreover, I selected him out of all the tribes of Israel to be My priest, to offer on My altar, to burn incense, to wear an ephod before Me. And I gave [from then on] to the house of your father [forefather] all the offerings of the Israelites made by fire.

29 Why then do you kick [trample upon, treat with contempt] My sacrifice and My offering which I commanded, and honor your sons above Me by fattening yourselves upon the choicest part of every offering of My people Israel?

30 Therefore the Lord, the God of Israel, says, I did promise that your house and that of your father [forefather Aaron] should go in and out before Me forever. But now the Lord says, Be it far from Me. For those who honor Me I will honor, and those who despise Me shall be lightly esteemed.

31 Behold, the time is coming when I will cut off your strength and the strength of your own father's house, that there shall not be an old man in your house.

32 And you shall behold the distress of My house, even in all the prosperity which God will give Israel, and there shall not be an old man in your house forever.

33 Yet I will not cut off from My altar every man of yours; some shall survive to weep and mourn [over the family's ruin], but all the increase of your house shall die in their best years. [I Sam. 22:17-20.]

34 And what befalls your two sons, Hophni and Phinehas, shall be a sign to you—in one day they both shall die. [Fulfilled in I Sam. 4:17, 18.]

35 And I will raise up for Myself a ᵈfaithful priest (Priest), who shall do according to what is in My heart and mind. And I will build him a sure house, and he shall walk before My anointed (Anointed) forever. [I Sam. 2:10.]

36 Everyone who is left in your house shall come crouching to him for a piece of silver and a bit of bread and say, Put me, I pray you, into a priest's office so I may have a piece of bread.

3 NOW THE boy Samuel ministered to the Lord before Eli. The word of the Lord was rare *and* precious in those days; there was no frequent *or* widely spread vision.

2 At that time Eli, whose eyesight had dimmed so that he could not see, was lying down in his own place.

3 The lamp of God had not yet gone out in the temple of the Lord, where the ark of God was, and Samuel was lying down

4 When the Lord called, Samuel! And he answered, Here I am.

5 He ran to Eli and said, Here I am, for you called me. Eli said, I did not call you; lie down again. So he went and lay down.

6 And the Lord called again, Samuel! And Samuel arose and went to Eli and said, Here am I; you did call me. Eli answered, I did not call, my son; lie down again.

7 Now Samuel did not yet know the Lord, and the word of the Lord was not yet revealed to him.

d This person is not identified, but this prophecy found its fulfillment from the standpoint of historical exposition in Samuel (J.P. Lange, *A Commentary*). Christian writers usually adopt also the Messianic interpretation. The text does not allow an exclusive reference to Christ, since it does look plainly to the then existing order of things; however, it also points to Christ as the consummation of the blessedness which it promises.

how to hear God's voice

When God started calling to Samuel, Samuel thought that his master, Eli, was speaking to him (see I Samuel 3:4–6). Both times Eli said to Samuel, "I did not call you." After this happened a third time, Eli finally realized God was calling Samuel. God spoke to Samuel in a voice that was familiar to him so that he would not be frightened.

Samuel was accustomed to hearing Eli's voice; therefore, when God called to him, it sounded like Eli. Likewise, God wants us to listen to Him, so He speaks to us through a voice that we will recognize. Sometimes it may sound like our own voice; sometimes it may sound like the voice of someone we know. But the point is that the voice will always bring peace when God speaks to us.

People who listen to my teaching tapes tell me that frequently when they are about to make a decision, they will hear me say something that gives them direction or correction. What they are really hearing is God speaking through His Word, but they have heard my voice speaking it to them for so long, it sounds like me when it comes to them.

A woman told me at a meeting, "I was in an intense situation with my husband. God spoke to me and told me what to do by reminding me of something you said on one of your tapes. All of a sudden I heard your voice saying just what I needed to remember. God reminded me of it as a *word in due season*." Even though she heard my voice playing back from her memory bank, it was the Holy Spirit Who called forth that memory just when she needed it.

When God speaks to us, He does not usually boom from heaven. Often He speaks to us through what His Word calls "a still, small voice" that comes from our inner man. In such situations, we may think we are talking to ourselves, but God's words in our spirit are always filled with a wisdom that we could never have on our own.

People have said to me, "You're always saying, 'God said.' You sound like you have conversations with God all the time." I do have fellowship with God regularly, and He speaks to me in many different ways—and God is trying to talk to everyone else all the time, too. We all can hear Him if we will simply ask Him to speak clearly to us, then listen to our "inner man" (our conscience), and wait for Him to speak (see Psalm 5:3).

God speaks to us in many different ways. Many people think they do not hear from God because they are looking for some kind of supernatural manifestation that is not likely to happen. Most of the time, God speaks in our hearts through peace or a lack of it. If we have peace, we may proceed with our intended action, but if we do not have peace, that is a word from God to stop. God also speaks through wisdom and common sense. He does not lead us to do foolish things. He speaks to us through His Word and never tells us to do anything that does not agree with His Word. He speaks to us through other people and even our circumstances. Let me encourage you to begin to ask God to speak to you and then listen for His voice. He has so many good things to say to you!

8 And the Lord called Samuel the third time. And he went to Eli and said, Here I am, for you did call me. Then Eli perceived that the Lord was calling the boy.

9 So Eli said to Samuel, Go, lie down. And if He calls you, you shall say, Speak, Lord, for Your servant is listening. So Samuel went and lay down in his place.

10 And the Lord came and stood and called as at other times, Samuel! Samuel! Then Samuel answered, Speak, Lord, for Your servant is listening.

11 The Lord told Samuel, Behold, I am about to do a thing in Israel at which both ears of all who hear it shall tingle.

12 On that day I will perform against Eli all that I have spoken concerning his house, from beginning to end.

13 And I [now] announce to him that I will judge *and* punish his house forever for the iniquity of which he knew, for his sons were bringing a curse upon themselves [blaspheming God], and he did not restrain them.

14 Therefore I have sworn to the house of Eli that the iniquity of Eli's house shall not be atoned for *or* purged with sacrifice or offering forever.

15 Samuel lay until morning; then he opened the doors of the Lord's house. And [he] was afraid to tell the vision to Eli.

16 But Eli called Samuel and said, Samuel, my son. And he answered, Here I am.

17 Eli said, What is it He told you? Pray do not hide it from me. May God do so to you, and more also, if you hide anything from me of all that He said to you.

18 And Samuel told him everything, hiding nothing. And Eli said, It is the Lord; let Him do what seems good to Him.

19 Samuel grew; the Lord was with him and let none of his words fall to the ground. [Josh. 23:14.]

20 And all Israel from Dan to Beersheba knew that Samuel was established to be a prophet of the Lord.

21 And the Lord continued to appear in Shiloh, for the Lord revealed Himself to Samuel in Shiloh through the word of the Lord.

4 AND THE word of [the Lord through] Samuel came to all Israel. Now Israel went out to battle against the Philistines and encamped beside Ebenezer; the Philistines encamped at Aphek.

2 The Philistines drew up against Israel, and when the battle spread, Israel was smitten by the Philistines, who slew about 4,000 men on the battlefield.

3 When the troops had come into the camp, the elders of Israel said, Why has the Lord smitten us today before the Philistines? Let us bring the ark of the covenant of the Lord here from Shiloh, that He may come among us and save us from the power of our enemies.

4 So the people sent to Shiloh and brought from there the ark of the

speak the Word

Speak to me, Lord. I am listening for Your voice.
ADAPTED FROM I SAMUEL 3:10

God, I thank You that as I continue to grow spiritually, You will be with me and let none of my words be wasted and fall to the ground.
ADAPTED FROM I SAMUEL 3:19

covenant of the Lord of hosts, Who dwells above the cherubim. And the two sons of Eli, Hophni and Phinehas, were with the ark of the covenant of God.

5   And when the ark of the covenant of the Lord came into the camp, all Israel shouted with a great shout, so that the earth resounded.

6   And when the Philistines heard the noise of the shout, they said, What does this great shout in the camp of the Hebrews mean? When they understood that the ark of the Lord had come into the camp,

7   The Philistines were afraid, for they said, God has come into the camp. And they said, Woe to us! For such a thing has not happened before.

8   Woe to us! Who shall deliver us out of the hand of these mighty gods? These are the gods that smote the Egyptians with every kind of plague in the wilderness.

9   Be strong, and acquit yourselves like men, O you Philistines, that you may not become servants to the Hebrews, as they have been to you; behave yourselves like men, and fight!

10   And the Philistines fought; Israel was smitten and they fled every man to his own home. There was a very great slaughter; for 30,000 foot soldiers of Israel fell.

11   And the ark of God was taken, and the two sons of Eli, Hophni and Phinehas, were slain. [Foretold in I Sam. 2:34.]

12   Now a man of Benjamin ran from the battle line and came to Shiloh that day, with his clothes torn and earth on his head.

13   When he arrived, Eli was sitting by the road watching, for his heart trembled for the ark of God. When the man told the news in the city, all the city [people] cried out.

14   When Eli heard the noise of the crying, he said, What is this uproar? And the man came hastily and told Eli.

15   Now Eli was 98 years old; his eyes were dim so that he could not see.

16   The man said to Eli, I have come from the battle; I fled from the battle today. Eli said, How did it go, my son?

17   The messenger replied, Israel fled before the Philistines, and there has been a great slaughter among the people. Also your two sons, Hophni and Phinehas, are dead, and the ark of God is captured.

18   And when he mentioned the ark of God, Eli fell off the seat backward by the side of the gate. His neck was broken and he died, for he was an old man and heavy. He had judged Israel forty years.

19   Now his daughter-in-law, Phinehas' wife, was with child, about to be delivered. And when she heard that the ark of God was captured and that her father-in-law and her husband were dead, she bowed herself and gave birth, for her pains came upon her.

20   And about the time of her death the women attending her said to her, Fear not, for you have borne a son. But she did not answer or notice.

21   And she named the child Ichabod, saying, The glory is departed from Israel!—because the ark of God had been captured and because of her father-in-law and her husband.

22   She said, The glory is gone from Israel, for the ark of God has been taken.

5 THE PHILISTINES brought the ark of God from Ebenezer to Ashdod.

2   They took the ark of God into the house of Dagon and set it beside Dagon [their idol].

3   When they of Ashdod arose early on the morrow, behold, Dagon had fallen upon his face on the ground before the ark of the Lord. So they took Dagon and set him in his place again.

4 But when they arose early the next morning, behold, Dagon had again fallen on his face on the ground before the ark of the Lord, and [his] head and both the palms of his hands were lying cut off on the threshold; only the trunk of Dagon was left him.
5 This is the reason neither the priests of Dagon nor any who come into Dagon's house tread on the threshold of Dagon in Ashdod to this day.
6 But the hand of the Lord was heavy upon the people of Ashdod, and He caused [mice to spring up and there was] very deadly destruction and He smote the people with [very painful] tumors or boils, both Ashdod and its territory.
7 When the men of Ashdod saw that it was so, they said, The ark of the God of Israel must not remain with us, for His hand is heavy on us and on Dagon our god.
8 So they sent and gathered all the lords of the Philistines to them and said, What shall we do with the ark of the God of Israel? They answered, Let [it] be carried around to Gath. So they carried the ark of the God of Israel there.
9 But after they had carried it to Gath, the hand of the Lord was against the city, causing an exceedingly great panic [at the deaths from the plague], for He afflicted the people of the city, both small and great, and tumors or boils broke out on them.
10 So they sent the ark of God to Ekron. And as [it] came, the people of Ekron cried out, They have brought the ark of the God of Israel to us to slay us and our people!
11 So they sent and assembled all the lords of the Philistines and said, Send away the ark of the God of Israel; let it return to its own place, that it may not slay us and our people. For there was a deadly panic throughout all the city; the hand of God was very heavy there.

12 The men who had not died were stricken with very painful tumors or boils, and the cry of the city went up to heaven.

6 THE ARK of the Lord was in the country of the Philistines seven months.
2 And the Philistines called for the priests and the diviners, saying, What shall we do to the ark of the Lord? Tell us with what we shall send it to its place.
3 And they said, If you send away the ark of the God of Israel, do not send it empty, but at least return to Him a guilt offering. Then you will be healed, and it will be known to you why His hand is not removed [and healing granted you].
4 Then they said, What shall be the guilt offering which we shall return to Him? They answered, Five golden tumors and five golden mice, according to the number of the Philistine lords, for one plague was on you all, even on your lords.
5 Therefore you must make images of your tumors and of your mice that destroy the land, and give glory to the God of Israel. Perhaps He will lighten His hand from off you and your gods and your land.
6 Why then do you harden your hearts as the Egyptians and Pharaoh hardened their hearts? When He had done wonders and made a mock of them, did they not let the people go, and they departed?
7 Now then, make and prepare a new cart and two milch cows on which no yoke has ever come; and yoke the cows to the cart, but take their calves home, away from them.
8 And take the ark of the Lord and place it upon the cart, and put in a box at its side the figures of gold which you are returning to Him as a guilt offering. Then send it away and let it be gone.

9 And watch. If it goes up by the way of its own land to Beth-shemesh, then He has done us this great evil. But if not, then we shall know that it was not His hand that struck us; it happened to us by chance.

10 And the men did so, and took two milch cows and yoked them to the cart and shut up their calves at home.

11 And they put the ark of the Lord on the cart and along with it the box with the mice of gold and the images of their tumors.

12 And the cows went straight toward Beth-shemesh along the highway, lowing as they went, and turned not aside to the right or the left. And the Philistine lords followed them as far as the border of Beth-shemesh.

13 Now the men of Beth-shemesh were reaping their wheat harvest in the valley, and they lifted up their eyes and saw the ark, and rejoiced to see it.

14 The cart came into the field of Joshua of Beth-shemesh and stopped there. A great stone was there; and the men split up the wood of the cart and offered the cows as a burnt offering to the Lord.

15 The Levites took down the ark of the Lord and the box beside it in which were the figures of gold and put them upon the great stone. And the men of Beth-shemesh offered burnt offerings and made sacrifices that day to the Lord.

16 When the five lords of the Philistines saw it, they returned that day to Ekron.

17 And these are the tumors of gold which the Philistines returned for a guilt offering to the Lord: one each for Ashdod, Gaza, Ashkelon, Gath and Ekron;

18 Also the mice of gold was according to the number of all the cities of the Philistines belonging to the five lords, both fortified cities and country villages. The great stone, on which they set the ark of the Lord, remains as a witness to this day in the field of Joshua of Beth-shemesh.

19 And the Lord slew some of the men of Beth-shemesh because they had looked into the ark of the Lord; He slew ᵉseventy men of them, and the people mourned because the Lord had made a great slaughter among them.

20 And the men of Beth-shemesh said, Who is able to stand before the Lord, this holy God? And to whom shall He go away from us?

21 And they sent messengers to the inhabitants of Kiriath-jearim, saying, The Philistines have returned the ark of the Lord. Come down and take it up to you.

7 SO THE men of Kiriath-jearim came and took the ark of the Lord and brought it into the house of Abinadab on the hill and consecrated Eleazar his son to have charge of the ark of the Lord.

2 And the ark remained in Kiriath-jearim a very long time [nearly 100 years, through Samuel's entire judgeship, Saul's reign, and well into David's, when it was brought to Jerusalem]. For it was twenty years before all the house of Israel lamented after the Lord. [I Chron. 13:5-7.]

3 Then Samuel said to all the house of Israel, If you are returning to the Lord with all your hearts, then put away the foreign gods and the Ashtaroth [female deities] from among you and direct your hearts to the Lord and serve Him only, and He will deliver you out of the hand of the Philistines.

4 So the Israelites put away the Baals and the Ashtaroth, and served the Lord only.

5 Samuel said, Gather all Israel to

e Most Hebrew manuscripts read 50,070.

Mizpah and I will pray to the Lord for you.

6 So they gathered at Mizpah and drew water and poured it out before the Lord and fasted on that day and said there, We have sinned against the Lord. And Samuel judged the Israelites at Mizpah.

7 Now when the Philistines heard that the Israelites had gathered at Mizpah, the lords of the Philistines went up against Israel. And when the Israelites heard of it, they were afraid of the Philistines.

8 And the Israelites said to Samuel, Do not cease to cry to the Lord our God for us, that He may save us from the hand of the Philistines.

9 So Samuel took a sucking lamb and offered it as a whole burnt offering to the Lord; and Samuel cried to the Lord for Israel, and the Lord answered him.

10 As Samuel was offering up the burnt offering, the Philistines drew near to attack Israel. But the Lord thundered with a great voice that day against the Philistines and threw them into confusion, and they were defeated before Israel.

11 And the men of Israel went out of Mizpah and pursued the Philistines and smote them as far as below Beth-car.

12 Then Samuel took a stone and set it between Mizpah and Shen, and he called the name of it Ebenezer [stone of help], saying, Heretofore the Lord has helped us.

13 So the Philistines were subdued and came no more into Israelite territory. And the hand of the Lord was against the Philistines all the days of Samuel.

14 The cities the Philistines had taken from Israel were restored to Israel, from Ekron to Gath, and Israel rescued [the cities'] territory from the Philistines. There was peace also between Israel and the Amorites.

15 And Samuel judged Israel all his days.

16 And he went from year to year on a circuit to Bethel, Gilgal, and Mizpah, and was judge for Israel in all those places.

17 Then he would return to Ramah, for his home was there; there he judged Israel, and there he built an altar to the Lord.

8 WHEN SAMUEL was old, he made his sons judges over Israel.

2 Now the name of his firstborn was Joel and the name of his second, Abijah. They were judges in Beersheba.

3 His sons did not walk in his ways, but turned aside after gain, took bribes, and perverted justice.

4 All the elders of Israel assembled and came to Samuel at Ramah

5 And said to him, Behold, you are old, and your sons do not walk in your ways; now appoint us a king to rule over us like all the other nations.

6 But it displeased Samuel when they said, Give us a king to govern us. And Samuel prayed to the Lord.

7 And the Lord said to Samuel, Hearken to the voice of the people in all they say to you; for they have not rejected you, but they have rejected Me, that I should not be King over them.

8 According to all the works which they have done since I brought them up out of Egypt even to this day, forsaking Me and serving other gods, so they also do to you.

9 So listen now to their voice; only solemnly warn them and show them the ways of the king who shall reign over them.

10 So Samuel told all the words of the Lord to the people who asked of him a king.

11 And he said, These will be the ways of the king who shall reign over you: he will take your sons and appoint them to his chariots and to be his horsemen and to run before his chariots.

12 He will appoint them for himself to be commanders over thousands and over fifties, and some to plow his ground and to reap his harvest and to make his implements of war and equipment for his chariots.

13 He will take your daughters to be perfumers, cooks, and bakers.

14 He will take your fields, your vineyards, and your olive orchards, even the best of them, and give them to his servants.

15 He will take a tenth of your grain and of your vineyards and give it to his officers and to his servants.

16 He will take your men and women servants and the best of your cattle and your donkeys and put them to his work.

17 He will take a tenth of your flocks, and you yourselves shall be his slaves.

18 In that day you will cry out because of your king you have chosen for yourselves, but the Lord will not hear you then.

19 Nevertheless, the people refused to listen to the voice of Samuel, and they said, No! We will have a king over us,

20 That we also may be like all the nations, and that our king may govern us and go out before us and fight our battles.

21 Samuel heard all the people's words and repeated them in the Lord's ears.

22 And the Lord said to Samuel, Hearken to their voice and appoint them a king. And Samuel said to the men of Israel, Go every man to his city.

9 THERE WAS a man of Benjamin whose name was Kish son of Abiel, the son of Zeror, the son of Becorath, the son of Aphiah, a Benjamite, a mighty man of wealth *and* valor.

2 Kish had a son named Saul, a choice young man and handsome; among all the Israelites there was not a man more handsome than he. He was a head taller than any of the people.

3 The donkeys of Kish, Saul's father, were lost. Kish said to Saul, Take a servant with you and go, look for the donkeys.

4 And they passed through the hill country of Ephraim and the land of Shalishah, but did not find them. Then they went through the land of Shaalim and the land of Benjamin, but did not find them.

5 And when they came to the land of Zuph, Saul said to his servant, Come, let us return, lest my father stop worrying about the donkeys and become concerned about us.

6 The servant said to him, Behold now, there is in this city a man of God, a man held in honor; all that he says surely comes true. Now let us go there. Perhaps he can show us where we should go.

7 Then Saul said to his servant, But if we go, what shall we bring the man? The bread in our sacks is gone, and there is no gift for the man of God. What have we?

8 The servant replied, I have here a quarter of a shekel of silver. I will give that to the man of God to tell us our way—

9 (Formerly in Israel, when a man went to inquire of God, he said, Come, let us go to the seer, for he that is now called a prophet was formerly called a seer.)

10 Saul said to his servant, Well said; come, let us go. So they went to the city where the man of God was.

11 As they went up the hill to the city, they met young maidens going out to draw water, and said to them, Is the seer here?

12 They answered, He is; behold, he is just beyond you. Hurry, for he came today to the city because the people have a sacrifice today on the high place.

13 As you enter the city, you will find him before he goes up to the high place to eat. The people will not eat until he comes to ask the blessing on the sacrifice. Afterward, those who are invited eat. So go on up, for about now you will find him.

14 So they went up to the city, and as they were entering, behold, Samuel came toward them, going up to the high place.

15 Now a day before Saul came, the Lord had revealed to Samuel in his ear,

16 Tomorrow about this time I will send you a man from the land of Benjamin, and you shall anoint him to be leader over My people Israel; and he shall save them out of the hand of the Philistines. For I have looked upon the distress of My people, because their cry has come to Me.

17 When Samuel saw Saul, the Lord told him, There is the man of whom I told you. He shall have authority over My people.

18 Then Saul came near to Samuel in the gate and said, Tell me where is the seer's house?

19 Samuel answered Saul, I am the seer. Go up before me to the high place, for you shall eat with me today, and tomorrow I will let you go and will tell you all that is on your mind.

20 As for your donkeys that were lost three days ago, do not be thinking about them, for they are found. And for whom are all the desirable things of Israel? Are they not for you and for all your father's house?

21 And Saul said, Am I not a Benjamite, of the smallest of the tribes of Israel? And is not my family the least of all the families of the clans of Benjamin? Why then do you speak this way to me?

22 Then Samuel took Saul and his servant and brought them into the guest room [at the high place] and had them sit in the chief place among the persons—about thirty of them—who were invited. [The other people feasted outside.]

23 And Samuel said to the cook, Bring the portion which I gave you, of which I said to you, Set it aside.

24 And the cook lifted high the shoulder and what was on it [indicating that it was the priest's honored portion] and set it before Saul. [Samuel] said, See what was reserved for you. Eat, for until the hour appointed it was kept for you, ever since I invited the people. So Saul ate that day with Samuel.

25 When they had come down from the high place into the city, Samuel conversed with Saul on the top of the house.

26 They arose early and about dawn Samuel called Saul [who was sleeping] on the top of the house, saying, Get up, that I may send you on your way. Saul arose, and both he and Samuel went out on the street.

27 And as they were going down to the outskirts of the city, Samuel said to Saul, Bid the servant pass on before us—and he passed on—but you stand still, first, that I may cause you to hear the word of God.

10 THEN SAMUEL took the vial of oil and poured it on Saul's head and kissed him and said, Has not the Lord anointed you to be prince over His heritage Israel?

2 When you have left me today, you will meet two men by Rachel's tomb in the territory of Benjamin at Zelzah, and they will say to you, The donkeys you sought are found. And your father has quit caring about them and is anxious for you, asking, What shall I do about my son?

3 Then you will go on from there and you will come to the oak of Tabor, and three men going up to God at Bethel will meet you there, one carrying three kids, another carrying three loaves of bread, and another carrying a skin bottle of wine.

4 They will greet you and give you two loaves of bread, which you shall accept from their hand.

5 After that you will come to the hill of God, where the garrison of the Philistines is; and when you come to the city, you will meet a company of prophets coming down from the high place with harp, tambourine, flute, and lyre before them, prophesying.

6 Then the Spirit of the Lord will come upon you mightily, and you will show yourself to be a prophet with them; and you will be turned into another man.

7 When these signs meet you, do whatever you find to be done, for God is with you.

8 You shall go down before me to Gilgal; and behold, I will come down to you to offer burnt offerings and to sacrifice peace offerings. You shall wait seven days until I come to you and show you what you shall do.

9 And when [Saul] had turned his back to leave Samuel, God gave him another heart, and all these signs came to pass that day.

10 When they came to the hill [Gibeah], behold, a band of prophets met him; and the Spirit of God came mightily upon him, and he spoke under divine inspiration among them.

11 And when all who knew Saul before saw that he spoke by inspiration among the [schooled] prophets, the people said one to another, What has come over [him, who is nobody

but] the son of Kish? Is Saul also among the prophets?

12 One from that same place answered, But who is the father of the others? So it became a proverb, Is Saul also among the prophets?

13 When [Saul] had ended his inspired speaking, he went to the high place.

14 Saul's uncle said to him and to his servant, Where did you go? And Saul said, To look for the donkeys, and when we found them nowhere, we went to Samuel.

15 Saul's uncle said, Tell me, what did Samuel say to you?

16 And Saul said to his uncle, He told us plainly that the donkeys were found. But of the matter of the kingdom of which Samuel spoke he told him nothing.

17 And Samuel called the people together to the Lord at Mizpah

18 And said to the Israelites, Thus says the Lord, the God of Israel: It was I Who brought up Israel out of Egypt and delivered you out of the hands of the Egyptians and of all the kingdoms that oppressed you.

19 But you have this day rejected your God, Who Himself saves you from all your calamities and distresses; and you have said to Him, No! Set a king over us. So now present yourselves before the Lord by your tribes and by your thousands.

20 And when Samuel had caused all the tribes of Israel to come near, the tribe of Benjamin was taken [probably by lot].

21 When he had caused the tribe of Benjamin to come near by their families, the family of Matri was taken.

speak the Word

God, I pray that Your Spirit will come upon me so mightily and make me so new that people will hardly recognize me!
ADAPTED FROM I SAMUEL 10:6

changed by the Holy Spirit

When the Spirit of God truly comes upon a person, that person will be changed. First Samuel 10:6 tells us that Saul would be "turned into another man," which really means that he would be so thoroughly changed that people would think he was someone else.

The most important evidences of the Spirit-filled life are a change of character and the development of the fruit of the Holy Spirit, which is described in Galatians 5:22, 23. God fills people with the Holy Spirit to enable them to live for Him. If they are not doing that, they are not showing forth the proper evidence of being a believer in Jesus Christ. Speaking in tongues was one of the evidences of the outpouring of the Holy Spirit at Pentecost, and it still is one today. But the most important evidence was then—and always will be—changed men and women (see Acts 2:1–4).

At Jesus' trial, Peter denied Christ three times because he was afraid of the Jews (see Luke 22:56–62); but after being filled with the Holy Spirit on the Day of Pentecost, he stood and preached an extremely bold message. Three thousand souls were added to the kingdom of God as the result of Peter's preaching that day (see Acts 2:14–41). The baptism in the Holy Spirit changed Peter; it turned him into another man. His fear suddenly disappeared, and he became as bold as a lion.

Peter was not the only person who took a courageous stand that day; all eleven of the remaining apostles did the same. They had all been hiding behind closed doors for fear of the Jews when Jesus came to them after His resurrection (see John 20:19–22), but suddenly, after being filled with the Holy Spirit, they all became fearless and brave.

There was a common thread that ran through the lives of Jesus' disciples—their fear was turned to boldness through the power of the Holy Spirit. Like them, you do not need to live with the torment of being afraid. Your fear can also be turned to boldness.

There is help available to you through the infilling of the Holy Spirit. The baptism in the Holy Spirit changed Saul; it changed Peter and the disciples; it changed me; and it continues to change earnest seekers all over the world. Ask God to fill you completely with His precious Holy Spirit. Surrender all of yourself to Him, holding nothing back. Paul prayed for the church that they would become bodies wholly filled with God Himself (see Ephesians 3:16). This is my desire, and I pray that it is also yours.

And Saul son of Kish was taken. But when they looked for him, he could not be found.

22 Therefore they inquired of the Lord further, if the man would yet come back. And the Lord answered, Behold, he has hidden himself among the baggage. [Exod. 28:30.]

23 They ran and brought him from there. And when he stood among the people, he was a head taller than any of them.

24 And Samuel said to all the people, Do you see him whom the Lord has chosen, that none like him is among all the people? And all the

people shouted and said, Long live the king!

25 Then Samuel told the people the manner of the kingdom [defining the position of the king in relation to God and to the people], and wrote it in a book and laid it up before the Lord. And Samuel sent all the people away, each one to his home.

26 Saul also went home to Gibeah; and there went with him a band of valiant men whose hearts God had touched.

27 But some worthless fellows said, How can this man save us? And they despised him and brought him no gift. But he held his peace *and* was as if deaf.

11 AND NAHASH the Ammonite went up and besieged Jabesh-gilead; and all the men of Jabesh said to Nahash, Make a treaty with us, and we will serve you.

2 But Nahash the Ammonite told them, On this condition I will make a treaty with you, that I thrust out all your right eyes and thus lay disgrace on all Israel.

3 The elders of Jabesh said to Nahash, Give us seven days' time, that we may send messengers through all the territory of Israel. Then, if there is no man to save us, we will come out to you.

4 Then messengers came to Gibeah of Saul and told the news in the ears of the people; and all the people wept aloud.

5 Now Saul came out of the field after the oxen, and [he] said, What ails the people that they are weeping? And they told him the words of the men of Jabesh.

6 The Spirit of God came mightily upon Saul when he heard those tidings, and his anger was greatly kindled.

7 And he took a yoke of oxen and cut them in pieces and sent them throughout all the territory of Israel by the hands of messengers, saying, Whoever does not come forth after Saul and Samuel, so shall it be done to his oxen! And terror from the Lord fell on the people, and they came out with one consent.

8 And he numbered them at Bezek, and the Israelites were 300,000 and the men of Judah 30,000.

9 The messengers who came were told, Say to the men of Jabesh-gilead, Tomorrow, by the time the sun is hot, you shall have help. The messengers came and reported to the men of Jabesh, and they were glad.

10 So the men of Jabesh said to Nahash, Tomorrow we will come out to you, and you may do to us all that seems good to you.

11 The next day Saul put the men in three companies; and they came into the midst of the enemy's camp in the [darkness of the] morning watch and slew the Ammonites until midday; and the survivors were scattered, so that no two of them remained together.

12 The people said to Samuel, Who is he who said, Shall Saul reign over us? Bring the men, that we may put them to death.

13 But Saul said, There shall not a man be put to death this day, for today the Lord has brought deliverance to Israel.

14 Samuel said to the people, Come, let us go to Gilgal and there renew the kingdom.

15 All the people went to Gilgal and there they made Saul king before the Lord. And there they sacrificed peace offerings before the Lord, and there Saul and all the men of Israel rejoiced greatly.

12 AND SAMUEL said to all Israel, I have listened to you in all that you have said to me and have made a king over you.

2 And now, behold, the king walks before you. And I am old and gray, and behold, my sons are with you. And I have walked before you from my childhood to this day.
3 Here I am; testify against me before the Lord and Saul His anointed. Whose ox or donkey have I taken? Or whom have I defrauded or oppressed? Or from whose hand have I received any bribe to blind my eyes? Tell me and I will restore it to you.
4 And they said, You have not defrauded us or oppressed us or taken anything from any man's hand.
5 And Samuel said to them, The Lord is witness against you, and His anointed is witness this day; that you have not found anything in my hand. And they answered, He is witness.
6 And Samuel said to the people, It is the Lord Who appointed Moses and Aaron and brought your fathers up out of Egypt.
7 Now present yourselves, that I may plead with you before the Lord concerning all the righteous acts of the Lord which He did for you and for your fathers.
8 When Jacob and his sons had come into Egypt [and the Egyptians oppressed them], and your fathers cried to the Lord, then the Lord sent Moses and Aaron, who brought forth your fathers out of Egypt and made them dwell in this place.
9 But when they forgot the Lord their God, He sold them into the hand of Sisera, commander of Hazor's army, and into the hands of the Philistines and of the king of Moab, and they fought those foes.
10 And they cried to the Lord, saying, We have sinned because we have for-saken the Lord and have served the Baals and the Ashtaroth; but now deliver us from the hands of our enemies; and we will serve You.
11 And the Lord sent Jerubbaal and Barak and Jephthah and Samuel, and He delivered you out of the hands of your enemies on every side, and you dwelt safely.
12 But when you saw that Nahash king of the Ammonites came against you, you said to me, No! A king shall reign over us—when the Lord your God was your King!
13 Now see the king whom you have chosen and for whom you have asked; behold, the Lord has set a king over you.
14 If you will revere *and* fear the Lord and serve Him and hearken to His voice and not rebel against His commandment, and if both you and your king will follow the Lord your God, it will be good!
15 But if you will not hearken to the Lord's voice, but rebel against His commandment, then the hand of the Lord will be against you, as it was against your fathers.
16 So stand still and see this great thing the Lord will do before your eyes now.
17 Is it not wheat harvest today? I will call to the Lord and He will send thunder and rain; then you shall know and see that your wickedness is great which you have done in the sight of the Lord in asking for a king for yourselves.
18 So Samuel called to the Lord, and He sent thunder and rain that day; and all the people greatly feared the Lord and Samuel.
19 And [they] all said to Samuel, Pray for your servants to the Lord

speak the Word

God, I declare that You are my King!
ADAPTED FROM I SAMUEL **12:12**

your God, that we may not die, for we have added to all our sins this evil—to ask for a king.

20 And Samuel said to the people, Fear not. You have indeed done all this evil; yet turn not aside from following the Lord, but serve Him with all your heart.

21 And turn not aside after vain *and* worthless things which cannot profit or deliver you, for they are empty *and* futile.

22 The Lord will not forsake His people for His great name's sake, for it has pleased Him to make you a people for Himself.

23 Moreover, as for me, far be it from me that I should sin against the Lord by ceasing to pray for you; but I will instruct you in the good and right way.

24 Only fear the Lord and serve Him faithfully with all your heart; for consider how great are the things He has done for you.

25 But if you still do wickedly, both you and your king shall be swept away.

13 SAUL WAS f[forty] years old when he began to reign; and when he had reigned two years over Israel,

2 Saul chose 3,000 men of Israel; 2,000 were with [him] in Michmash and the hill country of Bethel, and 1,000 with Jonathan in Gibeah of Benjamin. The rest of the men he sent away, each one to his home.

3 Jonathan smote the Philistine garrison at Geba, and the Philistines heard of it. And Saul blew the trumpet throughout all the land, saying, Let the Hebrews hear!

4 All Israel heard that Saul had defeated the Philistine garrison and also that Israel had become an abomination to the Philistines. And the people were called out to join Saul at Gilgal.

5 And the Philistines gathered to fight with Israel, 30,000 chariots and 6,000 horsemen and troops like sand on the seashore in multitude. They came up and encamped at Michmash, east of Beth-aven.

6 When the men of Israel saw that they were in a tight situation—for their troops were hard pressed—they hid in caves, holes, rocks, tombs, and pits *or* cisterns.

7 Some Hebrews had gone over the Jordan to the land of Gad and Gilead. As for Saul, he was still in Gilgal, and all the people followed him trembling.

8 Saul waited seven days, according to the set time Samuel had appointed. But Samuel had not come to Gilgal, and the people were scattering from Saul.

9 So Saul said, Bring me the burnt offering and the peace offerings. And he offered the burnt offering [which he was forbidden to do].

10 And just as he finished offering the burnt offering, behold, Samuel came! Saul went out to meet and greet him.

11 Samuel said, What have you done? Saul said, Because I saw that the people were scattering from me, and that you did not come within the days appointed, and that the Philistines were assembled at Michmash,

speak the Word

Lord, I give You reverence and I want to serve You faithfully, with my whole heart. Help me to always remember the great things You have done for me.
ADAPTED FROM I SAMUEL 12:24

f The complete numbers in this verse are missing in the Hebrew. The word "forty" is supplied by the best available estimate.

life point

First Samuel 13:1–14 gives us great insight into Saul's character. Saul was anointed king of Israel. He had an opportunity to enjoy a great and glorious future, but he had some character weaknesses that proved to be his downfall. Saul was a people-pleaser. He loved the approval of people so much that he disobeyed God's instructions in order to get it. God instructed Saul to wait until the prophet Samuel arrived to offer up a burnt offering. When Samuel did not arrive at the expected time, the people became restless and impatient. Although Saul knew in his heart that he was being disobedient, he went ahead and offered the sacrifice he had been forbidden to offer. Saul's reply to the question of why he had done this was, "Because I saw that the people were scattering from me . . ." (I Samuel 13:11). Samuel told Saul he had done a foolish thing, and because of his disobedience he would lose his kingdom. Saul was so addicted to approval that he did lose his kingdom because of it.

It is important that we do not follow Saul's example. We need to resist the urge to please others when they lead us contrary to God's ways. We need to be obedient to God, following Him wholeheartedly. When we aim to please God, and not man, we open the door for God's blessing.

12 I thought, The Philistines will come down now upon me to Gilgal, and I have not made supplication to the Lord. So I forced myself to offer a burnt offering.

13 And Samuel said to Saul, You have done foolishly! You have not kept the commandment of the Lord your God which He commanded you; for the Lord would have established your kingdom over Israel forever;

14 But now your kingdom shall not continue; the Lord has sought out [David] a man after His own ᵍheart, and the Lord has commanded him to be prince *and* ruler over His people, because you have not kept what the Lord commanded you.

15 And Samuel went up from Gilgal to Gibeah of Benjamin. And Saul numbered the people that were left with him, [only] about 600.

16 Saul and Jonathan his son and the people with them remained in Gibeah of Benjamin, but the Philistines encamped at Michmash.

17 And raiders came out of the Philistine camp in three companies; one company turned toward Ophrah, to the land of Shual,

18 Another turned toward Beth-horon, and another toward the border overlooking the Valley of Zeboim toward the wilderness.

19 Now there was no metal worker to be found throughout all the land of Israel, for the Philistines said, Lest the Hebrews make swords or spears.

20 But each of the Israelites had to go down to the Philistines to get his plowshare, mattock, axe, or sickle sharpened.

speak the Word

God, I pray that I will be like David and be a person after Your own heart.
ADAPTED FROM I SAMUEL **13:14**

g See footnote on I Sam. 27:10.

21 And the price for plowshares and mattocks was a pim, and a third of a shekel for axes and for setting goads [with resulting blunt edges on the sickles, mattocks, forks, axes, and goads.]
22 So on the day of battle neither sword nor spear was found in the hand of any of the men who were with Saul and Jonathan; but Saul and Jonathan his son had them.
23 And the garrison of the Philistines went out to the pass of Michmash.

14 ONE DAY Jonathan son of Saul said to his armor-bearer, Come, let us go over to the Philistine garrison on the other side. But he did not tell his father.
2 Saul was remaining in the outskirts of Gibeah under a pomegranate tree in Migron; and with him were about 600 men,
3 And Ahijah son of Ahitub, Ichabod's brother, the son of Phinehas, the son of Eli, the Lord's priest in Shiloh, was wearing the ephod. And the people did not know that Jonathan was gone.
4 Between the passes by which Jonathan sought to go over to the Philistine garrison there was a rocky crag on the one side and a rocky crag on the other side; one was named Bozez, and the other Seneh.
5 The one crag rose on the north in front of Michmash, and the other on the south in front of Geba.
6 And Jonathan said to his young armor-bearer, Come, and let us go over to the garrison of these uncircumcised; it may be that the Lord will work for us. For there is nothing to prevent the Lord from saving by many or by few.
7 And his armor-bearer said to him, Do all that is in your mind; I am with you in whatever you think [best].
8 Jonathan said, We will pass over to these men and we will let them see us.

9 If they say to us, Wait until we come to you, then we will stand still in our place and will not go up to them.
10 But if they say, Come up to us, we will go up, for the Lord has delivered them into our hand, and this will be our sign.
11 So both of them let the Philistine garrison see them. And the Philistines said, Behold, the Hebrews are coming out of the holes where they have hidden themselves.
12 The garrison men said to Jonathan and his armor-bearer, Come up to us and we will show you a thing. Jonathan said to his armor-bearer, Come up after me, for the Lord has given them into Israel's hand.
13 Then Jonathan climbed up on his hands and feet, his armor-bearer after him; and the enemy fell before Jonathan, and his armor-bearer killed them after him.
14 And that first slaughter which Jonathan and his armor-bearer made was about twenty men within about a half acre of land [which a yoke of oxen might plow].
15 And there was trembling *and* panic in the [Philistine] camp, in the field, and among all the men; the garrison, and even the raiders trembled; the earth quaked, and it became a terror from God.
16 Saul's watchmen in Gibeah of Benjamin looked, and behold, the multitude melted away and went hither and thither.
17 Then Saul said to the men with him, Number and see who is gone from us. When they numbered, behold, Jonathan and his armor-bearer were missing.
18 Saul said to Ahijah, Bring here the ark of God—for at that time the ark of God was with the children of Israel.
19 While Saul talked to the priest, the tumult in the Philistine camp kept increasing. Then Saul said to the priest, Withdraw your hand.

20 Then Saul and all the people with him rallied and went into the battle, and behold, every [Philistine's] sword was against his fellow in wild confusion.

21 Moreover, the Hebrews who were with the Philistines before that time, who went up with them into the camp from the country round about, even they also turned to be with the Israelites who were with Saul and Jonathan.

22 Likewise, all the men of Israel who had hid themselves in the hill country of Ephraim, when they heard that the Philistines fled, they also went after them in hot pursuit in the battle.

23 So the Lord delivered Israel that day, and the battle passed beyond Beth-aven.

24 But the men of Israel were distressed that day, for Saul had caused them to take an oath, saying, Cursed be the man who eats any food before evening and until I have taken vengeance on my enemies. So none of the men tasted any food.

25 And all the people of the land came to a wood, and there was honey on the ground.

26 When the men entered the wood, behold, the honey was dripping, but no man tasted it, for the men feared the oath.

27 But Jonathan had not heard when his father charged the people with the oath. So he dipped the end of the rod in his hand into a honeycomb and put it to his mouth, and his [weary] eyes brightened.

28 Then one of the men told him, Your father strictly charged the men with an oath, saying, Cursed be the man who eats any food today. And the people were exhausted *and* faint.

29 Then Jonathan said, My father has troubled the land. See how my eyes have brightened because I tasted a little of this honey.

30 How much better if the men had eaten freely today of the spoil of their enemies which they found! For now the slaughter of the Philistines has not been great.

31 They smote the Philistines that day from Michmash to Aijalon. And the people were very faint.

32 [When night came and the oath expired] the men flew upon the spoil. They took sheep, oxen, and calves, slew them on the ground, and ate them [raw] with the blood.

33 Then Saul was told, Behold, the men are sinning against the Lord by eating with the blood. And he said, You have transgressed; roll a great stone to me here.

34 Saul said, Disperse yourselves among the people and tell them, Bring me every man his ox or his sheep, and butcher them here and eat; and sin not against the Lord by eating the blood. So all the men brought each one his ox that night and butchered it there.

35 And Saul built an altar to the Lord; it was the first altar he built to the Lord.

36 Then Saul said, Let us go down after the Philistines by night and seize and plunder them until daylight, and let us not leave a man of them. They said, Do whatever seems good to you. Then the priest said, Let us draw near here to God.

37 And Saul asked counsel of God, Shall I go down after the Philistines? Will You deliver them into the hand of Israel? But He did not answer him that day.

38 Then Saul said, Draw near, all the chiefs of the people, and let us see how this sin [causing God's silence] arose today.

39 For as the Lord lives, Who delivers Israel, though it be in Jonathan my son, he shall surely die. But not a man among all the people answered him.

40 Then he said to all Israel, You be

on one side; and I and Jonathan my son will be on the other side. The people said to Saul, Do what seems good to you.

41 Therefore Saul said to the Lord, the God of Israel, Give a perfect lot *and* show the right. And Saul and Jonathan were taken [by lot], but the other men went free.

42 Saul said, Cast lots between me and Jonathan my son. And Jonathan was taken.

43 Saul said to Jonathan, Tell me what you have done. And Jonathan said, I tasted a little honey with the end of the rod that was in my hand. And behold, I must die.

44 Saul answered, May God do so, and more also, for you shall surely die, Jonathan.

45 But the people said to Saul, Shall Jonathan, who has wrought this great deliverance to Israel, die? God forbid! As the Lord lives, there shall not one hair of his head perish, for he has wrought this great deliverance with God this day. So the people rescued Jonathan, and he did not die.

46 Then Saul ceased pursuing the Philistines, and they went to their own place.

47 When Saul took over the kingdom of Israel, he fought against all his enemies on every side: Moab, the Ammonites, Edom, the kings of Zobah, and the Philistines. Wherever he turned, he made it worse for them.

48 He did valiantly and smote the Amalekites, and delivered Israel out of the hands of those who plundered them.

49 Now Saul's sons were Jonathan, Ishvi, and Malchi-shua; and the names of his two daughters were, of the firstborn, Merab; and of the younger, Michal.

50 The name of Saul's wife was Ahinoam daughter of Ahimaaz. The commander of his army was Abner son of Ner, Saul's uncle.

51 Kish the father of Saul and Ner the father of Abner were sons of Abiel.

52 There was severe war against the Philistines all the days of Saul, and whenever Saul saw any mighty or [outstandingly] courageous man, he attached him to himself.

15 SAMUEL TOLD Saul, The Lord sent me to anoint you king over His people Israel. Now listen and heed the words of the Lord.

2 Thus says the Lord of hosts, I have considered *and* will punish what Amalek did to Israel, how he set himself against him in the way when [Israel] came out of Egypt.

3 Now go and smite Amalek and utterly destroy all they have; do not spare them, but kill both man and woman, infant and suckling, ox and sheep, camel and donkey.

4 So Saul assembled the men and numbered them at Telaim—200,000 men on foot and 10,000 men of Judah.

5 And Saul came to the city of Amalek and laid wait in the valley.

6 Saul warned the Kenites, Go, depart, get down from among the Amalekites, lest I destroy you with them; for you showed kindness to all the Israelites when they came up out of Egypt. So the Kenites departed from among the Amalekites.

7 Saul smote the Amalekites from Havilah as far as Shur, which is east of Egypt.

8 And he took Agag king of the Amalekites alive, though he utterly destroyed all the rest of the people with the sword.

9 Saul and the people spared Agag and the best of the sheep, oxen, fatlings, lambs, and all that was good, and would not utterly destroy them; but all that was undesirable or worthless they destroyed utterly.

10 Then the word of the Lord came to Samuel, saying,

11 I regret making Saul king, for he has turned back from following Me and has not performed My commands. And Samuel was grieved *and* angry [with Saul], and he cried to the Lord all night.

12 When Samuel rose early to meet Saul in the morning, he was told, Saul came to Carmel, and behold, he set up for himself a monument or trophy [of his victory] and passed on and went down to Gilgal.

13 And Samuel came to Saul, and Saul said to him, Blessed are you of the Lord. I have performed what the Lord ordered.

14 And Samuel said, What then means this bleating of the sheep in my ears, and the lowing of the oxen which I hear?

15 Saul said, They have brought them from the Amalekites; for the people spared the best of the sheep and oxen to sacrifice to the Lord your God, but the rest we have utterly destroyed.

16 Then Samuel said to Saul, Stop! I will tell you what the Lord said to me tonight. Saul said to him, Say on.

17 Samuel said, When you were small in your own sight, were you not made the head of the tribes of Israel, and the Lord anointed you king over Israel?

18 And the Lord sent you on a mission and said, Go, utterly destroy the sinners, the Amalekites; and fight against them until they are consumed.

19 Why then did you not obey the voice of the Lord, but swooped down upon the plunder and did evil in the Lord's sight?

20 Saul said to Samuel, Yes, I have obeyed the voice of the Lord and have gone the way which the Lord sent me, and have brought Agag king of Amalek and have utterly destroyed the Amalekites.

21 But the people took from the spoil sheep and oxen, the chief of the things to be utterly destroyed, to sacrifice to the Lord your God in Gilgal.

22 Samuel said, Has the Lord as great a delight in burnt offerings and sacrifices as in obeying the voice of the Lord? Behold, to obey is better than sacrifice, and to hearken than the fat of rams.

life point

Saul had his own ideas about things. One time when Samuel the prophet was correcting Saul for not doing what he had been instructed to do, Saul's reply was, "I thought . . ." (I Samuel 13:12). He then proceeded to express his idea of how he "thought" things should have been done (compare I Samuel 10:6–8 with 13:8–14). Samuel's answer to King Saul's attitude is in this verse: " . . . to obey is better than sacrifice" (I Samuel 15:22).

How many of God's children fail to "reign as kings in life" (Romans 5:17; see also Revelation 1:6) because they substitute what God really requires with what they think He wants? When faced with a point of obedience, it is dangerous for us to say, "I think this" or "I want that." Rather we need to ask God, "What do You want me to do?" and be obedient to what He says. If Jesus is not Lord of all, then He is not our Lord at all. He may be our Savior, but not our Lord and Master. Let God take His rightful place in your life, which is "first place" in everything.

23 For rebellion is as the sin of witchcraft, and stubbornness is as idolatry and teraphim (household good luck images). Because you have rejected the word of the Lord, He also has rejected you from being king.

obedience is better than sacrifice

When the Lord called me into the ministry, He asked me to quit my job, trust Him to provide what we needed above my husband's salary, and spend my time preparing for my future teaching ministry. I struggled tremendously with the thought of not working, and, frankly, I was frightened by it. I had been working since I was thirteen years old and was accustomed to taking care of myself. Out of my fear, I decided to quit my full-time job and get a part-time job, instead of stopping work altogether as God had asked me to do. I had that job for only a short while before I was fired. I was normally a good employee and not the type who would be fired. Actually, the reason for my being fired was not related to my work; the office manager did not like me personally. I had disobeyed God, and He had withheld His favor in that job situation. I had tried to partially obey God and still needed to learn that obedience is not true obedience unless it is complete.

Like Saul, I had given a sacrifice instead of obedience (see I Samuel 15:22). God said, "Quit your job," and I did, but I got a part-time job to replace it. My part-time job represented part-time obedience. So often we think we can bargain with God, but it never works. There is only one way, and that is His way. It is all or nothing!

The Lord is very clear about disobedience. He says it is rebellion and that rebellion is like witchcraft (see I Samuel 15:23). We may think our ideas are better than God's, but He calls this attitude stubbornness and says it is equivalent to idolatry. Why idolatry? Because we are idolizing our own ideas, exalting them above God's command.

Saul rebelled and lost the opportunity to be king. I wonder how many people think they are obeying God when actually they are offering Him an unacceptable sacrifice. Those same people live miserable, unfulfilled lives and often blame God for what really is their own doing.

God requires prompt, complete obedience; nothing less is acceptable. We may feel that some of the things He asks us to do are too hard, but we must remember that He promises to give us grace to do whatever He asks of us; we need only to be willing.

24 And Saul said to Samuel, I have sinned; for I have transgressed the commandment of the Lord and your words, because I feared the people and obeyed their voice.
25 Now, I pray you, pardon my sin and go back with me, that I may worship the Lord.
26 And Samuel said to Saul, I will not return with you; for you have rejected the word of the Lord, and the Lord has rejected you from being king over Israel.
27 And as Samuel turned to go away, Saul seized the skirt of Samuel's mantle, and it tore.
28 And Samuel said to him, The Lord has torn the kingdom of Israel from you this day and has given it to a neighbor of yours who is better than you.
29 And also the Strength of Israel

breaking the cycle of abuse and rebellion

First Samuel 15:23 teaches us that "rebellion is as the sin of witchcraft." I believe a great deal of rebellion is the result of abuse. When a person has been repeatedly hurt by others, there usually comes a time when he makes up his mind, "Nobody is ever going to push me around again. As long as I live, nobody is going to tell me what to do. Why should I submit to somebody I can't trust to do what's best for me? From now on, I'm going to look out for myself and make my own decisions."

So often, the end result of abuse is willfulness, stubbornness, and rebellion. I know from my own bitter experience that being subjected to continual abuse has a lasting effect on a strong-willed person. It was a nightmare for someone of my personality type to be controlled and manipulated for years on end. In my case, I submitted to the Lord, and He used that experience to make me strong for ministry so that I could help others caught in similar situations.

The sad thing is that once people do manage to escape from an abusive environment, the effects of that abuse do not suddenly end. Many times, hurting, wounded people are drawn to other hurting, wounded people. Victims of long-term abuse often marry other such victims. The result is that they end up hurting and wounding each other. Their children pick up the tendency to abuse and pass it on from one generation to the next. The abusive tendency will go on until someone stops it with God's help.

Do you desire to break free from the pattern of abuse and rebellion? You do not have to end up like Saul. You can choose to follow God and His way rather than mindlessly following after your feelings and emotions. Boldly declare: "That's enough! This curse of abuse is not going any further! It is stopping right here!" Choose God's way, apply the victory that Jesus won at the cross to your life, and watch Him work for you.

You might feel that you have inherited some bad habits and character flaws through your bloodline, but the blood of Jesus, when applied to your life by faith, is able to erase the adverse effects of natural inheritance. Do not look back to your past and get stuck there; instead, look forward to the great future God has planned for you!

will not lie or repent; for He is not a man, that He should repent.

30 Saul said, I have sinned; yet honor me now, I pray you, before the elders of my people and before Israel, and return with me, that I may worship the Lord your God.

31 So Samuel turned back after Saul, and Saul worshiped the Lord.

32 Then Samuel said, Bring here to me Agag king of the Amalekites. And Agag came to him cheerfully. And Agag said, Surely the bitterness of death is past.

33 Samuel said, As your sword has made women childless, so shall your mother be childless among women. And Samuel hewed Agag in pieces before the Lord in Gilgal.

34 Then Samuel went to Ramah, but Saul went up to his house in Gibeah of Saul.

35 And Samuel came no more to see Saul until the day of his death, though Samuel grieved over Saul. And the Lord repented that He had made Saul king over Israel.

16 THE LORD said to Samuel, How long will you mourn for Saul, seeing I have rejected him from reigning over Israel? Fill your horn with oil; I will send you to Jesse the Bethlehemite. For I have provided for Myself a king among his sons.

2 Samuel said, How can I go? If Saul hears it, he will kill me. And the Lord said, Take a heifer with you and say, I have come to sacrifice to the Lord.

3 And invite Jesse to the sacrifice, and I will show you what you shall do; and you shall anoint for Me the one I name to you.

4 And Samuel did what the Lord said, and came to Bethlehem. And the elders of the town trembled at his coming and said, Have you come peaceably?

5 And he said, Peaceably; I have come to sacrifice to the Lord. Consecrate yourselves and come with me to the sacrifice. And he consecrated Jesse and his sons and called them to the sacrifice.

6 When they had come, he looked on Eliab [the eldest son] and said, Surely the Lord's anointed is before Him.

7 But the Lord said to Samuel, Look not on his appearance or at the height of his stature, for I have rejected him. For the Lord sees not as man sees; for man looks on the outward appearance, but the Lord looks on the heart.

life point

God is the God of hearts. He does not look at the exterior of a person—or even the things a person does—and judge an individual by that criterion. Man judges after the flesh, but I Samuel 16:7 teaches us that God judges according to the heart.

It is possible to put up a good front and still have an impure heart. It is also possible to be dealing with personality problems or bad habits on the outside and still have a right heart on the inside. God is much more inclined to use a person with a good heart and a few problems than He is to use a person who appears to be perfect outwardly, but who has a wicked heart.

If we want to have success as Christians or be used by God as leaders in His kingdom, it is important that we get in touch with our inner lives and our heart attitudes. Our motives, thoughts, and feelings need to be consistent with God's heart. Having a pure heart is vital. Start taking a regular inventory of your inner thoughts and attitudes, and work with the Holy Spirit to let the thoughts and attitudes of Jesus reside in you (see Philippians 2:5).

8 Then Jesse called Abinadab and made him pass before Samuel. But Samuel said, Neither has the Lord chosen this one.

9 Then Jesse made Shammah pass by. Samuel said, Nor has the Lord chosen him.

10 Jesse made seven of his sons pass before Samuel. And Samuel said to Jesse, The Lord has not chosen any of these.

11 Then [he] said to Jesse, Are all your sons here? [Jesse] said, There is yet the youngest; he is tending the sheep. Samuel said to Jesse, Send for him; for we will not sit down to eat until he is here.

12 Jesse sent and brought him. David had a healthy reddish complexion and beautiful eyes, and was fine-looking. The Lord said [to Samuel], Arise, anoint him; this is he.

13 Then Samuel took the horn of oil and anointed David in the midst of his brothers; and the Spirit of the Lord came mightily upon David from that day forward. And Samuel arose and went to Ramah.

14 But the Spirit of the Lord departed from Saul, and an evil spirit from the Lord tormented *and* troubled him.

15 Saul's servants said to him, Behold, an evil spirit from God torments you.

16 Let our lord now command your servants here before you to find a man who plays skillfully on the lyre; and when the evil spirit from God is upon you, he will play it, and you will be well.

17 Saul told his servants, Find me a man who plays well and bring him to me.

18 One of the young men said, I have seen a son of Jesse the Bethlehemite who plays skillfully, a valiant man, a man of war, prudent in speech *and* eloquent, an attractive person; and the Lord is with him.

19 So Saul sent messengers to Jesse and said, Send me David your son, who is with the sheep.

20 And Jesse took a donkey loaded with bread, a skin of wine, and a kid and sent them by David his son to Saul.

21 And David came to Saul and served him. Saul became very fond of him, and he became his armor-bearer.

22 Saul sent to Jesse, saying, Let David remain in my service, for he pleases me.

23 And when the evil spirit from God was upon Saul, David took a lyre and played it; so Saul was refreshed and became well, and the evil spirit left him.

17 NOW THE Philistines gathered their armies for battle and were assembled at Socoh, which belongs to Judah, and encamped between Socoh and Azekah in Ephes-dammim.

2 Saul and the men of Israel were encamped in the Valley of Elah and drew up in battle array against the Philistines.

3 And the Philistines stood on a mountain on one side and Israel stood on a mountain on the other side, with the valley between them.

4 And a champion went out of the camp of the Philistines named Goliath of Gath, whose height was six cubits and a span [almost ten feet].

5 And he had a bronze helmet on his head and wore a coat of mail, and the coat weighed 5,000 shekels of bronze.

6 He had bronze shin armor on his legs and a bronze javelin across his shoulders.

7 And the shaft of his spear was like a weaver's beam; his spear's head weighed 600 shekels of iron. And a shield bearer went before him.

8 Goliath stood and shouted to the ranks of Israel, Why have you come out to draw up for battle? Am I not a Philistine, and are you not servants of Saul? Choose a man for yourselves and let him come down to me.

9 If he is able to fight with me and kill me, then we will be your servants; but if I prevail against him and kill him, then you shall be our servants and serve us.

10 And the Philistine said, I defy the ranks of Israel this day; give me a man, that we may fight together.

11 When Saul and all Israel heard those words of the Philistine, they were dismayed and greatly afraid.

12 David was the son of an Ephrathite of Bethlehem in Judah named Jesse, who had eight sons. [Jesse] in the days of Saul was old, advanced in years.

13 [His] three eldest sons had followed Saul into battle. Their names were Eliab the firstborn; next, Abinadab; and third, Shammah.

14 David was the youngest. The three eldest followed Saul,

15 But David went back and forth from Saul to feed his father's sheep at Bethlehem.

16 The Philistine came out morning and evening, presenting himself for forty days.

17 And Jesse said to David his son, Take for your brothers an ephah of this parched grain and these ten loaves and carry them quickly to your brothers at the camp.

18 Also take these ten cheeses to the commander of their thousand. See how your brothers fare and bring some token from them.

19 Now Saul and the brothers and all the men of Israel were in the Valley of Elah, fighting with the Philistines.

20 So David rose up early next morning, left the sheep with a keeper, took the provisions, and went, as Jesse had commanded him. And he came to the encampment as the host going forth to the battleground shouted the battle cry.

21 And Israel and the Philistines put the battle in array, army against army.

22 David left his packages in the care of the baggage keeper and ran into the ranks and came and greeted his brothers.

23 As they talked, behold, Goliath, the champion, the Philistine of Gath, came forth from the Philistine ranks and spoke the same words as before, and David heard him.

24 And all the men of Israel, when they saw the man, fled from him, terrified.

25 And the Israelites said, Have you seen this man who has come out? Surely he has come out to defy Israel; and the man who kills him the king will enrich with great riches, and will give him his daughter and make his father's house free [from taxes and service] in Israel.

26 And David said to the men standing by him, What shall be done for the man who kills this Philistine and takes away the reproach from Israel? For who is this uncircumcised Philistine that he should defy the armies of the living God?

27 And the [men] told him, Thus shall it be done for the man who kills him.

28 Now Eliab his eldest brother heard what he said to the men; and Eliab's anger was kindled against David and he said, Why did you come here? With whom have you left those few sheep in the wilderness? I know your presumption and evilness of heart; for you came down that you might see the battle.

29 And David said, What have I done now? Was it not a harmless question?

30 And David turned away from Eliab to another and he asked the same question, and again the men gave him the same answer.

31 When David's words were heard, they were repeated to Saul, and he sent for him.

32 David said to Saul, Let no man's heart fail because of this Philistine; your servant will go out and fight with him.

33 And Saul said to David, You are not able to go to fight against this Philistine. You are only an adolescent, and he has been a warrior from his youth.

34 And David said to Saul, Your servant kept his father's sheep. And when there came a lion or again a bear and took a lamb out of the flock,

35 I went out after it and smote it and delivered the lamb out of its mouth;

reject rejection

David believed that with God's help, he could slay the giant Goliath, but his brother Eliab accused him of presumption and having an evil heart (see I Samuel 17:28). Eliab's accusation came from a jealous attitude toward David. He tried to make David feel small and worthless. David was a wise young man, and his response to Eliab was an important key to his future: "David turned away from Eliab" (I Samuel 17:30).

When we take a step of faith to do something for God or to help hurting people, Satan attacks. He often works through someone we love to make us feel worthless, rejected, unacceptable, inept, or out of place. We must stand against these attacks and keep our eyes on God and His direction to us. God fills our hearts with faith, enabling us to believe He can use us, but Satan comes against us with fears—often with fears about ourselves and our abilities.

David's older brothers did not include David in the things they did because they thought he was too young, and they probably were jealous of him. As a result, I am sure he felt rejected. Many times God will choose to use people who have felt rejected and been excluded. He selects those whom society would reject in order to show Himself strong. He also purposely chooses what the world would call "weak and foolish" so no one takes the credit that is due to Him alone (see I Corinthians 1:26–29).

If you have been rejected or ill-treated, I encourage you to do as David did. Turn away from it! Forgive your enemies, and do not let offense fill your heart. Do not pay attention to what the devil is trying to do; keep your eyes on God and follow His instructions. Yes, God can use you to do great things. God is not looking for someone with ability, but someone with availability. He is not looking for someone with perfect attributes, but someone with a perfect heart toward Him. Keep your heart pure by refusing to allow hatred, strife, offense, bitterness, resentment, or unforgiveness to dwell in it.

Always believe what God says about you above your own feelings about yourself and above what others have to say. God says you belong to Him. He loves you and will work through you if you will simply let Him. You are special to God. You have infinite worth and value. Perhaps the world would not consider you usable material for God, but He sees differently than the world does. Say, "Here I am God, use me," and watch Him go to work!

and when it arose against me, I caught it by its beard and smote it and killed it. **36** Your servant killed both the lion and the bear; and this uncircumcised Philistine shall be like one of them, for he has defied the armies of the living God! **37** David said, The Lord Who delivered me out of the paw of the lion and out of the paw of the bear, He will

life point

When David volunteered to go out and fight the giant Goliath, nobody encouraged him. Everyone told him, "You're too young. You don't have the right armor or weapons. He's much bigger and more experienced than you are," and on and on. Even King Saul questioned David's ability to overcome the boastful Philistine (see I Samuel 17:33). But David encouraged himself by recounting the victories God had given him in the past.

If you want to do something for God, you must understand that there will be hundreds, maybe thousands of times when Satan will come against you to discourage you. Why? Because he knows you must have courage to go forward and fulfill God's good plan for your life. When you become discouraged, you become weak and lose the courage you need to go forward. What must you do in times of discouragement? Shake it off in faith and recount the victories God has already given you. Have confidence that He will be strong in your weakness and use you for His glory.

deliver me out of the hand of this Philistine. And Saul said to David, Go, and the Lord be with you!
38 Then Saul clothed David with his armor; he put a bronze helmet on his head and clothed him with a coat of mail.
39 And David girded his sword over his armor. Then he tried to go, but could not, for he was not used to it. And David said to Saul, I cannot go

speak the Word

with these, for I am not used to them. And David took them off.
40 Then he took his staff in his hand and chose five smooth stones out of the brook and put them in his shepherd's [lunch] bag [a whole kid's skin slung from his shoulder], in his pouch, and his sling was in his hand, and he drew near the Philistine.
41 The Philistine came on and drew near to David, the man who bore the shield going before him.
42 And when the Philistine looked around and saw David, he scorned *and* despised him, for he was but an adolescent, with a healthy reddish color and a fair face.
43 And the Philistine said to David, Am I a dog, that you should come to me with sticks? And the Philistine cursed David by his gods.
44 The Philistine said to David, Come to me, and I will give your flesh to the birds of the air and the beasts of the field.
45 Then said David to the Philistine, You come to me with a sword, a spear, and a javelin, but I come to you in the name of the Lord of hosts, the God of the ranks of Israel, Whom you have defied.
46 This day the Lord will deliver you into my hand, and I will smite you and cut off your head. And I will give the corpses of the army of the Philistines this day to the birds of the air and the wild beasts of the earth, that all the earth may know that there is a God in Israel.
47 And all this assembly shall know that the Lord saves not with sword and spear; for the battle is the Lord's, and He will give you into our hands.
48 When the Philistine came forward to meet David, David ran quickly

Thank You, God, that in my battles You will give my enemies into my hands.
ADAPTED FROM I SAMUEL 17:47

life point

When young David looked at the giant, he "ran quickly toward the battle line" (I Samuel 17:48). I think David knew that if he thought about Goliath too long, he might run away. He took action and obeyed God immediately, and we need to always do the same. When God prompts you to take action, run to do it. His grace will be present to help you. Do not procrastinate! Frequently, those who do put things off never get around to obeying God. They have good intentions to do what God has asked of them at the right time, but, sadly, the "right time" never seems to come, and they lose out merely because they did not take faith-filled action at the right time.

toward the battle line to meet the Philistine.

49 David put his hand into his bag and took out a stone and slung it, and it struck the Philistine, sinking into his forehead, and he fell on his face to the earth.

50 So David prevailed over the Philistine with a sling and with a stone, and struck down the Philistine and slew him. But no sword was in David's hand.

51 So he ran and stood over the Philistine, took his sword and drew it out of its sheath, and killed him, and cut off his head with it. When the Philistines saw that their mighty champion was dead, they fled.

52 And the men of Israel and Judah rose with a shout and pursued the Philistines as far as Gath and the gates of Ekron. So the wounded Philistines fell along the way from Shaaraim as far as Gath and Ekron.

53 The Israelites returned from their pursuit of the Philistines and plundered their tents.

54 David took the head of the Philistine and brought it to Jerusalem, but he put his armor in his tent.

55 When Saul saw David go out against the Philistine, he said to Abner, the captain of the host, Abner, whose son is this youth? And Abner said, As your soul lives, O king, I cannot tell.

56 And the king said, Inquire whose son the stripling is.

57 When David returned from killing Goliath the Philistine, Abner brought him before Saul with the head of the Philistine in his hand.

58 And Saul said to him, Whose son are you, young man? And David answered, I am the son of your servant Jesse of Bethlehem.

18 WHEN DAVID had finished speaking to Saul, the soul of Jonathan was knit with the soul of David, and Jonathan loved him as his own life.

2 Saul took David that day and would not let him return to his father's house.

3 Then Jonathan made a covenant with David, because he loved him as his own life.

putting the Word to work

David and Jonathan were truly great friends to one another (see I Samuel 18:3). Do you have a great friend, someone you love as much as you love your own life? Thank God for that person today.

4 And Jonathan stripped himself of the robe that was on him and gave it to David, and his armor, even his sword, his bow, and his girdle.

5 And David went out wherever Saul sent him, and he prospered *and* behaved himself wisely; and Saul set him over the men of war. And it was

life point

One day I just happened to notice I Samuel 18:5, and I underlined it in my Bible. David was a man who was anointed to be king, yet he was put in the household of Saul for some training and some crucifixion of the flesh.

Anyone who is anointed for leadership has to be around a person like Saul sometime in his life. God uses the "Sauls" in our lives to get the "Saul" out of us. God always puts us around someone who is like sandpaper to smooth off our rough edges.

It's important we grasp this truth: *Just because we are anointed for leadership does not mean that we get to move immediately into a position of leadership.* There is a work that has to be done in us, a testing that has to take place before we get promoted.

After I had noticed and underlined this verse about David's serving under King Saul, my attention was drawn to 1 Samuel 18:14, which says, "David acted wisely in all his ways and succeeded, and the Lord was with him." Why did David succeed? Not just because he was anointed, but also because he acted wisely and allowed the Lord to be with him. If we want to lead, we must first serve in circumstances that may not be ideal and learn to behave wisely. This prepares us to be greatly used by God.

satisfactory both to the people and to Saul's servants.

6 As they were coming home, when David returned from killing the Philistine, the women came out of all the Israelite towns, singing and dancing, to meet King Saul with timbrels, songs of joy, and instruments of music.

7 And the women responded as they laughed *and* frolicked, saying, Saul has slain his thousands, and David his ten thousands.

8 And Saul was very angry, for the saying displeased him; and he said, They have ascribed to David ten thousands, but to me they have ascribed only thousands. What more can he have but the kingdom?

9 And Saul [jealously] eyed David from that day forward.

10 The next day an evil spirit from God came mightily upon Saul, and he raved [madly] in his house, while David played [the lyre] with his hand, as at other times; and there was a javelin in Saul's hand.

11 And Saul cast the javelin, for he thought, I will pin David to the wall. And David evaded him twice.

12 Saul was afraid of David, because the Lord was with him but had departed from Saul.

13 So Saul removed David from him and made him his commander over a thousand; and he went out and came in before the people.

14 David acted wisely in all his ways *and* succeeded, and the Lord was with him.

15 When Saul saw how capable *and* successful David was, he stood in awe of him.

speak the Word

God, I pray that I will act wisely in all my ways, and that I will honor You with all my behavior. I thank You that You will be with me, causing me to succeed.
ADAPTED FROM I SAMUEL 18:14

16 But all Israel and Judah loved David, for he went out and came in before them.

17 Saul said to David, My elder daughter Merab I will give you as wife; only serve me courageously and fight the Lord's battles. For Saul thought, Let not my hand, but the Philistines' hand, be upon him.

18 David said to Saul, Who am I, and what is my life or my father's family in Israel, that I should be the king's son-in-law?

19 But at the time when Merab, Saul's daughter, should have been given to David, she was given to Adriel the Meholathite as wife.

20 Now Michal, Saul's daughter, loved David; and they told Saul, and it pleased him.

21 Saul thought, I will give her to him that she may be a snare to him and that the hand of the Philistines may be against him. So Saul said to David a second time, You shall now be my son-in-law.

22 And Saul commanded his servants to speak to David privately and say, The king delights in you, and all his servants love you; now then, become [his] son-in-law.

23 Saul's servants told those words to David. David said, Does it seem to you a light thing to be a king's son-in-law, seeing I am a poor man and lightly esteemed?

24 And the servants of Saul told him what David said.

25 Saul said, Say this to David, The king wants no dowry but a hundred foreskins of the Philistines, to avenge himself of the king's enemies. But Saul thought to make David fall by the Philistines' hands.

26 When his servants told David these words, it pleased [him] well to become the king's son-in-law. Before the days expired,

27 David went, he and his men, and slew two hundred Philistine men, and brought their foreskins and gave them in full number to the king, that he might become the king's son-in-law. And Saul gave him Michal his daughter as wife.

28 When Saul saw and knew that the Lord was with David and that Michal [his] daughter loved him,

29 Saul was still more afraid of David; and Saul became David's constant enemy.

putting the Word to work

Is there anyone who treats you as a "constant enemy" (I Samuel 18:29), as Saul treated David? Remember the Bible's instructions about enemies: forgive them, love them, and pray for them (see Matthew 5:44).

30 Then the Philistine princes came out to battle, and when they did so, David had more success *and* behaved himself more wisely than all Saul's servants, so that his name was very dear *and* highly esteemed.

19 NOW SAUL told Jonathan his son and all his servants that they must kill David.

2 But Jonathan, Saul's son, delighted much in David, and he told David, Saul my father is seeking to kill you. Now therefore, take heed to yourself in the morning, and stay in a secret place and hide yourself.

3 And I will go out and stand beside my father in the field where you are; and I will converse with my father about you and if I learn anything, I will tell you.

4 And Jonathan spoke well of David to Saul his father and said to him, Let not the king sin against his servant David, for he has not sinned against you, and his deeds have been of good service to you.

5 For he took his life in his hands and slew the Philistine, and the Lord

wrought a great deliverance for all Israel; you saw it and rejoiced. Why then will you sin against innocent blood and kill David without a cause?
6 Saul heeded Jonathan and swore, As the Lord lives, David shall not be slain.
7 So Jonathan called David and told him all these things. And Jonathan brought David to Saul, and he was in his presence as in times past.
8 Then there was war again, and David went out and fought with the Philistines, and made a great slaughter among them and they fled before him.
9 Then an evil spirit from the Lord came upon Saul as he sat in his house with his spear in his hand; and David was playing [the lyre] with his hand.
10 Saul sought to pin David to the wall with the spear, but he slipped away, so that Saul struck the spear into the wall. Then David fled and escaped that night.
11 Saul sent messengers that night to David's house to watch him, that he might kill him in the morning. But Michal, David's wife, told him, If you do not save your life tonight, tomorrow you will be killed.
12 So Michal let David down through the window, and he fled and escaped.
13 And Michal took the teraph (household good luck image) and laid it in the bed, put a pillow of goats' hair at its head, and covered it with a bedspread.
14 And when Saul sent messengers to take David, she said, He is sick.
15 Then Saul sent the messengers again to see David, saying, Bring him up to me in the bed, that I may slay him.
16 And when the messengers came in, behold, there was an image in the bed, with a pillow of goats' hair at its head.
17 Saul said to Michal, Why have you deceived me so and sent away my

enemy so that he has escaped? Michal answered Saul, He said to me, Let me go. Why should I kill you?
18 So David fled and escaped and came to Samuel at Ramah and told him all that Saul had done to him. And he and Samuel went and dwelt in Naioth.
19 And it was told Saul, Behold, David is at Naioth in Ramah.
20 And Saul sent messengers to take David; and when they saw the company of the prophets prophesying, and Samuel standing as appointed head over them, the Spirit of God came upon the messengers of Saul and they also prophesied.
21 When it was told Saul, he sent other messengers, and they also prophesied. And Saul sent messengers again the third time, and they also prophesied.
22 Then Saul himself went to Ramah and came to a great well that is in Secu; and he asked, Where are Samuel and David? And he was told, They are at Naioth in Ramah.
23 So he went on to Naioth in Ramah; and the Spirit of God came upon him also, and as he went on he prophesied until he came to Naioth in Ramah.
24 He took off his royal robes and prophesied before Samuel and lay down stripped thus all that day and night. So they say, Is Saul also among the prophets? [I Sam. 10:10.]

20 DAVID FLED from Naioth in Ramah and came and said to Jonathan, What have I done? Of what am I guilty? What is my sin before your father, that he seeks my life?
2 Jonathan said, God forbid! You shall not die. My father does nothing great or small but what he tells me. And why should [he] hide this thing from me? It is not so.
3 But David replied, Your father

certainly knows that I have found favor in your eyes, and he thinks, Let not Jonathan know this, lest he be grieved. But truly as the Lord lives and as your soul lives, there is but a step between me and death.

4 Then Jonathan said to David, Whatever you desire, I will do for you.

5 David said to Jonathan, Tomorrow is the New Moon [festival], and I should not fail to sit at the table with the king; but let me go, that I may hide myself in the field till the third day at evening.

6 If your father misses me at all, then say, David earnestly asked leave of me that he might run to Bethlehem, his city, for there is a yearly sacrifice there for all the family.

7 If he says, All right, then it will be well with your servant; but if he is angry, then be sure that evil is determined by him.

8 Therefore deal kindly with your servant, for you have brought [me] into a covenant of the Lord with you. But if there is guilt in me, kill me yourself; for why should you bring me to your father?

9 And Jonathan said, Far be it from you! If I knew that evil was determined for you by my father, would I not tell you?

10 Then said David to Jonathan, Who will tell me if your father answers you roughly?

11 Jonathan said, Come, let us go into the field. So they went into the field.

12 Jonathan said to David, The Lord, the God of Israel, be witness. When I have sounded out my father about this time tomorrow, or the third day, behold, if he is well inclined toward David, and I do not send and let you know it,

13 The Lord do so, and much more, to Jonathan. But if it please my father to do you harm, then I will disclose it to you and send you away, that you may go in safety. And may the Lord be with you as He has been with my father.

14 While I am still alive you shall not only show me the loving-kindness of the Lord, so that I die not,

15 But also you shall not cut off your kindness from my house forever—no, not even when the Lord has cut off every enemy of David from the face of the earth.

16 So Jonathan made a covenant with the house of David, saying, And the Lord will require that this covenant be kept at the hands of David's enemies.

life point

In ancient Israel, when two people entered into a covenant relationship, everything they possessed as individuals was made freely available to the other. The covenant relationship also meant that they would help one another, fight for one another, and do anything necessary to meet each other's needs.

David and Jonathan had a covenant relationship that included all of their descendants (see I Samuel 20:14–16; 18:3). We know from later chapters that Jonathan was killed and David became king. David kept the covenant he made with Jonathan by actively searching for Jonathan's heirs so that he could bless them. King David found Jonathan's son, brought him to the royal palace, and restored him (see II Samuel 9:1–13). Just as David honored his covenant with Jonathan, God will honor the covenant He makes with us. God is looking for someone He can bless for Jesus' sake. It can be you, if you are willing.

17 And Jonathan caused David to swear again by his love for him, for Jonathan loved him as he loved his own life.

18 Then Jonathan said to David, Tomorrow is the New Moon festival; and you will be missed, for your seat will be empty.

19 On the third day you will go quickly and come to the place where you hid yourself when the matter was in hand, and remain by the stone Ezel.

20 And I will shoot three arrows on the side of it, as though I shot at a mark.

21 And I will send a lad, saying, Go, find the arrows. If I expressly say to the lad, Look, the arrows are on this side of you, take them—then you are to come, for it is safe for you and there is no danger, as the Lord lives.

22 But if I say to the youth, Look, the arrows are beyond you—then go, for the Lord has sent you away.

23 And as touching the matter of which you and I have spoken, behold, the Lord is between you and me forever.

24 So David hid himself in the field, and when the New Moon [festival] came, the king sat down to eat food.

25 The king sat, as at other times, on his seat by the wall, and Jonathan sat opposite, and Abner sat by Saul's side, but David's place was empty.

26 Yet Saul said nothing that day, for he thought, Something has befallen him and he is not clean—surely he is not clean.

27 But on the morrow, the second day after the new moon, David's place was empty; and Saul said to Jonathan his son, Why has not the son of Jesse come to the meal, either yesterday or today?

28 And Jonathan answered, David earnestly asked leave of me to go to Bethlehem.

29 He said, Let me go, I pray, for our family holds a sacrifice in the city and my brother commanded me to be there. Now, if I have found favor in your eyes, let me get away and see my brothers. That is why he has not come to the king's table.

30 Then Saul's anger was kindled against Jonathan and he said to him, You son of a perverse, rebellious woman, do not I know that you have chosen the son of Jesse to your own shame and to the shame of your mother who bore you?

31 For as long as the son of Jesse lives upon the earth, you shall not be established nor shall your kingdom. So now send and bring him to me, for he shall surely die.

32 Jonathan answered Saul his father, Why should he be killed? What has he done?

33 But Saul cast his spear at him to smite him, by which Jonathan knew that his father had determined to kill David.

34 So Jonathan arose from the table in fierce anger, and ate no food that second day of the month, for he grieved for David because his father had disgraced him.

35 In the morning Jonathan went out into the field at the time appointed with David, and a little lad was with him.

36 And he said to his lad, Run, find the arrows which I shoot. And as the lad ran, he shot an arrow beyond him.

37 When the lad came to the place where Jonathan had shot the arrow, Jonathan called to [him], Is not the arrow beyond you?

38 And Jonathan cried after the lad, Make speed, haste, stay not! The lad gathered up the arrow and came to his master.

39 But the lad knew nothing; only Jonathan and David knew the matter.

40 Jonathan gave his weapons to his lad and told him, Go, carry them to the city.

41 And as soon as the lad was gone, David arose from beside the heap of stones and fell on his face to the ground and bowed himself three times. And they kissed one another and wept with one another until David got control of himself.

42 And Jonathan told David, Go in peace, forasmuch as we have sworn to each other in the name of the Lord, saying, The Lord shall be between me and you, and between my descendants and yours forever. And Jonathan arose and departed into the city.

21 THEN DAVID went to Nob, to Ahimelech the priest; and Ahimelech was afraid at meeting David, and said to him, Why are you alone and no man with you?

2 David said to Ahimelech the priest, The king has charged me with a matter and has told me, Let no man know anything of the mission on which I send you and with what I have charged you. I have appointed the young men to a certain place.

3 Now what do you have on hand? Give me five loaves of bread, or whatever you may have.

4 And the priest answered David, There is no common bread on hand, but there is hallowed bread—if the young men have kept themselves at least from women.

5 And David told the priest, Truly women have been kept from us in these three days since I came out, and the food bags *and* utensils of the young men are clean, and although the bread will be used in a secular way, it will be set apart in the clean bags.

6 So the priest gave him holy bread, for there was no bread there but the showbread which was taken from before the Lord to put hot bread in its place the day when it was taken away.

7 Now a certain man of Saul's servants was there that day, detained before the Lord; his name was Doeg the Edomite, the chief of Saul's herdsmen.

8 David said to Ahimelech, Do you have at hand a sword or spear? The king's business required haste, and I brought neither my sword nor my weapons with me.

9 The priest said, The sword of Goliath the Philistine, whom you slew in the Valley of Elah, see, it is here wrapped in a cloth behind the ephod; if you will take that, do so, for there is no other here. And David said, There is none like that; give it to me.

10 David arose and fled that day from Saul and went to Achish king of Gath.

11 The servants of Achish said to him, Is not this David, the king of the land? Did they not sing one to another of him in their dances: Saul has slain his thousands, and David his ten thousands?

12 David took these words to heart and was much afraid of Achish king of Gath.

13 And he changed his behavior before them, and pretended to be insane in their [Philistine] hands, and scribbled on the gate doors, and drooled on his beard.

14 Then said Achish to his servants, You see the man is mad. Why then have you brought him to me?

15 Have I need of madmen, that you bring this fellow to play the madman in my presence? Shall this fellow come into my house?

22 SO DAVID departed and escaped to the cave of Adullam: and when his brothers and all his father's house heard it, they went down there to him.

2 And everyone in distress or in debt or discontented gathered to him, and he became a commander over them. And there were with him about 400 men.

3 And David went from there to Mizpah of Moab; and he said to the king of Moab, Let my father [of Moabite descent] and my mother, I pray you, come out [of Judah] and be with you till I know what God will do for me. [Ruth 4:13, 17.]

4 And he brought them before the king of Moab, and they dwelt with him all the while that David was in the stronghold [in Moab].

5 Then the prophet Gad said to David, Do not remain in the stronghold; leave, and get into the land of Judah. So David left and went into the forest of Hareth.

6 Saul heard that David was discovered, and the men that were with him. Saul was sitting in Gibeah under the tamarisk tree on the height, his spear in his hand and all his servants standing about him.

7 Saul said to his servants who stood about him, Hear now, you Benjamites! Will the son of Jesse give every one of you fields and vineyards and make you all commanders of thousands and hundreds,

8 That all of you have conspired against me? No one discloses to me when my son makes a league with the son of Jesse. None of you is sorry for me or discloses that my son has stirred up my servant against me to lie in wait, as he does this day?

9 Then Doeg the Edomite, who stood with Saul's servants, said, I saw the son of Jesse come to Nob, to Ahimelech son of Ahitub.

10 And [Ahimelech] inquired of the Lord for him, and gave him provisions and the sword of Goliath the Philistine.

11 Then the king sent to call Ahimelech the priest, the son of Ahitub, and all his father's house, the priests who were at Nob, and they all came to the king.

12 Saul said, Hear now, you son of Ahitub. He replied, Here I am, my lord.

13 Saul said to him, Why have you conspired against me, you and the son of Jesse, giving him bread and a sword

and inquiring of God for him, so he could rise against me to lie in wait, as he does this day?

14 Then Ahimelech answered the king, And who is so faithful among all your servants as David, who is the king's son-in-law, and is taken into your council and honored in your house?

15 Have I only today begun inquiring of God for him? No! Let not the king impute any wrong to his servant or to all the house of my father, for your servant has known nothing of all this, little or much.

16 [Saul] said, You shall surely die, Ahimelech, you and all your father's house.

17 And the king said to the guard that stood about him, Turn and slay the Lord's priests, because their hand also is with David and because they knew that he fled and did not disclose it to me. But the servants of the king would not put forth their hands against the Lord's priests.

18 The king said to Doeg, You turn and fall upon the priests. And Doeg the Edomite turned and attacked the priests and slew that day eighty-five persons who wore the priest's linen ephod.

19 And Nob, the city of the priests, he smote with the sword; both men and women, children and sucklings, oxen and donkeys and sheep, he put to the sword.

20 And one of the sons of Ahimelech son of Ahitub named Abiathar escaped and fled after David.

21 And Abiathar told David that Saul had slain the Lord's priests.

22 David said to Abiathar, I knew that day, when Doeg the Edomite was there, that he would surely tell Saul. I have occasioned the death of all your father's house.

23 Stay with me, fear not; for he who seeks my life seeks your life. But with me you shall be safeguarded.

23

THEN THEY told David, Behold, the Philistines are fighting against Keilah and are robbing the threshing floors.
2 So David inquired of the Lord, Shall I go and attack these Philistines? And the Lord said to David, Go,

putting the Word to work

In I Samuel 23:2, and throughout the biblical accounts of David's life, we see that David "inquired of the Lord." Do you inquire of God when faced with a need or a decision, or do you run to your friends for advice? "Don't run to the phone; run to the throne," as I like to say. Remember that God cares for you, and He will answer when you inquire of Him.

smite the Philistines and save Keilah.
3 David's men said to him, Behold, we are afraid here in Judah. How much more, then, if we come to Keilah against the armies of the Philistines?
4 Then David inquired of the Lord again. And the Lord answered him, Arise, go down to Keilah, for I will deliver the Philistines into your hand.
5 So David and his men went to Keilah and fought the Philistines with a great slaughter and brought away their cattle. So David delivered the people of Keilah.
6 When Abiathar son of Ahimelech fled to David at Keilah, he came with an ephod in his hand.
7 Now it was told Saul that David had come to Keilah. Saul said, God has delivered him into my hand, for he is shut in by going into a town that has gates and bars.
8 Saul summoned all the men for war, to go to Keilah to besiege David and his men.
9 David knew that Saul was plotting evil against him; and he said to Abiathar the priest, Bring the ephod here.

10 Then David said, O Lord, the God of Israel, Your servant has surely heard that Saul intends to come and destroy the city of Keilah on my account.
11 Will the men of Keilah deliver me into his hand? Will Saul come down, as Your servant has heard? O Lord, God of Israel, I beseech You, tell Your servant. And the Lord said, He will come down.
12 Then David asked, Will the men of Keilah deliver me and my men into Saul's hand? The Lord said, They will deliver you up.
13 Then David and his men, about 600, arose and left Keilah, going wherever they could go. When Saul was told that David had escaped from Keilah, he gave up going there.
14 David remained in the wilderness strongholds in the hill country of the Wilderness of Ziph. Saul sought him every day, but God did not give him into his hands.
15 David saw that Saul had come out to seek his life. David was in the Wilderness of Ziph in the wood [at Horesh].
16 And Jonathan, Saul's son, rose and went into the wood to David [at Horesh] and strengthened his hand in God.
17 He said to him, Fear not; the hand of Saul my father shall not find you. You shall be king over Israel, and I shall be next to you. Saul my father knows that too.
18 And the two of them made a covenant before the Lord. And David remained in the wood [at Horesh], and Jonathan went to his house.
19 Then the Ziphites came to Saul at Gibeah, saying, Does not David hide himself with us in strongholds in the wood [at Horesh], on the hill of Hachilah, which is south of Jeshimon?
20 Now come down, O king, according to all your heart's desire to come down, and our part shall be to deliver him into the king's hands.

21 And Saul said, The Lord bless you, for you have compassion on me.

22 Go, make yet more sure; and know and see where his haunt is and who has seen him there; for I am told he deals very craftily.

23 See and take note of all his hiding places and come back to me with the certain facts, and I will go with you. If he is in the land, I will search him out among all the thousands of Judah.

24 So they arose and went to Ziph ahead of Saul. Now David and his men were in the Wilderness of Maon, in the Arabah south of Jeshimon.

25 Saul and his men went to seek him. And David was told; so he went down to the rock in the Wilderness of Maon and stayed. When Saul heard that, he pursued David in the Wilderness of Maon.

26 And Saul went on one side of the mountain, and David and his men on the other side of the mountain. And David made haste to get away for fear of Saul, for Saul and his men were surrounding [him] and his men to capture them.

27 But a messenger came to Saul, saying, Make haste and come, for the Philistines have made a raid on the land.

28 So Saul returned from pursuing David and went against the Philistines. So they called that place the Rock of Escape.

29 David went up from there and dwelt in the strongholds of En-gedi.

24 WHEN SAUL returned from following the Philistines, he was told, Behold, David is in the Wilderness of En-gedi.

2 Then Saul took 3,000 chosen men out of all Israel and went to seek David and his men among the Rocks of the Wild Goats.

3 He came to the sheepfolds on the way, where there was a cave, and Saul went in to relieve himself. Now David and his men were sitting in the cave's innermost recesses.

4 David's men said to him, Behold the day of which the Lord said to you, Behold, I will deliver your enemy into your hands and you shall do to him as seems good to you. Then David arose [in the darkness] and stealthily cut off the skirt of Saul's robe.

5 Afterward, David's heart smote him because he had cut off Saul's skirt.

6 He said to his men, The Lord forbid that I should do this to my master, the Lord's anointed, to put my hand out against him, when he is the anointed of the Lord.

7 So David checked his men with these words and did not let them rise against Saul. But Saul rose up and left the cave and went on his way.

8 David also arose afterward and went out of the cave and called after Saul, saying, My lord the king! And when Saul looked behind him, David bowed with his face to the earth and did obeisance.

9 And David said to Saul, Why do you listen to the words of men who say, David seeks to do you harm?

10 Behold, your eyes have seen how the Lord gave you today into my hands in the cave. Some told me to kill you, but I spared you; I said, I will not put forth my hand against my lord, for he is the Lord's anointed.

11 See, my father, see the skirt of your robe in my hand! Since I cut off the skirt of your robe and did not kill you, you know and see that there is no evil or treason in my hands. I have not sinned against you, yet you hunt my life to take it.

12 May the Lord judge between me and you, and may the Lord avenge me upon you, but my hand shall not be upon you.

13 As the proverb of the ancients says, Out of the wicked comes forth wickedness; but my hand shall not be against you.

14 After whom has the king of Israel come out? After whom do you pursue? After a dead dog? After a flea?
15 May the Lord be judge and judge between me and you, and see and plead my cause, and deliver me out of your hands. [Ps. 142.]
16 When David had said this to Saul, Saul said, Is this your voice, my son David? And Saul lifted up his voice and wept.
17 He said to David, You are more upright in God's eyes than I, for you have repaid me good, but I have rewarded you evil.
18 You have declared today how you have dealt well with me; for when the Lord gave me into your hand, you did not kill me.
19 For if a man finds his enemy, will he let him go away unharmed? Therefore may the Lord reward you with good for what you have done for me this day.
20 And now, behold, I well know that you shall surely be king and that the kingdom of Israel shall be established in your hands.
21 Swear now therefore to me by the Lord that you will not cut off my descendants after me and that you will not destroy my name out of my father's house.
22 David gave Saul his oath; and Saul went home, but David and his men went up to the stronghold.

25 NOW SAMUEL died, and all the Israelites assembled and mourned for him, and buried him at his house in Ramah. David arose and went to the Wilderness of Paran.
2 A very rich man was in Maon, whose possessions *and* business were in Carmel. He had 3,000 sheep and 1,000 goats, and he was shearing his sheep in Carmel.
3 The man's name was Nabal and his wife's name was Abigail; she was a woman of good understanding, and beautiful. But the man was rough and evil in his doings; he was a Calebite.
4 David heard in the wilderness that Nabal was shearing his sheep.
5 And David sent out ten young men and said to [them], Go up to Carmel to Nabal and greet him in my name;
6 And salute him thus: Peace be to you and to your house and to all that you have.
7 I have heard that you have shearers. Now your shepherds have been with us and we did them no harm, and they missed nothing all the time they were in Carmel.
8 Ask your young men and they will tell you. Therefore let my young men find favor in your sight, for we come at an opportune time. I pray you, give whatever you have at hand to your servants and to your son David.
9 And when David's young men came, they said all this to Nabal in the name of David, and then paused.
10 And Nabal answered David's servants and said, Who is David? Who is the son of Jesse? There are many servants nowadays who are each breaking away from his master.
11 Shall I then take my bread and my water, and my meat that I have killed for my shearers, and give it to men when I do not know where they belong?
12 So David's young men turned away, and came and told him all that was said.
13 And David said to his men, Every man gird on his sword. And they did so, and David also girded on his sword; and there went up after David about 400 men, and 200 remained with the baggage.
14 But one of Nabal's young men told Abigail, Nabal's wife, Behold, David sent messengers out of the wilderness to salute our master, and he railed at them.

15 But David's men were very good to us, and we were not harmed, nor did we miss anything as long as we went with them, when we were in the fields.
16 They were a wall to us night and day, all the time we were with them keeping the sheep.
17 So know this and consider what you will do, for evil is determined against our master and all his house. For he is such a wicked man that one cannot speak to him.
18 Then Abigail made haste and took 200 loaves, two skins of wine, five sheep already dressed, five measures of parched grain, 100 clusters of raisins, and 200 cakes of figs, and laid them on donkeys.
19 And she said to her servants, Go on before me; behold, I come after you. But she did not tell her husband Nabal.
20 As she rode on her donkey, she came down hidden by the mountain, and behold, David and his men came down opposite her, and she met them.
21 Now David had said, Surely in vain have I protected all that this fellow has in the wilderness, so that nothing was missed of all that belonged to him; and he has repaid me evil for good.
22 May God do so, and more also, to David ʰif I leave of all who belong to him one male alive by morning.
23 When Abigail saw David, she hastened and lighted off the donkey, and fell before David on her face and did obeisance.
24 Kneeling at his feet she said, Upon me alone let this guilt be, my lord. And let your handmaid, I pray

you, speak in your presence, and hear the words of your handmaid.
25 Let not my lord, I pray you, regard this foolish *and* wicked fellow Nabal, for as his name is, so is he—Nabal [foolish, wicked] is his name, and folly is with him. But I, your handmaid, did not see my lord's young men whom you sent.
26 So now, my lord, as the Lord lives and as your soul lives, seeing that the Lord has prevented you from blood-guiltiness and from avenging yourself with your own hand, now let your enemies and those who seek to do evil to my lord be as Nabal.
27 And now this gift, which your handmaid has brought my lord, let it be given to the young men who follow my lord.
28 Forgive, I pray you, the trespass of your handmaid, for the Lord will certainly make my lord a sure house, because my lord is fighting the Lord's battles, and evil has not been found in you all your days.
29 Though man is risen up to pursue you and to seek your life, yet the life of my lord shall be bound in the living bundle with the Lord your God. And the lives of your enemies—them shall He sling out as out of the center of a sling.
30 And when the Lord has done to my lord according to all the good that He has promised concerning you and has made you ruler over Israel,
31 This shall be no staggering grief to you or cause for pangs of conscience to my lord, either that you have shed blood without cause or that my lord has avenged himself. And when the Lord has dealt well with my lord, then [ⁱearnestly] remember your handmaid.

---

h *The Septuagint* (Greek translation of the Old Testament) so reads. The Hebrew reads "David's enemies." **i** Whenever God's inspired Word says "[earnestly] remember," one is certain to miss something if he does not stop, look, and really listen to what the Holy Spirit is wanting to tell him—or her. "[Earnestly] remember" Abigail, the woman whom God has specifically held up as a pattern of right behavior in an unfortunate marriage. Here a dozen vital questions are answered through Abigail's example. She could not have known that thousands of years later people in similar circumstances

32 And David said to Abigail, Blessed be the Lord, the God of Israel, Who sent you this day to meet me.

33 And blessed be your discretion *and* advice, and blessed be you who have kept me today from bloodguiltiness and from avenging myself with my own hand.

34 For as the Lord, the God of Israel, lives, Who has prevented me from hurting you, if you had not hurried and come to meet me, surely by morning there would not have been left so much as one male to Nabal.

35 So David accepted what she had brought him and said to her, Go up in peace to your house. See, I have hearkened to your voice and have granted your petition.

36 And Abigail came to Nabal, and behold, he was holding a feast in his house like the feast of a king. And [his] heart was merry, for he was very drunk; so she told him nothing at all until the morning light.

37 But in the morning, when the wine was gone out of Nabal, and his wife told him these things, his heart died within him and he became [paralyzed, helpless as] a stone.

38 And about ten days after that, the Lord smote Nabal and he died.

39 When David heard that Nabal was dead, he said, Blessed be the Lord, Who has pleaded the cause of my reproach at the hand of Nabal, and kept His servant from evil. For the Lord has returned the wickedness of Nabal upon his own head. And David sent and communed with Abigail, to take her to him as his wife.

40 And when the servants of David had come to Abigail at Carmel, they said to her, David sent us to you to take you to him to be his wife.

41 And she arose and bowed herself to the earth and said, Behold, let your handmaid be a servant to wash the feet of the servants of my lord.

42 And Abigail hastened and arose and rode on a donkey, with five of her maids who followed her, and she went after the messengers of David and became his wife.

43 David also took Ahinoam of Jezreel, and they both became his wives.

44 Saul had given Michal his daughter, David's wife, to Phalti son of Laish, who was of Gallim.

26 THE ZIPHITES came to Saul at Gibeah, saying, Does not David hide himself on the hill of Hachilah, east of Jeshimon?

2 So Saul arose and went down to the Wilderness of Ziph, with 3,000 chosen men of Israel, to seek David [there].

3 Saul encamped on the hill of Hachilah, which is beside the road east of Jeshimon. But David remained in the wilderness. And when he saw that Saul came after him into the wilderness,

4 David sent out spies and learned that Saul had actually come.

5 David arose and came to the place where Saul had encamped, and saw where Saul lay with Abner son of Ner, commander of his army; and Saul was lying in the encampment, with the army encamped around him.

6 Then David said to Ahimelech the Hittite and to Abishai son of Zeruiah,

would become "more than conquerors" because of her, but God knew. Study her until you know her God-given secrets of success; then pass them on to the people who are letting an unfortunate marriage wreck them rather than sanctify them for service. F.B. Meyer (*Through the Bible Day by Day*) said, "Never let the evil disposition of one mate hinder the devotion and grace of the other. Never let the difficulties of your home lead you to abdicate your throne. Do not step down to the level of your circumstances, but lift them to your own high calling in Christ. 'Be not conformed . . . but be ye transformed' (Rom. 12:1, 2 KJV)."

brother of Joab, Who will go down with me into the camp of Saul? And Abishai said, I will go down with you.

7 So David and Abishai went to the army by night, and there Saul lay sleeping within the encampment with his spear stuck in the ground at his head; and Abner and the army lay round about him.

8 Then said Abishai to David, God has given your enemy into your hands this day. Now therefore let me smite him to the earth at once with one stroke of the spear, and I will not strike him twice.

9 David said to Abishai, Do not destroy him; for who can raise his hand against the Lord's anointed and be guiltless?

10 David said, As the Lord lives, [He] will smite him; or his day will come to die or he will go down in battle and perish.

11 The Lord forbid that I should raise my hand against the Lord's anointed; but take now the spear that is at his head and the bottle of water, and let us go.

12 So David took the spear and the bottle of water from Saul's head, and they got away. And no man saw or knew or wakened, for they were all asleep, because a deep sleep from the Lord had fallen upon them.

13 Then David went over to the other side and stood on the top of the mountain afar off, a great space being between them.

14 David called to the army and Abner son of Ner, Will you answer, Abner? Abner replied, Who are you, calling [and disturbing] the king?

15 David said to Abner, Are you not a valiant man? Who is like you in Israel? Why then have you not guarded your lord the king? For one of the people came in [to your camp] to destroy the king your lord.

16 This thing is not good that you have done. As the Lord lives, you

life point

David remained loyal and faithful to King Saul, recognizing and respecting God's anointing on him, even though Saul was trying to kill him. In his training for leadership, David learned to stay under God's protective hand by refusing to rise up against Saul—even when he had an opportunity (see I Samuel 26:7–11). Instead, he patiently waited for God to deliver him. If you are a leader, follow David's example and refuse to rebel against those in authority over you. Wait patiently for the Lord to deliver you, vindicate you, and raise you up as well.

deserve to die, because you have not guarded your master, the Lord's anointed. And now see where the king's spear is and the bottle of water that was at his head.

17 And Saul knew David's voice and said, Is this your voice, my son David? And David said, My voice, my lord O king!

18 And David said, Why does my lord thus pursue his servant? What have I done? Or what evil is in my hand [tonight]?

19 Now therefore, I pray you, let my lord the king hear the words of his servant. If the Lord has stirred you up against me, let Him accept an offering; but if it is men, may they be cursed before the Lord, for they have driven me out this day that I should have no share in the inheritance of the Lord, saying, Go, serve other gods.

20 Now therefore, let not my blood fall to the earth away from the presence of the Lord; for the king of Israel is come out to seek one flea, as when one hunts a partridge in the mountains.

21 Then said Saul, I have sinned. Return, my son David, for I will no more do you harm, because my life

was precious in your eyes this day. Behold, I have [j]played the fool and have erred exceedingly.

22 David answered, See the king's spear! Let one of the young men come and get it.

23 The Lord rewards every man for his righteousness and his faithfulness; for the Lord delivered you into my hands today, but I would not stretch forth my hand against the Lord's anointed.

24 And behold, as your life was precious today in my sight, so let my life be precious in the sight of the Lord, and let Him deliver me out of all tribulation.

25 Then Saul said to David, May you be blessed, my son David; you will both do mightily and surely prevail. So David went on his way, and Saul returned to his place.

27 BUT DAVID said in his heart, I shall now perish one day by the hand of Saul. There is nothing better for me than that I should escape into the land of the Philistines. Then Saul will despair of seeking me any more within the borders of Israel, and I shall escape out of his hand.

2 So David arose and went over with the 600 men who were with him to Achish son of Maoch, king of Gath.

3 And David dwelt with Achish at Gath, he and his men, every man with his household, and David with his two wives, Ahinoam the Jezreelitess and Abigail the Carmelitess, Nabal's widow.

4 When it was told Saul that David had fled to Gath, he sought for him no more.

5 And David said to Achish, If I have now found favor in your eyes, let me be given a place to dwell in some country town; for why should your servant live in the royal city with you?

6 Then Achish gave David the town of Ziklag that day. Therefore Ziklag belongs to the kings of Judah to this day.

7 The time David dwelt in the Philistines' country was a year and four months.

8 Now David and his men went up and made attacks on the Geshurites, Girzites, and Amalekites [enemies of Israel Joshua had failed to exterminate]. For from of old those nations inhabited the land, as one goes to Shur even to the land of Egypt. [Deut. 25:19; Josh. 13:1, 2, 13.]

9 And David smote the land and left neither man nor woman alive, and took away the sheep, oxen, donkeys, camels, and the apparel, and returned to Achish.

10 Achish would ask, Against whom have you made a raid today? And David would reply, [k]Against the South

j "When for a moment a man is off guard, in all probability you will know more truth about him than in all his attempts either to reveal himself or to hide himself. The ever-present consciousness, habitually hidden, flashes forth. Later he may apologize and say he did not mean what he said. The fact is that he was surprised into saying what he was constantly thinking. In all probability Saul had never said that before and would never say it again, but he had been thinking it for a long time—'I played the fool.' There is no escape for any man, as long as reason continues, from the naked truth about himself. He may practice deceit so skillfully as not only to hide himself from his fellowmen, but in his unutterable folly to imagine he has hidden himself from God; but he can never hide himself from **himself**. In some moment of stress and strain he says what he has been thinking all the time . . . . Ere Saul knew it, he had said, 'Behold, I have played the fool.' That is the whole story of the man" (G. Campbell Morgan, cited by J. Sidlow Baxter, *Explore the Book*). **k** How could David be "a man after His [God's] own heart" (I Sam. 13:14) and lie and deceive like that? God hates lying (Prov. 12:22), and those who deal in falsehood and deception are to be excluded from heaven (Rev. 22:15). The truth is that David had gone through such a long period of persecution and threatening circumstances that he had fallen into a bit of mistrust of God Himself. God had sworn to make him king, to rid him of his enemies, to give him a sure house; yet here he was in a panic, concluding that God had forsaken him and that if he was to remain alive he must manage it himself. It was very dishonoring to God. But God was standing by

(Negeb) of Judah, or of the Jerah-meelites, or of the Kenites.

11 And David saved neither man nor woman alive to bring tidings to Gath, thinking, Lest they should say about us, So did David, and so will he do as long as he dwells in the Philistines' country.

12 And Achish believed David, saying, He has made his people Israel utterly abhor him; so he shall be my servant always.

28 IN THOSE days the Philistines gathered their forces for war against Israel. Achish said to David, Understand that you and your men shall go with me to battle.

2 David said to Achish, All right, you shall know what your servant can do. Achish said to David, Therefore I will make you my bodyguard always.

3 Now Samuel was dead, and all Israel had mourned for him and buried him in Ramah, his own city. And Saul had put the mediums and the wizards out of the land.

4 And the Philistines assembled and came and encamped at Shunem; and Saul gathered all Israel and they encamped at Gilboa.

5 When Saul saw the Philistine host, he was afraid; his heart trembled greatly.

6 When Saul inquired of the Lord, He refused to answer him, either by dreams or by Urim [a symbol worn by the priest when seeking the will of God for Israel] or by the prophets. [Prov. 1:24-30.]

7 Then Saul said to his servants, Find me a woman who is a medium [between the living and the dead],

that I may go and inquire of her. His servants said, Behold, there is a woman who is a medium at Endor.

8 So Saul disguised himself, put on other raiment, and he and two men with him went and came to the woman at night. He said to her, Perceive for me by the familiar spirit and bring up for me the dead person whom I shall name to you.

9 The woman said, See here, you know what Saul has done, how he has cut off those who are mediums and wizards out of the land. Why then do you lay a trap for my life to cause my death?

10 And Saul swore to her by the Lord, saying, As the Lord lives, there shall no punishment come to you for this.

11 The woman said, Whom shall I bring up for you? He said, Bring up Samuel for me.

12 And when the woman saw Samuel, she screamed and she said to Saul, Why have you deceived me? For you are Saul!

13 The king said to her, Be not afraid; what do you see? The woman said to Saul, I see a god [terrifying superhuman being] coming up out of the earth!

14 He said to her, In what form is he? And she said, An old man comes up, covered with a mantle. And Saul perceived that it was Samuel, and he stooped with his face to the ground and made obeisance.

15 And Samuel said to Saul, Why have you disturbed me to bring me up? Saul answered, I am bitterly distressed; for the Philistines make war against me, and God has departed from me and answers me no more, either by prophets or by dreams. Therefore I

His stricken child, waiting for the moment when he would realize his own utter helplessness and turn in blessed surrender to the almighty arms of Him who had been watching over him all along. That time came at Ziklag, when, in the bitterest hour of his life, we are told, "But David encouraged *and* strengthened himself in the Lord his God" (I Sam. 30:6), truly "a man after God's own heart."

have called you, that you may make known to me what I should do.

16 Samuel said, Why then do you ask me, seeing that the Lord has turned from you and has become your enemy?

17 The Lord has done to you as He said through me He would do; for [He] has torn the kingdom out of your hands and given it to your neighbor David. [I Sam. 15:22-28.]

18 Because you did not obey the voice of the Lord or execute His fierce wrath upon Amalek, therefore the Lord has done this thing to you this day.

19 Moreover, the Lord will also give Israel with you into the hands of the Philistines, and tomorrow you and your sons shall be with me [among the dead]. The Lord also will give the army of Israel into the hands of the Philistines.

20 Then immediately Saul fell full length upon the earth floor [of the medium's house], and was exceedingly afraid because of Samuel's words. There was no strength in him, for he had eaten nothing all day and all night.

21 The woman came to Saul, and seeing that he was greatly troubled, she said to him, Behold, your handmaid has obeyed you, and I have put my life in my hands and have listened to what you said to me.

22 So now, I pray you, listen also to the voice of your handmaid and let me set a morsel of food before you, and eat, so you may have strength when you go on your way.

23 But he said, I will not eat. But his servants, together with the woman, urged him, and he heeded their words. So he arose from the ground and sat upon the bed.

24 The woman had a fat calf in the house; she hurried and killed it, and took flour, kneaded it, and baked unleavened bread.

25 Then she brought it before Saul and his servants, and they ate. Then they rose up and went away that night.

29 NOW THE Philistines gathered all their forces at Aphek, and the Israelites encamped by the fountain in Jezreel.

2 As the Philistine lords were passing on by hundreds and by thousands, and David and his men were in the rear with Achish,

3 The Philistine princes said, What are these Hebrews doing here? Achish said to the Philistine princes, Is not this David, the servant of Saul king of Israel, who has been with me these days and years, and I have found no fault in him since he deserted to me to this day?

4 And the Philistine princes were angry with Achish and they said to him, Make this fellow return, that he may go again to his place where you have assigned him, and let him not go down with us to battle, lest in the battle he become an adversary to us. For how could David reconcile himself to his master? Would it not be with the heads of the men here?

5 Is not this David, of whom they sang to one another in dances, Saul slew his thousands, and David his ten thousands?

6 Then Achish called David and said to him, As surely as the Lord lives, you have been honest *and* upright, and for you to go out and come in with me in the army is good in my sight; for I have found no evil in you from the day of your coming to me to this day. Yet the lords do not approve of you.

7 So return now and go peaceably, so as not to displease the Philistine lords.

8 David said to Achish, But what have I done? And what have you found in your servant as long as I have been with you to this day, that I may not go and fight against the enemies of my lord the king?

9 And Achish said to David, I know that you are as blameless in my sight as an angel of God; nevertheless the princes of the Philistines have said, He shall not go up with us to the battle.

10 So now rise up early in the morning, with your master's servants who have come with you, and as soon as you are up and have light, depart.

11 So David and his men rose up early in the morning to return to the land of the Philistines. But the Philistines went up to Jezreel [to fight against Israel].

30 NOW WHEN David and his men came home to Ziklag on the third day, they found that the Amalekites had made a raid on the South (the Negeb) and on Ziklag, and had struck Ziklag and burned it with fire,

2 And had taken the women and all who were there, both great and small, captive. They killed no one, but carried them off and went on their way.

3 So David and his men came to the town, and behold, it was burned, and their wives and sons and daughters were taken captive.

4 Then David and the men with him lifted up their voices and wept until they had no more strength to weep.

5 David's two wives also had been taken captive, Ahinoam the Jezreelitess and Abigail, the widow of Nabal the Carmelite.

6 David was greatly distressed, for the men spoke of stoning him because the souls of them all were bitterly grieved, each man for his sons and daughters. But David encouraged *and* strengthened himself in the Lord his God.

7 David said to Abiathar the priest, Ahimelech's son, I pray you, bring me the ephod. And Abiathar brought him the ephod.

putting the Word to work

Have you ever suffered loss, as David and the Israelites did in I Samuel 30? Remember that in God, you will "without fail recover all" (1 Samuel 30:8).

8 And David inquired of the Lord, saying, Shall I pursue this troop? Shall I overtake them? The Lord answered him, Pursue, for you shall surely overtake them and without fail recover all.

9 So David went, he and the 600 men with him, and came to the brook Besor; there those remained who were left behind.

10 But David pursued, he and 400 men, for 200 stayed behind who were too exhausted *and* faint to cross the brook Besor.

11 They found an Egyptian in the field and brought him to David, and gave him bread and he ate, and water to drink,

12 And a piece of a cake of figs and two clusters of raisins; and when he had eaten, his spirit returned to him, for he had eaten no food or drunk any water for three days and three nights.

13 And David said to him, To whom do you belong? And from where have you come? He said, I am a young man of Egypt, servant to an Amalekite; and my master left me because three days ago I fell sick.

14 We had made a raid on the South (Negeb) of the Cherethites and upon that which belongs to Judah and upon the South (Negeb) of Caleb. And we burned Ziklag with fire.

15 And David said to him, Can you take me down to this band? And he said, Swear to me by God that you will neither kill me nor deliver me into the hands of my master, and I will bring you down to this band.

16 And when he had brought David down, behold, the raiders were spread

encourage yourself!

If you need encouragement and no one is around to give it, encourage yourself as David did (see I Samuel 30:6). He had a positive attitude about himself, and you should also. We all should be careful of having a prideful attitude, but it is not wrong to have a good and confident attitude toward ourselves.

David was in a seemingly hopeless situation—his city was destroyed, its women and children captured, and his men blamed him for their misfortune. What did David do? He encouraged and strengthened himself in the Lord. Later on, that situation was totally turned around (see I Samuel 30:7–20).

Earlier in his life, when David was just a boy, everyone around him discouraged him concerning his ability to fight Goliath. David, however, was confident in God. He believed that God would be strong in his weakness and give him the victory. He went out in the name of the Lord, with a heart full of confidence, and became a giant-killer who was eventually crowned king (see I Samuel 17). David had no one to believe in him but God, so he believed about himself what God believed about him; he believed in God's ability in him.

The Lord once told me that if I did not have confidence in myself, I really did not have confidence in Him. He said, "I am in you; I am your confidence, but I can only do through you what you believe." Self-doubt is absolutely tormenting. I lived in it for many years, and I personally prefer confidence.

You may be thinking, *Well, Joyce, I wish I had confidence too*.

Confidence is something we decide to have. It is more than a feeling; it is a decision to step out boldly into whatever we feel God is leading us to do. We learn about God—about His love, His ways, and His Word—then ultimately we must *decide* whether we believe or not. If we do believe, then we have confidence. If we do not believe, we live in doubt about everything. Self-doubt makes us double-minded, and James 1:8 teaches us that a double-minded person is unstable and uncertain about everything. We really cannot go forward until we decide to have confidence in God and in ourselves.

I encourage you to take a big step of faith and *stop doubting yourself*. As the old saying goes, "Don't sell yourself short." You have more capabilities than you think you do. You are able to do a lot more than you have ever done in the past. God will help you, if you will put your trust in Him and stop doubting yourself.

Like everyone else, you will make mistakes—but God will allow you to learn from them and will actually work them out to your good if you will decide not to be defeated by them. When doubt begins to torment your mind, speak the Word of God and you will win the battle. Believe wholeheartedly in God, believe that He is in you, and believe you are able to do whatever you need to do through Him.

abroad over all the land, eating and drinking and dancing because of all the great spoil they had taken from the land of the Philistines and from the land of Judah.

17 And David smote them from twilight even to the evening of the next day, and not a man of them escaped, except 400 youths who rode camels and fled.

18 David recovered all that the Amalekites had taken and rescued his two wives.

19 Nothing was missing, small or great, sons or daughters, spoil or anything that had been taken; David recovered all.

20 Also David captured all the flocks and herds [which the enemy had], and the people drove those animals before him and said, This is David's spoil.

21 And David came to the 200 men who were so exhausted *and* faint that they could not follow [him] and had been left at the brook Besor [with the baggage]. They came to meet David and those with him, and when he came near to the men, he saluted them.

22 Then all the wicked and base men who went with David said, Because they did not go with us, we will give them nothing of the spoil we have recovered, except that every man may lead away his wife and children and depart.

23 David said, You shall not do so, my brethren, with what the Lord has given us. He has preserved us and has delivered into our hands the troop that came against us.

24 Who would listen to you in this matter? For as is the share of him who goes into the battle, so shall his share be who stays by the baggage. They shall share alike.

25 And from that day to this he made it a statute and ordinance for Israel.

26 When David came to Ziklag, he sent part of the spoil to the elders of Judah, his friends, saying, Here is a gift for you of the spoil of the enemies of the Lord:

27 For those in Bethel, Ramoth of the Negeb, Jattir,

28 Aroer, Siphmoth, Eshtemoa,

29 Racal, the cities of the Jerahmeelites, the cities of the Kenites,

30 Hormah, Bor-ashan, Athach,

31 Hebron, and for those in all the places David and his men had habitually haunted.

31 NOW THE Philistines fought against Israel; and the men of Israel fled before [them] and fell slain on Mount Gilboa.

2 And the Philistines pursued Saul and his sons, and slew Jonathan and Abinadab and Malchi-shua, Saul's sons.

3 The battle went heavily against Saul, and the archers severely wounded him.

4 Saul said to his armor-bearer, Draw your sword and thrust me through, lest these uncircumcised come and thrust me through and abuse *and* mock me. But his armor-bearer would not, for he was terrified. So [1]Saul took a sword and fell upon it.

5 When his armor-bearer saw that Saul was dead, he likewise fell upon his sword and died with him.

6 So Saul, his three sons, his armor-bearer, and all his men died that day together.

---

1 This account of Saul's death obviously contradicts that given by the Amalekite who came to David with Saul's spear and crown, claiming to have killed him (II Sam. 1:9ff). His story was probably a fabrication. He found the king's body on the battlefield, stripped it, and brought the spoil to David hoping for a reward, as *The Cambridge Bible* comments. However, it is possible that Saul was not entirely dead when the Amalekite found him, though his armor-bearer had thought him dead and had killed himself, in which case the Amalekite's story may have been true.

7 And when the men of Israel on the other side of the valley and beyond the Jordan saw that the Israelites had fled and that Saul and his sons were dead, they forsook the cities and fled; and the Philistines came and dwelt in them.

8 The next day, when the Philistines came to strip the slain, they found Saul and his three sons fallen on Mount Gilboa.

9 They cut off Saul's head and stripped off his armor and sent them round about the land of the Philistines to publish it in the house of their idols and among the people.

10 And they put Saul's armor in the house of the Ashtaroth [the idols representing the female deities Ashtoreth and Asherah], and they fastened his body to the wall of Beth-shan.

11 When the people of Jabesh-gilead heard what the Philistines had done to Saul,

12 All the valiant men arose and went all night, and they took the bodies of Saul and his sons from the wall of Beth-shan and came to Jabesh and cremated them there.

13 And they took their bones and buried them under a tree at Jabesh, and fasted seven days.

Second Samuel

Author:
Uncertain

Date:
Between 931 BC and 722 BC

Everyday Life Principles:
We position ourselves to receive God's blessings by getting into the places God has called us and staying there. Do not go to a place unless God leads you to go, and do not leave a place until God instructs you to leave.

Being in the wrong place at the wrong time can have serious consequences, both short-term and long-term.

God will help us get into proper position and stay there as we follow and obey Him.

One of the major life lessons we learn from II Samuel is that being in the right place at the right time brings God's blessings, and being out of position can keep God's blessings from flowing in our lives. In II Samuel, we learn this lesson primarily through people who were not in their proper places at the proper time.

Examples of people who were out of place include Uzzah, Mephibosheth, and even King David. Uzzah got out of position when, against God's instruction, he touched the ark when it became unstable. As a result, he died (see II Samuel 6:6, 7). Jonathan's son, Mephibosheth, was also in the wrong place, living in the wilderness of Lo-debar and thinking of himself as a "dead dog" (II Samuel 9:8), when his family's covenant with David entitled him to live in the palace and eat at the king's table (see II Samuel 9:1–13). We also see King David tragically out of place when he committed sin with Bathsheba. Second Samuel 11:1 tells us that he sinned with her "in the spring, when kings go forth to battle." If David had been at war where he was supposed to be instead of at home, he could have avoided falling into adultery and the tragedies that resulted from it.

Learn from those who were out of place in II Samuel. Ask God to help you hear His voice so that you will know where you are supposed to be and be there at the proper time.

1 NOW AFTER the death of Saul, when David returned from the slaughter of the Amalekites, he had stayed two days in Ziklag,

2 When on the third day a man came from Saul's camp with his clothes torn and dust on his head. When he came to David, he fell to the ground and did obeisance.

3 David said to him, Where have you come from? He said, I have escaped from the camp of Israel.

4 David said to him, How did it go? Tell me. He answered, The men have fled from the battle. Many have fallen and are dead; Saul and Jonathan his son are dead also.

5 David said to the young man, How do you know Saul and Jonathan his son are dead?

6 The young man said, By chance I happened to be on Mount Gilboa and I saw Saul leaning on his spear, and behold, the chariots and horsemen were close behind him.

7 When he looked behind him, he saw me and called to me. I answered, Here I am.

8 He asked me, Who are you? I answered, An Amalekite.

9 He said to me, Rise up against me and slay me; for terrible dizziness has come upon me, yet my life is still in me [and I will be taken alive].

10 So I stood up against him and slew him, because I was sure he could not live after he had fallen. So I took the crown on his head and the bracelet on his arm and have brought them here to my lord. [I Sam. 31:4.]

11 Then David grasped his own clothes and tore them; so did all the men with him.

12 They mourned and wept for Saul and Jonathan his son, and fasted until evening for the Lord's people and the house of Israel, because of their defeat in battle.

13 David said to the young man who told him, Where are you from? He

life point

David and Jonathan had a special bond (see I Samuel 18:1), and when Jonathan died, David lamented his death greatly (see II Samuel 1:11, 12).

Any time a person loses a loved one as David did or suffers a significant loss, he or she will need to grieve. The grieving *process* is necessary and healthy—mentally, emotionally, and even physically. Note that David rent his clothing and mourned his loss with weeping. Often a person who refuses to go through the grieving process is not facing reality, which ultimately has a devastating effect on his entire being.

A *spirit* of grief is another matter entirely. Usually a spirit of grief clings to an individual and brings with it severe regret and crushing guilt. A spirit of grief will not allow people to go on with their lives after their loss. If a person does not resist a spirit of grief, it will take over and destroy the life of the one who has suffered a loss. If not confronted and controlled, it will rob a person's health, strength, and vitality—and even life itself.

God's will is to comfort those who mourn. Are you having difficulty grieving a loss? I encourage you to face your grief with God's comfort. If need be, resist a spirit of grief with God's power. Stay in balance and receive the assurance Jesus gives: "Blessed . . . are those who mourn, for they shall be comforted!" (Matthew 5:4).

answered, I am the son of a foreigner, an Amalekite.

14 David said to him, Why were you not afraid to stretch forth your hand to destroy the Lord's anointed?

15 David called one of the young men and said, Go near and fall upon him. And he smote him so that he died.
16 David said to [the fallen man], Your blood be upon your own head; for you have testified against yourself, saying, I have slain the Lord's anointed.
17 David lamented with this lamentation over Saul and Jonathan his son,
18 And he commanded to teach it, [the lament of] the bow, to the Israelites. Behold, it is written in the Book of Jashar:
19 Your glory, O Israel, is slain upon your high places. How have the mighty fallen!
20 Tell it not in Gath, announce it not in the streets of Ashkelon, lest the daughters of the Philistines rejoice, lest the daughters of the uncircumcised exult.
21 O mountains of Gilboa, let there be no dew or rain upon you, or fields with offerings. For there the shield of the mighty was defiled, the shield of Saul, as though he were not anointed with oil.
22 From the blood of the slain, from the fat of the mighty, the bow of Jonathan turned not back, and the sword of Saul returned not empty.
23 Saul and Jonathan, beloved and lovely! In their lives and in their deaths they were not divided. They were swifter than eagles, they were stronger than lions.
24 You daughters of Israel, weep over Saul, who clothed you in scarlet with [other] delights, who put ornaments of gold upon your apparel.
25 How have the mighty fallen in the midst of the battle! Jonathan lies slain upon your high places.

26 I am distressed for you, my brother Jonathan; very pleasant have you been to me. Your love to me was wonderful, passing the love of women.
27 How have the mighty fallen, and the weapons of war perished!

2 AFTER THIS, David inquired of the Lord, saying, Shall I go up into any of the cities of Judah? And the Lord said to him, Go up. David said, To which shall I go up? And He said, To Hebron.
2 So David went up there with his two wives, Ahinoam the Jezreelitess and Abigail, the widow of Nabal of Carmel.
3 And David brought up his men who were with him, each one with his household, and they dwelt in the towns of Hebron.
4 And the men of Judah came and there they anointed David king over the house of Judah. They told David, The men of Jabesh-gilead buried Saul. [I Sam. 31:11-13.]
5 And David sent messengers to the men of Jabesh-gilead, saying, May the Lord bless you because you showed kindness *and* loyalty to Saul your king and buried him.
6 And now may the Lord show loving-kindness and faithfulness to you. I also will do well by you because you have done this.
7 So now, let your hands be strengthened and be valiant, for your master Saul is dead, and the house of Judah has anointed me king over them.
8 Now Abner son of Ner, commander of Saul's army, took Ish-bosheth son of Saul and brought him over to Mahanaim.

speak the Word

God, I pray that You would show me Your loving-kindness and Your faithfulness, and that You would strengthen my hands and cause me to be valiant.
ADAPTED FROM II SAMUEL 2:6, 7

9 And he made him king over Gilead, the Ashurites, Jezreel, Ephraim, Benjamin, and all Israel.

10 Ish-bosheth, Saul's son, was forty years old when he began his two-year reign over Israel. But the house of Judah followed David.

11 And David was king in Hebron over the house of Judah for seven years and six months.

12 And Abner son of Ner and the servants of Ish-bosheth son of Saul went out from Mahanaim to Gibeon.

13 Joab son of Zeruiah and the servants of David went out also; and the two groups met by the pool of Gibeon, seating themselves with one group on either side of the pool.

14 And Abner said to Joab, Let the young men now arise and have a contest before us. And Joab said, Let them arise.

15 Then there arose and went over by number—twelve of Benjamin who were with Ish-bosheth son of Saul, and twelve of the servants of David.

16 And each caught his opponent by the head and thrust his sword into his side; so they all fell together. Therefore that place was called the Field of Sharp Knives, which is at Gibeon.

17 A very fierce battle followed, and Abner and the men of Israel were beaten before the servants of David.

18 Three sons of Zeruiah [the half sister of David] were there: Joab, Abishai, and Asahel. Now Asahel was as light of foot as a wild roe *or* antelope.

19 Asahel pursued Abner, and as he ran he turned not to the right hand or to the left from following Abner.

20 Then Abner looked behind him and said, Are you Asahel? He answered, I am.

21 Abner said to him, Turn aside to your right or left, and seize one of the young men and take his armor. But Asahel would not turn aside from following him.

22 And Abner said again to Asahel, Turn aside from following me. Why should I strike you to the ground? How then should I be able to face Joab your brother?

23 Asahel refused to turn aside; so Abner with the rear end of his spear smote him through the abdomen, and he fell and died where he fell. And all who came to the place where Asahel fell and died stood still.

24 But Joab and Abishai [his brothers] pursued Abner; the sun was going down as they came to the hill of Ammah, before Giah on the way to the wilderness of Gibeon.

25 And the Benjamites gathered together behind Abner and became one troop and took their stand on the top of a hill.

26 Then Abner called to Joab, Shall the sword devour forever? Do you not know that bitterness will be the result? How long will it be then before you bid the people to stop pursuing their brethren?

27 Joab said, As God lives, if you had not spoken, surely the men would have stopped pursuing their brethren in the morning.

28 So Joab blew a trumpet, and all the people stood still and pursued Israel no more, nor did they fight any more.

29 Abner and his men went all night through the Arabah [plain], crossed the Jordan, and went through the whole Bithron [district of ravines] and came to Mahanaim.

30 Joab returned from pursuing Abner, and when he had gathered all the people together, there were missing of David's servants nineteen men besides Asahel.

31 But the servants of David had slain of Benjamin 360 of Abner's men.

32 And they took up Asahel and buried him in the tomb of his father at Bethlehem. And Joab and his men walked all night and came to Hebron at daybreak.

3 THERE WAS a long war between the house of Saul and the house of David. But David grew stronger and stronger, and the house of Saul grew weaker and weaker.

2 Sons were born to David in Hebron: his firstborn was Amnon, by Ahinoam the Jezreelitess;

3 His second, Chileab, by Abigail widow of Nabal of Carmel; the third, Absalom the son of Maacah daughter of Talmai king of Geshur;

4 The fourth, Adonijah the son of Haggith; the fifth, Shephatiah the son of Abital;

5 And the sixth, Ithream, by Eglah, David's wife. These were born to David in Hebron.

6 While there was war between the houses of Saul and David, Abner was making himself strong in the house of Saul.

7 Now Saul had a concubine whose name was Rizpah daughter of Aiah. And Ish-bosheth said to Abner, Why have you gone in to my father's concubine?

8 Then Abner was very angry at the words of Ish-bosheth and said, Am I a dog's head [despicable and hostile] against Judah? This day I keep showing kindness *and* loyalty to the house of Saul your father, to his brothers, and his friends, and have not delivered you into the hands of David; and yet you charge me today with a fault concerning this woman!

9 May God do so to Abner, and more also, if I do not do for David what the Lord has sworn to him,

10 To transfer the kingdom from the house of Saul and set the throne of David over Israel and Judah from Dan to Beersheba.

11 And Ish-bosheth could not answer Abner a word, because he feared him.

12 And Abner sent messengers to David where he was [at Hebron], saying, Whose is the land? Make your league with me, and my hand shall be with you to bring all Israel over to you.

13 And David said, Good. I will make a league with you. But I require one thing of you: that is, you shall not see my face unless you first bring Michal, Saul's daughter, when you come to see me.

14 And David sent messengers to Ish-bosheth, Saul's son, saying, Give me my wife Michal, whom I betrothed for a hundred foreskins of the Philistines.

15 And Ish-bosheth sent and took her from her [second] husband, from Paltiel son of Laish [to whom Saul had given her].

16 But her husband went with her, weeping behind her all the way to Bahurim. Then Abner said to him, Go back. And he did so.

17 Abner talked with the seniors of Israel, saying, In times past you sought to make David king over you.

18 Now then, do it! For the Lord has spoken of David, saying, By the hand of My servant David I will save My people Israel from the hands of the Philistines and of all their enemies. [I Sam. 9:16.]

19 Abner also spoke to [the men of] Benjamin. Then [he] went to Hebron to tell David all that seemed good to Israel and the whole house of Benjamin to do.

20 So Abner came to David at Hebron, and twenty men along with him. And David made Abner and the men with him a feast.

21 Abner said to David, I will go and gather all Israel to my lord the king, that they may make a league with you, and that you may reign over all that your heart desires. So David sent Abner away in peace.

22 Then the servants of David came with Joab from pursuing a troop and brought much spoil with them. But Abner was not with David in Hebron, for he had sent him away, and he had gone in peace.

23 When Joab and all the army with him had come, it was told to Joab, Abner son of Ner came to the king, and he has sent him away, and he is gone in peace.
24 Then Joab came to the king and said, What have you done? Behold, Abner came to you. Why is it you have sent him away and he is quite gone?
25 You know that Abner son of Ner came to deceive you and to know your going out and coming in and all you are doing.
26 When Joab came from seeing David, he sent messengers after Abner, and they brought him back from the well of Sirah; but David did not know it.
27 And when Abner returned to Hebron, Joab took him aside to the center of the gate to speak to him privately, and there he smote Abner in the abdomen, so that he died to avenge the blood of Asahel, Joab's brother.
28 When David heard of it, he said, I and my kingdom are guiltless before the Lord forever of the blood of Abner son of Ner.
29 Let it fall on the head of Joab and on all his father's house; and let the house of Joab never be without one who has a discharge or is a leper or walks with a crutch or is a distaff holder [unfit for war] or who falls by the sword or lacks food!
30 So Joab and Abishai his brother slew Abner because he had slain their brother Asahel at Gibeon in the battle.
31 And David said to Joab and to all the people with him, Rend your clothes, gird yourselves with sackcloth, and mourn before Abner. And King David followed the bier.
32 They buried Abner in Hebron. And the king lifted up his voice and wept at the grave of Abner, and all the people wept.
33 And the king lamented over Abner and said, Should Abner die as a fool dies?
34 Your hands were not bound or your feet put into fetters; as a man falls before wicked men, so you fell. And all the people wept again over him.
35 All the people came to urge David to eat food while it was yet day; but David took an oath, saying, May God do so to me, and more also, if I taste bread or anything else, till the sun is down.
36 And all the people took notice of it, and it pleased them, as whatever the king did pleased all the people.
37 For all the people and all Israel understood that day that it was not the king's will to slay Abner son of Ner.
38 King David said to his servants, Do you not know that a prince and a great man has fallen this day in Israel?
39 And I am this day weak, though anointed [but not crowned] king; these sons of Zeruiah are too hard for me. May the Lord repay the evildoer according to his wickedness!

4 WHEN ISH-BOSHETH, Saul's son [king over Israel], heard that Abner was dead in Hebron, his courage failed, and all the Israelites were troubled *and* dismayed.
2 Saul's son had two men who were captains of raiding bands. One was named Baanah and the other Rechab, sons of Rimmon the Beerothite of Benjamin—for Beeroth also was reckoned to Benjamin,
3 And the Beerothites fled to Gittaim and have been sojourners there to this day.
4 Jonathan, Saul's son, had a son who was a cripple in his feet. He was five years old when the news came out of Jezreel [of the deaths] of Saul and Jonathan. And the boy's nurse took him up and fled; and in her

haste, he fell and became lame. His name was Mephibosheth.

life point

Second Samuel 4:4 tells the story of Jonathan's young son named Mephibosheth. When his nurse heard the dreadful news that Saul and Jonathan had been killed in battle, she feared that David might try to take vengeance on the boy because of the terrible way Saul had treated David. She ran from the palace with the young child in her arms, dropping him in her escape attempt. This left him lame in both feet. He would have to live the rest of his life handicapped for something that was not even his fault.

Many of us have crippled self-images that prevent us from receiving all God has for us. If you have a poor self-image, as I did, I recommend that you read the end of Mephibosheth's story, which is found in II Samuel, chapter 9. The story of his restoration greatly affected my life, and I believe it will do the same for you. It will help you see not only why you are living far below the level that God intends for you now, but also why you are in danger of missing out on what He has in mind for you in the future—and I do not want you to miss the great things He has in store for you!

5 Now the sons of Rimmon the Beerothite, Rechab and Baanah, went about in the heat of the day to the house of Ish-bosheth, who lay resting on his bed at noon.
6 And they came into the interior of the house as though they were delivering wheat, and they smote him in the body; and Rechab and Baanah his brother escaped.
7 Now when they had come into the house and he lay on his bed in his bedroom, they [not only] smote and slew him, [but] beheaded him and took his head and went by the way of the plain all night.
8 And they brought the head of Ish-bosheth to David at Hebron and said to the king, Behold, the head of Ish-bosheth son of Saul, your enemy, who sought your life; and the Lord has avenged my lord the king this day on Saul and on his offspring.
9 And David answered Rechab and Baanah his brother, sons of Rimmon the Beerothite, As the Lord lives, Who redeemed my life out of all adversity,
10 When one told me, Behold, Saul is dead, thinking he was bringing good news, I seized and slew him in Ziklag who expected me to give him a reward for his news.
11 How much more—when wicked men have slain a just man in his own house on his bed—shall I not now require his blood of your hand and remove you from the earth!
12 David commanded his young men, and they slew them and cut off their hands and feet and hanged them over the pool in Hebron. But they took Ish-bosheth's head and buried it in Hebron in the tomb of Abner [his relative and once chief supporter].

5 THEN ALL the tribes of Israel came to David at Hebron and said, Behold, we are your bone and your flesh.
2 In times past, when Saul was king over us, it was you who led out and brought in Israel. And the Lord told you, You shall feed My people Israel and be prince over [them]. [I Sam. 15:27-29; 16:1.]
3 So all the elders of Israel came to the king at Hebron, and King David made a covenant with them [there] before the Lord, and they anointed [him] king over Israel.
4 David was thirty years old when he began his forty-year reign.

5 In Hebron he reigned over Judah seven years and six months, and in Jerusalem he reigned thirty-three years over all Israel and Judah.
6 And the king and his men went to Jerusalem against the Jebusites, the inhabitants of the land, who said to David, You shall not enter here, for the blind and the lame will prevent you; they thought, David cannot come in here.
7 Nevertheless, David took the stronghold of Zion, that is, the City of David.
8 David said on that day, Whoever smites the Jebusites, let him get up through the water shaft and smite the lame and the blind who are detested by David's soul. So they say, The blind and the lame shall not come into the house.
9 So David dwelt in the stronghold and called it the City of David. And he built round about from the Millo and inward.
10 David became greater and greater, for the Lord God of hosts was with him.
11 Hiram king of Tyre sent messengers to David, and cedar trees, carpenters, and masons; and they built David a house.
12 And David perceived that the Lord had established him king over Israel and that He had exalted his kingdom for His people Israel's sake.
13 And David took more concubines and wives out of Jerusalem, after he came from Hebron, and other sons and daughters were born to [him].

putting the Word to work

In II Samuel 5:12, we see that David "perceived that the Lord had established him king over Israel and that He had exalted his kingdom for His people Israel's sake." Can you perceive what God wants to do in you and through you and why? Ask Him to help you understand what He is establishing in you right now and what purposes of His can be served through you, just as His purposes were served through David.

14 And these are the names of those who were born to him in Jerusalem: Shammua, Shobab, Nathan, Solomon,
15 Ibhar, Elishua, Nepheg, Japhia,
16 Elishama, Eliada, and Eliphelet.
17 When the Philistines heard that David had been anointed king over Israel, they all went up to find [him], but [he] heard of it and went down to the stronghold.
18 The Philistines also came and spread themselves in the Valley of Rephaim.
19 David inquired of the Lord, saying, Shall I go up against the Philistines? Will You deliver them into my hand? And the Lord said to David, Go up, for I will surely deliver [them] into your hand.
20 And David came to Baal-perazim, and he smote them there, and said, The Lord has broken through my enemies before me, like the bursting out

speak the Word

God, I pray that You would make me greater and greater in You and for You because You are with me.
ADAPTED FROM II SAMUEL 5:10

Thank You, God, that You break through my enemies before me, like the bursting out of great waters.
ADAPTED FROM II SAMUEL 5:20

of great waters. So he called the name of that place Baal-perazim [Lord of breaking through].

21 There the Philistines left their [a]images, and David and his men took them away.

22 The Philistines came up again and spread themselves out in the Valley of Rephaim.

23 When David inquired of the Lord, He said, You shall not go up, but go around behind them and come upon them over opposite the mulberry (or balsam) trees.

24 And when you hear the sound of marching in the tops of the mulberry trees, then bestir yourselves, for then has the Lord gone out before you to smite the army of the Philistines.

25 And David did as the Lord had commanded him, and smote the Philistines from Geba to Gezer.

6 AGAIN DAVID gathered together all the chosen men of Israel, 30,000.

2 And [he] arose and went with all the people who were with him to Baale-judah [Kiriath-jearim] to bring up from there the ark of God, which is called by the name of the Lord of hosts, Who sits enthroned above the cherubim.

3 And they set the ark of God upon a new cart and brought it [b]out of the house of Abinadab, which was on the hill; and Uzzah and Ahio, sons of Abinadab, drove the new cart.

4 And they brought it out of the house of Abinadab, which was on the hill, with the ark of God; and Ahio went before the ark.

5 And David and all the house of Israel played before the Lord with all their might, with songs, lyres, harps, tambourines, castanets, and cymbals.

6 And when they came to Nacon's threshing floor, Uzzah put out his hand to the ark of God and took hold of it, for the oxen stumbled *and* shook it.

7 And the anger of the Lord was kindled against Uzzah; and God smote him there for touching the ark, and he died there by the ark of God.

life point

Uzzah disobeyed God by touching the ark, and, as a result, he was killed (see II Samuel 6:6, 7). I believe that Uzzah reached out to steady the ark because it had been kept in his father's house for a long time and had become familiar to him. We must not ever regard the holy as commonplace, but keep a reverent attitude toward sacred things (God's Word, prayer, worship, God's presence, etc.) and not allow them to become so familiar that we dishonor them.

We should always keep a sense of awe and wonder about the things of God.

8 David was grieved *and* offended because the Lord had broken forth upon Uzzah, and that place is called Perez-uzzah [the breaking forth upon Uzzah] to this day.

9 David was afraid of the Lord that day and said, How can the ark of the Lord come to me?

10 So David was not willing to take the ark of the Lord to him into the City of David; but he took it aside into the house of Obed-edom the Gittite.

11 And the ark of the Lord remained in the house of Obed-edom the Gittite for three months, and the Lord blessed Obed-edom and all his household.

a The Israelites took as spoil the images of the Philistines, perhaps to display in triumphal procession, though they were afterward burned (I Chron. 14:12) in compliance with the law of Deut. 7:5, 25. Thus the old disgrace of the capture of the ark by the Philistines was avenged (I Sam. 4:4, 10, 11) (*The Cambridge Bible*).   b How long had the ark been in the house of Abinadab (see I Sam. 7:2)?

putting the Word to work

When the ark of the Lord, which represents God's presence, was in Obed-edom's house, Obed-edom and all of his household were blessed (see II Samuel 6:11). Is God welcome in your home, and are you enjoying the blessings of His presence upon your house and your family? Tell Him today that you want His presence to fill your home and to be with everyone who lives there.

12 And it was told King David, The Lord has blessed the house of Obed-edom and all that belongs to him, because of the ark of God. So David went and brought up the ark of God from the house of Obed-edom into the City of David with rejoicing;

13 And when those who bore the ark of the Lord had gone six paces, he sacrificed an ox and a fatling.

14 And David danced before the Lord with all his might, clad in a linen ephod [a priest's upper garment].

15 So David and all the house of Israel brought up the ark of the Lord with shouting and with the sound of the trumpet.

16 As the ark of the Lord came into the City of David, Michal, Saul's daughter [David's wife], looked out of the window and saw King David leaping and dancing before the Lord, and she despised him in her heart.

17 They brought in the ark of the Lord and set it in its place inside the tent which David had pitched for it, and David offered burnt offerings and peace offerings before the Lord.

18 When David had finished offering the burnt offerings and peace offerings, he blessed the people in the name [and presence] of the Lord of hosts,

19 And distributed among all the people, the whole multitude of Israel, both to men and women, to each a cake of bread, a portion of meat, and a cake of raisins. So all the people departed, each to his house.

20 Then David returned to bless his household. And [his wife] Michal daughter of Saul came out to meet David and said, How glorious was the king of Israel today, who stripped himself of his kingly robes *and* uncovered himself in the eyes of his servants' maids as one of the worthless fellows shamelessly uncovers himself!

21 David said to Michal, It was before the Lord, Who chose me above your father and all his house to appoint me as prince over Israel, the people of the Lord. Therefore will I make merry [in pure enjoyment] before the Lord.

22 I will be still more lightly esteemed than this, and will humble *and* lower myself in my own sight [and yours]. But by the maids you mentioned, I will be held in honor.

putting the Word to work

In II Samuel 6:14–16, King David danced and worshipped God in a very demonstrative way, and his wife was embarrassed and despised him for his display of praise to God. In II Samuel 6:21–23, David tells her that he will continue to worship even more fervently and boldly than before. Are you expressing your worship to God as passionately as you possibly can, regardless of what people think? Go ahead; follow David's example in II Samuel 6:21, and express your "pure enjoyment" in God.

23 And Michal the daughter of Saul had no child to the day of her death.

7 WHEN KING David dwelt in his house and the Lord had given him rest from all his surrounding enemies,

2 The king said to Nathan the

prophet, See now, I dwell in a house of cedar, but the ark of God dwells within curtains.

3   And Nathan said to the king, Go, do all that is in your heart, for the Lord is with you.

4   That night the word of the Lord came to Nathan, saying,

5   Go and tell My servant David, Thus says the Lord: Shall you build Me a house in which to dwell?

6   For I have not dwelt in a house since I brought the Israelites out of Egypt to this day, but have moved about with a tent for My dwelling.

7   In all the places where I have moved with all the Israelites, did I speak a word to any from the tribes of Israel whom I commanded to be shepherd of My people Israel, asking, Why do you not build Me a house of cedar?

8   So now say this to My servant David, Thus says the Lord of hosts: I took you from the pasture, from following the sheep, to be prince over My people Israel.

9   And I was with you wherever you went, and have cut off all your enemies from before you; and I will make you a great name, like [that] of the great men of the earth.

10   And I will appoint a place for My people Israel and will plant them, that they may dwell in a place of their own and be moved no more. And wicked men shall afflict them no more, as formerly

11   And as from the time that I appointed judges over My people Israel; and I will cause you to rest from all your enemies. Also the Lord

declares to you that He will make for you a house:

12   And when your days are fulfilled and you sleep with your fathers, I will set up after you your offspring who shall be born to you, and I will establish his kingdom.

13   He shall build a house for My ᶜName [and My Presence], and I will establish the throne of his kingdom forever.

14   I will be his Father, and he shall be My son. When he commits iniquity, I will chasten him with the rod of men and with the stripes of the sons of men.

15   But My mercy *and* loving-kindness shall not depart from him, as I took [them] from Saul, whom I took away from before you.

16   And your house and your kingdom shall be made sure forever before you; your throne shall be established forever.

17   In accordance with all these words and all this vision Nathan spoke to David.

18   Then King David went in and sat before the Lord, and said, Who am I, O Lord God, and what is my house, that You have brought me this far?

19   Then as if this were a little thing in Your eyes, O Lord God, You have spoken also of Your servant's house in the far distant future. And this is the law for man, O Lord God!

20   What more can David say to You? For You know Your servant, O Lord God.

21   Because of Your promise and as Your own heart dictates, You have

speak the Word

c "Name" is equivalent to "Me" in II Sam. 7:5. See also footnote on Deut. 12:5.

done all these astounding things to make Your servant know *and* understand.

22 Therefore You are great, O Lord God; for none is like You, nor is there any God besides You, according to all [You have made] our ears to hear.

23 What [other] one nation on earth is like Your people Israel, whom God went to redeem to be a people for Himself and to make for Himself a name? You have done great and terrible things for Yourself *and* for Your land, before Your people, whom You redeemed *and* delivered for Yourself from Egypt, from the nations and their gods.

24 And You have established for Yourself Your people Israel to be Your people forever, and You, Lord, became their God.

25 Now, O Lord God, confirm forever the word You have given as to Your servant and his house; and do as You have said,

26 And Your name [and presence] shall be magnified forever, saying, The Lord of hosts is God over Israel; and the house of Your servant David will be made firm before You.

27 For You, O Lord of hosts, God of Israel, have revealed this to Your servant: I will build you a house. So Your servant has found courage to pray this prayer to You.

28 And now, O Lord God, You are God, and Your words are truth, and You have promised this good thing to Your servant.

29 Therefore now let it please You to bless the house of Your servant, that it may continue forever before You; for You, O Lord God, have spoken it, and with Your blessing let [his] house be blessed forever.

8 AFTER THIS David smote the Philistines and subdued them, and he took Metheg-ammah out of the hands of the Philistines.

2 He defeated Moab, and measured them with a line, making them lie down on the ground; two lines he measured to be put to death, and one full line to keep alive. And the Moabites became servants to David, bringing tribute.

3 David also defeated Hadadezer son of Rehob, king of Zobah, as he went to restore his power at the river [Euphrates].

4 David took from him 1,700 horsemen and 20,000 foot soldiers; and David hamstrung all the chariot horses, except he reserved enough of them for 100 chariots.

5 And when the Syrians of Damascus came to help Hadadezer king of Zobah, David slew 22,000 of them.

6 David put garrisons in Syrian Damascus, and the Syrians became [his] servants and brought tribute. The Lord preserved *and* gave victory to David wherever he went.

7 And David took the shields of gold that were on the servants of Hadadezer and brought them to Jerusalem.

8 And from Betah and Berothai, cities of Hadadezer, King David exacted an immense amount of bronze.

9 When Toi king of Hamath heard about David's defeat of all the forces of Hadadezer,

10 [He] sent Joram his son to King David to salute *and* congratulate him about his battle and defeat of Hadadezer. For Hadadezer had had wars with Toi. Joram brought vessels of silver, gold, and bronze.

11 These King David dedicated to the Lord, with the silver and gold that he had dedicated from all the nations he subdued:

12 From Syria, Moab, the Ammonites, the Philistines, Amalek, and from the spoil of Hadadezer son of Rehob, king of Zobah.

13 David won renown. When he returned he slew 18,000 Edomites in the Valley of Salt.

14 He put garrisons throughout all Edom, and all the Edomites became his servants. And the Lord preserved *and* gave victory to [him] wherever he went.

15 So David reigned over all Israel, and executed justice and righteousness for all his people.

16 Joab son of Zeruiah was over the army; Jehoshaphat son of Ahilud was recorder;

17 Zadok son of Ahitub and Ahimelech son of Abiathar were the [chief] priests, and Seraiah was the scribe;

18 Benaiah son of Jehoiada was over both the Cherethites and Pelethites [the king's bodyguards]; and David's sons were chief [confidential] assistants to the king.

9 AND DAVID said, Is there still anyone left of the house of Saul to whom I may show kindness for Jonathan's sake?

2 And of the house of Saul there was a servant whose name was Ziba. When they had called him to David, he said to him, Are you Ziba? He said, I, your servant, am he.

3 The king said, Is there not still someone of the house of Saul to whom I may show the [unfailing, unsought, unlimited] mercy *and* kindness of God? Ziba replied, Jonathan has yet a son who is lame in his feet. [I Sam. 20:14-17.]

4 And the king said, Where is he? Ziba replied, He is in the house of Machir son of Ammiel in Lo-debar.

5 Then King David sent and brought him from the house of Machir son of Ammiel at Lo-debar.

6 And Mephibosheth son of Jonathan, the son of Saul, came to David and fell on his face and did obeisance. David said, Mephibosheth! And he answered, Behold your servant!

7 David said to him, Fear not, for I will surely show you kindness for Jonathan your father's sake, and will restore to you all the land of Saul your father [grandfather], and you shall eat at my table always.

life point

Mephibosheth had been living for years in a small town called Lo-debar (see II Samuel 9:3, 4). The name *Lo-debar* means "pasture-less." In an agricultural society, a place without pastures was probably a place of poverty; it certainly was not a nice or popular town.

When our self-image is poor, we often choose surroundings that seem to fit the way we feel about ourselves. I have noticed that some people who are filled with self-loathing will not bother to fix themselves up or even try to dress or look nice. The way they feel about themselves inside shows on the outside. Other people go to the opposite extreme. They feel so bad about themselves inwardly that they try to hide it by becoming perfectionists outwardly. Everything around them has to appear to be perfect—their homes, personal appearance, children, spouse, and everything else. They live under tremendous pressure, and they put pressure on the people around them. We all need to realize that God wants to bless us in spite of our imperfections. Our worth and value are not found in outward things but knowing in our hearts who we are in Christ. Relax and learn to receive from God.

God wants you to have peace knowing that your imperfections will not and cannot stop Him from working in your life. God does not want you to live, like Mephibosheth, in a barren place, but to experience His unlimited kindness. He delights in being merciful!

8 And [the cripple] bowed himself and said, What is your servant, that you should look upon such a dead dog as I am?

looking for people to bless

David desired to bless someone in Saul's family because of a covenant he had made with his friend Jonathan (see I Samuel 18:3; 20:14–16). As he looked for Jonathan's descendants, he discovered that Jonathan's crippled son, Mephibosheth, was alive but living in less-than-desirable circumstances (see II Samuel 9:3, 4).

Just as David searched for someone he could be kind to for Jonathan's sake, God looks for people He can be kind to for Jesus' sake. God is merciful and kind; He is constantly extending His kindness toward us, but we must be willing to accept it.

David's covenant relationship with Jonathan included all of Jonathan's children. I believe Mephibosheth never exercised his covenant rights because of the negative way he felt about himself. Many of God's children do the same thing. They shrink back from God in fear rather than approaching Him boldly. They feel badly about themselves; they look at everything that is wrong with them instead of looking at Jesus and the righteousness He offers through faith in Him. Mephibosheth actually referred to himself as a "dead dog" (II Samuel 9:8). He had a poor self-image and, although David would have helped him at any time had he only asked, he never asked because he felt unworthy.

We can all learn a good lesson from Mephibosheth. God's goodness and mercy, and His willingness to help us, are not based on our perfection, but on our covenant with His Son, Jesus. When we are "in Christ," we are included in that covenant and can go boldly to the throne and receive mercy and help in plenty of time to meet all of our needs. Even though Mephibosheth was lame in both feet, he ultimately received the mercy David offered and ate at the king's table (see II Samuel 9:13).

We do not have to talk God into being good to us. He is good; and He is looking for someone to bless for Jesus' sake. Make a decision to start receiving what you do not deserve and have not earned. As you do, you will be living in God's awesome grace, which is freely available to all who will receive it.

9 Then the king called to Ziba, Saul's servant, and said to him, I have given your master's son [grandson] all that belonged to Saul and to all his house.

10 And you shall till the land for him, you, your sons, and your servants, and you shall bring in the produce, that your master's heir may have food to eat; but Mephibosheth, your master's son [grandson], shall eat always at my table. Now Ziba had fifteen sons and twenty servants.

11 Then Ziba said to the king, Your servant will do according to all my lord the king commands. So Mephibosheth ate at David's table as one of the king's sons.

12 Mephibosheth had a young son whose name was Micha. And all who dwelt in Ziba's house were servants to Mephibosheth.

13 So Mephibosheth dwelt in Jerusalem, for he ate continually at the king's table, [even though] he was lame in both feet.

no more dead dogs

Mephibosheth had a poor self-image, a dead-dog image (see II Samuel 9:8). He did not think very well of himself. Instead of seeing himself as the rightful heir of Jonathan (King David's covenant friend), he saw himself as someone who would be rejected. If this were not true, he would have already gone to the palace long before to claim his inheritance.

A poor self-image causes us to operate in fear instead of faith. We look at what is wrong with us instead of what is right with Jesus. He has taken our wrongness and given us His righteousness (see II Corinthians 5:21). We need to walk in the reality of that truth.

When I saw that Mephibosheth thought of himself as a "dead dog," I realized that I also had a dead-dog image that was hindering me from being all I could be and having all I could have in life. I started changing my attitude toward myself. It took time and a lot of help from the Holy Spirit, but I determined that I would not live below the blessed life Jesus had provided for me.

God's Word says that because of His covenant with you, you can be the "head, and not the tail . . . above only, and you shall not be beneath" (Deuteronomy 28:13). I am sure that, like me, you have been the tail long enough. It is time to take a stand and start receiving your rightful inheritance.

David blessed Mephibosheth. He gave him servants and provided for all of his needs. The story ends by saying that Mephibosheth dwelled in Jerusalem and ate at the king's table, even though "he was lame in both feet" (II Samuel 9:13).

I absolutely love the end of the story! I relate Mephibosheth's lameness to our own weaknesses. We may also fellowship and eat with our King, Jesus—even though we have faults and weaknesses. We still have a covenant with God, sealed and ratified in the blood of Jesus Christ. A blood covenant was, and still is, one of the strongest agreements that can be made between two parties.

In covenant, we offer God what we have, and He gives us what He has. He takes all of our sins, faults, weaknesses, and failures, and gives us His ability, His righteousness, and His strength. He takes our poverty and gives us His riches. He takes our diseases and sicknesses and gives us His healing and health. He takes our messed up, failure-filled pasts and gives us the hope of bright futures. In ourselves we are nothing; our own righteousness is like "filthy rags or a polluted garment" (Isaiah 64:6). But in Christ we have a future. We are in covenant with Almighty God. What an awesome truth!

10

LATER, THE king of the Ammonites died, and Hanun his son reigned in his stead.

2 David said, I will show kindness to Hanun son of Nahash, as his father did to me. So David sent his servants to console him for his father's death; and they came into the land of the Ammonites,

3 But the princes of the Ammonites said to Hanun their lord, Do you think that it is because David honors your father that he has sent comforters to you? Has he not rather sent his servants to you to search the city, spy it out, and overthrow it?

4 So Hanun took David's servants and shaved off half their beards and cut off their garments in the middle at their hips and sent them away.

5 When it was told David, he sent to meet them, for the men were greatly ashamed. And the king said, Tarry at Jericho until your beards are grown, and then return.

6 And when the Ammonites saw that they had made themselves obnoxious *and* disgusting to David, they sent and hired the Syrians of Beth-rehob and of Zobah, 20,000 foot soldiers, and of the king of Maacah 1,000 men, and of Tob 12,000 men.

7 When David heard of it, he sent Joab and all the army of the mighty men.

8 And the Ammonites came out and put the battle in array at the entrance of the gate, but the Syrians of Zobah and of Rehob and the men of Tob and Maacah were stationed by themselves in the open country.

9 When Joab saw that the battlefront was against him before and behind, he picked some of all the choice men of Israel and put them in array against the Syrians.

10 The rest of the men Joab gave over to Abishai his brother, that he might put them in array against the Ammonites.

11 Joab said, If the Syrians are too strong for me, then you shall help me; but if the Ammonites are too strong for you, I will come and help you.

12 Be of good courage; let us play the man for our people and the cities of our God. And may the Lord do what seems good to Him.

13 And Joab and the people who were with him drew near to battle against the Syrians, and they fled before him.

14 And when the Ammonites saw that the Syrians had fled, they also fled before Abishai and entered the city. So Joab returned from battling against the Ammonites and came to Jerusalem.

15 When the Syrians saw that they were defeated by Israel, they gathered together.

16 Hadadezer sent and brought the Syrians who were beyond the river [Euphrates]; and they came to Helam, with Shobach commander of the army of Hadadezer leading them.

17 When David was told, he gathered all Israel, crossed the Jordan, and came to Helam. Then the Syrians set themselves in array against David and fought with him.

18 The Syrians fled before Israel, and David slew of [them] the men of 700 chariots and 40,000 horsemen and smote Shobach captain of their army, who died there.

19 And when all the kings serving Hadadezer saw that they were defeated by Israel, they made peace with Israel and served them. So the Syrians were afraid to help the Ammonites any more.

11

IN THE spring, when kings go forth to battle, David sent Joab with his servants and all Israel, and they ravaged the

putting the Word to work

One of the reasons David fell into sin with Bathsheba was that he was not where he was supposed to be when he was supposed to be there. According to II Samuel 11:1, during the springtime, he should have been on the battlefield instead of in Jerusalem. Do you try to follow God's leading in every situation so that you will be at the right place at the right time? Ask Him to help you. He wants you to be perfectly positioned, far away from sin and in a place where you can receive His blessings.

Ammonites [country] and besieged Rabbah. But David remained in Jerusalem.

2 One evening David arose from his couch and was walking on the roof of the king's house, when from there he saw a woman bathing; and she was very lovely to behold.

3 David sent and inquired about the woman. One said, Is not this Bathsheba, the daughter of Eliam and the wife of Uriah the Hittite?

4 And David sent messengers and took her. And she came in to him, and he lay with her—for she was purified from her uncleanness. Then she returned to her house.

5 And the woman became pregnant and sent and told David, I am with child.

6 David sent to Joab, saying, Send me Uriah the Hittite. So Joab sent [him] Uriah.

7 When Uriah had come to him, David asked him how Joab was, how the people fared, and how the war progressed.

8 David said to Uriah, Go down to your house and wash your feet. Uriah went out of the king's house, and there followed him a mess of food [a gift] from the king.

9 But Uriah slept at the door of the king's house with all the servants of his lord and did not go down to his house.

10 When they told David, Uriah did not go down to his house, David said to Uriah, Have you not come from a journey? Why did you not go down to your house?

11 Uriah said to David, The ark and Israel and Judah live in tents, and my lord Joab and the servants of my lord are camping in the open field. Shall I then go to my house to eat and drink and lie with my wife? As you live and as my soul lives, I will not do this thing.

12 And David said to Uriah, Remain here today also, and tomorrow I will let you depart. So Uriah remained in Jerusalem that day and the next.

13 David invited him, and he ate with him and drank, so that he made him drunk; but that night he went out to lie on his bed with the servants of his lord and did not go down to his house.

14 In the morning David wrote a letter to Joab and sent it with Uriah.

15 And he wrote in the letter, Put Uriah in the front line of the heaviest fighting and withdraw from him, that he may be struck down and die.

16 So when Joab was besieging the city, he assigned Uriah opposite where he knew the enemy's most valiant men were.

17 And the men of the city came out and fought with Joab, and some of the servants of David fell. Uriah the Hittite died also.

18 Then Joab sent and told David all the things concerning the war.

19 And he charged the messenger, When you have finished reporting matters of the war to the king,

20 Then if the king's anger rises and he says to you, Why did you go so near to the city to fight? Did you not know they would shoot from the wall?

21 Who killed Abimelech son of

life point

Sin always leads to more sin, as it did when David ordered that Uriah be killed after he had committed adultery with his wife (see II Samuel 11:15). When we do sin, we must repent and receive God's forgiveness quickly. That way, we do not become ensnared in a web of sin, but we stay clean and pure before God. David did not repent for a long time, and, in God's eyes, the fact that he covered up his sin was worse than the original sin he had committed. We can receive forgiveness if we admit we have sinned and repent, but if we hide sin and make excuses, we remain in it and live deceived lives.

Jerubbesheth (Gideon)? Did not a woman cast an upper millstone upon him from the wall, so that he died in Thebez? Why did you go near the wall? Then say, Your servant Uriah the Hittite is dead also. [Judg. 9:35, 53.]
22 So the messenger went and told David all for which Joab had sent him.
23 The messenger said to David, Surely the men prevailed against us and came out to us in to the field, but we were upon them even to the entrance of the gate.
24 Then the archers shot at your servants from the wall. Some of the king's servants are dead, and your servant Uriah the Hittite is dead also.
25 Then David said to the messenger, Say to Joab, Let not this thing disturb you, for the sword devours one as well as another. Strengthen your attack upon the city and overthrow it. And encourage Joab.
26 When Uriah's wife heard that her husband was dead, she mourned for Uriah.
27 And when the mourning was past,

David sent and brought her to his house, and she became his wife and bore him a son. But the thing that David had done was evil in the sight of the Lord.

12 AND THE Lord sent Nathan to David. He came and said to him, There were two men in a city, one rich and the other poor.
2 The rich man had very many flocks and herds,
3 But the poor man had nothing but one little ewe lamb which he had bought and brought up, and it grew up with him and his children. It ate of his own morsel, drank from his own cup, lay in his bosom, and was like a daughter to him.
4 Now a traveler came to the rich man, and to avoid taking one of his own flock or herd to prepare for the wayfaring man who had come to him, he took the poor man's lamb and prepared it for his guest.
5 Then David's anger was greatly kindled against the man, and he said to Nathan, As the Lord lives, the man who has done this is a son [worthy] of death.
6 He shall restore the lamb fourfold, because he did this thing and had no pity.
7 Then Nathan said to David, You are the man! Thus says the Lord, the God of Israel: I anointed you king of Israel, and I delivered you out of the hand of Saul.
8 And I gave you your master's house, and your master's wives into your bosom, and gave you the house of Israel and of Judah; and if that had been too little, I would have added that much again.
9 Why have you despised the commandment of the Lord, doing evil in His sight? You have slain Uriah the Hittite with the sword and have taken his wife to be your wife. You have

the gift of repentance

David had committed adultery with Bathsheba and made arrangements to have her husband killed so that he could cover his sin (see II Samuel 11:1–15). Time had passed, and he was still ignoring the issue. He was probably doing what we are all tempted to do when we sin—he was making excuses and being deceived by his own reasoning. All of us may not deal with sins as serious as what David was facing, but sin is sin, and it has a similar effect on us, no matter what type of sin it is. The point is, until we admit it, confess and repent of our sin (which is to turn entirely away from it and go in another direction), we will not be able to worship God out of a pure heart or with a clean conscience. King David was quite miserable until he finally repented of his sin. His joy returned only after he repented (see Psalm 32:1–7).

I am very thankful for the gift of repentance. Why do I refer to repentance as a gift? I have seen people who could not feel sorry for their sins, and that is a terrible thing. When the conscience is seared (hardened), people are unable to feel the weight and seriousness of their wrong behavior. Because of this, we should all pray for a tender conscience toward God.

First John 1:9 states that we can admit our sins, confess them, and that God is faithful to completely cleanse us of all unrighteousness. What good news! We can live before God with a perfectly clear conscience.

murdered him with the sword of the Ammonites. [Lev. 20:10; 24:17.]

10 Now, therefore, the sword shall never depart from your house, because [you have not only despised My command, but] you have despised Me and have taken the wife of Uriah the Hittite to be your wife.

11 Thus says the Lord, Behold, I will raise up evil against you out of your ᵈown house; and I will take your wives before your eyes and give them to your neighbor, and he shall lie with your wives in the sight of this sun.

12 For you did it secretly, but I will do this thing before all Israel and before the sun. [Fulfilled in II Sam. 16:21, 22.]

13 And David said to Nathan, I have sinned against the Lord. And Nathan said to David, The Lord also has put away your sin; you shall not die. [Ps. 51.]

14 Nevertheless, because by this deed you have utterly scorned the Lord *and* given great occasion to the enemies of the Lord to blaspheme, the child that is born to you shall surely die.

15 Then Nathan departed to his

d This sentence was fulfilled in the agony brought on David by his lawless children: Amnon's scandalous behavior with his half sister Tamar (13:14) and his consequent murder by his brother Absalom (13:28, 29); Absalom's escape to a foreign land (13:38) and his return after three years; Absalom without recognition by David for two more years (14:28); Absalom's deliberate, rebellious attempt to win the hearts of the people and supplant his father (15:6); David's flight from Jerusalem, with the mass of the people against him (15:14), the terrible battle in the forest of Ephraim, won by David's forces, with Absalom killed in flight (18:6ff.). David's agony of heart is echoed repeatedly in the history of these tragedies [II Sam. 13:1–19:8] and in some of his psalms. Even when the great king was dying, his son Adonijah was attempting to usurp the throne, and was later executed as a traitor (II Kings 1:5; 2:25).

house. And the Lord struck the child that Uriah's widow bore to David, and he was very sick.

16 David therefore besought God for the child; and David fasted and went in and lay all night [repeatedly] on the floor.

17 His older house servants arose [in the night] and went to him to raise him up from the floor, but he would not, nor did he eat food with them.

18 And on the seventh day the child died. David's servants feared to tell him that the child was dead, for they said, While the child was yet alive, we spoke to him and he would not listen to our voices; will he then harm himself if we tell him the child is dead?

19 But when David saw that his servants whispered, he perceived that the child was dead. So he said to them, Is the child dead? And they said, He is.

20 Then David arose from the floor, washed, anointed himself, changed his apparel, and went into the house of the Lord and worshiped. Then he came to his own house, and when he asked, they set food before him, and he ate.

21 Then his servants said to him, What is this that you have done? You fasted and wept while the child was alive, but when the child was dead, you arose and ate food.

22 David said, While the child was still alive, I fasted and wept; for I said, Who knows whether the Lord will be gracious to me and let the child live?

23 But now he is dead; why should I fast? Can I bring him back again? I shall go to him, but he will not return to me.

24 David comforted Bathsheba his wife, and went to her and lay with her; and she bore a son, and she called his name Solomon. And the Lord loved [the child];

25 He sent [a message] by the hand of Nathan the prophet, and [Nathan] called the boy's [special] name Jedidi-

beyond grief

What was David saying in II Samuel 12:20–23? He was saying: "When my child was sick, I did everything I could to save him. Now that he is dead, there is nothing more I can do. Why should I sit around mourning over something I cannot change? It is much better for me if I get up and get on with my life."

That is what the Lord is encouraging us to do today. He is telling us to stop mourning over what has happened in the past and to make the decision to live today and every day for the rest of our lives. He is telling us not to ruin the time we have left by grieving what has been lost.

I am not saying that we should not go through a period of mourning when we experience loss. Going through a grief process is normal and right. What I *am* saying is that when we allow our grief to go on and on without a resolution, it becomes destructive and turns into self-pity.

Make a vow right now that from this moment on you are not going to waste any more of your valuable time feeling sorry for yourself and grieving over things you cannot change. Instead, pledge that you are going to live each day to the fullest, looking forward to what God has in store for you as you follow Him.

ah [beloved of the Lord], because the Lord [loved the child].

26 Now Joab fought against Rabbah of the Ammonites and took the royal city.

27 And Joab sent messengers to David and said, I have fought against Rabbah, and have taken the city of waters.

28 Now therefore assemble the rest of the men, encamp against the city, and take it, lest I take the city, and it be called after my name.

29 So David gathered all the men, went to Rabbah, fought against it, and took it.

30 And he took the crown of their king [of Malcham] from his head; the weight of it was a talent of gold, and in it were precious stones; and it was set on David's head. And he brought forth exceedingly much spoil from the city.

31 And he brought forth the people who were there, and put them to [work with] saws and iron threshing sledges and axes, and made them labor at the brickkiln. And he did this to all the Ammonite cities. Then [he] and all the men returned to Jerusalem.

13 ABSALOM SON of David had a fair sister whose name was Tamar, and Amnon [her half brother] son of David loved her.

2 And Amnon was so troubled that he fell sick for his [half] sister Tamar, for she was a virgin, and Amnon thought it impossible for him to do anything to her.

3 But Amnon had a friend whose name was Jonadab son of Shimeah, David's brother; and Jonadab was a very crafty man.

4 He said to Amnon, Why are you, the king's son, so lean and weak-looking from day to day? Will you not tell me? And Amnon said to him, I love Tamar, my [half] brother Absalom's sister.

5 Jonadab said to him, Go to bed and pretend you are sick; and when your father David comes to see you, say to him, Let my sister Tamar come and give me food and prepare it in my sight, that I may see it and eat it from her hand.

6 So Amnon lay down and pretended to be sick; and when the king came to see him, Amnon said to the king, I pray you, let my sister Tamar come and make me a couple of cakes in my sight, that I may eat from her hand.

7 Then David sent home and told Tamar, Go now to your brother Amnon's house and prepare food for him.

8 So Tamar went to her brother Amnon's house, and he was in bed. And she took dough and kneaded it and made cakes in his sight and baked them.

9 She took the pan and emptied it out before him, but he refused to eat. And Amnon said, Send everyone out from me. So everyone went out from him.

10 Then Amnon said to Tamar, Bring the food here into the bedroom, so I may eat from your hand. So Tamar took the cakes she had made and brought them into the room to Amnon her brother.

11 And when she brought them to him, he took hold of her and said, Come lie with me, my sister.

12 She replied, No, my brother! Do not force *and* humble me, for no such thing should be done in Israel! Do not do this foolhardy, scandalous thing! [Gen. 34:7.]

13 And I, how could I rid myself of my shame? And you, you will be [considered] one of the stupid fools in Israel. Now therefore, I pray you, speak to the king, for he will not withhold me from you.

14 But he would not listen to her, and being stronger than she, he forced her and lay with her.

the deepest kind of shame

The Bible does not ignore the issue of sexual abuse; we find it in II Samuel 13:1–14, in the story of Tamar. I believe that sexual abuse is the worst, most offensive, and most damaging of all types of abuse. When an individual is forced to engage in sex against his or her will, something that is meant to be given only willingly as a gift is violently taken from that person. If that individual is abused in a perverted manner, he or she may suffer lasting damage to the soul as well as to the physical body.

When people, especially children, are abused sexually, their minds, wills, and emotions may be tremendously damaged. They may become negative, suspicious, critical, judgmental, worried, and unsettled. They may also become what I would call "mentally deep," always reasoning, always trying to figure everything out, always asking, "How can I take care of myself? How can I keep life under control so I don't get hurt anymore?" The problem with such a deep thinker is that he or she never gets to enjoy life.

In almost every case, an abuse victim like Tamar will be rooted in shame and will develop a shame-based nature. Because my father sexually abused me, I felt shame, which I internalized. Along the way, I made an unhealthy transition in my thinking: I moved from being ashamed of what my father had done to me to being ashamed of myself because of what he did. This is a very common thought process for abuse victims.

The nature of shame is to be embarrassed or feel defective because of bad things that happen to us, and the only way to be healed of shame is to apply the medicine of God's Word to our lives. God's Word has healed me, not instantly, but over time. It will do the same for you if you diligently apply it to your life.

15 Then Amnon hated her exceedingly, so that his hatred for her was greater than the love with which he had loved her. And Amnon said to her, Get up and get out!

16 But she said, No! This great evil of sending me away is worse than what you did to me. But he would not listen to her.

17 He called the servant who served him and said, Put this woman out of my presence now, and bolt the door after her!

18 Now [Tamar] was wearing a long robe with sleeves *and* of various colors, for in such robes were the king's virgin daughters clad of old. Then Amnon's servant brought her out and bolted the door after her.

19 And [she] put ashes on her head and tore the long, sleeved robe which she wore, and she laid her hand on her head and went away shrieking *and* wailing.

20 And Absalom her brother said to her, Has your brother Amnon been with you? Be quiet now, my sister. He is your brother; take not this matter to heart. So Tamar dwelt in her brother Absalom's house, a desolate woman.

21 But when King David heard of all these things, he was very angry.

22 And Absalom spoke to Amnon neither good nor bad; for Absalom hated Amnon because he had humbled his sister Tamar.

23 After two full years Absalom had sheepshearers at Baal-hazor near Ephraim, and Absalom invited all the king's sons.

24 Absalom came to the king and said, Behold, your servant has sheepshearers; I pray you, let the king and his servants go with your servant.

25 And the king said to Absalom, No, my son, let us not all go, lest we be burdensome to you. Absalom urged David; still he would not go, but he blessed him.

26 Then said Absalom, If not, I pray you, let my brother Amnon go with us. And the king said to him, Why should he go with you?

27 But Absalom urged him, and he let Amnon and all the king's sons go with him.

28 Now Absalom commanded his servants, Notice now, when Amnon's heart is merry with wine and when I say to you, Strike Amnon, then kill him. Fear not; have I not commanded you? Be courageous and brave.

29 And the servants of Absalom did to Amnon as Absalom had commanded. Then all the king's sons arose and every man mounted his mule and fled.

30 While they were on the way, the word came to David, Absalom has killed all the king's sons, and not one of them is left.

31 Then the king arose and tore his garments and lay on the floor; and all his servants standing by tore their clothes.

32 But Jonadab son of Shimeah, David's brother, said, Let not my lord suppose they have killed all the king's sons; for Amnon only is dead. This purpose has shown itself on Absalom's determined mouth ever since the day Amnon humiliated his sister Tamar.

33 So let not my lord the king take the thing to heart and think all the king's sons are dead; for Amnon only is dead.

34 But Absalom fled. And the young man who kept the watch looked up, and behold, many people were coming by the way of the hillside behind him.

35 And Jonadab said to the king, See, the king's sons are coming. It is as your servant said.

36 And as he finished speaking, the king's sons came and lifted up their voices and wept; and the king also and all his servants wept very bitterly.

37 But Absalom fled and went to [his mother's father] Talmai son of Ammihud, king of Geshur. And David mourned for his son [Amnon] every day.

38 So Absalom fled to Geshur and was there three years.

39 And the spirit of King David longed to go forth to Absalom, for he was comforted about Amnon, seeing that he was dead.

14 NOW JOAB son of Zeruiah knew that the king's heart was toward Absalom.

2 And Joab sent to Tekoah and brought from there a wise woman and said to her, Pretend to be a mourner; put on mourning apparel, do not anoint yourself with oil, but act like a woman who has long been mourning for the dead.

3 And go to the king and speak thus to him. And Joab told her what to say.

4 When the woman of Tekoah spoke to the king, she fell on her face to the ground and did obeisance, and said, Help, O king!

5 The king asked her, What troubles you? She said, I am a widow; my husband is dead.

6 And your handmaid had two sons, and they quarreled with one another in the field. There was no one to separate them, and one struck the other and killed him.

7 And behold, our whole family has risen against your handmaid, and they say, Deliver him who slew his brother, that we may kill him for the life of his brother whom he slew; and so they would destroy the heir also. And so quenching my coal which is left, they would leave to my husband neither name nor remnant upon the earth.

8 David said to the woman, Go home, and I will give orders concerning you.

9 And the woman of Tekoah said to the king, My lord, O king, let the guilt be on me and on my father's house; let the king and his throne be guiltless.

10 The king said, If anyone says anything to you, bring him to me, and he shall not touch you again.

11 Then she said, I pray you, let the king remember the Lord your God, that the avenger of blood destroy not any more, lest they destroy my son. And David said, As the Lord lives, there shall not one hair of your son fall to the earth.

12 Then the woman said, Let your handmaid, I pray you, speak one word to my lord the king. He said, Say on.

13 [She] said, Why then have you planned such a thing against God's people? For in speaking this word the king is like one who is guilty, in that [he] does not bring home his banished one.

14 We must all die; we are like water spilled on the ground, which cannot be gathered up again. And God does not take away life, but devises means so that he who is banished may not be an utter outcast from Him.

15 And now I have come to speak of this thing to my lord the king because the people have made me afraid. And I thought, I will speak to the king; it may be that he will perform the request of his servant.

16 For the king will hear to deliver his handmaid from the hand of the man who would destroy me and my son together from [Israel] the inheritance of God.

17 And the woman said, The word of my lord the king will now give me rest *and* security, for as an angel of God is my lord the king to hear *and* discern good and evil. May the Lord your God be with you!

18 Then the king said to the woman, Hide not from me anything I ask you. And the woman said, Let my lord the king speak.

19 The king said, Is the hand of Joab with you in all this? And the woman answered, As your soul lives, my lord the king, none can turn to the right hand or to the left from anything my lord the king has said. It was your servant Joab who directed me; he put all these words in my mouth.

20 In order to change the course of matters [between Absalom and his father] your servant Joab did this. But my lord has wisdom like the wisdom of the angel of God—to know all things that are on the earth.

21 Then the king said to Joab, Behold now, I grant this; go, bring back the young man Absalom.

22 And Joab fell to the ground on his face and did obeisance and thanked the king. And Joab said, Today your servant knows that I have found favor in your sight, my lord, O king, in that the king has performed the request of his servant.

23 So Joab arose, went to Geshur, and brought Absalom to Jerusalem.

24 And the king said, Let him go to his own house, and let him not see my face. So Absalom went to his own house and did not see the king's face.

25 But in all Israel there was none so much to be praised for his beauty as Absalom; from the sole of his foot to the crown of his head there was no blemish in him.

26 And when he cut the hair of his

head, he weighed it—for at each year's end he cut it, because its weight was a burden to him—and it weighed 200 shekels by the king's weight.

27 There were born to Absalom three sons and one daughter whose name was Tamar; she was a beautiful woman.

28 Absalom dwelt two full years in Jerusalem and did not see the king's face.

29 So Absalom sent for Joab to send him to the king, but he would not come to him; even when he sent again the second time, he would not come.

30 Therefore Absalom said to his servants, See, Joab's field is near mine, and he has barley there; go and set it on fire. So Absalom's servants set the field afire.

31 Then Joab arose and went to Absalom at his house and said to him, Why have your servants set my field on fire?

32 Absalom answered Joab, I sent to you, saying, Come here, that I may send you to the king to ask, Why have I come from Geshur? It would be better for me to be there still. Now therefore [Joab], let me see the king, and if there is iniquity *and* guilt in me, let him kill me.

33 So Joab came to the king and told him. And when David had called for Absalom, he came to him and bowed himself on his face to the ground before the king; and [David] kissed Absalom.

15 AFTER THIS, Absalom got a chariot and horses, and fifty men to run before him.

2 And [he] rose up early and stood beside the gateway; and when any man who had a controversy came to the king for judgment, Absalom called to him, Of what city are you? And he would say, Your servant is of such and such a tribe of Israel.

3 Absalom would say to him, Your claims are good and right, but there is no man appointed as the king's agent to hear you.

4 Absalom added, Oh, that I were judge in the land! Then every man with any suit or cause might come to me and I would do him justice!

5 And whenever a man came near to do obeisance to him, he would put out his hand, take hold of him, and kiss him.

6 Thus Absalom did to all Israel who came to the king for judgment. So Absalom stole the hearts of the men of Israel.

7 And after [four] years, Absalom said to the king, I pray you, let me go to Hebron [his birthplace] and pay my vow to the Lord.

8 For your servant vowed while I dwelt at Geshur in Syria, If the Lord will bring me again to Jerusalem, then I will serve the Lord [by offering a sacrifice].

9 And the king said to him, Go in peace. So he arose and went to Hebron.

10 But Absalom sent secret messengers throughout all the tribes of Israel, saying, As soon as you hear the sound of the trumpet, then say, Absalom is king at Hebron.

11 With Absalom went 200 men from Jerusalem, who were invited [as guests to his sacrificial feast]; and they went in their simplicity, and they knew not a thing.

12 And while Absalom was offering the sacrifices, he sent for Ahithophel the Gilonite, David's counselor, from his city Giloh. And the conspiracy was strong; the people with Absalom increased continually.

13 And there came a messenger to David, saying, The hearts of the men of Israel have gone after Absalom.

14 David said to all his servants who were with him at Jerusalem, Arise and let us flee, or else none of us will escape from Absalom. Make haste to depart, lest he overtake us suddenly and bring evil upon us and smite the city with the sword.

15 And the king's servants said to the king, Behold, your servants are ready to do whatever my lord the king says.

16 So the king and all his household after him went forth. But he left ten women who were concubines to keep the house. [II Sam. 12:11; 20:3.]

17 The king went forth with all the people after him, and halted at the last house.

18 All David's servants passed on beside him, along with [his body-guards] all the Cherethites, Pelethites; also all the Gittites, 600 men who came after him from Gath, passed on before the king.

19 The king said to Ittai the Gittite, Why do you go with us also? Return to your place and remain with the king [Absalom], for you are a foreigner and an exile.

20 Since you came only yesterday, should I make you go up and down with us? Since I must go where I may, you return, and take back your brethren with you. May loving-kind-ness and faithfulness be with you.

21 But Ittai answered the king, As the Lord lives, and as my lord the king lives, wherever my lord the king shall be, whether for death or life, even there also will your servant be.

22 So David said to Ittai, Go on and pass over [the Kidron]. And Ittai the Gittite passed over and all his men and all the little ones who were with him.

23 All the country wept with a loud voice as all the people passed over. The king crossed the brook Kidron, and all the people went on toward the wilderness.

24 Abiathar [the priest] and behold, Zadok came also, and all the Levites with him, bearing the ark of the covenant of God. And they set down the ark of God until all the people had gone from the city.

25 Then the king told Zadok, Take back the ark of God to the city. If I find favor in the Lord's eyes, He will bring me back and let me see both it and His house.

26 But if He says, I have no delight in you, then here I am; let Him do to me what seems good to Him.

27 The king also said to Zadok the priest, Are you not a seer? [You and Abiathar] return to the city in peace, and your two sons with you, Ahimaaz your son and Jonathan son of Abi-athar.

28 See, I will wait at the fords [at the Jordan] of the wilderness until word comes from you to inform me.

29 Zadok, therefore, and Abiathar carried the ark of God back to Jeru-salem and they stayed there.

30 And David went up over the Mount of Olives and wept as he went, barefoot and his head covered. And all the people who were with him cov-ered their heads, weeping as they went.

31 David was told, Ahithophel [your counselor] is among the conspirators with Absalom. David said, O Lord, I pray You, turn Ahithophel's counsel into foolishness.

32 When David came to the summit [of Olivet], where he worshiped God, behold, Hushai the Archite came to meet him with his coat rent and earth upon his head.

33 David said to him, If you go with me, you will be a burden to me.

34 But if you return to the city and say to Absalom, I will be your servant, O king; as I have been your father's servant in the past, so will I be your servant now, then you may defeat for me the counsel of Ahithophel.

35 Will not Zadok and Abiathar the priests be with you? So whatever you hear from the king's house, just tell it to [them].

36 Behold, their two sons are there with them, Ahimaaz, Zadok's son and Jonathan, Abiathar's son; and by them send to me everything you hear.

37 So Hushai, David's friend, returned, and Absalom also came into Jerusalem.

16 WHEN DAVID was a little past the top [of Olivet], behold, Ziba, the servant of Mephibosheth, met him with a couple of donkeys saddled, and upon them 200 loaves of bread, 100 bunches of raisins, 100 summer fruits, and a skin of wine.

2 The king said to Ziba, What do you mean by these? Ziba said, The donkeys are for the king's household to ride on, the bread and summer fruit for the young men to eat, and the wine is for those to drink who become faint in the wilderness.

3 The king said, And where is your master's son [grandson Mephibosheth]? Ziba said to the king, Behold, he remains in Jerusalem, for he said, Today the house of Israel will give me back the kingdom of my father [grandfather Saul].

4 Then the king said to Ziba, Behold, all that belonged to Mephibosheth is now yours. Ziba said, I do obeisance; let me ever find favor in your sight, my lord O king.

5 When King David came to Bahurim, a man of the family of the house of Saul, Shimei son of Gera, came out and cursed continually as he came.

6 And he cast stones at David and at all the servants of King David; and all the people and all the mighty men were on his right hand and on his left.

7 Shimei said as he cursed, Get out, get out, you man of blood, you base fellow!

8 The Lord has avenged upon you all the blood of the house of Saul, in whose stead you have reigned; and

the Lord has delivered the kingdom into the hands of Absalom your son. Behold, the calamity is upon you because you are a bloody man!

9 Then said [David's nephew] Abishai son of Zeruiah to the king, Why should this dead dog curse my lord the king? Let me go over and take off his head.

10 The king said, What have I to do with you, you sons of Zeruiah? If he is cursing because the Lord said to him, Curse David, who then shall ask, Why have you done so?

11 And David said to Abishai and to all his servants, Behold, my son, who was born to me, seeks my life. With how much more reason now may this Benjamite do it? Let him alone; and let him curse, for the Lord has bidden him to do it.

12 It may be that the Lord will look on the iniquity done me and will recompense me with good for his cursing this day.

13 So David and his men went by the road, and Shimei went along on the hillside opposite David and cursed as he went and threw stones and dust at him.

14 And the king and all the people who were with him came [to the Jordan] weary, and he refreshed himself there.

15 And Absalom and all the people, the men of Israel, came to Jerusalem, and Ahithophel with him.

16 And when Hushai the Archite, David's friend, came to Absalom, Hushai said to [him], Long live the king! Long live the king!

17 Absalom said to Hushai, Is this your kindness *and* loyalty to your friend? Why did you not go with your friend?

18 Hushai said to Absalom, No, for whom the Lord and this people and all the men of Israel choose, his will I be, and with him I will remain.

19 And again, whom should I serve?

Should it not be his son? As I have served your father, so will I serve you.

20 Then Absalom said to Ahithophel, Give your counsel. What shall we do?

21 And Ahithophel said to Absalom, Go in to your father's concubines whom he has left to keep the house; and all Israel will hear that you are abhorred by your father. Then the hands of all who are with you will be made strong.

22 So they spread for Absalom a tent on the top of the [king's] house, and Absalom went in to his father's harem in the sight of all Israel.

23 And the counsel of Ahithophel in those days was as if a man had consulted the word of God; so was all Ahithophel's counsel considered both by David and by Absalom.

17 MOREOVER, Ahithophel said to Absalom, Let me choose 12,000 men and I will set out and pursue David this night.

2 I will come upon him while he is exhausted and weak, and cause him to panic; all the people with him will flee. Then I will strike down the king alone.

3 I will bring back all the people to you. [The removal of] the man whom you seek is the assurance that all will return; and all the people will be at peace.

4 And what he said pleased Absalom well and all the elders of Israel.

5 Absalom said, Now call Hushai the Archite also, and let us hear what he says.

6 When Hushai came, Absalom said to him, Ahithophel has counseled thus. Shall we do what he says? If not, speak up.

7 And Hushai said to Absalom, The counsel that Ahithophel has given is not good at this time.

8 For, said Hushai, you know your father and his men, that they are mighty men, and they are embittered *and* enraged like a bear robbed of her whelps in the field. And your father is a man of war, and will not lodge with the people.

9 Behold, he is hidden even now in some pit or other place; and when some of them are overthrown at the first, whoever hears it will say, There is a slaughter among the followers of Absalom.

10 And even he who is brave, whose heart is as the heart of a lion, will utterly melt, for all Israel knows that your father is a mighty man and that those who are with him are brave men.

11 Therefore I counsel that all [the men of] Israel be gathered to you, from Dan even to Beersheba, as the sand that is by the sea for multitude, and that you go to battle in your own person.

12 So shall we come upon [David] some place where he shall be found, and we will light upon him as the dew settles [unseen and unheard] on the ground; and of him and of all the men with him there shall not be left so much as one.

13 If he withdraws into a city, then shall all Israel bring ropes to that city, and we will drag it into the ravine until not one pebble is left there.

14 Absalom and all the men of Israel said, The counsel of Hushai the Archite is better than that of Ahithophel. For the Lord had ordained to defeat the good counsel of Ahithophel, so that the Lord might bring evil upon Absalom.

15 Then said Hushai to Zadok and Abiathar the priests, Thus and thus did Ahithophel counsel Absalom and the elders of Israel, and thus and thus have I counseled.

16 Now send quickly and tell David, Lodge not this night at the fords [at the Jordan] of the wilderness, but by all means pass over, lest the king be swallowed up and all the people with him.

17 Now [the youths] Jonathan and Ahimaaz stayed at En-rogel, for they must not be seen coming into the city. But a maidservant went and told them, and they went and told King David.

18 But a lad saw them and told Absalom; but they left quickly and came to the house of a man in Bahurim, who had a well in his court, and they went down into it.

19 And the woman spread a covering over the well's mouth and spread ground corn on it; and the thing was not discovered.

20 For when Absalom's servants came to the woman at the house, they said, Where are Ahimaaz and Jonathan? And the woman said to them, They went over the brook of water. When they had sought and could not find them, they returned to Jerusalem.

21 After they had departed, the boys came up out of the well and went and told King David, and said, Arise and pass quickly over the river Jordan; for thus and so has Ahithophel counseled against you.

22 David arose and all the people with him and passed over the Jordan. By daybreak, not one was left who had not crossed.

23 But when Ahithophel saw that his counsel was not followed, he saddled his donkey, went home to his city, put his household in order, and hanged himself and died, and was buried in the tomb of his father.

24 Then David came to Mahanaim. And Absalom passed over the Jordan, he and all the men of Israel with him.

25 Absalom made Amasa captain of the army instead of Joab. Amasa was the son of an [Ishmaelite] named Ithra, who married Abigail daughter of Nahash, [half sister of David and] sister of Zeruiah, Joab's mother.

26 So Israel and Absalom encamped in the land of Gilead.

27 When David came to Mahanaim, Shobi son of Nahash of Rabbah of the Ammonites, and Machir son of Ammiel of Lo-debar, and Barzillai the Gileadite of Rogelim

28 Brought beds, basins, earthen vessels, wheat, barley, meal, parched grain, beans, lentils, parched [pulse— seeds of peas and beans],

29 Honey, curds, sheep, and cheese of cows for David and the people with him to eat; for they said, The people are hungry, weary, and thirsty in the wilderness.

18 DAVID NUMBERED the men who were with him and set over them commanders of thousands and of hundreds.

2 David sent forth the army, a third under command of Joab, a third under Abishai son of Zeruiah, Joab's brother, and a third under Ittai the Gittite. [He] told the men, I myself will go out with you also.

3 But the men said, You shall not go out. For if we flee, they will not care about us; if half of us die, they will not care about us. But you are worth 10,000 such as we are. So now it is better that you be able to help us from the city.

4 The king said to them, Whatever seems best to you I will do. So he stood beside the gate, and all the army came out by hundreds and by thousands.

5 The king commanded Joab, Abishai, and Ittai, saying, Deal gently for my sake with the young man Absalom. And all the people heard when the king gave orders to all the commanders about Absalom.

6 So the army went out into the field against Israel, and the battle was fought in the forest of Ephraim.

7 [Absalom's] men of Israel were defeated by the servants of David, and there was a great slaughter that day of 20,000 men.

8 For the battle spread over the face of all the country, and the forest devoured more men that day than did the sword.

9 Then Absalom [unavoidably] met the servants of David. Absalom rode on a mule, and the mule went under the thick boughs of a great oak, and Absalom's head caught fast [in a fork] of the oak; and the mule under him ran away, leaving him hanging between the heavens and the earth.

10 A certain man saw it and told Joab, Behold, I saw Absalom hanging in an oak.

11 Joab said to the man, You saw him! Why did you not strike him down to the ground? I would have given you ten shekels of silver and a girdle.

12 The man told Joab, Though I should receive 1,000 pieces of silver, yet I would not put forth my hand against the king's son. For in our hearing the king charged you, Abishai, and Ittai, Have a care, whoever you be, for the young man Absalom.

13 Otherwise, if I had dealt falsely against his life—for nothing is hidden from the king—you yourself would have taken sides against me.

14 Joab said, I will not tarry thus with you. He took three darts in his hand and thrust them into the body of Absalom while he was yet alive in the midst of the oak.

15 And ten young men, Joab's armor-bearers, surrounded and struck Absalom and killed him.

16 Then Joab blew the trumpet, and the troops returned from pursuing Israel, for Joab restrained *and* spared them.

17 They took Absalom and cast him into a great pit in the forest and raised a very great heap of stones upon him. And all Israel fled, everyone to his own home.

18 Now Absalom in his lifetime had reared up for himself a pillar which is in the King's Valley, for he said, I have no son to keep my name in remembrance. He called the pillar after his own name, and to this day it is called Absalom's Monument.

19 Then said Ahimaaz son of Zadok, Let me now run and bear the king tidings of how the Lord has avenged David of his enemies.

20 Joab told him, You shall not carry news today, but another time. Today you shall bear no news, for the king's son is dead.

21 Then said Joab to the Cushite [an Ethiopian], Go tell the king what you have seen. And the Cushite bowed to Joab and ran.

22 Then said Ahimaaz son of Zadok again to Joab, But anyhow, let me, I pray you, also run after the Cushite. Joab said, Why should you run, my son, seeing you will have no reward, for you have not sufficient tidings?

23 But he said, Let me run anyhow. So Joab said to him, Run. Then Ahimaaz ran by the way of the plain and outran the Cushite.

24 Now David was sitting between the two gates; and the watchman went up to the roof over the gate by the wall, and when he looked, he saw a man running alone.

25 The watchman called out and told the king. The king said, If he is alone, he has news to tell. And he came on and drew near.

26 Then the watchman saw another man running, and the watchman called to the gatekeeper, Behold, another man running alone. The king said, He also brings news.

27 The watchman said, I think the man in front runs like Ahimaaz son of Zadok. The king said, He is a good man and comes with good tidings.

28 And Ahimaaz called and said to the king, All is well! And he fell down to the ground on his face before the king and said, Blessed be the Lord your God, Who has shut up the men who lifted up their hands against my lord the king.

29 The king said, Is the young man Absalom safe? Ahimaaz answered, When Joab sent the king's servant and me, your servant, I saw a great tumult, but I do not know what it was.

30 The king told him, Turn aside; stand here. And he turned aside and stood still.

31 And behold, the Cushite (Ethiopian) came, and he said, News, my lord the king! For the Lord has delivered you this day from all who rose up against you.

32 The king said to the Cushite, Is the young man Absalom safe? The Cushite replied, May the enemies of my lord the king and all who rise against you to do evil be like that young man is.

33 And the king was deeply moved and went up to the chamber over the gate and wept. And as he went, he said, O my son Absalom, my son, my son Absalom! Would to God I had died for you, O Absalom, my son, my son!

19 IT WAS told Joab, Behold, the king is weeping and mourning for Absalom.

2 So the victory that day was turned into mourning for all the people, for they heard it said, The king grieves for his son.

3 The people slipped into the city stealthily that day as humiliated people steal away when they flee in battle.

4 But the king covered his face and cried with a loud voice, O my son Absalom, O Absalom, my son, my son!

speak the Word

5 And Joab came into the house to the king and said, You have today covered the faces of all your servants with shame, who this day have saved your life and the lives of your sons and your daughters and the lives of your wives and concubines.

6 For you love those who hate you and hate those who love you. You have declared today that princes and servants are nothing to you; for today I see that if Absalom had lived and all the rest of us had died, you would be well pleased.

7 So now arise, go out and speak kindly and encouragingly to your servants; for I swear by the Lord that if you do not go, not a man will remain with you this night. And this will be worse for you than all the evil that has befallen you from your youth until now.

8 Then the king arose and sat in the gate. And all [his followers] were told, The king is sitting in the gate, and they all came before the king. Now Israel [Absalom's troops] had fled, every man to his home.

9 And all the people were at strife throughout all the tribes of Israel, saying, The king delivered us from the hands of our enemies, and he saved us from the hands of the Philistines. And now he has fled out of the land from Absalom.

10 And Absalom, whom we anointed over us, is dead in battle. So now, why do you say nothing about bringing back the king?

11 And King David sent to Zadok and to Abiathar the priests, saying, Say to the elders of Judah, Why are you the last to bring the king back to his house, when the word of all Israel has come to the king, to bring him to his house?

12 You are my kinsmen; you are my bone and my flesh. Why then are you the last to bring back the king?

13 And say to Amasa, Are you not of my bone and of my flesh? May God do so to me, and more also, if you are not commander of my army hereafter in place of Joab.

14 He inclined the hearts of all the men of Judah as one man, so they sent word to [him], Return, you and all your servants.

15 So [David] returned and came to the Jordan. And Judah came to Gilgal to meet the king, to conduct him over the Jordan.

16 And Shimei son of Gera, a Benjamite of Bahurim, hastily came down with the men of Judah to meet King David,

17 And 1,000 men of Benjamin with him. And Ziba, the servant of the house of Saul, and his fifteen sons and twenty servants with him, rushed to the Jordan *and* pressed quickly into the king's presence.

18 And there went over a ferryboat to bring over the king's household and to do what he thought good. And Shimei son of Gera fell down before the king as David came to the Jordan,

19 And said to the king, Let not my lord impute iniquity to me *and* hold me guilty, nor remember what your servant did the day my lord went out of Jerusalem [when Shimei grossly insulted David]; may the king not take it to heart.

20 For your servant knows that I have sinned; therefore, behold, I am today the first of all the house of Joseph to come down to meet my lord the king.

21 But Abishai son of Zeruiah said, Shall not Shimei be put to death for this, because he cursed the Lord's anointed?

22 David said, What have I to do with you, you sons of Zeruiah, that you should be an adversary to me today? Shall anyone be put to death today in Israel? For do not I know that I am this day king over Israel?

23 Therefore the king said to Shimei, You shall not die [at my hand]. And the king gave him his oath. [I Kings 2:44-46.]

24 Mephibosheth the son [grandson] of Saul came down to meet the king, and had not dressed his feet, trimmed his beard, or washed his clothes from the day the king left until he returned in peace *and* safety.

25 And when he came to Jerusalem to meet the king, David said to him, Why did you not go with me, Mephibosheth?

26 He said, My lord O king, my servant [Ziba] deceived me; for I said, Saddle me the donkey that I may ride on it and go to the king, for your servant is lame [but he took the donkey and left without me].

27 He has slandered your servant to my lord the king. But the king is as an angel of God; so do what is good in your eyes.

28 For all of my father's house were but doomed to death before my lord the king; yet you set your servant among those who ate at your own table. What right therefore have I to cry any more to the king?

29 The king said to him, Why speak any more of your affairs? I say, You and Ziba divide the land.

30 Mephibosheth said to the king, Oh, let him take it all, since my lord the king has returned home in safety *and* peace.

31 Now Barzillai the Gileadite came down from Rogelim and went on to the Jordan with the king to conduct him over the Jordan.

32 Now Barzillai was a very aged man, even eighty years old; and he had provided the king with food while he remained at Mahanaim, for he was a very great man.

33 And the king said to Barzillai, Come over with me, and I will provide for you with me in Jerusalem.

34 And Barzillai said to the king, How much longer have I to live, that it would be worthwhile for me to go up with the king to Jerusalem?

35 I am this day eighty years old. Could I now [be useful as a counselor to] discern between good and evil? Can your servant appreciate what I eat or drink? Can I any longer enjoy the voices of singing men and women? Why then should your servant be still a burden to my lord the king?

36 Your servant will only go over the Jordan with the king. Why should the king repay me with such a reward?

37 Let your servant turn back again, that I may die in my own city and be buried by the grave of my father and mother. But here is your servant Chimham; let him go over with my lord the king. And do to him what shall seem good to you.

38 The king answered, Chimham shall go over with me, and I will do to him what seems good to you; and whatever you ask of me I will do for you.

39 So all the people went over the Jordan. When the king had crossed over, he kissed Barzillai and blessed him, and [the great man] returned to his own place.

40 Then the king went on to Gilgal, and Chimham went with him; and all the people of Judah and also half the people of Israel escorted the king.

41 And all the men of Israel came to the king and said to him, Why have our kinsmen, the men of Judah, stolen you away and have brought the king and his household over the Jordan, and all David's men with him?

42 But all the men of Judah answered the men of Israel, Because the king is near of kin to us. Why then be angry about it? Have we eaten at all at the king's expense? Or has he given us any gift?

43 Then the men of Israel answered the men of Judah, We have ten [tribes'] shares in the king; and we have more right to David than you have. Why then did you despise *and* ignore us? Were we not the first to speak of our bringing back our king? But the words of the men of Judah were more violent than the charges of the men of Israel.

20 THERE HAPPENED to be there a base *and* contemptible fellow named Sheba son of Bichri, a Benjamite. He blew a trumpet and said, We have no portion in David and no inheritance in the son of Jesse! Every man to his tents, O Israel!

2 So all the men of Israel withdrew from David and followed Sheba son of Bichri; but the men of Judah stayed faithfully with their king, from the Jordan to Jerusalem.

3 So David came to his house at Jerusalem. And the king took the ten women, his concubines, whom he had left to keep the house, and put them away under guard and provided for them, but did not go in to them. So they were shut up to the day of their death, living in widowhood.

4 Then said the king to Amasa, Assemble the men of Judah to me within three days, and you be present here.

5 So Amasa went to assemble the men of Judah, but he tarried longer than the set time which had been appointed him.

6 And David said to Abishai, Now will Sheba son of Bichri do us more harm than Absalom did. Take your lord's servants and pursue him, lest he get for himself fenced cities and snatch away our very eyes.

7 And there went after him Joab's men and [David's bodyguards] the Cherethites and Pelethites and all the mighty men; they went out from Jerusalem to pursue Sheba son of Bichri.

8 When they were at the great stone in Gibeon, Amasa came to meet them. Joab was wearing a soldier's garment, and over it was a sheathed sword fastened around his hips; and as he went forward, it fell out.

9 Joab said to Amasa, Are you well, my brother? And Joab took Amasa by the beard with the right hand [as if] to kiss him.

10 But Amasa did not notice the sword in Joab's hand. So [Joab] struck him [who was to have been his successor] with it in the body, shedding his bowels to the ground without another blow; and [soon] he died. So Joab and Abishai his brother pursued Sheba son of Bichri.

11 And one of Joab's men stood by him and said, Whoever favors Joab and is for David, follow Joab!

12 And Amasa wallowed in his blood in the highway. And when the man saw that all the people who came by stood still, he removed Amasa out of the highway into the field and spread a cloth over him.

13 When Amasa was removed from the highway, all the people went on after Joab to pursue Sheba son of Bichri.

14 Joab went through all the tribes of Israel to Abel of Beth-maacah, and all the Berites assembled and also went after [Sheba] ardently.

15 And they came and besieged Sheba in Abel of Beth-maacah, and they cast up a siege mound against the city, and it stood against the rampart; and all the men with Joab battered *and* undermined the wall to make it fall.

16 Then a wise woman of the city cried, Hear, hear! Say to Joab, Come here so I can speak to you.

17 And when he came near her, the woman said, Are you Joab? He answered, I am. Then she said to him, Hear the words of your handmaid. He answered, I am listening.

18 Then she said, People used to say, Let them but ask counsel at Abel, and so they settled the matter.

19 I am one of the peaceable and faithful in Israel. You seek to destroy a city which is a mother in Israel. Why will you swallow up the inheritance of the Lord?

20 Joab answered, Far be it, far be it from me that I should swallow up or destroy!

21 That is not true. But a man of the hill country of Ephraim, Sheba son of Bichri, has lifted up his hand against King David. Deliver him only, and I will depart from the city. And the woman said, Behold, his head shall be thrown to you over the wall.

22 Then the woman in her wisdom went to all the people. And they cut off the head of Sheba son of Bichri and cast it down to Joab. So he blew the trumpet, and they retired from the city, every man to his own home. And Joab returned to Jerusalem to the king. [Eccl. 9:13-16.]

23 Joab was over the host of Israel; Benaiah son of Jehoiada was over [the king's bodyguards] the Cherethites and Pelethites;

24 Adoram was over the tribute; Jehoshaphat son of Ahilud was recorder;

25 Sheva was scribe; and Zadok and Abiathar were the priests;

26 Also Ira the Jairite was chief minister to David.

21 THERE WAS a three-year famine in the days of David, year after year; and David inquired of the Lord. The Lord replied, It is on account of Saul and his bloody house, for he put to death the Gibeonites.

2 So the king called the Gibeonites—now the Gibeonites were not Israelites but of the remnant of the Amorites. The Israelites had sworn to spare them, but Saul in his zeal for the people of Israel and Judah had sought to slay the Gibeonites—

3 So David said to the Gibeonites, What shall I do for you? How can I make atonement that you may bless the Lord's inheritance?

4 The Gibeonites said to him, We will accept no silver or gold of Saul or of his house; neither for us shall you kill any man in Israel. David said, I will do for you what you say.

5 They said to the king, The man who consumed us and planned to prevent us from remaining in any territory of Israel,

6 Let seven men of his sons be delivered to us and we will hang them up before the Lord at Gibeah of Saul, [on the mountain] of the Lord. And the king said, I will give them.

7 But the king spared Mephibosheth son of Jonathan, the son of Saul, because of the Lord's oath that was between David and Jonathan son of Saul.

8 But the king took the two sons of Rizpah daughter of Aiah, whom she bore to Saul, Armoni and Mephibosheth, and the five sons of [Merab] daughter of Saul, whom she bore to Adriel son of Barzillai the Meholathite.

9 He delivered them into the hands of the Gibeonites, and they hung them up on the hill before the Lord, and all seven perished together. They were put to death in the first days of barley harvest.

10 Rizpah daughter of Aiah took sackcloth and spread it for herself on the rock, from the beginning of harvest until rain fell on them, and she did not allow either the birds of the air to come upon them by day or the beasts of the field by night.

11 It was told David what Rizpah daughter of Aiah, the concubine of Saul, had done.

12 And David went and took the bones of Saul and Jonathan his son from the men of Jabesh-gilead, who had stolen them from the street of Beth-shan, where the Philistines had hung them up when the Philistines had slain Saul in Gilboa.

13 He brought from there the bones of Saul and of Jonathan his son, and they gathered the bones of those who were hung up.

14 And the bones of Saul and Jonathan his son they buried in the country of Benjamin in Zelah in the tomb of Kish, [Saul's] father, and they did all that the king commanded. And after that, God heard *and* answered when His people prayed for the land.

15 The Philistines had war again with Israel. And David went down and his servants with him and fought against the Philistines, and David became faint.

16 Ishbi-benob, who was of the sons of the giants, the weight of whose spear was 300 shekels of bronze, was girded with a new sword, and thought to kill David.

17 But Abishai son of Zeruiah came to David's aid, and smote and killed the Philistine. Then David's men charged him, You shall no more go out with us to battle, lest you quench the lamp of Israel.

18 After this, there was again war with the Philistines at Gob (Gezer). Then Sibbecai the Hushathite slew Saph (Sippai), who was a descendant of the giant.

19 There was again war at Gob with the Philistines, and Elhanan son of Jaare-oregim, a Bethlehemite, slew Goliath the Gittite, whose spear shaft was like a weaver's beam.

20 And there was again war at Gath, where there was a man of great stature who had six fingers on each hand and six toes on each foot, twenty-four in number; he also was a descendant of the giants.

21 And when he defied Israel, Jonathan son of Shimei, brother of David, slew him.

22 These four were descended from the giant in Gath, and they fell by the hands of David and his servants.

22 DAVID SPOKE to the Lord the words of this song on the day when the Lord delivered him from the hands of all his enemies and from the hand of Saul.

2 He said: The Lord is my Rock [of escape from Saul] and my Fortress [in the wilderness] and my Deliverer; [I Sam. 23:14, 25, 28.]

3 My God, my Rock, in Him will I take refuge; my Shield and the Horn of my salvation; my Stronghold and my Refuge, my Savior—You save me from violence. [Gen. 15:1.]

4 I call on the Lord, Who is worthy to be praised, and I am saved from my enemies.

5 For the waves of death enveloped me; the torrents of destruction made me afraid.

6 The cords of Sheol were entangling me; I encountered the snares of death.

7 In my distress I called upon the Lord; I cried to my God, and He heard my voice from His temple; my cry came into His ears.

8 Then the earth reeled and quaked, the foundations of the heavens trembled and shook because He was angry.

9 Smoke went up from His nostrils, and devouring fire from His mouth; coals were kindled by it.

speak the Word

life point

Why does praising the Lord and calling Him "worthy to be praised" (II Samuel 22:4) defeat our enemies? If you and I will go through the gates of praise into God's presence and begin to worship Him there, our enemies will become confused and destroy one another. When the devil tries to upset us and we react by singing praise to God, it confuses him and his demons so badly that they begin to attack each other. In the process we are delivered from the destruction they want to render to us, and we enter into new levels of joy.

10 He bowed the heavens and came down; thick darkness was under His feet.

11 He rode on a cherub and flew; He was seen upon the wings of the wind.

12 He made darkness His canopy around Him, gathering of waters, thick clouds of the skies.

13 Out of the brightness before Him coals of fire flamed forth.

14 The Lord thundered from heaven, and the Most High uttered His voice.

15 He sent out arrows and scattered them; lightning confused *and* troubled them.

16 The channels of the sea were visible, the foundations of the world were uncovered at the rebuke of the Lord, at the blast of the breath of His nostrils.

17 He sent from above, He took me; He drew me out of great waters.

18 He delivered me from my strong enemy, from those who hated me, for they were too mighty for me.

Thank You, God, for hearing me when I call upon You in times of distress. Thank You that my cry reaches Your ears and that You are listening to my voice when I cry out to You.
ADAPTED FROM II SAMUEL 22:7

19 They came upon me in the day of my calamity, but the Lord was my stay.
20 He brought me forth into a large place; He delivered me because He delighted in me.
21 The Lord rewarded me according to my uprightness with Him; He compensated *and* benefited me according to the cleanness of my hands.
22 For I have kept the ways of the Lord, and have not wickedly departed from my God.
23 For all His ordinances were before me; and from His statutes I did not turn aside.
24 I was also blameless before Him and kept myself from guilt *and* iniquity.
25 Therefore the Lord has recompensed me according to my righteousness, according to my cleanness in His [holy] sight.
26 Toward the loving *and* loyal You will show Yourself loving *and* loyal, and with the upright *and* blameless You will show Yourself upright *and* blameless.
27 To the pure You will show Yourself pure, and to the willful You will show Yourself willful.
28 And the afflicted people You will deliver, but Your eyes are upon the haughty, whom You will bring down.
29 For You, O Lord, are my Lamp; the Lord lightens my darkness.
30 For by You I run through a troop; by my God I leap over a wall.
31 As for God, His way is perfect; the word of the Lord is tried. He is a Shield to all those who trust *and* take refuge in Him.
32 For who is God but the Lord? And who is a Rock except our God?
33 God is my strong Fortress; He

life point

God is our Strength, our Rock and our Fortress (see II Samuel 22:32, 33). He asks us to put our faith in Him and to believe that we can do whatever He asks us to do. He is mighty to uphold us and make us stand. He will support us and keep us from failing. God's strength is readily available to us, and we receive it through believing the promise He has made to give it to us. If we believe we are weak, then we will only manifest weakness, but the Bible says, "Let the weak say, I am strong [a warrior]!" (Joel 3:10). When we can say we are strong with a heart of conviction—even though we are weak in ourselves—the Lord will be strong in us, and we will experience victory in our lives!

guides the blameless in His way *and* sets him free.
34 He makes my feet like the hinds' [firm and able]; He sets me secure *and* confident upon the heights.
35 He trains my hands for war, so that my arms can bend a bow of bronze.
36 You have also given me the shield of Your salvation; and Your condescension *and* gentleness have made me great.
37 You have enlarged my steps under me, so that my feet have not slipped.
38 I have pursued my enemies and destroyed them; and I did not turn back until they were consumed.
39 I consumed them and thrust them through, so that they did not arise; they fell at my feet.
40 For You girded me with strength

speak the Word

let God be your strength

David said, "God is my strong Fortress" (II Samuel 22:33). God does not want to just *give* us strength; He wants to *be* our Strength. In I Samuel 15:29, He is called "the Strength of Israel."

Many of the men and women in the Bible knew that God was their strength; they became examples to encourage us today to trust in God's strength. David wrote in Psalm 18:29 that by his God he could run through a troop and leap over a wall. In I Kings 19:4–8 an angel came and ministered to Elijah, who was tired and depressed, and he went forty days and nights in the strength that he received from that one visit. The apostle Paul found the strength of God so wonderful that in II Corinthians 12:9, 10 he wrote that he would glory in his weaknesses, knowing that when he was weak, the strength of God would rest upon him and fill up his weaknesses. To put it in our language today, Paul was saying that he was glad when he was weak because then he got to experience the strength of God.

How does a person receive strength from God? By faith. Start receiving the strength of God by *believing* His promise to strengthen you. That faith will quicken your body, as well as your spirit and soul. For example, if you have a weak back, it can be made strong. At our conferences, the Holy Spirit has strengthened weak knees, ankles, and backs as we have prayed for those who asked God for strength. His healing power came as we waited in His presence and received it from Him.

By faith you can receive strength to stay in a difficult marriage, raise a difficult child, or stick with a difficult job in which you have a difficult boss. You can receive strength to do great things even though you may have a physical impairment yourself.

Have you been trying to push through difficulties on your own? If so, make a change right now. Start getting strength from deep within you, where the Holy Spirit dwells. If that divine strength does not yet dwell in you, all you need to do to receive it is admit your sins, repent of them, and ask Jesus to be your Savior and Lord. Surrender your life, all that you are and all that you are not, to Him. Ask Him to baptize you in the Holy Spirit and to fill you through and through with the power of the Holy Spirit. Let God be your strength. Say with David, "My God, my Rock, in Him will I take refuge; my Shield and the Horn of my salvation; my Stronghold and my Refuge, my Savior" (II Samuel 22:3).

for the battle; those who rose up against me You subdued under me.

41 You have made my enemies turn their backs to me, that I might cut off those who hate me.

42 They looked, but there was none to save—even to the Lord, but He did not answer them.

43 Then I beat them small as the dust of the earth; I crushed them as the mire of the street and scattered them abroad.

44 You also have delivered me from strife with my people; You kept me as the head of the nations. People whom I had not known served me.

45 Foreigners yielded feigned obedience to me; as soon as they heard of me, they became obedient to me.

46 Foreigners faded away; they came limping *and* trembling from their strongholds.

47 The Lord lives; blessed be my Rock, and exalted be God, the Rock of my salvation.

48 It is God Who executes vengeance for me and Who brought down [and disciplined] the peoples under me,

49 Who brought me out from my enemies. You also lifted me up above those who rose up against me; You delivered me from the violent man.

50 For this I will give thanks *and* extol You, O Lord, among the nations; I will sing praises to Your name.

51 He is a Tower of salvation *and* great deliverance to His king, and shows loving-kindness to His anointed, to David and his offspring forever.

23 NOW THESE are the last words of David: David son of Jesse says, and the man who was raised on high, the anointed of the God of Jacob, and the sweet psalmist of Israel, says,

2 The Spirit of the Lord spoke in *and* by me, and His word was upon my tongue.

3 The God of Israel spoke, the Rock of Israel said to me, When one rules over men righteously, ruling in the fear of God,

4 He dawns on them like the morning light when the sun rises on a cloudless morning, when the tender grass springs out of the earth through clear shining after rain.

5 Truly does not my house stand so with God? For He has made with me an everlasting covenant, ordered in all things, and sure. For will He not

cause to prosper all my help and my desire?

6 But wicked, godless, *and* worthless lives are all like thorns to be thrust away, because they cannot be taken with the hand.

7 But the man who touches them arms himself with iron and the shaft of a spear, and they are utterly consumed with fire on the spot.

8 These are the names of the mighty men whom David had: Josheb-basshebeth, a Tahchemonite, chief of the Three [heroes], known also as Adino the Eznite; he wielded his spear and went against 800 men, who were slain at one time. [I Chron. 11:11.]

9 Next to him among the three mighty men was Eleazar son of Dodo, son of Ahohi. He was with David when they defied the Philistines assembled there for battle, and the men of Israel had departed.

10 [Eleazar] arose and struck down the Philistines until his hand was weary and clung to the sword. The Lord wrought a great deliverance *and* victory that day; the men returned after him only to take the spoil.

11 Next to [Eleazar] was Shammah son of Agee the Hararite. The Philistines were gathered at Lehi on a piece of ground full of lentils; and the [Israelites] fled from the Philistines.

12 But he stood in the midst of the ground and defended it and slew the Philistines; and the Lord wrought a great victory.

putting the Word to work

Second Samuel 23:3, 4 offers valuable insight to leaders. When we lead others in righteousness and in the fear of God, good things result. If you are a leader, ask God to help you increase more and more in righteousness and in the fear of the Lord as you lead those God has put under your care.

fear God, not people

David understood one of the essential qualities of a leader, as we see in II Samuel 23:3. Anyone who wants to lead well must fear the Lord. When we talk about fearing God, we are not talking about a wrong kind of fear. We are talking about the reverential fear that causes us to bow in His presence and even to prostrate ourselves before Him and say, "My God, there is none like You; Whom shall I fear? If You are for me, what can man do to me?"

The apostle Paul wrote something in Galatians 1:10 that has always gripped my heart. He said, "Now am I trying to win the favor of men, or of God? Do I seek to please men? If I were still seeking popularity with men, I should not be a bond servant of Christ (the Messiah)."

I know firsthand how Satan uses rejection to prevent us from going forward with the call of God on our lives. Have you ever been attacked by rejection? Of course you have; we all have. The devil uses it to keep us from making progress. He knows that we will be blessed if we are in the will of God, so he uses the fear of man's rejection to hold us back.

When I was filled with the Holy Spirit in 1976, I experienced rejection from most of my friends, my church, and my family. They did not understand my new zeal and enthusiasm and thought I was being deceived. The rejection grew even worse when God called me to teach and preach His Word. Everywhere I turned, I was being rejected by someone I loved and cared about. It was very difficult to go on. Many times I wanted to give in to the pressure and make decisions that would please people. I look back now and shudder to think what I might have sacrificed had I bowed down to the pressure. There have also been other important times in my life and ministry when the devil launched attacks of rejection against me, and each of them came at a time when God was trying to promote me into the next level of what He had for my life.

Anyone who is going to do the will of God must have more fear of God than of man. I wanted acceptance, but I did not want to be out of God's will, and I knew that I would be if I did what my friends wanted me to do. I thank God for His grace that sustained and strengthened me through those difficult times of testing.

Anyone who is going to do God's will must remember what Jesus told His disciples: "A servant is not greater than his master . . . If they persecuted Me, they will also persecute you" (John 15:20). He was saying, "If they reject you, in effect they are rejecting Me." I believe the Lord takes it personally when people reject you because you are trying to do the right thing. He knows how you feel about being rejected, because He felt the same thing. He is your Vindicator; your reward comes from Him, and you must reverentially fear and honor Him more than anything or anyone else.

13 And three of the thirty chief men went down at harvest time to David in the cave of Adullam, and a troop of Philistines was encamped in the Valley of Rephaim.

14 And David was then in the stronghold, and the garrison of the Philistines was then in Bethlehem.

15 And David said longingly, Oh, that someone would give me a drink of water from the well of Bethlehem by the gate!

16 And the three mighty men broke through the army of the Philistines and drew water out of the well of Bethlehem by the gate and brought it to David. But he would not drink it, but poured it out to the Lord.

17 And he said, Be it far from me, O Lord, to drink this. Is it not [the same as] the blood of the men who went at the risk of their lives? So he would not drink it. These things did the three mighty men.

18 Now Abishai the brother of Joab son of Zeruiah was chief of the Three. He wielded his spear against 300 men and slew them, and won a name beside the Three.

19 Was he not most renowned of the Three? So he was their captain; however, he did not attain to the Three.

20 And Benaiah son of Jehoiada, a valiant man of Kabzeel, who had done many notable acts, slew two lionlike men of Moab. He went down also and slew a lion in a pit on a snowy day.

21 And he slew an Egyptian, a handsome man. The Egyptian had a spear in his hand, but Benaiah went down to him with a staff, snatched the spear out of the Egyptian's hand, and slew the man with his own spear.

22 These things Benaiah son of Jehoiada did, and won a name beside the three mighty men.

23 He was more renowned than the Thirty, but he attained not to the [first] Three. David set him over his guard *or* council.

24 Asahel brother of Joab was one of the Thirty; then Elhanan son of Dodo of Bethlehem,

25 Shammah of Harod, Elika of Harod,

26 Helez the Paltite, Ira son of Ikkesh of Tekoa,

27 Abiezer of Anathoth, Mebunnai the Hushathite,

28 Zalmon the Ahohite, Maharai of Netophah,

29 Heleb son of Baanah of Netophah, Ittai son of Ribai of Gibeah of the Benjamites.

30 Benaiah of Pirathon, Hiddai of the brooks of Gaash,

31 Abi-albon the Arbathite, Azmaveth the Barhumite,

32 Eliahba of Shaalbon, the sons of Jashen, Jonathan,

33 Shammah the Hararite, Ahiam son of Sharar the Hararite,

34 Eliphelet son of Ahasbai, son of Maacah, Eliam son of Ahithophel of Giloh,

35 Hezro (Hezrai) of Carmel, Paarai the Arbite,

36 Igal son of Nathan of Zobah, Bani the Gadite,

37 Zelek the Ammonite, Naharai of Beeroth, armor-bearer of Joab son of Zeruiah,

38 Ira the Ithrite, Gareb the Ithrite,

39 Uriah the Hittite—thirty-seven in all.

24 AGAIN THE anger of the Lord was kindled against Israel, and He moved David against them, saying, Go, number Israel and Judah.

2 For the king said to Joab the captain of the host who was with him, Go now through all the tribes of Israel, from Dan even to Beersheba, and count the people, that I may know their number.

3 And Joab said to the king, May the Lord your God add a hundred times as many people as there are, and let the eyes of my lord the king see it; but why does my lord the king delight in this thing?

4 But the king's word prevailed against Joab and the commanders of the army. So they went from the king's presence to number the Israelites.

5 They passed over the Jordan and encamped in Aroer, on the south side of the city lying in the midst of the ravine [of the Arnon] toward Gad, and on to Jazer.

6 Then they came to Gilead, and to the land of Tahtim-hodshi, and they came to Dan-jaan [Dan in the forest] and around to Sidon,

7 And came to the stronghold of Tyre and to all the cities of the Hivites and Canaanites; and they went out to the South (the Negeb) of Judah at Beersheba.

8 So when they had gone through all the land [taking the census], they came to Jerusalem at the end of nine months and twenty days.

9 And Joab gave the sum of the numbering of the people to the king. There were in Israel 800,000 valiant men who drew the sword, and the men of Judah were 500,000.

10 But David's heart smote him after he had numbered the people. David said to the Lord, I have sinned greatly in what I have done. I beseech You, O Lord, take away the iniquity of Your servant, for I have done very foolishly.

11 When David arose in the morning, the word of the Lord came to the prophet Gad, David's seer, saying,

12 Go and say to David, Thus says the Lord, I hold over you three choices; select one of them, so I may bring it upon you.

13 So Gad came to David and told him and said, Shall seven years of famine come to your land? Or will you flee three months before your pursuing enemies? Or do you prefer three days of pestilence in your land? Con-

life point

David's heart "smote" him after he had sinned against the Lord (II Samuel 24:10). This means that his heart condemned him. A condemned heart steals confidence.

Anyone who wants to be a leader must learn how to handle condemnation. When he sins, he must know how to admit it, repent, and receive forgiveness. We must shake off mistakes from the past and go on, because no one is perfect. We may have perfect hearts, hearts after God's own, but still we will not be perfect in our every thought, word, and deed.

As a leader and teacher of God's Word, I know how condemning it is to teach others about what is right and then foul up in that very area myself. When we leaders do that, we feel a double dose of condemnation because the devil will say to us, "You, of all people, ought to know better." If we listen to him, he will make us feel that we are not worthy to be leaders of God's people.

God *convicts* us of our wrongdoing; He does not *condemn* us. Conviction helps us to repent and be lifted out of the problem; condemnation only pushes us down and makes us feel bad about ourselves. We must shake off the feeling of condemnation because if we don't, we won't have confidence before God. Without confidence, we will have no faith. And without faith, we cannot please God or receive His empowerment to fulfill His calling.

sider and see what answer I shall return to Him Who sent me.

14 And David said to Gad, I am in great distress. Let us fall into the hands of the Lord, for His mercies are many *and* great; but let me not fall into the hands of man.

15 So the Lord sent a pestilence upon Israel from the morning even to the time appointed; and there died of the people from Dan even to Beersheba 70,000 men.

16 And when the angel stretched out his hand upon Jerusalem to destroy it, the Lord relented of the evil *and* reversed His judgment and said to the destroying angel, It is enough; now stay your hand. And the angel of the Lord was by the threshing floor of Araunah the Jebusite.

17 When David saw the angel who was smiting the people, he spoke to the Lord and said, Behold, I have sinned and I have done wickedly; but these sheep, what have they done? Let Your hand, I pray You, be [only] against me and against my father's house.

18 Then Gad came to David and said, Go up, rear an altar to the Lord on the threshing floor of Araunah the Jebusite.

19 So David went up according to Gad's word, as the Lord commanded.

20 Araunah looked and saw the king and his servants coming toward him; and [he] went out and bowed himself before the king with his face to the ground.

21 Araunah said, Why has my lord the king come to his servant? And David said, To buy the threshing floor from you, to build there an altar to the Lord, that the plague may be stayed from the people.

22 And Araunah said to David, Let my lord the king take and offer up what seems good to him. Behold, here are oxen for burnt sacrifice, and threshing instruments and the yokes of the oxen for wood.

23 All this, O king, Araunah gives to the king. And Araunah said to the king, The Lord your God accept you.

24 But King David said to Araunah, No, but I will buy it of you for a price. I will not offer burnt offerings to the Lord my God of that which costs me nothing. So David bought the threshing floor and the oxen for fifty shekels of silver.

25 David built there an altar to the Lord and offered burnt offerings and peace offerings. So the Lord heeded the prayers for the land, and Israel's plague was stayed.

speak the Word

God, I pray that when I am in distress, I will fall into Your merciful hand and not into the hands of man.
ADAPTED FROM II SAMUEL **24:14**

First Kings

Author:
Unknown

Date:
600 BC–550 BC

Everyday Life Principles:
God values and works through relationships.

Honor your covenant with God. Your relationship with Him will be a powerful legacy for your descendants.

Remember that the character traits and standards of other people affect you, so be sure to associate with godly people.

In many ways, the everyday life lessons we learn from I Kings are woven through the stories of four men—the natural father-son team of David and Solomon, and the spiritual father-son team of Elijah and Elisha. Indeed, I Kings tells the stories of the division of the kingdom and of various rulers in the north and in the south, but much of its practical instruction for our lives is found in the context of relationships.

In David and Solomon, we see a son fulfilling his father's dream—the building of the temple. We also see God fulfilling to Solomon the covenant He made with David. Even when Solomon went astray and married foreign women, God left him on the throne for David's sake. In this, we see that a person who has a powerful relationship with God, as David did, will leave an awesome legacy for his or her descendants.

In the relationship between two prophets, Elijah and Elisha, we see Elisha learning from Elijah, observing him and doing everything he can to develop in his life the qualities he saw in his mentor. Elisha reminds us that other people affect us, and we can incorporate their character qualities into our lives. Elisha's faithfulness, as we learn in II Kings, resulted in his having a double portion of Elijah's spirit after Elijah was taken to heaven.

As you read I Kings, remember that relationships are important, and be sure to connect with godly people who can be a blessing in your life and whom you can bless in return.

1 AND KING David was old and advanced in years; they covered him with [bed]clothes, but he could not get warm.

2 So his servants [the [a]physicians] said to him, Let there be sought for my lord the king a young virgin, and let her wait on and be useful to the king; let her lie in your bosom, that my lord the king may get warm.

3 So they sought a fair maiden through all the territory of Israel and found Abishag the Shunammite, and brought her to the king.

4 The maiden was beautiful; and she waited on and nursed him. But the king had no intercourse with her.

5 Then Adonijah son of [David's wife] Haggith exalted himself, saying, I [the eldest living son] will be king. And he prepared for himself chariots and horsemen, with fifty men to run before him.

6 David his father had never in his life displeased him by asking, Why have you done so? He was also a very attractive man and was born after Absalom.

7 He conferred with [b]Joab son of Zeruiah [David's half sister] and with Abiathar the priest, and they followed Adonijah and helped him.

8 But Zadok the priest, Benaiah son of Jehoiada, Nathan the prophet, Shimei, Rei, and David's mighty men did not side with Adonijah.

9 Adonijah sacrificed sheep, oxen, and fatlings by the Stone of Zoheleth, which is beside [the well] En-rogel; and he invited all his brothers, the king's sons, and all the royal officials of Judah.

10 But Nathan the prophet, Benaiah, the mighty men, and Solomon his brother he did not invite.

11 Then Nathan said to Bathsheba the mother of Solomon, Have you not heard that Adonijah, the son of Haggith, reigns and David our lord does not know it?

12 Come now, let me advise you how to save your own life and your son Solomon's.

13 Go to King David and say, Did you not, my lord, O king, swear to your handmaid, saying, Assuredly Solomon your son shall reign after me, and he shall sit upon my throne? Why then does Adonijah reign?

14 Behold, while you are still talking there with the king, I also will come in after you and confirm your words.

15 So Bathsheba went in to the king in his chamber. Now the king was very old *and* feeble, and Abishag the Shunammite was ministering to [him].

16 Bathsheba bowed and did obeisance to the king. The king said, What do you wish?

17 And she said to him, My lord, you swore by the Lord your God to your handmaid, saying, Assuredly Solomon your son shall reign after me and sit upon my throne.

18 And now, behold, Adonijah is reigning, and, my lord the king, you do not know it.

19 He has sacrificed oxen and fatlings and sheep in abundance, and has invited all the king's sons and Abiathar the priest and Joab the commander of the army. But he did not invite Solomon your servant.

20 Now, my lord O king, the eyes of all Israel are on you, to tell who shall sit on the throne of my lord the king after you.

21 Otherwise, when my lord the king shall sleep with his fathers, I and my son Solomon shall be counted as offenders.

22 While she was still talking with the king, Nathan the prophet also came in.

23 The king was told, Here is Nathan

---

a Josephus, *Antiquities of the Jews* 14, 3.   b The commander of Israel's army.

the prophet. And when he came before the king, he bowed himself before him with his face to the ground.

24 And Nathan said, My lord the king, have you said, Adonijah shall reign after me, and he shall sit on my throne?

25 He has gone this day and sacrificed oxen, fatlings, and sheep in abundance, and has invited all the king's sons, the captains of the host, and Abiathar the priest; and they eat and drink before him and say, Long live King Adonijah!

26 But me your servant, and Zadok the priest, and Benaiah son of Jehoiada, and your servant Solomon he has not invited.

27 Is this done by my lord the king and you have not shown your servants who shall succeed my lord the king?

28 Then King David answered, Call Bathsheba. And she came into the king's presence and stood before him.

29 And the king took an oath and said, As the Lord lives, Who has redeemed my soul out of all distress,

30 Even as I swore to you by the Lord, the God of Israel, saying, Assuredly Solomon your son shall reign after me, and he shall sit upon my throne in my stead—even so will I certainly do this day.

31 Bathsheba bowed with her face to the ground and did obeisance to the king and said, Let my lord King David live forever!

32 King David said, Call Zadok the priest, Nathan the prophet, and Benaiah son of Jehoiada. And they came before the king.

33 The king told them, Take the servants of your lord and cause Solomon my son to ride on my own mule and bring him down to Gihon [in the Kidron Valley].

34 And let Zadok the priest and Nathan the prophet anoint him there king over Israel. Then blow the trumpet and say, Long live King Solomon!

35 Then you shall come up after him, and he shall come and sit on my throne, for he shall be king in my stead; I have appointed him ruler over Israel and Judah.

36 And Benaiah son of Jehoiada answered the king and said, Amen! May the Lord, the God of my lord the king, say so too.

37 As the Lord has been with my lord the king, even so may He be with Solomon and make his throne greater than the throne of my lord King David.

38 So Zadok the priest, Nathan the prophet, Benaiah son of Jehoiada, the Cherethites, and the Pelethites [the king's bodyguards] went down and caused Solomon to ride upon King David's mule and brought him to Gihon.

39 Zadok the priest took a horn of oil out of the tent and anointed Solomon. They blew the trumpet and all the people said, Long live King Solomon!

40 All the people followed him; they played on pipes and rejoiced greatly, so that the earth [resounded] with the joyful sound.

41 And Adonijah and all the guests with him heard it as they finished feasting. When Joab heard the trumpet sound, he said, What does this uproar in the city mean?

42 While he was still speaking, behold, Jonathan son of Abiathar the priest came. And Adonijah said, Come in, for you are a trustworthy man and bring good news.

43 Jonathan replied, Adonijah, truly our lord King David has made Solomon king!

44 The king has sent him with Zadok the priest, Nathan the prophet, Benaiah son of Jehoiada, the Cherethites and the Pelethites, and they have caused him to ride upon the king's mule.

45 Zadok the priest and Nathan the prophet have anointed him king in Gihon; they have come up from there

rejoicing, so the city resounds. This is the noise you heard.

46 Solomon sits on the royal throne.

47 Moreover, the king's servants came to congratulate our lord King David, saying, May God make the name of Solomon better than your name and make his throne greater than your throne. And the king bowed himself upon the bed

48 And said, Blessed be the Lord, the God of Israel, Who has granted me to see one of my offspring sitting on my throne this day.

49 And all the guests that were with Adonijah were afraid and rose up and went every man his way.

50 And Adonijah feared because of Solomon, and arose and went [to the tabernacle tent on Mt. Zion] and caught hold of the horns of the altar [as a fugitive's refuge].

51 And it was told Solomon, Behold, Adonijah fears King Solomon, for behold, he has caught hold of the horns of the altar, saying, Let King Solomon swear to me first that he will not slay his servant with the sword.

52 Solomon said, If he will show himself to be a worthy man, not a hair of him shall fall to the ground; but if wickedness is found in him, he shall die.

53 So King Solomon sent, and they brought Adonijah down from the altar [in front of the tabernacle]. He came and bowed himself to King Solomon, and Solomon said to him, Go to your house.

2 WHEN DAVID'S time to die was near, he charged Solomon his son, saying,

speak the Word

2 I go the way of all the earth. Be strong and show yourself a man;

3 Keep the charge of the Lord your God, walk in His ways, keep His statutes, His commandments, His precepts, and His testimonies, as it is written in the Law of Moses, that you may do wisely *and* prosper in all that you do and wherever you turn,

4 That the Lord may fulfill His promise to me, saying, If your sons take heed to their way, to walk before Me in truth with all their heart *and* mind and with all their soul, there shall not fail you [to have] a man on the throne of Israel.

5 You know also what Joab son of Zeruiah did to me, and what he did to the two captains of the hosts of Israel, Abner son of Ner and Amasa son of Jether, whom he murdered, avenging in time of peace blood shed in war, and putting innocent blood of war on the girdle on his loins and on the sandals of his feet.

6 Do therefore according to your wisdom, but let not his hoary head go down to Sheol (the place of the dead) in peace.

7 But show kindness to the sons of Barzillai the Gileadite and let them be among those who eat at your table; for with such kindness they met me when I fled because of Absalom your brother. [II Sam. 17:27-29.]

8 And you have with you Shimei son of Gera, the Benjamite of Bahurim, who cursed me with a grievous curse in the day when I went to Mahanaim. But he came down to meet me at the Jordan [on my return], and I swore to him by the Lord, saying, I will not put you to death with the sword.

God, I pray that I will keep Your charge, walk in Your ways, and keep Your statutes and commandments, that I may do wisely and prosper in all that I do, wherever I turn.
ADAPTED FROM II KINGS 2:3

9 So do not hold him guiltless; for you are a wise man and know what you should do to him. His hoary head bring down to the grave with blood.

10 So David slept with his fathers and was buried in the City of David.

11 David reigned over Israel forty years—seven years in Hebron and thirty-three years in Jerusalem.

12 Then Solomon sat on the throne of David his father, and his kingdom was firmly established.

13 Adonijah, the son of [David and] Haggith, came to Bathsheba, the mother of Solomon. She said, Do you come peaceably? And he said, Peaceably.

14 He said, I have something to say to you. And she said, Say on.

15 He said, You know that the kingdom belonged to me [as the eldest living son], and all Israel looked to me to reign. However, the kingdom has passed from me to my brother; for it was his from the Lord.

putting the Word to work

Today's world is full of examples of people who have maneuvered or manipulated their way into positions of authority that were not rightfully theirs. Have you ever felt that you have been cheated out of a promotion or a position of leadership? Like Solomon, you can rest confidently in the knowledge that if such a position is God's purpose for you, nothing or no one can keep you from being established in that place. Put your faith in God and His power to promote you, and do not ever let resentment or bitterness take root in your heart. Always remember that God's timing and ways are perfect!

16 Now I make one request of you; do not deny me. And she said, Say on.

17 He said, I pray you, ask King Solomon, for he will not refuse you, to give me Abishag the Shunammite to be my wife. [I Kings 1:1-4.]

18 And Bathsheba said, Very well; I will speak for you to the king.

19 So Bathsheba went to King Solomon to speak to him for Adonijah. The king rose to meet her, bowed to her, sat down on his throne, and caused a seat to be set at his right hand for her, the king's mother.

20 Then she said, I have one small request to make of you; do not refuse me. The king said to her, Ask on, my mother, for I will not refuse you.

21 She said, Give Abishag the Shunammite to Adonijah your brother to be his wife.

22 King Solomon answered his mother, And why do you ask Abishag the Shunammite for Adonijah? Ask for him the kingdom also—for he is my elder brother—[ask it] even for him and for [his supporters] Abiathar the priest and Joab son of Zeruiah.

23 Then King Solomon swore by the Lord, saying, May God do so to me, and more also, if Adonijah has not requested this against his own life.

24 Therefore, as the Lord lives, Who has established me and set me on the throne of David my father and Who has made me a house as He promised, Adonijah shall be put to death this day.

25 So King Solomon sent Benaiah son of Jehoiada, who attacked [Adonijah] and he died.

26 And to Abiathar the priest the king said, Get to Anathoth to your own estate; for you deserve death, but I will not put you to death now, because you bore the ark of the Lord God before my father David and were afflicted in all my father endured.

27 So Solomon expelled Abiathar [descendant of Eli] from being priest to the Lord, fulfilling the word of the Lord which He spoke concerning the house of Eli in Shiloh. [I Sam. 2:27-36.]

28 When the news came to Joab, for

Joab had followed Adonijah though he had not followed Absalom, [he] fled to the tent (tabernacle) of the Lord and caught hold of the horns of the altar [before it].

29 King Solomon was told that Joab had fled to the tent of the Lord and was at the altar. Then Solomon sent Benaiah son of Jehoiada, saying, Go, strike him down.

30 So Benaiah came to the tent of the Lord and told Joab, The king commands, Come forth. But Joab said, No, I will die here. Then Benaiah brought the king word again, Thus said Joab, and thus he answered me.

31 The king said to him, Do as he has said. Strike him down and bury him, that you may take away from [me and from] my father's house the innocent blood which Joab shed.

32 The Lord shall return his bloody deeds upon his own head, for he fell upon two men more [uncompromisingly] righteous and honorable than he and slew them with the sword, without my father knowing of it: Abner son of Ner, captain of the host of Israel, and Amasa son of Jether, captain of the host of Judah.

33 So shall their blood return upon the head of Joab and of his descendants forever. But upon David, his descendants, his house, and his throne, there shall be peace from the Lord forever.

34 So Benaiah son of Jehoiada went up and struck and killed Joab, and he was buried at his own house in the wilderness.

35 The king put Benaiah son of Jehoiada in Joab's place over the army and put Zadok the priest in place of Abiathar.

36 The king sent for Shimei and said to him, Build yourself a house in Jerusalem and dwell there, and do not leave there.

37 For on the day you go out and pass over the brook Kidron, know with certainty that you shall die; your blood shall be upon your own head.

38 And Shimei said to the king, The saying is good. As my lord the king has said, so your servant will do. And Shimei dwelt in Jerusalem many days.

39 But after three years, two of Shimei's servants ran away to Achish son of Maacah, king of Gath. And Shimei was told, Behold, your [runaway] servants are in Gath.

40 So Shimei arose, saddled his donkey, and went to Gath to King Achish to seek his servants, and brought them from Gath.

41 It was told Solomon that Shimei went from Jerusalem to Gath and had returned.

42 And the king sent for Shimei and said to him, Did I not make you swear by the Lord and warn you, saying, Know with certainty, on the day you go out and walk abroad anywhere, you shall surely die? And you said to me, I have heard your word. It is accepted.

43 Why then have you not kept the oath of the Lord and the command with which I have charged you?

44 The king also said to Shimei, You are aware in your own heart of all the evil you did to my father David; so the Lord will return your evil upon your own head.

45 But King Solomon shall be blessed, and the throne of David shall be established before the Lord forever.

46 So the king commanded Benaiah son of Jehoiada, who went out and struck down Shimei, and he died. And the kingdom was established in the hands of Solomon.

3 AND SOLOMON made an alliance with Pharaoh king of Egypt and took Pharaoh's daughter and brought her into the City of David until he had finished building his own house and the house of the Lord, and the wall around Jerusalem.

2 But the people sacrificed [to God] in the high places [as the heathen did to their idols], for there was no house yet built to the ᶜName of the Lord.

3 Solomon loved the Lord, walking [at first] in the statutes *and* practices of David his father, only he sacrificed and burned incense in the high places.

4 The king went to Gibeon [near Jerusalem, where stood the tabernacle and the bronze altar] to sacrifice there, for that was the great high place. One thousand burnt offerings Solomon offered on that altar.

5 In Gibeon the Lord appeared to Solomon in a dream by night. And God said, ᵈAsk what I shall give you.

6 Solomon said, You have shown to Your servant David my father great mercy *and* loving-kindness, according as he walked before You in faithfulness, righteousness, and uprightness of heart with You; and You have kept for him this great kindness *and* steadfast love, that You have given him a son to sit on his throne this day.

7 Now, O Lord my God, You have made Your servant king instead of David my father, and I am ᵉbut a lad [in wisdom and experience]; I know not how to go out (begin) or come in (finish).

8 Your servant is in the midst of Your people whom You have chosen, a great people who cannot be counted for multitude.

9 So give Your servant an understanding mind *and* a hearing heart to judge Your people, that I may discern between good and bad. For who is

speak the Word

putting the Word to work

If God came to you and said, "Ask! What shall I give you?" as He did to Solomon (see I Kings 3:5–10), how do you think you would respond? Solomon could have asked for riches beyond imagining, great fame, or unsurpassable power. Yet Solomon's response is an amazing demonstration of humility and recognition of his need for God and for wisdom. When you take your requests before God, ask Him to show you those things you truly need, and always remember that your greatest need is for *Him*, not the things He can do for you.

able to judge *and* rule this Your great people? [James 1:5.]

10 It pleased the Lord that Solomon had asked this.

11 God said to him, Because you have asked this and have not asked for long life or for riches, nor for the lives of your enemies, but have asked for yourself understanding to recognize what is just and right,

12 Behold, I have done as you asked. I have given you a wise, discerning mind, so that no one before you was your equal, nor shall any arise after you equal to you.

13 I have also given you what you have not asked, both riches and honor, so that there shall not be any among the kings equal to you all your days.

14 And if you will go My way, keep My statutes and My commandments

---

God, I pray that You would give me an understanding mind and heart that hears Your voice so that I can discern between good and evil.
ADAPTED FROM II KINGS 3:9

---

c See footnote on Deut. 12:5.   **d** This is the high privilege of the child of God. Each one's life tells what he has asked for—"in heaven above or in the earth beneath." Which shall it be, God's will and glory, or our own?   **e** Solomon was already a father (see I Kings 11:42; 14:21).

seek the best

If God were to tell you that you could ask for anything and He would give it to you, what would you ask for? Solomon had this opportunity, and God was extremely pleased with his request (see I Kings 3:5–10). He asked for wisdom, an understanding mind, and a hearing heart so that he might discern between good and evil.

It would be a great blessing if all God's children understood the value of wisdom, understanding, discretion, discernment, and prudence. Proverbs teaches us that these things are more valuable than anything else we could desire. They are more valuable than silver and gold, rubies, pearls, or other precious gems (see Proverbs 3:13–15).

What we seek after in life reveals so much about our character. Too many of us seek the wrong things, and, as a result, we are never satisfied and fulfilled. If we will seek God as our number one necessity in life and ask for understanding of His ways, we will be content and God will add other things, as He did for Solomon. God was so pleased with Solomon's request for wisdom that He also gave him popularity, fame, an abundance of wealth and possessions, friends, family, success, and anything else he could ever want in life.

What are you seeking? God confronted me with this question several years ago, and I discovered that my answer was not pleasing to Him. I was ashamed when I realized how much more concerned I was with my circumstances than with my spiritual life. At that point, God began to teach me what is truly valuable, and His grace enabled me to change my focus. I am eternally glad that God asked me that question, and I now ask it of myself on a regular basis. I always want to seek those things that are pleasing to my Lord, and I am sure you feel the same way.

Do not feel condemned if you find that the focus of your desires needs to be adjusted. Just ask God to help you make the necessary changes. Seek wisdom; seek to have a heart that understands other people's hurts and needs. Ask for the ability to discern between good and evil and the grace to always make the right choices. As you seek these things, you will enjoy a life that is beyond anything you could ever imagine.

as your father David did, then I will lengthen your days.

15 Solomon awoke, and behold, it was a dream. He came to Jerusalem, stood before the ark of the covenant of the Lord, and offered burnt offerings and peace offerings, and made a feast for all his servants.

16 Then two women who had become mothers out of wedlock came and stood before the king.

17 And one woman said, O my lord, I and this woman dwell in one house; and I was delivered of a child with her in the house.

18 And the third day after I was delivered, this woman also was delivered. And we were together; no stranger was with us, just we two in the house.

19 And this woman's child died in the night because she lay on him.

20 And she arose at midnight and took my son from beside me while your handmaid slept and laid him in her bosom and laid her dead child in my bosom.

21 And when I rose to nurse my child, behold, he was dead. But when I had considered him in the morning, behold, it was not the son I had borne.

22 But the other woman said, No! But the living one is my son, and the dead one is your son! And this one said, No! But the dead son is your son, and the living is my son. Thus they spoke before the king.

23 The king said, One says, This is my son that is alive and yours is the dead one. The other woman says, No! But your son is the dead one and mine is the living one.

24 And the king said, Bring me a sword. And they brought a sword to the king.

25 And the king said, Divide the living child in two and give half to the one and half to the other.

26 Then the mother of the living child said to the king, for she yearned over her son, O my lord, give her the living baby, and by no means slay him. But the other said, Let him not be mine or yours, but divide him.

27 Then the king said, Give her [who pleads for his life] the living baby, and by no means slay him. She is the child's mother.

28 And all Israel heard of the judgment which the king had made, and they stood in awe of him, for they saw that the wisdom of God was in him to do justice.

4 KING SOLOMON was king over all Israel.
2 These were his chief officials:

Azariah son of Zadok was the [high] priest;

3 Elihoreph and Ahijah, sons of Shisha, were secretaries; Jehoshaphat son of Ahilud was recorder;

4 Benaiah son of Jehoiada commanded the army; Zadok and Abiathar were priests;

5 Azariah son of Nathan was over the officers; Zabud son of Nathan was priest and the king's friend *and* private advisor;

6 Ahishar was in charge of the palace; and Adoniram son of Abda was in charge of the forced labor.

7 Solomon had twelve officers over all Israel, who secured provisions for the king and his household; each man had to provide for a month in a year.

8 These were their names: Ben-hur, in the hill country of Ephraim;

9 Ben-deker, in Makaz, Shaalbim, Beth-shemesh, and Elon-beth-hanan;

10 Ben-hesed, in Arubboth (to him belonged Socoh and all the land of Hepher);

11 Ben-abinadab, in Naphoth-dor (he had Taphath, Solomon's daughter, as wife);

12 Baana son of Ahilud, in Taanach,

putting the Word to work

Have you ever thought that a law or perhaps a court verdict was unfair or unjust? The Israelites ruled by Solomon were greatly blessed by his God-given wisdom in administering justice among them (see I Kings 3:28). Some governing officials today are like Solomon, but not all of them are. Remember to pray for those in the legislative and legal systems, that they might have great wisdom and discernment in matters of justice. Pray that they will all totally submit their lives to God and make laws based on His Word and principles.

Megiddo, and all Beth-shean which is beside Zarethan below Jezreel, from Beth-shean to Abel-meholah as far as beyond Jokmeam;

13 Ben-geber, in Ramoth-gilead (to him belonged the villages of Jair son of Manasseh which are in Gilead, also the region of Argob which is in Bashan, sixty great cities with walls and bronze bars);

14 Ahinadab son of Iddo, in Mahanaim;

15 Ahimaaz, in Naphtali (he had taken Basemath, Solomon's daughter, as his wife);

16 Baana son of Hushai, in Asher and Bealoth;

17 Jehoshaphat son of Paruah, in Issachar;

18 Shimei son of Ela, in Benjamin;

19 Geber son of Uri, in Gilead, the country of Sihon king of the Amorites and of Og king of Bashan; only one officer was over all the country [at one time, each serving for one month].

20 Judah and Israel were many, like the sand which is by the sea in multitude; they ate, drank, and rejoiced.

21 Solomon reigned ᶠover all the kingdoms from the [Euphrates] River to the land of the Philistines and to the border of Egypt; they brought tribute and served Solomon all the days of his life.

22 Solomon's provision for one day was thirty measures of fine flour, sixty measures of meal,

23 Ten fat oxen, twenty pasture-fed cattle, a hundred sheep, besides harts, gazelles, roebucks, and fatted fowl of choice kinds.

24 For he had dominion over all the region west of the [Euphrates] River, from Tiphsah to Gaza, over all the kings west of the River, and he had peace on all sides around him.

25 Judah and Israel dwelt safely, every man under his vine and fig tree, from Dan to Beersheba, all of Solomon's days.

26 Solomon also had 40,000 stalls of horses for his chariots, and 12,000 horsemen.

27 And those officers provided food for King Solomon and for all who came to his table, every man in his month; they let nothing be lacking.

28 Barley also and straw for the horses and swift steeds they brought to the place where it was needed, each according to his assignment.

29 And God gave Solomon exceptionally much wisdom and understanding, and breadth of mind like the sand of the seashore.

30 Solomon's wisdom excelled the wisdom of all the people of the East and all the wisdom of Egypt.

31 For he was wiser ᵍthan all other

speak the Word

Lord, I pray that You would do for me what You did for Solomon and give me exceedingly much wisdom and understanding, and breadth of mind like the sand of the seashore.
ADAPTED FROM I KINGS 4:29

f That King Solomon's empire was as great as is definitely indicated here and in II Chron. 9:26 has frequently been questioned because of the great empires of Assyria on the Euphrates and Egypt on the Nile. But archaeological discoveries prove that "precisely during the period 1100-900 BC, when the kingdom of Israel was being built up, 'the weak and inglorious twenty-first dynasty' was ruling in Egypt and at the same time Assyria went into a period of decline" (J.P. Free, *Archaeology and Bible History*, citing A.T. Olmstead, *History of Assyria*). **g** "Wiser than all other men," until Christ came. Jesus said, "Someone more *and* greater than Solomon is here" (Matt. 12:42).

men–than Ethan the Ezrahite, and Heman, Calcol, and Darda, the sons of Mahol. His fame was in all the nations round about.

32 He also originated 3,000 proverbs, and his songs were 1,005.

33 He spoke of trees, from the cedar that is in Lebanon to the hyssop that grows out of the wall; he spoke also of beasts, of birds, of creeping things, and of fish.

34 Men came from all peoples to hear the wisdom of Solomon, and from all kings of the earth who had heard of his wisdom.

5 HIRAM KING of Tyre sent his servants to Solomon, when he heard that he was anointed king in place of his father, for Hiram always loved David.

2 And Solomon sent to Hiram, saying,

3 You know how David my father could not build a house to the Name of the Lord his God because wars were about him on every side, until the Lord put his foes under his feet. [II Sam. 7:4ff.; I Chron. 22:8.]

4 But now the Lord my God has given me rest on every side, so that there is neither adversary nor evil confronting me.

5 And I purpose to build a house to the Name of the Lord my God, as the Lord said to David my father, Your son whom I will set on your throne in your place shall build the house to My Name *and* Presence.

6 So, Hiram, command them to hew me cedar trees out of Lebanon; my servants shall join yours, and I will give you whatever wages you set for your servants. For you know that no one among us can equal the skill of the Sidon men in cutting timber.

7 When Hiram heard the words of Solomon, he rejoiced greatly and said, Blessed be the Lord this day, Who has given David a wise son to be over this great people.

8 And Hiram sent to Solomon, saying, I have considered the things for which you sent to me; I will do all you wish concerning the cedar and cypress timber.

9 My servants shall bring the logs down from Lebanon to the sea, make them into rafts, and float them by sea to the place that you direct. I will have them released there, and you shall take them away. And you shall fulfill my desire by providing food for my household.

10 So Hiram gave Solomon all the cedar and cypress trees he desired,

11 And Solomon gave Hiram 20,000 measures of wheat for food for his household, and 20 measures of pure, beaten oil. He gave these to Hiram yearly.

12 The Lord gave Solomon wisdom, as He promised him; and there was peace between Hiram and Solomon, and they made a treaty.

13 King Solomon raised a levy [of forced labor] out of all Israel; and the levy was 30,000 men.

14 He sent them to Lebanon, 10,000 a month by divisions; one month they were in Lebanon and two months at home. Adoniram was over the levy.

15 And Solomon had 70,000 burden bearers and 80,000 hewers [of stone] in the hill country of Judah,

16 Besides Solomon's 3,300 overseers in charge of the people doing the work.

17 The king commanded, and they hewed *and* brought out ʰgreat, costly stones in order to lay the foundation of the house with dressed stone.

h These great foundation stones remain to this day. One of them is almost thirty-nine feet long, one of the most interesting stones of the world. It is the chief cornerstone of the Mosque of Omar's massive wall, placed in its present position 3,000 years ago. Markings on the stones represent the culture of Phoenicia, the region around Tyre from which Solomon received building materials for the temple.

handling your relationships wisely

Solomon asked God for wisdom, and God gave it to him (see I Kings 5:12). Solomon wrote the book of Proverbs, a collection of wise truths that have helped many people successfully live their day-to-day lives.

The Bible teaches us that it is hard to succeed at anything if we do not possess wisdom. Many people have gifts, but they do not operate in wisdom or develop good character because they simply will not grow up and allow God to do the things He needs to do in their lives. As believers in Jesus Christ, His wisdom is in us, but it does us no good if we do not use it. Nothing works right in life or relationships if we do not seek and walk in wisdom.

Let me give you an example of what can happen when people do not use wisdom in relationships. So many people get hurt because they tell friends what is on their hearts, and those friends betray them. Then they become angry with their friend. If they had used wisdom and kept their mouths shut in the first place, they would have avoided that whole situation. I know this is true because it has happened to me many times. God once told me, "Joyce, if you don't want your friends hurting your feelings and betraying you, then just learn to keep quiet about things you don't want anyone to know." If we expect God to share His secrets with us, we must be able to keep His secrets. Not telling people things I do not want repeated has taken a great deal of pressure out of my relationships. I no longer have to worry about their telling things I do not want known.

I cannot overemphasize the importance of using wisdom as we deal with other people—family, friends, coworkers, neighbors, and even casual acquaintances. Ask God to give you wisdom in your relationships. He'll do it!

18 Solomon's builders and Hiram's builders and the men of Gebal did the hewing and prepared the timber and stones to build the house.

6 AND 480 years after the Israelites came out of the land of Egypt, in the fourth year of Solomon's reign over Israel, in the second month, Ziv, he began to build the Lord's house.
2 The length of the house Solomon built for the Lord was sixty cubits, its breadth twenty, and its height thirty cubits.
3 The length of the vestibule in front of the temple was twenty cubits, equal to the width of the house, and

its depth in front of the house was ten cubits.
4 For the house he made narrow [latticed] windows.
5 Against the wall of the house he built chambers running round the walls of the house both of the Holy Place and of the Holy of Holies; and he made side chambers all around.
6 The first story's side chambers were five cubits wide, those of the middle story six cubits wide, and of the third story seven cubits wide; for around the outside of the wall of the house he made offsets in order that the supporting beams should not be thrust into the walls of the house.
7 When the house was being built,

its stone was made ready at the quarry, and no hammer, ax, or tool of iron was heard in the house while it was in building.

8 The entrance to the lowest side chamber was on the right [or south] side of the house; and one went up winding stairs into the middle chamber and from the middle into the third.

9 So Solomon built the temple building and finished it, and roofed the house with beams and boards of cedar.

10 Then he built the stories of chambers [the lean-to] against all the house, each [story] five cubits high; and it was joined to the house with timbers of cedar.

11 Now the word of the Lord came to Solomon, saying,

12 Concerning this house which you are building, if you will walk in My statutes, execute My precepts, and keep all My commandments to walk in them, then I will fulfill to you My promises which I made to David your father.

13 And I will dwell among the Israelites and will not forsake My people Israel.

14 So Solomon built the house and finished it.

15 He built the walls of the house (the Holy Place and the Holy of Holies) within with boards of cedar, from the floor of the house to the rafters of the ceiling. He covered the inside with wood, and the floor of the house with boards of cypress.

16 He built twenty cubits of the rear of the house with boards of cedar from the floor to the rafters; he built it within for the sanctuary, the Holy of Holies.

17 The [rest of the] house, that is, the temple in front of the Holy of Holies, was forty cubits long.

18 The cedar on the house within was carved with gourds and open flowers. All was cedar; no stone was visible.

putting the Word to work

Do you sometimes wonder whether God is concerned with the details of your life? Take heart in knowing that the God Who gave such precise instructions for the construction of the temple (see I Kings 6:14—7:51) is even more concerned about the particulars of your life. If something matters to you, it matters to Him!

19 And he prepared the Holy of Holies in the inner room in which to set the ark of the covenant of the Lord.

20 The Holy of Holies was twenty cubits in length, in breadth, and in height. He overlaid it with pure gold. He also overlaid the cedar altar.

21 Solomon overlaid the house within with pure gold, and he drew chains of gold across in front of the Holy of Holies and overlaid it with gold.

22 And the whole house he overlaid with gold, until all the house was finished. Also the whole [incense] altar that [stood outside the door but] belonged to the Holy of Holies he overlaid with gold.

23 Within the Holy of Holies he made two cherubim of olive wood, each ten cubits high.

life point

As you read about the construction of the temple, notice that God's house was built with extreme excellence (see I Kings 6:18–21). Today, we, His people, are His "house," the place where He lives and reveals Himself. We modern-day believers need to be diligent to follow the example of the Old Testament temple and provide excellence to the world around us by being excellent people.

24 Five cubits was the length of one wing of the cherub and five cubits its other wing; from the tip of one wing to the tip of the other was ten cubits.

25 The wings of the other cherub were also ten cubits. Both cherubim were the same,

26 The height of one cherub ten cubits, as was the other.

27 He put the cherubim within the inner sanctuary. Their wings were stretched out, so that the wing of one touched one wall, and the wing of the other cherub touched the other wall, and their inner wings touched in the midst of the room.

28 Solomon overlaid the cherubim with gold.

29 He carved all the walls of the house (these two holy rooms) round about with figures of cherubim, palm trees, and open flowers, within and without.

30 The floor of the house he overlaid with gold, inside and out.

31 For the Holy of Holies he made [folding] doors of olive wood; their entire width was one-fifth that of the wall.

32 On the two doors of olive wood he carved cherubim, palm trees, and open flowers; he overlaid them with gold, and spread gold on the cherubim and palm trees.

33 Also he made for the door of the Holy Place four-sided posts of olive wood.

34 The two doors were of cypress wood; the two leaves of each door were folding.

35 He carved on them cherubim, palm trees, and open flowers, covered with gold evenly applied on the carved work.

36 He built the inner court with three rows of hewn stone and a row of cedar beams.

37 In the fourth year the foundation of the Lord's house was laid, in the [second] month, Ziv.

38 In the eleventh year, in Bul, the eighth month, the house was finished throughout according to all its specifications. So he was seven years in building it.

7 SOLOMON WAS building his own house ithirteen years, and he finished all of it.

2 He built also the Forest of Lebanon House; its length was a hundred cubits, its breadth fifty, and its height thirty cubits, upon four rows of cedar pillars, with cedar beams upon the pillars.

3 And it was covered with cedar above the side chambers that were upon the forty-five pillars, fifteen in a row.

4 There were window frames in three rows, and window opposite window in three tiers.

5 All the doorways and windows were square cut, and window was opposite window in three tiers.

6 He also made the Hall of Pillars; its length was fifty cubits and its breadth thirty cubits. There was a porch in front, and pillars and a cornice before them.

7 He made the porch for the throne where he was to judge, the Porch of Judgment; it was covered with cedar from floor to ceiling.

8 His house where he was to dwell had another court behind the Porch of Judgment of similar work. Solomon also made a house like this porch for Pharaoh's daughter, whom he had married.

i Solomon built God's house first, then his own. That his took much longer is no reflection on Solomon, for David had made every possible preparation for building the temple, greatly reducing the time needed to finish it (I Chron. 22:2-5). David even left for Solomon plans and patterns for the temple and loyal friends eager to help (I Kings 5:1; I Chron. 28:14-19).

9 All were of costly stones hewn according to measure, sawed with saws back and front, even from foundation to coping, and from the outside to the great court.

10 The foundation was of costly stones, even great stones of eight and ten cubits.

11 And above were costly stones hewn according to measure, and cedar timbers.

12 Also the great encircling court had three courses of hewn stone and a course of cedar beams, like was around the inner court of the house of the Lord and the porch of the house.

13 King Solomon brought Hiram from Tyre.

14 He was the son of a widow of the tribe of Naphtali, and his father was a man of Tyre, a worker in bronze. He was full of wisdom, understanding, and skill to do any kind of work in bronze. So he came to King Solomon and did all his [bronze] work.

15 He fashioned the two pillars of bronze, each eighteen cubits high, and a line of twelve cubits measured its circumference.

16 He made two capitals of molten bronze to set upon the tops of the pillars; the height of each capital was five cubits.

17 Nets of checkerwork and wreaths of chainwork for the capitals were on the tops of the pillars, seven for each capital.

18 So Hiram made the pillars. There were two rows of pomegranates encircling each network to cover the capitals that were upon the top.

19 The capitals that were upon the top of the pillars in the porch were of lily work [design], four cubits.

20 The capitals were upon the two pillars and also above the rounded projection beside the network. There were 200 pomegranates in two rows round about, and so with the other capital.

21 Hiram set up the pillars of the porch of the temple; he set up the right pillar and called its name Jachin [he will establish], and he set up the left pillar and called its name Boaz [in strength].

22 On the tops of the pillars was lily work [design]. So the work of the pillars was finished.

23 He made a round molten Sea, ten cubits from brim to brim, five cubits high and thirty cubits in circumference. [Exod. 30:17-21; II Chron. 4:6.]

24 Under its brim were gourds encircling the Sea, ten to a cubit; the gourds were in two rows, cast in one piece with it.

25 It stood upon twelve oxen, three facing north, three west, three south, and three east; the Sea was set upon them, and all their rears pointed inward.

26 It was a handbreadth thick, and its brim was made like the brim of a cup, like a lily blossom. It held 2,000 baths [Hebrew liquid measurement].

27 Hiram made ten bronze bases [for the lavers]; their length and breadth were four cubits, and the height three cubits.

28 This is the way the bases were made: they had panels between the ledges.

29 On the panels between the ledges were lions, oxen, and cherubim; and upon the ledges there was a pedestal above. Beneath the lions and oxen were wreaths of hanging work.

30 And every base had four bronze wheels and axles of bronze, and at the four corners were supports for a laver. Beneath the laver the supports were cast, with wreaths at the side of each.

31 Its mouth within the capital projected upward a cubit, and its mouth was round like the work of a pedestal, a cubit and a half. Also upon its mouth were carvings, and their borders were square, not round.

32 Under the borders were four wheels, and the axles of the wheels were one piece with the base. And the height of a wheel was a cubit and a half.

33 The wheels were made like a chariot wheel: their axles, their rims, their spokes, and their hubs were all cast.

34 There were four supports to the four corners of each base; the supports were part of the base itself.

35 On the top of the base there was a circular elevation half a cubit high, and on the top of the base its stays and panels were of one piece with it.

36 And on the surface of its stays and its panels Hiram carved cherubim, lions, and palm trees, according to the space of each, with wreaths round about.

37 Thus he made the ten bases. They all had one casting, one measure, and one form.

38 Then he made ten lavers of bronze; each laver held forty baths and measured four cubits, and there was one laver on each of the ten bases.

39 He put the bases five on the south side of the house and five on the north side; and he set the Sea at the southeast corner of the house.

40 Hiram made the lavers, the shovels, and the basins. So Hiram finished all the work that he did for King Solomon on the house of the Lord:

41 The two pillars; and the two bowls of the capitals that were on the tops of the two pillars; and the two networks to cover the two bowls;

42 And the 400 pomegranates for the two networks, two rows of pomegranates for each network, to cover the two bowls of the capitals that were upon the pillars;

43 The ten bases and the ten lavers on the bases;

44 One Sea, and the twelve oxen under it;

45 The pots, the shovels, and the basins. All these vessels which Hiram made for King Solomon in the house of the Lord were of burnished bronze.

46 In the Jordan plain the king cast them, in clay ground between Succoth and Zarethan.

47 Solomon left all the vessels unweighed, because they were so many; the weight of the bronze was not found out.

48 Solomon made all the other vessels of the Lord's house: the [incense] altar of gold; the table of gold for the showbread;

49 The lampstands of pure gold, five on the right side and five on the left, in front of the Holy of Holies; with the flowers, the lamps, and the tongs of gold;

50 The cups, snuffers, basins, spoons, firepans—of pure gold; and the hinges of gold for the doors of the innermost room, the Holy of Holies, and for the doors of the Holy Place.

51 So all the work that King Solomon did on the house of the Lord was completed. Solomon brought in the things which David his father had dedicated—the silver, the gold, and the vessels—and put them in the treasuries of the Lord's house.

8 THEN SOLOMON assembled the elders of Israel and all the heads of the tribes, the chiefs of the fathers' houses of the Israelites, before the king in Jerusalem, to bring up the ark of the covenant of the Lord out of Zion, the City of David.

2 All the men of Israel assembled themselves before King Solomon at the feast in the seventh month, Ethanim.

3 All the elders of Israel came, and the priests took up the ark.

4 And they brought up the ark of the Lord, the Tent of Meeting, and all the holy vessels that were in the tent; the priests and the Levites brought them up.

5 King Solomon and all the congregation of Israel who had assembled before him were with him before the ark, sacrificing sheep and oxen, so many that they could not be reported or counted.

6 And the priests brought the ark of the covenant of the Lord to its place in the Holy of Holies of the house, under the wings of the cherubim.

7 For the cherubim spread forth their two wings over the place of the ark, and the cherubim covered the ark and its poles.

8 The poles were so long that the ends of them were seen from the Holy Place before the Holy of Holies, but they were not seen outside; they are there to this day.

9 There was nothing in the ark except the two tables of stone which Moses put there at Horeb, where the Lord made a covenant with the Israelites when they came out of the land of Egypt. [Deut. 10:2-5.]

10 When the priests had come out of the Holy Place, the cloud filled the Lord's house,

11 So the priests could not stand to minister because of the cloud, for the glory of the Lord had filled the Lord's house.

His awesome presence

In the Old Testament, the ark of the covenant represented the presence of the Lord. I cannot stress enough how much we need God's presence in our lives—in fact, we need His presence more than we need anything else.

When God called Moses to tell Pharaoh to let God's people go, Moses was scared and insecure about his lack of abilities. But God said to him, "I will surely be with you" (see Exodus 3:10–14). Later God told Moses, "My Presence shall go with you, and I will give you rest" (Exodus 33:14). I love Moses' reply: "If Your Presence does not go with me, do not carry us up from here!" (Exodus 33:15). In other words, "God, if You're not going to be there, don't send me!" That's exactly the way I feel when I start to minister to others.

We need to really understand the awesomeness of the presence of God and the magnitude of what is available to us as believers if only we will take the time to be in His presence! Why in the world would we not want to spend time with God? We spend time on the telephone, we hang out in the shopping center, we spend hours in front of the television—and we seem to have no problem investing our time in those pursuits. The truth is this: *The devil fights us more in the area of our spending time with God than he does in any other area of our Christian lives.* In fact, Satan would much prefer that we get involved in all kinds of religious activity rather than spend time with the Lord.

There is only one way I know to maintain the anointing on my life, and that is by spending time in the presence of God. You may be wondering, *But what do I do when I spend time with God?* You simply set aside a portion of your time for that purpose. Try not to be legalistic about it, but do try to be as regular with it as you can. During that time period, read the Bible and Christian books that minister to you. Talk to God. Sometimes you may want to listen to Christian music and worship; other times you may want to sit there and enjoy the silence. If you will do that, you will begin to feel and sense the presence of the Lord.

12 Then Solomon said, The Lord said that He would dwell in the thick darkness.

13 I have surely built You a house of habitation, a settled place for You to dwell in forever.

14 And the king turned his face about and blessed all the assembly of Israel, and all the assembly of Israel stood.

15 He said, Blessed be the Lord, the God of Israel, Who spoke with His mouth to David my father and has with His hand fulfilled it, saying,

16 Since the day that I brought forth My people Israel out of Egypt, I chose no city out of all the tribes of Israel in which to build a house that My Name [and My Presence] might be in it, but I chose David to be over My people Israel.

17 Now it was in the heart of David my father to build a house for the Name [the Presence] of the Lord, the God of Israel.

18 And the Lord said to David my father, Whereas it was in your heart to build a house for My Name, you did well that it was in your heart.

19 Yet you shall not build the house, but your son, who shall be born to you, shall build it to My Name [and My actively present Person].

20 And the Lord has fulfilled His promise which He made: I have risen up in the place of David my father, and sit on the throne of Israel, as the Lord promised, and have built a house for the Name (renown) of the Lord, the God of Israel.

21 And I have made there a place for the ark [the token of ʲHis presence], in which is the covenant [the Ten Commandments] of the Lord which He made with our fathers when He brought them out of the land of Egypt. [Exod. 34:28.]

22 Then Solomon stood [in the court] before the Lord's burnt offering altar in the presence of all the assembly of Israel, and spread forth his hands toward heaven

23 And he said, O Lord, the God of Israel, there is no God like You in heaven above or on earth beneath, keeping covenant and showing mercy *and* loving-kindness to Your servants who walk before You with all their heart.

life point

There are many facets of God's character, and each one of them seems to be more wonderful than the next. In I Kings 8:23, Solomon referred to God as covenant-keeping, merciful, loving, and kind. He is also faithful, true, long-suffering, just, and honest—among many other wonderful attributes. We need to get acquainted with God's qualities because they reveal God's character to us. The better we know His character, the better we know His heart for us, and the easier it becomes to trust and obey Him.

24 You have kept what You promised Your servant David my father. You also spoke with Your mouth and have fulfilled it with Your hand, as it is this day.

25 Therefore now, O Lord, the God of Israel, keep with Your servant David my father what You promised him when You said, There shall not fail you a man before Me to sit on the throne of Israel, if only your children take heed to their way, that they walk before Me as you have done.

26 Now, O God of Israel, let Your word which You spoke to Your servant

---

j God acknowledged the ark as a token of His presence (Matthew Henry, *Commentary on the Holy Bible*). The ark of the covenant is the pledge of the divine gracious presence, and the cloud that filled the house (I Kings 8:10) is the sign that Yahweh will dwell here (J.P. Lange, *A Commentary*).

David my father be confirmed [by experience].

27 But will God indeed dwell with men on the earth? Behold, the heavens and heaven of heavens [in its most extended compass] cannot contain You; how much less this house that I have built?

28 Yet graciously consider the prayer and supplication of Your servant, O Lord my God, to hearken to the [loud] cry and prayer which he prays before You today,

29 That Your eyes may be open toward this house night and day, toward the place of which You have said, My Name [and the token of My presence] shall be there, that You may hearken to the prayer which Your servant shall make in [or facing toward] this place.

30 Hearken to the prayer of Your servant and of Your people Israel when they pray in *or* toward this place. Hear in heaven, Your dwelling place, and when You hear, forgive.

31 Whenever a man sins against his neighbor and is made to take an oath and comes and swears the oath before Your altar in this house,

32 Then hear in heaven and do and judge Your servants, condemning the wicked by bringing his guilt upon his own head and justifying the [uncompromisingly] righteous by rewarding him according to his righteousness (his uprightness, right standing with God).

33 When Your people Israel are struck down before the enemy because they have sinned against You, and they turn again to You, confess Your [k]name (Your revelation of Yourself), and pray, beseeching You in this house,

34 Then hear in heaven and forgive the sin of Your people Israel and return them to the land You gave to their fathers.

35 When heaven is shut up and no rain falls because they have sinned against You, if they pray in [or toward] this place and confess Your name (Your revelation of Yourself) and turn from their sin when You afflict them,

36 Then hear in heaven and forgive the sin of Your servants, Your people Israel, when You teach them the good way in which they should walk. And give rain upon Your land which You have given to Your people as an inheritance.

37 If there is famine in the land or pestilence, blight, mildew, locust, or caterpillar, if their enemy besieges them in the land of their cities, whatever plague, whatever sickness there is,

38 Whatever prayer or supplication is made by any or all of Your people Israel—each man knowing the affliction of his own heart, and spreading forth his hands toward this house [and its pledge of Your presence]—

39 Then hear in heaven, Your dwelling place, and forgive and act and give to every man according to his ways, whose heart You know, for You and You only know the hearts of all the children of men,

40 That they may fear *and* revere

speak the Word

Thank You, God, for graciously considering my prayers and supplications and for hearing the requests that I make of You today.
ADAPTED FROM I KINGS 8:28

---

k See footnote on Exod. 3:15.

You all the days that they live in the land which You gave to our fathers.

41 Moreover, concerning a stranger who is not of Your people Israel but comes from a far country for the sake of Your name [and Your active Presence]—

42 For they will hear of Your great name (Your revelation of Yourself), Your strong hand, and outstretched arm—when he shall pray in [or toward] this house,

43 Hear in heaven, Your dwelling place, and do according to all that the stranger asks of You, so that all peoples of the earth may know Your name [and ¹Your revelation of Your presence] and fear *and* revere You, as do Your people Israel, and may know *and* comprehend that this house which I have built is called by Your Name [and contains the token of Your presence].

44 If Your people go out to battle against their enemy, wherever You shall send them, and shall pray to the Lord toward the city which You have chosen and the house that I have built for Your Name [and Your revelation of Yourself],

45 Then hear in heaven their prayer and supplication, and defend their cause *and* maintain their right.

46 If they sin against You—for there is no man who does not sin—and You are angry with them and deliver them to the enemy, so that they are carried away captive to the enemy's land, far or near;

47 Yet if they think *and* consider in the land where they were carried captive, and repent and make supplication to You there, saying, We have

speak the Word

sinned and have done perversely and wickedly;

48 If they repent *and* turn to You with all their mind and with all their heart in the land of their enemies who took them captive, and pray to You toward their land which You gave to their fathers, the city which You have chosen, and the house which I have built for Your Name;

49 Then hear their prayer and their supplication in heaven, Your dwelling place, and defend their cause *and* maintain their right.

50 And forgive Your people, who have sinned against You, and all their transgressions against You, and grant them compassion before those who took them captive, that they may have pity and be merciful to them;

51 For they are Your people and Your heritage, which You brought out of Egypt, from the midst of the iron furnace.

52 Let Your eyes be open to the supplication of Your servant and of Your people Israel, to hearken to them in all for which they call to You.

53 For You separated them from among all the peoples of the earth to be Your heritage, as You declared through Moses Your servant when You brought our fathers out of Egypt, O Lord God.

54 When Solomon finished offering all this prayer and supplication to the Lord, he arose from before the Lord's altar, where he had knelt with hands stretched toward heaven.

55 And he stood and blessed all the assembly of Israel with a loud voice, saying,

God, I pray that I will have a revelation of Your presence in my life.
ADAPTED FROM I KINGS 8:43

1 See footnote on Exod. 3:15.

56 Blessed be the Lord, Who has given rest to His people Israel, according to all that He promised. Not one word has failed of all His good promise which He promised through Moses His servant.

57 May the Lord our God be with us as He was with our fathers; may He not leave us or forsake us,

58 That He may incline our hearts to Him, to walk in all His ways and to keep His commandments, His statutes, and His precepts which He commanded our fathers.

59 Let these my words, with which I have made supplication before the Lord, be near to the Lord our God day and night, that He may maintain the cause *and* right of His servant and of His people Israel as each day requires

60 That all the earth's people may know that the Lord is God and that there is no other.

61 Let your hearts therefore be blameless *and* wholly true to the Lord our God, to walk in His statutes and to keep His commandments, as today.

62 And the king and all Israel with him offered sacrifice before the Lord.

63 Solomon offered as peace offerings to the Lord: 22,000 oxen and 120,000 sheep. So the king and all the Israelites dedicated the house of the Lord.

64 On that same day the king consecrated the middle of the court that was before the Lord's house; there he offered burnt offerings, cereal offerings, and the fat of the peace offerings, because the bronze altar that was before the Lord was too small to receive [all] the offerings.

65 So at that time Solomon held the feast, and all Israel with him, a great assembly, from the entrance of Hamath to the Brook of Egypt, before the Lord our God, for seven days [for the dedication] and seven days [for the Feast of Tabernacles], fourteen days in all.

66 On the eighth day he sent the people away; they blessed the king and went to their tents with greatest joy and gratitude for all the goodness the Lord had shown to David His servant and Israel His people.

9 WHEN SOLOMON finished the building of the Lord's house and the king's house, and all he desired and was pleased to do,

2 The Lord appeared to Solomon the second time, as He had appeared to him at Gibeon.

3 The Lord told him, I have heard your prayer and supplication which you have made before Me; I have hallowed this house which you have built, and I have put My Name [and My Presence] there forever. My eyes and My heart shall be there perpetually.

4 And if you will walk before Me, as David your father walked, in integrity of heart and uprightness, doing according to all that I have commanded you, keeping My statutes and My precepts,

5 Then I will establish your royal throne over Israel forever, as I promised David your father, saying, There shall not fail you [to have] a man upon the throne of Israel.

6 But if you turn away from following Me, you or your children, and will not keep My commandments and My statutes which I have set before you but go and serve other gods and worship them,

7 Then I will cut off Israel from the

speak the Word

Lord, I pray that my heart would be blameless and wholly true to You, my God.
ADAPTED FROM I KINGS 8:61

land I have given them, and this house I have hallowed for My Name (renown) I will cast from My sight. And Israel shall be a proverb and a byword among all the peoples.

8 This house shall become a heap of ruins; every passerby shall be astonished and shall hiss [with surprise] and say, Why has the Lord done thus to this land and to this house?

9 Then they will answer, Because they forsook the Lord their God, Who brought their fathers out of the land of Egypt, and have laid hold of other gods and have worshiped and served them; therefore the Lord has brought on them all this evil.

10 At the end of twenty years, in which Solomon had built the two houses, the Lord's house and the king's house,

11 For which Hiram king of Tyre had furnished Solomon with as much cedar and cypress timber and gold as he desired, King Solomon gave Hiram twenty cities in the land of Galilee.

12 And Hiram came from Tyre to see the cities which Solomon had given him, and they did not please him.

13 He said, What are these cities worth which you have given me, my brother? So they are called the Cabul [unproductive] Land to this day.

14 And Hiram sent to the king 120 talents of gold.

15 This is the account of the levy [of forced labor] which King Solomon raised to build the house of the Lord, his own house, the Millo, the wall of Jerusalem, Hazor, Megiddo, and Gezer.

16 For Pharaoh king of Egypt had gone up and taken Gezer, burned it with fire, slew the Canaanites who dwelt in the city, and had given it as dowry to his daughter, Solomon's wife.

17 So Solomon rebuilt Gezer and Lower Beth-horon,

18 Baalath and Tamar (Tadmor) in the wilderness, in the land of Judah,

19 And all the store cities which Solomon had and cities for his chariots and cities for his horsemen, and whatever Solomon desired to build ᵐfor his pleasure in Jerusalem, in Lebanon, and in all the land of his dominion.

20 As for all the people who were left of the Amorites, Hittites, Perizzites, Hivites, and Jebusites, who were not Israelites,

21 Their children who were left after them in the land, whom the Israelites were not able utterly to destroy, of them Solomon made a forced levy of slaves to this day.

22 But Solomon made no slaves of the Israelites; they were the soldiers, his officials, attendants, commanders, captains, chariot officers, and horsemen.

23 These were the chief officers over Solomon's work, 550 who had charge of the people who did the work.

24 But Pharaoh's daughter came up out of the City of David to her house which Solomon had built for her; then he built the Millo.

25 Three times a year Solomon offered burnt offerings and peace

m Once on the throne Solomon became a thoroughgoing despot. All political power was taken out of the hands of the tribal sheiks . . . and placed in the hands of officers who were simply puppets of Solomon. The resources of the nation were expended not on works of public utility but on the personal aggrandizement of the monarch. In the means he took to gratify his passions he showed himself to be little better than a savage (James Orr et al., eds., *The International Standard Bible Encyclopedia*). The division of the nation at Solomon's death with all the weakness and misery that it caused [idolatry, ignoring God, captivity, exile, the loss of the ten tribes] through the coming centuries was the direct outgrowth of Solomon's unholy self-indulgence (Amos R. Wells, *Bible Miniatures*). Because of his extensive building program and his extravagant expenditures in the maintenance of his luxurious court, he resorted to forced labor and heavy taxation. Bitter opposition to his rule thus engendered the division of the united kingdom after his death (*The New Jewish Encyclopedia*).

offerings on the altar he built to the Lord, and he burned incense with them before the Lord. So he finished the house.

26 And King Solomon made a fleet of ships in Ezion-geber, which is beside Eloth, on the shore of the Red Sea, in Edom.

27 And Hiram sent with the fleet his servants, shipmen who had knowledge of the sea, with the servants of Solomon.

28 They came to Ophir and got 420 talents of gold and brought it to King Solomon.

10 WHEN THE queen of Sheba heard of [the constant connection of] the fame of Solomon with the name of the Lord, she came to prove him with hard questions (problems and riddles).

2 She came to Jerusalem with a very great train, with camels bearing spices, very much gold, and precious stones. When she had come to Solomon, she communed with him about all that was in her mind.

3 Solomon answered all her questions; there was nothing hidden from

the king which he failed to explain to her.

4 When the queen of Sheba had seen all Solomon's wisdom *and* skill, the house he had built,

5 The food of his table, the seating of his officials, the standing at attention of his servants, their apparel, his cupbearers, his ascent by which he went up to the house of the Lord [or the burnt offerings he sacrificed], she was breathless *and* overcome.

6 She said to the king, It was a true report I heard in my own land of your acts *and* sayings and wisdom.

7 I did not believe it until I came and my eyes had seen. Behold, the half was not told me. You have added wisdom and goodness exceeding the fame I heard.

8 Happy are your men! Happy are these your servants who stand continually before you, hearing your wisdom!

9 Blessed be the Lord your God, Who delighted in you and set you on the throne of Israel! Because the Lord loved Israel forever, He made you king to execute justice and righteousness.

10 And she gave the king 120 talents of gold and of spices a very great store and precious stones. Never again came such abundance of spices as these the queen of Sheba gave King Solomon.

11 The navy also of Hiram brought from Ophir gold and a great plenty of almug (algum) wood and precious stones.

12 Of the almug wood the king made pillars for the house of the Lord and for the king's house, and lyres also and harps for the singers. No such almug wood came again or has been seen to this day.

13 King Solomon gave to the queen of Sheba all she wanted, whatever she asked, besides his gifts to her from his royal bounty. So she returned to her own country, she and her servants.

14 Now the weight of gold that came to Solomon in one [particular] year was 666 talents of gold,

15 Besides what the traders brought and the traffic of the merchants and from all the [tributary] kings and governors of the land of Arabia.

16 King Solomon made 200 large shields of beaten gold; 600 shekels of gold went into each shield.

17 And he made 300 shields of beaten gold; three minas of gold went into each shield. The king put them in the House of the Forest of Lebanon.

18 Also the king made a great throne of ivory and overlaid it with the finest gold.

19 The throne had six steps, and attached at the rear of the top of the throne was a round covering *or* canopy. On either side of the seat were armrests, and two lions stood beside the armrests.

20 Twelve lions stood there, one on either end of each of the six steps; there was nothing like it ever made in any kingdom.

21 All King Solomon's drinking vessels were of gold, and all vessels of the House of the Forest of Lebanon were of pure gold. None were of silver; it was accounted as nothing in the days of Solomon.

22 For the king had a fleet of ships of Tarshish at sea with the fleet of Hiram. Once every three years the fleet of ships of Tarshish came bringing gold, silver, ivory, apes, and peacocks.

23 So King Solomon exceeded all the kings of the earth in riches and in wisdom (skill).

24 And all the earth sought the presence of Solomon to hear his wisdom which God had put in his mind.

25 Every man brought tribute: vessels of silver and gold, garments, equipment, spices, horses, and mules, so much year by year.

26 Solomon collected chariots and horsemen; he had 1,400 chariots and 12,000 horsemen, which he stationed in the chariot cities and with the king in Jerusalem.

27 The king made silver as common in Jerusalem as stones, and cedars as plentiful as the sycamore trees in the lowlands.

28 Solomon's horses were brought out of Egypt, and the king's merchants received them in droves, each at a price. [Deut. 17:15, 16.]

29 A chariot could be brought out of Egypt for 600 shekels of silver, and a horse for 150. And so to all the kings of the Hittites and of Syria they were exported by the king's merchants.

11 BUT KING Solomon [defiantly] loved many foreign women—the [n]daughter of Pharaoh, women of the Moabites, Ammonites, Edomites, Sidonians, and Hittites.

2 They were of the very nations of whom the Lord said to the Israelites, You shall not mingle with them, neither shall they mingle with you, for surely they will turn away your hearts after their gods. Yet Solomon clung to these in love. [Deut. 17:17.]

3 He had 700 wives, princesses, and 300 concubines, and his wives turned away his heart from God.

4 For when Solomon was old, his wives turned away his heart after other gods, and his heart was not perfect (complete and whole) with the Lord his God, as was the heart of David his father.

n "Solomon brought the daughter of Pharaoh out of the City of David into the house he had built for her, for he said, My wife shall not dwell in the house of David king of Israel, because the places are holy to which the ark of the Lord has come" (II Chron. 8:11). God had given Solomon the name "Jedidiah [beloved of the Lord]" (II Sam. 12:25), yet he chose to be the beloved of heathen women instead, in defiance of God's covenant with him.

life point

Even though God had given Solomon a great gift of wisdom, he did not use wisdom in every area of his life (see I Kings 11:1). You see, godly wisdom does not automatically lead to obedience. Solomon defied God and loved foreign women. Having wisdom does not mean that a person uses wisdom. Let's thank God that His wisdom is in us as believers in Him, but let us also ask for the ability to act on the wisdom He gives us and to have hearts that are obedient to Him.

putting the Word to work

Even though Solomon did so much right, Scripture tells us that he did not *fully* follow God, and this was evil in God's sight (see I Kings 11:1–6). Ask God to identify anything in your life that is keeping you from following Him fully, repent and receive His forgiveness, and ask Him to help you to trust and follow Him completely.

5 For Solomon went after Ashtoreth the goddess of the Sidonians, and after Milcom the abominable idol of the Ammonites! [I Kings 9:6-9.]

6 Solomon did evil in the sight of the Lord, and went not fully after the Lord, as David his father did.

7 Then Solomon built a high place for Chemosh the abominable idol of Moab, on the hill opposite Jerusalem, and for Molech the abominable idol of the Ammonites.

8 And he did so °for all of his foreign wives, who burned incense and sacrificed to their gods.

9 And the Lord was angry with Solomon because his heart was turned from the Lord, the God of Israel, Who had appeared to him twice,

10 And had commanded him concerning this thing, that he should not go after other gods, but he did not do what the Lord commanded.

11 Therefore the Lord said to Solomon, Because you are doing this and have not kept My covenant and My statutes, which I have commanded you, I will surely rend the kingdom from you and will give it to your servant!

12 However, in your days I will not do it, for David your father's sake. But I will rend it out of the hand of your son!

13 However, I will not tear away all the kingdom, but will give one tribe to your son for David My servant's sake and for the sake of Jerusalem, which I have chosen.

14 The Lord stirred up an adversary against Solomon, Hadad the Edomite; he was of royal descent in Edom.

15 For when David was in Edom, and Joab the commander of Israel's army went up to bury the slain, he slew every male in Edom.

16 For Joab and all Israel remained there for six months, until he had cut off every male in Edom.

17 But Hadad fled, he and certain Edomites of his father's servants, to Egypt, Hadad being yet a little child.

18 They set out from Midian and came to Paran, and took men with them out of Paran and came to Egypt, to Pharaoh king of Egypt, who gave

o What all this did to Solomon's sweet fellowship with God is to be seen in Ecclesiastes. Take the sun out of the sky, and all earth's beauty and fruitfulness will go also. Take God out of your sky, and life's joys will be turned to dregs, bitterness, and futility. Solomon had deliberately chosen to live "under the sun" instead of under God. In the awareness of his own unquestionable greatness, he had become indifferent to the fact that "here is more than Solomon" (Luke 11:31) and that to scorn or ignore God is fatal. With all his wisdom he failed to recognize that "God will not allow Himself to be sneered at (scorned, disdained, or mocked by mere pretensions or professions or by His precepts being set aside) . . . For whatever a man sows, that *and* that only is what he will reap" (Gal. 6:7).

[young] Hadad a house and land and ordered provisions for him.

19 Hadad found great favor with Pharaoh, so that he gave him in marriage the sister of his own wife Tahpenes the queen.

20 The sister of Tahpenes bore Hadad Genubath his son, whom Tahpenes weaned in Pharaoh's house; and Genubath was in Pharaoh's household among the sons of Pharaoh.

21 But when Hadad heard in Egypt that David slept with his fathers and that Joab the commander of Israel's army was dead, Hadad said to Pharaoh, Let me depart, that I may go to my own country.

22 Then Pharaoh said to him, But what have you lacked with me that now you want to go to your own country? He replied, Nothing. However, let me go anyhow.

23 God raised up for [Hadad] another adversary, Rezon son of Eliada, who had fled from his master, Hadadezer king of Zobah.

24 Rezon gathered men about him and became leader of a marauding band after the slaughter by David. They went to Damascus and dwelt and made [Rezon] king in Damascus.

25 And Rezon was an adversary to Israel all the days of Solomon, besides the mischief that Hadad did. Rezon abhorred Israel and reigned over Syria.

26 Jeroboam son of Nebat, an Ephrathite of Zereda, Solomon's servant, whose mother's name was Zeruah, a widow woman, rebelled against the king—

27 And for this reason: Solomon built the Millo and repaired the breaches of the city of David his father.

28 The man Jeroboam was a mighty man of courage. Solomon, seeing that the young man was industrious, put him in charge over all the [forced] labor of the house of Joseph.

29 At that time, when Jeroboam went out of Jerusalem, the prophet Ahijah the Shilonite met him on the way. Ahijah had clad himself with a new garment; and they were alone in the field.

30 Ahijah caught the new garment he wore and tore it into twelve pieces.

31 He said to Jeroboam, You take ten pieces, for thus says the Lord, the God of Israel, Behold, I will tear the kingdom from the hand of Solomon and will give you ten tribes.

32 But he shall have one tribe, for My servant David's sake and for Jerusalem's sake, the city which I have chosen out of all the tribes of Israel,

33 Because they have forsaken Me and have worshiped Ashtoreth the goddess of the Sidonians, Chemosh the god of the Moabites, and Milcom the god of the Ammonites, and have not walked in My ways, to do what is right in My sight, keeping My statutes and My ordinances as did David his father.

34 However, I will not take the whole kingdom out of his hand; but I will make him ruler all the days of his life for David My servant's sake, whom I chose because he kept My commandments and My statutes.

35 But I will take the kingdom out of his son's hand and give it to you, ten tribes.

36 Yet to his son I will give one tribe, that David My servant may always have a light before Me in Jerusalem, the city where I have chosen to put My Name.

37 And I will take you, and you shall reign according to all that your soul desires; and you shall be king over Israel.

38 And if you will hearken to all I command you and will walk in My ways and do right in My sight, keeping My statutes and My commandments, as David My servant did, I will be with you and build you a sure house, as I built for David, and will give Israel to you.

39 And I will for this afflict the descendants of David, but not forever.

40 Solomon sought therefore to kill Jeroboam. But Jeroboam arose and fled into Egypt, to Shishak king of Egypt, and was in Egypt until Solomon died.

41 The rest of the acts of Solomon—and all that he did, and his wisdom (skill)—are they not written in the book of the acts of Solomon?

42 The time Solomon reigned in Jerusalem over all Israel was forty years.

43 And Solomon slept with his fathers and was buried in the city of David his father. Rehoboam his son reigned in his stead.

12 REHOBOAM WENT to Shechem, for all Israel had come to Shechem to make him king.

2 And when Jeroboam son of Nebat heard of it—for he still dwelt in Egypt, where he had fled from King Solomon—[he] returned from Egypt.

3 And they sent and called him, and Jeroboam and all the assembly of Israel came and said to Rehoboam,

4 Your father made our yoke heavy; now therefore lighten the hard service and the heavy yoke your father put upon us, and we will serve you.

5 He replied, Go away for three days and then return to me. So the people departed.

6 And King Rehoboam consulted with the old men who stood before Solomon his father while he yet lived and said, How do you advise me to answer this people?

7 And they said to him, If you will be a servant to this people today and serve them and answer them with good words, they will be your servants forever.

8 But he forsook the counsel the old men gave him and consulted the young men who grew up with him and stood before him.

9 He said to them, What do you advise that we answer this people who have said, Make the yoke your father put on us lighter?

10 The young men who grew up with him answered, To the people who told you, Your father made our yoke heavy, but you make it lighter for us—say this, My little finger shall be thicker than my father's loins.

11 And now whereas my father loaded you with a heavy yoke, I will add to your yoke. My father chastised you with whips, but I will chastise you with scorpions.

12 So Jeroboam and all the people came to Rehoboam on the third day, as the king had appointed.

13 And the king answered the people roughly and forsook the counsel the old men had given him,

14 And spoke to them after the counsel of the young men, saying, My father made your yoke heavy, but I will add to your yoke; he chastised you with whips, but I will chastise you with scorpions.

15 So the king did not hearken to the people, for the situation was from the Lord, that He might fulfill His word which He spoke by Ahijah the Shilonite to Jeroboam son of Nebat. [I Kings 11:29-33.]

16 So when all Israel saw that the king did not heed them, they answered the king, What portion have we in David? We have no inheritance in the son of Jesse. To your tents, O Israel! Look now to your own house, David! So Israel went to their tents.

17 But Rehoboam reigned over the Israelites who dwelt in the cities of Judah.

18 Then King Rehoboam sent Adoram, who was over the tribute [taskmaster over the forced labor], and all Israel stoned him to death with stones.

So King Rehoboam hastened to get into his chariot to flee to Jerusalem.

19 So Israel has rebelled against the house of David to this day.

20 When all Israel heard that Jeroboam had returned, they sent and called him to the assembly and made him king over all Israel. None followed the house of David except the tribe of Judah only.

21 And when Rehoboam had come to Jerusalem, he assembled all the house of Judah, with the tribe of Benjamin, 180,000 chosen warriors, to fight against the house of Israel to bring the kingdom back to Rehoboam son of Solomon.

22 But the word of God came to Shemaiah the man of God, saying,

23 Tell Rehoboam son of Solomon king of Judah and all the house of Judah and Benjamin and the remnant of the people,

24 Thus says the Lord, You shall not go up or fight against your brethren, the Israelites. Return every man to his house, for this thing is from Me. So they hearkened to the Lord's word and returned home, according to the Lord's word.

25 Then Jeroboam built Shechem in the hill country of Ephraim and lived there. He went out from there and built Penuel.

26 Jeroboam said in his heart, Now the kingdom will return to the house of David.

27 If this people goes up to the house of the Lord at Jerusalem to sacrifice, then the heart of this people will turn again to their lord, to Rehoboam king of Judah; and they will kill me and go back to Rehoboam king of Judah.

28 So the king took counsel and made two calves of gold. And he said to the people, It is too much for you to go [all the way] up to Jerusalem. Behold your gods, O Israel, who brought you up out of the land of Egypt.

29 And he set the one golden calf in Bethel, and the other he put in Dan.

30 And this thing became a sin; for the people went to worship each of them even as far as Dan.

31 Jeroboam also made houses on high places and made priests of people who were not Levites.

32 And Jeroboam appointed a feast on the fifteenth day of the eighth month, like the feast kept in Judah, and he offered sacrifices upon the altar. So he did in Bethel, sacrificing to the calves he had made. And he placed in Bethel the priests of the high places he had made.

33 So he offered upon the altar he had made in Bethel on the fifteenth day of the eighth month, a date which he chose individually; and he appointed a feast for the Israelites and he went up to the altar to burn incense [in defiance of God's law.]

13 AND BEHOLD, there came a man of God out of Judah by the word of the Lord to Bethel. Jeroboam stood by the altar to burn incense.

2 The man cried against the altar by the word of the Lord, O altar, altar, thus says the Lord: Behold, a son shall be born to the house of David, Josiah by name; and on you shall he offer the priests of the high places who burn incense on you, and men's bones shall be burned on you.

3 And he gave a sign the same day, saying, This is the sign which the Lord has spoken: Behold, the altar shall be split and the ashes that are upon it shall be poured out. [Fulfilled in II Kings 23:15, 16.]

4 When King Jeroboam heard the words the man of God cried against the altar in Bethel, he thrust out his hand, saying, Lay hold on him! And his hand which he put forth against him dried up, so that he could not draw it to him again.

5 The altar also was split and the ashes poured out from the altar according to the sign which the man of God had given by the word of the Lord.
6 And the king said to the man of God, Entreat now the favor of the Lord your God and pray for me, that my hand may be restored to me. And the man of God entreated the Lord, and the king's hand was restored and became as it was before.
7 And the king said to the man of God, Come home with me and refresh yourself, and I will give you a reward.
8 And the man of God said to the king, If you give me half your house, I will not go in with you, and I will not eat bread or drink water in this place.
9 For I was commanded by the word of the Lord, You shall eat no bread or drink water or return by the way you came.
10 So he went another way and did not return by the way that he came to Bethel.
11 Now there dwelt an old prophet in Bethel; and his sons came and told him all that the man of God had done that day in Bethel; the words which he had spoken to the king they told also to their father.
12 Their father asked them, Which way did he go? For his sons had seen which way the man of God who came from Judah had gone.
13 He said to his sons, Saddle the donkey for me. So they saddled the donkey and he rode on it
14 And went after the man of God. And he found him sitting under an oak, and he said to him, Are you the man of God who came from Judah? And he said, I am.
15 Then he said to him, Come home with me and eat bread.
16 He said, I may not return with you or go in with you, neither will I eat bread or drink water with you in this place.

17 For I was told by the word of the Lord, You shall not eat bread or drink water there or return by the way that you came.
18 He answered, I am a prophet also, as you are. And an angel spoke to me by the word of the Lord, saying, Bring him back with you to your house, that he may eat bread and drink water. But he lied to him.
19 So the man from Judah went back with him and ate and drank water in his house.
20 And as they sat at the table, the word of the Lord came to the prophet who brought him back.
21 And he cried to the man of God who came from Judah, Thus says the Lord: Because you have disobeyed the word of the Lord and have not kept the command which the Lord your God commanded you,
22 But have come back and have eaten bread and drunk water in the place of which the Lord said to you, Eat no bread and drink no water— your corpse shall not come to the tomb of your fathers.
23 And after the prophet of the house had eaten bread and drunk, he saddled the donkey for the man he had brought back.
24 And when he had gone, a lion met him by the road and slew him, and his corpse was cast in the way, and the donkey stood by it; the lion also stood by the corpse.
25 And behold, men passed by and saw the corpse thrown in the road, and the lion standing by the corpse, and they came and told it in the city where the old prophet dwelt.
26 When the prophet who brought him back from the way heard of it, he said, It is the man of God who was disobedient to the word of the Lord; therefore the Lord has given him to the lion, which has torn him and slain him, according to the word of the Lord which He spoke to him.

27 And he said to his sons, Saddle the donkey for me. And they saddled it.
28 And he went and found the corpse thrown in the road, and the donkey and the lion stood by the body; the lion had not eaten the corpse or torn the donkey.
29 The prophet took up the corpse of the man of God and laid it upon the donkey and brought it back, and the old prophet came into the city to mourn and to bury him.
30 And he laid the body in his own grave, and they mourned over him, saying, Alas, my brother!
31 After he had buried him, he said to his sons, When I am dead, bury me in the grave in which the man of God is buried; lay my bones beside his bones.
32 For the saying which he cried by the word of the Lord against the altar in Bethel and against all the houses of the high places which are in the cities of Samaria shall surely come to pass.
33 After this thing, Jeroboam turned not from his evil way, but made priests for the high places again from among all the people. Whoever would, he consecrated, that there might be priests for the high places.
34 And this thing became the sin of the dynasty of Jeroboam that caused it to be abolished and destroyed from the face of the earth.

14 THEN ABIJAH [the little] son of Jeroboam became sick.
2 And Jeroboam said to his wife, Arise, I pray you, and disguise yourself, that you may not be recognized as Jeroboam's wife, and go to Shiloh. Behold, Ahijah the prophet is there, who told me that I should be king over this people.
3 Take ten loaves, some cakes, and a bottle of honey, and go to him. He will tell you what shall happen to the child.
4 Jeroboam's wife did so. She arose and went [twenty miles] to Shiloh and came to the house of Ahijah. Ahijah could not see, for his eyes were dim because of his age.
5 And the Lord said to Ahijah, Behold, the ᴾwife of Jeroboam is coming to ask you concerning her son, for he is sick. Thus and thus shall you say to her. When she came, she pretended to be another woman.
6 But when Ahijah heard the sound of her feet as she came in at the door, he said, Come in, wife of Jeroboam. Why do you pretend to be another? For I am charged with heavy news for you.
7 Go, tell Jeroboam, Thus says the Lord, the God of Israel: Because I exalted you from among the people and made you leader over My people Israel
8 And rent the kingdom away from the house of David and gave it to you—and yet you have not been as My servant David, who kept My commandments and followed Me with all his heart, to do only what was right in My eyes,
9 But have done evil above all who

p The Hebrew text gives no particulars about the background of Jeroboam's wife, but there is an insertion in *The Septuagint* (Greek translation of the Old Testament), found in the Vatican manuscript after I Kings 12:24, in which we find further information about her. When Jeroboam, then taskmaster over the forced labor of the house of Joseph, fled to Egypt to escape death at the hands of King Solomon, he went to King Shishak of Egypt and was with him until the death of Solomon. Jeroboam asked permission of King Shishak to return to his own land, and the king told him, "Ask of me a request, and I will give it to you." And he gave to Jeroboam Ano, the elder sister of his own wife Thekemina (Tahpenes), to be his wife. She was great among the daughters of the king, and bore to Jeroboam Abias (Abijah) his son [who in this chapter lies dying in the palace of Jeroboam while Queen Ano, his mother, is about to hear what the old prophet has been required by God to tell her] (Charles Ellicott, *A Bible Commentary*).

were before you; for you have made yourself other gods, molten images, to provoke Me to anger and have cast Me behind your back—

10 Therefore behold, I will bring evil upon the house of Jeroboam and will cut off from [him] every male, both bond and free, in Israel, and will utterly sweep away the house of Jeroboam as a man sweeps away dung, till it is all gone.

11 Anyone belonging to Jeroboam who dies in the city the dogs shall eat, and any who dies in the field the birds of the heavens shall eat. For the Lord has spoken it.

12 Arise therefore [Ano, Jeroboam's wife], get to your own house. When your feet enter the city, the child shall die.

13 And all Israel shall mourn for him and bury him; for he only of Jeroboam's family shall come to the grave, because in him there is found something good *and* pleasing to the Lord, the God of Israel, in the house of Jeroboam.

14 Moreover, the Lord will raise up for Himself a king over Israel who shall cut off the house of Jeroboam this day. From now on

15 The Lord will smite Israel, as a reed is shaken in the water; and He will root up Israel out of this good land which He gave to their fathers and will scatter them beyond the [Euphrates] River, because they have made their Asherim [idolatrous symbols of the goddess Asherah], provoking the Lord to anger.

16 He will give Israel up because of the sins of Jeroboam which he has sinned and made Israel to sin.

17 So Jeroboam's wife departed and came to Tirzah. When she came to the threshold of the house, the child died.

18 And all Israel buried him and mourned for him, according to the word of the Lord spoken by His servant Ahijah the prophet.

19 The rest of the acts of Jeroboam, how he warred and how he reigned, behold, they are written in the Book of the Chronicles of the Kings of Israel.

20 Jeroboam reigned for twenty-two years; and he slept with his fathers; and Nadab his son reigned in his stead.

21 And Rehoboam son of Solomon reigned in Judah. Rehoboam was forty-one years old when he began to reign, and he reigned seventeen years in Jerusalem, the city the Lord chose out of all the tribes of Israel to put His Name [and the pledge of His presence] there. His mother's name was Naamah the Ammonitess.

22 And Judah did evil in the sight of the Lord, Whom they provoked to jealousy with the sins they committed, above all that their fathers had done.

23 For they also built themselves [idolatrous] high places, pillars, and Asherim [idolatrous symbols of the goddess Asherah] on every high hill and under every green tree.

24 There were also sodomites (male cult prostitutes) in the land. They did all the abominations of the nations whom the Lord cast out before the Israelites.

25 In the fifth year of King Rehoboam, Shishak king of Egypt [Jeroboam's brother-in-law] came up against Jerusalem.

26 He took away the treasures of the house of the Lord and of the king's house; he took away all, including all the shields of gold which Solomon had made.

27 King Rehoboam made in their stead bronze shields and committed them to the hands of the captains of the guard who kept the door of the king's house.

28 And as often as the king went into the house of the Lord, the guards bore them and brought them back into the guardroom.

29 The rest of the acts of Rehoboam, and all that he did, are they not written in the Book of the Chronicles of the Kings of Judah?
30 There was war between Rehoboam and Jeroboam continually.
31 Rehoboam slept with his fathers and was buried with them in the City of David. His mother's name was Naamah the Ammonitess. Abijam (Abijah) his son reigned in his stead.

15 IN THE eighteenth year of King Jeroboam son of Nebat, Abijam began to reign over Judah.
2 He reigned three years in Jerusalem. His mother was Maacah (Micaiah) daughter [granddaughter] of Abishalom (Absalom).
3 He walked in all the sins of his father [Rehoboam] before him; and his heart was not blameless with the Lord his God, as the heart of David his father [forefather].
4 Nevertheless, for David's sake the Lord his God gave him a lamp in Jerusalem, setting up his son after him and establishing Jerusalem,
5 Because David did what was right in the eyes of the Lord and turned not aside from anything that He commanded him all the days of his life, except in the matter of Uriah the Hittite.
6 There was war between [Abijam's father] Rehoboam and Jeroboam all the days of [Rehoboam's] life.
7 The rest of the acts of Abijam, and all that he did, are they not written in the Book of the Chronicles of the Kings of Judah? And there was war between Abijam and Jeroboam.

8 Abijam slept with his fathers and they buried him in the City of David. Asa his son reigned in his stead.
9 In the twentieth year of Jeroboam king of Israel, Asa began to reign over Judah.
10 Forty-one years he reigned in Jerusalem. His mother was [also named] Maacah (Micaiah) daughter of Abishalom (Absalom). [I Kings 15:2.]
11 And Asa did right in the eyes of the Lord, as did David his father [forefather].
12 He put away the sodomites (male cult prostitutes) out of the land and removed all the idols that his fathers [Solomon, Rehoboam, and Abijam] had made or promoted. [I Kings 11:5-11; 14:22.]
13 Also Maacah his mother he removed from being queen mother, because she had an image made for [the goddess] Asherah. Asa destroyed her image, burning it by the brook Kidron.
14 But the high places were not removed. Yet Asa's heart was blameless with the Lord all his days.
15 He brought the things which his father had dedicated and the things which he himself had dedicated into the house of the Lord—silver, gold, and vessels.
16 There was war between Asa and Baasha king of Israel all their days.
17 Baasha king of Israel went up against Judah and built up Ramah, that he might allow no one to go out or come in to Asa king of Judah.
18 Then Asa took all the silver and gold left in the treasuries of the house of the Lord and of the king's house and delivered them into the hands of his servants. And King Asa sent them

speak the Word

God, may I do what is right in Your eyes, turning not aside from anything You have commanded me all the days of my life.
ADAPTED FROM I KINGS 15:5

to Ben-hadad son of Tabrimmon, the son of Hezion, king of Syria, who dwelt at Damascus, saying,

19 Let there be a league between me and you, as was between my father and your father. Behold, I am sending you a present of silver and gold; go, break your league with Baasha king of Israel, that he may withdraw from me.

20 So Ben-hadad hearkened to king Asa and sent the commanders of his armies against the cities of Israel, and smote Ijon, Dan, Abel-beth-maacah, and all Chinneroth, with all the land of Naphtali.

21 When Baasha heard of it, he quit building up Ramah and dwelt in Tirzah.

22 Then King Asa made a proclamation to all Judah—none was exempted. They carried away the stones of Ramah and its timber with which Baasha had been building. And King Asa built up with them Geba of Benjamin, and also Mizpah.

23 The rest of all the acts of Asa, all his might, all that he did, and the cities which he built, are they not written in the Book of the Chronicles of the Kings of Judah? But in the time of his old age he was diseased in his feet.

24 Asa slept with his fathers and was buried with them in the city of David his father. Jehoshaphat his son reigned in his stead.

25 Nadab son of Jeroboam began to reign over Israel in the second year of Asa king of Judah, and reigned two years.

26 He did evil in the sight of the Lord and walked in the way of his father and in his sin, with which he made Israel sin.

27 Baasha son of Ahijah of the house of Issachar conspired against Nadab, and Baasha smote him at Gibbethon, which belonged to the Philistines, for Nadab and all Israel were laying siege to Gibbethon.

28 In the third year of Asa king of Judah Baasha slew Nadab and reigned in his stead.

29 As soon as he was king, Baasha killed all the household of Jeroboam. He left to [it] not one who breathed, until he had destroyed it, according to the word of the Lord which He spoke by His servant Ahijah the Shilonite— [I Kings 14:9-16.]

30 Because of the sins of Jeroboam which he sinned and by which he made Israel to sin, and because of his provocation of the Lord, the God of Israel, to anger.

31 The rest of Nadab's acts, and all that he did, are they not written in the Book of the Chronicles of the Kings of Israel?

32 There was war between Asa and Baasha king of Israel all their days.

33 In the third year of Asa king of Judah, Baasha son of Ahijah began his reign of twenty-four years over all Israel in Tirzah.

34 He did evil in the sight of the Lord and walked in the way of Jeroboam and in his sin, with which he made Israel sin.

16 AND THE word of the Lord came to Jehu son of Hanani against Baasha, saying,

2 Because I exalted you [Baasha] out of the dust and made you leader over My people Israel, and you have walked in the way of Jeroboam and have made My people Israel sin, to provoke Me to anger with their sins,

3 Behold, I will utterly sweep away Baasha and his house, and will make your house like [that] of Jeroboam son of Nebat.

4 Any of Baasha's family who dies in the city the dogs shall eat, and any who dies in the field the birds of the heavens shall eat.

5 Now the rest of the acts of Baasha, what he did and his might, are they not written in the Book of the Chronicles of the Kings of Israel?

6 Baasha slept with his fathers and was buried in Tirzah. Elah his son reigned in his stead.

7 Also the word of the Lord against Baasha and his house came through the prophet Jehu son of Hanani for all the evil that Baasha did in the sight of the Lord in provoking Him to anger with the work of his hands [idols], in being like the house of Jeroboam, and also because he destroyed it [the family of Jeroboam, of his own accord].

8 In the twenty-sixth year of Asa king of Judah, Elah son of Baasha began his reign of two years over Israel in Tirzah.

9 Elah's servant Zimri, captain of half his chariots, conspired against Elah. He was in Tirzah, drinking himself drunk in the house of Arza, who was over the household in Tirzah.

10 Zimri came in and smote and killed him in the twenty-seventh year of Asa king of Judah, and reigned in his stead.

11 When he began to reign, as soon as he sat on his throne, he killed all the household of Baasha; he left not one male of his kinsmen or his friends.

12 Thus Zimri destroyed all the house of Baasha, according to the word of the Lord which He spoke against Baasha through Jehu the prophet, [I Kings 16:3.]

13 For all the sins of Baasha and of Elah his son by which they sinned and made Israel sin, in provoking the Lord, the God of Israel, to anger with their idols.

14 The rest of the acts of Elah, and all he did, are they not written in the Book of the Chronicles of the Kings of Israel?

15 In the twenty-seventh year of Asa king of Judah, Zimri reigned for seven days in Tirzah. The troops were encamped against Gibbethon, which belonged to the Philistines,

16 And they heard the rumor, Zimri has conspired and slain the king! So all Israel made Omri, the commander of the army, king over Israel that day in the camp.

17 So Omri went up from Gibbethon, and all Israel with him, and they besieged Tirzah.

18 And when Zimri saw that the city was taken, he went into the stronghold of the king's house and burned the king's house over him with fire and died,

19 Because of his sins committed in doing evil in the sight of the Lord, in walking in the way of Jeroboam, and his sin in causing Israel to sin.

20 The rest of the acts of Zimri, and his deeds of treason, are they not written in the Book of the Chronicles of the Kings of Israel?

21 Then the people of Israel were divided into two factions. Half of the people followed Tibni son of Ginath, to make him king, and half followed Omri.

22 But the people who followed Omri prevailed against those who followed Tibni son of Ginath. So Tibni died and Omri reigned.

23 In the thirty-first year of Asa king of Judah, Omri began his reign of twelve years over Israel. He reigned six years in Tirzah.

24 Omri bought the hill Samaria from Shemer for two talents of silver. He built a city on the hill *and* fortified it, and called it Samaria (Shomeron), after the owner of the hill, Shemer.

25 But Omri did evil in the eyes of the Lord, even worse than all who were before him.

26 He walked in all the ways of Jeroboam son of Nebat and in his sin, by which he made Israel sin, to provoke the Lord, the God of Israel, to anger with their idols.

27 The rest of the acts of Omri, and

his might that he showed, are they not written in the Book of the Chronicles of the Kings of Israel?

28 So Omri slept with his fathers and was buried in Samaria. Ahab his son reigned in his stead.

29 In the thirty-eighth year of Asa king of Judah, Ahab son of Omri began his reign of twenty-two years over Israel in Samaria.

30 And Ahab son of Omri did evil in the sight of the Lord above all before him.

31 As if it had been a light thing for Ahab to walk in the sins of Jeroboam son of Nebat, he took for a wife Jezebel daughter of Ethbaal king of the Sidonians, and served Baal and worshiped him.

32 He erected an altar for Baal in the house of Baal which he built in Samaria.

33 And Ahab made an Asherah [idolatrous symbol of the goddess Asherah]. Ahab did more to provoke the Lord, the God of Israel, to anger than all the kings of Israel before him.

34 In his days, Hiel the Bethelite built Jericho. He laid its foundations at the cost of the life of Abiram his firstborn, and set up its gates with the loss of his youngest son Segub, according to the word of the Lord which He spoke through Joshua son of Nun. [Josh. 6:26.]

17 ELIJAH THE Tishbite, of the temporary residents of Gilead, said to Ahab, As the Lord, the God of Israel, lives, before Whom I stand, there shall not be dew or rain these years but according to My word.

2 And the word of the Lord came to him, saying,

3 Go from here and turn east and hide yourself by the brook Cherith, east of the Jordan.

4 You shall drink of the brook, and I

putting the Word to work

Have you ever wondered how all the bills were going to get paid, or perhaps even where your next meal was coming from? God can be very creative when it comes to providing for His people, as Elijah found out in I Kings 17:1–9. As you follow God, you can always trust Him to provide for you, even if it is in ways you don't expect! Be sure to thank Him for His faithful provision every day.

have commanded the ravens to feed you there.

5 So he did according to the word of the Lord; he went and dwelt by the brook Cherith, east of the Jordan.

6 And the ravens brought him bread and flesh in the morning and bread and flesh in the evening, and he drank of the brook.

7 After a while the brook dried up because there was no rain in the land.

8 And the word of the Lord came to him:

9 Arise, go to Zarephath, which belongs to Sidon, and dwell there. Behold, I have commanded a widow there to provide for you.

10 So he arose and went to Zarephath. When he came to the gate of the city, behold, a widow was there gathering sticks. He called to her, Bring me a little water in a vessel, that I may drink.

11 As she was going to get it, he called to her and said, Bring me a morsel of bread in your hand.

12 And she said, As the Lord your God lives, I have not a loaf baked but only a handful of meal in the jar and a little oil in the bottle. See, I am gathering two sticks, that I may go in and bake it for me and my son, that we may eat it—and die.

13 Elijah said to her, Fear not; go and do as you have said. But make me a little cake of [it] first and bring it to

life point

In the story that begins at I Kings 17:9, God sends Elijah to Zarephath. I believe God sent Elijah to the widow at Zarephath not because God wanted to do something in Elijah, but because God wanted to do something in the widow. If God relocates you or sends you into a situation you do not understand, He will bless you, but it may be for someone else's sake. If your "brook" dries up, as it did for Elijah in I Kings 17 before he went to Zarephath, that does not mean you have done anything wrong; it more likely means God needs you somewhere else. If God closes one door, you can always expect Him to open another one.

me, and afterward prepare some for yourself and your son.

14 For thus says the Lord, the God of Israel: The jar of meal shall not waste away or the bottle of oil fail until the day that the Lord sends rain on the earth.

15 She did as Elijah said. And she and he and her household ate for many days.

16 The jar of meal was not spent nor did the bottle of oil fail, according to the word which the Lord spoke through Elijah.

17 After these things, the son of the

putting the Word to work

Is there something that God is asking you to do that seems like a hardship or involves great personal cost, as it did for the widow at Zarephath (see I Kings 17:8–16)? Know that God's instructions may not seem to make sense, but when you obey you will discover, like the widow, that God will do amazing things in you, through you, and for you.

woman, the mistress of the house, became sick; and his sickness was so severe that there was no breath left in him.

18 And she said to Elijah, What have you against me, O man of God? Have you come to me to call my sin to remembrance and to slay my son?

19 He said to her, Give me your son. And he took him from her bosom and carried him up into the chamber where he stayed and laid him upon his own bed.

20 And Elijah cried to the Lord and said, O Lord my God, have You brought further calamity upon the widow with whom I sojourn, by slaying her son?

21 And he stretched himself upon the child three times and cried to the Lord and said, O Lord my God, I pray You, let this child's soul come back into him.

22 And the Lord heard the voice of Elijah, and the soul of the child came into him again, and he revived.

23 And Elijah took the child, and brought him down out of the chamber into the [lower part of the] house and gave him to his mother; and Elijah said, See, your son is alive!

24 And the woman said to Elijah, By this I know that you are a man of God and that the word of the Lord in your mouth is truth.

18 AFTER MANY days, the word of the Lord came to Elijah in the third year, saying, Go, show yourself to Ahab, and I will send rain upon the earth.

2 So Elijah went to show himself to Ahab. Now the famine was severe in Samaria.

3 And Ahab called Obadiah, who was the governor of his house. (Now Obadiah feared the Lord greatly;

4 For when Jezebel cut off the prophets of the Lord, Obadiah took a hundred prophets and hid them by

fifties in a cave and fed them with bread and water.)

5 And Ahab said to Obadiah, Go into the land to all the fountains of water and to all the brooks; perhaps we may find grass to keep the horses and mules alive, that we lose none of the beasts.

6 So they divided the land between them to pass through it. Ahab went one way and Obadiah went another way, each by himself.

7 As Obadiah was on the way, behold, Elijah met him. He recognized him and fell on his face and said, Are you my lord Elijah?

8 He answered him, It is I. Go tell your lord, Behold, Elijah is here.

9 And he said, What sin have I committed, that you would deliver your servant into the hands of Ahab to be slain?

10 As the Lord your God lives, there is no nation or kingdom where my lord has not sent to seek you. And when they said, He is not here, he took an oath from the kingdom or nation that they had not found you.

11 And now you say, Go tell your lord, Behold, Elijah is here.

12 And as soon as I have gone out from you, the Spirit of the Lord will carry you I know not where; so when I come and tell Ahab and he cannot find you, he will kill me. But I your servant have feared *and* revered the Lord from my youth.

13 Was it not told my lord what I did when Jezebel slew the prophets of the Lord, how I hid a hundred men of the Lord's prophets by fifties in a cave and fed them with bread and water?

14 And now you say, Go tell your lord, Behold, Elijah is here; and he will kill me.

15 Elijah said, As the Lord of hosts lives, before Whom I stand, I will surely show myself to Ahab today.

16 So Obadiah went to meet Ahab and told him, and Ahab went to meet Elijah.

17 When Ahab saw Elijah, Ahab said to him, Are you he who troubles Israel?

18 Elijah replied, I have not troubled Israel, but you have, and your father's house, by forsaking the commandments of the Lord and by following the Baals.

19 Therefore send and gather to me all Israel at Mount Carmel, and the 450 prophets of Baal and the 400 prophets of [the goddess] Asherah, who eat at [Queen] Jezebel's table.

20 So Ahab sent to all the Israelites and assembled the prophets at Mount Carmel.

21 Elijah came near to all the people and said, How long will you halt *and* limp between two opinions? If the Lord is God, follow Him! But if Baal, then follow him. And the people did not answer him a word.

22 Then Elijah said to the people, I, I only, remain a prophet of the Lord, but Baal's prophets are 450 men.

23 Let two bulls be given us; let them choose one bull for themselves and cut it in pieces and lay it on the wood but put no fire to it. I will dress the other bull, lay it on the wood, and put no fire to it.

24 Then you call on the name of your god, and I will call on the name of the Lord; and the One Who answers by fire, let Him be God. And all the people answered, It is well spoken.

25 Elijah said to the prophets of Baal,

putting the Word to work

Do you sometimes feel that God does not really hear you when you pray? The prophets of Baal went through quite a routine to try to get their god to hear them—without success (see I Kings 18:25–39). But you can have the confidence of Elijah when you pray, knowing that you pray to the living God, Who hears every prayer and is ready to act on your behalf.

the truth about doubt

When we read in I Kings 18:21 about halting and limping "between two opinions," we can interpret that phrase quite simply as "doubting." I once heard a story that offers valuable insight into the doubt that so often affects Christians.

There was a man who had a financial need and was confessing God's Word over his life, quoting Scriptures, and believing that God had already provided a way for him. He was just waiting for his breakthrough to become a reality. While doing so, he was intermittently attacked with thoughts of doubt. After he had suffered a particularly difficult time and was beginning to get discouraged, God opened his eyes to the spiritual world. This is what he saw: a demon (an evil spirit) speaking lies to him, telling him that he was not going to get the help he needed and that confessing God's Word was not going to work. But he also saw that each time he confessed the Word, light would come out of his mouth like a sword, and the demon would cower and fall backward.

As God showed him this vision, the man then understood why it is so important to keep speaking the Word. He saw that he did have faith, which was why the evil spirit was attacking him with doubt.

Doubt is not something God puts in us. Romans 12:3 says that God gives every man the "measure of faith" (KJV). God has placed faith in our hearts, but the devil tries to negate our faith by attacking us with doubt.

Doubt comes in the form of thoughts that are in opposition to the Word of God. This is why it is so important for us to know the Bible. If we know the Word, then we can recognize when the devil is lying to us. Be assured that he lies to us in order to steal what Jesus purchased for us through His death and resurrection.

I encourage you to be like that man who sought help from the Lord: speak God's Word because His Word is true, and because confessing the truth sends the demons of doubt away!

Choose one bull for yourselves and dress it first, for you are many; and call on the name of your god, but put no fire under it.

26 So they took the bull given them, dressed it, and called on the name of Baal from morning until noon, saying, O Baal, hear *and* answer us! But there was no voice; no one answered. And they leaped upon *or* limped about the altar they had made.

27 At noon Elijah mocked them, saying, Cry aloud, for he is a god; either he is musing, or he has gone aside, or he is on a journey, or perhaps he is asleep and must be awakened.

28 And they cried aloud and cut themselves after their custom with knives and lances until the blood gushed out upon them.

29 Midday passed, and they played the part of prophets until the time for offering the evening sacrifice, but there was no voice, no answer, no one who paid attention.

30 Then Elijah said to all the people, Come near to me. And all the people came near him. And he repaired the

[old] altar of the Lord that had been broken down [by Jezebel]. [I Kings 18:13; 19:10.]

31 Then Elijah took twelve stones, according to the number of the tribes of the sons of Jacob, to whom the word of the Lord came, saying, Israel shall be your name. [Gen. 32:28.]

32 And with the stones Elijah built an altar in the name [and self-revelation] of the Lord. He made a trench about the altar as great as would contain two measures of seed.

33 He put the wood in order and cut the bull in pieces and laid it on the wood and said, Fill four jars with water and pour it on the burnt offering and the wood.

34 And he said, Do it the second time. And they did it the second time. And he said, Do it the third time. And they did it the third time.

35 The water ran round about the altar, and he filled the trench also with water.

36 At the time of the offering of the evening sacrifice, Elijah the prophet came near and said, O Lord, the God of Abraham, Isaac, and Israel, let it be known this day that You are God in Israel and that I am Your servant and that I have done all these things at Your word.

37 Hear me, O Lord, hear me, that this people may know that You, the Lord, are God, and have turned their hearts back [to You].

38 Then the fire of the Lord fell and consumed the burnt sacrifice and the wood and the stones and the dust, and also licked up the water that was in the trench.

39 When all the people saw it, they fell on their faces and they said, The Lord, He is God! The Lord, He is God!

40 And Elijah said, Seize the prophets of Baal; let not one escape. They seized them, and Elijah brought them down to the brook Kishon, and [as God's law required] slew them there. [Deut. 13:5; 18:20.]

41 And Elijah said to Ahab, Go up, eat and drink, for there is the sound of abundance of rain.

42 So Ahab went up to eat and to

right as rain

God had brought drought and famine on Israel to show His power to Ahab. God was letting Ahab and his wicked wife, Jezebel, know that they needed to change their wicked ways, and if they did not, the circumstances were not going to be good. After three years of famine, God sent His prophet Elijah to tell Ahab it was going to rain. Elijah said to Ahab that he was hearing "the sound of abundance of rain" (I Kings 18:41). He told him to get ready because there was going to be a downpour.

Ahab and Jezebel could not stand the sight of Elijah because he was a prophet and servant of God. Have you ever noticed how wicked people hate righteous people for no reason at all? They will hate the righteous simply because we represent the One they are rebelling against. All Elijah did in I Kings 18 was to show up; that alone was enough to send Ahab into a rage. Although Ahab wanted rain, he did not want Elijah to be right or to be the one in control.

I do not believe Elijah really heard the sound of rain in the natural. He heard it in the Spirit by faith. He was listening to the Spirit of God; he believed what God said and began to act on it before he saw the manifestation of it. We need that kind of faith!

worship before the rain

After announcing to Ahab what was going to happen—rain was coming—Elijah went to the top of Mount Carmel. There he got down on his knees with his forehead on the ground (see I Kings 18:42). Can't you just see him? In that position of worship, Elijah sent his servant to run back and forth several times to see if it was starting to rain.

Seven times his servant came back with a bad report, but Elijah did not get out of his worship position. Imagine how Elijah must have felt every time the report came back that nothing was happening! But each time Elijah just said, "Go again" (see I Kings 18:43). Despite the repeated negative reports, Elijah never gave up. He stayed right where he was, worshipping God.

Worship strengthens our faith. Doubt could have caused Elijah to give up, but his worship kept him strong. Romans 4 tells us of another person in the Bible who had absolutely no human reason to hope. Doubt and unbelief came against Abraham but did not defeat him; he became strong as he gave praise and glory to God. If praise and worship worked for Abraham and Elijah, it will work for us also.

Elijah's servant could have been saying to him, "Elijah, you must have missed God this time because nothing is happening; there's not even a cloud out there." But each time Elijah refused to give up! Finally, Elijah's servant came back and reported that he saw a cloud as small as a man's hand. At that word, Elijah came up shouting, "Hallelujah! Go tell Ahab to hurry home and seek shelter because it's beginning to rain!" (see I Kings 18:44).

When you worship God, He will send the rain of His Spirit upon you, and it will drown all the "Ahabs" and all the other resistances in your life. Take your position and praise the Lord, worshipping before it begins to "rain" in your life.

drink. And Elijah went up to the top of Carmel; and he bowed himself down upon the earth and put his face between his knees

43 And said to his servant, Go up now, look toward the sea. And he went up and looked and said, There is nothing. Elijah said, Go again seven times.

44 And at the seventh time the servant said, A cloud as small as a man's hand is arising out of the sea. And Elijah said, Go up, say to Ahab, Hitch your chariot and go down, lest the rain stop you.

45 In a little while, the heavens were black with wind-swept clouds, and there was a great rain. And Ahab went to Jezreel.

46 The hand of the Lord was on Elijah. He girded up his loins and ran before Ahab to the entrance of Jezreel [nearly twenty miles].

19 AHAB TOLD Jezebel all that Elijah had done and how he had slain all the prophets [of Baal] with the sword.

2 Then Jezebel sent a messenger to Elijah, saying, So let the gods do to me, and more also, if I make not your life as the life of one of them by this time tomorrow.

keep your balance!

Why in the world would a man like Elijah, who the previous day had made absolute fools of 450 prophets of Baal and then personally slain every one of them, suddenly allow himself to become so intimidated by the threats of a solitary woman named Jezebel that he ran away in fear (see I Kings 19:1–3)? I doubt very much that Jezebel was so fearsome that Elijah had to do that. I believe he responded in such an unbalanced way because he was exhausted.

Many of the problems we face in relationships come from being out of balance, and often that imbalance is the result of simply being worn out. When we are totally exhausted, we respond to people differently than we do when we are fully rested. We tend to respond emotionally and get our feelings hurt easily. We are touchier and more likely to get upset over the slightest thing that goes wrong. Even our creative ability dries up when we are overly tired. Like Elijah, we become vulnerable to depression and discouragement. I know from personal experience that my faith is affected when I am too tired; it is even difficult to want to pray at those times.

In many of today's families, both husband and wife need to work full-time just to provide for themselves and their children. After working all day, they then have to go home and take care of the children, prepare meals, do laundry and housework, go grocery shopping, see to the yard work, pay bills, and on and on. Sooner or later, they may become exhausted. If they are Christians, they will want to attend church and may also take on other church commitments.

While many of these activities are good, they may not all be commitments that are Spirit-led. If the people are not careful, they may end up trying to be everything to everybody, which wears them out. They may begin to feel that they are being pulled apart because everywhere they look, someone wants them to do something. Although serving in church and community is a very important part of our overall duty and desire, we must be Spirit-led and simply realize that we can do some things, but we cannot do everything.

I know all about this because I have gone through it in my own life. Not only am I a minister with an international ministry to operate, I am also a wife, a mother of four grown children, a grandmother, and a friend with many other duties, responsibilities, and relationships.

I am extremely busy; we all are, which is why we need balance in our lives. That may mean having to cut off some things we do not really want to get rid of, but which will cause problems if we do not allow God to prune them. In some cases, that may mean giving up a second job. We may have told ourselves that we took the job for our families, but the truth may be that our family needs *us* more than they need the money we could earn for them.

Let Elijah's story in I Kings 19:1–3 remind you to maintain balance in every aspect of your life: physical, mental, emotional, social, and spiritual. God wants you blessed, and in order to receive, enjoy, and wisely steward His blessings, you need to be strong and refreshed, not stressed and exhausted.

3 Then he was afraid and arose and went for his life and came to Beersheba of Judah [over eighty miles, and out of Jezebel's realm] and left his servant there.
4 But he himself went a day's journey into the wilderness and came and sat down under a lone broom *or* juniper tree and asked that he might die. He said, It is enough; now, O Lord, take away my life; for I am no better than my fathers.

life point

Nothing in life looks good to us when we are exhausted. It seems that nobody loves us, nobody helps us, and nobody is concerned about us. We think that we have to do all the work. We think we are being abused, misused, misunderstood, and mistreated. Many times when we feel we have a deep problem, all that is wrong is that we (like Elijah) are just plain tired (see I Kings 19:4). When people are already exhausted and they continue to do more and more things, they usually become very confused and cranky. We must learn to listen to our bodies and rest when we need it. Rest is not a luxury; it is essential to living a balanced, fruitful life.

5 As he lay asleep under the broom *or* juniper tree, behold, an angel touched him and said to him, Arise and eat.
6 He looked, and behold, there was a cake baked on the coals, and a bottle of water at his head. And he ate and drank and lay down again.
7 The angel of the Lord came the second time and touched him and said, Arise and eat, for the journey is too great for you.
8 So he arose and ate and drank, and went in the strength of that food

life point

How did the Lord through His angel get Elijah to the place where he was strong enough to go on with the next phase of his ministry? He gave him two good meals and a nice long nap (see I Kings 19:5, 6). That was all He gave him, and in the strength of that food, Elijah went forty days and nights on a journey to Horeb! There was nothing great, spiritual, or supernatural about this. Elijah was worn out from everything he had done the day before and everything he had been through since. His body was broken down, and his emotions had fallen apart. He was not handling himself the way he normally would. He was afraid, depressed, discouraged, and even suicidal.

The Lord said to him, "You're worn out. You need a couple of hot meals and a good night's rest." And after Elijah was refreshed and made the journey to Horeb, the word of the Lord came to him there. With a fresh word from God, he was sent off again to do the work of the Lord.

Remember, staying spiritually strong does include natural wisdom. Take care of your body, exercise, and eat healthfully so that you will have the physical stamina and alertness necessary to complete God's next assignment for you.

forty days and nights to Horeb, the mount of God.
9 There he came to a cave and lodged in it; and behold, the word of the Lord came to him, and He said to him, What are you doing here, Elijah?
10 He replied, I have been very jealous for the Lord God of hosts; for the Israelites have forsaken Your

avoiding burnout

I have observed that after a person goes through a real emotional high, he will usually bottom out with an emotional low.

We see this in the life of Elijah the prophet. One day he is on Mount Carmel, in triumph and at the height of his victory. The next day he is sitting under a tree in the wilderness, asking God to let him die because he feels so depressed (see I Kings 19:4).

In my own life, I have noticed when I minister in a long series of meetings, I spend everything I have spiritually, emotionally, and mentally praying for people and meeting their needs. And when I return from something exciting like that to normal, everyday life, it is quite a transition. This might be compared to climbing an emotional mountain, then falling off it. Who would want to go from doing miracles one day to hiding from Jezebel the next?

Often we get the idea, *Oh, if I could just stay on this emotional high forever!* But God knows we could not stand to maintain that level of intense emotion. Too many emotional highs and lows wear us out in every way. When I have finished an extensive ministry trip and I feel completely drained, I have learned to rest. It usually takes about two days for me to totally recuperate physically, mentally, emotionally, and even spiritually. I need to sleep, have some quality food for nourishment, spend extra time with God, do something fun for my emotions, and not make decisions that would require any mental effort.

When you feel "low" after an emotional high, do not do as Elijah did and get down on yourself. Do not allow the devil to take advantage of you during those times. Use wisdom and get the rest you need—it will make a huge difference.

covenant, thrown down Your altars, and killed Your prophets with the sword. And I, I only, am left; and they seek my life, to take it away.

11 And He said, Go out and stand on the mount before the Lord. And behold, the Lord passed by, and a great and strong wind rent the mountains and broke in pieces the rocks before the Lord, but the Lord was not in the wind; and after the wind an earthquake, but the Lord was not in the earthquake;

12 And after the earthquake a fire, but the Lord was not in the fire; and after the fire [a sound of gentle stillness and] a still, small voice.

13 When Elijah heard the voice, he wrapped his face in his mantle and went out and stood in the entrance of the cave. And behold, there came a voice to him and said, What are you doing here, Elijah?

14 He said, I have been very jealous for the Lord God of hosts, because the Israelites have forsaken Your covenant, thrown down Your altars, and slain Your prophets with the

life point

The ways of the Holy Spirit are gentle; most of the time He speaks to us as He did to Elijah, in "a still, small voice" (I Kings 19:12).

hearing God's still, small voice

I was fascinated to learn that some horses have what their trainers call a "reining ear." While most horses are guided and led by a strap fastened to the bit in their mouth, some horses keep one ear turned to their master's voice. One ear is open for natural warnings; the other is sensitive to the trusted trainer.

Elijah needed to hear from God, and thankfully he had a reining ear toward God even though his circumstances had frightened him. He had experienced tremendous victory but afterward he ran for his life, hid in a cave, and prayed to God to die. Knowing Elijah's need, God taught Elijah a wonderful lesson about what His voice sounds like. As Elijah waited on God, He demonstrated His power through wind, earthquake, and fire. But God was not in those things; instead, He spoke to Elijah in a "still, small voice" (I Kings 19:12) and gave instructions for Elijah's next mission. Later in this chapter we will see that Elijah obeyed the still, small voice of the Lord.

Elijah's story helps us understand how to hear God when we need direction. God did not reassure Elijah with a showy, flashy manifestation of power, although He had already proven that He was capable of doing so. Instead, God spoke to His prophet through a still, small voice—and He still chooses to communicate directly to His children through a whisper deep within their spirits.

The Bible tells us that God is a spiritual Being, and those who worship Him must worship Him in spirit and truth (see John 4:24). Jesus explained that some people do not hear the voice of God because they do not believe Him and thus do not have His Word living in their hearts (see John 5:37–40). He taught us that we must be born again in order to hear God's voice: "You must all be born anew (from above). The wind blows (breathes) where it wills; and though you hear its sound, yet you neither know where it comes from nor where it is going. So it is with everyone who is born of the Spirit" (John 3:7, 8). When we are born again, we are made alive in our spirits to be sensitive to the voice of God. We hear His whisper even though we cannot tell where it comes from. Our ears become "tuned in" to hear our Master's voice. He whispers to convict, correct, and direct us by a still, small voice deep within our hearts.

sword. And I, I only, am left, and they seek my life, to destroy it.
15 And the Lord said to him, Go, return on your way to the Wilderness of Damascus; and when you arrive, anoint Hazael to be king over Syria.

16 And anoint Jehu son of Nimshi to be king over Israel, and anoint Elisha son of Shaphat of Abel-meholah to be prophet in your place.
17 And him who escapes from the sword of qHazael Jehu shall slay, and

q Ahab had again fallen under the sway of Jezebel. Therefore, Baal worship would recover from the blow dealt it by Elijah. Elijah is accordingly instructed to take the necessary steps for the destruction of Baal worship. They were three. First, Ahab was to be attacked from without by the Syrians, and for that purpose warlike Hazael was to take the Syrian throne. Second, when Ahab was thus weakened, Jehu was to seize his throne, since Jehu was a known opponent of Baal worship, and also him who escapes the sword of Jehu Elisha shall slay.

18 Yet I will leave Myself 7,000 in Israel, all the knees that have not bowed to Baal and every mouth that has not kissed him.

19 So Elijah left there and found Elisha son of Shaphat, whose plowing was being done with twelve yoke of oxen, and he drove the twelfth. Elijah crossed over to him and cast his mantle upon him.

20 He left the oxen and ran after Elijah and said, Let me kiss my father and mother, and then I will follow you. And he [testing Elisha] said, Go on back. What have I done to you? [Settle it for yourself.]

21 So Elisha went back from him. Then he took a yoke of oxen, slew them, boiled their flesh with the oxen's yoke [as fuel], and gave to the people, and they ate. Then he arose, followed Elijah, and served him. [II Kings 3:11.]

20 BEN-HADAD KING of Syria gathered all his army together; thirty-two kings were with him, and horses and chariots. And he went up and besieged Samaria, warring against it.

2 He sent messengers into Samaria to Ahab king of Israel and said to him, Thus says Ben-hadad:

3 Your silver and your gold are mine; your wives and your children, even the fairest, also are mine.

4 And the king of Israel answered and said, My lord, O king, according to what you say, I am yours, and all that I have.

5 The messengers came again and said, Thus says Ben-hadad: Although I have sent to you, saying, You shall deliver to me your silver, your gold, your wives, and your children—

6 Yet I will send my servants to you tomorrow about this time, and they shall search your house and the houses of your servants; and all the desire of your eyes they shall lay hands upon and take it away.

7 Then the king of Israel called all the elders of the land and said, Notice now and see how this man is seeking our destruction. He sent to me for my wives, my children, my silver, and my gold, and I did not refuse him.

8 And all the elders and all the people said to him, Do not heed him or consent.

9 So he said to Ben-hadad's messengers, Tell my lord the king, All you first sent for to your servant I will do, but this thing I cannot do. And the messengers left; then they brought him word again.

10 Ben-hadad sent to him and said, May the gods do so to me, and more also, if the rubbish of Samaria shall be enough for each one of all the people who are at my feet *and* follow me to get a handful.

11 The king of Israel answered, Tell him: Let not him who girds on his harness boast as he who puts it off.

12 When Ben-hadad heard this message as he and the kings were drinking in the booths, he said to his servants, Set the army in array. And they set themselves in array against [Samaria].

13 Then a prophet came to Ahab king of Israel and said, Thus says the Lord: Have you seen all this great multitude? Behold, I will deliver it into your hand today, and you shall know *and* realize that I am the Lord.

14 Ahab said, By whom? And he said, Thus says the Lord: By the young men [the attendants or bodyguards] of the governors of the districts. Then Ahab said, Who shall

a ruthless soldier. Third, Elijah was to appoint as his own successor the vigorous and wholehearted Elisha, who might be trusted under Jehu to complete the destruction of the adherents of Baal (*The Cambridge Bible*).

order the battle? And he answered, You.

15 Ahab numbered the attendants of the governors of the districts, and they were 232. After them he numbered all the people of [the army of] Israel, 7,000. [I Kings 19:18.]

16 And they went out at noon. But Ben-hadad was drinking himself drunk in the booths, he and the thirty-two kings who helped him.

17 The servants of the governors of the districts went out first; and Ben-hadad sent out, and they told him, saying, There are men come out of Samaria.

18 And he said, Whether they have come out for peace or for war, take them alive.

19 So these [strong young guards] of the governors of the districts went out of [Samaria], and the army followed them.

20 And each one killed his man; the Syrians fled, and Israel pursued them. Ben-hadad king of Syria escaped on a horse with the horsemen.

21 The king of Israel went out and smote [the riders of] the horses and chariots and slew the Syrians with a great slaughter.

22 The prophet came to the king of Israel and said to him, Go, fortify yourself and become strong and give attention to what you must do, for at the first of next year the king of Syria will return against you.

23 And the servants of the king of Syria said to him, Israel's gods are gods of the hills; therefore they were stronger than we. But let us fight against them in the plain, and surely we shall be stronger than they.

24 And do this thing: Remove the kings, each from his place, and put governors in their stead.

25 And muster yourself an army like the army you have lost, horse for horse and chariot for chariot. And we will fight against them in the plain,

and surely we shall be stronger than they. And he heeded their speech and did so.

26 And at the return of the year, Ben-hadad mustered the Syrians and went up to Aphek to fight against Israel.

27 The Israelites were counted and, all present, went against them. The Israelites encamped before the enemy like two little flocks of lost kids [absolutely everything against them but Almighty God], but the Syrians filled the country.

28 A man of God came and said to the king of Israel, Thus says the Lord: Because the Syrians have said, The Lord is God of the hills but He is not God of the valleys, therefore I will deliver all this great multitude into your hands, and you shall know and recognize by experience that I am the Lord. [Phil. 4:13.]

29 They encamped opposite each other seven days. Then the battle was joined; and the Israelites slew of the Syrians 100,000 foot soldiers in one day.

30 But the rest fled to the city of Aphek, and the wall fell upon 27,000 men who were left. Ben-hadad fled into the city and from chamber to chamber.

31 His servants said to him, We have heard that the kings of the house of Israel are merciful kings. Let us put sackcloth on our loins and ropes about our necks, and go out to the king of Israel; perhaps he will spare your life.

32 So they girded sackcloth on their loins and put ropes on their necks, and came to the king of Israel and said, Your servant Ben-hadad says, I pray you, let me live. And King [Ahab] said, Is he yet alive? He is my brother.

33 Now the men took it as an omen and they hastily took it up and said, Yes, your brother Ben-hadad. Then the king said, Go, bring him. Then Ben-hadad came forth to him, and the victorious king caused him to come up into the chariot.

34 Ben-hadad [tempting him] said, The cities which my father took from your father I will restore; and you may maintain bazaars of your own in Damascus, as my father did in Samaria. Then, said Ahab, I will send you away on these terms. So he made a covenant with him and sent him away.

35 And a certain man of the sons of the prophets said to his neighbor, At the command of the Lord, strike me, I pray you. And the man refused to strike him.

36 Then said he to him, Because you have not obeyed the voice of the Lord, behold, as soon as you have left me a lion will slay you. And as soon as he departed from him, a lion found him and killed him.

37 Then [the prophet] found another man and said, Strike me, I pray you. And the man struck him, so that in striking, he wounded him.

38 So the prophet departed and waited for King Ahab by the way, and disguised himself with ashes upon his face.

39 And as the king passed by, the [prophet] cried out to him, Your servant went out into the midst of the battle, and behold, a man turned aside and brought a man to me and said, Keep this man. If for any reason he is missing, then your life shall be required for his life, or else you shall pay a talent of silver.

40 But while your servant was busy here and there, he was gone. And the king of Israel said to him, Such is your own verdict; you yourself have decided it.

41 The man hastily removed the ashes from his face, and Ahab king of Israel recognized him as one of the prophets.

42 And he said to the king, Thus says the Lord: Because you have let go out of your hand the man I had devoted to destruction, therefore your life shall go for his life, and your people for his people.

43 And King [Ahab] of Israel went to his house resentful and sullen, and came to Samaria. [I Kings 22:34-36.]

21 NOW NABOTH the Jezreelite had a vineyard in Jezreel, close beside the palace of Ahab king of Samaria; and after these things,

2 Ahab said to Naboth, Give me your vineyard, that I may have it for a garden of herbs, because it is near my house. I will give you a better vineyard for it or, if you prefer, I will give you its worth in money.

3 Naboth said to Ahab, The Lord forbid that I should give the inheritance of my fathers to you.

4 And Ahab [already depressed by the Lord's message to him] came into his house [more] resentful and sullen because of what Naboth the Jezreelite had said to him; for he had said, I will not give you the inheritance of my fathers. And he lay down on his bed, turned away his face, and would eat no food.

5 But Jezebel his wife came and said to him, Why is your spirit so troubled that you eat no food?

6 And he said to her, Because I spoke to Naboth the Jezreelite and said to him, Give me your vineyard for money; or if you prefer, I will give you another vineyard for it. And he answered, I will not give you my vineyard.

7 Jezebel his wife said to him, Do you not govern Israel? Arise, eat food, and let your heart be happy. I will give you the vineyard of Naboth the Jezreelite.

8 So she wrote letters in Ahab's name and sealed them with his seal and sent them to the elders and nobles who dwelt with Naboth in his city.

9 And in the letters she said, Proclaim a fast and set Naboth up high among the people.

10 And set two men, base fellows, before him, and let them bear witness against him, saying, You cursed *and* renounced God and the king. Then carry him out and stone him to death.

11 And the men of his city, the elders and the nobles who dwelt there, did as Jezebel had directed in the letters sent them.

12 They proclaimed a fast and set Naboth on high among the people.

13 Two base fellows came in and sat opposite him and they charged Naboth before the people, saying, Naboth cursed *and* renounced God and the king. Then he was carried out of the city and stoned to death.

14 Then they sent to Jezebel, saying, Naboth has been stoned and is dead.

15 Then Jezebel said to Ahab, Arise, take possession of the vineyard of Naboth the Jezreelite which he refused to sell you, for Naboth is not alive, but dead.

16 When Ahab heard that, he arose to go down to the vineyard of Naboth the Jezreelite to take possession of it.

17 Then the word of the Lord came to Elijah the Tishbite, saying,

18 Arise, go down to meet Ahab king of Israel in Samaria. He is in the vineyard of Naboth, where he has gone to possess it.

19 Say to him, Thus says the Lord: Have you killed and also taken possession? Thus says the Lord: In the place where dogs licked the blood of Naboth shall dogs lick your blood, even yours.

20 And Ahab said to Elijah, Have you found me, O my enemy? And he answered, I have found you, because you have sold yourself to do evil in the sight of the Lord.

21 See [says the Lord], I will bring evil on you and utterly sweep away and cut off from Ahab every male, bond and free,

22 And will make your household like that of Jeroboam son of Nebat and like the household of Baasha son of Ahijah, for the provocation with which you have provoked Me to anger and made Israel to sin.

23 Also the Lord said of Jezebel: The dogs shall eat Jezebel by the wall of Jezreel.

24 Any belonging to Ahab who dies in the city the dogs shall eat, and any who dies in the field the birds of the air shall eat. [I Kings 14:11; 16:4.]

25 For there was no one who sold himself to do evil in the sight of the Lord as did Ahab, incited by his wife Jezebel.

26 He did very abominably in going after idols, as had the Amorites, whom the Lord cast out before the Israelites.

27 When Ahab heard those words of Elijah, he tore his clothes, put sackcloth on his flesh, fasted, lay in sackcloth, and went quietly.

28 And the word of the Lord came to Elijah the Tishbite, saying,

29 Do you see how Ahab humbles himself before Me? Because he humbles himself before Me, I will not bring the evil in his lifetime, but in his son's day I will bring the evil upon his house.

22 SYRIA AND Israel continued without war for three years.

2 In the third year Jehoshaphat king of Judah came down to the king of Israel.

3 And [Ahab] king of Israel said to his servants, Do you know that Ramoth in Gilead is ours, and we keep silence and do not take it from the king of Syria?

4 And [Ahab] said to Jehoshaphat, Will you go with me to Ramoth-gilead to battle? Jehoshaphat said to the king of Israel, I am as you are, my people as your people, my horses as your horses.

5   But Jehoshaphat said to the king of Israel, Inquire first, I pray you, for the word of the Lord today.

6   Then [Ahab] king of Israel gathered the prophets together, about 400 men, and said to them, Shall I go against Ramoth-gilead to battle, or shall I hold back? And they said, Go up, for the Lord will deliver it into the hand of the king.

7   Jehoshaphat said, Is there not another prophet of the Lord here whom we may ask?

8   [Ahab] king of Israel said to Jehoshaphat, There is yet one man, Micaiah son of Imlah, by whom we may inquire of the Lord, but I hate him, for he never prophesies good for me, but evil. Jehoshaphat said, Let not the king say that.

9   Then [Ahab] king of Israel told an officer, Bring quickly Micaiah son of Imlah.

10   Now the king of Israel and Jehoshaphat king of Judah were sitting in [royal] robes [or armor], each on his throne in an open place [on a threshing floor] at the entrance of the gate of Samaria; and all the prophets prophesied before them.

11   And Zedekiah son of Chenaanah made him horns of iron and said, Thus says the Lord: With these you shall push the Syrians until they are destroyed.

12   And all the prophets agreed, saying, Go up to Ramoth-gilead and prosper, for the Lord will deliver it into the king's hand.

13   The messenger who went to call Micaiah said to him, Behold now, the prophets unanimously declare good to the king. Let your answer, I pray you, be like theirs, and say what is good.

14   But Micaiah said, As the Lord lives, I will speak what the Lord says to me.

15   So he came to the king. King [Ahab] said, Micaiah, shall we go against Ramoth-gilead to battle, or shall we hold back? And he answered, Go and prosper, for the Lord will deliver it into the king's hand.

16   And the king said to him, How many times must I charge you to tell me nothing but the truth in the name of the Lord?

17   And he said, I saw all Israel scattered upon the hills as sheep that have no shepherd, and the Lord said, These have no master. Let them return every man to his house in peace.

18   Then the king of Israel said to Jehoshaphat, Did I not tell you that he would prophesy no good concerning me, but evil?

19   And Micaiah said, Hear the word of the Lord: I saw the Lord sitting on His throne, and all the host of heaven standing by Him on His right hand and on His left.

20   And the Lord said, Who will entice Ahab to go up and fall at Ramoth-gilead? One said this way, another said that way.

21   Then there came forth a spirit [of whom I am about to tell] and stood before the Lord and said, I will entice him.

22   The Lord said to him, By what means? And he said, I will go forth and be a lying spirit in the mouths of all his prophets. [The Lord] said, You shall entice him and succeed also. Go forth and do it.

speak the Word

Lord, may I be obedient and always speak what You say to me.
ADAPTED FROM I KINGS **22:14**

23 So the Lord has put a lying spirit in the mouths of all these prophets; and the Lord has spoken evil concerning you.

24 But Zedekiah son of Chenaanah went near and struck Micaiah on the cheek and said, Which way went the Spirit of the Lord from me to speak to you?

25 Micaiah said, Behold, you shall see on that day when you go into an inner chamber to hide yourself.

26 [Ahab] king of Israel said, Take Micaiah, carry him back to Amon the governor of the city and to Joash the king's son,

27 And say, The king says, Put this fellow in prison and feed him with bread and water of affliction until I come in peace.

28 Micaiah said, If you return at all in peace, the Lord has not spoken by me. He [added], Hear, O people, every one of you!

29 So [Ahab] king of Israel and Jehoshaphat the king of Judah went up to Ramoth-gilead.

30 And the king of Israel said to Jehoshaphat, I will disguise myself and enter the battle, but you put on your [royal] clothing. And the king of Israel disguised himself and went into the battle.

31 But the king of Syria had commanded the thirty-two captains of his chariots, Fight neither with small nor great, but only with [Ahab] king of Israel.

32 And when the captains of the chariots saw Jehoshaphat, they said, Surely it is the king of Israel. They turned to fight against him, but Jehoshaphat cried out.

33 And when the captains of the chariots saw that it was not the king of Israel, they turned back from pursuing him.

34 But a certain man drew a bow at a venture and smote [Ahab] the king of Israel between the joints of the armor.

So he said to the driver of his chariot, Turn around and carry me out of the army, for I am wounded.

35 The battle increased that day, and [Ahab] the king was propped up in his chariot facing the Syrians, and at nightfall he died. And the blood of his wound flowed onto the floor of the chariot.

36 And there went a cry throughout the army about sundown, saying, Every man to his city and his own country,

37 For the king is dead! And [Ahab] was brought to Samaria, where they buried him.

38 And they washed [his] chariot by the pool of Samaria, where the harlots bathed, and the dogs licked up his blood, as the Lord had predicted. [I Kings 21:19.]

39 The rest of Ahab's acts, all he did, the ivory palace and all the cities he built, are they not written in the Book of the Chronicles of the Kings of Israel?

40 So Ahab slept with his fathers. Ahaziah his son reigned in his stead.

41 Jehoshaphat son of Asa began to reign over Judah in the fourth year of Ahab king of Israel.

42 Jehoshaphat was thirty-five years old when he began to reign, and he reigned twenty-five years in Jerusalem. His mother was Azubah daughter of Shilhi.

43 He walked in all the ways *or* customs of Asa his father, never swerving from it, doing right in the sight of the Lord. However, the [idolatrous] high places were not taken away; for the people still sacrificed and burned incense in the high places.

44 And Jehoshaphat made peace with Israel's king.

45 The rest of the acts of Jehoshaphat, his might that he showed and how he warred, are they not written in the Book of the Chronicles of the Kings of Judah?

46 And the remnant of the sodomites (the male cult prostitutes) who remained in the days of his father Asa, [Jehoshaphat] expelled from the country.

47 There was no king in Edom; a deputy was acting king.

48 Jehoshaphat ordered ships of Tarshish to go to Ophir for gold, but they did not go, for the ships were wrecked at Ezion-geber.

49 When Ahaziah son of Ahab said to Jehoshaphat, Let my servants go with your servants in the ships, Jehoshaphat refused.

50 Jehoshaphat slept with his fathers and was buried with them in the city of David his father [forefather]. And Jehoram his son reigned in his stead.

51 Ahaziah son of Ahab began his two-year reign over Israel in Samaria in the seventeenth year of Jehoshaphat king of Judah.

52 He did evil in the sight of the Lord and walked in the ways of his father [Ahab] and of his mother [Jezebel] and of Jeroboam son of Nebat, who made Israel sin.

53 He served Baal and worshiped him and provoked the Lord, the God of Israel, to anger in all the ways his father had done.

Second Kings

Author:
Unknown

Date:
600 BC–550 BC

Everyday Life Principles:
Obeying God leads to blessings; disobeying or dishonoring Him brings curses.

The ministries of both Elijah and Elisha can remind us that God is a God of miracles and He still does miracles today.

A double portion awaits those who are faithful until the very end.

Second Kings, like I Kings, continues the biblical record of the names, reigns, and some of the actions of the rulers of the divided kingdom. On the time line of history, II Kings picks up where I Kings leaves off. Throughout II Kings, we see good kings and bad kings, those who sought to serve God and those who did not. We continue to see Israel as a nation go back and forth between honoring God and dishonoring Him.

One of the same truths we see throughout the Old Testament is reiterated yet again in II Kings: When we obey God, we are blessed; when we are living in disobedience to God, we cannot expect Him to bless us.

One noteworthy event in II Kings is the death of Elijah, which was not a typical death—he was simply caught up in a whirlwind and taken to heaven in a chariot of fire. Elisha remained faithful to Elijah until the very end, and after Elijah died, Elisha received a double portion of his spirit and went on to witness and be used by God in great signs, wonders, and miracles.

As you read II Kings, remember that obedience brings blessings and disobedience brings curses. Remember too that God will reward your faithfulness, just as He did Elisha's. Many people give up just prior to a breakthrough, but the double portion awaits those who will stay faithful until the end.

1 MOAB REBELLED against Israel after the death of Ahab.

2 [King] Ahaziah fell down through a lattice in his upper chamber in Samaria and lay sick. He sent messengers, saying, Go, ask Baal-zebub, the god of [Philistine] Ekron, if I shall recover from this illness.

3 But the angel of the Lord said to Elijah the Tishbite, Arise, go up to meet the messengers of the king in Samaria and say to them, Is it because there is no God in Israel that you are going to inquire of Baal-zebub, the god of Ekron?

4 Therefore the Lord says: You [Ahaziah] shall not leave the bed on which you lie, but shall surely die. And Elijah departed.

5 When the messengers returned to Ahaziah, he said, Why have you turned back?

6 They replied, A man came up to meet us who said, Go back to the king who sent you and tell him, Thus says the Lord: Is there no God in Israel that you send to inquire of Baal-zebub, the god of Ekron? Therefore you shall not leave the bed on which you lie, but shall surely die.

7 The king asked, What was the man like who came to meet you saying these things?

8 They answered, He was a hairy man with a girdle of leather about his loins. And he said, It is Elijah the Tishbite.

9 Then the king sent to Elijah a captain of fifty men with his fifty [to seize him]. He found Elijah sitting on a hilltop and said, Man of God, the king says, Come down.

10 Elijah said to the captain of fifty, If I am a man of God, then let fire come down from heaven and consume you and your fifty. And fire fell from heaven and consumed him and his fifty.

11 Again King [Ahaziah] sent to him another captain of fifty with his fifty. And he said to Elijah, Man of God, the king has said, Come down quickly!

12 And Elijah answered, If I am a man of God, let fire come down from heaven and consume you and your fifty. And the fire of God came down from heaven and consumed him and his fifty.

13 Ahaziah sent again a captain of a third fifty with his fifty. And the third captain of fifty went up and fell on his knees before Elijah and besought him and said to him, O man of God, I pray you, let my life and the lives of these fifty, your servants, be precious in your sight.

14 Behold, fire came down from heaven and burned up the two captains of the former fifties with their fifties. Therefore let my life now be precious in your sight.

15 The angel of the Lord said to Elijah, Go down with him; do not be afraid of him. So he arose and went with him to the king.

16 Elijah said to [King] Ahaziah, Thus says the Lord: Since you have sent messengers to inquire of Baal-zebub, god of Ekron, is it because there is no God in Israel of Whom to inquire His word? Therefore you shall not leave the bed on which you lie, but shall surely die.

17 So Ahaziah died according to the word of the Lord which Elijah had spoken. ªJoram [also a son of Ahab] reigned in Israel in his stead in the second year of Jehoram son of Jehoshaphat king of Judah, because Ahaziah had no son [but his brother].

18 Now the rest of the acts of Ahaziah, are they not written in the Book of the Chronicles of the Kings of Israel?

a Hebrew *Jehoram*, a variant of *Joram*.

2 WHEN THE Lord was about to take Elijah up to heaven by a whirlwind, Elijah and Elisha were going from Gilgal.

2 And Elijah said to Elisha, Tarry here, I pray you, for the Lord has sent me to Bethel. But Elisha replied, As the Lord lives and as your soul lives, I will not leave you. So they went down to Bethel.

3 The prophets' sons who were at Bethel came to Elisha and said, Do you know that the Lord will take your master away from you today? He said, Yes, I know it; hold your peace.

4 Elijah said to him, Elisha, tarry here, I pray you, for the Lord has sent me to Jericho. But he said, As the Lord lives and as your soul lives, I will not leave you. So they came to Jericho.

5 The sons of the prophets who were at Jericho came to Elisha and said, Do you know that the Lord will take your master away from you today? And he answered, Yes, I know it; hold your peace.

6 Elijah said to him, Tarry here, I pray you, for the Lord has sent me to the Jordan. But he said, As the Lord lives and as your soul lives, I will not leave you. And the two of them went on.

7 Fifty men of the sons of the prophets also went and stood [to watch] afar off; and the two of them stood by the Jordan.

putting the Word to work

Having a spiritual mentor is a great gift. Is there a more mature Christian in your life who is helping you to grow in your relationship with God? If not, ask God to identify someone who can be a mentor to you, as Elijah was to Elisha (see I Kings 2:2–8). If you do have a spiritual mentor, one way to show your appreciation is through faithful support of and loyalty to that individual.

8 And Elijah took his mantle and rolled it up and struck the waters, and they divided this way and that, so that the two of them went over on dry ground.

9 And when they had gone over, Elijah said to Elisha, Ask what I shall do for you before I am taken from you. And Elisha said, I pray you, let a double portion of your spirit be upon me.

10 He said, You have asked a hard thing. However, if you see me when I am taken from you, it shall be so for you—but if not, it shall not be so.

11 As they still went on and talked, behold, a chariot of fire and horses of fire parted the two of them, and Elijah went up by a whirlwind into heaven.

12 And Elisha saw it and he cried, My father, my father! The chariot of Israel and its horsemen! And he saw him no more. And he took hold of his own clothes and tore them in two pieces.

13 He took up also the mantle of Elijah that fell from him and went back and stood by the bank of the Jordan.

14 And he took the mantle that fell from Elijah and struck the waters and said, Where is the Lord, the God of Elijah? And when he had struck the waters, they parted this way and that, and Elisha went over.

15 When the sons of the prophets who were [watching] at Jericho saw him, they said, The spirit of Elijah rests on Elisha. And they came to meet him and bowed themselves to the ground before him.

16 And they said to him, Behold now, there are among your servants fifty strong men; let them go, we pray you, and seek your master. It may be that the Spirit of the Lord has taken him up and cast him on some mountain or into some valley. And he said, You shall not send.

17 But when they urged him till he was embarrassed, he said, Send. So

double-portion blessings

Seeing an assignment or a project from God through to the finish is extremely important. Many people start things enthusiastically but never finish them, and this is not pleasing to God. The Bible says in Luke 14:28–30 that we should count the cost before we begin to build and make sure we have what will be needed to finish the project.

Elisha was Elijah's servant and had been chosen and anointed to take Elijah's place when he was gone. As Elijah neared the end of his time on earth, he asked Elisha what he could do for him. We read in II Kings 2:9 that Elisha requested a double portion of his mentor's anointing. Elisha had asked for a hard thing, but was told he could have it if he saw Elijah when God took him away.

I have always felt that Elijah was saying, "If you stick with me until the very end, if you finish what you started many years ago—then you may have what you asked for." Many people ask for things and then are not willing to do what is required of them to have their requests granted. Asking is easy, but seeing things through to the finish is not. Beginnings are exciting, and they come with zeal and enthusiasm. Many times, in the beginning of an endeavor, lots of people are willing to help. However, the way becomes tougher when the newness wears off and some of the people who originally committed to help lose interest or grow weary.

We must be able to endure hard work, wait longer for results than we expected to, endure loneliness, betrayal, misunderstanding, and many other unpleasant things if needed. Jesus endured all these things in order to complete God's will for His life, and we are to follow in His footsteps. Jesus said, "Take up your cross and follow Me" (see Luke 9:23). I believe the cross we are called on to carry is the challenge of living an unselfish life. That means we cannot quit or give up just because we do not enjoy the difficult work of pressing on. We must live beyond how we feel, what we think or want, and, in the face of hardship, do all that God asks us to do.

Make a decision today that from now on, by God's grace, you will always finish what you start. It may be cleaning out your closet, or keeping a commitment at church or to a friend. It could be paying for the things you have purchased or going to a Bible college. Whatever it is, just do it! God has a double-portion blessing waiting for you, but you will find it at the finish line.

---

they sent fifty men, who sought for three days but did not find him.

18 When they returned to Elisha, who had waited at Jericho, he said to them, Did I not tell you, Do not go?

19 And the men of the city said to Elisha, Behold, inhabiting of this city is pleasant, as my lord sees, but the water is bad and the locality causes miscarriage *and* barrenness [in all animals].

20 He said, Bring me a new bowl and put salt [the symbol of God's purifying power] in it. And they brought it to him.

21 Then Elisha went to the spring of the waters and cast the salt in it and said, Thus says the Lord: I [not the salt] have healed these waters; there shall not be any more death, miscarriage *or* barrenness [and bereavement] because of it.
22 So the waters were healed to this day, as Elisha had said.
23 He went up from Jericho to Bethel. On the way, [b]young [maturing and accountable] boys came out of the city and mocked him and said to him, Go up [in a whirlwind], you baldhead! Go up, you baldhead!
24 And he turned around and looked at them and called a curse down on them in the name of the Lord. And two she-bears came out of the woods and ripped up forty-two of the boys.
25 Elisha went from there to Mount Carmel, and from there he returned to Samaria.

3 JORAM SON of Ahab began to reign over Israel in Samaria in the eighteenth year of Jehoshaphat king of Judah, and reigned twelve years.
2 He did evil in the sight of the Lord, but not like his father and mother; for he put away the pillar of Baal that his father had made.
3 Yet he clung to the sins of Jeroboam son of Nebat, which made Israel to sin; he departed not from them.
4 [c]Mesha king of Moab was a sheepmaster, and paid in tribute to the king of Israel [annually] 100,000 lambs and 100,000 rams, with the wool.
5 But when Ahab died, the king of Moab rebelled against the king of Israel.
6 So King Joram went out of Samaria at that time and mustered all Israel.
7 And he sent to Jehoshaphat king of Judah, saying, The king of Moab has rebelled against me. Will you go with me to war against Moab? And he said, I will go; I am as you are, my people as your people, my horses as your horses.
8 Joram said, Which way shall we go up? Jehoshaphat answered, The way through the Wilderness of Edom.
9 So the king of Israel went with the king of Judah and the king of Edom. They made a circuit of seven days' journey, but there was no water for the army or for the animals following them.
10 Then the king of Israel said, Alas! The Lord has called [us] three kings together to be delivered into Moab's hand!
11 But Jehoshaphat said, Is there no prophet of the Lord here by whom we may inquire of the Lord? One of the king of Israel's servants answered, Elisha son of Shaphat, who served Elijah, is here.
12 Jehoshaphat said, The word of the Lord is with him. So Joram king of Israel and Jehoshaphat and the king of Edom went down to Elisha.
13 And Elisha said to the king of Israel, What have I to do with you? Go to the prophets of your [wicked] father Ahab and your [wicked] mother Jezebel. But the king of Israel said to him, No, for the Lord has called [us] three kings together to be delivered into the hand of Moab.

b This incident has long been misunderstood because the Hebrew word "naar" was translated "little boys." That these characteristic juvenile delinquents were old enough to be fully accountable is obvious from the use of the word elsewhere. For example, it was used by David of his son Solomon and translated "young and inexperienced," when Solomon was a father (I Chron. 22:5; cf. I Kings 14:21 and II Chron. 9:30). It was used of Joseph when he was seventeen (Gen. 37:2). In fact, not less than seventy times in the *King James Version* this word "naar" is translated "young man" or "young men." **c** This name of the king of Moab occurs in the first line of the Moabite Stone. In that inscription the Moabite king mentions his successes against Omri and Omri's successor (I Kings 16:23).

14 And Elisha said, As the Lord of hosts lives, before Whom I stand, surely, were it not that I respect the presence of Jehoshaphat king of Judah, I would neither look at you nor see you [King Joram].

15 But now bring me a minstrel. And while the minstrel played, the hand *and* power of the Lord came upon [Elisha].

16 And he said, Thus says the Lord: Make this [dry] brook bed full of trenches.

17 For thus says the Lord: You shall not see wind or rain, yet that ravine shall be filled with water, so you, your cattle, and your beasts [of burden] may drink.

18 This is but a light thing in the sight of the Lord. He will deliver the Moabites also into your hands.

19 You shall smite every fenced city and every choice city, and shall fell every good tree and stop all wells of water and mar every good piece of land with stones.

20 In the morning, when the sacrifice was offered, behold, there came water by the way of Edom, and the country was filled with water.

21 When all the Moabites heard that the kings had come up to fight against them, all who were able to put on armor, young and old, gathered and drew up at the border.

22 When they rose up early next

flow freely again

In Old Testament times, stopping up wells with stones was one of the weapons used to defeat one's enemies (see I Kings 3:19). Our enemy, the devil, still uses that weapon against us today.

I believe that you and I are born open and free with an ability to flow. But over time our enemy, Satan, comes along and starts throwing stones into the well of our inner beings—stones of abuse, hurt, rejection, abandonment, misunderstanding, bitterness, rejection, resentment, self-pity, revenge, depression, hopelessness, and on and on. By the time we become adults, our wells are so filled with stones that they have become stopped up and no longer flow freely within us. Every now and then we may feel a little gurgle down inside, but we never seem to experience the full release that is needed for the waters of our souls to flow freely once again.

It is interesting that when Jesus went to raise His friend Lazarus from the dead, He ordered, "Take away the stone" (John 11:39). In a similar sense, I believe the Holy Spirit wants to take away the stones that have been clogging our wells of living water.

When speaking of living water in John 7:37–39, Jesus did not say that from those who believe in Him there will flow rivers of living water *once in a while*. He said these rivers of living water would flow *continuously*. That living water is the Holy Spirit. What Jesus was talking about here is the outpouring of the Holy Spirit, which we (who have accepted Jesus as Lord and Savior) have received. Let the power of the Holy Spirit remove the stones that block the wellspring of your life, and let the water of life within you be released to flow again.

morning, and the sun shone upon the water, the Moabites saw the water across from them as red as blood.

23 And they said, This is blood; the kings have surely been fighting and have slain one another. Now then, Moab, to the spoil!

24 But when they came to the camp of Israel, the Israelites rose up and smote the Moabites, so that they fled before them. And they went forward, slaying the Moabites as they went.

25 They beat down the cities [walls], and on every good piece of land every man cast a stone, covering it [with stones]. And they stopped all the springs of water and felled all the good trees, until only the stones [of the walls of Moab's capital city] of Kir-hareseth were left standing, and the slingers surrounded and took it.

26 And when the king of Moab saw that the battle was against him, he took with him 700 swordsmen to break through to the king of Edom, but they could not.

27 Then he [Moab's king] took his eldest son, who was to reign in his stead, and offered him for a burnt offering on the wall [in full view of the horrified enemy kings]. And there was great indignation, wrath, *and* bitterness against Israel; and they [his allies Judah and Edom] withdrew from [Joram] and returned to their own land.

4 NOW THE wife of a son of the prophets cried to Elisha, Your servant my husband is dead, and you know that your servant feared the Lord. But the creditor has come to take my two sons to be his slaves.

2 Elisha said to her, What shall I do for you? Tell me, what have you [of sale value] in the house? She said, Your handmaid has nothing in the house except a jar of oil.

3 Then he said, Go around and borrow vessels from all your neighbors, empty vessels—and not a few.

4 And when you come in, shut the door upon you and your sons. Then pour out [the oil you have] into all those vessels, setting aside each one when it is full.

5 So she went from him and shut the door upon herself and her sons, who brought to her the vessels as she poured the oil.

6 When the vessels were all full, she said to her son, Bring me another vessel. And he said to her, There is not a one left. Then the oil stopped multiplying.

7 Then she came and told the man of God. He said, Go, sell the oil and pay your debt, and you and your sons live on the rest.

8 One day Elisha went on to Shunem, where a rich and influential woman lived, who insisted on his eating a meal. Afterward, whenever he passed by, he stopped there for a meal.

9 And she said to her husband, Behold now, I perceive that this is a holy man of God who passes by continually.

10 Let us make a small chamber on the [housetop] and put there for him a bed, a table, a chair, and a lamp. Then whenever he comes to us, he can go [up the outside stairs and rest] here.

11 One day he came and turned into the chamber and lay there.

12 And he said to Gehazi his servant, Call this Shunammite. When he had called her, she stood before him.

13 And he said to Gehazi, Say now to her, You have been most painstakingly *and* reverently concerned for us; what is to be done for you? Would you like to be spoken for to the king or to the commander of the army? She answered, I dwell among my own people [they are sufficient].

14 Later Elisha said, What then is to be done for her? Gehazi answered, She has no child and her husband is old.

the first step to fullness

The key to value and worth is knowing who we are in Jesus. When we know that, there is nothing for us to do but stand in awe of the Lord and give Him thanks and praise for what He has done for us in Christ. Like the poor widow in II Kings 4:1–7, our first step to fullness is to recognize we are empty.

All of us are empty vessels. None of us has anything in us of any value except the power of God that is resident there to flow out of us. What do we have to offer to God? Nothing. God is not needy. He does not need you or me; He can do His own work without us. We are not indispensable. I do not make this observation to tear us down or make us feel bad about ourselves, but to remind us all that being used by God is a great privilege and an honor, not a right.

We do have value, but only the value the Lord assigns to us because of the blood of His Son, Jesus Christ. We have nothing in and of ourselves. In Christ, we exist and have everything. But in our flesh, there is nothing of any value or worth. What is born of the flesh is flesh, and it profits us nothing.

When I first started ministering, I wanted to help people. The Lord spoke to me then and said: "When you are empty of yourself so that all you have left within you is the ability to depend on the Holy Spirit, when you have learned that everything you are and have comes from Him, *then* I'll send you around to those you know to fill their empty vessels with the life I have poured into your empty vessel."

Arriving at the place of being empty of ourselves is not an easy task, and it does not happen quickly. I spent many years wondering if I would ever reach a place of manifesting humility instead of pride—of being dependent on God instead of independent—of trusting in the strength of His arm instead of my arm. If you feel the same way, let me encourage you that *as long as you don't give up, you are making progress.*

It may seem as though reaching the place you desire to go is taking forever, but "He Who began a good work in you will continue until the day of Jesus Christ [right up to the time of His return], developing [that good work] and perfecting and bringing it to full completion in you" (Philippians 1:6).

If we press on and are sincere about spiritual maturity, we will eventually be like the woman in II Kings 4:1–7—empty of ourselves and ready to be used by God to fulfill His great purposes for our lives.

15 He said, Call her. [Gehazi] called her, and she stood in the doorway.
16 Elisha said, At this season when the time comes round, you shall embrace a son. She said, No, my lord, you man of God, do not lie to your handmaid.
17 But the woman conceived and bore a son at that season the following year, as Elisha had said to her.

owe no man anything but love

The Bible teaches us that we are to owe no man anything except to love him (see Romans 13:8). In II Kings 4:7, we see that we are to pay our debts. When we allow debt to overwhelm us, we can quickly and easily become discouraged and depressed.

Have you realized that one of the main reasons people get into debt is that their emotions are out of control? When a desire for personal pleasure, a sense of prestige, or the ability to impress others causes us to live beyond our means, we end up in debt.

When Dave and I were young marrieds, we got into trouble with debt. We did it by running up our credit cards to their maximum limit, buying things we wanted for ourselves and our children. We made the minimum payments on our balances each month, but the interest was so high we never seemed to make any progress toward paying off what we owed. In fact, we just kept getting deeper and deeper into debt.

What caused that? Emotions and a lack of wisdom.

If you and I are ever going to get anywhere in the kingdom of God, we must learn to live by wisdom and not by our carnal desire, which is human emotion (Proverbs 3:13–15).

Wisdom makes the decision today that it will be comfortable with tomorrow. Emotion does what feels good today and takes no thought of tomorrow. When tomorrow arrives, the wise enjoy it in peace and security, but the foolish end up discouraged and depressed. Why? Because the wise have prepared for tomorrow and are able to enjoy the fruits of their labor, while the foolish, who have put pleasure first, now must pay for yesterday.

It is much better to work now and play later, than to play now and worry later!

It is so discouraging to go to the mailbox every day and find nothing there but bills, bills, and more bills. Eventually that discouragement leads to depression because of the pressure of not being able to see a way out. When we charge things we cannot pay for, we are spending tomorrow's prosperity today. Then when tomorrow comes, all we have is debt.

To live a disciplined life, which is what it takes to produce good fruit in our lives, we have to be willing to invest today so that we can reap tomorrow. To relieve the discouragement and depression that come from being in debt, we must get out of debt by becoming self-disciplined enough to think not of today's sacrifices, but of tomorrow's rewards.

putting the Word to work

Would you like to bless your pastor or some other Christian leader in your life? Offering hospitality in various forms is a wonderful way to demonstrate both your appreciation and God's love. As the Shunammite woman discovered (see II Kings 4:8–17), you can be sure that God honors those who provide hospitality!

18 When the child had grown, he went out one day to his father with the reapers.

19 But he said to his father, My head, my head! The man said to his servant, Carry him to his mother.

20 And when he was brought to his mother, he sat on her knees till noon, and then died.

21 And she went up and laid him on the bed of the man of God, and shut the door upon him and went out.

22 And she called to her husband and said, Send me one of the servants and one of the donkeys, that I may go quickly to the man of God and come back again.

23 And he said, Why go to him today? It is neither the New Moon nor the Sabbath. And she said, It will be all right.

24 Then she saddled the donkey and said to her servant, Ride fast; do not slacken your pace for me unless I tell you.

25 So she set out and came to the man of God at Mount Carmel. When the man of God saw her afar off, he said to Gehazi his servant, Behold, yonder is that Shunammite.

26 Run to meet her and say, Is it well with you? Well with your husband? Well with the child? And she answered, It is well.

27 When she came to the mountain to the man of God, she clung to his feet. Gehazi came to thrust her away, but the man of God said, Let her alone, for her soul is bitter *and* vexed within her, and the Lord has hid it from me and has not told me.

28 Then she said, Did I desire a son of my lord? Did I not say, Do not deceive me?

29 Then he said to Gehazi, Gird up your loins and take my staff in your hand and go lay my staff on the face of the child. If you meet any man, do not salute him. If he salutes you, do not answer him.

30 The mother of the child said, As the Lord lives and as my soul lives, I will not leave you. And he arose and followed her.

31 Gehazi passed on before them and laid the staff on the child's face, but the boy neither spoke nor heard. So he went back to meet Elisha and said to him, The child has not awakened.

32 When Elisha arrived in the house, the child was dead and laid upon his bed.

33 So he went in, shut the door on the two of them, and prayed to the Lord.

34 He went up and lay on the child, put his mouth on his mouth, his eyes on his eyes, and his hands on his hands. And as he stretched himself on him *and* embraced him, the child's flesh became warm.

35 Then he returned and walked in the house to and fro and went up again and stretched himself upon him. And the child sneezed seven times, and then opened his eyes.

36 Then [Elisha] called Gehazi and said, Call this Shunammite. So he called her. And when she came, he said, Take up your son.

37 She came and fell at his feet, bowing herself to the ground. Then she took up her son and went out.

38 Elisha came back to Gilgal during a famine in the land. The sons of the prophets were sitting before him, and he said to his servant, Set on the big pot and cook pottage for the sons of the prophets.

39 Then one went into the field to gather herbs and gathered from a wild vine his lap full of wild gourds, and returned and cut them up into the pot of pottage, for they were unknown to them.

40 So they poured it out for the men to eat. But as they ate of the pottage, they cried out, O man of God, there is death in the pot! And they could not eat it.

41 But he said, Bring meal [as a symbol of God's healing power]. And he cast it into the pot and said, Pour it out for the people that they may eat. Then there was no harm in the pot.

42 [At another time] a man from Baal-shalisha came and brought the man of God bread of the firstfruits, twenty loaves of barley, and fresh ears of grain [in the husk] in his sack. And Elisha said, Give to the men that they may eat.

43 His servant said, How am I to set [only] this before a hundred [hungry] men? He said, Give to the men that they may eat. For thus says the Lord: They shall be fed and have some left.

44 So he set it before them, and they ate and left some, as the Lord had said.

putting the Word to work

Do you ever feel that you do not have much to offer in ministry? The man from Baal-shalisha had only a little bit of food to offer one hundred men, but he gave it willingly (see II Kings 4:42–44). Not only did the men eat, but there was food left over! As you freely offer what you have to give in service to God, ask Him to multiply what you have given and make it a blessing beyond what you can imagine.

5 NAAMAN, COMMANDER of the army of the king of Syria, was a great man with his master, accepted [and acceptable], because by him the Lord had given victory to Syria. He was also a mighty man of valor, but he was a leper.

2 The Syrians had gone out in bands and had brought away captive out of the land of Israel a little maid, and she waited on Naaman's wife.

3 She said to her mistress, Would that my lord were with the prophet who is in Samaria! For he would heal him of his leprosy.

4 [Naaman] went in and told his king, Thus and thus said the maid from Israel.

5 And the king of Syria said, Go now, and I will send a letter to the king of Israel. And he departed and took with him ten talents of silver, 6,000 shekels of gold, and ten changes of raiment.

6 And he brought the letter to the king of Israel. It said, When this letter comes to you, I will with it have sent to you my servant Naaman, that you may cure him of leprosy.

7 When the king of Israel read the letter, he rent his clothes and said, Am I God, to kill and to make alive, that this man sends to me to heal a man of his leprosy? Just consider and see how he is seeking a quarrel with me.

8 When Elisha the man of God heard that the king of Israel had rent his clothes, he sent to the king, asking, Why have you rent your clothes? Let Naaman come now to me and he shall know that there is a prophet in Israel.

9 So Naaman came with his horses and chariots and stopped at Elisha's door.

10 Elisha sent a messenger to him, saying, Go and wash in the Jordan seven times, and your flesh shall be restored and you shall be clean.

putting the Word to work

Second Kings 5:9–14 tells the story of Naaman's healing. This man's pride almost kept him from receiving the healing God wanted to give him. Do you struggle with pride, perhaps thinking you should be treated a certain way because of your station in life? Ask God to identify areas of pride and to teach you humility. Do not let pride keep you from experiencing all God wants to do in your life.

11 But Naaman was angry and went away and said, Behold, I thought he would surely come out to me and stand and call on the name of the Lord his God, and wave his hand over the place and heal the leper.

12 Are not Abana and Pharpar, the rivers of Damascus, better than all the waters of Israel? May I not wash in them and be clean? So he turned and went away in a rage.

13 And his servants came near and said to him, My father, if the prophet had bid you to do some great thing, would you not have done it? How much rather, then, when he says to you, Wash and be clean?

14 Then he went down and dipped himself seven times in the Jordan, as the man of God had said, and his flesh was restored like that of a little child, and he was clean.

15 Then Naaman returned to the man of God, he and all his company, and stood before him. He said, Behold, now I know that there is no God in all the earth but in Israel. So now accept a gift from your servant.

16 Elisha said, As the Lord lives, before Whom I stand, I will accept none. He urged him to take it, but Elisha refused.

17 Naaman said, Then, I pray you, let there be given to me, your servant, two mules' burden of earth. For your servant will henceforth offer neither burnt offering nor sacrifice to other gods, but only to the Lord.

18 In this thing may the Lord pardon your servant: when my master [the king] goes into the house of [his god] Rimmon to worship there, and he leans on my hand and I bow myself in the house of Rimmon, when I bow down myself in the house of Rimmon, may the Lord pardon your servant in this thing.

19 Elisha said to him, Go in peace. So Naaman departed from him a little way.

20 But Gehazi, the servant of Elisha the man of God, said, Behold, my master spared this Naaman the Syrian, in not receiving from his hands what he brought. But as the Lord lives, I will run after him and get something from him.

21 So Gehazi followed after Naaman. When Naaman saw one running after him, he lighted down from the chariot to meet him and said, Is all well?

22 And he said, All is well. My master has sent me to say, There have just come to me from the hill country of Ephraim two young men of the sons of the prophets. I pray you, give them a talent of silver and two changes of garments.

23 And Naaman said, Be pleased to take two talents. And he urged him, and bound two talents of silver in two bags with two changes of garments and laid them upon two of his servants, and they bore them before Gehazi.

24 When he came to the hill, he took them from their hands and put them in the house; and he sent the men away, and they left.

25 He went in and stood before his master. Elisha said, Where have you been, Gehazi? He said, Your servant went nowhere.

26 Elisha said to him, Did not my spirit go with you when the man

putting the Word to work

Are you ever tempted to seek material gain even at the cost of your integrity? Elisha's servant Gehazi learned the hard way that greed is evil in the eyes of God (see II Kings 5:20–27). Ask God to teach you to be content and trust His provision for you.

turned from his chariot to meet you? Was it a time to accept money, garments, olive orchards, vineyards, sheep, oxen, menservants, and maidservants?

27 Therefore the leprosy of Naaman shall cleave to you and to your offspring forever. And Gehazi went from his presence a leper as white as snow.

6 THE SONS of the prophets said to Elisha, Look now, the place where we live before you is too small for us.

2 Let us go to the Jordan, and each man get there a [house] beam; and let us make us a place there where we may dwell. And he answered, Go.

3 One said, Be pleased to go with your servants. He answered, I will go.

4 So he went with them. And when they came to the Jordan, they cut down trees.

5 But as one was felling his beam, the axhead fell into the water; and he cried, Alas, my master, for it was borrowed!

6 The man of God said, Where did it fall? When shown the place, Elisha cut off a stick and threw it in there, and the iron floated.

7 He said, Pick it up. And he put out his hand and took it.

8 When the king of Syria was warring against Israel, after counseling with his servants, he said, In such and such a place shall be my camp.

9 Then the man of God sent to the king of Israel, saying, Beware that you pass not such a place, for the Syrians are coming down there.

10 Then the king of Israel sent to the place of which [Elisha] told *and* warned him; and thus he protected *and* saved himself there repeatedly.

11 Therefore the mind of the king of Syria was greatly troubled by this thing. He called his servants and said, Will you show me who of us is for the king of Israel?

12 One of his servants said, None, my lord O king; but Elisha, the prophet who is in Israel, tells the king of Israel the words that you speak in your bedchamber.

13 He said, Go and see where he is, that I may send and seize him. And it was told him, He is in Dothan.

14 So [the Syrian king] sent there horses, chariots, and a great army. They came by night and surrounded the city.

15 When the servant of the man of God rose early and went out, behold, an army with horses and chariots was around the city. Elisha's servant said to him, Alas, my master! What shall we do?

16 [Elisha] answered, Fear not; for those with us are more than those with them.

17 Then Elisha prayed, Lord, I pray You, open his eyes that he may see.

speak the Word

Thank You, God, that I do not need to fear because there are more with me than with my enemies.
ADAPTED FROM II KINGS **6:16**

And the Lord opened the young man's eyes, and he saw, and behold, the mountain was full of horses and chariots of fire round about Elisha.

18 And when the Syrians came down to him, Elisha prayed to the Lord, Smite this people with blindness, I pray You. And God smote them with blindness, as Elisha asked.

19 Elisha said to the Syrians, This is not the way or the city. Follow me, and I will bring you to the man whom you seek. And he led them to Samaria.

20 And when they had come into Samaria, Elisha said, Lord, open the eyes of these men that they may see. And the Lord opened their eyes, and they saw. Behold, they were in the midst of Samaria!

21 When the king of Israel saw them, he said to Elisha, My father, shall I slay them? Shall I slay them?

22 [Elisha] answered, You shall not slay them. Would you slay those you have taken captive with your sword and bow? Set bread and water before them, that they may eat and drink and return to their master.

23 So [the king] prepared great provision for them, and when they had eaten and drunk, he sent them away, and they went to their master. And the bands of Syria came no more into the land of Israel.

24 Afterward, Ben-hadad king of Syria gathered his whole army and went up and besieged Samaria,

25 And a great famine came to Samaria. They besieged it until a donkey's head was sold for eighty shekels of silver, and a fourth of a kab of dove's dung [a wild vegetable] for five shekels of silver.

26 As the king of Israel was passing by upon the wall, a woman cried to him, Help, my lord, O king!

27 He said, [For] if he does not help you [No, let the Lord help you!], from where can I get you help? Out of the threshing floor, or out of the winepress?

28 And the king said to her, What ails you? She answered, This woman said to me, Give me your son so we may eat him today, and we will eat my son tomorrow.

29 So we boiled my son and ate him. The next day I said to her, Give your son so we may eat him, but she had hidden her son.

30 When the king heard the woman's words, he rent his clothes. As he went on upon the wall, the people looked, and behold, he wore sackcloth inside on his flesh.

31 Then he said, May God do so to me, and more also, if the head of Elisha son of Shaphat shall stand on him this day!

32 Now Elisha sat in his house, and the elders sat with him. And the king sent a man from before him [to behead Elisha]. But before the messenger arrived, Elisha said to the elders, See how this son of [Jezebel] a murderer is sending to remove my head? Look, when the messenger comes, shut the door and hold it fast against him. Is not the sound of his master's feet [just] behind him?

33 And while Elisha was talking with them, behold, [the messenger] came to him [and then the king came also]. And [the relenting king] said, This evil is from the Lord! Why should I any longer wait [expecting Him to withdraw His punishment? What, Elisha, can be done now]?

7 THEN ELISHA said, Hear the word of the Lord. Thus says the Lord: Tomorrow about this time a measure of fine flour will sell for a shekel and two measures of barley for a shekel in the gate of Samaria!

2 Then the captain on whose hand the king leaned answered the man of God and said, If the Lord should make windows in heaven, could this thing be? But Elisha said, You shall see it with your own eyes, but you shall not eat of it.

3 Now four men who were lepers were at the entrance of the city's gate; and they said to one another, Why do we sit here until we die?

4 If we say, We will enter the city— then the famine is in the city, and we shall die there; and if we sit still here, we die also. So now come, let us go over to the army of the Syrians. If they spare us alive, we shall live; and if they kill us, we shall but die.

5 So they arose in the twilight and went to the Syrian camp. But when they came to the edge of the camp, no man was there.

6 For the Lord had made the Syrian army hear a noise of chariots and horses, the noise of a great army. They had said to one another, The king of Israel has hired the Hittite and Egyptian kings to come upon us.

7 So the Syrians arose and fled in the twilight and left their tents, horses, donkeys, even the camp as it was, and fled for their lives.

8 And when these lepers came to the edge of the camp, they went into one tent and ate and drank, and carried away silver, gold, and clothing, and went and hid them [in the darkness]. Then they entered another tent and carried from there also and went and hid it.

9 Then they said one to another, We are not doing right. This is a day of [glad] good news and we are silent and do not speak up! If we wait until daylight, some punishment will come upon us [for not reporting at once]. So now come, let us go and tell the king's household.

10 So they came and called to the gatekeepers of the city. They told them, We came to the camp of the Syrians, and behold, there was neither sight nor sound of man there—

only the horses and donkeys tied, and the tents as they were.

11 Then the gatekeepers called out, and it was told to the king's household within.

12 And the king rose in the night and said to his servants, I will tell you what the Syrians have done to us. They know that we are hungry; therefore they have gone out of the camp to hide themselves in the open country, thinking, When they come out of the city, we shall take them alive and get into the city.

13 One of his servants said, Let some men take five of the remaining horses; [if they are caught and killed] they will be no worse off than all the multitude of Israel left in the city to be consumed. Let us send and see.

14 So they took two chariot horses, and the king sent them after the Syrian army, saying, Go and see.

15 They went after them to the Jordan. All the way was strewn with clothing and equipment which the Syrians had cast away in their flight. And the messengers returned and told the king.

16 Then the people went out and plundered the tents of the Syrians. So a measure of fine flour was sold for a shekel, and two measures of barley for a shekel, as the Lord had spoken [through Elisha]. [II Kings 7:1.]

17 The king had appointed the captain on whose hand he leaned to have charge of the gate, and the [starving] people trampled him in the gate [as they struggled to get through for food], and he died, as the man of God had foretold when the king came down to him.

18 When the man of God had told the king, Two measures of barley shall sell for a shekel and a measure of fine flour for a shekel tomorrow about this time in the gate of Samaria,

19 The captain had told the man of God, If the Lord should make windows

in heaven, could such a thing be? And he said, You shall see it with your own eyes, but you shall not eat of it. [II Kings 7:2.]

20 And so it was fulfilled to him, for the people trampled on him in the gate, and he died.

8 NOW ELISHA had said to the woman whose son he had restored to life, Arise and go with your household and sojourn wherever you can, for the Lord has called for a famine, and moreover, it will come upon the land for seven years.

2 So the woman arose and did as the man of God had said. She went with her household and sojourned in the land of the Philistines seven years.

3 At the end of the seven years the woman returned from the land of the Philistines, and she went to appeal to the king for her house and land.

4 The king talked with Gehazi, the servant of the man of God, saying, Tell me all the great things Elisha has done.

5 And as Gehazi was telling the king how [Elisha] had restored the dead to life, behold, the woman whose son he had restored to life appealed to the king for her house and land. And Gehazi said, My lord O king, this is the woman, and this is her son whom Elisha brought back to life.

6 When the king asked the woman, she told him. So the king appointed to her a certain officer, saying, Restore all that was hers, and all the fruits of the field since the day that she left the land even until now.

7 Elisha came to Damascus, and Ben-hadad king of Syria was sick; and he was told, The man of God has come here.

8 And the king said to Hazael, Take a present in your hand and go meet the man of God, and inquire of the Lord by him, saying, Shall I recover from this disease?

9 So Hazael went to meet Elisha and took a present with him of every good thing of Damascus, forty camel loads, and came and stood before him and said, Your son Ben-hadad king of Syria has sent me to you, asking, Shall I recover from this disease?

10 And Elisha said, Go, say to him, You shall certainly recover; but the Lord has shown me that he shall certainly die.

11 Elisha stared steadily at him until Hazael was embarrassed. And the man of God wept.

12 And Hazael said, Why do you weep, my lord? He answered, Because I know the evil that you will do to the Israelites. You will burn their strongholds, slay their young men with the sword, dash their infants in pieces, and rip up their pregnant women.

13 And Hazael said, What is your servant, only a dog, that he should do this monstrous thing? And Elisha answered, The Lord has shown me that you will be king over Syria.

14 Then [Hazael] departed from Elisha and came to his master, who said to him, What did Elisha say to you? And he answered, He told me you would surely recover.

15 But the next day Hazael took the bedspread and dipped it in water and spread it on [the Syrian king's] face, so that he died. And Hazael reigned in his stead.

16 In the fifth year of Joram son of Ahab king of Israel, Jehoshaphat being then king of Judah, Jehoram son of Jehoshaphat king of Judah began to reign.

17 He was thirty-two years old when he began to reign, and he reigned eight years in Jerusalem.

18 He walked in the ways of the kings of Israel, as did the house of Ahab, for [Athaliah] the daughter of

Ahab was his wife. He did evil in the sight of the Lord.

19 Yet, for David His servant's sake, the Lord would not destroy Judah, for He promised to give him and his sons a lamp forever.

20 In his days, Edom revolted from the rule of Judah and set up a king over themselves.

21 So Jehoram [of Judah] went over to Zair with all his chariots. He and his chariot commanders rose up by night and slew the Edomites who had surrounded them; and [escaping] his army fled home.

22 So Edom revolted from the rule of Judah to this day. Then Libnah revolted at the same time.

23 The rest of the acts of Jehoram, and all that he did, are they not written in the Book of the Chronicles of the Kings of Judah?

24 Jehoram slept with his fathers and was buried with [them] in the City of David. Ahaziah his son reigned in his stead.

25 In the twelfth year of Joram son of Ahab king of Israel, Ahaziah son of Jehoram king of Judah began to reign.

26 Ahaziah was twenty-two years old when he began to reign, and he reigned one year in Jerusalem. His mother's name was Athaliah, the granddaughter of Omri king of Israel.

27 He walked in the ways of the house of Ahab and did evil in the sight of the Lord, as did the house of Ahab, for his father was son-in-law of Ahab.

28 Ahaziah went with Joram son of Ahab to war against Hazael king of Syria in Ramoth-gilead; and the Syrians wounded Joram.

29 King Joram returned to Jezreel to be healed of the wounds which the Syrians had given him at Ramah when he fought against Hazael king of Syria. And Ahaziah son of Jehoram king of Judah went down to see Joram son of Ahab in Jezreel, because he was sick.

9 AND ELISHA the prophet called one of the sons of the prophets and said to him, Gird up your loins, take this flask of oil in your hand, and go to Ramoth-gilead.

2 When you arrive, look there for Jehu son of Jehoshaphat son of Nimshi; and go in and have him arise from among his brethren and lead him to an inner chamber.

3 Then take the cruse of oil and pour it on his head and say, Thus says the Lord: I have anointed you king over Israel. Then open the door and flee; do not tarry.

4 So the young man, the young prophet, went to Ramoth-gilead.

5 And when he came, the captains of the army were sitting outside; and he said, I have a message for you, O captain. Jehu said, To which of us? And he said, To you, O captain.

6 And Jehu arose, and they went into the house. And the prophet poured the oil on Jehu's head and said to him, Thus says the Lord, the God of Israel: I have anointed you king over the people of the Lord, even over Israel.

7 You shall strike down the house of Ahab your master, that I may avenge the blood of My servants the prophets and of all the servants of the Lord [who have died] at the hands of Jezebel.

8 For the whole house of Ahab shall perish, and I will cut off from Ahab every male, bond or free, in Israel.

9 I will make the house of Ahab like the house of Jeroboam son of Nebat and like the house of Baasha son of Ahijah. [I Kings 21:22.]

10 And the dogs shall eat Jezebel in the portion of Jezreel, and none shall bury her. And he opened the door and fled. [Fulfilled in II Kings 9:33-37.]

11 When Jehu came out to the servants of his master, one said to him, Is all well? Why did this mad fellow come to you? And he said to them, You know that class of man and what he would say.

12 And they said, That is false; tell us now. And he said, Thus and thus he spoke to me, saying, Thus says the Lord: I have anointed you king over Israel.

13 Then they hastily took every man his garment and put it [for a cushion] under Jehu on the top of the [outside] stairs, and blew with trumpets, saying, Jehu is king!

14 So Jehu son of Jehoshaphat, the son of Nimshi, conspired against Joram [to dethrone and slay him]. Now Joram was holding Ramoth-gilead, he and all Israel, against Hazael king of Syria,

15 But King Joram had returned to be healed in Jezreel of the wounds which the Syrians had given him when he fought with Hazael king of Syria. And Jehu said, If this is your mind, let no one make his escape from the city [Ramoth-gilead] to go and tell it in Jezreel [the capital].

16 So Jehu rode in a chariot and went to Jezreel, for Joram lay there. And Ahaziah king of Judah had come down to see Joram.

17 A watchman on the tower in Jezreel spied the company of Jehu as he came, and said, I see a company. And Joram said, Send a horseman to meet them and have him ask, Do you come in peace?

18 So one on horseback went to meet him and said, Thus says the king: Is it peace? And Jehu said, What have you to do with peace? Rein in behind me. And the watchman reported, The messenger came to them, but he does not return.

19 Then Joram sent out a second man on horseback, who came to them and said, Thus says the king: Is it peace? Jehu replied, What have you to do with peace? Ride behind me.

20 And the watchman reported, He came to them, but does not return; also the driving is like the driving of Jehu son of Nimshi, for he drives furiously.

21 Joram said, Make ready. When his chariot was made ready, Joram king of Israel and Ahaziah king of Judah went out, each in his chariot. Thus they went out to meet Jehu and met him in the field of Naboth the Jezreelite.

22 When Joram saw Jehu, he said, Is it peace, Jehu? And he answered, How can peace exist as long as the fornications of your mother Jezebel and her witchcrafts are so many?

23 Then Joram reined about and fled, and he said to Ahaziah, Treachery, Ahaziah!

24 But Jehu drew his bow with his full strength and shot Joram between his shoulders; and the arrow went out through his heart, and he sank down in his chariot.

25 Then said Jehu to Bidkar his captain, Take [Joram] up and cast him in the plot of Naboth the Jezreelite's field; for remember how, when I and you rode together after Ahab his father, the Lord uttered this prophecy against him:

26 As surely as I saw yesterday the blood of Naboth and the blood of his sons, says the Lord, I will repay you on this plot of ground, says the Lord. Now therefore, take and cast Joram into the plot of ground [of Naboth], as the word of the Lord said. [I Kings 21:15-29.]

27 When Ahaziah king of Judah saw this, he fled by the way of the garden house. Jehu followed him and said, Smite him also in the chariot. And they did so at the ascent to Gur, which is by Ibleam. And [Ahaziah] fled to Megiddo and died there.

28 His servants took him in a chariot to Jerusalem, and buried him in his sepulcher with his fathers in the City of David.

29 In the eleventh year of Joram son of Ahab, Ahaziah's reign over Judah began.

30 Now when Jehu came to Jezreel, Jezebel heard of it, and she painted her eyes and beautified her head and looked out of [an upper] window.

31 And as Jehu entered in at the gate, she said, [Have you come in] peace, you Zimri, who slew his master? [I Kings 16:9, 10.]

32 Jehu lifted up his face to the window and said, Who is on my side? Who? And two or three eunuchs looked out at him.

33 And he said, Throw her down! So they threw her down, and some of her blood splattered on the wall and on the horses, and he drove over her.

34 When he came in, he ate and drank, and said, See now to this cursed woman and bury her, for she is a king's daughter.

35 They went to bury her, but they found nothing left of her except the skull, feet, and palms of her hands.

36 They came again and told Jehu. He said, This is the word of the Lord which He spoke by His servant Elijah the Tishbite, In the portion of Jezreel shall dogs eat the flesh of Jezebel. [I Kings 21:23.]

37 The corpse of Jezebel shall be like dung upon the face of the field in the portion of Jezreel, so that they shall not say, This is Jezebel.

10 AHAB HAD seventy [grandsons] in Samaria. So Jehu wrote letters and sent them from Jezreel to the rulers of Samaria, to the elders, and to those who brought up Ahab's [grandsons], saying,

2 Now as soon as this letter comes to you, seeing your master [Joram's] sons are with you and also chariots and horses, a fortified city, and weapons,

3 Select the best and most fit of your master's sons and set him on his father's throne; and fight for your master's house.

4 But they were exceedingly afraid and reasoned, The two kings could

not stand before [Jehu]; how then can we stand?

5 And he who was over the household, he who was over the city, the elders also, and the guardians *and* tutors sent to Jehu, saying, We are your servants and will do all that you bid us; [but] we will not make any man king; do what is good in your eyes.

6 Then [Jehu] wrote a second letter to them, saying, If you are with me and will obey me, take the heads of your master [Joram's] sons and come to me at Jezreel by tomorrow this time. Now the [dead] king's sons, seventy persons, were with the great men of the city, who were bringing them up.

7 When the letter came to these men, they took the king's sons and slew them, seventy persons, and put their heads in baskets and sent them to Jehu at Jezreel.

8 When a messenger came and told him, They have brought the heads of the king's sons, he said, Lay them in two heaps at the entrance of the city gate until morning.

9 The next morning he went out and stood and said to all the people, You are just *and* innocent. Behold, I conspired against my master and slew him, but who smote all these?

10 Know now that nothing which the Lord spoke concerning the house of Ahab shall be unfulfilled *or* ineffective; for the Lord has done what He said through His servant Elijah.

11 So Jehu slew all that remained of the house of Ahab in Jezreel, and all his great men, his familiar friends, and his priests, until he left him none remaining.

12 And he arose and went to Samaria. And as he was at the shearing house of the shepherds on the way,

13 Jehu met the kinsmen of Ahaziah king of Judah and said, Who are you? They answered, We are the kinsmen of Ahaziah, and we came down to visit the royal princes and the sons of [Jezebel] the queen mother.

14 He said, Take them alive. And they did so and slew them at the cistern of the shearing house, forty-two men; he left none of them.

15 When Jehu left there, he met Jehonadab son of Rechab coming to meet him. He saluted him and said to him, Is your heart right, as my heart is with yours? Jehonadab answered, It is. [Jehu said] If it is, give me your hand. He gave him his hand, and Jehu took him up into the chariot.

16 And he said, Come with me and see my zeal for the Lord. So they made [the Rechabite] ride in Jehu's chariot.

17 When Jehu came to Samaria, he slew all who remained of Ahab's family in Samaria, till he had destroyed them all, according to what the Lord said to Elijah.

18 Jehu assembled all the people and said to them, Ahab served Baal a little; but Jehu will serve him much.

19 So call to me all the prophets of Baal, all his worshipers, and all his priests. Let none be missing, for I have a great sacrifice to make to Baal; whoever is missing shall not live. But Jehu did it with trickery, intending to destroy the Baal worshipers.

20 Jehu said, Sanctify a solemn assembly for Baal. And they proclaimed it.

21 Jehu sent through all Israel, and all the worshipers of Baal came; not a man failed to come. They went to the house or temple of Baal, filling it from one end to the other.

22 And he said to the man over the vestry, Bring vestments for all the worshipers of Baal. And he brought them vestments.

23 Then Jehu with Jehonadab son of Rechab went into the house of Baal and said to the worshipers of Baal, Search and see that there are here with you none of the servants of the Lord—but Baal worshipers only.

24 And when they went in to offer sacrifices and burnt offerings, Jehu appointed eighty men outside and said, If any of the men whom I have brought into your hands escape, he who lets him go shall forfeit his own life for his life.

25 As soon as he had finished offering the burnt offering, Jehu said to the guards and to the officers, Go in and slay them; let none escape. And they smote them with the sword; and the guards or runners [before the king] and the officers threw their bodies out and went into the inner dwelling of the house of Baal.

26 They brought out the pillars or obelisks of the house of Baal and burned them.

27 They broke down the pillars of Baal and the house of Baal, and made it [forever unclean] a privy to this day.

28 Thus Jehu rooted Baal out of Israel.

29 But Jehu did not give up the sins of Jeroboam son of Nebat, by which he made Israel to sin, that is, the golden calves at Bethel and Dan. [I Kings 12:28ff.]

30 And the Lord said to Jehu, Because you have executed well what is right in My eyes and have done to the house of Ahab as I willed, your sons to the fourth generation shall sit on Israel's throne. [Fulfilled in II Kings 15:12.]

31 But Jehu paid no attention to walking in the law of the Lord, the

speak the Word

God of Israel, with all his heart. He did not quit the sins with which Jeroboam made Israel to sin.

32 [So] in those days the Lord began to cut off parts of Israel. Hazael [of Syria] defeated them in all the [across the Jordan] territory of Israel

33 From the Jordan east, all the land of Gilead, the Gadites, Reubenites, and Manassites, from Aroer which is by the Valley of the Arnon, even Gilead and Bashan.

34 The rest of the acts of Jehu, and all that he did, and all his might, are they not written in the Book of the Chronicles of the Kings of Israel?

35 Jehu slept with his fathers. They buried him in Samaria. Jehoahaz his son reigned in his stead.

36 The time that Jehu reigned over Israel in Samaria was twenty-eight years.

11 WHEN ATHALIAH the mother of [King] Ahaziah [of Judah] saw that her son was dead, she arose and destroyed all the royal descendants.

2 But Jehosheba, the daughter of King Jehoram, [half] sister of Ahaziah, stole Joash son of Ahaziah from among the king's sons, who were to be slain, even him and his nurse, and hid them from Athaliah in an inner storeroom for beds; so he was not slain.

3 Joash was with his nurse hidden in the house of the Lord for six years. And Athaliah reigned over the land.

4 In the seventh year Jehoiada [the priest, Jehosheba's husband] sent for the captains over hundreds of the Carites and of the guards *or* runners and brought them to him to the house of the Lord and made a covenant with them and took an oath from them in the house of the Lord and showed them the king's [hidden] son.

5 And he commanded them, saying, This is the thing you shall do: a third of you who come in on the Sabbath shall keep watch of the king's house,

6 A third shall be at the gate Sur, and a third at the gate behind the guard. So you shall keep watch of the palace [from three places] and be a barrier.

7 And two divisions of all you who should go off duty on the Sabbath shall keep the watch of the house of the Lord to [protect] the king.

8 You shall surround the [little] king, every man with his weapons in his hand. And let anyone who breaks through the ranks be put to death. You be with the king when he goes out and when he comes in.

9 The captains over the hundreds did all that Jehoiada the priest commanded; and they took every man his men who were to come on duty on the Sabbath with those who should go off duty on the Sabbath, and came to Jehoiada the priest.

10 To the captains over hundreds the priest gave the spears and shields that had been King David's, which were in the house of the Lord.

11 And the guards stood, every man with his weapons in his hand, from the right corner to the left corner of the temple area, along by the altar [in the court] and the temple proper.

12 And Jehoiada brought out the king's son and put the crown on him and gave him the Testimony [the Mosaic Law]; and they proclaimed him king and anointed him, and they clapped their hands and said, Long live the king!

13 When Athaliah heard the noise of the guards and the people, she went into the house of the Lord to the people.

14 When she looked, there stood the king [on the platform] by the pillar, as was customary [on such occasions], and the captains and the trumpeters beside the king, with all the people of the land rejoicing and blowing trumpets. And Athaliah rent her clothes and cried, Treason! Treason!

15 Then Jehoiada the priest commanded the captains of hundreds set over the army and said to them, Take her forth outside the ranks, and him who follows her kill with the sword. For the priest had said, Let her not be slain in the house of the Lord.

16 They seized her, and she went through the horses' entrance to the king's house, and there she was slain.

17 And Jehoiada made a covenant between the Lord, the king, and the people that they would be the Lord's people—and also between the king and the people.

18 Then all the people of the land went to the house of Baal and destroyed it. His altar and his images they broke completely in pieces, and Mattan the priest of Baal they slew before the altars. And [Jehoiada] the priest appointed watchmen to guard the house of the Lord.

19 Then he took the rulers over hundreds, the captains, the guard, and all the people of the land, and they brought the king down from the house of the Lord and came by way of the guards' gate to the king's house. And [little] Joash was seated on the throne of the kings.

20 So all the people of the land rejoiced, and the city was quiet after Athaliah had been slain with the sword beside the king's house.

21 Joash was seven years old when he began to reign.

12 IN THE seventh year of Jehu, ᵈJoash began to reign, and he reigned forty years in Jerusalem. His mother was Zibiah of Beersheba.

2 Joash did right in the sight of the Lord all his days in which Jehoiada the priest instructed him.

3 Yet the high places were not taken away; the people still sacrificed and burned incense in the high places.

4 And Joash said to the priests, All the current money brought into the house of the Lord to provide the dedicated things, also the money [which the priests by command have] assessed on all those bound by vows, also all the money that it comes into any man's heart voluntarily to bring into the house of the Lord,

5 Let the priests solicit *and* receive such contributions, every man from his acquaintance, and let them repair the Lord's house wherever any such need may be found.

6 But in the twenty-third year of King Joash's reign the priests had not made the needed repairs on the Lord's house.

7 Then King Joash called for Jehoiada the priest and the other priests and said to them, Why are you not repairing the [Lord's] house? Do not take any more money from your acquaintances, but turn it all over for the repair of the house. [You are no longer responsible for this work. I will take it into my own hands.]

8 And the priests consented to receive no more money from the people, nor to repair the breaches of the house.

9 Then Jehoiada the priest took a chest and bored a hole in the lid of it and set it beside the altar on the right side as one entered the house of the Lord; and the priests who guarded the door put in the chest all the money that was brought into the house of the Lord.

d Judah and Israel each had a king named Joash or Jehoash, and the Hebrew uses the two forms of the name interchangeably. Since the time of their reigns overlapped, it became difficult not to confuse them. So this version will call the first one Joash, referring to the king of Judah who began his reign at seven years of age, and the other one Jehoash (as the Hebrew does in II Kings 13:10 and 14:17), referring to the king of Israel who began his reign thirty-seven years later.

10 And whenever they saw that there was much money in the chest, the king's scribe and the high priest came up and counted the money that was found in the house of the Lord and tied it up in bags.

11 Then they gave the money, when it was weighed, into the hands of those who were doing the work, who had the oversight of the house of the Lord; and they paid it out to the carpenters and builders who worked on the house of the Lord

12 And to the masons and stonecutters, and to buy timber and hewn stone for making the repairs on the house of the Lord, and for all that was outlay for repairing the house.

13 However, there were not made for the house of the Lord basins of silver, snuffers, bowls, trumpets, any vessels of gold or of silver, from the money that was brought into the house of the Lord.

14 But they gave that to the workmen, and repaired with it the house of the Lord.

15 Moreover, they did not require an accounting from the men into whose hands they delivered the money to be paid to the workmen, for they dealt faithfully.

16 The money from the guilt offerings and sin offerings was not brought into the house of the Lord; it was the priests'.

17 Then Hazael king of Syria went up, fought against Gath [in Philistia], and took it. And Hazael set his face to go up to Jerusalem.

18 And Joash king of Judah took all the hallowed things that Jehoshaphat, Jehoram, and Ahaziah, his [forefathers], kings of Judah, had dedicated and his own hallowed things and all the gold that was found in the treasuries of the house of the Lord and in the king's house, and sent them to Hazael king of Syria; and Hazael went away from Jerusalem.

19 The rest of the acts of Joash, and all that he did, are they not written in the Book of the Chronicles of the Kings of Judah?

20 His servants arose and made a conspiracy and slew Joash [in revenge] in the house of Millo, on the way that goes down to Silla. [II Chron. 24:22-25.]

21 It was Jozachar son of Shimeath and Jehozabad son of Shomer, his servants, who smote him so that he died. They buried [Joash] with his fathers in the City of David. Amaziah his son reigned in his stead.

13 IN THE twenty-third year of Joash son of Ahaziah king of Judah, Jehoahaz son of Jehu began to reign over Israel in Samaria, and reigned seventeen years.

2 He did evil in the sight of the Lord and followed the sins of Jeroboam son of Nebat, which made Israel to sin, and did not depart from them.

3 The anger of the Lord was kindled against Israel, and He delivered them into the hand of Hazael king of Syria and of Ben-hadad son of Hazael continually.

4 But Jehoahaz besought the Lord, and the Lord hearkened to him, for He saw the oppression of Israel, how the king of Syria burdened them.

5 Then the Lord gave Israel a savior [one to rescue and give them peace], so that they escaped from under the hand of the Syrians; and the Israelites dwelt in their tents *or* homes as before.

6 Yet they did not depart from the sins of the house of Jeroboam, who made Israel sin; but the nation walked in them. And the Asherah [symbol of the goddess Asherah] remained in Samaria.

7 [Ben-hadad] of Syria did not leave to Jehoahaz of [Israel] an army of more than fifty horsemen, ten chariots, and

10,000 footmen, for the Syrian king had destroyed them and made them like dust to be trampled.

8 The rest of the acts of Jehoahaz, all that he did and his might, are they not written in the Book of the Chronicles of the Kings of Israel?

9 Jehoahaz slept with his fathers, and they buried him in Samaria. ᵉJehoash his son reigned in his stead.

10 In the thirty-seventh year of Joash king of Judah, Jehoash son of Jehoahaz began to reign over Israel in Samaria, and reigned sixteen years.

11 He did evil in the sight of the Lord; he departed not from all the sins of Jeroboam son of Nebat, who made Israel sin; he walked in them.

12 The rest of the acts of Jehoash, all that he did, and his might with which he fought against Amaziah king of Judah, are they not written in the Book of the Chronicles of the Kings of Israel?

13 Jehoash slept with his fathers, and Jeroboam [II] sat on his throne. Jehoash was buried in Samaria with the kings of Israel.

14 Now Elisha [previously] had become ill of the illness of which he died. And Jehoash king of Israel came down to him and wept over him and said, O my father, my father, the chariot of Israel and the horsemen of it! [II Kings 2:12.]

15 And Elisha said to him, Take bow and arrows. And he took bow and arrows.

16 And he said to the king of Israel, Put your hand upon the bow. And he put his hand upon it, and Elisha put his hands upon the king's hands.

17 And he said, Open the window to the east. And he opened it. Then Elisha said, Shoot. And he shot. And he said, The Lord's arrow of victory, the arrow of victory over Syria. For you shall smite the Syrians in Aphek till you have destroyed them.

18 Then he said, Take the arrows. And he took them. And he said to the king of Israel, Strike on the ground. And he struck three times and stopped.

19 And the man of God was angry with him and said, You should have struck five or six times; then you would have struck down Syria until you had destroyed it. But now you shall strike Syria down only three times.

20 Elisha died, and they buried him. Bands of the Moabites invaded the land in the spring of the next year.

21 As a man was being buried [on an open bier], such a band was seen coming; and the man was cast into Elisha's grave. And when the man being let down touched the bones of Elisha, he revived and stood on his feet.

22 Hazael king of Syria oppressed Israel all the days of Jehoahaz.

23 But the Lord was gracious to them and had compassion on them and turned toward them because of ᶠHis covenant with Abraham, Isaac, and Jacob, and would not destroy them or cast them from His presence yet. [Mal. 3:6.]

24 Hazael king of Syria died; Benhadad his son reigned in his stead.

25 Jehoash son of Jehoahaz recovered from Ben-hadad son of Hazael the cities which he had taken from Jehoahaz his father by war. Three times Jehoash defeated him, and recovered the cities of Israel. [II Kings 13:19.]

14 IN THE second year of Jehoash son of Jehoahaz king of Israel, Amaziah son of Joash king of Judah reigned.

---

e See footnote on II Kings 12:1. f Abraham, Isaac, and Jacob had been dead a thousand years, yet God's covenant with them was undiminishingly effective.

2 He was twenty-five years old when he began his twenty-nine-year reign in Jerusalem. His mother was Jehoaddin of Jerusalem.

3 He did right in the sight of the Lord, yet not like David his [forefather]. He did all things as Joash his father did.

4 But the high places were not removed; the people still sacrificed and burned incense on the high places.

5 As soon as the kingdom was established in Amaziah's hand, he slew his servants who had slain the king his father. [II Kings 12:20.]

6 But he did not slay the children of the murderers, in compliance with what is written in the Book of the Law of Moses, in which the Lord commanded, The fathers shall not be put to death for the children, nor the children for the fathers; but every man shall die for his own sin only.

7 Amaziah slew of Edom in the Valley of Salt 10,000, and took Sela (Greek *petra* [rock]) by war, and called it Joktheel, which is the name of it to this day.

8 Then Amaziah sent messengers to Jehoash son of Jehoahaz, the son of Jehu, king of Israel, saying, Come, let us look one another in the face *and* test each other.

9 Jehoash king of Israel replied to Amaziah king of Judah, The thistle in Lebanon sent to the cedar in Lebanon, saying, Give your daughter to my son as wife. And a wild beast of Lebanon passed by and trampled the thistle [leaving the cedar unharmed].

10 You have indeed smitten Edom, and your heart has lifted you up. Glory in that, and stay at home; for why should you meddle to your hurt *and* provoke calamity, causing you to fall, you and Judah with you?

11 But Amaziah would not hear. So Jehoash king of Israel went up; and he and Amaziah king of Judah measured swords at Beth-shemesh, which belongs to Judah.

12 But Judah was defeated by Israel, and every man fled home.

13 And Jehoash king of Israel captured Amaziah king of Judah, son of Joash, the son of Ahaziah, at Beth-shemesh, and came to Jerusalem and broke down the wall of Jerusalem from the Ephraim Gate to the Corner Gate, 400 cubits.

14 He seized all the gold and silver and all the vessels found in the Lord's house and in the treasuries of the king's house, also hostages, and returned to Samaria.

15 The rest of the acts of Jehoash, his might, and how he fought with Amaziah king of Judah, are they not written in the Book of the Chronicles of Israel's Kings?

16 Jehoash slept with his fathers, and was buried in Samaria with Israel's kings. Jeroboam [II] reigned in his stead.

17 Amaziah son of Joash king of Judah lived after the death of Jehoash son of Jehoahaz king of Israel fifteen years.

18 The rest of the acts of Amaziah, are they not written in the Book of the Chronicles of the Kings of Judah?

19 Now a conspiracy was made against him in Jerusalem, and Amaziah fled to Lachish, but they sent after him to Lachish and slew him there.

20 They brought him on horses and he was buried at Jerusalem with his fathers in the City of David.

21 And all the people of Judah took Azariah, sixteen years old, and made him king instead of his father Amaziah.

22 He built Elath and restored it to Judah after the king [his father] died.

23 In the fifteenth year of Amaziah son of Joash king of Judah Jeroboam [II] son of Jehoash king of Israel began to reign in Samaria, and reigned forty-one years.

24 He did evil in the sight of the Lord; he did not depart from all the sins of Jeroboam [I] son of Nebat, with which he made Israel to sin.

25 Jeroboam restored Israel's border from the entrance of Hamath to the [Dead] Sea of the Arabah, according to the word of the Lord, the God of Israel, which He spoke through His servant Jonah son of Amittai, the prophet from Gath-hepher.

26 For the Lord saw as very bitter the affliction of Israel; there was no one left, bond or free, nor any helper for Israel.

27 But the Lord had not said that He would blot out the name of Israel from under the heavens, so He saved them by the hand of Jeroboam [II] son of Jehoash.

28 The rest of the acts of Jeroboam [II], all that he did, his might, how he warred, and how he recovered for Israel Damascus and Hamath, which had belonged to Judah, are they not written in the Book of the Chronicles of the Kings of Israel?

29 Jeroboam [II] slept with his fathers, the kings of Israel. Zechariah his son reigned in his stead.

15 IN THE twenty-seventh year of Jeroboam [II] king of Israel, Azariah (Uzziah) son of Amaziah king of Judah began to reign.

2 He was sixteen years old when he began his fifty-two-year reign in Jerusalem. His mother was Jecoliah of Jerusalem.

3 He did right in the Lord's sight, in keeping with all his father Amaziah had done—

4 Except the high places were not removed; the people sacrificed and burned incense still on the high places.

5 And the Lord smote the king, so that he was a leper to his dying day,

and dwelt in a separate house. Jotham the king's son was over the household, judging the people of the land. [II Chron. 26:16-21.]

6 The rest of Azariah's acts, all that he did, are they not written in the Book of the Chronicles of the Kings of Judah?

7 Azariah slept with his fathers, and they buried him with them in the City of David. Jotham his son reigned in his stead.

8 In the thirty-eighth year of Azariah king of Judah Zechariah son of Jeroboam [II] reigned over Israel in Samaria six months.

9 He did evil in the sight of the Lord, as his fathers had done; he departed not from the sins of Jeroboam [I] son of Nebat, with which he made Israel to sin.

10 Shallum son of Jabesh conspired against Zechariah and struck and killed him before the people and reigned in his stead.

11 The rest of the acts of Zechariah, see, they are written in the Book of the Chronicles of the Kings of Israel.

12 This was the fulfillment of the promise to Jehu from the Lord: Your sons shall sit on the throne of Israel to the fourth generation. And so it came to pass. [II Kings 10:30.]

13 Shallum son of Jabesh, in the thirty-ninth year of Uzziah king of Judah, began his reign of a full month in Samaria.

14 For Menahem son of Gadi went up from Tirzah and came to Samaria, and smote and killed Shallum son of Jabesh in Samaria and reigned in his stead.

15 The rest of Shallum's acts, his conspiracy, see, they are written in the Book of the Chronicles of the Kings of Israel.

16 Then Menahem smote Tiphsah and all who were in it and its territory from Tirzah on; he attacked it because they did not open to him.

And all ^gthe women there who were with child he ripped up.

17 In the thirty-ninth year of Azariah king of Judah, Menahem son of Gadi began his ten-year reign over Israel in Samaria.

18 He did evil in the sight of the Lord; he did not depart all his days from the sins of Jeroboam son of Nebat, which he caused Israel to sin.

19 There came against the land Pul king of Assyria, and Menahem gave Pul 1,000 talents of silver, that he might help him to confirm his kingship.

20 Menahem exacted the money from Israel, from all the men of wealth, from each man fifty shekels of silver to give to the king of Assyria. So the king of Assyria turned back and did not stay in the land.

21 The rest of Menahem's acts, all that he did, are they not written in the Book of the Chronicles of the Kings of Israel?

22 Menahem slept with his fathers; Pekahiah his son reigned in his stead.

23 In the fiftieth year of Azariah king of Judah, Pekahiah son of Menahem began his two-year reign over Israel in Samaria.

24 He did evil in the sight of the Lord; he did not depart from the sins of Jeroboam [I] son of Nebat, which he made Israel sin.

25 But Pekah son of Remaliah, his captain, conspired against [Pekahiah] and attacked him in Samaria, in the citadel of the king's house, with Argob and Arieh; [for] with [Pekah] were fifty Gileadites. And he killed him and reigned in his stead.

26 The rest of the acts of Pekahiah, all he did, see, they are written in the Book of the Chronicles of the Kings of Israel.

27 In the fifty-second year of Azariah king of Judah, Pekah son of Remaliah began his twenty-year reign over Israel in Samaria.

28 He did evil in the Lord's sight; he did not depart from the sins of Jeroboam [I] son of Nebat, which he made Israel sin.

29 In the days of Pekah king of Israel, Tiglath-pileser king of Assyria came and took Ijon, Abel-beth-maacah, Janoah, Kedesh, Hazor, Gilead, and Galilee, all the land of Naphtali, and carried the people captive to Assyria.

30 Hoshea son of Elah conspired against Pekah son of Remaliah [of Israel]; he smote and killed him, and reigned in his stead in the twentieth year of Jotham son of Uzziah king of Judah.

31 The rest of Pekah's acts, all that he did, behold, they are written in the Book of the Chronicles of Israel's Kings.

32 In the second year of Pekah son of Remaliah king of Israel, Jotham son of Uzziah king of Judah became king.

33 When he was twenty-five years old, he began his reign of sixteen years in Jerusalem. His mother was Jerusha daughter of Zadok.

34 He did right in the Lord's sight, according to all his father Uzziah had done.

35 Yet the high places were not removed; the people sacrificed and burned incense still on the high places. He built the Upper Gate of the house of the Lord.

36 The rest of the acts of Jotham, all he did, are they not written in the Book of the Chronicles of Judah's Kings?

37 In those days the Lord began sending Rezin king of Syria and Pekah son of Remaliah against Judah.

---

g This savage conduct was among the enormities that a heathen ruler might perpetrate, but only here do we find such cruelty employed by an Israelite. It shows the great degradation and barbarity of the times (*The Cambridge Bible*).

38 Jotham slept with his fathers and was buried [with them] in the city of David his [forefather]. Ahaz his son succeeded him.

16 IN THE seventeenth year of Pekah son of Remaliah, Ahaz son of Jotham king of Judah became king.
2 Ahaz was twenty years old when he began his sixteen-year reign in Jerusalem. He did not do right in the sight of the Lord his God, like David his [forefather].
3 But he walked in the ways of Israel's kings, yes, and made his son pass through the fire [and offered him as a sacrifice], in accord with the abominable [idolatrous] practices of the [heathen] nations whom the Lord drove out before the Israelites.
4 He sacrificed and burned incense in the high places, on the hills, and under every green tree.
5 Then Rezin king of Syria and Pekah son of Remaliah king of Israel came up to Jerusalem to wage war; they besieged Ahaz, but could not conquer him.
6 At that time, Rezin king of Syria got back Elath [in Edom] for Syria and drove the Jews from [it]. The Syrians came to Elath and dwell there to this day.
7 So Ahaz sent messengers to Tiglath-pileser king of Assyria, saying, I am your servant and son. Come up and save me out of the hands of the kings of Syria and of Israel, who are attacking me.
8 And Ahaz took the silver and gold in the house of the Lord and in the treasuries of the king's house and sent a present to the king of Assyria.
9 Assyria's king hearkened to him; he went up against Damascus, took it, carried its people captive to Kir, and slew Rezin.
10 King Ahaz went to Damascus to meet Tiglath-pileser king of Assyria, and saw there their [heathen] altar. King Ahaz sent to Urijah the priest a model of the altar and an exact pattern for its construction.
11 So Urijah the priest built an altar according to all that King Ahaz had sent from Damascus, finishing it before King Ahaz returned.
12 When the king came from Damascus, he looked at the altar and offered on it.
13 King Ahaz burned his burnt offering and his cereal offering, poured his drink offering, and dashed the blood of his peace offerings upon that altar.
14 The bronze altar which was before the Lord he removed from the front of the house, from between his [new] altar and the house of the Lord, and put it on the north side of his altar.
15 And King Ahaz commanded Urijah the priest: Upon the principal (the new) altar, burn the morning burnt offering, the evening cereal offering, the king's burnt sacrifice and his cereal offering, with the burnt offering and cereal offering and drink offering of all the people of the land; and dash upon the [new] altar all the blood of the burnt offerings and the sacrifices. But the [old] bronze altar shall be kept for me to use to inquire by [of the Lord].
16 Urijah the priest did all this as King Ahaz commanded.
17 [To keep Assyria's king from getting them] King Ahaz cut off the panels of the bases [of the ten lavers] and removed the laver from each of them; and he took down the Sea from off the bronze oxen that were under it and put it upon stone supports.
18 And the covered way for the Sabbath that they had built in the temple court, and the king's outer entrance, he removed from the house of the Lord, because of the king of Assyria

[who if he heard of them might seize them].

19 The rest of the acts of Ahaz, are they not written in the Book of the Chronicles of the Kings of Judah?

20 Ahaz slept with his fathers and was buried [with them] in the City of David. Hezekiah his son reigned in his stead.

17 IN THE twelfth year of Ahaz king of Judah, Hoshea son of Elah began his nine-year reign in Samaria over Israel.

2 He did evil in the sight of the Lord, but not as Israel's kings before him did.

3 Against him came up Shalmaneser king of Assyria, and Hoshea became his servant and brought him tribute.

4 But the king of Assyria found treachery in Hoshea, for he had sent messengers to So king of Egypt and offered no tribute to the king of Assyria, as he had done year by year; therefore the king of Assyria shut him up and bound him in prison.

5 Then the king of Assyria invaded all the land and went up to Samaria and besieged it for three years.

6 In the ninth year of Hoshea, the king of Assyria took Samaria and carried the Israelites away into Assyria, and placed them in Halah and in Habor by the river of Gozan and in the cities of the Medes.

7 This was so because the Israelites had sinned against the Lord their God, Who had brought them out of the land of Egypt, from under the hand of Pharaoh king of Egypt; and they had feared other gods

speak the Word

putting the Word to work

We learn from II Kings 17:6–23 that the Lord allowed Israel to be taken captive and led away into exile because of their disobedience. Do you ever get careless about doing what God has asked you to do, letting sin creep into your life? Do not let our enemy, the devil, lead you into the captivity of sin and disobedience; it leads only to destruction.

8 And walked in the customs of the [heathen] nations whom the Lord drove out before the Israelites, customs the kings of Israel had introduced.

9 The Israelites did secretly against the Lord their God things not right. They built for themselves high places in all their towns, from [lonely] watchtower to [populous] fortified city.

10 They set up for themselves pillars and Asherim [symbols of the goddess Asherah] on every high hill and under every green tree.

11 There they burned incense on all the high places, as did the nations whom the Lord carried away before them; and they did wicked things provoking the Lord to anger.

12 And they served idols, of which the Lord had said to them, You shall not do this thing.

13 Yet the Lord warned Israel and Judah through all the prophets and all the seers, saying, Turn from your evil ways and keep My commandments and My statutes, according to all the Law which I commanded your fathers and which I sent to you by My servants the prophets.

14 Yet they would not hear, but hardened their necks as did their fathers who did not believe (trust in, rely on, and remain steadfast to) the Lord their God.

15 They despised *and* rejected His statutes and His covenant which He made with their fathers and His warnings to them, and they followed vanity (false gods—falsehood, emptiness, and futility) and [they themselves and their prayers] became false (empty and futile). They went after the heathen round about them, of whom the Lord had charged them that they should not do as they did.

16 And they forsook all the commandments of the Lord their God and made for themselves molten images, even two calves, and made an Asherah and worshiped all the [starry] hosts of the heavens and served Baal.

17 They caused their sons and their daughters to pass through the fire and used divination and enchantments and sold themselves to do evil in the sight of the Lord, provoking Him to anger.

18 Therefore the Lord was very angry with Israel and removed them out of His sight. None was left but the tribe of Judah.

19 Judah also did not keep the commandments of the Lord their God, but walked in the customs which Israel introduced.

20 The Lord rejected all the descendants of Israel and afflicted them and delivered them into the hands of spoilers, until He had cast them out of His sight.

21 For He tore Israel from the house of David; and they made Jeroboam son of Nebat king. And Jeroboam drew *and* drove Israel away from following the Lord and made them sin a great sin.

22 For the Israelites walked in all the sins Jeroboam committed; they departed not from them

23 Until the Lord removed Israel from His sight, as He had foretold by all His servants the prophets. So Israel was carried away from their own land to Assyria to this day.

24 The king of Assyria brought men from Babylon, Cuthah, Avva, Hamath, and Sepharvaim and placed them in the cities of Samaria instead of the Israelites. They possessed Samaria and dwelt in its cities.

25 At the beginning of their dwelling there, they did not fear *and* revere the Lord. Therefore the Lord sent lions among them, which killed some of them.

26 So the king of Assyria was told: The nations you removed and placed in the cities of Samaria do not know the manner in which the God of the land requires their worship. Therefore He has sent lions among them, and behold, they are killing them, because they do not know the manner of [worship demanded by] the God of the land.

27 Then the king of Assyria commanded, Take to Samaria one of the priests you brought from there, and let him [and his helpers] go and live there and let him teach the people the law of the God of the land.

28 So one of the priests whom they had carried away from Samaria came and dwelt in Bethel and taught them how they should fear *and* revere the Lord.

29 But every nationality still made gods of their own and put them in the shrines of the high places which the Samaritans had made, every nationality in the city in which they dwelt.

30 The men of Babylon made [and worshiped their deity] Succoth-benoth, the men of Cuth made Nergal, the men of Hamath made Ashima,

31 The Avvites made Nibhaz and Tartak, and the Sepharvites burned their children in the fire to Adram-

melech and Anammelech, the gods of Sepharvaim.
32 So they feared the Lord, yet appointed from among themselves, whether high or low, priests of the high places, who sacrificed for them in the shrines of the high places.
33 They feared the Lord, yet served their own gods, as did the nations from among whom they had been carried away.
34 Unto this day they do after their former custom: they do not fear the Lord [as God sees it], neither do they obey the statutes or the ordinances or the law and commandment which the Lord commanded the children of Jacob, whom He named Israel,
35 With whom the Lord had made a covenant and commanded them, You shall not fear other gods or bow yourselves to them or serve them or sacrifice to them.
36 But you shall [reverently] fear, bow yourselves to, and sacrifice to the Lord, Who brought you out of the land of Egypt with great power and an outstretched arm.
37 And the statutes, ordinances, law, and commandment which He wrote for you you shall observe and do forevermore; you shall not fear other gods.
38 And the covenant that I have made with you you shall not forget; you shall not fear other gods.
39 But the Lord your God you shall [reverently] fear; then He will deliver you out of the hands of all your enemies.

40 However, they did not listen, but they did as they had done formerly.
41 So these nations [vainly] feared the Lord and also served their graven images, as did their children and their children's children. As their fathers did, so do they to this day.

18 IN THE third year of Hoshea son of Elah king of Israel, Hezekiah son of Ahaz king of Judah began to reign.
2 He was twenty-five years old when he began his twenty-nine-year reign in Jerusalem. His mother was Abi daughter of Zechariah.
3 Hezekiah did right in the sight of the Lord, according to all that David his [forefather] had done.
4 He removed the high places, broke the images, cut down the Asherim, and broke in pieces the bronze serpent that Moses had made, for until then the Israelites had burned incense to it; but he called it Nehushtan [a bronze trifle].
5 Hezekiah trusted in, leaned on, *and* was confident in the Lord, the God of Israel; so that neither after him nor before him was any one of all the kings of Judah like him.
6 For he clung *and* held fast to the Lord and ceased not to follow Him, but kept His commandments, as the Lord commanded Moses.
7 And the Lord was with Hezekiah; he prospered wherever he went. And he rebelled against the king of Assyria and refused to serve him.

speak the Word

Thank You, God, that You will deliver me out of the hands of my enemies as I reverently fear You.
ADAPTED FROM II KINGS 17:39

God, may I be like Hezekiah, trusting in, leaning on, and being confident in You. May I cling to You and hold fast to You, never ceasing to follow You.
ADAPTED FROM II KINGS 18:5, 6

putting the Word to work

One of the first things Hezekiah did when he became king was to get rid of the things that kept his people from walking in obedience to God (see II Kings 18:1–7). What keeps you from obeying God? It may be something that seems very important to you, but there is nothing more important than obeying God. Ask God to help you do what is right in His eyes, and know that He will honor your obedience, as He did Hezekiah's (see II Kings 18:8).

8 He smote the Philistines, even to Gaza [the most distant city] and its borders, from the [isolated] watchtower to the [populous] fortified city.
9 In the fourth year of King Hezekiah, which was the seventh of Hoshea son of Elah king of Israel, Shalmaneser king of Assyria came up against Samaria and besieged it.
10 After three years it was taken; in the sixth year of Hezekiah, which was the ninth year of Hoshea king of Israel, Samaria was taken.
11 The king of Assyria carried Israel away to Assyria, and put them in Halah, and on the Habor, the river of Gozan, and in the cities of the Medes,
12 Because they did not obey the voice of the Lord their God, but transgressed His covenant, even all that Moses the servant of the Lord commanded, and would not hear it or do it.
13 In the fourteenth year of Hezekiah, Sennacherib king of Assyria came up against all the fortified cities of Judah and took them.
14 Then Hezekiah king of Judah sent to the king of Assyria at Lachish, saying, I have done wrong. Depart from me; what you put on me I will bear. And the king of Assyria exacted of Hezekiah king of Judah 300 talents of silver and thirty talents of gold.

15 And Hezekiah gave him all the silver that was found in the house of the Lord and in the treasuries of the king's house.
16 Then Hezekiah stripped off the gold from the doors of the temple of the Lord and from the doorposts which he as king of Judah had overlaid, and gave it to the king of Assyria.
17 And the king of Assyria sent the Tartan, the Rabsaris, and the Rabshakeh [the high officials] from Lachish to King Hezekiah at Jerusalem with a great army. They went up to Jerusalem, and when they arrived, they came and stood by the canal of the Upper Pool, which is on the highway to the Fuller's Field. [II Chron. 32:9-19; Isa. 36:1-22.]
18 When they called for the king, there came out to them Eliakim son of Hilkiah, who was over the king's household, and Shebna the scribe, and Joah son of Asaph the recorder.
19 The Rabshakeh told them, Say to Hezekiah, Thus says the great king of Assyria: What justifies this confidence of yours?
20 You say—but they are empty words—There is counsel and strength for war. Now on whom do you rely, that you rebel against me?
21 Behold, you are relying on Egypt, that broken reed of a staff; if a man leans on it, it will pierce his hand. So is Pharaoh king of Egypt to all who trust *and* rely on him.
22 But if you tell me, We trust in *and* rely on the Lord our God, is it not He Whose high places and altars Hezekiah has removed, saying to Judah and Jerusalem, You shall worship before this altar in Jerusalem?
23 So now, make a wager *and* give pledges to my lord the king of Assyria: I will deliver you 2,000 horses—if you can on your part put riders on them.
24 How then can you beat back one captain among the least of my mas-

ter's servants, when your trust is put in Egypt for chariots and horsemen?

25 Have I come up without the Lord against this place to destroy it? The Lord said to me, Go up against this land and destroy it.

26 Then Eliakim son of Hilkiah and Shebna and Joah said to the Rabshakeh, We pray you, speak to your servants in the Aramaic (Syrian) language, for we understand it; and do not speak to us in the Jews' language in the hearing of the people on the wall.

27 But the Rabshakeh said to them, Has my master sent me to your master and you only to say these things? Has he not sent me to the men who sit on the wall [whom Hezekiah has doomed to be forced] to eat their own dung and drink their own urine along with you?

28 Then the Rabshakeh stood and cried with a loud voice in the Jews' language, Hear the word of the great king of Assyria!

29 Thus says the king: Let not Hezekiah deceive you. For he will not be able to deliver you out of my hand.

30 Nor let Hezekiah make you trust in *and* rely on the Lord, saying, The Lord will surely deliver us, and this city will not be given into the hand of Assyria's king.

31 Hearken not to Hezekiah, for thus says the king of Assyria: Make your peace with me and come out to me, and eat every man from his own vine and fig tree and drink every man the waters of his own cistern,

32 Until I come and take you away to a land like your own, a land of grain and vintage fruit, of bread and vineyards, of olive trees and honey, that you may live and not die. Do not listen to Hezekiah when he urges you, saying, The Lord will deliver us.

33 Has any one of the gods of the nations ever delivered his land out of the hand of the king of Assyria?

34 Where are the gods of Hamath and Arpad [in Syria]? Where are the gods of Sepharvaim, Hena, and Ivvah [in the Euphrates Valley]? Have they delivered Samaria [Israel's capital] out of my hand?

35 Who of all the gods of the countries has delivered his country out of my hand, that the Lord should deliver Jerusalem out of my hand?

36 But the people were silent and answered him not a word, for Hezekiah had commanded, Do not answer him.

37 Then Eliakim son of Hilkiah, who was over the royal household, and Shebna the scribe, and Joah son of Asaph the recorder came to Hezekiah with their clothes rent, and told him what the Rabshakeh had said.

19 WHEN KING Hezekiah heard it, he rent his clothes and covered himself with sackcloth and went into the house of the Lord. [Isa. 37:1-13.]

2 And he sent Eliakim, who was over his household, Shebna the scribe, and the older priests, covered with sackcloth, to Isaiah the prophet the son of Amoz.

3 They said to him, Hezekiah says: This is a day of [extreme danger and] distress, of rebuke *and* chastisement, and blasphemous *and* insolent insult; for children have come to the birth, and there is no strength to bring them forth.

4 It may be that the Lord your God will hear all the words of the Rabshakeh, whom the king of Assyria has sent to mock, reproach, insult, *and* defy the living God, and will rebuke the words which the Lord your God has heard. So raise your prayer for the remnant [of His people] that is left.

5 So the servants of King Hezekiah came to Isaiah.

6 Isaiah said to them, Say to your

master, Thus says the Lord: Do not be afraid because of the words you have heard, with which the servants of the king of Assyria have reviled *and* blasphemed Me.

7 Behold, I will put a spirit in him so that he will hear a rumor and return to his own land, and I will cause him to fall by the sword in his own country.

8 So the Rabshakeh returned and found the king of Assyria fighting against Libnah [a fortified city of Judah]; for he had heard that the king had left Lachish.

9 And Sennacherib king of Assyria heard concerning Tirhakah king of Ethiopia, He has come to make war against you. And when he heard it, he sent messengers again to Hezekiah, saying,

10 Say this to Hezekiah king of Judah: Let not your God on Whom you rely deceive you by saying, Jerusalem shall not be delivered into the hand of the king of Assyria.

11 Behold, you have heard what the Assyrian kings have done to all lands, destroying them utterly. And shall you be delivered?

12 Have the gods of the nations delivered those whom my ancestors have destroyed, as Gozan, Haran [of Mesopotamia], Rezeph, and the people of Eden who were in Telassar?

13 Where are the kings of Hamath, of Arpad [of northern Syria], of the city of Sepharvaim, of Hena, and Ivvah?

14 Hezekiah received the letter from the hand of the messengers and read it. And he went up into the house of the Lord and spread it before the Lord. [Isa. 37:14-20.]

15 And Hezekiah prayed: O Lord, the God of Israel, Who [in symbol] is

enthroned above the cherubim [of the ark in the temple], You are the God, You alone, of all the kingdoms of the earth. You have made the heavens and the earth.

16 Lord, bow down Your ear and hear; Lord, open Your eyes and see; hear the words of Sennacherib which he has sent to mock, reproach, insult, *and* defy the living God.

17 It is true, Lord, that the Assyrian kings have laid waste the nations and their lands

18 And have cast the gods of those peoples into the fire, for they were not gods but the work of men's hands, wood and stone. So they [could destroy and] have destroyed them.

19 Now therefore, O Lord our God, I beseech You, save us out of his hand, that all the kingdoms of the earth may know *and* understand that You, O Lord, are God alone.

20 Then Isaiah son of Amoz sent to Hezekiah, saying, Thus says the Lord, the God of Israel: Your prayer to Me about Sennacherib king of Assyria I have heard. [Isa. 37:21-38.]

21 This is the word that the Lord has spoken concerning him: The Virgin Daughter of Zion has despised you and laughed you to scorn; the Daughter of Jerusalem has wagged her head behind you.

22 Whom have you mocked *and* reviled and insulted *and* blasphemed? Against Whom have you raised your voice and haughtily lifted your eyes? Against the Holy One of Israel!

23 By your messengers you have mocked, reproached, insulted, *and* defied the Lord, and have said, With my many chariots I have gone up to the heights of the mountains, to the far recesses of Lebanon. I cut down its

speak the Word

tall cedar trees and its choicest cypress trees. I entered its most distant retreat, its densest forest.

24 I dug wells and drank foreign waters, and with the sole of my feet have I dried up all [the defense and] the streams of Egypt.

25 [But, says the God of Israel] Have you not heard how I ordained long ago what now I have brought to pass? I planned it in olden times, that you [king of Assyria] should [be My instrument to] lay waste fortified cities, making them ruinous heaps.

26 That is why their inhabitants had little power, they were dismayed and confounded; they were like plants of the field, the green herb, the grass on the housetops, blasted before it is grown up.

27 But [O Sennacherib] I [the Lord] know your sitting down, your going out, your coming in, and your raging against Me.

28 Because your raging against Me and your arrogance *and* careless ease have come to My ears, therefore I will put My hook in your nose and My bridle in your lips, and I will turn you back by the way you came, O king of Assyria.

29 And [Hezekiah, says the Lord] this shall be the sign [of these things] to you: you shall eat this year what grows of itself, also in the second year what springs up voluntarily. But in the third year sow and reap, plant vineyards and eat their fruit.

30 And the remnant that has survived of the house of Judah shall again take root downward and bear fruit upward.

31 For out of Jerusalem shall go forth a remnant, and a band of survivors out of Mount Zion. The zeal of the Lord of hosts shall perform this.

32 Therefore thus says the Lord concerning the king of Assyria: He shall not come into this city or shoot an arrow here or come before it with shield or cast up a siege mound against it.

33 By the way that he came, by that way shall he return, and he shall not come into this city, says the Lord.

34 For I will defend this city to save it, for My own sake and for My servant David's sake.

35 And it all came to pass, for that night the ʰAngel of the Lord went forth and slew 185,000 in the camp of the Assyrians; and when [the living] arose early in the morning, behold, all these were dead bodies.

36 So Sennacherib king of Assyria departed and returned and dwelt at Nineveh.

37 And as he was worshiping in the house of Nisroch his god, Adrammelech and Sharezer his sons killed him with the sword, and they escaped to the land of Armenia *or* Ararat. Esarhaddon his son reigned in his stead.

20 IN THOSE days Hezekiah became deadly ill. The prophet Isaiah son of Amoz came and said to him, Thus says the Lord: Set your house in order, for you shall die; you shall not recover. [II Chron. 32:24-26; Isa. 38:1-8.]

2 Then Hezekiah turned his face to the wall and prayed to the Lord, saying,

3 I beseech You, O Lord, [earnestly] remember now how I have walked before You in faithfulness *and* truth and with a whole heart [entirely devoted to You] and have done what is good in Your sight. And Hezekiah wept bitterly.

4 Before Isaiah had gone out of the middle court, the word of the Lord came to him:

5 Turn back and tell Hezekiah, the

---

h See footnote on Gen. 16:7.

life point

God answered Hezekiah's prayer by healing him and adding fifteen years to his life (of course, God does not always respond this way, but in Hezekiah's case, He did). During that time, many horrible things happened (see II Kings 20:17), and Hezekiah suffered greatly. It seems that although God answered Hezekiah's request, it was not God's best for him. We need to remember that the only safe prayer policy is for God's will. The best prayer always acknowledges that we do not really know in most instances what is best for us; therefore, we must be willing to say, "Whatever You want, Lord." As Proverbs 16:9 reminds us: "A man's mind plans his way, but the Lord directs his steps."

leader of My people, Thus says the Lord, the God of David your [forefather]: I have heard your prayer, I have seen your tears; behold, I will heal you. On the third day you shall go up to the house of the Lord.

6 I will ¹add to your life fifteen years and deliver you and this city [Jerusalem] out of the hand of the king of Assyria; and I will defend this city for My own sake and for My servant David's sake.

7 And Isaiah said, Bring a cake of figs. Let them lay it on the burning inflammation, that he may recover.

8 Hezekiah said to Isaiah, What shall be the sign that the Lord will heal me and that I shall go up into the house of the Lord on the third day?

9 And Isaiah said, This is the sign to you from the Lord that He will do the thing He has promised: shall the shadow [denoting the time of day] go forward ten steps, or go back ten steps?

10 Hezekiah answered, It is an easy matter for the shadow to go forward ten steps; so let the shadow go back ten steps.

11 So Isaiah the prophet cried to the Lord, and He brought the shadow the ten steps backward by which it had gone down on the sundial of Ahaz.

12 At that time Merodach-baladan son of Baladan king of Babylon sent letters and a present to Hezekiah, for he had heard of Hezekiah's illness. [Isa. 39:1-8.]

13 And Hezekiah rejoiced *and* welcomed the embassy and showed them all his treasure-house—the silver, gold, spices, precious ointment, his armory, and all that was found in his treasuries. There was nothing in his house or in all his realm that Hezekiah did not show them.

14 Then Isaiah the prophet came to King Hezekiah and said, What did these men say? From where did they come to you? Hezekiah said, They are from a far country, from Babylon.

i Good King Hezekiah's prayer life holds a mighty challenge and a clear and terrible warning for every believer. In his nation's darkest hour (18:13-17), he prayed (19:15), and God performed a miracle, one He had foretold (19:20, 32-37). It is a wonderful thing to have such power as that with God! But in this chapter (20) and the next, that power has become a terrible thing; for Hezekiah had put himself on God's "ways and means committee," as chairman in fact. God virtually said, "Your time has come to die" (20:1). But Hezekiah's words and tears implied, "No! I want to live and have sons who will do mighty things, and I myself have my best years ahead of me!" Read this chapter and the next, and note at least ten terrible things (see also footnote on II Kings 20:17) that resulted which only God could foresee and that only Hezekiah's death executed at the time God intended it would have prevented. But Hezekiah interfered. The only safe prayer policy is "God's will; nothing more; nothing less; nothing else; at any cost" (see Luke 22:42, Acts 21:14). It pays triumphantly! Martin Luther is quoted as saying, "Blessed is he who submits to the will of God; he can never be unhappy. Men may deal with him as they will . . . ; he is without care; he knows that 'all things work together for good' for him" (Rom. 8:28) (Martin Luther, cited by J.P. Lange, *A Commentary*).

15 Isaiah said, What have they seen in your house? Hezekiah answered, They have seen all that is in my house. There is no treasure of mine that I have not shown them.
16 Then Isaiah said to Hezekiah, Hear the word of the Lord!
17 Behold, the time is coming when [j]all that is in your house, and that which your forefathers have stored up till this day, shall be carried to Babylon; nothing shall be left, says the Lord.
18 And some of your sons who shall be born to you shall be taken away, and they shall be eunuchs in the palace of Babylon's king.
19 Then said Hezekiah to Isaiah, The word of the Lord you have spoken is good. For he thought, Is it not good, if [all this evil is meant for the future and] peace and security shall be in my days?
20 The rest of the acts of Hezekiah, and all his might, and how he made the pool and the canal and brought water into the city, are they not written in the Book of the Chronicles of the Kings of Judah?
21 Hezekiah slept with his fathers. Manasseh his son reigned in his stead.

21 MANASSEH WAS twelve years old when he began his fifty-five-year [wicked] reign in Jerusalem. His mother's name was Hephzibah.
2 He [Hezekiah's son] did evil in the sight of the Lord, after the [idolatrous] practices of the [heathen] nations whom the Lord cast out before the Israelites.
3 For he built up again the high places which Hezekiah his father had destroyed; and he reared up altars for Baal and made an Asherah, as did Ahab king of Israel, and worshiped all the [starry] hosts of the heavens and served them!
4 And he built [heathen] altars in the house of the Lord, of which the Lord said, In Jerusalem will I put My [k]Name [and the pledge of My presence].
5 And he [good Hezekiah's son] built altars for all the hosts of the heavens in the two courts of the house of the Lord!
6 And he made his son pass through the fire *and* burned him as an offering [to Molech]; he practiced soothsaying and augury, and dealt with mediums and wizards! He did much wickedness in the sight of the Lord, provoking Him to anger.
7 He made a graven image of [the goddess] Asherah and set it in the house, of which the Lord said to David and to Solomon his son, In this house and in Jerusalem, which I have chosen out of all the tribes of Israel, will I put My Name [and the pledge of My presence] forever;
8 And I will not cause the feet of Israel to wander any more out of the land which I gave their fathers, if only they will observe to do according to all that I have commanded them and according to all the law that My servant Moses commanded them.
9 But they would not listen; and Manasseh seduced them to do more evil than the nations did whom the Lord destroyed before the Israelites!
10 And the Lord said through His servants the prophets:
11 Because Manasseh king of Judah has committed these abominations, and has done wickedly above all that the Amorites did who were before him, and has made Judah also to sin with his idols,

---

j This is the first of ten tragic results of Hezekiah's self-willed prayer, which God's plan for Hezekiah's death would have prevented (see the footnote on 20:6). For a listing of these results see II Kings 20:18; 21:1, 3, 4, 6, 9, 14, 16, 20. **k** See footnote on Deut. 12:5.

12 Therefore thus says the Lord, the God of Israel: Behold, I am bringing such evil upon Jerusalem and Judah, that whoever hears of it, both his ears shall tingle!
13 And I will stretch over Jerusalem the measuring line of Samaria and the plummet of the house of Ahab; and I will wipe Jerusalem as one wipes a dish, wiping it and turning it upside down.
14 And I will cast off the rest of My inheritance and deliver them into the hands of their enemies; and they shall become a prey and a spoil to all their enemies,
15 For they have done evil in My sight and have provoked Me to anger since their fathers came out of Egypt to this day.
16 Moreover, Manasseh shed very much innocent blood, filling Jerusalem from one end to another—besides his sin in making Judah sin, by doing evil in the sight of the Lord! [II Chron. 33:1-10.]
17 The rest of the acts of Manasseh, all that he did, and his sin that he committed, are they not written in the Book of the Chronicles of the Kings of Judah?
18 Manasseh slept with his fathers and was buried in the garden of his own house, in the garden of Uzza. Amon his son reigned in his stead.
19 Amon was twenty-two years old when he began his two-year reign in Jerusalem. His mother was Meshullemeth daughter of Haruz of Jotbah.
20 [But] he also did evil in the sight of the Lord, as his father Manasseh had done. [II Kings 23:26, 27; 24:3, 4.]
21 He walked in all the ways of his father; and he served the idols that his father served, and worshiped them;

speak the Word

22 He forsook the Lord, the God of his [forefathers], and did not walk in the way of the Lord.
23 The servants of Amon conspired against him and killed the king in his own house.
24 But the people of the land killed all those who had conspired against King Amon, and made Josiah his son king in his stead.
25 The rest of the acts of Amon, are they not written in the Book of the Chronicles of the Kings of Judah?
26 He was buried in his tomb in the garden of Uzza. Josiah his son succeeded him.

22 JOSIAH WAS eight years old when he began his thirty-one-year reign in Jerusalem. His mother was Jedidah daughter of Adaiah of Bozkath.

putting the Word to work

Have you ever doubted someone's spiritual leadership because he or she was young? Josiah was a young king (see II Kings 22:1), yet he led his people in great spiritual renewal, restoring worship and leading the people back into a right relationship with God. Encourage and pray for your children and other Christian young people, that they would walk in the destinies God has for them.

2 He did right in the sight of the Lord and walked in all the ways of David his [forefather], and turned not aside to the right hand or to the left.
3 In the eighteenth year of King Josiah, he sent Shaphan son of Azaliah, the son of Meshullam, the scribe, to the Lord's house, saying,

God, may I never forsake You or fail to walk in Your ways.
ADAPTED FROM II KINGS **21:22**

like a child

In II Kings 22:1, we see that Josiah became king when he was only eight years old. In II Kings 11:21, Joash became king at age seven; and in II Kings 21:1, Manasseh became king at age twelve. These boys were forced to grow up quickly!

Many people feel that they, like these young kings, were forced to grow up too fast. When that happened, they lost something, and that loss was detrimental to their enjoyment of adulthood.

As adults we should be able to accomplish things in our lives without feeling burdened. We should be responsible and yet lighthearted enough to enjoy our daily lives, even our work, as we read in Ecclesiastes 5:18: "Behold, what I have seen to be good and fitting is for one to eat and drink, and to find enjoyment in all the labor in which he labors under the sun all the days which God gives him—for this is his [allotted] part."

I believe we should be able to enjoy every single thing we do. Some years ago this fact was brought to my attention because I realized I was past forty years of age, married with four children, and yet I could not say I had ever really enjoyed much of my life.

John 10:10 tells us Jesus came to this earth so that you and I might have life and enjoy it to the full. I really think we have forgotten how to enjoy life. We need to learn how to be childlike, because if there is one thing a child knows how to do, it is to enjoy anything and everything! But when a child is forced to grow up too quickly without being permitted to be a child, he often ends up with tremendous emotional problems.

Not being permitted to play will steal a person's childhood and his enjoyment of adulthood. My problem was thinking I had to deserve every bit of fun, enjoyment, or blessing that came my way. Now I have learned to work until quitting time and then leave whatever I am doing for the next day. If you and I don't do that, we open ourselves up to burnout—and once we get burned-out, it is very hard to recover.

The good things that come to us in this life are given to us by the Lord (see James 1:17). He wants to give them to us. He wants us to enjoy life to the fullest. If you lost part of your childhood because you had to grow up too quickly, pray and ask God to restore your joy, your childlike faith, and your ability to celebrate life.

---

4 Go up to Hilkiah the high priest, that he may count the money brought into the house of the Lord, which the keepers of the door have gathered from the people. [II Kings 12:4ff.]

5 And let them deliver it into the hands of the workmen who have oversight of the Lord's house, to give to the laborers engaged in the repairing of the Lord's house—

6 That is, to the carpenters, builders, and masons—and to buy timber and hewn stone to repair the house.

7 However, there was no accounting required of them for the money delivered into their hands, because they dealt faithfully.

8 Hilkiah the high priest said to Shaphan the scribe, I have found the Book of the Law in the house of the Lord! Hilkiah gave the book to Shaphan, and he read it.

9 And Shaphan the scribe came to the king and reported to him: Your servants have gathered the money that was found in the house and have delivered it into the hands of the workmen who have oversight of the house of the Lord.

10 Then Shaphan the scribe told the king, Hilkiah the priest has given me a book. And Shaphan read it before the king.

11 And when the king heard the words of the Book of the Law, he rent his clothes.

12 And the king commanded Hilkiah the priest, Ahikam son of Shaphan, Achbor son of Micaiah, Shaphan the scribe, and Asaiah servant of the king,

13 Go, inquire of the Lord for me and for the people and for all Judah concerning the words of this book that has been found. For great is the wrath of the Lord that is kindled against us because our fathers have not listened *and* obeyed the words of this book, to do according to all that is written concerning us.

14 So Hilkiah the priest, Ahikam, Achbor, Shaphan, and Asaiah went to Huldah the prophetess, the wife of Shallum son of Tikvah, the son of Harhas, keeper of the wardrobe—now she dwelt in Jerusalem, in the Second Quarter—and they talked with her.

15 She said to them, Thus says the Lord, the God of Israel: Tell the man who sent you to me,

16 Thus says the Lord: Behold, I will bring evil upon this place and upon its inhabitants, according to all the words of the book which the king of Judah has read.

17 Because they have forsaken Me and have burned incense to other gods, provoking Me to anger with all the work of their hands, therefore My wrath will be kindled against this place and will not be quenched.

18 But to the king of Judah, who sent you to inquire of the Lord, say this, Thus says the Lord, the God of Israel, regarding the words you have heard:

19 Because your heart was [tender and] penitent and you humbled yourself before the Lord when you heard what I said against this place and against its inhabitants, that they should become a desolation, [an astonishment and] a curse, and you have rent your clothes and wept before Me, I also have heard you, says the Lord.

20 Behold, therefore [King Josiah], I

putting the Word to work

Do you ever wonder if it is just too late, or perhaps that your sin is too great, to receive forgiveness from God? Even though the sin of the people was enormous, God responded to Josiah's repentant heart (see II Kings 22:18, 19). Do not hesitate to seek God's forgiveness; He will not turn away a humble, tender heart.

speak the Word

God, help me to keep my heart tender, penitent, and humble before You.
ADAPTED FROM II KINGS 22:19

the gift of a tender heart

In II Kings 22:19, Huldah the prophetess, speaking for the Lord, declared that King Josiah had a tender heart. Having a tender heart is equivalent to having a tender conscience, and tenderness of conscience is vital to our being used by God.

It is dangerous to become hard-hearted and develop a seared conscience so that we cannot really tell if we are doing anything wrong or not. One way we develop a tender conscience is by repenting quickly if God convicts us of something and by not making excuses for our behavior.

When God shows us we have done something wrong, we need to say, "You're right, Lord, I'm wrong. There is no excuse, so please forgive me and help me not do it again." It is amazing how much that will help us have a tender conscience toward God. But as soon as we start trying to reason things out and make excuses for our wrongs, we start getting a little callous on our consciences. It becomes just a little bit harder for us to feel than it was the time before.

For example, if I mistreat someone without repenting, my conscience starts to become calloused. The next time I do it, my conscience becomes a little more calloused. Soon, although I go around presenting myself as a person who loves God, He cannot use me anymore because I am mistreating people and talking down to them and talking wrongly to them. The worst thing is that I don't even realize I am doing it, because I no longer have a tender heart and a tender conscience toward God.

We must remember that God does not care how gifted or talented we are; His primary concern is our heart attitude. If we have willing hearts, stirred-up hearts, wise hearts, perfect hearts, and tender consciences, then the devil is no real threat to us or our future, because nothing can stop God from using us.

Acts 23:1 describes the good conscience Paul had. He said, "Brethren, I have lived before God, doing my duty with a perfectly good conscience until this very day." How many of us can go to bed at night saying, "Well, Lord, I can go to sleep with a perfectly good conscience"? Paul goes on to describe what he did to keep his conscience tender: "Therefore I always exercise and discipline myself [mortifying my body, deadening my carnal affections, bodily appetites, and worldly desires, endeavoring in all respects] to have a clear (unshaken, blameless) conscience, void of offense toward God and toward men" (Acts 24:16).

Why did Paul strive to keep a clear conscience? Because he knew he could not minister to others out of a hard heart. He knew that if he wanted to help people, he had to keep a tender conscience toward God. I believe all of us should pray regularly, "Lord, help me to have a tender heart and a tender conscience toward You."

will gather you to your fathers, taken to your grave in peace, and your eyes shall not see all the evil which I will bring on this place. And they brought the king word.

23

KING JOSIAH sent and gathered to him all the elders of Judah and of Jerusalem.

2 The king went up to the house of the Lord, and with him all the men of Judah, all the inhabitants of Jerusalem, the priests, the prophets, and all the people, both small and great. And he read in their ears all the words of the Book of the Covenant, which was found in the Lord's house.

3 The king stood [on the platform] by the pillar and made a covenant before the Lord—to walk after the Lord and to keep His commandments, His testimonies, and His statutes with all his heart and soul, to confirm the words of this covenant that were written in this book. And all the people stood to join in the covenant.

putting the Word to work

Do you have difficulty in figuring out what it means to follow God or how He would want you to respond in certain situations? Josiah realized that if he and those he ruled were to know how they were to follow God, they had to know His law (see II Kings 23:1–3). Likewise, if you want to walk in God's ways, it is important that you learn all you can about God and His ways by reading Scripture and doing what it says.

4 And the king commanded Hilkiah the high priest and the priests of the second rank and the keepers of the threshold to bring out of the temple of the Lord all the vessels made for Baal, for [the goddess] Asherah, and for all the hosts of the heavens; and he burned them outside Jerusalem in the fields of the Kidron, and carried their ashes to Bethel [where Israel's idolatry began]. [I Kings 12:28, 29.]

5 He put away the idolatrous priests whom the kings of Judah had ordained to burn incense in the high places in Judah's cities and round about Jerusalem—also those who burned incense to Baal, to the sun, to the moon, to the constellations [or twelve signs of the zodiac], and to all the hosts of the heavens.

6 And Josiah brought the Asherah from the house of the Lord to outside Jerusalem to the brook Kidron and burned it there, and beat it to dust and cast its dust upon the graves of the common people [who had sacrificed to it].

7 And he broke down the houses of the male cult prostitutes, which were by the house of the Lord, where the women wove [tent] hangings for the Asherah [shrines].

8 And [Josiah] brought all the [idolatrous] priests out of the city of Judah and defiled the high places, where the priests had burned incense, from Geba to Beersheba [north to south], and broke down the high places both at the entrance of the Gate of Joshua the governor of the city and that which was on one's left at the city's gate.

9 However, the priests of the high places were not allowed to sacrifice upon the Lord's altar in Jerusalem, but they ate unleavened bread among their brethren.

10 And Josiah defiled Topheth, which is in the Valley of Ben-hinnom [son of Hinnom], that no man might ever burn there his son or his daughter as an offering to Molech. [Ezek. 16:21.]

11 And he removed the horses that the kings of Judah had devoted to the sun from the entrance of the house of

the Lord, by the chamber of Nathan-melech the chamberlain, which was in the area, and he burned the chariots of the sun with fire.

12 And the altars on the roof of the upper chamber of Ahaz, which the kings of Judah had made, and the altars which Manasseh had made in the two courts of the house of the Lord, [Josiah] pulled down and beat them in pieces, and he [ran and] cast their dust into the brook Kidron.

13 And the king defiled the high places east of Jerusalem, south of the Mount of Corruption, which Solomon the king of Israel had built for Ashtoreth the abominable [goddess] of the Sidonians, for Chemosh the abominable god of the Moabites, and for Milcom the abominable [god] of the Ammonites.

14 He broke in pieces the pillars (images) and cut down the Asherim and replaced them with the bones of men [to defile the places forever].

15 Moreover, the altar at Bethel, the high place made by Jeroboam son of Nebat, who made Israel to sin, that altar with the high place Josiah tore down *and* broke in pieces its stones, beating them to dust, and burned the Asherah.

16 And as Josiah turned, he saw the tombs across on the mount, and he sent and brought the bones out of the tombs and burned them upon the altar and defiled it, in fulfillment of the word of the Lord which the man of God prophesied, who predicted these things [about this altar, naming Josiah before he was born]. [I Kings 13:2-5.]

17 Josiah said, What is that monument I see? The men of the city told him, It is the tomb of the man of God who came from Judah and foretold these things that you have just done against the altar of Bethel.

18 He said, Let him alone; let no man move his bones. So they let his bones alone, with the bones of the prophet that came out of Samaria. [I Kings 13:31, 32.]

19 Also Josiah took away all the houses of the high places in the cities of Samaria which the kings of Israel had made, provoking the Lord to anger, and he did to them all that he had done in Bethel.

20 He slew all the priests of the high places that were there upon the altars and burned men's bones upon them [to defile the places forever]. Then he returned to Jerusalem.

21 The king commanded all the people, Keep the Passover to the Lord your God, as it is written in this Book of the Covenant.

22 Surely such a Passover was not held from the days of Israel's judges, even in all the days of the kings of Israel or Judah.

23 But in the eighteenth year of King Josiah, this Passover was kept to the Lord in Jerusalem.

24 Moreover, Josiah put away the mediums, the wizards, the teraphim (household gods), the idols, and all the abominations that were seen in Judah and in Jerusalem, that he might establish the words of the law written in the book found by Hilkiah the priest in the house of the Lord.

25 There was no king like him before or after [Josiah] who turned to the Lord with all his heart and all his soul and all his might, according to all the Law of Moses.

26 Still the Lord did not turn from the fierceness of His great wrath, kindled against Judah because of all the provocations with which Manasseh had provoked Him.

27 And the Lord said, I will remove Judah also out of My sight as I have removed Israel, and will cast off this city, Jerusalem, which I have chosen, and the house, of which I said, My Name [and the pledge of My presence] shall be there.

28 The rest of the acts of Josiah, all that he did, are they not written in the Book of the Chronicles of Judah's Kings?

29 In his days Pharaoh Necho king of Egypt went up against the king of Assyria to the river Euphrates. King Josiah went out against him, but he slew Josiah at Megiddo when he saw him.

30 Josiah's servants carried him dead in a chariot from Megiddo, brought him to Jerusalem, and buried him in his own tomb. The people of the land anointed Jehoahaz son of Josiah king in his stead.

31 Jehoahaz was twenty-three years old when he began his three-month reign in Jerusalem. His mother was Hamutal daughter of Jeremiah of Libnah.

32 He did evil in the sight of the Lord, according to all [the evil] his forefathers had done.

33 And Pharaoh Necho put him in bonds at Riblah in the land of Hamath, that he might not reign in Jerusalem, and laid a tribute of a hundred talents of silver and a talent of gold upon the land.

34 Pharaoh Necho made Eliakim son of Josiah king in place of Josiah and changed his name to Jehoiakim. But he took Jehoahaz away to Egypt, where he died.

35 Jehoiakim gave the silver and the gold to Pharaoh, but he taxed the land to give the money as Pharaoh commanded. He exacted the silver and gold of the people of the land, from everyone according to his assessment, to give it to Pharaoh Necho.

36 Jehoiakim was twenty-five years old when he began his eleven-year reign in Jerusalem. His mother was Zebidah daughter of Pedaiah of Rumah.

37 He did evil in the sight of the Lord, like all his [forefathers] had done.

24 IN HIS days, Nebuchadnezzar king of Babylon came up, and Jehoiakim became his servant for three years; then he turned and rebelled against him.

2 The Lord sent against Jehoiakim bands of Chaldeans, of Syrians, of Moabites, and of Ammonites. And He sent them against Judah to destroy it, according to the word of the Lord which He spoke by His servants the prophets.

3 Surely this came upon Judah at the command of the Lord, to remove them out of His sight because of the sins of Manasseh according to all he had done,

4 And also for the innocent blood that he shed. For he filled Jerusalem with innocent blood, and the Lord would not pardon.

5 The rest of the acts of Jehoiakim, all that he did, are they not written in the Book of the Chronicles of Judah's Kings?

6 So Jehoiakim slept with his fathers. Jehoiachin his son reigned in his stead.

7 The king of Egypt came no more out of his land, for the king of Babylon had taken all that belonged to Egypt's king, from the River of Egypt to the river Euphrates.

8 Jehoiachin was eighteen years old when he began his three-month reign in Jerusalem. His mother was Nehushta daughter of Elnathan of Jerusalem.

9 And he did evil in the sight of the Lord, in keeping with all his father had done.

10 At that time the servants of Nebuchadnezzar king of Babylon came up to Jerusalem, and the city was besieged.

11 Nebuchadnezzar king of Babylon came to the city while his servants were besieging it.

12 Jehoiachin king of Judah surrendered to the king of Babylon, he, his mother, his servants, princes, and palace officials. The king of Babylon took him prisoner in the eighth year of Nebuchadnezzar's reign.

13 He carried off all the treasures of the Lord's house and the king's house, and cut in pieces all the vessels of gold in the temple of the Lord, which Solomon king of Israel had made, as the Lord had said.

14 He carried away all Jerusalem, all the princes, all the mighty men of valor, 10,000 captives, and all the craftsmen and smiths. None remained except the poorest of the land.

15 Nebuchadnezzar took captive to Babylon King Jehoiachin; his mother, his wives, his officials, and the chief *and* mighty men of the land [the prophet Ezekiel included] he took from Jerusalem to Babylon into exile. [Ezek. 1:1.]

16 And the king of Babylon brought captive to Babylon all the men of valor, 7,000, and craftsmen and smiths, 1,000, all strong and fit for war.

17 And the king of Babylon made Mattaniah, Jehoiachin's uncle, king in his stead and changed his name to Zedekiah.

18 Zedekiah was twenty-one years old when he began his eleven-year reign in Jerusalem. His mother was Hamutal daughter of Jeremiah of Libnah.

19 He did evil in the sight of the Lord, in keeping with all Jehoiakim had done.

20 For because of the anger of the Lord it came to the point in Jerusalem and Judah that He cast them out of His presence. And Zedekiah rebelled against the king of Babylon.

25 IN THE ninth year of Zedekiah's reign, on the tenth day of the tenth month, Nebuchadnezzar king of Babylon came with all his army against Jerusalem and laid siege to it, and they built siege works against it round about.

2 The city was besieged [nearly two years] until the eleventh year of King Zedekiah.

3 On the ninth day of the fourth month the famine was complete in the city; there was no food for the people of the land.

4 Then the city was broken through; the king and all the warriors fled by night by way of the gate between the two walls by the king's garden, though the Chaldeans were round about the city. [The king] went by the way toward the Arabah (the plain).

5 The Chaldean army pursued the king and overtook him in the plains of Jericho. All his army was scattered from him.

6 So they captured Zedekiah and brought him to the king of Babylon at Riblah, and sentence was passed on him.

7 And they slew the sons of Zedekiah before his eyes and put out the eyes of Zedekiah and bound him in double fetters [hands and feet] and carried him to Babylon. [Foretold in Jer. 34:3; Ezek. 12:13.]

8 On the seventh day of the fifth month of the nineteenth year of King Nebuchadnezzar of Babylon, Nebuzaradan, captain of the Babylonian king's guard, came to Jerusalem.

9 He burned the house of the Lord, the king's house, and all the houses of Jerusalem; every great house he burned down.

10 All the army of the Chaldeans who were with the captain of the [Babylonian] guard broke down the walls around Jerusalem.

11 Now the rest of the people left in the city and the deserters who fell away to the king of Babylon, along with the rest of the multitude, Nebuzaradan the captain of the guard carried into exile.

12 But the captain of the guard left some of the poorest of the land to be vinedressers and soil tillers.

13 The bronze pillars in the Lord's house and [its] bases and the bronze Sea the Chaldeans smashed and carried the bronze to Babylon.

14 And they took away the pots, shovels, snuffers, dishes for incense, all the bronze vessels used in the temple service,

15 The firepans, and bowls. Such things as were of gold the captain of the guard took away as gold, and what was of silver [he took away] as silver.

16 The two pillars, the one Sea, and the bases, which Solomon had made for the house of the Lord, the bronze of all these articles was incalculable.

17 The height of the one pillar was eighteen cubits, and upon it was a capital of bronze. The height of the capital was three cubits; a network and pomegranates round about the capital were all of bronze. And the second pillar had the same as these, with a network.

18 The captain of the guard took Seraiah the chief priest, Zephaniah the second priest, and the three keepers of the threshold.

19 And out of the city he took an officer who was in command of the men of war and five men of the king's personal advisors, who were found in the city, and the scribe of the captain of the army who mustered the people of the land and sixty men of the people who were found in the city.

20 Nebuzaradan the captain of the guard took these and brought them to the king of Babylon at Riblah.

21 The king of Babylon smote and killed them at Riblah in the land of Hamath [north of Damascus]. So Judah was taken into exile.

22 Over the people whom Nebuchadnezzar king of Babylon had left in the land of Judah he appointed as governor Gedaliah son of Ahikam, the son of Shaphan.

23 And when all the captains of the forces and their men heard that the king of Babylon had made Gedaliah governor, they came with their men to Gedaliah at Mizpah, namely, Ishmael son of Nethaniah, Johanan son of Kareah, Seraiah son of Tanhumeth the Netophathite, and Jaazaniah son of the Maacathite.

24 And Gedaliah swore to them and their men, saying, Do not be afraid of the Chaldean officials. Dwell in the land and serve the king of Babylon, and it shall be well with you.

25 But in the seventh month Ishmael son of Nethaniah, the son of Elishama, of the royal family [so having a claim to be governor], came with ten men and smote and killed Gedaliah and the Jews and the Chaldeans who were with him at Mizpah.

26 Then all the people, both small and great, and the captains of the forces arose and went to Egypt, for they were afraid of the Chaldeans.

27 And in the thirty-seventh year of the captivity of Jehoiachin king of Judah, on the twenty-seventh day of the twelfth month, Evil-merodach king of Babylon, in the year that he began to reign, showed favor to Jehoiachin king of Judah and released him from prison;

28 He spoke kindly to him and ranked him above the kings with him in Babylon.

29 Jehoiachin put off his prison garments, and he dined regularly at the king's table the remainder of his life.

30 And his allowance, a continual one, was given him by the king, every day a portion, for the rest of his life.

First Chronicles

Author:
Attributed to Ezra

Date:
Probably between 425 BC and 400 BC

Everyday Life Principles:
God is faithful.

Faithfulness to God results in rewards from God.

God's presence makes all the difference in our everyday lives.

First Chronicles is full of encouragement to stay faithful to God. Its first nine chapters chronicle the family line of the godly King David, and its remaining twenty chapters tell the story of his righteous reign over God's people.

A key theme we find throughout I Chronicles is the theme of God's faithfulness to His people. His faithfulness brings blessings, which is why He continually calls for faithfulness and warns against unfaithfulness.

One of the highlights of this book is David's bringing the ark (the symbol of God's presence) back to Jerusalem. This ancient story reminds us of how desperately we need God's presence in every part of our lives today.

As you read I Chronicles, remember that faithfulness has its rewards, and unfaithfulness leads to trouble. When we are unfaithful, God always takes us back because of His mercy, but we often suffer the consequences of breaking fellowship with Him. Let me encourage you today to stay faithful to God in every situation in your life. Remember that He is faithful to you. He is always near you, always watching over you, always wanting the best for you.

When you come across the story of the ark's return to Jerusalem, consider the various aspects of your life—your family, your work, your friendships, your home, your spiritual life, your entertainment, your hobbies, your finances, and the other things that concern you—and ask God to increase His presence more and more in your life.

1 ADAM [his genealogical line], Seth, Enosh,

2 Kenan, Mahalalel, Jared,

3 Enoch, Methuselah, Lamech,

4 Noah, Shem, Ham, and Japheth.

5 The sons of Japheth: Gomer, Magog, Madai, Javan, Tubal, Meshech, and Tiras.

6 The sons of Gomer: Ashkenaz, Diphath, and Togarmah.

7 The sons of Javan: Elishah, Tarshish, Kittim, and Rodanim.

8 The sons of Ham: Cush, Mizraim (Egypt), Put, and Canaan.

9 The sons of Cush: Seba, Havilah, Sabta, Raamah, and Sabteca. The sons of Raamah: Sheba and Dedan.

10 Cush was the father of Nimrod; he began to be a mighty one upon the earth.

11 Mizraim (Egypt) was the father of the Ludim, Anamim, Lehabim, Naphtuhim,

12 Pathrusim, Casluhim, from whom came the Philistines, and the Caphtorim.

13 Canaan was the father of Sidon his firstborn, and Heth,

14 The Jebusites, Amorites, Girgashites,

15 Hivites, Arkites, Sinites,

16 Arvadites, Zemarites, and Hamathites.

17 The sons of Shem: Elam, Asshur, Arpachshad, Lud, Aram, Uz, Hul, Gether, and Meshech.

18 Arpachshad was the father of Shelah, Shelah of Eber.

19 To Eber were born two sons: the name of the one was Peleg, because in his days [the population of] the earth was divided [according to its languages], and his brother's name was Joktan.

20 Joktan was the father of Almodad, Sheleph, Hazarmaveth, Jerah,

21 Hadoram, Uzal, Diklah,

22 Ebal, Abimael, Sheba,

23 Ophir, Havilah, and Jobab. All these were the sons of Joktan.

24 Shem, Arpachshad, Shelah,

25 Eber, Peleg, Reu,

26 Serug, Nahor, Terah,

27 Abram, the same as Abraham.

28 The sons of Abraham: Isaac and Ishmael.

29 These are their descendants: The firstborn of Ishmael, Nebaioth; Kedar, Adbeel, Mibsam,

30 Mishma, Dumah, Massa, Hadad, Tema,

31 Jetur, Naphish, and Kedemah. These are the sons of Ishmael.

32 Now the sons of Keturah, Abraham's concubine: she bore Zimran, Jokshan, Medan, Midian, Ishbak, and Shuah. The sons of Jokshan: Sheba and Dedan.

33 The sons of Midian: Ephah, Epher, Hanoch, Abida, and Eldaah. All these are the sons [and grandsons] of Keturah.

34 Abraham was the father of Isaac. The sons of Isaac: Esau and Israel.

35 The sons of Esau: Eliphaz, Reuel, Jeush, Jalam, and Korah.

36 The sons of Eliphaz: Teman, Omar, Zephi, Gatam, Kenaz, Timna, and Amalek.

37 The sons of Reuel: Nahath, Zerah, Shammah, and Mizzah.

38 The sons of Seir: Lotan, Shobal, Zibeon, Anah, Dishon, Ezer, and Dishan.

39 The sons of Lotan: Hori and Homam; and Timna was Lotan's sister.

40 The sons of Shobal: Alian, Manahath, Ebal, Shephi, and Onam. The sons of Zibeon: Aiah and Anah.

41 The son of Anah: Dishon. The sons of Dishon: Hamran, Eshban, Ithran, and Cheran.

42 The sons of Ezer: Bilhan, Zaavan, [and] Jaakan. The sons of Dishan: Uz and Aran.

43 These are the kings who reigned in the land of Edom before any king reigned over the Israelites: Bela son of Beor; the name of his city was Dinhabah.

do things God's way

As believers, we need to be reminded of our heritage in God. The author of I Chronicles (presumed to be Ezra) provides us with a list of families among God's people, and as he does, we can remember and honor the legacy of faith in our own lives.

First Chronicles 1:27 mentions Abram. We recall that Genesis 12 teaches us that God called Abram to leave his family, his home, and all he was familiar with and go to a place God would show him. Just imagine—Abram left everything, not having any idea where he was supposed to go. As a result of his radical obedience, God made some very radical promises to him—promises of blessing, wealth, fame, leadership, descendants, and so on. God entered into covenant with Abram, changing his name to Abraham (see Genesis 17:5). Gold told Abraham that if he would believe, it would be counted unto him as right standing with God, and he would be taken care of in every way (see Genesis 15:5, 6).

Abraham believed God! That is all God asks of us: "Believe." Not just *for* things, but *in* and *through* things. Abraham believed God for a child that would be his heir, but he had to believe God "through" some difficult and lengthy things before he saw the promised child. You might say that those years of waiting were his "silent years," years during which he believed God, even though there was no outward evidence to him or anyone else that God had truly spoken to him.

During those silent years of waiting, Abraham took action that was not God-inspired when he followed his wife's advice and took her maid to be his secondary wife. Abraham's name has the prophetic meaning "father of a multitude" because God was planning to make him the father of many nations. But because Abraham and his wife, Sarah, got tired of waiting for God's promise, they took matters into their own hands, and Sarah's maid by Abraham gave birth to Ishmael. Although Abraham loved Ishmael, he was not the promised child and eventually brought great pain to Abraham and difficulty into his life.

There are times in our lives, as in Abraham's, when God simply lets us go our own way so we can learn by experience that "our way" does not work. We suffer during these years. We experience confusion and frustration, but we eventually emerge from our struggles as changed people, finally ready to do things God's way!

44 When Bela died, Jobab son of Zerah of Bozrah reigned in his stead. **45** When Jobab died, Husham of the land of the Temanites reigned in his stead. **46** When Husham died, Hadad [I of Edom] son of Bedad, who defeated Midian in the field of Moab, reigned in his stead; his city was Avith. **47** When Hadad [I] died, Samlah of Masrekah reigned in his stead. **48** When Samlah died, Shaul of Rehoboth on the River [Euphrates] reigned in his stead.

49 When Shaul died, Baal-hanan son of Achbor reigned in his stead.

50 When Baal-hanan died, Hadad [II] reigned in his stead; his city was Pai; his wife was Mehetabel daughter of Matred, the daughter of Mezahab.

51 Hadad died also. The chiefs of Edom were: chiefs Timna, Aliah, Jetheth,

52 Oholibamah, Elah, Pinon,

53 Kenaz, Teman, Mibzar,

54 Magdiel, and Iram. These are the chiefs of Edom.

2 THESE ARE the sons of Israel: Reuben, Simeon, Levi, Judah, Issachar, Zebulun,

2 Dan, Joseph, Benjamin, Naphtali, Gad, and Asher.

3 The sons of Judah: Er, Onan, and Shelah, whom Shua's daughter the Canaanitess bore him. Er, Judah's eldest, was evil in the Lord's sight, and He slew him.

4 Tamar, Judah's daughter-in-law, bore him Pharez and Zerah. All Judah's sons were five.

5 The sons of Pharez: Hezron and Hamul.

6 The sons of Zerah: Zimri, Ethan, Heman, Calcol, and Dara—five in all. [I Kings 4:31.]

7 The son of Carmi: Achar, the troubler of Israel, who transgressed in the matter of the devoted things. [Josh. 7:1.]

8 The son of Ethan: Azariah.

9 The sons of Hezron who were born to him: Jerahmeel, Ram, and Chelubai (that is, Caleb).

10 Ram was the father of Amminadab, and Amminadab of Nahshon, prince of the sons of Judah.

11 Nahshon was the father of Salma, Salma of Boaz,

be faithful and be blessed

One of the things we remember when we see Joseph's name in I Chronicles 2:2 is that he was faithful to God. Even though he was a slave in Potiphar's house, God blessed him and prospered him because He was with him everywhere he went (see Genesis 39:1–6).

Even when we are going through difficult times, God will bless us in them, not just when they are over. The important thing for us to do is keep a good attitude, which includes being thankful for what we do have and giving praise to God, worshipping Him for Who He is.

For example, even if your boss treats you improperly, does not recognize your true value, and will not let you do anything but sweep the floor, if God is with you, He can prosper you and make you successful in so many other ways. God can certainly promote you in His timing because all true promotion comes from the Lord (see Psalm 75:6, 7). Do not look to anything on this earth as your source; look only to God as your Source.

The world will soon recognize that God is with us. Some of those people who have rejected us in the past will come to see that God is with us; they will see the evidence of His presence in our lives. If we, like Joseph, will take our positions and be faithful in them while we wait on Him, God will raise us up in His timing, and it will become obvious that God's hand is upon us for good.

12 Boaz of Obed, and Obed of Jesse.
13 Jesse was the father of Eliab his firstborn, Abinadab second, Shimea third,
14 Nethanel fourth, Raddai fifth,
15 Ozem sixth, David seventh.
16 Their sisters were Zeruiah and Abigail. The sons of Zeruiah: Abishai, Joab, and Asahel, three.
17 Abigail bore Amasa, and the father of Amasa was Jether the Ishmaelite.
18 And Caleb son of Hezron had sons by his wife Azubah and by Jerioth. [Azubah's] sons were: Jesher, Shobab, and Ardon.
19 Azubah died, and Caleb married Ephrath, who bore him Hur.
20 Hur was the father of Uri, and Uri of Bezalel [the skillful craftsman who made the furnishings of the tabernacle]. [Exod. 31:2-5.]
21 Later, when Hezron was sixty years old, he married the daughter of Machir the father of Gilead, and she bore him Segub.
22 Segub was the father of Jair, who had twenty-three cities in the land of Gilead.
23 But Geshur and Aram took from them Havvoth-jair, with Kenath and its villages, sixty towns. All these were the descendants of Machir the father of Gilead.
24 After Hezron died in Caleb-ephrathah, Abiah, Hezron's wife, bore to him Ashhur the father of Tekoa.
25 The sons of Jerahmeel the first-born of Hezron: Ram the firstborn, Bunah, Oren, Ozem, and Ahijah.
26 Jerahmeel had another wife, named Atarah; she was the mother of Onam.
27 The sons of Ram the firstborn of Jerahmeel were: Maaz, Jamin, and Eker.
28 The sons of Onam: Shammai and Jada. The sons of Shammai: Nadab and Abishur.
29 Abishur's wife was Abihail; she bore him Ahban and Molid.

30 The sons of Nadab: Seled and Appaim. Seled died childless.
31 The son of Appaim: Ishi. The son of Ishi: Sheshan. The son of Sheshan: Ahlai.
32 The sons of Jada the brother of Shammai: Jether and Jonathan. Jether died childless.
33 The sons of Jonathan: Peleth and Zaza. These were the descendants of Jerahmeel.
34 Sheshan had no sons—only daughters. But Sheshan had a servant, an Egyptian, whose name was Jarha.
35 Sheshan gave his daughter to Jarha his servant as wife; she bore him Attai.
36 Attai was the father of Nathan, and Nathan of Zabad.
37 Zabad was the father of Ephlal, and Ephlal of Obed.
38 Obed was the father of Jehu, and Jehu of Azariah.
39 Azariah was the father of Helez, and Helez of Eleasah.
40 Eleasah was the father of Sismai, and Sismai of Shallum.
41 Shallum was the father of Jekamiah, and Jekamiah of Elishama.
42 The sons of Caleb the brother of Jerahmeel: Mesha his firstborn was the father of Ziph; and his son Mareshah [he was] the father of Hebron.
43 The sons of Hebron: Korah, Tappuah, Rekem, and Shema.
44 Shema was the father of Raham, the father of Jorkeam. And Rekem was the father of Shammai.
45 The son of Shammai was Maon; Maon's son was Beth-zur.
46 Ephah, Caleb's concubine, bore Haran, Moza, and Gazez; Haran was the father of Gazez.
47 The sons of Jahdai: Regem, Jotham, Geshan, Pelet, Ephah, and Shaaph.
48 Maacah, Caleb's concubine, bore Sheber and Tirhanah, and also
49 Shaaph the father of Madmannah

and Sheva the father of Machbenah and of Gibea; and the daughter of Caleb was Achsah.

50 These were the descendants of Caleb. The sons of Hur the firstborn of Ephrathah: Shobal the father of Kiriath-jearim,

51 Salma the father of Bethlehem, and Hareph the father of Beth-gader.

52 Shobal the father of Kiriath-jearim had [other] descendants: Ha-roeh, half [of the inhabitants] of Menuhoth [in Judah],

53 And the families of Kiriath-jearim: the Ithrites, Puthites, Shumathites, and Mishraites. From these came the Zorathites and the Eshtaolites.

54 The descendants of Salma: Bethlehem, the Netophathites, Atroth-beth-joab, and half of the Manahathites, [and] the Zorites,

55 And the families of scribes who dwelt at Jabez: the Tirathites, Shimeathites, and Sucathites. These are the Kenites who came from Hammath, the father of the house of Rechab.

3 THESE SONS of David were born to him in Hebron: the first-born was Amnon, of Ahinoam the Jezreelitess; second, Daniel (Chileab), of Abigail the Carmelitess;

2 Third, Absalom the son of Maacah daughter of Talmai king of Geshur; fourth, Adonijah, of Haggith;

3 Fifth, Shephatiah, of Abital; sixth, Ithream, of his wife Eglah.

4 These six were born to David in Hebron; there he reigned seven years and six months, and in Jerusalem he reigned thirty-three years.

5 These were born to [David] in Jerusalem: Shimea, Shobab, Nathan, Solomon—four of Bathshua (Bathsheba) daughter of Ammiel (Eliam);

6 Then Ibhar, Elishama, Eliphelet,

7 Nogah, Nepheg, Japhia,

8 Elishama, Eliada, and Eliphelet—nine in all.

9 These were all the sons of David, besides the sons of the concubines. And Tamar was their sister.

10 Solomon's descendants [omitting nonreigning offspring] were: his son Rehoboam. Abijah was his son, Asa his son, Jehoshaphat his son,

11 Jehoram (Joram) his son, Ahaziah his son, Joash his son,

12 Amaziah his son, Azariah his son, Jotham his son,

13 Ahaz his son, Hezekiah his son, Manasseh his son,

14 Amon his son, Josiah his son.

15 The descendants of Josiah: first-born, Johanan; second, Jehoiakim; third, Zedekiah; fourth, Shallum.

16 The descendants of Jehoiakim: Jehoiachin (Jeconiah) his son, Zedekiah his son.

17 The descendants of Jehoiachin the captive: Shealtiel his son,

18 Malchiram, Pedaiah, Shenazzar, Jekamiah, Hoshama, and Nedabiah.

19 The sons of Pedaiah: Zerubbabel and Shimei. The sons of Zerubbabel: Meshullam, Hananiah. And Shelomith was their sister;

20 And Hashubah, Ohel, Berechiah, Hasadiah, [and] Jushab-hesed—five [the sons of Meshullam?].

21 The sons of Hananiah: Pelatiah and Jeshaiah, whose son was Repha-iah, his son Arnan, his son Obadiah, his son Shecaniah.

22 The son of Shecaniah: Shemaiah.

putting the Word to work

Have you ever wondered why there are so many genealogies in the Bible? First Chronicles is full of them! Clearly, family is important to God. When you asked Jesus to forgive your sins and to come into your life, God adopted you into His family. Thank Him for your brothers and sisters in Christ, and ask Him to help you fully enjoy and experience the blessings of belonging to His family.

The sons of Shemaiah: Hattush, Igal, Bariah, Neariah, and Shaphat—six in all.

23 The sons of Neariah: Elioenai, Hizkiah, and Azrikam—three in all.

24 The sons of Elioenai: Hodaviah, Eliashib, Pelaiah, Akkub, Johanan, Delaiah, and Anani—seven in all.

4 THE SONS of Judah: Perez, Hezron, Carmi, Hur, and Shobal.

2 Reaiah son of Shobal was the father of Jahath, and Jahath of Ahumai and Lahad. These were the families of the Zorathites.

3 These were the sons of [Hur] the father of Etam: Jezreel, Ishma, and Idbash. And their sister was Hazzelelponi.

4 And Penuel was the father of Gedor, and Ezer the father of Hushah. These were the sons of Hur, the eldest of Ephrathah (Ephrath), the father of Bethlehem.

5 Ashur the father of Tekoa had two wives, Helah and Naarah.

6 Naarah bore him Ahuzzam, Hepher, Temeni, and Haahashtari. These were Naarah's sons.

7 The sons of Helah: Zereth, Izhar, and Ethnan.

8 Koz was the father of Anub, Zobebah, and the families of Aharhel son of Harum.

9 Jabez was honorable above his brothers; but his mother named him Jabez [sorrow maker], saying, Because I bore him in pain.

10 Jabez cried to the God of Israel, saying, Oh, that You would bless me and enlarge my border, and that Your hand might be with me, and You would keep me from evil so it might not hurt me! And God granted his request.

11 Chelub the brother of Shuhah was the father of Mehir, the father of Eshton.

12 Eshton was the father of Beth-rapha, Paseah, and Tehinnah the father of Ir-nahash. These are the men of Recah.

13 The sons of Kenaz: Othniel and Seraiah. The sons of Othniel: Hathath [and Meonothai].

14 Meonothai was father of Ophrah, and Seraiah of Joab the father of Geharashim [the Valley of Craftsmen], so named because they were craftsmen.

15 The sons of Caleb [Joshua's companion] son of Jephunneh: Iru, Elah, and Naam. The son of Elah: Kenaz.

16 The sons of Jehallelel: Ziph, Ziphah, Tiria, and Asarel.

17 The sons of Ezrah: Jether, Mered, Epher, and Jalon. aThese are the sons of Bithiah daughter of Pharaoh, whom Mered married: she bore Miriam, Shammai, and Ishbah the father of Eshtemoa.

18 And Mered's Jewish wife bore Jered the father of Gedor, Heber the father of Soco, and Jekuthiel the father of Zanoah.

19 The sons of the wife of Hodiah, the sister of Naham, were: the father of Keilah the Garmite, and Eshtemoa the Maacathite.

speak the Word

God, I pray like Jabez that You will bless me and enlarge my border, and that Your hand might be with me, and that You would keep me from evil.
ADAPTED FROM I CHRONICLES 4:10

---

a This clause, "These are the sons of Bithiah daughter of Pharaoh, whom Mered married," has been transposed from I Chron. 4:18 to I Chron. 4:17.

20 The sons of Shimon: Amnon, Rinnah, Ben-hanan, and Tilon. The sons of Ishi: Zoheth and Ben-zoheth.

21 The sons of Shelah son of Judah: Er the father of Lecah, and Laadah the father of Mareshah, and the families of the house of the linen workers at Beth-ashbea,

22 And Jokim, the men of Cozeba, Joash, and Saraph, who ruled in Moab, and returned to [Bethlehem]. These are ancient matters.

23 These were the potters and those who dwelt among plantations and hedges at Netaim and Gederah; there they dwelt with the king for his work.

24 The sons of Simeon: Nemuel, Jamin, Jarib, Zerah, and Shaul;

25 Shallum was his [Shaul's] son, Mibsam his son, Mishma his son.

26 The sons of Mishma: Hammuel his son, Zaccur his son, Shimei his son.

27 Shimei had sixteen sons and six daughters, but his brothers did not have many children; neither did all their family multiply like the children of Judah.

28 They dwelt at Beersheba, Moladah, Hazar-shual,

29 Bilhah, Ezem, Tolad,

30 Bethuel, Hormah, Ziklag,

31 Beth-marcaboth, Hazar-susim, Beth-biri, and at Shaaraim. These were their towns [and villages] until the reign of David.

32 There were also Etam, Ain, Rimmon, Tochen, and Ashan—five towns—

33 And all their villages that were round about these towns, as far as Baal[-ath-beer]. These were their settlements, and they had their genealogical record.

34 Meshobab, Jamlech, Joshah son of Amaziah,

35 Joel, Jehu son of Joshibiah, the son of Seraiah, the son of Asiel,

36 Also Elioenai, Jaakobah, Jeshohaiah, Asaiah, Adiel, Jesimiel, Benaiah,

37 Ziza son of Shiphi, the son of Allon, the son of Jedaiah, the son of Shimri, the son of Shemaiah.

38 These mentioned by name were princes in their families; and their fathers' houses increased greatly [so they needed more room].

39 And they journeyed to the entrance of Gedor to the east side of the valley to seek pasture for their flocks.

40 And they found rich, good pasture, and the [cleared] land was wide, quiet, and peaceful, because people of Ham had dwelt there of old [and had left it a better place for those who came after them].

41 And these registered by name came in the days of Hezekiah king of Judah and destroyed their tents and the Meunim [foreigners] who were found there and exterminated them to this day, and they settled in their stead, because there was pasture for their flocks.

42 And some of them from the sons of Simeon, 500 men, went to Mount Seir, having for their leaders Pelatiah, and Neariah, Rephaiah, and Uzziel, the sons of Ishi.

43 They destroyed the remnant of the Amalekites who had escaped, and they have dwelt there to this day.

5 NOW [we come to] the sons of Reuben the firstborn of Israel. For [Reuben] was the eldest, but because he polluted his father's couch [with Bilhah his father's concubine] his birthright was given to the sons of Joseph [favorite] son of Israel; so the genealogy is not to be reckoned according to the birthright. [Gen. 35:22; 48:15-22; 49:3, 4.]

2 Judah prevailed above his brethren, and from him came the prince *and* leader [and eventually the Messiah]; yet the birthright was Joseph's. [Gen. 49:10; Mic. 5:2.]

3 The sons of Reuben the firstborn

life point

Notice in I Chronicles 5:1 that Reuben's birthright was given to the sons of Joseph. Why? Because Reuben "polluted his father's couch" (I Chronicles 5:1) with his father's concubine. A birthright was an enormous and extremely valuable blessing to a man during Bible times. Whoever had the birthright inherited "the best of the best" from his father. But Reuben forfeited all the blessings of the birthright for a few moments with a concubine. He lost a great inheritance because he could not control his emotions.

Ask God to help you perceive what is truly valuable and to never allow the lust of the flesh or your emotions to cause you to miss out on a blessing.

of Israel: Hanoch, Pallu, Hezron, and Carmi.

4 The sons of Joel: Shemaiah his son, Gog his son, Shimei his son,

5 Micah his son, Reaiah his son, Baal his son,

6 Beerah his son, whom Tilgath-pilneser king of Assyria carried away captive; he was a prince of the Reubenites.

7 And his brethren by their families, when the genealogy of their generations was reckoned: the chief Jeiel, and Zechariah,

8 Bela son of Azaz, the son of Shema, the son of Joel, who dwelt in Aroer as far as Nebo and Baal-meon.

9 Eastward [Bela] inhabited the land as far as the entrance into the desert this [west] side of the river Euphrates, because their cattle had multiplied in the land of Gilead.

10 In the days of [King] Saul they made war with the Hagrites or Ishmaelites, who fell by their hands; they dwelt in their tents in all the land east of Gilead.

11 The children of Gad who dwelt opposite them in the land of Bashan, as far as Salecah:

12 Joel the chief, Shapham the next, Janai, and Shaphat in Bashan.

13 Their kinsmen of the houses of their fathers: Michael, Meshullam, Sheba, Jorai, Jacan, Zia, and Eber—seven in all.

14 These were the sons of Abihail son of Huri, the son of Jaroah, the son of Gilead, the son of Michael, the son of Jeshishai, the son of Jahdo, the son of Buz.

15 Ahi son of Abdiel, the son of Guni, was chief in their fathers' houses.

16 They dwelt in Gilead, in Bashan and in its towns, and in all the suburbs *and* pasturelands of Sharon to their limits.

17 All these were enrolled by genealogies in the days of Jotham king of Judah and in the days of Jeroboam [II] king of Israel.

18 The sons of Reuben, the Gadites, and the half-tribe of Manasseh—valiant men able to bear buckler and sword and to shoot with bow and skillful in war—were 44,760 able *and* ready to go forth to war.

19 And [these Israelites, on the east side of the Jordan River] made war with the Hagrites [a tribe of northern Arabia], Jetur, Naphish, and Nodab.

20 They were given help against them, and the Hagrites *or* Ishmaelites were delivered into their hands, and all who were allied with them, for they cried to God in the battle; and He granted their entreaty, because they relied on, clung to, *and* trusted in Him.

21 And [these Israelites] took away their adversaries' herds: of their camels 50,000, and of sheep 250,000, and of donkeys 2,000, and of the lives of men 100,000.

22 For a great number fell mortally wounded, because the battle was

God's. And [these Israelites] dwelt in their territory until the captivity [by Assyria more than five centuries later]. [II Kings 15:29.]

23 And the people of the half-tribe of Manasseh dwelt in the land; their settlements spread from Bashan to Baal-hermon, Senir, and Mount Hermon.

24 And these were the heads of their fathers' houses: Epher, Ishi, Eliel, Azriel, Jeremiah, Hodaviah, and Jahdiel, mighty men of strength of mind *and* spirit [enabling them to encounter danger with firmness and personal bravery], famous men, and heads of the houses of their fathers.

25 They transgressed against the God of their fathers and played the harlot [by unfaithfulness to their own God and running] after the gods of the native peoples, whom God had destroyed before them.

26 So the God of Israel stirred up the spirit of Pul king of Assyria, [that is,] the spirit of Tilgath-pilneser king of Assyria, and he carried them away, the Reubenites, Gadites, and half-tribe of Manasseh and brought them to Halah, Habor, Hara, and the river Gozan, to this day.

6 THE SONS of Levi: Gershom, Kohath, and Merari.
2 The sons of Kohath: Amram, Izhar, Hebron, and Uzziel.

3 The children of Amram: Aaron, Moses, and Miriam. The sons also of Aaron: Nadab, Abihu, Eleazar, and Ithamar.

4 Eleazar was the father of Phinehas, Phinehas of Abishua.

5 Abishua was the father of Bukki, and Bukki of Uzzi,

6 Uzzi of Zerahiah, and Zerahiah of Meraioth,

7 Meraioth of Amariah, and Amariah of Ahitub,

8 Ahitub of Zadok, and Zadok of Ahimaaz,

9 Ahimaaz of Azariah, and Azariah of Johanan,

10 Johanan of Azariah, who was priest in the temple Solomon built in Jerusalem,

11 Azariah of Amariah, and Amariah of Ahitub,

12 Ahitub of Zadok, and Zadok of Shallum,

13 Shallum of Hilkiah, and Hilkiah of Azariah,

14 Azariah of Seraiah, and Seraiah of Jehozadak;

15 Jehozadak went into captivity when the Lord sent Judah and Jerusalem into exile by the hand of Nebuchadnezzar.

16 The sons of Levi: Gershom, Kohath, and Merari.

17 These are the names of the sons of Gershom: Libni and Shimei.

18 The sons of Kohath: Amram, Izhar, Hebron, and Uzziel.

19 The sons of Merari: Mahli and Mushi. These are the families of the Levites according to their fathers:

20 Of Gershom: Libni his son, Jahath his son, Zimmah his son,

21 Joah his son, Iddo his son, Zerah his son, Jeatherai his son.

22 The sons of Kohath: Amminadab his son, Korah his son, Assir his son,

23 Elkanah his son, Ebiasaph his son, Assir his son,

24 Tahath his son, Uriel his son, Uzziah his son, and Shaul his son.

25 And the sons of Elkanah: Amasai, Ahimoth,

26 Elkanah his son, Zophai his son, Nahath his son,

27 Eliab his son, Jeroham his son, Elkanah [Samuel's father] his son.

28 The sons of Samuel: the firstborn [Joel] and Abijah.

29 The sons of Merari: Mahli, Libni his son, Shimei his son, Uzza his son,

30 Shimea his son, Haggiah his son, Asaiah his son.

31 These David put over the service of song in the house of the Lord after

the ark of the covenant rested there [after being taken by the Philistines and later placed in the house of Abinadab, where it remained for nearly 100 years during the rest of Samuel's judgeship and Saul's entire reign and into David's reign].

32 They ministered before the tabernacle of the Tent of Meeting with singing until Solomon had built the Lord's house in Jerusalem, performing their service in due order.

33 These and their sons served of the Kohathites: Heman, the singer, the son of Joel, the son of Samuel [the great prophet and judge],

34 The son of Elkanah [III], the son of Jeroham, the son of Eliel, the son of Toah,

35 The son of Zuph, the son of Elkanah [II], the son of Mahath, the son of Amasai,

36 The son of Elkanah [I], the son of Joel, the son of Azariah, the son of Zephaniah,

37 The son of Tahath, the son of Assir, the son of Ebiasaph, the son of Korah,

38 The son of Izhar, the son of Kohath, the son of Levi, the son of Israel (Jacob).

39 Heman's [tribal] brother Asaph stood at his right hand: Asaph son of Berechiah, the son of Shimea,

40 The son of Michael, the son of Baaseiah, the son of Malchijah,

41 The son of Ethni, the son of Zerah, the son of Adaiah,

42 The son of Ethan, the son of Zimmah, the son of Shimei,

43 The son of Jahath, the son of Gershom, the son of Levi.

44 Their kinsmen the sons of Merari stood at the left hand: Ethan son of Kishi, the son of Abdi, the son of Malluch,

45 The son of Hashabiah, the son of Amaziah, the son of Hilkiah,

46 The son of Amzi, the son of Bani, the son of Shemer,

47 The son of Mahli, the son of Mushi, the son of Merari, the son of Levi.

48 And their brethren the Levites [who were not descended from Aaron] were appointed for all other kinds of service of the tabernacle of the house of God.

49 But [the line of] Aaron and his sons offered upon the altar of burnt offering and the altar of incense, ministering for all the work of the Holy of Holies, and to make atonement for Israel, according to all that Moses, God's servant, had commanded.

50 The sons of Aaron: Eleazar his son, Phinehas his son, Abishua his son,

51 Bukki his son, Uzzi his son, Zerahiah his son,

52 Meraioth his son, Amariah his son, Ahitub his son,

53 Zadok his son, Ahimaaz his son.

54 Their dwelling places are according to their settlements within their borders: to the sons of Aaron of the families of the Kohathites, for theirs was the [first] lot—[Josh. 21:10.]

55 To them they gave Hebron in the land of Judah and its surrounding suburbs.

56 But the fields of the city and its villages they gave to Caleb son of Jephunneh.

57 To the sons of Aaron they gave the city of refuge, Hebron; also Libnah with its pasturelands, Jattir, Eshtemoa with its pasturelands, [Josh. 21:13.]

58 Hilen with its pasturelands, Debir with its pasturelands,

59 Ashan with its pasturelands, and Beth-shemesh with its pasturelands.

60 And out of the tribe of Benjamin: Geba, Alemeth, and Anathoth, with their pasturelands. All their cities according to their families were thirteen.

61 And to the rest of the Kohathites ten cities were given by lot out of the family of the tribe [of Ephraim and of Dan and], of the half-tribe, the half of Manasseh. [Josh. 21:5.]

62 To the Gershomites, according to their families, [were allotted] thirteen cities out of the tribes of Issachar, Asher, Naphtali, and Manasseh in Bashan.

63 To the Merarites were given by lot, according to their families, twelve cities out of the tribes of Reuben, Gad, and Zebulun.

64 And the Israelites gave to the Levites these cities with their pasturelands.

65 They gave by lot out of the tribes of Judah, Simeon, and Benjamin these cities whose names are mentioned.

66 Some of the families of the Kohathites had cities in the allotted territory out of the tribe of Ephraim.

67 And [the Ephraimites] gave to [the Levites] the city of refuge, Shechem in the hill country of Ephraim; also Gezer, [both] with their suburbs *and* pasturelands;

68 Jokmeam, Beth-horon,

69 Aijalon, and Gath-rimmon, with their suburbs *and* pasturelands;

70 And out of the half-tribe of Manasseh [these cities], with their suburbs *and* pasturelands: Aner and Bileam, for the rest of the families of the sons of Kohath.

71 To the Gershomites were given out of the half-tribe of Manasseh: Golan in Bashan and Ashtaroth, with their suburbs *and* pasturelands;

72 Out of the tribe of Issachar, with their suburbs *and* pasturelands: Kedesh, Daberath,

73 Ramoth, and Anem;

74 Out of the tribe of Asher, with their suburbs *and* pasturelands: Mashal, Abdon,

75 Hukok, and Rehob;

76 And out of the tribe of Naphtali, with their suburbs *and* pasturelands: Kedesh in Galilee, Hammon, and Kiriathaim.

77 To the rest of the Merarites were given from the tribe of Zebulun: Rimmono and Tabor, with their suburbs *and* pasturelands;

78 On the other side of the Jordan, on the east side by Jericho, the Levites were given out of the tribe of Reuben [these cities], with their suburbs *and* pasturelands: Bezer in the wilderness, Jahzah,

79 Kedemoth, and Mephaath;

80 Out of the tribe of Gad [these cities], with their suburbs *and* pasturelands: Ramoth in Gilead, Mahanaim,

81 Heshbon, and Jazer.

7 THE SONS of Issachar were: Tola, Puah, Jashub, and Shimron—four in all.

2 The sons of Tola: Uzzi, Rephaiah, Jeriel, Jahmai, Ibsam, Shemuel (Samuel)—heads of their fathers' houses, descendants of Tola. They were mighty men of valor in their generations; their number in David's days was 22,600.

3 The son of Uzzi: Izrahiah. The sons of Izrahiah: Michael, Obadiah, Joel, Isshiah—five, all of them chief men.

4 And with them by their generations according to their fathers' houses were units of the army for war, 36,000, for they had many wives and children [with them].

5 Their kinsmen from all the families of Issachar, mighty men of valor, registered by genealogies, were in all 87,000.

6 The sons of Benjamin: Bela, Becher, and Jediael—three in all.

7 The sons of Bela: Ezbon, Uzzi, Uzziel, Jerimoth, and Iri—five, heads of the houses of their fathers, mighty men of valor. By their genealogies they numbered 22,034.

8 The sons of Becher: Zemirah, Joash, Eliezer, Elioenai, Omri, Jeremoth, Abijah, Anathoth, and Alemeth, all sons of Becher.

9 The number of them by their genealogies by generations, as heads of their fathers' houses, mighty warriors, was 20,200.

10 The son of Jediael: Bilhan. The sons of Bilhan: Jeush, Benjamin, Ehud, Chenaanah, Zethan, Tarshish, and Ahishahar.

11 All these were the sons of Jediael, according to the heads of their fathers' houses, mighty men of valor, 17,200, able *and* fit for service in war.

12 Shuppim and Huppim were the sons of Ir, and Hushim the son of Aher.

13 The sons of Naphtali: Jahziel, Guni, Jezer, and Shallum, whose [grandmother] was Bilhah.

14 The sons of Manasseh: Ashriel, whom his concubine the Aramitess bore; she bore Machir the father of Gilead.

15 And Machir took as wife the sister of Huppim and Shuppim; her name was Maacah. The name of a second [and later descendant, the first being Gilead], was Zelophehad; and Zelophehad had daughters [only]. [Num. 27:1-7.]

16 Maacah the wife of Machir bore a son; she called his name Peresh. The name of his brother was Sheresh; his sons were Ulam and Rakem.

17 The son of Ulam: Bedan. These were the sons of Gilead son of Machir, the son of Manasseh.

18 His sister Hammolecheth bore Ishbod, Abiezer, and Mahlah.

19 The sons of Shemida were: Ahian, Shechem, Likhi, and Aniam.

20 The sons of Ephraim: Shuthelah, Bered his son, Tahath [I] his son, Eleadah his son, Tahath [II] his son,

21 Zabad his son, and Shuthelah his son. [During Ephraim's lifetime, his sons] Ezer and Elead were slain by men of Gath born in the land, who had come down to steal the cattle [of the Ephraimites, probably before the Israelites left Egypt].

22 And Ephraim their father mourned many days, and his brethren came to comfort him.

23 Then his wife conceived and bore a son, and he called his name Beriah [in evil], because calamity had befallen his house.

24 [Beriah's] daughter was Sheerah, who built both Lower and Upper Beth-horon, and also Uzzen-sheerah.

25 Rephah was his son, and Resheph [his son]; Resheph's son was Telah, Tahan his son,

26 Ladan his son, Ammihud his son, Elishama his son,

27 Nun his son, Joshua [Moses' successor] his son.

28 And their possessions and settlements were Bethel and its towns, and eastward Naaran, and westward Gezer, and Shechem, and as far as Azzah (Gaza) with all their towns,

29 And along the borders of the Manassites, Beth-shean, Taanach, Megiddo, Dor, with all their towns. In these dwelt the sons of Joseph son of Israel.

30 The sons of Asher: Imnah, Ishvah, Ishvi, Beriah; and Serah their sister.

31 The sons of Beriah: Heber and Malchiel, who was the father of Birzaith.

32 Heber was the father of Japhlet, Shomer, Hotham, and Shua their sister.

33 The sons of Japhlet: Pasach, Bimhal, and Ashvath. These were the sons of Japhlet.

34 The sons of Shemer (Shomer) his brother: Rohgah, Jehubbah, and Aram.

35 The sons of his brother Helem (Hotham): Zophah, Imna, Shelesh, and Amal.

36 The sons of Zophah: Suah, Harnepher, Shual, Beri, Imrah,

37 Bezer, Hod, Shamma, Shilshah, Ithran, and Beera.

38 The sons of Jether: Jephunneh, Pispa, and Ara.

39 The sons of Ulla: Arah, Hanniel, and Rizia.

40 All these were offspring of Asher, heads of their fathers' houses, approved men, mighty warriors, chief of the princes. Their number enrolled by genealogies for service in war, was 26,000 men.

8 BENJAMIN WAS the father of Bela his firstborn, Ashbel the second, Aharah the third,

2 Nohah the fourth, and Rapha the fifth.

3 Bela's sons were: Addar, Gera, Abihud,

4 Abishua, Naaman, Ahoah,

5 Gera, Shephuphan, and Huram.

6 The sons of Ehud: These are the heads of the fathers' houses of the inhabitants of Geba; they were exiled to Manahath:

7 Naaman, Ahijah, and Gera, that is, Heglam, who was the father of Uzza and Ahihud.

8 Shaharaim had sons in the country of Moab after he had [divorced and] sent away Hushim and Baara his wives.

9 And by Hodesh his [Moabitish] wife he was the father of Jobab, Zibia, Mesha, Malcam,

10 Jeuz, Sachia, and Mirmah. These were his sons, heads of fathers' houses.

11 By Hushim [divorced] he had had sons: Abitub and Elpaal.

12 The sons of Elpaal: Eber, Misham, and Shemed, who built Ono and Lod with its towns,

13 And Beriah and Shema, who were heads of fathers' houses of the inhabitants of Aijalon, who put to flight the inhabitants of Gath,

14 And Ahio, Shashak, and Jeremoth.

15 The sons of Beriah: Zebadiah, Arad, Eder,

16 Michael, Ishpah, and Joha.

17 Zebadiah, Meshullam, Hizki, Heber,

18 Ishmerai, Izliah, and Jobab were the sons of Elpaal.

19 Jakim, Zichri, Zabdi,

20 Elienai, Zillethai, Eliel,

21 Adaiah, Beraiah, and Shimrath were the sons of Shimei.

22 Ishpan, Eber, Eliel,

23 Abdon, Zichri, Hanan,

24 Hananiah, Elam, Anthothijah,

25 Iphdeiah, and Penuel were the sons of Shashak.

26 Shamsherai, Shehariah, Athaliah,

27 Jaareshiah, Elijah, and Zichri were the sons of Jeroham.

28 These were heads of the fathers' houses, according to their generations, chief men. These dwelt in Jerusalem.

29 At Gibeon dwelt [Jeiel] the father of Gibeon, whose wife's name was Maacah.

30 His firstborn son was Abdon, then Zur, Kish, Baal, Nadab,

31 Gedor, Ahio, Zecher,

32 And Mikloth the father of Shimeah. These dwelt together opposite their kinsmen in Jerusalem.

33 Ner was the father of Kish, and Kish of [King] Saul the father of Jonathan, Malchi-shua, Abinadab, and Esh-baal (Ish-bosheth).

34 The son of Jonathan was Meribbaal (Mephibosheth) the father of Micah.

35 The sons of Micah: Pithon, Melech, Tarea, and Ahaz.

36 Ahaz was the father of Jehoaddah, and Jehoaddah of Alemeth, Azmaveth, and Zimri; Zimri was the father of Moza.

37 Moza was the father of Binea; Raphah was his son, Eleasah his son, Azel his son.

38 Azel had six sons: Azrikam, Bocheru, Ishmael, Sheariah, Obadiah, and Hanan. All these were the sons of Azel.

39 The sons of Eshek his brother: Ulam his firstborn, Jehush the second, Eliphelet the third.

40 The sons of Ulam were mighty warriors, archers, with many sons and grandsons—150 in all. All these were Benjamites.

9 SO ALL Israel was enrolled by genealogies; and they are written in the Book of the Kings of Israel. And Judah was carried away captive to Babylon for their unfaithfulness to God.

2 Now the first [of the returned exiles] to dwell again in their possessions in the cities of Israel were the priests, Levites, and the Nethinim [the temple servants].

3 In Jerusalem dwelt some of the people of Judah, Benjamin, Ephraim, and Manasseh:

4 Uthai son of Ammihud, the son of Omri, the son of Imri, the son of Bani, of the sons of Pharez son of Judah.

5 Of the Shilonites: Asaiah the firstborn and his sons.

6 Of the sons of Zerah: Jeuel and their kinsmen, 690.

7 Of the Benjamites: Sallu son of Meshullam, the son of Hodaviah, the son of Hassenuah;

8 Ibneiah son of Jeroham; Elah son of Uzzi, the son of Michri; and Meshullam son of Shephatiah, the son of Reuel, the son of Ibnijah;

9 And their kinsmen, according to their generations, 956. All these were heads of fathers' houses according to their fathers' houses.

10 Of the priests: Jedaiah; Jehoiarib; Jachin;

11 Azariah son of Hilkiah, the son of Meshullam, the son of Zadok, the son of Meraioth, the son of Ahitub, the chief officer of God's house;

12 And Adaiah son of Jeroham, the son of Pashhur, the son of Malchijah; Massai son of Adiel, the son of Jahzerah, the son of Meshullam, the son of Meshillemith, the son of Immer;

13 And their kinsmen, heads of their fathers' houses, 1,760—very able men for the work of the service of the house of God.

14 Of the Levites: Shemaiah son of Hasshub, the son of Azrikam, the son of Hashabiah, of the sons of Merari;

15 And Bakbakkar, Heresh, Galal, and Mattaniah son of Mica, the son of Zichri, the son of Asaph;

16 Obadiah son of Shemaiah, the son of Galal, the son of Jeduthun; and Berechiah son of Asa, the son of Elkanah, who dwelt in the villages of the Netophathites [near Jerusalem].

17 The gatekeepers were: Shallum, Akkub, Talmon, Ahiman, and their kinsmen, Shallum being the chief

18 Who hitherto was assigned to the king's east side gate. They were the gatekeepers of the camp of the Levites.

19 Shallum son of Kore, the son of Ebiasaph, the son of Korah, and his kinsmen of his father's house, the Korahites, were in charge of the work of the service, keepers of the thresholds of the Tent, as their fathers had been in charge of the camp of the Lord, keepers of the entrance.

20 Phinehas son of Eleazar was ruler over them in times past, and the Lord was with him.

21 Zechariah son of Meshelemiah was gatekeeper at the entrance of the Tent of Meeting.

22 All these chosen to be keepers at the thresholds were 212. These were enrolled by their genealogies in their villages [around Jerusalem], these men [whose grandfathers] David and Samuel the seer had established to their office of trust.

23 So they and their sons had oversight of the gates of the Lord's house, that is, the house of the tabernacle, by wards.

24 The gatekeepers were stationed on the four sides [of the house of the Lord]—on the east, west, north, and south.

25 Their brethren in their villages were to come in every seven days to be with them.

26 But these Levites, the four chief gatekeepers, were in charge of the chambers and treasuries of the house of God.

27 They lodged round about God's house, for the duty [of watching] was theirs, as well as the opening of the house every morning.

28 Some of them had charge of the serving utensils, being required to count them when they brought them in or took them out.

29 Some of them also were appointed over the furniture and over all the sacred utensils, as well as over the fine flour, wine, oil, frankincense, and spices.

30 Other sons of the priests prepared the ointment of spices.

31 Mattithiah, one of the Levites, the firstborn of Shallum the Korahite, was responsible for the things baked in pans.

32 Of their Kohathite kinsmen, some were to prepare the showbread every Sabbath.

33 These are the singers, heads of the fathers' houses of the Levites, dwelling in the temple chambers, free from other service because they were on duty day and night.

34 These were heads of fathers' houses of the Levites, according to their generations, chief men, who lived in Jerusalem.

35 In Gibeon dwelt the father of Gibeon, Jeiel, whose wife's name was Maacah,

36 His firstborn son Abdon, then Zur, Kish, Baal, Ner, Nadab,

37 Gedor, Ahio, Zechariah, and Mikloth.

38 Mikloth was the father of Shimeam. They also dwelt beside their brethren, opposite their kinsmen in Jerusalem.

39 Ner was the father of Kish, Kish of [King] Saul, Saul of Jonathan, Malchishua, Abinadab, and Esh-baal.

40 The son of Jonathan was Merib-baal (Mephibosheth); Merib-baal was the father of Micah.

41 The sons of Micah: Pithon, Melech, Tahrea, and Ahaz.

42 Ahaz was the father of Jarah, and Jarah of Alemeth, Azmaveth, and Zimri; Zimri was the father of Moza,

43 Moza of Binea; Rephaiah was his son, Eleasah his son, Azel his son.

44 Azel had six sons: Azrikam, Bocheru, Ishmael, Sheariah, Obadiah, and Hanan. These were the sons of Azel.

10 NOW THE Philistines fought against Israel; and the men of Israel fled from before them and fell slain on Mount Gilboa.

2 And the Philistines followed close after Saul and his sons *and* overtook them, and the Philistines slew Jonathan, Abinadab, and Malchishua, the sons of Saul.

3 And the battle raged about Saul, and the archers found and wounded him.

4 Then Saul said to his armor-bearer, Draw your sword and thrust me through with it, lest these uncircumcised come and abuse *and* make sport of me. But his armor-bearer would not, for he was terrified. So Saul took his own sword and fell on it.

5 When his armor-bearer saw that Saul was dead, he also fell on his sword and died.

6 So Saul died; he and his three sons and all his house died together.

7 And when all the men of Israel who were in the valley saw that the army had fled and that Saul and his sons were dead, they forsook their cities and fled; and the Philistines came and dwelt in them.

8 The next day, when the Philistines came to strip the slain, they found Saul and his sons fallen on Mount Gilboa.

9 They stripped [Saul] and took his

head and his armor, and sent [them] round about in Philistia to carry the news to their idols and to the people. **10** And they put [Saul's] armor in the house of their gods and fastened his head in the temple of Dagon. **11** When all Jabesh-gilead heard all that the Philistines had done to Saul, **12** All the brave men arose, took away the bodies of Saul and his sons, brought them to Jabesh, and buried their bones under the oak in Jabesh; then they fasted seven days. [I Sam. 31:12.] **13** So Saul died for his trespass against the Lord [in sparing Amalek], for his unfaithfulness in not keeping God's word, and also for consulting [a medium with] a spirit of the dead to inquire pleadingly of it, **14** And inquired not so of the Lord [in earnest penitence]. Therefore the Lord slew him and turned the kingdom over to David son of Jesse. [I Sam. 28:6.]

11 THEN [after the death of Ish-bosheth, Saul's son, who ruled over eleven tribes of Israel for two troubled years after Saul's death] all Israel gathered at Hebron and said to David, Behold, we are your bone and your flesh. [II Sam. 2:8-10.] **2** In times past, even when Saul was king, it was you who led out and brought in Israel; and the Lord your God said to you, You shall be shepherd of My people Israel, and you shall be prince *and* leader over [them]. **3** So all the elders of Israel came to the king at Hebron, and David made a covenant with them there before the Lord, and they anointed [him] king over Israel, according to the word of the Lord through Samuel. [I Sam. 16:1, 12, 13.] **4** And David and all Israel went to

life point

Saul lost his kingdom because he did not keep God's Word and he consulted a medium (see I Chronicles 10:13, 14). No doubt he thought this person would speak truth to him, but such people are not only deceived themselves, they also speak deception to others and present it as truth. The world we live in would have us believe that there are many sources of truth. Remember to love, honor, know, study, and obey God's Word so that you can live by "the truth, the whole truth, and nothing but the truth," because it is "the Truth" that makes you free (see John 8:32).

Jerusalem, that is Jebus, where the Jebusites, the inhabitants of the land, were. **5** Then the Jebusites said to David, You shall not come in here! But David took the stronghold of Zion, that is, the City of David. **6** And David said, Whoever smites the Jebusites first shall be chief and commander. Joab son of Zeruiah [David's half sister] went up first, and so he was made chief. **7** David dwelt in the stronghold; so it was called the City of David. **8** He built the city from the Millo [a fortification] on around; and Joab repaired *and* revived the rest of the [old Jebusite] city. **9** And David became greater and greater, for the Lord of hosts was with him. **10** Now these are the chiefs of David's mighty men, who strongly supported him in his kingdom, together with all Israel, to make him king, according to the word of the Lord concerning Israel. **11** And this is the number [thirty, and list] of David's mighty men:

Jashobeam, a Hachmonite, the chief of the Thirty [captains]. He lifted up his spear against 300, whom he slew at one time.

12 Next to him in rank was Eleazar son of Dodo the Ahohite, one of the three mighty men.

13 He was with David at Pasdammim [where David had long before slain Goliath], and there the Philistines were gathered for battle, where there was a plot of ground full of barley *or* lentils; and the men [of Israel] fled before the Philistines.

14 And Eleazar [one of the Three] stood in the midst of that plot and defended it and slew the Philistines [until his hand was weary, and his hand cleaved to the sword], and the Lord saved by a great victory *and* deliverance. [II Sam. 23:9, 10.]

15 Three of the thirty chief men went down to the rock to David, into the cave of Adullam, and the army of the Philistines was encamped in the Valley of Rephaim.

16 David was then in the stronghold, and the Philistines' garrison was in Bethlehem.

17 And David longingly said, Oh, that someone would give me water to drink from the well of Bethlehem which is by the gate!

18 Then the Three [mighty men] broke through the camp of the Philistines and drew water out of the well of Bethlehem which was by the gate and brought it to David. But David would not drink it; he poured it out to the Lord,

19 And said, My God forbid that I should do this thing. Shall I drink the blood of these men who have put their lives in jeopardy? For at the risk of their lives they brought it. So he would not drink it. These things did these three mighty men.

20 Abishai the brother of Joab was chief of the Three. For he lifted up his spear against 300 and slew them, and was named among the Three.

21 Of the Three [in the second rank] he was more renowned than the two, and became their captain; however, he attained not to the first three.

22 Benaiah son of Jehoiada, whose father was a valiant man of Kabzeel, had done mighty deeds. He slew the two sons of Ariel of Moab. Also he went down and slew a lion in a pit in time of snow.

23 He slew an Egyptian also, a man of great stature, five cubits tall. The Egyptian held a spear like a weaver's beam, and [Benaiah] went to him with a staff and plucked the spear out of the Egyptian's hand and slew him with the man's own spear.

24 These things did Benaiah son of Jehoiada, and won a name beside the three mighty men.

25 He was renowned among the Thirty, but he did not attain to the rank of the first three. David put him over his guard *and* council.

26 Also the mighty men of the armies were: Asahel the brother of Joab, Elhanan son of Dodo of Bethlehem,

27 Shammoth of Harod, Helez the Pelonite,

28 Ira son of Ikkesh of Tekoa, Abiezer of Anathoth,

29 Sibbecai the Hushathite, Ilai the Ahohite,

30 Maharai of Netophah, Heled son of Baanah of Netophah,

31 Ithai son of Ribai of Gibeah of the Benjamites, Benaiah of Pirathon,

32 Hurai of the brooks of Gaash, Abiel the Arbathite,

33 Azmaveth of Baharum, Eliahba of Shaalbon,

34 The sons of Hashem the Gizonite, Jonathan son of Shagee the Hararite,

35 Ahiam son of Sacar the Hararite, Eliphal son of Ur,

36 Hepher the Mecherathite, Ahijah the Pelonite,

37 Hezro of Carmel, Naarai son of Ezbai,
38 Joel the brother of Nathan, Mibhar son of Hagri,
39 Zelek the Ammonite, Naharai the Berothite, the armor-bearer of Joab son of Zeruiah [David's half sister],
40 Ira the Ithrite, Gareb the Ithrite,
41 Uriah the Hittite [Bathsheba's husband], Zabad son of Ahlai,
42 Adina son of Shiza, a leader of the Reubenites, and thirty heroes with him,
43 Hanan son of Maacah, and Joshaphat the Mithnite,
44 Uzzia the Ashterathite, Shama and Jeiel the sons of Hotham the Aroerite,
45 Jediael son of Shimri, and Joha his brother, the Tizite,
46 Eliel the Mahavite, Jeribai and Joshaviah sons of Elnaam, Ithmah the Moabite,
47 Eliel, Obed, and Jaasiel the Mezobaite.

12 THESE ARE the ones who came to David at Ziklag, while he yet concealed himself because of Saul son of Kish; they were among the mighty men, his helpers in war.
2 They were bowmen and could use the right hand or the left to sling stones or shoot arrows from the bow; they were of Saul's kinsmen of Benjamin.
3 The chief was Ahiezer and then Joash the sons of Shemaah of Gibeah; Jeziel and Pelet the sons of Azmaveth; Beracah, and Jehu of Anathoth,
4 Ishmaiah of Gibeon, a mighty man among the Thirty and a [leader] over them; Jeremiah, Jahaziel, Johanan, Jozabad of Gederah,
5 Eluzai, Jerimoth, Bealiah, Shemariah, Shephatiah the Haruphite;
6 Elkanah, Isshiah, Azarel, Joezer, and Jashobeam, the Korahites;
7 Joelah and Zebadiah the sons of Jeroham of Gedor.
8 Of the Gadites there went over to David to the stronghold in the wilderness men of might, men trained for war who could handle shield and spear, whose faces were like the faces of lions, and who were swift as gazelles on the mountains:
9 Ezer the chief, Obadiah the second, Eliab the third,
10 Mishmannah the fourth, Jeremiah the fifth,
11 Attai the sixth, Eliel the seventh,
12 Johanan the eighth, Elzabad the ninth,
13 Jeremiah the tenth, Machbannai the eleventh.
14 These Gadites were officers of the army. The lesser was equal to *and* over a hundred, and the greater equal to *and* over a thousand.
15 These are the men who went over the Jordan in the first month when it had overflowed all its banks, and put to flight all those in the valleys, east and west.
16 There came some of the men of Benjamin and Judah to the stronghold to David.
17 David went out to meet them and said to them, If you have come peaceably to me to help me, my heart shall be knit to you; but if you have come to betray me to my adversaries, although there is no violence *or* wrong in my hands, may the God of our fathers look upon and rebuke you.
18 Then the Spirit came upon Amasai, who was chief of the captains, and he said, Yours we are, David, and on your side, you son of Jesse! Peace, peace be to you, and peace be to your

speak the Word

Thank You, God, that I have peace because You are helping me.
ADAPTED FROM I CHRONICLES **12:18**

helpers, for your God helps you. Then David received them and made them officers of his troops.

19 Some of the men of Manasseh deserted to David when he came with the Philistines for the battle against Saul. But [David's] men did not actually fight with them, for the lords of the Philistines, upon advisement, sent him away, saying, He will desert to his master Saul at the risk of our heads. [I Sam. 29:2-9.]

20 As David went to Ziklag, there deserted to him of Manasseh: Adnah, Jozabad, Jediael, Michael, Jozabad, Elihu, and Zillethai, chiefs of thousands in Manasseh.

21 They helped David against the band of raiders, for they were all mighty men of courage, and [all seven] became commanders in [his] army.

22 For at that time day by day men kept coming to David to help him, until there was a great army, like the army of God.

23 These are the numbers of the armed divisions who came to David at Hebron to turn the kingdom of Saul to him, according to the word of the Lord:

24 Those of Judah, who bore shield and spear, were 6,800 armed for war;

25 Those of Simeon, mighty and brave warriors, 7,100;

26 Those of Levi, 4,600—

27 Jehoiada was the leader of the Aaronite [priests], and with him were 3,700,

28 And Zadok, a young man mighty in valor, and twenty-two captains from his own father's house;

29 Of the Benjamites, the kindred of [King] Saul, 3,000—hitherto the majority of them had kept their allegiance [to Saul] *and* the charge of the house of Saul;

30 Of the Ephraimites, 20,800, mighty in valor, famous in their fathers' houses;

31 Of the half-tribe of Manasseh, 18,000, who were mentioned by name to come and make David king;

32 And of Issachar, men who had understanding of the times to know what Israel ought to do, 200 chiefs; and all their kinsmen were under their command;

33 Of Zebulun, 50,000 experienced troops, fitted out with all kinds of weapons *and* instruments of war that could order and set the battle in array, men not of double purpose *but* stable and trustworthy.

34 Of Naphtali, 1,000 captains, and with them 37,000 [of the rank and file armed] with shield and spear;

35 Of Dan, 28,600, men who could set the battle in array;

36 Of Asher, men able to go forth to battle, fit for active service, 40,000;

37 On the other [the east] side of the Jordan River, of Reuben and Gad and the half-tribe of Manasseh, 120,000 men, armed with all the weapons *and* instruments of war.

38 All these, being men of war arrayed in battle order, came with a perfect *and* sincere heart to Hebron to make David king over all Israel; and all the rest also of Israel were of one mind to make David king.

39 And they were there with David for three days, eating and drinking, for their brethren had prepared for them.

40 Also those who were near them from as far as Issachar, Zebulun, and Naphtali brought food on donkeys,

speak the Word

God, I pray that You would make me like the men of Issachar and give me understanding of the times, so that I will know what to do.
ADAPTED FROM I CHRONICLES **12:32**

the power of focus

In I Chronicles 12:33 the writer describes the brave men who helped David wage war. As we see, they were not double-hearted; they were focused, stable, and trustworthy. They stuck to their sole purpose in life.

God taught others in the Bible to be single-minded in purpose. When God called Abraham, He told him to leave the past behind and to focus on the place that God would show him (see Genesis 12:1). Being single-hearted was what Paul spoke of when he said to let go of what lies behind and press on to what lies ahead (see Philippians 3:13, 14). Being single in purpose was what the Lord was encouraging Israel to do through the prophet Isaiah: "Do not [earnestly] remember the former things; neither consider the things of old. Behold, I am doing a new thing!" (Isaiah 43:18, 19).

Our problem is that we always want to hold on to the past and still go into the future. There are times when God tells us to move on, but our souls are still tied to the place we need to leave behind. That causes a double heart, and when we are double-hearted it is difficult to find peace of mind.

Jesus said, "No one can serve two masters; for either he will hate the one and love the other, or he will stand by and be devoted to the one and despise and be against the other . . . " (Matthew 6:24). In James 1:8 we read that a person who is of two minds is hesitating, dubious, irresolute, unstable, unreliable, and uncertain about everything he thinks, feels, or decides.

We need to avoid having a double heart and a dual purpose in life. Instead, we should be decisive people. Leaders especially should be able to make decisions and then stick to them. If we make decisions and then continue to go back and forth in our minds about whether we did the right thing or not, we are unstable in our ways. We need to hear from God, and then make a decision based on what He has said to us. Once we have decided something, we need to do it with all our hearts, and totally commit to it.

Also, we need to be focused and single-hearted with respect to God's gifts and calling. In Romans 12 the Apostle Paul talks about the different gifts of grace that have been given to the individual members of the body of Christ. He says that if you are a teacher, you should give yourself to your teaching. If you are a giver, you should give yourself to your giving. If you are an exhorter, you should give yourself to exhortation. In other words, Paul says not to get overly involved in things God has not gifted you for and called you to do. Resist the temptation to get entangled in things that do not help you accomplish your goals. Do not be double-minded. If you believe you are supposed to do a specific thing with your life, then be consistent in your belief. Stay on track and remain focused and stable, always pressing toward your goal in the power of the Holy Spirit.

camels, mules, and oxen, abundant supplies of meal, cakes of figs, bunches of raisins, wine, oil, oxen, and sheep, for there was joy in Israel.

13

DAVID CONSULTED the captains of thousands and hundreds, even with every leader.

putting the Word to work

When you are facing a challenge, do you depend on your own wits to see you through or do you seek the counsel of others? David, even with all of his might and power, knew the value of trusted counsel (see I Chronicles 13:1). Seek people who can provide upright and reliable counsel to you, and avail yourself of their wisdom.

2   And David said to all the assembly of Israel, If it seems good to you and if it is of the Lord our God, let us send abroad everywhere to our brethren who are left in all the land of Israel, and with them to the priests and Levites in their cities that have suburbs *and* pasturelands, that they may gather together with us.
3   And let us bring again the ark of our God to us, for we did not seek it during the days of Saul.
4   And all the assembly agreed to do so, for the thing seemed right in the eyes of all the people.
5   So David gathered all Israel together, from the Shihor, the brook of Egypt [that marked the southeast border of Palestine], to the entrance of Hemath, to bring the ark of God from Kiriath-jearim.
6   And David and all Israel went up to Baalah, that is, to Kiriath-jearim which belonged to Judah, to bring up from there the ark of God the Lord, which is called by the name of Him Who sits [enthroned] above the cherubim.

7   And they carried the ark of God on a new cart and brought it out of the house of Abinadab, and Uzza and Ahio [his brother] drove the cart.
8   And David and all Israel merrily celebrated before God with all their might, with songs and lyres and harps and tambourines and cymbals and trumpets.
9   And when they came to the threshing floor of Chidon, Uzza put out his hand to steady the ark, for the oxen [that were drawing the cart] stumbled *and* were restive.
10 And the anger of the Lord was kindled against Uzza, and He smote him because he touched the ark; and there he died before God. [Num. 4:15.]
11 And David was offended because the Lord had broken forth upon Uzza; that place to this day is called Perez-uzza [the breaking forth upon Uzza].
12 And David was afraid of God that day, and he said, How can I bring the ark of God home to me?
13 So David did not bring the ark home to the City of David, but carried it aside into the house of Obed-edom the Gittite [a Levitical porter born in Gath-rimmon]. [Josh. 21:20, 24; I Chron. 15:24.]
14 And the ark of God remained with the family of Obed-edom in his house three months. And the Lord blessed the house of Obed-edom and all that he had.

14

AND HIRAM king of Tyre sent messengers to David, and cedar timbers, with masons and carpenters, to build him a house.
2   And David perceived that the Lord had established *and* confirmed him as king over Israel, for his kingdom was exalted highly for His people Israel's sake.
3   And David took more wives to

Jerusalem, and [he] became the father of more sons and daughters.

4 Now these are the names of the children whom he had in Jerusalem: Shammua, Shobab, Nathan, Solomon,

5 Ibhar, Elishua, Elpelet,

6 Nogah, Nepheg, Japhia,

7 Elishama, Beeliada, and Eliphelet.

8 And when the Philistines heard that David was anointed king over all Israel, [they] all went up to seek David. And [he] heard of it and went out before them.

9 Now the Philistines had come and made a raid in the Valley of Rephaim.

10 David asked God, Shall I go up against the Philistines? And will You deliver them into my hand? And the Lord said, Go up, and I will deliver them into your hand.

11 So [Israel] came up to Baal-perazim, and David smote [the Philistines] there. Then David said, God has broken my enemies by my hand, like the bursting forth of waters. Therefore they called the name of that place Baal-perazim [Lord of breaking through].

12 [The Philistines] left their gods there; David commanded and they were burned.

13 And the Philistines again made a raid in the valley.

14 And David inquired again of God, and God said to him, Do not go up after them; turn away from them and come [around] upon them over opposite the mulberry trees.

15 And when you hear a sound of marching in the tops of the mulberry *or* balsam trees, then go out to battle, for God has gone out before you to smite the Philistine host.

16 So David did as God commanded him, and they smote the army of the Philistines from Gibeon even to Gezer.

17 And the fame of David went out into all lands, and the Lord brought the fear of him upon all nations.

15 DAVID MADE for himself houses in the City of David, and he prepared a place for the ark of God and pitched a tent for it.

2 Then David said, None should carry the ark of God but the Levites, for the Lord chose them to carry the ark of God and to minister to Him forever.

3 And David assembled all Israel at Jerusalem to bring up the ark of the Lord to its place, which he had prepared for it.

4 And David gathered together the sons of Aaron and the Levites:

5 Of the sons of Kohath, Uriel the chief, with 120 kinsmen;

6 Of the sons of Merari, Asaiah the chief, with 220 kinsmen;

7 Of the sons of Gershom, Joel the chief, with 130 kinsmen;

8 Of the sons of Elizaphan, Shemaiah the chief, with 200 kinsmen;

9 Of the sons of Hebron, Eliel the chief, with 80 kinsmen;

10 Of the sons of Uzziel, Amminadab the chief, with 112 kinsmen.

11 And David called for Zadok and Abiathar the priests, and for the Levites—Uriel, Asaiah, Joel, Shemaiah, Eliel, and Amminadab,

12 And said to them, You are the heads of the fathers' houses of the Levites; sanctify yourselves, both you and your brethren, that you may bring up the ark of the Lord, the God of Israel, to the place that I have prepared for it.

13 For because you bore it not [as God directed] at the first, the Lord our God broke forth upon us—because we did not seek Him in the way He ordained. [Num. 1:50; I Chron. 13:7-10.]

14 So the priests and the Levites sanctified themselves to bring up the ark of the Lord, the God of Israel.

15 The Levites carried the ark of God on their shoulders with the poles, as

Moses commanded by the word of the Lord.

16 David told the chief Levites to appoint their brethren the singers with instruments of music—harps, lyres, and cymbals—to play loudly and lift up their voices with joy.

17 So the Levites appointed Heman son of Joel; and of his brethren, Asaph son of Berechiah; and of the sons of Merari their brethren, Ethan son of Kushaiah;

18 And with them their brethren of the second class: Zechariah, Ben, Jaaziel, Shemiramoth, Jehiel, Unni, Eliab, Benaiah, Maaseiah, Mattithiah, Eliphelehu, and Mikneiah, and also the gatekeepers, Obed-edom and Jeiel.

19 So the singers Heman, Asaph, and Ethan, were appointed to sound bronze cymbals;

20 Zechariah, Aziel, Shemiramoth, Jehiel, Unni, Eliab, Maaseiah, and Benaiah were to play harps [resembling guitars] set to Alamoth [probably the treble voice];

21 Mattithiah, Eliphelehu, Mikneiah, Obed-edom, Jeiel, and Azaziah were to lead with lyres set to Sheminith [the bass voice].

22 Chenaniah, leader of the Levites in singing, was put in charge of carrying the ark *and* lifting up song. He instructed about these matters because he was skilled *and* able.

23 Berechiah and Elkanah were gatekeepers for the ark.

24 Shebaniah, Joshaphat, Nethanel, Amasai, Zechariah, Benaiah, and Eliezer the priests were to blow the trumpets before the ark of God. And Obed-edom and Jehiah (Jeiel) were also gatekeepers for the ark.

25 So David, the elders of Israel, and the captains over thousands went to bring up the ark of the covenant of the Lord out of the house of Obed-edom with joy.

26 And when God helped the Levites who carried the ark of the covenant of

the Lord [with a safe start], they offered seven bulls and seven rams.

27 David was clothed with a robe of fine linen, as were the Levites who bore the ark, and the singers, and Chenaniah, director of the music of the singers. David also wore an ephod [a priestly upper garment] of linen.

28 Thus all Israel brought up the ark of the covenant of the Lord with shouting, sound of the cornet, trumpets, and cymbals, sounding aloud with harps and lyres.

29 As the ark of the covenant of the Lord came to the City of David, Michal [David's wife] daughter of Saul, looking from a window, saw King David leaping as in sport, and she despised him in her heart.

16 SO THEY brought the ark of God and set it in the midst of the tent which David had pitched for it, and they offered burnt offerings and peace offerings before God.

2 And when David had finished offering the burnt offerings and the peace offerings, he blessed the people in the name of the Lord.

3 And he distributed to everyone of Israel, both man and woman, to everyone a loaf of bread, a portion of meat, and a cake of raisins.

4 He appointed Levites to minister before the ark of the Lord and to celebrate [by calling to mind], thanking and praising the Lord, the God of Israel:

5 Asaph was the chief, next to him Zechariah, Jeiel (Jaaziel), Shemiramoth, Jehiel, Mattithiah, Eliab, and Benaiah, Obed-edom and Jeiel, who were to play harps and lyres; Asaph was to sound the cymbals;

6 Benaiah and Jahaziel the priests were to blow trumpets continually before the ark of the covenant of God.

7 Then on that day David first entrusted to Asaph and his brethren

take a praise pause

When the ark of God was placed in the tabernacle, David stopped everything and began to worship God (see I Chronicles 16:1–7). I do not think anything blesses God more than when we stop right in the middle of what we are doing and lift our hands to worship Him, or take a moment to bow down before Him and say, "I love You, Lord." In Psalm 119:164, the psalmist says he took time to praise God seven times a day and all day long too!

Think about a businessman, for example, maybe the president of a large company. Wouldn't it be wonderful if several times a day, he closed the door to his office, turned the lock, knelt, and said, "God, I just want to take some time to worship You. Father, all these things You are giving me—the business, the money, the success—are great, but I just want to worship You. I magnify You. You are so wonderful. I love You. You are all I need. Father, I worship You. Jesus, I worship You. Holy Spirit, I worship You." I do not think a businessman with such a habit would ever need to be concerned about his business, his finances, or his success. All of those things would be taken care of (see Matthew 6:33).

The same is true for students, stay-at-home moms, retired people, secretaries, flight attendants, brain surgeons, clerks, and salespeople—anyone you can think of. All of them would have many more fruitful, productive, and peaceful days if they took time to praise the Lord throughout the day.

We all would benefit greatly from taking a "praise pause." I encourage you to take one today.

the singing of thanks to the Lord [as their chief task]:

8 O give thanks to the Lord, call on His name; make known His doings among the peoples!

9 Sing to Him, sing praises to Him; meditate on *and* talk of all His wondrous works *and* devoutly praise them!

10 Glory in His holy name; let the hearts of those rejoice who seek the Lord!

11 Seek the Lord and His strength; yearn for *and* seek His face *and* to be in His presence continually!

12 [Earnestly] remember the marvelous deeds which He has done, His miracles, and the judgments He uttered [as in Egypt],

13 O you offspring of [Abraham and] of Israel His servants, you children of Jacob, His chosen ones!

14 He is the Lord our God; His judgments are in all the earth.

15 Be mindful of His covenant forever, the promise which He commanded *and* established to a thousand generations,

16 The covenant which He made

speak the Word

I give thanks to You, God, and I call upon Your name. I will make known Your deeds among the people around me. I will sing praise to You and meditate on all Your wondrous works!
ADAPTED FROM I CHRONICLES 16:8, 9

putting the Word to work

First Chronicles 16:7–36 helps us understand the value and necessity of thanksgiving. What are you most thankful for? Be sure to give thanks to God every day. Like David, remember to thank Him for His wondrous works, for His everlasting mercy, for the good news of His salvation, for His beauty and holiness, and for His goodness. Keep your thank-tank full and you, like David, will marvel at the greatness of God.

life point

Reverential fear, as is mentioned in I Chronicles 16:25, is to know that God is God and that He means business. He has called us His friends (see John 15:14, 15) and His children, but He is still an awesome, holy God. We need to honor Him, respect Him, obey Him, and revere Him in all things.

with Abraham, and His sworn promise to Isaac.

17 He confirmed it as a statute to Jacob, and to Israel for an everlasting covenant, [Gen. 35:11, 12.]

18 Saying, To you I will give the land of Canaan, the measured portion of your possession *and* inheritance.

19 When they were but few, even a very few, and only temporary residents *and* strangers in it,

20 When they went from nation to nation, and from one kingdom to another people,

21 He allowed no man to do them wrong; yes, He reproved kings for their sakes, [Gen. 12:17; 20:3; Exod. 7:15-18.]

22 Saying, Touch not My anointed, and do My prophets no harm. [Gen. 20:7.]

23 Sing to the Lord, all the earth; show forth from day to day His salvation.

24 Declare His glory among the nations, His marvelous works among all peoples.

25 For great is the Lord and greatly to be praised; He also is to be [rever-

ently] feared above all so-called gods.

26 For all the gods of the people are [lifeless] idols, but the Lord made the heavens.

27 Honor and majesty are [found] in His presence; strength and joy are [found] in His sanctuary.

28 Ascribe to the Lord, you families of the peoples, ascribe to the Lord glory and strength,

29 Ascribe to the Lord the glory due His name. Bring an offering and come before Him; worship the Lord in the beauty of holiness *and* in holy array.

30 Tremble *and* reverently fear before Him, all the earth's peoples; the world also shall be established, so it cannot be moved.

31 Let the heavens be glad and let the earth rejoice; and let men say among the nations, The Lord reigns!

32 Let the sea roar, and all the things that fill it; let the fields rejoice, and all that is in them.

33 Then shall the trees of the wood sing out for joy before the Lord, for He comes to judge *and* govern the earth.

34 O give thanks to the Lord, for He is good; for His mercy *and* lovingkindness endure forever!

35 And say, Save us, O God of our

speak the Word

Thank You, God, that honor, majesty, strength, and joy are found in Your presence.
ADAPTED FROM I CHRONICLES **16:27, 28**

life point

David loved God very much, yet he made serious mistakes. His passions gained mastery over him and caused him to commit adultery and have a man murdered. I believe David talked so much about the mercy of God (one example is in I Chronicles 16:34) because he had experienced it firsthand in his life and ministry. That same mercy is available today to all who will seek God for it.

salvation; gather us together and deliver us from the nations, that we may give thanks to Your holy name and glory in Your praise.

36 Blessed be the Lord, the God of Israel, forever and ever! And all the people said Amen! and praised the Lord.

37 So David left Asaph and his brethren before the ark of the covenant of the Lord to minister before the ark continually, as each day's work required,

38 And Obed-edom with [his] sixty-eight kinsmen. Also Obed-edom son of Jeduthun, and Hosah, were to be gatekeepers.

39 And David left Zadok the priest and his brethren the priests before the tabernacle of the Lord in the high place that was at Gibeon

40 To offer burnt offerings to the Lord upon the altar of burnt offering continually, morning and evening, and to do all that is written in the Law of the Lord which He commanded Israel.

41 With them were Heman and Jeduthun and the rest who were chosen and expressly named to give thanks to the Lord, for His mercy *and* loving-kindness endure forever.

42 With them were Heman and Jeduthun with trumpets and cymbals for those who should sound aloud, and instruments for accompanying the songs of God. And the sons of Jeduthun were to be at the gate.

43 Then all the people departed, each man to his house, and David returned home to bless his household.

17 AS DAVID sat in his house, he said to Nathan the prophet, Behold, I dwell in a house of cedars, but the ark of the covenant of the Lord remains under tent curtains.

life point

When I was learning to hear from God and desiring with all my heart to be led by the Spirit, I Chronicles 17:1–4 really helped me to realize that we can move about with some degree of freedom following our sanctified desires, as long as we are ready to immediately go in another direction if God shows us we need to do so. It is not wrong to have a plan and follow it if we are willing to give up that plan when God does not approve of it.

In John 15:7 Jesus said, "If you live in Me [abide vitally united to Me] and My words remain in you and continue to live in your hearts, ask whatever you will, and it shall be done for you." How can this be possible unless there really is a merging of our desires with God's as we mature in Him?

The goal of every true believer is to be one with God. This happens spiritually when we are born again; and it occurs in our minds, wills, and emotions as we grow and mature spiritually. In Ephesians 4:15 the Apostle Paul urges us, "Let us grow up in every way and in all things into Him Who is the Head." As we do so, our desires become His desires, and we are safe in following them.

words and actions

Must we always have a specific word from God before we take any action? I do not think so. David wanted to build a house for God, and the prophet Nathan told him to do all that was in his heart, for God was with him (see I Chronicles 17:1–4). That night, however, God spoke to David through Nathan and gave instructions that David was not to build His house, but that one of his sons would do it (see I Chronicles 17:11).

It seems to me that the general guideline on taking action is simply to follow our hearts unless God gives a specific word. We are told in Proverbs 3:6 to acknowledge God in all of our ways and He will direct our paths. To acknowledge God means to care about what He thinks. We are never told in Scripture that we must have specific direction from God before taking any action at all. God gives us wisdom, and He expects us to use it. As we study His Word we learn His ways, and He expects us to follow them. God gives us freedom; He believes in us and believes we can make good choices, so He lets us do so. In all our prayers we should tell our Lord that we want His will in all things and then trust Him to lead and guide us.

Note that David was planning to build God a house until the moment God said no. When He did, David immediately praised God for choosing one of his family members and never showed any disappointment or rebellion against God's choice. David had a heart after God. He wanted what God wanted.

This story was particularly helpful to me as a young believer who wanted God's will, but did not know what to do when God was not speaking. I learned that because we have His Spirit and heart, we should trust the inner witness that we sense about what we should or should not do. Do what you believe to be best based on the knowledge you have, and be willing to change if and when God shows you something definite.

2 Then Nathan said to David, Do all that is in your heart, for God is with you.

3 And that same night the word of God came to Nathan, saying,

4 Go and tell David My servant, Thus says the Lord: You shall not build Me a house to dwell in,

5 For I have not dwelt in a house since the day that I brought up Israel from Egypt until this day; but I have gone from tent to tent, and from one tabernacle to another.

6 Wherever I have walked with all Israel, did I say a word to any of the judges of Israel whom I commanded to feed My people, saying, Why have you not built Me a house of cedar?

7 Now therefore, thus shall you say to My servant David, Thus says the Lord of hosts: I took you from the sheepfold, from following the sheep, that you should be prince over My people Israel.

8 And I have been with you wherever you have gone, and I have cut off all your enemies from before you, and I will make your name like the name of the great ones of the earth.

9 Also I will appoint a place for My

people Israel and will plant them, that they may dwell in their own place and be moved no more; neither shall the children of wickedness waste them any more, as at the first,

10 Since the time that I commanded judges to be over My people Israel. Moreover, I will subdue all your enemies. Furthermore, I foretell to you that the Lord will build you a house (a blessed posterity).

11 And it shall come to pass that when your days are fulfilled to go to be with your fathers, I will raise up your offspring after you, one of your own sons, and I will establish his kingdom.

12 He shall build Me a house, and I will establish his throne forever. [I Chron. 28:7.]

13 I will be his father, and he shall be My son; and I will not take My mercy *and* steadfast love away from him, as I took it from him [King Saul] who was before you. [Heb. 1:5, 6.]

14 But I will settle ᵇhim (Him) in My house and in My kingdom forever; and his (His) throne shall be established forevermore. [Isa. 9:7.]

15 According to all these words and according to all this vision, so Nathan spoke to David.

16 And David the king went in and sat before the Lord and said, Who am I, O Lord God, and what is my house

and family, that You have brought me up to this?

17 And yet this was a small thing in Your eyes, O God; for You have spoken of Your servant's house for a great while to come, and have regarded me according to the estate of a man of high degree, O Lord God!

18 What more can David say to You for thus honoring Your servant? For You know Your servant.

19 O Lord, for Your servant's sake and in accord with Your own heart, You have wrought all this greatness, to make known all these great things.

20 O Lord, there is none like You, nor is there any God beside You, according to all that our ears have heard.

21 And what nation on the earth is like Your people Israel, whom God went to redeem to Himself as a people, making Yourself a name by great and terrible things, by driving out nations from before Your people, whom You redeemed out of Egypt?

22 You made Your people Israel Your own forever, and You, Lord, became their God.

23 Therefore now, Lord, let the word which You have spoken concerning Your servant and his house be established forever, and do as You have said.

24 Let it be established and let Your

speak the Word

God, I thank You that the word You have spoken concerning me and my household will be established.
ADAPTED FROM I CHRONICLES 17:23

b The "house" or "kingdom of God," in which this preservation or confirming of the seed of David is to take place, has two points of reference: first, the Old Testament theocracy [government of a state by the immediate direction of God], and second, the Messianic kingdom of the new covenant. The text of II Sam. 7:16 (KJV) differs: "And thine house and thy kingdom shall be established forever before thee, and thy throne shall be established forever." The sense of both is Messianic [though the writer in earlier verses definitely referred not to Christ but to Solomon (I Chron. 17:11-13 and II Sam. 7:13, 14)] (J.P. Lange, *A Commentary*). "The reference in this prophecy looks beyond Solomon to Him of Whom the greatest princes of the house of David were but imperfect types" (Charles Ellicott, *A Bible Commentary*).

name [and the character that name denotes] be magnified forever, saying, The Lord of hosts, the God of Israel, is Israel's God; and the house of David Your servant will be established before You.

25 For You, O my God, have told Your servant that You will build for him a house (a blessed posterity); therefore Your servant has found courage *and* confidence to pray before You.

26 And now, Lord, You are God, and have promised this good thing to Your servant.

27 Therefore may it please You to bless the house (posterity) of Your servant, that it may continue before You forever; for what You bless, O Lord, is blessed forever.

18 AFTER THIS, David smote and subdued the Philistines, and took Gath and its villages out of the hand of the Philistines.

2 He smote Moab, and the Moabites became David's servants and brought tribute.

3 Also David defeated Hadadezer king of Zobah toward Hamath, as he went to establish his dominion by the river Euphrates.

4 David took from him 1,000 chariots, 7,000 horsemen, and 20,000 foot soldiers. David also hamstrung all the chariot horses, but reserved enough for 100 chariots.

5 When the Syrians of Damascus came to help Hadadezer king of Zobah, David slew of the Syrians 22,000 men.

6 Then David put garrisons in Syria, [whose capital was] Damascus; the Syrians became David's servants and

brought tribute. Thus the Lord preserved *and* gave victory to David wherever he went.

7 David took the shields of gold that were carried by the servants of Hadadezer and brought them to Jerusalem.

8 Likewise from Tibhath and from Cun, cities of Hadadezer, David brought very much bronze, with which Solomon later made the bronze laver, the pillars, and the vessels of bronze.

9 When Tou king of Hamath heard how David had defeated all the hosts of Hadadezer king of Zobah,

10 He sent Hadoram his son to King David to salute him and to congratulate him because he had fought and defeated Hadadezer, for Hadadezer had had wars with Tou. And Hadoram brought with him all manner of vessels of gold, silver, and bronze.

11 King David dedicated them also to the Lord, with the silver and the gold he brought from all these nations: Edom, Moab, the Ammonites, the Philistines, and the Amalekites.

12 Also Abishai son of Zeruiah slew 18,000 of the Edomites in the Valley of Salt.

13 He put garrisons in Edom, and all the Edomites became David's servants. Thus the Lord preserved *and* gave victory to David wherever he went.

14 So David reigned over all Israel and executed judgment and justice among all his people.

15 Joab son of Zeruiah [David's half sister] was over the army; and Jehoshaphat son of Ahilud was the recorder;

16 Zadok son of Ahitub and Abimelech son of Abiathar were the

speak the Word

priests; and Shavsha was secretary [of state];

17 Benaiah son of Jehoiada was over [David's bodyguards] the Cherethites and the Pelethites; and David's sons were chiefs next to the king.

19 AFTER THIS, Nahash king of the Ammonites died, and his son reigned in his stead.

2 David said, I will show kindness to Hanun son of Nahash, because his father showed kindness to me. And David sent messengers to comfort him concerning his father's death. So the servants of David came into the land of the Ammonites to comfort Hanun.

3 But the princes of the Ammonites said to Hanun, Do you think that David has sent comforters to you because he honors your father? Have his servants not come to you to search, to overthrow, and to spy out the land?

4 Therefore Hanun took David's servants, shaved them, cut off their garments in the middle near their buttocks, and sent them away.

5 When David was told how the men were served, he sent to meet them, for [they] were greatly shamed *and* embarrassed. The king said, Stay in Jericho until your beards are grown, and then return.

6 When the Ammonites saw that they had made themselves hateful to David, Hanun and [his people] sent 1,000 talents of silver to hire chariots and horsemen from Mesopotamia and Aram-maacah and Zobah.

7 So they hired 32,000 chariots, and the king of Maacah and his troops, who came and pitched before Medeba. And the Ammonites gathered from their cities and came to battle.

8 When David heard of it, he sent Joab and all the army of mighty men.

9 And the Ammonites came out and lined up in battle array before the entrance of the city [Medeba], and the kings who had come were by themselves in the open country.

10 When Joab saw that the battle was set against him before and behind, he chose from all the choice men of Israel and put them in array against the Syrians.

11 The rest of the soldiers he delivered to Abishai his brother, and they were arrayed against the Ammonites.

12 And he said, If the Syrians are too strong for me, then you help me; but if the Ammonites are too strong for you, I will help you.

13 Be of good courage and let us behave ourselves courageously for our people and for the cities of our God; and may the Lord do what is good in His sight.

14 So Joab and the people who were with him drew near before the Syrians for battle, and they fled before him.

15 And when the Ammonites saw that the Syrians fled, they likewise fled before Abishai, Joab's brother, and entered into the city [Medeba]. Then Joab came to Jerusalem.

16 When the Syrians saw that they were defeated by Israel, they sent messengers and drew forth the Syrians who were beyond the Euphrates River, with Shophach the commander of the army of Hadadezer at their head.

17 It was told to David, and he gathered all Israel and crossed the Jordan and drew up his army against them. So when David set the battle in array against the Syrians, they fought with him.

18 But the Syrians fled before Israel, and David slew of the Syrians 7,000 men in chariots and 40,000 foot soldiers, and killed Shophach the commander of the army.

19 When the servants of Hadadezer saw that they were defeated before Israel, they made peace with David and became subject to him; nor would the Syrians any longer help the Ammonites.

20 AFTER THE end of the year, when kings go out to battle, Joab led forth the army and devastated the land of the Ammonites, and came and besieged Rabbah. But David tarried at Jerusalem. Joab smote Rabbah and overthrew it.

2 David took their king's crown from off his head and found that it weighed a talent of gold and that precious stones were in it. It was set upon David's head. He brought also very much spoil out of the city of Rabbah.

3 He brought out the people who were in it and set them at cutting with saws, iron wedges, and axes. So David dealt with all the Ammonite cities. And David and all the army returned to Jerusalem.

4 After this, there arose war at Gezer with the Philistines; then Sibbecai the Hushathite slew Sippai, of the sons of the giant, and they were subdued.

5 There was war again with the Philistines, and Elhanan son of Jair slew Lahmi the brother of Goliath the Gittite, the staff of whose spear was like a weaver's beam.

6 And again there was war at Gath, where was a man of great stature who had twenty-four fingers and toes, six on each hand and each foot. He also was born to the giant.

7 And when he reproached *and* defied Israel, Jonathan son of Shimea, David's brother, slew him.

8 These were born to the giant [clan] in Gath, and they fell by the hands of David and his servants.

21 SATAN [an adversary] stood up against Israel and stirred up David to number Israel.

2 David said to Joab and the rulers of the people, Go, number Israel from Beersheba to Dan, and bring me the total, that I may know it.

3 And Joab answered, May the Lord multiply His people a hundred times! But, my lord the king, are they not all my lord's servants? Why then does my lord require this? Why will he bring guilt upon Israel?

4 But the king's word prevailed against Joab. So Joab departed and went throughout all Israel and came to Jerusalem.

5 Joab gave the total number of the people to David. And all of Israel were 1,100,000 who drew the sword, and of Judah 470,000 who drew the sword.

6 But Levi and Benjamin he did not include among them, for the king's order was detestable to Joab.

7 And God was displeased with this [reliance on human resources], and He smote Israel.

8 And David said to God, I have sinned greatly because I have done this thing. But now, I beseech You, take away the hateful wickedness of Your servant; for I have done very foolishly.

9 And the Lord said to Gad, David's seer,

10 Go and tell David, Thus says the Lord: I offer you three things; choose one of them, that I may do it to you.

11 So Gad came to David and said to him, Thus says the Lord: Take which one you will:

12 Either three years of famine, or three months of devastation before your foes, while the sword of your enemies overtakes you, or else three days of the sword of the Lord and pestilence in the land, and the angel of the Lord destroying throughout all the borders of Israel. Now therefore, consider what answer I shall return to Him Who sent me.

13 And David said to Gad, I am in great *and* distressing perplexity; let

me fall, I pray you, into the hands of the Lord, for very great *and* many are His mercies; but let me not fall into the hands of man.

14 So the Lord sent a pestilence upon Israel, and there fell of Israel 70,000 men.

15 God sent an angel to Jerusalem to destroy it, and as he was destroying, the Lord beheld, and He regretted *and* relented of the evil and said to the destroying angel, It is enough; now stay your hand. And the angel of the Lord stood by the threshing floor of Ornan the Jebusite.

16 David lifted up his eyes and saw the angel of the Lord standing between earth and the heavens, having a drawn sword in his hand stretched out over Jerusalem. Then David and the elders, clothed in sackcloth, fell upon their faces.

17 And David said to God, Is it not I who commanded the people to be numbered? It is I who has sinned and done evil indeed; but as for these sheep, what have they done? Let Your hand, I pray You, O Lord my God, be on me and on my father's house, but not on Your people, that they should be plagued.

18 Then the angel of the Lord commanded Gad to say to David that David should go up and set up an altar to the Lord in the threshing floor of Ornan the Jebusite.

19 So David went up at Gad's word, which he spoke in the name of the Lord.

20 Now Ornan was threshing wheat, and he turned back and saw the angel; and his four sons hid themselves.

21 And as David came to Ornan, Ornan looked and saw him, and went out from the threshing floor and bowed himself to David with his face to the ground.

22 Then David said to Ornan, Grant me the site of this threshing floor, that I may build an altar on it to the Lord.

You shall charge me the full price for it, that the plague may be averted from the people.

23 Ornan said to David, Take it; and let my lord the king do what is good in his eyes. I give you the oxen also for burnt offerings and the threshing sledges for wood and the wheat for the meal offering. I give it all.

24 And King David said to Ornan, No, but I will pay the full price. I will not take what is yours for the Lord, nor offer burnt offerings which cost me nothing.

25 So David gave to Ornan for the site 600 shekels of gold by weight.

26 And David built there an altar to the Lord and offered burnt offerings and peace offerings and called upon the Lord; and He answered him by fire from heaven upon the altar of burnt offering.

27 Then the Lord commanded the [avenging] angel, and he put his sword back into its sheath.

28 When David saw that the Lord had answered him at the threshing floor of Ornan the Jebusite, he sacrificed there.

29 For the tabernacle of the Lord, which Moses made in the wilderness, and the altar of burnt offering were at that time in the high place at Gibeon.

30 But David could not go before it to inquire of God, for he was afraid of the sword of the angel of the Lord.

22 THEN DAVID said, Here shall be the house of the Lord God, and here the altar of the burnt offering for Israel.

2 David commanded to gather together the strangers who were in the land of Israel, and he set stonecutters to hew out stones to build the house of God.

3 David prepared iron in abundance for nails for the doors of the gates and for the couplings, and bronze in abundance without weighing,

putting the Word to work

Many of us spend hours preparing for a special event, a big project at work, or a test at school. David did all that he could to prepare for the building of the temple (see I Chronicles 22:1–5). Will you put the same diligent preparation into the work God calls you to?

4 Also cedar trees without number, for the Sidonians and they of Tyre brought much cedar timber to David.
5 David said, Solomon my son is young and inexperienced, and the house that is to be built for the Lord must be exceedingly magnificent, of fame and glory throughout all lands. I will therefore make preparation for it. So David prepared abundantly before his death.
6 Then he called for Solomon his son and charged him to build a house for the Lord, the God of Israel.
7 David said to Solomon, My son, it was in my heart to build a house to the ᶜName *and* [for the symbol of] the Presence of the Lord my God.
8 But the word of the Lord came to me, saying, You have shed much blood and have waged great wars; you shall not build a house to My Name,

putting the Word to work

Have you ever been disappointed when someone else was given the privilege of doing something in ministry that you wanted to do? Rather than be frustrated or discouraged, follow David's example in I Chronicles 22:6–11. Bless the efforts of others; pray for them that they might have wisdom; and encourage them to keep following the Lord in all they do, that they might prosper. God will be faithful to honor you.

c See footnote on Deut. 12:5.

because you have shed much blood on the earth in My sight.
9 Behold, a son shall be born to you who shall be a man of peace. I will give him rest from all his enemies round about; for his name shall be Solomon [peaceable], and I will give peace and quiet to Israel in his days. [II Sam. 12:24, 25.]
10 He shall build a house for My Name *and* [the symbol of My] Presence. He shall be My son, and I will be his father; and I will establish his royal throne over Israel forever.
11 Now, my son, the Lord be with and prosper you in building the house of the Lord your God, as He has spoken concerning you.
12 Only may the Lord give you wisdom and understanding as you are put in charge of Israel, that you may keep the law of the Lord your God.
13 Then you will prosper if you are careful to keep *and* fulfill the statutes and ordinances with which the Lord charged Moses concerning Israel. Be strong and of good courage. Dread not *and* fear not; be not dismayed.

life point

First Chronicles 22:13 warns us against dread. Dread will not only keep us from fulfilling God's Word, but will also hinder our prosperity. Dread is a forerunner of fear, and fear never brings a blessing. Instead of being dismayed over the things that frighten you, take courage in the Lord.

14 In my affliction *and* trouble I have provided for the house of the Lord 100,000 talents of gold, 1,000,000 talents of silver, and bronze and iron without weighing. I have also provided timber and stone; you must add to them.

life point

King David was an exceptional leader for many reasons, but what stands out to me about him in I Chronicles 22:14 is that he took a lead role in providing for the house of God even while he was troubled and afflicted. He did not expect others to do what he would not do, and he wanted to make sure that a good example for giving had been set so that all the people would follow. That's what an effective leader does—leads by example even when it requires pain or sacrifice.

15 You have workmen in abundance: hewers, workers of stone and timber, and all kinds of craftsmen without number, skillful in doing every kind of work

16 With gold, silver, bronze, and iron. So arise and be doing, and the Lord be with you!

17 David also commanded all the princes of Israel to help Solomon his son, saying,

18 Is not the Lord your God with you? And has He not given you peace on every side? For He has given the inhabitants of the land into my hand, and the land is subdued before the Lord and His people.

19 Now set your mind and heart to seek (inquire of and require as your vital necessity) the Lord your God. Arise and build the sanctuary of the Lord God, so that the ark of the covenant of the Lord and the holy vessels of God may be brought into the house built to the Name *and* renown of the Lord.

putting the Word to work

Are you looking for purpose and meaning in your life? Take heed of David's counsel in I Chronicles 22:19, and set your heart and soul to seek the Lord your God. As you do, you will find that God has plans and purposes for your life beyond anything you can dream of.

23 WHEN DAVID was old and full of days, he made Solomon his son king over Israel.

2 David assembled all the leaders of Israel, with the priests and Levites.

3 The Levites thirty years old and upward numbered, man by man, 38,000,

4 Of whom [d]24,000 were to oversee the work of the house of the Lord and 6,000 were to be officers and judges.

5 And, said David, 4,000 shall be gatekeepers and 4,000 are to praise the Lord with the instruments which I made for praise.

6 And David organized them in sections according to the sons of Levi: Gershon, Kohath, and Merari.

7 Of the Gershonites: Ladan (Libni) and Shimei.

8 The sons of Ladan: Jehiel the chief, Zetham, and Joel—three in all.

9 The sons of Shimei: Shelomoth, Haziel, and Haran—three in all. These were the heads of the fathers' houses of Ladan.

10 And the sons of Shimei: Jahath, Zina (Zizah), Jeush, and Beriah. Of these four sons of Shimei,

11 Jahath was chief and Zizah the

d The reader may be tempted to consider these figures absurdly high if he does not get the whole picture. Note these features of it: 1. The Levites were divided into twenty-four rotating divisions (I Chron. 24:6-19). 2. One thousand Levites on duty at one time for Solomon's temple, considering the many purposes and cost of the building, its ornate ritual, and the scale of the work, is not unreasonable according to authorities. 3. In the primitive simplicity of the wilderness, the worshiper killed the animal he brought for an offering, skinned it, cut it in pieces, and washed the entrails and legs. But now all these services were the duty of the Levites or Nethinim (servants of the temple); in addition, the number of worshipers had greatly increased (hence the need for a large number of Levites).

give when it hurts

God said that David was a man after His own heart—one who would do all of His will and carry out His program fully (see Acts 13:22). David was a giving man, and he gave generously toward the building of God's house. Even in his own times of trouble and affliction, he continued to give generously (see I Chronicles 22:14).

It is tempting to stop giving to others when we are hurting. During those times, we do not feel like being a blessing to someone else; we want someone to comfort us and make us feel better. But when we are hurting, we should behave as we would if we were not hurting. We should keep all our commitments, including our financial commitments to the work of God.

We all go through times of testing, and our behavior during those times clearly reveals our level of spiritual maturity. Spiritual babies do what is right only if they are quickly being noticed and rewarded. But mature Christians do what is right because it is right—and they never quit. They do not change when their circumstances change.

To me there is a big difference between giving and being a "giver." People who are givers look for opportunities to give to others; they do not look for reasons to get out of giving. It is easy to use personal problems as an excuse to be selfish, but I believe that seeds sown during hard times are more powerful than any other kind. God appreciates our faithfulness no matter what we are going through. Do not be an emotional giver, but choose to be one who does what is right on purpose, no matter how you feel.

If I am hurting from a trial I am going through and the devil tempts me not to give because of my personal pain, I purposely give a little extra, just to let the enemy know where I stand. When Jesus died for us He was hurting, yet He still gave His best. Let's always go the extra mile and never compromise on our commitments.

second, but Jeush and Beriah had not many sons [not enough for a father's house or clan]; so they were counted together as one father's house.

12 The sons of Kohath: Amram, Izhar, Hebron, and Uzziel—four in all.

13 The sons of Amram: Aaron and Moses. Aaron was set apart to sanctify him as most holy *and* to consecrate the most holy things, that he and his sons forever might burn incense before the Lord, minister to Him, and bless in His name [and the character which that name denotes] forever.

14 But the sons of Moses the man of God were named among the tribe of Levi.

15 The sons of Moses: Gershom and Eliezer.

16 The son of Gershom: Shebuel the chief.

17 The son of Eliezer: Rehabiah the chief. Eliezer had no other sons, but Rehabiah's sons were very many.

18 The sons of Izhar: Shelomith was the chief.

19 The sons of Hebron: Jeriah the first, Amariah the second, Jahaziel the third, and Jekameam the fourth.

20 The sons of Uzziel: Micah the first and Isshiah the second.

21 The sons of Merari: Mahli and Mushi. The sons of Mahli: Eleazar and Kish.

22 Eleazar died and had no sons, but daughters only, and their kinsmen, sons of Kish, took them as wives.

23 The sons of Mushi: Mahli, Eder, and Jeremoth—three in all.

24 These were the Levites by their fathers' houses, the heads of the fathers' houses of those registered, according to the number of names of the individuals who were the servants of the house of the Lord, from twenty years old and upward.

25 For David said, The Lord, the God of Israel has given peace *and* rest to His people, and He dwells in Jerusalem forever.

26 So the Levites no more have need to carry the tabernacle and all its vessels for its service.

27 For by the last words *and* acts of David, these were the number of the Levites from twenty years old and above.

28 But their duty should be to wait on [the priests] the sons of Aaron in the service of the house of the Lord, caring for the courts, the chambers, the cleansing of all holy things, and any work of the service of God's house,

29 For the showbread also, and for the fine flour for a cereal offering, whether of unleavened wafers or of what is baked on the griddle or soaked [in oil], and for all measuring of amount and size [as the Law of Moses required].

30 They are also to stand every morning to thank and praise the Lord, and likewise at evening,

31 And to assist in offering all burnt sacrifices to the Lord on Sabbaths, New Moon festivals, and set feast days by number according to the ordinance concerning them, continually before the Lord.

life point

First Chronicles 23:30 teaches us about those who were to worship the Lord morning and evening. I hope you will also begin to worship early in the morning. I suggest starting before you even get out of bed. Worship while you get ready for work; worship on the way to work; worship when you get home in the evening and as you go to sleep. You will be amazed to see how things begin to change. Worship creates an atmosphere where God can do mighty things in your life.

Worship is not difficult. It simply means to adore the Lord and be thankful for Him and all He does for you. Tell Him regularly how much you love Him and how wonderful He is!

32 So they shall keep charge of the Tent of Meeting and the Holy Place and shall attend to the sons of Aaron their kinsmen, for the service of the house of the Lord.

24 THE COURSES *or* divisions of the priests, the sons of Aaron, were these: The sons of Aaron: Nadab, and Abihu, Eleazar, and Ithamar.

2 But Nadab and Abihu died before their father and had no children; therefore Eleazar and Ithamar executed the priest's office.

3 And David, with Zadok of the sons of Eleazar and Ahimelech of the sons of Ithamar, divided *and* distributed them according to their assigned duties.

4 Since there were more chief men found among the sons of Eleazar [because of the misfortunes of Eli, and Saul's slaughter of the priests at Nob] than among the sons of Ithamar, they were divided thus: sixteen heads of fathers' houses of the sons of Eleazar and eight of the sons of Ithamar according to their fathers' houses.

5 Thus were they divided by lot, one group with the other, for there were chiefs of the sanctuary and chiefs of God [high priests] drawn both from the sons of Eleazar and from the sons of Ithamar.

6 Shemaiah the scribe, son of Nethanel, a Levite, recorded them in the presence of the king, the princes, Zadok the priest, Ahimelech son of Abiathar [the priest who escaped being killed at Nob by Saul and fled to David], and the heads of the fathers' houses of the priests and Levites— one father's house being taken alternately for Eleazar and one for Ithamar.

7 The lots fell, the first one to Jehoiarib, the second to Jedaiah,

8 The third to Harim, the fourth to Se-orim,

9 The fifth to Malchijah, the sixth to Mijamin,

10 The seventh to Hakkoz, the eighth to Abijah,

11 The ninth to Jeshua, the tenth to Shecaniah,

12 The eleventh to Eliashib, the twelfth to Jakim,

13 The thirteenth to Huppah, the fourteenth to Jeshebe-ab,

14 The fifteenth to Bilgah, the sixteenth to Immer,

15 The seventeenth to Hezir, the eighteenth to Happizzez,

16 The nineteenth to Pethahiah, the twentieth to Jehezkel,

17 The twenty-first to Jachin, the twenty-second to Gamul,

18 The twenty-third to Delaiah, the twenty-fourth to Maaziah.

19 This was their order for coming on duty to serve in the house of the Lord, according to the procedure ordered for them by their [forefather] Aaron, as the Lord, the God of Israel, had commanded him.

20 As for the rest of the sons of Levi:

of the sons of Amram: Shubael; of the sons of Shubael: Jehdeiah.

21 Of Rehabiah: of the sons of Rehabiah: Isshiah the chief.

22 Of the Izharites: Shelomoth; of the sons of Shelomoth: Jahath.

23 The sons of Hebron: Jeriah the first, Amariah the second, Jahaziel the third, Jekameam the fourth.

24 The son of Uzziel: Micah; of the sons of Micah: Shamir.

25 The brother of Micah: Isshiah; of the sons of Isshiah: Zechariah.

26 The sons of Merari: Mahli and Mushi. The son of Jaaziah: Beno.

27 The sons of Merari: by Jaaziah: Beno, Shoham, Zaccur, and Ibri.

28 Of Mahli: Eleazar, who had no sons.

29 Of Kish: the son of Kish: Jerahmeel.

30 The sons of Mushi: Mahli, Eder, and Jerimoth. These were the sons of the Levites, according to their fathers' houses.

31 These likewise cast lots, as did their kinsmen the sons of Aaron, in the presence of David the king, Zadok, Ahimelech, and the heads of the fathers' houses of the priests and Levites—the head of each father's house and his younger brother alike.

25 ALSO DAVID and the chiefs of the host [of the Lord] separated to the [temple] service some of the sons of Asaph, Heman, and Jeduthun, who should prophesy [being inspired] with lyres, harps, and cymbals. The list of the musicians according to their service was:

2 Of the sons of Asaph: Zaccur, Joseph, Nethaniah, and Asharelah, the sons of Asaph under the direction of Asaph, who prophesied (witnessed and testified under divine inspiration) in keeping with the king's order.

3 Of the sons of Jeduthun: Gedaliah, Zeri, Jeshaiah, Shimei, Hashabiah,

and Mattithiah, six in all, under the direction of their father Jeduthun, who witnessed *and* prophesied under divine inspiration with the lyre in thanksgiving and praise to the Lord.

4 Of Heman: the sons of Heman: Bukkiah, Mattaniah, Uzziel, Shebuel, Jerimoth, Hananiah, Hanani, Eliathah, Giddalti, Romamti-ezer, Joshbekashah, Mallothi, Hothir, and Mahazioth.

5 All these were the sons of Heman the king's seer [his mediator] in the words *and* things of God to exalt Him; for God gave to Heman fourteen sons and three daughters. [Ps. 68:25.]

6 All of whom were [in the choir] under the direction of their father for song in the house of the Lord, with cymbals, harps, and lyres, for the service of the house of God. Asaph, Jeduthun, and Heman were under the order of the king.

7 So the number of them [who led the remainder of the 4,000], with their kinsmen who were specially trained in songs for the Lord, all who were talented singers, was 288. [I Chron. 23:5.]

8 [The musicians] cast lots for their duties, small and great, teacher and scholar alike.

9 The first lot fell for Asaph to Joseph; the second to Gedaliah, to him, his brethren and his sons, twelve;

10 The third to Zaccur, his sons and his brethren, twelve;

11 The fourth to Izri, his sons and his brethren, twelve;

12 The fifth to Nethaniah, his sons and his brethren, twelve;

13 The sixth to Bukkiah, his sons and his brethren, twelve;

14 The seventh to Jesharelah, his sons and his brethren, twelve;

15 The eighth to Jeshaiah, his sons and his brethren, twelve;

16 The ninth to Mattaniah, his sons and his brethren, twelve;

17 The tenth to Shimei, his sons and his brethren, twelve;

18 The eleventh to Azarel, his sons and his brethren, twelve;

19 The twelfth to Hashabiah, his sons and his brethren, twelve;

20 The thirteenth to Shubael, his sons and his brethren, twelve;

21 The fourteenth to Mattithiah, his sons and his brethren, twelve;

22 The fifteenth to Jeremoth, his sons and his brethren, twelve;

23 The sixteenth to Hananiah, his sons and his brethren, twelve;

24 The seventeenth of Joshbekashah, his sons and his brethren, twelve;

25 The eighteenth to Hanani, his sons and his brethren, twelve;

26 The nineteenth to Mallothi, his sons and his brethren, twelve;

27 The twentieth to Eliathah, his sons and his brethren, twelve;

28 The twenty-first to Hothir, his sons and his brethren, twelve;

29 The twenty-second to Giddalti, his sons and his brethren, twelve;

30 The twenty-third to Mahazioth, his sons and his brethren, twelve;

31 The twenty-fourth to Romamti-ezer, his sons and his brethren, twelve.

26 FOR THE divisions of the gatekeepers: Of the Korahites was: Meshelemiah son of Kore, of the sons of Asaph.

2 And Meshelemiah had sons: Zechariah the firstborn, Jediael the second, Zebadiah the third, Jathniel the fourth,

3 Elam the fifth, Jehohanan the sixth, Eliehoenai the seventh.

4 Obed-edom had sons: Shemaiah the firstborn, Jehozabad the second, Joah the third, Sacar the fourth, Nethanel the fifth,

5 Ammiel the sixth, Issachar the seventh, Peullethai the eighth; for God blessed him.

6 Also to Shemaiah his son were sons born, who were rulers in their

fathers' houses, for they were mighty men of ability *and* courage.

7 The sons of Shemaiah: Othni, Rephael, Obed, and Elzabad, whose brethren were strong *and* able men, Elihu and Semachiah.

8 All these were sons of Obed-edom [in whose house the ark was kept], with their sons and brethren, strong *and* able men for the service—sixty-two in all. [I Chron. 13:13, 14.]

9 Meshelemiah had sons and brethren, strong *and* able men—eighteen in all.

10 Also Hosah, of the sons of Merari, had sons: Shimri the chief (he was not the firstborn, yet his father made him chief),

11 Hilkiah the second, Tebaliah the third, Zechariah the fourth; all the sons and brethren of Hosah were thirteen in all.

12 Of these were the divisions of the gatekeepers, even of the chief men, having duties, as did their brethren, to minister in the house of the Lord.

13 And they cast lots by fathers' houses, small and great alike, for every gate.

14 The lot for the east fell to Shelemiah. They cast lots also for Zechariah his son, a wise counselor, and his lot came out for the north.

15 To Obed-edom it came out for the south, and to his sons the storehouse was allotted.

16 To Shuppim and Hosah the lot fell for the west, by the refuse gate that goes into the ascending highway, post opposite post.

17 On the east were six Levites, on the north four a day, on the south four a day, and two by two at the storehouse.

18 At the ᵉcolonnade on the west side [of the outer court of the temple], there were four at the road and two at the colonnade.

19 These were the divisions of the gatekeepers among the Korahites and the sons of Merari.

20 Of the Levites, Ahijah was over the treasuries of the house of God and the treasuries of the dedicated gifts.

21 The sons of Ladan, the descendants of Gershon through Ladan, the heads of families of Ladan the Gershonite: Jehieli,

22 The sons of Jehieli, Zetham and Joel his brother, who were over the treasuries of the house of the Lord.

23 Of the Amramites, Izharites, Hebronites, and Uzzielites:

24 Shebuel son of Gershom, the son of Moses, was ruler over the treasuries.

25 His brethren from Eliezer were his son Rehabiah, his son Jeshaiah, his son Joram, his son Zichri, and his son Shelomoth.

26 This Shelomoth and his brethren were over all the treasuries of the dedicated gifts, which King David, the heads of the fathers' houses, the officers over thousands and hundreds, and the commanders of the army had dedicated.

27 From spoil won in battles they dedicated gifts to maintain the house of the Lord.

28 Also all that Samuel the seer, Saul son of Kish, Abner son of Ner, and Joab son of Zeruiah had dedicated, and whatever anyone had dedicated, it was in the charge of Shelomoth and his brethren.

29 Of the Izharites: Chenaniah and his sons were appointed to outside duties for Israel, as officers and judges.

30 Of the Hebronites: Hashabiah and his brethren, men of courage *and* ability, 1,700 in all, were officers over Israel on the west side of the Jordan in all the Lord's business and the king's service.

31 Of the Hebronites: Jerijah was the chief, according to their generations

---

e Hebrew *Parbar,* possibly court or colonnade.

by fathers' houses. In the fortieth year of David's reign a search was made, and men of great courage *and* ability were found among them at Jazer in Gilead.

32 Jerijah's kinsmen, men of courage *and* ability, were 2,700 heads of fathers' houses; King David made them overseers of the Reubenites, the Gadites, and the half-tribe of Manasseh, for everything pertaining to God and for the affairs of the king.

27 THIS IS the list of the Israelites, the heads of fathers' houses, the commanders of thousands and hundreds, and their officers who served the king in all matters of the divisions that came and went, month by month throughout the year, each division numbering 24,000.

2 Over the first division for the first month was Jashobeam son of Zabdiel. In his division were 24,000.

3 He was descended from Perez and was chief of all the commanders of the army for the first month.

4 Over the division for the second month was Dodai the Ahohite; and of his division Mikloth was the chief officer. In his division were 24,000.

5 The third commander of the army for the third month was Benaiah son of Jehoiada the priest, as chief. In his division were 24,000.

6 This is the Benaiah who was a mighty man of the Thirty and over the Thirty; and in his division was Ammizabad his son.

7 The fourth, for the fourth month, Asahel brother of Joab, and Zebadiah his son after him. In his division were 24,000.

8 The fifth, for the fifth month, Shamhuth the Izrahite. In his division were 24,000.

9 The sixth, for the sixth month, Ira son of Ikkesh the Tekoite. In his division were 24,000.

10 The seventh, for the seventh month, Helez the Pelonite, of the Ephraimites. In his division were 24,000.

11 The eighth, for the eighth month, Sibbecai the Hushathite, of the Zarahites. In his division were 24,000.

12 The ninth, for the ninth month, Abiezer of Anathoth, a Benjamite. In his division were 24,000.

13 The tenth, for the tenth month, Maharai from Netophah, of the Zerahites. In his division were 24,000.

14 The eleventh, for the eleventh month, Benaiah the Pirathonite, of the sons of Ephraim. In his division were 24,000.

15 The twelfth, for the twelfth month, Heldai the Netophathite, of Othniel. In his division were 24,000.

16 Also over the tribes of Israel: of the Reubenites: Eliezer son of Zichri was chief officer; of the Simeonites: Shephatiah son of Maachah;

17 Of Levi: Hashabiah son of Kemuel; of Aaron: Zadok;

18 Of Judah: Elihu, one of David's brothers; of Issachar: Omri son of Michael;

19 Of Zebulun: Ishmaiah son of Obadiah; of Naphtali: Jerimoth son of Azriel;

20 Of the Ephraimites: Hoshea son of Azaziah; of the half-tribe of Manasseh: Joel son of Pedaiah;

21 Of the half-tribe of Manasseh in Gilead: Iddo son of Zechariah; of Benjamin: Jaasiel son of Abner;

22 Of Dan: Azarel son of Jeroham. These were the leaders of the tribes of Israel.

23 But David did not number those under twenty years of age, for the Lord had promised to make Israel as the stars of the heavens.

24 Joab son of Zeruiah began a census but did not finish, because the census brought wrath upon Israel, and the number was not recorded in the chronicles of King David.

25 Over the king's treasuries was Azmaveth son of Adiel; and over the treasuries in the country, cities, villages, and towers *or* forts was Jonathan son of Uzziah;

26 Over those who did the work of the field of tilling the soil was Ezri son of Chelub;

27 Over the vineyards was Shimei the Ramathite; over the produce of the vineyards for the wine cellars, Zabdi the Shiphmite;

28 Over the olive and sycamore trees in the low plains, Baal-hanan the Gederite; over the stores of oil, Joash;

29 Over the herds pasturing in Sharon, Shitrai the Sharonite; over the herds in the valleys, Shaphat son of Adlai;

30 Over the camels, Obil the Ishmaelite; over the she-donkeys, Jehdeiah the Meronothite;

31 And over the flocks, Jaziz the Hagrite. All these were stewards of King David's property.

32 Also Jonathan, David's uncle, was a counselor, a wise man and a scribe; he and Jehiel son of Hachmoni attended the king's sons [as tutors]. [II Kings 10:6.]

33 Ahithophel was the king's counselor; Hushai the Archite was the king's companion *and* friend.

34 Ahithophel was succeeded by Jehoiada son of Benaiah and by Abiathar. Joab was the commander of the king's army.

28 DAVID ASSEMBLED at Jerusalem all the leaders of Israel and of the tribes, the officers of the divisions that served the king in courses, and those over thousands and hundreds, and the stewards over all the property and livestock of the king and his sons, with the palace officers, the mighty men, and all the mighty warriors.

2 Then David the king rose to his feet and said, Hear me, my brethren and my people. I myself intended to build a house of rest for the ark of the covenant of the Lord, as a footstool for our God, and I prepared materials for the building.

3 But God said to me, You shall not build a house for My Name [and Presence], because you have been a man of war and have shed blood.

4 However, the Lord, the God of Israel, chose me before all my father's house to be king over Israel forever. For He chose Judah to be the ruler; and of the house of Judah he chose the house of my father; and among the sons of my father He was pleased to make me king over all Israel;

5 And of all my sons, for the Lord has given me many sons, He has chosen Solomon my son to sit upon the throne of the kingdom of the Lord over Israel.

6 And He said to me, Solomon your son shall build My house and My courts, for I have chosen him to be My son, and I will be his father.

7 I will establish his kingdom forever if he loyally *and* continuously obeys My commandments and My ordinances, as he does today.

8 Now therefore, in the sight of all Israel, the assembly of the Lord, and in the hearing of our God, keep and seek [to be familiar with] all the commandments of the Lord your God, that you may possess this good land and

speak the Word

God, may I heed David's instructions and know You, cherish You, and serve You with a blameless heart and a willing mind. I know that if I seek You and require You as my first and vital necessity, I will find You.
ADAPTED FROM I CHRONICLES 28:9

leave it as an inheritance for your children after you forever.

9 And you, Solomon my son, know the God of your father [have personal knowledge of Him, be acquainted with, and understand Him; appreciate, heed, and cherish Him] and serve Him with a blameless heart and a willing mind. For the Lord searches all hearts *and* minds and understands all the wanderings of the thoughts. If you seek Him [inquiring for and of Him and requiring Him as your first and vital necessity] you will find Him; but f if you forsake Him, He will cast you off forever!

10 Take heed now, for the Lord has chosen you to build a house for the sanctuary. Be strong and do it!

11 Then David gave Solomon his son the plan of the vestibule of the temple, its houses, its treasuries, its upper chambers, its inner rooms, and of the place for the [ark and its] mercy seat;

12 And the plan of all that he had in mind [by the Spirit] for the courts of the house of the Lord, all the surrounding chambers, the treasuries of the house of God, and the treasuries for the dedicated gifts;

13 The plan for the divisions of the priests and the Levites, for all the work of the service in the house of the Lord; for all the vessels for service in the house of the Lord:

14 The weight of gold and silver for all the gold and silver articles of every kind of service—

15 The weight of the golden lampstands and their lamps, the weight of gold or silver for each lampstand and its lamps, according to the use of each lampstand;

16 The gold by weight for each table of showbread, and the silver for the tables of silver;

17 Also pure gold for the forks, basins, and cups; for the golden bowls by weight of each; for the silver bowls by weight of each;

18 For the incense altar refined gold by weight, and gold for the plan of the chariot of the cherubim that spread their wings and covered the ark of the Lord's covenant.

19 All this the Lord made me understand by the writing by His hand upon me, all the work to be done according to the plan.

20 Also David told Solomon his son,

speak the Word

> God, I will be strong and courageous and will do what You have asked me to do. I will not fear or be dismayed, because You are with me and You will not fail me or forsake me.
>
> ADAPTED FROM I CHRONICLES **28:20**

f God's promises to men and women invariably are dependent upon the other party to the covenant meeting His conditions, whether He says so at the time or not. In I Chron. 28:7 we find Him promising to establish Solomon's kingdom forever. Yet in I Kings 11:9-11 we find that God became angry with Solomon for all his degenerate and abominable conduct and his treachery of heart toward Him; and without mercy, except for David's sake, God declared that the kingdom would be torn from him. Was God breaking His covenant with Solomon? No, Solomon had broken and nullified that covenant long before; it no longer existed. There was now no promise for God to keep. Christians are prone to think that God will keep His part of a bargain whether they do or not, but the wisest man who ever lived died knowing that God is not mocked; "[He inevitably deludes himself who attempts to delude God.] For whatever a man sows, that *and* that only is what he will reap" (Gal. 6:7). "If you seek Him [inquiring for and of Him and requiring Him as your first and vital necessity], you will find Him; but if you forsake Him, He will cast you off forever!" David was telling Solomon all this, but as the new king grew in power, popularity, and personal aggrandizement, step by step he set himself up as privileged to ignore God. In all his wisdom he failed to comprehend that "Something greater *and* more exalted *and* more majestic than the temple is here! . . . Someone more *and* greater than Solomon is here" (Matt. 12:6, 42).

Be strong and courageous, and do it. Fear not, be not dismayed, for the Lord God, my God, is with you. He will not fail or forsake you until you have finished all the work for the service of the house of the Lord.

21 And see, [you have] the divisions of the priests and Levites for all the service of God's house, and with you in all the kinds of work will be every willing, skillful man for any kind of service. Also the officers and all the people will be wholly at your command.

29 AND KING David said to all the assembly, Solomon my son, whom alone God has chosen, is yet young, tender, and inexperienced; and the work is great, for the palace is not to be for man but for the Lord God.

2 So I have provided with all my might for the house of my God the gold for things to be of gold, silver for things of silver, bronze for things of bronze, iron for things of iron, and wood for things of wood, as well as onyx or beryl stones, stones to be set, stones of antimony, stones of various colors, and all sorts of precious stones, and marble stones in abundance.

3 Moreover, because I have set my affection on the house of my God, in addition to all I have prepared for the holy house, I have a private treasure of gold and silver which I give for the house of my God:

putting the Word to work

Have you ever had your heart set on something, only to be disappointed? David knew that only by fixing their hearts on God would the people he led prosper and have joy (see I Chronicles 29:3). Ask God to help you fix your heart on Him; He will never disappoint or fail you.

4 It is 3,000 talents of gold, gold of Ophir, 7,000 talents of refined silver for overlaying the walls of the house,

5 Gold for the uses of gold, silver for the uses of silver, and for every work to be done by craftsmen. Now who will offer willingly to fill his hand [and consecrate it] today to the Lord [like one consecrating himself to the priesthood]?

6 Then the chiefs of the fathers and princes of the tribes of Israel and the captains of thousands and of hundreds, with the rulers of the king's work, offered willingly

life point

It is important to look at our attitudes and motives for working. If we are lazy and do not want to work, we will not work. We will make all kinds of excuses and end up in ruin. But if we have strong desires, they will motivate us to work and work hard; we will do whatever it takes to get the job done, as the people mentioned in I Chronicles 29:6 did. Smart people realize that nothing worthwhile is ever accomplished without dedication and a lot of hard work.

7 And gave for the service of the house of God—of gold 5,000 talents and 10,000 darics, of silver 10,000 talents, of bronze 18,000 talents, and 100,000 talents of iron.

8 And whoever had precious stones gave them to the treasury of the house of the Lord in the care of Jehiel the Gershonite.

9 Then the people rejoiced because these had given willingly, for with a whole and blameless heart they had offered freely to the Lord. King David also rejoiced greatly.

10 Therefore David blessed the Lord before all the assembly and said, Be praised, adored, and thanked, O Lord,

be willing to be willing

Do you like it when people do something for you, but you know they do not really want to do it? I absolutely despise that. I believe that comes from my upbringing. It seemed to me that even when my father allowed me to do things, he really did not want me to do them. So to this day if people do not really want to do something for me, I would rather they just forget it.

If we are like that, how much more is God like that? We human beings do a halfway decent job of hiding our true feelings from people, but we cannot hide our hearts from God. We may as well start being honest about the way we feel and start doing things out of a willing heart—or at least start praying for God to give us a willing heart—so we can do them for the right reason.

Sometimes we may have to pray, "Lord, make me willing to be willing." And sometimes we may have to pray, "Lord, make me willing to be willing to be willing—because I don't even really feel that I want to be willing at all!"

God examines our heart attitudes, and whatever we do for Him needs to be done willingly. I particularly like I Chronicles 29:9 because it emphasizes that God really delights in those who give to Him willingly, joyfully, and cheerfully. He does not take pleasure in those who give legalistically or under compulsion.

There are times when we obey God even though it is difficult for us, but we still do it because we love Him and want to please Him. In those cases I still see us as willing. We are willing to go beyond our own fleshly feelings about a particular thing and honor God anyway. Even if you have to ask God to make you willing, be willing—and be one in whom God delights!

the God of Israel our [forefather], forever and ever.

11 Yours, O Lord, is the greatness and the power and the glory and the victory and the majesty, for all that is in the heavens and the earth is Yours; Yours

putting the Word to work

Do you regularly give of your finances to the work of God? As David's people willingly gave, they were filled with great joy (see I Chronicles 29:2–16)! Remember, anything you have to give came from God in the first place, and one way to honor Him is by joyfully giving of your resources.

is the kingdom, O Lord, and Yours it is to be exalted as Head over all.

12 Both riches and honor come from You, and You reign over all. In Your hands are power and might; in Your hands it is to make great and to give strength to all.

13 Now therefore, our God, we thank You and praise Your glorious name *and* those attributes which that name denotes.

14 But who am I, and what are my people, that we should retain strength *and* be able to offer thus so willingly? For all things come from You, and out of Your own [hand] we have given You.

15 For we are strangers before You,

and sojourners, as all our fathers were; our days on the earth are like a shadow, and there is no hope *or* expectation of remaining.

16 O Lord our God, all this store that we have prepared to build You a house for Your holy Name *and* the token of Your presence comes from Your hand, and is all Your own.

17 I know also, my God, that You try the heart and delight in uprightness. In the uprightness of my heart I have freely offered all these things. And now I have seen with joy Your people who are present here offer voluntarily *and* freely to You.

18 O Lord, God of Abraham, Isaac, and Israel, our fathers, keep forever such purposes *and* thoughts in the minds of Your people, and direct *and* establish their hearts toward You.

19 And give to Solomon my son a blameless heart to keep Your commandments, testimonies, and statutes, and to do all that is necessary to build the palace [for You] for which I have made provision.

20 And David said to all the assembly, Now adore (praise and thank) the Lord your God! And all the assembly blessed the Lord, the God of their fathers, and bowed down and did obeisance to the Lord and to the king [as His earthly representative].

21 The next day they offered sacrifices and burnt offerings to the Lord: 1,000 bulls, 1,000 rams, and 1,000 lambs, with their drink offerings, and sacrifices in abundance for all Israel.

22 They ate and drank before the Lord on that day with great rejoicing. They made Solomon son of David king a second time, and anointed him as prince for the Lord and Zadok to be high priest.

23 Then Solomon sat on the throne of the Lord as king instead of David his father; and he prospered, and all Israel obeyed him.

24 All the leaders and mighty men, and also all the sons of King David, pledged allegiance to King Solomon.

25 And the Lord magnified Solomon exceedingly in the sight of all Israel and bestowed upon him such royal majesty as had not been on any king before him in Israel.

26 Thus David son of Jesse reigned over all Israel.

27 The time he reigned over Israel was forty years—he reigned seven years in Hebron and thirty-three years in Jerusalem.

28 He died in a good old age [his seventy-first year], full *and* satisfied with days, riches, and honor. Solomon his son reigned in his stead.

29 Now the acts of King David, from first to last, are written in the recorded words of Samuel the seer, Nathan the prophet, and Gad the seer,

30 With accounts of all his reign and his might, and the times through which he and Israel passed, as did all the kingdoms of the countries.

Second Chronicles

Author:
Attributed to Ezra

Date:
Probably between 425 BC and 400 BC

Everyday Life Principles:
We need to see ourselves as a temple, a place where God is pleased to abide.

God blesses us when we seek Him.

Remember, the battle belongs to the Lord.

Just as I Chronicles recounts the reign of King David, II Chronicles records the rule of David's son, King Solomon, who is often called the wisest man who ever lived. No doubt, Solomon's greatest achievement was the completion of the temple—a permanent place where God would be pleased to dwell and be worshiped in the midst of His people.

One of the ongoing themes of II Chronicles is the instruction to seek God. Because of their history, God's people knew how miserable their lives could be when they did not seek Him and how blessed they could be when they did inquire of Him. Nevertheless, God continually reminded them in various ways throughout II Chronicles to consult Him in every situation.

I believe that one of the greatest truths in Scripture—one that we need to keep in the forefront of our minds as we go about our everyday lives—is found in II Chronicles 20: *The battle belongs to the Lord.* When we belong to God, our battles belong to Him too. We do not have to fight life's wars in our own strength, but we fight in the power of our God, Who always gains the victory.

I hope that II Chronicles will serve as a reminder to you to seek God continually and make a place for Him in every area of your life.

1 SOLOMON SON of David was strengthened in his kingdom, and the Lord his God was with him and made him exceedingly great.
2 Solomon spoke to all Israel, to the captains of thousands and of hundreds, and to the judges, and to every prince in all Israel, the heads of the fathers' houses.
3 And Solomon and all the assembly [a united nation] with him went to the high place that was at Gibeon, for the Tent of Meeting of God, which Moses the servant of the Lord had made in the wilderness, was there [where the Canaanites had habitually worshiped].
4 But David had brought up the ark of God from Kiriath-jearim to the place which David had prepared for it, for he had pitched a tent for it at Jerusalem.
5 Moreover, the bronze altar that Bezalel son of Uri, the son of Hur, had made was there before the tabernacle of the Lord, and Solomon and the assembly sought [the Lord].
6 Solomon went up there to the bronze altar before the Lord at the Tent of Meeting and offered 1,000 burnt offerings on it.
7 That night God appeared to Solomon and said to him, Ask what I shall give you.
8 And Solomon said to God, You have shown great mercy *and* lovingkindness to David my father and have made me king in his place.
9 Now, O Lord God, let Your promise to David my father be fulfilled, for you have made me king over a people like the dust of the earth in multitude.
10 Give me now wisdom and knowledge to go out and come in before this people, for who can rule this Your people who are so great?

putting the Word to work

Do you sometimes feel overwhelmed by everything you are supposed to be doing? Solomon certainly seemed to struggle with such feelings. Ask God, as Solomon did, for wisdom as to how you are to carry out your tasks (see II Chronicles 1:9, 10). He has promised to give wisdom to those who ask.

11 God replied to Solomon, Because this was in your heart and you have not asked for riches, possessions, honor, *and* glory, or the life of your foes, or even for long life, but have asked wisdom and knowledge for yourself, that you may rule *and* judge My people over whom I have made you king,
12 Wisdom and knowledge are granted you. And I will give you riches, possessions, honor, *and* glory, such as none of the kings had before you, and none after you shall have their equal.
13 Then Solomon came from the high place at Gibeon, from before the Tent of Meeting, to Jerusalem. And he reigned over Israel.
14 Solomon gathered chariots and horsemen; he had 1,400 chariots and 12,000 horsemen, which he placed in the cities [suited for the use] of chariots and with the king at Jerusalem.
15 And the king made silver and gold in Jerusalem as common as stones, and he made cedar as plentiful as the sycamores of the lowland.
16 Solomon's horses were brought out of Egypt; the king's merchants received them in droves, [a]each drove at a price.
17 They imported from Egypt a char-

a Solomon's actions were in violation of the commands given through Moses in Deut. 17:16, 17 (see also I Kings 4:26; I Kings 10:26—11:1-4).

iot for 600 shekels of silver, and a horse for 150; so they brought out horses for all the Hittite and Syrian kings as export agents.

2 SOLOMON DETERMINED to build a temple for the ᵇName of the Lord and a royal capitol.

2 And Solomon counted out 70,000 men to bear burdens, 80,000 to be stonecutters in the hill country, and 3,600 overseers.

3 And Solomon sent to Hiram king of Tyre, saying, As you dealt with David my father and sent him cedars to build himself a house in which to dwell, even so deal with me.

4 Behold, I am about to build a house for the Name of the Lord my God, dedicated to Him for the burning of incense of sweet spices before Him, for the continual showbread, and for the burnt offerings morning and evening, on the Sabbaths, New Moons, and on the solemn feasts of the Lord our God, as ordained forever for Israel.

5 The house which I am to build is great, for our God is greater than all gods.

6 But who is able to build Him a house, since heaven, even highest heaven, cannot contain Him? Who am I to build Him a house, except as a place to burn incense in worship before Him?

7 Now therefore, send a man skilled to work in gold, silver, bronze, and iron, and in purple, crimson, and blue colors, who is a trained engraver, to work with the skilled men who are with me in Judah and Jerusalem, whom David my father provided.

8 Send me also from Lebanon cedar, cypress, and algum timber, for I know your servants can skillfully cut timber in Lebanon; and my servants will be with your servants,

9 To prepare for me timber in abundance, for the house I am about to build shall be great and wonderful.

10 And I will give to your servants who cut timber 20,000 measures of crushed wheat and also of barley, and 20,000 baths of wine and also of oil.

11 Then Hiram king of Tyre replied in writing sent to Solomon, Because the Lord loves His people, He has made you king over them.

12 Hiram said also, Blessed be the Lord, the God of Israel, Who made heaven and earth, Who has given to David the king a wise son, endued with prudence and understanding, who should build a house for the Lord and a royal palace as his capitol.

13 Now I have sent a skilled man, endued with understanding, even Huram-abi, my trusted counselor,

14 The son of a woman of the daughters of ᶜDan; his father was a man of Tyre. He is a trained worker in gold, silver, bronze, iron, stone, and wood; in purple, blue, and crimson colors, and in fine linen; and also to engrave any type of engraving and to carry out any design given him, with your skilled men and those of my lord, David your father.

15 Now therefore, the wheat, barley, oil, and wine of which my lord has

speak the Word

I declare, God, that You are greater than all other so-called gods!
ADAPTED FROM II CHRONICLES 2:5

b See footnote on Deut. 12:5.   c I Kings 7:14 says that this woman was of the tribe of Naphtali. Doubtless her mother's marriage identified her with a tribe of which she was not a native.

life point

When Solomon was building the temple, a dwelling place for God, he chose laborers who were skilled in their crafts (see II Chronicles 2:7). These men knew what they were gifted to do, and they were skilled at doing it. When I think about them, I am reminded of how many people today are asking, *What am I supposed to do with my life? What is my purpose on earth? Does God have a calling on my life?* God answers these questions through our natural gifts and abilities, and He helps us discover our purposes through the natural skills and unique talents He bestows upon us.

God-given gifts are the skills a person easily performs without formal training. Although training and education may help to perfect our skills, they are readily recognized prior to the training. Many great artists know exactly how to put shapes and colors together, and so they enjoy designing buildings or sculpting beautiful and useful items. Many songwriters simply write down the music they hear in their heads. Some people are great at organizing, while others are natural counselors, helping people sort out their lives and their relationships. I have always been a good communicator. No matter what our gifts are, we all derive great pleasure from doing what we are naturally good at doing. We do not have to try to do it; it comes naturally.

If you are unsure of your purpose in life, just do what you are good at doing, and watch God confirm it by blessing your endeavors. Then be diligent to develop your gifts, so you can be skilled at what you are gifted to do.

spoken, let him send them to his servants,

16 And we will cut whatever timber you need from Lebanon and bring it to you in rafts by sea to Joppa, so you may take it up to Jerusalem.

17 Then Solomon took a census of all the aliens in the land of Israel, like the census of them which his father David had taken. They were found to be 153,600.

18 And he assigned 70,000 of them to be burden bearers, 80,000 to work in the mountain quarries, and 3,600 as overseers to direct the people's work.

3 THEN SOLOMON began to build the house of the Lord at Jerusalem on Mount Moriah, where the Lord appeared to David his father, in the place that David had appointed, on the threshing floor of Ornan the Jebusite. [I Chron. 21:20-22.]

2 And Solomon began to build on the second day of the second month in the fourth year of his reign.

3 Now these are the measurements for the foundations which Solomon laid for the house of God. The length in cubits by the former measure was sixty cubits, and the breadth twenty cubits.

4 The porch *or* vestibule across the front of the house was the same length as the house's breadth, twenty cubits, and the [d]height 120 cubits. He overlaid it inside with pure gold.

5 And the greater house (the Holy Place) he lined with cypress and overlaid it with fine gold and made palm trees and chains on it.

6 And he adorned the house with precious stones for beauty; and the gold was gold of Parvaim.

7 He lined the house (the Holy Place), its beams, thresholds, walls,

---

d This extreme height is believed by most scholars to be a copyist's error, but II Chron. 7:21 seems to confirm it. It reads, ". . . this house, which was so high . . ."

and doors with gold, and engraved cherubim on the walls.
8 He made the Most Holy Place, its length equaling the breadth of the house, twenty cubits, and its breadth twenty cubits; he overlaid it with 600 talents of fine gold.
9 The weight of the nails was fifty shekels of gold. And he lined the upper chambers with gold.
10 And in the Most Holy Place he made two cherubim of image work, and they were overlaid with gold.
11 And the wings of the cherubim [combined] extended twenty cubits: one wing of one cherub was five cubits, reaching to the wall of the house, and its other wing of five cubits touched the other cherub's wing.
12 And of the other cherub one wing of five cubits touched the wall of the house, and the other wing, also five cubits, joined the wing of the first cherub.
13 The wings of these cherubim extended twenty cubits; the cherubim stood on their feet, their faces toward the Holy Place.
14 And he made the veil [between the Holy Place and the Most Holy Place] of blue, purple, and crimson colors, and fine linen, and embroidered cherubim on it.
15 Before the house he made two pillars, 35 cubits high, with a capital on the top of each which was five cubits.
16 He made chains like a necklace and put them on the heads of the pillars, and he made 100 pomegranates and put them on the chains.
17 He erected the pillars before the temple, one on the right, the other on the left, and called the one on the right Jachin [he shall establish] and the one on the left Boaz [in it is strength].

4 ALSO SOLOMON made an altar of bronze, its top twenty by twenty cubits and its height ten cubits.

2 Also he made a round Sea of molten metal, ten cubits from brim to brim and five cubits high, and a line of thirty cubits measured around it.
3 Under it were figures of oxen encircling it, ten to a cubit. The oxen were in two rows, cast in one piece with it.
4 It stood upon twelve oxen, three looking north, three west, three south, three east; and the Sea rested upon them, and all their hind parts were inward.
5 Its thickness was a handbreadth; its brim was like the brim of a cup, like the flower of a lily; it held 3,000 baths (measures).
6 He made also ten lavers in which to wash and put five on the right (south) side and five on the left (north). Such things as they offered for the burnt offering they washed in them, but the Sea was for the priests to wash in.
7 And he made ten golden lampstands as directed and set them in the temple, five on the right side and five on the left.
8 He made also ten tables and placed them in the temple, five each on the right and left sides, and 100 basins of gold.
9 Moreover, he made the priests' court, and the great court and doors for the court, and overlaid their doors with bronze.
10 And he set the Sea at the southeast corner of the house.
11 And Huram made the pots, shovels, and basins. So Huram finished the work of God's house that he did for King Solomon:
12 The two pillars; the bowls; the capitals on top of the two pillars; and the two networks to cover the two bowls of the capitals on top of the pillars;
13 And 400 pomegranates for the two networks, two rows of pomegranates for each network, to cover the two bowls of the capitals upon the pillars.

14 He made also bases *or* stands and lavers upon the bases;

15 One Sea and the twelve oxen under it;

16 The pots, shovels, and fleshhooks, and all their equipment Huram his trusted counselor made of burnished bronze for King Solomon for the house of the Lord.

17 In the plain of the Jordan the king cast them, in the clay ground between Succoth and Zeredah.

18 Solomon made all these things in such great numbers that the weight of the bronze was not computed.

19 And Solomon made all the vessels for the house of God: the golden altar also; and the tables for the showbread (the bread of the Presence);

20 And the lampstands with their lamps of pure gold, to burn before the inner sanctuary (the Holy of Holies) as directed;

21 The flowers, lamps, and tongs, of purest gold;

22 The snuffers, basins, dishes for incense, and firepans, of pure gold; and for the temple entry, the inner doors for the Most Holy Place and the doors of the Holy Place were of gold.

5 THUS ALL the work that Solomon did for the house of the Lord was finished. He brought in all the things that David his father had dedicated, and the silver, the gold, and all the vessels he put in the treasuries of the house of God.

2 Then Solomon assembled the elders of Israel and all the heads of the tribes, the chiefs of the fathers' houses of the Israelites, to Jerusalem to bring up the ark of the covenant of the Lord out of the City of David, which is Zion.

3 All the men of Israel gathered to the king at the feast in the seventh month.

4 And all the elders of Israel came, and the Levites took up the ark.

5 And the priests and Levites brought up the ark, the Tent of Meeting, and all the holy vessels that were in the Tent.

6 Also King Solomon and all the assembly of Israel who were gathered to him before the ark sacrificed sheep and oxen so numerous that they could not be counted or reported.

7 And the priests brought the ark of the covenant of the Lord to its place, to the sanctuary of the house, into the Holy of Holies, under the wings of the cherubim;

8 For the cherubim spread out their wings over the place of the ark, making a covering above the ark and its poles.

9 And they drew out the poles of the ark, so that the ends of the poles protruding from the ark were visible from the front of the Holy of Holies, but were not visible from without. It is there to this day.

10 There was nothing in the ark except the two tables [the Ten Commandments] which Moses put in it at Mount Horeb, when the Lord made a covenant with the Israelites when they came out of Egypt.

11 And when the priests had come out of the Holy Place—for all the priests present had sanctified themselves, separating themselves from everything that defiles, without regard to their divisions;

12 And all the Levites who were singers—all of those of Asaph, Heman, and Jeduthun, with their sons and kinsmen, arrayed in fine linen, having cymbals, harps, and lyres—stood at the

putting the Word to work

Worship is a powerful way for us to draw near to God, just as it was in Solomon's day (see II Chronicles 5:11–14). Do you long to experience His presence in your life? Then worship, worship, worship!

east end of the altar, and with them 120 priests blowing trumpets;

13 And when the trumpeters and singers were joined in unison, making one sound to be heard in praising and thanking the Lord, and when they lifted up their voice with the trumpets and cymbals and other instruments for song and praised the Lord, saying, For He is good, for His mercy *and* loving-kindness endure forever, then the house of the Lord was filled with a cloud,

14 So that the priests could not stand to minister because of the cloud, for the glory of the Lord filled the house of God.

life point

In the Old Testament, God's glory visibly filled the temple and overwhelmed the priests to the point that they were unable to stand (see II Chronicles 5:13, 14). Today, under the New Covenant, you and I *are* God's temple (see I Corinthians 6:19). God wants to display His glory in and through us as dramatically as He did in the physical temple of Solomon's day. When God's glory is manifested in your life, others will look at you and say, "Wow, what a great God you serve," because the power of His goodness toward you is visibly evident to them. God wants to "wow" you as He fills your temple with His power and glory.

speak the Word

6 THEN SOLOMON said, The Lord has said that He would dwell in the thick darkness;

2 I have built You a house, [in which the dark Holy of Holies seems] a [fitting] abode for You, a place for You to dwell in forever.

3 And the king turned his face and blessed all the assembly of Israel, and they all stood.

4 And he said, Blessed be the Lord, the God of Israel, Who has fulfilled with His hands what He promised with His mouth to David my father, saying,

5 Since the day that I brought My people out of the land of Egypt, I chose no city among all the tribes of Israel to build a house in, that My Name might be there, ᵉneither chose I any man to be a ruler over My people Israel;

6 But I have chosen Jerusalem, that My Name [and the symbol of My presence] might be there, and I have chosen David to be over My people Israel.

7 Now it was in the heart of David my father to build a house for the Name *and* renown of the Lord, the God of Israel.

8 But the Lord said to David my father, Since it was in your heart to build a house for My Name *and* renown, you did well that it was in your heart.

9 Yet you shall not build the house, but your son, who shall be born to you—he shall build the house for My Name.

I bless You, Lord, because You fulfill with Your hands what You promise with Your mouth.
ADAPTED FROM II CHRONICLES 6:4

e God is plainly saying here that it was not His desire for Israel to have a king. To be sure, when to Samuel's attempt to dissuade them they replied, "No! We will have a king over us, that we also may be like all the nations" (I Sam. 8:19-20), God said to Samuel, "They have rejected Me, that I should not be King over them . . . appoint them a king" (I Sam. 8:7, 22). But Saul was originally the people's choice, not God's choice. The Bible nowhere teaches that "the voice of the people is the voice of

10 The Lord therefore has performed His word that He has spoken, for I have risen up in the place of David my father and sit on the throne of Israel, as the Lord promised, and have built the house for the Name of the Lord, the God of Israel.
11 In it have I put the ark [the symbol of His presence], in which is the covenant of the Lord [the Ten Commandments] which He made with the people of Israel.
12 And Solomon stood before the altar of the Lord in the presence of all the assembly of Israel and spread forth his hands.
13 For he had made a bronze scaffold, five cubits square and three cubits high, and had set it in the midst of the court; upon it he stood, and he knelt upon his knees before all the assembly of Israel and spread forth his hands toward heaven,
14 And said, O Lord, God of Israel, there is no God like You in the heavens or in the earth, keeping covenant and showing mercy *and* loving-kindness to Your servants who walk before You with all their hearts,
15 You Who have kept Your promises to my father David and fulfilled with Your hand what You spoke with Your mouth, as it is today.
16 Now therefore, O Lord, God of Israel, keep with Your servant David

putting the Word to work

God is faithful to fulfill every one of His promises to us. How do you respond to Him when He brings one of His promises to pass in your life? Be like Solomon; tell others about God's greatness and worship Him with thanksgiving (see II Chronicles 6:12–15).

my father that which You promised him, saying, There shall not fail a man in My sight to sit on the throne of Israel, provided your children are careful to walk in My law as you, David, have walked before Me.
17 Now then, O Lord, God of Israel, let Your word to Your servant David be verified.
18 But will God actually dwell with men on the earth? Behold, heaven and the heaven of heavens cannot contain You; how much less this house which I have built!
19 Yet have respect for the prayer of Your servant and for his supplication, O Lord my God, to listen to the cry and the prayer which Your servant prays before You,

life point

Throughout II Chronicles 6, we see Solomon crying out for God to hear his prayers. In order to accomplish what God has called us to do in this life, we need to be assured He does hear our prayers and does respond to them (see Psalm 65:2). Never neglect to pray, because God is always listening and ready to answer. Where there is prayer, there is power!

20 That Your eyes may be open upon this house day and night, toward the place in which You have said You would put Your Name [and the symbol of your presence], to listen to *and* heed the prayer which Your servant prays facing this place.
21 So listen to *and* heed the requests of Your servant and Your people Israel which they shall make facing this place. Hear from Your dwelling place, heaven; and when You hear, forgive.
22 If a man sins against his neighbor,

God." But it does teach that when people make demands of God that are not in harmony with His will, He may grant them to their sorrow, and send "leanness into their souls" (Ps. 106:15).

and he is required to take an oath, and the oath comes before Your altar in this house,

23 Then hear from heaven and do; and judge Your servants, requiting the wicked by bringing his conduct upon his own head, and justifying the [uncompromisingly] righteous by giving him according to his righteousness (his uprightness and right standing with God).

24 If Your people Israel have been defeated before the enemy because they have sinned against You, and shall return, confess Your name [and You Yourself], and pray and make supplication before You in this house,

25 Then hear from heaven and forgive the sin of Your people Israel and bring them again to the land which You gave to them and their fathers.

26 When the heavens are shut up and there is no rain because Your people have sinned against You, yet if they pray toward this place, confess your name [and You Yourself], and turn from their sin when You afflict them,

27 Then hear from heaven and forgive the sin of Your servants, [all of] Your people Israel, when You have taught them the good way in which they should walk. And send rain upon Your land which You have given to Your people for an inheritance.

28 If there is famine in the land, if there is pestilence, blight, mildew, locusts, or caterpillars, if their enemies besiege them in any of their cities, whatever plague or sickness there may be,

29 Then whatever prayer or supplication any man or all of Your people Israel shall make—each knowing his own affliction and his own sorrow and stretching out his hands toward this house—

30 Then hear from heaven, Your dwelling place, and forgive, and render to every man according to all his ways, whose heart You know; for You, You only, know men's hearts,

31 That they may fear You and walk in Your ways as long as they live in the land which You gave to our fathers.

32 Also concerning the stranger who is not of Your people Israel but has come from a far country for Your great name's sake and Your mighty power and Your outstretched arm—if he comes and prays toward this house,

33 Hear from heaven, from Your dwelling place, and do all for which the stranger calls to You, that all peoples of the earth may know Your name and fear You [reverently and worshipfully], as do Your people Israel, and may know that this house which I have built is called by Your Name.

34 If Your people go out to war against their enemies by the way that You send them, and they pray to You facing this city [Jerusalem] which You have chosen and the house which I have built for Your Name,

35 Then hear from heaven their prayer and supplication, and maintain their cause.

36 If they sin against You—for there is no man who does not sin—and You are angry with them and give them to enemies who take them captive to a land far or near;

37 Yet if they repent in the land to which they have been carried captive, and turn and pray there, saying, We

speak the Word

have sinned, we have done wrong, and have dealt wickedly;

38 If they return to You with all their heart and soul in the land of their captivity, and pray facing their land which You gave to their fathers and toward the city which You have chosen and the house which I have built for Your Name;

39 Then hear from heaven, Your dwelling place, their prayer and supplications, and maintain their cause; and forgive Your people, who have sinned against You.

40 Now, O my God, I beseech You, let Your eyes be open and Your ears attentive to the prayer offered in this temple.

41 So now arise, O Lord God, and come into Your resting place, You and the ark of Your strength *and* power. Let Your priests, O Lord God, be clothed with salvation, and let Your saints (Your zealous ones) rejoice in good *and* in Your goodness.

42 O Lord God, ᶠturn not away the face of [me] Your anointed one; [earnestly] remember Your good deeds, mercy, *and* steadfast love for David Your servant.

7 WHEN SOLOMON had finished praying, the fire came down from heaven and consumed the burnt offering and the sacrifices, and the glory of the Lord filled the house.

2 The priests could not enter the house of the Lord, because the glory of the Lord had filled the Lord's house.

3 And when all the people of Israel saw how the fire came down and the glory of the Lord upon the house, they bowed with their faces upon the pavement and worshiped and praised the Lord, saying, For He is good, for His mercy *and* loving-kindness endure forever.

4 Then the king and all the people offered sacrifices before the Lord.

5 King Solomon offered a sacrifice of 22,000 oxen and 120,000 sheep. So the king and all the people dedicated God's house.

6 The priests stood at their posts, and the Levites also, with instruments of music to the Lord, which King David had made to praise *and* give thanks to the Lord—for His mercy *and* loving-kindness endure forever— whenever David praised through their

speak the Word

Lord, I rejoice in You and in Your goodness!
ADAPTED FROM II CHRONICLES 6:41

f Young Solomon seems, and doubtless is, utterly sincere as he offers this prayer of which God shows His approval by the miraculous demonstration of His presence in the next verse. It raises the ever-present question, How could Solomon have begun his career like this, and have written his unquestionably divinely inspired books, and yet have fallen eventually into utter defiance of God's will? Not as the result of one false step, as with David, but as the habit of his life for the remainder of his days! Not broken with unspeakable sorrow for his awful sin, as was his penitent father (Ps. 51), but without ever apparently repenting or confessing his awful defiance of God and His explicit commands and warnings, given specifically to Solomon himself (II Chron. 7:17-22). Possibly in this closing sentence of Solomon's prayer we detect the fallacy in the young king's thinking. He seems to be saying in substance, "O Lord God, I am **Your responsibility** now; it will be for **You** to see that my face does not turn away from You; and not for my sake, but [since my name is identified with this temple as well as Yours, You must keep my face turned toward You] for Your own sake!" God lost no unnecessary time in attempting to set the young man straight as to whose is the responsibility for sin—in his case specifically (II Chron. 7:12, 17-22). But there is no evidence that Solomon applied it to himself; though he preached a bit to others, he seems to have considered himself exempt from obeying God's commands—an attitude which has brought disaster upon every person who has ever taken it, however great, or wise, or rich, or otherwise sufficient.

ministry; the priests blew trumpets before them, and all Israel stood.

7 Moreover, Solomon consecrated the middle of the court that was before the house of the Lord, for there he offered burnt offerings and the fat of the peace offerings, because the bronze altar which [he] had made was not sufficient to receive the burnt offerings, the cereal offerings, and the fat.

8 At that time Solomon held the feast for seven days, and all Israel with him, a very great assembly, from the entrance of Hamath to the Brook of Egypt.

9 The eighth day they made a solemn assembly, for they had kept the dedication of the altar and the feast, each for seven days.

10 And on the twenty-third day of the seventh month he sent the people away to their homes, glad and merry in heart for the goodness that the Lord had shown to David, to Solomon, and to Israel His people.

11 Thus Solomon finished the Lord's house and the king's house; all that [he] had planned to do in the Lord's house and his own house he accomplished successfully.

12 And the Lord appeared to Solomon by night and said to him: I have heard your prayer and have chosen this place for Myself as a house of sacrifice.

13 If I shut up heaven so no rain falls, or if I command locusts to devour the land, or if I send pestilence among My people,

14 If My people, who are called by My name, shall humble themselves, pray, seek, crave, *and* require of necessity My face and turn from their wicked ways, then will I hear from heaven, forgive their sin, and heal their land.

15 Now My eyes will be open and My ears attentive to prayer offered in this place.

16 For I have chosen and sanctified

putting the Word to work

God is very clear about what is necessary for a nation to receive His blessing (see II Chronicles 7:14). Did you know that you can help to bring about God's blessing upon your country? In humility, pray on behalf of your nation, identifying its sins and confessing them. Seek God's face, and pray that anyone who may be doing evil in your nation will turn from their wicked ways. God has promised forgiveness and healing to those nations that come to Him in humility and repentance.

(set apart for holy use) this house, that My Name may be here forever, and My eyes and My heart will be here perpetually.

17 As for you [Solomon], if you will walk before me as David your father walked, and do all I have commanded you, and observe My statutes and My ordinances, [I Kings 11:1-11.]

18 Then I will establish the throne of your kingdom, as I covenanted with David your father, saying, There shall not fail you a man to be ruler in Israel.

19 But if you [people] turn away and forsake My statutes and My commandments which I have set before you and go and serve other gods and worship them,

20 Then will I pluck [Israel] up by the roots out of My land which I have given [them]; and this house which I have hallowed for My Name will I cast out of My sight, and will make it to be a proverb and a byword among all nations. [Jer. 24:9, 10.]

21 And this house, which was so high, shall be an astonishment to everyone passing it, and they will say, Why has the Lord done thus to this land and to this house?

22 Then men will say, Because they forsook the Lord, the God of their fathers, Who brought them out of

Egypt, and they laid hold of other gods and worshiped and served them; therefore has He brought all this evil upon them.

8 AT THE end of twenty years, in which Solomon had built the house of the Lord and his own house,

2 The cities which Huram had given to [him] Solomon rebuilt *and* fortified, and caused the Israelites to dwell there.

3 And Solomon took Hamath-zobah.

4 He built Tadmor in the wilderness and all his store cities in Hamath.

5 Also he built Upper Beth-horon and Lower Beth-horon, fortified cities with walls, gates, and bars,

6 And Baalath and all the store cities [he] had, and all the cities for his chariots and the cities for his horsemen, and all that Solomon desired to build in Jerusalem, in Lebanon, and in all his dominion.

7 All the people who were left of the Hittites, Amorites, Perizzites, Hivites, and Jebusites, who were not of Israel,

8 But descendants of those who were left in the land, whom the Israelites had not destroyed—of them Solomon made a levy for forced labor to this day.

9 But of the Israelites Solomon made no slaves for his work; but they were men of war, chiefs of his captains, and captains of his chariots and horsemen.

10 These were the chiefs of King Solomon's officers, 250 in authority over the people.

11 Solomon brought the daughter of Pharaoh out of the City of David into the house he had built for her, for he said, My wife shall not dwell in the house of David king of Israel, because the places are holy to which the ark of the Lord has come.

12 Then Solomon offered burnt offerings to the Lord on the Lord's altar which he had built before the [temple] porch *or* vestibule,

13 A certain number every day, offering as Moses commanded for the Sabbaths, the New Moons, and the solemn feast days three times in the year—the Feasts of Unleavened Bread, of Weeks, and of Tabernacles.

14 And he appointed, as ordered by David his father, the divisions of the priests for their service, and the Levites to their offices to praise and to serve before the priests as the duty of every day required, and the gatekeepers also by their divisions at every gate; for so had David the man of God commanded.

15 And they did not turn from the command of the king to the priests and Levites in any respect or concerning the treasuries.

16 Thus all the work of Solomon was prepared from the day the foundation of the Lord's house was laid until it was finished. So the house of the Lord was completed.

17 Then Solomon went to Ezion-geber and to Eloth on the shore of the [Red] Sea in the land of Edom.

18 And Huram sent him by his servants ships and servants familiar with the sea; and they went with the servants of Solomon to Ophir and took from there 450 talents of gold and brought them to King Solomon.

9 WHEN THE queen of Sheba heard of the fame of Solomon, she came to Jerusalem to test him with hard questions, accompanied by very many attendants and camels bearing spices, much gold, and precious stones. And when she came to Solomon, she talked with him of all that was on her mind.

2 And Solomon answered all her questions; there was nothing hidden from [him] which he was unable to make clear to her.

3 And when the queen of Sheba had

seen Solomon's wisdom, the house he had built,

4 The food of his table, the seating of his officials, the [standing at] attention of his servants, their apparel, his cupbearers also and their apparel, and his burnt offerings which he offered at the house of the Lord, there was no more spirit in her.

5 She said to the king, The report which I heard in my own land of your acts *and* sayings and of your wisdom was true,

6 But I did not believe their words until I came and my eyes had seen it. Behold, the half of the greatness of your wisdom was not told me; you surpass the fame that I heard of you.

7 Happy are your wives *and* men, and happy are these your servants who stand continually before you and hear your wisdom!

8 Blessed be the Lord your God, Who delighted in you and set you on His throne to be king for the Lord your God! Because your God loved Israel and would establish them forever, He made you king over them, to do justice and righteousness.

9 She gave the king 120 talents of gold, a very large quantity of spices, and precious stones; such spice was not anywhere as that which the queen of Sheba gave King Solomon.

10 The servants of Huram and [those] of Solomon, who brought gold from Ophir, also brought algum trees and precious stones.

11 The king made of the algum trees terraces *or* walks to the house of the Lord and to the king's palace, and lyres and harps for the singers; none such had ever been seen before in the land of Judah.

12 And King Solomon gave to the queen of Sheba all her desire, whatever she asked, besides what she had brought to the king. So she with her servants returned to her own land.

13 Now the weight of gold that came to Solomon in one year was 666 talents,

14 Besides what traders and merchants brought; and all the kings of Arabia and governors of the country brought gold and silver to Solomon.

15 And King Solomon made 200 large shields *or* bucklers of beaten gold; 600 shekels of beaten gold went into each shield.

16 And he made 300 shields of beaten gold, with 300 shekels of gold spread on each shield. And the king put them in the House of the Forest of Lebanon.

17 Moreover, [he] made a great throne of ivory and overlaid it with pure gold.

18 There were six steps to the throne and a gold footstool attached to the throne, and arms on each side of the seat, with two lions standing beside the arms.

19 And twelve lions stood there one on either end of each of the six steps. The like of it was never made in any kingdom before.

20 King Solomon's drinking vessels were all of gold, and all the vessels of the House of the Forest of Lebanon were of pure gold; silver was not counted as anything in the days of Solomon.

21 For the king's ships went to Tarshish with Huram's servants; once every three years the ships of Tarshish came bringing gold, silver, ivory, apes, and peacocks.

22 King Solomon surpassed all the kings of the earth in riches and wisdom.

23 And all the kings of the earth sought the presence of Solomon to hear his wisdom which God had put into his mind.

24 And every man brought his tribute: silver and gold articles, robes, armor, spices, horses, and mules, so much year by year.

25 Solomon had 4,000 stalls for

putting the Word to work

If someone wanted to give you either wealth or wise counsel, which would you choose? Although the riches of Solomon surpassed those of all the kings of the earth, it was his wisdom that other rulers sought (see II Chronicles 9:23). Recognize, like the kings in Solomon's day, that God-given wisdom is far more valuable than wealth.

horses and chariots, and 12,000 horsemen, stationed in chariot cities or at Jerusalem with the king. [Deut. 17:16, 17.]

26 And he ruled over ᵍall the kings from the [Euphrates] River to the land of Philistia and to the frontier of Egypt.

27 The king made silver in Jerusalem as common as stones, and cedar wood as plentiful as sycamore trees in the lowlands.

28 And they imported horses for Solomon from Egypt and from all lands.

29 Now the rest of the acts of Solomon, from first to last, are they not written in the history of Nathan the prophet and in the prophecy of Ahijah the Shilonite and in the visions of Iddo the seer concerning Jeroboam the son of Nebat?

30 Solomon reigned in Jerusalem over all Israel forty years.

31 Then Solomon slept with his fathers; he was buried in the city of David his father. Rehoboam his son reigned in his stead.

10 REHOBOAM WENT to Shechem, for all Israel had gone to Shechem to make him king.

2 Jeroboam the son of Nebat was in Egypt, where he had fled from the presence of King Solomon, when he heard about the new king; so Jeroboam returned from Egypt.

3 And the people sent for him. So Jeroboam and all Israel came to Rehoboam, saying,

4 Your father [King Solomon] made our yoke grievous. So now make lighter the grievous service of your father and his heavy yoke that he put upon us, and we will serve you.

5 Rehoboam replied, Come again to me after three days. And the people departed.

6 King Rehoboam took counsel with the old men who stood before Solomon his father while he was alive, saying, What counsel do you give me in reply to the people?

7 And they answered him, If you are kind to [these] people and please them and speak good words to them, they will be your servants forever.

8 But the king forsook the counsel which the old men gave him and took counsel with the young men who were brought up with him and stood before him.

9 And he said to them, What answer do you advise that we give to the demand of [these] people, Make the yoke your father put upon us lighter?

10 The young men who were brought up with him said to him, Tell the people who said to you, Your father made our yoke heavy, but you make it lighter: My little finger is thicker than my father's loins.

11 For whereas my father put a heavy yoke upon you, I will add to your yoke. My father chastised you with whips, but I will chastise you with scorpions.

12 The third day Jeroboam and all the people returned to Rehoboam as he had said.

13 And the king answered them harshly, forsaking the counsel of the old men,

g See footnote on I Kings 4:21 for proof for this statement.

14 And answered them after the advice of the young men, saying, My father made your yoke heavy, but I will add to it; my father chastised you with whips, but I will chastise you with scorpions.

15 So the king did not heed the people, for it was ^hbrought about of God, that the Lord might perform His word which He spoke by Ahijah the Shilonite to Jeroboam son of Nebat. [I Kings 11:29-39.]

16 And when all Israel saw that the king would not listen to *and* heed them, they answered [him], What portion have we in David? We have no inheritance in the son of Jesse. Every man to your tents, O Israel! Now, David [tribe of Judah], see to your own house [under your tyrant King Rehoboam]! So all Israel went to their homes.

17 But as for the Israelites who dwelt in Judah's cities, Rehoboam ruled over them.

18 Then King Rehoboam sent Hadoram, who was over the forced labor, and the Israelites stoned him and he died. But King Rehoboam hastened to get up to his royal chariot to flee to Jerusalem.

19 And Israel has rebelled against the house of David to this day.

11 AND WHEN Rehoboam came to Jerusalem, he assembled of the house of Judah and Benjamin 180,000 chosen warriors to fight against [the ten rebellious tribes of] Israel to bring the kingdom again to Rehoboam.

2 But the word of the Lord came to Shemaiah the man of God, saying,

3 Say to Rehoboam son of Solomon king of Judah and to all Israel in Judah and Benjamin,

4 Thus says the Lord: You shall not go up or fight against your brethren. Return every man to his house, for this thing is from Me. And they obeyed the Lord and returned from going against Jeroboam.

5 Rehoboam dwelt in Jerusalem and built cities for defense in Judah.

6 He built Bethlehem, Etam, Tekoa,

7 Beth-zur, Soco, Adullam,

8 Gath, Mareshah, Ziph,

9 Adoraim, Lachish, Azekah,

10 Zorah, Aijalon, and Hebron, which are fortified cities in Judah and Benjamin.

11 He fortified the strongholds and put captains in them, with stores of food, oil, and vintage fruits.

12 And in each city he put shields and spears, and made them very strong. So he held Judah and Benjamin.

13 And the priests and the Levites who were in all Israel came over to Rehoboam from wherever they lived.

14 For the Levites left their suburbs and their possessions and came to Judah and Jerusalem, for Jeroboam and his sons had cast them out from executing the priest's office to the Lord.

15 And he appointed his own priests for the high places and for the [idols of demon] he-goats, and calves he had made. [I Kings 12:28.]

16 And after them out of all the tribes of Israel there came to Jerusalem those who set their hearts to seek *and* inquire of the Lord, the God of Israel, to sacrifice to the Lord, the God of their fathers.

17 So they strengthened the kingdom of Judah and upheld Rehoboam son of Solomon for three years; for they walked in the ways of David and Solomon for three years.

18 Rehoboam took as wife Mahalath, whose father was Jerimoth son of

h God permitted the revolt of the northern tribes, intending it as a punishment of the house of David for Solomon's apostasy (Robert Jamieson, A.R. Fausset and David Brown, *A Commentary*).

David; her mother was Abihail daughter of Eliab son of Jesse.

19 She bore him sons: Jeush, Shamariah, and Zaham.

20 And after her he took Maacah daughter [granddaughter] of Absalom, who bore him Abijah, Attai, Ziza, and Shelomith.

21 And Rehoboam loved Maacah daughter [granddaughter] of Absalom more than all his wives and concubines—for he took eighteen wives and sixty concubines, and he had twenty-eight sons and sixty daughters.

22 And Rehoboam made Abijah son of Maacah the chief prince among his brethren, for he intended to make him king.

23 And he dealt understandingly and dispersed his children throughout all Judah and Benjamin to every fortified city. He gave them abundant supplies, and he sought many wives for them.

12 WHEN REHOBOAM had established the kingdom and had strengthened himself, he forsook the law of the Lord, and all Israel with him.

2 And in the fifth year of King Rehoboam, because they had transgressed *and* been unfaithful to the Lord, Shishak king of Egypt came up against Jerusalem

3 With 1,200 chariots and 60,000 horsemen, and the people were without number who came with him from Egypt—the Libyans, Sukkiim, and Ethiopians.

4 And he took the fortified cities of Judah and came on to Jerusalem.

5 Then Shemaiah the prophet came to Rehoboam and the princes of Judah who had gathered at Jerusalem because of Shishak, and said to them, Thus says the Lord: You have forsaken Me, so I have abandoned you into the hands of Shishak.

6 Then the princes of Israel and the king humbled themselves and said, The Lord is righteous.

7 And when the Lord saw that they humbled themselves, the word of the Lord came to Shemaiah, saying, They have humbled themselves, so I will not destroy them, but I will grant them some deliverance; and My wrath shall not be poured out upon Jerusalem by the hand of Shishak.

8 Nevertheless, they shall be his servants, that they may know [the difference between] My service and the service of the kingdoms of the countries.

9 So Shishak king of Egypt came up against Jerusalem; he took away the treasures of the house of the Lord and of the king's house. He took everything. He took away also the shields of gold Solomon had made.

10 Instead of them King Rehoboam made shields of bronze and committed them to the hands of the officers of the guard who kept the door of the king's house.

11 And whenever the king entered the Lord's house, the guards came and got the shields of bronze and brought them again into the guard chamber.

12 When Rehoboam humbled himself, the wrath of the Lord turned from him, so as not to destroy him entirely; also in Judah conditions were good.

13 So King Rehoboam established *and* strengthened himself in Jerusalem and reigned. Rehoboam was forty-one years old when he began to reign, and he reigned seventeen years in Jerusalem, the city in which the Lord had chosen out of all the tribes of Israel to put His Name [and the symbol of His presence]. His mother was Naamah an Ammonitess.

14 And he did evil because he did not set his heart to seek (inquire of, yearn for) the Lord with all his desire.

15 Now the acts of Rehoboam, from

first to last, are they not written in the histories of Shemaiah the prophet and of Iddo the seer regarding genealogies? There were wars between Rehoboam of Judah and Jeroboam of Israel continually.

16 And Rehoboam slept with his fathers and was buried in the City of David; and Abijah his son reigned in his stead.

13

IN THE eighteenth year of King Jeroboam, Abijah began to reign over Judah.

2 He reigned three years in Jerusalem. His mother was Micaiah daughter of Uriel of Gibeah. And there was war between Abijah and Jeroboam of Israel.

3 And Abijah prepared for battle with an army of valiant men of war, 400,000 chosen men. Jeroboam set the battle in array against him with 800,000 chosen men, mighty men of valor.

4 And Abijah stood on Mount Zemaraim, in the hill country of Ephraim, and said, Hear me, O Jeroboam and all Israel!

5 Ought you not to know that the Lord, the God of Israel, gave the kingship over Israel to David forever, even to him and to his sons by a covenant of salt?

6 Yet Jeroboam son of Nebat, a servant of Solomon son of David, rose up and rebelled against his lord [the king].

7 And there gathered to him worthless men, base fellows, who strengthened themselves against Rehoboam son of Solomon when Rehoboam was young [as king], irresolute, and inexperienced and did not withstand them with firmness and strength.

8 And now you think to withstand the kingdom of the Lord which is in the hands of the sons of David, because you are a great multitude and you have with you the golden calves which Jeroboam made for you for gods.

9 Have you not driven out the priests of the Lord, the sons of Aaron, and the Levites, and made priests for yourselves like the peoples of other lands? So whoever comes to consecrate himself with a young bull and seven rams may be a priest of idols that are not gods.

10 But as for us, the Lord is our God, and we have not forsaken Him. We have priests ministering to the Lord who are sons of Aaron, and Levites for their service.

11 They offer to the Lord every morning and every evening burnt sacrifices and incense of sweet spices; they set in order the showbread on the table of pure gold and attend to the golden lampstand, that its lamps may be lighted every evening. For we keep the charge of the Lord our God, but you have forsaken Him.

12 Behold, God Himself is with us at our head, and His priests with their battle trumpets to sound an alarm against you. O Israelites, fight not against the Lord, the God of your fathers, for you cannot prosper.

13 But Jeroboam caused an ambushment to come around them from behind, so his troops were before Judah and the ambush behind.

14 When Judah looked, behold, the battle was before and behind; and they cried to the Lord, and the priests blew the trumpets.

15 Then the men of Judah gave a shout; and as they shouted, God smote Jeroboam and all Israel before Abijah and Judah.

16 And the Israelites fled before Judah, and God delivered them into their hands.

17 And Abijah and his people slew them with a great slaughter, so there fell of Israel 500,000 chosen men.

18 Thus the Israelites were brought low at that time, and the people of Judah prevailed because they relied upon the Lord, the God of their fathers.

19 And Abijah pursued Jeroboam and took some cities from him, Bethel, Jeshanah, and Ephraim (Ephron), with their towns.

20 Jeroboam did not recover strength again in the days of Abijah. And the Lord smote him and he died.

21 But Abijah became mighty. He married fourteen wives and had twenty-two sons and sixteen daughters.

22 And the rest of the acts of Abijah, his ways and his sayings, are written in the story of the prophet Iddo.

14 SO ABIJAH slept with his fathers, and they buried him in the City of David; and Asa his son reigned in his stead. In his days the land was at rest for ten years.

2 And Asa did what was good and right in the eyes of the Lord his God.

3 He took away the foreign altars and high places and broke down the idol pillars *or* obelisks and cut down the Asherim [symbols of the goddess Asherah]

4 And commanded Judah to seek the Lord, the God of their fathers [to inquire of and for Him and crave Him as a vital necessity], and to obey the law and the commandment.

5 Also Asa took out of all the cities of Judah the idolatrous high places and the incense altars. And the kingdom had rest under his reign.

6 And he built fortified cities in Judah, for the land had rest. He had no war in those years, for the Lord gave him peace.

7 Therefore he said to Judah, Let us build these cities and surround them with walls, towers, gates, and bars. The land is still ours, because we sought the Lord our God; we have sought Him [yearning for Him with all our desire] and He has given us rest *and* peace on every side. So they built and prospered.

8 Asa had an army of 300,000 men out of Judah, who bore bucklers and spears, and 280,000 out of Benjamin, who bore shields and drew bows, all mighty men of courage.

9 There came out against Judah Zerah the Ethiopian with a host of a million [that is, too many to be numbered] and 300 chariots, and came as far as Mareshah.

10 Then Asa went out against him, and they set up their lines of battle in the Valley of Zephathah at Mareshah.

11 Asa cried to the Lord his God, O Lord, there is none besides You to help, and it makes no difference to You whether the one You help is mighty or powerless. Help us, O Lord our God! For we rely on You, and we go against this multitude in Your name. O Lord, You are our God; let no man prevail against You!

12 So the Lord smote the Ethiopians before Asa and Judah, and the Ethiopians fled.

13 Asa and the people with him pursued them to Gerar; and the Ethiopians were overthrown, so that none remained alive; for they were destroyed before the Lord and His host, who carried away very much booty.

14 And they smote all the cities round about Gerar, for the fear of the Lord came upon them. They plundered all the cities, for there was much plunder in them.

speak the Word

God, there is none besides You to help me, and it makes no difference whether I am feeling mighty or powerless, I still need Your help. Help me, God; I am relying on You alone.

ADAPTED FROM II CHRONICLES **14:11**

15 They smote also the cattle encampments and carried away sheep in abundance and camels; and they returned to Jerusalem.

15

THE SPIRIT of God came upon Azariah son of Oded. **2** And he went out to meet Asa and said to him, Hear me, Asa, and all Judah and Benjamin: the Lord is with you while you are with Him. If you seek Him [inquiring for and of Him, craving Him as your soul's first necessity], He will be found by you; but if you [become indifferent and] forsake Him, He will forsake you. **3** Now for a long time Israel was without the true God, without a teaching priest, and without law. **4** But when they in their trouble turned to the Lord, the God of Israel, and [in desperation earnestly] sought Him, He was found by them.

putting the Word to work

Have you ever felt that God is hiding from you? Second Chronicles 15:1–4 provides us with encouragement as we seek God. He promises that when you seek Him, you *will* find Him. Always remember that He draws near to all those who draw near to Him.

5 And in those times there was no peace to him who went out nor to him who came in, but great *and* vexing afflictions *and* disturbances were upon all the inhabitants of the countries. **6** Nation was broke in pieces against nation, and city against city, for God vexed *and* troubled them with all sorts of adversity.

7 Be strong, therefore, and let not your hands be weak *and* slack, for your work shall be rewarded. **8** And when Asa heard these words, the prophecy of Oded the prophet, he took courage and put away the abominable idols from all the land of Judah and Benjamin and from the cities which he had taken in the hill country of Ephraim; and he repaired the altar [of burnt offering] of the Lord which was in front of the porch *or* vestibule [of the house] of the Lord. **9** And he gathered all Judah and Benjamin and the strangers with them out of Ephraim, Manasseh, and Simeon, for they came over to Asa out of Israel in large numbers when they saw that the Lord his God was with him. **10** So they gathered at Jerusalem in the third month of the fifteenth year of the reign of Asa. **11** And they sacrificed to the Lord on that day from the spoil which they had brought—700 oxen and 7,000 sheep. **12** And they entered into a covenant to seek the Lord, the God of their fathers, *and* to yearn for Him with all their heart's desire and with all their soul; **13** And that whoever would not seek the Lord, the God of Israel, should be put to death, whether young or old, man or woman. **14** They took an oath to the Lord with a loud voice, with shouting, with trumpets, and with cornets. **15** And all Judah rejoiced at the oath, for they had sworn with all their heart and sought Him [yearning for Him] with their whole desire, and He was found by them. And the Lord gave them rest *and* peace round about.

speak the Word

God, help me to be strong and not let my hands be weak or slack, knowing that my work will be rewarded.
ADAPTED FROM II CHRONICLES 15:7

16 Also Maacah, King Asa's mother, he removed from being queen mother, because she had made an abominable image for [the goddess] Asherah. Asa cut down her idol, crushed it, and burned it at the brook Kidron.

17 But the high places were not taken out of Israel. Nevertheless, the heart of Asa was blameless all his days.

18 And he brought into the house of God the things that his father [Abijah] had dedicated and those he himself had dedicated—silver and gold and vessels.

19 And there was no more war until the thirty-fifth year of the reign of Asa.

16 IN THE thirty-sixth year of Asa's reign, Baasha king of Israel came up against Judah, and built (fortified) Ramah intending to intercept anyone going out or coming in to Asa king of Judah.

2 Then Asa brought silver and gold out of the treasuries of the house of the Lord and of the king's house and sent them to Ben-hadad king of Syria, who dwelt at Damascus, saying,

3 Let there be a league between me and you, as was between my father and your father. Behold, I am sending you silver and gold; go, break your league with Baasha king of Israel, that he may withdraw from me.

4 And Ben-hadad hearkened to King Asa and sent the captains of his armies against the cities of Israel; and they smote Ijon, Dan, Abel-maim, and all the store cities of Naphtali.

5 And when Baasha heard it, he stopped building Ramah and let his work cease.

6 Then King Asa took all Judah, and they carried away the stones of Ramah and its timber with which Baasha had been building, and with them he built Geba and Mizpah.

7 At that time Hanani the seer came to Asa king of Judah and said to him, Because you relied on the king of Syria and not on the Lord your God, the army of the king of Syria has escaped you.

8 Were not the Ethiopians and Libyans a huge host with very many chariots and horsemen? Yet because you relied then on the Lord, He gave them into your hand.

9 For the eyes of the Lord run to and fro throughout the whole earth to show Himself strong in behalf of those whose hearts are blameless toward Him. You have done foolishly in this; therefore, from now on you shall have wars.

10 Then Asa was angry with the seer and put him in prison [in the stocks], for he was enraged with him because of this. Asa oppressed some of the people at the same time.

11 The acts of Asa, from first to last, are written in the Book of the Kings of Judah and Israel.

12 In the thirty-ninth year of his reign Asa was diseased in his feet—until his disease became very severe; yet in his disease he did not seek the Lord, but relied on the physicians.

13 And Asa slept with his fathers, dying in the forty-first year of his reign.

14 And they buried him in his own tomb which he had hewn out for himself in the City of David, and they laid him on a bier which was filled with sweet odors and various kinds [of spices] prepared by the perfumers' art; and they made a very great burning [of spices] in his honor.

speak the Word

Thank You, God, that You show Yourself strong in behalf of those whose hearts are blameless before You. Let my heart be blameless before You!
ADAPTED FROM II CHRONICLES **16:9**

how to have a "perfect" heart

God looks for those whose hearts are perfect or blameless toward Him. Earlier in my life, I misunderstood this truth. When I read that God's eyes roam to and fro looking for someone in whom He might show Himself strong (see II Chronicles 16:9), I always thought, *Boy, I had better straighten up.* Then I finally saw the remainder of that verse about God's looking for someone whose heart is perfect toward Him, and I began to understand what "perfect" really is. What does it mean to have a perfect or blameless heart? It does not mean to "perform" perfectly; it means to have a heartfelt desire to do right and to please God.

People who have a perfect heart truly love God, though they themselves may not be perfect. They may still have things in the flesh to deal with. They may say things they should not say. They may make mistakes or lose their tempers. But when they do, they are quick to repent and make things right with God again. If they have offended someone, they will humble themselves and apologize.

If we have perfect hearts toward God, He counts us as perfect and works with us while that perfection becomes more and more real in our lives.

I am not a perfect person, but I do believe I have a perfect heart toward God. I am sure there are things I am unaware of in my heart that need to be exposed and rooted out, but I believe God holds us responsible for only those things we are aware of. I do not have a perfect performance. Every day, I still do things I wish I did not do. But I love God with all my heart. There are many people with right hearts, and those are the ones God uses. Keep working on the things you need to work on in your life, and while you're at it, keep a perfect heart toward God.

17 JEHOSHAPHAT HIS son reigned in Asa's stead and strengthened himself against Israel.

2 And he placed forces in all the fortified cities of Judah and set garrisons in the land of Judah and in the cities of Ephraim which Asa his father had taken.

3 The Lord was with Jehoshaphat because he walked in the first ways of his father [David]. He did not seek the Baals

4 But sought *and* yearned with all his desire for the Lord, the God of his father, and walked in His commandments and not after the ways of Israel.

5 Therefore the Lord established the kingdom in his hand; and all Judah brought tribute to Jehoshaphat, and he had great riches and honor.

6 His heart was cheered *and* his courage was high in the ways of the Lord; moreover, he took away the high places and the Asherim out of Judah.

7 Also in the third year of his reign he sent his princes Ben-hail, Obadiah, Zechariah, Nethanel, and Micaiah to teach in the cities of Judah;

8 And with them were the Levites— Shemaiah, Nethaniah, Zebadiah, Asahel, Shemiramoth, Jehonathan, Adonijah, Tobijah, and Tob-adonijah; and with these Levites were the priests Elishama and Jehoram.

9 And they taught in Judah, and had the Book of the Law of the Lord with

them; they went about throughout all the cities of Judah and taught among the people.

10 And a terror from the Lord fell upon all the kingdoms of the lands that were round about Judah, so that they made no war against Jehoshaphat.

11 And some of the Philistines brought Jehoshaphat gifts and tribute silver, and the Arabs brought him flocks: 7,700 each of rams and of he-goats.

12 And Jehoshaphat became very great. He built in Judah fortresses and store cities,

13 And he had many works in the cities of Judah, and soldiers, mighty men of courage, in Jerusalem.

14 This was the number of them by their fathers' houses: Of Judah, the captains of thousands: Adnah the chief, with 300,000 mighty men of valor;

15 Next to him was Jehohanan the captain, with 280,000;

16 And next to him Amasiah son of Zichri, who willingly offered himself to the Lord, with 200,000 mighty men of valor.

17 Of Benjamin: Eliada, a mighty man of valor, with 200,000 men armed with bow and shield;

18 Next to him was Jehozabad with 180,000 armed for war.

19 These were in the king's service, besides those [he] had placed in fortified cities throughout all Judah.

18 NOW JEHOSHAPHAT had great riches and honor, but was allied [by marriage] with Ahab.

2 After some years he went down to Ahab in Samaria. And Ahab killed sheep and oxen for him in abundance and for the people with him and persuaded him to go up with him against Ramoth-gilead.

3 Ahab king of Israel said to Jehoshaphat king of Judah, Will you go with me to Ramoth-gilead? He answered, I am as you are, and my people as your people; we will be with you in the war.

4 And Jehoshaphat said to the king of Israel, Inquire first, I pray you, for the word of the Lord today.

5 So King [Ahab] of Israel gathered together the prophets, 400 men, and said to them, Shall we go to Ramoth-gilead to battle, or shall I forbear? And they said, Go up, for God will deliver it into the king's hand.

6 But Jehoshaphat said, Is there not another prophet of the Lord here by whom we may inquire?

7 King [Ahab] of Israel said to Jehoshaphat, There is another man, Micaiah son of Imla, by whom we may inquire of the Lord, but I hate him, for he never has prophesied good for me, but always evil. And Jehoshaphat said, Let not the king say so.

8 And King [Ahab] of Israel called for one of his officers and said, Bring quickly Micaiah son of Imla.

9 The king of Israel and Jehoshaphat king of Judah sat each on his throne, arrayed in their robes; they were sitting in an open place [at the threshing floor] at the entrance of the gate of Samaria; all the prophets were prophesying before them.

10 And Zedekiah son of Chenaanah had made himself horns of iron, and said, Thus says the Lord: With these you shall push the Syrians until they are destroyed.

11 All the prophets prophesied so, saying, Go up to Ramoth-gilead and prosper; the Lord will deliver it into the king's hand.

12 The messenger who went to call Micaiah said to him, Behold, the words of the prophets foretell good to the king with one accord. So let your word be like one of them, and speak favorably.

13 But Micaiah said, As the Lord lives, what my God says, that will I speak.

14 And when he had come to the king, King [Ahab] said to him, Micaiah, shall we go to Ramoth-gilead to battle, or shall I forbear? And he said, Go up and prosper, and they shall be delivered into your hand.

15 And the king said to him, How many times shall I warn you to tell nothing but the truth to me in the name of the Lord?

16 Then Micaiah said, I did see all Israel scattered upon the mountains as sheep that have no shepherd, and the Lord said, These have no master. Let each return to his house in peace.

17 And King [Ahab] of Israel said to Jehoshaphat, Did I not tell you that he would not prophesy good to me, but evil?

18 [Micaiah] said, Therefore hear the word of the Lord: I saw the Lord sitting on His throne, and all the host of heaven standing at His right hand and His left.

19 And the Lord said, Who shall entice Ahab king of Israel, that he may go up and fall at Ramoth-gilead? And one said this thing, and another that.

20 Then there came a spirit and stood before the Lord and said, I will entice him. The Lord said to him, By what means?

21 And he said, I will go out and be a lying spirit in the mouths of all his prophets. And the Lord said, You shall entice him and also succeed. Go forth and do so.

22 Now, you see, the Lord put a lying spirit in the mouths of your prophets; and the Lord has spoken evil concerning you.

23 Then Zedekiah the son of Chenaanah came near and smote Micaiah upon the cheek and said, Which way went the Spirit of the Lord from me to speak to you?

24 And Micaiah said, Behold, you shall see on that day when you shall go into an inner chamber to hide yourself.

25 Then King [Ahab] of Israel said, Take Micaiah back to Amon the governor of the city and to Joash the king's son,

26 And say, Thus says the king: Put this fellow in prison and feed him with bread and water of affliction until I return in peace.

27 Micaiah said, If you return at all in peace, the Lord has not spoken by me. And he [added], Hear it, you people, all of you!

28 So Ahab king of Israel and Jehoshaphat king of Judah went up to Ramoth-gilead.

29 And [Ahab] king of Israel said to Jehoshaphat, I will disguise myself and will go to the battle, but you put on your royal robes. So King Ahab of Israel disguised himself, and they went into the battle.

30 Now Syria's king had commanded his chariot captains, Fight not with small or great, but only with the king of Israel.

31 And when the captains of the chariots saw Jehoshaphat [of Judah], they said, It is the king of Israel. So they turned to fight against him, but Jehoshaphat cried out, and the Lord helped him; and God moved them to depart from him.

32 For when the captains of the chariots saw that it was not the king of Israel, they turned back from pursuing him.

33 A certain man drew his bow at a venture and smote King [Ahab] of Israel between the lower armor and the breastplate. So Ahab said to his chariot driver, Turn, carry me out of the battle, for I am wounded.

34 And the battle increased that day; however, King [Ahab] of Israel propped himself up in his chariot opposite the Syrians until evening, and about sunset he died.

19

JEHOSHAPHAT THE king of Judah returned safely to his house in Jerusalem.
2   Jehu son of Hanani, the seer, went out to meet him and said to Jehoshaphat, Should you help the ungodly and love those who hate the Lord? Because of this, wrath has gone out against you from the Lord.
3   But there are good things found in you, for you have destroyed the Asherim out of the land and have set your heart to seek God [with all your soul's desire].
4   Jehoshaphat dwelt at Jerusalem, and he went out again among the people from Beersheba to the hill country of Ephraim and brought them back to the Lord, the God of their fathers.
5   He appointed judges throughout all the fortified cities of Judah, city by city,
6   And said to the judges, Be careful what you do, for you judge not for man but for the Lord, and He is with you in the matter of judgment.
7   So now let the reverence *and* fear of the Lord be upon you; take heed what you do, for there is no injustice with the Lord our God, or partiality or taking of bribes.
8   Also in Jerusalem, Jehoshaphat set certain Levites, priests, and heads of families of Israel to give judgment for the Lord and decide controversies. When they [of the commission] returned to Jerusalem,
9   The king charged them, Do this in the fear of the Lord, faithfully, with integrity *and* a blameless heart.
10 Whenever any controversy shall come to you from your brethren who dwell in their cities, between blood and blood, between law and commandment, statutes and judgments, you shall warn *and* instruct them that they may not be guilty before the Lord; otherwise wrath will come upon you and your brethren. Do this and you will not be guilty.

11 And behold, Amariah the chief priest is over you in all matters of the Lord, and Zebadiah son of Ishmael, the governor of the house of Judah, in all the king's matters; also the Levites will serve you as officers. Deal courageously [be strong and do], and may the Lord be with the good!

20

AFTER THIS, the Moabites, the Ammonites, and with them the Meunites came against Jehoshaphat to battle.
2   It was told Jehoshaphat, A great multitude has come against you from beyond the [Dead] Sea, from Edom; and behold they are in Hazazontamar, which is En-gedi.
3   Then Jehoshaphat feared, and set himself [determinedly, as his vital need] to seek the Lord; he proclaimed a fast in all Judah.
4   And Judah gathered together to ask help from the Lord; even out of all the cities of Judah they came to seek the Lord [yearning for Him with all their desire].

putting the Word to work

Have you ever found yourself in circumstances that made you fearful? Jehoshaphat found himself surrounded by enemies, but instead of giving in to fear, he sought God's advice (see II Chronicles 20:1–4). When you are afraid or uncertain how to handle a difficult challenge, ask the Lord to help you know how to handle the situation correctly. He will give you the guidance you need.

5   And Jehoshaphat stood in the assembly of Judah and Jerusalem in the house of the Lord before the new court
6   And said, O Lord, God of our fathers, are You not God in heaven? And do You not rule over all the kingdoms of the nations? In Your hand

run to the throne

Are the "-ites" after you? In II Chronicles 20:1–3 it was the Moabites, the Ammonites, and the Meunites who were after King Jehoshaphat and the people of Judah. In other places in the Old Testament it was the Jebusites, the Hittites, and the Canaanites who were the troublemakers for God's people.

But with us it is the "fear-ites," "disease-ites," "poverty-ites," "bad marriage-ites," "stress-ites," "grouchy neighbor-ites," "insecurity-ites," "rejection-ites," and on and on.

How many "-ites" are chasing you around? However many there are, let's look at what King Jehoshaphat did to turn his attention on God instead of focusing on all those "-ites" that were trying to rise and rule.

When Jehoshaphat was told that the "-ites" were coming against him, the first thing he did was to fear. But then he did something else: He set himself to seek the Lord. Determined to hear from Him, he proclaimed a fast throughout the land for that very purpose. He knew he needed to hear from God. He needed a battle plan, and only God could give him one that was sure to succeed.

When we have trouble, we should develop the habit of running to God instead of to people. We should seek God rather than our own minds or other people's minds. Ask yourself, "When trouble comes, do I run to the phone or to the throne?" God might direct us to a person for advice, but we should always go to Him first to show that we honor and trust Him above all else.

are power and might, so that none is able to withstand You.

7 Did not You, O our God, drive out the inhabitants of this land before Your people Israel and give it forever to the descendants of Abraham Your friend?

8 They dwelt in it and have built You a sanctuary in it for Your Name, saying,

9 If evil comes upon us, the sword of judgment, or pestilence, or famine, we will stand before this house and before You—for Your Name [and the symbol of Your presence] is in this house—and cry to You in our affliction, and You will hear and save.

10 And now behold, the men of Ammon, Moab, and Mount Seir, whom You would not let Israel invade when they came from the land of Egypt, and whom they turned from and did not destroy—[Deut. 2:9.]

11 Behold, they reward us by coming to drive us out of Your possession which You have given us to inherit.

12 O our God, will You not exercise judgment upon them? For we have no might to stand against this great company that is coming against us. We do not know what to do, but our eyes are upon You.

13 And all Judah stood before the Lord, with their children and their wives.

14 Then the Spirit of the Lord came upon Jahaziel son of Zechariah, the son of Benaiah, the son of Jeiel, the son of Mattaniah, a Levite of the sons

these are fighting words

The words in II Chronicles 20:6–11 are fighting words! If we listen to what the Lord is saying to us through them, we will learn something that will change our battle plan forever and give us victory after victory.

After starting his prayer by acknowledging how great, awesome, powerful, and wonderful the Lord is, Jehoshaphat then began relating specific mighty acts God had performed in the past to protect His people and uphold the promises He had made to them. And in finally presenting his request, he expressed his confidence that God would handle the problem. Jehoshaphat said in so many words, "Oh, by the way, our enemies are coming against us to try to take away the possession that You gave us for our inheritance. I just thought I would mention this little problem. But You are so great; I know You already have it all under control."

When we do ask God for help, we should remember that He hears us the first time we ask Him for something. We do not need to spend our prayer time asking Him for the same things over and over. We may keep talking to Him about our needs until we have assurance in our hearts that we have a breakthrough, but we do not have to do that to move God.

God has a plan for our deliverance from every situation, even before those situations present themselves. He knows what we need before we ask Him. God is not surprised when the enemy attacks, and He is not in heaven wringing His hands, trying to figure out what to do. Our job is to focus on Him and His mighty power, worshipping Him and praising Him for the manifestation of His solution and listening for a word or direction from Him. He always has a winning battle plan!

of Asaph, in the midst of the assembly.

15 He said, Hearken, all Judah, you inhabitants of Jerusalem, and you King Jehoshaphat. The Lord says this to you: Be not afraid or dismayed at this great multitude; for the battle is not yours, but God's.

16 Tomorrow go down to them. Behold, they will come up by the Ascent of Ziz, and you will find them at the end of the ravine before the Wilderness of Jeruel.

17 You shall not need to fight in this battle; take your positions, stand still, and see the deliverance of the Lord [Who is] with you, O Judah and Jerusalem. Fear not nor be dismayed.

Tomorrow go out against them, for the Lord is with you.

18 And Jehoshaphat bowed his head with his face to the ground, and all Judah and the inhabitants of Jerusalem fell down before the Lord, worshiping Him.

19 And some Levites of the Kohathites and Korahites stood up to praise the Lord, the God of Israel, with a very loud voice.

20 And they rose early in the morning and went out into the Wilderness of Tekoa; and as they went out, Jehoshaphat stood and said, Hear me, O Judah, and you inhabitants of Jerusalem! Believe in the Lord your God and you shall be established;

rest in the storm

I love II Chronicles 20:12 because it tells us what to pray when we are facing a big battle: "We do not know what to do, but our eyes are upon You." The people in this war realized three things: (1) They had no might against their enemies; (2) they did not know what to do; (3) they needed to have their eyes focused on God.

The Lord responded with these powerful, assuring words: "You shall not need to fight in this battle; take your positions, stand still, and see the deliverance of the Lord [Who is] with you . . . Fear not nor be dismayed" (II Chronicles 20:17).

What is our position? It is one of abiding in Jesus and entering the rest of God. It is one of waiting on the Lord continually with our eyes focused upon Him, doing what He directs us to do. In other words, having a "reverential fear" of moving in the flesh.

Concerning entering God's rest, I would like to say this: There is no such thing as "the rest of God" without opposition. To illustrate, let me share a story I once heard involving two artists who were asked to paint pictures of "peace" as they perceived it. One painted a quiet, still lake, far back in the mountains. The other painted a raging, rushing waterfall that had a birch tree leaning out over it with a bird resting in a nest on one of the branches.

Which painting truly depicts peace? The second one does, because there is no such thing as peace without opposition. The first painting represents stagnation. The scene it sets forth may be serene; a person might be motivated to want to go there to recuperate. It may offer a pretty picture, but it does not depict "the rest of God."

Jesus said, "Peace I leave with you; My [own] peace I now give and bequeath to you. Not as the world gives do I give to you . . . " (John 14:27). His peace is a spiritual peace, and His rest is one that operates in the midst of the storm—not in its absence. Jesus did not come to remove all opposition from our lives, but rather to give us a different approach to the storms of life. As we learn His ways and approach life in the same way He did, we will experience His rest in the midst of our storms.

believe *and* remain steadfast to His prophets and you shall prosper.

21 When he had consulted with the people, he appointed singers to sing to the Lord and praise Him in their holy [priestly] garments as they went out before the army, saying, Give thanks to the Lord, for His mercy *and* loving-kindness endure forever!

22 And when they began to sing and to praise, the Lord set ambushments against the men of Ammon, Moab, and Mount Seir who had come against Judah, and they were [self-] slaughtered;

23 For [suspecting betrayal] the men of Ammon and Moab rose against those of Mount Seir, utterly destroying them. And when they had made an end of the men of Seir, they all helped to destroy one another.

24 And when Judah came to the

life point

When "all Judah" was assembled before the Lord in II Chronicles 20:13–17, Jahaziel began to prophesy and speak God's direction to them. I believe the Spirit of God came upon him because everyone was waiting on God.

When we learn to seek God and wait on Him, He will answer us. That answer may be very plain and simple, as Judah's was. The Lord told Judah to not be afraid because the battle was not to be their battle, but His. That does not sound too mystical or deeply spiritual, but it was all they needed to hear.

The battle is not yours, but God's. What good news! God did not say there was nothing for them to do in the battle; He was saying that He was going to show them their part. They could do it in the strength and wisdom of the Lord, but the battle was still His to win.

After God gave them that word of encouragement, He gave them a word of specific instruction (see II Chronicles 20:17). We are to wait on the Lord until He has told us what to do, and then we are to do it in the strength He gave us while we waited on Him.

watchtower of the wilderness, they looked at the multitude, and behold, they were dead bodies fallen to the earth, and none had escaped!
25 When Jehoshaphat and his people came to take the spoil, they found among them much cattle, goods, garments, and precious things which they took for themselves, more than they could carry away, so much they were three days in gathering the spoil.
26 On the fourth day they assembled in the Valley of Beracah. There they blessed the Lord. So the name of the place is still called the Valley of Beracah [blessing].
27 Then they returned, every man of Judah and Jerusalem, Jehoshaphat leading them, to Jerusalem with joy, for the Lord had made them to rejoice over their enemies.
28 They came to Jerusalem with harps, lyres, and trumpets to the house of the Lord.
29 And the fear of God came upon all the kingdoms of those countries when they heard that the Lord had fought against the enemies of Israel.
30 So the realm of Jehoshaphat was quiet, for his God gave him rest round about.
31 Thus Jehoshaphat reigned over Judah. He was thirty-five years old when he began his twenty-five-year reign in Jerusalem. His mother was Azubah daughter of Shilhi.
32 And he walked in the ways of Asa his father and departed not from it,

life point

Second Chronicles 20:22 says that while the people of Judah were singing praise to God, He set ambushments against their enemies. What happened next was astounding: The enemy soldiers slaughtered one another! Praise confused the enemy!

Just think about it. The people of Judah set themselves to seek God rather than live in fear. They told God how awesome He is; they stood and waited on God. He sent a prophet with a word for them, telling them the battle was not theirs but His. He told them to take their position and stand still. They worshiped and praised. Jehoshaphat appointed singers to sing and praise, and the Lord defeated their enemies by confusing them so much that they killed each other! What an awesome God we serve!

doing what was right in the sight of the Lord.

33 But the high places [of idolatry] were not taken away, for the people had not yet set their hearts on their fathers' God.

34 Now the rest of the acts of Jehoshaphat, from first to last, they are written in the records of Jehu son of Hanani, which are in the Book of the Kings of Israel.

35 After this, Jehoshaphat king of Judah joined with Ahaziah king of Israel, who did very wickedly.

36 He joined him in building ships to go to Tarshish, building them in Ezion-geber.

37 Then Eliezer son of Dodavahu of Mareshah prophesied against Jehoshaphat, saying, Because you have joined Ahaziah, the Lord will destroy your works. So the ships were wrecked and unable to go to Tarshish.

21 JEHOSHAPHAT SLEPT with his fathers and was buried with [them] in the City of David. Jehoram his son reigned in his stead.

2 He had brothers: Azariah, Jehiel, Zechariah, Azariah, Michael, and Shephatiah, all the sons of Jehoshaphat king of Israel.

3 Their father gave them great gifts of silver, gold, and precious things, together with fortified cities in Judah, but the kingdom he gave to Jehoram, the firstborn.

4 When Jehoram had ascended to the kingship of his father, he strengthened himself and slew all his brethren with the sword and also some of Israel's princes.

5 Jehoram at thirty-two years of age began his eight-year reign in Jerusalem.

6 He walked in the ways of the kings of Israel, as did the house of Ahab, for he married the daughter of Ahab and did what was evil in the eyes of the Lord.

7 But the Lord would not destroy the house of David, because He had made a covenant with David and promised to give a light to him and to his sons forever.

8 In Jehoram's days, the Edomites revolted from the rule of Judah and set up for themselves a king.

9 Then Jehoram passed over [the Jordan] with his captains and all his chariots, and rose up by night and smote the Edomites who had surrounded him and his chariot captains.

10 So Edom revolted from the rule of Judah to this day. Then Libnah also revolted from Jehoram's rule, because he had forsaken the Lord, the God of his fathers.

11 Moreover, he made idolatrous high places in the hill country of Judah and debauched spiritually the inhabitants of Jerusalem and led Judah astray [compelling the people's cooperation].

12 And there came a letter to Jehoram from Elijah the prophet, saying, Thus says the Lord, the God of David your father [forefather]: Because you have not walked in the ways of Jehoshaphat your father nor in the ways of Asa king of Judah,

13 But have walked in the ways of Israel's kings, and made Judah and the inhabitants of Jerusalem play the harlot like the [spiritual] harlotry of Ahab's house, and also have slain your brothers of your father's house, who were better than you,

14 Behold, the Lord will smite your people, and your children, your wives, and all your possessions with a great plague.

15 And you yourself shall have a severe illness because of an intestinal disease, until your bowels fall out because of the sickness, day after day.

16 And the Lord stirred up against Jehoram the anger of the Philistines and of the Arabs who were near the Ethiopians.

17 They came against Judah, invaded it, and carried away all the possessions found in *and* around the king's house, together with his sons and his wives; so there was not a son left to him except Jehoahaz, the youngest.

18 And after all this, the Lord smote [Jehoram] with an incurable intestinal disease.

19 In process of time, after two years, his bowels fell out because of his disease. So he died in severe distress. And his people made no funeral fire to honor him, like the fires for his fathers.

20 Thirty-two years old was Jehoram when he began to reign, and he reigned in Jerusalem eight years, and departed without being wanted. Yet they buried him in the City of David, but not in the tombs of the kings.

22 THE PEOPLE of Jerusalem made Ahaziah, his youngest son, king in his stead, for the troop that came with the Arabs to the camp had slain all the older sons. So Ahaziah son of Jehoram king of Judah reigned.

2 Forty-two years old was Ahaziah when he began his one-year reign in Jerusalem. His mother was Athaliah, a granddaughter of Omri. [II Kings 8:26.]

3 He also walked in the ways of the house of Ahab, for his mother was his counselor to do wickedly.

4 So he did evil in the sight of the Lord like the house of Ahab, for they were his counselors after his father's death, to his destruction.

5 He followed their counsel and even went with 'Joram son of Ahab king of Israel to war against Hazael king of Syria at Ramoth-gilead. And

the Syrians wounded Joram; [II Kings 8:28ff.]

6 And he returned to be healed in Jezreel of the wounds given him at Ramah when he fought against Hazael king of Syria. Azariah son of Jehoram king of Judah went down to see Joram son of Ahab in Jezreel because he was sick.

7 But the destruction of Ahaziah was ordained of God in his coming to visit Joram. For when he got there he went out with Joram against Jehu son of Nimshi, whom the Lord had anointed to destroy the house of Ahab.

8 And when Jehu was executing judgment upon the house of Ahab, he met the princes of Judah and the sons of Ahaziah's slain brothers, who attended Ahaziah, and he slew them.

9 And [Jehu] sought Ahaziah, who was hiding in Samaria; he was captured, brought to Jehu, and slain. They buried him, for they said, After all, he is the grandson of Jehoshaphat, who sought the Lord with all his heart. So the house of Ahaziah had no one left able to rule the kingdom.

10 But when Athaliah mother of Ahaziah saw that her son was dead, she arose and destroyed all the royal family of Judah.

11 But Jehosheba, the daughter of the king, took Joash [infant] son of Ahaziah and stole him away from among the king's sons who were to be slain, and she put him and his nurse in a bedchamber. So Jehosheba daughter of King Jehoram, sister of Ahaziah, and wife of Jehoiada the priest, hid [Joash] from [his grandmother] Athaliah, so that she did not slay him.

12 And Joash was with them hidden in the house of God six years, and Athaliah reigned over the land.

i See footnote on II Kings 1:17.

23 IN THE seventh year Jehoiada [the priest] took strength *and* courage and made a covenant with the captains of hundreds: Azariah son of Jeroham, Ishmael son of Jehohanan, Azariah son of Obed, Maaseiah son of Adaiah, and Elishaphat son of Zichri.

2 And they went about in Judah and gathered the Levites out of all the cities, and the chiefs of the fathers' houses of Israel, and they came to Jerusalem.

3 And all the assembly made a covenant in the house of God with the king [little Joash, to suddenly proclaim his sovereignty and overthrow Athaliah's tyranny]. And Jehoiada the priest said to them, Behold, the king's son shall reign, as the Lord has said of the offspring of David.

4 This is what you shall do: a third of you priests and Levites who are resuming service on the Sabbath shall be doorkeepers,

5 A [second] third shall be at the king's house, and [the final] third at the Foundation Gate; and all the people shall be in the courts [only] of the house of the Lord.

6 But let none come into the [main] house of the Lord except the priests and those of the Levites who minister; they may go in, for they are holy, but let all the rest of the people carefully observe the law against entering the holy place of the Lord.

7 And the Levites shall surround the young king, every man with his weapons in his hand; and whoever comes into the house [breaking through the ranks of the guard to get near Joash] shall be put to death. But you be with the king when he comes in [from the temple chamber where he is hiding] and when he goes out.

8 So the Levites and all Judah did according to all that Jehoiada the priest had commanded; and took every man his men who were to resume duty on the Sabbath, with those who were to go out on the Sabbath, for Jehoiada the priest did not dismiss the divisions [of priests and Levites].

9 Also Jehoiada the priest gave the captains of hundreds spears, bucklers, and shields that had been King David's, which were in the house of God.

10 And he set all the people as a guard for the king, every man having his weapon (missile) in his hand, from the right side to the left side of the temple, around the altar and the temple.

11 Then they brought out the king's son and put the crown on him and gave him the testimony *or* law and made him king. And Jehoiada and his sons anointed him and said, Long live the king!

12 When Athaliah heard the noise of the people running and praising the king, she went into the Lord's house to the people.

13 And behold, there the king stood by his pillar at the entrance, the captains and the trumpeters beside him; and all the people of the land rejoicing and blowing trumpets, and the singers with musical instruments led in singing of praise. Athaliah rent her clothes and cried, Treason! Treason!

14 Then Jehoiada the priest commanded the captains of hundreds who were over the army, Bring her out between the ranks, and whoever follows her, let him be slain with the sword. For the priest said, Do not slay her in the Lord's house.

15 So they made way for Athaliah, and she went into the entrance of the Horse Gate of the king's house; there they slew her.

16 Then Jehoiada made a covenant between himself, all the people, and the king, that they should be the Lord's people.

17 Then all the people went to the house of Baal, tore it down, and broke its altars and its images in pieces, and slew Mattan the priest of Baal before the altars.

18 Also Jehoiada appointed the offices *and* officers [for the care] of the house of the Lord under the direction of the Levitical priests, whom David had distributed [in his day] in the house of the Lord, to offer the burnt offerings of the Lord as written in the Law of Moses, with rejoicing and singing, as ordered by David.

19 Jehoiada set the gatekeepers at the gates of the house of the Lord so that no one should enter who was in any way unclean.

20 And he took the captains of hundreds and the nobles and governors of the people and all the people of the land and brought down the king from the house of the Lord; and they came through the Upper Gate to the king's house and set the king upon the throne of the kingdom.

21 So all the people of the land rejoiced, and the city was quiet after Athaliah had been slain with the sword.

24 JOASH WAS seven years old when he began his forty-year reign in Jerusalem. His mother was Zibiah of Beersheba.

2 And Joash did what was right in the sight of the Lord all the days of Jehoiada the priest [his uncle].

3 And Jehoiada took for him two wives, and he had sons and daughters.

4 After this, Joash decided to repair the Lord's house.

5 He gathered the priests and the Levites and said to them, Go out to the cities of Judah, and gather from all Israel money to repair the house of your God from year to year; and see that you hasten the matter. But the Levites did not hasten it.

6 So the king called for Jehoiada the high priest and said to him, Why have you not required the Levites to bring in from Judah and Jerusalem the tax authorized by Moses the servant of the Lord and of the assembly of Israel for the Tent of the Testimony?

7 For the sons of Athaliah, that wicked woman, had broken into the house of God and also had used for the Baals all the dedicated things of the house of the Lord.

8 And at the king's command they made a chest and set it outside the gate of the house of the Lord.

9 And they made a proclamation through Judah and Jerusalem to bring in for the Lord the tax that Moses the servant of God laid upon Israel in the wilderness.

10 And all the princes and people rejoiced and brought their tax and dropped it into the chest until they had finished.

11 When the Levites brought the chest to the king's office, and whenever they saw that there was much money, the king's secretary and the high priest's officer came and emptied the chest and carried it to its place again. Thus they did day by day and collected money in abundance.

12 And the king and Jehoiada gave it to those who did the work of the temple service; and they hired masons and carpenters and also those who worked in iron and bronze to repair the house of the Lord.

13 So the workmen labored, and the work of repairing went forward in their hands; and they set up the house of God according to its design and strengthened it.

14 When they had finished it, they brought the rest of the money before the king and Jehoiada; from it were made utensils for the Lord's house, vessels for ministering and for offerings, and cups and vessels of gold and silver. And they offered burnt offerings in the house of the Lord continually all the days of Jehoiada.

15 But Jehoiada became old and full of [the handicaps of great] age, and he died. He was 130 years old at his death.

16 They buried him in the City of David among the kings, because he had done good in Israel and toward God and His house.

17 Now after the death of Jehoiada [the priest, who had hidden Joash], the princes of Judah came and made obeisance to King Joash; then the king hearkened to them.

18 They forsook the house of the Lord, the God of their fathers, and served the Asherim and idols; and wrath came upon Judah and Jerusalem for their sin (guilt).

19 Yet [God] sent prophets to them to bring them again to the Lord; these testified against them, but they would not listen.

20 Then the Spirit of God came upon Zechariah son of Jehoiada the priest, who stood over the people, and he said to them, Thus says God: Why do you transgress the commandments of the Lord so that you cannot prosper? Because you have forsaken the Lord, He also has forsaken you.

21 They conspired against Zechariah the priest and stoned him at the command of the king in the court of the Lord's house!

22 Thus Joash the king did not remember the kindness which Jehoiada, Zechariah's father, had done him, but slew his son. And when [Zechariah the priest] was dying, he said, May the Lord see and avenge!

23 At the end of the year, the army of Syria came up against Joash. They came to Judah and Jerusalem and destroyed all the princes from among the people and sent all their spoil to the king of Damascus.

24 Though the army of the Syrians came with a small company of men,

the Lord delivered a very great host into their hands, because Joash and Judah had forsaken the Lord, the God of their fathers. So the Syrians executed judgment against Joash.

25 And when they had departed from Joash, leaving him very ill, his own servants conspired against him for the blood of the sons of Jehoiada the priest, and they slew him on his bed. So he died and they buried him in the City of David, but not in the tombs of the kings.

26 The conspirators against Joash were Zabad son of Shimeath the Ammonitess, and Jehozabad son of Shimrith the Moabitess.

27 Now concerning his sons and the greatness of the prophecies uttered against him and the rebuilding of the house of God, they are written in the commentary on the Book of Kings. And Amaziah his [Joash's] son reigned in his stead.

25 AMAZIAH WAS twenty-five years old when he began to reign, and he reigned twenty-nine years in Jerusalem. His mother was Jehoaddan of Jerusalem.

2 He did right in the Lord's sight, but not with a perfect *or* blameless heart.

3 When his kingdom was firmly established, he slew his servants who had killed the king his father.

4 But he did not slay their children; he did as it is written in the Law, in the Book of Moses, where the Lord commanded, The fathers shall not die for the children, or the children die for the fathers; but every man shall die for his own sin.

5 Amaziah assembled the men of Judah and set them by fathers' houses under commanders of thousands and of hundreds for all Judah and Benjamin. He numbered them from twenty years old and over and found them

doing the right thing with the right heart

There are many conditions of the heart. Some are positive, and some are negative. Of course, many people do have a right heart. They love God with all their hearts, and they really want to do the right thing in every situation. But there are others who have a wrong heart, and they do the right thing, but with the wrong motive.

In II Chronicles 25:1, 2 we read about a king who had a negative condition of the heart. This passage says that King Amaziah did all the right things, but his heart was not right. Therefore, God was not pleased with him. That's a scary situation. We can do the right thing, and yet it still will not be acceptable to God because we do it with a wrong heart.

Let's take giving, for example. In II Corinthians 9:7 we are told that God loves a cheerful giver, one who gives not out of compulsion or with a bad attitude, but out of a willing heart. God wants us to give joyfully. In fact, this verse says that God loves a cheerful giver so much, He is absolutely unwilling to abandon or do without a person whose heart is in his giving.

There is a physical heart and a spiritual heart, and the two are parallel. Physically speaking, the heart is the most important organ in our bodies. Spiritually speaking, I believe the heart of an individual is the most important aspect of his or her spiritual life. And it is the most important thing we can give to God. That is why the condition of our hearts is so important. Make sure that you are not only doing the right things, but also that the attitude of your heart is pleasing to the Lord.

to be 300,000 choice men fit for war and able to handle spear and shield.

6 He hired also 100,000 mighty men of valor from Israel for 100 talents of silver.

7 But a man of God came to him, saying, O king, do not let all this army of Ephraimites of Israel go with you [of Judah], for the Lord is not with you,

8 For if you go [in spite of warning], no matter how strong you are for battle, God will cast you down before the enemy, for God has power to help and to cast down.

9 And Amaziah said to the man of God, But what shall we do about the 100 talents which I have given to the army of Israel? The man of God answered, The Lord is able to give you much more than this.

10 So Amaziah discharged the army that came to him from Ephraim to go home. So their anger was greatly kindled against Judah; they returned home in fierce wrath.

11 And Amaziah took courage and led forth his people to the Valley of Salt and smote 10,000 of the men of Seir [Edom].

12 Another 10,000 the men of Judah captured alive and brought them to the top of a crag and cast them down from it, and they were all dashed to pieces.

13 But the soldiers of the band which Amaziah sent back, not allowing them to go with him to battle, fell upon the cities of Judah, from Samaria even to Beth-horon, and smote 3,000 [men] and took much spoil.

14 After Amaziah came back from

the slaughter of the Edomites, he brought their gods and set them up to be his gods and bowed before them and burned incense to them.

15 So the anger of the Lord was kindled against Amaziah, and He sent to him a prophet, who said, Why have you sought after the gods of the people, which could not deliver their own people out of your hand?

16 As he was talking, the king said to him, Have we made you the king's counselor? Stop it! Why should you be put to death? The prophet stopped but said, I know that God has determined to destroy you, because you have done this and ignored my counsel.

17 Then Amaziah king of Judah took counsel and sent to ʲJehoash son of Jehoahaz, the son of Jehu, king of Israel, saying, Come [to battle], let us look one another in the face. [II Kings 14:8-20.]

18 Jehoash king of Israel sent to Amaziah king of Judah, saying, A little thistle in Lebanon sent to a great cedar in Lebanon, saying, Give your daughter to my son as wife. And a wild beast of Lebanon passed by and trampled down the thistle.

19 You say, See, [I] have smitten Edom! Your heart lifts you up to boast. Stay at home; why should you meddle [and court disaster], so you will fall and Judah with you?

20 But Amaziah would not hear, for it came from God, that He might deliver Judah into the hands of their enemies, because they sought after the gods of Edom.

21 So Jehoash king of Israel went up; and he and Amaziah king of Judah faced one another at Beth-shemesh of Judah.

22 And Judah was defeated before Israel, and they fled every man to his tent.

23 And Jehoash king of Israel took Amaziah king of Judah, the son of Joash, the son of Jehoahaz, at Beth-shemesh and brought him to Jerusalem and broke down the wall of Jerusalem from the Ephraim Gate to the Corner Gate, 400 cubits.

24 And he took all the gold, the silver, and all the vessels found in God's house with [the doorkeeper] Obed-edom, and the treasures of the king's house and hostages also, and returned to Samaria.

25 And Amaziah son of Joash king of Judah lived after the death of Jehoash son of Jehoahaz king of Israel fifteen years.

26 The rest of the acts of Amaziah, from first to last, are they not written in the Book of the Kings of Judah and Israel?

27 Now after Amaziah turned away from the Lord, they made a conspiracy against him in Jerusalem, and he fled to Lachish. But they sent to Lachish and slew him there.

28 And they brought him upon horses and buried him with his fathers in the City of [David in] Judah.

26 THEN ALL the people of Judah took Uzziah, who was sixteen years old, and made him king in place of his father Amaziah.

2 He built Eloth and restored it to Judah after Amaziah slept with his fathers.

3 Uzziah was sixteen years old when he began his fifty-two-year reign in Jerusalem. His mother was Jecoliah of Jerusalem.

4 He did right in the Lord's sight, to the extent of all that his father Amaziah had done.

5 He set himself to seek God in the days of Zechariah, who instructed him in the things of God; and as long as he sought (inquired of, yearned

---

j Hebrew *Joash*, a variant of *Jehoash*.

for) the Lord, God made him prosper.
6 He went out against the Philistines and broke down the walls of Gath, of Jabneh, and of Ashdod, and built cities near Ashdod and elsewhere among the Philistines.
7 And God helped him against the Philistines, and the Arabs who dwelt in Gur-baal and the Meunim.
8 The Ammonites paid tribute to Uzziah, and his fame spread abroad even to the border of Egypt, for he became very strong.
9 Also Uzziah built towers in Jerusalem at the Corner Gate, the Valley Gate, and at the angle of the wall, and fortified them.
10 Also he built towers in the wilderness and hewed out many cisterns, for he had much livestock, both in the lowlands and in the tableland. And he had farmers and vinedressers in the hills and in the fertile fields [of Carmel], for he loved farming.
11 And Uzziah had a combat army for waging war by regiments according to the number as recorded by Jeiel the secretary and Maaseiah the officer under the direction of Hananiah, one of the king's commanders.
12 The whole number of the heads of fathers' houses of mighty men of valor was 2,600.
13 Under their command was an army of 307,500 who could fight with mighty power to help the king against the enemy.
14 Uzziah prepared for all the army shields, spears, helmets, coats of mail, bows, and stones to sling.
15 In Jerusalem he made machines invented by skillful men to be on the towers and the [corner] bulwarks, with which to shoot arrows and great stones. And his fame spread far, for he was marvelously helped till he was strong.

16 But when [King Uzziah] was strong, he became proud to his destruction; and he trespassed against the Lord his God, for he went ᵏinto the temple of the Lord to burn incense on the altar of incense.
17 And Azariah the priest went in after him and with him eighty priests of the Lord, men of courage.
18 They opposed King Uzziah and said to him, It is not for you, Uzziah, to burn incense to the Lord, but for the priests, the sons of Aaron, who are set apart to burn incense. Withdraw from the sanctuary; you have trespassed, and that will not be to your credit *and* honor before the Lord God.
19 Then Uzziah was enraged, and he had a censer in his hand to burn incense. And while he was enraged with the priests, leprosy broke out on his forehead before the priests in the house of the Lord, beside the incense altar.
20 And as Azariah the chief priest and all the priests looked upon him, behold, he was leprous on his forehead! So they forced him out of there; and he also made haste to get out, because the Lord had smitten him.
21 And King Uzziah was a leper to the day of his death, and, being a leper, he dwelt in a separate house, for he was excluded from the Lord's house. And Jotham his son took charge of the king's household, ruling the people of the land.
22 Now the rest of the acts of Uzziah, from first to last, Isaiah the prophet, the son of Amoz, wrote. [Isa. 1:1.]
23 So Uzziah slept with his fathers, and they buried him in the burial field of the kings [outside the royal tombs], for they said, He is a leper. Jotham his son reigned in his stead.

---

k No one but an ordained priest was permitted by law to enter the tabernacle or later the temple proper, even in Jesus' time. See footnote on Num. 3:38.

27

JOTHAM WAS twenty-five years old when he began to reign, and he reigned sixteen years in Jerusalem. His mother was Jerushah daughter of Zadok.

2 He did right in the sight of the Lord, to the extent of all that his father Uzziah had done. However, he did not invade the temple of the Lord. But the people still did corruptly.

3 He built the Upper Gate of the Lord's house and did much building on the wall of Ophel.

4 Moreover, he built cities in the hill country of Judah, and in the forests he built forts and towers.

5 He fought with the king of the Ammonites and prevailed against them. The Ammonites gave him that year 100 talents of silver and 10,000 measures each of wheat and of barley. That much the Ammonites paid to him also the second year and third year.

6 So Jotham grew mighty, for he ordered his ways in the sight of the Lord his God.

7 Now the rest of Jotham's acts, and all his wars and his ways, behold, they are written in the Book of the Kings of Israel and Judah.

8 He was twenty-five years old when he began to reign, and he reigned sixteen years in Jerusalem.

9 And Jotham slept with his fathers, and they buried him in the City of David. Ahaz his son reigned in his stead.

28

AHAZ WAS twenty years old when he began his sixteen-year reign in Jerusalem. He did not do right in the sight of the Lord, like David his father [forefather].

2 But he walked in the ways of the kings of Israel and even made molten images for the Baals.

3 And he burned incense in the Valley of Ben-hinnom [son of Hinnom] and burned his sons as an offering, after the abominable customs of the [heathen] nations whom the Lord drove out before the Israelites.

4 He sacrificed also and burnt incense in the high places, on the hills, and under every green tree.

5 Therefore the Lord his God gave Ahaz into the power of the king of Syria, who defeated him and carried away a great multitude of the Jews as captives, taking them to Damascus. And he was also delivered into the hands of the king of Israel, who smote Judah with a great slaughter.

6 For Pekah son of Remaliah slew in Judah 120,000 in one day, all courageous men, because they had forsaken the Lord, the God of their fathers.

7 And Zichri, a mighty man of Ephraim, slew Maaseiah, King Ahaz' son, and Azrikam the governor of the house, and Elkanah, who was second to the king.

8 And the Israelites carried away captive 200,000 of their kinsmen [of Judah]—women, sons, and daughters—and also took much plunder from them and brought it to Samaria.

9 But a prophet of the Lord was there whose name was Oded, and he went out to meet the army that was returning to Samaria and said to them, Behold, because the Lord, the God of your fathers, was angry with Judah, He delivered them into your hand; but you have slain them in a fury that reaches up to heaven.

10 And now you intend to suppress the people of Judah and Jerusalem, both men and women, as your slaves. But are not you yourselves guilty of crimes against the Lord your God?

11 Now hear me therefore, and set the prisoners free again whom you have taken captive of your kinsmen, for the fierce wrath of the Lord is upon you.

12 Then certain of the heads of the Ephraimites [Israel]—Azariah son of

Johanan, Berechiah son of Meshille-moth, Jehizkiah son of Shallum, and Amasa son of Hadlai—stood up against those returning from the war
13 And said, You shall not bring the captives in here; we are guilty before the Lord already, and what you intend will add more to our sins and our guilt. For our trespass (guilt) is great, and there is fierce anger against Israel.
14 So the armed men [of Israel] left the captives and the spoil [of Judah] before the princes and all the assembly.
15 And the men who have been mentioned by name rose up and took the captives, and with the spoil they clothed all who were naked among them; and having clothed them, shod them, given them food and drink, anointed them [as was a host's duty], and carried all the feeble of them upon donkeys, they brought them to Jericho, the City of Palm Trees, to their brethren. Then they returned to Samaria. [Luke 10:25-37.]
16 At that time King Ahaz sent to the king of Assyria to help him.
17 For again the Edomites had come and smitten Judah and carried away captives.
18 The Philistines had invaded the cities of the low country and of the South (the Negeb) of Judah, and had taken Beth-shemesh, Aijalon, Gede-roth, and Soco, and also Timnah and Gimzo, with their villages, and they settled there.
19 For the Lord brought Judah low because of Ahaz king of Israel, for Ahaz had dealt with reckless cruelty against Judah and had been faithless [had transgressed sorely] against the Lord.
20 So Tilgath-pilneser king of Assyria came to him and distressed him without strengthening him.
21 For Ahaz took [treasure] from the house of the Lord and out of the house of the king and from the princes and gave it as tribute to the king of Assyria, but it did not help Ahaz.
22 In the time of his distress he became still more unfaithful to the Lord—this same King Ahaz.
23 For he sacrificed to the gods of Damascus, which had defeated him, for he said, Since the gods of the kings of Syria helped them, I will sacrifice to them that they may help me. But they were the ruin of him and of all Israel.
24 And Ahaz collected the utensils of the house of God and cut them in pieces; and he shut up the doors of the Lord's temple [the Holy Place and the Holy of Holies] and made himself altars in every corner of Jerusalem.
25 In each city of Judah he made high places to burn incense to other gods, provoking to anger the Lord, the God of his fathers.
26 Now the rest of his acts and of all his ways, from first to last, behold, they are written in the Book of the Kings of Judah and Israel.
27 And Ahaz slept with his fathers, and they buried him in the city, in Jerusalem, but they did not bring him into the tombs of the kings of Israel. And Hezekiah his son reigned in his stead.

29 HEZEKIAH BEGAN to reign when he was twenty-five years old, and he reigned twenty-nine years in Jerusalem. His mother was Abijah daughter of Zechariah.
2 And he did right in the sight of the Lord, according to all that David his father [forefather] had done.
3 In the first year of his reign, in the first month, he opened the doors of the house of the Lord [which his father had closed] and repaired them.
4 He brought together the priests and Levites in the square on the east
5 And said to them, Levites, hear me! Now sanctify (purify and make

free from sin) yourselves and the house of the Lord, the God of your fathers, and carry out the filth from the Holy Place.

6 For our fathers have trespassed and have done what was evil in the sight of the Lord our God, and they have forsaken Him and have turned away their faces from the dwelling place of the Lord and have turned their backs.

7 Also they have closed the doors of the porch and put out the lamps, and they have not burned incense or offered burnt offerings in the place holy to the God of Israel. [II Kings 16:10-16.]

8 Therefore the wrath of the Lord was upon Judah and Jerusalem, and He has delivered them to be a terror *and* a cause of trembling, to be an astonishment, and a hissing, as you see with your own eyes.

9 For, behold, our fathers have fallen by the sword, and our sons, our daughters, and our wives are in captivity for this.

10 Now it is in my heart to make a covenant with the Lord, the God of Israel, that His fierce anger may turn away from us.

11 My sons, do not now be negligent, for the Lord has chosen you to stand in His presence, to serve Him, to be His ministers, and to burn incense to Him.

12 Then the Levites arose: Mahath son of Amasai, Joel son of Azariah, of the sons of the Kohathites; of the sons of Merari: Kish son of Abdi, Azariah son of Jehallelel; of the Gershonites: Joah son of Zimmah and Eden son of Joah;

13 Of the sons of Elizaphan: Shimri and Jeiel; of the sons of Asaph: Zechariah, and Mattaniah;

14 Of the sons of Heman: Jehiel and Shimei; and of the sons of Jeduthun: Shemaiah and Uzziel.

15 They gathered their brethren and sanctified themselves and went in, as the king had commanded by the words of the Lord, to cleanse the house of the Lord.

16 The priests went into the inner part of the house of the Lord to cleanse it, and brought out all the uncleanness they found in the temple of the Lord into the court of the Lord's house. And the Levites carried it out to the brook Kidron.

17 They began on the first day of the first month, and on the eighth day they came to the porch of the Lord. Then for eight days they sanctified the house of the Lord, and on the sixteenth day they finished.

18 Then they went to King Hezekiah and said, We have cleansed all the house of the Lord and the altar of burnt offering with all its utensils and the showbread table with all its utensils.

19 Moreover, all the utensils which King Ahaz in his reign cast away when he was transgressing [faithless] we have made ready and sanctified; and behold, they are before the altar of the Lord.

20 Then King Hezekiah rose early and gathered the officials of the city and went up to the house of the Lord.

21 They brought seven each of bulls, rams, lambs, and he-goats for a sin offering for the kingdom, the sanctuary, and Judah. He commanded the priests, the sons of Aaron, to offer them on the Lord's altar.

22 So they killed the bulls, and the priests received the blood and dashed it against the altar. Likewise, when they had killed the rams and then the lambs, they dashed the blood against the altar.

23 Then the he-goats for the sin offering were brought before the king and the assembly, and they laid their hands on them.

24 The priests killed them and made a sin offering with their blood upon the altar to make atonement for all

Israel, for the king commanded that the burnt offering and sin offering be made for all Israel.

25 Hezekiah stationed the Levites in the Lord's house with cymbals, harps, and lyres, as David [his forefather] and Gad the king's seer and Nathan the prophet had commanded; for the commandment was from the Lord through His prophets.

26 The Levites stood with the instruments of David, and the priests with the trumpets.

27 Hezekiah commanded to offer the burnt offering upon the altar. And when the burnt offering began, the song of the Lord began also with the trumpets and with the instruments ordained by King David of Israel.

28 And all the congregation worshiped, the singers sang, and the trumpeters sounded; all this continued until the burnt offering was finished.

29 When they had stopped offering, the king and all present with him bowed themselves and worshiped.

30 Also King Hezekiah and the princes ordered the Levites to sing praises to the Lord with the words of David and of Asaph the seer. And they sang praises with gladness and bowed themselves and worshiped.

31 Then Hezekiah said, Now you have consecrated yourselves to the Lord; come near and bring sacrifices and thank offerings into the house of the Lord. And the assembly brought in sacrifices and thank offerings, and as many as were of a willing heart brought burnt offerings.

32 And the number of the burnt offerings which the assembly brought was 70 bulls, 100 rams, and 200 lambs. All these were for a burnt offering to the Lord.

33 And the consecrated things were 600 oxen and 3,000 sheep.

34 But the priests were too few and could not skin all the burnt offerings. So until the other priests had sanctified themselves, their Levite kinsmen helped them until the work was done, for the Levites were more upright in heart than the priests in sanctifying themselves.

35 Also the burnt offerings were in abundance, with the fat of the peace offerings, and the drink offerings for every burnt offering. So the service of the Lord's house was set in order.

36 Thus Hezekiah rejoiced, and all the people, because of what God had prepared for the people, for it was done suddenly.

30 HEZEKIAH SENT to all Israel [as well as] Judah and wrote letters also to Ephraim and Manasseh to come to the Lord's house at Jerusalem to keep the Passover to the Lord, the God of Israel.

2 For the king and his princes and all the assembly in Jerusalem took counsel to keep the Passover in the ˡsecond month. [Num. 9:10, 11.]

3 For they could not keep it at the set time because not enough priests had sanctified themselves, neither had the people assembled in Jerusalem.

4 The new time pleased the king and all the assembly.

5 So they decreed to make a proclamation throughout all Israel, from Beersheba to Dan, that the people should come to keep the Passover to the Lord, the God of Israel, at Jerusalem. For they had not kept it collectively as prescribed for a long time.

6 So the posts went with the letters from the king and his princes throughout all Israel and Judah, as the king commanded, saying, O Israelites, return to the Lord, the God of

ˡ Postponement from the first month is graciously permitted by God (see Num. 9:10-11).

Abraham, Isaac, and Israel, that He may return to those left of you who escaped out of the hands of the kings of Assyria.

7 Do not be like your fathers and brethren, who were unfaithful to the Lord, the God of their fathers, so that He gave them up to desolation [to be an astonishment], as you see.

8 Now be not stiff-necked, as your fathers were, but yield yourselves to the Lord and come to His sanctuary, which He has sanctified forever, and serve the Lord your God, that His fierce anger may turn away from you.

9 For if you return to the Lord, your brethren and your children shall find compassion with their captors and return to this land. For the Lord your God is gracious and merciful, and He will not turn away His face from you if you return to Him.

10 So the posts passed from city to city through the country of Ephraim and Manasseh, even to Zebulun, but the people laughed them to scorn and mocked them.

11 Yet, a few of Asher, Manasseh, and Zebulun humbled themselves and came to Jerusalem.

12 Also the hand of God came upon Judah to give them one heart to do the commandment of the king and of the princes, by the word of the Lord.

13 And many people came to Jerusalem to keep the Feast of Unleavened Bread in the second month, a very great assembly.

14 They rose up and took away the altars [to idols] that were in Jerusalem, and all the altars *and* utensils for incense [to the gods] they took away and threw into the Kidron Val-

ley [dumping place for the ashes of such abominations].

15 Then they killed the Passover lamb on the fourteenth day of the second month. And the priests and the Levites were ashamed and sanctified themselves and brought burnt offerings to the Lord's house.

16 They stood in their accustomed places, as directed in the Law of Moses the man of God. The priests threw [against the altar] the blood they received from the hand of the Levites.

17 For many were in the assembly who had not sanctified themselves [become clean and free from all sin]. So the Levites had to kill the Passover lambs for all who were not clean, in order to make them holy to the Lord.

18 For a multitude of the people, many from Ephraim, Manasseh, Issachar, and Zebulun, had not cleansed themselves, yet they ate the Passover otherwise than Moses directed. For Hezekiah had prayed for them, saying, May the good Lord pardon everyone

19 Who sets his heart to seek *and* yearn for God—the Lord, the God of his fathers—even though not complying with the purification regulations of the sanctuary.

20 And the Lord hearkened to Hezekiah and healed the people.

21 And the Israelites who were in Jerusalem kept the Feast of Unleavened Bread for seven days with great joy. The Levites and priests praised the Lord day by day, singing with instruments of much volume to the Lord.

speak the Word

Help me, God, to not be stiff-necked or stubborn, but to always stay yielded to You.
ADAPTED FROM II CHRONICLES 30:8

22 Hezekiah spoke encouragingly to all the Levites who had good understanding in the Lord's work. So the people ate the seven-day appointed feast, offering peace offerings, making confession [and giving thanks] to the Lord, the God of their fathers.

23 And the whole assembly took counsel to prolong the feast another seven days; and they kept it another seven days with joy.

24 For Hezekiah king of Judah gave to the assembly 1,000 young bulls and 7,000 sheep, and the princes gave 1,000 young bulls and 10,000 sheep. And a great number of priests sanctified themselves [for service].

25 All the assembly of Judah, with the priests, the Levites, and all the assembly who with the sojourners came from the land of Israel to dwell in Judah, rejoiced.

26 So there was great joy in Jerusalem, for since the time of Solomon son of David king of Israel there was nothing like this in Jerusalem.

27 Then the priests and Levites arose and blessed the people; and their voice was heard and their prayer came up to [God's] holy habitation in heaven.

31 NOW WHEN all this was finished, all Israel present there went out to the cities of Judah and broke in pieces the pillars or obelisks, cut down the Asherim, and threw down the high places [of idolatry] and the altars in all Judah and Benjamin, in Ephraim and Manasseh, until they had utterly destroyed them all. Then all the Israelites returned to their own cities, every man to his possession.

2 And Hezekiah appointed the priests and the Levites after their divisions, each man according to his service, the priests and Levites for burnt offerings and for peace offer-ings, to minister, to give thanks, and to praise in the gates of the camp of the Lord.

3 King Hezekiah's personal contribution was for the burnt offerings: [those] of morning and evening, for the Sabbaths, for the New Moons, and for the appointed feasts, as written in the Law of the Lord.

4 He commanded the people living in Jerusalem to give the portion due the priests and Levites, that they might [be free to] give themselves to the Law of the Lord.

5 As soon as the command went abroad, the Israelites gave in abundance the firstfruits of grain, vintage fruit, oil, honey, and of all the produce of the field; and they brought in abundantly the tithe of everything.

6 The people of Israel and Judah who lived in Judah's cities also brought the tithe of cattle and sheep and of the dedicated things which were consecrated to the Lord their God, and they laid them in heaps.

7 In the third month [at the end of wheat harvest] they began to lay the foundation or beginning of the heaps and finished them in the seventh month.

8 When Hezekiah and the princes came and saw the heaps, they blessed the Lord and His people Israel.

9 Then Hezekiah questioned the priests and Levites about the heaps.

10 Azariah the high priest, of the house of Zadok, answered him, Since the people began to bring the offerings into the Lord's house, we have eaten and have plenty left, for the Lord has blessed His people, and what is left is this great store.

11 Then Hezekiah commanded them to prepare chambers [for storage] in the house of the Lord, and they prepared them

12 And brought in the offerings, tithes, and dedicated things faithfully. Conaniah the Levite was in charge of them, and Shimei his brother came next.

13 And Jehiel, Azaziah, Nahath, Asahel, Jerimoth, Jozabad, Eliel, Ismachiah, Mahath, and Benaiah were overseers directed by Conaniah and Shimei his brother, at the appointment of King Hezekiah and Azariah the chief officer of the house of God.

14 Kore son of Imnah the Levite, keeper of the East Gate, was over the freewill offerings to God, to apportion the contributions of the Lord and the most holy things.

15 Under him were Eden, Miniamin, Jeshua, Shemaiah, Amariah, and Shecaniah, in the priests' cities, in their office of trust faithfully to give to their brethren by divisions, to great and small alike,

16 Except those [Levites] registered as males from three years old and upward—who were consecrated to the temple service [in Jerusalem, for their daily portion] as the duty of every day required, for their service according to their offices by their divisions.

17 The registration of the priests was according to their fathers' houses; that of the Levites from twenty years old and upward was according to their offices by their divisions;

18 Also there was the registration of all their little ones, their wives, and their older sons and daughters through all the congregation. For in their office of trust they cleansed themselves *and* set themselves apart in holiness.

19 Also for the sons of Aaron the priests, who were in the fields of the suburbs of their cities or in every city, there were men who were mentioned by name to give portions to all the males among the priests and to all who were registered among the Levites.

20 Hezekiah did this throughout all Judah, and he did what was good, right, and faithful before the Lord his God.

21 And every work that he began in the service of the house of God, in keeping with the law and the commandments to seek his God [inquiring of and yearning for Him], he did with all his heart, and he prospered.

32 AFTER THESE things and this loyalty, Sennacherib king of Assyria came, invaded Judah, and encamped against the fortified cities, thinking to take them.

2 When Hezekiah saw that Sennacherib had come and intended to fight against Jerusalem,

3 He decided with his officers and his mighty men to stop up the waters of the fountains which were outside the city [by enclosing them with masonry and concealing them], and they helped him.

4 So many people gathered, and they stopped up all the springs and the brook which flowed through the land, saying, Why should the kings of Assyria come and find much water?

5 Also Hezekiah took courage and built up all the wall that was broken, and raised towers upon it, and he built another wall outside and strengthened the Millo in the City of David and made weapons and shields in abundance.

6 And he set captains of war over the people and gathered them together to him in the street of the gate of the city and spoke encouragingly to them, saying,

7 Be strong and courageous. Be not afraid or dismayed before the king of Assyria and all the horde that is with him, for there is Another with us greater than [all those] with him.

8 With him is an arm of flesh, but with us is the Lord our God to help us and to fight our battles. And the

God's strong arm

When the Assyrians came in great strength to invade Judah and lay siege to Jerusalem, King Hezekiah inspired courage in the people with strong words of encouragement saying basically, "Do not trust in the arm of flesh, but trust in the Lord" (see II Chronicles 32:7, 8).

That is the attitude you and I need to have in the face of seemingly overwhelming problems. Rather than looking at our past failures, our present fallacies, or our future fears, we need to be looking to the Lord and trusting in His wisdom, strength, and power. We should be reminding ourselves that no matter how many problems may be facing us, the One Who is with us is greater than all those who oppose us. With them is the arm of the flesh, but with us is the arm of the Lord.

In Jeremiah 17:5–8 we read that those who put their trust in the arm of the flesh are cursed with "great evil" (Jeremiah 17:5). They are like a plant in the desert that is dry and destitute. They will not see any good happen. But those who put their trust in the arm of the Lord are blessed. They are like a tree planted by a river that produces fruit even in the midst of a drought. No matter what comes, they will flourish and not be anxious. Jeremiah says, "Blessed is the man who believes in, trusts in, and relies on the Lord, and whose hope and confidence the Lord is" (Jeremiah 17:7).

If we lean on the arm of flesh, meaning other people or ourselves, we will end up being disappointed and perhaps devastated. We need to love and enjoy people, but we also need to realize that they have the ability to ultimately let us down. We must rely on the strong arm of the Lord to help us, because He will never fail us nor forsake us.

people relied on the words of Hezekiah king of Judah.

9 And this Sennacherib king of Assyria, while he himself with all his forces was before Lachish, sent his servants to Jerusalem, to Hezekiah king of Judah, and to all Judah who were at Jerusalem, saying,

10 Thus says Sennacherib king of Assyria: On what do you trust, that you remain in the strongholds in Jerusalem?

11 Is not Hezekiah leading you on in order to let you die by famine and thirst, saying, The Lord our God will deliver us out of the hand of the king of Assyria?

12 Has not the same Hezekiah taken away his high places and his altars, and commanded Judah and Jerusalem, You shall worship before one altar and burn incense upon it?

13 Do you not know what I and my fathers have done to all the peoples of other lands? Were the gods of the nations of those lands in any way able to deliver their lands out of my hand?

14 Who among all the gods of those nations that my fathers utterly destroyed was able to deliver his people out of my hand, that your God should be able to deliver you out of my hand?

15 So now, do not let Hezekiah deceive or mislead you in this way, and do not believe him, for no god of any nation or kingdom was able to deliver his people out of my hand or the hand of my fathers. How much less will your God deliver you out of my hand!

16 And his servants said still more against the Lord God and against His servant Hezekiah.

17 The Assyrian king also wrote letters insulting the Lord, the God of Israel, and speaking against Him, saying, As the gods of the nations of other lands have not delivered their people out of my hand, so shall not the God of Hezekiah deliver His people out of my hand.

18 And they shouted it loudly in the Jewish language to the people of Jerusalem who were on the wall, to frighten and terrify them, that they might take the city.

19 And they spoke of the God of Jerusalem as they spoke of the gods of the peoples of the earth, which are the work of the hands of men.

20 For this cause Hezekiah the king and the prophet Isaiah son of Amoz prayed and cried to heaven.

21 And the Lord sent an angel, who cut off all the mighty warriors and commanders and officers in the camp of the king of Assyria. So the Assyrian king returned with shamed face to his own land. And when he came into the house of his god, they who were his own offspring slew him there with the sword. [II Kings 19:35-37.]

22 Thus the Lord saved Hezekiah and the inhabitants of Jerusalem from the hand of Sennacherib the king of Assyria and from the hand of all his enemies, and He guided them on every side.

23 And many brought gifts to Jerusalem to the Lord and presents to Hezekiah king of Judah; so from then on he was magnified in the sight of all nations.

24 In those days Hezekiah was sick to the point of death; and he prayed to the Lord and He answered him and gave him a sign.

25 But Hezekiah did not make return [to the Lord] according to the benefit done to him, for his heart became proud [at such a spectacular response to his prayer]; therefore there was wrath upon him and upon Judah and Jerusalem.

26 But Hezekiah humbled himself for the pride of his heart, both he and the inhabitants of Jerusalem, so that the wrath of the Lord came not upon them in the days of Hezekiah.

27 And Hezekiah had very great wealth and honor, and he made for himself treasuries for silver, gold, precious stones, spices, shields, and all kinds of attractive vessels,

28 Storehouses also for the increase of grain, vintage fruits, and oil, and stalls for all kinds of cattle, and sheepfolds.

29 Moreover, he provided for himself cities and flocks and herds in abundance, for God had given him very great possessions.

30 This same Hezekiah also closed the upper springs of Gihon and directed the waters down to the west side of the City of David. And Hezekiah prospered in all his works.

31 And so in the matter of the ambassadors of the princes of Babylon who were sent to him to inquire

life point

Notice in II Chronicles 32:31 that God left Hezekiah "to himself to try him, that He might know all that was in his heart." Do not be discouraged if you feel there are times when God has left you "to yourself," when you do not sense His presence or hear His voice. Sometimes He is quiet and seemingly imperceptible, just to see if we will continue to be faithful to Him. Determine right now that you will always be faithful in hard times as well as in good times!

looking up

In answer to the prayers of King Hezekiah and the prophet Isaiah, the Lord intervened and saved Hezekiah and Judah from their enemies. As a result, Hezekiah began to be lifted up in the sight of the people (see II Chronicles 32:22, 23).

God is not against that. If you become a leader, people will look up to you and honor you. They may want to do nice things for you. That is not all bad, but it can be dangerous. As happened with Hezekiah, people's admiration for a leader, or the leader's view of that admiration, can lead to pride if not kept under control. In his pride, Hezekiah fell ill and almost died. But he humbled himself and repented of his proud heart and things were straightened out (see II Chronicles 32:24–26).

It is interesting that when Hezekiah turned to God, the Lord began to honor, promote, and bless him again (see II Chronicles 32:27). That is exactly what happens to people who commit wholeheartedly to the Lord. Sooner or later their ministry starts increasing, and they start moving up. People begin looking up to them. But if they become proud, God will deal with them about their pride. Like Hezekiah, they can quickly repent and come back to a place of humility; and God can continue to bless them in amazing ways. Or, if they refuse to repent, they will begin to lose God's blessing and eventually their place of honor.

This is a key issue in Christian leadership. Everyone who is doing anything of importance for the Lord must resist the attacks and temptations of the spirit of pride. That is why no one automatically always has a right heart; it takes effort to keep our hearts right. We have to work at it all the time. And one of the most powerful things we have to guard against is a spirit of self-righteousness, which is rooted in pride.

Our enemy Satan is going to use every opportunity he can to get us into places where our hearts are not right. When that happens, we need to repent to God immediately.

If you and I want to stand before God one day and say, as Jesus did in John 17:4, "I have glorified You down here on the earth by completing the work that You gave Me to do," then we must be careful to keep a right heart. Psalm 101:5 says that God will not tolerate anyone who has a haughty look and a proud and arrogant heart. We need to be diligent to guard against pride and make sure that we walk before God and others with a humbled heart. God's Word teaches us to guard our hearts with all diligence, for out of them flow the issues of life (see Proverbs 4:23).

about the wonder that was done in the land, God left him to himself to try him, that He might know all that was in his heart. [Isa. 39:1-7.]

32 Now the rest of the acts of Hezekiah and his good deeds, behold, they are written in the vision of Isaiah the prophet, the son of Amoz, and in the Book of the Kings of Judah and Israel.

33 And Hezekiah slept with his fathers and was buried in the ascent of the tombs of the descendants of David; and all Judah and the inhabitants of Jerusalem did him honor at his death. Manasseh his son reigned in his stead.

33 MANASSEH WAS twelve years old when he began to reign, and he reigned fifty-five years in Jerusalem.

2 But he did evil in the Lord's sight, like the abominations of the heathen whom the Lord drove out before the Israelites.

3 For he built again the [idolatrous] high places which Hezekiah his father had broken down, and he reared altars for the Baals and made the Asherim and worshiped all the hosts of the heavens and served them.

4 Also he built [heathen] altars in the Lord's house, of which the Lord had said, In Jerusalem shall My Name be forever.

5 He built altars for all the hosts of the heavens in the two courts of the Lord's house.

6 And he burned his children as an offering [to his god] in the Valley of Ben-hinnom [son of Hinnom], and practiced soothsaying, augury, and sorcery, and dealt with mediums and wizards. He did much evil in the sight of the Lord, provoking Him to anger.

7 And he set a carved image, the idol which he had made, in the house of God, of which God had said to David and to Solomon his son, In this

house and in Jerusalem, which I have chosen before all the tribes of Israel, will I put My Name [and Presence] forever;

8 And I will no more remove Israel from the land which I appointed for your fathers, if they will only take heed to do all that I have commanded them, the whole law, the statutes, and the ordinances given through Moses.

9 So Manasseh led Judah and the inhabitants of Jerusalem to do more evil than the heathen whom the Lord had destroyed before the Israelites.

10 The Lord spoke to Manasseh and to his people, but they would not hearken.

11 So the Lord brought against them the commanders of the host of the king of Assyria, who took Manasseh with hooks and in fetters and brought him to Babylon.

12 When he was in affliction, he besought the Lord his God and humbled himself greatly before the God of his fathers.

13 He prayed to Him, and God, entreated by him, heard his supplication and brought him again to Jerusalem to his kingdom. Then Manasseh knew that the Lord is God.

14 And he built an outer wall to the City of David west of Gihon in the valley, to the entrance of the Fish Gate, and ran it around Ophel, raising it to a very great height; and he put commanders of the army in all the fortified cities of Judah.

15 And he took away the foreign gods and the idol out of the house of the Lord and all the altars that he had built on the mount of the house of the Lord and in Jerusalem; and he cast them out of the city.

16 And he restored the Lord's altar and sacrificed on it offerings of peace and of thanksgiving; and he commanded Judah to serve the Lord, the God of Israel.

17 Yet the people still sacrificed in

the high places, but only to the Lord their God.

18 Now the rest of the acts of Manasseh, and his prayer to his God, and the words of the seers who spoke to him in the name of the Lord, the God of Israel, behold, they are written in the Book of the Kings of Israel.

19 His prayer and how God heard him, and all his sins and unfaithfulness, and the sites on which he built high places and set up the Asherim and graven images before he humbled himself, behold, they are written in the Chronicles of the Seers.

20 So Manasseh slept with his fathers, and they buried him in his own house [garden]. And Amon his son reigned in his stead.

21 Amon was twenty-two years old when he began his two-year reign in Jerusalem.

22 But he did evil in the sight of the Lord, as did Manasseh his father; for Amon sacrificed to all the images which Manasseh his father had made, and served them,

23 And he did not humble himself before the Lord, as Manasseh his father [finally] did; but Amon trespassed *and* became more and more guilty.

24 And his servants conspired against him and killed him in his own house.

25 But the people of the land slew all those who had conspired against King Amon, and they made Josiah his son king in his stead.

34 JOSIAH WAS eight years old when he began his thirty-one-year reign in Jerusalem.

2 He did right in the sight of the Lord and walked in the ways of David his father [forefather] and turned aside neither to the right hand nor to the left.

3 For in the eighth year of his reign, while he was yet young [sixteen], he began to seek after *and* yearn for the God of David his father [forefather]; and in the twelfth year he began to purge Judah and Jerusalem of the high places, the Asherim, and the carved and molten images.

4 They broke down the altars of the Baals in his presence; the sun-images that were high above them he hewed down; the Asherim and the graven images and the molten images he broke in pieces and made dust of them and strewed it upon the graves of those who sacrificed to them.

5 Josiah burned the bones of the [idolatrous] priests upon their altars, and so cleansed Judah and Jerusalem.

6 So he did in the cities of Manasseh, Ephraim, and Simeon, even to Naphtali, in their ruins round about [with their axes],

7 He broke down the altars and the Asherim and beat the graven images into powder and hewed down all the sun-images throughout all the land of Israel. Then he returned to Jerusalem.

8 In the eighteenth year of Josiah's reign, when he had purged the land and the [Lord's] house, he sent Shaphan son of Azaliah, and Maaseiah governor of the city, and Joah son of Joahaz, the recorder, to repair the house of the Lord his God.

9 When they came to Hilkiah the high priest, they delivered the money that had been brought into the house of God, which the Levites who kept the doors had collected from Manasseh, Ephraim, all the remnant of Israel, and from all Judah, Benjamin, and Jerusalem.

10 They delivered it to the workmen who had oversight of the Lord's house, who gave it to repair and restore the temple:

11 To the carpenters and builders to buy hewn stone, and timber for couplings and beams for the houses which the kings of Judah had destroyed [by neglect].

12 The men did the work faithfully. Their overseers were Jahath and Obadiah, Levites of the sons of Merari, and Zechariah and Meshullam, of the sons of the Kohathites. The Levites—all who were skillful with instruments of music—
13 Also had oversight of the burden bearers and all who did work in any kind of service; and some of the Levites were scribes, officials, and gatekeepers.
14 When they were bringing out the money that was brought into the house of the Lord, Hilkiah the priest found the Book of the Law of the Lord given by Moses.
15 Hilkiah told Shaphan the scribe, I have found the Book of the Law in the Lord's house. And [he] gave the book to Shaphan.
16 Shaphan took the book to King Josiah, but [first] reported to him, All that was committed to your servants they are doing.
17 They have emptied out the money that was found in the house of the Lord and have delivered it into the hand of the overseers and the workmen.
18 Then Shaphan the scribe said to the king, Hilkiah the priest has given me a book. And Shaphan read it before the king.
19 When King Josiah had heard the words of the Law, he rent his clothes.
20 And the king commanded Hilkiah, Ahikam son of Shaphan, Abdon son of Micah, Shaphan the scribe, and Asaiah a servant of the king, saying,
21 Go, inquire of the Lord for me and for those who are left in Israel and in Judah about the words of the book that is found. For great is the Lord's wrath that is poured out on us because our fathers have not kept the word of the Lord, to do according to all that is written in this book.
22 And Hilkiah and they whom the king had appointed went to Huldah the prophetess, the wife of Shallum son of Tokhath, the son of Hasrah, keeper of the wardrobe. She dwelt in Jerusalem, in the Second Quarter. They spoke to her to that effect.
23 And she answered them, Thus says the Lord, the God of Israel: Tell the man who sent you to me,
24 Thus says the Lord: Behold, I will bring evil upon this place and upon its inhabitants, even all the curses that are written in the book which they have read before the king of Judah.
25 Because they have forsaken Me and have burned incense to other gods, that they might provoke Me to anger with all the works of their hands, therefore My wrath shall be poured out upon this place and shall not be quenched.
26 But say to King Josiah of Judah, who sent you to inquire of the Lord, Thus says the Lord, the God of Israel, concerning the words which you have heard:
27 Because your heart was tender *and* penitent and you humbled yourself before God when you heard His words against this place and its inhabitants, and humbled yourself before Me and rent your clothes and wept before Me, I have heard you, says the Lord.
28 Behold, I will gather you to your fathers, and you shall be gathered to your grave in peace, and your eyes shall not see all the evil that I will bring upon this place and its inhabitants. So they brought the king word again.
29 Then King Josiah sent and gathered all the elders of Judah and Jerusalem.
30 And [he] went up into the house of the Lord, as did all the men of Judah, the inhabitants of Jerusalem, the priests, the Levites, and all the people, great and small; and he [the king] read in their hearing all the words of the Book of the Covenant that was found in the Lord's house.

31 Then the king stood in his place and made a covenant before the Lord—to walk after the Lord and to keep His commandments, His testimonies, and His statutes with all his heart and with all his soul, to perform the words of the covenant that are written in this book.

32 And he caused all who were present in Jerusalem and Benjamin to stand in confirmation of it. And the inhabitants of Jerusalem did according to the covenant of God, the God of their fathers.

33 Josiah removed all the [idolatrous] abominations from all the territory that belonged to the Israelites, and made all who were in Israel serve the Lord their God. All his days they did not turn from following the Lord, the God of their fathers.

35 JOSIAH KEPT the Passover to the Lord in Jerusalem; they killed the Passover lamb on the fourteenth day of the first month.

2 He appointed the priests to their positions and encouraged them in the service of the house of the Lord.

3 To the Levites who taught all Israel and were holy to the Lord he said: Put the holy ark in the house which Solomon son of David king of Israel, built; it shall no longer be a burden carried on your shoulders. Now serve the Lord your God and His people Israel.

4 Prepare yourselves according to your fathers' houses by your divisions, after the directions of David king of Israel and of Solomon his son.

5 And stand in the holy court of the priests according to the sections of the fathers' families of your kinsmen, the common people, and let there be a section of the Levites [to attend] to each division of the families of the people.

6 Kill the Passover lambs and sanctify yourselves and prepare for your brethren to do according to the word of the Lord by Moses.

7 Then Josiah contributed to the lay people lambs and kids of the flock as Passover offerings for all who were present, to the number of 30,000, and 3,000 young bulls—all from the king's possessions.

8 And his princes gave for a freewill offering to the people, to the priests, and the Levites. Hilkiah, Zechariah, and Jehiel, chief officers of God's house, gave the priests for the Passover offerings 2,600 [lambs and kids] and 300 bulls.

9 Conaniah also, and Shemaiah and Nethanel his brothers, and Hashabiah, Jeiel, and Jozabad, chiefs of the Levites, gave to the Levites for Passover offerings 5,000 [lambs and kids] and 500 bulls.

10 When the service was ready, the priests stood in their place and the Levites in their divisions as the king commanded.

11 They killed the Passover lambs, and the priests sprinkled the blood they received from the Levites who skinned the animals.

12 Then they removed the burnt offerings, that they might distribute them according to the divisions of the lay families to offer to the Lord, as directed in the Book of Moses. And so they did with the bulls.

13 And they roasted the Passover lambs with fire according to the ordinance; and they cooked the holy offerings in pots, in caldrons, and in pans and carried them quickly to all the people.

14 Afterward [the Levites] prepared for themselves and the priests, because the priests, the sons of Aaron, were busy in offering the burnt offerings and the fat until night; so the Levites prepared for themselves and also for the priests, the sons of Aaron.

15 The singers, the sons of Asaph, were in their places according to the command of David, Asaph, Heman, and Jeduthun the king's seer. And the gatekeepers were at every gate; they did not need to leave their service, for their brethren the Levites prepared for them.

16 So all the Lord's service was prepared the same day to keep the Passover and to offer burnt offerings upon the Lord's altar, as King Josiah commanded.

17 And the Israelites who were present kept the Passover at that time, and the Feast of Unleavened Bread for seven days.

18 No Passover like it had been kept in Israel since the days of Samuel the prophet, even by any of the kings of Israel, as was kept by Josiah and the priests, the Levites, and all Judah and Israel who were present, and the inhabitants of Jerusalem.

19 In the eighteenth year of the reign of Josiah this Passover was kept.

20 After all this, when Josiah had prepared the temple, Neco king of Egypt went out to fight against Carchemish on the Euphrates, and Josiah went out against him.

21 But [Neco] sent ambassadors to [Josiah], saying, What have I to do with you, you king of Judah? I come not against you this day, but against the house with which I am at war; and God has commanded me to make haste. Refrain from opposing God, Who is with me, lest He destroy you.

22 Yet Josiah would not turn away from him, but disguised himself in order to fight with him. He did not heed the words of Neco from the mouth of God, but came to fight with him in the valley of Megiddo.

23 And the archers shot King Josiah, and the king said to his servants, Take me away, for I am severely wounded.

24 So his servants took him out of the chariot and put him in his second chariot and brought him to Jerusalem. And he died and was buried in the tombs of his fathers. All Judah and Jerusalem mourned for Josiah.

25 Jeremiah gave a lament for Josiah, and all the singing men and women have spoken of Josiah in their laments to this day. They made them an ordinance in Israel; behold, they are written in the Laments. [Lam. 4:20.]

26 Now the rest of the acts of Josiah and his deeds, according to what is written in the Law of the Lord,

27 And his acts, from first to last, behold, they are written in the Book of the Kings of Israel and Judah.

36 THEN THE people of the land took Jehoahaz son of Josiah and made him king in his father's stead in Jerusalem.

2 Jehoahaz was [then] twenty-three years old; he reigned three months in Jerusalem.

3 Then the king of Egypt deposed him at Jerusalem and fined the land a hundred talents of silver and a talent of gold.

4 And the king of Egypt made Eliakim, Jehoahaz' brother, king over Judah and Jerusalem and changed his name to Jehoiakim. But Neco took Jehoahaz his brother and carried him to Egypt.

5 Jehoiakim was twenty-five years old when he began to reign, and he reigned eleven years in Jerusalem. He did evil in the sight of the Lord his God.

6 Against him came up Nebuchadnezzar king of Babylon and bound him in fetters to take him to Babylon.

7 Nebuchadnezzar also took some of the vessels of the house of the Lord to Babylon and put them in his temple *or* palace there.

8 Now the rest of the acts of Jehoiakim, and the abominations which he did, and what was found against him, behold, they are written in the Book of the Kings of Israel and Judah. And Jehoiachin his son reigned in his stead.

9 Jehoiachin was eight[een] years old then; he reigned three months and ten days in Jerusalem. He did evil in the Lord's sight. [II Kings 24:8.]

10 In the spring, King Nebuchadnezzar sent and brought him to Babylon, with the precious vessels of the house of the Lord, and made Zedekiah the [boy's] brother king over Judah and Jerusalem.

11 Zedekiah was twenty-one years old when he became king, and he reigned eleven years in Jerusalem.

12 He did evil in the sight of the Lord his God and did not humble himself before Jeremiah the prophet, who spoke at the dictation of the Lord.

13 He also rebelled against King Nebuchadnezzar, who made him swear by God. He stiffened his neck and hardened his heart against turning to the Lord, the God of Israel.

14 Also all the chiefs of the priests and the people trespassed greatly in accord with all the abominations of the heathen, and they polluted the house of the Lord which He had hallowed in Jerusalem.

15 And the Lord, the God of their fathers, sent to them persistently by His messengers, because He had compassion on His people and on His dwelling place.

16 But they kept mocking the messengers of God and despising His words and scoffing at His prophets till the wrath of the Lord rose against His people, till there was no remedy *or* healing.

17 Therefore He brought against them the king of the Chaldeans, who slew their young men with the sword in the house of their sanctuary, and had no compassion on young man or virgin, old man or hoary-headed; He gave them all into his hand.

18 And all the vessels of the house of God, great and small, and the treasures of the Lord's house, of the king, and of his princes, all these he brought to Babylon.

19 And they burned God's house and broke down Jerusalem's wall and burned all its palaces with fire and destroyed all its choice vessels.

20 Those who had escaped from the sword he took away to Babylon, where they were servants to him and his sons until the kingdom of Persia was established there,

21 To fulfill the Lord's word by Jeremiah, till the land had enjoyed its sabbaths; for as long as it lay desolate it kept sabbath to fulfill seventy years. [Lev. 25:4; 26:43; Jer. 25:11; 29:10.]

22 Now in the first year of Cyrus king of Persia, that the word of the Lord by the mouth of Jeremiah might be accomplished, the Lord stirred up the spirit of Cyrus king of Persia so that he made a proclamation throughout all his kingdom and also put it in writing:

23 Thus says Cyrus king of Persia: All the kingdoms of the earth the Lord, the God of heaven, has given me, and He has charged me to build Him a house in Jerusalem, which is in Judah. Whoever there is among you of all His people, may the Lord his God be with him, and let him go up [to Jerusalem].

Ezra

Author:
Probably Ezra

Date:
538 BC–457 BC

Everyday Life Principles:
The enemy always wants to oppose people who are doing something for God so that he can stop their work.

You do not have to be afraid when you experience opposition, because God is with you.

Even though the enemy does not give up easily, he is a defeated foe, and we will eventually overcome him if we stay "strong, alert, and courageous."

The events recounted in the book of Ezra cover a period of about eighty years and tell the story of diligent, faithful people who overcame opposition and resistance in order to rebuild God's temple and restore it to its former glory.

When the people grew weary and discouraged because of the taunts of their enemies, God sent the two prophets Haggai and Zechariah to remind them of God's faithfulness and to encourage them to finish the work. In fact, we can read some of the words that inspired the people and their leaders to continue in Haggai 2:4, 5: ". . . be strong, alert, and courageous, all you people of the land, says the Lord, and work! For I am with you, says the Lord of hosts . . . My Spirit stands and abides in the midst of you; fear not."

I believe that God has a great plan for your life and that you are called to do something special for Him. The enemy will resist you, but let the book of Ezra remind you that God is on your side and the enemy is a defeated foe. Whatever battles the enemy wages against you, do not become discouraged, but stay "strong, alert, and courageous" in God. Fear not, but remember that God is faithful and He is with you; He always wins and in Him, you do too.

1 NOW IN the first year of [a]Cyrus king of Persia [almost seventy years after the first Jewish captives were taken to Babylon], that the word of the Lord by the mouth of Jeremiah might begin to be accomplished, the Lord stirred up the spirit of Cyrus king of Persia so that he made a proclamation throughout all his kingdom and put it also in writing: [Jer. 29:10-14.]

2 Thus says Cyrus king of Persia: The Lord, the God of heaven, has given me all the kingdoms of the earth, and He has charged me to build Him a house at Jerusalem in Judah.

3 Whoever is among you of all His people, may his God be with him, and let him go up to Jerusalem in Judah and rebuild the house of the Lord, the God of Israel, in Jerusalem; He is God.

4 And in any place where a survivor [of the Babylonian captivity of the Jews] sojourns, let the men of that place assist him with silver and gold, with goods and beasts, besides freewill offerings for the house of God in Jerusalem.

5 Then rose up the heads of the fathers' houses of Judah and Benjamin, and the priests and Levites, with all those whose spirits God had stirred up, to go up to rebuild the house of the Lord in Jerusalem.

6 And all those who were around them aided them with vessels of silver, with gold, goods, beasts, and precious things, besides all that was willingly and freely offered.

7 Also Cyrus the king brought out the vessels of the house of the Lord, which Nebuchadnezzar had brought from Jerusalem [when he took that city] and had put in the house of his gods.

8 These Cyrus king of Persia directed Mithredath the treasurer to bring forth and count out to Sheshbazzar [who is Zerubbabel, recognized as the legitimate heir to the throne of David] the prince of Judah.

9 And they numbered: 30 basins of gold; 1,000 basins of silver; 29 sacrificial dishes;

10 Of gold bowls, 30; another sort of silver bowl, 410; and other vessels, 1,000.

11 All the vessels of gold and of silver were 5,400. All these Sheshbazzar [the governor] brought with the people of the captivity from Babylon to Jerusalem.

2 NOW THESE are the people of the province [of Judah] who went up out of the captivity of those exiles whom Nebuchadnezzar the king of Babylon had carried away to Babylon, but who came again to Jerusalem and Judah, everyone to his own city.

2 These came with Zerubbabel: Jeshua, Nehemiah [not the author], Seraiah, Reelaiah, Mordecai [not Esther's relative], Bilshan, Mispar, Bigvai, Rehum, Baanah. The number of the men of Israel:

3 The sons [meaning male descendants] of Parosh, 2,172.

4 The sons of Shephatiah, 372.

5 The sons of Arah, 775.

6 The sons of Pahath-moab, namely of the sons of Jeshua and Joab, 2,812.

---

a Cyrus, a heathen ruler of a heathen empire (Persia), was "twice named [before his birth] in the book of Isaiah as anointed of God and predestined to conquer kings and fortified places and to set the Jews free from captivity (Isa. 44:28; 45:1-14). Daniel . . . records that during the night that followed a great feast, Belshazzar, the king of the Chaldeans, was slain, and Darius the Mede received the kingdom (Dan. 5:30, 31). Darius was the predecessor of Cyrus, or his regent, in Babylonia (Dan. 6:28)" (John D. Davis, *A Dictionary of the Bible*). God gave Cyrus the resolution and the desire to execute His intention. That the Lord at this time chose a heathen as His instrument was in accordance with the new position that the empires of the world were henceforth to assume toward the kingdom of God (J.P. Lange, *A Commentary*).

7 The sons of Elam, 1,254.
8 The sons of Zattu, 945.
9 The sons of Zaccai, 760.
10 The sons of Bani, 642.
11 The sons of Bebai, 623.
12 The sons of Azgad, 1,222.
13 The sons of Adonikam, 666.
14 The sons of Bigvai, 2,056.
15 The sons of Adin, 454.
16 The sons of Ater, namely of Hezekiah, 98.
17 The sons of Bezai, 323.
18 The sons of Jorah, 112.
19 The sons of Hashum, 223.
20 The sons of Gibbar, 95.
21 The sons of Bethlehem, 123.
22 The men of Netophah, 56.
23 The men of Anathoth, 128.
24 The sons of Azmaveth, 42.
25 The sons of Kiriath-arim, Chephirah, and Beeroth, 743.
26 The sons of Ramah and Geba, 621.
27 The men of Michmas, 122.
28 The men of Bethel and Ai, 223.
29 The sons of Nebo, 52.
30 The sons of Magbish, 156.
31 The sons of the other Elam, 1,254.
32 The sons of Harim, 320.
33 The sons of Lod, Hadid, and Ono, 725.
34 The sons of Jericho, 345.
35 The sons of Senaah, 3,630.
36 The priests: the sons of Jedaiah, of the house of Jeshua, 973.
37 The sons of Immer, 1,052.
38 The sons of Pashhur, 1,247.
39 The sons of Harim, 1,017.
40 The Levites: the sons of Jeshua and Kadmiel, of the house of Hodaviah, 74.
41 The singers: the sons of Asaph, 128.
42 The sons of the gatekeepers: of Shallum, Ater, Talmon, Akkub, Hatita, and Shobai, in all 139.
43 The Nethinim [the temple servants]: the sons of Ziba, Hasupha, Tabbaoth,
44 The sons of Keros, Siaha, Padon,

45 The sons of Lebanah, Hagabah, Akkub,
46 The sons of Hagab, Shalmai, Hanan,
47 The sons of Giddel, Gahar, Reaiah,
48 The sons of Rezin, Nekoda, Gazzam,
49 The sons of Uzza, Paseah, Besai,
50 The sons of Asnah, Meunim, Nephisim,
51 The sons of Bakbuk, Hakupha, Harhur,
52 The sons of Bazluth, Mehida, Harsha,
53 The sons of Barkos, Sisera, Temah,
54 The sons of Neziah [and] of Hatipha.
55 The sons of [King] Solomon's servants: the sons of Sotai, Sophereth (Hassophereth), Peruda,
56 The sons of Jaalah, Darkon, Giddel,
57 The sons of Shephatiah, Hattil, Pochereth-hazzebaim, Ami.
58 All the Nethinim [the temple servants] and the sons of Solomon's servants were 392.
59 And these were they who came up from Tel-melah, Tel-harsha, Cherub, Addan, and Immer, but they could not show a record of their fathers' houses or prove their descent, whether they were of Israel:
60 The sons of Delaiah, Tobiah, and Nekoda, 652.
61 And of the sons of the priests: the sons of Habaiah, of Hakkoz, and of Barzillai, who had taken a wife from the daughters of Barzillai the [noted] Gileadite and had assumed their name. [II Sam. 17:27, 28; 19:31-39.]
62 These sought their names among those enrolled in the genealogies, but they were not found; so they were excluded from the priesthood as [ceremonially] unclean.
63 [Zerubbabel] the governor told them they should not eat of the most

holy things [the priests' food] until there should be a priest with Urim and Thummim [who by consulting these articles in his breastplate could ᵇknow God's will in the matter].

64 The whole congregation numbered 42,360,

65 Besides their menservants and maidservants, 7,337; and among them they had 200 men and women singers.

66 Their horses were 736; their mules, 245;

67 Their camels were 435; their donkeys, 6,720.

68 Some of the heads of families, when they came to the house of the Lord in Jerusalem, made freewill offerings for the house of God to [re]build it on its site.

69 They gave as they were able to the treasury for the work 61,000 darics of gold, 5,000 minas of silver, and 100 priests' garments.

70 So the priests, the Levites, some of the people, the singers, the gatekeepers, and the temple servants lived in their own towns, and all Israel [gradually settled] into their towns.

3 WHEN THE seventh month came and the Israelites were in the towns, the people gathered together as one man to Jerusalem.

2 Then stood up Jeshua son of Jozadak, and his brethren the priests, and Zerubbabel son of Shealtiel, and his brethren, and they built the altar

of the God of Israel to offer burnt offerings upon it, as it is written in the ᶜinstructions of Moses the man of God.

3 And they set the altar [in its place] upon its base, for fear was upon them because of the peoples of the countries; and they offered burnt offerings on it to the Lord morning and evening.

4 They kept also the Feast of Tabernacles, as it is written, and offered the daily burnt offerings by number according to the ordinances, as each day's duty required,

5 And after that, the continual burnt offering, the offering at the New Moon, and at all the appointed feasts of the Lord, and the offerings of everyone who made a freewill offering to the Lord.

6 From the first day of the seventh month they began to offer burnt offerings to the Lord, but the foundation of the temple of the Lord was not yet laid.

7 They gave money also to the masons and to the carpenters, and gave food, drink, and oil to the Sidonians and the Tyrians, to bring cedar trees from Lebanon to the seaport of Joppa, according to the grant they had from Cyrus king of Persia.

8 In the second year of their coming to God's house at Jerusalem, in the second month, Zerubbabel son of Shealtiel and Jeshua son of Jozadak

b But the effort doubtless would have been in vain. Long-standing disobedience had apparently caused Israel's priests to forfeit the divine gift of guidance through Urim and Thummim, and it was never recovered. Except for a similar incident in Neh. 7:65, Urim and Thummim are not again mentioned in the Scriptures. The higher revelation by the prophets superseded them as interpreters of the will of God (see also Exod. 28:30; Amos 3:7). **c** The Hebrew word here is *torah*, and although usually translated "law," that is only one phase of its meaning, and so to use it, to the exclusion of its fuller sense, may defeat its intended purpose at times. The word *torah* is used more than 200 times in the Old Testament. When capitalized, *Torah* means the whole of the Pentateuch, the five books of Moses. Says *Baker's Dictionary of Theology* (E.F. Harrison et al., eds.), "The Hebrew *torah* originally signified authoritative instruction (Prov. 1:8); hence it most commonly means an 'oracle' or 'word' of the Lord, whether delivered through an accredited spokesman such as Moses, or a prophet or priest. Thus *torah* comes to have the wider sense of 'instruction' (as in RV margin) from God. . . . It is therefore a synonym for the whole of the revealed will of God—the word, commandments, ways, judgments, precepts, etc., of the Lord, as in Gen. 26:5, and especially throughout Ps. 119."

life point

God moves on our behalf when we focus on Him instead of on our fears. The feeling of fear or fearful thoughts is simply our enemy Satan trying to distract us from God and His will for our lives. We would do well to follow the Israelites' example in Ezra 3:3 and focus on God, worshipping Him with all our hearts. The Israelites worshipped by offering burnt offerings, which was a requirement of the old covenant. Under the new covenant, we worship Him by offering everything we have and everything we are for His use and glory. He no longer wants dead animal sacrifices; now He wants us to come to Him as "living sacrifices," holy, well-pleasing, and devoted to Him (see Romans 12:1).

made a beginning, with the rest of their brethren—the priests and Levites and all who had come to Jerusalem out of the captivity. They appointed the Levites from twenty years old and upward to oversee the work of the Lord's house.
9   Then Jeshua with his sons and his kinsmen, Kadmiel and his sons, sons of Judah, together took the oversight of the workmen in the house of God—the sons of Henadad, with their sons and Levite kinsmen.
10 And when the builders laid the foundation of the temple of the Lord, the priests stood in their vestments with trumpets, and the Levite sons of Asaph with their cymbals, to praise the Lord, after the order of David king of Israel.
11 They sang responsively, praising and giving thanks to the Lord, saying, For He is good, for His mercy *and* loving-kindness endure forever toward Israel. And all the people shouted

putting the Word to work

Have you seen evidence of God fulfilling His plans in your life or ministry? Be sure to thank Him for His faithfulness from the very beginning, as the Israelites did when the foundation of the second temple was laid (see Ezra 3:10, 11).

with a great shout when they praised the Lord, because the foundation of the house of the Lord was laid!
12 But many of the priests and Levites and heads of fathers' houses, old men who had seen the first house [Solomon's temple], when the foundation of this house was laid before their eyes, wept with a loud voice, though many shouted aloud for joy.
13 So the people could not distinguish the shout of joy from the sound of the weeping of the people, for the

life point

The children of Israel faced much opposition as they worked to restore the temple, but they never lost sight of God's goodness (see Ezra 3:11). Like the Israelites, we need to remember that God is good all the time. He wants us to understand and experience His goodness in every situation.

When resistance attempts to stand in your way as you seek to obey God, remember to not question His goodness. Instead, let opposition provoke you to praise and declare the goodness of God. Be like the children of Israel and refuse to be discouraged. Instead, believe and proclaim God's goodness more aggressively. He *is* good, and His goodness is available to you, no matter what obstacles are in your way.

people shouted with a loud shout, and the sound was heard far off.

4 NOW WHEN [the Samaritans] the adversaries of Judah and Benjamin heard that the exiles from the captivity were building a temple to the Lord, the God of Israel,
2 They came to Zerubbabel [now governor] and to the heads of the fathers' houses and said, Let us build with you, for we seek *and* worship your God as you do, and we have sacrificed to Him since the days of Esarhaddon king of Assyria, who brought us here. [II Kings 17:24-29.]
3 But Zerubbabel and Jeshua and the rest of the heads of fathers' houses of Israel said to them, You have nothing to do with us in building a house to our God; but we ourselves will together build to the Lord, the God of Israel, as King Cyrus, the king of Persia, has commanded us.
4 Then [the Samaritans] the people of the land [continually] weakened the hands of the people of Judah and troubled *and* terrified them in building
5 And hired counselors against them to frustrate their purpose *and* plans all the days of Cyrus king of Persia, even until the reign of Darius [II] king of Persia.
6 And in the reign of Ahasuerus [or Xerxes], in the beginning of his reign, [the Samaritans] wrote to him an accusation against the [returned]

inhabitants of Judah and Jerusalem.
7 Later, in the days of King Artaxerxes, Bishlam, Mithredath, Tabeel, and the rest of their associates wrote to Artaxerxes king of Persia; and the letter was written in the Syrian *or* Aramaic script and interpreted in that language.
8 Rehum the [Persian] commander [of the Samaritans] and Shimshai the scribe wrote a letter against Jerusalem to Artaxerxes the king of this sort—
9 Then wrote Rehum the [Persian] commander, Shimshai the scribe, and the rest of their associates—the Dinaites, the Apharsathchites, the Tarpelites, the Apharsites, the Archevites, the Babylonians, the Susanchites, the Dehaites, the Elamites,
10 And the rest of the nations whom the great and noble Osnappar deported and settled in the city of Samaria and the rest of the country beyond [west of] the Euphrates River, and so forth.
11 This is a copy of the letter which they sent to King Artaxerxes: Your servants, the men beyond [that is, west of] the River [Euphrates], and so forth.
12 Be it known to the king that the Jews who came up from you to us have come to Jerusalem. This rebellious and bad city they are rebuilding, and have restored its walls and repaired the foundations.
13 Be it known now to the king that if this city is rebuilt and the walls finished, then they will not pay tribute, custom, or toll, and the royal revenue will be diminished.
14 Now because we eat the salt of the king's palace and it is not proper for us to witness the king's discredit, therefore we send to inform the king,
15 In order that a search may be made in the book of the records of your fathers, in which you will learn that this is a rebellious city, hurtful to kings and provinces, and that sedition

grace to overcome opposition

In Ezra 4:1–5, we read about the two tribes of Judah and Benjamin, who received permission from Cyrus, the king of Persia, to build a temple to the Lord. When the Samaritans heard what was going on, they went to the governor, Zerubbabel, and the other leaders of the people and asked to join in rebuilding the temple, because they claimed to worship the same God.

If we investigate, we will discover that although it is true that these Samaritans were worshipping the God of Israel, they were worshipping Him for the wrong reason. They were doing it because, basically, they had been taught to do so in order to keep evil out of their camp. These people were not Israelites; they were Assyrians who had simply added the Lord God of Israel to the list of other gods they worshipped. While they did worship the one true God, Jehovah, they also kept their false gods and idols.

Since the Israelites were well aware of this fact, they told the Samaritans, their longtime enemies, that they would have no part in building a temple to the Lord. This made the Samaritans so angry that they began to do everything in their power to harass and cause trouble for the Israelites, to frustrate their purpose and plans.

What should be the reaction of the godly to that kind of opposition and persecution? Jesus said we should "calm down" and "cheer up" (see John 14:27; 16:33). I believe the willingness to do that is a key to enjoying the life of grace that God provides and wants for His people.

If we think we can do anything for God without opposition, we are wrong. Jesus warned us that in this life we will have tribulation (see John 16:33). He said that if people hated and persecuted Him, they will also hate and persecute us, because we belong to Him (see John 15:18, 20). We know that we cannot go through life on this earth without encountering some kind of trouble. Yet so often it is trouble that frustrates us and makes us miserable and unhappy. If we know that trials are a fact of life, we should make the decision to not let them steal our peace and joy. If they do, they will also steal our power.

Often, when people first come to the Lord, they suddenly begin to be attacked in ways that are totally different from anything they have experienced before. Many times they do not understand what is happening to them or why. If they do not have proper instruction in this area, their misunderstanding and frustration can cause them to give up and fall away from God.

We must remember that the devil is not going to just sit back and allow us to take new ground without putting up a fight. Any time we begin to make progress in building the kingdom of God, our enemy will come against us. Many times the mistake we make is the one I made in my early Christian life—trying to use faith to get to the place where there is total freedom from trouble. I am sure you know by now that it just does not work that way.

The purpose of faith is not always to keep us *from* trouble; it is often to carry us *through* trouble. If we never had any trouble, we would not need any faith. What we need in the midst of trouble is grace—God's powerful, overcoming grace.

was stirred up in it of old. That is why [it] was laid waste.

16 We declare to the king that if this city is rebuilt and its walls finished, it will mean that you will have no portion on this side of the [Euphrates] River.

17 Then the king sent an answer: To Rehum the [Persian] official, to Shimshai the scribe, to the rest of their companions who dwell in Samaria and in the rest of the country beyond the River: Greetings.

18 The letter which you sent to us has been plainly read before me.

19 I commanded and search has been made, and it is found that this city [Jerusalem] of old time has made insurrection against kings and that rebellion and sedition have been made in it.

20 There have been mighty kings also over Jerusalem who have ruled over all countries beyond [west of] the [Euphrates] River, and tribute, custom, and toll were paid to them.

21 Therefore give a decree to make these men stop, that this city not be rebuilt, until a command is given by me.

22 Be sure that you do this. Why should damage grow, to the hurt of the kings?

23 When the copy of King Artaxerxes' letter was read before Rehum, Shimshai the scribe, and their companions, they went up in haste to Jerusalem to the Jews and by force and power made them cease.

24 Then the dwork on the house of God in Jerusalem stopped. It stopped until the second year of Darius [I] king of Persia.

5 NOW THE prophets, Haggai and Zechariah son [grandson] of Iddo, prophesied to the Jews in Judah and Jerusalem in the name of the God of Israel, Whose [Spirit] was upon them.

2 Then rose up Zerubbabel son of Shealtiel [heir to the throne of Judah] and Jeshua son of Jozadak and began to build the house of God in Jerusalem; and with them were the prophets of God [Haggai and Zechariah], helping them. [Hag. 1:12-14; Matt. 1:12, 13.]

3 Then Tattenai, governor on the west side of the [Euphrates] River, and Shethar-bozenai and their companions came to them and said, Who eauthorized you to build this house and to restore this wall?

4 Then we told them [in reply] the names of the men who were building this building.

5 But the eye of their God was upon the elders of the Jews, so the enemy could not make them stop until the matter came before Darius [I] and an answer was returned by letter concerning it.

6 This is a copy of the letter that Tattenai, governor on this side of the River, and Shethar-bozenai and his associates, the Apharsachites who were on this [west] side of the River, sent to Darius [I] the king.

7 They wrote: To Darius the king: All peace.

8 Be it known to the king that we went to the province of Judah, to the

---

d The long digression in Ezra 4:6-23 describes later opposition to Jewish efforts to restore the walls and rebuild the city during the reigns of Xerxes (486-465 BC) and Artaxerxes I (465-424). Here in Ezra 4:24 Ezra reverts back to the time of Darius I (522-486) and the rebuilding of the temple, which ceased because of the discouragement described in Ezra 4:4-5, resumed again (Ezra 5:2), and was completed in the sixth year of the reign of Darius I (Ezra 6:15).   **e** Seventeen or eighteen years had elapsed since Cyrus issued his decree. One other king had succeeded him. The second, Darius [I], was just assuring his position upon the throne after two years of incessant warring, and it was entirely possible that during this interval the affairs of a comparatively unimportant city . . . may well have been almost forgotten (*The Cambridge Bible*).

house of the great God. It is being built with huge stones, with timber laid in the walls; this work goes on with diligence *and* care and prospers in their hands.

9 Then we asked those elders, Who authorized you to build this house and restore these walls?

10 We asked their names also, that we might record the names of the men at their head and notify you.

11 They replied, We are servants of the God of heaven and earth, rebuilding the house which was erected and finished many years ago by a great king of Israel.

12 But after our fathers had provoked the God of heaven to wrath, He gave them into the hand of Nebuchadnezzar king of Babylon, the Chaldean, who destroyed this house and carried the people away into Babylon.

13 But in the first year of Cyrus king of Babylon, the same King Cyrus made a decree to rebuild this house of God.

14 And the vessels also of gold and silver of the house of God, which Nebuchadnezzar took from the temple in Jerusalem and brought into the temple of Babylon, King Cyrus took from the temple of Babylon and delivered to a man named Sheshbazzar, whom he had made governor.

15 And King Cyrus said to him, Go, take these vessels to Jerusalem and carry them into the temple, and let the house of God be built upon its site.

16 Then came this Sheshbazzar and laid the foundation of the house of God in Jerusalem; and since that time until now it has been in the process of being rebuilt and is not completed yet.

17 So now, if it seems good to the king, let a search be made in the royal archives there in Babylon to see if it is true that King Cyrus issued a decree to build this house of God at Jerusalem; and let the king send us his pleasure in this matter.

6 THEN KING Darius [I] decreed, and a search was made in Babylonia in the house where the treasured records were stored.

2 And at Ecbatana in the capital in the province of Media, a scroll was found on which this was recorded:

3 In the first year of King Cyrus, [he] made a decree: Concerning the house of God in Jerusalem, let the house, the place where they offer sacrifices, be built, and let its foundations be strongly laid, its height and its breadth each 60 cubits,

4 With three courses of great stones and one course of new timber. Let the cost be paid from the royal treasury.

5 Also let the gold and silver vessels of the house of God, which Nebuchadnezzar took from the temple in Jerusalem and brought to Babylon, be restored and brought back to the temple in Jerusalem, each put in its place in the house of God.

6 Now therefore, Tattenai, governor of the province [west of] the River, Shethar-bozenai, and your associates, the Apharsachites who are [west of] the River, keep far away from there.

7 Leave the work on this house of God alone; let the governor and the elders of the Jews build this house of God on its site.

8 Moreover, I make a decree as to what you shall do for these elders of the Jews for the rebuilding of this

speak the Word

Thank You, God, for giving me the diligence I need in order to press on in the work You have given me to do and for causing it to prosper in my hands.
ADAPTED FROM EZRA 5:8

house of God: the cost is to be paid in full to these men at once from the king's revenue, the tribute of the province [west of] the River, that they may not be hindered.

9 And all they need, including young bulls, rams, and lambs for the burnt offerings to the God of heaven, and wheat, salt, wine, and oil, according to the word of the priests at Jerusalem, let it be given them each day without fail,

10 That they may offer pleasing sacrifices to the God of heaven and pray for the life of the king and his sons.

11 Also I make a decree that whoever shall change *or* infringe on this order, let a beam be pulled from his house and erected; then let him be fastened to it, and let his house be made a dunghill for this.

12 May the God Who has caused His *f*Name to dwell there overthrow all kings and peoples who put forth their hands to alter this or to destroy this house of God in Jerusalem. I Darius make a decree; let it be executed speedily *and* exactly.

13 Then Tattenai, governor of the province this side of the River, with Shethar-bozenai and their associates, diligently did what King Darius had decreed.

14 And the elders of the Jews built and prospered through the prophesying of Haggai the prophet and Zechariah son of Iddo. They finished their building as commanded by the God of Israel and by decree of Cyrus and Darius and Artaxerxes king of Persia.

15 And this house was finished on the third day of the month of Adar, in the sixth year of the reign of King Darius.

16 And the Israelites—the priests, the Levites, and the rest of the returned exiles—celebrated the dedication of this house of God with joy.

17 They offered at the dedication of this house of God 100 young bulls, 200 rams, 400 lambs, and, for a sin offering for all Israel, 12 he-goats, according to the number of Israel's tribes.

18 And they set the priests in their divisions and the Levites in their courses for the service of God at Jerusalem, as it is written in the Book of Moses.

19 The returned exiles kept the Passover on the fourteenth day of the first month.

20 For the priests and the Levites had purified themselves together; all of them were clean. So they killed the Passover lamb for all the returned exiles, for their brother priests, and for themselves.

21 It was eaten by the Israelites who had returned from exile and by all who had joined them and separated themselves from the pollutions of the peoples of the land to seek the Lord, the God of Israel.

22 They kept the Feast of Unleavened Bread for seven days with joy, for the Lord had made them joyful and had turned the heart of the king of Assyria [referring to Darius king of Persia] to them, so that he strengthened their hands in the work of the house of God, the God of Israel.

7 NOW *g*AFTER this, in the reign of Artaxerxes [son of Xerxes, or Ahasuerus] king of Persia, Ezra son of Seraiah, the son of Azariah, the son of Hilkiah,

2 The son of Shallum, the son of Zadok, the son of Ahitub,

---

f See footnote on Deut. 12:5.   **g** There is about a sixty-year silence in the book of Ezra between chapters six and seven, including the years 516-458 BC. It is during this time that events of the book of Esther took place. The Ahasuerus of the book of Esther is identified with the Xerxes who invaded Greece, was stopped at Thermopylae, defeated at the naval battle at Salamis, and nearly annihilated at Plataea (479 BC). The French excavations at Susa in 1880-1890 disclosed the great palace of Xerxes (Ahasuerus), where Esther would have lived. The building covered two and one-half acres.

the truth about hard work

It is easy to drift backward amid obstacles and persecution, but we, like those who rebuilt the temple, need to press on and go forward. *Effortless living* is never effective. Everyone thinks that the more we can do with *less effort*, the better life is—but that is a lie!

Think about the number of buttons we push each day to make our lives easier. We push a button to get on an elevator and push another one to get to the next floor; we put dirty dishes in a washer and push a button and the dishes come out clean; we put the dirty clothes in a machine, push a button, and they are washed; throw them into another machine, push a button, and they are dried—and if we remove them from the dryer quickly enough, they do not even wrinkle enough to need ironing. Still, we complain and grumble because we have to load and unload the machines!

Speaking of effortless living and its effects, consider this story about a science experiment: Some bees were taken along on a space flight to see how they would do in a gravity-free environment. Because the bees floated in space, they did not have to make any effort to fly. When the astronauts were asked how the bees seemed to respond to the experiment, they replied, "They enjoyed the ride, but they died."

We may think we would enjoy an effortless life, but it would kill us. We are created to make effort. Whether we know it or not, we are created for work, involvement, participation, and struggle. We are not supposed to struggle with everything, but we are also not supposed to be the kind of people who always take the easy way out.

Look at what the people mentioned in Ezra accomplished with their hard work— they rebuilt God's beautiful temple, restoring worship to the Lord their God in Jerusalem (see Ezra 6:14, 15). Let their story restore diligence in your heart to faithfully serve the Lord.

3 The son of Amariah, the son of Azariah, the son of Meraioth,
4 The son of Zerahiah, the son of Uzzi, the son of Bukki,
5 The son of Abishua, the son of Phinehas, the son of Eleazar, the son of Aaron the chief priest—
6 This Ezra went up from Babylon. He was a skilled scribe in the five books of Moses, which the Lord, the God of Israel, had given. And the king granted him all he asked, for the hand of the Lord his God was upon him.
7 And also some of the Israelites, with some of the priests and Levites, the singers and gatekeepers, and the temple servants, went up [from Babylon] to Jerusalem in the seventh year of King Artaxerxes.
8 Ezra came to Jerusalem in the

The finds at Susa from this period were so astonishing that the Louvre in Paris devoted two large rooms to the exhibition of the treasures (J.P. Free, *Archaeology and Bible History*).

fifth month of the seventh year of the king.

9 On the first of the first month he started out from Babylon, and on the first of the fifth month he arrived in Jerusalem, for upon him was the good hand of his God.

10 For Ezra had [h]prepared *and* set his heart to seek the Law of the Lord [to inquire for it and of it, to require and yearn for it], and to do and teach in Israel its statutes and its ordinances.

11 Now this is the copy of the letter that King Artaxerxes gave to Ezra the priest, the scribe, even a scribe [occupied with] the words of the commands of the Lord and of His statutes to Israel:

12 Artaxerxes, king of kings, to Ezra the priest, scribe of the instructions of the God of heaven: Greetings.

13 I make a decree that all of the people of Israel and of their priests and Levites in my realm, who offer freely to go up to Jerusalem, may go with you.

14 For you are sent by the king and his seven counselors to inquire about Judah and Jerusalem according to the instruction of your God, which is in your hand,

15 And to carry the silver and gold which the king and his counselors have freely offered to the God of Israel, Whose dwelling is in Jerusalem,

16 And all the silver and gold that

you may find in all the province of Babylonia, with the freewill offerings of the people and of the priests, offered willingly for the house of their God in Jerusalem.

17 Therefore you shall with all speed *and* exactness buy with this money young bulls, rams, lambs, with their cereal offerings and drink offerings, and offer them on the altar of the house of your God in Jerusalem.

18 And whatever shall seem good to you and to your brethren to do with the rest of the silver and the gold, that do after the will of your God.

19 The vessels also that are given to you for the service of the house of your God, those deliver before the God of Jerusalem.

20 And whatever more shall be needful for the house of your God which you shall have occasion to provide, provide it out of the king's treasury.

21 And I, Artaxerxes the king, make a decree to all the treasurers in the province beyond the [Euphrates] River that whatever Ezra the priest, the scribe of the instructions of the God of heaven, shall require of you, it shall be done exactly *and* at once—

22 Up to 100 talents of silver, 100 measures of wheat, 100 baths of wine, 100 baths of oil, and salt not specified.

23 Whatever is commanded by the God of heaven, let it be done diligently

speak the Word

Lord, I pray that You would help me to prepare and set my heart to seek Your will, to inquire for it and to yearn for it.
ADAPTED FROM EZRA 7:10

God, whatever You command me to do, I will do it diligently and honorably.
ADAPTED FROM EZRA 7:23

h God can use mightily one whose whole heart craves a knowledge of Him and His Word like that. Watch Ezra throughout the remainder of his story, as he turns the homes of his nation back from heathendom to God—in the pouring rain! He was not merely righteous, he was "[uncompromisingly] righteous" (I Kings 8:32); he worshiped God, Who is not merely just and righteous, but "rigidly just *and* righteous" (Ezra 9:15.)

and honorably for the house of the God of heaven, lest His wrath be against the realm of the king and his sons.

24 Also we notify you that as to any of the priests and Levites, singers, gatekeepers, temple servants, or other servants of this house of God, it shall not be lawful to impose tribute, custom, or toll on them.

25 You, Ezra, after the wisdom of your God, which is [in His instructions] in your hand, set magistrates and judges who may judge all the people [west] of the River; choose those who know the instructions of your God, and teach him who does not know them.

26 And whoever will not do the law of your God and the law of the king, let judgment be executed upon him exactly *and* speedily, whether it be unto death or banishment or confiscation of goods or imprisonment.

27 Blessed be the Lord, the God of our fathers [said Ezra], Who put such a thing as this into the king's heart, to beautify the house of the Lord in Jerusalem,

28 And Who has extended His mercy *and* steadfast love to me before the king, his counselors, and all the king's mighty officers. I was strengthened and encouraged, for the hand of the Lord my God was upon me, and I gathered together outstanding men of Israel to go with me to Jerusalem.

8 THESE ARE the heads of their fathers' houses and this is the genealogy of those who went up with me from Babylonia in the reign of King Artaxerxes:

2 Of the sons of Phinehas, Gershom; of Ithamar, Daniel; of David, Hattush

3 Of the sons of Shecaniah; of the sons of Parosh, Zechariah, and with him were registered 150 men by genealogy;

4 Of the sons of Pahath-moab, Eliehoenai son of Zerahiah, with 200 men;

5 Of the sons of Zattu, Shecaniah son of Jahaziel, with 300 men;

6 Of the sons of Adin, Ebed son of Jonathan, with 50 men;

7 Of the sons of Elam, Jeshaiah son of Athaliah, with 70 men;

8 Of the sons of Shephatiah, Zebadiah son of Michael, with 80 men;

9 Of the sons of Joab, Obadiah son of Jehiel, with 218 men;

10 Of the sons of [Bani], Shelomith son of Josiphiah, with 160 men;

11 Of the sons of Bebai, Zechariah son of Bebai, with 28 men;

12 Of the sons of Azgad, Johanan son of Hakkatan, with 110 men;

13 Of the sons of Adonikam, the last to come, their names are Eliphelet, Jeuel, and Shemaiah, with 60 men;

14 Of the sons of Bigvai, Uthai and Zabbud [Zaccur], with 70 men.

15 I [Ezra] gathered them together at the river that runs to Ahava, and there we encamped three days. I reviewed the people and the priests, and found no Levites.

16 Then I sent for Eliezer, Ariel, Shemaiah, Elnathan, Jarib, Elnathan, Nathan, Zechariah, Meshullam, who were chief men, and also for Joiarib and Elnathan, who were teachers.

17 And I sent them to Iddo, the leading man at the place Casiphia, telling them to say to Iddo and his brethren the Nethinim [temple servants] at the place Casiphia, Bring to us servants for the house of our God.

18 And by the good hand of our God

speak the Word

God, I bless You because Your steadfast love and mercy are extended to me. I am strengthened and encouraged because Your hand is upon me.
ADAPTED FROM EZRA 7:27, 28

upon us, they brought us a man of understanding, of the sons of Mahli son of Levi, the son of Israel, named Sherebiah, with his sons and his kinsmen, 18;

19 And Hashabiah, and with him Jeshaiah of the sons of Merari, with his kinsmen and their sons, 20;

20 Also 220 of the Nethinim, whose forefathers David and the officials had set apart [with their descendants] to attend the Levites. They were all mentioned by name.

21 Then I proclaimed a fast there, at the river Ahava, that we might humble ourselves before our God to seek from Him a straight *and* right way for us, our little ones, and all our possessions.

22 For I was ashamed to request of the king a band of soldiers and horsemen to protect us against the enemy along the way, because we had told the king, The hand of our God is upon all them for good who seek Him, but His power and His wrath are against all those who forsake Him.

23 So we fasted and besought our God for this, and He heard our entreaty.

24 Then I set apart twelve leading priests, Sherebiah, Hashabiah, and ten of their kinsmen,

25 And weighed out to them the silver, the gold, and the vessels, the offering for the house of our God which the king, his counselors, his lords, and all Israel there present had offered.

26 I weighed into their hands 650 talents of silver, and silver vessels valued at 100 talents, and 100 talents of gold;

27 Also 20 basins of gold worth 1,000 darics, and two vessels of fine bright bronze, precious as gold.

putting the Word to work

Ezra knew that the exiled Jews needed guidance and protection as they prepared to return to Jerusalem (see Ezra 8:21–23). Are you facing a challenging situation and opposition from the enemy? Humble yourself before God, seek Him desperately and trust Him to honor your dependence on Him.

28 And I said to them, You are holy to the Lord, the vessels are holy also, and the silver and the gold are a freewill offering to the Lord, the God of your fathers.

29 Guard and keep them until you weigh them before the chief priests and Levites and heads of the fathers' houses of Israel in Jerusalem in the chambers of the house of the Lord.

30 So the priests and the Levites received the weight of the silver, the gold, and the vessels to bring them to Jerusalem into the house of our God.

31 We left the river Ahava on the twelfth day of the first month to go to Jerusalem; and the hand of our God was upon us, and He delivered us from the enemy and those who lay in wait by the way.

32 And we came to Jerusalem, and [had been] there three days.

33 On the fourth day, the silver, the gold, and the vessels were weighed in the house of our God into the hands of Meremoth the priest, son of Uriah, and with him was Eleazar son of Phinehas, and with them were Jozabad son of Jeshua and Noadiah son of Binnui—the Levites.

34 Every piece was counted and weighed, and all the weight was recorded at once.

speak the Word

God, I thank You that Your hand is upon me for good because I seek You.
ADAPTED FROM EZRA 8:22

seek God desperately

In Ezra 8:23, we read that Ezra proclaimed a fast to show his desperation to God when the Israelites required protection and needed to know what to do. Missing a few meals and taking that time to seek God is not a bad idea. Turning the television off and spending the time you would normally spend watching it with God instead is not a bad idea either. Stay home a few evenings and spend extra time with the Lord instead of going out with your friends and repeating your problem over and over to them.

Ezra and the Israelites "besought" God (Ezra 8:23), which simply means they sought Him, they inquired of Him. When we seek God we pursue, crave, and go after God with all our might. In other words, we act like a starving person in search of food to keep us alive. We need to seek God all the time, not just when we are in trouble.

God once spoke to me that the reason so many people have problems all the time is that the only time they seek Him is when they are in trouble. He showed me that if He removed the problems, the people would not spend any time with Him. He said, "Seek Me as if you were desperate all the time, and then you will not find yourself desperate as often in reality." I think this is good advice, and I highly recommend that we all follow it. Hearing from God is vital, and we need to do whatever it takes to hear His voice clearly.

35 Also those returned exiles whose parents had been carried into captivity offered burnt offerings to the God of Israel: twelve young bulls for all Israel, ninety-six rams, seventy-seven lambs, and twelve he-goats for a sin offering. All this was a burnt offering to the Lord.
36 And they delivered the king's commissions to the king's lieutenants and to the governors west of the River, and they aided the people and God's house.

9 AFTERWARD, THE officials came to me and said, The Israelites and the priests and Levites have not separated themselves from the peoples of the lands, but have committed the abominations of the Canaanites, Hittites, Perizzites, Jebusites, Ammonites, Moabites, Egyptians, and Amorites.
2 For they have taken as wives some of their daughters for themselves and for their sons, so that the holy offspring have mixed themselves with the peoples of the lands. Indeed, the officials and chief men have been foremost in this wicked act *and* direct violation [of God's will]. [Deut. 7:3, 4.]
3 When I heard this, I rent my undergarment and my mantle, I pulled hair from my head and beard and sat down appalled.
4 Then all those who trembled at the words of the God of Israel because of the offensive violation of His will by the returned exiles gathered around me as I sat astounded until the evening sacrifice.
5 At the evening sacrifice I arose from my depression, and, having rent my undergarment and my mantle, I fell on my knees and spread out my hands to the Lord my God,
6 Saying, O my God, I am ashamed and blush to lift my face to You, my

putting the Word to work

Have you ever been tempted to take sin lightly? Remember, in the eyes of the Lord, there is no distinction between "small" sins or "large" sins: sin is sin. We need to be like Ezra and approach God with true sorrow and humility when we ask for forgiveness (see Ezra 9:1–6).

God, for our iniquities have risen higher than our heads and our guilt has mounted to the heavens.

7 Since the days of our fathers we have been exceedingly guilty; and for our willfulness we, our kings, and our priests have been delivered into the hand of the kings of the lands, to the sword, captivity, plundering, and utter shame, as it is today.

8 And now, for a brief moment, grace has been shown us by the Lord our God, Who has left us a remnant to escape and has given us a secure hold in His holy place, that our God may brighten our eyes and give us a little reviving in our bondage.

9 For we are bondmen; yet our God has not forsaken us in our bondage, but has extended mercy *and* steadfast love to us before the kings of Persia, to give us some reviving to set up the house of our God, to repair its ruins, and to give us a wall [of protection] in Judah and Jerusalem.

10 Now, O our God, what can we say after this? For we have forsaken Your commands

11 Which You have commanded by Your servants the prophets, saying, 'The land which you are entering to possess is an unclean land with the pollutions of the peoples of the lands, through their abominations which have filled it from one end to the other with their filthiness.

12 Therefore, do not give your daughters to their sons or take their daughters for your sons; and never

seek their peace or prosperity, that you may be strong and eat the good of the land and leave it as an inheritance to your children always.

13 And after all that has come upon us for our evil deeds and for our great guilt, seeing that You, our God, have punished us less than our iniquities deserved and have given us such a remnant,

14 Shall we break Your commandments again and intermarry with the peoples who practice these abominations? Would You not be angry with us till You had consumed us, so that there would be no remnant nor any to escape? [Deut. 7:2-4.]

15 O Lord, the God of Israel, You are rigidly just *and* righteous, for we are left a remnant that is escaped, as it is this day. Behold, we are before You in our guilt, for none can stand before You because of this.

10 NOW WHILE Ezra prayed and made confession, weeping and casting himself down before the house of God, there gathered to him out of Israel a very great assembly of men, women, and children; for the people wept bitterly.

2 And Shecaniah [II] son of Jehiel [one of the congregation], of the sons of Elam, said to Ezra: We have broken faith *and* dealt treacherously against our God and have married foreign women of the peoples of the land; yet now there is still hope for Israel in spite of this thing.

3 Therefore let us make a covenant with our God to put away all the foreign wives and their children, according to the counsel of my lord and of those who tremble at the command of our God; and let it be done according to the Law.

4 Arise, for it is your duty, and we are with you. Be strong *and* brave and do it.

5 Then Ezra arose and made the chiefs of the priests, the Levites, and all Israel swear that they would do as had been said. So they took the oath. 6 Then Ezra came from before the house of God and went into the lodging place of Jehohanan son of Eliashib [for the night]. There he ate no bread and drank no water, for he mourned over the returned exiles' faithlessness [and violation of God's law].

7 And proclamation was made throughout Judah and Jerusalem to all the returned exiles, that they should assemble in Jerusalem,

8 And that whoever did not come within three days, by order of the officials and the elders, all his property should be forfeited and he himself banned from the assembly of the exiles.

9 Then all the men of Judah and Benjamin gathered at Jerusalem within three days. It was the twentieth day of the ninth month, and all the people sat in the open space before the house of God, trembling because of this matter and because of the heavy rain.

10 And Ezra the priest stood up and said to them, You have acted wickedly *and* broken faith [with God] and have married foreign (heathen) women, increasing the guilt of Israel.

11 So now make confession *and* give thanks to the Lord, the God of your fathers [for not consuming you], and do His will. ⁱSeparate yourselves from the peoples of the land and from [your] foreign (heathen) wives.

12 Then all the assembly answered with a loud voice, As you have said, so must we do.

13 But the people are many and it is a time of heavy rain; we cannot stand outside. Nor can this work be done in a day or two, for we have greatly transgressed in this matter.

14 Let our officials stand for the whole assembly; let all in our cities who have foreign wives come by appointment, and with each group the elders of that city and its judges, until the fierce wrath of our God over this matter is turned away from us.

15 Only Jonathan son of Asahel and Jahzeiah son of Tikvah opposed this, and Meshullam and Shabbethai the Levite supported them.

16 Then the returned exiles did so. Ezra the priest and certain heads of fathers' houses were selected, according to their fathers' houses, each of them by name; and they sat down on the first day of the tenth month to investigate the matter.

17 And by the first day of the first month they had come to the end of the cases of the men married to foreign wives.

18 Of the sons of the priests who had married non-Jewish women were found: of the sons of Jeshua [the high priest] son of Jozadak, and his

---

i The apparently great severity which characterized Ezra's divorce policy, as shown in chapters 9 and 10, becomes thoroughly justified when Israel's tragic experiences because of marriages with heathen women are considered. The consequent idolatry, first of King Solomon, for example, and then of the whole nation, was fatal. God's wrath had been so great that He not only took the kingship from Solomon, but eventually turned the Israelites over to their enemies and left the promised land desolate, while the people bewailed their fate as captives in a heathen country. Ezra, to whom the keeping of God's law was of constant concern, had been born in captivity among exiles who hung their harps on the willow trees and grieved for the country, for the peace and prosperity which their now justly offended God had once given them. Nothing could have been more abhorrent to Ezra than that the Jews should again fall into the snare of idolatry. His action in leading the exiles to give up their foreign wives and their children was the only way out if God's consuming wrath was not again to be incurred. That those still living of the 42,360 men who over eighty years before had made up the congregation (Ezra 2:64) also saw complete separation from the foreign women as the unavoidable solution is obvious from the fact that only four (Ezra 10:15) spoke against it. However, those who were now actually married to native heathen women were only 17 priests, 10 Levites, and 86 laymen—113 in all, according to the records, though the list may be incomplete.

brethren: Maaseiah, Eliezer, Jarib, and Gedaliah.

19 They solemnly vowed to put away their [heathen] wives, and, being guilty, [each] offered a ram of the flock for [his] guilt.

20 Of the sons of Immer: Hanani and Zebadiah.

21 Of the sons of Harim: Maaseiah, Elijah, Shemaiah, Jehiel, and Uzziah.

22 Of the sons of Pashhur: Elioenai, Maaseiah, Ishmael, Nethanel, Jozabad, and Elasah.

23 Of the Levites: Jozabad, Shimei, Kelaiah (Kelita), Pethahiah, Judah, and Eliezer.

24 Of the singers: Eliashib. Of the gatekeepers: Shallum, Telem, and Uri.

25 And of Israel: of the sons of Parosh: Ramiah, Izziah, Malchijah, Mijamin, Eleazar, Malchijah (Hashabiah), and Benaiah.

26 Of the sons of Elam: Mattaniah, Zechariah, Jehiel, Abdi, Jeremoth, and Elijah.

27 Of the sons of Zattu: Elioenai, Eliashib, Mattaniah, Jeremoth, Zabad, and Aziza.

28 Of the sons also of Bebai: Jehohanan, Hananiah, Zabbai, and Athlai.

29 Of the sons of Bani: Meshullam, Malluch, Adaiah, Jashub, Sheal, and Jeremoth.

30 Of the sons of Pahath-moab: Adna, Chelal, Benaiah, Maaseiah, Mattaniah, Bezalel, Binnui, and Manasseh.

31 Of the sons of Harim: Eliezer, Isshijah, Malchijah, Shemaiah, Shimeon,

32 Benjamin, Malluch, and Shemariah.

33 Of the sons of Hashum: Mattenai, Mattattah, Zabad, Eliphelet, Jeremai, Manasseh, and Shimei.

34 Of the sons of Bani: Maadai, Amram, Uel,

35 Benaiah, Bedeiah, Cheluhi (Cheluhu),

36 Vaniah, Meremoth, Eliashib,

37 Mattaniah, Mattenai, Jaasu [Jaasai],

38 Bani, Binnui, Shimei,

39 Shelemiah, Nathan, Adaiah,

40 Machnadebai, Shashai, Sharai,

41 Azarel, Shelemiah, Shemariah,

42 Shallum, Amariah, and Joseph.

43 Of the sons of Nebo: Jeiel, Mattithiah, Zabad, Zebina, Iddo (Jaddai), Joel, and Benaiah.

44 All these had married foreign women, and some of the wives had borne children.

Nehemiah

Author:
Nehemiah

Date:
Approximately 423 BC

Everyday Life Principles:
God wants to repair every broken thing in your life and restore everything that has been lost.

The enemy's resistance should be an encouragement that God is doing something significant in your life, because he never opposes anything that does not threaten him.

The enemy will oppose restoration in your life, but be like Nehemiah and stay focused and prayerful. You *will* overcome!

The book of Nehemiah is the story of a man who had a burden from God to rebuild the walls of the ruined city of Jerusalem. It is also the story of people who came together for a common purpose, worked and prayed in unity, resisted their enemies, responded to Nehemiah's good leadership, achieved their goal, celebrated their victory, enjoyed the rewards of their labors, and experienced spiritual renewal.

But in order to accomplish the task set before them, Nehemiah and the people had to be totally dedicated to the restoration to which God had called them. As their leader, Nehemiah stayed focused on his assignment, steadfastly refusing to be distracted or discouraged. Even in the midst of intense mocking and persecution and all kinds of resistance, he remained diligent and prayerful until his God-given assignment was complete.

Just as Nehemiah's enemies were relentless in their various efforts to stop the rebuilding of Jerusalem's walls, the devil will use multiple strategies as he repeatedly tries to thwart the restoration and rebuilding God wants to do in your life. The enemy does not oppose anything that does not threaten him, so let his resistance be a sign that God is indeed doing a great work in you. Be like Nehemiah; fight back with frequent, fervent prayer and with increased diligence as you partner with God to bring His purposes to pass in you.

1 THE WORDS *or* story of Nehemiah son of Hacaliah: Now in the month of Chislev in the twentieth year [of the Persian king], as I was in the castle of Shushan,

2 Hanani, one of my kinsmen, came with certain men from Judah, and I asked them about the surviving Jews who had escaped exile, and about Jerusalem.

3 And they said to me, The remnant there in the province who escaped exile are in great trouble and reproach; the wall of Jerusalem is broken down, and its [fortified] gates are destroyed by fire.

4 When I heard this, I sat down and wept and mourned for days and fasted and prayed [constantly] before the God of heaven,

life point

Nehemiah was not afraid of emotion; notice that he wept unashamedly in Nehemiah 1:4. Some people refuse to weep or show any kind of outward emotion, which is not healthy. Pent-up emotions are powerful and need to be released. If you do not release your emotions at appropriate times, as Nehemiah did when he heard that the walls of Jerusalem had been destroyed, then your emotions will eat away at you on the inside. Since God has given us tear glands and the ability to cry, that must mean there will be times in life when we, like Nehemiah, need to weep.

5 And I said, O Lord God of heaven, the great and terrible God, Who keeps covenant, loving-kindness, *and* mercy for those who love Him and keep His commandments,

6 Let Your ear now be attentive and

Your eyes open to listen to the prayer of Your servant which I pray before You day and night for the Israelites, Your servants, confessing the sins of the Israelites which we have sinned against You. Yes, I and my father's house have sinned.

7 We have acted very corruptly against You and have not kept the commandments, statutes, and ordinances which You commanded Your servant Moses. [Deut. 6:1-9.]

life point

Like Nehemiah, we are to confess our sins and failures to the Lord (see Nehemiah 1:6, 7), confident that He will forgive us of those sins and failures and cleanse us from all unrighteousness, as He has promised in His Word (see I John 1:9).

8 Remember [earnestly] what You commanded Your servant Moses: If you transgress *and* are unfaithful, I will scatter you abroad among the nations; [Lev. 26:33.]

9 But if you return to Me and keep My commandments and do them, though your outcasts were in the farthest part of the heavens [the expanse of outer space], yet will I gather them from there and will bring them to the place in which I have chosen to set My [a]Name. [Deut. 30:1-5.]

10 Now these are Your servants and

putting the Word to work

Nehemiah waited for God to respond to his prayers (see Nehemiah 1:5-11). When you pray, do you give God time to answer or do you try to push ahead? Remember Nehemiah, and always wait on God to respond to your prayers in His timing.

a See footnote on Deut. 12:5.

Your people, whom You have redeemed by Your great power and by
Your strong hand.
11 O Lord, let Your ear be attentive
to the prayer of Your servant and the
prayer of Your servants who delight
to revere *and* fear Your name (Your
nature and attributes); and prosper, I
pray You, Your servant this day and
grant him mercy in the sight of this
man. For I was cupbearer to the king.

2 IN THE month of Nisan in the
twentieth year of King Artaxerxes, when wine was before him,
I took up the wine and gave it to the
king. Now I had not been sad before
in his presence.
2 So the king said to me, Why do
you look sad, since you are not sick?
This is nothing but sorrow of heart.
Then I was very much afraid
3 And said to the king, Let the king
live forever! Why should I not be sad
faced when the city, the place of my
fathers' sepulchers, lies waste, and its
[fortified] gates are consumed by fire?
4 The king said to me, For what do
you ask? So I prayed to the God of
heaven.
5 And I said to [him], If it pleases
the king and if your servant has found
favor in your sight, I ask that you
will send me to Judah, to the city of
my fathers' sepulchers, that I may
rebuild it.
6 The king, beside whom the queen
was sitting, asked me, How long will
your journey take, and when will you
return? So it pleased [him] to send
me; and I set him a time.
7 Also I said to the king, If it pleases the king, let letters be given me for
the governors beyond the [Euphrates]

River, that they may let me pass
through to Judah,
8 And a letter to Asaph, keeper of
the king's forest *or* park, that he may
give me timber to make beams for the
gates of the fortress of the temple and
for the city wall and for the house that
I shall occupy. And the king granted
what I asked, for the good hand of my
God was upon me.
9 Then I came to the governors
beyond the River and gave them the
king's letters. Now the king had sent
captains of the army and horsemen
with me.
10 When Sanballat the Horonite and
Tobiah the servant, the Ammonite,
heard this, it distressed them exceedingly that a man had come to inquire
for *and* require the good *and* prosperity of the Israelites.
11 So I came to Jerusalem and had
been there three days.
12 Then I arose in the night, I and a
few men with me. And I told no one
what my God had put in my heart to
do for Jerusalem. No beast was with
me except the one I rode.
13 I went out by night by the Valley
Gate toward the Dragon's Well and to
the Dung Gate and inspected the
walls of Jerusalem, which were broken down, and its gates, which had
been destroyed by fire.
14 I passed over to the Fountain Gate
and to the King's Pool, but there was
no place for the beast that was under
me to pass.
15 So [gradually] I went up by the
brook [Kidron] in the night and
inspected the wall; then I turned back
and entered [the city] by the Valley
Gate, and so returned.
16 And the magistrates knew not

speak the Word

I thank You, Lord, that Your good hand is upon me.
ADAPTED FROM NEHEMIAH **2:8**

where I went or what I did; nor had I yet told the Jews, the priests, the nobles, the officials, or the rest who did the work.

17 Then I said to them, You see the bad situation we are in—how Jerusalem lies in ruins, and its gates are burned with fire. Come, let us build up the wall of Jerusalem, that we may no longer be a disgrace.

18 Then I told them of the hand of my God which was upon me for good, and also the words that the king had spoken to me. And they said, Let us rise up and build! So they strengthened their hands for the good work.

19 But when Sanballat the Horonite and Tobiah the servant, the Ammonite, and Geshem the Arab heard of it, they laughed us to scorn and despised us and said, What is this thing you are doing? Will you rebel against the king?

20 I answered them, The God of heaven will prosper us; therefore we His servants will arise and build, but you have no portion or right or memorial in Jerusalem.

3 THEN ELIASHIB the high priest rose up with his brethren the priests and built the Sheep Gate. They consecrated it and set up its doors; they consecrated it even to the Tower of Hammeah *or* the Hundred, as far as the Tower of Hananel.

2 And next to him [Eliashib] the men of Jericho built. Next to [them] Zaccur son of Imri built.

3 And the Fish Gate the sons of Hassenaah built; they laid its beams and set up its doors, its bolts, and its bars.

4 And next to them Meremoth son of Uriah, the son of Hakkoz, repaired. Next to them Meshullam son of Berechiah, the son of Meshezabel, repaired. Next to them Zadok son of Baana repaired.

5 Next to them the Tekoites repaired, but their nobles *or* lords did not put their necks to the work of their Lord.

6 Moreover, the Old Gate Joiada son of Paseah and Meshullam son of Besodeiah repaired. They laid its beams and set up its doors, its bolts, and its bars.

7 Next to them repaired Melatiah the Gibeonite and Jadon the Meronothite, the men of Gibeon and of Mizpah, [up] to the seat or residence of the governor [west of] the River [Euphrates, there in Jerusalem].

8 Next to them repaired Uzziel son of Harhaiah, one of the goldsmiths. Next to him repaired Hananiah, one of the perfumers, and they abandoned [fortification of] Jerusalem as far as the Broad Wall [omitting that part of the ancient city and reducing the area].

9 Next to them repaired Rephaiah son of Hur, ruler of half the district of Jerusalem.

10 Next to them repaired Jedaiah son of Harumaph, opposite his own house. And next to him repaired Hattush son of Hashabneiah.

11 Malchijah son of Harim and Hasshub son of Pahath-moab repaired another portion and the Tower of the Furnaces.

12 Next to [them] repaired Shallum son of Hallohesh, the ruler of half the district of Jerusalem, he and his daughters.

13 The Valley Gate [the main entrance in the west wall, the Jaffa Gate]

speak the Word

was repaired by Hanun and the inhabitants of Zanoah. They built it and set up its doors, its bolts, and its bars and repaired a thousand cubits of the wall, as far as the Dung Gate.

14 The Dung Gate was repaired by Malchijah son of Rechab, the ruler of the district of Beth-haccherem. He rebuilt it and set its doors, its bolts, and its bars.

15 The Fountain Gate was repaired by Shallum son of Col-hozeh, ruler of the district of Mizpah. He rebuilt and covered it and set up its doors, its bolts, and its bars, and the wall of the Pool of Shelah (Siloam), by the King's Garden, as far as the stairs that go down [the eastern slope] from the [portion of Jerusalem known as] the City of David.

16 After him Nehemiah [III] son of Azbuk, ruler of half the district of Beth-zur, repaired [the wall] to a point opposite the sepulchers of David, and to the artificial pool and the house of the guards.

17 After him the Levites: Rehum son of Bani. Next to him repaired Hashabiah, ruler of half the district of Keilah.

18 After him repaired their brethren under Bavvai son of Henadad, ruler of [the other] half of the district of Keilah.

19 Next to him repaired Ezer son of Jeshua, ruler of Mizpah, another district over opposite the ascent to the armory at the angle [in the wall].

20 After him Baruch son of Zabbai (Zaccai) earnestly repaired another portion [toward the hill] from the angular turning of the wall to the door of the house of Eliashib the high priest.

21 After him Meremoth son of Uriah, the son of Hakkoz, repaired from the door of Eliashib's house to the end of his house.

22 After him the priests, men of the plain, repaired.

23 After them Benjamin and Hasshub repaired opposite their house. After them repaired Azariah son of Maaseiah, the son of Ananiah beside his own house.

24 After him Binnui son of Henadad repaired another section [of the wall], from the house of Azariah to the angular turn of the wall and to the corner.

25 Palal son of Uzai repaired opposite the angular turn of the wall and the tower which stands out from the upper house of the king by the court of the guard. After him Pedaiah son of Parosh

26 And the servants of the priests dwelling on Ophel [the hill south of the temple] repaired to opposite the Water Gate on the east and the projecting tower.

27 After them the Tekoites repaired another portion opposite the great projecting tower to the wall of Ophel.

28 Above the Horse Gate the priests repaired, everyone opposite his own house.

29 After them repaired Zadok son of Immer opposite his house. Then Shemaiah son of Shecaniah, keeper of the East Gate, repaired.

30 After him Hananiah son of Shelemiah, and Hanun, the sixth son of Zalaph, repaired another section.

putting the Word to work

Do you ever struggle with your role, thinking others are called to more important or more valuable work? In Nehemiah 3:26–31, some workers were called to repair large portions of the wall, while others were to repair only the section in front of their own house. Be encouraged: All work done for God is significant; and the most important thing is to be obedient to do what God calls you to do.

After him Meshullam son of Berechiah repaired opposite his chamber.

31 After him Malchijah, one of the goldsmiths, repaired as far as the house of the temple servants and of the merchants, opposite the Muster Gate, and to the ascent *and* upper room of the corner.

32 And from the ascent *and* upper room of the corner to the Sheep Gate the goldsmiths and merchants repaired.

4 BUT WHEN Sanballat heard that we were building the wall, he was angry and in a great rage, and he ridiculed the Jews.

2 And he said before his brethren and the army of Samaria, What are these feeble Jews doing? Will they restore things [at will and by themselves]? Will they [try to bribe their God] with sacrifices? Will they finish up in a day? Will they revive the stones out of the heaps of rubbish, seeing they are burned?

3 Now Tobiah the Ammonite was near him, and he said, What they build—if a fox climbs upon it, he will break down their stone wall.

4 [And Nehemiah prayed] Hear, O our God, for we are despised. Turn their taunts upon their own heads, and give them for a prey in a land of their captivity.

5 Cover not their iniquity and let not their sin be blotted out before You, for they have vexed [with alarm] the builders *and* provoked You.

6 So we built the wall, and all [of it] was joined together to half its height, for the people had a heart *and* mind to work.

7 But when Sanballat, Tobiah, the Arabians, Ammonites, and Ashdodites heard that the walls of Jerusalem were going up and that the breaches were being closed, they were very angry.

8 And they all plotted together to

life point

When the enemy is coming against you, the most powerful thing you can do is refuse to let it upset you. Instead, be like Nehemiah in Nehemiah 4:9: intensify your prayers and increase your vigilance.

come and fight against Jerusalem, to injure *and* cause confusion *and* failure in it.

9 But because of them we made our prayer to our God and set a watch against them day and night.

10 And [the leaders of] Judah said, The strength of the burden bearers is weakening, and there is much rubbish; we are not able to work on the wall.

11 And our enemies said, They will not know or see till we come into their midst and kill them and stop the work.

12 And when the Jews who lived near them came, they said to us ten times, You must return [to guard our little villages]; from all places where they dwell they will be upon us.

13 So I set [armed men] behind the wall in places where it was least protected; I even thus used the people as families with their swords, spears, and bows.

14 I looked [them over] and rose up and said to the nobles and officials and the other people, Do not be afraid of the enemy; [earnestly] remember the Lord *and* imprint Him [on your minds], great and terrible, and [take from Him courage to] fight for your brethren, your sons, your daughters, your wives, and your homes.

15 And when our enemies heard that their plot was known to us and that God had frustrated their purpose, we all returned to the wall, everyone to his work.

16 And from that time forth, half of my servants worked at the task, and the other half held the spears, shields, bows, and coats of mail; and the leaders stood behind all the house of Judah.

17 Those who built the wall and those who bore burdens loaded themselves so that everyone worked with one hand and held a weapon with the other hand,

putting the Word to work

As we live and work for God, opposition will come. Do you find yourself under attack in your ministry? It is vitally important to have people in your life who will faithfully be at your side through prayer and other means of support (see Nehemiah 4:16, 17).

18 And every builder had his sword girded by his side, and so worked. And he who sounded the trumpet was at my side.

19 And I said to the nobles and officials and the rest of the people, The work is great and scattered, and we are separated on the wall, one far from another.

20 In whatever place you hear the sound of the trumpet, rally to us there. Our God will fight for us.

21 So we labored at the work while half of them held the spears from dawn until the stars came out.

22 At that time also I said to the people, Let everyone with his servant lodge within Jerusalem, that at night they may be a guard to us and a laborer during the day.

23 So none of us—I, my kinsmen, my servants, nor the men of the guard who followed me—took off our

clothes; each kept his weapon [in his hand for days].

5 NOW THERE arose a great cry of the [poor] people and of their wives [driven to borrowing] against their Jewish brethren [the few who could afford to lend].

2 For some said, We, our sons and daughters, are many; therefore allow us to take grain, that we may eat and live! If we are not given grain, let us take it!

3 Also some said, We are mortgaging our lands, vineyards, and houses to buy grain because of the scarcity.

4 Others said, We have borrowed money on our fields and vineyards to pay the [Persian] king's heavy tax.

5 Although our flesh is the same as that of our brethren and our children are as theirs, yet we are forced to sell our children as slaves; some of our daughters have already been thus sold, and we are powerless to redeem them, for others have our lands and vineyards.

6 I [Nehemiah] was very angry when I heard their cry and these words.

7 I thought it over and then rebuked the nobles and officials. I told them, You are exacting interest from your own kinsmen. And I held a great assembly against them.

8 I said to them, We, according to our ability, have bought back our Jewish brethren who were sold to the nations; but will you even sell your brethren, that they may be sold to us? Then they were silent and found not a word to say.

9 Also I said, What you are doing is not good. Should you not walk in the

speak the Word

When my enemies come against me, Lord, I pray that You will frustrate their purposes so that I can do as the Israelites and return to the task You have given me.
ADAPTED FROM NEHEMIAH 4:15

God will fight evil for you

When people or events come against us to destroy us, as Sanballat and Tobiah tried to destroy Nehemiah and his work, we are to stand firm, confident that everything is going to work out for the best (see Nehemiah 4:20). Whatever you are going through, remember, "this too shall pass."

When problems arise—and they will—we are not to assume that the Lord will intervene and take care of all our problems without our invitation. We are to pray and ask Him to change our circumstances. Then we are to remain constant and stable as Nehemiah did, and that will be a sign to the enemy of his impending downfall and destruction.

Do you know why our constancy and fearlessness are a sign to Satan that he will fail? Because he knows that the only way he can overcome a believer is through deception and intimidation. How can he threaten someone who is not afraid of him? How can he deceive someone who recognizes his lies and refuses to believe them? What good does it do him to try to stir up fear or anger or depression in someone who will not be moved by emotions but chooses to stand firmly on the Word of God?

When the devil sees his tactics are not working, he realizes he is failing and will be utterly defeated. God will fight for us as He did for Nehemiah, and we will have the victory.

fear of our God to prevent the taunts *and* reproach of the nations, our enemies? 10 I, my brethren, and my servants are lending them money and grain. Let us stop this forbidden interest! [Exod. 22:25.] 11 Return this very day to them their fields, vineyards, olive groves, and houses, and also a hundredth of all the money, grain, new wine, and oil that you have exacted from them. 12 Then they said, We will restore these and require nothing from them. We will do as you say. Then I called the priests and took an oath of the lenders that they would do according to this promise. 13 I shook out my lap and said, So may God shake out every man from his house and from [the exercise and fruits of] his labor who does not keep

this promise! So may he be shaken out and emptied. And all the assembly said, Amen, and praised the Lord.

life point

Nehemiah knew how to make the difficult choices that leadership demands. He had to be a leader, not a pal, to the Israelites. Because he related to them as not only a leader but also a comrade, he was able to confront them successfully in Nehemiah 5:7–10. The great end result of Nehemiah's correction was that the people praised the Lord and said, "We will do as you say" (see Nehemiah 5:12, 13). If we want to be leaders who make a difference in people's lives, we would be wise to follow Nehemiah's example.

And the people did according to this promise.

14 Also, in the twelve years after I was appointed to be their governor in Judah, from the twentieth to the thirty-second year of King Artaxerxes, neither I nor my kin ate the food allowed to [me] the governor.

15 But the former governors lived at the expense of the people and took from them food and wine, besides forty shekels of silver [a large monthly official salary]; yes, even their servants assumed authority over the people. But I did not so because of my [reverent] fear of God.

16 I also held fast to the work on this wall; and we bought no land. And all my servants were gathered there for the work.

17 And there were at my table 150 Jews and officials, besides those who came to us from the nations about us.

18 Now these were prepared for each day: one ox and six choice sheep; also fowls were prepared for me, and once in ten days a store of all sorts of wine. Yet for all this, I did not demand [my rights] the food allowed me as governor, for the [tribute] bondage was heavy upon this people.

19 O my God, [earnestly] remember me for good for all I have done for this people. [Heb. 6:10.]

6 NOW WHEN Sanballat, Tobiah, Geshem the Arab, and the rest of our enemies heard that I had built the wall and that there was no breach left in it, although at that time I had not set up the doors in the gates,

2 Sanballat and Geshem sent to me, saying, Come, let us meet together in one of the villages in the plain of Ono. But they intended to do me harm.

3 And I sent messengers to them, saying, I am doing a great work and cannot come down. Why should the work stop while I leave to come down to you?

4 They sent to me four times this way, and I answered them as before.

5 Then Sanballat sent his servant to me again the fifth time with an open letter.

6 In it was written: It is reported among the neighboring nations, and Gashmu says it, that you and the Jews plan to rebel; therefore you are building the wall, that you may be their king, according to the report.

7 Also you have set up prophets to announce concerning you in Jerusalem, There is a king in Judah. And now this will be reported to the [Persian] king. So, come now and let us take counsel together.

8 I replied to him, No such things as you say have been done; you are inventing them out of your own heart *and* mind.

9 For they all wanted to frighten us, thinking, Their hands will be so weak that the work will not be done. But now strengthen my hands!

10 I went into the house of Shemaiah son of Delaiah, the son of Mehetabel, who was shut up. He said, Let us meet together in the house of God, within the temple, and let us shut the doors of the temple, for they are coming to kill you—at night they are coming to kill you.

11 But I said, Should such a man as I flee? And what man such as I could go into the temple [where only the priests are allowed to go] and yet live? I will not go in.

putting the Word to work

Are you in a position of leadership or authority? Learn from Nehemiah's example as governor (see Nehemiah 5:14–19). Use your position to serve the people you lead, extend generosity in praise and in provision, and do not use your position for personal gain at the expense of those you lead.

life point

If we need help, we are to confidently ask God for it, as Nehemiah did when he cried out to God, "But now strengthen my hands!" (Nehemiah 6:9). Then we are to listen in faith for His answer. The Word explains that when we ask God for something, we must ask in faith with no wavering, no hesitating, and no doubting (see James 1:6). God wants us to be totally confident in Him to manifest His power and love in our lives.

12 And behold, I saw that God had not sent him, but he made this prophecy against me because Tobiah and Sanballat had hired him.
13 He was hired that I should be made afraid and do as he said and sin, that they might have matter for an evil report with which to taunt *and* reproach me.
14 My God, think on Tobiah and

life point

Nehemiah's enemies had hired someone to tempt him to fear and hide in the temple (see Nehemiah 6:11–13). This was yet another obstacle that Nehemiah refused to accept. He continued to move forward and do what God had called him to do.

Like Nehemiah, God has made a way for us to do everything He has put in our hearts. He does not put dreams and visions in us to frustrate us. We must be like Nehemiah and keep our confidence in God all the way through to the end, not just for a short while. When it looks like the obstacles in front of you are too formidable, do not give up! The completion of your project may be just one or two steps away, as it was for Nehemiah.

Sanballat according to these their works, and on the prophetess Noadiah and the rest of the prophets who would have put me in fear.
15 So the wall was finished on the twenty-fifth day of the month Elul, in fifty-two days.
16 When all our enemies heard of it, all the nations around us feared and fell far in their own esteem, for they saw that this work was done by our God.
17 Moreover, in those days the nobles of Judah sent many letters to Tobiah, and Tobiah's letters came to them.
18 For many in Judah were bound by oath to him, because he was the son-in-law of Shecaniah son of Arah, and his son Jehohanan had married the daughter of Meshullam son of Berechiah.
19 Also they spoke of [Tobiah's] good deeds before me and told him what I said. And Tobiah sent letters to frighten me.

life point

Tobiah was trying to frighten Nehemiah (see Nehemiah 6:19), but Nehemiah did not succumb to fear. Fear prevents us from receiving and doing all God has planned for us. Hear God's message to you: "Fear not, for I, the Lord, am with you."

7 NOW WHEN the wall was built and I had set up the doors, and the gatekeepers, singers, and Levites had been appointed,
2 I gave my brother Hanani, with Hananiah the ruler of the castle, charge over Jerusalem, for Hananiah was a more faithful and God-fearing man than many.
3 I said to them, Let not the gates of Jerusalem be opened until the sun is

finish well

Nehemiah knew how to finish what he started (see Nehemiah 6:15), and God uses people who know how to complete what they have begun. Many of us are good at starting, but not good at finishing. The reason is simple. Emotions motivate us and get us going, but it takes more than emotion to get us to the finish. Let's say we receive an encouraging word from God or someone else, and we are off and running. The question is, how long do we keep running after the emotions wear off? Many of us stop right that minute, as soon as we no longer *feel* anything.

I remember one time early in my Christian walk when I got so excited because of a word the Lord gave me. A guest speaker with the gift of prophecy came to our church, and as he was laying hands on people, praying for them and blessing them, he said to me, "I see you laying hands on multiplied thousands of people, and they are all coming under the power of God."

I went ballistic emotionally. To me, that word was confirmation of something I believed God had been speaking to me. I got so emotional about it that I think I scared the man! I usually do not respond with such enthusiasm, but I was so excited. After a few years, I was still going ballistic emotionally, but it was for another reason. It was not out of excitement; it was because I was still waiting for it to happen, and I thought, *I don't think I can stand this waiting another moment.* Emotions can be up and they can be down, but we must remember that they are fickle and do not speak truth to us. They can radically change overnight!

The beginning of a new thing is almost always exciting. But it is not those who start the race in excitement who win; it is those who stick to it and make it across the finish line—when nobody is excited anymore, when nobody is cheering them on, when their emotions are no longer supporting them, when they do not feel they can go on any longer, when it looks as if they will never make it to the end, when all they have left is that one word from God that got them started in the first place. Those people are called *finishers*, and Nehemiah was certainly a good one!

hot; and while the watchmen are still on guard, let them shut and bar the doors. Appoint guards from the people of Jerusalem, each to his watch [on the wall] and each opposite his own house.

4 Now the city was wide and large, but the people in it were few, and their houses were not yet built.

5 And my God put it into my mind *and* heart to assemble the nobles, the officers, and the people, that they might be counted by genealogy. And I found a register of the genealogy of those who came [from Babylon] at the first, and found written in it:

6 These are the people of the province who came up out of the captivity of those exiles whom Nebuchadnezzar the king of Babylon had carried away; they returned to Jerusalem and to Judah, each to his town,

7 Who came with Zerubbabel, Jeshua, Nehemiah [not the author], Azariah, Raamiah, Nahamani,

Mordecai, Bilshan, Mispereth, Bigvai, Nehum, Baanah. The men of Israel numbered:

8 The sons of Parosh, 2,172.

9 The sons of Shephatiah, 372.

10 The sons of Arah, 652.

11 The sons of Pahath-moab, namely the sons of Jeshua and Joab, 2,818.

12 The sons of Elam, 1,254.

13 The sons of Zattu, 845.

14 The sons of Zaccai, 760.

15 The sons of Binnui, 648.

16 The sons of Bebai, 628.

17 The sons of Azgad, 2,322.

18 The sons of Adonikam, 667.

19 The sons of Bigvai, 2,067.

20 The sons of Adin, 655.

21 The sons of Ater, namely of Hezekiah, 98.

22 The sons of Hashum, 328.

23 The sons of Bezai, 324.

24 The sons of Hariph, 112.

25 The sons of Gibeon, 95.

26 The men of Bethlehem and Netophah, 188.

27 The men of Anathoth, 128.

28 The men of Beth-azmaveth, 42.

29 The men of Kiriath-jearim, Chephirah, and Beeroth, 743.

30 The men of Ramah and Geba, 621.

31 The men of Michmas, 122.

32 The men of Bethel and Ai, 123.

33 The men of the other Nebo, 52.

34 The sons of the other Elam, 1,254.

35 The sons of Harim, 320.

36 The sons of Jericho, 345.

37 The sons of Lod, Hadid, and Ono, 721.

38 The sons of Senaah, 3,930.

39 The priests: the sons of Jedaiah, namely the house of Jeshua, 973.

40 The sons of Immer, 1,052.

41 The sons of Pashhur, 1,247.

42 The sons of Harim, 1,017.

43 The Levites: the sons of Jeshua, namely of Kadmiel of the sons of Hodevah, 74.

44 The singers: the sons of Asaph, 148.

45 The gatekeepers: the sons of Shallum, of Ater, of Talmon, of Akkub, of Hatita, and of Shobai, 138.

46 The Nethinim [temple servants]: the sons of Ziha, of Hasupha, of Tabbaoth,

47 Of Keros, of Sia, of Padon,

48 Of Lebana, of Hagaba, of Shalmai,

49 Of Hanan, of Giddel, of Gahar,

50 Of Reaiah, of Rezin, of Nekoda,

51 Of Gazzam, of Uzza, of Paseah,

52 Of Besai, of Meunim, of Nephushesim,

53 Of Bakbuk, of Hakupha, of Harhur,

54 Of Bazlith, of Mehida, of Harsha,

55 Of Barkos, of Sisera, of Temah,

56 Of Neziah, of Hatipha.

57 The sons of Solomon's servants: the sons of Sotai, of Sophereth, of Perida,

58 Of Jaala, of Darkon, of Giddel,

59 Of Shephatiah, of Hattil, of Pochereth-hazzebaim, of Amon.

60 All the Nethinim [temple servants] and the sons of Solomon's servants, 392.

61 And these were they who went up also from Tel-melah, Tel-harsha, Cherub, Addon, and Immer, but they [had no birth records and] could not prove their father's house nor their descent, whether they were of Israel:

62 The sons of Delaiah, of Tobiah, of Nekoda, 642.

63 Of the priests: the sons of Hobaiah, of Hakkoz, and of Barzillai, who [was so named because he] married one of the daughters of the [noted] Gileadite Barzillai and was called by their name.

64 These sought their registration among those recorded in the genealogies, but it was not found; so they were excluded from the priesthood as [ceremonially] unclean.

65 The governor told them that they should refrain from eating any of the most holy food until a priest with Urim and Thummim should arise [to determine the will of God in the matter].

66 The congregation all together was 42,360,

67 Besides their manservants and their maidservants, of whom there were 7,337; and they had 245 singers, men and women.

68 Their horses were 736; their mules, 245;

69 Their camels, 435; their donkeys, 6,720.

70 And some of the heads of fathers' houses gave to the work. The Tirshatha *or* governor gave to the treasury 1,000 darics of gold, 50 basins, 530 priests' garments.

71 Some of the heads of fathers' houses gave to the treasury for the work 20,000 darics of gold and 2,200 minas of silver.

72 What the rest of the people gave was 20,000 darics of gold, 2,000 minas of silver, and 67 priests' garments.

73 So the priests, the Levites, the gatekeepers, the singers, some of the people, the Nethinim [the temple servants], along with all Israel, dwelt in their towns, and were in them when the seventh month came.

8 THEN ALL the people gathered together as one man in the broad place before the Water Gate; and they asked Ezra the scribe to bring the Book of the Law of Moses, which the Lord had given to Israel.

2 And Ezra the priest brought the Law before the assembly of both men and women and all who could hear with understanding, on the first of the seventh month.

3 He read from it, facing the broad place before the Water Gate, from early morning until noon, in the presence of the men and women and those who could understand; and all the people were attentive to the Book of the Law.

4 Ezra the scribe stood on a wooden pulpit which they had made for the purpose. And beside him stood Mat-

tithiah, Shema, Anaiah, Uriah, Hilkiah, and Maaseiah on his right hand; and on his left hand, Pedaiah, Mishael, Malchijah, Hashum, Hashbaddana, Zechariah, and Meshullam.

5 Ezra opened the book in sight of all the people, for he was standing above them; and when he opened it, all the people stood up.

life point

When Ezra opened God's Word, all the people stood (see Nehemiah 8:5). I love this image of honoring the Word because the Word has the power to change people's lives. I enjoy teaching the Word, and one of my goals in life is to provoke tremendous respect and love for God's Word. If you have not experienced the transforming power of God's Word, I urge you to give it a try—and you will see why it is worthy of honor and respect.

6 And Ezra blessed the Lord, the great God. And all the people answered, Amen, Amen, lifting up their hands; and they bowed their heads and worshiped the Lord with faces to the ground.

7 Also Jeshua, Bani, Sherebiah, Jamin, Akkub, Shabbethai, Hodiah, Maaseiah, Kelita, Azariah, Jozabad, Hanan, Pelaiah—the Levites—helped the people to understand the Law, and the people [remained] in their place.

8 So they read from the Book of the Law of God distinctly, faithfully amplifying *and* giving the sense so that [the people] understood the reading.

9 And Nehemiah, who was the governor, and Ezra the priest and scribe, and the Levites who taught the people said to all of them, This day is holy to the Lord your God; mourn not nor weep. For all the people wept

life point

I believe that when we worship God, at least part of the time we need to assume a posture of worship, as the Israelites did in Nehemiah 8:6. We need to bend our knees and bow down before Him because those postures are signs of reverence and humility. They are outward representations of our inner heart attitudes. Satan cannot see what is in our hearts, but he can see our knees bent and our hands uplifted in worship to God.

Why should we make all these outward signs? Isn't what is in our hearts sufficient? As I have already written, the devil cannot see what is in our hearts, but he certainly can see our actions and hear our words. Satan can see the outward manifestation of our uplifted hands, and he knows what is going on when we bow down. That makes him afraid. He knows he cannot deceive and control a true worshiper.

I realize that our posture in worship is an outward form of worship, and outward appearance without a right heart attitude is useless. But both need to work together. Our heart attitude establishes things in the spiritual realm, and our actions and words establish things in this natural realm.

when they heard the words of the Law.
10 Then [Ezra] told them, Go your way, eat the fat, drink the sweet drink, and send portions to him for whom nothing is prepared; for this day is holy to our Lord. And be not grieved *and* depressed, for the joy of the Lord is your strength *and* stronghold.
11 So the Levites quieted all the people, saying, Be still, for the day is

b See footnote on Ezra 3:2.

holy. And do not be grieved *and* sad.
12 And all the people went their way to eat, drink, send portions, and make great rejoicing, for they had understood the words that were declared to them.
13 On the second day, all the heads of fathers' houses, with the priests and Levites, gathered to Ezra the scribe to study *and* understand the words of [b]divine instruction.
14 And they found written in the law, which the Lord had commanded through Moses, that the Israelites should dwell in booths during the feast of the seventh month
15 And that they should publish and proclaim in all their towns and in Jerusalem, saying, Go out to the hills and bring branches of olive, wild olive, myrtle, palm, and other leafy trees to make booths, as it is written. [Lev. 23:39, 40.]
16 So the people went out and brought them and made themselves booths, each on the roof of his house and in their courts and the courts of God's house and in the squares of the Water Gate and the Gate of Ephraim.
17 All the assembly of returned exiles made booths and dwelt in them; for since the days of Jeshua (Joshua) son of Nun up to that day,

life point

Isn't it easy to find things to worry about? It is indeed, but if we could learn to laugh a little more, our loads would be much lighter. In the world we live in, there is not a great deal to laugh about, so we will need to look for things to chuckle about on purpose! We need to laugh and have a good time as often as possible. Ask the Lord to help you be joyful and of good cheer. His joy will give you strength (see Nehemiah 8:10).

the joy of the Lord is your strength

When the people heard the words of the law they wept because of their sorrow. But Ezra spoke to them and said: " . . . be not grieved and depressed, for the joy of the Lord is your strength and stronghold" (Nehemiah 8:10).

The writer of Proverbs said that a merry heart does us good and acts just like a medicine (Proverbs 17:22). God has given us joy—it is a fruit of the Holy Spirit that is given to believers, but we must nurture and release it in our lives.

Satan is much more interested in stealing our joy than our goods. He knows that if he can sadden us, he can weaken us. He hopes that by causing the washing machine or other things to break down, he can steal our joy. Do not let him do it! No matter what kind of trouble Satan tries to use to distract you, do not pay attention to him. Each day that God gives us is holy and a precious gift from Him. We should enjoy it fully. We should not waste what God gives. Let the devil wear himself out starting fires in your life, but do not spend your time trying to put them out. Put your trust in God, and make a decision to rejoice.

Joy is powerful. Ezra knew that, and that is why he instructed the people to find their strength in God's joy. He also told them to eat, drink, and send portions to those who had nothing. They understood these words and got busy being a blessing and rejoicing. The Bible says it is more blessed to give than to receive (see Acts 20:35). Why? Because when we get something we only get the gift, but when we give, we receive the joy of giving. Nothing releases supernatural joy in our lives more than being a blessing to other people.

Selfishness and self-centeredness turn our focus in on ourselves and block our joy, but giving does just the opposite. People are happy when they are reaching out to others because they are functioning in the will of God. God has not called us to "in-reach," He has called us to outreach.

Be a blessing and be happy and rejoice on purpose. Satan comes to steal from us, but Jesus came that we might have and enjoy life in abundance (see John 10:10).

the Israelites had not done so. And there was very great rejoicing.
18 Also day by day, from the first day to the last, Ezra read from the Book of the Law of God. They kept the feast for seven days; the eighth day was a [closing] solemn assembly, according to the ordinance.

9 NOW ON the twenty-fourth day of this month, the Israelites were assembled with fasting and in sackcloth and with earth upon their heads.
2 And the Israelites separated themselves from all foreigners and stood and confessed their sins and the iniquities of their fathers.
3 And they stood in their place and read from the Book of the Law of the Lord their God for a fourth of the day, and for another fourth of it they confessed and worshiped the Lord their God.

4 On the stairs of the Levites stood Jeshua, Bani, Kadmiel, Shebaniah, Bunni, Sherebiah, Bani, and Chenani, and they cried with a loud voice to the Lord their God.

5 Then the Levites—Jeshua, Kadmiel, Bani, Hashabneiah, Sherebiah, Hodiah, Shebaniah, and Pethahiah—said, Stand up and bless the Lord your God from everlasting to everlasting. Blessed be Your glorious name which is exalted above all blessing and praise.

6 [And Ezra said], You are the Lord, You alone; You have made heaven, the heaven of heavens, with all their host, the earth, and all that is on it, the seas and all that is in them; and You preserve them all, and the hosts of heaven worship You.

7 You are the Lord, the God Who chose Abram and brought him out of Ur of the Chaldees and gave him the name Abraham.

8 You found his heart faithful before You, and You made the covenant with him to give his descendants the land of the Canaanite, Hittite, Amorite, Perizzite, Jebusite, and Girgashite. And You have fulfilled Your promise, for You are just *and* righteous.

9 You saw our fathers' affliction in Egypt, and You heard their cry at the Red Sea.

10 You performed signs and wonders against Pharaoh and all his servants and all the people of his land, for You knew that they dealt insolently against the Israelites. And You got for Yourself a name, as it is today.

11 You divided the sea before them, so that they went through its midst on dry land; their persecutors You threw into the depths, as a stone into mighty waters.

speak the Word

12 Moreover, by a pillar of cloud You led them by day, and by a pillar of fire by night to light the way they should go.

13 You came down also upon Mount Sinai and spoke with them from Heaven and gave them right ordinances and true laws, good statutes and commandments.

14 And You made known to them Your holy Sabbath and gave them commandments, statutes, and a law through Moses Your servant.

15 You gave them bread from heaven for their hunger and brought water for them out of the rock for their thirst; and You told them to go in and possess the land You had sworn to give them. [John 6:31-34.]

16 But they and our fathers acted presumptuously and stiffened their necks, and did not heed Your commandments.

17 They refused to obey, nor were they mindful of Your wonders *and* miracles which You did among them; but they stiffened their necks and in their rebellion appointed a captain, that they might return to their bondage [in Egypt]. But You are a God ready to

God, I will bless Your name continually. Your name is glorious and exalted above blessing and praise. You alone are my God!
ADAPTED FROM NEHEMIAH **9:5**

trusting day by day

In chapter 9 of Nehemiah, Ezra recounted the mighty miracles God had performed in Israel's past as a way of encouraging the people to believe Him for their present. In verse 20 he reminded them of God's faithfulness to provide food (manna) for His people when they were in the wilderness on their way to the Promised Land (see Exodus 16:15–25). During this time, God provided manna for them every day. He told them to gather each morning only what they needed for that specific day. He was teaching them that they were to live by faith, believing that what they needed each day would be supplied. The only exception to this was the Sabbath. On the day before the Sabbath, the people were to gather twice as much so they would not have to work on the day of rest.

There is a great lesson for us here. Have you ever thought that your future would be secure if you could stockpile God's provision? It is so easy to want to store up His grace to cover us for today as well as for tomorrow. But God teaches us that His provision of grace does not work that way. It comes one day at a time. God's grace, like His provision of manna, cannot be stored up because it doesn't take trust to live that way.

When you and I start fretting about what we are going to do tomorrow, we are "trying to gather manna for the future." That does not work! God wants us to know we can trust Him daily. Didn't Jesus teach us to pray, "Give us this day our daily bread" (Matthew 6:11)? Note that the Lord did not instruct us to ask for tomorrow's bread. He told us to request *today's* bread. God wants us to believe that when the time comes, He will provide what we need.

If you are concerned about what the future holds for you and your loved ones, the first thing you must do is make a decision not to worry. Believe God will show you what to do when the time comes. Trust Him to provide for you every day, one day at a time. If you feel overwhelmed when you think about what may happen tomorrow, just remember that you do not have tomorrow's grace today, but when tomorrow comes God's grace will be sufficient for all your needs.

pardon, gracious and merciful, slow to anger, and of great steadfast love; and You did not forsake them. **18** Even when they had made for themselves a molten calf and said, This is your god, who brought you out of Egypt, and had committed great *and* contemptible blasphemies, **19** You in Your great mercy forsook them not in the wilderness; the pillar of the cloud departed not from them by day to lead them in the way, nor the pillar of fire by night to light the way they should go. **20** You also gave Your good Spirit to instruct them, and withheld not Your manna from them, and gave water for their thirst.

speak the Word

21 Forty years You sustained them in the wilderness; they lacked nothing, their clothes did not wear out, and their feet did not swell.

22 Also You gave them kingdoms and peoples and allotted to them every corner. So they possessed the land of Sihon king of Heshbon and the land of Og king of Bashan.

23 Their children You also multiplied as the stars of heaven and brought them into the land which You told their fathers they should go in and possess.

24 So the descendants went in and possessed the land; and You subdued before them the inhabitants of the land, the Canaanites, and gave them into their hands, with their kings and the peoples of the land, that they might do with them as they would.

25 And they captured fortified cities and a rich land and took possession of houses full of all good things, cisterns hewn out, vineyards, olive orchards, and fruit trees in abundance. So they ate and were filled and became fat and delighted themselves in Your great goodness.

26 Yet they were disobedient and rebelled against You and cast Your law behind their back and killed Your prophets who accused *and* warned them to turn to You again; and they committed great *and* contemptible blasphemies.

27 Therefore You delivered them into the hand of their enemies, who distressed them. In the time of their suffering when they cried to You, You heard them from heaven, and according to Your abundant mercy You gave them deliverers, who saved them from their enemies.

28 But after they had rest, they did evil again before You; therefore You left them in the hand of their enemies, so that they had dominion over them. Yet when they turned and cried to You, You heard them from heaven, and many times You delivered them according to Your mercies,

29 And reproved *and* warned them, that You might bring them again to Your law. Yet they acted presumptuously and did not heed Your commandments, but sinned against Your ordinances, which by keeping, a man shall live. And they turned a stubborn shoulder, stiffened their neck, and would not listen.

30 Yet You bore with them many years more and reproved *and* warned them by Your Spirit through Your prophets; still they would not listen. Therefore You gave them into the power of the peoples of the lands.

31 Yet in Your great mercies You did not utterly consume them or forsake them, for You are a gracious and merciful God.

32 Now therefore, our God, the great, mighty, and terrible God, Who keeps covenant and mercy *and* loving-kindness, let not all the trouble *and* hardship seem little to You—the hardship that has come upon us, our kings, our princes, our priests, our prophets, our fathers, and on all Your people, since the time of the kings of Assyria to this day.

33 However, You are just in all that has come upon us; for You have dealt faithfully, but we have done wickedly;

34 Our kings, our princes, our priests, and our fathers have not kept Your law or hearkened to Your commandments and Your warnings *and* reproofs which You gave them.

35 They did not serve You in their

speak the Word

Thank You, Lord, for being gracious and merciful to me!
ADAPTED FROM NEHEMIAH 9:31

kingdom, and in Your great goodness that You gave them and in the large and rich land You set before them, nor did they turn from their wicked works. **36** Behold, we are slaves this day, and as for the land that You gave to our fathers to eat the fruit and the good of it, behold, we are slaves in it. **37** And its rich yield goes to the kings whom You have set over us because of our sins; they have power also over our bodies and over our livestock at their pleasure. And we are in great distress. **38** Because of all this, we make a firm *and* sure written covenant, and our princes, Levites, and priests set their seal to it.

10 THESE SET their seal: Nehemiah the governor, the son of Hacaliah. And Zedekiah,

2 Seraiah, Azariah, Jeremiah,

3 Pashhur, Amariah, Malchijah,

4 Hattush, Shebaniah, Malluch,

5 Harim, Meremoth, Obadiah,

6 Daniel, Ginnethon, Baruch,

7 Meshullam, Abijah, Mijamin,

8 Maaziah, Bilgai, Shemaiah—these were the priests.

9 And the Levites: Jeshua son of Azaniah, Binnui of the sons of Henadad, Kadmiel,

10 And their brethren: Shebaniah, Hodiah, Kelita, Pelaiah, Hanan,

11 Mica, Rehob, Hashabiah,

12 Zaccur, Sherebiah, Shebaniah,

13 Hodiah, Bani, Beninu.

14 The chiefs of the people: Parosh, Pahath-moab, Elam, Zattu, Bani,

15 Bunni, Azgad, Bebai,

16 Adonijah, Bigvai, Adin,

17 Ater, Hezekiah, Azzur,

18 Hodiah, Hashum, Bezai,

19 Hariph, Anathoth, Nebai,

20 Magpiash, Meshullam, Hezir,

21 Meshezabel, Zadok, Jaddua,

22 Pelatiah, Hanan, Anaiah,

23 Hoshea, Hananiah, Hasshub,

24 Hallohesh, Pilha, Shobek,

25 Rehum, Hashabnah, Maaseiah,

26 Ahiah, Hanan, Anan,

27 Malluch, Harim, Baanah.

28 And the rest of the people—the priests, Levites, gatekeepers, singers, Nethinim [temple servants], and all they who had separated themselves from the peoples of the lands to the Law of God, their wives, their sons, their daughters, all who had knowledge and understanding—

29 Join now, with their brethren, their nobles, and enter into a curse and an oath to walk in God's Law which was given to Moses the servant of God and to observe and do all the commandments of the Lord our Lord, and His ordinances and His statutes:

30 We shall not give our daughters to the peoples of the land or take their daughters for our sons.

31 And if the peoples of the land bring wares or any grain on the Sabbath day to sell, we shall not buy it on the Sabbath or on a holy day; and we shall forego raising crops the seventh year [letting the land lie fallow] and the compulsory payment of every debt. [Exod. 23:10, 11; Deut. 15:1, 2.]

32 Also we pledge ourselves to pay yearly a third of a shekel for the service expenses of the house of our God [which are]:

33 For the showbread; for the continual cereal offerings and burnt offerings; [for the offerings on] the Sabbaths, the New Moons, the set feasts; for the holy things, for the sin offerings to make atonement for Israel; and for all the work of the house of our God.

34 We also cast lots—the priests, the Levites, and the people—for the wood offering, to bring it into the house of our God, according to our fathers' houses, at appointed times year by year, to burn upon the altar of the Lord our God, as it is written in the Law.

35 And [we obligate ourselves] to

bring the firstfruits of our ground and the first of all the fruit of all trees year by year to the house of the Lord,

36 As well as the firstborn of our sons and of our cattle, as is written in the Law, and the firstlings of our herds and flocks, to bring to the house of our God, to the priests who minister in [His] house.

37 And we shall bring the first *and* best of our coarse meal, our contributions, the fruit of all kinds of trees, of new wine, and of oil to the priests, to the chambers of the house of our God. And we shall bring the tithes from our ground to the Levites, for they, the Levites, collect the tithes in all our rural towns.

38 And the priest, the son of Aaron, shall be with the Levites when [they] receive tithes, and [they] shall bring one-tenth of the tithes to the house of our God, to the chambers, into the storehouse.

39 For the Israelites and the sons of Levi shall bring the offering of grain, new wine, and oil to the chambers where the vessels of the sanctuary are, along with the priests who minister and the gatekeepers and singers. We will not forsake *or* neglect the house of our God.

11 NOW THE leaders of the people dwelt at Jerusalem; the rest of the people also cast lots to bring one of ten to dwell in Jerusalem, the holy city, while nine-tenths dwelt in other towns *and* villages.

2 And the people blessed all the men who willingly offered to live in Jerusalem.

3 These are the province chiefs who dwelt in Jerusalem, but in the towns of Judah everyone lived on his property there—Israelites, the priests, the Levites, the temple servants, and the descendants of Solomon's servants.

4 And at Jerusalem dwelt certain of the sons of Judah and Benjamin. Of Judah: Athaiah son of Uzziah, the son of Zechariah, the son of Amariah, the son of Shephatiah, the son of Mahalalel, of the sons of Perez;

5 Maaseiah son of Baruch, the son of Col-hozeh, the son of Hazaiah, the son of Adaiah, the son of Joiarib, the son of Zechariah, the son of the Shilonite.

6 All the sons of Perez who dwelt at Jerusalem were 468 valiant men.

7 These are the sons of Benjamin: Sallu son of Meshullam, the son of Joed, the son of Pedaiah, the son of Kolaiah, the son of Maaseiah, the son of Ithiel, son of Jeshaiah,

8 And after him Gabbai and Sallai, 928.

9 Joel son of Zichri was overseer, and Judah son of Hassenuah was second over the city.

10 Of the priests: Jedaiah son of Joiarib; Jachin;

11 Seraiah son of Hilkiah, the son of Meshullam, the son of Zadok, the son of Meraioth, the son of Ahitub, ruler of the house of God,

12 And their brethren, who did the work of the house, 822; and Adaiah son of Jeroham, the son of Pelaliah, the son of Amzi, the son of Zechariah, the son of Pashhur, the son of Malchijah,

13 And his brethren, chiefs of fathers' houses, 242; and Amashsai son of Azarel, the son of Ahzai, the son of Meshillemoth, the son of Immer,

14 And their brethren, mighty men of valor, 128. Their overseer was Zabdiel son of Haggedolim [one of the great men].

15 And of the Levites: Shemaiah son of Hasshub, the son of Azrikam, the son of Hashabiah, the son of Bunni;

16 And Shabbethai and Jozabad, of the chiefs of the Levites, who had charge of the outside work of the house of God;

17 Mattaniah son of Mica, the son of Zabdi, the son of Asaph, the leader to begin the thanksgiving in prayer; and Bakbukiah, second among his brethren; and Abda son of Shammua, the son of Galal, the son of Jeduthun.
18 The Levites in the holy city were 284.
19 The gatekeepers: Akkub, Talmon, and their brethren, who kept watch, were 172.
20 And the rest of Israel, with the priests and the Levites, were in all the cities of Judah, each in his inheritance.
21 But the temple servants dwelt on [the hill] Ophel; Ziha and Gishpa were over [them].
22 Overseer of the Levites in Jerusalem and the work of God's house was Uzzi son of Bani, the son of Hashabiah, the son of Mattaniah, the son of Mica, of Asaph's sons, the singers.
23 For the [Persian] king had ordered concerning them that a certain provision be made for the singers, as each day required.
24 Pethahiah son of Meshezabel, of the sons of Zerah son of Judah, was at the king's hand in all matters concerning the people.
25 As for the villages with their fields, some people of Judah dwelt in Kiriath-arba, Dibon, and Jekabzeel, and their villages,
26 In Jeshua, Moladah, Beth-pelet,
27 Hazar-shual, Beersheba and its villages,
28 Ziklag, Meconah and its villages,
29 En-rimmon, Zorah, Jarmuth,
30 Zanoah, Adullam, and their villages, Lachish and its fields, Azekah and its villages. So they encamped from Beersheba to the Hinnom Valley.
31 The people of Benjamin also dwelt from Geba onward, at Michmash, Aija, Bethel and its villages,
32 At Anathoth, Nob, Ananiah,
33 Hazor, Ramah, Gittaim,
34 Hadid, Zeboim, Neballat,
35 Lod, and Ono, the Valley of the Craftsmen.
36 And certain divisions of the Levites in Judah were joined to Benjamin.

12 NOW THESE are the priests and Levites who went up with Zerubbabel son of Shealtiel and with Jeshua: Seraiah, Jeremiah, Ezra,
2 Amariah, Malluch, Hattush,
3 Shecaniah, Rehum, Meremoth,
4 Iddo, Ginnethoi, Abijah,
5 Mijamin, Maadiah, Bilgah,
6 Shemaiah, Joiarib, Jedaiah,
7 Sallu, Amok, Hilkiah, and Jedaiah. These were the chiefs of the priests and their brethren in the days of Jeshua.
8 And the Levites were Jeshua, Binnui, Kadmiel, Sherebiah, Judah, and Mattaniah, who, with his brethren, was over the thanksgiving [choirs].
9 Bakbukiah and Unni, their brethren, stood opposite them according to their offices.
10 And Jeshua was the father of Joiakim, Joiakim of Eliashib, Eliashib of Joiada,
11 Joiada was the father of Jonathan, and Jonathan of Jaddua.
12 And in the days of Joiakim were priests, heads of fathers' houses: of Seraiah, Meraiah; of Jeremiah, Hananiah;
13 Of Ezra, Meshullam; of Amariah, Jehohanan;
14 Of Malluchi, Jonathan; of Shebaniah, Joseph;
15 Of Harim, Adna; of Meraioth, Helkai;
16 Of Iddo, Zechariah; of Ginnethon, Meshullam;
17 Of Abijah, Zichri; of Miniamin and of Moadiah, Piltai;
18 Of Bilgah, Shammua; of Shemaiah, Jehonathan;

19 Of Joiarib, Mattenai; of Jedaiah, Uzzi;

20 Of Sallai, Kallai; of Amok, Eber;

21 Of Hilkiah, Hashabiah; of Jedaiah, Nethanel.

22 As for the Levites in the days of Eliashib, Joiada, Johanan, and Jaddua, the heads of fathers' houses were recorded, as well as the priests, until the reign of Darius the Persian.

23 The sons of Levi, heads of fathers' houses, were recorded in the Book of the Chronicles until the days of Johanan son of Eliashib.

24 And the chiefs of the Levites were Hashabiah, Sherebiah, and Jeshua son of Kadmiel, with their brethren opposite them, to praise and to give thanks, as David, God's man, commanded, [one] watch [singing] in response to [the men in the opposite] watch.

25 Mattaniah, Bakbukiah, Obadiah, Meshullam, Talmon, and Akkub were gatekeepers guarding at the storehouses of the gates.

26 These were in the days of Joiakim son of Jeshua, the son of Jozadak, and in the days of Nehemiah the governor and of Ezra the priest and scribe.

27 And for the dedication of the wall of Jerusalem, they sought the Levites in all their places to bring them to Jerusalem to celebrate the dedication with gladness, with thanksgivings, and with singing, cymbals, harps, and lyres.

28 And the sons of the singers gathered together from the plain *and* circuit around Jerusalem and from the villages of the Netophathites,

29 And also from Beth-gilgal and the fields of Geba and Azmaveth, for the singers had built for themselves villages around Jerusalem.

30 And the priests and the Levites purified themselves, the people, the gates, and the wall.

31 Then I brought the princes of Judah up on the wall, and I appointed two great companies of them who gave thanks and went in procession. One went to the right upon the wall toward the Dung Gate.

32 And after them went Hoshaiah and half of the princes of Judah,

33 And Azariah, Ezra, Meshullam,

34 Judah, Benjamin, Shemaiah, and Jeremiah,

35 And certain of the priests' sons with trumpets, and Zechariah son of Jonathan, the son of Shemaiah, the son of Mattaniah, the son of Micaiah, the son of Zaccur, the son of Asaph,

36 And his kinsmen—Shemaiah, Azarel, Milalai, Gilalai, Maai, Nethanel, Judah, Hanani—with the musical instruments of David, God's man. And Ezra the scribe went before them.

37 At the Fountain Gate they went up straight ahead by the stairs of the City of David at the wall's ascent above David's house to the Water Gate on the east.

38 The other company of those who gave thanks went to the left; I followed with half of the people upon the wall, above the Tower of the Furnaces to the Broad Wall,

39 And above the Gate of Ephraim, and by the Old Gate and by the Fish Gate and by the Tower of Hananel and the Tower of Hammeah, even to the Sheep Gate; and they stopped at the Gate of the Guard.

putting the Word to work

When was the last time you celebrated God's goodness and faithfulness in your life? Nehemiah demonstrates the importance of both dedicating our work and accomplishments to the Lord and celebrating what the Lord has done for us. As individuals, families, and as the body of Christ, let's celebrate often the goodness of the Lord!

40 So the two companies of those who gave thanks stood in the house of God, and I, and the half of the officials with me;

41 And the priests Eliakim, Maaseiah, Miniamin, Micaiah, Elioenai, Zechariah, and Hananiah, with trumpets;

42 And Maaseiah, Shemaiah, Eleazar, Uzzi, Jehohanan, Malchijah, Elam, and Ezer. And the singers sang *and* made themselves heard, with Jezrahiah as leader.

43 Also that day they offered great sacrifices and rejoiced, for God had made them rejoice with great joy; the women also and the children rejoiced. The joy of Jerusalem was heard even afar off.

44 On that day men were appointed over the chambers for the stores, the contributions, the firstfruits, and the tithes, to gather into them the portions required by law for the priests and the Levites according to the fields of the towns, for Judah rejoiced over the priests and Levites who served [faithfully].

45 And they performed the due service of their God and of the purification; so did the singers and gatekeepers, as David and his son Solomon had commanded.

46 For in the days of David and Asaph of old, there was a chief of singers and songs of praise and thanksgiving to God.

47 And all Israel in the days of Zerubbabel and [later] of Nehemiah gave the daily portions for the singers and the gatekeepers; and they set apart what was for the Levites, and the Levites set apart what was for the sons of Aaron [the priests].

13 ON THAT day they read in the Book of Moses in the audience of the people, and in it was found written that no Ammonite or Moabite should ever come into the assembly of God,

2 For they met not the Israelites with food and drink but hired Balaam to curse them; yet our God turned the curse into a blessing. [Num. 22:3-11; Deut. 23:5, 6.]

3 When [the Jews] heard the law, they separated from Israel all who were of foreign descent.

4 Now before this, Eliashib the priest, who was appointed over the chambers of the house of our God, and was related [by marriage] to Tobiah [our adversary],

5 Prepared for Tobiah a large chamber where previously they had put the cereal offerings, the frankincense, the vessels, and the tithes of grain, new wine, and oil which were given by commandment to the Levites, the singers, and gatekeepers, and the contributions for the priests.

6 But in all this time I was not at Jerusalem, for in the thirty-second year of Artaxerxes [Persian] king of Babylon I went to the king. Then later I asked leave of him

7 And came to Jerusalem. Then I discovered the evil that Eliashib had done for Tobiah in preparing him [an adversary] a chamber in the courts of the house of God!

8 And it grieved me exceedingly, and I threw all the house furnishings of Tobiah out of the chamber.

9 Then I commanded, and they cleansed the chambers; and I brought back there the vessels of the house of

speak the Word

Thank You, God, for turning the curses in my life into blessings.
ADAPTED FROM NEHEMIAH **13:2**

God, with the cereal offerings and the frankincense.

10 And I perceived that the portions of the Levites had not been given them, so that the Levites and the singers who did the work [forced by necessity] had each fled to his field.

11 Then I contended with the officials and said, Why is the house of God neglected *and* forsaken? I gathered the Levites and singers and set them in their stations.

12 Then all Judah brought the tithe of the grain, the new wine, and the oil to the storerooms.

13 I set treasurers over the storerooms: Shelemiah the priest, Zadok the scribe, and Pedaiah of the Levites; assisting them was Hanan son of Zaccur, the son of Mattaniah, for they were counted faithful, and their task was to distribute to their brethren.

14 O my God, [earnestly] remember me concerning this and wipe not out my good deeds *and* kindnesses done for the house of my God and for His service.

15 In those days I saw in Judah men treading winepresses on the Sabbath, bringing in sheaves *or* heaps of grain with which they loaded donkeys, as well as wine, grapes, figs, and all sorts of burdens, which they brought into Jerusalem on the Sabbath day. And I protested *and* warned them on the day they sold the produce.

16 There dwelt men of Tyre there also who brought fish and all kinds of wares and sold on the Sabbath to the people of Judah and in Jerusalem.

17 Then I reproved the nobles of Judah and said, What evil thing is this that you do—profaning the Sabbath day?

18 Did not your fathers do thus, and did not our God bring all this evil upon us and upon this city? Yet you bring more wrath upon Israel by profaning the Sabbath.

19 And when it began to get dark at the gates of Jerusalem before the

life point

Because Nehemiah was a good leader, he chose faithful men as treasurers (see Nehemiah 13:13). It does not matter how gifted a person is, if he is not faithful, God cannot use him.

We must understand that God tests faithfulness. It is not enough to say, "Oh, yes, I'm faithful," because God will say, "Well, let's see." Do you know how God tests our faithfulness? He assigns us to do something for a period of time that we do not want to do, something that is not fun or exciting, something that may require us to submit to someone else's authority for a while, and He will speak to our hearts, "Just be faithful."

Faithfulness is not only showing up day after day; it is showing up day after day with a good attitude and an excellent spirit. God will reward that kind of faithfulness. Luke 16:12 tells us that if we are faithful over what belongs to someone else, God will give us our own. If you are being tested in the area of faithfulness, be unwavering in your resolve to be faithful and dependable. You will be glad you did.

life point

Nehemiah knew the importance of a Sabbath rest (see Nehemiah 13:19). When Elijah neglected to rest, he grew tired and became discouraged (see I Kings 19:1–4). He was depressed, and he wanted to be alone. This is an important lesson for all of us to learn. When we get overly tired and out of balance, depression and discouragement quickly try to come upon us. Whatever you do, remember to rest.

Sabbath [day began], I commanded that the gates should be shut and not be opened till after the Sabbath. And I set some of my servants at the gates to prevent any burden being brought in on the Sabbath day.

20 So the merchants and sellers of all kinds of wares lodged outside Jerusalem once or twice.

21 But I reproved *and* warned them, saying, Why do you lodge by the wall? If you do so again, I will lay hands on you. Then they stopped coming on the Sabbath.

22 And I commanded the Levites to cleanse themselves and come and guard the gates to keep the Sabbath day holy. O my God, [earnestly] remember me concerning this also and spare me according to the greatness of Your mercy *and* loving-kindness.

23 In those days also I saw Jews who had married wives from Ashdod, Ammon, and Moab.

24 And their children spoke half in the speech of Ashdod, and could not speak the Hebrew, but in the language of each people.

25 And I contended with them and reviled them and beat some of them and pulled out their hair and made them swear by God, saying, You shall not give your daughters to their sons, nor take their daughters for your sons or for yourselves.

26 Did not Solomon king of Israel act treacherously against God *and* miss the mark on account of such women? Among many nations there was no king like him. He was loved by his God, and God made him king over all Israel; yet strange women even caused him to sin [when he was old he turned treacherously away from the Lord to other gods, and God rent his kingdom from him]. [I Kings 11:1-11.]

27 Shall we then listen to you to do all this great evil and act treacherously against our God by marrying strange (heathen) women?

28 One of the sons of Joiada son of Eliashib the high priest was son-in-law to Sanballat the Horonite; therefore I chased him from me.

29 O my God, [earnestly] remember them, because they have defiled the priesthood and the covenant of the priests and Levites.

30 Thus I cleansed them from everything foreign (heathen), and I defined the duties of the priests and Levites, everyone in his work;

31 And I provided for the wood offering at appointed times, and for the firstfruits. O my God, [earnestly] remember me for good *and* imprint me [on Your heart]!

Esther

Author:
Unknown

Date:
Probably before the end of the fifth century BC

Everyday Life Principles:
Even though you are only one person, you can make a difference!

In order to fulfill a great calling, you will need great preparation.

When you do what God asks you to do, victory is sure.

I believe that the great encouragement the book of Esther offers us is the fact that one person can make a difference. Esther was certainly an unlikely candidate to become the queen of Persia and save the lives of an entire nation. First of all, she was not even Persian, and second, she was an orphan. No natural circumstances facilitated her marrying the king, but God intervened supernaturally and put her in a position of influence so that His purpose for her people, the Jews, would come to pass.

God called and chose Esther to bring deliverance to the Jews when they were marked for destruction. He appointed her for a difficult and dangerous work. Because her call was so significant, she needed thorough preparation. Without proper preparation, she could have faltered in her responsibilities or failed to obey God, but because she was thoroughly prepared and had an obedient heart, she succeeded gloriously. In Esther's case, the preparation included twelve months of beauty treatments and instruction from Hegai, the king's attendant. This type of preparation was necessary to assure that the king would respond favorably to her, which was what she needed in order to save her people.

I believe that God has a great call and purpose for your life, as He did for Esther's. Your assignment may not be the deliverance of a nation, but whatever God has called you to is extremely significant. Whatever it is, be diligent to embrace the preparation process it requires so that you will be well-equipped when the time comes for you to act.

1 IT WAS in the days of Ahasuerus [Xerxes], the Ahasuerus who reigned from India to Ethiopia over 127 provinces.

2 In those days when King Ahasuerus sat on his royal throne which was in Shushan *or* Susa [the capital of the Persian Empire] in the palace *or* castle,

3 In the third year of his reign he made a feast for all his princes and his courtiers. The chief officers of the Persian and Median army and the nobles and governors of the provinces were there before him

4 While he showed the riches of his glorious kingdom and the splendor and excellence of his majesty for many days, even 180 days.

5 And when these days were completed, the king made a feast for all the people present in Shushan the capital, both great and small, a seven-day feast in the court of the garden of the king's palace.

6 There were hangings of fine white cloth, of green and of blue [cotton], fastened with cords of fine linen and purple to silver rings *or* rods and marble pillars. The couches of gold and silver rested on a [mosaic] pavement of porphyry, white marble, mother-of-pearl, and [precious] colored stones.

7 Drinks were served in different kinds of golden goblets, and there was royal wine in abundance, according to the liberality of the king.

8 And drinking was according to the law; no one was compelled to drink, for the king had directed all the officials of his palace to serve only as each guest desired.

9 Also Queen Vashti gave a banquet for the women in the royal house which belonged to King Ahasuerus.

10 On the seventh day, when the king's heart was merry with wine, he commanded Mehuman, Biztha, Harbona, Bigtha, Abagtha, Zethar, and Carkas, the seven eunuchs who ministered to King Ahasuerus as attendants,

11 To bring Queen Vashti before the king, with her royal crown, to show the peoples and the princes her beauty, for she was fair to behold.

12 But Queen Vashti refused to come at the king's command conveyed by the eunuchs. Therefore the king was enraged, and his anger burned within him.

13 Then the king spoke to the wise men who knew the times—for this was the king's procedure toward all who were familiar with law and judgment—

14 Those next to him being Carshena, Shethar, Admatha, Tarshish, Meres, Marsena, and Memucan, the seven princes of Persia and Media who were in the king's presence and held first place in the kingdom.

15 [He said] According to the law, what is to be done to Queen Vashti because she has not done the bidding of King Ahasuerus conveyed by the eunuchs?

16 And Memucan answered before the king and the princes, Vashti the queen has not only done wrong to the king but also to all the princes and to all the peoples who are in all the provinces of King Ahasuerus.

17 For this deed of the queen will become known to all women, making their husbands contemptible in their eyes, since they will say, King Ahasuerus commanded Queen Vashti to be brought before him, but she did not come.

18 This very day the ladies of Persia and Media who have heard of the queen's behavior will be telling it to all the king's princes. So contempt and wrath in plenty will arise.

19 If it pleases the king, let a royal command go forth from him and let it be written among the laws of the Persians and Medes, so that it may not be changed, that Vashti is to [be divorced

and] come no more before King Ahasuerus; and let the king give her royal position to another who is better than she.

20 So when the king's decree is made and proclaimed throughout all his kingdom, extensive as it is, all wives will give honor to their husbands, high and low.

21 This advice pleased the king and the princes, and the king did what Memucan proposed.

22 He sent letters to all the royal provinces, to each in its own script and to every people in their own language, saying that every man should rule in his own house and speak there in the language of his own people. [If he had foreign wives, let them learn his language.]

2 AFTER THESE things, when the wrath of King Ahasuerus was pacified, he [earnestly] remembered Vashti and what she had done and what was decreed against her.

2 Then the king's servants who ministered to him said, Let beautiful young virgins be sought for the king.

3 And let the king appoint officers in all the provinces of his kingdom to gather all the beautiful young virgins to the capital in Shushan, to the harem under the custody of Hegai, the king's eunuch, who is in charge of the women; and let their things for purification be given them.

4 And let the maiden who pleases the king be queen instead of Vashti. This pleased the king, and he did so.

5 There was a certain Jew in the capital in Shushan whose name was Mordecai son of Jair, the son of Shimei, the son of Kish, a Benjamite,

6 Who had been carried away from Jerusalem with the captives taken away with Jeconiah king of Judah,

whom Nebuchadnezzar the king of Babylon had carried into exile.

7 He had brought up Hadassah, that is Esther, his uncle's daughter, for she had neither father nor mother. The maiden was beautiful and lovely, and when her father and mother died, Mordecai took her as his own daughter.

8 So when the king's command and his decree were proclaimed and when many maidens were gathered in Shushan the capital under the custody of Hegai, Esther also was taken to the king's house into the custody of Hegai, keeper of the women.

9 And the maiden pleased [Hegai] and obtained his favor. And he speedily gave her the things for her purification and her portion of food and the seven chosen maids to be given her from the king's palace; and he removed her and her maids to the best [apartment] in the harem.

10 Esther had not made known her nationality or her kindred, for Mordecai had charged her not to do so.

11 And Mordecai [who was an [a]attendant in the king's court] walked every day before the court of the harem to learn how Esther was and what would become of her.

12 Now when the turn of each maiden came to go in to King Ahasuerus, after the regulations for the women had been carried out for twelve months—since this was the regular period for their beauty treatments, six months with oil of myrrh and six months with sweet spices *and* perfumes and the things for the purifying of the women—

13 Then in this way the maiden came to the king: whatever she desired was given her to take with her from the harem into the king's palace.

14 In the evening she went and next day she returned into the second

a So says *The Septuagint* (Greek translation of the Old Testament).

putting the Word to work

Often God's assignments to us require preparation, as Esther's did (see Esther 2:12, 13). It may be spiritual preparation, or it may be that certain circumstances must first be in place, such as further training or others to help you. Are you confident that you are prepared for the work the Lord has for you at this time in your life? If not, ask God to show you the further preparation you need and, like Esther, embrace it.

harem in the custody of Shaashgaz, the king's eunuch who was in charge of the concubines. She came to the king no more unless the king delighted in her and she was called for by name.

15 Now when the turn for Esther the daughter of Abihail, the uncle of Mordecai who had taken her as his own daughter, had come to go in to the king, she required nothing but what Hegai the king's attendant, the keeper of the women, suggested. And Esther won favor in the sight of all who saw her.

16 So Esther was taken to King Ahasuerus into his royal palace in the tenth month, the month of Tebeth, in the seventh year of his reign.

17 And the king loved Esther more than all the women, and she obtained grace and favor in his sight more than all the maidens, so that he set the royal crown on her head and made her queen instead of Vashti.

18 Then the king gave a great feast for all his princes and his servants, Esther's feast; and he gave a holiday [or a lessening of taxes] to the provinces and gave gifts in keeping with the generosity of the king.

19 And when the maidens were gathered together the second time, Mordecai was sitting at the king's gate.

20 Now Esther had not yet revealed her nationality or her people, for she obeyed Mordecai's command to her [bto fear God and execute His commands] just as when she was being brought up by him.

21 In those days, while Mordecai sat at the king's gate, two of the king's eunuchs, Bigthan and Teresh, of those who guarded the door, were angry and sought to lay hands on King Ahasuerus.

22 And this was known to Mordecai, who told it to Queen Esther, and Esther told the king in Mordecai's name.

23 When it was investigated and found to be true, both men were hanged on the gallows. And it was recorded in the Book of the Chronicles in the king's presence.

putting the Word to work

Do you have a hard time asking for advice? Take a lesson from Esther, who recognized the source of wisdom that the Lord had given her in Hegai (see Esther 2:15). In seeking and heeding his counsel, she found favor that led to great deliverance and victory for her people. Ask the Lord to show you the people who are sources of wisdom and godly counsel in your life.

speak the Word

God, I pray that You will do for me what You did for Esther, and give me favor in the sight of everyone I meet.
ADAPTED FROM ESTHER 2:15

---

b So *The Septuagint* (Greek translation of the Old Testament) reads. The name of God is nowhere mentioned directly in the Hebrew text.

believe for God's favor

Do you know that there is a verse in the Bible that says God brings one person down and lifts up another (see I Samuel 2:7)? In Esther 2:15–17, He raised up Esther from obscurity to become the queen of the entire land. God gave her favor with everyone she met, including the king, because she had favor with Him.

Later on in the story, we will see that Esther drew upon that favor to save herself and her people, the Jews, from being murdered by the evil Haman, who was out to destroy them. She was not afraid to go to the king and ask him to intervene on behalf of herself and her people, even though such a bold request of the king could have cost her very life, because she knew that she had favor with God.

If you find yourself in a situation in which you are being harassed, persecuted, or discriminated against; if someone is trying to take something from you that rightfully belongs to you—whether it is your job, your home, your reputation, or anything else in life—do not try to retaliate by seeking natural favor. Instead, believe God for supernatural favor, because despite how hopeless things may look from a human perspective, God can lift you up and bring your enemies down.

Every single day when you go to work, let me encourage you to say, "I believe that I have favor in this place today. I believe that the light of the Lord shines upon me and that I have favor with everyone, with God and with men."

Do not go through life being afraid that nobody likes you. Do not harbor the fear of rejection. Instead, believe that God is causing everyone you come in contact with to like you, to want to be around you, to look upon you with favor.

life point

Mordecai was a man called and anointed by God to bring deliverance to His people, just as you and I are called and anointed by God to bring deliverance and help to others in our day.

3 AFTER THESE things, King ^cAhasuerus promoted Haman the son of Hammedatha the Agagite and advanced him and set his seat above all the princes who were with him.

2 And all the king's servants who were at the king's gate bowed down and did reverence to Haman, for the king had so commanded concerning him. But Mordecai did not bow down or do him reverence.

3 Then the king's servants who were at the king's gate said to Mordecai, Why do you transgress the king's command?

4 Now when they spoke to him day after day and he paid no attention to them, they told Haman to see whether Mordecai's conduct would stand, for he had told them that he was a Jew.

c There seems to be little doubt that King Ahasuerus is to be identified with the well-known Xerxes, who reigned from 486 to 465 BC. *The Zondervan Pictorial Bible Dictionary* (Merrill C. Tenney, ed.) gives four close similarities between them which support this identification. Also, "the Ahasuerus of Ezra 4:6, to whom were written accusations against the Jews of Jerusalem, is in all probability the same Xerxes, although sometimes identified with Cambyses son of Cyrus."

a better plan

If you are familiar with Esther's story, you know that Esther, the cousin and adopted daughter of a Jew named Mordecai, had been chosen by King Ahasuerus to be elevated to the position of queen of his kingdom. She was taken into the king's harem as a young maiden, and I feel sure that this was not the plan she had for her life. The situation probably frightened her and may even have seemed evil to her at the time. In the harem, her whole purpose was to prepare for a night with the king. Then when the time came, God gave her favor with the king, and he chose her to be the queen (see Esther 2:7–17). Little did she know that God was putting her in position to save a nation (see Esther 3:5, 6).

Often we have a plan in mind for our lives, but something happens to interrupt our plan. We often resist and are not happy about the change, but no matter what we do, this new thing seems to be God's will for us. We cannot imagine how it could turn out good, but God has a plan in mind that is much better than ours. In Esther's case, Mordecai told her that she was called to the kingdom "for such a time as this" (Esther 4:14) because the Jews were in danger of extinction. Her destiny was to save them from destruction, and if she did not do what God was asking her to do, she would perish along with everyone else (see Esther 4:14). She agreed to do whatever needed to be done.

I pray that you and I will be just as courageous as Esther was—even when we are led in a different direction than we had planned.

5 And when Haman saw that Mordecai did not bow down or do him reverence, he was very angry.
6 But he scorned laying hands only on Mordecai. So since they had told him Mordecai's nationality, Haman sought to destroy all the Jews, the people of Mordecai, throughout the whole kingdom of Ahasuerus.
7 In the first month, the month of Nisan, in the twelfth year of King Ahasuerus, Haman caused Pur, that is, lots, to be cast before him day after day [to find a lucky day for his venture], month after month, until the twelfth, the month of Adar.
8 Then Haman said to King Ahasuerus, There is a certain people scattered abroad and dispersed among the peoples in all the provinces of your kingdom; their laws are different from every other people, neither do they keep the king's laws. Therefore it is not for the king's profit to tolerate them.
9 If it pleases the king, let it be decreed that they be destroyed, and I will pay 10,000 talents of silver into the hands of those who have charge of the king's business, that it may be brought into the king's treasuries.
10 And the king took his signet ring from his hand [with which to seal his letters by the king's authority] and gave it to Haman son of Hammedatha the Agagite, the Jews' enemy.
11 And the king said to Haman, The silver is given to you, the people also, to do with them as it seems good to you.
12 Then the king's secretaries were called in on the thirteenth day of the first month, and all that Haman had commanded was written to the king's chief rulers and to the governors who

were over all the provinces and to the princes of each people, to every province in its own script and to each people in their own language; it was written in the name of King Ahasuerus and it was sealed with the king's [signet] ring.

13 And letters were sent by special messengers to all the king's provinces—to destroy, to slay, and to do away with all Jews, both young and old, little children and women, in one day, the thirteenth day of the twelfth month, the month of Adar, and to seize their belongings as spoil.

14 A copy of the writing was to be published *and* given out as a decree in every province to all the peoples to be ready for that day.

15 The special messengers went out in haste by order of the king, and the decree was given out in Shushan, the capital. And the king and Haman sat down to drink, but the city of Shushan was perplexed [at the strange and alarming decree].

4 NOW WHEN Mordecai learned all that was done, [he] rent his clothes and put on sackcloth with ashes and went out into the midst of the city and cried with a loud and bitter cry.

2 He came *and* stood before the king's gate, for no one might enter the king's gate clothed with sackcloth.

3 And in every province, wherever the king's commandment and his decree came, there was great mourning among the Jews, with fasting, weeping, and wailing, and many lay in sackcloth and ashes.

4 When Esther's maids and her attendants came and told it to her, the queen was exceedingly grieved *and* distressed. She sent garments to clothe Mordecai, with orders to take his sackcloth from off him, but he would not receive them.

5 Then Esther called for Hathach, one of the king's attendants whom he had appointed to attend her, and ordered him to go to Mordecai to learn what this was and why it was.

6 So Hathach went out to Mordecai in the open square of the city, which was in front of the king's gate.

7 And Mordecai told him of all that had happened to him, and the exact sum of money that Haman had promised to pay to the king's treasuries for the Jews to be destroyed.

8 [Mordecai] also gave him a copy of the decree to destroy them, that was given out in Shushan, that he might show it to Esther, explain it to her, and charge her to go to the king, make supplication to him, and plead with him for the lives of her people.

9 And Hathach came and told Esther the words of Mordecai.

10 Then Esther spoke to Hathach and gave him a message for Mordecai, saying,

11 All the king's servants and the people of the king's provinces know that any person, be it man or woman, who shall go into the inner court to the king without being called shall be put to death; there is but one law for him, except [him] to whom the king shall hold out the golden scepter, that he may live. But I have not been called to come to the king for these thirty days.

12 And they told Mordecai what Esther said.

13 Then Mordecai told them to return this answer to Esther, Do not flatter yourself that you shall escape in the king's palace any more than all the other Jews.

14 For if you keep silent at this time, relief and deliverance shall arise for the Jews from elsewhere, but you and your father's house will perish. And who knows but that you have come to the kingdom for such a time as this *and* for this very occasion?

15 Then Esther told them to give this answer to Mordecai,

for such a time as this

Queen Esther was asked to do something very difficult in order to help bring deliverance to her people. Most likely, she did not feel like being in the challenging place where God had put her. She probably did not want the responsibility, nor did she want to risk the personal harm she knew could come to her. Esther was a young maiden with her whole life ahead of her. Leaving her dreams behind, she was being asked to follow instructions from the Lord that seemed very dangerous. Esther was to go before the king to expose a wicked plot that had been launched against the Jews. No one was allowed to go before the king unless he or she was invited—not even the queen. Esther knew that unless God gave her favor, she would be killed (see Esther 4:16). I would say that Esther put everything on the line in order to obey God's will.

Mordecai, who was speaking to Esther on God's behalf, told her that she must not keep silent. If she did, people would perish. He reminded her that perhaps she had been called to the kingdom for the very task that lay before her.

You, too, may be alive today in order to fulfill the purposes of God in your generation. The timing and place of your birth are not accidental; God purposely and specifically places us all in certain time frames and places. Many people spend their entire lives never knowing what their purpose is, but perhaps it is because they try to choose their own destiny rather than follow the leading of the Holy Spirit. Following God requires sacrifices and a willingness to be uncomfortable. Esther reached a point of being willing to lay aside all her own thoughts, plans, and ideas. She was even willing to die if she needed to in order to obey God.

Because of Esther's sacrifice and bold step of faith, God did use her to save a nation. She was more blessed in God's will than she could ever have been anywhere else. God's will is not always easy, but it is always worth any sacrifice we need to make.

16 Go, gather together all the Jews that are present in Shushan, and fast for me; and neither eat nor drink for three days, night or day. I also and my maids will fast as you do. Then I will go to the king, though it is against the law; and if I perish, I perish. **17** So Mordecai went away and did all that Esther had commanded him.

5 ON THE third day [of the fast] Esther put on her royal robes and stood in the royal *or* inner court of the king's palace opposite his [throne room]. The king was sitting on his throne, facing the main entrance of the palace. **2** And when the king saw Esther the queen standing in the court, she

speak the Word

God, I pray that You will give me a heart like Esther's, willing to do Your will at any cost.
ADAPTED FROM ESTHER 4:16

obtained favor in his sight, and he held out to [her] the golden scepter that was in his hand. So Esther drew near and touched the tip of the scepter.

3 Then the king said to her, What will you have, Queen Esther? What is your request? It shall be given you, even to the half of the kingdom.

4 And Esther said, If it seems good to the king, let the king and Haman come this day to the dinner that I have prepared for the king.

life point

The Bible contains some very radical examples of things people did to obey God. It was radical of Esther to put everything on the line when she went before the king without being summoned. Her motive was right, and she did it in obedience; therefore, God gave her favor, and she was instrumental in saving her nation from disaster.

When we are called upon to make a sacrifice or do something radical for God, we should not feel deprived, but privileged. In the most radical act of human history, Jesus sacrificed His very life for us, and we are to follow in His footsteps. It is time to shake ourselves into reality and start doing what He asks us to do, no matter what the cost.

5 Then the king said, Cause Haman to come quickly, that what Esther has said may be done.

6 So the king and Haman came to the dinner that Esther had prepared.

7 And during the serving of wine, the king said to Esther, What is your petition? It shall be granted you. And what is your request? Even to the half of the kingdom, it shall be performed.

8 Then Esther said, My petition and my request is: If I have found favor in the sight of the king and if it pleases the king to grant my petition and to perform my request, let the king and Haman come tomorrow to the dinner that I shall prepare for them; and I will do tomorrow as the king has said.

9 Haman went away that day joyful and elated in heart. But when he saw Mordecai at the king's gate refusing to stand up or show fear before him, he was filled with wrath against Mordecai.

10 Nevertheless, Haman restrained himself and went home. There he sent and called for his friends and Zeresh his wife.

11 And Haman recounted to them the glory of his riches, the abundance of his [ten] sons, all the things in which the king had promoted him, and how he had advanced him above the princes and servants of the king.

12 Haman added, Yes, and today Queen Esther did not let any man come with the king to the dinner she

had prepared but myself; and tomorrow also I am invited by her together with the king.

13 Yet all this benefits me nothing as long as I see Mordecai the Jew sitting at the king's gate.

14 Then Zeresh his wife and all his friends said to him, Let a gallows be made, fifty cubits [seventy-five feet] high, and in the morning speak to the king, that Mordecai may be hanged on it; then you go in merrily with the king to the dinner. And the thing pleased Haman, and he caused the gallows to be made.

6 ON THAT night the king could not sleep; and he ordered that the book of memorable deeds, the chronicles, be brought, and they were read before the king.

2 And it was found written there how Mordecai had told of Bigthana and Teresh, two of the king's attendants who guarded the door, who had sought to lay hands on King Ahasuerus.

3 And the king said, What honor or distinction has been given Mordecai for this? Then the king's servants who ministered to him said, Nothing has been done for him.

4 The king said, Who is in the court? Now Haman had just come into the outer court of the king's palace to ask the king to hang Mordecai on the gallows he had prepared for him.

5 And the king's servants said to him, Behold, Haman is standing in the court. And the king said, Let him come in.

6 So Haman came in. And the king

God does not forget

I would like to share a truth with you. Whatever good thing you and I do, even in secret, God has recorded. He is not going to forget it. The day will come when our good deeds will be brought out into the open.

Every prayer we have prayed, every time we have submitted to authority when we wanted to rebel, every time we have confessed God's Word when our emotions were screaming at us to say negative things—each act of obedience is recorded and will be rewarded. Every time we have taken our position of faith, worship, and maintaining a good confession, every time we have offered up to God the sacrifice of praise, God remembers. He does not forget the things we have done right. He has them recorded in His book of memorable deeds, as we read in Hebrews 6:10: "For God is not unrighteous to forget or overlook your labor and the love which you have shown for His name's sake in ministering to the needs of the saints (His own consecrated people), as you still do."

Mordecai had been doing some good deeds, but he had not made a big deal about them. He had simply been doing them in secret, as unto the Lord. The Word teaches us that when we do good deeds, we are not to let our left hand know what our right hand is doing (see Matthew 6:3, 4). This means that we should do what we feel God is leading us to do—do it for His glory, then forget it and go on about our business. It means not patting ourselves on the back or telling others what we have done, but simply knowing that our reward will come from God when the time is right. When God's timing was right, He rewarded Mordecai (see Esther 6:1–3), and you can be sure He will do the same for you.

putting the Word to work

Has there ever been a time in your life when someone else tried to take credit for something you had done? Haman coveted the honor that rightfully belonged to Mordecai. When you do not receive the honor or credit that you know is rightfully yours, trust God; He does not forget, and He will be faithful to reward you.

said to him, What shall be done to the man whom the king delights to honor? Now Haman said to himself, To whom would the king delight to do honor more than to me?

7 And Haman said to the king, For the man whom the king delights to honor,

8 Let royal apparel be brought which the king has worn and the horse which the king has ridden, and a royal crown be set on his head.

9 And let the apparel and the horse be delivered to the hand of one of the king's most noble princes. Let him array the man whom the king delights to honor, and conduct him on horseback through the open square of the city, and proclaim before him, Thus shall it be done to the man whom the king delights to honor.

10 Then the king said to Haman, Make haste and take the apparel and the horse, as you have said, and do so to Mordecai the Jew, who sits at the

life point

The king, who represents God in this story, was telling Haman, "Every blessing you planned for yourself, you are going to confer on Mordecai. You are going to watch while I bless him" (see Esther 6:7–10). When God decides to bless someone, no person on earth or no devil in hell can stop Him.

king's gate. Leave out nothing that you have spoken.

11 Then Haman took the apparel and the horse and conducted Mordecai on horseback through the open square of the city, proclaiming before him, Thus shall it be done to the man whom the king delights to honor.

12 Then Mordecai came again to the king's gate. But Haman hastened to his house, mourning and having his head covered.

13 And Haman recounted to Zeresh his wife and all his friends everything that had happened to him. Then his wise men and Zeresh his wife said to him, If Mordecai, before whom you have begun to fall, is of the offspring of the Jews, you cannot prevail against him, but shall surely fall before him.

14 While they were yet talking with him, the king's attendants came and hastily brought Haman to the dinner that Esther had prepared.

7 SO THE king and Haman came to dine with Esther the queen.

2 And the king said again to Esther on the second day when wine was being served, What is your petition, Queen Esther? It shall be granted. And what is your request? Even to the half of the kingdom, it shall be performed.

3 Then Queen Esther said, If I have found favor in your sight, O king and if it pleases the king, let my life be given me at my petition and my people at my request.

4 For we are sold, I and my people, to be destroyed, slain, and wiped out of existence! But if we had been sold for bondmen and bondwomen, I would have held my tongue, for our affliction is not to be compared with the damage this will do to the king.

5 Then King Ahasuerus said to Queen Esther, Who is he, and where is he who dares presume in his heart to do that?

6 And Esther said, An adversary and an enemy, even this wicked Haman. Then Haman was afraid before the king and queen.

7 And the king arose from the feast in his wrath and went into the palace garden; and Haman stood up to make request for his life to Queen Esther, for he saw that there was evil determined against him by the king.

8 When the king returned out of the palace garden into the place of the drinking of wine, Haman was falling upon the couch where Esther was. Then said the king, Will he even forcibly assault the queen in my presence, in my own palace? As the king spoke the words, [the servants] covered Haman's face.

9 Then said Harbonah, one of the attendants serving the king, Behold, the gallows fifty cubits high, which Haman has made for Mordecai, whose warning saved the king, stands at the house of Haman. And the king said, Hang him on it!

10 So they hanged Haman on the gallows that he had prepared for Mordecai. Then the king's wrath was pacified.

8 ON THAT day King Ahasuerus gave the house of Haman, the Jews' enemy, to Queen Esther. And Mordecai came before the king, for Esther had told what he was to her.

2 And the king took off his [signet] ring, which he had taken from Haman, and gave it to Mordecai. And Esther set Mordecai over the house of Haman.

3 And Esther spoke yet again to the king and fell down at his feet and besought him with tears to avert the evil plot of Haman the Agagite and his scheme that he had devised against the Jews.

4 Then the king held out to Esther the golden scepter. So Esther arose and stood before the king.

life point

Esther had worshipped God by her obedience and willingness to stay in a situation that was unpleasant to her. She was willing to lay aside her plan and accept God's plan, even though she did not understand it for a period of time. Each act of obedience is a type of worship that God does not ignore. When we keep our eyes on God, stand firm in faith, continue to worship, and hold fast a good confession, we will always see the devil's plan for evil in our lives work for our good and to his demise, just as Esther did.

5 And she said, If it pleases the king and if I have found favor in his sight and the thing seems right before the king and I am pleasing in his eyes, let it be written to reverse the letters devised by Haman son of Hammedatha, the Agagite, which he wrote to destroy the Jews who are in all the king's provinces.

6 For how can I endure to see the evil that shall come upon my people? Or how can I endure to see the destruction of my kindred?

7 Then the King Ahasuerus said to Queen Esther and to Mordecai the Jew, Behold, I have given Esther the house of Haman, and him they have hanged upon the gallows because he laid his hand upon the Jews.

8 Write also concerning the Jews as it pleases you in the king's name, and seal it with the king's [signet] ring—for writing which is in the king's name and sealed with the king's ring no man can reverse.

9 Then the king's scribes were called, in the third month, the month of Sivan, on the twenty-third day, and it was written according to all that Mordecai commanded to the Jews, to the chief rulers, and the governors and princes of the provinces from India to Ethiopia, 127 provinces, to every province in its own script and to every people in their own language and to the Jews according to their writing and according to their language.

10 He wrote in the name of King Ahasuerus and sealed it with the king's ring and sent letters by messengers on horseback, riding on swift steeds, mules, and young dromedaries used in the king's service, bred from the [royal] stud.

11 In it the king granted the Jews who were in every city to gather and defend their lives; to destroy, to slay, and to wipe out any armed force that might attack them, their little ones, and women; and to take the enemies' goods for spoil.

12 On one day in all the provinces of King Ahasuerus, the thirteenth day of the twelfth month, the month of Adar,

13 A copy of the writing was to be issued as a decree in every province and as a proclamation to all peoples, and the Jews should be ready on that day to avenge themselves upon their enemies.

14 So the couriers, who were mounted on swift beasts that were used in the king's service, went out, being hurried and urged on by the king's command; and the decree was released in Shushan, the capital.

15 And Mordecai went forth from the presence of the king in royal apparel of blue and white, with a great crown of gold and with a robe of fine linen and purple; and the city of Shushan shouted and rejoiced.

16 The Jews had light [a dawn of new hope] and gladness and joy and honor.

17 And in every province and in every city, wherever the king's command and his decree came, the Jews had gladness and joy, a feast and a holiday. And many from among the peoples of the land [submitted themselves to Jewish rite and] became Jews, for the fear of the Jews had fallen upon them.

9 NOW IN the twelfth month, the month of Adar, on the thirteenth day of Adar when the king's command and his edict were about to be executed, on the [very] day that the enemies of the Jews had planned for a massacre of them, it was turned to the contrary and the Jews had rule over those who hated them.

2 The Jews gathered together in their cities throughout all the provinces of King Ahasuerus to lay hands on such as sought their hurt; and no man could withstand them, for the fear of them had fallen upon all the peoples.

3 And all the princes of the provinces and the chief rulers and the governors and they who attended to the king's business helped the Jews, because the fear of Mordecai had fallen upon them.

4 For Mordecai was great in the king's palace; and his fame went forth throughout all the provinces, for the man Mordecai became more and more powerful.

5 So the Jews smote all their enemies with the sword, slaughtering and destroying them, and did as they chose with those who hated them.

6 In Shushan, the capital itself, the Jews slew and destroyed 500 men.

7 And they killed Parshandatha,

8 Dalphon, Aspatha, Poratha, Adalia,

9 Aridatha, Parmashta, Arisai, Aridai,

10 And Vaizatha, the ten sons of Haman son of Hammedatha, the Jews' enemy; but on the spoil they laid not their hands.

11 On that day the number of those who were slain in Shushan, the capital, was brought before the king.

12 And the king said to Esther the queen, The Jews have slain and destroyed 500 men in Shushan, the capital, and the ten sons of Haman. What then have they done in the rest of the king's provinces! Now what is your petition? It shall be granted to you. Or what is your request further? It shall be done.

13 Then said Esther, If it pleases the king, let it be granted to the Jews which are in Shushan to do tomorrow also according to this day's decree, and let [the dead bodies of] Haman's ten sons be hanged on the gallows. [Esth. 9:10.]

14 And the king commanded it to be done; the decree was given in Shushan, and they hanged [the bodies of] Haman's ten sons.

15 And the Jews that were in Shushan gathered together on the fourteenth day also of the month of Adar and slew 300 men in Shushan, but on the spoil they laid not their hands.

16 And the other Jews who were in the king's provinces gathered to defend their lives and had relief *and* rest from their enemies and slew of them that hated them 75,000; but on the spoil they laid not their hands.

17 This was done on the thirteenth day of the month of Adar, and on the fourteenth day they rested and made it a day of feasting and gladness.

18 But the Jews who were in Shushan [Susa] assembled on the thirteenth day and on the fourteenth, and on the fifteenth day they rested and made it a day of feasting and gladness.

19 Therefore the Jews of the villages, who dwell in the unwalled towns, make the fourteenth day of the month of Adar a day of gladness and feasting, a holiday, and a day for sending choice portions to one another.

20 And Mordecai recorded these things, and he sent letters to all the Jews who were in all the provinces of the King Ahasuerus, both near and far,

21 To command them to keep the fourteenth day of the month of Adar and also the fifteenth, yearly,

22 As the days on which the Jews got rest from their enemies, and as the month which was turned for them from sorrow to gladness and from mourning into a holiday—that they should make them days of feasting and gladness, days of sending choice portions to one another and gifts to the poor.

23 So the Jews undertook to do as they had begun and as Mordecai had written to them—

24 Because Haman son of Hammedatha, the Agagite, the enemy of all the Jews, had plotted against the Jews to destroy them and had cast Pur, that is, the lot, [to find a lucky day] to crush *and* consume and destroy them.

25 But when Esther brought the matter before the king, he commanded in writing that Haman's wicked scheme which he had devised against the Jews should return upon his own head, and that he and his sons should be hanged on the gallows.

life point

Not only did the Lord turn the tables on Haman so that he had to give Mordecai the honor he had planned for himself (see Esther 6:11, 12), He also turned back on Haman the evil plan he had devised for Mordecai (see Esther 9:25). When Haman went to the dinner that Queen Esther gave for the king and for him, she revealed Haman's wicked plot to kill her and her people. As a result, the king had Haman hanged on the same gallows he had built for Mordecai (see Esther 7:9, 10). When we trust God, the evil that is planned against us will come to ruin and God will give us the ultimate victory.

26 Therefore they called these days Purim, after the name Pur [lot]. Therefore, because of all that was in this letter and what they had faced in this matter and what had happened to them,

27 The Jews ordained and took it

upon themselves and their descendants and all who joined them that without fail every year they would keep these two days at the appointed time and as it was written,

28 That these days should be remembered (imprinted on their minds) and kept throughout every generation in every family, province, and city, and that these days of Purim should never cease from among the Jews, nor the commemoration of them cease among their descendants.

29 Then Queen Esther, the daughter of Abihail, with Mordecai the Jew, gave full power [written authority], confirming this second letter about Purim.

30 And letters were sent to all the Jews, to the 127 provinces of the kingdom of Ahasuerus, in words of peace and truth,

31 To confirm that these days of Purim should be observed at their appointed times, as Mordecai the Jew and Queen Esther had commanded [the Jews], and as they had ordained for themselves and for their descendants in the matter of their fasts and their lamenting.

32 And the command of Esther confirmed these observances of Purim, and it was written in the book.

10 KING AHASUERUS laid a tribute (tax) on the land and on the coastlands of the sea.

2 And all the acts of his power and of his might, and the full account of the greatness of Mordecai to which

life point

I wholeheartedly believe that Esther 10:3 is a word in due season for our lives, one that we desperately need right now. Esther and Mordecai did receive honor and position at the end of the story, but first they had to be willing to sacrifice everything to avoid the extinction of their people. They did not seek position for themselves, but unselfishly laid their lives on the line in obedience to God's purpose. They did not give up until their people were saved and the victory was won.

I encourage you to take your position as Mordecai and Esther did. Do not give up. Stand still and trust God. Enter into God's rest. Like Mordecai, seek the welfare of others and speak peace to everyone you meet. Quit worrying and trying to figure out everything that is going on in your life. When you are tempted to waver, take your position and see the salvation God has planned for you.

the king advanced him, are they not written in the Book of the Chronicles of the Kings of Media and Persia?

3 For Mordecai the Jew was next to King Ahasuerus and great among the Jews, and was a favorite with the multitude of his brethren, for he sought the welfare of his people and spoke peace to his whole race.

Job

Author:
Uncertain

Date:
Probably written in the second millennium BC, but put in its present written form around the time of Solomon

Everyday Life Principles:
God does allow people to go through difficulties.

God loves us and helps us in the midst of our suffering.

When we suffer, we must be diligent to keep our faith strong and to maintain a good attitude. Faith in God and a positive attitude not only help us endure suffering, but also lead to restoration.

Simply put, the book of Job is about hard times. It teaches us that God does allow His people to suffer at times, but it also reminds us that God is with us in the midst of our suffering and encourages us to cling to Him through it all, no matter what we face in life.

Job endured almost every kind of loss imaginable—the loss of money, possessions, family, health, and the support of his friends. But he did not lose his hope in God. Even when things became so bad that his wife wanted him to "renounce God and die!" Job called her foolish and responded: "Shall we accept [only] good at the hand of God and shall we not accept [also] misfortune . . . ?" (Job 2:9, 10). Verse 10 continues, "In [spite of] all this, Job did not sin with his lips." He remained faithful to God despite devastating and difficult circumstances. In the end, God rewarded Job's faithfulness and restored double what he had lost. I want to repeat that he received *double* what he had lost.

I hope you will remember the lessons of Job when you face suffering in your life. Remember that God loves you, that your Redeemer lives and is working on your behalf, that nothing can steal God's presence from you, that you may have to close your ears to the skeptics in your life, that your persevering faith will ultimately cause you to triumph, and that God is able to restore far more than you have lost or suffered.

1 THERE WAS a man in the land of Uz whose name was Job; and that man was blameless and upright, and one who [reverently] feared God and abstained from *and* shunned evil [because it was wrong].

2 And there were born to him seven sons and three daughters.

3 He possessed 7,000 sheep, 3,000 camels, 500 yoke of oxen, 500 female donkeys, and a very great body of servants, so that this man was the greatest of all the men of the East.

4 His sons used to go and feast in the house of each on his day (birthday) in turn, and they invited their three sisters to eat and drink with them. [Gen. 21:8; 40:20.]

5 And when the days of their feasting were over, Job sent for them to purify *and* hallow them, and rose up early in the morning and offered burnt offerings according to the number of them all. For Job said, It may be that my sons have sinned and cursed *or* disowned God in their hearts. Thus did Job at all [such] times.

6 Now there was a day when the sons (the angels) of God came to present themselves before the Lord, and Satan (the adversary and accuser) also came among them. [Rev. 12:10.]

7 And the Lord said to Satan, From where did you come? Then Satan answered the Lord, From going to and fro on the earth and from walking up and down on it.

8 And the Lord said to Satan, Have you considered My servant Job, that there is none like him on the earth, a blameless and upright man, one who [reverently] fears God and abstains from *and* shuns evil [because it is wrong]?

9 Then Satan answered the Lord, Does Job [reverently] fear God for nothing?

10 Have You not put a hedge about him and his house and all that he has, on every side? You have conferred prosperity *and* happiness upon him in the work of his hands, and his possessions have increased in the land.

11 But put forth Your hand now and touch all that he has, and he will curse You to Your face.

12 And the Lord said to Satan (the adversary and the accuser), Behold, all that he has is in your power, only upon the man himself put not forth your hand. So Satan went forth from the presence of the Lord.

13 And there was a day when [Job's] sons and his daughters were eating and drinking wine in their eldest brother's house [on his birthday],

14 And there came a messenger to Job and said, The oxen were plowing and the donkeys feeding beside them,

15 And the Sabeans swooped down upon them and took away [the animals]. Indeed, they have slain the servants with the edge of the sword, and I alone have escaped to tell you.

16 While he was yet speaking, there came also another and said, The fire of God (lightning) has fallen from the heavens and has burned up the sheep and the servants and consumed them, and I alone have escaped to tell you.

17 While he was yet speaking, there came also another and said, The Chaldeans divided into three bands and made a raid upon the camels and have taken them away, yes, and have slain the servants with the edge of the sword, and I alone have escaped to tell you.

speak the Word

Help me, God, to be like Job—blameless and upright, fearing You and abstaining from evil.
ADAPTED FROM JOB 1:1

18 While he was yet speaking, there came also another and said, Your sons and your daughters were eating and drinking wine in their eldest brother's house,

19 And behold, there came a great [whirlwind] from the desert, and smote the four corners of the house, and it fell upon the young people and they are dead, and I alone have escaped to tell you.

20 Then Job arose and rent his robe and shaved his head and fell down upon the ground and worshiped

21 And said, Naked (without possessions) came I [into this world] from my mother's womb, and naked (without possessions) shall I depart. The Lord gave and the Lord has taken away; blessed (praised and magnified in worship) be the name of the Lord!

22 In all this Job sinned not nor charged God foolishly.

2 AGAIN THERE was a day when the sons of God [the angels] came to present themselves before the Lord, and Satan (the adversary and the accuser) came also among them to present himself before the Lord.

2 And the Lord said to Satan, From where do you come? And Satan (the adversary and the accuser) answered the Lord, From going to and fro on the earth and from walking up and down on it.

3 And the Lord said to Satan, Have you considered My servant Job, that there is none like him on the earth, a blameless and upright man, one who [reverently] fears God and abstains from and shuns all evil [because it is

wrong]? And still he holds fast his integrity, although you moved Me against him to destroy him without cause.

4 Then Satan answered the Lord, Skin for skin! Yes, all that a man has will he give for his life.

5 But put forth Your hand now, and touch his bone and his flesh, and he will curse *and* renounce You to Your face.

6 And the Lord said to Satan, Behold, he is in your hand; only spare his life.

7 So Satan went forth from the presence of the Lord and smote Job with loathsome *and* painful sores from the sole of his foot to the crown of his head.

8 And he took a piece of broken pottery with which to scrape himself, and he sat [down] among the ashes.

9 Then his wife said to him, Do you still hold fast your blameless uprightness? Renounce God and die!

10 But he said to her, You speak as one of the impious *and* foolish women would speak. What? Shall we accept [only] good at the hand of God and shall we not accept [also] misfortune *and* what is of a bad nature? In [spite of] all this, Job did not sin with his lips.

11 Now when Job's three friends heard of all this evil that was come upon him, they came each one from his own place, Eliphaz the Temanite and Bildad the Shuhite and Zophar the Naamathite; for they had made an appointment together to come to condole with him and to comfort him.

12 And when they looked from afar off and saw him [disfigured] beyond

speak the Word

God, I pray that no matter what I go through, I will not sin or make foolish accusations against You.
ADAPTED FROM JOB 1:22

putting the Word to work

Have you ever struggled to know what to say to someone who is grieving? After seeing Job's profound grief, his friends did not say anything for days, but they did stay with him and share in his grief.

Often the best thing to do for those who are grieving is simply to be present in the midst of their pain and pray for them.

recognition, they lifted up their voices and wept; and each one tore his robe, and they cast dust over their heads toward the heavens.

13 So they sat down with [Job] on the ground for seven days and seven nights, and none spoke a word to him, for they saw that his grief *and* pain were very great.

3 AFTER THIS, Job opened his mouth and cursed his day (birthday).

2 And Job said,

3 Let the day perish wherein I was born, and the night which announced, There is a man-child conceived.

4 Let that day be darkness! May not God above regard it, nor light shine upon it.

5 Let gloom and deep darkness claim it for their own; let a cloud dwell upon it; let all that blackens the day terrify it (the day that I was born).

6 As for that night, let thick darkness seize it; let it not rejoice among the days of the year; let it not come into the number of the months.

7 Yes, let that night be solitary *and* barren; let no joyful voice come into it.

8 Let those curse it who curse the day, who are skilled in rousing up Leviathan.

9 Let the stars of the early dawn of that day be dark; let [the morning] look in vain for the light, nor let it behold the day's dawning,

10 Because it shut not the doors of my mother's womb nor hid sorrow *and* trouble from my eyes.

11 Why was I not stillborn? Why did I not give up the ghost when my mother bore me?

12 Why did the knees receive me? Or why the breasts, that I should suck?

13 For then would I have lain down and been quiet; I would have slept; then would I have been at rest [in death]

14 With kings and counselors of the earth, who built up [now] desolate ruins for themselves,

15 Or with princes who had gold, who filled their houses with silver.

16 Or [why] was I not a miscarriage, hidden *and* put away, as infants who never saw light?

17 There [in death] the wicked cease from troubling, and there the weary are at rest.

18 There the [captive] prisoners rest together; they hear not the taskmaster's voice.

19 The small and the great are there, and the servant is free from his master. [Jer. 20:14-18.]

20 Why is light [of life] given to him who is in misery, and life to the bitter in soul,

21 Who long *and* wait for death, but it comes not, and dig for it more than for hidden treasures,

22 Who rejoice exceedingly and are elated when they find the grave?

23 [Why is the light of day given] to a man whose way is hidden, and whom God has hedged in?

24 For my sighing comes before my food, and my groanings are poured out like water.

25 For the thing which I greatly fear comes upon me, and that of which I am afraid befalls me.

26 I was not *or* am not at ease, nor had I *or* have I rest, nor was I *or* am I quiet, yet trouble came *and* still comes [upon me].

4 THEN ELIPHAZ the Temanite answered and said,
2 If we venture to converse with you, will you be offended? Yet who can restrain himself from speaking?
3 Behold, you have instructed many, and you have strengthened the weak hands.
4 Your words have held firm him who was falling, and you have strengthened the feeble knees.
5 But now it is come upon you, and you faint *and* are grieved; it touches you, and you are troubled *and* dismayed.

6 Is not your [reverent] fear of God your confidence and the integrity *and* uprightness of your ways your hope?
7 Think [earnestly], I beg of you: who, being innocent, ever perished? Or where were those upright *and* in right standing with God cut off?
8 As I myself have seen, those who plow iniquity and sow trouble *and* mischief reap the same.
9 By the breath of God they perish, and by the blast of His anger they are consumed.
10 The roaring of the lion and the voice of the fierce lion, and the teeth of the young lions are broken.

understanding misunderstanding

Job's friend Eliphaz gave him wrong advice because he totally misunderstood Job and the cause of his trouble. There are times when, like Job, we are misunderstood by people we thought would understand and comfort us. Sometimes even the people who are the closest to us do not understand our struggles, our dreams, our personalities, or our callings from God.

Before my ministry became established, I remember when people misunderstood me because I was too serious for them. They did not like the same things I did or do things the way I did. Instead, they would ask me, "Why do you act the way you do?"

I look back now and realize that everything I needed to do the work of Joyce Meyer Ministries was already in me. The personality type and qualities that God wanted me to have were already there. God just had to polish me and get me in good working order.

As God is preparing you for His use, and as you are discovering exactly what He wants you to do, you might also feel strange and out of place. You may feel that you do not fit into the regular regimen of what is going on around you. If you are already feeling strange, you may be tempted to be confused or bothered when people say things such as, "What's wrong with you? Why do you act the way you do?" Part of your training for leadership is realizing that people will misunderstand you. You have to make up your mind that you are going to stand with God and do what He says even if nobody understands you, agrees with you, or supports you.

I believe He wants to do great things through you, so stick with Him even when others do not understand. Most often, people who do not understand you do not mean to hurt you, they simply do not understand.

11 The old *and* strong lion perishes for lack of prey, and the whelps of the lioness are scattered abroad.

12 Now a thing was secretly brought to me, and my ear received a whisper of it.

13 In thoughts from the visions of the night, when deep sleep falls on men,

14 Fear came upon me and trembling, which made all my bones shake.

15 Then a spirit passed before my face; the hair of my flesh stood up!

16 [The spirit] stood still, but I could not discern the appearance of it. A form was before my eyes; there was silence, and then I heard a voice, saying,

17 Can mortal man be just before God, *or* be more right than He is? Can a man be pure before his Maker, *or* be more cleansed than He is? [I John 1:7; Rev. 1:5.]

18 Even in His [heavenly] servants He puts no trust *or* confidence, and His angels He charges with folly *and* error—

19 How much more those who dwell in houses (bodies) of clay, whose foundations are in the dust, who are crushed like the moth.

20 Between morning and evening they are destroyed; without anyone noticing it they perish forever.

21 Is not their tent cord plucked up within them [so that the tent falls]? Do they not die, and that without [acquiring] wisdom?

5 CALL NOW—is there any who will answer you? And to which of the holy [angels] will you turn?

2 For [a]vexation *and* rage kill the foolish man; jealousy *and* indignation slay the simple.

3 I have seen the foolish taking root [and outwardly prospering], but suddenly I saw that his dwelling was cursed [for his doom was certain].

4 His children are far from safety; [involved in their father's ruin] they are crushed in the [court of justice in the city's] gate, and there is no one to deliver them.

5 His harvest the hungry eat and take it even [when it grows] among the thorns; the snare opens for [his] wealth.

6 For affliction comes not forth from the dust, neither does trouble spring forth out of the ground.

7 But man is born to trouble as the sparks *and* the flames fly upward.

8 As for me, I would seek God *and* inquire of *and* require Him, and to God would I commit my cause—

9 Who does great things and unsearchable, marvelous things without number,

10 Who gives rain upon the earth and sends waters upon the fields,

11 So that He sets on high those who are lowly, and those who mourn He lifts to safety.

12 He frustrates the devices of the crafty, so that their hands cannot perform their enterprise *or* anything of [lasting] worth.

13 He catches the [so-called] wise in their own trickiness, and the counsel of the schemers is brought to a quick end. [I Cor. 3:19, 20.]

14 In the daytime they meet in darkness, and at noon they grope as in the night.

15 But [God] saves [the fatherless] from the sword of their mouth, and the needy from the hand of the mighty.

16 So the poor have hope, and iniquity shuts her mouth.

17 Happy *and* fortunate is the man

---

a This was written many centuries ago, but physicians and psychiatrists today are continually emphasizing the importance of recognizing the principle it lays down if one would avoid being among the constantly increasing number of the mentally ill and those killed by avoidable illnesses.

whom God reproves; so do not despise *or* reject the correction of the Almighty [subjecting you to trial and suffering].

18 For He wounds, but He binds up; He smites, but His hands heal.

19 He will rescue you in six troubles; in seven nothing that is evil [for you] will touch you.

20 In famine He will redeem you from death, and in war from the power of the sword.

21 You shall be hidden from the scourge of the tongue, neither shall you be afraid of destruction when it comes.

22 At destruction and famine you shall laugh, neither shall you be afraid of the living creatures of the earth.

23 For you shall be in league with the stones of the field, and the beasts of the field shall be at peace with you.

24 And you shall know that your tent shall be in peace, and you shall visit your fold *and* your dwelling and miss nothing [from them].

life point

Job 5:22 is one of my favorite passages on laughter as an expression of joy. It tells us that we will laugh at destruction and famine, which is what God would do in a similar situation. We see God laughing at His wicked enemies in Psalm 2:4: "He Who sits in the heavens laughs; the Lord has them in derision [and in supreme contempt He mocks them]." If God can laugh at His enemies, we can laugh at ours once in a while. When things come against you, do not be uptight and sensitive—just stay godly while you enjoy a good laugh! You are not laughing about the problem; you are laughing at the fact that it cannot do you any permanent harm because God is on your side.

25 You shall know also that your children shall be many, and your offspring as the grass of the earth.

26 You shall come to your grave in ripe old age, and as a shock of grain goes up [to the threshing floor] in its season.

27 This is what we have searched out; it is true. Hear *and* heed it and know for yourself [for your good].

6 THEN JOB answered,

2 Oh, that my impatience *and* vexation might be [thoroughly] weighed and all my calamity be laid up over against them in the balances, one against the other [to see if my grief is unmanly]!

3 For now it would be heavier than the sand of the sea; therefore my words have been rash *and* wild,

4 [But it is] because the arrows of the Almighty are within me, the poison which my spirit drinks up; the terrors of God set themselves in array against me.

5 Does the wild ass bray when it has grass? Or does the ox low over its fodder?

6 Can that which has no taste to it be eaten without salt? Or is there any flavor in the white of an egg?

7 [These afflictions] my soul refuses to touch! Such things are like diseased food to me [sickening and repugnant]!

8 Oh, that I might have my request, and that God would grant me the thing that I long for!

9 I even wish that it would please God to crush me, that He would let loose His hand and cut me off!

10 Then would I still have consolation—yes, I would leap [for joy] amid unsparing pain [though I shrink from it]—that I have not concealed *or* denied the words of the Holy One!

11 What strength have I left, that I should wait *and* hope? And what is ahead of me, that I should be patient?

12 Is my strength *and* endurance that of stones? Or is my flesh made of bronze?

13 Is it not that I have no help in myself, and that wisdom is quite driven from me?

14 To him who is about to faint *and* despair, kindness is due from his friend, lest he forsake the fear of the Almighty.

15 [You] my brethren have dealt deceitfully as a brook, as the channel of brooks that pass away,

16 Which are black *and* turbid by reason of the ice, *and* in which the snows hides itself;

17 When they get warm, they shrink *and* disappear; when it is hot, they vanish out of their place.

18 The caravans which travel by way of them turn aside; they go into the waste places and perish. [Such is my disappointment in you, the friends I fully trusted.]

19 The caravans of Tema looked [for water], the companies of Sheba waited for them [in vain].

20 They were confounded because they had hoped [to find water]; they came there and were bitterly disappointed.

21 Now to me you are [like a dried-up brook]; you see my dismay *and* terror, and [believing me to be a victim of God's anger] you are afraid [to sympathize with me].

22 Did I ever say, Bring me a gift, or Pay a bribe on my account from your wealth

23 To deliver me from the adversary's hand, or Redeem me from the hand of the oppressors?

24 Teach me, and I will hold my peace; and cause me to understand wherein I have erred.

25 How forcible are words of straightforward speech! But what does your arguing argue *and* prove *or* your reproof reprove?

26 Do you imagine your words to be an argument, but the speeches of one who is desperate to be as wind?

27 Yes, you would cast lots over the fatherless and bargain away your friend.

28 Now be pleased to look upon me, that it may be evident to you if I lie [for surely I would not lie to your face].

29 Return [from your suspicion], I pray you, let there be no injustice; yes, return again [to confidence in me], my vindication is in it.

30 Is there wrong on my tongue? Cannot my taste discern what is destructive?

7 IS THERE not an [appointed] warfare *and* hard labor to man upon earth? And are not his days like the days of a hireling?

2 As a servant earnestly longs for the shade *and* the evening shadows, and as a hireling who looks for the reward of his work,

3 So am I allotted months of futile [suffering], and [long] nights of misery are appointed to me.

4 When I lie down I say, When shall I arise and the night be gone? And I am full of tossing to and fro till the dawning of the day.

5 My flesh is clothed with worms and clods of dust; my skin is broken and has become loathsome, *and* it closes up and breaks out afresh.

6 My days are swifter than a weaver's shuttle, and are spent without hope.

7 Oh, remember that my life is but wind (a puff, a breath, a sob); my eye shall see good no more.

8 The eye of him who sees me shall see me no more; while your eyes are upon me, I shall be gone.

9 As the cloud is consumed and vanishes away, so he who goes down to Sheol (the place of the dead) shall come up no more.

10 He shall return no more to his

house, neither shall his place know him any more.

11 Therefore I will not restrain my mouth; I will speak in the anguish of my spirit, I will complain in the bitterness of my soul [O Lord]!

12 Am I the sea, or the sea monster, that You set a watch over me?

13 When I say, My bed shall comfort me, my couch shall ease my complaint,

14 Then You scare me with dreams and terrify me through visions,

15 So that I would choose strangling *and* death rather than these my bones.

16 I loathe my life; I would not live forever. Let me alone, for my days are a breath (futility).

17 What is man that You should magnify him *and* think him important? And that You should set Your mind upon him? [Ps. 8:4.]

18 And that You should visit him every morning and try him every moment?

19 How long will Your [plaguing] glance not look away from me, nor You let me alone till I swallow my spittle?

20 If I have sinned, what [harm] have I done You, O You Watcher *and* Keeper of men? Why have You set me as a mark for You, so that I am a burden to myself [and You]?

21 And why do You not pardon my transgression and take away my iniquity? For now shall I lie down in the dust; and [even if] You will seek me diligently, [it will be too late, for] I shall not be.

8 THEN ANSWERED Bildad the Shuhite,

2 How long will you say these things [Job]? And how long shall the words of your mouth be as a mighty wind?

3 Does God pervert justice? Or does the Almighty pervert righteousness?

4 If your children have sinned against Him, then He has delivered them into the power of their transgression.

5 If you will seek God diligently and make your supplication to the Almighty,

6 Then, if you are pure and upright, surely He will bestir Himself for you and make your righteous dwelling prosperous again.

7 And though your beginning was small, yet your latter end would greatly increase.

8 For inquire, I pray you, of the former age and apply yourself to that which their fathers have searched out,

9 For we are but of yesterday and know nothing, because our days upon earth are a shadow.

10 Shall not [the forefathers] teach you and tell you and utter words out of their hearts (the deepest part of their nature)?

11 Can the rush *or* papyrus grow up without marsh? Can the flag *or* reed grass grow without water?

12 While it is yet green, in flower, and not cut down, it withers before any other herb [when without water].

13 So are the ways of all who forget God; and the hope of the godless shall perish.

14 For his confidence breaks, and [the object of] his trust is a spider's web.

15 He shall lean upon his house, but it shall not stand; he shall hold fast to it, but it shall not last.

16 He is green before the sun, and his shoots go forth over his garden.

17 [Godless] his roots are wrapped about the [stone] heap, and see their way [promisingly] among the rocks.

18 But if [God] snatches him from his property, [then having passed into the hands of others] it [his property] will forget *and* deny him, [saying,] I have never seen you [before, as if ashamed of him—like his former friends].

19 See, this is the joy of going the

passing the frustration test

I cannot imagine anything more frustrating to Job than suffering as much as he did and never knowing why. We all experience frustration. It usually comes from trying to do something about a situation we cannot do anything about. We get frustrated because it seems things are taking too long, our task is too hard, or no one is willing to help us. We get frustrated because the money we need is not coming in, or the aches, pains, and burdens we have prayed to be removed from us keep going on and on.

I know what frustration is like because I spent a lot of years frustrated. I knew nothing of the grace of God. I have since discovered that when I get frustrated, it is almost always because I am trying to make something happen instead of waiting on the Lord to bring it to pass. My frustration is a sign that I am acting independently.

In order to pass the frustration test, we have to let go and trust God to do what only He can do. We have to let God be God.

Are you frustrated with your spiritual growth? Do you feel that you will never change? Does it seem that the more you pray and seek God, the worse you get? Are you wrestling with some area of your personality that is causing you problems, or are you dealing with some specific bondage in your life? If so, the reason you are getting so frustrated may be that you are trying to change yourself rather than trusting God to change you. The minute you sincerely say, "Lord, I can't do this, so I let it go," you can almost feel the frustration lift right off of you.

God is the only One Who can make things happen for you. He is the only One Who can bring the things you want and desire into your life. He is the only One Who can open doors of ministry for you; trying to knock them down on your own will not do you any good. The more you try to make your own way, the tighter the doors will stay closed. But when you do things God's way, suddenly He can open significant doors for you and do it so quickly that you will be amazed. You can end up running, trying just to keep up with God and all the good opportunities He is giving you. So do not give in to frustration. Wait on God, and you will see awesome results.

way [of the ungodly]! And from the dust others will spring up [to take his place].

20 Behold, as surely as God will never uphold wrongdoers, He will never cast away a blameless man.

21 He will yet fill your mouth with laughter [Job] and your lips with joyful shouting.

22 Those who hate you will be clothed with shame, and the tents of the wicked shall be no more.

9 THEN JOB answered and said,
2 Yes, I know it is true. But how can mortal man be right before God?

3 If one should want to contend with Him, he cannot answer one [of His questions] in a thousand.

4 [God] is wise in heart and mighty in strength; who has [ever] hardened himself against Him and prospered *or* even been safe?
5 [God] Who removes the mountains, and they know it not when He overturns them in His anger;
6 Who shakes the earth out of its place, and the pillars of it tremble;
7 Who commands the sun, and it rises not; Who seals up the stars [from view];
8 Who alone stretches out the heavens and treads upon the waves *and* high places of the sea;
9 Who made [the constellations] the Bear, Orion, and the [loose cluster] Pleiades, and the [vast starry] spaces of the south;
10 Who does great things past finding out, yes, marvelous things without number.
11 Behold, He goes by me, and I see Him not; He passes on also, but I perceive Him not.
12 Behold, He snatches away; who can hinder *or* turn Him back? Who will say to Him, What are You doing?
13 God will not withdraw His anger; the [proud] helpers of Rahab [arrogant monster of the sea] bow under Him.
14 How much less shall I answer Him, choosing out my words to reason with Him
15 Whom, though I were righteous (upright and innocent) yet I could not answer? I must appeal for mercy to my Opponent *and* Judge [for my right].
16 If I called and He answered me, yet would I not believe that He listened to my voice.
17 For He overwhelms *and* breaks me with a tempest and multiplies my wounds without cause.
18 He will not allow me to catch my breath, but fills me with bitterness.
19 If I speak of strength, behold, He is mighty! And if of justice, Who, says He, will summon Me?

20 Though I am innocent *and* in the right, my own mouth would condemn me; though I am blameless, He would prove me perverse.
21 Though I am blameless, I regard not myself; I despise my life.
22 It is all one; therefore I say, God [does not discriminate, but] destroys the blameless and the wicked.
23 When [His] scourge slays suddenly, He mocks at the calamity *and* trial of the innocent.
24 The earth is given into the hands of the wicked; He covers the faces of its judges [so that they are blinded to justice]. If it is not [God], who then is it [responsible for all this inequality]?
25 Now my days are swifter than a runner; they flee away, they see no good.
26 They are passed away like the swift rowboats made of reeds, or like the eagle that swoops down on the prey.
27 If I say, I will forget my complaint, I will put off my sad countenance, and be of good cheer *and* brighten up,
28 I become afraid of all my pains *and* sorrows [yet to come], for I know You will not pronounce me innocent [by removing them].
29 I shall be held guilty *and* be condemned; why then should I labor in vain [to appear innocent]?
30 If I wash myself with snow and cleanse my hands with lye,
31 Yet You will plunge me into the ditch, and my own clothes will abhor me [and refuse to cover so foul a body].
32 For [God] is not a [mere] man, as I am, that I should answer Him, that we should come together in court.
33 There is no umpire between us, who might lay his hand upon us both, [would that there were!] [I Tim. 2:5.]
34 That He might take His rod away from [threatening] me, and that the fear of Him might not terrify me.
35 [Then] would I speak and not fear Him, but I am not so in myself [to

putting the Word to work

In the midst of his trials and difficulties, Job felt as though there was no one to come to his aid or defense (see Job 9:32, 33). Have you ever felt this way? Thankfully, you have an Advocate, Jesus Christ, the one Mediator between God and man. Trust Him to intercede for you.

make me afraid, were only a fair trial given me].

10 I AM weary of my life *and* loathe it! I will give free expression to my complaint; I will speak in the bitterness of my soul.

2 I will say to God, Do not condemn me [do not make me guilty]! Show me why You contend with me.

3 Does it seem good to You that You should oppress, that You should despise *and* reject the work of Your hands, and favor the schemes of the wicked?

4 Have You eyes of flesh? Do You see as man sees?

5 Are Your days as the days of man, are Your years as man's [years],

6 That You inquire after my iniquity and search for my sin—

7 Although You know that I am not wicked *or* guilty and that there is none who can deliver me out of Your hand?

8 Your hands have formed me and made me. Would You turn around and destroy me?

9 Remember [earnestly], I beseech You, that You have fashioned me as clay [out of the same earth material, exquisitely and elaborately]. And will You bring me into dust again?

10 Have You not poured me out like milk and curdled me like cheese?

11 You have clothed me with skin and flesh and have knit me together with bones and sinews.

12 You have granted me life and

favor, and Your providence has preserved my spirit.

13 Yet these [the present evils] have You hid in Your heart [for me since my creation]; I know that this was with You [in Your purpose and thought].

14 If I sin, then You observe me, and You will not acquit me from my iniquity *and* guilt.

15 If I am wicked, woe unto me! And if I am righteous, yet must I not lift up my head, for I am filled with disgrace and the sight of my affliction.

16 If I lift myself up, You hunt me like a lion and again show Yourself [inflicting] marvelous [trials] upon me.

17 You renew Your witnesses against me and increase Your indignation toward me; I am as if attacked by a troop time after time.

18 Why then did You bring me forth out of the womb? Would that I had perished and no eye had seen me!

19 I should have been as though I had not existed; I should have been carried from the womb to the grave.

20 Are not my days few? Cease then and let me alone, that I may take a little comfort *and* cheer up

21 Before I go whence I shall not return, even to the land of darkness and the shadow of death,

22 The land of sunless gloom as intense darkness, [the land] of the shadow of death, without any order, and where the light is as thick darkness.

putting the Word to work

Do trials make you wonder if God really cares about you? Even in the midst of his suffering, Job knew he had to remember that it was God Who gave him life and preserved his spirit (see Job 10:12). Ask God to show you ways that He is caring for you even in the midst of your difficulty, so that you can be strengthened and encouraged.

11

THEN ZOPHAR the Naamathite replied,

2 Should not the multitude of words be answered? And should a man full of talk [and making such great professions] be pronounced free from guilt *or* blame?

3 Should your boastings *and* babble make men keep silent? And when you mock *and* scoff, shall no man make you ashamed?

4 For you have said, My doctrine [that God afflicts the righteous knowingly] is pure, and I am clean in [God's] eyes. [Job 10:7.]

5 But oh, that God would speak, and open His lips against you,

6 And that He would show you the secrets of wisdom! For He is manifold in understanding! Know therefore that God exacts of you less than your guilt *and* iniquity [deserve].

7 Can you find out the deep things of God, or can you by searching find out the limits of the Almighty [explore His depths, ascend to His heights, extend to His breadths, and comprehend His infinite perfection]?

8 His wisdom is as high as the heights of heaven! What can you do? It is deeper than Sheol (the place of the dead)! What can you know?

9 Longer in measure [and scope] is it than the earth, and broader than the sea.

10 If [God] sweeps in and arrests and calls into judgment, who can hinder Him? [If He is against a man, who shall call Him to account for it?]

11 For He recognizes *and* knows hollow, wicked, *and* useless men (men of falsehood); when He sees iniquity, will He not consider it?

12 But a stupid man will get wisdom [only] when a wild donkey's colt is born a man [as when he thinks himself free because he is lifted up in pride].

13 If you set your heart aright and stretch out your hands to [God],

14 If you put sin out of your hand *and* far away from you and let not evil dwell in your tents;

15 Then can you lift up your face to Him without stain [of sin, and unashamed]; yes, you shall be steadfast *and* secure; you shall not fear.

16 For you shall forget your misery; you shall remember it as waters that pass away.

17 And [your] life shall be clearer than the noonday *and* rise above it; though there be darkness, it shall be as the morning.

18 And you shall be secure *and* feel confident because there is hope; yes, you shall search about you, and you shall take your rest in safety.

19 You shall lie down, and none shall make you afraid; yes, many shall sue for your favor.

20 But the eyes of the wicked shall look [for relief] in vain, and they shall not escape [the justice of God]; and their hope shall be to give up the ghost.

12

THEN JOB answered,

2 No doubt you are the [only wise] people [in the world], and wisdom will die with you!

3 But I have understanding as well as you; I am not inferior to you. Who does not know such things as these [of God's wisdom and might]?

4 I am become one who is a laughingstock to his friend; I, one whom God answered when he called upon Him—a just, upright (blameless) man—laughed to scorn!

5 In the thought of him who is at ease there is contempt for misfortune—but it is ready for those whose feet slip.

6 The dwellings of robbers prosper; those who provoke God are [apparently] secure; God supplies them abundantly [who have no god but their own hands and power].

7 For ask now the animals, and they will teach you [that God does not deal

with His creatures according to their character]; ask the birds of the air, and they will tell you;

8 Or speak to the earth [with its other forms of life], and it will teach you; and the fish of the sea will declare [this truth] to you.

9 Who [is so blind as] not to recognize in all these [that good and evil are promiscuously scattered throughout nature and human life] that it is God's hand which does it [and God's way]?

10 In His hand is the life of every living thing and the breath of all mankind.

11 Is it not the task of the ear to discriminate between [wise and unwise] words, just as the mouth distinguishes [between desirable and undesirable] food?

12 With the aged [you say] is wisdom, and with length of days comes understanding.

13 But [only] with [God] are [perfect] wisdom and might; He [alone] has [true] counsel and understanding.

14 Behold, He tears down, and it cannot be built again; He shuts a man in, and none can open.

15 He withholds the waters, and the land dries up; again, He sends forth [rains], and they overwhelm the land *or* transform it.

16 With Him are might and wisdom; the deceived and the deceiver are His [and in His power].

17 He leads [great and scheming] counselors away stripped *and* barefoot and makes the judges fools [in

human estimation, by overthrowing their plans].

18 He looses the fetters [ordered] by kings and has [the] waistcloth [of a slave] bound about their [own] loins.

19 He leads away priests as spoil, and men firmly seated He overturns.

20 He deprives of speech those who are trusted and takes away the discernment *and* discretion of the aged.

21 He pours contempt on princes and loosens the belt of the strong [disabling them, bringing low the pride of the learned].

22 He uncovers deep things out of darkness and brings into light black gloom *and* the shadow of death.

23 He makes nations great, and He destroys them; He enlarges nations [and then straitens and shrinks them again], and leads them [away captive].

24 He takes away understanding from the leaders of the people of the land *and* of the earth, and causes them to wander in a wilderness where there is no path.

25 They grope in the dark without light, and He makes them to stagger *and* wander like a drunken man.

13 [JOB CONTINUED:] Behold, my eye has seen all this, my ear has heard and understood it.

2 What you know, I also know; I am not inferior to you.

3 Surely I wish to speak to the Almighty, and I desire to argue *and* reason my case with God [that He may explain the conflict between what I

speak the Word

Thank You, God, that my life is in Your hand.
ADAPTED FROM JOB **12:10**

God, I declare that wisdom and might are found only in You, and You alone can give me counsel and understanding.
ADAPTED FROM JOB **12:13**

believe of Him and what I see of Him].
4 But you are forgers of lies [you defame my character most untruthfully]; you are all physicians of no value *and* have no remedy to offer.
5 Oh, that you would altogether hold your peace! Then you would evidence your wisdom *and* you might pass for wise men.
6 Hear now my reasoning, and listen to the pleadings of my lips.
7 Will you speak unrighteously for God and talk deceitfully for Him?
8 Will you show partiality to Him [be unjust to me in order to gain favor with Him]? Will you act as special pleaders for God?
9 Would it be profitable for you if He should investigate your tactics [with me]? Or as one deceives *and* mocks a man, do you deceive *and* mock Him?
10 He will surely reprove you if you do secretly show partiality.
11 Shall not His majesty make you afraid, and should not your awe for Him restrain you?
12 Your memorable sayings are proverbs of ashes [valueless]; your defenses are defenses of clay [and will crumble].
13 Hold your peace! Let me alone, so I may speak; and let come on me what may.
14 Why should I take my flesh in my teeth and put my life in my hands [incurring the danger of God's wrath]?
15 [I do it because, though He slay me, yet will I wait for and trust Him and] behold, He will slay me; I have no hope—nevertheless, I will maintain *and* argue my ways before Him *and* even to His face.
16 This will be my salvation, that a

polluted *and* godless man shall not come before Him.
17 Listen diligently to my speech, and let my declaration be in your ears.
18 Behold now, I have prepared my case; I know that I shall be justified *and* vindicated.
19 Who is he who will argue against *and* refute me? For then I would hold my peace and expire.
20 Only [O Lord] grant two conditions to me, and then will I not hide myself from You:
21 Withdraw Your hand and take this bodily suffering far from me; and let not my [reverent] dread of You terrify me.
22 Then [Lord] call and I will answer, or let me speak, and You answer me.
23 How many are my iniquities and sins [that so much sorrow should come to me]? Make me recognize *and* know my transgression and my sin. [Rom. 8:1.]
24 Why do You hide Your face [as if offended] and alienate me as if I were Your enemy?
25 Will You harass *and* frighten a [poor, helpless] leaf driven to and fro, and will You pursue the chaff of the dry stubble?
26 For You write bitter things against me [in Your bill of indictment] and make me inherit *and* be accountable now for the iniquities of my youth.
27 You put my feet also in the stocks and observe critically all my paths; You set a circle *and* limit around the soles of my feet [which I must not overstep].
28 And he wastes away as a rotten thing, like a garment that is moth-eaten.

speak the Word

God, in the midst of suffering that threatens to defeat me, I will trust You and wait for You.
ADAPTED FROM JOB 13:15

14 MAN WHO is born of a woman is of few days and full of trouble.

2 He comes forth like a flower and withers; he flees also like a shadow and continues not.

3 And [Lord] do You open Your eyes upon such a one, and bring me into judgment with You?

4 Who can bring a clean thing out of an unclean? No one! [Isa. 1:18; I John 1:7.]

5 Since a man's days are already determined, and the number of his months is wholly in Your control, and he cannot pass the bounds of his allotted time—

6 [O God] turn from him [and cease to watch him so pitilessly]; let him rest until he has accomplished as does a hireling the appointed time for his day.

7 For there is hope for a tree if it is cut down, that it will sprout again and that the tender shoots of it will not cease. [But there is no such hope for man.]

8 Though its roots grow old in the earth and its stock dies in the ground,

9 Yet through the scent [and breathing] of water [the stump of the tree] will bud and bring forth boughs like a young plant.

10 But [the brave, strong] man must die and lie prostrate; yes, man breathes his last, and where is he?

11 As waters evaporate from the lake, and the river drains and dries up,

12 So man lies down and does not rise [to his former state]. Till the heavens are no more, men will not awake nor be raised [physically] out of their sleep.

13 Oh, that You would hide me in Sheol (the unseen state), that You would conceal me until Your wrath is past, that You would set a definite time and then remember me earnestly [and imprint me on your heart]!

14 If a man dies, shall he live again? All the days of my warfare *and* service I will wait, till my change *and* release

shall come. [John 5:25; 6:40; I Thess. 4:16.]

15 [Then] You would call and I would answer You; You would yearn for [me] the work of Your hands.

16 But now You number each of my steps and take note of my every sin.

17 My transgression is sealed up in a bag, and You glue up my iniquity [to preserve it in full for the day of reckoning].

18 But as a mountain, if it falls, crumbles to nothing, and as the rock is removed out of its place,

19 As waters wear away the stones and as floods wash away the soil of the earth, so You [O Lord] destroy the hope of man.

20 You prevail forever against him, and he passes on; You change his appearance [in death] and send him away [from the presence of the living].

21 His sons come to honor, and he knows it not; they are brought low, and he perceives it not.

22 But his body [lamenting its decay in the grave] shall grieve over him, and his soul shall mourn [over the body of clay which it once enlivened].

15 THEN ELIPHAZ the Temanite answered [Job],

2 Should a wise man utter such windy knowledge [as we have just heard] and fill himself with the east wind [of withering, parching, and violent accusations]?

3 Should he reason with unprofitable talk? Or with speeches with which he can do no good?

4 Indeed, you are doing away with [reverential] fear, and you are hindering *and* diminishing meditation *and* devotion before God.

5 For your iniquity teaches your mouth, and you choose the tongue of the crafty.

6 Your own mouth condemns you, and not I; yes, your own lips testify against you.

7 Are you the first man that was born [the original wise man]? Or were you created before the hills?

8 Were you present to hear the secret counsel of God? And do you limit [the possession of] wisdom to yourself?

9 What do you know that we know not? What do you understand that is not equally clear to us?

10 Among us are both the gray-haired and the aged, older than your father by far.

11 Are God's consolations [as we have interpreted them to you] too trivial for you? Is there any secret thing (any bosom sin) which you have not given up? [Or] were we too gentle [in our first speech] toward you to be effective?

12 Why does your heart carry you away [why allow yourself to be controlled by feeling]? And why do your eyes flash [in anger or contempt],

13 That you turn your spirit against God and let [such] words [as you have spoken] go out of your mouth?

14 What is man, that he could be pure *and* clean? And he who is born of a woman, that he could be right *and* just?

15 Behold, [God] puts no trust in His holy ones [the angels]; indeed, the heavens are not clean in His sight—

16 How much less that which is abominable and corrupt, a man who drinks iniquity like water?

17 I will show you, hear me; and that which I have seen I will relate,

18 What wise men have not hid but have freely communicated; it was told to them by their fathers,

19 Unto whom alone the land was given, and no stranger intruded *or* passed among them [corrupting the truth].

20 The wicked man suffers with [self-inflicted] torment all his days, through all the years that are numbered *and* laid up for him, the oppressor.

21 A [dreadful] sound of terrors is in his ears; in prosperity the destroyer shall come upon him [the dwellings of robbers are not at peace].

22 He believes that he will not return out of darkness, and [because of his guilt] he is waited for by the sword [of God's vengeance].

23 He wanders abroad for food, saying, Where is it? He knows that the day of darkness *and* destruction is already close upon him.

24 Distress and anguish terrify him; [he knows] they shall prevail against him, like a king ready for battle.

25 Because he has stretched out his hand against God and bids defiance *and* behaves himself proudly against the Almighty,

26 Running stubbornly against Him with a thickly ornamented shield;

27 Because he has covered his face with his fat, adding layers of fat on his loins [giving himself up to animal pleasures],

28 And has lived in desolate [God-forsaken] cities and in houses which no man should inhabit, which were destined to become heaps [of ruins];

29 He shall not be rich, neither shall his wealth last, neither shall his produce bend to the earth *nor* his possessions be extended on the earth.

30 He shall not depart out of darkness [and escape from calamity; the wrath of God] shall consume him as flame consumes a dry tree, and by the blast of His mouth he shall be swept away.

31 Let him not deceive himself and trust in vanity (emptiness, falseness, and futility), for these shall be his recompense [for such living].

32 It shall be accomplished *and* paid in full while he still lives, and his branch shall not be green [but shall wither away].

33 He shall fail to bring his grapes to maturity [leaving them to wither unnourished] on the vine and shall cast off blossoms [and fail to bring forth fruit] like the olive tree.

34 For the company of the godless shall be barren, and fire shall consume the tents of bribery (wrong and injustice).

35 They conceive mischief and bring forth iniquity, and their inmost soul hatches deceit.

16 THEN JOB answered, **2** I have heard many such things; wearisome *and* miserable comforters are you all!

3 Will your futile words of wind have no end? Or what makes you so bold to answer [me like this]?

4 I also could speak as you do, if you were in my stead; I could join words together against you and shake my head at you.

5 [But] I would strengthen *and* encourage you with [the words of] my mouth, and the consolation of my lips would soothe your suffering.

6 If I speak [to you miserable comforters], my sorrow is not soothed *or* lessened; and if I refrain [from speaking], in what way am I eased? [I hardly know whether to answer you or be silent.]

7 But now [God] has taken away my strength. You [O Lord] have made desolate all my family *and* associates.

8 You have laid firm hold on me *and* have shriveled me up, which is a witness against me; and my leanness [and wretched state of body] are further evidence [against me]; [they] testify to my face.

9 [[b]My adversary Satan] has torn [me] in his wrath and hated *and* persecuted me; he has gnashed upon me with his teeth; my adversary sharpens his eyes against me.

10 [The forces of evil] have gaped at me with their mouths; they have struck me upon the cheek insolently; they massed themselves together *and* conspired unanimously against me. [Ps. 22:13; 35:21.]

11 God has delivered me to the ungodly (to the evil one) and cast me [headlong] into the hands of the wicked (Satan's host).

12 I was living at ease, but [Satan] crushed me *and* broke me apart; yes, he seized me by the neck and dashed me in pieces; then he set me up for his target.

13 [Satan's] arrows whiz around me. He slashes open my vitals and does not spare; he pours out my gall on the ground.

14 [Satan] stabs me, making breach after breach *and* attacking again and again; he runs at me like a giant *and* irresistible warrior.

15 I have sewed sackcloth over my skin [as a sign of mourning] and have defiled my horn (my insignia of strength) in the dust.

16 My face is red *and* swollen with weeping, and on my eyelids is the shadow of death [my eyes are dimmed],

17 Although there is no guilt *or* violence in my hands and my prayer is pure.

18 O earth, cover not my blood, and let my cry have no resting-place [where it will cease being heard].

19 Even now, behold, my Witness is in heaven, and He who vouches for me is on high. [Rom. 1:9.]

b The next six verses leave the casual reader at a loss to know of whom Job is speaking—of God, of Eliphaz, or of Satan, each of whom has been the choice of various translators and commentators. But careful study of the text itself, particularly the eleventh verse, seems to leave no question that while Job is blaming God for abandoning him to Satanic forces, nevertheless the monstrous, appalling, and disgusting behavior which Job describes is by him being attributed to Satan himself. Verse eleven in any translation seems to reveal what the reader has known all along but which Job only now sees. He still does not understand God's motive, but he is facing the facts as they are: he is at the mercy of Satan! But God's thrilling and rewarding motive is still unknown to him.

20 My friends scorn me, but my eye pours out tears to God.
21 Oh, that there might be one who would plead for a man with God *and* that he would maintain his right with Him, as a son of man pleads with *or* for his neighbor! [I Tim. 2:5.]
22 For when a few years are come, I shall go the way from which I shall not return.

17 MY SPIRIT is broken, my days are spent (snuffed out); the grave is ready for me.
2 Surely there are mockers *and* mockery around me, and my eye dwells on their obstinacy, insults, *and* resistance.
3 Give me a pledge with Yourself [acknowledge my innocence before my death]; who is there that will give security for me?
4 But their hearts [Lord] You have closed to understanding; therefore You will not let them triumph [by giving them a verdict against me].
5 He who denounces his friends [in order to make them] a prey *and* get a share, the eyes of his children shall fail [to find food].
6 But He has made me a byword among the people, and they spit before my face.
7 My eye has grown dim because of grief, and all my members are [wasted away] like a shadow.
8 Upright men shall be astonished *and* appalled at this, and the innocent shall stir himself up against the godless *and* polluted.
9 Yet shall the righteous (those upright and in right standing with God) hold to their ways, and he who has clean hands shall grow stronger and stronger. [Ps. 24:4.]
10 But as for you, come on again, all of you, though I find not a wise man among you.
11 My days are past, my purposes

and plans are frustrated; even the thoughts (desires and possessions) of my heart [are broken off].
12 These [thoughts] extend from the night into the day, [so that] the light is short because of darkness.
13 But if I look to Sheol (the unseen state) as my abode, if I spread my couch in the darkness,
14 If I say to the grave *and* corruption, You are my father, and to the worm [that feeds on decay], You are my mother and my sister [because I will soon be closest to you],
15 Where then is my hope? And if I have hope, who will see [its fulfillment]?
16 [My hope] shall go down to the bars of Sheol (the unseen state) when once there is rest in the dust.

18 THEN BILDAD the Shuhite answered,
2 How long will you lay snares for words *and* have to hunt for your argument? Do some clear thinking, and then we will reply.
3 Why are we counted as beasts [as if we had no sense]? Why are we unclean in your sight?
4 You who tear yourself in your anger, shall the earth be forsaken for you, or the rock be removed out of its place?
5 Yes, the light of the wicked shall be put out, and the flame of his fire shall not shine. [Prov. 13:9; 24:20.]
6 The light shall be dark in his dwelling, and his lamp beside him shall be put out. [Ps. 18:28.]
7 The steps of his strength shall be shortened, and his own counsel *and* the plans in which he trusted shall bring about his downfall.
8 For the wicked is cast into a net by his own feet, and he walks upon a lattice-covered pit.
9 A trap will catch him by the heel, and a snare will lay hold on him.
10 A noose is hidden for him on the

ground and a trap for him in the way.
11 Terrors shall make him afraid on every side and shall chase him at his heels.
12 The strength [of the wicked] shall be hunger-bitten, and calamity is ready at his side [if he halts].
13 By disease his strength *and* his skin shall be devoured; the firstborn of death [the worst of diseases] shall consume his limbs.
14 He shall be rooted out of his dwelling place in which he trusted, and he shall be brought to the king of terrors [death].
15 There shall dwell in his tent that which is none of his [family]; sulphur shall be scattered over his dwelling [to purify it after his going].
16 The roots [of the wicked] shall be dried up beneath, and above shall his branch be cut off *and* wither.
17 His remembrance shall perish from the earth, and he shall have no name in the street.
18 He shall be thrust from light into darkness and driven out of the world.
19 He shall neither have son nor grandson among his people, nor any remaining where he sojourned.
20 They [of the west] that come after [the wicked man] shall be astonished *and* appalled at his day, as they [of the east] that went before were seized with horror.
21 Surely such are the dwellings of the ungodly, and such is the place of him who knows not (recognizes not and honors not) God.

19 THEN JOB answered:
2 How long will you vex *and* torment me and break me in pieces with words?
3 These ten times you have reproached me; you are not ashamed that you make yourselves strange [harden yourselves against me and deal severely with me].
4 And if it were true that I have

erred, my error would remain with me [I would be conscious of it].
5 If indeed you magnify yourselves against me and plead against me my reproach *and* humiliation,
6 Know that God has overthrown *and* put me in the wrong and has closed His net about me.
7 Behold, I cry out, Violence! but I am not heard; I cry aloud for help, but there is no justice.
8 He has walled up my way so that I cannot pass, and He has set darkness upon my paths.
9 He has stripped me of my glory and taken the crown from my head.
10 He has broken me down on every side, and I am gone; my hope has He pulled up like a tree.
11 He has also kindled His wrath against me, and He counts me as one of His adversaries.
12 His troops come together and cast up their way *and* siege works against me and encamp round about my tent.
13 He has put my brethren far from me, and my acquaintances are wholly estranged from me.
14 My kinsfolk have failed me, and my familiar friends have forgotten me.
15 Those who live temporarily in my house and my maids count me as a stranger; I am an alien in their sight.
16 I call to my servant, but he gives me no answer, though I beseech him with words.
17 I am repulsive to my wife and loathsome to the children of my own mother.

putting the Word to work

Are you facing great difficulty and feeling abandoned by all who care for you? Job certainly did. Like Job, realize that your Redeemer lives and that He will never fail you nor forsake you (see Job 19:25). Ask God to surround you with His presence and to give you His peace.

faith over feelings

Job endured many tests and trials, but his patience and faith triumphed in the end, as we will see in chapter 42. God tests us too. One of the ways He does so is by allowing us to go through dry times—times when nothing seems to minister to us or water our souls. We go to church, but we feel no different when we leave. We read the latest book or listen to the latest song, but it does us no good at all.

I have had those times in my life and ministry, and Job certainly had them—in what seems like extreme measure (see Job 19:7–11)! I have gone through mountaintop experiences, and I have been through valleys. I have had dry times in my prayer life and in my praise and worship. I have had times when I would go into a meeting or conference and be able to feel the presence of God, and I have had times when I would go and feel absolutely nothing. I have learned to believe that God is with me whether I feel it or not. There have also been times when I could hear from God so clearly and know that I had heard "a word in season" for me. There have been other times when I have not heard anything at all.

Looking back on my spiritual life, I realize that at times I have gone up and down, up and down. When I was up I felt that I was saved, and when I was down I felt that I was lost. When I felt sure God had called me, I was up, and when I was uncertain of my calling, I was down. When dry times came upon me, I let them affect me. At the time I did not know what was happening to me or why. Now I realize that God was working all the harmful things out of me and getting me to the point where I did not base my faith on my feelings.

I will be honest with you. I rarely go through those times now. I just love God, and that's it. I worship Him, and that's it. I pray, I believe He hears me, and that's it. I know I am called, and I go out and do what I am called to do, and I do not go through all the ups and downs I used to go through. Why? Because I have learned to stop basing everything on my feelings and to live by faith instead. I do not allow my emotions to determine whether I believe God is with me or not. I just choose to believe He is. That does not mean I never experience a rough time or have a bad day, but those times no longer control what I believe.

I do not believe God can allow us to go from one emotional high to another. If He did, we would depend too much on them and would probably start thinking more highly of ourselves than we should. God loves us and protects us from depending on emotions too much so that He can continue to use us.

We must learn to trust that God knows what He is doing in us. If we feel something in our emotions, that is fine. If we do not feel anything, that is fine too. We must remember that we are in this for the long haul—not just for those times when we feel good, but also for those times when we feel bad or do not feel anything at all. Be patient and stay faithful. God will come through for you, and you will be amazed!

18 Even young children despise me; when I get up, they speak against me.
19 All the men of my council *and* my familiar friends abhor me; those whom I loved are turned against me.
20 My bone clings to my skin and to my flesh, and I have escaped with the skin *or* gums of my teeth.
21 Have pity on me! Have pity on me, O you my friends, for the hand of God has touched me!
22 Why do you, as if you were God, pursue *and* persecute me? [Acting like wild beasts] why are you not satisfied with my flesh?
23 Oh, that the words I now speak were written! Oh, that they were inscribed in a book [carved on a tablet of stone]!
24 That with an iron pen and [molten] lead they were graven in the rock forever!
25 For I know that my Redeemer *and* Vindicator lives, and at last He [the Last One] will stand upon the earth. [Isa. 44:6; 48:12.]

life point

God is our Vindicator (see Job 19:25). As long as we behave properly toward others—even when they come against us or do not understand us—God will reward us for being steadfast toward Him.

26 And after my skin, even this body, has been destroyed, then from my flesh *or* without it I shall see God,
27 Whom I, even I, shall see for myself *and* on my side! And my eyes shall behold Him, and not as a stranger! My heart pines away *and* is consumed within me.
28 If you say, How we will pursue him! [and continue to persecute me with the claim] that the root [cause] of all these [afflictions] is found in me,
29 Then beware *and* be afraid of the sword [of divine vengeance], for wrathful are the punishments of that sword, that you may know there is a judgment.

20 THEN ZOPHAR the Naamathite answered,
2 Therefore do my thoughts give me an answer, and I make haste [to offer it] for this reason.
3 I have heard the reproof which puts me to shame, but out of my understanding my spirit answers me.
4 Do you not know from of old, since the time that man was placed on the earth,
5 That the triumphing of the wicked is short, and the joy of the godless *and* defiled is but for a moment? [Ps. 37:35, 36.]
6 Though his [proud] height mounts up to the heavens and his head reaches to the clouds,
7 Yet he will perish forever like his own dung; those who have seen him will say, Where is he?
8 He will fly away like a dream and will not be found; yes, he will be chased away as a vision of the night.
9 The eye which saw him will see him no more, neither will his [accustomed] place any more behold him.
10 The poor will oppress his children, and his hands will give back his [ill-gotten] wealth.
11 His bones are full of youthful energy, but it will lie down with him in the dust.
12 Though wickedness is sweet in his mouth, though he hides it under his tongue,
13 Though he is loath to let it go but keeps it still within his mouth,
14 Yet his food turns [to poison] in his stomach; it is the venom of asps within him.
15 He has swallowed down [his ill-gotten] riches, and he shall vomit them up again; God will cast them out of his belly.

16 He shall suck the poison of asps [which ill-gotten wealth contains]; the viper's tongue shall slay him.

17 He shall not look upon the rivers, the flowing streams of honey and butter [to enjoy his wealth].

18 That which he labored for shall he give back and shall not swallow it down [to enjoy it]; according to his wealth shall the restitution be, and he shall not rejoice in it.

19 For he has oppressed and forsaken the poor; he has violently taken away a house which he did not build.

20 Because his desire *and* greed knew no quietness within him, he will not save anything of that in which he delights.

21 There was nothing left that he did not devour; therefore his prosperity will not endure.

22 In the fullness of his sufficiency [in the time of his great abundance] he shall be poor and in straits; every hand of everyone who is in misery shall come upon him [he is but a wretch on every side].

23 When he is about to fill his belly [as in the wilderness when God sent the quails], God will cast the fierceness of His wrath upon him and will rain it upon him while he is eating. [Num. 11:33; Ps. 78:26-31.]

24 He will flee from the iron weapon, but the bow of bronze shall strike him through.

25 [The arrow] is drawn forth and it comes out after passing through his body; yes, the glittering point comes out of his gall. Terrors march in upon him;

26 Every misfortune is laid up for his treasures. A fire not blown by man shall devour him; it shall consume what is left in his tent [and it shall go ill with him who remains there].

27 The heavens shall reveal his iniquity, and the earth shall rise up against him.

28 The produce *and* increase of his house will go into exile [with the victors], dragged away in the day of [God's] wrath.

29 This is the wicked man's portion from God, and the heritage appointed to him by God.

21 THEN JOB answered,

2 Hear diligently my speech, and let this [your attention] be your consolation [given me].

3 Allow me, and I also will speak; and after I have spoken, mock on.

4 As for me, is my complaint to man *or* of him? And why should I not be impatient *and* my spirit be troubled?

5 Look at me and be astonished (appalled); and lay your hand upon your mouth.

6 Even when I remember, I am troubled *and* afraid; horror *and* trembling take hold of my flesh.

7 Why do the wicked live, become old, and become mighty in power?

8 Their children are established with them in their sight, and their offspring before their eyes.

9 Their houses are safe *and* in peace, without fear; neither is the rod of God upon them.

10 Their bull breeds and fails not; their cows calve and do not miscarry.

11 They send forth their little ones like a flock, and their children skip about.

12 They themselves lift up their voices *and* sing to the tambourine and the lyre and rejoice to the sound of the pipe.

13 They spend their days in prosperity and go down to Sheol (the unseen state) in a moment *and* peacefully.

14 Yet they say to God, Depart from us, for we do not desire the knowledge of Your ways.

15 Who is the Almighty, that we should serve Him? And what profit do we have if we pray to Him? [Exod. 5:2.]

16 But notice, [you say] the

prosperity of the wicked is not in their power; the mystery [of God's dealings] with the ungodly is far from my comprehension.

17 How often [then] is it that the lamp of the wicked is put out? That their calamity comes upon them? That God distributes pains *and* sorrows to them in His anger? [Luke 12:46.]

18 That they are like stubble before the wind and like chaff that the storm steals *and* carries away?

19 You say, God lays up [the punishment of the wicked man's] iniquity for his children. Let Him recompense it to the man himself, that he may know *and* feel it.

20 Let his own eyes see his destruction, and let him drink of the wrath of the Almighty.

21 For what pleasure *or* interest has a man in his house *and* family after he is dead, when the number of his months is cut off?

22 Shall any teach God knowledge, seeing that He judges those who are on high? [Rom. 11:34; I Cor. 2:16.]

23 One dies in his full strength, being wholly at ease and quiet;

24 His pails are full of milk [his veins are filled with nourishment], and the marrow of his bones is fresh *and* moist,

25 Whereas another man dies in bitterness of soul and never tastes of pleasure *or* good fortune.

26 They lie down alike in the dust, and the worm spreads a covering over them.

27 Behold, I know your thoughts *and* plans and the devices with which you would wrong me.

28 For you say, Where is the house of the rich *and* liberal prince [meaning me]? And where is the tent in which the wicked [Job] dwelt?

29 Have you not asked those who travel this way, and do you not accept their testimony *and* evidences—

30 That the evil man is [now] spared in the day of calamity *and* destruction, and they are led forth *and* away on the day of [God's] wrath?

31 But who declares [a man's] way [and rebukes] him to his face? And who pays him back for what he has done?

32 When he is borne to the grave, watch is kept over his tomb.

33 The clods of the valley are sweet to him, and every man shall follow him to a grave, as innumerable people [have gone] before him.

34 How then can you comfort me with empty *and* futile words, since in your replies there lurks falsehood?

22 THEN ELIPHAZ the Temanite answered [Job],

2 Can a man be profitable to God? Surely he that is wise is profitable to himself. [Ps. 16:2; Luke 17:10.]

3 Is it any pleasure *or* advantage to the Almighty that you are righteous (upright and in right standing with Him)? Or is it gain to Him that you make your ways perfect? [Isa. 62:3; Zech. 2:8; Mal. 3:17; Acts 20:28.]

4 Is it for your [reverential] fear of Him that He [thus] reproves you, that He enters with you into judgment?

5 Is not your wickedness great? There is no end to your iniquities.

6 For you have taken pledges of your brother for nothing, and stripped the naked of their clothing.

7 You have not given water to the weary to drink, and you have withheld bread from the hungry. [Matt. 25:42.]

8 But [you, Job] the man with power possessed the land, and the favored *and* accepted man dwelt in it.

9 You have sent widows away empty-handed, and the arms of the fatherless have been broken.

10 Therefore snares are round about you, and sudden fear troubles *and* overwhelms you;

11 Your light is darkened, so that you

cannot see, and a flood of water covers you.

12 Is not God in the height of heaven? And behold the height of the stars, how high they are!

13 Therefore you say, How *and* what does God know [about me]? Can He judge through the thick darkness?

14 Thick clouds are a covering to Him, so that He does not see, and He walks on the vault of the heavens.

15 Will you pay attention *and* keep to the old way that wicked men trod [in Noah's time], [II Pet. 2:5.]

16 Men who were snatched away before their time, whose foundations were poured out like a stream [during the flood]?

17 They said to God, Depart from us, and, What can the Almighty do for *or* to us?

18 Yet He filled their houses with good [things]. But the counsel of the ungodly is far from me.

19 The righteous see it and are glad; and the innocent laugh them to scorn [saying],

20 Surely those who rose up against us are cut off, and that which remained to them the fire has consumed.

21 Acquaint now yourself with Him [agree with God and show yourself to be conformed to His will] and be at peace; by that [you shall prosper and great] good shall come to you.

22 Receive, I pray you, the law *and* instruction from His mouth and lay up His words in your heart. [Ps. 119:11.]

23 If you return to the Almighty [and submit and humble yourself before Him], you will be built up; if you put away unrighteousness far from your tents,

24 If you lay gold in the dust, and the gold of Ophir among the stones of the brook [considering them of little worth],

25 And make the Almighty your gold and [the Lord] your precious silver treasure,

life point

There is a nugget of truth in the midst of the accusations of Job's friend Eliphaz in Job 22:21. It is true that when we are at peace, good comes to us. In fact, nothing is worth anything if we do not have peace.

Money is no good if we do not have peace. Fame is no good if we do not have peace. Having the most important, prestigious job in the whole company is not important if we do not have peace. How many people will spend their lives trying to climb the ladder of success, and every time they go up one more rung they lose more of their peace because of the pressure? They also lose more of their time to spend with their families. Everything about their lives is consumed with the stress of trying to play all the games to keep that job. They may have great positions, but they have to worry about keeping them all the time. Soon, their health is falling apart, and they do not have any peace of mind. Without peace, our lives are full of confusion and chaos, but when we are at peace, we have a good thing indeed!

26 Then you will have delight in the Almighty, and you will lift up your face to God.

27 You will make your prayer to Him, and He will hear you, and you will pay your vows.

28 You shall also decide *and* decree a thing, and it shall be established for you; and the light [of God's favor] shall shine upon your ways.

29 When they make [you] low, you will say, [There is] a lifting up; and the humble person He lifts up *and* saves.

30 He will even deliver the one [for whom you intercede] who is not innocent; yes, he will be delivered through the cleanness of your hands. [Job 42:7, 8.]

23

THEN JOB answered,
2   Even today is my complaint rebellious *and* bitter; my stroke is heavier than my groaning.

3   Oh, that I knew where I might find Him, that I might come even to His seat!

4   I would lay my cause before Him and fill my mouth with arguments.

5   I would learn what He would answer me, and understand what He would say to me.

6   Would He plead against me with His great power? No, He would give heed to me. [Isa. 27:4, 5; 57:16.]

7   There the righteous [one who is upright and in right standing with God] could reason with Him; so I should be acquitted by my Judge forever.

8   Behold, I go forward [and to the east], but He is not there; I go backward [and to the west], but I cannot perceive Him;

9   On the left hand [and to the north] where He works [I seek Him], but I cannot behold Him; He turns Himself to the right hand [and to the south], but I cannot see Him.

10 But He knows the way that I take [He has concern for it, appreciates, and pays attention to it]. When He has tried me, I shall come forth as refined gold [pure and luminous]. [Ps. 17:3; 66:10; James 1:12.]

11 My foot has held fast to His steps; His ways have I kept and not turned aside.

12 I have not gone back from the commandment of His lips; I have esteemed

and treasured the words of His mouth more than my necessary food.

13 But He is unchangeable, and who can turn Him? And what He wants to do, that He does.

14 For He performs [that which He has] planned for me, and of many such matters He is mindful.

15 Therefore am I troubled *and* terrified at His presence; when I consider, I am in dread *and* afraid of Him.

16 For God has made my heart faint, timid, *and* broken, and the Almighty has terrified me,

17 Because I was not cut off before the darkness [of these woes befell me], neither has He covered the thick darkness from my face.

24

WHY [seeing times are not hidden from the Almighty] does He not set seasons for judgment? Why do those who know Him see not His days [for punishment of the wicked]? [Acts 1:7.]

2   Some remove the landmarks; they violently take away flocks and pasture them [appropriating land and flocks openly].

3   They drive away the donkey of the fatherless; they take the widow's ox for a pledge.

4   They crowd the poor *and* needy off the road; the poor *and* meek of the earth all hide themselves.

5   Behold, as wild asses in the desert, [the poor] go forth to their work, seeking diligently for prey *and* food; the wilderness yields them bread for their children [in roots and herbage].

6   They reap each one his fodder in a field [that is not his own], and

speak the Word

trained to trust

One of the tests we can expect to encounter in our journey with God is the trust test. Like Job, we must learn to trust God when we do not understand what is going on in our lives (see Job 23:10).

How many times do we say to God, "What are You doing? What is happening? What is going on in my life? I don't understand this at all." At this point, many people get confused and give up or fail. They fall by the wayside and go back to something that will be quicker and easier for them.

If you are in a place right now where nothing in your life makes any sense, trust God anyway. Say to yourself, "This must be a test."

One of the things I have learned through the years is this: *There is no such thing as trusting God without unanswered questions.* If we have all the answers to all the questions, we have no need to trust because we already know everything.

As long as God is training us to trust, there are always going to be things in our lives we simply do not understand. That is why we have to learn to say, "God, I don't understand, but I trust You."

Sometimes I start to get frustrated and feel like saying, "Tell me something, Lord." But I have learned that if He does not tell me anything, I need to stay busy doing the last thing He told me to do, whatever it was, and just keep trusting Him. It may be five years before He gives me another direction. If He speaks something different to me, then I will do it. But until He does, I will just go on doing what He has already told me to do.

Without trusting God, our lives are miserable. So we, like Job, must learn to trust God when we do not understand and when heaven is silent.

they glean the vintage of the wicked man.

7 They lie all night naked, without clothing, and have no covering in the cold.

8 They are wet with the showers of the mountains and cling to the rock for want of shelter.

9 [The violent men whose wickedness seems unnoticed] pluck the fatherless infants from the breast [to sell or make them slaves], and take [the clothing on] the poor for a pledge,

10 So that the needy go about naked for lack of clothing, and though hungry, they must carry [but not eat from] the sheaves.

11 Among the olive rows [of the wicked, the poor] make oil; they tread [the fresh juice of the grape from] the presses, but suffer thirst.

12 From out of the populous city men groan, and the very life of the wounded cries for help; yet God [seemingly] regards not the wrong done them.

13 These wrongdoers are of those

who rebel against the light; they know not its ways nor stay in its paths.

14 The murderer rises with the light; he kills the poor and the needy, and in the night he becomes as a thief.

15 The eye also of the adulterer waits for the twilight, saying, No eye shall see me, and he puts a disguise upon his face.

16 In the dark, they dig through [the penetrable walls of] houses; by day they shut themselves up; they do not know the sunlight.

17 For midnight is morning to all of them; for they are familiar with the terrors of deep darkness.

18 [You say] Swiftly such men pass away on the face of the waters; their portion is cursed in the earth; [no treader] turns into their vineyards.

19 Drought and heat consume the snow waters; so does Sheol (the place of the dead) those who have sinned.

20 The womb shall forget him, the worm shall feed sweetly on him; he shall be no more remembered, and unrighteousness shall be broken like a tree [which cannot be healed]. [Prov. 10:7.]

21 [The evil man] preys upon the barren, childless woman and does no good to the widow.

22 Yet [God] prolongs the life of the [wicked] mighty by His power; they rise up when they had despaired of life.

23 God gives them security, and they rest on it; and His eyes are upon their ways.

24 They are exalted for a little while, and then are gone and brought low; they are taken out of the way as all others are and are cut off as the tops of the ears of grain.

25 And if this is not so, who will prove me a liar and make my speech worthless?

25 THEN BILDAD the Shuhite answered,

2 Dominion and fear are with [God]; He makes peace in His high places.

3 Is there any number to His armies? And upon whom does not His light arise?

4 How then can man be justified *and* righteous before God? Or how can he who is born of a woman be pure *and* clean? [Ps. 130:3; 143:2.]

5 Behold, even the moon has no brightness [compared to God's glory] and the stars are not pure in His sight—

6 How much less man, who is a maggot! And a son of man, who is a worm!

26 BUT JOB answered,

2 How you have helped him who is without power! How you have sustained the arm that is without strength!

3 How you have counseled him who has no wisdom! And how plentifully you have declared to him sound knowledge!

4 With whose assistance have you uttered these words? And whose spirit [inspired what] came forth from you?

5 The shades of the dead tremble underneath the waters and their inhabitants.

6 Sheol (the place of the dead) is naked before God, and Abaddon (the place of destruction) has no covering [from His eyes].

7 He it is Who spreads out the northern skies over emptiness and ᶜhangs the earth upon *or* over nothing.

---

c For millenniums, various theories of what supports the earth—elephants, giants, and other fantastic means—were accepted by mankind as truth. The Bible made no such absurd error. How could Job, more than 3,000 years ago, possibly have known that God "hangs the earth upon *or* over nothing," except by divine inspiration?

8 He holds the waters bound in His clouds [which otherwise would spill on earth all at once], and the cloud is not rent under them.

9 He covers the face of His throne and spreads over it His cloud.

10 He has placed an enclosing limit [the horizon] upon the waters at the boundary between light and darkness.

11 The pillars of the heavens tremble and are astonished at His rebuke.

12 He stills *or* stirs up the sea by His power, and by His understanding He smites proud Rahab.

13 By His breath the heavens are garnished; His hand pierced the [swiftly] fleeing serpent. [Ps. 33:6.]

14 Yet these are but [a small part of His doings] the outskirts of His ways *or* the mere fringes of His force, the faintest whisper of His voice! Who dares contemplate *or* who can understand the thunders of His full, magnificent power?

putting the Word to work

Do your troubles ever seem so great that you doubt God's power to act on your behalf? In the midst of his trials, Job recalled the greatness of God and recognized that he saw only the "outskirts of His ways" (Job 26:14). Be encouraged by the knowledge that the same God Who is powerful enough to "hang the earth on nothing" (see Job 26:7) has promised to act on your behalf!

27 JOB AGAIN took up his discourse and said,
2 As God lives, Who has taken away my right *and* denied me justice, and the Almighty, Who has vexed *and* embittered my life,
3 As long as my life is still whole within me, and the breath of God is [yet] in my nostrils,

4 My lips shall not speak untruth, nor shall my tongue utter deceit.

5 God forbid that I should justify you—saying you are right [in your accusations against me]; till I die, I will not put away my integrity from me.

6 My uprightness *and* my right standing with God I hold fast and will not let them go; my heart does not reproach me for any of my days *and* it shall not reproach me as long as I live.

7 Let my enemy be as the wicked, and let him who rises up against me be as the unrighteous.

8 For what is the hope of the godless *and* polluted, even though he has gained [in this world], when God cuts him off *and* takes away his life?

9 Will God hear his cry when trouble comes upon him?

10 Will he take delight in the Almighty? Will he call upon God at all times?

11 I will teach you regarding the hand *and* handiwork of God; that which is with the Almighty [God's actual treatment of the wicked man] will I not conceal.

12 Behold, all of you have seen it yourselves; why then have you become altogether vain [cherishing foolish notions]?

13 This [which I am about to tell] is the portion of a wicked man with God, and the heritage which oppressors shall receive from the Almighty:

14 If his children are multiplied, it is for the sword; and his offspring will not have sufficient bread.

15 Those who survive him, [the pestilence] will bury, and [their] widows will make no lamentation.

16 Though he heaps up silver like dust and piles up clothing like clay,

17 He may prepare it, but the just will wear it, and the innocent will divide the silver.

18 He builds his house like a moth *or* a spider, like a booth which a watchman makes [to last for a season].

19 [The wicked] will lie down rich, but does it not again; he opens his eyes, and [his wealth] is gone.
20 Terrors overtake him like a [suddenly loosened] flood; a windstorm steals him away in the night.
21 The east wind lifts him up, and he is gone; it sweeps him out of his place.
22 For [God and the storm] hurl at him without pity *and* unsparingly [their thunderbolts of wrath]; he flees in haste before His power.
23 [God causes] men to clap their hands at him [in malignant joy] and hiss him out of his place.

28 SURELY THERE is a mine for silver, and a place for gold where they refine it.
2 Iron is taken out of the earth, and copper is smelted from the stone ore.
3 Man sets an end to darkness, and he searches out the farthest bounds for the ore buried in gloom and deep darkness.
4 Men break open shafts away from where people sojourn, in places forgotten by [human] foot; and [descend into them], hanging afar from men, they swing *or* flit to and fro.
5 As for the earth, out of it comes bread, but underneath [its surface, down deep in the mine] there is dblasting, turning it up as by fire.
6 Its stones are the bed of sapphires; it holds dust of gold [which he wins].
7 That path no bird of prey knows, and the falcon's eye has not seen it.
8 The proud beasts [and their young] have not trodden it, nor has the fierce lion passed over it.
9 Man puts forth his hand upon the flinty rock; he overturns the mountains by the roots.
10 He cuts out channels *and* passages among the rocks; and his eye sees every precious thing.
11 [Man] binds the streams so that they do not trickle [into the mine], and the thing that is hidden he brings forth to light.
12 But where shall eWisdom be found? And where is the place of understanding?
13 Man knows not the price of it; neither is it found in the land of the living.
14 The deep says, [Wisdom] is not in me; and the sea says, It is not with me.
15 It cannot be gotten for gold, neither shall silver be weighed for the price of it.
16 It cannot be valued in [terms of] the gold of Ophir, in the precious onyx *or* beryl, or the sapphire.
17 Gold and glass cannot equal [Wisdom], nor can it be exchanged for jewels *or* vessels of fine gold.
18 No mention shall be made of coral or of crystal; for the possession of Wisdom is even above rubies *or* pearls.
19 The topaz of Ethiopia cannot compare with it, nor can it be valued in pure gold.
20 From where then does Wisdom come? And where is the place of understanding?
21 It is hidden from the eyes of all living, and knowledge of it is withheld from the birds of the heavens.
22 Abaddon (the place of destruction)

putting the Word to work

Where do you seek wisdom? Do you understand its value? Job knew that the value of wisdom is far beyond any wealth, and that wisdom is found in fearing the Lord (see Job 28:12–28). Ask the Lord to teach you what it means to fear Him and to help you grow in wisdom.

d Blasting of rocks is said to have been practiced on a large scale by the ancients (*Speaker's Commentary*).   **e** Wisdom is capitalized as a reminder of its divine implications. Note that the pronouns referring to wisdom are not capitalized. See footnote on Prov. 1:23.

and Death say, We have [only] heard the report of it with our ears.

23 God understands the way [to Wisdom] and He knows the place of it [Wisdom is with God alone].

24 For He looks to the ends of the earth and sees everything under the heavens.

25 When He gave to the wind weight *or* pressure and allotted the waters by measure,

26 When He made a decree for the rain and a way for the lightning of the thunder,

27 Then He saw [Wisdom] and declared it; He established it, yes, and searched it out [for His own use, and He alone possesses it].

28 But to man He said, Behold, the reverential *and* worshipful fear of the Lord—that is Wisdom; and to depart from evil is understanding.

29 AND JOB again took up his discussion and said,

2 Oh, that I were as in the months of old, as in the days when God watched over me, [Eccl. 7:10.]

3 When His lamp shone above *and* upon my head and by His light I walked through darkness;

4 As I was in the [prime] ripeness of my days, when the friendship *and* counsel of God were over my tent,

5 When the Almighty was yet with me and my children were about me,

6 When my steps [through rich pasturage] were washed with butter and the rock poured out for me streams of oil!

7 When I went out to the gate of the city, when I prepared my seat in the street [the broad place for the council at the city's gate],

8 The young men saw me and hid themselves; the aged rose up *and* stood;

9 The princes refrained from talking and laid their hands on their mouths;

10 The voices of the nobles were hushed, and their tongues cleaved to the roof of their mouths.

11 For when the ear heard, it called me happy *and* blessed me; and when the eye saw, it testified for me [approvingly],

12 Because I delivered the poor who cried, the fatherless and him who had none to help him.

13 The blessing of him who was about to perish came upon me, and I caused the widow's heart to sing for joy.

14 I put on ʳrighteousness, and it clothed me *or* clothed itself with me; my justice was like a robe and a turban *or* a diadem *or* a crown!

15 I was eyes to the blind, and feet was I to the lame.

16 I was a father to the poor *and* needy; the cause of him I did not know I searched out.

17 And I broke the jaws *or* the big teeth of the unrighteous and plucked the prey out of his teeth.

18 Then I said, I shall die in *or* beside my nest, and I shall multiply my days as the sand.

19 My root is spread out *and* open to

putting the Word to work

Do you ever struggle with the temptation to boast or brag? Ask the Lord for humility, so that you will not have to learn, as Job did, that those who exalt themselves will be humbled.

f Blameless and upright as Job had been—and God had so pronounced him—his misunderstood afflictions had caused him to get dangerously off-center. Instead of keeping his mind stayed on God and justifying Him, he is giving his whole thought to justifying himself. Instead of humility there is only self-righteousness. In this chapter he uses pronouns referring to himself fifty times. But when he was able to see himself as God saw him, he loathed himself and repented "in dust and ashes" (Job 42:6).

the waters, and the dew lies all night upon my branch.

20 My glory *and* honor are fresh in me [being constantly renewed], and my bow gains [ever] new strength in my hand.

21 Men listened to me and waited and kept silence for my counsel.

22 After I spoke, they did not speak again, and my speech dropped upon them [like a refreshing shower].

23 And they waited for me as for the rain, and they opened their mouths wide as for the spring rain.

24 I smiled on them when they had no confidence, and their depression did not cast down the light of my countenance.

25 I chose their way [for them] and sat as [their] chief, and dwelt like a king among his soldiers, like one who comforts mourners.

30 BUT NOW they who are younger than I have me in derision, whose fathers I disdained to set with the dogs of my flock.

2 Yes, how could the strength of their hands profit me? They were men whose ripe age *and* vigor had perished.

3 They are gaunt with want and famine; they gnaw the dry *and* barren ground *or* flee into the wilderness, into the gloom of wasteness and desolation.

4 They pluck saltwort *or* mallows among the bushes, and roots of the broom for their food *or* to warm them.

5 They are driven from among men, who shout after them as after a thief.

6 They must dwell in the clefts of frightful valleys (gullies made by torrents) and in holes of the earth and of the rocks.

7 Among the bushes they bray *and* howl [like wild animals]; beneath the prickly scrub they fling themselves *and* huddle together.

8 Sons of the worthless and name-

less, they have been scourged *and* crushed out of the land.

9 And now I have become their song; yes, I am a byword to them.

10 They abhor me, they stand aloof from me, and do not refrain from spitting in my face *or* at the sight of me.

11 For God has loosed my bowstring and afflicted *and* humbled me; they have cast off the bridle [of restraint] before me.

12 On my right hand rises the rabble brood; they jostle me *and* push away my feet, and they cast up against me their ways of destruction [like an advancing army].

13 They break up *and* clutter my path [embarrassing my plans]; they urge on my calamity, even though they have no helper [and are themselves helpless].

14 As through a wide breach they come in; amid the crash [of falling walls] they roll themselves upon me.

15 Terrors are turned upon me; my honor *and* reputation they chase away like the wind, and my welfare has passed away as a cloud.

16 And now my life is poured out within me; the days of affliction have gripped me.

17 My bones are pierced [with aching] in the night season, and the pains that gnaw me take no rest.

18 By the great force [of my disease] my garment is disguised *and* disfigured; it binds me about like the collar of my coat.

19 [God] has cast me into the mire, and I have become like dust and ashes.

20 I cry to You, [Lord,] and You do not answer me; I stand up, but You [only] gaze [indifferently] at me.

21 You have become harsh *and* cruel to me; with the might of Your hand You [keep me alive only to] persecute me.

22 You lift me up on the wind; You cause me to ride upon it, and You toss me about in the tempest.

23 For I know that You will bring me to death and to the house [of meeting] appointed for all the living.

24 However, does not one falling in a heap of ruins stretch out his hand? Or in his calamity will he not therefore cry for help?

25 Did not I weep for him who was in trouble? Was not my heart grieved for the poor *and* needy?

26 But when I looked for good, then evil came to me; and when I waited for light, there came darkness.

27 My heart is troubled and does not rest; days of affliction come to meet me.

28 I go about blackened, but not by the sun; I stand up in the congregation and cry for help.

29 I am a brother to jackals [which howl], and a companion to ostriches [which scream dismally].

30 My skin falls from me in blackened flakes, and my bones are burned with heat.

31 Therefore my lyre is turned to mourning, and my pipe into the voice of those who weep.

31 I DICTATED a covenant (an agreement) to my eyes; how then could I look [lustfully] upon a girl?

2 For what portion should I have from God above [if I were lewd], and what heritage from the Almighty on high?

3 Does not calamity [justly] befall the unrighteous, and disaster the workers of iniquity?

4 Does not [God] see my ways and count all my steps?

5 If I have walked with falsehood *or* vanity, or if my foot has hastened to deceit—

6 Oh, let me be weighed in a just balance *and* let Him weigh me, that God may know my integrity!

7 If my step has turned out of [God's] way, and my heart has gone

the way my eyes [covetously] invited, and if any spot has stained my hands with guilt,

8 Then let me sow and let another eat; yes, let the produce of my field *or* my offspring be rooted out.

9 If my heart has been deceived *and* I made a fool by a woman, or if I have [covetously] laid wait at my neighbor's door [until his departure],

10 Then let my wife grind [meal, like a bondslave] for another, and let others bow down upon her.

11 For [adultery] is a heinous *and* chief crime, an iniquity [to demand action by] the judges *and* punishment. [Deut. 22:22; John 8:5.]

12 For [uncontrolled passion] is a fire which consumes to Abaddon (to destruction, ruin, and the place of final torment); [that fire once lighted would rage until all is consumed] and would burn to the root all my [life's] increase.

13 If I have despised *and* rejected the cause of my manservant or my maidservant when they contended *or* brought a complaint against me,

14 What then shall I do when God rises up [to judge]? When He visits [to inquire of me], what shall I answer Him? [Ps. 44:21.]

15 Did not He Who made me in the womb make [my servant]? And did not One fashion us both in the womb? [Prov. 14:31; 22:2; Mal. 2:10.]

16 If I have withheld from the poor *and* needy what they desired, or have caused the eyes of the widow to look in vain [for relief],

17 Or have eaten my morsel alone and have not shared it with the fatherless—

18 No, but from my youth [the fatherless] grew up with me as a father, and I have been [the widow's] guide from my mother's womb—

19 If I have seen anyone perish for want of clothing, or any poor person without covering,

20 If his loins have not blessed me [for clothing them], and if he was not warmed with the fleece of my sheep,
21 If I have lifted my hand against the fatherless when I saw [that the judges would be favorable and be] my help at the [council] gate,
22 Then let my shoulder fall away from my shoulder blade, and my arm be broken from its socket.
23 For calamity from God was a terror to me, and because of His majesty I could not endure [to face Him] *and* could do nothing. [Isa. 13:6; Joel 1:15.]
24 If I have made gold my trust *and* hope or have said to fine gold, You are my confidence,
25 If I rejoiced because my wealth was great and because my [powerful] hand [alone] had gotten much,
26 If I beheld [as an object of worship] the sunlight when it shone or the moon walking in its brightness,
27 And my heart has been secretly enticed by them or my mouth has kissed my hand [in homage to them],
28 This also would have been [a heinous and principal] iniquity to demand the judges' action *and* punishment, for I would have denied *and* been false to the God Who is above. [Deut. 4:19; 17:2-7.]

29 If I rejoiced at the destruction of him who hated me or lifted myself up [in malicious triumph] when evil overtook him—
30 No, I have let my mouth sin nei-ther by cursing my enemy nor by praying that he might die—
31 [Just ask] if the men of my tent will not say, Who can find one in need who has not been satisfied with food he gave them?—
32 The temporary resident has not lodged in the street, but I have opened my door to the wayfaring man—
33 If like Adam *or* like [other] men I have concealed my transgressions, by hiding my iniquity in my bosom
34 Because I feared the great multitude and the contempt of families terrified me so that I kept silence and did not go out of the door—
35 Oh, for a hearing! Oh, for an answer from the Almighty! Let my adversary write out His indictment [and put His vague accusations in tangible form] in a book!
36 Surely I would [proudly] bear it on my shoulder and wind the scroll about my head as a diadem.
37 I would count out to Him the number of my steps [with every detail of my life], approaching His presence as a prince—
38 For if my land has cried out against me and its furrows have complained together with tears [that I have no right to them],
39 If I have eaten its fruits without paying for them or have caused its [rightful] owners to breathe their last,
40 Let thistles grow instead of wheat and cockleburs instead of barley. The [controversial] words of Job [with his friends] are ended.

32 SO THESE three men ceased to answer Job, because he was [rigidly] righteous (upright and in right standing with God) in his own eyes. [But there was a fifth man there also.]
2 Elihu son of Barachel the Buzite, of the family of Ram, became indignant. His indignation was

kindled against Job because he justified himself rather than God [even made himself out to be better than God].

3 Also against [Job's] three friends was [Elihu's] anger kindled, because they had found no answer [were unable to show his real error], and yet they had declared him to be in the wrong [and responsible for his own afflictions].

4 Now Elihu had waited to speak to Job because the others were older than he.

5 But when Elihu saw that there was no answer in the mouths of these three men, he became angry.

6 Then Elihu son of Barachel the Buzite said, I am young, and you are aged; for that reason I was timid *and* restrained and dared not declare my opinion to you.

7 I said, Age should speak, and a multitude of years should teach wisdom [so let it be heard].

8 But there is [a vital force] a spirit [of intelligence] in man, and the breath of the Almighty gives men understanding. [Prov. 2:6.]

9 It is not the great [necessarily] who are wise, nor [always] the aged who understand justice.

10 So I say, Listen to me; I also will give you my opinion [about Job's situation] *and* my knowledge.

putting the Word to work

Perhaps you have heard the saying "With age comes wisdom." In some cases this is true, but not always. Have you ever dismissed someone's counsel because he or she didn't seem to be old enough or at the proper stage of life to know what he or she was talking about? It is important to recognize, as Job's friend Elihu did, that it is the Spirit of the Lord Who gives people understanding and wisdom (see Job 32:8).

11 You see, I waited for your words, I listened to your wise reasons, while you searched out what to say.

12 Yes, I paid attention to what you said, and behold, not one of you convinced Job or made [satisfactory] replies to his words [you could not refute him].

13 Beware lest you say, We have found wisdom; God thrusts [Job] down [justly], not man [God alone is dealing with him].

14 Now [Job] has not directed his words against me [therefore I have no cause for irritation], neither will I answer him with speeches like yours. [I speak for truth, not for revenge.]

15 [Job's friends] are amazed *and* embarrassed, they answer no more; they have not a thing to say [reports Elihu].

16 And shall I wait, because they say nothing but stand still and answer no more?

17 I also will answer my [God-assigned] part; I also will declare my opinion *and* my knowledge.

life point

In Job 32:17–20, Job said that he was full of words to the point of feeling as though he would burst. But, he said, "the spirit within me constrains me" (Job 32:18). In the midst of everything he was going through, Job still exercised self-control. When you find yourself so hurt, angry, or stressed that you feel you could burst, be like Job and exercise self-control!

18 For I am full of words; the spirit within me constrains me.

19 My breast is as wine that has no vent; like new wineskins, it is ready to burst.

20 I must speak, that I may get relief *and* be refreshed; I will open my lips and answer.

21 I will not [I warn you] be influenced by respect for any man's person *and* show partiality, neither will I flatter any man.

22 For I know not how to flatter, [wasting my time in mere formalities, for then] my Maker would soon take me away.

33 BE THAT as it may, Job, I beg of you to hear what I have to say and give heed to all my words.

2 Behold, here I am with open mouth; here is my tongue talking.

3 My words shall express the uprightness of my heart, and my lips shall speak what they know with utter sincerity.

4 [It is] the Spirit of God that made me [which has stirred me up], and the breath of the Almighty that gives me life [which inspires me].

5 Answer me now, if you can; set your words in order before me; take your stand.

6 Behold, I am toward God *and* before Him even as you are; I also am formed out of the clay [though I speak with abnormal wisdom because of a divine illumination].

7 See my terror [for I am only a fellow mortal, not God]; I shall not make you afraid, neither shall my pressure be heavy upon you.

8 Surely you have spoken in my hearing, and I have heard the voice of your words, saying,

9 I am clean, without transgression; I am innocent, neither is there iniquity in me.

10 But behold, God finds occasions against me *and* causes of alienation *and* indifference; He counts me as His enemy.

11 He puts my feet in the stocks; He [untrustingly] watches all my paths [you say].

12 I reply to you, Behold, in this you are not just; God is superior to man.

13 Why do you contend against Him? For He does not give account of any of His actions. [Sufficient for us it should be to know that it is He Who does them.]

14 For God [does reveal His will; He] speaks not only once, but more than once, even though men do not regard it [including you, Job].

15 [One may hear God's voice] in a dream, in a vision of the night, when deep sleep falls on men while slumbering upon the bed,

16 Then He opens the ears of men and seals their instruction [terrifying them with warnings],

17 That He may withdraw man from his purpose and cut off pride from him [disgusting him with his own disappointing self-sufficiency].

18 He holds him back from the pit [of destruction], and his life from perishing by the sword [of God's destructive judgments].

19 [God's voice may be heard by man when] he is chastened with pain upon his bed and with continual strife in his bones *or* while all his bones are firmly set,

20 So that his desire makes him loathe food, and even dainty dishes [nauseate him].

21 His flesh is so wasted away that it cannot be seen, and his bones that were not seen stick out.

22 Yes, his soul draws near to corruption, and his life to the inflicters of death (the destroyers).

23 [God's voice may be heard] if there is for the hearer a messenger *or* an angel, an interpreter, one among a thousand, to show to man what is right for him [how to be upright and in right standing with God],

24 Then [God] is gracious to him and says, Deliver him from going down into the pit [of destruction]; I have found a ransom (a price of redemption, an atonement)!

25 [Then the man's] flesh shall be

restored; it becomes fresher *and* more tender than a child's; he returns to the days of his youth.

26 He prays to God, and He is favorable to him, so that he sees His face with joy; for [God] restores to him his righteousness (his uprightness and right standing with God—with its joys).

27 He looks upon other men *or* sings out to them, I have sinned and perverted that which was right, and it did not profit me, *or* He did not requite me [according to my iniquity]!

28 [God] has redeemed my life from going down to the pit [of destruction], and my life shall see the light!

29 [Elihu comments] Behold, God does all these things twice, yes, three times, with a man,

30 To bring back his life from the pit [of destruction], that he may be enlightened with the light of the living.

31 Give heed, O Job, listen to me; hold your peace, and I will speak.

32 If you have anything to say, answer me; speak, for I desire to justify you.

33 If [you do] not [have anything to say], listen to me; hold your peace, and I will teach you wisdom.

34 ELIHU ANSWERED (continued his discourse) and said,

2 Hear my words, you wise men, and give ear to me, you who have [so much] knowledge.

3 For the ear tries words as the palate tastes food.

4 Let us choose for ourselves that which is right; let us know among ourselves what is good.

5 For Job has said, I am [innocent and uncompromisingly] righteous, but God has taken away my right; [Job 33:9.]

6 Would I lie against my right? Yet, notwithstanding my right, I am counted a liar. My wound is incurable, though I am without transgression.

7 What man is like Job, who drinks up scoffing *and* scorning like water,

8 Who goes in company with the workers of iniquity and walks with wicked men?

9 For he has said, It profits a man nothing that he should delight himself with God *and* consent to Him.

10 Therefore hear me, you men of understanding. Far be it from God that He should do wickedness, and from the Almighty that He should commit iniquity.

11 For according to the deeds of a man God will [exactly] proportion his pay, and He will cause every man to find [recompense] according to his ways.

12 Truly God will not do wickedly, neither will the Almighty pervert justice.

13 Who put [God] in charge over the earth? Or who laid on Him the whole world?

14 If [God] should set His heart upon him [man] and withdraw His [life-giving] spirit and His breath [from man] to Himself,

15 All flesh would perish together, and man would turn again to dust. [Ps. 104:29; Eccl. 12:7.]

16 If now you have understanding, hear this; listen to my words.

17 Is it possible that an enemy of right should govern? And will you condemn Him Who is just *and* mighty?

18 [God] Who says to a king, You are worthless *and* vile, or to princes *and* nobles, You are ungodly *and* evil?

19 [God] is not partial to princes, nor does He regard the rich more than the poor, for they all are the work of His hands.

20 In a moment they die; even at midnight the people are shaken and pass away, and the mighty are taken away by no [human] hand.

21 For [God's] eyes are upon the ways of a man, and He sees all his steps. [Ps. 34:15; Prov. 5:21; Jer. 16:17.]

22 There is no darkness nor thick gloom where the evildoers may hide themselves.

23 [God] sets before man no appointed time, that he should appear before [Him] in judgment.

24 He breaks in pieces mighty men without inquiry [before a jury] *and* in ways past finding out and sets others in their stead. [Dan. 2:21.]

25 Therefore He takes knowledge of their works, and He overturns them in the night, so that they are crushed *and* destroyed.

26 God strikes them down as wicked men in the open sight of beholders,

27 Because they turned aside from Him and would not consider *or* show regard for any of His ways, [I Sam. 15:11.]

28 So that they caused the cry of the poor to come to Him, and He heard the cry of the afflicted. [Exod. 22:23; James 5:4.]

29 When He gives quietness (peace and security from oppression), who then can condemn? When He hides His face [withdrawing His favor and help], who then can behold Him [and make Him gracious], whether it be a nation or a man by himself?—

30 That the godless man may not reign, that there be no one to ensnare the people.

31 For has anyone said to God, I have borne my chastisement; I will not offend any more;

32 Teach me what I do not see [in regard to how I have sinned]; if I have done iniquity, I will do it no more?

33 Should [God's] recompense [for your sins] be as you will it, when you refuse to accept it? For you must do the choosing, and not I; therefore say what is your truthful conclusion.

34 Men of understanding will tell me, indeed, every wise man who hears me [will agree],

35 That Job speaks without knowl-edge, and his words are without wis-dom *and* insight.

36 [Would that Job's afflictions be continued and] he be tried to the end because of his answering like wicked men!

37 For he adds rebellion [in his unsubmissive, defiant attitude toward God] to his unacknowledged sin; he claps his hands [in open mockery and contempt of God] among us, and he multiplies his words of accusation against God.

35 ELIHU SPOKE further [to Job] and said,

2 Do you think this is your right, *or* are you saying, My righteousness is more than God's,

3 That you ask, What advantage have you? How am I profited more than if I had sinned?

4 I will answer you and your companions with you.

5 Look to the heavens and see; and behold the skies which are higher than you.

6 If you have sinned, how does that affect God? And if your transgressions are multiplied, what have you done to Him?

7 If you are righteous, what do you [by that] give God? Or what does He receive from your hand?

8 Your wickedness touches and affects a man such as you are, and your righteousness is for yourself, one of the human race [but it cannot touch God, Who is above such influence].

9 Because of the multitudes of oppressions the people cry out; they cry for help because of the violence of the mighty.

10 But no one says, Where is God my Maker, Who gives songs of rejoicing in the night, [Acts 16:25.]

11 Who teaches us more than the beasts of the earth and makes us wiser than the birds of the heavens?

12 [The people] cry out because of

the pride of evil men, but He does not answer.

13 Surely God will refuse to answer [the cry which is] vanity (vain and empty—instead of abiding trust); neither will the Almighty regard it—

14 How much less when [missing His righteous judgment on earth] you say that you do not see Him, that your cause is before Him, and you are waiting for Him!

15 But now because God has not [speedily] punished in His anger and seems to be unaware of the wrong *and* oppression [of which a person is guilty],

16 Job uselessly opens his mouth and multiplies words without knowledge [drawing the worthless conclusion that the righteous have no more advantage than the wicked].

36 ELIHU PROCEEDED and said, **2** Bear with me *and* wait a little longer, and I will show you, for I have something still to say on God's behalf.

3 I will bring my knowledge from afar and will ascribe righteousness to my Maker.

4 For truly my words shall not be false; He Who is perfect in knowledge is with you.

5 Behold! God is mighty, and yet despises no one nor regards anything as trivial; He is mighty in power of understanding *and* heart.

6 He does not prolong the life of the wicked, but gives the needy *and* afflicted their right.

7 He withdraws not His eyes from the righteous (the upright in right standing with God); but He sets them forever with kings upon the throne, and they are exalted.

8 And if they are bound in fetters [of adversity] and held by cords of affliction, [Ps. 107:10, 11.]

9 Then He shows to them [the true character of] their deeds and their transgressions, that they have acted arrogantly [with presumption and self-sufficiency].

10 He also opens their ears to instruction *and* discipline, and commands that they return from iniquity.

11 If they obey and serve Him, they shall spend their days in prosperity and their years in pleasantness *and* joy.

12 But if they obey not, they shall perish by the sword [of God's destructive judgments], and they shall die in ignorance of true knowledge.

13 But the godless *and* profane in heart heap up anger [at the divine discipline]; they do not cry to Him when He binds them [with cords of affliction]. [Rom. 2:5.]

14 They die in youth, and their life perishes among the unclean (those who are sodomites).

15 He delivers the afflicted in their affliction and opens their ears [to His voice] in adversity.

16 Indeed, God would have allured you out of the mouth of distress into a broad place where there is no situation of perplexity *or* privation; and that which would be set on your table would be full of fatness.

17 But if you [Job] are filled with the judgment of the wicked, judgment and justice will keep hold on you.

18 For let not wrath entice you into scorning chastisements; and let not the greatness of the ransom [the suffering, if rightly endured] turn you aside.

19 Will your cry be sufficient to keep you from distress, or will all the force of your strength do it?

20 Desire not the night, when peoples are cut off from their places;

21 Take heed, turn not to iniquity, for this [the iniquity of complaining against God] you have chosen rather than [submission in] affliction.

22 Behold, God exalts *and* does loftily

in His power; who is a ruler *or* a teacher like Him?

23 Who has appointed God His way? Or who can say, You have done unrighteousness?

24 Remember that [by submission] you magnify God's work, of which men have sung.

25 All men have looked upon God's work; man may behold it afar off.

26 Behold, God is great, and we know Him not! The number of His years is unsearchable. [I Cor. 13:12.]

27 For He draws up the drops of water, which distil as rain from His vapor,

28 Which the skies pour down and drop abundantly upon [the multitudes of] mankind.

29 Not only that, but can anyone understand the spreadings of the clouds *or* the thunderings of His pavilion? [Ps. 18:11; Isa. 40:22.]

30 Behold, He spreads His lightning against the dark clouds and covers the roots of the sea.

31 For by [His clouds] God executes judgment upon the peoples; He gives food in abundance.

32 He covers His hands with the lightning and commands it to strike the mark.

33 His thunderings speak [awesomely] concerning Him; the cattle are told of His coming storm.

37 INDEED, [at His thunderings] my heart also trembles and leaps out of its place.

2 Hear, oh, hear the roar of His voice and the sound of rumbling that goes out of His mouth!

3 Under the whole heaven He lets it loose, and His lightning to the ends of the earth.

4 After it His voice roars; He thunders with the voice of His majesty, and He restrains not [His lightnings against His adversaries] when His voice is heard.

5 God thunders marvelously with His voice; He does great things which we cannot comprehend.

6 For He says to the snow, Fall on the earth; likewise He speaks to the showers and to the downpour of His mighty rains.

7 God seals up (stops, brings to a standstill by severe weather) the hand of every man [and now under His seal their hands are forced to inactivity], that all men whom He has made may know His doings (His sovereign power and their subjection to it).

8 Then the beasts go into dens and remain in their lairs.

9 Out of its chamber comes the whirlwind, and cold from the scattering winds.

10 By the breath of God ice is given, and the breadth of the waters is frozen over. [Ps. 147:17, 18.]

11 He loads the thick cloud with moisture; He scatters the cloud of His lightning.

12 And it is turned round about by His guidance, that they may do whatever He commands them upon the face of the habitable earth.

13 Whether it be for correction or for His earth [generally] or for His mercy *and* loving-kindness, He causes it to come. [Exod. 9:18, 23; I Sam. 12:18, 19.]

14 Hear this, O Job; stand still and consider the wondrous works of God.

15 Do you know how God lays His command upon them and causes the lightning of His [storm] cloud to shine?

16 Do you know how the clouds are balanced [and poised in the heavens], the wonderful works of Him Who is perfect in knowledge?

17 [Or] why your garments are hot when He quiets the earth [in sultry summer] with the [oppressive] south wind?

life point

Even though Job's friend Elihu was critical and judgmental of Job, he did offer a good piece of advice in telling Job to "stand still" (Job 37:14). Standing still is action in God's economy. It is spiritual action. We usually take action in the natural realm and do nothing in the spiritual realm, but when we wait on God and stand before Him, we are taking spiritual action. Do you need God to move in a circumstance? Take spiritual action by saying, "Lord, I am going to wait on You until You do something about this situation."

18 Can you along with Him spread out the sky, [which is] strong as a molten mirror?
19 Tell us [Job] with what words of man we may address such a Being; we cannot state our case because we are in the dark [in the presence of the unsearchable God].
20 So shall it be told Him that I wish to speak? If a man speaks, shall he be swallowed up?
21 And now men cannot look upon the light when it is bright in the skies, when the wind has passed and cleared them.
22 Golden brightness *and* splendor come out of the north; [if men can scarcely look upon it, how much less upon the] terrible splendor *and* majesty God has upon Himself!
23 Touching the Almighty, we cannot find Him out; He is excellent in power; and to justice and plenteous righteousness He does no violence [He will disregard no right]. [I Tim. 6:16.]
24 Men therefore [reverently] fear Him; He regards *and* respects not any who are wise in heart [in their own understanding and conceit]. [Matt. 10:28.]

38 THEN THE Lord answered Job out of the whirlwind and said,
2 Who is this that darkens counsel by words without knowledge? [Job 35:16.]
3 Gird up now your loins like a man, and I will demand of you, and you declare to Me.
4 Where were you when I laid the foundation of the earth? Declare to Me, if you have *and* know understanding.
5 Who determined the measures of the earth, if you know? Or who stretched the measuring line upon it?
6 Upon what were the foundations of it fastened, or who laid its cornerstone,
7 When the morning stars sang together and all the sons of God shouted for joy?
8 Or who shut up the sea with doors when it broke forth *and* issued out of the womb?—
9 When I made the clouds the garment of it, and thick darkness a swaddling band for it,
10 And marked for it My appointed boundary and set bars and doors, [Jer. 5:22.]
11 And said, Thus far shall you come and no farther; and here shall your proud waves be stayed? [Ps. 89:9; 93:4.]
12 Have you commanded the morning since your days began and caused the dawn to know its place,
13 So that [light] may get hold of the corners of the earth and shake the wickedness [of night] out of it?
14 It is changed like clay into which a seal is pressed; and things stand out like a many-colored garment.
15 From the wicked their light is withheld, and their uplifted arm is broken.
16 Have you explored the springs of the sea? Or have you walked in the recesses of the deep?
17 Have the gates of death been

revealed to you? Or have you seen the doors of deep darkness?

18 Have you comprehended the breadth of the earth? Tell Me, if you know it all.

19 Where is the ᵍway where light dwells? And as for darkness, where is its abode,

life point

When God asked Job where light dwells and where the abode of darkness is (see Job 38:19), He was making a point about His limitless knowledge and about the mystery that surrounds Him. We will never know everything He knows, nor will we ever know everything there is to know about Him. But He knows everything there is to know about us, and in His awesomeness, He is doing great things for us and in our lives.

20 That you may conduct it to its home, and may know the paths to its house?

21 You must know, since you were born then! Or because you are so extremely old!

22 Have you entered the treasuries of the snow, or have you seen the treasuries of the hail,

23 Which I have reserved for the time of trouble, for the day of battle and war? [Exod. 9:18; Josh. 10:11; Isa. 30:30; Rev. 16:21.]

24 By what way is the light distributed, or the east wind spread over the earth?

25 Who has prepared a channel for the torrents of rain, or a path for the thunderbolt,

26 To cause it to rain on the uninhabited land [and] on the desert where no man lives,

27 To satisfy the waste *and* desolate ground and to cause the tender grass to spring forth?

28 Has the rain a father? Or who has begotten the drops of dew?

29 Out of whose womb came the ice? And the hoary frost of heaven, who has given it birth?

30 The waters are congealed like stone, and the face of the deep is frozen.

31 Can you bind the chains of [the cluster of stars called] Pleiades, or loose the cords of [the constellation] Orion?

32 Can you lead forth the signs of the zodiac in their season? Or can you guide [the stars of] the Bear with her young?

33 Do you know the ordinances of the heavens? Can you establish their rule upon the earth?

34 Can you lift up your voice to the clouds, so that an abundance of waters may cover you?

35 Can you send lightnings, that they may go and say to you, Here we are?

36 Who has put wisdom in the inward parts [or in the dark clouds]? Or who has given understanding to the mind [or to the meteor]?

37 Who can number the clouds by wisdom? Or who can pour out the [water] bottles of the heavens

38 When [heat has caused] the dust to run into a mass and the clods to cleave fast together?

39 Can you [Job] hunt the prey for the lion? Or satisfy the appetite of the young lions

40 When they couch in their dens or lie in wait in their hiding place?

41 Who provides for the raven its prey when its young ones cry to God and wander about for lack of food?

g How, except by divine inspiration, could Job have known that light does not dwell in a **place**, but a **way**? For light, as modern man has discovered, involves motion (wave motion). Traveling 186,000 miles a second, it can only dwell in a way.

39

DO YOU know the time when the wild goats of the rock bring forth [their young]? [Or] do you observe when the hinds are giving birth? [Do you attend to all this, Job?]

2 Can you number the months that they carry their offspring? Or do you know the time when they are delivered,

3 When they bow themselves, bring forth their young ones, [and] cast out their pains?

4 Their young ones become strong, they grow up in the open field; they go forth and return not to them.

5 Who has sent out the wild donkey, giving him his freedom? Or who has loosed the bands of the swift donkey [by which his tame brother is bound— he, the shy, the swift-footed, and the untamable],

6 Whose home I have made the wilderness, and the salt land his dwelling place?

7 He scorns the tumult of the city and hears not the shoutings of the taskmaster.

8 The range of the mountains is his pasture, and he searches after every green thing.

9 Will the wild ox be willing to serve you, or remain beside your manger?

10 Can you bind the wild ox with a harness to the plow in the furrow? Or will he harrow the furrows for you?

11 Will you trust him because his strength is great, or to him will you leave your labor?

12 Will you depend upon him to bring home your seed and gather the grain of your threshing floor? [Who, Job, was the author of this strange variance in the disposition of animals so alike in appearance? Was it you?]

13 The wings of the ostrich wave proudly, [but] are they the pinions and plumage of love?

14 The ostrich leaves her eggs on the ground and warms them in the dust,

15 Forgetting that a foot may crush them or that the wild beast may trample them.

16 She is hardened against her young ones, as though they were not hers; her labor is in vain because she has no sense of danger [for her unborn brood],

17 For God has deprived her of wisdom, neither has He imparted to her understanding.

18 Yet when she lifts herself up in flight, [so swift is she that] she can laugh to scorn the horse and his rider.

19 Have you given the horse his might? Have you clothed his neck with quivering *and* a shaking mane?

20 Was it you [Job] who made him to leap like a locust? The majesty of his [snorting] nostrils is terrible.

21 He paws in the valley and exults in his strength; he goes out to meet the weapons [of armed men].

22 He mocks at fear and is not dismayed *or* terrified; neither does he turn back [in battle] from the sword.

23 The quiver rattles upon him, as do the glittering spear and the lance [of his rider].

24 [He seems in running to] devour the ground with fierceness and rage; neither can he stand still at the sound of the [war] trumpet.

25 As often as the trumpet sounds he says, Ha, ha! And he smells the battle from afar, the thunder of the captains, and the shouting.

26 Is it by your wisdom [Job] that the hawk soars and stretches her wings toward the south [as winter approaches]?

27 Does the eagle mount up at your command and make his nest on [a] high [inaccessible place]?

28 On the cliff he dwells and remains securely, upon the point of the rock and the stronghold.

29 From there he spies out the prey; and his eyes see it afar off.

30 His young ones suck up blood, and where the slain are, there is he.

40 MOREOVER, THE Lord said to Job,

2 Shall he who would find fault with the Almighty contend with Him? He who disputes with God, let him answer it.

3 Then Job replied to the Lord:

4 Behold, I am of small account *and* vile! What shall I answer You? I lay my hand upon my mouth. [Ezra 9:6; Ps. 51:4.]

5 I have spoken once, but I will not reply again—indeed, twice [have I answered], but I will proceed no further.

6 Then the Lord answered Job out of the whirlwind, saying,

7 Gird up your loins now like a man; I will demand of you, and you answer Me.

8 Will you also annul (set aside and render void) My judgment? Will you condemn Me [your God], that you may [appear] righteous *and* justified?

9 Have you an arm like God? Or can you thunder with a voice like His?

10 [Since you question the manner of the Almighty's rule] deck yourself now with the excellency *and* dignity [of the Supreme Ruler, and yourself undertake the government of the world if you are so wise], *and* array yourself with honor and majesty.

11 Pour forth the overflowings of your anger, and look on everyone who is proud and abase him;

12 Look on everyone who is proud and bring him low, and tread down the wicked where they stand [if you are so able, Job].

13 [Bury and] hide them all in the dust together; [and] shut them up [in the prison house of death].

14 [If you can do all this, Job, proving yourself of divine might] then will I [God] praise you also [and acknowl-

edge that] your own right hand can save you.

15 Behold now the behemoth (the hippopotamus), which I created as I did you; he eats grass like an ox.

16 See now, his strength is in his loins, and his power is in the sinews of his belly.

17 He moves his tail like a cedar tree; the tendons of his thighs are twisted together [like a rope].

18 His bones are like tubes of bronze; his limbs [or ribs] are like bars of iron.

19 [The hippopotamus] is the first [in magnitude and power] of the works of God [in animal life]; [only] He Who made him provides him with his [swordlike tusks, or only God Who made him can bring near His sword to master him].

20 Surely the mountains bring him food, where all the wild animals play.

21 He lies under the lotus trees, in the covert of the reeds in the marsh.

22 The lotus trees cover him with their shade; the willows of the brook compass him about.

23 Behold, if a river is violent *and* overflows, he does not tremble; he is confident, though the Jordan [River] swells and rushes against his mouth.

24 Can any take him when he is on the watch, or pierce through his nose with a snare?

41 CAN YOU draw out the leviathan (the crocodile) with a fishhook? Or press down his tongue with a cord?

2 Can you put a rope into his nose? Or pierce his jaw through with a hook *or* a spike?

3 Will he make many supplications to you [begging to be spared]? Will he speak soft words to you [to coax you to treat him kindly]?

4 Will he make a covenant with you to take him for your servant forever?

5 Will you play with [the crocodile]

as with a bird? Or will you put him on a leash for your maidens?

6 Will traders bargain over him? Will they divide him up among the merchants?

7 Can you fill his skin with harpoons? Or his head with fishing spears?

8 Lay your hand upon him! Remember your battle with him; you will not do [such an ill-advised thing] again!

9 Behold, the hope of [his assailant] is disappointed; one is cast down even at the sight of him!

10 No one is so fierce [and foolhardy] that he dares to stir up [the crocodile]; who then is he who can stand before Me [the beast's Creator, or dares to contend with Me]?

11 Who has first given to Me, that I should repay him? Whatever is under the whole heavens is Mine. [Therefore, who can have a claim against God, God Who made the unmastered crocodile?] [Rom. 11:35.]

12 I will not keep silence concerning his limbs, nor his mighty strength, nor his goodly frame.

13 Who can strip off [the crocodile's] outer garment? [Who can penetrate his double coat of mail?] Who shall come within his jaws?

14 Who can open the doors of his [lipless] mouth? His [extended jaws and bare] teeth are terrible round about.

15 His scales are [the crocodile's] pride, [for his back is made of rows of shields] shut up together [as with] a tight seal;

16 One is so near to another that no air can come between them.

17 They are joined one to another; they stick together so that they cannot be separated.

18 His sneezings flash forth light, and his eyes are like the [reddish] eyelids of the dawn.

19 Out of his mouth go burning torches, [and] sparks of fire leap out.

20 Out of his nostrils goes forth smoke, as out of a seething pot over a fire of rushes.

21 His breath kindles coals, and a flame goes forth from his mouth.

22 In [the crocodile's] neck abides strength, and terror dances before him.

23 The folds of his flesh cleave together; they are firm upon him, and they cannot shake [when he moves].

24 His heart is as firm as a stone, indeed, as solid as a nether millstone.

25 When [the crocodile] raises himself up, the mighty are afraid; because of terror *and* the crashing they are beside themselves.

26 Even if one strikes at him with the sword, it cannot get any hold, nor does the spear, the dart, or the javelin.

27 He counts iron as straw and bronze as rotten wood.

28 The arrow cannot make [the crocodile] flee; slingstones are treated by him as stubble.

29 Clubs [also] are counted as stubble; he laughs at the rushing *and* the rattling of the javelin.

30 His underparts are like sharp pieces of broken pottery; he spreads [grooves like] a threshing sledge upon the mire.

31 He makes the deep boil like a pot; he makes the sea like a [foaming] pot of ointment.

32 [His swift darting] makes a shining track behind him; one would think the deep to be hoary [with foam].

33 Upon earth there is not [the crocodile's] equal, a creature made without fear *and* he behaves fearlessly.

34 He looks all mighty [beasts of prey] in the face [without terror]; he is monarch over all the sons of pride. [And now, Job, [h]who are you who dares

---

h This repeats the thought of verses ten and eleven of this chapter, which is the key and climax to God's argument with Job.

not arouse the unmastered crocodile, yet who dares resist Me, the beast's Creator, to My face? Everything under the heavens is Mine; therefore, who can have a claim against God?]

4 2 THEN JOB said to the Lord,
2 I know that You can do all things, and that no thought *or* purpose of Yours can be restrained *or* thwarted.
3 [You said to me] Who is this that darkens *and* obscures counsel [by words] without knowledge? Therefore [I now see] I have [rashly] uttered what I did not understand, things too wonderful for me, which I did not know. [Job 38:2.]
4 [I had virtually said to You what You have said to me:] Hear, I beseech You, and I will speak; I will demand of You, and You declare to me.
5 I had heard of You [only] by the hearing of the ear, but now my [spiritual] eye sees You.
6 Therefore I loathe [my words] *and* abhor myself and repent in dust and ashes.
7 After the Lord had spoken the previous words to Job, the Lord said to Eliphaz the Temanite, My wrath is kindled against you and against your two friends, for you have not spoken of Me the thing that is right, as My servant Job has.
8 Now therefore take seven bullocks and seven rams and go to My servant Job and offer up for yourselves a burnt offering; and My servant Job shall pray for you, for I will accept [his prayer] that I deal not with you after your folly, in that you have not spoken of Me the

speak the Word

life point

When others have betrayed us or done us wrong, we must pass the test of forgiveness. In Job 42:7–10 we read that Job prayed for his friends. These were the friends who had judged and criticized him. These were the friends who did not stand with him in his pain and suffering when he lost everything. What happened when Job prayed for them and forgave them? He received a double blessing from the Lord. Based on Job's story, I like to say: *If you do things God's way, He will give you double for your trouble.*

thing that is right, as My servant Job has.
9 So Eliphaz the Temanite and Bildad the Shuhite and Zophar the Naamathite went and did as the Lord commanded them; and the Lord accepted [Job's prayer].
10 And the Lord turned the captivity of Job *and* restored his fortunes, when he prayed for his friends; also the Lord gave Job twice as much as he had before. [Deut. 30:1-3; Ps. 126:1, 2.]
11 Then there came to him all his

putting the Word to work

Have you ever been wrongly accused and thus deeply wounded by others? Like Job, pray for those who have hurt you, and forgive them (see Job 42:10). When we forgive, God brings restoration.

God, I know that You can do all things, and that no thought or purpose of Yours can be held back or thwarted.
ADAPTED FROM JOB 42:2

brothers and sisters and all who had known him before, and they ate bread with him in his house; and they sympathized with him and comforted him over all the [distressing] calamities that the Lord had brought upon him. Every man also gave him a piece of money, and every man an earring of gold.

12 And the Lord blessed the latter days of Job more than his beginning; for he had 14,000 sheep, 6,000 camels, 1,000 yoke of oxen, and 1,000 female donkeys. [Job 1:3.]

13 He had also seven sons and three daughters.

14 And he called the name of the first Jemimah, and the name of the second Keziah, and the name of the third Keren-happuch.

life point

No matter what you are going through, God still has the same good plan for you right now that He had the moment you were born. He has never changed His mind. From the instant the enemy attacked you, God has had your restoration in mind.

15 And in all the land there were no women so fair as the daughters of Job, and their father gave them inheritance among their brothers.

16 After this, Job lived 140 years, and saw his sons and his sons' sons, even to four generations.

17 So Job died, an old man and full of days. [James 5:11.]

Psalms

Author:
David, Asaph, the sons of Korah, Moses, and others

Date:
1000 BC–300 BC

Everyday Life Principles:
The Psalms are full of practical advice for you, and they are easy to read and to pray.

When you need encouragement, instruction, or comfort, read the Psalms.

Express your heart to God freely and fully, just as the psalmists did.

The Psalms are a collection of 150 songs and poems written over a period of many years.

Because they were originally intended and used as worship songs for congregations or individuals, many of the psalms address God directly, and they are very easy to read and to pray. They are filled not only with praise and worship to God, but with practical advice and great insight into the various emotions, victories, and struggles that people face.

One thing I love about the Psalms is that the writers were very honest with God, and they communicated with Him from their hearts. Whether they were joyful, confident, depressed, angry, lonely, or afraid, they wrote about it. In the midst of expressing themselves freely and fully to Him, they also realized their need for God in fresh new ways and reaffirmed their trust in Him. Every emotion you or I could ever experience seems to be mentioned in the Psalms. No matter what you are going through, God wants to hear your heart.

Many people have a favorite psalm. For most, it is probably Psalm 23; for others, it is Psalm 91; and for others it is Psalm 100. I would have to say that my personal favorite is Psalm 27.

I encourage you to read the Psalms and read them often. Let them remind you to always tell God what is in your heart and receive comfort, strength, and direction from Him. Let them also remind you to praise and worship God with all your heart.

BOOK ONE

aPSALM 1

BLESSED (HAPPY, fortunate, prosperous, and enviable) is the man who walks *and* lives not in the counsel of the ungodly [following their advice, their plans and purposes], nor stands [submissive and inactive] in the path where sinners walk, nor sits down [to relax and rest] where the scornful [and the mockers] gather.

2 But his delight *and* desire are in the law of the Lord, and on His law (the precepts, the instructions, the teachings of God) he habitually meditates (ponders and studies) by day and by night. [Rom. 13:8-10; Gal. 3:1-29; II Tim. 3:16.]

3 And he shall be like a tree firmly planted [and tended] by the streams of water, ready to bring forth its fruit in its season; its leaf also shall not fade *or* wither; and everything he does shall prosper [and come to maturity]. [Jer. 17:7, 8.]

4 Not so the wicked [those disobedient and living without God are not so]. But they are like the chaff [worth-less, dead, without substance] which the wind drives away.

5 Therefore the wicked [those disobedient and living without God] shall not stand [justified] in the judgment, nor bsinners in the congregation of the righteous [those who are upright and in right standing with God].

6 For the Lord knows *and* is fully acquainted with the way of the righteous, but the way of the ungodly [those living outside God's will] shall perish (end in ruin and come to nought).

PSALM 2

WHY DO the nations assemble with commotion [uproar and confusion of voices], and why do the people imagine (meditate upon and devise) an empty scheme?

2 The kings of the earth take their places; the rulers take counsel together against the Lord and His Anointed One (the Messiah, the Christ). *They say,* [Acts 4:25-27.]

3 Let us break Their bands [of restraint] asunder and cast Their cords [of control] from us.

4 He Who sits in the heavens laughs; the Lord has them in derision [and in supreme contempt He mocks them].

5 He speaks to them in His deep anger and troubles (terrifies and confounds) them in His displeasure *and* fury, *saying,*

6 Yet have I anointed (installed and placed) My King [firmly] on My holy hill of Zion.

7 I will declare the decree of the

life point

Psalm 1 promises prosperity to those who delight in God's law (His precepts and instructions) and who meditate on His Word day and night. In other words, those who give God and His Word first place in their lives can expect to prosper in every way.

---

a This has been called "The Preface Psalm" because in some respects it may be considered "the text upon which the whole of the Psalms make up a divine sermon." It opens with a benediction, "Blessed," as does our Lord's Sermon on the Mount (Matt. 5:3). b Charles Haddon Spurgeon (*The Treasury of David*) said, "Sinners cannot live in heaven. They would be out of their element. Sooner could a fish live upon a tree than the wicked in paradise." The only way they will ever be able to endure heaven is to be born again and become new creatures with pure hearts able fully to enjoy the presence of God, His holy angels, and the redeemed.

Lord: He said to Me, You are My Son; this day [I declare] I have begotten You. [Heb. 1:5; 3:5, 6; II Pet. 1:17, 18.]

life point

I once saw a movie in which a king issued a royal decree. He wrote down his command and then sent forth riders on horseback throughout the country to "declare the decree" to the citizens of that kingdom. In the Scriptures we see the issuing of such royal decrees in Esther 8:8–14 and in Luke 2:1–3.

In Psalm 2:7, the psalmist wrote that he would "declare the decree of the Lord." What decree? The decree in which the Lord declares that He (Jesus) is God's only begotten Son (see Hebrews 1:1–5).

The written Word of God is the formal decree of the Lord, our King. When we declare God's Word out of our mouths, with hearts full of faith, those faith-filled words go forth to establish God's order in our lives. When the royal decree is pronounced, things begin to change!

8 Ask of Me, and I will give You the nations as Your inheritance, and the uttermost parts of the earth as Your possession.
9 You shall break them with a rod of iron; You shall dash them in pieces like potters' ware. [Rev. 12:5; 19:15.]
10 Now therefore, O you kings, act wisely; be instructed *and* warned, O you rulers of the earth.
11 Serve the Lord with reverent awe *and* worshipful fear; rejoice *and* be in high spirits with trembling [lest you displease Him].
12 Kiss the Son [pay homage to Him in purity], lest He be angry and you

perish in the way, for soon shall His wrath be kindled. O blessed (happy, fortunate, and to be envied) are all those who seek refuge *and* put their trust in Him!

PSALM 3
A Psalm of David. When he fled from Absalom his son.

LORD, HOW they are increased who trouble me! Many are they who rise up against me.
2 Many are saying of me, There is no help for him in God. Selah [pause, and calmly think of that]!
3 But You, O Lord, are a shield for me, my glory, and the lifter of my head.
4 With my voice I cry to the Lord, and He hears and answers me out of His holy hill. Selah [pause, and calmly think of that]!
5 I lay down and slept; I wakened again, for the Lord sustains me.
6 I will not be afraid of ten thousands of people who have set themselves against me round about.
7 Arise, O Lord; save me, O my God! For You have struck all my enemies on the cheek; You have broken the teeth of the ungodly.
8 Salvation belongs to the Lord; May Your blessing be upon Your people. Selah [pause, and calmly think of that]!

PSALM 4
To the Chief Musician; on stringed instruments. A Psalm of David.

ANSWER ME when I call, O God of my righteousness (uprightness, justice, and right standing with You)! You have freed me when I was hemmed in *and* enlarged me when I was in distress; have mercy upon me and hear my prayer.
2 O you sons of men, how long will you turn my honor *and* glory into

hold your head high

Although there are "downers" in this life, there are also "lifters." In Psalm 3:1–3, the psalmist says that despite his distressing situation, he is not despairing or becoming depressed because his confidence is in the Lord, the lifter of his head.

When we are depressed, it seems everything around us is falling apart. We lose strength; our heads and hands and hearts all begin to hang down. Even our eyes and our voices are lowered. We become downcast because we are looking at our problems rather than at the Lord.

No matter what is causing us to be downcast, the Lord encourages us throughout His Word to lift our heads and our hands and look to Him. We find one of these many examples in Genesis 13:14 when God told Abraham, who had been shortchanged by his nephew Lot, to "lift up" his eyes and look around him in all directions, for He was giving him all the land as far as he could see for his inheritance. In Psalm 24:7 the psalmist says, "Lift up your heads, O you gates; and be lifted up, you age-abiding doors, that the King of glory may come in." In I Timothy 2:8, the apostle Paul encouraged people to pray, "lifting up holy hands."

These instructions are good for us to remember today. When people disappoint us, God wants us, instead of becoming discouraged and depressed, to decide to lift up our heads and eyes and look at the possibilities, not the problems, around us, trusting Him to lead us into an even better situation—because He has one for us.

We may be tempted to say, "Oh, what's the use?" and just give up rather than moving in a new direction as Abraham did, but the Lord is constantly exhorting us to lift up our eyes and heads and hearts to take inventory of our blessings and not our problems. God encourages us to look at Him because He has plans to bless and increase us abundantly.

No matter how your life has turned out to this point, you have only two options. One is to give up and quit; the other is to keep going. If you decide to keep going, again you have only two choices. One is to live in constant depression and misery; the other is to live in hope and joy.

Choosing to live in hope and joy does not mean you will not face any more disappointments or discouraging situations; it just means you have decided not to let them get you down. Instead, you will lift up your eyes and hands and head and heart and look not at your problems, but at the Lord, Who has promised to see you through to abundance and victory.

shame? How long will you love vanity *and* futility *and* seek after lies? Selah [pause, and calmly think of that]!

3 But know that the Lord has set apart for Himself [and given distinction to] him who is godly [the man of loving-kindness]. The Lord listens *and* heeds when I call to Him.

4 Be angry [or stand in awe] and sin not; commune with your own hearts upon your beds and be silent (sorry for the things you say in your hearts). Selah [pause, and calmly think of that]! [Eph. 4:26.]

5 Offer just *and* right sacrifices; trust (lean on and be confident) in the Lord.

6 Many say, Oh, that we might see some good! Lift up the light of Your countenance upon us, O Lord.

7 You have put more joy *and* rejoicing in my heart than [they know] when their wheat and new wine have yielded abundantly.

8 In peace I will both lie down and sleep, for You, Lord, alone make me dwell in safety *and* confident trust.

PSALM 5

To the Chief Musician; on wind instruments. A Psalm of David.

LISTEN TO my words, O Lord, give heed to my sighing *and* groaning.

2 Hear the sound of my cry, my King and my God, for to You do I pray.

3 In the morning You hear my voice, O Lord; in the morning I prepare [a prayer, a sacrifice] for You and watch *and* wait [for You to speak to my heart].

4 For You are not a God Who takes pleasure in wickedness; neither will the evil [man] so much as dwell [temporarily] with You.

5 Boasters can have no standing in Your sight; You abhor all evildoers.

6 You will destroy those who speak lies; the Lord abhors [and rejects] the bloodthirsty and deceitful man.

7 But as for me, I will enter Your house through the abundance of Your steadfast love *and* mercy; I will worship toward *and* at Your holy temple in reverent fear *and* awe of You.

8 Lead me, O Lord, in Your righteousness because of my enemies; make Your way level (straight and right) before my face.

9 For there is nothing trustworthy *or* steadfast *or* truthful in their talk; their heart is destruction [or a destructive chasm, a yawning gulf]; their throat is an open sepulcher; they flatter and make smooth with their tongue. [Rom. 3:13.]

10 Hold them guilty, O God; let them fall by their own designs *and* counsels; cast them out because of the multitude of their transgressions, for they have rebelled against You.

11 But let all those who take refuge *and* put their trust in You rejoice; let them ever sing *and* shout for joy, because You make a covering over them *and* defend them; let those also who love Your name be joyful in You *and* be in high spirits.

12 For You, Lord, will bless the

speak the Word

Thank You, Lord, for listening and heeding me when I call to You.
ADAPTED FROM PSALM 4:3

Thank You, God, that I can take refuge in You and that I can trust You. Thank You for making a covering over me and for defending me.
ADAPTED FROM PSALM 5:11

[uncompromisingly] righteous [him who is upright and in right standing with You]; as with a shield You will surround him with goodwill (pleasure and favor).

PSALM 6

To the Chief Musician; on stringed instruments, set [possibly] an octave below. A Psalm of David.

O LORD, rebuke me not in Your anger nor discipline *and* chasten me in Your hot displeasure.

2 Have mercy on me *and* be gracious to me, O Lord, for I am weak (faint and withered away); O Lord, heal me, for my bones are troubled.

3 My [inner] self [as well as my body] is also exceedingly disturbed *and* troubled. But You, O Lord, how long [until You return and speak peace to me]?

4 Return [to my relief], O Lord, deliver my life; save me for the sake of Your steadfast love *and* mercy.

5 For in death there is no remembrance of You; in Sheol (the place of the dead) who will give You thanks?

6 I am weary with my groaning; all night I soak my pillow with tears, I drench my couch with my weeping.

7 My eye grows dim because of grief; it grows old because of all my enemies.

8 Depart from me, all you workers of iniquity, for the Lord has heard the voice of my weeping. [Matt. 7:23; Luke 13:27.]

9 The Lord has heard my supplication; the Lord receives my prayer.

10 Let all my enemies be ashamed and sorely troubled; let them turn back *and* be put to shame suddenly.

PSALM 7

An Ode of David, [probably] in a wild, irregular, enthusiastic strain, which he sang to the Lord concerning the words of Cush, a Benjamite.

O LORD my God, in You I take refuge *and* put my trust; save me from all those who pursue *and* persecute me, and deliver me,

2 Lest my foe tear my life [from my body] like a lion, dragging *me* away while there is none to deliver.

3 O Lord my God, if I have done this, if there is wrong in my hands,

4 If I have paid back with evil him who was at peace with me or without cause have robbed him who was my enemy,

5 Let the enemy pursue my life and take it; yes, let him trample my life to the ground and lay my honor in the dust. Selah [pause, and calmly think of that]!

6 Arise, O Lord, in Your anger; lift up Yourself against the rage of my enemies; and awake [and stir up] for me the justice *and* vindication [that] You have commanded.

7 Let the assembly of the peoples be gathered about You, and return on high over them.

8 The Lord judges the people; judge me, O Lord, *and* do me justice according to my righteousness [my rightness, justice, and right standing with You] and according to the integrity that is in me.

9 Oh, let the wickedness of the wicked come to an end, but establish the [uncompromisingly] righteous [those upright and in harmony with You]; for You, Who try the hearts and emotions *and* thinking powers, are a righteous God. [Rev. 2:23.]

speak the Word

God, I thank You for hearing my supplication and receiving my prayer.
ADAPTED FROM PSALM 6:9

when God tests your emotions

In Psalm 7:9 we read that God "tries" our emotions (Revelation 2:23 conveys a similar message). What does the word *try* mean in this context? It means "to test until purified."

A few years ago, as I was praying, God said to me, "Joyce, I am going to test your emotions." I had never heard of anything like that, and had not yet discovered the scriptures about this in the Bible.

About six months later, I became an emotional wreck. I cried for no reason. Everything hurt my feelings. There were times when I went to bed praying, feeling as sweet as could be, then I woke up the next morning in a really cranky mood, as if I had stayed up all night eating nails! I thought, *What is the problem here? What's going on?* Then the Lord reminded me of what He had spoken to me earlier: "I am going to test your emotions." As He led me to Psalm 7:9 and Revelation 2:23, He caused me to understand that He was doing a work in my emotional life for my own good. He was going to teach me how to be stable and continue walking in the fruit of the Holy Spirit, regardless of how I felt.

No matter who you are, there will be periods of time in which you feel more emotional than usual. You may wake up one morning and feel like breaking down and crying for no reason. You may feel sad or depressed; you may feel that nobody cares about you; or you might feel sorry for yourself. During those times you must learn how to manage your emotions and not allow them to manage you. At these times your feelings will probably get hurt very easily. The slightest thing might make you angry. Emotions are very fickle! They can be one way one day and entirely different the next day. God has to teach us not to live by our feelings, or we will never enjoy victorious living and we will not give God the glory He deserves.

What should you do when you start feeling that your emotions are being tested? (1) Do not allow yourself to fall under condemnation. (2) Do not even try to figure out what is happening. (3) Instead, simply say, "This is one of those times when my emotions are being tried. I'm going to trust God and learn to control them."

How are you and I ever going to learn to control ourselves emotionally unless God allows us to go through some trying times? Remember, the Bible says that God will never allow any more to come upon us than we are able to bear (see I Corinthians 10:13). If the Lord does not allow such testing times to come upon us, we will never grow, and we will never learn how to deal with Satan when he brings things against us—which he will sooner or later.

Trying times are learning times. They are testing times, and I always say, "Pass your test this time so you will not have to take it again."

10 My defense *and* shield depend on God, Who saves the upright in heart.
11 God is a righteous Judge, yes, a God Who is indignant every day.
12 If a man does not turn *and* repent, [God] will whet His sword; He has strung *and* bent His [huge] bow and made it ready [by treading it with His foot].
13 He has also prepared for him deadly weapons; He makes His arrows fiery shafts.
14 Behold, [the wicked man] conceives iniquity and is pregnant with mischief and gives birth to lies.
15 He made a pit and hollowed it out and has fallen into the hole which he made [before the trap was completed].
16 His mischief shall fall back in return upon his own head, and his violence come down [with the loose dirt] upon his own scalp.
17 I will give to the Lord the thanks due to His rightness *and* justice, and I will sing praise to the name of the Lord Most High.

PSALM 8

To the Chief Musician; set to a Philistine lute, or [possibly] to a particular Hittite tune. A Psalm of David.

O LORD, our Lord, how excellent (majestic and glorious) is Your name in all the earth! You have set Your glory on [or above] the heavens.
2 Out of the mouths of babes and unweaned infants You have established strength because of Your foes, that You might silence the enemy and the avenger. [Matt. 21:15, 16.]
3 When I view *and* consider Your

putting the Word to work

Have you ever looked into the vast, starry sky at night and felt very small in comparison? Consider the greatness of God as you observe His creation all around you, and remember that you are a masterpiece of God's creation, made in His very image! Take a moment and praise God for His excellence and thank Him for crowning you with glory and honor.

heavens, the work of Your fingers, the moon and the stars, which You have ordained *and* established,
4 What is man that You are mindful of him, and the son of [earthborn] man that You care for him?
5 Yet You have made him but a little lower than God [or heavenly beings], and You have crowned him with glory and honor.
6 You made him to have dominion over the works of Your hands; You have put all things under his feet: [I Cor. 15:27; Eph. 1:22, 23; Heb. 2:6-8.]
7 All sheep and oxen, yes, and the beasts of the field,
8 The birds of the air, and the fish of the sea, *and* whatever passes along the paths of the seas.
9 O Lord, our Lord, how excellent (majestic and glorious) is Your name in all the earth!

PSALM 9

To the Chief Musician; set for [possibly] soprano voices. A Psalm of David.

I WILL praise You, O Lord, with my whole heart; I will show forth (recount and tell aloud) all Your

speak the Word

I will praise You, God, with all my heart, and I will tell people about the wonderful things You have done for me. I will rejoice in You and be in high spirits!
ADAPTED FROM PSALM 9:1, 2

life point

You have been singled out by God, Who
has placed His crown of glory and honor,
or favor and excellence, upon your head,
according to Psalm 8:5. You may not see
your crown, but it is there—just like the
robe of righteousness in which you are
dressed. You may not see with your
physical eyes your robe of righteousness
or the crown of God's favor, but they
exist in the spiritual realm (see Isaiah
61:10). We need to remember that the
natural man cannot perceive the things
of God because they are spiritually
discerned (see I Corinthians 2:14).

Even though the Bible *says* we have
been crowned with God's favor and
excellence, often we do not act as
though we are. One reason we do not
tap into God's blessings is that we do
not believe we deserve them. Another
reason is that we have not been taught
that the blessings of God can be ours
and consequently have not activated our
faith in this area. So we wander through
life, taking whatever the devil throws at
us without ever resisting him and
claiming what is rightfully ours.

If you will reread Psalm 8:6, you will see
that all things have been placed under
our feet by God, Who has given us
dominion over all His creation. To me,
those words do not indicate that we are
supposed to allow our problems or the
devil and his demons to intimidate,
dominate, and oppress us. If we will
receive by faith the blessing of glory and
honor with which the Lord our God has
crowned us, not only will our faces shine
forth with the glory of the Lord, but we
will enjoy respect, esteem, favor, and a
good reputation.

marvelous works *and* wonderful deeds!

2   I will rejoice in You and be in high
spirits; I will sing praise to Your
name, O Most High!

3   When my enemies turned back,
they stumbled and perished before
You.

4   For You have maintained my right
and my cause; You sat on the throne
judging righteously.

5   You have rebuked the nations, You
have destroyed the wicked; You have
blotted out their name forever and
ever.

6   The enemy have been cut off *and*
have vanished in everlasting ruins,
You have plucked up *and* overthrown
their cities; the very memory of them
has perished *and* vanished.

7   But the Lord shall remain *and*
continue forever; He has prepared
and established His throne for judgment. [Heb. 1:11.]

8   And He will judge the world in
righteousness (rightness and equity);
He will minister justice to the peoples
in uprightness. [Acts 17:31.]

9   The Lord also will be a refuge *and* a
high tower for the oppressed, a refuge
and a stronghold in times of trouble
(high cost, destitution, and desperation).

10   And they who know Your name
[who have experience and acquaintance with Your mercy] will lean on
and confidently put their trust in You,
for You, Lord, have not forsaken those
who seek (inquire of and for) You [on
the authority of God's Word and the
right of their necessity]. [Ps. 42:1.]

11   Sing praises to the Lord, Who
dwells in Zion! Declare among the
peoples His doings!

12   For He Who avenges the blood [of
His people shed unjustly] remembers
them; He does not forget the cry of the
afflicted (the poor and the humble).

13   Have mercy upon me *and* be gracious *to me,* O Lord; consider how I
am afflicted by those who hate me,

You Who lift me up from the gates of death,

14 That I may show forth (recount and tell aloud) all Your praises! In the gates of the Daughter of Zion I will rejoice in Your salvation *and* Your saving help.

15 The nations have sunk down in the pit that they made; in the net which they hid is their own foot caught.

16 The Lord has made Himself known; He executes judgment; the wicked are snared in the work of their own hands. Higgaion [meditation]. Selah [pause, and calmly think of that]!

17 The wicked shall be turned back [headlong into premature death] into Sheol (the place of the departed spirits of the wicked), even all the nations that forget *or* are forgetful of God.

18 For the needy shall not always be forgotten, and the expectation *and* hope of the meek *and* the poor shall not perish forever.

19 Arise, O Lord! Let not man prevail; let the nations be judged before You.

20 Put them in fear [make them realize their frail nature], O Lord, that the nations may know themselves to be but men. Selah [pause, and calmly think of that]!

PSALM 10

WHY DO You stand afar off, O Lord? Why do You hide Yourself, [veiling Your eyes] in times of trouble (distress and desperation)?

2 The wicked in pride *and* arrogance hotly pursue *and* persecute the poor; let them be taken in the schemes which they have devised.

3 For the wicked *man* boasts (sings the praises) of his own heart's desire, and the one greedy for gain curses *and* spurns, yes, renounces *and* despises the Lord.

4 The wicked one in the pride of his countenance will not seek, inquire for, *and* yearn for God; all his thoughts are that there is no God [so He never punishes].

5 His ways are grievous [or persist] at all times; Your judgments [Lord] are far above *and* on high out of his sight [so he never thinks about them]; as for all his foes, he sniffs *and* sneers at them.

6 He thinks in his heart, I shall not be moved; for throughout all generations I shall not come to want *or* be in adversity.

7 His mouth is full of cursing, deceit, oppression (fraud); under his tongue are trouble and sin (mischief and iniquity).

8 He sits in ambush in the villages; in hiding places he slays the innocent; he watches stealthily for the poor (the helpless and unfortunate).

9 He lurks in secret places like a lion in his thicket; he lies in wait that he may seize the poor (the helpless and the unfortunate); he seizes the poor when he draws him into his net.

10 [The prey] is crushed, sinks down; and the helpless falls by his mighty [claws].

11 [The foe] thinks in his heart, God has quite forgotten; He has hidden His face; He will never see [my deed].

12 Arise, O Lord! O God, lift up Your hand; forget not the humble [patient and crushed].

13 Why does the wicked [man] condemn (spurn and renounce) God? Why has he thought in his heart, You will not call to account?

14 You have seen it; yes, You note trouble and grief (vexation) to requite it with Your hand. The unfortunate commits himself to You; You are the helper of the fatherless.

15 Break the arm of the wicked man; and as for the evil man, search out his wickedness until You find no more.

16 The Lord is King forever and ever; the nations will perish out of His land.

17 O Lord, You have heard the desire *and* the longing of the humble *and* oppressed; You will prepare *and* strengthen *and* direct their hearts, You will cause Your ear to hear,

18 To do justice to the fatherless and the oppressed, so that man, who is of the earth, may not terrify them any more.

PSALM 11

To the Chief Musician *or* Choir Leader. [A Psalm] of David.

I N THE Lord I take refuge [and put my trust]; how can you say to me, Flee like a bird to your mountain?

2 For see, the wicked are bending the bow; they make ready their arrow upon the string, that they [furtively] in darkness may shoot at the upright in heart.

3 If the foundations are destroyed, what can the [unyieldingly] righteous do, *or* what has He [the Righteous One] wrought *or* accomplished?

4 The Lord is in His holy temple; the Lord's throne is in heaven. His eyes behold; His eyelids test *and* prove the children of men. [Acts 7:49; Rev. 4:2.]

5 The Lord tests *and* proves the [unyieldingly] righteous, but His soul abhors the wicked and him who loves violence. [James 1:12.]

6 Upon the wicked He will rain quick burning coals *or* snares; fire, brimstone, and a [dreadful] scorching wind shall be the portion of their cup.

7 For the Lord is [rigidly] righteous, He loves righteous deeds; the upright shall behold His face, *or* He beholds the upright.

PSALM 12

To the Chief Musician; set [possibly] an octave below. A Psalm of David.

H ELP, LORD! For principled *and* godly people are here no more; faithfulness *and* the faithful vanish from among the sons of men.

2 To his neighbor each one speaks words without use *or* worth *or* truth; with flattering lips and double heart [deceitfully] they speak.

3 May the Lord cut off all flattering lips *and* the tongues that speak proud boasting,

4 Those who say, With our tongues we prevail; our lips are our own [to command at our will]—who is lord *and* master over us?

5 Now will I arise, says the Lord, because the poor are oppressed, because of the groans of the needy; I will set him in safety *and* in the salvation for which he pants.

6 The words *and* promises of the Lord are pure words, like silver refined in an earthen furnace, purified seven times over.

7 You will keep them and preserve them, O Lord; You will guard *and* keep us from this [evil] generation forever.

8 The wicked walk *or* prowl about on every side, as vileness is exalted [and baseness is rated high] among the sons of men.

PSALM 13

To the Chief Musician. A Psalm of David.

H OW LONG will You forget me, O Lord? Forever? How long will You hide Your face from me?

2 How long must I lay up cares within me and have sorrow in my heart day after day? How long shall my enemy exalt himself over me?

3 Consider and answer me, O Lord my God; lighten the eyes [of my faith to behold Your face in the pitchlike darkness], lest I sleep the sleep of death,

4 Lest my enemy say, I have prevailed over him, *and* those that trouble me rejoice when I am shaken.

the importance of faithfulness

In Psalm 12:1 we read that David asked the Lord for help because people were not being godly or faithful. Being faithful is as important today as it was then.

It is hard to find people who will be really faithful—people who will stick with you when they find out you are not perfect. The Bible says, "A friend loves at all times, and is born, as is a brother, for adversity" (Proverbs 17:17). In other words, a true friend is a person who is born to stick with you in your hard and not-so-nice times. I believe one of the saddest things in our society today is that we do not have this kind of loyalty and commitment. Many people miss out on so much because they are not faithful to see things through to the finish. Even sadder is that most of them will never even realize what incredible blessings they have missed.

David continues to say in the next verse of this psalm that people were speaking worthless, untrue words with deceitful, double hearts. We need single-minded men and women who can set their hearts on something and stick with it without being double-minded and speaking empty words. Double-hearted people believe one thing one day and something else the next. One day they like you and the next day they do not. They may be for you today, but against you tomorrow.

The Bible gives us many examples of faithful people. One of them was Moses, who was faithful in all the house of God (see Numbers 12:7). That means he was faithful to do exactly the duties God gave him to do day after day, month after month, year after year, even when he did not feel like being faithful. Moses was so faithful that even when his sister and brother, Miriam and Aaron, spoke against him, he loved them and remained faithful to them. He had so much faithfulness in his character that even when the people in his life did not treat him well, he remained the same way.

The Bible tells us that God remains faithful even when we are faithless (see II Timothy 2:13). That is the way God wants us to be. If everybody else is faithless, then we remain faithful. If you feel as though you are the only one who is being nice, the only one who apologizes or tries to do the right thing, keep on doing it. Determine in your heart to stay loyal to God and to keep bearing the fruit of faithfulness.

5 But I have trusted, leaned on, *and* been confident in Your mercy *and* loving-kindness; my heart shall rejoice *and* be in high spirits in Your salvation.
6 I will sing to the Lord, because He has dealt bountifully with me.

PSALM 14

To the Chief Musician. [A Psalm] of David.

THE [empty-headed] fool has said in his heart, There is no God. They are corrupt, they have done abominable deeds; there is none that does good *or* right. [Rom. 3:10.]

2 The Lord looked down from heaven upon the children of men to see if there were any who understood, dealt wisely, *and* sought after God, inquiring for *and* of Him *and* requiring Him [of vital necessity].

3 They are all gone aside, they have *all* together become filthy; there is none that does good *or* right, no, not one. [Rom. 3:11, 12.]

4 Have all the workers of iniquity no knowledge, who eat up my people as they eat bread and who do not call on the Lord?

5 There they shall be in great fear [literally—dreading a dread], for God is with the generation of the [uncompromisingly] righteous (those upright and in right standing with Him).

6 You [evildoers] would put to shame *and* confound the plans of the poor *and* patient, but the Lord is his safe refuge.

7 Oh, that the salvation of Israel would come out of Zion! When the Lord shall restore the fortunes of His people, then Jacob shall rejoice *and* Israel shall be glad. [Rom. 11:25-27.]

PSALM 15
A Psalm of David.

LORD, WHO shall dwell [temporarily] in Your tabernacle? Who shall dwell [permanently] on Your holy hill?

2 He who walks *and* lives uprightly *and* blamelessly, who works rightness *and* justice and speaks *and* thinks the truth in his heart,

3 He who does not slander with his tongue, nor does evil to his friend, nor takes up a reproach against his neighbor;

4 In whose eyes a vile person is despised, but he who honors those who fear the Lord (who revere and worship Him); who swears to his own hurt and does not change;

5 [He who] does not put out his money for ᶜinterest [to one of his own people] and who will not take a bribe against the innocent. He who does these things shall never be moved. [Exod. 22:25, 26.]

PSALM 16
A Poem of David; [probably] intended to record memorable thoughts.

KEEP *AND* protect me, O God, for in You I have found refuge, *and* in You do I put my trust *and* hide myself.

2 I say to the Lord, You are my Lord; I have no good beside *or* beyond You.

3 As for the godly (the saints) who are in the land, they are the excellent, the noble, *and* the glorious, in whom is all my delight.

4 Their sorrows shall be multiplied who choose another god; their drink offerings of blood will I not offer or take their names upon my lips.

5 The Lord is my chosen *and* assigned portion, my cup; You hold *and* maintain my lot.

6 The lines have fallen for me in pleasant places; yes, I have a good heritage.

---

c "Israel was originally not a mercantile people, and the law aimed at an equal diffusion of wealth, not at enriching some while others were poor. The spirit of the law still is obligatory—not to take advantage of a brother's distress to lend at interest ruinous to him—but the letter of the law is abrogated, and a loan at moderate interest is often of great service to the poor. Hence, it is referred to by our Lord in parables, apparently as a lawful as well as recognized usage. (Matt. 25:27; Luke 19:23)" (A.R. Fausset, *Bible Encyclopedia and Dictionary*).

7 I will bless the Lord, Who has given me counsel; yes, my heart instructs me in the night seasons.
8 I have set the Lord continually before me; because He is at my right hand, I shall not be moved.
9 Therefore my heart is glad and my glory [my inner self] rejoices; my body too shall rest *and* confidently dwell in safety,
10 For You will not abandon me to Sheol (the place of the dead), neither will You suffer Your holy one [Holy One] to see corruption. [Acts 13:35.]
11 You will show me the path of life; in Your presence is fullness of joy, at Your right hand there are pleasures forevermore. [Acts 2:25-28, 31.]

life point

We must learn to seek God's face and not just His hand. Seeking God for Who He is, not just for what He can do for us, assures us "fullness of joy" (Psalm 16:11) and is vital to our victory as believers.

PSALM 17
A Prayer of David.

HEAR THE right (my righteous cause), O Lord; listen to my shrill, piercing cry! Give ear to my prayer, that comes from unfeigned *and* guileless lips.
2 Let my sentence of vindication come from You! May Your eyes behold the things that are just *and* upright.
3 You have proved my heart; You have visited *me* in the night; You have tried me and find nothing [no evil purpose in me]; I have purposed that my mouth shall not transgress.
4 Concerning the works of men, by the word of Your lips I have avoided the ways of the violent (the paths of the destroyer).
5 My steps have held closely to Your paths [to the tracks of the One Who has gone on before]; my feet have not slipped.
6 I have called upon You, O God, for You will hear me; incline Your ear to me *and* hear my speech.
7 Show Your marvelous loving-kindness, O You Who save by Your right hand those who trust *and* take refuge in You from those who rise up against them.
8 Keep *and* guard me as the pupil of Your eye; hide me in the shadow of Your wings
9 From the wicked who despoil *and* oppress me, my deadly adversaries who surround me.
10 They are enclosed in their own prosperity *and* have shut up their hearts to pity; with their mouths they make exorbitant claims *and* proudly *and* arrogantly speak.
11 They track us down in each step we take; now they surround us; they set their eyes to cast us to the ground,
12 Like a lion greedy *and* eager to tear his prey, and as a young lion lurking in hidden places.
13 Arise, O Lord! Confront *and* forestall them, cast them down! Deliver my life from the wicked by Your sword,
14 From men by Your hand, O Lord, from men of *this* world [these poor moths of the night] whose portion in life is idle *and* vain. Their bellies are filled with Your hidden treasure [what You have stored up]; their children are satiated, and they leave the rest [of their] wealth to their babes.
15 As for me, I will continue beholding Your face in righteousness (rightness, justice, and right standing with You); I shall be fully satisfied, when I awake [to find myself] beholding Your form [and having sweet communion with You].

life point

Psalm 17:15 is one of my favorite verses because it teaches us how to wake up in the morning feeling satisfied in the Lord. Earlier in my life, I had many unhappy days because the minute I awoke each morning, I began to think about all the wrong things. But since I have learned the importance of seeking God's presence and not just His presents, I am a different person. I wake up with a thankful heart, and God has taught me to think of others and not just myself. Fellowshipping with God early in the morning is one sure way to begin enjoying every day of your life.

PSALM 18

To the Chief Musician. [A Psalm] of David the servant of the Lord, who spoke the words of this song to the Lord on the day when the Lord delivered him from the hand of all his enemies and from the hand of Saul. And he said:

I LOVE You fervently *and* devotedly, O Lord, my Strength.
2 The Lord is my Rock, my Fortress, and my Deliverer; my God, my keen *and* firm Strength in Whom I will trust *and* take refuge, my Shield, and the Horn of my salvation, my High Tower. [Heb. 2:13.]
3 I will call upon the Lord, Who is to be praised; so shall I be saved from my enemies. [Rev. 5:12.]
4 The cords *or* bands of death surrounded me, and the streams of ungodliness *and* the torrents of ruin terrified me.

speak the Word

5 The cords of Sheol (the place of the dead) surrounded me; the snares of death confronted *and* came upon me.
6 In my distress [when seemingly closed in] I called upon the Lord and cried to my God; He heard my voice out of His temple (heavenly dwelling place), and my cry came before Him, into His [very] ears.
7 Then the earth quaked and rocked, the foundations also of the mountains trembled; they moved *and* were shaken because He was indignant *and* angry.
8 There went up smoke from His nostrils; and lightning out of His mouth devoured; coals were kindled by it.
9 He bowed the heavens also and came down; and thick darkness was under His feet.
10 And He rode upon a cherub [a storm] and flew [swiftly]; yes, He sped on with the wings of the wind.
11 He made darkness His secret hiding place; as His pavilion (His canopy) round about Him were dark waters *and* thick clouds of the skies.
12 Out of the brightness before Him there broke forth through His thick clouds hailstones and coals of fire.
13 The Lord also thundered from the heavens, and the Most High uttered His voice, amid hailstones and coals of fire.
14 And He sent out His arrows and scattered them; and He flashed forth lightnings and put them to rout.
15 Then the beds of the sea appeared and the foundations of the world were laid bare at Your rebuke, O Lord, at the blast of the breath of Your nostrils.
16 He reached from on high, He took

Lord, I declare that You are my Rock, my Fortress, and my Deliverer. You are my keen and firm Strength, my Shield, the Horn of my salvation, and my High Tower!
ADAPTED FROM PSALM 18:2

me; He drew me out of many waters.
17 He delivered me from my strong enemy and from those who hated *and* abhorred me, for they were too strong for me.
18 They confronted *and* came upon me in the day of my calamity, but the Lord was my stay *and* support.
19 He brought me forth also into a large place; He was delivering me because He was pleased with me *and* delighted in me.
20 The Lord rewarded me according to my righteousness (my conscious integrity and sincerity with Him); according to the cleanness of my hands has He recompensed me.
21 For I have kept the ways of the Lord and have not wickedly departed from my God.
22 For all His ordinances were before me, and I put not away His statutes from me.
23 I was upright before Him *and* blameless with Him, ever [on guard] to keep myself free from my sin *and* guilt.
24 Therefore has the Lord recompensed me according to my righteousness (my uprightness and right standing with Him), according to the cleanness of my hands in His sight.
25 With the kind *and* merciful You will show Yourself kind *and* merciful, with an upright man You will show Yourself upright,
26 With the pure You will show Yourself pure, and with the perverse You will show Yourself contrary.
27 For You deliver an afflicted *and* humble people but will bring down those with haughty looks.
28 For You cause my lamp to be lighted *and* to shine; the Lord my God illumines my darkness.
29 For by You I can run through a

troop, and by my God I can leap over a wall.
30 As for God, His way is perfect! The word of the Lord is tested *and* tried; He is a shield to all those who take refuge *and* put their trust in Him.
31 For who is God except the Lord? Or who is the Rock save our God,
32 The God who girds me with strength and makes my way perfect?
33 He makes my feet like hinds' feet [able to stand firmly or make progress on the dangerous heights of testing and trouble]; He sets me securely upon my high places.
34 He teaches my hands to war, so that my arms can bend a bow of bronze.
35 You have also given me the shield of Your salvation, and Your right hand has held me up; Your gentleness *and* condescension have made me great.
36 You have given plenty of room for my steps under me, that my feet would not slip.
37 I pursued my enemies and overtook them; neither did I turn again till they were consumed.
38 I smote them so that they were not able to rise; they fell wounded under my feet.
39 For You have girded me with strength for the battle; You have subdued under me and caused to bow down those who rose up against me.
40 You have also made my enemies turn their backs to me, that I might cut off those who hate me.
41 They cried [for help], but there was none to deliver—even unto the Lord, but He answered them not.
42 Then I beat them small as the dust before the wind; I emptied them out as the dirt *and* mire of the streets.
43 You have delivered me from the strivings of the people; You made me

speak the Word

God, I know that Your way is perfect; Your word is tested and tried!
ADAPTED FROM PSALM 18:30

the head of the nations; a people I had not known served me.

44 As soon as they heard of me, they obeyed me; foreigners submitted themselves cringingly *and* yielded feigned obedience to me.

45 Foreigners lost heart and came trembling out of their caves *or* strongholds.

46 The Lord lives! Blessed be my Rock; and let the God of my salvation be exalted,

47 The God Who avenges me and subdues peoples under me,

48 Who delivers me from my enemies; yes, You lift me up above those who rise up against me; You deliver me from the man of violence.

49 Therefore will I give thanks *and* extol You, O Lord, among the nations, and sing praises to Your name. [Rom. 15:9.]

50 Great deliverances *and* triumphs gives He to His king; and He shows mercy *and* steadfast love to His anointed, to David and his offspring forever. [II Sam. 22:2-51.]

PSALM 19
To the Chief Musician. A Psalm of David.

THE HEAVENS declare the glory of God; and the firmament shows *and* proclaims His handiwork. [Rom. 1:20, 21.]

2 Day after day pours forth speech, and night after night shows forth knowledge.

3 There is no speech nor spoken word [from the stars]; their voice is not heard.

4 Yet their voice [in evidence] goes out through all the earth, their sayings to the end of the world. Of the heavens has God made a tent for the sun, [Rom. 10:18.]

5 Which is as a bridegroom coming out of his chamber; and it rejoices as a strong man to run his course.

6 Its going forth is from the end of the heavens, and its circuit to the ends of it; and nothing [yes, no one] is hidden from the heat of it.

7 The law of the Lord is perfect, restoring the [whole] person; the testimony of the Lord is sure, making wise the simple.

8 The precepts of the Lord are right, rejoicing the heart; the commandment of the Lord is pure *and* bright, enlightening the eyes.

9 The [reverent] fear of the Lord is clean, enduring forever; the ordinances of the Lord are true and righteous altogether.

10 More to be desired are they than gold, even than much fine gold; they are sweeter also than honey and drippings from the honeycomb.

11 Moreover, by them is Your servant warned (reminded, illuminated, and instructed); and in keeping them there is great reward.

putting the Word to work

Our everyday lives are governed by man-made laws that are for our benefit—obeying the speed limit, stopping at red lights, etc. Are you equally aware of the benefits of living by God's perfect law? Wisdom, joy, righteousness, rewards—all these things and more are benefits that come from living according to God's law. Spend time studying God's Word each day, and ask Him to help you live by it, so you can glorify Him and enjoy His blessings.

12 Who can discern his lapses *and* errors? Clear me from hidden [and unconscious] faults.

13 Keep back Your servant also from presumptuous sins; let them not have dominion over me! Then shall I be blameless, and I shall be innocent *and* clear of great transgression.

14 Let the words of my mouth and the meditation of my heart be acceptable

enjoy God's handiwork

God speaks to everyone through His handiwork. Even people living outside the will of God perceive right from wrong and the reality of God, because Psalm 19:1–4 tells us that nature itself testifies of God's power and divine plan.

I encourage you to take time to look at what God has created. The main message God speaks to us through nature is that *He is*. This is an important revelation because the Bible says that before we can get anywhere with God, we must first believe He is: "But without faith it is impossible to please and be satisfactory to Him. For whoever would come near to God must [necessarily] believe that God exists and that He is the rewarder of those who earnestly and diligently seek Him [out]" (Hebrews 11:6). We *can* believe God because the Bible says He has given every person a measure of faith to believe in Him (see Romans 12:3).

The very first words of the Bible give our first lesson of faith: "In the beginning God . . ." Many people acknowledge that God exists, but they have not learned to relate to Him on a day-to-day level. Through grace, God tries to reach us every day, and He places reminders of Himself everywhere. He leaves clues of Himself all around us, clues that bellow out clearly, "I am here. You do not have to live in fear; you do not have to worry, I am here." God wants to be involved in every aspect of your life. If He has taken time to keep all your tears in a bottle and count the very hairs on your head, then surely He cares about everything else.

Jesus said to consider the lilies of the field (see Matthew 6:28) and the birds of the air (see Luke 12:24). Meditating on how God adorns the fields and provides for the birds can remind us that He cares even more for us. A nice walk outdoors is a great opportunity to take a short vacation from the pressures of daily living and look at the trees, the birds, the flowers, and the children playing. Let me encourage you to take time to appreciate God's awesome handiwork today and to thank Him that He *is*.

Life is sometimes very complicated, but we can purposely learn to enjoy the simple yet powerful and beautiful things God has created!

in Your sight, O Lord, my [firm, impenetrable] Rock and my Redeemer.

PSALM 20
To the Chief Musician. A Psalm of David.

MAY THE Lord answer you in the day of trouble! May the name of the God of Jacob set you up on high [and defend you];

2 Send you help from the sanctuary and support, refresh, *and* strengthen you from Zion;

3 Remember all your offerings and accept your burnt sacrifice. Selah [pause, and think of that]!

4 May He grant you according to your heart's desire and fulfill all your plans.

5 We will [shout in] triumph at your salvation *and* victory, and in the name of our God we will set up our

life point

In Psalm 19:14, the psalmist prays: "Let the words of my mouth and the meditation of my heart be acceptable in Your sight, O Lord, my [firm, impenetrable] Rock and my Redeemer." Notice that he mentions both the mind and the mouth. This is because the two work together. We need to make sure that our meditations (our thoughts) are pleasing to God so that our words will be acceptable to Him as well.

banners. May the Lord fulfill all your petitions.

6 Now I know that the Lord saves His anointed; He will answer him from His holy heaven with the saving strength of His right hand.

7 Some trust in *and* boast of chariots and some of horses, but we will trust in *and* boast of the name of the Lord our God.

8 They are bowed down and fallen, but we are risen and stand upright.

9 O Lord, give victory; let the King answer us when we call.

PSALM 21
To the Chief Musician. A Psalm of David.

THE KING [David] shall joy in Your strength, O Lord; and in Your salvation how greatly shall he rejoice!

2 You have given him his heart's desire and have not withheld the request of his lips. Selah [pause, and think of that]!

3 For You send blessings of good things to meet him; You set a crown of pure gold on his head.

4 He asked life of You, *and* You gave it to him—long life forever and evermore.

5 His glory is great because of Your aid; splendor and majesty You bestow upon him.

6 For You make him to be blessed *and* a blessing forever; You make him exceedingly glad with the joy of Your presence. [Gen. 12:2.]

7 For the king trusts, relies on, *and* is confident in the Lord, and through the mercy *and* steadfast love of the Most High he will never be moved.

8 Your hand shall find all Your enemies; Your right hand shall find all those who hate You.

9 You will make them as if in a blazing oven in the time of Your anger; the Lord will swallow them up in His wrath, and the fire will utterly consume them.

10 Their offspring You will destroy from the earth, and their sons from among the children of men.

11 For they planned evil against You; they conceived a mischievous plot which they are not able to perform.

12 For You will make them turn their backs; You will aim Your bow [of divine justice] at their faces.

13 Be exalted, Lord, in Your strength; we will sing and praise Your power.

[d]PSALM 22
To the Chief Musician; set to [the tune of] Aijeleth Hashshahar [the hind of the morning dawn]. A Psalm of David.

MY GOD, my God, why have You forsaken me? Why are You so far from helping me, and from the words of my groaning? [Matt. 27:46.]

d "This is beyond all others 'The Psalm of the Cross.' It may have been actually repeated by our Lord when hanging on the tree; it would be too bold to say so, but even a casual reader may see that it might have been. It begins with, 'My God, my God, why hast thou forsaken me?' and ends [with the thought], 'It is finished.' For plaintive expressions uprising from unutterable depths of woe, we may say of this psalm, 'There is none like it' " (Charles Haddon Spurgeon, *The Treasury of David*). Quoted in the Gospels (Matt. 27:46; Mark 15:34; and alluded to in Matt. 27:35, 39, 43 and John 19:23-24, 28) as being fulfilled at Christ's crucifixion.

2 O my God, I cry in the daytime, but You answer not; and by night I am not silent *or* find no rest.

3 But You are holy, O You Who dwell in [the holy place where] the praises of Israel [are offered].

4 Our fathers trusted in You; they trusted (leaned on, relied on You, and were confident) and You delivered them.

5 They cried to You and were delivered; they trusted in, leaned on, *and* confidently relied on You, and were not ashamed *or* confounded *or* disappointed.

6 But I am a worm, and no man; I am the scorn of men, and despised by the people. [Matt. 27:39-44.]

7 All who see me laugh at me *and* mock me; they shoot out the lip, they shake the head, saying, [Matt. 27:43.]

8 He trusted *and* rolled himself on the Lord, that He would deliver him. Let Him deliver him, seeing that He delights in him! [Matt. 27:39, 43; Mark 15:29, 30; Luke 23:35.]

9 Yet You are He Who took me out of the womb; You made me hope *and* trust when I was on my mother's breasts.

10 I was cast upon You from my very birth; from my mother's womb You have been my God.

11 Be not far from me, for trouble is near and there is none to help.

12 Many [foes like] bulls have surrounded me; strong bulls of Bashan have hedged me in. [Ezek. 39:18.]

13 Against me they opened their mouths wide, like a ravening and roaring lion.

14 I am poured out like water, and all my bones are out of joint. My heart is like wax; it is softened [with anguish] *and* melted down within me.

15 My strength is dried up like a fragment of clay pottery; [with thirst] my tongue cleaves to my jaws; and You have brought me into the dust of death. [John 19:28.]

life point

God inhabits the praises of His people (see Psalm 22:3). That means He is comfortable in the midst of our sweet praises, but He is not comfortable in the midst of our sour attitudes.

I encourage you to take an inventory of your inner life because it is the dwelling place of God. When God dwelled in the portable tabernacle that the children of Israel carried through the wilderness, they understood that the inner court was a holy place. But now in the mystery of God's plan, we are like a portable tabernacle; we move from place to place, and God dwells inside us. There is still an outer court, a holy place, and a most holy place. The outer court is our body, the holy place is our soul, and the most holy place is our spirit.

When we examine our inner lives, we are looking at holy ground where the Spirit of God wants to make His home. God is much more interested in our inner lives than in our outer lives, and we need to be more concerned about what goes on *inside* us than about our external behavior. Praise, worship, and honor God in your inner life. When your "insides" are right, your "outsides" will follow!

16 For [like a pack of] dogs they have encompassed me; a company of evildoers has encircled me, they pierced my hands and my feet. [Isa. 53:7; John 19:37.]

17 I can count all my bones; [the evildoers] gaze at me. [Luke 23:27, 35.]

18 They part my clothing among them and cast lots for my raiment (a long, shirtlike garment, a seamless undertunic). [John 19:23, 24.]

19 But be not far from me, O Lord; O my Help, hasten to aid me!

20 Deliver my life from the sword, my dear life [my only one] from the power of the dog [the agent of execution].

21 Save me from the lion's mouth; for You have answered me [kindly] from the horns of the wild oxen.

22 I will declare Your name to my brethren; in the midst of the congregation will I praise You. [John 20:17; Rom. 8:29; Heb. 2:12.]

23 You who fear (revere and worship) the Lord, praise Him! All you offspring of Jacob, glorify Him. Fear (revere and worship) Him, all you offspring of Israel.

24 For He has not despised or abhorred the affliction of the afflicted; neither has He hidden His face from him, but when he cried to Him, He heard.

25 My praise shall be of You in the great congregation. I will pay to Him my vows [made in the time of trouble] before them who fear (revere and worship) Him.

26 The poor *and* afflicted shall eat and be satisfied; they shall praise the Lord—they who [diligently] seek for, inquire of *and* for Him, *and* require Him [as their greatest need]. May your hearts be quickened now *and* forever!

27 All the ends of the earth shall remember and turn to the Lord, and all the families of the nations shall bow down *and* worship before You,

28 For the kingship *and* the kingdom are the Lord's, and He is the ruler over the nations.

29 All the mighty ones upon earth shall eat [in thanksgiving] and wor-

ship; all they that go down to the dust shall bow before Him, even he who cannot keep himself alive.

30 Posterity shall serve Him; they shall tell of the Lord to the next generation.

31 They shall come and shall declare His righteousness to a people yet to be born—that He has done it [that it is finished]! [John 19:30.]

PSALM 23
A Psalm of David.

THE LORD is my Shepherd [to feed, guide, and shield me], I shall not lack.

2 He makes me lie down in [fresh, tender] green pastures; He leads me beside the still *and* restful waters. [Rev. 7:17.]

3 He refreshes *and* restores my life (my self); He leads me in the paths of righteousness [uprightness and right standing with Him—not for my earning it, but] for His name's sake.

4 Yes, though I walk through the [deep, sunless] valley of the shadow of death, I will fear *or* dread no evil, for You are with me; Your rod [to protect] and Your staff [to guide], they comfort me.

5 You prepare a table before me in the presence of my enemies. You anoint my head with ᵉoil; my [brimming] cup runs over.

6 Surely *or* only goodness, mercy, *and* unfailing love shall follow me all the days of my life, and through the length of my days the house of the Lord [and His presence] shall be my dwelling place.

---

e It is difficult for those living in a temperate climate to appreciate, but it was customary in hot climates to anoint the body with oil to protect it from excessive perspiration. When mixed with perfume, the oil imparted a delightfully refreshing and invigorating sensation. Athletes anointed their bodies as a matter of course before running a race. As the body, therefore, anointed with oil was refreshed, invigorated, and better fitted for action, so the Lord would anoint His "sheep" with the Holy Spirit, Whom oil symbolizes, to fit them to engage more freely in His service and run in the way He directs—in heavenly fellowship with Him.

God restores and leads

The Twenty-third Psalm is so comforting. In it the psalmist David tells us the Lord leads, feeds, guides, and shields us. He causes us to lie down and rest, and He "refreshes and restores" (Psalm 23:3) our lives. I like the way the Amplified Bible translates this verse, but I also like the way the beautiful old King James Version renders it: "He restoreth my soul." The soul is comprised of the mind, the will, and the emotions.

With our souls, we process our circumstances, we entertain our thoughts, we feel and express emotions, and we make decisions. What a wonderful promise—that God will restore our souls! The word *restore* means "to bring back into existence or use" or "to bring back to an original state or condition." The word is often used in a situation when a dethroned ruler is put back on his throne. *Restore* also means "to make restitution, to cause to return, or to refresh."

When David says God will restore our souls and our lives, I believe he means that God will return us to the state or condition we were in before we erred from following the good plan God had predestined for us before our birth, or before Satan attacked us to draw us out of God's plan for our lives.

We can take confidence that God will lead us in the path of righteousness, uprightness, and right standing with Him. I believe David is saying here that God individually leads each of us in the path that is right for us, a path that restores us in every way to the good places God has for us.

God has a path predestined for your restoration. If you will allow Him to do so, He will guide you by His Holy Spirit along the unique way that leads to restoration and to being able to fulfill the great purposes He has for your life.

putting the Word to work

At some point in our lives, all of us will walk through the valley of the shadow of death, either facing our own death, the death of a loved one, or some other extraordinarily difficult time (see Psalm 23:4). Are you or is someone you love walking through that valley right now? Remember, where there is a shadow, there must be light—and the Light of the world, Jesus, has promised to be with you always. Ask Him right now to comfort and guide you, and know that He is walking with you in every situation.

PSALM 24
A Psalm of David.

THE EARTH is the Lord's, and the fullness of it, the world and they who dwell in it. [I Cor. 10:26.]

2 For He has founded it upon the seas and established it upon the currents *and* the rivers.

3 Who shall go up into the mountain of the Lord? Or who shall stand in His Holy Place?

4 He who has clean hands and a pure heart, who has not lifted himself up to falsehood *or* to what is false, nor sworn deceitfully. [Matt. 5:8.]

life point

This last part of the beloved Psalm 23 describes the condition in which the Lord wants us to be continually. He wants us to be protected, guided, and comforted. He wants to set a table of blessings before us in the very face of our enemies. He wants to anoint us with the oil of joy instead of mourning. He wants our cup of blessings to overflow continually in thanksgiving and praise to Him for His goodness, mercy, and unfailing love toward us. And He wants us to live, moment by moment, in His presence.

All these things are part of His good plan for each of us. Regardless of how far we may have fallen, He wants to raise us up and restore us to that right and perfect plan He has for our lives.

5   He shall receive blessing from the Lord and righteousness from the God of his salvation.
6   This is the generation [description] of those who seek Him [who inquire of and for Him and of necessity require Him], who seek Your face, [O God of] Jacob. Selah [pause, and think of that]! [Ps. 42:1.]
7   Lift up your heads, O you gates; and be lifted up, you age-abiding doors, that the King of glory may come in.
8   Who is the King of glory? The Lord strong and mighty, the Lord mighty in battle.
9   Lift up your heads, O you gates; yes, lift them up, you age-abiding doors, that the King of glory may come in.
10 Who is [He then] this King of

glory? The Lord of hosts, He is the King of glory. Selah [pause, and think of that]!

PSALM 25
[A Psalm] of David.

UNTO YOU, O Lord, do I bring my life.
2   O my God, I trust, lean on, rely on, *and* am confident in You. Let me not be put to shame *or* [my hope in You] be disappointed; let not my enemies triumph over me.
3   Yes, let none who trust *and* wait hopefully *and* look for You be put to shame *or* be disappointed; let them be ashamed who forsake the right *or* deal treacherously without cause.
4   Show me Your ways, O Lord; teach me Your paths.
5   Guide me in Your truth *and* faithfulness and teach me, for You are the God of my salvation; for You [You only and altogether] do I wait [expectantly] all the day long.
6   Remember, O Lord, Your tender mercy and loving-kindness; for they have been ever from of old.
7   Remember not the sins (the lapses and frailties) of my youth or my transgressions; according to Your mercy *and* steadfast love remember me, for Your goodness' sake, O Lord.
8   Good and upright is the Lord; therefore will He instruct sinners in [His] way.
9   He leads the humble in what is right, and the humble He teaches His way.
10 All the paths of the Lord are mercy *and* steadfast love, even truth *and* faithfulness are they for those

speak the Word

God, I pray that You would show me Your ways and teach me Your paths. I am asking You to guide me in Your faithfulness. You are my salvation, and I am waiting expectantly on You.
ADAPTED FROM PSALM 25:4, 5

at ease

In order to live victorious lives, we need to be comfortable spiritually. That may sound strange to you, so let me share a story to explain what I mean.

In 1980, I had a job as the pastor's secretary at my church in St. Louis. After working one day, I got fired. Do you know why? Because I was not supposed to be a secretary; therefore, God would not bless me in that job.

You see, my desire to be a secretary was *my* idea, not God's; it was something *I* wanted to do, not something God wanted me to do. The job was not a "fit" for me; it was not comfortable for me, and I did not have grace to do it. It was not part of God's purpose for my life, and He would not allow me to stay in that job because He had other plans for me.

Trying to do things that are not part of God's plan for our lives is like trying to force our feet into shoes that are too small. I have been guilty of wanting to buy shoes that are slightly too tight, but I do not do that anymore. I have learned that tight shoes are not comfortable, and I want my feet to be comfortable.

During those days, I wanted to be comfortable spiritually too. I wanted to be relaxed in spirit; I wanted my inner life to be at ease, as though I were walking around in my most comfortable shoes. I wanted to be relaxed in my relationship with God and to feel at home in His presence. I also wanted to be comfortable around other people and not be afraid of their disapproval. All those things that I wanted I now enjoy because I have learned to follow God's plan rather than my own.

Do you feel the same way? Are you tired of being uncomfortable and being in places that do not fit God's call on your life? Are you tired of being spiritually uncomfortable, insecure, or anxious all the time?

I have good news for you. Psalm 25:12, 13 tell us that we can be at ease if we fear God, worship Him, and do only the things He has planned for us without trying to force our own agendas or striving to do what *we* want to do. God loves you, and He has awesome plans for your life. Surrender to His plans and His way—and you will find yourself at ease.

who keep His covenant and His testimonies.
11 For Your name's sake, O Lord, pardon my iniquity *and* my guilt, for [they are] great.
12 Who is the man who reverently fears *and* worships the Lord? Him shall He teach in the way that he should choose.

13 He himself shall dwell at ease, and his offspring shall inherit the land.
14 The secret [of the sweet, satisfying companionship] of the Lord have they who fear (revere and worship) Him, and He will show them His covenant *and* reveal to them its [deep, inner] meaning. [John 7:17; 15:15.]
15 My eyes are ever toward the Lord,

for He will pluck my feet out of the net.

16 [Lord] turn to me and be gracious to me, for I am lonely and afflicted.

17 The troubles of my heart are multiplied; bring me out of my distresses.

18 Behold my affliction and my pain and forgive all my sins [of thinking and doing].

19 Consider my enemies, for they abound; they hate me with cruel hatred.

20 O keep me, Lord, and deliver me; let me not be ashamed *or* disappointed, for my trust *and* my refuge are in You.

21 Let integrity and uprightness preserve me, for I wait for *and* expect You.

22 Redeem Israel, O God, out of all their troubles.

PSALM 26
[A Psalm] of David.

VINDICATE ME, O Lord, for I have walked in my integrity; I have [expectantly] trusted in, leaned on, *and* relied on the Lord without wavering *and* I shall not slide.

2 Examine me, O Lord, and prove me; test my heart and my mind.

3 For Your loving-kindness is before my eyes, and I have walked in Your truth [faithfully].

4 I do not sit with false persons, nor fellowship with pretenders;

5 I hate the company of evildoers and will not sit with the wicked.

6 I will wash my hands in innocence, and go about Your altar, O Lord,

7 That I may make the voice of thanksgiving heard and may tell of all Your wondrous works.

8 Lord, I love the habitation of Your house, and the place where Your glory dwells.

9 Gather me not with sinners *and* sweep me not away [with them], nor my life with bloodthirsty men,

10 In whose hands is wickedness, and their right hands are full of bribes.

11 But as for me, I will walk in my integrity; redeem me and be merciful *and* gracious to me.

12 My foot stands on an even place; in the congregations will I bless the Lord.

PSALM 27
[A Psalm] of David.

THE LORD is my Light and my Salvation—whom shall I fear *or* dread? The Lord is the Refuge *and* Stronghold of my life—of whom shall I be afraid?

2 When the wicked, even my enemies and my foes, came upon me to eat up my flesh, they stumbled and fell.

3 Though a host encamp against me, my heart shall not fear; though war arise against me, [even then] in this will I be confident.

4 One thing have I asked of the Lord, that will I seek, inquire for, *and* [insistently] require: that I may dwell in the house of the Lord [in His presence] all the days of my life, to behold *and* gaze upon the beauty [the sweet attractiveness and the delightful loveliness] of the Lord and to meditate, consider, *and* inquire in His temple. [Ps. 16:11; 18:6; 65:4; Luke 2:37.]

5 For in the day of trouble He will hide me in His shelter; in the secret place of His tent will He hide me; He will set me high upon a rock.

6 And now shall my head be lifted up above my enemies round about me; in His tent I will offer sacrifices *and* shouting of joy; I will sing, yes, I will sing praises to the Lord.

7 Hear, O Lord, when I cry aloud; have mercy *and* be gracious to me and answer me!

8 You have said, Seek My face [inquire for and require My presence as your vital need]. My heart says to

seek the "One Thing"

If you could ask for only one thing, what would it be? In Psalm 27:4, David said there was only one thing that he sought after—to dwell in God's presence. More than anything else, David wanted to know God, to see God as He really is and to be with Him. Truly, to know God is the highest calling we have.

Unfortunately, we can get so distracted with the busy details of our lives that we neglect the most important thing—spending time with God. Luke 10:38–42 illustrates this point well as it relates the story of busy Martha. When Jesus visited her home, she became preoccupied with serving, but her sister Mary stopped all work and sat at His feet. Jesus told Martha that only one thing was really important, and Mary had chosen it. Mary had decided she was not going to miss the opportunity to visit with the Master. I suppose Martha intended to work Jesus into her schedule somewhere, but Mary was willing to stop what she was doing and work her schedule around Him.

How foolish we are to spend our lives seeking those things that cannot satisfy while we ignore God, the "One Thing" Who can give us great joy, peace, satisfaction, and contentment. The world is filled with empty people who are trying to satisfy the void in their lives with the latest-model car, a promotion at work, a human relationship, a vacation, or some other thing. Their efforts to find fulfillment in those things never work. It is sad that so many people waste their entire lives and never realize it. They never know the joy of seeking the "One Thing" they really need. Each one of us has a God-shaped hole inside, and nothing can fill it except God Himself. No matter what else we try to fill it with, we will remain empty and frustrated.

If God is on your list of things to seek, but not at the top, I encourage you to move everything around and put it all *after* Him. If you will put Him first in everything you do, you will be so blessed. Investing your life in God is the very best thing you can do.

You, Your face (Your presence), Lord, will I seek, inquire for, *and* require [of necessity and on the authority of Your Word].

9 Hide not Your face from me; turn not Your servant away in anger, You Who have been my help! Cast me not off, neither forsake me, O God of my salvation!

10 Although my father and my mother have forsaken me, yet the Lord will take me up [adopt me as His child]. [Ps. 22:10.]

11 Teach me Your way, O Lord, and lead me in a plain *and* even path because of my enemies [those who lie in wait for me].

12 Give me not up to the will of my adversaries, for false witnesses have risen up against me; they breathe out cruelty *and* violence.

13 [What, what would have become of me] had I not believed that I would see the Lord's goodness in the land of the living!

14 Wait *and* hope for *and* expect the Lord; be brave *and* of good courage and let your heart be stout *and* enduring. Yes, wait for *and* hope for *and* expect the Lord.

the land of the living

In Psalm 27:13, David asked, basically, "What in the world would have happened to me? What kind of condition would I be in? What pit would I be in, had I not believed I would see the Lord's goodness in the land of the living?"

We spend a lot of time talking about what heaven will be like. That is great, but we are here on earth right now. We need to know something good is going to happen to us now. David said that he believed he would see God's goodness while he was alive, not just after he went to heaven.

I am looking forward to heaven, but I do not believe that God put us on earth to try to muddle through life until we get to heaven so we can finally have some joy. In John 10:10, Jesus says, "The thief comes only in order to steal and kill and destroy. I came that they may have and enjoy life, and have it in abundance (to the full, till it overflows)." God wants us to have abundant life right now, and one of the worst things we can do is fail to live lives that we enjoy. I have decided to enjoy my life while I am "in the land of the living." I want to have so much fun that the devil gets frustrated at my joy.

Let me encourage you to be like David and to believe that you will see and experience God's goodness not just in the "sweet by-and-by," but here on earth, every day, in the ordinary activities of your life. No matter what you are going through, put your hope in God's goodness and expect Him to move in your situation. Be brave and of good courage; let your heart be stout and enduring. Wait for and hope for and expect the Lord where you live today—in the land of the living.

PSALM 28
[A Psalm] of David.

UNTO YOU do I cry, O Lord my Rock, be not deaf *and* silent to me, lest, if You be silent to me, I become like those going down to the pit [the grave].

2 Hear the voice of my supplication as I cry to You for help, as I lift up my hands toward Your innermost sanctuary (the Holy of Holies).

3 Drag me not away with the wicked, with the workers of iniquity, who speak peace with their neighbors, but malice *and* mischief are in their hearts.

4 Repay them according to their work and according to the wickedness of their doings; repay them according to the work of their hands; render to them what they deserve. [II Tim. 4:14; Rev. 18:6.]

5 Because they regard not the works of the Lord nor the operations of His hands, He will break them down and not rebuild them.

6 Blessed be the Lord, because He has heard the voice of my supplications.

7 The Lord is my Strength and my

speak the Word

Lord, You are my Strength and my impenetrable Shield. My heart trusts in, relies on, and confidently leans on You.
ADAPTED FROM PSALM 28:7

[impenetrable] Shield; my heart trusts in, relies on, *and* confidently leans on Him, and I am helped; therefore my heart greatly rejoices, and with my song will I praise Him.

8 The Lord is their [unyielding] Strength, and He is the Stronghold of salvation to [me] His anointed.

9 Save Your people and bless Your heritage; nourish *and* shepherd them and carry them forever.

ᶠPSALM 29

A Psalm of David.

ASCRIBE TO the Lord, O sons of the mighty, ascribe to the Lord glory and strength.

2 Give to the Lord the glory due to His name; worship the Lord in the beauty of holiness *or* in holy array.

3 The voice of the Lord is upon the waters; the God of glory thunders; the Lord is upon many (great) waters.

4 The voice of the Lord is powerful; the voice of the Lord is full of majesty.

5 The voice of the Lord breaks the cedars; yes, the Lord breaks in pieces the cedars of Lebanon.

6 He makes them also to skip like a calf; Lebanon and Sirion (Mount Hermon) like a young, wild ox.

7 The voice of the Lord splits *and* flashes forth forked lightning.

8 The voice of the Lord makes the wilderness tremble; the Lord shakes the Wilderness of Kadesh.

9 The voice of the Lord makes the hinds bring forth their young, and His voice strips bare the forests, while in His temple everyone is saying, Glory!

10 The Lord sat as King over the deluge; the Lord [still] sits as King [and] forever!

11 The Lord will give [unyielding and impenetrable] strength to His people; the Lord will bless His people with peace.

PSALM 30

A Psalm; a Song at the Dedication of the Temple. [A Psalm] of David.

I WILL extol You, O Lord, for You have lifted me up and have not let my foes rejoice over me.

2 O Lord my God, I cried to You and You have healed me.

3 O Lord, You have brought my life up from Sheol (the place of the dead); You have kept me alive, that I should not go down to the pit (the grave).

4 Sing to the Lord, O you saints of His, and give thanks at the remembrance of His holy name.

5 For His anger is but for a moment, but His favor is for a lifetime *or* in His favor is life. Weeping may endure for a night, but joy comes in the morning. [II Cor. 4:17.]

6 As for me, in my prosperity I said, I shall never be moved.

7 By Your favor, O Lord, You have established me as a strong mountain; You hid Your face, and I was troubled.

8 I cried to You, O Lord, and to the Lord I made supplication.

9 What profit is there in my blood, when I go down to the pit (the grave)?

speak the Word

Thank You, God, that Your anger lasts for only a moment, but Your favor lasts for a lifetime. Thank You that weeping endures for only a night and that joy comes in the morning.
ADAPTED FROM PSALM 30:5

---

f This psalm has been called "The Song of the Thunderstorm," a glorious psalm of praise sung during an earthshaking tempest which reminds the psalmist of the time of Noah and the deluge (see Ps. 29:10).

Will the dust praise You? Will it declare Your truth *and* faithfulness to men?

10 Hear, O Lord, have mercy *and* be gracious to me! O Lord, be my helper!

11 You have turned my mourning into dancing for me; You have put off my sackcloth and girded me with gladness,

12 To the end that my tongue *and* my heart *and* everything glorious within me may sing praise to You and not be silent. O Lord my God, I will give thanks to You forever.

PSALM 31

To the Chief Musician. A Psalm of David.

IN YOU, O Lord, do I put my trust *and* seek refuge; let me never be put to shame *or* [have my hope in You] disappointed; deliver me in Your righteousness!

2 Bow down Your ear to me, deliver me speedily! Be my Rock of refuge, a strong Fortress to save me!

3 Yes, You are my Rock and my Fortress; therefore for Your name's sake lead me and guide me.

4 Draw me out of the net that they have laid secretly for me, for You are my Strength *and* my Stronghold.

5 Into Your hands I commit my spirit; You have redeemed me, O Lord, the God of truth *and* faithfulness. [Luke 23:46; Acts 7:59.]

6 [You and] I abhor those who pay regard to vain idols; but I trust in, rely on, *and* confidently lean on the Lord.

7 I will be glad and rejoice in Your mercy *and* steadfast love, because You have seen my affliction, You have taken note of my life's distresses,

8 And You have not given me into the hand of the enemy; You have set my feet in a broad place.

9 Have mercy *and* be gracious unto me, O Lord, for I am in trouble; with grief my eye is weakened, also my inner self and my body.

10 For my life is spent with sorrow and my years with sighing; my strength has failed because of my iniquity, and even my bones have wasted away.

11 To all my enemies I have become a reproach, but especially to my neighbors, and a dread to my acquaintances, who flee from me on the street.

12 I am forgotten like a dead man, and out of mind; like a broken vessel am I.

13 For I have heard the slander of many; terror is on every side! While they schemed together against me, they plotted to take my life.

14 But I trusted in, relied on, *and* was confident in You, O Lord; I said, You are my God.

15 My times are in Your hands; deliver me from the hands of my foes and those who pursue me *and* persecute me.

16 Let Your face shine on Your servant; save me for Your mercy's sake *and* in Your loving-kindness.

17 Let me not be put to shame, O Lord, *or* disappointed, for I am calling upon You; let the wicked be put to shame, let them be silent in Sheol (the place of the dead).

18 Let the lying lips be silenced, which speak insolently against the [consistently] righteous with pride and contempt.

19 Oh, how great is Your goodness, which You have laid up for those who fear, revere, *and* worship You, goodness which You have wrought for those who trust *and* take refuge in You before the sons of men!

20 In the secret place of Your presence You hide them from the plots of men; You keep them secretly in Your pavilion from the strife of tongues.

21 Blessed be the Lord! For He has shown me His marvelous loving favor when I was beset as in a besieged city.

22 As for me, I said in my haste *and* alarm, I am cut off from before Your eyes. But You heard the voice of my supplications when I cried to You for aid.

23 O love the Lord, all you His saints! The Lord preserves the faithful, and plentifully pays back him who deals haughtily.

24 Be strong and let your heart take courage, all you who wait for *and* hope for *and* expect the Lord!

PSALM 32

[A Psalm of David.] A skillful song, *or* a didactic *or* reflective poem.

BLESSED (HAPPY, fortunate, to be envied) is he who has forgiveness of his transgression continually exercised upon him, whose sin is covered.

everyday Christianity

God is good. All the time! Psalm 31:19 says that He stores up goodness for those who fear, revere, and worship Him. Notice also that this verse mentions the importance of trusting God *before the sons of men*. This phrase says to me that if I refuse to be what some might call a "closet Christian," but instead be open and live my Christianity before the sons of men, God will store up His goodness for me.

A number of people today profess to be Christians, but they do not want to admit it or live the principles of their faith outside their Christian circles. They are "Sunday morning" Christians, but on Monday morning they act no differently than unbelievers do. I call them "Sunday morning saints and Monday morning sinners."

I was once that way! I used to do all the "right" things in the right Christian circles, but I was not demonstrating vital faith elsewhere. I was on the church board, my husband was an elder in the church, our children went to Christian schools, our social life revolved around church, and we had a set of Christian bumper stickers for our cars. However, in my neighborhood, a person could not tell the difference between my behavior and the behavior of an unsaved person. At work, a person could not tell from my words or behavior that I was any different from my unsaved coworkers. Perhaps there was some difference, but not enough to notice! I was not taking the strong stand that I should have taken for God.

This is true for many of us. Because we are afraid of being rejected, isolated, or laughed at, we are afraid to take a stand and say, "I really don't want to hear a dirty joke. I'm a Christian, and I don't like to hear people take the Lord's name in vain. I'm not really interested in going to movies that leave wrong images in my mind or running to the bar every night after work for happy hour. That's not what I'm about. My life and my relationship with God are too important to me." That is what the scripture means when it says, "Those who trust and take refuge in You before the sons of men" will be blessed. We must care more about our reputation in heaven than our reputation among men on earth. Stand strong for God, and never be ashamed or embarrassed to live the Christian life openly and boldly before other people.

2 Blessed (happy, fortunate, to be envied) is the man to whom the Lord imputes no iniquity and in whose spirit there is no deceit. [Rom. 4:7, 8.]
3 When I kept silence [before I confessed], my bones wasted away through my groaning all the day long.
4 For day and night Your hand [of displeasure] was heavy upon me; my moisture was turned into the drought of summer. Selah [pause, and calmly think of that]!
5 I acknowledged my sin to You, and my iniquity I did not hide. I said, I will confess my transgressions to the Lord [continually unfolding the past till all is told]—then You [instantly] forgave me the guilt *and* iniquity of my sin. Selah [pause, and calmly think of that]!
6 For this [forgiveness] let everyone who is godly pray—pray to You in a time when You may be found; surely when the great waters [of trial] overflow, they shall not reach [the spirit in] him.
7 You are a hiding place for me; You, Lord, preserve me from trouble, You surround me with songs *and* shouts of deliverance. Selah [pause, and calmly think of that]!
8 I [the Lord] will instruct you and teach you in the way you should go; I will counsel you with My eye upon you.
9 Be not like the horse or the mule, which lack understanding, which must have their mouths held firm with bit and bridle, or else they will not come with you.
10 Many are the sorrows of the wicked, but he who trusts in, relies on, *and* confidently leans on the Lord shall be compassed about with mercy *and* with loving-kindness.

speak the Word

life point

Psalm 32:9 encourages us not to be like horses or mules, which need bits and bridles in order to follow their masters. Either a horse follows the pull of the bridle, which controls the bit in his mouth, or he experiences great pain by resisting it. The same principle applies to us and our relationship with the Holy Spirit. He is our bridle and the bit in our mouths. He should be controlling the reins of our lives. If we follow His promptings, we will end up at the right places and stay out of the wrong places. But if we do not follow Him, we will end up with a lot of pain. Determine today that you will let Him guide you and that you will not resist His leading in your life.

11 Be glad in the Lord and rejoice, you [uncompromisingly] righteous [you who are upright and in right standing with Him]; shout for joy, all you upright in heart!

PSALM 33

REJOICE IN the Lord, O you [uncompromisingly] righteous [you upright in right standing with God]; for praise is becoming *and* appropriate for those who are upright [in heart].
2 Give thanks to the Lord with the lyre; sing praises to Him with the harp of ten strings.
3 Sing to Him a new song; play skillfully [on the strings] with a loud *and* joyful sound.
4 For the word of the Lord is right;

God, I declare that Your Word is right and that all Your work is done in faithfulness.
ADAPTED FROM PSALM 33:4

and all His work is done in faithfulness.

5 He loves righteousness and justice; the earth is full of the lovingkindness of the Lord.

6 By the word of the Lord were the heavens made, and all their host by the breath of His mouth. [Heb. 11:3; II Pet. 3:5.]

7 He gathers the waters of the sea as in a bottle; He puts the deeps in storage places.

8 Let all the earth fear the Lord [revere and worship Him]; let all the inhabitants of the world stand in awe of Him.

9 For He spoke, and it was done; He commanded, and it stood fast.

10 The Lord brings the counsel of the nations to nought; He makes the thoughts *and* plans of the peoples of no effect.

11 The counsel of the Lord stands forever, the thoughts of His heart through all generations.

12 Blessed (happy, fortunate, to be envied) is the nation whose God is the Lord, the people He has chosen as His heritage.

13 The Lord looks from heaven, He beholds all the sons of men;

14 From His dwelling place He looks [intently] upon all the inhabitants of the earth—

15 He Who fashions the hearts of them all, Who considers all their doings.

16 No king is saved by the great size *and* power of his army; a mighty man is not delivered by [his] much strength.

17 A horse is devoid of value for victory; neither does he deliver any by his great power.

18 Behold, the Lord's eye is upon those who fear Him [who revere and worship Him with awe], who wait for Him *and* hope in His mercy *and* loving-kindness,

19 To deliver them from death and keep them alive in famine.

20 Our inner selves wait [earnestly] for the Lord; He is our Help and our Shield.

21 For in Him does our heart rejoice, because we have trusted (relied on and been confident) in His holy name.

22 Let Your mercy *and* loving-kindness, O Lord, be upon us, in proportion to our waiting *and* hoping for You.

PSALM 34

[A Psalm] of David; when he pretended to be insane before Abimelech, who drove him out, and he went away.

I WILL bless the Lord at all times; His praise shall continually be in my mouth.

2 My life makes its boast in the Lord; let the humble *and* afflicted hear and be glad.

3 O magnify the Lord with me, and let us exalt His name together.

4 I sought (inquired of) the Lord *and* required Him [of necessity and on the authority of His Word], and He heard me, and delivered me from all my fears. [Ps. 73:25; Matt. 7:7.]

5 They looked to Him and were radiant; their faces shall never blush for shame *or* be confused.

6 This poor man cried, and the Lord heard him, and saved him out of all his troubles.

7 ᵍThe Angel of the Lord encamps around those who fear Him [who revere and worship Him with awe] and each of them He delivers. [Ps. 18:1; 145:20.]

8 O taste and see that the Lord [our God] is good! Blessed (happy, fortunate, to be envied) is the man who trusts *and* takes refuge in Him. [I Pet. 2:2, 3.]

9 O fear the Lord, you His saints [revere and worship Him]! For there

g See footnote on Gen. 16:7.

at *all* times

Notice that the psalmist says he will bless the Lord *at all times*, not just when it is convenient or it feels good (see Psalm 34:1). Let me share with you a story that really emphasized this point for me.

One of my favorite things to do when I have finished a conference is to go to a restaurant, sit down, and have a good meal. I work hard, and that is one way I relax. One time, we called a restaurant and asked for a reservation. They sounded like they had taken our reservation, but when we got there, we found out they had not. The place was jam-packed, and we waited about forty-five minutes for a table. I felt irritation rise in me, but I told myself, *Joyce, you just finished preaching and telling people how to behave in hard times, so just practice what you preach.* (You know it is amazing how sometimes when you talk about what you believe, Satan will come around and test you on it!)

Finally we were seated and began ordering. The waitress came with our beverages on a large tray. The place was so crowded that she accidentally bumped the tray and dumped all the beverages on my husband, Dave. He had on a very nice suit, and it was soaked in water, coffee, iced tea, and soda pop. At that point he could have blown up. But Dave was so nice to the waitress about the whole ordeal. He said to her, "Don't worry about it. It was a mistake. I understand. I used to work at a restaurant, and one time I dumped malts inside a customer's car. He had on a really nice suit and was taking his date out. I know how you feel. Don't worry about it." Then he went to the manager and said, "I don't want her to get in trouble. The place is overly crowded. She is doing a good job. It was not her fault." He went to the extreme to be nice.

Soon the waitress came back with the second tray of beverages, and it was obvious she had been crying. She said to us, "I feel so bad that I dumped all those drinks on you." Then she looked right at me and said, "I think I'm just nervous because you're here. I watch you on television every day."

In my heart I said, *Oh, thank You, God, thank You, thank You, thank You, that we didn't act badly about this!* What would it have done to her—what would it have said to her about God, about leaders, about television evangelists—if she would have heard me preach every day on television and then seen Dave and me have a fit over her spilling the beverages on him?

Did I feel like blowing up? To be honest, yes. The Bible never says that our temptation to sin dies or goes away. It says that since Christ died for our sin we should consider ourselves dead to sin. And sometimes that means learning to bless Him at *all times*—especially when things are not going our way.

life point

Psalm 34:7 teaches us that "the Angel of the Lord encamps around those who fear Him . . .," Do you want angels to go to work in your life? Then start worshipping God, because the Bible says that the Angel of the Lord camps around those who revere and worship Him to watch over them and deliver them.

is no want to those who truly revere *and* worship Him *with* godly fear.

10 The young lions lack food and suffer hunger, but they who seek (inquire of and require) the Lord [by right of their need and on the authority of His Word], none of them shall lack any beneficial thing.

11 Come, you children, listen to me; I will teach you to revere *and* worshipfully fear the Lord.

12 What man is he who desires life *and* longs for many days, that he may see good?

13 Keep your tongue from evil and your lips from speaking deceit.

14 Depart from evil and do good; seek, inquire for, *and* crave peace and pursue (go after) it!

15 The eyes of the Lord are toward the [uncompromisingly] righteous and His ears are open to their cry.

16 The face of the Lord is against those who do evil, to cut off the

putting the Word to work

Psalm 34:8 encourages us to "taste and see" that the Lord is good. Think for a moment about your favorite food. Can you imagine how it tastes and the pleasure it brings? How infinitely greater is the pleasure of knowing the goodness of God! Let the sweetness of His praise be on your lips continually!

h See footnote on Gen. 16:7.

remembrance of them from the earth. [I Pet. 3:10-12.]

17 When the *righteous* cry for help, the Lord hears, and delivers them out of all their distress *and* troubles.

18 The Lord is close to those who are of a broken heart and saves such as are crushed with sorrow for sin *and* are humbly *and* thoroughly penitent.

19 Many evils confront the [consistently] righteous, but the Lord delivers him out of them all.

20 He keeps all his bones; not one of them is broken.

21 Evil shall cause the death of the wicked; and they who hate the just *and* righteous shall be held guilty *and* shall be condemned.

22 The Lord redeems the lives of His servants, and none of those who take refuge *and* trust in Him shall be condemned *or* held guilty.

PSALM 35
[A Psalm] of David.

CONTEND, O Lord, with those who contend with me; fight against those who fight against me!

2 Take hold of shield and buckler, and stand up for my help!

3 Draw out also the spear and javelin *and* close up the way of those who pursue *and* persecute me. Say to me, I am your deliverance!

4 Let them be put to shame and dishonor who seek *and* require my life; let them be turned back and confounded who plan my hurt!

5 Let them be as chaff before the wind, with the [h]Angel of the Lord driving them on!

6 Let their way be through dark and slippery places, with the Angel of the Lord pursuing *and* afflicting them.

7 For without cause they hid for me their net; a pit of destruction without cause they dug for my life.

8 Let destruction befall [my foe] unawares; let the net he hid for me catch him; let him fall into that very destruction.

9 Then I shall be joyful in the Lord; I shall rejoice in His deliverance.

10 All my bones shall say, Lord, who is like You, You Who deliver the poor *and* the afflicted from him who is too strong for him, yes, the poor and the needy from him who snatches away his goods?

11 Malicious *and* unrighteous witnesses rise up; they ask me of things that I know not.

12 They reward me evil for good to my personal bereavement.

13 But as for me, when they were sick, my clothing was sackcloth; I afflicted myself with fasting, and I prayed with head bowed on my breast.

14 I behaved as if grieving for my friend *or* my brother; I bowed down in sorrow, as one who bewails his mother.

15 But in my stumbling *and* limping they rejoiced and gathered together [against me]; the smiters (slanderers and revilers) gathered against me, and I knew them not; they ceased not to slander *and* revile me.

16 Like profane mockers at feasts [making sport for the price of a cake] they gnashed at me with their teeth.

17 Lord, how long will You look on [without action]? Rescue my life from their destructions, my dear *and* only life from the lions!

18 I will give You thanks in the great assembly; I will praise You among a mighty throng.

19 Let not those who are wrongfully my foes rejoice over me; neither let them wink with the eye who hate me without cause. [John 15:24, 25.]

20 For they do not speak peace, but they devise deceitful matters against those who are quiet in the land.

21 Yes, they open their mouths wide against me; they say, Aha! Aha! Our eyes have seen it!

22 You have seen this, O Lord; keep not silence! O Lord, be not far from me!

23 Arouse Yourself, awake to the justice due me, even to my cause, my God and my Lord!

24 Judge *and* vindicate me, O Lord my God, according to Your righteousness (Your rightness and justice); and let [my foes] not rejoice over me!

25 Let them not say in their hearts, Aha, that is what we wanted! Let them not say, We have swallowed him up *and* utterly destroyed him.

26 Let them be put to shame and confusion together who rejoice at my calamity! Let them be clothed with shame and dishonor who magnify *and* exalt themselves over me!

27 Let those who favor my righteous cause *and* have pleasure in my uprightness shout for joy and be glad and say continually, Let the Lord be magnified, Who takes pleasure in the prosperity of His servant.

28 And my tongue shall talk of Your righteousness, rightness, *and* justice, and of [my reasons for] Your praise all the day long.

PSALM 36

To the Chief Musician. [A Psalm] of David the servant of the Lord.

TRANSGRESSION [like an oracle] speaks to the wicked deep in his heart. There is no fear *or* dread of God before his eyes. [Rom. 3:18.]

2 For he flatters *and* deceives himself in his own eyes that his iniquity will not be found out and be hated.

3 The words of his mouth are wrong and deceitful; he has ceased to be wise *and* to do good.

4 He plans wrongdoing on his bed; he sets himself in a way that is not good; he does not reject *or* despise evil.
5 Your mercy *and* loving-kindness, O Lord, extend to the skies, *and* Your faithfulness to the clouds.
6 Your righteousness is like the mountains of God, Your judgments are like the great deep. O Lord, You preserve man and beast.
7 How precious is Your steadfast love, O God! The children of men take refuge *and* put their trust under the shadow of Your wings.
8 They relish *and* feast on the abundance of Your house; and You cause them to drink of the stream of Your pleasures.
9 For with You is the fountain of life; in Your light do we see light. [John 4:10, 14.]
10 O continue Your loving-kindness to those who know You, Your righteousness (salvation) to the upright in heart.
11 Let not the foot of pride overtake me, and let not the hand of the wicked drive me away.
12 There the workers of iniquity fall *and* lie prostrate; they are thrust down and shall not be able to rise.

PSALM 37
[A Psalm] of David.

FRET NOT yourself because of evildoers, neither be envious against those who work un-righteousness (that which is not upright or in right standing with God).
2 For they shall soon be cut down like the grass, and wither as the green herb.
3 Trust (lean on, rely on, and be confident) in the Lord and do good; so shall you dwell in the land and feed surely on His faithfulness, *and* truly you shall be fed.
4 Delight yourself also in the Lord, and He will give you the desires *and* secret petitions of your heart.
5 Commit your way to the Lord [roll and repose each care of your load on Him]; trust (lean on, rely on, and be confident) also in Him and He will bring it to pass.
6 And He will make your uprightness *and* right standing with God go forth as the light, and your justice *and* right as [the shining sun of] the noonday.
7 Be still *and* rest in the Lord; wait for Him *and* patiently lean yourself upon Him; fret not yourself because of him who prospers in his way, because of the man who brings wicked devices to pass.
8 Cease from anger and forsake wrath; fret not yourself—it tends only to evildoing.
9 For evildoers shall be cut off, but those who wait *and* hope *and* look for the Lord [in the end] shall inherit the earth. [Isa. 57:13c.]
10 For yet a little while, and the evildoers will be no more; though you

speak the Word

Thank You, Lord, that Your mercy and loving-kindness extend to the skies and Your faithfulness to the clouds. Your righteousness is like the mountains and Your judgments are like the sea.
ADAPTED FROM PSALM 36:5, 6

I declare, God, that the fountain of life is with You. In Your light, I see light.
ADAPTED FROM PSALM 36:9

delight yourself in God

Does a way exist for us to have our desires fulfilled? According to Psalm 37:4, 5, if we delight ourselves in the Lord, He will give us the desires of our hearts. I have learned that letting God give me something is so much better than trying to get it for myself. Most of us struggle greatly in our lives, trying to make things happen that only God can do. He wants us to seek Him, and He promises that He will add the things we desire if and when the time is right.

We are to commit our way unto Him and let Him bring the things that we desire to pass. Jesus said all those who labor and are heavy-laden should come to Him. He promised to ease, relieve, and refresh their souls (see Matthew 11:28, 29). His ways are higher than our ways, and His thoughts are higher than ours. In other words, God knows much better than we do what we need to do!

I spent much of my life frustrated and struggling, always trying to do something about things I could not do anything about. I worked really hard at life, but life still was not working for me.

My first Bible was a gift from my mother-in-law, and on the inside cover she wrote: "Commit your way to the Lord" from Psalm 37:5. Little did I know, when she gave me that Bible years ago, just how long it would take for me to let go of my ways and submit to God's.

I do not know why we tend to be so stubborn, but we do. I encourage you to let go of your ways and let God be God in your life. He wants to give you the desires of your heart as you commit your way to Him.

look with care where they used to be, they will not be found. [Heb. 10:36, 37; Rev. 21:7, 8.]

11 But the meek [in the end] shall inherit the earth and shall delight themselves in the abundance of peace. [Ps. 37:29; Matt. 5:5.]

12 The wicked plot against the [uncompromisingly] righteous (the upright in right standing with God); they gnash at them with their teeth.

13 The Lord laughs at [the wicked], for He sees that their own day [of defeat] is coming.

14 The wicked draw the sword and bend their bows to cast down the poor and needy, to slay those who walk uprightly (blameless in conduct and in conversation).

15 The swords [of the wicked] shall enter their own hearts, and their bows shall be broken.

16 Better is the little that the [uncompromisingly] righteous have than the abundance [of possessions] of many who are wrong *and* wicked. [I Tim. 6:6, 7.]

17 For the arms of the wicked shall be broken, but the Lord upholds the [consistently] righteous.

18 The Lord knows the days of the upright *and* blameless, and their heritage will abide forever.

19 They shall not be put to shame in the time of evil; and in the days of famine they shall be satisfied.

20 But the wicked shall perish, and the enemies of the Lord shall be as

the fat of lambs [that is consumed in smoke] *and* as the glory of the pastures. They shall vanish; like smoke shall they consume away.

21 The wicked borrow and pay not again [for they may be unable], but the [uncompromisingly] righteous deal kindly and give [for they are able].

22 For such as are blessed of God shall [in the end] inherit the earth, but they that are cursed of Him shall be cut off. [Isa. 57:13c.]

23 The steps of a [good] man are directed *and* established by the Lord when He delights in his way [and He busies Himself with his every step].

life point

God will tell us the way to go (see Psalm 37:23), but we have to do the walking. A walk with God develops by taking one step of obedience at a time. Some people want the entire blueprint for their lives before they will make one decision. God does not usually operate that way; He leads us one step at a time.

By faith, we take the step God has shown us, and then He gives us the next one. At times we may fall down and must get back up; we may stumble, but He always helps us. We continue on by His strength and His grace, knowing that every time we face a fork in the road (a place of decision), God will guide us.

24 Though he falls, he shall not be utterly cast down, for the Lord grasps his hand in support *and* upholds him.

25 I have been young and now am old, yet have I not seen the [uncompromisingly] righteous forsaken or their seed begging bread.

26 All day long they are merciful *and* deal graciously; they lend, and their offspring are blessed.

27 Depart from evil and do good; and you will dwell forever [securely].

28 For the Lord delights in justice and forsakes not His saints; they are preserved forever, but the offspring of the wicked [in time] shall be cut off.

29 [Then] the [consistently] righteous shall inherit the land and dwell upon it forever.

30 The mouth of the [uncompromisingly] righteous utters wisdom, and his tongue speaks with justice.

31 The law of his God is in his heart; none of his steps shall slide.

32 The wicked lie in wait for the [uncompromisingly] righteous and seek to put them to death.

33 The Lord will not leave them in their hands, or [suffer them to] condemn them when they are judged.

34 Wait for *and* expect the Lord and keep *and* heed His way, and He will exalt you to inherit the land; [in the end] when the wicked are cut off, you shall see it.

35 I have seen a wicked man in great power and spreading himself like a green tree in its native soil,

36 Yet he passed away, and behold, he was not; yes, I sought *and* inquired for him, but he could not be found.

37 Mark the blameless man and behold the upright, for there is a happy end for the man of peace.

38 As for transgressors, they shall be destroyed together; in the end the wicked shall be cut off.

39 But the salvation of the [consistently] righteous is of the Lord; He is their Refuge *and* secure Stronghold in the time of trouble.

40 And the Lord helps them and delivers them; He delivers them from the wicked and saves them, because they trust *and* take refuge in Him.

PSALM 38

A Psalm of David; to bring to remembrance *and* make memorial.

O LORD, rebuke me not in Your wrath, neither chasten me in Your hot displeasure.

2 For Your arrows have sunk into me *and* stick fast, and Your hand has come down upon me *and* pressed me sorely.

3 There is no soundness in my flesh because of Your indignation; neither is there any health *or* rest in my bones because of my sin.

4 For my iniquities have gone over my head [like waves of a flood]; as a heavy burden they weigh too much for me.

5 My wounds are loathsome and corrupt because of my foolishness.

6 I am bent and bowed down greatly; I go about mourning all the day long.

7 For my loins are filled with burning; and there is no soundness in my flesh.

8 I am faint and sorely bruised [deadly cold and quite worn out]; I groan by reason of the disquiet *and* moaning of my heart.

9 Lord, all my desire is before You; and my sighing is not hidden from You.

10 My heart throbs, my strength fails me; as for the light of my eyes, it also is gone from me.

11 My lovers and my friends stand aloof from my plague; and my neighbors *and* my near ones stand afar off. [Luke 23:49.]

12 They also that seek *and* demand my life lay snares for me, and they that seek *and* require my hurt speak crafty *and* mischievous things; they meditate treachery *and* deceit all the day long.

13 But I, like a deaf man, hear not; and I am like a dumb man who opens not his mouth.

14 Yes, I have become like a man who hears not, in whose mouth are no arguments *or* replies.

15 For in You, O Lord, do I hope; You will answer, O Lord my God.

16 For I pray, Let them not rejoice over me, who when my foot slips boast against me.

17 For I am ready to halt *and* fall; my pain *and* sorrow are continually before me.

18 For I do confess my guilt *and* iniquity; I am filled with sorrow for my sin. [II Cor. 7:9, 10.]

19 But my enemies are vigorous *and* strong, and those who hate me wrongfully are multiplied.

20 They also that render evil for good are adversaries to me, because I follow the thing that is good.

21 Forsake me not, O Lord; O my God, be not far from me.

22 Make haste to help me, O Lord, my Salvation.

PSALM 39

To the Chief Musician; for Jeduthun [founder of an official musical family]. A Psalm of David.

I SAID, I will take heed *and* guard my ways, that I may sin not with my tongue; I will muzzle my mouth as with a bridle while the wicked are before me.

2 I was dumb with silence, I held my peace without profit and had no comfort away from good, while my distress was renewed.

3 My heart was hot within me. While I was musing, the fire burned; then I spoke with my tongue:

4 Lord, make me to know my end and [to appreciate] the measure of my days—what it is; let me know *and* realize how frail I am [how transient is my stay here].

5 Behold, You have made my days as [short as] handbreadths, and my lifetime is as nothing in Your sight.

Truly every man at his best is merely a breath! Selah [pause, and think calmly of that]!

6 Surely every man walks to and fro—like a shadow in a pantomime; surely for futility *and* emptiness he is in turmoil; each one heaps up riches, not knowing who will gather them. [I Cor. 7:31; James 4:14.]

7 And now, Lord, what do I wait for *and* expect? My hope *and* expectation are in You.

8 Deliver me from all my transgressions; make me not the scorn *and* reproach of the [self-confident] fool!

9 I am dumb, I open not my mouth, for it is You Who has done it.

10 Remove Your stroke away from me; I am consumed by the conflict *and* the blow of Your hand.

11 When with rebukes You correct *and* chasten man for sin, You waste his beauty like a moth *and* what is dear to him consumes away; surely every man is a mere breath. Selah [pause, and think calmly of that]!

12 Hear my prayer, O Lord, and give ear to my cry; hold not Your peace at my tears! For I am Your passing guest, a temporary resident, as all my fathers were.

13 O look away from me *and* spare me, that I may recover cheerfulness *and* encouraging strength *and* know gladness before I go and am no more!

PSALM 40
To the Chief Musician. A Psalm of David.

I WAITED patiently *and* expectantly for the Lord; and He inclined to me and heard my cry.

2 He drew me up out of a horrible pit [a pit of tumult and of destruction], out of the miry clay (froth and slime), and set my feet upon a rock, steadying my steps *and* establishing my goings.

3 And He has put a new song in my mouth, a song of praise to our God. Many shall see and fear (revere and worship) and put their trust *and*

life point

When the Bible speaks of "the pit," as it does in Psalm 40, I always think of the depths of depression. The psalmist David often spoke of feeling as though he was going down into a pit and calling out to the Lord to rescue him and set his feet on solid, level ground.

Like David, nobody wants to be in the pit of depression. It is a terrible place. I cannot think of a worse place to be. When we are deeply depressed, we feel bad enough as it is. Then the devil comes along to add to our misery by bringing thoughts of every negative thing imaginable. He reminds us of every disappointing thing that has ever happened to us and tries to make us believe that nothing good will ever take place in our lives. His goal is to keep us so miserable and hopeless that we will never rise up to cause him any problems or to fulfill the call of God on our lives.

We must learn to resist descending into the pit of depression where we are at the mercy of the tormentor of our souls, who is determined to totally destroy us and our witness for Christ. Be like David; cry out to God and allow Him to set your feet upon a rock and bring stability to your life.

speak the Word

God, all of my hope and my expectation are in You.
ADAPTED FROM PSALM 39:7

confident reliance in the Lord. [Ps. 5:11.]

4 Blessed (happy, fortunate, to be envied) is the man who makes the Lord his refuge *and* trust, and turns not to the proud or to followers of false gods.

5 Many, O Lord my God, are the wonderful works which You have done, and Your thoughts toward us; no one can compare with You! If I should declare and speak of them, they are too many to be numbered.

6 Sacrifice and offering You do not desire, *nor* have You delight in them; You have given me the capacity to hear *and* obey [Your law, a more valuable service than] burnt offerings and sin offerings [which] You do not require.

7 Then said I, Behold, I come; in the volume of the book it is written of me;

8 I delight to do Your will, O my God; yes, Your law is within my heart. [Heb. 10:5-9.]

9 I have proclaimed glad tidings of righteousness in the great assembly [tidings of uprightness and right standing with God]. Behold, I have not restrained my lips, as You know, O Lord.

10 I have not concealed Your righteousness within my heart; I have proclaimed Your faithfulness and Your salvation. I have not hid away Your steadfast love and Your truth from the great assembly. [Acts 20:20, 27.]

11 Withhold not Your tender mercy from me, O Lord; let Your lovingkindness and Your truth continually preserve me!

12 For innumerable evils have compassed me about; my iniquities have taken such hold on me that I am not able to look up. They are more than the hairs of my head, and my heart has failed me *and* forsaken me.

13 Be pleased, O Lord, to deliver me; O Lord, make haste to help me!

14 Let them be put to shame and confounded together who seek *and* require my life to destroy it; let them be driven backward and brought to dishonor who wish me evil *and* delight in my hurt!

15 Let them be desolate by reason of their shame who say to me, Aha, aha!

16 Let all those that seek *and* require You rejoice and be glad in You; let such as love Your salvation say continually, The Lord be magnified!

17 [As for me] I am poor and needy, yet the Lord takes thought *and* plans for me. You are my Help and my Deliverer. O my God, do not tarry! [Ps. 70:1-5; I Pet. 5:7.]

PSALM 41

To the Chief Musician. A Psalm of David.

BLESSED (HAPPY, fortunate, to be envied) is he who considers the weak *and* the poor; the Lord will deliver him in the time of evil *and* trouble.

2 The Lord will protect him and keep him alive; he shall be called blessed in the land; and You will not deliver him to the will of his enemies.

3 The Lord will sustain, refresh, *and* strengthen him on his bed of languishing; all his bed You [O Lord] will turn, change, *and* transform in his illness.

4 I said, Lord, be merciful *and* gracious to me; heal my inner self, for I have sinned against You.

5 My enemies speak evil of me, [saying], When will he die and his name perish?

6 And when one comes to see me, he speaks falsehood *and* empty

speak the Word

pray and obey

God really wants us to hear and obey Him, and according to Psalm 40:6, He has given us the capacity to do so. In fact, God delights in the atmosphere of our obedience. Naturally, it does not do God any good to talk to us if we are not going to listen and obey!

For many years, I wanted God to talk to me, but I wanted to pick and choose what to obey. Like many others, I had "selective hearing." I wanted to do what God said to do *if* I thought it was a good idea. If I did not want to submit to what I was hearing, I could easily choose to think it was not from God.

God has given us the capacity both to hear Him and to obey Him, and obedience is the greatest sacrifice we can make to Him. Some of what God says to you will be exciting; other things may not be so thrilling to hear. But you can be assured that what God tells you will work out for good if you will just do it His way.

If God convicts you that you were rude to someone and instructs you to apologize, it is pointless to answer back, "Well, that person was rude to me too!" If you talk back with excuses, you may have prayed, and even heard, but you have not obeyed. Instead, go apologize. Say to that person, "I was rude to you, and I'm sorry." *Now* you have obeyed. Now God's anointing can flow through your life because you are obedient.

I was moved by a story about a message given at a pastors' conference by a pastor of a very large church. Hundreds of pastors had gathered from all over the nation to hear this man tell what he did to build his church. He told them simply, "I pray, and I obey. I pray, and I obey." One of the ministers who attended this meeting expressed to me his disappointment in the pastor's message. He said, "I spent all that money and went all that distance to hear this world-renowned leader tell me how his ministry grew to the point it has. For three hours, in various ways, he said the same thing, 'I pray. I obey. I pray. I obey. I pray. I obey. I pray. I obey.' I kept thinking, *Surely there is something else*."

Looking back over nearly three decades of walking with God, I would have to agree that if I put into words the simplest explanation for all the success we have enjoyed at Joyce Meyer Ministries, we too have learned to pray, hear from God, and then do what God tells us to do. Over the years, I have been seeking God about the call on my life and pressing forward in what I feel He has told me to do. The essence of it all is that I have prayed, and I have obeyed. My obedience has not always been popular with everyone else, but to the best of my ability I have prayed, I have obeyed—and it has worked. God's plan is not hard; *we* make it hard. Like everyone else I have made mistakes, but I have learned from them and have pressed on. Failing does not make you a failure. A person is a failure only if he gives up and refuses to try any longer.

If you want God's will for your life, I can give you the directions in their simplest form: *Pray and obey*. God has given you the capacity to do both.

words, while his heart gathers mischievous gossip [against me]; when he goes away, he tells it abroad.

7 All who hate me whisper together about me; against me do they devise my hurt [imagining the worst for me].

8 An evil disease, say they, is poured out upon him *and* cleaves fast to him; and now that he is bedfast, he will not rise up again.

9 Even my own familiar friend, in whom I trusted (relied on and was confident), who ate of my bread, has lifted up his heel against me. [John 13:18.]

10 But You, O Lord, be merciful *and* gracious to me, and raise me up, that I may requite them.

11 By this I know that You favor *and* delight in me, because my enemy does not triumph over me.

12 And as for me, You have upheld me in my integrity and set me in Your presence forever.

13 Blessed be the Lord, the God of Israel, from everlasting and to everlasting [from this age to the next, and forever]! Amen and Amen (so be it).

BOOK TWO

PSALM 42

To the Chief Musician. A skillful song, *or* a didactic *or* reflective poem, of the sons of Korah.

A S THE hart pants *and* longs for the water brooks, so I pant *and* long for You, O God.

putting the Word to work

Psalm 42:1 tells of a deer that longs for a refreshing stream. On a hot day, *knowing about* water does nothing to quench your thirst; only *drinking* water does. The same is true of our desire for God. Have you ever longed for more than just information about God? God wants you to experience Who He is. Seek Him, and He will satisfy your desire to know Him intimately.

2 My inner self thirsts for God, for the living God. When shall I come and behold the face of God? [John 7:37; I Thess. 1:9, 10.]

3 My tears have been my food day and night, while men say to me all day long, Where is your God?

4 These things I [earnestly] remember and pour myself out within me: how I went slowly before the throng and led them in procession to the house of God [like a bandmaster before his band, timing the steps to the sound of music and the chant of song], with the voice of shouting and praise, a throng keeping festival.

5 Why are you cast down, O my inner self? And why should you moan over me *and* be disquieted within me? Hope in God *and* wait expectantly for Him, for I shall yet praise Him, my Help and my God.

6 O my God, my life is cast down upon me [and I find the burden more than I can bear]; therefore will I

life point

In Psalm 42:5, we see the sons of Korah struggling with depression. I would like for us to examine how they handled their situation, because it shows us what to do when we are feeling depressed.

As we dissect this verse, we see three distinct responses the sons of Korah give to their depressed feelings. First, they put a question to their own souls and ask themselves: "Why are you downcast?" Then they give an instruction to their souls: "Put your hope in God." Finally, they declare what they are going to do: "I will praise the Lord." We might say the sons of Korah have a talk with themselves.

We must follow this same basic pattern of action as we confront our feelings of depression and come out of them and into victory.

how to deal with discouragement

In Psalm 42:5, the psalmist is discouraged. Discouragement destroys hope, so naturally the devil always tries to discourage us. Without hope we give up, which is exactly what the devil wants us to do.

The Bible repeatedly tells us not to be discouraged or dismayed. God knows that we will not be victorious if we get discouraged, so He always encourages us as we start out on a project by saying to us, "Do not get discouraged." God wants us to be *encouraged*, not *discouraged*.

When discouragement or condemnation tries to overtake you, the first thing to do is to examine your thought life. What kind of thoughts have you been thinking? Have they sounded something like this? *I am not going to make it; this is too hard. I always fail; it has always been the same. Nothing ever changes. I am sure other people do not have this much trouble getting their minds renewed. I may as well give up. I'm tired of trying. I pray, but it seems as if God doesn't hear. He probably doesn't answer my prayers because He is so disappointed in the way I act.*

If these examples represent your thoughts, then no wonder you get discouraged or feel condemned! Remember, you become what you think. Think discouraging thoughts, and you will get discouraged. Think condemning thoughts, and you will come under condemnation. Change your thinking and be set free!

Instead of thinking negatively, think more like this: *Well, things are going a little slowly, but, thank God, I am making some progress. I am sure glad I'm on the right path that will lead me to freedom. I had a rough day yesterday. I chose wrong thinking all day long. Father, forgive me, and help me to keep on keeping on. I made a mistake, but at least that is one mistake I won't have to make again. This is a new day. You love me, Lord. Your mercy is new every morning. I refuse to be discouraged. I refuse to be condemned. Father, the Bible says that You do not condemn me. You sent Jesus to die for me. I'll be fine—today will be a great day. I ask You to help me choose right thoughts today.*

I am sure you can already feel the victory in this type of cheerful, positive, God-like thinking. Practice this type of thinking today!

[earnestly] remember You from the land of the Jordan [River] and the [summits of Mount] Hermon, from the little mountain Mizar.

7 [Roaring] deep calls to [roaring] deep at the thunder of Your water-spouts; all Your breakers and Your rolling waves have gone over me.

8 Yet the Lord will command His loving-kindness in the daytime, and in the night His song shall be with me, a prayer to the God of my life.

9 I will say to God my Rock, Why have You forgotten me? Why go I mourning because of the oppression of the enemy?

10 As with a sword [crushing] in my bones, my enemies taunt *and* reproach me, while they say continually to me, Where is your God?

11 Why are you cast down, O my inner self? And why should you moan over me *and* be disquieted within me? Hope in God *and* wait expectantly for

Him, for I shall yet praise Him, Who is the help of my countenance, and my God.

PSALM 43

JUDGE *AND* vindicate me, O God; plead and defend my cause against an ungodly nation. O deliver me from the deceitful and unjust man!
2   For You are the God of my strength [my Stronghold—in Whom I take refuge]; why have You cast me off? Why go I mourning because of the oppression of the enemy?
3   O send out Your light and Your truth, let them lead me; let them bring me to Your holy hill and to Your dwelling.
4   Then will I go to the altar of God, to God, my exceeding joy; yes, with the lyre will I praise You, O God, my God!
5   Why are you cast down, O my inner self? And why should you moan over me *and* be disquieted within me? Hope in God *and* wait expectantly for Him, for I shall yet praise Him, Who is the help of my [sad] countenance, and my God.

PSALM 44

To the Chief Musician. [A Psalm] of the sons of Korah. A skillful song, *or* a didactic *or* reflective poem.

WE HAVE heard with our ears, O God; our fathers have told us [what] work You did in their days, in the days of old.
2   You drove out the nations with Your hand *and* it was Your power that gave [Israel] a home by rooting out the [heathen] peoples, but [Israel] You spread out.
3   For they got not the land [of Canaan] in possession by their own sword, neither did their own arm save them; but Your right hand and Your arm and the light of Your countenance [did it], because You were favorable toward *and* did delight in them.
4   You are my King, O God; command victories *and* deliverance for Jacob (Israel).
5   Through You shall we push down our enemies; through Your name shall we tread them under who rise up against us.
6   For I will not trust in *and* lean on my bow, neither shall my sword save me.
7   But You have saved us from our foes and have put them to shame who hate us.
8   In God we have made our boast all the day long, and we will give thanks to Your name forever. Selah [pause, and calmly think of that]!
9   But now You have cast us off and brought us to dishonor, and You go not out with our armies.
10   You make us to turn back from the enemy, and they who hate us take spoil for themselves.
11   You have made us like sheep intended for mutton and have scattered us in exile among the nations.
12   You sell Your people for nothing, and have not increased Your wealth by their price.
13   You have made us the taunt of our neighbors, a scoffing and a derision to those who are round about us.
14   You make us a byword among the nations, a shaking of the heads among the people.

speak the Word

God, send Your light and Your truth, and let them lead me. Let them bring me into Your presence.
ADAPTED FROM PSALM 43:3

be free from shame

Many people are "rooted" in shame. This means that their shame is so deep it functions as the root of a tree and actually produces "fruit" in the form of unhealthy thoughts and behaviors.

If you are rooted in shame, then you need to be aware that shame is different from guilt. I believe shame is a deeper problem than guilt. We may feel guilty over something we have done wrong, but shame makes us feel bad about who we are. There is also a difference between "normal" shame and "rooted" shame.

For example, if I knock over my water glass in a fancy restaurant, I feel ashamed or embarrassed because I have made a mess in front of everybody. That's normal. But I soon adjust to the mishap and go on. That incident does not mar my life.

In the Garden of Eden after the Fall, Adam and Eve were ashamed when they realized they were naked, and so they made aprons of fig leaves to cover themselves. But that too was a normal reaction.

When you and I make mistakes or commit sin, we feel bad for a while until we repent and are forgiven. Then we are able to put our mistakes and sins behind us and go on without any lasting harm.

But when an individual is rooted in shame, it affects his entire life. His bad attitude toward himself poisons everything he tries to accomplish. He is doomed to failure because he has no confidence. Jesus bore our shame for us on the cross (see Hebrews 12:2). Ask Jesus today to give you understanding of His work on the cross for you. Ask Him to heal you so that you can live free from shame.

15 My dishonor is before me all day long, and shame has covered my face

16 At the words of the taunter and reviler, by reason of the enemy and the revengeful.

17 All this is come upon us, yet have we not forgotten You, neither have we been false to Your covenant [which You made with our fathers].

18 Our hearts are not turned back, neither have our steps declined from Your path,

19 Though You have distressingly broken us in the place of jackals and covered us with deep darkness, even with the shadow of death.

20 If we had forgotten the name of our God or stretched out our hands to a strange god,

21 Would not God discover this? For He knows the secrets of the heart.

22 No, but for Your sake we are killed all the day long; we are accounted as sheep for the slaughter. [Rom. 8:35-39.]

23 Awake! Why do You sleep, O Lord? Arouse Yourself, cast us not off forever!

24 Why do You hide Your face and forget our affliction and our oppression?

25 For our lives are bowed down to the dust; our bodies cleave to the ground.

26 Rise up! Come to our help, and

deliver us for Your mercy's sake *and* because of Your steadfast love!

PSALM 45

To the Chief Musician; [set to the tune of] "Lilies" [probably a popular air. A Psalm] of the sons of Korah. A skillful song, *or* a didactic *or* reflective poem. A song of love.

M Y HEART overflows with a ¹goodly theme; I address my psalm to a King. My tongue is like the pen of a ready writer.

2   You are fairer than the children of men; graciousness is poured upon Your lips; therefore God has blessed You forever.

3   Gird Your sword upon Your thigh, O mighty One, in Your glory and Your majesty!

4   And in Your majesty ride on triumphantly for the cause of truth, humility, *and* righteousness (uprightness and right standing with God); and let Your right hand guide You to tremendous things.

5   Your arrows are sharp; the peoples fall under You; Your darts pierce the hearts of the King's enemies.

6   Your throne, O God, is forever and ever; the scepter of righteousness is the scepter of Your kingdom.

7   You love righteousness, uprightness, *and* right standing with God and hate wickedness; therefore God, Your God, has anointed You with the oil of gladness above Your fellows. [Heb. 1:8, 9.]

8   Your garments are all fragrant with myrrh, aloes, *and* cassia; stringed instruments make You glad.

9   Kings' daughters are among Your honorable women; at Your right hand stands the queen in gold of Ophir.

10   Hear, O daughter, consider, submit, *and* consent to my instruction: forget also your own people and your father's house;

11   So will the King desire your beauty; because He is your Lord, be submissive *and* reverence *and* honor Him.

12   And, O daughter of Tyre, the richest of the people shall entreat your favor with a gift.

13   The King's daughter in the inner part [of the palace] is all glorious; her clothing is inwrought with gold. [Rev. 19:7, 8.]

life point

What Psalm 45:13 means to me is that God puts the Holy Spirit inside us to work on our inner lives; our attitudes, our reactions, and our goals. Through His work in us, our inner lives can be tested and refined into an environment in which the Lord is comfortable to reside.

14   She shall be brought to the King in raiment of needlework; with the virgins, her companions that follow her, she shall be brought to You.

15   With gladness and rejoicing will they be brought; they will enter into the King's palace.

16   Instead of Your fathers shall be Your sons, whom You will make princes in all the land.

17   I will make Your name to be remembered in all generations; therefore shall the people praise and give You thanks forever and ever.

i Jesus spoke of what was written of Him "in the Psalms" (see Luke 24:44). This is one such Messianic psalm. However, the capitalization indicating the deity is offered provisionally. The chapter is written against the background of a secular royal wedding. But the New Testament reference to this psalm in Heb. 1:8, 9, where verses 6 and 7 of Psalm 45 are quoted and applied to Christ, makes any other interpretation seem incidental in importance.

PSALM 46

To the Chief Musician. [A Psalm] of
the sons of Korah, set to treble voices.
A song.

GOD IS our Refuge and Strength
[mighty *and* impenetrable to
temptation], a very present
and well-proved help in trouble.
2   Therefore we will not fear, though
the earth should change and though
the mountains be shaken into the
midst of the seas,
3   Though its waters roar and foam,
though the mountains tremble at its
swelling *and* tumult. Selah [pause,
and calmly think of that]!
4   There is a river whose streams
shall make glad the city of God, the
holy place of the tabernacles of the
Most High.
5   God is in the midst of her, she
shall not be moved; God will help her
right early [at the dawn of the morn-
ing].
6   The nations raged, the kingdoms
tottered *and* were moved; He uttered
His voice, the earth melted.
7   The Lord of hosts is with us; the
God of Jacob is our Refuge (our
Fortress and High Tower). Selah
[pause, and calmly think of that]!
8   Come, behold the works of the

life point

The Lord encourages us in Psalm 46:10
to be still and to know that He is God.
Often it is difficult for us to be still or
quiet because our flesh is full of energy
and usually wants to be active doing
something. Do not go to God and talk
to Him only when you want or need
something; also spend quiet time with
Him just listening for His voice. He will
give you great revelation and direction
if you will be still before Him and
simply listen.

Lord, Who has wrought desolations
and wonders in the earth.
9   He makes wars to cease to the end
of the earth; He breaks the bow into
pieces and snaps the spear in two; He
burns the chariots in the fire.
10 Let be *and* be still, and know
(recognize and understand) that I
am God. I will be exalted among
the nations! I will be exalted in the
earth!
11 The Lord of hosts is with us; the
God of Jacob is our Refuge (our High
Tower and Stronghold). Selah [pause,
and calmly think of that]!

PSALM 47

To the Chief Musician. A Psalm of the
sons of Korah.

O CLAP your hands, all you
peoples! Shout to God with
the voice of triumph *and*
songs of joy!
2   For the Lord Most High excites
terror, awe, *and* dread; He is a great
King over all the earth.
3   He subdued peoples under us,
and nations under our feet.
4   He chose our inheritance for us,
the glory *and* pride of Jacob, whom He
loves. Selah [pause, and calmly think
of that]! [I Pet. 1:4, 5.]
5   God has ascended amid shouting,
the Lord with the sound of a trumpet.
6   Sing praises to God, sing praises!
Sing praises to our King, sing praises!
7   For God is the King of all the
earth; sing praises in a skillful psalm
and with understanding.
8   God reigns over the nations; God
sits upon His holy throne.
9   The princes *and* nobles of the
peoples are gathered together, a
[united] people for the God of
Abraham, for the shields of the
earth belong to God; He is highly
exalted.

express yourself!

The Bible instructs us to dance, to play musical instruments, and to do all kinds of outward things to express worship to the Lord (see Psalm 47:1). We need to do this; it brings a release in our lives, it honors God, and it aids in defeating the devil.

It is not enough just to say, "Well, God knows how I feel about Him. I do not have to make a big display." That would be no different from saying, "Well, God knows I believe in Him; therefore, there is no real need for me to be baptized." Or to say, "God knows I am sorry for my sins; therefore, there is no need for me to admit my sins and repent of them." We readily see how foolish this would be, and people from all denominations would agree that we need to be baptized and confess our sins. Yet not all denominations teach people to have outward expression of their praise and worship. Some teach that quiet reverence is the only proper way to worship. We definitely need to be quiet and reverent before the Lord at times, but we also need to express our emotions in worship. I am convinced that God gave us emotions for more purposes than just being enthusiastic at a ball game or about a new car. Surely God wants us to employ our emotions in expressing our love and gratitude to Him.

I am not encouraging unbridled emotion. People who just get "emotional" all the time in worship can be distracting. What we need is balance. I personally believe that if we had a proper emotional release during praise and worship, we might not release emotions at other times in improper ways. Our emotions are just as much a part of us as our body, mind, will, or spirit. God gave us emotions, and they must be cared for, just like the rest of us. We are not to be controlled by emotions because they are known to be fickle or untrustworthy, but neither can we stifle them and not be adversely affected.

I think it is tragic not to allow people the freedom to express their hearts and their love for God in a balanced way. It is wrong to be so afraid of something getting out of balance that we cut it off altogether. It also is a bad idea to do things the same way every time because "that is the way we have always done them." We all must be open to growth, which always involves change. Jesus said that He could not pour new wine into old wineskins, meaning some of the people's old ways had to go (see Matthew 9:17). They had to "let go" of old things and take hold of the new, fresh things. Knowledge and revelation are progressive; if a thing (such as your worship) is not moving forward in your life, it is at the point of dying.

I encourage you to be expressive in your praise and worship. Do this at home if you attend a church where it would be unacceptable to do so in the public services. I also encourage you to pray that everyone will be taught to worship God as He truly deserves to be worshipped.

PSALM 48

A song; a Psalm of the sons of Korah.

GREAT IS the Lord, and highly to be praised in the city of our God! His holy mountain,
2 Fair *and* beautiful in elevation, is the joy of all the earth—[j]Mount Zion [the City of David], to the northern side [Mount Moriah and the temple], the [whole] city of the Great King! [Matt. 5:35.]
3 God has made Himself known in her palaces as a Refuge (a High Tower and a Stronghold).
4 For, behold, the kings assembled, they came onward *and* they passed away together.
5 They looked, they were amazed; they were stricken with terror *and* took to flight [affrighted and dismayed].
6 Trembling took hold of them there, and pain as of a woman in childbirth.
7 With the east wind You shattered the ships of Tarshish.
8 As we have heard, so have we seen in the city of the Lord of hosts, in the city of our God: God will establish it forever. Selah [pause, and calmly think of that]!
9 We have thought of Your steadfast love, O God, in the midst of Your temple.

life point

David frequently wrote of meditating on all the wonderful works of the Lord—the mighty acts of God. He said that he thought about the name of the Lord, the mercy of God, and many other such things. If you and I will do the same, we will stay encouraged, full of faith, and victorious in our everyday lives.

10 As is Your name, O God, so is Your praise to the ends of the earth; Your right hand is full of righteousness (rightness and justice).
11 Let Mount Zion be glad! Let the daughters of Judah rejoice because of Your [righteous] judgments!
12 Walk about Zion, and go round about her, number her towers (her lofty and noble deeds of past days),
13 Consider well her ramparts, go through her palaces *and* citadels, that you may tell the next generation [and cease recalling disappointments].
14 For this God is our God forever and ever; He will be our guide [even] until death.

PSALM 49

To the Chief Musician. A Psalm of the sons of Korah.

HEAR THIS, all you peoples; give ear, all you inhabitants of the world,
2 Both low and high, rich and poor together:
3 My mouth shall speak wisdom; and the meditation of my heart shall be understanding.
4 I will submit *and* consent to a parable *or* proverb; to the music of a lyre I will unfold my riddle (my problem).
5 Why should I fear in the days of evil, when the iniquity of those who would supplant me surrounds me on every side,
6 Even of those who trust in *and* lean on their wealth and boast of the abundance of their riches?
7 None of them can by any means redeem [either himself or] his brother, nor give to God a ransom for him—
8 For the ransom of a life is too

j Psalm 48 is a celebration of the security of Zion. See the beauty of Zion as God's unconquerable fortress.

costly, and [the price one can pay] can never suffice—

9 So that he should live on forever *and* never see the pit (the grave) *and* corruption.

10 For he sees that even wise men die; the [self-confident] fool and the stupid alike perish and leave their wealth to others.

11 Their inward thought is that their houses will continue forever, *and* their dwelling places to all generations; they call their lands their own [apart from God] *and* after their own names.

12 But man, with all his honor *and* pomp, does not remain; he is like the beasts that perish.

13 This is the fate of those who are foolishly confident, yet after them men approve their sayings. Selah [pause, and calmly think of that]!

14 Like sheep they are appointed for Sheol (the place of the dead); death shall be their shepherd. And the upright shall have dominion over them in the morning; and their form *and* beauty shall be consumed, for Sheol shall be their dwelling.

15 But God will redeem me from the power of Sheol (the place of the dead); for He will receive me. Selah [pause, and calmly think of that]!

16 Be not afraid when [an ungodly] one is made rich, when the wealth *and* glory of his house are increased;

17 For when he dies he will carry nothing away; his glory will not descend after him.

18 Though while he lives he counts himself happy *and* prosperous, and though a man gets praise when he does well [for himself],

19 He will go to the generation of his fathers, who will nevermore see the light.

20 A man who is held in honor and understands not is like the beasts that perish.

PSALM 50
A Psalm of [k]Asaph

THE MIGHTY One, God, the Lord, speaks and calls the earth from the rising of the sun to its setting.

2 Out of Zion, the perfection of beauty, God shines forth.

3 Our God comes and does not keep silence; a fire devours before Him, and round about Him a mighty tempest rages.

4 He calls to the heavens above and to the earth, that He may judge His people:

5 Gather together to Me My saints [those who have found grace in My sight], those who have made a covenant with Me by sacrifice.

6 And the heavens declare His righteousness (rightness and justice), for God, He is judge. Selah [pause, and calmly think of that]!

7 Hear, O My people, and I will speak; O Israel, I will testify to you *and* against you: I am God, your God.

8 I do not reprove you for your

speak the Word

Lord, You are not only God, but You are my God.
ADAPTED FROM PSALM 50:7

---

[k] Asaph was a Levite and one of the leaders of David's choir. He was the head of one of the three families permanently charged with the temple music. His family formed a guild which bore his name and is frequently mentioned (II Chron. 20:14; 29:13; 29:30). Twelve psalms (50: 73-83) are attributed in the titles to the family of Asaph. 128 of Asaph's members, all singers, came back from Babylon and took part when the foundations of Zerubbabel's temple were laid (Ezra 2:41; 3:10).

sacrifices; your burnt offerings are continually before Me.

9 I will accept no bull from your house nor he-goat out of your folds.

10 For every beast of the forest is Mine, *and* the cattle upon a thousand hills *or* upon the mountains where thousands are.

11 I know *and* am acquainted with all the birds of the mountains, and the wild animals of the field are Mine *and* are with Me, in My mind.

12 If I were hungry, I would not tell you, for the world and its fullness are Mine. [I Cor. 10:26.]

13 Shall I eat the flesh of bulls or drink the blood of goats?

14 Offer to God the sacrifice of thanksgiving, and pay your vows to the Most High,

15 And call on Me in the day of trouble; I will deliver you, and you shall honor *and* glorify Me.

16 But to the wicked, God says: What right have you to recite My statutes or take My covenant *or* pledge on your lips,

17 Seeing that you hate instruction *and* correction and cast My words behind you [discarding them]?

18 When you see a thief, you associate with him, and you have taken part with adulterers.

19 You give your mouth to evil, and your tongue frames deceit.

20 You sit and speak against your brother; you slander your own mother's son.

21 These things you have done and I kept silent; you thought I was once entirely like you. But [now] I will reprove you and put [the charge] in order before your eyes.

22 Now consider this, you who forget God, lest I tear you in pieces, and there be none to deliver.

23 He who brings an offering of praise *and* thanksgiving honors *and* glorifies Me; and he who orders his way aright [who prepares the way

that I may show him], to him I will demonstrate the salvation of God.

PSALM 51

To the Chief Musician. A Psalm of David; when Nathan the prophet came to him after he had sinned with Bathsheba.

HAVE MERCY upon me, O God, according to Your steadfast love; according to the multitude of Your tender mercy *and* lovingkindness blot out my transgressions.

2 Wash me thoroughly [and repeatedly] from my iniquity *and* guilt and cleanse me *and* make me wholly pure from my sin!

3 For I am conscious of my transgressions *and* I acknowledge them; my sin is ever before me.

4 Against You, You only, have I sinned and done that which is evil in Your sight, so that You are justified in Your sentence and faultless in Your judgment. [Rom. 3:4.]

5 Behold, I was brought forth in [a state of] iniquity; my mother was sinful who conceived me [and I too am sinful]. [John 3:6; Rom. 5:12; Eph. 2:3.]

6 Behold, You desire truth in the inner being; make me therefore to know wisdom in my inmost heart.

7 Purify me with hyssop, and I shall be clean [ceremonially]; wash me, and I shall [in reality] be whiter than snow.

8 Make me to hear joy and gladness *and* be satisfied; let the bones which You have broken rejoice.

9 Hide Your face from my sins and blot out all my guilt *and* iniquities.

10 Create in me a clean heart, O God, and renew a right, persevering, *and* steadfast spirit within me.

11 Cast me not away from Your presence and take not Your Holy Spirit from me.

12 Restore to me the joy of Your salvation and uphold me with a willing spirit.

life point

In Psalm 51, King David cries out to God for mercy and forgiveness because the Lord had been dealing with him about his sin with Bathsheba and the murder of her husband. Many people do not realize that David had done these things approximately one full year before he wrote this psalm. Apparently, he never really acknowledged this sin until long after it happened. He had not faced the truth, and as long as he refused to face the truth, he could not truly repent. And as long as he could not truly repent, he could not receive forgiveness from God.

Psalm 51:6 conveys a powerful message. It says that God desires truth "in the inner being." That means if we want to receive God's blessings, we must be honest with Him about our sins and ourselves. Let me encourage you not to let sin linger in your life. We all sin, and when we do, we need to be quick to repent.

13 Then will I teach transgressors Your ways, and sinners shall be converted *and* return to You.

14 Deliver me from bloodguiltiness *and* death, O God, the God of my salvation, *and* my tongue shall sing aloud of Your righteousness (Your rightness and Your justice).

15 O Lord, open my lips, and my mouth shall show forth Your praise.

16 For You delight not in sacrifice, or else would I give it; You find no pleasure in burnt offering. [I Sam. 15:22.]

17 My sacrifice [the sacrifice acceptable] to God is a broken spirit; a broken and a contrite heart [broken down with sorrow for sin and humbly and thoroughly penitent], such, O God, You will not despise.

18 Do good in Your good pleasure to Zion; rebuild the walls of Jerusalem.

19 Then will You delight in the sacrifices of righteousness, justice, *and* right, with burnt offering and whole burnt offering; then bullocks will be offered upon Your altar.

PSALM 52

To the Chief Musician. A skillful song, *or* a didactic *or* reflective poem. [A Psalm] of David, when Doeg the Edomite came and told Saul, David has come to the house of Ahimelech.

WHY BOAST you of mischief done against the loving-kindness of God [and the godly], O mighty [sinful] man, day after day?

2 Your tongue devises wickedness; it is like a sharp razor, working deceitfully.

3 You love evil more than good, and lying rather than to speak righteousness, justice, *and* right. Selah [pause, and calmly think of that]!

4 You love all destroying *and* devouring words, O deceitful tongue.

5 God will likewise break you down *and* destroy you forever; He will lay hold of you and pluck you out of your tent and uproot you from the land of the living. Selah [pause, and calmly think of that]!

6 The [uncompromisingly] righteous also shall see [it] and be in reverent fear *and* awe, but about you they will [scoffingly] laugh, saying,

7 See, this is the man who made not God his strength (his stronghold and high tower) but trusted in *and* confidently relied on the abundance of his riches, seeking refuge *and* security for himself through his wickedness.

8 But I am like a green olive tree in the house of God; I trust in *and* confidently rely on the loving-kindness *and* the mercy of God forever and ever.

9 I will thank You *and* confide in You forever, because You have done it [delivered me and kept me safe]. I will wait on, hope in *and* expect in Your name, for it is good, in the presence of Your saints (Your kind and pious ones).

PSALM 53

To the Chief Musician; in a mournful strain. A skillful song, or didactic or reflective poem of David.

THE [empty-headed] fool has said in his heart, There is no God. Corrupt *and* evil are they, and doing abominable iniquity; there is none who does good.
2 God looked down from heaven upon the children of men to see if there were any who understood, who sought (inquired after and desperately required) God.
3 Every one of them has gone back [backslidden and fallen away]; they have altogether become filthy *and* corrupt; there is none who does good, no, not one. [Rom. 3:10-12.]
4 Have those who work evil no knowledge (no understanding)? They eat up My people as they eat bread; they do not call upon God.
5 There they are, in terror *and* dread, where there was [and had been] no terror *and* dread! For God has scattered the bones of him who encamps against you; you have put them to shame, because God has rejected them.

speak the Word

6 Oh, that the salvation *and* deliverance of Israel would come out of Zion! When God restores the fortunes of His people, then will Jacob rejoice and Israel be glad.

PSALM 54

To the Chief Musician; with stringed instruments. A skillful song, or a didactic or reflective poem, of David, when the Ziphites went and told Saul, David is hiding among us.

SAVE ME, O God, by Your name; judge *and* vindicate me by Your mighty strength *and* power.
2 Hear my pleading *and* my prayer, O God; give ear to the words of my mouth.
3 For strangers *and* insolent men are rising up against me, and violent men *and* ruthless ones seek *and* demand my life; they do not set God before them. Selah [pause, and calmly think of that]!
4 Behold, God is my helper *and* ally; the Lord is my upholder *and* is with them who uphold my life.
5 He will pay back evil to my enemies; in Your faithfulness [Lord] put an end to them.
6 With a freewill offering I will sacrifice to You; I will give thanks *and* praise Your name, O Lord, for it is good.
7 For He has delivered me out of every trouble, and my eye has looked [in triumph] on my enemies.

Lord, I will thank You and confide in You forever because You have delivered me and kept me safe. I will wait on, hope in, and expect in Your name because it is good.
ADAPTED FROM PSALM 52:9

Thank You, God, for being my helper and my ally.
ADAPTED FROM PSALM 54:4

PSALM 55

To the Chief Musician; with stringed instruments. A skillful song, *or* a didactic *or* reflective poem, of David.

LISTEN TO my prayer, O God, and hide not Yourself from my supplication!

2 Attend to me and answer me; I am restless *and* distraught in my complaint and must moan

3 [And I am distracted] at the noise of the enemy, because of the oppression *and* threats of the wicked; for they would cast trouble upon me, and in wrath they persecute me.

4 My heart is grievously pained within me, and the terrors of death have fallen upon me.

5 Fear and trembling have come upon me; horror *and* fright have overwhelmed me.

6 And I say, Oh, that I had wings like a dove! I would fly away and be at rest.

7 Yes, I would wander far away, I would lodge in the wilderness. Selah [pause, and calmly think of that]!

8 I would hasten to escape *and* to find a shelter from the stormy wind and tempest.

9 Destroy [their schemes], O Lord, confuse their tongues, for I have seen violence and strife in the city.

10 Day and night they go about on its walls; iniquity and mischief are in its midst.

11 Violence *and* ruin are within it; fraud and guile do not depart from its streets *and* marketplaces.

12 For it is not an enemy who reproaches *and* taunts me—then I might bear it; nor is it one who has hated me who insolently vaunts himself against me—then I might hide from him.

13 But it was you, a man my equal, my companion and my familiar friend.

14 We had sweet fellowship together and used to walk to the house of God in company.

15 Let desolations *and* death come suddenly upon them; let them go down alive to Sheol (the place of the dead), for evils are in their habitations, in their hearts, *and* their inmost part.

16 As for me, I will call upon God, and the Lord will save me.

17 Evening and morning and at noon will I utter my complaint and moan *and* sigh, and He will hear my voice.

18 He has redeemed my life in peace from the battle that was against me [so that none came near me], for they were many who strove with me.

19 God will hear and humble them, even He Who abides of old—Selah [pause, and calmly think of that]!—because in them there has been no change [of heart], and they do not fear, revere, *and* worship God.

20 [My companion] has put forth his hands against those who were at peace with him; he has broken *and* profaned his agreement [of friendship and loyalty].

21 The words of his mouth were smoother than cream *or* butter, but war was in his heart; his words were softer than oil, yet they were drawn swords.

22 Cast your burden on the Lord [releasing the weight of it] and He will sustain you; He will never allow

speak the Word

God, I thank You that You have redeemed my life from the battles that are against me.
ADAPTED FROM PSALM 55:18

the [consistently] righteous to be moved (made to slip, fall, or fail). [I Pet. 5:7.]

23 But You, O God, will bring down the wicked into the pit of destruction; men of blood and treachery shall not live out half their days. But I will trust in, lean on, *and* confidently rely on You.

PSALM 56

To the Chief Musician; [set to the tune of] "Silent Dove Among Those Far Away." Of David. A record of memorable thoughts when the Philistines seized him in Gath.

BE MERCIFUL *and* gracious to me, O God, for man would trample me *or* devour me; all the day long the adversary oppresses me.

2 They that lie in wait for me would swallow me up *or* trample me all day long, for they are many who fight against me, O Most High!

3 What time I am afraid, I will have confidence in *and* put my trust *and* reliance in You.

4 By [the help of] God I will praise His word; on God I lean, rely, *and* confidently put my trust; I will not fear. What can man, who is flesh, do to me?

5 All day long they twist my words *and* trouble my affairs; all their thoughts are against me for evil *and* my hurt.

6 They gather themselves together, they hide themselves, they watch my steps, even as they have [expectantly] waited for my life.

7 They think to escape with iniquity, *and* shall they? In Your indignation bring down the peoples, O God.

8 You number *and* record my wanderings; put my tears into Your bottle—are they not in Your book?

9 Then shall my enemies turn back in the day that I cry out; this I know, for God is for me. [Rom. 8:31.]

10 In God, Whose word I praise, in the Lord, Whose word I praise,

11 In God have I put my trust *and* confident reliance; I will not be afraid. What can man do to me?

12 Your vows are upon me, O God; I will render praise to You *and* give You thank offerings.

13 For You have delivered my life from death, yes, and my feet from falling, that I may walk before God in the light of life *and* of the living.

PSALM 57

To the Chief Musician; [set to the tune of] "Do Not Destroy." A record of memorable thoughts of David when he fled from Saul in the cave.

BE MERCIFUL *and* gracious to me, O God, be merciful *and* gracious to me, for my soul takes refuge *and* finds shelter *and* confidence in You; yes, in the shadow of Your wings will I take refuge *and* be confident until calamities *and* destructive storms are passed.

2 I will cry to God Most High, Who performs on my behalf *and* rewards me [Who brings to pass His purposes for me and surely completes them]!

3 He will send from heaven and save me from the slanders *and* reproaches of him who would trample me down *or* swallow me up, *and* He will put him to shame. Selah [pause, and calmly think of that]! God will

speak the Word

God, I will release the weight of my burdens and cast them on You, knowing that You will sustain me. I declare, God, that You will not allow the righteous to be moved!

ADAPTED FROM PSALM 55:22

send forth His mercy *and* loving-kindness *and* His truth *and* faithfulness.

4 My life is among lions; I must lie among those who are aflame—the sons of men whose teeth are spears and arrows, their tongues sharp swords.

5 Be exalted, O God, above the heavens! Let Your glory be over all the earth!

6 They set a net for my steps; my very life was bowed down. They dug a pit in my way; into the midst of it they themselves have fallen. Selah [pause, and calmly think of that]!

7 My heart is fixed, O God, my heart is steadfast *and* confident! I will sing and make melody.

8 Awake, my glory (my inner self); awake, harp and lyre! I will awake right early [I will awaken the dawn]!

9 I will praise *and* give thanks to You, O Lord, among the peoples; I will sing praises to You among the nations.

10 For Your mercy *and* loving-kindness are great, reaching to the heavens, and Your truth *and* faithfulness to the clouds.

11 Be exalted, O God, above the heavens; let Your glory be over all the earth.

PSALM 58

To the Chief Musician; [set to the tune of] "Do Not Destroy." A record of memorable thoughts of David.

DO YOU indeed in silence speak righteousness, O you mighty ones? [Or is the righteousness, rightness, and justice you should speak quite dumb?] Do you judge fairly *and* uprightly, O you sons of men?

2 No, in your heart you devise wickedness; you deal out in the land the violence of your hands.

3 The ungodly are perverse *and* estranged from the womb; they go astray as soon as they are born, speaking lies.

4 Their poison is like the venom of a serpent; they are like the deaf adder *or* asp that stops its ear,

5 Which listens not to the voice of charmers *or* of the enchanter never casting spells so cunningly.

6 Break their teeth, O God, in their mouths; break out the fangs of the young lions, O Lord.

7 Let them melt away as water which runs on apace; when he aims his arrows, let them be as if they were headless *or* split apart.

8 Let them be as a snail dissolving slime as it passes on *or* as a festering sore which wastes away, like [the child to which] a woman gives untimely birth that has not seen the sun.

9 Before your pots can feel the thorns [that are placed under them for fuel], He will take them away as with a whirlwind, the green and the burning ones alike.

10 The [unyieldingly] righteous shall rejoice when he sees the vengeance; he will bathe his feet in the blood of the wicked.

11 Men will say, Surely there is a reward for the [uncompromisingly] righteous; surely there is a God Who judges on the earth.

PSALM 59

To the Chief Musician; [set to the tune of] "Do Not Destroy." Of David, a record of memorable thoughts when Saul sent men to watch his house in order to kill him.

DELIVER ME from my enemies, O my God; defend *and* protect me from those who rise up against me.

2 Deliver me from *and* lift me above those who work evil and save me from bloodthirsty men.

3 For, behold, they lie in wait for my life; fierce *and* mighty men are banding together against me, not for my transgression nor for any sin of mine, O Lord.

steadfast and confident

In Psalm 57:7, we read about a heart that is not only fixed and steadfast, but also confident.

I have discovered that staying confident at all times is vital to successful ministry and to an overcoming life. Even while I am in front of an audience teaching and ministering, the devil will try to introduce thoughts into my head to make me lose confidence. For example, there have been times when if I noticed two or three people glance at their watches, the devil whispered to me, "They are so bored they can't wait to get out of here." If a couple of people got up and left to go to the restroom, the devil would say, "They are leaving because they don't like your preaching."

I know that when people are singing or leading worship, it is not uncommon for the devil to tell them, "Nobody likes this. You picked the wrong music. You should have chosen a different song. Your voice sounds lousy. You are singing off-key," and on and on.

The mind is a battlefield, and the devil lies to us by putting wrong thoughts in our minds. He is constantly trying to steal our confidence. He does not want us to believe that we can hear from God or believe in the power of prayer. He does not want us to have any confidence concerning the call on our lives or to be confident that we look nice, that we have any wisdom, or that we know anything at all. He wants us to go around feeling that we are failures. That is why we need to keep our hearts confident within us all the time. I have learned that we do not have to *feel* confident to *be* confident. We can be confident by faith because our confidence should be in Christ, not in ourselves. No matter how I feel, I still believe that I can do whatever I need to do through Christ, Who strengthens me. If we do not feel confident, then we feel afraid, and I have learned at those times to "do it afraid."

We do not have to drag ourselves out of bed each day in fear or discouragement. Instead, we should get up every morning prepared to keep Satan under our feet. How do we do that? We do it by confidently declaring what the Word says about us, confessing scriptures such as, "I am more than a conqueror through Jesus. I can do all things through Christ Who strengthens me. I am triumphant in every situation because God always causes me to triumph" (see Romans 8:37; Philippians 4:13; II Corinthians 2:14). Speaking God's Word not only causes the devil to leave us alone, but it also strengthens our confidence—and confidence is essential if we are going to keep growing and keep going in God.

4 They run and prepare themselves, though there is no fault in me; rouse Yourself [O Lord] to meet *and* help me, and see!
5 You, O Lord God of hosts, the God of Israel, arise to visit all the nations; spare none *and* be not merciful to any who treacherously plot evil. Selah [pause, and calmly think of that]!
6 They return at evening, they howl *and* snarl like dogs, and go [prowling] about the city.
7 Behold, they belch out [insults] with their mouths; swords [of sarcasm,

ridicule, slander, and lies] are in their lips, for who, they think, hears us?

8 But You, O Lord, will laugh at them [in scorn]; You will hold all the nations in derision.

9 O my Strength, I will watch *and* give heed to You *and* sing praises; for God is my Defense (my Protector and High Tower).

10 My God in His mercy *and* steadfast love will meet me; God will let me look [triumphantly] on my enemies (those who lie in wait for me).

11 Slay them not, lest my people forget; scatter them by Your power *and* make them wander to and fro, and bring them down, O Lord our Shield!

12 For the sin of their mouths and the words of their lips, let them even be trapped *and* taken in their pride, and for the cursing and lying which they utter.

13 Consume them in wrath, consume them so that they shall be no more; and let them know unto the ends of the earth that God rules over Jacob (Israel). Selah [pause, and calmly think of that]!

14 And at evening let them return; let them howl *and* snarl like dogs, and go prowling about the city.

15 Let them wander up and down for food and tarry all night if they are not satisfied (not getting their fill).

16 But I will sing of Your mighty strength *and* power; yes, I will sing aloud of Your mercy *and* loving-kindness in the morning; for You have been to me a defense (a fortress and a high tower) and a refuge in the day of my distress.

17 Unto You, O my Strength, I will sing praises; for God is my Defense, my Fortress, *and* High Tower, the God

Who shows me mercy *and* steadfast love.

PSALM 60

To the Chief Musician; [set to the tune of] "The Lily of the Testimony." A poem of David intended to record memorable thoughts and to teach; when he had striven with the Arameans of Mesopotamia and the Arameans of Zobah, and when Joab returned and smote twelve thousand Edomites in the Valley of Salt.

O GOD, You have rejected us *and* cast us off, broken down [our defenses], *and* scattered us; You have been angry—O restore us *and* turn Yourself to us again!

2 You have made the land to quake *and* tremble, You have rent it [open]; repair its breaches, for it shakes *and* totters.

3 You have made Your people suffer hard things; You have given us to drink wine that makes us reel *and* be dazed.

4 [But now] You have set up a banner for those who fear *and* worshipfully revere You [to which they may flee from the bow], a standard displayed because of the truth. Selah [pause, and calmly think of that]!

5 That Your beloved ones may be delivered, save with Your right hand and answer us [or me].

6 God has spoken in His holiness [in His promises]: I will rejoice, I will divide and portion out [the land] Shechem and the Valley of Succoth [west to east].

7 Gilead is Mine, and Manasseh is Mine; Ephraim also is My helmet (the defense of My head); Judah is My scepter *and* My lawgiver.

speak the Word

Thank You, God, for always meeting me with mercy and steadfast love.
ADAPTED FROM PSALM **59:10**

8 Moab is My washpot [reduced to vilest servitude]; upon Edom I cast My shoe in triumph; over Philistia I raise the shout of victory.

9 Who will bring me [David] into the strong city [of Petra]? Who will lead me into Edom?

10 Have You not rejected us, O God? And will You not go forth, O God, with our armies?

11 O give us help against the adversary, for vain (ineffectual and to no purpose) is the help or salvation of man.

12 Through God we shall do valiantly, for He it is Who shall tread down our adversaries.

PSALM 61
To the Chief Musician; on stringed instruments. [A Psalm] of David.

HEAR MY cry, O God; listen to my prayer.
2 From the end of the earth will I cry to You, when my heart is overwhelmed *and* fainting; lead me to the rock that is higher than I [yes, a rock that is too high for me].

3 For You have been a shelter *and* a refuge for me, a strong tower against the adversary.

4 I will dwell in Your tabernacle forever; let me find refuge *and* trust in the shelter of Your wings. Selah [pause, and calmly think of that]!

5 For You, O God, have heard my vows; You have given me the heritage of those who fear, revere, *and* honor Your name.

6 May You prolong the [true] ¹King's life [adding days upon days], and may His years be to the last gen-

putting the Word to work

Has life ever seemed so overwhelming that you wanted to run and hide? You can be sure of God's eternal protection and ability to be your refuge (see Psalm 61:3, 4). Whether you need the strength of a rock or the comfort of His arms around you, cry out to God; He will answer in your time of need.

eration [of this world and the generations of the world to come].

7 May He sit enthroned forever before [the face of] God; O ordain that loving-kindness and faithfulness may watch over Him!

8 So will I sing praise to Your name forever, paying my vows day by day.

PSALM 62
To the Chief Musician; according to Jeduthun [Ethan, the noted musician, founder of an official musical family]. A Psalm of David.

FOR GOD alone my soul waits in silence; from Him comes my salvation.
2 He only is my Rock and my Salvation, my Defense *and* my Fortress, I shall not be greatly moved.

3 How long will you set upon a man that you may slay him, all of you, like a leaning wall, like a tottering fence?

4 They only consult to cast him down from his height [to dishonor him]; they delight in lies. They bless with their mouths, but they curse inwardly. Selah [pause, and calmly think of that]!

---

1 The thoughts of these verses (6-7) are fulfilled in Christ, David's great Son.

stability releases ability

Psalm 62:8 teaches us that we are not to have faith in God just once in a while, but at all times. We need to learn to live from faith to faith (see Romans 1:17), trusting the Lord when things are good and when things are bad.

It is easy to trust God when things are going well. But when things are not going well, we develop character by trusting God in our difficult situations. And the more character we develop, the more our ability can be released. That is why I say that *stability releases ability*. The more stable we become, the more our ability will be released because God will know that He can trust us.

Many people have gifts that can take them to places where their character cannot keep them. Gifts are *given*, but character is *developed*. I have learned this in my own life.

Throughout my childhood, one thing I could do well was talk. In school, I could talk enough to make the teacher think I understood everything she was teaching, when I really knew nothing about it. I have always been a communicator and a convincer. But in order for God to allow me in the pulpit to preach to millions every day, not only did I have to have a gift, I also had to have character so that He could trust me to use my mouth to teach His Word and communicate His heart. Otherwise, He could not allow me to teach that many people, because I might say one thing one day and something else the next day. Or, even worse, I might preach to others what I was unable to do in my own private life.

By disciplining our emotions, our moods, and our mouths, we become stable enough to remain peaceful, whatever our situation or circumstance, so that we can walk in the fruit of the Spirit—whether we feel like it or not. The more stable we become, the more ability can be released through us. Desire and pursue stability in every area of your life so that all the ability in you can be released!

5 My soul, wait only upon God *and* silently submit to Him; for my hope *and* expectation are from Him.
6 He only is my Rock and my Salvation; He is my Defense *and* my Fortress, I shall not be moved.
7 With God rests my salvation and my glory; He is my Rock of unyielding strength *and* impenetrable hardness, and my refuge is in God!

8 Trust in, lean on, rely on, *and* have confidence in Him at all times, you people; pour out your hearts before Him. God is a refuge for us (a fortress and a high tower). Selah [pause, and calmly think of that]!
9 Men of low degree [in the social scale] are emptiness (futility, a breath) *and* men of high degree [in the same scale] are a lie *and* a delusion. In

speak the Word

God, I am trusting in, leaning on, and relying on You; trusting You at all times. You are a fortress and a high tower for me!
ADAPTED FROM PSALM 62:8

the balances they go up; they are together lighter than a breath.

10 Trust not in *and* rely confidently not on extortion *and* oppression, and do not vainly hope in robbery; if riches increase, set not your heart on them.

11 God has spoken once, twice have I heard this: that power belongs to God.

12 Also to You, O Lord, belong mercy *and* loving-kindness, for You render to every man according to his work. [Jer. 17:10; Rev. 22:12.]

PSALM 63

A Psalm of David; when he was in the Wilderness of Judah.

O GOD, You are my God, earnestly will I seek You; my inner self thirsts for You, my flesh longs *and* is faint for You, in a dry and weary land where no water is.

life point

In Psalm 63:1, David cries out: "O God, You are my God, earnestly will I seek You . . ." Throughout the Psalms, David prayed similar prayers, which I call "seeking prayers." Many times per day, I find myself whispering in my heart or even aloud, "Oh, God, I need You." This is a very simple but very powerful way to pray. I encourage you to join me in seeking God in this quick and effective way.

2 So I have looked upon You in the sanctuary to see Your power and Your glory.

3 Because Your loving-kindness is better than life, my lips shall praise You.

4 So will I bless You while I live; I will lift up my hands in Your name.

5 My whole being shall be satisfied as with marrow and fatness; and my mouth shall praise You with joyful lips

life point

Sacrifice and Christianity have always been connected. In the Old Testament, the Law required sacrifices of various kinds. David speaks of lifting up the "hands as the evening sacrifice" in Psalm 141:2.

Other scriptures talk about the lifting up of hands in worship (see Psalm 28:2; 119:48; 134:2). Lifting our hands to God seems a natural thing to do when we are in His presence. To me, it is an expression of adoration, reverence, and surrender. We should continually surrender ourselves to God and His plan for us.

You can lift up your hands and speak a word of praise all throughout the day. Even at work, you can go to the bathroom and take a moment to praise God. When we willingly surrender and worship God as a sacrifice, He responds. God inhabits the praises of His people.

6 When I remember You upon my bed and meditate on You in the night watches.

7 For You have been my help, and in the shadow of Your wings will I rejoice.

8 My whole being follows hard after You *and* clings closely to You; Your right hand upholds me.

9 But those who seek *and* demand my life to ruin *and* destroy it shall [themselves be destroyed and] go into the lower parts of the earth [into the underworld of the dead].

10 They shall be given over to the power of the sword; they shall be a prey for foxes *and* jackals.

11 But the king shall rejoice in God; everyone who swears by Him [that is, who binds himself by God's authority, acknowledging His supremacy, and devoting himself to His glory and

life point

David spoke frequently about meditating on God, His goodness and His works and His ways. It is tremendously uplifting to think on the goodness of God and all the marvelous works of His hands.

I enjoy watching television shows about nature, animals, ocean life, and other things in the physical world because they depict the greatness and the awesomeness of God, His infinite creativity, and the fact that He is upholding all things by the might of His power (see Hebrews 1:3). Always remember that—and know that He is not only upholding and maintaining the moon, the stars, the planets including the earth, the animals, and all of creation, but that He is also upholding and maintaining everything about you and your life in the palm of His hand.

service alone; every such one] shall glory, for the mouths of those who speak lies shall be stopped.

PSALM 64
To the Chief Musician. A Psalm of David.

HEAR MY voice, O God, in my complaint; guard *and* preserve my life from the terror of the enemy.

2 Hide me from the secret counsel *and* conspiracy of the ungodly, from the scheming of evildoers,

3 Who whet their tongues like a sword, who aim venomous words like arrows,

4 Who shoot from ambush at the blameless man; suddenly do they shoot at him, without self-reproach *or* fear.

5 They encourage themselves in an evil purpose, they talk of laying snares secretly; they say, Who will discover *us*?

6 They think out acts of injustice and say, We have accomplished a well-devised thing! For the inward thought of each one [is unsearchable] and his heart is deep.

7 But God will shoot an unexpected arrow at them; and suddenly shall they be wounded.

8 And they will be made to stumble, their own tongues turning against them; all who gaze upon them will shake their heads *and* flee away.

9 And all men shall [reverently] fear *and* be in awe; and they will declare the work of God, for they will wisely consider *and* acknowledge that it is His doing.

10 The [uncompromisingly] righteous shall be glad in the Lord and shall trust *and* take refuge in Him; and all the upright in heart shall glory *and* offer praise.

PSALM 65
To the Chief Musician. A Psalm of David.
A song.

TO YOU belongs silence (the submissive wonder of reverence which bursts forth into praise) *and* praise is due *and* fitting to You, O God, in Zion; and to You shall the vow be performed.

2 O You Who hear prayer, to You shall all flesh come.

3 Iniquities *and* much varied guilt prevail against me; [yet] as for our transgressions, You forgive *and* purge them away [make atonement for them and cover them out of Your sight]!

4 Blessed (happy, fortunate, to be envied) is the man whom You choose and cause to come near, that he may dwell in Your courts! We shall be satisfied with the goodness of Your house, Your holy temple.

5 By fearful *and* glorious things [that terrify the wicked but make the godly sing praises] do You answer us

in righteousness (rightness and justice), O God of our salvation, You Who are the confidence and hope of all the ends of the earth and of those far off on the seas;

6 Who by [Your] might have founded the mountains, being girded with power,

7 Who still the roaring of the seas, the roaring of their waves, and the tumult of the peoples,

8 So that those who dwell in earth's farthest parts are afraid of [nature's] signs of Your presence. You make the places where morning and evening have birth to shout for joy.

9 You visit the earth and saturate it with water; You greatly enrich it; the river of God is full of water; You provide them with grain when You have so prepared the earth.

10 You water the field's furrows abundantly, You settle the ridges of it; You make the soil soft with showers, blessing the sprouting of its vegetation.

11 You crown the year with Your bounty and goodness, and the tracks of Your [chariot wheels] drip with fatness.

12 The [luxuriant] pastures in the uncultivated country drip [with moisture], and the hills gird themselves with joy.

13 The meadows are clothed with flocks, the valleys also are covered with grain; they shout for joy and sing together.

PSALM 66
To the Chief Musician. A song. A Psalm.

MAKE A joyful noise unto God, all the earth;

2 Sing forth the honor and glory of His name; make His praise glorious!

3 Say to God, How awesome and fearfully glorious are Your works! Through the greatness of Your power shall Your enemies submit themselves to You [with feigned and reluctant obedience].

4 All the earth shall bow down to You and sing [praises] to You; they shall praise Your name in song. Selah [pause, and calmly think of that]!

5 Come and see the works of God; see how [to save His people He smites their foes; He is] terrible in His doings toward the children of men.

6 He turned the sea into dry land, they crossed through the river on foot; there did we rejoice in Him.

7 He rules by His might forever, His eyes observe and keep watch over the nations; let not the rebellious exalt themselves. Selah [pause, and calmly think of that]!

8 Bless our God, O peoples, give Him grateful thanks and make the voice of His praise be heard,

9 Who put and kept us among the

life point

In his writings the psalmist often uses the word *selah*, which means "Pause, and calmly think of that." This phrase lets the reader know that this is a good place to stop and to slowly digest the meaning of what has just been said. The reader is given the opportunity to do this at the end of Psalm 66:4.

Jeremiah talked about stopping to feed on and digest the words of God. He said, "Your words were found, and I ate them; and Your words were to me a joy and the rejoicing of my heart" (Jeremiah 15:16). We must, so to speak, "chew" on the Word of God. Often we read the Bible for *quantity* when we should read for *quality*. Whatever passage you are reading, read in a manner that allows the Word to go down into your innermost being and feed your spirit.

living, and has not allowed our feet to slip.

10 For You, O God, have proved us; You have tried us as silver is tried, refined, *and* purified.

11 You brought us into the net (the prison fortress, the dungeon); You laid a heavy burden upon our loins.

12 You caused men to ride over our heads [when we were prostrate]; we went through fire and through water, but You brought us out into a broad, moist place [to abundance and refreshment and the open air].

13 I will come into Your house with burnt offerings [of entire consecration]; I will pay You my vows,

14 Which my lips uttered and my mouth promised when I was in distress.

15 I will offer to You burnt offerings of fat lambs, with rams consumed in sweet-smelling smoke; I will offer bullocks and he-goats. Selah [pause, and calmly think of that]!

16 Come and hear, all you who reverently *and* worshipfully fear God, and I will declare what He has done for me!

17 I cried aloud to Him; He was extolled *and* high praise was under my tongue.

18 If I regard iniquity in my heart, the Lord will not hear me; [Prov. 15:29; 28:9; Isa. 1:15; John 9:31; James 4:3.]

19 But certainly God has heard me; He has given heed to the voice of my prayer.

20 Blessed be God, Who has not rejected my prayer nor removed His mercy *and* loving-kindness from being [as it always is] with me.

PSALM 67

To the Chief Musician; on stringed instruments. A Psalm. A song.

GOD BE merciful *and* gracious to us and bless us and cause His face to shine upon us *and* among us—Selah [pause, and calmly think of that]!—

2 That Your way may be known upon earth, Your saving power (Your deliverances and Your salvation) among all nations.

3 Let the peoples praise You [turn away from their idols] *and* give thanks to You, O God; let all the peoples praise *and* give thanks to You.

4 O let the nations be glad and sing for joy, for You will judge the peoples fairly and guide, lead, *or* drive the nations upon earth. Selah [pause, and calmly think of that]!

5 Let the peoples praise You [turn away from their idols] *and* give thanks to You, O God; let all the peoples praise *and* give thanks to You!

6 The earth has yielded its harvest [in evidence of God's approval]; God, even our own God, will bless us.

7 God will bless us, and all the ends of the earth shall reverently fear Him.

PSALM 68

To the Chief Musician. A Psalm of David. A song.

GOD IS [already] beginning to arise, and His enemies to scatter; let them also who hate Him flee before Him!

2 As smoke is driven away, so drive them away; as wax melts before the

speak the Word

I bless You, Lord, because You have not rejected my prayer or removed Your mercy and loving-kindness from me.
ADAPTED FROM PSALM 66:20

God wants all nations and people to know Him, worship Him, and enjoy Him. How can you be involved in God's work in the world?

fire, so let the wicked perish before the presence of God.

3 But let the [uncompromisingly] righteous be glad; let them be in high spirits *and* glory before God, yes, let them [jubilantly] rejoice!

4 Sing to God, sing praises to His name, cast up a highway for Him Who rides through the deserts—His name is the Lord—be in high spirits *and* glory before Him!

5 A father of the fatherless and a judge *and* protector of the widows *is* God in His holy habitation.

6 God places the solitary in families *and* gives the desolate a home in which to dwell; He leads the prisoners out to prosperity; but the rebellious dwell in a parched land.

7 O God, when You went forth before Your people, when You marched through the wilderness—Selah [pause, and calmly think of that]!—

8 The earth trembled, the heavens also poured down [rain] at the presence of God; yonder Sinai quaked at the presence of God, the God of Israel.

9 You, O God, did send a plentiful rain; You did restore *and* confirm Your heritage when it languished *and* was weary.

10 Your flock found a dwelling place in it; You, O God, in Your goodness did provide for the poor *and* needy.

11 The Lord gives the word [of power]; the women who bear *and* publish [the news] are a great host.

12 The kings of the enemies' armies, they flee, they flee! She who tarries at home divides the spoil [left behind].

13 Though you [the slackers] may lie among the sheepfolds [in slothful ease, yet for Israel] the wings of a dove are covered with silver, its pinions excessively green with gold [are trophies taken from the enemy].

14 When the Almighty scattered kings in [the land], it was as when it snows on Zalmon [a wooded hill near Shechem].

15 Is Mount Bashan the high mountain of summits, Mount Bashan [east of the Jordan] the mount of God?

16 Why do you look with grudging *and* envy, you many-peaked mountains, at the mountain [of the city called Zion] which God has desired for His dwelling place? Yes, the Lord will dwell in it forever.

17 The chariots of God are twenty thousand, even thousands upon thousands. The Lord is among them as He was in Sinai, [so also] in the Holy Place (the sanctuary in Jerusalem).

18 [m]You have ascended on high. You have led away captive a train of vanquished foes; You have received gifts of men, yes, of the rebellious also, that the Lord God might dwell there with them. [Eph. 4:8.]

19 Blessed be the Lord, Who bears our burdens *and* carries us day by day, even the God Who is our salvation! Selah [pause, and calmly think of that]!

20 God is to us a God of deliverances

m David sang of the ark of the covenant, which after a great victory was transferred or brought back to Zion. In this fact he sees the principle of the history of the kingdom of God appearing in ever-widening circles and nobler manner. The earthly celebration of victory in battle, with the processional bearing of the ark into the temple, is to him a type of the method and course of the Messiah's kingdom, i.e., the certain triumph of God's kingdom and Christ's ascension to His place of enthronement. So the apostle Paul (in Eph. 4:8) is perfectly justified in finding the psalmist's eye directed toward Christ, and so interpreting it. The "on high" in the psalm is first of all Mount Zion, but this is a type of heaven, as Paul makes clear (J.P. Lange, *A Commentary*).

and salvation; and to God the Lord belongs escape from death [setting us free].

21 But God will shatter the heads of His enemies, the hairy scalp of such a one as goes on still in his trespasses *and* guilty ways.

22 The Lord said, I will bring back [your enemies] from Bashan; I will bring them back from the depths of the [Red] Sea,

23 That you may crush them, dipping your foot in blood, that the tongues of your dogs may have their share from the foe.

24 They see Your goings, O God, even the [solemn processions] of my God, my King, into the sanctuary [in holiness].

25 The singers go in front, the players on instruments last; between them the maidens are playing on tambourines.

26 Bless, give thanks, *and* gratefully praise God in full congregations, even the Lord, O you who are from [Jacob] the fountain of Israel.

27 There is little Benjamin in the lead [in the procession], the princes of Judah and their company, the princes of Zebulun, and the princes of Naphtali.

28 Your God has commanded your strength [your might in His service and impenetrable hardness to temptation]; O God, display Your might *and* strengthen what You have wrought for us!

29 [Out of respect] for Your temple at Jerusalem kings shall bring gifts to You.

30 Rebuke the wild beasts dwelling among the reeds [in Egypt], the herd of bulls (the leaders) with the calves of the peoples; trample underfoot those who lust for tribute money; scatter the peoples who delight in war.

31 Princes shall come out of Egypt; Ethiopia shall hasten to stretch out her hands [with the offerings of submission] to God.

32 Sing to God, O kingdoms of the earth, sing praises to the Lord! Selah [pause, and calmly think of that]!

33 [Sing praises] to Him Who rides upon the heavens, the ancient heavens; behold, He sends forth His voice, His mighty voice.

34 Ascribe power *and* strength to God; His majesty is over Israel, and His strength *and* might are in the skies.

35 O God, awe-inspiring, profoundly impressive, *and* terrible are You out of Your holy places; the God of Israel Himself gives strength and fullness of might to His people. Blessed be God!

PSALM 69

To the Chief Musician; [set to the tune of] "Lilies." [A Psalm] of David.

SAVE ME, O God, for the waters have come up to my neck [they threaten my life].

2 I sink in deep mire, where there is no foothold; I have come into deep waters, where the floods overwhelm me.

3 I am weary with my crying; my throat is parched; my eyes fail with waiting [hopefully] for my God.

4 Those who hate me without cause are more than the hairs of my head; those who would cut me off *and* destroy me, being my enemies wrongfully, are many *and* mighty. I am

speak the Word

[forced] to restore what I did not steal. [John 15:25.]

5 O God, You know my folly *and* blundering; my sins *and* my guilt are not hidden from You.

6 Let not those who wait *and* hope *and* look for You, O Lord of hosts, be put to shame through me; let not those who seek *and* inquire for *and* require You [as their vital necessity] be brought to confusion *and* dishonor through me, O God of Israel.

7 Because for Your sake I have borne taunt *and* reproach; confusion *and* shame have covered my face.

8 I have become a stranger to my brethren, and an alien to my mother's children. [John 7:3-5.]

9 For zeal for Your house has eaten me up, and the reproaches *and* insults of those who reproach *and* insult You have fallen upon me. [John 2:17; Rom. 15:3.]

10 When I wept *and* humbled myself with fasting, I was jeered at *and* humiliated;

11 When I made sackcloth my clothing, I became a byword (an object of scorn) to them.

12 They who sit in [the city's] gate talk about me, and I am the song of the drunkards.

13 But as for me, my prayer is to You, O Lord. At an acceptable *and* opportune time, O God, in the multitude of Your mercy *and* the abundance of Your loving-kindness hear me, *and* in the truth *and* faithfulness of Your salvation answer me.

14 Rescue me out of the mire, and let me not sink; let me be delivered from those who hate me and from out of the deep waters.

15 Let not the floodwaters overflow *and* overwhelm me, neither let the deep swallow me up nor the [dug] pit [with water perhaps in the bottom] close its mouth over me.

16 Hear *and* answer me, O Lord, for Your loving-kindness is sweet *and* comforting; according to Your plenteous tender mercy *and* steadfast love turn to me.

17 Hide not Your face from Your servant, for I am in distress; O answer me speedily!

18 Draw close to me and redeem me; ransom *and* set me free because of my enemies [lest they glory in my prolonged distress]!

19 You know my reproach and my shame and my dishonor; my adversaries are all before You [fully known to You].

20 Insults *and* reproach have broken my heart; I am full of heaviness *and* I am distressingly sick. I looked for pity, but there was none, and for comforters, but I found none.

21 They gave me also gall [poisonous and bitter] for my food, and in my thirst they gave me vinegar (a soured wine) to drink. [Matt. 27:34, 48.]

22 Let their own table [with all its abundance and luxury] become a snare to them; and when they are secure in peace [or at their sacrificial feasts, let it become] a trap to them.

23 Let their eyes be darkened so that they cannot see, and make their loins tremble continually [from terror, dismay, and feebleness].

24 Pour out Your indignation upon them, and let the fierceness of Your burning anger catch up with them.

25 Let their habitation *and* their encampment be a desolation; let no one dwell in their tents. [Matt. 23:38; Acts 1:20.]

26 For they pursue *and* persecute him whom You have smitten, and they gossip about those whom You have wounded, [adding] to their grief *and* pain.

27 Let one [unforgiven] perverseness *and* iniquity accumulate upon another for them [in Your book], and let them not come into Your righteousness *or* be justified and acquitted by You.

28 Let them be blotted out of the book of the living *and* the book of life and not be enrolled among the [uncompromisingly] righteous (those upright and in right standing with God). [Rev. 3:4, 5; 20:12, 15; 21:27.]
29 But I am poor, sorrowful, and in pain; let Your salvation, O God, set me up on high.
30 I will praise the name of God with a song and will magnify Him with thanksgiving,
31 And it will please the Lord better than an ox or a bullock that has horns and hoofs.
32 The humble shall see it and be glad; you who seek God, inquiring for *and* requiring Him [as your first need], let your hearts revive *and* live! [Ps. 22:26; 42:1.]
33 For the Lord hears the poor *and* needy and despises not His prisoners (His miserable and wounded ones).
34 Let heaven and earth praise Him, the seas and everything that moves in them.
35 For God will save Zion and rebuild the cities of Judah; and [His servants] shall remain *and* dwell there and have it in their possession;
36 The children of His servants shall inherit it, and those who love His name shall dwell in it.

PSALM 70

To the Chief Musician. [A Psalm] of David, to bring to remembrance *or* make memorial.

MAKE HASTE, O God, to deliver me; make haste to help me, O Lord!
2 Let them be put to shame *and*

speak the Word

confounded that seek *and* demand my life; let them be turned backward and brought to confusion *and* dishonor who desire *and* delight in my hurt.
3 Let them be turned back *and* appalled because of their shame *and* disgrace who say, Aha, aha!
4 May all those who seek, inquire of *and* for You, *and* require You [as their vital need] rejoice and be glad in You; and may those who love Your salvation say continually, Let God be magnified!
5 But I am poor and needy; hasten to me, O God! You are my Help and my Deliverer; O Lord, do not tarry!

PSALM 71

IN YOU, O Lord, do I put my trust *and* confidently take refuge; let me never be put to shame *or* confusion!
2 Deliver me in Your righteousness and cause me to escape; bow down Your ear to me and save me!
3 Be to me a rock of refuge in which to dwell, *and* a sheltering stronghold to which I may continually resort, which You have appointed to save me, for You are my Rock and my Fortress.
4 Rescue me, O my God, out of the hand of the wicked, out of the grasp of the unrighteous and ruthless man.
5 For You are my hope; O Lord God, You are my trust from my youth *and* the source of my confidence.
6 Upon You have I leaned *and* relied from birth; You are He Who took me from my mother's womb *and* You

God, I am seeking You, inquiring of You, requiring You as my vital need and rejoicing in You. I love Your salvation and I will say continually, "Let God be magnified!"
ADAPTED FROM PSALM 70:4

have been my benefactor from that day. My praise is continually of You.

7 I am as a wonder *and* surprise to many, but You are my strong refuge.

8 My mouth shall be filled with Your praise and with Your honor all the day.

9 Cast me not off *nor* send me away in the time of old age; forsake me not when my strength is spent *and* my powers fail.

10 For my enemies talk against me; those who watch for my life consult together,

11 Saying, God has forsaken him; pursue *and* persecute and take him, for there is none to deliver him.

12 O God, be not far from me! O my God, make haste to help me!

13 Let them be put to shame and consumed who are adversaries to my life; let them be covered with reproach, scorn, *and* dishonor who seek *and* require my hurt.

14 But I will hope continually, and will praise You yet more and more.

15 My mouth shall tell of Your righteous acts *and* of Your deeds of salvation all the day, for their number is more than I know.

16 I will come in the strength *and* with the mighty acts of the Lord God; I will mention *and* praise Your righteousness, even Yours alone.

17 O God, You have taught me from my youth, and hitherto have I declared Your wondrous works.

18 Yes, even when I am old and gray-headed, O God, forsake me not, [but keep me alive] until I have declared Your mighty strength to [this] generation, and Your might *and* power to all that are to come.

19 Your righteousness also, O God, is very high [reaching to the heavens], You Who have done great things; O God, who is like You, *or* who is Your equal?

20 You Who have shown us [all] troubles great and sore will quicken us again and will bring us up again from the depths of the earth.

21 Increase my greatness (my honor) and turn and comfort me.

22 I will also praise You with the harp, even Your truth and faithfulness, O my God; unto You will I sing praises with the lyre, O Holy One of Israel.

23 My lips shall shout for joy when I sing praises to You, and my inner being, which You have redeemed.

24 My tongue also shall talk of Your righteousness all the day long; for they are put to shame, for they are confounded, who seek *and* demand my hurt.

[n]**PSALM 72**

[A Psalm] for Solomon.

GIVE THE king [knowledge of] Your [way of] judging, O God, and [the spirit of] Your righteousness to the king's son [to control all his actions].

speak the Word

God, I will hope in You continually. I will praise You more and more.
ADAPTED FROM PSALM 71:14

[n] "This psalm, in highly wrought figurative style, describes the reign of a king as 'righteous, universal, beneficent, and perpetual.' By the older Jewish and most of the modern Christian interpreters it has been applied to Christ, Whose reign present and prospective alone corresponds with its statements. As the imagery of the Second Psalm was drawn from the martial character of David's reign, that of this is from the peaceful and prosperous state of Solomon's" (Robert Jamieson, A.R. Fausset

2 Let him judge *and* govern Your people with righteousness, and Your poor *and* afflicted ones with judgment *and* justice.

3 The mountains shall bring peace to the people, and the hills, through [the general establishment of] righteousness.

4 May he judge *and* defend the poor of the people, deliver the children of the needy, and crush the oppressor,

5 So that they may revere *and* fear You while the sun and moon endure, throughout all generations.

6 May he [Solomon as a type of King David's greater Son] be like rain that comes down upon the mown grass, like showers that water the earth.

7 In °His [Christ's] days shall the [uncompromisingly] righteous flourish and peace abound till there is a moon no longer. [Isa. 11:3-9.]

8 He [Christ] shall have dominion also from sea to sea and from the River [Euphrates] to the ends of the earth. [Zech. 14:9.]

9 Those who dwell in the wilderness shall bow before Him and His enemies shall lick the dust.

10 The kings of Tarshish and of the coasts shall bring offerings; the kings of Sheba and Seba shall offer gifts.

11 Yes, all kings shall fall down before Him, all nations shall serve Him. [Ps. 138:4.]

12 For He delivers the needy when he calls out, the poor also and him who has no helper.

13 He will have pity on the poor *and* weak and needy and will save the lives of the needy.

14 He will redeem their lives from oppression *and* fraud and violence, and precious *and* costly shall their blood be in His sight.

15 And He shall live; and to Him shall be given gold of Sheba; prayer also shall be made for Him *and* through Him continually, *and* they shall bless *and* praise Him all the day long.

16 There shall be abundance of grain in the soil upon the top of the mountains [the least fruitful places in the land]; the fruit of it shall wave like [the forests of] Lebanon, and [the inhabitants of] the city shall flourish like grass of the earth.

17 His name shall endure forever; His name shall continue as long as the sun [indeed, His name continues before the sun]. And men shall be blessed *and* bless themselves by Him; all nations shall call Him blessed!

18 Blessed be the Lord God, the God of Israel, Who alone does wondrous things!

19 Blessed be His glorious name forever; let the whole earth be filled with His glory! Amen and Amen!

20 The prayers of David son of Jesse are ended.

BOOK THREE

PSALM 73
A Psalm of Asaph.

TRULY GOD is [only] good to Israel, even to those who are upright *and* pure in heart.

2 But as for me, my feet were almost gone, my steps had well-nigh slipped.

3 For I was envious of the foolish *and* arrogant when I saw the prosperity of the wicked.

4 For they suffer no violent pangs in their death, but their strength is firm.

5 They are not in trouble as other men; neither are they smitten *and* plagued like other men.

6 Therefore pride is about their

and David Brown, *A Commentary*). "Jesus is here, beyond all doubt, in the glory of His reign, both as He now is and as He shall be revealed in the latter-day glory" (Charles Haddon Spurgeon, *The Treasury of David*). **o** See footnote on Ps. 72:1. The ideal concept of the king and the glorious effects of his reign are described, the fulfillment of which is experienced in Christ.

necks like a chain; violence covers them like a garment [like a long, luxurious robe].

7   Their eyes stand out with fatness, they have more than heart could wish; *and* the imaginations of their minds overflow [with follies].

8   They scoff, and wickedly utter oppression; they speak loftily [from on high, maliciously and blasphemously].

9   They set their mouths against *and* speak down from heaven, and their tongues swagger through the earth [invading even heaven with blasphemy and smearing earth with slanders]. [Rev. 13:6.]

10   Therefore His people return here, and waters of a full cup [offered by the wicked] are [blindly] drained by them.

11   And they say, How does God know? Is there knowledge in the Most High?

12   Behold, these are the ungodly, who always prosper *and* are at ease in the world; they increase in riches.

13   Surely then in vain have I cleansed my heart and washed my hands in innocency.

14   For all the day long have I been smitten *and* plagued, and chastened every morning.

15   Had I spoken thus [and given expression to my feelings], I would have been untrue *and* have dealt treacherously against the generation of Your children.

16   But when I considered how to understand this, it was too great an effort for me *and* too painful

17   Until I went into the sanctuary of God; then I understood [for I considered] their end.

18   [After all] You do set the [wicked] in slippery places; You cast them down to ruin *and* destruction.

19   How they become a desolation in a moment! They are utterly consumed with terrors!

20   As a dream [which seems real] until one awakens, so, O Lord, when

You arouse Yourself [to take note of the wicked], You will despise their outward show.

21   For my heart was grieved, embittered, *and* in a state of ferment, and I was pricked in my heart [as with the sharp fang of an adder].

22   So foolish, stupid, *and* brutish was I, and ignorant; I was like a beast before You.

23   Nevertheless I am continually with You; You do hold my right hand.

24   You will guide me with Your counsel, and afterward receive me to honor *and* glory.

25   Whom have I in heaven but You? And I have no delight *or* desire on earth besides You.

26   My flesh and my heart may fail, but God is the Rock *and* firm Strength of my heart and my Portion forever.

27   For behold, those who are far from You shall perish; You will destroy all who are false to You *and* like [spiritual] harlots depart from You.

28   But it is good for me to draw near to God; I have put my trust in the Lord God *and* made Him my refuge, that I may tell of all Your works.

putting the Word to work

Have you ever wondered who will be there for you when times are really tough? Even when you feel as though you cannot go on, God promises to be your strength (see Psalm 73:25–28). Ask God to draw you nearer to Himself, so you can experience His goodness and strength even more fully.

PSALM 74

A skillful song, or a didactic or reflective poem, of Asaph.

O GOD, why do You cast us off forever? Why does Your anger burn *and* smoke against the sheep of Your pasture?

2 [Earnestly] remember Your congregation which You have acquired of old, which You have redeemed to be the tribe of Your heritage; remember Mount Zion, where You have dwelt.

3 Direct Your feet [quickly] to the perpetual ruins *and* desolations; the foe has devastated *and* desecrated everything in the sanctuary.

4 In the midst of Your Holy Place Your enemies have roared [with their battle cry]; they set up their own [idol] emblems for signs [of victory].

5 They seemed like men who lifted up axes upon a thicket of trees to make themselves a record.

6 And then all the carved wood of the Holy Place they broke down with hatchets and hammers.

7 They have set Your sanctuary on fire; they have profaned the dwelling place of Your pName by casting it to the ground.

8 They said in their hearts, Let us make havoc [of such places] altogether. They have burned up all God's meetinghouses in the land.

9 We do not see our symbols; there is no longer any prophet, neither does any among us know for how long.

10 O God, how long is the adversary to scoff *and* reproach? Is the enemy to blaspheme *and* revile Your name forever?

11 Why do You hold back Your hand, even Your right hand? Draw it out of Your bosom *and* consume them [make an end of them]!

12 Yet God is my King of old, working salvation in the midst of the earth.

13 You did divide the [Red] Sea by Your might; You broke the heads of the [Egyptian] dragons in the waters. [Exod. 14:21.]

14 You crushed the heads of Leviathan (Egypt); You did give him as food for the creatures inhabiting the wilderness.

15 You did cleave open [the rock bringing forth] fountains and streams; You dried up mighty, ever-flowing rivers (the Jordan). [Exod. 17:6; Num. 20:11; Josh. 3:13.]

16 The day is Yours, the night also is Yours; You have established the [starry] light and the sun.

17 You have fixed all the borders of the earth [the divisions of land and sea and of the nations]; You have made summer and winter. [Acts 17:26.]

18 [Earnestly] remember how the enemy has scoffed, O Lord, *and* reproached You, and how a foolish *and* impious people has blasphemed Your name.

19 Oh, do not deliver the life of your turtledove to the wild beast (to the greedy multitude); forget not the life [of the multitude] of Your poor forever.

20 Have regard for the covenant [You made with Abraham], for the dark places of the land are full of the habitations of violence.

21 Oh, let not the downtrodden return in shame; let the oppressed and needy praise Your name.

22 Arise, O God, plead Your own cause; remember [earnestly] how the foolish *and* impious man scoffs *and* reproaches You day after day *and* all day long.

23 Do not forget the [clamoring] voices of Your adversaries, the tumult of those who rise up against You, which ascends continually.

PSALM 75

To the Chief Musician; [set to the tune of] "Do Not Destroy." A Psalm of Asaph. A song.

W E GIVE praise *and* thanks to You, O God, we praise *and* give thanks; Your

---

p See footnote on Deut. 12:5.

wondrous works declare that Your
qName is near *and* they who invoke
Your Name rehearse Your wonders.

2   When the proper time has come
[for executing My judgments], I will
judge uprightly [says the Lord].

3   When the earth totters, and all the
inhabitants of it, it is I Who will poise
and keep steady its pillars. Selah
[pause, and calmly think of that]!

4   I said to the arrogant *and* boastful,
Deal not arrogantly [do not boast];
and to the wicked, Lift not up the horn
[of personal aggrandizement].

5   Lift not up your [aggressive] horn
on high, speak not with a stiff neck
and insolent arrogance.

6   For not from the east nor from the
west nor from the south come promotion *and* lifting up. [Isa. 14:13.]

7   But God is the Judge! He puts
down one and lifts up another.

8   For in the hand of the Lord there
is a cup [of His wrath], and the wine
foams *and* is red, well mixed; and He
pours out from it, and all the wicked
of the earth must drain it and drink its
dregs. [Ps. 60:3; Jer. 25:15; Rev. 14:9,
10; 16:19.]

9   But I will declare *and* rejoice forever; I will sing praises to the God of
Jacob.

10 All the horns of the ungodly also
will I cut off [says the Lord], but the
horns of the [uncompromisingly]
righteous shall be exalted.

PSALM 76

To the Chief Musician; on stringed
instruments. A Psalm of Asaph. A song.

IN JUDAH God is known *and*
renowned; His name is highly
praised *and* is great in Israel.

2   In [Jeru]Salem also is His tabernacle, and His dwelling place is in
Zion.

3   There He broke the bow's flash-

ing arrows, the shield, the sword, and
the weapons of war. Selah [pause, and
calmly think of that]!

4   Glorious *and* excellent are You
from the mountains of prey [splendid
and majestic, more than the everlasting mountains].

5   The stouthearted are stripped of
their spoil, they have slept the sleep
[of death]; and none of the men of
might could raise their hands.

6   At Your rebuke, O God of Jacob,
both chariot [rider] and horse are cast
into a dead sleep [of death]. [Exod.
15:1, 21; Nah. 2:13; Zech. 12:4.]

7   You, even You, are to be feared
[with awe and reverence]! Who may
stand in Your presence when once
Your anger is roused?

8   You caused sentence to be heard
from heaven; the earth feared and
was still—

9   When God arose to [establish]
judgment, to save all the meek *and*
oppressed of the earth. Selah [pause,
and calmly think of that]!

10 Surely the wrath of man shall
praise You; the remainder of wrath
shall You restrain *and* gird *and* arm
Yourself with it.

11 Vow and pay to the Lord your
God; let all who are round about Him
bring presents to Him Who ought to
be [reverently] feared.

12 He will cut off the spirit [of pride
and fury] of princes; He is terrible to
the [ungodly] kings of the earth.

PSALM 77

To the Chief Musician; after the manner
of Jeduthun [one of David's three chief
musicians, founder of an official musical
family]. A Psalm of Asaph.

I WILL cry to God with my voice,
even to God with my voice, and He
will give ear *and* hearken to me.

2   In the day of my trouble I seek

q See footnote on Deut. 12:5.

(inquire of and desperately require) the Lord; in the night my hand is stretched out [in prayer] without slacking up; I refuse to be comforted.

3 I [earnestly] remember God; I am disquieted *and* I groan; I muse in prayer, and my spirit faints [overwhelmed]. Selah [pause, and calmly think of that]!

4 You hold my eyes from closing; I am so troubled that I cannot speak.

5 I consider the days of old, the years of bygone times [of prosperity].

6 I call to remembrance my song in the night; with my heart I meditate and my spirit searches diligently:

life point

In Psalm 77:6, David shows us how he sought God's leading. The next time you have a decision to make, do not try to figure it out with your mind. Go somewhere to get still and let your spirit search diligently for God's voice.

7 Will the Lord cast off forever? And will He be favorable no more?

8 Have His mercy *and* loving-kindness ceased forever? Have His promises ended for all time?

9 Has God [deliberately] abandoned *or* forgotten His graciousness? Has He in anger shut up His compassion? Selah [pause, and calmly think of that]!

10 And I say, This [apparent desertion of Israel by God] is my appointed lot *and* trial, but I will recall the years of the right hand of the Most High [in loving-kindness extended toward us], for this is my grief, that the right hand of the Most High changes.

11 I will [earnestly] recall the deeds of the Lord; yes, I will [earnestly] remember the wonders [You performed for our fathers] of old.

12 I will meditate also upon all Your works and consider all Your [mighty] deeds.

13 Your way, O God, is in the sanctuary [in holiness, away from sin and guilt]. Who is a great God like our God?

14 You are the God Who does wonders; You have demonstrated Your power among the peoples.

15 You have with Your [mighty] arm redeemed Your people, the sons of Jacob and Joseph. Selah [pause, and calmly think of that]!

16 When the waters [at the Red Sea and the Jordan] saw You, O God, they were afraid; the deep shuddered also, for [all] the waters saw You.

17 The clouds poured down water, the skies sent out a sound [of rumbling thunder]; Your arrows went forth [in forked lightning].

18 The voice of Your thunder was in the whirlwind, the lightnings illumined the world; the earth trembled and shook.

19 Your way [in delivering Your people] was through the sea, and Your paths through the great waters, yet Your footsteps were not traceable, *but* were obliterated.

20 You led Your people like a flock by the hand of Moses and Aaron.

PSALM 78

A skillful song, *or* a didactic *or* reflective poem, of Asaph.

GIVE EAR, O my people, to my teaching; incline your ears to the words of my mouth.

2 I will open my mouth in a parable (in instruction by numerous examples); I will utter dark sayings of old [that hide important truth] — [Matt. 13:34, 35.]

3 Which we have heard and known, and our fathers have told us.

4 We will not hide them from their children, but we will tell to the generation to come the praiseworthy deeds of the Lord, and His might, and the wonderful works that He has performed.

5 For He established a testimony

(an express precept) in Jacob and appointed a law in Israel, commanding our fathers that they should make [the great facts of God's dealings with Israel] known to their children,

6 That the generation to come might know them, that the children still to be born might arise and recount them to their children,

7 That they might set their hope in God and not forget the works of God, but might keep His commandments

8 And might not be as their fathers—a stubborn and rebellious generation, a generation that set not their hearts aright *nor* prepared their hearts to know God, and whose spirits were not steadfast *and* faithful to God.

9 The children of Ephraim were armed and carrying bows, yet they turned back in the day of battle.

10 They kept not the covenant of God and refused to walk according to His law

11 And forgot His works and His wonders that He had shown them.

12 Marvelous things did He in the sight of their fathers in the land of Egypt, in the field of Zoan [where Pharaoh resided].

13 He divided the [Red] Sea and caused them to pass through it, and He made the waters stand like a heap. [Exod. 14:22.]

14 In the daytime also He led them with a [pillar of] cloud and all the night with a light of fire. [Exod. 13:21; 14:24.]

15 He split rocks in the wilderness and gave them drink abundantly as out of the deep.

16 He brought streams also out of the rock [at Rephidim and Kadesh] and caused waters to run down like rivers. [Exod. 17:6; Num. 20:11.]

17 Yet they still went on to sin against Him by provoking *and* rebelling against the Most High in the wilderness (in the land of drought).

18 And they tempted God in their hearts by asking for food according to their [selfish] desire *and* appetite.

19 Yes, they spoke against God; they said, Can God furnish [the food for] a table in the wilderness?

20 Behold, He did smite the rock so that waters gushed out and the streams overflowed; but can He give bread also? Can He provide flesh for His people?

21 Therefore, when the Lord heard, He was [full of] wrath; a fire was kindled against Jacob, His anger mounted up against Israel,

22 Because in God they believed not [they relied not on Him, they adhered not to Him], and they trusted not in His salvation (His power to save).

23 Yet He commanded the clouds above and opened the doors of heaven;

24 And He rained down upon them manna to eat and gave them heaven's grain. [Exod. 16:14; John 6:31.]

25 Everyone ate the bread of the mighty [man ate angels' food]; God sent them meat in abundance.

26 He let forth the east wind to blow in the heavens, and by His power He guided the south wind.

27 He rained flesh also upon them like the dust, and winged birds [quails] like the sand of the seas. [Num. 11:31.]

28 And He let [the birds] fall in the midst of their camp, round about their tents.

29 So they ate and were well filled; He gave them what they craved *and* lusted after.

30 But scarce had they stilled their craving, and while their meat was yet in their mouths, [Num. 11:33.]

31 The wrath of God came upon them and slew the strongest *and* sturdiest of them and smote down Israel's chosen youth.

32 In spite of all this, they sinned still more, for they believed not in (relied not on and adhered not to Him for) His wondrous works.

leave your stubbornness behind

Psalm 78 describes some of the things that happened to the Israelites as they journeyed from Egypt to the Promised Land. Despite God's gracious and miraculous provision for them time and time again, verse 8 tells us that they were very stubborn and rebellious during their years in the wilderness. That is precisely what caused them to die out there. They simply would not do what God told them to do! They would cry out to God to get them out of trouble when they got into a mess. They would even respond to His instructions with obedience—until circumstances improved. Then, repeatedly, they would go right back into rebellion.

This same cycle is repeated and recorded so many times in the Old Testament that it is almost unbelievable. And yet, if we are not walking in wisdom, we will spend our lives doing the same thing. As we read about the Israelites and their time in the wilderness, let us learn from their mistakes and not repeat them in our own lives.

I suppose some of us are just, by nature, a little more strong-willed than others. And then, of course, we must consider our roots and how we got started in life, because that affects us too.

I was born with a strong personality. The years I spent being abused and controlled, plus my already-strong personality, combined to develop in me the mind-set that nobody was going to tell me what to do. Obviously, God had to deal with this bad attitude before He could use me.

The Lord demands that we learn to give up our own ways and be pliable and moldable in His hands. As long as we are stubborn and rebellious, He cannot use us.

I describe "stubborn" as obstinate, difficult to handle or work with; and "rebellious" as resisting control, resisting correction, unruly, refusing to follow ordinary guidelines. Both these definitions describe me as I used to be! The abuse I had suffered in my early life caused a lot of my out-of-balance attitudes toward authority. But in order to grow as a person and be successful in life, I could not allow my past to become an excuse to stay trapped in stubbornness, rebellion, or anything else.

Victorious living demands prompt and precise obedience to God. We grow in our ability and willingness to lay aside our will and do His. It is vital that we continue to make progress in this area. It is not enough to reach a certain plateau and think, *I have gone as far as I am going to go*. We must be obedient in all things—not holding back anything or keeping any doors in our lives closed to the Lord.

Let Him do a thorough work in you so that you can leave your "wilderness" behind and enter your Promised Land.

33 Therefore their days He consumed like a breath [in emptiness, falsity, and futility] and their years in terror *and* sudden haste.

34 When He slew [some of] them, [the remainder] inquired after Him diligently, and they repented *and* sincerely sought God [for a time].

35 And they [earnestly] remembered that God was their Rock, and the Most High God their Redeemer.

36 Nevertheless they flattered Him with their mouths and lied to Him with their tongues.

37 For their hearts were not right *or* sincere with Him, neither were they faithful *and* steadfast to His covenant. [Acts 8:21.]

38 But He, full of [merciful] compassion, forgave their iniquity and destroyed them not; yes, many a time He turned His anger away and did not stir up all His wrath *and* indignation.

39 For He [earnestly] remembered that they were but flesh, a wind that goes and does not return.

40 How often they defied *and* rebelled against Him in the wilderness *and* grieved Him in the desert!

41 And time and again they turned back *and* tempted God, provoking *and* incensing the Holy One of Israel.

42 They remembered not [seriously the miracles of the working of] His hand, nor the day when He delivered them from the enemy,

43 How He wrought His miracles in Egypt and His wonders in the field of Zoan [where Pharaoh resided]

44 And turned their rivers into blood, and their streams, so that they could not drink from them.

45 He sent swarms of [venomous] flies among them which devoured them, and frogs which destroyed them.

46 He gave also their crops to the caterpillar and [the fruit of] their labor to the locust.

47 He destroyed their vines with hail and their sycamore trees with frost *and* [great chunks of] ice.

48 He [caused them to shut up their cattle or] gave them up also to the hail and their flocks to hot thunderbolts. [Exod. 9:18-21.]

49 He let loose upon them the fierceness of His anger, His wrath and indignation and distress, by sending [a mission of] angels of calamity *and* woe among them.

50 He leveled *and* made a straight path for His anger [to give it free course]; He did not spare [the Egyptian families] from death but gave their beasts over to the pestilence *and* the life [of their eldest] over to the plague.

51 He smote all the firstborn in Egypt, the chief of their strength in the tents [of the land of the sons] of Ham.

52 But [God] led His own people forth like sheep and guided them [with a shepherd's care] like a flock in the wilderness.

53 And He led them on safely *and* in confident trust, so that they feared not; but the sea overwhelmed their enemies. [Exod. 14:27, 28.]

54 And He brought them to His holy border, the border of [Canaan] His sanctuary, even to this mountain [Zion] which His right hand had acquired.

55 He drove out the nations also before [Israel] and allotted their land as a heritage, measured out *and* partitioned; and He made the tribes of Israel to dwell in the tents of those dispossessed.

56 Yet they tempted and provoked *and* rebelled against the Most High God and kept not His testimonies.

57 But they turned back and dealt unfaithfully *and* treacherously like their fathers; they were twisted like a warped *and* deceitful bow [that will not respond to the archer's aim].

58 For they provoked Him to

[righteous] anger with their high places [for idol worship] and moved Him to jealousy with their graven images.

59 When God heard this, He was full of [holy] wrath; and He utterly rejected Israel, greatly abhorring *and* loathing [her ways],

60 So that He forsook the tabernacle at Shiloh, the tent in which He had dwelt among men [and never returned to it again],

61 And delivered His strength *and* power (the ark of the covenant) into captivity, and His glory into the hands of the foe (the Philistines). [I Sam. 4:21.]

62 He gave His people over also to the sword and was wroth with His heritage [Israel]. [I Sam. 4:10.]

63 The fire [of war] devoured their young men, and their bereaved virgins were not praised in a wedding song.

64 Their priests [Hophni and Phinehas] fell by the sword, and their widows made no lamentation [for the bodies came not back from the scene of battle, and the widow of Phinehas also died that day]. [I Sam. 4:11, 19, 20.]

65 Then the Lord awakened as from sleep, as a strong man whose consciousness of power is heightened by wine.

66 And He smote His adversaries in the back [as they fled]; He put them to lasting shame *and* reproach.

67 Moreover, He rejected the tent of Joseph and chose not the tribe of Ephraim [in which the tabernacle had been accustomed to stand].

68 But He chose the tribe of Judah [as Israel's leader], Mount Zion, which He loved [to replace Shiloh as His capital].

69 And He built His sanctuary [exalted] like the heights [of the heavens] and like the earth which He established forever.

70 He chose David His servant and took him from the sheepfolds; [I Sam. 16:11, 12.]

71 From tending the ewes that had their young He brought him to be the shepherd of Jacob His people, of Israel His inheritance. [II Sam. 7:7, 8.]

72 So [David] was their shepherd with an upright heart; he guided them by the discernment *and* skillfulness [which controlled] his hands.

PSALM 79

A Psalm of Asaph.

O GOD, the nations have come into [the land of Your people] Your inheritance; Your sacred temple have they defiled; they have made Jerusalem heaps of ruins.

2 The dead bodies of Your servants they have given as food to the birds of the heavens, the flesh of Your saints to the beasts of the earth.

3 Their blood they have poured out like water round about Jerusalem, and there was none to bury them.

4 [Because of such humiliation] we have become a taunt *and* reproach to our neighbors, a mocking and derision to those who are round about us.

5 How long, O Lord? Will You be angry forever? Shall Your jealousy [which cannot endure a divided allegiance] burn like fire?

6 Pour out Your wrath on the Gentile nations who do not acknowledge You, and upon the kingdoms that do not call on Your name. [II Thess. 1:8.]

7 For they have devoured Jacob and laid waste his dwelling *and* his pasture.

8 O do not [earnestly] remember against us the iniquities *and* guilt of our forefathers! Let Your compassion *and* tender mercy speedily come to meet us, for we are brought very low.

9 Help us, O God of our salvation, for the glory of Your name! Deliver us, forgive us, *and* purge away our sins for Your name's sake.

10 Why should the Gentile nations say, Where is their God? Let vengeance for the blood of Your servants which is poured out be known among the nations in our sight [not delaying until some future generation].

11 Let the groaning *and* sighing of the prisoner come before You; according to the greatness of Your power *and* Your arm spare those who are appointed to die!

12 And return into the bosom of our neighbors sevenfold the taunts with which they have taunted *and* scoffed at You, O Lord!

13 Then we Your people, the sheep of Your pasture, will give You thanks forever; we will show forth *and* publish Your praise from generation to generation.

PSALM 80

To the Chief Musician; [set to the tune of] "Lilies, a Testimony." A Psalm of Asaph.

GIVE EAR, O Shepherd of Israel, You Who lead Joseph like a flock; You Who sit enthroned upon the cherubim [of the ark of the covenant], shine forth

2 Before 'Ephraim and Benjamin and Manasseh! Stir up Your might, and come to save us!

3 Restore us again, O God; and cause Your face to shine [in pleasure and approval on us], and we shall be saved!

4 O Lord God of hosts, how long will You be angry with Your people's prayers?

5 You have fed them with the bread of tears, and You have given them tears to drink in large measure.

6 You make us a strife *and* scorn to our neighbors, and our enemies laugh among themselves.

7 Restore us again, O God of hosts; and cause Your face to shine [upon us with favor as of old], and we shall be saved!

8 You brought a vine [Israel] out of Egypt; You drove out the [heathen] nations and planted it [in Canaan].

9 You prepared room before it, and it took deep root and it filled the land.

10 The mountains were covered with the shadow of it, and the boughs of it were like the great cedars [cedars of God].

11 [Israel] sent out its boughs to the [Mediterranean] Sea and its branches to the [Euphrates] River. [I Kings 4:21.]

12 Why have You broken down its hedges *and* walls so that all who pass by pluck from its fruit?

13 The boar out of the wood wastes it and the wild beast of the field feeds on it.

14 Turn again, we beseech You, O God of hosts! Look down from heaven and see, visit, *and* have regard for this vine!

15 [Protect and maintain] the stock which Your right hand planted, and the branch (the son) that You have reared *and* made strong for Yourself.

16 They have burned it with fire, it is cut down; may they perish at the rebuke of Your countenance.

17 Let Your hand be upon the man of Your right hand, upon the son of man whom You have made strong for Yourself.

18 Then will we not depart from You; revive us (give us life) and we will call upon Your name.

19 Restore us, O Lord God of hosts; cause Your face to shine [in pleasure, approval, and favor on us], and we shall be saved!

r It is supposed that these three tribes represented the whole twelve tribes of Israel, Benjamin being incorporated with Judah, Manasseh embracing the country beyond the Jordan, and Ephraim the remainder. It was natural for the Israelites to think of the three in one group, for they had camped together on the west side of the tabernacle during the years in the wilderness, and also they were the only descendants of Jacob's wife Rachel.

PSALM 81

To the Chief Musician; set to Philistine lute, or [possibly] a particular Gittite tune. [A Psalm] of Asaph.

SING ALOUD to God our Strength! Shout for joy to the God of Jacob!

2 Raise a song, sound the timbrel, the sweet lyre with the harp.

3 Blow the trumpet at the New Moon, at the full moon, on our feast day.

4 For this is a statute for Israel, an ordinance of the God of Jacob.

5 This He ordained in Joseph [the ˢsavior] for a testimony when He went out over the land of Egypt. The speech of One Whom I knew not did I hear [saying],

6 I removed his shoulder from the burden; his hands were freed from the basket.

7 You called in distress and I delivered you; I answered you in the secret place of thunder; I tested you at the waters of Meribah. Selah [pause, and calmly think of that]! [Num. 20:3, 13, 24.]

8 Hear, O My people, and I will admonish you—O Israel, if you would listen to Me!

9 There shall no strange god be among you, neither shall you worship any alien god.

10 I am the Lord your God, Who brought you up out of the land of Egypt. Open your mouth wide and I will fill it.

11 But My people would not hearken to My voice, and Israel would have none of Me.

12 So I gave them up to their own hearts' lust *and* let them go after their own stubborn will, that they might follow their own counsels. [Acts 7:42, 43; 14:16; Rom. 1:24, 26.]

13 Oh, that My people would listen to Me, that Israel would walk in My ways!

14 Speedily then I would subdue their enemies and turn My hand against their adversaries.

15 [Had Israel listened to Me in Egypt, then] those who hated the Lord would have come cringing before Him, and their defeat would have lasted forever.

16 [God] would feed [Israel now] also with the finest of the wheat; and with honey out of the rock would I satisfy you.

PSALM 82

A Psalm of Asaph.

GOD STANDS in the assembly [of the representatives] of God; in the midst of the magistrates *or* judges He gives judgment [as] among the gods.

2 How long will you [magistrates or judges] judge unjustly and show partiality to the wicked? Selah [pause, and calmly think of that]!

3 Do justice to the weak (poor) and fatherless; maintain the rights of the afflicted and needy.

4 Deliver the poor and needy; rescue them out of the hand of the wicked.

5 [The magistrates and judges] know not, neither will they understand; they walk on in the darkness [of complacent satisfaction]; all the foundations of the earth [the fundamental principles upon which rests the administration of justice] are shaking.

6 I said, You are gods [since you judge on My behalf, as My representatives]; indeed, all of you are children

s Joseph had once gone out over Egypt with the title "Zaphenath-paneah," meaning, according to some, "Savior of the Age," to bring deliverance from famine to the Egyptians (Gen. 41:45). Later they forgot their benefactor and severely oppressed his family and their descendants. "Then Joseph's God arose and went forth over the land [of Egypt] in righteous judgment, yet still as Savior of that people [Israel], in whom dwelt the germ of blessing for all nations." (David M. Kay, cited by James C. Gray and George M. Adams, *Bible Commentary*).

of the Most High. [John 10:34-36; Rom. 13:1, 2.]

7 But you shall die as men and fall as one of the princes.

8 Arise, O God, judge the earth! For to You belong all the nations. [Rev. 11:15.]

PSALM 83
A song. A Psalm of Asaph.

KEEP NOT silence, O God; hold not Your peace or be still, O God.

2 For, behold, Your enemies are in tumult, and those who hate You have raised their heads. [Acts 4:25, 26.]

3 They lay crafty schemes against Your people and consult together against Your hidden *and* precious ones.

4 They have said, Come, and let us wipe them out as a nation; let the name of Israel be in remembrance no more.

5 For they have consulted together with one accord *and* one heart; against You they make a covenant—

6 The tents of Edom and the Ishmaelites, of Moab and the Hagrites,

7 Gebal and Ammon and Amalek, the Philistines, with the inhabitants of Tyre.

8 Assyria also has joined with them; they have helped the children of Lot [the Ammonites and the Moabites] *and* have been an arm to them. Selah [pause, and calmly think of that]!

9 Do to them as [You did to] the Midianites, as to Sisera and Jabin at the brook of Kishon, [Judg. 4:12-24.]

10 Who perished at Endor, who became like manure for the earth.

11 Make their nobles like Oreb and Zeeb, yes, all their princes as Zebah and Zalmunna, [Judg. 7:23-25; 8:10-21.]

12 Who say, Let us take possession for ourselves of the pastures of God.

13 O my God, make them like whirling dust, like stubble *or* chaff before the wind!

14 As fire consumes the forest, and as the flame sets the mountains ablaze,

15 So pursue *and* afflict them with Your tempest and terrify them with Your tornado *or* hurricane.

16 Fill their faces with shame, that they may seek, inquire for, *and* insistently require Your name, O Lord.

17 Let them be put to shame and dismayed forever; yes, let them be put to shame and perish,

18 That they may know that You, Whose name alone is the Lord, are the Most High over all the earth.

PSALM 84
To the Chief Musician; set to a Philistine lute, or [possibly] a particular Gittite tune. A Psalm of the sons of Korah.

HOW LOVELY are Your tabernacles, O Lord of hosts!

2 My soul yearns, yes, even pines *and* is homesick for the courts of the Lord; my heart and my flesh cry out *and* sing for joy to the living God.

3 Yes, the sparrow has found a house, and the swallow a nest for herself, where she may lay her young— even Your altars, O Lord of hosts, my King and my God.

4 Blessed (happy, fortunate, to be envied) are those who dwell in Your house *and* Your presence; they will be singing Your praises all the day long. Selah [pause, and calmly think of that]!

5 Blessed (happy, fortunate, to be envied) is the man whose strength is in You, in whose heart are the highways to Zion.

6 Passing through the Valley of Weeping (Baca), they make it a place of springs; the early rain also fills [the pools] with blessings.

7 They go from strength to strength

life point

When our strength is in God, the difficult places in life can be turned into blessings; the valleys of weeping can be turned into springs (see Psalm 84:5, 6). Whenever you face a tough situation or a place of sadness and despair, draw your strength from God. As you do, you will find yourself going "from strength to strength" and "increasing in victorious power," as Psalm 84:7 promises.

[increasing in victorious power]; each of them appears before God in Zion.

8 O Lord God of hosts, hear my prayer; give ear, O God of Jacob! Selah [pause, and calmly think of that]!

9 Behold our shield [the king as Your agent], O God, and look upon the face of Your anointed!

10 For a day in Your courts is better than a thousand [anywhere else]; I would rather be a doorkeeper *and* stand at the threshold in the house of my God than to dwell [at ease] in the tents of wickedness.

11 For the Lord God is a Sun and Shield; the Lord bestows [present] grace *and* favor and [future] glory

putting the Word to work

The Bible teaches us that God is our home. We view our homes as places of rest and comfort, shelters from all the other parts of life. Psalm 84:10 reminds us that dwelling in the presence of God is where the greatest blessing is to be found. Spend time every day with God through prayer, worship, and time in His Word, and you will find there is no place you would rather be than in His presence. When you are with Him, you will feel as though you are at home!

(honor, splendor, and heavenly bliss)! No good thing will He withhold from those who walk uprightly.

12 O Lord of hosts, blessed (happy, fortunate, to be envied) is the man who trusts in You [leaning and believing on You, committing all and confidently looking to You, and that without fear or misgiving]!

PSALM 85

To the Chief Musician. A Psalm of the sons of Korah.

LORD, YOU have [at last] been favorable *and* have dealt graciously with Your land [of Canaan]; You have brought back [from Babylon] the captives of Jacob.

2 You have forgiven *and* taken away the iniquity of Your people, You have covered all their sin. Selah [pause, and calmly realize what that means]!

3 You have withdrawn all Your wrath *and* indignation, You have turned away from the blazing anger [which You had let loose].

4 Restore us, O God of our salvation, and cause Your anger toward us to cease [forever].

5 Will You be angry with us forever? Will You prolong Your anger [and disfavor] *and* spread it out to all generations?

6 Will You not revive us again, that Your people may rejoice in You?

7 Show us Your mercy *and* lovingkindness, O Lord, and grant us Your salvation.

8 I will listen [with expectancy] to what God the Lord will say, for He will speak peace to His people, to His saints (those who are in right standing with Him)—but let them not turn again to [self-confident] folly.

9 Surely His salvation is near to those who reverently *and* worshipfully fear Him, [and is ready to be appropriated] that [the manifest presence

of God, His] glory may tabernacle *and* abide in our land.

10 Mercy *and* loving-kindness and truth have met together; righteousness and peace have kissed each other.

11 Truth shall spring up from the earth, and righteousness shall look down from heaven.

12 Yes, the Lord will give what is good, and our land will yield its increase.

13 Righteousness shall go before Him and shall make His footsteps a way in which to walk.

PSALM 86

A Prayer of David.

INCLINE YOUR ear, O Lord, and answer me, for I am poor *and* distressed, needy *and* desiring.

2 Preserve my life, for I am godly *and* dedicated; O my God, save Your servant, for I trust in You [leaning and believing on You, committing all and confidently looking to You, without fear or doubt].

3 Be merciful *and* gracious to me, O Lord, for to You do I cry all the day.

4 Make me, Your servant, to rejoice, O Lord, for to You do I lift myself up.

5 For You, O Lord, are good, and ready to forgive [our trespasses, sending them away, letting them go completely and forever]; and You are abundant in mercy *and* loving-kindness to all those who call upon You.

6 Give ear, O Lord, to my prayer; and listen to the cry of my supplications.

7 In the day of my trouble I will call on You, for You will answer me.

8 There is none like unto You among the gods, O Lord, neither are their works like unto Yours.

9 All nations whom You have made shall come and fall down before You, O Lord; and they shall glorify Your name.

10 For You are great and work wonders! You alone are God.

11 Teach me Your way, O Lord, that I may walk *and* live in Your truth; direct *and* unite my heart [solely, reverently] to fear *and* honor Your name. [Ps. 5:11; 69:36.]

12 I will confess *and* praise You, O Lord my God, with my whole (united) heart; and I will glorify Your name forevermore.

13 For great is Your mercy *and* loving-kindness toward me; and You have delivered me from the depths of

speak the Word

Sheol [from the exceeding depths of affliction].

14 O God, the proud *and* insolent are risen against me; a rabble of violent *and* ruthless men has sought *and* demanded my life, and they have not set You before them.

15 But You, O Lord, are a God merciful and gracious, slow to anger and abounding in mercy *and* loving-kindness and truth.

16 O turn to me and have mercy *and* be gracious to me; grant strength (might and inflexibility to temptation) to Your servant and save the son of Your handmaiden.

17 Show me a sign of [Your evident] goodwill *and* favor, that those who hate me may see it and be put to shame, because You, Lord, [will show Your approval of me when You] help and comfort me.

PSALM 87
A Psalm of the sons of Korah. A song.

O N THE holy hills stands the city [of Jerusalem and the temple] God founded.

2 The Lord loves the gates of Zion [through which the crowds of pilgrims enter from all nations] more than all the dwellings of Jacob (Israel).

3 Glorious things are spoken of you, O city of God. Selah [pause, and calmly realize what that means]!

4 I will make mention of Rahab [the poetic name for Egypt] and Babylon as among those who know [the city of God]—behold, Philistia and Tyre, with Ethiopia (Cush)—[saying], This man was born there.

5 Yes, of Zion it shall be said, This man and that man were born in her, for the Most High Himself will establish her.

6 The Lord shall count, when He registers the peoples, that this man was born there. Selah [pause, and calmly think of that]!

7 The singers as well as the players on instruments shall say, All my springs (my sources of life and joy) are in you [city of our God].

PSALM 88
A song. A Psalm of the sons of Korah. To the Chief Musician; set to chant mournfully. A didactic *or* reflective poem of Heman the Ezrahite.

O LORD, the God of my salvation, I have cried to You for help by day; at night I am in Your presence. [Luke 18:7.]

2 Let my prayer come before You *and* really enter into Your presence; incline Your ear to my cry!

3 For I am full of troubles, and my life draws near to Sheol (the place of the dead).

4 I am counted among those who go down into the pit (the grave); I am like a man who has no help *or* strength [a mere shadow],

5 Cast away among the dead, like the slain that lie in a [nameless] grave, whom You [seriously] remember no more, and they are cut off from Your hand.

6 You have laid me in the depths of the lowest pit, in darkness, in the deeps.

7 Your wrath lies hard upon me, and You have afflicted me with all Your waves. Selah [pause, and calmly think of that]! [Ps. 42:7.]

8 You have put my [familiar] friends far from me; You have made me an abomination to them. I am shut up, and I cannot come forth.

9 My eye grows dim because of sorrow *and* affliction. Lord, I have called daily on You; I have spread forth my hands to You.

10 Will You show wonders to the dead? Shall the departed arise and praise You? Selah [pause, and calmly think of that]!

11 Shall Your steadfast love be

declared in the grave? Or Your faithfulness in Abaddon (Sheol, as a place of ruin and destruction)?

12 Shall Your wonders be known in the dark? And Your righteousness in the place of forgetfulness [where the dead forget and are forgotten]?

13 But to You I cry, O Lord; and in the morning shall my prayer come to meet You.

14 Lord, why do You cast me off? Why do You hide Your face from me? [Matt. 27:46.]

15 I was afflicted and close to death from my youth up; while I suffer Your terrors I am distracted [I faint].

16 Your fierce wrath has swept over me; Your terrors have destroyed me.

17 They surround me like a flood all day long; together they have closed in upon me.

18 Lover and friend have You put far from me; my familiar friends are darkness *and* the grave.

PSALM 89

A skillful song, *or* a didactic *or* reflective poem, of Ethan the Ezrahite.

I WILL sing of the mercy *and* loving-kindness of the Lord forever; with my mouth will I make known Your faithfulness from generation to generation.

2 For I have said, Mercy *and* loving-kindness shall be built up forever; Your faithfulness will You establish in the very heavens [unchangeable and perpetual].

3 [You have said] I have made a ʰcovenant with My chosen one, I have sworn to David My servant,

4 Your Seed I will establish forever, and I will build up your throne for all generations. Selah [pause, and calmly think of that]! [Isa. 9:7; Luke 1:32, 33; Gal. 3:16]

5 Let heaven (the angels) praise Your wonders, O Lord, Your faithfulness also in the assembly of the holy ones (the holy angels).

6 For who in the heavens can be compared to the Lord? Who among the mighty [heavenly beings] can be likened to the Lord,

7 A God greatly feared *and* revered in the council of the holy (angelic) ones, and to be feared *and* worshipfully revered above all those who are round about Him?

8 O Lord God of hosts, who is a mighty one like unto You, O Lord? And Your faithfulness is round about You [an essential part of You at all times].

9 You rule the raging of the sea; when its waves arise, You still them.

10 You have broken Rahab (Egypt) in pieces; with Your mighty arm You have scattered Your enemies.

11 The heavens are Yours, the earth also is Yours; the world and all that is in it, You have founded them.

12 The north and the south, You have created them; Mount Tabor and

speak the Word

t "This covenant most incontestably had Jesus Christ in view. This is the Seed or Posterity Who would sit on the throne and reign forever and ever. David and his family have long since become extinct; none of his race has sat on the Jewish throne for more than two thousand years. But the Christ . . . will reign until all His enemies are put under His feet (Ps. 110:1; I Cor. 15:25, 27; Eph. 1:22); and to this the psalmist says, Selah." (One of many similar 19th-century comments.)

Mount Hermon joyously praise Your name.

13 You have a mighty arm; strong is Your hand, Your right hand is soaring high.

14 Righteousness and justice are the foundation of Your throne; mercy *and* loving-kindness and truth go before Your face.

15 Blessed (happy, fortunate, to be envied) are the people who know the joyful sound [who understand and appreciate the spiritual blessings symbolized by the feasts]; they walk, O Lord, in the light *and* favor of Your countenance!

16 In Your name they rejoice all the day, and in Your righteousness they are exalted.

17 For You are the glory of their strength [their proud adornment], and by Your favor our horn is exalted *and* we walk with uplifted faces!

18 For our shield belongs to the Lord, and our king to the Holy One of Israel.

19 Once You spoke in a vision to Your devoted ones and said, I have endowed one who is mighty [a hero, giving him the power to help—to be a champion for Israel]; I have exalted one chosen from among the people.

20 I have found David My servant; with My holy oil have I anointed him, [Acts 13:22.]

21 With whom My hand shall be established *and* ever abide; My arm also shall strengthen him.

22 The enemy shall not exact from him *or* do him violence *or* outwit him, nor shall the wicked afflict *and* humble him.

23 I will beat down his foes before his face and smite those who hate him.

24 My faithfulness and My mercy *and* loving-kindness shall be with him, and in My name shall his horn be

exalted [great power and prosperity shall be conferred upon him].

25 I will set his hand in control also on the [Mediterranean] Sea, and his right hand on the rivers [Euphrates with its tributaries].

26 He shall cry to Me, You are my Father, my God, and the Rock of my salvation!

27 Also I will make him the firstborn, the highest of the kings of the earth. [Rev. 1:5.]

28 My mercy *and* loving-kindness will I keep for him forevermore, and My covenant shall stand fast *and* be faithful with him.

29 His ᵘOffspring also will I make to endure forever, and his throne as the days of heaven. [Isa. 9:7; Gal. 3:16.]

30 If his children forsake My law and walk not in My ordinances,

31 If they break *or* profane My statutes and keep not My commandments,

32 Then will I punish their transgression with the rod [of chastisement], and their iniquity with stripes. [II Sam. 7:14.]

33 Nevertheless, My loving-kindness will I not break off from him, nor allow My faithfulness to fail [to lie and be false to him].

34 My covenant will I not break *or* profane, nor alter the thing that is gone out of My lips.

35 Once [for all] have I sworn by My holiness, which cannot be violated; I will not lie to David:

36 His Offspring shall endure forever, and his throne [shall continue] as the sun before Me. [Isa. 9:7; Gal. 3:16.]

37 It shall be established forever as the moon, the faithful witness in the heavens. Selah [pause, and calmly think of that]! [Rev. 1:5; 3:14.]

38 But [in apparent contradiction to all this] You [even You the faithful Lord] have cast off and rejected; You

u See footnote on Ps. 89:3.

have been full of wrath against Your anointed.

39 You have despised *and* loathed and renounced the covenant with Your servant; You have profaned his crown by casting it to the ground.

40 You have broken down all his hedges *and* his walls; You have brought his strongholds to ruin.

41 All who pass along the road spoil *and* rob him; he has become the scorn *and* reproach of his neighbors.

42 You have exalted the right hand of his foes; You have made all his enemies rejoice.

43 Moreover, You have turned back the edge of his sword and have not made him to stand in battle.

44 You have made his glory *and* splendor to cease and have hurled to the ground his throne.

45 The days of his youth have You shortened; You have covered him with shame. Selah [pause, and calmly think of that]!

46 How long, O Lord? Will You hide Yourself forever? How long shall Your wrath burn like fire?

47 O [earnestly] remember how short my time is *and* what a mere fleeting life mine is. For what emptiness, falsity, futility, *and* frailty You have created all men!

48 What man can live and shall not see death, or can deliver himself from the [powerful] hand of Sheol (the place of the dead)? Selah [pause, and calmly consider that]!

49 Lord, where are Your former loving-kindnesses [shown in the reigns of David and Solomon], which You swore to David in Your faithfulness?

50 Remember, Lord, *and* earnestly imprint [on Your heart] the reproach of Your servants, scorned *and* insulted, how I bear in my bosom the reproach of all the many *and* mighty peoples,

51 With which Your enemies have taunted, O Lord, with which they have mocked the footsteps of Your anointed.

52 Blessed be the Lord forevermore! Amen and Amen.

BOOK FOUR

PSALM 90

A Prayer of Moses the man of God.

LORD, YOU have been our dwelling place *and* our refuge in all generations [says Moses].

2 Before the mountains were brought forth or ever You had formed *and* given birth to the earth and the world, even from everlasting to everlasting You are God.

3 You turn man back to dust *and* corruption, and say, Return, O sons of the earthborn [to the earth]!

4 For a thousand years in Your sight are but as yesterday when it is past, or as a watch in the night. [II Pet. 3:8.]

5 You carry away [these disobedient people, doomed to die within forty years] as with a flood; they are as a sleep [vague and forgotten as soon as they are gone]. In the morning they are like grass which grows up—

6 In the morning it flourishes and springs up; in the evening it is mown down and withers.

7 For we [the Israelites in the wilderness] are consumed by Your anger, and by Your wrath are we troubled, overwhelmed, *and* frightened away.

8 Our iniquities, our secret heart *and* its sins [which we would so like to conceal even from ourselves], You have set in the [revealing] light of Your countenance.

9 For all our days [out here in this wilderness, says Moses] pass away in Your wrath; we spend our years as a tale that is told [for we adults know we are doomed to die soon, without reaching Canaan]. [Num. 14:26-35.]

10 The days of our years are ᵛthree-score years and ten (seventy years)— or even, if by reason of strength, fourscore years (eighty years); yet is their pride [in additional years] only labor and sorrow, for it is soon gone, and we fly away.

11 Who knows the power of Your anger? [Who worthily connects this brevity of life with Your recognition of sin?] And Your wrath, who connects it with the reverent *and* worshipful fear that is due You?

12 So teach us to number our days, that we may get us a heart of wisdom.

13 Turn, O Lord [from Your fierce anger]! How long—? Revoke Your sentence *and* be compassionate *and* at ease toward Your servants.

14 O satisfy us with Your mercy *and* loving-kindness in the morning [now, before we are older], that we may rejoice and be glad all our days.

15 Make us glad in proportion to the days in which You have afflicted us *and* to the years in which we have suffered evil.

16 Let Your work [the signs of Your power] be revealed to Your servants, and Your [glorious] majesty to their children.

17 And let the beauty *and* delightfulness *and* favor of the Lord our God be upon us; confirm *and* establish the work of our hands—yes, the work of our hands, confirm *and* establish it.

PSALM 91

H E WHO ʷdwells in the secret place of the Most High shall remain stable *and* fixed under the shadow of the Almighty [Whose power no foe can withstand].

2 I will say of the Lord, He is my Refuge and my Fortress, my God; on Him I lean *and* rely, *and* in Him I [confidently] trust!

3 For [then] He will deliver you from the snare of the fowler and from the deadly pestilence.

4 [Then] He will cover you with His pinions, and under His wings shall you trust *and* find refuge; His truth *and* His faithfulness are a shield and a buckler.

speak the Word

Lord, teach me to number my days, that I may develop a heart of wisdom.
ADAPTED FROM PSALM 90:12

God, let Your beauty and favor be upon me. Confirm and establish the work of my hands.
ADAPTED FROM PSALM 90:17

v This psalm is credited to Moses, who is interceding with God to remove the curse which made it necessary for every Israelite over twenty years of age (when they rebelled against God at Kadesh-barnea) to die before reaching the promised land (Num. 14:26-35). Moses says most of them are dying at seventy years of age. This number has often been mistaken as a set span of life for all mankind. It was not intended to refer to anyone except those Israelites under the curse during that particular forty years. Seventy years never has been the average span of life for humanity. When Jacob, the father of the twelve tribes, had reached 130 years (Gen. 47:9), he complained that he had not attained to the years of his immediate ancestors. In fact, Moses himself lived to be 120 years old, Aaron 123, Miriam several years older, and Joshua 110 years of age. Note as well that in the Millennium a person dying at 100 will still be thought a child (Isa. 65:20). **w** The rich promises of this whole chapter are dependent upon one's meeting exactly the conditions of these first two verses (see Exod. 15:26).

what do you say?

The psalmists frequently spoke about the goodness and character of God. In Psalm 91:2, one of them says God is his Refuge, his Fortress—a God he can really trust. It is interesting to note that the psalmist also wrote this verse, "I will *say* of the Lord . . ." (italics mine). Perhaps we should also regularly ask ourselves, "What am I saying of the Lord?"

We need to *say* right things, not just *think* them. We may think, *I believe all those good things about the Lord*, but are we also *saying* anything that is helping us? Often we claim to believe something, yet the opposite comes out of our mouths.

We need to speak aloud the goodness of God. We need to do it at proper times and in proper places, but we need to be sure we do it. I cannot encourage you strongly enough to make verbal confessions part of your fellowship time with God.

I often take walks in the morning. While I walk, I pray, I sing, and I confess the Word out loud. I say something like, "God is on my side. I can do whatever He assigns me to do." Or "God is good, and He has a good plan for my life. Blessings are chasing me and overflowing in my life." When I speak words like these, I am nullifying the evil plan Satan has for me.

Verbalize your thanksgiving, your praise, and your worship. Say aloud the things that are in your heart about God; sing songs that are filled with praise and worship. Take aggressive action against the enemy by speaking of the goodness of God!

5   You shall not be afraid of the terror of the night, nor of the arrow (the evil plots and slanders of the wicked) that flies by day,

life point

When you and I feel a tide of emotions beginning to swell within us, we need to return to the secret place of the Most High (see Psalm 91:1), crying out to Him: "Father, help me resist this surge of emotions that threatens to overwhelm me!" If we will do that, the Lord has promised to intervene on our behalf. We need to learn to take refuge under His shadow, where we will be safe and secure, knowing that no power in heaven or on earth can withstand Him.

6   Nor of the pestilence that stalks in darkness, nor of the destruction *and* sudden death that surprise *and* lay waste at noonday.
7   A thousand may fall at your side, and ten thousand at your right hand, but it shall not come near you.
8   Only a spectator shall you be [yourself inaccessible in the secret place of the Most High] as you witness the reward of the wicked.
9   Because you have made the Lord your refuge, and the Most High your dwelling place, [Ps. 91:1, 14.]
10   There shall no evil befall you, nor any plague *or* calamity come near your tent.
11   For He will give His angels [especial] charge over you to accompany *and* defend *and* preserve you in all your ways [of obedience and service].

12 They shall bear you up on their hands, lest you dash your foot against a stone. [Luke 4:10, 11; Heb. 1:14.]

13 You shall tread upon the lion and adder; the young lion and the serpent shall you trample underfoot. [Luke 10:19.]

14 Because he has set his love upon Me, therefore will I deliver him; I will set him on high, because he knows *and* understands My name [has a personal knowledge of My mercy, love, and kindness—trusts and relies on Me, knowing I will never forsake him, no, never].

15 He shall call upon Me, and I will answer him; I will be with him in trouble, I will deliver him and honor him.

16 With long life will I satisfy him and show him My salvation.

PSALM 92

A Psalm. A song for the Sabbath day.

IT IS a good *and* delightful thing to give thanks to the Lord, to sing praises [with musical accompaniment] to Your name, O Most High,

2 To show forth Your loving-kindness in the morning and Your faithfulness by night,

3 With an instrument of ten strings and with the lute, with a solemn sound upon the lyre.

4 For You, O Lord, have made me glad by Your works; at the deeds of Your hands I joyfully sing.

5 How great are Your doings, O Lord! Your thoughts are very deep.

6 A man in his rude *and* uncultivated state knows not, neither does a [self-confident] fool understand this:

7 That though the wicked spring up like grass and all evildoers flourish, they are doomed to be destroyed forever.

8 But You, Lord, are on high forever.

9 For behold, Your adversaries, O Lord, for behold, Your enemies shall perish; all the evildoers shall be scattered.

10 But my horn (emblem of excessive strength and stately grace) You have exalted like that of a wild ox; I am anointed with fresh oil.

11 My eye looks upon those who lie in wait for me; my ears hear the evildoers that rise up against me.

12 The [uncompromisingly] righteous shall flourish like the palm tree [be long-lived, stately, upright, useful, and fruitful]; they shall grow like a cedar in Lebanon [majestic, stable, durable, and incorruptible].

13 Planted in the house of the Lord, they shall flourish in the courts of our God.

14 [Growing in grace] they shall still bring forth fruit in old age; they shall be full of sap [of spiritual vitality] and [rich in the] verdure [of trust, love, and contentment].

15 [They are living memorials] to show that the Lord is upright *and* faithful to His promises; He is my Rock, and there is no unrighteousness in Him. [Rom. 9:14.]

PSALM 93

THE LORD reigns, He is clothed with majesty; the Lord is robed, He has girded Himself with strength *and* power; the world also is established, that it cannot be moved.

2 Your throne is established from of old; You are from everlasting.

3 The floods have lifted up, O Lord, the floods have lifted up their voice; the floods lift up the roaring of their waves.

4 The Lord on high is mightier *and* more glorious than the noise of many waters, yes, than the mighty breakers *and* waves of the sea.

5 Your testimonies are very sure; holiness [apparent in separation from sin, with simple trust and hearty obedience] is becoming to Your house, O Lord, forever.

PSALM 94

O LORD God, You to Whom vengeance belongs, O God, You to Whom vengeance belongs, shine forth!
2 Rise up, O Judge of the earth; render to the proud a fit compensation!
3 Lord, how long shall the wicked, how long shall the wicked triumph *and* exult?
4 They pour out arrogant words, speaking hard things; all the evildoers boast loftily. [Jude 14, 15.]
5 They crush Your people, O Lord, and afflict Your heritage.
6 They slay the widow and the transient stranger and murder the unprotected orphan.
7 Yet they say, The Lord does not see, neither does the God of Jacob notice it.
8 Consider *and* understand, you stupid ones among the people! And you [self-confident] fools, when will you become wise?
9 He Who planted the ear, shall He not hear? He Who formed the eye, shall He not see?
10 He Who disciplines *and* instructs the nations, shall He not punish, He Who teaches man knowledge?
11 The Lord knows the thoughts of man, that they are vain (empty and futile—only a breath). [I Cor. 3:20.]
12 Blessed (happy, fortunate, to be envied) is the man whom You discipline *and* instruct, O Lord, and teach out of Your law,
13 That You may give him power to keep himself calm in the days of

speak the Word

life point

In Psalm 94:12–15, God is saying that He deals with us and disciplines us for a reason. He wants us to come to the point where we can keep ourselves calm in the day of adversity.

In verses 14 and 15, notice the emphasis on God's faithfulness and justice toward His children. We can be sure that if we are being obedient to His Word and His will, and we are being led by His Holy Spirit, we have nothing to fear from our enemies, because the Lord Himself will fight our battles for us. Do you want God's help? If the answer is yes, then ask for His help and receive it by faith. Even God cannot help someone who does not want to be helped. Decide that you sincerely want God's help, and He will run to your aid and move mightily on your behalf.

adversity, until the [inevitable] pit of corruption is dug for the wicked.
14 For the Lord will not cast off *nor* spurn His people, neither will He abandon His heritage.
15 For justice will return to the [uncompromisingly] righteous, and all the upright in heart will follow it.
16 Who will rise up for me against the evildoers? Who will stand up for me against the workers of iniquity?
17 Unless the Lord had been my help, I would soon have dwelt in [the land where there is] silence.
18 When I said, My foot is slipping, Your mercy *and* loving-kindness, O Lord, held me up.
19 In the multitude of my [anxious]

God, when there are a multitude of anxious thoughts within me, Your comforts cheer and delight my soul.
ADAPTED FROM PSALM 94:19

thoughts within me, Your comforts cheer *and* delight my soul!

20 Shall the throne of iniquity have fellowship with You—they who frame *and* hide their unrighteous doings under [the sacred name of] law?

21 They band themselves together against the life of the [consistently] righteous and condemn the innocent to death.

22 But the Lord has become my High Tower *and* Defense, and my God the Rock of my refuge.

23 And He will turn back upon them their own iniquity and will wipe them out by means of their own wickedness; the Lord our God will wipe them out.

PSALM 95

O COME, let us sing to the Lord; let us make a joyful noise to the Rock of our salvation!

2 Let us come before His presence with thanksgiving; let us make a joyful noise to Him with songs of praise!

3 For the Lord is a great God, and a great King above all gods.

4 In His hand are the deep places of the earth; the heights *and* strength of the hills are His also.

5 The sea is His, for He made it; and His hands formed the dry land.

6 O come, let us worship and bow down, let us kneel before the Lord our Maker [in reverent praise and supplication].

7 For He is our God and we are the people of His pasture and the sheep of His hand. Today, if you will hear His voice, [Heb. 3:7-11.]

8 Harden not your hearts as at Meribah and as at Massah in the day of temptation in the wilderness, [Exod. 17:1-7; Num. 20:1-13; Deut. 6:16.]

9 When your fathers tried My patience *and* tested Me, proved Me, and saw My work [of judgment].

10 Forty years long was I grieved *and* disgusted with that generation, and I said, It is a people that do err in their hearts, and they do not approve, acknowledge, *or* regard My ways.

11 Wherefore I swore in My wrath that they would not enter My rest [the land of promise]. [Heb. 4:3-11.]

PSALM 96

O SING to the Lord a new song; sing to the Lord, all the earth!

2 Sing to the Lord, bless (affectionately praise) His name; show forth His salvation from day to day.

3 Declare His glory among the nations, His marvelous works among all the peoples.

4 For great is the Lord and greatly to be praised; He is to be reverently feared *and* worshiped above all [so-called] gods. [Deut. 6:5; Rev. 14:7.]

5 For all the gods of the nations are [lifeless] idols, but the Lord made the heavens.

6 Honor and majesty are before Him; strength and beauty are in His sanctuary.

7 Ascribe to the Lord, O you families of the peoples, ascribe to the Lord glory and strength.

8 Give to the Lord the glory due His name; bring an offering and come [before Him] into His courts.

9 O worship the Lord in the beauty of holiness; tremble before *and* reverently fear Him, all the earth.

10 Say among the nations that the Lord reigns; the world also is established, so that it cannot be moved; He shall judge *and* rule the people righteously *and* with justice. [Rev. 11:15; 19:6.]

11 Let the heavens be glad, and let the earth rejoice; let the sea roar, and all the things which fill it;

12 Let the field be exultant, and all that is in it! Then shall all the trees of the wood sing for joy

13 Before the Lord, for He comes, for He comes to judge *and* govern the earth! He shall judge the world with righteousness *and* justice and the peoples with His faithfulness *and* truth. [I Chron. 16:23-33; Rev. 19:11.]

PSALM 97

THE LORD reigns, let the earth rejoice; let the multitude of isles *and* coastlands be glad!
2   Clouds and darkness are round about Him [as at Sinai]; righteousness and justice are the foundation of His throne. [Exod. 19:9.]
3   Fire goes before Him and burns up His adversaries round about.
4   His lightnings illumine the world; the earth sees and trembles.
5   The hills melted like wax at the presence of the Lord, at the presence of the Lord of the whole earth.
6   The heavens declare His righteousness, and all the peoples see His glory.
7   Let all those be put to shame who serve graven images, who boast in idols. Fall prostrate before Him, all you gods. [Heb. 1:6.]
8   Zion heard and was glad, and the daughters of Judah rejoiced [in relief] because of Your judgments, O Lord.
9   For You, Lord, are high above all the earth; You are exalted far above all gods.
10 O you who love the Lord, hate evil; He preserves the lives of His saints (the children of God), He delivers them out of the hand of the wicked. [Rom. 8:13-17.]
11 Light is sown for the [uncompromisingly] righteous *and* strewn along their pathway, and joy for the upright in heart [the irrepressible joy which comes from consciousness of His favor and protection].
12 Rejoice in the Lord, you [consistently] righteous (upright and in right standing with God), and give thanks at the remembrance of His holiness.

PSALM 98
A Psalm.

O SING to the Lord a new song, for He has done marvelous things; His right hand and His holy arm have wrought salvation for Him.
2   The Lord has made known His salvation; His righteousness has He openly shown in the sight of the nations. [Luke 2:30, 31.]
3   He has [earnestly] remembered His mercy *and* loving-kindness, His truth *and* His faithfulness toward the house of Israel; all the ends of the earth have witnessed the salvation of our God. [Acts 13:47; 28:28.]
4   Make a joyful noise to the Lord, all the earth; break forth and sing for joy, yes, sing praises!
5   Sing praises to the Lord with the lyre, with the lyre and the voice of melody.
6   With trumpets and the sound of the horn make a joyful noise before the King, the Lord!
7   Let the sea roar, and all that fills it, the world, and those who dwell in it!
8   Let the rivers clap their hands; together let the hills sing for joy
9   Before the Lord, for He is coming to judge [and rule] the earth; with righteousness will He judge [and rule] the world, and the peoples with equity.

speak the Word

Thank You, God, for lighting the pathway for those who are uncompromisingly righteous and for giving irrepressible joy to those who are upright in heart.
ADAPTED FROM PSALM 97:11

PSALM 99

THE LORD reigns, let the peoples tremble [with reverential fear]! He sits [enthroned] above the cherubim, let the earth quake!

2 The Lord is great in Zion, and He is high above all the peoples.

3 Let them confess *and* praise Your great name, awesome *and* reverence inspiring! It is holy, *and* holy is He! [Rev. 15:4.]

4 The strength of the king who loves righteousness *and* equity You establish in uprightness; You execute justice and righteousness in Jacob (Israel).

5 Extol the Lord our God and worship at His footstool! Holy is He!

6 Moses and Aaron were among His priests, and Samuel was among those who called upon His name; they called upon the Lord, and He answered them.

7 He spoke to them in the pillar of cloud; they kept His testimonies and the statutes that He gave them. [Ps. 105:9, 10.]

8 You answered them, O Lord our God; You were a forgiving God to them, although avenging their evildoing *and* wicked practices.

9 Extol the Lord our God and worship at His holy hill, for the Lord our God is holy!

PSALM 100

A Psalm of thanksgiving and for the thank offering.

MAKE A joyful noise to the Lord, all you lands!

2 Serve the Lord with gladness! Come before His presence with singing!

3 Know (perceive, recognize, and understand with approval) that the Lord is God! It is He Who has made us, not we ourselves [and we are His]! We are His people and the sheep of His pasture. [Eph. 2:10.]

4 Enter into His gates with thanksgiving *and* a thank offering and into His courts with praise! Be thankful *and* say so to Him, bless *and* affectionately praise His name!

5 For the Lord is good; His mercy *and* loving-kindness are everlasting, His faithfulness *and* truth endure to all generations.

PSALM 101

A Psalm of David.

I WILL sing of mercy *and* loving-kindness and justice; to You, O Lord, will I sing.

2 I will behave myself wisely *and*

life point

When we have the mind of Christ, our thoughts will be filled with praise and thanksgiving. When we complain, we open many doors to the enemy. Complaining—either in thought or word—causes us to live weak, powerless lives and can sometimes bring on physical illness. Do you want to live a powerful life? Take the advice of Psalm 100; be thankful to God and *say* you are thankful. Realize that complaining is a death principle, but being thankful and saying so is a life principle that will bring joy to your everyday life.

speak the Word

Lord, I will behave wisely, and I will pay attention to Your blameless way. I will walk within my house in integrity and with a blameless heart.
ADAPTED FROM PSALM 101:2

give heed to the blameless way—O when will You come to me? I will walk within my house in integrity *and* with a blameless heart.

3 I will set no base *or* wicked thing before my eyes. I hate the work of them who turn aside [from the right path]; it shall not grasp hold of me.

4 A perverse heart shall depart from me; I will know no evil person *or* thing.

5 Whoso privily slanders his neighbor, him will I cut off [from me]; he who has a haughty look and a proud *and* arrogant heart I cannot *and* I will not tolerate.

6 My eyes shall [look with favor] upon the faithful of the land, that they may dwell with me; he who walks blamelessly, he shall minister to me.

7 He who works deceit shall not dwell in my house; he who tells lies shall not continue in my presence.

8 Morning after morning I will root up all the wicked in the land, that I may eliminate all the evildoers from the city of the Lord.

PSALM 102

A Prayer of the afflicted; when he is overwhelmed *and* faint and pours out his complaint to God.

HEAR MY prayer, O Lord, and let my cry come to You.

2 Hide not Your face from me in the day when I am in distress! Incline Your ear to me; in the day when I call, answer me speedily.

3 For my days consume away like smoke, and my bones burn like a firebrand *or* like a hearth.

4 My heart is smitten like grass and withered, so that [in absorption] I forget to eat my food.

5 By reason of my loud groaning [from suffering and trouble] my flesh cleaves to my bones.

6 I am like a melancholy pelican *or* vulture of the wilderness; I am like a [desolate] owl of the waste places.

7 I am sleepless *and* lie awake [mourning], like a bereaved sparrow alone on the housetop.

8 My adversaries taunt *and* reproach me all the day; and they who are angry with me use my name as a curse.

9 For I have eaten the ashes [in which I sat] as if they were bread and have mingled my drink with weeping,

10 Because of Your indignation and Your wrath, for You have taken me up and cast me away.

11 My days are like an evening shadow that stretches out *and* declines [with the sun]; and I am withered like grass.

12 But You, O Lord, are enthroned forever; and the fame of Your name endures to all generations.

13 You will arise *and* have mercy *and* loving-kindness for Zion, for it is time to have pity *and* compassion for her; yes, the set time has come [the moment designated]. [Ps. 12:5; 119:126.]

14 For Your servants take [melancholy] pleasure in the stones [of her ruins] and show pity for her dust.

15 So the nations shall fear *and* worshipfully revere the name of the Lord, and all the kings of the earth Your glory. [Ps. 96:9.]

16 When the Lord builds up Zion, He will appear in His glory;

17 He will regard the plea of the destitute and will not despise their prayer.

18 Let this be recorded for the generation yet unborn, that a people yet to be created shall praise the Lord.

19 For He looked down from the height of His sanctuary, from heaven did the Lord behold the earth,

20 To hear the sighing *and* groaning of the prisoner, to loose those who are appointed to death,

21 So that men may declare the name of the Lord in Zion and His praise in Jerusalem

22 When peoples are gathered together, and the kingdoms, to worship *and* serve the Lord.

23 He has afflicted *and* weakened my strength, humbling *and* bringing me low [with sorrow] in the way; He has shortened my days [aging me prematurely].

24 I said, O my God, take me not away in the midst of my days, You Whose years continue throughout all generations.

25 At the beginning You existed *and* laid the foundations of the earth; the heavens are the work of Your hands.

26 They shall perish, but You shall remain *and* endure; yes, all of them shall wear out *and* become old like a garment. Like clothing You shall change them, and they shall be changed *and* pass away.

27 But You remain the same, and Your years shall have no end. [Heb. 1:10-12.]

28 The children of Your servants shall dwell safely *and* continue, and their descendants shall be established before You.

PSALM 103
[A Psalm] of David.

BLESS (AFFECTIONATELY, gratefully praise) the Lord, O my soul; and all that is [deepest] within me, bless His holy name!

2 Bless (affectionately, gratefully praise) the Lord, O my soul, and forget not [one of] all His benefits—

3 Who forgives [every one of] all your iniquities, Who heals [each one of] all your diseases,

4 Who redeems your life from the pit *and* corruption, Who beautifies, dignifies, *and* crowns you with loving-kindness and tender mercy;

5 Who satisfies your mouth [your necessity and desire at your personal age and situation] with good so that your youth, renewed, is like the eagle's [strong, overcoming, soaring]! [Isa. 40:31.]

6 The Lord executes righteousness *and* justice [not for me only, but] for all who are oppressed.

7 He made known His ways [of righteousness and justice] to Moses, His acts to the children of Israel.

8 The Lord is merciful and gracious, slow to anger and plenteous in mercy *and* loving-kindness. [James 5:11.]

9 He will not always chide *or* be contending, neither will He keep His anger forever *or* hold a grudge.

10 He has not dealt with us after our sins nor rewarded us according to our iniquities.

11 For as the heavens are high above the earth, so great are His mercy *and* loving-kindness toward those who reverently *and* worshipfully fear Him.

12 As far as the east is from the west, so far has He removed our transgressions from us.

13 As a father loves *and* pities his children, so the Lord loves *and* pities those who fear Him [with reverence, worship, and awe].

14 For He knows our frame, He [earnestly] remembers *and* imprints [on His heart] that we are dust.

15 As for man, his days are as grass;

speak the Word

God, I am Your servant, and I declare that my children shall dwell safely and that their descendants shall be established before You.
ADAPTED FROM PSALM **102:28**

as a flower of the field, so he flourishes.

16 For the wind passes over it and it is gone, and its place shall know it no more.

17 But the mercy *and* loving-kindness of the Lord are from everlasting to everlasting upon those who reverently *and* worshipfully fear Him, and His righteousness is to children's children—[Deut. 10:12.]

18 To such as keep His covenant [hearing, receiving, loving, and obeying it] and to those who [earnestly] remember His commandments to do them [imprinting them on their hearts].

19 The Lord has established His throne in the heavens, and His kingdom rules over all.

20 Bless (affectionately, gratefully praise) the Lord, you His angels, you mighty ones who do His commandments, hearkening to the voice of His word.

21 Bless (affectionately, gratefully praise) the Lord, all you His hosts, you His ministers who do His pleasure.

22 Bless the Lord, all His works in all places of His dominion; bless (affectionately, gratefully praise) the Lord, O my soul!

PSALM 104

BLESS (AFFECTIONATELY, gratefully praise) the Lord, O my soul! O Lord my God, You are very great! You are clothed with honor and majesty—

2 [You are the One] Who covers Yourself with light as with a garment, Who stretches out the heavens like a curtain *or* a tent,

3 Who lays the beams of the upper room of His abode in the waters [above the firmament], Who makes the clouds His chariot, Who walks on the wings of the wind,

4 Who makes winds His messengers, flames of fire His ministers. [Heb. 1:7.]

5 You laid the foundations of the earth, that it should not be moved forever. [Job 38:4, 6.]

6 You covered it with the deep as with a garment; the waters stood above the mountains. [Gen. 1:2; II Pet. 3:5.]

7 At Your rebuke they fled; at the voice of Your thunder they hastened away.

8 The mountains rose, the valleys sank down to the place which You appointed for them.

9 You have set a boundary [for the waters] which they may not pass over, that they turn not again to deluge the earth.

10 He sends forth springs into the valleys; their waters run among the mountains.

11 They give drink to every [wild] beast of the field; the wild asses quench their thirst there.

12 Beside them the birds of the heavens have their nests; they sing among the branches. [Matt. 13:32.]

13 He waters the mountains from His upper rooms; the earth is satisfied *and* abounds with the fruit of His works.

14 He causes vegetation to grow for the cattle, and all that the earth produces for man to cultivate, that he may bring forth food out of the earth—

15 And wine that gladdens the heart of man, to make his face shine more than oil, and bread to support, refresh, *and* strengthen man's heart.

16 The trees of the Lord are watered abundantly *and* are filled with sap, the cedars of Lebanon which He has planted,

17 Where the birds make their nests; as for the stork, the fir trees are her house.

18 The high mountains are for the wild goats; the rocks are a refuge for the conies *and* badgers.

19 [The Lord] appointed the moon

for the seasons; the sun knows [the exact time of] its setting.

20 You [O Lord] make darkness and it becomes night, in which creeps forth every wild beast of the forest.

21 The young lions roar after their prey and seek their food from God.

22 When the sun arises, they withdraw themselves and lie down in their dens.

23 Man goes forth to his work and remains at his task until evening.

24 O Lord, how many *and* varied are Your works! In wisdom have You made them all; the earth is full of Your riches *and* Your creatures.

25 Yonder is the sea, great and wide, in which are swarms of innumerable creeping things, creatures both small and great.

26 There go the ships of the sea, and Leviathan (the sea monster), which You have formed to sport in it.

27 These all wait *and* are dependent upon You, that You may give them their food in due season.

28 When You give it to them, they gather it up; You open Your hand, and they are filled with good things.

29 When You hide Your face, they are troubled *and* dismayed; when You take away their breath, they die and return to their dust.

30 When You send forth Your Spirit *and* give them breath, they are created, and You replenish the face of the ground.

31 May the glory of the Lord endure forever; may the Lord rejoice in His works—

32 Who looks on the earth, and it quakes *and* trembles, Who touches the mountains, and they smoke!

33 I will sing to the Lord as long as I live; I will sing praise to my God while I have any being.

34 May my meditation be sweet to Him; as for me, I will rejoice in the Lord.

35 Let sinners be consumed from the earth, and let the wicked be no more. Bless (affectionately, gratefully praise) the Lord, O my soul! Praise the Lord! (Hallelujah!)

PSALM 105

O GIVE thanks unto the Lord, call upon His name, make known His doings among the peoples!

2 Sing to Him, sing praises to Him; meditate on *and* talk of all His marvelous deeds *and* devoutly praise them.

3 Glory in His holy name; let the hearts of those rejoice who seek *and* require the Lord [as their indispensable necessity].

4 Seek, inquire of *and* for the Lord, *and* crave Him and His strength (His might and inflexibility to temptation); seek *and* require His face *and* His presence [continually] evermore.

5 [Earnestly] remember the marvelous deeds that He has done, His miracles *and* wonders, the judgments *and* sentences which He pronounced [upon His enemies, as in Egypt]. [Ps. 78:43-51.]

putting the Word to work

Remembering God's faithfulness to us is an important means of building our faith. Psalm 105:5 encourages us to recall the things He has done for us. What are some of your favorite memories? Regularly take time to remember God's faithfulness in your life and what He has done for you, and thank Him. Share with others God's goodness to you so they too can hear what He has done!

6 O you offspring of Abraham His servant, you children of Jacob, His chosen ones,

7 He is the Lord our God; His judgments are in all the earth.

8 He is [earnestly] mindful of His covenant *and* forever it is imprinted on His heart, the word which He commanded *and* established to a thousand generations,

9 The covenant which He made with Abraham, and His sworn promise to Isaac, [Luke 1:72, 73.]

10 Which He confirmed to Jacob as a statute, to Israel as an everlasting covenant,

11 Saying, Unto you will I give the land of Canaan as your measured portion, possession, *and* inheritance.

12 When they were but a few men in number, in fact, very few, and were temporary residents *and* strangers in it,

13 When they went from one nation to another, from one kingdom to another people,

14 He allowed no man to do them wrong; in fact, He reproved kings for their sakes, [Gen. 12:17; 20:3-7.]

15 Saying, Touch not My anointed, and do My prophets no harm. [I Chron. 16:8-22.]

16 Moreover, He called for a famine upon the land [of Egypt]; He cut off every source of bread. [Gen. 41:54.]

17 He sent a man before them, even Joseph, who was sold as a servant. [Gen. 45:5; 50:20, 21.]

18 His feet they hurt with fetters; he was laid in chains of iron *and* his soul entered into the iron,

19 Until his word [to his cruel brothers] came true, until the word of the Lord tried *and* tested him.

20 The king sent and loosed him, even the ruler of the peoples, and let him go free.

21 He made Joseph lord of his house and ruler of all his substance, [Gen. 41:40.]

22 To bind his princes at his pleasure and teach his elders wisdom.

23 Israel also came into Egypt; and Jacob sojourned in the land of Ham. [Gen. 46:6.]

24 There [the Lord] greatly increased His people and made them stronger than their oppressors.

25 He turned the hearts [of the Egyptians] to hate His people, to deal craftily with His servants.

26 He sent Moses His servant, and Aaron, whom He had chosen.

27 They showed His signs among them, wonders *and* miracles in the land of Ham (Egypt).

28 He sent [thick] darkness and made the land dark, and they [God's two servants] rebelled not against His word. [Exod. 10:22; Ps. 99:7.]

29 He turned [Egypt's] waters into blood and caused their fish to die. [Exod. 7:20, 21.]

30 Their land brought forth frogs in abundance, even in the chambers of their kings. [Exod. 8:6.]

31 He spoke, and there came swarms of beetles *and* flies and mosquitoes *and* lice in all their borders. [Exod. 8:17, 24.]

32 He gave them hail for rain, with lightning like flaming fire in their land. [Exod. 9:23, 25.]

33 He smote their vines also and their fig trees and broke the [ice-laden] trees of their borders. [Ps. 78:47.]

34 He spoke, and the locusts came, and the grasshoppers, and that without number, [Exod. 10:4, 13, 14.]

35 And ate up all the vegetation in their land and devoured the fruit of their ground.

36 He smote also all the firstborn in their land, the beginning *and* chief substance of all their strength. [Exod. 12:29; Ps. 78:51.]

37 He brought [Israel] forth also with silver and gold, and there was not one feeble person among their tribes. [Exod. 12:35.]

38 Egypt was glad when they departed, for the fear of them had fallen upon the people. [Exod. 12:33.]

39 The Lord spread a cloud for a covering [by day], and a fire to give light in the night. [Exod. 13:21.]

remember Joseph

Psalm 105 is another wonderful place in the Bible where the writer takes time to recall God's working through history. Similar accounts can be found in Nehemiah 9 and in Hebrews 11. Each time a biblical writer recounts stories from the past, our faith is strengthened and our hearts are encouraged.

In Psalm 105:17–19, we are reminded of Joseph and of the unjust treatment he received from his brothers. They sold him into slavery and told his father that a wild animal had killed him. Meanwhile, Joseph was purchased by a wealthy man named Potiphar, who took him into his home as a slave. God gave Joseph favor everywhere he went, and soon he had favor with his new master.

Joseph kept getting promoted, but then something unjust would happen to him. Potiphar's wife tried to entice him into having an affair, but because he was a man of integrity, he would have nothing to do with her. Lying to her husband, she said that Joseph had attacked her, which caused him to be imprisoned for something he had not done!

Joseph tried to help others the entire time he was in prison. He never complained, and because he had a proper attitude in his suffering, God eventually delivered and promoted him. He ultimately had so much authority in Egypt that no one else in the entire land was above him except Pharaoh himself.

God also vindicated Joseph concerning the situation with his brothers, in that they had to come to Joseph for food when the whole land was in a state of famine. Once again, Joseph displayed a godly attitude by not mistreating them even though they deserved it. He told them what they had meant for his harm, God had worked out for his good—that they were in God's hands, not his, and that he had no right to do anything but bless them (see Genesis 37—45 for the details of this story). We can expect similar results when we stay patient through suffering and keep a positive, forgiving attitude.

40 [The Israelites] asked, and He brought quails and satisfied them with the bread of heaven. [Exod. 16:12-15.]
41 He opened the rock, and water gushed out; it ran in the dry places like a river. [Exod. 17:6; Num. 20:11.]
42 For He [earnestly] remembered His holy word *and* promise to Abraham His servant. [Gen. 15:14.]
43 And He brought forth His people with joy, and His chosen ones with gladness *and* singing,
44 And gave them the lands of the nations [of Canaan], and they reaped the fruits of those peoples' labor, [Deut. 6:10, 11.]
45 That they might observe His statutes and keep His laws [hearing, receiving, loving, and obeying them]. Praise the Lord! (Hallelujah!)

PSALM 106

PRAISE THE Lord! (Hallelujah!) O give thanks to the Lord, for He is good; for His mercy *and* loving-kindness endure forever! [I Chron. 16:34.]

2 Who can put into words *and* tell the mighty deeds of the Lord? *Or* who can show forth all the praise [that is due Him]?

3 Blessed (happy, fortunate, to be envied) are those who observe justice [treating others fairly] *and* who do right *and* are in right standing with God at all times.

4 [Earnestly] remember me, O Lord, when You favor Your people! O visit me also when You deliver them, *and* grant me Your salvation!—

5 That I may see *and* share the welfare of Your chosen ones, that I may rejoice in the gladness of Your nation, that I may glory with Your heritage.

6 We have sinned, as did also our fathers; we have committed iniquity, we have done wickedly. [Lev. 26:40-42.]

7 Our fathers in Egypt understood not nor appreciated Your miracles; they did not [earnestly] remember the multitude of Your mercies nor imprint Your loving-kindness [on their hearts], but they were rebellious *and* provoked the Lord at the sea, even at the Red Sea. [Exod. 14:21.]

8 Nevertheless He saved them for His name's sake [to prove the righteousness of the divine character], that He might make His mighty power known.

9 He rebuked the Red Sea also, and it dried up; so He led them through the depths as through a pastureland. [Exod. 14:21.]

10 And He saved them from the hand of him that hated them, and redeemed them from the hand of the [Egyptian] enemy. [Exod. 14:30.]

11 And the waters covered their adversaries; not one of them was left. [Exod. 14:27, 28; 15:5.]

12 Then [Israel] believed His words [trusting in, relying on them]; they sang His praise.

13 But they hastily forgot His works; they did not [earnestly] wait for His plans [to develop] regarding them,

14 But lusted exceedingly in the wilderness and tempted *and* tried to restrain God [with their insistent desires] in the desert. [Num. 11:4.]

15 And He gave them their request, but sent leanness into their souls *and* [thinned their numbers by] disease and death. [Ps. 78:29-31.]

16 They envied Moses also in the camp, and Aaron [the high priest], the holy one of the Lord. [Num. 16:1-32.]

17 Therefore the earth opened and swallowed up Dathan and closed over the company of Abiram. [Num. 16:31, 32.]

18 And a fire broke out in their company; the flame burned up the wicked. [Num. 16:35, 46.]

19 They made a calf in Horeb and worshiped a molten image. [Exod. 32:4.]

20 Thus they exchanged Him Who was their Glory for the image of an ox that eats grass [they traded their Honor for the image of a calf]!

21 They forgot God their Savior, Who had done such great things in Egypt,

22 Wonders *and* miracles in the land of Ham, dreadful *and* awesome things at the Red Sea.

23 Therefore He said He would destroy them. [And He would have done so] had not Moses, His chosen one, stepped into the breach before Him to turn away His threatening wrath. [Exod. 32:10, 11, 32.]

24 Then they spurned *and* despised the pleasant *and* desirable land [Canaan]; they believed not His word [neither trusting in, relying on, nor holding to it];

25 But they murmured in their tents *and* hearkened not to the voice of the Lord.

26 Therefore He lifted up His hand [as if taking an oath] against them, that He would cause them to fall in the wilderness,

be happy

Psalm 106:12–15 reminds us of the Israelites when they became greedy and demanding. It warns us of the dangers of a greedy, lustful heart because such a heart is never satisfied—and that is an unsafe spiritual condition.

Although God had led the Israelites out of bondage in Egypt and had destroyed Pharaoh and his army, who were chasing after them, the Israelites were not satisfied. They continued to gripe and complain every step of the way. No matter how much He provided for them, they always wanted more. They were on the way to the Promised Land, but they were not enjoying the journey. Many times, we have the same problem.

Early in my ministry, I taught twenty-five people every Tuesday evening in my living room. That was all I was mature enough to handle. I had a vision to do what I am doing now, so I grumbled, murmured, pleaded, prayed, and fasted, but I never got out of my living room. All my efforts were a waste of time and energy. I could have been relaxing, praising God, laughing, and enjoying my family and my life. But no, I had to be miserable all the time because I was not getting my way.

I finally got an opportunity to teach another Bible study. I was happy with that for a little while, but not for long. Then I went to work for a church where I was associate pastor for five years, but after a while I was not satisfied there anymore. Then I started my own ministry, and before long, I was unhappy with that. No matter what I was doing, I always wanted something else.

If people are not careful, they can waste their entire lives by always wanting what they do not have. They fall in love and cannot wait to get married. Then once they are married, they think about everything that is wrong with their spouses and they still are not happy. They have children and cannot wait for them to grow up and start school. As soon as the children are in school, they cannot wait until they graduate.

On and on it goes. No matter what their place in life, they always want something else. They keep murmuring and grumbling to God about what they want. Then as soon as He gives it to them, they start complaining again because they want something more.

The moral of the story of the Israelites is that they got what they asked for, but they were not really ready to handle it. Ask God to give you a heart that is satisfied and content at every point along your life's journey and to be able to handle increase when it comes. Learn to enjoy where you are on the way to where you are going!

27 Cast out their descendants among the nations, and scatter them in the lands [of the earth].

28 They joined themselves also to the [idol] Baal of Peor and ate sacrifices [offered] to the lifeless [gods].

29 Thus they provoked the Lord to anger with their practices, and a plague broke out among them.

30 Then stood up Phinehas [the priest] and executed judgment, and so the plague was stayed. [Num. 25:7, 8.]

31 And that was credited to him for righteousness (right doing and right standing with God) to all generations forever.

32 They angered the Lord also at the waters of Meribah, so that it went ill with Moses for their sakes; [Num. 20:3-13.]

33 For they provoked [Moses'] spirit, so that he spoke unadvisedly with his lips.

34 They did not destroy the [heathen] nations as the Lord commanded them,

35 But mingled themselves with the [idolatrous] nations and learned their ways and works

36 And served their idols, which were a snare to them.

37 Yes, they sacrificed their sons and their daughters to demons [II Kings 16:3.]

38 And shed innocent blood, even the blood of their sons and of their daughters, whom they sacrificed to the idols of Canaan; and the land was polluted with their blood.

39 Thus were they defiled by their own works, and they played the harlot and practiced idolatry with their own deeds [of idolatrous rites].

40 Therefore was the wrath of the Lord kindled against His people, insomuch that He abhorred and rejected His own heritage. [Deut. 32:17.]

41 And He gave them into the hands of the [heathen] nations, and they that hated them ruled over them.

42 Their enemies also oppressed them, and they were brought into subjection under the hand of their foes.

43 Many times did [God] deliver them, but they were rebellious in their counsel and sank low through their iniquity.

44 Nevertheless He regarded their distress when He heard their cry;

45 And He [earnestly] remembered for their sake His covenant and relented their sentence of evil [comforting and easing Himself] according to the abundance of His mercy and loving-kindness [when they cried out to Him].

46 He also caused [Israel] to find sympathy among those who had carried them away captive.

47 Deliver us, O Lord our God, and gather us from among the nations, that we may give thanks to Your holy name and glory in praising You.

48 Blessed (affectionately and gratefully praised) be the Lord, the God of Israel, from everlasting to everlasting! And let all the people say, Amen! Praise the Lord! (Hallelujah!) [I Chron. 16:35, 36.]

BOOK FIVE

PSALM 107

O GIVE thanks to the Lord, for He is good; for His mercy and loving-kindness endure forever!

2 Let the redeemed of the Lord say so, whom He has delivered from the hand of the adversary,

3 And gathered them out of the lands, from the east and from the west, from the north and from the [Red] Sea in the south.

4 Some wandered in the wilderness in a solitary desert track; they found no city for habitation.

5 Hungry and thirsty, they fainted;

their lives were near to being extinguished.

6 Then they cried to the Lord in their trouble, and He delivered them out of their distresses.

7 He led them forth by the straight *and* right way, that they might go to a city where they could establish their homes.

8 Oh, that men would praise [and confess to] the Lord for His goodness *and* loving-kindness and His wonderful works to the children of men!

9 For He satisfies the longing soul and fills the hungry soul with good.

10 Some sat in darkness and in the shadow of death, being bound in affliction and in irons, [Luke 1:79.]

11 Because they had rebelled against the words of God and spurned the counsel of the Most High.

12 Therefore He bowed down their hearts with hard labor; they stumbled *and* fell down, and there was none to help.

13 Then they cried to the Lord in their trouble, and He saved them out of their distresses.

14 He brought them out of darkness and the shadow of death and broke apart the bonds that held them. [Ps. 68:6; Acts 12:7; 16:26.]

15 Oh, that men would praise [and confess to] the Lord for His goodness *and* loving-kindness and His wonderful works to the children of men!

16 For He has broken the gates of bronze and cut the bars of iron apart.

17 Some are fools [made ill] because of the way of their transgressions and are afflicted because of their iniquities.

18 They loathe every kind of food, and they draw near to the gates of death.

19 Then they cry to the Lord in their trouble, and He delivers them out of their distresses.

20 He sends forth His word and heals them and rescues them from the pit *and* destruction. [II Kings 20:4, 5; Matt. 8:8.]

21 Oh, that men would praise [and confess to] the Lord for His goodness *and* loving-kindness and His wonderful works to the children of men! [Heb. 13:15.]

22 And let them sacrifice the sacrifices of thanksgiving and rehearse His deeds with shouts of joy *and* singing!

23 Some go down to the sea *and* travel over it in ships to do business in great waters;

24 These see the works of the Lord and His wonders in the deep.

25 For He commands and raises up the stormy wind, which lifts up the waves of the sea.

26 [Those aboard] mount up to the heavens, they go down again to the deeps; their courage melts away because of their plight.

27 They reel to and fro and stagger like a drunken man and are at their wits' end [all their wisdom has come to nothing].

28 Then they cry to the Lord in their trouble, and He brings them out of their distresses.

29 He hushes the storm to a calm *and* to a gentle whisper, so that the waves of the sea are still. [Ps. 89:9; Matt. 8:26.]

30 Then the men are glad because of the calm, and He brings them to their desired haven.

31 Oh, that men would praise [and confess to] the Lord for His goodness *and* loving-kindness and His wonderful works to the children of men!

32 Let them exalt Him also in the congregation of the people and praise Him in the company of the elders.

33 He turns rivers into a wilderness, water springs into a thirsty ground, [I Kings 17:1, 7.]

34 A fruitful land into a barren, salt waste, because of the wickedness of those who dwell in it. [Gen. 13:10; 14:3; 19:25.]

35 He turns a wilderness into a pool of water and a dry ground into water springs; [Isa. 41:18.]

36 And there He makes the hungry to dwell, that they may prepare a city for habitation,

37 And sow fields, and plant vineyards which yield fruits of increase.

38 He blesses them also, so that they are multiplied greatly, and allows not their cattle to decrease.

39 When they are diminished and bowed down through oppression, trouble, and sorrow,

40 He pours contempt upon princes and causes them to wander in waste places where there is no road.

41 Yet He raises the poor *and* needy from affliction and makes their families like a flock.

42 The upright shall see it and be glad, but all iniquity shall shut its mouth.

43 Whoso is wise [if there be any truly wise] will observe *and* heed these things; and they will diligently consider the mercy *and* loving-kindness of the Lord.

PSALM 108
A song. A Psalm of David.

O GOD, my heart is fixed (steadfast, in the confidence of faith); I will sing, yes, I will sing praises, even with my glory [all the faculties and powers of one created in Your image]!

2 Awake, harp and lyre; I myself will wake very early—I will waken the dawn!

3 I will praise *and* give thanks to You, O Lord, among the peoples; and I will sing praises unto You among the nations.

4 For Your mercy *and* loving-kindness are great *and* high as the heavens! Your truth *and* faithfulness reach to the skies! [Ps. 57:7-11.]

5 Be exalted, O God, above the heavens, and let Your glory be over all the earth.

6 That Your beloved [followers] may be delivered, save with Your right hand and answer us! [or me]!

7 God has promised in His holiness [regarding the establishment of David's dynasty]: I will rejoice, I will distribute [Canaan among My people], dividing Shechem and [the western region and allotting the eastern region which contains] the Valley of Succoth.

8 Gilead is Mine, Manasseh is Mine; Ephraim also is My stronghold *and* the defense of My head; Judah is My scepter *and* lawgiver. [Gen. 49:10.]

9 Moab is My washbasin; upon Edom [My slave] My shoe I cast [to be cleaned]; over Philistia I shout [in triumph].

10 Who will bring me [David] into the strong, fortified city [of Petra]? Who will lead me into Edom?

11 Have You not cast us off, O God? And will You not go forth, O God, with our armies?

12 Give us help against the adversary, for vain is the help of man.

13 Through *and* with God we shall do valiantly, for He it is Who shall tread down our adversaries. [Ps. 60:5-12.]

PSALM 109
To the Chief Musician. A Psalm of David.

O GOD of my praise! Keep not silence,

2 For the mouths of the wicked and the mouth of deceit are opened against me; they have spoken to me *and* against me with lying tongues.

3 They have compassed me about also with words of hatred and have fought against me without a cause.

4 In return for my love they are my adversaries, but I resort to prayer.

5 And they have rewarded *and* laid

upon me evil for good, and hatred for my love.

6 Set a wicked man over him [as a judge], and let [a malicious] accuser stand at his right hand.

7 When [the wicked] is judged, let him be condemned, and let his prayer [for leniency] be turned into a sin.

8 Let his days be few; and let another take his office *and* charge. [Acts 1:20.]

9 Let his children be fatherless and his wife a widow.

10 Let his children be continual vagabonds [as was Cain] and beg; let them seek their bread *and* be driven far from their ruined homes. [Gen. 4:12.]

11 Let the creditor *and* extortioner seize all that he has; and let strangers (barbarians and foreigners) plunder the fruits of his labor.

12 Let there be none to extend *or* continue mercy *and* kindness to him, neither let there be any to have pity on his fatherless children.

13 Let his posterity be cut off, and in the generation following let their names be blotted out.

14 Let the iniquity of his fathers be remembered by the Lord; and let not the sin of his mother be blotted out.

15 Let them be before the Lord continually, that He may cut off the memory of them from the earth!—

16 Because the man did not [earnestly] remember to show mercy, but pursued *and* persecuted the poor and needy man, and the broken in heart [he was ready] to slay.

17 Yes, he loved cursing, and it came [back] upon him; he delighted not in blessing, and it was far from him.

18 He clothed himself also with cursing as with his garment, and it seeped into his inward [life] like water, and like oil into his bones.

19 Let it be to him as the raiment with which he covers himself and as the girdle with which he is girded continually.

20 Let this be the reward of my adversaries from the Lord, and of those who speak evil against my life.

21 But You deal with me *and* act for me, O God the Lord, for Your name's sake; because Your mercy *and* loving-kindness are good, O deliver me.

22 For I am poor and needy, and my heart is wounded *and* stricken within me.

23 I am gone like the shadow when it lengthens *and* declines; I toss up and down *and* am shaken off as the locust.

24 My knees are weak *and* totter from fasting; and my body is gaunt *and* has no fatness.

25 I have become also a reproach *and* a taunt to others; when they see me, they shake their heads. [Matt. 26:39.]

26 Help me, O Lord my God; O save me according to Your mercy *and* loving-kindness!—

27 That they may know that this is Your hand, that You, Lord, have done it.

28 Let them curse, but do You bless. When adversaries arise, let them be put to shame, but let Your servant rejoice.

29 Let my adversaries be clothed with shame *and* dishonor, and let them cover themselves with their own disgrace *and* confusion as with a robe.

30 I will give great praise *and* thanks to the Lord with my mouth; yes, *and* I will praise Him among the multitude.

31 For He will stand at the right hand of the poor *and* needy, to save him from those who condemn his life.

PSALM 110
A Psalm of David.

THE LORD (God) says to my Lord (the Messiah), Sit at My right hand, until I make Your adversaries Your footstool. [Matt. 26:64; Acts 2:34; I Cor. 15:25; Col. 3:1; Heb. 12:2.]

2 The Lord will send forth from

healed healers

Psalm 109:22 speaks of a wounded heart. Is it wrong to have a wounded heart? No, a wounded heart is not wrong, but if you have one, I encourage you to receive God's healing and go on with your life.

In Old Testament days if a priest had a wound or a bleeding sore, he could not minister. I think we can learn from that today, because we have a lot of wounded people who are trying to minister and bring healing to others while they themselves still have unhealed wounds from the past. These people are still bleeding and hurting. They are what I call "wounded healers."

Am I saying such people cannot minister? No, but I am saying they need to be healed. Jesus said the blind cannot lead the blind because if they do, they will both fall into a ditch (see Matthew 15:14). There is a message in that statement. What is the use of my trying to minister victory to others if I have no victory in my own life? How can I minister emotional healing to others if I am not dealing with my emotional problems from my past? In order to minister properly, we first need to go to God and let Him heal us.

I have found that when I have a relationship problem, when I get wounded or when someone hurts my feelings, I cannot minister properly until I get that situation worked out because it takes away my strength and affects my faith. When I have unresolved problems in my life, I am not as strong as I could be.

God loves to use people who have been hurt or wounded and then healed because nobody can minister to someone else better than a person who has had the same problem or been in the same situation as the person he or she is trying to help. Ask God to heal you everywhere you hurt so that He can use you to help others. Ask Him to make you a healed healer!

Zion the scepter of Your strength; rule, then, in the midst of Your foes. [Rom. 11:26, 27.]

3 Your people will offer themselves willingly in the day of Your power, in the beauty of holiness *and* in holy array out of the womb of the morning; to You [will spring forth] Your young men, who are as the dew.

4 The Lord has sworn and will not revoke *or* change it: You are a priest forever, after the manner *and* order of Melchizedek. [Heb. 5:10; 7:11, 15, 21.]

5 The Lord at Your right hand will shatter kings in the day of His indignation.

6 He will execute judgment [in overwhelming punishment] upon the nations; He will fill the valleys with the dead bodies, He will crush the [chief] heads over lands many *and* far extended. [Ezek. 38:21, 22; 39:11, 12.]

7 He will drink of the brook by the way; therefore will He lift up His head [triumphantly].

PSALM 111

PRAISE THE Lord! (Hallelujah!)
I will praise *and* give thanks to
the Lord with my whole heart in
the council of the upright and in the
congregation.
2 The works of the Lord are great,
sought out by all those who have
delight in them.
3 His work is honorable and glorious, and His righteousness endures
forever.
4 He has made His wonderful works
to be remembered; the Lord is gracious, merciful, *and* full of loving compassion.
5 He has given food *and* provision to
those who reverently *and* worshipfully fear Him; He will remember His
covenant forever *and* imprint it [on
His mind]. [Deut. 10:12; Ps. 96:9.]
6 He has declared *and* shown to His
people the power of His works in giving them the heritage of the nations
[of Canaan].
7 The works of His hands are
[absolute] truth and justice [faithful
and right]; and all His decrees *and*
precepts are sure (fixed, established,
and trustworthy).
8 They stand fast *and* are established forever and ever and are done
in [absolute] truth and uprightness.
9 He has sent redemption to His
people; He has commanded His covenant to be forever; holy is His name,
inspiring awe, reverence, *and* godly
fear.
10 The reverent fear *and* worship of
the Lord is the beginning of ˣWisdom
and skill [the preceding and the first
essential, the prerequisite and the
alphabet]; a good understanding, wisdom, *and* meaning have all those who
do [the will of the Lord]. Their praise
of Him endures forever. [Job. 28:28;
Prov. 1:7; Matt. 22:37, 38; Rev. 14:7.]

x See footnote on Job 28:12.

life point

The Bible says that those who walk in
wisdom will be successful and live long
lives. They will be exceedingly happy.
They will be blessed, so blessed that
they will be envied (see Proverbs
3:1–18). But there is no such thing as
wisdom without worship. Psalm 111:10
says that reverence for God and worship
are the "beginning of Wisdom." In other
words, worship and reverence are
foundational to having a fruitful life.

Many people today are seeking
knowledge, and knowledge is good,
but wisdom is better. Wisdom is the
right use of knowledge. Knowledge
without wisdom can cause a person to
be puffed up or filled with pride, which
will ultimately ruin his or her life. A wise
person will always be knowledgeable,
but not all knowledgeable people are
wise.

God's Word tells us to cry out for
wisdom, to seek it as we would silver
and gold, to make it a vital necessity in
life. There is nothing more important
than wisdom, and wisdom starts with
reverence and worship.

PSALM 112

PRAISE THE Lord! (Hallelujah!)
Blessed (happy, fortunate, to be
envied) is the man who fears
(reveres and worships) the Lord, who
delights greatly in His commandments. [Deut. 10:12.]
2 His [spiritual] offspring shall be
mighty upon earth; the generation of
the upright shall be blessed.
3 Prosperity *and* welfare are in his
house, and his righteousness endures
forever.

your Provider

Do you need provision in an area of your life, and you are not really sure where it is going to come from? Be encouraged because, in Psalm 111:5, God promises to provide for those who "reverently and worshipfully fear Him." As long as we worship God, we are going to have His provision.

Perhaps you have been told that you are going to lose your job or housing. Maybe you are elderly and living on a pension or Social Security, and you wonder what is going to happen to you in the future. You see prices on everything rising all the time, and the devil whispers in your ear, "You are not going to have enough to live on." Or maybe the figures just do not add up; your income simply is not enough to support you, and yet you are doing all you know to do.

Whatever the reason for your concern about your provision, mark Psalm 111:5 in your Bible. Meditate on it and even memorize it, because it holds the key to having your needs met. That way when a need arises in your life, you will have hidden the Word of God in your heart, and it will strengthen you and help you remain in faith rather than fear.

Believe God's Word when He says He gives food and provision to those who reverently fear Him and worship Him. Whatever your situation may be, God will provide for you as you continue to worship and magnify Him.

Worship is actually fun and energizing; worry makes our hearts heavy and causes a loss of joy. Do not worry; worship and see God provide for your every need.

4 Light arises in the darkness for the upright, gracious, compassionate, *and* just [who are in right standing with God].
5 It is well with the man who deals generously and lends, who conducts his affairs with justice. [Ps. 37:26; Luke 6:35; Col. 4:5.]
6 He will not be moved forever; the [uncompromisingly] righteous (the upright, in right standing with God) shall be in everlasting remembrance. [Prov. 10:7.]
7 He shall not be afraid of evil tidings; his heart is firmly fixed, trusting (leaning on and being confident) in the Lord.
8 His heart is established *and* steady, he will not be afraid while he waits to see his desire established upon his adversaries.
9 He has distributed freely [he has given to the poor and needy]; his righteousness (uprightness and right standing with God) endures forever; his horn shall be exalted in honor. [II Cor. 9:9.]
10 The wicked man will see it and be grieved *and* angered, he will gnash his teeth and disappear [in despair]; the

speak the Word

Lord, I declare that because I fear You, prosperity and welfare will be in my house!
ADAPTED FROM PSALM 112:3

desire of the wicked shall perish *and* come to nothing.

PSALM 113

PRAISE THE Lord! (Hallelujah!) Praise, O servants of the Lord, praise the name of the Lord!
2   Blessed be the name of the Lord from this time forth and forever
3   From the rising of the sun to the going down of it *and* from east to west, the name of the Lord is to be praised!
4   The Lord is high above all nations, and His glory above the heavens!
5   Who is like the Lord our God, Who has His seat on high,
6   Who humbles Himself to regard the heavens and the earth! [Ps. 138:6; Isa. 57:15.]
7   [The Lord] raises the poor out of the dust *and* lifts the needy from the ash heap *and* the dung hill,
8   That He may seat them with princes, even with the princes of His people.
9   He makes the barren woman to be a homemaker *and* a joyful mother of [spiritual] children. Praise the Lord! (Hallelujah!)

PSALM 114

WHEN ISRAEL came forth out of Egypt, the house of Jacob from a people of strange language,
2   Judah became [God's] sanctuary (the Holy Place of His habitation), and Israel His dominion. [Exod. 29:45, 46; Deut. 27:9.]
3   The [Red] Sea looked and fled; the Jordan [River] was turned back. [Exod. 14:21; Josh. 3:13, 16; Ps. 77:16.]
4   The mountains skipped like rams, the little hills like lambs.
5   What ails you, O [Red] Sea, that you flee? O Jordan, that you turn back?

6   You mountains, that you skip like rams, and you little hills, like lambs?
7   Tremble, O earth, at the presence of the Lord, at the presence of the God of Jacob,
8   Who turned the rock into a pool of water, the flint into a fountain of waters. [Exod. 17:6; Num. 20:11.]

PSALM 115

NOT TO us, O Lord, not to us but to Your name give glory, for Your mercy *and* loving-kindness and for the sake of Your truth *and* faithfulness!
2   Why should the nations say, Where is now their God?
3   But our God is in heaven; He does whatever He pleases.
4   The idols of the nations are silver and gold, the work of men's hands.
5   They have mouths, but they speak not; eyes have they, but they see not;
6   They have ears, but they hear not; noses have they, but they smell not;
7   They have hands, but they handle not; feet have they, but they walk not; neither can they make a sound with their throats.
8   They who make idols are like them; so are all who trust in *and* lean on them. [Ps. 135:15-18.]
9   O Israel, trust *and* take refuge in the Lord! [Lean on, rely on, and be confident in Him!] He is their Help and their Shield.
10 O house of Aaron [the priest-hood], trust in *and* lean on the Lord! He is their Help and their Shield.
11 You who [reverently] fear the Lord, trust in *and* lean on the Lord! He is their Help and their Shield.
12 The Lord has been mindful of us, He will bless us: He will bless the house of Israel, He will bless the house of Aaron [the priesthood],
13 He will bless those who reverently *and* worshipfully fear the Lord,

both small and great. [Ps. 103:11; Rev. 11:18; 19:5.]

14 May the Lord give you increase more and more, you and your children.

15 May you be blessed of the Lord, Who made heaven and earth!

16 The heavens are the Lord's heavens, but the earth has He given to the children of men.

17 The dead praise not the Lord, neither any who go down into silence.

18 But we will bless (affectionately and gratefully praise) the Lord from this time forth and forever. Praise the Lord! (Hallelujah!)

PSALM 116

I LOVE the Lord, because He has heard [and now hears] my voice and my supplications.

2 Because He has inclined His ear to me, therefore will I call upon Him as long as I live.

3 The cords *and* sorrows of death were around me, and the terrors of Sheol (the place of the dead) had laid hold of me; I suffered anguish and grief (trouble and sorrow).

4 Then called I upon the name of the Lord: O Lord, I beseech You, save my life *and* deliver me!

5 Gracious is the Lord, and [rigidly] righteous; yes, our God is merciful.

6 The Lord preserves the simple; I was brought low, and He helped *and* saved me.

7 Return to your rest, O my soul, for the Lord has dealt bountifully with you. [Matt. 11:29.]

8 For You have delivered my life from death, my eyes from tears, and my feet from stumbling *and* falling.

9 I will walk before the Lord in the land of the living.

10 I believed (trusted in, relied on, and clung to my God), and therefore have I spoken [even when I said], I am greatly afflicted. [II Cor. 4:13.]

11 I said in my haste, All men are deceitful *and* liars.

12 What shall I render to the Lord for all His benefits toward me? [How can I repay Him for all His bountiful dealings?]

13 I will lift up the cup of salvation *and* deliverance and call on the name of the Lord.

14 I will pay my vows to the Lord, yes, in the presence of all His people.

15 Precious (important and no light matter) in the sight of the Lord is the death of His saints (His loving ones).

16 O Lord, truly I am Your servant; I am Your servant, the son of Your handmaid; You have loosed my bonds.

17 I will offer to You the sacrifice of thanksgiving and will call on the name of the Lord.

life point

Notice that in Psalm 116:17, the psalmist says that he will call on the name of the Lord, but only after he has offered the sacrifice of thanksgiving.

Many times I have attempted to call on the power of the name of Jesus to help me, while at the same time my life was filled with complaining—not thankfulness. I have discovered that there is no positive power in complaining. Complaining is filled with power, but it is negative (evil) power. If we want God's power to be released in our lives, we will have to stop complaining and be thankful.

18 I will pay my vows to the Lord, yes, in the presence of all His people,

19 In the courts of the Lord's house— in the midst of you, O Jerusalem. Praise the Lord! (Hallelujah!)

confess the Word

When we speak what we believe, as the psalmist did in Psalm 116:10, we are making a "confession."

I recommend having a list of confessions—statements or declarations that can be backed by the Word of God—things that you speak aloud over your life, your family, your circumstances, and your future. You can find a list of confessions in the back of this Bible.

Before learning to confess God's Word, I was terribly negative. I was a Christian and active in church work. My husband and I tithed and attended church regularly, but we did not know that we could do anything about any of our circumstances. God began teaching me that I should not think and say negative things. I felt He told me He could not work in my life until I stopped being so negative. I obeyed, and I became happier.

After some time had elapsed, I felt that my circumstances had not improved significantly. I asked the Lord about it, and He said, "You have stopped speaking negatively, but you are not saying anything positive." That was my first lesson in "calling those things which be not as if they were" (see Romans 4:17). I had not been taught it by anyone else; God was teaching me Himself, and it proved to be one of the major breakthroughs in my life. He showed me that confessing God's Word helps establish His life-giving truths in our hearts.

I made a list of the things that I had been learning were rightfully mine according to the Word of God. I had scriptures to support them. I confessed those truths aloud twice a day for approximately six months. I did this in my house, alone. I was not talking to any human person; I was declaring the Word of God and speaking it into the atmosphere I lived in. To this day, almost twenty years later, when I am praying and confessing the Word, I still hear many of those early confessions come out of my mouth.

I would like to share a few confessions from my list with you:

I am dead to sin but alive to God (see Romans 6:11); *I will study the Word of God; I will pray* (see II Timothy 2:15; Luke 18:1); *I take every thought captive unto the obedience of Jesus Christ, casting down every imagination, and every high and lofty thing that exalts itself against the knowledge of God* (see II Corinthians 10:5); *No weapon that is formed against me shall prosper, but every tongue that rises against me in judgment, I shall show to be in the wrong* (see Isaiah 54:17); *I do not think more highly of myself than I ought to in the flesh* (see Romans 12:3); *I am purposed that my mouth shall not transgress. I will speak forth the righteousness and praise of God all the day long* (see Psalm 17:3; 35:28); *God has not given me a spirit of fear, but one of power, love, and a sound mind* (see II Timothy 1:7).

I can look at my list now, and I am absolutely amazed at how many of the things have come to pass, and how impossible they seemed in the natural at the time.

I encourage you to make your own list, tailored to your situation. As you begin to confess God's Word, you will notice major changes in your life.

PSALM 117

O PRAISE the Lord, all you nations! Praise Him, all you people! [Rom. 15:11.]
2 For His mercy *and* loving-kindness are great toward us, and the truth *and* faithfulness of the Lord endure forever. Praise the Lord! (Hallelujah!)

PSALM 118

O GIVE thanks to the Lord, for He is good; for His mercy *and* loving-kindness endure forever!
2 Let Israel now say that His mercy *and* loving-kindness endure forever.
3 Let the house of Aaron [the priesthood] now say that His mercy *and* loving-kindness endure forever.
4 Let those now who reverently *and* worshipfully fear the Lord say that His mercy *and* loving-kindness endure forever.
5 Out of my distress I called upon the Lord; the Lord answered me and set me free *and* in a large place.
6 The Lord is on my side; I will not fear. What can man do to me? [Heb. 13:6.]
7 The Lord is on my side *and* takes my part, He is among those who help me; therefore shall I see my desire established upon those who hate me.
8 It is better to trust *and* take refuge in the Lord than to put confidence in man.
9 It is better to trust *and* take refuge in the Lord than to put confidence in princes.
10 All nations (the surrounding tribes) compassed me about, but in the name of the Lord I will cut them off!
11 They compassed me about, yes, they surrounded me on every side; but in the name of the Lord I will cut them off!

12 They swarmed about me like bees, they blaze up *and* are extinguished like a fire of thorns; in the name of the Lord I will cut them off! [Deut. 1:44.]
13 You [my adversary] thrust sorely at me that I might fall, but the Lord helped me.
14 The Lord is my Strength and Song; and He has become my Salvation.
15 The voice of rejoicing and salvation is in the tents *and* private dwellings of the [uncompromisingly] righteous: the right hand of the Lord does valiantly *and* achieves strength!
16 The right hand of the Lord is exalted; the right hand of the Lord does valiantly *and* achieves strength!
17 I shall not die but live, and shall declare the works *and* recount the illustrious acts of the Lord.
18 The Lord has chastened me sorely, but He has not given me over to death. [II Cor. 6:9.]
19 Open to me the [temple] gates of righteousness; I will enter through them, and I will confess *and* praise the Lord.
20 This is the gate of the Lord; the [uncompromisingly] righteous shall enter through it. [Ps. 24:7.]
21 I will confess, praise, *and* give thanks to You, for You have heard *and* answered me; and You have become my Salvation *and* Deliverer.
22 The stone which the builders rejected has become the chief cornerstone.
23 This is from the Lord *and* is His doing; it is marvelous in our eyes. [Matt. 21:42; Acts 4:11; I Pet. 2:7.]
24 This is the day which the Lord has brought about; we will rejoice and be glad in it.
25 Save now, we beseech You, O Lord; send now prosperity, O Lord, we beseech You, *and* give to us success!
26 Blessed is he who comes in the name of the Lord; we bless you from the house of the Lord [you who come

the right kind of fear

The psalmist says in Psalm 118:4 that he will reverence and worship God by declaring that His mercy and loving-kindness endure forever. As he worships God and talks about some of His great attributes, his faith is being strengthened.

Notice something interesting in Psalm 118:5. The psalmist tells how, in his distress, he called upon the Lord. But he did not do that until *after* he had worshipped the Lord and praised Him in verse 4 for the very attributes he was calling upon Him to display in his distressing situation. He continues by declaring: "The Lord is on my side; I will not fear. What can man do to me?" (Psalm 118:6).

Why should we fear? If Almighty God is for us, *and He is*, then what can mere human beings do to us? We definitely need to realize how big God is and how small our enemies are when compared to Him.

You may be worried about what man is going to do to you. You may be worried that man is going to take your job away, that man is not going to give you what you need. Man may treat you unfairly or may reject you. You may be worried about what man is going to think or say about you. I encourage you to be more concerned about what God thinks of you than what people think of you. The Bible tells us that we are not to fear man, but that we are to reverently and worshipfully fear the Lord. When we refuse to fear man, but instead reverently and worshipfully fear the Lord, then God moves on our behalf so that nothing man tries to do to us ever harms us permanently. Evil people may come against us one way, but they will have to flee before us seven ways (see Deuteronomy 28:7).

For a period of time it may seem as if someone is taking advantage of you. But if you keep your eyes on God and continue to worship Him, keeping your conversation in line with His Word, in the end God will reward you and bring justice because He is a God of justice. He loves justice and hates wrongdoing. God is our Vindicator, and He always makes wrong things right if we keep trusting Him long enough.

We need to retire from self-care and cast our cares upon the Lord. If we have our trust in God, nobody is going to take advantage of us—at least not for very long. God has thousands of ways to get His blessings to us. When a door closes, He opens another one. If there are no doors, He makes one!

Do you find yourself in distress or afraid of people? Then do what the psalmist did. First focus on God's mercy and loving-kindness, and encourage yourself with the knowledge that God is on your side.

into His sanctuary under His guardianship]. [Mark 11:9, 10.]

27 The Lord is God, Who has shown *and* given us light [He has illuminated us with grace, freedom, and joy]. Decorate the festival with leafy boughs *and* bind the sacrifices to be offered with thick cords [all over the priest's court, right up] to the horns of the altar.

28 You are my God, and I will confess, praise, *and* give thanks to You; You are my God, I will extol You.

29 O give thanks to the Lord, for He is good; for His mercy *and* lovingkindness endure forever.

PSALM 119

BLESSED (HAPPY, fortunate, to be envied) are the undefiled (the upright, truly sincere, and blameless) in the way [of the revealed will of God], who walk (order their conduct and conversation) in the law of the Lord (the whole of God's revealed will).

2 Blessed (happy, fortunate, to be envied) are they who keep His testimonies, and who seek, inquire for *and* of Him *and* crave Him with the whole heart.

3 Yes, they do no unrighteousness [no willful wandering from His precepts]; they walk in His ways. [I John 3:9; 5:18.]

4 You have commanded us to keep Your precepts, that we should observe them diligently.

5 Oh, that my ways were directed *and* established to observe Your statutes [hearing, receiving, loving, and obeying them]!

6 Then shall I not be put to shame [by failing to inherit Your promises] when I have respect to all Your commandments.

7 I will praise *and* give thanks to You with uprightness of heart when I learn [by sanctified experiences] Your

life point

Part of the reason many people backslide during tough times is that they have never learned how to speak in accordance with God's will. A trial is discouraging enough in itself, without adding insult to injury by depressing ourselves through negative speech. That is why we must learn to align our conversation with God's will and His Word.

When you find yourself in a time of trial, try not to simply focus on where you are right now and what is happening to you at the moment, but see yourself and your circumstances through the eyes of faith. You may feel as though you are out in the middle of an ocean with a storm raging around you, but *you will get to the other side.* There are blessings waiting for you there, *so do not jump overboard!* Learn, as the psalmist did, to order your conversation and conduct in accordance with God's plan (see Psalm 119:1). You will be blessed when you do!

righteous judgments [Your decisions against and punishments for particular lines of thought and conduct].

8 I will keep Your statutes; O forsake me not utterly.

9 How shall a young man cleanse his way? By taking heed *and* keeping watch [on himself] according to Your word [conforming his life to it].

10 With my whole heart have I sought You, inquiring for *and* of You *and* yearning for You; Oh, let me not wander *or* step aside [either in ignorance or willfully] from Your commandments. [II Chron. 15:15.]

11 Your word have I laid up in my heart, that I might not sin against You.

12 Blessed are You, O Lord; teach me Your statutes.

life point

I believe Psalm 119:6 says what we need to be saying in our hearts every day: "God, if I will just read Your Book and do what You say, everything in my life will work out for the best."

13 With my lips have I declared *and* recounted all the ordinances of Your mouth.
14 I have rejoiced in the way of Your testimonies as much as in all riches.
15 I will meditate on Your precepts and have respect to Your ways [the paths of life marked out by Your law]. [Ps. 104:34.]
16 I will delight myself in Your statutes; I will not forget Your word.
17 Deal bountifully with Your servant, that I may live; and I will observe Your word [hearing, receiving, loving, and obeying it]. [Ps. 119:97-101.]
18 Open my eyes, that I may behold wondrous things out of Your law.
19 I am a stranger *and* a temporary resident on the earth; hide not Your commandments from me. [Gen. 47:9; I Chron. 29:15; Ps. 39:12; II Cor. 5:6; Heb. 11:13.]
20 My heart is breaking with the longing that it has for Your ordinances *and* judgments at all times.
21 You rebuke the proud *and* arrogant, the accursed ones, who err *and* wander from Your commandments.
22 Take away from me reproach and contempt, for I keep Your testimonies.
23 Princes also sat *and* talked against me, but Your servant meditated on Your statutes.

putting the Word to work

Have you ever been lost? Do you remember the relief you felt when someone was able to give you good directions? The best directions we have for living an abundant life that is pleasing to God are found in the Bible. Hide God's Word in your heart by studying and even memorizing scripture verses and passages, so you will not sin against Him and will be able to live in His blessings (see Psalm 119:9–11).

24 Your testimonies also are my delight and my counselors.
25 My earthly life cleaves to the dust; revive *and* stimulate me according to Your word! [Ps. 143:11.]
26 I have declared my ways *and* opened my griefs to You, and You listened to me; teach me Your statutes.
27 Make me understand the way of Your precepts; so shall I meditate on *and* talk of Your wondrous works. [Ps. 145:5, 6.]
28 My life dissolves *and* weeps itself away for heaviness; raise me up *and* strengthen me according to [the promises of] Your word.
29 Remove from me the way of falsehood *and* unfaithfulness [to You], and graciously impart Your law to me.
30 I have chosen the way of truth *and* faithfulness; Your ordinances have I set before me.
31 I cleave to Your testimonies; O Lord, put me not to shame!
32 I will [not merely walk, but] run the way of Your commandments, when You give me a heart that is willing.

speak the Word

Lord, I pray that You would open my spiritual eyes so that I can have revelation of the wonderful things in Your Word.
ADAPTED FROM PSALM 119:18

33 Teach me, O Lord, the way of Your statutes, and I will keep it to the end [steadfastly].

34 Give me understanding, that I may keep Your law; yes, I will observe it with my whole heart. [Prov. 2:6; James 1:5.]

35 Make me go in the path of Your commandments, for in them do I delight.

36 Incline my heart to Your testimonies and not to covetousness (robbery, sensuality, unworthy riches). [Ezek. 33:31; Mark 7:21, 22; I Tim. 6:10; Heb. 13:5.]

37 Turn away my eyes from beholding vanity (idols and idolatry); and restore me to vigorous life *and* health in Your ways.

38 Establish Your word *and* confirm Your promise to Your servant, which is for those who reverently fear *and* devotedly worship You. [Deut. 10:12; Ps. 96:9.]

39 Turn away my reproach which I fear *and* dread, for Your ordinances are good.

40 Behold, I long for Your precepts; in Your righteousness give me renewed life.

41 Let Your mercy *and* loving-kindness come also to me, O Lord, even Your salvation according to Your promise;

42 Then shall I have an answer for those who taunt *and* reproach me, for I lean on, rely on, *and* trust in Your word.

43 And take not the word of truth utterly out of my mouth, for I hope in Your ordinances.

44 I will keep Your law continually, forever and ever [hearing, receiving, loving, and obeying it].

45 And I will walk at liberty *and* at ease, for I have sought and inquired for [and desperately required] Your precepts.

46 I will speak of Your testimonies also before kings and will not be put to shame. [Ps. 138:1; Matt. 10:18, 19; Acts 26:1, 2.]

47 For I will delight myself in Your commandments, which I love.

48 My hands also will I lift up [in fervent supplication] to Your commandments, which I love, and I will meditate on Your statutes.

49 Remember [fervently] the word *and* promise to Your servant, in which You have caused me to hope.

50 This is my comfort *and* consolation in my affliction: that Your word has revived me *and* given me life. [Rom. 15:4.]

51 The proud have had me greatly in derision, yet have I not declined in my interest in *or* turned aside from Your law.

52 When I have [earnestly] recalled Your ordinances from of old, O Lord, I have taken comfort.

53 Burning indignation, terror, *and* sadness seize upon me because of the wicked, who forsake Your law.

54 Your statutes have been my songs in the house of my pilgrimage.

55 I have [earnestly] remembered Your name, O Lord, in the night, and I have observed Your law.

56 This I have had [as the gift of Your grace and as my reward]: that I have kept Your precepts [hearing, receiving, loving, and obeying them].

57 You are my portion, O Lord; I have promised to keep Your words.

58 I entreated Your favor with my whole heart; be merciful *and* gracious to me according to Your promise.

59 I considered my ways; I turned my feet to [obey] Your testimonies.

60 I made haste and delayed not to keep Your commandments.

61 Though the cords of the wicked have enclosed *and* ensnared me, I have not forgotten Your law.

62 At midnight I will rise to give thanks to You because of Your righteous ordinances.

63 I am a companion of all those who fear, revere, *and* worship You, and of those who observe *and* give heed to Your precepts.

64 The earth, O Lord, is full of Your mercy *and* loving-kindness; teach me Your statutes.

65 You have dealt well with Your servant, O Lord, according to Your promise.

66 Teach me good judgment, wise *and* right discernment, and knowledge, for I have believed (trusted, relied on, and clung to) Your commandments.

67 Before I was afflicted I went astray, but now Your word do I keep [hearing, receiving, loving, and obeying it].

68 You are good *and* kind and do good; teach me Your statutes.

69 The arrogant *and* godless have put together a lie against me, but I will keep Your precepts with my whole heart.

70 Their hearts are as fat as grease [their minds are dull and brutal], but I delight in Your law.

71 It is good for me that I have been afflicted, that I might learn Your statutes.

72 The law from Your mouth is better to me than thousands of gold and silver pieces.

73 Your hands have made me, cunningly fashioned *and* established me; give me understanding, that I may learn Your commandments.

74 Those who reverently *and* worshipfully fear You will see me and be glad, because I have hoped in Your word *and* tarried for it.

75 I know, O Lord, that Your judgments are right *and* righteous, and that in faithfulness You have afflicted me. [Heb. 12:10.]

76 Let, I pray You, Your merciful kindness *and* steadfast love be for my comfort, according to Your promise to Your servant.

77 Let Your tender mercy *and* loving-kindness come to me that I may live, for Your law is my delight!

78 Let the proud be put to shame, for they dealt perversely with me without a cause; but I will meditate on Your precepts.

79 Let those who reverently *and* worshipfully fear You turn to me, and those who have known Your testimonies.

80 Let my heart be sound (sincere and wholehearted and blameless) in Your statutes, that I may not be put to shame.

81 My soul languishes *and* grows faint for Your salvation, but I hope in Your word.

82 My eyes fail, watching for [the fulfillment of] Your promise. I say, When will You comfort me?

83 For I have become like a bottle [a wineskin blackened and shriveled] in the smoke [in which it hangs], yet do I not forget Your statutes.

84 How many are the days of Your servant [which he must endure]? When will You judge those who pursue and persecute me? [Rev. 6:10.]

85 The godless *and* arrogant have dug pitfalls for me, men who do not conform to Your law.

86 All Your commandments are faithful *and* sure. [The godless] pursue *and* persecute me with falsehood; help me [Lord]!

87 They had almost consumed me upon earth, but I forsook not Your precepts.

88 According to Your steadfast love give life to me; then I will keep the testimony of Your mouth [hearing, receiving, loving, and obeying it].

89 Forever, O Lord, Your word is settled in heaven [stands firm as the heavens]. [Ps. 89:2; Matt. 24:34, 35; I Pet. 1:25.]

90 Your faithfulness is from generation to generation; You have established the earth, and it stands fast.

91 All [the whole universe] are Your servants; therefore they continue this day according to Your ordinances. [Jer. 33:25.]

92 Unless Your law had been my delight, I would have perished in my affliction.

93 I will never forget Your precepts, [how can I?] for it is by them You have quickened me (granted me life).

94 I am Yours, therefore save me [Your own]; for I have sought (inquired of and for) Your precepts *and* required them [as my urgent need]. [Ps. 42:1.]

95 The wicked wait for me to destroy me, but I will consider Your testimonies.

96 I have seen that everything [human] has its limits *and* end [no matter how extensive, noble, and excellent]; but Your commandment is exceedingly broad *and* extends without limits [into eternity]. [Rom. 3:10-19.]

97 Oh, how love I Your law! It is my meditation all the day. [Ps. 1:2.]

98 You, through Your commandments, make me wiser than my enemies, for [Your words] are ever before me.

99 I have better understanding *and* deeper insight than all my teachers, because Your testimonies are my meditation. [II Tim. 3:15.]

100 I understand more than the aged, because I keep Your precepts [hearing, receiving, loving, and obeying them].

101 I have restrained my feet from every evil way, that I might keep Your word [hearing, receiving, loving, and obeying it]. [Prov. 1:15.]

102 I have not turned aside from Your ordinances, for You Yourself have taught me.

103 How sweet are Your words to my taste, sweeter than honey to my mouth! [Ps. 19:10; Prov. 8:11.]

104 Through Your precepts I get

putting the Word to work

Wandering around in the dark can be scary and frustrating! Do you ever feel that you are wandering in life, not sure of which way to go? Learn God's Word; it is a lamp unto your feet and a light unto your path (see Psalm 119:105). God promises to use His Word to instruct you in the way you are to go, one step at a time!

understanding; therefore I hate every false way.

105 Your word is a lamp to my feet and a light to my path. [Prov. 6:23.]

106 I have sworn [an oath] and have confirmed it, that I will keep Your righteous ordinances [hearing, receiving, loving, and obeying them]. [Neh. 10:29.]

107 I am sorely afflicted; renew *and* quicken me [give me life], O Lord, according to Your word!

108 Accept, I beseech You, the freewill offerings of my mouth, O Lord, and teach me Your ordinances. [Hos. 14:2; Heb. 13:15.]

109 My life is continually in my hand, yet I do not forget Your law.

110 The wicked have laid a snare for me, yet I do not stray from Your precepts.

111 Your testimonies have I taken as a heritage forever, for they are the rejoicing of my heart. [Deut. 33:4.]

112 I have inclined my heart to perform Your statutes forever, even to the end.

113 I hate the thoughts of undecided [in religion], double-minded people, but Your law do I love.

114 You are my hiding place and my shield; I hope in Your word. [Ps. 32:7; 91:1.]

115 Depart from me, you evildoers, that I may keep the commandments of my God [hearing, receiving, loving, and obeying them]. [Ps. 6:8; 139:19; Matt. 7:23.]

116 Uphold me according to Your promise, that I may live; and let me not be put to shame in my hope! [Ps. 25:2; Rom. 5:5; 9:33; 10:11.]

117 Hold me up, that I may be safe and have regard for Your statutes continually!

118 You spurn *and* set at nought all those who stray from Your statutes, for their own lying deceives them *and* their tricks are in vain.

119 You put away *and* count as dross all the wicked of the earth [for there is no true metal in them]; therefore I love Your testimonies.

120 My flesh trembles *and* shudders for fear *and* reverential, worshipful awe of You, and I am afraid *and* in dread of Your judgments.

121 I have done justice and righteousness; leave me not to those who would oppress me.

122 Be surety for Your servant for good [as Judah was surety for the safety of Benjamin]; let not the proud oppress me. [Gen. 43:9.]

123 My eyes fail, watching for Your salvation and for the fulfillment of Your righteous promise.

124 Deal with Your servant according to Your mercy *and* loving-kindness, and teach me Your statutes.

125 I am Your servant; give me understanding (discernment and comprehension), that I may know (discern and be familiar with the character of) Your testimonies.

126 It is time for the Lord to act; they have frustrated Your law.

127 Therefore I love Your commandments more than [resplendent] gold, yes, more than [perfectly] refined gold.

128 Therefore I esteem as right all, yes, all Your precepts; I hate every false way.

129 Your testimonies are wonderful [far exceeding anything conceived by man]; therefore my [penitent] self

life point

According to Psalm 119:130, the entrance of God's Word brings light, which is something we all need. We do not always know or see what we need to do, and many times we do not recognize our own problems. We need God's light to understand ourselves and to see how we need to change and how we can cooperate with God to make things better. Reading God's Word is like looking in a mirror. It enables us to see what needs to be cleaned up in our lives.

keeps them [hearing, receiving, loving, and obeying them].

130 The entrance *and* unfolding of Your words give light; their unfolding gives understanding (discernment and comprehension) to the simple.

131 I opened my mouth and panted [with eager desire], for I longed for Your commandments.

132 Look upon me, be merciful unto me, *and* show me favor, as is Your way to those who love Your name.

133 Establish my steps *and* direct them by [means of] Your word; let not any iniquity have dominion over me.

134 Deliver me from the oppression of man; so will I keep Your precepts [hearing, receiving, loving, and obeying them]. [Luke 1:74.]

135 Make Your face shine [with pleasure] upon Your servant, and teach me Your statutes. [Ps. 4:6.]

136 Streams of water run down my eyes, because men do not keep Your law [they hear it not, nor receive it, love it, or obey it].

137 [Rigidly] righteous are You, O Lord, and upright are Your judgments *and* all expressions of Your will.

138 You have commanded *and* appointed Your testimonies in righteousness and in great faithfulness.

139 My zeal has consumed me *and*

cut me off, because my adversaries have forgotten Your words.

140 Your word is very pure (tried and well refined); therefore Your servant loves it.

141 I am small (insignificant) and despised, but I do not forget Your precepts.

142 Your righteousness is an everlasting righteousness, and Your law is truth. [Ps. 19:9; John 17:17.]

143 Trouble and anguish have found *and* taken hold on me, yet Your commandments are my delight.

144 Your righteous testimonies are everlasting *and* Your decrees are binding to eternity; give me understanding and I shall live [give me discernment and comprehension and I shall not die].

145 I cried with my whole heart; hear me, O Lord; I will keep Your statutes [I will hear, receive, love, and obey them].

146 I cried to You; save me, that I may keep Your testimonies [hearing, receiving, loving, and obeying them].

147 I anticipated the dawning of the morning and cried [in childlike prayer]; I hoped in Your word.

148 My eyes anticipate the night watches *and* I am awake before the cry of the watchman, that I may meditate on Your word.

149 Hear my voice according to Your steadfast love; O Lord, quicken me *and* give me life according to Your [righteous] decrees.

150 They draw near who follow after wrong thinking *and* persecute me with wickedness; they are far from Your law.

151 You are near, O Lord [nearer to me than my foes], and all Your commandments are truth.

152 Of old have I known Your testimonies, *and* for a long time, [therefore it is a thoroughly established conviction] that You have founded them forever. [Luke 21:33.]

153 Consider my affliction and deliver me, for I do not forget Your law.

154 Plead my cause and redeem me; revive me *and* give me life according to Your word.

155 Salvation is far from the wicked, for they seek not *nor* hunger for Your statutes.

156 Great are Your tender mercy *and* loving-kindness, O Lord; give me life according to Your ordinances.

157 Many are my persecutors and my adversaries, yet I do not swerve from Your testimonies.

158 I behold the treacherous and am grieved *and* loathe them, because they do not respect Your law [neither hearing, receiving, loving, nor obeying it].

159 Consider how I love Your precepts; revive me *and* give life to me, O Lord, according to Your loving-kindness!

160 The sum of Your word is truth [the total of the full meaning of all Your individual precepts]; and every one of Your righteous decrees endures forever.

161 Princes pursue *and* persecute me without cause, but my heart stands in awe of Your words [dreading violation of them far more than the force of prince or potentate]. [I Sam. 24:11, 14; 26:18.]

162 I rejoice at Your word as one who finds great spoil.

163 I hate and abhor falsehood, but Your law do I love.

164 Seven times a day *and* all day long do I praise You because of Your righteous decrees.

165 Great peace have they who love Your law; nothing shall offend them *or* make them stumble. [Prov. 3:2; Isa. 32:17.]

166 I am hoping *and* waiting [eagerly] for Your salvation, O Lord, and I do Your commandments. [Gen. 49:18.]

167 Your testimonies have I kept [hearing, receiving, loving, and obeying them]; I love them exceedingly!

168 I have observed Your precepts *and* Your testimonies, for all my ways are [fully known] before You.

169 Let my mournful cry *and* supplication come [near] before You, O Lord; give me understanding (discernment and comprehension) according to Your word [of assurance and promise].

170 Let my supplication come before You; deliver me according to Your word!

171 My lips shall pour forth praise [with thanksgiving and renewed trust] when You teach me Your statutes.

172 My tongue shall sing [praise for the fulfillment] of Your word, for all Your commandments are righteous.

173 Let Your hand be ready to help me, for I have chosen Your precepts.

174 I have longed for Your salvation, O Lord, and Your law is my delight.

175 Let me live that I may praise You, and let Your decrees help me.

176 I have gone astray like a lost sheep; seek, inquire for, *and* demand Your servant, for I do not forget Your commandments. [Isa. 53:6; Luke 15:4; I Pet. 2:25.]

PSALM 120
A Song of ʸAscents.

I N MY distress I cried to the Lord, and He answered me.

2 Deliver me, O Lord, from lying lips and from deceitful tongues.

3 What shall be given to you? Or

speak the Word

what more shall be done to you, you deceitful tongue?—

4 Sharp arrows of a [mighty] warrior, with [glowing] coals of the broom tree!

5 Woe is me that I sojourn with Meshech, that I dwell beside the tents of Kedar [as if among notoriously barbarous people]! [Gen. 10:2; 25:13; Jer. 49:28, 29.]

6 My life has too long had its dwelling with him who hates peace.

7 I am for peace; but when I speak, they are for war.

PSALM 121
A Song of ᶻAscents.

I WILL lift up my eyes to the hills [around Jerusalem, to sacred Mount Zion and Mount Moriah]— From whence shall my help come? [Jer. 3:23.]

2 My help comes from the Lord, Who made heaven and earth.

3 He will not allow your foot to slip *or* to be moved; He Who keeps you will not slumber. [I Sam. 2:9; Ps. 127:1; Prov. 3:23, 26; Isa. 27:3.]

4 Behold, He who keeps Israel will neither slumber nor sleep.

5 The Lord is your keeper; the Lord is your shade on your right hand [the side not carrying a shield]. [Isa. 25:4.]

6 The sun shall not smite you by day, nor the moon by night. [Ps. 91:5; Isa. 49:10; Rev. 7:16.]

God, I declare that my help comes from You. You will not allow my foot to slip. You do not slumber or sleep, but You are always watching over and keeping me. You are the shade on my right hand. You will keep me from all evil. You will keep my life and watch over my going out and my coming in.
ADAPTED FROM PSALM 121:2–8

y It is possible that the fifteen psalms known as the "Songs of Degrees or Ascents" were sung by the caravans of pilgrims going up to attend the annual feasts at Jerusalem. But it is equally possible that the title has reference to some peculiarity in connection with the music or the manner of using it. **z** See Psalm 120 title footnote.

seek God first

We should be mature enough in our faith that we do not run to somebody else every time we need to know what to do in a certain situation. I am not implying that it is wrong to go to people we feel are wiser than we are to ask for a word of counsel or advice. But I do believe it is wrong, and insulting to God, to go to people too often. Having someone give us advice is not necessarily a problem; the problem comes when we seek man rather than God. God is a jealous God (see James 4:5 and Deuteronomy 4:24), and He wants us to ask for His advice.

It is important to clearly establish in our hearts that we will seek God first, as the psalmist did in Psalm 121:1, 2. God wants to guide each one of us—not just pastors or ministers, but every person who truly trusts Him.

I encourage you to seek balance in this area and to wean yourself from seeking other people's opinions if you have a consistent habit of doing so. Discipline yourself to go to God first, and let Him choose whether He wants to speak to you Himself or use the counsel of other believers to clarify things for you.

7 The Lord will keep you from all evil; He will keep your life.

8 The Lord will keep your going out and your coming in from this time forth and forevermore. [Deut. 28:6; Prov. 2:8; 3:6.]

PSALM 122
A Song of ᵃAscents. Of David.

I WAS glad when they said to me, Let us go to the house of the Lord! [Isa. 2:3; Zech. 8:21.]

2 Our feet are standing within your gates, O Jerusalem!—

3 Jerusalem, which is built as a city that is compacted together—

4 To which the tribes go up, even the tribes of the Lord, as was decreed *and* as a testimony for Israel, to give thanks to the name of the Lord.

5 For there the thrones of judgment were set, the thrones of the house of David.

6 Pray for the peace of Jerusalem! May they prosper who love you [the Holy City]!

7 May peace be within your walls and prosperity within your palaces!

8 For my brethren and companions' sake, I will now say, Peace be within you!

9 For the sake of the house of the Lord our God, I will seek, inquire for, *and* require your good.

PSALM 123
A Song of ᵃAscents.

UNTO YOU do I lift up my eyes, O You Who are enthroned in heaven.

2 Behold, as the eyes of servants look to the hand of their master, and as the eyes of a maid to the hand of her mistress, so our eyes look to the Lord our God, until He has mercy *and* loving-kindness for us.

3 Have mercy on us, O Lord, have mercy on *and* loving-kindness for us, for we are exceedingly satiated with contempt.

4 Our life is exceedingly filled with the scorning *and* scoffing of those who

a See Psalm 120 title footnote.

are at ease and with the contempt of the proud (irresponsible tyrants who disregard God's law).

PSALM 124
A Song of ᵇAscents. Of David.

IF IT had not been the Lord Who was on our side—now may Israel say—
2 If it had not been the Lord Who was on our side when men rose up against us,
3 Then they would have quickly swallowed us up alive when their wrath was kindled against us;
4 Then the waters would have overwhelmed us *and* swept us away, the torrent would have gone over us;
5 Then the proud waters would have gone over us.
6 Blessed be the Lord, Who has not given us as prey to their teeth!
7 We are like a bird escaped from the snare of the fowlers; the snare is broken, and we have escaped!
8 Our help is in the name of the Lord, Who made heaven and earth.

PSALM 125
A Song of ᵇAscents.

THOSE WHO trust in, lean on, *and* confidently hope in the Lord are like Mount Zion, which cannot be moved but abides *and* stands fast forever.
2 As the mountains are round about Jerusalem, so the Lord is round about His people from this time forth and forever.
3 For the scepter of wickedness shall not rest upon the land of the [uncompromisingly] righteous, lest the righteous (God's people) stretch forth their hands to iniquity *and* apostasy.

b See Psalm 120 title footnote.

life point

God is for us; He is on our side (see Psalm 118:6). The devil has one position: he is against us. But God is over us, under us, through us, for us, and He surrounds us. So like Mount Zion, we should not be moved, because God is all around us (see Psalm 125:1, 2).

4 Do good, O Lord, to those who are good, and to those who are right [with You and all people] in their hearts.
5 As for such as turn aside to their crooked ways [of indifference to God], the Lord will lead them forth with the workers of iniquity. Peace be upon Israel!

PSALM 126
A Song of ᵇAscents.

WHEN THE Lord brought back the captives [who returned] to Zion, we were like those who dream [it seemed so unreal]. [Ps. 53:6; Acts 12:9.]
2 Then were our mouths filled with laughter, and our tongues with singing. Then they said among the nations, The Lord has done great things for them.
3 The Lord has done great things for us! We are glad!
4 Turn to freedom our captivity *and* restore our fortunes, O Lord, as the streams in the South (the Negeb) [are restored by the torrents].
5 They who sow in tears shall reap in joy *and* singing.
6 He who goes forth bearing seed and weeping [at needing his precious supply of grain for sowing] shall doubtless come again with rejoicing, bringing his sheaves with him.

fill your mouth with laughter

Psalm 126:2, 3 speak of laughter and gladness. I once watched a Christian television talk show in which the participants were talking about a laughing revival that took place in various parts of the world at one time. Someone asked the host of the show if he thought it was of God.

"Does it offend your mind?" the host asked.

"Yes, it does," answered the person who had raised the question.

"Well, then," responded the host, "it is probably of God."

Have you ever noticed that Jesus offended people who were falsely religious? It sometimes seemed He did it on purpose. In Matthew 15:12 Jesus' disciples said to Him, "Do You know that the Pharisees were displeased and offended and indignant when they heard this saying?" Jesus' answer to them was: "Let them alone and disregard them; they are blind guides and teachers. And if a blind man leads a blind man, both will fall into a ditch" (Matthew 15:14). If we are going to follow God, we need to realize that our minds may not always understand everything He does. Stop checking with your mind and start asking if you bear witness in your spirit to what is happening. We often reject things and movements that are genuinely of God simply because we have never seen them and do not understand them in our minds.

We must guard against "Pharisee-ism" in our hearts and attitudes. If the truth were known, the church today is full of Pharisees. I used to be one of them. In fact, I was a chief Pharisee. I was rigid, legalistic, boring, out to impress others, humorless, critical, and judgmental. I was on my way to heaven, but I was not enjoying the trip.

We need to stop being so rigid. Jesus was sent into this world, not to bind us up, but to set us free. We need to be free to laugh, enjoy life, love people, and not be afraid to step out and try new things.

Now, I do not mean we are to go through life trying to see how ridiculous we can act. I am not talking about weirdness and fanaticism; I am talking about freedom and joy. I am talking about freely following the leading of the Holy Spirit. Go ahead, laugh a little. God will not be offended; He wants you to be joyful!

PSALM 127
A Song of ᶜAscents. Of Solomon.

EXCEPT THE Lord builds the house, they labor in vain who build it; except the Lord keeps the city, the watchman wakes but in vain. [Ps. 121:1, 3, 5.]
2 It is vain for you to rise up early, to take rest late, to eat the bread of [anxious] toil—for He gives [blessings] to His beloved in sleep.
3 Behold, children are a heritage from the Lord, the fruit of the womb a reward. [Deut. 28:4.]
4 As arrows are in the hand of a warrior, so are the children of one's youth.

c See Psalm 120 title footnote.

life point

According to Psalm 127:1, unless the Lord builds the house, those who build it labor in vain. We may be able to build, but what we build will not last if God is not involved in it. He is our Partner in life, and as such, He desires to be a part of everything we do. God is interested in every facet of our lives. Believing that truth is the beginning of an exciting journey with Him.

5 Happy, blessed, *and* fortunate is the man whose quiver is filled with them! They will not be put to shame when they speak with their adversaries [in gatherings] at the [city's] gate.

PSALM 128
A Song of [d]Ascents.

BLESSED (HAPPY, fortunate, to be envied) is everyone who fears, reveres, *and* worships the Lord, who walks in His ways *and* lives according to His commandments. [Ps. 1:1, 2.]

2 For you shall eat [the fruit] of the labor of your hands; happy (blessed, fortunate, enviable) shall you be, and it shall be well with you.

3 Your wife shall be like a fruitful vine in the innermost parts of your house; your children shall be like olive plants round about your table.

4 Behold, thus shall the man be blessed who reverently *and* worshipfully fears the Lord.

5 May the Lord bless you out of Zion [His sanctuary], and may you see the prosperity of Jerusalem all the days of your life;

6 Yes, may you see your children's children. Peace be upon Israel!

PSALM 129
A Song of [d]Ascents.

MANY A time *and* much have they afflicted me from my youth up—let Israel now say—

2 Many a time *and* much have they afflicted me from my youth up, yet they have not prevailed against me.

3 The plowers plowed upon my back; they made long their furrows.

4 The Lord is [uncompromisingly] righteous; He has cut asunder the thick cords by which the wicked [enslaved us].

5 Let them all be put to shame and turned backward who hate Zion.

6 Let them be as the grass upon the housetops, which withers before it grows up,

7 With which the mower fills not his hand, nor the binder of sheaves his bosom—

8 While those who go by do not say, The blessing of the Lord be upon you! We bless you in the name of the Lord!

PSALM 130
A Song of [d]Ascents.

OUT OF the depths have I cried to You, O Lord.

2 Lord, hear my voice; let Your ears be attentive to the voice of my supplications.

3 If You, Lord, should keep account of *and* treat [us according to our] sins, O Lord, who could stand? [Ps. 143:2; Rom. 3:20; Gal. 2:16.]

4 But there is forgiveness with You [just what man needs], that You may be reverently feared *and* worshiped. [Deut. 10:12.]

d See Psalm 120 title footnote.

5 I wait for the Lord, I expectantly wait, and in His word do I hope.

6 I am looking *and* waiting for the Lord more than watchmen for the morning, I say, more than watchmen for the morning.

7 O Israel, hope in the Lord! For with the Lord there is mercy *and* loving-kindness, and with Him is plenteous redemption.

8 And He will redeem Israel from all their iniquities.

PSALM 131
A Song of ᵉAscents. Of David.

LORD, MY heart is not haughty, nor my eyes lofty; neither do I exercise myself in matters too great or in things too wonderful for me.

2 Surely I have calmed and quieted my soul; like a weaned child with his mother, like a weaned child is my soul within me [ceased from fretting].

3 O Israel, hope in the Lord from this time forth and forever.

PSALM 132
A Song of ᵉAscents.

LORD, [earnestly] remember to David's credit all his humiliations *and* hardships *and* endurance—

2 How he swore to the Lord and vowed to the Mighty One of Jacob:

3 Surely I will not enter my dwelling house or get into my bed—

4 I will not permit my eyes to sleep *or* my eyelids to slumber,

5 Until I have found a place for the Lord, a habitation for the Mighty One of Jacob. [Acts 7:46.]

6 Behold, at Ephratah we [first] heard of [the discovered ark]; we found it in the fields of the wood [at Kiriath-jearim]. [I Sam. 6:21.]

7 Let us go into His tabernacle; let us worship at His footstool.

8 Arise, O Lord, to Your resting-place, You and the ark [the symbol] of Your strength.

9 Let Your priests be clothed with righteousness (right living and right standing with God); and let Your saints shout for joy!

10 For Your servant David's sake, turn not away the face of Your anointed *and* reject not Your own king.

11 The Lord swore to David in truth; He will not turn back from it: One of the fruit of your body I will set upon your throne. [Ps. 89:3, 4; Luke 1:69; Acts 2:30, 31.]

12 If your children will keep My covenant and My testimony that I shall teach them, their children also shall sit upon your throne forever.

13 For the Lord has chosen Zion, He has desired it for His habitation:

14 This is My resting-place forever [says the Lord]; here will I dwell, for I have desired it.

15 I will surely *and* abundantly bless her provision; I will satisfy her poor with bread.

16 Her priests also will I clothe with salvation, and her saints shall shout aloud for joy.

17 There will I make a horn spring forth *and* bud for David; I have ordained *and* prepared a lamp for My anointed [fulfilling the promises of

speak the Word

Lord, I wait for You, and in Your Word I do hope.
ADAPTED FROM PSALM 130:5

e See Psalm 120 title footnote.

old]. [I Kings 11:36; 15:4; II Chron. 21:7; Luke 1:69.]

18 His enemies will I clothe with shame, but upon himself shall his crown flourish.

PSALM 133
A Song of ᶠAscents. Of David.

BEHOLD, HOW good and how pleasant it is for brethren to dwell together in unity!

2 It is like the precious ointment poured on the head, that ran down on the beard, even the beard of Aaron [the first high priest], that came down upon the collar *and* skirts of his garments [consecrating the whole body]. [Exod. 30:25, 30.]

3 It is like the dew of [lofty] Mount Hermon and the dew that comes on the hills of Zion; for there the Lord has commanded the blessing, even life forevermore [upon the high and the lowly].

PSALM 134
A Song of ᶠAscents.

BEHOLD, BLESS (affectionately and gratefully praise) the Lord, all you servants of the Lord, [singers] who by night stand in the house of the Lord. [I Chron. 9:33.]

2 Lift up your hands in holiness *and* to the sanctuary and bless the Lord [affectionately and gratefully praise Him]!

3 The Lord bless you out of Zion, even He Who made heaven and earth.

PSALM 135

PRAISE THE Lord! (Hallelujah!) Praise the name of the Lord; praise Him, O you servants of the Lord!

2 You who stand in the house of the Lord, in the courts of the house of our God,

3 Praise the Lord! For the Lord is good; sing praises to His name, for He is gracious *and* lovely!

4 For the Lord has chosen [the descendants of] Jacob for Himself, Israel for His peculiar possession *and* treasure. [Deut. 7:6.]

5 For I know that the Lord is great and that our Lord is above all gods.

6 Whatever the Lord pleases, that has He done in the heavens and on earth, in the seas and all deeps—

7 Who causes the vapors to arise from the ends of the earth, Who makes lightnings for the rain, Who brings the wind out of His storehouses;

8 Who smote the firstborn of Egypt, both of man and beast; [Exod. 12:12, 29; Ps. 78:51; 136:10.]

9 Who sent signs and wonders into the midst of you, O Egypt, upon Pharaoh and all his servants;

10 Who smote nations many *and* great and slew mighty kings—

11 Sihon king of the Amorites, Og king of Bashan, and all the kingdoms of Canaan.

12 [The Lord] gave their land as a heritage, a heritage to Israel His people.

13 Your name, O Lord, endures forever, Your fame, O Lord, throughout all ages.

14 For the Lord will judge *and* vindicate His people, and He will delay His judgments [manifesting His righteousness and mercy] *and* take into favor His servants [those who meet His terms of separation unto Him]. [Heb. 10:30.]

15 The idols of the nations are silver and gold, the work of men's hands.

16 [Idols] have mouths, but they speak not; eyes have they, but they see not;

ᶠ See Psalm 120 title footnote.

getting rid of "what if"

Our oldest son, David, and his wife once needed a place to live temporarily. They had just sold their mobile home, and their newly purchased house would not be ready for a month. Of course, my husband and I invited them to live with us, even though I was a bit wary. My son and I are alike in many ways—we are both strong-willed, which does not always mix well in close quarters. Nothing negative had happened between us, but in anticipation of this move my mind kept coming up with "what-ifs."

My husband and I would be driving down the road, and my mouth would want to start talking about negative things that could take place: "What if there is no hot water left for my shower in the morning after everyone else is finished? What if they leave messes for me to clean up?" David and his wife had not even moved in, and nothing bad had yet happened, but my mouth wanted to declare disaster ahead of time.

Satan wanted me to prophesy my future. He wanted me to be critical of the situation in advance.

If the devil can get us to be negative, he can provide us with negative circumstances. Often we call for our own problems. We "call those things which be not as though they were" (see Romans 4:17), only we do it in the negative sense by sowing negative seeds.

Look at it this way: My blender works regardless of what is placed in it. If I put ice cream and milk in it, I will get a milk shake. If I put in water and dirt, I will get mud. The blender works. It is created to work. It is up to me to decide what I will put in it. What I put in is what I will get out. The same is true with our minds and hearts and mouths. What goes in is what is going to come out—for good or for bad.

Our son and daughter-in-law did live with us for a month, and everything worked out fine. I knew enough biblical principles by then to resist the temptation to complain in advance, and I urge you to beware of this temptation also. When I was tempted to speak negative words, I would choose to say, "This will work out fine. I am sure everyone will cooperate and be sensitive to the needs of the others."

My son and I made a joke about our challenge of getting along for thirty days under the same roof. We both like to be right, so he said, "I'll tell you what, Mom. Let's take turns being right. During the thirty days we are together, you can be right fifteen days, and I will be right fifteen days." We both laughed and had a good time. But the point is that I learned to discard "what if" and accepted the blessing of pleasant unity in my home (see Psalm 133:1).

17 They have ears, but they hear not, nor is there any breath in their mouths. **18** Those who make [idols] are like them; so is everyone who trusts in *and* relies on them. [Ps. 115:4-8.] **19** Bless (affectionately and gratefully praise) the Lord, O house of Israel; bless the Lord, O house of Aaron [God's ministers]. **20** Bless the Lord, O house of Levi [the dedicated tribe]; you who reverently *and* worshipfully fear the Lord, bless the Lord [affectionately and gratefully praise Him]! [Deut. 6:5; Ps. 31:23.] **21** Blessed out of Zion be the Lord, Who dwells [with us] at Jerusalem! Praise the Lord! (Hallelujah!)

PSALM 136

O GIVE thanks to the Lord, for He is good; for His mercy *and* loving-kindness endure forever. **2** O give thanks to the God of gods, for His mercy *and* loving-kindness endure forever. **3** O give thanks to the Lord of lords, for His mercy *and* loving-kindness endure forever— **4** To Him Who alone does great wonders, for His mercy *and* loving-kindness endure forever; **5** To Him Who by wisdom *and* understanding made the heavens, for His mercy *and* loving-kindness endure forever; **6** To Him Who stretched out the earth upon the waters, for His mercy *and* loving-kindness endure forever; **7** To Him Who made the great lights, for His mercy *and* loving-kindness endure forever—

8 The sun to rule over the day, for His mercy *and* loving-kindness endure forever; **9** The moon and stars to rule by night, for His mercy *and* loving-kindness endure forever; **10** To Him Who smote Egypt in their firstborn, for His mercy *and* loving-kindness endure forever; [Exod. 12:29.] **11** And brought out Israel from among them, for His mercy *and* loving-kindness endure forever; [Exod. 12:51; 13:3, 17.] **12** With a strong hand and with an outstretched arm, for His mercy *and* loving-kindness endure forever; **13** To Him Who divided the Red Sea into parts, for His mercy *and* loving-kindness endure forever; [Exod. 14:21, 22.] **14** And made Israel to pass through the midst of it, for His mercy *and* loving-kindness endure forever; **15** But shook off *and* overthrew Pharaoh and his host into the Red Sea, for His mercy *and* loving-kindness endure forever; **16** To Him Who led His people through the wilderness, for His mercy *and* loving-kindness endure forever; **17** To Him Who smote great kings, for His mercy *and* loving-kindness endure forever; **18** And slew famous kings, for His mercy *and* loving-kindness endure forever—[Deut. 29:7.] **19** Sihon king of the Amorites, for His mercy *and* loving-kindness endure forever; [Num. 21:21-24.] **20** And Og king of Bashan, for His mercy *and* loving-kindness endure forever; [Num. 21:33-35.] **21** And gave their land as a heritage,

speak the Word

Thank You, Lord, that Your hand is strong and Your arm is outstretched toward me.
ADAPTED FROM PSALM 136:12

for His mercy *and* loving-kindness endure forever;
22 Even a heritage to Israel His servant, for His mercy *and* loving-kindness endure forever; [Josh. 12:1.]
23 To Him Who [earnestly] remembered us in our low estate *and* imprinted us [on His heart], for His mercy *and* loving-kindness endure forever;
24 And rescued us from our enemies, for His mercy *and* loving-kindness endure forever;
25 To Him Who gives food to all flesh, for His mercy *and* loving-kindness endure forever;
26 O give thanks to the God of heaven, for His mercy *and* loving-kindness endure forever!

PSALM 137

BY THE rivers of Babylon, there we [captives] sat down, yes, we wept when we [earnestly] remembered Zion [the city of our God imprinted on our hearts].
2 On the willow trees in the midst of [Babylon] we hung our harps.
3 For there they who led us captive required of us a song with words, and our tormentors *and* they who wasted us required of us mirth, saying, Sing us one of the songs of Zion.
4 How shall we sing the Lord's song in a strange land?
5 If I forget you, O Jerusalem, let my right hand forget its skill [with the harp].
6 Let my tongue cleave to the roof of my mouth if I remember you not, if I prefer not Jerusalem above my chief joy! [Ezek. 3:26.]
7 Remember, O Lord, against the Edomites, that they said in the day of Jerusalem's fall, Down, down to the ground with her!
8 O Daughter of Babylon [you devastator, you!], who [ought to be and] shall be destroyed, happy *and* blessed shall

he be who requites you as you have served us. [Isa. 13:1-22; Jer. 25:12, 13.]
9 Happy *and* blessed shall he be who takes and dashes your little ones against the rock!

PSALM 138
[A Psalm] of David.

I WILL confess *and* praise You [O God] with my whole heart; before the gods will I sing praises to You.
2 I will worship toward Your holy temple and praise Your name for Your loving-kindness and for Your truth *and* faithfulness; for You have exalted above all else Your name and Your word *and* You have magnified Your word above all Your name!
3 In the day when I called, You answered me; and You strengthened me with strength (might and inflexibility to temptation) in my inner self.
4 All the kings of the land shall give You credit *and* praise You, O Lord, for they have heard of the promises of Your mouth [which were fulfilled].
5 Yes, they shall sing of the ways of the Lord *and* joyfully celebrate His mighty acts, for great is the glory of the Lord.
6 For though the Lord is high, yet has He respect to the lowly [bringing them into fellowship with Him]; but the proud *and* haughty He knows *and* recognizes [only] at a distance. [Prov. 3:34; James 4:6; I Pet. 5:5.]
7 Though I walk in the midst of trouble, You will revive me; You will stretch forth Your hand against the wrath of my enemies, and Your right hand will save me. [Ps. 23:3, 4.]
8 The Lord will perfect that which concerns me; Your mercy *and* loving-kindness, O Lord, endure forever—forsake not the works of Your own hands. [Ps. 57:2; Phil. 1:6.]

PSALM 139
To the Chief Musician.
A Psalm of David.

O LORD, you have searched me [thoroughly] and have known me.

2 You know my downsitting and my uprising; You understand my thought afar off. [Matt. 9:4; John 2:24, 25.]

3 You sift *and* search out my path and my lying down, and You are acquainted with all my ways.

4 For there is not a word in my tongue [still unuttered], but, behold, O Lord, You know it altogether. [Heb. 4:13.]

5 You have beset me *and* shut me in—behind and before, and You have laid Your hand upon me.

6 Your [infinite] knowledge is too wonderful for me; it is high above me, I cannot reach it.

7 Where could I go from Your Spirit? Or where could I flee from Your presence?

8 If I ascend up into heaven, You are there; if I make my bed in Sheol (the place of the dead), behold, You are there. [Rom. 11:33.]

9 If I take the wings of the morning or dwell in the uttermost parts of the sea,

10 Even there shall Your hand lead me, and Your right hand shall hold me.

11 If I say, Surely the darkness shall cover me and the night shall be [the only] light about me,

12 Even the darkness hides nothing from You, but the night shines as the day; the darkness and the light are both alike to You. [Dan. 2:22.]

13 For You did form my inward parts; You did knit me together in my mother's womb.

14 I will confess *and* praise You *for You are fearful and wonderful and* for the awful wonder of my birth! Wonderful are Your works, and that my inner self knows right well.

15 My frame was not hidden from You when I was being formed in secret [and] intricately *and* curiously wrought [as if embroidered with various colors] in the depths of the earth [a region of darkness and mystery].

16 Your eyes saw my unformed substance, and in Your book all the days [of my life] were written before ever they took shape, when as yet there was none of them.

17 How precious *and* weighty also are Your thoughts to me, O God! How vast is the sum of them! [Ps. 40:5.]

18 If I could count them, they would be more in number than the sand. When I awoke, [could I count to the end] I would still be with You.

19 If You would [only] slay the wicked, O God, and the men of blood depart from me—[Isa. 11:4.]

20 Who speak against You wickedly, Your enemies who take Your name in vain! [Jude 15.]

21 Do I not hate them, O Lord, who hate You? And am I not grieved *and* do I not loathe those who rise up against You?

22 I hate them with perfect hatred; they have become my enemies.

23 Search me [thoroughly], O God, and know my heart! Try me and know my thoughts!

24 And see if there is any wicked *or* hurtful way in me, and lead me in the way everlasting.

speak the Word

Lord, I declare that You will perfect that which concerns me!
ADAPTED FROM PSALM **138:8**

God's good plan

God's plan for our lives has been established in the spiritual realm since before the foundation of the earth, and it is a good plan, as we see in Jeremiah 29:11: "For I know the thoughts and plans that I have for you, says the Lord, thoughts and plans for welfare and peace and not for evil, to give you hope in your final outcome."

Psalm 139:16 tells us that before we were even born, God had planned our days. However, Satan has worked hard to destroy the Lord's good plan in many of us, and he has had a high success rate.

God sent His Son, Jesus, to redeem us and to restore all things to proper order. He has written down His will for our lives, and as we believe it and confess it, it literally begins to become reality.

Some people believe for a great number of things but see very little manifestation of them. Perhaps the reason is because they are believing but not speaking. They may see some results of their faith, but not the radical results they would experience if they would bring their mouths along with their hearts into God's service (see Romans 10:9, 10).

Some people are trying to live in the blessings of the Lord while still talking like the devil. We must not make that mistake. We will not see positive results in our daily lives if we speak negative things. We should remember that what we are speaking, we are calling for. We are reaching into the spiritual realm and drawing out *something* according to our words. We can reach into Satan's realm, the realm of curses, and draw out evil, negative things, or we can reach into God's realm, the realm of blessings, and draw out good, positive things. Words are like containers; they carry creative or destructive power.

The choice is up to us.

PSALM 140
To the Chief Musician. A Psalm of David.

DELIVER ME, O Lord, from evil men; preserve me from violent men;

2 They devise mischiefs in their heart; continually they gather together *and* stir up wars.

3 They sharpen their tongues like a serpent's; adders' poison is under their lips. Selah [pause, and calmly think of that]! [Rom. 3:13.]

4 Keep me, O Lord, from the hands of the wicked; preserve me from the violent men who have purposed to thrust aside my steps.

5 The proud have hidden a snare for me; they have spread cords as a net by the wayside, they have set traps for me. Selah [pause, and calmly think of that]!

6 I said to the Lord, You are my God; give ear to the voice of my supplications, O Lord.

7 O God the Lord, the Strength of my salvation, You have covered my head in the day of battle.

8 Grant not, O Lord, the desires of the wicked; further not their wicked plot *and* device, lest they exalt themselves. Selah [pause, and calmly think of that]!

9 Those who are fencing me in raise their heads; may the mischief of their own lips *and* the very things they desire for me come upon them.

10 Let burning coals fall upon them; let them be cast into the fire, into floods of water *or* deep water pits, from which they shall not rise.

11 Let not a man of slanderous tongue be established in the earth; let evil hunt the violent man to overthrow him [let calamity follow his evildoings].

12 I know *and* rest in confidence upon it that the Lord will maintain the cause of the afflicted, and will secure justice for the poor *and* needy [of His believing children].

13 Surely the [uncompromisingly] righteous shall give thanks to Your name; the upright shall dwell in Your presence (before Your very face).

PSALM 141
A Psalm of David.

LORD, I call upon You; hasten to me. Give ear to my voice when I cry to You.

2 Let my prayer be set forth as incense before You, the lifting up of my hands as the evening sacrifice. [I Tim. 2:8; Rev. 8:3, 4.]

3 Set a guard, O Lord, before my mouth; keep watch at the door of my lips.

4 Incline my heart not to submit *or* consent to any evil thing or to be occupied in deeds of wickedness with men who work iniquity; and let me not eat of their dainties.

5 Let the righteous man smite and correct me—it is a kindness. Oil so choice let not my head refuse *or* discourage; for even in their evils *or*

---

calamities shall my prayer continue. [Prov. 9:8; 19:25; 25:12; Gal. 6:1.]

6 When their rulers are overthrown in stony places, [their followers] shall hear my words, that they are sweet (pleasant, mild, and just).

7 The unburied bones [of slaughtered rulers] shall lie scattered at the mouth of Sheol, [as unregarded] as the lumps of soil behind the plowman when he breaks open the ground. [II Cor. 1:9.]

8 But my eyes are toward You, O God the Lord; in You do I trust *and* take refuge; pour not out my life *nor* leave it destitute *and* bare.

9 Keep me from the trap which they have laid for me, and the snares of evildoers.

10 Let the wicked fall together into their own nets, while I pass over them *and* escape.

PSALM 142
A skillful song, *or* a didactic *or* reflective poem, of David; when he was in the cave. A Prayer.

I CRY to the Lord with my voice; with my voice to the Lord do I make supplication.

2 I pour out my complaint before Him; I tell before Him my trouble.

3 When my spirit was overwhelmed *and* fainted [throwing all its weight] upon me, then You knew my path. In the way where I walk they have hidden a snare for me.

when your mouth gets you in trouble

I pray Psalm 141:3 often because I know that I need help with my mouth on a daily basis. I want the Holy Spirit to convict me when I am talking too much, when I am saying things I should not, when I am speaking negatively, when I am complaining, when I am sounding harsh or engaging in any other kinds of "evil speaking."

Anything that offends God in our conversation needs to be eliminated. That is why we need to pray continually: "Set a guard, O Lord, before my mouth; keep watch at the door of my lips."

Another scripture on the importance of watching what we say is Psalm 17:3: "I have purposed that my mouth shall not transgress." This says we need to plan to keep our mouths from speaking bad or negative things. We *purpose* not to speak them. Whatever we do in this life of faith, we must do it on purpose. Discipline is a choice. It is not necessarily easy, but it begins with a quality decision. During difficult times when the storm is raging, we will need to purpose to keep our mouths from transgressing.

A third scripture that I pray regularly on this subject is Psalm 19:14: "Let the words of my mouth and the meditation of my heart be acceptable in Your sight, O Lord, my [firm, impenetrable] Rock and my Redeemer."

Are you having difficulty with your mouth? Pray the Word. It is God's Word that carries the power of the Holy Spirit. Let these scriptures be the cry of your heart. Be sincere in your desire to gain victory in this area, and as you seek God for His help, you will begin to notice that you are changing. This is what the Lord has done for me, and He can do it for you too; He is no respecter of persons (see Acts 10:34). All those who follow God-ordained guidelines get God-ordained results.

Pray this prayer of commitment to exercise control over your mouth: "Lord, I pray that You will help me to develop sensitivity to the Holy Spirit concerning all manner of my conversation. I do not want to be stubborn like a horse or mule that will not obey without a bridle and bit. I want to move in Your direction with only a gentle nudge from You. Place a guard over my lips and let all the words of my mouth be acceptable in Your sight, O Lord, my Strength and my Redeemer. In Jesus' name I pray, amen."

4 Look on the right hand [the point of attack] and see; for there is no man who knows me [to appear for me]. Refuge has failed me *and* I have no way to flee; no man cares for my life *or* my welfare.

5 I cried to You, O Lord; I said, You are my refuge, my portion in the land of the living.

6 Attend to my loud cry, for I am brought very low; deliver me from my persecutors, for they are stronger than I.

7 Bring my life out of prison, that I

may confess, praise, *and* give thanks to Your name; the righteous will surround me *and* crown themselves because of me, for You will deal bountifully with me.

PSALM 143
A Psalm of David.

HEAR MY prayer, O Lord, give ear to my supplications! In Your faithfulness answer me, and in Your righteousness.

2 And enter not into judgment with Your servant, for in Your sight no man living is [in himself] righteous *or* justified. [Ps. 130:3; Rom. 3:20-26; Gal. 2:16.]

3 For the enemy has pursued *and* persecuted my soul, he has crushed my life down to the ground; he has made me to dwell in dark places as those who have been long dead.

4 Therefore is my spirit overwhelmed *and* faints within me [wrapped in gloom]; my heart within my bosom grows numb.

5 I remember the days of old; I meditate on all Your doings; I ponder the work of Your hands.

6 I spread forth my hands to You; my soul thirsts after You like a thirsty land [for water]. Selah [pause, and calmly think of that]!

7 Answer me speedily, O Lord, for my spirit fails; hide not Your face from me, lest I become like those who go down into the pit (the grave).

8 Cause me to hear Your lovingkindness in the morning, for on You do I lean *and* in You do I trust. Cause me to know the way wherein I should walk, for I lift up my inner self to You.

speak the Word

life point

David's response to his feelings of depression and gloom was not to meditate on his problem. Instead, he literally came against the problem by *choosing* to remember the good times of past days—pondering the doings of God and the works of His hands (see Psalm 143:5). In other words, he thought about something good, and it helped him overcome his battle of depression.

Never forget this: *your mind plays an important role in your victory.*

I know it is the power of the Holy Spirit working through the Word of God that brings victory into our lives. But a large part of the work that needs to be done is for us to line up our thinking with God and His Word. If we refuse to do this or choose to think it is unimportant, we will never experience victory. But we will win if we discipline ourselves to meditate on the good things God has done.

9 Deliver me, O Lord, from my enemies; I flee to You to hide me.

10 Teach me to do Your will, for You are my God; let Your good Spirit lead me into a level country *and* into the land of uprightness.

11 Save my life, O Lord, for Your name's sake; in Your righteousness, bring my life out of trouble *and* free me from distress.

12 And in your mercy *and* lovingkindness, cut off my enemies and destroy all those who afflict my inner self, for I am Your servant.

Thank You, God, for dealing bountifully with me.
ADAPTED FROM PSALM 142:7

a biblical prescription for depression

Psalm 143:3–10 gives a description of depression and how to overcome it. Let's look at this passage in detail to see the steps we can take to defeat this attack of the enemy:

Psalm 143:3: *Identify the nature and cause of the problem*. David says he feels as if he is dwelling in "dark places as those who have been long dead." This certainly sounds to me like a description of someone who is depressed. I believe that the source of the depression described here is our enemy, Satan, who attacks the soul.

Psalm 143:4: *Recognize that depression steals life and light.* Depression oppresses a person's spiritual freedom and power. Our spirits (empowered and encouraged by God's Spirit) are powerful and free. Therefore, Satan seeks to oppress our spirits' power and liberty by filling our minds with darkness and gloom. Please realize that it is vital to resist the feeling called "depression" immediately when we begin to sense it. The longer it is allowed to remain, the harder it becomes to resist.

Psalm 143:5: *Remember the good times*. In this verse we see David's response to his condition. Remembering, meditating, and pondering are all functions of the mind. He obviously knows that his thoughts will affect his feelings, so he gets busy thinking about the kinds of things that will help overcome the attack upon his mind. He thinks about God and the good things He does.

Psalm 143:6: *Praise the Lord in the midst of the problem*. David knows the importance of praise; he lifts his hands in worship. He declares what his need truly is: He needs God. Far too often when people get depressed, it is because they are in need of something, and they seek it in the wrong place, which only adds to their problems. God alone can water a thirsty soul. Do not be deceived into thinking that anything else can satisfy you fully and completely. Chasing after the wrong thing will always leave you disappointed, and disappointment opens the door to depression.

Psalm 143:7: *Ask for God's help*. David asks for help. He is basically saying, "Hurry up, God, because I am not going to be able to hold on very much longer without You."

Psalm 143:8: *Listen to the Lord*. David knows that he needs to hear from God. He needs to be assured of God's love and kindness. He needs God's attention and direction.

Psalm 143:9: *Pray for deliverance*. Once again David declares that only God can help him. Please notice that throughout this discourse, he keeps his mind on God and not on the problem.

Psalm 143:10: *Seek God's wisdom, knowledge, and leadership*. Perhaps David is indicating that he has gotten out of the will of God and thus opened the door to the attack on his soul. He wants to be in God's will because he realizes that it is the only safe place to be. Then he requests that God help him to be stable. He wants his unsettled emotions to be level—not up and down.

I encourage you to meditate on God's Word and apply its principles to your life. Let it bring you freedom and peace.

life point

What is David doing in Psalm 143:5–8? He is crying out to God for help. When you and I feel ourselves sinking into the pit of depression, we can do what David did here. We can remember the days of old. We can meditate on all of the Lord's doings on our behalf. We can ponder the mighty works of His hands. We can spread forth our hands in prayer and supplication to Him. We can call upon Him to answer us speedily because we are leaning on and trusting in Him. We can lift up our souls, our inner beings, to Him.

All these things constitute an act of faith, and the Lord has promised to always respond to faith. If we are under a minor attack, it may take only a few hours or days. But if we are under a major attack, it may take much longer. However long it may be, we must stand firm and continue to cry out to God, receiving the help and encouragement that only He can give. We need to be confident that the Lord will deliver us, just as He delivered David from all his woes.

PSALM 144
[A Psalm] of David.

BLESSED BE the Lord, my Rock *and* my keen *and* firm Strength, Who teaches my hands to war and my fingers to fight—
2 My Steadfast Love and my Fortress, my High Tower and my Deliverer, my Shield and He in Whom I trust *and* take refuge, Who subdues my people under me.
3 Lord, what is man that You take notice of him? Or [the] son of man that You take account of him? [Job 7:17; Ps. 8:4; Heb. 2:6.]

life point

In the final verses of Psalm 143, David calls upon the Lord to deliver him from his enemies because he has run to Him for help and protection. He asks the Lord to teach him His will and to let His Spirit lead him into a "level country."

I believe that what David was asking for when he spoke of a level country was balanced emotions. Secure in who he was and in Whose he was, David was able to place himself into the hands of the Lord. David allowed God to bring his life out of trouble, free him from distress, punish his enemies, and cause him to win the victory over all those who were afflicting his soul, because he belonged to the Lord.

You and I are to place ourselves in God's hands. We need to withstand the devil's attempts to drag us down into the depths of depression and despair by allowing God to move on our behalf to win our victory.

4 Man is like vanity *and* a breath; his days are as a shadow that passes away.
5 Bow Your heavens, O Lord, and come down; touch the mountains, and they shall smoke.
6 Cast forth lightning and scatter [my enemies]; send out Your arrows and embarrass *and* frustrate them.
7 Stretch forth Your hand from above; rescue me and deliver me out of great waters, from the hands of hostile aliens (tribes around us)
8 Whose mouths speak deceit and whose right hands are right hands [raised in taking] fraudulent oaths.
9 I will sing a new song to You, O God; upon a harp, an instrument of ten strings, will I offer praises to You.
10 You are He Who gives salvation to

life point

In the opening verses of Psalm 144, David praises the Lord with strong, compelling words—Rock, Fortress, High Tower, and more. The Lord subdued his enemies under him, but David also did his part. We must always remember that we are partners with God. God has a part, and we have a part. We cannot do God's part, and He will not do our part. In verse 1, David said the Lord taught his hands to war and his fingers to fight. This is the key to conquering depression. We must do what David did. We must recognize depression, submit it to the Lord, call upon Him for His help, and then fight that depression in the strength and power of the Holy Spirit.

How do we fight depression? By spending time with God, by praying, and by speaking His Word. We also fight by lifting our eyes, heads, hands, and hearts and offering the sacrifice of praise and thanksgiving to the Lord, our Rock and Strength, our Steadfast Love and Fortress, our High Tower and Deliverer, our Shield and the One in Whom we trust and take refuge, the One Who subdues our enemies under us.

kings, Who rescues David His servant from the hurtful sword [of evil].

11 Rescue me and deliver me out of the power of [hostile] alien [tribes] whose mouths speak deceit and whose right hands are right hands [raised in taking] fraudulent oaths.

12 When our sons shall be as plants grown large in their youth and our daughters as sculptured corner pillars hewn like those of a palace;

13 When our garners are full, affording all manner of store, and our sheep bring forth thousands and ten thousands in our pastures;

14 When our oxen are well loaded; when there is no invasion [of hostile armies] and no going forth [against besiegers—when there is no murder or manslaughter] and no outcry in our streets;

15 Happy and blessed are the people who are in such a case; yes, happy (blessed, fortunate, prosperous, to be envied) are the people whose God is the Lord!

PSALM 145

[A Psalm] of praise. Of David.

I WILL extol You, my God, O King; and I will bless Your name forever and ever [with grateful, affectionate praise].

2 Every day [with its new reasons] will I bless You [affectionately and gratefully praise You]; yes, I will praise Your name forever and ever.

3 Great is the Lord and highly to be praised; and His greatness is [so vast and deep as to be] unsearchable. [Job 5:9; 9:10; Rom. 11:33.]

4 One generation shall laud Your works to another and shall declare Your mighty acts.

5 On the glorious splendor of Your majesty and on Your wondrous works I will meditate.

6 Men shall speak of the might of Your tremendous and terrible acts, and I will declare Your greatness.

7 They shall pour forth [like a fountain] the fame of Your great and abundant goodness and shall sing aloud of Your rightness and justice.

8 The Lord is gracious and full of compassion, slow to anger and abounding in mercy and loving-kindness.

9 The Lord is good to all, and His tender mercies are over all His works [the entirety of things created].

10 All Your works shall praise You, O Lord, and Your loving ones shall bless

You [affectionately and gratefully shall Your saints confess and praise You]!

11 They shall speak of the glory of Your kingdom and talk of Your power,

12 To make known to the sons of men God's mighty deeds and the glorious majesty of His kingdom.

13 Your kingdom is an everlasting kingdom, and Your dominion endures throughout all generations.

14 The Lord upholds all those [of His own] who are falling and raises up all those who are bowed down.

15 The eyes of all wait for You [looking, watching, and expecting] and You give them their food in due season.

16 You open Your hand and satisfy every living thing with favor.

17 The Lord is [rigidly] righteous in all His ways and gracious and merciful in all His works.

18 The Lord is near to all who call upon Him, to all who call upon Him sincerely and in truth.

19 He will fulfill the desires of those who reverently and worshipfully fear Him; He also will hear their cry and will save them.

20 The Lord preserves all those who love Him, but all the wicked will He destroy.

21 My mouth shall speak the praise of the Lord; and let all flesh bless (affectionately and gratefully praise) His holy name forever and ever.

PSALM 146

PRAISE THE Lord! (Hallelujah!) Praise the Lord, O my soul!

2 While I live will I praise the Lord; I will sing praises to my God while I have any being.

3 Put not your trust in princes, in a son of man, in whom there is no help.

4 When his breath leaves him, he returns to his earth; in that very day his [previous] thoughts, plans, and purposes perish. [I Cor. 2:6.]

5 Happy (blessed, fortunate, enviable) is he who has the God of [special revelation to] Jacob for his help, whose hope is in the Lord his God, [Gen. 32:30.]

6 Who made heaven and earth, the sea, and all that is in them, Who keeps truth and is faithful forever,

7 Who executes justice for the oppressed, Who gives food to the hungry. The Lord sets free the prisoners,

8 The Lord opens the eyes of the blind, the Lord lifts up those who are bowed down, the Lord loves the [uncompromisingly] righteous (those upright in heart and in right standing with Him). [Luke 13:13; John 9:7, 32.]

9 The Lord protects and preserves the strangers and temporary residents, He upholds the fatherless and the widow and sets them upright, but the way of the wicked He makes crooked (turns upside down and brings to ruin).

10 The Lord shall reign forever, even Your God, O Zion, from generation to generation. Praise the Lord! (Hallelujah!) [Ps. 10:16; Rev. 11:15.]

PSALM 147

PRAISE THE Lord! For it is good to sing praises to our God, for He is gracious and lovely; praise is becoming and appropriate.

2 The Lord is building up Jerusalem; He is gathering together the exiles of Israel.

3 He heals the brokenhearted and binds up their wounds [curing their

speak the Word

pains and their sorrows]. [Ps. 34:18; Isa. 57:15; 61:1; Luke 4:18.]

4 He determines *and* counts the number of the stars; He calls them all by their names.

5 Great is our Lord and of great power; His understanding is inexhaustible *and* boundless.

6 The Lord lifts up the humble *and* downtrodden; He casts the wicked down to the ground.

7 Sing to the Lord with thanksgiving; sing praises with the harp *or* the lyre to our God!—

8 Who covers the heavens with clouds, Who prepares rain for the earth, Who makes grass to grow on the mountains.

9 He gives to the beast his food, and to the young ravens that for which they cry.

10 He delights not in the strength of the horse, nor does He take pleasure in the legs of a man.

11 The Lord takes pleasure in those who reverently *and* worshipfully fear Him, in those who hope in His mercy *and* loving-kindness. [Ps. 145:20.]

12 Praise the Lord, O Jerusalem! Praise your God, O Zion!

13 For He has strengthened and made hard the bars of your gates, and He has blessed your children within you.

14 He makes peace in your borders; He fills you with the finest of the wheat.

15 He sends forth His commandment to the earth; His word runs very swiftly.

16 He gives [to the earth] snow like [a blanket of] wool; He scatters the hoarfrost like ashes.

17 He casts forth His ice like crumbs; who can stand before His cold?

18 He sends out His word, and melts [ice and snow]; He causes His wind to blow, and the waters flow.

19 He declares His word to Jacob, His statutes and His ordinances to Israel. [Mal. 4:4.]

20 He has not dealt so with any [other] nation; they have not known (understood, appreciated, given heed to, and cherished) His ordinances. Praise the Lord! (Hallelujah!) [Ps. 79:6; Jer. 10:25.]

PSALM 148

PRAISE THE Lord! Praise the Lord from the heavens, praise Him in the heights!

2 Praise Him, all His angels, praise Him, all His hosts!

3 Praise Him, sun and moon, praise Him, all you stars of light!

4 Praise Him, you highest heavens and you waters above the heavens!

5 Let them praise the name of the Lord, for He commanded and they were created.

6 He also established them forever and ever; He made a decree which shall not pass away [He fixed their bounds which cannot be passed over].

7 Praise the Lord from the earth, you sea monsters and all deeps!

8 You lightning, hail, fog, *and* frost, you stormy wind fulfilling His orders!

9 Mountains and all hills, fruitful trees and all cedars!

10 Beasts and all cattle, creeping things and flying birds!

11 Kings of the earth and all peoples, princes and all rulers *and* judges of the earth!

12 Both young men and maidens, old men and children!

13 Let them praise *and* exalt the name of the Lord, for His name alone is exalted *and* supreme! His glory *and* majesty are above earth and heaven!

14 He has lifted up a horn for His people [giving them power, prosperity, dignity, and preeminence], a song of praise for all His godly ones, for the people of Israel, who are near to Him. Praise the Lord! (Hallelujah!) [Ps. 75:10; Eph. 2:17.]

PSALM 149

PRAISE THE Lord! Sing to the Lord a new song, praise Him in the assembly of His saints!
2 Let Israel rejoice in Him, their Maker; let Zion's children triumph *and* be joyful in their King! [Zech. 9:9; Matt. 21:5.]
3 Let them praise His name in chorus *and* choir *and* with the [single or group] dance; let them sing praises to Him with the tambourine and lyre!
4 For the Lord takes pleasure in His people; He will beautify the humble with salvation *and* adorn the wretched with victory.
5 Let the saints be joyful in the glory *and* beauty [which God confers upon them]; let them sing for joy upon their beds.
6 Let the high praises of God be in their throats and a two-edged sword in their hands, [Heb. 4:12; Rev. 1:16.]
7 To wreak vengeance upon the nations and chastisement upon the peoples,
8 To bind their kings with chains, and their nobles with fetters of iron,
9 To execute upon them the judgment written. He [the Lord] is the honor of all His saints. Praise the Lord! (Hallelujah!)

PSALM 150

PRAISE THE Lord! Praise God in His sanctuary; praise Him in the heavens of His power!

---

putting the Word to work

If you have ever been to a professional sporting event, you have seen and experienced the exuberant enthusiasm of the fans. Do you praise God with that kind of intensity? While at times you may praise Him in the quietness of your heart, the psalmist tells us that we are also to praise God with instruments, with dancing, or with shouts of joy! He is worthy of your exuberant praise.

---

2 Praise Him for His mighty acts; praise Him according to the abundance of His greatness! [Deut. 3:24; Ps. 145:5, 6.]
3 Praise Him with trumpet sound; praise Him with lute and harp!
4 Praise Him with tambourine and [single or group] dance; praise Him with stringed and wind instruments *or* flutes!
5 Praise Him with resounding cymbals; praise Him with loud clashing cymbals!
6 Let everything that has breath *and* every breath of life praise the Lord! Praise the Lord! (Hallelujah!)

Proverbs

Author:
Solomon, with smaller portions by others

Date:
About 950 BC, with portions about 720 BC

Everyday Life Principles:
Whatever you do, seek wisdom.

Walking in wisdom means making decisions today that you will be happy with tomorrow.

Look to Proverbs to find godly, practical advice about many practical matters you face in your everyday life.

Proverbs was written by Solomon, who has been called the wisest man who ever lived, and is a book filled with wisdom and godly common sense about the practical matters of life. One of the most beneficial things we can seek in life is wisdom, which I like to define as "decisions you make now that you will be happy with later."

Within the pages of Proverbs, you will find sound guidance and advice on a multitude of situations you face on a regular basis, including how to:

- Think properly
- Control your mouth
- Manage your finances
- Plan for the future
- Treat people correctly
- Deal with offenses
- Receive correction
- Keep from being foolish and to handle those who are
- Be a good friend
- Behave as husbands and wives should
- Have good parent/child relationships

It also teaches us that our **words** are carriers of either **life or death**, that a **happy heart** does us good like a **medicine**, and that the **fear of the Lord** is the beginning of **wisdom**.

Because Proverbs has 31 chapters, many people read one chapter of Proverbs per day, each month of the year. Whether you read a chapter per day or the entire book at once, I encourage you to read Proverbs often and let its wisdom saturate your heart and direct your life.

1 THE PROVERBS (truths obscurely expressed, maxims, and parables) of Solomon son of David, king of Israel:

2 [a]That people may know skillful *and* godly [b]Wisdom and instruction, discern *and* comprehend the words of understanding *and* insight,

3 Receive instruction in wise dealing *and* the discipline of wise thoughtfulness, righteousness, justice, and integrity,

4 That prudence may be given to the simple, and knowledge, discretion, *and* discernment to the youth—

5 The wise also will hear and increase in learning, and the person of understanding will acquire skill *and* attain to sound counsel [so that he may be able to steer his course rightly]—[Prov. 9:9.]

6 That people may understand a proverb and a figure of speech *or* an enigma with its interpretation, and the words of the wise and their dark sayings *or* riddles.

7 The reverent *and* worshipful fear of the Lord is the beginning *and* the principal *and* choice part of knowledge [its starting point and its essence]; but fools despise skillful *and* godly Wisdom, instruction, *and* discipline. [Ps. 111:10.]

8 My son, hear the instruction of your father; reject not *nor* forsake the teaching of your mother.

life point

Proverbs 1:1–4 teaches us that wisdom is full of prudence. *Prudence* means "good management." Prudent people do not operate in extremes. They are balanced and conduct themselves wisely. I encourage you to be prudent in every situation!

9 For they are a [victor's] chaplet (garland) of grace upon your head and chains *and* pendants [of gold worn by kings] for your neck.

10 My son, if sinners entice you, do not consent. [Ps. 1:1; Eph. 5:11.]

11 If they say, Come with us; let us lie in wait [to shed] blood, let us ambush the innocent without cause [and show that his piety is in vain];

12 Let us swallow them up alive as does Sheol (the place of the dead), and whole, as those who go down into the pit [of the dead];

13 We shall find *and* take all kinds of precious goods [when our victims are put out of the way], we shall fill our houses with plunder;

14 Throw in your lot with us [they insist] *and* be a sworn brother *and* comrade; let us all have one purse in common—

15 My son, do not walk in the way with them; restrain your foot from their path;

speak the Word

God, I pray that You will help me to be wise. Help me to hear and increase in learning, to acquire skill, and to attain to sound counsel so that I may steer my course rightly.
ADAPTED FROM PROVERBS 1:5

a Over the doors of the school of Plato these words were written in Greek, "Let no one enter who is not a geometrician." But Solomon opens wide the doors of his proverbs with a special message of welcome to the unlearned, the simple, the foolish, the young, and even to the wise—that all "will hear and increase in learning" (Prov. 1:5). b A key term in the book of Proverbs, "Wisdom" is capitalized throughout, as God's design for living and as a reminder of Christ, Whom the apostle Paul calls "the wisdom of God . . . in Whom are hid all the treasures of wisdom and knowledge" (I Cor. 1:24; Col. 2:3 KJV).

16 For their feet run to evil, and they make haste to shed blood.
17 For in vain is the net spread in the sight of any bird!
18 But [when these men set a trap for others] they are lying in wait for their own blood; they set an ambush for their own lives.
19 So are the ways of everyone who is greedy of gain; such [greed for plunder] takes away the lives of its possessors. [Prov. 15:27; I Tim. 6:10.]
20 cWisdom cries aloud in the street, she raises her voice in the markets;
21 She cries at the head of the noisy intersections [in the chief gathering places]; at the entrance of the city gates she speaks:
22 How long, O simple ones [open to evil], will you love being simple? And the scoffers delight in scoffing and [self-confident] fools hate knowledge?
23 If you will turn (repent) *and* give heed to my reproof, behold, I [dWisdom] will pour out my spirit upon you, I will make my words known to you. [Isa. 11:2; Eph. 1:17-20.]

life point

God says in Proverbs 1:23 that He will make His words known to us if we listen to Him and repent when He corrects us. He will open up wisdom to us, and we will have more revelation than we could ever imagine.

All we need to do is obey what God has told us to do. He will reveal to us hidden treasures within His Word. We have not even scratched the surface of the revelation that is in the Word of God. If we obey Him, He will make His will clearly known to us. He will speak living words (*rhema*) to us—His personal word for our lives.

24 Because I have called and you have refused [to answer], have stretched out my hand and no man has heeded it, [Isa. 65:11, 12; 66:4; Jer. 7:13, 14; Zech. 7:11-13.]
25 And you treated as nothing all my counsel and would accept none of my reproof,
26 I also will laugh at your calamity; I will mock when the thing comes that shall cause you terror *and* panic—
27 When your panic comes as a storm *and* desolation and your calamity comes on as a whirlwind, when distress and anguish come upon you.
28 Then will they call upon me [Wisdom] but I will not answer; they will seek me early *and* diligently but they will not find me. [Job 27:9; 35:12, 13; Isa. 1:15, 16; Jer. 11:11; Mic. 3:4; James 4:3.]
29 Because they hated knowledge and did not choose the reverent *and* worshipful fear of the Lord, [Prov. 8:13.]
30 Would accept none of my counsel, and despised all my reproof,
31 Therefore shall they eat of the fruit of their own way and be satiated with their own devices.
32 For the backsliding of the simple shall slay them, and the careless ease of [self-confident] fools shall destroy them. [Isa. 32:6.]
33 But whoso hearkens to me [Wisdom] shall dwell securely *and* in confident trust and shall be quiet, without fear *or* dread of evil.

2 MY SON, if you will receive my words and treasure up my commandments within you,
2 Making your ear attentive to skillful *and* godly eWisdom *and* inclining and directing your heart *and* mind to understanding [applying all your powers to the quest for it];

---

c Wisdom here is personified. Read "the Wisdom of God" instead of "Wisdom" and see the wonderful power of this book. **d** See footnotes on Prov. 1:2 and 1:20. **e** See footnote on Prov. 1:2.

3 Yes, if you cry out for insight and raise your voice for understanding,

4 If you seek [Wisdom] as for silver and search for skillful *and* godly Wisdom as for hidden treasures,

5 Then you will understand the reverent *and* worshipful fear of the Lord and find the knowledge of [our omniscient] God. [Prov. 1:7.]

6 For the Lord gives skillful *and* godly Wisdom; from His mouth come knowledge and understanding.

7 He hides away sound *and* godly Wisdom *and* stores it for the righteous (those who are upright and in right standing with Him); He is a shield to those who walk uprightly *and* in integrity,

8 That He may guard the paths of justice; yes, He preserves the way of His saints. [I Sam. 2:9; Ps. 66:8, 9.]

9 Then you will understand righteousness, justice, and fair dealing [in every area and relation]; yes, you will understand every good path.

10 For skillful *and* godly Wisdom shall enter into your heart, and knowledge shall be pleasant to you.

11 Discretion shall watch over you, understanding shall keep you,

12 To deliver you from the way of evil *and* the evil men, from men who speak perverse things *and* are liars,

13 Men who forsake the paths of uprightness to walk in the ways of darkness,

14 Who rejoice to do evil and delight in the perverseness of evil,

15 Who are crooked in their ways, wayward *and* devious in their paths.

16 [Discretion shall watch over you, understanding shall keep you] to deliver you from the alien woman,

from the outsider with her flattering words, [Prov. 2:11.]

17 Who forsakes the husband *and* guide of her youth and forgets the covenant of her God.

18 For her house sinks down to death and her paths to the spirits [of the dead].

19 None who go to her return again, neither do they attain *or* regain the paths of life.

20 So may you walk in the way of good men, and keep to the paths of the [consistently] righteous (the upright, in right standing with God).

21 For the upright shall dwell in the land, and the men of integrity, blameless *and* complete [in God's sight], shall remain in it;

22 But the wicked shall be cut off from the earth, and the treacherous shall be rooted out of it.

3 MY SON, forget not my law *or* teaching, but let your heart keep my commandments;

2 For length of days and years of a life [worth living] and tranquility [inward and outward and continuing through old age till death], these shall they add to you.

3 Let not mercy and kindness [shutting out all hatred and selfishness] and truth [shutting out all deliberate hypocrisy or falsehood] forsake you; bind them about your neck, write them upon the tablet of your heart. [Col. 3:9-12.]

4 So shall you find favor, good understanding, *and* high esteem in the sight [or judgment] of God and man. [Luke 2:52.]

5 Lean on, trust in, *and* be confident

speak the Word

understanding people

Proverbs 2:1–5 teaches us about the necessity and rewards of understanding. We need to seek understanding—of God's Word and will, of ourselves, and of other people.

I would like to focus for a moment on the importance of really understanding others. In order to minister to them we must have an understanding heart, and how can we do that if we do not have a clue about their hurts and struggles?

One way to understand what people are going through is by going through it ourselves. We do not have to experience exactly the same thing, but I do not think anyone can understand a hurting person without having been hurt or having gone through a similar situation.

It is amazing how caring and compassionate we are when we have gone through a few problems of our own, and how flippant and judgmental we can be if we have not had the same problem ourselves. How easy our answers can be: "Well, now, sister, you just need to believe God." How different it is when *we* have been hurting for months, and somebody comes along with a problem. We throw our arms around that person and say, "Oh, I *understand* how you feel."

We all want understanding. It is one of the things we cry out to God for when we are going through rough times. We just want to be understood. Jesus understands, as we see in Hebrews 4:15: "For we do not have a High Priest Who is unable to understand and sympathize and have a shared feeling with our weaknesses and infirmities and liability to the assaults of temptation, but One Who has been tempted in every respect as we are, yet without sinning." Jesus can help us because He knows what we are going through. We can open up to Him without fear of judgment and rejection because He understands.

I am not sure that Jesus ever prayed for anybody until compassion was flowing. I recall an instance in the Bible in which a man came to Him asking for healing for his son who was possessed by a demon that caused him terrible suffering. Jesus asked the man, "How long has he had this?" (Mark 9:21). The answer did not affect whether or not Jesus would heal him. I believe Jesus asked the question because He wanted to have even more compassion than He already had for that father and the boy.

We need to be concerned enough about people to ask them questions about their situations: "How long have you been like this? Where does it hurt? What gives you comfort?"

When some of us ask a person how they are doing and they say that they are having a rough time, we tend to answer, "Well, praise the Lord anyway!" But when we are hurting or in trouble, that is not how we want others to respond to us. We want them to show us some real heartfelt understanding and compassion.

Be a person who seeks understanding and desires to be compassionate, and you will find yourself acting wisely toward others.

why not ask, "why?"

Proverbs 3:5, 6 is basically a passage that encourages us to have faith in God and not in our own thinking or reasoning. People who must reason out everything have a very hard time with faith because reasoning is not faith, and without faith it is impossible to please God (see Hebrews 11:6).

I can teach on reasoning because I used to be a "class A" chief "reasoner." I was the lady who had to have everything figured out. I had to have a plan. I had to know not only all about my own business but all about other people's business too—even God's. I was continually asking, "Why, God, why? When, God, when?"

In some respects, I had to reason everything out like the religious leaders of Jesus' day. We read about them in Mark 2:6–8: "Now some of the scribes were sitting there, holding a dialogue with themselves as they questioned in their hearts, Why does this Man talk like this? He is blaspheming! Who can forgive sins [remove guilt, remit the penalty, and bestow righteousness instead] except God alone? And at once Jesus, becoming fully aware in His spirit that they thus debated within themselves, said to them, Why do you argue (debate, reason) about all this in your hearts?"

Notice that the scribes were "holding a dialogue with themselves." Do you ever hold a dialogue with yourself? Realistically, you probably talk to yourself more than you talk to anybody else. I encourage you to examine what you are saying to yourself. These scribes were not saying those unkind things in Mark 2 aloud, but in their hearts. They were asking questions about Jesus within themselves. Immediately, He became aware in His Spirit of their arguing, debating, and reasoning and called it to their attention.

We need to be aware that trying to reason everything out by ourselves is a problem. It is a serious matter that we need to deal with, just as Jesus dealt with it in the hearts of those who followed Him. Ask God to help you stop reasoning and begin to live by faith, leaning on and trusting in Him and not on your own understanding.

in the Lord with all your heart *and* mind and do not rely on your own insight *or* understanding.

6 In all your ways know, recognize, *and* acknowledge Him, and He will direct *and* make straight *and* plain your paths.

7 Be not wise in your own eyes; reverently fear *and* worship the Lord and turn [entirely] away from evil. [Prov. 8:13.]

8 It shall be health to your nerves *and* sinews, and marrow *and* moistening to your bones.

9 Honor the Lord with your capital

life point

I believe what God meant when He said, "Be not wise in your own eyes" (Proverbs 3:7), was "Do not even think that you can run your life and do a good job without My help and direction!"

and sufficiency [from righteous labors] and with the firstfruits of all your income; [Deut. 26:2; Mal. 3:10; Luke 14:13, 14.]

10 So shall your storage places be filled with plenty, and your vats shall be overflowing with new wine. [Deut. 28:8.]

11 My son, do not despise *or* shrink from the chastening of the Lord [His correction by punishment or by subjection to suffering or trial]; neither be weary of *or* impatient about *or* loathe *or* abhor His reproof, [Ps. 94:12; Heb. 12:5, 6; Rev. 3:19.]

12 For whom the Lord loves He corrects, even as a father corrects the son in whom he delights.

13 Happy (blessed, fortunate, enviable) is the man who finds skillful *and* godly Wisdom, and the man who gets understanding [drawing it forth from God's Word and life's experiences],

14 For the gaining of it is better than the gaining of silver, and the profit of it better than fine gold.

15 Skillful *and* godly ᶠWisdom is more precious than rubies; and nothing you can wish for is to be compared to her. [Job 28:12-18.]

16 Length of days is in her right hand, and in her left hand are riches and honor. [Prov. 8:12-21; I Tim. 4:8.]

17 Her ways are highways of pleasantness, and all her paths are peace.

18 She is a tree of life to those who lay hold on her; and happy (blessed, fortunate, to be envied) is everyone who holds her fast.

19 The Lord by skillful *and* godly Wisdom has founded the earth; by understanding He has established the heavens. [Col. 1:16.]

20 By His knowledge the deeps were broken up, and the skies distill the dew.

21 My son, let them not escape from your sight, but keep sound *and* godly Wisdom and discretion,

22 And they will be life to your inner self, and a gracious ornament to your neck (your outer self).

23 Then you will walk in your way securely *and* in confident trust, and you shall not dash your foot *or* stumble. [Ps. 91:11, 12; Prov. 10:9.]

24 When you lie down, you shall not be afraid; yes, you shall lie down, and your sleep shall be sweet.

25 Be not afraid of sudden terror *and* panic, nor of the stormy blast *or* the storm and ruin of the wicked when it comes [for you will be guiltless],

26 For the Lord shall be your confidence, firm *and* strong, and shall keep your foot from being caught [in a trap or some hidden danger].

life point

As Christians, we should not place our confidence in our education, our looks, our position, our property, our gifts, our talents, our abilities, our accomplishments, or in other people's opinions. Through Proverbs 3:26, our heavenly Father is basically saying to us, "No more; it is time to let go of all those fleshly things to which you have been holding so firmly so long. It is time to put your trust and confidence in Me, and Me alone!"

27 Withhold not good from those to whom it is due [its rightful owners], when it is in the power of your hand to do it. [Rom. 13:7; Gal. 6:10.]

28 Do not say to your neighbor, Go, and come again; and tomorrow I will give it—when you have it with you. [Lev. 19:13; Deut. 24:15.]

29 Do not contrive *or* dig up *or* cultivate evil against your neighbor, who dwells trustingly *and* confidently beside you.

ᶠ See footnote on Prov. 1:20.

life point

We can have good intentions and still be disobedient. Procrastination is very deceptive and Proverbs 3:27, 28 instructs us not to do it. Often, we do not see putting things off as disobedience because we *intend* to obey God; it is just that we are going to do it *when*—when we have more money, when we are not so busy, as soon as Christmas is over, after we get the kids in school this year, when we return from vacation, etc. Remember, the best intentions do not produce results. Ask God to help you take action in a timely manner in every situation.

30 Contend not with a man for no reason—when he has done you no wrong. [Rom. 12:18.]
31 Do not resentfully envy *and* be jealous of an unscrupulous, grasping man, and choose none of his ways. [Ps. 37:1; 73:3; Prov. 24:1.]
32 For the perverse are an abomination [extremely disgusting and detestable] to the Lord; but His confidential communion *and* secret counsel are with the [uncompromisingly] righteous (those who are upright and in right standing with Him). [Ps. 25:14.]
33 The curse of the Lord is in *and* on the house of the wicked, but He declares blessed (joyful and favored with blessings) the home of the just *and* consistently righteous. [Ps. 37:22; Zech. 5:4; Mal. 2:2.]
34 Though He scoffs at the scoffers *and* scorns the scorners, yet He gives His undeserved favor to the low [in rank], the humble, *and* the afflicted. [James 4:6; I Pet. 5:5.]
35 The wise shall inherit glory (all honor and good) but shame is the highest rank conferred on [self-confident] fools. [Isa. 32:6.]

4 HEAR, MY sons, the instruction of a father, and pay attention in order to gain *and* to know intelligent discernment, comprehension, *and* interpretation [of spiritual matters].
2 For I give you good doctrine [what is to be received]; do not forsake my teaching.
3 When I [Solomon] was a son with my father [David], tender and the only son in the sight of my mother [Bathsheba],
4 He taught me and said to me, Let your heart hold fast my words; keep my commandments and live. [I Chron. 28:9; Eph. 6:4.]
5 Get skillful *and* godly Wisdom, get understanding (discernment, comprehension, and interpretation); do not forget and do not turn back from the words of my mouth.
6 Forsake not [Wisdom], and she will keep, defend, *and* protect you; love her, and she will guard you.
7 The beginning of Wisdom is: get Wisdom (skillful and godly Wisdom)! [For skillful *and* godly Wisdom is the principal thing.] And with all you have gotten, get understanding (discernment, comprehension, and interpretation). [James 1:5.]
8 Prize Wisdom highly *and* exalt her, and she will exalt *and* promote you; she will bring you to honor when you embrace her.
9 She shall give to your head a wreath of gracefulness; a crown of beauty *and* glory will she deliver to you.
10 Hear, O my son, and receive my sayings, and the years of your life shall be many.
11 I have taught you in the way of skillful *and* godly Wisdom [which is comprehensive insight into the ways and purposes of God]; I have led you in paths of uprightness.
12 When you walk, your steps shall not be hampered [your path will be clear and open]; and when you run, you shall not stumble.

the benefits of wisdom

Proverbs 4:5 instructs us to get "skillful and godly Wisdom," and I would like to share some of the results you can expect as you apply wisdom in your life.

Wisdom will always lead you to God's best. Wisdom teaches that you will not keep friends if you try to control and dominate everything that goes on in your life and theirs. You will not keep friends if you talk about them behind their backs or tell their secrets. Wisdom says, "Do not say things about others that you would not want people saying about you."

Wisdom will guide you in money matters. You will not get into debt if you do not spend more money than you make. A lot of people never have fruitful ministries because they think they can run a ministry without good business principles. The Holy Spirit does not need to speak in an audible voice to tell us that we cannot have more money going out than we have coming in. Wisdom tells us that we will get in trouble if we do that.

Wisdom will not let us get overextended in our commitments if we listen to her. No matter how anxious we may be to accomplish things, wisdom says we need to take time and wait on God to give us peace about what we are to do and not do. It has been very difficult for me over the years to learn to say no to certain speaking opportunities, but I have learned that it is not wise to wear myself out trying to do so much that I end up not doing a quality job.

To God, quality is more important than quantity. Many times wisdom leads us to say no to things we would like to say yes to. Wisdom may also lead us to say yes to something to which we would like to say no. For example, if a friend invites me to do something that is extremely important to her, and I have recently had to say no to her several times, even if I do not really want to accept the invitation, it might be wise for me to do so if I value her friendship and want to keep it.

Wisdom is our friend; it helps us not to live in regret. I think the saddest thing in the world would be to reach old age and look back at my life and feel nothing but regret about what I did or did not do. Wisdom helps us make choices now that we will be happy with later.

13 Take firm hold of instruction, do not let go; guard her, for she is your life.
14 Enter not into the path of the wicked, and go not in the way of evil men.
15 Avoid it, do not go on it; turn from it and pass on.
16 For they cannot sleep unless they have caused trouble or vexation; their sleep is taken away unless they have caused someone to fall.
17 For they eat the bread of wickedness and drink the wine of violence.
18 But the path of the [uncompromisingly] just and righteous is like the light of dawn, that shines more and more (brighter and clearer) until [it reaches its full strength and glory in] the perfect day [to be prepared]. [II Sam. 23:4; Matt. 5:14; Phil. 2:15.]
19 The way of the wicked is like deep darkness; they do not know over what they stumble. [John 12:35.]

life point

Proverbs 4:18 is so encouraging to me! This verse says to me that God is not angry with us because we have not yet "arrived." He is pleased that we are pressing on, that we are staying on the path. If you and I will just "keep on keeping on," God will be pleased with our progress.

Keep walking the walk. A walk is something taken one step at a time. This is an important thing to remember.

If I invited you to take a walk, you would think I was crazy if I became angry after the first few steps because we had not yet arrived at our destination. We can understand ordinary things like this, and yet we have a difficult time understanding that God expects our spiritual growth to take some time.

We do not think there is something wrong with one-year-old children because they cannot walk perfectly. They fall down frequently, but we pick them up, love them, bandage them if necessary, and keep working with them. Surely our awesome God can do even more for us than we do for our children. He is patient and stays with us until we reach our destination.

20 My son, attend to my words; consent *and* submit to my sayings.
21 Let them not depart from your sight; keep them in the center of your heart.
22 For they are life to those who find them, healing *and* health to all their flesh.
23 Keep *and* guard your heart with all vigilance *and* above all that you guard, for out of it flow the springs of life.
24 Put away from you false *and* dis-
honest speech, and willful *and* contrary talk put far from you.
25 Let your eyes look right on [with fixed purpose], and let your gaze be straight before you.
26 Consider well the path of your feet, and let all your ways be established *and* ordered aright.
27 Turn not aside to the right hand or to the left; remove your foot from evil.

5 MY SON, be attentive to my Wisdom [godly Wisdom learned by actual and costly experience], and incline your ear to my

life point

Proverbs 4:23 exhorts us to guard our hearts "with all vigilance." Practically, that means we need to examine our attitudes and our thoughts on a regular basis and make adjustments as needed.

Many people are deceived into believing they cannot help what they think, but we *can* choose our thoughts. We need to think about what we have been thinking about. When we do that, it doesn't take very long to discover the root cause of a bad attitude.

Satan will always try to fill our minds with wrong thinking, but we do not have to receive everything he tries to give us. I would not take a spoonful of poison just because someone offered it to me, and neither would you. If we are smart enough not to swallow poison, we should also be smart enough not to allow Satan to poison our minds, attitudes, and, ultimately, our lives.

Guard your heart aggressively. Let your thoughts be good thoughts. Think about things that are honorable and true (see Philippians 4:8), and watch your heart attitude change.

understanding [of what is becoming and prudent for you],

2 That you may exercise proper discrimination *and* discretion and your lips may guard *and* keep knowledge *and* the wise answer [to temptation].

3 For the lips of a loose woman drip honey as a honeycomb, and her mouth is smoother than oil; [Ezek. 20:30; Col. 2:8-10; II Pet. 2:14-17.]

4 But in the end she is bitter as wormwood, sharp as a two-edged *and* devouring sword.

5 Her feet go down to death; her steps take hold of Sheol (Hades, the place of the dead).

6 She loses sight of *and* walks not in the path of life; her ways wind about aimlessly, and you cannot know them.

7 Now therefore, my sons, listen to me, and depart not from the words of my mouth.

8 Let your way in life be far from her, and come not near the door of her house [avoid the very scenes of temptation], [Prov. 4:15; Rom. 16:17; I Thess. 5:19-22.]

9 Lest you give your honor to others and your years to those without mercy,

10 Lest strangers [and false teachings] take their fill of your strength *and* wealth and your labors go to the house of an alien [from God]—

11 And you groan *and* mourn when your end comes, when your flesh and body are consumed,

12 And you say, How I hated instruction *and* discipline, and my heart despised reproof!

13 I have not obeyed the voice of my teachers nor submitted *and* consented to those who instructed me.

14 [The extent and boldness of] my sin involved almost all evil [in the estimation] of the congregation *and* the community.

life point

As believers, you and I should not hate instruction as we read about in Proverbs 5:12, but we should be teachable. If we ever get to the point where we think we know everything, then we can be assured that we know nothing! We need to stop hating and despising things—even little things. People use the words *hate* and *despise* quite casually, making comments such as: "I hate going to the grocery store," or "I hate traffic," or "I despise my job." We are not supposed to hate anything but sin.

We all are tempted to hate certain things, just as we are prone to dread certain things. God has taught me that dread is a close relative of fear. We do not need to dread doing the dishes, getting up, going to work, exercising, or anything else. Satan uses those feelings of dread and our feelings of hatred to deceive us. We simply are not to have hearts that despise anyone or anything. If you have hatred in your heart, repent and then ask God to replace your despising attitude with His love and grace.

15 ᵍDrink waters out of your own cistern [of a pure marriage relationship], and fresh running waters out of your own well.

16 Should your offspring be dispersed abroad as water brooks in the streets?

17 [Confine yourself to your own wife] let your children be for you alone, and not the children of strangers with you.

18 Let your fountain [of human life] be blessed [with the rewards of

---

g All of the Ten Commandments are reflected in the book of Proverbs; here it is the seventh, "You shall not commit adultery."

fidelity], and rejoice in the wife of your youth.

19 Let her be as the loving hind and pleasant doe [tender, gentle, attractive]—let her bosom satisfy you at all times, and always be transported with delight in her love.

20 Why should you, my son, be infatuated with a loose woman, embrace the bosom of an outsider, *and* go astray?

21 For the ways of man are directly before the eyes of the Lord, and He [Who would have us live soberly, chastely, and godly] carefully weighs all man's goings. [II Chron. 16:9; Job 31:4; 34:21; Prov. 15:3; Jer. 16:17; Hos. 7:2; Heb. 4:13.]

22 His own iniquities shall ensnare the wicked man, and he shall be held with the cords of his sin.

23 He will die for lack of discipline *and* instruction, and in the greatness of his folly he will go astray *and* be lost.

6 MY SON, if you have become security for your neighbor, if you have given your pledge for a stranger *or* another,

2 You are snared with the words of your lips, you are caught by the speech of your mouth.

3 Do this now [at once and earnestly], my son, and deliver yourself when you have put yourself into the ʰpower of your neighbor; go, bestir *and* humble yourself, and beg your neighbor [to pay his debt and thereby release you].

4 Give not [unnecessary] sleep to your eyes, nor slumber to your eyelids;

5 Deliver yourself, as a roe *or* gazelle from the hand of the hunter, and as a bird from the hand of the fowler.

6 Go to the ant, you sluggard; consider her ways and be wise!—[Job 12:7.]

7 Which, having no chief, overseer, or ruler,

8 Provides her food in the summer and gathers her supplies in the harvest.

9 How long will you sleep, O sluggard? When will you arise out of your sleep? [Prov. 24:33, 34.]

10 Yet a little sleep, a little slumber, a little folding of the hands to lie down *and* sleep—

11 So will your poverty come like a robber *or* one who travels [with slowly but surely approaching steps] and your want like an armed man [making you helpless]. [Prov. 10:4; 13:4; 20:4.]

12 A worthless person, a wicked man, is he who goes about with a perverse (contrary, wayward) mouth.

13 He winks with his eyes, he speaks by shuffling *or* tapping with his feet, he makes signs [to mislead and deceive] *and* teaches with his fingers.

14 Willful *and* contrary in his heart, he devises trouble, vexation, *and* evil continually; he lets loose discord *and* sows it.

15 Therefore upon him shall the crushing weight of calamity come suddenly; suddenly shall he be broken, and that without remedy.

16 These six things the Lord hates, indeed, seven are an abomination to Him:

17 A proud look [the spirit that makes one overestimate himself and underestimate others], a lying tongue,

h The Bible consistently teaches that one is not to forsake a friend, and this passage is not to be otherwise construed. But it is one thing to lend a friend money, and quite another thing to promise to pay his debts for him if he fails to do so himself. It might cost one, under the rigid customary laws governing debt, his money, his land, his bed, and his clothing—and if these were not sufficient, he and his wife and children could be sold as slaves, not to be released until the next Year of Jubilee— fifty years after the previous one. God's Word is very plain on the subject of not underwriting another person's debts (see Prov. 11:15; 17:18; 22:26).

and hands that shed innocent blood,
[Ps. 120:2, 3.]
18 A heart that manufactures wicked
thoughts *and* plans, feet that are swift
in running to evil,
19 A false witness who breathes out
lies [even under oath], and he who
sows discord among his brethren.
20 My son, keep your father's [God-
given] commandment and forsake not
the law of [God] your mother [taught
you]. [Eph. 6:1-3.]
21 Bind them continually upon your
heart and tie them about your neck.
[Prov. 3:3; 7:3.]
22 When you go, they [the words of
your parents' God] shall lead you;
when you sleep, they shall keep you;
and when you waken, they shall talk
with you.
23 For the commandment is a lamp,
and the whole teaching [of the law] is
light, and reproofs of discipline are
the way of life, [Ps. 19:8; 119:105.]
24 To keep you from the evil woman,
from the flattery of the tongue of a
loose woman.
25 Lust not after her beauty in your
heart, neither let her capture you with
her eyelids.
26 For on account of a harlot a man is
brought to a piece of bread, and the
adulteress stalks *and* snares [as with a
hook] the precious life [of a man].
27 Can a man take fire in his bosom
and his clothes not be burned?
28 Can one go upon hot coals and his
feet not be burned?
29 So he who cohabits with his
neighbor's wife [will be tortured with
evil consequences and just retribu-
tion]; he who touches her shall not be
innocent *or* go unpunished.
30 Men do not despise a thief if he
steals to satisfy himself when he is
hungry;
31 But if he is found out, he must
restore seven times [what he stole]; he
must give the whole substance of his
house [if necessary—to meet his fine].

32 But whoever commits adultery
with a woman lacks heart *and* understanding (moral principle and prudence); he who does it is destroying
his own life.
33 Wounds and disgrace will he get,
and his reproach will not be wiped
away.
34 For jealousy makes [the wronged]
man furious; therefore he will not
spare in the day of vengeance [upon
the detected one].
35 He will not consider any ransom
[offered to buy him off from demanding full punishment]; neither will he
be satisfied, though you offer him
many gifts *and* bribes.

7 MY SON, keep my words; lay
up within you my command-
ments [for use when needed]
and treasure them.
2 Keep my commandments and
live, and keep my law *and* teaching as
the apple (the pupil) of your eye.
3 Bind them on your fingers; write
them on the tablet of your heart.
4 Say to skillful *and* godly Wisdom,
You are my sister, and regard understanding *or* insight as your intimate
friend—
5 That they may keep you from the
loose woman, from the adventuress
who flatters with *and* makes smooth
her words.
6 For at the window of my house I
looked out through my lattice.
7 And among the simple (empty-
headed and emptyhearted) ones, I
perceived among the youths a young
man void of good sense,
8 Sauntering through the street
near the [loose woman's] corner; and
he went the way to her house
9 In the twilight, in the evening;
night black and dense was falling
[over the young man's life].
10 And behold, there met him a
woman, dressed as a harlot and sly
and cunning of heart.

11 She is turbulent *and* willful; her feet stay not in her house;

12 Now in the streets, now in the marketplaces, she sets her ambush at every corner.

13 So she caught him and kissed him and with impudent face she said to him,

14 Sacrifices of peace offerings were due from me; this day I paid my vows.

15 So I came forth to meet you [that you might share with me the feast from my offering]; diligently I sought your face, and I have found you.

16 I have spread my couch with rugs *and* cushions of tapestry, with striped sheets of fine linen of Egypt.

17 I have perfumed my bed with myrrh, aloes, and cinnamon.

18 Come, let us take our fill of love until morning; let us console *and* delight ourselves with love.

19 For the man is not at home; he is gone on a long journey;

20 He has taken a bag of money with him and will come home at the day appointed [at the full moon].

21 With much justifying *and* enticing argument she persuades him, with the allurements of her lips she leads him [to overcome his conscience and his fears] *and* forces him along.

22 Suddenly he [yields and] follows her reluctantly like an ox moving to the slaughter, like one in fetters going to the correction [to be given] to a fool or ¹*like a dog enticed by food to the muzzle*

23 Till a dart [of passion] pierces *and* inflames his vitals; then like a bird fluttering straight into the net [he hastens], not knowing that it will cost him his life.

24 Listen to me now therefore, O you sons, and be attentive to the words of my mouth.

25 Let not your heart incline toward her ways, do not stray into her paths.

26 For she has cast down many wounded; indeed, all her slain are a mighty host. [Neh. 13:26.]

27 Her house is the way to Sheol (Hades, the place of the dead), going down to the chambers of death.

8 DOES NOT skillful *and* godly Wisdom cry out, and understanding raise her voice [in contrast to the loose woman]?

2 On the top of the heights beside the way, where the paths meet, stands Wisdom [skillful and godly];

3 At the gates at the entrance of the town, at the coming in at the doors, she cries out:

4 To you, O men, I call, and my voice is directed to the sons of men.

5 O you simple *and* thoughtless ones, understand prudence; you [self-confident] fools, be of an understanding heart. [Isa. 32:6.]

6 Hear, for I will speak excellent *and* princely things; and the opening of my lips shall be for right things.

7 For my mouth shall utter truth, and wrongdoing is detestable *and* loathsome to my lips.

8 All the words of my mouth are righteous (upright and in right standing with God); there is nothing contrary to truth or crooked in them.

9 They are all plain to him who understands [and opens his heart], and right to those who find knowledge [and live by it].

10 Receive my instruction in preference to [striving for] silver, and knowledge rather than choice gold,

11 For skillful *and* godly Wisdom is better than rubies *or* pearls, and all the things that may be desired are not to be compared to it. [Job 28:15; Ps. 19:10; 119:127.]

12 I, Wisdom [from God], make prudence my dwelling, and I find out knowledge and discretion. [James 1:5.]

---

i *The Septuagint* (Greek translation of the Old Testament) so reads at this point.

life point

Proverbs 8:6–9 describes what should be our confession, our testimony, and our reputation. Our reputation involves not only what we say about ourselves, but also what others say about us.

Unfortunately, many of us have learned in this life to "talk in circles," and often when we finish talking, others still do not have the slightest idea what we have just said. We need to learn how to engage in plain, straightforward, honest, truthful communication.

James 3:10 tells us that we should not let both blessings and cursings come from our mouths. Instead, we ought to be like the virtuous woman in Proverbs 31:26, in whose mouth is the law of kindness. As children of God, we need to be excellent in our speech and speak words that are righteous and true.

13 The reverent fear *and* worshipful awe of the Lord [includes] the hatred of evil; pride, arrogance, the evil way, and perverted *and* twisted speech I hate.
14 I have counsel and sound knowledge, I have understanding, I have might *and* power.
15 By me kings reign and rulers decree justice. [Dan. 2:21; Rom. 13:1.]
16 By me princes rule, and nobles, even all the judges *and* governors of the earth.
17 I love those who love me, and those who seek me early *and* diligently shall find me. [I Sam. 2:30; Ps. 91:14; John 14:21; James 1:5.]
18 Riches and honor are with me, enduring wealth and righteousness (uprightness in every area and rela-

tion, and right standing with God). [Prov. 3:16; Matt. 6:33.]
19 My fruit is better than gold, yes, than refined gold, and my increase than choice silver.
20 I [Wisdom] walk in the way of righteousness (moral and spiritual rectitude in every area and relation), in the midst of the paths of justice,
21 That I may cause those who love me to inherit [true] riches and that I may fill their treasuries.
22 The Lord formed *and* brought me [Wisdom] forth at the beginning of His way, before His acts of old.
23 I [Wisdom] was inaugurated *and* ordained from everlasting, from the beginning, before ever the earth existed. [John 1:1; I Cor. 1:24.]
24 When there were no deeps, I was brought forth, when there were no fountains laden with water.
25 Before the mountains were settled, before the hills, I was brought forth, [Job 15:7, 8.]
26 While as yet He had not made the land or the fields or the first of the dust of the earth.
27 When He prepared the heavens, I [Wisdom] was there; when He drew a circle upon the face of the deep *and* stretched out the firmament over it,
28 When He made firm the skies above, when He established the fountains of the deep,
29 When He gave to the sea its limit *and* His decree that the waters should not transgress [across the boundaries set by] His command, when He appointed the foundations of the earth—[Job 38:10, 11; Ps. 104:6-9; Jer. 5:22.]
30 Then I [Wisdom] was ʲbeside Him as a master *and* director of the work; and I was daily His delight, rejoicing before Him always, [Matt. 3:17; John 1:2, 18.]

j See Wisdom here present and involved at creation as an attribute of God.

a little common sense goes a long way

In Proverbs 8:15, 16, Wisdom is speaking, and she says that through her, leaders rule. Wisdom brings us to places of leadership, and if we want to be good leaders, we need wisdom and common sense!

People are constantly asking me, "How were you able to build a ministry like yours?" I share with them a ministry success principle—one of the most positive aspects of our ministry, the thing that has brought us to where we are today: *common sense!*

My husband, Dave, and I use common sense in everything we do in our ministry. You might call it "sanctified common sense." It is not merely reason or logic. Romans 8:6 states that the mind of the flesh is sense and reason without the Holy Spirit. Dave and I strive not to walk according to the mind of the flesh, because we are aware that sense and reason alone can cause a lot of trouble. We seek godly, Spirit-filled, sanctified common sense. We believe common sense leads us to present a balanced gospel. We do not buy things we do not have the money to pay for. We do not hire people if we cannot afford to pay their salaries. We know that we cannot try to control our friends if we want to keep them. We have enough common sense to know what to do to stay out of trouble.

Living by common sense is really not difficult; just do what you would want others to do to you. Pay your bills on time; communicate properly; mix encouragement with correction so a person's spirit is not broken—these are just a few examples of good common sense.

As you use more and more common sense, things will get better and better for you. Do not do things that are foolish; ask God for wisdom. While you are at it, ask Him to help you also use good, sanctified common sense in every situation.

31 Rejoicing in His inhabited earth and delighting in the sons of men. [Ps. 16:3.]
32 Now therefore listen to me, O you sons; for blessed (happy, fortunate, to be envied) are those who keep my ways. [Ps. 119:1, 2; 128:1, 2; Luke 11:28.]
33 Hear instruction and be wise, and do not refuse *or* neglect it.
34 Blessed (happy, fortunate, to be envied) is the man who listens to me, watching daily at my gates, waiting at the posts of my doors.
35 For whoever finds me [Wisdom] finds life and draws forth *and* obtains favor from the Lord.

36 But he who misses me *or* sins against me wrongs *and* injures himself; all who hate me love *and* court death.

9 WISDOM HAS built her house; she has hewn out *and* set up her seven [perfect number of] pillars.
2 She has killed her beasts, she has mixed her [spiritual] wine; she has also set her table. [Matt. 22:2-4.]
3 She has sent out her maids to cry from the highest places of the town:
4 Whoever is simple (easily led astray and wavering), let him turn in

life point

We can miss God by being in a hurry to get what we want. If we do not wait, especially in important areas, we will bring trouble into our lives (see Proverbs 8:34–36). I am "fine-tuning" patience in my life all the time.

I am a natural-born confronter. In the past, if I wanted something solved, I confronted the issue and forced a solution. It took me years to learn that sometimes it was not good for me to deal with issues that directly. I learned that I could make matters worse, or get in God's way and end up having to go through the same situation again because I did not wait for God's timing. Because I was impatient, I did not give God a chance to solve things for me.

I have learned that when I feel overly anxious to handle something, I should let it rest for at least twenty-four hours. It is amazing how we can change our minds if we will just let things settle for a few hours. We can save ourselves so much trouble if we will learn to wait on God.

here! As for him who lacks understanding, [God's] Wisdom says to him,

5 Come, eat of my bread and drink of the [spiritual] wine which I have mixed. [Isa. 55:1; John 6:27.]

6 Leave off, simple ones [forsake the foolish and simpleminded] and live! And walk in the way of insight *and* understanding.

7 He who rebukes a scorner heaps upon himself abuse, and he who reproves a wicked man gets for himself bruises.

8 Reprove not a scorner, lest he hate you; reprove a wise man, and he will love you. [Ps. 141:5.]

9 Give instruction to a wise man and he will be yet wiser; teach a righ-

teous man (one upright and in right standing with God) and he will increase in learning.

10 The reverent *and* worshipful fear of the Lord is the beginning (the chief and choice part) of Wisdom, and the knowledge of the Holy One is insight *and* understanding.

11 For by me [Wisdom from God] your days shall be multiplied, and the years of your life shall be increased.

12 If you are wise, you are wise for yourself; if you scorn, you alone will bear it *and* pay the penalty.

13 The foolish woman is noisy; she is simple *and* open to all forms of evil, she [willfully and recklessly] knows nothing whatever [of eternal value].

14 For she sits at the door of her house *or* on a seat in the conspicuous places of the town,

15 Calling to those who pass by, who go uprightly on their way:

16 Whoever is simple (wavering and easily led astray), let him turn in here! And as for him who lacks understanding, she says to him,

17 Stolen waters (pleasures) are sweet [because they are forbidden]; and bread eaten in secret is pleasant. [Prov. 20:17.]

18 But he knows not that the shades of the dead are there [specters haunting the scene of past transgressions], and that her invited guests are [already sunk] in the depths of Sheol (the lower world, Hades, the place of the dead).

10 THE PROVERBS of Solomon: A wise son makes a glad father, but a foolish *and* self-confident son is the grief of his mother.

2 Treasures of wickedness profit nothing, but righteousness (moral and spiritual rectitude in every area and relation) delivers from death.

3 The Lord will not allow the [uncompromisingly] righteous to famish,

but He thwarts the desire of the wicked. [Ps. 34:9, 10; 37:25.]

4 He becomes poor who works with a slack *and* idle hand, but the hand of the diligent makes rich.

5 He who gathers in summer is a wise son, but he who sleeps in harvest is a son who causes shame.

6 Blessings are upon the head of the [uncompromisingly] righteous (the upright, in right standing with God) but the mouth of the wicked conceals violence.

7 The memory of the [uncompromisingly] righteous is a blessing, but the name of the wicked shall rot. [Ps. 112:6; 9:5.]

8 The wise in heart will accept *and* obey commandments, but the foolish of lips will fall headlong.

9 He who walks uprightly walks securely, but he who takes a crooked way shall be found out *and* punished.

10 He who winks with the eye [craftily and with malice] causes sorrow; the foolish of lips will fall headlong *but* ᵏ*he who boldly reproves makes peace.*

11 The mouth of the [uncompromisingly] righteous man is a well of life, but the mouth of the wicked conceals violence.

12 Hatred stirs up contentions, but love covers all transgressions.

13 On the lips of him who has discernment skillful *and* godly ¹Wisdom is found, but discipline *and* the rod are for the back of him who is without sense *and* understanding.

14 Wise men store up knowledge [in mind and heart], but the mouth of the foolish is a present destruction.

15 The rich man's wealth is his strong city; the poverty of the poor is their ruin. [Ps. 52:7; I Tim. 6:17.]

16 The earnings of the righteous (the upright, in right standing with God) lead to life, but the profit of the wicked leads to further sin. [Rom. 6:21; I Tim. 6:10.]

17 He who heeds instruction *and* correction is [not only himself] in the way of life [but also] is a way of life for others. And he who neglects *or* refuses reproof [not only himself] goes astray [but also] causes to err *and* is a path toward ruin for others.

18 He who hides hatred is of lying lips, and he who utters slander is a [self-confident] fool. [Prov. 26:24-26.]

19 In a multitude of words transgression is not lacking, but he who restrains his lips is prudent.

20 The tongues of those who are upright *and* in right standing with God are as choice silver; the minds of those who are wicked *and* out of harmony with God are of little value.

21 The lips of the [uncompromisingly] righteous feed *and* guide many, but fools die for want of understanding *and* heart.

22 The blessing of the Lord—it makes [truly] rich, and He adds no sorrow with it [neither does toiling increase it].

23 It is as sport to a [self-confident] fool to do wickedness, but to have skillful *and* godly Wisdom is pleasure *and* relaxation to a man of understanding.

24 The thing a wicked man fears shall come upon him, but the desire of

speak the Word

Thank You, God, that blessings are on the heads of the uncompromisingly righteous and that I am righteous through Your Son!
ADAPTED FROM PROVERBS 10:6

k *The Septuagint* (Greek translation of the Old Testament) so reads at this point.   l Recall that "Wisdom" is capitalized throughout the book of Proverbs as a reminder of its divine implications. See footnotes on Prov. 1:2 and Prov. 1:20.

the [uncompromisingly] righteous
shall be granted.

25 When the whirlwind passes, the
wicked are no more, but the [uncom-
promisingly] righteous have an everlasting foundation. [Ps. 125:1; Matt.
7:24-27.]

26 As vinegar to the teeth and as
smoke to the eyes, so is the sluggard
to those who employ *and* send him.

27 The reverent *and* worshipful fear
of the Lord prolongs one's days, but
the years of the wicked shall be made
short.

28 The hope of the [uncompromis-
ingly] righteous (the upright, in right
standing with God) is gladness, but
the expectation of the wicked (those
who are out of harmony with God)
comes to nothing.

29 The way of the Lord is strength
and a stronghold to the upright, but it
is destruction to the workers of iniquity.

30 The [consistently] righteous shall
never be removed, but the wicked
shall not inhabit the earth [eventual-
ly]. [Ps. 37:22; 125:1.]

31 The mouths of the righteous
(those harmonious with God) bring
forth skillful *and* godly Wisdom, but
the perverse tongue shall be cut down
[like a barren and rotten tree].

32 The lips of the [uncompromising-
ly] righteous know [and therefore
utter] what is acceptable, but the
mouth of the wicked knows [and
therefore speaks only] what is obstinately willful *and* contrary.

11 A FALSE balance *and*
unrighteous dealings are
extremely offensive *and*
shamefully sinful to the Lord, but a

just weight is His delight. [Lev. 19:35,
36; Prov. 16:11.]

2 When swelling *and* pride come,
then emptiness *and* shame come also,
but with the humble (those who are
lowly, who have been pruned or chis-
eled by trial, and renounce self) are
skillful *and* godly Wisdom *and* soundness.

3 The integrity of the upright shall
guide them, but the willful contrariness *and* crookedness of the treacherous shall destroy them.

4 Riches provide no security in any
day of wrath *and* judgment, but righteousness (uprightness and right
standing with God) delivers from
death. [Prov. 10:2; Zeph. 1:18.]

5 The righteousness of the blameless shall rectify *and* make plain their
way *and* keep it straight, but the
wicked shall fall by their own wickedness.

6 The righteousness of the upright
[their rectitude in every area and
relation] shall deliver them, but the
treacherous shall be taken in their
own iniquity *and* greedy desire.

7 When the wicked man dies, his
hope [for the future] perishes; and the
expectation of the godless comes to
nothing.

8 The [uncompromisingly] righteous is delivered out of trouble, and
the wicked gets into it instead.

9 With his mouth the godless man
destroys his neighbor, but through
knowledge *and* superior discernment
shall the righteous be delivered.

10 When it goes well with the
[uncompromisingly] righteous, the
city rejoices, but when the wicked
perish, there are shouts of joy.

11 By the blessing of the influence of

speak the Word

the upright *and* God's favor [because of them] the city is exalted, but it is overthrown by the mouth of the wicked.

12 He who belittles *and* despises his neighbor lacks sense, but a man of understanding keeps silent.

13 He who goes about as a talebearer reveals secrets, but he who is trustworthy *and* faithful in spirit keeps the matter hidden.

14 Where no wise guidance is, the people fall, but in the multitude of counselors there is safety.

putting the Word to work

Proverbs 11:14 teaches us that there is safety in a multitude of counselors. Do you have wise, godly people who can provide sound counsel in your life? If so, consult them often. Never put them ahead of God, and do not let them make your final decisions, because those should be made between you and God. However, wise counselors are very valuable, and if you do not have such people in your life, ask God to send them.

15 He who becomes security for an outsider shall smart for it, but he who hates suretyship is secure [from its penalties].

16 A gracious *and* good woman wins honor [for her husband], and violent men win riches *but* ᵐ*a woman who hates righteousness is a throne of dishonor for him.*

17 The merciful, kind, *and* generous man benefits himself [for his deeds return to bless him], but he who is cruel *and* callous [to the wants of others] brings on himself retribution.

18 The wicked man earns deceitful wages, but he who sows righteousness (moral and spiritual rectitude in every area and relation) shall have a sure reward [permanent and satisfying]. [Hos. 10:12; Gal. 6:8, 9; James 3:18.]

19 He who is steadfast in righteousness (uprightness and right standing with God) attains to life, but he who pursues evil does it to his own death.

20 They who are willfully contrary in heart are extremely disgusting *and* shamefully vile in the eyes of the Lord, but such as are blameless *and* wholehearted in their ways are His delight!

21 Assuredly [I pledge it] the wicked shall not go unpunished, but the multitude of the [uncompromisingly] righteous shall be delivered.

22 As a ring of gold in a swine's snout, so is a fair woman who is without discretion.

23 The desire of the [consistently] righteous brings only good, but the expectation of the wicked brings wrath.

24 There are those who [generously] scatter abroad, and yet increase more; there are those who withhold more than is fitting *or* what is justly due, but it results only in want.

25 The liberal person shall be enriched, and he who waters shall himself be watered. [II Cor. 9:6-10.]

26 The people curse him who holds back grain [when the public needs it], but a blessing [from God and man] is upon the head of him who sells it.

27 He who diligently seeks good seeks [God's] favor, but he who searches after evil, it shall come upon him.

putting the Word to work

Proverbs 11:25 says that people who are generous will be enriched and that when we "water" others, we will be "watered" in return. In what ways can you be generous to someone today?

m *The Septuagint* (Greek translation of the Old Testament) so reads at this point.

28 He who leans on, trusts in, *and* is confident in his riches shall fall, but the [uncompromisingly] righteous shall flourish like a green bough.

29 He who troubles his own house shall inherit the wind, and the foolish shall be servant to the wise of heart.

30 The fruit of the [uncompromisingly] righteous is a tree of life, and he who is wise captures human lives [for God, as a fisher of men—he gathers and receives them for eternity]. [Matt. 4:19; I Cor. 9:19; James 5:20.]

31 Behold, the [uncompromisingly] righteous shall be recompensed on earth; how much more the wicked and the sinner! *And* nif the righteous *are barely saved, what will become of the ungodly and wicked?* [I Pet. 4:18.]

12 WHOEVER LOVES instruction *and* correction loves knowledge, but he who hates reproof is like a brute beast, stupid *and* indiscriminating.

2 A good man obtains favor from the Lord, but a man of wicked devices He condemns.

3 A man shall not be established by wickedness, but the root of the [uncompromisingly] righteous shall never be moved.

4 A virtuous *and* worthy wife [earnest and strong in character] is a crowning joy to her husband, but she who makes him ashamed is as rottenness in his bones. [Prov. 31:23; I Cor. 11:7.]

5 The thoughts *and* purposes of the [consistently] righteous are honest *and* reliable, but the counsels *and* designs of the wicked are treacherous.

6 The words of the wicked lie in wait for blood, but the mouth of the upright shall deliver them *and* the innocent ones [thus endangered].

7 The wicked are overthrown and are not, but the house of the [uncompromisingly] righteous shall stand.

8 A man shall be commended according to his Wisdom [godly Wisdom, which is comprehensive insight into the ways and purposes of God], but he who is of a perverse heart shall be despised.

9 Better is he who is lightly esteemed but works for his own support than he who assumes honor for himself and lacks bread.

10 A [consistently] righteous man regards the life of his beast, but even the tender mercies of the wicked are cruel. [Deut. 25:4.]

11 He who tills his land shall be satisfied with bread, but he who follows worthless pursuits is lacking in sense *and* is without understanding.

12 The wicked desire the booty of evil men, but the root of the [uncompromisingly] righteous yields [richer fruitage].

13 The wicked is [dangerously] snared by the transgression of his lips, but the [uncompromisingly] righteous shall come out of trouble.

14 From the fruit of his words a man shall be satisfied with good, and the work of a man's hands shall come back to him [as a harvest].

15 The way of a fool is right in his own eyes, but he who listens to counsel is wise. [Prov. 3:7; 9:9; 21:2.]

16 A fool's wrath is quickly *and* openly known, but a prudent man ignores an insult.

17 He who breathes out truth shows forth righteousness (uprightness and right standing with God), but a false witness utters deceit.

18 There are those who speak rashly, like the piercing of a sword, but the tongue of the wise brings healing.

19 Truthful lips shall be established forever, but a lying tongue is [credited] but for a moment.

n *The Septuagint* (Greek translation of the Old Testament) so reads at this point.

20 Deceit is in the hearts of those who devise evil, but for the counselors of peace there is joy.
21 No [actual] evil, misfortune, *or* calamity shall come upon the righteous, but the wicked shall be filled with evil, misfortune, *and* calamity. [Job 5:19; Ps. 91:3; Prov. 12:13; Isa. 46:4; Jer. 1:8; Dan. 6:27; II Tim. 4:18.]
22 Lying lips are extremely disgusting *and* hateful to the Lord, but they who deal faithfully are His delight. [Prov. 6:17; 11:20; Rev. 22:15.]
23 A prudent man is reluctant to display his knowledge, but the heart of [self-confident] fools proclaims their folly. [Isa. 32:6.]
24 The hand of the diligent will rule, but the slothful will be put to forced labor.
25 Anxiety in a man's heart weighs it down, but an encouraging word makes it glad. [Ps. 50:4; Prov. 15:13.]
26 The [consistently] righteous man is a guide to his neighbor, but the way of the wicked causes others to go astray.
27 The slothful man does not catch his game *or* roast it once he kills it, but the diligent man gets precious possessions.
28 Life is in the way of righteousness (moral and spiritual rectitude in every area and relation), and in its pathway there is no death *but* immortality (perpetual, eternal life). [John 3:36; 4:36; 8:51; 11:26; I Cor. 15:54; Gal. 6:8.]

13 A WISE son heeds [and is the fruit of] his father's instruction *and* correction, but a scoffer listens not to rebuke.
2 A good man eats good from the fruit of his mouth, but the desire of the treacherous is for violence.
3 He who guards his mouth keeps his life, but he who opens wide his lips comes to ruin.
4 The appetite of the sluggard craves and gets nothing, but the

life point

I believe every Christian should keep his heart light. The King James Version of Proverbs 12:25 says, "Heaviness in the heart of man maketh it stoop: but a good word maketh it glad."

We do not have to go around with a troubled, heavy heart or with a spirit of heaviness on us. In John 14:1 Jesus told His disciples, "Do not let your hearts be troubled (distressed, agitated)." Isaiah 61:3 gives a wonderful promise to those who need the Lord to lift the heaviness from them. It says that God wants to "grant [consolation and joy] to those who mourn in Zion—to give them an ornament (a garland or diadem) of beauty instead of ashes, the oil of joy instead of mourning, the garment [expressive] of praise instead of a heavy, burdened, and failing spirit . . ."

The Lord does not want us to have heavy or troubled hearts. The next time things are not going well for you, remember to release your burdens and anxieties to the Lord. He wants you to be lighthearted and to enjoy life.

appetite of the diligent is abundantly supplied. [Prov. 10:4.]
5 A [consistently] righteous man hates lying *and* deceit, but a wicked man is loathsome [his very breath spreads pollution] and he comes [surely] to shame.
6 Righteousness (rightness and justice in every area and relation) guards him who is upright in the way, but wickedness plunges into sin *and* overthrows the sinner.
7 One man considers himself rich, yet has nothing [to keep permanently]; another man considers himself poor, yet has great [and indestructible] riches. [Prov. 12:9; Luke 12:20, 21.]

8 A rich man can buy his way out of threatened death by paying a ransom, but the poor man does not even have to listen to threats [from the envious].
9 The light of the [uncompromisingly] righteous [is within him—it grows brighter and] rejoices, but the lamp of the wicked [furnishes only a derived, temporary light and] shall be put out shortly.
10 By pride *and* insolence comes only contention, but with the well-advised is skillful *and* godly Wisdom.
11 Wealth [not earned but] won in haste *or* unjustly *or* from the production of things for vain *or* detrimental use [such riches] will dwindle away, but he who gathers little by little will increase [his riches].
12 Hope deferred makes the heart sick, but when the desire is fulfilled, it is a tree of life.

from disappointment to reappointment

Proverbs 13:12 says that "hope deferred makes the heart sick." What is "hope deferred"? I believe it is what we call disappointment.

We all are disappointed when things do not work out the way we want them to. We become disappointed when we have a plan that fails, a hope that does not materialize, or a goal that is not reached. We are disappointed by everything from a picnic that is rained out to the loss of a job. We are disappointed when the new watch we were given will not keep time correctly, or when the child we had hoped would turn out right shows no signs of doing so.

When things like that happen, for a certain period of time we experience a letdown—one that can lead to depression if it is not handled properly. That is when we have to make the decision to adapt and adjust, to take a new approach and just keep going despite our feelings. That is when we must remember that we have the Greater One residing within us, so that no matter what may happen to frustrate us, or how long it may take for our dreams and goals to become realities, we are not going to give up and quit just because of our emotions.

That is when we must remember what God once told me in just such a moment: *"When you get disappointed, you can always make the decision to get reappointed!"*

Disappointment often leads to discouragement, which is even more of a "downer." We have all experienced the depressing feeling that comes after we have tried our very best to do something and either nothing happens or it all falls totally apart.

How disappointing and discouraging it is to see the things we love senselessly destroyed by others or, even worse, by our own neglect or failure. Regardless of how it may happen or who may be responsible, it is hard to go on when everything we have counted on falls down around us. That is when those of us who have the creative power of the Holy Spirit on the inside can get a new vision, a new direction, and a new goal to help us overcome the frustrating, downward pull of disappointment. Hope deferred does make the heart sick, but hope can be rekindled, and our hearts can be made whole again by the power of the Holy Spirit.

13 Whoever despises the word *and* counsel [of God] brings destruction upon himself, but he who [reverently] fears *and* respects the commandment [of God] is rewarded.
14 The teaching of the wise is a fountain of life, that one may avoid the snares of death.
15 Good understanding wins favor, but the way of the transgressor is hard [like the barren, dry soil or the impassable swamp].
16 Every prudent man deals with knowledge, but a [self-confident] fool exposes *and* flaunts his folly.
17 A wicked messenger falls into evil, but a faithful ambassador brings healing.
18 Poverty and shame come to him who refuses instruction *and* correction, but he who heeds reproof is honored.
19 Satisfied desire is sweet to a person; therefore it is hateful *and* exceedingly offensive to [self-confident] fools to give up evil [upon which they have set their hearts].
20 He who walks [as a companion] with wise men is wise, but he who associates with [self-confident] fools is [a fool himself and] shall smart for it. [Isa. 32:6.]
21 Evil pursues sinners, but the consistently upright *and* in right standing with God is recompensed with good.
22 A good man leaves an inheritance [of moral stability and goodness] to his children's children, and the wealth of the sinner [finds its way eventually] into the hands of the righteous, for whom it was laid up.
23 Much food is in the tilled land of the poor, but there are those who are destroyed because of injustice.
24 He who spares his rod [of discipline] hates his son, but he who loves him disciplines diligently *and* punishes him early. [Prov. 19:18; 22:15; 23:13; 29:15, 17.]
25 The [uncompromisingly] righteous eats to his own satisfaction, but the stomach of the wicked is in want.

life point

A prudent person is balanced; he avoids extremes in the management of his life and faith. It seems to me, after many years of observation in the kingdom of God, that people have a difficult time with balance. Ideas concerning the power of words, the mouth, confession, calling those things that be not as though they are, and speaking things into existence, is one example of an area in which I have seen people move into extremes. It seems that the flesh wants to live in the ditch on one side of the road or the other, but it has a difficult time staying in the middle of the highway between the lines of safety. We should speak positively about our lives and our futures. We should agree with what God says about us in His Word. Our confession does have a lot to do with our possession, but we should not ever think that we can have whatever we want just because we say it. We are to speak forth God's Word, not our carnal desires.

Extremes are actually the devil's playground. If he cannot get a believer to totally ignore a truth and live in deception, his next tactic will be to get him so one-sided and out of balance with the truth that he is no better off than he was before. Sometimes he is even worse off than he was.

Wisdom is a central theme of God's Word. As a matter of fact, there is no real victory without it, and we are wise to remain balanced in our everyday lives.

14 EVERY WISE woman builds her house, but the foolish one tears it down with her own hands.

2 He who walks in uprightness reverently *and* worshipfully fears the Lord, but he who is contrary *and* devious in his ways despises Him.

3 In the °fool's own mouth is a rod [to shame] his pride, but the wise men's lips preserve them.

4 Where no oxen are, the grain crib is empty, but much increase [of crops] comes by the strength of the ox.

5 A faithful witness will not lie, but a false witness breathes out falsehoods.

6 A scoffer seeks Wisdom in vain [for his very attitude blinds and deafens him to it], but knowledge is easy to him who [being teachable] understands.

7 Go from the presence of a foolish *and* self-confident man, for you will not find knowledge on his lips.

8 The Wisdom [godly Wisdom, which is comprehensive insight into the ways and purposes of God] of the prudent is to understand his way, but the folly of [self-confident] fools is to deceive.

9 Fools make a mock of sin *and* sin mocks the fools [who are its victims; a sin offering made by them only mocks them, bringing them disappointment and disfavor], but among the upright there is the favor of God. [Prov. 10:23.]

10 The heart knows its own bitterness, and no stranger shares its joy.

11 The house of the wicked shall be overthrown, but the tent of the upright shall flourish.

12 There is a way which seems right to a man *and* appears straight before him, but at the end of it is the way of death.

13 Even in laughter the heart is sorrowful, and the end of mirth is heaviness *and* grief.

14 The backslider in heart [from God and from fearing God] shall be filled with [the fruit of] his own ways, and a good man shall be satisfied with [the fruit of] his ways [with the holy thoughts and actions which his heart prompts and in which he delights].

15 The simpleton believes every word he hears, but the prudent man looks *and* considers well where he is going.

16 A wise man suspects danger and cautiously avoids evil, but the fool bears himself insolently and is [presumptuously] confident.

17 He who foams up quickly *and* flies into a passion deals foolishly, and a man of wicked plots *and* plans is hated.

18 The simple acquire folly, but the prudent are crowned with knowledge.

19 The evil men bow before the good, and the wicked [stand suppliantly] at the gates of the [uncompromisingly] righteous.

speak the Word

Help me, Lord, to speak wisely, because wise words will preserve me.
ADAPTED FROM PROVERBS 14:3

Thank You, God, for making me upright and giving me Your favor.
ADAPTED FROM PROVERBS 14:9

o The word "fool" in the Old Testament seldom, if ever, is used to describe the feebleminded, imbecile, idiot, or moron. Rather, it always has within it the meaning of **a rebel**, especially against God and the laws of order, decency, and justice. Notice in Proverbs how many such characteristics of rebelliousness are listed against the fool, and see God's attitude toward them.

20 The poor is hated even by his own neighbor, but the rich has many friends.

21 He who despises his neighbor sins [against God, his fellowman, and him-

self], but happy (blessed and fortunate) is he who is kind *and* merciful to the poor.

22 Do they not err who devise evil *and* wander from the way of life? But

free from bitterness

Proverbs 14:10 speaks of bitterness in our hearts. Bitterness (harboring unforgiveness) in our hearts is extremely dangerous because the Bible tells us very plainly that if we will not forgive other people, then God cannot forgive us (see Mark 11:26). If we do not forgive others, our faith will not work. And everything that comes from God comes by faith. If our faith does not work, we cannot receive from God and we are in serious trouble.

When I preach on the subject of forgiveness, I often ask members of the audience to stand if they have been offended and need to forgive someone. I have never seen less than 80 percent of the congregation stand up.

It does not take a genius to figure out why we are lacking the power we need in the body of Christ. Power comes from love, not from hatred, bitterness, and unforgiveness.

"But you don't know what was done to me," people say when trying to excuse their bitterness, resentment, and unforgiveness. Based on what the Bible says, it really does not matter how great the offense was. We serve a God Who is greater, and if we will handle the offense in the right way, He will bring us justice and recompense when we allow Him to do so.

In Isaiah 61:7 the Lord promises us, "Instead of your [former] shame you shall have a twofold recompense." A recompense is a reward. It is a payback for past hurts. It is like worker's compensation. The Lord once told me, "Joyce, you work for Me, and as long as you do, if you get hurt on the job, I will pay you back."

In Romans 12:19 we are told, "Beloved, never avenge yourselves, but leave the way open for [God's] wrath; for it is written, Vengeance is Mine, I will repay (requite), says the Lord." Do not try to get people back for what they have done to you. Leave it in God's hands.

Jesus taught us that we are to forgive those who hurt us, pray for those who spitefully use us, and bless those who curse us (see Matthew 5:44). That is hard. But there is something harder: being full of hatred, bitterness, and resentment.

Quite often, people do not even know that they have hurt us. Do not spend your life hating someone who is probably out having a good time while you are all upset! Rather, choose to allow God to work forgiveness in you so that you may be released from your bitterness and set free to enjoy life.

loving-kindness *and* mercy, loyalty *and* faithfulness, shall be to those who devise good.

23 In all labor there is profit, but idle talk leads only to poverty.

24 The crown of the wise is their wealth of Wisdom, but the foolishness of [self-confident] fools is [nothing but] folly.

25 A truthful witness saves lives, but a deceitful witness speaks lies [and endangers lives].

26 In the reverent *and* worshipful fear of the Lord there is strong confidence, and His children shall always have a place of refuge.

27 Reverent *and* worshipful fear of the Lord is a fountain of life, that one may avoid the snares of death. [John 4:10, 14.]

28 In a multitude of people is the king's glory, but in a lack of people is the prince's ruin.

29 He who is slow to anger has great understanding, but he who is hasty of spirit exposes *and* exalts his folly. [Prov. 16:32; James 1:19.]

30 A calm *and* undisturbed mind *and* heart are the life *and* health of the body, but envy, jealousy, *and* wrath are like rottenness of the bones.

31 He who oppresses the poor reproaches, mocks, *and* insults his

Maker, but he who is kind *and* merciful to the needy honors Him. [Prov. 17:5; Matt. 25:40, 45.]

32 The wicked is overthrown through his wrongdoing *and* calamity, but the [consistently] righteous has hope *and* confidence even in death.

33 Wisdom rests [silently] in the mind *and* heart of him who has understanding, but that which is in the inward part of [self-confident] fools is made known. [Isa. 32:6.]

34 Uprightness *and* right standing with God (moral and spiritual rectitude in every area and relation) elevate a nation, but sin is a reproach to any people.

35 The king's favor is toward a wise *and* discreet servant, but his wrath is against him who does shamefully. [Matt. 24:45, 47.]

15 A SOFT answer turns away wrath, but grievous words stir up anger. [Prov. 25:15.]

life point

The Bible teaches us in Proverbs 15:1 that a "soft answer turns away wrath." In other words, if someone is angry and yelling, then responding to that person calmly and gently will change the situation and stop an argument. How awesome! The next time angry words seem to be flying around you, respond with soft, gentle words. That's the best way to diffuse an argument.

2 The tongue of the wise utters knowledge rightly, but the mouth of the [self-confident] fool pours out folly.

life point

Think about it: a person who has a calm and undisturbed mind has health for his body. But as we see in Proverbs 14:30, envy, jealousy, and anger can actually destroy the physical body. Keeping these negative emotions far from you is good for your health!

speak the Word

Thank You, God, that I have strong confidence as I hold you in fear and reverence. In You, I will always have a place of refuge.
ADAPTED FROM PROVERBS **14:26**

3 The eyes of the Lord are in every place, keeping watch upon the evil and the good. [Job 34:21; Prov. 5:21; Jer. 16:17; 32:19; Heb. 4:13.]

4 A gentle tongue [with its healing power] is a tree of life, but willful contrariness in it breaks down the spirit.

life point

Throughout the Word of God we are told to be careful how we use our mouths. We are to pay attention to our words. We are never to speak things that are going to make people want to give up or quit. We are not to pollute one another or ourselves with negative words from our lips.

Proverbs 15:4 tells us that willful contrariness breaks down the spirit. Notice that the word *spirit* is spelled with a small *s*. This verse is not talking about the Holy Spirit; it is referring to our own human spirits. Depression of the human spirit is another problem created and magnified by wrong thoughts and words—our own or those of others.

We are not to use our mouths to hurt, break down, or depress, but rather to heal, restore, and uplift. The tongue has healing power, and we need to use it to bring healing.

5 A fool despises his father's instruction *and* correction, but he who regards reproof acquires prudence.

6 In the house of the [uncompromisingly] righteous is great [priceless] treasure, but with the income of the wicked is trouble *and* vexation.

7 The lips of the wise disperse knowledge [sifting it as chaff from the grain]; not so the minds *and* hearts of the self-confident *and* foolish.

8 The sacrifice of the wicked is an abomination, hateful *and* exceedingly

life point

Those who are wise in heart use their lips to spread knowledge (see Proverbs 15:7), but those who are foolish in heart speak whatever comes to mind. I believe one of the biggest problems with people is that they do not use wisdom when they think and thus say or do foolish things. Ask God to help you identify and correct any foolishness in your life and to enable you to use wisdom in everything you do.

offensive to the Lord, but the prayer of the upright is His delight! [Isa. 1:11; Jer. 6:20; Amos 5:22.]

9 The way of the wicked is an abomination, extremely disgusting *and* shamefully vile to the Lord, but He loves him who pursues righteousness (moral and spiritual rectitude in every area and relation).

10 There is severe discipline for him who forsakes God's way; and he who hates reproof will die [physically, morally, and spiritually].

11 Sheol (the place of the dead) and Abaddon (the abyss, the final place of the accuser Satan) are both before the Lord—how much more, then, the hearts of the children of men? [Job 26:6; Ps. 139:8; Rev. 9:2; 20:1, 2.]

12 A scorner has no love for one who rebukes him; neither will he go to the wise [for counsel].

13 A glad heart makes a cheerful countenance, but by sorrow of heart the spirit is broken. [Prov. 17:22.]

14 The mind of him who has understanding seeks knowledge and inquires after *and* craves it, but the mouth of the [self-confident] fool feeds on folly. [Isa. 32:6.]

15 All the days of the desponding *and* afflicted are made evil [by anxious thoughts and forebodings], but he who has a glad heart has a continual feast [regardless of circumstances].

life point

Proverbs 15:13 says that a glad, happy heart makes a cheerful countenance. The Bible uses the word *countenance* in many places, so I think we should pay attention to it. Your countenance is your face, the way you look. God is concerned about how we look because either we are walking advertisements for Jesus or we are walking advertisements for Satan. That is why it is important that we learn how to have a cheerful countenance and a pleasant look on our faces.

My husband has a secretary who is always smiling. Everything he asks her to do, she does it with a smile. I think that is the way God wants all of us to be. When we smile, it puts other people at ease. It gives them freedom and liberty and a sense of confidence.

It is amazing how much more comfortable and secure we are when we smile at one another and how much discomfort and insecurity we cause one another when we go around with a sour look on our faces.

Sometimes our problems are not caused by the devil as we might like to assume—they are the results of the way we feel and act. We need to cheer up. When we relax and smile, it makes us (and everyone around us) feel better.

16 Better is little with the reverent, worshipful fear of the Lord than great *and* rich treasure and trouble with it. [Ps. 37:16; Prov. 16:8; I Tim. 6:6.]
17 Better is a dinner of herbs where love is than a fatted ox and hatred with it. [Prov. 17:1.]
18 A hot-tempered man stirs up strife, but he who is slow to anger appeases contention.
19 The way of the sluggard is over-grown with thorns [it pricks, lacer-ates, and entangles him], but the way of the righteous is plain *and* raised like a highway.
20 A wise son makes a glad father, but a self-confident *and* foolish man despises his mother *and* puts her to shame.
21 Folly is pleasure to him who is without heart *and* sense, but a man of understanding walks uprightly [mak-ing straight his course]. [Eph. 5:15.]
22 Where there is no counsel, pur-poses are frustrated, but with many counselors they are accomplished.
23 A man has joy in making an apt answer, and a word spoken at the right moment—how good it is!
24 The path of the wise leads upward to life, that he may avoid [the gloom] in the depths of Sheol (Hades, the place of the dead). [Phil. 3:20; Col. 3:1, 2.]
25 The Lord tears down the house of the proud, but He makes secure the boundaries of the [consecrated] widow.
26 The thoughts of the wicked are shamefully vile *and* exceedingly of-fensive to the Lord, but the words of the pure are pleasing words to Him.
27 He who is greedy for unjust gain troubles his own household, but he who hates bribes will live. [Isa. 5:8; Jer. 17:11.]
28 The mind of the [uncompromis-ingly] righteous studies how to answer, but the mouth of the wicked pours out evil things. [I Pet. 3:15.]
29 The Lord is far from the wicked, but He hears the prayer of the [con-sistently] righteous (the upright, in right standing with Him).
30 The light in the eyes [of him whose heart is joyful] rejoices the hearts of others, and good news nour-ishes the bones.
31 The ear that listens to the reproof [that leads to or gives] life will remain among the wise.
32 He who refuses *and* ignores

instruction *and* correction despises himself, but he who heeds reproof gets understanding.

33 The reverent *and* worshipful fear of the Lord brings instruction in Wisdom, and humility comes before honor.

16 THE PLANS of the mind *and* orderly thinking belong to man, but from the Lord comes the [wise] answer of the tongue.

2 All the ways of a man are pure in his own eyes, but the Lord weighs the spirits (the thoughts and intents of the heart). [I Sam. 16:7; Heb. 4:12.]

3 Roll your works upon the Lord [commit and trust them wholly to Him; He will cause your thoughts to become agreeable to His will, and] so shall your plans be established *and* succeed.

the wise answer of the tongue

Sometimes the Lord gives us "the [wise] answer of the tongue" (Proverbs 16:1) from our very own lips. I learned this truth when I was in a situation where I did not know what to do and my own thoughts left me confused. I was not getting anywhere with my circumstances until I took a walk with a friend.

I was facing a major decision that needed a godly answer, but I could not find God's leading. My friend and I discussed the issue for about an hour as we walked together, enjoying the fresh air and each other's company. That is when I learned that sometimes wisdom comes out of our own mouths as we begin to talk to someone about a situation.

We talked about the circumstance and discussed several different possible solutions and their potential outcomes. We talked about how good it might be if we handled the situation one way and how bad it might be if we handled it another way. Suddenly, one particular answer settled in my heart.

What I decided I needed to do was not something I naturally wanted to do. A stubborn mind-set is a great enemy of peace. Some of my struggle was because I wanted to convince God that my situation should be dealt with differently from the way He was leading me. His voice was difficult to discern because my mind was already set against His plan.

We have to be willing to lay aside our own desires or we may miss a clear word from God. Our natural inclination is to manipulate things to work the way we want them to work. Some of our best childhood toys taught us that square pegs will not fit into round holes, and we must remember that our plans do not always fit God's ways—no matter how forcefully we try to make the two work together.

While my friend and I considered the situation together, a wise answer came out of my mouth that I knew was from the Lord. It did not come from my mind, but it rose from my inner being. God promises that if we open our mouths, He will fill them (see Psalm 81:10), and Jesus promises to give us words and wisdom that none of our adversaries will be able to resist or contradict (see Luke 21:15).

life point

Proverbs 16:2 says that all our ways are pure in our own eyes. In other words, most of us do not see our own faults.

It would do us good to choose about three of our most trusted friends, sit down with them several times a year, and ask them, "How do you see me?" This is because we see ourselves a whole lot differently than others see us. Ask this question of mature, trustworthy, honest people. Take their answers seriously and pray about them, asking God to help you in your weaknesses.

4 The Lord has made everything [to accommodate itself and contribute] to its own end *and* His own purpose— even the wicked [are fitted for their role] for the day of calamity *and* evil.
5 Everyone proud *and* arrogant in heart is disgusting, hateful, *and* exceedingly offensive to the Lord; be assured [I pledge it] they will not go unpunished. [Prov. 8:13; 11:20-21.]
6 By mercy *and* love, truth *and* fidelity [to God and man—not by sacrificial offerings], iniquity is purged out of the heart, and by the reverent, worshipful fear of the Lord men depart from *and* avoid evil.
7 When a man's ways please the Lord, He makes even his enemies to be at peace with him.
8 Better is a little with righteousness (uprightness in every area and relation and right standing with God) than great revenues with injustice. [Ps. 37:16; Prov. 15:16.]
9 A man's mind plans his way, but

the Lord directs his steps *and* makes them sure. [Ps. 37:23; Prov. 20:24; Jer. 10:23.]
10 Divinely directed decisions are on the lips of the king; his mouth should not transgress in judgment.
11 A just balance *and* scales are the Lord's; all the weights of the bag are His work [established on His eternal principles].
12 It is an abomination [to God and men] for kings to commit wickedness, for a throne is established *and* made secure by righteousness (moral and spiritual rectitude in every area and relation).
13 Right *and* just lips are the delight of a king, and he loves him who speaks what is right.
14 The wrath of a king is as messengers of death, but a wise man will pacify it.
15 In the light of the king's countenance is life, and his favor is as a cloud bringing the spring rain.
16 How much better it is to get skillful *and* godly Wisdom than gold! And to get understanding is to be chosen rather than silver. [Prov. 8:10, 19.]
17 The highway of the upright turns aside from evil; he who guards his way preserves his life.
18 Pride goes before destruction, and a haughty spirit before a fall.
19 Better it is to be of a humble spirit with the meek *and* poor than to divide the spoil with the proud.
20 He who deals wisely *and* heeds [God's] word *and* counsel shall find good, and whoever leans on, trusts in, *and* is confident in the Lord—happy, blessed, *and* fortunate is he.
21 The wise in heart are called prudent, understanding, *and* knowing,

speak the Word

Thank You, God, that as I roll my works on You and trust You, You will cause my thoughts to agree with Your will and make my plans succeed.
ADAPTED FROM PROVERBS 16:3

humble people are happy people

People who are proud are hard to deal with because they refuse correction and good advice. In fact, Proverbs 16:5 says they are "disgusting, hateful, and exceedingly offensive to the Lord." They cannot be told anything because they think they already know everything. Since they are so opinionated, they are always on the defensive, which makes it hard for them to receive correction. To them that would seem to be an admission that they are wrong—and that is something they find almost impossible to do.

In my ministry, the Lord uses me to bring correction from His Word. Generally, the flesh does not care for that, but it is what makes us grow up in the Lord. Although I try to do it in a loving way, sometimes it still causes people to react against me because, being proud, they resist the truth. Yet Jesus told us that it is the Truth that sets us free (see John 8:32). Remember: free people are happy people.

It was good for me to learn that when the Lord does lead me to correct people, it is not my job to convince them. That is the job of the Holy Spirit. In John 16:8 Jesus said that it is the Holy Spirit Who convicts and convinces people of the truth. That means you and I do not have to try to "play God" in other people's lives.

Proud people feel they have to convince others that they are right and everyone else is wrong. They try to tell people how they need to change or what they need to do. As Proverbs 16:5 tells us, that kind of domineering, superior approach is not pleasing to God. He wants His children to walk in kindness and humility, not arrogance and pride.

Proud people are also usually very rigid, which explains why they are often such strict disciplinarians. They have their own way of doings things, and if anyone does not do it their way, they react strongly, sometimes even violently: "This is it! This is the way it has to be done—or else!"

Finally, proud people are often complicated people. Although the Bible calls us to a life of simplicity, proud people feel that they have to make a big deal out of everything, to make a mountain out of every molehill. Part of the reason is because they think they have to figure out everything, that they have to know the "ins and outs" of every situation and know the reason for everything that happens in life. To put it simply, they want to be in control because deep down inside they feel that nobody can handle things as well as they can!

All these things help to explain why proud people are usually not very happy people. And unhappy people do not make very many other people happy either. Cultivate humility in your life so that you can be happy and bring joy to others.

and winsome speech increases learning [in both speaker and listener].

22 Understanding is a wellspring of life to those who have it, but to give instruction to fools is folly.

23 The mind of the wise instructs his mouth, and adds learning *and* persuasiveness to his lips.

24 Pleasant words are as a honeycomb, sweet to the mind and healing to the body.

25 There is a way that seems right to a man *and* appears straight before him, but at the end of it is the way of death.

26 The appetite of the laborer works for him, for [the need of] his mouth urges him on.

27 A worthless man devises *and* digs up mischief, and in his lips there is as a scorching fire.

28 A perverse man sows strife, and a whisperer separates close friends. [Prov. 17:9.]

29 The exceedingly grasping, covetous, *and* violent man entices his neighbor, leading him in a way that is not good.

30 He who shuts his eyes to devise perverse things and who compresses his lips [as if in concealment] brings evil to pass.

31 The hoary head is a crown of beauty *and* glory if it is found in the way of righteousness (moral and spiritual rectitude in every area and relation). [Prov. 20:29.]

32 He who is slow to anger is better than the mighty, he who rules his [own] spirit than he who takes a city.

33 The lot is cast into the lap, but the decision is wholly of the Lord [even the events that seem accidental are really ordered by Him].

17 BETTER IS a dry morsel with quietness than a house full of feasting [on offered sacrifices] with strife.

2 A wise servant shall have rule over a son who causes shame, and shall share in the inheritance among the brothers.

3 The refining pot is for silver and the furnace for gold, but the Lord tries the hearts. [Ps. 26:2; Prov. 27:21; Jer. 17:10; Mal. 3:3.]

4 An evildoer gives heed to wicked lips; and a liar listens to a mischievous tongue.

5 Whoever mocks the poor reproaches his Maker, and he who is glad at calamity shall not be held innocent *or* go unpunished. [Job 31:29; Prov. 14:31; Obad. 12.]

6 Children's children are the crown of old men, and the glory of children is their fathers. [Ps. 127:3; 128:3.]

7 Fine *or* arrogant speech does not befit [an empty-headed] fool—much less do lying lips befit a prince.

8 A bribe is like a bright, precious stone that dazzles the eyes *and* affects the mind of him who gives it; [as if by magic] he prospers, whichever way he turns.

9 He who covers *and* forgives an offense seeks love, but he who repeats *or* harps on a matter separates even close friends.

10 A reproof enters deeper into a man of understanding than a hundred lashes into a [self-confident] fool. [Isa. 32:6.]

11 An evil man seeks only rebellion; therefore a stern *and* pitiless messenger shall be sent against him.

12 Let [the brute ferocity of] a bear robbed of her whelps meet a man rather than a [self-confident] fool in his folly [when he is in a rage]. [Hos. 13:8.]

13 Whoever rewards evil for good, evil shall not depart from his house. [Ps. 109:4, 5; Jer. 18:20.]

14 The beginning of strife is as when water first trickles [from a crack in a dam]; therefore stop contention before it becomes worse *and* quarreling breaks out.

15 He who justifies the wicked and

he who condemns the righteous are both an abomination [exceedingly disgusting and hateful] to the Lord. [Exod. 23:7; Prov. 24:24; Isa. 5:23.]

16 Of what use is money in the hand of a [self-confident] fool to buy skillful *and* godly Wisdom—when he has no understanding *or* heart for it?

17 A friend loves at all times, and is born, as is a brother, for adversity.

18 A man void of good sense gives a pledge and becomes security for another in the presence of his neighbor.

19 He who loves strife *and* is quarrelsome loves transgression *and* involves himself in guilt; he who raises high his gateway *and* is boastful *and* arrogant invites destruction.

20 He who has a wayward *and* crooked mind finds no good, and he who has a willful *and* contrary tongue will fall into calamity. [James 3:8.]

21 He who becomes the parent of a [self-confident] fool does it to his sorrow, and the father of [an empty-headed] fool has no joy [in him].

22 A happy heart is good medicine

people who laugh, last

We need to enjoy life while we work and perform the things we think we are supposed to do. Proverbs 17:22 teaches us that happiness in our hearts is like a good medicine.

Because my childhood was stolen from me through abuse, I never learned to be childlike. I never learned to "lighten up" and "live a little." I was so serious that I thought I should not have anything to do with things I considered to be "frivolous." I was always uptight about everything, and I rarely laughed because I was so busy working and taking life seriously. On the other hand, my husband, Dave, is the type who enjoys life regardless of what is going on around him. Although I may never have the ability to be just like he is because of our different personalities, I have learned I can be much happier and more lighthearted than I used to be.

As a minister of the Gospel, I have a huge responsibility. I have to work hard at what I have been called to do, and I love it. I really do enjoy my work. But if I am not careful, I can become stressed and burned out. That is why I have to make an effort to apply to my life verses such as Proverbs 17:22 and develop a happy heart and a cheerful mind.

You and I need a balance of fun and responsibility. If we are not emotionally balanced, our entire lives will be affected. I truly believe if we do not learn to laugh more, we are going to get into serious trouble because, as the Bible teaches, a happy heart is like medicine. There have been many articles written in recent years stating that medical science now confirms that laughter can be instrumental in bringing healing to the body. Laughter is like internal jogging—it exercises our inner soul, bringing health to it.

We need to find more humor in our everyday lives. We ought to laugh at ourselves, not taking ourselves too seriously. We all need to laugh more—and sometimes we need to do it on purpose. Remember, a happy heart is good medicine!

and a cheerful mind works healing, but a broken spirit dries up the bones. [Prov. 12:25; 15:13, 15.]

23 A wicked man receives a bribe out of the bosom (pocket) to pervert the ways of justice.

24 A man of understanding sets skillful *and* godly Wisdom before his face, but the eyes of a [self-confident] fool are on the ends of the earth.

25 A self-confident *and* foolish son is a grief to his father and bitterness to her who bore him.

26 Also, to punish *or* fine the righteous is not good, nor to smite the noble for their uprightness.

27 He who has knowledge spares his words, and a man of understanding has a cool spirit. [James 1:19.]

28 Even a fool when he holds his peace is considered wise; when he closes his lips he is esteemed a man of understanding.

18 HE WHO willfully separates *and* estranges himself [from God and man] seeks his own desire *and* pretext to break out against all wise *and* sound judgment.

2 A [self-confident] fool has no delight in understanding but only in revealing his personal opinions *and* himself.

3 When the wicked comes in [to the depth of evil], he becomes a contemptuous despiser [of all that is pure and good], and with inner baseness comes outer shame *and* reproach.

4 The words of a [discreet and wise] man's mouth are like deep waters [plenteous and difficult to fathom], and the fountain of skillful *and* godly Wisdom is like a gushing stream [sparkling, fresh, pure, and life-giving].

5 To respect the person of the wicked *and* be partial to him, so as to deprive the [consistently] righteous of justice, is not good.

6 A [self-confident] fool's lips bring contention, and his mouth invites a beating.

7 A [self-confident] fool's mouth is his ruin, and his lips are a snare to himself.

8 The words of a whisperer *or* talebearer are as dainty morsels; they go down into the innermost parts of the body.

9 He who is loose *and* slack in his work is brother to him who is a destroyer *and* ᵖ*he who does not use his endeavors to heal himself is brother to him who commits suicide.*

10 The name of the Lord is a strong tower; the [consistently] righteous man [upright and in right standing with God] runs into it and is safe, high [above evil] *and* strong.

11 The rich man's wealth is his strong city, and as a high protecting wall in his own imagination *and* conceit.

12 Haughtiness comes before disaster, but humility before honor.

13 He who answers a matter before he hears the facts—it is folly and shame to him. [John 7:51.]

14 The strong spirit of a man sustains him in bodily pain *or* trouble, but a weak *and* broken spirit who can raise up *or* bear?

15 The mind of the prudent is ever

speak the Word

God, I declare that Your name is a strong tower. I can run into it and be safe!
ADAPTED FROM PROVERBS 18:10

---

p This verse so reads in *The Septuagint* (Greek translation of the Old Testament). Its statement squarely addresses the problem of whether one has a moral right to neglect his body by "letting nature take its unhindered course" in illness.

strengthen the weak

Do you realize what Proverbs 18:14 is saying? Regardless of what comes into a person's life, he can bear up under it if he has a strong spirit within to sustain him in those times of trouble. But if his spirit is weak or wounded, he is going to have a hard time bearing anything in life.

Do you know what is wrong with many in the body of Christ today, why they cannot seem to handle their problems? It is not because their problems are any worse than those of anybody else. It is because they are weak in spirit. The Bible says that we are to bear with the failings and the frailties of the weak (see Romans 15:1). We are to lift them up and support them (see I Thessalonians 5:14).

Romans 12:8 tells us that one of the ministry gifts God gives to the church is the encourager or exhorter. Such people are usually easy to recognize because every time we get around them, they make us feel better by the things they say and do. It just seems to come naturally to them to uplift, encourage, and strengthen others by their very presence and personality.

If you are like I am and would not call yourself a naturally gifted encourager, then form a habit of being more encouraging. That is what I have done, and it not only makes others feel better, it also increases my joy level. We all can give compliments, and we all can say, "Thank you." We all can refuse to be slanderers. We all can refuse to allow evil things to come out of our mouths that tear people down. We all can build up, edify, lift up, and speak life to others.

getting knowledge, and the ear of the wise is ever seeking (inquiring for and craving) knowledge.

16 A man's gift makes room for him and brings him before great men. [Gen. 32:20; I Sam. 25:27; Prov. 17:8; 21:14.]

17 He who states his case first seems right, until his rival comes and cross-examines him.

18 To cast lots puts an end to disputes and decides between powerful contenders.

19 A brother offended is harder to be won over than a strong city, and [their] contentions separate them like the bars of a castle.

20 A man's [moral] self shall be filled with the fruit of his mouth; and with the consequence of his words he must be satisfied [whether good or evil].

21 Death and life are in the power of the tongue, and they who indulge in it shall eat the fruit of it [for death or life]. [Matt. 12:37.]

22 He who finds a [true] wife finds a

life point

Proverbs 18:21 teaches us that "death and life are in the power of the tongue." I do not believe we can overestimate the importance of our words, because they truly can make the difference between life and death. Determine today to use the power of your words to speak life everywhere you go!

power in your mouth

Proverbs 18:21 is a verse I have known for years and am very familiar with, but I am blessed every time I read it. I do not think we can read it too often, know it too well, or apply it too much. As you can tell by reading this verse, it teaches us that death and life are in the power of the tongue, and those who indulge in it will eat its fruit, either for death or for life.

Basically, the writer of Proverbs is saying in this verse: "Every time you open your mouth, you are ministering death or life, and whatever you dish out is what you are going to eat."

We have heard the phrase "You're going to have to eat your words," and Proverbs 18:21 confirms this truth. The words we speak have power to influence our lives. In fact, you may be eating your words right now, and that may be why you are not happy with your life. Your mouth may be getting you in trouble with yourself!

Proverbs 18:21 teaches us that words are so awesome. They are containers for power; they carry either a life-giving force or a destructive force.

For example, in my conferences I speak words, and those who hear those words receive life—life in their relationships, in their ministries, in their thoughts, and in all the areas that God uses me to speak to them about.

I have written a book called *Me and My Big Mouth!*, which deals with the words we speak and how to make them work for us instead of against us. The subtitle of the book is "Your Answer Is Right Under Your Nose." Perhaps you are desperately looking for an answer to what is happening in your life. Do you believe it is even remotely possible that your answer could be found in changing the way you talk? Go ahead and try it. I know the truth of Proverbs 18:21 and have experienced it many times in my own life. I believe if you will begin to speak positive, encouraging words of life and blessing, you will see blessing in your life!

good thing and obtains favor from the Lord. [Prov. 19:14; 31:10.]

23 The poor man uses entreaties, but the rich answers roughly.

24 The man of many friends [a friend of all the world] will prove himself a bad friend, but there is a friend who sticks closer than a brother.

19 BETTER IS a poor man who walks in his integrity than a rich man who is perverse in his speech and is a [self-confident] fool.

2 Desire without knowledge is not good, and to be overhasty is to sin *and* miss the mark.

3 The foolishness of man subverts his way [ruins his affairs]; then his

life point

Jesus is a friend who sticks closer than a brother (see Proverbs 18:24). Let Him be your best friend. If you do, you will be blessed, and your relationships will be more peaceful and balanced.

heart is resentful *and* frets against the Lord.

4 Wealth makes many friends, but the poor man is avoided by his neighbor. [Prov. 14:20.]

5 A false witness shall not be unpunished, and he who breathes out lies shall not escape. [Exod. 23:1; Deut. 19:16-19; Prov. 6:19; 21:28.]

6 Many will entreat the favor of a liberal man, and every man is a friend to him who gives gifts.

7 All the brothers of a poor man detest him—how much more do his friends go far from him! He pursues them with words, but they are gone.

8 He who gains Wisdom loves his own life; he who keeps understanding shall prosper *and* find good.

9 A false witness shall not be unpunished, and he who breathes forth lies shall perish.

10 Luxury is not fitting for a [self-confident] fool—much less for a slave to rule over princes.

11 Good sense makes a man restrain his anger, and it is his glory to overlook a transgression *or* an offense.

12 The king's wrath is as terrifying as the roaring of a lion, but his favor is as [refreshing as] dew upon the grass. [Hos. 14:5.]

13 A self-confident *and* foolish son is the [multiplied] calamity of his father, and the contentions of a wife are like a continual dripping [of water through a chink in the roof].

14 House and riches are the inheritance from fathers, but a wise, understanding, *and* prudent wife is from the Lord. [Prov. 18:22.]

15 Slothfulness casts one into a deep sleep, and the idle person shall suffer hunger.

16 He who keeps the commandment [of the Lord] keeps his own life, but he who despises His ways shall die. [Luke 10:28; 11:28.]

17 He who has pity on the poor lends to the Lord, and that which he has given He will repay to him. [Prov. 28:27; Eccl. 11:1; Matt. 10:42; 25:40; II Cor. 9:6-8; Heb. 6:10.]

18 Discipline your son while there is hope, but do not [indulge your angry resentments by undue chastisements and] set yourself to his ruin.

19 A man of great wrath shall suffer the penalty; for if you deliver him [from the consequences], he will [feel free to] cause you to do it again.

20 Hear counsel, receive instruction, *and* accept correction, that you may be wise in the time to come.

21 Many plans are in a man's mind, but it is the Lord's purpose for him that will stand. [Job 23:13; Ps. 33:10, 11; Isa. 14:26, 27; 46:10; Acts 5:39; Heb. 6:17.]

22 That which is desired in a man is loyalty *and* kindness [and his glory and delight are his giving], but a poor man is better than a liar.

23 The reverent, worshipful fear of the Lord leads to life, and he who has it rests satisfied; he cannot be visited with [actual] evil. [Job 5:19; Ps. 91:3; Prov. 12:13; Isa. 46:4; Jer. 1:8; Dan. 6:27; II Tim. 4:8.]

24 The sluggard buries his hand in the dish, and will not so much as bring it to his mouth again.

25 Strike a scoffer, and the simple will learn prudence; reprove a man of understanding, and he will increase in knowledge.

26 He who does violence to his father and chases away his mother is a son who causes shame and brings reproach.

speak the Word

Thank You, Lord, that Your purpose for me will stand.
ADAPTED FROM PROVERBS 19:21

27 Cease, my son, to hear instruction only to ignore it *and* stray from the words of knowledge.

28 A worthless witness scoffs at justice, and the mouth of the wicked swallows iniquity.

29 Judgments are prepared for scoffers, and stripes for the backs of [self-confident] fools. [Isa. 32:6.]

20 WINE IS a mocker, strong drink a riotous brawler; and whoever errs *or* reels because of it is not wise. [Prov. 23:29, 30; Isa. 28:7; Hos. 4:11.]

2 The terror of a king is as the roaring of a lion; whoever provokes him to anger *or* angers himself against him sins against his own life.

3 It is an honor for a man to cease from strife *and* keep aloof from it, but every fool will quarrel.

4 The sluggard does not plow when winter sets in; therefore he begs in harvest and has nothing.

5 Counsel in the heart of man is like water in a deep well, but a man of understanding draws it out. [Prov. 18:4.]

6 Many a man proclaims his own loving-kindness *and* goodness, but a faithful man who can find?

7 The righteous man walks in his integrity; blessed (happy, fortunate, enviable) are his children after him.

8 A king who sits on the throne of judgment winnows out all evil [like chaff] with his eyes.

9 Who can say, I have made my heart clean, I am pure from my sin? [I Kings 8:46; II Chron. 6:36; Job 9:30; 14:4; Ps. 51:5; I John 1:8.]

10 Diverse weights [one for buying and another for selling] and diverse measures—both of them are exceed-ingly offensive *and* abhorrent to the Lord. [Deut. 25:13; Mic. 6:10, 11.]

11 Even a child is known by his acts, whether [or not] what he does is pure and right.

12 The hearing ear and the seeing eye—the Lord has made both of them.

13 Love not sleep, lest you come to poverty; open your eyes and you will be satisfied with bread.

14 It is worthless, it is worthless! says the buyer; but when he goes his way, then he boasts [about his bargain].

15 There is gold, and a multitude of pearls, but the lips of knowledge are a vase of preciousness [the most precious of all]. [Job 28:12, 16-19; Prov. 3:15; 8:11.]

16 [The judge tells the creditor] Take the garment of one who is security for a stranger; and hold him in pledge when he is security for foreigners.

17 Food gained by deceit is sweet to a man, but afterward his mouth will be filled with gravel.

18 Purposes *and* plans are established by counsel; and [only] with good advice make *or* carry on war.

19 He who goes about as a talebearer reveals secrets; therefore associate not with him who talks too freely. [Rom. 16:17, 18.]

20 Whoever curses his father or his mother, his lamp shall be put out in complete darkness.

21 An inheritance hastily gotten [by greedy, unjust means] at the beginning, in the end it will not be blessed. [Prov. 28:20; Hab. 2:6.]

22 Do not say, I will repay evil; wait [expectantly] for the Lord, and He will rescue you. [II Sam. 16:12; Rom. 12:17-19; I Thess. 5:15; I Pet. 3:9.]

23 Diverse *and* deceitful weights are

speak the Word

shamefully vile *and* abhorrent to the Lord, and false scales are not good.

24 Man's steps are ordered by the Lord. How then can a man understand his way?

25 It is a snare to a man to utter a vow [of consecration] rashly and [not until] afterward inquire [whether he can fulfill it].

26 A wise king winnows out the wicked [from among the good] and brings the threshing wheel over them [to separate the chaff from the grain].

27 The spirit of man [that factor in human personality which proceeds immediately from God] is the lamp of the Lord, searching all his innermost parts. [I Cor. 2:11.]

28 Loving-kindness *and* mercy, truth *and* faithfulness, preserve the king, and his throne is upheld by [the people's] loyalty.

29 The glory of young men is their strength, and the beauty of old men is their gray head [suggesting wisdom and experience].

30 Blows that wound cleanse away evil, and strokes [for correction] reach to the innermost parts.

21 THE KING'S heart is in the hand of the Lord, as are the watercourses; He turns it whichever way He wills.

2 Every way of a man is right in his own eyes, but the Lord weighs *and* tries the hearts. [Prov. 24:12; Luke 16:15.]

3 To do righteousness and justice is more acceptable to the Lord than sacrifice. [I Sam. 15:22; Prov. 15:8; Isa. 1:11; Hos. 6:6; Mic. 6:7, 8.]

4 Haughtiness of eyes and a proud heart, even the tillage of the wicked *or* the lamp [of joy] to them [whatever it may be], are sin [in the eyes of God].

5 The thoughts of the [steadily] diligent tend only to plenteousness, but everyone who is impatient *and* hasty hastens only to want.

6 Securing treasures by a lying tongue is a vapor driven to and fro; those who seek them seek death.

7 The violence of the wicked shall sweep them away, because they refuse to do justice.

8 The way of the guilty is exceedingly crooked, but as for the pure, his work is right *and* his conduct is straight.

9 It is better to dwell in a corner of the housetop [on the flat oriental roof, exposed to all kinds of weather] than in a house shared with a nagging, quarrelsome, *and* faultfinding woman.

10 The soul *or* life of the wicked craves *and* seeks evil; his neighbor finds no favor in his eyes. [James 2:16.]

11 When the scoffer is punished, the fool gets a lesson in being wise; but men of [godly] Wisdom *and* good sense learn by being instructed.

12 The [uncompromisingly] righteous man considers well the house of the wicked—how the wicked are cast down to ruin.

13 Whoever stops his ears at the cry of the poor will cry out himself and not be heard. [Matt. 18:30-34; James 2:13.]

14 A gift in secret pacifies *and* turns away anger, and a bribe in the lap, strong wrath.

15 When justice is done, it is a joy to the righteous (the upright, in right standing with God), but to the evildoers it is dismay, calamity, *and* ruin.

16 A man who wanders out of the way of understanding shall abide in the congregation of the spirits (of the dead).

17 He who loves pleasure will be a poor man; he who loves wine and oil will not be rich.

18 The wicked become a ransom for the [uncompromisingly] righteous, and the treacherous for the upright [because the wicked themselves fall into the traps and pits they have dug for the good].

19 It is better to dwell in a desert

land than with a contentious woman and with vexation.

20 There are precious treasures and oil in the dwelling of the wise, but a self-confident *and* foolish man swallows it up *and* wastes it.

21 He who earnestly seeks after *and* craves righteousness, mercy, *and* loving-kindness will find life in addition to righteousness (uprightness and right standing with God) and honor. [Prov. 15:9; Matt. 5:6.]

22 A wise man scales the city walls of the mighty and brings down the stronghold in which they trust.

23 He who guards his mouth and his tongue keeps himself from troubles. [Prov. 12:13; 13:3; 18:21; James 3:2.]

24 The proud *and* haughty man— Scoffer is his name—deals *and* acts with overbearing pride.

25 The desire of the slothful kills him, for his hands refuse to labor.

26 He covets greedily all the day long, but the [uncompromisingly] righteous gives and does not withhold. [II Cor. 9:6-10.]

27 The sacrifice of the wicked is exceedingly disgusting *and* abhorrent [to the Lord]—how much more when he brings it with evil intention?

28 A false witness will perish, but the word of a man who hears attentively will endure *and* go unchallenged.

29 A wicked man puts on the bold, unfeeling face [of guilt], but as for the upright, he considers, directs, *and* establishes his way [with the confidence of integrity].

30 There is no [human] wisdom or understanding or counsel [that can prevail] against the Lord.

31 The horse is prepared for the day

of battle, but deliverance *and* victory are of the Lord.

22 A GOOD name is rather to be chosen than great riches, and loving favor rather than silver and gold.

2 The rich and poor meet together; the Lord is the Maker of them all. [Job 31:15; Prov. 14:31.]

3 A prudent man sees the evil and hides himself, but the simple pass on and are punished [with suffering].

4 The reward of humility *and* the reverent *and* worshipful fear of the Lord is riches and honor and life.

5 Thorns and snares are in the way of the obstinate *and* willful; he who guards himself will be far from them.

6 Train up a child in the way he should go [and in keeping with his individual gift or bent], and when he is old he will not depart from it. [Eph. 6:4; II Tim. 3:15.]

putting the Word to work

Proverbs 22:6 teaches that children will not depart from good training. If you are a parent, how can you train your children in godly ways? Ask God to help you. He will!

7 The rich rule over the poor, and the borrower is servant to the lender.

8 He who sows iniquity will reap calamity *and* futility, and the rod of his wrath [with which he smites others] will fail.

9 He who has a bountiful eye shall be blessed, for he gives of his bread to the poor. [II Cor. 9:6-10.]

10 Drive out the scoffer, and

speak the Word

God, I declare that no human wisdom, understanding, or counsel can prevail against You. Deliverance and victory come from You alone.
ADAPTED FROM PROVERBS 21:30, 31

contention will go out; yes, strife and abuse will cease.

11 He who loves purity *and* the pure in heart *and* who is gracious in speech—because of the grace of his lips will he have the king for his friend.

12 The eyes of the Lord keep guard over knowledge *and* him who has it, but He overthrows the words of the treacherous.

13 The sluggard says, There is a lion outside! I shall be slain in the streets!

14 The mouth of a loose woman is a deep pit [for ensnaring wild animals]; he with whom the Lord is indignant *and* who is abhorrent to Him will fall into it.

15 Foolishness is bound up in the heart of a child, but the rod of discipline will drive it far from him.

16 He who oppresses the poor to get gain for himself *and* he who gives to the rich—both will surely come to want.

17 Listen (consent and submit) to the words of the wise, and apply your mind to my knowledge;

18 For it will be pleasant if you keep them in your mind [believing them]; your lips will be accustomed to [confessing] them.

19 So that your trust (belief, reliance, support, and confidence) may be in the Lord, I have made known these things to you today, even to you.

20 Have I not written to you [long ago] excellent things in counsels and knowledge,

21 To make you know the certainty of the words of truth, that you may give a true answer to those who sent you? [Luke 1:3, 4.]

22 Rob not the poor [being tempted by their helplessness], neither oppress the afflicted at the gate [where the city court is held], [Exod. 23:6; Job 31:16, 21.]

23 For the Lord will plead their cause and deprive of life those who deprive [the poor or afflicted]. [Zech. 7:10; Mal. 3:5.]

24 Make no friendships with a man given to anger, and with a wrathful man do not associate,

25 Lest you learn his ways and get yourself into a snare.

26 Be not one of those who strike hands *and* pledge themselves, or of those who become security for another's debts.

27 If you have nothing with which to pay, why should he take your bed from under you?

28 Remove not the ancient landmark which your fathers have set up.

29 Do you see a man diligent *and* skillful in his business? He will stand before kings; he will not stand before obscure men.

23 WHEN YOU sit down to eat with a ruler, consider who *and* what are before you;

2 For you will put a knife to your throat if you are a man given to desire.

3 Be not desirous of his dainties, for it is deceitful food [offered with questionable motives].

4 Weary not yourself to be rich; cease from your own [human] wisdom. [Prov. 28:20; I Tim. 6:9, 10.]

5 Will you set your eyes upon wealth, when [suddenly] it is gone? For riches certainly make themselves wings, like an eagle that flies toward the heavens.

6 Eat not the bread of him who has a hard, grudging, *and* envious eye, neither desire his dainty foods;

7 For as he thinks in his heart, so is he. As one who reckons, he says to you, eat and drink, yet his heart is not with you [but is grudging the cost].

8 The morsel which you have eaten you will vomit up, and your complimentary words will be wasted.

9 Speak not in the ears of a [self-confident] fool, for he will despise the [godly] Wisdom of your words. [Isa. 32:6.]

think as God thinks

Proverbs 23:7 teaches us that we become what we think, and I have certainly learned this truth over the years. Indeed, "where the mind goes, the man follows." One of the first principles believers must learn if we intend to walk in real victory is that our minds must be renewed according to the Word of God. We must learn to think like God!

Sadly, we believe many things that simply are not true. For example, some people believe they have no worth and value because people have said they do not or have treated them in a way that made them feel worthless and devalued. However, the Bible makes clear that we are so valuable to God that He sent His only Son, Jesus Christ, to die and suffer in our place in order that we might be redeemed from our sins and have an intimate relationship with Him.

As we learn to think as God thinks, we exchange depression and hopelessness for joyful expectation. We believe God has a wonderful future planned for us, no matter what our past has been like. We believe God wants to bless us.

When we have negative thoughts, we end up with negative results. But positive thoughts open the door for God to work in our lives. If we think we are unable to do certain things, we will be rendered unable—even though God's Word says that we can do anything God asks us to do because of His ability in us (see Philippians 4:13). Our thoughts are *that* powerful.

We must all change our way of thinking before our lives will change. Romans 12:2 says we are not to conform to the world and its ways, but we are to completely renew our minds and attitudes so we can prove for ourselves the good and perfect will of God. In other words, God has good plans for us, but we will not experience them if we cling to old ways of thinking.

We must cast down wrong thinking and replace it with thinking that God approves of. The mind is the battlefield on which our war with Satan is won or lost. Satan is a liar and a deceiver. His lies become our reality only when we believe them. Stop allowing your mind to be a garbage dump for Satan's trash and instead, make it available for God's ideas. Then you will enjoy a life worth living and have the testimony of bearing good fruit for God's glory.

---

10 Remove not the ancient landmark and enter not into the fields of the fatherless, [Deut. 19:14; 27:17; Prov. 22:28.]
11 For their Redeemer is mighty; He will plead their cause against you.
12 Apply your mind to instruction *and* correction and your ears to words of knowledge.
13 Withhold not discipline from the child; for if you strike *and* punish him with the [reedlike] rod, he will not die.
14 You shall whip him with the rod and deliver his life from Sheol (Hades, the place of the dead).
15 My son, if your heart is wise, my heart will be glad, even mine;
16 Yes, my heart will rejoice when your lips speak right things.
17 Let not your heart envy sinners,

life point

Proverbs 23:7 lets us know how crucial it is for us to think properly. Thoughts are powerful, and according to the writer of Proverbs, they have creative ability. If our thoughts are going to affect what we become (and they will), then thinking right thoughts should be a high priority in our lives.

but continue in the reverent *and* worshipful fear of the Lord all the day long.

18 For surely there is a latter end [a future and a reward], and your hope *and* expectation shall not be cut off.

19 Hear, my son, and be wise, and direct your mind in the way [of the Lord].

20 Do not associate with winebibbers; be not among them *nor* among gluttonous eaters of meat, [Isa. 5:22; Luke 21:34; Rom. 13:13; Eph. 5:18.]

21 For the drunkard and the glutton shall come to poverty, and drowsiness shall clothe a man with rags.

22 Hearken to your father, who begot

life point

Proverbs 23:12 instructs us to apply our minds to "instruction and correction." Correction is probably one of the most difficult things for most of us to receive, especially when it comes through another person. Even if we have problems, we do not want others to know we have them. I believe God prefers to correct us privately. However, if we will not accept His correction, or if we do not know how to allow Him to correct us privately, He will correct us publicly, using whatever source or means He needs to use. God's correction, even if it is uncomfortable to us, is always intended for our good.

you, and despise not your mother when she is old.

23 Buy the truth and sell it not; not only that, but also get discernment *and* judgment, instruction and understanding.

24 The father of the [uncompromisingly] righteous (the upright, in right standing with God) shall greatly rejoice, and he who becomes the father of a wise child shall have joy in him.

25 Let your father and your mother be glad, and let her who bore you rejoice.

26 My son, give me your heart and let your eyes observe *and* delight in my ways,

27 For a harlot is a deep ditch, and a loose woman is a narrow pit.

28 She also lies in wait as a robber *or* as one waits for prey, and she increases the treacherous among men.

29 Who has woe? Who has sorrow? Who has strife? Who has complaining? Who has wounds without cause? Who has redness *and* dimness of eyes?

30 Those who tarry long at the wine, those who go to seek *and* try mixed wine. [Prov. 20:1; Eph. 5:18.]

31 Do not look at wine when it is red, when it sparkles in the wineglass, when it goes down smoothly.

32 At the last it bites like a serpent and stings like an adder.

33 [Under the influence of wine] your eyes will behold strange things [and loose women] and your mind will utter things turned the wrong way [untrue, incorrect, and petulant].

34 Yes, you will be [as unsteady] as he who lies down in the midst of the sea, and [as open to disaster] as he who lies upon the top of a mast.

35 You will say, They struck me, but I was not hurt! They beat me [as with a hammer], but I did not feel it! When shall I awake? I will crave *and* seek more wine again [and escape reality].

24

BE NOT envious of evil men, nor desire to be with them;

2 For their minds plot oppression *and* devise violence, and their lips talk of causing trouble *and* vexation.

3 Through skillful *and* godly Wisdom is a house (a life, a home, a family) built, and by understanding it is established [on a sound and good foundation],

4 And by knowledge shall its chambers [of every area] be filled with all precious and pleasant riches.

5 A wise man is strong *and* ᑫ*is better than a strong man*, and a man of knowledge increases *and* strengthens his power; [Prov. 21:22; Eccl. 9:16.]

6 For by wise counsel you can wage your war, and in an abundance of counselors there is victory *and* safety.

7 Wisdom is too high for a ʳfool; he opens not his mouth in the gate [where the city's rulers sit in judgment].

8 He who plans to do evil will be called a mischief-maker.

9 The plans of the foolish *and* the thought of foolishness are sin, and the scoffer is an abomination to men.

10 If you faint in the day of adversity, your strength is small.

11 Deliver those who are drawn away to death, and those who totter to the slaughter, hold them back [from their doom].

12 If you [profess ignorance and] say, Behold, we did not know this, does not He Who weighs *and* ponders the heart perceive *and* consider it? And He Who guards your life, does not He know it? And shall not He render to [you and] every man according to his works?

13 My son, eat honey, because it is good, and the drippings of the honeycomb are sweet to your taste.

life point

Proverbs 24:10 tells us that our strength is small if we faint when we encounter hard times or difficult situations. The Bible never promises that we will not face adversities; it promises us the strength and grace we need in order to overcome those adversities. With God's strength, we never have to become fainthearted or give up, no matter what trials or tribulations come our way.

14 So shall you know skillful *and* godly Wisdom to be thus to your life; if you find it, then shall there be a future *and* a reward, and your hope *and* expectation shall not be cut off.

15 Lie not in wait as a wicked man against the dwelling of the [uncompromisingly] righteous (the upright, in right standing with God); destroy not his resting-place;

16 For a righteous man falls seven times and rises again, but the wicked are overthrown by calamity. [Job 5:19; Ps. 34:19; 37:24; Mic. 7:8.]

17 Rejoice not when your enemy falls, and let not your heart be glad when he stumbles *or* is overthrown,

18 Lest the Lord see it and it be evil in His eyes *and* displease Him, and He turn away His wrath from him [to expend it upon you, the worse offender].

19 Fret not because of evildoers, neither be envious of the wicked,

20 For there shall be no reward for the evil man; the lamp of the wicked shall be put out.

21 My son, [reverently] fear the Lord and the king, and do not associate with those who are given to change [of allegiance, and are revolutionary],

22 For their calamity shall rise suddenly, and who knows the punishment

q Several other texts, including *The Septuagint* (Greek translation of the Old Testament), so read.
r See footnote on Proverbs 14:3.

life point

Have people done you wrong and then later had problems themselves? Proverbs 24:17, 18 strongly warns us to keep a right heart attitude and not be happy about their affliction. Basically these verses say that if we rejoice and think they deserve what they are getting, our offense becomes worse than theirs, and we will experience the wrath they would have experienced.

That is really an awesome scripture. All of us will have to admit that when someone has done us wrong, it takes a lot of "heart work" for us not to be at least a little bit glad to see that person get what is coming to him. We may pretend we do not feel this way, but I believe we all have problems with spiteful attitudes from time to time.

We need to see that God is supremely concerned about our heart attitudes. It is so important for us not to be petty and small-minded about offenses against us. We need to just keep a right heart attitude and let God take care of everybody else. We should always remember that "hurting people hurt people." Those who hurt us are usually hurting within themselves, and their pain may be so strong that they are not even aware they are hurting us.

and ruin which both [the Lord and the king] will bring upon [the rebellious]?

23 These also are sayings of the wise: To discriminate *and* show partiality, having respect of persons in judging, is not good.

24 He who says to the wicked, You are righteous *and* innocent—peoples will curse him, nations will defy *and* abhor him.

25 But to those [upright judges] who rebuke the wicked, it will go well with them *and* they will find delight, and a good blessing will be upon them.

26 He kisses the lips [and wins the hearts of men] who give a right answer.

27 [Put first things first.] Prepare your work outside and get it ready for yourself in the field; and afterward build your house *and* establish a home.

28 Be not a witness against your neighbor without cause, and deceive not with your lips. [Eph. 4:25.]

29 Say not, I will do to him as he has done to me; I will pay the man back for his deed. [Prov. 20:22; Matt. 5:39, 44; Rom. 12:17, 19.]

30 I went by the field of the lazy man, and by the vineyard of the man void of understanding;

31 And, behold, it was all grown over with thorns, and nettles were covering its face, and its stone wall was broken down.

32 Then I beheld *and* considered it well; I looked *and* received instruction.

33 Yet a little sleep, a little slumber, a little folding of the hands to sleep—

34 So shall your poverty come as a robber, and your want as an armed man.

25 THESE ARE also the proverbs of Solomon, which the men of Hezekiah king of Judah copied: [I Kings 4:32.]

2 It is the glory of God to conceal a thing, but the glory of kings is to search out a thing. [Deut. 29:29; Rom. 11:33.]

3 As the heavens for height and the earth for depth, so the hearts *and* minds of kings are unsearchable.

4 Take away the dross from the silver, and there shall come forth [the

material for] a vessel for the silver-smith [to work up]. [II Tim. 2:21.]

5 Take away the wicked from before the king, and his throne will be established in righteousness (moral and spiritual rectitude in every area and relation).

6 Be not forward (self-assertive and boastfully ambitious) in the presence of the king, and stand not in the place of great men;

7 For better it is that it should be said to you, Come up here, than that you should be put lower in the presence of the prince, whose eyes have seen you. [Luke 14:8-10.]

8 Rush not forth soon to quarrel [before magistrates or elsewhere], lest you know not what to do in the end when your neighbor has put you to shame. [Prov. 17:14; Matt. 5:25.]

9 Argue your cause with your neighbor himself; discover not *and* disclose not another's secret, [Matt. 18:15.]

10 Lest he who hears you revile you *and* bring shame upon you and your ill repute have no end.

11 A word fitly spoken *and* in due season is like apples of gold in settings of silver. [Prov. 15:23; Isa. 50:4.]

12 Like an earring *or* nose ring of gold or an ornament of fine gold is a wise reprover to an ear that listens *and* obeys.

13 Like the cold of snow [brought from the mountains] in the time of harvest, so is a faithful messenger to those who send him; for he refreshes the life of his masters.

14 Whoever falsely boasts of gifts [he does not give] is like clouds and wind without rain. [Jude 12.]

15 By long forbearance *and* calmness of spirit a judge *or* ruler is persuaded, and soft speech breaks down the most bonelike resistance. [Gen. 32:4; I Sam. 25:24; Prov. 15:1; 16:14.]

life point

Spending too much time with any one person or group of people is usually not a good idea. In fact, Proverbs 25:17 says that people can get tired of us if we overdo it. We can appreciate one another more if we stay balanced in our relationships.

16 Have you found [pleasure sweet like] honey? Eat only as much as is sufficient for you, lest, being filled with it, you vomit it.

17 Let your foot seldom be in your neighbor's house, lest he become tired of you and hate you.

18 A man who bears false witness against his neighbor is like a heavy sledgehammer and a sword and a sharp arrow.

19 Confidence in an unfaithful man in time of trouble is like a broken tooth or a foot out of joint.

20 He who sings songs to a heavy heart is like him who lays off a garment in cold weather *and* like vinegar upon soda. [Dan. 6:18; Rom. 12:15.]

21 If your enemy is hungry, give him bread to eat; and if he is thirsty, give him water to drink; [Matt. 5:44; Rom. 12:20.]

22 For in doing so, you will ˢheap coals of fire upon his head, and the Lord will reward you.

23 The north wind brings forth rain;

ˢ This is not to be understood as a revengeful act intended to embarrass its victim, but just the opposite. The picture is that of the high priest (Lev. 16:12) who, on the Day of Atonement, took his censer and filled it with "coals of fire" from off the altar of burnt offering, and then put incense on the coals to create a pleasing, sweet-smelling fragrance. The cloud or smoke of the incense covered the mercy seat and was acceptable to God for atonement. Samuel Wesley wrote: / "So artists melt the sullen ore of lead, / By heaping coals of fire upon its head: / In the kind warmth the metal learns to glow, / And pure from dross the silver runs below."

so does a backbiting tongue bring forth an angry countenance.

24 It is better to dwell in the corner of the housetop than to share a house with a disagreeing, quarrelsome, *and* scolding woman. [Prov. 21:9.]

25 Like cold water to a thirsty soul, so is good news from a far [home] country.

26 Like a muddied fountain and a polluted spring is a righteous man who yields, falls down, *and* compromises his integrity before the wicked.

27 It is not good to eat much honey; so for men to seek glory, their own glory, causes suffering *and* is not glory.

28 He who has no rule over his own spirit is like a city that is broken down and without walls. [Prov. 16:32.]

26 LIKE SNOW in summer and like rain in harvest, so honor is not fitting for a [self-confident] fool. [Isa. 32:6.]

2 Like the sparrow in her wandering, like the swallow in her flying, so the causeless curse does not alight. [Num. 23:8.]

3 A whip for the horse, a bridle for the donkey, and a [straight, slender] rod for the backs of [self-confident] fools.

4 Answer not a [self-confident] fool according to his folly, lest you also be like him.

5 Answer a [self-confident] fool according to his folly, lest he be wise in his own eyes *and* conceit. [Matt. 16:1-4; 21:24-27.]

6 He who sends a message by the hand of a †fool cuts off the feet [of satisfactory delivery] and drinks the damage. [Prov. 13:17.]

7 Like the legs of a lame man which hang loose, so is a parable in the mouth of a fool.

8 Like he who binds a stone in a

sling, so is he who gives honor to a [self-confident] fool.

9 Like a thorn that goes [without being felt] into the hand of a drunken man, so is a proverb in the mouth of a [self-confident] fool.

10 [But] like an archer who wounds all, so is he who hires a fool or chance passers-by.

11 As a dog returns to his vomit, so a fool returns to his folly.

12 Do you see a man wise in his own eyes *and* conceit? There is more hope for a [self-confident] fool than for him. [Prov. 29:20; Luke 18:11; Rom. 12:16; Rev. 3:17.]

13 The sluggard says, There is a lion in the way! A lion is in the streets! [Prov. 22:13.]

14 As the door turns on its hinges, so does the lazy man [move not from his place] upon his bed.

15 The slothful *and* self-indulgent buries his hand in his bosom; it distresses *and* wearies him to bring it again to his mouth. [Prov. 19:24.]

16 The sluggard is wiser in his own eyes *and* conceit than seven men who can render a reason *and* answer discreetly.

17 He who, passing by, stops to meddle with strife that is none of his business is like one who takes a dog by the ears.

18 Like a madman who casts firebrands, arrows, and death,

19 So is the man who deceives his neighbor and then says, Was I not joking? [Eph. 5:4.]

20 For lack of wood the fire goes out, and where there is no whisperer, contention ceases.

21 As coals are to hot embers and as wood to fire, so is a quarrelsome man to inflame strife. [Prov. 15:18; 29:22.]

22 The words of a whisperer *or* slanderer are like dainty morsels *or* words

† See footnote on Proverbs 14:3.

of sport [to some, but to others are like deadly wounds]; and they go down into the innermost parts of the body [or of the victim's nature].

23 Burning lips [uttering insincere words of love] and a wicked heart are like an earthen vessel covered with the scum thrown off from molten silver [making it appear to be solid silver].

24 He who hates pretends with his lips, but stores up deceit within himself.

25 When he speaks kindly, do not trust him, for seven abominations are in his heart.

26 Though his hatred covers itself with guile, his wickedness shall be shown openly before the assembly.

27 Whoever digs a pit [for another man's feet] shall fall into it himself, and he who rolls a stone [up a height to do mischief], it will return upon him. [Ps. 7:15, 16; 9:15; 10:2; 57:6; Prov. 28:10; Eccl. 10:8.]

28 A lying tongue hates those it wounds and crushes, and a flattering mouth works ruin.

27 DO NOT boast of [yourself and] tomorrow, for you know not what a day may bring forth. [Luke 12:19, 20; James 4:13.]

2 Let another man praise you, and not your own mouth; a stranger, and not your own lips.

3 Stone is heavy and sand weighty, but a fool's [unreasoning] wrath is heavier and more intolerable than both of them.

4 Wrath is cruel and anger is an overwhelming flood, but who is able to stand before jealousy?

5 Open rebuke is better than love that is hidden. [Prov. 28:23; Gal. 2:14.]

6 Faithful are the wounds of a friend, but the kisses of an enemy are lavish and deceitful.

7 He who is satiated [with sensual pleasures] loathes and treads under-foot a honeycomb, but to the hungry soul every bitter thing is sweet.

8 Like a bird that wanders from her nest, so is a man who strays from his home.

9 Oil and perfume rejoice the heart; so does the sweetness of a friend's counsel that comes from the heart.

10 Your own friend and your father's friend, forsake them not; neither go to your brother's house in the day of your calamity. Better is a neighbor who is near [in spirit] than a brother who is far off [in heart].

11 My son, be wise, and make my heart glad, that I may answer him who reproaches me [as having failed in my parental duty]. [Prov. 10:1; 23:15, 24.]

12 A prudent man sees the evil and hides himself, but the simple pass on and are punished [with suffering].

13 [The judge tells the creditor] Take the garment of one who is security for a stranger; and hold him in pledge when he is security for foreigners. [Prov. 20:16.]

14 The flatterer who loudly praises and glorifies his neighbor, rising early in the morning, it shall be counted as cursing him [for he will be suspected of sinister purposes].

15 A continual dripping on a day of violent showers and a contentious woman are alike; [Prov. 19:13.]

16 Whoever attempts to restrain [a contentious woman] might as well try to stop the wind—his right hand encounters oil [and she slips through his fingers].

17 Iron sharpens iron; so a man sharpens the countenance of his friend [to show rage or worthy purpose].

18 Whoever tends the fig tree shall eat its fruit; so he who patiently and faithfully guards and heeds his master shall be honored. [I Cor. 9:7, 13.]

19 As in water face answers to and reflects face, so the heart of man to man.

20 Sheol (the place of the dead) and

Abaddon (the place of destruction) are never satisfied; so [the lust of] the eyes of man is never satisfied. [Prov. 30:16; Hab. 2:5.]

21 As the refining pot for silver and the furnace for gold [bring forth all the impurities of the metal], so let a man be in his trial of praise [ridding himself of all that is base or insincere; for a man is judged by what he praises and of what he boasts].

22 Even though like grain you should pound a fool in a mortar with a pestle, yet will not his foolishness depart from him.

23 Be diligent to know the state of your flocks, and look well to your herds;

24 For riches are not forever; does a crown endure to all generations?

25 When the hay is gone, the tender grass shows itself, and herbs of the mountain are gathered in,

26 The lambs will be for your clothing, and the goats [will furnish you] the price of a field.

27 And there will be goats' milk enough for your food, for the food of your household, and for the maintenance of your maids.

28 THE WICKED flee when no man pursues them, but the [uncompromisingly] righteous are bold as a lion. [Lev. 26:17, 36; Ps. 53:5.]

2 When a land transgresses, it has many rulers, but when the ruler is a man of discernment, understanding, *and* knowledge, its stability will long continue.

3 A poor man who oppresses the poor is like a sweeping rain which leaves no food [plundering them of their last morsels]. [Matt. 18:28.]

4 Those who forsake the law [of God and man] praise the wicked, but those who keep the law [of God and man] contend with them. [Prov. 29:18.]

5 Evil men do not understand jus-

tice, but they who crave *and* seek the Lord understand it fully. [John 7:17; I Cor. 2:15; I John 2:20, 27.]

6 Better is the poor man who walks in his integrity than he who willfully goes in double *and* wrong ways, though he is rich.

7 Whoever keeps the law [of God and man] is a wise son, but he who is a companion of gluttons *and* the carousing, self-indulgent, *and* extravagant shames his father.

8 He who by charging excessive interest *and* who by unjust efforts to get gain increases his material possession gathers it for him [to spend] who is kind *and* generous to the poor. [Job 27:16, 17; Prov. 13:22; Eccl. 2:26.]

9 He who turns away his ear from hearing the law [of God and man], even his prayer is an abomination, hateful *and* revolting [to God]. [Ps. 66:18; 109:7; Prov. 15:8; Zech. 7:11.]

10 Whoever leads the upright astray into an evil way, he will himself fall into his own pit, but the blameless will have a goodly inheritance.

11 The rich man is wise in his own eyes *and* conceit, but the poor man who has understanding will find him out.

12 When the [uncompromisingly] righteous triumph, there is great glory *and* celebration; but when the wicked rise [to power], men hide themselves.

13 He who covers his transgressions will not prosper, but whoever confesses and forsakes his sins will obtain mercy. [Ps. 32:3, 5; I John 1:8-10.]

14 Blessed (happy, fortunate, and to be envied) is the man who reverently *and* worshipfully fears [the Lord] at all times [regardless of circumstances], but he who hardens his heart will fall into calamity.

15 Like a roaring lion or a ravenous *and* charging bear is a wicked ruler over a poor people.

16 A ruler who lacks understanding is [like a wicked one] a great oppressor, but he who hates covetousness

bold as a lion

If we intend to succeed at being ourselves and truly enjoy our everyday lives, we must reach a point where we allow the Holy Spirit to lead us. Only God, through His Spirit, can lead us to succeed and be all we can be. Other people usually will not, the devil *certainly* will not, and we are not able to do it ourselves without God.

Being led by the Spirit does not mean we never make mistakes. The Holy Spirit does not make mistakes, but we do. Following the Spirit's leading is a process that can be learned only by *doing*. We start by stepping out into things we believe God is putting on our hearts; and we learn by wisdom and experience how to hear more clearly and definitely. I always say, "Step out and find out." That is one way to discover if what is in your heart is from God. If it works it is God, and if it doesn't work it is not God, and there is no shame in stepping out to find out. Take little "baby steps" and see if the first one produces good fruit; if it does, then take another step. If it does not, then back off and pray some more.

I say that boldness is required to be led by the Spirit because only boldness steps out and only boldness can survive making mistakes. We must remember that the "righteous are bold as a lion" (Proverbs 28:1). When insecure people make mistakes, often they will not try again. Bold people make many mistakes, but their attitude is, "I am going to keep trying until I learn to do this right."

Those who suffer from condemnation usually do not believe they can hear from God. Even if they think they may have heard from God and do step out, a minor failure is a major setback to them. Each time they make a mistake, they come under a new load of guilt and condemnation. They end up spending all their time in the cycle. They make a mistake, feel condemned, make another mistake, feel condemned, and on and on. Finally they become frozen with fear and never fulfill their destinies.

I encourage you to step out in faith and be all that God has called you to be. If you do step out and two weeks later discover that you made a mistake, are you going to be bold enough to pray, wise enough to learn from your mistakes, and determined enough to go on? Or are you going to feel condemned and go back to wasting your life? There is no point in learning to be led by the Holy Spirit if you do not understand that you will make some mistakes while on the journey.

Be as bold as a lion in your faith. Do not hide behind fears, insecurities, and mistakes any longer. If you have already made major blunders in your life and have been living under condemnation because of them, this is the time to forgive yourself and press on!

You can be all God planned for you, in Christ. Do not be half of it or three-quarters of it, but be *all* that God designed you to be. Do all He wants you to do, and have all He wants you to have. You will not enjoy God's fullness without His boldness. Remember, condemnation destroys boldness, so do not stay under condemnation.

Proverbs 28:1 says that the wicked flee when no one is even pursuing them. The wicked are running all the time. They run from everything. But the uncompromisingly righteous are as bold as a lion. And whether you feel it or not, you are righteous!

and unjust gain shall prolong his days.
17 If a man willfully sheds the blood of a person [and keeps the guilt of murder upon his conscience], he is fleeing to the pit (the grave) *and* hastening to his own destruction; let no man stop him!

18 He who walks uprightly shall be safe, but he who willfully goes in double *and* wrong ways shall fall in one of them.

19 He who cultivates his land will have plenty of bread, but he who follows worthless people *and* pursuits will have poverty enough.

20 A faithful man shall abound with blessings, but he who makes haste to be rich [at any cost] shall not go unpunished. [Prov. 13:11; 20:21; 23:4; I Tim. 6:9.]

21 To have respect of persons *and* to

life point

A life of faithfully serving and obeying God allows Him to place us in a position to be consistently blessed. As we learn from Proverbs 28:20, a person who is faithful abounds with blessings.

show partiality is not good, neither is it good that man should transgress for a piece of bread.

22 He who has an evil *and* covetous eye hastens to be rich and knows not that want will come upon him. [Prov. 21:5; 28:20.]

23 He who rebukes a man shall afterward find more favor than he who flatters with the tongue.

24 Whoever robs his father or his mother and says, This is no sin—he is in the same class as [an open, lawless robber and] a destroyer.

25 He who is of a greedy spirit stirs up strife, but he who puts his trust in the Lord shall be enriched *and* blessed.

26 He who leans on, trusts in, *and* is

confident of his own mind *and* heart is a [self-confident] fool, but he who walks in skillful *and* godly Wisdom shall be delivered. [James 1:5.]

27 He who gives to the poor will not want, but he who hides his eyes [from their want] will have many a curse. [Deut. 15:7; Prov. 19:17; 22:9.]

28 When the wicked rise [to power], men hide themselves; but when they perish, the [consistently] righteous increase *and* become many. [Prov. 28:12.]

29 HE WHO, being often reproved, hardens his neck shall suddenly be destroyed—and that without remedy.

2 When the [uncompromisingly] righteous are in authority, the people rejoice; but when the wicked man rules, the people groan *and* sigh.

3 Whoever loves skillful *and* godly Wisdom rejoices his father, but he who associates with harlots wastes his substance.

4 The king by justice establishes the land, but he who exacts gifts *and* tribute overthrows it.

5 A man who flatters his neighbor spreads a net for his own feet.

6 In the transgression of an evil man there is a snare, but the [uncompromisingly] righteous man sings and rejoices.

7 The [consistently] righteous man knows *and* cares for the rights of the poor, but the wicked man has no interest in such knowledge. [Job 29:16; 31:13; Ps. 41:1.]

8 Scoffers set a city afire [inflaming the minds of the people], but wise men turn away wrath.

9 If a wise man has an argument with a foolish man, the fool only rages or laughs, and there is no rest.

10 The bloodthirsty hate the blameless man, but the upright care for *and* seek [to save] his life. [Gen. 4:5, 8; I John 3:12.]

11 A [self-confident] fool utters all his anger, but a wise man holds it back and stills it.

12 If a ruler listens to falsehood, all his officials will become wicked.

13 The poor man and the oppressor meet together—the Lord gives light to the eyes of both.

14 The king who faithfully judges the poor, his throne shall be established continuously.

15 The rod and reproof give wisdom, but a child left undisciplined brings his mother to shame.

16 When the wicked are in authority, transgression increases, but the [uncompromisingly] righteous shall see the fall of the wicked.

17 Correct your son, and he will give you rest; yes, he will give delight to your heart.

18 Where there is no vision [no redemptive revelation of God], the people perish; but he who keeps the law [of God, which includes that of man]—blessed (happy, fortunate, and enviable) is he. [I Sam. 3:1; Amos 8:11, 12.]

19 A servant will not be corrected by words alone; for though he understands, he will not answer [the master who mistreats him].

20 Do you see a man who is hasty in his words? There is more hope for a [self-confident] fool than for him.

21 He who pampers his servant from childhood will have him expecting the rights of a son afterward.

22 A man of wrath stirs up strife, and a man given to anger commits *and* causes much transgression.

23 A man's pride will bring him low, but he who is of a humble spirit will obtain honor. [Prov. 15:33; 18:12; Isa. 66:2; Dan. 4:30; Matt. 23:12; James 4:6, 10; I Pet. 5:5.]

24 Whoever is partner with a thief

the importance of vision

People who have a sad past need to be able to believe in a bright future. Proverbs 29:18 says that where there is no vision, people perish.

A vision is something we see in our minds—"a mental sight," as one definition puts it. It may be something God plants in us supernaturally or something we see on purpose. It involves the way we think about our past, our future, and ourselves.

Some people are afraid to believe God for a vision. They think they may be setting themselves up for disappointment. They have not realized they will be perpetually disappointed if they do not believe. If I am describing you, remember this truth: *it does not cost anything to believe*. I feel that if I believe for a lot and get even half of it, I am better off than I would be to believe for nothing and get all of nothing.

I challenge you to start believing that something good is going to happen to you. Ask God for a vision to pursue, and believe you can do whatever you need to do in life through Christ. Do not have a "give-up-easily" attitude. Let your faith soar. Be creative with your thoughts. Take an inventory and ask yourself, "What have I been believing lately?" An honest answer may help you understand why you have not been receiving what you have wanted to receive. Allow God's redemptive revelation to lead you away from the dead ends of your life and give you vision for your future.

hates his own life; he falls under the curse [pronounced upon him who knows who the thief is] but discloses nothing.

25 The fear of man brings a snare, but whoever leans on, trusts in, *and* puts his confidence in the Lord is safe *and* set on high.

26 Many crave *and* seek the ruler's favor, but the wise man [waits] for justice from the Lord.

27 An unjust man is an abomination to the righteous, and he who is upright in the way [of the Lord] is an abomination to the wicked.

30 THE WORDS of Agur son of Jakeh of Massa: The man says to Ithiel, to Ithiel and to Ucal:

2 Surely I am too brutish *and* stupid to be called a man, and I have not the understanding of a man [for all my secular learning is as nothing].

3 I have not learned skillful *and* godly Wisdom, that I should have the knowledge *or* burden of the Holy One.

4 Who has ascended into heaven and descended? Who has gathered the wind in His fists? Who has bound the waters in His garment? Who has established all the ends of the earth? What is His name, and what is His Son's name, if you know? [John 3:13; Rev. 19:12.]

5 Every word of God is tried *and* purified; He is a shield to those who trust *and* take refuge in Him. [Ps. 18:30; 84:11; 115:9-11.]

6 Add not to His words, lest He reprove you, and you be found a liar.

7 Two things have I asked of You [O Lord]; deny them not to me before I die:

8 Remove far from me falsehood and lies; give me neither poverty nor riches; feed me with the food that is needful for me,

9 Lest I be full and deny You and say, Who is the Lord? Or lest I be poor and steal, and so profane the name of my God. [Deut. 8:12, 14, 17; Neh. 9:25, 26; Job 31:24; Hos. 13:6.]

10 Do not accuse *and* hurt a servant before his master, lest he curse you, and you be held guilty [of adding to the burdens of the lowly].

11 There is a class of people who curse their fathers and do not bless their mothers.

12 There is a class of people who are pure in their own eyes, and yet are not washed from their own filth.

13 There is a class of people—oh, how lofty are their eyes and their raised eyelids!

14 There is a class of people whose teeth are as swords and whose fangs as knives, to devour the poor from the earth and the needy from among men.

15 The leech has two daughters, crying, Give, give! There are three things that are never satisfied, yes, four that do not say, It is enough:

16 Sheol (the place of the dead), the barren womb, the earth that is not satisfied with water, and the fire that says not, It is enough.

17 The eye that mocks a father and scorns to obey a mother, the ravens of the valley will pick it out, and the young vultures will devour it. [Lev. 20:9; Prov. 20:20; 23:22.]

18 There are three things which are too wonderful for me, yes, four which I do not understand:

19 The way of an eagle in the air, the

speak the Word

God, every word of Yours is tried and purified; You are a shield to me because I trust You.
ADAPTED FROM PROVERBS 30:5

way of a serpent upon a rock, the way of a ship in the midst of the sea, and the way of a man with a maid.

20 This is the way of an adulterous woman: she eats and wipes her mouth and says, I have done no wickedness.

21 Under three things the earth is disquieted, and under four it cannot bear up:

22 Under a servant when he reigns, a [empty-headed] fool when he is filled with food,

23 An unloved *and* repugnant woman when she is married, and a maidservant when she supplants her mistress.

24 There are four things which are little on the earth, but they are exceedingly wise:

25 The ants are a people not strong, yet they lay up their food in the summer; [Prov. 6:6.]

26 The conies are but a feeble folk, yet they make their houses in the rocks; [Ps. 104:18.]

27 The locusts have no king, yet they go forth all of them by bands;

28 The lizard you can seize with your hands, yet it is in kings' palaces.

29 There are three things which are stately in step, yes, four which are stately in their stride:

30 The lion, which is mightiest among beasts and turns not back before any;

31 The war horse [well-knit in the loins], the male goat also, and the king [when his army is with him and] against whom there is no uprising.

32 If you have done foolishly in exalting yourself, or if you have thought evil, lay your hand upon your mouth. [Job 21:5; 40:4.]

33 Surely the churning of milk brings forth butter, and the wringing of the nose brings forth blood; so the forcing of wrath brings forth strife.

31 THE WORDS of Lemuel king of Massa, which his mother taught him:

2 What, my "son? What, son of my womb? What [shall I advise you], son of my vows *and* dedication to God?

3 Give not your strength to [loose] women, nor your ways to those who *and* that which ruin *and* destroy kings.

4 It is not for kings, O Lemuel, it is not for kings to drink wine, or for rulers to desire strong drink, [Eccl. 10:17; Hos. 4:11.]

5 Lest they drink and forget the law *and* what it decrees, and pervert the justice due any of the afflicted.

6 Give strong drink [as medicine] to him who is ready to pass away, and wine to him in bitter distress of heart.

7 Let him drink and forget his poverty and [seriously] remember his want *and* misery no more.

8 Open your mouth for the dumb [those unable to speak for themselves], for the rights of all who are left desolate *and* defenseless; [I Sam. 19:4; Esth. 4:16; Job 29:15, 16.]

9 Open your mouth, judge righteously, and administer justice for the poor and needy. [Lev. 19:15; Deut. 1:16; Job 29:12; Isa. 1:17; Jer. 22:16.]

10 A capable, intelligent, *and* "virtuous woman—who is he who can find her? She is far more precious than jewels *and* her value is far above rubies *or* pearls. [Prov. 12:4; 18:22; 19:14.]

11 The heart of her husband trusts in

---

u It is important to the purpose of this invaluable chapter that one realizes that it is first of all intended for young men. It is the mother's God-given task to provide youth with this information directly from its inspired source, letting them grow up with it in their consciousness. **v** It is most unfortunate that this description of God's ideal woman is usually confined in readers' minds merely to its literal sense—her ability as a homemaker, as in the picture of Martha of Bethany in Luke 10:38-42. But it is obvious that far more than that is meant. When the summary of what makes her value "far above rubies" is given (in Prov. 31:30), it is her spiritual life only that is mentioned. One can almost hear the voice of Jesus saying, "Mary has chosen the good portion . . . which shall not be taken away from her" (Luke 10:42).

her confidently *and* relies on and believes in her securely, so that he has no lack of [honest] gain or need of [dishonest] spoil.

12 She comforts, encourages, *and* does him only good as long as there is life within her.

13 She seeks out wool and flax and works with willing hands [to develop it].

14 She is like the merchant ships loaded with foodstuffs; she brings her household's food from a far [country].

15 She rises while it is yet night and gets [spiritual] food for her household and assigns her maids their tasks. [Job 23:12.]

16 She considers a [new] field before she buys or accepts it [expanding prudently and not courting neglect of her present duties by assuming other duties]; with her savings [of time and strength] she plants fruitful vines in her vineyard. [S. of Sol. 8:12.]

kindness on your lips

One of my biggest problems in learning to control my anger and my words was the fact that I had been mistreated and abused in the earlier years of my life. As a result, I ended up with a harsh, hard spirit. I was determined that nobody was ever going to hurt me again, and that attitude influenced the things I said. Although I tried to say things that were right and pleasing to others, by the time my thoughts had passed through my soul and picked up the hardness and bitterness hidden there, my words came out harsh and hard.

No matter how right you think your heart is before the Lord, if you have pride or anger or resentment in your spirit, you cannot open your mouth without expressing those negative traits and emotions. Why is that? Because, as Jesus told us, it is out of the abundance of the heart or the spirit that the mouth speaks (see Matthew 12:34).

I began to realize that the Lord had an important work to do in me. Gentleness became a key issue in my life. Part of what God revealed to me in His Word on this subject was in Proverbs 31, the chapter that speaks of the "capable, intelligent, and virtuous" woman (verse 10). In verse 26, the writer says that on her tongue is the "law of kindness."

When I read that, I thought, *Oh, God, I've got anything in my mouth but the law of kindness!* It seemed to me that I was so hard inside that whenever I opened my mouth, out came a hammer.

You may relate to that situation. You may have been mistreated and abused as I was so that you are full of hatred, resentment, distrust, anger, and hostility. Instead of kindness and gentleness, you are filled with harshness and bitterness.

Ask God to heal you from all the pain of your past and to help you develop the kindness and gentleness He wants you to possess. Let His healing words flow from your mouth and keep kindness on your lips.

17 She girds herself with strength [spiritual, mental, and physical fitness for her God-given task] and makes her arms strong *and* firm.

18 She tastes *and* sees that her gain from work [with and for God] is good; her lamp goes not out, but it burns on continually through the night [of trouble, privation, or sorrow, warning away fear, doubt, and distrust].

19 She lays her hands to the spindle, and her hands hold the distaff.

20 She opens her hand to the poor, yes, she reaches out her filled hands to the needy [whether in body, mind, or spirit].

21 She fears not the snow for her family, for all her household are doubly clothed in scarlet. [Josh. 2:18, 19; Heb. 9:19-22.]

22 She makes for herself coverlets, cushions, *and* rugs of tapestry. Her clothing is of linen, pure *and* fine, and of purple [such as that of which the clothing of the priests and the hallowed cloths of the temple were made]. [Isa. 61:10; I Tim. 2:9; Rev. 3:5; 19:8, 14.]

23 Her husband is known in the [city's] gates, when he sits among the elders of the land. [Prov. 12:4.]

24 She makes fine linen garments *and* leads others to buy them; she delivers to the merchants girdles [or sashes that free one up for service].

25 Strength and dignity are her clothing *and* her position is strong and secure; she rejoices over the future [the latter day or time to come, knowing that she and her family are in readiness for it]!

26 She opens her mouth in skillful and godly Wisdom, and on her tongue is the law of kindness [giving counsel and instruction].

27 She looks well to how things go in her household, and the bread of idleness (gossip, discontent, and self-pity) she will not eat. [I Tim. 5:14; Tit. 2:5.]

28 Her children rise up and call her blessed (happy, fortunate, and to be envied); and her husband boasts of *and* praises her, [saying],

29 ᵂMany daughters have done virtuously, nobly, *and* well [with the strength of character that is steadfast in goodness], but you excel them all.

30 Charm *and* grace are deceptive, and beauty is vain [because it is not lasting], but a woman who reverently *and* worshipfully fears the Lord, she shall be praised!

31 Give her of the fruit of her hands, and let her own works praise her in the gates [of the city]! [Phil. 4:8.]

---

w "Many daughters have done . . . nobly and well . . . but you excel them all." What a glowing description here recorded of this woman in private life, this "capable, intelligent, and virtuous woman" of Prov. 31! It means she had done more than Miriam, the one who led a nation's women in praise to God (Exod. 15:20, 21); Deborah, the patriotic military advisor (Judg. 4:4-10); Ruth, the woman of constancy (Ruth 1:16); Hannah, the ideal mother (I Sam. 1:20; 2:19); the Shunammite, the hospitable woman (II Kings 4:8-10); Huldah, the woman who revealed God's secret message to national leaders (II Kings 22:14); and even more than Queen Esther, the woman who risked sacrificing her life for her people (Esth. 4:16). In what way did she "excel them all"? In her spiritual and practical devotion to God, which permeated every area and relationship of her life. All seven of the Christian virtues (II Pet. 1:5) are there, like colored threads in a tapestry. Her secret, which is open to everyone, is the Holy Spirit's climax to the story, and to this book. In Prov. 31:30, it becomes clear that the "reverent *and* worshipful fear of the Lord," which is "the beginning (the chief and choice part) of Wisdom" (Prov. 9:10), is put forth as the true foundation for a life which is valued by God and her husband as "far above rubies *or* pearls" (Prov. 31:10).

Ecclesiastes

Author:
Traditionally, Solomon

Date:
Traditionally, near Solomon's death
(about 931 BC)

Everyday Life Principles:
We need to accept what God gives us
and be happy with our lives.

Fearing God and keeping His commandments is the solution to every problem
we face in life.

God is the ultimate Judge. We need to
do things His way; and He will reward us
accordingly.

Solomon, the wise king who wrote
Ecclesiastes, had tried everything.
After he had exhausted almost every
imaginable worldly pursuit, he finally realized that everything on earth
is an exercise in vanity if we do not
fear God and obey His Word. He
makes this point in one of my
favorite Bible verses, Ecclesiastes
12:13: "All has been heard; the end of
the matter is: Fear God [revere and
worship Him, knowing that He is]
and keep His commandments, for
this is the whole of man [the full,
original purpose of his creation, the
object of God's providence, the root
of character, the foundation of all
happiness, the adjustment to all
inharmonious circumstances and
conditions under the sun] and the
whole [duty] for every man."

On the way to his conclusion that
everything about our lives comes
down to fearing God and keeping His
commandments, Solomon learned
some other lessons that are important for us. He learned that being
happy in life and in work is one of
the best things we can do. He
learned that there is a time and a
season for everything that needs to
be done. And he learned that God
will bring all of our works, good or
evil, into judgment.

As you read Solomon's words in
Ecclesiastes, remember to take his
advice: enjoy your life, be happy
with your work, fear God, and keep
His Word.

1 THE WORDS of the Preacher, the son of David and king in Jerusalem.

2 Vapor of vapors *and* futility of futilities, says the Preacher. Vapor of vapors *and* futility of futilities! All is vanity (emptiness, falsity, and vainglory). [Rom. 8:20.]

3 What profit does man have left from all his toil at which he toils ªunder the sun? [Is life worth living?]

4 One generation goes and another generation comes, but the earth remains forever. [Ps. 119:90.]

5 The sun also rises and the sun goes down, and hastens to the place where it rises.

6 The wind goes to the south and circles about to the north; it circles *and* circles about continually, and on its circuit the wind returns again. [John 3:8.]

7 All the rivers run into the sea, yet the sea is not full. To the place from which the rivers come, to there *and* from there they return again.

8 All things are weary with toil *and* all words are feeble; man cannot utter it. The eye is not satisfied with seeing, nor the ear filled with hearing. [Prov. 27:20.]

9 The thing that has been—it is what will be again, and that which has been done is that which will be done again; and there is nothing new under the sun.

10 Is there a thing of which it may be said, See, this is new? It has already been, in the vast ages of time

[recorded or unrecorded] which were before us.

11 There is no remembrance of former happenings *or* men, neither will there be any remembrance of happenings of generations that are to come by those who are to come after them.

12 I, the Preacher, have been king over Israel in Jerusalem.

13 And I applied myself by heart *and* mind to seek and search out by [human] ᵇwisdom all human activity under heaven. It is a miserable business which ᶜGod has given to the sons of man with which to busy themselves.

14 I have seen all the works that are done under the sun, and behold, all is vanity, a striving after the wind *and* a feeding on wind.

15 What is crooked cannot be made straight, and what is defective *and* lacking cannot be counted.

16 I entered into counsel with my own mind, saying, Behold, I have acquired great [human] wisdom, yes,

life point

I like the way Solomon summarized the earthly pursuits so many of us run after. He said that trying to find fulfillment in anything the world has to offer is like chasing the wind (see Ecclesiastes 1:14). No matter how hard we chase after it, it always evades us. No matter how fast we run, we will never catch it.

a Ecclesiastes is the book of the natural man whose interests are confined to the unstable, vanishing pleasures and empty satisfactions of those who live merely "under the sun." The natural man is not aware that all the affirmative answers to life are to be found in Him Who is above, not "under," the sun. The natural man grovels in the dust and finds only earthworms, while the spiritual man may soar on wings like eagles (Isa. 40:31) above all that is futile and disappointing, and may live in the consciousness of God's companionship, favor, and incomparable, everlasting rewards. b The "Wisdom" of Proverbs is not the "wisdom" of Ecclesiastes. The former is Godlike, the latter is usually human. c Throughout this book not once is the Supreme Being recognized as "Lord" [of lords and King of kings]. The word used to designate Him is invariably the one that may be applied to God or to idols—"Elohim," the God recognized "under the sun." The wisdom which is thus limited can end only in "a miserable business" and in vexation of spirit until it finds "the wisdom that is from above" (James 3:17 KJV), "the hidden wisdom, which God ordained before the world unto our glory" (I Cor. 2:7 KJV).

more than all who have been over Jerusalem before me; and my mind has had great experience of [moral] wisdom and [scientific] knowledge.

17 And I gave my mind to know [practical] wisdom and to discern [the character of] madness and folly [in which men seem to find satisfaction]; I perceived that this also is a searching after wind *and* a feeding on it. [I Thess. 5:21.]

18 For in much [human] wisdom is much vexation, and he who increases knowledge increases sorrow.

2 I SAID in my mind, Come now, I will prove you with mirth *and* test you with pleasure; so have a good time [enjoy pleasure]. But this also was vanity (emptiness, falsity, and futility)! [Luke 12:19, 20.]

2 I said of laughter, It is mad, and of pleasure, What does it accomplish?

3 I searched in my mind how to cheer my body with wine—yet at the same time having my mind hold its course *and* guide me with [human] wisdom—and how to lay hold of folly, till I might see what was good for the sons of men to do under heaven all the days of their lives.

4 I made great works; I built myself houses, I planted vineyards.

5 I made for myself gardens and orchards and I planted in them all kinds of fruit trees.

6 I made for myself pools of water from which to water the forest *and* make the trees bud.

7 I bought menservants and maidservants and had servants born in my house. Also I had great possessions of herds and flocks, more than any who had been before me in Jerusalem.

8 I also gathered for myself silver and gold and the treasure of kings and of the provinces. I got for myself men singers and women singers, and the delights of the sons of men—dconcubines very many. [I Kings 9:28; 10:10, 14, 21.]

9 So I became great and increased more than all who were before me in Jerusalem. Also my wisdom remained with me *and* stood by me.

10 And whatever my eyes desired I kept not from them; I withheld not my heart from any pleasure, for my heart rejoiced in all my labor, and this was my portion *and* reward for all my toil.

11 Then I looked on all that my hands had done and the labor I had spent in doing it, and behold, all was vanity and a striving after the wind *and* a feeding on it, and there was no profit under the sun. [Matt. 16:26.]

12 So I turned to consider [human] wisdom and madness and folly; for what can the man do who succeeds the king? Nothing but what has been done already.

13 Then I saw that even [human] wisdom [that brings sorrow] is better than [the pleasures of] folly as far as light is better than darkness.

14 The wise man's eyes are in his head, but the fool walks in darkness; and yet I perceived that [in the end] one event happens to them both. [Prov. 17:24.]

15 Then said I in my heart, As it happens to the fool, so it will happen even to me. And of what use is it then for me to be more wise? Then I said in my heart, This also is vanity (emptiness, vainglory, and futility)!

16 For of the wise man, the same as of the fool, there is no permanent remembrance, since in the days to come all

d Solomon's reign began under most promising conditions: he "loved the Lord, walking in the statutes of David his father . . . All Israel . . . feared the king [Solomon], for they saw that the wisdom of God was in him, to do judgment" (I Kings 3:3, 28 KJV). But soon his own "wisdom" alone was guiding him. He openly affronted God by taking many wives, including even heathen women. They seduced him into tolerating and even practicing idolatry (I Kings 11:1ff.).

the secret of fulfillment

Solomon writes in Ecclesiastes 2:17, 18: "So I hated life, because what is done under the sun was grievous to me; for all is vanity and a striving after the wind and a feeding on it. And I hated all my labor in which I had toiled under the sun, seeing that I must leave it to the man who will succeed me."

Solomon was a busy man; he tried everything that could be tried and did everything there was to do, but at the end of his experience, he was unfulfilled and bitter. Many people today have this same problem; they try everything they can think of to find satisfaction and joy in life, but in the end, they are exhausted, disappointed, and frustrated.

So what is the secret to happiness and fulfillment in life? I believe it is making sure that we are obeying God's will and giving ourselves to what He has called us to do. Will that always be easy? No. Doing God's will is not without challenge. We will struggle at times. We will get tired, but it will be a "good kind of tired" that comes from doing what we are supposed to do.

Let me encourage you today to take a serious inventory of the way you spend your time. Get out the pruning shears and, as God leads you, cut activities and commitments out of your life until you no longer go through every day at such a frantic pace.

Realizing that you cannot do everything, then deciding with God's help what you can and cannot do, will make you more effective at the things you are supposed to do and will greatly increase the level of peace in your life. Peace equals power; without it, you will stay frustrated and weak.

As you evaluate how you are spending your time and what you are doing with your life, use this simple rule: If you have peace about it, keep doing it. If you do not have peace about it, stop. Hearing yourself complaining about it on a regular basis indicates that you need to make an adjustment.

God does not want you to end up like Solomon, hating your life and being bitter. No, His great desire is for you to enjoy being in His will and to be satisfied and at peace as you fulfill His call on your life.

will be long forgotten. And how does the wise man die? Even as the fool! **17** So I hated life, because what is done under the sun was grievous to me; for all is vanity and a striving after the wind *and* a feeding on it. **18** And I hated all my labor in which I had toiled under the sun, seeing that I must leave it to the man who will succeed me. [Ps. 49:10.] **19** And who knows whether he will be a wise man or a fool? Yet he will have dominion over all my labor in which I have toiled and in which I have shown myself wise under the sun. This is also vanity (emptiness, falsity, and futility)!

20 So I turned around and gave my heart up to despair over all the labor of my efforts under the sun.

21 For here is a man whose labor is with wisdom and knowledge and skill; yet to a man who has not toiled for it he must leave it all as his portion. This also is vanity (emptiness, falsity, and futility) and a great evil!

22 For what has a man left from all his labor and from the striving *and* vexation of his heart in which he has toiled under the sun?

23 For all his days are but pain *and* sorrow, and his work is a vexation *and* grief; his mind takes no rest even at night. This is also vanity (emptiness, falsity, and futility)!

24 There is nothing better for a man than that he should eat and drink and make himself enjoy good in his labor. Even this, I have seen, is from the hand of God.

25 For who can eat or who can have enjoyment any more than I can— ᵉ*apart from Him*?

26 For to the person who pleases Him God gives wisdom and knowledge and

putting the Word to work

Ecclesiastes 2:24 tells us that there is nothing better than enjoying what we do. Are you enjoying what you do or are you tired, weary, or bored? Ask God to refresh you and enable you to enjoy your work.

joy; but to the sinner He gives the work of gathering and heaping up, that he may give to one who pleases God. This also is vanity and a striving after the wind *and* a feeding on it.

3 TO EVERYTHING there is a season, and a time for every matter *or* purpose under heaven:

2 A time to be born and a time to die, a time to plant and a time to pluck up what is planted, [Heb. 9:27.]

3 A time to kill and a time to heal, a time to break down and a time to build up,

4 A time to weep and a time to laugh, a time to mourn and a time to dance,

5 A time to cast away stones and a time to gather stones together, a time to embrace and a time to refrain from embracing,

6 A time to get and a time to lose, a time to keep and a time to cast away,

7 A time to rend and a time to sew, a time to keep silence and a time to speak, [Amos 5:13.]

8 A time to love and a time to hate, a time for war and a time for peace. [Luke 14:26.]

9 What profit remains for the worker from his toil?

10 I have seen the painful labor *and* exertion *and* miserable business which God has given to the sons of men with which to exercise *and* busy themselves.

11 He has made everything beautiful in its time. He also has planted eternity

speak the Word

God, I want to please You and have Your wisdom, knowledge, and joy flowing in my life.
ADAPTED FROM Ecclesiastes 2:26

e According to *The Septuagint* (Greek translation of the Old Testament) and *The Syriac* reading: Jesus recognized the unprecedented glory which Solomon's human wisdom had brought him, but He said that Solomon arrayed in all of it was not equal in glory to one tiny lily of the field—which God's wisdom had made (Matt. 6:29).

life point

God has shown me that the devil offers us two lies: the "forever" lie and the "never" lie. The enemy tells us the negative things in our lives will "never" change and will "forever" be the way they are. He tells us we will "never" get what we want, and we will "never" experience the freedom or healing we desire. He says you will be the way you are right now "forever." The devil is a liar! These lies create fear in our hearts, and they are untrue because sooner or later, everything changes. If we continue to believe God and place our trust in Him, bad things ultimately give way to better things. As Ecclesiastes 3 reminds us, there is a time for everything. The good things you are believing God for are on their way!

in men's hearts *and* minds [a divinely implanted sense of a purpose working through the ages which nothing under the sun but God alone can satisfy], yet so that men cannot find out what God has done from the beginning to the end.

12 I know that there is nothing better for them than to be glad and to get *and* do good as long as they live;

13 And also that every man should eat and drink and enjoy the good of all his labor—it is the gift of God.

14 I know that whatever God does, it endures forever; nothing can be added to it nor anything taken from it. And God does it so that men will [reverently] fear Him [revere and worship Him, knowing that He is]. [Ps. 19:9; James 1:17.]

15 That which is now already has been, and that which is to be already has been; and God seeks that which has passed by [so that history repeats itself].

16 Moreover, I saw under the sun that in the place of justice there was wickedness, and that in the place of righteousness wickedness was there also.

17 I said in my heart, God will judge the righteous and the wicked, for there is a time [appointed] for every matter *and* purpose and for every work.

putting the Word to work

Ecclesiastes 3:17 declares that there is a time appointed for every matter, every purpose, and every work. In other words, God has an appointed time in which to do everything He has planned. Are you submitted to His timing in your life, or have you grown impatient waiting for something to happen? I encourage you today to repent for any impatience you have had and to make a fresh surrender to God's perfect timing for everything He wants to do in your life.

18 I said in my heart regarding the subject of the sons of men, God is trying (separating and sifting) them, that they may see that by themselves [under the sun, without God] they are but like beasts.

19 For that which befalls the sons of men befalls beasts; even [in the end] one thing befalls them both. As the one dies, so dies the other. Yes, they all have one breath *and* spirit, so that a ᶠman has no preeminence over a beast; for all is vanity (emptiness, falsity, and futility)!

20 All go to one place; all are of the dust, and all turn to dust again.

f Does the Bible really teach that "a man has no preeminence over a beast"? No! The Bible only records that the book of Ecclesiastes says it. Then why is this book in the Bible? Can it possibly be called inspired by God when it makes such "under the sun" pronouncements, some only partially

21 Who knows the spirit of man, whether it goes upward, and the spirit of the beast, whether it goes downward to the earth?
22 So I saw that there is nothing better than that a man should rejoice in his own works, for that is his portion. For who shall bring him back to see what will happen after he is gone?

4 THEN I returned and considered all the oppressions that are practiced under the sun: And I beheld the tears of the oppressed, and they had no comforter; and on the side of their oppressors was power, but they [too] had no comforter.
2 So I praised *and* thought more fortunate those who have been long dead than the living, who are still alive.
3 But better than them both [I thought] is he who has not yet been born, who has not seen the evil deeds that are done under the sun.
4 Then I saw that all painful effort in labor and all skill in work comes from man's rivalry with his neighbor. This is also vanity, a vain striving after the wind *and* a feeding on it.
5 The fool folds his hands together and eats his own flesh [destroying himself by indolence].
6 Better is a handful with quietness than both hands full with painful effort, a vain striving after the wind *and* a feeding on it.
7 Then I returned, and I saw vanity under the sun [in one of its peculiar forms].

8 Here is one alone—no one with him; he neither has child nor brother. Yet there is no end to all his labor, neither is his eye satisfied with riches, neither does he ask, For whom do I labor and deprive myself of good? This is also vanity (emptiness, falsity, and futility); yes, it is a painful effort *and* an unhappy business. [Prov. 27:20; I John 2:16.]
9 Two are better than one, because they have a good [more satisfying] reward for their labor;
10 For if they fall, the one will lift up his fellow. But woe to him who is alone when he falls and has not another to lift him up!
11 Again, if two lie down together, then they have warmth; but how can one be warm alone?
12 And though a man might prevail against him who is alone, two will withstand him. A threefold cord is not quickly broken.
13 Better is a poor and wise youth than an old and foolish king who [g]no longer knows how to receive counsel (friendly reproof and warning)—
14 Even though [the youth] comes out of prison to reign, while the other, born a king, becomes needy.
15 I saw all the living who walk under the sun with the youth who was to stand up in the king's stead.
16 There was no end to all the people; he was over all of them. Yet those who come later will not rejoice in him. Surely this also is vanity (emptiness, falsity, vainglory) and a striving after the wind *and* a feeding on it.

true, others entirely false? Here is the tested answer: "Every scripture inspired of God is also profitable for teaching . . . reproof . . . correction, for instruction . . . in righteousness." (II Tim. 3:16 ASV.) The divine purpose in including Ecclesiastes in the Bible is obvious. It gives a startling picture of how fatal it is for even the wisest of men to substitute man's "wisdom" for God's wisdom, and to attempt to live by it. Solomon's reign began with God, gold, and glory. It ended with bafflement, brass, and bewildered acceptance of man's having "no preeminence over a beast"!—man, who was made "in the image *and* likeness of God" (Gen. 1:27) and "but little lower than God [or heavenly beings]"! (Ps. 8:5.)
g "Christianity calls upon us to make our old age into an aspect of youth. There is to be no old age in the sense of spiritual exhaustion or moral decrepitude or misanthropic isolation; old age is to be equivalent to increase of kingliness and bounty and holy influence." "The path of the righteous is as the dawning light that shineth more and more unto the perfect day" (Prov. 4:18 ASV).

5 KEEP YOUR foot [give your mind to what you are doing] when you go [as Jacob to sacred Bethel] to the house of God. For to draw near to hear *and* obey is better than to give the sacrifice of fools [carelessly, irreverently] too ignorant to know that they are doing evil. [Gen. 35:1-4; Exod. 3:5.]

life point

Ecclesiastes 5:1 instructs us to give our minds to what we are doing, and to "keep [our] foot"—meaning our footing. We must learn to focus on what we are doing. If we do not, we will "lose our footing" and end up anxious and worried because we will always be mentally dealing with yesterday or tomorrow when we should be living today.

2 Be not rash with your mouth, and let not your heart be hasty to utter a word before God. For God is in heaven, and you are on earth; therefore let your words be few.
3 For a dream comes with much business *and* painful effort, and a fool's voice with many words.
4 When you vow a vow *or* make a pledge to God, do not put off paying it; for God has no pleasure in fools (those who witlessly mock Him). Pay what you vow. [Ps. 50:14; 66:13, 14; 76:11.]
5 It is better that you should not vow than that you should vow and not pay. [Prov. 20:25; Acts 5:4.]
6 Do not allow your mouth to cause your body to sin, and do not say before the messenger [the priest] that it was an error *or* mistake. Why should God be [made] angry at your voice and destroy the work of your hands? [Mal. 2:7.]
7 For in a multitude of dreams there is futility *and* worthlessness, and ruin in a flood of words. But [reverently]

life point

We can be led of the Spirit through internal peace every day of our lives, but we do need to beware of false peace. A strong desire to do something can produce a false peace that actually comes only from excitement. As time passes, this false peace disappears, and God's *true will* emerges in our lives. For this reason we should never move too quickly on important decisions. A little time of waiting is always wise and prudent. This is why Ecclesiastes 5:2 tells us not to be rash in what we say or hasty in the commitments we make. Excited emotions are often mistaken for God's will. However, emotions rise and fall, and if our desire and determination rise and fall with them, we will end up in real trouble. I always say, "Let emotions subside and then decide!"

fear God [revere and worship Him, knowing that He is].
8 If you see the oppression of the poor and the violent taking away of justice and righteousness in the state *or* province, do not marvel at the matter. [Be sure that there are those who will attend to it] for a higher [official]

life point

Ecclesiastes 5:3 teaches us that we need to put effort into seeing our dreams come true. I hope you have a dream or a vision in your heart for something greater than you have now. Though you will likely have to work in order to see your dream come to pass, I know that God is for you and He will help you. If you are not dreaming of anything, you are cheating yourself. We all need to think big thoughts, hope big hopes, and dream big dreams!

stay on track

I believe the expression "keep your foot" in Ecclesiastes 5:1 means "Do not lose your balance or get off track." The amplification of this phrase indicates that one stays on track by keeping his mind on what he is doing.

I used to have a wandering mind, and I had to train it by discipline. It was not easy, and sometimes I still have a relapse. While trying to complete a project, I will suddenly realize that my mind has just wandered off to something else that has nothing to do with the issue at hand. I have not yet arrived at a place of perfect concentration, but at least I understand how important it is not to allow my mind to go wherever it wishes, whenever it desires.

The word *wander* means "to move about aimlessly; to roam or ramble." It implies that a person is taking an irregular course of action at no particular pace and in no particular direction. If you are like I am, you could be sitting in a church service listening to the speaker, really enjoying and benefiting from what is being said, when suddenly your mind begins to wander. After a while you "wake up" to find that you do not remember a thing that has been going on. Even though your body stayed in church, your mind was at the shopping center browsing through the stores or at home cooking dinner.

Remember, in spiritual warfare the mind is the battlefield. That is where the enemy makes his attack. He knows very well that if we cannot keep our minds on what is being taught, we will gain absolutely nothing by being in a church service. The devil knows that we cannot complete a project if we cannot discipline our minds and focus on what we are doing.

This mind-wandering phenomenon also occurs during conversation. There are times when my husband, Dave, is talking to me and I listen for a while; then all of a sudden I realize that I have not heard a thing he has been saying. Why? Because I allowed my mind to wander off to something else. My body was standing there appearing to listen, yet in my mind I heard nothing.

For many years, when this sort of thing happened, I would pretend that I knew exactly what Dave was saying. Now I stop and say, "Can you back up and repeat that? I let my mind wander off, and I did not hear a thing you said."

In this way, I feel that at least I am dealing with the problem. Confronting issues is the only way to get on the victorious side of them! Staying focused is not only important in our church lives, our professional lives, our social lives, and our relationships; it is also vital in our spiritual lives if we want to overcome the enemy. I encourage you to pay attention to your thoughts and not let your mind wander. Defend your mental battlefield by staying focused!

than the high is observing, and higher ones are over them.

9 Moreover, the profit of the earth is for all; the king himself is served by the field *and* in all, a king is an advantage to a land with cultivated fields.

10 He who loves silver will not be satisfied with silver, nor he who loves abundance with gain. This also is vanity (emptiness, falsity, and futility)!

11 When goods increase, they who eat them increase also. And what gain is there to their owner except to see them with his eyes?

12 The sleep of a laboring man is sweet, whether he eats little or much, but the fullness of the rich will not let him sleep.

13 There is a serious *and* severe evil which I have seen under the sun: riches were kept by their owner to his hurt.

14 But those riches are lost in a bad venture; and he becomes the father of a son, and there is nothing in his hand [with which to support the child].

15 As [the man] came forth from his mother's womb, so he will go again, naked as he came; and he will take away nothing for all his labor which he can carry in his hand.

16 And this also is a serious *and* severe evil—that in all points as he came, so shall he go; and what gain has he who labors for the wind? [I Tim. 6:6.]

17 All his days also he eats in darkness [cheerlessly, with no sweetness and light in them], and much sorrow and sickness and wrath are his.

18 Behold, what I have seen to be good and fitting is for one to eat and drink, and to find enjoyment in all the labor in which he labors under the sun all the days which God gives

enjoy your journey

Years ago my husband and I enrolled in a nine-month Bible study course because we felt that God's will for us was to start training for ministry. The course met two or three nights a week, which was quite a commitment, especially for Dave because he worked so hard in the engineering field during the day.

That course seemed like a major undertaking until the Lord gave me a vision about having goals and reaching them. In the vision I saw the horizon ahead of me, which in this case represented graduating from the course. As I began moving toward the horizon in the vision, it faded from sight and another would rise up.

The Lord was showing me that we will always be moving toward some goal or objective in our lives. As soon as we finish one, another will take its place. As believers, we are always extending our faith for something. Whatever we believe God for right now could happen a year from now, but by that time we will be believing God for something else. The Lord was teaching me that since we are going to spend the majority of our lives waiting for something, we should learn to enjoy life as it unfolds. If we do not, life will pass us by, and we will never enjoy where we are right now.

Let me encourage you, as the writer of Ecclesiastes does (see Ecclesiastes 5:18), to enjoy everything you do to the fullest extent, for as long as you live!

him—for this is his [allotted] part. [I Tim. 6:17.]

19 Also, every man to whom God has given riches and possessions, and the power to enjoy them and to accept his appointed lot and to rejoice in his toil—this is the gift of God [to him].

20 For he shall not much remember [seriously] the days of his life, because God [Himself] answers *and* corresponds to the joy of his heart [the tranquillity of God is mirrored in him].

6 THERE IS an evil which I have seen under the sun, and it lies heavily upon men:

2 A man to whom God has given riches, possessions, and honor, so that he lacks nothing for his soul of all that he might desire, yet God does not give him the power *or* capacity to enjoy them [things which are gifts from God], but a stranger [in whom he has no interest succeeds him and] consumes *and* enjoys them. This is vanity (emptiness, falsity, and futility); it is a sore affliction! [Luke 12:20.]

3 If a man begets a hundred children and lives many years so that the days of his years are many, but his life is not filled with good, and also he is given no burial [honors nor is laid to rest in the sepulcher of his fathers], I say that [he who had] an untimely birth [resulting in death] is better off than he, [Job 3:16.]

4 For [the untimely one] comes in futility and goes into darkness, and in darkness his name is covered.

5 Moreover, he has not seen the sun nor had any knowledge, yet he [the stillborn child] has rest rather than he [who is aware of all that he has missed and all that he would not have had to suffer].

6 Even though he lives a thousand years twice over and yet has seen no good *and* experienced no enjoyment—do not all go to one place [the place of the dead]?

7 All the labor of man is for his mouth [for self-preservation and enjoyment], and yet his desire is not satisfied. [Prov. 16:26.]

8 For what advantage has the wise man over the fool [being worldly-wise is not the secret to happiness]? What advantage has the poor man who has learned how to walk before the living [publicly, with men's eyes upon him; being poor is not the secret to happiness either]?

9 Better is the sight of the eyes [the enjoyment of what is available to one] than the cravings of wandering desire. This is also vanity (emptiness, falsity, and futility) and a striving after the wind *and* a feeding on it!

10 Whatever [man] is, he has been named that long ago, and it is known that it is man [h][Adam]; nor can he contend with Him who is mightier than he [whether God or death].

11 Seeing that there are [all these and] many other things *and* words that increase the emptiness, falsity, vainglory, *and* futility [of living], what profit *and* what outcome is there for man?

12 For who [i][limited to human wisdom] knows what is good for man in his life, all the days of his vain life which he spends as a shadow [going through the motions but accomplishing nothing]? For who can tell a man what will happen [to his work, his treasure, his plans] under the sun after he is gone?

---

h The Hebrew "Adam" means man, of the ground. The very name witnesses to his frailty.   i How impressive throughout Ecclesiastes is the evidence that, while Solomon is doing his utmost to prove that life is futile and not worth living, the Holy Spirit is using him to show that these conclusions are the tragic effect of living "under the sun"—ignoring the Lord, dwelling away from God the Father, oblivious of the Holy Spirit—and yet face to face with the mysteries of life and nature!

7 A GOOD name is better than precious perfume, and the day of death better than the day of one's birth.

2 It is better to go to the house of mourning than to go to the house of feasting, for that is the end of all men; and the living will lay it to heart.

3 Sorrow is better than laughter, for by the sadness of the countenance the heart is made better *and* gains gladness. [II Cor. 7:10.]

4 The heart of the wise is in the house of mourning, but the heart of fools is in the house of mirth *and* sensual joy.

5 It is better for a man to hear the rebuke of the wise than to hear the song of fools.

6 For like the crackling of thorns under a pot, so is the laughter of the fool. This also is vanity (emptiness, falsity, and futility)!

7 Surely oppression *and* extortion make a wise man foolish, and a bribe destroys the understanding *and* judgment.

8 Better is the end of a thing than the beginning of it, and the patient in spirit is better than the proud in spirit.

9 Do not be quick in spirit to be

be slow to anger

Ecclesiastes 7:9 exhorts: "Do not be quick in spirit to be angry or vexed, for anger and vexation lodge in the bosom of fools." Not being "quick in spirit to be angry" speaks to me of self-control. We cannot ever develop into victorious, overcoming believers if we do not learn to exercise self-control by managing our emotions, especially the emotion of anger.

Ecclesiastes 7:9 is only one of many Bible verses that address the subject of anger. For example, Proverbs 14:17 says, "He who foams up quickly and flies into a passion deals foolishly." In Proverbs 16:32, we read that someone who is slow to get angry is better than one who is mighty. Proverbs further addresses anger by stating that "Good sense makes a man restrain his anger" (Proverbs 19:11). And in James 1:19, 20, we read: "Let every man be quick to hear [a ready listener], slow to speak, slow to take offense and to get angry. For man's anger does not promote the righteousness God [wishes and requires]."

Notice in James 1:19, 20 that "man's anger does not promote" righteousness. Part of righteousness, or the right way of being what God wants us to be, is fulfilling our potential—and we cannot do that unless we learn to restrain our anger.

We all want more than we have in various areas of our lives, but we do not always want to operate within the boundaries of self-control. If we really want to grow spiritually, we must keep our passions under control. That does not mean we have to be perfect or that we can never make mistakes. Although the Holy Spirit will give us power to control our emotions, we may still lose our tempers at times. But as soon as we do, we should immediately confess and repent.

A disciplined, self-controlled life not only requires time, determination, and hard work; it also requires self-denial, but the rewards are worth the effort.

angry *or* vexed, for anger *and* vexation lodge in the bosom of fools. [James 1:19, 20.]

10 Do not say, Why were the old days better than these? For it is not wise *or* because of wisdom that you ask this.

11 Wisdom is as good as an inheritance, yes, more excellent it is for those [the living] who see the sun.

12 For wisdom is a defense even as money is a defense, but the excellency of knowledge is that wisdom shields *and* preserves the life of him who has it.

13 Consider the work of God: who can make straight what He has made crooked?

14 In the day of prosperity be joyful, but in the day of adversity consider that God has made the one side by side with the other, so that man may not find out anything that shall be after him.

15 I have seen everything in the days of my vanity (my emptiness, falsity, vainglory, and futility): there is a righteous man who perishes in his righteousness, and there is a wicked man who prolongs his life in [spite of] his evildoing.

16 Be not [morbidly exacting and externally] righteous overmuch, neither strive to make yourself [pretentiously appear] overwise—why should you [get puffed up and] destroy yourself [with presumptuous self-sufficiency]?

17 [Although all have sinned] be not wicked overmuch *or* willfully, neither be foolish—why should you die before your time?

18 It is good that you should take hold of this and from that withdraw not your hand; for he who [reverently] fears *and* worships God will come forth from them all.

19 [True] wisdom is a strength to the wise man more than ten rulers *or* valiant generals who are in the city. [Ps. 127:1; II Tim. 3:15.]

20 Surely there is not a righteous man upon earth who does good and never sins. [Isa. 53:6; Rom. 3:23.]

21 Do not give heed to everything that is said, lest you hear your servant cursing you—

22 For often your own heart knows that you have likewise cursed others.

23 All this have I tried *and* proved by wisdom. I said, I will be wise [independently of God]—but it was far from me.

24 That which is is far off, and that which is deep is very deep—who can find it out [true wisdom independent of the fear of God]? [Job 28:12-28; I Cor. 2:9-16.]

25 I turned about [penitent] and my heart was set to know and to search out and to seek [true] wisdom and the reason of things, and to know that wickedness is folly and that foolishness is madness [and what had led me into such wickedness and madness].

26 And I found that [of all sinful follies none has been so ruinous in seducing one away from God as idolatrous women] more bitter than death is the woman whose heart is snares and nets and whose hands are bands. Whoever pleases God shall escape from her, but the sinner shall be taken by her.

27 Behold, this I have found, says the Preacher, while weighing one thing after another to find out the right estimate [and the reason]—

28 Which I am still seeking but have not found—one upright man among a thousand have I found, but an upright woman among all those [one thousand in my harem] have I not found. [I Kings 11:3.]

29 Behold, this is the only [reason for it that] I have found: God made man upright, but they [men and women] have sought out many devices [for evil].

8 WHO IS like the wise man? And who knows the interpretation of a thing? A man's wisdom makes his face shine, and the hardness of his countenance is changed.

2 I counsel you to keep the king's command, and that in regard to the oath of God [by which you swore to him loyalty]. [II Sam. 21:7.]

3 Be not panic-stricken *and* hasty to get out of his presence. Persist not in an evil thing, for he does whatever he pleases.

4 For the word of a king is authority *and* power, and who can say to him, What are you doing?

5 Whoever observes the [king's] command will experience no harm, and a wise man's mind will know both when and what to do.

6 For every purpose *and* matter has its [right] time and judgment, although the misery *and* wickedness of man lies heavily upon him [who rebels against the king].

7 For he does not know what is to be, for who can tell him how *and* when it will be?

8 There is no man who has power over the spirit to retain the breath of life, neither has he power over the day of death; and there is no discharge in battle [against death], neither will wickedness deliver those who are its possessors *and* given to it.

9 All this have I seen while applying my mind to every work that is done under the sun. There is a time in which one man has power over another to his own hurt *or* to the other man's.

10 And so I saw the wicked buried— those who had come and gone out of the holy place [but did not thereby escape their doom], and they are [praised and] forgotten in the city where they had done such things. This also is vanity (emptiness, falsity, vainglory, and futility)!

11 Because the sentence against an evil work is not executed speedily, the hearts of the sons of men are fully set to do evil.

12 Though a sinner does evil a hundred times and his days [seemingly] are prolonged [in his wickedness], yet surely I know that it will be well with those who [reverently] fear God, who revere *and* worship Him, realizing His continual presence. [Ps. 37:11, 18, 19; Isa. 3:10, 11; Matt. 25:34.]

life point

If we seek God only when we are desperate, then He will keep us in desperate circumstances because He deeply desires to fellowship with us.

God *will* rescue us and get us out of trouble when we come to Him. But, according to Ecclesiastes 8:12, if we want to stay in a place of constant victory, we must diligently seek Him *at all times* and desire to experience His continual presence in our everyday lives. We must never forget that relationship is built on fellowship.

13 But it will not be well with the wicked, neither will he prolong his days like a shadow, because he does not [reverently] fear *and* worship God. [Matt. 25:41.]

14 Here also is a futility that goes on upon the earth: there are righteous men who fare as though they were wicked, and wicked men who fare as though they were righteous. I say that this also is vanity (emptiness, falsity, and futility)!

15 Then I commended enjoyment, because a man has no better thing under the sun [without God] than to eat and to drink and to be joyful, for that will remain with him in his toil through the days of his life which God gives him under the sun.

16 When I applied my mind to know wisdom and to see the business

activity *and* the painful effort that take place upon the earth—how neither day nor night some men's eyes sleep—

17 Then I saw all the work of God, that man cannot find out the work that is done under the sun—because however much a man may toil in seeking, yet he will not find it out; yes, more than that, though a wise man thinks *and* claims he knows, yet will he not be able to find it out. [Deut. 29:29; Rom. 11:33.]

9 FOR ALL this I took to heart, exploring *and* examining it all, how the righteous (the upright, in right standing with God) and the wise and their works are in the hands of God. Whether it is to be love or hatred no man knows; all that is before them.

2 All things come alike to all. There is one event to the righteous and to the wicked, to the good and to the clean and to the unclean; to him who sacrifices and to him who does not sacrifice. As is the good man, so is the sinner; and he who swears is as he who fears *and* shuns an oath.

3 This evil is in all that is done under the sun: one fate comes to all. Also the hearts of men are full of evil, and madness is in their hearts while they live, and after that they go to the dead.

4 [There is no exemption] but he who is joined to all the living has hope—for a living dog is better than a dead lion.

5 For the living know that they will die, but the dead know nothing; and they have no more reward [here], for the memory of them is forgotten.

6 Their love and their hatred and their envy have already perished; neither have they any more a share in anything that is done under the sun.

7 Go your way, eat your bread with joy, and drink your wine with a cheerful heart [if you are righteous, wise, and in the hands of God], for God has already accepted your works.

8 Let your garments be always white [with purity], and let your head not lack [the] oil [of gladness].

9 Live joyfully with the wife whom you love all the days of your vain life which He has given you under the sun—all the days of futility. For that is your portion in this life and in your work at which you toil under the sun.

10 Whatever your hand finds to do, do it with all your might, for there is no work or device or knowledge or wisdom in Sheol (the place of the dead), where you are going.

11 I returned and saw under the sun that the race is not to the swift nor the battle to the strong, neither is bread to the wise nor riches to men of intelligence *and* understanding nor favor to men of skill; but time and chance happen to them all. [Ps. 33:16-19; Rom. 9:16.]

12 For man also knows not his time [of death]: as the fishes are taken in an evil net, and as the birds are caught in the snare, so are the sons of men snared in an evil time when [calamity] falls suddenly upon them.

13 This [illustration of] wisdom have I seen also under the sun, and it seemed great to me:

14 There was a little city with few men in it. And a great king came against it and besieged it and built great bulwarks against it.

speak the Word

15 But there was found in it a poor wise man, and he by his wisdom delivered the city. Yet no man [seriously] remembered that poor man.

16 But I say that wisdom is better than might, though the poor man's wisdom is despised and his words are not heeded.

17 The words of wise men heard in quiet are better than the shouts of him who rules among fools.

18 Wisdom is better than weapons of war, but one sinner destroys much good.

10 DEAD FLIES cause the ointment of the perfumer to putrefy [and] send forth a vile odor; so does a little folly [in him who is valued for wisdom] outweigh wisdom and honor.

2 A wise man's heart turns him toward his right hand, but a fool's heart toward his left. [Matt. 25:31-41.]

3 Even when he who is a fool walks along the road, his heart *and* understanding fail him, and he says of everyone *and* to everyone that he is a fool.

4 If the temper of the ruler rises up against you, do not leave your place [or show a resisting spirit]; for gentleness *and* calmness prevent *or* put a stop to great offenses.

5 There is an evil which I have seen under the sun, like an error which proceeds from the ruler:

6 Folly is set in great dignity *and* in high places, and the rich sit in low places.

7 I have seen slaves on horses, and princes walking like slaves on the earth.

8 He who digs a pit [for others] will fall into it, and whoever breaks through a fence *or* a [stone] wall, a serpent will bite him. [Ps. 57:6.]

9 Whoever removes [landmark] stones *or* hews out [new ones with

similar intent] will be hurt with them, *and* he who fells trees will be endangered by them. [Prov. 26:27.]

10 If the ax is dull and the man does not whet the edge, he must put forth more strength; but wisdom helps him to succeed.

11 If the serpent bites before it is charmed, then it is no use to call a charmer [and the slanderer is no better than the uncharmed snake].

12 The words of a wise man's mouth are gracious *and* win him favor, but the lips of a fool consume him.

13 The beginning of the words of his mouth is foolishness, and the end of his talk is wicked madness.

14 A fool also multiplies words, though no man can tell what will be— and what will happen after he is gone, who can tell him?

15 The labor of fools wearies every one of them, because [he is so ignorant of the ordinary matters that] he does not even know how to get to town.

16 Woe to you, O land, when your king is a child *or* a servant and when your officials feast in the morning!

17 Happy (fortunate and to be envied) are you, O land, when your king is a free man *and* of noble birth *and* character and when your officials feast at the proper time—for strength and not for drunkenness! [Isa. 32:8.]

18 Through indolence the rafters [of state affairs] decay *and* the roof sinks in, and through idleness of the hands the house leaks.

19 [Instead of repairing the breaches, the officials] make a feast for laughter, serve wine to cheer life, and [depend on tax] money to answer for all of it.

20 Curse not the king, no, not even in your thoughts, and curse not the rich in your bedchamber, for a bird of the air will carry the voice, and a winged creature will tell the matter. [Exod. 22:28.]

11

CAST YOUR bread upon the waters, for you will find it after many days.

2 Give a portion to seven, yes, even [divide it] to eight, for you know not what evil may come upon the earth.

3 If the clouds are full of rain, they empty themselves upon the earth; and if a tree falls toward the south or toward the north, in the place where the tree falls, there it will lie.

4 He who observes the wind [and waits for all conditions to be favorable] will not sow, and he who regards the clouds will not reap.

5 As you know not what is the way of the wind, or how the spirit comes to the bones in the womb of a pregnant woman, even so you know not the work of God, Who does all.

6 In the morning sow your seed, and in the evening withhold not your

the pitfall of procrastination

In 1993, when God showed my husband, Dave, and me that He wanted our ministry to begin television broadcasts, He said, "I am giving you an opportunity to go on television; but if you procrastinate and do not take the opportunity now, it will never pass by you again." Perhaps if God had not told us this opportunity was open only for that particular moment, we might have put off pursuing it. After all, we were finally in a position where we could be comfortable and perhaps not have to work as hard as we had in the past.

For nine years, we had been in the process of "birthing" Joyce Meyer Ministries. Now, suddenly, God was giving us an opportunity to reach more people, which is something we wanted to do with all our hearts. However, in order to do it, we would need to take on new responsibility.

When the Lord asks any of us to do something, we can be tempted to wait for a convenient season, a time when "all conditions are favorable," as we read in Ecclesiastes 11:4. There is always the tendency to hold back until it will not cost anything or be so difficult.

I encourage you to be a person who is not afraid of responsibility and who does not procrastinate when God speaks. If you do only what is easy, you will always remain weak; but as you meet resistance and overcome, you will build your strength.

God expects you and me to be responsible and take care of what He gives us; He wants us to do something with His gifts that will produce good fruit. If we do not use the gifts and talents He has given us when He directs us to do so, then we are not being responsible over what He has entrusted to us.

If you are a procrastinator, I urge you to heed the instruction of Ecclesiastes 11:4. You do not have to wait until everything is perfect to obey God. Do what He says to do, when He says to do it, and you will reap the blessings of obedience.

hands, for you know not which shall prosper, whether this or that, or whether both alike will be good.

7 Truly the light is sweet, and a pleasant thing it is for the eyes to behold the sun.

8 Yes, if a man should live many years, let him rejoice in them all; yet let him [seriously] remember the days of darkness, for they will be many. All that comes is vanity (emptiness, falsity, vainglory, and futility)!

9 Rejoice, O young man, in your adolescence, and let your heart cheer you in the days of your [full-grown] youth. And walk in the ways of your heart and in the sight of your eyes, but know that for all these things God will bring you into judgment.

10 Therefore remove [the lusts that end in] sorrow *and* vexation from your heart *and* mind and put away evil from your body, for youth and the dawn of life are vanity [transitory, idle, empty, and devoid of truth]. [II Cor. 7:1; II Tim. 2:22.]

12 REMEMBER [earnestly] also your Creator [that you are not your own, but His property now] in the days of your youth, before the evil days come or the years draw near when you will say [of physical pleasures], I have no enjoyment in them—[II Sam. 19:35.]

2 Before the sun and the light and the moon and the stars are darkened [sight is impaired], and the clouds [of depression] return after the rain [of tears];

3 In the day when the keepers of the house [the hands and the arms] tremble, and the strong men [the feet and the knees] bow themselves, and the grinders [the molar teeth] cease because they are few, and those who look out of the windows [the eyes] are darkened;

4 When the doors [the lips] are shut in the streets and the sound of the

grinding [of the teeth] is low, and one rises up at the voice of a bird *and* the crowing of a cock, and all the daughters of music [the voice and the ear] are brought low;

5 Also when [the old] are afraid of danger from that which is high, and fears are in the way, and the almond tree [their white hair] blooms, and the grasshopper [a little thing] is a burden, and desire *and* appetite fail, because man goes to his everlasting home and the mourners go about the streets *or* marketplaces. [Job 17:13.]

6 [Remember your Creator earnestly now] before the silver cord [of life] is snapped apart, or the golden bowl is broken, or the pitcher is broken at the fountain, or the wheel broken at the cistern [and the whole circulatory system of the blood ceases to function];

7 Then shall the dust [out of which God made man's body] return to the earth as it was, and the spirit shall return to God Who gave it.

8 Vapor of vapors *and* futility of futilities, says the Preacher. All is futility (emptiness, falsity, vainglory, and transitoriness)!

9 And furthermore, because the Preacher was wise, he [Solomon] still taught the people knowledge; and he pondered and searched out and set in order many proverbs.

10 The Preacher sought acceptable words, even to write down rightly words of truth *or* correct sentiment.

11 The words of the wise are like prodding goads, and firmly fixed [in the mind] like nails are the collected sayings which are given [as proceeding] from one Shepherd. [Ezek. 37:24.]

12 But about going further [than the words given by one Shepherd], my son, be warned. Of making many books there is no end [so do not believe everything you read], and much study is a weariness of the flesh.

13 All has been heard; the end of the matter is: Fear God [revere and worship Him, knowing that He is] and keep His commandments, for this is the whole of man [the full, original purpose of his creation, the object of God's providence, the root of character, the foundation of all happiness, the adjustment to all inharmonious circumstances and conditions under the sun] *and* the whole [duty] for every man.

14 For God shall bring every work into judgment, with every secret thing, whether it is good or evil. [Matt. 12:36; Acts 17:30, 31; Rom. 2:16; I Cor. 4:5.]

life point

After a lifetime of trying everything the world had to offer, Solomon finally concluded that the only thing that made any sense at all was God. He realized that no one can find any lasting enjoyment apart from Him. Solomon said what he had learned from all his searching was that the best way to spend our lives is to fear God and obey Him. This is our highest purpose and our most noble duty, so I encourage you to make a priority of it in your life.

Song of Solomon

Author:
Attributed to Solomon

Date:
Probably between 970 BC and 930 BC

Everyday Life Principles:
The lessons we learn about love in the Song of Solomon can be applied spiritually and naturally.

We need to abandon ourselves to those we love in committed, intimate relationships. This is true for believers in relationship with God and for husbands and wives within the marriage covenant.

True love is worth pursuing, and it should be expressed with passion.

Some people believe the Song of Solomon applies only to a physical love relationship between husband and wife; others believe it is entirely symbolic of God's love for His people. I believe its principles and lessons can be applied both naturally and spiritually. It does provide insight and guidance for marriage and for the sexual relationship within marriage, but it also reveals the passion with which God loves us.

This book is a beautiful story about pursuing love, expressing love, and enjoying love. It teaches us to abandon ourselves to the Lover of our souls (God) and to the husbands or wives to whom we are joined in the marriage covenant. It encourages us to love God and our spouses wholeheartedly and passionately, holding nothing back. It also reminds us that God is chasing us, wooing us, pursuing us with the same type of tenderness and zeal that a young man employs when trying to win the heart of the woman he loves.

As you read through the Song of Solomon, I encourage you to learn from it on two levels. First, let it stir your passion for God and inspire your gratitude for His relentless pursuit of you. Second, if you are married or hope to marry some day, let this book teach you lessons of intimacy that will serve your marriage well. Above all, intensely enjoy and celebrate the beauty and the richness of your love relationship with God and with your mate.

NOTE: *Among the multitudes who read the Bible there are comparatively few who have a clear understanding of the Song of Solomon. Some have thought it to be a collection of songs, but it is more generally understood to be a sort of drama, the positive interpretation of which is impossible because the identity of the speakers and the length of the speeches are not disclosed.*

1 THE SONG of songs [the most excellent of them all] which is Solomon's. [I Kings 4:32.]
2   Let him kiss me with the kisses of his mouth! [she cries. Then, realizing that Solomon has arrived and has heard her speech, she turns to him and adds] For your love is better than wine!
3   [And she continues] The odor of your ointments is fragrant; your name is like perfume poured out. Therefore do the maidens love you.
4   Draw me! We will run after you! The king brings me into his apartments! We will be glad and rejoice in you! We will recall [when we were favored with] your love, more fragrant than wine. The upright [are not offended at your choice, but sincerely] love you.
5   I am so black; but [you are] lovely *and* pleasant [the ladies assured her]. O you daughters of Jerusalem, [I am as dark] as the tents of [the Bedouin tribe] Kedar, like the [beautiful] curtains of Solomon!
6   [Please] do not look at me, [she said, for] I am swarthy. [I have worked out] in the sun *and* it has left its mark upon me. My stepbrothers were angry with me, and they made

speak the Word

life point

The maiden portrayed in the Song of Solomon says, "Draw me! We will run after You" (Song of Solomon 1:4). In attempting to have a close intimate relationship with God, we must first ask Him to draw us by His Holy Spirit. No matter how much we want to come to Him, He must be drawing us, wooing us, and leading us to be closer to Him. The maiden does not say, "I" will run after you, she says, "we" will run after you. I think there is a strong possibility that she is talking about the various components of her personality. She may be saying that her mind, will, emotions, heart, and every other faculty she possesses will run after him if he will only draw her. She is ready to abandon herself to him and hold nothing back! Have you come to that place yet? Do you want a visitation from God? Make a decision to give all of yourself, and ask Him to draw you to Himself.

me keeper of the vineyards; but my own vineyard [my complexion] I have not kept.
7   [Addressing her shepherd, she said] Tell me, O ᵃyou whom my soul loves, where you pasture your flock, where you make it lie down at noon. For why should I [as I think of you] be as a veiled one straying beside the flocks of your companions? [Ps. 23:1, 2.]
8   If you do not know [where your lover is], O you fairest among women,

a Does my spirit crave the Divine Shepherd, even in the presence of the best that the world can offer me?

run along, follow the tracks of the flock, and [amuse yourself by] pasturing your kids beside the shepherds' tents.

9 O my love [he said as he saw her], you remind me of my [favorite] mare in the chariot spans of Pharaoh.

10 Your cheeks are comely with ornaments, your neck with strings of jewels.

11 We will make for you chains *and* ornaments of gold, studded with silver.

12 While the king sits at his table [she said], my spikenard [my absent lover] sends forth [his] fragrance [over me].

13 My beloved [shepherd] is to me like a [scent] bag of myrrh that lies in my bosom.

14 My beloved [shepherd] is to me a cluster of henna flowers in the vineyards of En-gedi [famed for its fragrant shrubs].

15 Behold, you are beautiful, my love! Behold, you are beautiful! You have doves' eyes.

16 [She cried] Behold, you are beautiful, my beloved [shepherd], yes, delightful! Our arbor *and* couch are green *and* leafy.

17 The beams of our house are cedars, and our rafters *and* panels are cypresses *or* pines.

2 [SHE SAID] I am only a little rose *or* autumn crocus of the plain of Sharon, or a [humble] lily of the valleys [that grows in deep and difficult places].

2 But Solomon replied, Like the lily among thorns, so are you, my love, among the daughters.

speak the Word

3 Like an apple tree among the trees of the wood, so is my beloved [shepherd] among the sons [cried the girl]! Under his shadow I delighted to sit, and his fruit was sweet to my taste.

4 He brought me to the banqueting house, and his banner over me was love [for love waved as a protecting and comforting banner over my head when I was near him].

5 Sustain me with raisins, refresh me with apples, for I am sick with love.

6 [I can feel] ᵇhis left hand under my head and his right hand embraces me! [Deut. 33:27; Matt. 28:20.]

7 [He said] I charge you, O you daughters of Jerusalem, by the gazelles or by the hinds of the field [which are free to follow their own instincts] that you not try to stir up or awaken [my] love until it pleases.

8 [Vividly she pictured it] The voice of my beloved [shepherd]! Behold, he comes, leaping upon the mountains, bounding over the hills. [John 10:27.]

9 My beloved is like a gazelle or a young hart. Behold, he stands behind the wall of our house, he looks in through the windows, he glances through the lattice.

10 My beloved speaks and says to me, Rise up, my love, my fair one, and come away.

11 For, behold, the winter is past; the rain is over and gone.

12 The flowers appear on the earth; the time of the singing [of birds] has come, and the voice of the turtledove is heard in our land.

13 The fig tree puts forth *and* ripens her green figs, and the vines are in blossom and give forth their fragrance.

b Do I have a constant sense of my Shepherd's presence, regardless of my surroundings?

ᶜArise, my love, my fair one, and come away.

14 [So I went with him, and when we were climbing the rocky steps up the hillside, my beloved shepherd said to me] O my dove, [while you are here] in the seclusion of the clefts in the solid rock, in the sheltered *and* secret place of the cliff, let me see your face, ᵈlet me hear your voice; for your voice is sweet, and your face is lovely.

15 [My heart was touched and I fervently sang to him my desire] Take for us the foxes, the ᵉlittle foxes that spoil the vineyards [of our love], for our vineyards are in blossom.

16 [She said distinctly] My beloved is mine and I am his! He pastures his flocks among the lilies. [Matt. 10:32; Acts 4:12.]

17 [Then, longingly addressing her absent shepherd, she cried] Until the day breaks and the shadows flee away, return hastily, O my beloved, and be like a gazelle or a young hart as you cover the mountains [which separate us].

3 IN THE night I dreamed that I sought the one whom I love. [She said] I looked for him but could not find him. [Isa. 26:9.]

2 So I decided to go out into the city, into the streets and broad ways [which are so confusing to a country girl], and seek him whom my soul loves. I sought him, but I could not find him.

3 The watchmen who go about the city found me, to whom I said, Have you seen him whom my soul loves?

4 I had gone but a little way past them when I found him whom my soul loves. I held him and would not let him go until I had brought him into

life point

Tucked away in the midst of the romance of the Song of Solomon is an extremely valuable piece of wisdom for everyday life: It is "the little foxes" that spoil the vine (Song of Solomon 2:15). What this means is that people's lives are typically not destroyed by what we would consider "big" issues, but by a series of smaller, seemingly insignificant choices or compromises.

Watch the "little foxes" in your life; forgive even the most minor offense so that your heart stays clean, do not cut corners in your finances or on the job when you think no one will notice, do not expose yourself to ungodly influences, thinking, *It won't hurt me if I do it just this once.* Little things add up to big things, and before you know it, little foxes can ruin a strong, healthy vine.

my mother's house, and into the chamber of her who conceived me. [Rom. 8:35; I Pet. 2:25.]

5 I adjure you, O daughters of Jerusalem, by the gazelles or by the hinds of the field that you stir not up nor awaken love until it pleases.

6 Who *or* what is this [she asked] that comes gliding out of the wilderness like stately pillars of smoke per-

life point

Just as the woman in Song of Solomon 3:4 who found her beloved and "would not let him go," we need to do everything possible to honor the legally and spiritually binding covenant of marriage.

---

c Do I take time to meet my Good Shepherd each day, letting Him tell me of His love, and cheering His heart with my interest in Him?   **d** Do I realize that my voice lifted in praise and song is sweet to Him, or do I withhold it?   **e** What is my greatest concern, the thing about which most of all I want Christ's help? When He asks to hear my voice, what do I tell Him?

fulfillment in marriage

Solomon uses rich and unusual imagery to portray the love between a man and a woman in marriage. In Song of Solomon 2:16 and in other passages throughout this book, the married couple share a oneness that can be found in no other relationship.

The Bible says that when a man and a woman are married, "they shall become one flesh" (Genesis 2:24). Notice the word *become*. When you and your spouse are married, you are "one" before God, as well as legally, but in your relationship you are still in the process of *becoming* one. While you work this process out between you, you should hold your marriage in honor, and esteem your partner as worthy and precious.

Many couples get stumped when trying to work on their marriage because men and women are so different. It helps to understand that God made us different on purpose. Do not confuse weaknesses with differences. We are to help build up each other's frailties, but we are not called to change one another's differences. It certainly is not God's plan for us to try to make our partners be like we are. But we are in each other's lives to help build each other up to become all that God has in mind for us to be.

I exhort you to treat your spouse as if you were still courting each other because, in effect, you *are* still courting. If you do not work at your marriage, you will not have a good one. Make a fresh commitment today to be diligent in your relationship with your spouse and to keep becoming one. It will take effort, but the rewards are sweet!

fumed with myrrh, frankincense, and all the fragrant powders of the merchant?

7 [Someone answered] Behold, it is the traveling litter (the bridal car) of Solomon. Sixty mighty men are around it, of the mighty men of Israel.

8 They all handle the sword and are expert in war; every man has his sword upon his thigh, that fear be not excited in the night.

9 King Solomon made himself a car *or* a palanquin from the [cedar] wood of Lebanon.

10 He made its posts of silver, its back of gold, its seat of purple, the inside of it lovingly *and* intricately wrought in needlework by the daughters of Jerusalem.

11 Go forth, O you daughters of Zion, and gaze upon King Solomon wearing the crown with which his mother [Bathsheba] crowned him on the day of his wedding, on the day of his gladness of heart.

4 HOW FAIR you are, my love [he said], how very fair! Your eyes behind your veil [remind me] of those of a dove; your hair [makes me think of the black, wavy fleece] of a flock of [the Arabian] goats which one sees trailing down Mount Gilead [beyond the Jordan on the frontiers of the desert].

2 Your teeth are like a flock of shorn ewes which have come up from the washing, of which all are in pairs, and none is missing among them.

3 Your lips are like a thread of

first a wedding, then a marriage

Song of Solomon 3:11 mentions Solomon's wedding day and refers to it as "the day of his gladness of heart."

Wedding days are happy indeed, but after every wedding comes a marriage. The Bible says that marriage is a union—such an intimate joining together of two separate entities that they become one. We tend to be somewhat casual in our use of the word *union* today. We know that the Father, Son, and Holy Spirit are in a union known as "the Godhead"; we know that there is supposed to be a union among all believers; and we know that when a man and a woman marry, a union is supposed to take place. But what does this marriage union really mean?

Let me suggest a word picture that may help you understand. Picture an empty glass. Beside that empty glass is a cup of strong coffee and a glass of water. Of course, the coffee is dark and black, while the water is clear. Many times, when two people marry, they are as different as the coffee and the water. Occasionally a husband and a wife are very similar, but typically they are quite different when they first join together.

Now, envision pouring both the coffee and the water into the empty glass. This is a great image of what happens in a marriage. Once you have done that, could you ever possibly separate those two liquids again?

Once the coffee and the water have been poured into the previously empty glass, you cannot even call the substance all-coffee or all-water; it is a mixture of both. It looks and tastes different from 100 percent coffee or 100 percent water—and you would have no idea how to separate one from the other.

When a man and a woman marry, God intends for their lives to blend together in an inseparable way. They become one new person joined together in Christ Jesus. That is the way God planned for our marriages to be. Do everything you can to cultivate a true union in your marriage, and you will enjoy not only your wedding day, but a wonderful life as one with your husband or wife.

scarlet, and your mouth is lovely. Your cheeks are like halves of a pomegranate behind your veil.
4 Your neck is like the tower of David, built for an arsenal, whereon hang a thousand bucklers, all of them shields of warriors.
5 Your two breasts are like two fawns, like twins of a gazelle that feed among the lilies.

6 Until the day breaks and the shadows flee away, [in my thoughts] I will get to the mountain of myrrh and the hill of frankincense [to him whom my soul adores].
7 [He exclaimed] O my love, how beautiful you are! There is no flaw in you! [John 14:18; Eph. 5:27.]
8 Come ᶠaway with me from Lebanon, my [promised] bride, come with

f Do I heed Christ when He bids me to come away from the lions' den of temptation and dwell with Him?

putting the Word to work

The man in Song of Solomon 4:7 is so in love with his bride that he sees "no flaw" in her. We know that no one is perfect, but love does enable us to overlook people's faults. Is there anyone for whom you need to "cut some slack" in your life right now? Remember to always look for the best in people.

me from Lebanon. Depart from the top of Amana, from the peak of Senir and Hermon, from the lions' dens, from the mountains of the leopards. [II Cor. 11:2, 3.]

9 You have ravished my heart *and* given me courage, my sister, my [promised] bride; you have ravished my heart *and* given me courage with one look from your eyes, with one jewel of your necklace.

10 How beautiful is your love, my sister, my [promised] bride! How much better is your love than wine! And the fragrance of your ointments than all spices! [John 15:9; Rom. 8:35.]

11 Your lips, O my [promised] bride, drop honey as the honeycomb; honey and milk are under your tongue. And the odor of your garments is like the odor of Lebanon.

12 A garden enclosed *and* barred is

life point

Marriage is more than a sexual union, and it is more than a legal institution that binds the property accumulated by two people to an equal right of ownership. Marriage is a promise of companionship and provision for the spiritual, emotional, and physical needs of two people.

my sister, my [promised] bride—a spring shut up, a fountain sealed.

13 Your shoots are an orchard of pomegranates *or* a paradise with precious fruits, henna with spikenard plants, [John 15:5; Eph. 5:9.]

14 Spikenard and saffron, calamus and cinnamon, with all trees of frankincense, myrrh, and aloes, with all the chief spices.

15 You are a fountain [springing up] in a garden, a well of living waters, and flowing streams from Lebanon. [John 4:10; 7:37, 38.]

16 [You have called me a garden, she said] Oh, I pray that the [cold] �g north wind and the [soft] south wind may blow upon my garden, that its spices may flow out [in abundance for you in whom my soul delights]. Let my beloved come into his garden and eat its choicest fruits.

life point

Regarding the sexual relationship in marriage, unless it is perverted outside marriage, sexuality is to be holy, fun, and wholesome. It is a stress reliever that brings two people into a closeness that cannot be found in any other way except through a right relationship in a marriage union. Being single-hearted toward a person's spouse brings great fulfillment for both partners in marriage.

5 I HAVE come into my garden, my sister, my [promised] bride; I have gathered my myrrh with my balsam *and* spice [from your sweet words I have gathered the richest perfumes and spices]. I have eaten my honeycomb with my honey; I have drunk my wine with my milk. Eat, O friends [feast on, O revelers of the

g Am I willing to have the north wind of adversity blow upon me, if it will better fit me for Christ's presence and companionship?

palace; you can never make my lover disloyal to me]! Drink, yes, drink abundantly of love, O precious one [for now I know you are mine, irrevocably mine! With his confident words still thrilling her heart, through the lattice she saw her shepherd turn away and disappear into the night]. [John 16:33.]

2 I went to sleep, but my heart stayed awake. [I dreamed that I heard] the voice of my beloved as he knocked [at the door of my mother's cottage]. Open to me, my sister, my love, my dove, my spotless one [he said], for I am wet with the [heavy] night dew; my hair is covered with it. [Job 11:13-15.]

3 [But weary from a day in the vineyards, I had already sought my rest] I had put off my garment—ʰhow could I [again] put it on? I had washed my feet—how could I [again] soil them? [Isa. 32:9; Heb. 3:15.]

4 My beloved put in his hand by the hole of the door, and my heart was moved for him.

5 I rose up to open for my beloved, and my hands dripped with myrrh, and my fingers with liquid [sweet-scented] myrrh, [which he had left] upon the handles of the bolt.

6 I opened for my beloved, but my beloved had turned away *and* withdrawn himself, and was gone! My soul went forth [to him] when he spoke, but it failed me [and now he was gone]! I sought him, but I could not find him; I called him, but he gave me no answer.

7 The watchmen who go about the city found me. They struck me, they wounded me; the keepers of the walls took my veil *and* my mantle from me.

8 I charge you, O daughters of Jerusalem, if you find my beloved, that you tell him that I am sick from love [simply sick to be with him]. [Ps. 63:1.]

9 What is your beloved more than another beloved, O you fairest among women [taunted the ladies]? What is your beloved more than another beloved, that you should give us such a charge? [John 10:26.]

10 [She said] My beloved is fair and ruddy, the chief among ten thousand! [Ps. 45:2; John 1:14.]

11 His head is [as precious as] the finest gold; his locks are curly *and* bushy and black as a raven.

12 His eyes are like doves beside the water brooks, bathed in milk *and* fitly set.

13 His cheeks are like a bed of spices *or* balsam, like banks of sweet herbs yielding fragrance. His lips are like bloodred anemones or lilies distilling liquid [sweet-scented] myrrh.

14 His hands are like rods of gold set with [nails of] beryl *or* topaz. His body is a figure of bright ivory overlaid with [veins of] sapphires.

15 His legs are like strong and steady pillars of marble set upon bases of fine gold. His appearance is like Lebanon, excellent, stately, *and* majestic as the cedars.

16 His voice *and* speech are exceedingly sweet; yes, he is altogether lovely [the whole of him delights and is precious]. ⁱThis is my beloved, and this is my friend, O daughters of Jerusalem! [Ps. 92:15; Col. 1:15.]

6 WHERE HAS your beloved gone, O you fairest among women? [Again the ladies showed their interest in the remarkable person whom the Shulammite had championed with such unstinted praise; they too wanted to know him,

---

h In my weariness from earthly cares, do I hesitate to answer when the Divine Shepherd knocks at my door, and so turn Him from me?   i Is my Savior unquestionably the One altogether lovely, the One above all others most precious to me? Can I tell how and why Christ is more to me than any human being or than all earthly possessions?

they insisted.] Where is your beloved hiding himself? For we would seek him with you.

2 [She replied] My beloved has gone down to his garden, to the beds of spices, to feed in the gardens and to gather lilies.

3 I am my beloved's [garden] and my beloved is mine! He feeds among the lilies [which grow there].

4 [He said] You are as beautiful as Tirzah [capital of the northern kingdom's first king], my love, and as comely as Jerusalem, [but you are] as terrible as a bannered host!

5 Turn away your [flashing] eyes from me, for they have overcome me! Your hair is like a flock of goats trailing down from Mount Gilead.

6 Your teeth are like a flock of ewes coming from their washing, of which all are in pairs, and not one of them is missing.

7 Your cheeks are like halves of a pomegranate behind your veil.

8 There are sixty queens and eighty concubines, and virgins without number;

9 But my dove, my undefiled *and* perfect one, stands alone [above them all]; she is the only one of her mother, she is the choice one of her who bore her. The daughters saw her and called her blessed *and* happy, yes, the queens and the concubines, and they praised her. [Col. 2:8, 9.]

10 [The ladies asked] Who is this that looks forth like the dawn, fair as the moon, clear *and* pure as the sun, *and* terrible as a bannered host?

11 [The Shulammite replied] I went down into the nut orchard [one day] to look at the green plants of the valley, to see whether the grapevine had budded and the pomegranates were in flower.

12 Before I was aware [of what was happening], my desire [to roam about] had brought me into the area of the princes of my people [the king's retinue].

13 [I began to flee, but they called to me] Return, return, O Shulammite; return, return, that we may look upon you! [I replied] What is there for you to see in the [poor little] Shulammite? [And they answered] As upon a dance before two armies *or* a dance of Mahanaim.

7 [THEN HER companions began noticing and commenting on the attractiveness of her person] How beautiful are your feet in sandals, O queenly maiden! Your rounded limbs are like jeweled chains, the work of a master hand.

2 Your body is like a round goblet in which no mixed wine is wanting. Your abdomen is like a heap of wheat set about with lilies.

3 Your two breasts are like two fawns, the twins of a gazelle.

4 Your neck is like a tower of ivory, your eyes like the pools of Heshbon by the gate of Bath-rabbim. Your nose is like the tower of Lebanon which looks toward Damascus.

5 Your head crowns you like Mount Carmel, and the hair of your head like purple. [Then seeing the king watching the girl in absorbed admiration, the speaker added] The king is held captive by its tresses.

6 [The king came forward, saying] How fair and how pleasant you are, O love, with your delights!

7 Your stature is like that of a palm

tree, and your bosom like its clusters [of dates, declared the king].

8 I resolve that I will climb the palm tree; I will grasp its branches. Let your breasts be like clusters of the grape-vine, and the scent of your breath like apples,

9 And your kisses like the best wine—[then the Shulammite inter-rupted] that goes down smoothly *and* sweetly for my beloved [shepherd, kisses] gliding over his lips while he sleeps!

10 [She proudly said] I am my beloved's, and his desire is toward me! [John 10:28.]

11 [She said] Come, my beloved! Let us go forth into the field, let us lodge in the villages. [Luke 14:33.]

12 Let us go out early to the vine-yards and see whether the vines have budded, whether the grape blossoms have opened, and whether the pome-granates are in bloom. There I will give you my love.

13 The mandrakes give forth fra-grance, and over our doors are all manner of choice fruits, new and old, which I have laid up for you, O my beloved!

8 [LOOKING FORWARD to the shepherd's arrival, the eager girl pictures their meeting and says] Oh, that you were like my brother, who nursed from the breasts of my mother! If I should find you without, I would kiss you, yes, and none would despise me [for it]. [Ps. 143:6.]

2 I would lead you and bring you into the house of my mother, who would instruct me. I would cause you to drink spiced wine and of the juice of my pomegranates.

3 [Then musingly she added] Oh, that his left hand were under my head and that his right hand embraced me! [Exod. 19:4; Deut. 33:27.]

4 I adjure you, O daughters of Jeru-salem, that you never [again attempt to] stir up or awaken love until it pleases.

5 Who is this who comes up from the wilderness leaning upon her beloved? [And as they sighted the home of her childhood, the bride said] Under the apple tree I awakened you; there your mother gave you birth, there she was in travail and bore you.

6 Set me like a seal upon your heart, like a seal upon your arm; for love is as strong as death, jealousy is as hard *and* cruel as Sheol (the place of the dead). Its flashes are flashes of fire, a most vehement flame [the very flame of the Lord]! [Deut. 4:24; Isa. 49:16; I Cor. 10:22.]

7 Many waters cannot quench love, neither can floods drown it. If a man would offer all the goods of his house for love, he would be utterly scorned *and* despised.

8 [Gathered with her family and the wedding guests in her mother's cot-tage, the bride said to her stepbroth-ers, When I was a little girl, you said] We have a little sister and she has no breasts. What shall we do for our sis-ter on the day when she is spoken for in marriage?

9 If she is a wall [discreet and wom-anly], we will build upon her a turret [a dowry] of silver; but if she is a door [bold and flirtatious], we will enclose her with boards of cedar.

10 [Well] I am a wall [with battle-ments], and my breasts are like the towers of it. Then was I in [the king's] eyes as one [to be respected and to be allowed] to find peace.

11 Solomon had a vineyard at Baal-hamon; he let out the vineyard to keepers; everyone was to bring him a thousand pieces of silver for its fruit.

12 You, O Solomon, can have your thousand [pieces of silver], and those who tend the fruit of it two hundred; but my vineyard, which is mine [with all its radiant joy], is before me!

13 O you who dwell in the gardens, your companions have been listening to your voice—now cause me to hear it.

14 [Joyfully the radiant bride turned to him, the one altogether lovely, the chief among ten thousand to her soul, and with unconcealed eagerness to begin her life of sweet companionship with him, she answered] Make haste, my beloved, *and* come quickly, like a gazelle or a young hart [and take me to our waiting home] upon the mountains of spices!

Isaiah

Author:
Isaiah

Date:
Approximately 700 BC–690 BC

Everyday Life Principles:
Sin cannot be tolerated; it must be dealt with. God forgives sin.

God is in the business of redemption and restoration.

God will comfort and guide you.

Isaiah is the first book in a series of books (which make up the remainder of the Old Testament) written by prophets. Prophets are spokespeople for God, and they communicate the things that are on God's heart. They are His mouthpieces, sharing what God wants people to know, informing people of what God intends to do, speaking words of warning and offering encouragement from the Lord. They often prophesy doom and gloom to people who will not obey, and words of comfort, direction, and assurance to those who do obey.

Isaiah's ministry as a prophet included warnings to kings who ignored him, but it also included several prophetic references to Jesus. One such reference is Isaiah 9:6, which declares: "For to us a Child is born, to us a Son is given; and the government shall be upon His shoulder, and His name shall be called Wonderful Counselor, Mighty God, Everlasting Father [of Eternity], Prince of Peace."

Isaiah's writing is not soft on sin, but it points to Jesus and gives people clear hope for salvation. This book is loaded with comfort, inspiration, and variety. It speaks of God's love for us, reminds us that He redeems and restores us, encourages us to trust Him, and promises that He will guide us.

Whether you need comfort, strength, hope, peace, or a reminder of God's loving, forgiving heart toward you, you will find it in Isaiah.

1 THE VISION [seen by spiritual perception] of Isaiah son of Amoz, which he saw concerning Judah [the kingdom] and Jerusalem [its capital] in the days of Uzziah, Jotham, Ahaz, and Hezekiah, kings of Judah.

2 Hear, O heavens, and give ear, O earth! For the Lord has spoken: I have nourished and brought up sons *and* have made them great and exalted, but they have rebelled against Me *and* broken away from Me.

3 The ox [instinctively] knows his owner, and the donkey his master's crib, but Israel does not know *or* recognize Me [as Lord], My people do not consider *or* understand.

4 Ah, sinful nation, a people loaded with iniquity, offspring of evildoers, sons who deal corruptly! They have forsaken the Lord, they have despised *and* shown contempt *and* provoked the Holy One of Israel to anger, they have become utterly estranged (alienated).

5 Why should you be stricken *and* punished any more [since it brings no correction]? You will revolt more and more. The whole head is sick, and the whole heart is faint (feeble, sick, and nauseated).

6 From the sole of the foot even to the head there is no soundness *or* health in [the nation's body]—but wounds and bruises and fresh *and* bleeding stripes; they have not been pressed out *and* closed up or bound up or softened with oil. [No one has troubled to seek a remedy.]

7 [Because of your detestable disobedience] your country lies desolate, your cities are burned with fire; your land—strangers devour it in your very presence, and it is desolate, as overthrown by aliens.

8 And the Daughter of Zion [Jerusalem] is left like a [deserted] booth in a vineyard, like a lodge in a garden of cucumbers, like a besieged city [spared, but in the midst of desolation].

9 Except the Lord of hosts had left us a very small remnant [of survivors], we should have been like Sodom, and we should have been like Gomorrah. [Gen. 19:24, 25; Rom. 9:29.]

10 Hear [O Jerusalem] the word of the Lord, you rulers *or* judges of [another] Sodom! Give ear to the law *and* the teaching of our God, you people of [another] Gomorrah!

11 To what purpose is the multitude of your sacrifices to Me [unless they are the offering of the heart]? says the Lord. I have had enough of the burnt offerings of rams and the fat of fed beasts [without obedience]; and I do not delight in the blood of bulls or of lambs or of he-goats [without righteousness].

12 When you come to appear before Me, who requires of you that your [unholy feet] trample My courts?

13 Bring no more offerings of vanity (emptiness, falsity, vainglory, and futility); [your hollow offering of] incense is an abomination to Me; the New Moons and Sabbaths, the calling of assemblies, I cannot endure—[it is] iniquity *and* profanation, even the solemn meeting.

14 Your New Moon festivals and your [hypocritical] appointed feasts My soul hates. They are an oppressive burden to Me; I am weary of bearing them.

15 And when you spread forth your hands [in prayer, imploring help], I will hide My eyes from you; even though you make many prayers, I will not hear. Your hands are full of blood!

16 Wash yourselves, make yourselves clean; put away the evil of your doings from before My eyes! Cease to do evil,

17 Learn to do right! Seek justice, relieve the oppressed, *and* correct the oppressor. Defend the fatherless, plead for the widow.

18 Come now, and let us reason together, says the Lord. Though your sins are like scarlet, they shall be as white as snow; though they are red

like crimson, they shall be like wool.
19 If you are willing and obedient,
you shall eat the good of the land;
20 But if you refuse and rebel, you
will be devoured by the sword. For the
mouth of the Lord has spoken it.
21 How the faithful city has become
an [idolatrous] harlot, she who was
full of justice! Uprightness *and* right
standing with God [once] lodged in
her—but now murderers.
22 Your silver has become dross,
your wine is mixed with water.
23 Your princes are rebels and companions of thieves; everyone loves
bribes and runs after compensation
and rewards. They judge not for the
fatherless *nor* defend them, neither
does the cause of the widow come to
them [for they delay or turn a deaf ear].
24 Therefore says the Lord, the Lord
of hosts, the Mighty One of Israel, Ah, I
will appease Myself on My adversaries
and avenge Myself on My enemies.
25 And I will bring My hand again
upon you and thoroughly purge away
your dross [as with lye] and take away
all your tin *or* alloy.
26 And I will restore your judges as
at the first, and your counselors as at
the beginning; afterward you shall be
called the City of Righteousness, the
Faithful City.
27 Zion shall be redeemed with justice, and her [returned] converts with
righteousness (uprightness and right
standing with God).
28 But the crushing *and* destruction
of rebels and sinners shall be together, and they who forsake the Lord
shall be consumed.
29 For you will be ashamed [of the
folly and degradation] of the oak *or*
terebinth trees in which you found
[idolatrous] pleasure, and you will

blush with shame for the [idolatrous
worship which you practice in the
passion-inflaming] gardens which
you have chosen.
30 For you shall be like an oak *or*
terebinth whose leaf withers, and like
a garden that has no water.
31 And the strong shall become like
tow *and* become tinder, and his work
like a spark, and they shall both burn
together, with none to quench them.

2 THE WORD which Isaiah son of
Amoz saw [revealed] concerning
Judah and Jerusalem.
2 It shall come to pass in the latter
days that the mountain of the Lord's
house shall be [firmly] established as
the highest of the mountains and shall
be exalted above the hills, and all
nations shall flow to it.
3 And many people shall come and
say, Come, let us go up to the mountain of the Lord, to the house of the
God of Jacob, that He may teach us
His ways and that we may walk in His
paths. For out of Zion shall go forth
the law *and* instruction, and the word
of the Lord from Jerusalem.
4 And He shall judge between the
nations and shall decide [disputes] for
many peoples; and they shall beat
their swords into plowshares and their
spears into pruning hooks. Nation
shall not lift up sword against nation,
neither shall they learn war any more.
[Mic. 4:1-3.]
5 O house of Jacob, come, let us
walk in the light of the Lord.
6 Surely [Lord] You have rejected
and forsaken your people, the house
of Jacob, because they are filled [with
customs] from the east and with
soothsayers [who foretell] like the
Philistines; also they strike hands *and*

speak the Word

make pledges *and* agreements with the children of aliens. [Deut. 18:9-12.]

7 Their land also is full of silver and gold; neither is there any end to their treasures. Their land is also full of horses; neither is there any end to their chariots. [Deut. 17:14-17.]

8 Their land also is full of idols; they worship the work of their own hands, what their own fingers have made.

9 And the common man is bowed down [before idols], also the great man is brought low *and* humbles himself—therefore forgive them not [O Lord].

10 Enter into the rock and hide yourself in the dust from before the terror of the Lord and from the glory of His majesty.

11 The proud looks of man shall be brought low, and the haughtiness of men shall be humbled; and the Lord alone shall be exalted in that day.

12 For there shall be a day of the Lord of hosts against all who are proud and haughty and against all who are lifted up—and they shall be brought low—[Zeph. 2:3; Mal. 4:1.]

13 [The wrath of God will begin by coming down] against all the cedars of Lebanon [west of the Jordan] that are high and lifted up, and against all the oaks of Bashan [east of the Jordan],

14 And [after that] against all the high mountains and all the hills that are lifted up,

15 And against every high tower and every fenced wall,

16 And against all the ships of Tarshish and all the picturesque *and* desirable imagery [designed for mere ornament and luxury].

17 Then the loftiness of man shall be bowed down, and the haughtiness of men shall be brought low; and the Lord alone shall be exalted in that day.

18 And the idols shall utterly pass away (be abolished).

19 Then shall [the stricken, deprived of all in which they had trusted] go into the caves of the rocks and into

the holes of the earth from before the terror *and* dread of the Lord and from before the glory of His majesty, when He arises to shake mightily *and* terribly the earth. [Luke 23:30.]

20 In that day men shall cast away to the moles and to the bats their idols of silver and their idols of gold, which they made for themselves to worship,

21 To go into the caverns of the rocks and into the clefts of the ragged rocks from before the terror *and* dread of the Lord and from before the glory of His majesty, when He rises to shake mightily *and* terribly the earth.

22 Cease to trust in [weak, frail, and dying] man, whose breath is in his nostrils [for so short a time]; in what sense can he be counted as having intrinsic worth?

3 FOR BEHOLD, the Lord, the Lord of hosts, is taking away from Jerusalem and from Judah the stay and the staff [every kind of prop], the whole stay of bread and the whole stay of water,

2 The mighty man and the man of war, the judge *and* the [professional] prophet, the one who foretells by divination and the old man,

3 The captain of fifty and the man of rank, the counselor and the expert craftsman and the skillful enchanter.

4 And I will make boys their princes, and with childishness shall they rule over them [with outrage instead of justice].

5 And the people shall be oppressed, each one by another, and each one by his neighbor; the child shall behave himself proudly *and* with insolence against the old man, and the lowborn against the honorable [person of rank].

6 When a man shall take hold of his brother in the house of his father, saying, You have a robe, you shall be our judge *and* ruler, and this heap of ruins shall be under your control—

when God removes your props

In Isaiah 2:22 God asks, "Why are you putting your trust in frail people who are only alive for so short a time?" Then in the next verse, God says that He is removing from His people their props—the external things on which they depend. The reason? He wants His people to trust Him.

What happens to us when our props are pulled out from under us? We discover what we are *really* leaning on, what we are really rooted and grounded in. Let me give you an example.

My husband and I play golf frequently. On the golf course are little twigs that will someday grow into trees. Those little plants have no strength or roots, and they are so tiny and weak that usually, there are sticks set on either side of them as props to hold them up. Without those sticks to hold them up, they would be destroyed when the wind and rain come.

That is the way we are as new believers. When we begin our walk with God we need a prop system, something to help us stand up straight and strong. We need a group of people around us to keep us studying the Bible, praying, and seeking the Lord. If we do not have that support system, when the storms of life come against us, they will blow us over.

Our support system may take many forms, but whatever it is, sooner or later God is going to start taking it away by removing the props from under us. At first, this is pretty scary because we do not understand it, and we do not like it. Our props may be things from which we derive pleasure and satisfaction—things like singing, playing an instrument, being part of the worship team, or being a recognized leader or pastor in the ministry. Then suddenly, for whatever reason, we lose that position or God requires us to give it up. It is then that we discover how much of our sense of value and worth depends on the things we are doing.

In order for us to grow, God sometimes has to strip away everything we put our security in—everything else but Him. This is because He is a God of restoration. He restores our minds, our emotions, our souls, and our health. When we start to restore a beautiful, expensive piece of antique furniture, we have to first strip away the old paint or varnish before we apply a new finish. We have to sand it so the new application will stick. If you are going through that stripping process, do not be upset. Cooperate with God while He does the work.

Do not be like a twig thrashing about in the wind because its props have been taken away. Instead, put down some roots so that one day you can stand tall and steady and be a tree of righteousness. And remember that whatever God takes away from you or requires you to give up, He will give you more than you previously had, and everything will be better than before.

7 In that day he will answer, saying, I will not be a healer *and* one who binds up; [a]*I am not a physician*. For in my house is neither bread nor clothing; you shall not make me judge *and* ruler of the people.

8 For Jerusalem is ruined and Judah is fallen, because their speech and their deeds are against the Lord, to provoke the eyes of His glory *and* defy His glorious presence.

9 Their respecting of persons *and* showing of partiality witnesses against them; they proclaim their sin like Sodom; they do not hide it. Woe to them! For they have brought evil [as a reward upon themselves].

10 Say to the righteous that it shall be well with them, for they shall eat the fruit of their deeds.

11 Woe to the wicked! It shall be ill with them, for what their hands have done shall be done to them.

12 As for My people, children are their oppressors, and women rule over them. O My people, your leaders cause you to err, and they confuse (destroy and swallow up) the course of your paths.

13 The Lord stands up to contend, and stands to judge the peoples *and* His people.

14 The Lord enters into judgment with the elders of His people and their princes: For [by your exactions and oppressions you have robbed the people and ruined the country] you have devoured the vineyard; the spoil of the poor is in your houses.

15 What do you mean by crushing My people and grinding the faces of the poor? says the Lord God of hosts.

16 Moreover, the Lord said, Because the daughters of Zion are haughty and walk with outstretched necks and with undisciplined (flirtatious and alluring) eyes, tripping along with mincing *and* affected gait, and making a tinkling noise with [the anklets on] their feet,

17 Therefore the Lord will smite with a scab the crown of the heads of the daughters of Zion [making them bald], and the Lord will cause them to be [taken as captives and to suffer the indignity of being] stripped naked.

18 In that day the Lord will take away the finery of their tinkling anklets, the caps of network, the crescent head ornaments,

19 The pendants, the bracelets *or* chains, and the spangled face veils *and* scarfs,

20 The headbands, the short ankle chains [attached from one foot to the other to insure a measured gait], the sashes, the perfume boxes, the amulets *or* charms [suspended from the ears or neck],

21 The signet rings and nose rings,

22 The festal robes, the cloaks, the stoles *and* shawls, and the handbags,

23 The hand mirrors, the fine linen [undergarments], the turbans, and the [whole body-enveloping] veils.

24 And it shall come to pass that instead of the sweet odor of spices there shall be the stench of rottenness; and instead of a girdle, a rope; and instead of well-set hair, baldness; and instead of a rich robe, a girding of sackcloth; and searing [of captives by the scorching heat] instead of beauty.

25 Your men shall fall by the sword, and your mighty men in battle.

26 And [Jerusalem's] gates shall lament and mourn [as those who wail for the dead]; and she, being ruined *and* desolate, shall sit upon the ground.

4 AND IN that day [b]seven women shall take hold of one man, saying, We will eat our own bread and provide our own apparel; only let us be called by your name to take away our reproach [of being unmarried].

2 In that day the Branch of the Lord shall be beautiful and glorious, and the fruit of the land shall be excellent and lovely to those of Israel who have escaped. [Jer. 23:5; 33:15; Zech. 3:8; 6:12.]

3 And he who is left in Zion and remains in Jerusalem will be called holy, everyone who is recorded for life in Jerusalem *and for* ᶜ*eternal life,* [Joel 3:17; Phil. 4:3.]

4 After the Lord has washed away the [moral] filth of the daughters of Zion [pride, vanity, haughtiness] and has purged the bloodstains of Jerusalem from the midst of it by the spirit *and* blast of judgment and by the spirit *and* blast of burning *and* sifting.

5 And the Lord will create over the whole site, over every dwelling place of Mount Zion and over her assemblies, a cloud and smoke by day and the shining of a flaming fire by night; for over all the glory shall be a canopy (a defense of divine love and protection).

6 And there shall be a pavilion for shade in the daytime from the heat, and for a place of refuge and a shelter from storm and from rain.

5 LET ME [as God's representative] sing of *and* for my greatly Beloved [God, the Son] a tender song of my Beloved concerning His vineyard [His chosen people]. My greatly Beloved had a vineyard on a very fruitful hill. [S. of Sol. 6:3; Matt. 21:33-40.]

2 And He dug *and* trenched the ground and gathered out the stones from it and planted it with the choicest vine and built a tower in the midst of it and hewed out a winepress in it. And He looked for it to bring forth grapes, and it brought forth wild grapes.

3 And now, O inhabitants of Jerusalem and men of Judah, judge, I pray you, between Me and My vineyard [My people, says the Lord].

4 What more could have been done for My vineyard that I have not done in it? When I looked for it to bring forth grapes, why did it yield wild grapes?

5 And now I will tell you what I will do to My vineyard: I will take away its hedge, and it shall be eaten *and* burned up; and I will break down its wall, and it shall be trodden down [by enemies].

6 And I will lay it waste; it shall not be pruned or cultivated, but there shall come up briers and thorns. I will also command the clouds that they rain no rain upon it.

7 For the vineyard of the Lord of hosts is the house of Israel, and the men of Judah His pleasant planting [the plant of His delight]. And He looked for justice, but behold, [He saw] oppression *and* bloodshed; [He looked] for righteousness (for uprightness and right standing with God), but behold, [He heard] a cry [of oppression and distress]!

8 Woe to those who join house to house [and by violently expelling the poorer occupants enclose large acreage] and join field to field until there is no place for others and you are made to dwell alone in the midst of the land!

9 In my [Isaiah's] ears the Lord of hosts said, Of a truth many houses

in World War I became casualties (according to *The World Almanac*), and the casualties in World War II have been estimated at 33 million. Not counting deaths in the armed forces, the ratio of deaths between males and females was (as of 1960) nine to seven. This had not been true in previous centuries. Isaiah here foresees a time when the ratio between marriageable men and women will be one to seven in Jerusalem. **c** *The Chaldee Translation* reads "eternal life."

shall be desolate, even great and beautiful ones shall be without inhabitant.

10 For ten acres of vineyard shall yield only about eight gallons, and ten bushels of seed will produce but one bushel.

11 Woe unto those who rise early in the morning, that they may pursue strong drink, who tarry late into the night till wine inflames them!

12 They have lyre and harp, tambourine and flute and wine at their feasts, but they do not regard the deeds of the Lord, neither do they consider the operation of His hands [in mercy and in judgment].

13 Therefore My people go into captivity [to their enemies] without knowing it and because they have no knowledge [of God]. And their honorable men [their glory] are famished, and their common people are parched with thirst.

14 Therefore Sheol (the unseen state, the realm of the dead) has enlarged its appetite and opened its mouth without measure; and [Jerusalem's] nobility and her multitude and her pomp and tumult and [the drunken reveler] who exults in her descend into it.

15 And the common man is bowed down, and the great man is brought low, and the eyes of the haughty are humbled.

16 But the Lord of hosts is exalted in justice, and God, the Holy One, shows Himself holy in righteousness and through righteous judgments.

17 Then shall the lambs feed [among the ruins] as in their own pasture, and [among] the desolate places of the [exiled] rich shall sojourners and aliens eat.

18 Woe to those who draw [calamity] with cords of iniquity and falsehood, who bring punishment to themselves with a cart rope of wickedness,

19 Who say, Let [the Holy One] make haste and speed His [prophesied] vengeance, that we may see it; and let the purpose of the Holy One of Israel draw near and come, that we may know it!

20 Woe to those who call evil good and good evil, who put darkness for light and light for darkness, who put bitter for sweet and sweet for bitter!

21 Woe to those who are wise in their own eyes and prudent and shrewd in their own sight!

22 Woe to those who are mighty heroes at drinking wine and men of strength in mixing alcoholic drinks!—

23 Who justify and acquit the guilty for a bribe, but take away the rights of the innocent and righteous from them!

24 Therefore, as the tongue of fire devours the stubble, and as the dry grass sinks down in the flame, so their root shall be like rottenness and their blossom shall go up like fine dust—because they have rejected and cast away the law and the teaching of the Lord of hosts and have not believed but have treated scornfully and have despised the word of the Holy One of Israel.

25 Therefore is the anger of the Lord kindled against His people, and He has stretched forth His hand against them and has smitten them. And the mountains trembled, and their dead bodies were like dung and sweepings in the midst of the streets. For all this, His anger is not turned away, but His hand is still stretched out [in judgment].

26 And He will lift up a signal to call together a hostile people from afar [to execute His judgment on Judea], and will hiss for them from the end of the earth [as bees are hissed from their hives], and behold, they shall come with speed, swiftly!

27 None is weary or stumbles among them, none slumbers or sleeps; nor is the girdle of their loins loosed or the latchet (thong) of their shoes broken;

28 Their arrows are sharp, and all their bows bent; their horses' hoofs seem like flint, and their wheels like a whirlwind.

29 Their roaring is like that of a lioness, they roar like young lions; they growl and seize their prey and carry it safely away, and there is none to deliver it.

30 And in that day they [the army from afar] shall roar against [the Jews] like the roaring of the sea. And if one looks to the land, behold, there is darkness and distress; and the light [itself] will be darkened by the clouds of it.

6 IN THE year that King Uzziah died, [in a vision] I saw the Lord sitting upon a throne, high and lifted up, and the skirts of His train filled the [most holy part of the] temple. [John 12:41.]

2 Above Him stood the seraphim; each had six wings: with two [each] covered his [own] face, and with two [each] covered his feet, and with two [each] flew.

3 And one cried to another and said, Holy, holy, holy is the Lord of hosts; the whole earth is full of His glory!

4 And the foundations of the thresholds shook at the voice of him who cried, and the house was filled with smoke.

5 Then said I, Woe is me! For I am undone *and* ruined, because I am a man of unclean lips, and I dwell in the midst of a people of unclean lips; for my eyes have seen the King, the Lord of hosts!

6 Then flew one of the seraphim [heavenly beings] to me, having a live coal in his hand which he had taken with tongs from off the altar;

7 And with it he touched my mouth and said, Behold, this has touched your lips; your iniquity *and* guilt are taken away, and your sin is completely atoned for *and* forgiven.

8 Also I heard the voice of the Lord, saying, Whom shall I send? And who will go for Us? Then said I, Here am I; send me.

9 And He said, Go and tell this people, Hear *and* hear continually, but understand not; and see *and* see continually, but do not apprehend with your mind.

10 Make the heart of this people fat; and make their ears heavy and shut their eyes, lest they see with their eyes and hear with their ears and understand with their hearts and turn again and be healed.

11 Then said I, Lord, how long? And He answered, Until cities lie waste without inhabitant and houses without man, and the land is utterly desolate,

12 And the Lord removes [His] people far away, and the forsaken places are many in the midst of the land.

13 And though a tenth [of the people] remain in the land, it will be for their destruction [eaten up and burned] like a terebinth tree or like an oak whose stump *and* substance remain when they are felled *or* have cast their leaves. The holy seed [the elect remnant] is the stump *and* substance [of Israel].

speak the Word

God, I declare that You are holy. The whole earth is full of Your glory.
ADAPTED FROM ISAIAH 6:3

Lord, here I am. Send me wherever You want to send me.
ADAPTED FROM ISAIAH 6:8

cleansed, then used

Before God can use us, He needs to cleanse us. In Isaiah 6:1–9, Isaiah realized he had a sinful, unclean mouth that needed to be dealt with. I believe that because Isaiah's heart cried for change, God sent help.

The coming forward of the seraphim with a coal of fire is recorded in verse 6 as an instantaneous happening, but answers may not always come so quickly to us. We all would prefer miraculous deliverance, but most of the time the Lord puts us through a cleansing process.

Notice that God forgave Isaiah's sin and then issued a call: "Who will go for Us?" (Isaiah 6:8). Isaiah responded, "Here am I; send me" (verse 9). Isaiah's heart wanted to serve the Lord, and God knew that. God will always look for someone who has a perfect *heart* toward Him, not necessarily someone who has a perfect *performance* before Him. When the Lord has the heart, He can always change the behavior.

This truth should encourage those of us who want to be used by God, but who often feel that we just have too many flaws. God uses "cracked pots," as the saying goes. We come to Him as we are, and He molds and makes us into vessels fit for His use (see II Timothy 2:21).

After Isaiah's mouth had been cleansed, God called him, saying, "Go and tell this people . . ." (Isaiah 6:9). The call, the anointing, and the appointment can occur in different time periods, but no matter how they take place or in what order, the process of preparation is as important to us today as it was to Isaiah long ago. One thing is sure: when God calls us into His presence, He is going to deal with us, and we must let Him do that. He is doing a good work!

7 IN THE days of Ahaz son of Jotham, the son of Uzziah, king of Judah, Rezin the king of Syria and Pekah son of Remaliah king of Israel went up to Jerusalem to wage war against it, but they could not conquer it.

2 And the house of David [Judah] was told, Syria is allied with Ephraim [Israel]. And the heart [of Ahaz] and the hearts of his people trembled *and* shook, as the trees of the forest tremble *and* shake with the wind.

3 Then said the Lord to Isaiah, Go forth now to meet *Judah's King* Ahaz, you and your son Shear-jashub [a remnant shall return], at the end of the aqueduct *or* canal of the Upper Pool on the highway to the Fuller's Field;

4 And say to him, Take heed and be quiet; fear not, neither be fainthearted because of these two stumps of smoking firebrands—at the fierce anger of [the Syrian King] Rezin and Syria and of the son of Remaliah [Pekah, usurper of the throne of Israel].

5 Because Syria, Ephraim [Israel], and the son of Remaliah have purposed evil against you [Judah], saying,

6 Let us go up against Judah and

harass *and* terrify it; and let us cleave it asunder [each of us taking a portion], and set a [vassal] king in the midst of it, namely the son of Tabeel,

7 Thus says the Lord God: It shall not stand, neither shall it come to pass.

8 For the head [the capital] of Syria is Damascus, and the head of Damascus is [King] Rezin. Within sixty-five years Ephraim will be broken to pieces so that it will no longer be a people.

9 And the head (the capital) of Ephraim is Samaria, and the head of Samaria is Remaliah's son [Pekah]. If you will not believe *and* trust *and* rely [on God and on the words of God's prophet instead of Assyria], surely you will not be established *nor* will you remain.

10 Moreover, the Lord spoke again to King Ahaz, saying,

11 Ask for yourself a sign (a token or proof) of the Lord your God [one that will convince you that God has spoken and will keep His word]; ask it either in the depth below or in the height above [let it be as deep as Sheol or as high as heaven].

12 But Ahaz said, I will not ask, neither will I tempt the Lord.

13 And [Isaiah] said, Hear then, O house of David! Is it a small thing for you to weary *and* try the patience of men, but will you weary *and* try the patience of my God also?

14 Therefore the Lord Himself shall give you a sign: Behold, the young woman who is unmarried *and* a virgin shall conceive and bear a son, and shall call his name Immanuel [God with us]. [Isa. 9:6; Jer. 31:22; Mic. 5:3-5; Matt. 1:22, 23.]

15 Butter *and* curds and wild honey shall he eat when he knows [enough] to refuse the evil and choose the good.

16 For before the child shall know [enough] to refuse the evil and choose the good, the land [Canaan] whose two kings you abhor *and* of whom you are in sickening dread shall be forsaken [both Ephraim and Syria]. [Isa. 7:2.]

17 The Lord shall bring upon you and upon your people and upon your father's house such days as have not come since the day that Ephraim [the ten northern tribes] departed from Judah—even the king of ᵈAssyria.

18 And in that day the Lord shall whistle for the fly [the numerous and troublesome foe] that is in the whole extent of the canal country of Egypt and for the bee that is in the land of Assyria.

19 And these [enemies like flies and bees] shall come and shall rest all of them in the desolate *and* rugged valleys *and* deep ravines and in the clefts of the rocks, and on all the thornbushes and on all the pastures.

20 In the same day [will the people of Judah be utterly stripped of belongings], the Lord will shave with the razor that is hired from the parts beyond the River [Euphrates]—even with the king of Assyria—[that razor will shave] the head and the hair of the legs, and it shall also consume the beard [leaving Judah with open shame and scorn]. [II Kings 16:7, 8; 18:13-16.]

21 And [because of the desolation brought on by the invaders] in that day, a man will [be so poor that he will] keep alive only a young milk cow and two sheep.

22 And because of the abundance of milk that they will give, he will eat butter *and* curds, for [only] butter *and* curds and [wild] honey [no vegetables] shall everyone eat who is left in

d "Jesus was actually born in a time when the Holy Land found itself under the supremacy of [Assyria, when looked upon as] the universal empire, a condition which went back to the unbelief of Ahaz as its ultimate cause" (F. Delitzsch, cited by *The New Bible Commentary*).

the land [these products provided from the extensive pastures and the plentiful wild flowers upon which the bees depend].

23 And in that day, in every place where there used to be a thousand vines worth a thousand silver shekels, there will be briers and thorns.

24 With arrows and with bows shall a man come [to hunt] there, because all the land will be briers and thorns.

25 And as for all the hills that were formerly cultivated with mattock and hoe, you will not go there for fear of briers and thorns; but they will become a place where oxen are let loose to pasture and where sheep tread.

8 THEN THE Lord said to me, Take a large tablet [of wood, metal, or stone] and write upon it with a graving tool and in ordinary characters [which the humblest man can read]: Belonging to Maher-shalal-hash-baz [they (the Assyrians) hasten to the spoil (of Syria and Israel), they speed to the prey].

2 And I took faithful witnesses to record and attest [this prophecy] for me, Uriah the priest and Zechariah son of Jeberechiah.

3 And I approached [my wife] the prophetess, and when she had conceived and borne a son, the Lord said to me, Call his name Maher-shalal-hash-baz [as a continual reminder to the people of the prophecy],

4 For before the child knows how to say, My father or my mother, the riches of Damascus [Syria's capital] and

the spoil of Samaria [Israel's capital] eshall be carried away before the king of Assyria.

5 The Lord spoke to me yet again and said,

6 Because this people [Israel and Judah] have refused and despised the waters of Shiloah [Siloam, the only perennial fountain of Jerusalem, and symbolic of God's protection and sustaining power] that go gently, and rejoice in and with Rezin [the king of Syria] and Remaliah's son [Pekah the king of Israel],

7 Now therefore, behold, the Lord brings upon them the waters of the River [Euphrates], strong and many—even the king of Assyria and all the glory [of his gorgeous retinue]; and it will rise over all its channels, brooks, valleys, and canals and extend far beyond its banks; [Isa. 7:17.]

8 And it will fsweep on into Judah; it will overflow and go over [the hills], reaching even [but only] to the neck [of which Jerusalem is the head], and the outstretched wings [of the armies of Assyria] shall fill the breadth of Your land, O Immanuel g[Messiah, God is with us]! [Num. 14:9; Ps. 46:7.]

9 Make an uproar and be broken in pieces, O you peoples [rage, raise the war cry, do your worst, and be utterly dismayed]! Give ear, all you [our enemies] of far countries. Gird yourselves [for war], and be thrown into consternation! Gird yourselves, and be [utterly] dismayed!

10 Take counsel together [against Judah], but it shall come to nought;

speak the Word

e Samaria was overthrown by Assyria in 722 BC, ten years after the downfall of Damascus, fulfilling this prophecy.   f This prophecy was literally fulfilled, and although Syria and Israel were conquered and led into captivity, the kingdom of Judah was spared and continued for over 130 years.
g In its fullest sense 'Immanuel' [God with us] can apply only to the Messiah; the fact that Judah is His was and still is a pledge that, no matter how sorely overwhelmed, it shall be saved at last.

speak the word, but it will not stand, for God is with us [Immanuel]!

11 For the Lord spoke thus to me with His strong hand [upon me], and warned *and* instructed me not to walk in the way of this people, saying,

12 Do not call conspiracy [or hard, or holy] all that this people will call conspiracy [or hard, or holy]; neither be in fear of what they fear, nor [make others afraid and] in dread.

13 The Lord of hosts—regard Him as holy *and* honor His holy name [by regarding Him as your only hope of safety], and let Him be your fear and let Him be your dread [lest you offend Him by your fear of man and distrust of Him].

14 And He shall be a sanctuary [a sacred and indestructible asylum to those who reverently fear and trust in Him]; but He shall be a Stone of stumbling and a Rock of offense to both the houses of Israel, a trap and a snare to the inhabitants of Jerusalem. [Isa. 28:6; Rom. 9:33; I Pet. 2:6-8.]

15 And many among them shall stumble thereon; and they shall fall and be broken, and be snared and taken.

16 Bind up the testimony, seal the law *and* the teaching among my [Isaiah's] disciples.

17 And I will wait for the Lord, Who is hiding His face from the house of Jacob; and I will look for *and* hope in Him.

18 Behold, I and the children whom the Lord has given me are [h]signs and wonders [that are to take place] in Israel from the Lord of hosts, Who dwells on Mount Zion.

19 And when the people [instead of putting their trust in God] shall say to you, Consult for direction mediums and wizards who chirp and mutter, should not a people seek *and* consult their God? Should they consult the dead on behalf of the living?

20 [Direct such people] to the teaching and to the testimony! If their teachings are not in accord with this word, it is surely because there is no dawn *and* no morning for them.

21 And they [who consult mediums and wizards] shall pass through [the land] sorely distressed and hungry; and when they are hungry, they will fret, and will curse by their king and their God; and whether they look upward

22 Or look to the earth, they will behold only distress and darkness, the gloom of anguish, and into thick darkness *and* widespread, obscure night they shall be driven away.

9 BUT [in the midst of judgment there is the promise and the certainty of the Lord's deliverance and] there shall be no gloom for her who was in anguish. In the former time [the Lord] brought into contempt the land of Zebulun and the land of Naphtali, but in the latter time He will make it glorious, by the way of the Sea [of Galilee, the land] beyond the Jordan, Galilee of the nations.

2 The people who walked in darkness have seen a great Light; those who dwelt in the land of intense darkness *and* the shadow of death, upon them has the Light shined. [Isa. 42:6; Matt. 4:15, 16.]

3 You [O Lord] have multiplied the nation and increased their joy; they rejoice before You like the joy in harvest, as men rejoice when they divide the spoil [of battle].

4 For the yoke of [Israel's] burden, and the staff *or* rod for [goading] their shoulders, the rod of their oppressor, You have broken as in the day of

---

h Isaiah's own name means "Salvation of the Lord." His two children's names were "signs" pointing to the coming crisis and the need for God's help: *Shear-jashub* means "A remnant shall return" (Isa. 7:3), and *Maher-shalal-hash-baz* means "They hasten to the spoil; they speed to the prey," referring to the Assyrians (Isa. 8:1).

[Gideon with] Midian. [Judg. 7:8-22.] **5** For every [tramping] warrior's war boots *and* all his armor in the battle tumult and every garment rolled in blood shall be burned as fuel for the fire. **6** For to us a Child is born, to us a Son is given; and the government shall be upon His shoulder, and His name shall be called Wonderful Counselor, Mighty God, Everlasting Father [of Eternity], Prince of Peace. [Isa. 25:1; 40:9-11; Matt. 28:18; Luke 2:11.] **7** Of the increase of His government and of peace there shall be no end, upon the throne of David and over his kingdom, to establish it and to uphold it with justice and with righteousness from the [latter] time forth, even forevermore. The zeal of the Lord of hosts will perform this. [Dan. 2:44; I Cor. 15:25-28; Heb. 1:8.] **8** The Lord has sent a word against Jacob [the ten tribes], and it has lighted upon Israel [the ten tribes, the kingdom of Ephraim]. **9** And all the people shall know it— even Ephraim and the inhabitants of Samaria [its capital]—who said in pride and stoutness of heart, **10** The bricks have fallen, but we will build [all the better] with hewn stones; the sycamores have been cut down, but we will put [costlier] cedars in their place. **11** Therefore the Lord has stirred up the adversaries [the Assyrians] of Rezin [king of Syria] against [Ephraim], and He will stir up their enemies *and* arm *and* join them together, **12** The Syrians [compelled to fight with their enemies, going] before [on the east] and the Philistines behind [on the west]; and they will devour Israel with open mouth. For all this, [God's] anger is not [then] turned away, but His hand is still stretched out [in judgment].

13 Yet the people turn not to Him Who smote them, neither do they seek [inquire for or require as their vital need] the Lord of hosts. **14** Therefore the Lord will cut off from Israel head and tail [the highest and the lowest]—[high] palm branch and [low] rush in one day; **15** The elderly and honored man, he is the head; and the prophet who teaches lies, he is the tail. **16** For they who lead this people cause them to err, and they who are led [astray] by them are swallowed up (destroyed). **17** Therefore the Lord will not rejoice over their young men, neither will He have compassion on their fatherless and widows, for everyone is profane and an evildoer, and every mouth speaks folly. For all this, [God's] anger is not turned away, but His hand is still stretched out [in judgment]. **18** For wickedness burns like a fire; it devours the briers and thorns, and it kindles in the thickets of the forest; they roll upward in a column of smoke. **19** Through the wrath of the Lord of hosts the land is darkened *and* burned up, and the people are like fuel for the fire; no man spares his brother. **20** They snatch in discord on the right hand, but are still hungry [their cruelty not diminished]; and they devour *and* destroy on the left hand, but are not satisfied. Each devours *and* destroys his own flesh [and blood] *or* his neighbor's.

speak the Word

God's government

Isaiah 9:6, 7 reveals so much about the character and nature of Jesus because it lists some of the names by which we know Him. Verse 7 also declares that *"of the increase of His government and of peace there shall be no end"* (italics mine).

The government that is upon Jesus' shoulders is not a political government; no, this verse refers to the governing of our lives. We are not supposed to be running our own lives. In fact, we are not even capable or qualified to do so. None of us are intelligent enough to know what is best, and that is why we need to be so thankful for God's intervention and His willingness to lovingly guide our lives.

The more God's government increases in my life (the more He directs my thoughts, conversations, decisions, and actions), the more my peace will increase. Peace does not come from success, professional position or promotions, social status, educational achievements, money, or an engaging personality. No, we find peace as we live according to the kingdom of God, which is defined as righteousness, peace, and the joy of the Holy Spirit (see Romans 14:17). Being right with God, knowing we are right with God, and doing right things out of knowing who we are in Christ is a process, but it leads us to peace, and peace leads us to joy.

If we do not have righteousness, peace, and joy, then we are not enjoying the kingdom of God as we should. Occasionally, we may need to take a break from all our other pursuits and simply seek God's kingdom. Matthew 6:33 exhorts us to "seek (aim at and strive after) *first of all* His kingdom and His righteousness (His way of doing and being right), and then all these things taken together will be given you besides" (italics mine).

Many times, we work, struggle, and strive for "all these things," such as food, clothing, a relationship we desire, pleasure, and position in society, when we should be diligently seeking God's kingdom, loving Jesus, and making sure that His government is established in our lives.

21 Manasseh [thirsts for the blood of his brother] Ephraim, and Ephraim [for that of] Manasseh; but together they are against Judah. For all this, [God's] anger is not turned away, but His hand is still stretched out [in judgment].

10 WOE TO those [judges] who issue unrighteous decrees, and to the magistrates who keep causing unjust *and* oppressive decisions to be recorded,

2 To turn aside the needy from justice and to make plunder of the rightful claims of the poor of My people, that widows may be their spoil, and that they may make the fatherless their prey!

3 And what will you do in the day of visitation [of God's wrath], and in the desolation which shall come from afar? To whom will you flee for help? And where will you deposit [for safekeeping] your wealth *and* with whom leave your glory?

4 Without Me they shall bow down among the prisoners, and they shall

fall [overwhelmed] under the heaps of the slain [on the battlefield]. For all this, [God's] anger is not turned away, but His hand is still stretched out [in judgment].

5 Woe to the Assyrian, the rod of My anger, the staff in whose hand is My indignation *and* fury [against Israel's disobedience]!

6 I send [the Assyrian] against a hypocritical *and* godless nation and against the people of My wrath; I command him to take the spoil and to seize the prey and to tread them down like the mire in the streets.

7 However, this is not his intention [nor is the Assyrian aware that he is doing this at My bidding], neither does his mind so think *and* plan; but it is in his mind to destroy and cut off many nations.

8 For [the Assyrian] says, Are not my officers all either [subjugated] kings *or* their equal?

9 Is not Calno [of Babylonia conquered] like Carchemish [on the Euphrates]? Is not Hamath [in Upper Syria] like Arpad [her neighbor]? Is not Samaria [in Israel] like Damascus [in Syria]? [Have any of these cities been able to resist Assyria? Not one!]

10 As my hand has reached to the kingdoms of the idols [which were unable to defend them,] whose graven images were more to be feared *and* dreaded *and* more mighty than those of Jerusalem and of Samaria—

11 Shall I not be able to do to Jerusalem and her images as I have done to Samaria and her idols? [says the Assyrian]

12 Therefore when the Lord has completed all His work [of chastisement and purification to be executed] on Mount Zion and on Jerusalem, it shall be that He will inflict punishment on the fruit [the thoughts, words, and deeds] of the stout *and* arrogant heart of the king of Assyria and the haughtiness of his pride.

13 For [the Assyrian king] has said, I have done it solely by the power of my own hand and wisdom, for I have insight *and* understanding. I have removed the boundaries of the peoples and have robbed their treasures; and like a bull I have brought down those who sat on thrones *and* the inhabitants.

14 And my hand has found like a nest the wealth of the people; and as one gathers eggs that are forsaken, so I have gathered all the earth; and there was none that moved its wing, or that opened its mouth or chirped.

15 Shall the ax boast itself against him who chops with it? Or shall the saw magnify itself against him who wields it back and forth? As if a rod should wield those who lift it up, or as if a staff should lift itself up as if it were not wood [but a man of God]!

16 Therefore will the Lord, the Lord of hosts, send leanness among [the Assyrian's] fat ones; and instead of his glory *or* under it He will kindle a burning like the burning of fire.

17 And the Light of Israel shall become a fire and His Holy One a flame, and it will ¹burn and devour [the Assyrian's] thorns and briers in one day. [II Kings 19:35-37; Isa. 31:8-9; 37:36.]

18 [The Lord] will consume the glory of the [Assyrian's] forest and of his fruitful field, both soul and body; and it shall be as when a sick man pines away *or* a standard-bearer faints.

19 And the remnant of the trees of his forest shall be few, so that a child may make a list of them.

20 And it shall be in that day that the remnant of Israel, and such as are

---

i During a single night this prophecy was fulfilled, when "the Angel of the Lord went forth and slew 185,000 in the camp of the Assyrians; and when the living arose early in the morning, behold, all these were dead bodies" (II Kings 19:35)—just when their victory over God's people had seemed certain.

escaped of the house of Jacob, shall no more lean upon him who smote them, but will lean upon the Lord, the Holy One of Israel, in truth.

21 A remnant will return [Shear-jashub, name of Isaiah's son], a remnant of Jacob, to the mighty God.

22 For though your population, O Israel, be as the sand of the sea, only a remnant of it will return [and survive]. The [fully completed] destruction is decreed (decided upon and brought to an issue); it overflows with justice and righteousness [the infliction of just punishment]. [Rom. 9:27, 28.]

23 For the Lord, the Lord of hosts, will make a full end, whatever is determined or decreed [in Israel], in the midst of all the earth.

24 Therefore thus says the Lord, the Lord of hosts, O My people who dwell in Zion, do not be afraid of the Assyrian, who smites you with a rod and lifts up his staff against you, as [the king of] Egypt did. [Exod. 5.]

25 For yet a little while and My indignation against you shall be accomplished, and My anger shall be directed to destruction [of the Assyrian].

26 And the Lord of hosts shall stir up and brandish a scourge against them as when He smote Midian at the rock of Oreb; and as His rod was over the [Red] Sea, so shall He lift it up as He did in [the flight from] Egypt. [Exod. 14:26-31; Judg. 7:24, 25.]

27 And it shall be in that day that the burden of [the Assyrian] shall depart from your shoulders, and his yoke from your neck. The yoke shall be destroyed because of fatness [which prevents it from going around your neck]. [Deut. 32:15.]

28 [The Assyrian with his army comes to Judah]. He arrives at Aiath; he passes through Migron; at Michmash he gets rid of his baggage [by storing it].

29 They go through the pass, they make Geba their camping place for the night; Ramah is afraid and trembles, Gibeah [the city] of [King] Saul flees.

30 Cry aloud [in consternation], O Daughter of Gallim! Hearken, O Laishah! [Answer her] O you poor Anathoth!

31 Madmenah is in flight; the inhabitants of Gebim seize their belongings and make their households flee for safety.

32 This very day [the Assyrian] will halt at Nob [the city of priests], shaking his fist at the mountain of the Daughter of Zion, at the hill of Jerusalem.

33 [But just when the Assyrian is in sight of his goal] behold, the Lord, the Lord of hosts, will lop off the beautiful boughs with terrorizing force; the high in stature will be hewn down and the lofty will be brought low.

34 And He will cut down the thickets of the forest with an ax, and Lebanon [the Assyrian] with its majestic trees shall fall by the Mighty One and mightily. [Gen. 49:24; Isa. 9:6.]

11 AND THERE shall come forth a Shoot out of the stock of Jesse [David's father], and a Branch out of his roots shall grow and bear fruit. [Isa. 4:2; Matt. 2:23; Rev. 5:5; 22:16.]

2 And the Spirit of the Lord shall rest upon Him—the Spirit of wisdom and understanding, the Spirit of counsel and might, the Spirit of knowledge and of the reverential and obedient fear of the Lord—

3 And shall make Him of quick understanding, and His delight shall be in the reverential and obedient fear of the Lord. And He shall not judge by the sight of His eyes, neither decide by the hearing of His ears;

4 But with righteousness and justice shall He judge the poor and decide with fairness for the meek, the poor, and the downtrodden of the earth; and

putting the Word to work

Isaiah 11:2 declares that God's Spirit is the Spirit of wisdom and understanding, the Spirit of counsel and might, the Spirit of knowledge and of the reverential and obedient fear of the Lord. How have you experienced the Holy Spirit's ministry in each of these ways? If you have not, ask God to give you such experiences with His Spirit.

He shall smite the earth *and* the oppressor with the rod of His mouth, and with the breath of His lips He shall slay the wicked.

5 And righteousness shall be the girdle of His waist and faithfulness the girdle of His loins.

6 And the wolf shall dwell with the lamb, and the leopard shall lie down with the kid, and the calf and the young lion and the fatted domestic animal together; and a little child shall lead them.

7 And the cow and the bear shall feed side by side, their young shall lie down together, and the lion shall eat straw like the ox.

8 And the sucking child shall play over the hole of the asp, and the weaned child shall put his hand on the adder's den.

9 They shall not hurt or destroy in all My holy mountain, for the earth shall be full of the knowledge of the Lord as the waters cover the sea.

10 And it shall be in that day that the Root of Jesse shall stand as a signal for the peoples; of Him shall the nations inquire *and* seek knowledge, and His dwelling shall be glory [His rest glorious]! [John 12:32.]

11 And in that day the Lord shall again lift up His hand a second time to recover (acquire and deliver) the remnant of His people which is left, from Assyria, from Lower Egypt, from Pathros, from Ethiopia, from Elam [in Persia], from Shinar [Babylonia], from Hamath [in Upper Syria], and from the countries bordering on the [Mediterranean] Sea. [Jer. 23:5-8.]

12 And He will raise up a signal for the nations and will assemble the out-casts of Israel and will gather togeth-er the dispersed of Judah from the four corners of the earth.

13 The envy *and* jealousy of Ephraim also shall depart, and they who vex *and* harass Judah from outside *or* inside shall be cut off; Ephraim shall not envy Judah, and Judah shall not vex *and* harass Ephraim.

14 But [with united forces Ephraim and Judah] will swoop down upon the shoulders of the Philistines' [land sloping] toward the west; together they will strip the people on the east [the Arabs]. They will lay their hands upon Edom and Moab, and the Ammonites will obey them.

15 And the Lord will utterly destroy (doom and dry up) the tongue of the Egyptian sea [the west fork of the Red Sea]; and with His [mighty] scorching wind He will wave His hand over the river [Nile] and will smite it into seven channels and will cause men to cross over dry-shod.

16 And there shall be a highway from Assyria for the remnant left of His people, as there was for Israel when they came up out of the land of Egypt.

life point

We see in Isaiah 11:3, 4 that Jesus did not make decisions "by the sight of His eyes" or "the hearing of His ears," yet He was of "quick understanding." If we follow His example, not relying on what we see or hear with our natural senses, but watching and listening for the Holy Spirit to lead us in our hearts, we will also understand quickly what we would otherwise not learn in a lifetime.

12 AND IN that day you will say, I will give thanks to You, O Lord; for though You were angry with me, Your anger has turned away, and You comfort me.

2 Behold, God, my salvation! I will trust and not be afraid, for the Lord God is my strength and song; yes, He has become my salvation.

3 Therefore with joy will you draw water from the wells of salvation.

4 And in that day you will say, Give thanks to the Lord, call upon His name and by means of His name [in solemn entreaty]; declare and make known His deeds among the peoples of the earth, proclaim that His name is exalted!

5 Sing praises to the Lord, for He has done excellent things [gloriously]; let this be made known to all the earth.

6 Cry aloud and shout joyfully, you women and inhabitants of Zion, for great in your midst is the Holy One of Israel.

13 THE MOURNFUL, inspired prediction (a burden to be lifted up) concerning Babylon which Isaiah son of Amoz saw [with prophetic insight]:

2 Raise up a signal banner upon the high and bare mountain, summon them [the Medes and Persians] with loud voice and beckoning hand that they may enter the gates of the [Babylonian] nobles.

3 I Myself [says the Lord] have commanded My designated ones and

have summoned My mighty men to execute My anger, even My proudly exulting ones [the Medes and Persians]—those who are made to triumph for My honor.

4 Hark, the uproar of a multitude in the mountains, like that of a great people! The noise of the tumult of the kingdoms of the nations gathering together! The Lord of hosts is mustering the host for the battle.

5 They come from a distant country, from the uttermost part of the heavens [the far east]—even the Lord and the weapons of His indignation—to seize and destroy the whole land. [Ps. 19:4-6; Isa. 5:26.]

6 Wail, for the day of the Lord is at hand; as destruction from the Almighty and Sufficient One [Shaddai] will it come! [Gen. 17:1.]

7 Therefore will ʲall hands be feeble, and every man's heart will melt.

8 And they [of Babylon] shall be dismayed and terrified, pangs and sorrows shall take hold of them; they shall be in pain as a woman in childbirth. They will gaze stupefied and aghast at one another, their faces will be aflame [from the effects of the unprecedented warfare].

9 Behold, the day of the Lord is coming!—fierce, with wrath and raging anger—to make the land and the [whole] earth a desolation and to destroy out of it its sinners. [Isa. 2:10-22; Rev. 19:11-21.]

10 For the stars of the heavens and their constellations will not give their light; the sun will be darkened at its rising and the moon will not shed its light.

speak the Word

God, You are my salvation! I will trust and not be afraid, for You are my strength and my song.
ADAPTED FROM ISAIAH **12:2**

---

j Babylon was taken by surprise on the night of Belshazzar's sacrilegious feast, when Belshazzar was slain and Darius the Mede was made king over the realm of the Chaldeans (Dan. 5:30).

11 And I, the Lord, will punish the world for its evil, and the wicked for their guilt *and* iniquity; I will cause the arrogance of the proud to cease and will lay low the haughtiness of the terrible *and* the boasting of the violent *and* ruthless.

12 I will make a man more rare than fine gold, and mankind scarcer than the pure gold of Ophir.

13 Therefore I will make the heavens tremble; and the ᵏearth shall be shaken out of its place at the wrath of the Lord of hosts in the day of His fierce anger.

14 And like the chased roe *or* gazelle, and like sheep that no man gathers, each [foreign resident] will turn to his own people, and each will flee to his own land.

15 Everyone who is found will be thrust through, and everyone who is connected with the slain *and* is caught will fall by the sword.

16 Their infants also will be dashed to pieces before their eyes; their houses will be plundered and their wives ravished.

17 Behold, I will stir up the Medes against them, who have no regard for silver and do not delight in gold [and thus cannot be bribed].

18 Their bows will cut down the young men [of Babylon]; and they will have no pity on the fruit of the womb, their eyes will not spare children.

19 And Babylon, the glory of kingdoms, the beauty of the Chaldeans' pride, shall be like Sodom and Gomorrah when God overthrew them.

20 [Babylon] shall never be inhabited or dwelt in from generation to generation; neither shall the Arab pitch his tent there, nor shall the shepherds make their sheepfolds there.

21 But wild beasts of the desert will lie down there, and the people's houses will be full of dolefully howling creatures; and ostriches will dwell there, and wild goats [like demons] will dance there.

22 And ˡwolves *and* howling creatures will cry *and* answer in the deserted castles, and jackals in the pleasant palaces. And [Babylon's] time has nearly come, and her days will not be prolonged.

14 FOR THE Lord will have mercy on Jacob [the captive Jews in Babylon] and will again choose Israel and set them in their own land; and foreigners [who are proselytes] will join them and will cleave to the house of Jacob (Israel). [Esth. 8:17.]

2 And the peoples [of Babylonia] shall ᵐtake them and bring them to their own country [of Judea] *and* help restore them. And the house of Israel will possess [the foreigners who prefer to stay with] them in the land of the Lord as male and female servants; and they will take captive [not by physical but by moral might] those whose captives they have been, and

---

k "By the outbreak of [the Lord's] wrath the material universe is [to be] shaken to its foundations. Such representations are common in the descriptions of the day of the Lord, and are not to be dismissed as merely figurative" (*The Cambridge Bible*). See also I Thess. 5:2; II Thess. 1:7, 8; II Pet. 3:10.
l This whole prophecy is generally conceded to have been written well over a century (170 years, according to archbishop James Ussher) before Babylon's downfall, when the circumstances necessary for its fulfillment seemed most improbable—but it has been literally fulfilled in detail. Human keenness of foresight could not possibly have foreseen that great Babylon would be wiped from the face of the earth (Isa. 13:19), become ruins infested by wild animals (Isa. 13:21, 22), be feared because of superstition by the Arabs (Isa. 13:20)—with only a small village near the area to mark the place where, since the days of Nimrod, mighty kings had exalted themselves above the God of heaven. Various conquerors during the centuries contributed to Babylon's downfall until, by the first century BC, it was as utterly and hopelessly destroyed as Sodom and Gomorrah (Isa. 13:19).
m This prophecy (Isa. 14:1, 2) was fulfilled literally and in detail under King Cyrus of Persia and Babylonia. (Ezra 1.)

they will rule over their [former] oppressors. [Ezra 1.]

3 When the Lord has given you rest from your sorrow *and* pain and from your trouble *and* unrest and from the hard service with which you were made to serve,

4 You shall take up this [taunting] parable against the king of Babylon and say, How the oppressor has stilled [the restless insolence]! The golden *and* exacting city has ceased!

5 The Lord has broken the staff of the wicked, the scepter of the [tyrant] rulers,

6 Who smote the peoples in anger with incessant blows *and* trod down the nations in wrath with unrelenting persecution—[until] he who smote is persecuted and no one hinders any more.

7 The whole earth is at rest and is quiet; they break forth into singing.

8 Yes, the fir trees *and* cypresses rejoice at you [O kings of Babylon], even the cedars of Lebanon, saying, Since you have been laid low, no woodcutter comes up against us.

9 Sheol (Hades, the place of the dead) below is stirred up to meet you at your coming [O tyrant Babylonian rulers]; it stirs up the shades of the dead to greet you—even all the chief ones of the earth; it raises from their thrones [in astonishment at your humbled condition] all the kings of the nations.

10 All of them will [tauntingly] say to you, Have you also become weak as we are? Have you become like us?

11 Your pomp *and* magnificence are brought down to Sheol (the under-world), along with the sound of your harps; the maggots [which prey upon dead bodies] are spread out under you and worms cover you [O Babylonian rulers].

12 How have you fallen from heaven, O [n]light-bringer *and* daystar, son of the morning! How you have been cut down to the ground, you who weakened *and* laid low the nations [O blasphemous, satanic king of Babylon!]

13 And you said in your heart, I will ascend to heaven; I will exalt my throne above the stars of God; I will sit upon the mount of assembly in the uttermost north.

14 I will ascend above the heights of the clouds; I will make myself like the Most High.

15 Yet you shall be brought down to Sheol (Hades), to the innermost recesses of the pit (the region of the dead).

16 Those who see you will gaze at you *and* consider you, saying, Is this the man who made the earth tremble, who shook kingdoms?—

17 Who made the world like a wilderness and overthrew its cities, who would not permit his prisoners to return home?

18 All the kings of the nations, all of them lie sleeping in glorious array, each one in his own sepulcher.

19 But you are cast away from your tomb like a loathed growth *or* premature birth *or* an abominable branch [of the family] *and* like the raiment of the slain; and you are clothed with the slain, those thrust through with the

---

n The Hebrew for this expression—"light-bringer" or "shining one"—is translated "Lucifer" in *The Latin Vulgate*, and is thus translated in the *King James Version*. But because of the association of that name with Satan, it is not now used in this and other translations. Some students feel that the application of the name Lucifer to Satan, in spite of the long and confident teaching to that effect, is erroneous. The application of the name to Satan has existed since the third century AD, and is based on the supposition that Luke 10:18 is an explanation of Isa. 14:12, which many authorities believe is not true. "Lucifer," the light-bringer, is the Latin equivalent of the Greek word "Phosphoros," which is used as a title of Christ in II Pet. 1:19 and corresponds to the name "radiant *and* brilliant Morning Star" in Rev. 22:16, a name Jesus called Himself. This passage here in Isa. 14:13 clearly applies to the king of Babylon.

vote against yourself

Notice in Isaiah 14:12–15 that self-will destroyed Lucifer. In exalting himself, he said, "I will" five times. God had an answer for him: "You shall be brought down to Sheol (Hades), to the innermost recesses of the pit (the region of the dead)" (Isaiah 14:15). In other words, "You will be cast down to hell."

We need to guard against self-will by following Jesus's example. Sooner or later God will ask us to do something contrary to our will, and we will need to remember what Jesus said, "My Father, if it is possible, let this cup pass away from Me; nevertheless, not what I will [not what I desire], but as You will and desire" (Matthew 26:39).

Not getting our own way is one of the most painful things we ever go through in life. When we want something, we really want it, and we do not give up easily. We do not like to vote against our own desires! It takes a lot of work and a lot of humility and brokenness to bring us to the place where we are pliable and moldable in the hands of God, to the point where we can say, "Well, God, I'd rather not do this, but I'm willing to do whatever You want."

The lesson here is that we must be willing to do whatever God says, and not what we think, feel, or want. We must deny ourselves if we are going to follow Him. We need to say, "Your will, God, be done in my life," and really mean it!

We are afraid that we will never get the things we want if we deny ourselves, but God will give us what we desire, and even better, in due time. Do not be afraid to delay gratification and trust God to give you what you really need.

sword, who go down to the stones of the pit [into which carcasses are thrown], like a dead body trodden underfoot.

20 You shall not be joined with them in burial, because you have destroyed your land and have slain your people. May the descendants of evildoers nevermore be named!

21 Prepare a slaughtering place for his sons because of the guilt *and* iniquity of their fathers, so that they may not rise, possess the earth, and fill the face of the world with cities.

22 And I will rise up against them, says the Lord of hosts, and cut off from Babylon name and remnant, and son and son's son, says the Lord.

23 I will also make it a possession of the hedgehog *and* porcupine, and of °marshes *and* pools of water, and I will sweep it with the broom of destruction, says the Lord of hosts.

24 The Lord of hosts has sworn, saying, Surely, as I have thought *and* planned, so shall it come to pass, and as I have purposed, so shall it stand—

25 That I will break the Assyrian in My land, and upon My mountains I

o The city of Babylon was in the midst of a very fertile area, and it would have seemed reasonable to suppose that, regardless of what happened to the population, the region would always furnish pasturage for flocks. But Isaiah said it would become the possession of wild animals and would be covered with "marshes *and* pools of water." This is how that prophecy was literally fulfilled: after Babylon was taken, the whole area around the city was put under water from neglect of the canals and dikes of the Euphrates River. It became stagnant "marshes *and* pools of water" among ruins haunted by wild animals, proclaiming to any who might see it that "surely, as [the Lord has] thought *and* planned, so shall it come to pass" (Isa. 14:24).

will tread him underfoot. Then shall the [Assyrian's] Pyoke depart from [the people of Judah], and his burden depart from their shoulders.

26 This is the [Lord's] purpose that is purposed upon the whole earth [regarded as conquered and put under tribute by Assyria]; and this is [His omnipotent] hand that is stretched out over all the nations.

27 For the Lord of hosts has purposed, and who can annul it? And His hand is stretched out, and who can turn it back?

28 In the year that King Ahaz [of Judah] died there came this mournful, inspired prediction (a burden to be lifted up):

29 Rejoice not, O Philistia, all of you, because the rod [of Judah] that smote you is broken; for out of the serpent's root shall come forth an adder [King Hezekiah of Judah], and its [the serpent's] offspring will be a fiery, flying serpent. [II Kings 18:1, 3, 8.]

30 And the firstborn of the poor *and* the poorest of the poor [of Judah] shall feed on My meadows, and the needy will lie down in safety; but I will kill your root with famine, and your remnant shall be slain.

31 Howl, O gate! Cry, O city! Melt away, O Philistia, all of you! For there is coming a smoke out of the north, and there is no straggler in his ranks *and* none stands aloof [in Hezekiah's battalions].

32 What then shall one answer the messengers of the [Philistine] nation? That the Lord has founded Zion, and in her shall the poor *and* afflicted of His people trust *and* find refuge.

15 THE MOURNFUL, inspired prediction (a burden to be lifted up) concerning Moab:

Because in a night Ar of Moab is laid waste and brought to silence! Because in a night Kir of Moab is laid waste and brought to silence!

2 They are gone up to Bayith and to Dibon, to the high places to weep. Moab wails over Nebo and over Medeba; on all their heads is baldness, and every beard is cut off [as a sign of deep sorrow and humiliation]. [Jer. 48:37.]

3 In their streets they gird themselves with sackcloth; on the tops of their houses and in their broad places everyone wails, weeping abundantly.

4 And Heshbon and Elealeh [cities in possession of Moab] cry out; their voice is heard even to Jahaz. Therefore the armed soldiers of Moab cry out; [Moab's] life is grievous *and* trembles within him.

5 My heart cries out for Moab; his nobles *and* other fugitives flee to Zoar, to Eglath-shelishiyah [like a heifer three years old]. For with weeping they go up the ascent of Luhith; for on the road to Horonaim they raise a cry of destruction. [Jer. 48:5.]

6 For the waters of Nimrim are desolations, for the grass is withered away and the new growth fails; there is no green thing.

7 Therefore the abundance [of possessions] they have acquired and stored away they [now] carry over the willow brook *and* to the valley of the Arabians.

8 For the cry [of distress] has gone round the borders of Moab; the wailing has reached to Eglaim, and the prolonged *and* mournful cry to Beer-elim.

9 For the waters of Dimon are full of blood; yet I [the Lord] will bring even more on Dimon—a lion upon those of Moab who escape and upon the remnant of the land.

p The prophecy against Assyria had actually by this time already been fulfilled, but Isaiah attached it to the as yet unfulfilled prophecy against Babylon as a pledge or guarantee of the fulfillment of the latter.

a person of purpose

Isaiah 14:26, 27 tell us that God is a God of purpose, and that when He purposes something, it *will* come to pass.

Jesus knew His purpose. As we know from John 10:10, He said that He came into the world that we might have life. In John 18:37 He told Pilate, "This is why I was born, and for this I have come into the world, to bear witness to the Truth." John wrote that Jesus's purpose was to destroy the works of the devil (see I John 3:8).

If we do not have a purpose in life, we feel useless, worthless, and frustrated. So it is very important for us to see that God has designed us with a purpose in mind (see Psalm 139:16). Generally, He wants us to enjoy ourselves and to enjoy the life He has given us. But as far as our specific purpose, that varies from individual to individual and from one season of life to the next, so we must seek to discover what it is.

Right now you may be in a time of transition from one season to the next. If so, do not be discouraged. God will show you what He has for you to do next. Sometimes you may have to step out and try a few things until you find what you are comfortable with. But you can be assured that whatever it may be, you do have a purpose, and you are never going to be fulfilled until you find it and start flowing in it.

Not only do we need to know our purpose, we need to do it "on purpose." This involves making decisions to live right. We need to love on purpose. We do not love because we feel like it; we love because we purpose to do so. Love is not a gooey feeling we get about people; it is a decision we make about how we relate to people. Giving is also a decision. We do not give just because we feel like giving. We give because we are convinced it is what God wants us to do. We give on purpose and for a purpose.

The same is true of being merciful, being kind, and walking in the Spirit. We do those things not because we necessarily always feel like it, but because we are called to do them. Love, joy, peace, patience, kindness, goodness, and all the other fruit of the Spirit are characteristics of the Holy Spirit that we have within us when we accept Jesus as our Savior. And we can release them if we do it on purpose. Make a choice to let the good things God has placed in your spirit flow through your soul and body so others may be blessed and God will be glorified.

Our flesh is not always going to agree with us to do these things. But we must choose to love on purpose, give on purpose, and stay at peace on purpose. If we want to have peace, we must purpose to have peace, because the devil will try to steal it.

Everything we do for others, and everything we do in life, needs to be done on purpose. Ask God to help you increasingly become a person of purpose!

16 YOU [Moabites, now fugitives in Edom, which is ruled by the king of Judah] send qlambs to the ruler of the land, from Sela or Petra through the desert *and* wilderness to the mountain of the Daughter of Zion [Jerusalem]. [II Kings 3:4, 5.]

2 For like wandering birds, like a brood cast out *and* a scattered nest, so shall the daughters of Moab be at the fords of the [river] Arnon.

3 [Say to the ruler] Give counsel, execute justice [for Moab, O king of Judah]; make your shade [over us] like night in the midst of noonday; hide the outcasts, betray not the fugitive to his pursuer.

4 Let our outcasts of Moab dwell among you; be a sheltered hiding place to them from the destroyer. When the extortion *and* the extortioner have been brought to nought, and destruction has ceased, and the oppressors *and* they who trample men are consumed *and* have vanished out of the land,

5 Then in mercy *and* loving-kindness shall a throne be established, and rOne shall sit upon it in truth *and* faithfulness in the tent of David, judging and seeking justice and being swift to do righteousness. [Ps. 96:13; Jer. 48:47.]

6 We have heard of the pride of Moab, that he is very proud—even of his arrogance, his conceit, his wrath, his untruthful boasting.

7 Moab therefore shall wail for Moab; everyone shall wail. For the ruins, flagons of wine, *and* the raisin cakes of Kir-hareseth you shall sigh and mourn, utterly stricken *and* discouraged.

8 For the fields of Heshbon languish *and* wither, and the vines of Sibmah; the lords of the nations have broken down [Moab's] choice vine branches, which reached even to Jazer, wandering into the wilderness; its shoots stretched out abroad, they passed over [the shores of] the [Dead] Sea.

9 Therefore I [Isaiah] will weep with the weeping of Jazer for the vines of Sibmah. I will drench you with my tears, O Heshbon and Elealeh; for upon your summer fruits and your harvest the shout [of alarm and the cry of the enemy] has fallen.

10 And gladness is taken away, and joy out of the plentiful field; and in the vineyards there is no singing, nor is there joyful sound; the treaders tread out no wine in the presses, for the shout of joy has been made to cease.

11 Wherefore my heart sounds like a harp [in mournful compassion] for Moab, and my inner being [goes out] for Kir-hareseth [for those brick-walled citadels of his].

12 It shall be that when Moab presents himself, when he wearies himself [worshiping] on the high place [of idolatry], he will come to his sanctuary [of Chemosh, god of Moab], but he will not prevail. [Then will he be ashamed of his god.] [Jer. 48:13.]

13 This is the word that the Lord has spoken concerning Moab since that time [when Moab's pride and resistance to God were first known].

14 But now the Lord has spoken, saying, Within sthree years, as the

q As King Mesha sent 100,000 lambs each year to King Ahab of Israel (II Kings 3:4), so now the Moabites are advised to win the king's favor and protection by diverting their tribute to the king in Jerusalem, as an acknowledgment of subjection. r Isaiah apparently puts these words in the mouths of the Moabite ambassadors to the king of Judah, but in "language so divinely framed as to apply to 'the latter days' under King Messiah, when the Lord shall bring again [reverse] the captivity of Moab" (Robert Jamieson, A.R. Fausset and David Brown, *A Commentary*). s This prophecy was fulfilled after the death of King Ahaz of Judah (Isa. 14:28), somewhere around the third year of King Hezekiah's reign. Moab was not left completely without population at this time; there was still a "remnant." The final desolation of Moab was reserved for King Nebuchadnezzar of Babylon in years of a hireling [who will not serve longer than the allotted time], the glory of Moab shall be brought into contempt, in spite of all his mighty multitudes of people; and the remnant that survives will be very small, feeble, *and* of no account.

17 THE MOURNFUL, inspired prediction (a burden to be lifted up) concerning Damascus [capital of Syria, and Israel's bulwark against Assyria]. Behold, Damascus will cease to be a city and will become a heap of ruins.
2 The cities of Aroer [east of the Jordan] are forsaken; they shall be for flocks, which shall lie down, and none shall make them afraid.
3 His bulwark [Syria] *and* the fortress shall disappear from Ephraim, and the kingdom from Damascus; and the remnant of Syria will be like the [departed] glory of the children of Israel [her ally], says the Lord of hosts.
4 And in that day the former glory of Jacob [Israel—his might, his population, his prosperity] shall be enfeebled, and the fat of his flesh shall become lean.
5 And it shall be as when the reaper gathers the standing grain and his arm harvests the ears; yes, it shall be as when one gathers the ears of grain in the fertile Valley of Rephaim.
6 Yet gleanings [of grapes] shall be left in it [the land of Israel], as after the beating of an olive tree [with a stick], two or three berries in the top of the uppermost bough, four or five in the outermost branches of the fruitful tree, says the Lord, the God of Israel.
7 In that day will men look to their Maker, and their eyes shall regard the Holy One of Israel.

8 And they will not look to the [idolatrous] altars, the work of their hands, neither will they have respect for what their fingers have made—either the Asherim [symbols of the goddess Asherah] or the sun-images.
9 In that day will their [Syria's and Israel's] strong cities be like the forsaken places in the wood and on the mountaintop, as they [the 'Amorites and the Hivites] forsook their [cities] because of the children of Israel; and there will be desolation.
10 Because you have forgotten the God of your salvation [O Judah] and have not been mindful of the Rock of your strength, your Stronghold—therefore, you have planted pleasant nursery grounds *and* plantings [to Adonis, pots of quickly withered flowers used to set by their doors or in the courts of temples], and have set [the grounds] with vine slips of a strange [God],
11 And in the day of your planting you hedge it in, and in the morning you make your seed to blossom, yet [promising as it is] the harvest shall be a heap of ruins *and* flee away in the day of expected possession and of desperate sorrow *and* sickening, incurable pain.
12 Hark, the uproar of a multitude of peoples! They roar *and* thunder like the noise of the seas! Ah, the roar of nations! They roar like the roaring of rushing *and* mighty waters!
13 The nations will rush *and* roar like the rushing *and* roaring of many waters—but [God] will rebuke them, and they will flee far off and will be chased like chaff on the mountains before the wind, and like rolling thistledown *or* whirling dust of the stubble before the storm.
14 At evening time, behold, terror!

around 582 BC, some five years after the taking of Jerusalem. The ruins of Elealeh, Heshbon, Medeba, Dimon, etc., still exist to confirm through modern research the accuracy of the fulfillment of this prophecy. **t** *The Septuagint* (Greek translation of the Old Testament) so reads.

And ᵘbefore the morning, they [the terrorizing Assyrians] are not. This is the portion of those who strip us [the Jews] of what belongs to us, and the lot of those who rob us. [Fulfilled in Isa. 37:36.]

18 WOE TO the land whirring with wings which is beyond the rivers of Cush *or* Ethiopia,

2 That sends ambassadors by the Nile, even in vessels of papyrus upon the waters! Go, you swift messengers, to a nation tall and polished, to a people terrible from their beginning [feared and dreaded near and far], a nation strong and victorious, whose land the rivers divide!

3 All you inhabitants of the world, you who dwell on the earth, when a signal is raised on the mountains—look! When a trumpet is blown—hear!

4 For thus the Lord has said to me: I will be still and I will look on from My dwelling place, like clear *and* glowing heat in sunshine, like a fine cloud of mist in the heat of harvest.

5 For before the harvest, when the blossom is over and the flower becomes a ripening grape, He will cut off the sprigs with pruning hooks, and the spreading branches He will remove and cut away.

6 They [the dead bodies of the slain warriors] shall be left together to the ravenous birds of the mountains and to the beasts of the earth; and the ravenous birds will summer upon them, and all the beasts of the earth will winter upon them.

7 At that time shall a present be brought to the Lord of hosts from a people tall and polished, from a people terrible from their beginning *and* feared *and* dreaded near and far, a nation strong and victorious, whose land the rivers *or* great channels divide—to the place [of worship] of the ᵛName of the Lord of hosts, to Mount Zion [in Jerusalem]. [Deut. 12:5; II Chron. 32:23; Isa. 16:1; 45:14; Zeph. 3:10.]

19 THE MOURNFUL, inspired prediction (a burden to be lifted up) concerning Egypt: Behold, the Lord is riding on a swift cloud and comes to Egypt; and the idols of Egypt will tremble at His presence, and the hearts of the Egyptians will melt within them.

2 And I will stir up Egyptians against Egyptians, and they will fight, every one against his brother and every one against his neighbor, city against city, kingdom against kingdom.

3 And the spirit of the Egyptians within them will become exhausted and emptied out *and* will fail, and I will destroy their counsel *and* confound their plans; and they will seek counsel from the idols and the sorcerers, and from those having familiar spirits (the mediums) and the wizards.

4 And I will give over the Egyptians into the hand of a hard *and* cruel master, and a fierce king will rule over them, says the Lord, the Lord of hosts.

5 And the waters shall fail from the Nile, and the river shall be wasted and become dry.

6 And the rivers shall become foul, the streams *and* canals of Egypt shall be diminished and dried up, the reeds and the rushes shall wither *and* rot away.

---

u Isaiah foretells (in Isa. 14:25) that God will break the Assyrian conqueror and tread him underfoot. Now (in Isa. 17:14) further details seem to be furnished—"terror" (because the enemy has all but been victorious), but "before the morning, they [the terrorizing Assyrians] are not." The startling fulfillment of this prophecy (cf. also Isa. 10:33-34; 30:31; 31:8) is found in Isa. 37:36, following the repetition of the prophecy first recorded in II Kings 19:29-36. Just when an overwhelming victory by the Assyrian Sennacherib seemed inevitable, during a single night 185,000 of his army died, and Judah was spared—as the Lord through Isaiah had promised. **v** See footnote on Deut. 12:5.

7 The meadows by the Nile, by the brink of the Nile, and all the sown fields of the Nile shall become dry, be blown away, and be no more.

8 The fishermen will lament, and all who cast a hook into the Nile will mourn; and they who spread nets upon the waters will languish.

9 Moreover, they who work with combed flax and they who weave white [cotton] cloth will be confounded *and* in despair.

10 [Those who are] the pillars *and* foundations of Egypt will be crushed, and all those who work for hire *or* who build dams will be grieved.

11 The princes of Zoan [ancient capital of the Pharaohs] are utterly foolish; the counsel of the wisest counselors of Pharaoh has become witless (stupid). How can you say to Pharaoh, I am a son of the wise, a son of ancient kings?

12 Where then are your wise men? Let them tell you now [if they are so wise], and let them make known what the Lord of hosts has purposed against Egypt [if they can].

13 The princes of Zoan have become fools, and the princes of Memphis are confused *and* deceived; those who are the cornerstones of her tribes have led Egypt astray.

14 The Lord has mingled a spirit of perverseness, error, *and* confusion within her; [her leaders] have caused Egypt to stagger in all her doings, as a drunken man staggers in his vomit.

15 Neither can any work [done singly or by concerted action] accomplish anything for Egypt, whether by head or tail, palm branch or rush [high or low].

16 In that day will the Egyptians be like women [timid and helpless]; and they will tremble and fear because of the shaking of the hand of the Lord of hosts which He shakes over them.

17 And the land of Judah [allied to Assyria] shall become a terror to the Egyptians; everyone to whom mention of it is made will be afraid *and*

everyone who mentions it—to him will they turn in fear, because of the purpose of the Lord of hosts which He purposes against Egypt.

18 In that day there will be five cities in the land of Egypt that speak the language of [the Hebrews of] Canaan and swear allegiance to the Lord of hosts. One of them will be called the City of the Sun *or* Destruction.

19 In that day there will be an altar to the Lord in the midst of the land of Egypt, and a pillar to the Lord at its border.

20 And it will be a sign and a witness to the Lord of hosts in the land of Egypt; for they will cry to the Lord because of oppressors, and He will send them a savior, even a mighty one, and he will deliver them. [Judg. 2:18; 3:9, 15.]

21 And the Lord will make Himself known to Egypt, and the Egyptians will know (have knowledge of, be acquainted with, give heed to, and cherish) the Lord in that day and will worship with sacrifices of animal *and* vegetable offerings; they will vow a vow to the Lord and perform it.

22 And the Lord shall smite Egypt, smiting and healing it; and they will return to the Lord, and He will listen to their entreaties and heal them.

23 In that day shall there be a highway out of Egypt to Assyria, and the Assyrian will come into Egypt and the Egyptian into Assyria; and the Egyptians will worship [the Lord] with the Assyrians.

24 In that day Israel shall be the third, with Egypt and with Assyria [in a Messianic league], a blessing in the midst of the earth,

25 Whom the Lord of hosts has blessed, saying, Blessed be Egypt My people and Assyria the work of My hands and Israel My heritage.

20 IN THE year that the Tartan [Assyrian commander in chief] came to Ashdod in Philistia, sent by Sargon king of Assyria, he fought against Ashdod and took it.

2 At that time the Lord spoke by Isaiah son of Amoz, saying, Go, loose the sackcloth from off your loins and take your shoes off your feet. And he had done so, walking around stripped [to his loincloth] and barefoot.

3 And the Lord said, As My servant Isaiah has walked [comparatively] naked and barefoot for three years, as a sign and forewarning concerning Egypt and concerning Cush (Ethiopia),

4 So shall the king of Assyria lead away the Egyptian captives and the Ethiopian exiles, young and old, naked and barefoot, even with buttocks uncovered—to the shame of Egypt.

5 And they shall be dismayed and confounded because of Ethiopia their hope and expectation and Egypt their glory and boast.

6 And the inhabitants of this coastland [the Israelites and their neighbors] will say in that day, See! This is what comes to those in whom we trusted and hoped, to whom we fled for help to deliver us from the king of Assyria! But we, how shall we escape [captivity and exile]?

21 THE MOURNFUL, inspired prediction (a burden to be lifted up) concerning the Desert of the Sea [which was Babylon after great dams were raised to control the waters of the Euphrates River which overflowed it like a sea—and would do so again]: As whirlwinds in the South (the Negeb) sweep through, so it [the judgment of God by hostile armies] comes from the desert, from a terrible land.

2 A hard and grievous vision is declared to me: the treacherous dealer deals treacherously, and the destroyer destroys. Go up, O Elam! Besiege, O Media! All the sighing [caused by Babylon's ruthless oppres-

sions] I will cause to cease [says the Lord]. [Isa. 11:11; 13:17.]

3 Therefore are my [Isaiah's] loins filled with anguish, pangs have seized me like the pangs of a woman in childbirth; I am bent and pained so that I cannot hear, I am dismayed so that I cannot see.

4 My mind reels and wanders, horror terrifies me. [In my mind's eye I am at the feast of Belshazzar. I see the defilement of the golden vessels taken from God's temple, I watch the handwriting appear on the wall—I know that Babylon's great king is to be slain.] The twilight I looked forward to with pleasure has been turned into fear and trembling for me. [Dan. 5.]

5 They prepare the table, they spread the rugs, [and having] set the watchers [the revelers take no other precaution], they eat, they drink. Arise, you princes, and oil your shields [for your deadly foe is at the gates]!

6 For thus has the Lord said to me: Go, set [yourself as] a watchman, let him declare what he sees.

7 And when he sees a troop, horsemen in pairs, a troop of donkeys, and a troop of camels, he shall listen diligently, very diligently.

8 And [the watchman] cried like a lion, O Lord, I stand continually on the watchtower in the daytime, and I am set in my station every night.

9 And see! Here comes a troop of men and chariots, horsemen in pairs! And he [the watchman] tells [what it foretells]: Babylon has fallen, has fallen! And all the graven images of her gods lie shattered on the ground [in my vision]!

10 O you my threshed and winnowed ones [my own people the Jews, who must be trodden down by Babylon], that which I have heard from the Lord of hosts, the God of Israel, I have [joyfully] announced to you [Babylon is to fall]!

11 The mournful, inspired prediction

(a burden to be lifted up) concerning Dumah (Edom): One calls to me from Seir (Edom), Watchman, what of the night? [How far is it spent? How long till morning?] Guardian, what of the night?

12 The watchman said, The morning comes, but also the night. [Another time, if Edom earnestly wishes to know] if you will inquire [of me], inquire; return, come again.

13 The mournful, inspired prediction (a burden to be lifted up) concerning Arabia: In the forests *and* thickets of Arabia you shall lodge, O you caravans of Dedanites [from northern Arabia].

14 To the thirsty [Dedanites] bring water, O inhabitants of the land of Tema [in Arabia]; meet the fugitive with bread [suitable] for him.

15 For they have fled from the swords, from the drawn sword, from the bent bow, and from the grievousness of war [the press of battle].

16 For the Lord has said this to me, Within a year, according to the years of a hireling [who will work no longer than was agreed], all the glory of Kedar [an Arabian tribe] will fail.

17 And the remainder of the number of archers *and* their bows, the mighty men of the sons of Kedar, will be diminished *and* few; for the Lord, the God of Israel, has spoken it.

22 THE MOURNFUL, inspired prediction (a burden to be lifted up) concerning the Valley of Vision: What do you mean [I wonder] that you have all gone up to the housetops,

2 You who are full of shouting, a tumultuous city, a joyous *and* exultant city? [O Jerusalem] your slain warriors have not met [a glorious] death with the sword or in battle.

3 All your [military] leaders have fled together; without the bow [which they had thrown away] they have been taken captive *and* bound by the archers. All of you who were found were bound together [as captives], though they had fled far away.

4 Therefore I [Isaiah] said, Look away from me; I will weep bitterly. Do not hasten *and* try to comfort me over the destruction of the daughter of my people.

5 For it is a day of discomfiture *and* of tumult, of treading down, of confusion *and* perplexity from the Lord God of hosts in the Valley of Vision, a day of breaking down the walls and of crying to the mountains.

6 And [in my vision I saw] Elam take up the quiver, with troops in chariots, infantry, *and* horsemen; and Kir [with Elam subject to Assyria] uncovered the shield.

7 And it came to pass that your choicest valleys were full of chariots, and the horsemen took their station [and set themselves in offensive array at the gate of Jerusalem]. [Fulfilled in II Chron. 32; Isa. 36.]

8 Then [God] removed the protective covering of Judah; and you looked to the weapons in the House of the Forest [the king's armory] in that day. [I Kings 7:2; 10:17, 21.]

9 You saw that the breaches [in the walls] of the City of David [the citadel of Zion] were many; [since the water supply was still defective] you collected [within the city's walls] the waters of the Lower Pool.

10 And you numbered the houses of Jerusalem, and you broke down the houses [to get materials] to fortify the [city] wall.

11 You also made a reservoir between the two walls for the water of the Old Pool, but you did not look to the Maker of it, nor did you recognize Him Who planned it long ago.

12 And in that day the Lord God of hosts called you to weeping and mourning, to the shaving off of all your hair [in humiliation] and to the girding with sackcloth.

13 But instead, see the pleasure and mirth, slaying oxen and killing sheep, eating flesh and drinking wine, [with the idea] Let us eat and drink, for tomorrow we die!

14 And the Lord of hosts revealed Himself in my ears [as He said], Surely this unatoned sin shall not be purged from you until [you are punished—and the punishment will be] death, says the Lord God of hosts.

15 Come, go to this [contemptible] steward *and* treasurer, to Shebna, who is over the house [but who is presumptuous enough to be building himself a tomb among those of the mighty, a tomb worthy of a king], and say to him,

16 What business have you here? And whom have you entombed here, that you have the right to hew out for yourself a tomb here? He hews out a sepulcher for himself on the height! He carves out a dwelling for himself in the rock!

17 Behold, the Lord will hurl you away violently, O you strong man; yes, He will take tight hold of you *and* He will surely cover you [with shame].

18 He will surely roll you up in a bundle [Shebna] and toss you like a ball into a large country; there you will die and there will be your splendid chariots, you disgrace to your master's house!

19 And I will thrust you from your office, and from your station will you be pulled down.

20 And in that day I will call My servant, Eliakim son of Hilkiah.

21 And I will clothe him with your robe and will bind your girdle on him and will commit your authority to his hand; he shall be a father to the inhabitants of Jerusalem and to the house of Judah.

22 And the key of the house of David I will lay upon his shoulder; he shall open and no one shall shut, he shall shut and no one shall open.

23 And I will fasten him like a peg *or* nail in a firm place; and he will become a throne of honor *and* glory to his father's house.

24 And they will hang on him the honor *and* the whole weight of [responsibility for] his father's house: the offspring and issue [of the family, high and low], every small vessel, from the cups even to all the flasks *and* big bulging bottles.

25 In that day, says the Lord of hosts, the nail *or* peg that was fastened into the sure place shall give way *and* be moved and be hewn down and fall, and the burden that was upon it shall be cut off; for the Lord has spoken it.

23 THE MOURNFUL, inspired prediction (a burden to be lifted up) concerning Tyre: Wail, you ships of [Tyre returning from trading with] Tarshish, for Tyre is laid waste, so that there is no house, no harbor; from the land of Kittim (Cyprus) they learn of it.

2 Be still, you inhabitants of the coast, you merchants of Sidon, **ʷ*your messengers*** passing over the sea have replenished you [with wealth and industry],

3 And were on great waters. The seed *or* grain of the Shihor, the harvest [due to the overflow] of the Nile River, was [Tyre's] revenue, and she became the merchandise of the nations.

4 Be ashamed, O Sidon [mother-city of Tyre, now a widow bereaved of her children], for the sea has spoken, the stronghold of the sea, saying, I have neither travailed nor brought forth children; I have neither nourished *and* reared young men nor brought up virgins.

w *The Dead Sea Scrolls* so read.

5 When the report comes to Egypt, they will be sorely pained over the report about Tyre.

6 Pass over to Tarshish [to seek safety as exiles]! Wail, you inhabitants of the [Tyre] coast!

7 Is this your jubilant city, whose origin dates back into antiquity, whose own feet are accustomed to carry her far off to settle [daughter cities]?

8 Who has purposed this against Tyre, the bestower of crowns, whose merchants were princes, whose traders were the honored of the earth?

9 The Lord of hosts has purposed it [in accordance with a fixed principle of His government], to defile the pride of all glory and to bring into dishonor *and* contempt all the honored of the earth.

10 Overflow your land like [the overflow of] the Nile River, O Daughter of Tarshish; there is no girdle of restraint [on you] any more [to make you pay tribute or customs or duties to Tyre].

11 He stretched out His hand over the sea, He shook the kingdoms; the Lord has given a command concerning Canaan to destroy her strongholds *and* fortresses [Tyre, Sidon, etc.].

12 And He said, You shall no more exult, you oppressed *and* crushed one, O Virgin Daughter of Sidon. Arise, pass over to Kittim (Cyprus); but even there you will have no rest.

13 Look at the land of the Chaldeans! That people and not the Assyrians designed *and* assigned [Tyre] for the wild beasts *and* those who [previously] dwelt in the wilderness. They set up their siege works, they overthrew its palaces, they made it a ruin!

14 Howl, you ships of Tarshish, for your stronghold [of Tyre] is laid waste [your strength has been destroyed].

15 And in that day Tyre will be in obscurity *and* forgotten for seventy years, according to the days of one dynasty. After the end of seventy years will Tyre sing as a harlot [who has been forgotten but again attracts her lovers].

16 Take a harp, go about the city, forgotten harlot; play skillfully *and* make sweet melody, sing many songs, that you may be remembered.

17 And after the end of seventy years the Lord will remember Tyre; and she will return to her hire and will play the harlot [resume her commerce] with all the kingdoms of the world on the face of the earth.

18 But her gain and her hire [the profits of Tyre's new prosperity] will be ˣdedicated to the Lord [eventually]; it will not be treasured or stored up, for her gain will be used for those who dwell in the presence of the Lord [the ministers], that they may eat sufficiently and have durable *and* stately clothing [suitable for those who minister at God's altar].

24 BEHOLD, THE Lord will make the land *and* the ʸearth empty and make it waste and turn it upside down (twist the face of it) and scatter abroad its inhabitants.

---

x This whole prophecy (Isa. 23:14-18) was literally fulfilled in following centuries. Tyre was destroyed by Nebuchadnezzar in 572 BC and lay desolate for seventy years. The new city built on the island was taken by Alexander the Great in 332 BC (see footnotes on Ezek. 26:4, 14). Eventually the true religion prevailed at Tyre. Jesus visited there (Matt. 15:21) and so did Paul (Acts 21:3-6). Eusebius (Hist. 10:4) says that "when the church of God was founded in Tyre . . . ., much of its wealth was consecrated to God . . . and was presented for the support of the ministry." Jerome, also writing in the fourth century AD, says that the wealth of the churches of Tyre "was not treasured up or hidden but was given to those who dwelt before the Lord."   **y** "The prophet transports himself in spirit to the end of all things. He describes the destruction of the world. He sees, however, that this destruction will be gradually accomplished. He here depicts the first scene: the destruction of all that exists on

2 And it shall be—as [what happens] with the people, so with the priest; as with the servant, so with his master; as with the maid, so with her mistress; as with the buyer, so with the seller; as with the lender, so with the borrower; as with the creditor, so with the debtor.

3 The land *and* the earth shall be utterly laid waste and utterly pillaged; for the Lord has said this.

4 The land *and* the earth mourn and wither, the world languishes and withers, the high ones of the people [and the heavens with the earth] languish.

5 The land *and* the earth also are defiled by their inhabitants, because they have transgressed the laws, disregarded the statutes, and broken the everlasting covenant. [Gen. 9:1-17; Deut. 29:20.]

6 Therefore a curse devours the land *and* the earth, and they who dwell in it suffer the punishment of their guilt. Therefore the inhabitants of the land *and* the earth are scorched *and* parched [under the curse of God's wrath], and few people are left. [Rom. 1:20.]

7 The new wine mourns, the vine languishes; all the merrymakers sigh.

8 The mirth of the timbrels is stilled, the noise of those who rejoice ends, the joy of the lyre is stopped.

9 No more will they drink wine with a song; strong drink will be bitter to those who drink it.

10 The wasted city of emptiness *and* confusion is broken down; every house is shut up so that no one may enter.

11 There is crying in the streets for wine; all joy is darkened, the mirth of the land is banished *and* gone into captivity.

12 In the city is left desolation, and its gate is battered *and* destroyed.

13 For so shall it be in the midst of the earth among the peoples, as the shaking *and* beating of an olive tree, or as the gleaning when the vintage is done [and only a small amount of the fruit remains].

14 [But] these [who have escaped and remain] lift up their voices, they shout; for the majesty of the Lord they cry aloud from the [Mediterranean] Sea.

15 Wherefore glorify the Lord in the east [whether in the region of daybreak's lights and fires, or in the west]; [glorify] the name of the Lord, the God of Israel in the isles *and* coasts of the [Mediterranean] Sea.

16 From the uttermost parts of the earth have we heard songs: Glory to the Righteous One [and to the people of Israel]! But I say, Emaciated I pine away, I pine away. Woe is me! The treacherous dealers deal treacherously! Yes, the treacherous dealers deal very treacherously.

17 Terror and pit [of destruction] and snare are upon you, O inhabitant of the earth!

18 And he who flees at the noise of the terror will fall into the pit; and he who comes up out of the pit will be caught in the snare. For the windows of the heavens are opened [as in the deluge], and the foundations of the earth tremble *and* shake.

19 The earth is utterly broken, the earth is rent asunder, the earth is shaken violently.

20 The earth shall stagger like a drunken man and shall sway to and

the surface of the earth . . . as even now occurs [in limited areas] as a consequence of wars . . . . Jehovah empties, devastates, depopulates the surface of the earth . . . ." (Johan P. Lange, *A Commentary*). "The writer feels that he is living in the last days, and in the universal wretchedness and confusions of the age he seems to discern the 'beginning of sorrows.' His thoughts glide almost imperceptibly from the one point of view to the other, now describing the distress and depression which exist, and now the more terrible visitation which is imminent" (*The Cambridge Bible*).

fro like a hammock; its transgression shall lie heavily upon it, and it shall fall and not rise again.

21 And in that day the Lord will visit *and* punish the host of the high ones on high [the host of heaven in heaven, celestial beings] and the kings of the earth on the earth. [I Cor. 15:25; Eph. 3:10; 6:12.]

22 And they will be gathered together as prisoners are gathered in a pit *or* dungeon; they will be shut up in prison, and after many days they will be visited, inspected, *and* punished *or* ᶻpardoned. [Zech. 9:11, 12; II Pet. 2:4; Jude 6.]

23 Then the moon will be confounded and the sun ashamed, when [they compare their ineffectual fire to the light of] the Lord of hosts, Who will reign on Mount Zion and in Jerusalem, and before His elders will show forth His glory.

25 O LORD, You are my God; I will exalt You, I will praise Your name, for You have done wonderful things, even purposes planned of old [and fulfilled] in faithfulness and truth.

2 For You have made a city a heap, a fortified city a ruin, a palace of aliens without a city [is no more a city]; it will never be rebuilt.

3 Therefore [many] a strong people will glorify You, [many] a city of terrible *and* ruthless nations will [reverently] fear You.

4 For You have been a stronghold for the poor, a stronghold for the needy in his distress, a shelter from the storm, a shade from the heat; for the blast of the ruthless ones is like a rainstorm against a wall.

5 As the heat in a dry land [is reduced by the shadow of a cloud, so] You will bring down the noise of aliens [exultant over their enemies]; and as the heat is brought low by the shadow of a cloud, so the song of the ruthless ones is brought low.

6 And on this Mount [Zion] shall the Lord of hosts make for all peoples a feast of rich things [symbolic of His coronation festival inaugurating the reign of the Lord on earth, in the wake of a background of gloom, judgment, and terror], a feast of wines on the lees—of fat things full of marrow, of wines on the lees well refined.

7 And He will destroy on this mountain the covering of the face that is cast over the heads of all peoples [in mourning], and the veil [of profound wretchedness] that is woven *and* spread over all nations.

8 He will swallow up death [in victory; He will abolish death forever]. And the Lord God will wipe away tears from all faces; and the reproach of His people He will take away from off all the earth; for the Lord has spoken it. [I Cor. 15:26, 54; II Tim. 1:10.]

9 It shall be said in that day, Behold our God upon Whom we have waited *and* hoped, that He might save us! This is the Lord, we have waited for Him; we will be glad and rejoice in His salvation.

10 For the hand of the Lord shall rest

speak the Word

God, I declare that You are my God and I exalt You. I praise Your name because You have done wonderful things planned from long ago for me. You continue to fulfill those purposes in faithfulness and truth in my life.

ADAPTED FROM ISAIAH 25:1

---

z The Hebrew word used here may mean **visit in mercy** as well as **visit in punishment**, but the context does not seem to indicate the possibility of mercy in this case.

on this Mount [Zion], and Moab shall be threshed *and* trodden down in his place as straw is trodden down in the [filthy] water of a [primitive] cesspit.
11 And though [Moab] stretches forth his hands in the midst of [the filthy water] as a swimmer stretches out his hands to swim, the Lord will bring down [Moab's] pride in spite of the skillfulness of his hands *and* together with the spoils of his hands.
12 And the high fortifications of your walls [the Lord] will bring down, lay low, and bring to the ground, even to the dust.

26 IN THAT day shall this song be sung in the land of Judah: ªWe have a strong city; [the Lord] sets up salvation as walls and bulwarks.
2 Open the gates, that the [uncompromisingly] righteous nation which keeps her faith *and* her troth [with God] may enter in.
3 You will guard him *and* keep him in perfect *and* constant peace whose mind [both its inclination and its character] is stayed on You, because he commits himself to You, leans on You, *and* hopes confidently in You.

putting the Word to work

Isaiah 26:3 promises that God will keep us in perfect and constant peace when our minds are stayed on Him. Are you anxious or worried today? Then turn your thoughts toward Him so that you will experience His perfect peace.

life point

Peace of mind must precede peace in every other area of our lives. Isaiah 26:3 promises perfect peace to those who keep their minds on God. When we allow our minds to wander and when we think too much about everything we do, we push ourselves out of peace and into turmoil; when we think about the future and the responsibilities we will have, we can be overwhelmed. This kind of thinking is called anxiety. Likewise, we grow anxious and lose our peace when we spend today trying to figure out tomorrow or when we try to live tomorrow in our minds today.

We will never enjoy the rich and fruitful lives God intends for us unless we learn to discipline our thoughts and resist anxiety by keeping our minds on God. I often say: "Where the mind goes, the man follows." Let your mind lead you into peace!

4 So trust in the Lord (commit yourself to Him, lean on Him, hope confidently in Him) forever; for the Lord God is an everlasting Rock [the Rock of Ages].
5 For He has brought down the inhabitants of the height, the lofty city; He lays it low, lays it low to the ground; He brings it even to the dust.
6 The foot has trampled it down—even the feet of the poor, and the steps of the needy.

speak the Word

God, I trust You. I lean on You and hope confidently in You. You are my everlasting Rock!
ADAPTED FROM Isaiah 26:4

a *The Dead Sea Scrolls* read, "You [Lord] have been to me a strong wall."

7 The way of the [consistently] righteous (those living in moral and spiritual rectitude in every area and relationship of their lives) is level *and* straight; You, O [Lord], Who are upright, direct aright *and* make level the path of the [uncompromisingly] just *and* righteous.

8 Yes, in the path of Your judgments, O Lord, we wait [expectantly] for You; our heartfelt desire is for Your name and for the remembrance of You.

9 My soul yearns for You [O Lord] in the night, yes, my spirit within me seeks You earnestly; for [only] when Your judgments are in the earth will the inhabitants of the world learn righteousness (uprightness and right standing with God).

10 Though favor is shown to the wicked, yet they do not learn righteousness; in the land of uprightness they deal perversely and refuse to see the majesty of the Lord.

11 Though Your hand is lifted high to strike, Lord, they do not see it. Let them see Your zeal for Your people and be ashamed; yes, let the fire reserved for Your enemies consume them.

12 Lord, You will ordain peace (God's favor and blessings, both temporal and spiritual) for us, for You have also wrought in us *and* for us all our works.

13 O Lord, our God, other masters besides You have ruled over us, but we will acknowledge *and* mention Your name only.

14 They [the former tyrant masters] are dead, they shall not live *and* reappear; they are powerless ghosts, they shall not rise *and* come back. Therefore You have visited and made an end of them and caused every memory of them [every trace of their supremacy] to perish.

15 You have increased the nation, O Lord; You have increased the nation.

You are glorified; You have enlarged all the borders of the land.

16 Lord, when they were in trouble *and* distress, they sought *and* visited You; they poured out a prayerful whisper when Your chastening was upon them.

17 As a woman with child drawing near the time of her delivery is in pain *and* writhes and cries out in her pangs, so we have been before You (at Your presence), O Lord.

18 We have been with child, we have been writhing *and* in pain; we have, as it were, brought forth [only] wind. We have not wrought any deliverance in the earth, and the inhabitants of the world [of Israel] have not yet been born.

19 Your dead shall live [O Lord]; the bodies of our dead [saints] shall rise. You who dwell in the dust, awake and sing for joy! For Your dew [O Lord] is a dew of [sparkling] light [heavenly, supernatural dew]; and the earth shall cast forth the dead [to life again; for on the land of the shades of the dead You will let Your dew fall]. [Ezek. 37:11-12.]

20 Come, my people, enter your chambers and shut your doors behind you; hide yourselves for a little while until the [Lord's] wrath is past.

21 For behold, the Lord is coming out of His place [heaven] to punish the inhabitants of the earth for their iniquity; the earth also will disclose the blood shed upon her and will no longer cover her slain *and* conceal her guilt.

27 IN THAT day [the Lord will deliver Israel from her enemies and also from the rebel powers of evil and darkness] His sharp *and* unrelenting, great, and strong sword will visit *and* punish Leviathan the swiftly fleeing serpent, Leviathan the twisting *and* winding serpent; and He will slay the monster that is in the sea.

2 In that day [it will be said of the redeemed nation of Israel], A vineyard beloved *and* lovely; sing a responsive song to it *and* about it!

3 I, the Lord, am its Keeper; I water it every moment; lest anyone harm it, I guard *and* keep it night and day.

4 Wrath is not in Me. Would that the briers *and* thorns [the wicked internal foe] were lined up against Me in battle! I would stride in against them; I would burn them up together.

5 Or else [if all Israel would escape being burned up together there is but one alternative], let them take hold of My strength *and* make complete surrender to My protection, that they may make peace with Me! Yes, let them make peace with Me!

6 In the days *and* generations to come Jacob shall take root; Israel shall blossom and send forth shoots and fill the whole world with fruit [of the knowledge of the true God]. [Hos. 14:1-6; Rom. 11:12.]

7 Has [the Lord] smitten [Israel] as He smote those who smote them? Or have [the Israelites] been slain as their slayers were slain?

8 By driving them out of Canaan, by exile, You contended with them in a measure [O Lord]—He removed them with His rough blast as in the day of the east wind.

9 Only on this condition shall the iniquity of Jacob (Israel) be forgiven *and* purged, and this shall be the full fruit [God requires] for taking away his sin: that [Israel] should make all the stones of the [idol] altars like chalk stones crushed to pieces, so that the Asherim and the sun-images shall not remain standing *or* rise again.

10 For the fortified city is solitary, a habitation deserted and forsaken like the wilderness; there the calf grazes, and there he lies down; he strips its branches *and* eats its twigs.

11 When its boughs are withered *and* dry, they are broken off; the women come *and* set them afire. For they are a people of no understanding *or* discernment—[b]*witless folk*; therefore He Who made them will not have compassion on them, and He Who formed them will show them no favor.

12 And it shall be in that day that the Lord will thresh out His grain from the flood of the River [Euphrates] to the Brook of Egypt, and you will be gathered one by one *and* one to another, O children of Israel!

13 And it shall be in that day that a great trumpet will be blown; and they will come who were lost *and* ready to perish in the land of Assyria and those who were driven out to the land of Egypt, and they will worship the Lord on the holy mountain at Jerusalem. [Zech. 14:16; Matt. 24:31; Rev. 11:15.]

28 WOE TO [Samaria] the crown of pride of the drunkards of Ephraim [the ten tribes], and to the fading flower of its glorious beauty, which is on the head of the rich valley of those overcome *and* smitten down with wine!

2 Behold, the Lord has a strong and mighty one [the Assyrian]; like a tempest of hail, a destroying storm, like a flood of mighty overflowing waters, he will cast it down to the earth with violent hand.

3 With [alien] feet [Samaria] the proud crown of the drunkards of Ephraim will be trodden down.

4 And the fading flower of its glorious beauty, which is on the head of the rich valley, will be like the early fig before the fruit harvest, which, when anyone sees it, he snatches and eats it up greedily at once. [So in an amazingly short time will the Assyrians devour Samaria, Israel's capital.]

b *The Dead Sea Scrolls* so read.

5 [But] in that [future ᶜMessianic] day the Lord of hosts shall become a crown of glory and a diadem of beauty to the [converted] remnant of His people,

6 And a spirit of justice to him who sits in judgment *and* administers the law, and strength to those who turn back the battle at the gate.

7 But even these reel from wine and stagger from strong drink: the priest and the prophet reel from strong drink; they are confused from wine, they stagger *and* are gone astray through strong drink; they err in vision, they stumble when pronouncing judgment.

8 For all the tables are full of filthy vomit, so that there is no place that is clean.

9 To whom will He teach knowledge? [Ask the drunkards.] And whom will He make to understand the message? Those who are babies, just weaned from the milk and taken from the breasts? [Is that what He thinks we are?]

10 For it is [His prophets repeating over and over]: precept upon precept, precept upon precept, rule upon rule, rule upon rule; here a little, there a little.

11 No, but [the Lord will teach the rebels in a more humiliating way] by men with stammering lips and another tongue will He speak to this people [says Isaiah, and teach them His lessons].

12 To these [complaining Jews the Lord] had said, This is the true rest [the way to true comfort and happiness] that you shall give to the weary, and, This is the [true] refreshing—yet they would not listen [to His teaching].

13 Therefore the word of the Lord will be to them [merely monotonous repeatings of]: precept upon precept, precept upon precept, rule upon rule, rule upon rule; here a little, there a little—that they may go and fall backward, and be broken and snared and taken.

14 Therefore hear the word of the Lord, you scoffers who rule this people in Jerusalem!

15 Because you have said, We have made a covenant with death, and with Sheol (the place of the dead) we have an agreement—when the overflowing scourge passes through, it will not come to us, for we have made lies our refuge, and in falsehood we have taken shelter.

16 Therefore thus says the Lord God, Behold, I am laying in Zion for a foundation a Stone, a tested Stone, a precious Cornerstone of sure foundation; he who believes (trusts in, relies on, and adheres to that Stone) will not ᵈ*be ashamed or* give way *or* hasten away [in sudden panic]. [Ps. 118:22; Matt. 21:42; Acts 4:11; Rom. 9:33; Eph. 2:20; I Pet. 2:4-6.]

17 I will make justice the measuring line and righteousness the plummet; and hail will sweep away the refuge of lies, and waters will overwhelm the hiding place (the shelter).

18 And your covenant with death shall be annulled, and your agreement with Sheol (the place of the dead) shall not stand; when the overwhelming scourge passes through, then you will be trodden down by it.

19 As often as it passes through, it [the enemy's scourge] will take you; for morning by morning will it pass through, by day and by night. And it will be utter terror merely to hear *and* comprehend the report *and* the message of it [but only hard treatment and

---

c *The Bible in Aramaic: The Latter Prophets According to Targum Jonathan* reads, "In that time Messiah, the Lord of hosts, shall be a crown of joy and a diadem of praise to the residue of His people." Commentators generally agree that this is the meaning of the passage. d *The Septuagint* (Greek translation of the Old Testament) reads "be ashamed."

dispersion will make you understand God's instruction].

20 For [they will find that] the bed is too short for a man to stretch himself on and the covering too narrow for him to wrap himself in. [All their sources of confidence will fail them.]

21 For the Lord will rise up as on Mount Perazim, He will be wrathful as in the Valley of Gibeon, that He may do His work, His strange work, and bring to pass His act, His strange act. [II Sam. 5:20; I Chron. 14:16.]

22 Now therefore do not be scoffers, lest the bands which bind you be made strong; for a decree of destruction have I heard from the Lord God of hosts upon the whole land *and* the whole earth.

23 Give ear and hear my [Isaiah's] voice; listen and hear my words.

24 Does he who plows for sowing plow continually? Does he continue to plow and harrow the ground after it is smooth?

25 When he has leveled its surface, does he not cast abroad [the seed of] dill *or* fennel and scatter cummin [a seasoning], and put the wheat in rows, and barley in its intended place, and spelt [an inferior kind of wheat] as the border?

26 [And he trains each of them correctly] for his God instructs him correctly and teaches him.

27 For dill is not threshed with a sharp threshing instrument, nor is a cartwheel rolled over cummin; but dill is beaten off with a staff, and cummin with a rod [by hand].

28 Does one crush bread grain? No, he does not thresh it continuously. But when he has driven his cartwheel and his horses over it, he scatters it

[tossing it up to the wind] without having crushed it.

29 This also comes from the Lord of hosts, Who is wonderful in counsel [and] excellent in wisdom *and* effectual working.

29 WOE TO Ariel [Jerusalem], to Ariel, the city where David encamped! Add yet another year; let the feasts run their round [but only one year more].

2 Then will I distress Ariel; and there shall be mourning and lamentation, yet she shall be to Me like an Ariel [an altar hearth, a hearth of burning, the altar of God].

3 And I will encamp against you round about; and I will hem you in with siege works and I will set up fortifications against you.

4 And you shall be laid low [Jerusalem], speaking from beneath the ground, and your speech shall come humbly from the dust. And your voice shall be like that of a ghost [produced by a medium] coming from the earth, and your speech shall whisper *and* squeak as it chatters from the dust.

5 But the multitude of your [enemy] strangers that assail you shall be like small dust, and the multitude of the ruthless *and* terrible ones like chaff that blows away. And in an instant, suddenly,

6 You shall be visited *and* delivered by the Lord of hosts with thunder and earthquake and great noise, with whirlwind and tempest and the flame of a devouring fire.

7 And the multitude of all the nations that fight against Ariel [Jerusalem], even all that fight against her

speak the Word

God, I declare that You are wonderful in counsel and excellent in wisdom. You are working effectively in my life!

ADAPTED FROM ISAIAH **28:29**

and her stronghold and that distress her, shall be as a dream, a vision of the night.

8 It shall be as when a hungry man dreams that he is eating, but he wakens with his craving not satisfied; or as when a thirsty man dreams that he is drinking, but he wakens and is faint, and his thirst is not quenched. So shall the multitude of all the nations be that fight against Mount Zion.

9 Stop and wonder [at this prophecy, if you choose, whether you understand it or not; soon you will witness the actual event] and be confounded [reluctantly]! Blind yourselves [now, if you choose; take your pleasure] and then be blinded [at the actual occurrence]. They are drunk, but not from wine; they stagger, but not from strong drink [but from spiritual stupor].

10 For the Lord has poured out on you the spirit of deep sleep. And He has closed your eyes, the prophets; and your heads, the seers, He has covered *and* muffled.

11 And the vision of all this has become for you like the words of a book that is sealed. When men give it to one who can read, saying, Read this, I pray you, he says, I cannot, for it is sealed.

12 And when the book is given to him who is not learned, saying, Read this, I pray you, he says, I cannot read.

13 And the Lord said, Forasmuch as this people draw near Me with their mouth and honor Me with their lips but remove their hearts *and* minds far from Me, and their fear *and* reverence for Me are a commandment of men that is learned by repetition [without any thought as to the meaning],

14 Therefore, behold! I will again do marvelous things with this people, marvelous and astonishing things; and the wisdom of their wise men will perish, and the understanding of their discerning men will vanish *or* be hidden.

15 Woe to those who [seek to] hide deep from the Lord their counsel, whose deeds are in the dark, and who say, Who sees us? Who knows us?

16 [Oh, your perversity!] You turn things upside down! Shall the potter be considered of no more account than the clay? Shall the thing that is made say of its maker, He did not make me; or the thing that is formed say of him who formed it, He has no understanding?

17 Is it not yet a very little while until Lebanon shall be turned into a fruitful field and the fruitful field esteemed as a forest?

18 And in that day shall the deaf hear the words of the book, and out of obscurity *and* gloom and darkness the eyes of the blind shall see.

19 The meek also shall increase their joy in the Lord, and the poor among men shall rejoice *and* exult in the Holy One of Israel.

20 For the terrible one [the Assyrian enemy] shall come to nought, and the scoffer shall cease, and all those who watch for iniquity [as an occasion for accusation] shall be cut off—

21 Those who make a man an offender *and* bring condemnation upon him with a word, and lay a trap for him who upholds justice at the city gate, and thrust aside the innocent *and* truly righteous with an empty plea.

22 Therefore thus says the Lord, Who redeemed Abraham [out of Ur and idolatry], concerning the house of Jacob: Jacob shall not then be ashamed; not then shall his face become pale [with fear and disappointment because of his children's degeneracy].

23 For when he sees his children [walking in the way of piety and virtue], the work of My hands in his midst, they will revere My name; they will revere the Holy One of Jacob and reverently fear the God of Israel.

24 Those who err in spirit will come to understanding, and those who murmur [discontentedly] will accept instruction.

30 WOE TO the rebellious children, says the Lord, who take counsel *and* carry out a plan, but not Mine, and who make a league *and* pour out a drink offering, but not of My Spirit, thus adding sin to sin;

2 Who set out to go down into Egypt, and have not asked Me—to flee to the stronghold of Pharaoh *and* to strengthen themselves in his strength and to trust in the shadow of Egypt!

life point

Isaiah 30:1, 2 is another of those "woe" passages we see from time to time in the Bible. In it the Lord pronounces a curse upon those rebellious children who turn from trusting in Him to take counsel of themselves, carry out their own plans, and flee to "the shadow of Egypt," rather than resting under the "shadow of the Almighty."

In this case, fleeing to the "shadow of Egypt" refers to turning to the arm of the flesh rather than leaning on the arm of the Lord. In other words, we are not to trust in others, in ourselves, or in the world, but only in the Lord. We are to acknowledge Him in all our ways so that He may direct our paths. We are to find our strength in Him alone.

3 Therefore shall the strength *and* protection of Pharaoh turn to your shame, and the refuge in the shadow of Egypt be to your humiliation *and* confusion.

4 For though [Pharaoh's] officials

life point

In Isaiah 30:3–7 the Lord continues to warn against relying on the strength of Egypt—the superpower of that day. I believe the Lord is saying to us, "Do not run away from trusting in Me to trusting in your own plans and devices. They will not work, and you will only end up humiliated and confused. Before you do anything, check with Me to see if it is what you should be doing. Do not look to the world for answers, because it has none to give. The help it has to offer is absolutely worthless. Salvation and deliverance are with Me, and Me alone."

are at Zoan and his ambassadors arrive at Hanes [in Egypt],

5 Yet will all be ashamed because of a people [the Egyptians] who cannot profit them, who are not a help or benefit, but a shame and disgrace.

6 A mournful, inspired prediction (a burden to be lifted up) concerning the beasts of the South (the Negeb): Oh, the heavy burden, the load of treasures going to Egypt! Through a land of trouble and anguish, in which are lioness and lion, viper and fiery flying serpent, they carry their riches upon the shoulders of young donkeys, and their treasures upon the humps of camels, to a people that will not *and* cannot profit them.

7 For Egypt's help is worthless and toward no purpose. Therefore I have called her Rahab Who Sits Still.

8 Now, go, write it before them on a tablet and inscribe it in a book, that it may be as a witness for the time to come forevermore.

9 For this is a rebellious people, faithless *and* lying sons, children who will not hear the law *and* instruction of the Lord;

10 Who [virtually] say to the seers [by their conduct], See not! and to the

prophets, Prophesy not to us what is right! Speak to us smooth things, prophesy deceitful illusions.

11 Get out of the true way, turn aside out of the path, cease holding up before us the Holy One of Israel.

12 Therefore thus says the Holy One of Israel: Because you despise *and* spurn this [My] word and trust in cunning *and* oppression, in crookedness *and* perverseness, and rely on them,

13 Therefore this iniquity *and* guilt will be to you like a broken section of a high wall, bulging out and ready [at some distant day] to fall, whose crash will [then] come suddenly *and* swiftly, in an instant.

14 And he shall break it as a potter's

from brokenness to blessing

When you and I make our own plans or run to other people instead of trusting in the Lord, we leave a weak spot in our wall of divine protection. At a time when we least expect it, the enemy will break through that weak spot. When that happens, we will indeed be like the "broken section of a high wall" mentioned in Isaiah 30:13.

God does not want us to have weak spots in our lives. He wants us to rely on Him and be obedient to Him so our "walls" will remain strong and thick and our lives will be blessed and full.

The more we depend on God, the more He can do through us. But sometimes we go through brokenness before we enter His blessings.

Once, for about a year and a half, I thought I might be going mad. All day long I walked around in my house, praying, "Help me, Lord!" I did not even know what kind of help I needed, or why I needed it. Now as I look back on that experience, I know what was happening. God was breaking off my spirit of independence, and He was bringing me to the point where I knew I could do nothing apart from Him.

I remember one night as I was getting ready to go to sleep, I picked up a little book and started reading it. Suddenly I had a visitation from God. For about forty-five minutes I sat there on the edge of my bed and wept. Finally, the Lord spoke to me and said, "Anything good you do has nothing to do with you. I am the One Who is good. When you see yourself doing anything good, it is only because I have wrestled with you to get your flesh under subjection long enough to allow My glory to shine through it."

Sometimes before God can promote us, He has to remind us of our place. In my own case, my ministry was just about to experience a sudden growth spurt. God was preparing me in advance by telling me, "I'm going to do something marvelous in your life and ministry, and when it happens you must remember that it is I and not you who is bringing it to pass."

God was teaching me what He is teaching all of us today: He is the answer to *all* of our problems.

vessel is broken, breaking it in pieces without sparing so that there cannot be found among its pieces one large enough to carry coals of fire from the hearth or to dip water out of the cistern.

15 For thus said the Lord God, the Holy One of Israel: In returning [to Me] and resting [in Me] you shall be saved; in quietness and in [trusting] confidence shall be your strength. But you would not,

16 And you said, No! We will speed [our own course] on horses! Therefore you will speed [in flight from your enemies]! You said, We will ride upon swift steeds [doing our own way]! Therefore will they who pursue you be swift, [so swift that]

17 One thousand of you will flee at the threat of one of them; at the threat of five you will flee till you are left like a beacon *or* a flagpole on the top of a mountain, and like a signal on a hill.

18 And therefore the Lord [earnestly] waits [expecting, looking, and longing] to be gracious to you; and therefore He lifts Himself up, that He may have mercy on you *and* show loving-kindness to you. For the Lord is a God of justice. Blessed (happy, fortunate, to be envied) are all those who [earnestly] wait for Him, who expect *and* look *and* long for Him [for His victory, His favor, His love, His peace, His joy, and His matchless, unbroken companionship]! [John 14:3, 27; II Cor. 12:9; Heb. 12:2; I John 3:16; Rev. 3:5.]

19 O people who dwell in Zion at Jerusalem, you will weep no more. He will surely be gracious to you at the sound of your cry; when He hears it, He will answer you.

speak the Word

life point

Isaiah 30:18 is one of my favorite scriptures. If you will meditate on it, it will begin to bring you great hope.

In this verse, God says that He is actively looking for someone to be good to. In fact, He *waits* and *expects* and *looks* and *longs* to be gracious to you! But He cannot pour out His goodness on anyone who has a negative attitude. He is looking for someone who is expecting His goodness, someone who is on the lookout all the time, someone who is full of faith and trust, someone who is eagerly anticipating His gracious gifts. He wants to be good to you, so be expecting an outpouring of His goodness!

20 And though the Lord gives you the bread of adversity and the water of affliction, yet your Teacher will not hide Himself any more, but your eyes will constantly behold your Teacher.

21 And your ears will hear a word behind you, saying, This is the way; walk in it, when you turn to the right hand and when you turn to the left.

22 Then you will defile your carved images overlaid with silver and your molten images plated with gold; you will cast them away as a filthy bloodstained cloth, and you will say to them, Be gone!

23 Then will He give you rain for the seed with which you sow the soil, and bread grain from the produce of the ground, and it will be rich and plentiful. In that day your cattle will feed in large pastures.

24 The oxen likewise and the young

Thank You, God, for saving me as I return to and rest in You. In quietness and confidence, You give me strength.
ADAPTED FROM ISAIAH **30:15**

this is the way

No matter what has happened to you in your lifetime—even if you have been abandoned by your spouse or abused by your parents or hurt by your children or others—if you will stay on the narrow path as God directs you and leave all your excess fleshly baggage behind, you will find the peace, joy, and fulfillment you seek. As you walk through this process, you can find comfort in God's promise from Isaiah 30:21 to guide you.

Jesus is the Way, and He has shown us the way in which we are to walk. The Lord has sent upon us His Holy Spirit to lead and guide us in the way we are to go, the narrow way that leads to life and not the broad way that leads to destruction.

Whatever happens, we must keep walking in the ways of the Lord. Galatians 6:9 encourages us: "And let us not lose heart and grow weary and faint in acting nobly and doing right, for in due time and at the appointed season we shall reap, if we do not loosen and relax our courage and faint." The Bible does not promise that when we do right we will reap the rewards immediately. But it does assure us that if we keep doing right, eventually we will be rewarded.

God says that as long as the earth remains, there will be "seedtime and harvest" (see Genesis 8:22). We might paraphrase it like this: "As long as the earth remains, there will be *seed*, *time*, and *harvest*." When we walk in God's path, we must be patient like the farmer, who plants the seed and expectantly waits for the harvest. He looks forward to reaping the harvest, but he knows that time will elapse between seed planting and harvest. He does not allow that God-ordained process to frustrate him.

God promises in Isaiah 30:21 that "your ears will hear a word behind you, saying, This is the way; walk in it." If you continue to walk in the way the Lord has prescribed for you in His Word and by His Spirit, you will enjoy great blessing both in this life and in eternity.

So keep walking the narrow path that leads to life—life in all its fullness and abundance!

donkeys that till the ground will eat savory *and* salted fodder, which has been winnowed with shovel and with fork.
25 And upon every high mountain and upon every high hill there will be brooks and streams of water in the day of the great slaughter [the day of the Lord], when the towers fall [and all His enemies are destroyed].

26 Moreover, the light of the moon will be like the light of the sun, and the light of the sun will be sevenfold, like the light of seven days [concentrated in one], in the day that the Lord binds up the hurt of His people, and heals their wound [inflicted by Him because of their sins].
27 Behold, the ᵉName of the Lord comes from afar, burning with His

e The revelation of the power and glory of God.

anger, and in thick, rising smoke. His lips are full of indignation, and His tongue is like a consuming fire.

28 And His breath is like an overflowing stream that reaches even to the neck, to sift the nations with the sieve of destruction; and a bridle that causes them to err will be in the jaws of the people.

29 You shall have a song as in the night when a holy feast is kept, and gladness of heart as when one marches in procession with a flute to go to the temple on the mountain of the Lord, to the Rock of Israel.

30 And the Lord shall cause His glorious voice to be heard and the descending blow of His arm to be seen, coming down with indignant anger and with the flame of a devouring fire, amid crashing blast *and* cloudburst, tempest, and hailstones.

31 At the voice of the Lord the Assyrians will be stricken with dismay *and* terror, when He smites them with His rod.

32 And every passing stroke of the staff of punishment *and* doom which the Lord lays upon them shall be to the sound of [Israel's] timbrels and lyres, when in battle He attacks [Assyria] with swinging *and* menacing arms.

33 For Topheth [a place of burning and abomination] has already been laid out *and* long ago prepared; yes, for the [Assyrian] king *and* [the god] Molech it has been made ready, its pyre made deep *and* large, with fire and much wood; the breath of the Lord, like a stream of brimstone, kindles it. [Jer. 7:31, 32; Matt. 5:22; 25:41.]

31 WOE TO those who go down to Egypt for help, who rely on horses and trust in chariots because they are many and in horsemen because they

are very strong, but they look not to the Holy One of Israel, nor seek *and* consult the Lord!

2 And yet He is wise and brings calamity and does not retract His words; He will arise against the house (the whole race) of evildoers and against the helpers of those who work iniquity.

3 Now the Egyptians are men and not God, and their horses are flesh and not spirit; and when the Lord stretches out His hand, both [Egypt] who helps will stumble, and [Judah] who is helped will fall, and they will all perish *and* be consumed together.

4 For the Lord has said to me, As the lion or the young lion growls over his prey—and though a large band of shepherds is called out against him, he will not be terrified at their voice or daunted at their noise—so the Lord of hosts will come down to fight upon Mount Zion and upon its hills.

5 Like birds hovering, so will the Lord of hosts defend Jerusalem; He will protect and deliver it, He will pass over *and* spare and preserve it.

6 Return, O children of Israel, to Him against Whom you have so deeply plunged into revolt.

7 For in that day every man of you will cast away [in contempt and disgust] his idols of silver and his idols of gold, which your own hands have sinfully made for you.

8 Then the Assyrian shall fall by a sword not of man; and a sword, not of men [but of God], shall devour him. And he shall flee from the sword, and his young men shall be subjected to forced labor.

9 [In his flight] he shall pass beyond his rock [refuge and stronghold] because of terror; even his officers shall desert the standard in fear *and* panic, says the Lord, Whose fire is in Zion and Whose furnace is in Jerusalem.

32

BEHOLD, A [f]King will reign in righteousness, and princes will rule with justice.

2 And each one of them shall be like a hiding place from the wind and a shelter from the storm, like streams of water in a dry place, like the shade of a great rock in a weary land [to those who turn to them].

3 Then the eyes of those who see will not be closed or dimmed, and the ears of those who hear will listen.

4 And the mind of the rash will understand knowledge and have good judgment, and the tongue of the stammerers will speak readily and plainly.

5 The fool (the unbeliever and the ungodly) will no more be called noble, nor the crafty and greedy [for gain] said to be bountiful and princely.

6 For the fool speaks folly and his mind plans iniquity: practicing profane ungodliness and speaking error concerning the Lord, leaving the craving of the hungry unsatisfied and causing the drink of the thirsty to fail.

7 The instruments and methods of the fraudulent and greedy [for gain] are evil; he devises wicked devices to ruin the poor and the lowly with lying words, even when the plea of the needy is just and right.

8 But the noble, openhearted, and liberal man devises noble things; and he stands for what is noble, open-hearted, and generous.

9 Rise up, you women who are at ease! Hear my [Isaiah's] voice, you confident and careless daughters! Listen to what I am saying!

10 In little more than a year you will be shaken with anxiety, you careless and complacent women; for the vintage will fail, and the ingathering will not come.

11 Tremble, you women who are at ease! Shudder with fear, you complacent ones! Strip yourselves bare and gird sackcloth upon your loins [in grief]!

12 They shall beat upon their breasts for the pleasant fields, for the fruitful vine,

13 For the land of my people growing over with thorns and briers—yes, for all the houses of joy in the joyous city.

14 For the palace shall be forsaken, the populous city shall be deserted; the hill and the watchtower shall become dens [for wild animals] endlessly, a joy for wild donkeys, a pasture for flocks,

15 Until the Spirit is poured upon us from on high, and the wilderness becomes a fruitful field, and the fruitful field is valued as a forest. [Ps. 104:30; Ezek. 36:26, 27; 39:29; Zech. 12:10.]

16 Then justice will dwell in the wilderness, and righteousness (moral and spiritual rectitude in every area and relation) will abide in the fruitful field.

17 And the effect of righteousness will be peace [internal and external], and the result of righteousness will be quietness and confident trust forever.

18 My people shall dwell in a peaceable habitation, in safe dwellings, and in quiet resting-places.

19 But it [the wrath of the Lord] shall

speak the Word

Thank You, God, that the effect of righteousness is internal and external peace in my life.
ADAPTED FROM ISAIAH **32:17**

f The Messianic age is again in view (Isa. 9:7; 11:4; 16:5; 33:17).

hail, coming down overpoweringly on the forest [the army of the Assyrians], and the capital ^gcity shall be utterly humbled *and* laid prostrate.

20 Happy *and* fortunate are you who cast your seed upon all waters [when the river overflows its banks; for the seed will sink into the mud and when the waters subside, the plant will spring up; you will find it after many days and reap an abundant harvest], you who safely send forth the ox and the donkey [to range freely].

33 WOE TO you, O destroyer, you who were not yourself destroyed, who deal treacherously though they [your victims] did not deal treacherously with you! When you have ceased to destroy, you will be destroyed; and when you have stopped dealing treacherously, they will deal treacherously with you.

2 O Lord, be gracious to us; we have waited [expectantly] for You. Be the arm [of Your servants—their strength and defense] every morning, our salvation in the time of trouble.

3 At the noise of the tumult [caused by Your voice at which the enemy is overthrown], the peoples flee; at the lifting up of Yourself, nations are scattered.

4 And the spoil [of the Assyrians] is gathered [by the inhabitants of Jerusalem] as the caterpillar gathers; as locusts leap *and* run to and fro, so [the Jews spoil the Assyrians' forsaken camp as they] leap upon it.

5 The Lord is exalted, for He dwells on high; He will fill Zion with justice and righteousness (moral and spiritual rectitude in every area and relation).

6 And there shall be stability in your times, an abundance of salvation, wisdom, and knowledge; the reverent fear *and* worship of the Lord is your treasure *and* His.

7 Behold, their valiant ones cry without; the ambassadors of peace weep bitterly.

8 The highways lie waste, the wayfaring man ceases. The enemy has broken the covenant, he has despised the cities *and* ^h*the witnesses*, he regards no man.

9 The land mourns and languishes, Lebanon is confounded and [its luxuriant verdure] withers away; Sharon [a fertile pasture region south of Mount Carmel] is like a desert, and Bashan [a broad, fertile plateau east of the Jordan River] and [Mount] Carmel shake off their leaves.

10 Now will I arise, says the Lord. Now will I lift up Myself; now will I be exalted.

11 You conceive chaff, you bring forth stubble; your breath is a fire that consumes you.

12 And the people will be burned as if to lime, like thorns cut down that are burned in the fire.

13 Hear, you who are far off [says the Lord], what I have done; and you who are near, acknowledge My might!

14 The sinners in Zion are afraid; trembling seizes the godless ones. [They cry] Who among us can dwell with that devouring fire? Who among

speak the Word

Thank You, God, for the stability You bring to my life. Thank You for the abundance of wisdom and knowledge You give me. I treasure You.
ADAPTED FROM ISAIAH **33:6**

g Authorities find it impossible to be sure whether the "city" here means Nineveh, Jerusalem, or even Babylon. Some say it could be a composite of all the cities opposed to God. h *The Dead Sea Scrolls* read "the witnesses."

us can dwell with those everlasting burnings?

15 He who walks righteously and speaks uprightly, who despises gain from fraud *and* from oppression, who shakes his hand free from the taking of bribes, who stops his ears from hearing of bloodshed and shuts his eyes to avoid looking upon evil.

16 [Such a man] will dwell on the heights; his place of defense will be the fortresses of rocks; his bread will be given him; water for him will be sure.

17 Your eyes will see the King in His beauty; [your eyes] will behold a land of wide distances that stretches afar.

18 Your mind will meditate on the terror: [asking] Where is he who counted? Where is he who weighed the tribute? Where is he who counted the towers?

19 You will see no more the fierce *and* insolent people, a people of a speech too deep *and* obscure to be comprehended, of a strange *and* stammering tongue that you cannot understand.

20 Look upon Zion, the city of our set feasts *and* solemnities! Your eyes shall see Jerusalem, a quiet habitation, a tent that shall not be taken down; not one of its stakes shall ever be pulled up, neither shall any of its cords be broken.

21 But there the Lord will be for us in majesty *and* splendor a place of broad rivers and streams, where no oar-propelled boat can go, and no mighty *and* stately ship can pass.

22 For the Lord is our Judge, the Lord is our Lawgiver, the Lord is our King; He will save us. [Isa. 2:3-4; 11:4; 32:1; James 4:12.]

23 Your hoisting ropes hang loose; they cannot strengthen *and* hold firm the foot of their mast or keep the sail spread out. Then will prey and spoil in abundance be divided; even the lame will take the prey.

24 And no inhabitant [of Zion] will say, I am sick; the people who dwell there will be forgiven their iniquity *and* guilt.

34 COME NEAR, you nations, to hear; and hearken, you peoples! Let the earth hear, and all that is in it; the world, and all things that come forth from it.

2 For the Lord is indignant against all nations, and His wrath is against all their host. He has utterly doomed them, He has given them over to slaughter.

3 Their slain also shall be cast out, and the stench of their dead bodies shall rise, and the mountains shall flow with their blood.

4 All the host of the heavens shall be dissolved *and* crumble away, and the skies shall be rolled together like a scroll; and all their host [the stars and the planets] shall drop like a faded leaf from the vine, and like a withered fig from the fig tree. [Rev. 6:13, 14.]

5 Because My sword has been bathed *and* equipped in heaven, behold, it shall come down upon Edom [the descendants of Esau], upon the people whom I have doomed for judgment. [Obad. 8-21.]

6 The sword of the Lord is filled with blood [of sacrifices], it is gorged *and* greased with fatness—with the blood of lambs and goats, with the fat of the kidneys of rams. For the Lord has a sacrifice in Bozrah [capital of Edom] and a great slaughter in the land of Edom.

7 And the wild oxen shall fall with them, and the [young] bullocks with the [old and mighty] bulls; and their land shall be drunk *and* soaked with blood, and their dust made rich with fatness.

8 For the Lord has a day of vengeance, a year of recompense, for the cause of Zion.

9 And the streams [of Edom] will be

turned into pitch and its dust into brimstone, and its land will become burning pitch.

10 [The burning of Edom] shall not be quenched night or day; its smoke shall go up forever. From generation to generation it shall lie waste; none shall pass through it forever and ever. [Rev. 19:3.]

11 But the pelican and the porcupine will possess it; the owl *and* the bittern and the raven will dwell in it. And He will stretch over it [Edom] the measuring line of confusion and the plummet stones of chaos [over its nobles].

12 They shall call its nobles to proclaim the kingdom, but nothing shall be there, and all its princes shall be no more.

13 And thorns shall come up in its palaces *and* strongholds, nettles and brambles in its fortresses; and it shall be a habitation for jackals, an abode for ostriches.

14 And the wild beasts of the desert will meet here with howling creatures [wolves and hyenas] and the [shaggy] wild goat will call to his fellow; the night monster will settle there and find a place of rest.

15 There shall the arrow snake make her nest and lay her eggs and hatch them and gather her young under her shade; there shall the kites be gathered [also to breed] every one with its mate.

16 Seek out of the book of the Lord and read: not one of these [details of prophecy] shall fail, none shall want *and* lack her mate [in fulfillment]. For the mouth [of the Lord] has commanded, and His Spirit has gathered them.

17 And He has cast the lot for them, and His hand has portioned [Edom] to [the wild beasts] by measuring line. They shall possess it forever; from generation to generation they shall dwell in it.

35 THE WILDERNESS and the dry land shall be glad; the desert shall rejoice and blossom like the rose *and* the autumn crocus.

2 It shall blossom abundantly and rejoice even with joy and singing. The glory of Lebanon shall be given to it, the excellency of [Mount] Carmel and [the plain] of Sharon. They shall see the glory of the Lord, the majesty *and* splendor *and* excellency of our God.

3 Strengthen the weak hands and make firm the feeble *and* tottering knees. [Heb. 12:12.]

4 Say to those who are of a fearful *and* hasty heart, Be strong, fear not! Behold, your God will come with vengeance; with the recompense of God He will come and save you.

5 Then the eyes of the blind shall be opened, and the ears of the deaf shall be unstopped.

6 Then shall the lame man leap like a hart, and the tongue of the dumb shall sing for joy. For waters shall break forth in the wilderness and streams in the desert. [Matt. 11:5.]

7 And the burning sand *and* the mirage shall become a pool, and the thirsty ground springs of water; in the haunt of jackals, where they lay resting, shall be grass with reeds and rushes.

8 And a highway shall be there, and a way; and it shall be called the Holy Way. The unclean shall not pass over it, but it shall be for the redeemed; the wayfaring men, yes, the simple ones *and* fools, shall not err in it *and* lose their way.

9 No lion shall be there, nor shall any ravenous beast come up on it; they shall not be found there. But the redeemed shall walk on it.

10 And the ransomed of the Lord shall return and come to Zion with singing, and everlasting joy shall be upon their heads; they shall obtain joy and gladness, and sorrow and sighing shall flee away.

36 NOW IN the fourteenth year of King Hezekiah, Sennacherib king of Assyria came up against all the fortified cities of Judah and took them. [II Kings 18:13, 17-37; II Chron. 32:9-19.]
2 And the king of Assyria sent the Rabshakeh [the military official] from Lachish [the Judean fortress commanding the road from Egypt] to King Hezekiah at Jerusalem with a great army. And he stood by the canal of the Upper Pool on the highway to the Fuller's Field.
3 Then came out to meet him Eliakim son of Hilkiah, who was over the [royal] household, and Shebna the secretary, and Joah son of Asaph, the recording historian.
4 And the Rabshakeh said to them, Say to Hezekiah, Thus says the great king, the king of Assyria: What reason for confidence is this in which you trust?
5 Do you suppose that mere words of the lips can pass for warlike counsel and strength? Now in whom do you trust *and* on whom do you rely, that you rebel against me? [II Kings 18:7.]
6 Behold, you trust in the staff of this bruised *and* broken reed, Egypt, which will pierce the hand of any man who leans on it. So is Pharaoh king of Egypt to all who trust *and* rely on him.
7 But if you say to me, We trust in *and* rely on the Lord our God—is it not He Whose high places and Whose altars Hezekiah has taken away, saying to Judah and to Jerusalem, You shall worship before this altar? [II Kings 18:4, 5.]
8 Now therefore, I pray you, make a wager with my master the king of Assyria *and* give him pledges, and I will give you two thousand horses—if

you are able on your part to put riders on them.
9 How then can you repulse the attack of a single captain of the least of my master's servants, when you put your reliance on Egypt for chariots and for horsemen?
10 Moreover, is it without the Lord that I have now come up against this land to destroy it? The Lord said to me, Go up against this land and destroy it.
11 Then Eliakim and Shebna and Joah said to the Rabshakeh, We pray you, speak to your servants in the Aramaic *or* Syrian language, for we understand it; and do not speak to us in the language of the Jews in the hearing of the people on the wall.
12 But the Rabshakeh said, Has my master sent me to speak these words only to your master and to you? Has he not sent me to the men sitting on the wall, who are doomed with you to eat their own dung and drink their own urine?
13 Then the Rabshakeh stood and cried with a loud voice in the language of the Jews: Hear the words of the great king, the king of Assyria!
14 Thus says the king: Let not Hezekiah deceive you, for he will not be able to deliver you.
15 Nor let Hezekiah make you trust in *and* rely on the Lord, saying, The Lord will surely deliver us; this city will not be delivered into the hand of the king of Assyria.
16 Do not listen to Hezekiah, for thus says the king of Assyria: Make your peace with me and come out to me; and eat every one from his own vine and every one from his own fig tree and drink every one the water of his own cistern,
17 Until I come and take you away to a land like your own land, a land of grain and wine, a land of bread and vineyards.
18 Beware lest Hezekiah persuade

and mislead you by saying, The Lord will deliver us. Has any one of the gods of the nations ever delivered his land out of the hand of the king of Assyria?

19 Where are the gods of Hamath and Arpad [in Syria]? Where are the gods of Sepharvaim [a place from which the Assyrians brought colonists to inhabit evacuated Samaria]? And have [the gods] delivered Samaria [capital of the ten northern tribes of Israel] out of my hand?

20 Who among all the gods of these lands has delivered his land out of my hand, that [you should think that] the Lord can deliver Jerusalem out of my hand?

21 But they kept still and answered him not a word, for the king's [Hezekiah's] command was, Do not answer him.

22 Then Eliakim son of Hilkiah, who was over the household, and Shebna the secretary, and Joah son of Asaph, the recording historian came to Hezekiah with their clothes rent, and told him the words of the Rabshakeh [the Assyrian military official].

37 AND WHEN King Hezekiah heard it, he rent his clothes and covered himself with sackcloth and went into the house of the Lord. [II Kings 19:1-13.]

2 And he sent Eliakim, who was over the [royal] household, and Shebna the secretary, and the older priests, clothed with sackcloth, to Isaiah the prophet, the son of Amoz.

3 And they said to him, Thus says Hezekiah: This day is a day of trouble *and* distress and of rebuke and of disgrace; for children have come to the birth, and there is no strength to bring them forth.

4 It may be that the Lord your God will hear the words of the Rabshakeh, whom the king of Assyria, his master, has sent to mock, reproach, insult, *and* defy the living God, and will rebuke the words which the Lord your God has heard. Therefore lift up your prayer for the remnant [of His people] that is left.

5 So the servants of King Hezekiah came to Isaiah.

6 And Isaiah said to them, You shall say to your master, Thus says the Lord: Do not be afraid because of the words which you have heard, with which the servants of the king of Assyria have reviled *and* blasphemed Me.

7 Behold, I will put a spirit in him so that he will hear a rumor and return to his own land, and I will cause him to fall by the sword in his own land.

8 So the Rabshakeh returned and found the king of Assyria fighting against Libnah [a fortified city of Judah]; for he had heard that the king had departed from Lachish.

9 And [Sennacherib king of Assyria] heard concerning Tirhakah king of Ethiopia, He has come forth to make war with you. And when he heard it, he sent messengers to Hezekiah, saying,

10 Thus shall you speak to Hezekiah king of Judah: Let not your God in Whom you trust deceive you by saying, Jerusalem shall not be given into the hand of the king of Assyria.

11 Behold, you have heard what the kings of Assyria have done to all lands, destroying them utterly. And shall you be delivered?

12 Have the gods of the nations delivered those whom my predecessors have destroyed, as ⁱGozan, Haran [of Mesopotamia], Rezeph, and the children of Eden who were in Telassar?

13 Where is the king of Hamath, and the king of Arpad [of northern Syria],

---

i The place-names in this verse are all found on the Assyrian monuments. For further information, see E.S. Schrader, *Cuneiform Inscriptions and the Old Testament,* and his comments on II Kings 19:12.

and the king of the city of Sephar-vaim, the king of Hena, or the king of Ivvah?

14 And Hezekiah received the letter from the hand of the messengers and read it. And Hezekiah went up to the house of the Lord and spread it before the Lord. [II Kings 19:14-19.]

15 And Hezekiah prayed to the Lord:

16 O Lord of hosts, God of Israel, Who [in symbol] are enthroned above the cherubim [of the ark in the temple], You are the God, You alone, of all the kingdoms of the earth. You have made heaven and earth.

17 Incline Your ear, O Lord, and hear; open Your eyes, O Lord, and see; and hear all the words of Sennacherib which he has sent to mock, reproach, insult, *and* defy the living God.

18 It is true, Lord, that the kings of Assyria have laid waste all the nations and their lands

19 And have cast the gods of those peoples into the fire, for they were not gods but the work of men's hands, wood and stone. Therefore they have destroyed them.

20 Now therefore, O Lord our God, save us from his hand, that all the kingdoms of the earth may know (understand and realize) that You are the Lord, even You only.

21 Then Isaiah son of Amoz sent to Hezekiah, saying, Thus says the Lord, the God of Israel: Because you have prayed to Me against Sennacherib king of Assyria, [II Kings 19:20-37; II Chron. 32:20-21.]

22 This is the word which the Lord has spoken concerning him: The Virgin Daughter of Zion has despised you and laughed you to scorn; the Daughter of Jerusalem has shaken her head behind you.

23 Whom have you mocked and reviled [insulted and blasphemed]? And against Whom have you raised your voice and haughtily lifted your eyes? Against the Holy One of Israel!

24 By your servants you have mocked, reproached, insulted, *and* defied the Lord, and you have said, With my many chariots I have gone up to the height of the mountains, to the inner recesses of Lebanon. I cut down its tallest cedars *and* its choicest cypress trees; I came to its remotest height, its most luxuriant *and* dense forest;

25 I dug wells and drank foreign waters, and with the sole of my feet I have dried up all the rivers [the Nile streams] of Egypt.

26 [But, says the God of Israel] have you not heard that I purposed to do it long ago, that I planned it in ancient times? Now I have brought it to pass, that you [king of Assyria] should [be My instrument to] lay waste fortified cities, making them ruinous heaps.

27 Therefore their inhabitants had little power, they were dismayed and confounded; they were like the grass of the field and like the green herb, like the grass on the housetops and like a field of grain blasted before it is grown *or* is in stalk.

28 But I [the Lord] know your sitting down and your going out and your coming in and your raging against Me.

29 Because your raging against Me and your arrogance *and* careless ease have come to My ears, therefore will I put My hook in your nose and My bridle in your lips, and I will turn you back by the way you came.

30 And [now, Hezekiah, says the Lord] this shall be the sign [of these things] to you: you shall eat this year what grows of itself, and in the second year that which springs from the same. And in the third year sow and reap, and plant vineyards and eat the fruit of them.

31 And the remnant that has survived of the house of Judah shall again take root downward and bear fruit upward.

32 For out of Jerusalem will go forth a remnant, and a band that survives out of Mount Zion. The zeal of the Lord of hosts will perform this.
33 Therefore thus says the Lord concerning the king of Assyria: He shall not come into this city or shoot an arrow here or come before it with shield or cast up a siege mound against it.
34 By the way that he came, by the same way he shall return, and he shall not come into this city, says the Lord.
35 For I will defend this city to save it, for My own sake and for the sake of My servant David.
36 And the ʲAngel of the Lord went forth, and ᵏslew 185,000 in the camp of the Assyrians; and when [the living] arose early in the morning, behold, all these were dead bodies. [II Kings 19:35.]
37 So Sennacherib king of Assyria departed and returned and dwelt at Nineveh.
38 And as he was worshiping in the house of Nisroch his god, Adrammelech and Sharezer his sons killed him with the sword, and they escaped into the land of Armenia or Ararat. And Esarhaddon his son reigned in his stead.

speak the Word

38 IN THOSE days King Hezekiah of Judah became ill and was at the point of death. And Isaiah the prophet, the son of Amoz, came to him and said, Thus says the Lord: Set your house in order, for you shall die and not live. [II Kings 20:1-11; II Chron. 32:24-26.]
2 Then Hezekiah turned his face to the wall and prayed to the Lord
3 And said, Remember [earnestly] now, O Lord, I beseech You, how I have walked before You in faithfulness *and* in truth, with a whole heart [absolutely devoted to You], and have done what is good in Your sight. And Hezekiah wept bitterly.
4 Then came the word of the Lord to Isaiah, saying,
5 Go, and say to Hezekiah, Thus says the Lord, the God of David your father: I have heard your prayer, I have seen your tears; behold, I will ˡadd to your life fifteen years.
6 And I will deliver you and this city out of the hand of the king of Assyria; and I will defend this city [Jerusalem].
7 And this will be the sign to you from the Lord that the Lord will do this thing that He has spoken:
8 Behold, I will turn the shadow [denoting the time of day] on the

Thank You, God, for seeing my tears and hearing my prayer.
ADAPTED FROM ISAIAH **38:5**

j See footnote on Gen. 16:7.   **k** A startling, literal fulfillment of the prophecy made in Isaiah 31:8, 9. See also Isa. 10:33-34; 14:25; 17:14; 30:31.   **l** God's time for Hezekiah to die had come (Isa. 38:1), but he had no son. It was unthinkable to him, apparently, that he should die and leave no heir to his throne. As devout as he was, he could not trust the Lord to give His faithful servant what was best for him. So he took matters into his own hands and begged to be allowed to live on. The Lord granted his request—sons were born. How immense the grief that resulted! One of his sons, Manasseh, became Hezekiah's disgraceful and ruthless successor, not for just a few years, but for fifty-five! (II Kings 21:1ff.) He undid everything reformatory that had been done, established idol worship, caused his son to go through the fire as an offering to the pagan god, defied God's prophets, and caused the slaughter of those who opposed him (including perhaps Isaiah, his father's best friend who, according to Jewish tradition, was sawed in half during Manasseh's reign). How little Hezekiah knew of what was best for him or for Judah! How presumptuous is anyone who demands that his own shortsighted vision replace the wisdom of God's plan for his own life or for that of others! See also footnote on II Kings 20:6.

steps *or* degrees, which has gone down on the steps *or* sundial of Ahaz, backward ten steps *or* degrees. And the sunlight turned back ten steps on the steps on which it had gone down.

9 This is the writing of Hezekiah king of Judah after he had been sick and had recovered from his sickness:

10 I said, In the noontide *and* tranquillity of my days I must depart; I am to pass through the gates of Sheol (the place of the dead), deprived of the remainder of my years.

11 I said, I shall not see the Lord, even the Lord, in the land of the living; I shall behold man no more among the inhabitants of the world.

12 My [fleshly] dwelling is plucked up *and* is removed from me like a shepherd's tent. I have rolled up my life as a weaver [rolls up the finished web]; [the Lord] cuts me free from the loom; from day to night You bring me to an end.

13 I thought *and* quieted myself until morning. Like a lion He breaks all my bones; from day to night You bring me to an end.

14 Like a twittering swallow *or* a crane, so do I chirp *and* chatter; I moan like a dove. My eyes are weary *and* dim with looking upward. O Lord, I am oppressed; take my side *and* be my security [as of a debtor being sent to prison].

15 But what can I say? For He has both spoken to me and He Himself has done it. I must go softly [as in solemn procession] all my years *and* my sleep has fled because of the bitterness of my soul.

16 O Lord, by these things men live; and in all these is the life of my spirit. O give me back my health and make me live!

17 Behold, it was for my peace that I had intense bitterness; but You have loved back my life from the pit of corruption *and* nothingness, for You have cast all my sins behind Your back.

18 For Sheol (the place of the dead) cannot confess *and* reach out the hand to You, death cannot praise *and* rejoice in You; they who go down to the pit cannot hope for Your faithfulness [to Your promises; their probation is at an end, their destiny is sealed].

19 The living, the living—they shall thank *and* praise You, as I do this day; the father shall make known to the children Your faithfulness *and* Your truth.

20 The Lord is ready to save (deliver) me; therefore we will sing my songs with [my] stringed instruments all the days of our lives in the house of the Lord.

21 Now Isaiah had said, Let them take a cake of figs and lay it for a plaster upon the boil, that he may recover.

22 Hezekiah also had said, What is the sign that I shall go up to the house of the Lord?

39 AT THAT time Merodachbaladan son of Baladan king of Babylon sent [messengers with] letters and a present to Hezekiah, for he had heard that he had been sick and had recovered. [II Kings 20:12-19.]

2 And Hezekiah was glad *and* welcomed them and showed them the house of his spices *and* precious things—the silver, the gold, the spices, the precious ointment, all the house of his armor *and* his jewels, and all that was found in his treasuries. There was nothing in his house nor in all his dominion that Hezekiah did not show them.

3 Then came Isaiah the prophet to King Hezekiah and said to him, What did these men say? From where did they come to you? And Hezekiah said, They came to me from a far country, even from Babylon.

4 Then Isaiah said, What have they seen in your house? And Hezekiah answered, They have seen all that is in my house; there is nothing among my treasures that I have not shown them.

5 Then said Isaiah to Hezekiah, Hear the word of the Lord of hosts:

6 Behold, the days are coming when all that is in your house, and that which your predecessors have stored up till this day, shall be carried to Babylon. Nothing shall be left, says the Lord.

7 And some of your own sons who are born to you shall be taken away, and they shall be eunuchs in the palace of the king of Babylon.

8 Then said Hezekiah to Isaiah, The word of the Lord which you have spoken is good. And he added, For there will be peace and faithfulness [to His promises to us] in my days.

40 COMFORT, COMFORT My people, says your God. 2 Speak tenderly to the heart of Jerusalem, and cry to her that her time of service *and* her warfare are ended, that [her punishment is accepted and] her iniquity is pardoned, that she has received [punishment] from the Lord's hand double for all her sins.

3 A voice of one who cries: Prepare in the wilderness the way of the Lord [clear away the obstacles]; make straight *and* smooth in the desert a highway for our God! [Mark 1:3.]

4 Every valley shall be lifted *and* filled up, and every mountain and hill shall be made low; and the crooked *and* uneven shall be made straight *and* level, and the rough places a plain.

speak the Word

putting the Word to work

We all have "mountaintop" experiences and valleys (low moments) in our lives; we all have crooked places that seem confusing, times that are uneven (up and down), and situations that are rough and difficult (see Isaiah 40:4). In what ways has God brought stability and evenness to your life? How has He made crooked places straight and given you grace for the rough spots along your journey? Remember how He has helped you and thank Him today.

5 And the glory (majesty and splendor) of the Lord shall be revealed, and all flesh shall see it together; for the mouth of the Lord has spoken it. [Luke 3:5, 6.]

6 A voice says, Cry [prophesy]! And I said, What shall I cry? [The voice answered, Proclaim:] All flesh is as frail as grass, and all that makes it attractive [its kindness, its goodwill, its mercy from God, its glory and comeliness, however good] is transitory, like the flower of the field.

7 The grass withers, the flower fades, when the breath of the Lord blows upon it; surely [all] the people are like grass.

8 The ᵐgrass withers, the flower fades, but the word of our God will stand forever. [James 1:10, 11; I Pet. 1:24, 25.]

9 O you who bring good tidings to Zion, get up to the high mountain. O you who bring good tidings to Jerusalem, lift up your voice with

Thank You, God, that Your Word stands forever!
ADAPTED FROM ISAIAH **40:8**

---

m The apostle Peter quotes this verse (I Pet. 1:24-25) and then adds, "and this Word is the good news which was preached to you"—which confirms as fact that Isaiah is here referring to the times of Christ, the Messiah, the Anointed One.

magnets for His power

Isaiah 40:6, 7 teaches us that the flesh (people, just like you and me) is like puffs of smoke or blades of grass. We are here on earth for a very short time; we tend to be fragile, unsure, and shaky during our relatively brief lifetimes. God knows that and has no problem with it, because He is willing to work through us and to show Himself strong in our weaknesses. Actually, the Bible teaches that God's strength shows itself most effectively through our weaknesses (see II Corinthians 12:9). Our weaknesses and shortcomings are like magnets for His power.

God can handle knowing what we lack and knowing that we fail. We, on the other hand, tend to beat ourselves up over our imperfections. We try to make excuses for them, try to compensate for them, and try to keep other people from seeing them. Instead, we need to admit our weaknesses and face them, not feel badly about them. We need to be honest about what we can do, but we need to be equally honest about what we cannot do, recognizing that those things are great opportunities for God to work through us.

Let me encourage you to get up every morning, love God, and do your best in every situation. He will do the rest! Remember that God is not surprised by your inabilities, imperfections, or faults. He has always known about those areas of your life, even if you are just now discovering them. Only God is perfect; He chose you anyway, and He loves you in spite of all your shortcomings!

strength, lift it up, be not afraid; say to the cities of Judah, Behold your God! [Acts 10:36; Rom. 10:15.]

10 Behold, the Lord God will come with might, and His arm will rule for Him. Behold, His reward is with Him, and His recompense before Him. [Rev. 22:7, 12.]

11 He will feed His flock like a shepherd: He will gather the lambs in His arm, He will carry them in His bosom and will gently lead those that have their young.

12 Who has measured the waters in the hollow of his hand, marked off the heavens with a [nine-inch] span, enclosed the dust of the earth in a measure, and weighed the mountains in scales and the hills in a balance?

13 Who has directed the Spirit of the Lord, or as His counselor has taught Him? [Rom. 11:34.]

14 With whom did He take counsel, that instruction might be given Him?

Who taught Him the path of justice and taught Him knowledge and showed Him the way of understanding?

15 Behold, the nations are like a drop from a bucket and are counted as small dust on the scales; behold, He takes up the isles like a very little thing.

16 And all Lebanon's [forests] cannot supply sufficient fuel, nor all its wild beasts furnish victims enough to burn sacrifices [worthy of the Lord].

17 All the nations are as nothing before Him; they are regarded by Him as less than nothing and emptiness (waste, futility, and worthlessness).

18 To whom then will you liken God? Or with what likeness will you compare Him? [Acts 17:29.]

19 The graven image! A workman casts it, and a goldsmith overlays it with gold and casts silver chains for it.

20 He who is so impoverished that he

has no offering *or* oblation *or* rich gift to give [to his god is constrained to make a wooden offering, an idol; so he] chooses a tree that will not rot; he seeks out a skillful craftsman to carve *and* set up an image that will not totter *or* deteriorate.

21 [You worshipers of idols, you are without excuse.] Do you not know? Have you not heard? Has it not been told you from the beginning? [These things ought to convince you of God's omnipotence and of the folly of bowing to idols.] Have you not understood from the foundations of the earth? [Rom. 1:20, 21.]

22 It is God Who sits above the circle (the horizon) of the earth, and its inhabitants are like grasshoppers; it is He Who stretches out the heavens like [gauze] curtains and spreads them out like a tent to dwell in,

23 Who brings dignitaries to nothing, Who makes the judges *and* rulers of the earth as chaos (emptiness, falsity, and futility).

24 Yes, these men are scarcely planted, scarcely are they sown, scarcely does their stock take root in the earth, when [the Lord] blows upon them and they wither, and the whirlwind *or* tempest takes them away like stubble.

25 To whom then will you liken Me, that I should be equal to him? says the Holy One.

26 Lift up your eyes on high and see! Who has created these? He Who brings out their host by number and calls them all by name; through the greatness of His might and because He is strong in power, not one is missing *or* lacks anything.

27 Why, O Jacob, do you say, and declare, O Israel, My way *and* my lot are hidden from the Lord, and my right is passed over without regard from my God?

28 Have you not known? Have you not heard? The everlasting God, the Lord, the Creator of the ends of the earth, does not faint or grow weary; there is no searching of His understanding.

29 He gives power to the faint *and* weary, and to him who has no might He increases strength [causing it to multiply and making it to abound]. [II Cor. 12:9.]

30 Even youths shall faint and be weary, and [selected] young men shall feebly stumble *and* fall exhausted;

31 But those who wait for the Lord [who expect, look for, and hope in Him] shall change *and* renew their

life point

I have experienced the truth of Isaiah 40:29, and I honestly believe that being filled with the Holy Spirit actually gives us physical energy.

Many times I have been quickened by the Holy Spirit and have suddenly gone from being extremely tired to feeling as if I could run around the city. This is a good reason to keep ourselves filled with the Holy Spirit; we need all the energy we can get! I firmly believe we can make ourselves feel drained by the way we think and talk. Likewise, we can help ourselves feel energetic by following biblical guidelines for everyday living.

It seems that most people in the world today are tired. Part of their fatigue comes from being too busy, but another large part of it is due to the way they live—how they think, talk, and act toward other people.

The Holy Spirit will not energize us to be mean, hateful, selfish, or self-centered. He will give us strength and energy to do the things God has called us to do and to be kind, loving, diligent, and focused in the process.

strength *and* power; they shall lift their wings *and* mount up [close to God] as eagles [mount up to the sun]; they shall run and not be weary, they shall walk and not faint *or* become tired. [Heb. 12:1-3.]

life point

Quietly waiting on God (spending time alone with Him in prayer, worship, or Bible reading), as Isaiah 40:31 encourages us, does more to restore our bodies, minds, and emotions than anything else we can do. We need to do this regularly. I urge you to insist on quiet time with God; do not let anyone take those consecrated moments from you. In those times, God empowers you to face everything you need to do with renewed physical, emotional, mental, and spiritual strength.

41 LISTEN IN silence before Me, O islands *and* regions bordering on the sea! And let the people gather *and* renew their strength [for the argument; let them offer their strongest arguments]! Let them come near, then let them speak; let us come near together for judgment [and decide the point at issue between us concerning the enemy advancing from the east].
2   Who has roused up one [Cyrus] from the east, whom He calls in righteousness to His service *and* whom victory meets at every step? He [the Lord] subdues nations before him and makes him ruler over kings. He turns them to dust with the sword [of Cyrus], and to driven straw *and* chaff with his bow. [Ezra 1:2.]
3   He [Cyrus] pursues them and passes safely *and* unhindered, even by a way his feet had not trod *and* so swiftly that his feet do not touch the ground.

4   Who has prepared and done this, calling forth *and* guiding the destinies of the generations [of the nations] from the beginning? I, the Lord—the first [existing before history began] and with the last [an ever-present, unchanging God]—I am He.
5   The islands *and* coastlands have seen and fear; the ends of the earth tremble. They draw near and come;
6   They help every one his neighbor and say to his brother [in his tiresome idol making], Be of good courage!
7   So the carpenter encourages the goldsmith, *and* he who smooths [the metal] with the hammer [encourages] him who smites the anvil, saying of the soldering, That is good! And he fastens it with nails so that it cannot be moved.
8   But you, Israel, My servant, Jacob, whom I have chosen, the offspring of Abraham My friend, [Heb. 2:16; James 2:23.]
9   You whom I [the Lord] have taken from the ends of the earth and have called from the corners of it, and said to you, You are My servant—I have chosen you and not cast you off [even though you are exiled].
10   Fear not [there is nothing to fear], for I am with you; do not look around you in terror *and* be dismayed, for I am your God. I will strengthen *and* harden you to difficulties, yes, I will

life point

If there is something we are supposed to be doing, the Lord will give us the ability to do it. He will not lead us into a situation and then leave us there to face it alone in our own weak, human power. No, because as Isaiah 41:10 reminds us, He is with us. He is our great God; He will harden us to difficulties, help us, and uphold us with His hand of victory.

waiting on God

Isaiah 40:31 teaches us that waiting on God is expecting, looking for, and hoping in Him. It is spending time with Him in His Word and in His presence. We do not worry while we wait on God; we do not get frustrated while we wait on God; we do not get upset while we wait on God. We rest.

Sometimes when you start to get nervous and upset, anxious, or worried, you just need to tell yourself, "Sit down." That does not mean just your physical body; it also means your soul—your mind, will, and emotions. It is important to let your entire being rest.

Under the Old Covenant, when the high priest went into the Holy of Holies to make blood sacrifices for the sins of the people, he did not sit down. It seems very unlikely that there was a chair in there because the Bible does not mention it, even though it offers detailed descriptions of the Israelites' place of worship. The requirements on the high priest were so stringent that he did what he had to do and left. He could not rest in the presence of God.

I have been told that the high priest wore bells on his robe and that he had a rope tied to his waist. As he moved around the Holy of Holies, people outside could hear the bells. If the bells stopped ringing, the people knew he had done something wrong and had died, so they pulled him out by the rope.

There is such a powerful lesson in that. It teaches us that people could not rest in God's presence under the Old Covenant. The Old Covenant had many laws and was based on works. But thank God, the New Covenant is based on the work Jesus has accomplished, not on our own merits or works.

Jesus, our High Priest Who went into the Holy of Holies with His own blood, put the blood on the mercy seat in heaven and sat down. Now the atonement for the sins of the world is finished.

If you are struggling in your life, take a seat and rest in God's presence. The promise of God's peace is not made to those who work and struggle in their own strength but to those who sit and rest in Christ Jesus. Wait on Him, and your strength will be renewed.

help you; yes, I will hold you up *and* retain you with My [victorious] right hand of rightness *and* justice. [Acts 18:10.]

11 Behold, all they who are enraged *and* inflamed against you shall be put to shame and confounded; they who strive against you shall be as nothing and shall perish.

12 You shall seek those who contend with you but shall not find them; they who war against you shall be as nothing, as nothing at all.

13 For I the Lord your God hold your right hand; I am the Lord, Who says to you, Fear not; I will help you!

14 Fear not, you worm Jacob, you men of Israel! I will help you, says the

Lord; your Redeemer is the Holy One of Israel.

15 Behold, I will make you to be a new, sharp, threshing instrument which has teeth; you shall thresh the mountains and beat them small, and shall make the hills like chaff.

16 You shall winnow them, and the wind shall carry them away, and the tempest *or* whirlwind shall scatter them. And you shall rejoice in the Lord, you shall glory in the Holy One of Israel.

17 The poor and needy are seeking water when there is none; their tongues are parched with thirst. I the Lord will answer them; I, the God of Israel, will not forsake them.

18 I will open rivers on the bare heights, and fountains in the midst of the valleys; I will make the wilderness a pool of water, and the dry land springs of water.

19 I will plant in the wilderness the cedar, the acacia, the myrtle, and the wild olive; I will set the cypress in the desert, the plane [tree] and the pine [tree] together,

20 That men may see and know and consider and understand together that the hand of the Lord has done this, that the Holy One of Israel has created it.

21 [You idols made by men's hands, prove your divinity!] Produce your cause [set forth your case], says the Lord. Bring forth your strong proofs, says the King of Jacob.

22 Let them bring them forth and tell us what is to happen. Let them tell us the former things, what they are, that we may consider them and know the outcome of them; or declare to us the things to come.

23 Tell us the things that are to come hereafter, that we may know that you are gods; yes, do good or do evil

[something or other], that we may stare in astonishment *and* be dismayed as we behold [the miracle] together!

24 Behold, you [idols] are nothing, and your work is nothing! The worshiper who chooses you is an abomination [extremely disgusting and shamefully vile in God's sight]. [I Cor. 8:4.]

25 I have raised up *and* impelled to action one from the north [n][Cyrus], and he comes; from the rising of the sun he calls upon My name [recognizing that his victories have been granted to him by Me]. And he shall tread upon rulers *and* deputies as upon mortar and as the potter treads clay. [He comes with the suddenness of a comet, but none of the idol oracles of the nations has anticipated it.] [II Chron. 36:23; Ezra 1:1-3.]

26 [What idol] has declared this from the beginning, that we could know? And beforetime, that we could say that he is [unquestionably] right? Yes, there is none who declares it, yes, there is none who proclaims it; yes, [for the truth is, O you dumb idols] there is none who hears you speak!

27 I [the Lord] first gave to Zion the announcement, Behold, [the Jews will be restored to their own land, and the man Cyrus shall be raised up who will deliver them] behold them! And to Jerusalem I gave a herald [Isaiah] bringing the good news. [Isa. 40:9; 52:7.]

28 For I look [upon the heathen prophets and the priests of pagan practices] and there is no man among them [who could predict these events], and among these [idols] there is no counselor who, when I ask of him, can answer a word.

29 Behold, these [pagan prophets

n Cyrus came from the east (Isa. 41:2), but defeated a number of kingdoms north of Babylon early in his reign. Palestinian authors frequently perceived invasions as coming primarily from the north.

and priests] are all emptiness (falseness and futility)! Their works are worthless; their molten images are empty wind (confusion and waste).

42 BEHOLD MY °Servant, Whom I uphold, My elect in Whom My soul delights! I have put My Spirit upon Him; He will bring forth justice *and* right *and* reveal truth to the nations. [Matt. 3:16, 17.]

2 He will not cry or shout aloud or cause His voice to be heard in the street.

3 A bruised reed He will not break, and a dimly burning wick He will not quench; He will bring forth justice in truth. [Matt. 12:17-21.]

4 He will not fail *or* become weak or be crushed *and* discouraged till He has established justice in the earth; and the islands *and* coastal regions shall wait hopefully for Him *and* expect His direction *and* law. [Rom. 8:22-25.]

5 Thus says God the Lord—He Who created the heavens and stretched them forth, He Who spread abroad the earth and that which comes out of it, He Who gives breath to the people on it and spirit to those who walk in it:

6 I the Lord have called You [the Messiah] for a righteous purpose *and* in righteousness; I will take You by the hand and will keep You; I will give You for a covenant to the people [Israel], for a light to the nations [Gentiles],

7 To open the eyes of the blind, to bring out prisoners from the dungeon, and those who sit in darkness from the prison. [Matt. 12:18-21.]

8 I am the Lord; that is My name! And My glory I will not give to another, nor My praise to graven images.

9 Behold, the former things have come to pass, and new things I now declare; before they spring forth I tell you of them.

10 Sing to the Lord a new song, and His praise from the end of the earth! You who go down to the sea, and all that is in it, the islands *and* coastal regions and the inhabitants of them [sing a song such as has never been heard in the heathen world]!

11 Let the wilderness and its cities lift up their voices, the villages that Kedar inhabits. Let the inhabitants of the rock [Sela or Petra] sing; let them shout from the tops of the mountains!

12 Let them give glory to the Lord and declare His praise in the islands *and* coastal regions.

13 The Lord will go forth like a mighty man, He will rouse up His zealous indignation *and* vengeance like a warrior; He will cry, yes, He will shout aloud, He will do mightily against His enemies.

14 [Thus says the Lord] I have for a long time held My peace, I have been still and restrained Myself. Now I will cry out like a woman in travail, I will gasp and pant together.

15 I will lay waste the mountains and hills and dry up all their herbage; I will turn the rivers into islands, and I will dry up the pools.

16 And I will bring the blind by a way that they know not; I will lead them in paths that they have not known. I will make darkness into light before them and make uneven places into a plain. These things I have determined to do [for them]; and I will not leave them forsaken.

o This is the first of the famous prophecies concerning the great future "Servant of the Lord" (Isa. 42:1-7; 49:1-9a; 50:4-9; 52:13-53:12). Interpreters have struggled with the question, "Who is meant by 'the servant'?" Some think the "servant of the Lord" is the people of Israel. Others think it makes reference to the faithful part of the people, the "ideal" people of Israel. Still others think of the prophets as a group. Another large group of scholars believes that the "Servant of the Lord" is the Messiah, the One Who will establish God's kingdom on earth.

God declares new things

In Isaiah 42:9 God speaks to His people and declares new things before they happen. If you are like I am, you may be ready and waiting for some new things in your life. You need some changes, and those changes may be coming soon.

Even though I know the principles I am about to share with you, I too need to be reminded of them occasionally. Sometimes we all need to be "stirred up" in things we already know. That encourages us to begin operating once again in powerful principles that we have let slip away.

If you are tired of the old things, then stop speaking the old things. Do you want some new things? Then start speaking some new things. Spend some time with God. Set aside some special time to study His Word. Find out what His will is for your life. Do not let the devil push you around anymore.

Find out what God's Word promises you, and begin to declare the end from the beginning. Instead of saying, "Nothing will ever change," say, "God is making changes in my life and circumstances every day."

I heard the story of a doctor who was not a believer but who had discovered the power of the principle I am sharing with you. His prescription to his patients was to go home and repeat several times daily: "I am getting better and better every day." He had such marvelous results that people traveled from all over the world to avail themselves of his services. How much better, then, is it when we say God's Word in anticipation of the new thing He says He is going to do. Remember, unlike the words of man, God's Word is eternal and true; it does not return to Him void: "Behold, the former things have come to pass, and new things I now declare."

17 They shall be turned back, they shall be utterly put to shame, who trust in graven images, who say to molten images, You are our gods.

life point

Many people have 20/20 vision in their physical eyes, but they are spiritually blind. If you feel that you are just stumbling around in the darkness and do not know what to do, I encourage you to take the promise from God in Isaiah 42:16 for yourself. God wants to turn your darkness into light. He has determined to do good for you, and He will not leave you forsaken.

18 Hear, you deaf! And look, you blind, that you may see!
19 Who is blind but My servant [Israel]? Or deaf like My messenger whom I send? Who is blind like the one who is at peace with Me [who has been admitted to covenant relationship with Me]? Yes, who is blind like the Lord's servant?
20 You have seen many things, but you do not observe *or* apprehend their true meaning. His ears are open, but he hears not!
21 It was the Lord's pleasure for His righteousness' sake [in accordance with a steadfast and consistent purpose] to magnify instruction *and* revelation and glorify them.

22 But this is a people robbed and plundered; they are all of them snared in holes and hidden in houses of bondage. They have become a prey, with no one to deliver them, a spoil, with no one to say, Restore them! [This shows the condition that will ensue as Israel's punishment for not recognizing the Servant of the Lord and the day of His visit among them.] [Luke19:41-44.]

23 Who is there among you who will give ear to this? Who will listen and hear in the time to come?

24 Who gave up Jacob [the kingdom of Judah] for spoil, and [the kingdom of] Israel to the robbers? Was it not the Lord, He against Whom we [of Judah] have sinned and in Whose ways they [of Israel] would not walk, neither were they obedient to His law *or* His teaching?

25 Therefore He poured out upon [Israel] the fierceness of His anger and the strength of battle. And it set him on fire round about, yet he knew not [the lesson of repentance which the Assyrian conquest was intended to teach]; it burned him, but he did not lay it to heart.

43 BUT NOW [in spite of past judgments for Israel's sins], thus says the Lord, He Who created you, O Jacob, and He Who formed you, O Israel: Fear not, for I have redeemed you [ransomed you by paying a price instead of leaving you captives]; I have called you by your name; you are Mine.

2 When you pass through the waters, I will be with you, and through the rivers, they will not overwhelm you. When you walk through the fire, you will not be burned *or* scorched, nor will the flame kindle upon you.

3 For I am the Lord your God, the Holy One of Israel, your Savior; I give Egypt [to the Babylonians] for your ransom, Ethiopia and Seba [a province of Ethiopia] in exchange [for your release].

4 Because you are precious in My sight and honored, and because I love you, I will give men in return for you and peoples in exchange for your life.

5 Fear not, for I am with you; I will bring your offspring from the east [where they are dispersed] and gather you from the west. [Acts 18:10.]

6 I will say to the north, Give up! and to the south, Keep not back. Bring My sons from afar and My daughters from the ends of the earth—

7 Even everyone who is called by My name, whom I have created for My glory, whom I have formed, whom I have made.

8 Bring forth the blind people who have eyes and the deaf who have ears.

9 Let all the nations be gathered together and let the peoples be assembled. Who among [the idolaters] could predict this [that Cyrus would be the deliverer of Israel] and show us the former things? Let them bring their witnesses, that they may be justified, or let them hear and acknowledge, It is the truth. [Ps. 123:3, 4.]

10 You are My witnesses, says the Lord, and My servant whom I have chosen, that you may know Me, believe Me *and* remain steadfast to Me, and understand that I am He. Before Me there was no God formed, neither shall there be after Me.

11 I, even I, am the Lord, and besides Me there is no Savior.

12 I have declared [the future] and have saved [the nation in times of

speak the Word

Thank You, God, for redeeming me and for calling me by name. I am Yours!
ADAPTED FROM ISAIAH 43:1

through it all

In Isaiah 43:2, God tells us that He will be with us as we go through the water and through the fire. This means that we will have to face some tests and trials in our lives; they cannot be avoided. There will be some difficult things that we have to go through.

I do not know what specific form your challenges may take, but I know that they are intended to strengthen you, to develop your character, to cause you to persevere, to sanctify you, to purify you, to teach you the unique lessons of suffering, to teach you the benefits and disciplines of sacrifice, and to make you a better person. You may cringe as you think about these things, but if you really want to fulfill your potential, you simply must be prepared to go through them.

I have been through many tests and trials. I have faced loneliness, obstacles, and persecution. There have been times when I wanted to give up, and in the midst of those times, God often put someone in my life I did not particularly like or want to deal with. I now know that He placed those people near me because I needed them. He used them to be the sandpaper that was needed to smooth my rough edges.

Has God put someone or something in your life as sandpaper? That situation may feel like a flood or a fire to you, but it is serving a great purpose, and God is going to take you through the difficulty to the other side. He is going to use it to strengthen you, change you, and advance His purpose for your life.

God must take us through hard things because He must change us in order to use us. We must become like Jesus in our character; we must follow His example and walk in His ways. Gifts are given to us by God, but good fruit and godly character must be developed.

I struggled with the process of change for a long time, but finally realized that I was not going to succeed in getting God to do things my way. He did not want to hear an argument from me; He wanted to hear, "Yes, Lord. Your will be done."

We will always face obstacles and difficulties—"floods and fires"—as God continues to strengthen us and prepare us to be used in His service in greater and greater ways. We would be wise to settle down and deal with the challenges He puts before us. Whatever they are, if we will receive them as His training for us and submit to His will, we will not get stuck, but go through to victory.

---

danger], and I have shown [that I am God]—when there was no strange and alien god among you; therefore you are My witnesses, says the Lord, that I am God.

13 Yes, from the time of the first exis-

tence of day *and* from this day forth I am He; and there is no one who can deliver out of My hand. I will work, and who can hinder *or* reverse it?

14 Thus says the Lord, your Redeemer, the Holy One of Israel: For your sake I have sent [one] to Babylon, and I will bring down all of them as fugitives, [with] all their nobles, even the Chaldeans, into the ships over which they rejoiced.

15 I am the Lord, your Holy One, the Creator of Israel, your King.

16 Thus says the Lord, Who makes a way through the sea and a path through the mighty waters,

17 Who brings forth chariot and horse, army and mighty warrior. They lie down together, they cannot rise; they are extinguished, they are quenched like a lampwick:

18 Do not [earnestly] remember the former things; neither consider the things of old.

19 Behold, I am doing a new thing! Now it springs forth; do you not perceive *and* know it *and* will you not give heed to it? I will even make a way in the wilderness and rivers in the desert.

20 The beasts of the field honor Me, the jackals and the ostriches, because I give waters in the wilderness *and* rivers in the desert, to give drink to My people, My chosen, [Isa. 41:17, 18; 48:21.]

21 The people I formed for Myself, that they may set forth My praise [and they shall do it].

22 Yet you have not called upon Me [much less toiled for Me], O Jacob; but you have been weary of Me, O Israel!

23 You have not brought Me your sheep *and* goats for burnt offerings, or honored Me with your sacrifices. I have not required you to serve with an offering *or* treated you as a slave by demanding tribute or wearied you with offering incense.

24 You have not bought Me sweet

speak the Word

life point

Careful consideration of Isaiah 43:18, 19 seems to indicate that you and I can cooperate with God's plan, for He says, "Will you not give heed to it?"

We can release God's plan for our lives by no longer thinking about the things of old, believing that God has a good plan for our future. Since what we think about eventually comes out of our mouths, we will never get our mouths straightened out unless we do something about our thoughts.

I believe that if we stop mentally living in the past, we can begin to think in agreement with God. Then once we do that, we can begin to speak in agreement with Him. By so doing we can actually prophesy our own future.

If God can make a way in the wilderness and rivers in the desert, He can make a way for you.

cane with money, or satiated Me with the fat of your sacrifices. But you have only burdened Me with your sins; you have wearied Me with your iniquities.

25 I, even I, am He Who blots out *and* cancels your transgressions, for My own sake, and I will not remember your sins.

26 Put Me in remembrance [remind Me of your merits]; let us plead *and* argue together. Set forth your case, that you may be justified (proved right).

27 Your first father [Jacob, in particular] sinned, and your teachers [the priests and the prophets—your mediators] transgressed against Me.

Thank You, God, for blotting out and canceling my transgressions and for forgetting my sins completely.
ADAPTED FROM ISAIAH 43:25

28 And so I will profane the chief ones of the sanctuary and will deliver Jacob to the curse (the ban, a solemn anathema or excommunication) and [will subject] Israel to reproaches *and* reviling.

44 YET NOW hear, O Jacob, My servant and Israel, whom I have chosen.
2 Thus says the Lord, Who made you and formed you from the womb, Who will help you: Fear not, O Jacob, My servant, and you Jeshurun [the upright one—applied to Israel as a type of the Messiah], whom I have chosen.
3 For I will pour water upon him who is thirsty, and floods upon the dry ground. I will pour My Spirit upon your offspring, and My blessing upon your descendants. [Isa. 32:15; 35:6, 7; Joel 2:28; John 7:37-39.]
4 And they shall spring up among the grass like willows *or* poplars by the watercourses.
5 One will say, I am the Lord's; and another will call himself by the name of Jacob; and another will write [even brand or tattoo] upon his hand, I am the Lord's, and surname himself by the [honorable] name of Israel.
6 Thus says the Lord, the King of Israel and his Redeemer, the Lord of hosts: I am the First and I am the Last; besides Me there is no God. [Rev. 1:17; 2:8; 22:13.]
7 Who is like Me? Let him [stand and] proclaim it, declare it, and set [his proofs] in order before Me, since I made *and* established the people of antiquity. [Who has announced from of old] the things that are coming? Then let them declare yet future things.
8 Fear not, nor be afraid [in the coming violent upheavals]; have I not told it to you from of old and declared it? And you are My witnesses! Is there a God besides Me? There is no [other] Rock; I know not any.

9 All who make graven idols are confusion, chaos, *and* worthlessness. Their objects (idols) in which they delight do not profit them, and their own witnesses (worshipers) do not see or know, so that they are put to shame.
10 Who is [such a fool as] to fashion a god or cast a graven image that is profitable for nothing?
11 Behold, all his fellows shall be put to shame, and the craftsmen, [how can they make a god?] they are but men. Let them all be gathered together, let them stand forth; they shall be terrified, they shall be put to shame together.
12 The ironsmith sharpens *and* uses a chisel and works it over the coals; he shapes [the core of the idol] with hammers and forges it with his strong arm. He becomes hungry and his strength fails; he drinks no water and is faint.
13 The carpenter stretches out a line, he marks it out with a pencil *or* red ocher; he fashions [an idol] with planes and marks it out with the compasses; and he shapes it to have the figure of a man, with the beauty of a man, that it may dwell in a house.
14 He hews for himself cedars, and takes the holm tree and the oak and lets them grow strong for himself among the trees of the forest; he plants a fir tree *or* an ash, and the rain nourishes it.
15 Then it becomes fuel for a man to burn; a part of it he takes and warms himself, yes, he kindles a fire and bakes bread. [Then out of the remainder, the leavings] he also makes a god and worships it! He [with his own hands] makes it into a graven image and falls down and worships it!
16 He burns part of the wood in the fire; with part of it he [cooks and] eats flesh, he roasts meat and is satisfied. Also he warms himself and says, Aha! I am warm, I have seen the fire!
17 And from what is left [of the log]

he makes a god, his graven idol. He falls down to it, he worships it and prays to it and says, Deliver me, for you are my god!

18 They do not know or understand, for their eyes God has let become besmeared so that they cannot see, *and* their minds as well so that they cannot understand.

19 And no one considers in his mind, nor has he knowledge and understanding [enough] to say [to himself], I have burned part of this log in the fire, and also I have baked bread on its coals and have roasted meat and eaten it. And shall I make the remainder of it into an abomination [the very essence of what is disgusting, detestable, and shamefully vile in the eyes of a jealous God]? Shall I fall down *and* worship the stock of a tree [a block of wood without consciousness or life]?

20 That kind of man feeds on ashes [and finds his satisfaction in ashes]! A deluded mind has led him astray, so that he cannot release *and* save himself, or ask, Is not [this thing I am holding] in my right hand a lie?

21 Remember these things [earnestly], O Jacob, O Israel, for you are My servant! I formed you, you are My servant; O Israel, you shall not be forgotten by Me.

22 I have blotted out like a thick cloud your transgressions, and like a cloud your sins. Return to Me, for I have redeemed you.

23 Sing, O heavens, for the Lord has done it; shout, you depths of the earth; break forth into singing, you mountains, O forest and every tree in it! For the Lord has redeemed Jacob, and He glorifies Himself in Israel.

24 Thus says the Lord, your Redeemer, and He Who formed you from the womb: I am the Lord, Who made all things, Who alone stretched out the heavens, Who spread out the earth by Myself [who was with Me]?—

25 [I am the Lord] Who frustrates the signs *and* confounds the omens [upon which the false prophets' forecasts of the future are based] of the [boasting] liars and makes fools of diviners, Who turns the wise backward and makes their knowledge foolishness, [I Cor. 1:20.]

26 [The Lord] Who confirms the word of His servant and performs the counsel of His messengers, Who says of Jerusalem, She shall [again] be inhabited, and of the cities of Judah, They shall [again] be built, and I will raise up their ruins,

27 Who says to the deep, Be dry, and I will dry up your rivers,

28 Who says of Cyrus, He is My shepherd (ruler), and he shall perform all My pleasure *and* fulfill all My purpose—even saying of Jerusalem, She shall [again] be built, and of the temple, Your foundation shall [again] be laid.

45 THUS SAYS the Lord to His anointed, to Cyrus, whose right hand I have held to subdue nations before him, and I will unarm *and* ungird the loins of kings to open doors before him, so that gates will not be shut.

2 I will go before you and level the mountains [to make the crooked places straight]; I will break in pieces the doors of bronze and cut asunder the bars of iron.

3 And I will give you the treasures of darkness and hidden riches of secret places, that you may know that it is I, the Lord, the God of Israel, Who calls you by your name.

4 For the sake of Jacob My servant, and of Israel My chosen, I have called you by your name. I have surnamed you, though you have not known Me.

5 I am the Lord, and there is no one else; there is no God besides Me. I will gird *and* arm you, though you have not known Me,

6 That men may know from the east *and* the rising of the sun and from the west *and* the setting of the sun that there is no God besides Me. I am the Lord, and no one else [is He].

7 I form the light and create darkness, I make peace [national well-being] and I create [physical] Pevil (calamity); I am the Lord, Who does all these things.

8 Let fall in showers, you heavens, from above, and let the skies rain down righteousness [the pure, spiritual, heaven-born possibilities that have their foundation in the holy being of God]; let the earth open, and let them [skies and earth] sprout forth salvation, and let righteousness germinate *and* spring up [as plants do] together; I the Lord have created it.

9 Woe to him who strives with his Maker!—a worthless piece of broken pottery among other pieces equally worthless [and yet presuming to strive with his Maker]! Shall the clay say to him who fashions it, What do you think you are making? or, Your work has no handles? [Rom. 9:20.]

10 Woe to him [who complains against his parents that they have begotten him] who says to a father, What are you begetting? or to a woman, With what are you in travail?

11 Thus says the Lord, the Holy One of Israel, and its Maker: Would you question Me about things to come concerning My children, and concerning the work of My hands [would you] command Me?

12 I made the earth and created man upon it. I, with My hands, stretched out the heavens, and I commanded all their host.

13 I will raise [Cyrus] up in righteousness [willing in every way that which is right and proper], and I will direct all his ways; he will build My city, and he will let My captives go, not for hire or for a bribe, says the Lord of hosts.

14 Thus says the Lord: The labor *and* wealth of Egypt and the merchandise of Ethiopia and the Sabeans, men of stature, shall come over to you and they shall be yours; they shall follow you; in chains [of subjection to you] they shall come over, and they shall fall down before you; they shall make supplication to you, saying, Surely God is with you, and there is no other, no God besides Him. [I Cor. 14:25.]

15 Truly You are a God Who hides Himself, O God of Israel, the Savior.

16 They shall be put to shame, yes, confounded, all of them; they who are makers of idols shall go off into confusion together.

17 But Israel shall be saved by the Lord with an everlasting salvation; you shall not be put to shame or confounded to all eternity. [Heb. 5:9.]

18 For thus says the Lord—Who created the heavens, God Himself, Who formed the earth and made it, Who established it and did not create it to be a worthless waste; He formed it to be inhabited—I am the Lord, and there is no one else.

19 I have not spoken in secret, in a corner of the land of darkness; I did not call the descendants of Jacob [to a fruitless service], saying, Seek Me for nothing [but I promised them a just reward]. I, the Lord, speak righteousness (the truth—trustworthy, straightforward correspondence between deeds and words); I declare things that are right. [John 18:20.]

20 Assemble yourselves and come; draw near together, you survivors of the nations! They have no knowledge who carry about [in religious processions or into battle] their wooden

p Moral evil proceeds from the will of men, but physical evil proceeds from the will of God.

idols and keep on praying to a god that cannot save.

21 Declare and bring forward your strong arguments [for praying to gods that cannot save]; yes, take counsel together. Who announced this [the rise of Cyrus and his conquests] beforehand (long ago)? [What god] declared it of old? Was it not I, the Lord? And there is no other God besides Me, a rigidly *and* uncompromisingly just *and* righteous God and Savior; there is none besides Me.

22 Look to Me and be saved, all the ends of the earth! For I am God, and there is no other.

23 I have sworn by Myself, the word is gone out of My mouth in righteousness and shall not return, that unto Me every knee shall bow, every tongue shall swear [allegiance]. [Rom. 14:11; Phil. 2:10, 11; Heb. 6:13.]

24 Only in the Lord shall one say, I have righteousness (salvation and victory) and strength [to achieve]. To Him shall all come who were incensed against Him, and they shall be ashamed. [I Cor. 1:30, 31.]

25 In the Lord shall all the offspring of Israel be justified (enjoy righteousness, salvation, and victory) and shall glory.

46 BEL BOWS down, Nebo stoops [gods of Babylon, whose idols are being carried off]; their idols are on the beasts [of burden] and on the cattle. These things that you carry about are loaded as burdens on the weary beasts.

2 [The gods] stoop, they bow down together; they cannot save [their own idols], but are themselves going into captivity.

3 Listen to Me [says the Lord], O house of Jacob, and all the remnant of the house of Israel, you who have been borne by Me from your birth, carried from the womb:

4 Even to your old age I am He, and even to hair white with age will I carry you. I have made, and I will bear; yes, I will carry and will save you.

5 To whom will you liken Me and make Me equal and compare Me, that we may be alike? [Isa. 40:18-20.]

6 They lavish gold out of the cup *or* bag, weigh out silver on the scales, and hire a goldsmith, and he fashions it into a god; [then] they fall down, yes, they worship it!

7 They bear it upon their shoulders [in religious processions or into battle]; they carry it and set it down in its place, and there it stands. It cannot move from its place. Even if one cries to it for help, yet [the idol] cannot answer or save him out of his distress.

8 [Earnestly] remember this, be ashamed *and* own yourselves guilty; bring it again to mind *and* lay it to heart, O you rebels!

9 [Earnestly] remember the former things, [which I did] of old; for I am God, and there is no one else; I am God, and there is none like Me,

10 Declaring the end *and* the result from the beginning, and from ancient times the things that are not yet done, saying, My counsel shall stand, and I will do all My pleasure *and* purpose,

11 Calling a ravenous bird from the east—the man [Cyrus] who executes My counsel from a far country. Yes, I have spoken, and I will bring it to pass; I have purposed it, and I will do it.

12 Listen to Me, you stiff-hearted *and* you who have lost heart, you who are far from righteousness (from uprightness and right standing with God, and from His righteous deliverance).

13 I bring near My righteousness [in the deliverance of Israel], it will not be far off; and My salvation shall not tarry. And I will put salvation in Zion, for Israel My glory [yes, give salvation in Zion and My glory to Israel].

life point

In Isaiah 46:9, 10 the Lord says that He is the same God Who has helped us in the past; He is able to declare in the beginning how things will turn out in the end.

The Word says the Lord is the Alpha and Omega, the Beginning and the End (see Revelation 1:8). He is also everything in between. He knows before trouble ever shows up that we can be victorious if we fight the battle His way. His way is not a negative way, but a good and right way. God already has an answer before we have a problem.

Romans 8:37 affirms that we are "more than conquerors . . . through Him Who loved us." I believe that means we can know we will win before the battle even begins. Through Him we can see the end from the beginning, and we know that victory is sure.

47 COME DOWN, and sit in the dust, O Virgin Daughter of Babylon; sit on the ground [in abject humiliation]; there is no throne for you, O Daughter of the Chaldeans, for you shall no longer be called dainty and delicate.

2   Take the millstones [like the poorest female slave of the household does] and grind meal; take off your veil *and* uncover your hair. Remove your skirt, bare your leg, wade through the rivers [at the command of your captors].

3   Your nakedness shall be exposed, and your shame shall be seen. I will take vengeance, and I will spare no man [none I encounter will be able to resist Me],

4   [Says] our Redeemer—the Lord of hosts is His name—the Holy One of Israel.

5   Sit in silence and go into dark-

ness, O Daughter of the Chaldeans; for you shall no more be called the lady *and* mistress of kingdoms.

6   I was angry with My people, I profaned My inheritance [Judah]; and I gave them into your hand [Babylon]. You showed them no mercy; upon the old people you made your yoke very heavy.

7   And you said, I shall be the mistress forever! So you did not lay these things to heart, nor did you [seriously] remember the certain, ultimate end of such conduct.

8   Therefore now, hear this, you who love pleasures *and* are given over to them, you who dwell safely *and* sit securely, who say in your mind, I am [the mistress] and there is no one else besides me. I shall not sit as a widow, nor shall I know the loss of children.

9   But these two things shall come to you in a moment, in one day: loss of

life point

We learn in Isaiah 46:10 that God knows the beginning from the end of all things. He already knows what our thoughts are, and He already hears every word we will speak. He is acquainted with all our ways (see Psalm 139:1–4). Sometimes we act as though God is shocked to discover that we make mistakes. We need to remember that He is not in heaven wringing His hands, saying, "Oh, no! I had no idea you would act this way when I chose you!" God has a big eraser, and He uses it to keep our records clear and clean. Even with His foreknowledge of our weaknesses and mistakes, He still chose us on purpose and brought us into relationship with Himself through Jesus Christ. When you make a mistake, relax. God knew long ago that you would do so and has provided full forgiveness for you through His Son.

children and widowhood. They shall come upon you in full measure, in spite of the multitude of [your claims to] power given you by the assistance of evil spirits, in spite of the great abundance of your enchantments. [Rev. 18:7, 8.]

10 For you [Babylon] have trusted in your wickedness; you have said, No one sees me. Your wisdom and your knowledge led you astray, and you said in your heart and mind, I am, and there is no one besides me.

11 Therefore shall evil come upon you; you shall not know the dawning of it or how to charm it away. And a disaster and evil shall fall upon you that you shall not be able to atone for [with all your offerings to your gods]; and desolation shall come upon you suddenly, about which you shall know nothing or how to avert it.

12 Persist, then, with your enchantments and the multitude of your sorceries [Babylon], in which you have labored from your youth; and see if perhaps you will be able to profit, if you will prevail and strike terror!

13 You are wearied with your many counsels and plans. Let now the astrologers, the stargazers, and the monthly prognosticators stand up and make known to you and save you from the things that shall come upon you [Babylon].

14 Behold, they are like stubble; the fire consumes them. They cannot even deliver themselves from the power of the flame [much less deliver the nation]. There is no coal for warming or fire before which to sit!

15 Such to you shall they [the astrologers and their kind] be, those with whom you have labored and such their fate, those who have done business with you from your youth; they will wander, every one to his own quarter and in his own direction. No one will save you.

48 HEAR THIS, O house of Jacob, who are called by the name of Israel and who come forth from the seed of Judah, you who swear allegiance by the name of the Lord and make mention of the God of Israel—but not in truth and sincerity, nor in righteousness (rightness and moral and spiritual rectitude in every area and relation)—

2 For they call themselves [citizens] of the holy city and depend on the God of Israel—the Lord of hosts is His name.

3 I have declared from the beginning the former things [which happened in times past to Israel]; they went forth from My mouth and I made them known; then suddenly I did them, and they came to pass [says the Lord].

4 Because I knew that you were obstinate, and your neck was an iron sinew and your brow was brass,

5 Therefore I have declared things to come to you from of old; before they came to pass I announced them to you, so that you could not say, My idol has done them, and my graven image and my molten image have commanded them.

6 You have heard [these things foretold], now you see this fulfillment. And will you not bear witness to it? I show you specified new things from this time forth, even hidden things [kept in reserve] which you have not known.

7 They are created now [called into being by the prophetic word], and not long ago; and before today you have never heard of them, lest you should say, Behold, I knew them!

8 Yes, you have never heard, yes, you have never known; yes, from of old your ear has not been opened. For I, the Lord, knew that you, O house of Israel, dealt very treacherously; you were called a transgressor and a rebel [in revolt] from your birth.

9 For My name's sake I defer My

life point

Notice the basic principle of God's method of operation: first He declares things; then He does them.

This principle explains why God sent the prophets. They spoke God-inspired, God-instructed words that brought forth God's will from the spiritual realm into the natural realm on earth. Jesus did not come to the earth until first the prophets had spoken about Him for hundreds of years. God operates on spiritual laws that He has set in place, and we cannot ignore them.

"Sowing and reaping" is an example of a law that operates in the natural earth, but it also operates in the spiritual realm. We sow material seed, and we reap material blessings of all kinds. Words are also seeds. We sow word seeds and reap according to what we have sown.

God wanted stubborn Israel to know that it was He Who was doing great works in their lives, so He announced them ahead of time. What was the end result? The things God declared came to pass. His Word is always true, and He always does what He says He will do.

anger, and for the sake of My praise I restrain it for you, that I may not cut you off.

10 Behold, I have refined you, but not as silver; I have tried *and* chosen you in the furnace of affliction.

11 For My own sake, for My own sake, I do it [I refrain and do not utterly destroy you]; for why should I permit My name to be polluted *and* profaned [which it would be if the Lord completely destroyed His chosen people]? And I will not give My glory to another [by permitting the wor-

shipers of idols to triumph over you].

12 Listen to Me, O Jacob, and Israel, My called [ones]: I am He; I am the First, I also am the Last. [Isa. 41:4.]

13 Yes, My hand has laid the foundation of the earth, and My right hand has spread out the heavens; when I call to them, they stand forth together [to execute My decrees].

14 Assemble yourselves, all of you, and hear! Who among them [the gods and Chaldean astrologers] has foretold these things? The Lord has loved him [Cyrus of Persia]; he will do His pleasure *and* purpose on Babylon, and his arm will be against the Chaldeans.

15 I, even I, have foretold it; yes, I have called him [Cyrus]; I have brought him, and [the Lord] shall make his way prosperous.

16 Come near to me and listen to this: I have not spoken in secret from the beginning; from the time that it happened, I was there. And now the Lord God has sent His Spirit in *and* with me.

17 Thus says the Lord, your Redeemer, the Holy One of Israel: I am the Lord your God, Who teaches you to profit, Who leads you in the way that you should go.

18 Oh, that you had hearkened to My commandments! Then your peace *and* prosperity would have been like a flowing river, and your righteousness

life point

God has an individual plan for each person. If you will go to Him and submit to Him, He will come into your heart and commune with you. He will teach you and guide you in the way you should go. Do not try to be someone else. Do not try to do what someone else does. Just allow the Lord to show *you* how to fellowship with Him. Then follow Him step-by-step as He directs your life.

[the holiness and purity of the nation] like the [abundant] waves of the sea.

19 Your offspring would have been like the sand, and your descendants like the offspring of the sea; their name would not be cut off or destroyed from before Me. [Gen. 13:16; Jer. 33:22; Luke 19:42.]

20 Go forth out of Babylon, flee from the Chaldeans! With a voice of singing declare, tell this, cause it to go forth even to the end of the earth; say, The Lord has redeemed His servant Jacob!

21 And they thirsted not when He led them through the deserts; He caused the waters to flow out of the rock for them; He split the rock also, and the waters gushed out.

22 There is no peace, says the Lord, for the wicked.

49 LISTEN TO me, O isles *and* coastlands, and hearken, you peoples from afar. The Lord has called me from the womb; from the body of my mother He has named my name.

2 And He has made my mouth like a sharp sword; in the shadow of His hand has He hid me and made me a polished arrow; in His quiver has He kept me close *and* concealed me.

3 And [the Lord] said to me, You are My �q servant, Israel [you who strive with God and with men and prevail], in whom I will be glorified. [Gen. 32:28; Deut. 7:6; 26:18, 19; Eph. 1:4-6.]

4 Then I said, I have labored in vain, I have spent my strength for nothing and in empty futility; yet surely my right is with the Lord, and my recompense is with my God.

5 And now, says the Lord—Who formed me from the womb to be His servant to bring Jacob back to Him and that Israel might be gathered to Him *and* not be swept away, for I am honorable in the eyes of the Lord and my God has become my strength—

6 He says, It is too light a thing that you should be My servant to raise up the tribes of Jacob and to restore the survivors [of the judgments] of Israel; I will also give you for a light to the nations, that My salvation may extend to the end of the earth.

7 Thus says the Lord, the Redeemer of Israel, Israel's Holy One, to him whom man rejects *and* despises, to him whom the nations abhor, to the servant of rulers: Kings shall see you and arise; princes, and they shall prostrate themselves, because of the Lord, Who is faithful, the Holy One of Israel, Who has chosen you.

8 Thus says the Lord, In an acceptable *and* favorable time I have heard *and* answered you, and in a day of salvation I have helped you; and I will preserve you and give you for a covenant to the people, to raise up *and* establish the land [from its present state of ruin] and to apportion *and* cause them to inherit the desolate [moral wastes of heathenism, their] heritages, [II Cor. 6:2.]

9 Saying to those who are bound, Come forth, and to those who are in [spiritual] darkness, Show yourselves [come into the light of the Sun of righteousness]. They shall feed in ʳall the ways [in which they go], and their pastures shall be [not in deserts, but] on all the bare [grass-covered] hills.

10 They will not hunger or thirst, neither will mirage [mislead] or scorching wind or sun smite them; for He Who has mercy on them will lead

q It is difficult to know positively to whom the Lord is speaking in these next verses—whether (1) to the Messiah, (2) to Israel, or (3) to Isaiah. The large majority of early authorities favored interpretation (1); later scholars incline toward interpretation (2). See also footnote on Isa. 42:1. **r** *The Septuagint* (Greek translation of the Old Testament) here reads, "In all the highways they shall be fed, and there shall be pasture for them in all the paths."

them, and by springs of water will He guide them. [Rev. 7:16, 17.]

11 And I will make all My mountains a way, and My highways will be raised up.

12 Behold, these shall come from afar—and, behold, these from the north and from the west, and these from the land of Sinim (China).

13 Sing for joy, O heavens, and be joyful, O earth, and break forth into singing, O mountains! For the Lord has comforted His people and will have compassion upon His afflicted.

14 But Zion [Jerusalem, her people as seen in captivity] said, The Lord has forsaken me, and my Lord has forgotten me.

15 [And the Lord answered] Can a woman forget her nursing child, that she should not have compassion on the son of her womb? Yes, they may forget, yet I will not forget you.

16 Behold, I have indelibly imprinted (tattooed a picture of) you on the palm of each of My hands; [O Zion] your walls are continually before Me.

17 Your children *and* your builders make haste; your destroyers and those who laid you waste go forth from you.

18 Lift up your eyes round about and see [the returning exiles, ready to rebuild Jerusalem]; all these gather together and come to you. As I live, says the Lord, you [Zion] shall surely clothe yourself with them all as with an ornament and bind them on you as a bride does.

19 For your waste and desolate places and your land [once the scene] of destruction surely now [in coming years] will be too narrow to accommodate the population, and those who once swallowed you up will be far away.

20 The children of your bereavement [born during your captivity] shall yet say in your ears, The place is too narrow for me; make room for me, that I may live.

21 Then [Zion], you will say in your heart, Who has borne me all these children, seeing that I lost my offspring and am alone *and* barren *and* unfruitful, an exile put away and wandering hither and thither? And who brought them up? Behold, I was left alone [put away by the Lord, my Husband]; from where then did all these children come?

22 Thus says the Lord God: Behold, I will lift up My hand to the Gentile nations and set up My standard *and* raise high My signal banner to the peoples; and they will bring your sons in the bosom of their garments, and your daughters will be carried upon their shoulders.

23 And kings shall be your foster fathers *and* guardians, and their queens your nursing mothers. They shall bow down to you with their faces to the earth and lick up the dust of your feet; and you shall know [with an acquaintance and understanding based on and grounded in personal experience] that I am the Lord; for they shall

speak the Word

Thank You, God, for imprinting me on Your hand. That way, I know that You will not forget me!
ADAPTED FROM ISAIAH **49:16**

God, I wait for, look for, hope for, and expect You in my life. I know that I will not be put to shame.
ADAPTED FROM ISAIAH **49:23**

not be put to shame who wait for, look for, hope for, *and* expect Me.

24 Shall the prey be taken from the mighty, or the lawful captives of the just be delivered?

25 For thus says the Lord: Even the captives of the mighty will be taken away, and the prey of the terrible will be delivered; for I will contend with him who contends with you, and I will give safety to your children *and* ease them.

26 And I will make those who oppress you consume themselves [in mutually destructive wars], thus eating their own flesh; and they will be drunk with their own blood, as with sweet wine; and all flesh will know [with a knowledge grounded in personal experience] that I, the Lord, am your Savior and your Redeemer, the Mighty One of Jacob.

50 THUS SAYS the Lord: Where is the bill of your mother's divorce with which I put her away, O Israel? Or which of My creditors is it to whom I have sold you? Behold, for your iniquities you were sold, and for your transgressions was your mother put away.

2 Why, when I came, was there no man? When I called, why was there no one to answer? Is My hand shortened at all, that it cannot redeem? Or have I no power to deliver? Behold, at My rebuke I dry up the sea, I make the rivers a desert; their fish stink because there is no water, and they die of thirst.

3 I clothe the heavens with [the] blackness [of murky storm clouds],

and I make sackcloth [of mourning] their covering.

4 [The ˢServant of God says] The Lord God has given Me the tongue of a disciple *and* of one who is taught, that I should know how to speak a word in season to him who is weary. He wakens Me morning by morning, He wakens My ear to hear as a disciple [as one who is taught].

5 The Lord God has opened My ear, and I have not been rebellious or turned backward.

6 I gave My back to the smiters and My cheeks to those who plucked off the hair; I hid not My face from shame and spitting. [Matt. 26:67; 27:30; John 19:1.]

life point

The prophet said that the Lord had given him the tongue of a disciple—a learner, one who is taught—so that he would know how to "speak a word in season" to the weary (Isaiah 50:4).

Do you see weary people in the body of Christ? While the world has serious problems that can wear us down, we can experience joy from God, Who lifts us up. According to the Bible, the joy of the Lord is our strength (see Nehemiah 8:10). Joy is not found in our circumstances; it is found in Christ, the Mystery of the Ages, Who dwells within us. You and I are learning to find our joy in Christ alone. While we are in the process, speaking words in due season to one another will keep us from growing weary.

speak the Word

Thank You, God, for contending with those who contend with me.
ADAPTED FROM ISAIAH **49:25**

s See footnote on Isa. 42:1.

7 For the Lord God helps Me; therefore have I not been ashamed *or* confounded. Therefore have I set My face like a flint, and I know that I shall not be put to shame. [Luke 9:51; Isa. 52:13; 53:10-12.]

8 He is near Who declares Me in the right. Who will contend with Me? Let us stand forth together! Who is My adversary? Let him come near to Me. [Rom. 8:33-35; I Tim. 3:16.]

9 Behold, the Lord God will help Me; who is he who will condemn Me? Behold, they all will wax old *and* be worn out as a garment; the moth will eat them up. [Heb. 1:11, 12.]

10 Who is among you who [reverently] fears the Lord, who obeys the voice of His Servant, yet who walks in darkness *and* deep trouble and has no shining splendor [in his heart]? Let him rely on, trust in, *and* be confident in the name of the Lord, and let him lean upon *and* be supported by his God.

11 Behold, all you [enemies of your own selves] who attempt to kindle your own fires [and work out your own plans of salvation], who surround *and* gird yourselves with momentary sparks, darts, *and* firebrands that you set aflame!—walk by the light of your self-made fire and of the sparks that you have kindled [for yourself, if you will]! But this shall you have from My hand: you shall lie down in grief *and* in torment. [Isa. 66:24.]

51 HEARKEN TO Me, you who follow after rightness *and* justice, you who seek *and* inquire of [and require] the Lord [claiming Him by necessity and by right]: look to the rock from which you were hewn and to the hole in the quarry from which you were dug;

2 Look to Abraham your father and to Sarah who bore you; for I called him when he was but one, and I blessed him and made him many.

3 For the Lord will comfort Zion; He will comfort all her waste places. And He will make her wilderness like Eden, and her desert like the garden of the Lord. Joy and gladness will be found in her, thanksgiving and the voice of song *or* instrument of praise.

4 Listen to Me [the Lord], O My people, and give ear to Me, O My nation; for a [divine] law will go forth from Me, and I will establish My justice for a light to the peoples.

5 My rightness *and* justice are near, My salvation is going forth, and My arms shall rule the peoples; the islands shall wait for *and* expect Me, and on My arm shall they trust *and* wait with hope.

6 Lift up your eyes to the heavens, and look upon the earth beneath; for the heavens shall be dissolved *and* vanish away like smoke, and the earth shall wax old like a garment, and they that dwell therein shall die in like manner [like gnats]. But My salvation shall be forever, and My rightness *and* justice [and faithfully fulfilled promise] shall not be abolished. [Matt. 24:35; Heb. 1:11; II Pet. 3:10.]

7 Listen to Me, you who know rightness *and* justice *and* right standing with God, the people in whose heart is My law *and* My instruction: fear not the reproach of men, neither be afraid *nor* dismayed at their revilings.

8 For [in comparison with the Lord they are so weak that things as insignificant as] the moth shall eat them up like a garment, and the worm shall eat them like wool. But My rightness *and* justice [and faithfully fulfilled promise] shall be forever, and My salvation to all generations.

9 [Zion now cries to the Lord, the God of Israel] Awake, awake, put on strength *and* might, O arm of the Lord; awake, as in the ancient days, as in the generations of long ago. Was it not You Who cut Rahab [Egypt] in pieces, Who pierced the dragon [symbol of Egypt]? [Isa. 30:7.]

10 Was it not You Who dried up the Red Sea, the waters of the great deep, Who made the depths of the sea a way for the redeemed to pass over? [Why then are we left so long in captivity?]

11 [The Lord God says] And the redeemed of the Lord shall return and come with singing to Zion; everlasting joy shall be upon their heads. They shall obtain joy and gladness, and sorrow and sighing shall flee away. [Rev. 7:17; 21:1, 4.]

12 I, even I, am He Who comforts you. Who are you, that you should be afraid of man, who shall die, and of a son of man, who shall be made [as destructible] as grass,

13 That you should forget the Lord your Maker, Who stretched forth the heavens and laid the foundations of the earth, and fear continually every day because of the fury of the oppressor, when he makes ready to destroy or even though he did so? And where is the fury of the oppressor?

14 The captive exile *and* he who is bent down by chains shall speedily be released; and he shall not die and go down to the pit of destruction, nor shall his food fail.

15 For I am the Lord your God, Who stirs up the sea so that its waves roar *and* Who by rebuke restrains it—the Lord of hosts is His name.

16 And I have put My words in your mouth and have covered you with the shadow of My hand, that I may fix the [new] heavens as a tabernacle and lay the foundations of a [new] earth and say to Zion, You are My people. [Isa. 65:17; 66:22; Rev. 21:1.]

17 Arouse yourself, awake! Stand up, O Jerusalem, you who have drunk at the hand of the Lord the cup of His wrath, you who have drunk the cup of staggering *and* intoxication to the dregs.

18 There is none to guide her among all the sons she has borne; neither is there anyone to take her by the hand

among all the sons whom she has brought up.

19 Two kinds of calamities have befallen you—but who feels sorry for *and* commiserates you?—they are desolation and destruction [on the land and city], and famine and sword [on the inhabitants]—how shall I comfort you *or* by whom?

20 Your sons have fainted; they lie [like corpses] at the head of all the streets, like an antelope in a net; they are full [from drinking] of the wrath of the Lord, the rebuke of your God.

21 Therefore, now hear this, you who are afflicted, and [who are] drunk, but not with wine [but thrown down by the wrath of God].

22 Thus says your Lord, the Lord, and your God, Who pleads the cause of His people: Behold, I have taken from your hand the cup of staggering *and* intoxication; the cup of My wrath you shall drink no more.

23 And I will put it into the hands of your tormentors *and* oppressors, those who said to you, Bow down, that we may ride *or* tread over you; and you have made your back like the ground and like the street for them to pass over.

52 AWAKE, AWAKE, put on your strength, O Zion; put on your beautiful garments, O Jerusalem, the holy city; for henceforth there shall no more come into you the uncircumcised and the unclean. [Rev. 21:27.]

2 Shake yourself from the dust; arise, sit [erect in a dignified place], O Jerusalem; loose yourself from the bonds of your neck, O captive Daughter of Zion.

3 For thus says the Lord: You were sold for nothing, and you shall be redeemed without money.

4 For thus says the Lord God: My people went down at the first into Egypt to sojourn there; and [many years later Sennacherib] the Assyrian oppressed them for nothing. [Now I delivered you from both Egypt and Assyria; what then can prevent Me from delivering you from Babylon?]

5 But now what have I here, says the Lord, seeing that My people have been taken away for nothing? Those who rule over them howl [with joy], says the Lord, and My name continually is blasphemed all day long. [Rom. 2:24.]

6 Therefore My people shall know what My name is *and* what it means; therefore they shall know in that day that I am He who speaks; behold, I AM! [Exod. 3:13, 14.]

7 How beautiful upon the mountains are the feet of him who brings good tidings, who publishes peace, who brings good tidings of good, who publishes salvation, who says to Zion, Your God reigns! [Acts 10:36; Rom. 10:15; Eph. 6:14-16.]

8 Hark, your watchmen lift up their voices; together they sing for joy; for they shall see eye to eye the return of the Lord to Zion.

9 Break forth joyously, sing together, you waste places of Jerusalem, for the Lord has comforted His people, He has redeemed Jerusalem!

10 The Lord has made bare His holy arm before the eyes of all the nations [revealing Himself as the One by Whose direction the redemption of Israel from captivity is accomplished], and all the ends of the earth shall witness the salvation of our God. [Luke 2:29-32; 3:6.]

11 Depart, depart, go out from there [the lands of exile]! Touch no unclean thing! Go out of the midst of her [Babylon]; cleanse yourselves *and* be clean, you who bear the vessels of the Lord [on your journey from there]. [II Cor. 6:16, 17.]

12 For you will not go out with haste, nor will you go in flight [as was necessary when Israel left Egypt]; for the Lord will go before you, and the God of Israel will be your rear guard.

13 Behold, My 'Servant shall deal wisely *and* shall prosper; He shall be exalted and extolled and shall stand very high.

14 [For many the Servant of God became an object of horror; many were astonished at Him.] His face *and* His whole appearance were marred more than any man's, and His form beyond that of the sons of men—but just as many were astonished at Him,

15 So shall He startle *and* sprinkle many nations, and kings shall shut their mouths because of Him; for that which has not been told them shall they see, and that which they have not heard shall they consider *and* understand. [Rom. 15:21.]

53 WHO HAS believed (trusted in, relied upon, and clung to) our message [of that which was revealed to us]? And to whom has the arm of the Lord been disclosed? [John 12:38-41; Rom. 10:16.]

2 For [the Servant of God] grew up before Him like a tender plant, and like a root out of dry ground; He has no form or comeliness [royal, kingly pomp], that we should look at Him,

speak the Word

Thank You, God, for always going before me and behind me. I know that I am safe in Your presence!
ADAPTED FROM ISAIAH 52:12

t See footnote on Isa. 42:1.

and no beauty that we should desire Him.

3 He was despised and rejected *and* forsaken by men, a Man of sorrows *and* pains, and acquainted with grief *and* sickness; and like One from Whom men hide their faces He was despised, and we did not appreciate His worth *or* have any esteem for Him.

life point

Jesus did not seem to let the fact that He was despised and rejected bother Him (see Isaiah 53:3). He certainly did not complain about it. I am sure He felt intense pain, just as you and I do when we are rejected, but He did not allow it to prevent Him from fulfilling His purpose. Do not let it hinder you either!

4 Surely He has borne our griefs (sicknesses, weaknesses, and distresses) and carried our sorrows *and* pains [of punishment], yet we [ignorantly] considered Him stricken, smitten, and afflicted by God [as if with leprosy]. [Matt. 8:17.]

5 But He was wounded for our transgressions, He was bruised for our guilt *and* iniquities; the chastisement [needful to obtain] peace *and* well-being for us was upon Him, and with the stripes [that wounded] Him we are healed *and* made whole.

6 All we like sheep have gone astray, we have turned every one to his own way; and the Lord has made to light upon Him the guilt *and* iniquity of us all. [I Pet. 2:24, 25.]

7 He was oppressed, [yet when] He was afflicted, He was submissive *and* opened not His mouth; like a lamb that is led to the slaughter, and as a sheep before her shearers is dumb, so He opened not His mouth.

8 By oppression and judgment He was taken away; and as for His generation, who among them considered that He was cut off out of the land of the living [stricken to His death] for the transgression of my [Isaiah's] people, to whom the stroke was due?

9 And they assigned Him a grave with the wicked, and with a rich man in His death, although He had done no violence, neither was any deceit in His mouth. [Matt. 27:57-60; I Pet. 2:22, 23.]

10 Yet it was the will of the Lord to bruise Him; He has put Him to grief *and* made Him sick. When You *and* He make His life an offering for sin [and He has risen from the dead, in time to come], He shall see His [spiritual] offspring, He shall prolong His days, and the will *and* pleasure of the Lord shall prosper in His hand.

11 He shall see [the fruit] of the travail of His soul and be satisfied; by His knowledge of Himself [which He possesses and imparts to others] shall My [uncompromisingly] righteous One, My Servant, justify many *and* make many righteous (upright and in right standing with God), for He shall bear their iniquities *and* their guilt [with the consequences, says the Lord].

12 Therefore will I divide Him a portion with the great [kings and rulers], and He shall divide the spoil with the mighty, because He poured out His life unto death, and [He let Himself]

speak the Word

Thank You, Jesus, for bearing my griefs and sicknesses, for carrying my pain and sorrow, for being wounded for my sin and obtaining peace and well-being for me. I declare today that by Your stripes, I am healed.

ADAPTED FROM ISAIAH **53:4, 5**

condemnation or conviction?

If condemnation is filling our consciences, it is not from God. He sent Jesus to die for us to pay the price for our sins. According to Isaiah 53:3–6 and many passages in the New Testament, Jesus bore our sin and the guilty condemnation that accompanies sin. We should get rid of the sin and not keep the guilt. Once God breaks the yoke of sin from us, He removes the guilt too. He is faithful and just to forgive all of our sins and to continuously cleanse us from all unrighteousness (see I John 1:9).

How does condemnation differ from conviction? Let me explain it this way: We need forgiveness every day of our lives. The Holy Spirit sets off the alarm in our consciences so we can recognize sin, and He gives us the power of the blood of Jesus to continuously cleanse us from sin and keep us right before Him. This process is called "conviction," and it is of the Lord, while condemnation is from the enemy.

Often when we are convicted of sin, we become grouchy while God is dealing with us. Until we admit our sin, become ready to turn from it, and ask for forgiveness, we feel a pressure that squeezes out the worst we have in us. As soon as we come into agreement with God, our peace returns and our behavior improves.

The devil knows that condemnation and shame keep us from approaching God in prayer so our needs can be met and we can once again enjoy fellowship with God. Feeling bad about ourselves or thinking that God is angry with us separates us from His presence. God does not leave us, but we withdraw from Him because of our guilt or fear.

That is why it is so important to discern the truth and know the difference between conviction and condemnation. Remember, if you heed conviction, it lifts you up and out of sin; condemnation only makes you feel bad about yourself.

When you pray for people to change, the Holy Spirit convicts them of their sin, and many times they will start acting worse than they did before. But do not let that make you believe your prayers are ineffective. Their behavior is actually a good sign that God is indeed working, convicting them of sin and convincing them of their need to change. So keep praying!

As you pray, regularly ask God to convict you of your own sin. Realize that conviction is a blessing, not a problem. If only perfect people could pray and receive answers, nobody would pray. We do not need to be perfect, but we do need to be cleansed of sin. As we begin our prayer time, it is good to ask the heavenly Father to cleanse us of all sin and unrighteousness. When we pray in Jesus' name, we are presenting to our Father all that Jesus is, not all that we are.

Experiencing conviction through the Holy Spirit's work in our lives is necessary for a vital walk with God. Remember that conviction is a gift from God because it leads us to hear from Him. Do not make the mistake of letting it condemn you, as I did for years. Let conviction lift you to a new level in God. Do not resist it; receive it.

be regarded as a criminal *and* be numbered with the transgressors; yet He bore [and took away] the sin of many and made intercession for the transgressors (the rebellious). [Luke 22:37.]

54 SING, ᵘO barren one, you who did not bear; break forth into singing and cry aloud, you who did not travail with child! For the [spiritual] children of the desolate one will be more than the children of the married wife, says the Lord. [Gal. 4:27.]

2 Enlarge the place of your tent, and let the curtains of your habitations be stretched out; spare not; lengthen your cords and strengthen your stakes,

3 For you will spread abroad to the right hand and to the left; and your offspring will possess the nations and make the desolate cities to be inhabited.

4 Fear not, for you shall not be ashamed; neither be confounded *and* depressed, for you shall not be put to shame. For you shall forget the shame of your youth, and you shall not [seriously] remember the reproach of your widowhood any more.

5 For your Maker is your Husband—the Lord of hosts is His name—and the Holy One of Israel is your Redeemer; the God of the whole earth He is called.

6 For the Lord has called you like a woman forsaken, grieved in spirit, *and* heartsore—even a wife [wooed and won] in youth, when she is [later] refused *and* scorned, says your God.

7 For a brief moment I forsook you, but with great compassion *and* mercy I will gather you [to Me] again.

8 In a little burst of wrath I hid My face from you for a moment, but with age-enduring love *and* kindness I will have compassion *and* mercy on you, says the Lord, your Redeemer.

9 For this is like the days of Noah to Me; as I swore that the waters of Noah should no more go over the earth, so have I sworn that I will not be angry with you or rebuke you.

10 For though the mountains should depart and the hills be shaken *or* removed, yet My love *and* kindness shall not depart from you, nor shall My covenant of peace *and* completeness be removed, says the Lord, Who has compassion on you.

11 O you afflicted [city], storm-tossed and not comforted, behold, I

speak the Word

Thank You, God, for being my Redeemer, the God of the whole earth.
ADAPTED FROM ISAIAH **54:5**

God, I declare today that Your love and kindness will never depart from me and that Your covenant of peace and completeness will never be removed.
ADAPTED FROM ISAIAH **54:10**

u Although this chapter is primarily intended to express Zion's joy over redemption, it has also a very personal, long-neglected, and often overlooked message for women—the lonely, the disappointed, the childless, the widow. It has all the glorious confidence and assurance, the incentive and understanding, for which feminine hearts have longed throughout the ages! Every woman who will read it every week for a year with receptive heart and mind will find herself not only spiritually prepared for her own childlessness or widowhood, should it come, but also supplied with rich treasure with which to address the similar needs of countless other aching hearts to whom the Holy Spirit is here speaking.

free from shame

Do you have a shame-based nature? Are you rooted or grounded in shame? The curse and power of shame can be broken off from you through the power of God.

We know from Isaiah 54:4 that the Lord has promised to remove the shame and dishonor from us so that we remember it no more. In fact, God has promised that in their place He will pour out upon us a twofold blessing. We will possess double what we have lost, and we will have everlasting joy (see Isaiah 61:7).

Take your stand on the Word of God. Become rooted and grounded, not in shame and dishonor, but in the love of Christ, being complete in Him.

Ask the Lord to work a healing miracle in your mind, will, and emotions. Let Him come in and fulfill what He came to do: heal your broken heart, bind up your wounds, give you beauty for ashes, joy for mourning, a garment of praise instead of heaviness, and a double honor for a double shame (see Isaiah 61:1–3).

Determine that from this moment on you are going to reject the roots of bitterness, shame, negativism, and perfectionism, and nourish the roots of joy, peace, love, and power.

By faith, draw the bloodline of Jesus Christ across your life and boldly declare that you are healed from the pains and wounds of your past; you have been set free to live a new life of health and wholeness. Continue to praise the Lord and confess His Word over yourself, claiming His forgiveness, cleansing, and healing.

Stop blaming yourself and feeling guilty, unworthy, and unloved. Instead begin to say, "If God is for me, who can be against me? God loves me, and I love myself. Praise the Lord, I am free in Jesus' name, amen!"

will set your stones in fair colors [in antimony to enhance their brilliance] and lay your foundations with sapphires.

12 And I will make your windows *and* pinnacles of [sparkling] agates *or* rubies, and your gates of [shining] carbuncles, and all your walls [of your enclosures] of precious stones. [Rev. 21:19-21.]

13 And all your [spiritual] children shall be disciples [taught by the Lord and obedient to His will], and great shall be the peace *and* undisturbed composure of your children. [John 6:45.]

14 You shall establish yourself in righteousness (rightness, in conformity with God's will and order): you shall be far from even the thought of oppression *or* destruction, for you shall not fear, and from terror, for it shall not come near you.

15 Behold, they may gather together

speak the Word

God, I declare that all my children shall be taught by You and that great shall be their peace.
ADAPTED FROM ISAIAH 54:13

and stir up strife, but it is not from Me. Whoever stirs up strife against you shall fall *and* surrender to you.

16 Behold, I have created the smith who blows on the fire of coals and who produces a weapon for its purpose; and I have created the devastator to destroy.

17 But no weapon that is formed against you shall prosper, and every tongue that shall rise against you in judgment you shall show to be in the wrong. This [peace, righteousness, security, triumph over opposition] is the heritage of the servants of the Lord [those in whom the ideal Servant of the Lord is reproduced]; this is the righteousness *or* the vindication which they obtain from Me [this is that which I impart to them as their justification], says the Lord.

55 WAIT *and* listen, everyone who is thirsty! Come to the waters; and he who has no money, come, buy and eat! Yes, come, buy [priceless, spiritual] wine and milk without money and without price [simply for the self-surrender that accepts the blessing]. [Rev. 21:6, 7; 22:17.]

2 Why do you spend your money for that which is not bread, and your earnings for what does not satisfy? Hearken diligently to Me, and eat what is good, and let your soul delight itself in fatness [the profuseness of spiritual joy]. [Jer. 31:12-14.]

3 Incline your ear [submit and consent to the divine will] and come to Me; hear, and your soul will revive; and I will make an everlasting covenant *or* league with you, even the sure mercy (kindness, goodwill, and compassion) promised to David. [II Sam. 7:8-16; Acts 13:34; Heb. 13:20.]

4 Behold, I have appointed him (Him) [David, as a representative of the Messiah, or the Messiah Himself] to be a witness [one (One) who shall testify of salvation] to the nations, a prince (Prince) and commander (Commander) to the peoples.

5 Behold, you v[Israel] shall call nations that you know not, and nations that do not know you shall run to you because of the Lord your God, and of the Holy One of Israel, for He has glorified you.

6 Seek, inquire for, *and* require the Lord while He may be found [claiming Him by necessity and by right]; call upon Him while He is near.

7 Let the wicked forsake his way and the unrighteous man his thoughts; and let him return to the Lord, and He will have love, pity, *and* mercy for him, and to our God, for He will multiply to him His abundant pardon.

8 For My thoughts are not your thoughts, neither are your ways My ways, says the Lord.

9 For as the heavens are higher than the earth, so are My ways higher than your ways and My thoughts than your thoughts.

10 For as the rain and snow come

speak the Word

I declare today, God, that no weapon formed against me will prosper and that every tongue that rises against me in judgment will be proved wrong. This is my heritage in You!

ADAPTED FROM ISAIAH **54:17**

---

v The identification of the one here addressed is uncertain. A proportionately large number of authorities believe it to be Israel, as here indicated, but other interpreters think it is the Messiah [the second David], or David as His representative.

down from the heavens, and return not there again, but water the earth and make it bring forth and sprout, that it may give seed to the sower and bread to the eater, [II Cor. 9:10.]

11 So shall My word be that goes forth out of My mouth: it shall not return to Me void [without producing any effect, useless], but it shall accomplish that which I please *and* purpose, and it shall prosper in the thing for which I sent it.

life point

The prophets were mouthpieces for God. They were called to speak God's words to people, situations, cities, dry bones, mountains, or whatever God told them to speak to. To fulfill their God-ordained mission, they had to be submitted to the Lord, and their mouths had to be consecrated to Him.

Those who desire to be used by God need to allow Him to deal with them concerning their mouths and the things they say. If you want Him to use you, be prepared for Him to deal with you concerning your words so that you are able to represent Him well with your mouth when the time comes for you to speak His Word.

12 For you shall go out [from the spiritual exile caused by sin and evil into the homeland] with joy and be led forth [by your Leader, the Lord Himself, and His word] with peace; the mountains and the hills shall break forth before you into singing, and all the trees of the field shall clap their hands.

13 Instead of the thorn shall come up the cypress tree, and instead of the brier shall come up the myrtle tree; and it shall be to the Lord for a name of renown, for an everlasting sign [of

jubilant exaltation] *and* memorial [to His praise], which shall not be cut off.

56 THUS SAYS the Lord: Keep justice, do *and* use righteousness (conformity to the will of God which brings salvation), for My salvation is soon to come and My righteousness (My rightness and justice) to be revealed. [Isa. 62:1, 11; Matt. 3:2; Luke 21:31; Rom. 13:11, 12.]

2 Blessed, happy, *and* fortunate is the man who does this, and the son of man who lays hold of it *and* binds himself fast to it, who keeps sacred the Sabbath so as not to profane it, and keeps his hand from doing any evil.

3 Let not the foreigner who has joined himself to the Lord say, The Lord will surely separate me from His people. And let not the eunuch say, Behold, I am a dry tree.

4 For thus says the Lord: To the eunuchs who keep My Sabbaths and choose the things which please Me and hold firmly My covenant—

5 To them I will give in My house and within My walls a memorial and a name better [and more enduring] than sons and daughters; I will give them an everlasting name that will not be cut off.

6 Also the foreigners who join themselves to the Lord to minister to Him and to love the name of the Lord and to be His servants, everyone who keeps the Sabbath so as not to profane it and who holds fast My covenant [by conscientious obedience]—

7 All these I will bring to My holy mountain and make them joyful in My house of prayer. Their burnt offerings and their sacrifices will be accepted on My altar; for My house will be called a house of prayer for all peoples.

8 Thus says the Lord God, Who gathers the outcasts of Israel: I will

the power of God's Word

God's Word is filled with inherent power. When God speaks, powerful things take place. As we read in Isaiah 55:11, His Word never returns void; it always accomplishes its purpose. When we learn to speak God's Word instead of rehearsing how we feel or declaring what we think, we are also releasing power. The Word of God spoken in faith from a believer's mouth can change circumstances. We may experience negative facts in our lives, but God's Word is truth, and truth is more powerful than facts.

Lazarus was dead; that was a fact. But when Jesus, Who is the Truth, walked up to the tomb and spoke, that truth changed the facts. Throughout the Gospels, we repeatedly read of people who were sick and demon-possessed who went to Jesus. When He spoke, their facts changed. They were healed, delivered, and set free. We must never magnify the facts of our circumstances above God and the power of His Word. When God speaks, things change!

Actually, God has spoken, and all we need to do is believe what He has said. His Word is loaded with promises that are for anyone who will believe them and act accordingly. Just as you may have, I had a set of unpleasant facts in my life. I had been badly abused. I was emotionally wounded and experienced various personality disorders as a result of enduring a very dysfunctional life. I had a sour attitude, a chip on my shoulder, and was filled with bitterness and unforgiveness. But Jesus came into my life, and I learned to believe and speak His Word in faith, and today I am free from all those things that were definitely negative facts years ago.

God compares His Word to seed. When we plant the seed by speaking it, praying it, believing it, and acting upon it, it will produce what it says. God promises us that it will produce! Begin to speak God's Word regularly and believe what it says more than you believe your circumstances. Hold fast your confession of faith in Him (see Hebrews 4:14), and soon you will be sharing your testimony of victory with others.

gather yet others to [Israel] besides those already gathered.

9 All you beasts of the field, come to devour, all you beasts (hostile nations) in the forest.

10 [Israel's] watchmen are blind, they are all without knowledge; they are all dumb dogs, they cannot bark; dreaming, lying down, they love to slumber.

11 Yes, the dogs are greedy; they never have enough. And such are the shepherds who cannot understand;

they have all turned to their own way, each one to his own gain, from every quarter [one and all].

12 Come, say they, We will fetch wine, and we will fill ourselves with strong drink! And tomorrow shall be as this day, a day great beyond measure.

57 THE RIGHTEOUS man perishes, and no one lays it to heart; and merciful *and* devout men are taken away, with no

life point

Under the old covenant, the temple was the house of God, the place of prayer for His people. Under the new covenant, *we* are now God's house because He dwells within us (see I Corinthians 3:16; 6:19). We may still be under construction, but nonetheless we are His house, His tabernacle, His dwelling place. Therefore, we should consider ourselves "houses of prayer."

Ephesians 6:18 gives some practical instruction on how to be a true house of prayer. It lets us know that we can pray anywhere at any time about anything, and that we should be watchful to do so: "Pray at all times (on every occasion, in every season) in the Spirit, with all [manner of] prayer and entreaty. To that end keep alert and watch with strong purpose and perseverance, interceding in behalf of all the saints (God's consecrated people)." Believing and practicing Ephesians 6:18 can be life-changing. This kind of continual communion with God helps us truly become the living "houses of prayer" that God speaks of in Isaiah 56:7.

one considering that the uncompromisingly upright *and* godly person is taken away from the calamity *and* evil to come [even through wickedness].

2 He [in death] enters into peace; they rest in their beds, each one who walks straight *and* in his uprightness.

3 But come close, you sons of a sorceress [nursed in witchcraft and superstition], you offspring of an adulterer and a harlot.

4 Against whom do you make sport *and* take your delight? Against whom do you open wide your mouth and put out your tongue? Are you not your-

selves the children of transgression, the offspring of deceit—

5 You who burn with lust [inflaming yourselves with idols] among the oaks, under every green tree, you who slay the children [in sacrifice] in the valleys under the clefts of the rocks?

6 Among the smooth stones of the valley is your portion; they, they [the idols] are your lot; to them you have poured out a drink offering, you have offered a cereal offering. Should I be quiet in spite of all these things [and leave them unpunished—bearing them with patience]?

7 Upon a lofty and high mountain you have openly *and* shamelessly set your [idolatrous and adulterous] bed; even there you went up to offer sacrifice [in spiritual unfaithfulness to your divine Husband].

8 Behind the door and the doorpost you have set up your [idol] symbol [as a substitute for the Scripture text God ordered]. Deserting Me, you have uncovered and ascended and enlarged your bed; and you have made a [fresh] bargain for yourself with [the adulterers], and you loved their bed, where you saw [a beckoning hand or a passion-inflaming image]. [Deut. 6:5, 6, 9; 11:18, 20.]

9 And you went to the king [of foreign lands with gifts] *or* to Molech [the god] with oil and increased your perfumes *and* ointments; you sent your messengers far off and debased yourself even to Sheol (Hades) [symbol of an abysmal depth of degradation].

10 You were wearied with the length of your way [in trying to find rest and satisfaction in alliances apart from the true God], yet you did not say, There is no result *or* profit. You found quickened strength; therefore you were not faint *or* heartsick [or penitent].

11 Of whom have you been so afraid

and in dread that you lied *and* were treacherous and did not [seriously] remember Me, did not even give Me a thought? Have I not been silent, even for a long time, and so you do not fear Me?

12 I will expose your [pretended] righteousness and your doings, but they will not help you.

13 When you cry out, let your [rabble] collection of idols deliver you! But the wind shall take them all, a breath shall carry them away. But he who takes refuge in Me shall possess the land [Judea] and shall inherit My holy mountain [Zion, also the heavenly inheritance and the spiritual Zion]. [Ps. 37:9, 11; 69:35, 36; Isa. 49:8; Matt. 5:5; Heb. 12:22.]

14 And the word of One shall go forth, Cast up, cast up, prepare the way! Take up the stumbling block out of the way [of the spiritual return] of My people.

15 For thus says the high and lofty One—He Who inhabits eternity, Whose name is Holy: I dwell in the high and holy place, but with him also who is of a thoroughly penitent and humble spirit, to revive the spirit of the humble and to revive the heart of the thoroughly penitent [bruised with sorrow for sin]. [Matt. 5:3.]

16 For I will not contend forever, neither will I be angry always, for [if I did stay angry] the spirit [of man]

would faint *and* be consumed before Me, and [My purpose in] creating the souls of men would be frustrated.

17 Because of the iniquity of his [Judah's] covetousness *and* unjust gain I was angry and smote him. I hid my face and was angry, and he went on turning away *and* backsliding in the way of his [own willful] heart.

18 I have seen his [willful] ways, but I will heal him; I will lead him also and will recompense him and restore comfort to him and to those who mourn for him. [Isa. 61:1, 2; 66:10.]

19 Peace, peace, to him who is far off [both Jew and Gentile] and to him who is near! says the Lord; I create the fruit of his lips, and I will heal him [make his lips blossom anew with speech in thankful praise]. [Acts 2:39; Eph. 2:13-17, 18; Heb. 13:15.]

20 But the wicked are like the troubled sea, for it cannot rest, and its waters cast up mire and dirt.

21 There is no peace, says my God, for the wicked.

58 CRY ALOUD, spare not. Lift up your voice like a trumpet and declare to My people their transgression and to the house of Jacob their sins!

2 Yet they seek, inquire for, *and* require Me daily and delight [externally] to know My ways, as [if they were in reality] a nation that did righteousness and forsook not the ordinance of their God. They ask of Me righteous judgments, they delight to draw near to God [in visible ways].

3 Why have we fasted, they say, and You do not see it? Why have we afflicted ourselves, and You take no knowledge [of it]? Behold [O Israel], on the day of your fast [when you should be grieving for your sins], you find profit in your business, and [instead of stopping all work, as the law implies you and your workmen should do] you

putting the Word to work

Isaiah 57:15 tells us that God dwells in a high and holy place, but that He also dwells with those who have a penitent and humble spirit. Do you have a penitent and humble spirit? Are you struggling with stubbornness or pride in any area of your life? If so, repent and ask God to forgive you. Then He will revive your heart, as He promises in this verse.

extort from your hired servants a full amount of labor. [Lev. 16:29.]

4 [The facts are that] you fast only for strife and debate and to smite with the fist of wickedness. Fasting as you do today will not cause your voice to be heard on high.

5 Is such a fast as yours what I have chosen, a day for a man to humble himself with sorrow in his soul? [Is true fasting merely mechanical?] Is it only to bow down his head like a bulrush and to spread sackcloth and ashes under him [to indicate a condition of heart that he does not have]? Will you call this a fast and an acceptable day to the Lord?

6 [Rather] is not this the fast that I have chosen: to loose the bonds of wickedness, to undo the bands of the yoke, to let the oppressed go free, and that you break every [enslaving] yoke? [Acts 8:23.]

7 Is it not to divide your bread with the hungry and bring the homeless poor into your house—when you see the naked, that you cover him, and that you hide not yourself from [the needs of] your own flesh *and* blood?

8 Then shall your light break forth like the morning, and your healing (your restoration and the power of a new life) shall spring forth speedily; your righteousness (your rightness, your justice, and your right relationship with God) shall go before you [conducting you to peace and prosperity], and the glory of the Lord shall be your rear guard. [Exod. 14:19, 20; Isa. 52:12.]

9 Then you shall call, and the Lord will answer; you shall cry, and He will say, Here I am. If you take away from your midst yokes of oppression [wherever you find them], the finger pointed in scorn [toward the oppressed or the godly], and every form of false, harsh, unjust, *and* wicked speaking, [Exod. 3:14.]

10 And if you pour out that with

life point

The scene we read about in Isaiah 58:5 is an exchange between the Israelites and God. The people had been fasting, and they felt that God had not noticed. He told them that they were fasting with the wrong motives, and that they had things in their lives that needed to be dealt with.

True fasting is for the purpose of breaking the power of the flesh in our lives. It is supposed to be a special, consecrated time of prayer in which God's people seek Him seriously and sacrificially for themselves or for others. True fasting, with right motives, *is* effective.

which you sustain your own life for the hungry and satisfy the need of the afflicted, then shall your light rise in darkness, and your obscurity *and* gloom become like the noonday.

11 And the Lord shall guide you continually and satisfy you in drought *and* in dry places and make strong your bones. And you shall be like a watered garden and like a spring of water whose waters fail not.

12 And your ancient ruins shall be rebuilt; you shall raise up the foundations

life point

What wonderful promises we find in Isaiah 58:9–12! When can we expect these blessings of the Lord to come upon us and overtake us? When we stop judging others and put away every form of vain, false, harsh, unjust, and wicked speaking. We should not expect God's blessings when our mouths are speaking curses, but when we begin to speak blessings to others from a sincere heart, blessings begin to flow toward us.

first things first

Some people become so involved in ministry that they overlook their own family members and friends, but the Lord makes clear in Isaiah 58:7 that we are not to neglect one in order to attend to the other.

In this verse, God tells us that we are not only to meet the needs of those around us in the world (the poor, needy, and disadvantaged), but that we are also to meet the needs of our immediate and extended families.

I have a widowed aunt to whom I minister quite often. I once thought I was too busy to help her, but God showed me that she is my "flesh and blood." She is part of my family, and I am responsible to minister to her needs just as I am responsible to minister to thousands of people in many locations all over the world. If I ignore my responsibilities toward my relatives, I will pay the price of losing an aspect of God's anointing in other areas of my life.

In Isaiah 58:7, the Word says that we must not only feed the hungry and clothe the naked, but that we must also not hide ourselves from the needs of our own flesh and blood. *After* we have done these things, then Isaiah 58:8 will work for us: our light shall break forth like the morning, our healing (our restoration and the power of a new life) will spring forth speedily, our righteousness (our rightness, our justice, and our right relationship with God) will go before us (conducting us to peace and prosperity), and God's glory will guard us from behind. Those are awesome promises, and I encourage you to do what is necessary for you to be in position to receive them in your life.

of [buildings that have laid waste for] many generations; and you shall be called Repairer of the Breach, Restorer of Streets to Dwell In.

13 If you turn away your foot from [traveling unduly on] the Sabbath, from doing your own pleasure on My holy day, and call the Sabbath a [spiritual] delight, the holy day of the Lord honorable, and honor Him *and* it, not going your own way or seeking *or* finding your own pleasure or speaking with your own [idle] words,

14 Then will you delight yourself in the Lord, and I will make you to ride on the high places of the earth, and I will feed you with the heritage [promised for you] of Jacob your father; for the mouth of the Lord has spoken it. [Gen. 27:28, 29; 28:13-15.]

59 BEHOLD, THE Lord's hand is not shortened at all, that it cannot save, nor His ear dull with deafness, that it cannot hear.

2 But your iniquities have made a separation between you and your God, and your sins have hidden His face from you, so that He will not hear.

3 For your hands are defiled with blood and your fingers with iniquity; your lips have spoken lies, your tongue mutters wickedness.

4 None sues *or* calls in righteousness [but for the sake of doing injury to others—to take some undue advantage]; no one goes to law honestly *and* pleads [his case] in truth; they trust in emptiness, worthlessness *and* futility,

and speaking lies! They conceive mischief and bring forth evil!

5   They hatch adders' eggs and weave the spider's web; he who eats of their eggs dies, and [from an egg] which is crushed a viper breaks out [for their nature is ruinous, deadly, evil].

6   Their webs will not serve as clothing, nor will they cover themselves with what they make; their works are works of iniquity, and the act of violence is in their hands.

7   Their feet run to evil, and they make haste to shed innocent blood. Their thoughts are thoughts of iniquity; desolation and destruction are in their paths *and* highways.

8   The way of peace they know not, and there is no justice *or* right in their goings. They have made them into crooked paths; whoever goes in them does not know peace. [Rom. 3:15-18.]

9   Therefore are justice *and* right far from us, and righteousness *and* salvation do not overtake us. We expectantly wait for light, but [only] see darkness; for brightness, but we walk in obscurity *and* gloom.

10 We grope for the wall like the blind, yes, we grope like those who have no eyes. We stumble at noonday as in the twilight; in dark places *and* among those who are full of life *and* vigor, we are as dead men.

11 We all groan *and* growl like bears and moan plaintively like doves. We look for justice, but there is none; for salvation, but it is far from us.

12 For our transgressions are multiplied before You [O Lord], and our sins testify against us; for our transgressions are with us, and as for our iniquities, we know *and* recognize them [as]:

13 Rebelling against and denying the Lord, turning away from following our God, speaking oppression and revolt, conceiving in and muttering *and* moaning from the heart words of falsehood.

14 Justice is turned away backward, and righteousness (uprightness and right standing with God) stands far off; for truth has fallen in the street (the city's forum), and uprightness cannot enter [the courts of justice].

15 Yes, truth is lacking, and he who departs from evil makes himself a prey. And the Lord saw it, and it displeased Him that there was no justice.

16 And He saw that there was no man and wondered that there was no intercessor [no one to intervene on behalf of truth and right]; therefore His own arm brought Him victory, and His own righteousness [having the Spirit without measure] sustained Him. [Isa. 53:11; Col. 2:9; I John 2:1, 2.]

17 For [the Lord] put on righteousness as a breastplate *or* coat of mail, and salvation as a helmet upon His head; He put on garments of vengeance for clothing and was clad with zeal [and furious divine jealousy] as a cloak. [Eph. 6:14, 17; I Thess. 5:8.]

18 According as their deeds deserve, so will He repay wrath to His adversaries, recompense to His enemies; on the foreign islands *and* coastlands He will make compensation.

19 So [as the result of the Messiah's intervention] they shall [reverently] fear the name of the Lord from the west, and His glory from the rising of the sun. When the enemy shall come in like a flood, the Spirit of the Lord will lift up a standard against him *and* put him to flight [for He will come like a rushing stream which the breath of the

speak the Word

Thank You, God, for raising up a standard against the enemy and putting him to flight when he comes against me.
ADAPTED FROM ISAIAH **59:19**

Lord drives]. [Matt. 8:11; Luke 13:29.]
20 He shall come as a Redeemer to Zion and to those in Jacob (Israel) who turn from transgression, says the Lord.
21 As for Me, this is My covenant *or* league with them, says the Lord: My Spirit, Who is upon you [and Who writes the law of God inwardly on the heart], and My words which I have put in your mouth shall not depart out of your mouth, or out of the mouths of your [true, spiritual] children, or out of the mouths of your children's children, says the Lord, from henceforth and forever. [Jer. 31:33; Rom. 11:26, 27; Gal. 3:29; Heb. 12:22-24.]

60 ARISE [from the depression and prostration in which circumstances have kept you—rise to a new life]! Shine (be radiant with the glory of the Lord), for your light has come, and the glory of the Lord has risen upon you! [Zech. 8:23.]
2 For behold, darkness shall cover the earth, and dense darkness [all] peoples, but the Lord shall arise upon you [O Jerusalem], and His glory shall be seen on you. [Isa. 60:19-22; Mal. 4:2; Rev. 21:2, 3.]
3 And nations shall come to your light, and kings to the brightness of your rising. [Isa. 2:2, 3; Jer. 3:17.]
4 Lift up your eyes round about you and see! They all gather themselves together, they come to you. Your sons shall come from afar, and your daughters shall be carried *and* nursed in the arms.

5 Then you shall see and be radiant, and your heart shall thrill *and* tremble with joy [at the glorious deliverance] and be enlarged; because the abundant wealth of the [Dead] ᵂSea shall be turned to you, unto you shall the nations come with their treasures. [Ps. 119:32.]
6 A multitude of camels [from the eastern trading tribes] shall cover you [Jerusalem], the young camels of Midian and Ephah; all the men from Sheba [who once came to trade] shall come, bringing gold and frankincense and proclaiming the praises of the Lord. [Matt. 2:11.]
7 All the flocks of Kedar shall be gathered to you [as the eastern pastoral tribes join the trading tribes], the rams of Nebaioth shall minister to you; they shall come up with acceptance on My altar, and My glorious house I will glorify.
8 Who are these who fly like a cloud, and like doves to their windows?
9 Surely the isles *and* distant coastlands shall wait for *and* expect Me; and the ships of Tarshish [shall come] first, to bring your sons from afar, their silver and gold with them, for the name of the Lord your God, for the Holy One of Israel, because He has beautified *and* glorified you.
10 Foreigners shall build up your walls, and their kings shall minister to you; for in My wrath I smote you, but in My favor, pleasure, *and* goodwill I have had mercy, love, *and* pity for you.
11 And your gates shall be open continually, they shall not be shut day or

w Prior to well into the twentieth century, scholars could only speculate as to what Isaiah might have meant here by "the abundant wealth of the [Dead] Sea" that would one day be turned over to Jerusalem. Of course, the Dead Sea, which for ages had been considered only a place of death and desolation, was ruled out as a possible meaning. Then suddenly it was discovered that the waters of the Dead Sea contain important chemicals. In AD 1935 G.T.B. Davis wrote, "One is almost staggered by the computed wealth of the chemical salts of the Dead Sea. It is estimated that the potential value of the potash, bromine, and other chemical salts of its waters is . . . four times the wealth of the United States!" (G.T.B. Davis, *Rebuilding Palestine*) Isaiah himself did not know this, but the God who caused the Dead Sea to play a part in His program in the last days knew all about it, and He led the prophet to so prophesy here in this verse.

night, that men may bring to you the wealth of the nations—and their kings led in procession [your voluntary captives]. [Rev. 21:24-27.]

12 For the nation and kingdom that will not serve you in that day [Jerusalem] shall perish; yes, those nations shall be utterly laid waste.

13 The glory of Lebanon shall come to you, the cypress, the plane, and the pine [trees] together, to beautify the place of My sanctuary; and I will make the place of My feet glorious.

14 The sons of those who afflicted you shall come bending low to you, and all those who despised you shall bow down at your feet, and they shall call you the City of the Lord, the Zion of the Holy One of Israel. [Rev. 3:9.]

15 Whereas you have been forsaken and hated, so that no man passed through you, I will make you [Jerusalem] an eternal glory, a joy from age to age.

16 You shall suck the milk of the [Gentile] nations and shall suck the breast of kings; and you shall recognize *and* know that I, the Lord, am your Savior and your Redeemer, the Mighty One of Jacob.

17 Instead of bronze I will bring gold, and instead of iron I will bring silver; and instead of wood, bronze, and instead of stones, iron. [Instead of the tyranny of the present] I will appoint peace as your officers and righteousness as your taskmasters.

18 Violence shall no more be heard in your land, nor devastation or destruction within your borders, but you shall call your walls Salvation and your gates Praise.

19 The sun shall no more be your light by day, nor for brightness shall the moon give light to you, but the Lord shall be to you an everlasting light, and your God your glory *and* your beauty. [Jer. 9:23, 24; Rev. 21:23.]

20 Your sun shall no more go down, nor shall your moon withdraw itself, for the Lord shall be your everlasting light, and the days of your mourning shall be ended.

21 Your people also shall all be [uncompromisingly and consistently] righteous; they shall possess the land forever, the branch of My planting, the work of My hands, that I may be glorified.

22 The least one shall become a thousand [a clan], and the small one a strong nation. I, the Lord, will hasten it in its [appointed] time.

61 THE SPIRIT of the Lord God is upon me, because the Lord has anointed *and* qualified me to preach the Gospel *of* good tidings to the meek, the poor, *and* afflicted; He has sent me to bind up *and* heal the brokenhearted, to proclaim liberty to the [physical and spiritual] captives and the opening of

life point

In Luke 4:18 Jesus stood up in the temple to read the prophetic passage from Isaiah 61:1, and after doing so He said, "Today this Scripture has been fulfilled" (Luke 4:21). One of the things said in Isaiah 61:1 is that Jesus has come to open prison doors and set captives free. I believe this refers to the prison of sin, guilt, and condemnation. Jesus died so that our sins could be forgiven and completely removed along with any sense of guilt and condemnation.

speak the Word

God, You are an everlasting light to me. You are my glory and my beauty.
ADAPTED FROM ISAIAH **60:19**

healing in every way

Jesus can heal us everywhere we hurt! He wants to help us mentally and emotionally, as well as spiritually and physically. For a long time, I did not know that, and my lack of knowledge caused me to live a dysfunctional life. Abuse and rejection had left me emotionally wounded until I discovered that Jesus wanted to give me—and all of us—beauty for ashes.

When we accept Jesus as Savior and Lord, a great exchange takes place in the spirit realm. He gives us everything He has and is—and we are supposed to give Him not only everything we are, but even what we are not. He takes our weakness and gives us His strength. He takes our sickness and gives us His health and healing. We give Him our sin, and He gives us His righteousness. He will give us beauty for ashes, but we must be willing to give up our ashes. We cannot live in the past and press into the future at the same time. Let go of what lies behind and start enjoying the new life that Jesus has for you.

When I married my husband in 1967, I had no automobile, but he did, so suddenly I had one too. My poverty was swallowed up in his abundance. Similarly, when we accept Jesus our sin-filled, miserable, hopeless lives are swallowed up in His goodness, mercy, and grace. If you have problems, you are just the person Jesus died for. He came for the sick and needy, not for those who need nothing. It is not a shame to be needy. The greatest need that most people have is to admit they have a need!

It is time for you to enjoy God's favor (see Isaiah 61:2). That means He will bless you even though you do not deserve it, if you place your faith in Him. God wants you to enjoy yourself and your life. He wants to heal you everywhere you hurt! He wants to heal you spiritually, mentally, emotionally, physically, financially, and socially. Do not close off any part of your life to His healing touch. Invite Jesus into every area and ask Him to make you whole.

the prison *and* of the eyes to those who are bound. [Rom. 10:15.]

2 To proclaim the acceptable year of the Lord [the year of His favor] ˣand the day of vengeance of our God, to comfort all who mourn, [Matt. 11:2-6; Luke 4:18, 19; 7:22.]

3 To grant [consolation and joy] to those who mourn in Zion—to give them an ornament (a garland or diadem) of beauty instead of ashes, the oil of joy instead of mourning, the garment [expressive] of praise in-stead of a heavy, burdened, *and* failing spirit—that they may be called oaks of righteousness [lofty, strong, and magnificent, distinguished for uprightness, justice, and right standing with God], the planting of the Lord, that He may be glorified.

4 And they shall rebuild the ancient ruins; they shall raise up the former desolations and renew the ruined cities, the devastations of many generations.

5 Aliens shall stand [ready] and

x See footnote on Ezek. 34:28.

life point

If we consistently believe God's Word, He will turn circumstances from negative to positive—from ashes to beauty (see Isaiah 61:3)—in His perfect timing.

A lot of negative things have happened to me, and Satan used them to sour my attitude toward life and people. I was trapped in my past because I did not believe I had a future. As soon as I believed in Jesus Christ, I was released from the past and began making progress toward the good things God had in mind for me. It did not all come to me immediately in manifested form, but believing in God gave me renewed hope that kept me going from day to day. Slowly but surely I began to see changes take place in my life, and each change encouraged me to believe God more.

Believing God is the key to receiving from Him. No matter what has happened to you in the past, if you believe, you can receive beauty for your ashes too. You can begin to enjoy the good future that is set aside for you in Jesus Christ, Who came to do the will of His Father in heaven.

feed your flocks, and foreigners shall be your plowmen and your vine-dressers. 6 But you shall be called the priests of the Lord; people will speak of you as the ministers of our God. You shall eat the wealth of the nations, and the glory [once that of your captors] shall be yours. [Exod. 19:6; I Pet. 2:5; Rev. 1:6; 5:10; 20:6.]

speak the Word

7 Instead of your [former] shame you shall have a twofold recompense; instead of dishonor *and* reproach [your people] shall rejoice in their portion. Therefore in their land they shall possess double [what they had forfeited]; everlasting joy shall be theirs.
8 For I the Lord love justice; I hate robbery *and* wrong with violence *or* a burnt offering. And I will faithfully give them their recompense in truth, and I will make an everlasting covenant *or* league with them.
9 And their offspring shall be known among the nations and their descendants among the peoples. All who see them [in their prosperity] will recognize *and* acknowledge that they are the people whom the Lord has blessed.
10 I will greatly rejoice in the Lord, my soul will exult in my God; for He has clothed me with the garments of salvation, He has covered me with the robe of righteousness, as a bridegroom decks himself with a garland, and as a bride adorns herself with her jewels.
11 For as [surely as] the earth brings forth its shoots, and as a garden causes what is sown in it to spring forth, so [surely] the Lord God will cause rightness *and* justice and praise to spring forth before all the nations [through the self-fulfilling power of His word].

62 FOR ZION'S sake will I [Isaiah] not hold my peace, and for Jerusalem's sake I will not rest until her imputed righteousness *and* vindication go forth as brightness, and her salvation radiates as does a burning torch.
2 And the nations shall see your

God, I will greatly rejoice in You. My soul will exult in You because You have clothed me with garments of salvation and with a robe of righteousness.
ADAPTED FROM ISAIAH 61:10

double for your trouble

The word *recompense,* which we see in Isaiah 61:7, means "repayment." So when Isaiah says that the Lord will recompense us for our shame, dishonor, and reproach, he means that God will make up for all the hurts we have experienced in life.

One of the greatest mistakes we make is trying to avenge ourselves, to get even, to bring the scales of justice into balance rather than trusting God to do that for us. If we try to do this ourselves, we only wind up making a huge mess. The Bible says, "Beloved, never avenge yourselves, but leave the way open for [God's] wrath; for it is written, Vengeance is Mine, I will repay (requite), says the Lord" (Romans 12:19).

When the Bible talks about recompense or justice, it simply means that you and I will get what is right for us, what is coming to us. Now, as blood-bought children of God, we know that as long as we trust in the Lord and are obedient to Him and repentant of our sins and failures, we will not get what is coming to us in the form of punishment for our sins, but we will get rewards for our righteousness. Jesus took our punishment, and we receive His inheritance.

The Bible says in Psalm 37:1, 2, "Fret not yourself because of evildoers, neither be envious against those who work unrighteousness (that which is not upright or in right standing with God). For they shall soon be cut down like the grass, and wither as the green herb." We should not want anyone to "be cut down" and "wither," even those people who have harmed us. Instead, we need to allow God's love to be "poured out in our hearts through the Holy Spirit" (Romans 5:5).

In my own life, I thank God I have come to the place of not wanting to see my tormentors have a miserable life. But what God has promised us who belong to Him and follow Him is that those who have hurt us will one day pay for their transgressions against us, unless they come to a place of repentance. But God *will* make it up to us if we trust Him to do so.

Too often believers do not seem to realize they are not to take matters into their own hands. Many of them are angry at what has been done to them—and that anger manifests itself in many destructive ways.

Part of the problem is that we as Christians have not yet learned that everybody experiences difficulties in life. The Bible says, "Many evils confront the [consistently] righteous" (Psalm 34:19). We fail to realize that even though we are God's children, not everything will go just the way we want, and not everyone will treat us the way we would like to be treated. However, the Bible teaches that if we continue to trust God no matter what happens to us, if we keep our eyes on Him and have faith and confidence in Him, He will balance out the scales. The second half of Psalm 34:19 says a person may have problems, "but the Lord delivers him out of them all."

The time will come when everything will be set straight. Our enemies will be repaid for all their treachery, and we will be paid back double for all we have lost and suffered. True justice is worth waiting for.

righteousness *and* vindication [your rightness and justice—not your own, but His ascribed to you], and all kings shall behold your salvation and glory; and you shall be called by a new name which the mouth of the Lord shall name. [Rev. 2:17.]

3 You shall also be [so beautiful and prosperous as to be thought of as] a crown of glory *and* honor in the hand of the Lord, and a royal diadem [exceedingly beautiful] in the hand of your God.

4 You [Judah] shall no more be termed Forsaken, nor shall your land be called Desolate any more. But you shall be called Hephzibah [My delight is in her], and your land be called Beulah [married]; for the Lord delights in you, and your land shall be married [owned and protected by the Lord].

5 For as a young man marries a virgin [O Jerusalem], so shall your sons marry you; and as the bridegroom rejoices over the bride, so shall your God rejoice over you.

6 I have set watchmen upon your walls, O Jerusalem, who will never hold their peace day or night; you who [are His servants and by your prayers] put the Lord in remembrance [of His promises], keep not silence,

7 And give Him no rest until He establishes Jerusalem and makes her a praise in the earth.

8 The Lord has sworn by His right hand and by His mighty arm: Surely I will not again give your grain as food for your enemies, and [the invading sons of] aliens shall not drink your new wine for which you have toiled;

9 But they who have gathered it shall eat it and praise the Lord, and they who have brought in the vintage shall drink it [at the feasts celebrated] in the courts of My sanctuary (the temple of My holiness).

10 Go through, go through the gates! Prepare the way for the people. Cast up, cast up the highway! Gather out the stones. Lift up a standard *or* ensign over *and* for the peoples.

11 Behold, the Lord has proclaimed to the end of the earth: Say to the Daughter of Zion, Behold, your salvation comes [in the person of the Lord]; behold, His reward is with Him, and His work *and* recompense before Him. [Isa. 40:10.]

12 And they shall call them the Holy People, the Redeemed of the Lord; and you shall be called Sought Out, a City Not Forsaken.

63 WHO IS this Who comes from Edom, with crimson-stained garments from Bozrah [in Edom]? This One Who is glorious in His apparel, striding triumphantly in the greatness of His might? It is I, [the One] Who speaks in righteousness [proclaiming vindication], mighty to save!

2 Why is Your apparel splashed with red, and Your garments like the one who treads in the winepress?

3 I have trodden the winepress alone, and of the peoples there was no one with Me. I trod them in My anger and trampled them in My wrath; and their lifeblood is sprinkled upon My garments, and I stained all My raiment.

4 For the day of vengeance was in My heart, and My year of redemption [the year of My redeemed] has come.

5 And I looked, but there was no one to help; I was amazed *and* appalled that there was no one to uphold [truth and right]. So My own arm brought Me victory, and My wrath upheld Me.

6 I trod down the peoples in My anger and made them drink of the cup of My wrath until they were intoxicated, and I spilled their lifeblood upon the earth.

7 I will recount the loving-kindnesses of the Lord and the praiseworthy deeds of the Lord, according to all

that the Lord has bestowed on us, and the great goodness to the house of Israel, which He has granted them according to His mercy and according to the multitude of His loving-kindnesses.

8 For He said, Surely they are My people, sons who will not lie [who will not deal falsely with Me]; and so He was to them a Savior [in all their distresses].

9 In all their affliction He was afflicted, and the ʸAngel of His presence saved them; in His love and in His pity He redeemed them; and He lifted them up and carried them all the days of old. [Exod. 23:20-23; 33:14-15; Deut. 1:31; 32:10-12.]

10 But they rebelled and grieved His Holy Spirit; therefore He turned to become their enemy and Himself fought against them.

11 Then His people [seriously] remembered the days of old, of Moses and his people [and they said], Where is He Who brought [our fathers] up out of the [Red] Sea, with [Moses and the other] shepherds of His flock? Where is He Who put His Holy Spirit within their midst,

12 Who caused His glorious arm to go at the right hand of Moses, dividing the waters before them, to make for Himself an everlasting name,

13 Who led them through the depths, like a horse in the wilderness, so that they did not stumble?

14 Like the cattle that go down into the valley [to find better pasturage, refuge, and rest], the Spirit of the Lord caused them to rest. So did You lead Your people [Lord] to make for Yourself a beautiful *and* glorious name [to prepare the way for the acknowledgment of Your name by all nations].

15 Look down from heaven and see from the dwelling place of Your holiness and Your glory. Where are Your zeal *and* Your jealousy and Your mighty acts [which you formerly did for Your people]? Your yearning pity and the [multitude of] compassions of Your heart are restrained *and* withheld from me.

16 For [surely] You are our Father, even though Abraham [our ancestor] does not know us and Israel (Jacob) does not acknowledge us; You, O Lord, are [still] our Father, our Redeemer from everlasting is Your name.

17 O Lord, why have You made us [able] to err from Your ways and hardened our hearts to [reverential] fear of You? Return [to bless us] for Your servants' sake, the tribes of Your heritage.

18 Your holy people possessed Your sanctuary but a little while; our adversaries have trodden it down.

19 We have become [to You] like those over whom You never exercised rule, like those who were not called by Your name.

64 OH, THAT You would rend the heavens and that You would come down, that the mountains might quake *and* flow down at Your presence—

2 As when fire kindles the brushwood and the fire causes the waters to boil—to make Your name known to Your adversaries, that the nations may tremble at Your presence!

3 When You did terrible things which we did not expect, You came down; the mountains quaked at Your presence.

4 For from of old no one has heard nor perceived by the ear, nor has the eye seen a God besides You, Who works *and* shows Himself active on behalf of him who [earnestly] waits for Him.

5 You meet *and* spare him who

y See footnote on Genesis 16:7.

joyfully works righteousness (uprightness and justice), [earnestly] remembering You in Your ways. Behold, You were angry, for we sinned; we have long continued in our sins [prolonging Your anger]. And shall we be saved?

6 For we have all become like one who is unclean [ceremonially, like a leper], and all our righteousness (our best deeds of rightness and justice) is like filthy rags *or* a polluted garment; we all fade like a leaf, and our iniquities, like the wind, take us away [far from God's favor, hurrying us toward destruction]. [Lev. 13:45, 46.]

7 And no one calls on Your name and awakens *and* bestirs himself to take *and* keep hold of You; for You have hidden Your face from us and have delivered us into the [consuming] power of our iniquities. [Rom. 1:21-24.]

8 Yet, O Lord, You are our Father; we are the clay, and You our Potter, and we all are the work of Your hand.

9 Do not be exceedingly angry, O Lord, or [seriously] remember iniquity forever. Behold, consider, we beseech You, we are all Your people.

10 Your holy cities have become a wilderness; Zion has become a wilderness, Jerusalem a desolation.

11 Our holy and our beautiful house, [the temple] where our fathers praised You, is burned with fire, and all our pleasant *and* desirable places are in ruins.

12 Considering these [calamities], will You restrain Yourself, O Lord [and not come to our aid]? Will You keep silent *and* not command our deliverance but humble *and* afflict us exceedingly?

65 I WAS [ready to be] inquired of by those who asked not; I was [ready to be] found by those who sought Me not. I said, Here I am, here I am

[says I AM] to a nation [Israel] that has not called on My name. [Exod. 3:14; Isa. 58:9.]

2 I have spread out My hands all the day long to a rebellious people, who walk in a way that is not good, after their own thoughts—

3 A people who provoke Me to My face continually, sacrificing [to idols] in gardens and burning incense upon bricks [instead of at God's prescribed altar];

4 Who sit among the graves [trying to talk with the dead] and lodge among the secret places [or caves where familiar spirits were thought to dwell]; who eat swine's flesh, and the broth of abominable *and* loathsome things is in their vessels;

5 Who say, Keep to yourself; do not come near me, for I am set apart from you [and lest I sanctify you]! These are smoke in My nostrils, a fire that burns all the day.

6 Behold, it is written before Me: I will not keep silence but will repay; yes, I will repay into their bosom

7 Both your own iniquities and the iniquities of your fathers, says the Lord. Because they too burned incense upon the mountains and reviled *and* blasphemed Me upon the hills, therefore will I measure *and* stretch out their former doings into their own bosom.

8 Thus says the Lord: As the juice [of the grape] is found in the cluster, and one says, Do not destroy it, for there is a blessing in it, so will I do for My servants' sake, that I may not destroy them all.

9 And I will bring forth an offspring from Jacob, and from Judah an inheritor of My mountains; My chosen *and* elect will inherit it, and My servants will dwell there.

10 And [the plain of] Sharon shall be a pasture *and* fold for flocks, and the Valley of Achor a place for herds to lie down, for My people who seek Me,

inquire of Me, *and* require Me [by right of their necessity and by right of My invitation].

11 But you who forsake the Lord, who forget *and* ignore My holy Mount [Zion], who prepare a table for Gad [the Babylonian god of fortune] and who furnish mixed drinks for Meni [the god of destiny]—

12 I will destine you [says the Lord] for the sword, and you shall all bow down to the slaughter, because when I called, you did not answer; when I spoke, you did not listen *or* obey. But you did what was evil in My eyes, and you chose that in which I did not delight.

13 Therefore thus says the Lord God: Behold, My servants shall eat, but you shall be hungry; behold, My servants shall drink, but you shall be thirsty; behold, My servants shall rejoice, but you shall be put to shame.

14 Behold, My servants shall sing for joy of heart, but you shall cry out for pain *and* sorrow of heart and shall wail *and* howl for anguish, vexation, *and* breaking of spirit.

15 And you will leave your name to My chosen [to those who will use it] for a curse; and the Lord God will slay you, but He will call His servants by another name [as much greater than the former name as the name Israel was greater than the name Jacob]. [Gen. 32:28; Jer. 29:22.]

16 So [it shall be] that he who invokes a blessing on himself in the land shall do so by saying, May the God of truth *and* fidelity [the Amen] bless me; and he who takes an oath in the land shall swear by the God of truth *and* faithfulness to His promises [the Amen], because the former troubles are forgotten and because they are hidden from My eyes. [II Cor. 1:20; Rev. 3:14.]

17 For behold, I create [z]new heavens and a new earth. And the former things shall not be remembered or come into mind. [Isa. 66:22; II Pet. 3:13; Rev. 21:1.]

18 But be glad and rejoice forever in that which I create; for behold, I create Jerusalem to be a rejoicing and her people a joy.

19 And I will rejoice in Jerusalem and be glad in My people; and the sound of weeping will no more be heard in it, nor the cry of distress.

20 There shall no more be in it an infant who lives but a few days, or an old man who dies prematurely; for the child shall die a hundred years old, and the sinner who dies when only a hundred years old shall be [thought only a child, cut off because he is] accursed.

21 They shall build houses and inhabit them, and they shall plant vineyards and eat the fruit of them.

22 They shall not build and another inhabit; they shall not plant and another eat [the fruit]. For as the days of a tree, so shall be the days of My people, and My chosen *and* elect shall long make use of *and* enjoy the work of their hands.

23 They shall not labor in vain or bring forth [children] for sudden terror *or* calamity; for they shall be the descendants of the blessed of the Lord, and their offspring with them.

24 And it shall be that before they call I will answer; and while they are yet speaking I will hear. [Isa. 30:19; 58:9; Matt. 6:8.]

25 The wolf and the lamb shall feed together, and the lion shall eat straw like the ox; and dust shall be the serpent's food. They shall not hurt or destroy in all My holy Mount [Zion], says the Lord.

---

z A new universe is meant here. The Hebrew language has no single word to express the concept of cosmos or universe, so heavens and earth are substituted.

66 THUS SAYS the Lord: Heaven is My throne, and the earth is My footstool. What kind of house would you build for Me? And what kind can be My resting-place? [Acts 17:24.]

2 For all these things My hand has made, and so all these things have come into being [by and for Me], says the Lord. But this is the man to whom I will look *and* have regard: he who is humble and of a broken *or* wounded spirit, and who trembles at My word *and* reveres My commands. [John 4:24.]

3 [The acts of the hypocrite's worship are as abominable to God as if they were offered to idols.] He who kills an ox [then] will be as guilty as if he slew *and* sacrificed a man; he who sacrifices a lamb *or* a kid, as if he broke a dog's neck *and* sacrificed him; he who offers a cereal offering, as if he offered swine's blood; he who burns incense [to God], as if he blessed an idol. [Such people] have chosen their own ways, and they delight in their abominations;

4 So I also will choose their delusions *and* mockings, their calamities *and* afflictions, and I will bring their fears upon them—because when I called, no one answered; when I spoke, they did not listen *or* obey. But they did what was evil in My sight and chose that in which I did not delight.

5 Hear the word of the Lord, you who tremble at His word: Your brethren who hate you, who cast you out for My name's sake, have said, Let the Lord be glorified, that we may see your joy! But it is they who shall be put to shame.

6 [Hark!] An uproar from the city! A voice from the temple! The voice of the Lord, rendering recompense to His enemies!

7 Before [Zion] travailed, she gave birth; before her pain came upon her, she was delivered of a male child.

8 Who has heard of such a thing? Who has seen such things? Shall a land ᵃbe born in one day? Or shall a nation be brought forth in a moment? For as soon as Zion was in labor, she brought forth her children.

9 Shall I bring to the [moment of] birth and not cause to bring forth? says the Lord. Shall I Who causes to bring forth shut the womb? says your God.

10 Rejoice with Jerusalem and be glad for her, all you who love her; rejoice for joy with her, all you who mourn over her,

11 That you may nurse and be satisfied from her consoling breasts, that you may drink deeply and be delighted with the abundance *and* brightness of her glory.

12 For thus says the Lord: Behold, I will extend peace to her like a river, and the glory of the nations like an overflowing stream; then you will be nursed, you will be carried on her hip and trotted [lovingly bounced up and down] on her [God's maternal] knees.

13 As one whom his mother comforts, so will I comfort you; you shall be comforted in Jerusalem.

14 When you see this, your heart shall rejoice; your bones shall flourish like green *and* tender grass. And the [powerful] hand of the Lord shall be revealed *and* known to be with His

---

a Never in the history of the world had such a thing happened before—but God keeps His word. As definitely foretold here and in Ezekiel 37:21, 22, Israel became a recognized nation, actually "born in one day." After being away from their homeland for almost 2,000 years, the Jews were given a national homeland in Palestine by the Balfour Declaration in November, 1917. In 1922, the League of Nations gave Great Britain the mandate over Palestine. On May 14, 1948, Great Britain withdrew her mandate, and immediately Israel was declared a sovereign state, and her growth and importance among nations became astonishing.

servants, but His indignation [shown] to be against His enemies.

15 For behold, the Lord will come in fire, and His chariots will be like the stormy wind, to render His anger with fierceness, and His rebuke with flames of fire.

16 For by fire and by His sword will the Lord execute judgment upon all flesh, and the slain of the Lord will be many.

17 Those who [attempt to] sanctify themselves and cleanse themselves to enter [and sacrifice to idols] in the gardens, following after [b]one in the midst, eating hog's flesh and the abomination [creeping things] and the [mouse—their works and their thoughts] shall come to an end together, says the Lord.

18 For I know their works and their thoughts. And the time is coming when I will gather all nations and tongues, and they will come and see My glory.

19 And I will set up a [miraculous] sign among them, and from them I will send survivors to the nations—to Tarshish, Pul (Put), and Lud, who draw the bow, to Tubal and Javan, to the isles *and* coastlands afar off that

have not heard of My fame nor seen My glory. And they will declare *and* proclaim My glory among the nations.

20 And they shall bring all your brethren from all the nations as an offering to the Lord—upon horses and in chariots and in litters and upon mules and upon camels—to My holy mountain Jerusalem, says the Lord, just as the children of Israel bring their cereal offering in a clean vessel to the house of the Lord.

21 And I will also take some of them for priests and for Levites, says the Lord.

22 For as the new [c]heavens and the new earth which I make shall remain before Me, says the Lord, so shall your offspring and your name remain.

23 And it shall be that from one New Moon to another New Moon and from one Sabbath to another Sabbath, all flesh shall come to worship before Me, says the Lord.

24 And they shall go forth and gaze upon the dead bodies of the [rebellious] men who have stepped over against Me; for their worm shall not die, their fire shall not be quenched, and they shall be an abhorrence to all mankind.

a Several in the history of the world had such a thing happened before—but God keeps His word, as definitely foretold here and in Ezekiel 37:21. 22. Israel became a recognized nation, actually "born in one day." After being away from their homeland for almost 2,000 years, they were given a national homeland in Palestine by the Balfour Declaration in November, 1917. In 1922, the League among nations became astonishing.

b Perhaps referring to the image of the Syrian god Adad. Some commentators also suggest that this may refer to the cultic leader in the center who shows by his example how to conduct the ceremonies. **c** See footnote on Isa. 65:17.

Jeremiah

Author:
Jeremiah

Date:
626 BC–586 BC

Everyday Life Principles:
Remember that you were born with a God-given purpose. Stay focused on Him, even amid opposition, and you will prevail in fulfilling your purpose.

Trust God with all of your heart.

Make a priority of seeking God above and before everything else.

Have you ever met someone you considered "a born leader," "a born athlete," or "a born salesman"? Well, Jeremiah was truly "a born prophet." God called him in his mother's womb, before he ever breathed his first breath, for the specific purpose of giving His message to the people of Judah. Jeremiah enjoyed good times during the reign of a good king, Josiah; he also endured persecution and hostility when he had to deliver difficult messages and warnings to bad kings. Even though he did not quickly embrace his call as a prophet in his younger days, he did obey God and stay faithful to Him.

Some of Jeremiah's key themes include obeying God's call, trusting God and not putting faith in people, staying faithful to a covenant relationship with God, seeking God wholeheartedly, continuing to obey God in the face of opposition, and remembering that God loves us with an everlasting love. In addition to these great themes, Jeremiah also includes some beloved Bible verses, such as Jeremiah 29:11, which says: "For I know the thoughts and plans that I have for you, says the Lord, thoughts and plans for welfare and peace and not for evil, to give you hope in your final outcome."

I hope you will read the book of Jeremiah and be encouraged in God's purpose for your life as you continue to trust and seek Him.

1 THE WORDS of Jeremiah son of Hilkiah, of the priests who were in Anathoth in the land of Benjamin [two or three miles north of Jerusalem],

2 To whom the word of the Lord came in the days of Josiah son of Amon king of Judah in the thirteenth year of his reign.

3 It came also in the days of Jehoiakim son of Josiah king of Judah until the end of the eleventh year of Zedekiah son of Josiah king of Judah, until the carrying away of Jerusalem into captivity in the fifth month. [II Kings 25:8-11.]

4 Then the word of the Lord came to me [Jeremiah], saying,

5 Before I formed you in the womb I knew [and] approved of you [as My chosen instrument], and before you were born I separated *and* set you apart, consecrating you; [and] I appointed you as a prophet to the nations. [Exod. 33:12; Isa. 49:1, 5; Rom. 8:29.]

6 Then said I, Ah, Lord God! Behold, I cannot speak, for I am only a youth. [Exod. 4:10; 6:12, 30; I Kings 3:7.]

7 But the Lord said to me, Say not, I am only a youth; for you shall go to all

approved!

God told Jeremiah that He knew him and approved of him before he was formed in his mother's womb (see Jeremiah 1:5). When God said He *knew* Jeremiah, He was not speaking of a casual acquaintance, but of the deepest, most intimate knowledge. God knows us the same way. He knows everything about us, even things we will never discover about ourselves. He knows every mistake we will ever make—and He loves us and approves of us anyway.

God does not always approve of our behavior and choices, but He does approve of us as His chosen instruments. There is a big difference between *who* we are and *what* we do. Jeremiah was a child of God, and God knew his heart. He did not "do" everything right. For one thing, he was afraid of what people would think of him. The fear of man displeases God. He wants us to realize that when He is on our side, it does not matter who is against us. We should strive to be God-pleasers, not man-pleasers.

If we live with feelings that God disapproves of us, we will always have the wrong kind of fear of Him, and that will hinder us from enjoying an intimate relationship and rich fellowship with Him. God wants us to have a reverential fear and awe of Him, but He does not want us to be afraid of Him in a wrong way. He wants us to come boldly to the throne of grace and ask Him to meet our needs and help us in every situation we face (see Hebrews 4:16). Ephesians 3:12 teaches us that we should have an unreserved approach to God, with freedom and without fear.

Do not shrink back in fear, but press forward in faith. Without faith we cannot please God (see Hebrews 11:6), and without fear we cannot please Satan. Whom do you want to please? I am sure it is God, so begin right now by living in the freedom of realizing that God *knows* you and approves of you as His chosen instrument.

to whom I shall send you, and whatever I command you, you shall speak.
8 Be not afraid of them [their faces], for I am with you to deliver you, says the Lord.
9 Then the Lord put forth His hand and touched my mouth. And the Lord said to me, Behold, I have put My words in your mouth.
10 See, I have this day appointed you to the oversight of the nations and of the kingdoms to root out and pull down, to destroy and to overthrow, to build and to plant.

11 Moreover, the word of the Lord came to me, saying, Jeremiah, what do you see? And I said, I see a branch *or* shoot of an almond tree [the emblem of alertness and activity, blossoming in late winter].
12 Then said the Lord to me, You have seen well, for I am alert *and* active, watching over My word to perform it.
13 And the word of the Lord came to me the second time, saying, What do you see? And I said, I see a boiling pot, and the face of it is [tipped away]

you are chosen

We all want other people to like us and approve of us. However, our desire for approval can truly be met only by receiving God's acceptance and approval of us. God told Jeremiah that before He formed him in the womb of his mother, He knew him and approved of him as His chosen instrument (see Jeremiah 1:5). When God says He knows us, He means He really *knows* us. This is a knowing that leaves nothing out.

I am amazed that God chose me. I do not think I would have chosen myself. But God's tool chest has some interesting things in it. He works with what the world would reject as useless and throw away as trash (see I Corinthians 1:27, 28).

Yes, God chooses and uses what the world would reject! Was Jeremiah perfect? Absolutely not! Jeremiah was fearful, and God had to correct him about his fear of people. Jeremiah was afraid of being rejected and disapproved of. God corrected him about speaking negatively and encouraged him to go forward and not give up.

It is interesting to note that God actually told Jeremiah in Jeremiah 1:8 not to be afraid of people's faces. Why is that? We tend to watch people's faces to see if they approve or disapprove of everything about us—what we are wearing, our hair, our performance, etc. We pay too much attention to how people respond to us.

Yes, Jeremiah had problems just as we do. When God saw Jeremiah, He did not see perfection, but He obviously did see someone with a right heart who believed in Him. He saw in Jeremiah two main ingredients essential to pleasing God: (1) faith in God, and (2) a deep desire to please Him. Although Jeremiah was not perfect, he did submit to the call of God on his life. Jeremiah, despite criticism, unpopularity, and attacks against him, faithfully delivered God's message to the nation of Judah. By doing so, he honored God, demonstrated faith and courage, and chose obedience over his personal preferences. I encourage you to do likewise!

from the north [its mouth about to pour forth on the south, on Judea].

14 Then the Lord said to me, Out of the north the evil [which the prophets had foretold as the result of national sin] shall disclose itself *and* break forth upon all the inhabitants of the land.

15 For, behold, I will call all the tribes of the kingdoms of the north, says the Lord; and they will come and set every one his throne at the entrance of the gates of Jerusalem, against all its walls round about, and against all the cities of Judah [as God's judicial act, a consequence of Judah's wickedness].

16 And I will utter My judgments against them for all the wickedness of those who have forsaken Me, burned incense to other gods, and worshiped the works of their own hands [idols].

17 But you [Jeremiah], gird up your loins! Arise and tell them all that I command you. Do not be dismayed *and* break down at the sight of their faces, lest I confound you before them *and* permit you to be overcome.

18 For I, behold, I have made you this day a fortified city and an iron pillar and bronze walls against the whole land—against the [successive] kings of Judah, against its princes, against its priests, and against the people of the land [giving you divine strength which no hostile power can overcome]. [Isa. 50:7; 54:17; Jer. 6:27; 15:20; Luke 21:15; Acts 6:10.]

19 And they shall fight against you, but they shall not [finally] prevail against you, for I am with you, says the Lord, to deliver you.

2 AND THE word of the Lord came to me [Jeremiah], saying, 2 Go and cry in the ears of Jerusalem, saying, Thus says the Lord: I [earnestly] remember the kindness *and* devotion of your youth, your love after your betrothal [in Egypt] *and* marriage [at Sinai] when you followed Me in the wilderness, in a land not sown.

3 Israel was holiness [something set apart from ordinary purposes, dedicated] to the Lord, the firstfruits of His harvest [of which no stranger was allowed to partake]; all who ate of it [injuring Israel] offended *and* became guilty; evil came upon them, says the Lord.

4 Hear the word of the Lord, O house of Jacob, and all the families of the house of Israel.

5 Thus says the Lord: What unrighteousness did your fathers find in Me, that they went far from Me and [habitually] went after emptiness, falseness, *and* futility and themselves became fruitless *and* worthless?

6 Nor did they say, Where is the Lord, Who brought us up out of the land of Egypt, Who led us through the wilderness, through a land of deserts and pits, through a land of drought and of the shadow of death *and* deep darkness, through a land that no man passes through and where no man dwells?

7 And I brought you into a plentiful land to enjoy its fruits and good things. But when you entered, you defiled My land and made My heritage an abomination [detestable and loathsome].

8 [Even] the priests did not say, Where is the Lord? And those who handle the law [given by God to Moses] knew Me not. The rulers *and* secular shepherds also transgressed against Me, and the prophets prophesied by [the authority and in the name of] Baal and followed after things that do not profit.

9 Therefore I will still contend with you [by inflicting further judgments on you], says the Lord, and with your children's children will I contend.

10 For cross over to the coasts of Cyprus [to the west] and see, send

make your work succeed

The people in Jeremiah 2:13 worked hard to dig wells for themselves, but their wells could not hold water. I am sure they were very disappointed when they did not get the result they wanted after working so hard. I know what it is like to work hard with no results. I have spent many years of my life digging "*empty wells*" like these, and that frustrated and discouraged me. It took me a long time to realize that unless "the Lord builds the house, they labor in vain who build it" (Psalm 127:1).

You may be digging an empty well right now. You may be working on something or somebody. You may have your own little project going on, but you are doing it your way. You may be following your own little plan, trying to make things happen in your own strength and ability. If so, it is not going to work if you have left God out of your plan.

There is nothing more frustrating than trying to do something about something you cannot do anything about. It is similar to having your car stuck in the mud and continuing to press the accelerator down and spin your wheels until you burn up the engine. We often burn out from weariness due to "works of the flesh," which are works that do not work!

Many times we make a plan and then pray for it to work. God wants us to pray *first* and ask Him for His plan. After we have His plan, then He wants us to trust Him to bring it to pass.

Our activity birthed out of the flesh actually prevents God from showing Himself strong in our lives. That is not the way to live the higher life that God has prepared for us. Ask God to help you and lead you as you work, so that your efforts will be productive.

---

also to Kedar [to the east] and carefully consider; and see whether there has been such a thing as this:
11 Has a nation [ever] changed its gods, even though they are not gods? But My people have changed their Glory [God] for that which does not profit.
12 Be astonished *and* appalled, O heavens, at this; be shocked *and* shrivel up with horror, says the Lord [at the behavior of the people].
13 For My people have committed two evils: they have forsaken Me, the Fountain of living waters, *and* they have hewn for themselves cisterns, broken cisterns which cannot hold water.

14 Is Israel a servant? Is he a homeborn slave? Why has he become a captive *and* a prey?
15 The young lions have roared over him *and* made their voices heard. And they have made his land a waste; his cities are burned ruins without inhabitant.
16 Moreover, the children of Memphis and Tahpanhes (Egypt) [have in times past shown their power as a foe; they] have broken *and* fed on the crown of your head [Israel]—so do not rely on them as an ally now.
17 Have you not brought this upon yourself by forsaking the Lord your God when He led you in the way?

18 And now what have you to gain by allying yourself with Egypt *and* going her way, to drink the [black and roiled] waters of the Nile? Or what have you to gain in going the way of Assyria, to drink the waters of the Euphrates?

19 Your own wickedness shall chasten *and* correct you, and your backslidings *and* desertion of faith shall reprove you. Know therefore *and* recognize that this is an evil and bitter thing: [first,] you have forsaken the Lord your God; [second,] you are indifferent to Me *and* the fear of Me is not in you, says the Lord of hosts.

20 For long ago [in Egypt] I broke your yoke and burst your bonds [not that you might be free, but that you might serve Me] ªand long ago you shattered the yoke and snapped the bonds [of My law which I put upon you]; you said, I will not serve *and* obey You! For upon every high hill and under every green tree you [eagerly] prostrated yourself [in idolatrous worship], playing the harlot.

21 Yet I had planted you [O house of Israel] a choice vine, wholly of pure seed. How then have you turned into degenerate shoots of wild vine alien to Me?

22 For though you wash yourself with lye and use much soap, yet your iniquity *and* guilt are still [upon you; you are] spotted, dirty, *and* stained before Me, says the Lord.

23 How can you say, I am not defiled; I have not gone after the Baals [other gods]? Look at your way in the valley; know what you have done. You are a restive young female camel [in the uncontrollable violence of her brute passion eagerly] running hither and thither,

24 Or [you have the untamed and reckless nature of] a wild donkey used to the desert, in her heat sniffing the wind [for the scent of a male]. In her mating season who can restrain her? No males seeking her need weary themselves; in her month they will find her [seeking them].

25 [Cease from your mad running after idols, from which you get nothing but bitter injury.] Keep your feet from being unshod and your throat from thirst. But you said, It is hopeless! For I have loved strangers *and* foreigners, and after them I will go.

26 As the thief is brought to shame when he is caught, so shall the house of Israel be brought to shame—they, their kings, their princes, their priests, and their prophets—

27 [Inasmuch as] they say to a tree, You are my father, and to a stone, You gave me birth. For they have turned their backs to Me and not their faces; but in the time of their trouble, they say, Arise [O Lord] and save us!

28 But where are your gods that you made for yourself? Let them arise if they can save you in the time of your trouble! For [as many as] the number of your cities are your gods, O Judah. [Surely so many handmade idols should be able to help you!]

29 Why do you complain *and* remonstrate against My wrath? You all have rebelled *and* revolted against Me, says the Lord.

30 In vain have I stricken your children (your people); they received no discipline (no correction). Your own sword devoured your prophets like a destroying lion.

31 O generation [that you are]! Behold, consider, *and* regard the word of the Lord: Have I been a wilderness to Israel [like a land without food]? A land of deep darkness [like a way without light]? Why do My people say, We have broken loose [we are free and will roam at large]; we will come no more to You?

a Another translation of the previous statement.

32 Can a maid forget *and* neglect [to wear] her ornaments, or a bride her [marriage] girdle [with its significance like that of a wedding ring]? Yet My people have forgotten Me, days without number.

33 How you deck yourself *and* direct your way to procure [adulterous] love! Because of it even wicked women have learned [indecent] ways from you.

34 Also on your skirts is found the lifeblood of the persons of the innocent poor; you did not find them housebreaking, *nor* have I found it out by secret search. But it is because of [your lust for idolatry that you have done] all these things—[that is everywhere evident.]

35 Yet you keep saying, I am innocent; surely His anger has turned away from Me. Behold, I will bring you to judgment *and* will plead against you because you say, I have not sinned.

36 Why do you gad *or* wander about so much to change your way? You shall be put to shame by Egypt as you were put to shame by Assyria.

37 From [Egypt] also you will come away with your hands upon your head, for the Lord has rejected those in whom you confide, and you will not prosper with [respect to] them.

3 THAT IS to say, If a man puts away his wife and she goes from him and becomes another man's, will he return to her again? [Of course not!] Would not that land [where such a thing happened] be greatly polluted? But you have played the harlot [against Me] with many lovers—yet would you now return to Me? says the Lord [or do you even think to return to Me?]

2 Lift up your eyes to the bare heights and see. Where have you not been adulterously lain with? By the wayside you have sat waiting for lovers [eager for idolatry], like an Arabian [desert tribesman who waits to plunder] in the wilderness; and you have polluted the land with your vile harlotry and your wickedness (unfaithfulness and disobedience to God).

3 Therefore the showers have been withheld, and there has been no spring rain. Yet you have the brow of a prostitute; you refuse to be ashamed.

4 Have you not just now cried to Me: My Father, You were the guide *and* companion of my youth?

5 Will He retain His anger forever? Will He keep it to the end? Behold, you have so spoken, but you have done all the evil things you could *and* have had your way *and* have carried them through.

6 Moreover, the Lord said to me [Jeremiah] in the days of Josiah the king [of Judah], Have you seen what that faithless *and* backsliding Israel has done—how she went up on every high hill and under every green tree and there played the harlot?

7 And I said, After she has done all these things, she will return to Me; but she did not return, and her faithless *and* treacherous sister Judah saw it.

8 And I saw, even though [Judah knew] that for this very cause of committing adultery (idolatry) I [the Lord] had put faithless Israel away and given her a bill of divorce; yet her faithless *and* treacherous sister Judah was not afraid, but she also went and played the harlot [following after idols].

9 And through the infamy *and* unseemly frivolity of Israel's whoredom [because her immorality mattered little to her], she polluted *and* defiled the land, [by her idolatry] committing adultery with [idols of] stones and trees.

10 But in spite of all this, her faithless *and* treacherous sister Judah did not return to Me in sincerity *and* with her whole heart, but only in sheer hypocrisy [has she feigned obedience to King Josiah's reforms], says the Lord. [II Chron. 34:33; Hos. 7:13, 14.]

11 And the Lord said to me, Backsliding *and* faithless Israel has shown herself less guilty than false *and* treacherous Judah.

12 Go and proclaim these words toward the north [where the ten tribes have been taken as captives] and say, Return, faithless Israel, says the Lord, *and* I will not cause My countenance to fall *and* look in anger upon you, for I am merciful, says the Lord; I will not keep My anger forever.

13 Only know, understand, *and* acknowledge your iniquity *and* guilt— that you have rebelled *and* transgressed against the Lord your God and have scattered your favors among strangers under every green tree, and you have not obeyed My voice, says the Lord.

14 Return, O faithless children [of the whole twelve tribes], says the Lord, for I am Lord *and* Master *and* Husband to you, and I will take you [not as a nation, but individually]— one from a city and two from a tribal family—and I will bring you to Zion. [Luke 15:20-22.]

15 And I will give you [spiritual] shepherds after My own heart [in the final time], who will feed you with knowledge and understanding *and* judgment.

16 And it shall be that when you have multiplied and increased in the land in those days, says the Lord, they shall no more say, The ark of the covenant of the Lord. It shall not

come to mind, nor shall they [seriously] remember it, nor shall they miss *or* visit it, nor shall it be repaired *or* made again [for instead of the ark, which represented God's presence, He will show Himself to be present throughout the city]. [Isa. 65:17; Rev. 21:3, 22, 23.]

17 At that time they shall call Jerusalem The Throne of the Lord, and all the nations shall be gathered to it, in the renown *and* name of the Lord, to Jerusalem; nor shall they walk any more after the stubbornness of their own evil hearts.

18 In those days the house of Judah shall walk with the house of Israel, and together they shall come out of the land of the north to the land that I gave as an inheritance to your fathers.

19 And I thought how [gloriously and honorably] I would set you among My children and give you a pleasant land, a goodly heritage, the most beautiful *and* best [inheritance] among all nations! And I thought you would call Me My Father and would not turn away from following Me.

20 Surely, as a wife treacherously *and* faithlessly departs from her husband, so have you dealt treacherously *and* faithlessly with Me, O house of Israel, says the Lord.

21 A voice is heard on the bare heights, the weeping *and* pleading of the sons of Israel, because they have perverted their ways, they have [eagerly] forgotten the Lord their God.

22 Return, O faithless sons, [says the Lord, and] I will heal your faithlessness. [And they answer] Behold, we come to You, for You are the Lord our God.

23 Truly in vain is the hope of salvation from the hills and from the tumult *and* noisy throng on the mountains; truly in *and* with the Lord our God rests the salvation of Israel.

24 [We have been ruined as a nation

---

putting the Word to work

Do you have a "spiritual shepherd" (a spiritual leader) who has God's heart, as mentioned in Jeremiah 3:15? If so, thank God for that person. If not, ask God to give you such a leader.

by our faithlessness and idolatry] for the shameful thing has consumed all for which our fathers toiled from our youth—their flocks and their herds, their sons and their daughters.
25 Let us lie prostrate in our shame, and let our dishonor *and* confusion cover us; for we have sinned against the Lord our God, we and our fathers; from our youth even to this day we have not obeyed the voice of the Lord our God.

4 IF YOU will return, O Israel, says the Lord, if you will return to Me, and if you will put away your abominable false gods out of My sight and not stray *or* waver,
2 And if you swear, As the Lord lives, in truth, in judgment *and* justice, and in righteousness (uprightness in every area and relation), then the nations will bless themselves in Him and in Him will they glory.
3 For thus says the Lord to the men of Judah and to Jerusalem: Break up your ground left uncultivated for a season, so that you may not sow among thorns.
4 Circumcise yourselves to the Lord and take away the foreskins of your hearts, you men of Judah and inhabitants of Jerusalem, lest My wrath go forth like fire [consuming all that gets in its way] and burn so that no one can quench it because of the evil of your doings.
5 Declare in Judah and publish in Jerusalem and say: Blow the trumpet in the land; cry aloud and say: Assemble yourselves, and let us go into the fortified cities.

6 Raise a standard toward Zion [to mark out the safest route to those seeking safety within Jerusalem's walls]! Flee for safety, stay not, for I bring evil from the north, and great destruction.
7 A lion has gone up from his thicket, and a destroyer of nations is on his way. He has gone forth from his place to make your land a desolate waste; and your cities shall be left in ruins without an inhabitant.
8 For this, gird yourselves with sackcloth, lament and wail, for the fierce anger of the Lord has not turned back from us.
9 And it shall be in that day, says the Lord, that the understanding *and* courage of the king shall fail (be paralyzed), and also that of the princes; the priests shall be appalled and the prophets astounded *and* dazed with horror.
10 Then I [Jeremiah] said, *b*Alas, Lord God! Surely You have greatly deceived *and* misled this people and Jerusalem, [for the prophets represented You as] saying [to Your people], You shall have peace, whereas the sword has reached to [their very] life.
11 At that time it will be said to this people and to Jerusalem, A hot wind from the bare heights in the wilderness [comes at My command] against the daughter of My people—not [a wind] to fan or cleanse [from chaff, as when threshing, but]
12 A wind too strong *and* full for winnowing comes at My word. Now I will also speak in judgment against [My people].
13 Behold, [the enemy] comes up

---

b Jeremiah could not reconcile the doom he was now commanded to pronounce either with his own previous prophecy or with what he had read in the writings of the previous prophets. We have the apostle Peter's comment on the perplexity of the prophets in I Pet. 1:10-12: "The prophets, who prophesied of the grace (divine blessing) which was intended for you, searched and inquired earnestly about this salvation. They sought [to find out] to whom or when this was to come which the Spirit of Christ working within them was indicating when He predicted the sufferings of Christ and the glories that should follow [them]. It was then disclosed to them that the services they were rendering were not meant for themselves *and* their period of time, but for you. . . . Into these things [the very] angels long to look!"

like clouds, his chariots like the whirlwind; his horses are swifter than eagles. Woe to us, for we are ruined (destroyed)!

14 O Jerusalem, wash your heart from wickedness, that you may be saved! How long shall your iniquitous *and* grossly offensive thoughts lodge within you?

15 For a voice declares from Dan [in the north] and proclaims evil from Mount Ephraim [the range dividing Israel from Judah].

16 Warn the [neighboring] nations [that our adversary is coming]; announce to Jerusalem that besiegers are coming from a far country, and they shout against the cities of Judah.

17 Like keepers of a field they are against her round about, because she has been rebellious against Me, says the Lord.

18 Your ways and your doings have brought these things upon you. This is your calamity *and* doom; surely it is bitter, for surely it reaches your very heart!

19 [It is not only the prophet but also the people who cry out in their thoughts] My anguish, my anguish! I writhe in pain! Oh, the walls of my heart! My heart is disquieted *and* throbs aloud within me; I cannot be silent! For I have heard the sound of the trumpet, the alarm of war.

20 News of one violent disaster *and* calamity comes close after another, for the whole land is laid waste; suddenly are my tents spoiled *and* destroyed, and my [tent] curtains ruined in a moment.

21 [O Lord] how long must I see the flag [marking the route for flight] and hear the sound of the trumpet [urging the people to flee for refuge]?

22 [Their chastisement will continue until it has accomplished its purpose] for My people are stupid, says the Lord [replying to Jeremiah]; they do not know *and* understand Me. They are thickheaded children, and they have no understanding. They are wise to do evil, but to do good they have no knowledge [and know not how].

23 [In a vision Jeremiah sees Judah laid waste by conquest and captivity.] I looked at the land, and behold, it was [as at the time of creation] waste and vacant (void); and at the heavens, and they had no light.

24 I looked at the mountains, and behold, they trembled, and all the hills moved lightly to and fro.

25 I looked, and behold, there was no man, and all the birds of the air had fled.

26 I looked, and behold, the fruitful land was a desert, and all its cities were laid waste before the Lord's presence, before His fierce anger.

27 For thus says the Lord: The whole land will be a desolation, yet I will not make a full *and* complete end of it. [Jer. 5:10, 18; 30:11; 46:28.]

28 For this will the earth mourn and the heavens above be black; because I have spoken, I have purposed, and I will not relent, nor will I turn back [from it].

29 Every city flees because of the noise of the horsemen and bowmen. They go into the thickets and climb among the rocks; every city is forsaken, and not a man dwells in them.

30 And you [plundered one], when you are made desolate, what will you do? Though you clothe yourself with scarlet, though you deck yourself with ornaments of gold, though you paint your eyelids *and* make them look farther apart, in vain you beautify yourself. Your lovers (allies) despise you; they seek your life.

31 For I have heard a cry as of a woman in travail, the anguish as of one who brings forth her first child—the cry of the Daughter of Zion, who gasps for breath, who spreads her hands, saying, Woe is me now! I am fainting before the murderers.

5 RUN TO and fro through the streets of Jerusalem, and see now and take notice! Seek in her broad squares to see if you can find a man [as Abraham sought in Sodom], one who does justice, who seeks truth, sincerity, *and* faithfulness; and I will pardon [Jerusalem—for one uncompromisingly righteous person]. [Gen. 18:22-32.]

2   And though they say, As the Lord lives, surely they swear falsely.

3   O Lord, do not your eyes look on the truth? [They have meant to please You outwardly, but You look on their hearts.] You have stricken them, but they have not grieved; You have consumed them, but they have refused to take correction *or* instruction. They have made their faces harder than a rock, they have refused to repent *and* return to You.

4   Then I said, Surely these are only the poor; they are [sinfully] foolish *and* have no understanding, for they know not the way of the Lord, the judgment (the just and righteous law) of their God.

5   I will go to the great men and will speak to them, for they must know the way of the Lord, the judgment (the just and righteous law) of their God. But [I found the very reverse to be true] these had all alike broken the yoke [of God's law] and had burst the bonds [of obedience to Him].

6   Therefore a lion out of the forest shall slay them, a wolf of the desert shall destroy them, a leopard *or* panther shall lie in wait against their cities. Everyone who goes out of them shall be torn in pieces, because their transgressions are many, their backslidings *and* total desertion of faith are increased *and* have become great *and* mighty.

7   Why should I *and* how can I pass over this *and* forgive you for it? Your children have forsaken Me and sworn by those that are no gods. When I had fed them to the full *and* bound them to Me by oath, they committed [spiritual] adultery, assembling themselves in troops at the houses of [idol] harlots.

8   They were like fed stallions roaming at large; each one neighed after his neighbor's wife.

9   Shall I not punish them for these things? says the Lord; and shall I not avenge Myself on such a nation as this?

10 Go up within [Jerusalem's] walls and destroy [her vines], but do not make a full *and* complete end. Trim away the tendrils [of her vines], for they are not the Lord's.

11 For the house of Israel and the house of Judah have dealt very faithlessly *and* treacherously against Me, says the Lord.

12 They have lied about *and* denied the Lord by saying, It is not He [Who speaks through His prophets]! Evil shall not come upon us; nor shall we see war or famine.

13 And [say they] the prophets will become wind [what they prophesy will not come to pass], and the word [of God] is not in them. Thus shall it be done to them [as they threatened would be done to us].

14 Therefore thus says the Lord God of hosts: Because you [the people] have spoken this word, behold, I will make My words fire in your mouth [Jeremiah] and this people wood, and it will devour them.

15 Behold, I am bringing a nation upon you from afar, O house of Israel, says the Lord. It is a mighty *and* enduring nation, it is an ancient nation, a nation whose language you do not know, nor can you understand what they say.

16 Their quiver is [filled with deadly missiles] like an open sepulcher [filled with dead bodies; the foes] are all mighty men (heroes).

17 They shall consume your harvest and your food; they shall consume

words of fire

In Jeremiah 5:14, we see that God was calling Jeremiah to a new level where his words would be mighty and powerful, like fire.

God is also calling you and me to experience a higher level of His power and blessing, and we need to realize that with every new level comes new opposition. In the face of that opposition, we should choose our words carefully. We must realize that wrong words can open doors for the enemy that we do not want to open.

For years God spoke to me about not opening doors to Satan. Then one day He said, "Joyce, forget about doors; Satan is looking for any tiny crack he can crawl through in your life." God was actually telling me that I would need to live more carefully than ever before.

Whatever Jeremiah had been doing previously was not as aggressive against the kingdom of darkness as what God had planned. I believe the same thing holds true in your life and mine. Things that God was patient with in the past, He will have to deal with now. We cannot walk in the flesh until it is time to exercise our ministry gifts and then quickly try to get in the Spirit. There will be no power, no anointing, released through such a life.

Remember that God told Jeremiah He would make His words like fire in his mouth, and that He would make the people like wood. I have read books that spoke of past revivals and explained how the anointing of the Lord was so strong on the preaching at times that hundreds of people fell out of their chairs onto the floor and began crying out for deliverance and salvation. I believe that is a manifestation of God, making the words of the speakers' mouths like fire and the people like wood. But we will not see such signs and wonders as long as we intentionally allow a mixture in our lives and in the words of our mouths. We may never experience complete perfection in this area, but it is time to deal with this issue very seriously.

When I speak God's Word, I want it to have a dramatic effect on people, changing them radically. Let me encourage you to do likewise. Ask God to put His fire in your mouth so that your words will be life-changing for those who hear them.

your sons and your daughters; they shall consume your flocks and your herds; they shall consume your vines and your fig trees. They shall break down *and* impoverish your fortified cities in which you trust, with the sword [they shall destroy them].

18 But even in those days, says the Lord, I will not make a full *and* complete end of you.

19 And when your people say, Why has the Lord our God done all these things to us? then you shall answer them, As you have forsaken Me, says the Lord, and have served strange gods in your land, so shall you serve strangers (gods) in a land that is not yours.

20 Declare this in the house of Jacob and publish it in Judah:

21 Hear now this, O foolish people without understanding *or* heart, who have eyes and see not, who have ears and hear not: [Isa. 6:9, 10; Matt. 13:10-15; Mark 8:17, 18.]

22 Do you not fear *and* reverence Me? says the Lord. Do you not tremble before Me? *I* placed the sand for the boundary of the sea, a perpetual barrier beyond which it cannot pass *and* by an everlasting ordinance beyond which it cannot go? And though the waves of the sea toss *and* shake themselves, yet they cannot prevail [against the feeble grains of sand which God has ordained by nature to be sufficient for His purpose]; though [the billows] roar, yet they cannot pass over that [barrier]. [Is not such a God to be reverently feared and worshiped?]

23 But these people have hearts that draw back from God and wills that rebel against Him; they have revolted *and* quit His service and have gone away [into idolatry].

24 Nor do they say in their hearts, Let us now reverently fear *and* worship the Lord our God, Who gives rain, both the autumn and the spring rain in its season, Who reserves *and* keeps for us the appointed weeks of the harvest.

25 Your iniquities have turned these blessings away, and your sins have kept good [harvests] from you.

26 For among My people are found wicked men; they watch like fowlers who lie in wait; they set a trap, they catch men.

27 As a cage is full of birds, so are their houses full of deceit *and* treachery; therefore they have become great and grown rich,

28 They have grown fat *and* sleek. Yes, they surpass in deeds of wickedness; they do not judge *and* plead with justice the cause of the fatherless, that they may prosper, and they do not defend the rights of the needy.

29 Shall I not punish them for these things? says the Lord. Shall I not avenge Myself on such a nation as this?

30 An appalling and horrible thing [bringing desolation and destruction] has come to pass in the land:

31 The prophets prophesy falsely, and the priests exercise rule at their own hands *and* by means of the prophets. And My people love to have it so! But what will you do when the end comes?

6 FLEE FOR safety, you children of Benjamin, out of the midst of Jerusalem! And blow the trumpet in Tekoa [a town far south in Judah], and raise a [fire] signal over Beth-haccherem [a town near Jerusalem]! For evil is looking forth with eagerness from the north, and great destruction.

2 The comely and delicate one, [Jerusalem] the Daughter of Zion, I will destroy. [To a pasturage, yes, a luxurious pasturage, have I likened her.]

3 Shepherds with their flocks shall come against her; they shall pitch their tents round about her; they shall pasture, each one in his place [eating up all her luxurious herbage on every side].

4 Prepare yourselves for war against her [they cry]; up, let us attack her at noon! But alas, the day declines, the evening shadows lengthen.

5 Arise, let us go by night and destroy her palaces!

6 For the Lord of hosts has said, Hew down her trees and cast up a siege mound against Jerusalem. This is the city which must be punished; there is nothing but oppression within her.

7 As a fountain wells up *and* casts forth its waters *and* keeps them fresh, so she is [continually] casting forth [fresh] wickedness. Violence and destruction are heard within her; sickness and wounds are continually before Me.

8 Be corrected, reformed, instructed, *and* warned, O Jerusalem, lest I be alienated *and* parted from you, lest I make you a desolation, an uninhabited land.

9 Thus says the Lord of hosts: They shall thoroughly glean as a vine what is left of Israel; turn back your hand again *and* again [O minister of destruction] into the baskets, like a grape gatherer, *and* strip the tendrils [of the vine].

10 To whom shall I [Jeremiah] speak and give warning, that they may hear? Behold, their ears are uncircumcised [never brought into covenant with God or consecrated to His service], and they cannot hear *or* obey. Behold, the word of the Lord has become to them a reproach *and* the object of their scorn; they have no delight in it.

life point

In the sixth chapter of Jeremiah, the Lord told Jeremiah to warn His children of the impending destruction of the city that was full of oppression. God wants to protect and provide for His people, and it is so tragic when they cannot hear His voice because they have not consecrated their ears to His service (see Jeremiah 6:10). Ask God to make your ears sensitive to His voice.

11 Therefore I am full of the wrath of the Lord; I am weary of restraining it. I will pour it out on the children in the street and on the gathering of young men together; for even the husband with the wife will be taken, the aged with the very old.

12 And their houses will be turned over to others, their fields and their wives together; for I will stretch out My hand against the inhabitants of the land, says the Lord.

13 For from the least of them even to the greatest of them, everyone is given to covetousness (to greed for unjust gain); and from the prophet even to the priest, everyone deals falsely.

14 They have healed also the wound of the daughter of My people lightly *and* neglectfully, saying, Peace, peace, when there is no peace.

15 Were they brought to shame because they had committed abominations (extremely disgusting and vile things)? No, they were not at all ashamed, nor could they blush [at their idolatry]. Therefore they shall fall among those who fall; at the time that I punish them they shall be overthrown, says the Lord.

16 Thus says the Lord: Stand by the roads and look; and ask for the eternal paths, where the good, old way is; then walk in it, and you will find rest for your souls. But they said, We will not walk in it! [Matt. 11:29.]

17 Also I set watchmen over you, saying, Hear *and* obey the sound of the trumpet! But they said, We will not listen *or* obey.

18 Therefore hear, O [Gentile] nations, and know, O congregation [of believing ones], what [great things I will do] to them.

19 Hear, O earth: behold, I am bringing evil upon this people, the fruit of their thoughts (their schemes and devices) because they have not listened *and* obeyed My words, and as for My law, they have rejected it.

20 To what purpose does frankincense come to Me from Sheba [in southwestern Arabia] and the sweet cane from a far country? Your burnt offerings are not acceptable, nor are your sacrifices sweet *or* pleasing to Me.

21 Therefore thus says the Lord: Behold, I will lay stumbling blocks before this people. And the fathers and the sons together will stumble against them; the neighbor and his friend will perish.

22 Thus says the Lord: Behold, a people is coming from the north country, and a great nation is arousing itself from the ends of the earth.

23 They lay hold on bow and spear; they are cruel (ruthless and inhuman) and have no mercy. Their voice sounds like the roaring sea; they ride on horses, every one set in array as a man for battle against you, O Daughter of Zion!

24 We have heard the report of it; our hands become feeble *and* helpless. Anguish has taken hold of us, pangs like that of a woman in childbirth.

25 Go not out into the field nor walk on the road, for the enemy is armed with the sword; terror is on every side.

26 O daughter of my people [says Jeremiah], gird yourself with sackcloth and wallow in ashes; make mourning as for an only son, a most bitter lamentation, for the destroyer will suddenly come upon us [on prophet and people].

27 I [says the Lord] have set you [Jeremiah] as an assayer *and* a prover of ore among My people, that you may know and try their doings and be like a watchtower.

28 They are all the worst [kind] of rebels *and* utter and total revolters against God, going about publishing slander. They are [not gold and silver ore, but] bronze and iron; they are all corrupters.

29 The bellows blow fiercely, the lead is consumed by the fire; in vain do they continue refining, for the wicked [the dross] are not removed.

30 Men will call them reprobate *and* rejected silver [only dross, without good metal], because the Lord has rejected them.

7 THE WORD that came to Jeremiah from the Lord, saying,

2 Stand in the gate of the Lord's house and proclaim there this word and say, Hear the word of the Lord, all you of Judah who enter in at these gates to worship the Lord.

3 Thus says the Lord of hosts, the God of Israel: Amend your ways and your doings, and I will cause you to dwell in this place.

4 Trust not in the lying words [of the false prophets who maintain that God will protect Jerusalem because His temple is there], saying, This is the temple of the Lord, the temple of the Lord, the temple of the Lord.

5 For if you thoroughly amend your ways and your doings, if you thoroughly *and* truly execute justice between every man and his neighbor,

6 If you do not oppress the transient *and* the alien, the fatherless, and the widow or shed innocent blood [by oppression and by judicial murders] in [Jerusalem] or go after other gods to your own hurt,

7 Then I will cause you to dwell in this place, in the land that I gave of old to your fathers to dwell in forever.

8 Behold, you trust in lying words that cannot benefit [so that you do not profit].

9 Will you steal, murder, commit adultery, swear falsely, burn incense to Baal, and go after other gods that you have not known,

10 And [then dare to] come and stand before Me in this house, which is called by My ᶜName, and say, [By the discharge of this religious formality] we are set free!—only to go on with this wickedness *and* these abominations?

c See footnote on Deut. 12:5.

11 Has this house, which is called by My Name, become a den of robbers in your eyes [a place of retreat for you between acts of violence]? Behold, I Myself have seen it, says the Lord.

12 But go now to My place which was in Shiloh [in Ephraim], where I set My Name at the first, and see what I did to it for the wickedness of My people Israel. [I Sam. 4:10-18.]

13 And now, because you have done all these things, says the Lord, and [because] when I spoke to you persistently [even rising up early and speaking], you did not listen, and when I called you, you did not answer,

14 Therefore will I do to this house (the temple), which is called by My Name *and* in which you trust, to the place which I gave to you and to your fathers, as I did to Shiloh.

15 And I will cast you out of My sight, as I have cast out all your brethren, even the whole posterity of Ephraim.

16 Therefore do not pray for this people [of Judah] or lift up a cry or entreaty for them or make intercession to Me, for I will not listen to *or* hear you.

17 Do you not see what they are doing in the cities of Judah and in the streets of Jerusalem?

18 The children gather wood, the fathers kindle the fire, and the women knead the dough, to make cakes for the ᵈqueen of heaven; and they pour out drink offerings to other gods, that they may provoke Me to anger!

19 Am I the One Whom they provoke to anger? says the Lord. Is it not themselves [whom they provoke], to their own confusion *and* vexation *and* to their own shame?

20 Therefore thus says the Lord God: Behold, My anger and My wrath will be poured out on this place, on man and beast, on the trees of the field and the fruit of the ground; it will burn and not be quenched.

21 Thus says the Lord of hosts, the God of Israel: Add your burnt offerings to your sacrifices and eat the flesh [if you will. It will avail you nothing].

22 For in the day that I brought them out of the land of Egypt, I did not speak to your fathers or command them concerning burnt offerings or sacrifices.

23 But this thing I did command them: Listen to *and* obey My voice, and I will be your God and you will be My people; and walk in the whole way that I command you, that it may be well with you.

24 But they would not listen to *and* obey Me or bend their ear [to Me], but followed the counsels *and* the stubborn promptings of their own evil hearts *and* minds, and they turned their backs *and* went in reverse instead of forward.

25 Since the day that your fathers came forth out of the land of Egypt to this day, I have persistently sent to you all My servants the prophets, sending them daily, early and late.

26 Yet the people would not listen to *and* obey Me or bend their ears [to Me], but stiffened their necks and behaved worse than their fathers.

27 Speak all these words to them, but they will not listen to *and* obey you; also call to them, but they will not answer you.

28 Yet you shall say to them, This is the nation that did not obey the voice of the Lord their God or receive instruction *and* correction *and* warning; truth *and* faithfulness have perished and have completely vanished from their mouths.

29 Cut off your hair [your crown, O Jerusalem] and cast it away, and take

d A goddess of fertility, probably the Babylonian title for Ishtar. She is identified with the planet Venus. Offerings to this goddess included cakes made in the shape of a star (Jer. 44:19).

up a lamentation on the bare heights, for the Lord has rejected and forsaken the generation of His wrath.

30 For the children of Judah have done evil in My sight, says the Lord; they have set their abominations (extremely disgusting and shamefully vile things) in the house which is called by My Name to defile it.

31 And they have built the high places of Topheth, which is in the Valley of Ben-hinnom [son of Hinnom], to burn their sons and their daughters in the fire [in honor of Molech, the fire god]—which I did not command, nor did it come into My mind or heart. [Lev. 18:21; Josh. 15:8; II Kings 16:2-3; 21:1, 6; Isa. 30:33.]

32 Therefore, behold, the days are coming, says the Lord, when it shall no more be called Topheth or the Valley of Ben-hinnom [son of Hinnom], but the Valley of Slaughter, for [in bloody warfare] they will bury in Topheth till there is no more room and no place else to bury. [Jer. 19:6.]

33 And the dead bodies of this people will be meat for the fowls of the air and for the beasts of the earth, and none will frighten them away.

34 Then will I cause to cease from the cities of Judah and from the streets of Jerusalem the voice of mirth and the voice of gladness, the voice of the bridegroom and the voice of the bride; for the land will become a waste.

8 AT THAT time, says the Lord, [the Babylonian army will break open the sepulchers, and] they shall bring out the ᵉbones of the kings of Judah, the bones of its princes, the bones of the priests, the bones of the prophets, and the bones of the inhabitants of Jerusalem from their graves.

2 And they will [carelessly] scatter [the corpses] before the sun and the moon and all the host of heaven, which [the dead] have loved and which they have served and after which they have walked and which they have sought, inquired of, and required and which they have worshiped. They shall not be gathered, or be buried; they shall be like ᶠdung upon the face of the earth.

3 And death shall be chosen rather than life by all the residue of those who remain of this evil family (nation), who remain in all the places to which I have driven them, says the Lord of hosts.

4 Moreover, you [Jeremiah] shall say to them, Thus says the Lord: Shall men fall and not rise up again? Shall one turn away [from God] and not repent and return [to Him]?

5 Why then is this people of Jerusalem turned away with a perpetual turning away [from Me]? They hold fast to ᵍdeceit (idolatry); they refuse to repent and return [to God].

6 I have listened and heard, but they have not spoken aright; no man repents of his wickedness, saying, What have I done? Everyone turns to his [individual] course, as the horse rushes like a torrent into battle.

7 [Even the migratory birds are punctual to their seasons.] Yes, the stork [excelling in the great height of her flight] in the heavens knows her appointed times [of migration], and the turtledove, the swallow, and the crane observe the time of their return. But My people do not know the law of

---

e "Of the motive of the disinterment [on the part of the Babylonian conquerors] the prophet says nothing. He had certainly no idea of its being the search for booty. He has in mind only the justice of God [which is concerned with punishment or penalties upon the rebellious people of God]" (Johan P. Lange, *A Commentary*). f "Observe the irony. The stars look powerlessly down on the bones of their worshipers—while these send up a stench!" (Johan P. Lange, *A Commentary*). g Idolatry is deceitful and false because in their idolatry men and women worship what is false, and it merely deludes the worshipers and causes them to believe a lie.

the Lord [which the lower animals instinctively recognize in so far as it applies to them].

8 How can you say, We are wise, and we have the written law of the Lord [and are learned in its language and teachings]? Behold, the truth is, the lying pen of the scribes has made of the law a falsehood (a mere code of ceremonial observances). [Mark 7:13.]

9 The wise men shall be put to shame; they shall be dismayed and taken [captive]. Behold, they have rejected the word of the Lord, and what wisdom *and* broad, full intelligence is in them?

10 Therefore will I give their wives to others and their fields to those who gain possession of them; for everyone, from the least even to the greatest, is given to covetousness (is greedy for unjust gain); from the prophet even to the priest, everyone deals falsely.

11 For they have healed the wound of the daughter of My people only lightly *and* slightingly, saying, Peace, peace, when there is no peace.

12 They are brought to shame because they have committed abominations (extremely disgusting and shamefully vile things). And yet they were not at all ashamed, nor could they blush. Therefore they shall fall among those who fall; at the time of their punishment they shall be overthrown, says the Lord. [Jer. 6:12-15.]

13 I will gather *and* sweep them away, utterly consuming them, says the Lord. [I will find] no grapes on the vine, nor figs on the fig tree, and even the leaf is withered; and the things that I have given them shall pass away from them [for I have appointed to them those who shall pass over them]. [Matt. 21:18, 19.]

14 [Then say the people to each other] Why do we sit still? Assemble yourselves, and let us enter into the fortified cities and be silent *or* perish there! For the Lord our God has decreed our ruin and given us bitter *and* poisonous water to drink, because we have sinned against the Lord.

15 We looked for peace *and* completeness, but no good came, and for a time of healing, but behold, dismay, trouble, *and* terror!

16 The snorting of [Nebuchadnezzar's] horses is heard from Dan [on the northern border of Palestine]. At the sound of the neighing of his strong war-horses the whole land quakes; for they come and devour the land and all that is in it, the city and those who dwell in it.

17 For behold, I am sending among you serpents, adders which cannot be charmed, and they shall bite you, says the Lord.

18 Oh, that I [Jeremiah] could comfort myself against sorrow, [for my grief is beyond healing], my heart is sick *and* faint within me!

19 Behold [says the prophet, listen to the voice of] the cry of the daughter of my people [for help] because of those who dwell in a far country: Is not the Lord in Zion? Is not her King in her? [But the Lord answers] Why have they provoked Me to anger with their carved images and with foreign idols?

20 The harvest is past, the summer has ended *and* the gathering of fruit is over, yet we are not saved! [comes again the voice of the people.]

21 For the hurt of the daughter of my people am I [Jeremiah] hurt; I go around mourning; dismay has taken hold on me.

22 Is there no balm in Gilead? Is there no physician there? Why then is not the health of the daughter of my people restored? [Because Zion no longer enjoyed the presence of the Great Physician!] [Exod. 15:26.]

9 OH, THAT my head were waters and my eyes a reservoir of tears, that I might weep day and night

for the slain of the daughter of my people!

2 Oh, that I had in the wilderness a lodging place (a mere shelter) for wayfaring men, that I might leave my people and go away from them! For they are all adulterers [rendering worship to idols instead of to the Lord, Who has espoused the people to Himself]; they are a gang of treacherous men [faithless even to each other].

3 And they bend their tongue, [which is] their bow for the lies [they shoot]. And not according to faithfulness do they rule *and* become strong in the land; for they proceed from evil to evil, and they do not know *and* understand *and* acknowledge Me, says the Lord.

4 Let everyone beware of his neighbor and put no trust in any brother. For every brother is an utter *and* complete supplanter (one who takes by the heel and trips up, a deceiver, a Jacob), and every neighbor goes about as a slanderer. [Gen. 25:26.]

5 And they deceive *and* mock every one his neighbor and do not speak the truth. They have taught their tongues to speak lies; they weary themselves committing iniquity.

6 Your habitation is in the midst of deceit [oppression upon oppression and deceit upon deceit]; through deceit they refuse to know *and* understand Me, says the Lord.

7 Therefore thus says the Lord of hosts: Behold, I will melt them [by the process of affliction to remove the dross] and test them, for how else should I deal with the daughter of My people?

8 Their tongue is a murderous arrow; it speaks deceitfully; one speaks peaceably to his neighbor with his mouth, but in his heart he lays snares and waits in ambush for him.

9 Shall I not punish them for these things? says the Lord. Shall I not avenge Myself on such a nation as this?

10 For the mountains I will take up a weeping and wailing and for the pastures of the wilderness a lament, because they are burned up *and* desolated, so that no one passes through [them]; neither can men hear [any longer] the lowing of cattle. Both the fowls of the air and the beasts have fled, they are gone!

11 I will make Jerusalem heaps [of ruins], a dwelling place of jackals; and I will make the cities of Judah a desolation, without inhabitant.

12 Who is the wise man who may understand this? To whom has the mouth of the Lord spoken, that he may declare it? Why is the land ruined *and* laid waste like a wilderness, so that no one passes through it?

13 And the Lord says, Because they have forsaken My law, which I set before them, and have not listened to *and* obeyed My voice or walked in accordance with it

14 But have walked stubbornly after their own hearts and after the Baals, as their fathers taught them,

15 Therefore thus says the Lord of hosts, the God of Israel: Behold, I will feed them, even this people, with wormwood and give them bitter *and* poisonous water to drink.

16 I will scatter them also among nations that neither they nor their fathers have known, and I will send the sword among them *and* after them until I have consumed them.

17 Thus says the Lord of hosts: Consider and call for the mourning women to come; send for the skillful women to come.

18 Let them make haste and raise a wailing over us *and* for us, that our eyes may run down with tears and our eyelids gush with water.

19 For a sound of wailing is heard [coming] out of Zion: How we are plundered *and* ruined! We are greatly confounded *and* utterly put to shame, because we have forsaken the land,

because they have cast down our dwellings [our dwellings that have cast us out].

20 Yet hear the word of the Lord, O you women, and let your ears receive the word of His mouth; teach your daughters a lament, and each one [teach] her neighbor a dirge.

21 For death has come up into our windows; it has entered into our palaces, cutting off the children from outdoors and the young men from the streets.

22 Speak, Thus says the Lord: The dead bodies of men shall fall like dung on the open field and like sheaves [of grain] behind the reaper, and none shall gather them. [Jer. 8:2.]

23 Thus says the Lord: Let not the wise *and* skillful person glory *and* boast in his wisdom *and* skill; let not the mighty *and* powerful person glory *and* boast in his strength *and* power; let not the person who is rich [in physical gratification and earthly wealth] glory *and* boast in his [temporal satisfactions and earthly] riches;

24 But let him who glories glory in this: that he understands and knows Me [personally and practically, directly discerning and recognizing My character], that I am the Lord, Who practices loving-kindness, judgment, and righteousness in the earth, for in these things I delight, says the Lord. [I Cor. 1:31; II Cor. 10:17.]

25 Behold, the days are coming, says the Lord, when I will punish all who though circumcised [outwardly, in the flesh] are still uncircumcised [in corresponding inward purity] — [Rom. 2:25-29.]

26 Egypt, Judah, Edom, the children of Ammon, Moab [all of whom are

related except Egypt], and all who live in the desert and who clip off the corners of their hair *and* beards; for all these nations are uncircumcised [in heart], and all the house of Israel is uncircumcised in heart.

10 HEAR THE word which the Lord speaks to you, O house of Israel.

2 Thus says the Lord: Learn not the way of the [heathen] nations and be not dismayed at the signs of the heavens, though they are dismayed at them,

3 For the customs *and* ordinances of the peoples are false, empty, *and* futile; it is but a tree which one cuts out of the forest [to make for himself a god], the work of the hands of the craftsman with the ax *or* other tool.

4 They deck [the idol] with silver and with gold; they fasten it with nails and with hammers so it will not fall apart *or* move around.

5 [Their idols] are like pillars of turned work [as upright and stationary and immobile as a palm tree], like scarecrows in a cucumber field; they cannot speak; they have to be carried, for they cannot walk. Do not be afraid of them, for they cannot do evil, neither is it possible for them to do good [and it is not in them].

6 None at all is like You, O Lord; You are great, and Your name is great in might.

7 Who would not fear You, O King of the nations? For it is fitting to You *and* Your due! For among all the wise [men or gods] of the nations and in all their kingdoms, there is none like You.

8 But they are altogether irrational

speak the Word

God, I glory only in the fact that I know You, that I understand You are the Lord,
Who practices loving-kindness, judgment, and righteousness.
ADAPTED FROM JEREMIAH 9:24

and stupid and foolish. Their instruction is given by idols who are but wood [it is a teaching of falsity, emptiness, futility]!

9 Silver beaten [into plates] is brought from Tarshish and gold from Uphaz, the work of the craftsman and of the hands of the goldsmith; the [idols'] clothing is violet and purple—they are all the work of skillful men.

10 But the Lord is the true God *and* the God of truth (the God Who is Truth). He is the living God and the everlasting King. At His wrath the earth quakes, and the nations are not able to bear His indignation.

11 Thus shall you say to them: The gods, who did not make the heavens and the earth, shall perish from the earth and from under the heavens.

12 God made the earth by His power; He established the world by His wisdom and by His understanding *and* skill stretched out the heavens.

13 When He utters His voice, there is a tumult of waters in the heavens, and He causes the vapors to ascend from the ends of the earth. He makes lightnings for the rain and brings forth the wind out from His treasuries *and* from His storehouses.

14 Every man has become like a brute, irrational *and* stupid, without knowledge [of God]; every goldsmith is brought to shame by his graven idols; for his molten images are frauds *and* falsehood, and there is no breath in them.

15 They are devoid of worth, usefulness, *or* truth, a work of delusion *and* mockery; in their time of trial *and* punishment they shall [helplessly] perish.

16 The Portion of Jacob [the true God on Whom Israel has a claim] is not like these, for He is the Fashioner *and* Maker of all things, and Israel is the tribe of His inheritance—the Lord of hosts is His name.

17 Gather up your bundle [of baggage] from the ground, O you who dwell under siege.

18 For thus says the Lord: Behold, I will sling out the inhabitants of the land at this time and will bring distress on them, that they may feel it *and* find it [to be as I have said, and turn to Me].

19 Woe is me because of my hurt! [says Jeremiah, speaking for the nation.] My wound is grievous *and* incurable. But I said, Surely this sickness *and* suffering *and* grief are mine, and I must endure, tolerate, *and* bear them.

20 My tent (home) is taken by force *and* plundered, and all my [tent] cords are broken. My children have gone forth [as captives] from me, and they are no more; there is no one to stretch forth my tent any more and to set up my [tent] curtains.

21 For the shepherds [of the people] have become like brutes, irrational *and* stupid, and have not sought the Lord *or* inquired of Him *or* required Him [by necessity and by right of His word]. Therefore they have not dealt prudently *and* have not prospered, and all their flocks are scattered.

22 Hark, the sound of a rumor! [The invading army] comes!—a great commotion out of the north country—to make the cities of Judah a desolation, a dwelling place of jackals.

23 O Lord [pleads Jeremiah in the name of the people], I know that [the determination of] the way of a man is not in himself; it is not in man [even in a strong man or in a man at his best] to direct his [own] steps. [Ps. 37:23; Prov. 20:24.]

24 O Lord, correct, instruct, *and* chastise me, but with judgment *and* in just measure—not in Your anger, lest You diminish me *and* bring me to nothing.

25 Pour out Your wrath upon the nations that do not know *or* recognize You and upon the peoples that do not

life point

Life would be so much easier if we would believe God's Word and act accordingly, but most of us have to find out the hard way what works and what does not work. God's Word says in Jeremiah 10:23 that we do not have it in us to run our own lives, but we still try. Let me encourage you to give up trying to control your own life or someone else's. God is in control, so relax and let Him direct your steps.

call upon Your name. For they have devoured Jacob, yes, devoured him and consumed him and made his habitation a desolate waste.

11 THE WORD that came to Jeremiah from the Lord:
2 Hear the words of this covenant or solemn pledge, and speak to the men of Judah and the inhabitants of Jerusalem.
3 Say to them, Thus says the Lord, the God of Israel: Cursed is the man who does not heed the words of this covenant or solemn pledge
4 Which I commanded your fathers at the time that I brought them out of the land of Egypt, from the iron furnace, saying, Listen to My voice and do according to all that I command you. So will you be My people, and I will be your God,
5 That I may perform the oath which I swore to your fathers, to give them a land flowing with milk and honey, as it is this day. Then I answered, Amen (so be it), O Lord.
6 And the Lord said to me, Proclaim all these words in the cities of Judah and in the streets of Jerusalem: Hear the words of this covenant or solemn pledge and do them.
7 For I earnestly protested to and warned your fathers at the time that I

brought them up out of the land of Egypt, even to this day, protesting to and warning them persistently, saying, Obey My voice.
8 Yet they did not obey or incline their ear [to Me], but everyone walked in the stubbornness of his own evil heart. Therefore I brought upon them all [the calamities threatened in] the words of this covenant or solemn pledge, which I had commanded, but they did not do.
9 And the Lord said to me, A conspiracy is found among the men of Judah and among the inhabitants of Jerusalem.
10 They have turned back to the iniquities of their forefathers, who refused to hear My words; they have gone after other gods to serve them. The house of Israel and the house of Judah have broken My covenant or solemn pledge which I made with their fathers.
11 Therefore thus says the Lord: Behold, I am bringing evil and calamity upon them which they will not be able to escape; though they cry to Me, I will not listen to them.
12 Then the cities of Judah and the inhabitants of Jerusalem will go and cry out to the gods to whom they offer incense, but they cannot save them at all in the time of their evil trouble.
13 For [as many as] the number of your cities are your gods, O Judah; and [as many as] the number of the streets of Jerusalem are the altars you have set up to the shameful thing, even altars to burn incense to Baal.
14 Therefore do not pray for this people or lift up a cry or prayer for them, for I will not listen when they cry out to Me in the time of their evil trouble.
15 What right has My beloved [to be] in My house when she has wrought lewdness and done treacherously many times? Can vows and the holy flesh [of your sacrifices] remove from

you your wickedness *and* avert your calamity? Can you by these [escape your doom and] rejoice exultantly?

16 The Lord [acknowledged you once to be worthy to be] called a green olive tree, fair *and* of good fruit; but with the roar of a great tempest He will set fire to it, and its branches will be consumed. [Ps. 52:8; Jer. 21:14.]

17 For the Lord of hosts, Who planted you, has pronounced evil *and* calamity against you because of the evil which the house of Israel and the house of Judah have done against themselves in provoking Me to anger by offering incense to Baal.

18 And the Lord gave me [Jeremiah] knowledge of it [their plot], and I knew it; then You [O Lord] showed me their doings.

19 But I was like a tame lamb that is brought to the slaughter; I did not know that they had devised inventions *and* schemes against me, saying, Let us destroy the tree with its fruit; let us cut him off from the land of the living, that his name may be no more remembered.

20 But, O Lord of hosts, Who judges rightly *and* justly, Who tests the heart and the mind, let me see Your vengeance on them, for to You I have revealed *and* committed my cause [rolling it upon You].

life point

Every time God gives us a test, we can tell how far we have come and how far we still have to go by how we react in that test. Attitudes of the heart that we did not know we had often come out through tests and trials. Embrace your tests as opportunities for growth and development.

21 Therefore thus says the Lord about the men of Anathoth [Jeremiah's hometown], who seek your life

[Jeremiah] and say, Prophesy not in the name of the Lord, that you die not by our hands—

22 Therefore thus says the Lord of hosts: Behold, I will punish them. Their young men will die by the sword, their sons and their daughters will die by famine;

23 And there will be no remnant [of the conspirators] left, for I will bring evil *and* calamity upon the men of Anathoth in the year of their punishment.

12 UNCOMPROMISINGLY righteous *and* rigidly just are You, O Lord, when I complain against *and* contend with You. Yet let me plead *and* reason the case with You: Why does the way of the wicked prosper? Why are all they at ease *and* thriving who deal very treacherously *and* deceitfully?

2 You have planted them, yes, they have taken root; they grow, yes, they bring forth fruit. You are near in their mouths but far from their hearts.

3 But You, O Lord, know *and* understand me *and* my devotion to You; You see me and try my heart toward You. [O Lord] pull [these rebellious ones] out like sheep for the slaughter and devote *and* prepare them for the day of slaughter.

4 How long must the land mourn and the grass *and* herbs of the whole country wither? Through the wickedness of those who dwell in it, the beasts and the birds are consumed *and* are swept away [by the drought], because men [mocked] me, saying, He shall not [live to] see our final end.

5 [But the Lord rebukes Jeremiah's impatience, saying] If you have raced with men on foot and they have tired you out, then how can you compete with horses? And if [you take to flight] in a land of peace where you feel secure, then what will you do [when you tread the tangled maze of

how to pass life's tests

Jeremiah 11:20 tells us that God tests our hearts, emotions, and thinking powers. When we want to test something, how do we do it? We put pressure on it to see if it will do what it says it will do; we look to see if it will hold up under the stress. God does the same thing with us. When we pray, asking Him to use us and to put us into positions of leadership, His answer is, "Let Me try you out first. Let Me put you to the test."

I am saddened when I realize how many people never make it past the trying point. They never pass the test. They spend their whole lives going around and around the same proverbial mountains. But in God's school we do not flunk; we get to keep taking the test again and again until we pass it.

To test something means to prove its truth or genuineness by an experiment, a trial, or an examination. It also means to compare something against a standard. One of the ways God tests us is by requiring us to manifest what we say we know. Head knowledge alone is not enough. If we cannot produce the goods, head knowledge means nothing.

Deuteronomy 8:2 says that God led the Israelites in the wilderness for forty years to humble them, to prove them, and to see if they would keep His commandments. Tests usually do not come in good times. They come in hard times because not everything God asks us to do is going to be easy. That is why He tests us to see if we are ready and able before He promotes us to a higher level of responsibility.

So many things come our way every day that are just nothing more than tests. For example, sometimes when we have to wait to be seated at a table in a restaurant and then we get a bad meal, it is a test. Sometimes when we are going to pull into a parking space and someone zooms in and takes it, it is a test. Sometimes when our boss tells us to do something we do not want to do, it is a test.

James 1:2–4 says that tests bring out what is in us. In times of trial we become best acquainted with ourselves and with what we are capable of doing. Peter did not think he would ever deny Jesus, but when he was put to the test, that is exactly what he did (see Luke 22:60–62). God is not impressed with what we say we will do; He is impressed with what we prove we will do under pressure. We do not get promoted in ministry because we have our Bible underlined in two colors. We are raised up in life and ministry because we have been tested and tried, and we have passed our tests.

jungle haunted by lions] in the swelling *and* flooding of the Jordan?

6 For even your brethren and the house of your father—even they have dealt treacherously with you; yes,

even they are [like a pack of hounds] in full cry after you. Believe them not, though they speak fair words *and* promise good things to you.

7 I have forsaken My house, I have

cast off My heritage; I have given the dearly beloved of My life into the hands of her enemies.

8 My heritage has become to Me like a lion in the forest; she has uttered her voice against Me; therefore I have [treated her as if I] hated her.

9 Is My heritage to Me like a speckled bird of prey? Are the birds of prey against her round about? Go, assemble all the wild beasts of the field; bring them to devour.

10 Many shepherds [of an invading host] have destroyed My vineyard, they have trampled My portion underfoot; they have made My pleasant portion a desolate wilderness.

11 They have made it a desolation, and desolate it mourns before Me; the whole land has been made desolate, but no man lays it to heart.

12 Destroyers have come upon all the bare heights in the desert, for the sword of the Lord devours from one end of the land even to the other; no flesh has peace *or* can find the means to escape.

13 They have sown wheat but have reaped thorns; they have worn themselves out but without profit. And they shall be ashamed of your [lack of] harvests *and* revenues because of the fierce *and* glowing anger of the Lord.

14 Thus says the Lord against all My evil neighbor [nations] who touch the inheritance which I have caused My people Israel to inherit: Behold, I will pluck them up from their land and I will pluck up the house of Judah from among them.

15 And after I have plucked them up, I will return and have compassion on them and will bring them back again, every man to his heritage and every man to his land.

16 And if these [neighbor nations] will diligently learn the ways of My people, to swear by My name, saying, As the Lord lives—even as they taught My people to swear by Baal—then will

they be built up in the midst of My people.

17 But if any nation will not hear and obey, I will utterly pluck up and destroy that nation, says the Lord.

13 THUS THE Lord said to me: Go and buy yourself a linen girdle and put it on your loins, but do not put it in water.

2 So I bought a girdle *or* waistcloth, according to the word of the Lord, and put it on my loins.

3 And the word of the Lord came to me the second time, saying,

4 Take the girdle which you have bought, which is on your loins, and arise, go to the [river] Euphrates, and hide it there in a cleft of the rock.

5 So I went and hid it by the Euphrates, as the Lord commanded me.

6 And after many days the Lord said to me, Arise, go to the Euphrates, and take from there the girdle which I commanded you to hide there.

7 Then I went to the Euphrates and dug and took the girdle *or* waistcloth from the place where I had hidden it. And behold, the girdle was decayed *and* spoiled; it was good for nothing.

8 Then the word of the Lord came to me, saying,

9 Thus says the Lord: After this manner will I mar the pride of Judah and the great pride of Jerusalem.

10 These evil people, who refuse to hear My words, who walk in the stubbornness of their hearts and have gone after other gods to serve them and to worship them, shall even be like this girdle *or* waistcloth, which is profitable for nothing.

11 For as the girdle clings to the loins of a man, so I caused the whole house of Israel and the whole house of Judah to cling to Me, says the Lord, that they might be for Me a people, a name, a praise, and a glory; but they would not listen *or* obey.

12 Therefore you shall speak to them

this word: Thus says the Lord, the God of Israel: Every bottle *and* jar should be filled with wine. [The people] will say to you, Do we not certainly know that every bottle *and* jar should be filled with wine?

13 Then say to them, Thus says the Lord: Behold, I will fill with drunkenness all the inhabitants of this land, even the kings who sit upon David's throne, the priests, the prophets, and all the inhabitants of Jerusalem.

14 And I will dash them one against another, even the fathers and the sons together, says the Lord. I will not pity or spare or have compassion, that I should not destroy them.

15 Hear and give ear, do not be proud, for the Lord has spoken [says Jeremiah].

16 Give glory to the Lord your God before He brings darkness and before your feet stumble upon the dark *and* twilit mountains, and [before], while you are looking for light, He turns it into the shadow of death and makes it thick darkness.

17 But if you will not hear *and* obey, I will weep in secret for your pride; my eyes will weep bitterly and run down with tears, because the Lord's flock has been taken captive.

18 Say to the king and the queen mother, Humble yourselves *and* take a lowly seat, for down from your head has come your beautiful crown (the crown of your glory).

19 The cities of the South (the Negeb) have been shut up, and there is no one to open them; all Judah has been carried away captive, it has been wholly taken captive *and* into exile.

20 Lift up your eyes and behold those [the eruption of a hostile army] who come from the north. Where is the flock that was given to you [to shepherd], your beautiful flock?

21 What will you say [O Jerusalem] when He [the Lord] sets over you as head those [tyrannical foreign na-tions] whom you yourselves [at inter-vals] have taught to be lovers (allies) with you [instructing them, even your friends, to be head over you]? Will not pangs take hold of you like that of a woman in travail?

22 And if you say in your heart, Why have these things come upon me?— [the answer is], Because of the great-ness of your iniquity has your long robe been pulled aside [showing you in the garb of a menial] *and* have you [barefooted and treated like a slave] suffered violence.

23 Can the Ethiopian change his skin or the leopard his spots? Then also can you do good who are accustomed *and* taught [even trained] to do evil.

24 Therefore I will scatter you like chaff driven away by the wind from the desert.

25 This is your lot, the portion mea-sured to you from Me, says the Lord, because you have forgotten Me and trusted in falsehood [false gods and alliances with idolatrous nations].

26 Therefore I Myself will [retaliate], throwing your skirts up over your face, that your shame [of being clad like a slave] may be exposed.

27 I have seen your detestable acts, even your adulteries and your lustful neighings [after idols], and the lewd-ness of your harlotry on the hills in the field. Woe to you, O Jerusalem! For how long a time yet will you not [meet My conditions and] be made clean?

14 THE WORD of the Lord that came to Jeremiah con-cerning the drought:

2 Judah mourns and her gates lan-guish; [her people] sit in black [mourn-ing garb] upon the ground, and the cry of Jerusalem goes up.

3 And their nobles send their little ones *and* their inferiors for water; they come to the cisterns and find no water. They return with empty vessels; they are put to shame and confounded and cover their heads.

4 Because the ground is cracked *and* the tillers are dismayed, since there has been no rain on the land, the plowmen are put to shame, and they cover their heads.

5 Yes, even the hind gives birth to her calf in the field and forsakes it, because there is no grass *or* herbage.

6 And the wild donkeys stand on the bare heights; they pant for air like jackals *or* crocodiles; their eyesight fails because there is no grass.

7 O Lord, though our iniquities testify against us [prays Jeremiah], deal *and* work with us for Your own name's sake [that the heathen may witness Your might and faithfulness]! For our backslidings are many; we have sinned against You.

8 O Hope of Israel, her Savior in time of trouble, why should You be like a sojourner in the land and like a wayfaring man who turns aside *and* spreads his tent to tarry [only] for a night?

9 Why should You be [hesitant and inactive] like a man stunned *and* confused, like a mighty man who cannot save? Yet You, O Lord, are in the midst of us, and we are called by Your name; do not leave us!

10 [And the Lord replied to Jeremiah] Thus says the Lord to this people [Judah]: In the manner *and* to the degree already pointed out have they loved to wander; they have not restrained their feet. Therefore the Lord does not accept them; He will now [seriously] remember their iniquity and punish them for their sins.

11 The Lord said to me, Do not pray for this people for their good.

12 Though they fast, I will not hear their cry; and though they offer burnt offering and cereal offering [without heartfelt surrender to Me, or by offering it too late], I will not accept them.

But I will consume them by the sword, by famine, and by pestilence.

13 Then said I, Alas, Lord God! Behold, the [false] prophets say to them, You will not see the sword, nor will you have famine; but I [the Lord] will give you assured peace (peace that lasts, the peace of truth) in this place.

14 Then the Lord said to me, The [false] prophets prophesy lies in My name. I sent them not, neither have I commanded them, nor have I spoken to them. They prophesy to you a false *or* pretended vision, a worthless divination [conjuring or practicing magic, trying to call forth the responses supposed to be given by idols], and the deceit of their own minds.

15 Therefore thus says the Lord concerning the [false] prophets who prophesy in My name—although I did not send them—and who say, Sword and famine shall not be in this land: By sword and famine shall those prophets be consumed.

16 And the people to whom they prophesy shall be cast out in the streets of Jerusalem, victims of famine and sword; and they shall have none to bury them—them, their wives, their sons, and their daughters. For I will pour out their wickedness upon them [and not on their false teachers only, for the people could not have been deceived except by their own consent].

17 Therefore [Jeremiah] you shall say to them, Let my eyes run down with tears night and day, and let them not cease; for the virgin daughter of my people has been smitten with a great wound, with a very grievous blow.

18 If I go out into the field, then behold, those slain with the sword! And if I enter the city, then behold, those tormented with the diseases of famine! For both prophet and priest go about not knowing what to do *or* as beggars [exiled] in a land that they know not, and they have no knowledge.

19 [O Lord] have You utterly rejected Judah? Do You loathe Zion? Why have You smitten us so that there is no healing for us? We looked for peace *and* completeness, but no good came, and for a time of healing, but behold, dismay, disaster, *and* terror!

20 We know *and* acknowledge, O Lord, our wickedness and the iniquity of our fathers; for we have sinned against You.

21 Do not abhor, condemn, *and* spurn us, for Your name's sake; do not dishonor, debase, *and* lightly esteem Your glorious throne; [earnestly] remember, break not Your covenant *or* solemn pledge with us.

22 Are there any among the false gods of the nations who can cause rain? Or can the heavens [of their own will] give showers? Are You [alone] not He, O Lord our God? Therefore we will wait [expectantly] for You, for You have made all these things [the heavens and the rain].

15 THEN THE Lord said to me, Though Moses and Samuel stood [interceding for them] before Me, yet My mind could not be turned with favor toward this people [Judah]. Send them out of My sight and let them go!

2 And if they say to you, Where shall we go? then tell them, Thus says the Lord: Such as are [destined] for death, to death; and such as are for the sword, to the sword; and such as are for famine, to famine; and such as are for captivity, to captivity.

3 And I will appoint over them four kinds [of destroyers], says the Lord: the sword to slay, the dogs to tear *and* drag away, and the birds of the air and the beasts of the earth to devour and to destroy.

4 And I will cause them to be tossed to and fro among all the kingdoms of the earth *and* to be made a horror to all nations because of Manasseh son of Hezekiah king of Judah, for [the horrible wickedness] which he did in Jerusalem. [II Kings 21:3-7.]

5 For who will have pity on you, O Jerusalem? Or who will bemoan you? Or who will turn aside to ask about your welfare?

6 You have rejected *and* forsaken Me, says the Lord. You keep going in reverse. Therefore I will stretch out My hand against you and destroy you; I am weary of relenting [concerning your punishment].

7 I will winnow them with a fan *and* a winnowing fork in the gates of the land; I will bereave them [of children], I will destroy My people; from their [evil] ways they did not return.

8 I will increase the number of their widows more than the sand of the seas. I will bring upon them, [both] against the mother of young men *and* the young men [themselves], a destroyer at noonday. I will cause anguish and terrors to fall upon her [Jerusalem] suddenly.

9 She who has borne seven languishes; she has expired. Her sun has gone down while it was yet day; she has been put to shame, confounded, *and* disgraced. And the rest of them I will deliver to the sword before their enemies, says the Lord.

10 Woe is me, my mother, that you bore me to be a man of strife and a man of contention to the whole earth! I have neither loaned, nor have men loaned to me, yet everyone curses me. [Jer. 1:18, 19.]

11 The Lord said, Truly your release, affliction, *and* strengthening will be for good [purposes]; surely [Jeremiah] I will intercede for you with the enemy *and* I will cause the enemy to ask for your aid in the time of evil and in the time of affliction. [Jer. 21:1, 2; 37:3; 42:2; Rom. 8:28.]

12 Can iron break the iron from the north and the bronze?

13 Your [nation's] substance and your treasures will I give as spoil, without price, and that for all your sins, even in all your territory.

14 And I will make [your possessions] to pass with your enemies into a land which you do not know *and* I will make you to serve [your conquerors] there, for a fire is kindled in My anger which will burn upon you [Israel].

15 [Jeremiah said] O Lord, You know *and* understand; [earnestly] remember me and visit me and avenge me on my persecutors. Take me not away [from joy or from life itself] in Your long-suffering [to my enemies]; know that for Your sake I suffer *and* bear reproach.

16 Your words were found, and I ate them; and Your words were to me a joy and the rejoicing of my heart, for I am called by Your name, O Lord God of hosts.

17 I sat not in the assembly of those who make merry, nor did I rejoice; I sat alone because Your [powerful] hand was upon me, for You had filled me with indignation.

18 Why is my pain perpetual and my wound incurable, refusing to be healed? Will you indeed be to me like a deceitful brook, like waters that fail *and* are uncertain?

19 Therefore thus says the Lord [to Jeremiah]: If you return [and give up this mistaken tone of distrust and despair], then I will give you again a settled place of quiet *and* safety, and you will be My minister; and if you separate the precious from the vile [cleansing your own heart from

unworthy and unwarranted suspicions concerning God's faithfulness], you shall be My mouthpiece. [But do not yield to them.] Let them return to you—not you to [the people].

20 And I will make you to this people a fortified, bronze wall; they will fight against you, but they will not prevail over you, for I am with you to save *and* deliver you, says the Lord.

21 And I will deliver you out of the hands of the wicked, and I will redeem you out of the palms of the terrible *and* ruthless tyrants.

16 THE WORD of the Lord came also to me, saying,
2 You shall not take a wife or have sons and daughters in this place [Jerusalem].

3 For thus says the Lord concerning the sons and daughters who are born in this place and concerning the mothers who bore them and the fathers who begot them in this land:

4 They shall die of deadly diseases. They shall not be lamented, nor shall they be buried, but they shall be like dung upon the face of the ground. They shall perish *and* be consumed by the sword and by famine, and their dead bodies shall be food for the fowls of the air and for the beasts of the earth.

5 For thus says the Lord: Enter not into the house of mourning, nor go to lament or bemoan [the dead], for I have taken away My peace from this people, says the Lord, even My steadfast love *and* loving-kindness and tender mercy.

6 Both the great and the small shall die in this land. They shall not be buried, neither shall men lament for

speak the Word

them or cut themselves or make themselves bald for them.

7 Neither shall men prepare food for the mourners to comfort them for the dead; nor shall men give them the cup of consolation to drink for their father or for their mother.

8 And you [Jeremiah] shall not go into the house of feasting to sit with them to eat and drink.

9 For thus says the Lord of hosts, the God of Israel: Behold, I will cause to cease from this place before your very eyes and in your days the voice of mirth and the voice of gladness, the voice of the bridegroom and the voice of the bride.

10 And when you tell these people all these words and they inquire of you, Why has the Lord decreed all this enormous evil against us? Or, What is our iniquity? Or, What is the sin that we have committed against the Lord our God?

11 Then you shall say to them, [It is] because your fathers have forsaken Me, says the Lord, and have walked after other gods and have served and worshiped them and have forsaken Me and have not kept My law,

12 And because you have done worse than your fathers. For behold, every one of you walks after the stubbornness of his own evil heart, so that you do not listen to and obey Me.

13 Therefore I will cast you out of this land [of Judah] into the land [of the Babylonians] neither you nor your fathers have known, and there you will serve other gods day and night, for I will show you no favor there.

14 Therefore, behold, the days are coming, says the Lord, when it shall no more be said, As the Lord lives, Who brought up the children of Israel out of the land of Egypt,

15 But, As the Lord lives, Who brought up the children of Israel from the land of the north and from all the countries to which He had driven

them. And I will bring them again to their land which I gave to their fathers.

16 Behold, I will send for many fishers, says the Lord, and they will fish them out; and afterward I will send for many hunters, and they will hunt them from every mountain and from every hill and out of the clefts of the rocks.

17 For My eyes are on all their ways; they are not hidden from My face, neither is their iniquity concealed from My eyes.

18 First [before I bring them back to their land] I will doubly recompense and punish them for their iniquity and their sin, because they have polluted My land with the carcasses of their detestable idols and with the abominable things offered to false gods with which they have filled My inheritance.

19 [Then said Jeremiah] O Lord, my Strength and my Stronghold, and my Refuge in the day of affliction, to You shall the nations come from the ends of the earth and shall say, Surely our fathers have inherited nothing but lies, emptiness, and futility, worthless things in which there is no profit!

20 Can a man make gods for himself? Such are not gods!

21 Therefore [says the Lord] behold, I will make them know—[yes] this once I will make them know My power and My might; and they will know and recognize that My name is the Lord.

17 THE SIN of Judah is written with a pen or stylus of iron and with the point of a diamond; it is engraved on the tablets of their hearts and on the horns of their altars,

2 While their children [earnestly] remember their [heathen] altars and their Asherim [wooden symbols of the goddess Asherah] beside the green trees upon the high hills.

3 O [Jerusalem] My mountain in the field, I will give your wealth *and* all your treasures to the spoil and your high places for sin [as the price of your sin] throughout all your territory.

4 And you, through your own fault, will loosen your hand *and* discontinue from your heritage which I gave you; and I will cause you to serve your enemies in a land which you do not know, for you have kindled a fire in My anger which will burn throughout the ages.

5 Thus says the Lord: Cursed [with great evil] is the strong man who trusts in *and* relies on frail man, making weak [human] flesh his arm, and whose mind *and* heart turn aside from the Lord.

6 For he shall be like a shrub *or* a person naked and destitute in the desert; and he shall not see any good come, but shall dwell in the parched places in the wilderness, in an uninhabited salt land.

7 [Most] blessed is the man who believes in, trusts in, *and* relies on the Lord, and whose hope *and* confidence the Lord is.

8 For he shall be like a tree planted by the waters that spreads out its roots by the river; and it shall not see *and* fear when heat comes; but its leaf shall be green. It shall not be anxious *and* full of care in the year of drought, nor shall it cease yielding fruit.

9 The heart is deceitful above all things, and it is exceedingly perverse *and* corrupt and severely, mortally sick! Who can know it [perceive, understand, be acquainted with his own heart and mind]? [Matt. 13:15-17; Mark 7:21-23; Eph. 4:20-24.]

10 I the Lord search the mind, I try the heart, even to give to every man according to his ways, according to the fruit of his doings.

11 Like the partridge that gathers a brood which she did not hatch *and* sits on eggs which she has not laid, so is he who gets riches by unjust means *and* not by right. He will leave them, *or* they will leave him, in the midst of his days, and at his end he will be a fool.

12 A glorious throne, set on high from the beginning, is the place of our sanctuary (the temple).

13 O Lord, the Hope of Israel, all who forsake You shall be put to shame. They who depart from You *and* me [Your prophet] shall [disappear like] writing upon the ground, because they have forsaken the Lord, the Fountain of living waters.

14 Heal me, O Lord, and I shall be healed; save me, and I shall be saved, for You are my praise.

15 Behold, they say to me, Where is the word of the Lord [predicting the disaster that you said would befall us]? Let it come now!

16 But as for me, I have not sought to escape from being a shepherd after You, nor have I desired the woeful day [of judgment]; You know that. Whatever I said was spoken in Your presence *and* was from You.

17 Be not a terror to me; You are my refuge *and* my hope in the day of evil.

18 Let those be put to shame who persecute me, but let me not be put to shame; let them be dismayed, but let me not be dismayed. Bring on them the day of evil, and destroy them with double destruction.

19 Thus said the Lord to me: Go and stand in the gate of the sons of the people, through which the kings of

speak the Word

Lord, heal me and I shall be healed; save me and I shall be saved. You are my praise.
ADAPTED FROM JEREMIAH **17:14**

live deeper

Jeremiah 17:9 teaches us that our hearts are deceitful above all things. Self-deception is one of the easiest traps of the enemy that we can fall into. The self always helps the self get whatever it wants. When we have a strong desire for something, we can easily deceive ourselves by telling ourselves whatever we want to hear. If my will wants a thing, my mind will give me a variety of reasons I should have it, and my emotions will certainly produce ample feelings that agree with my will's wants!

We must learn to live deeper than the shallowness of our own minds, wills, and feelings. Deeper living means that we go beyond what we want, what we think, and how we feel and live by the Word of God. We must bow our knees in humility to God's Word and His will because that is where we find true blessings.

I encourage you to have regular times of waiting in God's presence, asking Him to reveal any impure motives you might have. Pray against deception, for Satan is the great deceiver. When we believe something that is not true, we are deceived. Satan also seeks to lead us astray through reasoning that is contrary to the truth.

When you believe a lie, it becomes truth to you even though it is not actually truth at all. Do not trust yourself too much. Realize that not everything you want is best for you. Ask God for what you want, but always be willing to change if you discover that you are not in agreement with God's will. If what you ask God for is His will, it will come in due time. If it does not come, then believe that He has something better in mind for you.

Above all, hold your peace and remain at rest. God can easily lead the believer who is not frustrated and anxious. Pray as David in Psalm 51: "Behold, You desire truth in the inner being; make me therefore to know wisdom in my inmost heart" (Psalm 51:6). The more you truly know God's wisdom in your heart, the less likely you are to be deceived.

Judah enter and through which they go out, and also [stand] in all the gates of Jerusalem.

20 Say to them, Hear the word of the Lord, you kings of Judah, and all Judah, and all the inhabitants of Jerusalem who enter through these gates.

21 Thus says the Lord: Take heed to yourselves *and* for the sake of your lives bear no burden on the Sabbath day or bring it in through the gates of Jerusalem.

22 And do not carry a burden out of your houses on the Sabbath day or do any work, but keep the Sabbath day holy (set apart to the worship of God), as I commanded your fathers.

23 Yet they would not listen *and* obey or incline their ears; but they stiffened their necks, that they might not hear and might not receive instruction.

24 But if you diligently listen to *and* obey Me, says the Lord, and bring in no burden through the gates of this city on the Sabbath day, but keep the Sabbath day holy (set apart to the

worship of God), to do no work on it,
25 Then there will enter through the gates of this city kings and princes who will sit upon the throne of David, riding in chariots and on horses—the kings and their princes, the men of Judah and the inhabitants of Jerusalem; and this city will be inhabited *and* last throughout the ages.
26 And people shall come from the cities of Judah and the places round about Jerusalem, from the land of Benjamin, from the lowland, from the hill country, and from the South (the Negeb), bringing burnt offerings and sacrifices, cereal offerings and frankincense, and bringing sacrifices of thanksgiving to the house of the Lord.
27 But if you will not listen to Me to keep the Sabbath day holy (set apart to the worship of God), and not to bear a burden and enter in at the gates of Jerusalem [with one] on the Sabbath day, then I will kindle a fire in her gates, and it shall devour the palaces of Jerusalem, and it shall not be quenched.

18 THE WORD which came to Jeremiah from the Lord:
2 Arise and go down to the potter's house, and there I will cause you to hear My words.
3 Then I went down to the potter's house, and behold, he was working at the wheel.
4 And the vessel that he was making from clay was spoiled in the hand of the potter; so he made it over, reworking it into another vessel as it seemed good to the potter to make it.
5 Then the word of the Lord came to me:
6 O house of Israel, can I not do with you as this potter does? says the Lord. Behold, as the clay is in the potter's hand, so are you in My hand, O house of Israel.
7 At one time I will suddenly speak

life point

In Jeremiah 18:1–4 we read of the potter who had to remake his vessel because it had been marred. That is a picture of us in the hands of the Lord, the Master Potter.

When we enter into a relationship with Christ, the Bible tells us that we become new creations (see II Corinthians 5:17). Old things have passed away, and we are given an opportunity for a new beginning. We become new spiritual clay for the Holy Spirit to work with. I believe that He is shaping you into a beautiful vessel, perfectly designed for the great purposes He has for your life.

concerning a nation or kingdom, that I will pluck up and break down and destroy it;
8 And if [the people of] that nation concerning which I have spoken turn from their evil, I will relent *and* reverse My decision concerning the evil that I thought to do to them.
9 At another time I will suddenly speak concerning a nation or kingdom, that I will build up and plant it;
10 And if they do evil in My sight, obeying not My voice, then I will regret *and* reverse My decision concerning the good with which I said I would benefit them.
11 Now therefore say to the men of Judah and to the inhabitants of Jerusalem, Thus says the Lord: Behold, I am shaping evil against you and devising a plan against you. Return now each one from his evil way; reform your [accustomed] ways *and* make your [individual] actions good *and* right.
12 But they will say, That is in vain! For we will walk after our own devices, and we will each do as the stubbornness of his own evil heart dictates.

13 Therefore thus says the Lord: Ask now among the nations: Who has heard such things? Virgin Israel has done a very vile *and* horrible thing.

14 Will the snow of Mount Lebanon fail *and* vanish from its rocks [which tower above the land of Israel]? Will the cold, rushing waters of strange lands [that dash down from afar] be dried up?

15 Yet My people have forgotten Me; they burn incense to false gods, they have been caused to stumble in their ways and in the ancient roads, to walk in bypaths, in a way not graded *and* built up [not on a highway],

16 Making their land a desolation *and* a horror, a thing to be hissed at perpetually; everyone who passes by shall be astounded *and* horrified and shake his head.

17 I will scatter them as with an east wind before the enemy; I will show them My back and not My face in the day of their calamity [says the Lord].

18 Then [my enemies] said, Come and let us devise schemes against Jeremiah; for the law [of Moses] shall not perish from the priest [as this false prophet Jeremiah predicts], nor will counsel from the wise, nor the word from the prophet. Come, let us smite him with the tongue [making a charge against him to the king], and let us not pay any attention to his words.

19 Give heed to me, Lord; listen to [what] my adversaries [are plotting to do to me—and intercede].

20 Shall evil be recompensed for good? Yet they have dug a pit for my life. [Earnestly] remember that I stood before You to speak good for them, to turn away Your anger from them.

21 Therefore deliver up their children to the famine; give them over to the power of the sword. And let their wives become childless and widows; let their men meet death by pestilence, their young men be slain by the sword in battle.

22 Let a cry be heard from their houses when You suddenly bring a troop upon them, for they have dug a pit to take me and have hidden snares for my feet.

23 Yet, Lord, You know all their plotting against me to slay me. Forgive not their iniquity, nor blot out their sin from Your sight. But let them be overthrown before You; deal with them in the time of Your anger.

19 THUS SAYS the Lord: Go and get a potter's earthen bottle, and take some of the old people and some of the elderly priests

2 And go out to the Valley of Ben-hinnom [son of Hinnom], which is by the entrance of the Potsherd Gate; and proclaim there the words that I shall tell you,

3 And say, Hear the word of the Lord, O kings of Judah and inhabitants of Jerusalem. Thus says the Lord of hosts, the God of Israel: Behold, I am going to bring such evil upon this place that the ears of whoever hears of it will tingle.

4 Because the people have forsaken Me and have estranged *and* profaned this place [Jerusalem] by burning incense in it to other gods that neither they nor their fathers nor the kings of Judah ever knew, and because they have filled this place with the blood of innocents

5 And have built the high places of Baal to burn their sons in the fire as burnt offerings to Baal, which I commanded not nor spoke of it, nor did it come into My mind *and* heart—

6 Therefore, behold, the days are coming, says the Lord, when this place shall no more be called Topheth or the Valley of Ben-hinnom [son of Hinnom], but the Valley of Slaughter. [Jer. 7:31-32.]

7 And I will pour out *and* make void the counsel *and* the plans of [the men of] Judah and Jerusalem in this place, and I will cause their people to fall by the sword before their enemies and by the hands of those who seek their lives, and their dead bodies I will give to be food for the birds of the air and for the beasts of the earth.

8   And I will make this city an astonishment *and* a horror and a hissing; everyone who passes by it will be horrified and will hiss [in scorn] because of all its plagues *and* disasters.

9   And I will cause them to eat the flesh of their sons and their daughters, and they shall eat each one the flesh of his neighbor *and* friend in the siege and in the distress with which their enemies and those who seek their lives distress them.

10   Then you shall break the bottle in the sight of the men who accompany you,

11   And say to them, Thus said the Lord of hosts: Even so will I break this people and this city as one breaks a potter's vessel, so that it cannot be mended. Men will bury in Topheth because there will be no other place for burial *and* until there is no more room to bury.

12   Thus will I do to this place, says the Lord, and to its inhabitants; and I will even make this city like Topheth.

13   And the houses of Jerusalem and the houses of the kings of Judah, which are defiled, shall be like the place of Topheth—even all the houses upon whose roofs incense has been burned to all the host of the heavens and drink offerings have been poured out to other gods. [Acts 7:42, 43.]

14   Then came Jeremiah from Topheth, where the Lord had sent him to prophesy, and he stood in the court of the Lord's house and said to all the people,

15   Thus says the Lord of hosts, the God of Israel: Behold, I will bring upon this city and upon all its towns all the evil that I have pronounced against it, because they have stiffened their necks, refusing to hear My words.

20 NOW PASHHUR son of Immer, the priest, who was [also] chief officer in the house of the Lord, heard Jeremiah prophesying these things.

2   Then Pashhur beat Jeremiah the prophet and put him in the stocks that were at the upper Benjamin Gate by the house of the Lord. [Jer. 1:19; 15:15.]

3   And the next day Pashhur brought Jeremiah out of the stocks. Then Jeremiah said to him, The Lord does not call your name Pashhur, but Magor-missabib [terror on every side].

4   For thus says the Lord: Behold, I will make you a terror to yourself and to all your friends; they will fall by the sword of their enemies while you look on. And I will give all Judah into the hand of the king of Babylon; he will carry them captive to Babylon and will slay them with the sword.

5   Moreover, I will deliver all the riches of this city—all the results of its labors, all its precious things, and all the treasures of the kings of Judah—into the hand of their enemies, who will make them a prey *and* plunder them and seize them and carry them to Babylon.

6   And you, Pashhur, and all who dwell in your house shall go into captivity; you shall go to Babylon, and there you shall die and be buried, you and all your friends to whom you have prophesied falsely.

7   [But Jeremiah said] O Lord, You have persuaded *and* deceived me, and I was persuaded *and* deceived; You are stronger than I am and You have prevailed. I am a laughingstock all the day; everyone mocks me.

8   For whenever I speak, I must cry out *and* complain; I shout, Violence and destruction! For the word of the

Lord has become to me a reproach and a derision *and* has brought me insult all day long.

9   If I say, I will not make mention of [the Lord] or speak any more in His name, in my mind *and* heart it is as if there were a burning fire shut up in my bones. And I am weary of enduring *and* holding it in; I cannot [contain it any longer].

10 For I have heard many whispering *and* defaming, [There is] terror on every side! Denounce him! Let us denounce him! Say all my familiar friends, they who watch for my fall, Perhaps he will be persuaded *and* deceived; then we will prevail against him, and we will get our revenge on him.

11 But the Lord is with me as a mighty *and* terrible One; therefore my persecutors will stumble, and they will not overcome [me]. They will be utterly put to shame, for they will not deal wisely *or* prosper [in their schemes]; their eternal dishonor will never be forgotten.

12 But, O Lord of hosts, You Who try the righteous, Who see the heart and the mind, let me see Your vengeance on them, for to You have I revealed *and* committed my cause.

13 Sing to the Lord! Praise the Lord! For He has delivered the life of the poor *and* needy from the hands of evildoers.

14 Cursed be the day on which I was born! Let not the day on which my mother bore me be blessed!

15 Cursed be the man who brought the tidings to my father, saying, A son is born to you!—making him very glad.

16 And let that man be like the cities which the Lord overthrew, and did not relent. Let him hear the [war] cry in the morning and the shouting of alarm at noon,

17 Because he did not slay me in the womb, so that my mother might have been my grave, and her womb always great.

18 Why did I come out of the womb to see labor and sorrow, that my days should be consumed in shame?

21 THE WORD which came to Jeremiah from the Lord when King Zedekiah sent to him Pashhur son of Malchiah, and Zephaniah the priest, the son of Maaseiah, saying,

2   Inquire, I pray you, of the Lord for us, for ᵸNebuchadrezzar king of Babylon is making war against us. Perhaps the Lord will deal with us according to all His wonderful works, forcing him to withdraw from us.

3   Then said Jeremiah to them, Say this to Zedekiah:

4   Thus says the Lord, the God of Israel: Behold, I will turn back *and* dull the edge of the weapons of war that are in your hands, with which you fight against the king of Babylon and the Chaldeans who are besieging you outside the walls; and I will bring them into the midst of this city [Jerusalem].

5   And I Myself will fight against you

speak the Word

ᵸ The reader will no doubt notice that the name of the Babylonian ruler Nebuchadnezzar is frequently spelled Nebuchadrezzar in the book of Jeremiah, as well as on several occasions in the book of Ezekiel (Ezek. 26:7; 29:18-19; 30:10, 24). "The two forms represent different Hebrew methods of reproducing the name" (John D. Davis, *A Dictionary of the Bible*).

with an outstretched hand and with a strong arm in anger, in fury, and in great indignation *and* wrath.

6 And I will smite the inhabitants of this city, both man and beast; they will die of a great pestilence.

7 And afterward, says the Lord, I will deliver Zedekiah king of Judah and his servants and the people in this city who survive the pestilence, the sword, and the famine, into the hand of Nebuchadrezzar king of Babylon and into the hands of their enemies, into the hands of those who seek their lives. And he will smite them with the edge of the sword; he will not spare them nor have pity or mercy *and* compassion upon them.

8 And to this people you [Jeremiah] shall say, Thus says the Lord: Behold, I set before you the way of life and the way of death.

9 He who remains in this city [Jerusalem] shall die by the sword and by famine and by pestilence. But he who goes out and passes over to the Chaldeans who besiege you, he shall live, and his life shall be to him his only booty [as a prize of war].

10 For I have set My face against this city for evil and not for good, says the Lord. It shall be given into the hand of the king of Babylon, and he shall burn it with fire.

11 And concerning the royal house of the king of Judah, hear the word of the Lord:

12 O house of David, thus says the Lord: Execute justice in the morning, and deliver from the hand of the oppressor him who has been robbed, lest My wrath go forth like fire and burn so that none can quench it—because of the evil of your doings.

13 Behold, I am against you, O inhabitant of the valley, O rock of the plain, says the Lord—you who say, Who shall come down against us? Or, Who shall enter into our dwelling places?

14 And I will punish you according to the fruit of your doings, says the Lord. I will kindle a fire in your forest, and it will devour all that is round about you.

22 THUS SAYS the Lord: Go down to the house of the king of Judah and speak there this word:

2 Hear the word of the Lord, O king of Judah, you who sit upon the throne of David—you and your servants and your people who enter by these gates.

3 Thus says the Lord: Execute justice and righteousness, and deliver out of the hand of the oppressor him who has been robbed. And do no wrong; do no violence to the stranger *or* temporary resident, the fatherless, or the widow, nor shed innocent blood in this place.

4 For if you will indeed obey this word, then will there enter in through the gates of this [the king's] house kings sitting [for David] upon David's throne, riding in chariots and on horses—they and their servants and their people.

5 But if you will not hear these words, I swear by Myself, says the Lord, that this house will become a desolation.

6 For thus says the Lord concerning the house of the king of Judah: [If you will not listen to Me, though] you are [as valuable] to Me as [the fat pastures of] Gilead [east of the Jordan] or as the [plentiful] summit of Lebanon [west of the Jordan], yet surely I will make you a wilderness and uninhabited cities.

7 And I will prepare, solemnly set apart, *and* appoint [to execute My judgments against you] destroyers, each with his weapons, and they will cut down your [palaces built of] choicest cedars and cast them into the fire.

8 And many nations will pass by this city, and every man will say to his neighbor, Why has the Lord done this to this great city?

9 Then they will answer, Because [the people] forsook the covenant *or* solemn pledge with the Lord their God and worshiped other gods and served them.

10 Weep not for him who is dead nor bemoan him; but weep bitterly for him who goes away [into captivity], for he shall return no more nor see his native country [again].

11 For thus says the Lord concerning Shallum son of Josiah king of Judah, who reigned instead of Josiah his father and who went forth out of this place: [Shallum] shall not return here any more;

12 But he shall die in the place where they have led him captive, and he shall see this land no more.

13 Woe to him who builds his house by unrighteousness and his [upper] chambers by injustice, who uses his neighbor's service without wages and does not give him his pay [for his work],

14 Who says, I will build myself a wide house with large rooms, and he cuts himself out windows, and it is ceiled *or* paneled with cedar and painted with vermilion.

15 Do you think that being a king [merely] means [self-indulgent] vying [with Solomon] *and* striving to excel in cedar [palaces]? Did not your father [Josiah], as he ate and drank, do justice and righteousness [being upright and in right standing with God]? Then it was well with him.

16 He judged *and* defended the cause of the poor and needy; then it was well. Was not [all] this [what it means] to know *and* recognize Me? says the Lord.

17 But your eyes and your heart are only for your covetousness *and* dishonest gain, for shedding innocent blood, for oppression and doing violence.

18 Therefore thus says the Lord concerning Jehoiakim son of Josiah king of Judah: [Relatives] shall not lament for him, saying, Ah, my brother! or, Ah, sister, [how great our loss! Subjects] shall not lament for him saying, Ah, lord! or Ah, his majesty! *or* Ah, [how great was] his glory!

19 [No] he shall be buried with the burial of a donkey—dragged out and cast forth beyond the gates of Jerusalem.

20 Go up [north] to Lebanon and cry out, and raise your voice in [the hills] of Bashan [across the Jordan], and cry out from Abarim [a range of mountains southeast of Palestine], for all your lovers (the king's chosen allies) are destroyed. [Jer. 27:6-7.]

21 I spoke to you in your [times of] prosperity, but you said, I will not listen! This has been your attitude from your youth; you have not obeyed My voice.

22 The wind [of adversity] shall pasture upon *and* consume all your shepherds (your princes and statesmen), and your lovers (allies) shall go into captivity. Surely then shall you be ashamed and confounded *and* dismayed because of all your wickedness.

23 O inhabitant of Lebanon [Jerusalem, whose palaces are made of Lebanon's trees], you who make your nest among the cedars, how you will groan *and* how pitiable you will be when pangs come upon you, pain like that of a woman in childbirth! [I Kings 7:2.]

24 As I live, says the Lord, though Coniah [also called Jeconiah and Jehoiachin] son of Jehoiakim king of Judah were the signet [ring] upon My right hand, yet would I tear you off.

25 And I will give you into the hands of those who seek your life and into the hand of those of whom you are afraid, even into the hand of Nebuchadrezzar king of Babylon and into the hands of the Chaldeans.

26 And I will hurl you and the mother who bore you into another country, where you were not born, and there you will die.

27 But to the land to which they will yearn to return, there they will not return.

28 Is this man [King] Coniah a despised, broken pot? Is he a vessel in which no one takes pleasure? Why are they hurled out, he and his royal offspring, and cast into a land which they do not know, understand, *or* recognize?

29 O land, land, land, hear the word of the Lord!

30 Thus says the Lord: Write this man [Coniah] down as childless, a man who shall not prosper in his days, for no man of his offspring shall succeed in sitting upon the throne of David and ruling any more in Judah.

23

WOE TO the shepherds (the civil leaders) who destroy and scatter the sheep of My pasturing! says the Lord.

2 Therefore thus says the Lord, the God of Israel, concerning the shepherds who care for *and* feed My people: You have scattered My flock and driven them away and have not visited *and* attended to them; behold, I will visit *and* attend to you for the evil of your doings, says the Lord.

3 And I will gather the remnant of My flock out of all the countries to which I have driven them and will bring them again to their folds *and* pastures; and they will be fruitful and multiply.

4 And I will set up shepherds over them who will feed them. And they will fear no more nor be dismayed, neither will any be missing *or* lost, says the Lord.

5 Behold, the days are coming, says the Lord, when I will raise up to David a righteous Branch (Sprout), and He will reign as King and do wisely and will execute justice and righteousness in the land.

6 In His days Judah shall be saved and Israel shall dwell safely: and this is His name by which He shall be called: The Lord Our Righteousness. [Matt. 1:21-23; Rom. 3:22.]

7 Therefore behold, the days are coming, says the Lord, when they shall no more say, As the Lord lives, Who brought up the children of Israel out of the land of Egypt,

8 But, As the Lord lives, Who brought up and led the offspring of the house of Israel from the north country and from all the countries to which I had driven them. And they shall dwell in their own land. [Jer. 16:14-15.]

9 Concerning the prophets: My heart [says Jeremiah] is broken within me, all my bones shake; I am like a drunken man, a man whom wine has overcome, because of the Lord and because of His holy words [which He has pronounced against unfaithful leaders].

10 For the land is full of adulterers (forsakers of God, Israel's true Husband). Because of the curse [of God upon it] the land mourns, the pastures of the wilderness are dried up. They [both false prophets and people] rush into wickedness; *and* their course is evil, their might is not right.

11 For both [false] prophet and priest are ungodly *and* profane; even in My house have I found their wickedness, says the Lord.

12 Therefore their way will be to them like slippery paths in the dark; they will be driven on and fall into them. For I will bring evil upon them in the year of their punishment, says the Lord.

13 And I have seen folly in the prophets of Samaria: they prophesied by Baal and caused My people Israel to err *and* go astray.

14 I have seen also in the prophets of Jerusalem a horrible thing: they commit adultery and walk in lies; they encourage *and* strengthen the hands of evildoers, so that none returns from his wickedness. They have all of them become to Me like Sodom, and her inhabitants like Gomorrah.

15 Therefore thus says the Lord of hosts concerning the prophets: Behold, I will feed them with [the bitterness of] wormwood and make them drink the [poisonous] water of gall, for from the [false] prophets of Jerusalem profaneness *and* ungodliness have gone forth into all the land.

16 Thus says the Lord of hosts: Do not listen to the words of the [false] prophets who prophesy to you. They teach you vanity (emptiness, falsity, and futility) *and* fill you with vain hopes; they speak a vision of their own minds and not from the mouth of the Lord.

17 They are continually saying to those who despise Me *and* the word of the Lord, The Lord has said: You shall have peace; and they say to everyone who walks after the stubbornness of his own mind *and* heart, No evil shall come upon you.

18 For who among them has stood in the council of the Lord, that he should perceive and hear His word? Who has marked His word [noticing and observing and giving attention to it] and has [actually] heard it?

19 Behold, the tempest of the Lord has gone forth in wrath, a whirling tempest; it shall whirl *and* burst upon the heads of the wicked.

20 The anger of the Lord shall not turn back until He has executed *and* accomplished the thoughts *and* intents of His mind *and* heart. In the latter days you shall consider *and* understand it perfectly.

21 I did not send these [false] prophets, yet they ran; I did not speak to them, yet they prophesied.

22 But if they had stood in My council, then they would have caused My people to hear My words, then they would have turned them [My people] from their evil way and from the evil of their doings.

23 Am I a God at hand, says the Lord, and not a God afar off?

24 Can anyone hide himself in secret places so that I cannot see him? says the Lord. Do not I fill heaven and earth? says the Lord.

25 I have heard what the prophets have said who prophesy lies in My name, saying, I have dreamed, I have dreamed [visions on my bed at night].

26 [How long shall this state of things continue?] How long yet shall it be in the minds of the prophets who prophesy falsehood, even the prophets of the deceit of their own hearts,

27 Who think that they can cause My people to forget My name by their dreams which every man tells to his neighbor, just as their fathers forgot My name because of Baal?

28 The prophet who has a dream, let him tell his dream; but he who has My word, let him speak My word faithfully. What has straw in common with wheat [for nourishment]? says the Lord.

29 Is not My word like fire [that consumes all that cannot endure the test]? says the Lord, and like a hammer that breaks in pieces the rock [of most stubborn resistance]?

30 Therefore behold, I am against

speak the Word

God, I declare that I do have Your word and I ask you to help me to speak it faithfully.
ADAPTED FROM JEREMIAH **23:28**

the [false] prophets, says the Lord, [I am even now descending upon them with punishment, these prophets] who steal My words from one another [imitating the phrases of the true prophets].

31 Behold, I am against the prophets, says the Lord, who use their [own deceitful] tongues and say, Thus says the Lord.

32 Behold, I am against those who prophesy lying dreams, says the Lord, and tell them and cause My people to err *and* go astray by their lies and by their vain boasting *and* recklessness— when I did not send them or command them; nor do they profit these people at all, says the Lord.

33 And when these people, or a prophet or a priest, ask you, What is the burden of the Lord [the thing to be lifted up now]? then you shall say to them, What burden [indeed]! [You are the burden!] And I will disburden Myself of you *and* I will cast you off, says the Lord.

34 And as for the prophet, the priest, or [any of these] the people, whoever [in mockery calls the word of the Lord a burden and] says, The burden of the Lord, I will even visit in wrath *and* punish that man and his house.

35 [For the future, in speaking of the utterances of the Lord] thus shall you say every one to his neighbor and every one to his brother: What has the Lord answered? or, What has the Lord spoken?

36 But the burden of the Lord you must mention no more, for every man's burden is his own response *and* word [for as they mockingly call all prophecies burdens, whether good or bad, so will it prove to be to them; God will take them at their own word]; for you pervert the words [not of a lifeless idol, but] of the living God, the Lord of hosts, our God!

37 Thus shall you [reverently] say to the prophet: What has the Lord answered you? Or, What has the Lord spoken?

38 But if you say, The burden of the Lord, therefore thus says the Lord: Because you said these words, The burden of the Lord, when I sent to you, saying, You shall not say, The burden of the Lord,

39 Therefore behold, I, even I, will assuredly take you up and cast you away from My presence, you and the city [Jerusalem] which I gave to you and to your fathers.

40 And I will bring an everlasting reproach upon you and a perpetual shame which will not be forgotten.

24 AFTER NEBUCHADREZ-ZAR king of Babylon had taken into exile Jeconiah [also called Coniah and Jehoiachin] son of Jehoiakim king of Judah and the princes of Judah, with the craftsmen and smiths from Jerusalem, and had brought them to Babylon, the Lord showed me [in a vision] two baskets of figs set before the temple of the Lord.

2 One basket had very good figs, like the figs that are first ripe; but the other basket had very bad figs, so bad that they could not be eaten.

3 Then the Lord said to me, What do you see, Jeremiah? And I said, Figs—the good figs very good, and the bad very bad, so bad that they cannot be eaten.

4 Again the word of the Lord came to me, saying,

5 Thus says the Lord, the God of Israel: Like these good figs, so will I regard the captives of Judah whom I have sent out of this place into the land of the Chaldeans for their good.

6 For I will set My eyes upon them for good, and I will bring them again to this land; and I will build them up and not pull them down, and I will plant them and not pluck them up.

7 And I will give them a heart to know (recognize, understand, and be acquainted with) Me, that I am the Lord; and they will be My people, and I will be their God, for they will return to Me with their whole heart.

8 And as for the bad figs, which are so bad that they cannot be eaten, surely thus says the Lord, So will I give up Zedekiah king of Judah and his princes and the residue of Jerusalem who remains in this land and those who dwell in the land of Egypt.

9 I will even give them up to be a dismay *and* a horror *and* to be tossed to and fro among all the kingdoms of the earth for evil, to be a reproach, a byword *or* proverb, a taunt, and a curse in all places where I will drive them.

10 And I will send the sword, famine, and pestilence among them until they are consumed from off the land that I gave to them and to their fathers.

2 5 THE WORD that came to Jeremiah concerning all the people of Judah in the fourth year of the reign of Jehoiakim son of Josiah king of Judah—which was the first year of the reign of Nebuchadrezzar king of Babylon—

2 Which Jeremiah the prophet spoke to all the people of Judah and to all the inhabitants of Jerusalem:

3 For these twenty-three years— from the thirteenth year of Josiah son of Amon king of Judah, even to this day—the word of the Lord has come to me and I have spoken to you persistently early and late, but you have not listened *and* obeyed.

4 Although the Lord persistently

speak the Word

sent you all the prophets, His servants, yet you have not listened and obeyed or [even] inclined your ear to hear.

5 [The prophets came on My behalf] saying, Turn again now every one from his evil way and wrongdoing; [that you may not forfeit the right to] dwell in the land that the Lord gave to you and to your fathers from of old *and* forevermore.

6 Do not go after other gods to serve and worship them, and do not provoke Me to anger with the works of your hands. Then I will do you no harm.

7 Yet you have not listened to *and* obeyed Me, says the Lord, that you might provoke Me to anger with the works (idols) made by your hands to your own hurt.

8 Therefore thus says the Lord of hosts: Because you have not heard *and* obeyed My words,

9 Behold, I will send for all the tribes of the north, says the Lord, and I will send for Nebuchadrezzar king of Babylon, My servant [or agent to fulfill My designs], and I will bring them against this land and its inhabitants and against all these nations round about; and I will devote them [to God] *and* utterly destroy them and make them an amazement, a hissing, and perpetual *and* agelong desolations.

10 Moreover, I will take from them the voice of mirth and the voice of gladness, the voice of the bridegroom and the voice of the bride, the sound of the millstones [grinding out the meal] and the light of the candle [which every home burned throughout the night]. [Jer. 7:34.]

11 And this whole land shall be a

waste and an astonishment, and these nations shall serve the king of Babylon ¹seventy years. [II Chron. 36:20-23; Jer. 4:27; 12:11, 12; Dan. 9:2.]

12 Then when seventy years are completed, I will punish the king of Babylon and that nation, the land of the Chaldeans, says the Lord, for their iniquity, and will make the land [of the Chaldeans] a perpetual waste. [Jer. 29:10.]

13 And I will bring upon that land all My words which I have pronounced against it, even all that is written in this book, which Jeremiah has prophesied against all the nations.

14 For many nations and great kings shall make bondmen of them, even them [the Chaldeans who enslaved other nations]; and I will recompense [all of] them according to their deeds and according to the work of their [own] hands.

15 For thus says the Lord, the God of Israel, to me: Take this cup of the wine of wrath from My hand and cause all the nations to whom I send you to drink it.

16 They shall drink and reel to and fro and be crazed because of the sword that I will send among them.

17 Then I [Jeremiah] took the cup from the Lord's hand and made all the nations drink it to whom the Lord had sent me: [that is,]

18 Jerusalem and the cities of Judah [being most guilty because their privileges were greatest], its kings and princes, to make them a desolation, an astonishment, a hissing, and a curse, as it is to this day; [I Pet. 4:17.]

19 Pharaoh king of Egypt, his servants, his princes, all his people,

20 And all the mixed foreign popula-

tion; all the kings of the land of Uz; and all the kings of the land of the Philistines and [their cities of] Ashkelon, Gaza, Ekron, and the remnant of Ashdod;

21 Edom, Moab, and the children of Ammon;

22 All the kings of Tyre, all the kings of Sidon, and the kings of the islands *and* the coastlands across the [Mediterranean] Sea;

23 Dedan, Tema, Buz [neighboring tribes north of Arabia], and all who clip off the corners of their hair *and* beards; [Lev. 19:27; Jer. 9:26.]

24 All the kings of Arabia and all the kings of the mixed foreign people who dwell in the desert;

25 All the kings of Zimri, all the kings of Elam (Persia), and all the kings of Media;

26 All the kings of the north, far and near, one after another—and all the kingdoms of the world which are on the face of the earth. And after them the king of Sheshach (Babel or Babylon) shall drink.

27 Then you shall say to them, Thus says the Lord of hosts, the God of Israel: Drink, be drunk, vomit, and fall to rise no more because of the sword which I am sending among you.

28 And if they refuse to take the cup from your hand to drink, then you shall say to them, Thus says the Lord of hosts: You shall surely drink!

29 For behold, I am beginning to work evil in the city which is called by My Name, and shall you go unpunished? You shall not go unpunished, for I am calling for a sword against all the inhabitants of the earth, says the Lord of hosts. [Jer. 7:10.]

30 Therefore prophesy against them

i As both sacred and secular history show, this prophecy was approximately literally fulfilled, whether it refers to the duration of the Babylonian Empire (with its heyday from the beginning of Nebuchadnezzar's reign in 605 BC till its downfall in 539), or to the length of the Jewish captivity in Babylon (with the first deportation in 605 BC and the first return in 538). For the marvelous literal fulfillment of specific details concerning the destruction and perpetual desolation of Babylon, see footnotes on Isa. 13:22 and 14:23.

all these words and say to them: The Lord shall roar from on high and utter His voice from His holy habitation; He shall roar mightily against His fold *and* pasture. He shall give a shout like those who tread grapes [in the winepress, but His shout will be] against all the inhabitants of the earth.

31 A noise will come even to the ends of the earth, for the Lord has a controversy and an indictment against the nations; He will enter into judgment with all mankind; as for the wicked, He will give them to the sword, says the Lord.

32 Thus says the Lord of hosts: Behold, evil will go forth from nation to nation, and a great whirling tempest will rise from the uttermost parts of the earth.

33 And those slain by the Lord shall be at that day from one end of the earth even to the other end of the earth. They shall not be lamented or gathered or buried; their [dead bodies] shall be dung upon the ground. [Jer. 8:2; 16:4.]

34 Wail, you shepherds, and cry; and roll in ashes, you principal ones of the flock. For the days of your slaughter and of your dispersions have fully come, and you shall fall *and* be dashed into pieces like a choice vessel.

35 And the shepherds shall have no way to flee, nor the principal ones of the flock any means of escape.

36 A voice! The cry of the shepherds and the wailing of the principal ones of the flock! For the Lord is laying waste *and* destroying their pasture.

37 And the peaceable folds are devastated *and* brought to silence because of the fierce anger of the Lord.

38 He has left His shelter like the lion; for their land has become a waste *and* an astonishment because of the fierceness of the oppressor and because of [the Lord's] fierce anger.

26 IN THE beginning of the reign of Jehoiakim son of Josiah king of Judah came this word from the Lord:

2 Thus says the Lord: Stand in the court of the Lord's house [Jeremiah] and speak to all [the people of] the cities of Judah who come to worship in the Lord's house all the words that I command you to speak to them; subtract not a word.

3 It may be that they will listen and turn every man from his evil way, that I may relent *and* reverse My decision concerning the evil which I purpose to do to them because of their evil doings.

4 And you will say to them, Thus says the Lord: If you will not listen to *and* obey Me, to walk in My law, which I have set before you,

5 And to hear *and* obey the words of My servants the prophets, whom I have sent to you urgently *and* persistently—though you have not listened *and* obeyed—

6 Then will I make this house [the temple] like Shiloh [the home of the Tent of Meeting, abandoned and later destroyed after the ark was captured by the Philistines], and I will make this city subject to the curses of all nations of the earth [so vile in their sight will it be]. [I Sam. 4; Jer. 7:12.]

7 And the priests and the [false] prophets and all the people heard Jeremiah speaking these words in the house of the Lord.

8 Now when Jeremiah had finished speaking all that the Lord had commanded him to speak to all the people, the priests and the [false] prophets and all the people seized him, saying, You shall surely die!

9 Why have you prophesied in the name of the Lord, saying, This house shall be like Shiloh [after the ark of the Lord had been taken by our enemies] and this city [Jerusalem] shall be desolate, without inhabitant? And all the people were gathered around

Jeremiah in the [outer area of the] house of the Lord.

10 When the princes of Judah heard these things, they came up from the king's house to the house of the Lord and sat down in the entry of the New Gate of the house of the Lord.

11 Then the priests and the prophets said to the princes and to all the people, This man is deserving of death, for he has prophesied against this city, as you have heard with your own ears.

12 Then Jeremiah said to all the princes and to all the people: The Lord sent me to prophesy against this house and against this city all the words that you have heard.

13 Therefore now amend your ways and your doings and obey the voice of the Lord your God; then the Lord will relent *and* reverse the decision concerning the evil which He has pronounced against you.

14 As for me, behold, I am in your hands; do with me as seems good and suitable to you.

15 But know for certain that if you put me to death, you will bring innocent blood upon yourselves and upon this city and upon its inhabitants, for in truth the Lord has sent me to you to speak all these words in your hearing.

16 Then said the princes and all the people to the priests and to the prophets: This man is not deserving of death, for he has spoken to us in the name of the Lord our God.

17 Then certain of the elders of the land arose and said to all the assembly of the people,

18 Micah of Moresheth prophesied in the days of Hezekiah king of Judah and said to all the people of Judah, Thus says the Lord of hosts: Zion shall be ʲplowed like a field, and Jerusalem shall become heaps [of ruins], and the mountain of the house [of the Lord— Mount Moriah, on which stands the temple, shall become covered not with buildings, but] like a densely wooded height. [Mic. 3:12.]

19 Did Hezekiah king of Judah and all Judah put [Micah] to death? Did he not [reverently] fear the Lord and entreat the Lord? And did not the Lord relent *and* reverse the decision concerning the evil which He had pronounced against them? But [here] we are thinking of committing what will be a great evil against ourselves.

20 And there was also a man who prophesied in the name of the Lord, Uriah son of Shemaiah of Kiriath-jearim, who prophesied against this city and against this land in words similar to those of Jeremiah.

21 And when Jehoiakim the king, with all his mighty men and all the princes, heard his words, the king sought to put [Uriah] to death; but when Uriah heard of it, he was afraid and fled and escaped to Egypt.

22 And Jehoiakim the king sent men into Egypt, namely, Elnathan son of Achbor and certain other men [who went] with him into Egypt.

23 And they fetched Uriah from Egypt and brought him to Jehoiakim the king, who slew him [God's spokesman] with the sword and cast his dead body among the graves of the common people.

24 But the hand of Ahikam son of Shaphan was with Jeremiah, that he

---

j This prophecy of Micah, made in the days of King Hezekiah, that Mount Zion would become a plowed field, was literally fulfilled. When Nebuchadnezzar and the Chaldeans took Jerusalem, they broke down the walls (II Kings 25:10). That was in 586 BC In AD 1542 the present walls of Jerusalem were built by Suleiman the Magnificent, the greatest of the sultans of the Turks. By some strange error, the part of the city known as Mount Zion was omitted from the enclosure and remained outside the walls; for centuries it was literally "plowed like a field." That Mount Zion is the only part of Jerusalem ever known to be plowed is conclusive evidence of the divine inspiration and infinite foreknowledge of the word of the Lord which came to His prophet Micah. See also footnote on Mic. 3:12.

might not be given into the hands of the people to put him [also] to death.

27 IN THE beginning of the reign of Zedekiah son of Josiah king of Judah, this word came to Jeremiah from the Lord:

2 Thus says the Lord to me: Make for yourself thongs and yoke bars and put them on your neck,

3 And send them to the king of Edom, to the king of Moab, to the king of the Ammonites, to the king of Tyre, and to the king of Sidon by the hand of the messengers who have come to Jerusalem to Zedekiah king of Judah.

4 And command them to say to their masters, Thus says the Lord of hosts, the God of Israel: Thus shall you say to your masters:

5 I have made the earth, the men, and the beasts that are upon the face of the earth by My great power and by My outstretched arm, and I give it to whomever it seems right *and* suitable to Me.

6 And now I have given all these lands into the hand of Nebuchadnezzar king of Babylon, My servant *and* instrument, and the beasts of the field also I have given him to serve him.

7 And all nations shall serve him and his son and his grandson until the [God-appointed] time [of punishment] of his own land comes; and then many nations and great kings shall make him their slave.

8 But any nation or kingdom that will not serve this same Nebuchadnezzar king of Babylon and put its neck under the yoke of the king of Babylon, that nation will I punish, says the Lord, with the sword, with famine, and with pestilence, until I have consumed it by [Nebuchadnezzar's] hand.

9 So do not listen to your [false] prophets, your diviners, your dreamers [and your dreams, whether your own or others'], your soothsayers, your sorcerers, who say to you, You shall not serve the king of Babylon.

10 For they prophesy a lie to you which will cause you to be removed far from your land; and I will drive you out, and you will perish.

11 But any nation that brings its neck under the yoke of the king of Babylon and serves him, that nation will I let remain on its own land, says the Lord, to cultivate it and dwell in it.

12 I spoke also to Zedekiah king of Judah in the same way: Bring your necks under the yoke of the king of Babylon, and serve him and his people, and live.

13 Why will you and your people die by the sword, by the famine, and by the pestilence, as the Lord has spoken concerning any nation that will not serve the king of Babylon?

14 Do not listen to *and* believe the words of the [false] prophets who are saying to you, You shall not serve the king of Babylon, for it is a lie that they prophesy to you.

15 For I have not sent them, says the Lord; but they are prophesying falsely in My name. [It will only end when] I will drive you out to perish together with the [false] prophets who prophesy to you.

16 Also I said to the priests and to all these people, Thus says the Lord: Do not listen to the words of your [false] prophets who are prophesying to you, saying, Behold, the vessels of the Lord's house shall now shortly be brought ᵏback from Babylon; for they are prophesying a lie to you.

17 Do not listen to them *or* heed them;

---

k Nebuchadnezzar besieged Jerusalem three times. The second time was during the reign of Jeconiah (Jehoiachin or Coniah), whom he took captive with all the nobles of Judah and Jerusalem (Jer. 27:20), at which time he carried away some of the sacred vessels of the temple. The third siege was now imminent.

serve the king of Babylon, and live. Why should this city be laid waste?

18 But if they are true prophets and if the word of the Lord is really spoken by them, let them now make intercession to the Lord of hosts, that the vessels which are [still] left in the house of the Lord, in the house of the king of Judah, and in Jerusalem may not go to Babylon.

19 For thus says the Lord of hosts concerning the [bronze] pillars [each twenty-seven feet high], the [bronze] Sea [the laver at which the priests cleansed their hands and feet before ministering at the altar], the [bronze] bases [of the ten lavers in Solomon's temple used for washing animals to be offered as sacrifices], and the remainder of the vessels which are left in this city [Jerusalem], [I Kings 7:23-37; II Chron. 4:6; Jer. 52:17.]

20 Which Nebuchadnezzar king of Babylon did not take when he carried into exile from Jerusalem to Babylon Jeconiah [also called Coniah and Jehoiachin] son of Jehoiakim king of Judah, with all the nobles of Judah and Jerusalem—

21 Yes, thus says the Lord of hosts, the God of Israel, concerning the vessels which [still] remain in the house of the Lord, in the house of the king of Judah, and in Jerusalem:

22 They will be ¹carried to Babylon and there will they be until the day that I visit them [with My favor], says the Lord. Then I will bring them back and restore them to this place.

28 IN THAT same year, in the beginning of the reign of Zedekiah king of Judah, in the fourth year and the fifth month, Hananiah son of Azzur, the [false] prophet, who was from Gibeon [one of the priests' cities], said [falsely] to me in the house of the Lord in the presence of the priests and all the people:

2 Thus says the Lord of hosts, the God of Israel: I have broken the yoke of the king of Babylon.

3 Within two [full] years will I bring back into this place all the vessels of the Lord's house that Nebuchadnezzar king of Babylon took away from this place and carried to Babylon.

4 And I will also bring back to this place Jeconiah [also called Coniah and Jehoiachin] son of Jehoiakim king of Judah, with all the exiles from Judah who went to Babylon, says the Lord, for I will break the yoke of the king of Babylon. [Jer. 22:10, 24-27; 52:34]

5 Then the prophet Jeremiah spoke to the prophet Hananiah in the presence of the priests and all the people who stood in the house of the Lord.

6 The prophet Jeremiah said, Amen! May the Lord do so; may the Lord perform your words which you have prophesied to bring back to this place from Babylon the vessels of the Lord's house and all who were carried away captive.

7 Nevertheless, listen now to *and* hear this word which I speak in your hearing and in the hearing of all the people:

8 The prophets who were before me and before you from of old prophesied against many countries and against great kingdoms, of war, of evil, and of pestilence.

9 But as for the prophet who [on the contrary] prophesies of peace, when that prophet's word comes to pass, [only] then will it be known that the Lord has truly sent him.

10 Then Hananiah the prophet took the yoke bar off the prophet Jeremiah's neck and smashed it.

---

1 This prophecy was literally fulfilled. The remaining sacred vessels were carried to Babylon (II Kings 25:13; II Chron. 36:18; Jer. 52:17-23), where they were kept for seventy years (II Chron. 36:21), the length of the captivity as Jeremiah had foretold it (Jer. 29:10), and then brought back to Jerusalem (Ezra 1:7; 7:19).

11 And Hananiah said in the presence of all the people, Thus says the Lord: Even so will I break the yoke bars of Nebuchadnezzar king of Babylon from the neck of all the nations within the space of two [full] years. But the prophet Jeremiah went his way.

12 The word of the Lord came to Jeremiah the prophet [some time] after Hananiah the prophet had broken the yoke bar from the neck of the prophet Jeremiah:

13 Go, tell Hananiah, Thus says the Lord: You have broken yoke bars of wood, but you have made in their stead bars of iron.

14 For thus says the Lord of hosts, the God of Israel: I have put upon the neck of all these nations the iron yoke of servitude of Nebuchadnezzar king of Babylon, and they shall serve him. For I have given him even the beasts of the field. [Jer. 27:6-7.]

15 Then said the prophet Jeremiah to Hananiah the prophet, Listen now, Hananiah, The Lord has not sent you, but you have made this people trust in a lie.

16 Therefore thus says the Lord: Behold, I will cast you from the face of the earth. This year you will die, because you have uttered *and* taught rebellion against the Lord.

17 So Hananiah the prophet died [two months later], the same year, in the seventh month.

29 NOW THESE are the words of the letter that Jeremiah the prophet sent from Jerusalem to the rest of the elders in exile and to the priests, the prophets, and all the people whom Nebuchadnezzar had carried away captive from Jerusalem to Babylon.

2 This was after King Jeconiah [also called Coniah and Jehoiachin] and the queen mother, the eunuchs, the princes of Judah and Jerusalem, the craftsmen and the smiths had departed from Jerusalem.

3 [The letter was sent] by the hand of Elasah son of Shaphan and Gemariah son of Hilkiah, whom Zedekiah king of Judah sent to Babylon to Nebuchadnezzar king of Babylon. It said:

4 Thus says the Lord of hosts, the God of Israel, to all the captives whom I have caused to be carried into exile from Jerusalem to Babylon:

5 Build yourselves houses and dwell in them; plant gardens and eat the fruit of them.

6 Take wives and have sons and daughters; take wives for your sons and give your daughters in marriage, that they may bear sons and daughters; multiply there, and do not be diminished.

7 And seek (inquire for, require, and request) the peace *and* welfare of the city to which I have caused you to be carried away captive; and pray to the Lord for it, for in the welfare of [the city in which you live] you will have welfare.

8 For thus says the Lord of hosts, the God of Israel: Let not your [false] prophets and your diviners who are in your midst deceive you; pay no attention *and* attach no significance to your dreams which you dream *or* to theirs,

9 For they prophesy falsely to you in My name. I have not sent them, says the Lord.

10 For thus says the Lord, When seventy years are completed for Babylon, I will visit you and keep My good promise to you, causing you to return to this place.

11 For I know the thoughts *and* plans that I have for you, says the Lord, thoughts *and* plans for welfare *and* peace and not for evil, to give you hope in your final outcome.

12 Then you will call upon Me, and you will come and pray to Me, and I will hear *and* heed you.

13 Then you will seek Me, inquire

life point

The Lord sees not only what you are right now, but also what you can become. He knows the plans He has for you, and, according to Jeremiah 29:11, they are good plans for progress and success, not defeat and failure. Let me encourage you to give God everything about yourself. He will be patient with you as He works His good plans in you.

for, *and* require Me [as a vital necessity] and find Me when you search for Me with all your heart. [Deut. 4:29-30.]

14 I will be found by you, says the Lord, and I will release you from captivity and gather you from all the nations and all the places to which I have driven you, says the Lord, and I will bring you back to the place from which I caused you to be carried away captive.

15 [But as for those still in Jerusalem] because you have said, The Lord has raised up prophets for us in Babylon,

16 Thus says the Lord concerning the king who sits upon the throne of

God's good plan

According to Jeremiah 29:11, God has a plan for each of us, a plan that should give us great hope for our future. It is our destiny. But that plan is a possibility, not a "positively."

If someone prophesies over us wonderful things in the name of the Lord, what they say to us may express the heart, the will, and the desire of God for us. But that does not mean it is positively going to happen just as it is prophesied. This is because it cannot and will not come to pass if we choose to refuse to cooperate with God or to stray away from His will.

God does have a plan for our lives, but we have to participate in that plan for it to come true. God is not likely to do anything in our lives without our cooperation.

We need to cooperate with God every single day of our lives in order for our potential to be developed. Every day we ought to learn something. Every day we ought to grow. Every day we ought to discover something. Every day we ought to be a bit further along than we were the day before. We should be "lifetime learners."

We must understand that no other human being on the face of the earth can develop our potential for us. We must each discover our own God-given gifts and talents, what we are truly capable of, and then put ourselves to the task of developing those gifts, talents, and capabilities to their fullest extent.

God has a plan for each of us. It is a good plan, an uncommon plan, a great plan; it is not an average, mediocre plan. I encourage you to seek that plan and cooperate with God so that it will be wonderfully fulfilled in your life.

life point

Jeremiah 29:13 is an awesome promise; God says, "Then you will seek Me, inquire for, and require Me [as a vital necessity] and find Me when you search for Me with all your heart." Notice that we are to require God "as a vital necessity." In other words, the wonderful life Jesus died for us to have depends on our personal relationship with God. We need Him just as we need food, water, and air to breathe.

When you spend time with God, everyone knows. You become calmer; you are easier to get along with; you do not lose control of your emotions as quickly. Your patience increases, wisdom is manifested through you, and your heart soon understands what God likes and what offends Him. As with any friend, the more time you spend with God, the more you become like Him. Spend time with God today. Make it a priority. Your life depends on it because He is your vital necessity.

David and concerning all the people who dwell in this city, your brethren who did not go forth with you into captivity—

17 Thus says the Lord of hosts: Behold, I am sending on them the sword, famine, and pestilence, and I will make them like vile figs which are so bad they cannot be eaten.

18 And I will pursue them with the sword, famine, and pestilence and will give them up to be tossed to and fro *and* to be a horror to all the kingdoms of the earth, to be a curse, an astonishment, *and* a terror, a hissing and a reproach among all the nations to which I have driven them,

19 Because they have not listened to *and* heeded My words, says the Lord, which I sent to them persistently by My servants the prophets; but you [exiles] would not listen [either], says the Lord. [Ezek. 2:5, 7.]

20 Hear therefore the word of the Lord, all you exiles whom I have sent away from Jerusalem to Babylon.

21 Thus says the Lord of hosts, the God of Israel, concerning Ahab son of Kolaiah and concerning Zedekiah son of Maaseiah, who are prophesying lies to you in My name: Behold, I will deliver them into the hand of ^mNebuchadrezzar king of Babylon, and he will slay them [those false prophets whom you say I have raised up for you in Babylon] before your eyes! [Jer. 29:15.]

22 And because of them, this curse shall be taken up *and* used by all from Judah who are in captivity in Babylon: The Lord make you like Zedekiah and like Ahab, whom the king of Babylon roasted in the fire—

23 Because they have committed folly in Israel and have committed adultery with their neighbors' wives and have spoken words in My name falsely, which I had not commanded them. I am the One Who knows and I am witness, says the Lord.

24 Also you shall say this concerning *and* to Shemaiah of Nehelam [among the exiles in Babylon]:

25 Thus says the Lord of hosts, the God of Israel: Because you have sent letters in your [own] name to all the people who are in Jerusalem and to Zephaniah son of Maaseiah the priest and to all the priests, saying,

26 The Lord has made you [Zephaniah] priest instead of Jehoiada the [deputy] priest, that you should have oversight in the house of the Lord over every madman who makes himself a prophet, that you should put him in the stocks and collar.

m See footnote on Jer. 21:2.

27 Now therefore [continued the letter from Shemaiah in Babylon to Zephaniah in Jerusalem], why have you not rebuked Jeremiah of Anathoth, who makes himself a prophet to you?

28 For he has sent to us in Babylon, saying, [This captivity of yours] is to be long; build houses and dwell in them; plant gardens and eat the fruit of them.

29 And Zephaniah the priest read this letter in the hearing of Jeremiah the prophet.

30 Then came the word of the Lord to Jeremiah:

31 Send [this message] to all those in captivity, saying, Thus says the Lord concerning Shemaiah of Nehelam: Because Shemaiah has prophesied to you, though I did not send him, and has caused you to trust in a lie,

32 Therefore thus says the Lord: Behold, I will punish Shemaiah of Nehelam and his offspring. He will not have anyone [born] to dwell among this people, nor will he see the good that I will do to My people, says the Lord, because he has spoken *and* taught rebellion against the Lord.

30 THE WORD that came to Jeremiah from the Lord:

2 Thus says the Lord, the God of Israel: Write all the words that I have spoken to you in a book.

3 For, note well, the days are coming, says the Lord, when I will release from captivity My people Israel and Judah, says the Lord, and I will cause them to return to the land that I gave to their fathers, and they will possess it.

4 And these are the words the Lord spoke concerning Israel and Judah:

5 Thus says the Lord: We have heard a voice of trembling *and* panic—of terror, and not peace.

6 Ask now and see whether a man can give birth to a child? Why then do I see every man with his hands on his loins like a woman in labor? Why are all faces turned pale?

7 Alas! for that day will be great, so that none will be like it; it will be the time of Jacob's [unequaled] trouble, but he will be saved out of it. [Matt. 24:29, 30; Rev. 7:14.]

8 For it will come to pass in that day, says the Lord of hosts, that I will break [the oppressor's] yoke from your neck, and I will burst your bonds; and strangers will no more make slaves of [the people of Israel].

9 But they will serve the Lord their God and David's [descendant] their King, Whom I will raise up for them. [Jer. 23:5.]

10 Therefore fear not, O My servant Jacob, says the Lord, nor be dismayed *or* cast down, O Israel; for behold, I will save you out of a distant land [of exile] and your posterity from the land of their captivity. Jacob will return and will be quiet and at ease, and none will make him afraid *or* cause him to be terrorized *and* to tremble.

11 For I am with you, says the Lord, to save you; for I will make a full *and* complete end of all the nations to which I have scattered you, but I will not make a full *and* complete end of you. But I will correct you in measure *and* with judgment and will in no sense hold you guiltless *or* leave you unpunished.

12 For thus says the Lord: Your hurt is incurable and your wound is grievous.

13 There is none to plead your cause; for [the pressing together of] your wound you have no healing [device], no binding plaster.

14 All your lovers (allies) have forgotten you; they neither seek, inquire of, *or* require you. For I have hurt you with the wound of an enemy, with the chastisement of a cruel *and* merciless foe, because of the greatness of your perversity *and* guilt, because your sins are glaring *and* innumerable.

15 Why do you cry out because of your hurt [the natural result of your sins]? Your pain is deadly (incurable). Because of the greatness of your perversity *and* guilt, because your sins are glaring *and* innumerable, I have done these things to you.

16 Therefore all who devour you will be devoured; and all your adversaries, every one of them, will go into captivity. And they who despoil you will become a spoil, and all who prey upon you will I give for a prey.

17 For I will restore health to you, and I will heal your wounds, says the Lord, because they have called you an outcast, saying, This is Zion, whom no one seeks after *and* for whom no one cares!

18 Thus says the Lord: Behold, I will release from captivity the tents of Jacob and have mercy on his dwelling places; the city will be rebuilt on its own [old] moundlike site, and the palace will be dwelt in after its former fashion.

19 Out of them [city and palace] will come songs of thanksgiving and the voices of those who make merry. And I will multiply them, and they will not be few; I will also glorify them, and they will not be small.

20 Their children too shall be as in former times, and their congregation shall be established before Me, and I will punish all who oppress them.

21 And their prince will be one of them, and their ruler will come from the midst of them. I will cause him to draw near and he will approach Me,

for who is he who would have the boldness *and* would dare [on his own initiative] to approach Me? says the Lord.

22 Then you will be My people, and I will be your God. [Jer. 7:23.]

23 Behold, the tempest of the Lord has gone forth with wrath, a sweeping *and* gathering tempest; it shall whirl *and* burst upon the heads of the wicked.

24 The fierce anger *and* indignation of the Lord shall not turn back until He has executed *and* accomplished the thoughts *and* intents of His mind *and* heart. In the latter days you shall understand this.

31 AT THAT time, says the Lord, will I be the God of all the families of Israel, and they will be My people.

2 Thus says the Lord: The people who survived the sword found favor in the wilderness [place of exile]— when Israel sought to find rest.

3 The Lord appeared from of old to me [Israel], saying, Yes, I have loved you with an everlasting love; therefore with loving-kindness have I drawn you *and* continued My faithfulness to you. [Deut. 7:8.]

4 Again I will build you and you will be built, O Virgin Israel! You will again be adorned with your timbrels [small one-headed drums] and go forth in the dancing [chorus] of those who make merry. [Isa. 37:22; Jer. 18:13.]

5 Again you shall plant vineyards upon the mountains of Samaria; the planters shall plant and make the fruit common *and* enjoy it [undisturbed].

speak the Word

Thank You, God, for restoring health to me and for healing my wounds.
ADAPTED FROM JEREMIAH 30:17

Thank You, Lord, for loving me with an everlasting love, for drawing me with Your loving-kindness, and for continuing Your faithfulness to me.
ADAPTED FROM JEREMIAH 31:3

6 For there shall be a day when the watchmen on the hills of Ephraim shall cry out, Arise, and let us go up to Zion, to the Lord our God.

7 For thus says the Lord: Sing aloud with gladness for Jacob, and shout for the head of the nations [on account of the chosen people, Israel]. Proclaim, praise, and say, The Lord has saved His people, the remnant of Israel!

8 Behold, I will bring them from the north country and gather them from the uttermost parts of the earth, and among them will be the blind and the lame, the woman with child and she who labors in childbirth together; a great company, they will return here to Jerusalem.

9 They will come with weeping [in penitence and for joy], pouring out prayers [for the future]. I will lead them back; I will cause them to walk by streams of water and bring them in a straight way in which they will not stumble, for I am a Father to Israel, and Ephraim [Israel] is My firstborn.

10 Hear the word of the Lord, O you nations, and declare it in the isles *and* coastlands far away, and say, He Who scattered Israel will gather him and will keep him as a shepherd keeps his flock.

11 For the Lord has ransomed Jacob and has redeemed him from the hand of him who was too strong for him.

12 They shall come and sing aloud on the height of Zion and shall flow together *and* be radiant with joy over the goodness of the Lord—for the corn, for the juice [of the grape], for the oil, and for the young of the flock and the herd. And their life shall be like a watered garden, and they shall not sorrow *or* languish any more at all.

13 Then will the maidens rejoice in the dance, and the young men and old together. For I will turn their mourning into joy and will comfort them and make them rejoice after their sorrow.

14 I will satisfy fully the life of the priests with abundance [of offerings shared with them], and My people will be satisfied with My goodness, says the Lord.

15 Thus says the Lord: A [n]voice is heard in Ramah, lamentation and bitter weeping. Rachel is weeping for her children; she refuses to be comforted for her children, because they are no more. [Matt. 2:18.]

16 Thus says the Lord: Restrain your voice from weeping and your eyes from tears, for your work shall be rewarded, says the Lord; and [your children] shall return from the enemy's land.

17 And there is hope for your future, says the Lord; your children shall come back to their own country.

speak the Word

Thank You, God, for turning my mourning into joy and for comforting me in my sorrow.
ADAPTED FROM JEREMIAH **31:13**

God, I declare today that there is hope in my future!
ADAPTED FROM JEREMIAH **31:17**

n The mourning at Ramah is a forecast of that bitter wailing which would be raised by the mothers of the slaughtered babes of Bethlehem centuries later when Herod would attempt to kill the Christ Child (Matt. 2:17, 18). Rachel's name, used in the prophecy, is naturally associated with Bethlehem by the fact that her tomb was in that neighborhood (*The Cambridge Bible*).

18 I have surely heard Ephraim [Israel] moaning thus: You have chastised me, and I was chastised, like a bullock unaccustomed to the yoke; bring me back, that I may be restored, for You are the Lord my God. **19** Surely after I [Ephraim] was turned [from You], I repented; and after I was instructed, I penitently smote my thigh. I was ashamed, yes, even confounded, because I bore the disgrace of my youth [as a nation]. **20** Is Ephraim My dear son? Is he a darling child *and* beloved? For as often as I speak against him, I do [earnestly] remember him still. Therefore My affection is stirred *and* My heart yearns for him; I will surely have mercy, pity, *and* loving-kindness for him, says the Lord. **21** Set up for yourselves highway markers [back to Canaan], make for yourselves guideposts; turn your thoughts *and* attention to the way by which you went [into exile]. Retrace your steps, O Virgin Israel, return to these your cities. **22** How long will you waver *and* hesitate [to return], O you backsliding daughter? For the Lord has created a °new thing in the land [of Israel]: a female shall compass (woo, win, and protect) a man. **23** Thus says the Lord of hosts, the God of Israel: Once more they shall use these words in the land of Judah and in her cities when I release them from exile: The Lord bless you, O

habitation of justice *and* righteousness, O holy mountain! **24** And [the people of] Judah and all its cities shall dwell there together— [nomad] farmers and those who wander about with their flocks. **25** For I will [fully] satisfy the weary soul, and I will replenish every languishing *and* sorrowful person. **26** Thereupon I [Jeremiah] awoke and looked, and my [trancelike] sleep was sweet [in the assurance it gave] to me. **27** Behold, the days are coming, says the Lord, when I will sow the house of Israel and the house of Judah with the seed (offspring) of man and of beast. **28** And it will be that as I have watched over them to pluck up and to break down, and to overthrow, destroy, and afflict [with evil], so will I watch over them to build and to plant [with good], says the Lord. **29** In those days they shall say no more, The fathers have eaten sour grapes, and the children's teeth are set on edge. [Ezek. 18:2.] **30** But everyone shall die for his own iniquity [only]; every man who eats sour grapes—his [own] teeth shall be set on edge. **31** Behold, the days are coming, says the Lord, when I will make a new covenant with the house of Israel and with the house of Judah, [Luke 22:20; I Cor. 11:25.] **32** Not according to the covenant which I made with their fathers in the

speak the Word

God, You satisfy my weary soul, and You replenish me.
ADAPTED FROM JEREMIAH **31:25**

o The early church fathers believed this passage had reference to the mystery of Christ's incarnation, but that interpretation is now generally rejected for various reasons. It is sufficient to say that the word "female" here used for "woman" absolutely excludes the idea that this refers to the virgin birth (for this was to be a "new thing"). To "compass" is to woo and win. That the early translators attached that meaning to it is clear from the fact that Shakespeare, their contemporary, so used it (Charles Ellicott, *A Bible Commentary*). Probably the implication is that Israel, the erring but deeply penitent wife, instead of going about after other lovers will devote herself to winning back and being worthy of the love of her divine Husband and Lord, Who had rejected her.

day when I took them by the hand to bring them out of the land of Egypt, My covenant which they broke, although I was their Husband, says the Lord.

33 But this is the covenant which I will make with the house of Israel: After those days, says the Lord, I will put My law within them, and on their hearts will I write it; and I will be their God, and they will be My people.

34 And they will no more teach each man his neighbor and each man his brother, saying, Know the Lord, for they will all know Me [recognize, understand, and be acquainted with Me], from the least of them to the greatest, says the Lord. For I will forgive their iniquity, and I will [seriously] remember their sin no more. [Heb. 8:8-12; 10:16, 17.]

35 Thus says the Lord, Who gives the sun for a light by day and the fixed order of the moon and of the stars for a light by night, Who stirs up the sea's roaring billows *or* stills the waves when they roar—the Lord of hosts is His name:

36 If these ordinances [of fixed order] depart from before Me, says the Lord, then the posterity of Israel also shall cease from being a nation before Me throughout the ages.

37 Thus says the Lord: If the heavens above can be measured and the foundations of the earth searched out beneath, then I will cast off all the offspring of Israel for all that they have done, says the Lord.

38 Behold, the days are coming, says the Lord, when the city [of Jerusalem]

"I will remember your sin no more"

No matter what your problem is or how badly you feel about yourself as a result of it, God loves you. In Jesus Christ He has given you a new life. He will provide new friends to love, accept, appreciate, and uphold you. You are okay, and you are going to make it because of the One Who lives inside you and cares for you.

Regardless of what you may have done, you need a deeper revelation of what God means when He says in Jeremiah 31:34, "I will remember your sins no more." Once you have confessed your sins and asked for God's forgiveness, if you continue to bring them up to Him every time you go to Him in prayer, you are reminding Him of something He has promised to forget—something He has removed from you as far as the east is from the west (see Psalm 103:12). You need to realize that once you have confessed your sins to God and asked Him to forgive you of them, He has not only *forgiven* them, but He has actually *forgotten* them.

You may have to look at yourself in the mirror and confess your deepest failure. You may need to say to God something like, "I had an abortion." Or, "I committed adultery. I did that, Lord, and it is a marvel to me to realize that I can stand here and look myself in the eye. But I can do so because I know that even though I did something so wrong, You have put my sins as far away from me as the east is from the west, and You remember them no more!"

Whatever your sin or failure, you need to confess it to God and then let it go. Stop punishing yourself for something that is in the past. Refuse to remember something God has chosen to forget.

shall be built [again] for the Lord from the ᴾTower of Hananel to the Corner Gate.

39 And the measuring line shall go out farther straight onward to the hill Gareb and shall then turn to Goah [exact location unknown].

40 And the whole valley [Hinnom] of the dead bodies and [the hill] of the ashes [long dumped there from the temple sacrifices], and all the fields as far as the brook Kidron, to the corner of the Horse Gate toward the east, shall be holy to the Lord. It [the city] shall not be plucked up or overthrown any more to the end of the age. [Zech. 14:10-11.]

32 THE WORD that came to Jeremiah from the Lord in the tenth year of Zedekiah king of Judah, which was the eighteenth year of �qNebuchadrezzar.

2 For the king of Babylon's army was then besieging Jerusalem, and Jeremiah the prophet was shut up in the court of the guard, which was in the house of the king of Judah.

3 For Zedekiah king of Judah had locked him up, saying, Why do you prophesy and say, Thus says the Lord: Behold, I am giving this city into the hand of the king of Babylon, and he shall take it;

4 And Zedekiah king of Judah shall not escape out of the hands of the Chaldeans but shall surely be delivered into the hand of the king of Babylon, and shall speak with him

face to face and see him eye to eye;

5 And he shall lead Zedekiah to Babylon, and there shall he be until I visit him [for evil], says the Lord; and though you fight against the Chaldeans, you shall not prosper [why do you thus prophesy]? [Jer. 21:3-7; 34:2-5; 37:17; 52:7-14.]

6 And Jeremiah said, The word of the Lord came to me, saying,

7 Behold, Hanamel son of Shallum your uncle shall come to you and say, Buy my field that is in Anathoth, for the right of redemption is yours to buy it.

8 So Hanamel my uncle's son came to me in the court of the guard in accordance with the word of the Lord, and he said to me, I pray you, buy my field that is in Anathoth, which is in the land of Benjamin, for the right of inheritance is yours and the redemption is yours; buy it for yourself. Then I knew that this was the word of the Lord.

9 And I bought the field that was in Anathoth from Hanamel my uncle's son and weighed out for him the money—seventeen shekels of silver.

10 And I signed the deed and sealed it, called witnesses, and weighed out for him the money on the scales.

11 So I took the deed of the purchase—both that which was sealed, containing the terms and conditions, and the copy which was unsealed—

12 And I gave the purchase deed to Baruch son of Neriah, the son of Mahseiah, in the sight of Hanamel my uncle's son and the witnesses who signed the purchase deed, in the

---

p Many times after the days of the Old Testament, Jerusalem was destroyed. Travelers in recent centuries reported it to be an almost deserted city—its buildings were ruins filled with rubble, its inhabitants numbered barely enough to populate a village. Yet not only did God's word declare that it would be rebuilt, but also definitely and in detail it drew a word map of the exact outline which the future city would follow—from a well-known tower to the gate at a certain corner, then on over a particular hill, coming now outside the walls of the original city and taking in a large area definitely marked out by familiar landmarks. Eight details are unmistakably given here, and Zechariah adds another (Zech. 14:10). Moreover, the city's enlargement was to be in one general direction—to the northwest. Twenty-five hundred years later, in AD 1935, the prophecy had been fulfilled to the letter, as if indeed with God's "measuring line" (Jer. 31:39). What a God, and what a Book! So unlikely seemed this prophecy's fulfillment that some commentators were of the opinion that it should be interpreted spiritually!   q See footnote on Jer. 21:2.

presence of all the Jews who were sitting in the court of the guard.

13 And I charged Baruch before them, saying,

14 Thus says the Lord of hosts, the God of Israel: Take these deeds, both this purchase deed which is sealed and this unsealed deed, and put them in an earthen vessel, that they may last a long time.

15 For thus says the Lord of hosts, the God of Israel: Houses and fields and vineyards shall be purchased yet again in this land.

16 Now when I had delivered the purchase deed to Baruch son of Neriah, I prayed to the Lord, saying:

17 Alas, Lord God! Behold, You have made the heavens and the earth by Your great power and by Your outstretched arm! There is nothing too hard *or* too wonderful for You—

18 You Who show loving-kindness to thousands but recompense the iniquity of the fathers into the bosoms of their children after them. The great, the mighty God; the Lord of hosts is His name—

19 Great [are You] in counsel and mighty in deeds, Whose eyes are open to all the ways of the sons of men, to reward *or* repay each one according to his ways and according to the fruit of his doings,

20 Who wrought signs and wonders in the land of Egypt, and even to this day [continues to do so], both in Israel and among other men, and made for Yourself a name, as at this day.

21 And You brought forth Your people Israel out of the land of Egypt with signs and wonders, with a strong hand and outstretched arm and with great terror;

22 And You gave them this land which You swore to their fathers to give them, a land flowing with milk and honey;

23 And they entered and took possession of it, but they obeyed not Your voice, nor walked in Your law; they have done nothing of all that You commanded them to do. Therefore You have caused all this evil to come upon them.

24 See the siege mounds [of earth which the foe has heaped against the walls]; they have come up to the city to take it. And the city is given into the hand of the Chaldeans who fight against it, because [the people are overcome] by the sword and the famine and the pestilence. What You have spoken has come to pass, and behold, You see it.

25 Yet, O Lord God, You said to me, Buy the field with money and get witnesses, even though the city is given into the hands of the Chaldeans.

26 Then came the word of the Lord to Jeremiah, saying,

27 Behold, I am the Lord, the God of all flesh; is there anything too hard for Me?

28 Therefore thus says the Lord: Behold, I am giving this city into the hands of the Chaldeans and into the hand of Nebuchadrezzar king of Babylon, and he shall take it;

29 And the Chaldeans who are fighting against this city shall come in and set this city on fire and burn it, along with the houses on whose roofs incense has been offered to Baal and drink offerings have been poured out to other gods to provoke Me to anger. [Jer. 19:13.]

30 For the children of Israel and the children of Judah have done only evil before Me from their youth; for the children of Israel have only provoked Me to anger with the work of their hands [the idols], says the Lord.

31 For this city has been to Me a [such a] provocation of My anger and My wrath from the day that they [finished] building it [in the time of Solomon, who was the first Israelite king who turned to idolatry] even to this day that I must remove it from before My face—[I Kings 11:1-13.]

32 Because of all the evil of the children of Israel and of the children of Judah which they have done to provoke Me to anger—they, their kings, their princes, their priests, their prophets, the men of Judah, and the inhabitants of Jerusalem.

33 And they have turned their backs to Me and not their faces; though I taught them persistently, yet they would not listen and receive instruction.

34 But they set their abominations [of idol worship] in the house which is called by My ʳName to defile it.

35 And they built the high places [for worship] of Baal in the Valley of Ben-hinnom [son of Hinnom] to cause their sons and their daughters to pass through the fire [in worship also of and] to Molech—which I did not command them, nor did it come into My mind or heart that they should do this abomination, to cause Judah to sin. [Jer. 7:30-31.]

36 And now therefore thus says the Lord, the God of Israel, concerning this city of which you say, It shall be delivered into the hand of the king of Babylon by sword and by famine and by pestilence:

37 Behold, I will gather them out of all countries to which I drove them in My anger and in My wrath and in great indignation; I will bring them again to this place, and I will make them dwell safely.

38 And they will be My people, and I will be their God.

39 And I will give them one heart and one way, that they may [reverently] fear Me forever for the good of themselves and of their children after them.

40 And I will make an everlasting covenant with them: I will not turn

away from following them to do them good, and I will put My [reverential] fear in their hearts, so that they will not depart from Me. [Jer. 31:31-34.]

41 Yes, I will rejoice over them to do them good, and I will plant them in this land assuredly and in truth with My whole heart and with My whole being.

42 For thus says the Lord: As I have brought all this great evil upon this people, so will I bring upon them all the good that I have promised them.

43 And fields shall be bought in this land of which you say, It is desolate, without man or beast; it is given into the hands of the Chaldeans.

44 Men shall buy fields for money and shall sign deeds, seal them, and call witnesses in the land of Benjamin, in the places around Jerusalem, in the cities of Judah, in the cities of the hill country, in the cities of the lowland, and in the cities of the South (the Negeb), for I will cause them to be released from their exile, says the Lord.

33 MOREOVER, THE word of the Lord came to Jeremiah the second time, while he was still shut up in the court of the guard, saying,

2 Thus says the Lord Who made [the earth], the Lord Who formed it to establish it—the Lord is His name:

3 Call to Me and I will answer you and show you great and mighty things, fenced in and hidden, which you do not know (do not distinguish and recognize, have knowledge of and understand).

4 For thus says the Lord, the God of Israel, concerning the houses of this city and the houses of the kings of Judah which are torn down to make a defense against the siege mounds and before the sword: [Isa. 22:10; Jer. 6:6.]

ʳ See footnote on Deut. 12:5.

5 They [the besieged Jews] are coming in to fight against the Chaldeans, and they [the houses] will be filled with the dead bodies of men whom I shall slay in My anger and My wrath; for I have hidden My face [in indignation] from this city because of all their wickedness.

6 Behold, [in the future restored Jerusalem] I will lay upon it health and healing, and I will cure them and will reveal to them the abundance of peace (prosperity, security, stability) and truth.

7 And I will cause the captivity of Judah and the captivity of Israel to be reversed and will rebuild them as they were at first.

8 And I will cleanse them from all the guilt *and* iniquity by which they have sinned against Me, and I will forgive all their guilt *and* iniquities by which they have sinned and rebelled against Me.

9 And [Jerusalem] shall be to Me a name of joy, a praise and a glory before all the nations of the earth that hear of all the good I do for it, and they shall fear and tremble because of all the good and all the peace, prosperity, security, *and* stability I provide for it.

10 Thus says the Lord: Yet again there shall be heard in this place of which you say, It is a desolate waste, without man and without beast—even in the cities of Judah and in the streets of Jerusalem that are desolate, without man and without inhabitant and without beast—

11 [There shall be heard again] the voice of joy and the voice of gladness, the voice of the bridegroom and the voice of the bride, the voices of those who sing as they bring sacrifices of thanksgiving into the house of the Lord, Give praise *and* thanks to the Lord of hosts, for the Lord is good; for His mercy *and* kindness *and* steadfast love endure forever! For I will cause the captivity of the land to be reversed *and* return to be as it was at first, says the Lord.

12 Thus says the Lord of hosts: In this place which is desolate, without man and without beast, and in all its cities, there shall again be dwellings *and* pastures of shepherds resting their flocks.

13 In the cities of the hill country, in the cities of the lowland, in the cities of the South (the Negeb), in the land of Benjamin, in the places around Jerusalem, and in the cities of Judah shall flocks pass again under the hands of him who counts them, says the Lord.

14 Behold, the days are coming, says the Lord, when I will fulfill the good promise I have made to the house of Israel and the house of Judah.

15 In those days and at that time will I cause a righteous Branch [the Messiah] to grow up to David; and He shall execute justice and righteousness in the land. [Isa. 4:2; Jer. 23:5; Zech. 3:8; 6:12.]

16 In those days Judah shall be saved and Jerusalem shall dwell safely. And this is the name by which it will be called, The Lord is Our Righteousness (our Rightness, our Justice).

17 For thus says the Lord: David shall never fail [to have] a man [descendant] to sit on the throne of the house of Israel,

18 Nor shall the Levitical priests fail [to have] a man [descendant] to offer

speak the Word

Thank You, God, that a time is coming when You will fulfill every good promise You have made to me.
ADAPTED FROM JEREMIAH 33:14

burnt offerings before Me and to burn cereal offerings and to make sacrifices continually (all day long).

19 And the word of the Lord came to Jeremiah, saying,

20 Thus says the Lord: If you can break My covenant with the day, and My covenant with the night, so that there should not be day and night in their season,

21 Then can also My covenant be broken with David My servant, so that he shall not have a son to reign upon his throne, and [My league be broken also] with the Levitical priests, My ministers.

22 As the host of [the stars of] the heavens cannot be numbered nor the sand of the sea be measured, so will I multiply the offspring of David My servant and the Levites who minister to Me.

23 Moreover, the word of the Lord came to Jeremiah, saying,

24 Have you not noticed that these people [the Jews] are saying, The Lord has cast off the two families [Israel and Judah] which He chose? Thus My people have despised [themselves in relation to God as His covenant people], so that they are no more a nation in their [own] sight.

25 Thus says the Lord: If My covenant with day and night does not stand, and if I have not appointed the ordinances of the heavens and the earth [the whole order of nature],

26 Then will I also cast away the descendants of Jacob and David My servant and will not choose one of his offspring to be ruler over the descendants of Abraham, Isaac, and Jacob. For I will cause their captivity to be reversed, and I will have mercy, kindness, *and* steadfast love on *and* for them. [Gen. 49:10.]

34

THE WORD that came to Jeremiah from the Lord when Nebuchadnezzar king of Babylon and all his army and all the kingdoms of the earth under his dominion and all the people were fighting against Jerusalem and all of its cities:

2 Thus says the Lord, the God of Israel: Go and speak to Zedekiah king of Judah and tell him, Thus says the Lord: Behold, I am giving this city into the hand of the king of Babylon, and he will burn it with fire.

3 And you will not escape out of his hand but will surely be taken and delivered into his hand; you will see the king of Babylon eye to eye, and he will speak with you face to face; and you will go to Babylon.

4 Yet hear the word of the Lord, O Zedekiah king of Judah! Thus says the Lord concerning you: You shall not die by the sword;

5 But you shall die in peace. And as with the burnings of [spices and perfumes on wood that were granted as suitable for and in honor of] your fathers, the former kings who were before you, so shall a burning be made for you; and [people] shall lament for you, saying, Alas, lord! For I have spoken the word, says the Lord.

6 Then Jeremiah the prophet spoke all these words to Zedekiah king of Judah, in Jerusalem,

7 When the army of the king of Babylon was fighting against Jerusalem and against all the cities of Judah that were left, against Lachish and Azekah, for these were the only fortified cities remaining of the cities of Judah.

8 [This is] the word that came to Jeremiah from the Lord after King Zedekiah had made a covenant with all the people who were at Jerusalem to proclaim liberty to them:

9 Every man should let his Hebrew slaves, male and female, go free, so that no one should make a slave of a Jew, his brother.

10 And all the princes and all the

people obeyed, who had entered into the covenant that everyone would let his manservant and his maidservant go free, so that none should make bondmen of them any more; they obeyed, and let them go.

11 But afterward they turned around and caused the servants and the handmaids whom they had let go free to return [to their former masters] and brought them into subjection for servants and for handmaids.

12 Therefore the word of the Lord came to Jeremiah from the Lord, saying,

13 Thus says the Lord, the God of Israel: I made a covenant with your fathers in the day that I brought them forth out of the land of Egypt, out of the house of bondage, saying,

14 At the end of seven years you shall let every man his brother who is a Hebrew go free who has sold himself *or* has been sold to you and has served you six years; but your fathers did not listen to *and* obey Me or incline their ear [submitting and consenting to Me]. [Deut. 15:12.]

15 And you recently turned around *and* repented, doing what was right in My sight by proclaiming liberty each one to his neighbor [who was his bond servant]; and you made a covenant *or* pledge before Me in the house which is called by My ˢName.

16 But then you turned around and defiled My name; each of you caused to return to you your servants, male and female, whom you had set free as they might desire; and you brought them into subjection again to be your slaves.

17 Therefore thus says the Lord: You have not listened to Me *and* obeyed Me in proclaiming liberty each one to his brother and neighbor. Behold, I proclaim to you liberty—to the sword, to pestilence, and to famine, says the

s See footnote on Deut. 12:5.

putting the Word to work

Jeremiah 34:17 declares that God proclaims liberty to us. In what ways has He set you free? Thank Him today for the liberty He brings to your life.

Lord; and I will make you to be tossed to and fro *and* to be a horror among all the kingdoms of the earth!

18 And the men who have transgressed My covenant, who have not kept the terms of the covenant *or* solemn pledge which they had made before Me, I will make them [like] the [sacrificial] calf which they cut in two and then passed between its separated parts [solemnizing their pledge to Me]—I will make those men the calf! [Gen. 15:9, 10, 17.]

19 The princes of Judah, the princes of Jerusalem, the eunuchs, the priests, and all the people of the land who passed between the parts of the calf,

20 I will give them into the hands of their enemies and into the hands of those who seek their life. And their dead bodies will be food for the birds of the heavens and the beasts of the earth.

21 And Zedekiah king of Judah and his princes will I give into the hands of their enemies and into the hands of those who seek their life, and into the hand of the king of Babylon's army which has withdrawn from you.

22 Behold, I will command, says the Lord, and cause them [the Chaldeans] to return to this city; and they shall fight against it and take it and burn it with fire. I will make the cities of Judah a desolation without inhabitant.

35 THE WORD that came to Jeremiah from the Lord in the days of Jehoiakim son of Josiah king of Judah:

2 Go to the house of the Rechabites

proclaim liberty

I encourage you to give the gift of freedom and "proclaim liberty" to your family, friends, neighbors, and coworkers. People will love you for it. Obviously, this does not mean letting others do whatever they want to do. But it does mean that you stop trying to control people and situations and let God be God.

For years I tried desperately to control and remold my husband and children, until I finally realized that my efforts were acts of selfishness, not love. I told myself that I simply wanted God's best for them; however, I had decided what His best was and was trying to force it upon them.

Unknowingly, I was ignoring scriptures that shed light on the proper attitude parents should have toward their children. Proverbs 22:6 tells us that we are to train up our children in the way they should go, and when they are old, they will not depart from it. Ephesians 6:4 tells us that we are not to irritate and provoke our children or exasperate them to resentment, but to bring them up tenderly and in the training, discipline, counsel, and admonition of the Lord. Quite frequently we have plans for our children. We have our own ideas about what they should do with their lives, and we pressure them to go in the direction we desire for them.

At one point in my life, I wanted all of my children to preach, just as I do. That did not happen, and, actually, I now realize that was not even what would have blessed me after all. Each of my grown children performs a different function that fulfills a great need for me in the ministry, and I would really be missing something if I had gotten my way with them. God is in control, and I am glad. Trying to control others is hard work, and it *does not work*!

Make sure the atmosphere in your home and your business is free and relaxed, not one that makes people feel that if they do not please you all the time, tension will fill the air and tempers will explode. When people make mistakes, do not make them feel rejected, but go the extra mile to make them feel forgiven and accepted. Treat others the way you want to be treated.

Relax. Loosen up a bit. Proclaim liberty as Jeremiah 34:15 instructs, and give everyone around you the gift of freedom.

and speak to them and bring them into the house of the Lord, into one of the chambers; then give them [who are pledged to drink no wine] some wine to drink.

3 So I took Jaazaniah son of Jeremiah, the son of Habazziniah, and his brothers and all his sons, and the whole house of the Rechabites,

4 And I brought them into the house of the Lord, into the chamber of the sons of Hanan son of Igdaliah the man of God, which was by the chamber of the princes, above the chamber of Maaseiah son of Shallum the keeper of the door.

5 And I set before the sons of the house of the Rechabites pitchers full

of wine, and cups, and I said to them, Drink wine.

6 But they said, We will drink no wine, for Jonadab son of Rechab, our father, commanded us: You shall not drink wine, neither you nor your sons, forever.

7 Neither shall you build a house or sow seed or plant a vineyard or have them; but you shall dwell all your days in tents, that you may live many days in the land where you are temporary residents.

8 And we have obeyed the voice of Jonadab son of Rechab, our father, in all that he charged us, to drink no wine all our days—we, our wives, our sons, and our daughters—

9 And not to build ourselves houses to live in; nor do we have vineyard or field or seed.

10 But we have dwelt in tents and have obeyed and done according to all that Jonadab our ancestor commanded us.

11 But when 'Nebuchadrezzar king of Babylon came up against the land, we said, Come and let us go to Jerusalem for fear of the army of the Chaldeans and the army of the Syrians. So we are living in Jerusalem.

12 Then came the word of the Lord to Jeremiah:

13 Thus says the Lord of hosts, the God of Israel: Go and say to the men of Judah and the inhabitants of Jerusalem, Will you not receive instruction and listen to My words *and* obey them? says the Lord.

14 The command which Jonadab son of Rechab gave to his sons not to drink wine, has been carried out *and* established [as a custom for more than two hundred years]. To this day they drink no wine, but they have obeyed their father's command. But I, even I, have persistently spoken to

you, but you have not listened to *and* obeyed Me.

15 I have sent also to you all My servants the prophets earnestly *and* persistently, saying, Return now every man from his evil way and amend your doings and go not after other gods to serve them; and then you shall dwell in the land which I have given to you and to your fathers. But you did not submit *and* consent to Me or listen to *and* obey Me.

16 Since the sons of Jonadab son of Rechab have fulfilled *and* established the command of their father which he commanded them, but these people have not listened to and obeyed Me,

17 Therefore thus says the Lord God of hosts, the God of Israel: Behold, I am bringing upon Judah and all the inhabitants of Jerusalem all the evil that I have pronounced against them, because I have spoken to them, but they have not listened, and I have called to them, but they have not answered.

18 And Jeremiah said to the house of the Rechabites, Thus says the Lord of hosts, the God of Israel: Because you have obeyed the command of Jonadab your father and have kept all his precepts and have done according to all that he commanded you,

19 Therefore thus says the Lord of hosts, the God of Israel: Jonadab son of Rechab shall never fail [to have] a man [descendant] to stand before Me.

36 IN THE fourth year of Jehoiakim son of Josiah king of Judah, this word came to Jeremiah from the Lord:

2 Take a scroll [of parchment] for a book and write on it all the words I have spoken to you against Israel and Judah and all the nations from the day I spoke to you in the days of [King] Josiah until this day.

---

t See footnote on Jer. 21:2.

3 It may be that the house of Judah will hear all the evil which I purpose to do to them, so that each one may turn from his evil way, that I may forgive their iniquity and their sin. [Jer. 18:7-10; 26:3.]

4 Then Jeremiah called Baruch son of Neriah, and Baruch wrote upon the scroll of the book all the words which Jeremiah dictated, [words] that the Lord had spoken to him.

5 And Jeremiah commanded Baruch, saying, I am [in hiding, virtually] restrained *and* shut up; I cannot go into the house of the Lord.

6 Therefore you go, and on a day of fasting, in the hearing of all the people in the Lord's house, you shall read the words of the Lord which you have written on the scroll at my dictation. Also you shall read them in the hearing of all who come out of the cities of Judah.

7 It may be that they will make their supplication [for mercy] before the Lord, and each one will turn back from his evil way, for great is the anger and the wrath that the Lord has pronounced against this people.

8 And Baruch son of Neriah did according to all that Jeremiah the prophet commanded him, reading from [Jeremiah's] book the words of the Lord in the Lord's house.

9 And in the fifth year of Jehoiakim son of Josiah king of Judah, in the ninth month, a fast was proclaimed before the Lord for all the people in Jerusalem and all the people who came to Jerusalem from the cities of Judah.

10 Then Baruch read in the hearing of all the people the words of Jeremiah from the scroll of the book in the house of the Lord, in the chamber of Gemariah son of Shaphan the scribe, in the upper court at the entry of the New Gate of the Lord's house.

11 When Micaiah son of Gemariah, the son of Shaphan, had heard out of the book all the words of the Lord,

12 He went down to the king's house into the scribe's chamber, and behold, all the princes were sitting there: Elishama the scribe, Delaiah son of Shemaiah, Elnathan son of Achbor, Gemariah son of Shaphan, Zedekiah son of Hananiah, and all the [other] princes.

13 Then Micaiah declared to them all the words that he had heard when Baruch read the book in the hearing of the people.

14 Therefore all the princes sent Jehudi son of Nethaniah, the son of Shelemiah, the son of Cushi, to Baruch, saying, Take in your hand the scroll from which you have read in the hearing of the people and come [to us]. So Baruch son of Neriah took the scroll in his hand and came to them.

15 And they said to him, Sit down now and read it in our hearing. So Baruch read it in their hearing.

16 Now when they had heard all the words, they turned one to another in fear and said to Baruch, We must surely tell the king of all these words.

17 And they asked Baruch, Tell us now, how did you write all these words? At [Jeremiah's] dictation?

18 Then Baruch answered them, He dictated all these words to me, and I wrote them with ink in the book.

19 Then the princes said to Baruch, Go and hide, you and Jeremiah, and let no one know where you are.

20 Then they went into the court to the king, but they [first] put the scroll in the chamber of Elishama the scribe; then they reported all the words to the king.

21 So the king sent Jehudi to get the scroll, and he took it out of the chamber of Elishama the scribe. And Jehudi read it in the hearing of the king and of all the princes who stood beside the king.

22 Now it was the ninth month, and the king was sitting in the winter house, and a fire was burning there before him in the brazier.

23 And [each time] when Jehudi had read three or four columns [of the scroll], he [King Jehoiakim] would cut them off with a penknife and cast them into the fire that was in the brazier, until the entire scroll was consumed in the fire that was in the brazier.

24 Yet they were not afraid, nor did they rend their garments—neither the king, nor any of his servants who heard all these words.

25 Even though Elnathan and Delaiah and Gemariah tried to persuade the king not to burn the scroll, he would not listen to them.

26 And the king commanded Jerahmeel the king's son and Seraiah son of Azriel and Shelemiah son of Abdeel to seize Baruch the scribe and Jeremiah the prophet, but the Lord hid them.

27 Now the word of the Lord came to Jeremiah after the king had burned the scroll with the words which Baruch wrote at the dictation of Jeremiah, [and the Lord] said:

28 Take another scroll and write on it all the former words that were on the first scroll, which Jehoiakim the king of Judah burned.

29 And concerning Jehoiakim king of Judah you shall say, Thus says the Lord: You have burned this scroll, saying, Why have you written on it that the king of Babylon shall surely come and destroy this land and shall cut off man and beast from it?

30 Therefore thus says the Lord concerning Jehoiakim king of Judah: ᵘHe shall have no [heir] to sit upon the throne of David, and his dead body shall be cast out to the heat by day and to the frost by night.

31 And I will punish him and his offspring and his servants for their iniquity; and I will bring upon them and the inhabitants of Jerusalem and the men of Judah all the evil that I have pronounced against them—but they would not hear.

32 Then Jeremiah took another scroll and gave it to Baruch the scribe, the son of Neriah, who wrote on it at the dictation of Jeremiah all the words of the book which Jehoiakim king of Judah had burned in the fire; and besides them many similar words were added.

37 AND ZEDEKIAH son of Josiah, whom ᵛNebuchadrezzar king of Babylon made king in the land of Judah, reigned instead of Coniah [also called Jeconiah and Jehoiachin] son of Jehoiakim.

2 But neither he nor his servants nor the people of the land listened to *and* obeyed the words of the Lord which He spoke through the prophet Jeremiah.

3 Zedekiah the king sent Jehucal son of Shelemiah with Zephaniah son of Maaseiah, the priest, to the prophet Jeremiah, saying, Pray now to the Lord our God for us.

4 Now Jeremiah was coming in and going out among the people, for they had not [yet] put him in prison.

5 And Pharaoh's army had come forth out of Egypt, and when the Chaldeans who were besieging Jerusalem heard the news about them,

---

u This prophecy against King Jehoiakim was literally fulfilled. Several years after these events, the king rebelled against Babylon (II Kings 24:1) and was attacked by numerous bands from various nations subject to Babylon (II Kings 24:2). He thus came to a violent death and a disgraceful burial such as Jeremiah had foretold several chapters before this one (Jer. 22:13-19). There, after a stern and scathing censure of the king, the Lord foretells through his prophet that Jehoiakim will "be buried with the burial of a donkey—dragged out and cast forth beyond the gates of Jerusalem" (Jer. 22:19). How could Jeremiah possibly have foreseen these events except by divine inspiration?
v See footnote on Jer. 21:2.

do it again!

Even though Jeremiah was in prison, he still received prophecies from the Lord and recorded them, according to Jeremiah 36. God would give him a message, and he would record it on parchment that was rolled up into a scroll. Then one of his servants would come and carry the message throughout the land, since Jeremiah was unable to go personally. From this we see that God is not put off by inconveniences; He always finds another way to get the job done.

The people of those days did not have computers and printers, typewriters, or even ballpoint pens and pads of paper, so imagine how tedious their job of writing was! Everything had to be taken down by a quill and ink on a scroll. If more than one copy was needed, then it had to be made by hand from the original, which was a long, tiresome, painstaking process.

In Jeremiah 36:1, 2, God gave Jeremiah a specific prophecy about Israel and Judah, and He told him to record it on a scroll. Jeremiah called his secretary, Baruch, who wrote while Jeremiah dictated (see Jeremiah 36:4). When the king heard about the scroll, he ordered it to be brought to the royal palace and read to him. As his attendant Jehudi was reading it to him, the king would take a few columns that had been read, cut them off the scroll with a knife, and then burn them in a fire (see Jeremiah 36:22, 23).

It was wintertime. Maybe the king was sitting there by the fire, warming his toes and eating an apple. Whatever the case, the king did not like what Jehudi was reading because he liked his unrighteous lifestyle and did not want to change it. So he cut up and burned section after section from the scroll until he burned up all Jeremiah's prophecies.

Can you imagine how Jeremiah must have felt when he learned that all of his hard work had been burned up? Can you relate to that experience? Have you ever worked on something for a long time and struggled and tried and done everything you knew how to do and somehow the devil got in and destroyed it all? The word to you is: *Do it again!*

That is what Jeremiah did. God's answer to Jeremiah's terrible dilemma and discouragement was: "Take another scroll and write on it all the former words that were on the first scroll" (Jeremiah 36:28). God said, basically, "Jeremiah, go get yourself another scroll and write the thing over."

In other words, *do it again*.

If you and I want to be strong and victorious in the kingdom of God, we must be willing to do it—and then do it again and again and again, if necessary—until we get a breakthrough and what God has called us to do is completed.

they withdrew from Jerusalem *and* departed.

6 Then came the word of the Lord to the prophet Jeremiah:

7 Thus says the Lord, the God of Israel: Thus shall you say to the king of Judah, who sent you to Me to inquire of Me: Behold, Pharaoh's army, which has come forth to help you, will return to Egypt, to their own land.

8 And the Chaldeans shall come again and fight against this city, and they shall take it and burn it with fire.

9 Thus says the Lord: Do not deceive yourselves, saying, The Chaldeans will surely stay away from us—for they will not stay away.

10 For though you should defeat the whole army of the Chaldeans who fight against you, and there remained only the wounded *and* men stricken through among them, every man confined to his tent, yet they would rise up and burn this city with fire.

11 And when the army of the Chaldeans had departed from Jerusalem for fear of Pharaoh's approaching army,

12 Jeremiah went forth out of Jerusalem to go into the land of Benjamin [to slip away during the brief lull in the Chaldean invasion] to receive [the title to] his portion [of land, which the Lord had promised would eventually be valuable] there among the people.

13 And when he was at the Gate of Benjamin, a sentry was [on guard] there, whose name was Irijah son of Shelemiah, the son of Hananiah; and he seized Jeremiah the prophet, saying, You are deserting to the Chaldeans.

14 Then said Jeremiah, It is false! I am not deserting to the Chaldeans. But the sentry would not listen to him. So Irijah took Jeremiah and brought him to the princes.

15 Therefore the princes were enraged with Jeremiah and beat him and put him in prison in the house of Jonathan the scribe—for they had made that the prison.

16 When Jeremiah had come into ^wthe cells in the dungeon and had remained there many days,

17 Zedekiah the king sent and brought him out; and the king asked him secretly in his house, Is there any word from the Lord? And Jeremiah said, There is! And he said also, You shall be delivered into the hand of the king of Babylon.

18 Moreover, Jeremiah said to King Zedekiah, In what have I sinned against you or against your servants or against this people, that you have put me in prison?

19 Where now are your prophets who prophesied to you, saying, The king of Babylon shall not come against you or against this land?

20 Therefore hear now, I pray you, O my lord the king. Let my supplication, I pray you, come before you *and* be acceptable, that you do not cause me to return to the house of Jonathan the scribe, lest I die there.

21 Then Zedekiah the king commanded, and they committed Jeremiah to the court of the guard, and a round loaf of bread from the bakers' street was given to him daily until all the bread in the city was gone. So Jeremiah remained [imprisoned] in the court of the guard.

38

NOW SHEPHATIAH son of Mattan, Gedaliah son of Pashhur, Jucal [also called Jehucal] son of Shelemiah, and Pashhur son of Malchiah heard the words that Jeremiah spoke to all the people, saying,

2 Thus says the Lord: He who remains in this city shall die by the sword, by famine, and by pestilence,

---

w Literally, "the house of the cistern."

but he who goes out to the Chaldeans shall live; for he shall have his life as his only booty [as a prize of war], and he shall live. [Jer. 21:9.]

3 Thus says the Lord: This city shall surely be given into the hand of the army of the king of Babylon, and he shall take it.

4 Therefore the princes said to the king, We beseech you, let this man [Jeremiah] be put to death; for [talking] thus he weakens the hands of the soldiers who remain in this city and the hands of all the people by speaking such words to them. For this man is not seeking the welfare of these people, but [to do them] harm.

5 Then Zedekiah the king said, Behold, he is in your hands; for the king is in no position to do anything against you.

6 So they took Jeremiah and cast him into the dungeon or cistern pit [in the charge] of Malchiah the king's son, which was in the court of the guard; and they let Jeremiah down [into the pit] with ropes. And in the dungeon or cistern pit there was no water, but only mire, and Jeremiah sank in the mire.

7 Now when Ebed-melech the Ethiopian [a Cushite], one of the eunuchs who was in the king's house, heard that they had put Jeremiah in the dungeon or cistern pit; and while the king was then sitting in the Gate of Benjamin,

8 Ebed-melech went out of the king's house and spoke to the king, saying,

9 My lord the king, these men have done evil in all that they have done to Jeremiah the prophet, whom they have cast into the dungeon or cistern pit; and he is liable to die of hunger and is [as good as] dead in the place where he is, for there is no more bread left in the city.

10 Then the king commanded Ebed-melech the Ethiopian, saying, Take from here thirty men with you and raise Jeremiah the prophet out of the dungeon or cistern pit before he dies.

11 So Ebed-melech took the men with him and went into the house of the king [to a room] under the treasury, and took along from there old rags and worn-out garments and let them down by ropes into the dungeon or cistern pit to Jeremiah.

12 And Ebed-melech the Ethiopian said to Jeremiah, Put now these old rags and worn-out garments under your armpits under the ropes. And Jeremiah did so.

13 So they drew up Jeremiah with the ropes and took him up out of the dungeon or cistern pit; and Jeremiah remained in the court of the guard.

14 Then Zedekiah the king sent and brought Jeremiah the prophet to him into the third entrance that is in the house of the Lord. And the king said to Jeremiah, I am going to ask you something; hide nothing from me.

15 Then Jeremiah said to Zedekiah, If I tell you, will you not surely put me to death? And even if I did give you counsel, you would not listen to me.

16 So Zedekiah the king swore secretly to Jeremiah, As the Lord lives, Who made our lives, I will not put you to death or give you into the hands of these men who seek your life.

17 Then said Jeremiah to Zedekiah, Thus says the Lord God of hosts, the God of Israel: If you will go forth and surrender to the princes of the king of Babylon, then you will live and this city will not be burned with fire; and you will live—you and your house.

18 But if you will not go forth and surrender to the princes of the king of Babylon, then this city will be given into the hands of the Chaldeans and they will burn it with fire; and you will not escape out of their hands.

19 And Zedekiah the king said to Jeremiah, I am afraid of the Jews who have deserted to the Chaldeans, lest the enemy deliver me into their [these former subjects'] hands and they mock me *and* abuse me.

20 But Jeremiah said, They will not deliver you [to them]. Obey, I beg of you, the voice of the Lord, Who speaks to you through me. Then it will be well with you, and you will live.

21 But if you refuse to go forth *and* surrender to them, this is the word [the vision] that the Lord has shown me:

22 Behold, [in it] all the women who are left in the house of the king of Judah will be brought forth to the king of Babylon's princes and will say [to you, King Zedekiah], Your friends have prevailed against your better judgment *and* have deceived you. Now when your feet are sunk in the mire [of trouble], they have turned their backs.

23 All your wives and your children will be brought out to the Chaldeans; and you [yourself] will not escape out of their hands, but you will be seized by the king of Babylon, and you will cause this city [Jerusalem] to be burned with fire.

24 Then Zedekiah said to Jeremiah, Let no man know of this conversation and you will not die.

25 But if the princes hear that I have talked with you, and they come to you and say, Tell us what you said to the king and what he said to you; hide it not from us and we will not put you to death,

26 Then you shall say to them, I was presenting to the king my humble plea that he would not send me back to Jonathan's house to die there.

27 Then came all the princes to Jeremiah and asked him [just what King Zedekiah had anticipated they would ask], and he told them all that the king had commanded. So they left off speaking with him, for what the con-versation [with the king] had been was not discovered.

28 So Jeremiah remained in the court of the guard until the day that Jerusalem was taken [by the Chaldeans].

39 IN THE ninth year of Zedekiah king of Judah, in the tenth month, ˣNebuchadrezzar king of Babylon and all his army came against Jerusalem and besieged it. [Jer. 52:4-27.]

2 And in the eleventh year of Zedekiah, in the fourth month, on the ninth day of the month, they broke into the city.

3 [ʸWhen Jerusalem was taken] all the princes of the king of Babylon came in and sat in the Middle Gate: Nergal-sharezer, Samgar-nebo, Sar-sechim [the Rabsaris] a chief of the eunuchs, and Nergal-sharezer [II, the Rabmag] a chief of the magicians, with all the rest of the officials of the king of Babylon.

4 And when Zedekiah king of Judah and all the men of war saw them, they fled and went forth out of the city at night by way of the king's garden, through the gate between the two walls, and [the king] went out toward the Arabah (the Jordan Valley).

5 But the Chaldean army pursued them and overtook Zedekiah in the plains of Jericho. And when they had taken him, they brought him up to Nebuchadrezzar king of Babylon at Riblah in the [Syrian] land of Hamath, where he pronounced sentence upon him.

6 Then the king of Babylon slew the sons of Zedekiah at Riblah before his eyes; also the king of Babylon slew all the nobles of Judah.

7 Moreover, he put out Zedekiah's eyes and bound him with shackles to take him to Babylon. [Ezek. 12:13.]

---

x See footnote on Jer. 21:2.   **y** This clause has been supplied from the end of chapter 38, where, according to many authorities, many translations have wrongly placed it.

8 And the Chaldeans burned the king's house and the houses of the people and broke down the walls of Jerusalem.

9 Then Nebuzaradan the [chief executioner and] captain of the guard carried away captive to Babylon the rest of the people who remained in the city, along with those who deserted to him, and the remainder of the [so-called better class of] people who were left.

10 But Nebuzaradan the [Babylonian] captain of the guard left in the land of Judah some of the poor of the people who had nothing, giving them vineyards and fields at the same time.

11 Nebuchadrezzar king of Babylon gave command concerning Jeremiah to Nebuzaradan the captain of the guard, saying,

12 Take him and look after him well; do him no harm but deal with him as he may ask of you.

13 So Nebuzaradan the captain of the guard, Nebushasban [the Rabsaris] a chief of the eunuchs, Nergal-sharezer [II, the Rabmag] a chief of the magicians, and all the chief officers of the king of Babylon

14 Sent and took Jeremiah out of the court of the guard and entrusted him to Gedaliah [a prominent man whose father had once saved the prophet's life] son of Ahikam, the son of Shaphan, that he should take him home [with him to Mizpah]. So Jeremiah was released *and* dwelt among the people. [Jer. 26:24.]

15 Now the word of the Lord came to Jeremiah while he was [still] shut up in the court of the guard, saying,

16 Go and say to Ebed-melech the Ethiopian, Thus says the Lord of hosts, the God of Israel: Behold, I will bring to pass My words against this city for evil and not for good; and they will be accomplished before you on that day.

17 But I will deliver you [Ebed-melech] on that day, says the Lord, and you will not be given into the hands of the men of whom you are afraid. [Jer. 38:7-13.]

18 For I will surely deliver you; and you will not fall by the sword, but your life will be [as your only booty and] as a reward of battle to you, because you have put your trust in Me, says the Lord.

40 THE WORD that came to Jeremiah from the Lord after Nebuzaradan the captain of the guard had let him go from Ramah, when he had taken him bound in chains among all who were carried away captive from Jerusalem and Judah, who were taken as exiles to Babylon.

2 And the captain of the guard took Jeremiah and said to him, The Lord your God pronounced evil upon this place.

3 Now the Lord has brought it about and has done as He said: [It is] because you [of Judah] have sinned against the Lord and have not obeyed His voice, therefore this thing has come upon you.

4 Now, see, I am freeing you today [Jeremiah] from the chains upon your hands. If it seems good to you to come with me to Babylon, come, and I will keep an eye on you *and* look after you well. But if it seems bad to you to come with me to Babylon, then do not do it. Behold, all the land is before you; wherever it seems good, right, *and* convenient for you to go, go there.

5 While [Jeremiah] was hesitating, [the captain of the guard] said, Go back then to Gedaliah son of Ahikam, the son of Shaphan, whom the king of Babylon made governor over the cities of Judah, and dwell with him among the people; or go wherever it seems right for you to go. So the captain of the guard gave him an allowance of food and a present and let him go.

6 Then Jeremiah went to Gedaliah son of Ahikam at Mizpah and dwelt with him among the people who were left in the land.

7 Now when all the captains of the forces that were in the open country [of Judah] and their men heard that the king of Babylon had made Gedaliah son of Ahikam governor in the land [of Judah] and had committed to him men, women, and children, those of the poorest of the land who had not been taken into exile to Babylon,

8 They went to Gedaliah at Mizpah—Ishmael son of Nethaniah, Johanan and Jonathan the sons of Kareah, Seraiah son of Tanhumeth, the sons of Ephai the Netophathite, and Jezaniah the son of the Maacathite, they and their men.

9 And Gedaliah son of Ahikam, the son of Shaphan, swore to them and their men, saying, Do not be afraid to serve the Chaldeans; dwell in [this] land and serve the king of Babylon, and it shall be well with you.

10 As for me, I will dwell at Mizpah to stand [for you] before the Chaldeans who come to us [ministering to them and looking after the king's interests]; but as for you, gather the juice [of the grape], summer fruits and oil, and store them in your utensils [chosen for such purposes], and dwell in your cities that you have seized.

11 Likewise, when all the Jews who were in Moab and among the people of Ammon and in Edom and who were in all the other countries heard that the king of Babylon had left a remnant in Judah and had set over them [as governor] Gedaliah son of Ahikam, the son of Shaphan,

12 Then all the Jews returned from all the places to which they had been driven and came to the land of Judah, to Gedaliah at Mizpah, and gathered a great abundance of juice [of the grape] and summer fruits.

13 Moreover, Johanan son of Kareah and all the captains of the forces that were in the open country came to Gedaliah at Mizpah

14 And said to him, Do you know that Baalis king of the Ammonites has sent Ishmael son of Nethaniah to take your life? But Gedaliah son of Ahikam did not believe them.

15 Then Johanan son of Kareah spoke to Gedaliah in Mizpah secretly, saying, Let me go, I pray you, and I will slay Ishmael son of Nethaniah, and no man will know it. Why should he slay you and cause all the Jews who are gathered to you to be scattered and the remnant of Judah to perish?

16 But Gedaliah son of Ahikam said to Johanan son of Kareah, You shall not do this thing, for you speak falsely of Ishmael.

41 NOW IN the seventh month [of that year] Ishmael son of Nethaniah, the son of Elishama, of the royal descendants and one of the princes of the king, came [at the instigation of the Ammonites] with ten men to Gedaliah son of Ahikam in Mizpah. As they were eating a meal together there in Mizpah,

2 Ishmael son of Nethaniah and the ten men who were with him arose and struck down Gedaliah son of Ahikam, the son of Shaphan, with the sword and killed him, the one whom the king of Babylon had made governor over the land. [II Kings 25:25.]

3 Ishmael [manipulated by the Ammonites] also slew all the Jews who were with Gedaliah at Mizpah, and the Chaldean soldiers who were found there.

4 And the second day after the slaying of Gedaliah, before anyone knew about it,

5 There came eighty men from

Shechem, from Shiloh, and from Samaria, having their beards shaved off and their clothes torn and having cut themselves, bringing cereal offerings and incense, going up [to Jerusalem] to present them in the house of the Lord.

6 And Ishmael son of Nethaniah went out from Mizpah to meet them, weeping all the way as he went. As he met them, he said to them, Come to Gedaliah son of Ahikam.

7 And when they came into the city, Ishmael son of Nethaniah slew them, and cast them into the midst of the [city] cistern pit—he and the men with him.

8 But ten men were among them who said to Ishmael, Do not kill us! For we have stores hidden in the field—of wheat and barley and oil and honey. So he refrained and did not slay them with their brethren.

9 Now the cistern pit into which Ishmael had cast all the dead bodies of the men whom he had slain in addition to Gedaliah was the one which Asa the king [of Judah] had once made for fear of Baasha king of Israel [should Baasha lay siege to Mizpah]. Ishmael son of Nethaniah filled it with those who were slain.

10 Then Ishmael carried away captive all the rest of the people who were in Mizpah—even the king's daughters and all the people who remained in Mizpah, whom Nebuzaradan the captain of the guard had committed to Gedaliah son of Ahikam. Ishmael son of Nethaniah carried them away captive and departed to cross over [the Jordan] to the Ammonites.

11 But when Johanan son of Kareah and all the captains of the forces that were with him heard of all the evil that Ishmael son of Nethaniah had done,

12 They took all their men and went to fight with Ishmael son of Nethaniah and found him by the great pool that is in Gibeon.

13 Now when all the people who were [captives] with Ishmael saw Johanan son of Kareah and all the captains of the forces that were with him, they were glad.

14 So all the people whom Ishmael had carried away captive from Mizpah turned around and came back, and went to Johanan son of Kareah.

15 But Ishmael son of Nethaniah escaped from Johanan with eight men and went to the Ammonites.

16 Then Johanan son of Kareah and all the captains of the forces that were with him took from Mizpah all the remainder of the people whom he had recovered from Ishmael son of Nethaniah after he had slain Gedaliah son of Ahikam: [they were] the soldiers, the women, the children, and the eunuchs whom [Johanan] had brought back from Gibeon.

17 And they departed and stayed at the lodging place of Chimham, which is near Bethlehem, [intending] to go to Egypt

18 Because of the Chaldeans; for they were afraid of them because Ishmael son of Nethaniah had slain Gedaliah son of Ahikam, whom the king of Babylon had made governor over the land [and whose death the king could avenge without much discrimination].

42 THEN ALL the captains of the forces, and Johanan son of Kareah and Jezaniah [Azariah] son of Hoshaiah, and all the people from the least even to the greatest came near

2 And said to Jeremiah the prophet, We beseech you that you will let our supplication be presented before you and that you will pray to the Lord your God for us, even for all this remnant [of the people of Judah]; for whereas we were once many, there are but a few of us left, as you see with your [own] eyes.

3 [Pray] that the Lord your God may

show us the way in which we should walk and the thing that we should do.

4 Then Jeremiah the prophet said to them, I have heard you. Behold, I will pray to the Lord your God according to your words; and it will be that whatever thing the Lord will answer you, I will declare it to you; I will keep nothing back from you.

5 Then they said to Jeremiah, May the Lord be a true and faithful witness against us if we fail to do according to all the things that the Lord your God sends you to tell us.

6 Whether it is good or evil, we will obey the voice of the Lord our God, to Whom we are sending you [to inquire], that it may be well with us when we obey the voice of the Lord our God.

7 And after ten days the word of the Lord came to Jeremiah.

8 Then he called Johanan son of Kareah and all the captains of the forces that were with him and all the people from the least even to the greatest,

9 And said to them, Thus says the Lord, the God of Israel, to Whom you sent me to present your supplication before Him:

10 If you will remain in this land, then I will build you up and not pull you down, and I will plant you and not pull you up; for I will relent *and* comfort *and* ease Myself concerning the evil that [in chastisement] I have done to you [and I will substitute mercy and loving-kindness for judgment]. [Jer. 31:4, 28.]

11 Be not afraid of the king of Babylon, of whom you are fearful [with the profound and reverent dread inspired by deity]; be not afraid of him, says

speak the Word

the Lord, for [he is a mere man, while I am the all-wise, all-powerful, and ever-present God] I [the Lord] am with you to save you and to deliver you from his hand.

12 And I will grant mercy to you, that he may have mercy on you and permit you to remain in your own land.

13 But if you say, We will not dwell in this land, and so disobey the voice of the Lord your God,

14 Saying, No, but we will go to the land of Egypt, where we will not see war or hear the sound of the trumpet or be hungry for bread, and we will dwell there,

15 Then hear the word of the Lord, O remnant of Judah. Thus says the Lord of hosts, the God of Israel: If you are fully determined to go to Egypt and you do go to dwell there temporarily,

16 Then the sword which you fear shall overtake you there in the land of Egypt, and the famine of which you are afraid shall follow close after you to Egypt *and* in it, and there you shall die.

17 So will it be with all the men who set their faces to go to Egypt to dwell there temporarily; they will die by the sword, by famine, and by pestilence; none of them will remain or survive the evil that I will bring upon them.

18 For thus says the Lord of hosts, the God of Israel: As My anger and My wrath have been poured forth upon the inhabitants of Jerusalem, so shall My wrath be poured forth upon you when you enter Egypt. You shall be a detested thing, an astonishment *and* horror, a curse, a thing lightly esteemed *and* a taunt *and* a reproach; you shall see this place no more.

19 The Lord has said to you, O

God, I pray that You would show me the way in which I should walk and the things that I should do.
ADAPTED FROM JEREMIAH **42:3**

remnant of Judah, Do not go to Egypt. Know for a certainty that I [Jeremiah] have warned *and* testified to you this day

20 That you have dealt deceitfully against your own lives; for you sent me [Jeremiah] to the Lord your God, saying, Pray for us to the Lord our God; and whatever the Lord our God says, declare it to us and we will do it. **21** And I have this day declared it to you, but you have not obeyed the voice of the Lord your God in anything that He sent me to tell you. **22** Now therefore know for a certainty that you shall die by the sword, by famine, and by pestilence in the place [Egypt] where you desire to go to dwell temporarily.

43

AND WHEN Jeremiah had finished speaking to all the people all these words of the Lord their God—everything for which the Lord their God had sent him to them— **2** Then Azariah son of Hoshaiah and Johanan son of Kareah and all the proud *and* insolent men said to Jeremiah, You are not telling the truth! The Lord our God has not sent you to say, Do not go into Egypt to dwell there temporarily. **3** But Baruch son of Neriah is setting you against us to deliver us into the hands of the Chaldeans, so they may put us to death or carry us away captive to Babylon. **4** So Johanan son of Kareah and all the captains of the forces and all the people did not obey the voice of the Lord to remain in the land of Judah. **5** But Johanan son of Kareah and all the captains of the forces took all the remnant of Judah who had returned to dwell in the land of Judah from all the nations to which they had been driven—

6 Even men, women, and children, the king's daughters, and every person whom Nebuzaradan the captain of the guard had left with Gedaliah son of Ahikam, the son of Shaphan; also he took Jeremiah the prophet and Baruch son of Neriah. **7** So they came into the land of Egypt—for they obeyed not the voice of the Lord. And they came to Tahpanhes. **8** Then came the word of the Lord to Jeremiah in Tahpanhes, saying, **9** Take large stones in your hands and hide them in the mortar in the pavement of brick which is at the entrance of Pharaoh's house in Tahpanhes, in the sight of the men of Judah; **10** And say to them, Thus says the Lord of hosts, the God of Israel: Behold, I will send and take ᶻNebuchadrezzar king of Babylon, My servant [because he works for Me], and I [through him] will set his throne upon these stones that I have hidden; and his [glittering, royal] canopy will be stretched over them. [Ezek. 29:19, 20.] **11** And he shall come and smite the land of Egypt, giving such as are [destined] for death, to death, and such as are [destined] for captivity, to captivity, and such as are [destined] for the sword, to the sword. **12** And I [through him] will kindle a fire in the temples of the gods of Egypt; and he will burn [the houses] and carry [the people] away captive. And he will array himself with the land of Egypt, as a shepherd puts on his garment [as he wills and when he chooses]; and he will go away from there in peace. **13** [Nebuchadrezzar] shall break also the images *and* obelisks of Heliopolis [called On or Beth-shemesh—house of the sun] in the land of Egypt, and the temples of the gods of Egypt shall he burn with fire.

z See footnote on Jer. 21:2.

44

THE WORD that came to Jeremiah concerning all the Jews who were dwelling in the land of Egypt—at Migdol, at Tahpanhes, at Memphis—and in the country of Pathros, saying,

2 Thus says the Lord of hosts, the God of Israel: You have seen all the evil that I brought upon Jerusalem and upon all the cities of Judah; and see, this day they are a desolation and no man dwells in them

3 Because of the wickedness which they committed, provoking Me to anger in that they went to burn incense to serve other gods that they did not know—neither they, nor you, nor your fathers.

4 Yet I sent to you all My servants the prophets earnestly *and* persistently, saying, Oh, do not do this loathsome *and* shamefully vile thing that I hate *and* abhor!

5 But they did not listen *and* obey or submit *and* consent to turn from their wickedness and burn no incense to other gods.

6 Therefore My wrath and My anger were poured out and were kindled in the cities of Judah and in the streets of Jerusalem; and they became wasted and desolate, as it is this day.

7 Therefore now thus says the Lord God of hosts, the God of Israel: Why do you commit this great evil against yourselves that will cut off from you man and woman, infant and weaned child, out of Judah, to leave yourselves with none remaining?

8 Why do you provoke Me to anger with the works (idols) of your own hands, burning incense to other gods in the land of Egypt, where you [of your own accord] have come to dwell temporarily, that you might be cut off and become a curse and a reproach (an object of reviling and taunts) among all the nations of the earth?

9 Have you forgotten the wickedness of your fathers, the wickedness of the kings of Judah, the wickedness of their wives [who clung to their foreign gods], your own wickedness, and the wickedness of your wives [who imitated their queens], which they committed in the land of Judah and in the streets of Jerusalem?

10 They are not humbled (contrite, penitent, and bruised for their guilt and iniquities) even to this day, neither have they feared *and* revered [Me] nor walked in My law or My statutes which I set before you and before your fathers. [Jer. 6:15; 26:4-6; 44:23.]

11 Therefore thus says the Lord of hosts, the God of Israel: Behold, I will set My face against you for evil—even to cut off all Judah [from the land].

12 And I will take away the remnant of Judah who have set their faces to come into the land of Egypt to dwell here temporarily [fleeing to Egypt instead of surrendering to the Chaldeans as directed by the Lord through Jeremiah], and they will all be consumed and will fall in the land of Egypt; they will be consumed by the sword and by famine. From the least even to the greatest, they shall die by the sword and by famine. And they will be a detestable thing, an astonishment, a curse, and a reproach (an object of horror, reviling, and taunts).

13 For I will punish all the inhabitants of the land of Egypt as I have punished Jerusalem—by the sword, by famine, and by pestilence—

14 So that none of the remnant of Judah who have come to the land of Egypt to dwell temporarily shall escape or survive or return to the land of Judah, to which they desire *and* lift up their souls to return to dwell there; for none shall return except [a few] fugitives.

15 Then all the men who knew that their wives were burning incense to other gods, and all the women who stood by—a great assembly—even all

the people who dwelt in Pathros in the land of Egypt, answered Jeremiah: **16** As for the word that you have spoken to us in the name of the Lord, we will not listen to *or* obey you.

17 But we will certainly perform every word of the vows we have made: to burn incense to the ªqueen of heaven and to pour out drink offerings to her as we have done—we and our fathers, our kings and our princes—in the cities of Judah and in the streets of Jerusalem; for then we had plenty of food and were well off *and* prosperous and saw no evil.

18 But since we stopped burning incense to the queen of heaven and pouring out drink offerings to her, we have lacked everything and have been consumed by the sword and by famine.

19 [And the wives said] When we burned incense to the queen of heaven and poured out drink offerings to her, did we make cakes [in the shape of a star] to represent *and* honor her and pour out drink offerings to her without [the knowledge and approval of] our husbands?

20 Then Jeremiah said to all the people—to the men and to the women and to all the people who had given him that answer—

21 The incense that you burned in the cities of Judah and in the streets of Jerusalem—you and your fathers, your kings and your princes, and the people of the land—did not the Lord [earnestly] remember [your idolatrous wickedness] and did it not come into His mind?

22 The Lord could no longer endure the evil of your doings and the abominations which you have committed; because of them therefore has your land become a desolation and an [astonishing] waste and a curse, without inhabitants, as it is this day.

23 Because you have burned incense

[to idols] and because you have sinned against the Lord and have not obeyed the voice of the Lord or walked in His law and in His statutes and in His testimonies, therefore this evil has fallen upon you, as it is this day.

24 Moreover, Jeremiah said to all the people, including all the women, Hear the word of the Lord, all you of Judah who are in the land of Egypt,

25 Thus says the Lord of hosts, the God of Israel: You and your wives have both declared with your mouths and fulfilled it with your hands, saying, We will surely perform our vows that we have vowed to burn incense to the queen of heaven and to pour out drink offerings to her. [Surely] then confirm your vows and [surely] perform your vows! [If you will defy all My warnings to you, then, by all means, go ahead!]

26 Therefore hear the word of the Lord, all [you people of] Judah who dwell in the land of Egypt: Behold, I have sworn by My great name, says the Lord, that My name shall no more be invoked by the mouth of any man of Judah in all the land of Egypt, saying, As the Lord God lives.

27 Behold, I am watching over them for evil and not for good; and all the men of Judah who are in the land of Egypt shall be consumed by the sword and by famine until there is an end of them *and* they are all destroyed.

28 Yet a small number who escape the sword shall return out of the land of Egypt to the land of Judah; and all the remnant of Judah who came to the land of Egypt to dwell temporarily shall know whose words shall stand, Mine or theirs.

29 And this will be the sign to you, says the Lord, that I will punish you in this place, so that you may know that My words will surely stand against you for evil.

a See footnote on Jer. 7:18.

30 Thus says the Lord: Behold, I will give Pharaoh Hophra king of Egypt into the hands of his enemies and into the hands of those who seek his life, just as I gave Zedekiah king of Judah into the hand of [b]Nebuchadrezzar king of Babylon, who was his enemy and was seeking his life.

45

THE WORD that Jeremiah the prophet spoke to Baruch son of Neriah, when he had written these words in a book at the dictation of Jeremiah, in the fourth year of Jehoiakim son of Josiah king of Judah, saying,

2 Thus says the Lord, the God of Israel, unto you, O Baruch:

3 You said, Woe is me now! For the Lord has added sorrow to my pain; I am weary with my groaning *and* sighing and I find no rest.

4 Say this to him: The Lord speaks thus: Behold, what I have built I will break down, and that which I have planted I will pluck up—and this means the whole land.

5 And should you [c]seek great things for yourself? Seek them not; for behold, I will bring evil upon all flesh, says the Lord, but your life I will give to you [as your only booty and] as a [snatched] prize of war wherever you go.

46

THE WORD of the Lord that came to Jeremiah the prophet concerning *and* against the [Gentile] nations.

2 Concerning *and* against Egypt: against the army of Pharaoh Necho king of Egypt, which was by the river Euphrates at Carchemish, which [d]Nebuchadrezzar king of Babylon smote *and* defeated in the fourth year of Jehoiakim son of Josiah king of Judah: [Isa. 19-20; Ezek. 29-32; Zech. 14:18, 19.]

3 Put in order the buckler and shield, and advance for battle!

4 Harness the horses, and mount, you horsemen! Stand forth with your helmets! Polish the spears, put on the coats of mail!

5 Why have I seen it? They are dismayed and have turned backward, and their mighty warriors are beaten down. They flee in haste and look not back; terror is on every side! says the Lord. [Ps. 31:13; Jer. 6:25; 20:3, 10; 49:29.]

6 Let not the swift flee nor the mighty man escape; in the north by the river Euphrates they stumble and fall.

7 Who is this that rises up like the Nile [River], like the branches [of the Nile in the delta of Egypt] whose waters surge *and* toss?

8 Egypt rises like the Nile, like the rivers whose waters surge *and* toss. She says, I will rise, I will cover the earth; I will destroy cities and their inhabitants.

9 Go up, you horses, and drive furiously, you chariots! Let the warriors go forth—men of Ethiopia and Put who handle the shield, men of Lud who are skilled in handling and stringing the bow.

b See footnote on Jer. 21:2. **c** Baruch plays a role familiar in normal human life today—that of having to take second place, having to play second fiddle. He was of high birth; his grandfather Maaseiah was governor of Jerusalem in the days of King Josiah (II Chron. 34:8). Considering all that Baruch was doing to make Jeremiah's prophecies permanent by recording them for posterity, it is not surprising that he seems to have expected to share the prophet's rewards. "To play a prominent part in the impending crisis, to be the hero of a national revival, to gain the favor of the conqueror he announced," seems to have been his high ideal, his glorious dream. When its realization was denied him, "he sank in despair at the seeming fruitlessness of his efforts" (Sir William Smith, *A Dictionary of the Bible*). Yet Baruch is an excellent illustration of how little the gift of prophecy depended on men, and how completely it remained for God to grant or deny prominence and recognition to His perhaps equally deserving servants. But each man's eternal rewards are proportioned according to his faithfulness, and not according to his earthly recognition or the lack of it (Matt. 25:14-30). **d** See footnote on Jer. 21:2.

10 But that day is a day of the Lord, the Lord of hosts—a day of vengeance, that He may avenge Himself on His adversaries. And the sword shall devour, and it shall be satiated and shall drink its fill of their blood; for the Lord, the Lord of hosts has a sacrifice [like that of a great sin offering] in the north country by the river Euphrates.

11 Go up into Gilead and take [healing] balm, O Virgin Daughter of Egypt! In vain do you use many medicines; for you there is no healing *or* remedy.

12 The nations have heard of your disgrace *and* shame, and your cry has filled the earth. For warrior has stumbled against *and* thrown down warrior, and they have fallen both of them together.

13 The word that the Lord spoke to Jeremiah the prophet concerning the coming of ᵈNebuchadrezzar king of Babylon and his smiting of the land of Egypt:

14 Declare in Egypt and proclaim in Migdol; and publish in Memphis and in Tahpanhes; say, Stand forth and get yourself ready, for the sword devours round about you.

15 Why is your strong one [the sacred bull-god Apis] swept *and* dragged away? He stood not, because the Lord drove him *and* thrust him down.

16 [The Lord] made many to stumble *and* fall; yes, they fell one upon another. And they said, Arise, and let us go back to our own people and to the land of our birth, away from the sword of the oppressor.

17 They cried there, Pharaoh king of Egypt is destroyed *and* is only a noise; he has let the appointed time [in which God had him on probation] pass by!

18 As I live, says the King, Whose name is the Lord of hosts, surely like Tabor among the mountains and like Carmel by the sea, so shall he [the

king of Babylon, standing out above other rulers] come.

19 O you daughter who dwells in Egypt *and* you who dwell with her, furnish yourselves [with all you will need] to go into exile, for Memphis will be waste, desolate, *and* burned up, without inhabitant.

20 Egypt is a very fair heifer [like Apis the bull-god, to which the country is, so to speak, espoused], but destruction [a gadfly] is coming—out of the north it is coming [against her]!

21 Also her hired troops in the midst of her are like fatted calves [in the stall], for they also are turned back and are fleeing together; they do not stand, because the day of their calamity is coming upon them, the time of their visitation (their inspection and punishment).

22 The sound [of Egypt fleeing from the enemy] is like the rustling of an escaping serpent, for her foes advance with a mighty army and come against her with axes, like those who fell trees *and* cut wood.

23 They shall cut down her forest, says the Lord, though it is impenetrable, because they [the invading army] are more numerous than locusts and cannot be counted.

24 The Daughter of Egypt shall be disgraced; she shall be delivered into the hands of the people of the north [the Chaldeans].

25 The Lord of hosts, the God of Israel, says: Behold, I will visit punishment upon Amon [the chief god of the sacred city, the capital of Upper Egypt] of No *or* Thebes, and upon Pharaoh and Egypt, with her gods and her kings—even Pharaoh and all those [Jews and others] who put their trust in [Pharaoh as a support against Babylon].

26 And I will deliver them into the hands of those who seek their lives, and into the hand of Nebuchadrezzar king of Babylon, and into the hands of his servants. Afterward [Egypt] will be ᵉinhabited as in the days of old, says the Lord.

27 But fear not, O My servant Jacob, and be not dismayed, O Israel. For behold, I will save you from afar, and your offspring from the land of their exile; and Jacob will return and be quiet and at ease, and none will make him afraid.

28 Fear not, O Jacob My servant, says the Lord, for I am with you. For I will make a full *and* complete end of all the nations to which I have driven you; yet I will not make a full end of you. But I will chasten *and* correct you in just measure, and I will not hold you guiltless by any means *or* leave you unpunished.

47 THE WORD of the Lord that came to Jeremiah the prophet concerning the Philistines before Pharaoh smote [the Philistine city] Gaza. [Isa. 14:29-31; Ezek. 25:15-17; Amos 1:6-8; Zeph. 2:4-7; Zech. 9:5-7.]

2 Thus says the Lord: Behold, waters are rising out of the north and shall become an overflowing stream and shall overflow the land and all that is in it, the city and those who dwell in it. Then the men shall cry, and all the inhabitants of the land [of Philistia] shall wail.

3 At the noise of the stamping of the hoofs of [the Chaldean king's] war-horses, at the rattling of his chariots, and at the rumbling of his wheels, the fathers do not look back to their children, so feeble are their hands [with terror]

4 Because of the day that is coming to destroy all the Philistines and to cut off from Tyre and Sidon every helper who remains. For the Lord is destroying the Philistines, the remnant [still surviving] of the isle *or* coastland of Caphtor [where the Philistines originated]. [Amos 9:7.]

5 Baldness [as a token of mourning] will come upon Gaza; Ashkelon will be cut off *and* be dumb. O remnant of their valley *and* of the giants, how long will you gash yourselves [as a token of mourning]?

6 O you sword of the Lord, how long will it be before you are quiet? Put yourself into your scabbard; rest and be still.

7 How can it [the sword of the Lord] be quiet when the Lord has given it an assignment to discharge? Against Ashkelon and against the [whole Philistine] seashore He has appointed it.

48 CONCERNING MOAB: Thus says the Lord of hosts, the God of Israel: Woe to [the city of] Nebo, for it is laid

speak the Word

God, I will not fear, because You are with me.
ADAPTED FROM JEREMIAH 46:28

ᵉ It is startling to realize that God, through His prophets, accurately foretold in detail the future of every one of the prominent nations of Old Testament times, often specifying the fate of particular rulers and chief cities as well. It will greatly increase the reader's interest if he or she will look up the literal fulfillment of these prophecies as he or she comes to them, as indicated in the textual references or the footnotes. Notice how definite and specific the prophecies are; what was said of Babylon, for instance, would not have been applicable to Egypt or Ammon or Sidon. And history proves their fulfillment. If there was no other evidence that there is a God and that the Bible is inspired by Him, the fulfillment of prophecy in history should be sufficient proof for any person capable of thinking it through. Nor are the prophecies against some nations recorded by only one writer, but a number of them, widely separated by time and circumstances, set them down in writing. Let us approach these records with awe and awakened vision; we are on holy ground.

waste! Kiriathaim is put to shame and taken; Misgab [the high fortress] is put to shame, broken down, *and* crushed. [Isa. 15-16; 25:10-12; Ezek. 25:8-11; Amos 2:1-3; Zeph. 2:8-11.]

2 The glory of Moab is no more; in Heshbon [a border town between Reuben and Gad, east of the Jordan River] they planned evil against her, saying, Come, let us cut her off from being a nation. You also, O [town of] Madmen, shall be brought to silence; the sword shall pursue you.

3 The sound of a cry from Horonaim, [a cry of] desolation and great destruction!

4 Moab is destroyed; her little ones have caused a cry to be heard [as far as Zoar].

5 For the ascent of Luhith will be climbed [by successive bands of fugitives] with continual weeping; for on the descent of Horonaim they have heard the distress of the cry of destruction.

6 Flee! Save your lives! But they shall be like a destitute *and* forsaken person in the wilderness.

7 For because you have trusted in your works [your bungling idol images] and in your treasures [instead of in God], you shall also be taken. And Chemosh [your god] shall go into captivity, his priests and his princes together.

8 And the destroyer shall come upon every city; no city shall escape. The [Jordan] valley also shall perish, and the plain shall be devastated, as the Lord has said.

9 Give wings to Moab, for [by that means only] she will flee and get away; her cities will be desolate, without any to dwell in them.

10 Cursed be he who does the work of the Lord negligently [with slackness, deceitfully]; and cursed be he who keeps back his sword from blood [in executing judgment pronounced by the Lord].

11 Moab has been at ease from his youth, and he has settled on his lees [like wine] and has not been drawn off from one vessel to another, neither has he gone into exile. Therefore his taste remains in him, and his scent has not changed.

12 Therefore behold, the days are coming, says the Lord, when I shall send to [Moab] tilters who shall tilt him up and shall empty his vessels and break his bottles (earthenware) in pieces.

13 And Moab shall be ashamed of Chemosh [his god], as the house of Israel was ashamed of Bethel, their confidence. [I Kings 12:28, 29.]

14 How can you say, We are heroes and mighty men in the war?

15 Moab has been made desolate, and his cities have gone up [in smoke and flame]; and his chosen young men have gone down to the slaughter, says the King, Whose name is the Lord of hosts.

16 The destruction of Moab is coming near, and his calamity hastens swiftly.

17 Bemoan him, all you [nations] who are around him, and all you [nations more remote] who know his name; say, How broken is the mighty scepter [of national power] and the splendid rod [of glory]!

18 Come down from your glory, you inhabitant of the Daughter of 'Dibon, and sit on the ground among the thirsty! For the destroyer of Moab is advancing against you; he will destroy your strongholds.

19 O inhabitant of Aroer, stand by

f Dibon, known today as Dhiban, stands on two hills. The "Moabite Stone," which contains a record of Moabite history, was found among the ruins of Dibon. The Aroer mentioned in this chapter (Jer. 48:19) stood on the north side of the river Arnon (Jer. 48:20), just south of Dibon. Mesha records on the "Moabite Stone" that he "built [restored] the city [Aroer] and made the road over the Arnon" (*The Cambridge Bible*).

the way and watch! Ask him who flees and her who escapes, What has happened?

20 Moab is put to shame, for she is broken down. Wail and cry out! Tell by [the banks of] the Arnon that Moab is laid waste (destroyed).

21 Judgment has come upon the land of the plain—upon Holon and Jahzah and Mephaath,

22 And upon Dibon and Nebo and Beth-diblathaim,

23 And upon Kiriathaim and Beth-gamul and Beth-meon,

24 And upon Kerioth and Bozrah—and all the cities of the land of Moab, far and near.

25 The horn (strength) of Moab is cut off, and his arm [of authority] is shattered, says the Lord.

26 Make him drunk, for he has magnified himself against the Lord [by resisting Reuben's occupation of the land the Lord had assigned him]. Moab also shall splash in his vomit, and he too shall be held in derision. [Num. 22:1-7.]

27 For was not Israel [an object of] derision to you? Was he found among thieves—since whenever you speak of him you wag your head [in scorn]?

28 O you inhabitants of Moab, leave the cities and dwell among the rocks, and be like the dove that makes her nest in the walls of the yawning ravine.

29 We have heard of the [giddy] pride of Moab, the extremely proud one—his loftiness, his arrogance, his conceit, and the haughtiness of his heart.

30 I know his insolent wrath, says the Lord, and the nothingness of his boastings *and* his deeds; they are false *and* have accomplished nothing.

31 Therefore I will wail over Moab, and I will cry out over the whole of Moab. Over the men of Kir-heres (Kir-hareseth) there will be sighing *and* mourning. [Isa. 15:1; 16:7, 11.]

32 O vines of Sibmah, I weep for you more than the weeping of Jazer [over its ruins and wasted vineyards]. Your tendrils [of influence] have gone over the sea, reaching even to Jazer. The destroyer has fallen upon your summer fruit harvest and your [season's] crop of grapes.

33 Joy and gladness are taken away from the fruitful orchards *and* fields and from the land of Moab. And I have made the juice [of the grape] to fail from what is pressed out in the vats; no one treads [the grapes] with shouting. Their shouting is no shouting [of joy, but is a battle cry].

34 From the cry of Heshbon even to Elealeh even to Jahaz have they uttered their voice, from Zoar even to Horonaim and Eglath-shelishiyah [like a three-year-old heifer], for even the waters of Nimrim have become desolations.

35 Moreover, I will cause to cease in Moab, says the Lord, the one who ascends *and* offers in the high place and the one who burns incense to his gods.

36 Therefore My heart moans *and* sighs for Moab like flutes, and My heart moans *and* sighs like flutes for the men of Kir-heres (Kir-hareseth); therefore [the remnant of] the abundant riches they gained has perished.

37 For every head is shaven bald and every beard cut off; upon all the hands are cuts (slashes) and upon the loins is sackcloth [all to express mourning]. [Isa. 15:2, 3.]

38 On all the housetops of Moab and in its streets there is lamentation everywhere, for I have broken Moab like a vessel in which there is no pleasure, says the Lord.

39 How it is broken down! How they wail! How Moab has turned his back in shame! So Moab has become [an object of] a derision and a [horrifying] terror to all who are round about him.

40 For thus says the Lord: Behold, he

[Babylon] shall fly swiftly like an eagle and shall spread out his wings against Moab. [Ezek. 17:3.]

41 Kerioth [and the cities] shall be taken and the strongholds seized; and the hearts of the mighty warriors of Moab in that day shall be as the heart of a woman in her pangs [in child-birth].

42 And Moab shall be ᵍdestroyed from being a nation, because he has magnified himself against the Lord.

43 Terror and pit and snare are before you, O inhabitant of Moab, says the Lord. [Isa. 24:7.]

44 He who flees from the terror will fall into the pit, and he who gets up out of the pit will be taken *and* caught in the trap *or* snare; for I will bring upon it, even upon Moab, the year of their visitation (their inspection and inflic-tion of punishment), says the Lord.

45 In the shadow of Heshbon the fugi-tives stand powerless (stopped in their tracks, helpless and without strength), for a fire has gone forth from Heshbon, a flame from the midst of Sihon; it has destroyed the corner of Moab and the crowns of the heads of the ones in tumult [the proud Moabites].

46 Woe to you, O Moab! The people of [the god] Chemosh *are* undone; for your sons are taken away captive and your daughters into captivity.

47 Yet will I reverse the captivity *and* ᵍrestore the fortunes of Moab in the latter days, says the Lord. Thus far is the judgment on Moab.

49

CONCERNING *and* against the Ammonites: Thus says the Lord: Has Israel no sons [to return after their captivity and claim the territory of Gad east of the Jordan which the Ammonites have taken over]? Has [Israel's Gad] no heir? Why then has Milcom [the god the Ammonites call their king] dispos-sessed *and* inherited Gad, and [why do] his people dwell in Gad's cities?

2 Therefore behold, the days are coming, says the Lord, when I will cause an alarm of war to be heard against Rabbah of the Ammonites; and it [the high ground on which it stands] will become a desolate heap, and its daughter [villages] will be burned with fire. Then will Israel dis-possess those who dispossessed him, says the Lord. [Ezek. 21:28-32; 25:1-7, 11; Amos 1:13-15; Zeph. 2:8-11.]

3 Wail, O Heshbon [in Moab, just south of Ammon], for Ai [in Ammon] is laid waste! Cry out, you daughter [villages] of Rabbah! Gird yourselves with sackcloth, lament, and run to and fro inside the [sheepfold] enclosures; for Milcom [the god-king] shall go into exile, together with his priests and his princes.

4 Why do you boast of your valleys? Your valley flows away, O [Ammon] rebellious *and* faithless daughter, who trusted in her treasures, who said, Who can come against me?

5 Behold, I will bring terror upon you, says the Lord, the Lord of hosts, from all who are round about you; and you will be driven out, each man fleeing straight before him [without thought of his neighbor], and there will be no one to gather together the fugitives.

6 And ʰafterward I will reverse the

---

g Nebuchadnezzar (605-562 BC) subjugated the Moabites, but they continued to exist as a race into the first century AD (though the national existence of both Moab and Ammon seems to have ended long before the time of Christ). This in itself is a remarkable fulfillment of prophecy; but the fact that Moab's fortunes are to be restored "in the latter days" (Jer. 48:47), and have proceeded toward that end before our very eyes, is even more startling. Yet Moab is only one of the numerous nations whose fate was accurately written down in advance by the ancient prophets of God. h As complete and continuous as the desolation of Moab and Ammon was for so many long centuries, yet God is keeping His word for their restoration "in the latter days" (Jer. 48:47) in a remarkable manner. For instance, Amman, the capital of the Hashemite Kingdom of Jordan (formerly called Transjordania, captivity of the children of Ammon *and* restore their fortunes, says the Lord.

7 Concerning *and* against Edom: Thus says the Lord of hosts: Is there no longer wisdom in Teman [a district in Edom]? Has counsel vanished from the intelligent *and* prudent? Is their wisdom all poured out *and* used up? [Isa. 34; 63:1-6; Ezek. 25:12-14; 35; Amos 1:11, 12; Obad. 1-16; Mal. 1:2-5.]

8 Flee, turn back, dwell deep [in the deserts to escape the Chaldeans], O inhabitants of Dedan [neighbor of Edom]! For I will bring the calamity *and* destruction of Esau upon him [Edom] when I inspect *and* punish him.

9 If grape gatherers came to you, would they not leave some ungleaned grapes? If thieves came by night, would they not destroy only what is enough [for them]?

10 But I have stripped Esau (Edom) bare; I have uncovered his hiding places, and he cannot hide himself. His offspring will be destroyed, with his brethren and his neighbors; and he will be no more.

11 Leave your fatherless children; I will [do what is necessary to] preserve them alive. And let [those who have been made] your widows trust *and* confide in Me.

12 For thus says the Lord: Behold, they [Israel] whose rule was not to drink the cup [of wrath] shall assuredly drink—and are you to remain unpunished? You shall not go unpunished, but you shall surely drink. [Jer. 25:28, 29.]

13 For I have sworn by Myself, says the Lord, that Bozrah [in Edom, between Petra and the Dead Sea] shall become a horror, a reproach, a waste, and a curse; and all its cities shall be ¹perpetual wastes.

14 I have heard a report from the Lord, and a messenger is sent to the nations, saying, Gather together and come against her! And rise up for the battle.

15 For, behold, I will make you [Edom] small among the nations and despised among men. [Ezek. 35:9.]

16 Your [object of] horror (your idol) has deceived you, and the pride of your heart [has deceived you], O you who dwell in the clefts of the rock [Sela or ʲPetra], who hold *and* occupy the height of the hill. Though you make your nest as high as the eagle's, I will bring you down from there, says the Lord.

17 And Edom shall be an astonishment *and* a horror; everyone who goes by it shall be astonished *and* shall hiss with horror at all its plagues *and* disasters.

18 As [it was] in the overthrow of Sodom and Gomorrah and their neighboring cities, says the Lord, no man shall dwell there; neither shall a son of man live in it temporarily.

19 See, there comes up one [Nebuchadnezzar] like a lion from [lurking in] the jungles (the pride) of the Jordan against the strong habitation [of Edom] *and* into the permanent pastures; for in a twinkling I will drive

---

and in Bible times the ancient Rabbah of Ammon), was a mere village in 1900, but by 1960 it was a city of 200,000 inhabitants. One can only stand in awe and reverent amazement at the precision with which the prophecies of the Word of God are being carried out in the present day and age. **i** How except by divine inspiration could the prophets have foretold that Edom's desolation would be perpetual? After 2,500 years the statement is so literally true that in the land of Edom, where millions once lived, there are only a few people barely existing, and the land is in ruins. For there was no prophecy that Edom would recover "in the latter days" (Jer. 48:47), as was predicted for Moab and Ammon, but Edom's desolation was to be lasting. The short book of Obadiah presents an interesting further clarification of God's reason for this exceptional treatment of Edom. It was all the outcome of a mere quarrel, a family feud, between two brothers, Jacob and Esau, which erupted into acts of violence and which continued from Genesis to the Gospels. (Gen. 27 and footnote on Gen. 27:41). **j** Petra, once an important Roman province in Edom, was lost for many centuries but rediscovered in 1812. On the height above its ruins is the great high place, and other evidences of idolatry stand on neighboring heights.

him [Edom] from there. And I will appoint over him the one whom I choose. For who is like Me? And who will appoint for Me the time *and* prosecute Me for this proceeding? And what [earthly, national] shepherd can stand before Me *and* defy Me?

20 Therefore hear the plan of the Lord which He has made against Edom, and His purposes which He has formed against the inhabitants of Teman: Surely they shall be dragged away [by Nebuchadnezzar], even the little ones of the flock; surely He shall make their habitation desolate because of them *and* their fold shocked at their fate.

21 At the sound of their fall the earth shall tremble; at their crying the sound shall be heard at the Red Sea.

22 Behold, one will come up and fly swiftly like an eagle and spread his wings against [the Edomite city of] Bozrah; and in that day the hearts of the mighty warriors of Edom will be like the heart of a woman in her pangs [in childbirth]. [Jer. 48:41.]

23 Concerning *and* against Damascus [in Syria]: Hamath and Arpad are confounded *and* put to shame, for they have heard bad news; they are fainthearted *and* wasting away; there is trouble *and* anxiety [like] on a [storm-tossed] sea which cannot rest.

24 Damascus has become feeble; she has turned to flee, and terror *and* panic have seized her; anguish and sorrow have taken hold of her, like a woman in childbirth.

25 How [remarkable that] the renowned city is not deserted, the city of my joy! [exclaims one from Damascus].

26 Therefore her young men shall fall in her streets, and all her soldiers shall be destroyed in that day, says the Lord of hosts. [Isa. 17:1-3; Amos 1:3-5; Zech. 9:1.]

27 And I will kindle a fire in the wall of Damascus, and it will consume the palaces of Ben-hadad [title of several kings of Syria].

28 Concerning Kedar [a tribe of nomad Arabs] and concerning the kingdoms of ^kHazor, which Nebuchadrezzar king of Babylon shall smite: Thus says the Lord [to him]: Arise, go up against Kedar and destroy the sons of the east.

29 Their tents and their flocks shall they [the Chaldeans] take—their tent hangings and all their utensils and their camels. And men shall cry to them, Terror on every side! [Ps. 31:13; Jer. 6:25; 20:3, 10; 46:5.]

30 Flee, wander far off, dwell deep [in the deserts], O you inhabitants of Hazor [in the Arabian Desert] says the Lord, for ^lNebuchadrezzar king of Babylon has planned a course against you and has conceived a purpose against you.

31 Arise [Nebuchadrezzar], get up into a nation which is at ease, which dwells without care, says the Lord, [a nation] which has neither gates nor bars, which dwells apart *and* alone.

32 And their camels will be booty, and their herds of cattle a spoil; and I will scatter to all [the four] winds those who [as evidence of their idolatry] clip off the corners of their hair, and I will bring their calamity from every side, says the Lord. [Lev. 19:27.]

33 And Hazor shall become a dwelling place of jackals, a desolation forever; no man shall dwell there; neither shall a son of man live in it temporarily.

k This Hazor is not to be confused with three others mentioned elsewhere (Josh. 11:1; 15:23; Neh. 11:33). It was a region in the Arabian Desert east of Palestine. Jeremiah's prophecy concerning it was literally fulfilled. Nebuchadnezzar conquered Arabia, according to historians, and Hazor's exact situation is long since unknown. Hazor is also known as that part of the Arab nation which used fixed dwellings in unwalled towns, in contrast to nomad Arabs. l See footnote on Jer. 21:2.

34 The word of the Lord that came to Jeremiah the prophet concerning *and* against Elam, in the beginning of the reign of Zedekiah king of Judah, saying,

35 Thus says the Lord of hosts: Behold, I will break the bow of Elam, the chief [weapon and part] of their strength.

36 And upon Elam will I bring the four winds from the four corners of heaven; and I will scatter them toward all those winds, and there will be no nation to which the outcasts of Elam will not come.

37 And I will cause ᵐElam to be dismayed *and* terrified before their enemies and before those who seek *and* demand their lives; and I will bring evil *and* disaster upon them, even My fierce anger, says the Lord. And I will send the sword after them until I have consumed them.

38 And I will set My throne [of judgment] in Elam [whose capital city was Shushan, from which God wrought wonders through Nehemiah, Esther, and Daniel]; and I will destroy from their king and princes, says the Lord. [Neh. 1:1; Esth. 1:2; Dan. 8:1, 2.]

39 But it shall be ᵐin the latter days (the end of days) that I will reverse the captivity and restore the fortunes of Elam, says the Lord.

50 THE WORD that the Lord spoke concerning *and* against Babylon and concerning *and* against the land of the Chaldeans through Jeremiah the prophet: [Isa. 13:1-14:23; 47; Hab. 1, 2.]

2 Declare it among the nations and publish it and set up a signal [to spread the news]—publish and conceal it not; say, Babylon has been taken; Bel [the patron god] is put to shame, Merodach (Bel) is dismayed *and* broken down. [Babylon's] images are put to shame, her [senseless] idols are thrown down!

3 For out of the north there has come up a nation [Media] against her which will make her land desolate, and none will dwell there. They will have fled, they will be gone—from man even to beast.

4 In those days and at that time, says the Lord, the children of Israel shall come, they and the children of Judah together; they shall come up weeping as they come and seek the Lord their God [inquiring for and of Him and requiring Him, both by right of necessity and of the promises of God's Word].

5 They shall ask the way to Zion, with their faces in that direction, saying, Come, let us join ourselves to the Lord in a perpetual covenant that shall not be forgotten.

6 My people have been lost sheep; their shepherds have led them astray [to favorite places of idolatry] on mountains [that seduce]. They have gone from [one sin to another] mountain to hill; they have forgotten their [own] resting-place. [Isa. 53:6; I Pet. 2:25.]

7 All who found them devoured them; and their adversaries said, We are not guilty, because they have sinned against the Lord [and are no longer holy to Him], their true habitation of righteousness *and* justice, even

---

m Elam was a region beyond the Tigris River. After a long period of subjugation to foreign powers, it joined with Media and ultimately captured Babylon (Isa. 21:2, 9). Elam became a province of the Persian Empire. Elamites had been settled as colonists in Samaria long before the return of the Jews from Babylon, and they joined with others in attempting to prevent the rebuilding of Jerusalem and the temple (Ezra 4:9). There were also Elamites present on the Day of Pentecost (Acts 2:9), but they became extinct in the eleventh century. Elam in modern times is a province of modern Iran, bearing the name Khuzistan. Thus this prophecy of that nation's destruction is long since fulfilled, with the restoration of Elam's fortunes predicted in Jer. 49:39, the fulfillment of which we anticipate and await.

the Lord, the hope of their fathers.
8 Flee out of the midst of Babylon,
and go forth out of the land of the
Chaldeans; and be as the he-goats
[who serve as examples and as leaders in the flight] before the flocks.
[Jer. 51:6, 9, 45; II Cor. 6:17; Rev. 18:4.]
9 For behold, I will raise and cause
to come up against Babylon an assembly of great nations from the north
country. They will equip *and* set
themselves against her; from there
she will be taken. Their arrows will be
like [both] an expert, mighty warrior
and like his arrows—none [of them]
will return in vain.
10 And Chaldea shall become plunder; all who plunder her shall be satisfied, says the Lord.
11 Though you are glad, though you
rejoice, O you who plunder My heritage, though you are wanton *and* skip
about like a heifer at grass and neigh
like strong stallions,
12 Your mother [Babylon] shall be
put to great shame; she who bore you
shall blush *and* be disgraced. Behold,
she shall be at the rear of the nations
[least of the nations]—a wilderness,
waste, and desert.
13 Because of the wrath of the Lord
she shall not be inhabited but shall be
wholly desolate; everyone who goes by
Babylon shall be appalled and hiss *and*
mock at all her wounds *and* plagues.
14 Set yourselves in array against
Babylon round about, all you archers.
Shoot at her! Spare not the arrows, for
she has sinned against the Lord.
15 Raise the battle cry against her
round about! She gives her hand [in
agreement] *and* surrenders; her supports *and* battlements fall, her walls
are thrown down. For this is the
vengeance of the Lord: take vengeance
on her; as she has done [to others], do
to her.
16 Exterminate the sower from

Babylon, and the one who handles the
sickle in the time of harvest. For fear
of the sword of the oppressor everyone shall return to his people, and
everyone shall flee to his own land.
17 Israel is a hunted *and* scattered
sheep [driven hither and thither and
preyed upon by savage beasts]; the
lions have chased him. First the king
of Assyria devoured him, and now at
last ⁿNebuchadrezzar king of Babylon
has broken *and* gnawed his bones.
18 Therefore thus says the Lord of
hosts, the God of Israel: Behold, I will
visit *and* punish the king of Babylon
and his land, just as I visited *and* punished the king of Assyria.
19 And I will bring Israel [home]
again to his fold *and* pasturage, and
he will feed on Carmel and Bashan [in
the most fertile districts both west and
east], and his soul will be satisfied
upon the hills of Ephraim and Gilead.
20 In those days and at that time, says
the Lord, the iniquity of Israel will be
sought, but there will be none, and the
sins of Judah [will be sought], but none
will be found, for I will pardon those
whom I cause to remain as a remnant
(the preserved ones who come forth
after a long tribulation). [Isa. 1:9; 43:25;
Jer. 31:34; 33:8; Rom. 9:27.]
21 Go up against [Babylon] the land
of Merathaim [two rebellions, double
or intense defiance], even against it
and against the inhabitants of Pekod
[visitation and punishment]. Slay and
utterly destroy them, says the Lord,
and do according to all that I have
commanded you.
22 The cry *and* noise of battle is in
the land, and [the noise] of great
destruction.
23 How the hammer of the whole
earth is crushed and broken! How
Babylon has become a horror of desolation among the nations!
24 I set a trap for you, and you also

n See footnote on Jer. 21:2.

were taken, O Babylon, and you did not know it; you were found and also caught because you have struggled *and* contended against the Lord.

25 The Lord has opened His armory and has brought forth [the nations who unknowingly are] the weapons of His indignation *and* wrath, for the Lord God of hosts has work to do in the land of the Chaldeans.

26 Come against her from every quarter *and* from the utmost border. Open her granaries *and* storehouses; pile up [their contents] like heaps of rubbish. Burn *and* destroy her utterly; let nothing be left of her.

27 Slay all her bullocks (her choice youths, the strength of her army); let them go down to the slaughter! Woe to [the Chaldeans]! For their day has come, the time of their visitation (their inspection and punishment).

28 Listen! The voice of those [Jews] who flee and escape out of the land of Babylon proclaiming in Zion the vengeance of the Lord our God, the vengeance [of the Lord upon the Chaldeans] for [the plundering and destruction of] His temple.

29 Call together [many] archers against Babylon, all those who bend the bow. Encamp against her round about; let none from there escape. Recompense her according to her deeds; just as she has done, do to her. For against the Lord, against the Holy One of Israel, has she been proudly defiant *and* presumptuous.

30 Therefore shall her young men fall in her streets *and* squares, and all her soldiers shall be destroyed on that day, says the Lord.

31 Behold, I am against you, O Babylon [you who are pride and presumption personified], says the Lord, the Lord of hosts, for your day has come, the time when I will visit *and* punish you.

32 And Pride (the arrogant one) shall stumble (totter) and fall, and none shall raise him up. And I will kindle a fire in his cities, and it shall devour all who are round about him.

33 Thus says the Lord of hosts: The children of Israel and the children of Judah are oppressed together; all who took them captive have held them fast; they refuse to let them go.

34 Their Redeemer is strong; the Lord of hosts is His name. He will surely *and* thoroughly plead their case *and* defend their cause, that He may give rest to [the land of Israel and to the Babylonian-enslaved nations of] the earth, but unrest to the inhabitants of Babylon.

35 A sword upon the Chaldeans, says the Lord—upon the inhabitants of Babylon and upon her princes (rulers in civic matters) and upon her wise men (the astrologers and rulers in religious affairs)!

36 A sword upon the babbling liars (the diviners), that they may become fools! A sword upon her mighty warriors, that they may be dismayed *and* destroyed!

37 A sword upon their horses and upon their chariots and upon all the mixed foreign troops that are in the midst of her, that they may become [as weak and defenseless as] women! A sword upon her treasures, that they may be plundered!

38 A sword *and* a drought upon her waters, that they may be dried up! For it is a land of images, and they are mad over idols (objects of terror in which they foolishly trust).

39 Therefore °wild beasts of the desert shall dwell [in Babylon] with the jackals, and ostriches shall dwell there. And it shall never again be inhabited with people, even from generation to generation. [Isa. 13:20-22.]

40 As when God overthrew Sodom

o See footnote on Isa. 13:22 for this prophecy's fulfillment.

and Gomorrah and their neighboring cities, says the Lord, so no man shall dwell there; neither shall any son of man live there temporarily. [Jer. 49:18.]

41 Behold, a people is coming from the north; and a great nation and many kings are stirring from the uttermost parts of the earth.

42 They lay hold of bow, lance, *and* spear; they are cruel *and* have no mercy *or* compassion. They sound like the roaring of the sea; they ride upon horses, every man equipped like a man [ready] for the battle against you, O Daughter of Babylon!

43 The king of Babylon has heard the news about them, and his hands fall feeble *and* helpless; anguish has seized him, and pangs like that of a woman in childbirth.

44 See, there comes up one like a lion from the jungles (the pride) of the Jordan against the strong habitation [of Babylon] *and* into the permanent pasturage *and* sheepfold; for in a twinkling I will drive him [Babylon] from there. And I will appoint over him the one whom I choose. For who is like Me? And who will challenge Me *and* prosecute Me for this proceeding? And what [earthly, national] shepherd can stand before Me *and* defy Me? [Jer. 49:19.]

45 Therefore hear the plan of the Lord which He has made against Babylon, and His purposes which He has formed against the land of the Chaldeans: Surely they shall be dragged away, even the little ones of the flock; surely He shall make their habitation desolate because of them *and* their fold amazed *and* appalled at their fate.

46 At the cry, Babylon has been taken! the earth shall tremble, and the cry shall be heard among the nations.

51 THUS SAYS the Lord: Behold, I will raise up against Babylon and against those who dwell among those rebelling against Me a destroying wind *and* spirit;

2 And I will send to Babylon strangers *or* winnowers who will winnow her and will empty her land; for in the day of calamity they will be against her on every side.

3 Against him who bends let the archer bend his bow, and against him who lifts himself up in his coat of mail. And spare not her young men; devote [to God] and utterly destroy her entire host.

4 Thus they shall fall down slain in the land of the Chaldeans, and wounded in her streets.

5 For Israel has not been widowed *and* forsaken, nor has Judah, by his God, the Lord of hosts, though their land is full of guilt against the Holy One of Israel.

6 Flee out of the midst of Babylon! Let every man save his life! Let not destruction come upon you through her [punishment for] sin *and* guilt. For it is the time of the Lord's vengeance; He will render to her a recompense. [Jer. 50:28; II Cor. 6:17; Rev. 18:4.]

7 Babylon was a golden cup in the Lord's hand, making all the earth drunken. The nations drank of her wine; therefore the nations have gone mad. [Rev. 14:8; 17:4.]

8 Babylon has suddenly fallen and is shattered (destroyed)! Wail for her [if you care to]! Get balm for her [incurable] pain; if [you do] so she may [possibly] be healed! [Jer. 25:15; Rev. 14:8-10; 16:19; 18:2, 3.]

9 We would have healed Babylon, but she is not healed. Forsake her and let us each go to his own country, for her guilt *and* the judgment against her reach to heaven and are lifted even to the skies. [Gen. 18:20, 21.]

10 The Lord has brought forth *and* made known the righteousness [of our cause]; come and let us declare in Zion the work of the Lord our God.

11 Make clean *and* sharp the arrows, take up the shields *or* coats of armor [and cover your bodies with them]! The Lord has stirred up the spirit of the kings of the Medes [who with the Persians will destroy the Babylonian Empire], for His purpose concerning Babylon is to destroy it; for that is the vengeance of the Lord, the vengeance [upon Babylon for the plundering and destruction] of His temple.

12 Set up a standard *or* signal [to spread the news] upon the walls of Babylon! Make the watch *and* blockade strong, set the guards, prepare the ambushes! For the Lord has both purposed and done that which He spoke against the inhabitants of Babylon.

13 O [Babylon] you who dwell by many waters, rich in treasures, your end has come, and the line measuring your life is cut. [Rev. 17:1-6.]

14 The Lord of hosts has sworn by Himself, saying, Surely I will fill you with men, as with [a swarm of] locusts [who strip a land clean], and they will lift up a song *and* shout [of victory] over you.

15 He made the earth by His power; He established the world by His wisdom and stretched out the heavens by His understanding.

16 When He utters His voice, there is a tumult of waters in the heavens, and He causes the vapors to ascend from the ends of the earth. He makes lightnings for the rain and brings forth the wind from His treasuries.

17 Every man has become stupid *and* brutelike, without knowledge [of God]; every goldsmith is put to shame by the images he has made; for his molten idols are a lie, and there is no breath [of life] in them.

18 They are worthless (emptiness, falsity, futility), a work of delusion *and* worthy of derision; in the time of their inspection *and* punishment they shall [helplessly] perish.

19 Not like these [gods] is He Who is the Portion of Jacob [the true God on Whom Israel has a claim], for He is the One Who formed all things, and Israel is the tribe of His inheritance— the Lord of hosts is His name. [Jer. 10:12-16.]

20 You [Cyrus of Persia, soon to conquer Babylon] are My battle-ax *or* maul and weapon of war—for with you I break nations in pieces, with you I destroy kingdoms,

21 With you I break in pieces the horse and his rider, with you I break in pieces the chariot and the charioteer,

22 With you I break in pieces man and woman, with you I break in pieces old man and youth, with you I break in pieces young man and maiden,

23 With you I break in pieces the shepherd and his flock, with you I break in pieces the farmer and his yoke of oxen, and with you I break in pieces governors and commanders.

24 And I will [completely] repay Babylon and all the inhabitants of Chaldea for all the evil that they have done in Zion—before your very eyes [I will do it], says the Lord.

25 Behold, I am against you, says the Lord, O destroying mountain [which is burning out, you who will be as barren and desolate as an extinct volcano], you who [would] destroy the whole earth. I will stretch out My hand over *and* against you and roll you down from the [burnt] crags and will make you a burnt-out mountain [of combustive fires],

26 And [O Babylon] they shall not take your cracked stones for a cornerstone, or any stone for foundations, but you shall be waste *and* ᴾdesolate forever, says the Lord.

27 Set up a standard *or* signal in the

p See footnote on Isa. 13:22 for this prophecy's fulfillment.

land [to spread the news]! Blow the trumpet among the nations! Prepare *and* dedicate the nations for war against her; call against her the kingdoms of Ararat, Minni, and Ashkenaz. Appoint a marshal against her; cause the horses to come up like [a swarm of] locusts [when their wings are not yet released from their horny cases].

28 Prepare *and* dedicate the nations for war against her—the kings of Media, with their governors and commanders (deputies), and every land of their dominion.

29 [I foresee this:] The land trembles and writhes in pain *and* sorrow, for the purposes of the Lord against Babylon stand—to make the land of Babylon a desolation without inhabitant.

30 The mighty warriors of Babylon have ceased to fight; they have remained in their holds. Their might has failed; they have become [weak and helpless] like women. Her dwelling places are burned up; her bars [and defenses generally] are broken.

31 One post shall run to meet another and one messenger to meet another to show the king of Babylon that his city is taken on every side *and* to its farthest end,

32 And that the passages [or ferries across the Euphrates] are stopped, and the great marshes they [the Medes] have burned with fire, and the men of war are frightened.

33 For thus says the Lord of hosts, the God of Israel: The Daughter of Babylon is like a threshing floor at the time it is [being prepared]; yet a little while and the time of harvest shall come to her.

34 [The inhabitants of Zion say] qNebuchadrezzar king of Babylon has devoured us, he has crushed us, he has made us an empty vessel. Like a monster he has swallowed us up, he has filled his belly with our delicacies; he has rinsed us out *and* cast us away.

35 May the violence done to me and to my flesh *and* blood be upon Babylon, will the inhabitant of Zion say; and, May my blood be upon the inhabitants of Chaldea, will Jerusalem say.

36 Therefore thus says the Lord: Behold, I will plead your cause and take vengeance for you. I will dry up her lake *or* great reservoir and make her fountain dry.

37 And Babylon shall become heaps [of ruins], a dwelling place of jackals, a horror (an astonishing desolation) and a hissing [of amazement], without inhabitant.

38 They [the Chaldean lords] shall be roaring together [before their sudden capture] like young lions [over their prey], they [the princes] shall be growling like lions' whelps.

39 When the revelers are rinflamed [with wine and lust during their drinking bouts], I will prepare them a feast [of My wrath] and make them drunk, that they may rejoice and fall asleep to a perpetual sleep and not waken, says the Lord.

40 I will bring them down like lambs to the slaughter, like rams together with he-goats.

41 How Sheshach [Babylon] is taken! And the praise of the whole earth is surprised *and* seized! How Babylon has become an astonishing desolation *and* a horror among the nations!

42 The sea has come up upon

q See footnote on Jer. 21:2. **r** Here is God's forecast through Jeremiah of what was going to happen to great Babylon, of whom Herodotus said she had been "embellished with ornaments more than any city" of his acquaintance. The fact that all of the details of the prophecy were carried out is recorded by Daniel (5:1-30), and becomes more and more amazing and awe-inspiring as one reflects on it all after twenty-five verifying centuries. Truly only an "[empty-headed] fool" could say in his heart, "There is no God" (Ps. 14:1).

Babylon; she is covered with the tumult *and* multitude of its waves.

43 Her cities have become a desolation *and* a horror, a land of drought and a wilderness, a land in which no one lives, nor does any son of man pass through it.

44 And I will punish *and* execute judgment upon Bel [the god] in Babylon and take out of his mouth what he has swallowed up [the sacred vessels and the people of Judah and elsewhere who were taken captive]. The nations will not flow any more to him. Yes, the wall of Babylon has fallen!

45 My people, come out of the midst of her! And let every man save his life from the fierce anger of the Lord! [Jer. 50:8; II Cor. 6:17; Rev. 18:4.]

46 And beware, lest your heart faint and you be afraid at the report (rumor) heard in the land; for in one year shall one report come and in another year another report, and violence shall be in the land, ruler against ruler.

47 Therefore behold, the days will come when I will execute judgment *and* punishment upon the idols of Babylon; her whole land will be confounded *and* put to shame, and all her slain will fall in the midst of her.

48 Then heaven and earth and all that is in them shall sing for joy over Babylon, for the [Median] destroyers shall come against her from the north, says the Lord. [Isa. 44:23; Jer. 51:11; Rev. 12:12; 18:20.]

49 As Babylon caused the slain of Israel to fall, so at Babylon shall fall the slain of all [her] land.

50 You who have escaped the sword, go away, stand not still! [Seriously and earnestly] remember the Lord from afar [Babylon], and let [desolate] Jerusalem come into your mind.

51 We are confounded *and* ashamed, for we have heard reproach; confusion *and* shame have covered our faces, for strangers have come into the [most] sacred parts of the sanctuary of the Lord [even those forbidden for entrance by all but the high priest or the appointed priests].

52 Therefore behold, the days are coming, says the Lord, when I will execute judgment upon [Babylon's] idols *and* images, and throughout all her land the wounded will groan.

53 Though Babylon should mount up to heaven, and though she should fortify her strong height (her lofty stronghold), yet destroyers will come upon her from Me, says the Lord.

54 The sound of a cry [comes] from Babylon, and [the sound of] great destruction *and* ruin from the land of the Chaldeans!

55 For the Lord is destroying Babylon *and* laying her waste and stilling her great voice [the hum of the city's life]. And the waves [of her conquerors] roar like great waters, the noise of their voices is raised up [like the tramping of an army].

56 For the destroyer is coming upon her, upon Babylon; and her mighty warriors are taken, their bows are broken in pieces; for the Lord is a God of recompense; He will surely requite.

57 And I will make drunk her princes and her wise men, her governors and her commanders (deputies) and her mighty warriors; and they will sleep a perpetual sleep and not waken, says the King—the Lord of hosts is His name.

58 Thus says the Lord of hosts: The broad walls of Babylon shall be utterly overthrown *and* [the foundations] made bare, and her high gates shall be burned with fire; the peoples shall labor in vain, and the nations [only] to satisfy the fire, and they shall be weary. [Hab. 2:13.]

59 The word that Jeremiah the prophet commanded Seraiah son of Neriah, the son of Mahseiah, when he went with Zedekiah king of Judah to Babylon in the fourth year of his reign. Now this Seraiah was chief chamberlain *or* quartermaster [and brother of Baruch].

60 So Jeremiah wrote in a book all the evil that would come upon Babylon—even all these words that are written against Babylon.

61 And Jeremiah said to Seraiah, When you come to Babylon, see to it that you read all these words.

62 Then say, O Lord, You have spoken concerning this place that it shall be cut off, so that nothing shall remain and dwell in it, neither man nor beast; but it shall be desolate forever.

63 And it shall be that when you have finished reading this book, you shall bind a stone to it and cast it into the midst of the Euphrates.

64 Then say, Thus will Babylon sink and not rise because of the evil that I will bring upon her; and [the Babylonians] will be weary (hopelessly exhausted). Thus far are the words of Jeremiah. [Rev. 18:21.]

52 ZEDEKIAH WAS twenty-one years old when he began to reign, and he reigned eleven years in Jerusalem. And his mother's name was Hamutal daughter of Jeremiah [not the prophet] of Libnah. [II Kings 24:18-25:21.]

2 And he did that which was evil in the sight of the Lord, according to all that Jehoiakim had done.

3 For all this came to pass in Jerusalem and Judah because of the anger of the Lord, and [in the end] He cast them out from His presence. And Zedekiah rebelled against the king of Babylon.

4 And in the ninth year of his reign, in the tenth month, on the tenth day of the month, ˢNebuchadrezzar king of Babylon came, he and all his army, against Jerusalem; and they pitched against it and built moveable towers *and* siege mounds against it round about. [Jer. 39:1-10.]

5 So the city was besieged until the eleventh year of King Zedekiah. [II Chron. 36:11-13.]

6 And in the fourth month, on the ninth day of the month, the famine was so severe in the city that there was no bread for the people of the land.

7 Then the city [wall] was broken through, so that all the men of war might flee, and they went forth out of the city by night [as Ezekiel had foretold] by way of the gate between the two walls by the king's garden, though the Chaldeans were round about the city. And they [the Jewish soldiers fled] by way of the Arabah (the Jordan Valley). [Ezek. 12:12.]

8 But the army of the Chaldeans pursued the king and overtook Zedekiah in the plains of Jericho; and all his army was scattered from him.

9 Then they seized the king and brought him up to the king of Babylon at Riblah in the [Syrian] land of Hamath [on the northern border of Israel], where he pronounced sentence upon him.

10 And the king of Babylon slew the sons of Zedekiah before his eyes; he slew also all the princes of Judah at Riblah.

11 Then he put out the eyes of Zedekiah; and the king of Babylon bound him with shackles and carried him to Babylon and put him in prison ᵗ[mill] till the day of his death. [Ezek. 12:13.]

12 Now in the fifth month, on the tenth day of the month, which was the nineteenth year of Nebuchadrezzar

s See footnote on Jer. 21:2. **t** *The Septuagint* (Greek translation of the Old Testament) renders this word "mill." Hence it has been inferred that the Chaldeans ascribed to Zedekiah in his old age the same fate as that to which the Philistines assigned Samson (Judg. 16:21) (*The Cambridge Bible*).

king of Babylon, there came to Jerusalem Nebuzaradan captain of the guard, who stood *and* served before the king of Babylon.

13 And he burned the house of the Lord and the king's house and all the houses of Jerusalem; every great house he consumed with fire.

14 And all the army of the Chaldeans who were with the captain of the guard broke down all the walls round about Jerusalem.

15 Then Nebuzaradan the captain of the guard carried away captive some of the poorest of the people and those who were left in the city [at the time it was captured], along with those who went out to the king of Babylon [during the siege] and the remnant of the multitude [the country's working people].

16 But Nebuzaradan the captain of the guard left some of the poorest of the land to be vinedressers and tillers of the soil.

17 Also the pillars of bronze that belonged to the house of the Lord, and the bronze bases *or* pedestals [which supported the ten basins] and the bronze Sea *or* huge laver that were in the house of the Lord, the Chaldeans broke into pieces and carried all the bronze of them to Babylon.

18 The pots [for carrying away ashes] also and the shovels and the snuffers and the bowls and the spoons and all the vessels of bronze used in the temple service they took away.

19 Also the small bowls and the firepans and the basins and the pots and the lampstands and the incense cups and the bowls for the drink offerings—whatever was of gold the captain of the guard took away as gold, and whatever was of silver as silver.

20 The two pillars, one Sea *or* huge laver, and [u]twelve bronze bulls *or* oxen under the Sea, which King Solomon had made in the house of the Lord—the bronze of all these things was beyond weighing.

21 Concerning the pillars, the height of the one pillar was eighteen cubits (twenty-seven feet), and an ornamental molding of twelve cubits (eighteen feet) went around its circumference; it was four fingers thick, and it [the pillar] was hollow.

22 An upper part *or* capital of bronze was on top of it. The height of one capital was five cubits (seven and one-half feet), with a network and pomegranates around it, all of bronze. The second pillar also, with its pomegranates, was similar to these.

23 And there were ninety-six pomegranates on the sides; and all the pomegranates upon the network were a hundred round about.

24 And the captain of the guard took [as prisoners] Seraiah the chief priest and Zephaniah the second priest and the three keepers of the door.

25 He took also out of the city a court officer who had been overseer of the soldiers, and seven men of them who were next to the king [as advisers] *and* saw his face, who were found in the city, and the scribe of the prince *or* captain of the army who mustered the people of the land, and sixty men of the people of the land who were found in the midst of the city.

26 And Nebuzaradan the captain of the guard took them and brought them to the king of Babylon at Riblah.

27 And the king of Babylon smote them and put them to death at Riblah in the land of Hamath. Thus Judah was carried away captive out of his own land.

28 This is the number of people whom

u King Ahaz had previously removed the twelve bronze bulls or oxen (I Kings 7:25) from under the big laver and had replaced them with a substructure of stone (II Kings 16:17), but obviously he had not put them beyond the reach of the Chaldeans when they set their minds to find them.

Nebuchadrezzar carried away captive: in the seventh year, 3,023 Jews;

29 In the eighteenth year of Nebuchadrezzar, he carried away captive from Jerusalem 832 persons;

30 In the twenty-third year of Nebuchadrezzar, Nebuzaradan the captain of the [Babylonian] guard carried away captive of the Jews 745 persons. All the persons were 4,600.

31 And in the thirty-seventh year of the captivity of Jehoiachin [also called Coniah and Jeconiah] king of Judah, in the twelfth month, on the twenty-fifth day of the month, Evil-merodach king of Babylon in the first year of his reign lifted up the head of Jehoiachin king of Judah [and showed favor to him] and brought him out of prison. [II Kings 25:27-30.]

32 He spoke kindly to him and gave him a seat above the seats of the kings who were [captives] with him in Babylon,

33 Jehoiachin put off his prison garments, and he dined regularly at the king's table all the days of his life.

34 And his allowance, a continual one, was given him by the king of Babylon, a portion according to his requirements until the day of his death, ᵛall the days of his life.

---

v The latter of these clauses is probably an afterthought in order to prevent ending the book with the word "death." The general object too of the paragraph [the last four verses] seems to have been to leave the reader with a parting ray of comfort and encouragement in the thought that even in exile the Lord remembered His people and softened the heart of the heathen tyrant toward David's seed (*The Cambridge Bible*). Note also the contrast between Zedekiah, who remained in prison till the day he died (Jer. 52:11), and Jehoiachin, who was released from prison and treated well by the Babylonian kings till the day he died.

Lamentations

Author:
Traditionally, Jeremiah

Date:
587 BC

Everyday Life Principles:
Bad things—even devastating things—happen. When they do, run to God and find comfort.

Even when we know we do not deserve God's mercy, we can still call upon Him. Because of His great compassion, He *will* hear us and help us.

Never stop hoping in God's mercy.

To "lament" is to feel intense sorrow, sadness, or grief, even to cry or to wail. This book, entitled Lamentations, focuses on suffering, loss, and hopelessness. It acknowledges the reality of pain, grief, and tragedy, not only in Old Testament times (pain and grief resulting from Israel's turning away from God), but in our lives today. Even though some of the circumstances of our suffering may be different from the Israelites' experience, the pain of suffering is just as real.

Against the dismal backdrop of Lamentations, a ray of hope begins to shine. Having written extensively about the destruction in the beginning of Lamentations, the writer admits in Lamentations 3:17, "I have forgotten what good and happiness are." But then he begins to come out of his misery, saying: "But this I recall and therefore have I hope and expectation" (Lamentations 3:21). He then moves into one of the best-known, best-loved scriptures I know of: "It is because of the Lord's mercy and loving-kindness that we are not consumed, because His [tender] compassions fail not. They are new every morning; great and abundant is Your stability and faithfulness" (Lamentations 3:22, 23).

No matter what you are facing today, let Lamentations remind you of God's faithfulness to you. Recall God's mercy in every situation, and let it give you hope and expectation!

1 HOW SOLITARY *and* lonely sits the city [Jerusalem] that was [once] full of people! How like a widow has she become! She who was [a]great among the nations and princess among the provinces has become a tributary [in servitude]!

2 She weeps bitterly in the night, and her tears are [constantly] on her cheeks. Among all her lovers (allies) she has no one to comfort her. All her friends have dealt treacherously with her; they have become her enemies. [Jer. 3:1; 4:30.]

3 Judah has gone into exile [to escape] from the affliction and laborious servitude [of the homeland]. She dwells among the [heathen] nations, but she finds no rest; all her persecutors overtook her amid the [dire] straits [of her distress].

4 The roads to Zion mourn, because no one comes to the solemn assembly *or* the appointed feasts. All her gates are desolate, her priests sigh *and* groan, her maidens are grieved *and* vexed, and she herself is in bitterness.

5 Her adversaries have become the head; her enemies prosper. For the Lord has afflicted her for the multitude of her transgressions; her young children have gone into captivity before the enemy. [Jer. 30:14, 15; 52:28; Dan. 9:7-14.]

6 From the Daughter of Zion all her beauty *and* majesty have departed. Her princes have become like harts that find no pasture; they have fled without strength before the pursuer.

7 Jerusalem [earnestly] remembers in the days of her affliction, in the days of her [compulsory] wanderings *and* her bitterness, all the pleasant *and* precious things that she had from the days of old. When her people fell into *and* at the hands of the adversary, and there was none to help her, the enemy [gloated as they] looked at her, and they mocked at her desolations *and* downfall.

8 Jerusalem has grievously sinned; therefore she has become an unclean thing *and* has been removed. All who honored her despise her, because they have seen her nakedness; yes, she herself groans *and* sighs and turns [her face] away.

9 Her filthiness was in *and* on her skirts; she did not [seriously and earnestly] consider her final end. Therefore she has come down [from throne to slavery] singularly *and* astonishingly; she has no comforter. O Lord [cries Jerusalem], look at my affliction, for the enemy has magnified himself [in triumph]!

10 The adversary has spread out his hand upon all her precious *and* desirable things; for she has seen the nations enter her sanctuary [of the temple]—[b]when You commanded that they should not even enter Your

a It is possible to read the writings of the prophets only as valuable contributions to Old Testament history. And the reader may be enriched by familiarity with their forecasts of events which have been startlingly fulfilled, thus proclaiming the divine inspiration of the books and the wisdom and power of the God Who prompted their writings. But to stop there is by no means to grasp their full and outstanding purpose for today. Through the prophets God is speaking definitely and definitively to every individual and nation on earth, even right now demanding that we see ourselves as He sees us—a world of nations and individuals tobogganing toward disaster; and He declares that there is no alternative unless we repent and come to terms with Him.   b The Ammonites and Moabites, descendants of Lot and kinsmen of Israel, were forbidden to enter the congregation of the Lord, "even to their tenth generation," because they refused assistance to the Israelites when they were fleeing from Egypt, and because they hired Balaam to curse Israel (Deut. 23:3, 4). The Israelites themselves never assembled any closer to the sanctuary of the temple than in the court outside its door. No Jew—not even David or Jesus Himself or any of His apostles—ever ventured into the sanctuary or temple proper except for certain Levites to whom such service was assigned. Two Greek words have customarily been translated "temple" in the New Testament. One (*hieron*) always means the temple enclosure (the porches, courts, chambers, and the like); the other word (*naos*) means the

congregation [in the outer courts]. [Deut. 23:3; Jer. 51:51; Ezek. 44:7, 9.]
11 All her people groan *and* sigh, seeking for bread; they have given their desirable *and* precious things [in exchange] for food to revive their strength *and* bring back life. See, O Lord, and consider how wretched *and* lightly esteemed, how vile *and* abominable, I have become!
12 Is it nothing to you, all you who pass by? Look and see if there is any sorrow like my sorrow which was dealt out to me, with which the Lord has afflicted me in the day of His fierce anger!
13 From above He has sent fire into my bones, and it prevailed against them. He has spread a net for my feet; He has turned me back. He has made me hopelessly miserable and faint all the day long.
14 The yoke of my transgressions is bound by His hand; they were twined together; they were set upon my neck. He has made my strength fail *and* [me to] stumble; the Lord has delivered me into the hands of those I am unable to resist *or* withstand. [Deut. 28:48.]
15 The Lord has made of no account all my [Jerusalem's] mighty men in the midst of me; He has proclaimed a set time against me to crush my young men. The Lord has trodden as in a winepress the Virgin Daughter of Judah.
16 For these things I weep; my eyes overflow with tears, because a comforter, one who could refresh *and* restore my soul, is far from me. My children are desolate *and* perishing, for the enemy has prevailed. [Lam. 1:21.]
17 Zion stretches forth her hands,

but there is no comforter for her. The Lord has commanded concerning *and* against Jacob that his neighbors should be his adversaries; Jerusalem has become a filthy thing among them [an object of contempt].
18 The Lord is righteous (just and in the right); for I have rebelled against His commandment (His word). Hear, I pray you, all you peoples, and look at my sorrow *and* suffering; my maidens and my young men have gone into captivity.
19 I [Jerusalem] called to my lovers [allies], but they deceived me. My priests and my elders expired in the city while they sought food to save their lives.
20 Behold, O Lord, how distressed I am! My vital parts (emotions) are in tumult *and* are deeply disturbed; my heart cannot rest *and* is violently agitated within me, for I have grievously rebelled. Outside the house the sword bereaves, at home there is [famine, pestilence] death!
21 [My foes] have heard that I [Jerusalem] sigh *and* groan, that I have no comforter [in You]. All my enemies have heard of my trouble; they are glad [O Lord] that You have done it. You will bring the day [of Judah's punishment] that you have foretold *and* proclaimed; [it involves also my foes' punishment] and they will become like me. [Isa. 14:5, 6; Jer. 30:16.]
22 Let all their wickedness come before You; and deal with them as You have dealt with me because of all my transgressions; for my sighs *and* groans are many and my heart is faint.

2 HOW THE Lord has covered the Daughter of Zion with a cloud in His anger! He has cast down

sanctuary proper—the Holy Place and the Holy of Holies—into which none but the authorized priests might go, and then only at stated times. But now, Jeremiah says, the forbidden heathen nations enter the very Holy of Holies for plunder! Nothing more humiliating could happen for a Jew than this.

from heaven to the earth the beauty *and* splendor of Israel and has not [earnestly] remembered His footstool in the day of His anger!

2 The Lord has swallowed up all the country places *and* habitations of Jacob and has spared not *nor* pitied; He has demolished in His wrath the strongholds of the Daughter of Judah. He has cast down to the ground the kingdom and its rulers, polluting them *and* depriving them of their sanctity.

3 He has broken off in His fierce anger every horn (means of defense) of Israel. He has drawn back His right hand from before the enemy. And He has burned amidst Jacob like a flaming fire consuming all around.

4 He has bent His bow like an enemy; He has stood with His right hand set like a foe and has slain all the delights *and* pride of the eye; on *and* in the tent of the Daughter of Zion He has poured out His wrath like fire.

5 The Lord has become like an enemy; He has destroyed Israel. He has destroyed all its palaces, has laid in ruins its strongholds, and has multiplied in the Daughter of Judah groaning and moaning and lamentation.

6 And He has violently broken down His temple like a booth *or* hedge of a garden; He has destroyed the place of His appointed assembly. The Lord has caused the solemn appointed feasts and Sabbaths to be forgotten in Zion and has spurned *and* rejected in the indignation of His anger the king and the priest.

7 The Lord has scorned, rejected, *and* cast off His altar; He has abhorred *and* disowned His sanctuary. He has given into the hand of the enemy the walls of her palaces [and high buildings]; they have raised a clamor in the house of the Lord as on a day of a solemn appointed feast.

8 The Lord purposed to lay in ruins the [city] wall of the Daughter of Zion.

He marked it off by measuring line; He restrained not His hand from destroying. He made rampart and wall lament; they languished together.

9 Her gates have sunk into the ground; He has destroyed and broken her bars. Her king and her princes are [exiled] among the nations; the law is no more; her prophets also obtain no vision from the Lord.

10 The elders of the Daughter of Zion sit on the ground keeping silent; they have cast dust on their heads, they have girded themselves with sackcloth. The maidens of Jerusalem have bowed their heads to the ground [says Jeremiah].

11 My eyes fail from weeping, my emotions are deeply disturbed, my heart is poured out upon the ground [in grief] because of the destruction of the daughter of my people, because infants and nurslings faint in the streets of the city.

12 They keep crying to their mothers, Where is corn and wine [food and drink]? as they faint like wounded men in the streets of the city, as their lives ebb away on their mothers' bosom.

13 What [example of suffering in the past] is sufficient for me to remind you for your [comfort]? To what shall I liken you, O Daughter of Jerusalem? With what shall I compare you, that I may comfort you, O Virgin Daughter of Zion? For your ruin is as measureless as the sea! Who can heal you? [Lam. 1:12; Dan. 9:12.]

14 Your prophets have predicted for you falsehood and delusion *and* foolish things; and they have not exposed your iniquity *and* guilt to avert your captivity [by causing you to repent]. But they have divined *and* declared to you false *and* deceptive prophecies, worthless *and* misleading.

15 All who pass by clap their hands at you; they hiss and wag their heads at the Daughter of Jerusalem, saying, Is this the city which was called the

perfection of beauty, the joy of all the earth?

16 All your enemies have opened wide their mouths against you; they scornfully hiss and gnash their teeth. They cry, We have swallowed her up! Certainly this is the day we have looked for; we have it, we see it!

17 The Lord has done what He planned; He has carried out *and* finished His word which He threatened *and* decreed ᶜin the days of old. He has demolished without pity; He has made the enemy rejoice over you and has exalted the might of your foes. [Lev. 26:14-39; Deut. 28:15-68.]

18 The hearts [of the inhabitants of Jerusalem] cried to the Lord. [Then to the congregation, I, Jeremiah, cried, addressing the wall as its symbol] O wall of the Daughter of Zion, let tears run down like a river day and night; give yourself no rest, let not your eyes stop [shedding tears].

19 Arise [from your bed], cry out in the night, at the beginning of the watches; pour out your heart like water before the face of the Lord. Lift up your hands toward Him for the lives of your young children, who faint from hunger at the head of every street. [Ps. 62:8.]

20 Behold, O Lord, and consider [carefully] to whom You have done this. Should *and* shall women eat the fruit of their own bodies, the children whom they have tended *and* swaddled with their hands? Should *and* shall priest and prophet be slain in the

place set apart [for the worship] of the Lord?

21 The young and the old lie on the ground in the streets; my maidens and my young men have fallen by the sword. You have slain them in the day of Your anger, slaughtering them without pity.

22 You [Lord] called together, as on an appointed feast day of solemn assembly, my terrors (dangers) from every side. And there was not one in the day of God's wrath who escaped or survived; those I have nursed and brought up, my enemy has destroyed.

3 I AM [Jeremiah] the man who has seen affliction under the rod of His wrath.

2 He has led me and brought me into darkness and not light.

3 Surely He has turned away from me; His hand is against me all the day.

4 My flesh and my skin has He worn out *and* made old; He has shattered my bones.

5 He has built up [siege mounds] against me and surrounded me with bitterness, tribulation, *and* anguish.

6 He has caused me to dwell in dark places like those long dead.

7 He walled me in so that I cannot get out; He has weighted down my chain.

8 Even when I cry and shout for help, He shuts out my prayer.

9 He has enclosed my ways with hewn stone; He has made my paths crooked.

speak the Word

God, I will pour out my heart like water before You. I will freely and fully express my feelings to You.
ADAPTED FROM LAMENTATIONS 2:19

---

c "This reference to the ancient predictions of judgment against Israel for their sins is of great importance, both because it shows that these prophecies were then extant and well known among the Jews, and because it shows that they were understood by the pious remnant exactly as we now explain them" (Johan P. Lange, *A Commentary*).

10 He is to me like a bear lying in wait, and like a lion [hiding] in secret places.

11 He has turned me off my ways and pulled me in pieces; He has made me desolate.

12 He has bent His bow and set me as a mark for the arrow.

13 He has caused the arrows of His quiver to enter into my heart [the seat of my affections and desires].

14 I have become a derision to all my people, and [the subject of] their singsong all the day.

15 He has filled me with bitterness; He has made me drink to excess *and* until drunken with wormwood [bitterness].

16 He has also broken my teeth with gravel (stones); He has covered me with ashes.

17 And You have bereaved my soul *and* cast it off far from peace; I have forgotten what good *and* happiness *are*.

18 And I say, Perished is my strength and my expectation from the Lord.

19 [O Lord] remember [earnestly] my affliction and my misery, my wandering *and* my outcast state, the wormwood and the gall.

20 My soul has them continually in remembrance and is bowed down within me.

21 But this I recall and therefore have I hope *and* expectation:

22 It is because of the Lord's mercy *and* loving-kindness that we are not consumed, because His [tender] compassions fail not. [Mal. 3:6.]

23 They are new every morning; great *and* abundant is Your stability *and* faithfulness. [Isa. 33:2.]

24 The Lord is my portion *or* share, says my living being (my inner self); therefore will I hope in Him *and* wait expectantly for Him. [Num. 18:20.]

25 The Lord is good to those who wait hopefully *and* expectantly for Him, to those who seek Him [inquire

life point

In Lamentations 3:19, 20, we read about the writer of this book, who has his mind on all his problems and whose soul is bowed down within him with sorrow. However, he declares in Lamentations 3:21: "But this I recall and therefore have I hope and expectation." Now he makes a turn. He says, "Okay, I am going to get something else in my mind that gives me hope and the expectation of good." The thing that he begins to think about pulls him out of this pit. Then in verses 22–24 he talks about the Lord's mercy, His compassion, and His faithfulness.

The writer's positive thoughts about God brought him out of the depressed, miserable state he was in. When we think about our problems, we sink lower and lower, but thoughts about the goodness, mercy, kindness, and faithfulness of God give us hope.

of and for Him and require Him by right of necessity and on the authority of God's word].

26 It is good that one should hope in *and* wait quietly for the salvation (the safety and ease) of the Lord.

27 It is good for a man that he should bear the yoke [of divine disciplinary dealings] in his youth.

28 Let him sit alone uncomplaining *and* keeping silent [in hope], because [God] has laid [the yoke] upon him [for his benefit]. [Rom. 8:28.]

life point

Lamentations 3:25 says that God is good to those who wait for Him and expect Him to be good to them. We do not deserve His goodness, but it is available to all who *expect* it.

new every morning

Thank God for His great and abundant mercy! His mercies are new every morning (see Lamentations 3:22, 23). Surely we would all live miserable, defeated, wretched lives separated from His presence if it were not for His compassion and willingness to forgive us.

When we meditate on God's mercy and truly realize how much He willingly forgives us, we can much more easily show mercy to others. Good relationships are impossible unless we are generous with mercy and forgiveness. Being merciful simply means that we are good to those who do not deserve goodness. We have received unmerited blessings from God, and He expects us to give to others what we have received from Him. Let the goodness of God flow through you, because He has created you to be blessed and to be a blessing.

Jesus said that we are to forgive our enemies (see Luke 6:37) and be kind, doing favors in such a way that people derive benefit from them. In this way we show ourselves to be like our Father in heaven, for He is merciful, kind, and good. He promised that we would lose nothing and our reward would be great. God is our Vindicator, and we always come out on top when we do things His way.

God's mercy is new every morning, and I am glad—because I am sure I use my allotted portion every day. I am grateful for a new, fresh start each day. God desires mercy, not sacrifice. When we make mistakes, He does not want our sacrifice. Jesus is the only sacrifice ever needed. He wants us to admit our mistakes, repent, and receive forgiveness and mercy. When others make mistakes and hurt or offend us, He wants us to give them mercy and not require sacrifices from them. What this means is that we are not to try to make people feel guilty or pay for their errors, but to give them the gift of mercy instead, just as we receive that gift from God.

We are wise to give mercy today because none of us know how much mercy we will need tomorrow. Learn to give and receive mercy regularly. Let mercy become a way of life for you.

29 Let him put his mouth in the dust [in abject recognition of his unworthiness]—there may yet be hope. [Mic. 7:17.]

30 Let him give his cheek to the One Who smites him [even through His human agents]; let him be filled [full] with [men's] reproach [in meekness].

31 For the Lord will not cast off forever! [Ps. 94:14.]

32 But though He causes grief, yet will He be moved to compassion according to the multitude of His loving-kindness and tender mercy.

33 For He does not willingly and from His heart afflict or grieve the children of men. [Ezek. 18:23, 32; Hos. 11:8; Heb. 12:5-10; II Pet. 3:9.]

34 To trample and crush underfoot all the prisoners of the earth,

35 To turn aside and deprive a man of his rights before the face of the Most High or a superior [acting as God's representative],

36 To subvert a man in his cause—

[of these things] the Lord does not approve.

37 Who is he who speaks and it comes to pass, if the Lord has not authorized *and* commanded it?

38 Is it not out of the mouth of the Most High that evil and good both proceed [adversity and prosperity, physical evil or misfortune and physical good or happiness]?

39 Why does a living man sigh [one who is still in this life's school of discipline]? [And why does] a man complain for the punishment of his sins?

40 Let us test and examine our ways, and let us return to the Lord!

putting the Word to work

In Lamentations 3:40, the people decided to "test and examine" their ways, and return to the Lord. Have you examined your ways lately? Ask God to show you whether or not you have strayed from Him in any area of your life. Then turn back to Him through repentance and receive His great mercy.

41 Let us lift up our hearts and our hands [and then with them mount up in prayer] to God in heaven:

42 We have transgressed and rebelled and You have not pardoned.

43 You have covered Yourself with wrath and pursued *and* afflicted us; You have slain without pity.

44 You have covered Yourself with a cloud so that no prayer can pass through.

speak the Word

45 You have made us offscouring and refuse among the nations.

46 All our enemies have gaped at us *and* railed against us.

47 Fear and pitfall have come upon us, devastation and destruction.

48 My eyes overflow with streams of tears because of the destruction of the daughter of my people.

49 My eyes overflow continually and will not cease

50 Until the Lord looks down and sees from heaven.

51 My eyes cause me grief at the fate of all the maidens [and the daughter-towns] of my city [Jerusalem].

52 I have been hunted down like a bird by those who were my enemies without cause.

53 They [thought they had] destroyed my life in the dungeon (pit) and cast a stone [over it] above me. [Jer. 38.]

54 The waters ran down on my head; I said, I am gone.

55 I called upon Your name, O Lord, out of the depths [of the mire] of the dungeon. [Jer. 38:6.]

56 You heard my voice [then]: [Oh] hide not Your ear [now] at my prayer for relief.

57 You drew near on the day I called to You; You said, Fear not. [James 4:8.]

58 O Lord, You have pleaded the causes of my soul [You have managed my affairs and You have protected my person and my rights]; You have rescued *and* redeemed my life!

59 O Lord, You have seen my wrong [done to me]; judge *and* maintain my cause.

60 You have seen all their vengeance, all their devices against me.

61 You have heard their reproach *and* revilings, O Lord, and all their devices against me—

62 The lips *and* thoughts of my assailants are against me all day long.

63 Look at their sitting down and their rising up [their movements, doings, and secret counsels]; I am their singsong [the subject of their derision and merriment]. [Ps. 139:2; Isa. 37:28.]

64 Render to them a recompense, O Lord, according to the work of their hands.

65 You will give them hardness *and* blindness of heart; Your curse will be upon them.

66 You will pursue *and* afflict them in anger and destroy them from under Your heavens, O Lord.

4 HOW THE gold has become dim! How the most pure gold has changed! The hallowed stones [of the temple] are poured out at the head of every street.

2 The noble *and* precious sons of Zion, [once] worth their weight in fine gold—how they are esteemed [merely] as earthen pots *or* pitchers, the work of the hands of the potter! [Isa. 30:14; Jer. 19:11; II Cor. 4:7.]

3 Even the jackals draw out the breast, they give suck to their young ones, but the daughter of my people has become cruel like ostriches in the wilderness [that desert their young].

4 The tongue of the nursing babe cleaves to the roof of its mouth because of thirst; the young children beg for food, but no one gives it to them.

5 Those who feasted on dainties are perishing in the streets; those who were brought up in purple lie cleaving to refuse *and* ash heaps.

6 For the punishment of the iniquity of the daughter of my people is greater than the punishment of the sin of Sodom, which was overthrown in a moment, and no hands had come against her *or* been laid on her. [Gen. 19:25.]

7 [In physical appearance] her princes were purer than snow, they were whiter than milk; they were more ruddy in body than rubies *or* corals, their shapely figures [suggested a carefully cut] sapphire.

8 [Prolonged famine has made] them look blacker than soot and darkness; they are not recognized in the streets. Their skin clings to their bones; it is withered and it has become [dry] like a stick.

9 Those who are slain with the sword are more fortunate than those who are the victims of hunger [slain by the famine]; for they [the hungry] pine *and* ebb away, stricken through for want of the fruits of the field.

10 The hands of [heretofore] compassionate women have boiled their own children; they were their food during the destruction of the daughter of my people [Judah].

11 The Lord has fulfilled His wrath; He has poured out His fierce anger and has kindled a fire in Zion that has consumed her foundations.

12 The kings of the earth did not believe, nor did any of the inhabitants of the earth, that the oppressor and enemy could enter the gates of Jerusalem.

speak the Word

Thank You, God, for drawing near when I call to You and for pleading the causes of my soul—managing my affairs and protecting me. You have rescued and redeemed my life!
ADAPTED FROM LAMENTATIONS 3:57, 58

13 [But this happened] because of the sins of her [false] prophets and the iniquities of her priests, who shed the blood of the just *and* righteous in the midst of her.

14 [The false prophets and priests] wandered [staggering] in the streets as if blind; they had so polluted themselves with blood it was not [lawful] for men to touch their garments.

15 [People] cried to them, Go away! Unclean! Depart! Depart! Touch not! When they fled away, then they wandered [as fugitives]; men said among the nations, They shall not stay here any longer.

16 The anger of the Lord has scattered [and divided them among the nations]; He will no longer look after them. They did not respect the persons of the priests; they did not favor the elders.

17 As for us, our eyes yet failed *and* wasted away in looking for our worthless help. In our watching [on our watchtower] we have watched *and* waited expectantly for a nation [Egypt or some other one to come to our rescue] that could not save us. [Ezek. 29:16.]

18 [The missiles of the enemy] dog our steps, so that we cannot go into our streets; our end is near, our days are fulfilled—yes, our end has come.

19 Our pursuers were swifter than the eagles of the sky; they pursued us on the mountains, they lay in wait for us in the wilderness.

20 The breath of our nostrils, the anointed of the Lord [our king], was taken in their snares—he of whom we said, Under his shadow we shall live among the nations.

21 Rejoice and be glad, O Daughter of Edom, you who dwell in the land of Uz. But the cup [of the wine of God's wrath] also shall pass to you; you shall become drunk and make yourself naked. [Jer. 25:17.]

22 The punishment of your iniquity will be accomplished *and* completed, O Daughter of Zion; [the Lord] will no more carry you away *or* keep you in exile. But He will inspect *and* punish your iniquity *and* guilt, O Daughter of Edom; He will uncover your sins. [Ps. 137:7.]

5 O LORD, [earnestly] remember what has come upon us! Look down and see our reproach (our national disgrace)!

2 Our inheritance has fallen over to strangers, our houses to foreigners.

3 We have become orphans and fatherless; our mothers are like widows.

4 We have had to pay money to drink the water that belongs to us; our [own] wood is sold to us.

5 Our pursuers are upon our necks [like a yoke]; we are weary and are allowed no rest.

6 We have given the hand [as a pledge of fidelity and submission] to the Egyptians and to the Assyrians [merely] to get food to satisfy [our hunger].

7 Our fathers sinned *and* are no more, and [d]we have borne their iniquities. [Isa. 65:7; Jer. 16:11-12; 31:29; Ezek. 18:2-4.]

8 Servants *and* slaves rule over us; there is none to deliver us out of their hands. [Neh. 5:15.]

9 We get our bread at the peril of our lives because of the sword of the wilderness [the wild Arabs, who may attack if we venture into the fields to reap our harvests].

10 Our skin glows *and* is parched as

d Fathers and sons alike are responsible for the calamity that has befallen Jerusalem. The truth of the matter is: this generation too deserved their punishment. "Woe to us, for we have sinned! Because of this our hearts are faint and sick; because of these things our eyes are dim *and* see darkly" (Lam. 5:16, 17).

from [the heat of] an oven because of the burning heat of [the fever of] famine.

11 They ravished the women in Zion, the virgins in the cities of Judah.

12 They hung princes by their hands; the persons of elders were not respected.

13 Young men carried millstones, and boys fell [staggering] under [burdens of] wood.

14 The elders have ceased from [congregating at] the city's gate, the young men from their music.

15 Ceased is the joy of our hearts; our dancing has turned into mourning.

16 The crown has fallen from our head [our honor is brought to the dust]! Woe to us, for we have sinned!

17 Because of this our hearts are faint *and* sick; because of these things our eyes are dim *and* see darkly.

18 As for Mount Zion, which lies desolate, the jackals prowl over it!

19 But You, O Lord, remain *and* reign forever; Your throne endures from generation to [all] generations.

20 Why do You forget us forever? Why do You forsake us so long?

21 Turn us to Yourself, O Lord, and we shall be turned *and* restored! Renew our days as of old!—

22 Or have You utterly rejected us? ^eOr are You exceedingly angry with us [still]?

---

e "The Book of Lamentations, like so many of even the saddest of the psalms, does in fact end with the language of hope, a hope that is so little apparent on the first reading of the conclusion to Lamentations that in many Hebrew manuscripts the words of Lam. 5:21 are repeated at the end, right after Lam. 5:22, so that its words of hope and restoration rather than the somber ending of "Or are You exceedingly angry with us [still]?" may be the last to fall upon the ear. A similar expedient is used in the case of Ecclesiastes, Isaiah, and Malachi" (*The Cambridge Bible*). See also footnote on Jer. 52:34.

Ezekiel

Author:
Ezekiel

Date:
593 BC–571 BC

Everyday Life Principles:
Hope and restoration are always available in God.

Hard, stony hearts can be made soft and tender again by the touch of the Holy Spirit.

"Dry bones"—things that seem to be dead in your life—can live again!

The name *Ezekiel* means "God is strong," and throughout the book that bears Ezekiel's name, we see the strength of God. Ezekiel was a righteous man, called by God to be a preacher of righteousness in a pagan culture. In the midst of idolatry and sin, he trumpeted a prophetic message of God's unending, unbreakable covenant with His people. He called them to return to God and be changed and restored.

Though Ezekiel's message was intended for an entire nation, it can be applied in very personal ways. I believe that one of the most hopeful, personal promises we can find in the Bible is found in Ezekiel 11:19: "And I will give them one heart [a new heart] and I will put a new spirit within them; and I will take the stony [unnaturally hardened] heart out of their flesh, and will give them a heart of flesh [sensitive and responsive to the touch of their God]." Similarly, God promises in Ezekiel 36:26: "A new heart will I give you and a new spirit will I put within you, and I will take away the stony heart out of your flesh and give you a heart of flesh."

As you read through Ezekiel, you will find fascinating stories and some interesting prophetic content. More than anything, I hope this book will encourage and remind you that, as a believer, you are in covenant with God. His hope and restoration are always near to you!

1 NOW [when I was] in [my] thirtieth year, in the fourth month, in the fifth day of the month, as I was in the midst of captivity beside the river Chebar [in Babylonia], the heavens were opened and I saw visions of God.

2 On the fifth day of the month, which was in the fifth year of King Jehoiachin's captivity,

3 The word of the Lord came expressly to Ezekiel the priest, the son of Buzi, in the land of the Chaldeans by the river Chebar; and the hand of the Lord was there upon him. [I Kings 18:46; II Kings 3:15.]

4 As I looked, behold, a stormy wind came out of the north, and a great cloud with a fire enveloping it *and* flashing continually; a brightness was about it and out of the midst of it there seemed to glow amber metal, out of the midst of the fire.

5 And out of the midst of it came the likeness of four living creatures [or cherubim]. And this was their appearance: they had the likeness of a man,

6 But each one had four faces and each one had four wings.

7 And their legs were straight legs, and the sole of their feet was like the sole of a calf's foot, and they sparkled like burnished bronze.

8 And they had the hands of a man under their wings on their four sides. And the four of them had their faces and their wings thus:

9 Their wings touched one another; they turned not when they went but went every one straight forward.

10 As for the ᵃlikeness of their faces, they each had the face of a man [in front], and each had the face of a lion on the right side and the face of an ox on the left side; the four also had the face of an eagle [at the back of their heads]. [Rev. 4:7.]

11 Such were their faces. And their wings were stretched out upward [each creature had four wings]; two wings of each one were touching the [adjacent] wing of the creatures on either side of it, and [the remaining] two wings of each creature covered its body.

12 And they went every one straight forward; wherever the spirit would go, they went, and they turned not when they went.

13 In the midst of the living creatures there was what looked like burning coals of fire, like torches moving to and fro among the living creatures; the fire was bright and out of the fire went forth lightning.

14 And the living creatures darted back and forth like a flash of lightning.

15 Now as I was still looking at the living creatures, I saw one wheel upon the ground beside each of the living creatures with its four faces.

16 As to the appearance of the wheels and their construction: in appearance they gleamed like chrysolite; and the four were formed alike, and their construction work was as it were a wheel within a wheel.

17 When they went, they went in one of their four directions without turning [for they were faced that way].

18 As for their rims, they were so high that they were dreadful, and the four had their rims full of eyes round about.

19 And when the living creatures went, the wheels went beside them; and when the living creatures were lifted up from the earth, the wheels were lifted up.

---

a It is noteworthy that the four faces of the living creatures as here described are symbolic of "the four portraits of Jesus" as given in the four Gospels. Matthew represents our Lord as the King (the lion), Mark portrays Him as the Servant (the ox), Luke emphasizes His humanity (man), and John proclaims especially His deity (the eagle).

20 Wherever the spirit went, the creatures went and the wheels rose along with them, for the spirit *or* life of the [four living creatures acting as one] living creature was in the wheels.

21 When those went, these went; and when those stood, these stood; and when those were lifted up from the earth, the wheels were lifted up high beside them, for the spirit *or* life of the [combined] living creature was in the wheels.

22 Over the head of the [combined] living creature there was the likeness of a firmament, looking like the terrible *and* awesome [dazzling of shining] crystal *or* ice stretched across the expanse of sky over their heads.

23 And under the firmament their wings were stretched out straight, one toward another. Every living creature had two wings which covered its body on this side and two which covered it on that side.

24 And when they went, I heard the sound of their wings like the noise of great waters, like the voice of the Almighty, the sound of tumult like the noise of a host. When they stood, they let down their wings.

25 And there was a voice above the firmament that was over their heads; when they stood, they let down their wings.

26 And above the firmament that was over their heads was the likeness of a throne in appearance like a sapphire stone, and seated above the likeness of a throne was a likeness with the appearance of a Man. [Phil. 2:5-8.]

27 From what had the appearance of His waist upward, I saw a lustre as it were glowing metal with the appearance of fire enclosed round about within it; and from the appearance of His waist downward, I saw as it were the appearance of fire, and there was brightness [of a halo] round about Him.

28 Like the appearance of the bow that is in the cloud on the day of rain, so was the appearance of the brightness round about. This was the appearance of the likeness of the glory of the Lord. And when I saw it, I fell upon my face and I heard a voice of One speaking. [Rev. 4:3.]

2 AND HE said to me [Ezekiel], Son of man, stand upon your feet and I will speak to you.

2 And the Spirit entered into me when He spoke to me and set me upon my feet, and I heard Him speaking to me.

3 And He said to me, I send you, son of man, to the children of Israel, two rebellious nations that have rebelled against Me. They and their fathers have transgressed against Me even to this very day.

4 And the children are impudent and hard of heart. I send you to them and you shall say to them, Thus says the Lord God.

5 And they, whether they will hear or refuse to hear—for they are a rebellious house—yet shall they know *and* realize that there has been a prophet among them.

6 And you, son of man, be not afraid of them, neither be afraid of their words; though briers and thorns are all around you and you dwell *and* sit among scorpions, be not afraid of their words nor be dismayed at their looks, for they are a rebellious house.

7 And you shall speak My words to them whether they will hear or refuse

speak the Word

Lord, I pray that I will be like Ezekiel and hear You when You speak to me.
ADAPTED FROM EZEKIEL 2:2

to hear, for they are most rebellious.

8 As for you, son of man, hear what I say to you; be not rebellious like that rebellious house; open your mouth and eat what I give you.

9 And when I looked, behold, a hand was stretched out to me and behold, a scroll of a book was in it.

10 And He spread it before me and it was written within and on the back, and written on it were words of lamentation and mourning and woe.

3 HE SAID to me, Son of man, eat what you find [in this book]; eat this scroll; then go and speak to the house of Israel.

2 So I opened my mouth, and He caused me to eat the scroll.

3 And He said to me, Son of man, eat this scroll that I give you and fill your stomach with it. Then I ate it, and it was as sweet as honey in my mouth.

4 And He said to me, Son of man, go, get you to the house of Israel and speak to them with My words.

5 For you are not sent to a people of a foreign speech and of a difficult language but to the house of Israel;

6 Not to many peoples of foreign speech and of a hard language, whose words you cannot understand. Surely, had I sent you to such people, they would have listened to you *and* heeded My words.

7 But the house of Israel will not listen to you *and* obey you since they will not listen to Me *and* obey Me, for all the house of Israel are impudent and stubborn of heart.

8 Behold, I have made your face strong *and* hard against their faces and your forehead strong *and* hard against their foreheads.

9 Like an adamant harder than flint *or* a diamond point have I made your forehead; fear them not, neither be dismayed at their looks, for they are a rebellious house. [Isa. 50:7; Jer. 1:18; 15:20; Mic. 3:8.]

10 Moreover, He said to me, Son of man, all My words that I shall speak to you, receive in your heart and hear with your ears.

11 And go, get you to the [Jewish] captives [in Babylon], to the children of your people, and speak to them and tell them, Thus says the Lord God, whether they will hear or refuse to hear.

12 Then the Spirit lifted me up, and I heard behind me a voice of a great rushing [saying], Blessed be the glory of the Lord from His place [above the firmament].

13 I heard the noise of the wings of the living creatures as they touched *and* joined each one the other [its sister wing], and I heard the noise of the wheels beside them and the noise of a great rushing.

14 So the Spirit lifted me up and took me away [in the vision], and I went in bitterness [of discouragement] in the heat of my spirit; and the hand of the Lord was strong upon me.

15 Then I came to them of the captivity at Tel-abib, who sat *and* dwelt by the river of Chebar, and I sat where they sat and remained there among them seven days, overwhelmed with astonishment *and* silent.

16 And at the end of seven days, the word of the Lord came to me:

17 Son of man, I have made you a watchman to the house of Israel; therefore hear the word at My mouth and give them warning from Me. [Isa. 52:8; 56:10; 62:6; Jer. 6:17.]

speak the Word

God, every word that You speak to me I will not only hear with my ears, but I will also receive in my heart.
ADAPTED FROM EZEKIEL **3:10**

18 If I say to the wicked, You shall surely die, and you do not give him warning or speak to warn the wicked to turn from his wicked way, to save his life, the same wicked man shall die in his iniquity, but his blood will I require at your hand.

19 Yet if you warn the wicked and he turn not from his wickedness or from his wicked way, he shall die in his iniquity, but you have delivered yourself.

20 Again, if a righteous man turns from his righteousness (right doing and right standing with God) and some gift or providence which I lay before him he perverts into an occasion to sin and he commits iniquity, he shall die; because you have not given him warning, he shall die in his sin and his righteous deeds which he has done shall not be remembered, but his blood will I require at your hand.

21 Nevertheless if you warn the righteous man not to sin and he does not sin, he shall surely live because he is warned; also you have delivered yourself from guilt.

22 And the hand of the Lord was there upon me, and He said to me, Arise, go forth into the plain and I will talk with you there.

23 Then I arose and went forth into the plain, and behold, the glory of the Lord stood there, like the glory I had seen by the river Chebar, and I fell on my face.

24 Then the Spirit entered into me and set me on my feet; He spoke and said to me, Go, shut yourself up in your house.

25 But you, O son of man, behold, ropes will be put upon you and you will be bound with them, and you cannot go out among people.

26 And I will make your tongue cleave to the roof of your mouth so that you cannot talk and be a reprover of the people, for they are a rebellious house.

27 But when I speak with you, I will open your mouth and you shall say to the people, Thus says the Lord God; he who hears, let him hear, and he who refuses to hear, let him refuse; for they are a rebellious house.

4 AND YOU, son of man, take a tile and lay it before you, and make upon it a drawing of a city, even Jerusalem.

2 And put siege works against it, build a siege wall against it, and cast up a mound against it; set camps also against it and set battering rams against it round about.

3 Moreover, take a plate of iron and place it for an iron wall between you and the city; and set your face toward it and it shall be besieged, and you shall press the siege against it. This is a sign to the house of Israel.

4 Then [bound as you are] lie upon your left [and north] side to bear symbolically the iniquity of the house of the ten tribes of Israel upon that side. According to the number of days that you shall lie upon it you shall bear their iniquity.

5 For I have laid upon you the years of their iniquity, according to the number of the days, 390 days [representing 390 years]; so you shall bear the iniquity of the house of Israel.

6 And when you have fulfilled the days for Israel, lie again, but on your right [and south] side, and you shall bear the iniquity of the house of Judah forty days. I have appointed you one day for each year.

7 Therefore you shall set your face toward the siege of Jerusalem and your arm shall be uncovered [ready for battle], and you shall prophesy against [the city].

8 And, behold, I will lay bands upon you and you shall not turn yourself from one side to another till you have ended the days of your siege.

9 Also take wheat, barley, beans,

lentils, millet, and spelt, and put them into one vessel and make bread of them. According to the number of the days that you shall lie upon your side, 390 days you shall eat of it.

10 And the food you eat shall be by weight, twenty shekels *or* a full half pound a day, to be eaten at a fixed time each day.

11 You shall drink water by measure also, about one quart *or* the sixth part of a hin; you shall drink at a fixed time each day.

12 And you shall eat your food as barley cakes and you shall bake it with human dung as fuel in the sight of the people.

13 And the Lord said, Even thus shall the children of Israel eat their defiled bread among the nations to whom I will drive them. [Hos. 9:3.]

14 Then said I, Ah, Lord God! Behold, I have never defiled myself. From my youth up even till now have I not eaten of that which dies of itself or is torn in pieces; neither did there ever come abominable flesh into my mouth. [Acts 10:14.]

15 Then He said to me, Behold, I will let you use cow's dung instead of human dung, and you shall prepare your food with it.

16 Moreover, He said to me, Son of man, behold, I will break the staff of bread [by which life is supported] in Jerusalem; and they shall eat bread rationed by weight and with fearfulness, and they shall drink water rationed by measure and with dismay (silent, speechless grief caused by the impending starvation), [Lev. 26:26; Ps. 105:16; Isa. 3:1.]

17 In order that they may lack bread and water and look at one another in dismay and waste away [in their punishment] for their iniquity.

5 AND YOU, son of man [Ezekiel], take a sharp sword and use it as a barber's razor and shave your head and your beard. Then take balances for weighing and divide the hair into three parts.

2 You shall burn one part with fire in the midst of the city, when the days of the siege are fulfilled; and you shall take a second part and strike with the sword round about it; and a third part you shall scatter to the wind, and I will draw out a sword after them.

3 You shall also take from these a small number of hairs and bind them in the skirts of your robe.

4 And of these again take some hairs and cast them into the midst of the fire and burn them in the fire; from there a fire shall come forth into all the house of Israel.

5 Thus says the Lord God: This is Jerusalem; in the center of the nations I have set her, and countries are round about her.

6 And she has changed *and* rebelled against My ordinances more wickedly than the [heathen] nations, and against My statutes more than the countries that are round about her; for [Israel] rejected My ordinances, and as for My statutes, they have not walked in them. [Rom. 2:14, 15.]

7 Therefore thus says the Lord God: Because you were more turbulent *and* raged [against Me] more than the nations that are round about you and have not walked in My statutes, neither have kept My ordinances, nor have done according to the ordinances [concerning] the nations that are round about you; [Deut. 7:2-6; Josh. 23:7; Judg. 2:2.]

8 Therefore thus says the Lord God: Behold, I, even I, am against you, and I will execute judgments in the midst of you in the sight of the nations.

9 And because of all your abominations, I will do in you that which I have not done and the like of which I will never do again. [Lam. 4:6; Dan. 9:12; Amos 3:2.]

10 Therefore fathers shall eat their

sons in your midst, and sons shall eat their fathers; and I will execute judgments on you and all who are left of you I will scatter to all the winds. [Lev. 26:33; Deut. 28:64; Ezek. 12:14; Zech. 2:6.]

11 Therefore, as I live, says the Lord God, surely because you have defiled My sanctuary with all your detestable things and with all your abominations, therefore will I also diminish you *and* withdraw My eye that it shall not spare you. And I also will have no pity.

12 And a third of you shall die of pestilence and be consumed by famine in the midst of you; a third shall fall by the sword round about you; and I will scatter a third to all the winds and will draw out a sword after them.

13 Thus shall My anger be spent and I will cause My wrath toward them to rest and I will be eased *and* comforted. And they shall know, understand, *and* realize that I the Lord have spoken in My zeal, when I have accomplished My wrath upon them. [Ezek. 36:6; 38:19.]

14 Moreover, I will make you a desolation and a reproach among the nations that are round about you and in the sight of all who pass by. [Lev. 26:31, 32; Neh. 2:17.]

15 So it shall be a reproach and a taunt, a warning and a horror *and* an astonishment to the [heathen] nations around you when I shall execute judgments upon you in anger and in wrath and in furious chastisements *and* rebukes—I the Lord have spoken it. [Deut. 28:37; Ps. 79:4; Jer. 24:9.]

16 When I shall loose against them the evil arrows of hunger that are for destruction, which I will send to destroy you, then I will increase the famine upon you and will break your staff of bread.

17 And I will send upon you hunger and wild beasts, and they shall bereave you [of your loved ones]; and pestilence and blood shall pass through you, and I will bring the sword upon you. I the Lord have spoken it.

6 AND THE word of the Lord came to me, saying,

2 Son of man, set your face toward the mountains of Israel and prophesy against them,

3 And say, You mountains of Israel, hear the word of the Lord God! Thus says the Lord God to the mountains and the hills, to the river ravines and the valleys: Behold, I, even I, will bring a sword upon you, and I will destroy your high places [of idolatrous worship],

4 And your altars shall be made desolate and your sun-pillars shall be broken in pieces, and I will cast down your slain before your idols. [Lev. 26:30.]

5 And I will lay the dead bodies of the children of Israel before their idols, and I will scatter your bones round about your altars.

6 In all your dwelling places the cities shall be laid waste and the high places shall be made desolate, that your altars may bear their guilt *and* be laid waste and made desolate, your idols may be broken and destroyed, your sun-images may be hewn down, and your handiworks may be wiped away *and* blotted out.

7 And the slain shall fall in the midst of you, and you shall ᵇknow,

b On the basis of the fact that God uses it more often than any other important word in the Bible, the word "Lord" becomes the most essential term in any language for the welfare of any person. It is not enough that one knows that God is God, and that He is, for only a fool would deny that (Ps. 53:1), but God demands of every person who is to be recognized by Him that he accepts Him as Lord of his life, his Sovereign Ruler, to Whom he yields implicit obedience. When Thomas was able to say of Jesus, "My Lord and my God!" (John 20:28), his doubts ceased to exist. Nothing short of that kind understand, *and* realize that I am the Lord.

8 Yet will I leave some of you alive. When you have some that shall escape the sword among the nations, when you shall be scattered through the countries,

9 Then those of you who escape shall [earnestly] remember Me among the nations to which they shall be carried captive, how that I have been broken by their lewdness *and* have Myself broken their wanton heart which has departed from Me and blinded their eyes which turn after their idols wantonly; and they shall be loathsome in their own sight for the evils which they have committed in all their abominations.

10 And they shall know, understand, *and* realize that I am the Lord. I have not said in vain that I would bring this evil calamity [in punishment] upon them.

11 Thus says the Lord God: Strike with your fist, stamp with your foot, and say, Alas! over all the vile abominations of the house of Israel for which [Israel] shall fall by sword, by famine, and by pestilence.

12 He who is far off shall die of the pestilence, and he that is near shall fall by the sword, and he who remains and is preserved shall die by the famine. Thus will I accomplish My wrath upon them.

13 Then shall you know, understand, *and* realize that I am the Lord, when their slain shall lie among their idols round about their altars upon every high hill, on all the tops of the mountains, under every green tree, and under every thickly leafed oak, the places where they were accustomed to offer sweet incense to all their idols.

14 And I will stretch out My hand upon them and make the land desolate and waste, yes, more desolate than the wilderness toward Diblah [a Moabite city], throughout all their dwelling places; and they shall know, understand, *and* realize that I am the Lord.

7 MOREOVER, THE word of the Lord came to me, saying,

2 Also, son of man, thus says the Lord God to the land of Israel: An end! The end has come upon the four corners of the land. [Ezek. 11:13; Amos 8:2.]

3 Now is the end upon you, and I will send My anger upon you and will judge you according to your ways and will bring upon you retribution for all your abominations.

4 And My eye will not spare you, neither will I have pity; but I will bring recompense for your evil ways upon you, while your abominations are in the midst of you [calling down punishment from a righteous God]; and you shall know (recognize, understand, and realize) that I am the Lord.

5 Thus says the Lord God: Behold, an evil is coming, [an evil so destructive and injurious, so sudden and violent, that it stands alone, not as a succession but as] only one evil.

6 An end has come! The end has come! [The end—after sleeping so long] awakes against you. See, it has come!

7 Your turn (your doom) has come upon you, O inhabitant of the land; the time has come, the day is near, a day not of joyful shouting, but a day of tumult upon the mountains.

8 Now will I shortly pour out My wrath upon you and finish spending My anger against you, and I will judge

---

of expression of Christ's lordship meets God's demands. Watch for the word "Lord" in the Bible; it occurs around 5,000 times. Watch also for this phrase ("you shall know, understand, *and* realize that I am the Lord") throughout the book of Ezekiel.

you according to your ways and will recompense you with punishment for all your abominations.

9 And My eye will not spare, nor will I have pity. I will punish you according to your ways while your abominations are right in the midst of you. And you shall know, understand, *and* realize that it is I the Lord Who smites you.

10 Behold, the day! Behold, it has come! Your doom has gone forth, the rod has blossomed, pride has budded.

11 Violence has grown up into a rod of wickedness; none of [Israel] shall remain, none of their abundance, none of their wealth; neither shall there be preeminence among them *or* wailing for them.

12 The time has come, the day draws near. Let not the buyer rejoice nor the seller mourn, for wrath is upon all their multitude.

13 For the seller shall not return to that which is sold, even were they yet alive. For the vision [of punishment] is touching [Israel's] whole multitude; he shall not come back, neither shall any strengthen himself whose life is in his iniquity.

14 They have blown the trumpet and have made all ready, but none goes to the battle, for My wrath is upon all their multitude.

15 The sword is without and pestilence and famine are within. He who is in the field shall die by the sword, and him who is in the city shall famine and pestilence devour.

16 But those of them that escape shall escape, but shall be on the mountains like doves of the valleys, all of them moaning, every one in his iniquity's [punishment].

17 All hands shall be feeble and all knees shall be weak as water. [Isa. 13:7; Jer. 6:24; Ezek. 21:7.]

18 They shall also gird themselves with sackcloth; horror *and* dismay shall cover them, and shame shall be upon all faces and baldness upon all their heads [as evidence of grief].

19 They shall cast their silver into the streets, and their gold shall be [discarded] like an unclean thing *or* rubbish; their silver and their gold shall not be able to deliver them in the day of the wrath of the Lord; they shall not satisfy their animal cravings nor fill their stomachs with them, for [wealth] has been the stumbling block of their iniquity. [Prov. 11:4; Zeph. 1:18.]

20 As for the beauty of gold for ornament, they turned it to pride and made of it the images of their abominations (idols) and of their detestable things. Therefore I will make it to them as an unclean thing.

21 And I will give it for plunder into the hands of strangers and to the wicked of the earth for a spoil, and they shall profane it.

22 Also I will turn My face from them and they shall profane My secret treasure [the temple]; and robbers shall enter into it and profane it.

23 Prepare the chain [of imprisonment], for the land is full of bloodguiltiness [murders committed with pretended formalities of justice] and the city is full of violence.

24 Therefore I will bring in the worst of the [heathen] nations, who will take possession of the houses [of the people of Judah]; I will also silence their strongholds *and* put an end to their proud might, and their holy places *and* those who sanctify them shall be profaned.

25 Distress, panic, *and* destruction shall come, and they [of Judah] shall seek peace, and there shall be none.

26 Calamity shall come upon calamity and rumor shall be upon rumor, and they shall seek a vision of the prophet; and the law *and* instruction shall cease from the [distracted] priest and counsel from the [dismayed] elders. [Ps. 74:9; Lam. 2:9.]

27 The king [of Judah] shall wear

mourning and the prince shall clothe himself with garments of despair *and* desolation, while the hands of the people of the land shall tremble [palsied by terror]; for I will do to them in accordance with their ways, and according to their deserts will I judge them; and they shall know, recognize, *and* realize that I am the Lord.

8 AND IN the sixth year [of the capitivity of King Jehoiachin], in the sixth month, on the fifth day of the month, as I sat in my house [a captive of the Babylonians] with the elders of Judah sitting before me, the hand of the Lord God fell there upon me.

2   Then I beheld, and lo, a likeness of a Man with the appearance of fire; from His waist downward He was like fire, and from His waist upward He had the appearance of brightness like gleaming bronze.

3   And He put forth the form of a hand and took me by a lock of my head; and the Spirit lifted me up between the earth and the heavens and brought me in the visions of God to Jerusalem, to the entrance of the door of the inner [court] which faces toward the north, where was the seat of the idol (image) of jealousy, which provokes to jealousy. [II Kings 16:10-16; 21:4, 5.]

4   And behold, there was the glory of the God of Israel [Who had loved and chosen them], like the vision I saw in the plain. [Ezek. 1:28; 3:22, 23.]

5   Then He [the Spirit] said to me, Son of man, now lift up your eyes toward the north. So I lifted up my eyes toward the north, and behold, on the north of the altar gate was that idol (image) of jealousy in the entrance.

6   Furthermore, [the Spirit] said to me, Son of man, do you see what they are doing? The great abominations that the house of Israel is committing here to drive Me far from My sanctu-

ary? But you shall again see greater abominations.

7   And He brought me to the door of the court; and when I looked, behold, there was a hole in the wall.

8   Then He said to me, Son of man, dig now in the wall. And when I had dug in the wall, behold, there was a door.

9   And He said to me, Go in and see the wicked abominations that they do here.

10 So I went in and saw there pictures of every form of creeping things and loathsome beasts and all the idols of the house of Israel, painted round about on the wall.

11 And there stood before these [pictures] seventy men of the elders of the house of Israel, and in the midst of them stood Jaazaniah the son of Shaphan [the scribe], with every man his censer in his hand, and a thick cloud of incense was going up [in prayer to these their gods].

12 Then said He to me, Son of man, have you seen what the elders of the house of Israel do in the dark, every man in his [secret] chambers of [idol] pictures? For they say, The Lord does not see us; the Lord has forsaken the land.

13 He also said to me, Yet again you shall see greater abominations which they are committing.

14 Then He brought me to the entrance of the north gate of the Lord's house; and behold, there sat women weeping for Tammuz [a Babylonian god, who was supposed to die annually and subsequently be resurrected].

15 Then said [the Spirit] to me, Have you seen this, O son of man? Yet again you shall see greater abominations that they are committing.

16 And He brought me to the inner court of the Lord's house; and behold, at the door of the temple of the Lord, between the porch and the bronze

altar, were about twenty-five men with their backs to the temple of the Lord and their faces toward the east, and they were bowing themselves toward the east *and* worshiping the sun.

17 Then [the Spirit] said to me, Have you seen this, O son of man? Is it too slight a thing to the house of Judah to commit the abominations which they commit here, that they must fill the land with violence and turn back afresh to provoke Me to anger? And behold, they put the branch to their nose [actually, before their mouths, in superstitious worship]!

18 Therefore I will deal in wrath; My eye will not spare, nor will I have pity; and though they cry in My ears with a loud voice, yet will I not hear them. [Prov. 1:28; Isa. 1:15; Jer. 11:11; 14:12; Mic. 3:4; Zech. 7:13.]

9 [THE SPIRIT] cried in my ears [in the vision] with a loud voice, saying, Cause those to draw near who have charge over the city [as executioners], every man with his destroying weapon in his hand.

2 And behold, six men came from the direction of the Upper Gate, which faces north, every man with his battle-ax in his hand; and one man among them was clothed in linen, with a writer's ink bottle at his side. And they went in and stood beside the bronze altar.

3 And the glory of the God of Israel [the Shekinah, cloud] had gone up from the cherubim upon which it had rested to [stand above] the threshold of the [Lord's] house. And [the Lord] called to the man clothed with linen, who had the writer's ink bottle at his side.

4 And the Lord said to him, Go through the midst of the city, through the midst of Jerusalem, and set a mark upon the foreheads of the men who sigh and groan over all the abominations that are committed in the midst of it.

5 And to the others He said in my hearing, Follow [the man with the ink bottle] through the city and smite; let not your eye spare, neither have any pity.

6 Slay outright the elderly, the young man and the virgin, the infant and the women; but do not touch *or* go near anyone on whom is the mark. Begin at My sanctuary. So they began with the old men who were in front of the temple [who did not have the Lord's mark on their foreheads]. [I Pet. 4:17.]

7 And He said to [the executioners], Defile the temple and fill its courts with the slain. Go forth! And they went forth and slew in the city.

8 And while they were slaying them and I was left, I fell upon my face and cried, Ah, Lord God! Will You destroy all that is left of Israel in Your pouring out of Your wrath *and* indignation upon Jerusalem?

9 Then said He to me, The iniquity *and* guilt of the house of Israel and Judah are exceedingly great; the land is full of blood and the city full of injustice *and* perverseness; for they say, The Lord has forsaken the land; the Lord does not see [what we are doing].

10 And as for Me, My eye will not spare, neither will I have pity, but I will recompense their wicked doings upon their own heads.

11 And behold, the man clothed in linen, who had the ink bottle at his side, reported the matter, saying, I have done as You have commanded me.

10 THEN I looked and behold, in the firmament that was over the heads of the cherubim there appeared above them something looking like a sapphire stone, in form resembling a throne.

2 And [the Lord] spoke to the man clothed in linen and said, Go in among the whirling wheels under the cherubim; fill your hands with coals of fire from between the cherubim and scatter them over the city. And he went in before my eyes. [Rev. 8:5.]

3 Now the cherubim stood on the south side of the house when the man went in; and the cloud [the Shekinah] filled the inner court.

4 Then the glory of the Lord mounted up from the cherubim to stand over the threshold of the [Lord's] house; and the house was filled with the cloud, and the court was full of the brightness of the Lord's glory. [I Kings 8:10, 11; Ezek. 43:5.]

5 And the sound of the wings of the cherubim was heard even to the outer court, like the voice of God Almighty when He speaks. [Ps. 29:3, 4.]

6 And when He commanded the man clothed in linen, saying, Take fire from between the whirling wheels, from between the cherubim, [the man] went in and stood beside a wheel.

7 And a cherub stretched forth his hand from between the cherubim to the fire that was between the cherubim, and took some of it and put it into the hands of the man clothed in linen, who took it and went out.

8 And the cherubim seemed to have the form of a man's hand under their wings.

9 And I looked and behold, there were four wheels beside the cherubim, one wheel beside one cherub and another wheel beside another cherub; and the appearance of the wheels was like sparkling chrysolite.

10 And as for their appearance, they four looked alike, as if a wheel had been within a wheel.

11 When they went, they went in any one of the four directions [in which their four individual faces were turned]; they did not turn as they went, but to the place to which the front wheel faced the others followed; they turned not as they went.

12 And their whole body, their backs, their hands, and their wings, and the wheels, were full of eyes round about, even the wheels that each had.

13 As regarding the wheels [attached to them], they were called in my hearing the whirling wheels.

14 And every one had four faces: the first face was the face of the cherub, the second the face of a man, the third the face of a lion, and the fourth the face of an eagle.

15 And the cherubim mounted upward. This is the [same] living creature [the four regarded as one] that I saw by the river Chebar [in Babylonia]. [Ezek. 1:5.]

16 And when the cherubim went, the wheels went beside them; and when the cherubim lifted up their wings to mount up from the earth, the wheels did not turn from beside them.

17 When those stood still, these stood still; and when those mounted up, these [the wheels] mounted up also, for the spirit of life was in these [wheels]. [Ezek. 1:21.]

18 Then the glory of the Lord [the Shekinah, cloud] went forth from above the threshold of the temple and stood over the cherubim.

19 And the cherubim lifted up their wings and mounted up from the earth in my sight, and they went forth with the wheels beside them; and they stood at the entrance of the East Gate of the house of the Lord, and the glory of the God of Israel [the Shekinah, cloud] was over them.

20 This is the living creature [of four combined creatures] that I saw beneath the God of Israel by the river Chebar, and I knew that they were cherubim.

21 Each one had four faces and each one had four wings, and what looked like the hands of a man was under their wings.

22 And as for the likeness of their faces, they were the same faces which I saw by the river Chebar, with regard

to their appearances and themselves; they went every one straight forward.

11 MOREOVER, THE Spirit lifted me up and brought me to the East Gate of the Lord's house, which faces east. And behold, at the door of the gateway there were twenty-five men; and I saw in the midst of them Jaazaniah the son of Azzur and Pelatiah the son of Benaiah, princes of the people.

2 Then [the Spirit] said to me, Son of man, these are the men who devise iniquity and give wicked counsel in this city,

3 Who say, [The time] is not near to build houses; this city is the boiling pot and we are the flesh.

4 Therefore prophesy against them; prophesy, O son of man!

5 And the Spirit of the Lord fell upon me, and He said to me, Speak. Say, Thus says the Lord: This is what you thought, O house of Israel, for I know the things that come into your mind.

6 You have multiplied your slain in this city and you have filled its streets with the slain.

7 Therefore thus says the Lord God: Your slain whom you have laid in your midst; they are the flesh and this city is the boiling pot, but you shall be brought forth out of the midst of it.

8 You have feared the sword, and I will bring a sword upon you, says the Lord God.

9 And I will bring you forth out of the midst of it and deliver you into the hands of foreigners and execute judgments among you.

10 You shall fall by the sword; I will judge *and* punish you [before your neighbors] at the border *or* outside the land of Israel, and you shall know (understand and realize) that I am the Lord.

11 This city shall not be your boiling pot, neither shall you be the flesh in the midst of it; I will judge you at the border *or* outside of Israel;

12 And you shall know (understand and realize) that I am the Lord; for you have not walked in My statutes nor executed My ordinances, but have acted according to the ordinances of the nations around you.

13 And while I was prophesying, Pelatiah the son of Benaiah died. Then I fell down upon my face and cried with a loud voice, Ah, Lord God! Will You make a complete end of the remnant of Israel?

14 And the word of the Lord came to me, saying,

15 Son of man, your brethren, even your kindred, your fellow exiles, and all the house of Israel, all of them, are they of whom the [present] inhabitants of Jerusalem have said, They have gone far from the Lord [and from this land]; therefore this land is given to us for a possession.

16 Therefore say, Thus says the Lord God: Whereas I have removed [Israel] far off among the nations, and whereas I have scattered them among the countries, yet I have been to them a sanctuary for a little while in the countries to which they have come.

17 Therefore say, Thus says the Lord God: I will gather you from the peoples and assemble you out of the countries where you have been scattered, and I will give back to you the land of Israel.

18 And when they return there, they shall take away from it all traces of its detestable things and all its abominations (sex impurities and heathen religious practices).

19 And I will give them one heart [a new heart] and I will put a new spirit within them; and I will take the stony [unnaturally hardened] heart out of their flesh, and will give them a heart of flesh [sensitive and responsive to the touch of their God], [Ezek. 18:31; 36:26; II Cor. 3:3.]

life point

In Ezekiel 11:19, God says He will replace the stony hearts in His people with new hearts that are sensitive to His touch.

When we give our lives to God, He puts a sense of right and wrong deep within our consciences. But if we rebel against our consciences too many times, we can become hard-hearted. If that happens, we need to let God soften our hearts so we can be spiritually sensitive to the leadership of the Holy Spirit.

I was very hard-hearted before I really began fellowshipping with God. Being in His presence regularly developed the new heart in me—the new heart that Jesus died to give me. Without a heart sensitive to God's touch, we will not recognize many of the times He is speaking to us. He speaks gently, in a still, small voice, or with gentle conviction about a matter.

Those who are hard-hearted and busy "doing their own thing" will not be sensitive to God's voice. I am grateful that He has softened my heart with His Word, because a hardened heart cannot receive the blessings He wants to give.

20 That they may walk in My statutes and keep My ordinances, and do them. And they shall be My people, and I will be their God.
21 But as for those whose heart yearns for *and* goes after their detestable things and their loathsome abominations [associated with idolatry], I will repay their deeds upon their own heads, says the Lord God.
22 Then the cherubim lifted up their wings with the wheels which were beside them, and the glory of the God of Israel [the Shekinah, cloud] was over them.

23 Then the glory of the Lord rose up from over the midst of the city and stood over the mountain which is on the east side of the city.
24 And the Spirit lifted me up and brought me in a vision by the Spirit of God into Chaldea, to the exiles. Then the vision that I had seen went up from me.
25 And I told the exiles everything that the Lord had shown me.

12 THE WORD of the Lord also came to me, saying,
2 Son of man, you dwell in the midst of the house of the rebellious, who have eyes to see and see not, who have ears to hear and hear not, for they are a rebellious house. [Mark 8:18.]
3 Therefore, son of man, prepare your belongings for removing *and* going into exile, and move out by day in their sight; and you shall remove from your place to another place in their sight. It may be they will consider *and* perceive that they are a rebellious house.
4 And you shall bring forth your baggage by day in their sight, as baggage for removing into exile; and you shall go forth yourself at evening in their sight, as those who go forth into exile.
5 Dig through the wall in their sight and carry the stuff out through the hole.
6 In their sight you shall bear your baggage upon your shoulder and carry it forth in the dark; you shall cover your face so that you cannot see the land, for I have set you as a sign for the house of Israel.
7 And I did as I was commanded. I brought forth my baggage by day, as baggage for exile, and in the evening I dug through the wall with my own hands. I brought out my baggage in the dark, carrying it upon my shoulder in their sight.

the cure for hard-heartedness

I believe the secret to being happy is to walk in love. And walking in love is impossible unless we allow the Holy Spirit to tenderize our hearts. As God says in Ezekiel 11:19, it is not His will for us to be hard-hearted.

I had a hard heart because I had been abused as a child and abandoned by people who said they loved me. It seemed that all my life, people had taken advantage of me and used me for their own selfish purposes. My response was to become hard-hearted in an attempt to block further emotional pain.

Once our hearts become hardened, it is nearly impossible to change them by decision alone. That type of change requires a supernatural working of the Holy Spirit. He is the only One Who can get inside our souls and heal the wounds and bruises there. He alone can restore us to the condition we were in prior to our injuries. He is the One Who sheds God's love abroad in our hearts. He is also the One Who teaches us, convicting us of wrong conduct when we mistreat others; and He works in us to give us tender hearts.

When I realized that I grieved the Holy Spirit when I was sharp, angry, or hateful toward someone, I began to take that kind of behavior more seriously. I love God, and I certainly do not want to grieve His Spirit.

When you and I do grieve the Holy Spirit, we also feel grieved. Even though we may not realize what is wrong with us, we know that we feel sad or depressed, or that something is just not right.

I have come to believe that much of the sadness, depression, and heaviness we experience is most likely linked to our own behavior toward other people. Galatians 6:7 says that whatever we sow, we will reap. If we sow words and actions that sadden others, we will reap sadness. But if we sow happiness in the lives of others, we will reap happiness in our own lives.

Do not ever allow yourself to remain hard-hearted. Pray for God to soften your heart and give you a tender conscience—one that is responsive to His touch. Ask Him to allow you to feel what He feels and to work His character in you. Learn how to walk in love with a heart that is open to God and sensitive to the needs of others.

8 And in the morning came the word of the Lord to me, saying,
9 Son of man, has not the house of Israel, the rebellious house, asked you what you are doing?
10 Say to them, Thus says the Lord God: This oracle *or* revelation concerns the prince in Jerusalem and all the house of Israel who are in it.
11 Say, I am your sign; as I have done, so shall it be done to them; into banishment, into captivity, they shall go.
12 And the prince who is in their midst shall lift up his luggage to his

shoulder in the dark; then shall he go forth. They shall dig through the wall to carry out through the hole in it. He shall cover his face so that he will ᶜnot see with his eyes the land.

13 My net also will I spread over him, and he shall be taken in My snare, and I will bring him to Babylonia, to the land of the Chaldeans; yet shall he ᵈnot see it, though he shall die there. [II Kings 25:1-7; 39:5; Jer. 52:7-11.]

14 And I will scatter toward every wind all who are about him to help him, even all his bands; and I will draw out the sword after them.

15 And they shall know (recognize, understand, and realize) that I am the Lord, when I shall scatter them among the nations and disperse them in the countries.

16 But I will leave a few survivors who will escape the sword, the famine, and the pestilence, that they may declare *and* confess all their [idolatrous] abominations among the nations to which they go, and [thus God's punishment of them will be justified before everyone and] they shall know (understand and realize) that I am the Lord.

17 Moreover, the word of the Lord came to me, saying,

18 Son of man, eat your bread with shaking, and drink water with trembling and with fearfulness;

19 And say to the people of the land, Thus says the Lord God concerning the inhabitants of Jerusalem in the land of Israel: They shall eat their bread with fearfulness and drink water with dismay, for their land will be stripped *and* plundered of all its fullness, because of the violence of all those who dwell in it.

20 And the cities that are inhabited shall be laid waste, and the land shall be deserted *and* become a desolation; and you shall know (understand and realize) that I am the Lord.

21 And the word of the Lord came to me, saying,

22 Son of man, what is this proverb that you have in the land of Israel, saying, The days drag on and every vision comes to nothing *and* is not fulfilled?

23 Tell them therefore, Thus says the Lord God: I will put an end to this proverb, and they shall use it no more as a proverb in Israel. But say to them, The days are at hand and the fulfillment of every vision.

24 For there shall be no more any false, empty, *and* fruitless vision or flattering divination in the house of Israel.

25 For I am the Lord; I will speak, and the word that I shall speak shall be performed (come to pass); it shall be no more delayed *or* prolonged, for in your days, O rebellious house, I will speak the word and will perform it, says the Lord God.

26 Again the word of the Lord came to me, saying,

27 Son of man, behold, they of the house of Israel say, The vision that [Ezekiel] sees is for many days to come, and he prophesies of the times that are far off.

28 Therefore say to them, Thus says the Lord God: There shall none of My words be deferred any more, but the word which I have spoken shall be performed, says the Lord God.

13 AND THE word of the Lord came to me, saying, **2** Son of man, prophesy against the prophets of Israel who prophesy, and say to those who

---

c This prophecy was literally fulfilled as recorded in Jer. 52:7-11. King Zedekiah's eyes were put out in Riblah, Palestine, before he was carried to Babylon, where he died. Thus he did "not see it," even though he died there. **d** This prophecy was literally fulfilled as recorded in several Old Testament passages (see textual references).

prophesy out of their own mind *and* heart, Hear the word of the Lord!

3 Thus says the Lord God: Woe to the foolish prophets who follow their own spirit [and things they have not seen] and have seen nothing!

4 O Israel, your prophets have been like foxes among ruins *and* in waste places.

5 You have not gone up into the gaps *or* breeches, nor built up the wall for the house of Israel that it might stand in the battle in the day of the Lord.

6 They have seen falsehood and lying divination, saying, The Lord says; but the Lord has not sent them. Yet they have hoped *and* made men to hope for the confirmation of their word.

7 Have you not seen a false vision and have you not spoken a lying divination when you say, The Lord says, although I have not spoken?

8 Therefore thus says the Lord God: Because you have spoken empty, false, *and* delusive words and have seen lies, therefore behold, I am against you, says the Lord God.

9 And My hand shall be against the prophets who see empty, false, *and* delusive visions and who give lying prophecies. They shall not be in the secret council of My people, nor shall they be recorded in the register of the house of Israel, nor shall they enter into the land of Israel; and you shall know (understand and realize) that I am the Lord God.

10 Because, even because they have seduced My people, saying, Peace, when there is no peace, and because when one builds a [flimsy] wall, behold, [these prophets] daub it over with whitewash,

11 Say to them who daub it with whitewash that it shall fall! There shall be a downpour of rain; and you, O great hailstones, shall fall, and a violent wind shall tear apart [the whitewashed, flimsy wall].

12 Behold, when the wall is fallen, will you not be asked, Where is the coating with which you [prophets] daubed it?

13 Therefore thus says the Lord God: I will even rend it with a stormy wind in My wrath, and there shall be an overwhelming rain in My anger and great hailstones in wrath to destroy [that wall].

14 So will I break down the wall that you have daubed with whitewash and bring it down to the ground, so that its foundations will be exposed; when it falls, you will perish *and* be consumed in the midst of it. And you will know (understand and realize) that I am the Lord.

15 Thus will I accomplish My wrath upon the wall and upon those who have daubed it with whitewash, and I will say to you, The wall is no more, neither are they who daubed it,

16 The [false] prophets of Israel who prophesied deceitfully about Jerusalem, seeing visions of peace for her when there is no peace, says the Lord God.

17 And you, son of man, set your face against the daughters of your people who prophesy out of [the wishful thinking of] their own minds *and* hearts; prophesy against them,

18 And say, Thus says the Lord God: Woe to the women who sew pillows to all armholes and fasten magic, protective charms to all wrists, and deceptive veils upon the heads of those of every stature to hunt *and* capture human lives! Will you snare the lives of My people to keep your own selves alive?

19 You have profaned Me among My people [in payment] for handfuls of barley and for pieces of bread, slaying persons who should not die and giving [a guaranty of] life to those who should not live, by your lying to My people, who give heed to lies.

20 Therefore thus says the Lord God:

Behold, I am against your pillows *and* charms *and* veils with which you snare human lives like birds, and I will tear them from your arms and will let the lives you hunt go free, the lives you are snaring like birds.

21 Your [deceptive] veils also will I tear and deliver My people out of your hand, and they shall be no more in your hand to be hunted *and* snared. Then you shall know (understand and realize) that I am the Lord.

22 Because with lies you have made the righteous sad *and* disheartened, whom I have not made sad *or* disheartened, and because you have encouraged *and* strengthened the hands of the wicked, that he should not return from his wicked way and be saved [in that you falsely promised him life],

23 Therefore you will no more see false visions or practice divinations, and I will deliver My people out of your hand. Then you will know (understand and realize) that I am the Lord.

14 THEN CAME certain of the elders of Israel to me and sat before me.

2 And the word of the Lord came to me:

3 Son of man, these men have set up their idols in their hearts and put the stumbling block of their iniquity *and* guilt before their faces; should I permit Myself to be inquired of at all by them?

4 Therefore speak to them and say to them, Thus says the Lord God: Every man of the house of Israel who takes his idols [of self-will and unsubmissiveness] into his heart and puts the stumbling block of his iniquity [idols of silver and gold] before his face, and yet comes to the prophet [to inquire of him], I the Lord will answer him, answer him according to the multitude of his idols,

5 That I may lay hold of the house of Israel in the thoughts of their own mind *and* heart, because they are all estranged from Me through their idols.

6 Therefore say to the house of Israel, Thus says the Lord God: Repent *and* turn away from your idols, and turn away your faces from all your abominations.

putting the Word to work

In Ezekiel 14:6, God calls Israel to repent and turn away from idols. An idol is anything we worship by giving it too much attention or anything that is more important to us than God. Do you have any idols—social status, money, your job, your house or car, your children? Obey God's Word and ask Him to forgive you and to help you put Him in first place in your life. He will gladly do it!

7 For anyone of the house of Israel or of the strangers who sojourn in Israel who separates himself from Me, taking his idols into his heart and putting the stumbling block of his iniquity *and* guilt before his face, and [yet] comes to the prophet to inquire for himself of Me, I the Lord will answer him Myself!

8 And I will set My face against that [false worshiper] and will make him a sign and a byword, and I will cut him off from the midst of My people; and you shall know (understand and realize) that I am the Lord.

9 [The prophet has not been granted permission to give an answer to the hypocritical inquirer] but if the prophet does give the man the answer he desires [thus allowing himself to be a party to the inquirer's sin], I the Lord will see to it that the prophet is deceived in his answer, and I will stretch out My hand against him and will destroy him from the midst of My people Israel.

10 And they both shall bear the punishment of their iniquity: the iniquity of the [presumptuous] prophet shall be the same as the iniquity of the [hypocritical] inquirer,

11 That the house of Israel may go no more astray from Me, neither defile themselves any more with all their transgressions, but that they may be My people, and I may be their God, says the Lord God.

12 The word of the Lord came [again] to me, saying,

13 Son of man, when a land sins against Me by committing a trespass, and I stretch out My hand against it and break its staff of bread and send famine upon it and cut off from it man and beast,

14 Even if these three men, Noah, Daniel, and Job were in it, they would save but their own lives by their righteousness (their uprightness and right standing with Me), says the Lord God.

15 If I cause ferocious *and* evil wild animals to pass through the land and they ravage *and* bereave it, and it becomes desolate so that no man may pass through because of the beasts;

16 Though these three men were in it, as I live, says the Lord God, they would deliver neither sons nor daughters; they themselves alone would be delivered but the land would be desolate (laid waste and deserted).

17 Or if I bring a sword upon that land and say, Sword, go through the land, so that I cut off man and beast from it,

18 Though these three men were in it, as I live, says the Lord God, they would deliver neither sons nor daughters, but they themselves alone would be delivered.

19 Or if I send a pestilence into that land and pour out My wrath upon it in blood, to cut off from it man and beast,

20 Though Noah, Daniel, and Job were in it, as I live, says the Lord God, they would deliver neither son nor daughter; they would but deliver their own lives by their righteousness (their moral and spiritual rectitude in every area and relation).

21 For thus says the Lord God: How much more when I send My four sore acts of judgment upon Jerusalem—the sword, the famine, the evil wild beasts, and the pestilence—to cut off from it man and beast! [Lev. 26:21-33.]

22 And yet, behold, in it shall be left a remnant (an escaped portion), both sons and daughters. They shall be carried forth to you [in Babylon], and when you see their [ungodly] walk and their [wicked] doings, you will be consoled for the evil that I have brought upon Jerusalem, even concerning all that I have brought upon it.

23 And they shall console you when you see their evil ways and their rebellious actions. Then you shall know (understand and realize) that I have not done without cause all that I have done in Jerusalem, says the Lord God.

15 AND THE word of the Lord came to me, saying,

2 Son of man, How is the wood of the grapevine [Israel] more than that of any tree, the vine branch which was among the trees of the forest? [Ps. 80:8-13; Jer. 2:21.]

3 Shall wood be taken from it to do any work? Or will men take a peg of it on which to hang any vessel?

4 Behold, it is cast into the fire for fuel; the fire consumes both ends of it and the middle of it is charred. Is it suitable *or* profitable for any work?

5 Notice, even when it was whole, it was good for no work; how much less shall it be useful *and* profitable when the fire has devoured it and it is charred?

6 Therefore thus says the Lord God: Like the wood of the grapevine among the trees of the forest, which I have given to the fire for fuel, so will I give up the inhabitants of Jerusalem.

7 And I will set My face against them; they shall go out from one fire and another fire shall devour them, and you shall know (understand and realize) that I am the Lord, when I set My face against them.

8 And I will make the land desolate (laid waste and deserted) because they have acted faithlessly [through their idolatry], says the Lord.

16 AGAIN THE word of the Lord came to me, saying, 2 Son of man, cause Jerusalem to know, understand, and realize her [idolatrous] abominations [that they] are disgusting, detestable, and shamefully vile.

3 And say, Thus says the Lord God to Jerusalem [representing Israel]: Your [spiritual] origin and your birth are thoroughly Canaanitish; your [spiritual] father was an Amorite and your [spiritual] mother a Hittite. [Ezek. 16:45; John 8:44.]

4 And as for your birth, on the day you were born your navel cord was not cut, nor were you washed with water to cleanse you, nor rubbed with salt or swaddled with bands at all.

5 No eye pitied you to do any of these things for you, to have compassion on you; but you were cast out in the open field, for your person was abhorrent and loathsome on the day that you were born.

6 And when I passed by you and saw you rolling about in your blood, I said to you in your blood, Live! Yes, I said to you still in your natal blood, Live!

7 I caused you [Israel] to multiply as the bud which grows in the field, and you increased and became tall and you came to full maidenhood and beauty; your breasts were formed and your hair had grown, yet you were naked and bare.

8 Now I passed by you again and looked upon you; behold, you were maturing and at the time for love, and I spread My skirt over you and covered your nakedness. Yes, I plighted My troth to you and entered into a covenant with you, says the Lord, and you became Mine.

9 Then I washed you with water; yes, I thoroughly washed away your [clinging] blood from you and I anointed you with oil.

10 I clothed you also with embroidered cloth and shod you with [fine seal] leather; and I girded you about with fine linen and covered you with silk.

11 I decked you also with ornaments and I put bracelets on your wrists and a chain on your neck.

12 And I put a ring on your nostril and earrings in your ears and a beautiful crown upon your head!

13 Thus you were decked with gold and silver, and your raiment was of fine linen and silk and embroidered cloth; you ate fine flour and honey and oil. And you were exceedingly beautiful and you prospered into royal estate.

14 And your renown went forth among the nations for your beauty, for it was perfect through My majesty and splendor which I had put upon you, says the Lord God.

15 But you trusted in and relied on your own beauty and were unfaithful to God and played the harlot [in idolatry] because of your renown, and you poured out your fornications upon anyone who passed by [as you worshiped the idols of every nation which prevailed over you] and your beauty was his.

16 And you took some of your garments and made for yourself gaily decorated high places or shrines and played the harlot on them—things which should not come and that which should not take place.

17 You did also take your fair jewels *and* beautiful vessels of My gold and My silver which I had given you and made for yourself images of men, and you played the harlot with them;

18 And you took your embroidered garments and covered them and set My oil and My incense before them.

19 My bread also which I gave you—fine flour and oil and honey with which I fed you—you have even set it before the idols for a sweet odor. Thus it was, says the Lord God.

20 Moreover, you have taken your sons and your daughters whom you have borne to Me, and you have sacrificed them [to your idols] to be destroyed. Were your harlotries too little,

21 That you have slain My children and delivered them up, in setting them apart *and* causing them to pass through the fire for [your idols]?

22 And in all your abominations and idolatrous whoredoms you have not [earnestly] remembered the days of your youth when you were naked and bare, rolling about in your natal blood.

23 And after all your wickedness—Woe, woe to you! says the Lord God—

24 You have built also for yourself a vaulted chamber (brothel) and have made a high place [of idol worship] in every street.

25 At every crossway you built your high place [for idol worship] and have made your beauty an abomination [abhorrent, loathsome, extremely disgusting, and detestable]; and you have made your body available to every passerby and multiplied your [idolatry and spiritual] harlotry.

26 You have also played the harlot with the Egyptians, your neighbors, [by adopting their idolatries] whose worship is thoroughly sensuous, and you have multiplied your harlotry to provoke Me to anger.

27 Behold therefore, I have stretched out My hand against you, diminished your ordinary allowance of food, and delivered you over to the will of those who hate *and* despise you, the daughters of the Philistines, who turned away in shame from your despicable policy *and* lewd behavior [for they are faithful to their gods]!

28 You played the harlot also with the Assyrians because you were unsatiable; yes, you played the harlot with them, and yet you were not satisfied.

29 Moreover, you multiplied your harlotry with the land of trade, with Chaldea, and yet even with this you were not satisfied.

30 How weak *and* spent with longing *and* lust is your heart *and* mind, says the Lord God, seeing you do all these things, the work of a bold, domineering harlot,

31 In that you build your vaulted place (brothel) at the head of every street and make your high place at every crossing. But you were not like a harlot because you scorned pay.

32 Rather, you were as an adulterous wife who receives strangers instead of her husband!

33 Men give gifts to all harlots, but you give your gifts to all your lovers and hire them, bribing [the nations to ally themselves with you], that they may come to you on every side for your harlotries (your idolatrous unfaithfulnesses to God).

34 And you are different [the reverse] from other women in your harlotries, in that nobody follows you to lure you into harlotry and in that you give hire when no hire is given you; and so you are different.

35 Therefore, O harlot [Israel], hear the word of the Lord!

36 Thus says the Lord God: Because your brass [coins and gifts] *and* your filthiness were emptied out and your nakedness uncovered through your harlotries with your lovers, and because of all the [filthy] idols of your abominations, and the blood of your children that you gave to them,

37 Therefore behold, I will gather all your lovers with whom you have taken pleasure, and all those whom you have loved with all those whom you have hated; I will even gather them [the allies you have courted] against you on every side and will uncover your nakedness to them, that they may see all your nakedness [making you, Israel, an object of loathing and of mockery, a spectacle among the nations].

38 And I the Lord will judge you as women who break wedlock and shed blood are judged, and I will bring upon you the blood of [your divine Husband's] wrath and jealousy. [Num. 5:18.]

39 And I will also give you into the hand of those [your enemies], and they shall throw down your vaulted place (brothel) and shall demolish your high places [of idolatry]; they shall strip you of your clothes and shall take your splendid jewels and leave you naked and bare.

40 They shall also bring up a company against you, and they shall stone you with stones and hew down *and* thrust you through with their swords.

41 And they shall burn your houses with fire and execute judgments upon you before the eyes of many women spectators [the nations]. And I will cause you to cease playing the harlot, and you also shall give hire no more.

42 So will I make My wrath toward you to rest and My jealousy shall depart from you [My adulterous wife], and I will be quiet and will be no more angry.

43 Because you have not [earnestly] remembered the days of your youth but have enraged Me with all these things, therefore behold, I also will bring your deeds down on your own head, says the Lord God. Did you not commit this lewdness above *and* in addition to all your other abominations?

44 Behold, everyone who uses proverbs will use this proverb against you: As is the mother, so is her daughter.

45 You are your [spiritual] mother's daughter who loathed her husband and her children, and you are the sister of your sisters who loathed their husbands and their children. Your mother was a Hittite and your father an Amorite.

46 And your elder sister is Samaria, she and her daughters who dwelt in the north *and* at your left hand; and your younger sister who dwelt in the south *and* at your right hand is Sodom and her daughters.

47 Yet you were not satisfied to walk after their ways or to do after their abominations, but very soon you were more corrupt in all your ways than they were [for your sin, as those taught of God, is far blacker than theirs]. [Matt. 11:20-24.]

48 As I live, says the Lord God, Sodom your sister has not done, she nor her daughters, as you have done, you and your daughters.

49 Behold, this was the iniquity of your sister Sodom: pride, overabundance of food, prosperous ease, *and* idleness were hers and her daughters'; neither did she strengthen the hand of the poor and needy.

50 And they were haughty and committed abominable offenses before Me; therefore I removed them when I saw it *and* I saw fit. [Gen. 13:13; 18:20; 19:5.]

51 Neither has Samaria committed half of your sins, but you have multiplied your [idolatrous] abominations more than they and have seemed to justify your sisters [Samaria and Sodom] in all their wickedness by all the abominable things which you have done—you even make them appear righteous in comparison with you.

52 Take upon you *and* bear your own shame *and* disgrace [in your punishment], you also who called in question

the sin of ignoring the needy

Sodom and Gomorrah are usually known for their sexual sin, but we see in Ezekiel 16:49 that God actually considered other sins to be the root of all their problems. First of all, they had such an overabundance of everything that their hearts grew proud. This still happens today. When people do not have any needs, they frequently turn away from God.

According to Ezekiel 16:49, life was too easy for the people in Sodom. They were idle, and idleness always leads to trouble. Yes, these two cities had many problems, but one of the worst was that they did not help the poor and the needy.

God's Word explicitly teaches us to help those less fortunate than we are. He instructs us to share some of what we have with those who are in need. When we do not share, I believe we invite a curse onto our lives. God is always giving. Something good is always flowing out of Him to those in need—and He expects us, as His children, to be the same way.

Pure religion that is unblemished in God's sight is to visit and help and care for the orphans and widows in their affliction and need (see James 1:27). This simply means we should be involved in helping people who are hurting and needy. Our religion is worthless if we are not.

God has not called the church to "in-reach"; He has called us to "out-reach." I frequently find that I cannot solve my own problems, but I can always reach out and help someone else. When I do, I am sowing seeds for the harvest I need in my own life. Proverbs 11 teaches us that when we are merciful to the poor and needy we benefit ourselves. Do not be like Sodom and become proud in your abundance. Instead, make giving and helping others in need part of your daily life.

and judged your sisters, for you have virtually absolved them by your sins in which you behaved more abominably than they; they are more right than you. Yes, be ashamed *and* confounded and bear your shame *and* disgrace, you also, for you have seemed to justify your sisters *and* make them appear righteous.

53 I will restore them again from their captivity, restore the fortunes of Sodom and her daughters and the fortunes of Samaria and her daughters, and I will restore your own fortunes in the midst of them [in the day of the Lord], [Isa. 1:9.]

54 That you [Judah], amid your shame *and* disgrace, may be compelled to recognize your wickedness *and* be thoroughly ashamed *and* confounded at all you have done, becoming [converted and bringing] consolation *and* comfort to [your sisters.]

55 And your sisters, Sodom and her daughters shall return to their former estate, and Samaria and her daughters shall return to their former estate; then you and your daughters shall return to your former estate.

56 For was your sister Sodom not mentioned by you [except] as a byword in the day of your pride,

57 Before your own wickedness was uncovered? Now you have become

like her, an object of reproach *and* a byword for the daughters of Syria *and* of Edom and for all who are round about them and for the daughters of the Philistines—those round about who despise you.

58 You bear the penalty of your lewdness and your [idolatrous] abominations, says the Lord.

59 Yes, thus says the Lord God: I will even deal with you as you have done, who have despised the oath in breaking the covenant;

60 Nevertheless, I will [earnestly] remember My covenant with you in the days of your youth and I will establish with you an everlasting covenant. [Ps. 106:45.]

61 Then you will [earnestly] remember your ways and be ashamed *and* confounded when you shall receive your sisters, both your elder and your younger; I will give them to you as daughters, but not on account of your covenant [with Me]. [John 10:16.]

62 And I will establish My covenant with you, and you shall know (understand and realize) that I am the Lord, [Hos. 2:19, 20.]

63 That you may [earnestly] remember and be ashamed *and* confounded and never open your mouth again because of your shame, when I have forgiven you all that you have done, says the Lord God.

17 AND THE word of the Lord came to me, saying,

2 Son of man, put forth a riddle and speak a parable *or* allegory to the house of Israel;

3 Say, Thus says the Lord God: A great eagle [Nebuchadnezzar] with great wings and long pinions, rich in

feathers of various colors, came to Lebanon [symbolic of Jerusalem] and took the top of the cedar [tree].

4 He broke off the topmost of its young twigs [the youthful King Jehoiachin] and carried it into a land of trade [Babylon]; he set it in a city of merchants.

5 He took also of the seedlings of the land [Zedekiah, one of the native royal family] and planted it in fertile soil *and* a fruitful field; he placed it beside abundant waters and set it as a willow tree [to succeed Zedekiah's nephew Jehoiachin in Judah as vassal king].

6 And it grew and became a spreading vine of low [not Davidic] stature, whose branches turned [in submission] toward him, and its roots remained under *and* subject to him [the king of Babylon]; so it became a vine and brought forth branches and shot forth leafy twigs.

7 There was also another great eagle [the Egyptian king] with great wings and many feathers; and behold, this vine [Zedekiah] bent its roots [languishingly] toward him and shot forth its branches toward him, away from the beds of its planting, for him to water.

8 Though it was planted in good soil where water was plentiful for it to produce leaves and to bear fruit, it was transplanted, that it might become a splendid vine.

9 Thus says the Lord God: Ask, Will it thrive? Will he [the insulted Nebuchadnezzar] not pluck up its roots and strip off its fruit so that all its fresh sprouting leaves will wither? It will not take a strong arm or many people to pluck it up by its roots

speak the Word

Thank You, God, for establishing Your covenant with me and helping me know, understand, and realize that You are the Lord.
ADAPTED FROM EZEKIEL 16:62

[totally ending Israel's national existence]. [II Kings 25:1-7.]

10 Yes, behold, though transplanted, will it prosper? Will it not utterly wither when the east wind touches it? It will wither in the furrows *and* beds where it sprouted *and* grew. [Hos. 13:9-12, 15.]

11 Moreover, the word of the Lord came to me, saying,

12 Say now to the rebellious house, Do you not know *and* realize what these things mean? Tell them, Behold, the king of Babylon came to Jerusalem and took its king [Jehoiachin] and its princes and brought them with him to Babylon. [II Kings 24:11-16.]

13 And he took one of the royal family [the king's uncle, Zedekiah] and made a covenant with him, putting him under oath. He also took the mighty *and* chief men of the land, [II Kings 24:17.]

14 That the kingdom might become low *and* base and be unable to lift itself up, but that by keeping his [Nebuchadnezzar's] covenant it might stand.

15 But he [Zedekiah] rebelled against him [Nebuchadnezzar] in sending his ambassadors into Egypt, that they might give him horses and much people. Will he prosper? Will he escape who does such things? Can he break the covenant with [Babylon] and yet escape?

16 As I live, says the Lord God, surely in the place where the king [Nebuchadnezzar] dwells who made [Zedekiah as vassal] king, whose oath [Zedekiah] despised and whose covenant he broke, even with him in the midst of Babylon shall [Zedekiah] die.

17 Neither shall Pharaoh with his mighty army and great company help him in the war when the [Babylonians] cast up mounds and build forts to destroy many lives.

18 For [Zedekiah] despised the oath and broke the covenant and behold, he

had given his hand, and yet has done all these things; he shall not escape.

19 Therefore thus says the Lord God: As I live, surely My oath [made for Me by Nebuchadnezzar] that [Zedekiah] has despised and My covenant with him that he has broken, I will even bring down on his own head.

20 And I will spread My net over him, and he shall be taken in My snare; and I will bring him to Babylon and will enter into judgment *and* punishment with him there for his trespass *and* treason that he has committed against Me.

21 And all his fugitives [from Judah] in all his bands shall fall by the sword, and they that remain shall be scattered toward every wind. And you shall know (understand and realize) that I the Lord have spoken it.

22 Thus says the Lord God: I Myself will take a twig from the lofty top of the cedar and will set it out; I will crop off from the topmost of its young twigs a tender one and will plant it upon a mountain high and exalted. [Isa. 11:1, 10; 53:2; Jer. 23:5; Zech. 3:8.]

23 On the mountain height of Israel will I plant it, that it may bring forth boughs and bear fruit and be a noble cedar, and under it shall dwell all birds of every feather; in the shade of its branches they shall nestle *and* find rest.

24 And all the trees of the field shall know (understand and realize) that I the Lord have brought low the high tree, have exalted the low tree, have dried up the green tree, and have made the dry tree flourish. I the Lord have spoken, and I will do it.

18 THE WORD of the Lord came to me again, saying,
2 What do you mean by using this proverb concerning the land of Israel, The fathers have eaten sour grapes, and the children's teeth are set on edge?

3 As I live, says the Lord God, you shall not have occasion any more to use this proverb in Israel.

4 Behold, all souls are Mine; as the soul of the father, so also the soul of the son is Mine; the soul that sins, it shall die. [Rom. 6:23.]

5 But if a man is [uncompromisingly] righteous (upright and in right standing with God) and does what is lawful and right,

6 And has not eaten [at the idol shrines] upon the mountains nor lifted up his eyes to the idols of the house of Israel, has not defiled his neighbor's wife nor come near to a woman in her time of impurity,

7 And has not wronged anyone but has restored to the debtor his pledge, has taken nothing by robbery but has given his bread to the hungry and has covered the naked with a garment,

8 Who does not charge interest or percentage of increase on what he lends [in compassion], who withholds his hand from iniquity, who executes true justice between man and man,

9 Who has walked in My statutes and kept My ordinances, to deal justly; [then] he is [truly] righteous; he shall surely live, says the Lord God. [Ezek. 20:11; Amos 5:4.]

10 If he begets a son who is a robber or a shedder of blood, who does to a brother either of these sins of violence,

11 And leaves undone all of the duties [of a righteous man], and has even eaten [the food set before idols] on the mountains and defiled his neighbor's wife,

12 Has wronged the poor and needy, has taken by robbery, has not restored [to the debtor] his pledge, has lifted up his eyes to the idols, has committed abomination (things hateful and exceedingly vile in the eyes of God),

13 And has charged interest or percentage of increase on what he has loaned [in supposed compassion]; shall he then live? He shall not live! He has done all these abominations; he shall surely die; his blood shall be upon him.

14 But if this wicked man begets a son who sees all the sins which his father has committed, and considers *and* fears [God] and does not do like his father,

15 Who has not eaten [food set before idols] upon the mountains nor has lifted up his eyes to the idols of the house of Israel, has not defiled his neighbor's wife,

16 Nor wronged anyone, nor has taken anything in pledge, nor has taken by robbery but has given his bread to the hungry and has covered the naked with a garment,

17 Who has withdrawn his hand from [oppressing] the poor, who has not received interest or increase [from the needy] but has executed My ordinances and has walked in My statutes; he shall not die for the iniquity of his father; he shall surely live.

18 As for his father, because he cruelly oppressed, robbed his brother, and did that which is not good among his people, behold, he shall die for his iniquity *and* guilt.

19 Yet do you say, Why does not the son bear the iniquity of the father? When the son has done that which is lawful and right and has kept all My statutes and has done them, he shall surely live.

20 The soul that sins, it [is the one that] shall die. The son shall not bear *and* be punished for the iniquity of the father, neither shall the father bear *and* be punished for the iniquity of the son; the righteousness of the righteous shall be upon him only, and the wickedness of the wicked shall be upon the wicked only.

21 But if the wicked man turns from all his sins that he has committed and keeps all My statutes and does that which is lawful and right, he shall surely live; he shall not die.

22 None of his transgressions which he has committed shall be remembered against him; for his righteousness which he has executed [for his moral and spiritual rectitude in every area and relation], he shall live.

23 Have I any pleasure in the death of the wicked? says the Lord, and not rather that he should turn from his evil way *and* return [to his God] and live?

24 But if the righteous man turns away from his righteousness and commits iniquity and does according to all the abominations that the wicked man does, shall he live? None of his righteous deeds which he has done shall be remembered. In his trespass that he has trespassed and in his sin that he has sinned, in them shall he die.

25 Yet you say, The way of the Lord is not fair *and* just. Hear now, O house of Israel: Is not My way fair *and* just? Are not your ways unfair *and* unjust?

26 When a righteous man turns away from his righteousness and commits iniquity and dies in his sins, for his iniquity that he has done he shall die.

27 Again, when the wicked man turns away from his wickedness which he has committed and does that which is lawful and right, he shall save his life.

28 Because he considers and turns away from all his transgressions which he has committed, he shall surely live; he shall not die.

29 Yet says the house of Israel, The way of the Lord is not fair and just! O house of Israel, are not My ways fair and just? Are not your ways unfair and unjust?

30 Therefore I will judge you, O house of Israel, every one according to his ways, says the Lord God. Repent and turn from all your transgressions, lest iniquity be your ruin

and so shall they not be a stumbling block to you. [Matt. 3:2; Rev. 2:5.]

31 Cast away from you all your transgressions by which you have transgressed against Me, and make you a new mind *and* heart and a new spirit. For why will you die, O house of Israel? [Eph. 4:22, 23.]

32 For I have no pleasure in the death of him who dies, says the Lord God. Therefore turn (be converted) and live!

19 MOREOVER, TAKE up a lamentation for the princes of Israel,

2 And say, What a lioness was your mother [Jerusalem-Judah]! She couched among lions; in the midst of young lions she nourished her cubs.

3 And she [the royal mother-city] brought up one of her cubs [Jehoahaz]; he became a young lion and he learned to catch the prey; he devoured men. [II Kings 23:30, 32.]

4 The nations also heard of him; he was taken in their pit, and they brought him with hooks to the land of Egypt. [II Chron. 36:1, 4.]

5 Now when she had waited, she saw her hope was lost. Then she took another of her cubs [Jehoiachin] and made him a young lion. [II Kings 23:34; 24:1, 6.]

6 And he [Jehoiachin] went up and down among the lions; he became a young lion and learned to catch prey, and he devoured men.

7 And he knew *and* ravaged their strongholds and he laid waste their cities, and the land was appalled and all who were in it by the noise of his roaring.

8 Then the nations set against [the king] on every side from the provinces, and they spread their net over him [Jehoiachin]; he was taken in their pit. [II Kings 24:8-15.]

9 With hooks they put him in a cage and brought him to the king of

Babylon; they brought him into custody *and* put him in strongholds, that his voice should no more be heard upon the mountains of Israel.

10 Your mother [the mother-city Jerusalem] was like a vine [like you, Zedekiah, and in your blood] planted by the waters; it was fruitful and full of branches by reason of abundant water. [II Kings 24:17; Ezek. 17:7.]

11 And it had strong rods for the scepters of those who bore rule and its height was exalted among the thick branches *and* into the clouds, and it was seen in its height among the multitude of its branches *and* was conspicuous.

12 But the vine was plucked up in God's wrath [by His agent the Babylonian king] and it was cast down to the ground; the east wind dried up its fruit; its strong rods were broken off and withered; the fire [of God's judgment] consumed them.

13 And now it is transplanted in the wilderness, in a dry and thirsty land [Babylon].

14 And fire went out of a rod [Zedekiah] of its branches which has consumed the vine's fruit, so that it has in it no [longer a] strong rod to be a scepter for ruling. This is a lamentation and shall be for a lamentation *and* a dirge.

20 IN THE seventh year, in the fifth [month], on the tenth [day] of the month [after the beginning of the Babylonian captivity, which was to last seventy years], certain of the elders of Israel came to inquire of the Lord and sat down before me [Ezekiel, in Babylonia]. [Jer. 25:11; 29:10.]

2 Then came the word of the Lord to me, saying,

3 Son of man, speak to the elders of Israel and say to them, Thus says the Lord God: Have you come to inquire of Me? As I live, says the Lord God, I will not be inquired of by you!

4 Will you judge them, son of man [Ezekiel], will you judge them? Then cause them to know, understand, *and* realize the abominations of their fathers. [Matt. 23:29-33; Acts 7:51, 52.]

5 And say to them, Thus says the Lord God: In the day when I chose Israel and lifted up My hand *and* swore to the offspring of the house of Jacob and made Myself known to them in the land of Egypt, when I lifted up My hand *and* swore to them, saying, I am the Lord your God,

6 On that day I lifted up My hand *and* swore to them to bring them out of the land of Egypt to a land that I had searched out for them, flowing with milk and honey, [a land] which is an ornament *and* a glory to all lands.

7 Then said I to them, Let every man cast away the abominable things on which he feasts his eyes, and defile not yourselves with the idols of Egypt; I am the Lord your God.

8 But they rebelled against Me and would not listen to Me; they did not every man cast away the abominable things on which they feasted their eyes, nor did they forsake the idols of Egypt. Then I [thought], I will pour out My wrath upon them and finish My anger against them in the midst of the land of Egypt.

9 But I acted for My name's sake, that it should not be profaned in the sight of the [heathen] nations among whom they dwelt, in whose sight I made Myself known to them by bringing them out of the land of Egypt.

10 So I caused them to go out from the land of Egypt and brought them into the wilderness.

11 And I gave them My statutes and showed *and* made known to them My judgments, which, if a man keeps, he must live in *and* by them.

12 Moreover, also I gave them My Sabbaths to be a sign between Me and them, that they might understand *and* realize that I am the Lord Who sanctifies them [separates and sets them apart].

13 But the house of Israel rebelled against Me in the wilderness; they walked not in My statutes and they despised *and* cast away My judgments, which, if a man keeps, he must even live in *and* by them; and they grievously profaned My Sabbaths. Then I thought I would pour out My wrath on them in the wilderness and uproot *and* consume them.

14 But I acted for My name's sake, that it should not be profaned before the [heathen] nations in whose sight I brought them out.

15 Yet also I lifted up My hand to swear to them in the wilderness that I would not bring them into the land which I had given them, flowing with milk and honey, which is the ornament *and* glory of all lands—

16 Because they despised *and* rejected My ordinances and walked not in My statutes and profaned My Sabbaths, for their hearts went after their idols.

17 Yet My eye pitied them instead of destroying them, and I did not make a full end of them in the wilderness.

18 But I said to their sons in the wilderness, You shall not walk in the statutes of your fathers nor observe their ordinances nor defile yourselves with their idols.

19 I the Lord am your God; walk in My statutes and keep My ordinances,

20 And hallow (separate and keep holy) My Sabbaths, and they shall be a sign between Me and you, that you may know, understand, *and* realize that I am the Lord your God.

21 Yet the sons rebelled against Me; they walked not in My statutes, nei-

ther kept My ordinances which, if a man does, he must live in *and* by them; they profaned My Sabbaths. Then I thought I would pour out My wrath on them and finish My anger against them in the wilderness.

22 Yet I withheld My hand and acted for My name's sake, that it should not be debased and profaned in the sight of the [heathen] nations, in whose sight I had brought them forth [from bondage].

23 Moreover, I lifted up My hand *and* swore to them in the wilderness that I would scatter them among the [heathen] nations and disperse them in the countries,

24 Because they had not executed My ordinances but had despised *and* rejected My statutes and had profaned My Sabbaths, and their eyes were set on their fathers' idols.

25 Wherefore also I gave them [over to] statutes that were not good and ordinances whereby they should not live *and* could not have life, [Ps. 81:12; Isa. 66:4; Rom. 1:21-25, 28.]

26 And I [let them] pollute *and* make themselves unclean in their own offerings [to their idols], in that they caused to pass through the fire all the firstborn, that I might make them desolate, to the end that they might know, understand, *and* realize that I am the Lord. [Lev. 20:2-5.]

27 Therefore, son of man, speak to the house of Israel and say to them, Thus says the Lord God: Again in this your fathers blasphemed Me, in that they dealt faithlessly *and* treacherously with Me and committed a treasonous trespass against Me.

28 For when I had brought them into

speak the Word

Thank You, God, for the gift of the Sabbath. Help me to live a balanced life, not wearing myself out or overworking, but regularly observing the times of rest and refreshment that You provide.
ADAPTED FROM EZEKIEL **20:12**

the land which I lifted up My hand *and* swore to give to them, then they saw every high hill and every dark *and* leafy tree [as a place for idol worship], and they offered there their sacrifices and there they presented their offering that provoked My anger *and* sadness; there also they made their sweet-smelling savor and poured out there their drink offerings.

29 Then I said to them, What is the high place to which you go? And the name of it is called Bamah [high place] to this day.

30 Therefore say to the house of Israel, Thus says the Lord God: Do you [exiles] debase *and* defile yourselves after the manner of your fathers? And do you play the harlot after their loathsome *and* detestable things?

31 And when you offer your gifts, when you make your sons pass through the fire, do you not debase *and* defile yourselves with all your idols to this day? And shall I be inquired of by you, O house of Israel? As I live, says the Lord God, I will not be inquired of by you!

32 And that which has come up in your mind shall never happen, in that you think, We will be as the nations, as the tribes of the countries, to serve idols of wood and stone.

33 As I live, says the Lord God, surely with a mighty hand and an outstretched arm and with wrath poured out will I be King over you.

34 And I will bring you out from the peoples and will gather you out of the countries in which you are scattered, with a mighty hand and an outstretched arm and with wrath poured out.

35 And I will bring you into the wilderness of the peoples, and there will I enter into judgment with you *and* contend with you face to face.

36 As I entered into judgment *and* contended with your fathers in the wilderness of the land of Egypt, so will I enter into judgment *and* contend with you, says the Lord God. [Num. 11; Ps. 106:15; I Cor. 10:5-10.]

37 And I will cause you to pass under the rod [as the shepherd does his sheep when he counts them, and I will count you as Mine and I will constrain you] and bring you into the covenant to which you are permanently bound. [Lev. 27:32.]

38 And I will purge out *and* separate from among you the rebels and those who transgress against Me; I will bring them out of the country where they temporarily dwell, but they shall not enter the land of Israel. Then you shall know, understand, *and* realize that I am the Lord. [Heb. 4:2, 3.]

39 As for you, O house of Israel, thus says the Lord God: Go, serve every one of you his idols, now and hereafter, if you will not listen to Me! But you shall not profane My holy name any more with your sacrificial gifts and your idols!

40 For on My holy mountain, on the mountain height of Israel, says the Lord God, there all the house of Israel, all of them in the land, shall serve Me. There will I [graciously] accept them, and there will I require your offerings and the firstfruits *and* the choicest of your contributions, with all your sacred things.

41 I will accept you [graciously] as a pleasant odor when I lead you out from the peoples and gather you out of the countries in which you have been scattered, and I will manifest My holiness among you in the sight of the nations [who will seek Me because of My power displayed in you]. [Eph. 5:2; Phil. 4:18.]

42 And you shall know, understand, *and* realize that I am the Lord, when I bring you into the land of Israel, into the country which I lifted up My hand *and* swore to give to your fathers.

put God first

Ezekiel 20:40 says that we should bring to the Lord our firstfruits, the choicest selections of all our offerings. To stay in perfect peace, we should give God the best of our time and our goods. We must be honest with ourselves about what our priorities really are and start making changes that will enable us to keep God in first place.

Being too busy is not an acceptable excuse for not staying focused on what is truly important. Everyone sets his or her own schedule. We need to establish boundaries, and we need to learn to say no when people ask us to do something that leads us away from peace.

Be honest with yourself as you examine how you spend your time. Do not give God your leftovers; do not give Him the part of your day when you are worn out and you cannot think straight or keep your eyes open. Give God the firstfruits of your attention. Give Him the best part of your day.

God needs to be your priority in *everything* you do. From getting dressed to setting your schedule, you can ask God for wisdom to make choices that will glorify Him. You can intermingle your time with God into everything you do to such a degree that you can pray without ceasing by praying your way through your day. As you become aware of His presence, it will not be possible to separate secular activities from sacred ones. Even ordinary events will become sacred because He is involved in them.

You can just talk to God as you go about your day, asking Him to direct you in the choices you are making and to empower you for the jobs you need to get done. As you acknowledge that God is always with you, you will keep Him first in everything you set out to do, and He will show you a direct path that will lead you to peace. You will experience great pleasure in your life, knowing you are keeping God first and thereby partnering with Him in everything you do.

43 And there you shall [earnestly] remember your ways and all your doings with which you have defiled yourselves, and you shall loathe yourselves in your own sight for all your evil deeds which you have done.
44 And you shall know, understand, *and* realize that I am the Lord, when I deal with you for My name's sake, not according to your evil ways nor according to your corrupt doings, O house of Israel, says the Lord God.
45 Moreover, the word of the Lord came to me, saying,

46 Son of man, set your face toward the south, preach against the south, and prophesy against the forest land of the South (the Negeb),
47 And say to the forest of the South (the Negeb), Hear the word of the Lord; Thus says the Lord God: Behold, I will kindle a fire in you and it shall devour every green tree in you and every dry tree. The blazing flame shall not be quenched, and all faces from the south to the north shall be scorched by it.
48 All flesh shall see that I the Lord

have kindled it; it shall not be quenched.

49 Then said I, Ah, Lord God! They are saying of me, Does he not speak in parables *and* make allegories?

21 AND THE word of the Lord came to me, saying, **2** Son of man, set your face toward Jerusalem and direct your [prophetic] word against the holy places; prophesy against the land of Israel

3 And say to the land of Israel, Thus says the Lord: Behold, I am against you and will draw forth My sword out of its sheath and will cut off from you both the righteous and the wicked.

4 Because I will cut off from you both the righteous and the wicked, therefore shall My sword go out of its sheath against all flesh from the south to the north,

5 And all living shall know, understand, *and* realize that I the Lord have drawn My sword out of its sheath; it shall not be sheathed any more.

6 Sigh therefore, son of man! With breaking heart and with bitterness shall you sigh before their eyes.

7 And it shall be that when they say to you, Why do you sigh? that you shall answer, Because of the tidings. When it comes, every heart will melt and all hands will be feeble, and every spirit will faint and all knees will be weak as water. Behold, it comes and it shall be fulfilled, says the Lord God.

8 Again the word of the Lord came to me, saying,

9 Son of man, prophesy and say, Thus says the Lord: Say, A sword, a sword is sharpened and also polished;

10 It [the sword of Babylon] is sharpened that it may make a slaughter, polished that it may flash *and* glitter like lightning! Shall we then rejoice *and* make mirth [when such a calamity is impending]? But the rod *or* scepter of My son [Judah] rejects *and* views with contempt every tree [that is, since God's promise long ago to Judah is certain, he believes Judah's scepter must remain no matter what power arises against it]! [Gen. 49:9, 10; II Sam. 7:23.]

11 And the sword [of Babylon] is given to be polished that it may be put to use; the sword is sharpened and polished to be given into the hand of the slayer.

12 Cry and wail, son of man, for it is against My people; it is against all the princes of Israel; they are thrown to the sword along with My people, *and* terrors by reason of the sword are upon My people. Therefore smite your thigh [in dismay].

13 For this sword has been tested *and* proved [on others], and what if the rejecting *and* despising rod *or* scepter of Judah shall be no more but completely swept away? says the Lord God.

14 Therefore, son of man, prophesy and smite your hands together and let the sword be doubled, yes, trebled in intensity—the sword for those to be overthrown *and* pierced through; it is the sword of great slaughter which encompasses them [so that none can escape, even by entering into their inner chambers].

15 I have set the threatening *and* glittering sword against all their gates, that their hearts may melt and their stumblings be multiplied. Ah! It is made [to flash] like lightning; it is pointed *and* sharpened for slaughter.

16 Turn [O sword] and cut right or cut left, whichever way your lust for blood *and* your edge direct you.

17 I will also clap My hands, and I will cause My wrath to rest. I the Lord have said it.

18 The word of the Lord came to me again, saying,

19 Also, son of man, mark out two ways by which the sword of the king of Babylon may come; both shall come forth from the same land. And make a signpost (a hand); make it at the head of the way to a city.

20 You shall point out a way for the [Babylonian] sword to come to Rabbah [the capital] of the sons of Ammon and to Judah with Jerusalem, the fortified *and* inaccessible.

21 For the king of Babylon stands at the parting of the way, at the fork of the two ways, to use divination. He shakes the arrows to and fro, he consults the teraphim (household gods), he looks at the liver.

22 In his right hand is the lot marked for Jerusalem: to set battering rams, to open the mouth calling for slaughter, to lift up the voice with a war cry, to set battering rams against the gates, to cast up siege mounds, and to build siege towers.

23 And it shall seem like a lying divination to them who have sworn oaths [of allegiance to Nebuchadnezzar]. [Will he now fight against their homeland?] But he will remind them of their guilt *and* iniquity [in violating those oaths], that they may be caught. [II Chron. 36:10, 13; Ezek. 17:15, 18-21.]

24 Therefore thus says the Lord God: Because you have made your guilt *and* iniquity to be remembered, in that your transgressions are uncovered, so that in all your doings your sins appear—because, I say, you have come to remembrance, you shall be taken with the [enemy's] hand.

25 And you, O dishonored and wicked one [Zedekiah], the prince of Israel, whose day will come at the time of your final reckoning *and* punishment,

26 Thus says the Lord God: Remove the [high priest's] miter *or* headband and take off the [king's] crown; things shall not remain as they have been; the low is to be exalted and the high is to be brought low.

27 I will overthrow, overthrow, over-throw it; this also shall be no more until He comes Whose right it is [to reign in judgment and in righteousness], and I will give it to Him. [Gen. 49:10; Isa. 9:6, 7; 11:1-4; Dan. 7:14; Luke 1:31-33.]

28 And you, son of man, prophesy and say, Thus says the Lord God concerning the sons of Ammon and concerning their reproach: Say, A sword, a sword is drawn for the slaughter; it is polished to cause it to devour to the uttermost *and* to flash like lightning,

29 While they see for you false visions, while they divine lies for you to lay you [of Ammon] upon the headless trunks of those who are slain, of the wicked whose day is coming at the time of the final reckoning *and* punishment.

30 Return [the sword] to its sheath. In the place where you were created, in the land of your origin *and* of your birth, I will judge you.

31 And I will pour out My indignation upon you [O sons of Ammon]; I will blow upon you with the fire of My wrath and will deliver you into the hand of brutish men, skillful to destroy.

32 You shall be for fuel to the fire; your blood shall be in the midst of the land; you shall be no more remembered, for I the Lord have spoken it. [Jer. 49:1-6; Ezek. 25:1-7; Amos 1:13-15; Zeph. 2:8-11.]

22 MOREOVER, THE word of the Lord came to me, saying,

2 And you son of man [Ezekiel], will you judge, will you judge the bloodshedding city? Then cause her to know all her abominations,

3 And say, Thus says the Lord God: A city that sheds blood in the midst of her so that her time [of doom] will come, and makes idols [over those who worship them] to defile her!

4 In your blood which you have

shed you have become guilty, and you are defiled by the idols which you have made, and you have caused your time [of judgment and punishment] to draw near and have arrived at the full measure of your years. Therefore have I made you a reproach to the [heathen] nations and a mocking to all countries.

5 Those who are near and those who are far from you will mock you, you infamous one, full of tumult.

6 Behold, the princes of Israel in you, every one according to his power, have been intending to shed blood.

7 In you have they treated father and mother lightly; in the midst of you they have dealt unjustly *and* by oppression in relation to the stranger; in you they have wronged the fatherless and the widow.

8 You have despised *and* scorned My sacred things and have profaned My Sabbaths.

9 In you are slanderous men who arouse suspicions to shed blood, and in you are they who have eaten [food offered to idols] upon the mountains; in the midst of you they have committed lewdness.

10 In you men have uncovered their fathers' nakedness [the nakedness of mother or stepmother]; in you they have humbled women who are [ceremonially] unclean [during their periods or because of childbirth].

11 And one has committed abomination with his neighbor's wife, another has lewdly defiled his daughter-in-law, and another in you has humbled his sister, his father's daughter.

12 In you they have accepted bribes to shed blood; you have taken [forbidden] interest and [percentage of] increase, and you have greedily gained from your neighbors by oppression *and* extortion and have forgotten Me, says the Lord God.

13 Behold therefore, I have struck My hands together at your dishonest gain which you have made and at the blood which has been in the midst of you.

14 Can your heart *and* courage endure or can your hands be strong in the days that I shall deal with you? I the Lord have spoken it, and I will do it.

15 And I will scatter you among the nations and disperse you through the countries, and I will consume your filthiness out of you.

16 And you shall be dishonored *and* profane yourself in the sight of the nations, and you shall know (understand and realize) that I am the Lord.

17 And the word of the Lord came to me, saying,

18 Son of man, the house of Israel has become to Me scum *and* waste matter. All of them are bronze and tin and iron and lead in the midst of the furnace; they are the dross of silver.

19 Therefore thus says the Lord God: Because you have all become scum *and* waste matter, behold therefore, I will gather you [O Israel] into the midst of Jerusalem.

20 As they gather silver and bronze and iron and lead and tin into the midst of the furnace, to blow the fire upon it in order to melt it, so will I gather you in My anger and in My wrath, and I will put you in and melt you.

21 Yes, I will gather you and blow upon you with the fire of My wrath, and you shall be melted in the midst of it.

22 As silver is melted in the midst of the furnace, so shall you be melted in the midst of it, and you shall know, understand, *and* realize that I the Lord have poured out My wrath upon you [O Israel].

23 And the word of the Lord came to me, saying,

24 Son of man, say to her, You are a land that is not cleansed nor rained upon in the day of indignation.

25 There is a conspiracy of [Israel's

false] prophets in the midst of her, like a roaring lion tearing the prey; they have devoured human lives; they have taken [in their greed] treasure and precious things; they have made many widows in the midst of her.

26 Her priests have done violence to My law and have profaned My holy things. They have made no distinction between the sacred and the secular, neither have they taught people the difference between the unclean and the clean and have hid their eyes from My Sabbaths, and I am profaned among them.

27 Her princes in the midst of her are like wolves rending *and* devouring the prey, shedding blood and destroying lives to get dishonest gain.

28 And her prophets have daubed them over with whitewash, seeing false visions and divining lies to them, saying, Thus says the Lord God—when the Lord has not spoken.

29 The people of the land have used oppression *and* extortion and have committed robbery; yes, they have wronged *and* vexed the poor and needy; yes, they have oppressed the stranger *and* temporary resident wrongfully.

30 And I sought a man among them who should build up the wall and stand in the gap before Me for the land, that I should not destroy it, but I found none.

31 Therefore have I poured out My indignation upon them; I have consumed them with the fire of My wrath; their own way have I repaid [by bringing it] upon their own heads, says the Lord God.

23 THE WORD of the Lord came again to me, saying, 2 Son of man, there were two women, the daughters of one mother;

3 And they played the harlot in Egypt. There they played the harlot in their youth; there their bosoms were pressed and there their virgin breasts were handled.

4 And the names of them were Aholah the elder and Aholibah her sister, and they became Mine and they bore sons and daughters. As for the identity of their names, Aholah is Samaria and Aholibah is Jerusalem.

5 And Aholah played the harlot when she was Mine, and she was foolishly fond of her lovers *and* doted on the Assyrians her neighbors,

6 Who were clothed with blue, governors and deputies, all of them attractive young men, horsemen riding upon horses.

7 And she bestowed her harlotries upon them, the choicest men of Assyria all of them; and on whomever she doted, with all their idols she defiled herself.

8 Neither has she left her harlotries since the days of Egypt [from where she brought them], for in her youth men there lay with her and handled her girlish bosom, and they poured out their sinful desire upon her.

9 Wherefore I delivered her into the hand of her lovers, into the hand of the Assyrians upon whom she doted.

10 These uncovered her nakedness *and* shame; they took her sons and her daughters and they slew her with the sword, and her name became notorious *and* a byword among women when judgments were executed upon her.

11 And her sister Aholibah saw this; yet she was more corrupt in her foolish fondness than she, and in her harlotries she was more wanton than her sister in her harlotries.

12 She doted upon the Assyrians—governors and deputies, her neighbors, clothed most gorgeously, horsemen riding upon horses, all of them desirable young men.

13 And I saw that she was defiled, that both [of the sisters] took one way.

stand in the gap

God is looking for people today who will "stand in the gap" for others, just as He was in Ezekiel's time (see Ezekiel 22:30). If there is a gap in a person's relationship with God due to a particular sin in his life, we have the privilege of placing ourselves in that breach and praying for him. If he has needs, we can intercede for him and expect to see him comforted and encouraged while he waits. We can also expect a timely breakthrough for this person concerning his needs being met.

I do not know what I would do if people did not intercede for me. Literally thousands of people have told me over the years that they pray for me. I actually ask God for intercessors. I petition Him to give me people to intercede for me and for the fulfillment of the ministry to which He has called me.

If our prayers are filled with only petition for the things we want and are void of intercession, that makes a statement about our character—just as when petition outweighs praise and thanksgiving in our prayer lives. I have discovered that the more I am delivered from selfishness, the more I pray for others.

Praying for others is equivalent to sowing seed. We all know that we must sow seed if we are to reap a harvest (see Galatians 6:7). Sowing seed into the lives of other people is one sure way to reap a harvest in our own lives. Each time we pray for someone else, we are assuring our own success.

If you want to succeed as a believer, I highly recommend that you include ample intercession for others in your prayer life. Give away what you need or want.

If you want to be a success, help someone else succeed by praying for him or her. If you want your ministry to succeed, pray for someone else's ministry. If you want your business to succeed, pray for someone else's business. If you need a breakthrough over some bad habit that is hindering you and holding you back, pray for someone who has a need in a similar area.

Remember, we are often tempted to judge others, and that only holds us in bondage. Give people *prayer* instead of *judgment*, and stand in the gap for them as often and as fervently as you possibly can. Then you will be a blessing to them, and you will make much faster progress toward the fulfillment of your destiny.

14 But [Aholibah] carried her harlotries further, for she saw men pictured upon the wall, the pictures of the Chaldeans sketched in bright red pigment,

15 Girded with girdles on their loins, with flowing turbans on their heads, all of them looking like officers, a picture of Babylonian men whose native land was Chaldea,

16 Then as soon as she saw [the sketches of] them, she doted on them and sent messengers to them in Chaldea.

17 And the Babylonians came to her into the bed of love, and they defiled her with their evil desire; and when she was polluted by them, she [Jerusalem] broke the relationship *and* pushed them away from her in disgust.

18 So she flaunted her harlotries and exposed her nakedness, and I was disgusted and turned from her, as I had turned in disgust from her sister.

19 Yet she multiplied her harlotries, remembering the days of her youth in which she had played the harlot in the land of Egypt.

20 For she doted upon her paramours there, whose lust was sensuous *and* vulgar like that of asses *or* stallions.

21 Thus you yearned for the lewdness of your youth, when those of Egypt handled your bosom on account of your girlish breasts.

22 Therefore, O Aholibah, thus says the Lord God: Behold, I will rouse up your lovers against you, from whom you turned in disgust, and I will bring them against you on every side:

23 The Babylonians and all the Chaldeans, Pekod and Shoa and Koa, and all the Assyrians with them, desirable young men, governors and officers all of them, princes, men of renown *and* counselors, all of them riding on horses.

24 And they shall come against you with weapons, chariots, wagons *and* wheels, and with a host of infantry which shall array themselves against you with buckler and shield and helmet round about; and I will commit the judgment *and* punishment to them, and they shall judge *and* punish you according to their [heathen] customs in such matters.

25 And I will set My jealous indignation against you, and they shall deal with you in fury; they shall take away your nose and your ears, and those who are left of you shall fall by the sword; they shall take your sons and your daughters, and the remainder shall be devoured by the fire.

26 They shall also strip you [Judah] of your clothes and take away your fine jewels.

27 Thus I will put an end to your lewdness and your harlotry brought from the land of Egypt, so that you will not lift up your eyes to them nor [earnestly] remember Egypt any more.

28 For thus says the Lord God: Behold, I will deliver you into the hands of those whom you hate, into the hands of those from whom you turned away in disgust.

29 They shall deal with you in hatred and shall take away all [the earnings of] your labor and shall leave you naked and bare, and the nakedness of your harlotry shall be uncovered, both your lewdness and your wanton ways.

30 These things shall be done to you, because you have played the harlot after the nations and because you have defiled yourself with their idols.

31 You have walked in the way of your sister [Samaria, Israel's capital]; therefore I will give her cup into your hand.

32 Thus says the Lord God: You shall drink of your sister's cup which is deep and wide *and* brimful; you shall be laughed to scorn and held in derision, for it contains much [too much to endure].

33 You shall be filled with drunkenness and sorrow, with the cup of wasting astonishment *and* horror and desolation, with the cup of your sister Samaria.

34 You shall drink it and drain it out, and then gnaw the pieces of it [which in your drunkenness you have broken] and shall tear your [own] breasts; for I have spoken it, says the Lord God.

35 Therefore thus says the Lord God: Because you have forgotten Me [your divine Husband] and cast Me behind your back, therefore bear also [the consequences of] your lewdness and your harlotry.

36 The Lord said, moreover, to me: Son of man, will you judge Aholah and Aholibah? Then declare *and* show to them their abominations (the detestable, loathsome, and shamefully vile things they do),

37 For they have committed adultery and blood is on their hands, even with their idols have they committed adultery [against Me]. And they have also caused their sons, whom they bore to Me, to pass through the fire to their images [as an offering of food] to be devoured [by them].

38 Moreover, this they have done to Me: they have defiled My sanctuary on the same day [of their idolatries] and have profaned My Sabbaths.

39 For when they had slain their children [as offerings] to their idols, then they came the same day into My sanctuary to profane it [by daring to offer sacrifice there also]! And behold, thus have they done in the midst of My house!

40 And furthermore, you have sent for men to come from afar, to whom a messenger was sent; and behold, they came—those for whom you washed yourself, painted your eyelids, and decked yourself with ornaments;

41 And you sat upon a stately couch with a table spread before it upon which you set My incense and My oil.

42 And the sound of a careless crowd was with her, and with men of the common sort were brought drunkards from the wilderness, who put bracelets upon the hands of both sisters and beautiful crowns upon their heads.

43 Then I said of the one [Aholah] worn out with adulteries, Will they now play the harlot with her [now that she is old] and she with them?

44 Yet they went in to her as they go in to a woman who plays the harlot; so they went in to Aholah and to

Aholibah [Israel and Judah], the lewd women.

45 And the righteous men, they shall judge *and* condemn them to the punishment due to adulteresses, to women who shed blood, for they are adulteresses and blood is upon their hands.

46 For thus says the Lord God: I will bring up a host upon them and will give them over to be tossed to and fro and robbed.

47 And the host shall stone them with stones and cut them down with their swords; they shall slay their sons and their daughters and burn up their houses with fire.

48 Thus will I cause lewdness to cease out of the land, that all women may be taught not to do after your lewdness.

49 Thus your lewdness shall be recompensed upon you and you shall suffer the penalty for your sinful idolatry; and you shall know (understand and realize) that I am the Lord God.

24 AGAIN IN the ninth year [of King Jehoiachin's captivity by Nebuchadnezzar of Babylon], in the tenth month, on the tenth day of the month, the word of the Lord came to me, saying,

2 Son of man, record the name of the day, even of this same day; the king of Babylon set himself against *and* assailed Jerusalem this same day.

3 And utter a parable against the rebellious house [of Judah] and say to them, Thus says the Lord God: Put on a pot; put it on and also pour water into it.

4 Put into it the pieces [of meat], all the good pieces, the thigh and the shoulder; fill it with the choice of the bones.

5 Take the choicest of the flock and burn also the unused bones under it, and make it boil well and seethe its bones in [the pot].

6 Therefore thus says the Lord God:

Woe to the bloody city, to the pot whose rust *and* scum are in it and whose rust *and* scum have not gone out of it! Take out of it piece by piece, without making any choice.

7 For the blood she has shed remains in the midst of her; she put it upon the bare rock; she did not pour it on the ground to cover it with dust.

8 That it may cause wrath to come up to take vengeance, I have put her blood [guilt for her children sacrificed to Molech] upon the bare rock, that it would not be covered.

9 Therefore thus says the Lord God: Woe to the bloodguilty city! Also I will make the pile [of fuel] great.

10 Heap on wood, kindle the fire *and* make it hot, boil well the meat *and* mix the spices, pour out the broth when thick, and let the bones be burned up.

11 Then set [the pot Jerusalem] back empty upon the coals, that the bronze of it may be hot and may glow and the filthiness of it may be melted in it and the rust *and* scum of it may be consumed.

12 She has wearied herself *and* Me with toil; yet her great rust *and* scum go not forth out of her, for however hotly the fire burns, her thick rust *and* filth will not go out of her by fire.

13 In your filthiness is abomination; [and therefore] because I would have cleansed you and you were not cleansed, you shall not be cleansed from your filthiness any more until I have satisfied My wrath against *and* upon you.

14 I the Lord have spoken it; it shall come to pass and I will do it; I will not go back, neither will I spare, neither will I relent; according to your ways and according to your doings shall they judge *and* punish you, says the Lord God.

15 Also the word of the Lord came to me, saying,

16 Son of man [Ezekiel], behold, I take away from you the desire of your eyes [your wife] at a single stroke. Yet you shall neither mourn nor weep, neither shall your tears flow.

17 Sigh *and* groan, but not aloud [be silent]; make no mourning for the dead; bind your turban upon your head and put your shoes on your feet, and do not cover your beard or eat the bread of mourners [furnished by others].

18 So I spoke to the people in the morning and in the evening my wife died, and I did the next morning as I was commanded.

19 And the people said to me, Will you not tell us what these things are supposed to mean to us, that you are acting as you do?

20 Then I answered them, The word of the Lord came to me, saying,

21 Speak to the house of Israel, Thus says the Lord God: Behold, I will profane My sanctuary—[in which you take] pride as your strength, the desire of your eyes, and the pity *and* sympathy of your soul [that you would spare with your life]; and your sons and your daughters whom you have left behind shall fall by the sword.

22 And you shall do as I [Ezekiel] have done; you shall not cover your beard nor eat the bread of mourning [brought to you by others],

23 And your turbans shall be upon your heads and your shoes upon your feet; you shall not mourn or weep, but you shall pine away for your iniquities (your guilt) and sigh *and* groan to one another. [Lev. 26:39.]

24 Thus Ezekiel is to you a sign; according to all that he has done you shall do. And when this [destruction of the temple] comes, you shall know, understand, *and* realize that I am the Lord God [the Sovereign Ruler, Who calls forth loyalty and obedient service].

25 And you, son of man, on the day when I take from them [My temple] their strength *and* their stronghold, their joy and their glory, the delight

of their eyes and their hearts' chief desire, and also [take] their sons and their daughters—

26 On that day an escaped fugitive shall come to you to cause you to hear of it [the destruction of Jerusalem] with your own ears.

27 In that day your mouth shall be open to him who has escaped, and you shall speak and be no more speechless, and you shall be a sign to them and they shall know, understand, *and* realize that I am the Lord.

25 THE WORD of the Lord came again to me, saying, **2** Son of man, set your face toward the Ammonites and prophesy against them.

3 And say to the Ammonites, Hear the word of the Lord God, for thus says the Lord God: Because you said Aha! over My sanctuary when it was profaned and over the land of Israel when it was made desolate and over the house of Judah when it went into captivity *and* exile,

4 Therefore behold, I am delivering you to the people of the East for a possession, and they shall set their encampments among you and make their dwellings in your midst; they shall eat your fruit and they shall drink your milk.

5 And I will make Rabbah [your chief city] a stable for camels and [the cities of] the Ammonites a fold for flocks. And you shall know (understand and realize) that I am the Lord [the Sovereign Ruler, Who calls forth loyalty and obedient service].

6 For thus says the Lord God: Because you have clapped your hands and stamped with the feet and rejoiced [in heart] with all the contempt, malice, *and* spite that is in you against the land of Israel,

7 Therefore behold, I have stretched out My hand against you and will hand you over for a prey *and*

a spoil to the nations, and I will cut you off from the peoples and will cause you to perish *and* be lost out of the countries; I will destroy you. Then will you know (understand and realize) that I am the Lord [the Sovereign Ruler, Who calls forth loyalty and obedient service]. [Jer. 49:1-6; Ezek. 21:28-32; Amos 1:13-15; Zeph. 2:8-11.]

8 Thus says the Lord God: Because Moab says, as does Seir [Edom], Behold, the house of Judah is like all the [heathen] nations,

9 Therefore behold, I will lay open the flank of Moab from the cities, from its cities on its frontiers *and* in every quarter, the glory of the country, Beth-jeshimoth, Baal-meon, and Kiriathaim.

10 I will give it along with the children of Ammon to the people of the East for a possession, that it *and* the children of Ammon may not be [any more seriously] remembered among the nations.

11 And I will execute judgments *and* punishments upon Moab, and they shall know (understand and realize) that I am the Lord [the Sovereign Ruler, Who calls forth loyalty and obedient service]. [Isa. 15, 16; Jer. 48; Amos 2:1-3; Zeph. 2:8-11.]

12 Thus says the Lord God: Because Edom has dealt against the house of Judah by taking vengeance and has greatly offended *and* has become doubly guilty by taking revenge upon them,

13 Therefore thus says the Lord God: I will also stretch out My hand against Edom and will cut off *and* root out man and beast from it, and I will make it desolate; from Teman even to Dedan they shall fall by the sword.

14 And I will lay My vengeance upon Edom by the hand of My people Israel, and they shall do upon Edom according to My anger and according to My wrath, and they shall know My vengeance, says the Lord God. [Isa. 34; Ezek. 35; Amos 1:11, 12; Obad.]

15 Thus says the Lord God: Because the Philistines have dealt revengefully and have taken vengeance contemptuously, with malice *and* spite in their hearts, to destroy in perpetual enmity,

16 Therefore thus says the Lord God: Behold, I will stretch out My hand against the Philistines, and I will cut off the Cherethites [an immigration in Philistia] and destroy the remainder of the seacoast.

17 And I will execute great vengeance upon them with wrathful rebukes *and* chastisements, and they shall know (understand and realize) that I am the Lord, when I lay My vengeance upon them. [Isa. 14:29-31; Jer. 47; Amos 1:6-8; Zeph. 2:4-7; Zech. 9:5-7.]

life point

Basically, what God was saying in Ezekiel 25:15–17 was that He would take vengeance on the Philistines because they had taken vengeance upon their enemies with spite and malice in their hearts. When people hurt us, we are wise to not take our own vengeance upon them; instead, we need to turn them over to God. Waiting on God to make things right is an act of trust, and it is also the smartest response we can make.

26 AND IN the eleventh year, on the first day of the month [after the carrying away of King Jehoiachin], the word of the Lord came to me, saying,

2 Son of man, because Tyre has said against Jerusalem, Aha! She is broken that has been the gate of the people; she is open to me [Tyre]; I shall become full now that she is desolate *and* a wasteland,

3 Therefore thus says the Lord God: Behold, I am against you, O Tyre, and will cause many nations to come up against you as the sea mounts up by its waves.

4 And they shall destroy the walls of Tyre and break down her towers; I will also escrape her dust from her and make her bare like the top of a rock.

5 Her island in the midst of the sea shall become a place for the spreading of nets, for I have spoken it, says the Lord God; and she shall become a prey *and* a spoil to the nations.

6 And Tyre's daughters [her towns and villages on the mainland] in the level place shall be slain by the sword, and they shall know (understand and realize) that I am the Lord [the Sovereign Ruler, Who calls forth loyalty and obedient service].

7 For thus says the Lord God: Behold, I will bring from the north upon Tyre fNebuchadrezzar king of Babylon, a king of kings, with horses and chariots and with horsemen and a host of many people.

8 He shall slay with the sword your daughters [the towns and villages] in the level area [on the mainland], and he shall make a fortified wall against you and cast up a siege mound against you and raise up a roof of bucklers *and* shields as a defense against you.

9 And he shall set his battering engines in shock against your walls, and with his axes he will break down your towers.

10 Because of the great number of [Nebuchadrezzar's] horses, their dust will cover you; your walls [O Tyre] will shake at the noise of the horsemen and of the wagon wheels and of the chariots, when he enters into your gates as

e To prevent Nebuchadnezzar from getting her valuables, Tyre transported herself to an island a half mile out in the sea. The conqueror destroyed the city on the mainland and left. But more than two centuries later, Alexander the Great took the ruins of the old city, even scraping up the dust, and made a causeway to the island, thus fulfilling the prophecy exactly.   f See footnote on Jer. 21:2.

men enter into the city in whose walls there has been made a breach.

11 With the hoofs of his horses [Nebuchadrezzar] will trample all your streets; he will slay your people with the sword and your strong pillars *or* obelisks will fall to the ground.

12 And [your adversaries] shall make a spoil of your riches and make booty of your merchandise. And they shall break down your walls and destroy your pleasant houses, and they shall lay the stones and the timber and the very dust from your demolished city out in the midst of the water [between the island and the mainland city site to make a causeway].

13 And I will cause the noise of your songs to cease, and the sound of your lyres shall be no more heard.

14 And I will make you [Tyre] a ᵍbare rock; you shall be a place upon which to spread nets; you shall never be rebuilt, for I the Lord have spoken it, says the Lord God.

15 Thus says the Lord God to Tyre: Shall not the isles *and* coastlands shake at the sound of your fall when the wounded groan, when the slaughter is made in the midst of you?

16 Then all the princes of the sea shall come down from their thrones and lay aside their robes and strip off their embroidered garments; they shall clothe themselves with tremblings; they shall sit upon the ground and shall tremble every moment and be astonished at you *and* appalled.

17 They shall take up a lamentation over you and say to you, How you are destroyed *and* vanished, O renowned city that was won from the seas *and* inhabited by seafaring men, renowned city that was mighty on the sea, she and her inhabitants who caused their terror to fall upon all who dwell there!

18 Now the isles *and* coastlands tremble in the day of your fall; yes, the isles that are in the sea are troubled *and* dismayed at your departure.

19 For thus says the Lord God: When I make you a desolate city like the cities that are not inhabited, when I bring up the deep over you and great waters cover you,

20 Then I will thrust you down with those who descend into the pit (the place of the dead) to the people of olden times, and I will make you [Tyre] to dwell in the lower world like the places that were desolate of old, with those who go down to the pit, that you be not inhabited or shed forth your glory *and* renown in the land of the living.

21 I will make you a terror [bring you to a dreadful end] and you shall be no more. Though you be sought, yet you shall never be found again, says the Lord God.

27 THE WORD of the Lord came again to me, saying,
2 Now you, son of man, take up a lamentation over Tyre,
3 And say to Tyre, O you who dwell at the entrance to the sea, who are merchant of the peoples of many

g According to Herodotus, Tyre's history began in 2750 BC It was a fortified city in Joshua's time (Josh. 19:29), and later became a great maritime commercial center (Isa. 23:8). Yet Jeremiah (27:2-7; 47:4) and Ezekiel (26:3-21; 28:6-10) foretold utter destruction for Tyre, naming not less than twenty-five separate details, each of which in the following centuries came true literally. Mathematicians have estimated, according to the "Law of Compound Probabilities," that if a prophecy concerning a person, place, or event has twenty-five details beyond the possibility of human collusion, calculation, coincidence, and comprehension, there is only one chance in more than thirty-three and one-half million of its accidental fulfillment. Yet Tyre's history at the hands of Nebuchadnezzar, and then more than two centuries later at the hands of Alexander the Great, and centuries after that at the hands of the Crusaders, was the striking fulfillment of each detail of the prophets' forecasts. No other city in the world's history could have fulfilled them. The authenticity and credibility of God's Word leaves no chance for sane denial. See footnote on Zeph. 2:7 for information about a similar fulfillment of details of Bible prophecy with regard to Palestine and to the end of Christ's life.

islands *and* coastlands, thus says the Lord God: O Tyre, you have thought *and* said, I am perfect in beauty.

4 Your borders are in the heart of the seas; your builders have perfected your beauty.

5 They have made all your planks *and* boards of fir trees from Senir [a peak of Mount Hermon]; they have taken a cedar from Lebanon to make a mast for you.

6 Of the oaks of Bashan they have made your oars; they have made your deck *and* benches of boxwood from the coasts of Cyprus, inlaid with ivory.

7 Of fine linen with embroidered work from Egypt was your sail, that it might be an ensign for you; blue and purple from the coasts of Elishah [of Asia Minor] was the [ship's] awning which covered you.

8 The inhabitants of Sidon and [the island] of Arvad were your oarsmen; your skilled *and* wise men, O Tyre, were in you; they were your pilots.

9 The old men of Gebal [a city north of Sidon] and its skilled *and* wise men in you were your calkers; all the ships of the sea with their mariners were in you to deal in your merchandise *and* trading.

10 Persia and Lud and Put were in your army as your men of war; they hung the shield and helmet in you; they gave you beauty *and* splendor.

11 The men of Arvad with your army were upon your walls round about and valorous men [of Gamad] were in your towers; they hung their shields upon your walls round about; they have perfected your beauty *and* splendor.

12 Tarshish [in Spain] carried on traffic with you because of the abundance of your riches of all kinds; with silver, iron, tin, and lead they traded for your wares.

13 Javan (Greece), Tubal, and Meshech [in the mountainous region between the Black and Caspian Seas] traded with you. They exchanged the lives of men [taken as slaves] and vessels of bronze for your merchandise.

14 They of the house of Togarmah (Armenia) traded for your wares with [chariot] horses, cavalry horses, and mules.

15 The men of Dedan [in Arabia] traded with you; many islands *and* coastlands were your own markets; they brought you in payment *or* as presents ivory tusks and ebony.

16 Aram (Syria or Mesopotamia) *and* Edom traded with you because of the multitude of the wares of your making. They exchanged for your merchandise emeralds, purple, embroidered work, fine linen, coral, and agate *or* rubies.

17 Judah and the land of Israel, they were your traders; they exchanged in your market wheat of Minnith [in Ammon], olives *or* early figs, honey, oil, and balm.

18 Damascus traded with you because of the abundance of supplies of your handiworks and the immense wealth of every kind, with wine of Helbon [Aleppo] and white wool [of Sachar in Syria].

19 Vedan also and [Arabic] Javan traded with yarn from Uzal [in Arabia] for your wares; wrought iron, cassia, and calamus were exchanged for your merchandise.

20 Dedan supplied you with precious [saddle] cloths for riding.

21 Arabia and all the princes of Kedar, they were the merchants in lambs, rams, and goats favored by you; in these they traded with you.

22 The merchants of Sheba and Raamah [in Arabia] traded with you; they exchanged for your wares the choicest of all kinds of spices and all precious stones and gold.

23 Haran and Canneh and Eden [in Mesopotamia], the merchants of Sheba [on the Euphrates], Asshur, and Chilmad [near Bagdad] were your traders.

24 These traded with you in choice

fabrics, in bales of garments of blue and embroidered work, and in treasures of many colored rich damask *and* carpets bound with cords and made firm; in these they traded with you.
25 The ships of Tarshish were your caravans for your merchandise, and you were replenished [Tyre] and were heavily loaded *and* made an imposing fleet [in your location] in the heart of the seas.
26 Your rowers have brought you out into great *and* deep waters; the east wind has broken *and* wrecked you in the heart of the seas.
27 Your riches, your wares, your merchandise, your oarsmen and your pilots, your caulkers, your dealers in merchandise, and all your men of war who are in you, with all your company which is in your midst, sink in the heart of the seas on the day of your ruin!
28 The waves *and* the countryside shake at the [piercing] sound of the [hopeless, wailing] cry of your pilots.
29 And down from their ships come all who handle the oar. The mariners and all the pilots of the sea stand upon the shore
30 And are heard wailing loudly over you, and they cry bitterly. They cast up dust on their heads; they wallow in ashes,
31 And they make themselves [utterly] bald for you and gird themselves with sackcloth, and they weep over you in bitterness of heart and with bitter mourning *and* wailing.
32 And in their wailing they take up a lamentation for you and lament over you, saying, Who was ever like Tyre, the destroyed (the annihilated), [who has become so still] in the heart of the sea?

33 When your wares came forth from the seas, you met the desire, the demand, *and* the necessities of many people; you enriched the kings of the earth with your abundant wealth and merchandise.
34 Now you are shattered by the seas in the depths of the waters; your merchandise and all your crew have gone down with you.
35 All the inhabitants of the isles *and* coastlands are astonished *and* appalled at you, and their kings are horribly frightened *and* shudder greatly; their faces quiver.
36 The merchants among the people hiss over you [with malicious joy]; you have become a horror *and* a source of terrors. You shall be [h]no more [forever].

28 THE WORD of the Lord came again to me, saying,
2 Son of man, say to the prince of Tyre, Thus says the Lord God: Because your heart is lifted up and you have said *and* thought, I am a god, I sit in the seat of the gods, in the heart of the seas; yet you are only man [weak, feeble, made of earth] and not God, though you imagine yourself to be almost more than mortal with your mind as the mind of God;
3 Indeed, you are [imagining yourself] wiser than Daniel; there is no secret [you think] that is hidden from you;
4 With your own wisdom and with your own understanding you have gotten you riches *and* power and have brought gold and silver into your treasuries;
5 By your great wisdom and by your traffic you have increased your riches

h Down to the thirteenth century AD the grandeur of the ancient city of Tyre was still visible. But God's Word does not fail. Soon Tyre had become an almost uninhabited pile of ruins. A large part of the western section of "the island" became covered by the sea, and early travelers told of seeing "houses, towers, and streets far down in the deep." In modern times the population of Tyre, made up largely of fishermen who spread their nets on its beaches, has increased to around 6,000, but the city as such has never been revived, and the original site has long since become obliterated.

and power, and your heart is proud *and* lifted up because of your wealth;

6 Therefore thus says the Lord God: Because you have imagined your mind as the mind of God [having thoughts and purposes suitable only to God Himself], [Obad. 3.]

7 Behold therefore, I am bringing strangers upon you, the most terrible of the nations, and they shall draw their swords against the beauty of your wisdom [O Tyre], and they shall defile your splendor.

8 They shall bring you down to the pit [of destruction] and you shall die the [many] deaths of all the Tyrians that are slain in the heart of the seas.

9 Will you still say, I am a god, before him who slays you? But you are only a man [made of earth] and no god in the hand of him who wounds *and* profanes you.

10 You shall die the death of the uncircumcised by the hand of strangers, for I have spoken it, says the Lord God.

11 Moreover, the word of the Lord came to me, saying,

12 Son of man, take up a lamentation over the king of Tyre and say to him, Thus says the Lord God: You are the full measure *and* pattern of exactness [giving the finishing touch to all that constitutes completeness], full of wisdom and perfect in beauty.

13 You were in Eden, the garden of God; every precious stone was your covering, the carnelian, topaz, jasper, chrysolite, beryl, onyx, sapphire, carbuncle, and emerald; and your settings and your sockets *and* engravings were wrought in gold. On the day that you were created they were prepared. [Gen. 3:14, 15; Isa. 14:12-15; Matt. 16:23.]

14 You were the anointed cherub that covers with overshadowing [wings], and I set you so. You were upon the holy mountain of God; you walked up and down in the midst of the stones of fire [like the paved work of gleaming sapphire stone upon which the God of Israel walked on Mount Sinai]. [Exod. 24:10.]

15 You were blameless in your ways from the day you were created until iniquity *and* guilt were found in you.

16 Through the abundance of your commerce you were filled with lawlessness *and* violence, and you sinned; therefore I cast you out as a profane thing from the mountain of God and the guardian cherub drove you out from the midst of the stones of fire.

17 Your heart was proud *and* lifted up because of your beauty; you corrupted your wisdom for the sake of your splendor. I cast you to the ground; I lay you before kings, that they might gaze at you.

18 You have profaned your sanctuaries by the multitude of your iniquities *and* the enormity of your guilt, by the unrighteousness of your trade. Therefore I have brought forth a fire from your midst; it has consumed you, and I have reduced you to ashes upon the earth in the sight of all who looked at you.

19 All who know you among the people are astonished and appalled at you; you have come to a horrible end and shall never return to being. [Isa. 23; Joel 3:4-8; Amos 1:9, 10; Zech. 9:3, 4.]

20 Again the word of the Lord came to me, saying,

21 Son of man, set your face toward Sidon and prophesy against her.

22 And say, Thus says the Lord God:

---

i This speech, though not addressed to Satan in and of himself, seems to be ironically spoken against his evil genius fulfilling itself in and through the human ruler who appropriates to himself the honors due only to God, as in the case of the king of Babylon (Isa. 14:12-15). Here is to be seen a foreshadowing of "the beast" who is to attribute to himself divine rights in the time of the end (Dan. 7:8-28; II Thess. 2:1-12; Rev. 13; 19:20).

Behold, I am against you, O Sidon, and I will show forth My glory *and* be glorified in the midst of you. And they shall know (understand and realize) that I am the Lord when I execute judgments *and* punishments in her, and am set apart *and* separated *and* My holiness is manifested in her.

23 For I will send pestilence into her and blood into her streets, and the wounded shall be judged *and* fall by the sword in the midst of her on every side, and they shall know (understand and realize) that I am the Lord [the Sovereign Ruler, Who calls forth loyalty and obedient service].

24 And there shall be no more a brier to prick the house of Israel or a hurting thorn of all those around them who have treated them with contempt, and they shall know (understand and realize) that I am the Lord God [the Sovereign Ruler, Who calls forth loyalty and obedient service].

25 Thus says the Lord God: When I gather the house of Israel from the peoples among whom they are scattered, and I shall be set apart *and* separated *and* My holiness made apparent in them in the sight of the nations, then shall they dwell in their own land which I gave to My servant Jacob.

26 And they shall dwell safely in it and shall build houses and plant vineyards; yes, they shall dwell securely *and* with confidence when I have executed judgments *and* punishments upon all those round about them who have despised *and* trodden upon them *and* pushed them away, and they shall know (understand and realize) that I am the Lord their God [their Sovereign Ruler, Who calls forth loyalty and obedient service].

29 IN THE tenth year [of the captivity of King Jehoiachin by the king of Babylon], in the tenth [month], on the twelfth [day] of the month, the word of the Lord came to me, saying,

2 Son of man, set your face toward Pharaoh king of Egypt and prophesy against him and against all Egypt.

3 Say, Thus says the Lord God: Behold, I am against you, Pharaoh king of Egypt, the great monster [of sluggish and unwieldy strength] that lies in the midst of his [delta] streams, [boastfully] declaring, My river Nile is my own and I have made it for myself.

4 But I will put hooks in your jaws [O Egyptian dragon] and I will cause the fish of your rivers to stick to your scales, and I will draw you up out of the midst of your streams with all the fish of your streams which stick to your scales.

5 And I will cast you forth into the wilderness, you and all the fish of your rivers; you shall fall upon the open field and not be gathered up or buried. I have given you for food to the [wild] beasts of the earth and the birds of the heavens.

6 And all the inhabitants of Egypt shall know (understand and realize) that I am the Lord [the Sovereign Ruler, Who calls forth loyalty and obedient service], because they have been a [deceitful] staff [made of fragile] reeds to the house of Israel.

7 When they grasped you with the hand *and* leaned upon you, you broke and tore their whole shoulder, and [by injuring their muscles made them so stiff and rigid that] they could do no more than stand.

8 Therefore thus says the Lord God: Behold, I will bring a sword upon you and cut off man and beast from you,

9 And the land of Egypt shall be a desolation and a waste. And they shall know (understand and realize) that I am the Lord [the Sovereign Ruler, Who calls forth loyalty and obedient service]. Because you have said, The river is mine and I have made it,

10 Behold therefore, I am against you and against your streams, and I will make the land of Egypt an utter [plundered] waste and desolation [of subjection] from [northern] Migdol to [southern] Syene, even as far as the border of Ethiopia.

11 No foot of man shall pass through it [in travel], no foot of beast shall pass through it [in trade with other countries], neither shall [Egypt] be [truly] inhabited [again] for forty years.

12 And I will make the land of Egypt a desolation [plundered and reduced to subjection] in the midst of desolated (plundered and reduced to subjection) countries, and her cities among the cities that are laid waste shall be a desolation forty years. I will scatter the Egyptians among the nations and will disperse them through the countries.

13 Yet thus says the Lord God: At the end of [their] forty years will I gather the Egyptians from the peoples among whom they were scattered, [Jer. 46:25, 26.]

14 And I will reverse the captivity of Egypt [as I will that of Israel] and will cause them to return into the land of Pathros [under Egypt], the land of their origin, and they shall be there a lowly kingdom.

15 It shall be the lowliest of the kingdoms, neither shall it [j]exalt itself any more above the nations; I will diminish [the Egyptians] so they shall never again rule over the nations.

16 And never again shall Egypt have the confidence *and* be the reliance of the house of Israel; their iniquity will be brought to remembrance whenever [Israel] looks toward them [for help]. They shall know (understand and realize) that I am the Lord God

[Who demands loyalty and obedient service].

17 In the twenty-seventh year [after King Jehoiachin was taken to Babylon], in the first month, on the first day of the month, the word of the Lord came to me, saying,

18 Son of man, [k]Nebuchadrezzar king of Babylon caused his army to render heavy service [at My bidding] against Tyre; every [soldier's] head became bald and every shoulder was worn *and* peeled [with carrying loads of earth and stones for siege works]. Yet he had no remuneration from Tyre [in proportion to the time and labor expended in the thirteen years' siege], either for himself or his army, for the work that he had done against it [for Me].

19 Therefore thus says the Lord God: Behold, I will give the land of Egypt to Nebuchadrezzar king of Babylon, and he shall carry off her great mass of people *and* of things (her riches) and take her spoil and take her prey, and it shall be the wages for his army.

20 I have given him the land of Egypt for his labor with which he served [against Tyre] because they did it for Me, says the Lord God.

21 In that day will I cause a horn to spring forth to the house of Israel and I will open your lips among them, and they shall know (understand and realize) that I am the Lord [the Sovereign Ruler, Who calls forth loyalty and obedient service].

30 THE WORD of the Lord came again to me, saying,

2 Son of man, prophesy and say, Thus says the Lord God: Wail, Alas for the day!

3 For the day is near, even the day of the Lord is near, a cloudy day; it

---

j For a little while Egypt struggled against its oppressors, but its power was already broken. From the time of its conquest by Cambyses, it has never been for any length of time independent. There are few stronger contrasts in any inhabited country than between the ancient glory, dignity, power, and wealth of Egypt and its later [lack of] significance (Charles J. Ellicott, *A Bible Commentary*).

k See footnote on Jer. 21:2.

shall be the time [of doom] for the nations.

4 And a sword shall come upon Egypt, and anguish *and* great sorrow shall be in Ethiopia (Cush), when the slain fall in Egypt and they [of Babylon] carry away her great mass of people *and* of things and her foundations are broken down.

5 Ethiopia (Cush) and Put, Lud and all the mingled people [foreigners living in Egypt], Cub (Lub, Libya) and the children of the land of the covenant [the Jews who had taken refuge in Egypt] shall fall with [the Egyptians] by the sword.

6 Thus says the Lord: They also who uphold *or* lean upon *and* are supported by Egypt shall fall, and the pride of her power shall come down; from Migdol [in the north] to Syene [in the south] they shall fall within her by the sword, says the Lord God.

7 And they shall be desolated in the midst of countries that are desolated, and her cities shall be in the midst of cities that are wasted [by plunder and subjection].

8 And they shall know (understand and realize) that I am the Lord [the Sovereign Ruler, Who calls forth loyalty and obedient service], when I have set a fire in Egypt and all her helpers are broken *and* destroyed.

9 In that day shall [swift] messengers go forth from Me in ships to terrify the careless *and* unsuspecting Ethiopians, and there shall be anguish *and* great sorrow upon them as in the day of Egypt's [doom], for behold, [their day] comes!

10 Thus says the Lord God: I will also make the tumult *and* the wealth *and* the large population of Egypt to cease by the hand of ¹Nebuchadrezzar king of Babylon.

11 He and his people with him, the [most] terrible of the nations, shall be brought in to destroy the land, and they shall draw their swords against Egypt and fill the land with the slain.

12 And I will make the [artificial] streams [of the Nile delta] dry and will sell the land into the hand of evil men, and I will make the land desolate, and all that is in it, by the hand of strangers. I the Lord [the Sovereign Ruler, Who calls forth loyalty and obedient service] have spoken it.

13 Thus says the Lord God: I will also destroy the idols and I will put an end to the images in Noph *or* Memphis, and there shall be no longer a prince of the land of Egypt. And I will put fear in the land of Egypt.

14 And I will make Pathros desolate and will set fire to Zoan and will execute judgments *and* punishments upon No *or* Thebes.

15 And I will pour My wrath upon Pelusium, the stronghold of Egypt, and I will cut off the tumult, the prosperity *and* the population of No *or* Thebes.

16 And I will set fire to Egypt; Pelusium shall have great anguish and No *or* Thebes shall be torn open and Noph *or* Memphis shall have adversaries in the daytime *and* all the day long.

17 The young men of Aven *or* On and of Pibeseth shall fall by the sword, and the [women and children] shall go into captivity.

18 At Tehaphnehes also the day shall withdraw itself *and* be dark when I break there the yokes *and* dominion of Egypt, and the pride of her power shall come to an end. As for her, a cloud [of calamities] shall cover her and her daughters shall go into captivity.

19 Thus will I execute judgments *and* punishments upon Egypt. Then shall they know (understand and realize) that I am the Lord [the Sovereign Ruler, Who calls forth loyalty and obedient service].

1 See footnote on Jer. 21:2.

20 And in the eleventh year [after King Jehoiachin was taken to Babylon], in the first month, on the seventh day of the month, the word of the Lord came to me, saying,

21 Son of man, I have broken the arm of Pharaoh king of Egypt, and behold, it has not been bound up to heal it by binding it with a bandage, to make it strong to hold *and* wield the sword.

22 Therefore thus says the Lord God: Behold, I am against Pharaoh king of Egypt and will break his arms, both the strong one and the one which was broken, and I will cause the sword to fall from his hand.

23 And I will scatter the Egyptians among the nations and will disperse them throughout the countries.

24 And I will strengthen the arms of the king of Babylon and put My sword in his hand, but I will break Pharaoh's arms and he will groan before [Nebuchadrezzar] with the groanings of a mortally wounded man.

25 But I will strengthen *and* hold up the arms of the king of Babylon and the arms of Pharaoh shall fall down, and they [of Egypt] shall know (understand and realize) that I am the Lord [the Sovereign Ruler, Who calls forth loyalty and obedient service], when I put My sword into the hand of the king of Babylon and he shall stretch it out upon the land of Egypt.

26 And I will scatter the Egyptians among the nations and disperse them through the countries, and they shall know (understand and realize) that I am the Lord [the Sovereign Ruler, Who calls forth loyalty and obedient service].

31 AND IN the eleventh year [after King Jehoiachin was taken captive to Babylon], in the third month, on the first day of the month, the word of the Lord came to me, saying,

2 Son of man, say to Pharaoh king of Egypt and to his multitude: Whom are you like in your greatness?

3 Behold, [I will liken you to] Assyria, a cedar in Lebanon, with fair branches and with forestlike shade and of high stature, with its top among the thick boughs [even among the clouds].

4 The waters nourished it; the deep made it grow tall; its rivers ran round about its planting, sending out its streams to all the trees of the forest [the other nations].

5 Therefore it towered higher than all the trees of the forest; its boughs were multiplied and its branches became long, because there was much water when they were shot forth.

6 All the birds of the heavens made their nests in its boughs, and under its branches all the wild beasts of the field brought forth their young and under its shadow dwelt all of the great nations.

7 Thus was it beautiful in its greatness, in the length of its branches, for its root was by many *and* great waters.

8 The cedars in the garden of God could not hide *or* rival it; the cypress trees did not have boughs like it and the plane trees did not have branches like it, nor was any tree in the garden of God like it in its beauty.

9 I made it beautiful with the multitude of its branches, so that all the trees of ᵐEden that were in the garden of God envied it [Assyria].

10 Therefore thus said the Lord God: Because it is exalted in stature and has set its top among the thick boughs *and* the clouds, and its heart is proud of its height, [II Kings 18:31-35.]

---

m The traditional site of Eden was within the bounds of the Assyrian Empire. However, this in no sense implies that Assyria was in the garden of God told about in Gen. 2:8.

11 I will even ⁿdeliver it into the hand of a mighty one of the nations; he shall surely deal with it. I have driven it out for its wickedness *and* lawlessness.

12 And strangers, the most terrible of the nations, will cut it off and leave it; upon the mountains and in all the valleys its branches will fall and its boughs will lie broken by all the watercourses of the land, and all the peoples of the earth will go down out of its shade and leave it.

13 Upon its ruins all the birds of the heavens will dwell, and all the wild beasts of the field will be upon [Assyria's fallen] branches.

14 All this is so that none of the trees by the waters may exalt themselves because of their height or shoot up their top among the thick boughs *and* the clouds, and that none of their mighty ones should stand upon [their own estimate of] themselves for their height, all that drink water. For they are all delivered over to death, to the lower world, in the midst of the children of men, with those who go down to the pit (the grave).

15 Thus says the Lord God: When [Assyria] goes down to Sheol (the place of the dead), I will cause a mourning; I will cover the deep for it and I will restrain its floods, and the many waters [that contributed to its prosperity] will be stayed; and I will cause Lebanon to be in black gloom *and* to mourn for it, and all the trees of the field, dismayed, will faint because of it.

16 I will make the nations quake at the sound of its fall when I cast it down to Sheol with those who descend into the pit, and all the trees of Eden, the choice and best of Lebanon, all [the trees] that drink water, will be comforted in the netherworld [at Assyria's downfall].

17 They also shall go down into Sheol with it to those who were slain by the sword—yes, those who were its arm, who dwelt under its shadow in the midst of the nations.

18 To whom [O Egypt] among the trees of Eden are you thus like in glory and in greatness? Yet you [also] shall be brought down with the trees of Eden to the netherworld. You shall lie among the ᵒuncircumcised heathen with those who are slain by the sword. This is ᵖhow it shall be with Pharaoh and all the multitude of his strength, his tumult, *and* his store [of wealth and glory], says the Lord God. [Ezek. 28:10; 32:19.]

32 IN THE twelfth year [after King Jehoiachin of Judah was taken into exile by the king of Babylon], in the twelfth month, on the first day of the month, the word of the Lord came to me, saying,

2 Son of man, take up a lamentation over Pharaoh king of Egypt and say to him, You have likened [yourself] to a young lion, leader of the nations, but you are like a [monster] dragon in the seas; you break forth in your rivers

---

n The effectiveness of this comparison [of Egypt] with Assyria becomes clear when it is remembered that Assyria had conquered and held Egypt in vassalage, and had then herself been conquered and annihilated only thirty-seven years before the date of this prophecy—by the same Chaldean [Babylonian] power [then controlled by the father of Nebuchadnezzar, which is] now foretold as about to execute judgment upon Egypt. Egypt could not hope to resist the conqueror of her conqueror (Charles Ellicott, *A Bible Commentary*). o Though there were other circumcised peoples besides the Hebrews, especially the Egyptians (and they as early as 3000 BC), yet the Philistines, the Moabites, the Ammonites, the Syrians, the Assyrians, the Babylonians, and various other nationalities with whom the Jews were in contact were uncircumcised, so that the word "uncircumcised" as a term of reproach meant practically (though not etymologically) almost the same thing as heathen (John D. Davis, *A Dictionary of the Bible*). p *The Septuagint* (Greek translation of the Old Testament) so reads at this point.

and trouble the waters with your feet, and you make foul their rivers [the sources of their prosperity].

3 Thus says the Lord God: I will therefore throw out My net over you with a host of many peoples, and they shall bring you up in My dragnet.

4 Then I will leave you [Egypt] upon the shore; I will cast you on the open field and will cause all the birds of the heavens to settle upon you, and I will fill the beasts of the whole earth with you.

5 And I will scatter your flesh upon the mountains and fill the valleys with your high heap of corpses *and* their worms.

6 I will also water with your flowing blood the land, even to the mountains, and the hollows *and* water channels shall be full of you.

7 And when I have extinguished you, I will cover the heavens [of Egypt] and make their stars dark; I will cover the sun with a cloud and the moon shall not give her light.

8 All the bright lights of the heavens I will make dark over you and set darkness upon your land, says the Lord God.

9 I will also trouble *and* vex the hearts of many peoples when I bring your breaking *and* trembling *and* destruction *and* carry you captive among the nations, into the countries which you have not known.

10 I will make many peoples amazed *and* appalled at you [Egypt], and their kings shall shudder *and* be horribly afraid because of you when I brandish My sword before them; they shall tremble every moment, every man for his own life, in the day of your downfall.

11 For thus says the Lord God: The sword of the king of Babylon shall come upon you.

12 I will cause your multitude, your tumult, *and* your store [of wealth, strength, and glory] to fall by the swords of the mighty—the most terrible among the nations are they all. And they shall bring to nothing the pomp *and* pride of Egypt, and all its multitude [with its activity and its wealth in every sphere] shall be destroyed.

13 I will destroy also all its beasts from beside many *and* great waters, and no foot of man shall trouble them any more, nor shall the hoofs of beasts trouble them.

14 Then will I make their waters sink down (subside, be quiet, and become clear); their rivers I will cause to run [slowly and smoothly] like oil, says the Lord God.

15 When I make the land of Egypt desolate, and the country is stripped *and* destitute of all that of which it was full when I smite all those who dwell in it, then will they know, understand, *and* realize that I am the Lord [the Sovereign Ruler, Who requires and calls forth loyalty and obedient service].

16 This is the lamentation with which they shall intone *or* chant the lament for her; the daughters of the nations shall chant their lament with it; over Egypt and over all her multitude, her tumult, *and* her wealth in every sphere shall they chant it, says the Lord God.

17 In the twelfth year [after King Jehoiachin of Judah was taken into exile], on the fifteenth day of the month, the word of the Lord came to me, saying,

18 Son of man, wail over the multitude of Egypt and cast them down, even her and the daughters of the famous *and* majestic nations, to the netherworld, with those who go down to the pit;

19 Whom [among them] do you surpass in beauty? Go down and be laid with the uncircumcised (the heathen).

20 They shall fall in the midst of those who are slain by the sword; she [Egypt] is delivered to the sword; they

draw her down [to her judgment], and all her multitudes [with their noise and stores].

21 The strong among the mighty shall speak of [Pharaoh] out of the midst of Sheol (the place of the dead, the netherworld) with those who helped him; they are gone down; they lie still, even the uncircumcised (the heathen) slain by the sword.

22 Assyria is there and all her company; their graves are round about her, all of them slain, fallen by the sword,

23 Whose graves are set in the uttermost parts of the pit and whose company is round about her grave, all of them slain, fallen by the sword, who caused terror to spread in the land of the living.

24 Elam [an auxiliary of Assyria] is there and all her multitude round about her grave, all of them slain, fallen by the sword, who have gone down uncircumcised into the netherworld, who caused their terror to spread in the land of the living and have borne their shame with those who go down to the pit.

25 They have set her a bed (a sepulcher) among the slain with all her multitude—their graves round about her, all of them uncircumcised, slain by the sword, for their terror had spread in the land of the living, and they henceforth bear their shame with those who go down to the pit; they are laid in the midst of the slain.

26 Meshech, Tubal, and all their multitude are there; their graves are round about [Pharaoh], all of them uncircumcised, slain by the sword, for they caused their terror to be spread in the land of the living.

27 And they shall not lie with the mighty who have fallen of the uncircumcised [and] who have gone down to Sheol (the place of the dead, the netherworld) with their weapons of war, whose swords were laid [with honors] under their heads and whose iniquities are upon their bones, for they caused their terror to spread in the land of the living.

28 But you [Meshech and Tubal] shall be broken in the midst of the uncircumcised and shall lie [without honors] with those who are slain with the sword.

29 Edom is there, her kings and all her princes, who for all their might are laid with those who were slain by the sword; they shall lie with the �q̃uncircumcised (the heathen) and with those who go down to the pit.

30 The princes of the north are there, all of them, and all the Sidonians, who have gone down with the slain; for all the terror which they caused by their might they are put to shame, and they lie uncircumcised with those who are slain by the sword and henceforth bear their shame with those who go down to the pit.

31 When Pharaoh sees them, he will comfort himself for all his multitude—even Pharaoh and all his army, slain by the sword, says the Lord God.

32 For I have put his *and* My terror in the land of the living, and he shall be laid in the midst of the uncircumcised (the heathen) with those slain by the sword, even Pharaoh and all his multitude, says the Lord God. [Isa. 19; Jer. 46; Zech. 14:18, 19.]

33

AND THE word of the Lord came to me, saying,

2 Son of man, speak to your people [the Israelite captives in Babylon] and say to them, When I bring the sword upon a land and the people of the land take a man from among them and make him their watchman,

3 If when he sees the sword coming

q The Edomites observed the rite of circumcision, but they were not spared because of that.

upon the land, he blows the trumpet and warns the people,

4 Then whoever hears the sound of the trumpet and does not take warning, and the sword comes and takes him away, his blood shall be upon his own head.

5 He heard the sound of the trumpet and did not take warning; his blood shall be upon himself. But he who takes warning shall save his life.

6 But if the watchman sees the sword coming and does not blow the trumpet and the people are not warned, and the sword comes and takes any one of them, he is taken away in and for his perversity and iniquity, but his blood will I require at the watchman's hand.

7 So you, son of man, I have made you a watchman for the house of Israel; therefore hear the word at My mouth and give them warning from Me.

8 When I say to the wicked, O wicked man, you shall surely die, and you do not speak to warn the wicked from his way, that wicked man shall die in his perversity and iniquity, but his blood will I require at your hand.

9 But if you warn the wicked to turn from his evil way and he does not turn from his evil way, he shall die in his iniquity, but you will have saved your life.

10 And you, son of man, say to the house of Israel, Thus you have said: Truly our transgressions and our sins are upon us, and we waste away because of them; how then can we live?

11 Say to them, As I live, says the Lord God, I have no pleasure in the death of the wicked, but rather that the wicked turn from his way and live. Turn back, turn back from your evil ways, for why will you die, O house of Israel?

12 And you, son of man, say to your people, The uprightness and justice of the [uncompromisingly] righteous shall not deliver him in the day of his transgression; and as for the wicked lawlessness of the wicked lawless, he shall not fall because of it in the day that he turns from his wickedness, neither shall the rigidly upright and just be able to live because of his past righteousness in the day that he sins and misses the mark [in keeping in harmony and right standing with God].

13 When I shall say to the [uncompromisingly] righteous that he shall surely live, and he trusts to his own righteousness [to save him] and commits iniquity (heinous sin), all his righteous deeds shall not be [seriously] remembered; but for his perversity and iniquity that he has committed he shall die.

14 Again, when I have said to the wicked, You shall surely die, if he turns from his sin and does that which is lawful and right—

15 If the wicked restores [what he took in] pledge, gives back what he had taken in robbery, walks in the statutes of life [right relationship with God], without committing iniquity, he shall surely live; he shall not die.

16 None of his sins that he has committed shall be [seriously] remembered against him; he has done that which is lawful and right; he shall surely live.

17 Yet your people say, The way of the Lord is not perfect or even just; but as for them, it is their own way that is not perfect or even just.

18 When the righteous turns back from his [uncompromising] righteousness and commits perverseness and iniquity, he shall even die in and because of it.

19 But if the wicked turns back from his wickedness and does what is lawful and right, he shall live because of it.

20 Yet you say, The way of the Lord is not perfect or [even] just. O you house of Israel, I will judge you, every one according to his own ways!

21 In the twelfth year of our captivity [in Babylon], in the tenth [month], on the fifth [day] of the month, a man who had escaped out of Jerusalem came to me [Ezekiel], saying, The city [Jerusalem] is taken.

22 Now the hand of the Lord had been upon me in the evening before this one who had escaped came, and He had opened my mouth [in readiness for the fugitives] coming to me in the morning, and my mouth was opened and I was no longer dumb.

23 Then the word of the Lord came to me, saying,

24 Son of man, those [back in Palestine] who inhabit those wastes of the ground of Israel are saying, Abraham was only one man and he inherited the land, but we are many; the land is surely given to us to possess as our inheritance.

25 Therefore say to them, Thus says the Lord God: You eat meat with the blood [as an idolatrous rite] and lift up your eyes to your [filthy] idols and shed blood; shall you then possess the land? [Gen. 9:4; Lev. 3:17; 7:27; Acts 15:28, 29.]

26 You stand upon your sword [as your dependence]; you commit abominations and each of you defiles your neighbor's wife; shall you then possess the land?

27 Say this to them, Thus says the Lord God: As I live, surely those who are in the waste places shall fall by the sword, and him that is in the open field will I give to the beasts to be devoured, and those who are in strongholds and in caves shall die by pestilence.

28 And I will make the land [of Israel] a desolation and a waste, and her proud might shall cease, and the mountains of Israel shall be so desolate that no one will pass through them.

29 Then shall they know, understand, *and* realize that I am the Lord, when I have made the land a desola-

tion and a waste because of all their abominations which they have committed.

30 As for you, son of man, your people who talk of you by the walls and in the doors of the houses say one to another, every one to his brother, Come and hear what the word is that comes forth from the Lord.

31 And they come to you as people come, and they sit before you as My people, and they hear the words you say, but they will not do them; for with their mouths they show much love, but their hearts go after *and* are set on their [idolatrous greed for] gain.

32 Behold, you are to them as a very lovely [love] song of one who has a pleasant voice and can play well on an instrument, for they hear your words but do not do them.

33 When this comes to pass—for behold, it will come!—then shall they know, understand, *and* realize that a prophet has been among them.

34 AND THE word of the Lord came to me, saying, **2** Son of man, prophesy against the shepherds of Israel; prophesy and say to them, even to the [spiritual] shepherds, Thus says the Lord God: Woe to the [spiritual] shepherds of Israel who feed themselves! Should not the shepherds feed the sheep?

3 You eat the fat, you clothe yourselves with the wool, you kill the fatlings, but you do not feed the sheep.

4 The diseased *and* weak you have not strengthened, the sick you have not healed, the hurt *and* crippled you have not bandaged, those gone astray you have not brought back, the lost you have not sought to find, but with force and hardhearted harshness you have ruled them.

5 And they were scattered because there was no shepherd, and when they were scattered they became food for all the wild beasts of the field.

6 My sheep wandered through all the mountains and upon every high hill; yes, My sheep were scattered upon all the face of the earth and no one searched or sought for them. [Matt. 9:36.]

7 Therefore, you [spiritual] shepherds, hear the word of the Lord:

8 As I live, says the Lord God, surely because My sheep became a prey, and My sheep became food for every beast of the field because there was no shepherd—neither did My shepherds search for My sheep, but the shepherds fed themselves and fed not My sheep—

9 Therefore, O you [spiritual] shepherds, hear the word of the Lord:

10 Thus says the Lord God: Behold, I am against the shepherds, and I will require My sheep at their hand and cause them to cease feeding the sheep, neither shall the shepherds feed themselves any more. I will rescue My sheep from their mouths, that they may not be food for them.

11 For thus says the Lord God: Behold, I, I Myself, will search for My sheep and will seek them out.

12 As a shepherd seeks out his sheep in the day that he is among his flock that are scattered, so will I seek out My sheep; and I will rescue them out of all places where they have been scattered in the day of clouds and thick darkness.

13 And I will bring them out from the peoples and gather them from the countries and will bring them to their own land; and I will feed them upon the mountains of Israel, by the watercourses, and in all the inhabited places of the country.

14 I will feed them with good pas-ture, and upon the high mountains of Israel shall their fold be; there shall they lie down in a good fold, and in a fat pasture shall they feed upon the mountains of Israel.

15 I will feed My sheep and I will cause them to lie down, says the Lord God.

16 I will seek that which was lost and bring back that which has strayed, and I will bandage the hurt *and* the crippled and will strengthen the weak *and* the sick, but I will destroy the fat and the strong [who have become hardhearted and perverse]; I will feed them with judgment *and* punishment. [Luke 19:10.]

17 And as for you, O My flock, thus says the Lord God: Behold, I judge between sheep and sheep, between the rams and the great he-goats [the malicious and the tyrants of the pasture].

18 Is it too little for you that you feed on the best pasture, but you must tread down with your feet the rest of your pasture? And to have drunk of the waters clarified by subsiding, but you must foul the rest of the water with your feet?

19 And My flock, must they feed on what your feet have trodden and drink what your feet have fouled?

20 Therefore thus says the Lord God to them: Behold, I, I Myself, will judge between fat sheep and impoverished sheep, *or* fat goats and lean goats.

21 Because you push with side and with shoulder and thrust with your horns all those that have become weak *and* diseased, till you have scattered them abroad,

22 Therefore will I rescue My flock, and they shall no more be a prey; and

speak the Word

Thank You, God, for seeking what is lost and bringing back what has strayed in my life. Thank You for bandaging my hurts and strengthening me.
ADAPTED FROM EZEKIEL **34:16**

I will judge between sheep and sheep.
23 And I will raise up over them one Shepherd and He shall feed them, even My Servant 'David; He shall feed them and He shall be their Shepherd. [Ezek. 37:24; John 10:14-18.]
24 And I the Lord will be their God and My Servant David a Prince among them; I the Lord have spoken it.
25 And I will confirm with them a covenant of peace and will cause the evil beasts to cease out of the land, and [My people] shall dwell safely in the wilderness, desert, *or* pastureland and sleep [confidently] in the woods. [Ps. 127:2b; Isa. 11:6-9; John 14:27; 16:33.]
26 And I will make them and the places round about My hill a blessing, and I will cause the showers to come down in their season; there shall be showers of blessing [of good insured by God's favor].
27 And the tree of the field shall yield its fruit and the earth shall yield its increase; and [My people] shall be secure in their land, and they shall be confident *and* know (understand and realize) that I am the Lord, when I have broken the bars of their yoke and have delivered them out of the hand of those who made slaves of them.
28 And they shall no more be a prey to the nations, nor shall the beasts of the earth devour them, but they shall dwell safely and none shall make them afraid [in the ˢday of the Messiah's reign]. [Isa. 60:21; 61:3.]
29 And I will raise up for them a planting of crops for renown, and they shall be no more consumed with hunger in the land nor bear the reproach of the nations any longer.
30 Then shall they know [positively] that I, the Lord their God, am with them and that they, the house of Israel, are My people, says the Lord God,
31 And that you, My sheep, the sheep of My pasture, are [only] men and I am your God, says the Lord God.

35 MOREOVER, THE word of the Lord came to me, saying,
2 Son of man, set your face against the mountain [range of] Seir [in Edom] and prophesy against it,
3 And say to it, Thus says the Lord God: Behold, O Mount Seir, I am against you, and I will stretch out My hand against you and I will make you a desolation and an astonishment.
4 I will lay your cities waste and you shall be desolate, and you shall know, understand, *and* realize that I am the Lord [the Sovereign Ruler, Who calls forth loyalty and obedient service].
5 Because you [of Esau] have had a perpetual enmity [for Jacob] and you

---

r The name of David is here put simply, as well as in Ezek. 34:24; Ezek. 37:24, 25; Jer. 30:9; Hos. 3:5, instead of the more usual designations of the Messiah as the Son (Matt. 1:1), the Branch (Jer. 23:5), the Offspring of David (Rev. 22:16). But there can be no possible doubt as to the meaning . . . . David, as the head of the theocracy and the ancestor of our Lord according to the flesh, constantly appears in the Scriptures as a type of the Messiah, and there can be no reasonable doubt that the prophecy would have been so understood, even at the time it was uttered (Charles Ellicott, *A Bible Commentary*). **s** One day when Jesus visited the synagogue in Nazareth (Luke 4:16-21), He was handed the roll of the book of Isaiah to read aloud. He deliberately turned to Isaiah 61, which tells in its eleven verses what His coming to the world would mean. But Jesus read only a few lines of the chapter, stopping in the midst of a sentence, and said, "This day is this scripture fulfilled in your ears" (Luke 4:21 KJV). He had just read of His coming to preach the Gospel, to proclaim release to the captives [of Satan], to give sight to the blind, to set at liberty the bruised, and to proclaim the acceptable year of the Lord. But He had to stop there, for the rest of the chapter could not be fulfilled until His second coming, of which Isaiah's prophecy tells. This section before us in Ezekiel (34:24-31) is telling of the same Messianic reign of which so many Scripture passages speak, the Messianic reign for which Jesus definitely promised to return to earth. [Matt. 25:31-34; 24:30; Rev. 1:7, 8. (See also Luke 1:32, 33; Acts 1:10, 11).]

gave over the sons of Israel to the power of the sword at the time of their calamity, when they were suffering their final punishment [the Babylonian conquest], [Ezek. 25:12-14; 36:5.]

6 Therefore, as I live, says the Lord God, I will expose you to slaughter and slaughter shall pursue you; since you could not bear to live without bloodshed, therefore bloodshed shall pursue you.

7 Thus will I make Mount Seir an astonishment and a desolation, and I will cut off from it him who passes through it and him who returns [that way].

8 And I will fill [Edom's] mountains with his slain men; on your hills and in your valleys and in all your ravines shall those fall who are slain with the sword.

9 I will make you a perpetual desolation and your 'cities shall not be inhabited. Then you will know, understand, *and* realize that I am the Lord [the Sovereign Ruler, Who calls forth loyalty and obedient service].

10 Because you [Edom] said, These two nations [Israel and Judah] and these two countries shall be mine and we will take possession of them— although the Lord was there,

11 Therefore, as I live, says the Lord God, I will deal with you according to the anger and envy you showed because of your enmity for them, and I will make Myself known among them [as He Who will judge and punish] when I judge *and* punish you.

12 And you shall know, understand, *and* realize that I am the Lord [the Sovereign Ruler, Who calls forth loyalty and obedient service], and that I have heard all your revilings *and* scornful speeches that you have uttered against the mountains of Israel, saying, They are laid waste *and* desolate; they are given to us to devour.

13 Thus you have boasted *and* magnified yourselves against Me with your mouth, multiplying your words against Me; I have heard it.

14 Thus says the Lord God: While the whole earth rejoices, I will make you a waste *and* desolation.

15 As you rejoiced over the inheritance of the house of Israel because it was desolate, so will I deal with you; you shall be a waste *and* desolation, O Mount Seir and all Edom, all of it. Then they shall know, understand, *and* realize that I am the Lord [the Sovereign Ruler, Who calls forth loyalty and obedient service].

36 ALSO YOU, son of man, prophesy to the mountains of Israel and say, You mountains of Israel, hear the word of the Lord.

2 Thus says the Lord God: Because the enemy has said over you, Aha! and, The ancient heights have become our possession,

3 Therefore prophesy and say, Thus says the Lord God: Because, yes, because they made you a desolation, and they snapped after *and* crushed

---

t The Edomites gave whatever help they could to Nebuchadnezzar when he captured Judah (Ps. 137:7; Obad. 11-14). Later these cousins of the Israelites were pushed out of their own country into southern Judea; Hebron became their chief city. When in AD 70 the Romans under Titus besieged Jerusalem, Josephus says that the Edomites joined the Jews in rebellion against the attackers, and 20,000 were admitted into the city as defenders of the Holy City. But once in, they pillaged the city, raping and killing, not even sparing the priests—though these traitors themselves had been previously forced to become circumcised and recognized as Jews. The Roman conqueror slew them, and Edom ceased to be. The forecasts of the prophets regarding Edom are in striking contrast to those of their neighbors, Moab and Ammon. The latter two countries were to suffer great and severe judgments, as was Edom. But restoration and renewed prosperity were promised to them "in the latter days" (Jer. 48:47; 49:6), while Edom was never to be rebuilt. This is all obviously nearing fulfillment in the twenty-first century. Truly Edom is the scene of "a perpetual desolation," with no hint of restoration.

you from every side so that you became the possession of the rest of the nations and you became the talk and evil gossip of the people,

4   Therefore, O mountains of Israel, hear the word of the Lord God: Thus says the Lord God to the mountains and hills, to the ravines and valleys, to the desolate wastes and the cities that are forsaken, that have become a prey and derision to the rest of the nations that are round about;

5   Therefore thus says the Lord God: Surely in the fire of My hot jealousy have I spoken against the rest of the nations and against all Edom, who have given to themselves My land with wholehearted joy and with uttermost contempt, that they might empty it out *and* possess it for a prey *and* a spoil.

6   Prophesy therefore concerning the land of Israel and say to the mountains and hills, to the ravines and valleys, Thus says the Lord God: Behold, I have spoken in My jealousy and in My wrath because you have suffered the shame *and* reproach of the nations;

7   Therefore thus says the Lord God: I have lifted up My hand *and* sworn, Surely the nations that are round about you shall themselves suffer shame and reproach.

8   But you, O mountains of Israel, shall shoot forth your branches and yield your fruit to My people Israel, for they are soon to come [home].

9   For behold, I am for you and I will turn to you; and you shall be tilled and sown,

10   And I will multiply men upon you, the whole house of Israel, even all of it; the cities shall be inhabited and the waste places shall be rebuilt,

11   And I will multiply upon you man and beast, and they shall increase and be fruitful. And I will cause you to be inhabited according to your former estate and I will do better for you than at your beginnings; and you shall know, understand, *and* realize that I am the Lord [the Sovereign Ruler, Who calls forth loyalty and obedient service].

12   Yes, [O mountains of Israel] I will cause men to walk upon you, even My people Israel, and they shall possess you, and you shall be their inheritance; and you shall no more after this bereave them of children [for idol sacrifices].

13   Thus says the Lord God: Because they say to you, You [O land] are a devourer of men and have bereaved your nation of children [offered to idols],

14   Therefore you shall devour men no more, neither bereave your nation *or* cause it to stumble any more, says the Lord God.

15   Neither will I let you hear any more the reproach of the nations, nor shall you suffer the dishonor of the peoples any more, nor shall you cause your nation to stumble *and* fall any more [through idolatry], says the Lord God.

16   Moreover, the word of the Lord came to me, saying,

17   Son of man, when the house of Israel dwelt in their own land, they defiled it by [doing] their [own] way and by their [idolatrous] doings. Their conduct before Me was like the uncleanness of a woman during her [physical] impurity.

18   So I poured out My wrath upon them for the blood that they had shed upon the land and for their idols with which they had defiled it.

speak the Word

Thank You, God, that You are for me!
ADAPTED FROM EZEKIEL 36:9

19 And I scattered them among the nations, and they were dispersed through the countries; according to their conduct and their [idolatrous] deeds I judged *and* punished them.
20 And when they came to the nations to which they went, they profaned My holy name in that men said of them, These are the people of the Lord, and yet they had to go forth out of His land.
21 But I had regard, concern, *and* compassion for My holy name, which the house of Israel had profaned among the nations to which they went.
22 Therefore say to the house of Israel, Thus says the Lord God: I do not do this for your sakes, O house of Israel, but for My holy name's sake, which you have profaned among the nations to which you went.
23 And I will vindicate the holiness of My great name *and* separate it for its holy purpose from all that defiles it—My name, which has been profaned among the nations, which you have profaned among them—and the nations will know, understand, *and* realize that I am the Lord [the Sovereign Ruler, Who calls forth loyalty and obedient service], when I shall be set apart by you *and* My holiness vindicated in you before their eyes *and* yours.
24 For I will ᵘtake you from among the nations and gather you out of all countries and bring you into your own land.
25 Then will I sprinkle clean water upon you, and you shall be clean from all your uncleanness; and from all your idols will I cleanse you.

26 A new heart will I give you and a new spirit will I put within you, and I will take away the stony heart out of your flesh and give you a heart of flesh.
27 And I will put my Spirit within you and cause you to walk in My statutes, and you shall heed My ordinances and do them.

life point

Ezekiel 36:26, 27 contains God's promise that the day would come when He would give people a new heart and put His Spirit *within* them. Under the old covenant, the Holy Spirit was with people and came upon people for special purposes, but He did not live inside them. God dwelt in a tabernacle made with human hands during that dispensation. But under the new covenant, signed and sealed in the blood of Jesus Christ (see Hebrews 13:20), He no longer dwells in a tabernacle made by human hands, but in the hearts of people who have committed their lives to Him.

28 And you shall dwell in the land that I gave to your fathers; and you shall be My people, and I will be your God.
29 I will also save you from all your uncleannesses, and I will call forth the grain and make it abundant and lay no famine on you.
30 And I will multiply the fruit of the tree and the increase of the field, that you may no more suffer the reproach

---

u No person needs to be reminded of the startling way in which this prophecy has been in the process of fulfillment since World War II. The Jews have for centuries been dispersed among all the nations with only a few left in the homeland which lay waste and desolate. It was said that travelers in Palestine had no difficulty in recognizing the appropriateness of Ezekiel's label for the country: a "valley . . . full of bones" (Ezek. 37:1). But by AD 1960 one-sixth of the Jewish population of the world was in Palestine. Already they had been made "one nation" (Ezek. 37:22a)—between sunrise of one day and sunset of the next—"a nation born in one day" (Isa. 66:8)! But the greatest event of all is yet to come (Ezek. 37:22b-25). This prophecy will be fulfilled in its entirety.

an exchange of hearts

You and I may have similar backgrounds. I had lived a hard life, and my heart was hardened because of it. I suffered many years of abuse. I built invisible walls around myself and decided that people could not hurt me if I did not let them into my life.

When we receive Jesus as our Savior, He takes our old hard hearts and gives us His heart instead (see Ezekiel 36:26, 27). The new heart God gives is one that desires to love and be involved with people. It usually takes time, and we go through a process of change before our actions and behavior catch up with our new hearts, but God does give us new desires. He gives us a heart to obey Him and, for this reason, we can no longer be comfortable with sin. We still sin, but we do not want to. Our consciences are bothered when we go against God and His Word. Our new hearts war against the flesh; the two are continually antagonistic toward each other. But thank God, we submit areas of our lives to Him little by little, and as we do, He changes our behavior to match our new hearts.

God gives us His Spirit, and only because of His Spirit within us can we obey God and His Word. The Holy Spirit, Who dwells in us, strengthens us, and enables us to do the will of God. We must learn to lean on Him and not be independent, trying to do things in our own strength.

Galatians 3:3 teaches us a wonderful lesson. It asks: "Having begun [your new life spiritually] with the [Holy] Spirit, are you now reaching perfection [by dependence] on the flesh?" In other words, why do we think we can perfect ourselves by our own effort? We need to learn to "let go and let God be God," and that is one of the biggest challenges we face. Jesus said that we can do absolutely nothing apart from Him (see John 15:5). Our job is to believe, and God's job is to perform. If we were called to achieve we would be called achievers, not believers. God said, "I will put My Spirit within you and cause you to walk in My statutes" (Ezekiel 36:27). Learn to depend more on the Holy Spirit within you and less on yourself. If you do, you will love the results. Your peace and joy will greatly increase, and your progress will be apparent to you and to everyone around you.

and disgrace of famine among the nations.

31 Then you shall [earnestly] remember your own evil ways and your doings that were not good, and shall loathe yourselves in your own sight for your iniquities and for your abominable deeds.

32 Not for your sake do I do this, says the Lord God; let that be known to you. Be ashamed and confounded for your [own] wicked ways, O house of Israel!

33 Thus says the Lord God: In the day that I cleanse you from all your iniquities I will [also] cause [Israel's] cities to be inhabited, and the waste places shall be rebuilt.

34 And the desolate land shall be tilled, that which had lain desolate in the sight of all who passed by.

35 And they shall say, This land that was desolate has become like the garden of Eden, and the waste and desolate and ruined cities are fortified and inhabited.

36 Then the nations that are left round about you shall know that I the Lord have rebuilt the ruined places and replanted that which was desolate. I the Lord have spoken it, and I will do it.

37 Thus says the Lord God: For this also I will let the house of Israel inquire of Me to do it for them; I will increase their men like a flock.

38 Like the flock of holy things for sacrifice, like the flock of Jerusalem in her [solemn] appointed feasts, so shall the waste cities be filled with flocks of men; and they shall know, understand, *and* realize that I am the Lord [the Sovereign Ruler, Who calls forth loyalty and obedient service].

37 THE HAND of the Lord was upon me, and He brought me out in the Spirit of the Lord and set me down in the midst of the valley; and it was full of bones.

2 And He caused me to pass round about among them, and behold, there were very many [human bones] in the open valley *or* plain, and behold, they were very dry.

3 And He said to me, Son of man,

life point

You may feel as if your life is no better than the dead, dry bones described by the prophet in Ezekiel 37:1–4. Your circumstances may be so dead that they stink. Your hope may seem lost, but God has a way out.

As this passage continues, the prophet does as God instructs, and he sees God totally revive and bring breath and spirit back into what once were dead, dry bones (see Ezekiel 37:5–10). The same can happen to you. God can revive things that have been dry, brittle, and dead in your life.

can these bones live? And I answered, O Lord God, You know! [I Cor. 15:35.]

4 Again He said to me, Prophesy to these bones and say to them, O you dry bones, hear the word of the Lord. [John 5:28.]

5 Thus says the Lord God to these bones: Behold, I will cause breath *and* spirit to enter you, and you shall live;

6 And I will lay sinews upon you and bring up flesh upon you and cover you with skin, and I will put breath *and* spirit in you, and you [dry bones] shall live; and you shall know, understand, *and* realize that I am the Lord [the Sovereign Ruler, Who calls forth loyalty and obedient service].

7 So I prophesied as I was commanded; and as I prophesied, there was a [thundering] noise and behold, a shaking *and* trembling *and* a rattling, and the bones came together, bone to its bone.

8 And I looked and behold, there were sinews upon [the bones] and flesh came upon them and skin covered them over, but there was no breath *or* spirit in them.

9 Then said He to me, Prophesy to the breath *and* spirit, son of man, and say to the breath *and* spirit, Thus says the Lord God: Come from the four winds, O breath *and* spirit, and breathe upon these slain that they may live.

10 So I prophesied as He commanded me, and the breath *and* spirit came into [the bones], and they lived and stood up upon their feet, an exceedingly great host. [Rev. 11:11.]

11 Then He said to me, Son of man, these bones are the whole house of Israel. Behold, they say, Our bones are dried up and our hope is lost; we are completely cut off.

12 Therefore prophesy and say to them, Thus says the Lord God: Behold, I will open your graves and cause you to come up out of your graves, O My people; and I will bring

hear the word of the Lord

I am sure that at one time or another in your life, you have felt that everywhere you looked you saw a pile of dead, dry bones, such as the scene in Ezekiel 37:1–4.

God showed a pile of such brittle bones to Ezekiel and asked him, "Can these bones live?" (Ezekiel 37:3). In other words, He was asking, "Can anything be done with this mess? Can this situation change?"

Then He told Ezekiel to speak to the bones and say to them, "Oh, you dry bones, hear the word of the Lord" (Ezekiel 37:4).

If you have a big mess in your life and you are trying to run the devil off your property and keep him under your feet, you can do it with words. You can say, "Listen, you big mountain, hear the word of the Lord! Listen, you big mess, hear the word of the Lord! Listen, poverty, hear the word of the Lord! Listen, sickness and disease, hear the word of the Lord! Listen, you tormenting spirit, hear the word of the Lord!"

As you read the remainder of the story in Ezekiel 37, you will find that after Ezekiel had done as God told him to do and prophesied to those dry bones, they came together, sinews and flesh came upon them, and skin covered them.

Then, in Ezekiel 37:9, the Lord told Ezekiel to prophesy and command that breath and spirit come into them. In verse 10 Ezekiel said, "So I prophesied as He commanded me, and the breath and spirit came into [the bones], and they lived and stood up upon their feet, an exceedingly great host." All of that happened because one man prophesied God's Word over a situation that needed to be changed.

Let me ask you: What are you saying to the dead, dry circumstances in your life? Are you prophesying to your dead bones? Or is what you are saying making them more dead and dry?

Maybe this sounds familiar to you: "Nothing in my life is ever going to change. Every time I get a dollar the devil takes it away from me. It never fails; every time I think something good is going to happen, I get attacked." If that is what you are saying, then you are just asking for more trouble. Every time you speak that way, you are giving the devil the right to use his power. Instead, learn how to speak God's Word and neutralize Satan's power.

Do not talk about how you feel or what you think; do not look at your life and what you do not have. Open your mouth and talk about what God has promised you! Once you change your words, it's all over for the devil. There is nothing he can do against God's Word. The victory belongs to you!

you [back home] to the land of Israel. [Hos. 13:14.]

13 And you shall know that I am the Lord [your Sovereign Ruler], when I have opened your graves and caused you to come up out of your graves, O My people.

14 And I shall put My Spirit in you and you shall live, and I shall place you in your own land. Then you shall know, understand, *and* realize that I the Lord have spoken it and performed it, says the Lord.

15 The word of the Lord came again to me, saying,

16 Son of man, take a stick and write on it, For Judah and the children of Israel his companions; then take another stick and write upon it, For Joseph, the stick of Ephraim, and all the house of Israel his companions;

17 And join them together into one stick that they may become one in your hand.

18 And when your people say to you, Will you not show us what you mean by these?

19 Say to them, Thus says the Lord God: Behold, I will take the stick of Joseph—which is in the hand of Ephraim—and the tribes of Israel his associates, and will join with it the stick of Judah and make them one stick, and they shall be one in My hand.

20 When the sticks on which you write shall be in your hand before their eyes,

21 Then say to them, Thus says the Lord God: Behold, I will take the children of Israel from among the nations to which they have gone, and will

ᵛgather them from every side and bring them into their own land.

22 And I will make them one nation in the land, upon the mountains of Israel, and one ʷKing shall be King over them all; and they shall be no longer two nations, neither be divided into two kingdoms any more. [Jer. 50:4.]

23 They shall not defile themselves any more with their idols and their detestable things or with any of their transgressions, but I will save them out of all their dwelling places *and* from all their backslidings in which they have sinned, and I will cleanse them. So shall they be My people, and I will be their God.

24 And ˣDavid My Servant shall be King over them, and they all shall have one Shepherd. They shall also walk in My ordinances and heed My statutes and do them.

25 They shall dwell in the land in which your fathers dwelt, that I gave to My servant Jacob, and they shall dwell there, they and their children and their children's children, forever; and My Servant David shall be their Prince forever. [Isa. 60:21; Joel 3:20; Amos 9:15.]

26 I will make a covenant of peace with them; it shall be an everlasting covenant with them, and I will give blessings to them and multiply them and will set My sanctuary in the midst of them forevermore.

27 My tabernacle *or* dwelling place also shall be with them; and I will be their God, and they shall be My people.

28 Then the nations shall know, understand, *and* realize that I the Lord

speak the Word

Thank You, God, for putting Your Spirit in me!
ADAPTED FROM EZEKIEL **37:14**

v See footnote on Ezek. 36:24.   **w** Reference to the coming Messianic ruler, Who would achieve for Israel what David had—only more fully. See also footnote on Ezek. 34:23.   **x** See footnote on Ezek. 34:23.

do set apart *and* consecrate Israel for holy use, when My sanctuary shall be in their midst forevermore.

38 AND THE word of the Lord came to me, saying, 2 Son of man, set your face against Gog, of the land of ᵞMagog, the prince of Rosh, of Meshech, and of Tubal, and prophesy against him,

3 And say, Thus says the Lord God: Behold, I am against you, O Gog, chief prince (ruler) of Rosh, of Meshech, and of Tubal.

4 And I will turn you back and put hooks into your jaws, and I will bring you forth and all your army, horses and horsemen, all of them clothed in full armor, a great company with buckler and shield, all of them handling swords—

5 Persia, Cush, and Put *or* Libya with them, all of them with shield and helmet,

6 Gomer and all his hordes, the house of Togarmah in the uttermost parts of the north and all his hordes— many people are with you.

7 You [Gog] be prepared; yes, prepare yourself, you and all your companies that are assembled about you, and you be a guard *and* a commander for them.

8 After many days you shall be visited *and* mustered [for service]; in the latter years you shall go against the land that is restored from the ravages of the sword, where people are gathered out of many nations upon the mountains of Israel, which had been a continual waste; but its [people] are brought forth out of the nations and they shall dwell securely, all of them. [Isa. 24:22.]

9 You shall ascend and come like a storm; you shall be like a cloud to cover the land, you and all your hosts and many people with you.

10 Thus says the Lord God: At the same time thoughts shall come into your mind, and you will devise an evil plan.

11 And you will say, I will go up against an open country [the land of unwalled villages]; I will fall upon those who are at rest, who dwell securely, all of them dwelling without walls and having neither bars nor gates,

12 To take spoil and prey, to turn your hand upon the desolate places now inhabited and assail the people gathered out of the nations, who have obtained livestock and goods, who dwell at the center of the earth [Palestine].

13 Sheba and Dedan and the merchants of Tarshish, with all their lionlike cubs [or satellite areas], shall say to you, Have you come to take spoil? Have you gathered your hosts to take the prey? To carry away silver and gold, to take away livestock and goods, to take a great spoil?

14 Therefore, son of man, prophesy and say to Gog, Thus says the Lord God: In that day when My people Israel dwell securely, will you not know it *and* be aroused?

15 And you will come from your place out of the uttermost parts of the north, you and many peoples with you, all of them riding on horses, a great host, a mighty army.

16 And you shall come up against My people Israel like a cloud to cover the land. In the latter days I will bring you against My land, that the

---

y Gog is a symbolic name, representing the leader of the world powers antagonistic to God (see also Rev. 20:8). Meshech and Tubal are understood to have been the same as the Moschi and Tibareni of the Greeks—tribes that inhabited regions in the Caucasus. Rosh, which some would identify with Russia, must have designated a land and people somewhere in the same area. And therefore the Gog of Ezekiel must be viewed as in some sense the head of the high regions in the northwest of Asia. (Patrick Fairbairn, *The Imperial Bible-dictionary*).

nations may know, understand, *and* realize Me when My holiness shall be vindicated through you [vindicated and honored in your overwhelming destruction], O Gog, before their eyes.

17 Thus says the Lord God: Are you he of whom I have spoken in olden times by My servants the prophets of Israel, who prophesied in those days for years that I would bring you [Gog] against them?

18 But in that day when Gog shall come against the land of Israel, says the Lord God, My wrath shall come up into My nostrils.

19 For in My jealousy and in the fire of My wrath have I said, Surely in that day there shall be a great shaking *or* cosmic catastrophe in the land of Israel,

20 So that the fishes of the sea and the birds of the heavens, the beasts of the field and all creeping things that creep upon the earth, and all the men that are upon the face of the earth, shall tremble *and* shake at My presence; and the mountains shall be thrown down and the steep places shall fall and every wall [natural or artificial] shall fall to the ground.

21 And I will call for a sword against [Gog] throughout all My mountains, says the Lord God, every man's sword shall be against his brother [over the dividing of booty].

22 And with pestilence and with bloodshed will I enter into judgment with [Gog], and I will rain upon him and upon his hordes and upon the many peoples that are with him torrents of rain and great hailstones, fire and brimstone. [Ps. 11:6.]

23 Thus will I demonstrate My greatness and My holiness, and I will be recognized, understood, *and* known in the eyes of many nations; yes, they shall know that I am the Lord [the Sovereign Ruler, Who calls forth loyalty and obedient service].

39 AND YOU, son of man, prophesy against Gog, Thus says the Lord God: Behold, I am against you, O Gog, chief prince (ruler) of Rosh, of Meshech, and of Tubal.

2 And I will turn you about and will lead you on, and will cause you to come up from the uttermost parts of the north and will lead you against the mountains of Israel;

3 And I will smite your bow from your left hand and will cause your arrows to fall out of your right hand.

4 You shall fall [dead] upon the mountains of Israel, you and all your hosts and the peoples who are with you. I will give you to the ravenous birds of every sort and to the beasts of the field to be devoured.

5 You shall fall in the open field, for I have spoken [it], says the Lord God.

6 I will send fire on Magog and upon those who dwell securely in the coastlands, and they shall know, understand, *and* realize that I am the Lord [the Sovereign Ruler, Who calls forth loyalty and obedient service].

7 And I will make My holy name known in the midst of My people Israel, and I will not let them profane My holy name any more; and the nations shall know, understand, *and* realize that I am the Lord, the Holy One of Israel.

8 Behold, it is coming and it will be done, says the Lord God; that is the day of which I have spoken.

9 And [when you, Gog, are no longer] they who dwell in the cities of Israel shall go forth and shall set on fire and burn the battle gear, the shields and the bucklers, the bows and the arrows, the handspikes *or* riding whips and the spears; and they shall burn them as fuel for seven years,

10 So that My people shall take no firewood out of the field or cut down any out of the forests, for they shall make their fires of the weapons. And they shall despoil those who despoiled them and plunder those who plundered them, says the Lord God.

11 And in that day, I will give to Gog a place for burial there in Israel, the valley of those who pass through on the east side in front of the [Dead] Sea [the highway between Syria, Petra, and Egypt], and it will delay *and* stop those who pass through. And there shall they ᶻbury Gog and all his multitude, and they shall call it the Valley of Hamon-gog [multitude of Gog].

12 For seven months the house of Israel will be burying them, that they may cleanse the land.

13 Yes, all the people of the land will bury them, and it shall bring them renown in the day that I shall be glorified, says the Lord God.

14 And they shall set apart men to work continually who shall pass through the land, men commissioned to bury, with the help of those who are passing by, those bodies that lie unburied on the face of the ground, in order to cleanse the land. After the end of seven months they shall make their search.

15 And when these pass through the land and anyone sees a human bone, he shall set up a marker by it as a sign to the buriers, until they have buried it in the Valley of Hamon-gog *or* of Gog's multitude.

16 And Hamonah [multitude] shall also be the name of the city [of the dead]. Thus shall they cleanse the land.

17 And you, son of man, thus says the Lord God: Say to the birds of prey of every sort and to every beast of the field, Assemble yourselves and come, gather from every side to the sacrificial feast that I am preparing for you, even a great sacrificial feast on the mountains of Israel at which you may eat flesh and drink blood.

18 You shall eat the flesh of the mighty and drink the blood of the princes of the earth, of rams, of lambs, of goats, and of bullocks, all of them fatlings of Bashan [east of the Jordan].

19 And you shall eat fat till you are filled and drink blood till you are drunk at the sacrificial feast which I am preparing for you.

20 And you shall be filled at My table with horses and riders, with mighty men, and with soldiers of every kind, says the Lord God.

21 And I will manifest My honor *and* glory among the nations, and all the nations shall see My judgment *and* justice [in the punishment] which I have executed and My hand which I have laid on them.

22 So the house of Israel shall know, understand, *and* realize beyond all question that I am the Lord their God from that day forward.

23 And the nations shall know, understand, *and* realize positively that the house of Israel went into captivity for their iniquity, because they trespassed against Me; and I hid My face from them. So I gave them into the hand of their enemies and they all fell [into captivity or were slain] by the power of the sword. [Deut. 31:17.]

24 According to their uncleanness and according to their transgressions I dealt with them and hid My face from them.

z The number of dead bodies left after the great catastrophe which God will send upon Gog and his hosts would necessarily amount to several millions. Their graves would naturally interfere with traffic on the interstate highway. The dead will not be slain in battle. God will slay them by a great "cosmic catastrophe" (Ezek. 38:18-23). And not just some, but "all" of Gog's multitude will die then (Ezek. 39:4, 11); before they have had a chance to use their weapons, God will strike them from their hands (Ezek. 39:3). That one-sixth of the horde from the north will be left alive, as the *King James Version* says (Ezek. 39:2), is without noted exception conceded to be a mistaken translation by all authorities of modern times.

25 Therefore thus says the Lord God: Now will I reverse the captivity of Jacob and have mercy upon the whole house of Israel and will be jealous for My holy name.
26 They shall forget their shame *and* self-reproach and all their treachery *and* unfaithfulness in which they have transgressed against Me, when they dwell securely in their land and there is none who makes them afraid.
27 When I have brought them again from the peoples and gathered them out of their enemies' lands, and My justice *and* holiness are set apart *and* vindicated through them in the sight of many nations,
28 Then shall they know, understand, *and* realize positively that I am the Lord their God, because I sent them into captivity *and* exile among the nations and then gathered them to their own land. I will leave none of them remaining among the nations any more [in the latter days].
29 Neither will I hide My face any more then from them, when I have poured out My Spirit upon the house of Israel, says the Lord God.

40 IN THE twenty-fifth year of our captivity [by Babylon], in the beginning of the year, on the tenth day of the month, in the fourteenth year after the city [of Jerusalem] was taken, on the very same day the hand of the Lord was upon me and He brought me to that place.
2 In the visions of God He brought me into the land of Israel and set me down upon a very high mountain, on the south side of which there was what seemed to be the structure of a city.

3 He brought me there, and behold, there was a man [an angel] whose appearance was like bronze, with a line of flax and a measuring reed in his hand, and he stood in the gateway.
4 And the man said to me, Son of man, look with your eyes and hear with your ears and set your heart *and* mind on all that I will show you, for you are brought here that I may show them to you. Declare all that you see to the house of Israel.
5 And behold, there was a wall all around the outside area of the house [of the Lord], and in the man's hand a measuring reed six long cubits in length, each cubit being longer [than the usual one] by a handbreadth; so he measured the thickness of the wall, one reed, and the height, one reed.
6 Then he came to the gate which faced the east and went up its [seven] steps and measured the threshold of the gateway, one reed broad, and the other threshold of the gateway [inside the thick wall], one reed broad.
7 And every room for the guards was one reed long and one reed broad, and the space between the guardrooms *or* lodges was five cubits. And the threshold of the gate by the porch *or* vestibule of the gateway within was one reed.
8 He measured also the porch *or* vestibule of the gate toward the house [of the Lord], one reed.
9 Then he measured the porch *or* vestibule of the gateway, eight cubits, and its posts *or* jambs, two cubits. And the porch *or* vestibule of the gate was inside [toward the house of the Lord].
10 And the guardrooms *or* lodges of the east gateway were three on this side and three on that side; the three

speak the Word

were the same size, and the posts *or* jambs were the same size on either side.

11 And he measured the breadth of the opening of the gateway, ten cubits, and the length of the gateway, thirteen cubits.

12 And a border *or* barrier before the guardrooms was one cubit on this side, and a border *or* barrier, one cubit on that side. And the guardrooms *or* lodges were six cubits on this side and six cubits on that side.

13 And ᵃ*the man* [an angel] measured the gate from the outer wall of one chamber *or* guardroom to the outer wall of another—a breadth of twenty-five cubits from door to door.

14 And ᵃthe open part of the porch *or* vestibule of the gateway on the outside was twenty cubits, the chambers *or* guardrooms of the gate being round about.

15 And including this porch *or* vestibule of the gate on the outside and the porch *or* vestibule on the inside, the extent was fifty cubits.

16 And there were closed windows to the guardrooms *or* chambers and to their posts *or* pillars within the gate round about, and likewise to the archway *or* vestibule; and windows were round about facing into the court, and upon each post *or* pillar were palm tree [decorations].

17 Then he brought me into the outward court, and behold, there were chambers and a pavement round about the court; thirty chambers fronted on the pavement.

18 And the pavement was along by the side of the gates, answerable to the length of the gateways; this was the lower pavement.

19 Then *the man* measured the distance from the inner front before the lower gate to the outer front of the inner court, a hundred cubits, both on the east and on the north.

20 And the gate of the outward court which faced the north, of it he measured both the length and the breadth.

21 And its guardrooms *or* lodges, three on this side and three on that side, and its posts *or* pillars and archway *or* vestibule were the same size as those of the first gate; the length was fifty cubits and the breadth twenty-five cubits.

22 And its windows and its archway *or* vestibule and its palm trees were of the same size as those of the gate that faces toward the east. It was reached by going up seven steps, and the archway of its vestibule was on the inner side.

23 Opposite the gate on the north and on the east was a gate to the inner court, and he [the man with the measuring rod of reed] measured from gate to gate, a hundred cubits.

24 After that *the man* brought me toward the south, and behold, there was a gate on the south, and he measured its posts *or* pillars and its archway *or* vestibule; they measured as the others did.

25 And there were windows round about in it and in its archway *or* vestibule, like those windows in the other gateways; its length was fifty cubits and its breadth twenty-five cubits.

26 And there were seven steps going up to the gate, and its archway *or* vestibule was on the inside. And it had palm trees, one on this side and another on that side, carved on its posts *or* pillars.

27 And there was a gate to the inner court on the south, and he measured from gate to gate toward the south, a hundred cubits.

28 And *the man* [an angel] brought

---

a As *The Septuagint* (Greek translation of the Old Testament) renders these verses. The Hebrew is obscure.

me into the inner court by the south gate, and he measured the south gate; its measurements were the same as those of the other gateways.

29 And its guardrooms *or* chambers and its posts *or* pillars and its archway *or* vestibule measured as did the others. And there were windows in the gateway and in its archway *or* vestibule round about; its length was fifty cubits and its breadth twenty-five cubits.

30 And there was an archway *or* a vestibule round about, twenty-five cubits long and five cubits wide.

31 And its [arched] vestibule faced the outer court; and palm trees were carved upon its posts *or* pillars, and the steps going up to it were eight.

32 And he brought me into the inner court toward the east and he measured the gate; it measured the same as the others.

33 And its guardrooms *or* chambers and its posts *or* pillars and its archway *or* vestibule measured as did the others. And there were windows in it and in its [arched] vestibule round about; the gateway was fifty cubits long and twenty-five cubits wide.

34 And its [arched] vestibule faced the outer court; and palm trees were carved upon its posts *or* pillars on either side, and the steps leading to it were eight.

35 And *the man* [an angel] brought me to the north gate and measured it; the measurements were the same as those of the other gates.

36 Its guardrooms *or* chambers, its posts *or* pillars, its [arched] vestibule, and the windows to it round about [were of the same size as the others]. The length of the gateway was fifty cubits and the width was twenty-five cubits.

37 And its posts *or* pillars were toward the outer court, and palm trees were carved upon them on either side.

And the approach to it had eight steps.

38 There was an attached chamber with its door beside the posts *or* pillars of the gates where the burnt offering was to be washed.

39 And in the porch *or* vestibule of the gate were two tables on this side and two tables on that side, on which to slay the burnt offering and the sin offering and the trespass *or* guilt offering.

40 And on the one side without, as one goes up to the entrance of the gate to the north, were two tables; and on the other side at the vestibule of the gate were two tables.

41 Four tables were on the inside and four tables on the outside of the side of the gate, eight tables upon which the sacrifices were to be slain.

42 Moreover, there were four tables of hewn stone for the burnt offering, a cubit and a half long, a cubit and a half broad, and one cubit high. Upon them were to be laid the instruments with which were slain the burnt offering and the sacrifice.

43 And slabs *or* hooks a handbreadth long were fastened within [the room] round about. Upon the tables was to be placed the flesh of the offering.

44 [b]Then *the man* [an angel] led me [from without] into the inner court, and behold, there were two chambers in the inner court: one beside the north gate but facing the south, and one beside the south gate but looking toward the north.

45 And *the man* [an angel who was guiding me] said, This chamber with its view to the south is for the priests who have charge of the house [of the Lord],

46 And the chamber with its view to the north is for the priests who have charge of the altar. These are the sons of Zadok, who alone among the sons

b Taken from *The Septuagint* (Greek translation of the Old Testament) for a clearer description.

of Levi may come near to the Lord to minister to Him.

47 And he measured the court, a hundred cubits long and a hundred cubits broad, foursquare; and the altar was in front of the house [of the Lord].

48 Then he brought me to the porch *or* vestibule of the temple proper, and he measured each post *or* pillar of the porch, five cubits on either side. And the width of the gate was three cubits for this [leaf] and three cubits for that one.

49 And the length of the porch *or* vestibule was twenty cubits and the breadth eleven cubits; and he brought me by the steps by which it was reached, and there were two pillars standing on the posts [as bases] *or* beside them, one on either side of the entrance.

41 AND *the man* [an angel] brought me to [the Holy Place of] the temple and measured the wall pillars, six cubits broad on one side [of the ten-cubit door] and six cubits broad on the other side, cwhich was the breadth of the tabernacle *or* tent [later called the temple].

2 And the breadth of the entrance was ten cubits, and the leaves of the door were five cubits on the one side and five cubits on the other side; and he measured its length, forty cubits, and its breadth, twenty cubits.

3 Then *the man* [being an angel, and unrestricted] went inside [the inner room, but went alone] and measured each post of the door, two cubits, the doorway, six cubits, and the breadth of the entrance, seven cubits. [Heb. 9:6, 7; 10:19-25.]

4 And he measured the length [of the interior of the second room] in the temple proper, twenty cubits, and the breadth, twenty cubits; and he [came

out and] said to me, This is the Most Holy Place (the Holy of Holies).

5 Then he measured the wall of the temple, six cubits thick [to accommodate side chambers]; and the breadth of every side chamber, four cubits, round about the temple proper on every side.

6 These side chambers were three stories high, one over another and thirty in each story; and they entered into the wall which belonged to the house for the side chambers round about, that they might have hold of the wall [of the house], but they did not have hold of the wall of the temple.

7 And the side rooms became broader as they encompassed the temple higher and higher, for the encircling of the house went higher and higher round about the temple; therefore the breadth of the house continued upward, and so one went up from the lowest story to the highest one by way of the middle story [on a winding stairway].

8 I saw also that the temple had an elevation *or* foundation platform round about it. The foundations of the side chambers measured a full reed measure of six long cubits.

9 The thickness of the outer wall of the side chamber was five cubits, as was the width of that part of the foundation that was left free of the side chambers that belonged to the house.

10 And between [the free space of the foundation platform and] the chambers was a breadth of twenty cubits round about the temple on every side.

11 And the doors of the attached side chambers opened on the free space that was left, one door toward the north and another door toward the south; and the breadth of the space on

c *The Septuagint* (Greek translation of the Old Testament) does not contain this phrase, "which was the breadth of the tabernacle," but most Hebrew manuscripts do contain it.

the foundation platform that was left free was five cubits round about.

12 And the building that faced the temple yard on the west side was seventy cubits broad, and the wall of the building was five cubits thick round about, and its length ninety cubits.

13 And *the man* [an angel in my vision] measured the temple, a hundred cubits long; and the yard and the building with its walls, a hundred cubits long;

14 Also the breadth of the east front of the temple and the yard, a hundred cubits.

15 Then *the man* [an angel] measured the length of the building on the west side of the yard with its walls on either side, a hundred cubits. The Holy Place of the temple, the inner Holy of Holies, and the outer vestibule

16 Were roofed over, and all three had latticed windows all around. The inside walls of the temple were paneled with wood round about from the floor up to the windows and from the windows to the roof,

17 Including the space above the door leading to the inner room, inside and out. And on the walls round about in the inner room and the Holy Place were carvings,

18 With figures of cherubim and palm trees, so that a palm tree was between a cherub and a cherub; and every cherub had two faces,

19 So that the face of a man was toward the palm tree on the one side, and the face of a young lion toward the palm tree on the other side. It was made this way through all the house round about.

20 From the floor to above the entrance were cherubim and palm trees made, and also on the wall of the temple [the Holy Place].

21 The door frames of the temple were squared, and in front [outside of the sanctuary or Holy of Holies] was what appeared to be

22 An altar of wood, three cubits high and two cubits long [and wide]; and its corners, its base, and its sides were of wood. And *the man* [an angel] said to me, This is the table that is before the Lord.

23 And the temple *or* Holy Place and the sanctuary *or* Holy of Holies, had two doors [one for each of them].

24 And the doors had two leaves apiece, two folding leaves—two leaves for the one door and two leaves for the other door.

25 And there were carved on them, on the doors of the temple, cherubim and palm trees, like those carved upon the walls; and there was also a canopy of wood in front of the porch outside.

26 And there were recessed windows and palm trees on the one side and on the other side of the porch. Thus were the side chambers and the canopies of the house.

42 THEN *the man* [an angel] brought me forth into the outer court northward, and he brought me to the attached chambers that were opposite the temple yard and were opposite the building on the north.

2 Before the long side of one hundred cubits was the door toward the north, and the breadth was fifty cubits.

3 Adjoining the twenty cubits which belonged to the inner court, and opposite the pavement which belonged to the outer court, was balcony facing balcony in three stories.

4 And before the attached chambers was a walk inward of ten cubits breadth and a hundred cubits long, and their doors were on the north.

5 Now the upper chambers were shorter, for the balconies took off from these more than from the lower and middle chambers of the building.

6 For they were in three stories, but

did not have pillars as the pillars of the [outer] court; therefore the upper chambers were set back more than the lower and the middle ones from the ground.

7 And the wall *or* fence that was outside, opposite *and* parallel to the chambers, toward the outer court before the chambers, was fifty cubits long,

8 For the length of the [combined] chambers that were on the outer court was fifty cubits, while [the length] of those opposite the temple was a hundred cubits.

9 And under these chambers was the entrance on the east side, as one approached them from the outer court.

10 In the breadth of the wall of the court going toward the east, before the yard and before the building, were the chambers

11 With a passage before them that gave the appearance of the attached chambers on the north, of the same length and breadth, with similar exits and arrangements and doors.

12 And like the doors of the chambers that were toward the south there was an entrance at the head of the way, the way before the dividing wall toward the east, as one enters them.

13 Then said *the man* [an angel] to me, The north chambers and the south chambers, which are opposite the yard, are the holy chambers where the priests who approach the Lord shall eat the most holy offerings; there shall they lay the most holy things—the meal offering, the sin offering, and the trespass *or* guilt offering—for the place is holy.

14 When the priests enter the Holy Place, they shall not go out of it into the outer court unless they lay aside there the garments in which they minister, for these are holy, separate, *and* set apart. They shall put on other garments before they approach that which is for the people.

15 Now when he had finished measuring the inner temple area, he brought me forth toward the gate which faces east and measured it [the outer area] round about.

16 He measured the east side with the measuring reed, five hundred reeds with the measuring reed round about.

17 He measured the north side, five hundred reeds with the measuring reed round about.

18 He measured the south side, five hundred reeds with the measuring reed.

19 He turned about to the west side and measured five hundred reeds with the measuring reed.

20 He measured it on the four sides; it had a wall round about, the length five hundred reeds and the breadth five hundred, to make a separation between that which was holy [the temple proper] and that which was common [the outer area].

43 AFTERWARD *the man* [an angel] brought me to the gate, the gate that faces east.

2 And behold, the glory of the God of Israel came from the east and His voice was like the sound of many waters, and the earth shone with His glory. [Rev. 1:15; 14:2.]

3 And the vision which I saw was like the vision I had seen when I came to foretell the destruction of the city and like the vision I had seen beside the river Chebar [near Babylon]; and I fell on my face. [Ezek. 1:4; 3:23; 10:15, 22.]

4 And the glory of the Lord entered the temple by the gate facing east.

5 Then the Spirit caught me up and brought me into the inner court, and behold, the glory of the Lord filled the temple.

6 And I heard One speaking to me

out of the temple, and a Man stood by me.

7 And He [the Lord] said to me, Son of man, this is the place of My throne and the place of the soles of My feet, where I will dwell in the midst of the children of Israel forever; and My holy name the house of Israel shall no more profane, neither they nor their kings, by their [idolatrous] harlotry, nor by the dead bodies *and* monuments of their kings,

8 Nor by setting their threshold by My thresholds and their doorposts by My doorposts, with a mere wall between Me and them. They have profaned My holy name by their abominations which they have committed; therefore I have consumed them in My anger.

9 Now let them put away their [idolatrous] harlotry and the dead bodies *and* monuments of their kings far from Me, and I will dwell in their midst forever.

10 Son of man, show the temple by your description of it to the house of Israel, that they may be ashamed of their iniquities; and let them measure accurately its appearance and plan.

11 And if they are ashamed of all that they have done, make known to them the form of the temple and the arrangement of it—its exits and its entrances and the whole form of it—all its ordinances and all its forms and all its laws. And write it down in their sight so that they may keep the whole form of it and all the ordinances of it and do them.

12 This is the law of the house [of the Lord]: The whole area round about on the top of the mountain ᵈ[Mount Moriah] shall be most holy, separated, *and* set apart. Behold, this is the law of the house [of the Lord].

13 And these are the measurements of the altar [of burnt offering] in cubits. The cubit is a royal cubit [the length of a forearm and a palm of the hand]; the bottom *or* gutter shall be a cubit deep and a cubit wide, with a rim or lip round about it of a span's breadth. And this shall be the height of the altar:

14 From the bottom *or* gutter on the ground to the lower ledge *or* brim shall be two cubits, and the breadth one cubit; and from the lesser ledge to the greater ledge shall be four cubits, and the breadth one cubit.

15 And the altar hearth shall be four cubits high, and from the altar hearth reaching upward there shall be four horns one cubit high.

16 And the altar hearth shall be square—twelve cubits long, twelve broad, square in its four sides.

17 And the ledge shall be fourteen cubits long and fourteen cubits broad on its four sides, and the border about it shall be half a cubit; and its bottom *or* gutter shall be a cubit deep and wide, and its ascent [not steps] shall face the east. [Exod. 20:26.]

18 And [the Lord] said to me, Son of man, thus says the Lord God: These are the regulations for the use of the altar in the day that it is erected, upon which to offer burnt offerings and to sprinkle blood against it:

19 You shall give to the priests, the Levites who are of the offspring of Zadok, who are near to Me to minister to Me, says the Lord God, a young bull for a sin offering.

20 And you shall take of its blood and put it on the four horns of [the altar of burnt offering] and on the four corners of the ledge and on the rim *or* border round about. Thus shall you cleanse *and* make atonement for [the altar].

21 You shall also take the bullock of

---

d Moriah is identified in Gen. 22:2 as the region where Abraham prepared to sacrifice Isaac, and is identified in II Chron. 3:1 as the site of the temple built by Solomon.

the sin offering, and it shall be burned in the appointed place of the temple, outside the sacred enclosure. [Heb. 13:11.]

22 And on the second day you shall offer a male goat without blemish for a sin offering. Thus the altar shall be cleansed, as it was cleansed with the bullock.

23 When you have finished cleansing it, you shall offer a young bull without blemish and a ram out of the flock without blemish.

24 And you shall bring them near before the Lord, and the priests shall cast salt upon them and they shall offer them up for a burnt offering to the Lord.

25 Seven days you shall prepare every day a goat for a sin offering; also a young bull and a ram out of the flock, without blemish, shall be prepared.

26 For seven days shall they make atonement for the altar and purify it; so the priests shall consecrate, separate, *and* set it apart to receive offerings. [Exod. 29:37.]

27 And when these days have been accomplished, on the eighth day and from then on, the priests shall offer your burnt offerings upon the altar and your peace offerings; and I will accept you, says the Lord God. [Rom. 12:1; I Pet. 2:5.]

44 THEN *the man* [an angel] brought me back the way of the outer gate of the sanctuary which faces the east, and it was shut.

2 Then the Lord said to me, This gate shall be ᵉshut; it shall not be opened and no man shall enter in by it, for the Lord, the God of Israel, has entered in by it; therefore it shall remain shut.

3 As for the prince, being the prince, he shall sit in it to eat bread before the Lord; he shall enter by way of the porch *or* vestibule of the gate and shall go out the same way.

4 Then he brought me by way of the north gate to the front of the temple; I looked, and behold, the glory of the Lord filled the house of the Lord, and I fell upon my face. [Rev. 15:8.]

5 And the Lord said to me, Son of man, mark well *and* set your heart to see with your eyes and hear with your ears all that I say to you concerning all the ordinances of the house of the Lord and all its laws, and mark well *and* set your heart to know who are allowed to enter the temple and all those who are excluded from the sanctuary.

6 And you shall say to the rebellious, even to the house of Israel, Thus says the Lord God: O you house of Israel, let all your previous abominations be enough for you! [Do not repeat them!]

7 You have brought into My sanctuary aliens, uncircumcised in heart and uncircumcised in flesh, to be in My sanctuary to pollute *and* profane it, even My house, when you offer My bread, the fat and the blood; and through it all *and* in addition to all your abominations, they *and* you have broken My covenant.

8 And you have not kept charge of My holy things, but you have chosen foreign keepers to please yourselves and have set them in charge of My sanctuary.

9 Therefore thus says the Lord God: No foreigner uncircumcised in heart and flesh shall enter into My

---

e In Christ's time the Golden Gate was the principal eastside thoroughfare. Through it the Prince of Peace would naturally make His triumphal entry. But by AD 1542-3, when Sultan Suleiman the Magnificent rebuilt the wall of Jerusalem, tradition says that the road which once led to this gate had fallen into disuse, and what is now St. Stephen's Gate was the accepted entrance. So the Sultan walled up the Golden Gate with its double entrance, and it has remained so ever since.

sanctuary [where no one but the priests might enter], of any foreigners who are among the children of Israel.

10 But the Levites who went far away from Me when Israel went astray, who went astray from Me after their idols, they shall bear [the punishment for] their iniquity *and* guilt.

11 They shall minister in My sanctuary, having oversight as guards at the gates of the temple and ministering in the temple. They shall slay the burnt offering and the sacrifice for the people, and they shall attend the people to serve them.

12 Because [the priests] ministered to [the people] before their idols and became a stumbling block of iniquity *and* guilt to the house of Israel, therefore I have lifted up My hand *and* have sworn against them, says the Lord God, that they shall bear the punishment for their iniquity *and* guilt.

13 And they shall not come near to Me to do the office of a priest to Me, nor come near to any of My holy things that are most sacred; but they shall bear their shame *and* their punishment for the abominations which they have committed.

14 Yet I will appoint them as caretakers to have charge of the temple, for all the service of the temple and for all that will be done in it.

15 But the Levitical priests, the sons of Zadok, who kept the charge of My sanctuary when the children of Israel went astray from Me, shall come near to Me to minister to Me, and they shall attend Me to offer to Me the fat and the blood, says the Lord God.

16 They shall enter into My sanctuary; and they shall come near to My table to minister to Me, and they shall keep My charge.

17 When they enter the gates of the inner court, they shall be clothed in linen garments; no wool shall be on them while they minister at the gates of the inner court and within the temple.

18 They shall have linen turbans on their heads and linen breeches upon their loins; they shall not gird themselves with anything that causes [them to] sweat.

19 And when they go out into the outer court to the people, they shall put off the garments in which they ministered and lay them in the holy chambers, and they shall put on other garments, lest by contact of their garments with the people they should consecrate (separate and set apart for holy use) such persons [unintentionally and unfittingly].

20 Neither shall they shave their heads or allow their locks to grow long; they shall only cut short *or* trim the hair of their heads.

21 Neither shall any priest drink wine when he enters the inner court.

22 Neither shall they take for their wives a widow or a woman separated *or* divorced from her husband; but they shall marry maidens [who are virgins] of the offspring of the house of Israel or a widow previously married to a priest.

23 The priests shall teach My people the difference between the holy and the common *or* profane, and cause them to distinguish between the unclean and the clean.

speak the Word

God, I pray that You would help me to know the difference between the holy and the common, between the clean and the unclean. I want to live a life that is holy and clean before You.
ADAPTED FROM EZEKIEL **44:23**

24 And in a controversy they shall act as judges, and they shall judge according to My judgments; and they shall keep My laws and My statutes in all My appointed feasts, and they shall keep My Sabbaths holy.

25 And they shall go near to no dead person to defile themselves, except for father or for mother, for son or for daughter, for brother or for sister who has had no husband; for them they may defile themselves. [Lev. 21:1, 2.]

26 And after he is cleansed [from the defilement of a dead body] they shall reckon to him seven days more before returning to the temple.

27 And on the day that he goes into the sanctuary, into the inner court to minister in the sanctuary, he shall offer his sin offering, says the Lord God.

28 This [their ministry to Me] shall be to them as an inheritance, for I am their inheritance; and you shall give them no possession in Israel, for I am their possession. [Josh. 13:14, 33.]

29 They shall eat the meal offering and the sin offering and the trespass offering, and every offering in Israel dedicated by a solemn vow to God shall be theirs.

30 And the first of all the firstfruits of all kinds, and every offering of all kinds from all your offerings, shall belong to the priests. You shall also give to the priest the first of your coarse meal *and* bread dough, that a blessing may rest on your house.

31 The priests shall not eat of anything that has died of itself or is torn, whether it be bird or beast.

45 MOREOVER, WHEN you shall divide the land by apportioned *and* assigned lots for inheritance, you shall set apart as an offering to the Lord a por-tion of the land to be used for holy purposes. The length shall be 25,000 *cubits,* and the breadth 20,000. It shall be holy (set apart and consecrated to sacred use) in its every area. [Ezek. 48:9, 12, 13.]

2 Of this there shall belong to the sanctuary a square plot 500 by 500, and 50 *cubits* for the open space around it.

3 And in this sacred section you shall measure off a portion 25,000 *cubits* in length and 10,000 *cubits* in breadth. And in it shall be the sanctu-ary which is most holy.

4 It is a holy portion of the land; it shall be for the priests, the ministers of the sanctuary, who come near to minister to the Lord; and it shall be a place for their houses and a holy place (set apart as sacred) for the sanctuary.

5 And another portion of land, 25,000 *cubits* long and 10,000 *cubits* wide, shall also be for the Levites, the ministers of the temple, and they shall possess it as a place in which to live.

6 And you shall appoint for the pos-session of the city an area of 5,000 *cubits* wide and 25,000 *cubits* long, along beside the portion set aside as a holy section. It shall belong to the whole house of Israel.

7 And to the prince shall belong the land on the one side and on the other side of the portion set aside as a holy section and the property of the city, in front of the holy section and the prop-erty of the city, from the west side westward and from the east side east-ward; and the length shall be answer-able to that of one of the tribal portions *and* parallel to it from the western boundary to the eastern boundary of the land.

8 It shall be for the prince—his pos-session in Israel. And My princes shall no more oppress My people, but

---

f *The Septuagint* (Greek translation of the Old Testament) so reads. The term "cubits" rather than "reeds" is supplied throughout this chapter only as the more probable reading. Neither is definitely designated in the Hebrew.

they shall give the rest of the land to the house of Israel according to their tribes.

9 Thus says the Lord God: That is enough for you, O princes of Israel! Stop the violence and plundering *and* oppression [that you did when you were given no property], and do justice and righteousness, and take away your exactions *and* cease your evictions of My people, says the Lord God.

10 You shall have just weights on your scales and just measures—both a just ephah measure and a just bath measure.

11 The ephah and the bath measures shall both be the same size, the bath containing one tenth of a homer and the ephah one tenth of a homer; the standard measure shall be the homer.

12 And the shekel shall be twenty gerahs; twenty shekels and twenty-five shekels and fifteen shekels shall be your maneh.

13 This is the offering which you shall make: a sixth of an ephah from each homer of wheat and a sixth of an ephah from each homer of barley.

14 And as to the set portion of oil, you shall offer the tenth part of a bath of oil out of each cor, which is a homer of ten baths, for ten baths make [both a cor and] a homer.

15 And [you shall offer] one lamb out of every flock of two hundred, out of the well-watered pastures of Israel *and* from all the families of Israel, to provide for a meal offering and for a burnt offering and for peace offerings, to make atonement for those who brought them, says the Lord God.

16 All the people of the land shall give this offering for the prince in Israel.

17 And it shall be the prince's part to furnish [from the contributions of the people] the burnt offerings, meal offerings, and drink offerings at the feasts and on the New Moons and on the Sabbaths, at all the appointed feasts of the house of Israel. He shall prepare *and* make the sin offering, the meal offering, the burnt offering, and the peace offerings to make atonement for, bringing forgiveness *and* reconciliation to, the house of Israel.

18 Thus says the Lord God: In the first [month], on the first [day] of the month, you shall take a young bull without blemish and you shall cleanse the sanctuary.

19 And the priest shall take some of the blood of the sin offering and put it upon the doorposts of the temple and upon the four corners of the ledge of the altar and upon the posts of the gate of the inner court.

20 You shall do this on the seventh day of the month for everyone who has sinned through error *or* ignorance and for him who is simple-minded. So shall you make atonement for the temple.

21 In the first month on the fourteenth day of the [month]; you shall have the Passover, a feast of seven days; unleavened bread shall be eaten.

22 Upon that day the prince shall prepare for himself and for all the people of the land a bullock for a sin offering.

23 And for the seven days of the feast he shall prepare a burnt offering to the Lord, seven bullocks and seven rams without blemish daily for the seven days, and a he-goat daily for a sin offering.

24 And he shall prepare as a meal offering to be offered with each bullock an ephah of meal, an ephah for each ram, and a hin of oil for each ephah of meal.

25 In the seventh [month], on the fifteenth day of the month, he shall make the same provision *and* preparation for the seven days of the feast, for sin offerings, burnt offerings, bloodless *or* meal offerings, and for the oil.

46

THUS SAYS the Lord God: The gate of the inner court that faces east shall be shut during the six working days, but on the Sabbath it shall be opened, and also on the day of the New Moon it shall be opened.

2   And the prince shall enter by the porch *or* vestibule of the gate from without and shall stand by the side-post of the gate. The priests shall prepare *and* offer his burnt offering and his peace offerings, and he shall worship at the threshold of the gate. Then he shall go out, but the gate shall not be shut until evening.

3   The people of the land shall worship at the entrance of that gate before the Lord on the Sabbaths and on the New Moons.

4   And the burnt offering that the prince shall offer to the Lord on the Sabbath day shall be six lambs without blemish and a ram without blemish.

5   And the bloodless *or* meal offering with the ram shall be an ephah, and the meal offering with the lambs shall be as much as he is able *and* willing to give, and a hin of oil with each ephah.

6   And on the day of the New Moon the offering shall be a young bull without blemish and six lambs and a ram without blemish.

7   And the prince shall provide *and* make a meal *or* bloodless offering, an ephah for the bullock and an ephah for the ram, and for the lambs as he is able *and* willing according to what has been made available to his hand, and a hin of oil to each ephah.

8   And when the prince shall enter, he shall go in by the porch *or* vestibule of that gate and he shall go out by way of it.

9   But when the people of the land shall come before the Lord at the appointed solemn feasts, he who enters the north gate to worship shall go out by the south gate, and he who enters by the south gate shall go out by the north gate; he shall not return by the gate by which he came in but shall go out by the opposite gate [straight ahead]. [Phil. 3:13.]

10   And the prince, when they go in, shall go in with them, and when they go out, he shall go out.

11   And in the appointed and solemn feasts the meal *or* bloodless offering shall be with a bullock an ephah, and with a ram an ephah, and with the lambs as much as the prince is willing *and* able to give [from what has been made available to him], and a hin of oil with each ephah.

12   When the prince shall prepare *and* make a freewill burnt offering or peace offerings voluntarily to the Lord, the gate that faces east shall be opened for him, and he shall offer his burnt offering and his peace offerings as he does on the Sabbath day. Then he shall go out, and after he has gone out, the gate shall be shut.

13   And a lamb a year old without blemish shall you [the priests, for the congregation] offer daily to the Lord; you shall prepare *and* offer it every morning.

14   And you [the priests] shall prepare a meal offering to go with it every morning, one-sixth of an ephah with one-third of a hin of oil to moisten the fine flour. This is a perpetual ordinance for a continual meal offering to the Lord.

15   Thus shall they prepare *and* offer the lamb and the meal offering and the oil every morning for a continual burnt offering.

16   Thus says the Lord God: If the prince gives a gift to any of his sons out of his inheritance, it shall belong to his sons; it is their property by inheritance.

17   But if he gives a gift out of his inheritance to one of his servants,

then it shall be his until the year of liberty [the Year of Jubilee]; after that it shall be returned to the prince; only his sons may keep a gift from his inheritance [permanently].

18 Moreover, the prince shall not take of the people's inheritance by oppression, thrusting them out of their property; what he gives to his sons he shall take out of his own possession, so that none of My people shall be separated from his [inherited] possession.

19 Then he [my guide] led me through the entrance which was at the side of the gate into the holy chambers for the priests, which faced the north; and behold, there was a place at the extreme western end of them.

20 And he said to me, This is the place where the priests shall boil the guilt offering and the sin offering, and where they shall bake the [bloodless] meal offering, to prevent their having to bring them into the outer court, lest they should thereby wrongfully sanctify (separate and consecrate for holy service) the people who are there.

21 And he brought me out into the outer court and caused me to pass by the four corners of the court, and behold, in every corner of the court there was a court.

22 In the four corners of the court there were courts joined on *and* enclosed, forty cubits long and thirty broad; these four in the corners were the same size.

23 And there was a row of masonry inside them, round about [each of] the four courts, and it was made with hearths for boiling at the bottom of the rows round about.

24 Then said he to me, These are the kitchens of those who do the boiling, where the ministers [the Levites] of the temple shall boil the sacrifices of the people.

47 THEN HE [my guide] brought me again to the door of the house [of the Lord—the temple], and behold, waters issued out from under the threshold of the temple toward the east, for the front of the temple was toward the east; and the waters came down from under, from the right side of the temple, on the south side of the altar.

2 Then he brought me out by way of the north gate and led me around outside to the outer gate by the way that faces east, and behold, waters were running out on the right side. [Zech. 14:8; Rev. 22:1, 2.]

3 And when the man went on eastward with the measuring line in his hand, he measured a thousand cubits, and he caused me to pass through the waters, waters that were ankle-deep.

4 Again he measured a thousand cubits and caused me to pass through the waters, waters that reached to the knees. Again he measured a thousand cubits and caused me to pass through the waters, waters that reached to the loins.

5 Afterward he measured a thousand, and it was a river that I could not pass through, for the waters had risen, waters to swim in, a river that could not be passed over *or* through.

6 And he said to me, Son of man, have you seen this? Then he led me and caused me to return to the bank of the river.

7 Now when I had returned, behold, on the bank of the river were very many trees on the one side and on the other.

8 Then he said to me, These waters pour out toward the eastern region and go down into the Arabah (the Jordan Valley) and on into the Dead Sea. And when they shall enter into the sea [the sea of putrid waters], the waters shall be healed *and* made fresh.

9 And wherever the double river shall go, every living creature which swarms shall live. And there shall be a very great number of fish, because these waters go there that [the waters of the sea] may be healed *and* made fresh; and everything shall live wherever the river goes.

10 The fishermen shall stand on [the banks of the Dead Sea]; from En-gedi even to En-eglaim shall be a place to spread nets; their fish shall be of very many kinds, as the fish of the Great *or* Mediterranean Sea.

11 But its swamps and marshes will not become wholesome for animal life; they shall [as the river subsides] be left encrusted with salt *and* given over to it.

12 And on the banks of the river on both its sides, there shall grow all kinds of trees for food; their leaf shall not fade nor shall their fruit fail [to meet the demand]. Each tree shall bring forth new fruit every month, [these supernatural qualities being] because their waters came from out of the sanctuary. And their fruit shall be for food and their leaves for healing.

13 Thus says the Lord God: These shall be the boundaries by which you shall divide the land among the twelve tribes of Israel: Joseph shall have two portions.

14 And you shall divide it equally. I lifted up My hand *and* swore to give it to your fathers, and this land shall fall to you as your inheritance.

15 And this shall be the boundary of the land on the north side: from the Great *or* Mediterranean Sea by way of Hethlon to the entrance of Zedad,

16 Hamath, Berothah, Sibraim, which is on the border between Damascus and Hamath, as far as Hazer-hatticon on the border of Hauran.

17 So the boundary shall extend from the [Mediterranean] Sea to Hazar-enan, at the boundary of Damascus on the north, together with the boundary of Hamath to the north. This is the north side.

18 And on the east side you shall measure the boundary from between Hauran and Damascus, and Gilead on one side and the land of Israel on the other, with the Jordan forming the boundary down to the East *or* Dead Sea. And this [from Damascus to the Dead Sea and including it] is the east side.

19 And the south side [boundary] southward, from Tamar [near the Dead Sea] shall run as far as the waters of Meribath-kadesh, then along the Brook of Egypt to the Great *or* Mediterranean Sea. And this is the south side.

20 On the west side [the boundary] shall be the Great *or* Mediterranean Sea to a point opposite the entrance of Hamath [north of Mount Hermon]. This is the west side.

21 So you shall divide this land among you according to the tribes of Israel.

22 You shall divide it by allotment as an inheritance for yourselves and for the foreigners who reside among you and shall have children born among you. They shall be to you as those born in the country among the children of Israel; they shall inherit with you among the tribes of Israel.

23 In whatever tribe the foreigner resides, there shall you give him his inheritance, says the Lord God.

48 NOW THESE are the names of the tribes: From the north end, beside the way of Hethlon to the entrance of Hamath as far as Hazar-enan, which is on the northern border of Damascus opposite Hamath, and reaching from the east border to the west, Dan, one [portion].

2 And beside the border of Dan, from the east side to the west side, Asher, one [portion].

3 And beside the border of Asher,

from the east side to the west side, Naphtali, one [portion].

4 And beside the border of Naphtali, from the east side to the west side, Manasseh, one [portion].

5 And beside the border of Manasseh, from the east side to the west side, Ephraim, one [portion].

6 And beside the border of Ephraim, from the east side to the west side, Reuben, one [portion].

7 And beside the border of Reuben, from the east side to the west side, Judah, one [portion].

8 And beside the border of Judah, from the east side to the west side, shall be the offering of land which you shall offer: 25,000 reeds in breadth, and in length as one of the tribal portions from the east side to the west side; and the sanctuary shall be in the midst of it.

9 The portion of land that you shall set apart and offer to the Lord shall be 25,000 [measures] in length and 10,000 in breadth [for each of the two districts].

10 And for these, even for the priests, shall be this holy offering of land: toward the north 25,000 [measures] in length, and toward the west 10,000 in breadth, and toward the east 10,000 in breadth, and toward the south 25,000 in length, and the sanctuary of the Lord shall be in the midst of it.

11 The set-apart *and* sacred portion shall be for the consecrated priests of the sons of Zadok, who have kept My charge and who did not go astray when the children of Israel went astray, as the other Levites did.

12 And this land offering shall be for the priests as a thing most holy beside the border of the [other] Levites.

13 And opposite the border of the priests the [other] Levites shall have 25,000 [measures] in length and 10,000 in breadth. The whole length shall be 25,000 and the breadth 10,000.

14 And they shall not sell any of it or exchange it; they shall not convey *or* transfer this the firstfruits of the land, for it has been offered to the Lord and is holy to Him.

15 And the remaining strip of 5,000 [measures] in breadth and 25,000 in length shall be for the city's secular use, for a place in which to dwell and for open country *or* suburbs. The city shall be in the midst of the plot.

16 And these shall be the dimensions of it: the north side 4,500 [measures] and the south side 4,500, the east side 4,500 and the west side 4,500. [Rev. 21:16.]

17 And the city shall have suburbs *or* open country: toward the north 250 [measures] and toward the south 250, toward the east 250 and toward the west 250.

18 The remainder of the length along beside the holy portion shall be 10,000 [measures] to the east and 10,000 to the west, and it shall be along beside the holy portion. The produce from it shall be for food for those who work in the city.

19 And the workers of the city from all the tribes of Israel shall till the open land.

20 The whole portion that you shall set apart as an offering to God shall be 25,000 [measures] by 25,000; you shall set apart the holy portion foursquare, together with the property of the city.

21 And what is left unallotted, on both sides of the holy portion and of that possessed by the city, shall belong to the prince. Reaching eastward from the 25,000 [measures] of the holy portion to the east border, and westward from the 25,000 [measures] to the west border, parallel to the tribal allotments, it belongs to the prince. The holy portion with the sanctuary of the temple in its midst,

22 And the possession of the Levites and the property of the city [of Jerusalem] shall be in the midst of that which belongs to the prince. What lies between the border of Judah and the border of Benjamin shall be for the prince.

23 As for the rest of the tribes, from the east side to the west side, Benjamin, one [portion].

24 And beside the border of Benjamin, from the east side to the west side, Simeon, one [portion].

25 And beside the border of Simeon, from the east side to the west side, Issachar, one [portion].

26 And beside the border of Issachar, from the east side to the west side, Zebulun, one [portion].

27 And beside the border of Zebulun, from the east side to the west side, Gad, one [portion].

28 And beside the border of Gad, at the south side southward, the border shall extend from Tamar to the waters of Meribath-kadesh and on along the Brook [of Egypt] to the Great *or* Mediterranean Sea.

29 This is the land which you shall divide by allotment among the tribes of Israel as their inheritance, and these are their several portions, says the Lord God.

30 And these shall be the exits of the city: On the north side, which is to extend 4,500 measures,

31 Three gates: one gate of Reuben, one gate of Judah, one gate of Levi, the gates of the city being called after the names of the tribes of Israel;

32 And on the east side's 4,500 measures, three gates: one gate of Joseph, one gate of Benjamin, one gate of Dan;

33 And on the south side's 4,500 measures, three gates: one gate of Simeon, one gate of Issachar, one gate of Zebulun;

34 On the west side's 4,500 measures, three gates: one gate of Gad, one gate of Asher, one gate of Naphtali.

35 The distance around the city shall be 18,000 [4 x 4,500] measures; and the name of the city from that day *and* ever after shall be, THE LORD IS THERE. [Rev. 21:12, 13, 16.]

Daniel

Author:
Daniel

Date:
Late sixth century BC

Everyday Life Principles:

Like Daniel, we must determine in our hearts that we will not defile ourselves, but that we will stay faithful to the Lord.

An excellent spirit is one of the best character qualities a person can have.

We must refuse to compromise or to allow the world's influence to cause us to turn from God.

Daniel is one of several biblical books that teach their lessons through a person's life. Two of the great lessons we learn from Daniel are excellence and courage.

Daniel 5:12 and Daniel 6:3 both tell us that Daniel had "an excellent spirit." Throughout the book of Daniel, we see him making excellent choices, and we read that he did things in an excellent way. But his choices and his actions were "fruits," not roots. The fruit of excellent decisions and behavior was rooted in his excellent spirit. As believers, you and I have God's Spirit living in us and we, like Daniel, can live with excellence because God is an excellent God!

Daniel also teaches us about courage. He was always willing to stand up to the authorities in Babylon who did not share his devotion to God. He was willing to suffer and even die for his beliefs. His courageous refusal to compromise landed him in a den of hungry lions, but God delivered him! Daniel ended up in a high government position; and the king of Babylon forsook his old ways, turned to God, and required his subjects to believe in God as well.

As you read the book of Daniel, I pray that you will be inspired to reach for higher levels of excellence in everything you do and that your courage will be stirred. As we learn from Daniel, one uncompromising and brave person can change a nation!

1 IN THE third year of the reign of Jehoiakim king of Judah, Nebuchadnezzar king of Babylon came to Jerusalem and besieged it.

2   And the Lord gave Jehoiakim king of Judah into his hand, along with a part of the vessels of the house of God; and he carried them into the land of Shinar [Babylonia] to the house of his god and placed the vessels in the treasury of his god. [II Chron. 36:5-7; Jer. 27:19, 20; Dan. 5:1-3.]

3   And the [Babylonian] king told Ashpenaz, the master of his eunuchs, to bring in some of the children of Israel, both of the royal family and of the nobility—[II Kings 20:17, 18.]

4   Youths without blemish, well-favored in appearance and skillful in all wisdom, discernment, *and* understanding, apt in learning knowledge, competent to stand *and* serve in the king's palace—and to teach them the literature and language of the Chaldeans.

5   And the king assigned for them a daily portion of his own rich *and* dainty food and of the wine which he drank. They were to be so educated

life point

After the fall of Judah to Babylon, Nebuchadnezzar—the king of Babylon at that time—decided to bring in some young Hebrew men and train them as his attendants. His purpose was for them to conform to the lifestyle of his court.

But Daniel, one of the devout young men of Judah who loved the Lord, was determined to be a God-pleaser and not a man-pleaser. He refused to conform to what the king and others thought he should be.

Daniel stood his ground and won favor with the king and his court. As a result of his fearless stand, God ended up using him in a very powerful way.

putting the Word to work

Daniel had the opportunity to eat "rich and dainty" food from the king's table (Daniel 1:8), but he determined not to defile himself with those delicacies. You and I have similar opportunities to defile ourselves today, especially in the area of entertainment. We can be defiled by the ungodly influences of television shows or movies we watch or the music we listen to. We can also defile ourselves by compromising and going along with friends who are making wrong choices. Are you willing to be like Daniel and determine not to defile yourself? Ask God to help you make godly choices and stay faithful to Him.

and so nourished for three years that at the end of that time they might stand before the king.

6   Among these were of the children of Judah: Daniel, Hananiah, Mishael, and Azariah.

7   The chief of the eunuchs gave them names: Daniel he called Belteshazzar [the king's attendant], Hananiah he called Shadrach, Mishael he called Meshach, and Azariah he called Abednego.

8   But Daniel determined in his heart that he would not defile himself by [eating his portion of] the king's rich *and* dainty food or by [drinking] the wine which he drank; therefore he requested of the chief of the eunuchs that he might [be allowed] not to defile himself. [Num. 6:1-4; I Cor. 10:21.]

9   Now God made Daniel to find favor, compassion, *and* loving-kindness with the chief of the eunuchs.

10   And the chief of the eunuchs said to Daniel, I fear, lest my lord the king, who has appointed your food and your drink, should see your faces worse looking *or* more sad than the other youths of your age. Then you

the blessings of wholehearted commitment

Because of their sins against the Lord, the nation of Judah was carried away into captivity in Babylon. There, some of the most promising young men, including Daniel and three of his friends, were chosen to become attendants to the Babylonian king. As part of their three-year period of training and preparation, these young men were supposed to follow a diet of rich meat and wine provided from the king's table. However, Daniel and his friends had apparently made a previous commitment to God concerning their diet, and they determined that they would not defile themselves by eating the king's food and drinking his wine (see Daniel 1:8). Instead, Daniel asked the eunuch who oversaw them if it would be possible for them to follow their own diet of vegetables and water.

The Bible tells us that the Lord gave Daniel favor (compassion and loving-kindness) with the eunuch, who agreed to allow them to follow their diet as long as it did not harm them. Of course, not only did it not harm them, it made them stronger and healthier than all the other young men in training as royal attendants. In fact, the king was so impressed by their wisdom that he chose them out of all the young men to serve as his trusted counselors (see Daniel 1:10–20).

God's favor rested on Daniel and his friends so strongly that eventually Daniel rose to become the chief governor of Babylon—the world's greatest power at that time—and the other three were made high officials in the kingdom.

What was the key to Daniel's success? He followed God with his whole heart and refused to compromise, and as a result, God gave him wisdom, skill, and favor.

would endanger my head with the king.

11 Then said Daniel to the steward whom the chief of the eunuchs had set over Daniel, Hananiah, Mishael, and Azariah,

12 Prove your servants, I beseech you, for ten days and let us be given a vegetable diet and water to drink.

13 Then let our appearance and the appearance of the youths who eat of the king's [rich] dainties be observed *and* compared by you, and deal with us your servants according to what you see.

14 So [the man] consented to them in this matter and proved them ten days.

15 And at the end of ten days it was seen that they were looking better and had taken on more flesh than all the youths who ate of the king's rich dainties.

16 So the steward took away their [rich] dainties and the wine they were to drink and gave them vegetables.

17 As for these four youths, God gave them knowledge and skill in all learning and wisdom, and Daniel had understanding in all [kinds of] visions and dreams. [Luke 21:15; James 1:5-7.]

speak the Word

God, I pray that You would give me knowledge, skill, and understanding in all the things I need to know.
ADAPTED FROM DANIEL 1:17

18 Now at the end of the time which the king had set for bringing [all the young men in], the chief of the eunuchs brought them before Nebuchadnezzar.
19 And the king conversed with them, and among them all none was found like Daniel, Hananiah, Mishael, and Azariah; therefore they were assigned to stand before the king.
20 And in all matters of wisdom and understanding concerning which the king asked them, he found them ten times better than all the [learned] magicians and enchanters who were in his whole realm.
21 And Daniel continued there even to the first year of King Cyrus [at the close of the seventy years' exile of Judah in Babylonia, which Jeremiah had foretold]. [Ezra 1:1-3; Jer. 25:11, 12; 29:10.]

2 IN THE second year of the reign of Nebuchadnezzar, Nebuchadnezzar had dreams by which his spirit was troubled *and* agitated and his sleep went from him.
2 Then the king commanded to call the magicians, the enchanters *or* soothsayers, the sorcerers, and the Chaldeans [diviners], to tell the king his dreams. So they came and stood before the king.
3 And the king said to them, I had a dream and my spirit is troubled to know the dream.
4 Then said the Chaldeans [diviners] to the king in Aramaic [the Syrian language], O king, live forever! Tell your servants the dream, and we will show the interpretation.
5 The king answered the Chaldeans, The thing is gone from me! And the decree goes forth from me *and* I say it with all emphasis: if you do not make known to me the dream with its interpretation, you shall be cut in pieces and your houses shall be made a dunghill!

6 But if you show the dream and its interpretation, you shall receive from me gifts and rewards and great honor. So show me the dream and the interpretation of it.
7 They answered again, Let the king tell his servants the dream, and we will show the interpretation of it.
8 The king answered, I know with certainty that you are trying to gain time, because you see the thing is gone from me *and* because you see that my word [against you] is sure:
9 If you will not make known to me the dream, there is but one sentence for you; for you have prepared lying and corrupt words to speak before me [hoping to delay your execution] until the time is changed. Therefore tell me the dream, and I will know that you can tell me the interpretation of it.
10 The Chaldeans [diviners] answered before the king and said, There is not a man on earth who can show the king this matter, for no king, lord, or ruler has [ever] asked such a thing of any magician or enchanter or Chaldean.
11 A rare *and* weighty thing indeed the king requires! None except the gods can reveal it to the king, and their dwelling is not with [human] flesh.
12 For this cause the king was angry and very furious and commanded that all the wise men of Babylon be destroyed.
13 So the decree went forth that the wise men were to be killed, and [the officers] sought Daniel and his companions to be slain.
14 Then Daniel returned an answer which was full of prudence and wisdom to Arioch the captain *or* executioner of the king's guard, who had gone forth to slay the wise men of Babylon.
15 He said to Arioch, the king's captain, Why is the decree so urgent *and* hasty from the king? Then Arioch explained the matter to Daniel.

16 And Daniel went in and desired of the king that he would set a date *and* give him time, and he would show the king the interpretation.

17 Then Daniel went to his house and made the thing known to Hananiah, Mishael, and Azariah, his companions,

18 So that they would desire *and* request mercy of the God of heaven concerning this secret, that Daniel and his companions should not perish with the rest of the wise men of Babylon.

19 Then the secret was revealed to Daniel in a vision of the night, and Daniel blessed the God of heaven.

20 Daniel answered, Blessed be the name of God forever and ever! For wisdom and might are His!

21 He changes the times and the seasons; He removes kings and sets up kings. He gives wisdom to the wise and knowledge to those who have understanding! [Dan. 4:35.]

putting the Word to work

Daniel 2:21 tells us that "God changes the times and the seasons." This is not only true in the natural world, but in our lives. His timing and His ways are always perfect. Are you fully trusting Him to bring the changes you need in your life at the time that is right? He is doing a good work in you, so I encourage you to cooperate with the changes He brings. You will be glad you did.

22 He reveals the deep and secret things; He knows what is in the darkness, and the light dwells with Him! [Job 15:8; Ps. 25:14; Matt. 6:6.]

23 I thank You and praise You, O God of my fathers, Who has given me wisdom and might and has made known to me now what we desired of You, for You have made known to us the solution to the king's problem.

24 Therefore Daniel went to Arioch, whom the king had appointed to destroy the wise men of Babylon; he went and said thus to him: Do not destroy the wise men of Babylon! Bring me in before the king, and I will show to the king the interpretation.

25 Then Arioch brought in Daniel before the king in haste and said thus to him: I have found a man of the captives of Judah who will make known to the king the interpretation [of his dream].

26 The king said to Daniel, whose name was Belteshazzar, Are you able to make known to me the dream which I have seen and the interpretation of it?

27 Daniel answered the king, The [mysterious] secret which the king has demanded neither the wise men, enchanters, magicians, nor astrologers can show the king,

28 But there is a God in heaven Who reveals secrets, and He has made known to King Nebuchadnezzar what it is that shall be in the latter days (at the end of days). Your dream and the visions in your head upon your bed are these:

29 As for you, O king, as you were lying upon your bed thoughts came into your mind about what should come to pass hereafter, and He Who reveals secrets was making known to you what shall come to pass.

30 But as for me, this secret is not revealed to me for any wisdom that I have more than anyone else living, but in order that the interpretation may be made known to the king and that you may know the thoughts of your heart *and* mind.

31 You, O king, saw, and behold, [there was] a great image. This image which was mighty and of exceedingly great brightness stood before you, and the appearance of it was frightening *and* terrible.

32 As for this ªimage, its head was of fine gold, its breast and its arms of silver, its belly and its thighs of bronze,
33 Its legs of iron, its feet partly of iron and partly of clay [the baked clay of the potter].
34 As you looked, a ᵇStone was cut out without human hands, which smote the image on its feet of iron and [baked] clay [of the potter] and broke them to pieces. [I Pet. 2:3-8.]
35 Then the iron, the [baked] clay [of the potter], the bronze, the silver, and the gold were broken *and* crushed together and became like the chaff of the summer threshing floors, and the wind carried them away so that not a trace of them could be found. And the Stone that smote the image became a great mountain *or* rock and filled the whole earth.
36 This was the dream, and we will tell the interpretation of it to the king.
37 You, O king, are king of the [earthly] kings to whom the God of heaven has given the kingdom, the power, the might, and the glory. [Jer. 25:9; 27:6; 28:14.]
38 And wherever the children of men dwell, and the beasts of the field, and the birds of the heavens—He has given them into your hand and has made you to rule over them all. You [king of Babylon] are the head of gold.
39 And after you shall arise another kingdom [the Medo-Persian], inferior to you, and still a third kingdom of bronze [Greece under Alexander the Great] which shall bear rule over all the earth.
40 And the fourth kingdom [Rome] shall be strong as iron, since iron

breaks to pieces and subdues all things; and like iron which crushes, it shall break and crush all these. [Dan. 7:7, 23.]
41 And as you saw the feet and toes, partly of [baked] clay [of the potter] and partly of iron, it shall be a divided kingdom; but there shall be in it some of the firmness *and* strength of iron, just as you saw the iron mixed with miry [earthen] clay.
42 And as the toes of the feet were partly of iron and partly of [baked] clay [of the potter], so the kingdom shall be partly strong and partly brittle *and* broken.
43 And as you saw the iron mixed with miry *and* earthen clay, so they shall mingle themselves in the seed of men [in marriage bonds]; but they will not hold together [for two such elements or ideologies can never harmonize], even as iron does not mingle itself with clay.
44 And in the days of these [final ten] kings shall the God of heaven set up a kingdom which shall never be destroyed, nor shall its sovereignty be left to another people; but it shall break *and* crush and consume all these kingdoms and it shall stand forever. [Dan. 7:14-17; Luke 1:31-33; Rev. 11:15.]
45 Just as you saw that the Stone was cut out of the mountain without hands and that it broke in pieces the iron, the bronze, the clay, the silver, and the gold, the great God has made known to the king what shall come to pass hereafter. The dream is certain and the interpretation of it is sure.
46 Then King Nebuchadnezzar fell on his face and paid homage to Daniel

a Daniel's interpretation of Nebuchadnezzar's dream outlines the further history of Gentile world power. The four metals of which the image was made represented four successive empires, each with the power to possess the whole inhabited earth—though each stopped short of that. They were: (1) Babylon (Jer. 51:7) (2) Medo-Persia (3) Greece under Alexander (4) Rome. The latter power was divided first into the two legs, corresponding to the eastern and western Roman empires, and then (after a very long time apparently) into the ten toes, a confederacy made up largely of European nations (Dan. 7:24-27). **b** The eternal kingdom of God, the Messianic kingdom, will extend over "the whole earth," and all who reject Jesus, the Messiah, the Stone, will be crushed. See also Ps. 118:22-23; Isa. 8:14; Matt. 21:44; Luke 2:34; 20:18; I Pet. 2:3-8.

refuse to conform

Daniel went through a period of testing and trial, but in the end, the same king who tried to get him to conform had such respect for him that he exalted him to a high position in the kingdom (see Daniel 2:48).

The same thing happened to me years ago in the work world. My boss wanted me to help him steal some money, in a roundabout way. I was a bookkeeper, and he wanted me to write off a customer's credit balance. The customer had paid a bill twice, and my employer did not want that fact reflected on the client's statement.

I refused.

Several years later, I ended up having great favor in that company. I was made second-in-command of the office, the warehouse, all of the inventory, and all the truck drivers. I was called upon to solve problems I did not even understand, and God gave me the wisdom I needed to do the job accurately.

As a young woman, I had a major position of leadership in the company. I did not really have the education or even the training for the position. How did that happen? It came about because, like Daniel, I refused to conform to a lower standard. I was respected in the company and was exalted to a higher position of honor.

Those who try to get you to conform will not respect you if you do conform. In fact, they will despise your weakness. They will know they are controlling you and that what they are doing is wrong. But if you will stand your ground, you will be the one who ends up with the respect. For a while they may treat you as though you were the lowest creature on earth. But when all is said and done, you will gain their respect. Integrity and godly convictions lead to blessing and favor.

[as a great prophet of the highest God] and ordered that an offering and incense should be offered up to him [in honor of his God].
47 The king answered Daniel, Of a truth your God is the God of gods and the Lord of kings and a Revealer of secret mysteries, seeing that you could reveal this secret mystery! [Prov. 3:32; Rev. 19:16.]
48 Then the king made Daniel great and gave him many great gifts, and he made him to rule over the whole province of Babylon and to be chief governor over all the wise men of Babylon.

49 And Daniel requested of the king and he appointed Shadrach, Meshach, and Abednego over the affairs of the province of Babylon. But Daniel remained in the gate of the king [at the king's court].

3 NEBUCHADNEZZAR THE king [caused to be] made an image of gold, whose height was sixty cubits *or* ninety feet and its breadth six cubits *or* nine feet. He set it up on the plain of Dura in the province of Babylon.
2 Then Nebuchadnezzar the king sent to gather together the satraps, the

deputies, the governors, the judges *and* chief stargazers, the treasurers, the counselors, the sheriffs *and* lawyers, and all the chief officials of the provinces to come to the dedication of the image which King Nebuchadnezzar had [caused to be] set up.

3 Then the satraps, the deputies, the governors, the judges *and* chief stargazers, the treasurers, the counselors, the sheriffs *and* lawyers, and all the chief officials of the provinces were gathered together for the dedication of the image that King Nebuchadnezzar had set up, and they stood before the image that Nebuchadnezzar had set up.

4 Then the herald cried aloud, You are commanded, O peoples, nations, and languages,

5 That when you hear the sound of the horn, pipe, lyre, trigon, harp, dulcimer *or* bagpipe, and every kind of music, you are to fall down and worship the golden image that King Nebuchadnezzar has set up.

6 And whoever does not fall down and worship shall that very hour be cast into the midst of a burning fiery furnace.

7 Therefore, when all the peoples heard the sound of the horn, pipe, lyre, trigon, dulcimer *or* bagpipe, and every kind of music, all the peoples, nations, and languages fell down and worshiped the golden image that King Nebuchadnezzar had set up.

8 Therefore at that time certain men of Chaldean descent came near and brought [malicious] accusations against the Jews.

9 They said to King Nebuchadnezzar, O king, live forever!

10 You, O king, have made a decree that every man who hears the sound of the horn, pipe, lyre, trigon, harp, dulcimer *or* bagpipe, and every kind of music shall fall down and worship the golden image,

11 And that whoever does not fall down and worship shall be cast into the midst of a burning fiery furnace.

12 There are certain Jews whom you have appointed *and* set over the affairs of the province of Babylon—Shadrach, Meshach, and Abednego. These men, O king, pay no attention to you; they do not serve your gods or worship the golden image which you have set up.

13 Then Nebuchadnezzar in rage and fury commanded to bring Shadrach, Meshach, and Abednego; and these men were brought before the king.

14 [Then] Nebuchadnezzar said to them, Is it true, O Shadrach, Meshach, and Abednego, that you do not serve my gods or worship the golden image which I have set up?

15 Now if you are ready when you

life point

King Nebuchadnezzar set up a huge golden image in Babylon and required everyone to bow down before it and worship it (see Daniel 3:14). Anybody who refused to do so would be thrown into a fiery furnace.

Shadrach, Meshach, and Abednego, three of Daniel's close friends, refused to bow down. They had the same excellent, godly spirit that Daniel had, so they refused. The king said to them, basically, "If you do not do as I say, I am going to burn you alive" (see Daniel 3:15).

Isn't that basically what the world says to you and me? If we refuse to conform to its standards, the world threatens us by saying, "If you do not bow down and do what we want you to do, if you do not fit into our mold, we are going to hurt you in some way." The world may threaten us, but with God, we will always emerge victorious.

life point

Do you know what I like about Shadrach, Meshach, and Abednego? Their absolute refusal to be frightened or intimidated. They told the king: "We believe God is going to deliver us, but even if He *does not*, we are not conforming to your image of what you think we ought to be. We are going to do what God is telling us to do. You can do what you want to with your furnace. But whatever happens to us, we will have peace" (see Daniel 3:17, 18).

That is the attitude we ought to have toward those who try to pressure us into disobeying what we know to be the will of God for us. Pray for that kind of courage and faith.

hear the sound of the horn, pipe, lyre, trigon, harp, dulcimer *or* bagpipe, and every kind of music to fall down and worship the image which I have made, very good. But if you do not worship, you shall be cast at once into the midst of a burning fiery furnace, and who is that god who can deliver you out of my hands?

16 Shadrach, Meshach, and Abednego answered the king, O Nebuchadnezzar, it is not necessary for us to answer you on this point.

17 If our God Whom we serve is able to deliver us from the burning fiery furnace, He will deliver us out of your hand, O king.

18 But if not, let it be known to you, O king, that we will not serve your gods or worship the golden image which you have set up! [Job 13:15; Acts 4:19, 20.]

19 Then Nebuchadnezzar was full of fury and his facial expression was changed [to antagonism] against Shadrach, Meshach, and Abednego. Therefore he commanded that the furnace should be heated seven times hotter than it was usually heated.

20 And he commanded the strongest men in his army to bind Shadrach, Meshach, and Abednego and to cast them into the burning fiery furnace.

21 Then these [three] men were bound in their cloaks, their tunics *or* undergarments, their turbans, and their other clothing, and they were cast into the midst of the burning fiery furnace.

22 Therefore because the king's commandment was urgent and the furnace exceedingly hot, the flame *and* sparks from the fire killed those men who handled Shadrach, Meshach, and Abednego.

23 And these three men, Shadrach, Meshach, and Abednego, fell down bound into the burning fiery furnace.

24 Then Nebuchadnezzar the king [saw and] was astounded, and he jumped up and said to his counselors, Did we not cast three men bound into the midst of the fire? They answered, True, O king.

25 He answered, Behold, I see four men loose, walking in the midst of the fire, and they are not hurt! And the form of the fourth is like a son of the gods! [Phil. 2:5-8.]

26 Then Nebuchadnezzar came near to the mouth of the burning fiery furnace and said, Shadrach, Meshach, and Abednego, you servants of the Most High God, come out and come here. Then Shadrach, Meshach, and Abednego came out from the midst of the fire.

27 And the satraps, the deputies, the governors, and the king's counselors gathered around together and saw these men—that the fire had no power upon their bodies, nor was the hair of their head singed; neither were their garments scorched *or* changed in color *or* condition, nor had even the smell of smoke clung to them.

28 Then Nebuchadnezzar said,

life point

Shadrach, Meshach, and Abednego experienced affliction when they remained firm in their commitment to the one true God. When they refused the command of the wicked king Nebuchadnezzar to worship the golden image he had set up, Nebuchadnezzar cast them into the fiery furnace, which he heated seven times hotter than usual!

Nebuchadnezzar was "astounded" to see that Shadrach, Meshach, and Abednego were joined by a fourth man in the fiery furnace—one who was, according to the King James Version, "like the Son of God" (Daniel 3:25). Not only did the three come out of the fiery furnace loosed from their bonds and totally unharmed, they did not even smell like smoke!

Just as God was with these men in their furnace of affliction, so He will be with you in whatever situation you may have to face in life.

Blessed be the God of Shadrach, Meshach, and Abednego, Who has sent His angel and delivered His servants who believed in, trusted in, *and* relied on Him! And they set aside the king's command and yielded their bodies rather than serve or worship any god except their own God.
29 Therefore I make a decree that any people, nation, and language that speaks anything amiss against the God of Shadrach, Meshach, and Abednego shall be cut in pieces and their houses be made a dunghill, for there is no other God who can deliver in this way!
30 Then the king promoted Shadrach, Meshach, and Abednego in the province of Babylon.

4 NEBUCHADNEZZAR THE king, to all people, nations, and languages that dwell on all the earth: May peace be multiplied to you!
2 It seemed good to me to show the signs and wonders that the Most High God has performed toward me.
3 How great are His signs! And how mighty His wonders! His kingdom is an everlasting kingdom, and His dominion is from generation to generation. [Dan. 7:13, 14; Luke 1:31-33.]
4 I, Nebuchadnezzar, was at rest in my house and prospering in my palace.
5 I had a dream which made me afraid, and the thoughts *and* imaginations and the visions of my head as I was lying upon my bed troubled *and* agitated me.
6 Therefore I made a decree to bring in all the wise men of Babylon before me, that they might make known to me the interpretation of the dream.
7 Then the magicians, the enchanters, the Chaldeans, and the astrologers came in, and I told them the dream, but they could not make known to me the interpretation of it.
8 But at last Daniel came in before me—he who was named Belteshazzar, after the name of my god, and in whom is the Spirit of the Holy God—and I told the dream before him, saying,
9 O Belteshazzar, chief of the magicians, because I know that the Spirit of the Holy God is in you and no secret mystery is a burden *or* troubles you, tell me the visions of my dream that I have seen and the interpretation of it.
10 The visions of my head [as I lay] on my bed were these: I saw, and behold, [there was] a tree in the midst of the earth, and its height was great.
11 The tree grew and was strong and its height reached to the heavens, and the sight of it reached to the end of the whole earth.

12 Its leaves were fair and its fruit abundant, and in it was food for all. The living creatures of the field found shade under it, and the birds of the sky dwelt in its branches; and all flesh was fed from it.

13 I saw in the visions of my head [as I lay] on my bed, and behold, a watcher, a holy one, came down from heaven.

14 He cried aloud [with might] and said, Cut down the tree and cut off its branches; shake off its leaves and scatter its fruit. Let the living creatures flee from under it and the fowls from its branches.

15 Nevertheless leave the stump of its roots in the earth, bound with a band of iron and bronze, in the midst of the tender grass of the field. Let him be wet with the dew of the heavens, and let him share the lot of the living creatures in the grass of the earth.

16 Let his nature *and* understanding be changed from a man's and let a beast's nature *and* understanding be given him, and let seven times [or years] pass over him.

17 This sentence is by the decree of the [heavenly] watchers and the decision is by the word of the holy ones, to the intent that the living may know that the Most High [God] rules the kingdom of mankind and gives it to whomever He will and sets over it the humblest *and* lowliest of men. [Dan. 2:21; 5:21.]

18 This dream I, King Nebuchadnezzar, have seen. And you, O Belteshazzar [Daniel], declare now its interpretation, since all the wise men of my kingdom are not able to make known to me the interpretation; but you are able, for the Spirit of the Holy God is in you.

19 Then Daniel, whose name was Belteshazzar, was astonished *and* dismayed *and* stricken dumb for a while [concerned about the king's destiny],

and his thoughts troubled, agitated, *and* alarmed him. The king said, Belteshazzar, let not the dream or its interpretation trouble *or* alarm you. Belteshazzar answered, My lord, may the dream be for those who hate you and its message for your enemies.

20 The tree that you saw, which grew [great] and was strong, whose height reached to the heavens and which was visible to all the earth,

21 Whose foliage was beautiful and its fruit abundant, on which was food for all, under which the living creatures of the field dwelt, and on whose branches the birds of the sky had their nests—

22 It is you, O king, who have grown and become strong; your greatness has increased and it reaches to the heavens, and your dominion to the ends of the earth.

23 And whereas the king saw a watcher, a holy one, coming down from heaven and saying, Cut the tree down and destroy it, but leave the stump of its roots in the earth with a band of iron and bronze around it, in the tender grass of the field; and let him be wet with the dew of the heavens, and let his portion be with the living creatures of the field until seven times [or years] pass over him—

24 This is the interpretation, O king: It is the decree of the Most High [God] which has come upon my lord the king:

25 You shall be driven from among men and your dwelling shall be with the beasts of the field; you shall be made to eat grass as do the oxen and you shall be wet with the dew of the heavens; and seven times [or years] shall pass over you until you learn *and* know *and* recognize that the Most High [God] rules the kingdom of mankind and gives it to whomever He will.

26 And in that it was commanded to leave the stump of the roots of the tree, your kingdom shall be sure to you after you have learned *and* know that [the God of] heaven rules.

27 Therefore, O king, let my counsel be acceptable to you; break off your sins *and* show the reality of your repentance by righteousness (right standing with God and moral and spiritual rectitude and rightness in every area and relation) *and* liberate yourself from your iniquities by showing mercy *and* loving-kindness to the poor *and* oppressed, that [if the king will repent] there may possibly be a continuance *and* lengthening of your peace *and* tranquility *and* a healing of your error.

28 All this was fulfilled *and* came upon King Nebuchadnezzar.

29 At the end of twelve months he was walking in the royal palace of Babylon.

30 The king said, Is not this the great Babylon that I have built as the royal residence *and* seat of government by the might of my power and for the honor *and* glory of my majesty?

31 While the words were still in the king's mouth, there fell a voice from heaven, saying, O King Nebuchadnezzar, to you it is spoken: The kingdom has departed from you,

32 And you shall be driven from among men and your dwelling will be with the living creatures of the field. You will be made to eat grass like the oxen, and seven times [or years] shall pass over you until you have learned *and* know that the Most High [God] rules in the kingdom of men and gives it to whomever He will.

33 That very hour the thing was [in process of] being fulfilled upon Nebuchadnezzar. He was driven from among men and did eat grass like oxen [as Daniel had said he would], and his body was wet with the dew of the heavens until his hair grew like eagles' [feathers] and his nails [were] like birds' [claws].

34 And at the end of the days [seven years], I, Nebuchadnezzar, lifted up my eyes to heaven, and my understanding *and* the right use of my mind returned to me; and I blessed the Most High [God] and I praised and honored *and* glorified Him Who lives forever, Whose dominion is an everlasting dominion; and His kingdom endures from generation to generation.

35 And all the inhabitants of the earth are accounted as nothing. And He does according to His will in the host of heaven and among the inhabitants of the earth, and none can stay His hand or say to Him, What are You doing?

36 Now at the same time my reason *and* understanding returned to me; and for the glory of my kingdom, my majesty and splendor returned to me, and my counselors and my lords sought me out; I was reestablished in my kingdom, and still more greatness [than before] was added to me.

37 Now I, Nebuchadnezzar, praise and extol and honor the King of heaven, Whose works are all faithful *and* right and Whose ways are just. And those who walk in pride He is able to abase *and* humble.

5 BELSHAZZAR THE king [descendant of Nebuchadnezzar] made a great feast for a thousand of his lords, and he drank his wine in the presence of the thousand.

speak the Word

2 Belshazzar, while he was tasting the wine, commanded that the gold and silver vessels which his father Nebuchadnezzar had taken out of the temple [out of the sacred area—the Holy Place and the Holy of Holies] which was in Jerusalem be brought, that the king and his lords, his wives, and his concubines might drink from them.

3 Then they brought in the gold *and* silver vessels which had been taken out of the temple, the house of God which was in Jerusalem; and the king and his lords, his wives, and his concubines drank from them.

4 They drank wine and praised the gods of gold and silver, of bronze, iron, wood, and stone.

5 Immediately *and* suddenly there appeared the fingers of a man's hand and wrote on the plaster of the wall opposite the candlestick [so exposed especially to the light] in the king's palace, and the king saw the part of the hand that wrote.

6 Then the color *and* the [drunken] hilarious brightness of the king's face was changed, and his [terrifying] thoughts troubled *and* alarmed him; the joints *and* muscles of his hips *and* back gave way and his knees smote together.

7 The king cried aloud [mightily] to bring in the enchanters *or* soothsayers, the Chaldeans [diviners], and the astrologers. The king said to the wise men of Babylon, Whoever will read this writing and show me the interpretation of it will be clothed with purple and have a chain of gold put about his neck and will be the third ruler in the kingdom.

8 And all the king's wise men came in, but they could not read the writing or make known to the king the interpretation of it.

9 Then King Belshazzar was greatly perplexed *and* alarmed and the color faded from his face, and his lords were puzzled *and* astounded.

10 Now the queen [mother], overhearing the exciting words of the king and his lords, came into the banquet house. The queen [mother] said, O king, live forever! Do not be alarmed at your thoughts or let your cheerful expression *and* the color of your face be changed.

11 There is a man in your kingdom in whom is the Spirit of the holy God [or gods], and in the days of your father light and understanding and wisdom like the wisdom of the gods were found in him; and King Nebuchadnezzar, your father—the king, I say, your father—appointed him master of the magicians, enchanters *or* soothsayers, Chaldeans, and astrologers,

12 Because an excellent spirit, knowledge, and understanding to interpret dreams, clarify riddles, and solve knotty problems were found in this same Daniel, whom the king named Belteshazzar. Now let Daniel be called, and he will show the interpretation.

life point

Daniel 5:12 tells us that "an excellent spirit" was found in Daniel. We must make up our minds and get into agreement with God that we, like Daniel, are going to be excellent, not mediocre. We must take an inventory of our lives and prune off anything that entangles us or simply steals our time. We must be determined, work hard, and refuse to quit or give up—drawing strength from God and not depending on ourselves. If we will do these things persistently and with an excellent spirit, we will eventually be victorious.

13 Then Daniel was brought in before the king. And the king said to Daniel, Are you that Daniel of the children of the captivity of Judah, whom the king my father brought out of Judah?

14 I have heard of you, that the Spirit of the holy God [or gods] is in you and that light and understanding and superior wisdom are found in you.

15 Now the wise men, the enchanters, have been brought in before me that they might read this writing and make known to me the interpretation of it, but they could not show the interpretation of the matter.

16 But I have heard of you, that you can make interpretations and solve knotty problems. Now if you can read the writing and make known to me its interpretation, you shall be clothed with purple and have a chain of gold put around your neck and shall be the third ruler in the kingdom.

17 Then Daniel answered before the king, Let your gifts be for yourself and give your rewards to another. However, I will read the writing to the king and make known to him the interpretation.

18 O king, the Most High God gave Nebuchadnezzar your father a kingdom and greatness and glory and majesty;

19 And because of the greatness that He gave him, all peoples, nations, and languages trembled and feared before him. Whom he would he slew, and whom he would he kept alive; whom he would he set up, and whom he would he put down.

20 But when his heart was lifted up and his mind *and* spirit were hardened so that he dealt proudly, he was deposed from his kingly throne and his glory was taken from him;

21 He was driven from among men, and his heart *or* mind was made like the beasts, and his dwelling was with the wild asses. He was fed with grass like oxen, and his body was wet with the dew of the heavens until he learned *and* knew that the Most High God rules in the kingdom of men and that He appoints *and* sets over it whomever He will.

22 And you his son, O Belshazzar, have not humbled your heart *and* mind, though you knew all this [knew it and were defiant].

23 And you have lifted yourself up against the Lord of heaven, and the vessels of His house have been brought before you, and you and your lords, your wives, and your concubines have drunk wine from them; and you have praised the gods of silver and gold, of bronze, iron, wood, and stone, which do not see or hear or know; but the God in Whose hand your breath is and Whose are all your ways you have not honored *and* glorified [but have dishonored and disgraced].

24 Then was the part of the hand sent from the presence of [the Most High God], and this writing was inscribed.

25 And this is the ᶜinscription that was written, MENE, MENE, TEKEL, UPHARSIN—numbered, numbered, weighed, divisions.

26 This is the interpretation of the matter: MENE, God has numbered the days of your kingship and brought them to an end;

27 TEKEL, You are weighed in the balances and are found wanting;

28 ᵈPERES, Your kingdom *and* your

---

c For many people it may be difficult to understand why all the wise men, the magicians, the soothsayers, the Chaldeans, and the astrologers were unable to translate a few simple words, especially when Daniel's prescribed education in languages was the same as their own—and he had no difficulty translating. The answer is that any wise man who was present there probably could recognize the four inscribed words, but only the uncompromising man of God—who knew God through daily fellowship and communion with Him, who was so dedicated to Him that God could speak to him and through him—only such a man could tell what the words really meant. Blessed (happy, fortunate, prosperous, and enviable) are those who dare to be a Daniel! **d** The singular of UPHARSIN (see Dan. 5:25).

kingship are divided and given to the Medes and Persians. [Foretold in Isa. 21:2, 5, 9.]

29 Then Belshazzar commanded, and Daniel was clothed with purple and a chain of gold put about his neck, and a proclamation was made concerning him that he should be the third ruler in the kingdom.

30 During that night Belshazzar the king of the Chaldeans was slain,

31 And Darius the Mede took the kingdom; he was about sixty-two years old.

6 IT PLEASED [King] Darius [successor to Belshazzar] to set over the kingdom 120 satraps who should be [in charge] throughout all the kingdom,

2 And over them three presidents— of whom Daniel was one—that these satraps might give account to them and that the king should have no loss *or* damage.

3 Then this Daniel was distinguished above the presidents and the satraps because an excellent spirit was in him, and the king thought to set him over the whole realm.

4 Then the presidents and satraps sought to find occasion [to bring accusation] against Daniel concerning the kingdom, but they could find no occasion or fault, for he was faithful, nor was there any error or fault found in him.

5 Then said these men, We shall not find any occasion [to bring accusation] against this Daniel except we find it against him concerning the law of his God. [Acts 24:13-21; I Pet. 4:12-16.]

6 Then these presidents and satraps came [tumultuously] together to the king and said to him, King Darius, live forever!

7 All the presidents of the kingdom, the deputies and the satraps, the counselors and the governors, have

consulted *and* agreed that the king should establish a royal statute and make a firm decree that whoever shall ask a petition of any god or man for thirty days, except of you, O king, shall be cast into the den of lions.

8 Now, O king, establish the decree and sign the writing that it may not be changed, according to the law of the Medes and Persians, which cannot be altered.

9 So King Darius signed the writing and the decree.

10 Now when Daniel knew that the writing was signed, he went into his house, and his windows being open in his chamber toward Jerusalem, he got down upon his knees three times a day and prayed and gave thanks before his God, as he had done previously. [Ps. 5:7.]

life point

We know by reading Daniel 6:10 that Daniel certainly believed in the importance of prayer. The king had issued a royal decree saying that for thirty days, anyone asking a petition of any god or man other than the king would be cast into a den of lions.

Daniel continued to pray as he always had. He apparently knew that God's protection could render men's threats totally null and void. If we believe we are doing God's will and then run into opposition, we need to be like Daniel and boldly continue to do as God has instructed us, trusting Him to protect us.

11 Then these men came thronging [by agreement] and found Daniel praying and making supplication before his God.

12 Then they came near and said before the king concerning his prohibitory decree, Have you not signed an edict that any man who shall make

be excellent!

Daniel was a man of excellence, and because of that, the king promoted him to a position of great influence and authority (see Daniel 6:3). Daniel was also a man who refused to compromise. Even if his choices endangered his life, he would not compromise. He believed strongly in keeping his commitments, promises, and vows, and he was willing to endure personal discomfort to do so. The Bible says we should swear to our own hurt and change not. In other words, we should do what we say we are going to do even if it is hard or brings negative consequences.

Ecclesiastes 5:4, 5 says: "When you vow a vow or make a pledge to God, do not put off paying it; for God has no pleasure in fools (those who witlessly mock Him). Pay what you vow. It is better that you should not vow than that you should vow and not pay."

In Daniel chapter 1, we see that Daniel requested to not have to eat the king's rich and dainty food because he felt it would defile him. Obviously, he had made a commitment to not eat that type of food. Because of his convictions, God caused Daniel to find favor with the man in charge, and no harm came to him.

In Daniel chapter 6, the king signed a decree stating that anyone who asked a petition of any god or person besides the king for thirty days would be cast into a den of lions. Daniel refused to stop praying to God and was indeed sent into the lions' den; however, no harm came to him because God miraculously shut the lions' mouths. The king was so impressed with Daniel's decision and the miraculous way God took care of him that he issued a decree that all the people had to fear and tremble before Daniel's God, for He was indeed the living God. After this, Daniel prospered in the reign of King Darius and in the reign of Cyrus.

Our God is an excellent God, and He has called us to be excellent too. To be excellent is a decision we must make, and it means we should always go the extra mile to do things the very best way they can be done. And, we should strive to do what we believe God would do in a situation similar to the one we are in. Make a decision today to be excellent!

a petition to any god or man within thirty days, except of you, O king, shall be cast into the den of lions? The king answered and said, The thing is true, according to the law of the Medes and Persians, which cannot be changed *or* repealed.

13 Then they said before the king, That Daniel, who is one of the exiles from Judah, does not regard *or* pay any attention to you, O king, or to the decree that you have signed, but makes his petition three times a day.

14 Then the king, when he heard these words, was much distressed [over what he had done] and set his mind on Daniel to deliver him; and he labored until the sun went down to rescue him.

15 Then these same men came thronging [by agreement] to the king and said, Know, O king, that it is a law

uncompromising worship

Daniel's enemies were jealous of him and of his high position in the kingdom. Because Daniel was a righteous man, they knew there was no way to bring a true accusation against him because of any wrong behavior. Therefore, they sought to find a way to stop his worship and devotion to God through fear of harm.

Daniel's enemies knew that his habit was to go into his room three times a day, open the windows toward Jerusalem, and kneel down to pray and worship God (see Daniel 6:10). With this in mind, they persuaded King Darius to issue a decree that for a thirty-day period, no one would be allowed to petition any god or man other than the king. Anyone caught disobeying this order would be thrown into a den of lions.

Daniel continued to worship after the decree had been issued. I love the part of this story that says he prayed with his windows open as he had done previously. In other words, he was not trying to keep his worship a secret. He had reverential fear and awe for God that far exceeded any fear of man.

Because Daniel refused to compromise his worship, his enemies brought him before the king for not honoring the decree (see Daniel 6:13). The king had no choice but to have him thrown into the den of lions. King Darius spent a sleepless night and in the morning cried out in front of the den, "O Daniel, servant of the living God, is your God, Whom you serve continually, able to deliver you from the lions?" (Daniel 6:20). In triumph Daniel came out of that lions' den totally unharmed and refreshed in his faith because God had shut the mouths of the lions. Afterward, Daniel's enemies were thrown into the same den and were all destroyed by the hungry lions.

If you and I will trust God and worship Him when our enemies conspire to bring harm to us, then, like Daniel, we will come out unharmed.

of the Medes and Persians that no decree or statute which the king establishes may be changed *or* repealed.

16 Then the king commanded, and Daniel was brought and cast into the den of lions. The king said to Daniel, May your God, Whom you are serving continually, deliver you! [Ps. 34:7, 19; 37:39, 40; 50:15.]

17 And a stone was brought and laid upon the mouth of the den, and the king sealed it with his own signet and with the signet of his lords, that there might be no change of purpose concerning Daniel.

speak the Word

God, I pray that as You did for Daniel, You will deliver me as I continually serve you.
ADAPTED FROM DANIEL 6:16

18 Then the king went to his palace and passed the night fasting, neither were instruments of music or dancing girls brought before him; and his sleep fled from him.
19 Then the king arose very early in the morning and went in haste to the den of lions.
20 And when he came to the den and to Daniel, he cried out in a voice of anguish. The king said to Daniel, O Daniel, servant of the living God, is your God, Whom you serve continually, able to deliver you from the lions?
21 Then Daniel said to the king, O king, live forever!
22 My God has sent His angel and has shut the lions' mouths so that they have not hurt me, because I was found innocent *and* blameless before Him; and also before you, O king, [as you very well know] I have done no harm *or* wrong. [II Tim. 4:17.]
23 Then the king was exceedingly glad and commanded that Daniel should be taken up out of the den. So Daniel was taken up out of the den, and no hurt of any kind was found on him because he believed in (relied on, adhered to, and trusted in) his God.
24 And the king commanded, and those men who had accused Daniel were brought and cast into the den of lions, they, their children, and their wives; and before they ever reached the bottom of the den, the lions had overpowered them and had broken their bones in pieces.
25 Then King Darius wrote to all peoples, nations, and languages [in his realm] that dwelt in all the

earth: May peace be multiplied to you!
26 I make a decree that in all my royal dominion men must tremble and fear before the God of Daniel, for He is the living God, enduring *and* steadfast forever, and His kingdom shall not be destroyed and His dominion shall be even to the end [of the world].
27 He is a Savior and Deliverer, and He works signs and wonders in the heavens and on the earth—He Who has delivered Daniel from the power of the lions.
28 So this [man] Daniel prospered in the reign of Darius and in the reign of Cyrus the Persian.

life point

Daniel's life was characterized by pressure to conform to what others wanted him to do and be. He refused to yield to pressure. After a period of trial and tribulation, God exalted him, and he was put in charge of the entire kingdom.

Have the courage to be different. It will change your life, and God will exalt you in the process.

7 IN THE first year of Belshazzar king of Babylon [e]Daniel had a dream and visions in his head as he was lying upon his bed. Then he wrote down the dream and told the gist of the matter.
2 Daniel said, I saw in my vision by night, and behold, the four winds of the heavens [political and social agitations] were stirring up the great sea [the nations of the world].

e This chapter, in its subject matter as well as its position in the central part of the book, is to the book of Daniel what the eighth chapter of Romans is to that epistle. Next to the fifty-third chapter of Isaiah (and perhaps the ninth chapter also), we have here the most precious and prominent portion of the sure word of prophecy concerning the coming of the Messiah. The chapter is worthy of the most careful prayer and study. It is referred to directly or indirectly by Christ and His apostles perhaps more than other portions of the Old Testament of similar extent. It appears to have been regarded by the Old Testament saints in the centuries preceding the Messiah's first advent as preeminently the "word of prophecy" (*Homiletical Commentary*).

3 And four great beasts came up out of the sea in succession, and different from one another.

4 The first [the Babylonian empire under Nebuchadnezzar] was like a lion and had eagle's wings. I looked till the wings of it were plucked, and it was lifted up from the earth and made to stand upon two feet as a man, and a man's heart was given to it. [Dan. 2:37, 38.]

5 And behold another beast, a second one [the Medo-Persian empire], was like a bear, and it raised up itself on one side [or one dominion] and three ribs were in its mouth between its teeth; and it was told, Arise, devour much flesh.

6 After this I looked, and behold, another [the Grecian empire of Alexander the Great], like a leopard which had four wings of a bird on its back. The beast had also four heads [Alexander's generals, his successors], and dominion was given to it. [Dan. 2:39; 8:20-22.]

7 After this I saw in the night visions, and behold, a fourth beast [the Roman empire] — terrible, powerful *and* dreadful, and exceedingly strong. And it had great iron teeth; it devoured and crushed and trampled what was left with its feet. And it was different from all the beasts that came before it, and it had ten horns [symbolizing ten kings]. [Dan. 2:40-43; 7:23.]

8 I considered the horns, and behold, there came up among them another horn, a little one, before which three of the first horns were plucked up by the roots; and behold, in this horn were eyes like the eyes of a man and a mouth speaking great things.

9 I kept looking until thrones were placed [for the assessors with the Judge], and the Ancient of Days [God, the eternal Father] took His seat, Whose garment was white as snow and the hair of His head like pure wool. His throne was like the fiery flame; its wheels were burning fire. [I Kings 22:19; Ps. 90:2; Ezek. 1:26-28; Dan. 7:13, 22; Matt. 19:28; Rev. 20:4.]

10 A stream of fire came forth from before Him; a thousand thousands ministered to Him and ten thousand times ten thousand rose up *and* stood before Him; the Judge was seated [the court was in session] and the books were opened.

11 I looked then because of the sound of the great words which the horn was speaking. I watched until the beast was slain and its body destroyed and given over to be burned with fire.

12 And as for the rest of the beasts, their power of dominion was taken away; yet their lives were prolonged [for the duration of their lives was fixed] for a season and a time.

13 I saw in the night visions, and behold, ᶠon the clouds of the heavens came One like a Son of man, and He came to the Ancient of Days and was presented before Him.

14 And there was given Him [the Messiah] dominion and glory and kingdom, that all peoples, nations, and languages should serve Him. His dominion is an everlasting dominion which shall not pass away, and His kingdom is one which shall not be destroyed. [Rev. 5:1-10.]

15 As for me, Daniel, my spirit was grieved *and* anxious within me, and

---

f Notice that the four beasts of this seventh chapter of Daniel symbolize the same world kingdoms that were pictured by the images in Dan. 2, and the ten horns of the last beast correspond to the ten toes of the legs of iron (Dan. 2:41-42). Much of both prophecies has been fulfilled, and at this writing "the blessed hope" (Tit. 2:13) of the ages is also showing every evidence of nearing realization. Both visions portray the end of Gentile world power. View the events of the present in the light of these disclosures, and they fall into focus and make sense. The individual child of God is challenged as never before in the world's history to let go of the trivial and the transient, and to yield himself unreservedly to Him Who is coming back to fulfill the longings of every true believer—forever and ever!

the visions of my head alarmed *and* agitated me.

16 I came near to one of those who stood there and asked him the truth of all this. So he told me and made known to me the interpretation of the things.

17 These four great beasts are four kings who shall arise out of the earth.

18 But the saints of the Most High [God] shall receive the kingdom and possess the kingdom forever, even forever and ever. [Rom. 8:17; I Pet. 2:9; Rev. 3:21.]

19 Then I wished to know the truth about the fourth beast—which was different from all the others, exceedingly terrible *and* shocking, whose teeth were of iron and its nails of bronze, which devoured, broke *and* crushed, and trampled what was left with its feet—

20 And about the ten horns [representing kings] that were on its head, and the other horn which came up later and before which three of [the horns] fell, the horn which had eyes and a mouth that spoke great things and which looked greater than the others.

21 As I looked, this horn made war with the saints and prevailed over them [Rev. 13:7-9.]

22 Until the Ancient of Days came, and judgment was given to the saints of the Most High [God], and the time came when the saints possessed the kingdom.

23 Thus [the angel] said, The fourth beast shall be a fourth kingdom on earth, which shall be different from all other kingdoms and shall devour the whole earth, tread it down, and break it in pieces *and* crush it.

24 And as for the ten horns, out of this kingdom ten kings shall arise; and another shall arise after them, and he shall be different from the former ones, and he shall subdue *and* put down three kings.

25 And he shall speak words against

life point

Daniel 7:21 speaks of the king who made "war with the saints." Daniel 7:25 tells us that in the end times Satan will wear out the saints! But it also tells us in verse 27 what happens after that: "And the kingdom and the dominion and the greatness of the kingdom under the whole heavens shall be given to the people of the saints of the Most High."

Even though Satan is releasing an attack of weariness against the saints, Jesus came to give us victory over the attacks of Satan and "to undo (destroy, loosen, and dissolve) the works the devil [has done]" (I John 3:8).

Let this truth sink in: *Jesus came to destroy the works of the devil.* Even though Satan will try to attack those of us who have received Jesus, "He Who lives in you is greater (mightier) than he who is in the world" (I John 4:4). Always remember that!

the Most High [God] and shall wear out the saints of the Most High and think to change the time [of sacred feasts and holy days] and the law; and the saints shall be given into his hand for a time, two times, and half a time [three and one-half years]. [Rev. 13:1-6.]

26 But the judgment shall be set [by the court of the Most High], and they shall take away his dominion to consume it [gradually] and to destroy it [suddenly] in the end.

27 And the kingdom and the dominion and the greatness of the kingdom under the whole heavens shall be given to the people of the saints of the Most High; His kingdom is an everlasting kingdom, and all the dominions shall serve and obey Him.

how to resist satan

Satan works diligently to cause trouble in virtually every area of our lives. He does not attack every area at one time, but eventually he gets to everything. He will bring inconvenience of every kind. Problems never come when we are ready to deal with them.

Daniel 7:25 says that Satan seeks to wear out the saints of the Most High God. How does this "wearing out" take place? Often Satan's work is barely noticeable because he tries to wear us down gradually—a little here and a little there. Satan knows it takes more than one attack to wear us out, so he relentlessly comes again and again. One way Satan seeks to wear us out is by stealing our time, forcing us to deal with trouble that he starts. He would like us to spend our lives trying to put out the little fires he starts.

What is the answer? James 4:7 says we are to submit ourselves to God, resist the devil, and he will flee. We see that we have to *resist* the devil. But when should we resist him? How long should we wait? How much should we put up with before coming against him? While the Bible teaches Christians to be patient with one another, we are not to be patient with the devil. First Peter 5:9 shares a wonderful and most important principle: "Withstand him; be firm in faith [against his onset—rooted, established, strong, immovable, and determined]." We are to resist the devil *at his onset*.

When Satan attacks, we should immediately begin to praise God; in this way, we resist Satan. When he speaks lies, we should speak truth. The instant we sense an attack, we should draw near to God and pray. The Bible tells us to be alert for when we can practice prayer. Several times the Word of God instructs us to "watch and pray." This means to watch for things going wrong in our own lives or the lives of others and to pray immediately. As I like to say: "Do not delay, *pray right away!*"

Another way to resist Satan is to apply the blood of Jesus by faith to the situation. Just as the Israelites were delivered from death by putting the blood of the lamb on the lintels and doorframes of their homes during Passover (see Exodus 12:1–13), so we can apply the blood of our Passover Lamb, Jesus, by faith and be protected.

Remind Satan of the cross on which Jesus totally defeated him; remind him that he is already a defeated foe and that you will not be deceived or deluded in any way. Let Satan know that you recognize it is he who is coming against you and that you will not blame people, God, or life for what he is doing.

Satan wants us weak and worn out; that way we have no power to resist him. He knows that if he gains a foothold, he can get a stronghold. As I said before, *resist the devil at his onset!* Be aggressive; do not wait to see what will happen. If you wait, you will not like it. Stir yourself up in the Holy Spirit, fan the embers of your inner fire, and do not let it go out during trouble. Remember that Jesus, the Victor, lives inside you—you have the victory!

28 Here is the end of the matter. As for me, Daniel, my [waking] thoughts troubled and alarmed me much and my cheerfulness of countenance was changed in me; but I kept the matter [of the interpreting angel's information] in my heart *and* mind.

8 IN THE third year of the reign of King Belshazzar a vision appeared to me, Daniel, after the one that appeared to me at the first.
2 And I saw in the vision and it seemed that I was at Shushan the palace *or* fortress [in Susa, the capital of Persia], which is in the province of Elam, and I saw in the vision and I was by the river of Ulai.
3 And I lifted up my eyes and saw, and behold, there stood before the river a [single] ram which had two horns [representing two kings of Medo-Persia: Darius the Mede, then Cyrus]; and the two horns were high, but one [Persia] was higher than the other, and the higher one came up last.
4 I looked *and* saw the ram [Medo-Persia] pushing *and* charging westward and northward and southward; no beast could stand before him, neither could anyone rescue from his power, but he did according to his [own] will *and* pleasure and magnified himself. [Dan. 8:20.]
5 As I was considering, behold, a he-goat [the king of Greece] came from the west across the face of the whole earth without touching the ground, and the goat had a conspicuous *and* remarkable horn between his eyes [symbolizing Alexander the Great]. [Dan. 8:21.]
6 And he came to the ram that had

the two horns which I had seen standing on the bank of the river and ran at him in the heat of his power.
7 [In my vision] I saw him come close to the ram [Medo-Persia], and he was moved with anger against him and he [Alexander the Great] struck the ram and broke his two horns; and there was no power in the ram to stand before him, but the goat threw him to the ground and trampled on him. And there was no one who could rescue the ram from his power.
8 And the he-goat [Alexander the Great] magnified himself exceedingly, and when he was [young and] strong, the ᵍgreat horn [he] was [suddenly] broken; and instead of [him] there came up four notable horns [to whom the kingdom was divided, one] toward [each of] the four winds of the heavens.
9 Out of littleness *and* small beginnings one of them came forth [Antiochus Epiphanes], a ʰhorn whose [impious presumption and pride] grew exceedingly great toward the south and toward the east and toward the ornament [the precious, blessed land of Israel]. [Dan. 8:23.]
10 And [in my vision this horn] grew great, even against the host of heaven [God's true people, the saints], and some of the host and of the stars [priests] it cast down to the ground and trampled on them,
11 Yes, [this horn] magnified itself, even [matching itself] against the Prince of the host [of heaven]; and from Him the continual [burnt offering] was taken away and the place of [God's] sanctuary was cast down *and* profaned.
12 And the host [the chosen people]

g Alexander the Great suddenly died at the height of his power, and his empire was divided into four parts—east, west, north, and south—ruled over by his four generals. h This horn of Dan. 8:9-12 is not to be confused with the "little horn" of Dan. 7:8. This one is a prophetic forecast of Antiochus Epiphanes, who came out of Syria, one of the four dynasties into which Alexander's empire was divided, and became a great conqueror. Hating God, he profaned the temple and persecuted the Jews terribly. However, he serves as a type of the "little horn" of Dan. 7:8, the even more ruthless beast of the last days (Rev. 13:4-9).

was given [to the wicked horn] together with the continual burnt offering because of the transgression [of God's people—their abounding irreverence, ungodliness, and lack of piety]. And righteousness *and* truth were cast down to the ground, and it [the wicked horn] accomplished this [by divine permission] and prospered.

13 Then I heard a holy one speaking, and another holy one said to the one that spoke, For how long is the vision concerning the continual offering, the transgression that makes desolate, and the giving over of both the sanctuary and the host [of the people] to be trampled underfoot? [Luke 21:24.]

14 And he said to him *and* to me, For 2,300 evenings and mornings; then the sanctuary shall be cleansed *and* restored.

15 When I, even I, Daniel, had seen the vision, I sought to understand it; then behold, there stood before me one [Gabriel] with the appearance of a man.

16 And I heard a man's voice between the banks of the [river] Ulai which called and said, Gabriel, make this man [Daniel] understand the vision. [Dan. 9:21; Luke 1:19, 26.]

17 So he came near where I stood, and when he came, I was frightened and fell on my face. But he said to me, Understand, O son of man, for the [fulfillment of the] vision belongs to [events that shall occur in] the time of the end.

18 Now as he [Gabriel] was speaking with me, I fell stunned *and* in deep unconsciousness with my face to the ground; but he touched me and set me upright [where I had stood].

19 And he said, Behold, I will make you know what will be in the latter time of the indignation [of God upon the ungodly], for it has to do with the time of the end.

20 The ram you saw having two horns, they are the kings of Media and Persia.

21 And the shaggy *and* rough he-goat is the king of Greece, and the great horn between his eyes is the first king [who consolidated the whole realm, Alexander the Great].

22 And as for the horn which was shattered, in whose place four others arose, four kingdoms shall arise out of his nation but not having his [Alexander's] power.

23 And at the latter end of their kingdom, when the transgressors [the apostate Jews] have reached the fullness [of their wickedness, taxing the limits of God's mercy], a king of fierce countenance and understanding dark trickery *and* craftiness shall stand up.

24 And his power shall be mighty, but not by his own power; and he shall corrupt *and* destroy astonishingly and shall prosper and do his own pleasure, and he shall corrupt *and* destroy the mighty men and the holy people (the people of the saints). [Dan. 8:9-12; II Thess. 2:3-10; Rev. 13:4-10.]

25 And through his policy he shall cause trickery to prosper in his hand; he shall magnify himself in his heart *and* mind, and in their security he will corrupt *and* destroy many. He shall also stand up against the Prince of princes, but he shall be broken and that by no [human] hand. [Rev. 19:19, 20.]

26 The vision of the evenings and the mornings which has been told you is true. But seal up the vision, for it has to do with *and* belongs to the [now] distant future.

27 And I, Daniel, fainted and was sick [for several] days. Afterward I rose up and did the king's business; and I wondered at the vision, but there was no one who understood it *or* could make it understood.

9 IN THE first year of Darius son of Ahasuerus, of the offspring of the Medes, who was made king over the realm of the Chaldeans—

2 In the first year of his reign, I,

Daniel, understood from the books the number of years which, according to the word of the Lord to Jeremiah the prophet, must pass by before the desolations [which had been] pronounced on Jerusalem should end; and it was seventy years. [Jer. 25:11, 12; 29:10.]

3 And I set my face to the Lord God to seek Him by prayer and supplications, with fasting and sackcloth and ashes;

4 And I prayed to the Lord my God and made confession and said, O Lord, the great and dreadful God, Who keeps covenant, mercy, *and* loving-kindness with those who love Him and keep His commandments,

5 We have sinned and dealt perversely and done wickedly and have rebelled, turning aside from Your commandments and ordinances.

6 Neither have we listened to *and* heeded Your servants the prophets, who spoke in Your name to our kings, our princes and our fathers, and to all the people of the land.

7 O Lord, righteousness belongs to You, but to us confusion *and* shame of face, as at this day—to the men of Judah, to the inhabitants of Jerusalem, and to all Israel, to those who are near and those who are far off, through all the countries to which You have driven them because of the [treacherous] trespass which they have committed against You.

8 O Lord, to us belong confusion *and* shame of face—to our kings, to our princes, and to our fathers—

because we have sinned against You.

9 To the Lord our God belong mercy *and* loving-kindness and forgiveness, for we have rebelled against Him;

10 And we have not obeyed the voice of the Lord our God by walking in His laws which He set before us through His servants the prophets.

11 Yes, all Israel has transgressed Your law, even turning aside that they might not obey Your voice. Therefore the curse has been poured out on us and the oath that is written in the Law of Moses the servant of God, because we have sinned against Him. [Lev. 26:14-45; Deut. 28:15-68.]

12 And He has carried out intact His [threatening] words which He threatened against us and against our judges [the kings, princes, and rulers generally] who ruled us, and He has brought upon us a great evil; for under the whole heavens there has not been done before [anything so dreadful] as [He has caused to be] done against Jerusalem.

13 Just as it is written in the Law of Moses as to all this evil [that would surely come upon transgressors], so it has come upon us. Yet we have not earnestly begged for forgiveness *and* entreated the favor of the Lord our God, that we might turn from our iniquities and have understanding *and* become wise in Your truth. [Deut. 4:29; 28:15ff.]

14 Therefore the Lord has kept ready the calamity (evil) and has brought it upon us, for the Lord our God is [uncompromisingly] righteous *and*

speak the Word

God, to You belong mercy and loving-kindness and forgiveness!
ADAPTED FROM DANIEL 9:9

God, I declare that You are uncompromisingly righteous and rigidly just in all Your works and that You always keep Your word.
ADAPTED FROM DANIEL 9:14

rigidly just in all His works which He does [keeping His word]; and we have not obeyed His voice.

15 And now, O Lord our God, Who brought Your people forth out of the land of Egypt with a mighty hand and secured Yourself renown *and* a name as at this day, we have sinned, we have done wickedly!

16 O Lord, according to all Your rightness *and* justice, I beseech You, let Your anger and Your wrath be turned away from Your city Jerusalem, Your holy mountain. Because of our sins and the iniquities of our fathers, Jerusalem and Your people have become a reproach *and* a byword to all who are around about us.

17 Now therefore, O our God, listen to *and* heed the prayer of Your servant ⁱ[Daniel] and his supplications, and for Your own sake cause Your face to shine upon Your sanctuary which is desolate.

18 O my God, incline Your ear and hear; open Your eyes and look at our desolations and the city which is called by Your name; for we do not present our supplications before You for our own righteousness *and* justice, but for Your great mercy *and* lovingkindness.

19 O Lord, hear! O Lord, forgive! O Lord, give heed and act! Do not delay, for Your own sake, O my God, because Your city and Your people are called by Your name.

20 While I was speaking and praying, confessing my sin and the sin of my people Israel, and presenting my supplication before the Lord my God for the holy hill of my God—

21 Yes, while I was speaking in prayer, the man Gabriel, whom I had seen in the former vision, being caused to fly swiftly, came near to me *and* touched me about the time of the evening sacrifice. [Dan. 8:16.]

22 He instructed me *and* made me understand; he talked with me and said, O Daniel, I am now come forth to give you skill *and* wisdom and understanding.

23 At the beginning of your prayers, the word [giving an answer] went forth, and I have come to tell you, for you are greatly beloved. Therefore consider the matter and understand the vision.

24 Seventy weeks [of years, or 490 years] are decreed upon your people and upon your holy city [Jerusalem], to finish *and* put an end to transgression, to seal up *and* make full the measure of sin, to purge away *and* make expiation *and* reconciliation for sin, to bring in everlasting righteousness (permanent moral and spiritual rectitude in every area and relation) to seal up vision and prophecy *and* prophet, and to anoint a Holy of Holies.

25 Know therefore and understand that from the going forth of the commandment to restore and to build Jerusalem until [the coming of] the Anointed One, a Prince, shall be seven weeks [of years] and sixty-two weeks [of years]; it shall be built again with [city] square and moat, but in troublous times.

26 And after the sixty-two weeks [of years] shall the Anointed One be cut off *or* killed and shall have nothing [and no one] belonging to [and defending] Him. And the people of the [other] prince who will come will destroy the city and the sanctuary. Its end shall come with a flood; and even to the end there shall be war, and desolations are decreed. [Isa. 53:7-9; Nah. 1:8; Matt. 24:6-14.]

27 And he shall enter into a strong *and* firm covenant with the many for one week [seven years]. And in the midst of the week he shall cause the sacrifice

---

ⁱ Compare this verse with Ezek. 14:12-20.

and offering to cease [for the remaining three and one-half years]; and upon the wing *or* pinnacle of abominations [shall come] one who makes desolate, until the full determined end is poured out on the desolator.

10 IN THE third year of Cyrus king of Persia a word was revealed to Daniel, who was called Belteshazzar. And the word was true and it referred to great tribulation (conflict and wretchedness). And he understood the word and had understanding of the vision. [Dan. 8:26; Rev. 19:9.]

2 In those days I, Daniel, was mourning for three whole weeks.

3 I ate no pleasant *or* desirable food, nor did any meat or wine come into my mouth; and I did not anoint myself at all for the full three weeks.

4 On the twenty-fourth day of the first month, as I was on the bank of the great river Hiddekel [which is the Tigris],

5 I lifted up my eyes and looked, and behold, a man clothed in linen, whose loins were girded with pure gold of Uphaz.

6 His body also was [a golden luster] like beryl, his face had the appearance of lightning, his eyes were like flaming torches, his arms and his feet like glowing burnished bronze, and the sound of his words was like the noise of a multitude [of people or the roaring of the sea]. [Rev. 1:12-16; 19:6.]

7 And I, Daniel, alone saw the vision [of this heavenly being], for the men who were with me did not see the vision, but a great trembling fell upon them so that they fled to hide themselves.

8 So I was left alone and saw this great vision, and no strength was left in me, for my fresh appearance was turned to pallor; I grew weak *and* faint [with fright].

9 Then I heard the sound of his words; and when I heard the sound of his words, I fell on my face in a deep sleep, with my face [sunk] to the ground.

10 And behold, a hand touched me, which set me [unsteadily] upon my knees and upon the palms of my hands.

11 And [the angel] said to me, O Daniel, you greatly beloved man, understand the words that I speak to you and stand upright, for to you I am now sent. And while he was saying this word to me, I stood up trembling.

12 Then he said to me, Fear not, Daniel, for from the first day that you set your mind *and* heart to understand and to humble yourself before your God, your words were heard, and I have come as a consequence of [and in response to] your words.

13 But the prince of the kingdom of Persia withstood me for twenty-one days. Then Michael, one of the chief [of the celestial] princes, came to help me, for I remained there with the kings of Persia.

14 Now I have come to make you understand what is to befall your people in the latter days, for the vision is for [many] days yet to come.

15 When he had spoken to me according to these words, I turned my face toward the ground and was dumb.

16 And behold, one in the likeness of the sons of men touched my lips. Then I opened my mouth and spoke. I said to him who stood before me, O my lord, by reason of the vision sorrows *and* pains have come upon me, and I retain no strength.

17 For how can my lord's servant [who is so feeble] talk with this my lord? For now no strength remains in me, nor is there any breath left in me.

18 Then there touched me again one whose appearance was like that of a man, and he strengthened me.

19 And he said, O man greatly beloved, fear not! Peace be to you! Be

strong, yes, be strong. And when he had spoken to me, I was strengthened and said, Let my lord speak, for you have strengthened me.

20 Then he said, Do you know why I have come to you? And now I will return to fight with the [hostile] prince of Persia; and when I have gone, behold, the [hostile] prince of Greece will come.

21 But I will tell you what is inscribed in the writing of truth or the Book of Truth. There is no one who holds with me and strengthens himself against these [hostile spirit forces] except Michael, your prince [national guardian angel].

11 ALSO I [the angel], in the first year of Darius the Mede, even I, stood up to confirm and to strengthen him [Michael, the angelic prince].

2 And now I will show you the truth. Behold, there shall arise three more kings in Persia, and a fourth shall be far richer than they all. And when he has become strong through his riches he shall stir up and stake all against the realm of Greece.

3 Then a ʲmighty [warlike, threatening] king shall arise who shall rule with great dominion and do according to his [own] will.

4 And as soon as he has fully arisen, his [Alexander the Great's] kingdom shall be broken [by his death] and divided toward the four winds [the east, west, north, and south] of the heavens, but not to his posterity, nor according to the [Grecian] dominion which he ruled, for his kingdom shall

be torn out and uprooted and go to others [to his four generals] to the exclusion of these.

5 Then the king of the South (Egypt) shall be strong, but one of his princes shall be stronger than he is and have dominion; his dominion shall be a great dominion.

6 At the end of some years they [the king of the North, Syria, and the king of the South, Egypt] shall make an alliance; the daughter of the king of the South shall come to the king of the North to make [a just and peaceful marriage] agreement; but she shall not retain the power of her might, neither shall he and his might endure. She shall be handed over with her attendants, her child, and him who strengthened her in those times.

7 But out of a branch of the [same ancestral] roots as hers shall one [her brother] stand up in his place or office, who shall come against the [Syrian] army and shall enter into the fortress of the king of the North and shall deal against them and shall prevail.

8 And also he shall carry off to Egypt their [Syria's] gods with their molten images and with their precious vessels of silver and of gold, and he shall refrain for some years from [waging war against] the king of the North.

9 And he [the king of Syria] shall come into the kingdom of the king of the South but shall return to his own land.

10 But his sons shall be stirred up and shall prepare for war and shall assemble a multitude of great forces,

---

j There are many good reasons for identifying this mighty king as Alexander the Great, as well as identifying the other characters according to their relationship to the events of those times. "But the mere similarity which exists between certain things predicted here and what actually occurred in the times of the Ptolemies of Egypt is not sufficient to limit the fulfillment of the prophecy to those times—certainly [we find here what] was characteristic of Alexander, but there is nothing in the context which makes it necessary to limit the passage to him. Some autocrat may arise 'in the latter days' to whom it will apply with greater force than it did to Alexander." (Charles Ellicott, *A Bible Commentary*).

which shall come on and overflow and pass through and again shall make war even to the fortress [of the king of the South].

11 And the king of the South (Egypt) shall be moved with anger and shall come forth and fight with the king of the North (Syria); and he [the Syrian king] shall set forth a great multitude, but the multitude shall be given into his [the Egyptian king's] hand.

12 When the multitude is taken *and* carried away, the heart *and* mind [of the Egyptian king] shall be exalted, and he shall cast down tens of thousands, but he shall not prevail.

13 For the king of the North shall raise a multitude greater than [he had] before, and after some years shall certainly return, coming with a great army and much substance *and* equipment.

14 In those times many shall rise up against the king of the South (Egypt); also the men of violence among your own people shall lift themselves up in order to fulfill the visions [of Dan. 8 and 9], but they shall fail *and* fall.

15 Then the king of the North shall come and cast up siege works and take a well-fortified city, and the forces of the South shall not stand, or even his chosen troops, for there shall be no strength to stand [against the Syrian king].

16 But he [Antiochus the Great] who comes against him [from Syria] shall do according to his own will, and none shall stand before him; he shall stand in the glorious land [of Israel], and in his hand shall be destruction *and* all the land shall be in his power.

17 He [Antiochus the Great] shall set his face to come with the strength of his whole kingdom, and with him upright conditions *and* terms of peace, and he shall perform them [by making an agreement with the king of the South]. He shall give him [his] daughter to corrupt *and* destroy it [his league with Egypt] *and* the kingdom, but it shall not succeed or be to his advantage.

18 After this he shall turn his attention to the islands *and* coastlands and shall take over many of them. But a prince *or* commander shall teach him [Antiochus the Great] to put an end to the insults offered by him; in fact he shall turn his insolence *and* reproaches back upon him.

19 Then he shall turn his face back toward the fortresses of his own land [of Syria], but he shall stumble and fall and not be found.

20 Then shall [k]stand up in his place *or* office one who shall send an exactor of tribute to pass through the glory of the kingdom, but within a few days he shall be destroyed, [yet] neither in anger nor in battle.

21 And in his place *or* office [in Syria] shall arise a [l]contemptuous *and* contemptible person, to whom royal majesty *and* honor of the kingdom have not been given. But he shall come in without warning in time of security and shall obtain the kingdom by flatteries, intrigues, *and* cunning hypocritical conduct. [Dan. 8:9-12, 23-25.]

22 Before him the overwhelming forces of invading armies shall be broken *and* utterly swept away; yes, and a prince of the covenant [with those who

---

k The reference here is undoubtedly to Seleucus Philopator [a king of Syria], the eldest son of Antiochus the Great and his immediate successor (Albert Barnes, *Notes on the Old Testament*). l This contemptible conqueror is generally identified as Antiochus Epiphanes, the younger son of Antiochus the Great, king of Syria, and is a type of the final antichrist referred to in Dan. 11:36; II Thess. 2:3-12; I John 4:3; II John 7; and Rev. 13:5-8. "He [Antiochus Epiphanes] stirred up the Jews by robbing the temple and setting up a statue of Jupiter in the Holy of Holies. He also pulled down the walls of Jerusalem, commanded the sacrifice of [forbidden] swine, forbade circumcision, and destroyed all the sacred books that could be found" (John D. Davis, *A Dictionary of the Bible*).

were at peace with him] also [shall be broken and swept away].

23 And from the time that an alliance is made with him he shall work deceitfully, and he shall come up unexpectedly and shall become strong with a small people.

24 Without warning *and* stealthily he shall come into the most productive places of a province *or* among the richest men of a province [of Egypt], and he shall do that which his fathers have not done nor his fathers' fathers; he shall distribute among them plunder, spoil, and goods. He shall devise plans against strongholds—but only for a time [the period decreed by God].

25 And he shall stir up his power and his courage against the king of the South [Egypt] with a great army; and the king of the South shall wage war with an exceedingly great and mighty army, but he shall not stand, for schemes shall be devised against [the king of the South].

26 Yes, those who eat of his rich *and* dainty food shall break *and* destroy him, and his army shall drift *or* turn away to flee, and many shall fall down slain.

27 And as for both of these kings, their hearts *and* minds shall be set on doing mischief; they shall speak lies over the same table, but it will not succeed, for the end is yet to be at the time appointed.

28 Then shall [the vile conqueror from the North] return into his land with much booty; and his heart *and* purpose shall be set against [God's] holy covenant [with His people], and he shall accomplish [his malicious intention] and return to his own land [Syria].

29 At the time appointed [God's own time] he shall return and come into the South, but it shall not be successful as were the former invasions [of Egypt].

30 For the ships of Kittim [or Cyprus, in Roman hands] shall come against him; therefore he shall be grieved *and* discouraged and turn back [to Palestine] and carry out his rage *and* indignation against the holy covenant *and* God's people, and he shall do his own pleasure; he shall even turn back and make common cause with those [Jews] who abandon the holy covenant [with God].

31 And armed forces of his shall appear [in the holy land] and they shall pollute the sanctuary, the [spiritual] stronghold, and shall take away the continual [daily burnt offering]; and they shall set up [in the sanctuary] the abomination that astonishes *and* makes desolate [probably an altar to a pagan god].

32 And such as violate the covenant he shall pervert *and* seduce with flatteries, but the people who know their God shall prove themselves strong *and* shall stand firm and do exploits [for God].

33 And they who are wise *and* understanding among the people shall instruct many *and* make them understand, though some [of them and their followers] shall fall by the sword and flame, by captivity and plunder, for many days.

34 Now when they fall, they shall receive a little help. Many shall join themselves to them with flatteries *and* hypocrisies.

35 And some of those who are wise, prudent, *and* understanding shall be weakened *and* fall, [thus, then, the

speak the Word

insincere among the people will lose courage and become deserters. It will be a test] to refine, to purify, and to make those among [God's people] white, even to the time of the end, because it is yet for the time [God] appointed.

36 And the ᵐking shall do according to his will; he shall exalt himself and magnify himself above every god and shall speak astonishing things against the God of gods and shall prosper till the indignation be accomplished, for that which is determined [by God] shall be done.

37 He shall not regard the gods of his fathers or Him [to Whom] women desire [to give birth—the Messiah] or any other god, for he shall magnify himself above all.

38 But in their place he shall honor the god of fortresses; a god whom his fathers knew not shall he honor with gold and silver, with precious stones, and with pleasant *and* expensive things.

39 And he shall deal with the strongest fortresses by the help of a foreign god. Those who acknowledge him he shall magnify with glory *and* honor, and he shall cause them to rule over many and shall divide the land for a price.

40 And at the time of the end the king of the South shall push at *and* attack him, and the king of the North shall come against him like a whirlwind, with chariots and horsemen and with many ships; and he shall enter into the countries and shall overflow and pass through.

41 He shall enter into the Glorious Land [Palestine] and many shall be overthrown, but these shall be delivered out of his hand: Edom, Moab, and the main [core] of the people of Ammon.

42 He shall stretch out his hand also against the [other] countries, but the land of Egypt shall not be among the escaped ones.

43 But he shall have power over the treasures of gold and of silver and over all the precious things of Egypt, and the Libyans and the Ethiopians shall accompany him [compelled to follow his steps].

44 But rumors from the east and from the north shall alarm *and* hasten him. And he shall go forth with great fury to destroy and utterly to sweep away many.

45 And he shall pitch his palatial tents between the seas and the glorious holy Mount [Zion]; yet he shall come to his end with none to help him. [II Thess. 2:4; Rev. 13:5-8.]

12 AND AT that time [of the end] Michael shall arise, the great [angelic] prince who defends *and* has charge of your [Daniel's] people. And there shall be a time of trouble, straitness, *and* distress such as never was since there was a nation till that time. But at that time your people shall be delivered, everyone whose name shall be found written in the Book [of God's plan for His own].

2 And many of those who sleep in the dust of the earth shall awake: some to everlasting life and some to shame and everlasting contempt *and* abhorrence. [John 5:29.]

3 And the teachers *and* those who are wise shall shine like the brightness of the firmament, and those who turn many to righteousness (to uprightness and right standing with God) [shall give forth light] like the stars forever and ever. [Matt. 13:43.]

4 But you, O Daniel, shut up the words and seal the Book until the time

---

m The antichrist is in view from this point in the prophecy to the end of the chapter. The details listed here do not fit what is known of Antiochus Epiphanes. See II Thess. 2:4; Rev. 13:5-8.

of the end. [Then] many shall run to and fro *and* search anxiously [through the Book], and knowledge [of God's purposes as revealed by His prophets] shall be increased *and* become great. [Amos 8:12.]

5 Then I, Daniel, looked, and behold, there stood two others, the one on the brink of the river on this side and the other on the brink of the river on that side.

6 And one said to the man clothed in linen, who was above the waters of the river, How long shall it be to the end of these wonders? [Dan. 10:5.]

7 And I heard the man clothed in linen, who was above the waters of the river, when he held up his right and his left hand toward the heavens and swore by Him Who lives forever that it shall be for a time, times, and a half a time [or three and one-half years]; and when they have made an end of shattering *and* crushing the power of the holy people, all these things shall be finished.

8 And I heard, but I did not understand. Then I said, O my lord, what shall be the issue *and* final end of these things?

9 And he [the angel] said, Go your way, Daniel, for the words are shut up and sealed till the time of the end.

10 Many shall purify themselves and make themselves white and be tried, smelted, *and* refined, but the wicked shall do wickedly. And none of the wicked shall understand, but the teachers *and* those who are wise shall understand. [Dan. 11:33-35.]

11 And from the time that the continual burnt offering is taken away and the abomination that makes desolate is set up, there shall be 1,290 days. [Dan. 11:31.]

12 Blessed, happy, fortunate, spiritually prosperous, *and* to be envied is he who waits expectantly *and* earnestly [who endures without wavering beyond the period of tribulation] and comes to the 1,335 days!

13 But you [Daniel, who was now over ninety years of age], go your way until the end; for you shall rest and shall stand [fast] in your allotted place at the end of the days. [Heb. 11:32-40.]

Hosea

Author:
Hosea

Date:
About 750 BC

Everyday Life Principles:
God loves us unconditionally.

God is faithful, even when we are faithless.

God's love and mercy never stop reaching out to us. We can always have a new beginning in Him, no matter what we have done.

Sometimes, people who are prophets of God must live the messages they preach. That was certainly the case with Hosea. God had called Hosea, whose name means "salvation" or "deliverance," to proclaim His love and faithfulness to the people of Israel, who had turned their backs on Him, forgotten His goodness, and forsaken Him as a man forsakes his wife for a prostitute. In fact, God said through Hosea that Israel had "played the harlot" (Hosea 2:5).

In order to understand and demonstrate God's love for backsliding Israel, God required Hosea to marry a prostitute, named Gomer, who continually turned her back on him and lived as a harlot. Hosea, in response, repeatedly rescued Gomer from her sinful, low-class living, took her back home, and loved and cared for her. But after a while, she would leave him again and return to prostitution. The cycle of her unfaithfulness and Hosea's unconditional love continues throughout this book to show God's people that He never, ever gives up on us. It also teaches us that love cannot be bought; it must be received as a gift, for God says in Hosea 14:4, "I will love them freely."

As you read the book of Hosea, let it remind you of God's unconditional love and unfailing mercy. He will never leave you or let you down, no matter how you have sinned or turned away from Him. In God, you can always have a fresh start.

1 THE WORD of the Lord that came to Hosea son of Beeri in the days of Uzziah, Jotham, Ahaz, and Hezekiah, kings of Judah, and in the days of Jeroboam son of Joash king of Israel.

2 When the Lord first spoke with *and* through Hosea, the Lord said to him, Go, take to yourself a wife of harlotry and have children of [her] harlotry, for the land commits great whoredom by departing from the Lord.

3 So he went and took Gomer the daughter of Diblaim, and she became pregnant and bore him a son.

4 And the Lord said to him, Call his name Jezreel *or* God-sows, for yet a little while and I will avenge the blood of Jezreel *and* visit the punishment for it upon the house of Jehu, and I will put an end to the kingdom of the house of Israel. [II Kings 10:11.]

5 And on that day I will break the bow of Israel in the Valley of Jezreel.

6 And [Gomer] conceived again and bore a daughter. And the Lord said to Hosea, Call her name Lo-Ruhamah *or* Not-pitied, for I will no more have love, pity, *and* mercy on the house of Israel, that I should in any way pardon them.

7 But I will have love, pity, *and* mercy on the house of Judah and will deliver them by the Lord their God and will [a]not save them by bow, nor by sword, nor by equipment of war, nor by horses, nor by horsemen. [Isa. 31:8; 37:33-35.]

8 Now when [Gomer] had weaned Lo-Ruhamah [Not-pitied], she became pregnant [again] and bore a son.

9 And the Lord said, Call his name Lo-Ammi [Not-my-people], for you are not My people and I am not your God.

10 Yet the number of the children of Israel shall be as the sand of the sea, which cannot be measured or numbered; and instead of it being said to them, You are not My people, it shall be said to them, Sons of the Living God! [Rom. 9:26.]

11 Then shall the children of Judah and the children of Israel be gathered together and appoint themselves one head, and they shall go up out of the land, for great shall be the day of Jezreel [for the spiritually reborn Israel, a divine offspring, the people whom the Lord has blessed.] [Isa. 11:12, 13; Ezek. 37:15-28.]

2 [HOSEA], SAY to your brethren, Ammi [or You-are-my-people], and to your sisters, Ruhamah [or You-have-been-pitied-and-have-obtained-mercy].

2 Plead with your mother [your nation]; plead, for she is not My wife and I am not her Husband; [plead] that she put away her [marks of] harlotry from her face and her adulteries from between her breasts, [Isa. 50:1.]

3 Lest I strip her naked and make her as in the day she was born, and make her as a wilderness and set her like a parched land and slay her with thirst.

4 Yes, for her children I will have no love *nor* pity *nor* mercy, for they are the children of harlotry.

5 For their mother has played the harlot; she who conceived them has done shamefully, for she said, I will go after my lovers that give me my food and my water, my wool and my flax, my oil and my refreshing drinks.

6 Therefore, behold, I [the Lord God] will hedge up her way [even yours, O Israel] with thorns; and I will build a wall against her that she shall not find her paths.

7 And she shall follow after her lovers but she shall not overtake

---

a Isaiah also made this prophecy (Isa. 31:8-9) and both he and Hosea lived to see its remarkable, literal fulfillment (Isa. 37:36). See also II Kings 19:35-37.

them; and she shall seek them [inquiring for and requiring them], but shall not find them. Then shall she say, Let me go and return to my first husband, for then was it better with me than now.

8 For she has not noticed, understood, *or* realized that it was I [the Lord God] Who gave her the grain and the new wine and the fresh oil, and Who lavished upon her silver and gold which they used for Baal *and* made into his image.

9 Therefore will I return *and* take back My grain in the time for it and My new wine in the season for it, and will pluck away *and* recover My wool and My flax which were to cover her [Israel's] nakedness.

10 And now will I uncover her lewdness *and* her shame in the sight of her lovers, and no one shall rescue her out of My hand.

11 I will also cause to cease all her mirth, her feastmaking, her New Moons, her Sabbaths, and all her solemn feasts *and* appointed festive assemblies.

12 And I will lay waste *and* destroy her vines and her fig trees of which she has said, These are my reward *or* loose woman's hire that my lovers have given me; and I will make [her plantations] an inaccessible forest, and the wild beasts of the open country shall eat them.

13 And I will visit [punishment] upon her for the feast days of the Baals, when she burned incense to them and decked herself with her earrings *and* nose rings and her jewelry and went after her lovers and forgot Me, says the Lord.

14 Therefore, behold, I will allure her [Israel] and bring her into the wilderness, and I will speak tenderly *and* to her heart.

15 There I will give her her vineyards and make the Valley of Achor [troubling] to be for her a door of hope *and* expectation. And she shall sing there *and* respond as in the days of her youth and as at the time when she came up out of the land of Egypt. [Exod. 15:2; Josh. 7:24-26.]

16 And it shall be in that day, says the Lord, that you will call Me Ishi [my Husband], and you shall no more call Me Baali [my Baal].

17 For I will take away the names of Baalim [the Baals] out of her mouth, and they shall no more be mentioned *or* seriously remembered by their name.

18 And in that day will I make a covenant for Israel with the living creatures of the open country and with the birds of the heavens and with the creeping things of the ground. And I will break the bow and the sword and [abolish battle equipment and] conflict out of the land and will make you lie down safely.

19 And I will betroth you to Me forever; yes, I will betroth you to Me in righteousness and justice, in steadfast love, and in mercy.

20 I will even betroth you to Me in stability *and* in faithfulness, and you shall know (recognize, be acquainted with, appreciate, give heed to, and cherish) the Lord.

21 And in that day I will respond, says the Lord; I will respond to the heavens [which ask for rain to pour on the earth], and they shall respond to the earth [which begs for the rain it needs],

speak the Word

22 And the earth shall respond to the grain and the wine and the oil [which beseech it to bring them forth], and these shall respond to Jezreel [restored Israel, who prays for a supply of them].

23 And I will sow her for Myself anew in the land, and I will have love, pity, *and* mercy for her who had not obtained love, pity, *and* mercy; and I will say to those who were not My people, You are My people, and they shall say, You are my God! [I Pet. 2:9, 10.]

3 THEN SAID the Lord to me, Go again, love [the same] woman [Gomer] who is beloved of a paramour and is an adulteress, even as the Lord loves the children of Israel, though they turn to other gods and love cakes of raisins [used in the sacrificial feasts in idol worship].

2 So I bought her for ᵇfifteen pieces of silver and a homer and a half of barley [the price of a slave].

3 And I said to her, You shall be [betrothed] to me for many days; you shall not play the harlot and you shall not belong to another man. So will I also be to you [until you have proved your loyalty to me and our marital relations may be resumed].

4 For the children of Israel shall dwell *and* sit deprived many days, without king or prince, without sacrifice or [idolatrous] pillar, and without ephod [a garment worn by priests when seeking divine counsel] or teraphim (household gods).

speak the Word

5 Afterward shall the children of Israel return and seek the Lord their God, [inquiring of and requiring Him] and [from the line of] David, their King [of kings]; and they shall come in [anxious] fear to the Lord and to His goodness *and* His good things in the latter days. [Jer. 30:9; Ezek. 34:24.]

4 HEAR THE word of the Lord, you children of Israel, for the Lord has a controversy (a pleading contention) with the inhabitants of the land, because there is no faithfulness, love, pity *and* mercy, or knowledge of God [from personal experience with Him] in the land.

2 There is nothing but [false] swearing and breaking faith and killing and stealing and committing adultery; they break out [into violence], one [deed of] bloodshed following close on another.

3 Therefore shall the land [continually] mourn, and all who dwell in it shall languish, together with the wild beasts of the open country and the birds of the heavens; yes, the fishes of the sea also shall [perish because of the drought] be collected *and* taken away.

4 Yet let no man strive, neither let any man reprove [another—do not waste your time in mutual recriminations], for with you is My contention, O priest.

5 And you shall stumble in the daytime, and the [false] prophet also shall stumble with you in the night; and I will destroy your mother [the priestly nation]. [Exod. 19:6.]

Thank You, Lord, for betrothing me to You forever in righteousness and justice, in steadfast love and in mercy, in stability and faithfulness. I will know, be acquainted with, appreciate, give heed to, and cherish You.
ADAPTED FROM HOSEA **2:19, 20**

b Hosea bought Gomer back after she had become a slave. The combination of fifteen pieces of silver and a homer and a half of barley totaled the standard price of a slave (30 pieces of silver). See Exod. 21:7, 32; II Kings 7:1, 16, 18.

6   My people are destroyed for lack of knowledge; because you [the priestly nation] have rejected knowledge, I will also reject you that you shall be no priest to Me; seeing you have forgotten the law of your God, I will also forget your children.

7   The more they increased *and* multiplied [in prosperity and power], the more they sinned against Me; I will change their glory into shame.
8   They feed on the sin of My people and set their heart on their iniquity.
9   And it shall be: Like people, like priest; I will punish them for their ways and repay them for their doings.
10   For they shall eat and not have enough; they shall play the harlot and beget no increase, because they have forsaken the Lord for harlotry;
11   Harlotry and wine and new wine take away the heart *and* the mind *and* the spiritual understanding.
12   My people [habitually] ask counsel of their [senseless] wood [idols], and their staff [of wood] gives them oracles *and* instructs them. For the spirit of harlotry has led them astray and they have played the harlot, withdrawing themselves from subjection to their God.
13   They sacrifice on the tops of the mountains, and they burn incense upon the hills and under oaks, poplars, and terebinths, because there the shade is good. Therefore your daughters play the harlot and your sons' wives commit adultery.
14   I will not punish your daughters when they play the harlot nor your daughters-in-law when they commit adultery, for [the fathers and husbands] themselves go aside in order to be alone with women who prostitute themselves for gain, and they sacrifice at the altar with dedicated harlots [who surrender their chastity in honor of the goddess]. Therefore the people without understanding shall stumble *and* fall *and* come to ruin.
15   Though you, Israel, play the harlot *and* worship idols, let not Judah offend *and* become guilty; come not to Gilgal, neither go up to Beth-aven [contemptuous reference to Bethel, then noted for idolatry], nor swear [in idolatrous service, saying], As the Lord lives.
16   For Israel has behaved stubbornly, like a stubborn heifer. How then should he expect to be fed *and* treated by the Lord like a lamb in a large pasture?
17   Ephraim is joined [fast] to idols, [so] let him alone [to take the consequences].
18   Their drinking carousal over, they go habitually to play the harlot; [Ephraim's] rulers [continue to] love shame more than her glory [which is the Lord, Israel's God].
19   The resistless wind [of God's wrath] has bound up [Israel] in its wings *or* skirts, and [in captivity] they *and* their altars shall be put to shame because of their sacrifices [to calves, to sun, moon, and stars, and to heathen gods].

5   HEAR THIS, O you priests! And listen, O house of Israel! And give ear, O house of the king! For the judgment pronounced pertains to you *and* is meant for you, because you have been a snare at Mizpah and a net spread upon Tabor [military strongholds on either side of the Jordan River].
2   The revolters are deeply sunk in corruption *and* slaughter, but I [the

when we know right, we can choose to do right

We cannot do what is right if we do not know what is right. We must learn God's Word and, by it, learn His will and His ways. Righteousness is, first of all, a position given to us by Jesus Christ when we accept Him as our Savior. It is then to be worked out in our lives and is said to be "conforming to the will of God in purpose, thought, and action." (I John 2:29).

We learn from Hosea 4:6 that people are deceived and thereby destroyed through a lack of knowledge. Satan is the great deceiver. When people do not know better, they believe Satan's lies and live miserable lives. Satan comes only to kill, steal, and destroy; but Jesus came that we might have and enjoy our lives in abundance (see John 10:10). For many years Satan stole from me while I blamed other people; sometimes I even blamed God.

As a child I was filled with fear and torment. I did not know that Satan was the source of all my problems. I did not know that even though people had hurt me, the pain was actually inflicted by Satan as he worked through them. I did not know that although I had a painful past, I could have a wonderful future. There was so much I did not know! I had a genuine lack of knowledge and I was perishing—living in darkness and bondage—because of it.

In 1976, God gave me a strong desire to study and understand His Word (the Bible), and my life has been changing for the better ever since. Once I knew that God loved me and wanted me to have a good life, my outlook on everything changed. Prior to knowing truth, I felt hopeless and trapped; I was very bitter. I blamed everyone for my pain except Satan, the real culprit. Yes, people had hurt me, and they were responsible too, but I learned that "hurting people, hurt people." The people who hurt me had done so because someone had hurt them. This knowledge helped me forgive my enemies, and my healing began.

When you take time and make the effort to gain knowledge, you not only help yourself but all your descendants. My children have better lives than I did because of the knowledge I have. We never know so much that we do not need to keep learning. Make a decision to be a "lifetime learner" so that a lack of knowledge will not cause you to suffer.

Lord God] am a rebuke *and* a chastisement for them all.

3 I know Ephraim, and Israel is not hid from Me; for now, O Ephraim, you have played the harlot *and* have worshiped idols; Israel is defiled.

4 Their doings will not permit them to return to their God, for the spirit of harlotry is within them and they know not the Lord [they do not recognize,

appreciate, give heed to, or cherish the Lord].

5 But the pride *and* self-reliance of Israel testifies before his [own] face. Therefore shall [all] Israel, and [especially] Ephraim [the northern ten tribes], totter *and* fall in their iniquity *and* guilt, and Judah shall stumble *and* fall with them.

6 They shall go with their flocks and

with their herds to seek the Lord [inquiring for and requiring Him], but they will not find Him; He has withdrawn Himself from them.

7 They have dealt faithlessly *and* treacherously with the Lord [their espoused Husband], for they have borne alien children. Now shall a [single] New Moon (one month) devour them with their fields.

8 Blow the horn in Gibeah and the trumpet in Ramah [both lofty hills on Benjamin's northern border]. Sound the alarm at Beth-aven: [the enemy is] behind you *and* after you, O Benjamin [be on your guard]!

9 Ephraim shall become a desolation in the day of rebuke *and* punishment. Among the tribes of Israel I declare what shall surely be.

10 The princes of Judah are like those who remove the landmark [the barrier between right and wrong]; I will pour out My wrath upon them like water. [Deut. 19:14; Prov. 22:28.]

11 Ephraim is oppressed; he is broken *and* crushed by [divine] judgment, because he was content to walk after idols (images) *and* man's [evil] command c(*vanities and filth*).

12 Therefore I am like a moth to Ephraim and like dry rot to the house of Judah [in My judgment against them].

13 When Ephraim saw his sickness and Judah saw his wound, then Ephraim went to Assyria and sent to [Assyria's] great King Jareb [for help]. Yet he cannot heal you nor will he cure you of your wound [received in divine judgment].

14 For I will be to Ephraim like a lion, and like a young lion to the house of Judah. I, even I, will rend and go on [rending]; I will carry off and there will be no one to deliver.

15 I will return to My place [on high]

life point

The Bible is filled with scriptures inviting us to seek God in whatever circumstances we find ourselves. Hosea 5:15 encourages us to seek Him when we need forgiveness and healing from the distress and affliction of our guilt.

Exactly how do we seek God? One way is to think about Him and to consider what matters to Him and what He says about certain situations. When we seek Him, we find much more than His answers to our problems. We also find joy, peace, love, wisdom, and everything else we need in our lives. Let me urge you to seek Him in every area of your life today.

until they acknowledge their offense *and* feel their guilt and seek My face; in their affliction *and* distress they will seek, inquire for, *and* require Me earnestly, saying,

6 COME AND let us return to the Lord, for He has torn so that He may heal us; He has stricken so that He may bind us up.

2 After two days He will revive us (quicken us, give us life); on the third day He will raise us up that we may live before Him. [Isa. 26:19; Ezek. 37:1-10.]

3 Yes, let us know (recognize, be acquainted with, and understand) Him; let us be zealous to know the Lord [to appreciate, give heed to, and cherish Him]. His going forth is prepared *and* certain as the dawn, and He will come to us as the [heavy] rain, as the latter rain that waters the earth.

4 O Ephraim, what shall I do with you? [says the Lord] O Judah, what shall I do with you? For your

c "Vanities" is the rendering of *The Septuagint* (Greek translation of the Old Testament); "filth," the rendering of *The Dead Sea Scrolls.*

life point

Hosea 6:1 contains one of God's promises to heal us. Unless we receive a miracle, all healing is a process that takes time, especially emotional healing. Healing does not come easily and can be quite painful. Sometimes we have wounds that are still infected, and before we can be thoroughly healed, those wounds must be opened and the infection removed. Only God knows how to do this properly. As you seek God for the healing from your hurts, there are two main things you can do to facilitate the process: spend time with God in His Word and wait in His presence. I guarantee you will find healing there!

[wavering] love *and* kindness are like the night mist *or* like the dew that goes early away.

5　Therefore have I hewn down *and* smitten them by means of the prophets; I have slain them by the words of My mouth; My judgments [pronounced upon them by you prophets] are like the light that goes forth.

6　For I desire *and* delight in dutiful steadfast love *and* goodness, not sacrifice, and the knowledge of *and* acquaintance with God more than burnt offerings. [Matt. 9:13; 12:7.]

7　But they, like [less-privileged] men *and* like Adam, have transgressed the covenant; there have they dealt faithlessly *and* treacherously with Me.

8　Gilead is a city of evildoers; it is tracked with bloody [footprints].

9　And as troops of robbers lie in wait for a man, so the company of priests murder on the road toward Shechem; yes, they commit villainy *and* outrages.

10　I have seen a horrible thing in the house of Israel! There harlotry *and* idolatry are found in Ephraim; Israel is defiled.

11　Also, O Judah, there is a harvest [of divine judgment] appointed for you; when I would return My people from their captivity [in which they are slaves to the misery brought on by their own sins],

7 WHEN I would heal Israel, then Ephraim's guilt is uncovered, and the wickedness of Samaria; how they practice falsehood, and the thief enters and the troop of bandits ravage *and* raid without.

2　But they do not consider *and* say to their minds *and* hearts that I [earnestly] remember all their wickedness. Now their own doings surround and entangle them; they are before My face.

3　They make the king glad with their wickedness, and the princes with their lies.

4　They are all [idolatrous] adulterers; their passion smolders like heat of an oven when the baker ceases to stir the fire from the kneading of the dough until it is leavened.

5　On the [special] day of our king the princes made themselves *and* him sick with the heat of wine; [the king] stretched out his hand with scoffers *and* lawless men.

6　For they have made ready their heart, *and* their mind burns [with intrigue] like an oven while they lie in wait. Their anger smolders all night; in the morning it blazes forth as a flaming fire.

speak the Word

7 They are all hot as an oven and devour their judges; all their kings are fallen; there is none among them who calls to Me.

8 Ephraim mixes himself among the peoples [courting the favor of first one country, then another]; Ephraim is a cake not turned.

9 Strangers have devoured his strength, and he knows it not; yes, gray hairs are sprinkled here and there upon him, and he does not know it.

10 And the pride of Israel testifies against him *and* to his face. But they do not return to the Lord their God, nor seek *nor* inquire of *nor* require Him in spite of all this.

11 Ephraim also is like a silly dove without heart *or* understanding; they call to Egypt; they go to Assyria.

12 As they go, I will spread My net over them; I will bring them down like birds of the heavens. I will chastise them according to the announcement [or prediction made] to their congregation [in the Scriptures]. [Lev. 26:14-39.]

13 Woe to them, for they have wandered from Me! Destruction to them, because they have rebelled *and* trespassed against Me! Though I would redeem them, yet they have spoken lies against Me.

14 They do not cry to Me from their heart, but they wail upon their beds; they gash *and* distress *and* assemble themselves [in mourning] for grain and new wine; they rebel against Me.

15 Although I have chastened them *and* trained and strengthened their arms, yet they think *and* devise evil against Me.

16 They turn back, shift, *or* change, but not upwards [to the Most High]. They are like a deceitful bow; their princes shall fall by the sword for the insolence *and* rage of their tongue. This shall be [cause for] their derision *and* scorning in the land of Egypt.

8 SET THE trumpet to your lips! [The enemy] comes as a [great] vulture against the house of the Lord, because they have broken My covenant and transgressed against My law.

2 Then they will cry to Me, My God, we [of Israel] know You!

3 Israel has rejected the good [with loathing]; the enemy shall pursue him.

4 They set up kings, but not from Me [therefore without My blessing]; they have made princes or removed them [without consulting Me; therefore], I knew *and* recognized [them] not. With their silver and their gold they made idols for themselves, that they [the silver and the gold] may be destroyed.

5 Your calf [idol], O Samaria, is loathsome *and* I have spurned it. My wrath burns against them. How long will it be before they attain purity?

6 For this [calf] too is from Israel; a craftsman made it; therefore it is not God. The calf of Samaria shall be broken to shivers *and* go up in flames.

7 For they sow the wind and they shall reap the whirlwind. The standing grain has no heads; it shall yield no meal; if it were to yield, strangers *and* aliens would eat it up.

8 Israel is [as if] swallowed up. Already they have become among the nations as a vessel [of cheap, coarse pottery] that is useless.

9 For they are gone up to Assyria, a wild ass taking her own way by herself; Ephraim has hired lovers.

10 Yes, though with presents they hire [allies] among the nations, now will I gather them up, and in a little while they will sorrow *and* begin to diminish [their gifts] because of the burden (tribute) imposed by the king of princes [the king of Assyria].

11 For Ephraim has multiplied altars for sinning; yes, to him altars are intended for sinning.

12 I wrote for him the ten thousand things of My law, but they are counted as a strange thing [as something which does not concern him].
13 My sacrificial gifts they sacrifice [as a mere form]; yes, they sacrifice flesh and eat it, but the Lord does not accept them. Now He will [earnestly] remember their guilt *and* iniquity and will punish their sins. They shall return to [another] Egypt [Assyria]. [Deut. 28:68.]
14 For Israel has forgotten his Maker and built palaces *and* idol temples, and Judah has multiplied fortified cities; but I will send a fire upon his cities and it shall devour his palaces *and* fortified buildings. [Amos 1:4, 7, 10, 12, 14; 2:2, 5.]

9 REJOICE NOT, O Israel, with exultation as do the peoples, for you have played the harlot, forsaking your God. You have loved [a harlot's] hire upon every threshing floor [ascribing the harvest to the Baals instead of to God].
2 The threshing floor and the winevat shall not feed them, and the new wine shall fail them.
3 They shall not remain in the Lord's land, but Ephraim shall return to [another] Egypt and they shall eat unclean food in Assyria. [Ezek. 4:13.]
4 They shall not pour out wine offerings to the Lord, neither shall they be pleasing to Him. Their sacrifices shall be to them as the bread of mourners; all who eat of them shall be defiled, for their bread shall be [only] for their appetite; it shall not come into the house of the Lord [to be offered first to Him].
5 What will you do on the day of the appointed solemn assembly *or* festival and on the day of the feast of the Lord [when you are in exile]?
6 For behold, they are gone away from devastation *and* destruction; Egypt shall gather them in; Memphis shall bury them. Their precious things of silver shall be in the possession of nettles; thorns shall be [growing] in their tents.
7 The days of visitation *and* punishment have come; the days of recompense have come; Israel shall know it. The prophet is [considered] a crazed fool and the man who is inspired is [treated as if] mad *or* a fanatic, because of the abundance of your iniquity and because the enmity, hostility, *and* persecution are great. [Luke 21:22.]
8 Ephraim was [intended to be] a watchman with my God [and a prophet to the surrounding nations]; but he, that prophet, has become a fowler's snare in all his ways. There is enmity, hostility, *and* persecution in the house of his God.
9 They have deeply corrupted themselves as in the days of Gibeah. The Lord will [earnestly] remember their iniquity; He will punish their sins. [Judg. 20.]
10 I found Israel like grapes in the wilderness; I saw your fathers as the first ripe fruit on the fig tree in its first season, but they went to Baal-peor and consecrated themselves to that shameful thing [Baal], and they became detestable *and* loathsome like that which they loved.
11 As for Ephraim, their glory shall fly away like a bird; there shall be no birth, no being with child, and [because of their impurity] no becoming pregnant.
12 Though they bring up their children, yet will I bereave them so that not a man shall be left; yes, woe also to them when I look away *and* depart from them!
13 Ephraim, as I have seen with Tyre, is planted in a pleasant place, but Ephraim shall bring out his children to the slayer.
14 Give them [their due], O Lord! [But] what will You give? Give them a miscarrying womb and dry breasts.

15 All their wickedness [says the Lord] is focused in Gilgal, for there I hated them; for the wickedness of their [idolatrous] doings I will drive them out of My house [the Holy Land]; I will love them no more; all their princes are rebels. [Hos. 4:15; 12:11.]

16 Ephraim is smitten, their root is dried up, they shall bear no fruit. Yes, though they bring forth, yet will I slay even their beloved children.

17 My God will cast them away because they did not listen to *and* obey Him, and they shall be wanderers *and* fugitives among the nations.

10 ISRAEL IS a luxuriant vine that puts forth its [material] fruit. According to the abundance of his fruit he has multiplied his altars [to idols]; according to the goodness *and* prosperity of their land they have made goodly pillars *or* obelisks [to false gods].

2 Their heart is divided *and* deceitful; now shall they be found guilty *and* suffer punishment. The Lord will smite *and* break down [the horns of] their altars; He will destroy their [idolatrous] pillars.

3 Surely now they shall say, We have no [actual] king because we fear not the Lord; and as for the king, what can he do for us?

4 They have spoken mere words of the lips, swearing falsely in making covenants; therefore judgment springs up like hemlock [or other poisonous plants] in the furrows of the field.

5 The inhabitants of Samaria shall be in terror for the calf [idol] of Bethaven [the house of idolatry, contemptuously meaning Bethel], for its people shall mourn over it and its [idolatrous] priests who rejoiced over it [shall tremble] for the glory of [their calf god], because it is departed from it.

6 [The golden calf] shall also be carried into Assyria as a tribute-gift to the fighting King Jareb; Ephraim shall be put to shame and Israel shall be ashamed of his own counsel [to set up calf worship and detach Israel from Judah].

7 As for Samaria, her king *and* her whole monarchy are cut off like twigs *or* foam upon the water.

8 The high places also of Aven [once Beth(el), house of God, now (Beth-) aven, house of idolatry], the sin of Israel, shall be destroyed; the thorn and the thistle shall come up on their [idol] altars, and they shall say to the mountains, Cover us! And to the hills, Fall on us! [Luke 23:30; Rev. 6:16; 9:6.]

9 O Israel, you have [willfully] sinned from the days of Gibeah [when you all but wiped out the tribe of Benjamin]! There [Israel] stood [then, only] that the battle against the sons of unrighteousness might not overtake *and* turn against them at Gibeah [but now the kingdom of the ten tribes and the name of Ephraim shall be utterly blotted out]. [Judg. 20.]

10 When I please I will chastise them, and hostile peoples shall be gathered against them when I shall bind *and* yoke them for their two transgressions [revolt from the Lord their God and the worship of idols]. [Jer. 2:13; Lam. 3:31-33.]

11 Ephraim indeed is a heifer broken in *and* loving to tread out the grain, but I have [heretofore] spared the beauty of her fair neck. I will now set a rider upon Ephraim *and* make him to draw; Judah shall plow and Jacob shall break his clods.

12 Sow for yourselves according to righteousness (uprightness and right standing with God); reap according to mercy *and* loving-kindness. Break up your uncultivated ground, for it is time to seek the Lord, to inquire for *and* of Him, *and* to require His favor, till He comes and teaches you righteousness *and* rains His righteous gift of salvation upon you. [II Cor. 9:10.]

13 You have plowed *and* plotted wickedness, you have reaped the [willful] injustice [of oppressors], you have eaten the fruit of lies. Because you have trusted in your [own] way *and* your chariots, in the multitude of your mighty men,

14 Therefore shall a tumult arise against your people and all your fortresses shall be wasted *and* destroyed, as Shalmaneser wasted *and* destroyed Beth-arbel on the day of battle; the mother was dashed in pieces with her children. [II Kings 17:3.]

15 So shall it be done to you at [idolatrous] Bethel because of your great wickedness; at daybreak shall the king of Israel be utterly cut off.

11 WHEN ISRAEL was a child, then I loved him and called My son out of Egypt. [Matt. 2:15.]

2 The more [the prophets] called to them, the more they went from them; they kept sacrificing to the Baals and burning incense to the graven images.

3 Yet I taught Ephraim to walk, taking them by their arms *or* taking them up in My arms, but they did not know that I healed them.

4 I drew them with cords of a man, with bands of love, and I was to them as one who lifts up *and* eases the yoke over their cheeks, and I bent down to them *and* gently laid food before them.

5 They shall not [literally] return into [another bondage in] the land of Egypt, but the Assyrian shall be their king because they refused to return to Me.

6 And the sword shall rage against *and* fall upon their cities and shall consume the bars of their gates and shall make an end [of their defenses], because of their own counsels *and* devices.

7 My people are bent on backsliding from Me; though [the prophets] call them to Him Who is on high, none at all will exalt Him *or* lift himself up [to come to Him].

8 How can I give you up, O Ephraim! How can I surrender you *and* cast you off, O Israel! How can I make you as Admah *or* how can I treat you as Zeboiim [both destroyed with Sodom]! My heart recoils within Me; My compassions are kindled together. [Deut. 29:23.]

9 I will not execute the fierceness of My anger; I will not bring back Ephraim to nothing *or* again destroy him. For I am God and not man, the Holy One in the midst of you, and I will not come in wrath *or* enter into the city.

10 They shall walk after the Lord, Who will roar like a lion; He Himself will roar and [His] sons shall come trembling *and* eagerly from the west.

11 They shall come trembling *but* hurriedly like a bird out of Egypt and like a dove out of the land of Assyria, and I will cause them to dwell in their houses, says the Lord.

12 Ephraim surrounds Me with lies and the house of Israel with deceit, and Judah is not yet steadfast with God, with the faithful Holy One.

speak the Word

God, I will sow for myself according to righteousness and reap according to mercy and loving-kindness. I will allow You to break up the fallow ground in my heart, for it is time to seek You, to inquire for and of You, and to require Your favor, till You come and rain righteousness on me.

ADAPTED FROM HOSEA 10:12

12

EPHRAIM HERDS *and* feeds on the wind and pursues the [parching] east wind; every day he increases lies and violence, and a covenant is made with Assyria and oil is carried to Egypt. [Isa. 30:6, 7.]

2 The Lord has also a controversy (a pleading contention) with Judah, and will punish Jacob by visiting upon him according to his ways; according to his doings will He recompense him.

3 He took his brother by the heel in [their mother's] womb, and in the strength [of his manhood] he contended *and* had power with God. [Gen. 25:26; 27:36.]

4 Yes, he had power over the ^dAngel [of the Lord] and prevailed; he wept and sought His favor. He met Him in Bethel, and there [God] spoke with [him and through him with] us— [Gen. 28:12-19; 32:28; Gen. 35:1-15.]

5 Even the Lord the God of hosts, the name of Him [Who spoke with Jacob] is the Lord.

6 Therefore return to your God! Hold fast to love *and* mercy, to righteousness *and* justice, and wait [expectantly] for your God continually!

7 Canaan [Israel—whose ideals have sunk to those of Canaan] is a trader; the balances of deceit are in his hand; he loves to oppress *and* defraud.

8 Ephraim has said, Ah, but I have become rich; I have gained for myself

life point

Hosea 12:6 teaches us to wait expectantly for the Lord. Waiting for God means spending time with Him in His Word and in His presence. When we wait expectantly for God, we are anticipating something good from our time with Him.

wealth. All my profits shall bring on me no iniquity that would be sin. [But all his profits will never offset nor suffice to expiate the guilt which he has incurred.] [Rev. 3:17.]

9 But I [Who] am the Lord your God from [when you became a nation in] the land of Egypt will yet make you to dwell in tents, as in the days of the appointed *and* solemn Feast [of Tabernacles]. [Lev. 23:39-43.]

10 I have also spoken to [you by] the prophets, and I have multiplied visions [for you] and [have appealed to you] through parables acted out by the prophets.

11 If Gilead is given over to idolatry, they shall come to nought *and* be mere waste; if they [insult God by] sacrificing bullocks in Gilgal [on heathen altars], their altars shall be like heaps in the furrows of the fields.

12 Jacob fled into the open country of Aram *or* Padan-aram, and [there] Israel served for a wife, and for a wife he herded sheep. [Gen. 29:18-20; 30:31; 31:38-41.]

13 And by a prophet the Lord brought Israel out of Egypt, and by a prophet was [Israel] preserved.

14 Ephraim has provoked most bitter anger; therefore shall his blood [guilt] be left upon him, and his disgrace *and* reproach shall his Lord return upon him.

13

WHEN EPHRAIM spoke with trembling, he exalted himself in Israel; but when he offended *and* became guilty in Baal worship, he died [spiritually, and then outward ruin came also, sealing Israel's doom as a nation].

2 And now they sin more and more and have made for themselves molten images of their silver, even idols according to their own understanding [as it pleased them], all of them the

d See footnotes on Gen. 16:7 and Gen. 32:28.

work of the craftsmen. To these [very works of their hands] they speak *or* pray who sacrifice to them; they kiss *and* show homage to the calves [as if they were alive]!

3 Therefore they shall be like the morning mist or like the dew that passes early away, like the chaff that swirls with the whirlwind from the threshing floor and as the smoke out of the chimney *or* through the window.

4 Yet I am the Lord your God from [the time you became a nation in] the land of Egypt, and you shall know *or* recognize no God but Me, for there is no Savior besides Me.

5 I knew (recognized, understood, and had regard for) you in the wilderness, in the land of great drought.

6 According to their pasture, so were they filled [when they fed, they grew full], and their heart was lifted up; therefore have they forgotten Me.

7 Therefore I have become to them like a lion; like a leopard I will lurk by the way [to Assyria] *and* watch them.

8 I will meet them like a bear that is robbed of her cubs, and I will rend the covering of their heart, and there will I devour them like a lioness, as a wild beast would tear them.

9 It is your destruction, O Israel, that you have been against Me, for in Me is your help.

10 Where now is your king that he may save you in all your cities? And your judges of whom you said, Give me a king and princes?

11 I have given you a king in My anger, and I have taken him away in My wrath.

12 The iniquity of Ephraim [not fully punished yet] is bound up [as in a bag]; his sin is laid up in store [for judgment and destruction].

13 The pains of a woman in childbirth are coming on for him [to be born]; but he is an unwise son, for now when it is time [to be born], he comes not to the place where [unborn] children break forth [he needs new birth but makes no effort to acquire it].

14 Should I ransom them from the power of Sheol (the place of the dead)? Should I redeem them from death? [e]O death, where are your plagues? O Sheol, where is your destruction? Relenting *and* compassion are hidden from My eyes. [I Cor. 15:55.]

15 For though among his brethren [his fellow tribes] he may be fruitful, an east wind [Assyria] will come, the breath of the Lord rising from the desert; and Ephraim's spring shall become dry and his fountain be dried up. [Assyria] shall plunder his treasury of every precious vessel.

16 Samaria shall bear her guilt *and* become desolate, for she rebelled against her God; they shall fall by the sword, their infants shall be dashed in pieces, and their pregnant women shall be ripped up.

speak the Word

Lord, I declare that there is no Savior besides You.
ADAPTED FROM HOSEA **13:4**

God, in You is my help.
ADAPTED FROM HOSEA **13:9**

e The apostle Paul in I Cor. 15:55 brings to mind this passage—but with a triumphant reversal of meaning made possible by our Lord's resurrection.

God loves you freely

Do you ever wonder how God can love us, as imperfect as we are? He can because He *wants to*; it pleases Him. Hosea 14:4 tells us that God wants to heal our faithlessness and freely love us.

God's Word is full of verses about His love. Ephesians 1:5 teaches: "He foreordained us (destined us, planned in love for us) to be adopted (revealed) as His own children through Jesus Christ, in accordance with the purpose of His will [because it pleased Him and was His kind intent]."

God loves because love is His nature—God is love (see I John 4:8). If He were otherwise, He would not be Who He is.

God always loves us! He may not always love everything we do, but He does love us. His love is unconditional. It is love based on Him, not on us; we receive God's love without deserving it. God's unconditional love is the power that forgives our sins, heals our emotional wounds, and mends our broken hearts (see Psalm 147:3).

Once you realize that you are loved by God, not because of anything you are or anything you have done, then you can quit trying to deserve or earn His love and simply receive and enjoy it. Remember, He loves you freely—without requiring or asking anything of you.

If you struggle to believe or accept God's unconditional love for you, start by confessing that God loves you. Say, "God loves me" aloud several times a day when you are alone. Speak it out into the atmosphere and become accustomed to hearing it. Get comfortable with the thought of it. Bask in His love, soak in it, and let it saturate your soul, your thinking and emotions. Imagine how awesome it is: *"God loves me!"*

Once your heart is filled with the knowledge of God's awesome, unconditional love, you can begin to love Him in return and to express His love to others too.

14 O ISRAEL, return to the Lord your God, for you have stumbled *and* fallen, [visited by calamity] due to your iniquity.

2 Take with you words and return to the Lord. Say to Him, Take away all *our* iniquity; accept what is good *and* receive us graciously; so will we render [our thanks] as bullocks [to be sacrificed] *and* pay the confession of our lips. [Heb. 13:15.]

3 Assyria shall not save us; we will not ride upon horses, neither will we say any more to the work of our hands [idols], You are our gods. For in You [O Lord] the fatherless find love, pity, *and* mercy.

4 I will heal their faithlessness; I will love them freely, for My anger is turned away from [Israel].

5 I will be like the dew *and* the night mist to Israel; he shall grow *and* blossom like the lily and cast forth his

roots like [the sturdy evergreens of] Lebanon.

6 His suckers *and* shoots shall spread, and his beauty shall be like the olive tree and his fragrance like [the cedars and aromatic shrubs of] Lebanon.

7 They that dwell under his shade shall return; they shall revive like the grain and blossom like the vine; the scent of it shall be like the wine of Lebanon.

8 Ephraim shall say, What have I to do any more with idols? I have answered [him] and will regard *and* watch over him; I am like a green fir *or* cypress tree; with Me is the

putting the Word to work

In what ways has God shown you love, pity, and mercy (see Hosea 14:3)? How has He healed you and loved you (see Hosea 14:4)? Thank Him today!

fruit found [which is to nourish you].

9 Who is wise, that he may understand these things? Prudent, that he may know them? For the ways of the Lord are right and the [uncompromisingly] just shall walk in them, but transgressors shall stumble *and* fall in them. [Ps. 107:43; Isa. 26:7; Jer. 9:12; Dan. 12:10.]

Joel

Author:
Joel

Date:
Traditional view is about 830 BC

Everyday Life Principles:
Sin requires repentance.

Continual sin and lack of repentance lead to God's judgment.

God does execute judgment, but He also brings restoration.

In modern-day language, the basic message of the book of Joel is: "Straighten up!" Joel wrote during difficult days, a time when the entire land of Judah suffered under a massive locust plague, in which crops failed, livestock died, and people perished. Joel interpreted this destruction as God's judgment and declared that to the people. Joel went on to urge the people to repent and to encourage them by telling them God wanted to bring restoration to their devastation.

Perhaps the most familiar passage in Joel is God's promise of restoration in Joel 2:25, 26: "And I will restore or replace for you the years that the locust has eaten—the hopping locust, the stripping locust, and the crawling locust, My great army which I sent among you. And you shall eat in plenty and be satisfied and praise the name of the Lord, your God, Who has dealt wondrously with you. And My people shall never be put to shame."

Whatever has been lost in your life, I pray that the book of Joel will remind you that God is a God of restoration. He is able to restore what has been lost or stolen from you. He wants to make the words of Joel 2:26 a reality in your life, so that you are able to declare that the Lord your God has dealt wondrously with you.

1 THE WORD of the Lord that came to [a]Joel the son of Pethuel.
2 Hear this, you aged men, and give ear, all you inhabitants of the land! Has such a thing as this occurred in your days or even in the days of your fathers?

3 Tell your children of it, and let your children tell their children, and their children another generation.

4 What the crawling locust left, the swarming locust has eaten; and what the swarming locust left, the hopping locust has eaten; and what the hopping locust left, the stripping locust has eaten.

5 Awake, you drunkards, and weep; wail, all you drinkers of wine, because of the [fresh] sweet juice [of the grape], for it is cut off *and* removed from your mouth.

6 For a [heathen and hostile] nation [of locusts, illustrative of a human foe] has invaded My land, mighty and without number; its teeth are the teeth of a lion, and it has the jaw teeth of a lioness. [Rev. 9:7, 8.]

7 It has laid waste My vine [symbol of God's people] and barked *and* broken My fig tree; it has made them completely bare and thrown them down; their branches are made white. [Isa. 5:5, 6.]

8 Lament like a virgin [bride] girded with sackcloth for the husband of her youth [who has died].

9 The meal *or* cereal offering and the drink offering are cut off from the house of the Lord; the priests, the Lord's ministers, mourn.

10 The field is laid waste, the ground mourns; for the grain is destroyed, the new juice [of the grape] is dried up, the oil fails.

11 Be ashamed, O you tillers of the soil; wail, O you vinedressers, for the wheat and for the barley, because

the harvest of the field has perished.
12 The vine is dried up and the fig tree fails; the pomegranate tree, the palm tree also, and the apple *or* quince tree, even all the trees of the field are withered, so that joy has withered *and* fled away from the sons of men.

13 Gird yourselves and lament, you priests; wail, you ministers of the altar; come, lie all night in sackcloth, you ministers of my [Joel's] God, for the cereal *or* meal offering and the drink offering are withheld from the house of your God.

14 Sanctify a fast, call a solemn assembly, gather the elders and all the inhabitants of the land in the house of the Lord, your God, and cry to the Lord [in penitent pleadings].

15 Alas for the day! For the day of [the judgment of] the Lord is at hand, and as a destructive tempest from the Almighty will it come. [Zeph. 1:14-18.]

16 Is not the food cut off before our eyes, joy and gladness from the house of our God?

17 The seed [grain] rots *and* shrivels under the clods, the garners are desolate *and* empty, the barns are in ruins because the grain has failed.

18 How the beasts groan! The herds of cattle are perplexed *and* huddle together because they have no pasture; even the flocks of sheep suffer punishment (are forsaken and made wretched).

19 O Lord, to You will I cry, for the fire has devoured the pastures *and* folds of the plain *and* the wilderness, and flame has burned all the trees of the field.

20 Even the wild beasts of the field pant *and* cry to You, for the water brooks are dried up and fire has consumed the pastures *and* folds of the wilderness *and* the plain.

---

a Joel was a prophet of Judah and possibly a contemporary of Elisha.

2 BLOW THE trumpet in Zion; sound an alarm on My holy Mount [Zion]. Let all the inhabitants of the land tremble, for the day of [the judgment of] the Lord is coming; it is close at hand—[Ezek. 7:2-4; Amos 5:16-20.]

2 A day of darkness and gloom, a day of clouds and of thick mists *and* darkness, like the morning dawn spread upon the mountains; so there comes a [heathen, hostile] people numerous and mighty, the like of which has never been before and shall not be again even to the years of many generations.

3 A fire devours before them, and behind them a flame burns; the land is as the garden of Eden before them, and behind them a desolate wilderness; yes, and none has escaped [the ravages of the devouring hordes].

4 Their appearance is like the appearance of horses, and like war horses *and* horsemen, so do they run.

5 Like the noise of chariots on the tops of the mountains they leap—like the noise of a flame of fire devouring the stubble, like a mighty people set in battle array. [Rev. 9:7, 9.]

6 Before them the peoples are in anguish; all faces become pale.

7 They run like mighty men; they climb the wall like men of war. They march each one [straight ahead] on his ways, and they do not break their ranks.

8 Neither does one thrust upon another; they walk every one in his path. And they burst through *and* upon the weapons, yet they are not wounded *and* do not change their course.

9 They leap upon the city; they run upon the wall; they climb up on *and* into the houses; they enter in at the windows like a thief.

10 The earth quakes before them; the heavens tremble. The sun and the moon are darkened and the stars withdraw their shining. [Rev. 9:2-4; 16:14.]

11 And the Lord utters His voice before His army, for His host is very great, and [they are] strong *and* powerful who execute [God's] word. For the day of the Lord is great and very terrible, and who can endure it? [Isa. 26:20, 21; 34:1-4, 8; Rev. 6:16, 17.]

12 Therefore also now, says the Lord, turn *and* keep on coming to Me with all your heart, with fasting, with weeping, and with mourning [until every hindrance is removed and the broken fellowship is restored].

13 Rend your hearts and not your garments and return to the Lord, your God, for He is gracious and merciful, slow to anger, and abounding in loving-kindness; and He revokes His sentence of evil [when His conditions are met].

14 Who knows but what He will turn, revoke your sentence [of evil], and leave a blessing behind Him [giving you the means with which to serve Him], even a cereal *or* meal offering and a drink offering for the Lord, your God?

15 Blow the trumpet in Zion; set apart a fast [a day of restraint and humility]; call a solemn assembly.

16 Gather the people, sanctify the congregation; assemble the elderly people, gather the children and the nursing infants; let the bridegroom [who is legally exempt from attending] go forth from his chamber and

speak the Word

When I sin, I repent and return to You, my God, for You are gracious and merciful, slow to anger, and abounding in loving-kindness.
ADAPTED FROM JOEL 2:13

putting the Word to work

Have you ever received a halfhearted apology? Repentance is not just a matter of going through the motions; it is honest confession and a conscious decision to return to following God. Do not take for granted God's grace, kindness, and mercy, but recognize your sin and be wholehearted and sincere in asking for forgiveness. God will be merciful to you (see Joel 2:12–14)!

the bride out of her closet. [None is exempt from the humiliation.]

17 Let the priests, the ministers of the Lord, weep between the porch and the altar; and let them say, Have pity *and* spare Your people, O Lord, and give not Your heritage to reproach, that the [heathen] nations should rule over them *or* use a byword against them. Why should they say among the peoples, Where is their God?

18 Then was the Lord jealous for His land and had pity on His people.

19 Yes, the Lord answered and said to His people, Behold, I am sending you grain and juice [of the grape] and oil, and you shall be satisfied with them; and I will no more make you a reproach among the [heathen] nations.

20 But I will remove far off from you the northern [destroyer's] army and will drive it into a land barren and desolate, with its front toward the eastern [Dead] Sea and with its rear toward the western [Mediterranean]

Sea. And its stench shall come up [like that of a decaying mass of locusts, a symbol and forecast of the fate of the northern army in the final day of the Lord], and its foul odor shall come up, because ᵇHe has done great things [the Lord will have destroyed the invaders]! [Isa. 34:1-4, 8; Jer. 25:31-35; Joel 2:11.]

21 Fear not, O land; be glad and rejoice, for the Lord has done great things! [Zech. 12:8-10.]

22 Be not afraid, you wild beasts of the field, for the pastures of the wilderness have sprung up *and* are green; the tree bears its fruit, and the fig tree and the vine yield their [full] strength.

23 Be glad then, you children of Zion, and rejoice in the Lord, your God; for He gives you the former *or* early rain in just measure *and* in righteousness, and He causes to come down for you the rain, the former rain and the latter rain, as before.

24 And the [threshing] floors shall be full of grain and the vats shall overflow with juice [of the grape] and oil.

25 And I will restore *or* replace for you the years that the locust has eaten—the hopping locust, the stripping locust, and the crawling locust, My great army which I sent among you.

26 And you shall eat in plenty and be satisfied and praise the name of the Lord, your God, Who has dealt wondrously with you. And My people shall never be put to shame.

27 And you shall know, understand,

speak the Word

God, I will not fear. I will be glad and rejoice, for You have done great things.
ADAPTED FROM JOEL **2:21**

---

b The capitalization here is suppositional. Interpreters are divided as to whether it is the northern destroyer who has "done great things," or the Lord; either, in different senses, is true. However, the latter view is strongly supported by the parallel phrase to the same effect in the next verse (Joel 2:21).

All of us have experienced the consequences of sin. Is there an area in your life where you are still feeling the ramifications of your sin? Be encouraged; God can bring healing and restoration (see Joel 2:25–27). Remember to thank Him for His grace and mercy.

and realize that I am in the midst of Israel and that I the Lord am your God and there is none else. My people shall never be put to shame.

28 And afterward I will pour out My Spirit upon all flesh; and your sons and your daughters shall prophesy, your old men shall dream dreams, your young men shall see visions.

life point

Joel 2:28 states that in the last days the old men shall dream dreams, and the young men shall see visions.

Dreams are certainly one of the valid ways God speaks, but this is also an area in which people can easily get out of balance. This is because dreaming is common to all of us, and not all dreams are from God. If you want to know whether or not a dream is from God, use discernment, wisdom, and balance, and I believe you will have confirmation in your heart if God is trying to speak to you or show you something.

29 Even upon the menservants and upon the maidservants in those days will I pour out My Spirit.
30 And I will show signs *and* wonders in the heavens, and on the earth, blood and fire and columns of smoke.
31 The sun shall be turned to darkness and the moon to blood before

the great and terrible day of the Lord comes. [Isa. 13:6, 9-11; 24:21-23; Ezek. 32:7-10; Matt. 24:29, 30; Rev. 6:12-17.]
32 And whoever shall call on the name of the Lord shall be delivered *and* saved, for in Mount Zion and in Jerusalem there shall be those who escape, as the Lord has said, and among the remnant [of survivors] shall be those whom the Lord calls. [Acts 2:17-21; Rom. 10:13.]

Have you ever called on someone for help who was either too busy to lend a hand or could not provide the help you needed? No matter how desperate your situation, God's promise is sure: He will save and deliver whoever calls upon Him (see Joel 2:32).

3 FOR BEHOLD, in those days and at that time when I shall reverse the captivity *and* restore the fortunes of Judah and Jerusalem,
2 I will gather all nations and will bring them down into the Valley of Jehoshaphat, and there will I deal with *and* execute judgment upon them for [their treatment of] My people and of My heritage Israel, whom they have scattered among the nations and [because] they have divided My land.
3 And they have cast lots for My people, and have given a boy for a

Have you ever been discriminated against because of your age, gender, or situation in life? God does not discriminate, and He continues to pour out His Spirit. Ask God today for a fresh outpouring of His Spirit in your life (See Joel 2:28, 29).

rejoice!

Joel 2:23 instructs us to rejoice in the Lord our God. Joy is one of the most powerful weapons we have against the devil. He has evil intentions to destroy our lives, but joy is a great source of strength that God has given us to interrupt Satan's plan. The devil wants us down because he knows if we lose our joy, we will lose our strength, and if we lose our strength, he will be able to walk all over us. But the Lord wants to lift us up, and He does that through the joy of the Lord, which is our strength (see Nehemiah 8:10).

The Bible says to be "glad-hearted continually" (I Thessalonians 5:16). It is not godly to be joyless all the time. Instead, I believe we need to aim to be joyful on a regular, ongoing basis. Let me urge you not to wait to feel joyful, but to be joyful on purpose. Think about right things; smile and laugh as often as possible. Believing releases joy. Believe in God, believe His promises, and believe that He really wants you to enjoy your life.

I was not raised in a joyful atmosphere. I was made to feel that if I was having fun, I was doing something wrong. So I was frequently discouraged and sad. I worked hard and was a responsible person, but I did not really enjoy my life.

Satan robbed me of many things through my ignorance of God's Word (see Hosea 4:6). Because I lacked proper spiritual knowledge, for a while Satan deceived me and stole the victorious, joy-filled life Jesus had already provided in His plan for me. Now I live a life of joy because the Lord has helped me.

The next time you feel as if you have lost your joy, I encourage you to remember that joy is a fruit of the Holy Spirit. However, it is released only by making a decision not to allow adverse circumstances to rule your emotional and mental attitudes.

Through joy, you can receive strength to do things that would otherwise be impossible. Through joy, you can overcome problems the devil will tell you are impossible to overcome. You can be defeated only if you lose your joy. No matter what happens in your life, remember this: You have the ability to maintain and release joy in your life, and there is nothing Satan can do to stop you when your heart is full of joy. So, take Joel's advice and rejoice in the Lord your God!

harlot and have sold a girl for juice [of the grape] and have drunk it.

4 Yes, and what are you to Me, O Tyre and Sidon and all the [five small] divisions of Philistia? Will you pay Me back for something? Even if you pay Me back, swiftly and speedily I will return your deed [of retaliation] upon your own head, [Isa. 23; Ezek. 26:1-18; Amos 1:6-10; Zeph. 2:4-7; Zech. 9:2-7.]

5 Because you have taken My silver and My gold and have carried into your temples *and* palaces My precious treasures,

6 And have sold the children of Judah and the children of Jerusalem to the sons of the Grecians, that you

may remove them far from their border.

7 Behold, I will stir them up out of the place to which you have sold them and will return your deed [of retaliation] upon your own head.

8 I will sell your sons and your daughters into the hand of the children of Judah, and they will sell them to the Sabeans, to a nation far off, for the Lord has spoken it. [Isa. 14:2; 60:14.]

9 Proclaim this among the nations: Prepare war! Stir up the mighty men! Let all the men of war draw near, let them come up.

10 Beat your plowshares into swords, and your pruning hooks into spears;

let the weak say, I am strong [a warrior]! [Isa. 2:4; Mic. 4:3.]

11 Hasten and come, all you nations round about, and assemble yourselves; there You, O Lord, will bring down Your mighty ones (Your warriors).

12 Let the nations bestir themselves and come up to the Valley of Jehoshaphat, for there will I sit to judge all the nations round about.

13 Put in the sickle, for the [vintage] harvest is ripe; come, get down and tread the grapes, for the winepress is full; the vats overflow, for the wickedness [of the peoples] is great. [Mark 4:29; Rev. 14:15, 18-20.]

14 Multitudes, multitudes in the valley

God of restoration

God is a God of restoration (see Joel 2:25, 26). He makes worn-out and destroyed things brand-new. In fact, many words that begin with "re" describe actions of God: He re-news, re-wards, re-deems, re-fines, brings re-compense, re-surrects, re-stores, re-vives, re-leases, and He teaches us to re-pent.

The *pent*house is the highest place in an apartment building or hotel. When we re-pent, God takes us back to the highest place, where we belong and from which we have fallen through sin. God is the God of mercy, Who continues to work with us as long as we desire change in our lives. He never gives up on us. He is not a harsh taskmaster Who is angry and impatient. Actually, God is just the opposite. He is merciful, gracious, kind, patient, slow to anger, compassionate, good, faithful, and every other wonderful thing.

When something has been lost or stolen from us, we become bitter unless we know there is hope of restoration. God not only gives back what was lost but promises us "double for our trouble." Isaiah 61:6, 7 says that for our former shame He will give us a twofold recompense. God promises that, instead of suffering with dishonor and reproach, we will rejoice, for He loves justice, and He hates robbery, wrongdoing, and violence.

Job went through a very difficult time, but he remained faithful to God—and God restored to him twice as much as he had lost. How can a person be bitter about their past when God promises such a bright future? Forget what lies behind, remember that God loves to restore, and press on into the new things He has for you.

of decision! For the day of the Lord is near in the valley of decision. [Zech. 14:1-9.]

15 The sun and the moon are darkened and the stars withdraw their shining.

16 The Lord will thunder *and* roar from Zion and utter His voice from Jerusalem, and the heavens and the earth shall shake; but the Lord will be a refuge for His people and a stronghold to the children of Israel. [Amos 9:11-15; Mic. 4:1-3; 5:2; Zeph. 3:13-20; Zech. 6:12, 13; 12:8, 9.]

17 So shall you know, understand, *and* realize that I am the Lord your God, dwelling in Zion, My holy mountain. Then shall Jerusalem be holy, and strangers *and* foreigners [not born into the family of God] shall no more pass through it.

18 And in that day, the mountains shall drip with fresh juice [of the grape] and the hills shall flow with milk; and all the brooks *and* riverbeds of Judah shall flow with water, and a fountain shall come forth from the house of the Lord and shall water the Valley of Shittim. [Ezek. 47:1-12; Amos 9:13; Zech. 14:8.]

putting the Word to work

Do you remember the day you decided to follow Jesus? Perhaps it was a quick decision, or perhaps you spent months or even years thinking about that decision. Joel's message is both timely and urgent for today: As you once were, there are countless people still in that "valley of decision" (Joel 3:14), weighing whether or not to follow God. Pray earnestly both for those you know personally and for those you do not know who are in the valley, that they will decide to follow Him.

19 Egypt shall be a desolation and Edom shall be a desolate wilderness for their violence against the children of Judah, because they have shed innocent blood in their land.

20 But Judah shall remain *and* be inhabited forever, and Jerusalem from generation to generation.

21 And I will cleanse *and* hold as innocent their blood *and* avenge it, blood which I have not cleansed, held innocent, *and* avenged, for the Lord dwells in Zion.

speak the Word

Lord, I declare that in You I am strong!
ADAPTED FROM JOEL **3:10**

Lord, You are a refuge and a stronghold for me.
ADAPTED FROM JOEL **3:16**

Amos

Author:
Amos

Date:
760 BC–750 BC

Everyday Life Principles:
Guard your heart during good or prosperous times so that you do not forget God.

Continue to seek the Lord in the midst of blessing, when everything seems to be wonderful and you may not feel a need for God.

True life is not found in prosperity or ease, but in seeking and finding the Lord.

Amos prophesied during a time of great prosperity in Israel and Judah. The nations were powerful politically, economically, and militarily—and everything appeared to be going better than ever. Because the people enjoyed such power, wealth, and material abundance, they assumed that God was pleased with them and that their prosperity was a sign of His blessing.

The truth was that in the midst of seemingly good times, there was much corruption, idolatry, injustice, and immorality. God sent Amos into this situation to declare to His people that their prosperity did not indicate His pleasure. Instead, He was displeased with their hearts and their behavior, and judgment was inevitable unless they changed their ways and began to seek Him again.

Amos teaches us that God will judge corruption and immorality in a society. He is not looking for cities or nations that will be merely "religious," but for those who value and practice righteousness and justice, for people who will love one another, stand up for the oppressed, and seek Him.

Remember as you read the book of Amos that material prosperity is not always a sign of God's blessing and that it can cause people to think they do not need God. Let this book remind you of your desperate need to seek Him, because, as Amos 5 repeatedly affirms, we live not by material abundance, but by truly seeking God.

1 THE WORDS of Amos, who was among the herdsmen *and* sheep masters of Tekoa, which he saw [in divine revelation] concerning Israel in the days of Uzziah king of Judah and in the days of Jeroboam the son of Joash, king of Israel, two years before the earthquake. [Zech. 14:5.]

putting the Word to work

The name *Amos* means "Burden-Bearer." Do you know the meaning of your name? If you are a follower of Jesus, "Christian" is one of your names, and it means "one belonging to or resembling Christ." Like Amos, seek to serve the Lord your God with all your heart.

2 And he said, The Lord roars out of Zion and utters His voice from Jerusalem; then the pastures of the shepherds mourn and the top of [Mount] Carmel dries up. [Isa. 42:13; Jer. 25:30; Joel 3:16.]
3 Thus says the Lord: For three transgressions of Damascus [the capital of Syria] and for four [for multiplied delinquencies], I will not reverse the punishment of it *or* revoke My word concerning it, because they have threshed Gilead [east of the Jordan River] with iron sledges. [II Kings 10:32, 33.]
4 So I will send a fire [of war, conquest, and destruction] upon the house of Hazael [who killed and succeeded King Ben-hadad] which shall devour the palaces *and* strongholds of Ben-hadad.
5 I will break also the bar [of the gate] of Damascus and cut off the inhabitant from the plain of Aven *or* On, and him who holds the scepter from Beth-eden; and the people of Syria [conquered by the Assyrians] shall go into exile to Kir, says the Lord. [Ezek. 30:17.]
6 Thus says the Lord: For three transgressions of Gaza [a city in Philistia] and for four [for multiplied delinquencies], I will not reverse the punishment of it *or* revoke My word concerning it, because [as slave traders] they carried away captive the whole [Jewish] population [of defenseless Judean border villages, of which none was spared, none left behind] and delivered them up to Edom [for the slave trade]. [Joel 3:6.]
7 So I will send a fire on the wall of Gaza which shall devour its strongholds.
8 And I will cut off the inhabitants from Ashdod and him who holds the scepter from Ashkelon, and I will turn My hand against Ekron; and the rest of the Philistines [in Gath and the towns dependent on these four Philistine cities] shall perish, says the Lord God. [Josh. 13:3.]
9 Thus says the Lord: For three transgressions of Tyre and for four [for multiplied delinquencies], I will not reverse the punishment of it *or* revoke My word concerning it, because they [as middlemen] delivered up a whole [Jewish] population to Edom and did not [seriously] remember their brotherly covenant. [I Kings 5:1, 12; 9:12, 13.]
10 So I will send a fire on the wall of Tyre which shall devour its strongholds.
11 Thus says the Lord: For three transgressions of Edom [descendants of Esau] and for four [for multiplied delinquencies], I will not reverse the punishment of it *or* revoke My word concerning it, because he pursued his brother Jacob (Israel) with the sword, corrupting his compassions *and* casting off all pity, and his anger tore perpetually and his wrath he kept *and* heeded forever.
12 So I will send a fire upon Teman which shall devour the strongholds of Bozrah [in Edom].
13 Thus says the Lord: For three

transgressions of the children of Ammon [descendants of Lot] and for four [for multiplied delinquencies], I will not reverse the punishment of it *or* revoke My word concerning it, because [the Ammonites] have ripped up women with child in Gilead, that they might enlarge their border.

14 So I will kindle a fire in the wall of Rabbah [in Ammon] and it shall devour the strongholds of it, with shouting in the day of battle, with a tempest in the day of the whirlwind;

15 And their king shall go into exile, he and his princes together, says the Lord.

2 THUS SAYS the Lord: For three transgressions of Moab [descendants of Lot] and for four [for multiplied delinquencies], I will not reverse the punishment of it *or* revoke My word concerning it, because he burned the bones of the king of Edom [Esau's descendant] into lime.

2 So I will send a fire upon Moab and it shall devour the strongholds of Kerioth, and Moab shall die amid uproar, shouting, and the sound of the trumpet.

3 And I will cut off the ruler from its midst and will slay all its princes with him, says the Lord.

4 Thus says the Lord: For three transgressions of Judah and for four [for multiplied delinquencies], I will not reverse the punishment of it *or* revoke My word concerning it, because they have despised *and* rejected the law of the Lord and have not kept His commandments, but their lies, after which their fathers have walked, caused them to err *and* go astray.

5 So I will send a fire upon Judah and it shall devour the strongholds of Jerusalem.

6 Thus says the Lord: For three transgressions of Israel and for four [for multiplied delinquencies], I will not reverse the punishment of it *or*

putting the Word to work

The people of Judah despised God's Word and did not keep His commandments (see Amos 2:4). Most of us would be quick to say we do not despise God's Word, but do you know that the word *despise* also means "to regard as unimportant"? Know that living by God's Word is important in every area of your life, and make every effort to keep His commandments.

revoke My word concerning it, because they have sold the [strictly] just *and* uncompromisingly righteous for silver and the needy for a pair of sandals;

7 They pant after [the sight of] the poor [reduced to such misery that they will be throwing] dust of the earth on their heads [in token of their grief]; they defraud *and* turn aside the humble [who are too meek to defend themselves]; and a man and his father will have sexual relations with the same maiden, so that My holy name is profaned.

8 And they lay themselves down beside every [pagan] altar upon clothes they have taken in pledge [for indebtedness], and in the house of their God [in daring contempt of Him] they frivolously drink the wine which has been exacted from those [unjustly] fined.

9 Yet I destroyed the Amorite before them, whose height was like the height of the cedars and he was strong as the oaks; yet I destroyed his fruit from above and his roots from beneath.

10 Also I brought you up out of the land of Egypt and led you forty years through the wilderness to possess the land of the Amorite.

11 And I raised up some of your sons for prophets and some of your young men for dedicated ones [Nazirites]. Is

this not true, O you children of Israel? says the Lord. [Num. 6:1-8.]

12 But you gave the dedicated ones [the Nazirites] wine to drink and commanded the prophets, saying, Prophesy not.

13 Behold, I am pressed under you *and* I will press you down in your place as a cart presses that is full of sheaves.

14 And flight shall be lost to the swift *and* refuge shall fail him; the strong shall not retain *and* confirm his strength, neither shall the mighty deliver himself.

15 Neither shall he stand who handles the bow, and he who is swift of foot shall not deliver himself; neither shall he who rides the horse deliver his life.

16 And he who is courageous among the mighty shall flee away naked on that day, says the Lord.

3 HEAR THIS word that the Lord has spoken against you, O children of Israel, against the whole family which I brought up from the land of Egypt:

2 You only have I known (chosen, sympathized with, and loved) of all the families of the earth; therefore I will visit upon you all your wickedness *and* punish you for all your iniquities.

3 Do two walk together except they make an appointment *and* have agreed?

4 Will a lion roar in the forest when

life point

In Amos 3:3 we read, "Do two walk together except they make an appointment and have agreed?" To walk with God, we must agree with God. This means agreeing with His Word, with His heart, and with His character. We need to agree with everything He says, everything He does, and everything He is. As we do, we will be empowered to live victorious, blessed, overcoming lives.

he has no prey? Will a young lion cry out of his den if he has taken nothing?

5 Can a bird fall in a snare upon the earth where there is no trap for him? Does a trap spring up from the ground when nothing at all has sprung it?

6 Shall a trumpet be blown in the city and the people not be alarmed *and* afraid? Shall misfortune *or* evil occur [as punishment] and the Lord has not caused it?

7 Surely the Lord God will do nothing ªwithout revealing His secret to His servants the prophets. [Rev. 10:7.]

8 The lion has roared; who will not fear? The Lord God has spoken; who can but prophesy? [Acts 4:20; 5:20, 29; I Cor. 9:16.]

9 Publish to the strongholds in Ashdod [Philistia] and to the strongholds in the land of Egypt, and say, Assemble yourselves upon the mountains of Samaria, and behold what great tumults (confusion and disorder) are

a God has always warned the world of coming judgments in order that it may not bring them upon itself. He warned Noah of the coming flood (Gen. 6:13ff.); Abraham and Lot of the future destruction of Sodom (Gen. 18:17; 19:14); Joseph of the seven-year famine (Gen. 41:30); Moses of the ten plagues on Egypt (Exod. 7:1ff.); Jonah of the destruction of Nineveh (Jonah 1:2; 3:4); Amos of the downfall of Syria, Philistia, Tyre, Edom, Ammon, Moab, Judah, and Israel (Amos 1 and 2). Various prophets were told in detail about the final events in connection with the captivities of the chosen people, and in every case the warnings were startlingly executed. Jonah announced the destruction of Nineveh, but judgment was postponed following repentance. When later generations of Ninevites backslid and reverted to extreme wickedness, the warning of Nahum was carried out completely against them. Christ's coming was foretold throughout the Old Testament, from Genesis to Malachi. Equally plain and inevitable of fulfillment are the warnings of Jesus and the prophets concerning the future that each day comes nearer to every nation on earth.

in her and what oppressions are in the midst of her.

10 For they know not how to do right, says the Lord, they who store up violence and robbery in their strongholds.

11 Therefore thus says the Lord God: An adversary shall surround the land, and he shall bring down your defenses from you and your strongholds shall be plundered.

12 Thus says the Lord: As the shepherd rescues out of the mouth of the lion two legs or a piece of an ear [of a sheep], so shall the children of Israel who dwell in Samaria be rescued with the corner of a couch and [part of] the damask covering of a bed.

13 Hear and bear witness in the house of Jacob, says the Lord God, the God of hosts,

14 That in the day when I visit Israel's transgressions upon him I will also visit [with punishment] the altars of Bethel [with its golden calf], and the horns of the altar shall be cut off and fall to the ground.

15 And I will smite the winter house with the summer house, and the houses of ivory shall perish and the many *and* great houses shall come to an end, says the Lord.

4 HEAR THIS word, you cows [women] of Bashan who are in the mountain of Samaria, who oppress the poor, who crush the needy, who say to their husbands, Bring and let us drink! [Ps. 22:12; Ezek. 39:18.]

2 The Lord God has sworn by His holiness that behold, the days shall come upon you when they shall take you away with hooks and the last of you with fishhooks. [Ps. 89:35.]

3 And you shall go out through the breaches [made in the city's wall], every [woman] straight before her, and you shall be cast forth into Harmon [an unknown place of exile], says the Lord.

4 Come to Bethel [where the golden calf is] and transgress; at Gilgal [another idol worship center] multiply transgression; and bring your sacrifices every morning and your tithes every three days.

5 And offer [by burning] a sacrifice of thanksgiving of that which is leavened, and proclaim and publish freewill offerings, for this you like to do, O children of Israel! says the Lord God.

6 I also gave you cleanness of teeth in all your cities and want of bread in all your places; yet you did not return to Me, says the Lord.

7 And also I withheld the rain from you when there were yet three months to the harvest. I caused it to rain upon one city and caused it not to rain upon another city; one piece of ground was rained upon, and the piece upon which it did not rain withered.

8 So [the people of] two or three cities wandered *and* staggered into one city to drink water, but they were not satisfied; yet you did not return to Me, says the Lord.

9 I smote you with blight [from the poisonous east wind] and with mildew; I laid waste the multitude of your gardens and your vineyards; your fig trees and your olive trees the palmerworm [a form of locust] devoured; yet you did not return to Me, says the Lord.

10 I have sent among you the pestilence [which I made] epidemic in Egypt; your young men I slew with the sword and I took into exile your horses, and I made the stench of your camp come up into your nostrils; yet you did not return to Me, says the Lord. [II Kings 8:12; 13:3, 7.]

11 I have overthrown some among you as when God overthrew Sodom and Gomorrah, and you were as a brand plucked out of the burning; yet you did not return to Me, says the

Lord. [Gen. 19:24, 25; Isa. 13:19; Jer. 49:18.]

12 Therefore thus will I do to you, O Israel; and because I will do this to you, prepare to meet your God, O Israel!

13 For behold, He Who forms the mountains and creates the wind and declares to man what is his thought, Who makes the morning darkness and treads on the heights of the earth—the Lord, the God of hosts, is His name! [Ps. 139:2; Dan. 2:28.]

5 HEAR THIS word which I take up concerning you in lamentation, O house of Israel:

2 The Virgin of Israel has fallen; she shall no more rise; she lies cast down and forsaken on her land; there is no one to raise her up.

3 For thus says the Lord God: The city that went forth a thousand shall have a hundred left, and that which went forth a hundred shall have ten left to the house of Israel.

4 For thus says the Lord to the house of Israel: Seek Me [inquire for and of Me and require Me as you require food] and you shall live! [II Chron. 15:2; Jer. 29:13.]

5 But seek not [the golden calf at] Bethel nor enter into [idolatrous] Gilgal, and pass not over to [the idols of] Beersheba; for Gilgal shall surely go into captivity and exile, and Bethel [house of God] shall become Beth-aven [house of vanity, emptiness, falsity, and futility] and come to nothing.

6 Seek the Lord [inquire for and of Him and require Him] and you shall live, lest He rush down like fire upon the house of Joseph [representing the ten tribes] and devour it, and there be

none to quench it in Bethel [the center of their idol hopes].

7 You who turn justice into [the bitterness of] wormwood and cast righteousness (uprightness and right standing with God) down to the ground,

8 Seek Him Who made the [cluster of stars called] Pleiades and [the constellation] Orion, Who turns the shadow of death or deep darkness into the morning and darkens the day into night, Who calls for the waters of the sea and pours them out upon the face of the earth—the Lord is His name—

9 Who causes sudden destruction to flash forth upon the strong so that destruction comes upon the fortress.

10 They hate him who reproves in the [city] gate [holding him as an abomination and rejecting his rebuke], and they abhor him who speaks uprightly.

11 Therefore because you tread upon the poor and take from him exactions of wheat, you have built houses of hewn stone, but you shall not dwell in them; you have planted pleasant vineyards, but you shall not drink their wine.

12 For I know how manifold are your transgressions and how mighty are your sins—you who afflict the [uncompromisingly] righteous, who take a bribe, and who turn aside the needy in the [court of the city] gate from their right.

13 Therefore he who is prudent will keep silence in such a time, for it is an evil time.

14 Seek (inquire for and require) good and not evil that you may live, and so the Lord, the God of hosts, will be with you, as you have said.

15 Hate the evil and love the good and establish justice in the [court of

speak the Word

a healthy kind of anger

Amos 5:15 tells us to hate what is evil and love what is good. Since the devil is the source of all evil, being angry at him and the devastation he causes can be healthy—if that anger is expressed in a biblical manner. In Ephesians 6:12 we are told that we war against "the world rulers of this present darkness, against the spirit forces of wickedness." So we see that our war is definitely not against God or against people, but against the enemy of our souls. How can anger at the devil be effectively expressed? Let me give you an example from my own personal life.

For many years, I was angry with Satan because of the fifteen years of child abuse I had endured, but I was venting my anger in the wrong way. I became hard-hearted and harsh in dealing with others. I have since learned that we defeat and overcome evil with good (see Romans 12:21).

I was angry at the devil because he had stolen my childhood from me, but my being bitter and resentful was not repaying him for my loss. Now I am preaching the gospel, helping people who are hurting, and seeing countless lives restored. As I do these things I am overcoming the evil Satan did to me by being good to others through bringing the good news of God to them. *This is the way to get back at the devil!*

When you have been hurt, you will be better off if you help someone else. Reaching out to other hurting people helps you forget about your own pain.

The only way to repay the devil for hurt and devastation in your personal life is to aggressively and passionately seek to do the work of Jesus. Hate evil, and be angry with the devil, who causes it; just express that anger in a godly, productive way.

the city's] gate. It may be that the Lord, the God of hosts, will be gracious to the remnant of Joseph [the northern kingdom].

16 Therefore thus says the Lord, the God of hosts, the Lord: There shall be wailing in all the broad ways, and in all the streets they shall say, Alas! Alas! And they shall call the farmers to mourning and such as are skilled in lamentation to wailing.

17 And in all vineyards there shall be wailing, for I will pass through the midst of you, says the Lord.

18 Woe to you who desire the day of the Lord! Why would you want the day of the Lord? It is darkness and not light;

19 It is as if a man fled from a lion and a bear met him, or went into the house and leaned with his hand against the wall and a serpent bit him.

20 Shall not the day of the Lord be darkness, not light? Even very dark with no brightness in it?

21 I hate, I despise your feasts, and I will not smell a savor *or* take delight in your solemn assemblies.

22 Though you offer Me your burnt offerings and your cereal offerings, I will not accept them, neither will I look upon the peace *or* thank offerings of your fatted beasts.

23 Take away from Me the noise of your songs, for I will not listen to the melody of your harps.

24 But let justice run down like waters and righteousness as a mighty *and* ever-flowing stream.

25 Did you bring to Me sacrifices and cereal offerings during those forty years in the wilderness, O house of Israel?

26 [No] but [instead of bringing Me the appointed sacrifices] you carried about the tent of your king Sakkuth and Kaiwan [names for the gods of the planet Saturn], your images of your star-god which you made for yourselves [and you will do so again].

27 Therefore I will cause you to go into exile beyond Damascus, says the Lord, whose name is the God of hosts. [Acts 7:42, 43.]

6 WOE TO those who are at ease in Zion and to those on the mountain of Samaria who are careless *and* feel secure, the notable men of the chief [because chosen by God] of the nations, to whom the house of Israel comes! [Luke 6:24, 25.]

2 Pass over to Calneh and see, and from there go to Hamath the great [city, north of Damascus]; then go down to Gath of the Philistines. Are they better than these [your] kingdoms? Or are their boundaries greater than your boundaries,

3 O you who put far away the evil day [of punishment], yet cause the sitting of violence [upon you] to come near?

4 Woe to those who lie upon beds of ivory and stretch themselves upon their couches, and eat the lambs out of the flock and the calves out of the midst of the stall,

5 Who sing idle songs to the sound of the harp and invent for themselves

instruments of music like David's, [I Chron. 23:5.]

6 Who drink wine in bowls and anoint themselves with the finest oils, but are not grieved *and* sick at heart over the affliction *and* ruin of Joseph (Israel)! [Gen. 49:22, 23.]

7 Therefore now shall they go captive with the first who go into exile, and the revelry *and* banqueting of those who stretch themselves shall be ended.

8 The Lord God has sworn by Himself—the Lord, the God of hosts, says: I abhor, reject, *and* despise the pride *and* false, futile glory of Jacob (Israel), and I hate his palaces *and* strongholds; and I will deliver up the city [idol-worshiping Samaria] with all that is in it.

life point

Amos 6:8 tells us that God hates pride. Pride is a hideous monster that prevents us from asking for help. We want to be self-sufficient and independent. However, God created us in such a way that although we do have strengths, we also have weaknesses and will always need help from Him in those areas. He knows how much we need Him, and He wants us to recognize our need for Him. When we are proud, we do not acknowledge our need for Him, and that keeps Him from blessing us. That is one of the reasons God hates pride.

9 And it shall come to pass that if there remain ten men in one house, they shall die [by the pestilence that comes with war].

10 And then a man's uncle *or*

speak the Word

God, I pray that as Your Word says, justice will run down like waters, and righteousness will run as a mighty and ever-flowing stream.
ADAPTED FROM AMOS 5:24

kinsman, he who is to make a burning to cremate *and* dispose [of his pestilence-infected body], comes in to bring the bones out of the house, and he shall say to another still alive in the farthest parts of the house, Is there anyone else with you? and he shall say, No. Then shall the newcomer say, Hush! Hold your [cursing] tongue! We dare not so mention the name of the Lord [lest we invoke more punishment]. [I Sam. 31:12.]

11 For behold, the Lord commands and He will smite the great house into ruins and the little house into fragments.

12 Do horses run upon rocks? Do men plow the ocean with oxen? But you have turned justice into [the poison of] gall and the fruit of righteousness into [the bitterness of] wormwood—

13 You who rejoice in Lo-debar [a thing of nought], who say, Have we not by our own strength taken Karnaim *or* horns [of resistance] for ourselves?

14 For behold, I will raise up against you a nation, O house of Israel, says the Lord, the God of hosts; and they shall afflict *and* oppress you [to the entire limits of Israel] from the entrance of Hamath to the brook of the Arabah.

7 THUS THE Lord God showed me [Amos], and behold, He formed locusts in the beginning of the shooting up of the second crop, and behold, it was the second crop after the king's mowings.

2 And when [the locusts] had finished eating the plants of the land, then I said, O Lord God, forgive, I pray You. How can Jacob stand? For he is so small!

3 The Lord relented *and* revoked this sentence: It shall not take place, said the Lord [and He was eased and comforted concerning it].

4 Thus the Lord God showed me, and behold, the Lord God called for punishment with fire, and it devoured the great deep and would have eaten up the land.

5 Then said I, O Lord God, cease, I pray You! How can Jacob stand? He is so little!

6 The Lord relented *and* revoked this sentence: This also shall not be, said the Lord [and He was eased and comforted concerning it].

7 Thus He showed me, and behold, the Lord stood upon a wall with a plumb line, with a plumb line in His hand. [II Kings 21:13; Isa. 34:11.]

8 And the Lord said to me, Amos, what do you see? And I said, A plumb line. Then said the Lord, Behold, I am setting a plumb line as a standard in the midst of My people Israel. I will not pass by *and* spare them any more [the door of mercy is shut].

9 And the [idolatrous] high places of Isaac (Israel) shall be desolate and the sanctuaries of Israel shall be laid waste, and I will rise with the sword against the house of King Jeroboam [who set up the golden calf shrines].

putting the Word to work

A plumb line provides a true measure for a vertical line or for depth. Amos is telling the Israelites that God is going to measure them by His standard (see Amos 7:7–9). How do you measure your life? I encourage you to spend time in God's Word, so you can learn about His standards and His promises for your life.

10 Then Amaziah the priest of [the golden calf shrine at] Bethel sent to Jeroboam king of Israel, saying, Amos has conspired against you in the midst of the house of Israel; the land is not able to bear all his words. [I Kings 12:31, 32.]

11 For thus Amos has said, Jeroboam

shall die by the sword and Israel shall surely be led away captive out of his land.

12 Also Amaziah said to Amos, O you seer, go! Flee back to the land of Judah [your own country], and eat your bread and live out your profession as a prophet there [as I perform my duties here].

13 But do not prophesy any more at Bethel, for it is the king's sanctuary and a seat of his kingdom. [Luke 10:10-12.]

14 Then Amos said to Amaziah, I was no prophet [by profession]! Neither was I a prophet's son; [but I had my occupation] I was a herdsman and a dresser of sycamore trees and a gatherer of sycamore figs.

15 And the Lord took me as I followed the flock and the Lord said to me, Go, prophesy to My people Israel.

16 Now therefore listen to the word of the Lord: You say, Do not prophesy against Israel and drop no statements not complimentary to the house of Isaac.

17 Therefore thus says the Lord: Your wife shall be a harlot in the city and your sons and your daughters shall fall by the sword, and your land shall be divided up by line; you yourself shall die in an unclean and defiled land, and Israel shall surely go forth out of his land into exile.

8 THUS THE Lord God showed to me, and behold, a basket of [ripe and therefore soon to perish] summer fruit.

2 And He said, Amos, what do you see? And I said, A basket of summer fruit. Then said the Lord to me, The end has come upon My people Israel; I will not pass by and spare them any more.

3 And the songs of the temple shall become wailings in that day, says the Lord God. The dead bodies shall be many; in every place they shall be cast forth in silence.

4 Hear this, O you who would swallow up and trample down the needy, even to make the poor of the land to fail and come to an end,

5 Saying, When will the New Moon festival be past that we may sell grain? And the Sabbath that we may offer wheat for sale, making the ephah [measure] small and the shekel [measure] great and falsifying the scales by deceit,

6 That we may buy [into slavery] the poor for silver and the needy for a pair of sandals; yes, and sell the refuse of the wheat [as if it were good grade]?

7 The Lord has sworn by [Himself Who is] the Glory and Pride of Jacob, Surely I will never forget any of their [rebellious] deeds.

8 Shall not the land tremble on this account, and everyone mourn who dwells in it? Yes, it shall rise like the river [Nile], all of it, and it shall be tossed about and sink back again to normal level, as does the Nile of Egypt.

9 And in that day, says the Lord God, I will cause the sun to go down at noon, and I will darken the earth in the broad daylight. [Ezek. 32:7-10.]

10 And I will turn your feasts into mourning and all your songs into lamentation, and I will cause sackcloth to be put upon all loins and baldness [for mourning] shall come on every head; and I will make that time as the mourning for an only son, and the end of it as a bitter day.

11 Behold, the days are coming, says the Lord God, when I will send a famine in the land, not a famine of bread, nor a thirst for water, but [a famine] for hearing the words of the Lord.

12 And [the people] shall wander from sea to sea and from the north even to the east; they shall run to and fro to seek the word of the Lord [inquiring for and requiring it as one requires food], but shall not find it.

13 In that day shall the fair virgins and young men faint for thirst.

14 Those who swear by Ashimah *or* the sin of Samaria and say, By the life of your god [the golden calf], O Dan! and [swear], By the life of the way of [idolatrous] Beersheba, they shall fall and rise no more.

9 I SAW the Lord standing at the altar, and He said, Smite the tops of the pillars until the thresholds tremble, and shatter them on the heads of all of the people; and the remainder of them I will slay with the sword. He who flees of them shall not get away, and he who escapes of them shall not be delivered.

2 Though they dig into Sheol (Hades, the dark abode of the gathered dead), from there shall My hand take them; though they climb up to heaven [the abode of light], from there will I bring them down;

3 And though they hide themselves on the top of [Mount] Carmel, from there I will search out and take them; and though they [try to] hide from My sight at the bottom of the sea, there I will command the serpent and it shall bite them.

4 And though they go into captivity before their enemies, there will I command the sword and it shall slay them, and I will set My eyes upon them for evil and not for good.

5 The Lord God of hosts, it is He Who touches the earth and it melts, and all who dwell in it mourn; it shall rise like the [river] Nile, all of it, and it shall sink again like the Nile of Egypt.

6 It is He Who builds His upper chambers in the heavens and Who founds His vault over the earth, Who calls to the waters of the sea and pours them out on the face of the earth—The Lord is His name.

7 You [O degenerate children of Israel] are no more to Me than these [despised] Cushites, says the Lord. I brought up Israel out of the land of Egypt, but have I not [also] brought the Philistines out of Caphtor and the Syrians from Kir?

8 Behold, the eyes of the Lord God are upon the sinful kingdom [of Israel's ten tribes] and I will destroy it from the surface of the ground, except that I will not utterly destroy the house of Jacob, says the Lord.

9 For behold, I will command, and I will sift the house of Israel among all nations *and* cause it to move to and fro as grain is sifted in a sieve, yet shall not the least kernel fall upon the earth *and* be lost [from My sight]. [Lev. 26:33; Deut. 28:64; Hos. 9:17.]

10 All the sinners of My people shall die by the sword, who say, The evil shall not overtake or meet [and assail] us.

11 In that day will I raise up the tabernacle of David, the fallen hut *or* booth, and close up its breaches; and I will raise up its ruins, and I will build it as in the days of old,

12 That they may possess the remnant of Edom and of all the nations that are called by My name, says the Lord Who does this. [Acts 15:15-17.]

13 Behold, the days are coming, says the Lord, that the plowman shall overtake the reaper, and the treader

of grapes him who sows the seed; and the mountains shall drop sweet wine and all the hills shall melt [that is, everything heretofore barren and unfruitful shall overflow with spiritual blessing]. [Lev. 26:5; Joel 3:18.]

14 And I will bring back the exiles of My people Israel, and they shall build the waste cities and inhabit them; and they shall plant vineyards and drink the wine from them; they shall also make gardens and eat the fruit of them.

15 And I will plant them upon their land, and they shall no more be torn up out of their land which I gave them, says the Lord your God.

Obadiah

Author:
Obadiah

Date:
Between the ninth century and the fourth century BC

Everyday Life Principles:
The pride of our hearts does deceive us.

Pride will cause us to mistreat other people.

Judgment comes as a result of mistreating others.

Obadiah is the shortest book in the Old Testament, but it conveys a powerful message that is as valid today as it was when the prophet Obadiah, whose name means "servant of the Lord," wrote it centuries ago. Obadiah prophesied God's judgment against the kingdom of Edom, which was formed by the descendants of Esau. The Edomites were strong people who were enemies of God's people Israel, just as their founder, Esau, had been opposed to his brother, the Israelite patriarch, Jacob. The rivalry between the two brothers extended to their descendants, and the Edomites seemed to take great pleasure in invading and plundering Jerusalem.

Simply put, the Edomites had a problem with pride, just as many nations and individuals do today. Obadiah declared God's warning of destruction to Edom, saying, "Behold, I will make you small among the nations [Edom]; you shall be despised exceedingly. The pride of your heart has deceived you" (Obadiah 2, 3).

In the end, the Edomites' pride did lead to their destruction. God did execute His judgment against them, and these people are never mentioned in Scripture again after the fall of Jerusalem in AD 70.

I hope the message of Obadiah will remind us that pride is deadly. God wants us to live before Him and before others with a humble, tender heart. Pride, whether it is in a nation or in an individual, will not escape God's judgment, but humility brings His blessing and favor.

1 THE VISION of Obadiah. Thus says the Lord God concerning ªEdom: We have heard tidings from the Lord, and an ambassador is sent forth among the nations [saying], Arise, and let us rise up against [Edom] for battle! [Ps. 137:7; Isa. 34:1-15; 63:1-6; Jer. 49:7-22; Ezek. 25:8-14.]

2 Behold, I will make you small among the nations [Edom]; you shall be despised exceedingly. [Ezek. 35.]

3 The pride of your heart has deceived you, you dweller in the refuges of the rock [Petra, Edom's capital], whose habitation is high, who says in his heart, Who can bring me down to the ground?

4 Though you mount on high as the eagle and though you set your nest among the stars, I will bring you down from there, says the Lord.

5 If thieves came to you, if robbers by night—how you are brought to nothing!—would they not steal only enough for themselves? If grape gatherers came to you, would they not leave some grapes for gleaning? [But this ravaging was done by God, not men.] [Jer. 49:9.]

6 How are the things of Esau [Edom] searched out! How are his hidden treasures sought out!

7 All the men of your confederacy (your allies) have brought you on your way, even to the border; the men who were at peace with you have deceived you and prevailed against you; they who eat your bread have laid a snare under you. There is no understanding [in Edom, or] of it.

8 Will not I in that day, says the Lord, destroy the wise men out of Edom and [men of] understanding out

life point

The pride spoken of in Obadiah 3 says, "Who can bring me down?" This kind of pride says, "I am better than you; I am smarter than you. My opinion matters; yours does not. Everything I do is better."

Did you know that "me, myself, and I" are the greatest problems we have? We spend our time and energy admiring ourselves and simply being full of ourselves, when in reality we are supposed to be full of God and empty of ourselves—totally empty.

God can use only humble men and women. I have heard it said that it is yet to be seen what God can do through a man or a woman who will give Him all the glory.

Pride and love do not mix. Love is not proud and haughty. It is not boastful or conceited. It is not puffed up. Love does not look down on others; it does not see others as little and insignificant. Because love values every individual, everyone who comes in contact with a person who is full of love will be made to feel special, valuable, and encouraged.

Do you want God to use you? Ask Him to deal with your pride and give you love for people. Look to your example, Jesus, Who humbled Himself and gave Himself for you.

of Mount Esau [Idumea, a mountainous region]?

9 And your mighty men, O Teman,

---

a Edom, or Seir, was the country southeast of Judah extending from the Dead Sea to the eastern arm of the Red Sea. It included the city of Petra. The country of Moab formed Edom's boundary on the north, and the descendants of Esau constituted its population. Edom and Moab have a remarkably prominent place in prophecy as "the scene of the final destruction of Gentile world power in the day of the Lord," as revealed in the Scripture references accompanying Obad. 1 (which are important for the full, vivid picture of what lies ahead for the nations of the world).

who, me?

Pride is a difficult problem for us to deal with because it hides. As Obadiah 3 says, it deceives us and causes us to think we do not have it. It hides in our thinking, in the deepest recesses of our minds. It will not admit that it is present because it is too proud to do so!

For years, Joyce Meyer Ministries has had teaching resources available on the subject of pride. They are not our best sellers! I believe that is because those people who need them are too proud to admit it and begin getting the help they need. After all, someone might see them or hear about it and wonder if they have a problem with pride!

Luke 18:9–14 describes somebody who was full of pride, and I doubt he even realized it. He was a religious leader who looked down on a tax collector he considered to be lowly and unworthy of God. If we are not careful, the spirit of pride can deceive us in that same way.

Satan wants our minds and attitudes to be filled with pride so he can bring destruction into our lives. Ask God to show you anywhere pride may be hiding in your life and to help you develop the humble attitude He wants you to have.

shall be dismayed, to the end that everyone from Mount Esau will be cut off by slaughter.

10 For the violence you did against your brother Jacob, shame shall cover you, and you shall be cut off forever.

11 On the day that you stood aloof [from your brother Jacob] — on the day that strangers took captive his forces *and* carried off his wealth, and foreigners entered into his gates and cast lots for Jerusalem—you were even as one of them. [Num. 20:18-20; Amos 1:11, 12.]

12 But you should not have gloated over your brother's day, the day when his misfortune came *and* he was made a stranger; you should not have rejoiced over the sons of Judah in the day of their ruin; you should not have spoken arrogantly in the day of their distress.

13 You should not have entered the gate of My people in the day of their calamity *and* ruin; yes, you should not have looked [with delight] on their misery in the day of their calamity *and* ruin, and not have reached after their army *and* their possessions in the day of their calamity *and* ruin.

14 And you should not have stood at the crossway to cut off those of Judah who escaped, neither should you have delivered up those [of Judah] who remained in the day of distress.

15 For the day of the Lord is near upon all the nations. As you have done, it shall be done to you; your dealings will return upon your own head. [Isa. 2:10-22; Zeph. 3:8-20; Zech. 12:1-14; Rev. 19:11-21.]

putting the Word to work

Have you ever been tempted to be glad about someone else's hardship? Clearly this is displeasing to God. When someone near you is facing adversity, extend the same mercy and compassion to him or her as God extends to you.

life point

In Obadiah 17, God expresses through the prophet His desire for His people to be holy—and that comes by the Holy Spirit. The Holy Spirit is in the conviction business and He works out the process of sanctification and holiness in us.

16 For as you [Edom] have drunk upon the mountain of My holiness [desecrating it in the wild revelry of the destroyers], so shall all the nations drink continually [in turn, of My wrath]; yes, they shall drink, talk foolishly, *and* swallow down [the full measure of punishment] and they shall be [destroyed] as though they had not been. [Rev. 16:14-16.]

17 But on Mount Zion [in Jerusalem] there shall be deliverance [for those who escape], and it shall be holy; and the house of Jacob shall possess its [own former] possessions. [Ezek. 36; Joel 2:32.]

18 The house of Jacob shall be a fire and the house of Joseph a flame, but the house of Esau shall be stubble; they shall kindle *and* burn them and consume them, and there shall be no survivor of the house of Esau, for the Lord has spoken it. [Ezek. 25:12-14.]

19 They of the South (the Negeb) shall possess Mount Esau, and they of the lowland the land of the Philistines; they shall possess the land of Ephraim and the fields of Samaria, and Benjamin shall possess Gilead [across the Jordan River]. [Amos 9:12; Zeph. 2:7.]

20 And the exiles of this host of the children of Israel who are among the Canaanites shall possess [Phoenicia] as far as Zarephath, and the exiles of Jerusalem who are in Sepharad shall possess the cities of the South (the Negeb).

21 And deliverers shall go up on Mount Zion to rule *and* judge Mount Esau, and the kingdom *and* the kingship shall be the Lord's. [Zech. 12:8, 9; Mal. 1:2-5; Matt. 24:27-30; Luke 1:31-33; Acts 15:14-17.]

putting the Word to work

Most of us struggle with loss and brokenness in our lives. Has your enemy the devil robbed you of joy? Has he turned your peace into doubt or insecurity? Do you know that God wants to bring healing and restoration to you? Ask God to come into those broken places in your life, and trust Him in His perfect ways and timing to bring wholeness again.

Jonah

Author:
Jonah

Date:
About 760 BC or after 612 BC

Everyday Life Principles:
Whatever God sends you to do, do it without delay.

Remember that you cannot successfully run from God or His call.

God loves everyone and desires to be merciful to every person, city, and nation on earth.

The message of the book of Jonah centers on obedience. God specifically called the prophet Jonah to go and call the people of Nineveh to repentance and announce that God's mercy would follow their repentance. The problem was that Jonah was a devout patriot of Israel, and Nineveh belonged to the Assyrians, who were dreaded and despised enemies of Israel. Jonah was bullish on Israel and did not want to tell the Ninevites that God wanted to be merciful to them, so he tried to run away.

You will read in the book of Jonah that the prophet had to endure all kinds of unpleasant circumstances and hardship as a result of his disobedience. In the end, he finally obeyed God and went to Nineveh. The Ninevites did repent, and God was merciful to them, proving to Jonah that God loves everyone, not just particular races or nationalities.

Let the story of Jonah remind you that God requires obedience. He can wait patiently for us to do as He asks, but we are wise to respond promptly. We can try to run away, but in the end we must obey, or we will be miserable. When God calls us to do something, He is serious. We may not want to do it, but no matter how we resist, He will not change His mind. When He calls you, be quick to obey.

1 NOW THE word of the Lord came to ªJonah son of Amittai, saying,

2 Arise, go to ᵇNineveh, that great city, and proclaim against it, for their wickedness has come up before Me. [Gen. 10:11, 12.]

3 But Jonah rose up to flee to Tarshish from being in the presence of the Lord [as His prophet] and went down to Joppa and found a ship going to Tarshish [the most remote of the Phoenician trading places then known]. So he paid the appointed fare and went down into the ship to go with them to Tarshish from being in the presence of the Lord [as His servant and minister]. [Gen. 4:16; Job 1:12; 2:7.]

life point

In Jonah 1:1–3 we read that God told Jonah to go to Nineveh and preach repentance to the people there. But Jonah did not want to go, so he ran away to Tarshish, a city in the opposite direction from Nineveh. Running from God does not help us to be at peace with Him. If God gives you an assignment, embrace it. If you do not want to do it or if you find it exceedingly difficult, ask Him to help you have the right attitude about it and give you strength to fulfill it.

4 But the Lord sent out a great wind upon the sea, and there was a violent tempest on the sea so that the ship was about to be broken. [Ps. 107:23-27.]

5 Then the mariners were afraid, and each man cried to his god; and they cast the goods that were in the ship into the sea to lighten it for them. But Jonah had gone down into the inner part of the ship and had lain down and was fast asleep.

6 So the captain came and said to him, What do you mean, you sleeper? Arise, call upon your God! Perhaps your God will give a thought to us so that we shall not perish.

7 And they each said to one another, Come, let us cast lots, that we may know on whose account this evil has come upon us. So they cast lots and the lot fell on Jonah.

8 Then they said to him, Tell us, we pray you, on whose account has this evil come upon us? What is your occupation? Where did you come from? And what is your country and nationality?

9 And he said to them, I am a Hebrew, and I [reverently] fear *and* worship the Lord, the God of heaven, Who made the sea and the dry land.

10 Then the men were exceedingly afraid and said to him, What is this that you have done? For the men knew that he fled from being in the presence of the Lord [as His prophet and servant], because he had told them.

11 Then they said to him, What shall we do to you, that the sea may subside *and* be calm for us? For the sea became more and more [violently] tempestuous.

---

a That Jonah was a historical character is evidenced beyond question by the reference to him in II Kings 14:25: "Jeroboam restored Israel's border . . . according to the word of the Lord . . . which He spoke through His servant Jonah son of Amittai, the prophet from Gath-hepher." **b** In spite of the fact that Nineveh is called a "great city" three times in the Old Testament (Gen. 10:11, 12; Jonah 1:2; 3:3) and once in the Apocrypha (Judith 1:1), skeptical Bible critics long believed the statement to be greatly exaggerated. When the walled city was first excavated, it was found to be less than nine miles in circumference. That sparked cynical claims that the author, Jonah, did not know what he was talking about. But the real author, the Holy Spirit, was being overlooked. Later excavations have revealed that Nineveh had many suburbs, three of which are mentioned along with Nineveh in Gen. 10:11, 12. One first-century writer (Diodorus of Sicily) justifiably says that Nineveh was a quadrangle measuring about sixty miles in circuit—a "great city" indeed.

putting the Word to work

Have you ever been tempted to think that disobeying God will not affect anyone but you? Jonah's story paints a very different picture (see Jonah 1:10–16)! By not obeying God, he put the lives of others in jeopardy. In contrast, his later obedience was a blessing to a whole city! When you are tempted to disobey God, remember that you, and others as well, will face consequences. Ask God to help you to obey Him, so that you, like Jonah, can be a blessing to many!

12 And [Jonah] said to them, Take me up and cast me into the sea; so shall the sea become calm for you, for I know that it is because of me that this great tempest has come upon you. 13 Nevertheless the men rowed hard to bring the ship to the land, but they could not, for the sea became more and more violent against them. 14 Therefore they cried to the Lord, We beseech You, O Lord, we beseech You, let us not perish for this man's life, and lay not upon us innocent blood; for You, O Lord, have done as it pleased You. 15 So they took up Jonah and cast him into the sea, and the sea ceased from its raging. 16 Then the men [reverently and worshipfully] feared the Lord exceedingly, and they offered a sacrifice to the Lord and made vows. 17 Now the Lord had prepared and appointed a great fish to swallow up Jonah. And Jonah was in the belly of the fish three days and three nights. [Matt. 12:40.]

2 THEN JONAH prayed to the Lord his God from the fish's belly, 2 And said, I cried out of my distress to the Lord, and He heard me; out of the belly of Sheol cried I, and You heard my voice. [Ps. 120:1; 130:1; 142:1; Lam. 3:55-58.] 3 For You cast me into the deep, into the heart of the seas, and the floods surrounded me; all Your waves and Your billows passed over me. [Ps. 42:7.] 4 Then I said, I have been cast out of Your presence and Your sight; yet I will look again toward Your holy temple. [Ps. 31:22.] 5 The waters compassed me about, even to [the extinction of] life; the abyss surrounded me, the seaweed was wrapped about my head. [Ps. 69:1; Lam. 3:54.] 6 I went down to the bottoms and the very roots of the mountains; the earth with its bars closed behind me forever. Yet You have brought up my life from the pit and corruption, O Lord my God. 7 When my soul fainted upon me [crushing me], I earnestly and seriously remembered the Lord; and my prayer came to You, into Your holy temple.

putting the Word to work

Are you currently in unusual or difficult circumstances? Jonah certainly felt that way in the belly of the whale, yet God was using those circumstances to get his attention. No matter how desperate or hopeless your situation, no matter how far away God seems, know that God hears your prayer and will help you.

speak the Word

Thank You, God, for hearing me in my distress. I know that You hear my voice, no matter where I am.
ADAPTED FROM JONAH 2:2

never too late

What happens when we go in the opposite direction from where God has directed us? What happened to Jonah? Jonah 1 tells us that when he boarded a ship and headed in his own direction, a storm arose. Many of the storms we face in life are the results of our own stubbornness, nothing else. We may try to blame them on other things and people, but the truth is that in many instances, we have been disobedient to the voice and leadership of God.

The violent storm that came upon Jonah frightened the men on the ship, and they knew that they would all die if something did not change. They cast lots to see who was causing the trouble, and the lot fell on Jonah. They asked Jonah what he had done that made God so angry. He knew he had disobeyed God, so he told the men to throw him overboard in order to deliver them from danger. They did as he requested; the storm stopped, and a great fish swallowed Jonah. From the fish's belly (not a pleasant place), he cried out to God for deliverance and repented of his stubborn ways.

Even though Jonah was in a bad place—seaweed was wrapped around his head and the "abyss" surrounded him—he turned to the Lord.

Jonah did the right thing. He did not say to himself, *Well, I've really blown it now. I've disobeyed God so much that there is no turning back*. Instead, Jonah turned to the Lord, praised Him, and expressed faith in His delivering power.

It is never too late for us to pray to God, even when we may have run the opposite direction from Him. God is a God of mercy and grace. He heard Jonah's prayer and spoke to the fish to vomit him out on dry land. While this was not pleasant for Jonah, his life was spared. His story speaks to us that we can never stray so far from God that He cannot hear us. He will respond when we cry out to Him. We will be able to say, as Jonah: "I cried out of my distress to the Lord, and He heard me" (Jonah 2:2).

8 Those who pay regard to false, useless, *and* worthless idols forsake their own [Source of] mercy *and* loving-kindness.

9 But as for me, I will sacrifice to You with the voice of thanksgiving; I will pay that which I have vowed. Salvation *and* deliverance belong to the Lord!

10 And the Lord spoke to the fish, and it vomited out Jonah upon the dry land.

3 AND THE word of the Lord came to Jonah the second time, saying,

2 Arise, go to Nineveh, that great

speak the Word

God, You have brought up my life from the pit. When my soul fainted, I remembered You, and You heard my prayer.
ADAPTED FROM JONAH 2:6, 7

city, and preach *and* cry out to it the preaching that I tell you.

3 So Jonah arose and went to Nineveh according to the word of the Lord. Now Nineveh was an exceedingly great city of three days' journey [sixty miles in circumference].

4 And Jonah began to enter into the city a day's journey, and he cried, Yet forty days and Nineveh shall be overthrown!

5 So the people of Nineveh believed in God and proclaimed a fast and put on sackcloth [in penitent mourning], from the greatest of them even to the least of them.

putting the Word to work

Have you ever needed a second chance? God went to great lengths to give Jonah a second chance, and when Jonah availed himself of the opportunity God gave him, lives were changed for eternity (see Jonah 3:1–5). God is still the God of second chances today! Ask Him for yours, and then be faithful to follow through.

6 For word came to the king of Nineveh [of all that had happened to Jonah, and his terrifying message from God], and he arose from his throne and he laid his robe aside, covered himself with sackcloth, and sat in ashes.

7 And he made proclamation and published through Nineveh, By the decree of the king and his nobles: Let neither man nor beast, herd nor flock, taste anything; let them not feed nor drink water.

8 But let man and beast be covered with sackcloth and let them cry mightily to God. Yes, let every one turn from his evil way and from the violence that is in his hands.

9 Who can tell, God may turn and revoke His sentence against us [when

putting the Word to work

When you share with people about your faith, do you ever feel that your words are falling on deaf ears? Ask God what you are to say to people when you talk with them, and then pray that they will have hearts ready to respond to God as wholeheartedly as the Ninevites did (see Jonah 3:5–10).

we have met His terms], and turn away from His fierce anger so that we perish not. [Joel 2:13, 14.]

10 And God saw their works, that they turned from their evil way; and God revoked His [sentence of] evil that He had said that He would do to them and He did not do it [for He was comforted and eased concerning them].

4 BUT IT displeased Jonah exceedingly and he was very angry.

2 And he prayed to the Lord and said, I pray You, O Lord, is not this just what I said when I was still in my country? That is why I fled to Tarshish, for I knew that You are a gracious God and merciful, slow to anger and of great kindness, and [when sinners turn to You and meet Your conditions] You revoke the [sentence of] evil against them. [Exod. 34:6.]

life point

As Jonah noted in Jonah 4:2, one of God's awesome character traits is mercy. Mercy chooses to be kind and good to people who deserve to be punished. Always remember that God is a merciful God and that, according to Lamentations 3:22, His mercies are new every morning. We may deserve to be punished, but God has extended His mercy through Jesus Christ, and His mercy never runs out!

the God of the second chance

In Jonah 3:1 we see that the word of the Lord came to Jonah a second time, and it was no different from the first time (recorded in Jonah 1:2). God told him to go to Nineveh and preach to the people there. God gave Jonah a second chance.

No matter how long we avoid God's instruction, it is still there for us to deal with when we stop running. Eventually we see that being *in* God's will, not *out* of His will, is what brings peace and joy to us. We have to surrender our own wills because walking in our self-centered ways keeps us unhappy.

Running from difficult things never works in the long term. I know a woman who ran from everything in life that was difficult. She ignored things she needed to deal with, including abuse in her home. She lived in fear and had a very miserable life. She ultimately carried so much turmoil, she had a complete mental and emotional breakdown. Pretending that her problems did not exist did not make them go away. They were there, pressuring her all the time. God was trying to lead her to deal with her conflicts, but she would not trust Him enough to do so.

God never leads us anywhere He cannot keep us. If God is leading you to deal with an unpleasant situation in your life, do not run from it. He promises to be with you at all times and never to leave you or forsake you.

Surrender to God can be frightening when we first begin to practice it because we do not know what the outcome will be if we yield ourselves to God's will. However, once we have surrendered and begin to experience God's faithfulness and the peace that passes understanding, we learn quickly that God's way is better than any plan we could ever devise.

Not knowing exactly what will happen in the future, but trusting God to take care of us and enjoying peace, is far better than erroneously thinking we have life all figured out while continuing to live in fear and anxiety. To enjoy peace with God, we must become comfortable with not always knowing what the future holds.

There is no such thing as trust without unanswered questions. If God is leading you to do something difficult, just begin to take baby steps of faith, and after each one He will show you what to do next. We do not have to have an entire blueprint for the future; we do not need to have all the answers. All we need is to know the One Who knows, and that is Jesus Himself.

3 Therefore now, O Lord, I beseech You, take my life from me, for it is better for me to die than to live.

4 Then said the Lord, Do you do well to be angry?

5 So Jonah went out of the city and sat to the east of the city, and he made a booth there for himself. He sat there under it in the shade till he might see what would become of the city.

6 And the Lord God prepared a gourd and made it to come up over

Jonah, that it might be a shade over his head, to deliver him from his evil situation. So Jonah was exceedingly glad [to have the protection] of the gourd.

7 But God prepared a cutworm when the morning dawned the next day, and it smote the gourd so that it withered.

8 And when the sun arose, God prepared a sultry east wind, and the sun beat upon the head of Jonah so that he fainted and wished in himself to die and said, It is better for me to die than to live.

9 And God said to Jonah, Do you do well to be angry for the loss of the gourd? And he said, I do well to be angry, angry enough to die!

10 Then said the Lord, You have had pity on the gourd, for which you have not labored nor made it grow, which came up in a night and perished in a night.

11 And should not I spare Nineveh, that great city, in which there are more than 120,000 persons not [yet old enough to] know their right hand from their left, and also many cattle [not accountable for sin]?

Micah

Author:
Micah

Date:
Between 704 BC and 696 BC

Everyday Life Principles:
Leaders must practice what they preach.

God does not require strict adherence to rules and regulations; He requires us to practice justice, to be kind and merciful to others, and to live in humility.

Waiting on God is always worth it.

Micah, whose name means "who is like the Lord?" declares in his prophecy that God has no equal, especially when it comes to His compassion and faithfulness. Against that backdrop, Micah calls attention to the poor leadership that prevailed in his day among not only civic authorities, but also among priests and prophets. These leaders did not do as they commanded the people to do, and they failed to honor God as they carried out their responsibilities. Their disregard for God and lack of holiness demanded judgment, but Micah continually contrasts their sin with God's mercy.

Though God's mercy and the importance of good leadership are prevailing themes in Micah, this book also stresses holiness, not tolerating injustice, the importance of practicing what we preach, and the rewards of waiting on God. It also emphasizes God's promise of restoration, reminding us that there are no dead ends in God, that there is always hope.

Perhaps the best-known verse in this book is Micah 6:8, which says: "He has showed you, O man, what is good. And what does the Lord require of you but to do justly, and to love kindness and mercy, and to humble yourself and walk humbly with your God?"

I hope you will learn from the various lessons of the book of Micah. Above all, remember to act justly, to love mercy, and to walk humbly before God and others.

1 THE WORD of the Lord that came to Micah of Moresheth in the days of Jotham, Ahaz, and Hezekiah, kings of Judah, which he saw [through divine revelation] concerning Samaria and Jerusalem.

2 Hear, all you people; listen closely, O earth and all that is in it, and let the Lord God be witness among you *and* against you, the Lord from His holy temple. [I Kings 22:28.]

3 For behold, the Lord comes forth out of His place and will come down and tread upon the high places of the earth. [Zech. 14:3, 4; Mal. 4:2, 3; Matt. 24:27-30; Rev. 1:7; 19:11-16.]

4 And the mountains shall melt under Him and the valleys shall be cleft like wax before the fire, like waters poured down a steep place.

5 All this is because of the transgression of Jacob and the sins of the house of Israel. What is the transgression of Jacob? Is it not [the idol worship of] Samaria? And what are the high places [of idolatry] in Judah? Are they not Jerusalem?

6 Therefore I [the Lord] will make Samaria a ªheap in the open country, a place for planting vineyards; and I will pour down into the ravine her stones and lay bare her foundations. [II Kings 19:25; Ezek. 13:14.]

7 And all her carved images shall be broken in pieces, and all her hires [all that man would gain from desertion of God] shall be burned with fire, and all her idols will be laid waste; for from the hire of [one] harlot she gathered them, and to the hire of [another] harlot they shall return.

8 Therefore I [Micah] will lament and wail; I will go stripped and [virtually] naked; I will make a wailing like the jackals and a lamentation like the ostriches.

9 For [Samaria's] wounds are incurable and they come even to Judah; He [the Lord] has reached to the gate of my people, to Jerusalem.

10 In Gath [a city in Philistia] announce it not; *in* ᵇ*Acco* weep not at all, [betraying your grief to foreigners; but among your own people] in Bethle-aphrah [house of dust] roll yourself in the dust.

11 Pass on your way [into exile], dwellers of Shaphir, in shameful nakedness. The dwellers of Zaanan dare not come forth; the wailing of Beth-ezel takes away from you the place on which it stands.

12 For the inhabitant of Maroth [bitterness] writhes in pain [at its losses] and waits anxiously for good, because evil comes down from the Lord to the gate of Jerusalem.

13 Bind the chariot to the swift steed, O lady inhabitant of Lachish; you were the beginning of sin to the Daughter of Zion, for the transgressions of Israel were found in you.

14 Therefore you must give parting gifts to Moresheth-gath [Micah's home town]; the houses of Achzib [place of deceit] shall be a deception to the kings of Israel.

15 Yet will I bring a conqueror upon you, O lady inhabitant of Mareshah, who shall possess you; the glory *and* nobility of Israel shall come to Adullam [to hide in the caves, as did David]. [I Sam. 22:1.]

16 Make yourself bald in mourning

---

a Samaria was captured by the king of Assyria around 722 BC (II Kings 17:6), and was besieged and demolished by John Hyrcanus around 128 BC In his book *Syria and Palestine,* written in the nineteenth century, Van de Velde, after visiting Sebaste or Samaria, wrote: "Samaria, a heap of stones! Her foundations discovered, her streets plowed up and covered with corn fields and olive gardens! Samaria has been destroyed; her rubbish has been thrown down into the valley; her foundation stones lie scattered about on the slope of the hill." Through the inspiration of the omniscient and omnipotent God, Micah was able to foretell all this more than 2,000 years before. b *The Septuagint* (Greek translation of the Old Testament) suggests this rendering: "in Acco weep not at all." Acco was a coastal city about 25 miles south of Tyre.

and cut off your hair for the children of your delight; enlarge your baldness as the eagle, for [your children] shall be carried from you into exile.

2 WOE TO those who devise iniquity and work out evil upon their beds! When the morning is light, they perform *and* practice it because it is in their power.

2 They covet fields and seize them, and houses and take them away; they oppress *and* crush a man and his house, a man and his inheritance. [Isa. 5:8.]

3 Therefore thus says the Lord: Behold, against this family I am planning a disaster from which you cannot remove your necks, nor will you be able to walk erect; for it will be an evil time.

4 In that day shall they take up a [taunting] parable against you and wail with a doleful *and* bitter lamentation and say, We are utterly ruined *and* laid waste! [God] changes the portion of my people. How He removes it from me! He divides our fields [to the rebellious, our captors].

5 Therefore you shall have no one to cast a line by lot upon a plot [of ground] in the assembly of the Lord. [Rev. 21:27.]

6 Do not preach, say the prophesying false prophets; one should not babble *and* harp on such things; disgrace will not overtake us [the reviling has no end].

7 O house of Jacob, shall it be said, Is the Spirit of the Lord restricted, impatient, *and* shortened? Or are these [prophesied plagues] His doings? Do not My words do good to him who walks uprightly?

8 But lately (yesterday) My people have stood up as an enemy [and have made Me their antagonist]. Off from the garment you strip the cloak of those who pass by in secure confidence of safety *and* are averse to war.

9 The women of My people you cast out from their pleasant houses; from their young children you take away My glory forever.

10 Arise and depart, for this is not the rest [which was promised to the righteous in Canaan], because of uncleanness that works destruction, even a sharp *and* grievous destruction.

11 If a man walking in a spirit [of vanity] and in falsehood should lie and say, I will prophesy to you of wine and strong drink, O Israel, he would even be the acceptable prophet of this people! [Jer. 5:31.]

12 I will surely gather all of you, O Jacob; I will surely collect the remnant of Israel. I will bring them [Israel] together like sheep in a fold, like a flock in the midst of their pasture. They [the fold and the pasture] shall swarm with men *and* hum with much noise.

13 The Breaker [the Messiah] will go up before them. They will break through, pass in through the gate and go out through it, and their King will pass on before them, the Lord at their head. [Exod. 23:20, 21; 33:14; Isa. 63:8, 9; Hos. 3:5; Amos 9:11.]

3 AND I [Micah] said, Hear, I pray you, you heads of Jacob and rulers of the house of Israel! Is it not for you to know justice?—

2 You who hate the good and love the evil, who pluck *and* steal the skin from off [My people] and their flesh from off their bones;

3 Yes, you who eat the flesh of my people and strip their skin from off them, who break their bones and

c Over and again the prophets unveiled the full dimensions of God's judgment and salvation. God must punish His rebellious people but will afterward redeem them. Israel will be carried into captivity, yet a remnant will return. The Messiah, the One who breaks open the way, will lead them back home, and will restore the kingdom of David.

chop them in pieces as for the pot, like meat in a big kettle.

4 Then will they cry to the Lord, but He will not answer them; He will even hide His face from them at that time, because they have made their deeds evil. [Isa. 1:15.]

5 Thus says the Lord: Concerning the false prophets who make My people err, when they have anything good to bite with their teeth they cry, Peace; and whoever gives them nothing to chew, against him they declare a sanctified war.

6 Therefore it shall be night to you, so that you shall have no vision; yes, it shall be dark to you without divination. And the sun shall go down over the false prophets, and the day shall be black over them.

7 And the seers shall be put to shame and the diviners shall blush *and* be confounded; yes, they shall all cover their lips, for there is no answer from God.

8 But truly I [Micah] am full of power, of the Spirit of the Lord, and of justice and might, to declare to Jacob his transgression and to Israel his sin.

9 Hear this, I pray you, you heads of the house of Jacob and rulers of the house of Israel, who abhor *and* reject justice and pervert all equity,

10 Who build up Zion with blood and Jerusalem with iniquity.

11 Its heads judge for reward *and* a bribe and its priests teach for hire and its prophets divine for money; yet they lean on the Lord and say, Is not the Lord among us? No evil can come upon us. [Isa. 1:10-15.]

12 Therefore shall Zion on your

life point

Micah 3:8 tells us that we can be full of power by the Holy Spirit. I believe any common, ordinary, everyday person can be *mightily* used by God. I believe we can do great and mighty things, things that will totally amaze us, if we believe God can use us and if we are daring enough to have uncommon goals and visions. What I mean by "uncommon" is things that we could never do without divine help. Our vision does not always make sense to the mind, but it is solidly planted in our hearts.

Ephesians 3:20 teaches us that God is able to do exceedingly abundantly above and beyond all that we could dare to ask, think, or hope, according to His great power that is at work in us. God does it, but He does it through us, so we need to cooperate with Him. That means we need to be daring in our faith and in our prayers.

Some of us do not believe for enough. We need to stretch our faith into new realms. We need to be people with uncommon goals because we are full of power by the Spirit of the Lord.

account be ᵈplowed like a field, Jerusalem shall become heaps [of ruins], and the mountain of the house [of the Lord] like a densely wooded height. [Jer. 26:17-19.]

4 BUT IN the latter days it shall come to pass that the mountain of the house of the Lord shall be

---

d In his book *The Land and the Book*, Dr. William Thomson wrote, "Mount Zion is now [in the eighteenth century], for the most part, a rough field. From the tomb of David I passed on through the fields of ripe grain. It is the only part of Jerusalem that is now or ever has been plowed." When Sultan Suleiman the Magnificent rebuilt the walls of Jerusalem in AD 1542, the architect omitted Mount Zion, the City of David, from the area he enclosed, and strangely enough it was only partly built up again. How, except by divine inspiration, could Micah have foretold that this particular part of Jerusalem would be "plowed like a field"?

established as the highest of the mountains; and it shall be exalted above the hills, and peoples shall flow to it.

2   And many nations shall come and say, Come, let us go up to the mountain of the Lord, to the house of the God of Jacob, that He may teach us His ways, and we may walk in His paths. For the law shall go forth out of Zion and the word of the Lord from Jerusalem.

3   And He shall judge between many peoples and shall decide for strong nations afar off, and they shall beat their swords into plowshares and their spears into pruning hooks; nation shall not lift up sword against nation, neither shall they learn war any more. [Isa. 2:2-4; Joel 3:10.]

4   But they shall sit every man under his vine and under his fig tree, and none shall make them afraid, for the mouth of the Lord of hosts has spoken it. [Zech. 3:10.]

putting the Word to work

Do you sometimes dread watching the news because of the overwhelming amount of evil we see played out before us? Micah 4:1–4 reminds us that a day is coming when the kingdom of God will be fully established, and injustice, violence, and war will cease. Pray for the nations of the world as you wait for this day to come.

5   For all the peoples [now] walk every man in the name of his god, but we will walk in the name of the Lord our God forever and ever.

6   In that day, says the Lord, I will assemble the lame, and I will gather those who have been driven away and those whom I have afflicted.

7   And I will make the lame a remnant, and those who were cast off a strong nation; and the Lord shall reign over them in Mount Zion from this time forth and forever.

8   And you, O tower of the flock, the hill *and* stronghold of the Daughter of Zion, unto you the former dominion shall come, the kingdom of the Daughter of Jerusalem.

9   Now why do you cry aloud? Is there no king among you? Has your counselor perished, that pains have taken you like a woman in labor?

10 Writhe in pain and labor to bring forth, O Daughter of Zion, like a woman in childbirth; for now you shall go forth out of the city and you shall live in the open country. You shall go to Babylon; there you shall be rescued. There the Lord shall redeem you from the hand of your enemies.

11 Now many nations are assembled against you, saying, Let her be profaned and let our eyes gaze upon Zion.

12 But they know not the thoughts of the Lord, neither do they understand His plan, for He shall gather them as the sheaves to the threshing floor.

13 Arise and thresh, O Daughter of Zion! For I will make your horn iron and I will make your hoofs bronze; you shall beat in pieces many peoples, and I will devote their gain to the Lord and their treasure to the Lord of all the earth. [Zech. 12:1-8; 14:14.]

5 NOW GATHER yourself in troops, O daughter of troops; a state of siege has been placed against us. They shall smite the ruler of Israel with a rod (a scepter) on the cheek.

2   But you, Bethlehem Ephratah, you are little to be among the clans of Judah; [yet] out of you shall One come forth for Me Who is to be Ruler in Israel, Whose goings forth have been from of old, from ancient days (eternity). [Gen. 49:10; Matt. 2:5-12; John 7:42.]

3   Therefore shall He give them up

until the time that she who travails has brought forth; then what is left of His brethren shall return to the children of Israel.

4 And He shall stand and feed His flock in the strength of the Lord, in the majesty of the name of the Lord His God; and they shall dwell [secure], for then shall He be great [even] to the ends of the earth. [Ps. 72:8; Isa. 40:11; Zech. 9:10; Luke 1:32, 33.]

5 And this [One] shall be our peace. When the Assyrian comes into our land and treads upon our soil *and* in our palaces, then will we raise against him seven shepherds and eight princes among men. [Isa. 9:6; Eph. 2:14.]

6 And they shall rule *and* waste the land of Assyria with the sword and the land of Nimrod within her [Assyria's own] gates. Thus shall He [the Messiah] deliver us from the Assyrian [representing the opposing powers] when he comes into our land and when he treads on our borders.

7 Then the remnant of Jacob shall be in the midst of many peoples like dew from the Lord, like showers upon the grass which [come suddenly and] tarry not for man nor wait for the sons of men. [Ps. 72:6; 110:3.]

8 And the remnant of Jacob shall be among the nations in the midst of many peoples like a lion among the beasts of the forest, like a young lion [suddenly appearing] among the flocks of sheep which, when it goes through, treads down and tears in pieces, and there is no deliverer.

9 Your hand will be lifted up above your adversaries, and all your enemies shall be cut off.

10 And in that day, says the Lord, I will cut off your horses [on which you depend] from among you and will destroy your chariots. [Ps. 20:7, 8; Zech. 9:10.]

11 And I will cut off the cities of your land and throw down all your strongholds.

12 And I will cut off witchcrafts *and* sorceries from your hand, and you shall have no more soothsayers.

13 Your carved images also I will cut off and your statues *or* pillars out of your midst, and you shall no more worship the work of your hands.

14 And I will root out your Asherim [symbols of the goddess Asherah] and I will destroy your cities [the seats of false worship]. [Deut. 16:21.]

15 And in anger and wrath I will execute vengeance upon the nations which would not obey [vengeance such as they have not heard of before].

6 HEAR NOW what the Lord says: Arise, contend *and* plead your case before the mountains, and let the hills hear your voice.

2 Hear, O mountains, the Lord's controversy, and you strong *and* enduring foundations of the earth, for the Lord has a controversy (a pleading contention) with His people, and He will [pleadingly] contend with Israel.

3 O My people, what have I done to you? And in what have I wearied you? Testify against Me [answer Me]!

4 For I brought you up out of the land of Egypt and redeemed you out of the house where you were bond servants, and I sent before you Moses, Aaron, and Miriam.

5 O My people, [earnestly] remember now what Balak king of Moab devised and what Balaam the son of Beor answered him; [remember what the Lord did for you] from

speak the Word

Thank You, God, that Jesus, the prophesied Messiah, is my peace.
ADAPTED FROM MICAH 5:5

eShittim to Gilgal, that you may know the righteous *and* saving acts of the Lord. [Num. 23:7-24; 24:3-24; Josh. 3:1; 4:19.]

6 With what shall I come before the Lord and bow myself before God on high? Shall I come before Him with burnt offerings, with calves a year old?

7 Will the Lord be pleased with thousands of rams or with ten thousands of rivers of oil? Shall I give my firstborn for my transgression, the fruit of my body for the sin of my soul?

8 He has showed you, O man, what is good. And what does the Lord require of you but to do justly, and to love kindness *and* mercy, and to humble yourself *and* walk humbly with your God? [Deut. 10:12, 13.]

9 The voice of the Lord calls to the city [Jerusalem]—and it is sound wisdom to hear *and* fear Your name—Hear (heed) the rod and Him Who has appointed it.

10 Are there not still treasures gained by wickedness in the house of the wicked, and a scant measure [a false measure for grain] that is abominable *and* accursed?

11 Can I be pure [Myself, and acquit the man] with wicked scales and with a bag of deceitful weights? [I Thess. 4:6.]

12 For [the city's] rich men are full of violence; her inhabitants have spoken lies and their tongues are deceitful in their mouths.

13 Therefore I have also smitten you with a deadly wound *and* made you sick, laying you desolate, waste, *and* deserted because of your sins.

14 You shall eat but not be satisfied, and your emptiness *and* hunger shall remain in you; you shall carry away [goods and those you love] but fail to save them, and those you do deliver I will give to the sword.

15 You shall sow but not reap; you shall tread olives but not anoint yourselves with oil, and [you shall extract juice from] the grapes but not drink the wine.

16 For the statutes of [idolatrous] Omri you have kept, and all the works of the house of [wicked] Ahab, and you walk in their counsels. Therefore I will make you a desolation *and* an astonishment and your [city's] inhabitants a hissing, and you shall bear the reproach *and* scorn of My people.

7 WOE IS me! For I am as when the summer fruits have been gathered, as when the vintage grapes have been gleaned and there is no cluster to eat, no first-ripe fig for which my appetite craves.

2 The godly man has perished from the earth, and there is none upright among men. They all lie in wait for blood; each hunts his brother with a net.

3 Both their hands are put forth *and* are upon what is evil to do it diligently; the prince and the judge ask for a bribe, and the great man utters his

speak the Word

God, I know what is good and what You require of me: to do justice, to love kindness and mercy, and to humble myself and to walk humbly with You.
ADAPTED FROM MICAH 6:8

---

e God reminds His people of His gracious acts in their behalf—how Balak sought to oppose Israel through pagan divination, sending for Balaam to put a curse on the Israelites; how God saved Israel by causing Balaam to bless instead of curse; and how God later led them across the Jordan River into the promised land, from Shittim (Josh. 3:1) to Gilgal (Josh. 4:19).

God's requirements

What we think God requires of us and what He actually requires can often be very different. We might think God requires us to do a lot of church work or a certain number of good deeds. We might think He requires extreme sacrifices or perfection from us. We might even think He requires us to read the Bible from Genesis to Revelation every year and spend hours each day in prayer and meditation. Although all of these things can be good and have their place, we may do them and still miss what God considers to be important.

His requirements have a lot to do with how we treat people. According to Micah 6:8, we are to do what is just, love mercy and kindness, and walk humbly with our God. God is just, which means that He is always fair and that He works to make wrong things right. We should treat people justly and work to see that justice is done in their lives. Many people have been terribly mistreated and abused, and we have the opportunity as God's representatives to help them enjoy what Jesus died for them to have. We can help restore them to the knowledge of God and His love for them, as well as bringing practical aid and help in areas where it is needed.

God also requires us to love mercy and kindness. We certainly need more kindness and mercy in the world! People do not need to be pressured to perform perfectly; they need to be loved and accepted. It is the goodness of God—not the judgment of God—that leads people to repentance. Our job is not to be faultfinders, but to be dispensers of God's mercy and kindness. God is merciful and kind toward us, and He expects us to give to others what we have received from Him.

Finally, as shown in Micah 6:8, humility is the attitude of heart and mind that God requires of us. Never, under any circumstances, view yourself as better than or above other people. According to Proverbs 6:17 a proud person overestimates himself and underestimates others. If we think more highly of ourselves than we ought, having an exaggerated opinion of our own importance, we will see others as beneath us. This can cause us to have a disrespectful attitude and harsh behavior toward other people, even our family and friends. Strive to give God what He truly requires, which is to do what is just, love mercy and kindness, and walk humbly with Him.

evil desire. Thus they twist between them [the course of justice].

4   The best of them is like a brier; the most upright *or* the straightest is like a thorn hedge. The day of your watchmen, even of [God's] judgment *and* your punishment, has come; now shall be their perplexity *and* confusion.

5   Trust not in a neighbor; put no confidence in a friend. Keep the doors of your mouth from her who lies in your bosom. [Luke 12:51-53.]

6   For the son dishonors the father, the daughter rises up against her mother, the daughter-in-law against her mother-in-law—a man's enemies are the men (members) of his own house. [Matt. 10:21, 35, 36; Mark 13:12, 13.]

7   But as for me, I will look to the

outlast the devil

Your enemy, Satan, may come against you, but when you fall, you will arise (see Micah 7:7, 8)! Make a decision to endure whatever comes against you. That literally means you will outlast the devil. Greater is He Who is in you than he who is in the world (see I John 4:4). You are more than a conqueror through Jesus Christ (see Romans 8:37).

Even during times of intense trouble, believers should live with expectancy. Expect God to work something good out of your situation, and expect Him to bless you even in the presence of your enemies. David said in Psalm 23:5, "You prepare a table before me in the presence of my enemies. You anoint my head with oil; my [brimming] cup runs over." In the midst of trouble, keep a positive attitude and talk about the possibilities, not the problem.

Being positive is very important because it leads to progress or forward motion. We cannot go forward or overcome negative situations unless we choose to be positive. I believe there is something good in everything that happens to us; we just need to look for it. If you are stuck in traffic and in a hurry, you may become frustrated or angry, but the delay might have caused you to avoid being involved in an accident. God may have saved your life!

God hears us when we pray in faith. Put your confidence in Him and expect something good to happen to you. Expect your situation to change for the better, and know that in the meantime, God will use whatever you are going through to help you be a better person in the end. You can choose to let every trial you encounter make you bitter or better. Trials and tribulations are a part of life, and the way we handle them reveals our level of spiritual maturity. Be stable and do not let Satan intimidate you. This will be a sign to him of his impending destruction. Satan cannot do any real harm to a person he cannot manipulate and control. God has a good plan for your life, and He never changes His mind about it. Make a decision right now that you will never give up; once you have made that decision, your victory is sure.

Lord *and* confident in Him I will keep watch; I will wait with hope *and* expectancy for the God of my salvation; my God will hear me.
8 Rejoice not against me, O my enemy! When I fall, I shall arise; when I sit in darkness, the Lord shall be a light to me.
9 I will bear the indignation of the Lord because I have sinned against Him, until He pleads my cause and executes judgment for me. He will

speak the Word

God, I will look to You. Confident in You, I will keep watch. I will wait with hope and expectancy for the God of my salvation. I know that You will hear me. When I fall I will arise; when I sit in darkness You will be a light to me.
ADAPTED FROM MICAH 7:7, 8

putting the Word to work

Micah 7:7 teaches us how to wait. Whether we are sitting in traffic, waiting for an appointment, or waiting in line at the grocery store, waiting is a part of everyday life for most of us. Is it hard for you to wait? When you wait on God, you can wait with hopeful expectation that He hears your every prayer and is working for your good.

bring me forth to the light, and I shall behold His righteous deliverance. [Rom. 10:1-4; 11:23-27.]
10 Then my enemy will see it, and shame will cover her who said to me, Where is the Lord your God? My eyes will see my desire upon her; now she will be trodden down as the mire of the streets.
11 In the day that your walls are to be built [a day for building], in that day shall the boundary [of Israel] be far extended *and* the decree [against her] be far removed. [Isa. 33:17; Amos 9:11.]
12 In that day they will come to you from Assyria and from the cities of Matzor [Egypt] and from Egypt even to the river [Euphrates], from sea to sea and from mountain to mountain.
13 Yet shall the earth be desolate because of those who dwell in it, for the fruit of their doings.
14 Rule *and* feed Your people with

Your rod *and* scepter, the flock of Your inheritance who dwell alone in a forest in the midst of Carmel [a garden land]; they shall feed in Bashan and Gilead, as in the days of old.
15 As in the days of your coming forth from the land of Egypt, I will show them marvelous things.
16 The nations shall see [God's deliverance] and be ashamed of all their might [which cannot be compared to His]. They shall lay their hands upon their mouths in consternation; their ears shall be deaf.
17 They shall lick the dust like a serpent; like crawling things of the earth they shall come trembling out of their strongholds *and* close places. They shall turn *and* come with fear *and* dread to the Lord our God and shall be afraid *and* stand in awe because of You [O Lord]. [Jer. 33:9.]
18 Who is a God like You, Who

putting the Word to work

Do you ever have a hard time forgiving someone? When it is hard to forgive, focus on God's forgiveness and remember His mercy toward you (see Micah 7:18–20). Ask Him to help you let go of your anger, to extend compassion and forgiveness to those who have wronged you. You may not be able to quickly forget the wrong or hurt that you have experienced, but you can quickly forgive, as God does.

speak the Word

Thank You, God, that You do not retain Your anger forever, because You delight in mercy and loving-kindness.
ADAPTED FROM MICAH **7:18**

Thank You, God, for showing Your faithfulness to me and for performing Your promises.
ADAPTED FROM MICAH **7:20**

forgives iniquity and passes over the transgression of the remnant of His heritage? He retains not His anger forever, because He delights in mercy *and* loving-kindness.

19 He will again have compassion on us; He will subdue *and* tread underfoot our iniquities. You will cast all *our* sins into the depths of the sea. [Ps. 103:12.]

20 You will show Your faithfulness *and* perform the sure promise to Jacob and loving-kindness *and* mercy to Abraham, as You have sworn to our fathers from the days of old. [Luke 1:54, 55.]

Nahum

Author:
Nahum

Date:
Shortly before 612 BC

Everyday Life Principles:
God will not tolerate evil forever.

Trouble comes to every life.

God never gives us more than we can bear with His help.

The message of Nahum is that even though evil may seem to prevail for a period of time, God will not tolerate it forever. As we read in Psalm 37:2, evildoers will "be cut down like the grass." Sin is extremely serious; it is not something God ignores or takes lightly, even if it seems to go unpunished for a season. Nahum 1:3 teaches us that the Lord is slow to anger, but He is also great in power. When He does execute His judgment, it is so fierce that nothing can stand against it.

The primary theme of Nahum is God's judgment on the Assyrian city of Nineveh, but it also contains a message of great comfort to the people of Judah. This is appropriate, since it was written by a man whose name, Nahum, means "consolation" or "comfort."

One of the verses of comfort in Nahum is 1:7: "The Lord is good, a Strength and Stronghold in the day of trouble; He knows (recognizes, has knowledge of, and understands) those who take refuge and trust in Him." Even when our enemies seem to prevail and a "day of trouble comes," God will intervene, and He will not give us more than we can bear.

I encourage you to remember that God is your strength and your stronghold when trouble comes, and He knows you intimately if you have put your trust in Him.

1 THE BURDEN *or* oracle (the thing to be lifted up) concerning aNineveh [the capital of Assyria]. The book of the vision of Nahum of Elkosh.

2 The Lord is a jealous God and avenging; the Lord avenges and He is full of wrath. The Lord takes vengeance on His adversaries and reserves wrath for His enemies. [Exod. 20:5.]

3 The Lord is slow to anger and great in power and will by no means clear the guilty. The Lord has His way in the whirlwind and in the storm, and the clouds are the dust of His feet. [Exod. 34:6, 7.]

4 He rebukes *and* threatens the sea and makes it dry, and dries up all the rivers. Bashan [on the east] and Mount Carmel [on the west] wither, and [in the north] the blossom of Lebanon fades.

5 The mountains tremble *and* quake before Him and the hills melt away, and the earth is upheaved at His presence—yes, the world and all that dwell in it.

6 Who can stand before His indignation? And who can stand up *and* endure the fierceness of His anger? His wrath is poured out like fire, and the rocks are broken asunder by Him.

putting the Word to work

Do you know someone, perhaps even yourself, with a quick temper? Those bursts of temper can be frightening, but they are nothing compared to the anger of God as described in Nahum 1:2–6. It is important to recognize that God has been slow to anger in your life, reaching out to you with His mercy, grace, and compassion through Jesus Christ. Although God is merciful and long-suffering, justice ultimately must be satisfied. If we continue in willful sin, God's judgment will eventually come into our lives, but if we admit we are sinners, ask God to forgive us, and receive Jesus Christ as our Savior, we can be spared and enjoy the abundant life He has promised.

7 The Lord is good, a Strength *and* Stronghold in the day of trouble; He knows (recognizes, has knowledge of, and understands) those who take refuge *and* trust in Him. [Ps. 1:6; Hos. 13:5; John 10:14, 27.]

8 But with an boverrunning flood He will make a full end of [Nineveh's very] site and pursue His enemies into darkness.

speak the Word

Lord, I thank You that You are slow to anger and great in power.
ADAPTED FROM NAHUM 1:3

a Under the preaching of Jonah, the king of Nineveh and all its people repented (Jonah 3:5). They must not only have heard his startling testimony of the terrible suffering which running away from obedience to God had cost him, but they must have been terrified at the evidence of the truth of his near-death experience in the belly of the great fish. So the whole city turned to God. But when Nahum came to Nineveh some 150 years later, all that was forgotten, and the later generations had become hopelessly godless. God's wrath was not to be turned away this time. Jonah had been sent to preach, "Repent!" But Nahum's one "burden (the thing to be lifted up)" is the message that Nineveh is to be destroyed—utterly. b Countless authorities confirm the literal accuracy of this reference. Diodorus of Sicily refers to a legend that Nineveh could never be taken until the river became its enemy. Arbaces the Scythian had besieged the city in vain for two years, but in the third year, the river Khoser during a flood season washed away a considerable section of the very great wall, and through this opening the besiegers gained entrance. Nah. 2:6 refers to the devastating flood, and 3:13, 15 probably to the destruction of Nineveh by fire. The vivid descriptions of chapter 3 "are true to their records and their sculptures."

in the day of trouble

What will you do in the "day of trouble" (Nahum 1:7)? I believe we are wise to make up our minds ahead of time concerning what we will do when trouble comes. Let me encourage you to decide to be stable before trouble ever comes. Decide to stay in faith and remain thankful for what God is doing in your life. When difficulties arise, keep praising Him, and do not ever give up.

Do not be surprised by trouble. Jesus said that in the world we would have tribulation and trials (see John 16:33), but we know that He will also strengthen us and enable us to do whatever we need to do in life (see Philippians 4:13). God is our Strength, our Refuge, and our Stronghold in the day of trouble.

God knows those who trust Him, and He already has a plan for our deliverance before our trouble ever begins. The Bible teaches us that we are more than conquerors through Christ, Who loves us (see Romans 8:37). I have thought a lot about what that means, and I believe one way to explain it is to say, "In Christ, we have won the battle before it ever begins." Therefore, we have no reason to be afraid of anything that comes our way.

You may be tempted to think God will not help you in your times of trouble if you have made mistakes or been less than perfect, but that is not true. James 1:5 tells us that if we ask for wisdom in our times of trial, He will help us without faultfinding or reproaching us. Yes, the Lord is good, and, thankfully, our weaknesses cannot change that. He loves us unconditionally and looks for a heart that trusts and loves Him, not for perfect performance. Trust in the Lord with all your heart and mind, and lean not on your own understanding (see Proverbs 3:5). You may not know how your problem will be solved, but as long as you know God and He knows you, then you know all you really need to know.

life point

Nahum 1:7 reminds us that God is good. Goodness is one of His many wonderful character traits. When something is part of an individual's character, we can expect him to always respond in ways that are consistent with that trait. God is good all the time—not just some of the time, *all* the time.

9   What do you devise *and* [how mad is your attempt to] plot against the Lord? He will make a full end [of Nin-eveh]; affliction [which My people shall suffer from Assyria] shall not rise up the second time.
10 For [the Ninevites] are as bundles of thorn branches [for fuel], and even while drowned in their drunken [carousing] they shall be consumed like stubble fully dry [in the day of the Lord's wrath]. [Mal. 4:1.]
11 There is one gone forth out of you [O Nineveh] who plots evil against the Lord, a villainous ᶜcounselor [the king of Assyria, who counsels for wicked-ness and worthlessness]. [II Kings 19:20-23; Isa. 10:5-7; 36:15-20.]

c The reference here may be to Sennacherib, who reigned over Assyria from 705-681 BC.

putting the Word to work

Have you ever seen or visited a castle and been impressed by the strength of its fortifications? Although the city of Nineveh had remarkable protection— immense walls, moats, armed guards, and more—in the face of God's wrath, those defenses drastically failed (see Nahum 1:8). No matter how great the trouble or calamity you face, as one who trusts in God, you are protected by the ultimate Stronghold—the Lord Himself (see Nahum 1:7). His protection will never fail you.

12 Thus says the Lord: Though they be in full strength and likewise many, even so shall [the Assyrians] be cut down when [their evil counselor] shall pass away. Though I have afflicted you [Jerusalem], I will not cause you to be afflicted [for your past sins] any more. [II Kings 19:35-37; John 5:14.]
13 For now will I break his yoke from off you and will burst your bonds asunder. [Isa. 14:25.]
14 And the Lord has given a commandment concerning you [evil Assyrian counselor], that no more of your name shall be born *nor* shall your name be perpetuated. Out of the house of your gods I will cut off the graven and molten images; I will make [their temple] your tomb, for you are vile *and* despised. [Isa. 37:38.]
15 Behold! upon the mountains the feet of him who brings good tidings [telling of the Assyrian's death], who publishes peace! Celebrate your feasts, O Judah; perform your vows. For the wicked counselor [the king of Assyria] shall no more come against you *or* pass through your land; he is utterly cut off. [Isa. 52:7; Rom. 10:15.] [Then the prophet Nahum sarcastically addresses his message to Nineveh:]

2 HE WHO dashes in pieces [that is, the king of Medo-Babylon] is come up before your face [Nineveh]. Keep the fortress *and* ramparts manned, watch the road, gird your loins, collect *and* fortify all your strength *and* power mightily.
2 For the Lord restores the excellency of Jacob as the excellency of [ancient] Israel, for plunderers have plundered them *and* emptied them out and [outrageously] destroyed their vine branches. [Isa. 10:12.]
3 The shields of the mighty men [of Media and Babylon] are [dyed] red; the valiant men are [clothed] in dyed scarlet. The chariots blaze with fire of steel on the day of his preparation [for battle], and the officers' horses prance like a cypress forest [reeling in the wind].
4 The chariots rage in confusion in the streets; they run to and fro [in wild terror] in the broad ways. They flash with steel [making them appear like torches]; they rush [in various directions] like forked lightnings.
5 [The Assyrian leader] remembers *and* summons his bravest men; they stumble in their march. They hasten to the city's wall, and their movable defense shelter is prepared *and* set up.
6 The gates *or* dams of the rivers [surrounding and guarding Nineveh] are opened and the [imperial] palace

putting the Word to work

Do you remember the last time you received good news? Just as the bearer of good news in Nahum 1:15 brought word of deliverance from the tyranny of the enemy, the good news of the gospel of Jesus Christ was delivered to you. You too have been set free from the enemy! Ask God to show you people to whom you can deliver this good news, that they too might enjoy freedom from the enemy and new life in Christ!

[of sun-dried brick] is dissolved [by the torrents] *and* is in dismay.

7 It is decreed. She [Nineveh] is stripped and removed, and her maids are lamenting *and* moaning like doves [softly for fear], beating upon their breasts [and hearts].

8 And Nineveh, like a standing pool are her waters and [her inhabitants] are fleeing away! Stand! Stand [firm! a few cry], but no one looks back *or* causes them to return.

9 Take the spoil of silver; take the spoil of gold! For there is no end of the treasure, the glory *and* wealth of all the precious furnishings.

10 Emptiness! Desolation! Utter waste! Hearts faint and knees smite together, and anguish is in all loins, and the faces of all grow pale! [Isa. 13:7, 8.]

11 Where is the den of the lions which was the feeding place of the young lions, where the lion and the lioness walked, and the lion's whelp, and none made them afraid?

12 The lion tore in pieces enough for his whelps and strangled [prey] for his lionesses; he filled his caves with prey and his dens with what he had seized *and* carried off.

13 Behold, I am against you [Nineveh], says the Lord of hosts, and I will burn *your* chariots in the smoke, and the sword shall devour your young lions. And I will cut off your prey from the earth, and the voice of your messengers shall no more be heard.

3 WOE TO the bloody city! It is full of lies and booty and [there is] no end to the plunder! [Ezek. 24:6, 9, 10; Hab. 2:12.]

2 The cracking of the whip, the noise of the rattling of wheels, and prancing horses and chariots rumbling *and* bounding,

3 Horsemen mounting *and* charging, the flashing sword, the gleaming spear, a multitude of slain and a great number of corpses, no end of corpses! [The horsemen] stumble over the corpses!

4 All because of the multitude of the harlotries [of Nineveh], the well-favored harlot, the mistress of deadly charms who betrays *and* sells nations through her whoredoms [idolatry] and peoples through her enchantments.

5 Behold, I am against you, says the Lord of hosts, and I will lift up your skirts over your face, and I will let the nations look on your nakedness [O Nineveh] and the kingdoms on your shame.

6 I will cast abominable things at you *and* make you filthy, treat you with contempt, and make you a gazingstock.

7 And all who look on you will shrink *and* flee from you and say, Nineveh is laid waste; who will pity *and* bemoan her? Where [then] shall I seek comforters for you?

8 Are you better than No-amon [Thebes, capital of Upper Egypt], that dwelt by the rivers *or* canals, that had the waters round about her, whose rampart was a sea [the Nile] and water her wall?

9 Ethiopia and Egypt were her strength, and that without limit. Put and the Libyans were *her* helpers.

10 Yet she was carried away; she went into captivity. Her young children also were dashed in pieces at all the street corners; lots were cast [by the Assyrian officers] for her nobles, and all her great men were bound with chains.

11 You will be drunk [Nineveh, with the cup of God's wrath]; you will be dazed. You will seek *and* require a refuge because of the enemy.

12 All your fortresses are fig trees with early figs; if they are shaken they will fall into the mouth of the eater.

13 Behold, your troops in the midst of you are [as weak and helpless as]

women; the gates of your land are set wide open to your enemies [without effort]; fire consumes your bars.

14 Draw for yourself the water [necessary] for a [long continued] siege, make strong your fortresses! Go down into the clay pits and trample the mortar; make ready the brickkiln [to burn bricks for the bulwarks]!

15 [But] there [in the very midst of these preparations] will the fire devour you; the sword will cut you off; it will destroy you as the locusts [destroy]. Multiply yourselves like the licking locusts; make yourselves many like the swarming locusts!

16 You increased your merchants more than the [visible] stars of the heavens. The swarming locust spreads itself *and* destroys, and then flies away.

17 Your princes are like the grasshoppers and your marshals like the swarms of locusts which encamp in the hedges on a cold day—but when the sun rises, they fly away, and no one knows where they are.

18 Your shepherds are asleep, O king of Assyria; your nobles are lying still [in death]. Your people are scattered on the mountains and there is no one to gather them.

19 There is no healing of your hurt; your wound is grievous. All who hear the news about you clap their hands over [what has happened to] you. For upon whom has not your [unceasing] evil come continually?

Habakkuk

Author:
Habakkuk

Date:
Probably between 612 BC and 586 BC

Everyday Life Principles:
Remember that righteous people live by faith.

God always does what is right.

God will give us opportunities to grow.

The book of Habakkuk was written as a dialogue, or conversation, between God and the prophet Habakkuk. In the beginning of this book, Habakkuk is overwhelmed by the devastation that surrounds him. He cannot seem to get his focus off his circumstances and the bad things that are happening in his country.

In Habakkuk 2, God tells Habakkuk that righteous people live by faith and that even in the midst of suffering, oppression, and destruction, the righteous know and trust that God is doing what is right.

One of the verses many people know from Habakkuk is 3:19, which says: "The Lord God is my Strength, my personal bravery, and my invincible army; He makes my feet like hinds' feet and will make me to walk [not to stand still in terror, but to walk] and make [spiritual] progress upon my high places [of trouble, suffering, or responsibility]!"

As you read the book of Habakkuk, be reminded that God is your very own invincible army and that He is helping you make spiritual progress by giving you opportunities to grow, which may include trouble, suffering, or responsibility, but which are designed to make you stronger. No matter what happens around you or in your own life, live by faith and trust God to do what is right.

1 THE BURDEN *or* oracle (the thing to be lifted up) which Habakkuk the prophet saw.

2 O Lord, how long shall I cry for help and You will not hear? Or cry out to You of violence and You will not save?

3 Why do You show me iniquity *and* wrong, and Yourself look upon *or* cause me to see perverseness *and* trouble? For destruction and violence are before me; and there is strife, and contention arises.

4 Therefore the law is slackened and justice *and* a righteous sentence never go forth, for the [hostility of the] wicked surrounds the [uncompromisingly] righteous; therefore justice goes forth perverted.

5 Look around [you, Habakkuk, replied the Lord] among the nations and see! And be astonished! Astounded! For I am putting into effect a work in your days [such] that you would not believe it if it were told you. [Acts 13:40, 41.]

6 For behold, I am rousing up the Chaldeans, that bitter and impetuous nation who march through the breadth of the earth to take possession of dwelling places that do not belong to them. [II Kings 24:2.]

7 [The Chaldeans] are terrible and dreadful; their justice and dignity proceed [only] from themselves.

8 Their horses also are swifter than leopards and are fiercer than the evening wolves, and their horsemen spread themselves *and* press on proudly; yes, their horsemen come from afar; they fly like an eagle that hastens to devour.

9 They all come for violence; their faces turn eagerly forward, and they gather prisoners together like sand.

10 They scoff at kings, and rulers are a derision to them; they ridicule every stronghold, for they heap up dust [for earth mounds] and take it.

11 Then they sweep by like a wind and pass on, and they load themselves with guilt, [as do all men] whose own power is their god.

12 Are not You from everlasting, O Lord my God, my Holy One? We shall not die. O Lord, You have appointed [the Chaldean] to execute [Your] judgment, and You, O Rock, have established him for chastisement *and* correction. [Deut. 32:4.]

13 You are of purer eyes than to behold evil and can not look [inactively] upon injustice. Why then do You look upon the plunderer? Why are you silent when the wicked one destroys him who is more righteous than [the Chaldean oppressor] is?

14 Why do You make men like the fish of the sea, like reptiles *and* creeping things that have no ruler [and are defenseless against their foes]?

15 [The Chaldean] brings all of them

putting the Word to work

When you see evidence of violence and injustice in the world, do you ever wonder why God does not put a stop to such evils? Habakkuk asked God such questions, and found that God answered him in unexpected ways (see Habakkuk 1:2–6). God wants us to bring our questions to Him, but we may not always get the answers we expect. We can, however, always trust that God's ways are best, even when we do not fully understand them.

speak the Word

God, I know that You are of purer eyes than to behold evil and that You cannot look inactively upon injustice.
ADAPTED FROM HABAKKUK 1:13

up with his hook; he catches and drags them out with his net, he gathers them in his dragnet; so he rejoices and is in high spirits.

16 Therefore he sacrifices [offerings] to his net and burns incense to his dragnet, because from them he lives luxuriously and his food is plentiful *and* rich.

17 Shall he therefore continue to empty his net and mercilessly go on slaying the nations forever?

2 [OH, I know, I have been rash to talk out plainly this way to God!] I will [in my thinking] stand upon my post of observation and station myself on the tower *or* fortress, and will watch to see what He will say within me and what answer I will make [as His mouthpiece] to the perplexities of my complaint against Him.

2 And the Lord answered me and said, Write the vision and engrave it so plainly upon tablets that everyone who passes may [be able to] read [it easily and quickly] as he hastens by.

3 For the vision is yet for an appointed time and it hastens to the end [fulfillment]; it will not deceive *or* disappoint. Though it tarry, wait [earnestly] for it, because it will surely come; it will not be behindhand on its appointed day. [Heb. 10:37, 38.]

4 Look at the proud; his soul is not

straight *or* right within him, but the [rigidly] just *and* the [uncompromisingly] righteous man shall [a]live by his faith *and* in his faithfulness. [Rom. 1:17; Gal. 3:11.]

5 Moreover, wine *and* [b]wealth are treacherous; the proud man [the Chaldean invader] is restless *and* cannot stay at home. His appetite is large like that of Sheol and [his greed] is like death and cannot be satisfied; he gathers to himself all nations and collects all people as if he owned them.

6 Shall not all these [victims of his greed] take up a taunt against him and in scoffing derision of him say, Woe to him who piles up that which is not his! [How long will he possess it?] And [woe to him] who loads himself with promissory notes for usury!

7 Shall [your debtors] not rise up

a There is a curious passage in the Talmud [the body of Jewish civil and religious law] which says that Moses gave six hundred injunctions to the Israelites. As these commands might prove too numerous to commit to memory, David brought them down to eleven in Psalm 15. Isaiah reduced these eleven to six in [his] chapter 33:15. Micah (6:8) further reduced them to three; and Isaiah (56:1) once more brought them down to two. These two Amos (5:4) reduced to one. However, lest it might be supposed from this that God could be found only in the fulfillment of the law, Habakkuk (2:4 KJV) said, "The just shall live by his faith" (William H. Saulez, *The Romance of the Hebrew Language*). **b** *The Dead Sea Scrolls* read "wealth."

discovering your vision

Do you know what God's will is for you? Do you have a vision? Do you know what you are going to do with your life? You should! Having a vision for your life is very important, as God's Word declares in Habakkuk 2:2, 3.

When young people start out in life, they may not know what their futures are going to hold. There is nothing wrong with that because many times God unfolds His plan as we start to move in a direction and trust Him to lead. What young people need to do is to seek God's plans for their lives and then write down what they believe God is saying to them. As they begin to move in a certain direction, what they are supposed to do with their lives will become increasingly clear.

People who are older should have figured out their purposes in life. However, many of them still do not know what they want to be when they "grow up" because issues in their lives have blocked the formation of their vision.

Too many people concentrate on what they cannot do. They focus on everything they do wrong and never on what they do right. They get so caught up in their mistakes and inabilities that they lose sight of the fact that we serve a great God. If this is you, I encourage you to study Hebrews 12:2. This verse tells you to look away from the things that distract you and focus on Jesus. Even if you are being sidetracked by your own inabilities and weaknesses, stop looking at those things and start looking up to Jesus. If you believe you can do only one thing, make up your mind that you are going to do that one thing well. Decide that you are going to be the best you can be at that one thing.

Take an inventory of your life and decide what you have that you can use to fulfill God's purpose for you. What are you doing with your time, your energy, and your abilities? Stop looking at what you do not have and begin using what you do have.

Become a person of purpose. Know why you are doing what you are doing. Make sure you do not lose sight of your goals. In order to do that, you may need to heed the advice of Habakkuk: write your vision and make it plain!

suddenly who shall bite you, exacting usury of you, and those awake who will vex you [toss you to and fro and make you tremble violently]? Then you will be booty for them.

8 Because you [king of Babylon] have plundered many nations, all who are left of the people shall plunder you—because of men's blood and for the violence done to the earth, to the city and all the people who live in each city.

9 Woe to him who obtains wicked gain for his house, [who thinks by so doing] to set his nest on high that he may be preserved from calamity *and* delivered from the power of evil!

10 You have devised shame to your house by cutting off *and* putting an end to many peoples, and you have sinned against *and* forfeited your own life.

11 For the stone shall cry out of the wall [built in sin, to accuse you], and the beam out of the woodwork will answer it [agreeing with its charge against you].

12 Woe to him who builds a town

life point

Habakkuk 2:3 speaks of an "appointed time" for a vision to come to pass. "Appointed time" simply means that God knows the time is right. We must humble ourselves and our ideas to His wisdom and power; and we must trust Him when He says He will not be late.

"Appointed time" also means a time already established and decided for certain reasons. It is like having an appointment. We cannot have access to a doctor, a dentist, or a mechanic until our appointment time has come. Similarly, God has "appointments" for specific things in our lives. Those things will happen at their appointed times; they will not be early, but they will not be even one minute late. Be encouraged. God will keep the appointments He has for you!

putting the Word to work

Have you ever been tempted to cheat on your taxes or to not be completely honest in your business practices (see Habakkuk 2:9, 10)? While such actions may bring short-term gain, they lead to shame and seriously damage your relationships with others and God. Be intentional about acting with integrity and honesty in your business practices.

with blood and establishes a city by iniquity!

13 Behold, is it not by appointment of the Lord of hosts that the nations toil only to satisfy the fire [that will consume their work], and the peoples weary themselves only for emptiness, falsity, and futility?

14 But [the time is coming when] the earth shall be filled with the knowledge of the glory of the Lord as the waters cover the sea. [Isa. 11:9.]

15 Woe to him who gives his neighbors drink, who pours out your bottle to them and adds to it your poisonous and blighting wrath and also makes them drunk, that you may look on their stripped condition and pour out foul shame [on their glory]!

16 You [yourself] will be filled with shame and contempt instead of glory. Drink also and be like an uncircumcised [heathen]! The cup [of wrath] in the Lord's right hand will come around to you [O destroyer], and foul

shame shall be upon your own glory! [Rev. 16:19.]

17 For the violence done to Lebanon will cover and overwhelm you; the destruction of the animals [which the violence frightened away] will terrify you on account of men's blood and the violence done to the land, to the city and all its inhabitants.

18 What profit is the graven image when its maker has formed it? It is only a molten image and a teacher of lies. For the maker trusts in his own creations [as his gods] when he makes dumb idols.

19 Woe to him who says to the wooden image, Awake! and to the dumb stone, Arise, teach! [Yet, it cannot, for] behold, it is laid over with gold and silver and there is no breath at all inside it!

20 But the Lord is in His holy temple; let all the earth hush and keep silence before Him. [Zeph. 1:7; Zech. 2:13.]

3 A PRAYER of Habakkuk the prophet, set to wild, enthusiastic, and triumphal music.

2 O Lord, I have heard the report of You and was afraid. O Lord, revive Your work in the midst of the years, in the midst of the years make [Yourself] known! In wrath [earnestly] remember love, pity, and mercy.

3 God [approaching from Sinai] came from Teman [which represents Edom] and the Holy One from Mount

life point

Habakkuk 2:20 instructs us to "keep silence" before the Lord. I believe that sitting silently in God's presence is a type of prayer and is one aspect of what we define as "waiting on God." Waiting is a vital part of prayer, and learning to wait on the Lord is extremely important. Prayer is not talking to God all the time—it is also listening to Him, which may require waiting. Take time today to be quiet before God and to wait on Him to speak to you.

Paran [in the Sinai region]. Selah [pause, and calmly think of that]! His glory covered the heavens and the earth was full of His praise.

life point

In Habakkuk 3:2, the prophet prays for God to remember mercy in the midst of His wrath.

Some people cannot appreciate God's mercy until they have experienced a bit of His wrath. It is important for us to understand that God is never wrathful against His people personally; He directs His anger toward the sin in their lives. He hates sin, and we must learn to hate it also. Like God, we must hate sin but love the sinner.

If we do not receive God's mercy for our sins and failures, we will not have any mercy to give to others when they fail us and disappoint us. We cannot lead people into powerful relationships with the Lord through harshness, hardness, rigidity, and legalism. We must show them that the God we serve is merciful, patient, and long-suffering. In His wrath, He does remember mercy.

4 And His brightness was like the sunlight; rays streamed from His hand, and there [in the sunlike splendor] was the hiding place of His power.
5 Before Him went the pestilence [as in Egypt], and burning plague followed His feet [as in Sennacherib's army]. [Exod. 7:2-4; II Kings 19:32-35.]
6 He stood and measured the earth; He looked and shook the nations, and the eternal mountains were scattered and the perpetual hills bowed low. His ways are everlasting *and* His goings are of old.
7 I [Habakkuk, in vision] saw the tents of Cushan [probably Ethiopia] in affliction; the [tent] curtains of the land of Midian trembled.
8 Were You displeased with the rivers, O Lord? Or was Your anger against the rivers [You divided]? Was Your wrath against the [Red] Sea, that You rode [before] upon Your horses and Your chariots of victory *and* deliverance?
9 Your bow was made quite bare; sworn to the tribes [of Israel] by Your sure word were the rods of chastisement, scourges, *and* calamities. Selah [pause, and calmly think of that]!

life point

The prophet proclaims in Habakkuk 3:18 that he *will* rejoice in God. Similarly, the psalmist said, "This is the day which the Lord has brought about; we will rejoice and be glad in it" (Psalm 118:24). I believe the psalmist had chosen to rejoice, and he was establishing this attitude not only for himself but also for everyone who wanted to listen.

Joy is not just a feeling; it is a decision. We can decide to declare: "God has given me this day. And if He has decided to let me breathe another day, then I am going to enjoy it." Choose today, like Habakkuk and the psalmist, to rejoice!

With rivers You cleaved the earth [bringing forth waters in dry places]. [Exod. 17:6; Num. 20:11.]
10 The mountains saw You; they trembled *and* writhed [as if in pain]. The overflowing of the water passed by [as at the deluge]; the deep uttered its voice and lifted its hands on high.
11 The sun and moon stood back [as before Joshua] in their habitation at the light of Your arrows as they sped, at the flash of Your glittering spear. [Josh. 10:12, 13.]

12 You marched through the land in indignation; You trampled *and* threshed the nations in anger.
13 You went forth *and* have come for the salvation of Your people, for the deliverance *and* victory of Your anointed [people Israel]; You smote the head of the house of the wicked, laying bare the foundation even to the neck. Selah [pause, and calmly think of that]!
14 You pierced with his own arrows the head of [the enemy's] hordes; they came out as a whirlwind to

the Lord is your strength

What shall we do when everything in life seems to be going wrong? What if we have several problems all at one time, like the situation mentioned in Habakkuk 3:17? Perhaps you are having problems in any number of areas: your children, your marriage, your finances, your health, your job, your neighbors, or your mind and emotions. If so, I am sure you need to be encouraged.

God promises to be your Strength. He is the God of our salvation. That means He delivers us and provides a way out of the troubles in which we find ourselves. It is important to keep rejoicing even in times of trouble, because the joy of the Lord is our strength (see Nehemiah 8:10). Depression, discouragement, and despair only weaken us, but being positive and finding something to rejoice about adds energy to our lives. Even if you cannot find something to rejoice about, you can rejoice over your relationship with the Lord. *He* is your joy, not your circumstances.

When we trust in God, He enables us to make spiritual progress even during times of trouble. Through Him we can keep on walking forward. I have said in the past, "Keep on walking when the devil is stalking." Satan's favorite tool to use against God's children is fear. Fear immobilizes us if we let it, and it prevents us from making progress. But thank God that in Him we can still make progress even in times that are hard to endure.

We tend to think that the highest place to be is on the mountaintop with no problems and everything going our way, but that is not true according to God's Word. He says that our high places are trouble, suffering, and responsibility, and He promises that He will give us hinds' feet. A hind is a type of mountain goat that can leap about freely on the rocky, difficult slopes. Hinds climb mountains with seemingly no effort at all because of the way God has made them.

Look to God as your Strength, and trust Him to help you make progress during trouble.

scatter me [the people], rejoicing as if to devour the poor [Israel] secretly.

15 You have trodden the sea with Your horses, [beside] the heap of great *and* surging waters. [Exod. 15:8.]

16 I heard and my [whole inner self] trembled; my lips quivered at the sound. Rottenness enters into my bones and under me [down to my feet]; I tremble. I will wait quietly for the day of trouble and distress when there shall come up against [my] people him who is about to invade *and* oppress them.

17 Though the fig tree does not blossom and there is no fruit on the vines, [though] the product of the olive fails and the fields yield no food, though the flock is cut off from the fold and there are no cattle in the stalls,

18 Yet I will rejoice in the Lord; I will exult in the [victorious] God of my salvation! [Rom. 8:37.]

19 The Lord God is my Strength, my personal bravery, *and* my invincible army; He makes my feet like hinds' feet and will make me to walk [not to stand still in terror, but to walk] *and*

life point

Whatever obstacles you may have right now in your life, I encourage you to go through them and not give up!

Habakkuk 3:19 says that we need to allow our difficulties to help us develop "hinds' feet." When we have hinds' feet, we will not stand still in terror in the face of our problems. Instead, we will walk and make progress through our trouble, suffering, responsibility, or whatever is trying to hold us back.

It is easy to quit in hard times; it takes faith to go through those hard times. Know that God wants to be with you to help you make spiritual progress. He wants to strengthen you and encourage you to "keep on keeping on" through the storms of your life.

make [spiritual] progress upon my high places [of trouble, suffering, or responsibility]!

For the Chief Musician; with my stringed instruments.

Zephaniah

Author:
Zephaniah

Date:
About 630 BC

Everyday Life Principles:
God is the God of history.

After repentance comes restoration.

God is singing over you.

One of Zephaniah's key themes is that God is the God of history—and that He has always been and will always be deeply involved in human affairs. Like other Old Testament prophets, Zephaniah recognized the sin that surrounded him. Specifically, his prophecy was a message of impending judgment against Judah, Jerusalem, and surrounding nations. He urged repentance, knowing that sin demands judgment; and He knew that God was merciful and eager to forgive. He believed that God would always have a remnant of faithful people who would seek Him, who would go after Him with all their might. Zephaniah knew that God's wrath is severe; but he also knew that God's love is awesome.

Zephaniah gives us a beloved Old Testament verse, one that has encouraged people in God's love for generations: "The Lord your God is in the midst of you, a Mighty One, a Savior [Who saves]! He will rejoice over you with joy; He will rest [in silent satisfaction] and in His love He will be silent and make no mention [of past sins, or even recall them]; He will exult over you with singing" (Zephaniah 3:17).

I urge you to learn from Zephaniah that repentance is the only appropriate response to sin and that restoration follows. I also encourage you to remember that no matter what happens in life, God loves you and is always singing over you.

1 THE WORD of the Lord which came to Zephaniah son of Cushi, the son of Gedaliah, the son of Amariah, the son of Hezekiah, in the days of Josiah king of Judah and son of Amon.

2 By taking away I will make an end *and* I will utterly consume *and* sweep away all things from the face of the earth, says the Lord.

3 I will consume *and* sweep away man and beast; I will consume *and* sweep away the birds of the air and the fish of the sea. I will overthrow the stumbling blocks (the idols) with the wicked [worshipers], and I will cut off mankind from the face of the earth, says the Lord.

4 I will also stretch out My hand over Judah and over all the inhabitants of Jerusalem, and I will cut off the remnant of Baal from this place and the name of the idol priests with the [false] priests,

5 And those who worship the starry host of the heavens upon their housetops and those who [pretend to] worship the Lord and swear by *and* to Him and yet swear by *and* to [the heathen god Molech or] Malcam [their idol king],

6 And those who have drawn back from following the Lord and those who have not sought the Lord nor inquired for, inquired of, *and* required the Lord [as their first necessity].

7 [Hush!] Be silent before the Lord God, for the day [of the vengeance] of the Lord is near; for the Lord has prepared a sacrifice, and He has set apart [for His use] those who have accepted His invitation. [Hab. 2:20.]

8 And on the day of the Lord's sacrifice, I will punish the officials and the king's sons and all who are clothed in [lavish] foreign apparel [instead of the Jewish dress, with its reminders to obey God's commandments]. [Num. 15:38, 39.]

9 In the same day also will I punish all those who leap swiftly on *or* over the threshold [upon entering houses to steal], who fill their master's house with violence and deceit *and* fraud.

10 And in that day, says the Lord, there shall be heard the voice of crying from the Fish Gate [in the wall of Jerusalem] and a wailing from the Second Quarter *or* Lower City and a great crashing *and* sound of destruction from the hills.

11 Wail, you inhabitants of the Mortar [those located in the hollow part of the city]! For all the merchant people, like the people of Canaan, will be silent [entirely destroyed]; all those who weighed out silver *and* were loaded with it will be cut off.

12 And at that time I will search Jerusalem with lamps and punish the men who [like old wine] are thickening *and* settling on their lees, who say in their hearts, The Lord will not do good, nor will He do evil.

13 And their wealth shall become plunder and their houses a desolation. Though they build houses, they shall not inhabit them; though they plant vineyards, they shall not drink the wine from them. [Deut. 28:30, 39; Amos 5:11, 12.]

14 The great day of the Lord is near—near and hastening fast. Hark! the voice of the day of the Lord! The mighty man [unable to fight or to flee] will cry then bitterly.

15 That day is a day of wrath, a day of distress and anguish, a day of ruin

putting the Word to work

Have you ever heard someone say, "All religions are alike; it doesn't really matter what you believe," or something like that? The truth is that it *does* matter whom you believe in, and Zephaniah 1:4–6 illustrates that following and worshipping God alone is what is acceptable.

putting the Word to work	putting the Word to work

Although we do not know the specific time, the day of God's judgment is coming, and Zephaniah 1:14 helps us understand how terrible that day will be. Do you regularly pray for people who do not yet know God and salvation in Jesus Christ? Let me encourage you to do so.

Many people are driven by the pursuit of money, convinced that it is both necessary for fulfillment in life and also the ultimate protection against calamity, but that is not true (see Zephaniah 1:18).

Do you invest more time and effort in pursuing money or intimacy with God? While making a living is admirable, remember that it is your relationship with God that brings the greatest reward and the ultimate security.

and devastation, a day of darkness and gloom, a day of clouds and thick darkness, [Jer. 30:7; Joel 2:11; Amos 5:18.]

16 A day of the blast of trumpet and battle cry against the fortified cities and against the high towers *and* battlements.

17 And I will bring distress upon men, so that they shall walk like blind men, because they have sinned against the Lord; their blood shall be poured out like dust and their flesh like dung.

18 Neither their silver nor their gold shall be able to deliver them in the day of the Lord's indignation *and* wrath. But the whole earth shall be consumed in the fire of His jealous [a]wrath, for a full, yes, a sudden, end will He make of all the inhabitants of the earth. [Luke 21:35, 36; II Pet. 3:10-13.]

2 COLLECT YOUR thoughts, yes, unbend yourselves [in submission and see if there is no sense of shame and no consciousness of sin left in you], O shameless nation [not desirous or desired]!

speak the Word

2 [The time for repentance is speeding by like chaff whirled before the wind!] Therefore consider, before God's decree brings forth [the curse upon you], before the time [to repent] is gone like the drifting chaff, before the fierce anger of the Lord comes upon you—yes, before the day of the wrath of the Lord comes upon you!

3 Seek the Lord [inquire for Him, inquire of Him, and require Him as the foremost necessity of your life], all you humble of the land who have acted in compliance with His revealed will *and* have kept His commandments; seek righteousness, seek humility [inquire for them, require them as vital]. It may be you will be hidden in the day of the Lord's anger.

4 For [hear the fate of the Philistines:] Gaza shall be forsaken and Ashkelon shall become a desolation; the people of Ashdod shall be driven out at noonday and Ekron shall be uprooted.

Lord, I seek You. I inquire of You and for You; I seek You as the foremost necessity in my life.
ADAPTED FROM ZEPHANIAH 2:3

---

a God's judgment, God's mercy—the twin themes of the prophets. In this dramatic passage, the Lord describes the destruction that will sweep the earth in the day of God's wrath. Yet the Lord is true to His promises—the remnant will be restored (Zeph. 3:18-20); the last day is also "the day of redemption" (Eph. 4:30). See also Matt. 24:31; John 14:3; I Thess. 4:15-17.

5 Woe to the inhabitants of the sea-coast, the nation of the Cherethites [in Philistia]! The word of the Lord is against you, O Canaan, land of the Philistines; I will destroy you until no inhabitant is left.

6 And the seacoast shall be pastures, with [deserted] dwelling places *and* caves for shepherds and folds for flocks.

7 The ᵇseacoast shall belong to the remnant of the house of Judah; they shall pasture their flocks upon it; in the houses of [deserted Philistine] Ashkelon shall they of Judah lie down in the evening. For the Lord their [Judah's] God shall visit them [for their relief] and restore them from their captivity. [Isa. 14:29-31; Amos 1:6-8.]

8 I have heard the taunts of Moab and the revilings of the Ammonites by which they have reproached My people, and magnified themselves *and* made boasts against their territory.

9 Therefore, as I live, says the Lord of hosts, the God of Israel, Moab shall become like Sodom and the Ammonites like Gomorrah, a land possessed by nettles *and* wild vetches and salt pits, and a perpetual desolation. The remnant of My people shall make a prey of them and what is left of My nation shall possess them.

10 This shall they have for their pride, because they have taunted and boasted against the people of the Lord of hosts.

11 The Lord will be terrible to them, for He will make lean *and* famish all the gods of the earth; and men shall worship Him, every one from his place, even all the isles *and* coastlands of the nations. [Joel 2:11; Zeph. 1:4; 3:9.]

12 You Ethiopians also, you shall be slain by My sword. [Isa. 18.]

13 And [the Lord] will stretch out His hand against the north and destroy Assyria and will make Nineveh a desolation, dry as the desert. [Isa. 10:12; Nah. 1:1.]

14 Herds shall lie down in the midst of [Nineveh], all the [wild] beasts of the nations *and* of every kind; both the pelican and the hedgehog shall lodge on the upper part of her [fallen] pillars; the voice [of the nesting bird] shall sing in the windows; desolation *and* drought shall be on the thresholds, for her cedar paneling will He lay bare.

15 This is the joyous *and* exultant city that dwelt carelessly [feeling so secure], that said in her heart, I am and there is none beside me. What a desolation she has become, a lair for [wild] beasts! Everyone who passes by her shall hiss and wave his hand [indicating his gratification]. [Isa. 10:5-34; 47:8, 10.]

3 WOE TO her that is rebellious and polluted, the oppressing city [Jerusalem]!

2 She did not listen to *and* heed the voice [of God]; she accepted no correction *or* instruction; she trusted not in the Lord [nor leaned on or was confident in Him, but was confident in her own wealth]; she drew not near to her God [but to the god of Baal or Molech].

b This is one of the more than twenty-five details of Bible prophecy concerning the land of Palestine that has been literally fulfilled. Probability computers estimate that if a prophecy concerning a person, place, or event has twenty-five details, there is one chance in more than thirty-three million of its accidental fulfillment. And such prophecy must be (1) above the possibility of human collusion; (2) beyond the ability of human calculation; (3) proof against human coincidence; (4) above all possibility of human comprehension. What inconceivable omniscience was behind the writing of the Bible! Twenty-five details also concerning the betrayal, trial, death, and burial of our Lord were fulfilled, fulfilled within twenty-four hours! And the fulfillment of the most remarkable prophecies of all time is predicted in the Bible for the rapidly approaching future! See footnote on Ezek. 26:14 for information about a similar fulfillment of details of Bible prophecy with regard to Tyre.

3 Her officials in the midst of her are roaring lions; her judges are evening wolves; they gnaw not the bones on the morrow, for nothing is left by morning.

4 Her prophets are light [lacking truth, gravity, and steadiness] and men of treachery; her priests have profaned the sanctuary; [defrauding God and man by pretending their own word is God's word] they have done violence to the law. [Jer. 23:11; Ezek. 22:26; Hos. 9:7.]

5 The Lord in the midst of her is [uncompromisingly] righteous; He will not do iniquity. Every morning He brings His justice to light; He fails not, but the unjust [person] knows no shame.

6 I [the Lord] have cut off nations; their battlements *and* corner towers are desolate *and* in ruins. I laid their streets waste so that none passes over them; their cities are destroyed so that there is no man, there is no inhabitant.

7 I said, Only let her [reverently and worshipfully] fear Me, receive correction and instruction, and [Jerusalem's] dwelling shall not be cut off. However, I have punished her [according to all that I have appointed concerning her in the way of punishment], but all the more they are eager to make all their doings corrupt *and* infamous.

8 Therefore [earnestly] wait for Me, says the Lord, [waiting] for the day when I rise up to the attack [as a witness, accuser, or judge, and a testimony]. For My decision *and* determination *and* right it is to gather the nations together, to assemble the kingdoms, to pour upon them My indignation, even all [the heat of] My fierce anger; for [in that day] all the earth shall be consumed with the fire of My zeal *and* jealousy.

9 For then [changing their impure language] I will give to the people a clear *and* pure speech from pure lips, that they may all call upon the name of the Lord, to serve Him with one unanimous consent *and* one united shoulder [bearing the yoke of the Lord].

10 From beyond the rivers of Cush *or* Ethiopia those who pray to Me, the daughter of My dispersed people, will bring *and* present My offering.

11 In that day you [the congregation of Israel] shall not be put to shame for all your deeds by which you have rebelled *and* transgressed against Me, for then I will take away out of your midst those who exult in your majesty *and* pride; and you shall no more be haughty [and carry yourselves arrogantly on or] because of My holy mountain.

12 For I will leave in the midst of you a people afflicted and poor, and they shall trust, seek refuge, *and* be confident in the name of the Lord.

13 What is left of Israel shall not do iniquity or speak lies, neither shall a deceitful tongue be found in their mouth, for they shall feed and lie down and none shall make them afraid.

14 Sing, O Daughter of Zion; shout, O Israel! Rejoice, be in high spirits *and* glory with all your heart, O Daughter of Jerusalem [in that day].

15 [For then it will be that] the Lord has taken away the judgments against you; He has cast out your enemy. The King of Israel, even the Lord [Himself], is in the midst of you; [and after He has come to you] you shall not experience *or* fear evil any more.

16 In that day it shall be said to

speak the Word

Thank You, God, that You are uncompromisingly righteous. Every morning You bring Your justice to light. You never fail me.
ADAPTED FROM ZEPHANIAH 3:5

putting the Word to work

Do you ever wonder how much God really loves you? Zephaniah 3:17, in Hebrew, gives us the image that God literally "spins around" with joy over you and that He sings and shouts over *you* with joy! God has not only saved you from His wrath through Jesus, but He delights in you! Thank God for His great love for you, and ask Him to help you understand the depths of His love for you even more fully.

Jerusalem, Fear not, O Zion. Let not your hands sink down *or* be slow *and* listless.
17 The Lord your God is in the midst of you, a Mighty One, a Savior [Who saves]! He will rejoice over you with joy; He will rest [in silent satisfaction] *and* in His love He will be silent *and* make no mention [of past sins, or even recall them]; He will exult over you with singing.
18 I will gather those belonging to you [those Israelites in captivity] who yearn *and* grieve for the solemn assembly [and the festivals], on whom

[their exile and inability to attend services at Jerusalem have brought derision and] the reproach of it is a burden.
19 Behold, at that time I will deal with all those who afflict you; I will save the limping [ones] and gather the outcasts and will make them a praise and a name in every land of their shame. [Mic. 4:6, 7.]
20 At that time I will bring you in; yes, at that time I will gather you, for I will make you a name and a praise among all the nations of the earth when I reverse your captivity before your eyes, says the Lord.

life point

Zephaniah 3:19 says that God wants to bless those who would appear to be outcasts, those with "limps" in their lives. He has determined to gather and bless those who are imperfect—and that includes all of us. He promises to cast out the enemy, which is in many cases shame, blame, or disgrace. God does not want you to "limp" through life anymore. He wants you to have peace and enjoy your life.

Haggai

Author:
Haggai

Date:
520 BC

Everyday Life Principles:
We can be deceived into thinking we are obeying God simply because we have good intentions.

Good intentions do not equal obedience.

We need to obey God quickly.

After the Jews returned to Jerusalem from exile, much restoration was needed in the city. The prophet Haggai, along with Zechariah, realized the importance of having a place to worship and encouraged the Jews to rebuild the temple, as God had directed them. The Jews were slow to obey God, and after He told them to rebuild the temple, they spent eighteen years rebuilding their own homes and ignoring God's house. They had good intentions of rebuilding the temple, but they had not done it. They thought their good intentions and plans to rebuild the temple would satisfy God's request; they thought they were being obedient to Him because they knew they would eventually get around to doing what He had told them to do. But after eighteen years of putting off obedience to God, they began to suffer drought, crop failure, and all kinds of discomfort and trouble because of their procrastination (see Haggai 1:6, 10, 11).

Haggai knew that the people were struggling because they had not obeyed God promptly. They had put their own desire for comfortable homes ahead of their desire to complete the task God had assigned to them.

We must learn from the Jews' mistake to prioritize God's work and respond quickly to the assignments He gives us. Good intentions will not get the job done; we must act. Let the book of Haggai remind you to obey without delay when God asks you to do something for Him.

1 IN THE second year of Darius king [of Persia], in the sixth month, on the first day of the month, the word of the Lord came by means of Haggai the prophet [in Jerusalem after the Babylonian captivity] to Zerubbabel son of Shealtiel, governor of Judah, and to Joshua son of Jehozadak, the high priest, saying,

2 Thus says the Lord of hosts: These people say, The time is not yet come that the aLord's house should be rebuilt [although Cyrus had ordered it done eighteen years before]. [Ezra 1:1-6; 4:1-6, 24; 5:1-3.]

putting the Word to work

Some people believe the Bible is simply a collection of stories and legends. Others view it solely as a historical document. Yet in Haggai 1:1, 2 we see that Scripture is set in history and also that God is actively involved in human affairs, speaking to His people. How do you view God's Word? As you read the Bible, ask God to reveal Himself to you even more fully through His living Word.

3 Then came the word of the Lord by Haggai the prophet, saying,

4 Is it time for you yourselves to dwell in your paneled houses while this house [of the Lord] lies in ruins?

5 Now therefore thus says the Lord of hosts: Consider your ways *and* set your mind on what has come to you.

6 You have sown much, but you have reaped little; you eat, but you do not have enough; you drink, but you do not have your fill; you clothe yourselves, but no one is warm; and he who earns wages has earned them to put them in a bag with holes in it.

7 Thus says the Lord of hosts: Consider your ways (your previous and present conduct) *and* how you have fared.

a See footnote on Ezra 4:24.

putting the Word to work

Have you ever heard the saying "You have to look out for number one"? Our culture emphasizes putting self over anything or anyone else. Yet God, through Haggai, told the people that as they trusted Him and gave to Him of their time and money, He would see to their needs. "Consider your ways," as Haggai 1:7 instructs, and ask God to show you areas in your life where you still need to put Him first. You will be blessed as you honor and trust Him.

8 Go up to the hill country and bring lumber and rebuild [My] house, and I will take pleasure in it and I will be glorified, says the Lord [by accepting it as done for My glory and by displaying My glory in it].

9 You looked for much [harvest], and behold, it came to little; and even when you brought that home, I blew it away. Why? says the Lord of hosts. Because of My house, which lies waste while you yourselves run each man to his own house [eager to build and adorn it].

10 Therefore the heavens above you [for your sake] withhold the dew, and the earth withholds its produce.

11 And I have called for a drought upon the land and the hill country, upon the grain, the fresh wine, the oil, upon what the ground brings forth, upon men and cattle, and upon all the [wearisome] toil of [men's] hands.

12 Then Zerubbabel son of Shealtiel and Joshua son of Jehozadak, the high priest, with all the remnant of the people [who had returned from captivity], listened to *and* obeyed the voice of the Lord their God [not vaguely or partly, but completely, according to] the

consider your ways

The first chapter of Haggai introduces us to a group of people who had ignored an instruction from God. He had told them to rebuild the temple eighteen years earlier, but they told themselves it was not the right time to do it. Instead of rebuilding God's house, they built their own houses during those eighteen years and experienced fruitlessness and frustration as a result. They found themselves in desperate circumstances. They never had enough money. Things were not working out for them. Whatever they did gain, they quickly lost.

God spoke to them through the prophet Haggai and said, "Consider your ways" (Haggai 1:7). In other words, "Look at your situation and ask yourselves why you are in such dire straits; it is because you are trying to take care of yourselves instead of obeying Me and working together to provide something for everyone. It will not work!"

Selfishness did not work for the people of Haggai's day, and it will not work for us today. It stops up every avenue of blessing that would otherwise flow into our lives.

Selfish people are quite miserable and usually think if they could just get what they want, they would feel better. Satan has them on a treadmill of striving to make themselves happy and never succeeding.

words of Haggai the prophet, since the Lord their God had sent him, and the people [reverently] feared *and* [worshipfully] turned to the Lord.
13 Then Haggai, the Lord's messenger, spoke the Lord's message to the people saying, I am with you, says the Lord.
14 And the Lord aroused the spirit of Zerubbabel son of Shealtiel, governor of Judah, and the spirit of Joshua son of Jehozadak, the high priest, and the spirit of all the remnant of the people, so that they came and labored on the house of the Lord of hosts, their God,
15 On the twenty-fourth day of the sixth month.

2 IN THE seventh month, on the twenty-first day of the month, in the second year of Darius king [of Persia], came the word of the Lord by the prophet Haggai, saying,
2 Speak now to Zerubbabel son of Shealtiel, governor of Judah, and to Joshua son of Jehozadak, the high priest, and to the remainder of the people, saying,
3 Who is left among you who saw this house in its former glory? And how do you see it now? Is not this in your sight as nothing in comparison to that?
4 Yet now be strong, alert, *and* courageous, O Zerubbabel, says the Lord; be strong, alert, *and* courageous,

speak the Word

God, I will be strong, alert, and courageous because You are with me.
ADAPTED FROM Haggai 2:4

Haggai 2:3, 4 really are verses about dealing with change. When changes come in the life of a church, some people are unhappy. They will say, "I wish we could go back to the way we did it before," or "I liked the old way better." How do you handle change in your church? Pray for your church leaders, that they will have wisdom in making decisions concerning the church, and continue to be actively involved in the life and ministry of the church, remembering that God is with you.

O Joshua son of Jehozadak, the high priest; and be strong, alert, *and* courageous, all you people of the land, says the Lord, and work! For I am with you, says the Lord of hosts.

5 According to the promise that I covenanted with you when you came out of Egypt, so My Spirit stands *and* abides in the midst of you; fear not.

6 For thus says the Lord of hosts: Yet once more, in a little while, I will shake *and* make tremble the [starry] heavens, the earth, the sea, and the dry land; [Heb. 12:26.]

7 And I will shake all nations and the ᵇdesire *and* the precious things of all nations shall come in, and I will fill this house with splendor, says the Lord of hosts. [Isa. 60:5; Matt. 2:1-12.]

speak the Word

8 The silver is Mine and the gold is Mine, says the Lord of hosts.

9 The latter glory of this house [with its successor, to which Jesus came] shall be greater than the former, says the Lord of hosts; and in this place will I give peace *and* prosperity, says the Lord of hosts.

10 On the twenty-fourth day of the ninth month, in the second year of Darius, came the word of the Lord by Haggai the prophet, saying,

11 Thus says the Lord of hosts: Ask now the priests to decide this question of law:

12 If one carries in the skirt of his garment flesh that is holy [because it has been offered in sacrifice to God], and with his skirt *or* the flaps of his garment he touches bread, or pottage, or wine, or oil, or any kind of food, does what he touches become holy [dedicated to God's service exclusively]?

life point

As we see in Haggai 2:11-13, unholiness is infectious; holiness is not. This means that when you and I associate with someone who is living a sinful life, that individual's sinfulness can rub off on us. We can catch it like a disease. But holiness is not like that. It cannot be picked up by contact or exposure; it has to be chosen on purpose. Choose to be holy today!

Thank You, God, for giving me peace and prosperity.
ADAPTED FROM HAGGAI 2:9

b It is with great reluctance that we refrain from capitalizing the word "desire" here, thus making the phrase point directly to the Messiah, as has been the accepted interpretation through many centuries until modern times. But the verb "shall come" has a plural referent, and, as many commentators agree, refers to the most desired treasures that all nations will bring as gifts to adorn the temple where the Messiah will one day come. Thus the Messianic reference of the prophecy is neither questioned nor obscured, but the picture presented is like that of the coming of the Magi (Matt. 2:1-12) to find the Babe of Bethlehem, the Desire of all of them; and when they found Him they fell down and worshiped Him, bringing Him their most desirable treasures—gold, frankincense, and myrrh.

more and more glory

In Haggai 2:9, God promises that the glory of the latter house will be greater than the glory of the former temple.

Do you know that you and I are the temple of God today (see II Corinthians 6:16) and that God's glory (His manifest excellence) is upon us? Just as the temple in Haggai would increase in glory, so you and I also increase in glory as we grow in God. The glory we had in the past (the former glory) is not as great as what we have today or will have tomorrow.

In II Corinthians 3:18, Paul states that God changes us "from one degree of glory to another." In other words, the changes in us personally, as well as in our circumstances, take place in degrees.

You are in the glory right now! If you are born again, then you are somewhere on the path of the righteous. You may not be as far along as you would like to be, but thank God, you are on the path. There was a time when you were totally outside covenant relationship with God through unbelief (see Ephesians 2:11, 12). But now you belong to the household of God and are being transformed by Him day by day. Enjoy the glory you have right now, and do not feel jealous of where others may be. They may have already passed through the place where you are now.

We have a strong tendency to compare our glory with everybody else's, but this is fleshly thinking. The devil arranges for us to think that way, but it is not God's way. God wants us to realize that each of us is a unique individual and that He has a unique plan for every one of us. Satan wants to make sure that we never enjoy where we are at the moment. He wants us in competition with one another, always wanting what someone else has. When we do not know how to enjoy the glory we are in right now, all we do is slow down the maturity process. I do not believe we pass into the next degree of glory until we have learned to enjoy the one we are in at the moment.

In this sense, a "glory" is simply a place that is better than the previous one. I had so many flaws in my personality and character that even after five years of trying to walk with the Lord, I still felt that I had made practically no progress. Yet, all that time I was gradually becoming a little more "glorious."

We are usually too hard on ourselves. We would grow faster if we relaxed more. We cannot live by our feelings in these matters. Satan makes sure we frequently "feel" that we are an unredeemable mess or that God is not working in our lives. We must learn to live by God's Word and not by how we feel. His Word states that as long as we believe, He is working in us! Your latter glory will be greater than your former!

And the priests answered, No! [Holiness is not infectious.]

13 Then said Haggai, If one who is [ceremonially] unclean because he has come in contact with a dead body should touch any of these articles of food, shall it be [ceremonially] unclean? And the priests answered, It shall be unclean. [Unholiness is infectious.]

14 Then answered Haggai, So is this people and so is this nation before Me, says the Lord; and so is every work of their hands, and what they offer there [on the altar] is unclean [because they who offer it are themselves unclean].

15 And now, I pray you, consider what will happen from this day onward. Since the time before a stone was laid upon a stone in the temple of the Lord, how have you fared?

16 Through all that time [the harvests have not fulfilled expectations, for] when one has gone expecting to find a heap [of sheaves] of twenty measures, there were but ten; when he has gone to the wine vat to draw out fifty bucketfuls from the press, there were only twenty.

17 I smote you with blight and with mildew and with hail in all [the products of] the labors of your hands; yet you returned not *nor* were converted to Me, says the Lord.

18 Consider, I pray you, from this day onward, from the twenty-fourth day of the ninth month, even from the day that the foundation of the Lord's temple was [re]laid, consider this:

19 Is the harvested grain any longer in the barn? As to the grapevine, the fig tree, the pomegranate, and the olive tree—they have not yet borne. From this day on I will bless you.

20 And again the word of the Lord came to Haggai on the twenty-fourth *day* of the month, saying,

21 Speak to Zerubbabel [the representative of the Davidic monarchy and covenant and in direct line of the ancestry of Jesus Christ] governor of Judah, saying, I will shake the heavens and the earth; [Hag. 2:6; Matt. 1:12, 13.]

22 And I will [in the distant future] overthrow the throne of kingdoms and I will destroy the strength of the kingdoms of the [ungodly] nations, and I will overthrow the chariots and those who ride in them, and the horses and their riders shall go down, every one by the sword of his brother. [Dan. 2:34, 35, 44, 45; Rev. 19:11-21.]

23 In that day, says the Lord of hosts, will I take you, O Zerubbabel, My servant, the son of Shealtiel, says the Lord, and will make you [through the Messiah, your descendant] *My* signet ring; for I have chosen you [as the one with whom to renew My covenant to David's line], says the Lord of hosts. [II Sam. 7:12, 16.]

putting the Word to work

Haggai 2:15–19 illustrates the importance of making God's purposes for your life top priority. Without priorities, it is difficult to live with any sense of purpose or to accomplish much. What are your priorities in your life?

speak the Word

Thank You, God, that You are blessing me today and from this day on.
ADAPTED FROM HAGGAI 2:19

Zechariah

Author:
Zechariah

Date:
Between 520 BC and 475 BC

Everyday Life Principles:
The only way to overcome the enemy is by God's Spirit.

Rely on God's grace and on the power of the Holy Spirit to overcome obstacles.

We make progress little by little.

Zechariah is a book of encouragement to Jews who were rebuilding the temple after their return to Jerusalem from exile. Zechariah's encouragement is as relevant to us today as it was to them centuries ago. Whatever work you have set your hand to, these truths from Zechariah 4 will serve you well.

First, the only way to defeat an enemy or accomplish God's purpose is through His Spirit (see Zechariah 4:6). One of the biggest mistakes we make is trying to obey God in our own strength rather than by His Spirit. We will fail if we try to achieve anything by human effort, but when we work by His Spirit, we always succeed.

Second, we will encounter obstacles as we seek to obey God, and we need God's grace in order to overcome them. As we rely on the Holy Spirit to help us, those mountain-sized obstacles become as molehills.

Third, we make progress step-by-step. We are not to despise small things (see Zechariah 4:10) or look upon seemingly minor accomplishments as insignificant. Everything big has to start small, and in fact includes many, many small parts.

As you read Zechariah's words, I hope you will be encouraged in the work God has given you to do. Just as He encouraged the Jews in the rebuilding of the temple through the prophet, He is encouraging you today by His Spirit. Just as He brought about the restoration of the temple in their day, He wants to bring restoration to every area of your life today.

1 IN THE eighth month, in the second year [of the reign] of Darius, came the word of the Lord to Zechariah son of Berechiah, the son of Iddo, the prophet, saying, [Ezra 5:1.]

2 The Lord was very angry with your fathers.

3 Therefore say to them [the Jews of this day], Thus says the Lord of hosts: Return to Me, says the Lord of hosts, and I will return to you; it is the utterance of the Lord of hosts.

4 Be not as your fathers to whom the former prophets cried, Thus says the Lord of hosts: Return now from your evil ways and your evil doings; but they would not hear or listen to Me, says the Lord. [II Kings 17:13; Isa. 45:22; Jer. 18:11; Ezek. 33:11.]

5 Your fathers, where are they? And the prophets, do they live forever?

6 But My words and My statutes, which I commanded My servants the prophets, did they not overtake *and* take hold of your fathers? So they repented and said, As the Lord of hosts planned *and* purposed to do to us, according to our ways and according to our doings, so has He dealt with us.

7 Upon the twenty-fourth day of the eleventh month, which is the month of Shebat, in the second year of the reign of Darius, the word of the Lord came to Zechariah son of Berechiah, the son of Iddo, the prophet. Zechariah said,

8 I saw in the night [vision] and behold, a ᵃMan riding upon a red horse, and He stood among the myrtle trees that were in a low valley *or* bottom, and behind Him there were horses, red, bay *or* flame-colored, and white.

9 Then said I, O my lord, what are these? And the ᵇangel who talked with me said, I will show you what these are.

10 And the Man who stood among the myrtle trees answered and said, These are they whom the Lord has sent to walk to and fro through the earth *and* patrol it.

11 And the men on the horses answered ᶜthe Angel of the Lord Who stood among the myrtle trees and said, We have walked to and fro through the earth [patrolling it] and behold, all the earth sits at rest [in peaceful security].

12 Then the Angel of the Lord said, O Lord of hosts, how long will You not have mercy *and* lovingkindness for Jerusalem and the cities of Judah, against which You have had indignation these seventy years [of the Babylonian captivity]?

13 And the Lord answered the angel who talked with me with gracious and comforting words.

14 So the angel who talked with me said to me, Cry out, Thus says the Lord of hosts: I am jealous for Jerusalem and for Zion with a great jealousy.

15 And I am very angry with the nations that are at ease; for while I was but a little displeased, they helped forward the affliction *and* disaster.

16 Therefore thus says the Lord: I have returned to Jerusalem with compassion (lovingkindness and mercy).

---

a The Angel of the Lord of Zech. 1:11.   **b** The interpreting angel, mentioned in Zech. 1:9, 13-14; 2:3; 4:1, 4-5; 5:5, 10; 6:4-5, not to be confused with the Man of Zech. 1:8 or the Angel of the Lord of Zech. 1:11.   **c** That the Angel of the Lord is an uncreated angel distinguished from other angels, and in many places identified with the Lord God, is undeniable. On the other hand there are passages in which He seems to be distinguished from God the Father. The simplest way of reconciling these two classes is to adopt the old view that this Angel is Christ, the second person of the Godhead, even at that early period appearing as the Revealer of the Father (Johan P. Lange, *A Commentary*). See also footnote on Gen. 16:7.

My house shall be built in it, says the Lord of hosts, and a measuring line shall be stretched out over Jerusalem [with a view to rebuilding its walls].

17 Cry yet again, saying, Thus says the Lord of hosts: My cities shall yet again overflow with prosperity, and the Lord shall yet comfort Zion and shall yet choose Jerusalem.

18 Then I lifted up my eyes and saw, and behold, four horns [symbols of strength].

19 And I said to the angel who talked with me, What are these? And he answered me, These are the horns or powers which have scattered Judah, Israel, and Jerusalem.

20 Then the Lord showed me four smiths or workmen [one for each enemy horn, to beat it down].

21 Then said I, What are these [horns and smiths] coming to do? And he said, These are the horns or powers that scattered Judah so that no man lifted up his head. But these smiths or workmen have come to terrorize them and cause them to be panic-stricken, to cast out the horns or powers of the nations who lifted up their horn against the land of Judah to scatter it.

2 AND I lifted up my eyes and saw, and behold, a man with a measuring line in his hand.

2 Then said I, Where are you going? And he said to me, To measure Jerusalem, to see what is its breadth and what is its length.

3 And behold, the angel who talked with me went forth and another angel went out to meet him,

4 And he said to the second angel, Run, speak to this young man, saying, Jerusalem shall be inhabited and dwell as villages without walls, because of the multitude of people and livestock in it.

5 For I, says the Lord, will be to her a wall of fire round about, and I will be the glory in the midst of her.

6 Ho! ho! [Hear and] flee from the land of the north, says the Lord, and from the four winds of the heavens, for to them have I scattered you, says the Lord.

7 Ho! Escape to Zion, you who dwell with the daughter of Babylon!

8 For thus said the Lord of hosts, after [His] glory had sent me [His messenger] to the nations who plundered you—for he who touches you touches the apple or pupil of His eye:

9 Behold, I will swing my hand over them and they shall become plunder for those who served them. Then you shall know (recognize and understand) that the Lord of hosts has sent me [His messenger].

10 Sing and rejoice, O Daughter of Zion; for behold, I come, and I will dwell in the midst of you, says the Lord.

11 And many nations shall join themselves to the Lord in that day and shall be My people. And I will dwell in the midst of you, and you shall know (recognize and understand) that the Lord of hosts has sent me [His messenger] to you. [Isa. 2:3; Mic. 4:2.]

12 And the Lord shall inherit Judah as His portion in the holy land and shall again choose Jerusalem.

13 Be still, all flesh, before the Lord, for He is aroused and risen from His holy habitation. [Hab. 2:20; Zeph. 1:7.]

speak the Word

3 THEN [the guiding angel] showed me Joshua the high priest standing before ᵈthe Angel of the Lord, and Satan standing at Joshua's right hand to be his adversary *and* to accuse him.

2 And the Lord said to Satan, The Lord rebuke you, O Satan! Even the Lord, Who [now and habitually] chooses Jerusalem, rebuke you! Is not this [returned captive Joshua] a brand plucked out of the fire? [Jude 9.]

3 Now Joshua was clothed with filthy garments and was standing before the Angel [of the Lord].

4 And He spoke to those who stood before Him, saying, Take away the filthy garments from him. And He said to [Joshua], Behold, I have caused your iniquity to pass from you, and I will clothe you with rich apparel.

5 And I [Zechariah] said, Let them put a clean turban on his head. So they put a clean turban on his head and clothed him with [rich] garments. And the Angel of the Lord stood by.

6 And the Angel of the Lord [solemnly and earnestly] protested *and* affirmed to Joshua, saying,

7 Thus says the Lord of hosts: If you will walk in My ways and keep My charge, then also you shall rule My house and have charge of My courts, and I will give you access [to My presence] *and* places to walk among these who stand here.

8 Hear now, O Joshua the high priest, you and your colleagues who [usually] sit before you—for they are men who are a sign *or* omen [types of what is to come]—for behold, I will bring forth My servant the ᵉBranch. [Isa. 4:2; Jer. 23:5; 33:15; Zech. 6:12.]

9 For behold, upon the stone which I have set before Joshua, upon that one stone are seven eyes *or* facets [the all-embracing providence of God and the sevenfold radiations of the

putting the Word to work

Zechariah 3:3–5 is a brief illustration of God's power and desire to cleanse us from sin. Have you ever had a piece of clothing ruined by a stain that would not come out? Our lives are stained by sin, and there is nothing we can do on our own to cleanse that stain. Yet God removed the stain of sin in our lives through the sacrifice of His Son, Jesus. If you have not already done so, acknowledge that your life is stained by sin, and ask God for forgiveness. Rejoice that He will remove the stain of sin and clothe you with righteousness!

Spirit of God]. Behold, I will carve upon it its inscription, says the Lord of hosts, and I will remove the iniquity *and* guilt of this land in a single day. [II Chron. 16:9; Jer. 50:20; Zech. 4:10.]

10 In that day, says the Lord of hosts, you shall invite each man his neighbor under his own vine and his own fig tree. [Mic. 4:1-4.]

4 AND THE angel who talked with me came again and awakened me, like a man who is wakened out of his sleep.

2 And said to me, What do you see? I said, I see, and behold, a lampstand all of gold, with its bowl [for oil] on the top of it and its seven lamps on it, and [there are] seven pipes to each of the seven lamps which are upon the top of it. [Matt. 5:14, 16; Luke 12:35; Phil. 2:15; Rev. 1:20.]

3 And there are two olive trees by it, one upon the right side of the bowl and the other upon the left side of it [feeding it continuously with oil]. [Rev. 11:4-13.]

4 So I asked the angel who talked with me, What are these, my lord?

---

d See footnote on Zechariah 1:11. **e** A Messianic title.

5 Then the angel who talked with me answered me, Do you not know what these are? And I said, No, my lord.

6 Then he said to me, This [addition of the bowl to the candlestick, causing it to yield a ceaseless supply of oil from the olive trees] is the word of the Lord to Zerubbabel, saying, Not by might, nor by power, but by My Spirit [of Whom the oil is a symbol], says the Lord of hosts.

life point

Are you faced with a difficult obstacle? Like the Israelites, you cannot overcome any situation by determination alone. You do need to be determined, but as Zechariah 4:6 teaches, be *determined in the Holy Spirit*—not in the effort of your own flesh. The Holy Spirit is your Helper; seek His help. Lean on Him. You cannot make it alone. You need Him.

7 For who are you, O great mountain [of human obstacles]? Before Zerubbabel [who with Joshua had led the return of the exiles from Babylon and was undertaking the rebuilding of the temple, before him] you shall become a plain [a mere ᶠmolehill]! And he shall bring forth the finishing gable stone [of the new temple] with loud shoutings of the people, crying, Grace, grace to it! [Ezra 4:1-5, 24; Isa. 40:4.]

8 Moreover, the word of the Lord came to me, saying,

9 The hands of Zerubbabel have laid the foundations of this house; his hands shall also finish it. Then you shall know (recognize and understand) that the Lord of hosts has sent me [His messenger] to you.

10 Who [with reason] despises the day of small things? For these seven shall rejoice when they see the plum-

life point

In Zechariah 4:7, the Lord tells Zechariah that the problem facing the Israelites, although it may appear to be a mountain, is actually a molehill. How would you like for all your mountains to become molehills? They can, if you will do what God is saying here and look not at the problems, but at the Lord and His power.

If God has told you to do something, it certainly is His will that you begin it. But it is His will that you finish it as well. You will never complete your God-given task if you do not understand grace— the power of the Holy Spirit—and shout, "Grace, Grace!" to the obstacles in front of you.

Remember, it is not by power or by might, but by the Spirit that we win the victory over our enemy. We overcome *through* faith, *by* grace.

met in the hand of Zerubbabel. [These seven] are the eyes of the Lord which run to and fro throughout the whole earth. [Rev. 5:6.]

11 Then I said to him [the angel who

life point

Zechariah 4:10 instructs us not to despise "the day of small things." When we despise something, we take it lightly; we disregard it and count it as nothing.

When we are believing God for something "big," we need to remember that great things start small. We need to appreciate "the day of small things," because the little things will grow if we recognize them, appreciate them, and honor them as gifts from God and indicators of greater things to come.

---

f This recalls the familiar proverb about "making mountains out of molehills," with a surprising twist.

by His Spirit

Have you ever been frustrated because you were doing everything right you knew to do in a situation, but no matter what you did, nothing worked? I have certainly had times like that, and I believe everyone else has too. After many years of being frustrated most of the time, I finally learned that I was placing too much trust in myself and my own efforts and not trusting God enough.

God's Word refers to us as "believers," and our job is to believe. We usually think we should be doing or achieving something, but if that were the case we would be called "achievers" instead of "believers." We are certainly responsible to do certain things, but most of us go far beyond our God-given responsibility and try to do things that only God can do.

What needs to be accomplished in our lives and circumstances is not going to happen by might or power on our part, but it will be done by the Spirit of God as we place our trust in Him (see Zechariah 4:6). God gives us the Holy Spirit as our divine Helper. He enables us to do what we need to do, and He does what we cannot do. We are partners with God; He has a part and we have a part. Our part is to trust God and do whatever He leads us to do, and His part is to accomplish what needs to be done in our lives and work on our behalf. God will not do our part, and we cannot do His part. This is one of the most important lessons we must learn in life unless we want to be frustrated most of the time.

When I begin to feel frustrated, I know that I have slipped over into trying to make things happen by my own efforts and have stopped fully trusting God. As soon as I get my trust back where it belongs, which is in God and not in myself, I start to feel relaxed again. Jesus said if we labor and are heavy-laden and overburdened, we should come to Him (see Matthew 11:28). He put it very simply, and we need to very simply do what He said. What needs to be done in our lives will not be done by might or power, but by the Holy Spirit.

---

talked with me], What are these two olive trees on the right side of the lampstand and on the left side of it?
12 And a second time I said to him, What are these two olive branches which are beside the two golden tubes *or* spouts by which the golden oil is emptied out?
13 And he answered me, Do you not know what these are? And I said, No, my lord.

14 Then said he, These are the two ᵍsons of oil [Joshua the high priest and Zerubbabel the prince of Judah, the two anointed ones] who stand before the Lord of the whole earth [as His anointed instruments]. [Rev. 11:4.]

5 AGAIN I lifted up my eyes and behold, I saw a scroll flying *or* floating in the air!
2 And the angel said to me, What do

---

g The oil used in anointing symbolizes the Holy Spirit (Zech. 4:6). The combination of priest and ruler points ultimately to the Messianic Priest-King (Ps. 110; Zech. 6:13; Heb. 7).

small things lead to big things

As I look back on the early days of my ministry, I can remember "the day of small things" (Zechariah 4:10), which would have been so easy to despise! When I first started out, my meetings would draw just a handful of people, maybe fifty at the most. It is just as hard to preach to fifty as it is to preach to five thousand, so I had to put the same amount of time and effort into my lessons then as I do now.

When my ministry team started traveling, we needed a vehicle to transport all our equipment and all of the team. The first van we bought cost twenty-six hundred dollars. It had bald tires and rust spots on it. We would leave our hometown and drive to a little town several hours away, where there would be 70 to 125 people in attendance at our meeting.

Since we did not have enough money to spend the night in a motel, we would drive back home that same evening after the services had ended. We would usually get back about three o'clock in the morning. On the way home we would get so tired we would have to pull off on the side of the road and get ten or fifteen minutes of sleep before driving on.

Those days frustrated me while I was living them, but now I can see their value. They were important because they were times of preparation for the greater days the Lord knew lay ahead. I sincerely believe Joyce Meyer Ministries would not have grown to the point of reaching the number of people it does today if we had not been faithful enough to press through those early hardships. We need to remember that God anointed David to be king long before he actually became king, and David was tested in many ways while he waited. Patience must be tested, humility must be manifested, and faith must grow. Only after we pass our tests do we get promoted into the next level of what God has in mind for us.

I hate to see people give up in the hard times and never get to enjoy the fruit of all their labors. Starting an endeavor is easy, but finishing it is much harder. In the beginning, we are excited, and usually people give us all kinds of enthusiastic support. But as the days go by and the "great and glorious cause" becomes a matter of daily, consistent hard work, often we are left with nobody to urge us on except God and ourselves.

That is when we have to decide if we are going to see it through to the finish. That is when we have to realize everything we are going through at the moment will one day pass and we will enjoy the fruit of our labors. In the meantime, we need to enjoy where we are while we are on the way to where we are going and be sure to appreciate the small things.

you see? And I answered, I see a flying scroll; its length is twenty cubits *or* thirty feet and its breadth is ten cubits *or* fifteen feet.

3 Then he said to me, This is the curse that goes out over the face of the whole land; for everyone who steals shall be cut off from henceforth according to it [the curse written on this subject on the scroll], and everyone who swears falsely shall be cut off from henceforth according to it. [Isa. 24:6; Mal. 3:8, 9.]

4 I will bring [the curse] forth, says the Lord of hosts, and it shall enter into the house of the thief and into the house of him who swears falsely by My name; and it shall abide in the midst of his house and shall consume it, both its timber and its stones.

5 Then the angel who talked with me came forward and said to me, Lift up now your eyes and see what this is that goes forth.

6 And I said, What is it? [What does it symbolize?] And he said, This that goes forth is an ephah[-sized vessel for separate grains all collected together]. This, he continued, is the symbol of the sinners mentioned above *and* is the resemblance of their iniquity throughout the whole land. [Amos 8:5.]

7 And behold, a round, flat weight of lead was lifted and there sat a woman in the midst of the ephah[-sized vessel].

8 And he said, This is lawlessness (wickedness)! And he thrust her back into the ephah[-sized vessel] and he cast the weight of lead upon the mouth of it!

9 Then lifted I up my eyes and looked, and behold, there were two women coming forward! The wind was in their wings, for they had wings like the wings of a stork, and they lifted up the ephah[-sized vessel] between the earth and the heavens.

10 Then said I to the angel who talked with me, Where are they taking the ephah[-sized vessel]?

11 And he said to me, To the land of Shinar [Babylonia] to build it a house, and when it is finished, to set up the ephah[-sized vessel—the symbol of such sinners and their guilt] there upon its own base.

6 AND AGAIN I lifted up my eyes and saw, and behold, four chariots came out from between two mountains; and the mountains were mountains of firm, immovable bronze.

2 The first chariot had red *or* bay horses, the second chariot had black horses,

3 The third chariot had white horses, and the fourth chariot had dappled, active, *and* strong horses.

4 Then I said to the angel who talked with me, What are these, my lord?

5 And the angel answered me, These are the four winds *or* spirits of the heavens, which go forth from presenting themselves before the Lord of all the earth. [Ps. 104:4; Matt. 24:31.]

6 The chariot with the black horses is going forth into the north country, and the white ones are going forth after them [because there are two northern powers to overcome], and the dappled ones are going forth toward the south country.

7 And [the chariots with] the strong [horses] went forth and sought to go that they might patrol the earth. And [the Lord] said to them, Go, walk to and fro through the earth *and* patrol it. So they walked about through the earth [watching and protecting it].

8 Then He summoned me and said to me, Behold, these that go toward the north country have quieted My Spirit [of wrath] *and* have caused it to rest in the north country.

9 And the word of the Lord came to me, saying,

10 Accept donations *and* offerings from these [as representatives of the]

exiles, from Heldai, from Tobijah, and from Jedaiah, who have come from Babylon; and come the same day and go to the house of Josiah the son of Zephaniah.

11 Yes, take from them silver and gold, and make crowns and set [one] upon the head of Joshua the son of Jehozadak, the high priest,

12 And say to him, Thus says the Lord of hosts: [You, Joshua] behold (look at, keep in sight, watch) the Man [the Messiah] whose name is the Branch, for He shall grow up in His place and He shall build the [true] temple of the Lord. [Isa. 4:2; Jer. 23:5; 33:15; Zech. 3:8.]

13 Yes, [you are building a temple of the Lord, but] it is He Who shall build the [true] temple of the Lord, and He shall bear the honor *and* glory [as of the only begotten of the Father] and shall sit and rule upon His throne. And He shall be a ʰPriest upon His throne, and the counsel of peace shall be between the two [offices—Priest and King]. [John 1:14; 17:5; Heb. 2:9.]

14 And the [other] crown shall be [credited] to Helem (Heldai), to Tobijah, and to Jedaiah, and to the kindness *and* favor of Josiah the son of Zephaniah, and shall be in the temple of the Lord for a reminder *and* memorial. [Matt. 10:41.]

15 And those who are far off shall come and help build the temple of the Lord, and you shall know (recognize and understand) that the Lord sent me [Zechariah] to you. And [your part in this] shall come to pass if you will diligently obey the voice of the Lord your God.

7 AND IN the fourth year of the reign of King Darius, the word of the Lord came to Zechariah on the fourth day of the ninth month, Chislev.

2 Now the people of Bethel had sent Sharezer and Regem-melech and their men to pray *and* entreat the favor of the Lord

3 And to speak to the priests of the house of the Lord of hosts and to the prophets, saying, [Now that I am returned from exile] should I weep in the fifth month, separating myself as I have done these so many years [in Babylon]?

4 Then came the word of the Lord of hosts to me [Zechariah], saying,

5 Speak to all the people of the land and to the priests, saying, When you fasted and mourned in the fifth and seventh months, even those seventy years you were in exile, was it for Me that you fasted, for Me?

6 And when you ate and when you drank, did you not eat for yourselves and drink for yourselves?

7 Should you not hear the words which the Lord cried by the former prophets when Jerusalem was inhabited and in prosperity with her cities round about her, and the South (the Negeb) and the lowlands were inhabited?

8 And the word of the Lord came to Zechariah, saying,

9 Thus has the Lord of hosts spoken: Execute true judgment and show mercy *and* kindness and tender compassion, every man to his brother;

10 And oppress not the widow or the fatherless, the temporary resident or the poor, and let none of you devise *or* imagine *or* think evil against his brother in your heart.

11 But they refused to listen and turned a rebellious *and* stubborn shoulder and made heavy *and* dull their ears that they might not hear.

12 Yes, they made their hearts as an adamant stone *or* diamond point, lest they should hear the law and the words which the Lord of hosts had

h The coming Davidic King will also be a Priest.

sent by His Spirit through the former prophets. Therefore there came great wrath from the Lord of hosts.

13 So it came to pass that as He cried and they would not hear [He said], So they shall cry and I will not answer, says the Lord of hosts,

14 But I will scatter them with a whirlwind among all the nations whom they know not *and* who know not them. Thus the land was desolate after they had gone, so that no man passed through or returned, for they [the Jews by their sins] had [caused to be] laid waste *and* forsaken the pleasant land (the land of desire).

8 AND THE word of the Lord of hosts came to me, saying, **2** Thus says the Lord of hosts: I am jealous for Zion with great jealousy, and I am jealous for her with great wrath [against her enemies].

3 Thus says the Lord: I shall return to Zion and will dwell in the midst of Jerusalem, and Jerusalem shall be called the [faithful] City of Truth, and the mountain of the Lord of hosts, the Holy Mountain.

4 Thus says the Lord of hosts: Old men and old women shall again dwell in Jerusalem *and* sit out in the streets, every man with his staff in his hand for very [advanced] age.

5 And the streets of the city shall be full of boys and girls playing in its streets.

6 Thus says the Lord of hosts: Because it will be marvelous in the eyes of the remnant of this people in those days [in which it comes to pass], should it also be marvelous in My eyes? says the Lord of hosts. [Gen. 18:14; Jer. 32:17, 27; Luke 18:27.]

7 Thus says the Lord of hosts: Behold, I will save My people from the east country and from the west [the country of the going down of the sun]. [Isa. 43:5, 6.]

8 And I will bring them [home] and

they shall dwell in the midst of Jerusalem; and they shall be My people, and I will be their God in truth *and* faithfulness and in righteousness.

9 Thus says the Lord of hosts: Let your hands be strong *and* hardened, you who in these days hear these words from the mouths of the prophets who on the day that the foundation of the house of the Lord of hosts was laid foretold that the temple should be rebuilt.

10 For before those days there was no hire for man nor any hire for beast, neither was there any peace *or* success to him who went out or came in because of the adversary *and* oppressor, for I set (let loose) all men, every one against his neighbor.

11 But now [in this period since you began to build] I am not to the remnant of this people as in the former days, says the Lord of hosts.

12 For there shall the seed produce peace *and* prosperity; the vine shall yield her fruit and the ground shall give its increase and the heavens shall give their dew; and I will cause the remnant of this people to inherit *and* possess all these things.

13 And as you have been a curse *and* a byword among the nations, O house of Judah and house of Israel, so will I save you, and you shall be a blessing. Fear not, but let your hands be strong *and* hardened. [Jer. 22:8, 9.]

14 For thus says the Lord of hosts: As I thought to bring calamity upon you when your fathers provoked Me to wrath, says the Lord of hosts, and I did not relent *or* revoke your sentence,

15 So again have I purposed in these days to do good to Jerusalem and to the house of Judah. Fear not!

16 These are the things that you shall do: speak every man the truth with his neighbor; render the truth and pronounce the judgment *or* verdict that makes for peace in [the courts at] your gates. [Eph. 4:25.]

putting the Word to work

Clearly, acting with integrity and peace and for the good of our neighbors is important to God (see Zechariah 8:16, 17). Do you know who your neighbors are? Take an opportunity to reach out to a neighbor with a word of encouragement or an act of kindness. Ask God to show you how to be a good neighbor and pray for those in your neighborhood to be blessed.

17 And let none of you think *or* imagine *or* devise evil *or* injury in your hearts against his neighbor, and love no false oath, for all these things I hate, says the Lord.

18 And the word of the Lord of hosts came to me [Zechariah], saying,

19 Thus says the Lord of hosts: The fast of the fourth month and the fast of the fifth, the fast of the seventh and the fast of the tenth, shall be to the house of Judah times of joy and gladness and cheerful, appointed seasons; therefore [in order that this may happen to you, as the condition of fulfilling the promise] love truth and peace.

20 Thus says the Lord of hosts: It shall yet come to pass that there shall come [to Jerusalem] peoples and the inhabitants of many *and* great cities,

21 And the inhabitants of one city shall go to them of another, saying, Let us go speedily to pray *and* entreat the favor of the Lord and to seek, inquire of, *and* require [to meet our

own most essential need] the Lord of hosts. I will go also.

22 Yes, many people and strong nations shall come to Jerusalem to seek, inquire of, *and* require [to fill their own urgent need] the Lord of hosts and to pray to the Lord for His favor.

23 Thus says the Lord of hosts: In those days ten men out of all languages of the nations shall take hold of the robe of him who is a Jew, saying, Let us go with you, for we have heard that God is with you.

9 THE BURDEN *or* oracle (the thing to be lifted up) of the word of the Lord is against the land of Hadrach [in Syria], and Damascus shall be its resting place, for the Lord has an eye upon mankind as upon all the tribes of Israel,

2 And Hamath also, which borders on [Damascus], Tyre with Sidon, though they are very wise.

3 And Tyre has built herself a stronghold [on an island a half mile from the shore, which seems impregnable], and heaped up silver like dust and fine gold like the mire of the streets.

4 Behold, the Lord will ¹cast her out *and* dispossess her; He will smite her power in the sea *and* into it and [Tyre] shall be devoured by fire.

5 [The strong cities of Philistia] shall see it and fear; ʲAshkelon, Gaza also, and be sorely pained, and Ekron, for her confidence *and* expectation

---

i Tyre was utterly destroyed by Alexander the Great and has never been rebuilt. History records that after he had slain everyone except those who had fled to the temples, Alexander ordered the houses to be set afire. Yet Sidon, Tyre's sister city (Zech. 9:2), though meeting with many adversities, has survived and has kept her identity (modern Saida) for an estimated 4,000 years (Gen. 10:15, 19). How did Zechariah know that it was Tyre, not Sidon, that was to be permanently destroyed? Ezekiel wrote of Tyre, after telling the details of her destruction, "You shall never be rebuilt, for I the Lord have spoken it, says the Lord God" (Ezek. 26:14). j Ashkelon was one of the five strong, leading Philistine cities (Josh. 13:3)—Gath and Ashdod being the ones not named here in this verse. Ashkelon was the birthplace of Herod the Great, and the residence of his sister Salome. It was not until AD 1270 that Zechariah's prophecy of its total destruction was fulfilled, when the Sultan Bibars reduced it to ruins and filled the harbor with stones. Nearly 700 years later the city is still uninhabited, and the seacoast has been and continues to be the site of "dwellings and cottages for shepherds and folds for flocks" (Zeph. 2:6 KJV).

shall be put to shame, and a king [monarchial government] shall perish from Gaza, and Ashkelon shall not be inhabited.

6 And a mongrel people shall dwell in Ashdod, and I will put an end to the pride of the Philistines.

7 And I will take out of [the Philistines'] mouths and from between their teeth the abominable idolatrous sacrifices eaten with the blood. And they too shall remain *and* be a remnant for our God, and they shall be like chieftains (the head over a thousand) in Judah, and Ekron shall be like one of the Jebusites [who at last were merged and had lost their identity in Israel].

8 Then I will encamp about My house as a guard *or* a garrison so that none shall march back and forth, and no oppressor *or* demanding collector shall again overrun them, for now My eyes are upon them.

9 Rejoice greatly, O Daughter of Zion! Shout aloud, O Daughter of Jerusalem! Behold, your King comes to you; He is [uncompromisingly] just and having salvation [triumphant and victorious], patient, meek, lowly, and riding on a donkey, upon a colt, the foal of a donkey. [Matt. 21:5; John 12:14, 15.]

10 And I will cut off *and* exterminate the war chariot from Ephraim and the [war] horse from Jerusalem, and the battle bow shall be cut off; and He shall speak the word and peace shall come to the nations, and His dominion shall be from the [Mediterranean] Sea to [any other] sea, and from the River [Euphrates] to the ends of the earth! [Ps. 72:8.]

11 As for you also, because of *and* for the sake of the [covenant of the Lord with His people, which was sealed with sprinkled] covenant blood, I have released *and* sent forth your imprisoned people out of the waterless pit. [Gen. 37:24; Exod. 24:4-8; Heb. 9:16.]

12 Return to the stronghold [of security and prosperity], you prisoners of hope; even today do I declare that I will restore double your former prosperity to you. [Ps. 40:2; Isa. 40:2.]

life point

As "prisoners of hope" (Zechariah 9:12), we must allow ourselves to be captured by and filled with hope. We must think hope and we must talk hope. When you face a seemingly hopeless situation, remember that in God, you are a prisoner of hope; there is no way to get away from the hope that is in Him.

13 For I have bent Judah for Myself as My bow, filled the bow with Ephraim as My arrow, and will stir up your sons, O Zion, against your sons, O Greece, and will make you [Israel] as the sword of a mighty man.

14 And the Lord shall be seen over them and His arrow shall go forth as the lightning, and the Lord God will blow the trumpet and will go forth in the windstorms of the south.

15 The Lord of hosts shall defend *and* protect them; and they shall devour and they shall tread on [their fallen enemies] as on slingstones [that have missed their aim], and they shall drink [of victory] and be noisy *and* turbulent as from wine and become full like bowls [used to catch the sacrificial blood], like the corners of the [sacrificial] altar.

16 And the Lord their God will save them on that day as the flock of His people, for they shall be as the [precious] jewels of a crown, lifted high over *and* shining glitteringly upon His land.

17 For how great is God's goodness and how great is His beauty! And how great [He will make Israel's] goodliness and [Israel's] beauty! Grain shall make the young men thrive and fresh wine the maidens.

prisoners of hope

What is a prisoner of hope (see Zechariah 9:12)? It is someone who refuses to stop hoping in God, no matter how bad his or her circumstances are. Abraham was such a man. We learn from God's Word that all human reason for hope being gone, Abraham hoped on in faith that God's promise would come to pass in his life (see Romans 4:18).

Godly hope is not the same quality as what the world calls "hope." Usually when we hear people say they are "hoping" something will or will not happen, they are vaguely hoping, but clearly doubting. They speak negatively and complain about almost everything and then wonder why nothing works out for them. True biblical hope is a solid foundation; it is a springboard for our faith to take off from and actually take hold of the promises of God.

I know this may sound simple, but I think we can say real hope is a constant positive attitude that no matter what is happening currently, things will change for the better. Satan cannot defeat a person who refuses to stop hoping in God. Abraham refused to give up hope, and just as God had told him, he did become a father when he was far too old to father children. Hope is powerful. It opens the door for the impossible to become possible. All things are possible with God, but we must cooperate with Him by being hopeful and full of faith.

God promises that He will restore double what we have lost or had stolen if we will stay hopeful. It does no good at all to be hopeless. It only makes us unhappy, critical, and grouchy. Hopelessness leads to depression and many other problems. Become a prisoner of hope. Be the kind of person who absolutely refuses to be negative, and get ready to receive a double blessing for your former trouble.

10 ASK OF the Lord rain in the time of the latter *or* spring rain. It is the Lord Who makes lightnings which usher in the rain *and* give men showers, and grass to everyone in the field.
2 For the teraphim (household idols) have spoken vanity (emptiness, falsity, and futility) and the diviners have seen a lie and the dreamers have told false dreams; they comfort in vain. Therefore the people go their way like sheep; they are afflicted *and* hurt because there is no shepherd.
3 My anger is kindled against the shepherds [who are not true shepherds] and I will punish the goat leaders, for the Lord of hosts has visited His flock, the house of Judah, and will make them as His beautiful *and* majestic horse in the battle. [Ezek. 34:1-10.]
4 Out of him [Judah] shall come forth the kCornerstone, out of him the tent peg, out of him the battle bow; every ruler shall proceed from him. [Jer. 30:21.]
5 And they shall be like mighty men treading down their enemies in the mire of the streets in the battle, and

k This Messianic referent reminds one of the "Cornerstone" imagery of Ps. 118:22-23; Isa. 28:16; Matt. 21:42; Acts 4:11; Eph. 2:19-22; I Pet. 2:6-8.

they shall fight because the Lord is with them, and the [oppressor's] riders on horses shall be confounded *and* put to shame.

6   And I will strengthen the house of Judah and I will save the house of Joseph [Ephraim]. I will bring them back *and* cause them to dwell securely, for I have mercy, loving-kindness, *and* compassion for them. They shall be as though I had not cast them off, for I am the Lord their God, and I will hear them.

7   Then Ephraim [the ten tribes] shall become like a mighty warrior, and their hearts shall rejoice as through wine; yes, their children shall see it and rejoice; their hearts shall feel great delight *and* glory triumphantly in the Lord!

8   I will hiss for them [as the keeper does for his bees] and gather them in, for I have redeemed them, and they shall increase [again] as they have increased [before, in Egypt]. [Ezek. 36:10, 11.]

9   And though I sow them among the nations, yet they shall [earnestly] remember Me in far countries, and with their children they shall live and shall return [to God and the land He gave them].

10 I will bring them [all Israel] home again from the land of Egypt and gather them out of Assyria, and I will bring them into the land [on the east and on the west of the Jordan, into] Gilead and Lebanon, and room enough shall not be found for them.

11 And [the Lord] will pass through the sea of distress *and* affliction [at the head of His people, as He did at the Red Sea]; and He will smite down the waves of the sea, and all the depths of

speak the Word

the [river] Nile shall be dried up *and* put to shame; and the pride of Assyria shall be brought down and the scepter *or* rod [of the taskmasters of Egypt] shall pass away.

12 And I will strengthen [Israel] in the Lord, and they shall walk up and down *and* glory in His name, says the Lord.

11 OPEN YOUR doors, O Lebanon, that the fire may devour your cedars!

2   Wail, O fir tree *and* cypress, for the cedar has fallen, because the glorious *and* lofty trees are laid waste! Wail, O you oaks of Bashan, for the thick *and* inaccessible forest [on the steep mountainside] has in flames been felled!

3   A voice of the wailing of the shepherds, for their glory, the broad pasturage, is laid waste! A voice of the roaring of young lions, for the pride of the Jordan [the jungle or thickets] is ruined!

4   Thus says the Lord my God: Shepherd the flock [destined] for slaughter,

5   Whose buyers *or* possessors slay them and hold themselves not guilty; and they who sell them say, Blessed be the Lord, for I have become rich! And their own shepherds neither pity *nor* spare them [from the wolves].

6   For I will no more pity *or* spare the inhabitants of the land, says the Lord; but behold, I will deliver every man into his neighbor's hand and into the hand of his [foreign] king. And [the enemy] shall lay waste the land, and I will not deliver [the people] out of the hand [of the foreign oppressor].

7   So I [Zechariah] shepherded the

Thank You, Lord, that I am being strengthened in You. I will walk in and glory in Your name.
ADAPTED FROM ZECHARIAH 10:12

flock of slaughter, truly [as the name implies] the most miserable of sheep. And I took two [shepherd's] staffs, the one I called Beauty or Grace and the other I called Bands or Union; and I fed and shepherded the flock.

8 And I cut off the three shepherds [the civil authorities, the priests, and the prophets] in one month, for I was weary and impatient with them, and they also loathed me. [Jer. 2:8, 26; 18:18.]

9 So I [Zechariah] said, I will not be your shepherd. What is to die, let it die, and what is to be destroyed, let it be destroyed; and let the survivors devour one another's flesh.

10 And I took my staff, Beauty or Grace, and broke it in pieces to show that I was annulling the covenant or agreement which I had made with all the peoples [not to molest them].

11 So the covenant was annulled on that day, and thus the most wretched of the flock and the traffickers in the sheep who were watching me knew (recognized and understood) that it was truly the word of the Lord.

12 And I said to them, If it seems just and right to you, give me my wages; but if not, withhold them. So they weighed out for my price thirty pieces of silver.

13 And the Lord said to me, Cast it to the potter [as if He said, To the dogs!]—the munificently [miserable] sum at which I [and My shepherd] am priced by them! And I [Zechariah] took the thirty pieces of silver and cast them to the potter in the house of the Lord. [Matt. 26:14, 15; 27:3-10.]

14 Then I broke into pieces my other staff, Bands or Union, indicating that I was annulling the brotherhood between Judah and Israel.

15 And the Lord said to me, Take up once more the implements [the staff and rod of a shepherd, but this time] of a worthless and wicked shepherd. [Ezek. 34:2-6.]

16 For behold, I will raise up a false shepherd in the land; the lost and perishing he will not miss or visit, the young and scattered he will not go to seek, the wounded and broken he will not heal, nor will he feed those that are sound and strong; but he will eat the flesh of the fat ones and break off their hoofs [to consume all the flesh].

17 Woe to the worthless and foolish shepherd who deserts the flock! The sword shall smite his arm and his right eye; his arm shall be utterly withered and his right eye utterly blinded. [Jer. 23:1; John 10:12, 13.]

12 THE BURDEN or oracle (the thing to be lifted up) of the word of the Lord concerning Israel: Thus says the Lord, Who stretches out the heavens and lays the foundation of the earth and forms the spirit of man within him:

2 Behold, I am about to make Jerusalem a cup or bowl of reeling to all the peoples round about, and in the siege against Jerusalem will there also be a siege against and upon Judah.

3 And in that day I will make Jerusalem a burdensome stone for all peoples; all who lift it or burden themselves with it shall be sorely wounded. And all the nations of the earth shall come and gather together against it.

4 In that day, says the Lord, I will smite every horse [of the armies that contend against Jerusalem] with terror and panic and his rider with madness; and I will open My eyes and regard with favor the house of Judah and will smite every horse of the opposing nations with blindness.

5 And the chiefs of Judah shall say in their hearts, The inhabitants of Jerusalem are our strength in the Lord of hosts, their God.

6 In that day will I make the chiefs of Judah like a big, blazing pot among [sticks of] wood and like a flaming torch among sheaves [of grain], and they shall devour all the peoples round about, on the right hand and on the left; and they of Jerusalem shall yet again dwell *and* sit securely in their own place, in Jerusalem.

7   And the Lord shall save *and* give victory to the tents of Judah first, that the glory of the house of David and the glory of the inhabitants of Jerusalem may not be magnified *and* exalted above Judah.

8   In that day will the Lord guard *and* defend the inhabitants of Jerusalem, and he who is [spiritually] feeble *and* stumbles among them in that day [of persecution] shall become [strong and noble] like David; and the house of David [shall maintain its supremacy] like God, like the ¹Angel of the Lord Who is before them.

9   And it shall be in that day that I will make it My aim to destroy all the nations that come against Jerusalem.

10 And I will pour out upon the house of David and upon the inhabitants of Jerusalem the Spirit of grace *or* unmerited favor and supplication. And they shall look [earnestly] upon Me Whom they have pierced, and they shall mourn for Him as one mourns for his only son, and shall be in bitterness for Him as one who is in bitterness for his firstborn. [John 19:37; Rev. 1:7.]

11 In that day shall there be a great mourning in Jerusalem, as the mourning of [the city of] Hadadrimmon in the Valley of Megiddo [over beloved King ᵐJosiah]. [II Chron. 35:22-25.]

12 And the land shall mourn, every family apart: the [kingly] family of the house of David apart and their wives apart; the family of the house of

life point

The Holy Spirit not only leads us to pray, He also helps us pray. He shows us how to pray when we do not know what to pray for (see Romans 8:26, 27). Welcome the Spirit of supplication (see Zechariah 12:10) into your life and allow the ministry of prayer to be fulfilled through you. It is quite wonderful to watch the miraculous things that take place in response to prayer.

Nathan [David's son] apart and their wives apart;

13 The [priestly] family of the house of Levi apart and their wives apart; the family of Shimei [grandson of Levi] apart and their wives apart;

14 All the families that are left, each by itself, and their wives by themselves [each with an overwhelming individual sorrow over having blindly rejected their unrecognized Messiah].

13 IN THAT day there shall be a fountain opened for the house of David and for the inhabitants of Jerusalem [to cleanse them from] sin and uncleanness.

2   And in that day, says the Lord of hosts, I will cut off the names of the idols from the land, and they shall no more be remembered; and also I will remove from the land the [false] prophets and the unclean spirit.

3   And if anyone again appears [falsely] as a prophet, then his father and his mother who bore him shall say to him, You shall not live, for you speak lies in the name of the Lord; and his father and his mother who

---

1 See footnote on Zech. 1:11. See also Exod. 14:19; 23:20; 32:34; 33:2, 14-15, 22; Hos. 12:3-4. **m** King Josiah was mortally wounded at the age of thirty-nine. His death sparked an extraordinarily deep sense of grief among the people. That same kind of deep grief will characterize the mourning of Israel when they recognize as their once-crucified Messiah Him Who has come to reign.

the Spirit of grace and supplication

In Zechariah 12:1–10 God is saying to His people that He will destroy all their enemies and give them a great victory by pouring out upon them His Spirit of grace (or unmerited favor) and supplication.

There is no way to live in victory without an understanding of the Spirit of grace and supplication. These two words, *grace* and *supplication*, go together because the Spirit of supplication is the Holy Spirit. That means He is the Spirit of prayer. Each time we sense a desire to pray, the Holy Spirit is giving us that desire.

We may not realize when people or situations come to mind that the Holy Spirit is leading us to pray for them. We may wonder why we are thinking of them so much, but we neglect to pray for them. We do not grasp the fact that the Holy Spirit is at work in our thoughts.

Recognizing when we are being led by the Holy Spirit to pray is often a lesson that takes a long time to learn. We attribute too many things to coincidence or chance rather than understanding that God is attempting to lead us by His Spirit.

It is important that we realize the Spirit of supplication and grace accomplishes what we cannot do in our flesh if we will trust God's leading. We can relax and let God intercede through us as we pray. I believe what God is saying in Zechariah 12:10 is: "When the Spirit of supplication comes upon you and you begin to pray in faith, then My Spirit of grace will come flooding into your life. Through that channel of prayer I will, by My power, accomplish in your life what needs to be done, that which you cannot do alone."

bore him shall thrust him through when he prophesies.

4 And in that day the [false] prophets shall each be ashamed of his vision when he prophesies, nor will he wear a hairy or rough garment to deceive,

5 But he will [deny his identity and] say, I am no prophet. I am a tiller of the ground, for I have been made a bond servant from my youth.

6 And one shall say to him, What are these wounds on your breast or between your hands? Then he will answer, Those with which I was wounded [when disciplined] in the house of my [loving] friends.

7 Awake, O sword, against My shepherd and against the man who is My associate, says the Lord of hosts;

smite the shepherd and the sheep [of the flock] shall be scattered, and I will turn back My hand *and* stretch it out again upon the little ones [of the flock]. [Matt. 26:31, 32.]

8 And in all the land, says the Lord, two-thirds shall be cut off and perish, but one-third shall be left alive. [Hos. 2:23; Rom. 11:5.]

9 And I will bring the third part through the fire, and will refine them as silver is refined and will test them as gold is tested. They will call on My name, and I will hear *and* answer them. I will say, It is My people; and they will say, The Lord is my God.

14 BEHOLD, A day of the Lord is coming when the spoil [taken from you]

putting the Word to work

Have you ever heard the phrase "trial by fire"? God says that He tests us by fire to refine us, to remove the impurities of sin (see Zechariah 13:9). If you are in a season of testing or trials in your life, call upon God, for He has promised to answer you. Trust Him as He refines you, and know that He is at work to accomplish His purposes in you.

shall be divided [among the victors] in the midst of you.

2　For I will gather all nations against Jerusalem to battle, and the city shall be taken and the houses rifled and the women ravished; and half of the city shall go into exile, but the rest of the people shall not be cut off from the city.

3　Then shall the Lord go forth and fight against those nations, as when He fought in the day of battle.

4　And His feet shall stand in that day upon the Mount of Olives, which lies before Jerusalem on the east, and the Mount of Olives shall be split in two from the east to the west by a very great valley; and half of the mountain shall remove toward the north and half of it toward the south. [Isa. 64:1, 2.]

5　And you shall flee by the valley of My mountains, for the valley of the mountains shall reach to Azal, and you shall flee as you fled from before

the earthquake in the days of Uzziah king of Judah; and the Lord my [Zechariah's] [n]God shall come, and all the holy ones [saints and angels] with *Him*. [Amos 1:1; Col. 3:4; I Thess. 4:14; Jude 14, 15.]

6　And it shall come to pass in that day that there shall not be light; the glorious *and* bright ones [the heavenly bodies] shall be darkened.

7　But it shall be one continuous day, known to the Lord—not day and not night, but at evening time there shall be light.

8　And it shall be in that day that living waters shall go out from Jerusalem, half of them to the eastern [Dead] Sea and half of them to the western [Mediterranean] Sea; in summer and in winter shall it be.

9　And the Lord shall be King over all the earth; in that day the Lord shall be one [in the recognition and worship of men] and His name one.

10　All the land shall be turned into a plain from Geba to Rimmon, [the Rimmon that is] south of Jerusalem. But Jerusalem shall remain lifted up on its site and dwell in its place, from Benjamin's gate to the place of the First Gate, to the Corner Gate, and from the Tower of Hananel to the king's winepresses.

11　And it shall be inhabited, for there shall be no more curse *or* ban of utter destruction, but Jerusalem shall dwell securely. [Rev. 22:3.]

12　And this shall be the plague

speak the Word

Thank You, God, that You hear me and answer me when I call upon Your name. You say that I am Yours, and I say that You are mine.
ADAPTED FROM ZECHARIAH **13:9**

n The second advent of Christ is the coming of **God** to earth—hence the emphasis placed upon it in the Scriptures. It is heralded not just once, but many times—plainly, without opportunity for misinterpretation, such as in Deut. 30:3; Zech. 14:3, 4; Matt. 16:27; 24:3-14, 27, 36-39; 25:31, 32; 26:64; Luke 21:25-28; Acts 1:9-11; I Cor. 1:7, 8; 4:5; I Tim. 6:14; II Tim. 4:1; Tit. 2:13; Heb. 9:28; I John 2:28; Rev. 3:11; 16:15; 22:7, 20.

wherewith the Lord will smite all the peoples that have warred against Jerusalem: their flesh shall rot away while they stand upon their feet and their eyes shall corrode away in their sockets and their tongue shall decay away in their mouth.

13 And in that day there shall be a great confusion, discomfiture, *and* panic among them from the Lord; and they shall seize each his neighbor's hand, and the hand of the one shall be raised against the hand of the other.

14 And Judah also shall fight at Jerusalem, and the wealth of all the nations round about shall be gathered together—gold and silver and apparel in great abundance.

15 And as that plague on men, so shall be the plague on the horse, on the mule, on the camel, on the donkey, and on all the livestock *and* beasts that may be in those camps.

16 And everyone who is left of all the nations which came against Jerusalem shall even go up from year to year to worship the King, the Lord of hosts, and to keep the Feast of Tabernacles *or* Booths.

17 And it shall be that whoso of the families of the earth shall not go up to Jerusalem to worship the King, the Lord of hosts, upon them there shall be no rain.

18 And if the family of Egypt does not go up to Jerusalem and present themselves, upon them there shall be no rain, but there shall be the plague with which the Lord will smite the nations that go not up to keep the Feast of Tabernacles.

19 This shall be the consequent punishment of the sin of Egypt and the consequent punishment of the sin of all the nations that do not go up to keep the Feast of Tabernacles.

20 In that day there shall be [written] upon the [little] bells on the horses, HOLY TO THE LORD, and the pots in the Lord's house shall be holy to the Lord like the bowls before the altar.

21 Yes, every pot in all the houses of Jerusalem and in Judah shall be dedicated *and* holy to the Lord of hosts, and all who sacrifice may come and take of them and boil their sacrifices in them [and traders in such wares will no longer be seen at the temple]. And in that day there shall be no more a Canaanite [that is, any godless or unclean person, whether Jew or Gentile] in the house of the Lord of hosts. [Eph. 2:19-22.]

Malachi

Author:
Malachi

Date:
About 450 BC

Everyday Life Principles:
Even when there is a place of worship in our lives, we still must have hearts that worship and honor God.

Christian leaders must live holy lives, not causing others to sin but setting worthy examples for them to follow.

Christianity is about relationship, not religion.

The name Malachi means "my messenger," and indeed Malachi was God's messenger to the Jews in the years following the rebuilding of the temple. Even though the temple had finally been rebuilt, the people were not worshipping and relating to God as they should have been. Some had turned to idolatry, some had disobeyed God by marrying foreigners, and some were neglecting to pay their tithes. These practices and others combined to create a general dishonor toward God and disregard for the things of God—and these attitudes demand judgment unless people repent.

Malachi does rebuke the people for their attitudes and behavior, but he also addresses leaders extensively, rebuking the priests for causing the people to stumble and for not living holy lives. He promises that God will come "like a refiner's fire" and like launderers' soap (see Malachi 3:2) to purify the priests and restore them to a place of being able to serve Him in righteousness, with right heart attitudes and right actions.

As you read the book of Malachi, remember that being a Christian is not about religion, but about relationship. It is not *only* about having or going to a "temple," which in today's society would be equal to going to church, but about developing and maintaining the heart attitudes that keep you in close relationship with God.

1 THE BURDEN *or* oracle (the thing to be lifted up) of the word of the Lord to Israel by Malachi [My messenger].

2 I have loved you, says the Lord. Yet you say, How *and* in what way have You loved us? Was not Esau Jacob's brother? says the Lord; yet I loved Jacob (Israel),

3 But [in comparison with the degree of love I have for Jacob] I have hated Esau [Edom] and have laid waste his mountains, and his heritage I have given to the jackals of the wilderness. [Rom. 9:13, 16.]

4 Though [impoverished] Edom should say, We are beaten down, but we will return and build the waste places—thus says the Lord of hosts: They may build, but I will tear *and* throw down; and men will call them the Wicked Country, the people against whom the Lord has indignation forever.

5 Your own eyes shall see this and you shall say, The Lord is great *and* will be magnified over *and* beyond the border of Israel! [Isa. 34; 63:1-6; Jer. 49:7-22; Ezek. 25:12-14; Obad. 1.]

6 A son honors his father, and a servant his master. If then I am a Father, where is My honor? And if I am a Master, where is the [reverent] fear due Me? says the Lord of hosts to you, O priests, who despise My name. You say, How *and* in what way have we despised Your name?

7 By offering polluted food upon My altar. And you ask, How have we polluted it *and* profaned You? By thinking that the table of the Lord is contemptible *and* may be despised.

8 When you [priests] offer blind [animals] for sacrifice, is it not evil? And when you offer the lame and the sick, is it not evil? Present such a thing [a blind or lame or sick animal] now to your governor [in payment of your taxes, and see what will happen]. Will he be pleased with you? Or will he receive you graciously? says the Lord of hosts.

9 Now then, I [Malachi] beg [you priests], entreat God [earnestly] that He will be gracious to us. With such a gift from your hand [as a defective animal for sacrifice], will He accept it *or* show favor to any of you? says the Lord of hosts.

10 Oh, that there were even one among you [whose duty it is to minister to Me] who would shut the doors, that you might not kindle fire on My altar to no purpose [an empty, futile, fruitless pretense]! I have no pleasure in you, says the Lord of hosts, nor will I accept an offering from your hand.

11 For from the rising of the sun to its setting My name shall be great among the nations, and in every place incense shall be offered to My name, and indeed a pure offering; for My name shall be great among the nations, says the Lord of hosts.

12 But you [priests] profane it when [by your actions] you say, The table of the Lord is polluted, and the fruit of it, its food, is contemptible *and* may be despised.

13 You say also, Behold, what a

putting the Word to work

Many things in life—our studies, our work, our relationships—demand or expect our best. Do you give your best to God in worship? I encourage you to commit to worshipping Him wholeheartedly and always doing your very best for Him (see Malachi 1:11–14).

speak the Word

God, You are my Father and my Master. I honor You and I fear You.
ADAPTED FROM MALACHI 1:6

drudgery *and* weariness this is! And you have sniffed at it, says the Lord of hosts. And you have brought that which was [a]taken by violence, or the lame or the sick; this you bring as an offering! Shall I accept this from your hand? says the Lord. [Lev. 1:3; Deut. 15:21.]

14 But cursed is the [cheating] deceiver who has a male in his flock and vows to offer it, yet sacrifices to the [sovereign] Lord a blemished *or* diseased thing! For I am a great King, says the Lord of hosts, and My name is terrible[´] *and* to be [reverently] feared among the nations.

life point

There is power in the name of the Lord, and His name is to be reverently feared (see Malachi 1:14). You and I need to have such reverence for the Lord and for His name that we are afraid to speak His holy name casually or without purpose.

2 AND NOW, O you priests, this commandment is for you.

2 If you will not hear and if you will not lay it to heart to give glory to My name, says the Lord of hosts, then I will send the curse upon you, and I will curse your blessings; yes, I have already turned them to curses because you do not lay it to heart.

3 Behold, I will rebuke your seed [grain—which will prevent due harvest], and I will spread the [b]dung from the festival offerings upon your faces, and you shall be taken away with it.

4 And you shall know, recognize, *and* understand that I have sent this [new] decree to you priests, to be My [new] covenant with Levi [the priestly tribe], says the Lord of hosts.

5 My covenant [on My part with Levi] was to give him life and peace, because [on his part] of the [reverent and worshipful] fear with which [the priests] would revere Me and stand in awe of My name.

6 The law of truth was in [Levi's] mouth, and unrighteousness was not found in his lips; he walked with Me in peace and uprightness and turned many away from iniquity.

7 For the priest's lips should guard *and* keep pure the knowledge [of My law], and the people should seek (inquire for and require) instruction

life point

Malachi 2:5–7 deals with priests and the way they are supposed to speak. Since I am a minister of the gospel, this subject naturally interests me. But in reality, according to Revelation 1:6, all believers are kings and priests because Jesus Christ has "formed us into a kingdom (a royal race), priests to His God and Father."

Notice that in Malachi 2:5, God says He will make a covenant with His priests. In the Bible, whenever there is a covenant between two individuals, each has a part to play in that agreement or contract. In our covenant with the Lord, He has a part to play, and we have a part to play. He covenants to give us life and peace; our part is to give Him reverence and worshipful fear, to revere Him, and to stand in awe of His name.

If we have reverential and worshipful fear of the Lord—if we revere Him and stand in awe of His name—then we will not use our mouths to speak evil against His people, whom we serve as His priests and ministers.

---

a Animals with defects or serious flaws were unacceptable as sacrifices. **b** Instead of the edible portions of the sacrificed animals—the shoulder, cheeks, and stomach—which were the wages for the work of the priests (Deut. 18:3).

at his mouth; for he is the messenger of the Lord of hosts.

8 But you have turned aside out of the way; you have caused many to stumble by your instruction [in the law]; you have corrupted the covenant of Levi [with Me], says the Lord of hosts.

9 Therefore have I also made you despised and abased before all the people, inasmuch as you have not kept My ways but have shown favoritism to persons in your administration of the law [of God].

10 Have we not all one Father? Has not one God created us? Why then do we deal faithlessly and treacherously each against his brother, profaning the covenant of [God with] our fathers?

11 Judah has been faithless and dealt treacherously, and an abomination has been committed in Israel and in Jerusalem; for Judah [that is, Jewish men] has profaned the holy sanctuary of the Lord which He loves, and has married the daughter of a foreign god [having divorced his Jewish wife]. [Ezra 9:2; Jer. 2:3.]

12 The Lord will cast out of the tents of Jacob to the last man those who do this [evil thing], the master and the servant [or the pupil] alike, even him who brings an offering to the Lord of hosts.

13 And this you do with double guilt; you cover the altar of the Lord with tears [shed by your unoffending wives, divorced by you that you might take heathen wives], and with [your own] weeping and crying out because the Lord does not regard your offering any more or accept it with favor at your hand.

14 Yet you ask, Why does He reject it? Because the Lord was witness [to the covenant made at your marriage] between you and the wife of your youth, against whom you have dealt

life point

In Malachi 2:13–17, the prophet is addressing the issue of marriage. In Malachi 2:16, he writes: "Keep a watch upon your spirit [that it may be controlled by (God's) Spirit]." We cannot expect anything to go well for us or in our marriages if we do not allow ourselves to be controlled by God's Spirit. But if we will listen to God and be diligent to obey, our lives and our marriages can be wonderful.

treacherously and to whom you were faithless. Yet she is your companion and the wife of your covenant [made by your marriage vows].

15 And did not God make [you and your wife] one [flesh]? Did not One make you and preserve your spirit alive? And why [did God make you two] one? Because He sought a godly offspring [from your union]. Therefore take heed to yourselves, and let no one deal treacherously and be faithless to the wife of his youth.

16 For the Lord, the God of Israel, says: I hate divorce and marital separation and him who covers his garment [his wife] with violence. Therefore keep a watch upon your spirit [that it may be controlled by My Spirit], that you deal not treacherously and faithlessly [with your marriage mate].

17 You have wearied the Lord with your words. Yet you say, In what way have we wearied Him? [You do it when by your actions] you say, Everyone who does evil is good in the sight of the Lord and He delights in them. Or [by asking], Where is the God of justice?

3 BEHOLD, I send My ᶜmessenger, and he shall prepare the way before Me. And the Lord

---

c This is fulfilled in John the Baptist (Matt. 11:10; Mark 1:2; Luke 1:76).

[the Messiah], Whom you seek, will suddenly come to His temple; the [d]Messenger *or* Angel of the covenant, Whom you desire, behold, He shall come, says the Lord of hosts. [Matt. 11:10; Luke 1:13-17, 76.]

2   But who can endure the day of His coming? And who can stand when He appears? For He is like a refiner's fire and like fullers' soap; [Rev. 6:12-17.]

3   He will sit as a refiner and purifier of silver, and He will purify the priests, the sons of Levi, and refine them like gold and silver, that they may offer to the Lord offerings in righteousness.

4   Then will the offering of Judah and Jerusalem be pleasing to the Lord as in the days of old and as in ancient years.

5   Then I will draw near to you for judgment; I will be a swift witness against the sorcerers, against the adulterers, against the false swearers, and against those who oppress the hireling in his wages, the widow and the fatherless, and who turn aside the temporary resident from his right and fear not Me, says the Lord of hosts.

6   For I am the Lord, I do not change; that is why you, O sons of Jacob, are not consumed.

7   Even from the days of your fathers you have turned aside from My ordinances and have not kept them. Return to me, and I will return to you, says the Lord of hosts. But you say, How shall we return?

8   Will a man rob *or* defraud God? Yet you rob *and* defraud Me. But you say, In what way do we rob *or* defraud You? [You have withheld your] tithes and offerings.

9   You are cursed with the curse, for you are robbing Me, even this whole nation. [Lev. 26:14-17.]

10   Bring all the tithes (the whole tenth of your income) into the storehouse,

life point

In our daily relationship with God, one of the things we appreciate most about Him is the fact that we can count on Him not to change.

We love God and can trust Him because He never changes. He says in Malachi 3:6, basically, "This is the way I have always been, and this is the way I'm always going to be." If you can count on anything, you can count on Jesus never changing. He can change anything else that needs to be changed, but He always remains constant, steady, and eternal. Hallelujah!

that there may be food in My house, and prove Me now by it, says the Lord of hosts, if I will not open the windows of heaven for you and pour you out a blessing, that there shall not be room enough to receive it. [Mal. 2:2.]

11   And I will rebuke the devourer [insects and plagues] for your sakes and he shall not destroy the fruits of your ground, neither shall your vine drop its fruit before the time in the field, says the Lord of hosts.

12   And all nations shall call you happy *and* blessed, for you shall be a land of delight, says the Lord of hosts.

13   Your words have been strong *and* hard against Me, says the Lord. Yet you say, What have we spoken against You?

14   You have said, It is useless to serve God, and what profit is it if we keep His ordinances and walk gloomily *and* as if in mourning apparel before the Lord of hosts?

15   And now we consider the proud *and* arrogant to be happy *and* favored; evildoers are exalted *and* prosper; yes, and when they test God, they escape [unpunished].

d The Messiah as God's representative will confirm and establish the covenant (see Isa. 42:6).

the refiner's fire

God desires to consume everything in our lives that does not bring Him glory. He sends the Holy Spirit to live inside us believers, to be in close fellowship with us, and to bring conviction of our every wrong thought, word, or action. We must all go through the "refiner's fire" (Malachi 3:2).

What does that mean? It means God will deal with us. He will change our attitudes, desires, ways, thoughts, and conversations. Those of us who go through the fire instead of running from it are the ones who will bring great glory to God.

Going through fire sounds frightening. It reminds us of pain and even death. However, in Romans 8:17 Paul said that if we want to share Christ's inheritance, we must also share His suffering. Because of that truth, it is important for us to think about how Jesus suffered. We know He suffered horribly on the cross, so are we expected to go to the cross also? The answer is yes and no. We do not have to physically go to a cross and be nailed to it for our sins, but in Mark 8:34 Jesus did say that we should take up our crosses and follow Him. What does that mean? Taking up our crosses means laying aside selfish, self-centered lifestyles. Believe me, getting rid of selfishness takes some fire (difficult times)—and usually a lot of it—but it is worth it in the end.

16 Then those who feared the Lord talked often one to another; and the Lord listened and heard it, and a book of remembrance was written before Him of those who reverenced *and* worshipfully feared the Lord and who thought on His name.

17 And they shall be Mine, says the Lord of hosts, in that day when I publicly recognize *and* openly declare them to be My jewels (My special possession, My peculiar treasure). And I will spare them, as a man spares his own son who serves him.

18 Then shall you return and discern

life point

Verses 10–12 of Malachi chapter 3, a chapter known for its teaching on tithing and giving, describe the blessings God tells Israel tithing will bring: God will rebuke the devourer for the tithers' sake! The fruit of their ground will not be destroyed, and all nations will call them happy and blessed. By obeying God's directions rather than following the world's system, they will be blessed.

The Lord wants His people to bring their tithes to the storehouse to prove Him. When we bring tithes in obedience to His Word, He promises to pour out a blessing so enormous that there will not be room to contain it.

putting the Word to work

Do you ever wonder if faithfully serving God is really worth it, as people said in Malachi 3:14? Sometimes it may seem as though it really does not make a difference. But be encouraged! Know that God sees your faithfulness and remembers. Ask God to help you to trust that He is always at work in you and through you for your good and for His purposes.

are you angry with God?

Many times people blame God for their unhappiness. They develop bitterness and resentment toward God, especially if they have had a lot of disappointments in their lives.

The devil wants us to blame God if we are not happy. He wants to create a rift between God and us so that we will lose our joy. In Malachi 3:13–15, we read about people who were angry with God and spoke harshly against Him. Similarly, we may become angry with God and if so, then we need to take steps to get rid of that anger.

Sometimes we try to get things we want from God by imitating what we have seen others do. Then we get upset when He does not answer the way we think He should. But by copying others' actions, we may be doing things God never told us to do. Do not be angry with God for not blessing something He did not tell you to do. And do not blame Him for the things the devil has brought into your life.

This may sound odd to you, but if you are angry with God, you need to "forgive" Him. God does not need your forgiveness—He has done nothing wrong—but you need to be released from the harsh results of the unforgiveness and bitterness you may have directed toward God. If you have unforgiveness in your heart against God, give it up and let it go. God is your friend, not your enemy. Let faith and joy fill that place where unforgiveness once was.

You will not be disappointed with God if you wait in faith to hear from Him. Romans 10:17 teaches: "So faith comes by hearing [what is told], and what is heard comes by the preaching [of the message that came from the lips] of Christ (the Messiah Himself)." If you want joy in your life, you have to believe that God is good and that He rewards those who diligently seek Him (see Hebrews 11:6). Joy will fill you when you quit demanding answers to your questions about why bad things have happened to you. Trust God's ways and His timing, and remember that trust always requires some unanswered questions.

God wants to bless every person. No matter what is going on in your life right now, no matter how badly it hurts, do not blame God. You may not always understand what is happening, but God is perfect. He is good, and He is right. Fault and error are either caused by people or instigated by the devil.

If you have been upset with God, I encourage you to release your anger to Him. Pray with me, "God, I have held anger against You. I know You have done nothing wrong, and I am in need of *Your* forgiveness. But I believe that my saying, 'I forgive You,' will help me let go of unforgiveness that I have misdirected toward You. I forgive You. My problems are not Your fault. You are my *answer*."

a book of remembrance

The Lord listens to every conversation we have. A greater awareness of that fact would probably cause us to change some of our conversations. When our conversations please Him, He records them in a book called a "book of remembrance" (Malachi 3:16).

I keep a book of remembrance, and I believe keeping such a book is a good habit for anyone to form. In my book, which is more like a journal, I record things God has done for me, special things that clearly remind me that His favor and love are upon me. Writing them down helps me to remember them. We are to be thankful and to give God praise at all times. Keeping a record of God's awesome deeds is beneficial to us because we can read them anytime we want to and bring to our minds how good He is to us.

Why would God keep a book of remembrance of the things we say in conversation to others? I believe He does so because our words come from our hearts. Words are very important; they are containers for power. Our words can bless or they can curse; they can build up or tear down. Obviously our words are extremely important to God, they are important enough for Him to record the good ones. I wonder if He also reads over His book of remembrance and gets pleasure when He thinks of His children who have sat at lunch having conversations that included praise and a grateful attitude or loving and kind words for others.

God actually indicates that a day will come when He will openly and publicly declare that type of person to be His special treasure, or His jewel. All righteous deeds bring a reward in due time, and all unrighteous deeds bring a curse in due time. We reap what we sow. Start today guarding your conversations, and let the words of your mouth be filled with good things so God can record them in His special book of remembrance.

---

between the righteous and the wicked, between him who serves God and him who does not serve Him.

4 FOR BEHOLD, the day comes that shall burn like an oven, and all the proud *and* arrogant, yes, and all that do wickedly *and* are lawless, shall be stubble; the day that comes shall burn them up, says the Lord of hosts, so that it will leave them neither root nor branch. [Isa. 5:21-25; Matt. 3:12.]

2 But unto you who revere *and* worshipfully fear My name shall the Sun of Righteousness arise with healing in His wings *and* His beams, and you shall go forth and gambol like calves [released] from the stall *and* leap for joy.

3 And you shall tread down the lawless *and* wicked, for they shall be ashes under the soles of your feet in the day that I shall do this, says the Lord of hosts.

4 [Earnestly] remember the law of Moses, My servant, the statutes and the ordinances which I commanded him on [Mount] Horeb [to give] to all Israel.

5 Behold, I will send you Elijah the prophet before the great and terrible day of the Lord comes. [Matt. 11:14; 17:10-13.]

6 And he shall turn *and* reconcile the hearts of the [estranged] fathers to the [ungodly] children, and the hearts of the [rebellious] children to [the piety of] their fathers [a reconciliation produced by repentance of the ungodly], lest I come and smite the land with a curse *and* a ban of utter destruction. [Luke 1:17.]

putting the Word to work

All of us have areas of brokenness in our lives or wounded hearts. These wounds may be from a broken relationship, a difficult experience, or disappointments. Is there a particular area in your life where you need healing? God promises to bring healing; ask Him to cover you with His wings of healing and to bring restoration and wholeness to your life.

New Testament

Matthew

Author:
Attributed to Matthew

Date:
Probably shortly before AD 70

Everyday Life Principles:
Jesus' teachings in the book of Matthew and in the other Gospels are as relevant and as important to your life today as they were while He lived on earth.

Jesus taught us with words, with stories, and by personal example. I strongly encourage you to study His teachings and to imitate His attitudes and actions.

One way to be blessed is to cultivate the heart attitudes and character qualities Jesus taught in The Beatitudes and throughout the book of Matthew.

The book of Matthew begins the New Testament and is the first of the four Gospels—accounts of Jesus' life and ministry, which include stories He told (called parables), lessons He taught, and miracles He worked. The Gospels also include the teachings, insights, and instructions Jesus gave to the people who followed Him so many centuries ago—and to those who follow Him today.

Matthew focuses on Jesus as the fulfillment of the Old Testament law, on Jesus as the Messiah Who was prophesied for so long, and on the kingdom of heaven. There are so many treasures in Matthew; it is especially rich with Jesus' practical instructions for our lives. This book emphasizes Jesus' teaching ministry, and as we read it, we see Jesus teaching people, both through the spoken word and by example: how to live, how to think, how to treat people, how to pray, and how to be wise and godly in everyday life.

In Matthew chapters 5—7, we find a collection of teachings called The Sermon on the Mount. In this great sermon are The Beatitudes (a list of heart attitudes and character qualities that bring blessing to our lives, found in 5:1–12) and The Lord's Prayer (6:9–13).

I hope you will take time to read, meditate on, and apply to your life the teachings and truths in Matthew. As you do, you will be blessed.

1 THE BOOK of the ancestry (genealogy) of Jesus Christ (the Messiah, the Anointed), the son (descendant) of David, the son (descendant) of Abraham. [Ps. 132:11; Isa. 11:1.]

2 Abraham was the father of Isaac, Isaac the father of Jacob, Jacob the father of Judah and his brothers,

3 Judah the father of Perez and Zerah, whose mother was Tamar, Perez the father of Hezron, Hezron the father of Aram,

4 Aram the father of Aminadab, Aminadab the father of Nahshon, Nahshon the father of Salmon,

5 Salmon the father of Boaz, whose mother was Rahab, Boaz the father of Obed, whose mother was Ruth, Obed the father of Jesse,

6 Jesse the father of King David, King David the father of Solomon, whose mother had been the wife of Uriah, [Ruth 4:18-22; I Chron. 2:13-15.]

7 Solomon the father of Rehoboam, Rehoboam the father of Abijah, Abijah the father of Asa,

8 Asa the father of Jehoshaphat, Jehoshaphat the father of Joram [Jehoram], Joram the father of Uzziah,

9 Uzziah the father of Jotham, Jotham the father of Ahaz, Ahaz the father of Hezekiah,

10 Hezekiah the father of Manasseh, Manasseh the father of Amon, Amon the father of Josiah,

11 And Josiah became the father of Jeconiah [also called Coniah and Jehoiachin] and his brothers about the time of the removal (deportation) to Babylon. [II Kings 24:14; I Chron. 3:15, 16.]

12 After the exile to Babylon, Jeconiah became the father of Shealtiel [Salathiel], Shealtiel the father of Zerubbabel,

13 Zerubbabel the father of Abiud,

Abiud the father of Eliakim, Eliakim the father of Azor,

14 Azor the father of Sadoc, Sadoc the father of Achim, Achim the father of Eliud,

15 Eliud the father of Eleazar, Eleazar the father of Matthan, Matthan the father of Jacob,

16 Jacob the father of Joseph, the husband of Mary, of whom was born Jesus, Who is called the Christ. (the Messiah, the Anointed)

17 So all the generations from Abraham to David are fourteen, from David to the Babylonian exile (deportation) fourteen generations, from the Babylonian exile to the Christ fourteen generations.

18 Now the birth of Jesus Christ took place under these circumstances: When His mother Mary had been promised in marriage to Joseph, before they came together, she was found to be pregnant [through the power] of the Holy Spirit.

19 And her [promised] husband Joseph, being a just *and* upright man and not willing to expose her publicly *and* to shame *and* disgrace her, decided to repudiate *and* dismiss (divorce) her quietly *and* secretly.

20 But as he was thinking this over, behold, an angel of the Lord appeared to him in a dream, saying, Joseph, descendant of David, do not be afraid to take Mary [as] your wife, for that which is conceived in her is of (from, out of) the Holy Spirit.

21 She will bear a Son, and you shall call His name Jesus [the Greek form of the Hebrew Joshua, which means Savior], for He will save His people from their sins [that is, prevent them from [a]failing and missing the true end and scope of life, which is God].

22 All this took place that it might be fulfilled which the Lord had spoken through the prophet,

---

a Marvin Vincent, *Word Studies in the New Testament.*

23 Behold, the virgin shall become pregnant and give birth to a Son, and they shall call His name Emmanuel—which, when translated, means, God with us. [Isa. 7:14.]
24 Then Joseph, being aroused from his sleep, did as the angel of the Lord had commanded him: he took [her to his side as] his wife.
25 But he had no union with her as her husband until she had borne *her firstborn* Son; and he called His name Jesus.

2 NOW WHEN Jesus was born in Bethlehem of Judea in the days of Herod the king, behold, wise men [astrologers] from the east came to Jerusalem, asking,
2 Where is He Who has been born King of the Jews? For we have seen His star in the east ᵇat its rising and have come to worship Him. [Num. 24:17; Jer. 23:5; Zech. 9:9.]
3 When Herod the king heard this, he was disturbed *and* troubled, and the whole of Jerusalem with him.
4 So he called together all the chief priests and learned men (scribes) of the people and ᶜanxiously asked them where the Christ was to be born.
5 They replied to him, In Bethlehem of Judea, for so it is written by the prophet:
6 And you Bethlehem, in the land of Judah, you are not in any way least *or* insignificant among the ᵈchief cities of Judah; for from you shall come a Ruler (ᵉLeader) Who will govern *and* ᶠshepherd My people Israel. [Mic. 5:2.]
7 Then Herod sent for the wise men [astrologers] secretly, and ᶠaccurately to the last point ascertained from them the time of the appearing of the star [that is, ᶠhow long the star had made itself visible since its rising in the east].
8 Then he sent them to Bethlehem, saying, Go and search for the Child carefully *and* diligently, and when you have found ᵍHim, bring me word, that I too may come and worship Him.
9 When they had listened to the king, they went their way, and behold, the star which had been seen in the east ᵇin its rising went before them until it came and stood over the place where the young Child was.
10 When they saw the star, they were thrilled with ecstatic joy.
11 And on going into the house, they saw the Child with Mary His mother, and they fell down and worshiped Him. Then opening their treasure bags, they presented to Him gifts—gold and frankincense and myrrh.
12 And ᶠreceiving an answer to their asking, they were divinely instructed *and* warned in a dream not to go back to Herod; so they departed to their own country by a different way.
13 Now after they had gone, behold, an angel of the Lord appeared to Joseph in a dream and said, Get up! [ʰTenderly] take *unto you* the young Child and His mother and flee to Egypt; and remain there till I tell you [otherwise], for Herod intends to search for the Child in order to destroy Him.
14 And having risen, he took the Child and His mother by night and withdrew to Egypt
15 And remained there until Herod's death. This was to fulfill what the Lord had spoken by the prophet, Out of Egypt have I called My Son. [Hos. 11:1.]
16 Then Herod, when he realized that he had been misled by the wise men, was furiously enraged, and he

---

b Alternate translation.   **c** Charles B. Williams, *The New Testament: A Translation in the Language of the People*.   **d** Joseph Henry Thayer, *A Greek-English Lexicon of the New Testament*.   **e** James Hope Moulton and George Milligan, *The Vocabulary of the Greek Testament*.   **f** Marvin Vincent, *Word Studies*.   **g** Capitalized because of what He is, the spotless Son of God, not what the speaker may have thought He was.   **h** Charles B. Williams, *The New Testament: A Translation*.

sent and put to death all the male children in Bethlehem and in all that territory who were two years old and under, reckoning according to the date which he had investigated diligently *and* had learned exactly from the wise men.

life point

Satan is always out to kill things in their infancy, which is why he planted the thought in Herod's mind to order every male child in Bethlehem, two years old and under, put to death. Because Herod was frightened of the newborn Christ Child—the "King of the Jews" Whom the wise men sought—he wanted to kill Him (see Matthew 2:1–16).

I find it interesting that Satan was afraid of a child, and that a child was the King of the Jews. Kings rule, and perhaps one lesson here is that if we desire to rule and reign as kings in life (see Romans 5:17; Revelation 1:6), we must also become like little children. When we become childlike (humble, trusting, lowly, and forgiving), we frighten the devil just as the Christ Child frightened Herod. If you want to be a threat to the enemy, become childlike in your faith.

17 Then was fulfilled what was spoken by the prophet Jeremiah:
18 A voice was heard in Ramah, wailing and loud lamentation, Rachel weeping for her children; she refused to be comforted, because they were no more. [Jer. 31:15.]
19 But when Herod died, behold, an angel of the Lord appeared in a dream to Joseph in Egypt
20 And said, Rise, [ᶦtenderly] take

unto you the Child and His mother and go to the land of Israel, for those who sought the Child's life are dead.
21 Then he awoke and arose and [ᶦtenderly] took the Child and His mother and came into the land of Israel.
22 But because he heard that Archelaus was ruling over Judea in the place of his father Herod, he was afraid to go there. And being divinely warned in a dream, he withdrew to the region of Galilee.
23 He went and dwelt in a town called Nazareth, so that what was spoken through the prophets might be fulfilled: He shall be called a Nazarene [Branch, Separated One]. [Isa. 11:1.]

3 IN THOSE days there appeared John the Baptist, preaching in the Wilderness (Desert) of Judea
2 And saying, Repent (ʲthink differently; change your mind, regretting your sins and changing your conduct), for the kingdom of heaven is at hand.
3 This is he who was mentioned by the prophet Isaiah when he said, The voice of one crying in the wilderness (shouting in the desert), Prepare the road for the Lord, make His highways straight (level, ᵏdirect). [Isa. 40:3.]
4 This *same* John's garments were made of camel's hair, and he wore a leather girdle about his waist; and his food was locusts and wild honey. [Lev. 11:22; II Kings 1:8; Zech. 13:4.]
5 Then Jerusalem and all Judea and all the country round about the Jordan went out to him;
6 And they were baptized in the Jordan by him, confessing their sins.
7 But when he saw many of the Pharisees and Sadducees coming for baptism, he said to them, You brood of vipers! Who warned you to flee *and*

---

i Charles B. Williams, *The New Testament: A Translation.* **j** Marvin Vincent, *Word Studies.* **k** G. Abbott-Smith, *Manual Greek Lexicon of the New Testament.*

escape from the wrath *and* indignation [of God against disobedience] that is coming?

8 Bring forth fruit that is consistent with repentance [let your lives prove your change of heart];

9 And do not presume to say to yourselves, We have Abraham for our forefather; for I tell you, God is able to raise up descendants for Abraham from these stones!

10 And already the ax is lying at the root of the trees; every tree therefore that does not bear good fruit is cut down and thrown into the fire.

11 I indeed baptize you [l]in (with) water [m]because of repentance [that is, because of your [n]changing your minds for the better, heartily amending your ways, with abhorrence of your past sins]. But He Who is coming after me is mightier than I, Whose sandals I am not worthy *or* fit to take off *or* carry; He will baptize you with the Holy Spirit and with fire.

12 His winnowing fan (shovel, fork) is in His hand, and He will thoroughly clear out *and* clean His threshing floor and gather *and* store His wheat in His barn, but the chaff He will burn up with fire that cannot be put out.

13 Then Jesus came from Galilee to the Jordan to John to be baptized by him.

14 But John [o]protested strenuously, having in mind to prevent Him, saying, It is I who have need to be baptized by You, and do You come to me?

15 But Jesus replied to him, [n]Permit it just now; for this is the fitting way for [both of] us to fulfill all righteousness [that is, to [n]perform completely whatever is right]. Then he permitted Him.

16 And when Jesus was baptized, He went up at once out of the water; and behold, the heavens were opened, and he [John] saw the Spirit of God descending like a dove and alighting on Him.

17 And behold, a voice from heaven said, This is My Son, My Beloved, in Whom I delight! [Ps. 2:7; Isa. 42:1.]

4 THEN JESUS was led (guided) by the [Holy] Spirit into the wilderness (desert) to be tempted (tested and tried) by the devil.

2 And He went without food for forty days and forty nights, and later

putting the Word to work

Do you ever struggle with wondering if you do enough to please God? When Jesus was baptized, He had not yet publicly taught, performed any miracles, or "done" any sort of ministry. Yet God called Him "My Son, My Beloved Son, in Whom I delight!" (Matthew 3:17). Likewise, God is delighted with you because you are His child. That pleases Him far more than anything you can do. Ask Him to show you more and more how delighted He is in you.

speak the Word

God, I pray that my life will bring forth fruit that is consistent with the change of heart that You have worked in me.
ADAPTED FROM MATTHEW 3:8

---

l *En*, the preposition used here, is translated both "in" and "with" in the Greek lexicons and concordances generally. The *King James Version* (the *Authorized Version*) gives preference to "with," putting "in" in the margin; the *American Standard Version* gives preference to "in," putting "with" in the margin. Many modern versions choose one or the other about equally. **m** Charles B. Williams, *The New Testament: A Translation.* **n** Joseph Thayer, *A Greek-English Lexicon.* **o** Marvin Vincent, *Word Studies.*

He was hungry. [Exod. 34:28; I Kings 19:8.]

3 And the tempter came and said to Him, If You are God's Son, command these stones to be made [ᵖloaves of] bread.

4 But He replied, It has been written, Man shall not live *and* be upheld *and* sustained by bread alone, but by every word that comes forth from the mouth of God. [Deut. 8:3.]

5 Then the devil took Him into the holy city and placed Him on �۹a turret (pinnacle, ʳgable) of the temple ˢsanctuary. [Neh. 11:1; Dan. 9:24.]

6 And he said to Him, If You are the Son of God, throw Yourself down; for it is written, He will give His angels charge over you, and they will bear you up on their hands, lest you strike your foot against a stone. [Ps. 91:11, 12.]

7 Jesus said to him, ᵗOn the other hand, it is written also, You shall not tempt, ᵘtest thoroughly, *or* ᵛtry exceedingly the Lord your God. [Deut. 6:16.]

8 Again, the devil took Him up on a very high mountain and showed Him all the kingdoms of the world and the glory (the splendor, magnificence, preeminence, and excellence) of them.

9 And he said to Him, These things, all taken together, I will give You, if You will prostrate Yourself before me and do homage *and* worship me.

10 Then Jesus said to him, Begone, Satan! For it has been written, You shall worship the Lord your God, and Him alone shall you serve. [Deut. 6:13.]

11 Then the devil departed from Him, and behold, angels came and ministered to Him.

12 Now when Jesus heard that John had been arrested *and* put in prison, He withdrew into Galilee.

putting the Word to work

We should not be surprised when temptation comes. Satan deliberately tried to tempt Jesus, and he tries to tempt us. How do you respond to temptation? Every time Jesus was tempted, He responded with the Word of God (see Matthew 4:1–11). Be diligent to study God's Word, so that when temptation comes, you too will know what action to take in order to resist and overcome it.

13 And leaving Nazareth, He went *and* dwelt in Capernaum by the sea, in the country of Zebulun and Naphtali—

14 That what was spoken by the prophet Isaiah might be brought to pass:

15 The land of Zebulun and the land of Naphtali, in the ʷway to the sea, beyond the Jordan, Galilee of the Gentiles [of the ʷpeoples who are not of Israel]—[Isa. 9:1-2.]

16 The people who sat ᵖ(dwelt enveloped) in darkness have seen a great Light, and for those who sat in the land and shadow of death Light has dawned.

17 From that time Jesus began to preach, ᵗcrying out, Repent (ᵘchange your mind for the better, heartily amend your ways, with abhorrence of your past sins), for the kingdom of heaven is at hand.

18 As He was walking by the Sea of Galilee, He noticed two brothers, Simon who is called Peter and Andrew his brother, throwing a dragnet into the sea, for they were fishermen.

19 And He said to them, Come ᵘafter Me [as disciples—letting Me be your

p John Wycliffe, *The Wycliffe Bible.* **q** G. Abbott-Smith, *Manual Greek Lexicon.* **r** James Moulton and George Milligan, *The Vocabulary.* **s** Richard Trench, *Synonyms of the New Testament.* **t** Marvin Vincent, *Word Studies.* **u** Joseph Thayer, *A Greek-English Lexicon.* **v** Robert Young, *Analytical Concordance to the Bible.* **w** Hermann Cremer, *Biblico-Theological Lexicon of New Testament Greek.*

Guide], follow Me, and I will make you fishers of men!

20 At once they left their nets and [x]became His disciples [sided with His party and followed Him].

21 And going on further from there He noticed two other brothers, James son of Zebedee and his brother John, in the boat with their father Zebedee, mending their nets *and* putting them right; and He called them.

22 At once they left the boat and their father and [x]joined Jesus as disciples [sided with His party and followed Him].

23 And He went about all Galilee, teaching in their synagogues and preaching the good news (Gospel) of the kingdom, and healing every disease and every weakness *and* infirmity among the people.

24 So the report of Him spread throughout all Syria, and they brought Him all who were sick, those afflicted with various diseases and torments, those under the power of demons, and epileptics, and paralyzed people, and He healed them.

25 And great crowds joined *and* accompanied Him about, coming from Galilee and Decapolis [the district of the ten cities east of the Sea of Galilee] and Jerusalem and Judea and from the other [the east] side of the Jordan.

5 SEEING THE crowds, He went up on the mountain; and when He was seated, His disciples came to Him.

2 Then He opened His mouth and taught them, saying:

3 Blessed (happy, [y]to be envied, and [z]spiritually prosperous—[a]with life-joy and satisfaction in God's favor and salvation, regardless of their outward

conditions) are the poor in spirit (the humble, who rate themselves insignificant), for theirs is the kingdom of heaven!

4 Blessed *and* enviably happy [with a [a]happiness produced by the experience of God's favor and especially conditioned by the revelation of His matchless grace] are those who mourn, for they shall be comforted! [Isa. 61:2.]

5 Blessed (happy, blithesome, joyous, [z]spiritually prosperous—[a]with life-joy and satisfaction in God's favor and salvation, regardless of their outward conditions) are the meek (the mild, patient, long-suffering), for they shall inherit the earth! [Ps. 37:11.]

6 Blessed *and* fortunate *and* happy *and* [z]spiritually prosperous (in that state in which the born-again child of God [a]enjoys His favor and salvation) are those who hunger and thirst for righteousness (uprightness and right standing with God), for they shall be [z]completely satisfied! [Isa. 55:1, 2.]

7 Blessed (happy, [b]to be envied, and

life point

In Matthew 5:4, Jesus said that those who mourn are blessed and that they will be comforted. The comfort of God, which is administered by His Holy Spirit, is so awesome that it is almost worth having a problem just to be able to experience it. As with most of the things of God, it goes far beyond any kind of ordinary comfort.

Let God be your source of comfort. When you are hurting, just ask Him to comfort you. Then wait in His presence while He works in your heart and emotions. He will not fail you.

---

x Joseph Thayer, *A Greek-English Lexicon.*   **y** Alexander Souter, *Pocket Lexicon of the Greek New Testament.*   **z** Marvin Vincent, *Word Studies.*   **a** Hermann Cremer, *Biblico-Theological Lexicon.*
b Alexander Souter, *Pocket Lexicon.*

pure-hearted and powerful

God is seeking people who are pure in heart (see Matthew 5:8). A person who has a pure heart, who is wholeheartedly serving God, is truly powerful. In Psalm 51:6, David tells us that having a pure heart means having truth in our "inner being," which is who we really are deep in our hearts. Having a pure heart starts with paying attention to our thoughts, because from our thoughts come our words, our emotions, our attitudes, and our motives.

It took me a long time to realize that God will not bless actions that are done out of wrong motives or an impure heart.

Purity of heart is not a natural trait; in most of us, it is something we must work on. First Thessalonians 4:3 teaches us to desire and work toward purity of heart because that is God's will. This is a challenge that every believer should be excited about accepting, but we do not have to face it alone.

God has created us to be dependent upon Him, to bring Him our challenges and allow Him to help us with them. Only He knows what is in our hearts, and He is an expert at removing the worthless things from us while retaining the valuable.

There is a price to pay to have a pure heart, but there is also a reward. We do not have to be afraid to make the commitment to allow God to do a deep purifying work in us. We may not always feel comfortable about the truth He brings us, but if we do our part—facing it, accepting it, and allowing it to change us—He will make sure that we are blessed.

cspiritually prosperous—dwith life-joy and satisfaction in God's favor and salvation, regardless of their outward conditions) are the merciful, for they shall obtain mercy!

8 Blessed (happy, eenviably fortunate, and cspiritually prosperous—possessing the dhappiness produced by the experience of God's favor and especially conditioned by the revelation of His grace, regardless of their outward conditions) are the pure in heart, for they shall see God! [Ps. 24:3, 4.]

9 Blessed (enjoying eenviable happiness, cspiritually prosperous—dwith life-joy and satisfaction in God's favor and salvation, regardless of their out-ward conditions) are the makers and fmaintainers of peace, for they shall be called the sons of God!

10 Blessed and happy and eenviably fortunate and cspiritually prosperous d(in the state in which the born-again child of God enjoys and finds satisfaction in God's favor and salvation, regardless of his outward conditions) are those who are persecuted for righteousness' sake (for being and doing right), for theirs is the kingdom of heaven!

11 Blessed (happy, eto be envied, and cspiritually prosperous—dwith life-joy and satisfaction in God's favor and salvation, regardless of your outward conditions) are you when people

c Marvin Vincent, *Word Studies*. d Hermann Cremer, *Biblico-Theological Lexicon*. e Alexander Souter, *Pocket Lexicon*. f William Tyndale, *The Tyndale Bible*.

revile you and persecute you and say all kinds of evil things against you falsely on My account.

12 Be glad *and* supremely joyful, for your reward in heaven is great (strong and intense), for in this same way people persecuted the prophets who were before you. [II Chron. 36:16.]

13 You are the salt of the earth, but if salt has lost its taste (its strength, its quality), how can its saltness be restored? It is not good for anything any longer but to be thrown out and trodden underfoot by men.

14 You are the light of the world. A city set on a hill cannot be hidden.

15 Nor do men light a lamp and put it under a peck measure, but on a lampstand, and it gives light to all in the house.

16 Let your light so shine before men that they may see your ᵍmoral excellence *and* your praiseworthy, noble, *and* good deeds and ᵍrecognize *and* honor *and* praise *and* glorify your Father Who is in heaven.

17 Do not think that I have come to do away with *or* ʰundo the Law or the Prophets; I have come not to do away with *or* undo but to complete *and* fulfill them. [Lev. 19:1; Num. 30:2; Deut.

18 For truly I tell you, until the sky and earth pass away *and* perish, not one smallest letter nor one little hook [identifying certain Hebrew letters] will pass from the Law until all things [it foreshadows] are accomplished.

19 Whoever then breaks *or* does away with *or* relaxes one of the least [important] of these commandments and teaches men so shall be called least [important] in the kingdom of heaven, but he who practices them and teaches others to do so shall be called great in the kingdom of heaven.

20 For I tell you, unless your righ-

life point

In Matthew 5:13, Jesus tells us we are the salt of the earth, but if salt loses its flavor it is not good for anything.

I say that all of life is tasteless without love. Even acts of generosity that are done out of obligation, but without sincere love, leave us empty. Love represents the salt; it is the energy and the flavor of our lives.

Every day can be exciting if we see ourselves as God's secret agents, waiting in the shadows to sprinkle some salt on the tasteless lives of the people we encounter. For example, we might see a woman behind a counter in a fast food restaurant who looks unhappy, tired, and angry. A simple comment such as, "Your hair is really pretty," can add flavor to her day.

Love is an effort, and sometimes we allow ourselves to become lazy in dispersing this gift. I hope you will actively express God's love everywhere you go, sprinkling "salt" on everyone you meet because God has placed you where you are for that very purpose.

teousness (your uprightness and your right standing with God) is more than that of the scribes and Pharisees, you will never enter the kingdom of heaven.

21 You have heard that it was said to the men of old, You shall not kill, and whoever kills shall be ⁱliable to *and* unable to escape the punishment imposed by the court. [Exod. 20:13; Deut. 5:17; 16:18.]

22 But I say to you that everyone who continues to be ʲangry with his

---

g Hermann Cremer, *Biblico-Theological Lexicon*. **h** John Wycliffe, *The Wycliffe Bible*. **i** Joseph Thayer, *A Greek-English Lexicon*. **j** Some manuscripts insert here: "without cause."

brother *or* harbors malice (enmity of heart) against him shall be ᵏliable to *and* unable to escape the punishment imposed by the court; and whoever speaks contemptuously *and* insultingly to his brother shall be ᵏliable to *and* unable to escape the punishment imposed by the Sanhedrin, and whoever says, You ˡcursed fool! [You empty-headed idiot!] shall be ᵏliable to *and* unable to escape the hell (Gehenna) of fire.

23 So if when you are offering your gift at the altar you there remember that your brother has any [grievance] against you,

24 Leave your gift at the altar and go. First make peace with your brother, and then come back *and* present your gift.

25 Come to terms quickly with your accuser while you are on the way traveling with him, lest your accuser hand you over to the judge, and the judge to the guard, and you be put in prison.

26 Truly I say to you, you will not be released until you have paid the last fraction of a penny.

27 You have heard that it was said, You shall not commit adultery. [Exod. 20:14; Deut. 5:18.]

28 But I say to you that everyone who so much as looks at a woman with evil desire for her has already committed adultery with her in his heart.

29 If your right eye serves as a trap to ensnare you *or* is an occasion for you to stumble *and* sin, pluck it out and throw it away. It is better that you lose one of your members than that your whole body be cast into hell (Gehenna).

30 And if your right hand serves as a trap to ensnare you *or* is an occasion for you to stumble *and* sin, cut it off and cast it from you. It is better that

you lose one of your members than that your entire body should be cast into hell (Gehenna).

31 It has also been said, Whoever divorces his wife must give her a certificate of divorce.

32 But I tell you, Whoever dismisses *and* repudiates *and* divorces his wife, except on the grounds of unfaithfulness (sexual immorality), causes her to commit adultery, and whoever marries a woman who has been divorced commits adultery. [Deut. 24:1-4.]

33 Again, you have heard that it was said to the men of old, You shall not swear falsely, but you shall perform your oaths to the Lord [as a religious duty].

34 But I tell you, Do not bind yourselves by an oath at all: either by heaven, for it is the throne of God;

35 Or by the earth, for it is the footstool of His feet; or by Jerusalem, for it is the city of the Great King. [Ps. 48:2; Isa. 66:1.]

36 And do not swear by your head, for you are not able to make a single hair white or black.

37 Let your Yes be simply Yes, and your No be simply No; anything more than that comes from the evil one. [Lev. 19:12; Num. 30:2; Deut. 23:21.]

38 You have heard that it was said, An eye for an eye, and a tooth for a tooth. [Exod. 21:24; Lev. 24:20; Deut. 19:21.]

39 But I say to you, Do not resist the evil man [who injures you]; but if anyone strikes you on the right jaw *or* cheek, turn to him the other one too.

40 And if anyone wants to sue you and take your undershirt (tunic), let him have your coat also.

41 And if anyone forces you to go one mile, go with him two [miles].

42 Give to him who keeps on begging from you, and do not turn away from

---

k Joseph Thayer, *A Greek-English Lexicon.* l Charles B. Williams, *The New Testament: A Translation.*

him who would borrow [mat interest] from you. [Deut. 15:8; Prov. 24:29.]

43 You have heard that it was said, You shall love your neighbor and hate your enemy; [Lev. 19:18; Ps. 139:21, 22.]
44 But I tell you, Love your enemies and pray for those who persecute you, [Prov. 25:21, 22.]
45 nTo show that you are the children of your Father Who is in heaven; for He makes His sun rise on the wicked and on the good, and makes the rain fall upon the upright and the wrong-doers [alike].
46 For if you love those who love you, what reward can you have? Do not even the tax collectors do that?
47 And if you greet only your brethren, what more than others are you doing? Do not even the Gentiles (the heathen) do that?
48 You, therefore, must be perfect [growing into complete omaturity of godliness in mind and character, nhaving reached the proper height of virtue and integrity], as your heavenly Father is perfect. [Lev. 19:2, 18.]

6 TAKE CARE not to do your good deeds publicly *or* before men, in order to be seen by them; otherwise you will have no reward [mreserved for and awaiting you] with *and* from your Father Who is in heaven.
2 Thus, whenever you give to the poor, do not blow a trumpet before you, as the hypocrites in the synagogues and in the streets like to do, that they may be precognized *and* honored *and* praised by men. Truly I tell you, they have their reward min full already.
3 But when you give to charity, do not let your left hand know what your right hand is doing,
4 So that your deeds of charity may

life point

Pharisees and hypocrites want to be "recognized and honored and praised by men," according to Matthew 6:2. I call this kind of desire "approval addiction."

Many people never receive God's best for them because they are addicted to the approval of others. Even if they know God's will for them, they will not walk in it because they are afraid their friends may not understand or agree.

Not everyone approves of the way God moves in our lives. In fact, almost everyone I knew rejected me when I began following His will for my life. It was hard to stand alone against so much disapproval, but during that time I learned that other people's opinions do not really matter; it is what *God* thinks that is important.

In Galatians 1:10, Paul wrote, "Now am I trying to win the favor of men, or of God? Do I seek to please men? If I were still seeking popularity with men, I should not be a bond servant of Christ (the Messiah)."

Do not be addicted to approval. Follow your heart. Do what you believe God is telling you to do, and stand firm in Him and Him alone.

be in secret; and your Father Who sees in secret will reward you *openly*.
5 Also when you pray, you must not be like the hypocrites, for they love to pray standing in the synagogues and on the corners of the streets, that they may be seen by people. Truly I tell you, they have their reward min full already.
6 But when you pray, go into your

---

m Marvin Vincent, *Word Studies.*   **n** Joseph Thayer, *A Greek-English Lexicon.*   **o** Kenneth Wuest, *Word Studies in the New Testament.*   **p** Hermann Cremer, *Biblico-Theological Lexicon.*

secret goodness

In Matthew 6:1, Jesus warns us against trying to impress people with our good deeds and encourages us to wait for our reward from God. God really brought this point home for me once through something that happened in my own life.

I was having my nails done in a shop where I went regularly, and I happened to be wearing a rhinestone "Jesus" pin. God prompted me to give it to a nurse, who was sitting nearby talking about ministering to cancer patients in the hospital where she worked. She said that she was not allowed to preach to them openly, but wanted to be able to give them something.

The Lord spoke to my heart and told me to give her my pin so that when she wore it on her lapel as she bent over her patients, just the name of Jesus would minister to them. I hesitated because I felt the Lord wanted me to do that privately, but saw no way to do so because of the girl who was doing my nails.

Suddenly the manicurist stopped and said, "Oh, I ran out of something. I have to run next door to get some more. I will be right back."

I knew God was making a way for me to give the nurse my pin discreetly and without any fanfare, but my flesh wanted some credit. So instead of doing what God wanted me to do the way He wanted me to do it, I kept putting it off, reasoning to myself, *I think it would really bless this manicurist to see my generosity*.

I waited until the manicurist came back. Then I took off the pin and made a big deal about giving it to the nurse. Just as I envisioned, the ladies expounded on my generosity, going on and on about how kind it was of me to give my pin away. As I left the shop thinking about how generous I had been, the Holy Spirit spoke to my heart and said, "Well, I hope you enjoyed that because it is all the reward you are going to get. Whatever reward you would have had from Me, you just traded for those compliments."

I often wonder what God would have done for me if I had obeyed and done what He told me to do, letting Him have all the glory and credit. Let me urge you not to make the same mistake I did. Obey God and do what He wants you to do, when He wants you to do it, the way He wants you to do it.

[most] private room, and, closing the door, pray to your Father, Who is in secret; and your Father, Who sees in secret, will reward you *in the open*.

7 And when you pray, do not heap up phrases (multiply words, repeating the same ones over and over) as the Gentiles do, for they think they will be heard for their much speaking. [I Kings 18:25-29.]

8 Do not be like them, for your Father knows what you need before you ask Him.

9 Pray, therefore, like this: Our

life point

Although some prayers are meant to be public prayers or group prayers, most of our prayer lives should be conducted in secret. In other words, we do not have to broadcast how much we pray and everything we pray about. Jesus encourages us in Matthew 6:5, 6 to practice "secret prayer."

"Secret prayer" means a number of things. It means that we do not tell everyone our personal experiences in prayer. We pray about the things and people God places on our hearts, and we keep our prayers between Him and us unless we have a really good reason to do otherwise.

There is nothing wrong with saying to a friend, "I have been praying for the youth of our nation a lot lately," or, "I have been praying for people to enter into a more serious relationship with God." Sharing of this type is simply a part of friendship, but there are things God places on our hearts to pray about that we should keep to ourselves.

"Secret prayer" means that we do not make a display of our prayers to impress people. True secret prayer from a humble, fervent heart results in awesome answers from God.

Father Who is in heaven, hallowed (kept holy) be Your name.
10 Your kingdom come, Your will be done on earth as it is in heaven.
11 Give us this day our daily bread.
12 And forgive us our debts, as we also have forgiven (qleft, remitted, and

let go of the debts, and have rgiven up resentment against) our debtors.
13 And lead (bring) us not into temptation, but deliver us from the evil one. *For Yours is the kingdom and the power and the glory forever. Amen.*
14 For if you forgive people their trespasses [their sreckless and willful sins, qleaving them, letting them go, and rgiving up resentment], your heavenly Father will also forgive you.
15 But if you do not forgive others their trespasses [their sreckless and willful sins, qleaving them, letting them go, and rgiving up resentment], neither will your Father forgive you your trespasses.
16 And whenever you are fasting, do not look gloomy *and* tsour *and* udreary like the hypocrites, for they put on a dismal countenance, that their fasting may be apparent to *and* seen by men. Truly I say to you, they have their reward sin full already. [Isa. 58:5.]
17 But when you fast, perfume your head and wash your face,
18 So that your fasting may not be noticed by men but by your Father, Who sees in secret; and your Father, Who sees in secret, will reward you *in the open.*
19 Do not vgather *and* heap up *and* store up for yourselves treasures on earth, where moth and rust *and* worm consume *and* destroy, and where thieves break through and steal.
20 But tgather *and* heap up *and* store for yourselves treasures in heaven, where neither moth nor rust *nor* worm consume *and* destroy, and where thieves do not break through and steal;
21 For where your treasure is, there will your heart be also.
22 The eye is the lamp of the body.

q James Moulton and George Milligan, *The Vocabulary.* **r** *Webster's New International Dictionary* offers this phrase as a definition of the word "forgive." **s** Marvin Vincent, *Word Studies.* **t** Martin Luther, cited by Marvin Vincent, *Word Studies.* **u** Richard Trench, *Synonyms of the New Testament.* **v** Joseph Thayer, *A Greek-English Lexicon.*

short and simple

I believe God has instructed me to make my requests of Him with as few words as possible. As I follow this practice, I understand more and more why He has asked me to pray this way. I find if I can keep my requests simple and not confuse the issue by trying to come up with too many words, my prayers actually are more clear and powerful.

We need to spend our energy releasing our faith, not repeating phrases over and over when they only serve to make our prayers long and involved.

I am not advocating praying only for a short period of time, but I am suggesting that each prayer be simple, direct, to the point and filled with faith. Let me give you an example. If I need forgiveness, I can pray, "Lord, I lost my temper, and I am sorry. I ask You to forgive me. I receive Your forgiveness, and I thank You for it, in Jesus' name. Amen."

Keeping my prayers short and simple was difficult when I first began praying that way. Then I realized that my problem was a lack of faith that my prayer would get to God if it was short, simple, and to the point. I fell into the same trap that many people do—"the-longer-the-better" mentality. However, after praying that way, most of the time I felt confused and unsure, as though I still had not gotten the job done.

Now as I follow God's direction to keep it simple and make my request without unnecessary and excessive words, I experience a much greater release of my faith, and I know that God has heard me and will answer.

Confidence in prayer is vital to our lives as believers. Be really honest with yourself about your prayer life and make adjustments wherever they are needed. If you are not praying enough, pray more. If your prayers are complicated, simplify them. God wants to hear what you have to say through prayer and He wants to answer. I encourage you to become more effective in prayer by keeping it short and simple.

So if your eye is sound, your entire body will be full of light.

23 But if your eye is unsound, your whole body will be full of darkness. If then the very light in you [your ʷconscience] is darkened, how dense is that darkness!

24 No one can serve two masters; for either he will hate the one and love the other, or he will stand by *and* be devoted to the one and despise and be ˣagainst the other. You cannot serve God and mammon (ʷdeceitful riches, money, possessions, or ʸwhatever is trusted in).

25 Therefore I tell you, stop being ᶻperpetually uneasy (anxious and worried) about your life, what you shall eat *or what you shall drink;* or about your body, what you shall put

w Hermann Cremer, *Biblico-Theological Lexicon.* **x** Marvin Vincent, *Word Studies.* **y** Joseph Thayer, *A Greek-English Lexicon.* **z** Kenneth Wuest, *Word Studies.*

putting the Word to work

Do you have a savings account or a financial portfolio? Even if you do not, you are probably very aware of your financial situation. It is wise to plan and be financially responsible. Being greedy, however, is a different story. Do not let the pursuit of money or material possessions keep you from pursuing the treasures of God's kingdom, which have far greater worth and eternal value than anything on earth (see Matthew 6:19–21).

putting the Word to work

Are you worried about something right now? Jesus understood how burdensome and destructive worry can be in our lives, and He *commands* us not to worry (see Matthew 6:25–31, 34). Instead, He calls us to look to God's sure and faithful provision as the antidote to our worry (see Matthew 6:33). Encourage yourself by remembering other times when God has provided for you and ask Him to help you trust Him for your every need instead of worrying.

on. Is not life greater [in quality] than food, and the body [far above and more excellent] than clothing?

26 Look at the birds of the air; they neither sow nor reap nor gather into barns, and yet your heavenly Father keeps feeding them. Are you not worth much more than they?

27 And who of you by worrying *and* being anxious can add one unit of measure (cubit) to his stature *or* to the ªspan of his life? [Ps. 39:5-7.]

28 And why should you be anxious about clothes? Consider the lilies of the field *and* ᵇlearn thoroughly how they grow; they neither toil nor spin.

29 Yet I tell you, even Solomon in all his ᵇmagnificence (excellence, dignity, and grace) was not arrayed like one of these. [I Kings 10:4-7.]

30 But if God so clothes the grass of the field, which today is alive *and* green and tomorrow is tossed into the furnace, will He not much more surely clothe you, O you of little faith?

31 Therefore do not worry *and* be anxious, saying, What are we going to have to eat? or, What are we going to have to drink? or, What are we going to have to wear?

32 For the Gentiles (heathen) wish

for *and* crave *and* diligently seek all these things, and your heavenly Father knows well that you need them all.

33 But seek (ᵇaim at and strive after) first of all His kingdom and His righteousness (ᶜHis way of doing and being right), and then all these things ᵇtaken together will be given you besides.

34 So do not worry *or* be anxious about tomorrow, for tomorrow will have worries *and* anxieties of its own. Sufficient for each day is its own trouble.

life point

God gives us enough grace for one day at a time, and to avoid fatigue and burnout, weariness and fainting in our minds, we must learn to live one day at a time. That is why Jesus teaches us in Matthew 6:34 to meet each day's challenges as they come and not to borrow trouble from tomorrow. If we will do that, then at the appointed time God's grace will be available to us in sufficient supply to help us face and overcome whatever may occur in our lives.

a Alexander Souter, *Pocket Lexicon*: the word translated "cubit" is used as a measurement of time, as well as a measurement of length. **b** Joseph Thayer, *A Greek-English Lexicon*. **c** Charles B. Williams, *The New Testament: A Translation.*

first place

Simply put, I believe Matthew 6:33 teaches that "the main thing is to keep the main thing the main thing." We must know what the most important thing in our lives is and keep our priorities in line. In our society today we see a huge emphasis on commerce and material things, but we must remember that things are not most important to God. He wants us to have and enjoy nice things, but He demands first place in our lives. We are taught to seek the kingdom of God and His way of being and doing before we seek anything else.

The word *seek* is a very strong word. It means "to pursue," "to crave," and "to go after with all your might." When we seek something, we think about it often; we talk about it; and we are willing to pay a price to have it. Some people even fall into the trap of seeking God so He will give them the things they want. When they do that, their motives are wrong and God withholds what they want.

We must form a habit of seeking God's face and not His hand. In other words, we are to seek His "presence," not His "presents." I urge you to seek Him for who He is, not for what He can do for you.

God is pleased immensely when we want to spend time with Him just because we love Him. He is also pleased when we praise and worship Him just because He *is*. Everyone enjoys having their "being" celebrated, not just their "doing." I do not want friends who are only interested in what I can do for them; I want them to be interested in who I am and to like me for me. I am sure you feel the same way—and so does God.

When we put Him first, keep Him there and seek to do things His way, we are showing that we delight in Him. Then He gives us the desires of our hearts (see Psalm 37:4).

7 DO NOT judge *and* criticize *and* condemn others, so that you may not be judged *and* criticized *and* condemned yourselves.

2 For just as you judge *and* criticize *and* condemn others, you will be judged *and* criticized *and* condemned, and in accordance with the measure you [use to] deal out to others, it will be dealt out again to you.

3 Why do you ᵈstare from without at the ᵉvery small particle that is in your brother's eye but do not become aware of *and* consider the beam ᶠof timber that is in your own eye?

4 Or how can you say to your brother, Let me get the tiny particle out of your eye, when there is the beam ᶠof timber in your own eye?

5 You hypocrite, first get the beam of timber out of your own eye, and then you will see clearly to take the tiny particle out of your brother's eye.

6 Do not give that which is holy (the sacred thing) to the dogs, and do not throw your pearls before hogs, lest

d Marvin Vincent, *Word Studies*. e James Moulton and George Milligan, *The Vocabulary*. f G. Abbott-Smith, *Manual Greek Lexicon*.

life point

Matthew 7:1, 2 plainly tells us that we will reap what we sow (see Galatians 6:7). Sowing and reaping do not apply solely to the agricultural and financial realms, they also apply to the mental realm. We can sow and reap an attitude as well as a crop or an investment.

One pastor wisely says that when he hears that someone has talked about him in an unkind or judgmental way, he asks himself, "Are they sowing, or am I reaping?" Many times we are reaping in our lives what we have previously sown into someone else's life. Be sure you sow good seeds!

they trample upon them with their feet and turn *and* tear you in pieces.

7   gKeep on asking and it will be given you; gkeep on seeking and you will find; gkeep on knocking [reverently] and [the door] will be opened to you.

8   For everyone who keeps on asking receives; and he who keeps on seeking finds; and to him who keeps on knocking, [the door] will be opened.

9   Or what man is there of you, if his son asks him for a loaf of bread, will hand him a stone?

10 Or if he asks for a fish, will hand him a serpent?

11 If you then, evil as you are, know how to give good *and* hadvantageous gifts to your children, how much more will your Father Who is in heaven [perfect as He is] give good *and* hadvantageous things to those who gkeep on asking Him!

12 So then, whatever you desire that others would do to *and* for you, even so do also to *and* for them, for this is (sums up) the Law and the Prophets.

13 Enter through the narrow gate; for wide is the gate and spacious *and* broad is the way that leads away to destruction, and many are those who are entering through it.

14 But the gate is narrow (contracted iby pressure) and the way is straitened *and* compressed that leads away to life, and few are those who find it. [Deut. 30:19; Jer. 21:8.]

15 Beware of false prophets, who come to you dressed as sheep, but inside they are devouring wolves. [Ezek. 22:27.]

16 You will jfully recognize them by their fruits. Do people pick grapes from thorns, or figs from thistles?

17 Even so, every healthy (sound) tree bears good fruit [hworthy of admiration], but the sickly (decaying, worthless) tree bears bad (worthless) fruit.

life point

The devil loves to keep us busy, identifying and judging the faults of others in our minds. That way, we never see or deal with what is wrong with us!

When we focus our thoughts and conversations on the shortcomings of others, we are usually being deceived about our own conduct. Therefore, Jesus commanded that we not concern ourselves with the wrongs of others when we have so much wrong with ourselves (see Matthew 7:3–5).

We cannot change others; only God can. We cannot change ourselves either, but we can cooperate with the Holy Spirit and allow Him to do the work. Allow God to deal with you first, and then you will be able to humbly, lovingly, and effectively help others.

g Kenneth Wuest, *Word Studies*. h Hermann Cremer, *Biblico-Theological Lexicon*. i Alexander Souter, *Pocket Lexicon*. j Marvin Vincent, *Word Studies*.

do not judge

I believe Matthew 7:6 refers to our God-given ability to love each other.

If we have the ability to love others and know that God has commanded us to love them, but we judge and criticize them instead, we have taken the holy thing (love) and cast it before dogs and hogs (evil spirits). We have opened a door for those spirits to trample on holy things and turn and tear us to pieces.

When I became pregnant with our fourth child, I was a Christian, baptized in the Holy Spirit, called into ministry, and a diligent Bible student. I had learned about exercising my faith for healing. Yet, during the first three months of the pregnancy, I was very, very sick. I lost weight and energy. I spent most of my time lying on the couch, so nauseated and tired that I could barely move.

This situation was really confusing to me since I had felt wonderful during my other three pregnancies. I was also sincerely trusting God that I would not be sick during this fourth pregnancy.

One day as I lay in bed listening to my husband and children having a good time in the backyard, I aggressively asked God, "What in the world is wrong with me? Why am I so sick? And why am I not getting well?"

The Holy Spirit prompted me to read Matthew 7, and as I did, He reminded me of an event that had happened a couple of years earlier.

As I lay in my bed that day, I recalled that a Christian friend and I had talked about, judged, and criticized another Christian friend who was pregnant and had stopped attending our weekly Bible study because she said she felt so bad. We believed her problem was that she was unwilling to "press through" her circumstances and come to Bible study. We never offered to help her in any way. We just decided that she was a weakling and was using her pregnancy as an excuse to be lazy and self-indulgent.

Now, I was in the same circumstance that woman had been in. God showed me that although I was healthy during my first three pregnancies, I had opened a huge door for the devil by my judgment and criticism. I took my pearls, the holy things (my ability to love the woman), threw them before the dogs and hogs, and now they were turned and tearing me to pieces. I can tell you, I was quick to repent. As soon as I did, my health was completely restored.

From this incident I learned an important lesson about the dangers of judging and criticizing others. Jesus tells us not to judge others for our own good; He does not want us to be judged in return. Resist the temptation to criticize and judge, and thereby enable yourself and others to enjoy blessings instead of judgment.

persistent, not repetitious

It is difficult to lay down strict rules on the subject of how often to pray about the same situation. I have heard some people say, "Pray repeatedly until you see the breakthrough." I have heard others say, "If you pray more than once for something, then you do not believe you got it the first time."

I do not believe we can make any strict rules, but I do think there are some guidelines we can apply that will help us have more confidence in the power of prayer.

If my children told me their shoes were worn out and asked me to get them some new ones, I would probably respond, "Okay, I will get them as soon as I can."

What I would want from my children is trust. I would want them to trust me to do what they asked me to do. I would not mind, and might even like it, if they occasionally said, "Mom, I am sure looking forward to those new shoes," or "I am excited about my new shoes, Mom; I will be glad when I get them and can wear them." Both of those statements would declare to me that they believed I would do as I promised. They would actually be reminding me of my promise, but in a way that would not question my integrity.

On the other hand, if they came back to me an hour later and made the same request again, I might be irritated. If they said, "Mom, my shoes are worn out, and I am asking you to get me some new ones," I would think, "I heard you the first time, and I told you I would get them as soon as I can. What is your problem?"

I believe that, sometimes, asking God for the same thing repeatedly is a sign of doubt and unbelief, not of faith and persistence.

When I ask the Lord for something, and that thing comes to my mind or heart again later, I talk to Him about it again. But when I do, I try to refrain from asking Him the same thing as if I think He did not hear me the first time. I believe we honor God when we demonstrate faith and persistence by thanking Him for hearing and answering us.

Jesus said in Matthew 7:7: "Keep on asking . . . keep on seeking . . . keep on knocking." We should be persistent, but not repetitious in prayer. Keep pressing on and do not give up, and keep expressing your faith and gratitude to God for answering you.

---

18 A good (healthy) tree cannot bear bad (worthless) fruit, nor can a bad (diseased) tree bear ᵏexcellent fruit [worthy of admiration].

19 Every tree that does not bear good fruit is cut down and cast into the fire. **20** Therefore, you will ˡfully know them by their fruits.

---

k Hermann Cremer, *Biblico-Theological Lexicon*. l Marvin Vincent, *Word Studies*.

life point

In Matthew 7:13, 14, Jesus speaks of two different paths we can take in our lives: the broad way that leads to destruction and the narrow way that leads to life.

As I meditated on this passage, the Lord quickened it to me by saying, "Joyce, on the broad way there is room for all kinds of fleshly things like bitterness, unforgiveness, resentment, and vindictiveness. But on the narrow way there is only room for the Spirit."

In the flesh it is easy to take the broad path, but the end result is destruction. It is much harder to take the narrow path, but in the end it leads to life.

Emotions tempt us to take the easy way, to do what feels good for the moment. Wisdom moves us to take the way that seems hard at first, but later on we find that it leads to life.

21 Not everyone who says to Me, Lord, Lord, will enter the kingdom of heaven, but he who does the will of My Father Who is in heaven.
22 Many will say to Me on that day, Lord, Lord, have we not prophesied in Your name and driven out demons in Your name and done many mighty works in Your name?
23 And then I will say to them openly (publicly), I never knew you; depart from Me, you who act wickedly [disregarding My commands]. [Ps. 6:8.]
24 So everyone who hears these words of Mine and acts upon them [obeying them] will be like a ^msensible (prudent, practical, wise) man who built his house upon the rock.
25 And the rain fell and the floods came and the winds blew and beat against that house; yet it did not fall, because it had been founded on the rock.
26 And everyone who hears these words of Mine and does not do them will be like a stupid (foolish) man who built his house upon the sand.
27 And the rain fell and the floods came and the winds blew and beat against that house, and it fell—and great *and* complete was the fall of it.
28 When Jesus had finished these sayings [the Sermon on the Mount], the crowds were astonished *and* overwhelmed with bewildered wonder at His teaching,
29 For He was teaching as *One* Who had [and was] authority, and not as [did] the scribes.

8 WHEN JESUS came down from the mountain, great throngs followed Him.
2 And behold, a leper came up to Him and, prostrating himself, worshiped Him, saying, Lord, if You are willing, You are able to ⁿcleanse me by curing me.
3 And He reached out His hand and touched him, saying, I am willing; be cleansed ⁿby being cured. And instantly his leprosy was cured *and* cleansed.
4 And Jesus said to him, See that you tell nothing about this to anyone; but go, show yourself to the priest and present the offering that Moses commanded, for a testimony [to your healing] *and* as an evidence to the people. [Lev. 14:2.]
5 As Jesus went into Capernaum, a centurion came up to Him, begging Him,
6 And saying, Lord, my servant boy is lying at the house paralyzed *and* ⁿdistressed with intense pains.
7 And Jesus said to him, I will come and restore him.

m G. Abbott-Smith, *Manual Greek Lexicon*.   **n** Joseph Thayer, *A Greek-English Lexicon*.

known by our fruit

One time my husband and I were in Florida, and I saw a tree that I thought was very attractive. I asked, "What kind of tree is that?" Before anyone could answer, I saw oranges beginning to blossom on the branches, and I realized that it was an orange tree. I knew it by its fruit.

Jesus teaches in Matthew 7:20 that we will know people by their fruit. Let me encourage you to examine your own fruit to see if it is good. I did that in my own life and discovered that I was like an apple tree that sat all day long and yelled, "I am an apple tree! I am an apple tree!" but I never produced any apples.

Believers often carry outward signs of their Christianity in an attempt to share their faith. Bumper stickers on automobiles are a good example. These signs say that the drivers are Christians, but what kind of fruit do they bear in traffic? Are they obeying the speed limit or are they speeding? How do they react to other drivers, especially to those who cut them off in traffic? Their actions are *true* signs of who they are.

You and I can carry big Bibles, wear Christian jewelry, and display large collections of Christian books in our homes—and still not be producing any good fruit. We must be concerned about producing the fruit of the Holy Spirit, because the Holy Spirit is concerned with that. One of His main purposes in making us His home is to continually work His fruit in us and display it through us.

In John 15, Jesus compares our relationship with Him to that of a living plant. He is the Vine, we are the branches. Although it is not stated in John 15, we could also say the Holy Spirit is the Gardener who prunes us and keeps the weeds in us from choking the fruit.

God has planted a garden in each of us (see I Corinthians 3:9) and He has assigned the Holy Spirit the job of Gardener. A gardener aids in the production of fruit. That is what the Holy Spirit was sent to do in us—help us bear good fruit.

Examine your own fruit regularly. If any of it is diseased or rotten, ask the Gardener to help you get rid of it and produce a new crop. He will gladly do it!

---

8 But the centurion replied to Him, Lord, I am not worthy *or* fit to have You come under my roof; but only speak the word, and my servant boy will be cured.

9 For I also am a man subject to authority, with soldiers subject to me.

And I say to one, Go, and he goes; and to another, Come, and he comes; and to my slave, Do this, and he does it.

10 When Jesus heard him, He marveled and said to those who followed Him [°who adhered steadfastly to Him, conforming to His example in

o Joseph Thayer, *A Greek-English Lexicon.*

living and, if need be, in dying also], I tell you truly, I have not found so much faith as this ᴾwith anyone, even in Israel.

11 I tell you, many will come from east and west, and will sit at table with Abraham, Isaac, and Jacob in the kingdom of heaven,

12 While the sons *and* heirs of the kingdom will be driven out into the darkness outside, where there will be weeping and grinding of teeth. [Ps. 107:2, 3; Isa. 49:12; 59:19; Mal. 1:11.]

13 Then to the centurion Jesus said, Go; it shall be done for you as you have believed. And the servant boy was restored to health at that very �q̇moment.

14 And when Jesus went into Peter's house, He saw his mother-in-law lying ill with a fever.

15 He touched her hand and the fever left her; and she got up and began waiting on Him.

16 When evening came, they brought to Him many who were ʳunder the power of demons, and He drove out the spirits with a word and restored to health all who were sick.

17 And thus He fulfilled what was spoken by the prophet Isaiah, He Himself took [ʳin order to carry away] our weaknesses *and* infirmities and bore ˢaway our diseases. [Isa. 53:4.]

18 Now Jesus, when He saw the great throngs around Him, gave orders to cross to the other side [of the lake].

19 And a scribe came up and said to Him, Master, I will accompany You wherever You go.

20 And Jesus replied to him, Foxes have holes and the birds of the air have lodging places, but the Son of Man has nowhere to lay His head.

21 Another of the disciples said to Him, Lord, let me first go and bury [ᵗcare for till death] my father.

22 But Jesus said to him, Follow Me, and leave the dead [ᵘin sin] to bury their own dead.

23 And after He got into the boat, His disciples followed Him.

24 And ᵛsuddenly, behold, there arose a violent storm on the sea, so that the boat was being covered up by the waves; but He was sleeping.

25 And they went and awakened Him, saying, Lord, rescue *and* preserve us! We are perishing!

26 And He said to them, Why are you timid *and* afraid, O you of little faith? Then He got up and rebuked the winds and the sea, and there was a great *and* wonderful calm (ʷa perfect peaceableness).

27 And the men were stunned with bewildered wonder *and* marveled, saying, What kind of Man is this, that even the winds and the sea obey Him!

28 And when He arrived at the other side in the country of the Gadarenes, two men under the control of demons went to meet Him, coming out of the tombs, so fierce *and* savage that no one was able to pass that way.

29 And behold, they shrieked *and* screamed, What have You to do with us, *Jesus,* Son of God? Have You come to torment us before the appointed time? [Judg. 11:12; II Sam. 16:10.]

30 Now at some distance from there a drove of many hogs was grazing.

31 And the demons begged Him, If You drive us out, send us into the drove of hogs.

32 And He said to them, Begone! So they came out and went into the hogs, and behold, the whole drove rushed

p Some manuscripts add "with anyone." **q** James Moulton and George Milligan, *The Vocabulary.* **r** Joseph Thayer, *A Greek-English Lexicon.* **s** G. Abbott-Smith, *Manual Greek Lexicon;* George Ricker Berry, *Greek-English New Testament Lexicon;* Alexander Souter, *Pocket Lexicon;* Joseph Thayer, *A Greek-English Lexicon;* W.J. Hickie, *Greek-English Lexicon.* **t** Many commentators interpret it thus. **u** Albert Barnes, *Notes on the New Testament.* **v** Marvin Vincent, *Word Studies.* **w** John Wycliffe, *The Wycliffe Bible.*

as you have believed

In Matthew 8:13, Jesus told the centurion that the healing he requested would be done as he believed. The centurion had a positive, believing attitude and Jesus did what he asked Him to do.

Do you know that positive minds produce positive lives? Negative minds produce negative lives. Positive thoughts are always full of faith and hope. Negative thoughts are always full of fear and doubt.

Some people are afraid to hope because they have been hurt so much in their lives. They experience so many disappointments that they do not think they can face the pain of another one. Therefore, they refuse to hope so they will not be disappointed in case things do not work out as they hoped.

Disappointment hurts! But this type of behavior sets up a negative lifestyle. Everything becomes negative because the thoughts are negative. Remember, Proverbs 23:7 says, "For as he thinks in his heart, so is he . . . "

Many years ago, I was extremely negative. I always say that if I thought two positive thoughts in a row my mind would cramp. My whole philosophy was this: "If you do not expect anything good to happen, then you will not be disappointed when it does not."

I thought that my avoidance of hope would protect me from being hurt. I had encountered so many disappointments in life—so many devastating things had happened to me—that I was afraid to believe that anything good might happen. I had a terribly negative outlook on everything. Since my thoughts were all negative, so were my words and therefore, so was my life.

When I really began to study God's Word and to trust Him to restore me, one of the first things I realized was that the negativism had to go. I began to see the truth of Matthew 8:13—that it will be done for me as I have believed.

I do not mean to imply that you and I can get anything we want by just thinking about it. God has a perfect plan for each of us, and we cannot control Him with our thoughts and words. But, we must think and speak in agreement with His will and plan for us.

If you do not have any idea what God's will is for you at this point, at least begin by thinking, "I may not know God's plan for me, but I know He loves me. Whatever He does will be good, and I will be blessed."

Begin to think positively about your life: practice being positive in each situation that arises. Even if whatever is taking place in your life at the moment is not so good, expect God to bring good out of it, as He has promised in His Word.

down the steep bank into the sea and died in the water.

33 The herdsmen fled and went into the town and reported everything, including what had happened to the men under the power of demons.

34 And behold, the whole town went out to meet Jesus; and as soon as they saw Him, they begged Him to depart from their locality.

9 AND JESUS, getting into a boat, crossed to the other side and came to His own town [Capernaum].

2 And behold, they brought to Him a man paralyzed *and* prostrated by illness, lying on a sleeping pad; and when Jesus saw their faith, He said to the paralyzed man, Take courage, son; your sins are forgiven *and* the ˣpenalty remitted.

3 And behold, some of the scribes said to themselves, This man blasphemes [He claims the rights and prerogatives of God]!

4 But Jesus, knowing (ʸseeing) their thoughts, said, Why do you think evil *and* harbor ˣmalice in your hearts?

5 For which is easier: to say, Your sins are forgiven *and* the ˣpenalty remitted, or to say, Get up and walk?

6 But in order that you may know that the Son of Man has authority on earth to forgive sins *and* ˣremit the penalty, He then said to the paralyzed man, Get up! Pick up your sleeping pad and go to your own house.

7 And he got up and went away to his own house.

8 When the crowds saw it, they were struck with fear *and* awe; and they ᶻrecognized God *and* praised *and* thanked Him, Who had given such power *and* authority to men.

9 As Jesus passed on from there, He saw a man named Matthew sitting at the tax collector's office; and He said to him, ˣBe My disciple [side with My party and follow Me]. And he rose and followed Him.

10 And as Jesus reclined at table in the house, behold, many tax collectors and ᵃ[especially wicked] sinners came and sat (reclined) with Him and His disciples.

11 And when the Pharisees saw this, they said to His disciples, Why does your Master eat with tax collectors and those [preeminently] sinful?

12 But when Jesus heard it, He replied, Those who are strong *and* well (healthy) have no need of a physician, but those who are weak *and* sick.

13 Go and learn what this means: I desire mercy [that is, ˣreadiness to help those in trouble] and not sacrifice *and* sacrificial victims. For I came not to call *and* invite [to repentance] the righteous (those who are upright and in right standing with God), but sinners (the erring ones and all those not free from sin). [Hos. 6:6.]

14 Then the disciples of John came to Jesus, inquiring, Why is it that we and the Pharisees fast ʸoften, [that is, abstain from food and drink as a religious exercise], but Your disciples do not fast?

15 And Jesus replied to them, Can the wedding guests mourn while the bridegroom is still with them? The days will come when the bridegroom is taken away from them, and then they will fast.

16 And no one puts a piece of cloth that has not been shrunk on an old garment, for such a patch tears away from the garment and a worse rent (tear) is made.

17 Neither is new wine put in old wineskins; for if it is, the skins burst and are ˣtorn in pieces, and the wine is spilled and the skins are ruined. But

---

x Joseph Thayer, *A Greek-English Lexicon.* **y** Many manuscripts so read. **z** Hermann Cremer, *Biblico-Theological Lexicon.* **a** G. Abbott-Smith, *Manual Greek Lexicon.*

treasure mercy

As a young woman, born again, filled with the Spirit and in ministry, I had no idea that I had a problem with mercy. I had probably preached messages on mercy, but God began impressing upon me that I needed to experience the truth of Matthew 9:13. In my heart, I could hear Him say over and over again: "Go and learn what this means: *I desire mercy.*"

Mercy is kindness. It took a long time for me to understand what I am sharing with you, but slowly I discovered two things about myself: I was not a merciful person, and I was not merciful to others because I was raised in an atmosphere in which I had not experienced much mercy in my own life.

I became very legalistic and rigid. I had a way I wanted things done and that was the way I wanted them done. I was not too willing to give an inch in either direction. If I did not get it the way I wanted it, although the other person did their best and really could not give me what I wanted, I became upset with them. I was not merciful. I refused to give people any room for error.

Although I reached a place where I wanted to be merciful with all my heart, I was not able to be. I got angry because I saw other people show mercy, and I wanted to do the same. Then God showed me that there are two sides to mercy. We have to learn how to *receive* God's mercy before we can *give* God's mercy.

I had a hard time being merciful because I would not receive mercy. I was very legalistic with myself, and therefore, very legalistic with everyone else. The Bible says you are to love your neighbor as you love yourself (see Matthew 22:39). It is important to look at how you treat yourself because sometimes you try to give something to someone that you yourself do not have.

If you do not receive God's love and then love yourself in a balanced way, how can that love flow through you to anybody else? If you do not receive God's mercy when you make mistakes, you do not have a reservoir of mercy from which to draw for others.

I have learned to be a merciful person, and I enjoy the mercy of God every day in my own life. When I sin, I receive mercy immediately. I am sorry for the mistakes I make, but I refuse to live under condemnation (see Romans 8:1). We should admit our sins, repent, ask God to forgive us, receive His mercy, and press forward. Mercy is for people who do not deserve it. Remember that for yourself and for others.

new wine is put into fresh wineskins, and so both are preserved. **18** While He was talking this way to them, behold, a ruler entered and, kneeling down, worshiped Him, saying, My daughter has just ᵇnow died; but come and lay Your hand on her, and she will come to life.

b Marvin Vincent, *Word Studies*.

19 And Jesus got up and accompanied him, with His disciples.

20 And behold, a woman who had suffered from a flow of blood for twelve years came up behind Him and touched the fringe of His garment; [Matt. 14:36.]

21 For she kept saying to herself, If I only touch His garment, I shall be restored to health.

22 Jesus turned around and, seeing her, He said, Take courage, daughter! Your faith has made you well. And at once the woman was restored to health.

23 And when Jesus came to the ruler's house and saw the flute players and the crowd making an uproar *and* din,

24 He said, Go away; for the girl is not dead but sleeping. And they laughed *and* jeered at Him.

25 But when the crowd had been ordered to go outside, He went in and took her by the hand, and the girl arose.

26 And the news about this spread through all that district.

27 As Jesus passed on from there, two blind men followed Him, shouting loudly, Have pity *and* mercy on us, Son of David!

28 When He reached the house and went in, the blind men came to Him, and Jesus said to them, Do you believe that I am able to do this? They said to Him, Yes, Lord.

29 Then He touched their eyes, saying, According to your faith *and* trust *and* reliance [on the power invested in Me] be it done to you;

30 And their eyes were opened. And Jesus earnestly *and* sternly charged them, See that you let no one know about this.

31 But they went off and blazed *and* spread His fame abroad throughout that whole district.

32 And while they were going away,

behold, a dumb man under the power of a demon was brought to Jesus.

33 And when the demon was driven out, the dumb man spoke; and the crowds were stunned with bewildered wonder, saying, Never before has anything like this been seen in Israel.

34 But the Pharisees said, He drives out demons through *and* with the help of the prince of demons.

35 And Jesus went about all the cities and villages, teaching in their synagogues and proclaiming the good news (the Gospel) of the kingdom and curing all kinds of disease and every weakness *and* infirmity.

36 When He saw the throngs, He was moved with pity *and* sympathy for them, because they were bewildered (harassed and distressed and dejected and helpless), like sheep without a shepherd. [Zech. 10:2.]

37 Then He said to His disciples, The harvest is indeed plentiful, but the laborers are few.

38 So pray to the Lord of the harvest to ᶜforce out *and* thrust laborers into His harvest.

10 AND JESUS summoned to Him His twelve disciples and gave them power *and* authority over unclean spirits, to drive them out, and to cure all kinds of disease and all kinds of weakness *and* infirmity.

2 Now these are the names of the twelve apostles (special messengers): first, Simon, who is called Peter, and Andrew his brother; James son of Zebedee, and John his brother;

3 Philip and Bartholomew [Nathaniel]; Thomas and Matthew the tax collector; James son of Alphaeus, and Thaddaeus [Judas, not Iscariot];

4 Simon the Cananaean, and Judas Iscariot, who also betrayed Him.

5 Jesus sent out these twelve,

c Marvin Vincent, *Word Studies.*

charging them, Go nowhere among the Gentiles and do not go into any town of the Samaritans;

6 But go rather to the lost sheep of the house of Israel.

7 And as you go, preach, saying, The kingdom of heaven is at hand!

8 Cure the sick, raise the dead, cleanse the lepers, drive out demons. Freely (without pay) you have received, freely (without charge) give.

9 Take no gold nor silver nor [even] copper money in your purses (belts);

10 And do not take a provision bag *or* a ᵈwallet for a collection bag for your journey, nor two undergarments, nor sandals, nor a staff; for the workman deserves his support (his living, his food).

11 And into whatever town or village you go, inquire who in it is deserving, and stay there [at his house] until you leave [that vicinity].

12 As you go into the house, give your greetings *and* wish it well.

13 Then if indeed that house is deserving, let come upon it your peace [that is, ᵉfreedom from all the distresses that are experienced as the result of sin]. But if it is not deserving, let your peace return to you.

14 And whoever will not receive *and* accept *and* welcome you nor listen to your message, as you leave that house or town, shake the dust [of it] from your feet.

15 Truly I tell you, it shall be more tolerable on the day of judgment for the land of Sodom and Gomorrah than for that town.

16 Behold, I am sending you out like sheep in the midst of wolves; be ᶠwary *and* wise as serpents, and be innocent (harmless, guileless, and ᵍwithout falsity) as doves. [Gen. 3:1.]

17 Be on guard against men [whose ᵉway or nature is to act in opposition to God]; for they will deliver you up to councils and flog you in their synagogues,

18 And you will be brought before governors and kings for My sake, as a witness to bear testimony before them and to the Gentiles (the nations).

19 But when they deliver you up, do not be anxious about how *or* what you are to speak; for what you are to say will be given you in that very hour *and* ᵈmoment,

20 For it is not you who are speaking, but the Spirit of your Father speaking through you.

21 Brother will deliver up brother to death, and the father his child; and children will take a stand against their parents and will have them put to death.

22 And you will be hated by all for My name's sake, but he who perseveres *and* endures to the end will be saved [ʰfrom spiritual disease and death in the world to come].

23 When they persecute you in one town [that is, pursue you in a manner that would injure you and cause you to suffer because of your belief], flee to another town; for truly I tell you, you will not have gone through all the towns of Israel before ⁱthe Son of Man comes.

speak the Word

d James Moulton and George Milligan, *The Vocabulary*. **e** Hermann Cremer, *Biblico-Theological Lexicon*. **f** John Wycliffe, *The Wycliffe Bible*. **g** Martin Luther, cited by Marvin Vincent, *Word Studies*. **h** G. Abbott-Smith, *Manual Greek Lexicon*. **i** Believed by many to mean the coming of the Holy Spirit at Pentecost. Other commentators observe that the saying seems to teach that the Gospel

24 A disciple is not above his teacher, nor is a servant *or* slave above his master.

25 It is sufficient for the disciple to be like his teacher, and the servant *or* slave like his master. If they have called the Master of the house Beelzebub [ʲmaster of the dwelling], how much more will they speak evil of those of His household. [II Kings 1:2.]

26 So have no fear of them; for nothing is concealed that will not be revealed, or kept secret that will not become known.

27 What I say to you in the dark, tell in the light; and what you hear whispered in the ear, proclaim upon the housetops.

28 And do not be afraid of those who kill the body but cannot kill the soul; but rather be afraid of Him who can destroy both soul and body in hell (Gehenna).

29 Are not two ᵏlittle sparrows sold for a penny? And yet not one of them will fall to the ground without your Father's leave (consent) *and* notice.

30 But even the very hairs of your head are all numbered.

31 Fear not, then; you are of more value than many sparrows.

32 Therefore, everyone who acknowledges Me before men *and* confesses Me [ᵏout of a state of oneness with Me], I will also acknowledge him before My Father Who is in heaven *and* ᵏconfess [that I am abiding in] him.

33 But whoever denies *and* disowns Me before men, I also will deny *and* disown him before My Father Who is in heaven.

34 Do not think that I have come to bring peace upon the earth; I have not come to bring peace, but a sword.

35 For I have come to part asunder a man from his father, and a daughter from her mother, and a ᵏnewly married wife from her mother-in-law—

36 And a man's foes will be they of his own household. [Mic. 7:6.]

37 He who loves [and ˡtakes more pleasure in] father or mother more than [in] Me is not worthy of Me; and he who loves [and takes more pleasure in] son or daughter more than [in] Me is not worthy of Me;

38 And he who does not take up his cross and follow Me [ᵐcleave steadfastly to Me, conforming wholly to My example in living and, if need be, in dying also] is not worthy of Me.

39 Whoever finds his [ˡlower] life will lose it [the higher life], and whoever loses his [lower] life on My account will find it [the higher life].

putting the Word to work

The Bible tells us that we love because God first loved us. Who do you love most? Your love for God should exceed even the strongest love you have for another person. As a follower of Jesus, you demonstrate your love for Him by placing His purposes before your own interests. Ask God to show you what it means to pick up your cross daily to follow Him (see Matthew 10:38).

40 He who receives *and* welcomes *and* accepts you receives *and* welcomes *and* accepts Me, and he who receives *and* welcomes *and* accepts Me receives *and* welcomes *and* accepts Him Who sent Me.

41 He who receives *and* welcomes *and* accepts a prophet because he is a prophet shall receive a prophet's reward, and he who receives *and* welcomes *and* accepts a righteous man because he is a righteous man shall

will continue to be preached to the Jews until Christ's second coming. **j** John D. Davis, *A Dictionary of the Bible*. **k** Marvin Vincent, *Word Studies*. **l** Kenneth Wuest, *Word Studies*. **m** Joseph Thayer, *A Greek-English Lexicon*.

receive a righteous man's reward.
42 And whoever gives to one of these little ones [in rank or influence] even a cup of cold water because he is My disciple, surely I declare to you, he shall not lose his reward.

11 WHEN JESUS had finished His charge to His twelve disciples, He left there to teach and to preach in their [Galilean] cities.
2 Now when John in prison heard about the activities of Christ, he sent a message by his disciples
3 And asked Him, Are You the One Who was to come, or should we keep on expecting a different one? [Gen. 49:10; Num. 24:17.]
4 And Jesus replied to them, Go and report to John what you hear and see:
5 The blind receive their sight and the lame walk, lepers are cleansed (by healing) and the deaf hear, the dead are raised up and the poor have good news (the Gospel) preached to them. [Isa. 35:5, 6; 61:1.]
6 And blessed (happy, fortunate, and ⁿto be envied) is he who takes no offense at Me *and* finds no cause for stumbling in *or* through Me *and* is not hindered from seeing the Truth.
7 Then as these men went their way, Jesus began to speak to the crowds about John: What did you go out in the wilderness (desert) to see? A reed swayed by the wind?
8 What did you go out to see then? A man clothed in soft garments? Behold, those who wear soft clothing are in the houses of kings.
9 But what did you go out to see? A prophet? Yes, I tell you, and one [°out of the common, more eminent, more remarkable, and] °superior to a prophet.

10 This is the one of whom it is written, Behold, I send My messenger ahead of You, who shall make ready Your way before You. [Mal. 3:1.]
11 Truly I tell you, among those born of women there has not risen anyone greater than John the Baptist; yet he who is least in the kingdom of heaven is greater than he.
12 And from the days of John the Baptist until the present time, the kingdom of heaven has endured violent assault, and violent men seize it by force [as a precious prize—a Pshare in the heavenly kingdom is sought with most ardent zeal and intense exertion].
13 For all the Prophets and the Law prophesied up until John.
14 And if you are willing to receive *and* accept it, John himself is Elijah who was to come [before the kingdom]. [Mal. 4:5.]
15 He who has ears to hear, let him be listening *and* let him consider *and* °perceive *and* comprehend by hearing.
16 But to what shall I liken this generation? It is like little children sitting in the marketplaces who call to their playmates,
17 We piped to you [playing wedding], and you did not dance; we wailed dirges [playing funeral], and you did not mourn *and* beat your breasts *and* weep aloud.
18 For John came neither eating nor drinking [with others], and they say, He has a demon!
19 The Son of Man came eating and drinking [with others], and they say, Behold, a glutton and a wine drinker, a friend of tax collectors *and* [°especially wicked] sinners! Yet wisdom is justified *and* vindicated by what she does (her deeds) *and* by �q*her children.*
20 Then He began to censure *and*

---

n Alexander Souter, *Pocket Lexicon.* o G. Abbott-Smith, *Manual Greek Lexicon.* p Joseph Thayer, *A Greek-English Lexicon.* q Many manuscripts read "children" here, as in Luke 7:35.

reproach the cities in which most of His mighty works had been performed, because they did not repent [and their hearts were not changed].

21 Woe to you, Chorazin! Woe to you, Bethsaida! For if the mighty works done in you had been done in Tyre and Sidon, they would long ago have repented in sackcloth and ashes [and their hearts would have been changed].

22 I tell you [further], it shall be more endurable for Tyre and Sidon on the day of judgment than for you.

23 And you, Capernaum, are you to be lifted up to heaven? You shall be brought down to Hades [the region of the dead]! For if the mighty works done in you had been done in Sodom, it would have continued until today.

24 But I tell you, it shall be more endurable for the land of Sodom on the day of judgment than for you.

25 At that time Jesus began to say, I thank You, Father, Lord of heaven and earth [and ʳI acknowledge openly *and* joyfully to Your honor], that You have hidden these things from the wise *and* clever and learned, and revealed them to babies [to the ʳchildish, untaught, and unskilled].

26 Yes, Father, [I praise You that] such was Your gracious will *and* good pleasure.

27 All things have been entrusted *and* delivered to Me by My Father; and no one ˢfully knows *and* ʳaccu-

rately understands the Son except the Father, and no one ˢfully knows *and* ʳaccurately understands the Father except the Son and anyone to whom the Son ʳdeliberately wills to make Him known.

28 Come to Me, all you who labor and are heavy-laden *and* overburdened, and I will cause you to rest. [I will ᵗease and relieve and ᵘrefresh ʳyour souls.]

29 Take My yoke upon you and learn of Me, for I am gentle (meek) and humble (lowly) in heart, and you will find rest (ᵛrelief and ease and refreshment and ʳrecreation and blessed quiet) for your souls. [Jer. 6:16.]

30 For My yoke is wholesome (useful, ʷgood—not harsh, hard, sharp, or pressing, but comfortable, gracious, and pleasant), and My burden is light *and* easy to be borne.

12 AT THAT ˢparticular time Jesus went through the fields of standing grain on the Sabbath; and His disciples were hungry, and they began to pick off the spikes of grain and to eat. [Deut. 23:25.]

2 And when the Pharisees saw it, they said to Him, See there! Your disciples are doing what is unlawful *and* not permitted on the Sabbath.

3 He said to them, Have you not even read what David did when he was hungry, and those who accompanied him—[Lev. 24:9; I Sam. 21:1-6.]

4 How he went into the house of

speak the Word

Thank You, Jesus, that You will ease and refresh my soul when I am weary and that You will cause me to rest. Thank You that Your yoke is not harsh, hard, sharp, or pressing, but comfortable, gracious, and pleasant and that Your burden is light and easy for me to bear.
ADAPTED FROM MATTHEW 11:28–30

---

r Joseph Thayer, *A Greek-English Lexicon*. **s** Marvin Vincent, *Word Studies*. **t** William Tyndale, *The Tyndale Bible*. **u** John Wycliffe, *The Wycliffe Bible*. **v** Alexander Souter, *Pocket Lexicon*. **w** James Moulton and George Milligan, *The Vocabulary*.

lighten your load

God will give you the power and the strength you need to serve Him. Matthew 11:28–30 teaches us that Jesus is not a hard taskmaster.

In this passage, Jesus is saying that He is good and His system is good, not burdensome or difficult. Religious rules and regulations can be harsh and pressing, and you can easily get overburdened if you do not know how to do everything you feel is expected of you. But Jesus is saying here: "I am not that way. My ways are not like that. They are not hard, harsh, sharp, and pressing, but they are comfortable, gracious, and pleasant."

God not only tells us what to do, He gives us the strength and wisdom to do it. If God did not give me the power to run Joyce Meyer Ministries, I would be burdened and in way over my head. But it is not hard for me. I am comfortable doing what God has equipped me to do. I would not be equipped with any power to get it done if I tried to serve God from the standpoint of mere rules and regulations, and I would be miserable. But I serve Him because I deeply love Him; therefore, I have joy in what I do.

Jesus leads us to a place that is comfortable, gracious, and pleasant. I believe that serving God is easy if we learn to hear from Him and simply obey rather than struggle to do things He never asked us to do for Him.

Take time and seek God about whether your works are His works. Is He leading you to do them? If you discover that you are involved in works of the flesh and that God has not given you the grace to do them, do not be afraid to lay them down and seek Him about His will for your life. Remember, it will not always be easy, but there will be comfort, grace, and pleasure associated with doing His works. Jesus wants to lighten the load you have been carrying all by yourself and give you rest.

God and ate the loaves of the show-bread—which was not lawful for him to eat, nor for the men who accompanied him, but for the priests only?

5 Or have you never read in the Law that on the Sabbath the priests in the temple violate the sanctity of the Sabbath [breaking it] and yet are guiltless? [Num. 28:9, 10.]

6 But I tell you, Something greater and ˣmore exalted and more majestic than the temple is here!

7 And if you had only known what this saying means, I desire mercy [readiness to help, to spare, to forgive] rather than sacrifice *and* sacrificial victims, you would not have condemned the guiltless. [Hos. 6:6; Matt. 9:13.]

8 For the Son of Man is Lord [even] of the Sabbath.

9 And going on from there, He went into their synagogue.

10 And behold, a man was there with one withered hand. And they said to Him, Is it lawful *or* allowable to cure

ˣ Joseph Thayer, *A Greek-English Lexicon*.

people on the Sabbath days?—that they might accuse Him.

11 But He said to them, What man is there among you, if he has only one sheep and it falls into a pit *or* ditch on the Sabbath, will not take hold of it and lift it out?

12 How much better *and* of more value is a man than a sheep! So it is lawful *and* allowable to do good on the Sabbath days.

13 Then He said to the man, Reach out your hand. And the man reached it out and it was restored, as sound as the other one.

14 But the Pharisees went out and held a consultation against Him, how they might do away with Him.

15 But being aware of this, Jesus went away from there. And many people ʸjoined *and* accompanied Him, and He cured all of them,

16 And strictly charged them *and* sharply warned them not to make Him ᶻpublicly known.

17 This was in fulfillment of what was spoken by the prophet Isaiah,

18 Behold, My Servant Whom I have chosen, My Beloved in *and* with Whom My soul is well pleased *and* ᶻhas found its delight. I will put My Spirit upon Him, and He shall proclaim *and* ᶻshow forth justice to the nations.

19 He will not strive *or* wrangle or cry out loudly; nor will anyone hear His voice in the streets;

20 A bruised reed He will not break, and a smoldering (dimly burning) wick He will not quench, till He brings ʸjustice *and* a just cause to victory.

21 And in *and* on His name will the Gentiles (the ᵃpeoples outside of Israel) set their hopes. [Isa. 42:1-4.]

22 Then a blind and dumb man under the power of a demon was brought to Jesus, and He cured him, so that the blind and dumb man both spoke and saw.

23 And all the [crowds of] people were stunned with bewildered wonder and said, This cannot be the Son of David, can it?

24 But the Pharisees, hearing it, said, This ᵇMan drives out demons only by *and* with the help of Beelzebub, the prince of demons.

25 And knowing their thoughts, He said to them, Any kingdom that is divided against itself is being brought to desolation *and* laid waste, and no city *or* house divided against itself will last *or* continue to stand.

26 And if Satan drives out Satan, he has become divided against himself *and* disunified; how then will his kingdom last *or* continue to stand?

27 And if I drive out the demons by [help of] Beelzebub, by whose [help] do your sons drive them out? ᶻFor this reason they shall be your judges.

28 But if it is by the Spirit of God that I drive out the demons, then the kingdom of God has come upon you [ᶜbefore you expected it].

29 Or how can a person go into a strong man's house and carry off his goods (the entire equipment of his house) without first binding the strong man? Then indeed he may plunder his house.

30 He who is not with Me [definitely ʸon My side] is against Me, and he who does not [definitely] gather with Me *and* for ʸMy side scatters.

31 Therefore I tell you, every sin and blasphemy (every evil, abusive, ᵈinjurious speaking, or indignity against sacred things) can be forgiven men, but blasphemy against the [Holy] Spirit shall not *and* ᵈcannot be forgiven.

---

y Joseph Thayer, *A Greek-English Lexicon.* **z** John Darby, *The New Testament, a New Translation.* **a** Hermann Cremer, *Biblico-Theological Lexicon.* **b** Capitalized because of what He is, the spotless Son of God, not what the speakers may have thought He was. **c** Marvin Vincent, *Word Studies.* **d** Charles B. Williams, *The New Testament: A Translation.*

32 And whoever speaks a word against the Son of Man will be forgiven, but whoever speaks against the Spirit, the Holy One, will not be forgiven, either in this world *and* age or in the world *and* age to come.
33 Either make the tree sound (healthy and good), and its fruit sound (healthy and good), or make the tree rotten (diseased and bad), and its fruit rotten (diseased and bad); for the tree is known *and* recognized *and* judged by its fruit.

life point

Matthew 12:33 says that a tree is known by its fruit. The same is true in our lives. Thoughts bear fruit. If we think good thoughts, the fruit in our lives will be good. If we think bad thoughts, the fruit in our lives will be bad.

We can look at a person's attitude and know what kind of thinking is prevalent in his life. A sweet, kind person does not have mean, vindictive thoughts. By the same token, a truly evil person does not have good, loving thoughts. Your thoughts determine your results in life, so think good thoughts and bear good fruit!

34 You offspring of vipers! How can you speak good things when you are evil (wicked)? For out of the fullness (the overflow, the [e]superabundance) of the heart the mouth speaks.
35 The good man from his inner good treasure [f]flings forth good things, and the evil man out of his inner evil storehouse [f]flings forth evil things.
36 But I tell you, on the day of judgment men will have to give account for every [f]idle (inoperative, nonworking) word they speak.
37 For by your words you will be justified *and* acquitted, and by your

life point

Matthew 12:34 teaches us that "out of the fullness (the overflow, the superabundance) of heart the mouth speaks." If we permit wrong thoughts to dwell in our hearts, we will ultimately speak them. Whatever is hidden in our hearts will sooner or later be expressed openly through our mouths.

words you will be condemned *and* sentenced.
38 Then some of the scribes and Pharisees said to Him, Teacher, we desire to see a sign *or* miracle from You [proving that You are what You claim to be].
39 But He replied to them, An evil and adulterous generation (a generation [f]morally unfaithful to God) seeks *and* demands a sign; but no sign shall be given to it except the sign of the prophet Jonah.
40 For even as Jonah was three days and three nights in the belly of the sea monster, so will the Son of Man be

life point

As parents, employers, friends, husbands, wives, and children—all of us need to make a commitment to love with our words and to build confidence in others. Every word we speak can be a brick to build with or a bulldozer to destroy.

Choose your words carefully because according to Matthew 12:36, you will have to account for the idle, thoughtless things you say. Remember, words are seeds; they are containers for power. They carry creative or destructive power and they produce a good harvest or a bad harvest in your life and in the lives of those you love.

e Alexander Souter, *Pocket Lexicon*.   **f** Marvin Vincent, *Word Studies*.

three days and three nights in the heart of the earth. [Jonah 1:17.]

41 The men of Nineveh will stand up at the judgment with this generation and condemn it; for they repented at the preaching of Jonah, and behold, Someone more *and* greater than Jonah is here! [Jonah 3:5.]

42 The queen of the South will stand up at the judgment with this generation and condemn it; for she came from the ends of the earth to listen to the wisdom of Solomon, and behold, Someone more *and* greater than Solomon is here. [I Kings 10:1; II Chron. 9:1.]

43 But when the unclean spirit has gone out of a man, it roams through dry [arid] places in search of rest, but it does not find any.

44 Then it says, I will go back to my house from which I came out. And when it arrives, it finds the place unoccupied, swept, put in order, *and* decorated.

45 Then it goes and brings with it seven other spirits more wicked than itself, and they go in and make their home there. And the last condition of that man becomes worse than the first. So also shall it be with this wicked generation.

46 Jesus was still speaking to the people when behold, His mother and brothers stood outside, seeking to speak to Him.

47 [g]*Someone said to Him, Listen! Your mother and Your brothers are standing outside, seeking to speak to You.*

48 But He replied to the man who told Him, Who is My mother, and who are My brothers?

49 And stretching out His hand toward [not only the twelve disciples but all] [h]His adherents, He said, Here are My mother and My brothers.

50 For whoever does the will of My Father in heaven is My brother and sister and mother!

13 THAT SAME day Jesus went out of the house and was sitting beside the sea.

2 But such great crowds gathered about Him that He got into a boat and remained sitting there, while all the throng stood on the shore.

3 And He told them many things in parables (stories by way of illustration and comparison), saying, A sower went out to sow.

4 And as he sowed, some seeds fell by the roadside, and the birds came and ate them up.

5 Other seeds fell on rocky ground, where they had not much soil; and at once they sprang up, because they had no depth of soil.

6 But when the sun rose, they were scorched, and because they had no root, they dried up *and* withered away.

7 Other seeds fell among thorns, and the thorns grew up and choked them out.

8 Other seeds fell on good soil, and yielded grain—some a hundred times as much as was sown, some sixty times as much, and some thirty.

9 He who has ears [to hear], let him be listening *and* let him [i]consider *and* [j]perceive *and* comprehend by hearing.

10 Then the disciples came to Him and said, Why do You speak to them in parables?

11 And He replied to them, To you it has been given to know the secrets *and* mysteries of the kingdom of heaven, but to them it has not been given.

12 For whoever has [spiritual knowledge], to him will more be given *and* he will [g]be furnished richly so that he will have abundance; but from him who has not, even what he has will be taken away.

---

g Some manuscripts omit verse 47.   **h** Hermann Cremer, *Biblico-Theological Lexicon.*   **i** Joseph Thayer, *A Greek-English Lexicon.*   **j** G. Abbott-Smith, *Manual Greek Lexicon.*

13 This is the reason that I speak to them in parables: because ᵏhaving the power of seeing, they do not see; and ᵏhaving the power of hearing, they do not hear, nor do they grasp *and* understand.

14 In them indeed is ˡthe process of fulfillment of the prophecy of Isaiah, which says: You shall indeed hear *and* hear but never grasp *and* understand; and you shall indeed look *and* look but never see *and* perceive.

15 For this nation's heart has grown gross (fat and dull), and their ears heavy *and* difficult of hearing, and their eyes they have tightly closed, lest they see *and* perceive with their eyes, and hear *and* comprehend the sense with their ears, and grasp *and* understand with their heart, and turn *and* I should heal them. [Isa. 6:9, 10.]

16 But blessed (happy, fortunate, and ᵐto be envied) are your eyes because they do see, and your ears because they do hear.

17 Truly I tell you, many prophets and righteous men [men who were upright and in right standing with God] yearned to see what you see, and did not see it, and to hear what you hear, and did not hear it.

18 Listen then to the [meaning of the] parable of the sower:

19 ˡWhile anyone is hearing the Word of the kingdom and does not grasp *and* comprehend it, the evil one comes and snatches away what was sown in his heart. This is what was sown along the roadside.

20 As for what was sown on thin (rocky) soil, this is he who hears the Word and at once welcomes *and* accepts it with joy;

21 Yet it has no real root in him, but is temporary (inconstant, ⁿlasts but a little while); and when affliction *or* trouble *or* persecution comes on account of the Word, at once he is caused to stumble [he is repelled and ᵏbegins to distrust and desert Him Whom he ought to trust and obey] *and* he falls away.

22 As for what was sown among thorns, this is he who hears the Word, but the cares of the world and the pleasure *and* delight *and* glamour *and* deceitfulness of riches choke *and* suffocate the Word, and it yields no fruit.

23 As for what was sown on good soil, this is he who hears the Word and grasps *and* comprehends it; he indeed bears fruit and yields in one case a hundred times as much as was sown, in another sixty times as much, and in another thirty.

24 Another parable He set forth before them, saying, The kingdom of heaven is like a man who sowed good seed in his field.

25 But while he was sleeping, his enemy came and sowed also darnel (weeds resembling wheat) among the wheat, and went on his way.

26 So when the plants sprouted and formed grain, the darnel (weeds) appeared also.

27 And the servants of the owner came to him and said, Sir, did you not sow good seed in your field? Then how does it have darnel shoots in it?

28 He replied to them, An enemy has done this. The servants said to him,

speak the Word

God, I pray that I will be one who hears the Word and grasps it. As the Word takes root in my heart, I pray that I will bear much fruit.
ADAPTED FROM MATTHEW 13:23

---

k Joseph Thayer, *A Greek-English Lexicon.*   **l** Marvin Vincent, *Word Studies.*   **m** Alexander Souter, *Pocket Lexicon.*   **n** John Wycliffe, *The Wycliffe Bible.*

Then do you want us to go and weed them out?
29 But he said, No, lest in gathering the wild wheat (weeds resembling wheat), you root up the [true] wheat along with it.
30 Let them grow together until the harvest; and at harvest time I will say to the reapers, Gather the darnel first and bind it in bundles to be burned, but gather the wheat into my granary.
31 Another story by way of comparison He set forth before them, saying, The kingdom of heaven is like a grain of mustard seed, which a man took and sowed in his field.
32 Of all the seeds it is the smallest, but when it has grown it is the largest of the garden herbs and becomes a tree, so that the birds of the air come and find shelter in its branches.
33 He told them another parable: The kingdom of heaven is like leaven (°sour dough) which a woman took and covered over in three measures of meal or flour till all of it was leavened. [Gen. 18:6.]
34 These things Pall taken together Jesus said to the crowds in parables; indeed, without a parable He said nothing to them.
35 This was in fulfillment of what was spoken by the prophet: I will open My mouth in parables; I will utter things that have been hidden since the foundation of the world. [Ps. 78:2.]
36 Then He left the throngs and went into the house. And His disciples came to Him saying, Explain to us the parable of the darnel in the field.
37 He answered, He Who sows the good seed is the Son of Man.
38 The field is the world, and the good seed means the children of the kingdom; the darnel is the children of the evil one,
39 And the enemy who sowed it is the devil. The harvest is the close *and* consummation of the age, and the reapers are angels.
40 Just as the darnel (weeds resembling wheat) is gathered and burned with fire, so it will be at the close of the age.
41 The Son of Man will send forth His angels, and they will gather out of His kingdom all causes of offense [Ppersons by whom others are drawn into error or sin] and all who do iniquity *and* act wickedly,
42 And will cast them into the furnace of fire; there will be weeping *and* wailing and grinding of teeth.
43 Then will the righteous (those who are upright and in right standing with God) shine forth like the sun in the kingdom of their Father. Let him who has ears [to hear] be listening, *and* let him Pconsider *and* perceive *and* understand by hearing. [Dan. 12:3.]
44 The kingdom of heaven is like Psomething precious buried in a field, which a man found and hid again; then in his joy he goes and sells all he has and buys that field.
45 Again the kingdom of heaven is like a man who is a dealer in search of fine *and* Pprecious pearls,
46 Who, on finding a single pearl of great price, went and sold all he had and bought it.
47 Again, the kingdom of heaven is like a qdragnet which was cast into the sea and gathered in fish of every sort.
48 When it was full, men dragged it up on the beach, and sat down and sorted out the good fish into baskets, but the worthless ones they threw away.
49 So it will be at the close *and* consummation of the age. The angels will go forth and separate the wicked from the righteous (those who are upright and in right standing with God)
50 And cast them [the wicked] into

---

o John Wycliffe, *The Wycliffe Bible.*   **p** Joseph Thayer, *A Greek-English Lexicon.*   **q** Marvin Vincent, *Word Studies.*

the furnace of fire; there will be weeping *and* wailing and grinding of teeth.

51 Have you understood ᵗall these things [parables] taken together? They said to Him, Yes, *Lord.*

52 He said to them, Therefore every ᵗteacher *and* interpreter of the Sacred Writings who has been instructed about *and* trained for the kingdom of heaven and has ˢbecome a disciple is like a householder who brings forth out of his storehouse treasure that is new and [treasure that is] old [the fresh as well as the familiar].

53 When Jesus had finished these parables (these comparisons), He left there.

54 And coming to His own country [Nazareth], He taught in their synagogue so that they were amazed with bewildered wonder, and said, Where did this ᵗMan get this wisdom and these miraculous powers?

55 Is not this the carpenter's Son? Is not His mother called Mary? And are not His brothers James and Joseph and Simon and Judas?

56 And do not all His sisters live here among us? Where then did this Man get all this?

57 And they took offense at Him [they were repelled and hindered from acknowledging His authority, and caused to stumble]. But Jesus said to them, A prophet is not without honor except in his own country and in his own house.

58 And He did not do many works of power there, because of their unbelief (their lack of faith ˢin the divine mission of Jesus).

14 AT THAT time Herod the governor heard the reports about Jesus,

2 And he said to his attendants, This is John the Baptist; He has been raised from the dead, and that is why the powers ˢof performing miracles are at work in Him.

3 For Herod had arrested John and bound him and put him in prison [to ᵘstow him out of the way] on account *and* for the sake of Herodias, his brother Philip's wife,

4 For John had said to him, It is not lawful *or* right for you to have her. [Lev. 18:16; 20:21.]

5 Although he wished to have him put to death, he was afraid of the people, for they regarded John as a prophet.

6 But when Herod's birthday came, the daughter of Herodias danced in the midst [before the company] and pleased *and* fascinated Herod,

7 And so he promised with an oath to give her whatever she might ask.

8 And she, being put forward *and* prompted by her mother, said, Give me the head of John the Baptist right here on a ᵛplatter.

9 And the king was distressed *and* sorry, but because of his oaths and his guests, he ordered it to be given her;

10 He sent and had John beheaded in the prison.

11 And his head was brought in on a ᵛplatter and given ʷto the little maid, and she brought it to her mother.

12 And John's disciples came and took up the body and buried it. Then they went and told Jesus.

13 When Jesus heard it, He withdrew from there privately in a boat to a solitary place. But when the crowds heard of it, they followed Him [by land] on foot from the towns.

14 When He went ashore and saw a great throng of people, He had

---

r Joseph Thayer, *A Greek-English Lexicon.* **s** Marvin Vincent, *Word Studies.* **t** See footnote on Matt. 2:8. **u** G. Abbott-Smith, *Manual Greek Lexicon.* **v** William Tyndale, *The Tyndale Bible.* **w** Martin Luther, cited by Marvin Vincent, *Word Studies.*

1514

compassion (pity and deep sympathy) for them and cured their sick.

15 When evening came, the disciples came to Him and said, This is a remote *and* barren place, and the day is now over; send the throngs away into the villages to buy food for themselves.

16 Jesus said, They do not need to go away; you give them something to eat.

17 They said to Him, We have nothing here but five loaves and two fish.

18 He said, Bring them here to Me.

19 Then He ordered the crowds to recline on the grass; and He took the five loaves and the two fish, and, looking up to heaven, He gave thanks *and* blessed and broke the loaves and handed the pieces to the disciples, and the disciples gave them to the people.

20 And they all ate and were satisfied. And they picked up twelve [ˣsmall hand] baskets full of the broken pieces left over.

21 And those who ate were about 5,000 men, not including women and children.

22 Then He directed the disciples to get into the boat and go before Him to the other side, while He sent away the crowds.

23 And after He had dismissed the multitudes, He went up into the hills by Himself to pray. When it was evening, He was still there alone.

24 But the boat was by this time out on the sea, *many furlongs* [a furlong is one-eighth of a mile] *distant from the land,* beaten and tossed by the waves, for the wind was against them.

25 And in the fourth watch [between 3:00—6:00 a.m.] of the night, Jesus came to them, walking on the sea.

26 And when the disciples saw Him walking on the sea, they were terrified and said, It is a ghost! And they screamed out with fright.

27 But instantly He spoke to them, saying, Take courage! I AM! Stop being afraid! [Exod. 3:14.]

28 And Peter answered Him, Lord, if it is You, command me to come to You on the water.

29 He said, Come! So Peter got out of the boat and walked on the water, and he came toward Jesus.

30 But when he perceived *and* felt the strong wind, he was frightened, and as he began to sink, he cried out, Lord, save me [from death]!

31 Instantly Jesus reached out His hand and caught *and* held him, saying to him, O you of little faith, why did you doubt?

32 And when they got into the boat, the wind ceased.

33 And those in the boat knelt and worshiped Him, saying, Truly You are the Son of God!

34 And when they had crossed over to the other side, they went ashore at Gennesaret.

35 And when the men of that place recognized Him, they sent around into all the surrounding country and brought to Him all who were sick

36 And begged Him to let them merely touch the fringe of His garment; and as many as touched it were perfectly restored. [Matt. 9:20.]

speak the Word

Jesus, I pray that I will be like Peter and always trust You enough to step out in faith when You call. Help me to keep my faith strong and not doubt.
ADAPTED FROM MATTHEW 14:28–30

---

x Marvin Vincent, *Word Studies*. But according to James Moulton and George Milligan, *The Vocabulary*, the term refers to the type of material of which the basket is constructed (perhaps a wicker basket) and not necessarily the size of the basket.

15

THEN FROM Jerusalem came scribes and Pharisees and said,

2 Why do Your disciples transgress *and* violate the rules handed down by the elders of the past? For they do not practice [ceremonially] washing their hands before they eat.

3 He replied to them, And why also do you transgress *and* violate the commandment of God for the sake of the rules handed down to you by your forefathers (the elders)?

4 For God commanded, Honor your father and your mother, and, He who curses *or* reviles *or* speaks evil of *or* abuses *or* treats improperly his father or mother, let him surely come to his end by death. [Exod. 20:12; 21:17; Lev. 20:9; Deut. 5:16.]

5 But you say, If anyone tells his father or mother, What you would have gained from me [that is, the money and whatever I have that might be used for helping you] is already dedicated as a gift to God, then he is exempt *and* no longer under obligation to honor *and* help his father *or his mother.*

6 So for the sake of your tradition (the rules handed down by your forefathers), you have set aside the Word of God [depriving it of force and authority and making it of no effect].

7 You pretenders (hypocrites)! Admirably *and* truly did Isaiah prophesy of you when he said:

8 These people *draw near Me with their mouths and* honor Me with their lips, but their hearts hold off *and* are far away from Me.

9 Uselessly do they worship Me, for they teach as doctrines the commands of men. [Isa. 29:13.]

10 And Jesus called the people to Him and said to them, Listen and grasp *and* comprehend this:

11 It is not what goes into the mouth of a man that makes him unclean *and* defiled, but what comes out of the mouth; this makes a man unclean *and* defiles [him].

12 Then the disciples came and said to Him, Do You know that the Pharisees were displeased *and* offended *and* indignant when they heard this saying?

13 He answered, Every plant which My heavenly Father has not planted will be torn up by the roots. [Isa. 60:21.]

14 Let them alone *and* disregard them; they are blind guides *and* teachers. And if a blind man leads a blind man, both will fall into a ditch.

15 But Peter said to Him, Explain this ʸproverb (this ᶻmaxim) to us.

16 And He said, Are you also even yet dull *and* ignorant [without understanding and ᵃunable to put things together]?

17 Do you not see *and* understand that whatever goes into the mouth passes into the ᵇabdomen and so passes on into the place where discharges are deposited?

18 But whatever comes out of the mouth comes from the heart, and this is what makes a man unclean *and* defiles [him].

19 For out of the heart come evil thoughts (reasonings and disputings and designs) such as murder, adultery, sexual vice, theft, false witnessing, slander, *and* irreverent speech.

20 These are what make a man unclean *and* defile [him]; but eating with unwashed hands does not make him unclean *or* defile [him].

21 And going away from there, Jesus withdrew to the district of Tyre and Sidon.

22 And behold, a woman who was a Canaanite from that district came out and, with a [loud, troublesomely

y G. Abbott-Smith, *Manual Greek Lexicon.* **z** Joseph Thayer, *A Greek-English Lexicon.* **a** Hermann Cremer, *Biblico-Theological Lexicon.* **b** James Moulton and George Milligan, *The Vocabulary.*

urgent] cry, begged, Have mercy on me, O Lord, Son of David! My daughter is miserably *and* distressingly *and* cruelly possessed by a demon!

23 But He did not answer her a word. And His disciples came and implored Him, saying, Send her away, for she is crying out after us.

24 He answered, I was sent only to the lost sheep of the house of Israel.

25 But she came and, kneeling, worshiped Him and kept praying, Lord, help me!

26 And He answered, It is not right (proper, becoming, or fair) to take the children's bread and throw it to the ᶜlittle dogs.

27 She said, Yes, Lord, yet even the little pups (ᵈlittle whelps) eat the crumbs that fall from their [young] masters' table.

28 Then Jesus answered her, O woman, great is your faith! Be it done for you as you wish. And her daughter was cured from that ᵉmoment.

29 And Jesus went on from there and passed along the shore of the Sea of Galilee. Then He went up into the hills and kept sitting there.

30 And a great multitude came to Him, bringing with them the lame, the maimed, the blind, the dumb, and many others, and they put them down at His feet; and He cured them,

31 So that the crowd was amazed when they saw the dumb speaking, the maimed made whole, the lame walking, and the blind seeing; and they ᶠrecognized *and* praised *and* thanked *and* glorified the God of Israel.

32 Then Jesus called His disciples to Him and said, I have pity *and* sympathy *and* am deeply moved for the crowd, because they have been with Me now three days and they have nothing [at all left] to eat; and I am not willing to send them away hungry, lest they faint *or* become exhausted on the way.

33 And the disciples said to Him, Where are we to get bread sufficient to feed so great a crowd in this isolated *and* desert place?

34 And Jesus asked them, How many loaves of bread do you have? They replied, Seven, and a few small fish.

35 And ordering the crowd to recline on the ground,

36 He took the seven loaves and the fish, and when He had given thanks, He broke them and gave them to the disciples, and the disciples gave them to the people.

37 And they all ate and were satisfied. And they gathered up seven [ᵍlarge provision] baskets full of the broken pieces that were left over.

38 Those who ate were 4,000 men, not including the women and the children.

39 Then He dismissed the crowds, got into the boat, and went to the district of Magadan.

16 NOW THE Pharisees and Sadducees came up to Jesus, and they asked Him to show them a sign (spectacular miracle) from heaven [attesting His divine authority].

2 He replied to them, ʰ*When it is evening you say, It will be fair weather, for the sky is red,*

3 *And in the morning, It will be stormy today, for the sky is red and has a gloomy and threatening look. You know how to interpret the appearance of the sky, but you cannot interpret the signs of the times.*

4 A wicked and morally unfaithful generation craves a sign, but no sign shall be given to it except the sign of

c Marvin Vincent, *Word Studies*. d John Wycliffe, *The Wycliffe Bible*. e James Moulton and George Milligan, *The Vocabulary*. f Hermann Cremer, *Biblico-Theological Lexicon*. g Marvin Vincent, *Word Studies*. See also footnote on Matt. 14:20. h Some manuscripts do not have the rest of verse 2 and all of verse 3.

the prophet Jonah. Then He left them and went away. [Jonah 3:4, 5.]

5 When the disciples reached the other side of the sea, they found that they had forgotten to bring any bread.

6 Jesus said to them, Be careful *and* on your guard against the leaven (ferment) of the Pharisees and Sadducees.

7 And they reasoned among themselves about it, saying, *It is* because we did not bring any bread.

8 But Jesus, aware of this, asked, Why are you discussing among yourselves the fact that you have no bread? O you [men, how little trust you have in Me, how] little faith!

9 Do you not yet discern (perceive and understand)? Do you not remember the five loaves of the five thousand, and how many ['small hand] baskets you gathered?

10 Nor the seven loaves for the four thousand, and how many ['large provision] baskets you took up?

11 How is it that you fail to understand that I was not talking to you about bread? But beware of the leaven (ferment) of the Pharisees and Sadducees.

12 Then they discerned that He did not tell them to beware of the leaven of bread, but of the teaching of the Pharisees and Sadducees.

13 Now when Jesus went into the region of Caesarea Philippi, He asked His disciples, Who do people say that the Son of Man is?

14 And they answered, Some say John the Baptist; others say Elijah; and others Jeremiah or one of the prophets.

15 He said to them, But who do you [yourselves] say that I am?

16 Simon Peter replied, You are the Christ, the Son of the living God.

17 Then Jesus answered him, Blessed (happy, fortunate, and [j]to be envied) are you, Simon Bar-Jonah. For flesh and blood [men] have not revealed this to you, but My Father Who is in heaven.

18 And I tell you, you are [k]Peter [Greek, *Petros*—a large piece of rock], and on this rock [Greek, *petra*—a [l]huge rock like Gibraltar] I will build My church, and the gates of Hades (the powers of the [l]infernal region) shall [m]not overpower it [or be strong to its detriment or hold out against it].

life point

What rock is Jesus talking about in Matthew 16:17, 18? He is talking about the rock of faith. He tells Simon Peter that on the faith he has just displayed He will build His Church, and " . . . the gates of hell shall not prevail against it", (KJV). That means that the powers of hell shall not prevail against the person who walks in faith.

19 I will give you the keys of the kingdom of heaven; and whatever you bind (declare to be improper and unlawful) on earth [n]must be what is already bound in heaven; and whatever you loose (declare lawful) on earth [n]must be what is already loosed in heaven. [Isa. 22:22.]

20 Then He sternly *and* strictly charged *and* warned the disciples to tell no one that He was *Jesus* the Christ.

21 From that time forth Jesus began [clearly] to show His disciples that He

i Marvin Vincent, *Word Studies.* See also footnote on Matt. 14:20. **j** Alexander Souter, *Pocket Lexicon.* **k** The rock on which the church is built is traditionally interpreted as either Peter's inspired confession of faith in Jesus as the Messiah, or it may be Peter himself (see Eph. 2:20). **l** Kenneth Wuest, *Word Studies.* **m** Joseph Thayer, *A Greek-English Lexicon.* **n** Charles B. Williams, *The New Testament: A Translation:* "The perfect passive participle, here referring to a state of having been already forbidden [or permitted]."

life point

Matthew 16:19 says that we have authority as believers to bring heaven's will to earth by acting in partnership with God. He is in heaven, and we are on earth. Because His Spirit is in us, and because we have His Word, we can know what His will is. We have authority on earth to bring heaven's will into action. What God binds or looses in heaven—what He allows or disallows—is all that we can allow or disallow here in the earth.

must go to Jerusalem and suffer many things at the hands of the elders and the high priests and scribes, and be killed, and on the third day be raised °from death.

22 Then Peter took Him aside Pto speak to Him privately and began to reprove and ᑫcharge Him sharply, saying, God forbid, Lord! This must never happen to You!

23 But Jesus turned Paway from Peter and said to him, Get behind Me, Satan! You are in My way [an offense and a hindrance and a snare to Me]; for you are Pminding what partakes not of the nature *and* quality of God, but of men.

24 Then Jesus said to His disciples, If anyone desires to be My disciple, let him deny himself [disregard, lose sight of, and forget himself and his own interests] and take up his cross and follow Me [ᑫcleave steadfastly to Me, conform wholly to My example in living and, if need be, in dying, also].

25 For whoever is bent on saving his [temporal] life [his comfort and security here] shall lose it [eternal life]; and whoever loses his life [his comfort and security here] for My sake shall find it [life everlasting].

26 For what will it profit a man if he gains the whole world and forfeits his life [his blessed ᑫlife in the kingdom of God]? Or what would a man give as an exchange for his [blessed] ᑫlife [in the kingdom of God]?

27 For the Son of Man is going to come in the glory (majesty, splendor) of His Father with His angels, and then He will render account *and* reward every man in accordance with what he has done.

28 Truly I tell you, there are some standing here who will not taste death before they see the Son of Man coming in (into) His kingdom.

17 AND SIX days after this, Jesus took with Him Peter and James and John his brother, and led them up on a high mountain by themselves.

2 And His appearance underwent a change in their presence; and His face shone °clear and bright like the sun, and His clothing became as white as light.

3 And behold, there appeared to them Moses and Elijah, who kept talking with Him.

4 Then Peter began to speak and said to Jesus, Lord, it is good *and* delightful that we are here; if You approve, I will put up three booths here—one for You and one for Moses and one for Elijah.

5 While he was still speaking, behold, a shining cloud [ᑫcomposed of light] overshadowed them, and a voice from the cloud said, This is My Son, My Beloved, with Whom I am [and ʳhave always been] delighted. Listen to Him! [Ps. 2:7; Isa. 42:1.]

6 When the disciples heard it, they fell on their faces and were ᑫseized with alarm *and* struck with fear.

o Hermann Cremer, *Biblico-Theological Lexicon*. **p** Marvin Vincent, *Word Studies*. **q** Joseph Thayer, *A Greek-English Lexicon*. **r** Charles B. Williams, *The New Testament: A Translation*: "suggested by the aorist (past) tense."

"not me!"

In Matthew 16:22, Peter rebuked Jesus. Anyone who rebukes Jesus has a problem with pride, and Peter had a big problem with pride. He was full of himself. He thought he had a better idea than Jesus did.

Jesus had just said He was going to Jerusalem to be killed and to be raised from the dead. Peter's response was something like, "Oh, no Jesus. You must not go. No, that is not the thing to do." How did Jesus respond to Peter's remark? He said in verse 23: "Get behind Me, Satan! You are in My way [an offense and a hindrance and a snare to Me]."

Later Jesus told Peter that Satan was going to try to sift him like grain and that Peter would deny his Lord three times. Jesus told Peter He had prayed for him that his faith would not fail (see Luke 22:31–34). Peter did not believe that. He did not say, "Oh, thank You, Jesus. Please pray for me." He essentially said, "Oh, I would never deny You. No, not me."

Have you ever said, "I will never do that!"? It is amazing the number of things we think we will never do that we end up doing.

It is interesting that when Jesus was being accused, Peter was the only disciple recognized as having been with Jesus. Others were present, but the spotlight shined on Peter. Peter vehemently denied this and started cursing to prove that he did not know Jesus (see Matthew 26:69–74). I believe that God arranged for Peter to be recognized because Peter needed to be humbled. God had a plan for Peter's life.

Peter loved Jesus, but he was still full of himself. He argued with Jesus on these occasions. I do not think he did it maliciously, but that always happens when someone has a spirit of pride. They think they know more than others do and will always argue, attempting to prove they are right.

Jesus knew that Peter was useable material, but he needed some work. You might say that Peter was a diamond in the rough. Peter needed some polishing, he needed some time on the Potter's wheel—but he was blind to his own faults and weaknesses, just as we usually are. Jesus had to teach him a lesson, and teach him He did. Peter ended up very meek, very repentant, and very submissive after his humbling experience.

God has a plan for your life and He will deal with every bad attitude and character flaw in you in order to prepare you to fulfill and enjoy the great purpose He has for your life, just as He did with Peter.

7   But Jesus came and touched them and said, Get up, and do not be afraid.

8   And when they raised their eyes, they saw no one but Jesus only.

9   And as they were going down the mountain, Jesus cautioned *and* commanded them, Do not mention to anyone what you have seen, until the Son of Man has been raised from the dead.

10 The disciples asked Him, Then why do the scribes say that Elijah must come first?

11 He replied, Elijah does come and will get everything restored *and* ready.

12 But I tell you that Elijah has come already, and they did not know *or* recognize him, but did to him as they liked. So also the Son of Man is going to be treated *and* suffer at their hands.

13 Then the disciples understood that He spoke to them about John the Baptist. [Mal. 4:5.]

14 And when they approached the multitude, a man came up to Him, kneeling before Him and saying,

15 Lord, do pity *and* have mercy on my son, for he has epilepsy (is ˢmoon-struck) and he suffers terribly; for frequently he falls into the fire and many times into the water.

16 And I brought him to Your disciples, and they were not able to cure him.

17 And Jesus answered, O you unbelieving (ᵗwarped, wayward, rebellious) and ᵘthoroughly perverse generation! How long am I to remain with you? How long am I to bear with you? Bring him here to Me.

18 And Jesus rebuked the demon, and it came out of him, and the boy was cured instantly.

19 Then the disciples came to Jesus and asked privately, Why could we not drive it out?

20 He said to them, Because of the littleness of your faith [that is, your lack of ᵛfirmly relying trust]. For truly I say to you, if you have faith [ᵂthat is living] like a grain of mustard seed, you can say to this mountain, Move from here to yonder place, and it will move; and nothing will be impossible to you.

21 ˣ*But this kind does not go out except by prayer and fasting.*

22 When they were going about here and there in Galilee, Jesus said to them, The Son of Man is going to be turned over into the hands of men.

23 And they will kill Him, and He will be raised [to life] again on the third day. And they were deeply *and* exceedingly grieved *and* distressed.

24 When they arrived in Capernaum, the collectors of the half shekel [the temple tax] went up to Peter and said, Does not your Teacher pay the half shekel? [Exod. 30:13; 38:26.]

25 He answered, Yes. And when he came home, Jesus spoke to him [about it] first, saying, What do you think, Simon? From whom do earthly rulers collect duties *or* tribute—from their own sons or from others ʸnot of their own family?

26 And when Peter said, From other people ʸnot of their own family, Jesus said to him, Then the sons are exempt.

27 However, in order not to give offense *and* cause them to stumble [that is, to cause them ʸto judge unfavorably and unjustly] go down to the sea and throw in a hook. Take the first fish that comes up, and when you open its mouth you will find there a shekel. Take it and give it to them to pay the temple tax for Me and for yourself.

---

s Joseph Thayer, *A Greek-English Lexicon*: "Epilepsy is supposed to return and increase with the increase of the moon." **t** Marvin Vincent, *Word Studies*. **u** Literally, "throughout" *(dia)*. **v** Hermann Cremer, *Biblico-Theological Lexicon*. **w** Charles B. Williams, *The New Testament: A Translation*. **x** Some manuscripts do not contain this verse. **y** Joseph Thayer, *A Greek-English Lexicon*

18 AT THAT time the disciples came up and asked Jesus, Who then is [really] the greatest in the kingdom of heaven?

2 And He called a little child to Himself and put him in the midst of them,

3 And said, Truly I say to you, unless you repent (change, turn about) and become like little children [trusting, lowly, loving, forgiving], you can never enter the kingdom of heaven [at all].

4 Whoever will humble himself therefore and become like this little child [trusting, lowly, loving, forgiving] is greatest in the kingdom of heaven.

5 And whoever receives *and* accepts *and* welcomes one little child like this for My sake and in My name receives *and* accepts *and* welcomes Me.

6 But whoever causes one of these little ones who believe in *and* ᶻacknowledge *and* cleave to Me to stumble and sin [that is, who entices him or hinders him in right conduct or thought], it would be better (ᵃmore expedient and profitable or advantageous) for him to have a great millstone fastened around his neck and to be sunk in the depth of the sea.

7 Woe to the world for such temptations to sin *and* influences to do wrong! It is necessary that temptations come, but woe to the person on whose account *or* by whom the temptation comes!

8 And if your hand or your foot causes you to stumble *and* sin, cut it off and throw it away from you; it is better (more profitable and wholesome) for you to enter life maimed or lame than to have two hands or two feet and be thrown into everlasting fire.

9 And if your eye causes you to stumble *and* sin, pluck it out and throw it away from you; it is better (more profitable and wholesome) for you to enter life with only one eye than to have two eyes and be thrown into the hell (Gehenna) of fire.

10 Beware that you do not despise *or* feel scornful toward *or* think little of one of these little ones, for I tell you that in heaven their angels always are in the presence of *and* look upon the face of My Father Who is in heaven.

11 ᵇ*For the Son of man came to save* [ᶻfrom the penalty of eternal death] *that which was lost.*

12 What do you think? If a man has a hundred sheep, and one of them has gone astray *and* gets lost, will he not leave the ninety-nine on the mountain and go in search of the one that is lost?

13 And if it should be that he finds it, truly I say to you, he rejoices more over it than over the ninety-nine that did not get lost.

14 Just so it is not the will of My Father Who is in heaven that one of these little ones should be lost *and* perish.

15 If your brother wrongs you, go and show him his fault, between you

putting the Word to work

When another Christian wrongs or offends you, what do you do? Your first inclination may be to run and tell someone else all about it or to let anger or hurt build up inside of you. However, Jesus teaches us the appropriate method for bringing correction and reconciliation in Matthew 18:15–17. The next time you are hurt or wronged by another believer, be sure to go to that person first. Ask God to help you forgive.

z Hermann Cremer, *Biblico-Theological Lexicon.* a G. Abbott-Smith, *Manual Greek Lexicon.*
b Many manuscripts do not contain this verse.

and him privately. If he listens to you, you have won back your brother.

16 But if he does not listen, take along with you one or two others, so that every word may be confirmed *and* upheld by the testimony of two or three witnesses.

17 If he pays no attention to them [refusing to listen and obey], tell it to the church; and if he refuses to listen even to the church, let him be to you as a pagan and a tax collector. [Lev. 19:17; Deut. 19:15.]

18 Truly I tell you, whatever you forbid *and* declare to be improper and unlawful on earth must be ᶜwhat is already forbidden in heaven, and whatever you permit *and* declare proper and lawful on earth must be ᶜwhat is already permitted in heaven.

19 Again I tell you, if two of you on earth agree (harmonize together, make a symphony together) about whatever [anything and ᵈeverything]

life point

The Amplified Bible makes clear in Matthew 18:18, 19 that God gives us authority in order to bring His will to earth, not to bring our own will to pass.

As believers, we have spiritual authority and we should exercise it. One of the ways we do that is in prayer. God desires to use His surrendered servants to pray His will down from heaven to earth, as we are taught by Jesus to pray: "Your will be done on earth as it is in heaven" (Matthew 6:10).

What an awesome privilege. Our prayers can affect our own lives as well as the lives of other people. God can use us to help them experience the fullness of all He has planned for them in life.

they may ask, it will come to pass *and* be done for them by My Father in heaven.

20 For wherever two or three are gathered (drawn together as My followers) in (into) My name, there I AM in the midst of them. [Exod. 3:14.]

21 Then Peter came up to Him and said, Lord, how many times may my brother sin against me and I forgive him *and* ᵉlet it go? [As many as] up to seven times?

22 Jesus answered him, I tell you, not up to seven times, but seventy times seven! [Gen. 4:24.]

23 Therefore the kingdom of heaven is like a human king who wished to settle accounts with his attendants.

24 When he began the accounting, one was brought to him who owed him 10,000 talents [probably about $10,000,000],

25 And because he could not pay, his master ordered him to be sold, with his wife and his children and everything that he possessed, and payment to be made.

26 So the attendant fell on his knees, begging him, Have patience with me and I will pay you everything.

27 And his master's heart was moved with compassion, and he released him

putting the Word to work

Sometimes forgiving someone can be very difficult, especially if that person has repeatedly hurt or offended us. Is there someone in your life you are having a hard time forgiving? Remember the gracious gift of God's forgiveness to you. As you have received forgiveness, you are called to extend forgiveness to others (see Matthew 18:21–35). Ask God to help you forgive as you have been forgiven.

c See footnote on Matt. 16:19.   **d** John Wycliffe, *The Wycliffe Bible*.   **e** Joseph Thayer, *A Greek-English Lexicon*.

how many times?

As believers, we will never experience joy-filled, victorious lives unless we are ready to forgive people. This is something we are going to have to do frequently, and according to Matthew 18:21, 22, even repeatedly. The Lord tells us plainly in the Bible that if we will not forgive other people for the wrong things they have done against us, then God will not forgive us for the wrong things we have done against Him (see Matthew 6:14, 15).

What kind of condition would we be in if God refused to forgive us? We could not possibly have a proper relationship with Him. Everything in our lives would be stopped up. We like to think that we can stay angry with other people and yet go to God and receive forgiveness for our sins. But the Lord tells us in the Bible that this is not so.

Jesus taught us to pray, "And forgive us our debts, as we also have forgiven (left, remitted, and let go of the debts, and have given up resentment against) our debtors" (Matthew 6:12). God is a God of mercy, and this issue of forgiveness is very important to Him. He tells us repeatedly in His Word that if we want mercy, we have to give mercy.

In Matthew 18:21, 22, Peter asked Jesus how many times he had to forgive his brother: "up to seven times?" Jesus' answer was not seven times, but seventy times that many.

I do not know about you, but I am glad that God does not put a limit on how many times He will forgive us. How many of us have done the same wrong thing at least seventy times seven, and God has still forgiven us for it? We are willing to keep taking and taking forgiveness from God, but it is amazing how little we want to extend forgiveness to others. We freely accept mercy, yet it is surprising how rigid, legalistic, and merciless we can be toward others, especially if they have wronged us in some way. Yet the Bible says that the debt we owe God is much greater than any debt anyone may owe us. Always remember how great God's generosity is, especially in the area of forgiveness. Aim to forgive others as quickly, as often, and as generously as God forgives you.

and forgave him [cancelling] the debt.
28 But that same attendant, as he went out, found one of his fellow attendants who owed him a hundred denarii [about twenty dollars]; and he caught him by the throat and said, Pay what you owe!
29 So his fellow attendant fell down and begged him earnestly, Give me time, and I will pay you *all*!

30 But he was unwilling, and he went out and had him put in prison till he should pay the debt.
31 When his fellow attendants saw what had happened, they were greatly distressed, and they went and told everything that had taken place to their master.
32 Then his master called him and said to him, You contemptible *and*

wicked attendant! I forgave *and* cancelled all that [great] debt of yours because you begged me to.

33 And should you not have had pity *and* mercy on your fellow attendant, as I had pity *and* mercy on you?

34 And in wrath his master turned him over to the torturers (the jailers), till he should pay all that he owed.

35 So also My heavenly Father will deal with every one of you if you do not freely forgive your brother from your heart *his offenses.*

19 NOW WHEN Jesus had finished saying these things, He left Galilee and went into the part of Judea that is beyond the Jordan;

2 And great throngs accompanied Him, and He cured them there.

3 And Pharisees came to Him and put Him to the test by asking, Is it lawful *and* right to dismiss *and* repudiate *and* divorce one's wife for any *and* [f]every cause?

4 He replied, Have you never read that He Who made them from the beginning made them male and female,

5 And said, For this reason a man shall leave his father and mother and shall be united firmly (joined inseparably) to his wife, and the two shall become one flesh? [Gen. 1:27; 2:24.]

6 So they are no longer two, but one flesh. What therefore God has joined together, let not man put asunder (separate).

7 They said to Him, Why then did Moses command [us] to give a certificate of divorce and thus to dismiss *and* repudiate a wife? [Deut. 24:1-4.]

8 He said to them, Because of the hardness (stubbornness and perversity) of your hearts Moses permitted you to dismiss *and* repudiate *and* divorce your wives; but from the beginning it has not been [g]so [ordained].

9 I say to you: whoever dismisses (repudiates, divorces) his wife, except for unchastity, and marries another commits adultery, [h]*and he who marries a divorced woman commits adultery.*

10 The disciples said to Him, If the case of a man with his wife is like this, it is neither profitable *nor* advisable to marry.

11 But He said to them, Not all men can accept this saying, but it is for those to whom [the capacity to receive] it has been given.

12 For there are eunuchs who have been born incapable of marriage; and there are eunuchs who have been made so by men; and there are eunuchs who have made themselves incapable of marriage for the sake of the kingdom of heaven. Let him who is able to accept this accept it.

13 Then little children were brought to Jesus, that He might put His hands on them and pray; but the disciples rebuked those who brought them.

14 But He said, Leave the children alone! Allow the little ones to come to Me, and do not forbid *or* restrain *or* hinder them, for of such [as these] is the kingdom of heaven *composed.*

15 And He put His hands upon them, and then went on His way.

16 And behold, there came a man up to Him, saying, Teacher, what excellent *and* perfectly *and* essentially good deed must I do to possess eternal life? [Lev. 18:5.]

17 And He said to him, Why do you ask Me about the perfectly *and* essentially good? There is only One Who is good [perfectly and essentially]—God. If you would enter into the Life, you must continually keep the commandments.

---

f Marvin Vincent, *Word Studies.* **g** Joseph Thayer, *A Greek-English Lexicon.* **h** Some manuscripts do not contain this phrase.

love yourself

One of the greatest problems many people have today is that they do not think well of themselves. They need to know that God's Word teaches them to love themselves!

Since the Lord commands us to love our neighbors as we love ourselves (see Matthew 19:19), He must think that it is as important to love ourselves as it is to love others. But it is not enough just to love ourselves; we must also *like* ourselves.

I learned this truth several years ago when I was having a terrible time getting along with other people. I discovered the reason I had so much trouble getting along with others was that I was not getting along with myself.

If you do not like yourself, you will have a hard time liking anyone else. You may pretend you do, but pretense does not alter fact. Sooner or later, the truth will come out.

Every one of us is supposed to be a powerhouse for God, living in balance and harmony within ourselves and with others. In order to do that, we must have not only the right attitude toward others but also the right attitude toward ourselves. We need to be at peace with our past, content with our present and sure about our future, knowing it is all in God's hands. We need to be stable, rooted, and grounded in the love of God as expressed in His Son Jesus Christ.

Because we are rooted and grounded in love, we can be relaxed and at ease, knowing that our acceptance is not based on our performance or our perfect behavior. We can be secure in the knowledge that our value and worth are not dependent upon who we are or what we think or say or do. It is based on who we are in Christ Jesus and what He has done for us.

Secure in our knowledge of who we are in Him, we can give up our masks and façades. We do not have to pretend anymore. We do not have to be phony. Instead, we are free to simply be ourselves—just as we are. We are also free to love ourselves, and that will enable us to love others too.

---

18 He said to Him, What ¹sort of commandments? [Or, which ones?] And Jesus answered, You shall not kill, You shall not commit adultery, You shall not steal, You shall not bear false witness, [Exod. 20:12-16; Deut. 5:16-20.]

19 Honor your father and your mother, and, You shall love your neighbor as [you do] yourself. [Lev. 19:18; Matt. 22:39.]

20 The young man said, I have observed all these *from my youth;* what still do I lack?

---

i Charles B. Williams, *The New Testament: A Translation*: "Interrogative of quality."

21 Jesus answered him, If you would be perfect [that is, ʲhave that spiritual maturity which accompanies self-sacrificing character], go and sell what you have and give to the poor, and you will have riches in heaven; and come, ᵏbe My disciple [side with My party and follow Me].

22 But when the young man heard this, he went away sad (grieved and in much distress), for he had great possessions.

23 And Jesus said to His disciples, Truly I say to you, it will be difficult for a rich man to get into the kingdom of heaven.

24 Again I tell you, it is easier for a camel to go through the eye of a needle than for a rich man to go into the kingdom of heaven.

25 When the disciples heard this, they were utterly puzzled (astonished, bewildered), saying, Who then can be saved [ˡfrom eternal death]?

26 But Jesus looked at them and said, With men this is impossible, but all things are possible with God. [Gen. 18:14; Job 42:2.]

27 Then Peter answered Him, saying, Behold, we have left [our] all and have become ᵏYour disciples [sided with Your party and followed You]. What then shall we receive?

28 Jesus said to them, Truly I say to you, in the new age [the ᵐMessianic rebirth of the world], when the Son of Man shall sit down on the throne of His glory, you who have [become My disciples, sided with My party and] followed Me will also sit on twelve thrones and judge the twelve tribes of Israel.

29 And anyone *and* everyone who has left houses or brothers or sisters or father or mother or children or lands for My name's sake will receive ⁿmany [even a hundred] times more and will inherit eternal life.

30 But many who [now] are first will be last [then], and many who [now] are last will be first [then].

20

FOR THE kingdom of heaven is like the owner of an estate who went out in the morning ᵒalong with the dawn to hire workmen for his vineyard.

2 After agreeing with the laborers for a denarius a day, he sent them into his vineyard.

3 And going out about the third hour (nine o'clock), he saw others standing idle in the marketplace;

4 And he said to them, You go also into the vineyard, and whatever is right I will pay you. And they went.

5 He went out again about the sixth hour (noon), and the ninth hour (three o'clock) he did the same.

6 And about the eleventh hour (five o'clock) he went out and found still others standing around, and said to them, Why do you stand here idle all day?

7 They answered him, Because nobody has hired us. He told them, You go out into the vineyard also ᵖ*and you will get whatever is just and fair.*

8 When evening came, the owner of the vineyard said to his manager, Call the workmen and pay them their wages, beginning with the last and ending with the first. [Lev. 19:13; Deut. 24:15.]

9 And those who had been hired at the eleventh hour (five o'clock) came and received a denarius each.

10 Now when the first came, they supposed they would get more, but each of them also received a denarius.

11 And when they received it, they grumbled at the owner of the estate,

---

j Kenneth Wuest, *Word Studies.* k Joseph Thayer, *A Greek-English Lexicon.* l Hermann Cremer, *Biblico-Theological Lexicon.* m James Moulton and George Milligan, *The Vocabulary.* n Some manuscripts read "manifold." o Marvin Vincent, *Word Studies.* p Some manuscripts do not contain this phrase.

all things are possible

It is exciting to know that with God all things are possible (see Matthew 19:26). In our human thinking we hit brick walls, so to speak, when we come up against something that is impossible for us. We feel frustrated and hopeless. But with God, that never has to happen. When we put our trust in Him another world opens up to us, a world of possibilities that we would have never thought possible in the natural.

You may have practically worn yourself out trying to accomplish something and, when you finally gave up and turned it over to God, you saw Him do with ease what you had struggled with for a long time. I know that has happened to me over and over again.

I am so glad that we serve a God of possibilities. Even the word *impossible* makes me feel hopeless and frustrated. I always like to believe there is hope, no matter how bad things may look.

If God can take a hard, sinful, hateful, bitter heart, and make it soft, holy, loving, and forgiving, then, as far as I am concerned, He can do anything. I think that sometimes we do not realize what a miracle our salvation is. We become completely new creatures and are given a brand-new start in life by accepting Jesus Christ as our Savior (see II Corinthians 5:17). How much more awesome could anything be? No wonder the Gospel is called the "good news"!

God can change hearts, heal a sick body, rekindle a marriage, or restore finances. He can feed five thousand people with a little boy's lunch, walk on water, read men's hearts, and anything else He wants to do. Nothing is impossible with God. Do not ever look at a situation and think or say, "This is impossible." It may be impossible with men, but with God all things are possible.

If we keep praying and believing, God can keep working, but if we give up, we close the door on the miracle God has in mind for us. You may say, "You just don't realize what a mess I have in my life." My advice to you is to ask God to take your mess and turn it into your greatest miracle. He can work it out for your good and you will have a testimony that encourages others. With God, all things *are* possible.

12 Saying, These [men] who came last worked no more than an hour, and yet you have made them rank with us who have borne the burden and the qscorching heat of the day.
13 But he answered one of them,

Friend, I am doing you no injustice. Did you not agree with me for a denarius?
14 Take what belongs to you and go. I choose to give to this man hired last the same as I give to you.

q Marvin Vincent, *Word Studies.*

15 Am I not permitted to do what I choose with what is mine? [Or do you begrudge my being generous?] Is your eye evil because I am good?
16 So those who [now] are last will be first [then], and those who [now] are first will be last [then]. [r]*For many are called, but few chosen.*

life point

I once heard a Bible teacher say that Matthew 20:16 means that many are called or given an opportunity to do something for the Lord, but very few are willing to take the responsibility to answer that call. God's call does come with responsibility, but it also comes with rewards. I believe that you are called for a very special purpose. I hope you will say yes to Him!

17 And as Jesus was going up to Jerusalem, He took the twelve disciples aside along the way and said to them,
18 Behold, we are going up to Jerusalem, and the Son of Man will be handed over to the chief priests and scribes; and they will sentence Him to death
19 And deliver Him over to the Gentiles to be mocked and whipped and crucified, and He will be raised [to life] on the third day.
20 Then the mother of Zebedee's children came up to Him with her sons and, kneeling, worshiped Him and asked a favor of Him.
21 And He asked her, What do you wish? She answered Him, Give orders that these two sons of mine may sit, one at Your right hand and one at Your left in Your kingdom.
22 But Jesus replied, You do not realize what you are asking. Are you able to drink the cup that I am about to drink [r]*and to be baptized with the bap-*

tism with which I am baptized? They answered, We are able.
23 He said to them, You will drink My cup, but seats at My right hand and at My left are not Mine to give, but they are for those for whom they have been [s]ordained *and* prepared by My Father.
24 But when the ten [other disciples] heard this, they were indignant at the two brothers.
25 And Jesus called them to Him and said, You know that the rulers of the Gentiles lord it over them, and their great men hold them in subjection [tyrannizing over them].
26 Not so shall it be among you; but whoever wishes to be great among you must be your servant,
27 And whoever desires to be first among you must be your slave—
28 Just as the Son of Man came not to be waited on but to serve, and to give His life as a ransom for many [the price paid to set them free].
29 And as they were going out of Jericho, a great throng accompanied Him.
30 And behold, two blind men were sitting by the roadside, and when they heard that Jesus was passing by, they cried out, Lord, have pity *and* mercy on us, [You] Son of David!
31 The crowds reproved them and told them to keep still; but they cried out all the more, Lord, have pity *and* mercy on us, [You] Son of David!
32 And Jesus stopped and called them, and asked, What do you want Me to do for you?
33 They answered Him, Lord, we want our eyes to be opened!
34 And Jesus, in pity, touched their eyes; and instantly they received their sight and followed Him.

21 AND WHEN they came near Jerusalem and had reached Bethphage at the

---

r Some manuscripts do not contain this phrase.　**s** Joseph Thayer, *A Greek-English Lexicon.*

Mount of Olives, Jesus sent two disciples on ahead,

2 Saying to them, Go into the village that is opposite you, and at once you will find a donkey tied, and a colt with her; untie [them] and bring [them] to Me.

3 If anyone says anything to you, you shall reply, The Lord needs them, and he will let them go without delay.

4 This happened that what was spoken by the prophet might be fulfilled, saying,

5 Say to the Daughter of Zion [inhabitants of Jerusalem], Behold, your King is coming to you, lowly and riding on a donkey, and on a colt, the foal of a donkey [a beast of burden]. [Isa. 62:11; Zech. 9:9.]

6 Then the disciples went and did as Jesus had directed them.

7 They brought the donkey and the colt and laid their coats upon them, and He seated Himself on them [the clothing].

8 And most of the crowd kept spreading their garments on the road, and others kept cutting branches from the trees and scattering them on the road.

9 And the crowds that went ahead of Him and those that followed Him kept shouting, Hosanna ('O be propitious, graciously inclined) to the Son of David, ['the Messiah]! Blessed (praised, glorified) is He Who comes in the name of the Lord! Hosanna (O be favorably disposed) in the highest [heaven]! [Ps. 118:26.]

10 And when He entered Jerusalem, all the city became agitated and u[trembling with excitement] said, Who is vThis?

11 And the crowds replied, This is the prophet Jesus from Nazareth of Galilee.

12 And Jesus went into the temple (wwhole temple enclosure) and drove out all who bought and sold in the 'sacred place, and He turned over the xfour-footed tables of the money changers and the chairs of those who sold doves.

13 He said to them, The Scripture says, My house shall be called a house of prayer; but you have made it a den of robbers. [Isa. 56:7; Jer. 7:11.]

14 And the blind and the lame came to Him in the wporches and courts of the temple, and He cured them.

15 But when the chief priests and the scribes saw the wonderful things that He did and the boys and the girls and the yyouths and the maidens crying out in the wporches and courts of the temple, Hosanna (O be propitious, graciously inclined) to the Son of David! they were indignant.

16 And they said to Him, Do You hear what these are saying? And Jesus replied to them, Yes; have you never read, Out of the mouths of babes and unweaned infants You have made (provided) perfect praise? [Ps. 8:2.]

17 And leaving them, He departed from the city and went out to Bethany and lodged there.

18 In the early dawn the next morning, as He was coming back to the city, He was hungry.

19 And as He saw uone single leafy fig tree 'above the roadside, He went to it but He found nothing but leaves on it [zseeing that in the fig tree the fruit appears at the same time as the leaves]. And He said to it, Never again shall fruit grow on you! And the fig tree withered up at once.

---

t Joseph Thayer, *A Greek-English Lexicon.* u Literal meaning. v Capitalized because of what He is, the spotless Son of God, not what the speakers may have thought He was. w Richard Trench, *Synonyms of the New Testament.* x James Moulton and George Milligan, *The Vocabulary.* y G. Abbott-Smith, *Manual Greek Lexicon.* z James Orr et al., eds., *International Standard Bible Encyclopedia.*

20 When the disciples saw it, they marveled greatly and asked, How is it that the fig tree has withered away all at once?

21 And Jesus answered them, Truly I say to you, if you have faith (a ªfirm relying trust) and do not doubt, you will not only do what has been done to the fig tree, but even if you say to this mountain, Be taken up and cast into the sea, it will be done.

22 And whatever you ask for in prayer, having faith *and* [really] believing, you will receive.

23 And when He entered the sacred ᵇenclosure of the temple, the chief priests and elders of the people came up to Him as He was teaching and said, By what ᶜpower of authority are You doing these things, and who gave You this power of authority?

24 Jesus answered them, I also will ask you a question, and if you give Me the answer, then I also will tell you by what ᶜpower of authority I do these things.

25 The baptism of John—from where was it? From heaven or from men? And they reasoned *and* argued with one another, If we say, From heaven, ᵈHe will ask us, Why then did you not believe him?

26 But if we say, From men—we are afraid of *and* must reckon with the multitude, for they all regard John as a prophet.

27 So they answered Jesus, We do not know. And He said to them, Neither will I tell you by what ᶜpower of authority I do these things.

28 What do you think? There was a man who had two sons. He came to the first and said, Son, go and work today in the vineyard.

29 And he answered, I will not; but afterward he changed his mind and went.

30 Then the man came to the second and said the same [thing]. And he replied, I will [go], sir; but he did not go.

31 Which of the two did the will of the father? They replied, The first one. Jesus said to them, Truly I tell you, the tax collectors and the harlots will get into the kingdom of heaven before you.

32 For John came to you walking in the way of an upright man in right standing with God, and you did not believe him, but the tax collectors and the harlots did believe him; and you, even when you saw that, did not afterward change your minds and believe him [adhere to, trust in, and rely on what he told you].

33 Listen to another parable: There was a master of a house who planted a vineyard and put a hedge around it and dug a wine vat in it and built a watchtower. Then he let it out [for rent] to tenants and went into another country.

34 When the fruit season drew near, he sent his servants to the tenants to get his [share of the] fruit.

35 But the tenants took his servants and beat one, killed another, and stoned another.

36 Again he sent other servants, more than the first time, and they treated them the same way.

37 Finally he sent his own son to them, saying, They will respect *and* give heed to my son.

38 But when the tenants saw the son, they said to themselves, This is the heir; come on, let us kill him and have his inheritance.

39 And they took him and threw him out of the vineyard and killed him.

40 Now when the owner of the vineyard comes back, what will he do to those tenants?

---

a Hermann Cremer, *Biblico-Theological Lexicon*. **b** Richard Trench, *Synonyms of the New Testament*. **c** Joseph Thayer, *A Greek-English Lexicon*. **d** Capitalized because of what He is, the spotless Son of God, not what the speakers may have thought He was.

41 They said to Him, He will put those wretches to a miserable death and rent the vineyard to other tenants ᵉof such a character that they will give him the fruits promptly in their season. [Isa. 5:1-7.]

42 Jesus asked them, Have you never read in the Scriptures: The very Stone which the builders rejected *and* threw away has become the Cornerstone; this is the Lord's doing, and it is marvelous in our eyes? [Ps. 118:22, 23.]

43 I tell you, for this reason the kingdom of God will be taken away from you and given to a people who will produce the fruits of it.

44 ᶠ*And whoever falls on this Stone will be broken to pieces, but he on whom It falls will be crushed to powder* [and It will ᵍwinnow him, ᵉscattering him like dust]. [Isa. 8:14; Dan. 2:34, 35.]

45 And when the chief priests and the Pharisees heard His parables (comparisons, stories used to illustrate and explain), they perceived that He was talking about them.

46 And although they were trying to arrest Him, they feared the throngs because they regarded Him as a prophet.

22 AND AGAIN Jesus spoke to them in parables (comparisons, stories used to illustrate and explain), saying,

2 The kingdom of heaven is like a king who gave a wedding banquet for his son

3 And sent his servants to summon those who had been invited to the wedding banquet, but they refused to come.

4 Again he sent other servants, saying, Tell those who are invited, Behold, I have prepared my banquet; my bullocks and my fat calves are killed, and everything is prepared; come to the wedding feast.

5 But they were not concerned *and* paid no attention [they ignored and made light of the summons, treating it with contempt] and they went away— one to his farm, another to his business,

6 While the others seized his servants, treated them shamefully, and put them to death.

7 [Hearing this] the king was infuriated; and he sent his soldiers and put those murderers to death and burned their city.

8 Then he said to his servants, The wedding [feast] is prepared, but those invited were not worthy.

9 So go to the thoroughfares where they leave the city [where the main roads and those from the country end] and invite to the wedding feast as many as you find.

10 And those servants went out on the crossroads and got together as many as they found, both bad and good, so [the room in which] the wedding feast [was held] was filled with guests.

11 But when the king came in to view the guests, he looked intently at a man there who had on no wedding garment.

12 And he said, Friend, how did you come in here without putting on the [appropriate] wedding garment? And he was speechless (ʰmuzzled, gagged).

13 Then the king said to the attendants, Tie him hand and foot, and throw him into the darkness outside; there will be weeping and grinding of teeth.

14 For many are called (invited and summoned), but few *are* chosen.

15 Then the Pharisees went and consulted *and* plotted together how they might entangle Jesus in His talk.

16 And they sent their disciples to Him along with the Herodians, saying,

---

e Marvin Vincent, *Word Studies*.   f Some manuscripts do not contain verse 44.   g Joseph Thayer, *A Greek-English Lexicon*.   h Literal translation.

Teacher, we know that You are [i]sincere *and* what You profess to be and that You teach the way of God truthfully, regardless of consequences *and* being afraid of no man; for You are impartial *and* do not regard either the person *or* the position of anyone.

17 Tell us then what You think about this: Is it lawful to pay tribute [levied on individuals and to be paid yearly] to Caesar or not?

18 But Jesus, aware of their malicious plot, asked, Why do you put Me to the test *and* try to entrap Me, you pretenders (hypocrites)?

19 Show me the money *used* for the tribute. And they brought Him a denarius.

20 And Jesus said to them, Whose likeness and title are these?

21 They said, Caesar's. Then He said to them, Pay therefore to Caesar the things that are due to Caesar, and pay to God the things that are due to God.

22 When they heard it they were amazed *and* marveled; and they left Him and departed.

23 The same day some Sadducees, who say that there is no resurrection [of the dead], came to Him and they asked Him a question,

24 Saying, Teacher, Moses said, If a man dies, leaving no children, his brother shall marry the widow and raise up a family for his brother. [Deut. 25:5.]

25 Now there were seven brothers among us; the first married and died, and, having no children, left his wife to his brother.

26 The second also died childless, and the third, down to the seventh.

27 Last of all, the woman died also.

28 Now, in the resurrection, to which of the seven will she be wife? For they all had her.

29 But Jesus replied to them, You are wrong because you know neither the Scriptures nor God's power.

30 For in the resurrected state neither do [men] marry nor are [women] given in marriage, but they are like the angels in heaven.

31 But as to the resurrection of the dead—have you never read what was said to you by God,

32 I am the God of Abraham, and the God of Isaac, and the God of Jacob? He is not the God of the dead but of the living! [Exod. 3:6.]

33 And when the throng heard it, they were astonished *and* filled with [i]glad] amazement at His teaching.

34 Now when the Pharisees heard that He had silenced ([k]muzzled) the Sadducees, they gathered together.

35 And one of their number, a lawyer, asked Him a question to test Him.

36 Teacher, which [l]kind of commandment is great and important (the principal kind) in the Law? [Some commandments are light—which are heavy?]

37 And He replied to him, You shall love the Lord your God with all your heart and with all your soul and with all your mind (intellect). [Deut. 6:5.]

38 This is the great (most important, principal) and first commandment.

39 And a second is like it: You shall love your neighbor as [you do] yourself. [Lev. 19:18.]

40 These two commandments [j]sum up *and* upon them depend all the Law and the Prophets.

41 Now while the Pharisees were still assembled there, Jesus asked them a question,

42 Saying, What do you think of the Christ? Whose Son is He? They said to Him, The Son of David.

43 He said to them, How is it then

i Hermann Cremer, *Biblico-Theological Lexicon.*   j Joseph Thayer, *A Greek-English Lexicon.*   k Literal translation.   l Marvin Vincent, *Word Studies.*

that David, under the influence of the [Holy] Spirit, calls Him Lord, saying,

44 The Lord said to My Lord, Sit at My right hand until I put Your enemies under Your feet? [Ps. 110:1.]

45 If then David thus calls Him Lord, how is He his Son?

46 And no one was able to answer Him a word, nor from that day did anyone venture *or* dare to question Him.

23

THEN JESUS said to the multitudes and to His disciples,

2 The scribes and Pharisees sit on Moses' seat [of authority].

3 So observe and practice all they tell you; but do not do what they do, for they preach, but do not practice.

4 They tie up heavy loads, *hard to bear*, and place them on men's shoulders, but they themselves will not lift a finger to help bear them.

5 They do all their works to be seen of men; for they make wide their phylacteries (ᵐsmall cases enclosing certain Scripture passages, worn during prayer on the left arm and forehead) and make long their fringes [worn by all male Israelites, according to the command]. [Exod. 13:9; Num. 15:38; Deut. 6:8.]

6 And they ⁿtake pleasure in *and* [thus] love the place of honor at feasts and the best seats in the synagogues,

7 And to be greeted with honor in the marketplaces and to have people call them rabbi.

8 But you are not to be called rabbi (teacher), for you have one Teacher and you are all brothers.

9 And do not call anyone [in the church] on earth father, for you have one Father, Who is in heaven.

10 And you must not be called mas-

ters (leaders), for you have one Master (Leader), the Christ.

11 He who is greatest among you shall be your servant.

12 Whoever exalts himself [°with haughtiness and empty pride] shall be humbled (brought low), and whoever humbles himself [whoever has a modest opinion of himself and behaves accordingly] shall be °raised to honor.

13 But woe to you, scribes and Pharisees, pretenders (hypocrites)! For you shut the kingdom of heaven in men's faces; for you neither enter yourselves, nor do you allow those who are about to go in to do so.

14 ᵖ*Woe to you, scribes and Pharisees, pretenders (hypocrites)! For you swallow up widows' houses and for a pretense to cover it up make long prayers; therefore you will receive the greater condemnation and the heavier sentence.*

15 Woe to you, scribes and Pharisees, pretenders (hypocrites)! For you travel over sea and land to make a single proselyte, and when he becomes one [a proselyte], you make him doubly as much a child of hell (Gehenna) as you are.

16 Woe to you, blind guides, who say, If anyone swears by the �q sanctuary of the temple, it is nothing; but if anyone swears by the gold of the �q sanctuary, he is a debtor [bound by his oath].

17 You blind fools! For which is greater: the gold, or the �q sanctuary of the temple that has made the gold sacred? [Exod. 30:29.]

18 You say too, Whoever swears by the altar is not duty bound; but whoever swears by the offering on the altar, his oath is binding.

19 You blind men! Which is greater: the gift, or the altar which makes the gift sacred?

20 So whoever swears by the altar

---

m John D. Davis, *A Dictionary of the Bible*. **n** Kenneth Wuest, *Word Studies*. **o** Joseph Thayer, *A Greek-English Lexicon*. **p** Some manuscripts do not contain verse 14. **q** Richard Trench, *Synonyms of the New Testament*.

swears by it and by everything on it.
21 And he who swears by the ʳsanctuary of the temple swears by it and by Him Who dwells in it. [I Kings 8:13; Ps. 26:8.]
22 And whoever swears by heaven swears by the throne of God and by Him Who sits upon it.
23 Woe to you, scribes and Pharisees, pretenders (hypocrites)! For you give a tenth of your mint and dill and cummin, and have neglected *and* omitted the weightier (more important) matters of the Law—right *and* justice and mercy and fidelity. These you ought [particularly] to have done, without neglecting the others.
24 You blind guides, filtering out a gnat and gulping down a ˢcamel! [Lev. 27:30; Mic. 6:8.]
25 Woe to you, scribes and Pharisees, pretenders (hypocrites)! For you clean the outside of the cup and of the plate, but within they are full of extortion (prey, spoil, plunder) and grasping self-indulgence.
26 You blind Pharisee! First clean the inside of the cup and of the plate, so that the outside may be clean also.
27 Woe to you, scribes and Pharisees, pretenders (hypocrites)! For you are like tombs that have been whitewashed, which look beautiful on the outside but inside are full of dead men's bones and everything impure.
28 Just so, you also outwardly seem to people to be just *and* upright but inside you are full of pretense and lawlessness *and* iniquity. [Ps. 5:9.]
29 Woe to you, scribes and Pharisees, pretenders (hypocrites)! For you build tombs for the prophets and decorate the monuments of the righteous,
30 Saying, If we had lived in the days of our forefathers, we would not have

aided them in shedding the blood of the prophets.
31 Thus you are testifying against yourselves that you are the descendants of those who murdered the prophets.
32 Fill up, then, the measure of your fathers' sins to the brim [so ᵗthat nothing may be wanting to a full measure].
33 You serpents! You spawn of vipers! How can you escape the ᵗpenalty to be suffered in hell (Gehenna)?
34 Because of this, take notice: I am sending you prophets and wise men (interpreters and teachers) and scribes (men learned in the Mosaic Law and the Prophets); some of them you will kill, even crucify, and some you will flog in your synagogues and pursue *and* persecute from town to town,
35 So that upon your heads may come all the blood of the righteous (ᵘthose who correspond to the divine standard of right) shed on earth, from the blood of the righteous Abel to the blood of Zechariah son of Barachiah, whom you murdered between the sanctuary and the altar [of burnt offering]. [Gen. 4:8; II Chron. 24:21.]
36 Truly I declare to you, all these [ᵗevil, calamitous times] will come upon this generation. [II Chron. 36:15, 16.]
37 O Jerusalem, Jerusalem, murdering the prophets and stoning those who are sent to you! How often would I have gathered your children together as a mother fowl gathers her brood under her wings, and you refused!
38 Behold, your house is forsaken and desolate (abandoned and left destitute of God's help). [I Kings 9:7; Jer. 22:5.]
39 For I declare to you, you will not see Me again until you say, Blessed

---

r Richard Trench, *Synonyms of the New Testament.*   s The camel was also unclean, one of the largest of unclean animals, whereas the gnat was the smallest of unclean animals (Lev. 11:4). t Joseph Thayer, *A Greek-English Lexicon.*   u G. Abbott-Smith, *Manual Greek Lexicon.*

(magnified in worship, adored, and exalted) is He Who comes in the name of the Lord! [Ps. 118:26.]

24 JESUS DEPARTED from the temple ᵛarea and was going on His way when His disciples came up to Him to call His attention to the buildings of the temple *and* point them out to Him.
2 But He answered them, Do you see all these? Truly I tell you, there will not be left here one stone upon another that will not be thrown down.
3 While He was seated on the Mount of Olives, the disciples came to Him privately and said, Tell us, when will this take place, and what will be the sign of Your coming and of the end (the completion, the consummation) of the age?
4 Jesus answered them, Be careful that no one misleads you [deceiving you and leading you into error].
5 For many will come in (on the strength of) My name [ᵂappropriating the name which belongs to Me], saying, I am the Christ (the Messiah), and they will lead many astray.
6 And you will hear of wars and rumors of wars; see that you are not frightened *or* troubled, for this must take place, but the end is not yet.
7 For nation will rise against nation, and kingdom against kingdom, and there will be famines and earthquakes in place after place;
8 All this is but the beginning [the early pains] of the ˣbirth pangs [of the ᵂintolerable anguish].
9 Then they will hand you over to suffer affliction *and* tribulation and put you to death, and you will be hated by all nations for My name's sake.
10 And then many will be offended *and* repelled *and* will ᵂbegin to distrust

and desert [Him Whom they ought to trust and obey] *and* will stumble and fall away and betray one another *and* pursue one another with hatred.
11 And many false prophets will rise up and deceive *and* lead many into error.
12 And the love of ʸthe great body of people will grow cold because of the multiplied lawlessness *and* iniquity,
13 But he who endures to the end will be saved.
14 And this good news of the kingdom (the Gospel) will be preached throughout the whole world as a testimony to all the nations, and then will come the end.
15 So when you see the appalling sacrilege [the abomination that astonishes and makes desolate], spoken of by the prophet Daniel, standing in the Holy Place—let the reader take notice *and* ᵂponder *and* consider *and* heed [this]—[Dan. 9:27; 11:31; 12:11.]
16 Then let those who are in Judea flee to the mountains;
17 Let him who is on the housetop not come down *and* go into the house to take anything;
18 And let him who is in the field not turn back to get his overcoat.
19 And alas for the women who are pregnant and for those who have nursing babies in those days!
20 Pray that your flight may not be in winter or on a Sabbath.
21 For then there will be great tribulation (affliction, distress, and oppression) such as has not been from the beginning of the world until now—no, and never will be [again]. [Dan. 12:1; Joel 2:2.]
22 And if those days had not been shortened, no human being would endure *and* survive, but for the sake of the elect (God's chosen ones) those days will be shortened.

---

v Richard Trench, *Synonyms of the New Testament.* w Joseph Thayer, *A Greek-English Lexicon.*
x Literal translation. y Marvin Vincent, *Word Studies.*

keep love from growing cold

The twenty-fourth chapter of Matthew deals with signs of the end times. Most of them we are very familiar with—wars and rumors of wars, earthquakes, famines, and widespread deception. But there is another sign of the end times. Matthew 24:12 says that "the love of the great body of people will grow cold" due to the lawlessness and wickedness in the land.

The "great body" is the church, not the world. The pressure of rampant evil, difficult circumstances, and even the stress of our modern-day lifestyle produce an atmosphere so supercharged with problems that most people totally ignore their love walk with God. Instead they concentrate on themselves, look out for themselves, and try to solve their own problems.

This is something that God never told us to do. If we tend to His business, He will tend to ours. We are to concentrate on representing Him properly, and that is impossible to do unless we are walking in love. As we do that, He gives us wisdom to deal with our problems and brings deliverance from our foes.

Have you ever noticed that God does not always give us the ability to solve our own problems, yet when we are powerless to solve our own, He enables us to solve someone else's?

At one point in my own life, I realized I was spinning my wheels, so to speak. I was trying to solve all my problems, thinking that when my life got straightened out I could go forward in ministry to others. The fact is I had it backwards, as do so many others. I needed to cast my care on the Lord. I needed to do what He showed me concerning my situations in life without getting entangled in them. I needed to sow seeds in other people's lives by helping them, and then God would bring a harvest in my own life.

Refuse to let your love grow cold. Stir up the love in your life—toward your spouse and toward your family, friends, neighbors, and coworkers. Reach out to others who are hurting and in need. Pray for people and bless them. Grow to the point that one of your first thoughts each morning in your heart is about how you can bless someone else that day.

23 If anyone says to you then, Behold, here is the Christ (the Messiah)! or, There He is!—do not believe it.
24 For false Christs and false prophets will arise, and they will show great signs and wonders so as to deceive *and* lead astray, if possible, even the elect (God's chosen ones).

25 See, I have warned you beforehand.
26 So if they say to you, Behold, He is in the wilderness (desert)—do not go out there; if they tell you, Behold, He is in the secret places *or* inner rooms—do not believe it.
27 For just as the lightning flashes from the east and shines *and* ᶻis seen

z Marvin Vincent, *Word Studies.*

as far as the west, so will the coming of the Son of Man be.

28 Wherever there is a fallen body (a corpse), there the vultures (or eagles) will flock together. [Job 39:30.]

29 Immediately after the tribulation of those days the sun will be darkened, and the moon will not shed its light, and the stars will fall from the sky, and the powers of the heavens will be shaken. [Isa. 13:10; 34:4; Joel 2:10, 11; Zeph. 1:15.]

30 Then the sign of the Son of Man will appear in the sky, and then all the tribes of the earth will mourn *and* ªbeat their breasts *and* lament in anguish, and they will see the Son of Man coming on the clouds of heaven with power and great glory [in brilliancy and splendor]. [Dan. 7:13; Rev. 1:7.]

31 And He will send out His angels with a loud trumpet call, and they will gather His elect (His chosen ones) from the four winds, [even] from one end of the ᵇuniverse to the other. [Isa. 27:13; Zech. 9:14.]

32 From the fig tree learn this lesson: as soon as its ªyoung shoots become soft and tender and it puts out its leaves, you know ᶜof a surety that summer is near.

33 So also when you see these signs, ᶜall taken together, coming to pass, you may know ᶜof a surety that He is near, at the very doors.

34 Truly I tell you, this generation (ᶜthe whole multitude of people living at the same time, ᵈin a definite, ᵇgiven period) will not pass away till all these things ᶜtaken together take place.

35 ᵉSky and earth will pass away, but My words will not pass away.

36 But of that [exact] day and hour no one knows, not even the angels of heaven, nor the Son, but only the Father.

37 As were the days of Noah, so will be the coming of the Son of Man.

38 For just as in those days before the flood they were eating and drinking, [men] marrying and [women] being given in marriage, until the [very] day when Noah went into the ark,

39 And they did not know *or* understand until the flood came and swept them all away—so will be the coming of the Son of Man. [Gen. 6:5-8; 7:6-24.]

40 At that time two men will be in the field; one will be taken and one will be left.

41 Two women will be grinding at the hand mill; one will be taken and one will be left.

42 Watch therefore [ᶜgive strict attention, be cautious and active], for you do not know in what kind of a day [ªwhether a near or remote one] your Lord is coming.

43 But understand this: had the householder known in what [part of the night, whether in a ªnight or a morning] watch the thief was coming, he would have watched and would not have allowed his house to be ᶠundermined *and* broken into.

44 You also must be ready therefore, for the Son of Man is coming at an hour when you do not expect Him.

45 Who then is the faithful, thoughtful, *and* wise servant, whom his master has put in charge of his household to give to the others the food *and* supplies at the proper time?

46 Blessed (happy, fortunate, and ᵉto be envied) is that servant whom, when his master comes, he will find so doing.

47 I solemnly declare to you, he will set him over all his possessions.

48 But if that servant is wicked and says to himself, My master is delayed *and* is going to be gone a long time,

a Marvin Vincent, *Word Studies*. b G. Abbott-Smith, *Manual Greek Lexicon*. c Joseph Thayer, *A Greek-English Lexicon*. d Hermann Cremer, *Biblico-Theological Lexicon*. e James Moulton and George Milligan, *The Vocabulary*. f John Wycliffe, *The Wycliffe Bible*. g Alexander Souter, *Pocket Lexicon*.

49 And begins to beat his fellow servants and to eat and drink with the drunken,

50 The master of that servant will come on a day when he does not expect him and at an hour of which he is not aware,

51 And will punish him [hcut him up by scourging] and put him with the pretenders (hypocrites); there will be weeping and grinding of teeth.

25 THEN THE kingdom of heaven shall be likened to ten virgins who took their lamps and went to meet the bridegroom.

2 Five of them were foolish (thoughtless, without forethought) and five were wise (sensible, intelligent, and prudent).

3 For when the foolish took their lamps, they did not take any [extra] oil with them;

4 But the wise took flasks of oil along with them [also] with their lamps.

5 While the bridegroom lingered *and* was slow in coming, they all began nodding their heads, and they fell asleep.

6 But at midnight there was a shout, Behold, the bridegroom! Go out to meet him!

7 Then all those virgins got up and put their own lamps in order.

8 And the foolish said to the wise, Give us some of your oil, for our lamps are going out.

9 But the wise replied, There will not be enough for us and for you; go instead to the dealers and buy for yourselves.

10 But while they were going away to buy, the bridegroom came, and those who were prepared went in with him to the marriage feast; and the door was shut.

11 Later the other virgins also came

life point

All ten of the virgins in Matthew 25:1–10 had the same opportunity, but only half of them were prepared to take it.

In a society where people needed oil to provide light, five virgins were wise and had extra oil on hand; the other five were foolish and lost out because they did not keep their lamps filled with oil. When the bridegroom came, the five virgins without the oil missed their opportunity to go with him because they were lazy when they should have been working and were out trying to buy more oil for their lamps at the wrong time.

God is an "equal-opportunity employer." It does not matter to Him what kind of background we come from, what kind of parents or family life we have, what color or gender we are, what kind of education we received, or what our physical handicaps may be. None of those things make any difference to Him. In Him, we all have equal opportunity. Anyone who will follow His guidelines and do what He tells them to do can be blessed and used by Him. All ten of the virgins had the same opportunity, but only five were willing to do their part.

God puts potential in all of us and if we are willing to develop it, we will see wonderful things take place in our lives. Do your part and don't be left out as the five foolish virgins were.

and said, Lord, Lord, open [the door] to us!

12 But He replied, I solemnly declare to you, I do not know you [I am not acquainted with you].

13 Watch therefore [give strict

h Joseph Thayer, *A Greek-English Lexicon.*

attention and be cautious and active], for you know neither the day nor the hour *when the Son of Man will come.*

14 For it is like a man who was about to take a long journey, and he called his servants together and entrusted them with his property.

15 To one he gave five talents [probably about $5,000], to another two, to another one—to each in proportion to his own ᶦpersonal ability. Then he departed *and* left the country.

16 He who had received the five talents went at once and traded with them, and he gained five talents more.

17 And likewise he who had received the two talents—he also gained two talents more.

18 But he who had received the one talent went and dug a hole in the ground and hid his master's money.

19 Now after a long time the master of those servants returned and settled accounts with them.

20 And he who had received the five talents came and brought him five more, saying, Master, you entrusted to me five talents; see, here I have gained five talents more.

21 His master said to him, Well done, you upright (honorable, ʲadmirable) and faithful servant! You have been faithful *and* trustworthy over a little; I will put you in charge of much. Enter into *and* share the joy (the delight, the ᵏblessedness) which your master enjoys.

22 And he also who had the two talents came forward, saying, Master, you entrusted two talents to me; here I have gained two talents more.

23 His master said to him, Well done, you upright (honorable, ʲadmirable) and faithful servant! You have been faithful *and* trustworthy over a little; I will put you in charge of much. Enter into *and* share the joy (the delight, the ᵏblessedness) which your master enjoys.

24 He who had received one talent also came forward, saying, Master, I knew you to be a harsh *and* hard man, reaping where you did not sow, and gathering where you had not winnowed [the grain].

25 So I was afraid, and I went and hid your talent in the ground. Here you have what is your own.

26 But his master answered him, You wicked *and* lazy *and* idle servant! Did you indeed know that I reap where I have not sowed and gather [grain] where I have not winnowed?

27 Then you should have invested my money with the bankers, and at my coming I would have received what was my own with interest.

28 So take the talent away from him and give it to the one who has the ten talents.

29 For to everyone who has will more be given, and he will be ᵏfurnished richly so that he will have an abundance; but from the one who does not have, even what he does have will be taken away.

30 And throw the good-for-nothing servant into the outer darkness; there will be weeping and grinding of teeth.

31 When the Son of Man comes in His glory (His majesty and splendor), and all the *holy* angels with Him, then He will sit on the throne of His glory.

32 All nations will be gathered before Him, and He will separate them [the people] from one another as a shepherd separates his sheep from the goats; [Ezek. 34:17.]

33 And He will cause the sheep to stand at His right hand, but the goats at His left.

34 Then the King will say to those at His right hand, Come, you blessed of My Father [you ᵏfavored of God and

---

i Marvin Vincent, *Word Studies.*   **j** Hermann Cremer, *Biblico-Theological Lexicon.*   **k** Joseph Thayer, *A Greek-English Lexicon.*

use it or lose it

In Matthew 25:14, 15, Jesus tells the story of a man who was going on a long journey. He called his servants together and gave them different amounts of money to handle, according to their abilities.

No, we do not all have the same talents and abilities. We cannot all do the same things, but we can all be what God has called us individually to be. I cannot be what you are, and you cannot be what I am, but we can each be all that God wants us to be.

Many people are frustrated and miserable because they do not feel fulfilled. They are not being all they can be and are not doing all they know they are supposed to be doing. They are letting the devil or other people talk them out of their callings and their blessings.

This is what happened to one of the servants in Matthew 25. The man who was going on the journey gave talents to three of his servants before he left. While he was gone, one servant invested what he was given and received it back with interest. When the man returned and found out what the servant did with the talent, he said, "Well done, you upright (honorable, admirable) and faithful servant! You have been faithful and trustworthy over a little; I will put you in charge of much" (Matthew 25:21). The second servant did the same, and was told the same thing by the man (see Matthew 25:22, 23). But the third servant buried his talent in the ground because he was afraid. When the man found out what that servant did, he was so upset with him that he took away his talent and gave it to the servant who had the ten talents (see Matthew 25:24–28).

Many people are like that third servant. They hide their talents because they are afraid—afraid of responsibility, afraid of judgment, afraid of what people will think. They are afraid to step out; afraid they might fail, afraid of criticism, afraid of other people's opinions, afraid of being misunderstood. They are afraid of the sacrifice and hard work involved.

I do not want you to be afraid to take the talent God gave you and use it for His glory. I do not want you to end up unhappy, unfulfilled, and dissatisfied because you are compromising what He has placed in you.

Let me encourage you to use your talents to the greatest possible extent and to do your best in every area of your life. Then you will hear your Master say, "Well done!"

appointed to eternal salvation], inherit (receive as your own) the kingdom prepared for you from the foundation of the world.

35 For I was hungry and you gave Me food, I was thirsty and you gave Me something to drink, I was a stranger and you [1]brought Me together with

1 Literal meaning.

yourselves *and* welcomed *and* entertained *and* ^mlodged Me,

36 I was naked and you clothed Me, I was sick and you visited Me ⁿwith help *and* ministering care, I was in prison and you came to see Me. [Isa. 58:7.]

37 Then the just *and* upright will answer Him, Lord, when did we see You hungry and gave You food, or thirsty and gave You something to drink?

38 And when did we see You a stranger and welcomed *and* entertained You, or naked and clothed You?

39 And when did we see You sick or in prison and came to visit You?

40 And the King will reply to them, Truly I tell you, in so far as you did it for one of the least [^oin the estimation of men] of these My brethren, you did it for Me. [Prov. 19:17.]

41 Then He will say to those at His left hand, Begone from Me, you cursed, into the eternal fire prepared for the devil and his angels!

42 For I was hungry and you gave Me no food, I was thirsty and you gave Me nothing to drink,

43 I was a stranger and you did not welcome Me *and* entertain Me, I was naked and you did not clothe Me, I was sick and in prison and you did not visit Me ⁿwith help *and* ministering care.

44 Then they also [in their turn] will answer, Lord, when did we see You hungry or thirsty or a stranger or naked or sick or in prison, and did not minister to You?

45 And He will reply to them,

speak the Word

Solemnly I declare to you, in so far as you failed to do it for the least [^oin the estimation of men] of these, you failed to do it for Me. [Prov. 14:31; 17:5.]

46 Then they will go away into eternal punishment, but those who are just *and* upright *and* in right standing with God into eternal life. [Dan. 12:2.]

26 WHEN JESUS had ended this discourse, He said to His disciples,

2 You know that the Passover is in two days—and the Son of Man will be delivered up ^otreacherously to be crucified.

3 Then the chief priests and the elders of the people gathered in the [^popen] court of the palace of the high priest, whose name was Caiaphas,

4 And consulted together in order to arrest Jesus by stratagem secretly and put Him to death.

5 But they said, It must not be during the Feast, for fear that there will be a riot among the people.

6 Now when Jesus came back to Bethany and was in the house of Simon the leper,

7 A woman came up to Him with an alabaster flask of very precious perfume, and she poured it on His head as He reclined at table.

8 And when the disciples saw it, they were indignant, saying, For what purpose is all this waste?

9 For this perfume might have been sold for a large sum and the money given to the poor.

10 But Jesus, fully aware of this, said to them, Why do you bother the

---

Jesus, I declare that You are worth so much more than the most precious thing I have. Help me to love You extravagantly.
ADAPTED FROM MATTHEW 26:7

---

m William Tyndale, *The Tyndale Bible*. **n** Kenneth Wuest, *Word Studies*. **o** Joseph Thayer, *A Greek-English Lexicon*. **p** Marvin Vincent, *Word Studies*.

woman? She has done a noble (praise-worthy and beautiful) thing to Me.

11 For you always have the poor among you, but you will not always have Me. [Deut. 15:11.]

12 In pouring this perfume on My body she has done something to prepare Me for My burial.

13 Truly I tell you, wherever this good news (the Gospel) is preached in the whole world, what this woman has done will be told also, in memory of her.

14 Then one of the Twelve [apostles], who was called Judas Iscariot, went to the chief priests

15 And said, What are you willing to give me if I hand Him over to you? And they weighed out for *and* paid to him thirty pieces of silver [about twenty-one dollars and sixty cents]. [Exod. 21:32; Zech. 11:12.]

16 And from that moment he sought a fitting opportunity to betray Him.

17 Now on the first day of Unleavened Bread [Passover week], the disciples came to Jesus and said *to Him,* Where do You wish us to prepare for You to eat the Passover supper?

18 He said, Go into the city to a certain man and say to him, The Master says: My time is near; I will keep the Passover at your house with My disciples.

19 And accordingly the disciples did as Jesus had directed them, and they made ready the Passover supper. [Deut. 16:5-8.]

20 When it was evening, He was reclining at table with the twelve disciples.

21 And as they were eating, He said, Solemnly I say to you, one of you will betray Me!

22 They were exceedingly pained *and* distressed *and* deeply hurt *and* sorrowful and began to say to Him one after another, qSurely it cannot be I, Lord, can it?

23 He replied, He who has [just] dipped his hand in the same dish with Me will betray Me!

24 The Son of Man is going just as it is written of Him; but woe to that man by whom the Son of Man is betrayed! It would have been better (more profitable and wholesome) for that man if he had never been born! [Ps. 41:9.]

25 Judas, the betrayer, said, qSurely it is not I, is it, Master? He said to him, You have stated [the fact].

26 Now as they were eating, Jesus took bread and, rpraising God, gave thanks *and* asked Him to bless it to their use, and when He had broken it, He gave it to the disciples and said, Take, eat; this is My body.

27 And He took a cup, and when He had given thanks, He gave it to them, saying, Drink of it, all of you;

28 For this is My blood of the *new* covenant, which [rratifies the agreement and] is qbeing poured out for many for the forgiveness of sins. [Exod. 24:6-8.]

29 I say to you, I shall not drink again of this fruit of the vine until that day when I drink it with you new *and* rof superior quality in My Father's kingdom.

30 And when they had sung a hymn, they went out to the Mount of Olives.

31 Then Jesus said to them, You will all be offended *and* stumble *and* fall away because of Me this night [distrusting and deserting Me], for it is written, I will strike the Shepherd, and the sheep of the flock will be scattered. [Zech. 13:7.]

32 But after I am raised up [to life again], I will go ahead of you to Galilee.

33 Peter declared to Him, Though they all are offended *and* stumble *and* fall away because of You [and distrust and desert You], I will never do so.

34 Jesus said to him, Solemnly I

---

q Marvin Vincent, *Word Studies.* r Joseph Thayer, *A Greek-English Lexicon.*

declare to you, this very night, before a ˢsingle rooster crows, you will deny *and* disown Me three times.

35 Peter said to Him, Even if I must die with You, I will not deny *or* disown You! And all the disciples said the same thing.

36 Then Jesus went with them to a place called Gethsemane, and He told His disciples, Sit down here while I go over yonder and pray.

37 And taking with Him Peter and the two sons of Zebedee, He began to ˢshow grief *and* distress of mind and was ᵗdeeply depressed.

38 Then He said to them, My soul is very sad *and* deeply grieved, so that ᵘI am almost dying of sorrow. Stay here and keep awake *and* keep watch with Me.

39 And going a little farther, He threw Himself upon the ground on His face and prayed saying, My Father, if it is possible, let this cup pass away from Me; nevertheless, not what I will [not what I desire], but as You will *and* desire.

40 And He came to the disciples and found them sleeping, and He said to Peter, What! Are you so utterly unable to stay awake *and* keep watch with Me for one hour?

41 All of you must keep awake (give strict attention, be cautious and active) *and* watch and pray, that you may not come into temptation. The spirit indeed is willing, but the flesh is weak.

42 Again a second time He went away and prayed, My Father, if this cannot pass by unless I drink it, Your will be done.

43 And again He came and found them sleeping, for their eyes were weighed down with sleep.

44 So, leaving them again, He went

life point

We need to apply Jesus' admonition to "watch and pray" (Matthew 26:41) to our own lives. Watch for the attacks of the enemy in your life and then pray immediately. Come against Satan when he is trying to get a foothold, and he will never get a stronghold!

away and prayed for the third time, using the same words.

45 Then He returned to the disciples and said to them, Are you still sleeping and taking your rest? Behold, the hour is at hand, and the Son of Man is betrayed into the hands of ᵛespecially wicked sinners [ʷwhose way or nature it is to act in opposition to God].

46 Get up, let us be going! See, My betrayer is at hand!

47 As He was still speaking, Judas, one of the Twelve [apostles], came up, and with him a great crowd with swords and clubs, from the chief priests and elders of the people.

48 Now the betrayer had given them a sign, saying, The One I shall kiss is the Man; seize Him.

49 And he came up to Jesus at once and said, Hail (greetings, good health to You, long life to You), Master! And he ˣembraced Him and kissed Him ʸwith [pretended] warmth and devotion.

50 Jesus said to him, Friend, for what are you here? Then they came up and laid hands on Jesus and arrested Him.

51 And behold, one of those who were with Jesus reached out his hand and drew his sword and, striking the body servant of the high priest, cut off his ear.

52 Then Jesus said to him, Put your sword back into its place, for all who

---

s Marvin Vincent, *Word Studies.* **t** George R. Berry, *Greek-English New Testament Lexicon.* **u** Joseph Thayer, *A Greek-English Lexicon.* **v** G. Abbott-Smith, *Manual Greek Lexicon.* **w** Hermann Cremer, *Biblico-Theological Lexicon.* **x** H.A.W. Meyer, *Critical and Exegetical Handbook to the Gospel of Matthew.* **y** Kenneth Wuest, *Word Studies.*

draw the sword will die by the sword. [Gen. 9:6.]

53 Do you suppose that I cannot appeal to My Father, and He will immediately provide Me with more than twelve legions [²more than 80,000] of angels?

54 But how then would the Scriptures be fulfilled, that it must come about this way?

55 At that moment Jesus said to the crowds, Have you come out with swords and clubs as [you would] against a robber to capture Me? Day after day I was ªaccustomed to sit in the ᵇporches *and* courts of the temple teaching, and you did not arrest Me.

56 But all this has taken place in order that the Scriptures of the prophets might be fulfilled. Then all the disciples deserted Him and, fleeing, escaped.

57 But those who had seized Jesus took Him away to Caiaphas, the high priest, where the scribes and the elders had assembled.

58 But Peter followed Him at a distance, as far as the courtyard of the high priest's home; he even went inside and sat with the guards to see the end.

59 Now the chief priests and the whole council (the Sanhedrin) sought to get false witnesses to testify against Jesus, so that they might put Him to death;

60 But they found none, though many witnesses came forward [to testify]. At last two men came forward

61 And testified, This ᶜFellow said, I am able to tear down the ᵇsanctuary of the temple of God and to build it up again in three days.

62 And the high priest stood up and said, Have You no answer to make?

What about this that these men testify against You?

63 But Jesus kept silent. And the high priest said to Him, ªI call upon you to swear by the living God, and tell us whether you are the Christ, the Son of God.

64 Jesus said to him, ªYou have stated [the fact]. More than that, I tell you: You will in the future see the Son of Man seated at the right hand of ²the Almighty and coming on the clouds of the sky. [Ps. 110:1; Dan. 7:13.]

65 Then the high priest tore his clothes and exclaimed, He has uttered blasphemy! What need have we of further evidence? You have now heard His blasphemy. [Lev. 24:16; Num. 14:6.]

66 What do you think now? They answered, He deserves to be put to death.

67 Then they spat in His face and struck Him with their fists; and some ᶻslapped Him in the face, [Isa. 50:6.]

68 Saying, Prophesy to us, You Christ (the Messiah)! Who was it that struck You?

69 Now Peter was sitting outside in the courtyard, and ªone maid came up to him and said, You were also with Jesus the Galilean!

70 But he denied it ᵈfalsely before them all, saying, I do not know what you mean.

71 And when he had gone out to the porch, another maid saw him, and she said to the bystanders, This fellow was with Jesus the Nazarene!

72 And again he denied it and ᵈdisowned Him with an oath, saying, I do not know the Man!

73 After a little while, the bystanders came up and said to Peter, You

---

z Joseph Thayer, *A Greek-English Lexicon.* **a** Marvin Vincent, *Word Studies.* **b** Richard Trench, *Synonyms of the New Testament.* **c** Capitalized because of what He is, the spotless Son of God, not what the speakers may have thought He was. **d** Hermann Cremer, *Biblico-Theological Lexicon.*

certainly are one of them too, for even your accent betrays you.

74 Then Peter began to invoke a curse on himself and to swear, I do not even know the Man! And at that moment a rooster crowed.

75 And Peter remembered Jesus' words, when He had said, Before a ^esingle rooster crows, you will deny *and* disown Me three times. And he went outside and wept bitterly.

27 WHEN IT was morning, all the chief priests and the elders of the people held a consultation against Jesus to put Him to death;

2 And they bound Him and led Him away and handed Him over to Pilate the governor.

3 When Judas, His betrayer, saw that [Jesus] was condemned, [Judas was ^fafflicted in mind and troubled for his former folly; and] with remorse [with little more than a selfish dread of the consequences] he brought back the thirty pieces of silver to the chief priests and the elders, [Exod. 21:32.]

4 Saying, I have sinned in betraying innocent blood. They replied, What is that to us? See to that yourself.

5 And casting the pieces of silver [forward] into the [Holy Place of the ^gsanctuary of the] temple, he departed; and he went off and hanged himself.

6 But the chief priests, picking up the pieces of silver, said, It is not legal to put these in the [consecrated] treasury, for it is the price of blood.

7 So after consultation they bought with them [the pieces of silver] the potter's field [as a place] in which to bury strangers.

8 Therefore that piece of ground has been called the Field of Blood to the present day.

9 Then were fulfilled the words spoken by Jeremiah the prophet when he said, And they took the thirty pieces of silver, the price of Him on Whom a price had been set by some of the sons of Israel, [Zech. 11:12, 13.]

10 And they gave them for the potter's field, as the Lord directed me.

11 Now Jesus stood before the governor [Pilate], and the governor asked Him, Are you the King of the Jews? Jesus said to him, You have stated [the fact].

12 But when the charges were made against Him by the chief priests and elders, He made no answer. [Isa. 53:7.]

13 Then Pilate said to Him, Do You not hear how many *and* how serious are the things they are testifying against You?

14 But He made no reply to him, not even to a single accusation, so that the governor marveled greatly.

15 Now at the Feast [of the Passover] the governor was in the habit of setting free for the people any one prisoner whom they chose.

16 And at that time they had a notorious prisoner whose name was Barabbas.

17 So when they had assembled for this purpose, Pilate said to them, Whom do you want me to set free for you, Barabbas, or Jesus Who is called Christ?

18 For he knew that it was because of envy that they had handed Him over to him.

19 Also, while he was seated on the judgment bench, his wife sent him a message, saying, Have nothing to do with that just *and* upright Man, for I have had a painful experience today in a dream because of Him.

20 But the chief priests and the elders prevailed on the people to ask for Barabbas, and put Jesus to death.

e Marvin Vincent, *Word Studies*. **f** Jeremy Taylor and Aristotle, cited by Richard Trench, *Synonyms of the New Testament*. **g** Richard Trench, *Synonyms of the New Testament*.

21 Again the governor said to them, Which of the two do you wish me to release for you? And they said, Barabbas!

22 Pilate said to them, Then what shall I do with Jesus Who is called Christ?

23 They all replied, Let Him be crucified! And he said, Why? What has He done that is evil? But they shouted all the louder, Let Him be crucified!

24 So when Pilate saw that he was getting nowhere, but rather that a riot was about to break out, he took water and washed his hands in the presence of the crowd, saying, I am not guilty of nor responsible for this ʰrighteous Man's blood; see to it yourselves. [Deut. 21:6-9; Ps. 26:6.]

25 And all the people answered, Let His blood be on us and on our children! [Josh. 2:19.]

26 So he set free for them Barabbas; and he [had] Jesus whipped, and delivered Him up to be crucified.

27 Then the governor's soldiers took Jesus into the palace, and they gathered the whole battalion about Him.

28 And they stripped off His clothes and put a scarlet robe (ⁱgarment of dignity and office worn by Roman officers of rank) upon Him,

29 And, weaving a crown of thorns, they put it on His head and put a reed (staff) in His right hand. And kneeling before Him, they made sport of Him, saying, Hail (greetings, good health to You, long life to You), King of the Jews!

30 And they spat on Him, and took the reed (staff) and struck Him on the head.

31 And when they finished making sport of Him, they stripped Him of the robe and put His own garments on Him and led Him away to be crucified.

32 As they were marching forth, they came upon a man of Cyrene named Simon; this man they forced to carry the cross of Jesus.

33 And when they came to a place called Golgotha [Latin: Calvary], which means The Place of a Skull,

34 They offered Him wine mingled with gall to drink; but when He tasted it, He refused to drink it.

35 And when they had crucified Him, they divided and distributed His garments [among them] by casting lots ʲso that the prophet's saying was fulfilled, They parted My garments among them and over My apparel they cast lots. [Ps. 22:18.]

36 Then they sat down there and kept watch over Him.

37 And over His head they put the accusation against Him (ᵏthe cause of His death), which read, This is Jesus, the King of the Jews.

38 At the same time two robbers were crucified with Him, one on the right hand and one on the left.

39 And those who passed by spoke reproachfully and abusively and jeered at Him, wagging their heads, [Ps. 22:7, 8; 109:25.]

40 And they said, You Who would tear down the ⁱsanctuary of the temple and rebuild it in three days, rescue Yourself ˡfrom death. If You are the Son of God, come down from the cross.

41 In the same way the chief priests, with the scribes and elders, made sport of Him, saying,

42 He rescued others ˡfrom death; Himself He cannot rescue ˡfrom death. He is the King of Israel? Let Him come down from the cross now, and we will believe in and ˡacknowledge and cleave to Him.

43 He trusts in God; let God deliver

---

h Some manuscripts so read. i Richard Trench, *Synonyms of the New Testament*. j Many manuscripts do not contain this part of verse 35. k William Tyndale, *The Tyndale Bible*. l Hermann Cremer, *Biblico-Theological Lexicon*.

Him now if He cares for Him *and* will have Him, for He said, I am the Son of God.

44 And the robbers who were crucified with Him also abused *and* reproached *and* made sport of Him in the same way.

45 Now from the sixth hour (noon) there was darkness over all the land until the ninth hour (three o'clock).

46 And about the ninth hour (three o'clock) Jesus cried with a loud voice, Eli, Eli, lama sabachthani?—that is, My God, My God, why have You abandoned Me [leaving Me [m]helpless, forsaking and failing Me in My need]? [Ps. 22:1.]

47 And some of the bystanders, when they heard it, said, This Man is calling for Elijah!

48 And one of them immediately ran and took a sponge, soaked it with vinegar (a sour wine), and put it on a reed (staff), and was [n]about to give it to Him to drink. [Ps. 69:21.]

49 But the others said, Wait! Let us see whether Elijah will come to save Him [n]from death.

50 And Jesus cried again with a loud voice and gave up His spirit.

51 And at once the curtain of the [o]sanctuary of the temple was torn in two from top to bottom; the earth shook and the rocks were split. [Exod. 26:31-35.]

52 The tombs were opened and many bodies of the saints who had fallen asleep [p]in death were raised [to life];

53 And coming out of the tombs after His resurrection, they went into the holy city and appeared to many people.

54 When the centurion and those who were with him keeping watch over Jesus observed the earthquake and all that was happening, they were terribly frightened *and* filled with awe, and said, Truly this was God's Son!

55 There were also numerous women there, looking on from a distance, who were of those who had accompanied Jesus from Galilee, ministering to Him.

56 Among them were Mary of Magdala, and Mary the mother of James and Joseph, and the mother of Zebedee's sons.

57 When it was evening, there came a rich man from Arimathea, named Joseph, who also was a disciple of Jesus.

58 He went to Pilate and asked for the body of Jesus, and Pilate ordered that it be given to him.

59 And Joseph took the body and [q]rolled it up in a clean linen cloth [r]used for swathing dead bodies

60 And laid it in his own fresh ([n]undefiled) tomb, which he had hewn in the rock; and he rolled a big boulder over the door of the tomb and went away.

61 And Mary of Magdala and the other Mary kept sitting there opposite the tomb.

62 The next day, that is, the day after the day of Preparation [for the Sabbath], the chief priests and the Pharisees assembled before Pilate

63 And said, Sir, we have just remembered how that [n]vagabond Imposter said while He was still alive, After three days I will rise again.

64 Therefore give an order to have the tomb made secure *and* safeguarded until the third day, for fear that His disciples will come and steal Him away and tell the people that He has risen from the dead, and the last deception *and* fraud will be worse than the first.

---

m Kenneth Wuest, *Word Studies.*   **n** Marvin Vincent, *Word Studies.*   **o** Richard Trench, *Synonyms of the New Testament.*   **p** Hermann Cremer, *Biblico-Theological Lexicon.*   **q** Robert Young, *Analytical Concordance.*   **r** James Moulton and George Milligan, *The Vocabulary.*

65 Pilate said to them, You have a guard [of soldiers; take them and] go, make it as secure as you can.
66 So they went off and made the tomb secure by sealing the boulder, a guard of soldiers being with them *and* remaining to watch.

28 NOW AFTER the Sabbath, near dawn of the first day of the week, Mary of Magdala and the other Mary went to take a look at the tomb.
2 And behold, there was a great earthquake, for an angel of the Lord descended from heaven and came and rolled the boulder back and sat upon it.
3 His appearance was like lightning, and his garments as white as snow.
4 And those keeping guard were so frightened at the sight of him that they were agitated *and* they trembled and became like dead men.
5 But the angel said to the women, Do not be alarmed *and* frightened, for I know that you are looking for Jesus, Who was crucified.
6 He is not here; He has risen, as He said [He would do]. Come, see the place where He lay.
7 Then go quickly and tell His disciples, He has risen from the dead, and behold, He is going before you to Galilee; there you will see Him. Behold, I have told you.
8 So they left the tomb hastily with fear and great joy and ran to tell the disciples.
9 And *as they went,* behold, Jesus met them and said, Hail (greetings)! And they went up to Him and clasped His feet and worshiped Him.
10 Then Jesus said to them, Do not

be alarmed *and* afraid; go and tell My brethren to go into Galilee, and there they will see Me.
11 While they were on their way, behold, some of the guards went into the city and reported to the chief priests everything that had occurred.
12 And when they [the chief priests] had gathered with the elders and had consulted together, they gave a sufficient sum of money to the soldiers,
13 And said, Tell people, His disciples came at night and stole Him away while we were sleeping.
14 And if the governor hears of it, we will appease him and make you safe *and* free from trouble *and* care.
15 So they took the money and did as they were instructed; and this story has been current among the Jews to the present day.
16 Now the eleven disciples went to Galilee, to the mountain to which Jesus had directed *and* made appointment with them.
17 And when they saw Him, they fell down and worshiped Him; but some doubted.

putting the Word to work

Have you ever wondered about your purpose in life? Know that you have been called by God to teach others about Who He is and what it means to follow Him. God gave you the authority to do so, and has promised to not leave you on your own, but to be with you always (see Matthew 28:18–20). Ask God to show you where He wants you to go—to someone in your office, in your neighborhood, perhaps even in your own family—so that you can help others follow Him too.

speak the Word

Thank You, Jesus, that You rose from the dead, just as You promised!
ADAPTED FROM MATTHEW 28:6

18 Jesus approached and, [s]breaking the silence, said to them, All authority (all power of rule) in heaven and on earth has been given to Me.
19 Go then and make disciples of all the nations, baptizing them [s]into the name of the Father and of the Son and of the Holy Spirit,

20 Teaching them to observe everything that I have commanded you, and behold, I am with you [t]all the days ([u]perpetually, uniformly, and on every occasion), to the [very] close *and* consummation of the age. [v]*Amen (so let it be).*

s Marvin Vincent, *Word Studies.* **t** John Wycliffe, *The Wycliffe Bible.* **u** *Webster's New International Dictionary* offers this phrase as a definition of "always." **v** Some manuscripts do not contain this ending.

Mark

Author:
Mark

Date:
Possibly AD 55–65

Everyday Life Principles:
In order to follow Jesus, we must deny ourselves and lose sight of our own interests.

We must continually and steadfastly cling to Jesus in every aspect of our lives.

The only way to experience true joy is to allow God to work through you to bless others.

Mark is the shortest of the four Gospels and tells the story of Jesus in a style that is simple and concise, yet detailed. It focuses on facts more than on themes and on actions more than attitudes. Because of Mark's straightforward and unadorned approach, many believe this book gives a much more vivid account of Jesus' life and ministry than the other Gospels.

Scholars believe Mark's Gospel was written during a time when Christians were viciously persecuted and killed for their faith. This may be the reason for the sense of urgency we feel in Mark and for its emphasis on the cost of following Jesus. Mark 8:34 records Jesus' words: "If anyone intends to come after Me, let him deny himself [forget, ignore, disown, and lose sight of himself and his own interests] and take up his cross, and [joining Me as a disciple and siding with My party] follow with Me [continually, cleaving steadfastly to Me]."

I do not believe the "cross" we are to carry is a burden of disaster, disease, and misery, but is a sacrificial life of allowing God to work through us to bless others. This kind of cross is the only way to truly experience the joy that Jesus gives.

As you read Mark's vivid presentation of Jesus' life and ministry, I pray that you will see Him more clearly and follow Him, as Mark 8:34 says, "continually, cleaving steadfastly to [Him]" all the days of your life.

1 THE BEGINNING [of the facts] of the good news (the Gospel) of Jesus Christ, [a]*the Son of God.*

2 [b]Just as it is written in the prophet Isaiah: Behold, I send My messenger before Your face, who will make ready Your way—[Mal. 3:1.]

3 A voice of one crying in the wilderness [shouting in the desert], Prepare the way of the Lord, make His [c]beaten tracks straight (level and passable)! [Isa. 40:3.]

4 John the Baptist appeared in the wilderness (desert), preaching a baptism [[d]obligating] repentance ([e]a change of one's mind for the better, heartily amending one's ways, with abhorrence of his past sins) in order [f]to obtain forgiveness of *and* release from sins.

5 And there kept going out to him [continuously] all the country of Judea and all the inhabitants of Jerusalem; and they were baptized by him in the river Jordan, [d]as they were confessing their sins.

6 And John wore clothing woven of camel's hair and had a leather girdle around his loins and ate locusts and wild honey.

7 And he preached, saying, After me comes He Who is stronger (more powerful and more valiant) than I, the strap of Whose sandals I am not worthy *or* fit to stoop down and unloose.

8 I have baptized you with water, but He will baptize you with the Holy Spirit.

9 In those days Jesus came from Nazareth of Galilee and was baptized by John in the Jordan.

10 And when He came up out of the water, at once he [John] saw the heavens torn open and the [Holy]

life point

Before Jesus' public ministry began, He was immersed in water and anointed with the Holy Spirit and with power (see Mark 1:10). This enabled Him to do the task His Father sent Him to do. Similarly, when we are filled with the Holy Spirit, we are equipped for service in the kingdom of God because we are able to draw on the power of the Holy Spirit, Whom we received when He came upon us to be His witnesses. According to Acts 1:8, His power can be defined as "ability, efficiency, and might" that enable us to be what God wants us to be as His witnesses.

Spirit like a dove coming down [[d]to enter] [g]into Him. [John 1:32.]

11 And there came a voice [d]out from within heaven, You are My Beloved Son; in You I am well pleased. [Ps. 2:7; Isa. 42:1.]

12 Immediately the [Holy] Spirit [from within] drove Him out into the wilderness (desert),

13 And He stayed in the wilderness (desert) forty days, being tempted [all the while] by Satan; and He was with the wild beasts, and the angels ministered to Him [continually].

14 Now after John was arrested *and* put in prison, Jesus came into Galilee, preaching the good news (the Gospel) *of the kingdom* of God,

15 And saying, The [appointed period of] time is fulfilled (completed), and the kingdom of God is at hand; repent ([h]have a change of mind which issues in regret for past sins and in change of conduct for the better) and believe (trust in, rely on, and adhere to) the good news (the Gospel).

---

a Some manuscripts do not contain this phrase.   b Kenneth Wuest, *Word Studies in the Greek New Testament.*   c James Moulton and George Milligan, *The Vocabulary of the Greek Testament.*   d Kenneth Wuest, *Word Studies.*   e Joseph Thayer, *A Greek-English Lexicon of the New Testament.*   f Charles B. Williams, *The New Testament: A Translation in the Language of the People.*   g Literal translation of *eis.*   h Marvin Vincent, *Word Studies in the New Testament.*

16 And passing along the shore of the Sea of Galilee, He saw Simon [Peter] and Andrew the brother of Simon casting a net [to and fro] in the sea, for they were fishermen.

17 And Jesus said to them, Come after Me *and* [i]be My disciples, and I will make you to become fishers of men.

18 And at once they left their nets and [[i]yielding up all claim to them] followed [with] Him [[i]joining Him as disciples and siding with His party].

19 He went on a little farther and saw James the *son* of Zebedee, and John his brother, who were in [their] boat putting their nets in order.

20 And immediately He called out to them, and [[i]abandoning all mutual claims] they left their father Zebedee in the boat with the hired men and went off after Him [[i]to be His disciples, side with His party, and follow Him].

21 And they entered into Capernaum, and immediately on the Sabbath He went into the synagogue and began to teach.

putting the Word to work

Several of Jesus' disciples were fishermen by trade (see Mark 1:16–20). Have you ever been fishing? Even if you have not, you probably know that people use many different types of bait to catch a fish. As a "fisher" of men and women, God asks you to demonstrate through your life, words, and actions the blessing of following Him. Some people will respond to hearing about God, others will respond to your actions that demonstrate His love and grace, and still others by seeing the joy and peace you have in your life. Remember, every day brings opportunities to fish!

22 And they were completely astonished at His teaching, for He was teaching as One Who possessed authority, and not as the scribes.

23 Just at that time there was in their synagogue a man [who was in the power] of an unclean spirit; and now [immediately] he raised a deep *and* terrible cry from the depths of his throat, saying,

24 What have You to do with us, Jesus of Nazareth? Have You come to destroy us? I know who You are—the Holy One of God!

25 And Jesus rebuked him, saying, Hush up (be muzzled, gagged), and come out of him!

26 And the unclean spirit, throwing the man into convulsions and [j]screeching with a loud voice, came out of him.

27 And they were all so amazed *and* [k]almost terrified that they kept questioning *and* demanding one of another, saying, What is this? What new (fresh) teaching! With authority He gives orders even to the unclean spirits and they obey Him!

28 And immediately rumors concerning Him spread [everywhere] throughout all the region surrounding Galilee.

29 And at once He left the synagogue and went into the house of Simon [Peter] and Andrew, accompanied by James and John.

30 Now Simon's mother-in-law [l]had for some time been lying sick with a fever, and at once they told Him about her.

31 And He went up to her and took her by the hand and raised her up; and the fever left her, and she began to wait on them.

32 Now when it was evening, after the sun had set, they brought to Him all who were sick and those under the power of demons,

i Joseph Thayer, *A Greek-English Lexicon*. **j** A.T. Robertson, *Word Pictures in the New Testament*. **k** Alexander Souter, *Pocket Lexicon of the Greek New Testament*. **l** Kenneth Wuest, *Word Studies*.

33 Until the whole town was gathered together about the door.
34 And He cured many who were afflicted with various diseases; and He drove out many demons, but would not allow the demons to talk because they knew Him [[m]intuitively].
35 And in the morning, long before daylight, He got up and went out to a [n]deserted place, and there He prayed.

life point

Surely prayer was important to Jesus; otherwise, He would have stayed in bed! Most of us do not get up early for anything unless it is very important.

But, Jesus did not make a big display of prayer. In Mark 1:35, He went to a private place, where the Bible simply says, "He prayed." Prayer is vital and powerful, but needs to be kept simple in our lives.

36 And Simon [Peter] and those who were with him followed Him [[o]pursuing Him eagerly and hunting Him out],
37 And they found Him and said to Him, Everybody is looking for You.
38 And He said to them, Let us be going on into the neighboring country towns, that I may preach there also; for that is why I came out.
39 [So] He went throughout the whole of Galilee, preaching in their synagogues and driving out demons.
40 And a leper came to Him, begging Him on his knees and saying to Him, If You are willing, You are able to make me clean.
41 And being moved with pity *and* sympathy, Jesus reached out His hand and touched him, and said to him, I am willing; be made clean!

42 And at once the leprosy [completely] left him and he was made clean [by being healed].
43 And Jesus charged him sternly (sharply and threateningly, and with earnest admonition) and [acting with deep feeling thrust him forth and] sent him away at once,
44 And said to him, See that you tell nothing [of this] to anyone; but begone, show yourself to the priest, and offer for your purification what Moses commanded, as a proof (an evidence and witness) to the people [that you are really healed]. [Lev. 13:49; 14:2-32.]
45 But he went out and began to talk so freely about it and blaze abroad the news [spreading it everywhere] that [Jesus] could no longer openly go into a town but was outside in [lonely] desert places. But the people kept on coming to Him from [n]all sides *and* every quarter.

2 AND JESUS having returned to Capernaum, after some days it was rumored about that He was in the house [probably Peter's].
2 And so many people gathered together there that there was no longer room [for them], not even around the door; and He was discussing the Word.
3 Then they came, bringing a paralytic to Him, who had been picked up *and* was being carried by four men.
4 And when they could not get him to a place in front of Jesus because of the throng, they dug through the roof above Him; and when they had [o]scooped out an opening, they let down the [[o]thickly padded] quilt *or* mat upon which the paralyzed man lay.
5 And when Jesus saw their faith [their confidence in God through Him], He said to the paralyzed man,

m Charles B. Williams, *The New Testament: A Translation.*　**n** James Moulton and George Milligan, *The Vocabulary.*　**o** Marvin Vincent, *Word Studies.*

putting the Word to work

Some people have a hard time coming to Jesus, just as the man mentioned in Mark 2:1–4. They may be "paralyzed" by their doubts, their questions, or even their fears. Is there anyone in your life like this? Make a commitment to do whatever it takes to help this person see Jesus. Ask the Holy Spirit to break through the walls of their unbelief.

Son, your sins are forgiven [you] *and* put away [that is, the ᵖpenalty is remitted, the sense of guilt removed, and you are made upright and in right standing with God].

6 Now some of the scribes were sitting there, holding a dialogue with themselves as they questioned in their hearts,

7 Why does this �q Man talk like this? He is blaspheming! Who can forgive sins [ᵖremove guilt, remit the penalty, and bestow righteousness instead] except God alone?

8 And at once Jesus, becoming fully aware in His spirit that they thus debated within themselves, said to them, Why do you argue (debate, reason) about all this in your hearts?

9 Which is easier: to say to the paralyzed man, Your sins are forgiven *and* ᵖput away, or to say, Rise, take up your sleeping pad *or* mat, and start walking about [and ᵖkeep on walking]?

10 But that you may know positively *and* beyond a doubt that the Son of Man has right *and* authority *and* power on earth to forgive sins—He said to the paralyzed man,

11 I say to you, arise, pick up *and* carry your sleeping pad *or* mat, and be going on home.

12 And he arose at once and picked up the sleeping pad *or* mat and went out

before them all, so that they were all amazed and ʳrecognized *and* praised *and* thanked God, saying, We have never seen anything like this before!

13 [Jesus] went out again along the seashore; and all the multitude kept gathering about Him, and He kept teaching them.

14 And as He was passing by, He saw Levi (Matthew) son of Alphaeus sitting at the tax office, and He said to him, Follow Me! [Be ˢjoined to Me as a disciple, side with My party!] And he arose and joined Him as His disciple *and* sided with His party *and* accompanied Him.

15 And as Jesus, together with His disciples, sat at table in his [Levi's]

life point

Do you ever hold a negative dialogue with yourself as the scribes were doing in Mark 2:6? The fact is that you probably talk to yourself more than you talk to anybody else. The question is, what are you saying to yourself?

These scribes were questioning Jesus' authority to be God's Son by asking, "Who does this Man think He is?" They did not speak those words out loud, but said them deep within their hearts.

Without a word being spoken, Jesus picked up right away that they were arguing, debating, and reasoning within themselves. As believers we need to avoid this kind of negative self-talk. It is a serious matter that we need to deal with, just as Jesus dealt with it. We need to learn to have simple faith, to be discerning, and to be led by the Spirit instead of by our own divisive thoughts and reasoning.

---

p Kenneth Wuest, *Word Studies*. q Capitalized because of what He is, the spotless Son of God, not what the speakers may have thought He was. r Hermann Cremer, *Biblico-Theological Lexicon*. s Joseph Thayer, *A Greek-English Lexicon*.

house, many tax collectors and persons ['definitely stained] with sin were dining with Him, for there were many who walked the same road (followed) with Him.

16 And the scribes [belonging to the party] of the Pharisees, when they saw that He was eating with [those 'definitely known to be especially wicked] sinners and tax collectors, said to His disciples, Why does He eat *and drink* with tax collectors and [notorious] sinners?

17 And when Jesus heard it, He said to them, Those who are strong *and* well have no need of a physician, but those who are weak *and* sick; I came not to call the righteous ones *to repentance,* but sinners (the "erring ones and 'all those not free from sin).

18 Now John's disciples and the Pharisees were observing a fast; and [some people] came and asked Jesus, Why are John's disciples and the disciples of the Pharisees fasting, but Your disciples are not doing so?

19 Jesus answered them, Can the wedding guests fast (abstain from food and drink) while the bridegroom is with them? As long as they have the bridegroom with them, they cannot fast.

20 But the days will come when the bridegroom will be taken away from them, and they will fast in that day.

21 No one sews a patch of unshrunken (new) goods on an old garment; if he does, the patch tears away from it, the new from the old, and the rent (tear) becomes bigger *and* worse [than it was before].

22 And no one puts new wine into old wineskins; if he does, the wine will burst the skins, and the wine is lost and the bottles destroyed; but new wine is to be put in new (fresh) wineskins.

23 One Sabbath He was going along beside the fields of standing grain, and as they made their way, His disciples began to ⱽpick off the grains. [Deut. 23:25.]

24 And the Pharisees said to Him, Look! Why are they doing what is not permitted *or* lawful on the Sabbath?

25 And He said to them, Have you never [even] read what David did when he was in need and was hungry, he and those who were accompanying him?—

26 How he went into the house of God when Abiathar was the high priest, and ate the sacred loaves set forth [before God], which it is not permitted *or* lawful for any but the priests to eat, and [how he] also gave [them] to those who were with him? [I Sam. 21:1-6; II Sam. 8:17.]

27 And Jesus said to them, The Sabbath was made on account *and* for the sake of man, not man for the Sabbath; [Exod. 23:12; Deut. 5:14.]

28 So the Son of Man is Lord even of the Sabbath.

3 AGAIN JESUS went into a synagogue, and a man was there who had one withered hand [ᵂas the result of accident or disease].

2 And [the Pharisees] kept watching Jesus [closely] to see whether He would cure him on the Sabbath, so that they might get a charge to bring against Him [ᵛformally].

3 And He said to the man who had the withered hand, Get up [and stand here] in the midst.

4 And He said to them, Is it lawful *and* right on the Sabbath to do good or to do evil, to save life or to take it? But they kept silence.

5 And He glanced around at them with vexation *and* anger, grieved at

t Joseph Thayer, *A Greek-English Lexicon.* **u** Robert Young, *Analytical Concordance to the Bible.* **v** Kenneth Wuest, *Word Studies.* **w** Marvin Vincent, *Word Studies.*

the hardening of their hearts, and said to the man, Hold out your hand. He held it out, and his hand was [completely] restored.

6 Then the Pharisees went out and immediately held a consultation with the Herodians against Him, how they might [devise some means to] put Him to death.

7 And Jesus retired with His disciples to the lake, and a great throng from Galilee followed Him. Also from Judea

8 And from Jerusalem and Idumea and from beyond the Jordan and from about Tyre and Sidon—a vast multitude, hearing all the many things that He was doing, came to Him.

9 And He told His disciples to have a little boat in [constant] readiness for Him because of the crowd, lest they press hard upon Him *and* crush Him.

10 For He had healed so many that all who had distressing bodily diseases kept falling upon Him *and* pressing upon Him in order that they might touch Him.

11 And the spirits, the unclean ones, ˣas often as they might see Him, fell down before Him and kept screaming out, You are the Son of God!

12 And He charged them strictly *and* severely under penalty again *and* again that they should not make Him known.

13 And He went up on the hillside and called to Him [ʸfor Himself] those whom He wanted *and* chose, and they came to Him.

14 And He appointed twelve to ʸcontinue to be with Him, and that He might send them out to preach [as apostles or special messengers]

15 And to have authority *and* power to *heal the sick and to* drive out demons:

16 [They were] Simon, and He surnamed [him] Peter;

17 James son of Zebedee and John the brother of James, and He surnamed them Boanerges, that is, Sons of Thunder;

18 And Andrew, and Philip, and Bartholomew (Nathaniel), and Matthew, and Thomas, and James son of Alphaeus, and Thaddaeus (Judas, not Iscariot), and Simon the Cananaean [also called Zelotes],

19 And Judas Iscariot, he who betrayed Him.

20 Then He went to a house [probably Peter's], but a throng came together again, so that Jesus and His disciples could not even take food.

21 And when those ᶻwho belonged to Him (ᵃHis kinsmen) heard it, they went out to take Him by force, for they kept saying, He is out of ᵇHis mind (beside Himself, deranged)!

22 And the scribes who came down from Jerusalem said, He is possessed by Beelzebub, and, By [the help of] the prince of demons He is casting out demons.

23 And He summoned them to Him and said to them in parables (illustrations or comparisons put beside truths to explain them), How can Satan drive out Satan?

24 And if a kingdom is divided *and* rebelling against itself, that kingdom cannot stand.

25 And if a house is divided (split into factions and rebelling) against itself, that house will not be able to last.

26 And if Satan has raised an insurrection against himself and is divided, he cannot stand but is [surely] coming to an end.

27 But no one can go into a strong man's house and ransack his house-

---

x Marvin Vincent, *Word Studies*. **y** Kenneth Wuest, *Word Studies*. **z** William Tyndale, *The Tyndale Bible*. **a** John Wycliffe, *The Wycliffe Bible*. **b** Capitalized for what He is, the spotless Son of God, not what the speakers may have thought He was.

life point

Jesus teaches us in Mark 3:27 that we must bind the strong man if we want to plunder his house. The strong man represents the devil. Do not ever become passive as a Christian and forget that Jesus instructs us to take authority over and bind the enemy.

---

hold goods right and left *and* seize them as plunder unless he first binds the strong man; then indeed he may [thoroughly] plunder his house. [Isa. 49:24, 25.]

28 Truly *and* solemnly I say to you, all sins will be forgiven the sons of men, and whatever abusive *and* blasphemous things they utter;

29 But whoever speaks abusively against *or* maliciously misrepresents the Holy Spirit can never get forgiveness, but is guilty of *and* is in the grasp of ᶜan everlasting trespass.

30 For they ᵈpersisted in saying, ᵉHe has an unclean spirit.

31 Then His mother and His brothers came and, standing outside, they sent word to Him, calling [for] Him.

32 And a crowd was sitting around Him, and they said to Him, Your mother and Your brothers *and Your sisters* are outside asking for You.

33 And He replied, Who are My mother and My brothers?

34 And looking around on those who sat in a circle about Him, He said, See! Here are My mother and My brothers;

35 For whoever does the things God wills is My brother and sister and mother!

4 AGAIN JESUS began to teach beside the lake. And a very great crowd gathered about Him, so that He got into a ship in order to sit in it on the sea, and the whole crowd was at the lakeside on the shore.

2 And He taught them many things in parables (illustrations or comparisons put beside truths to explain them), and in His teaching He said to them:

3 Give attention to this! Behold, a sower went out to sow.

4 And as he was sowing, some seed fell along the path, and the birds came and ate it up.

5 Other seed [of the same kind] fell on ground full of rocks, where it had not much soil; and at once it sprang up, because it had no depth of soil;

6 And when the sun came up, it was scorched, and because it had not taken root, it withered away.

7 Other seed [of the same kind] fell among thorn plants, and the thistles grew *and* pressed together *and* utterly choked *and* suffocated it, and it yielded no grain.

8 And other seed [of the same kind] fell into good (well-adapted) soil and brought forth grain, growing up and increasing, and yielded up to thirty times as much, and sixty times as much, and even a hundred times as much as had been sown.

9 And He said, He who has ears to hear, let him be hearing [and let him ᶠconsider, and comprehend].

10 And as soon as He was alone, those who were around Him, with the Twelve [apostles], began to ask Him about the parables.

11 And He said to them, To you has been entrusted the mystery of the kingdom of God [that is, ᵍthe secret counsels of God which are hidden from the ungodly]; but for those outside [ᵈof our circle] everything becomes a parable,

c John Wycliffe, *The Wycliffe Bible.* d Marvin Vincent, *Word Studies.* e Capitalized for what He is, the spotless Son of God, not what the speakers may have thought He was. f Joseph Thayer, *A Greek-English Lexicon.* g Kenneth Wuest, *Word Studies.*

12 In order that they may [indeed] look *and* look but not see *and* perceive, and may hear *and* hear but not grasp *and* comprehend, [h]lest haply they should turn again, and it [[i]their willful rejection of the truth] should be forgiven them. [Isa. 6:9, 10; Matt. 13:13-15.]

13 And He said to them, Do you not discern *and* understand this parable? How then is it possible for you to discern *and* understand all the parables?

14 The sower sows the Word.

15 The ones along the path are those who have the Word sown [in their hearts], but when they hear, Satan comes at once and [by force] takes away the message which is sown in them.

16 And in the same way the ones sown upon stony ground are those who, when they hear the Word, at once receive *and* accept *and* welcome it with joy;

17 And they have no real root in themselves, and so they endure for a little while; then when trouble or persecution arises on account of the Word, they immediately are offended (become displeased, indignant, resentful) *and* they stumble *and* fall away.

18 And the ones sown among the thorns are others who hear the Word;

19 Then the cares *and* anxieties of the world *and* distractions of the age, and the pleasure *and* delight *and* false glamour *and* deceitfulness of riches, and the craving *and* passionate desire for other things creep in and choke *and* suffocate the Word, and it becomes fruitless.

20 And those sown on the good (well-adapted) soil are the ones who hear the Word and receive *and* accept *and* welcome it and bear fruit—some thirty times as much as was sown, some sixty times as much, and some [even] a hundred times as much.

21 And He said to them, Is the lamp brought in to be put under a [j]peck measure or under a bed, and not [to be put] on the lampstand?

22 [[k]Things are hidden temporarily only as a means to revelation.] For there is nothing hidden except to be revealed, nor is anything [temporarily] kept secret except in order that it may be made known.

23 If any man has ears to hear, let him be listening *and* let him perceive *and* comprehend.

24 And He said to them, Be careful what you are hearing. The measure [l][of thought and study] you give [to [m]the truth you hear] will be the measure [l][of virtue and knowledge] that comes back to you—and more [besides] will be given to you *who hear.*

25 For to him who has will more be given; and from him who has nothing, even what he has will be taken away [[n]by force],

life point

Mark 4:24 is a great scripture! It tells us that the more time we spend thinking about the Word we read and hear, the more power and ability we will have to obey it—the more revelation knowledge we will have about what we have read or heard. Basically this tells us that we will get out of God's Word what we put into it. I want you to receive maximum benefit from God's awesome Word, so be diligent to read it, study it, and apply it to your life.

h A.T. Robertson, *Word Pictures.* **i** Kenneth Wuest, *Word Studies.* **j** James Moulton and George Milligan, *The Vocabulary.* **k** Henry Swete, *The Gospel According to Saint Mark*; A.T. Robertson, *Word Pictures*; Marvin Vincent, *Word Studies*; and others. **l** W. Robertson Nicoll, ed., *The Expositor's Greek New Testament.* **m** James C. Gray and George M. Adams, *Bible Commentary*; Kenneth Wuest, *Word Studies*; Albert Barnes, *Notes on the New Testament*; and others. **n** Joseph Thayer, *A Greek-English Lexicon.*

when your breakthrough is delayed

I discovered a long time ago that when I became impatient, frustrated, and fretful it was because I tried to make something happen that only God could make happen. I was caught up in works of the flesh, which I define as "human energy attempting to do God's job."

Sometimes when we pray and believe for a breakthrough, it seems like nothing happens. If we really want to know how to act during those times, we can receive much help from the story of the patient farmer Jesus spoke of in Mark 4:26–28.

The farmer sows his seed in the ground and then goes on his way, sleeping and rising. Eventually, the ground brings forth its yield on its own. The farmer does not know how the harvest will come or exactly when it will come, but his job is to get up in the morning, do his work, and go to bed at night. He keeps up his patient vigil over the seed he has sown until he receives the harvest.

Jesus was telling us that this is the way we should respond to God. Our problem is that we are often impatient. We continually ask God, "How are You going to do this? When are You going to do that?"

A farmer never knows exactly when his crop will come in. He just keeps sleeping and rising, does what he can to enrich his soil and cultivate his crops, but leaves the rest in the hands of the Creator. Let me encourage you to do likewise.

26 And He said, The kingdom of God is like a man who scatters seed upon the ground,

27 And then continues sleeping and rising night and day while the seed sprouts and grows *and* °increases—he knows not how.

28 The earth produces [acting] by itself—first the blade, then the ear, then the full grain in the ear.

29 But when the grain is ripe *and* permits, immediately he ᴾsends forth [the reapers] *and* puts in the sickle, because the harvest stands ready.

30 And He said, With what can we compare the kingdom of God, or what parable shall we use to illustrate *and* explain it?

31 It is like a grain of mustard seed, which, when sown upon the ground, is the smallest of all seeds upon the earth;

32 Yet after it is sown, it grows up and becomes the greatest of all garden herbs and puts out large branches, so that the birds of the air are able to make nests *and* dwell in its shade.

33 With many such parables [Jesus] spoke the Word to them, as they were able to hear *and* °to comprehend *and* understand.

34 He did not tell them anything without a parable; but privately to His disciples (�q those who were peculiarly His own) He explained everything [fully].

35 On that same day [when] evening

o Joseph Thayer, *A Greek-English Lexicon*.   p Marvin Vincent, *Word Studies*.   q Kenneth Wuest, *Word Studies*.

had come, He said to them, Let us go over to the other side [of the lake].

36 And leaving the throng, they took Him with them, [just] as He was, in the boat [in which He was sitting]. And other boats were with Him.

37 And a furious storm of wind [ʳof hurricane proportions] arose, and the waves kept beating into the boat, so that it was already becoming filled.

38 But He [Himself] was in the stern [of the boat], asleep on the [leather] cushion; and they awoke Him and said to Him, Master, do You not care that we are perishing?

39 And He arose and rebuked the wind and said to the sea, Hush now! Be still (muzzled)! And the wind ceased (ˢsank to rest as if exhausted by its beating) and there was [immediately] a great calm (ᵗa perfect peacefulness).

life point

When Jesus and the disciples were crossing the lake and a storm arose, the disciples panicked, but Jesus was able to stand up in the boat and rebuke the storm (see Mark 4:39).

You cannot rebuke the storms in your life if you have a storm on the inside of you. The disciples could not rebuke the storm because they lost their peace and were as "stormy" as the storm. But when Jesus spoke out of His reservoir of peace for the wind and waves to be still, immediately there was calm.

40 He said to them, Why are you so timid *and* fearful? How is it that you have no faith (no ᵘfirmly relying trust)?

41 And they were filled with great awe *and* ˢfeared exceedingly and said one to another, Who then is this, that even wind and sea obey Him?

5 THEY CAME to the other side of the sea to the region of the Gerasenes.

2 And as soon as He got out of the boat, there met Him out of the tombs a man [under the power] of an unclean spirit.

3 This man ʳcontinually lived among the tombs, and no one could subdue him any more, even with a chain;

4 For he had been bound often with shackles for the feet and ᵛhandcuffs, but the handcuffs of [light] chains he wrenched apart, and the shackles he rubbed *and* ground together *and* broke in pieces; and no one had strength enough to restrain *or* tame him.

5 Night and day among the tombs and on the mountains he was always ᵛshrieking *and* screaming and ʷbeating *and* bruising *and* ˣcutting himself with stones.

6 And when from a distance he saw Jesus, he ran and fell on his knees before Him in homage,

7 And crying out with a loud voice, he said, What have You to do with me, Jesus, Son of the Most High God? [What is there in common between us?] I ʳsolemnly implore you by God, do not begin to torment me!

8 For Jesus was commanding, Come out of the man, you unclean spirit!

9 And He asked him, What is your name? He replied, My name is Legion, for we are many.

10 And he kept begging Him urgently not to send them [himself and the

---

r Kenneth Wuest, *Word Studies.* s Marvin Vincent, *Word Studies.* t John Wycliffe, *The Wycliffe Bible.* u Hermann Cremer, *Biblico-Theological Lexicon.* v Joseph Thayer, *A Greek-English Lexicon.* w James Moulton and George Milligan, *The Vocabulary.* x G. Abbott-Smith, *Manual Greek Lexicon.*

what to do on a sinking boat

It is always exciting when Jesus says to us, "Let's do a new thing." To me the phrase, "Let us go over to the other side" (Mark 4:35), is equivalent to saying, "Promotion is coming," or, "Blessings are on their way," or "Come up higher," or any variety of phrases God uses to communicate to us that it is time for a change.

I am sure the disciples were excited to see what would happen on "the other side." What they did not expect or foresee was a raging storm on the way!

The disciples probably were not nearly as excited in the middle of their voyage as they may have been in the beginning.

Although God often calls us to launch out to a new destination, He usually does not let us know what is going to happen on the way. We leave the security of where we are and start out for the blessings of the other side, but it is often in the middle where we encounter the storms.

The middle is often a place of testing.

The storm that the disciples experienced was no little "April shower" or harmless summer squall, but a *storm of hurricane proportions*.

The waves were not gently rolling and tossing, they were beating into the boat with such fury that it quickly filled with water. That would be enough to frighten anyone.

The storm was in full force, and Jesus was asleep! Does that sound familiar? Have you ever had times when you felt that you were sinking fast, and Jesus was asleep? You prayed and prayed and heard nothing from God. You spent time with Him and tried to sense His presence, and yet you felt nothing. You searched for an answer, but no matter how hard you struggled against the wind and waves, the storm raged on and you did not know what to do about it.

We sometimes refer to those seasons as "the midnight hour" or "the dark night of the soul."

At times like these, when it looks like the boat is sinking with us in it, we must use our faith. Jesus simply wanted His disciples to believe Him. He said, "Let us go to the other side." He expected them to believe that if He said it, it would happen. But, like us, they were afraid. Jesus calmed the storm, but He rebuked the disciples for their lack of faith.

It is vital to our future that we grow in faith, which shows confidence and trust in God. We must learn to conquer our fear and press on to the other side. We must also learn to have peace and joy in the midst of the storm, not only when it has passed.

other demons] away out of that region.
11 Now a great herd of hogs was grazing there on the hillside.
12 And *the demons* begged Him, saying, Send us to the hogs, that we may go into them!
13 So He gave them permission. And the unclean spirits came out [of the man] and entered into the hogs; and the herd, numbering about 2,000, rushed headlong down the steep slope into the sea and were drowned in the sea.
14 The hog feeders ran away, and told [it] in the town and in the country. And [the people] came to see what it was that had taken place.
15 And they came to Jesus and looked intently *and* searchingly at the man who had been a demoniac, sitting there, clothed and in his right mind, [the same man] who had had the legion [of demons]; and they were ʸseized with alarm *and* struck with fear.
16 And those who had seen it related in full what had happened to the man possessed by demons and to the hogs.
17 And they began to beg [Jesus] to leave their neighborhood.
18 And when He had stepped into the boat, the man who had been controlled by the unclean spirits kept begging Him that he might be with Him.
19 But Jesus refused to permit him, but said to him, Go home to your own [family and relatives and friends] and bring back word to them of how much the Lord has done for you, and [how He has] had sympathy for you *and* mercy on you.
20 And he departed and began to publicly proclaim in Decapolis [the region of the ten cities] how much Jesus had done for him, and all the people were astonished *and* marveled. [Matt. 4:25.]

21 And when Jesus had recrossed in the boat to the other side, a great throng gathered about Him, and He was at the lakeshore.
22 Then one of the rulers of the synagogue came up, Jairus by name; and seeing Him, he prostrated himself at His feet
23 And begged Him earnestly, saying, My little daughter is at the point of death. Come and lay Your hands on her, so that she may be healed *and* live.
24 And Jesus went with him; and a great crowd kept following Him and pressed Him ʸfrom all sides [so as almost to suffocate Him].
25 And there was a woman who had had a flow of blood for twelve years,
26 And who had endured much ᶻsuffering under [the hands of] many physicians and had spent all that she had, and was no better but instead grew worse.
27 She had heard the reports concerning Jesus, and she came up behind Him in the throng and touched His garment,
28 For she kept saying, If I only touch His garments, I shall be restored to health.
29 And immediately her flow of blood was dried up at the source, and [ᵃsuddenly] she felt in her body that she was healed of her [ʸdistressing] ailment.
30 And Jesus, recognizing in Himself that the power proceeding from Him had gone forth, turned around immediately in the crowd and said, Who touched My clothes?
31 And the disciples kept saying to Him, You see the crowd pressing hard around You ʸfrom all sides, and You ask, Who touched Me?
32 Still He kept looking around to see her who had done it.

y Joseph Thayer, *A Greek-English Lexicon.* **z** Marvin Vincent, *Word Studies.* **a** Kenneth Wuest, *Word Studies.*

life point

The woman with the issue of blood, whose story is told in Mark 5:25-29, had the same problem for twelve years. She had suffered greatly, and no one was able to help her.

Surely this woman was attacked with thoughts of hopelessness. When she thought about going to Jesus, surely she must have heard, "What's the use?" But she pressed on past the crowd that was so thick on all sides that it was suffocating. As she touched the hem of Jesus' garment, His healing virtue flowed to her and she was made well.

Whatever you are facing today—no matter how long you have struggled with it—let me encourage you to press on. Whatever it takes, reach out and touch Jesus!

33 But the woman, knowing what had been done for her, though alarmed *and* frightened and trembling, fell down before Him and told Him the whole truth.
34 And He said to her, Daughter, your faith (your ᵇtrust and confidence in Me, springing from faith in God) has restored you to health. Go in ᶜ(into) peace and be continually healed *and* freed from your [ᵇdistressing bodily] disease.
35 While He was still speaking, there came some from the ruler's house,

who said [to Jairus], Your daughter has died. Why bother *and* distress the Teacher any further?
36 ᵈ*Overhearing* but ignoring what they said, Jesus said to the ruler of the synagogue, Do not be seized with alarm *and* struck with fear; only keep on believing.
37 And He permitted no one to accompany Him except Peter and James and John the brother of James.
38 When they arrived at the house of the ruler of the synagogue, He ᶜlooked [carefully and with understanding] at [the] tumult and *the people* weeping and wailing loudly.
39 And when He had gone in, He said to them, Why do you make an uproar and weep? The little girl is not dead but is sleeping.
40 And they laughed *and* ᵉjeered at Him. But He put them all out, and, taking the child's father and mother and those who were with Him, He went in where the little girl was *lying*.
41 Gripping her [firmly] by the hand, He said to her, Talitha cumi—which translated is, Little girl, I say to you, arise [ᵇfrom the sleep of death]!
42 And instantly the girl got up and started walking around—for she was twelve years old. And they were utterly astonished *and* overcome with amazement.
43 And He strictly commanded *and* warned them that no one should know this, and He [ᵇexpressly] told them to give her [something] to eat.

speak the Word

God, when I am tempted to be afraid, may I remember Jesus' words to the ruler of the synagogue: "Do not be seized with alarm and struck with fear; only keep on believing."
ADAPTED FROM MARK 5:36

b Joseph Thayer, *A Greek-English Lexicon*. **c** Kenneth Wuest, *Word Studies*. **d** Some manuscripts so read. **e** G. Abbott-Smith, *Manual Greek Lexicon*.

6 JESUS WENT away from there and came to His [own] country *and* hometown [Nazareth], and His disciples followed [with] Him.

2 And on the Sabbath He began to teach in the synagogue; and many who listened to Him were utterly astonished, saying, Where did this [f]Man acquire all this? What is the wisdom [the broad and full intelligence which has been] given to Him? What mighty works *and* exhibitions of power are wrought by His hands!

3 Is not this the Carpenter, the son of Mary and the brother of James and Joses and Judas and Simon? And are not His sisters here among us? And they took offense at Him *and* [g]were hurt [that is, they [h]disapproved of Him, and it hindered them from acknowledging His authority] *and* they were caused to stumble *and* fall.

4 But Jesus said to them, A prophet is not without honor (deference, reverence) except in his [own] country and among [his] relatives and in his [own] house.

5 And He was not able to do [h]even one work of power there, except that He laid His hands on a few sickly people [and] cured them.

6 And He marveled because of their unbelief (their lack of faith in Him). And He went about among the surrounding villages and continued teaching.

7 And He called to Him the Twelve [apostles] and began to send them out [as His ambassadors] two by two and gave them authority *and* power over the unclean spirits.

8 He charged them to take nothing for their journey except a walking stick—no bread, [i]no wallet for a collection bag, no money in their belts (girdles, purses)—

9 But to go with sandals on their feet and not to put on two tunics (undergarments).

10 And He told them, Wherever you go into a house, stay there until you leave that place.

11 And if any community will not receive *and* accept *and* welcome you, and they refuse to listen to you, when you depart, shake off the dust that is on your feet, for a testimony against them. [j]*Truly I tell you, it will be more tolerable for Sodom and Gomorrah in the judgment day than for that town.*

12 So they went out and preached that men should repent [[k]that they should change their minds for the better and heartily amend their ways, with abhorrence of their past sins].

13 And they drove out many unclean spirits and anointed with oil many who were sick and cured them.

14 King Herod heard of it, for [Jesus'] name had become well known. [l]He *and* they [of his court] said, John the Baptist has been raised from the dead; that is why these mighty powers [[m]of performing miracles] are at work in Him.

15 [But] others kept saying, It is Elijah! And others said, It is a prophet, like one of the prophets [of old].

16 But when Herod heard [of it], he said, [[n]This very] John, whom I beheaded, has been raised [from the dead].

17 For [this] Herod himself had sent and seized John and bound him in prison for the sake of Herodias, his brother Philip's wife, because he [Herod] had married her.

---

f Capitalized because of what He is, the spotless Son of God, not what the speakers may have thought He was. g William Tyndale, *The Tyndale Bible*. h Kenneth Wuest, *Word Studies*. i James Moulton and George Milligan, *The Vocabulary*. j Some manuscripts do not contain the last section of verse 11. k Joseph Thayer, *A Greek-English Lexicon*. l Some ancient manuscripts read "he," while others read "they." m G. Abbott-Smith, *Manual Greek Lexicon*. n Marvin Vincent, *Word Studies*.

shake off rejection

Mark 6:11 speaks of rejection. When I first started preaching, I was extremely insecure and often felt rejected. If a few people got up and walked out of the service, the devil told me they were leaving because they did not like to see a woman preaching. That did happen a few times in churches whose pastors warned me ahead of time that they had never had a woman in their pulpit and were not sure how their congregations would react. When it did happen, I was always embarrassed and I felt bad.

Then God gave me this scripture from Luke 10:16: "He who hears and heeds you [disciples] hears and heeds Me; and he who slights and rejects you slights and rejects Me; and he who slights and rejects Me slights and rejects Him who sent Me."

The Lord simply told me, "I am the One who called you. Do not worry about what people think. If you do, you are going to worry all your life because the devil will never stop finding people who will think something unkind about you."

In Mark 6:7–11 when Jesus sent His disciples out into the towns to preach, He told them what to do if people rejected them. He did not tell them to stand around and cry and be wounded, hurt, bleeding, and embarrassed. He told them to "shake it off!"

You and I need to take Jesus' advice and learn to shake off our troubles, problems, disappointments, and rejections. So if there is a call on your life, and one person or group of people rejects you, there will be others who will accept you.

Just shake off the rejection and move on.

18 For John had told Herod, It is not lawful *and* you have no right to have your brother's wife.

19 And Herodias was angry (enraged) with him *and* held a grudge against him and wanted to kill him; but she could not,

20 For Herod had [°a reverential] fear of John, knowing that he was a righteous and holy man, and [continually] kept him safe [Punder guard]. When he heard [John speak], he was much perplexed; and [yet] he heard him gladly.

21 But an opportune time came [for Herodias] when Herod on his birthday gave a banquet for his nobles and the high military commanders and chief men of Galilee.

22 For when the daughter qof Herodias herself came in and danced, she pleased *and* qfascinated Herod and his guests; and the king said to the girl, Ask me for whatever you desire, and I will give it to you.

23 And he put himself under oath to her, Whatever you ask me, I will give it to you, even to the half of my kingdom. [Esth. 5:3, 6.]

24 Then she left the room and said to

o G. Abbott-Smith, *Manual Greek Lexicon.*   p Marvin Vincent, *Word Studies.*   q Kenneth Wuest, *Word Studies.*

her mother, What shall I ask for [myself]? And she replied, The head of John the Baptist!

25 And she rushed back instantly to the king and requested, saying, I wish you to give me right now the head of John the Baptist on a platter.

26 And the king was deeply pained *and* grieved *and* exceedingly sorry, but because of his oaths and his guests, he did not want to slight her [by breaking faith with her].

27 And immediately the king sent off one [of the soldiers] of his bodyguard and gave him orders to bring [John's] head. He went and beheaded him in the prison

28 And brought his head on a platter and handed it to the girl, and the girl gave it to her mother.

29 When his disciples learned of it, they came and took [John's] body and laid it in a tomb.

30 The apostles [sent out as missionaries] came back *and* gathered together to Jesus, and told Him all that they had done and taught.

31 And He said to them, [ʳAs for you] come away by yourselves to a deserted place, and rest a while—for many were [continually] coming and going, and they had not even leisure enough to eat.

32 And they went away in a boat to a solitary place by themselves.

33 Now many [people] saw them going and recognized them, and they ran there on foot from all the surrounding towns, and they got there ahead [of those in the boat].

34 As Jesus landed, He saw a great crowd waiting, and He was moved with compassion for them, because they were like sheep without a shepherd; and He began to teach them many things.

35 And when ʳthe day was already far gone, His disciples came to Him and said, This is a desolate *and* isolated place, and the hour is now late.

36 Send the crowds away to go into the country and villages round about and buy themselves something to eat.

37 But He replied to them, Give them something to eat yourselves. And they said to Him, Shall we go and buy 200 ˢdenarii [about forty dollars] worth of bread and give it to them to eat? [II Kings 4:42-44.]

38 And He said to them, How many loaves do you have? Go and see. And when they [had looked and] knew, they said, Five [loaves] and two fish.

39 Then He commanded the people all to recline on the green grass by companies.

40 So they threw themselves down in ranks of hundreds and fifties [with the ᵗregularity of an arrangement of beds of herbs, looking ᵘlike so many garden plots].

41 And taking the five loaves and two fish, He looked up to heaven and, praising God, gave thanks and broke the loaves and kept on giving them to the disciples to set before the people; and He [also] divided the two fish among [them] all.

putting the Word to work

Do you ever feel like you do not have much to offer in ministry? As you willingly offer Jesus what you do have, He will bless and multiply it to meet the needs of others, as He did in the story found in Mark 6:30–44. What may seem to you like a small contribution of time, treasure or talent, can become an enormous blessing when you put it in God's hands.

---

r Kenneth Wuest, *Word Studies*. **s** The usual pay for a day's work was one denarius. **t** James Moulton and George Milligan, *The Vocabulary*. **u** Richard Trench, *Notes on the Miracles of our Lord*.

the lonely leader

In Mark 6:45–47, we see that Jesus sent the disciples and the crowds away and ended up "by Himself." Apparently Jesus chose to have a few moments of solitude. All leaders need solitude at times, but there will also be times when we face loneliness. That is part of leadership. I do not know what you think about people who are "at the top" in leadership, but let me share a little secret with you: Sometimes it can get pretty lonely up there.

The relationship between a Christian leader and those who work with him is similar to an employer/employee relationship. There may be some exceptions, but usually it is not a workable situation for the boss or leader to become extremely close to those under his authority. Sometimes employees do not realize this fact and think their employer separates himself from them because he thinks he is better than they are.

The fact is that usually, if a spiritual leader tries to be really chummy with the people who work for him, they frequently develop a spirit of familiarity that causes them to take liberties with him they should not take and to assume things about the relationship they should not assume. Through years of experience I have learned that I simply cannot become close buddies with most of my employees because it inevitably causes problems. As I said earlier, there are exceptions, but they are rare.

When you are in a position of leadership, people tend to look up to you. They may even develop expectations of you that are not realistic. They know you are only human, as they are, but they really do not want to see your human flaws and weaknesses. For example, they do not want to ever see you lose your temper or say anything negative about anything or anybody. The first time something like that happens, the devil whispers in their ear, "How can you receive ministry from someone who acts like that?"

Whatever position of leadership you may fill, realize that you must depend upon God to bring what I call "divine connections" into your life. By that I mean people who are right for you, people to whom you can get close, people who understand your call and how they should relate to you and your ministry.

One of the things about leadership you need to understand is that if you really want to be a key leader, then you will probably experience some loneliness.

---

42 And they all ate and were satisfied.

43 And they took up twelve [ᵛsmall hand] baskets full of broken pieces [from the loaves] and of the fish.

44 And those who ate the loaves were 5,000 men.

45 And at once He insisted that the disciples get into the boat and go ahead of Him to the other side to

v Marvin Vincent, *Word Studies*. See also footnote on Matt. 14:20.

Bethsaida, while He was sending the throng away.

46 And after He had taken leave of them, He went off into the hills to pray.

47 Now when evening had come, the boat was out in the middle of the lake, and He was by Himself on the land.

48 And having seen that they were troubled *and* tormented in [their] rowing, for the wind was against them, about the fourth watch of the night [between 3:00-6:00 a.m.] He came to them, walking [directly] on the sea. And He acted as if He meant to pass by them,

49 But when they saw Him walking on the sea they thought it was a ghost, and ᵂraised a [deep, throaty] shriek of terror.

50 For they all saw Him and were agitated (troubled and filled with fear and dread). But immediately He talked with them and said, Take heart! I AM! Stop being alarmed *and* afraid. [Exod. 3:14.]

51 And He went up into the boat with them, and the wind ceased (ˣsank to rest as if exhausted by its own beating). And they were astonished exceedingly [beyond measure],

52 For they failed to consider *or* understand [the teaching and meaning of the miracle of] the loaves; [in fact] their hearts had ᵂgrown callous [had become dull and had ᵂlost the power of understanding].

53 And when they had crossed over, they reached the land of Gennesaret and ᵂcame to [anchor at] the shore.

54 As soon as they got out of the boat, [the people] recognized Him,

55 And they ran about the whole countryside, and began to carry around sick people on their sleeping pads *or* mats to any place where they heard that He was.

56 And wherever He came into villages or cities or the country, they would lay the sick in the marketplaces and beg Him that they might touch even the fringe of His outer garment, and as many as touched Him were restored to health.

7 NOW THERE gathered together to [Jesus] the Pharisees and some of the scribes who had come from Jerusalem,

2 For they had seen that some of His disciples ate with ʸcommon hands, that is, unwashed [with hands defiled and unhallowed, because they had not given them a ᶻceremonial washing]—

3 For the Pharisees and all of the Jews do not eat unless [merely for ceremonial reasons] they wash their hands [diligently ᵃup to the elbow] with clenched fist, adhering [carefully and faithfully] to the tradition of [practices and customs handed down to them by] their forefathers [to be observed].

4 And [when they come] from the marketplace, they do not eat unless they purify themselves; and there are many other traditions [oral, man-made laws handed down to them, which they observe faithfully and diligently, such as], the washing of cups and wooden pitchers and wide-mouthed jugs and utensils of copper and ᵇbeds—

5 And the Pharisees and scribes kept asking [Jesus], Why do Your disciples not order their way of living according to the tradition handed down by the forefathers [to be observed], but eat

---

w Joseph Thayer, *A Greek-English Lexicon*. **x** Marvin Vincent, *Word Studies*. **y** William Tyndale, *The Tyndale Bible*. **z** Charles B. Williams, *The New Testament: A Translation*. **a** G. Abbott-Smith, *Manual Greek Lexicon*. **b** James Moulton and George Milligan, *The Vocabulary* and Robert Young, *Analytical Concordance* agree with most lexicons in reading "beds" here. Some manuscripts end verse 4 after "utensils of copper."

with hands unwashed *and* ceremonially not purified?

6 But He said to them, Excellently *and* truly [^c^so that there will be no room for blame] did Isaiah prophesy of you, the pretenders *and* hypocrites, as it stands written: These people [constantly] honor Me with their lips, but their hearts hold off *and* are far distant from Me.

7 In vain (fruitlessly and without profit) do they worship Me, ordering *and* teaching [to be obeyed] as doctrines the commandments *and* precepts of men. [Isa. 29:13.]

8 You disregard *and* give up *and* ask to depart from you the commandment of God and cling to the tradition of men [keeping it carefully and faithfully].

9 And He said to them, You have a fine way of rejecting [thus thwarting and nullifying and doing away with] the commandment of God in order to keep your tradition (your own human regulations)!

10 For Moses said, Honor (revere with tenderness of feeling and deference) your father and your mother, and, He who curses *or* reviles *or* speaks evil of *or* abuses *or* treats improperly his father or mother, let him surely die. [Exod. 20:12; 21:17; Lev. 20:9; Deut. 5:16.]

11 But [as for you] you say, A man is exempt if he tells [his] father or [his] mother, What you would otherwise have gained from me [everything I have that would have been of use to you] is Corban, that is, is a gift [already given as an offering to God],

12 Then you no longer are permitting him to do anything for [his] father or mother [but are letting him off from helping them].

13 Thus you are nullifying *and* mak-

ing void *and* of no effect [the authority of] the Word of God through your tradition, which you [in turn] hand on. And many things of this kind you are doing.

14 And He called the people to [Him] again and said to them, Listen to Me, all of you, and understand [what I say].

15 There is not [even] one thing outside a man which by going into him can pollute *and* defile him; but the things which come out of a man are what defile him *and* make him unhallowed *and* unclean.

16 ^d^If any man has ears to hear, let him be listening [and let him ^e^perceive and comprehend by hearing].

17 And when He had left the crowd and had gone into the house, His disciples began asking Him about the parable.

18 And He said to them, Then are you also unintelligent *and* dull *and* without understanding? Do you not discern *and* see that whatever goes into a man from the outside cannot make him unhallowed *or* unclean,

19 Since it does not reach *and* enter his heart but [only his] digestive tract, and so passes on [into the place designed to receive waste]? Thus He was making *and* declaring all foods [ceremonially] clean [that is, ^f^abolishing the ceremonial distinctions of the Levitical Law].

20 And He said, What comes out of a man is what makes a man unclean *and* renders [him] unhallowed.

21 For from within, [that is] out of the hearts of men, come base *and* wicked thoughts, sexual immorality, stealing, murder, adultery,

22 Coveting (a greedy desire to have more wealth), dangerous *and* destructive wickedness, deceit; ^g^unrestrained

c Joseph Thayer, *A Greek-English Lexicon.* **d** Many manuscripts do not contain this verse. **e** G. Abbott-Smith, *Manual Greek Lexicon.* **f** W. Robertson Nicoll, ed., *The Expositor's Greek New Testament.* **g** Alexander Souter, *Pocket Lexicon of the Greek New Testament.*

(indecent) conduct; an evil eye (envy), slander (evil speaking, malicious misrepresentation, abusiveness), pride ([h]the sin of an uplifted heart against God and man), foolishness (folly, lack of sense, recklessness, thoughtlessness).

23 All these evil [purposes and desires] come from within, and they make the man unclean *and* render him unhallowed.

24 And Jesus arose and went away from there to the region of Tyre *and Sidon*. And He went into a house and did not want anyone to know [that He was there]; but it was not possible for Him to be hidden [from public notice].

25 Instead, at once, a woman whose little daughter had (was under the control of) an unclean spirit heard about Him and came and flung herself down at His feet.

26 Now the woman was a Greek (Gentile), a Syrophoenician by nationality. And she kept begging Him to drive the demon out of her little daughter.

27 And He said to her, First let the children be fed, for it is not becoming *or* proper *or* right to take the children's bread and throw it to the [little house] dogs.

28 But she answered Him, Yes, Lord, yet even the small pups under the table eat the little children's scraps of food.

29 And He said to her, Because of this saying, you may go your way; the demon has gone out of your daughter [permanently].

30 And she went home and found the child thrown on the couch, and the demon departed.

31 Soon after this, Jesus, coming back from the region of Tyre, passed through Sidon on to the Sea of Galilee, through the region of Decapolis [the ten cities].

32 And they brought to Him a man who was deaf and had difficulty in speaking, and they begged Jesus to place His hand upon him.

33 And taking him aside from the crowd [privately], He thrust His fingers into the man's ears and spat and touched his tongue;

34 And looking up to heaven, He sighed as He said, Ephphatha, which means, Be opened!

35 And his ears were opened, his tongue was loosed, and he began to speak distinctly *and* as he should.

36 And Jesus [[i]in His own interest] admonished *and* ordered them sternly *and* expressly to tell no one; but the more He commanded them, the more zealously they proclaimed it.

37 And they were overwhelmingly astonished, saying, He has done everything excellently (commendably and nobly)! He even makes the deaf to hear and the dumb to speak!

8 IN THOSE days when [again] an immense crowd had gathered and they had nothing to eat, Jesus called His disciples to Him and told them,

2 I have pity *and* sympathy for the people *and* My heart goes out to them, for they have been with Me now three days and have nothing [left] to eat;

3 And if I send them away to their homes hungry, they will be feeble through exhaustion *and* faint along the road; and some of them have come a long way.

4 And His disciples replied to Him, How can anyone fill *and* satisfy [these people] with loaves of bread here in [this] desolate *and* uninhabited region?

5 And He asked them, How many

h Marvin Vincent, *Word Studies.* i Kenneth Wuest, *Word Studies:* The Greek uses the middle voice here to show that the charge is given with the speaker's personal interest in view.

loaves have you? They said, Seven.

6 And He commanded the multitude to recline upon the ground, and He [then] took the seven loaves [of bread] and, having given thanks, He broke them and kept on giving them to His disciples to put before [the people], and they placed them before the crowd.

7 And they had a few small fish; and when He had [j]praised God *and* given thanks *and* asked Him to bless them [to their use], He ordered that these also should be set before [them].

8 And they ate and were satisfied; and they took up seven [[k]large provision] baskets full of the broken pieces left over.

9 And there were about 4,000 people. And He dismissed them,

10 And at once He got into the boat with His disciples and went to the district of Dalmanutha (or Magdala).

11 The Pharisees came and began to argue with *and* question Him, demanding from Him a sign (an attesting miracle from heaven) [maliciously] to test Him.

12 And He groaned *and* sighed deeply in His spirit and said, Why does this generation demand a sign? Positively I say to you, no sign shall be given this generation.

13 And He went away *and* left them and, getting into the boat again, He departed to the other side.

14 Now they had [[l]completely] forgotten to bring bread, and they had only one loaf with them in the boat.

15 And Jesus [repeatedly and expressly] charged *and* admonished them, saying, Look out; keep on your guard *and* beware of the leaven of the Pharisees and the leaven of Herod [m]*and the Herodians*.

16 And they discussed it *and* reasoned with one another, It is because we have no bread.

17 And being aware [of it], Jesus said to them, Why are you reasoning *and* saying it is because you have no bread? Do you not yet discern or understand? Are your hearts in [a settled state of] hardness? [Isa. 6:9, 10; Jer. 5:21.]

18 Having eyes, do you not see [with them], and having ears, do you not hear *and* perceive *and* understand the sense of what is said? And do you not remember?

19 When I broke the five loaves for the 5,000, how many [[k]small hand] baskets full of broken pieces did you take up? They said to Him, Twelve.

20 And [when I broke] the seven loaves for the 4,000, how many [[k]large provision] baskets full of broken pieces did you take up? And they said to Him, Seven.

21 And He [n]kept repeating, Do you not yet understand?

22 And they came to Bethsaida. And [people] brought to Him a blind man and begged Him to touch him.

23 And He [o]caught the blind man by the hand and led him out of the village; and when He had spit on his eyes and put His hands upon him, He asked him, Do you [n]possibly] see anything?

24 And he looked up and said, I see people, but [they look] like trees, walking.

25 Then He put His hands on his eyes again; and the man looked intently [that is, fixed his eyes on definite objects], and he was restored and saw everything distinctly [even what was [j]at a distance].

26 And He sent him away to his house, telling [him], Do not [even] enter the village [p]*or tell anyone there.*

---

j Joseph Thayer, *A Greek-English Lexicon.* **k** Marvin Vincent, *Word Studies.* See also footnote on Matt. 14:20. **l** Kenneth Wuest, *Word Studies.* **m** Some ancient manuscripts add "and the Herodians." **n** W. Robertson Nicoll, ed., *The Expositor's Greek New Testament.* **o** William Tyndale, *The Tyndale Bible.* **p** Some manuscripts add this phrase.

reasoning robs your peace

In Mark 8:14–17, as in other Bible passages, we see that Jesus was able to discern the reasoning in the hearts of His disciples, who frequently did not act wisely. They needed revelation, not reasoning.

For all their reasoning, they failed, as we often do, to understand what the Lord was saying to them. Jesus was not talking about literal bread; He was talking about spiritual leaven—about the legalistic teachings and practices of the Pharisees. He warned His disciples to stay away from hypocritical attitudes that say, "Do what I say, not what I do." Jesus knew that a person is poisoned when he does not practice the good things he preaches and hides behind a legalistic front.

But the disciples just did not understand what Jesus meant, and so they "reasoned with one another" about it. Notice in verse 17 that Jesus' response was, "Why are you reasoning . . . Do you not yet discern or understand?"

That is what I used to do. I used to have a lot of problems with reasoning. I was always trying to figure things out. Then one day the Lord said something interesting to me: "As long as you continue to reason, you will never have discernment."

Discernment starts in the heart and enlightens the mind. As long as my mind was so busy reasoning, God could not get through to me, just as Jesus could not get through to His disciples.

This is an important issue. Reasoning is such a huge problem because reasoning is not faith. Romans 8:6 says that the mind of the flesh is sense and reason without the Holy Spirit. It goes on to say that those operating in the mind of the flesh will experience a miserable life, but those who flow in the mind of the Holy Spirit will have life and peace. Reasoning belongs to the mind of the flesh and does not produce good fruit.

The "reasoning" I refer to is reasoning that is *contrary* to the truth in the Word of God. God wants us to use common sense! There is nothing wrong with using our minds in an attempt to understand something. However, when we reason to a point of being confused we need to recognize that we have gone too far. At that point we need to pray for discernment and wait on God to reveal to us what we need to know.

You cannot have peace of mind and heart if you reason without God's truth to enlighten you. If you lack peace in your life, it may be that you are trying to figure out too many things. Stop asking, "Why, God, why?" Just say, "Lord, You know, and I need to be satisfied with that. When You are ready to show me, do so. Until then, with Your help, I am going to enjoy my life, trusting that You are in charge and that You will take care of everything that concerns me."

27 And Jesus went on with His disciples to the villages of Caesarea Philippi; and on the way He asked His disciples, Who do people say that I am?
28 And they answered [Him], John the Baptist; and others [say], Elijah; but others, one of the prophets.
29 And He asked them, But who do you yourselves say that I am? Peter replied to Him, You are the Christ (the Messiah, the Anointed One).
30 And He charged them sharply to tell no one about Him.
31 And He began to teach them that the Son of Man must of necessity suffer many things and be tested *and* disapproved *and* rejected by the elders and the chief priests and the scribes, and be put to death, and after three days rise again [qfrom death].
32 And He said this freely (frankly, plainly, and explicitly, making it unmistakable). And Peter took Him rby the hand *and* led Him aside and then [facing Him] began to rebuke Him.
33 But turning around [His back to Peter] and seeing His disciples, He rebuked Peter, saying, Get behind Me, Satan! For you do not have a mind rintent on promoting what God wills, but what pleases men [you are not on God's side, but that of men].
34 And Jesus called [to Him] the throng with His disciples and said to them, If anyone intends to come after Me, let him deny himself [forget, ignore, disown, and rlose sight of himself and his own interests] and take up his cross, and [sjoining Me as a disciple and siding with My party] follow swith Me [continually, cleaving steadfastly to Me].
35 For whoever wants to save his [thigher, spiritual, eternal] life, will lose it [the tlower, natural, temporal

life point

Jesus heard clearly from His Father that He needed to go to the cross. In Mark 8:31, Jesus told the disciples that it was necessary for Him to suffer many things: be tested, disapproved, rejected by the elders and the chief priests and scribes, and be put to death, but, after three days, rise again from the dead. In response, Peter "took Him by the hand and led Him aside and then [facing Him] began to rebuke Him" (Mark 8:32). But Jesus disregarded Peter's comments and rebuked him. Jesus honored whatever His Father said, no matter what it cost. He was a God-pleaser, not a people-pleaser.

Sometimes we only listen to God if what He says will not cost us anything, or if He tells us what we want to hear. Most of the time, if we receive a discomforting word, we act like Peter and say, "Oh no, this cannot be God!" We cannot have what I call "selective hearing," only paying attention to those things that please us. We must hear and obey all of what God says to us through His Word.

life rwhich is lived only on earth]; and whoever gives up his life [which is lived only on earth] for My sake and the Gospel's will save it [his thigher, spiritual life rin the eternal kingdom of God].
36 For what does it profit a man to gain the whole world, and forfeit his life [rin the eternal kingdom of God]?
37 For what can a man give as an exchange (qa compensation, a ransom, in return) for his [blessed] life [rin the eternal kingdom of God]?

q Hermann Cremer, *Biblico-Theological Lexicon.* **r** Joseph Thayer, *A Greek-English Lexicon.* **s** Kenneth Wuest, *Word Studies.* **t** Robert Jamieson, A.R. Fausett and David Brown, *A Commentary on the Old and New Testaments.*

the cross we bear

Jesus died on the cross for us and He said that those of us who want to follow Him will also have to carry a cross in life (see Mark 8:34). What is the cross that we are expected to bear as believers in Jesus Christ? It's not disasters, disease, devastation, or any other miserable thing we can think of. Some people like to make Christianity seem like a burden to bear rather than a relationship to enjoy.

We do carry a cross, but Jesus said our cross is to live unselfish lives. He said we are to forget about ourselves, losing sight of ourselves and our own interests. That literally means we must live for God and other people. We must lay our lives down and do what is for the good of other people and the kingdom of God. When we think of the choice to live an unselfish life, something deep within us cries out, "What about me?" The good news is that God takes care of us if we do what He asks us to do. Each act of obedience to God's will is a seed we sow that reaps an abundant harvest of peace, joy, and blessing in our own lives.

We can spend our lives trying to take care of ourselves and we will end up needy and unhappy. God has not called us to take care of ourselves. He has not called us to "in-reach," but to "out-reach." Reach out to others, and God will reach into your life and take care of all of your needs.

God's ways sometimes seem to be upside-down from what we think. He says that the first will be last, the greatest of all is the servant of all, and that the way to get more money is to give away some of what you have. None of these statements seem to make sense; they do not make sense to the natural mind, but they do work. God's ways work!

Do not be afraid to trust God with yourself. Give yourself away, sow yourself as a seed and get ready for a great life. Jesus said that unless the grain of wheat falls into the ground and dies, it would abide alone, but if it dies, it will bear much fruit (see John 12:24).

38 For whoever [u]is ashamed [here and now] of Me and My words in this adulterous (unfaithful) and [preeminently] sinful generation, of him will the Son of Man also be ashamed when He comes in the glory (splendor and majesty) of His Father with the holy angels.

9 AND JESUS said to them, Truly *and* solemnly I say to you, there are some standing here who will in no way taste death before they see the kingdom of God come in [its] power.

2 Six days after this, Jesus took with Him Peter and James and John and led them up on a high mountain apart by themselves. And He was transfigured before them *and* became resplendent with divine brightness.

3 And His garments became glistening, intensely white, as no fuller (cloth dresser, launderer) on earth could bleach them.

4 And Elijah appeared [there] to

u A.T. Robertson, *Word Pictures*.

them, accompanied by Moses, and they were [v]holding [a protracted] conversation with Jesus.

5   And [w]Peter took up the conversation, saying, Master, it is good *and* suitable *and* beautiful for us to be here. Let us make three booths (tents)—one for You and one for Moses and one for Elijah.

6   For he did not [really] know what to say, for they were in a violent fright ([x]aghast with dread).

7   And a cloud threw a shadow upon them, and a voice came out of the cloud, saying, This is My Son, the [[x]most dearworthy] Beloved One. Be [v]constantly listening to *and* obeying Him!

8   And looking around, they suddenly no longer saw anyone with them except Jesus only.

9   And as they were coming back down the mountain, He admonished *and* [y]expressly ordered them to tell no one what they had seen until the Son of Man should rise from among the dead.

10 So they carefully *and* faithfully kept the matter to themselves, questioning *and* disputing with one another about what rising from among the dead meant.

11 And they asked Him, Why do the scribes say that it is necessary for Elijah to come first? [Mal. 4:5, 6.]

12 And He said to them, Elijah, it is true, does come first to restore all things *and* [z]set them to rights. And how is it written of the Son of Man that He will suffer many things *and* be utterly despised *and* be treated with contempt *and* rejected? [Isa. 53:3.]

13 But I tell you that Elijah has already come, and [people] did to him whatever they desired, as it is written of him.

14 And when they came to the [nine] disciples, they saw a great crowd around them and scribes questioning *and* disputing with them.

15 And immediately all the crowd, when they saw Jesus [[a]returning from the holy mount, His face and person yet glistening], they were greatly amazed and ran up to Him [and] greeted Him.

16 And He asked them, About what are you questioning *and* discussing with them?

17 And one of the throng replied to Him, Teacher, I brought my son to You, for he has a dumb spirit.

18 And wherever it lays hold of him [so as to make him its own], it dashes him down *and* convulses him, and he foams [at the mouth] and grinds his teeth, *and* he [[v]falls into a motionless stupor and] is wasting away. And I asked Your disciples to drive it out, and they were not able [to do it].

19 And He answered them, O unbelieving generation [without any faith]! How long [v]shall I [have to do] with you? How long am I to bear with you? Bring him to Me.

20 So they brought [the boy] to Him, and when the spirit saw Him, at once

putting the Word to work

Most of us can relate to this man who asked Jesus, " . . . help my weakness of faith!" in Mark 9:24. The man's honesty is so refreshing, and Jesus immediately acts on his behalf. Is there an area of your life where you need more faith? Be honest with God and know that He is compassionate and will meet you where you are. Ask Him to increase your faith daily, that you will know with certainty that all things are possible when you believe.

v Kenneth Wuest, *Word Studies*. **w** H.A.A. Kennedy, *Sources of New Testament Greek*. **x** John Wycliffe, *The Wycliffe Bible*. **y** G. Abbott-Smith, *Manual Greek Lexicon*. **z** Matthew Henry, *Commentary on the Holy Bible*. **a** Richard Trench, *Notes on the Miracles*.

it completely convulsed the boy, and he fell to the ground and kept rolling about, foaming [at the mouth].

21 And [Jesus] asked his father, How long has he had this? And he answered, From the time he was a little boy.

22 And it has often thrown him both into fire and into water, intending to kill him. But if You can do anything, do have pity on us and help us.

23 And Jesus said, [You say to Me], If You can do anything? [Why,] all things can be (are possible) to him who believes!

life point

Mark 9:23 teaches us that "all things can be (are possible) to him who believes!" Spiritually speaking, when you and I believe something, we receive it into our hearts. If a physical manifestation is needed, it will come after we have believed, not before. In the world we are taught to believe what we see. In God's kingdom, we must learn to believe first, and then in due time we will see manifested what we have believed.

24 At once the father of the boy gave [an [b]eager, [c]piercing, inarticulate] cry *with tears,* and he said, Lord, I believe! [Constantly] help my [d]weakness of faith!

25 But when Jesus noticed that a crowd [of people] came running together, He rebuked the unclean spirit, saying to it, You dumb and deaf spirit, I charge you to come out of him and never go into him again.

26 And after giving a [hoarse, clamoring, fear-stricken] shriek of anguish and convulsing him terribly, it came out; and the boy lay [pale and motion-less] like a corpse, so that many of them said, He is dead.

27 But Jesus took [[e]a strong grip of] his hand and began lifting him up, and he stood.

28 And when He had gone indoors, His disciples asked Him privately, Why could not we drive it out?

29 And He replied to them, This kind cannot be driven out by anything but prayer [f]*and fasting.*

30 They went on from there and passed along through Galilee. And He did not wish to have anyone know it,

31 For He was [engaged for the time being in] teaching His disciples. He said to them, The Son of Man is being delivered into the hands of men, and they will put Him to death; and when He has been killed, after three days He will rise [[g]from death].

32 But they did not comprehend what He was saying, and they were afraid to ask Him [what this statement meant].

33 And they arrived at Capernaum; and when [they were] in the house, He asked them, What were you discussing *and* arguing about on the road?

34 But they kept still, for on the road they had discussed *and* disputed with one another as to who was the greatest.

35 And He sat down and called the Twelve [apostles], and He said to them, If anyone desires to be first, he must be last of all, and servant of all.

36 And He took a little child and put him in the center of their group; and taking him in [His] arms, He said to them,

37 Whoever in My name *and* for My sake accepts *and* receives *and* welcomes one such child also accepts *and* receives *and* welcomes Me; and

b W. Robertson Nicoll, ed., *The Expositor's Greek New Testament.* **c** Henry Swete, *The Gospel According to Saint Mark.* **d** Joseph Thayer, *A Greek-English Lexicon.* **e** Kenneth Wuest, *Word Studies.* **f** Some manuscripts add "and fasting." **g** Hermann Cremer, *Biblico-Theological Lexicon.*

whoever so receives Me receives not only Me but Him Who sent Me.

38 John said to Him, Teacher, we saw a man who does not follow along with us driving out demons in Your name, and we forbade him to do it, because he [h]is not one of our band [of Your disciples].

39 But Jesus said, Do not restrain *or* hinder *or* forbid him; for no one who does a mighty work in My name will soon afterward be able to speak evil of Me.

40 For he who is not against us is for us. [Num. 11:27-29.]

41 For I tell you truly, whoever gives you a cup of water to drink because you belong to *and* bear the name of Christ will by no means fail to get his reward.

42 And whoever causes one of these little ones (these believers) who [j]acknowledge *and* cleave to Me to stumble *and* sin, it would be better (more profitable *and* wholesome) for him if a [huge] millstone were hung about his neck, and he were thrown into the sea.

43 And if your hand puts a stumbling block before you *and* causes you to sin, cut it off! It is more profitable *and* wholesome for you to go into life [[l]that is really worthwhile] maimed than with two hands to go to hell (Gehenna), into the fire that cannot be put out.[k]

45 And if your foot is a cause of stumbling *and* sin to you, cut it off! It is more profitable *and* wholesome for you to enter into life [that is really worthwhile] crippled than, having two feet, to be cast into hell (Gehenna).[l]

47 And if your eye causes you to stumble *and* sin, pluck it out! It is more profitable *and* wholesome for you to enter the kingdom of God with

one eye than with two eyes to be thrown into hell (Gehenna),

48 Where their worm [[m]which preys on the inhabitants and is a symbol of the wounds inflicted on the man himself by his sins] does not die, and the fire is not put out. [Isa. 66:24.]

49 For everyone shall be salted with fire.

50 Salt is good (beneficial), but if salt has lost its saltness, how will you restore [the saltness to] it? Have salt within yourselves, and be at peace *and* live in harmony with one another.

10 AND [Jesus] left there [Capernaum] and went to the region of Judea and beyond [east of] the Jordan; and crowds [constantly] gathered around Him again, and as was His custom, He began to teach them again.

2 And some Pharisees came up, and, in order to test Him *and* try to find a weakness in Him, asked, Is it lawful for a man to [h]dismiss *and* repudiate *and* divorce his wife?

3 He answered them, What did Moses command you?

4 They replied, Moses allowed a man to write a bill of divorce and to put her away. [Deut. 24:1-4.]

5 But Jesus said to them, Because of your hardness of heart [[n]your condition of insensibility to the call of God] he wrote you this [h]precept in your Law.

6 But from the beginning of creation God made them male and female. [Gen. 1:27; 5:2.]

7 For this reason a man shall leave [behind] his father and his mother [o]*and be [p]joined to his wife and cleave closely to her permanently,*

---

h Joseph Thayer, *A Greek-English Lexicon.* **i** Hermann Cremer, *Biblico-Theological Lexicon.* **j** Kenneth Wuest, *Word Studies.* **k** Verses 44 and 46, which are identical with verse 48, are not found in the best ancient manuscripts. **l** See footnote on Mark 9:43. **m** Ezra Palmer Gould, cited by A.T. Robertson, *Word Pictures* and Henry Swete, *The Gospel According to Saint Mark.* **n** Henry Swete, *The Gospel According to Saint Mark.* **o** Some manuscripts do not contain this last section of verse 7. **p** James Moulton and George Milligan, *The Vocabulary.*

8 And the two shall become one flesh, so that they are no longer two, but one flesh. [Gen. 2:24.]
9 What therefore God has united (joined together), let not man separate *or* divide.
10 And indoors the disciples questioned Him again about this subject.
11 And He said to them, Whoever qdismisses (repudiates and divorces) his wife and marries another commits adultery against her;
12 And if a woman dismisses (repudiates and divorces) her husband and marries another, she commits adultery.
13 And they kept bringing young children to Him that He might touch them, and the disciples were reproving them [for it].
14 But when Jesus saw [it], He was indignant *and* rpained and said to them, Allow the children to come to Me—do not forbid *or* prevent *or* hinder them—for to such belongs the kingdom of God.
15 Truly I tell you, whoever does not receive *and* accept *and* welcome the kingdom of God like a little child [does] positively shall not enter it at all.
16 And He took them [the children up sone by one] in His arms and [tfervently invoked a] blessing, placing His hands upon them.
17 And as He was setting out on His journey, a man ran up and knelt before Him and asked Him, Teacher, [You are uessentially and perfectly vmorally] good, what must I do to inherit eternal life [that is, uto partake of eternal salvation in the Messiah's kingdom]?
18 And Jesus said to him, Why do you call Me [uessentially and perfectly vmorally] good? There is no one [uessentially and perfectly vmorally] good—except God alone.
19 You know the commandments: Do not kill, do not commit adultery, do not steal, do not bear false witness, do not defraud, honor your father and mother. [Exod. 20:12-16; Deut. 5:16-20.]
20 And he replied to Him, Teacher, I have carefully guarded *and* observed all these *and* taken care not to violate them from my boyhood.
21 And Jesus, looking upon him, loved him, and He said to him, You lack one thing; go and sell all you have and give [the money] to the poor, and you will have treasure in heaven; and come [and] accompany Me [wwalking the same road that I walk].
22 At that saying the man's countenance fell *and* was gloomy, and he went away grieved *and* sorrowing, for he was holding great possessions.
23 And Jesus looked around and said to His disciples, With what difficulty will those who possess wealth *and* xkeep on holding it enter the kingdom of God!
24 And the disciples were amazed *and* bewildered *and* perplexed at His words. But Jesus said to them again, Children, how hard it is yfor those who trust (place their confidence, their sense of safety) in riches to enter the kingdom of God!
25 It is easier for a camel to go through the eye of a needle than for a rich man to enter the kingdom of God.
26 And they were shocked *and* exceedingly astonished, and said to Him *and* zto one another, Then who can be saved?
27 Jesus glanced around at them and said, With men [it is] impossible, but not with God; for all things are possible with God.

---

q Henry Swete, *The Gospel According to Saint Mark*. **r** A.T. Robertson, *Word Pictures*. **s** W. Robertson Nicoll, ed., *The Expositor's Greek New Testament*. **t** Henry Alford, *The Greek New Testament*. **u** Joseph Thayer, *A Greek-English Lexicon*. **v** Hermann Cremer, *Biblico-Theological Lexicon*. **w** Literal translation. **x** Kenneth Wuest, *Word Studies*. **y** Some manuscripts do not contain this phrase. **z** Many ancient manuscripts add "to one another."

28 Peter started to say to Him, Behold, we have [a]yielded up *and* abandoned everything [once and for all and [b]joined You as Your disciples, siding with Your party] and accompanied You [[c]walking the same road that You walk].

29 Jesus said, Truly I tell you, there is no one who has given up *and* left house or brothers or sisters or mother or father or children or lands for My sake and for the Gospel's

30 Who will not receive a hundred times as much now in this time— houses and brothers and sisters and mothers and children and lands, with persecutions—and in the age to come, eternal life.

31 But many [who are now] first will be last [then], and many [who are now] last will be first [then].

32 They were on the way going up to Jerusalem, and Jesus was walking on in front of them; and they were bewildered *and* perplexed *and* greatly astonished, and those [who were still] following were seized with alarm *and* were afraid. And He took the Twelve [apostles] again and began to tell them what was about to happen to Him,

33 [Saying], Behold, we are going up to Jerusalem, and the Son of Man will be turned over to the chief priests and the scribes; and they will condemn *and* sentence Him to death and turn Him over to the Gentiles.

34 And they will mock Him and spit on Him, and whip Him and put Him to death; but after three days He will rise again [[d]from death].

35 And James and John, the sons of Zebedee, approached Him and said to Him, Teacher, we desire You to do for us whatever we ask of You.

36 And He replied to them, What do you desire Me to do for you?

37 And they said to Him, Grant that we may sit, one at Your right hand and one at [Your] left hand, in Your glory (Your majesty and splendor).

38 But Jesus said to them, You do not know what you are asking. Are you able to drink the cup that I drink or be baptized with the baptism [of affliction] with which I am baptized?

39 And they replied to Him, We are able. And Jesus told them, The cup that I drink you will drink, and you will be baptized with the baptism with which I am baptized,

40 But to sit at My right hand or at My left hand is not Mine to give; but [it will be given to those] for whom it is ordained *and* prepared.

41 And when the other ten [apostles] heard it, they began to be indignant with James and John.

42 But Jesus called them to [Him] and said to them, You know that those

putting the Word to work

If God asked you today, "What do you want me to do for you?" how would you respond? James and John wanted positions of honor for themselves (see Mark 10:35–37). Bartimaeus, however, wanted to *see* and the first thing he saw was Jesus Himself (see Mark 10:46–51). What do you want God to do for you? Ask God to help you to see—more of Him, His purposes for your life, and what you are to do as you follow Him.

speak the Word

God, I declare that all things are possible with You!
ADAPTED FROM MARK 10:27

---

a Kenneth Wuest, *Word Studies*.   b Joseph Thayer, *A Greek-English Lexicon*.   c Literal translation.
d Hermann Cremer, *Biblico-Theological Lexicon*.

when obedience means sacrifice

Several years ago, our ministry needed two couples to go to Australia and manage our office there. In order to move that distance, they basically had to give up everything they owned and start over. It was too expensive to ship a lot of personal belongings that far.

The two couples who responded to God's call to go to Australia took a big step of obedience. In stepping out, they made huge personal sacrifices. They sold their cars and furniture, left behind family and friends, and separated themselves from churches where they were deeply rooted. They left everything and everyone they loved in order to obey God and move to a faraway place. Despite their love for God and their desire to do His will, it was a difficult transition.

When we go to a new place, often we feel that everything and everyone around us is strange. We are lonely and do not feel comfortable or "at home." But that kind of radical obedience pays great dividends—not only in the personal happiness and contentment that comes from knowing we are in the will of God, but also in the material blessings that God provides according to the promises of His Word.

When we take steps of faith and obedience and give up important things for the sake of the Gospel, we will find the promise of Mark 10:29, 30 to be true. We will experience great rewards now and for eternity.

who are recognized as governing *and* are supposed to rule the Gentiles (the nations) lord it over them [ruling with absolute power, holding them in subjection], and their great men exercise authority *and* dominion over them.
43 But this is not to be so among you; instead, whoever desires to be great among you must be your servant,
44 And whoever wishes to be most important *and* first in rank among you must be slave of all.
45 For even the Son of Man came not to have service rendered to Him, but to serve, and to give His life as a ransom for (°instead of) many.
46 Then they came to Jericho. And as He was leaving Jericho with His disciples and a great crowd, Bartimaeus, a blind beggar, a son of Timaeus, was sitting by the roadside.

47 And when he heard that it was Jesus of Nazareth, he began to shout, saying, Jesus, Son of David, have pity *and* mercy on me [ᶠnow]!
48 And many ᵍseverely censured *and* reproved him, telling him to keep still, but he kept on shouting out all the more, You Son of David, have pity *and* mercy on me [now]!
49 And Jesus stopped and said, Call him. And they called the blind man, telling him, Take courage! Get up! He is calling you.
50 And throwing off his outer garment, he leaped up and came to Jesus.
51 And Jesus said to him, What do you want Me to do for you? And the blind man said to Him, Master, let me receive my sight.
52 And Jesus said to him, Go your way; your faith has healed you. And at

e Marvin Vincent, *Word Studies*.　f Kenneth Wuest, *Word Studies*: The Greek aorist (past tense) imperative.　g Joseph Thayer, *A Greek-English Lexicon*.

Jesus loves to be merciful

I believe that mercy must precede healing. My favorite story about mercy and healing is the story of blind Bartimaeus in Mark 10:46–52. In this passage, Bartimaeus cried out to Jesus, "Son of David, have pity and mercy on me [now]!" (Mark 10:47).

I can just imagine the scene. Jesus was on His way somewhere and this guy shouted out, "Jesus! Have mercy on me." The crowd urged the blind man, "Shut up. Quit bothering Him. He does not want to be bothered with you." But this made Bartimaeus all the more determined to have Jesus hear him, so he continued to cry out for Jesus' mercy. What did Jesus do? He stopped. He could have listened to the crowd and ignored the man, but He responded to the man's plea for mercy. Jesus healed Him.

We do not cry out for God's mercy enough. We spend too much time trying to deserve God's goodness. In Luke 17:12–19, lepers cried out for mercy, and they all received healing, but only one came back to give Him thanks. In Matthew 15:22–28, a woman from the Canaanite district said with a loud and urgent cry, "Have mercy on me, O Lord, Son of David! My daughter is miserably and distressingly and cruelly possessed by a demon!" Her daughter was delivered. In Matthew 17:15, we see a man whose son had epilepsy, and he came to Jesus and said, "Have mercy on my son, for he has epilepsy." Jesus stopped again and cured the boy.

It seems wherever Jesus traveled, somebody asked Him for mercy. In response to them, He stopped, talked to them, and met their needs.

Let me assure you that Jesus will listen to and respond to your cry for mercy, just as He did for blind Bartimaeus and many others.

once he received his sight and accompanied Jesus on the road. [Isa. 42:6, 7.]

11 WHEN THEY were getting near to Jerusalem, to Bethphage and Bethany at the Mount of Olives, He sent ahead two of His disciples

2 And instructed them, Go into the village in front of you, and as soon as you enter it, you will find a colt tied, which has never been ridden by anyone; unfasten it and bring it [here].

3 If anyone asks you, Why are you doing this? answer, The Lord needs it, and He will send it back here presently.

4 So they went away and found a colt tied at the door out in the [winding] open street, and they loosed it.

5 And some who were standing there said to them, What are you doing, untying the colt?

6 And they replied as Jesus had directed them, and they allowed them to go.

7 And they brought the colt to Jesus and threw their outer garments upon it, and He sat on it.

8 And many [of the people] spread their garments on the road, and others [scattered a layer of] leafy branches which they had cut from the fields.

9 And those who went before and

those who followed cried out [[h]with a cry of happiness], Hosanna! [Be graciously inclined and propitious to Him!] Praised *and* blessed is He Who comes in the name of the Lord! [Ps. 118:26.]

10 Praised *and* blessed *in the name of the Lord* is the coming kingdom of our father David! Hosanna (O save us) in the highest [heaven]!

11 And Jesus went into Jerusalem and entered the temple [[i]enclosure]; and when He had looked around, surveying *and* observing everything, as it was already late, He went out to Bethany together with the Twelve [apostles].

putting the Word to work

When world leaders or other famous dignitaries gather, there is often a great deal of pomp and pageantry involved. Most people in Jesus' day would expect a king to arrive in Jerusalem on a great horse with a large entourage, surrounded by evidence of military might and wealth. Jesus entered the city on the back of a colt (see Mark 11:1–11). Does God always work in your life in ways you expect? Ask God to help you recognize Him at work in your life, and enjoy His presence even when He works in unexpected ways.

12 On the day following, when they had come away from Bethany, He was hungry.

13 And seeing in the distance a fig tree [covered] with leaves, He went to see if He could find any [fruit] on it [[j]for in the fig tree the fruit appears at the same time as the leaves]. But when He came up to it, He found nothing but leaves, for the fig season had not yet come.

14 And He said to it, No one ever again shall eat fruit from you. And His disciples were listening [to what He said].

15 And they came to Jerusalem. And He went into the temple [area, the [i]porches and courts] and began to drive out those who sold and bought in the temple area, and He overturned the [[k]four-footed] tables of the money changers and the seats of those who dealt in doves;

16 And He would not permit anyone to carry any household equipment through the temple enclosure [thus making the temple area a short-cut traffic lane].

17 And He taught and said to them, Is it not written, My house shall be called a house of prayer for all the nations? But you have turned it into a den of robbers. [Isa. 56:7; Jer. 7:11.]

18 And the chief priests and the scribes heard [of this] and kept seeking some way to destroy Him, for they feared Him, because the entire multitude was struck with astonishment at His teaching.

19 And when evening came on, *He and* [l]His disciples, as accustomed, went out of the city.

20 In the morning, when they were passing along, they noticed that the fig tree was withered [completely] away to its roots.

21 And Peter remembered and said to Him, Master, look! The fig tree which You doomed has withered away!

22 And Jesus, replying, said to them, Have faith in God [constantly].

23 Truly I tell you, whoever says to this mountain, Be lifted up and thrown into the sea! and does not doubt at all in his heart but believes that what he says will take place, it will be done for him.

---

h Alexander Souter, *Pocket Lexicon.* **i** Richard Trench, *Synonyms of the New Testament.* **j** James Orr et al., eds., *The International Standard Bible Encyclopedia.* **k** James Moulton and George Milligan, *The Vocabulary.* **l** Some manuscripts read "they."

walk the talk

In Mark 11:13, 14, when the hungry Jesus saw that the fig tree did not have any figs on it, He said to it, "No one ever again shall eat fruit from you." Mark 11:20 tells us that the next morning the fig tree completely withered.

One day when I read this story in *The Amplified Bible*, I finally understood what happened here because this translation makes the point that *the fruit of the fig tree appears at the same time as the leaves.*

With most fruit trees, if there are leaves, there is fruit under the leaves. When Jesus saw that it had leaves but no fruit, He cursed it because it was a phony. Where there are leaves, there is supposed to be fruit also!

If our lives revolve around the church but we have no fruit, we are not living our faith. We can have Christian bumper stickers on our cars, wear Jesus pins, carry our Bibles around, spend the lunch break sitting alone reading our Bibles, have plaques listing the fruit of the Spirit hanging on our walls, and listen to teaching tapes and say, "Praise the Lord! Hallelujah," but if we do not have time to help anybody else or even show kindness, we are like the fig tree with leaves but no fruit.

If a friend calls and says, "Could you do me a favor and watch my children for half an hour? I have a problem and need to run somewhere quickly," and we respond, "I would like to help you, but I just can't right now. I have plans. I'm sorry. I hope you understand." If we could have changed our plans but were simply too selfish to do so, we are like that phony fig tree.

People with a spiritual outward appearance but no fruit are hard to get along with and never allow themselves to be inconvenienced by anybody else. I know because I used to be that way! But I decided a long time ago that I am not going to be a phony Christian.

I want people to see that Christians are genuine. I want them to see that our ministry is real and what we do behind the scenes is the same thing we preach outwardly.

If we have leaves, we need to also have fruit.

Many people who are searching for God will be watching us. They will want to know Jesus like we do when they see that our fruit is real and that we are not pretenders that only look good on the outside. We will be the ambassadors for Christ that He intends us to be.

life point

Notice in Mark 11:22 that the first thing Jesus tells us to do is to have faith in God constantly. We must beware of putting our faith in anything other than God Himself and His Word. There was a time in my life when I had my faith in my faith. I relied on my ability to believe God rather than relying on God Himself. Then I read in God's Word that even when we are faithless He remains faithful (see II Timothy 2:13). None of us has perfect faith. Although we should strive to have faith in God constantly, there will be times when we allow doubt to creep in. I am comforted by the knowledge that even in those times God is still God and He does not change. He is always faithful!

24 For this reason I am telling you, whatever you ask for in prayer, believe (trust and be confident) that it is granted to you, and you will [get it]. 25 And whenever you stand praying, if you have anything against anyone, forgive him *and* ^mlet it drop (leave it, let it go), in order that your Father Who is in heaven may also forgive you your [own] failings *and* shortcomings *and* let them drop. 26 ^nBut if you do not forgive, neither will your Father in heaven forgive your failings and shortcomings. 27 And they came again to Jerusalem. And when Jesus was walking about in the [°courts and porches of the] temple, the chief priests and the scribes and the elders came to Him, 28 And they kept saying to Him, By what [sort of] authority are You doing these things, or who gave You this authority to do them? 29 Jesus told them, I will ask you a question. Answer Me, and then I will tell you by what [sort of] authority I do these things.

30 Was the baptism of John from heaven or from men? Answer Me. 31 And they reasoned *and* argued with one another, If we say, From heaven, He will say, Why then did you not believe him? 32 But [on the other hand] can we say, From men? For they were afraid of the people, because everybody considered *and* held John actually to be a prophet. 33 So they replied to Jesus, We do not know. And Jesus said to them, Neither am I going to tell you what [sort of] authority I have for doing these things.

12 AND [Jesus] started to speak to them in parables [with comparisons and illustrations]. A man planted a vineyard and put a hedge around it and dug a pit for the winepress and built a tower and let it out [for rent] to vinedressers and went into another country. 2 When the season came, he sent a bond servant to the tenants to collect from them some of the fruit of the vineyard. 3 But they took him and beat him and sent him away without anything. 4 Again he sent to them another bond servant, and they *stoned him and* wounded him in the head and treated him shamefully [sending him away with insults]. 5 And he sent another, and that one they killed; then many others—some they beat, and some they put to death. 6 He had still one left [to send], a beloved son; last of all he sent him to them, saying, They will respect my son. 7 But those tenants said to one

---

m James Moulton and George Milligan, *The Vocabulary*. n Some manuscripts do not contain verse 26. o Richard Trench, *Synonyms of the New Testament*.

what to do with your mountain

Usually when we have mountains in our lives we talk *about* them, but God's Word instructs us to talk *to* them, as we see in Mark 11:22, 23.

When Jesus said that we are to speak to our mountains in faith, commanding them to be lifted up and thrown into the sea, He made a radical statement and one that deserves some study.

First of all, what do we say to the mountains in our lives? It is obvious that we should not hurl our will at them; we are to hurl God's will at them—and His will is His Word.

Speaking the Word of God is powerful and absolutely necessary in conquering our mountains. However, it is only the beginning. Obedience is equally important. If a person thinks he can live in disobedience, but speak God's Word to his mountains and get results, he will be sadly disappointed, as Jesus clearly stated in this passage.

Mark 11:22–26 must be considered as a whole. In verse 22 Jesus said to constantly have faith in God. In verse 23 He talked about releasing faith by speaking to mountains. In verse 24 He spoke of prayer and the importance of praying believing prayers. In verse 25 He gave a command to forgive. And in verse 26 He stated plainly that if we do not forgive, neither will our Father in heaven forgive us our failings and shortcomings.

There is no power in speaking to a mountain if our hearts are full of unforgiveness. Yet the problem of unforgiveness is rampant among God's children. Multitudes of people who have accepted Christ as their personal Savior fall into the deception of trying to operate under one of God's principles while completely ignoring another.

Ask God to help you understand the whole counsel of the Word so that you can live a balanced, victorious life as a believer.

another, Here is the heir; come on, let us put him to death, and [then] the inheritance will be ours.

8 And they took him and killed him, and threw [his body] outside the vineyard.

9 Now what will the owner of the vineyard do? He will come and destroy the tenants, and give the vineyard to others.

10 Have you not even read this [passage of] Scripture: The very Stone which [ᵖafter putting It to the test] the builders rejected has become the Head of the corner [Cornerstone];

11 This is from the Lord *and* is His doing, and it is marvelous in our eyes? [Ps. 118:22, 23.]

12 And they were trying to get hold of Him, but they were afraid of the people, for they knew that He spoke this parable with reference to *and* against them. So they left Him and departed. [Isa. 5:1-7.]

p Kenneth Wuest, *Word Studies.*

13 But they sent some of the Pharisees and of the Herodians to Him for the purpose of entrapping Him in His speech.

14 And they came up and said to Him, Teacher, we know that You are [q]sincere *and* what You profess to be, that You cannot lie, *and* that You have no personal bias for anyone; for You are not influenced by partiality *and* have no [r]regard for anyone's external condition *or* position, but in [and on the basis of] truth You teach the way of God. Is it lawful (permissible and right) to give tribute ([r]poll taxes) to Caesar or not?

15 Should we pay [them] or should we not pay [them]? But knowing their hypocrisy, He asked them, Why do you put Me to the test? Bring Me a coin (a denarius), so I may see it.

16 And they brought [Him one]. Then He asked them, Whose image (picture) is this? And whose superscription ([s]title)? They said to Him, Caesar's.

17 Jesus said to them, Pay to Caesar the things that are Caesar's and to [t]God the things that are God's. And they [s]stood marveling *and* greatly amazed at Him.

18 And [some] Sadducees came to Him, [of that party] who say there is no resurrection, and they asked Him a question, saying,

19 Teacher, Moses gave us [a law] that if a man's brother died, leaving a wife but no child, the man must marry the widow and raise up offspring for his brother. [Deut. 25:5.]

20 Now there were seven brothers; the first one took a wife and died, leaving no children.

21 And the second [brother] married her, and died, leaving no children; and the third did the same;

22 And all seven, leaving no children. Last of all, the woman died also.

23 Now in the resurrection, whose wife will she be? For the seven were married to her.

24 Jesus said to them, Is not this where you wander out of the way *and* go wrong, because you know neither the Scriptures nor the power of God?

25 For when they arise from among the dead, [men] do not marry nor are [women] given in marriage, but are like the angels in heaven.

26 But concerning the dead being raised—have you not read in the book of Moses, [in the passage] about the [burning] bush, how God said to him, I am the God of Abraham and the God of Isaac and the God of Jacob? [Exod. 3:2-6.]

27 He is not the God of [the] dead, but of [the] living! You are very wrong.

28 Then one of the scribes came up and listened to them disputing with one another, and, noticing that Jesus answered them fitly *and* admirably, he asked Him, Which commandment is first *and* most important of all [[u]in its nature]?

29 Jesus answered, The first *and* principal *one of all commands* is: Hear, O Israel, The Lord our God is one Lord;

30 And you shall love the Lord your God [u]out of *and* with your whole heart and out of *and* with all your soul (your [q]life) and out of *and* with all your mind (with [u]your faculty of thought and your moral understanding) and out of *and* with all your strength. [v]*This is the first and principal commandment.* [Deut. 6:4, 5.]

31 The second *is like it and* is this, You shall love your neighbor as yourself. There is no other commandment greater than these. [Lev. 19:18.]

---

q Hermann Cremer, *Biblico-Theological Lexicon.* **r** Joseph Thayer, *A Greek-English Lexicon.*
s Kenneth Wuest, *Word Studies.* **t** A rebuke of emperor worship. **u** Marvin Vincent, *Word Studies.*
v Some manuscripts do not contain this part of verse 30.

32 And the scribe said to Him, Excellently *and* fitly *and* admirably answered, Teacher! You have said truly that He is One, and there is no other but Him;

33 And to love Him out of *and* with all the heart and with all the understanding [with the ʷfaculty of quick apprehension and intelligence and keenness of discernment] and with all the strength, and to love one's neighbor as oneself, is much more than all the whole burnt offerings and sacrifices. [I Sam. 15:22; Hos. 6:6; Mic. 6:6-8; Heb. 10:8.]

34 And when Jesus saw that he answered intelligently (discreetly and ʷhaving his wits about him), He said to him, You are not far from the kingdom of God. And after that no one ventured *or* dared to ask Him any further question.

35 And as Jesus taught in [a ˣporch or court of] the temple, He said, How can the scribes say that the Christ is David's Son?

36 David himself, [inspired] in the Holy Spirit, declared, The Lord said to my Lord, Sit at My right hand until I make Your enemies [a footstool] under Your feet. [Ps. 110:1.]

37 David himself calls Him Lord; so how can it be that He is his Son? Now the great mass of the people heard [Jesus] gladly [listening to Him with delight].

38 And in [the course of] His teaching, He said, Beware of the scribes, who like to go around in long robes and [to get] greetings in the marketplaces [public forums],

39 And [have] the front seats in the synagogues and the ˣchief couches (places of honor) at feasts,

40 Who devour widows' houses and to cover it up make long prayers. They will receive the heavier [sentence of] condemnation.

41 And He sat down opposite the treasury and saw how the crowd was casting money into the treasury. Many rich [people] were throwing in large sums.

42 And a widow who was poverty-stricken came and put in two copper mites [the smallest of coins], which together make ʸhalf of a cent.

43 And He called His disciples [to Him] and said to them, Truly *and* surely I tell you, this widow, [she who is] poverty-stricken, has put in more than all those contributing to the treasury.

44 For they all threw in out of their abundance; but she, out of her deep poverty, has put in everything that she had—[even] all she had on which to live.

13 AND AS [Jesus] was coming out of the temple [ˣarea], one of His disciples said to Him, Look, Teacher! Notice the sort *and* quality of these stones and buildings!

2 And Jesus replied to him, You see these great buildings? There will not be left here one stone upon another that will not be loosened *and* torn down.

3 And as He sat on the Mount of Olives opposite the temple [ˣenclosure],

speak the Word

w Marvin Vincent, *Word Studies.* **x** Richard Trench, *Synonyms of the New Testament.* **y** John D. Davis, *A Dictionary of the Bible.*

Peter and James and John and Andrew asked Him privately,

4 Tell us when is this to take place and what will be the sign when these things, all [of them], are about to be accomplished?

5 And Jesus began to tell them, Be careful *and* watchful that no one misleads you [about it].

6 Many will come in [²appropriating to themselves] the name [of Messiah] which belongs to Me [ᵃbasing their claims on the use of My name], saying, I am [He]! And they will mislead many.

7 And when you hear of wars and rumors of wars, do not get alarmed (troubled and frightened); it is necessary [that these things] take place, but the end is not yet.

8 For nation will rise against nation, and kingdom against kingdom. There will be earthquakes in various places; there will be famines *and calamities.* This is but the beginning of the ᶻintolerable anguish *and* suffering [only the first of the ᵇbirth pangs].

9 But look to yourselves; for they will turn you over to councils, and you will be beaten in the synagogues, and you will stand before governors and kings for My sake as a testimony to them.

10 And the good news (the Gospel) must first be preached to all nations.

11 Now when they take you [to court] and put you under arrest, do not be anxious beforehand about what you are to say ᶜnor [*even*] *meditate about it;* but say whatever is given you in that hour *and* at ᵈthe moment, for it is not you who will be speaking, but the Holy Spirit.

12 And brother will hand over brother to death, and the father his child; and children will take a stand against their parents and [have] them put to death.

13 And you will be hated *and* detested by everybody for My name's sake, but he who patiently perseveres *and* endures to the end will be saved (ᶻmade a partaker of the salvation by Christ, and delivered ᶻfrom spiritual death).

14 But when you see the abomination of desolation *mentioned by Daniel the prophet* standing where it ought not to be— [and] let the one who reads take notice *and* consider *and* understand *and* heed [this]—then let those who are in Judea flee to the mountains. [Dan. 9:27; 11:31; 12:11.]

15 Let him who is on the housetop not go down *into the house* nor go inside to take anything out of his house;

16 And let him who is in the field not turn back again to get his mantle (cloak).

17 And alas for those who are pregnant and for those who have nursing babies in those days!

18 Pray that it may not occur in winter,

19 For at that time there will be such affliction (oppression and tribulation) as has not been from the beginning of the creation which God created until this particular time—and ᵉpositively never will be [again].

20 And unless the Lord had shortened the days, no human being would be saved (rescued); but for the sake of the elect, His chosen ones (those whom He ᶠpicked out for Himself), He has shortened the days. [Dan. 12:1.]

21 And then if anyone says to you, See, here is the Christ (the Messiah)! or, Look, there He is! do not believe it.

22 False Christs (Messiahs) and false prophets will arise and show signs and

---

z Joseph Thayer, *A Greek-English Lexicon.* **a** Marvin Vincent, *Word Studies.* **b** Literal meaning. **c** Most manuscripts do not contain this phrase. **d** James Moulton and George Milligan, *The Vocabulary.* **e** Kenneth Wuest, *Word Studies.* **f** G. Abbott-Smith, *Manual Greek Lexicon.*

[work] miracles to deceive *and* lead astray, if possible, even the elect (those God has chosen out for Himself).

23 But look to yourselves *and* be on your guard; I have told you everything beforehand.

24 But in those days, after [the affliction and oppression and distress of] that tribulation, the sun will be darkened, and the moon will not give its light; [Isa. 13:10.]

25 And the stars will be falling from the sky, and the powers in the heavens will be shaken. [Isa. 34:4.]

26 And then they will see the Son of Man coming in clouds with great (kingly) power and glory (majesty and splendor). [Dan. 7:13, 14.]

27 And then He will send out the angels and will gather together His elect (those He has ᵍpicked out for Himself) from the four winds, from the farthest bounds of the earth to the farthest bounds of heaven.

28 Now learn a lesson from the fig tree: as soon as its branch becomes tender and it puts forth its leaves, you recognize *and* know that summer is near.

29 So also, when you see these things happening, you may recognize *and* know that He is near, at [the very] door.

30 Surely I say to you, this generation (ʰthe whole multitude of people living at that one time) positively will not perish *or* pass away before all these things take place.

31 Heaven and earth will perish *and* pass away, but My words will not perish *or* pass away.

32 But of that day or that hour not a [single] person knows, not even the angels in heaven, nor the Son, but only the Father.

33 Be on your guard [constantly alert], and watch ⁱ*and pray;* for you do not know when the time will come.

34 It is like a man [ʲalready] going on a journey; when he leaves home, he puts his servants in charge, each with his particular task, and he gives orders to the doorkeeper to be constantly alert *and* on the watch.

35 Therefore watch (give strict attention, be cautious and alert), for you do not know when the Master of the house is coming—in the evening, or at midnight, or at cockcrowing, or in the morning—

36 [Watch, I say] lest He come suddenly *and* unexpectedly and find you asleep.

37 And what I say to you I say to everybody: Watch (give strict attention, be cautious, active, and alert)!

putting the Word to work

When your boss is away from the office, what do you spend your time doing? As a good employee, you should spend your time working diligently to continue the work you were assigned to do. The same principle applies as you wait for Jesus' return. Do not waste time speculating about when He is coming back, but serve Him wholeheartedly every day, as Mark 13:33 instructs.

14 IT WAS now two days before the Passover and the Feast of Unleavened Bread, and the chief priests and the scribes were all the while seeking to arrest [Jesus] by secrecy *and* deceit and put [Him] to death,

2 For they kept saying, It must not be during the Feast, for fear that there might be a riot of the people.

3 And while He was in Bethany, [a guest] in the house of Simon the

---

g G. Abbott-Smith, *Manual Greek Lexicon*.   **h** Hermann Cremer, *Biblico-Theological Lexicon*; Joseph Thayer, *A Greek-English Lexicon*; and G. Abbott-Smith, *Manual Greek Lexicon*.   **i** Some manuscripts add "and pray."   **j** John Wycliffe, *The Wycliffe Bible*; William Tyndale, *The Tyndale Bible*.

leper, as He was reclining [at table], a woman came with an alabaster jar of ointment (ᵏperfume) of pure nard, very costly *and* precious; and she broke the jar and poured [the perfume] over His head.

4 But there were some who were moved with indignation and said to themselves, To what purpose was the ointment (ᵏperfume) thus wasted?

5 For it was possible to have sold this [perfume] for more than 300 denarii [a laboring man's wages for a year] and to have given [the money] to the poor. And they censured *and* reproved her.

6 But Jesus said, Let her alone; why are you troubling her? She has done a good *and* beautiful thing to Me [praiseworthy and noble].

7 For you always have the poor with you, and whenever you wish you can do good to them; but you will not always have Me. [Deut. 15:11.]

8 She has done what she could; she came beforehand to anoint My body for the burial.

9 And surely I tell you, wherever the good news (the Gospel) is proclaimed in the entire world, what she has done will be told in memory of her.

10 Then Judas Iscariot, who was one of the Twelve [apostles], went off to the chief priests in order to betray *and* hand Him over to them.

11 And when they heard it, they rejoiced *and* were delighted, and they promised to give him money. And he [busying himself continually] sought an opportunity to betray Him.

12 On the first day [of the Feast] of Unleavened Bread, when [as was customary] they killed the Passover lamb, [Jesus'] disciples said to Him, Where do You wish us to go [and] prepare the Passover [supper] for You to eat?

13 And He sent two of His disciples and said to them, Go into the city, and a man carrying an [earthen] jar *or* pitcher of water will meet you; follow him.

14 And whatever [house] he enters, say to the master of the house, The Teacher says: Where is My guest room, where I may eat the Passover [supper] with My disciples?

15 And he will [himself] show you a large upper room, furnished [with carpets and with dining couches properly spread] and ready; there prepare for us.

16 Then the disciples set out and came to the city and found [everything] just as He had told them; and they prepared the Passover.

17 And when it was evening, He came with the Twelve [apostles].

18 And while they were at the table eating, Jesus said, Surely I say to you, one of you will betray Me, [one] who is eating [here] with Me. [Ps. 41:9.]

19 And they began to show that they were sad *and* hurt, and to say to Him one after another, Is it I? *or,* It is not I, is it?

20 He replied to them, It is one of the Twelve [apostles], one who is dipping [bread] into the [same deep] dish with Me.

21 For the Son of Man is going as it stands written concerning Him; but woe to that man by whom the Son of Man is betrayed! It would have been good (profitable and wholesome) for that man if he had never been born. [Ps. 41:9.]

22 And while they were eating, He took a loaf [of bread], praised God *and* gave thanks *and* asked Him to bless it to their use. [Then] He broke [it] and gave to them and said, Take. *Eat.* This is My body.

23 He also took a cup [of the juice of grapes], and when He had given thanks, He gave [it] to them, and they all drank of it.

k James Moulton and George Milligan, *The Vocabulary.*

the meaning of Communion

The scene in Mark 14:22–24 is what we commonly refer to as "The Last Supper." Jesus wanted to eat a final meal with His disciples and be strengthened in their fellowship before facing all the agony that was ahead. During this last meal He spoke prophetically, instructing them to partake of His broken body and shed blood by eating and drinking the bread and wine. In verse 24 He made clear that His blood would seal and ratify, or validate, the New Covenant they were to have with Almighty God. Today we remember Jesus' shed blood and broken body through our taking of Communion.

Like many others, I received and participated in Communion services for years without truly understanding what I was doing. I knew the bread and juice represented the body and blood of the Lord Jesus. I knew He instructed that we eat it and drink it in remembrance of Him. But there is a much deeper and more glorious meaning of Communion.

Holy Communion was never intended to be an empty ritual with little or no meaning to those participating in it. First, we take the bread: Jesus is the Bread of Life, He is the Word made flesh (John 6:35; 1:14). As we partake of the bread, we take Him as our Living Bread, the only source that can truly satisfy our hunger in life. We remember what He has done for us. We take Him as our Living Drink, the only source that can satisfy our thirst. As we drink of the cup, it is the equivalent of "sprinkling blood" or "shedding blood" on the sacrifice of His body. It is important that we take both the bread and the cup. If people attempt to remove the blood, they are removing the power of the Gospel.

Communion can and should be a fresh dedication of our lives to the Lord, a reminder of the blood covenant that we have with God because Jesus stood in our place. In His great love for us, He took our sins upon Himself and remembers them no more. His sacrifice on the cross made it possible for us to receive His salvation, mercy, grace, and favor.

When you take Communion, realize that Jesus has given you His best. Remember that He shed His blood and gave His life for you. Communion is a time to examine your life and ask for forgiveness in areas where it is needed. It is also a good time to release your faith and ask God for healing in your physical body, as well as every other area of your life.

---

24 And He said to them, This is My blood [which ratifies] the *new* covenant, [the blood] which is being poured out for (on account of) many. [Exod. 24:8.]

25 Solemnly *and* surely I tell you, I shall not again drink of the fruit of the vine till that day when I drink it [1]of a new *and* a higher quality in God's kingdom.

---

1 Marvin Vincent, *Word Studies*.

26 And when they had sung a hymn, they went out to the Mount of Olives.
27 And Jesus said to them, You will all fall away *this night* [that is, you will be caused to stumble and will begin to distrust and desert Me], for it stands written, I will strike the Shepherd, and the sheep will be scattered. [Zech. 13:7.]
28 But after I am raised [to life], I will go before you into Galilee.
29 But Peter said to Him, Even if they all fall away *and* are caused to stumble *and* distrust *and* desert You, yet I will not [do so]!
30 And Jesus said to him, Truly I tell you, this very night, before a cock crows twice, you will utterly deny Me [disclaiming all connection with Me] three times.
31 But [Peter] said more vehemently *and* repeatedly, [Even] if it should be necessary for me to die with You, I will not deny *or* disown You! And they all kept saying the same thing.
32 Then they went to a place called Gethsemane, and He said to His disciples, Sit down here while I pray.
33 And He took with Him Peter and James and John, and began to be ᵐstruck with terror *and* amazement and deeply troubled *and* depressed.
34 And He said to them, My soul is exceedingly sad (overwhelmed with grief) so that it almost kills Me! Remain here and keep awake *and* be watching.
35 And going a little farther, He fell on the ground and kept praying that if it were possible the [ᵐfatal] hour might pass from Him.
36 And He was saying, Abba, [which means] Father, everything is possible for You. Take away this cup from Me; yet not what I will, but what You [will].
37 And He came back and found them sleeping, and He said to Peter, Simon, are you asleep? Have you not

the strength to keep awake *and* watch [with Me for] one hour?
38 Keep awake *and* watch and pray [constantly], that you may not enter into temptation; the spirit indeed is willing, but the flesh is weak.
39 He went away again and prayed, saying the same words.
40 And again He came back and found them sleeping, for their eyes were very heavy; and they did not know what answer to give Him.
41 And He came back a third time and said to them, Are you still sleeping and resting? It is enough [of that]! The hour has come. The Son of Man is betrayed into the hands of sinful men (men ⁿwhose way or nature is to act in opposition to God).
42 Get up, let us be going! See, My betrayer is at hand!
43 And at once, while He was still speaking, Judas came, one of the Twelve [apostles], and with him a crowd of men with swords and clubs, [who came] from the chief priests and the scribes and the elders [of the Sanhedrin].
44 Now the betrayer had given them a signal, saying, The One I shall kiss is [the Man]; seize Him and lead [Him] away safely [so as to prevent His escape].
45 And when he came, he went up to Jesus immediately and said, Master! *Master!* and he ᵒembraced Him *and* kissed Him fervently.
46 And they threw their hands on Him and arrested Him.
47 But one of the bystanders drew his sword and struck the bond servant of the high priest and cut off his ear.
48 And Jesus said to them, Have you come out with swords and clubs as [you would] against a robber to capture Me?
49 I was with you daily in the temple

---

m Joseph Thayer, *A Greek-English Lexicon*. **n** Hermann Cremer, *Biblico-Theological Lexicon*.
o H.A.W. Meyer, *Critical and Exegetical Handbook to the Gospel of Mark*.

life point

Those of us who are leaders on any level at all may encounter what I call the "Judas-kiss test," that is, the test of being betrayed by friends, as happened to Jesus in Mark 14:43–46.

Some time ago I talked with a person who went through something that was emotionally hard because it involved rejection and betrayal by people this individual considered close and trusted friends. I told this person the same thing I share with you now.

There were certain things Jesus did for us that we should not have to go through. For example, He bore our sins so we do not have to bear them. But there are other things that Jesus went through and that He endured as an example for us, things we will have to follow in His footsteps and go through. One of those things is betrayal.

To be honest with you, I do not know very many key leaders—people who have been in positions of leadership for a very long time—who have not at one time or another in their lives been betrayed by someone they really loved, respected, and trusted. If and when that happens to you, do as Jesus did and stay focused on your purpose. Forgive the offender and do not allow him or her to cause you to fail or delay in doing what God has called you to do.

[Pporches and courts] teaching, and you did not seize Me; but [this has happened] that the Scriptures might be fulfilled.
50 Then [His disciples], forsaking Him, fled, all [of them].

51 And a young man was following Him, with nothing but a linen cloth (qsheet) thrown about [his] naked [body]; and they laid hold of him,
52 But, leaving behind the linen cloth (qsheet), he fled from them naked.
53 And they led Jesus away to the high priest, and all the chief priests and the elders and the scribes were gathered together.
54 And Peter followed Him at a distance, even right into the courtyard of the high priest. And he was sitting [rin the firelight] with the guards and warming himself at the fire.
55 Now the chief priests and the entire council (the Sanhedrin) were constantly seeking [to get] testimony against Jesus with a view to condemning Him *and* putting Him to death, but they did not find any.
56 For many were repeatedly bearing false witness against Him, but their testimonies did not agree.
57 And some stood up and were bearing false witness against Him, saying,
58 We heard Him say, I will destroy this temple (sanctuary) which is made with hands, and in three days I will build another, made without hands.
59 Still not even [in this] did their testimony agree.
60 And the high priest stood up in the midst and asked Jesus, Have You not even one answer to make? What [about this which] these [men] are testifying against You?
61 But He kept still and did not answer at all. Again the high priest asked Him, Are You the Christ (the Messiah, the Anointed One), the Son of the Blessed?
62 And Jesus said, I AM; and you will [all] see the Son of Man seated at the right hand of Power (sthe Almighty) and coming on the clouds of heaven. [Ps. 110:1; Dan. 7:13.]

p Richard Trench, *Synonyms of the New Testament*.   q Alexander Souter, *Pocket Lexicon*.   r Marvin Vincent, *Word Studies*.   s Joseph Thayer, *A Greek-English Lexicon*.

63 Then the high priest tore his garments and said, What need have we for more witnesses? [Num. 14:6.]

64 You have heard His blasphemy. What is your decision? And they all condemned Him as being guilty *and* deserving of death. [Lev. 24:16.]

65 And some of them began to spit on Him and to blindfold Him and to strike Him with their fists, saying to Him, Prophesy! And the guards received Him with blows *and* by slapping Him.

66 While Peter was down below in the courtyard, one of the [serving] maids of the high priest came;

67 And when she saw Peter warming himself, she gazed intently at him and said, You were with Jesus of Nazareth too.

68 But he denied it ᵗfalsely *and* disowned Him, saying, I neither know nor understand what you say. Then he went outside [the courtyard and was] into the ᵘvestibule. ᵛ*And a cock crowed.*

69 And the maidservant saw him, and began again to say to the bystanders, This [man] is [one] of them.

70 But again he denied it ᵗfalsely *and* disowned Him. And after a short while, again the bystanders said to Peter, ᵗReally, you are one of them, for you are a Galilean ᵂ*and your dialect shows it.*

71 Then he commenced invoking a curse on himself [should he not be telling the truth] and swearing, I do not know the Man about Whom you are talking!

72 And at once for the second time a cock crowed. And Peter remembered how Jesus said to him, Before a cock crows twice, you will ˣutterly deny Me [disclaiming all connection with Me]

three times. And ˣhaving put his thought upon it [and remembering], he broke down *and* wept aloud *and* ʸlamented.

15 AND IMMEDIATELY when it was morning, the chief priests, with the elders and scribes and the whole council, held a consultation; and when they had bound Jesus, they took Him away [ʸviolently] and handed Him over to Pilate. [Isa. 53:8.]

2 And Pilate inquired of Him, Are You the King of the Jews? And He replied, It is as you say.

3 And the chief priests kept accusing Him of many things.

4 And Pilate again asked Him, Have ᶻYou no answer to make? See how many charges they are bringing against You!

5 But Jesus made no further answer at all, so that Pilate wondered *and* marveled. [Isa. 53:7.]

6 Now at the Feast he [was accustomed to] set free for them any one prisoner whom they requested.

7 And among the rioters in the prison who had committed murder in the insurrection there was a man named Barabbas.

8 And the throng came up and began asking Pilate to do as he usually did for them.

9 And he replied to them, Do you wish me to set free for you the King of the Jews?

10 For he was aware that it was [ʸbecause they were prompted] by envy that the chief priests had delivered Him up.

11 But the chief priests stirred up the crowd to get him to release for them Barabbas instead.

12 And again Pilate said to them,

t Hermann Cremer, *Biblico-Theological Lexicon.* **u** Marvin Vincent, *Word Studies.* **v** Some manuscripts add this sentence. **w** Some manuscripts contain this phrase instead. **x** Kenneth Wuest, *Word Studies.* **y** Joseph Thayer, *A Greek-English Lexicon.* **z** Capitalized because of what He is, the spotless Son of God, not what the speaker may have thought He was.

Then what shall I do with the Man Whom you call the King of the Jews? **13** And they shouted back again, Crucify Him!

14 But Pilate said to them, Why? What has He done that is evil? But they shouted with all their might all the more, Crucify Him [ªat once]!

15 So Pilate, wishing to satisfy the crowd, set Barabbas free for them; and after having Jesus whipped, he handed [Him] over to be crucified. [Isa. 53:5.]

16 Then the soldiers led Him away to the courtyard inside the palace, that is, the Praetorium, and they called the entire detachment of soldiers together.

17 And they dressed Him in [a] purple [robe], and, weaving together a crown of thorns, they placed it on Him. **18** And they began to salute Him, Hail (greetings, good health to You, long life to You), King of the Jews!

19 And they struck His head with a staff made of a [bamboo-like] reed and spat on Him and kept bowing their knees in homage to Him. [Isa. 50:6.]

20 And when they had [finished] making sport of Him, they took the purple [robe] off of Him and put His own clothes on Him. And they led Him out [of the city] to crucify Him.

21 And they forced a passerby, Simon of Cyrene, the father of Alexander and Rufus, who was coming in from the field (country), to carry His cross.

22 And they led Him to Golgotha [in Latin: Calvary], meaning The Place of a Skull.

23 And they [attempted to] give Him wine mingled with myrrh, but He would not take it.

24 And they crucified Him; and they divided His garments *and* distributed them among themselves, throwing lots for them to decide who should take what. [Ps. 22:18.]

25 And it was the third hour (about nine o'clock in the morning) when they crucified Him. [Ps. 22:14-16.]

26 And the inscription of the accusation against Him was written above, The King of the Jews.

27 And with Him they crucified two robbers, one on [His] right hand and one on His left.

28 *ᵇAnd the Scripture was fulfilled which says, He was counted among the transgressors.* [Isa. 53:12.]

29 And those who passed by kept reviling Him *and* reproaching Him abusively in harsh *and* insolent language, wagging their heads and saying, Aha! You Who would destroy the temple and build it in three days,

30 Now rescue ᶜYourself [ᵈfrom death], coming down from the cross!

31 So also the chief priests, with the scribes, made sport of Him to one another, saying, He rescued others [ᵈfrom death]; Himself He is unable to rescue. [Ps. 22:7, 8.]

32 Let the Christ (the Messiah), the King of Israel, come down now from the cross, that we may see [it] and trust in *and* rely on Him *and* adhere to Him! Those who were crucified with Him also reviled *and* reproached Him [speaking abusively, harshly, and insolently].

33 And when the sixth hour (about midday) had come, there was darkness over the whole land until the ninth hour (about three o'clock).

34 And at the ninth hour Jesus cried with a loud voice, Eloi, Eloi, lama sabachthani?—which means, My God, My God, why have You forsaken Me [ᵉdeserting Me and leaving Me helpless and abandoned]? [Ps. 22:1.]

---

a Kenneth Wuest, *Word Studies.* **b** Many manuscripts do not contain this verse. **c** Capitalized because of what He is, the spotless Son of God, not what the speakers may have thought He was. **d** Hermann Cremer, *Biblico-Theological Lexicon.* **e** Joseph Thayer, *A Greek-English Lexicon.*

35 And some of those standing by, [and] hearing it, said, See! He is calling Elijah!

36 And one man ran, and, filling a sponge with vinegar (a ᶠmixture of sour wine and water), put it on a staff made of a [bamboo-like] reed and gave it to Him to drink, saying, Hold off! Let us see whether Elijah [does] come to take Him down. [Ps. 69:21.]

37 And Jesus uttered a loud cry, and breathed out His life.

38 And the curtain [of the Holy of Holies] of the temple was torn in two from top to bottom.

39 And when the centurion who stood facing Him saw Him expire this way, he said, ᵍReally, this Man was God's Son!

40 Now some women were there also, looking on from a distance, among whom were Mary Magdalene, and Mary the mother of James the younger and of Joses, and Salome,

41 Who, when [Jesus] was in Galilee, were in the habit of accompanying and ministering to Him; and [there were] also many other [women] who had come up with Him to Jerusalem.

42 As evening had already come, since it was the day of Preparation, that is, [the day] before the Sabbath, [Deut. 21:22, 23.]

43 Joseph, he of Arimathea, noble *and* honorable in rank *and* a respected member of the council (Sanhedrin), who was himself waiting for the kingdom of God, daring the consequences, took courage *and* ventured to go to Pilate and asked for the body of Jesus.

44 But Pilate wondered whether He was dead so soon, and, having called the centurion, he asked him whether [Jesus] was already dead.

45 And when he learned from the

life point

When Jesus died, the veil that separated the Holy Place from the Most Holy Place in the temple was torn from the top to the bottom (see Mark 15:37, 38). That opened the way for every believer to go into God's presence. Prior to Jesus' death, only the high priest could go into God's presence, and then only once a year with the blood of slain animals, to cover and atone for his sins and the sins of the people.

It is significant that the tear in the veil of the temple was from top to bottom. The veil or curtain was so high and thick that no human could have torn it. It was torn supernaturally by the power of God, showing that He was opening up a new and living way for His people to approach Him.

centurion [that He was indeed dead], he gave the body to Joseph.

46 And Joseph bought a [fine] linen cloth [ʰfor swathing dead bodies], and, taking Him down from the cross, he ⁱrolled Him up in the [fine] linen cloth and placed Him in a tomb which had been hewn out of a rock. Then he rolled a [very large] stone against the door of the tomb. [Isa. 53:9; Matt. 16:4.]

47 And Mary Magdalene and Mary [the mother] of Joses were [ʲattentively] observing where He was laid.

16 AND WHEN the Sabbath was past [that is, after the sun had set], Mary Magdalene, and Mary [the mother] of James, and Salome purchased sweetsmelling spices, so that they might go and anoint [Jesus' body].

---

f Joseph Thayer, *A Greek-English Lexicon.* **g** Hermann Cremer, *Biblico-Theological Lexicon.* **h** James Moulton and George Milligan, *The Vocabulary.* **i** Robert Young, *Analytical Concordance.* **j** Marvin Vincent, *Word Studies.*

2 And very early on the first day of the week they came to the tomb; [by then] the sun had risen.

3 And they said to one another, Who will roll back the stone for us out of [the groove across the floor at] the door of the tomb?

4 And when they looked up, they [distinctly] saw that the stone was already rolled back, for it was very large.

5 And going into the tomb, they saw a young man sitting [there] on the right [side], clothed in a [klong, stately, sweeping] robe of white, and they were utterly amazed *and* struck with terror.

6 And he said to them, Do not be amazed *and* terrified; you are looking for Jesus of Nazareth, Who was crucified. He has risen; He is not here. See the place where they laid Him. [Ps. 16:10.]

7 But be going; tell the disciples and Peter, He goes before you into Galilee; you will see Him there, [just] as He told you. [Mark 14:28.]

8 Then they went out [and] fled from the tomb, for trembling and bewilderment *and* consternation had seized them. And they said nothing about it to anyone, for they were held by alarm *and* fear.

9 lNow Jesus, having risen [mfrom death] early on the first day of the week, appeared first to Mary Magdalene, from whom He had driven out seven demons.

10 She went and reported it to those who had been with Him, as they grieved and wept.

11 And when they heard that He was alive and that she had seen Him, they did not believe it.

12 After this, He appeared in a different form to two of them as they were walking [along the way] into the country.

13 And they returned [to Jerusalem] and told the others, but they did not believe them either.

14 Afterward He appeared to the Eleven [apostles themselves] as they reclined at table; and He reproved *and* reproached them for their unbelief (their lack of faith) and their hardness of heart, because they had refused to believe those who had seen Him *and* looked at Him attentively after He had risen [mfrom death].

15 And He said to them, Go into all the world and preach *and* publish openly the good news (the Gospel) to

life point

Mark 16:15 records what we commonly call the Great Commission: "And He said to them, Go into all the world and preach and publish openly the good news (the Gospel) to every creature [of the whole human race]." People from every Christian church accept and attempt to carry out this verse. Yet two verses later, in Mark 16:17 and 18, Jesus says believers will cast out demons, speak in new tongues, and lay hands on the sick. Some churches do not practice these things, and many teach against them.

I honestly believe that a few moments of sincere thought will reveal to the seeking soul that if Jesus meant for us to carry out Mark 16:15, then He intended for us to carry out verses 17 and 18 as well. It is dangerous business to pick and choose among scriptures. If we are going to follow the full Gospel, we cannot take the scriptures we are comfortable with and ignore the rest. We need the whole counsel of God's Word, not just bits and pieces of it.

---

k Richard Trench, *Synonyms of the New Testament*. **l** Some of the earliest manuscripts do not contain verses 9-20. **m** Hermann Cremer, *Biblico-Theological Lexicon*.

every creature [of the whole ⁿhuman race].

16 He who believes [who adheres to and trusts in and relies on the Gospel and Him Whom it sets forth] and is baptized will be saved [°from the penalty of eternal death]; but he who does not believe [who does not adhere to and trust in and rely on the Gospel and Him Whom it sets forth] will be condemned.

17 And these attesting signs will accompany those who believe: in My name they will drive out demons; they will speak in new languages;

18 They will pick up serpents; and [even] if they drink anything deadly, it will not hurt them; they will lay their hands on the sick, and they will get well.

19 So then the Lord Jesus, after He had spoken to them, was taken up into heaven and He sat down at the right hand of God. [Ps. 110:1.]

20 And they went out and preached everywhere, while the Lord kept working with them and confirming the message by the attesting signs *and* miracles that closely accompanied [it]. Amen (so be it).

life point

Mark 16:20 says that the apostles went everywhere preaching the Word, and God confirmed the Word with "signs and miracles."

I always believed those signs and wonders to be miraculous healings until God began showing me to believe not only for miraculous healings to confirm the Word preached, but also to believe for and expect miraculous breakthroughs and abundant fruit in whatever area I was ministering.

Whatever you do to serve the Lord, whether it is at home taking care of your family, as an employee of a corporation, as a public servant, as a volunteer at a hospital or nursing home—whatever you do, wherever you do it—believe God for miraculous breakthroughs to follow the things you do to serve Him. Jesus heals us everywhere we hurt! When we are about His business, we can expect signs and wonders to follow us.

ⁿ Joseph Thayer, *A Greek-English Lexicon.* ° Hermann Cremer, *Biblico-Theological Lexicon.*

Luke

Author:
Luke

Date:
Around AD 60

Everyday Life Principles:

As you read Luke and see its emphasis on the ministry of the Holy Spirit, remember that He wants to be actively involved in every aspect of your life today.

Nothing is impossible with God.

Do not let the devil intimidate you. Talk back to him, using the Word of God.

Each Gospel is unique. These four books are written in different styles, to different audiences, from different points of view, and with different emphases on certain aspects of Jesus' life and ministry.

Luke's Gospel is the longest of the four Gospels and presents Jesus as the Savior of the world; it highlights the ministry of the Holy Spirit; and it pays particular attention to women, children, the poor, and the oppressed.

Luke contains many wonderful stories and lessons, including one of the greatest and most important truths for any Christian's life: "For with God nothing is ever impossible and no word from God shall be without power or impossible of fulfillment" (Luke 1:37). No matter how difficult our situations are, God can always bring change and restoration.

In Luke 4, we learn another critical lesson. Here, we see the devil tempting Jesus in the wilderness and every time the devil says something, Jesus immediately responds, "It is written, . . ." and fights back with a verse or passage of Scripture. This teaches us that we too must know the Word and use it as our weapon against the enemy. Jesus overcame him that way, and we will too.

As you read the book of Luke, I pray you will remember that nothing is impossible with God, that the Holy Spirit is always there to help you, and that you can have victory over the enemy as you use the weapon of the Word against him.

1 SINCE [[a]as is well known] many have undertaken to put in order *and* draw up a [[a]thorough] narrative of the surely established deeds which have been accomplished *and* fulfilled [b]in *and* among us,

2 Exactly as they were handed down to us by those who from the [[a]official] beginning [of Jesus' ministry] were eyewitnesses and ministers of the Word [that is, of [c]the doctrine concerning the attainment through Christ of salvation in the kingdom of God],

3 It seemed good *and* desirable to me, [and so I have determined] also after [d]having searched out diligently *and* followed all things closely *and* traced accurately the course from the highest to the minutest detail from the very first, to write an orderly account for you, most excellent Theophilus, [Acts 1:1.]

4 [My purpose is] that you may know the full truth *and* understand with certainty *and* security against error the accounts (histories) *and* doctrines of the faith of which you have been informed *and* in which you have been [a]orally instructed.

5 In the days when Herod was king of Judea there was a certain priest whose name was Zachariah, [a]of the daily service (the division) of Abia; and his wife was also a descendant of Aaron, and her name was Elizabeth.

6 And they both were righteous in the sight of God, walking blamelessly in all the commandments and requirements of the Lord.

7 But they had no child, for Elizabeth was barren; and both were [b]far advanced in years.

8 Now while on duty, serving as priest before God in the order of his division,

9 As was the custom of the priesthood, it fell to him by lot to enter [the [e]sanctuary of] the temple of the Lord and burn incense. [Exod. 30:7.]

10 And all the throng of people were praying outside [in the court] at the hour of incense [burning].

11 And there appeared to him an angel of the Lord, standing at the right side of the altar of incense.

12 And when Zachariah saw him, he was troubled, and fear took possession of him.

13 But the angel said to him, Do not be afraid, Zachariah, because your petition [d]was heard, and your wife Elizabeth will bear you a son, and you must call his name John [God is favorable].

14 And you shall have joy and exultant delight, and many will rejoice over his birth,

15 For he will be great *and* distinguished in the sight of the Lord. And he must drink no wine nor strong drink, and he will be filled with *and* controlled by the Holy Spirit even [d]in *and* from his mother's womb. [Num. 6:3.]

16 And he will turn back *and* cause to return many of the sons of Israel to the Lord their God,

17 And he will [himself] go before Him in the spirit and power of Elijah, to turn back the hearts of the fathers to the children, and the disobedient *and* incredulous *and* unpersuadable to the wisdom of the upright [which is [f]the knowledge and holy love of the will of God]—in order to make ready for the Lord a people [perfectly] prepared [in spirit, [g]adjusted and disposed and placed in the right moral state]. [Isa. 40:3; Mal. 4:5, 6.]

18 And Zachariah said to the angel, By what shall I know *and* be sure of this? For I am an old man, and my wife is well advanced in years.

a Marvin Vincent, *Word Studies in the New Testament.* b John Wycliffe, *The Wycliffe Bible.* c Joseph Thayer, *A Greek-English Lexicon of the New Testament.* d William Tyndale, *The Tyndale Bible.* e Richard Trench, *Synonyms of the New Testament.* f Joseph Thayer, *A Greek-English Lexicon.* g Marvin Vincent, *Word Studies.*

19 And the angel replied to him, I am Gabriel. I stand in the [very] presence of God, and I have been sent to talk to you and to bring you this good news. [Dan. 8:16; 9:21.]

20 Now behold, you will be *and* [h]will continue to be silent and not able to speak till the day when these things take place, because you have not believed what I told you; but my words are [h]of a kind which will be fulfilled in the appointed *and* proper time.

21 Now the people kept waiting for Zachariah, and they wondered at his delaying [so long] in the [i]sanctuary.

22 But when he did come out, he was unable to speak to them; and they [h]clearly] perceived that he had seen a vision in the [i]sanctuary; and he kept making signs to them, still he remained dumb.

23 And when his time of performing priestly functions was ended, he returned to his [own] house.

24 Now after this his wife Elizabeth became pregnant, and for five months she secluded herself [i]entirely, saying, [I have hid myself]

25 [h]Because thus the Lord has dealt with me in the days when He deigned to look on me to take away my reproach among men. [Gen. 30:23; Isa. 4:1.]

26 Now in the sixth month [after that], the angel Gabriel was sent from God to a town of Galilee named Nazareth,

27 To a girl never having been married *and* a [j]virgin engaged to be married to a man whose name was Joseph, a descendant of the house of David; and the virgin's name was Mary.

28 And he came to her and said, Hail, O favored one [[k]endued with grace]! The Lord is with you! [l]Blessed (favored of God) are you before all other women!

29 But *when she saw him,* she was greatly troubled *and* disturbed *and* confused at what he said and kept revolving in her mind what such a greeting might mean.

30 And the angel said to her, Do not be afraid, Mary, for you have found grace ([h]free, spontaneous, absolute favor and loving-kindness) with God.

31 And listen! You will become pregnant and will give birth to a Son, and you shall call His name Jesus.

32 He will be great (eminent) and will be called the Son of the Most High; and the Lord God will give to Him the throne of His forefather David,

33 And He will reign over the house of Jacob throughout the ages; and of His reign there will be no end. [Isa. 9:6, 7; Dan. 2:44.]

34 And Mary said to the angel, How can this be, since I have no [intimacy with any man as a] husband?

35 Then the angel said to her, The Holy Spirit will come upon you, and the power of the Most High will overshadow you [like a shining cloud]; and so the holy (pure, sinless) Thing (Offspring) which shall be born *of you* will be called the Son of God. [Exod. 40:34; Isa. 7:14.]

putting the Word to work

Has God ever asked you to do something you never expected to do? No doubt, Mary was very surprised when the angel told her she would give birth to the Son of God (see Luke 1:26–34). Mary's trust in God, and her obedience and cooperation with God's plans and purposes, is a great example to follow. Allow God to work in you as He wants to, and know that all His plans for you are for your good. When unexpected things happen, keep trusting Him!

---

h Marvin Vincent, *Word Studies.*   **i** Richard Trench, *Synonyms of the New Testament.*   **j** This Greek word *parthenos* (virgin) is used in Isa. 7:14 in *The Septuagint*, the Greek Old Testament translation which Jesus read and quoted.   **k** Literal translation.   **l** Some manuscripts do not contain this phrase.

36 And listen! Your relative Elizabeth in her old age has also conceived a son, and this is now the sixth month with her who was called barren.

37 For with God nothing is ever impossible *and* no word from God shall be without power *or* impossible of fulfillment.

38 Then Mary said, Behold, I am the handmaiden of the Lord; let it be done to me according to what you have said. And the angel left her.

39 And at that time Mary arose and went with haste into the hill country to a town of Judah,

40 And she went to the house of Zachariah and, entering it, saluted Elizabeth.

41 And it occurred that when Elizabeth heard Mary's greeting, the baby leaped in her womb, and Elizabeth was filled with *and* controlled by the Holy Spirit.

42 And she cried out with a loud cry, and then exclaimed, Blessed (favored of God) above all other women are you! And blessed (favored of God) is the Fruit of your womb!

43 And how [have I deserved that this honor should] be granted to me, that the mother of my Lord should come to me?

44 For behold, the instant the sound of your salutation reached my ears, the baby in my womb leaped for joy.

45 And blessed (happy, ᵐto be envied) is she who believed that there would be a fulfillment of the things that were spoken to her from the Lord.

46 And Mary said, My soul magnifies *and* extols the Lord,

47 And my spirit rejoices in God my Savior,

48 For He has looked upon the low station *and* humiliation of His handmaiden. For behold, from now on all generations [of all ages] will call me blessed *and* declare me happy *and* ⁿto be envied!

49 For He Who is almighty has done great things for me—and holy is His name [to be venerated in His purity, majesty and glory]!

50 And His mercy (His compassion and kindness toward the miserable and afflicted) is on those who fear Him with godly reverence, from generation to generation *and* age to age. [Ps. 103:17.]

51 He has shown strength *and* ᵒmade might with His arm; He has scattered the proud *and* haughty in *and* by the imagination *and* purpose *and* designs of their hearts.

52 He has put down the mighty from their thrones and exalted those of low degree.

53 He has filled *and* satisfied the hungry with good things, and the rich He has sent away empty-handed [without a gift].

54 He has laid hold on His servant Israel [to help him, to espouse his cause], in remembrance of His mercy,

55 Even as He promised to our forefathers, to Abraham and to his descendants forever. [Gen. 17:7; 18:18; 22:17; I Sam. 2:1-10; Mic. 7:20.]

56 And Mary remained with her [Elizabeth] for about three months and [then] returned to her [own] home.

57 Now the time that Elizabeth

speak the Word

m Alexander Souter, *Pocket Lexicon of the Greek New Testament.* **n** Alexander Souter, *Pocket Lexicon.* **o** John Wycliffe, *The Wycliffe Bible.*

should be delivered came, and she gave birth to a son.

58 And her neighbors and relatives heard that the Lord had shown great mercy on her, and they rejoiced with her.

59 And it occurred that on the eighth day, when they came to circumcise the child, they were intending to call him Zachariah after his father, [Gen. 17:12; Lev. 12:3.]

60 But his mother answered, Not so! But he shall be called John.

61 And they said to her, None of your relatives is called by that name.

62 And they inquired with signs to his father [as to] what he wanted to have him called.

63 Then Zachariah asked for a writing tablet and wrote, His name is John. And they were all astonished.

64 And at once his mouth was opened and his tongue loosed, and he began to speak, blessing *and* praising *and* thanking God.

65 And awe *and* reverential fear came on all their neighbors; and all these things were discussed throughout the hill country of Judea.

66 And all who heard them laid them up in their hearts, saying, Whatever will this little boy be then? For the hand of the Lord was [Pso evidently] with him [protecting and aiding him].

67 Now Zachariah his father was filled with *and* controlled by the Holy Spirit and prophesied, saying,

68 Blessed (praised and extolled and thanked) be the Lord, the God of Israel, because He has come and brought deliverance *and* redemption to His people!

69 And He has raised up a Horn of salvation [a mighty and valiant Helper, the Author of salvation] for us in the house of David His servant—

70 This is as He promised by the mouth of His holy prophets from the most ancient times [in the memory of man]—

71 That we should have deliverance *and* be saved from our enemies and from the hand of all who detest *and* pursue us with hatred;

72 To make true *and* show the mercy *and* compassion *and* kindness [promised] to our forefathers and to remember *and* carry out His holy covenant [to bless, which is qall the more sacred because it is made by God Himself],

73 That covenant He sealed by oath to our forefather Abraham:

74 To grant us that we, being delivered from the hand of our foes, might serve Him fearlessly

75 In holiness (divine consecration) and righteousness [in accordance with the everlasting principles of right] within His presence all the days of our lives.

76 And you, little one, shall be called a prophet of the Most High; for you shall go on before the face of the Lord to make ready His ways, [Isa. 40:3; Mal. 4:5.]

77 To bring *and* give the knowledge of salvation to His people in the forgiveness *and* remission of their sins.

78 Because of *and* through the heart of tender mercy *and* loving-kindness of our God, a Light from on high will dawn upon us *and* visit [us] [Mal. 4:2.]

79 To shine upon *and* give light to those who sit in darkness and in the shadow of death, to direct *and* guide our feet in a straight line into the way of peace. [Isa. 9:2.]

80 And the little boy grew and became strong in spirit; and he was in the deserts (wilderness) until the day of his appearing to Israel [the commencement of his public ministry].

---

p Albert Barnes, *Notes on the New Testament.*   **q** Joseph Thayer, *A Greek-English Lexicon.*

2 IN THOSE days it occurred that a decree went out from Caesar Augustus that the whole ʳRoman empire should be registered.

2 This was the first enrollment, and it was made when Quirinius was governor of Syria.

3 And all the people were going to be registered, each to his own city *or* town.

4 And Joseph also went up from Galilee from the town of Nazareth to Judea, to the town of David, which is called Bethlehem, because he was of the house and family of David,

5 To be enrolled with Mary, his espoused (ˢmarried) wife, who was about to become a mother. [Matt. 1:18-25.]

6 And while they were there, the time came for her delivery,

7 And she gave birth to her Son, her Firstborn; and she wrapped Him in swaddling clothes and laid Him in a manger, because there was no room *or* place for them in the inn.

8 And in that vicinity there were shepherds living [out under the open sky] in the field, watching [in shifts] over their flock by night.

9 And *behold*, an angel of the Lord stood by them, and the glory of the Lord flashed *and* shone all about them, and they were terribly frightened.

10 But the angel said to them, Do not be afraid; for behold, I bring you good news of a great joy which will come to all the people.

11 For to you is born this day in the town of David a Savior, Who is Christ (the Messiah) the Lord! [Mic. 5:2.]

12 And this will be a sign for you [by which you will recognize Him]: you will find [ᵗafter searching] a Baby wrapped in swaddling clothes and

lying in a manger. [I Sam. 2:34; II Kings 19:29; Isa. 7:14.]

13 Then suddenly there appeared with the angel an army of the troops of heaven (ᵘa heavenly knighthood), praising God and saying,

14 Glory to God in the highest [heaven], and on earth peace among men with whom He is well pleased [ᵘmen of goodwill, of His favor].

15 When the angels went away from them into heaven, the shepherds said one to another, Let us go over to Bethlehem and see this thing (ᵛsaying) that has come to pass, which the Lord has made known to us.

16 So they went with haste and [ᵗby searching] found Mary and Joseph, and the Baby lying in a manger.

17 And when they saw it, they made known what had been told them concerning this Child,

18 And all who heard it were astounded *and* marveled at what the shepherds told them.

19 But Mary was keeping ᵛwithin herself all these things (ᵛsayings), weighing *and* pondering them in her heart.

20 And the shepherds returned, glorifying and praising God for all the things they had heard and seen, just as it had been told them.

21 And at the end of eight days, when [the Baby] was to be circumcised, He was called Jesus, the name given by the angel before He was conceived in the womb.

22 And when the time for their purification [the mother's purification and the Baby's dedication] came according to the Law of Moses, they brought Him up to Jerusalem to present Him to the Lord — [Lev. 12:1-4.]

23 As it is written in the Law of the Lord, Every [firstborn] male that opens the womb shall be set apart *and*

r George R. Berry, *Greek-English New Testament Lexicon.* s Marvin Vincent, *Word Studies.* t Joseph Thayer, *A Greek-English Lexicon.* u John Wycliffe, *The Wycliffe Bible.* v Marvin Vincent, *Word Studies.*

when *not* to speak

Mary had some pretty serious things happen in her life. She was a sweet, ordinary girl who loved God when an angel of the Lord appeared to her and told her she was going to become the mother of the Son of God.

She had to have thought about Joseph, the man she was engaged to marry. She had to have wondered how she was going to tell him this news and how he would react. She had to have questioned whether her parents and friends would believe her story.

Then time passed and the birth took place. The angels appeared to the shepherds and told them to come to the stable and worship the Christ Child. The shepherds told Mary and Joseph and everyone else what happened. These are the things that Mary did not speak about. She kept them in her heart and pondered them, according to Luke 2:19.

Whatever Mary may have thought or felt, she controlled it because she said to the angel who first brought the news, " . . . . let it be done to me according to what you have said" (Luke 1:38).

I believe that when God speaks something to us, many times we need to keep it to ourselves. He gives us the faith to believe what He has said to us, but if we try to tell it to others, they may think we have lost our minds.

You should have heard some of the things people said to me when I told them that God spoke to my heart and called me into the ministry. Knowing my background and the condition I was in at the time, they were not encouraging at all.

That is one of the problems with sharing too much with others; we get discouraged instead of encouraged. Other people do not always have the faith to believe what God has told us.

When God calls you to do something, He also gives you the faith to do it.

You do not have to live in fear all the time, thinking that you are not able to do what He has given you to do. When you have a gift of faith, things seem easy to you. But to someone else without that gift of faith, these things seem impossible.

When God spoke to Mary through the angel, there was a gift of faith that came with that word to her from the Lord so that she was able to say, "Let it be done." But she was also wise enough not to go around knocking on doors saying, "I just had a visitation from an angel who told me I am going to give birth to the Son of God. I am going to get pregnant by the Holy Spirit, and the Child I will bear will be the Savior of the world." Mary knew how to keep her mouth shut and her heart open. I encourage you to do likewise!

dedicated *and* called holy to the Lord—[Exod. 13:1, 2, 12; Num. 8:17.]

24 And [they came also] to offer a sacrifice according to what is said in the Law of the Lord: a pair of turtledoves or two young pigeons. [Lev. 12:6-8.]

25 Now there was a man in Jerusalem whose name was Simeon, and this man was righteous and devout [cautiously and carefully observing the divine Law], and looking for the Consolation of Israel; and the Holy Spirit was upon him.

26 And it had been divinely revealed (communicated) to him by the Holy Spirit that he would not see death before he had seen the Lord's Christ (the Messiah, the Anointed One).

27 And prompted by the [Holy] Spirit, he came into the temple [ʷenclosure]; and when the parents brought in the little child Jesus to do for Him what was customary according to the Law,

28 [Simeon] took Him up in his arms and praised *and* thanked God and said,

29 And now, Lord, You are releasing Your servant to depart (leave this world) in peace, according to Your word.

30 For with my [own] eyes I have seen Your Salvation, [Isa. 52:10.]

31 Which You have ordained *and* prepared before (in the presence of) all peoples,

32 A Light for ˣrevelation to the Gentiles [to disclose what was before unknown] and [to bring] praise *and* honor *and* glory to Your people Israel. [Isa. 42:6; 49:6.]

33 And His [legal] father and [His] mother were marveling at what was said about Him.

34 And Simeon blessed them and said to Mary His mother, Behold, this Child is appointed *and* destined for the fall and rising of many in Israel, and for a sign that is spoken against— [Isa. 8:14, 15.]

35 And a sword will pierce through your own soul also—that the secret thoughts *and* purposes of many hearts may be brought out *and* disclosed.

36 And there was also a prophetess, Anna, the daughter of Phanuel, of the tribe of Asher. She was very old, having lived with her husband seven years from her maidenhood, [Josh. 19:24.]

37 And as a widow even for eighty-four years. She did not go out from the temple ʷenclosure, but was worshiping night and day with fasting and prayer.

38 And she too came up at that same hour, and she returned thanks to God and talked of [Jesus] to all who were looking for the redemption (deliverance) of Jerusalem.

39 And when they had done everything according to the Law of the Lord, they went back into Galilee to their own town, Nazareth.

40 And the Child grew and became strong *in spirit,* filled with wisdom; and the grace (favor and spiritual blessing) of God was upon Him. [Judg. 13:24; I Sam. 2:26.]

41 Now His parents went to Jerusalem every year to the Passover Feast. [Deut. 16:1-8; Exod. 23:15.]

42 And when He was twelve years [old], they went up, as was their custom.

43 And when the Feast was ended, as they were returning, the boy Jesus remained behind in Jerusalem. Now His parents did not know this,

44 But, supposing Him to be in the caravan, they traveled on a day's journey; and [then] they sought Him [diligently, looking up and down for Him] among their kinsfolk and acquaintances.

45 And when they failed to find Him,

ʷ Richard Trench, *Synonyms of the New Testament.*   ˣ Marvin Vincent, *Word Studies.*

they went back to Jerusalem, looking for Him [up and down] all the way.

46 After three days they found Him [came upon Him] in the ʸ[court of the] temple, sitting among the teachers, listening to them and asking them questions.

47 And all who heard Him were astonished *and* overwhelmed with bewildered wonder at His intelligence *and* understanding and His replies.

48 And when they [Joseph and Mary] saw Him, they were amazed; and His mother said to Him, Child, why have You treated us like this? Here Your father and I have been anxiously looking for You [distressed and tormented].

49 And He said to them, How is it that you had to look for Me? Did you not see *and* know that it is necessary [as a duty] for Me ᶻto be in My Father's house *and* [occupied] about My Father's business?

50 But they did not comprehend what He was saying to them.

51 And He went down with them and came to Nazareth and was [habitually] obedient to them; and his mother kept *and* closely and persistently guarded all these things in her heart.

52 And Jesus increased in wisdom (in broad and full understanding) and in stature *and* years, and in favor with God and man.

3 IN THE fifteenth year of Tiberius Caesar's reign—when Pontius Pilate was governor of Judea, and Herod was tetrarch of Galilee, and his brother Philip tetrarch of the region of Ituraea and Trachonitis, and Lysanias tetrarch of Abilene—

2 In the high priesthood of Annas and Caiaphas, the Word of God [ᵃcon-

putting the Word to work

Throughout the Bible, we see that children hold a special place in God's heart. Think for a moment about a child who is important to you. Do you pray regularly for him or her? Praying for children as they grow up is one of the greatest gifts that you can give to them. Pray that he or she, like Jesus, will increase in wisdom and in stature and in favor with God and with people (see Luke 2:52).

cerning the attainment through Christ of salvation in the kingdom of God] came to John son of Zachariah in the wilderness (desert).

3 And he went into all the country round about the Jordan, preaching a baptism of repentance (ᵃof hearty amending of their ways, with abhorrence of past wrongdoing) unto the forgiveness of sin.

4 As it is written in the book of the words of Isaiah the prophet, The voice of one crying in the wilderness [shouting in the desert]: Prepare the way of the Lord, make His beaten paths straight.

5 Every valley *and* ravine shall be filled up, and every mountain and hill shall be leveled; and the crooked places shall be made straight, and the rough roads shall be made smooth;

6 And all mankind shall see (behold and ᵇunderstand and at last acknowledge) the salvation of God (the deliverance from eternal death ᵃdecreed by God). [Isa. 40:3-5.]

7 So he said to the crowds who came out to be baptized by him, You offspring of vipers! Who ᶜsecretly warned you to flee from the coming wrath?

---

y Richard Trench, *Synonyms of the New Testament.*　**z** Literally, "in the things of My Father."
a Joseph Thayer, *A Greek-English Lexicon.*　**b** James Gray and George Adams, *Bible Commentary.*
c Literal translation.

8 Bear fruits that are deserving *and* consistent with [your] repentance [that is, ᵈconduct worthy of a heart changed, a heart abhorring sin]. And do not begin to say to yourselves, We have Abraham as our father; for I tell you that God is able from these stones to raise up descendants for Abraham.
9 Even now the ax is laid to the root of the trees, so that every tree that does not bear good fruit is cut down and cast into the fire.
10 And the multitudes asked him, Then what shall we do?
11 And he replied to them, He who has two tunics (undergarments), let him share with him who has none; and he who has food, let him do it the same way.
12 Even tax collectors came to be baptized, and they said to him, Teacher, what shall we do?
13 And he said to them, Exact *and* collect no more than the fixed amount appointed you.
14 Those serving as soldiers also asked him, And we, what shall we do? And he replied to them, Never demand *or* enforce ᵉby terrifying people or by accusing wrongfully, and always be satisfied with your rations (supplies) *and* with your allowance (wages).
15 As the people were in suspense *and* waiting expectantly, and everybody reasoned *and* questioned in their hearts concerning John, whether he perhaps might be the Christ (the Messiah, the Anointed One).
16 John answered them all by saying, I baptize you with water; but He Who is mightier than I is coming, the strap

speak the Word

of Whose sandals I am not fit to unfasten. He will baptize you with the Holy Spirit and with fire.
17 His winnowing shovel (fork) is in His hand to thoroughly clear *and* cleanse His [threshing] floor and to gather the wheat *and* store it in His granary, but the chaff He will burn with fire that cannot be extinguished.
18 So with many other [various] appeals and admonitions he preached the good news (the Gospel) to the people.
19 But Herod the tetrarch, who had been [repeatedly] told about his fault *and* reproved *with* rebuke ᵉproducing conviction by [John] for [having] Herodias, his brother's wife, and for all the wicked things that Herod had done,
20 Added this to them all—that he shut up John in prison.
21 Now when all the people were baptized, and when Jesus also had been baptized, and [while He was still] praying, the [visible] heaven was opened
22 And the Holy Spirit descended upon Him in bodily form like a dove, and a voice came from heaven, *saying,* You are My Son, My Beloved! In You I am well pleased *and* find delight! [Ps. 2:7; Isa. 42:1.]
23 Jesus Himself, when He began [His ministry], was about thirty years of age, being the Son, as was supposed, of Joseph, the son of Heli,
24 The son of Matthat, the son of Levi, the son of Melchi, the son of Jannai, the son of Joseph,
25 The son of Mattathias, the son of Amos, the son of Nahum, the son of Esli, the son of Naggai,

God, I believe by faith that because I am in Christ, You say to me as You said to Him: "You are . . . My Beloved! In You I am well pleased and find delight!"
ADAPTED FROM LUKE **3:22**

d Joseph Thayer, *A Greek-English Lexicon.*   **e** Marvin Vincent, *Word Studies.*

26 The son of Maath, the son of Mattathias, the son of Semein, the son of Josech, the son of Joda,
27 The son of Joanan, the son of Rhesa, the son of Zerubbabel, the son of Shealtiel, the son of Neri,
28 The son of Melchi, the son of Addi, the son of Cosam, the son of Elmadam, the son of Er,
29 The son of Jesus, the son of Eliezer, the son of Jorim, the son of Matthat, the son of Levi,
30 The son of Simeon, the son of Judah, the son of Joseph, the son of Jonam, the son of Eliakim,
31 The son of Melea, the son of Menna, the son of Mattatha, the son of Nathan, the son of David,
32 The son of Jesse, the son of Obed, the son of Boaz, the son of Salmon (Sala), the son of Nahshon,
33 The son of Aminadab, the son of Admin, the son of Arni, the son of Hezron, the son of Perez, the son of Judah,
34 The son of Jacob, the son of Isaac, the son of Abraham, the son of Terah, the son of Nahor,
35 The son of Serug, the son of Reu, the son of Peleg, the son of Eber, the son of Shelah,
36 The son of Cainan, the son of Arphaxad, the son of Shem, the son of Noah, the son of Lamech,
37 The son of Methuselah, the son of Enoch, the son of Jared, the son of Mahalaleel, the son of Cainan,
38 The son of Enos, the son of Seth, the son of Adam, the son of God. [Gen. 5:3-32; 11:10-26; Ruth 4:18-22; I Chron. 1:1-4, 24-28; 2:1-15.]

4 THEN JESUS, full of *and* controlled by the Holy Spirit, returned from the Jordan and was led in [by] the [Holy] Spirit
2 For (during) forty days in the wilderness (desert), where He was tempted (ᶠtried, tested exceedingly) by the devil. And He ate nothing during those days, and when they were completed, He was hungry. [Deut. 9:9; I Kings 19:8.]
3 Then the devil said to Him, If You are the Son of God, order this stone to turn into a loaf [of bread].
4 And Jesus replied to him, It is written, Man shall not live *and* be sustained by (on) bread alone ᵍ*but by every word and expression of God.* [Deut. 8:3.]
5 Then the devil took Him up to a high mountain and showed Him all the kingdoms of the habitable world

life point

Jesus answered every temptation the devil used against Him with God's Word. Throughout Luke 4:1–12, we read that He repeatedly said, "It is written . . . " and then quoted scriptures that directly addressed the enemy's lies and tempting schemes.

We may start to fight the devil with the Word, but when we do not see quick results, many times we stop speaking the Word and begin talking about our feelings or our circumstances.

Let me encourage you to be persistent as you wage war against the enemy by speaking the Word. A stonecutter may strike a rock ninety-nine times without even making a crack in the rock. But the hundredth strike may split the rock in two. Each blow weakened the rock, even though there were no outward signs of it.

Persistence is vital to victory in our lives just as it is in the stonecutter's work. Do not relent in speaking the Word against the enemy. The next time you do, it may deal him a deathblow!

f Robert Young, *Analytical Concordance to the Bible.*   **g** Some manuscripts add this phrase.

in a moment of time [[h]in the twinkling of an eye].

6 And he said to Him, To You I will give all this power *and* authority and their glory (all their magnificence, excellence, preeminence, dignity, and grace), for it has been turned over to me, and I give it to whomever I will.

7 Therefore if You will do homage to *and* worship me [[i]just once], it shall all be Yours.

8 And Jesus replied to him, [j]*Get behind Me, Satan!* It is written, You shall do homage to *and* worship the Lord your God, and Him only shall you serve. [Deut. 6:13; 10:20.]

9 Then he took Him to Jerusalem and set Him on [k]a gable of the temple, and said to Him, If You are the Son of God, cast Yourself down from here;

10 For it is written, He will give His angels charge over you to guard *and* watch over you closely *and* carefully;

11 And on their hands they will bear you up, lest you strike your foot against a stone. [Ps. 91:11, 12.]

12 And Jesus replied to him, [The Scripture] says, You shall not tempt (try, [l]test exceedingly) the Lord your God. [Deut. 6:16.]

13 And when the devil had ended every [the complete cycle of] temptation, he [temporarily] left Him [that is, [m]stood off from Him] until another more opportune *and* favorable time.

14 Then Jesus went back full of *and* under the power of the [Holy] Spirit into Galilee, and the fame of Him spread through the whole region round about.

15 And He Himself conducted [[n]a course of] teaching in their syna-gogues, being [o]recognized *and* honored *and* praised by all.

16 So He came to Nazareth, [[k]that Nazareth] where He had been brought up, and He entered the syna-gogue, as was His custom on the Sabbath day. And He stood up to read.

17 And there was handed to Him [the roll of] the book of the prophet Isaiah. He opened (unrolled) the book and found the place where it was written, [Isa. 61:1, 2.]

18 The Spirit of the Lord [is] upon Me, because He has anointed Me [the Anointed One, the Messiah] to preach the good news (the Gospel) to the poor; He has sent Me to announce release to the captives and recovery of sight to the blind, to send forth as delivered those who are oppressed [who are downtrodden, bruised, crushed, and broken down by calamity],

19 To proclaim the accepted *and* acceptable year of the Lord [the day [p]when salvation and the free favors of God profusely abound]. [Isa. 61:1, 2.]

20 Then He rolled up the book and gave it back to the attendant and sat down; and the eyes of all in the syna-gogue were gazing [attentively] at Him.

21 And He began to speak to them: Today this Scripture has been ful-filled [p]while you are present *and* hear-ing.

22 And all spoke well of Him and marveled at the words of grace that came forth from His mouth; and they said, Is not this Joseph's [q]Son?

23 So He said to them, You will doubtless quote to Me this proverb: Physician, heal Yourself! What we have learned by hearsay that You did

h William Tyndale, *The Tyndale Bible.* **i** Charles B. Williams, *The New Testament: A Translation in the Language of the People*: "expressed by the Greek aorist tense." **j** Some manuscripts add this phrase. **k** James Moulton and George Milligan, *The Vocabulary of the Greek Testament.* **l** Robert Young, *Analytical Concordance.* **m** Kenneth Wuest, *Word Studies in the Greek New Testament.* **n** Marvin Vincent, *Word Studies*: in Greek imperfect tense. **o** Hermann Cremer, *Biblico-Theological Lexicon of New Testament Greek.* **p** Joseph Thayer, *A Greek-English Lexicon.* **q** Capitalized because of what He is, the spotless Son of God, not what the speakers may have thought He was.

in Capernaum, do here also in Your [own] town.

24 Then He said, Solemnly I say to you, no prophet is acceptable *and* welcome in his [own] town (country).

25 But in truth I tell you, there were many widows in Israel in the days of Elijah, when the heavens were closed up for three years and six months, so that there came a great famine over all the land;

26 And yet Elijah was not sent to a single one of them, but only to Zarephath in the country of Sidon, to a woman who was a widow. [I Kings 17:1, 8-16; 18:1.]

27 And there were many lepers in Israel in the time of Elisha the prophet, and yet not one of them was cleansed [by being healed]—but only Naaman the Syrian. [II Kings 5:1-14.]

28 When they heard these things, all the people in the synagogue were filled with rage.

29 And rising up, they pushed *and* drove Him out of the town, and [laying hold of Him] they led Him to the [projecting] upper part of the hill on which their town was built, that they might hurl Him headlong down [over the cliff].

30 But passing through their midst, He went on His way.

31 And He descended to Capernaum, a town of Galilee, and there He continued to teach the people on the Sabbath days.

32 And they were amazed at His teaching, for His word was with authority *and* ability *and* weight *and* power.

33 Now in the synagogue there was a man who was possessed by the foul spirit of a demon; and he cried out with a loud (deep, terrible) cry,

34 Ah, ʳ*let us alone!* What have You to do with us [What have ˢwe in common], Jesus of Nazareth? Have You come to destroy us? I know Who You are—the Holy One of God!

35 But Jesus rebuked him, saying, Be silent (muzzled, gagged), and come out of him! And when the demon had thrown the man down in their midst, he came out of him without injuring him in any ᵗpossible way.

36 And they were all amazed and said to one another, What kind of talk is this? For with authority and power He commands the foul spirits and they come out!

37 And a rumor about Him spread into every place in the surrounding country.

38 Then He arose and left the synagogue and went into Simon's (Peter's) house. Now Simon's mother-in-law was suffering in the grip of a burning fever, and they pleaded with Him for her.

39 And standing over her, He rebuked the fever, and it left her; and immediately she got up and began waiting on them.

40 Now at the setting of the sun [indicating the end of the Sabbath], all those who had any [who were] sick with various diseases brought them to Him, and He laid His hands upon every one of them and cured them.

41 And demons even came out of many people, screaming *and* crying out, You are the Son of God! But He rebuked them and would not permit them to speak, because they knew that He was the Christ (the Messiah).

42 And when daybreak came, He left [Peter's house] and went into an isolated [desert] place. And the people looked for Him until they came up to Him and tried to prevent Him from leaving them.

43 But He said to them, I must preach the good news (the Gospel) of the kingdom of God to the other cities

---

r Some manuscripts so read.   **s** John Wycliffe, *The Wycliffe Bible*.   **t** Literal translation.

[and towns] also, for I was sent for this [purpose].

44 And He continued to preach in the synagogues of Galilee.

5 NOW IT occurred that while the people pressed upon Jesus to hear the message of God, He was standing by the Lake of Gennesaret (Sea of Galilee).

2 And He saw two boats drawn up by the lake, but the fishermen had gone down from them and were washing their nets.

3 And getting into one of the boats, [the one] that belonged to Simon (Peter), He requested him to draw away a little from the shore. Then He sat down and continued to teach the crowd [of people] from the boat.

4 When He had stopped speaking, He said to Simon (Peter), Put out into the deep [water], and lower your nets for a haul.

step out and find out

The only way we ever fulfill our destinies and succeed at being our true selves is to take many, many steps of faith. Stepping out into the unknown and launching out into the deep water, as we read about in Luke 5:4, can be frightening.

Because of feelings of fear, many people never *step out*; therefore they never *find out* what they are capable of.

Each of us needs to obey God when He wants us to step out into something new or challenging. We are living in the dispensation of grace and many doors of opportunity are open to share the Gospel of Jesus Christ with others. Make a decision that you will not miss any opportunity that God gives you. Do what God asks you to do even if you must "do it afraid." Feel the fear and do it anyway!

Many people miss God's will for their lives because they play it safe. I do not want to come to the end of my life and say, "I was safe, but I am sorry."

"Better safe than sorry" does not always work in God's economy. If I tried to be safe all the time, I am sure I would not be where I am today. I would never have sown the seeds of obedience that produced the harvest I now enjoy in my ministry and in many other areas of my life. Nothing feels better than knowing you are in the will of God—and nothing feels worse than knowing you are not.

I am not suggesting we all start doing foolish things that are unwise, but I know for a fact that not everything God wants us to do makes sense to the natural mind. You and I must learn to be led by discernment in the inner man (the spirit) and not by our own carnal minds or what other people suggest to us. When we step out, we should do all we can to be sure that we respond in faith and obedience to God's leadership—and not act on some wild thought we have or on a lie of Satan to try to lure us into destruction. I encourage you to be willing to go into deep waters for God. Ask Him to make clear what He wants you to do and then obey.

5 And Simon (Peter) answered, Master, we toiled all night [ᵘexhaustingly] and caught nothing [in our nets]. But ᵘon the ground of Your word, I will lower the nets [again].

6 And when they had done this, they caught a great number of fish; and as their nets were [ᵛat the point of] breaking,

7 They signaled to their partners in the other boat to come and take hold with them. And they came and filled both the boats, so that they began to sink.

8 But when Simon Peter saw this, he fell down at Jesus' knees, saying, Depart from me, for I am a sinful man, O Lord.

9 For he was gripped with bewildering amazement [allied to terror], and all who were with him, at the haul of fish which they had made;

10 And so also were James and John, the sons of Zebedee, who were partners with Simon (Peter). And Jesus said to Simon, Have no fear; from now on you will be catching men!

11 And after they had run their boats on shore, they left everything and ʷjoined Him as His disciples *and* sided with His party *and* accompanied Him.

12 While He was in one of the towns, there came a man full of (covered with) leprosy; and when he saw Jesus, he fell on his face and implored Him, saying, Lord, if You are willing, You are able to cure me *and* make me clean.

13 And [Jesus] reached out His hand and touched him, saying, I am willing; be cleansed! And immediately the leprosy left him.

14 And [Jesus] charged him to tell no one [ᵘthat he might chance to meet], ˣuntil [He said] you go and show yourself to the priest, and make an offering for your purification, as Moses commanded, for a testimony *and* proof to the people, that they may have evidence [of your healing]. [Lev. 13:49; 14:2-32.]

15 But so much the more the news spread abroad concerning Him, and great crowds kept coming together to hear [Him] and to be healed by Him of their infirmities.

16 But He Himself withdrew [in retirement] to the wilderness (desert) and prayed.

life point

Jesus made sure He had seasons of peace and time alone (see Luke 5:15, 16). He ministered to the people, but He slipped away regularly from the crowds to be alone and pray. Surely if Jesus needed this type of lifestyle, we do also.

17 One of those days, as He was teaching, there were Pharisees and teachers of the Law sitting by, who had come from every village *and* town of Galilee and Judea and from Jerusalem. And the power of the Lord was [present] with Him to heal ʸ*them*.

18 And behold, some men were bringing on a stretcher a man who was paralyzed, and they tried to carry him in and lay him before [Jesus].

19 But finding no way to bring him in because of the crowd, they went up on the roof and lowered him with his stretcher through the tiles into the midst, in front of Jesus.

20 And when He saw [their confidence in Him, springing from] their faith, He said, Man, your sins are forgiven you!

21 And the scribes and the Pharisees began to reason *and* question *and*

---

u Marvin Vincent, *Word Studies.* **v** Richard Trench, *Synonyms of the New Testament.* **w** Joseph Thayer, *A Greek-English Lexicon.* **x** Richard Trench, *Notes on the Miracles of our Lord.* **y** Some ancient manuscripts so read.

argue, saying, Who is this [Man] Who speaks blasphemies? Who can forgive sins but God alone?

22 But Jesus, knowing their thoughts *and* questionings, answered them, Why do you question in your hearts?

23 Which is easier: to say, Your sins are forgiven you, or to say, Arise and walk [about]?

24 But that you may know that the Son of Man has the [ᶻpower of] authority *and* right on earth to forgive sins, He said to the paralyzed man, I say to you, arise, pick up your litter (stretcher), and go to your own house!

25 And instantly [the man] stood up before them and picked up what he had been lying on and went away to his house, ᵃrecognizing *and* praising *and* thanking God.

26 And overwhelming astonishment *and* ecstasy seized them all, and they ᵃrecognized *and* praised *and* thanked God; and they were filled with *and* controlled by reverential fear and kept saying, We have seen wonderful *and* strange *and* incredible *and* unthinkable things today!

27 And after this, Jesus went out and looked [attentively] at a tax collector named Levi sitting at the tax office; and He said to him, ᶻJoin Me as a disciple *and* side with My party *and* accompany Me.

28 And he forsook everything and got up and followed Him [becoming His disciple and siding with His party].

29 And Levi (Matthew) made a great banquet for Him in his own house, and there was a large company of tax collectors and others who were reclining [at the table] with them.

30 Now the Pharisees and their scribes were grumbling against Jesus' disciples, saying, Why are you eating and drinking with tax collectors and [preeminently] sinful people?

31 And Jesus replied to them, It is not those who are healthy who need a physician, but those who are sick.

32 I have not come to arouse *and* invite *and* call the righteous, but ᵇthe erring ones (ᶻthose not free from sin) to repentance [ᶻto change their minds for the better and heartily to amend their ways, with abhorrence of their past sins].

33 Then they said to Him, The disciples of John practice fasting often and offer up prayers of [special] petition, and so do [the disciples] of the Pharisees also, but Yours eat and drink.

34 And Jesus said to them, Can you make the wedding guests fast as long as the bridegroom is with them?

35 But the days will come when the bridegroom will be taken from them; and then they will fast in those days.

36 He told them a ᶜproverb also: No one puts a patch from a new garment on an old garment; if he does, he will both tear the new one, and the patch from the new [one] will not match the old [garment].

37 And no one pours new wine into old wineskins; if he does, the fresh wine will burst the skins and it will be spilled and the skins will be ruined (destroyed).

38 But new wine must be put into fresh wineskins.

39 And no one after drinking old wine immediately desires new wine, for he says, The old is good *or* ᵈ*better*.

6 ONE SABBATH while Jesus was passing through the fields of standing grain, it occurred that His disciples picked some of the spikes and ate [of the grain], rubbing it out in their hands. [Deut. 23:25.]

---

z Joseph Thayer, *A Greek-English Lexicon.* **a** Hermann Cremer, *Biblico-Theological Lexicon.* **b** Robert Young, *Analytical Concordance.* **c** G. Abbott-Smith, *Manual Greek Lexicon of the New Testament.* **d** Many ancient manuscripts read "better."

give Jesus all you are not

If you are needy, you are just the person that Jesus died for (see Luke 5:31). So often we feel we must hide our weaknesses and always pretend that we are strong and in need of nothing, but that attitude only closes the door to God's help. He said, "Ask and it shall be given you" (see Luke 11:9). Do not be ashamed of yourself or your needs.

I suggest that when people receive Jesus Christ as their Savior, they give Him not only all they are, but especially all they are not. We try to impress God and other people with what we are while we hide what we are not. I do not believe people can become all that God wants them to be until they face what they are not and no longer have a problem with it.

I am a teacher, but I am not a singer, or a musician. I tried for a period of time to learn to play the guitar and to sing, but I just did not have the ability. I struggled and wasted time—precious time I could have spent developing the gift of teaching that I do have. Many people never fulfill their God-ordained destiny because they keep trying to be something or somebody they were never meant to be. All God wants us to be is who we are!

We do not have to compare ourselves with others or compete with them. We *all* have weaknesses and inabilities. Satan would like for you to think you are the only one with the problem or weakness you have, but that simply is not true. If we were all perfect, Jesus would not have needed to come to earth. According to Luke 5:31, He came for those who were sick (needy) not those who were healthy (not needy).

When the apostle Paul finally saw this truth, he stopped struggling with his weaknesses and said that he would "all the more gladly glory in [them]" from that point on (see II Corinthians 12:7–10). God's strength is made perfect in our weaknesses. Whatever we are not, He is, and He is what He is, for us.

Go ahead and be needy. Tell God everything you need. He already knows anyway and is waiting for you to ask for help.

2   But some of the Pharisees asked them, Why are you doing what is not permitted to be done on the Sabbath days? [Exod. 20:10; 23:12; Deut. 5:14.]

3   And Jesus replied to them, saying, Have you never so much as read what David did when he was hungry, he and those who were with him?— [I Sam. 21:1-6.]

4   How he went into the house of God and took and ate the [sacred] loaves of the showbread, which it is not permitted for any except only the priests to eat, and also gave to those [who were] with him? [Lev. 24:9.]

5   And He said to them, The Son of Man is Lord even of the Sabbath.

6   And it occurred on another Sabbath that when He went into the synagogue and taught, a man was present whose right hand was withered.

7   And the scribes and the Pharisees

kept watching Jesus to see whether He would [actually] heal on the Sabbath, in order that they might get [some ground for] accusation against Him.

8 But He was aware all along of their thoughts, and He said to the man with the withered hand, Come and stand here in the midst. And he arose and stood there.

9 Then Jesus said to them, I ask you, is it lawful *and* right on the Sabbath to do good [eso that someone derives advantage from it] or to do evil, to save a life [and fmake a soul safe] or to destroy it?

10 Then He glanced around at them all and said to the man, Stretch out your hand! And he did so, and his hand was fully restored glike the other one.

11 But they were filled with lack of understanding *and* senseless rage and discussed (consulted) with one another what they might do to Jesus.

12 Now in those days it occurred that He went up into a mountain to pray, and spent the whole night in prayer to God.

13 And when it was day, He summoned His disciples and selected from them twelve, whom He named apostles (special messengers):

14 They were Simon, whom He named Peter, and his brother Andrew; and James and John; and Philip and Bartholomew;

15 And Matthew and Thomas; and James son of Alphaeus, and Simon who was called the Zealot,

16 And Judas son of James; and Judas Iscariot, who became a traitor (a treacherous, basely faithless person).

17 And Jesus came down with them and took His stand on a level spot, with a great crowd of His disciples and a vast throng of people from all over Judea and Jerusalem and the seacoast of Tyre and Sidon, who came to listen to Him and to be cured of their diseases—

18 Even those who were disturbed *and* troubled with unclean spirits, and they were being healed [also].

19 And all the multitude were seeking to touch Him, for healing power was all the while going forth from Him and curing them all [hsaving them from severe illnesses or calamities].

20 And solemnly lifting up His eyes on His disciples, He said: Blessed (happy—ewith life-joy and satisfaction in God's favor and salvation, apart from your outward condition— and ito be envied) are you poor *and* jlowly *and* afflicted (destitute of wealth, influence, position, and honor), for the kingdom of God is yours!

21 Blessed (happy—ewith life-joy and satisfaction in God's favor and salvation, apart from your outward condition—and ito be envied) are you who hunger *and* seek with eager desire now, for you shall be filled *and* completely satisfied! Blessed (happy—ewith life-joy and satisfaction in God's favor and salvation, apart from your outward condition— and ito be envied) are you who weep *and* sob now, for you shall laugh!

22 Blessed (happy—ewith life-joy and satisfaction in God's favor and salvation, apart from your outward condition—and ito be envied) are you when people despise (hate) you, and when they exclude *and* excommunicate you [as disreputable] and revile *and* denounce you and defame *and* cast out *and* spurn your name as evil (wicked) on account of the Son of Man.

23 Rejoice *and* be glad at such a time

---

e Hermann Cremer, *Biblico-Theological Lexicon.*　**f** John Wycliffe, *The Wycliffe Bible.*　**g** Some manuscripts add this phrase.　**h** Marvin Vincent, *Word Studies.*　**i** Alexander Souter, *Pocket Lexicon.*　**j** Joseph Thayer, *A Greek-English Lexicon.*

and exult *and* leap for joy, for behold, your reward is rich *and* great *and* strong *and* intense *and* abundant in heaven; for even so their forefathers treated the prophets.

24 But woe to (alas for) you who are rich (*abounding in material resources), for you already are receiving your consolation (the solace and sense of strengthening and cheer that come from prosperity) *and* have taken and enjoyed your comfort in full [having nothing left to be awarded you].

25 Woe to (alas for) you who are full now (completely filled, luxuriously gorged and satiated), for you shall hunger *and* suffer want! Woe to (alas for) you who laugh now, for you shall mourn and weep *and* wail!

26 Woe to (alas for) you when everyone speaks fairly *and* handsomely of you *and* praises you, for even so their forefathers did to the false prophets.

27 But I say to you who are listening now to Me: [ʲin order to heed, make it a practice to] love your enemies, treat well (do good to, act nobly toward) those who detest you *and* pursue you with hatred,

28 Invoke blessings upon *and* pray for the happiness of those who curse you, implore God's blessing (favor) upon those who abuse you [who revile, reproach, disparage, and high-handedly misuse you].

29 To the one who strikes you on the ᵏjaw *or* cheek, offer the other ᵏjaw *or* cheek also; and from him who takes away your outer garment, do not withhold your undergarment as well.

30 Give away to everyone who begs of you [who is ᵏin want of necessities], and of him who takes away from you your goods, do not demand *or* require them back again.

31 And as you would like *and* desire that men would do to you, do exactly so to them.

32 If you [merely] love those who love you, what ˡquality of credit *and* thanks is that to you? For even ᵐthe [very] sinners love their lovers (those who love them).

33 And if you are kind *and* good *and* do favors to *and* benefit those who are kind *and* good *and* do favors to *and* benefit you, what ˡquality of credit *and* thanks is that to you? For even ᵏthe preeminently sinful do the same.

34 And if you lend money ˡat interest to those from whom you hope to receive, what ˡquality of credit *and* thanks is that to you? Even notorious sinners lend money ˡat interest to sinners, so as to recover as much again.

35 But love your enemies and be kind *and* do good [doing favors ⁿso that someone derives benefit from them] and lend, expecting *and* hoping for nothing in return *but* ˡconsidering nothing as lost *and* despairing of no one; and then your recompense (your reward) will be great (rich, strong, intense, and abundant), and you will be sons of the Most High, for He is kind *and* charitable *and* good to the ungrateful *and* the selfish and wicked.

36 So be merciful (sympathetic, tender, responsive, and compassionate) even as your Father is [all these].

37 Judge not [neither pronouncing judgment nor subjecting to censure],

speak the Word

Help me, God, to be merciful—sympathetic, tender, responsive, and compassionate—to others, even as You are all of these to me.
ADAPTED FROM LUKE 6:36

k Joseph Thayer, *A Greek-English Lexicon*. **l** Marvin Vincent, *Word Studies*. **m** William Tyndale, *The Tyndale Bible*. **n** Hermann Cremer, *Biblico-Theological Lexicon*.

further than forgiveness

Luke 6:27, 28 teaches how to deal with our enemies. Something is missing when we say we forgive those who have hurt or offended us and go no further.

Let me share with you a lesson I learned from ministering on the subject of forgiveness. I once asked the Lord, "Father, why is it that people come to our meetings and pray for the ability to forgive, and yet in just a short time they are right back again still having the same problems with bitterness, anger, and hypersensitivity, and asking for help?"

The first thing the Lord told me is that these types of people are not doing what He instructs in His Word.

You see, though God tells us in His Word to *forgive* others, He does not stop there. He goes on to instruct us to *bless* them. In this context, the word "bless" means "to speak well of." So one of our problems is though we pray and try to forgive those who offend us, we turn right around and curse them with our tongues or we rehash the offense again and again with others.

This will not work!

To work through the process of forgiveness and enjoy the peace we seek, we must do what God tells us to do, which is not only to forgive but also to bless.

One reason we find it so hard to pray for those who hurt us and mistreat us is that we tend to think we are asking God to bless them physically or materially. The truth is that we are not praying for them to make more money or have more possessions; we are praying for them to be blessed spiritually. What we are doing is asking God to bring truth and revelation to them about their attitude and behavior so they will be willing to repent and be freed from their sins.

It is not enough to merely say we forgive others; we must be careful not to curse them or speak evil of them even if we think they deserve it. Instead, we must do as Jesus did and pray for them, bless them, and speak well of them. Why? Because by doing so, we bless not only them, but ourselves too. Hating those who hurt you is like taking poison and hoping your enemy will die. Obviously, anyone who did that would only be hurting himself. Why spend your life angry at people who probably do not even know or care that you are angry? These people are thoroughly enjoying their lives while you are miserable. Release them, let the offense go, drop it, and have the same attitude toward them that Jesus had toward His enemies. By doing this, you will experience wonderful freedom and God will show Himself strong as your Vindicator.

and you will not be judged; do not condemn *and* pronounce guilty, and you will not be condemned *and* pronounced guilty; acquit *and* forgive *and* °release (give up resentment, let it drop), and you will be acquitted *and* forgiven *and* ᵖreleased.

38 Give, and [gifts] will be given to you; good measure, pressed down, shaken together, and running over, will they pour �q into [the pouch formed by] the bosom [of your robe and used as a bag]. For with the measure you deal out [with the measure you use when you confer benefits on others], it will be measured back to you.

39 He further told them ʳa proverb: Can a blind [man] guide *and* direct a blind [man]? Will they not both stumble into a ditch *or* a ˢhole in the ground?

life point

The blind cannot lead the blind—if they try to do so, they will both fall into a ditch (see Luke 6:39). Think of it another way: trying to help others while ignoring our own problems never helps anyone.

40 A pupil is not superior to his teacher, but everyone [when he is] completely trained (readjusted, restored, set to rights, and perfected) will be like his teacher.

41 Why do you see the speck that is in your brother's eye but do not notice *or* consider the beam [of timber] that is in your own eye?

42 Or how can you say to your brother, Brother, allow me to take out the speck that is in your eye, when you yourself do not see the beam that is in your own eye? You actor (pretender, hypocrite)! First take the beam out of your own eye, and then you will see clearly to take out the speck that is in your brother's eye.

43 For there is no good (healthy) tree that bears decayed (worthless, stale) fruit, nor on the other hand does a decayed (worthless, sickly) tree bear good fruit.

44 For each tree is known *and* identified by its own fruit; for figs are not gathered from thornbushes, nor is a cluster of grapes picked from a bramblebush.

45 The upright (honorable, intrinsically good) man out of the good treasure [stored] in his heart produces what is upright (honorable and intrinsically good), and the evil man out of the evil storehouse brings forth that which is depraved (wicked and intrinsically evil); for out of the abundance (overflow) of the heart his mouth speaks.

46 Why do you call Me, Lord, Lord, and do not [practice] what I tell you?

47 For everyone who comes to Me and listens to My words [in order to heed their teaching] and does them, I will show you what he is like:

48 He is like a man building a house, who dug and went down deep and laid a foundation upon the rock; and when a flood arose, the torrent broke against that house and could not shake *or* move it, because it had been securely built *or* ᵗfounded on a rock.

putting the Word to work

Luke 6:43–45 teaches us that our actions reflect what is in our hearts. Does any of your behavior indicate a need for a change in your heart? Ask God to continue to transform you more and more into His image, so your actions will reflect His work and His presence in your heart.

---

o Literal translation. **p** Literal meaning. **q** Marvin Vincent, *Word Studies.* **r** G. Abbott-Smith, *Manual Greek Lexicon.* **s** Alexander Souter, *Pocket Lexicon.* **t** Some manuscripts so read.

the root of unhealthy attitudes

Jesus said that every tree is known and identified by its fruit (see Luke 6:44). Imagine looking at a fruit tree that depicts all the bad things produced in the life of someone who is unhealthy emotionally. If you look at the roots of that person's life you will see things like rejection, abuse, guilt, negativism, and shame.

If you have a problem with unhealthy attitudes in your life, they are the bitter fruit of what has rooted into your thinking. You may be the product of improper mirroring and imaging of your parents and others. You may suffer from the bad example you were exposed to in your earlier years.

If parents, teachers, or other authority figures told you over and over in your youth that you were no good, that there was something wrong with you, that you could not do anything right, that you were worthless and would never amount to anything, you may actually believe it. Satan reinforces that message by repeating it in your mind again and again until it becomes such a part of your self-image that you actually become on the outside the way you envision yourself on the inside.

It has been proven that if people believe something about themselves strongly enough, they will actually begin to behave the way they perceive themselves to be. But I have good news: Your mind can be renewed by the Word of God (see Romans 12:2). This does not happen instantly, but it is possible with the help of the Holy Spirit. God wants you to bear good fruit, and He will help you do so by replacing bad roots with good roots as you meditate on His Word. Jesus invites us to be rooted and grounded in Him and in His love (see Ephesians 3:17, Colossians 2:7).

49 But he who merely hears and does not practice doing My words is like a man who built a house on the ground without a foundation, against which the torrent burst, and immediately it collapsed *and* fell, and the breaking *and* ruin of that house was great.

7 AFTER JESUS had finished all that He had to say in the hearing of the people [on the mountain], He entered Capernaum.
2 Now a centurion had a bond servant who was held in honor *and* highly valued by him, who was sick and at the point of death.
3 And when the centurion heard of Jesus, he sent some Jewish elders to Him, requesting Him to come and make his bond servant well.
4 And when they reached Jesus,

putting the Word to work

What do you think is the most important part of a house? It's the foundation, of course, as we learn from Luke 6:47–49. Without a firm foundation, a house is constantly in danger of collapsing. The same is true in your life as a Christian. Knowing God's Word and obeying it is the foundation of the Christian life. Ask God to teach you His Word and to help you obey Him in every area of your life, so you can stand strong in all circumstances.

they begged Him earnestly, saying, He is worthy that You should do this for him,

5 For he loves our nation and he built us our synagogue [at his own expense].

6 And Jesus went with them. But when He was not far from the house, the centurion sent [some] friends to Him, saying, Lord, do not trouble [Yourself], for I am not ⁿsufficiently worthy to have You come under my roof;

7 Neither did I consider myself worthy to come to You. But [just] speak a word, and my servant boy will be healed.

8 For I also am a man [daily] subject to authority, with soldiers under me. And I say to one, Go, and he goes; and to another, Come, and he comes; and to my bond servant, Do this, and he does it.

9 Now when Jesus heard this, He marveled at him, and He turned and said to the crowd that followed Him, I tell you, not even in [all] Israel have I found such great faith [as this].

10 And when the messengers who had been sent returned to the house, they found the bond servant *who had been ill* quite well again.

11 *Soon afterward, Jesus went to a town called Nain, and His disciples and a great throng accompanied Him.

12 [Just] as He drew near the gate of the town, behold, a man who had died was being carried out—the only son of his mother, and she was a widow; and a large gathering from the town was accompanying her.

13 And when the Lord saw her, He had compassion on her and said to her, Do not weep.

14 And He went forward and touched the funeral bier, and the pallbearers stood still. And He said, Young man, I say to you, arise [ˣfrom death]!

15 And the man [who was] dead sat up and began to speak. And [Jesus] gave him [back] to his mother.

16 Profound *and* reverent fear seized them all, and they began ʸto recognize God *and* praise *and* give thanks, saying, A great ᶻProphet has appeared among us! And God has visited His people [in order to help and care for and provide for them]!

17 And this report concerning [Jesus] spread through the whole of Judea and all the country round about. [I Kings 17:17-24; II Kings 4:32-37.]

18 And John's disciples brought him [who was now in prison] word of all these things.

19 And John summoned to him a certain two of his disciples and sent them to the Lord, saying, Are You He Who is to come, or shall we [continue to] look for another?

20 So the men came to Jesus and said, John the Baptist sent us to You to ask, Are You the One Who is to come, or shall we [continue to] look for another?

21 In that very hour Jesus was healing many [people] of sicknesses and distressing bodily plagues and evil spirits, and to many who were blind He gave [ᵃa free, gracious, joy-giving gift of] sight.

22 So He replied to them, Go and tell John what you have seen and heard: the blind receive their sight, the lame walk, the lepers are cleansed, the deaf hear, the dead are raised up, and the poor have the good news (the Gospel) preached to them. [Isa. 29:18, 19; 35:5, 6; 61:1.]

23 And blessed (happy—ˣwith life-joy and satisfaction in God's favor and salvation, apart from outward

---

u Literal translation: "sufficient." **v** Some manuscripts add this phrase. **w** Many ancient manuscripts read "the next day." **x** Hermann Cremer, *Biblico-Theological Lexicon.* **y** Joseph Thayer, *A Greek-English Lexicon.* **z** Capitalized because of what He is, the spotless Son of God, not what the speakers may have thought He was. **a** Marvin Vincent, *Word Studies.*

conditions—and [b]to be envied) is he who takes no offense in Me *and* who is not hurt *or* resentful *or* annoyed *or* repelled *or* made to stumble [[c]whatever may occur].

24 And the messengers of John having departed, Jesus began to speak to the crowds about John: What did you go out into the desert to gaze on? A reed shaken *and* swayed by the wind?

25 Then what did you go out to see? A man dressed up in soft garments? Behold, those who wear fine apparel and live in luxury are in the courts *or* palaces of kings.

26 What then did you go out to see? A prophet (a forthteller)? Yes, I tell you, and far more than a prophet.

27 This is the one of whom it is written, Behold, I send My messenger before Your face, who shall make ready Your way before You. [Mal. 3:1.]

28 I tell you, among those born of women there is no one greater than John; but [d]he that is inferior [to the other citizens] in the kingdom of God is greater [in incomparable privilege] than he.

29 And all the people who heard Him, even the tax collectors, acknowledged the justice of God [in [d]calling them to repentance and in pronouncing future wrath on the impenitent], being baptized with the baptism of John.

30 But the Pharisees and the lawyers [of the Mosaic Law] annulled *and* rejected *and* brought to nothing God's purpose concerning themselves, by [refusing and] not being baptized by him [John].

31 So to what shall I compare the men of this generation? And what are they like?

32 They are like little children sitting in the marketplace, calling to one another and saying, We piped to you [playing wedding], and you did not dance; we sang dirges *and* wailed [playing funeral], and you did not weep.

33 For John the Baptist has come neither eating bread nor drinking wine, and you say, He has a demon.

34 The Son of Man has come eating and drinking, and you say, Behold, a Man Who is a glutton and a wine drinker, a friend of tax collectors and notorious sinners.

35 Yet wisdom is vindicated ([e]shown to be true and divine) by all her children [[e]by their life, character, and deeds].

36 One of the Pharisees asked Jesus to dine with him, and He went into the Pharisee's house and reclined at table.

37 And behold, a woman of the town who was [d]an especially wicked sinner, when she learned that He was reclining at table in the Pharisee's house, brought an alabaster flask of ointment (perfume).

38 And standing behind Him at His feet weeping, she began to wet His feet with [her] tears; and she wiped them with the hair of her head and kissed His feet [affectionately] and anointed them with the ointment (perfume).

39 Now when the Pharisee who had invited Him saw it, he said to himself, If this Man were a prophet, He would surely know who and what sort of woman this is who is touching Him—for she is a notorious sinner (a social outcast, devoted to sin).

40 And Jesus, replying, said to him, Simon, I have something to say to you. And he answered, Teacher, say it.

41 A certain lender of money [at interest] had two debtors: one owed him five hundred denarii, and the other fifty.

---

b Alexander Souter, *Pocket Lexicon.* c Marvin Vincent, *Word Studies.* d Joseph Thayer, *A Greek-English Lexicon.* e Albert Barnes, *Notes on the New Testament.*

the woman with a past

The woman in Luke 7:37 was a woman with a past. She sold her love by the hour; she was a prostitute. The Pharisee called her "an especially wicked sinner." I believe her presence in the Bible and in Jesus' life shows us that God does not always call people with wonderful pasts to serve Him. But we also learn from this woman that He does call people with a negative past to a powerful, blessed future. Just because you did not have a good beginning in life does not mean that you cannot have a great finish.

In Luke 7:38, we see the account of the woman anointing Jesus' feet with a bottle of very expensive perfume, washing them with her tears and drying them with her hair. Since she was a prostitute, the perfume was probably either a gift from one of her clients or purchased with money she earned from her profession. Other people probably viewed her act of love as erotic because of her past, but Jesus knew it was an act of pure love.

When we have an unpleasant past, people often misjudge our actions, and we find ourselves caught up in the approval game, trying to convince others that we are acceptable. People do not forget our past as easily as God does. The Pharisee could not understand why Jesus allowed the woman to even touch Him (see Luke 7:39). But Jesus responded to this by saying that those who have been forgiven much will love much (see Luke 7:47).

This woman knew her past well; she loved Jesus greatly because He forgave her greatly for her sins. She wanted to give Him the most expensive thing she owned; she wanted to serve Him. He saw her heart, not her past. This is what He sees in you too.

42 When they had no means of paying, he freely forgave them both. Now which of them will love him more?
43 Simon answered, The one, I take it, for whom he forgave *and* cancelled more. And Jesus said to him, You have decided correctly.
44 Then turning toward the woman, He said to Simon, Do you see this woman? When I came into your house, you gave Me no water for My feet, but she has wet My feet with her tears and wiped them with her hair.
45 You gave Me no kiss, but she from the moment I came in has not ceased [[f]intermittently] to kiss My feet tenderly *and* caressingly.
46 You did not anoint My head with [g][cheap, ordinary] oil, but she has anointed My feet with [g][costly, rare] perfume.
47 Therefore I tell you, her sins, many [as they are], are forgiven her—because she has loved much. But he who is forgiven little loves little.
48 And He said to her, Your sins are forgiven!
49 Then those who were at table with Him began to say among themselves, Who is this Who even forgives sins?
50 But Jesus said to the woman, Your faith has saved you; go (enter) [f]into peace [[g]in freedom from all the distresses that are experienced as the result of sin].

f Marvin Vincent, *Word Studies*.   **g** Hermann Cremer, *Biblico-Theological Lexicon*.

8 SOON AFTERWARD, [Jesus] went on through towns and villages, preaching and bringing the good news (the Gospel) of the kingdom of God. And the Twelve [apostles] were with Him,

2 And also some women who had been cured of evil spirits and diseases: Mary, called Magdalene, from whom seven demons had been expelled;

3 And Joanna, the wife of Chuza, Herod's household manager; and Susanna; and many others, who ministered to *and* provided for hHim and them out of their property *and* personal belongings.

4 And when a very great throng was gathering together and people from town after town kept coming to Jesus, He said in a parable:

5 A sower went out to sow seed; and as he sowed, some fell along the traveled path and was trodden underfoot, and the birds of the air ate it up.

6 And some [seed] fell on the rock, and as soon as it sprouted, it withered away because it had no moisture.

7 And other [seed] fell in the midst of the thorns, and the thorns grew up with it and choked it [off].

8 And some seed fell into good soil, and grew up and yielded a crop a hundred times [as great]. As He said these things, He called out, He who has ears to hear, let him be listening *and* let him iconsider *and* understand by hearing!

9 And when His disciples asked Him the meaning of this parable,

10 He said to them, To you it has been given to [come progressively to] know (to recognize and understand more strongly and clearly) the mysteries *and* secrets of the kingdom of God, but for others they are in parables, so that, [though] looking, they

may not see; and hearing, they may not comprehend. [Isa. 6:9, 10; Jer. 5:21; Ezek. 12:2.]

11 Now the meaning of the parable is this: The seed is the Word of God.

12 Those along the traveled road are the people who have heard; then the devil comes and carries away the message out of their hearts, that they may not believe (iacknowledge Me as their Savior and devote themselves to Me) and be saved [here and hereafter].

13 And those upon the rock [are the people] who, when they hear [the Word], receive *and* welcome it with joy; but these have no root. They believe for a while, and in time of trial *and* temptation fall away (withdraw and stand aloof).

14 And as for what fell among the thorns, these are [the people] who hear, but as they go on their way they are choked *and* suffocated with the anxieties *and* cares and riches and pleasures of life, and their fruit does not ripen (come to maturity and perfection).

15 But as for that [seed] in the good soil, these are [the people] who, hearing the Word, hold it fast in a just (jnoble, virtuous) and worthy heart, and steadily bring forth fruit with patience.

16 No one after he has lighted a lamp covers it with a vessel or puts it under a [dining table] couch; but he puts it on a lampstand, that those who come in may see the light.

17 For there is nothing hidden that shall not be disclosed, nor anything secret that shall not be known and come out into the open.

18 Be careful therefore how you listen. For to him who has [spiritual knowledge] will more be given; and from him who does not have

---

h Some ancient manuscripts read "Him" instead of "them." i Joseph Thayer, *A Greek-English Lexicon.* j Marvin Vincent, *Word Studies.*

[spiritual knowledge], even what he thinks *and* ᵏguesses *and* ˡsupposes that he has will be taken away.

19 Then Jesus' mother and His brothers came along toward Him, but they could not get to Him because of the crowd.

20 And it was told Him, Your mother and Your brothers are standing outside, desiring to have an interview with You.

21 But He answered them, My mother and My brothers are those who listen to the Word of God and do it!

22 One of those days He and His disciples got into a boat, and He said to them, Let us go across to the other side of the lake. So they put out to sea.

23 But as they were sailing, He fell off to sleep. And a ᵐwhirlwind revolving from below upwards swept down on the lake, and the boat was filling with water, and they were in great danger.

24 And the disciples came and woke Him, saying, Master, Master, we are perishing! And He, being thoroughly awakened, ⁿcensured *and* ᵏblamed *and* rebuked the wind and the raging waves; and they ceased, and there came a calm.

25 And He said to them, [Why are you so fearful?] Where is your faith (your trust, your confidence in Me—in My veracity and My integrity)? And they were seized with alarm *and* profound *and* reverent dread, and they marveled, saying to one another, Who then is this, that He commands even wind and sea, and they obey Him?

26 Then they came to the country of the Gerasenes, which is opposite Galilee.

27 Now when Jesus stepped out on land, there met Him a certain man out of the town who had [was possessed by] demons. For a long time he had worn no clothes, and he lived not in a house but in the tombs.

28 And when he saw Jesus, he raised a deep (terrible) cry [from the depths of his throat] and fell down before Him [in terror] and shouted loudly, What have You [to do] with me, Jesus, Son of the Most High God? [ᵏWhat have we in common?] I beg You, do not torment me!

29 For Jesus was already commanding the unclean spirit to come out of the man. For many times it had snatched *and* held him; he was kept under guard and bound with chains and fetters, but he would break the bonds and be driven by the demon into the wilderness (desert).

30 Jesus then asked him, What is your name? And he answered, Legion; for many demons had entered him.

31 And they begged [Jesus] not to command them to depart into the Abyss (bottomless pit). [Rev. 9:1.]

32 Now a great herd of swine was there feeding on the hillside; and [the demons] begged Him to give them leave to enter these. And He allowed them [to do so].

33 Then the demons came out of the man and entered into the swine, and the herd rushed down the steep cliff into the lake and were drowned.

34 When the herdsmen saw what had happened, they ran away and told it in the town and in the country.

35 And [people] went out to see what had occurred, and they came to Jesus and found the man from whom the demons had gone out, sitting at the feet of Jesus, clothed and in his right (sound) mind; and they were seized with alarm *and* fear.

36 And those [also] who had seen it told them how he who had been

k John Wycliffe, *The Wycliffe Bible*. **l** William Tyndale, *The Tyndale Bible*. **m** J.H. Heinrich Schmidt, cited by Joseph Thayer, *A Greek-English Lexicon*. **n** James Moulton and George Milligan, *The Vocabulary*.

possessed with demons was restored [to health].

37 Then all the people of the country surrounding the Gerasenes' district asked [Jesus] to depart from them, for they were possessed *and* suffering with dread *and* terror; so He entered a boat and returned [to the west side of the Sea of Galilee].

38 But the man from whom the demons had gone out kept begging *and* °praying that he might accompany Him *and* be with Him, but [Jesus] sent him away, saying,

39 Return to your home, and recount [the story] of how many *and* great things God has done for you. And [the man] departed, proclaiming throughout the whole city how much Jesus had done for him.

40 Now when Jesus came back [to Galilee], the crowd received *and* welcomed Him gladly, for they were all waiting *and* looking for Him.

41 And there came a man named Jairus, who had [for a ᵖlong time] been a director of the synagogue; and falling at the feet of Jesus, he begged Him to come to his house,

42 For he had an only daughter, about twelve years of age, and she was dying. As [Jesus] went, the people pressed together around Him [almost suffocating Him].

43 And a woman who had suffered from a flow of blood for twelve years �q*and had spent all her living upon physicians*, and could not be healed by anyone,

44 Came up behind Him and touched the fringe of His garment, and immediately her flow of blood ceased.

45 And Jesus said, Who is it who touched Me? When all were denying it, Peter ʳ*and those who were with him* said, Master, the multitudes surround You *and* press You on every side!

46 But Jesus said, Someone did touch Me; for I perceived that [healing] power has gone forth from Me.

47 And when the woman saw that she had not escaped notice, she came up trembling, and, falling down before Him, she declared in the presence of all the people for what reason she had touched Him and how she had been instantly cured.

48 And He said to her, Daughter, your faith (your confidence and trust in Me) has made you well! Go (enter) ˢinto peace (ᵗuntroubled, undisturbed well-being).

49 While He was still speaking, a man from the house of the director of the synagogue came and said [to Jairus], Your daughter is dead; do not ˢweary *and* trouble the Teacher any further.

50 But Jesus, on hearing this, answered him, Do not be seized with alarm *or* struck with fear; simply believe [ᵘin Me as able to do this], and she shall be made well.

51 And when He came to the house, He permitted no one to enter with Him except Peter and John and James, and the girl's father and mother.

52 And all were weeping for and bewailing her; but He said, Do not weep, for she is not dead but sleeping.

53 And they laughed Him to scorn, knowing full well that she was dead.

54 And grasping her hand, He called, saying, Child, arise [ᵘfrom the sleep of death]!

55 And her spirit returned [ᵗfrom death], and she arose immediately; and He directed that she should be given something to eat.

56 And her parents were amazed, but He charged them to tell no one what had occurred.

---

o Marvin Vincent, *Word Studies*. p Charles B. Williams, *The New Testament: A Translation*: "The Greek imperfect tense expresses this idea of duration." q Many manuscripts add this phrase. r Some manuscripts add this phrase. s Richard Trench, *Synonyms of the New Testament*. t Hermann Cremer, *Biblico-Theological Lexicon*. u Joseph Thayer, *A Greek-English Lexicon*.

9 THEN JESUS called together the Twelve [apostles] and gave them power and authority over all demons, and to cure diseases,

2 And He sent them out to announce *and* preach the kingdom of God and to bring healing.

3 And He said to them, Do not take anything for your journey—neither walking stick, nor ᵛwallet [for a collection bag], nor food of any kind, nor money, and do not have two undergarments (tunics).

4 And whatever house you enter, stay there until you go away [from that place].

5 And wherever they do not receive *and* accept *and* welcome you, when you leave that town shake off [even] the dust from your feet, as a testimony against them.

6 And departing, they went about from village to village, preaching the Gospel and restoring the afflicted to health everywhere.

7 Now Herod the tetrarch heard of all that was being done by [Jesus], and he was [thoroughly] perplexed *and* troubled, because it was said by some that John [the Baptist] had been raised from the dead,

8 And by others that Elijah had appeared, and by others that one of the prophets of old had come back to life.

9 But Herod said, John I beheaded; but Who is this about Whom I [learn] such things by hearsay? And he sought to see Him.

10 Upon their return, the apostles reported to Jesus all that they had done. And He took them [along with Him] and withdrew into privacy near a town called Bethsaida.

11 But when the crowds learned of it, [they] followed Him; and He welcomed them and talked to them about the kingdom of God, and healed those who needed restoration to health.

12 Now the day began to decline, and the Twelve came and said to Him, Dismiss the crowds *and* send them away, so that they may go to the neighboring hamlets *and* villages and the surrounding country and find lodging and get a ʷsupply of provisions, for we are here in an uninhabited (barren, solitary) place.

13 But He said to them, You [yourselves] give them [food] to eat. They said, We have no more than five loaves and two fish—unless we are to go and buy food for all this crowd, [II Kings 4:42-44.]

14 For there were about 5,000 men. And [Jesus] said to His disciples, Have them [sit down] reclining in table groups (companies) of about fifty each.

15 And they did so, and made them all recline.

16 And taking the five loaves and the two fish, He looked up to heaven and [praising God] gave thanks *and* asked Him to bless them [to their use]. Then He broke them and gave them to the disciples to place before the multitude.

17 And all the people ate and were satisfied. And they gathered up what remained over—twelve [ˣsmall hand] baskets of broken pieces.

18 Now it occurred that as Jesus was praying privately, the disciples were with Him, and He asked them, Who do men say that I am?

19 And they answered, John the Baptist; but some say, Elijah; and others, that one of the ancient prophets has come back to life.

20 And He said to them, But who do you [yourselves] say that I am? And Peter replied, The Christ of God!

21 But He strictly charged and

---

v James Moulton and George Milligan, *The Vocabulary*. **w** Marvin Vincent, *Word Studies*. **x** Marvin Vincent, *Word Studies*. See also footnote on Matt. 14:20.

sharply commanded them [ʸunder penalty] to tell this to no one [no one, ʸwhoever he might be].

22 Saying, The Son of Man must suffer many things and be [ʸdeliberately] disapproved *and* repudiated *and* rejected on the part of the elders and chief priests and scribes, and be put to death and on the third day be raised [again].

23 And He said to all, If any person wills to come after Me, let him deny himself [ᶻdisown himself, ᵃforget, lose sight of himself and his own interests, ᵇrefuse and give up himself] and take up his cross daily and follow Me [ᵃcleave steadfastly to Me, conform wholly to My example in living and, if need be, in dying also].

24 For whoever would preserve his life *and* save it will lose *and* destroy it, but whoever loses his life for My sake, he will preserve *and* save it [ᵇfrom the penalty of eternal death].

25 For what does it profit a man, if he gains the whole world and ruins or forfeits (loses) himself?

26 Because whoever is ashamed of Me and of My teachings, of him will the Son of Man be ashamed when He comes in the [ʸthreefold] glory (the splendor and majesty) of Himself and of the Father and of the holy angels.

27 However I tell you truly, there are some of those standing here who will not taste death before they see the kingdom of God.

28 Now about eight days after these teachings, Jesus took with Him Peter and John and James and went up on the mountain to pray.

29 And as He was praying, the appearance of His countenance became altered (different), and His raiment became dazzling white [ʸflashing with the brilliance of lightning].

30 And behold, two men were conversing with Him—Moses and Elijah,

31 Who appeared in splendor *and* majesty *and* brightness and were speaking of His exit [from life], which He was about to bring to realization at Jerusalem.

32 Now Peter and those with him were weighed down with sleep, but when they fully awoke, they saw His glory (splendor and majesty and brightness) and the two men who stood with Him.

33 And it occurred as the men were parting from Him that Peter said to Jesus, Master, it is delightful *and* good that we are here; and let us construct three booths *or* huts—one for You and one for Moses and one for Elijah! not noticing *or* knowing what he was saying.

34 But even as he was saying this, a cloud came and began to overshadow them, and they were seized with alarm *and* struck with fear as they entered into the cloud.

35 Then there came a voice out of the cloud, saying, This is My Son, My Chosen One *or* ᶜ*My Beloved*; listen to *and* yield to *and* obey Him!

36 And when the voice had died away, Jesus was found there alone. And they kept still, and told no one at that time any of these things that they had seen.

37 Now it occurred the next day, when they had come down from the mountain, that a great multitude met Him.

38 And behold, a man from the crowd shouted out, Master, I implore You to look at my son, for he is my only child;

39 And behold, a spirit seizes him and suddenly he cries out; it convulses him so that he foams at the mouth;

---

y Marvin Vincent, *Word Studies*. **z** James Moulton and George Milligan, *The Vocabulary*. **a** Joseph Thayer, *A Greek-English Lexicon*. **b** Hermann Cremer, *Biblico-Theological Lexicon*. **c** Many ancient manuscripts so read.

and he is sorely shattered, and it will scarcely leave him.
40 And I implored Your disciples to drive it out, but they could not.
41 Jesus answered, O [faithless ones] unbelieving *and* without trust in God, a perverse (dwayward, ecrooked and fwarped) generation! Until when *and* how long am I to be with you and bear with you? Bring your son here [to Me].
42 And even while he was coming, the demon threw him down and [completely] convulsed him. But Jesus censured *and* severely rebuked the unclean spirit and healed the child and restored him to his father.
43 And all were astounded at the evidence of God's mighty power *and* His majesty *and* magnificence. But [while] they were all marveling at everything Jesus was doing, He said to His disciples,
44 Let these words sink into your ears: the Son of Man is about to be delivered into the hands of men [gwhose conduct is opposed to God].
45 However, they did not comprehend this saying; and it was kept hidden from them, so that they should not grasp it *and* understand, and they were afraid to ask Him about the statement.
46 But a controversy arose among them as to which of them might be the greatest [surpassing the others in excellence, worth, and authority].
47 But Jesus, as He perceived the thoughts of their hearts, took a little child and put him at His side
48 And told them, Whoever receives *and* accepts *and* welcomes this child in My name *and* for My sake receives *and* accepts *and* welcomes Me; and whoever so receives Me so also receives Him Who sent Me. For he who is least *and* lowliest among you

all—he is [the one who is truly] great.
49 John said, Master, we saw a man driving out demons in Your name and we commanded him to stop it, for he does not follow along with us.
50 But Jesus told him, Do not forbid [such people]; for whoever is not against you is for you.
51 Now when the time was almost come for Jesus to be received up [to heaven], He steadfastly *and* determinedly set His face to go to Jerusalem.
52 And He sent messengers before Him; and they reached and entered a Samaritan village to make [things] ready for Him;
53 But [the people] would not welcome *or* receive *or* accept Him, because His face was [set as if He was] going to Jerusalem.
54 And when His disciples James and John observed this, they said, Lord, do You wish us to command fire to come down from heaven and consume them, h*even as Elijah did*? [II Kings 1:9-16.]
55 But He turned and rebuked *and* severely censured them. i*He said, You do not know of what sort of spirit you are,*
56 *For the Son of Man did not come to destroy men's lives, but to save them* g[from the penalty of eternal death]. And they journeyed on to another village.
57 And it occurred that as they were going along the road, a man said to Him, *Lord,* I will follow You wherever You go.
58 And Jesus told him, Foxes have lurking holes and the birds of the air have roosts *and* nests, but the Son of Man has no place to lay His head.
59 And He said to another, jBecome My disciple, side with My party, and

d John Wycliffe, *The Wycliffe Bible.* **e** William Tyndale, *The Tyndale Bible.* **f** Marvin Vincent, *Word Studies.* **g** Hermann Cremer, *Biblico-Theological Lexicon.* **h** Some manuscripts add this phrase. **i** Some manuscripts add this to verse 55 and continue into verse 56. **j** Joseph Thayer, *A Greek-English Lexicon.*

accompany Me! But he replied, *Lord,* permit me first to go and bury ([k]await the death of) my father.

60 But Jesus said to him, Allow the dead to bury their own dead; but as for you, go *and* publish abroad [l]throughout all regions the kingdom of God.

61 Another also said, I will follow You, Lord, *and* become Your disciple *and* side with Your party; but let me first say good-bye to those at my home.

62 Jesus said to him, No one who puts his hand to the plow and looks back [to the things behind] is fit for the kingdom of God.

10 NOW AFTER this the Lord chose *and* appointed seventy others and sent them out ahead of Him, two by two, into every town and place where He Himself was about to come (visit).

2 And He said to them, The harvest indeed is abundant [[m]there is much ripe grain], but the farmhands are few. Pray therefore the Lord of the harvest to send out laborers into His harvest.

3 Go your way; behold, I send you out like lambs into the midst of wolves.

4 Carry no purse, no provisions bag, no [change of] sandals; refrain from [retarding your journey by] saluting *and* wishing anyone well along the way.

5 Whatever house you enter, first say, Peace be to this household! [[n]Freedom from all the distresses that result from sin be with this family].

6 And if anyone [worthy] of peace *and* blessedness is there, the peace *and* blessedness you wish shall come upon him; but if not, it shall come back to you.

7 And stay on in the same house, eating and drinking what they provide, for the laborer is worthy of his wages. Do not keep moving from house to house. [Deut. 24:15.]

life point

When Jesus sent His followers out two by two to do His kingdom work (see Luke 10:1–11), He said to them, basically, "Go and find a house and say, 'Peace be unto you.' And if your peace settles on that house, then you can stay there. If it does not, shake the dust off your feet and go on" (see Luke 10:5–11, Matthew 10:12–14).

One time God kept leading me to these scriptures, and I did not know what He was trying to get across to me. Then finally I saw it. He was trying to help me understand the same thing that Jesus was saying to His disciples: "I want you to minister with My power and anointing, Joyce, but to do that you need to live in peace."

In Luke 10:5–7, Jesus was essentially saying, "Once you find a peaceful place, it can be your base of operations, and you can go out and come back, go out and come back. If it is not peaceful, you need to do whatever you can to gain and maintain a peaceful atmosphere because strife and confusion adversely affect the anointing and power of God that rests on your life."

Let me encourage you to do all you can do to ensure peace in your "home base." That way, everyone who lives and works from that place will do so in God's power and with His anointing—and they will have success.

---

k Many commentators interpret it thus. **l** Marvin Vincent, *Word Studies.* **m** John Wycliffe, *The Wycliffe Bible.* **n** Hermann Cremer, *Biblico-Theological Lexicon.*

intimacy with Jesus

We know from Luke 10:1 that Jesus appointed at least seventy people to travel ahead of Him to every place He went. We know that Jesus chose twelve disciples to share a deeper level of intimacy with Him, and out of the twelve there were three—Peter, James, and John—who were taken by Jesus into situations that none of the others shared (see Matthew 17:1, 2). But of these three, who was closest to Jesus? Only John felt comfortable enough to rest his head on Jesus' chest (an act of intimacy) as he listened to the Lord talk at the Passover Feast (see John 13:23). When Jesus was dying on the cross, he told John to take care of His mother. He knew that John loved Him enough to do whatever He asked of Him.

Jesus had seventy acquaintants, twelve disciples, three close friends, and one who loved Him even more deeply than all the others. Jesus loved them all, and they all loved Jesus, but there were few willing to make the same level of commitment as those who entered into a more intimate relationship with Him.

Not everyone is willing to obey God and pay the price required to be close to Him. Intimacy with God requires an investment of time and not everyone is willing to invest the same amount of it.

God does not ask for *all* of our time, but He does ask to be kept in first place at all times (see I John 5:21). Some people think the only way to be close to God is to do nothing but spiritual things. However, God designed us with a body, a soul, and a spirit; and He expects us to take care of each area of our being. If we keep God first, then everything we do can be *spiritual*. Even something like cooking breakfast can be an act of worship if we do it unto the Lord and for His glory.

However, I believe the main issue of intimacy with God involves how we *prioritize* our time.

We may say we do not have time to seek God, but we take time to do the things that are the most important to us. "I am busy" can be an excuse. We all have to fight distractions every day to protect our time to seek God. He is the most important requirement in our lives, so why does He not have that place of importance in our time? Perhaps it is because when we start making a spiritual investment, we want instant gratification. But to seek God means to *continue* craving, pursuing, and going after Him.

We will not experience instant gratification when we seek God. We must sow before we reap; we must invest before we get a return. In other words, we must lose before we gain; we must give up time before we can experience intimacy with God.

8 Whenever you go into a town and they receive *and* accept *and* welcome you, eat what is set before you;

9 And heal the sick in it and say to them, The kingdom of God has come close to you.

10 But whenever you go into a town and they do not receive *and* accept *and* welcome you, go out into its streets and say,

11 Even the dust of your town that clings to our feet we are wiping off against you; yet know *and* understand this: the kingdom of God has come near *you*.

12 I tell you, it shall be more tolerable in that day for Sodom than for that town. [Gen. 19:24-28.]

13 Woe to you, Chorazin! Woe to you, Bethsaida! For if the mighty miracles performed in you had been performed in Tyre and Sidon, they would have repented long ago, sitting in sackcloth and ashes.

14 However, it shall be more tolerable in the judgment for Tyre and Sidon than for you.

15 And you, Capernaum, will you be exalted unto heaven? You shall be brought down to Hades (the regions of the dead).

16 He who hears *and* heeds you [disciples] hears *and* heeds Me; and he who slights *and* rejects you slights *and* rejects Me; and he who slights *and* rejects Me slights *and* rejects Him who sent Me.

17 The seventy returned with joy, saying, Lord, even the demons are subject to us in Your name!

18 And He said to them, I saw Satan falling like a lightning [flash] from heaven.

19 Behold! I have given you authority *and* power to trample upon serpents and scorpions, and [physical and mental strength and ability] over all the power that the enemy [pos-

sesses]; and nothing shall in any way harm you.

20 Nevertheless, do not rejoice at this, that the spirits are subject to you, but rejoice that your names are enrolled in heaven. [Exod. 32:32; Ps. 69:28; Dan. 12:1.]

21 In that same hour He rejoiced *and* gloried in the Holy Spirit and said, I thank You, Father, Lord of heaven and earth, that You have concealed these things [relating to salvation] from the wise and understanding *and* learned, and revealed them to babes (the childish, unskilled, and untaught). Yes, Father, for such was Your gracious °will *and* choice *and* good pleasure.

22 All things have been given over into My power by My Father; and no one knows Who the Son is except the Father, or Who the Father is except the Son and anyone to whom the Son may choose to reveal *and* make Him known.

23 Then turning to His disciples, He said privately, Blessed (happy, ᴾto be envied) are those whose eyes see what you see!

24 For I tell you that many prophets and kings longed to see what you see and they did not see it, and to hear what you hear and they did not hear it.

25 And then a certain lawyer arose to try (test, tempt) Him, saying, Teacher, what am I to do to inherit everlasting life [that is, to partake of eternal salvation in the Messiah's kingdom]?

26 Jesus said to him, What is written in the Law? How do you read it?

27 And he replied, You must love the Lord your God with all your heart and with all your soul and with all your strength and with all your mind; and your neighbor as yourself. [Lev. 19:18; Deut. 6:5.]

28 And Jesus said to him, You have answered correctly; do this, and you

o Joseph Thayer, *A Greek-English Lexicon.*   p Alexander Souter, *Pocket Lexicon.*

will live [enjoy active, blessed, endless life in the kingdom of God].

29 And he, [q]determined to acquit himself of reproach, said to Jesus, And who is my neighbor?

30 Jesus, [q]taking him up, replied, A certain man was going from Jerusalem down to Jericho, and he fell among robbers, who stripped him of his clothes and belongings and beat him and went their way, [[q]unconcernedly] leaving him half dead, as it happened.

31 Now by [q]coincidence a certain priest was going down along that road, and when he saw him, he passed by on the other side.

32 A Levite likewise came down to the place and saw him, and passed by on the other side [of the road].

33 But a certain Samaritan, as he traveled along, came down to where he was; and when he saw him, he was moved with pity *and* sympathy [for him],

34 And went to him and dressed his wounds, pouring on [them] oil and wine. Then he set him on his own beast and brought him to an inn and took care of him.

35 And the next day he took out two denarii [two day's wages] and gave [them] to the innkeeper, saying, Take care of him; and whatever more you spend, I [myself] will repay you when I return.

36 Which of these three do you think proved himself a neighbor to him who fell among the robbers?

37 He answered, The one who

speak the Word

putting the Word to work

When you see people in need, do you know how to help? The parable of the Good Samaritan in Luke 10:29–37 provides some valuable insight. First, it is necessary to draw near to people in difficulty to be able to offer comfort and assess their needs. Second, be aware that you may not be able to meet all of their needs, and that you may need others to help. Pray that God will help you see the needs of those around you and give you wisdom regarding who to help and how best to care for them.

showed pity *and* mercy to him. And Jesus said to him, Go and do likewise.

38 Now while they were on their way, it occurred that Jesus entered a certain village, and a woman named Martha received *and* welcomed Him into her house.

39 And she had a sister named Mary, who seated herself at the Lord's feet and was listening to His teaching.

40 But Martha [overly occupied and too busy] was distracted with much serving; and she came up to Him and said, Lord, is it nothing to You that my sister has left me to serve alone? Tell her then to help me [to lend a hand and do her part along with me]!

41 But the Lord replied to her by saying, Martha, Martha, you are anxious and troubled about many things;

42 There is need of only one *or but* [r]a few things. Mary has chosen the good portion [[s]that which is to her

Jesus, help me be like Mary and choose to put anxieties aside and spend time with You.
ADAPTED FROM LUKE **10**:39

---

q Marvin Vincent, *Word Studies.*   **r** Some ancient manuscripts read "a few things," while others read "only one," and still others read "a few and only one."   **s** Hermann Cremer, *Biblico-Theological Lexicon.*

take time to enjoy Jesus

Are you too busy? It seems today that almost everyone is. Quite often I run into people I have not seen for a long time and when I ask them how they have been they reply, "Busy." I think that is a shame and a problem. Martha was also busy (see Luke 10:40). She was too busy to take time to enjoy Jesus when He came to her home. She was busy working and trying to impress Jesus and everyone else. She wanted everything to be just right, and everything was just right—except her motives.

Mary, on the other hand, seized the opportunity to sit at the feet of Jesus and learn (see Luke 10:39). She knew the work would always be there, but that Jesus would not. We need to spend regular, quality time with God. Do not make the mistake of trying to work Him into your schedule, but make a decision to put Him first and work the rest of your schedule around your time with Him.

Not spending time with God is the biggest mistake we make in our spiritual lives. Isaiah 40:31 tells us that those who wait upon the Lord shall change and renew their strength. They shall mount up with wings as eagles, run and not be weary, walk and not faint. Spending time studying God's Word, praying, and fellowshipping with Him changes us and makes us strong enough to endure whatever challenges come our way in life. The truth of the matter is that we really cannot get along well at all unless we do this one thing that Jesus told Martha was so very important. He told her there was need of only one thing and "Mary has chosen the good portion" (Luke 10:42).

Nobody on a deathbed has ever said, "I wish I spent more time working at the office." Most people wish they spent more time on relationships. If we make right decisions now, we will not live in the agony of regret later on in life. Learn to recognize the time of your visitation, those special times when God calls you to come and spend time with Him. When Jesus knocks at the door of your heart, do not answer with, "I'm busy. Come back another time." Welcome Him in and enjoy His presence.

advantage], which shall not be taken away from her.

1 1 THEN HE was praying in a certain place; and when He stopped, one of His disciples said to Him, Lord, teach us to pray, [just] as John taught his disciples.

2 And He said to them, When you pray, say: *Our* Father *Who is in heaven,* hallowed be Your name, Your kingdom come. *Your will be done* [held holy and revered] on earth as it is in heaven.

3 Give us daily our bread ['food for the morrow].

4 And forgive us our sins, for we ourselves also forgive everyone who is indebted to us [who has offended us or done us wrong]. And bring us not into temptation *but rescue us from evil.*

5 And He said to them, Which of you who has a friend will go to him at

t James Moulton and George Milligan, *The Vocabulary.*

life point

In Luke 10:41, Jesus implied more than we sometimes realize when He spoke the two words, "Martha, Martha." Martha was too busy for relationships; she chose work and worry over intimacy. As a result, she misused her time and missed what was vital to her.

Mary operated in wisdom; she took advantage of the moment. She could spend the rest of her life cleaning, but Jesus was there and she wanted Him to feel welcome. He came to see her and Martha, not their clean house. This does not mean that a clean house is not important, but there is a time for everything—and this was not the time for cleaning house. Let us use wisdom and not miss God's presence when it is available.

midnight and will say to him, Friend, lend me three loaves [of bread],

6 For a friend of mine who is on a

putting the Word to work

Do you ever struggle with how to pray or what to pray for? You are not alone—even the disciples needed to learn how to pray (see Luke 11:1–4)! Although there is no one "right way" to pray, the prayer that Jesus taught His disciples is an excellent model.

Worship, intercession, repentance, surrender, praise, and petition are all important elements of prayer. Even as the disciples did, ask God to teach you about these different aspects of prayer and be sure to spend time with Him in prayer. Daily.

journey has just come, and I have nothing to put before him;

7 And he from within will answer, Do not disturb me; the door is now closed, and my children are with me in bed; I cannot get up and supply you [with anything]?

8 I tell you, although he will not get up and supply him anything because he is his friend, yet because of his shameless persistence *and* insistence he will get up and give him as much as he needs.

9 So I say to you, Ask *and* ᵘkeep on asking and it shall be given you; seek *and* ᵘkeep on seeking and you shall find; knock *and* ᵘkeep on knocking and the door shall be opened to you.

life point

Our asking, seeking, and knocking (see Luke 11:9) must be sincere and we should always be ready to make a deeper commitment to God. When this happens, He will move and send His Holy Spirit to touch each of us in a special way. Ask and believe by faith that God will do something wonderful. While you wait for Him to do it, keep thanking Him and offering Him praise.

10 For everyone who asks *and* ᵘkeeps on asking receives; and he who seeks *and* ᵘkeeps on seeking finds; and to him who knocks *and* ᵘkeeps on knocking, the door shall be opened.

11 What father among you, if his son asks for ᵛ*a loaf of bread, will give him a stone; or if he asks for* a fish, will instead of a fish give him a serpent?

12 Or if he asks for an egg, will give him a scorpion?

13 If you then, evil as you are, know how to give good gifts [gifts ʷthat are

---

u Charles B. Williams, *The New Testament: A Translation*: The idea of continuing or repeated action is often carried by the present imperative and present participles in Greek.   **v** Some manuscripts contain this portion within verse 11.   **w** Hermann Cremer, *Biblico-Theological Lexicon*.

to their advantage] to your children, how much more will your heavenly Father give the Holy Spirit to those who ask *and* ˣcontinue to ask Him!

14 Now Jesus was driving out a demon that was dumb; and it occurred that when the demon had gone out, the dumb man spoke. And the crowds marveled.

15 But some of them said, He drives out demons [because He is in league with and] by Beelzebub, the prince of demons,

16 While others, to try *and* test *and* tempt Him, demanded a sign of Him from heaven.

17 But He, [well] aware of their intent *and* purpose, said to them, Every kingdom split up against itself is doomed *and* brought to desolation, and so house falls upon house. [The disunited household will collapse.]

18 And if Satan also is divided against himself, how will his kingdom last? For you say that I expel demons with the help of *and* by Beelzebub.

19 Now if I expel demons with the help of *and* by Beelzebub, with whose help *and* by whom do your sons drive them out? Therefore they shall be your judges.

20 But if I drive out the demons by the finger of God, then the kingdom of God has [already] come upon you.

21 When the strong man, fully armed, [ʸfrom his courtyard] guards his own dwelling, his belongings are undisturbed [his property is at peace and is secure].

22 But when one stronger than he attacks him and conquers him, he robs him of his whole armor on which he had relied and divides up *and* distributes all his goods as plunder (spoil).

23 He who is not with Me [siding and believing with Me] is against Me, and he who does not gather with Me [engage in My interest], scatters.

24 When the unclean spirit has gone out of a person, it roams through waterless places in search [of a place] of rest (release, refreshment, ease); and finding none it says, I will go back to my house from which I came.

25 And when it arrives, it finds [the place] swept *and* put in order and furnished *and* decorated.

26 And it goes and brings other spirits, seven [of them], more evil than itself, and they enter in, settle down, *and* dwell there; and the last state of that person is worse than the first.

27 Now it occurred that as He was saying these things, a certain woman in the crowd raised her voice and said to Him, Blessed (happy and ᶻto be envied) is the womb that bore You and the breasts that You sucked!

28 But He said, Blessed (happy and ᶻto be envied) rather are those who hear the Word of God and obey *and* practice it!

29 Now as the crowds were [increasingly] thronging Him, He began to say, This present generation is a wicked one; it seeks *and* demands a sign (miracle), but no sign shall be given to it

speak the Word

God, I know that You are faithful and that if I ask and keep on asking, I will receive from You. If I seek and keep on seeking, I will find. If I knock and keep on knocking, the door will be opened.
ADAPTED FROM LUKE **11:10**

---

x Charles B. Williams, *The New Testament: A Translation*: The idea of continuing or repeated action is often carried by the present imperative and present participles in Greek. **y** Marvin Vincent, *Word Studies*. **z** Alexander Souter, *Pocket Lexicon*.

ask, seek, knock

Luke 11:9–13, just as in Matthew 7:7–11, encourages us to keep on asking, seeking, and knocking on a continual basis, day in and day out, 365 days a year, so that we may keep receiving what we need.

How many times do we stay awake all night wrestling with our problems and losing sleep over them, instead of simply casting our cares upon the Lord and asking Him to meet our needs—then trusting Him to do so?

How often do we *try* to make something happen in our lives without asking God for help? How often do we *try* to prosper in some area without asking God for prosperity? And how often do we *try* to handle our own problems without asking God to work them out for us?

Our mistake is failing to ask and seek and knock, failing to trust God, our loving heavenly Father, to give us all the good things that we ask of Him. We struggle and frustrate ourselves with *works of the flesh* when we should humble ourselves under God's mighty hand knowing that in due time He will bring to pass what is right for us (see I Peter 5:5, 6).

In Matthew 7:11, Jesus says, "If you then, evil as you are, know how to give good and advantageous gifts to your children, how much more will your Father Who is in heaven [perfect as He is] give *good and advantageous things* to those who keep on asking Him!" (emphasis mine). In Luke 11:13, Jesus says, ". . . how much more will your heavenly Father give *the Holy Spirit* to those who ask and continue to ask Him!" (emphasis mine).

Notice that both passages say that if we who are evil know how to bless our children with good gifts, how much more will our heavenly Father who is perfect be willing to bless His children with good things. The most important of those "good things" that God wants to give us is His own Holy Spirit. This is a truly awesome gift!

except the sign of Jonah [the prophet]. [Jonah 1:17; Matt. 12:40.]
30 For [just] as Jonah became a sign to the people of Nineveh, so will also the Son of Man be [a sign] to this age *and* generation. [Jonah 3:4-10.]
31 The queen of the South will arise in the judgment with the people of this age *and* generation and condemn them; for she came from the ends of the [inhabited] earth to listen to the wisdom of Solomon, and notice, ªhere is more than Solomon. [I Kings 10:1-13; II Chron. 9:1-12.]
32 The men of Nineveh will appear as witnesses at the judgment with this generation and will condemn it; for they repented at the preaching of Jonah, and behold, ªhere is more than Jonah. [Jonah 3:4-10.]
33 No one after lighting a lamp puts it in a cellar *or* crypt or under a bushel

a John Wycliffe, *The Wycliffe Bible*.

measure, but on a lampstand, that those who are coming in may see the light.

34 Your eye is the lamp of your body; when your eye (ᵇyour conscience) is sound *and* fulfilling its office, your whole body is full of light; but when it is not sound *and* is not fulfilling its office, your body is full of darkness.

35 Be careful, therefore, that the light that is in you is not darkness.

36 If then your entire body is illuminated, having no part dark, it will be wholly bright [with light], as when a lamp with its bright rays gives you light.

37 Now while Jesus was speaking, a Pharisee invited Him to take dinner with him, so He entered and reclined at table.

38 The Pharisee noticed and was astonished [to see] that Jesus did not first wash before dinner.

39 But the Lord said to him, Now you Pharisees cleanse the outside of the cup and of the plate, but inside you yourselves are full of greed *and* robbery *and* extortion and malice *and* wickedness.

40 You senseless (foolish, stupid) ones [acting without reflection or intelligence]! Did not He Who made the outside make the inside also?

41 But [dedicate your inner self and] give as donations to the poor of those things which are within [of inward righteousness] and behold, everything is purified *and* clean for you.

42 But woe to you, Pharisees! For you tithe mint and rue and every [little] herb, but disregard *and* neglect justice and the love of God. These you ought to have done without leaving the others undone. [Lev. 27:30; Mic. 6:8.]

43 Woe to you, Pharisees! For you love the best seats in the synagogues and [you love] to be greeted *and* bowed down to in the [public] marketplaces.

44 Woe to you! For you are like graves which are not marked *or* seen, and men walk over them without being aware of it [and are ceremonially defiled].

45 One of the experts in the [Mosaic] Law answered Him, Teacher, in saying this, You reproach *and* outrage *and* affront even us!

46 But He said, Woe to you, the lawyers, also! For you load men with oppressive burdens hard to bear, and you do not personally [even ᶜgently] touch the burdens with one of your fingers.

47 Woe to you! For you are ᵈrebuilding *and* repairing the tombs of the prophets, whom your fathers killed (destroyed).

48 So you bear witness and give your full approval *and* consent to the deeds of your fathers; for they actually killed them, and you rebuild *and* repair monuments to them.

49 For this reason also the wisdom of God said, I will send them prophets and apostles, [some] of whom they will put to death and persecute,

50 So that the blood of all the prophets shed from the foundation of the world may be charged against *and* required of this age *and* generation,

51 From the blood of Abel to the blood of Zechariah, who was slain between the altar and the sanctuary. Yes, I tell you, it shall be charged against *and* required of this age *and* generation. [Gen. 4:8; II Chron. 24:20, 21; Zech. 1:1.]

52 Woe to you, lawyers (experts in the Mosaic Law)! For you have taken away the key to knowledge; you did not go in yourselves, and you hindered *and* prevented those who were entering.

---

b Hermann Cremer, *Biblico-Theological Lexicon.* **c** Marvin Vincent, *Word Studies.* **d** Joseph Thayer, *A Greek-English Lexicon.*

uncovering the treasures in God's Word

God's Word contains incredible hidden treasures, powerful life-giving secrets that God wants to reveal to us, and Luke 12:2 confirms that whatever is hidden to us will be revealed. How does this happen? These treasures are disclosed to those who meditate, ponder, study, think about, mentally practice, and declare the Word of God.

As a teacher of God's Word, I know personally the truth of this principle. It seems there is no end to what God can show me out of one verse from His Word. I will study it one time and gain an understanding, and later I will see something new that I did not even notice before.

The Lord reveals His secrets to those who are diligent to study and meditate on the Word. Do not be the kind of person who always wants to live off someone else's revelation. Study the Word yourself and allow the Holy Spirit to bless your life with truth. Love God's Word and give it a place of priority in your daily life, and you will walk in wisdom and power.

Meditating on God's Word is one of the most important things that you and I can learn to do. As you go about your daily life, ask the Holy Spirit to remind you of certain scriptures so you can meditate on them. You will be amazed at how much power will be released into your life from this practice. The more you meditate on the Word of God, the more you can readily draw upon its strength in times of trouble. Remember: *the power to do the Word comes from the practice of meditating on it* (see Joshua 1:8).

53 As He left there, the scribes and the Pharisees [followed Him closely, and they] began [e]to be enraged with *and* set themselves violently against Him and to draw Him out *and* provoke Him to speak of many things,
54 Secretly watching *and* plotting *and* lying in wait for Him, to seize upon something He might say [that they might accuse Him].

12 IN THE meanwhile, when so many thousands of the people had gathered that they were trampling on one another, Jesus commenced by saying primarily to His disciples, Be on your guard against the leaven (ferment) of the Pharisees, which is hypocrisy [producing unrest and violent agitation].
2 Nothing is [so closely] covered up that it will not be revealed, or hidden that it will not be known.
3 Whatever you have spoken in the darkness shall be heard *and* listened to in the light, and what you have whispered in [people's] ears and behind closed doors will be proclaimed upon the housetops.
4 I tell you, My friends, do not dread *and* be afraid of those who kill the body and after that have nothing more that they can do.
5 But I will warn you whom you should fear: fear Him Who, after killing, has power to hurl into hell

e Joseph Thayer, *A Greek-English Lexicon.*

(Gehenna); yes, I say to you, fear Him!

6 Are not five sparrows sold for two pennies? And [yet] not one of them is forgotten *or* uncared for in the presence of God.

7 But [even] the very hairs of your head are all numbered. Do not be struck with fear *or* seized with alarm; you are of greater worth than many [flocks] of sparrows.

8 And I tell you, Whoever declares openly [speaking out freely] *and* confesses that he is My worshiper *and* acknowledges Me before men, the Son of Man also will declare *and* confess *and* acknowledge him before the angels of God.

9 But he who disowns *and* denies *and* rejects *and* refuses to acknowledge Me before men will be disowned *and* denied *and* rejected *and* refused acknowledgement in the presence of the angels of God.

10 And everyone who makes a statement *or* speaks a word against the Son of Man, it will be forgiven him; but he who blasphemes against the Holy Spirit [that is, whoever [f]intentionally comes short of the reverence due the Holy Spirit], it will not be forgiven him [for him there is no forgiveness].

11 And when they bring you before the synagogues and the magistrates and the authorities, do not be anxious [beforehand] how you shall reply in defense or what you are to say.

12 For the Holy Spirit will teach you in that very hour *and* [g]moment what [you] ought to say.

13 Someone from the crowd said to Him, Master, order my brother to divide the inheritance *and* share it with me.

14 But He told him, Man, who has

appointed Me a judge or umpire *and* divider over you?

15 And He said to them, Guard yourselves and keep free from all covetousness (the immoderate desire for wealth, the greedy longing to have more); for a man's life does not consist in *and* is not derived from possessing [h]overflowing abundance *or* that which is [i]over and above his needs.

16 Then He told them a parable, saying, The land of a rich man was fertile *and* yielded plentifully.

17 And he considered *and* debated within himself, What shall I do? I have no place [in which] to gather together my harvest.

18 And he said, I will do this: I will pull down my storehouses and build larger ones, and there I will store all [j]my grain *or produce* and my goods.

19 And I will say to my soul, Soul, you have many good things laid up, [enough] for many years. Take your ease; eat, drink, *and* enjoy yourself merrily.

20 But God said to him, You fool! This very night [k]they [the messengers of God] will demand your soul of you; and all the things that you have prepared, whose will they be? [Job 27:8; Jer. 17:11.]

21 So it is with the one who continues to lay up *and* hoard possessions for himself and is not rich [in his relation] to God [this is how he fares].

22 And [Jesus] said to His disciples, Therefore I tell you, do not be anxious *and* troubled [with cares] about your life, as to what you will [have to] eat; or about your body, as to what you will [have to] wear.

23 For life is more than food, and the body [more] than clothes.

24 Observe *and* consider the ravens;

f Joseph Thayer, *A Greek-English Lexicon*. **g** James Moulton and George Milligan, *The Vocabulary*. **h** Alexander Souter, *Pocket Lexicon*. **i** G. Abbott-Smith, *Manual Greek Lexicon*. **j** Some ancient manuscripts read "grain;" some read "produce" or "fruits." **k** Marvin Vincent, *Word Studies*: "The indefiniteness is impressive."

for they neither sow nor reap, they have neither storehouse nor barn; and [yet] God feeds them. Of how much more worth are you than the birds!

25 And which of you by being overly anxious *and* troubled with cares can add a [l]cubit to his stature *or* a moment [unit] of time to his [l]age [the length of his life]?

26 If then you are not able to do such a little thing as that, why are you anxious *and* troubled with cares about the rest?

27 Consider the lilies, how they grow. They neither [wearily] toil nor spin *nor* [m]*weave;* yet I tell you, even Solomon in all his glory (his splendor and magnificence) was not arrayed like one of these. [I Kings 10:4-7.]

28 But if God so clothes the grass in the field, which is alive today, and tomorrow is thrown into the furnace, how much more will He clothe you, O you [people] of little faith?

29 And you, do not seek [by meditating and reasoning to inquire into] what you are to eat and what you are to drink; nor be of anxious (troubled) mind [[n]unsettled, excited, worried, and [o]in suspense];

30 For all the pagan world is [greedily] seeking these things, and your Father knows that you need them.

31 Only aim at *and* strive for *and* seek His kingdom, and all these things shall be supplied to you also.

32 Do not be seized with alarm *and* struck with fear, little flock, for it is your Father's good pleasure to give you the kingdom!

speak the Word

life point

God's children are not to be like the world. The world seeks after things, but we are to seek the Lord and His kingdom. He promises that if we will do that, He will add to us everything else He knows we need (see Luke 12:31).

33 Sell what you possess and give donations to the poor; provide yourselves with purses *and* handbags that do not grow old; an unfailing *and* inexhaustible treasure in the heavens, where no thief comes near and no moth destroys.

34 For where your treasure is, there will your heart be also.

35 Keep your loins girded and your lamps burning,

36 And be like men who are waiting for their master to return home from the marriage feast, so that when he returns from the wedding and comes and knocks, they may open to him immediately.

37 Blessed (happy, fortunate, and [p]to be envied) are those servants whom the master finds awake *and* alert *and* watching when he comes. Truly I say to you, he will gird himself and have them recline at table and will come and serve them!

38 If he comes in the second watch (before midnight) or the third watch (after midnight), and finds them so, blessed (happy, fortunate, and [p]to be envied) are those servants!

39 But of this be assured: if the

God, I will not be anxious and troubled with cares about my life, because I know that I am very valuable to You and that You will take care of me.
ADAPTED FROM LUKE 12:22–24

---

l G. Abbott-Smith, *Manual Greek Lexicon*: "A stage of growth, whether measured by age or stature."
m Some ancient manuscripts read "weave."   **n** Marvin Vincent, *Word Studies*.   **o** G. Abbott-Smith, *Manual Greek Lexicon*.   **p** Alexander Souter, *Pocket Lexicon*.

householder had known at what time the burglar was coming, he would have been awake *and* alert *and* watching and would not have permitted his house to be dug through *and* broken into.

40 You also must be ready, for the Son of Man is coming at an hour *and* a ᑫmoment when you do not anticipate it.

41 Peter said, Lord, are You telling this parable for us, or for all alike?

42 And the Lord said, Who then is that faithful steward, the wise man whom his master will set over those in his household service to supply them their allowance of food at the appointed time?

43 Blessed (happy and ʳto be envied) is that servant whom his master finds so doing when he arrives.

44 Truly I tell you, he will set him in charge over all his possessions.

45 But if that servant says in his heart, My master is late in coming, and begins to strike the menservants and the maids and to eat and drink and get drunk,

46 The master of that servant will come on a day when he does not expect him and at an hour of which he does not know, and will punish him *and* cut him off and assign his lot with ˢthe unfaithful.

47 And that servant who knew his master's will but did not get ready or act as he would wish him to act shall be beaten with many [lashes].

48 But he who did not know and did things worthy of a beating shall be beaten with few [lashes]. For everyone to whom much is given, of him shall much be required; and of him to whom men entrust much, they will require *and* demand all the more. [Num. 15:29, 30; Deut. 25:2, 3.]

49 I have come to cast fire upon the earth, and how I wish that it were already kindled!

50 I have a baptism with which to be baptized, and how greatly *and* sorely I am urged on (impelled, ˢconstrained) until it is accomplished!

51 Do you suppose that I have come to give peace upon earth? No, I say to you, but rather division;

52 For from now on in one house there will be five divided [among themselves], three against two and two against three.

53 They will be divided, father against son and son against father, mother against daughter and daughter against mother, mother-in-law against her daughter-in-law and daughter-in-law against her mother-in-law. [Mic. 7:6.]

54 He also said to the crowds of people, When you see a cloud rising in the west, at once you say, It is going to rain! And so it does.

55 And when [you see that] a south wind is blowing, you say, There will be severe heat! And it occurs.

56 You playactors (hypocrites)! You know how [intelligently] to discern *and* interpret *and* ˢprove the looks of the earth and sky; but how is it that you do not know how to discern *and* interpret *and* apply the proof to this present time?

57 And why do you not judge what is just *and* personally decide what is right?

58 Then as you go with your accuser before a magistrate, on the way make a diligent effort to settle *and* be quit (free) of him, lest he drag you to the judge, and the judge turn you over to the officer, and the officer put you in prison.

59 I tell you, you will never get out until you have paid the very last [fraction of a] cent.

---

q James Moulton and George Milligan, *The Vocabulary*. **r** Alexander Souter, *Pocket Lexicon*. **s** John Wycliffe, *The Wycliffe Bible*.

13

JUST AT that time there [arrived] some people who informed Jesus about the Galileans whose blood Pilate had mixed with their sacrifices.

2 And He replied by saying to them, Do you think that these Galileans were greater sinners than all the other Galileans because they have suffered in this way?

3 I tell you, No; but unless you repent (ᵗchange your mind for the better and heartily amend your ways, with abhorrence of your past sins), you will all likewise perish *and* be lost ᵘeternally.

4 Or those eighteen on whom the tower in Siloam fell and killed them—do you think that they were more guilty offenders (debtors) than all the others who dwelt in Jerusalem?

5 I tell you, No; but unless you repent (ᵗchange your mind for the better and heartily amend your ways, with abhorrence of your past sins), you will all likewise perish *and* be lost ᵘeternally.

6 And He told them this parable: A certain man had a fig tree, planted in his vineyard, and he came looking for fruit on it, but did not find [any].

7 So he said to the vinedresser, See here! For these three years I have come looking for fruit on this fig tree and I find none. Cut it down! Why should it continue also to use up the ground [to ᵛdeplete the soil, intercept the sun, and take up room]?

8 But he replied to him, Leave it alone, sir, [just] this one more year, till I dig around it and put manure [on the soil].

9 Then perhaps it will bear fruit after this; but if not, you can cut it down *and* out.

10 Now Jesus was teaching in one of the synagogues on the Sabbath.

11 And there was a woman there who for eighteen years had had an ʷinfirmity caused by a spirit (ˣa demon of sickness). She was ᵗbent completely forward and utterly unable to straighten herself up *or* to ʸlook upward.

12 And when Jesus saw her, He called [her to Him] and said to her, Woman, you are released from your infirmity!

13 Then He laid [His] hands on her, and instantly she was made straight, and she ᶻrecognized *and* thanked *and* praised God.

14 But the ʸleader of the synagogue, indignant because Jesus had healed on the Sabbath, said to the crowd, There are six days on which work ought to be done; so come on those days and be cured, and not on the Sabbath day. [Exod. 20:9, 10.]

15 But the Lord replied to him, saying, You playactors (hypocrites)! Does not each one of you on the Sabbath loose his ox or his donkey from the stall and lead it out to water it?

16 And ought not this woman, a daughter of Abraham, whom Satan has kept bound for eighteen years, be loosed from this bond on the Sabbath day?

17 Even as He said this, all His opponents were put to shame, and all the people were rejoicing over all the glorious things that were being done by Him.

18 This led Him to say, What is the kingdom of God like? And to what shall I compare it?

19 It is like a grain of mustard seed, which a man took and planted in his own garden; and it grew and became a tree, and the wild birds ᵃfound

---

t Joseph Thayer, *A Greek-English Lexicon.* u Robert Jamieson, A.R. Fausett and David Brown, *A Commentary on the Old and New Testaments.* v Johann Bengel, cited by Marvin Vincent, *Word Studies.* w Marvin Vincent, *Word Studies.* x Hermann Cremer, *Biblico-Theological Lexicon.* y Alexander Souter, *Pocket Lexicon.* z Johann Bengel, cited by Marvin Vincent, *Word Studies.* a James Moulton and George Milligan, *The Vocabulary.*

shelter *and* roosted *and* nested in its branches.

20 And again He said, To what shall I liken the kingdom of God?

21 It is like leaven which a woman took and hid in three measures of wheat flour *or* meal until it was all leavened (fermented).

22 [Jesus] journeyed on through towns and villages, teaching, and making His way toward Jerusalem.

23 And someone asked Him, Lord, will only a few be saved (rescued, delivered from the penalties of the last judgment, and made partakers of the salvation by Christ)? And He said to them,

24 Strive to enter by the narrow door [force yourselves through it], for many, I tell you, will try to enter and will not be able.

25 When once the Master of the house gets up and closes the door, and you begin to stand outside and to knock at the door [again and again], saying, Lord, open to us! He will answer you, I do not know where [ᵇwhat household—certainly not Mine] you come from.

26 Then you will begin to say, We ate and drank in Your presence, and You taught in our streets.

27 But He will say, I tell you, I do not know where [ᵇwhat household—certainly not Mine] you come from; depart from Me, all you wrongdoers!

28 There will be weeping and grinding of teeth when you see Abraham and Isaac and Jacob and all the prophets in the kingdom of God, but you yourselves being cast forth (banished, driven away).

29 And [people] will come from east and west, and from north and south, and sit down (feast at table) in the kingdom of God.

30 And behold, there are some [now] last who will be first [then], and there are some [now] first who will be last [then].

31 At that very hour some Pharisees came up and said to Him, Go away from here, for Herod is determined to kill You.

32 And He said to them, Go and tell that fox [sly and crafty, skulking and cowardly], Behold, I drive out demons and perform healings today and tomorrow, and on the third day I finish (complete) My course.

33 Nevertheless, I must continue on My way today and tomorrow and the day after that—for it will never do for a prophet to be destroyed away from Jerusalem!

34 O Jerusalem, Jerusalem, you who continue to kill the prophets and to stone those who are sent to you! How often I have desired *and* yearned to gather your children together [around Me], as a hen [gathers] her young under her wings, but you would not!

35 Behold, your house is forsaken (abandoned, left to you destitute of God's help)! And I tell you, you will not see Me again until the time comes when you shall say, Blessed (to be celebrated with praises) is He Who comes in the name of the Lord! [Ps. 118:26; Jer. 22:5.]

14 IT OCCURRED one Sabbath, when [Jesus] went for a meal at the house of one of the ruling Pharisees, that they were [engaged in] watching Him [closely].

2 And behold, [just] in front of Him there was a man who had dropsy.

3 And Jesus asked the lawyers and the Pharisees, Is it lawful *and* right to cure on the Sabbath or not?

4 But they kept silent. Then He took hold [of the man] and cured him and ᶜsent him away.

5 And He said to them, Which of

you, having a son ᵈor a donkey or an ox that has fallen into a well, will not at once pull him out on the Sabbath day?

6 And they were unable to reply to this.

7 Now He told a parable to those who were invited, [when] He noticed how they were selecting the places of honor, saying to them,

8 When you are invited by anyone to a marriage feast, do not recline on the chief seat [in the place of honor], lest a more distinguished person than you has been invited by him, [Prov. 25:6, 7.]

9 And he who invited both of you will come to you and say, Let this man have the place [you have taken]. Then, with humiliation and a guilty sense of impropriety, you will begin to take the lowest place.

10 But when you are invited, go and recline in the lowest place, so that when your host comes in, he may say to you, Friend, go up higher! Then you will be honored in the presence of all who sit [at table] with you.

11 For everyone who exalts himself will be humbled (ranked below others who are honored or rewarded), and he who humbles himself (keeps a modest opinion of himself and behaves accordingly) will be exalted (elevated in rank).

12 Jesus also said to the man who had invited Him, When you give a dinner or a supper, do not invite your friends or your brothers or your relatives or your wealthy neighbors, lest perhaps they also invite you in return, and so you are paid back.

13 But when you give a banquet or a reception, invite the poor, the disabled, the lame, and the blind.

14 Then you will be blessed (happy, fortunate, and ᵉto be envied), because they have no way of repaying you, and you will be recompensed at the resurrection of the just (upright).

15 When one of those who reclined [at the table] with Him heard this, he said to Him, Blessed (happy, fortunate, and ᵉto be envied) is he who shall eat bread in the kingdom of God!

16 But Jesus said to him, A man was once giving a great supper and invited many;

17 And at the hour for the supper he sent his servant to say to those who had been invited, Come, for all is now ready.

18 But they all alike began to make excuses and to beg off. The first said to him, I have bought a piece of land, and I have to go out and see it; I beg you, have me excused.

19 And another said, I have bought five yoke of oxen, and I am going to examine and ᶠput my approval on them; I beg you, have me excused.

20 And another said, I have married a wife, and because of this I am unable to come. [Deut. 24:5.]

21 So the servant came and reported these [answers] to his master. Then the master of the house said in wrath to his servant, Go quickly into the ᵍgreat streets and the small streets of the city and bring in here the poor and the disabled and the blind and the lame.

22 And the servant [returning] said, Sir, what you have commanded me to do has been done, and yet there is room.

23 Then the master said to the servant, Go out into the highways and hedges and urge and constrain [them] to yield and come in, so that my house may be filled.

24 For I tell you, not one of those who were invited shall taste my supper.

---

d Many ancient manuscripts so read. **e** Alexander Souter, *Pocket Lexicon*. **f** Kenneth Wuest, *Word Studies*. **g** John Wycliffe, *The Wycliffe Bible*.

25 Now huge crowds were going along with [Jesus], and He turned and said to them,
26 If anyone comes to Me and does not hate his [own] father and mother [[h]in the sense of indifference to or relative disregard for them in comparison with his attitude toward God] and [likewise] his wife and children and brothers and sisters—[yes] and even his own life also—he cannot be My disciple.
27 Whoever does not persevere *and* carry his own cross and come after (follow) Me cannot be My disciple.
28 For which of you, wishing to build a [i]farm building, does not first sit down and calculate the cost [to see] whether he has sufficient means to finish it?
29 Otherwise, when he has laid the foundation and is unable to complete [the building], all who see it will begin to mock *and* jeer at him,
30 Saying, This man began to build and was not able ([j]worth enough) to finish.
31 Or what king, going out to engage in conflict with another king, will not first sit down and consider *and* take counsel whether he is able with ten thousand [men] to meet him who comes against him with twenty thousand?
32 And if he cannot [do so], when the other king is still a great way off, he sends an envoy and asks the terms of peace.
33 So then, any of you who does not forsake (renounce, surrender claim to, give up, [j]say good-bye to) all that he has cannot be My disciple.
34 Salt is good [an excellent thing], but if salt has lost its strength *and* has become saltless (insipid, flat), how shall its saltness be restored?
35 It is fit neither for the land nor for the manure heap; men throw it away.

He who has ears to hear, let him listen *and* consider *and* comprehend by hearing!

15 NOW THE tax collectors and [notorious and [k]especially wicked] sinners were all coming near to [Jesus] to listen to Him.
2 And the Pharisees and the scribes kept muttering *and* indignantly complaining, saying, This man accepts *and* receives *and* welcomes [[k]preeminently wicked] sinners and eats with them.
3 So He told them this parable:
4 What man of you, if he has a hundred sheep and should lose one of them, does not leave the ninety-nine in the wilderness (desert) and go after the one that is lost until he finds it?
5 And when he has found it, he lays it on his [own] shoulders, rejoicing.
6 And when he gets home, he summons together [his] friends and [his] neighbors, saying to them, Rejoice with me, because I have found my sheep which was lost.
7 Thus, I tell you, there will be more joy in heaven over one [[k]especially] wicked person who repents ([k]changes his mind, abhorring his errors and misdeeds, and determines to enter upon a better course of life) than over ninety-nine righteous persons who have no need of repentance.
8 Or what woman, having ten [silver] drachmas [each one equal to a day's wages], if she loses one coin, does not light a lamp and sweep the house and look carefully *and* diligently until she finds it?
9 And when she has found it, she summons her [women] friends and neighbors, saying, Rejoice with me, for I have found the silver coin which I had lost.

h G. Abbott-Smith, *Manual Greek Lexicon.* **i** James Moulton and George Milligan, *The Vocabulary.* **j** Marvin Vincent, *Word Studies.* **k** Joseph Thayer, *A Greek-English Lexicon.*

putting the Word to work

Have you ever lost something of great value, like the man and the woman that Jesus talks about in Luke 15:1–10? If so, you probably spent some frenzied moments searching, retracing your steps, and may have even asked others to help you look for your lost valuable. Do you remember the joy you experienced when you found what was lost? That joy pales in comparison to the joy in heaven when even one sinner repents. If there is someone in your life who does not yet know God, pray often that he or she will soon come to know Jesus as Savior and Lord.

10 Even so, I tell you, there is joy among *and* in the presence of the angels of God over one [[especially] wicked person who repents ([changes his mind for the better, heartily amending his ways, with abhorrence of his past sins).

11 And He said, There was a certain man who had two sons;

12 And the younger of them said to his father, Father, give me the part of the property that falls [to me]. And he divided the estate between them. [Deut. 21:15-17.]

13 And not many days after that, the younger son gathered up all that he had and journeyed into a distant country, and there he wasted his fortune in reckless *and* loose [from restraint] living.

14 And when he had spent all he had, a ^m^mighty famine came upon that country, and he began to fall behind *and* be in want.

15 So he went and forced (glued) himself upon one of the citizens of that country, who sent him into his fields to feed hogs.

16 And he would gladly have fed on *and* ^n^*filled his belly with* the ^m^carob pods that the hogs were eating, but [they could not satisfy his hunger and] nobody gave him anything [better]. [Jer. 30:14.]

17 Then when he came to himself, he said, How many hired servants of my father have enough food, and [even food] to spare, but I am perishing (dying) here of hunger!

18 I will get up and go to my father, and I will say to him, Father, I have sinned against heaven and in your sight.

19 I am no longer worthy to be called your son; [just] make me like one of your hired servants.

20 So he got up and came to his [own] father. But while he was still a long way off, his father saw him and was moved with pity *and* tenderness [for him]; and he ran and embraced him and kissed him [^m^fervently].

21 And the son said to him, Father, I have sinned against heaven and in your sight; I am no longer worthy to be called your son [I no longer deserve to be recognized as a son of yours]!

22 But the father said to his bond servants, Bring quickly the best robe (the festive robe of honor) and put it on him; and give him a ring for his hand and sandals for his feet. [Gen. 41:42; Zech. 3:4.]

23 And bring out ^o^that [wheat-]fattened calf and kill it; and let us ^p^revel *and* feast *and* be happy *and* make merry,

24 Because this my son was dead and is alive again; he was lost and is found! And they began to ^p^revel *and* feast *and* make merry.

l Joseph Thayer, *A Greek-English Lexicon.* m G. Abbott-Smith, *Manual Greek Lexicon.* n Many ancient manuscripts so read. o William Tyndale, *The Tyndale Bible.* p Alexander Souter, *Pocket Lexicon.*

25 But his older son was in the field; and as he returned and came near the house, he heard music and dancing.
26 And having called one of the servant [boys] to him, he began to ask what this meant.
27 And he said to him, Your brother has come, and your father has killed qthat [wheat-]fattened calf, because he has received him back safe and well.
28 But [the elder brother] was angry [with deep-seated wrath] and resolved not to go in. Then his father came out and began to plead with him,
29 But he answered his father, Look! These many years I have served you, and I have never disobeyed your command. Yet you never gave me [so much as] a [little] kid, that I might rrevel *and* feast *and* be happy *and* make merry with my friends;
30 But when this son of yours arrived, who has devoured your estate with immoral women, you have killed for him qthat [wheat-] fattened calf!
31 And the father said to him, Son, you are always with me, and all that is mine is yours.
32 But it was fitting to make merry, to rrevel *and* feast and rejoice, for this brother of yours was dead and is alive again! He was lost and is found!

16 ALSO [Jesus] said to the disciples, There was a certain rich man who had a smanager of his estate, and accusations [against this man] were brought to him, that he was squandering his [master's] possessions.
2 And he called him and said to him, What is this that I hear about you? Turn in the account of your management [of my affairs], for you can be [my] manager no longer.

3 And the manager of the estate said to himself, What shall I do, seeing that my master is taking the management away from me? I am not able to dig, and I am ashamed to beg.
4 I have come to know what I will do, so that they [my master's debtors] may accept *and* welcome me into their houses when I am put out of the management.
5 So he summoned his master's debtors one by one, and he said to the first, How much do you owe my master?
6 He said, A hundred measures [about 900 gallons] of oil. And he said to him, Take back your written acknowledgement of tobligation, and sit down quickly and write fifty [about 450 gallons].
7 After that he said to another, And how much do you owe? He said, A hundred measures [about 900 bushels] of wheat. He said to him, Take back your written acknowledgement of tobligation, and write eighty [about 700 bushels].
8 And [his] master praised the dishonest (unjust) manager for acting ushrewdly *and* tprudently; for the sons of this age are shrewder *and* more prudent *and* wiser in [urelation to] their own generation [to their own age and qkind] than are the sons of light.
9 And I tell you, make friends for yourselves by means of unrighteous mammon (rdeceitful riches, money, possessions), so that when it fails, they [those you have favored] may receive *and* welcome you into the everlasting habitations (dwellings).
10 He who is faithful in a very little [thing] is faithful also in much, and he who is dishonest *and* unjust in a very little [thing] is dishonest *and* unjust also in much.

---

q William Tyndale, *The Tyndale Bible*. r Alexander Souter, *Pocket Lexicon*. s James Moulton and George Milligan, *The Vocabulary*. t John Wycliffe, *The Wycliffe Bible*. u Marvin Vincent, *Word Studies*.

11 Therefore if you have not been faithful in the [case of] unrighteous mammon (ᵛdeceitful riches, money, possessions), who will entrust to you the true riches?

12 And if you have not proved faithful in that which belongs to another [whether God or man], who will give you that which is your own [that is, ʷthe true riches]?

13 No servant is able to serve two masters; for either he will hate the one and love the other, or he will stand by *and* be devoted to the one and despise the other. You cannot serve God and mammon (riches, or ˣanything in which you trust and on which you rely).

14 Now the Pharisees, who were covetous *and* lovers of money, heard all these things [taken together], and they began to sneer at *and* ridicule *and* scoff at Him.

15 But He said to them, You are the ones who declare yourselves just *and* upright before men, but God knows your hearts. For what is exalted *and* highly thought of among men is detestable *and* abhorrent (an abomination) in the sight of God. [I Sam. 16:7; Prov. 21:2.]

16 Until John came, there were the Law and the Prophets; since then the good news (the Gospel) of the kingdom of God is being preached, and everyone strives violently to go in [would force his ʸown way rather than God's way into it].

17 Yet it is easier for heaven and earth to pass away than for one dot of the Law to fail *and* become void.

18 Whoever divorces (dismisses and repudiates) his wife and marries another commits adultery, and he who marries a woman who is divorced from her husband commits adultery.

19 There was a certain rich man who [habitually] clothed himself in purple and fine linen and ᵛreveled *and* feasted *and* made merry in splendor every day.

20 And at his gate there ʷwas [carelessly] dropped down *and* left a certain ʷutterly destitute man named Lazarus, [reduced to begging alms and] covered with [ʷulcerated] sores.

21 He [eagerly] desired to be satisfied with what fell from the rich man's table; moreover, the dogs even came and licked his sores.

22 And it occurred that the man [reduced to] begging died and was carried by the angels to Abraham's bosom. The rich man also died and was buried.

23 And in Hades (the realm of the dead), being in torment, he lifted up his eyes and saw Abraham far away, and Lazarus in his bosom.

24 And he cried out and said, Father Abraham, have pity *and* mercy on me and send Lazarus to dip the tip of his finger in water and cool my tongue, for I am in anguish in this flame.

25 But Abraham said, Child, remember that you in your lifetime fully received [what is due you in] comforts *and* delights, and Lazarus in like manner the discomforts *and* distresses; but now he is comforted here and you are in anguish.

26 And besides all this, between us and you a great chasm has been fixed, in order that those who want to pass from this [place] to you may not be able, and no one may pass from there to us.

27 And [the man] said, Then, father, I beseech you to send him to my father's house—

28 For I have five brothers—so that he may give [solemn] testimony *and* warn them, lest they too come into this place of torment.

v Alexander Souter, *Pocket Lexicon*. **w** Marvin Vincent, *Word Studies*. **x** Joseph Thayer, *A Greek-English Lexicon*. **y** Gerrit Verkuyl, *The Berkeley Version in Modern English*.

the problem with a double purpose

In Luke 16:13, Jesus talked about not serving "two masters." Let me give you an example from a time in my life when I wrestled with this truth.

Some years ago I served at a church as an associate pastor. I loved this ministry and the people of the church, but the Lord told me to leave my job there and start my own ministry.

I knew that when the Lord calls you to do something, you need to do it. If you do not move forward to answer that call, everything else in your life will dry up.

I also knew that I was no longer enjoying what I was doing and eventually realized it was because God was finished with it. And when God gets finished, we may as well get finished too or we will end up essentially miserable trying to serve "two masters." The job I once thoroughly enjoyed, I now dreaded, simply because God was calling me to something new.

Even though I knew all this, I stayed in that position for another year. During that time I experienced all kinds of things that I did not like. I was not happy at all, and I did not know why. Nothing seemed to be right any longer.

Finally, the Lord spoke to me and said, "Take your ministry and go north, south, east, and west." I obeyed that direction, but for three years I deeply felt the loss of what I left behind. I experienced excitement about the future and sorrow over the past at the same time. I could not understand why I felt the sadness and sorrow I did since I thought I had heard from God and was doing His will. My pastor felt the same way I did and we kept trying to work out ways that I could have my own ministry but still work at the church and be heavily involved in all they were doing.

Through all of this, God really dealt with me. Finally, He said to me, "Joyce, I cannot do anything else in your ministry until you set your heart fully and completely on what I have called you to do." I came to realize that I had "soul ties" to that old job. I invested five years of my life there. God told me to move on, but my soul (mind, will, and emotions) was still tied to the place I left behind. My basic problem was that I tried to serve two masters. As long as I was torn between my past and my future, I could not find peace of mind. I made the same mistake that multitudes of others make. I tried to press into the future while holding on to the past.

That is why, when God called Abraham, He told him to get away from his country, his family, his relatives, and everything he knew, and go to a place that God would show him (see Genesis 12:1). This does not mean we must all leave our family members behind to serve God. However, some scholars believe that many of Abraham's relatives were idol worshippers and, for that reason, God did not want anything from the past influencing him. Paul said we must let go of what lies behind and press on to what lies ahead (see Philippians 3:13). The Lord told Israel through the prophet Isaiah, "Do not [earnestly] remember the former things; neither consider the things of old. Behold, I am doing a new thing!" (Isaiah 43:18, 19).

Our problem is that when we want to hold on to the past and still go into the future, we are double-minded and serving "two masters." Let me encourage you today to let go of the past and embrace the good things God has ahead for you!

29 But Abraham said, They have Moses and the Prophets; let them hear *and* listen to them.

30 But he answered, No, father Abraham, but if someone from the dead goes to them, they will repent (^zchange their minds for the better and heartily amend their ways, with abhorrence of their past sins).

31 He said to him, If they do not hear *and* listen to Moses and the Prophets, neither will they be persuaded *and* convinced *and* believe [even] if someone should rise from the dead.

17 AND [Jesus] said to His disciples, Temptations (snares, traps set to entice to sin) are sure to come, but woe to him by *or* through whom they come!

2 It would be more profitable for him if a millstone were hung around his neck and he were hurled into the sea than that he should cause to sin *or* be a snare to one of these little ones [^alowly in rank or influence].

3 ^bPay attention *and* always be on your guard [looking out for one another]. If your brother sins (misses the mark), solemnly tell him so *and* reprove him, and if he repents (feels sorry for having sinned), forgive him.

4 And even if he sins against you seven times in a day, and turns to you seven times and says, I repent [I am sorry], you must forgive him (give up resentment and consider the offense as recalled and annulled).

5 The apostles said to the Lord, Increase our faith (that trust and confidence that spring from our belief in God).

6 And the Lord answered, If you had faith (trust and confidence in God) even [so small] like a grain of mustard seed, you could say to this mulberry tree, Be pulled up by the roots, and be planted in the sea, and it would obey you.

7 Will any man of you who has a servant plowing or tending sheep say to him when he has come in from the field, Come at once and take your place at the table?

8 Will he not instead tell him, Get my supper ready and gird yourself and serve me while I eat and drink; then afterward you yourself shall eat and drink?

9 Is he grateful *and* does he praise the servant because he did what he was ordered to do?

10 Even so on your part, when you have done everything that was assigned *and* commanded you, say, We are unworthy servants [possessing no merit, for we have not gone beyond our obligation]; we have [merely] done what was our duty to do.

11 As He went on His way to Jerusalem, it occurred that [Jesus] was passing [along the border] between Samaria and Galilee.

12 And as He was going into one village, He was met by ten lepers, who stood at a distance.

13 And they raised up their voices and called, Jesus, Master, take pity *and* have mercy on us!

putting the Word to work

When was the last time you thanked God for working in your life? Even if you have not seen your breakthrough yet, it is important to cultivate an attitude of gratitude for all that God has done and is doing for you. Be like the leper in Luke 17:11–19 and be sure to take time to thank God for His work in your life, for His unfailing love and grace, and for all that He means to you.

z Joseph Thayer, *A Greek-English Lexicon*. **a** G. Abbott-Smith, *Manual Greek Lexicon*. **b** James Moulton and George Milligan, *The Vocabulary*.

how to increase your faith

People often pray for "great faith," yet they do not understand that faith grows through challenges like stepping out to do things they do not fully understand or have experience with. I do not believe anyone is automatically a person of great faith; faith becomes great through experience. It develops as it is used.

In Luke 17:5 the apostles said to the Lord, "Increase our faith." Jesus responded in the next verse by encouraging them to have faith like a small mustard seed; then they could say to a mulberry tree, "Be pulled up by the roots, and be planted in the sea," (Luke 17:6) and the tree would obey them. I believe what Jesus meant was that if you have any faith, you will plant it by doing something. One of the ways we release our faith is by doing something God asks of us. Faith often requires us to take action. The apostles were doing nothing in this situation, and yet they wanted great faith.

I am not saying to take action without God's leading. There are times when God does not want us to take action because He wants us to wait for Him to take action for us. However, we need to understand that trust is active rather than passive. It includes being active in prayer, praise, and confession of God's Word. We should actively trust God, pray, and confess His Word in our situation while we wait on Him to act on our behalf. As we do, our faith will increase.

14 And when He saw them, He said to them, Go [at once] and show yourselves to the priests. And as they went, they were cured *and* made clean. [Lev. 14:2-32.]
15 Then one of them, upon seeing that he was cured, turned back, °recognizing *and* thanking *and* praising God with a loud voice;
16 And he fell prostrate at Jesus' feet, thanking Him [over and over]. And he was a Samaritan.
17 Then Jesus asked, Were not [all] ten cleansed? Where are the nine?
18 Was there no one found to return and to °recognize *and* give thanks *and* praise to God except this alien?
19 And He said to him, Get up and go on your way. Your faith (your trust and confidence that spring from your belief in God) has restored you to health.

20 Asked by the Pharisees when the kingdom of God would come, He replied to them by saying, The kingdom of God does not come with signs to be observed *or* with visible display,
21 Nor will people say, Look! Here [it is]! or, See, [it is] there! For behold, the kingdom of God is within you [in your hearts] *and* among you [surrounding you].
22 And He said to the disciples, The time is coming when you will long to see [even] one of the days of the Son of Man, and you will not see [it].
23 And they will say to you, Look! [He is] there! or, Look! [He is] here! But do not go out or follow [them].
24 For like the lightning, that flashes and lights up the sky from one end to the other, so will the Son of Man be in His [own] day.
25 But first He must suffer many

c Hermann Cremer, *Biblico-Theological Lexicon.*

things and be disapproved *and* repudiated *and* rejected by this age *and* generation.

26 And [just] as it was in the days of Noah, so will it be in the time of the Son of Man.

27 [People] ate, they drank, they married, they were given in marriage, right up to the day when Noah went into the ark, and the flood came and destroyed them all. [Gen. 6:5-8; 7:6-24.]

28 So also [it was the same] as it was in the days of Lot. [People] ate, they drank, they bought, they sold, they planted, they built;

29 But on the [very] day that Lot went out of Sodom, it rained fire and brimstone from heaven and destroyed [them] all.

30 That is the way it will be on the day that the Son of Man is revealed. [Gen. 18:20-33; 19:24, 25.]

31 On that day let him who is on the housetop, with his belongings in the house, not come down [and go inside] to carry them away; and likewise let him who is in the field not turn back.

32 Remember Lot's wife! [Gen. 19:26.]

33 Whoever tries to preserve his life will lose it, but whoever loses his life will preserve and ᵈquicken it.

34 I tell you, in that night there will be two men in one bed; one will be taken and the other will be left.

35 There will be two women grinding together; one will be taken and the other will be left.

36 ᵉ*Two men will be in the field; one will be taken and the other will be left.*

37 Then they asked Him, Where, Lord? He said to them, Wherever the dead body is, there will the vultures *or* eagles be gathered together.

18 ALSO [Jesus] told them a parable to the effect that they ought always to pray and not to ᶠturn coward (faint, lose heart, and give up).

2 He said, In a certain city there was a judge who neither reverenced *and* feared God nor respected *or* considered man.

3 And there was a widow in that city who kept coming to him and saying, Protect *and* defend *and* give me justice against my adversary.

4 And for a time he would not; but later he said to himself, Though I have neither reverence *or* fear for God nor respect *or* consideration for man,

5 Yet because this widow continues to bother me, I will defend *and* protect *and* avenge her, lest she give me ᵍintolerable annoyance *and* wear me out by her continual coming *or* ʰat the last she come and rail on me *or* ᶠassault me *or* ᵈstrangle me.

6 Then the Lord said, Listen to what the unjust judge says!

7 And will not [our just] God defend *and* protect *and* avenge His elect (His chosen ones), who cry to Him day and night? Will He ᶦdefer them *and* ᶠdelay help on their behalf?

8 I tell you, He will defend *and* protect *and* avenge them speedily. However, when the Son of Man comes, will He find [ᶠpersistence in] faith on the earth?

9 He also told this parable to some people who trusted in themselves *and* were confident that they were righteous [that they were upright and in right standing with God] and scorned *and* made nothing of all the rest of men:

10 Two men went up into the temple [ᶦenclosure] to pray, the one a Pharisee and the other a tax collector.

---

d John Wycliffe, *The Wycliffe Bible.* **e** Many manuscripts do not contain this verse. **f** Marvin Vincent, *Word Studies.* **g** Joseph Thayer, *A Greek-English Lexicon.* **h** William Tyndale, *The Tyndale Bible.* **i** Richard Trench, *Synonyms of the New Testament.*

life point

In Luke 18:8, Jesus asks whether He will find faith on the earth when He returns. We need to remember that God is pleased with us as long as we believe. We need to maintain a high level of confidence in Him. We must deal sternly with our flesh and not allow it to rule, remembering that Jesus wants to find us full of faith!

11 The Pharisee ʲtook his stand ostentatiously and began to pray thus before *and* with himself: God, I thank You that I am not like the rest of men—extortioners (robbers), swindlers [unrighteous in heart and life], adulterers—or even like this tax collector here.
12 I fast twice a week; I give tithes of all that I gain.
13 But the tax collector, [merely] standing at a distance, would not even lift up his eyes to heaven, but kept striking his breast, saying, O God, be favorable (be gracious, be merciful) to me, the ᵏespecially wicked sinner that I am!
14 I tell you, this man went down to his home justified (forgiven and made upright and in right standing with God), rather than the other man; for everyone who exalts himself will be humbled, but he who humbles himself will be exalted.
15 Now they were also bringing [even] babies to Him that He might touch them, and when the disciples noticed it, they reproved them.
16 But Jesus called them [ˡthe parents] to Him, saying, Allow the little children to come to Me, and do not hinder them, for to such [as these] belongs the kingdom of God.
17 Truly I say to you, whoever does

life point

In Luke 18:17, Jesus stressed the importance of being childlike in our faith. What are children like? Matthew 18:3 states they are "trusting, lowly, loving, and forgiving." Oh, how much more would we enjoy our lives if we only operated in these four virtues! I encourage you to develop them in your life.

not accept *and* receive *and* welcome the kingdom of God like a little child [does] shall not in any way enter it [at all].
18 And a certain ruler asked Him, Good Teacher [You who are ᵏessentially and perfectly ᵐmorally good], what shall I do to inherit eternal life [to partake of eternal salvation in the Messiah's kingdom]?
19 Jesus said to him, Why do you call Me [ᵏessentially and perfectly ᵐmorally] good? No one is [ᵏessentially and perfectly ᵐmorally] good—except God only.
20 You know the commandments: Do not commit adultery, do not kill, do not steal, do not witness falsely, honor your father and your mother. [Exod. 20:12-16; Deut. 5:16-20.]
21 And he replied, All these I have kept from my youth.
22 And when Jesus heard it, He said to him, One thing you still lack. Sell everything that you have and ᵏdivide [the money] among the poor, and you will have [rich] treasure in heaven; and come back [and] follow Me [become My disciple, join My party, and accompany Me].
23 But when he heard this, he became distressed *and* very sorrowful, for he was rich—exceedingly so.
24 Jesus, observing him, said, How

j Marvin Vincent, *Word Studies.* **k** Joseph Thayer, *A Greek-English Lexicon.* **l** Matthew Henry, *Commentary on the Holy Bible.* **m** Hermann Cremer, *Biblico-Theological Lexicon.*

the trap of trusting yourself

In Luke 18:9–14, Jesus tells a parable to people who "trusted in themselves." This means they were proud; they felt confident they were righteous, upright, and in right standing with God because of their own works.

The parable describes two people who came to the temple to pray. One was a Pharisee and one was a tax collector. The Pharisees were revered because they were religious, and the tax collectors were hated because many of them extorted money from their own people. Tax collectors were considered very wicked.

I love the way the *Amplified Bible* depicts this Pharisee. I can almost picture him: "The Pharisee took his stand ostentatiously and began to pray thus before and with himself . . . " (Luke 18:11). Do you see that? The Pharisee was not even talking to God; he was really talking to himself. This portion of Scripture helped me realize that there were times in my own life when I also prayed publicly but I was not truly talking to God. My only concern was how I sounded in front of people. Now when I lead a prayer in front of other people, I always try to keep my attention fully on God, not what the people think about how I sound. We spend too much time being concerned about what everyone thinks.

The Pharisee continued his monologue with himself. He favorably compared himself to others he considered lowly—robbers, swindlers, and adulterers—"or even this tax collector here." Ouch! This Pharisee was saying, "Thank You God that I am not like he is; thank You that I am so holy."

I have never prayed that prayer, but that does not mean I never thought it. You probably have a friend in your life right now that you consider yourself spiritually superior to. This could be a Christian friend who does not practice his or her spirituality the way you do. You attend early-morning prayer three times a week and this person does not. Your tithe even includes money you received as a birthday gift and you are sure theirs does not.

Those Pharisees were such good little tithers. They gave ten percent of every little mint and leaf, every little grain of spice. They would not miss giving their tithes, but they were rotten to the core. Jesus referred to them as a bunch of whitewashed tombs full of dead men's bones. Jesus had a problem with the Pharisees because they put on a good show, but they had rotten hearts (see Matthew 23:23–27). God tells us to give a tithe of all of our increase, but He does not tell us to presume that we know what others are doing.

It is so easy to develop an "I'm better-than-you" attitude when we compare ourselves to others. Guard your heart against self-righteous attitudes. Be like the man in this parable who trusted in the mercy of God—not in himself or his own goodness.

difficult it is for those who have wealth to enter the kingdom of God!

25 For it is easier for a camel to enter through a needle's eye than [for] a rich man to enter the kingdom of God.

26 And those who heard it said, Then who can be saved?

27 But He said, What is impossible with men is possible with God. [Gen. 18:14; Jer. 32:17.]

28 And Peter said, See, we have left our own [things—home, family, and business] and have followed You.

29 And He said to them, I say to you truly, there is no one who has left house or wife or brothers or parents or children for the sake of the kingdom of God

30 Who will not receive in return many times more in this world and, in the coming age, eternal life.

31 Then taking the Twelve [apostles]

life point

Do you have a miserable past? Are your current circumstances negative and depressing? Do you face situations that are so bad it seems you have no real reason to hope? I say to you boldly, *your future is not determined by your past or your present!*

Let me encourage you today to believe that with God all things are possible (see Luke 18:27). Humanly speaking, some things may *be* impossible, but we serve a God who created everything we see out of nothing (see Hebrews 11:3). Give Him your nothingness and watch Him go to work. All He needs is your faith in Him. He needs for you to believe, and He will do the rest.

aside, He said to them, Listen! We are going up to Jerusalem, and all things that are written about the Son of Man through *and* by the prophets will be fulfilled. [Isa. 53:1-12.]

32 For He will be handed over to the Gentiles and will be made sport of *and* scoffed *and* jeered at and insulted and spit upon. [Isa. 50:6.]

33 They will flog Him and kill Him; and on the third day He will rise again. [Ps. 16:10.]

34 But they understood nothing of these things; His words were a mystery *and* hidden from them, and they did not comprehend what He was telling them.

35 As He came near to Jericho, it occurred that a blind man was sitting by the roadside begging.

36 And hearing a crowd going by, he asked what it meant.

37 They told him, Jesus of Nazareth is passing by.

38 And he shouted, saying, Jesus, Son of David, take pity *and* have mercy on me!

39 But those who were in front reproved him, telling him to keep quiet; yet he [n]screamed *and* shrieked so much the more, Son of David, take pity *and* have mercy on me!

40 Then Jesus stood still and ordered that he be led to Him; and when he came near, Jesus asked him,

41 What do you want Me to do for you? He said, Lord, let me receive my sight!

42 And Jesus said to him, Receive your sight! Your faith ([o]your trust and confidence that spring from your faith in God) has healed you.

43 And instantly he received his sight and began to follow Jesus, [p]recognizing, praising, *and* honoring God; and all the people, when they saw it, praised God.

n Marvin Vincent, *Word Studies.*   **o** Joseph Thayer, *A Greek-English Lexicon.*   **p** Hermann Cremer, *Biblico-Theological Lexicon.*

19

AND [Jesus] entered Jeri-cho and was passing through it.

2 And there was a man called Zac-chaeus, a chief tax collector, and [he was] rich.

3 And he was trying to see Jesus, which One He was, but he could not on account of the crowd, because he was small in stature.

4 So he ran on ahead and climbed up in a sycamore tree in order to see Him, for He was about to pass that way.

5 And when Jesus reached the place, He looked up and said to him, Zacchaeus, hurry and come down; for I must stay at your house today.

6 So he hurried and came down, and he received *and* welcomed Him joyfully.

7 And when the people saw it, they all ^q^muttered among themselves *and* indignantly complained, He has gone in to be the guest of *and* lodge with a man who is devoted to sin *and* preem-inently a sinner.

8 So then Zacchaeus stood up and solemnly declared to the Lord, See, Lord, the half of my goods I [now] give [by way of restoration] to the poor, and if I have cheated anyone out of anything, I [now] restore four times as much. [Exod. 22:1; Lev. 6:5; Num. 5:6, 7.]

9 And Jesus said to him, Today is [^r^Messianic and spiritual] salvation come to [all the members of] this household, since Zacchaeus too is a [real spiritual] son of Abraham;

10 For the Son of Man came to seek and to save that which was lost.

11 Now as they were listening to these things, He proceeded to tell a parable, because He was approaching Jerusalem and because they thought that the kingdom of God was going to

life point

Notice that Luke 19:10 says "that which," not "those who." In the previous verse we see that the chief tax collector, Zacchaeus, and his household just received salvation. They were lost and were now saved, but their salvation was not going to end there. The statement Jesus made about coming to save that which was lost tells me He intends to save us not only from our sins, but also from everything Satan tries to do to ruin our lives.

be brought to light *and* shown forth immediately.

12 He therefore said, A certain nobleman went into a distant country to obtain for himself a kingdom and then to return.

13 Calling ten of his [own] bond ser-vants, he gave them ten minas [each equal to about one hundred days' wages or nearly twenty dollars] and said to them, ^s^Buy *and* sell with these while I go *and* then return.

14 But his citizens detested him and sent an embassy after him to say, We do not want this man to become ruler over us.

15 When he returned after having received the kingdom, he ordered these bond servants to whom he had given the money to be called to him, that he might know how much each one had made by ^s^buying *and* selling.

16 The first one came before him, and he said, Lord, your mina has made ten [additional] minas.

17 And he said to him, Well done, excellent bond servant! Because you have been faithful *and* trustworthy in a very little [thing], you shall have authority over ten cities.

---

q G. Abbott-Smith, *Manual Greek Lexicon*.   r James Moulton and George Milligan, *The Vocabulary*.
s William Tyndale, *The Tyndale Bible*.   t Marvin Vincent, *Word Studies*.

18 The second one also came and said, Lord, your mina has made five more minas.

19 And he said also to him, And you will take charge over five cities.

20 Then another came and said, Lord, here is your mina, which I have kept laid up in a ᵘhandkerchief.

21 For I was [constantly] afraid of you, because you are a stern (hard, severe) man; you pick up what you did not lay down, and you reap what you did not sow.

22 He said to the servant, I will judge *and* condemn you out of your own mouth, you wicked slave! You knew [did you] that I was a stern (hard, severe) man, picking up what I did not lay down, and reaping what I did not sow?

23 Then why did you not put my money in a bank, so that on my return, I might have collected it with interest?

24 And he said to the bystanders, Take the mina away from him and give it to him who has the ten minas.

25 And they said to him, Lord, he has ten minas [already]!

26 And [said Jesus,] I tell you that to everyone who gets *and* has will more be given, but from the man who does not get *and* does not have, even what he has will be taken away.

27 [The indignant king ended by saying] But as for these enemies of mine who did not want me to reign over them—bring them here and ᵛslaughter them in my presence!

28 And after saying these things, Jesus went on ahead of them, going up to Jerusalem.

29 When He came near Bethphage and Bethany at the mount called [the Mount of] Olives, He sent two of His disciples,

30 Telling [them], Go into the village yonder; there, as you go in, you will find a donkey's colt tied, on which no man has ever yet sat. Loose it and bring [it here].

31 If anybody asks you, Why are you untying [it]? you shall say this: Because the Lord has need of it.

32 So those who were sent went away and found it [just] as He had told them.

33 And as they were loosening the colt, its owners said to them, Why are you untying the colt?

34 And they said, The Lord has need of it.

35 And they brought it to Jesus; then they threw their garments over the colt and set Jesus upon it. [Zech. 9:9.]

36 And as He rode along, the people kept spreading their garments on the road. [II Kings 9:13.]

37 As He was approaching [the city], at the descent of the Mount of Olives, the whole crowd of the disciples began to rejoice and to praise God [extolling Him exultantly and] loudly for all the mighty miracles *and* works of power that they had witnessed,

38 Crying, Blessed (celebrated with praises) is the King Who comes in the name of the Lord! Peace in heaven [ʷfreedom there from all the distresses that are experienced as the result of sin] and glory (majesty and splendor) in the highest [heaven]! [Ps. 118:26.]

39 And some of the Pharisees from the throng said to Jesus, Teacher, reprove Your disciples!

40 He replied, I tell you that if these keep silent, the very stones will cry out. [Hab. 2:11.]

41 And as He approached, He saw the city, and He wept [ᵛaudibly] over it,

42 Exclaiming, Would that you had known personally, even at least in this your day, the things that make for peace (for ʷfreedom from all the

---

u James Moulton and George Milligan, *The Vocabulary*.   **v** Marvin Vincent, *Word Studies*.   **w** Hermann Cremer, *Biblico-Theological Lexicon.*

distresses that are experienced as the result of sin and upon which your peace—your ˣsecurity, safety, prosperity, and happiness—depends)! But now they are hidden from your eyes.

43 For a time is coming upon you when your enemies will throw up a ʸbank [with pointed stakes] about you and surround you and shut you in on every side. [Isa. 29:3; Jer. 6:6; Ezek. 4:2.] **44** And they will dash you down to the ground, you [Jerusalem] and your children within you; and they will not leave in you one stone upon another, [all] because you did not come progressively to recognize *and* know *and* understand [from observation and experience] the time of your visitation [that is, when God was visiting you, the time ˣin which God showed Himself gracious toward you and offered you salvation through Christ].

45 Then He went into the temple [ᶻenclosure] and began to drive out those who were selling,

46 Telling them, It is written, My house shall be a house of prayer; but you have made it a ᵃcave of robbers. [Isa. 56:7; Jer. 7:11.]

47 And He continued to teach day after day in the temple [ᶻporches and courts]. The chief priests and scribes and the leading men of the people were seeking to put Him to death,

48 But they did not discover anything they could do, for all the people hung upon His words *and* ᵇstuck by Him.

20 ONE DAY as Jesus was instructing the people in the temple [ᶻporches] and preaching the good news (the Gospel), the chief priests and the scribes came up with the elders (members of the Sanhedrin)

2 And said to Him, Tell us by what [sort of] authority You are doing these things? Or who is it who gave You this authority?

3 He replied to them, I will also ask you a question. Now answer Me:

4 Was the baptism of John from heaven, or from men?

5 And they argued *and* discussed [it] *and* reasoned together ʸwith themselves, saying, If we reply, From heaven, He will say, Why then did you not believe him?

6 But if we answer, From men, all the people will stone us ʸto death, for they are ʸlong since firmly convinced that John was a prophet.

7 So they replied that they did not know from where it came.

8 Then Jesus said to them, Neither will I tell you by what authority I do these things.

9 Then He began to relate to the people this parable (ˣthis story to figuratively portray what He had to say): A man planted a vineyard and leased it to some vinedressers and went into another country for a long stay. [Isa. 5:1-7.]

10 When the [right] season came, he sent a bond servant to the tenants, that they might give him [his part] of the fruit of the vineyard; but the tenants beat (ˣthrashed) him and sent him away empty-handed.

11 And he sent still another servant; him they also beat (ˣthrashed) and dishonored *and* insulted him ᶜdisgracefully and sent him away empty-handed.

12 And he sent yet a third; this one they wounded and threw out [of the vineyard].

13 Then the owner of the vineyard said, What shall I do? I will send my beloved son; it is ʸprobable that they will respect him.

---

x Joseph Thayer, *A Greek-English Lexicon*. **y** Marvin Vincent, *Word Studies*. **z** Richard Trench, *Synonyms of the New Testament*. **a** James Moulton and George Milligan, *The Vocabulary*. **b** William Tyndale, *The Tyndale Bible*. **c** Alexander Souter, *Pocket Lexicon*.

14 But when the tenants saw him, they argued among themselves, saying, This is the heir; let us kill him, so that the inheritance may be ours.

15 So they drove him out of the vineyard and killed him. What then will the owner of the vineyard do to them?

16 He will come and [ᵈutterly] put an end to those tenants and will give the vineyard to others. When they [the chief priests and the scribes and the elders] heard this, they said, May it never be!

17 But [Jesus] looked at them and said, What then is [the meaning of] this that is written: The [very] Stone which the builders rejected has become the chief Stone of the corner [Cornerstone]? [Ps. 118:22, 23.]

18 Everyone who falls on that Stone will be broken [in pieces]; but upon whomever It falls, It will crush him [winnow him and ᵉscatter him as dust]. [Isa. 8:14, 15; Dan. 2:34, 35.]

19 The scribes and the chief priests desired *and* tried to find a way to arrest Him at that very hour, but they were afraid of the people; for they discerned that He had related this parable against them.

20 So they watched [for an opportunity to ensnare] Him, and sent spies who pretended to be upright (honest and sincere), that they might lay hold of something He might say, so as to turn Him over to the control and authority of the governor.

21 They asked Him, Teacher, we know that You speak and teach what is right, and that You show no partiality to anyone but teach the way of God honestly *and* in truth.

22 Is it lawful for us to give tribute to Caesar or not?

23 But He recognized *and* under-

stood their cunning *and* ᶠunscrupulousness and said to them,

24 Show Me a denarius (a coin)! Whose image and inscription does it have? They answered, Caesar's.

25 He said to them, Then render to Caesar the things that are Caesar's, ᵍand to God the things that are God's.

26 So they could not in the presence of the people take hold of anything He said to turn it against Him; but marveling at His reply, they were silent.

27 Also there came to Him some Sadducees, those who say that there is no resurrection.

28 And they asked Him a question, saying, Teacher, Moses wrote for us [a law] that if a man's brother dies, leaving a wife and no children, the man shall take the woman and raise up offspring for his brother. [Deut. 25:5, 6.]

29 Now there were seven brothers; and the first took a wife and died without [having any] children.

30 And the second

31 And then the third took her, and in like manner all seven, and they died, leaving no children.

32 Last of all, the woman died also.

33 Now in the resurrection whose wife will the woman be? For the seven married her.

34 And Jesus said to them, The people of this world *and* present age marry and are given in marriage;

35 But those who are considered worthy to gain that other world *and* that future age and to attain to the resurrection from the dead neither marry nor are given in marriage;

36 For they cannot die again, but they are ʰangel-like *and* ⁱequal to angels. And being sons of *and* ᵈsharers in the resurrection, they are sons of God.

37 But that the dead are raised [ᵈfrom death]—even Moses made known *and*

showed in the passage concerning the [burning] bush, where he calls the Lord, The God of Abraham, the God of Isaac, and the God of Jacob. [Exod. 3:6.] **38** Now He is not the God of the dead, but of the living, for to Him all men are alive [whether in the body or out of it] *and* they are alive [not dead] unto Him [in definite relationship to Him].

39 And some of the scribes replied, Teacher, you have spoken well *and* expertly [ʲso that there is no room for blame].

40 For they did not dare to question Him further.

41 But He asked them, How can people say that the Christ (the Messiah, the Anointed One) is David's Son?

42 For David himself says in [the] Book of Psalms, The Lord said to my Lord, Sit at My right hand

43 Until I make Your enemies a footstool for Your feet. [Ps. 110:1.]

44 So David calls Him Lord; how then is He his Son?

45 And with all the people listening, He said to His disciples,

46 Beware of the scribes, who like to walk about in long robes and love to be saluted [with honor] in places where people congregate and love the front *and* best seats in the synagogues and places of distinction at feasts,

47 Who make away with *and* devour widows' houses, and [to cover it up] with pretense make long prayers. They will receive the greater condemnation (the heavier sentence, the severer punishment).

21 LOOKING UP, [Jesus] saw the rich people putting their gifts into the treasury.

2 And He saw also a poor widow putting in two mites (copper coins).

3 And He said, Truly I say to you, this poor widow has put in more than all of them;

4 For they all gave out of their abundance (their surplus); but she has contributed out of her lack *and* her want, putting in all that she had on which to live.

5 And as some were saying of the temple that it was decorated with handsome (shapely and magnificent) stones and consecrated offerings [ˡlaid up to be kept], He said,

6 As for all this that you [thoughtfully] look at, the time will come when there shall not be left here one stone upon another that will not be thrown down.

7 And they asked Him, Teacher, when will this happen? And what sign will there be when this is about to occur?

8 And He said, Be on your guard *and* be careful that you are not led astray; for many will come in My name [ʲappropriating to themselves the name Messiah which belongs to Me], saying, I am He! and, The time is at hand! Do not go out after them.

9 And when you hear of wars and insurrections (disturbances, disorder, and confusion), do not become alarmed *and* panic-stricken *and* terrified; for all this must take place first, but the end will not [come] immediately.

10 Then He told them, Nation will rise against nation, and kingdom against kingdom. [II Chron. 15:6; Isa. 19:2.]

11 There will be mighty *and* violent earthquakes; and in various places famines and pestilences (plagues: ᵏmalignant and contagious or infectious epidemic diseases which are deadly and devastating); and there will be sights of terror and great signs from heaven.

---

j Joseph Thayer, *A Greek-English Lexicon*. k *Webster's New International Dictionary* offers this phrase as a definition of "plague" and "pestilence."

12 But previous to all this, they will lay their hands on you and persecute you, turning you over to the synagogues and prisons, and you will be led away before kings and governors for My name's sake.

13 This will be a time (an opportunity) for you to bear testimony.

14 Resolve *and* settle it in your minds not to meditate *and* prepare beforehand how you are to make your defense *and* how you will answer.

15 For I [Myself] will give you a mouth *and* such utterance and wisdom that all of your foes combined will be unable to stand against or refute.

16 You will be delivered up *and* betrayed even by parents and brothers and relatives and friends, and [some] of you they will put to death.

17 And you will be hated (despised) by everyone because [you bear] My name *and* for its sake.

18 But not a hair of your head shall perish. [I Sam. 14:45.]

19 By your steadfastness *and* patient endurance you [l]shall win the [m]true life of your souls.

20 But when you see Jerusalem surrounded by armies, then know *and* understand that its desolation has come near.

21 Then let those who are in Judea flee to the mountains, and let those who are inside [the city] get out of it, and let not those who are out in the country come into it;

22 For those are days of vengeance [of rendering full justice or satisfaction], that all things that are written may be fulfilled.

23 Alas for those who are pregnant and for those who have babies which they are nursing in those days! For great misery *and* anguish *and* distress shall be upon the land and indigna-

tion *and* punishment *and* retribution upon this people.

24 They will fall by [n]the mouth *and* the edge of the sword and will be led away as captives to *and* among all nations; and Jerusalem will be trodden down by the Gentiles until the times of the Gentiles are fulfilled (completed). [Isa. 63:18; Dan. 8:13.]

25 And there will be signs in the sun and moon and stars; and upon the earth [there will be] distress (trouble and anguish) of nations in bewilderment *and* perplexity [[m]without resources, left wanting, embarrassed, in doubt, not knowing which way to turn] at the roaring ([l]the echo) of the tossing of the sea, [Isa. 13:10; Joel 2:10; Zeph. 1:15.]

26 Men swooning away *or* expiring with fear *and* dread *and* apprehension and expectation of the things that are coming on the world; for the [very] powers of the heavens will be shaken *and* [m]caused to totter.

27 And then they will see the Son of Man coming in a cloud with great (transcendent and overwhelming) power and [all His kingly] glory (majesty and splendor). [Dan. 7:13, 14.]

28 Now when these things begin to occur, look up and lift up your heads, because your redemption (deliverance) is drawing near.

29 And He told them a parable: Look at the fig tree and all the trees;

30 When they put forth their buds *and* come out in leaf, you see for yourselves and perceive *and* know that summer is already near.

31 Even so, when you see these things taking place, understand *and* know that the kingdom of God is at hand.

32 Truly I tell you, this generation ([o]those living at that definite period of time) will not perish *and* pass away until all has taken place.

---

l Marvin Vincent, *Word Studies*. m Joseph Thayer, *A Greek-English Lexicon*. n John Wycliffe, *The Wycliffe Bible*. o Hermann Cremer, *Biblico-Theological Lexicon*.

33 The psky and the earth (qthe universe, the world) will pass away, but My words will not pass away.

34 But take heed to yourselves *and* be on your guard, lest your hearts be overburdened *and* depressed (weighed down) with the qgiddiness *and* headache *and* rnausea of self-indulgence, drunkenness, and worldly worries *and* cares pertaining to [the sbusiness of] this life, and [lest] that day come upon you suddenly like a trap *or* a noose;

35 For it will come upon all who live upon the face of the entire earth.

36 Keep awake then *and* watch at all times [be discreet, attentive, and ready], praying that you may have the full strength *and* ability *and* be accounted worthy to escape all these things [taken together] that will take place, and to stand in the presence of the Son of Man.

37 Now in the daytime Jesus was teaching in [tthe porches and courts of] the temple, but at night He would go out and stay on the mount called Olivet.

38 And early in the morning all the people came to Him in the temple [tporches or courts] to listen to Him.

22 NOW THE Festival of Unleavened Bread was drawing near, which is called the Passover.

2 And the chief priests and the scribes were seeking how to do away with [Jesus], for they feared the people.

3 But [then] Satan entered into Judas, called Iscariot, who was one of the Twelve [apostles].

4 And he went away and discussed with the chief priests and captains how he might betray Him *and* deliver Him up to them.

life point

Judas was one of Jesus' twelve disciples, yet we read that Satan entered into him (see Luke 22:3). We must understand that Satan can work through anyone, even those who are close to us. That is why it is dangerous to expect too much of the people around us. When we expect them never to hurt us, we set ourselves up for severe disappointment.

That does not mean we should adopt a sour, bitter, cynical attitude toward everyone and say, "Well, a person cannot trust anybody these days." I am not saying that at all. I like people, and I trust people. I do not go through life being suspicious of everyone I meet. At the same time, I also do not go through life expecting never to be hurt by anyone because I know that other people are flesh and blood, just as I am. I realize that they are going to fail just as I fail. Therefore, I put my trust not in people but in Jesus, the Friend who sticks closer than a brother. I encourage you to do the same. He will never disappoint you!

5 And they were delighted and pledged [themselves] to give him money.

6 So he agreed [to this], and sought an opportunity to betray Him to them [without an uprising] in the absence of the throng.

7 Then came the day of Unleavened Bread on which the Passover [lamb] had to be slain. [Exod. 12:18-20; Deut. 16:5-8.]

8 So Jesus sent Peter and John,

---

p James Moulton and George Milligan, *The Vocabulary*.   q Joseph Thayer, *A Greek-English Lexicon*. r G. Abbott-Smith, *Manual Greek Lexicon*.   s John Wycliffe, *The Wycliffe Bible*.   t Richard Trench, *Synonyms of the New Testament*.

saying, Go and prepare for us the Passover meal, that we may eat it.

9 They said to Him, Where do You want us to prepare [it]?

10 He said to them, Behold, when you have gone into the city, a man carrying an earthen jug *or* pitcher of water will meet you; follow him into the house which he enters,

11 And say to the master of the house, The Teacher asks you, Where is the guest room, where I may eat the Passover [meal] with My disciples?

12 And he will show you a large room upstairs, furnished [with carpets and with couches properly spread]; there make [your] preparations.

13 And they went and found it [just] as He had said to them; and they made ready the Passover [supper].

14 And when the hour came, [Jesus] reclined at table, and the apostles with Him.

15 And He said to them, I have earnestly *and* intensely desired to eat this Passover with you before I suffer;

16 For I say to you, I shall eat it no more until it is fulfilled in the kingdom of God.

17 And He took a cup, and when He had given thanks, He said, Take this and divide *and* distribute it among yourselves;

18 For I say to you that from now on I shall not drink of the fruit of the vine at all until the kingdom of God comes.

19 Then He took a loaf [of bread], and when He had given thanks, He broke [it] and gave it to them saying, This is My body which is given for you; do this in remembrance of Me.

20 And in like manner, He took the cup after supper, saying, This cup is the new testament *or* covenant [ratified] in My blood, which is shed (poured out) for you.

21 But, behold, the hand of him who

[u]is now engaged in betraying Me is with Me on the table. [Ps. 41:9.]

22 For the Son of Man is going as it has been determined *and* appointed, but woe to that man by whom He is betrayed *and* delivered up!

23 And they began to inquire among themselves which of them it was who was about to do this. [Ps. 41:9.]

24 Now [u]an eager contention arose among them [as to] which of them was considered *and* reputed to be the greatest.

25 But Jesus said to them, The kings of the Gentiles [v]are deified by them *and* exercise lordship [[v]ruling as emperor-gods] over them; and those in authority over them are called benefactors *and* well-doers.

26 But this is not to be so with you; on the contrary, let him who is the greatest among you become like the youngest, and him who is the chief *and* leader like one who serves.

27 For who is the greater, the one who reclines at table (the master), or the one who serves? Is it not the one who reclines at table? But I am in your midst as One Who serves.

28 And you are those who have remained [throughout] *and* persevered with Me in My trials;

29 And as My Father has appointed a kingdom *and* conferred it on Me, so do I confer on you [the privilege and decree],

30 That you may eat and drink at My table in My kingdom and sit on thrones, judging the twelve tribes of Israel.

31 Simon, Simon (Peter), listen! Satan [w]has asked excessively that [all of] you be given up to him [out of the power and keeping of God], that he might sift [all of] you like grain, [Job 1:6-12; Amos 9:9.]

32 But I have prayed especially for you [Peter], that your [own] faith may

---

u Marvin Vincent, *Word Studies*.   **v** Kenneth Wuest, *Word Studies*.   **w** Joseph Thayer, *A Greek-English Lexicon*.

who is the greatest?

Early in my life, I struggled with jealousy and envy as I compared myself to other people. This is a common habit of the insecure. If we are not secure concerning our own worth and value as a unique individual, we will find ourselves competing with anyone who appears to be successful and doing well.

Learning that I was an individual with a God-ordained, unique, personal plan for my life has indeed been one of the most valuable and precious freedoms the Lord has granted me. I am assured that I do not need to compare myself, or my ministry, to anyone.

I am always encouraged that there is hope for me when I look at Jesus' disciples and realize that they struggled with many of the same things I do. In Luke 22:24 we find the disciples arguing over which of them was the greatest. Jesus responded to them by saying that the greatest was actually the one who was willing to be considered the least or the one who was willing to be a servant. Our Lord spent a great deal of His time trying to teach His disciples that life in the kingdom of God is usually the direct opposite of the way of the world or the flesh.

Jesus taught His disciples great principles like these: Many who are first will be last, and the last will be first (see Mark 10:31); rejoice with the lost who have been found (see Luke 15:6, 32); love your enemies and pray for people who persecute you (see Matthew 5:44); it is more blessed to give than to receive (see Acts 20:35). The world says this is foolishness—but Jesus says it is true power. Be a disciple and determine to live your life by Jesus' kingdom principles.

not fail; and when you yourself have turned again, strengthen *and* establish your brethren.

33 And [Simon Peter] said to Him, Lord, I am ready to go with You both to prison and to death.

34 But Jesus said, I tell you, Peter, before a [single] cock shall crow this day, you will three times [utterly] deny that you know Me.

35 And He said to them, When I sent you out with no purse or [provision] bag or sandals, did you lack anything? They answered, Nothing!

36 Then He said to them, But now let him who has a purse take it, and also [his provision] bag; and let him who has no sword sell his mantle and buy a sword.

37 For I tell you that this Scripture must yet be fulfilled in Me: And He was counted *and* classed among the wicked (the outlaws, the criminals); for what is written about Me has its fulfillment [has reached its end and is finally settled]. [Isa. 53:12.]

38 And they said, Look, Lord! Here are two swords. And He said to them, It is enough.

39 And He came out and went, as was His habit, to the Mount of Olives, and the disciples also followed Him.

40 And when He came to the place, He said to them, Pray that you may not [at all] enter into temptation.

41 And He withdrew from them about a stone's throw and knelt down and prayed,

42 Saying, Father, if You are willing,

putting the Word to work

Jesus struggled when faced with the reality of going to the cross, yet He chose God's will over His own (see Luke 22:39–42). How will you respond when God asks you to choose His will over what you want to do? You may never be asked to sacrifice your life for your faith; yet in every sacrifice whether great or small, ask God for the strength to do His will, His way.

remove this cup from Me; yet not My will, but [ˣalways] Yours be done.

43 And there appeared to Him an angel from heaven, strengthening Him in spirit.

44 And being in an agony [of mind], He prayed [all the] more earnestly *and* intently, and His sweat became like great ʸclots of blood dropping down upon the ground.

45 And when He got up from prayer, He came to the disciples and found them sleeping from grief,

46 And He said to them, Why do you sleep? Get up and pray that you may not enter [at all] into temptation.

47 And while He was still speaking, behold, there came a crowd, and the man called Judas, one of the Twelve [apostles], was going before [leading] them. He drew near to Jesus to kiss Him,

48 But Jesus said to him, Judas! Would you betray *and* deliver up the Son of Man with a kiss?

49 And when those who were around Him saw what was about to happen, they said, Lord, shall we strike with the sword?

50 And one of them struck the bond servant of the high priest and cut off his ear, the right one.

51 But Jesus said, Permit ʸthem to go so far [as to seize Me]. And He touched the ᶻlittle (insignificant) ear and healed him.

52 Then Jesus said to those who had come out against Him—the chief priests and captains of the temple and elders [of the Sanhedrin]—Have you come out with swords and clubs as [you would] against a robber?

53 When I was with you day after day in the temple [ᵃenclosure], you did not stretch forth [your] hands against Me. But this is your hour—and the power [which] darkness [gives you has its way].

54 Then they seized Him and led Him away, bringing Him into the house of the high priest. Peter was following at a distance.

55 And when they had kindled a fire in the middle of the courtyard and were seated together, Peter sat among them.

56 Then a servant girl, seeing him as he sat in the firelight and gazing [intently] at him, said, This man too was with ᵇHim.

57 But he denied it and said, Woman, I do not know Him!

58 And a little later someone else saw him and said, You are one of them also. But Peter said, Man, I am not!

59 And when about an hour more had elapsed, still another emphatically insisted, It is the truth that this man also was with Him, for he too is a Galilean!

60 But Peter said, Man, I do not know what you are talking about. And instantly, while he was still speaking, the cock crowed.

61 And the Lord turned and looked at Peter. And Peter recalled the Lord's words, how He had told him,

---

x Charles B. Williams, *The New Testament: A Translation*: "in the Greek present imperative, denoting continued action." **y** Marvin Vincent, *Word Studies*. **z** John Wycliffe, *The Wycliffe Bible*. **a** Richard Trench, *Synonyms of the New Testament*. **b** Capitalized because of what He is, the spotless Son of God, not what the speaker may have thought He was.

Before the cock crows today, you will deny Me thrice.

62 And he went out and wept bitterly [that is, with painfully moving grief].

63 Now the men who had Jesus in custody treated Him with contempt *and* scoffed at *and* ridiculed Him and beat Him;

64 They blindfolded Him also and asked Him, Prophesy! Who is it that struck ᶜYou?

65 And they said many other evil *and* slanderous *and* insulting words against Him, reviling Him.

66 As soon as it was day, the assembly of the elders of the people gathered together, both chief priests and scribes; and they led Him into their council (the Sanhedrin), and they said,

67 If You are the Christ (the Messiah), tell us. But He said to them, If I tell you, you will not believe (trust in, cleave to, and rely on what I say),

68 And if I question you, you will not answer.

69 But hereafter (from this time on), the Son of Man shall be seated at the right hand of the power of God. [Ps. 110:1.]

70 And they all said, You are the Son of God, then? And He said to them, ᵈIt is just as you say; I AM.

71 And they said, What further evidence do we need? For we have heard [it] ourselves from His own mouth!

23 THEN THE whole assembly of them got up and conducted [Jesus] before Pilate.

2 And they began to accuse Him, asserting, We found this ᶜMan per-

verting (misleading, corrupting, and turning away) our nation and forbidding to pay tribute to Caesar, saying that He Himself is Christ (the Messiah, the Anointed One), a King!

3 So Pilate asked Him, Are You the King of the Jews? And He answered him, [ᵈIt is just as] you say. [I AM.]

4 And Pilate said to the chief priests and the throngs, I find no guilt *or* crime in this Man.

5 But they were urgent *and* emphatic, saying, He stirs up *and* excites the people, teaching throughout all Judea—from Galilee, where He began, even to this place.

6 Upon hearing this, Pilate asked whether the Man was a Galilean.

7 And when he found out [certainly] that He belonged to Herod's jurisdiction, he sent Him up to Herod [a higher authority], who was also in Jerusalem in those days.

8 Now when Herod saw Jesus, he was exceedingly glad, for he had eagerly desired to see Him for a long time because of what he had heard concerning Him, and he was hoping to witness some sign (some striking evidence or spectacular performance) done by Him.

9 So he asked Him many questions, but He made no reply. [Isa. 53:7.]

10 Meanwhile, the chief priests and the scribes stood by, continuing vehemently *and* violently to accuse Him.

11 And Herod, with his soldiers, treated Him with contempt and scoffed at *and* ridiculed Him; then, dressing Him up in bright *and* gorgeous apparel, he sent Him back to Pilate. [Isa. 53:8.]

speak the Word

c Capitalized because of what He is, the spotless Son of God, not what the speaker may have thought He was.   d Joseph Thayer, *A Greek-English Lexicon.*

12 And that very day Herod and Pilate became friends with each other—[though] they had been at enmity before this.

13 Pilate then called together the chief priests and the rulers and the people,

14 And said to them, You brought this Man before me as One Who was perverting *and* misleading *and* eturning away *and* corrupting the people; and behold, after examining Him before you, I have not found any offense (crime or guilt) in this Man in regard to your accusations against Him;

15 No, nor indeed did Herod, for he sent Him back to us; behold, He has done nothing deserving of death.

16 I will therefore chastise Him *and* edeliver Him amended (reformed, taught His lesson) and release Him.

17 *fFor it was necessary for him to release to them one prisoner at the Feast.*

18 But they all together raised a deep cry [from the depths of their throats], saying, Away with this Man! Release to us Barabbas!

19 He was a man who had been thrown into prison for raising a riot in the city, and for murder.

20 Once more Pilate called to them, wishing to release Jesus;

21 But they kept shouting out, Crucify, crucify Him!

22 A third time he said to them, Why? What wrong has He done? I have found [no offense or crime or guilt] in Him nothing deserving of death; I will therefore chastise Him [gin order to teach Him better] and release Him.

23 But they were insistent *and* urgent, demanding with loud cries that He should be crucified. And their voices prevailed (accomplished their purpose).

24 And Pilate gave sentence, that what they asked should be done.

25 So he released the man who had been thrown into prison for riot and murder, for whom they continued to ask, but Jesus he delivered up to be done with as they willed.

26 And as they led Him away, they seized one Simon of Cyrene, who was coming in from the country, and laid on him the cross and made him carry it behind Jesus.

27 And there accompanied [Jesus] a great multitude of the people, [including] women who bewailed and lamented Him.

28 But Jesus, turning toward them, said, Daughters of Jerusalem, do not weep for Me, but weep for yourselves and for your children.

29 For behold, the days are coming during which they will say, Blessed (happy, fortunate, and hto be envied) are the barren, and the wombs that have not borne, and the breasts that have never nursed [babies]!

30 Then they will begin to say to the mountains, Fall on us! and to the hills, Cover (conceal, hide) us!

31 For if they do these things when the timber is green, what will happen when it is dry?

32 Two others also, who were criminals, were led away to be executed with Him. [Isa. 53:12.]

33 And when they came to the place which is called The Skull [Latin: Calvary; Hebrew: Golgotha], there they crucified Him, and [along with] the criminals, one on the right and one on the left.

34 And Jesus prayed, Father, forgive them, for they know not what they do. And they divided His garments *and* distributed them by casting lots for them. [Ps. 22:18.]

35 Now the people stood by [gcalmly and leisurely] watching; but the rulers

---

e John Wycliffe, *The Wycliffe Bible.* f Many manuscripts do not contain this verse. g Marvin Vincent, *Word Studies.* h Alexander Souter, *Pocket Lexicon.*

scoffed *and* sneered ([i]turned up their noses) at Him, saying, He rescued others [[i]from death]; let Him now rescue Himself, if He is the Christ (the Messiah) of God, His Chosen One!

36 The soldiers also ridiculed *and* made sport of Him, coming up and offering Him vinegar (a sour wine mixed with water) [Ps. 69:21.]

37 And saying, If you are the King of the Jews, save (rescue) Yourself [[i]from death].

38 For there was also an inscription above Him [k]*in letters of Greek and Latin and Hebrew*: This is the King of the Jews.

39 One of the criminals who was suspended kept up a railing at Him, saying, Are You not the Christ (the Messiah)? Rescue Yourself and us [[i]from death]!

40 But the other one reproved him, saying, Do you not even fear God, seeing you yourself are under the same sentence of condemnation *and* suffering the same penalty?

41 And we indeed suffer it justly, receiving the due reward of our actions; but this Man has done nothing out of the way [nothing [l]strange or eccentric or perverse or unreasonable].

42 Then he said to Jesus, *Lord,* remember me when You come [l]in Your kingly glory!

43 And He answered him, Truly I tell you, today you shall be with Me in Paradise.

44 It was now about the sixth hour (midday), and darkness enveloped the whole land *and* earth until the ninth hour (about three o'clock in the afternoon),

45 While the sun's light faded *or* [m]*was darkened*; and the curtain [of the Holy of Holies] of the temple was torn in two. [Exod. 26:31-35.]

46 And Jesus, crying out with a loud voice, said, Father, into Your hands I commit My spirit! And with these words, He expired. [Ps. 31:5.]

47 Now the centurion, having seen what had taken place, [j]recognized God *and* thanked *and* praised Him, and said, Indeed, without question, this Man was upright (just and innocent)!

48 And all the throngs that had gathered to see this spectacle, when they saw what had taken place, returned to their homes, beating their breasts.

49 And all the acquaintances of [Jesus] and the women who had followed Him from Galilee stood at a distance and watched these things.

50 Now notice, there was a man named Joseph from the Jewish town of Arimathea. He was a member of the council (the Sanhedrin), and a good (upright, [j]advantageous) man, and righteous (in right standing with God and man),

51 Who had not agreed with *or* assented to the purpose and action of the others; and he was expecting *and* waiting for the kingdom of God.

52 This man went to Pilate and asked for the body of Jesus.

53 Then he took it down and [n]rolled it up in a linen cloth [o]for swathing dead bodies and laid Him in a rock-hewn tomb, where no one had ever yet been laid.

---

i Literal translation. **j** Hermann Cremer, *Biblico-Theological Lexicon*. **k** Some manuscripts add this phrase. **l** Marvin Vincent, *Word Studies*. **m** Many ancient manuscripts so read. **n** Robert Young, *Analytical Concordance*. **o** James Moulton and George Milligan, *The Vocabulary*.

54 It was the day of Preparation [for the Sabbath], and the Sabbath was dawning (approaching).

55 The women who had come with [Jesus] from Galilee followed closely and saw the tomb and how His body was laid.

56 Then they went back and made ready spices and ointments (perfumes). On the Sabbath day they rested in accordance with the commandment. [Exod. 12:16; 20:10.]

24 BUT ON the first day of the week, at early dawn, [the women] went to the tomb, taking the spices which they had made ready.

2 And they found the stone rolled back from the tomb,

3 But when they went inside, they did not find the body of the Lord Jesus.

4 And while they were perplexed *and* wondering what to do about this, behold, two men in dazzling raiment suddenly stood beside them.

5 And as [the women] were frightened and were bowing their faces to the ground, the men said to them, Why do you look for the living among [those who are] dead?

6 He is not here, but has risen! Remember how He told you while He was still in Galilee

7 That the Son of Man must be given over into the hands of sinful men (men Pwhose way or nature is to act in opposition to God) and be crucified and on the third day rise [Pfrom death]. [Ps. 16:10.]

8 And they remembered His words.

9 And having returned from the tomb, they reported all these things [taken together] to the eleven apostles and to all the rest.

10 Now it was Mary Magdalene and Joanna and Mary the mother of James, and the other women with them, who reported these things to the apostles.

11 But these reports seemed to the men an idle tale (qmadness, rfeigned things, snonsense), and they did not believe the women.

12 But Peter got up and ran to the tomb; and stooping down and looking in, he saw the linen cloths alone by themselves, and he went away, wondering about *and* marveling at what had happened.

13 And behold, that very day two of [the disciples] were going to a village called Emmaus, [which is] about seven miles from Jerusalem.

14 And they were talking with each other about all these things that had occurred.

15 And while they were conversing and discussing together, Jesus Himself caught up with them and was already accompanying them.

16 But their eyes were held, so that they did not recognize Him.

17 And He said to them, What is this discussion that you are exchanging (throwing back and forth) between yourselves as you walk along? And they stood still, looking sad *and* downcast.

18 Then one of them, named Cleopas, answered Him, Do you alone dwell as a stranger in Jerusalem and not know the things that have occurred there in these days?

19 And He said to them, What [kind of] things? And they said to Him, About Jesus of Nazareth, Who was a Prophet mighty in work and word before God and all the people—

20 And how our chief priests and rulers gave Him up to be sentenced to death, and crucified Him.

---

p Hermann Cremer, *Biblico-Theological Lexicon.* **q** John Wycliffe, *The Wycliffe Bible.* **r** William Tyndale, *The Tyndale Bible.* **s** James Moulton and George Milligan, *The Vocabulary.* **t** Literal translation.

21 But we were hoping that it was He Who would redeem *and* set Israel free. Yes, and besides all this, it is now the third day since these things occurred.

22 And moreover, some women of our company astounded us *and* ᵘdrove us out of our senses. They were at the tomb early [in the morning]

23 But did not find His body; and they returned saying that they had [even] seen a vision of angels, who said that He was alive!

24 So some of those [who were] with us went to the tomb and they found it just as the women had said, but Him they did not see.

25 And [Jesus] said to them, O foolish ones [sluggish in mind, dull of perception] and slow of heart to believe (adhere to and trust in and rely on) everything that the prophets have spoken!

26 Was it not necessary *and* ᵛessentially fitting that the Christ (the Messiah) should suffer all these things before entering into His glory (His majesty and splendor)?

27 Then beginning with Moses and [throughout] all the Prophets, He went on explaining *and* interpreting to them in all the Scriptures the things concerning *and* referring to Himself.

28 Then they drew near the village to which they were going, and He acted as if He would go further.

29 But they urged *and* insisted, saying to Him, Remain with us, for it is toward evening, and the day is now far spent. So He went in to stay with them.

30 And it occurred that as He reclined at table with them, He took [a loaf of] bread and praised [God] *and* gave thanks *and* asked a blessing, and then broke it and was giving it to them

31 When their eyes were [instantly] opened and they [clearly] recognized Him, and He vanished (ᵛdeparted invisibly).

32 And they said to one another, Were not our hearts greatly moved *and* burning within us while He was talking with us on the road and as He opened *and* explained to us [the sense of] the Scriptures?

33 And rising up that very hour, they went back to Jerusalem, where they found the Eleven [apostles] gathered together and those who were with them,

34 Who said, The Lord really has risen and has appeared to Simon (Peter)!

35 Then they [themselves] ᵛrelated [in full] what had happened on the road, and how He was known *and* recognized by them in the breaking of bread.

36 Now while they were talking about this, Jesus Himself took His stand among them and said to them, Peace (ʷfreedom from all the distresses that are experienced as the result of sin) be to you!

37 But they were so startled and terrified that they thought they saw a spirit.

38 And He said to them, Why are you disturbed *and* troubled, and why do such doubts *and* questionings arise in your hearts?

39 See My hands and My feet, that it is I Myself! Feel *and* handle Me and see, for a spirit does not have flesh and bones, as you see that I have.

40 And when He had said this, He showed them His hands and His feet.

41 And while [since] they still could not believe it for sheer joy and marveled, He said to them, Have you anything here to eat?

42 They gave Him a piece of broiled fish,

---

u Literal translation.   **v** Marvin Vincent, *Word Studies*.   **w** Hermann Cremer, *Biblico-Theological Lexicon*.

43 And He took [it] and ate [it] before them.

44 Then He said to them, This is what I told you while I was still with you: everything which is written concerning Me in the Law of Moses and the Prophets and the Psalms must be fulfilled.

45 Then He [thoroughly] opened up their minds to understand the Scriptures,

46 And said to them, Thus it is written that the Christ (the Messiah) should suffer and on the third day rise from (*among) the dead, [Hos. 6:2.]

47 And that repentance [with a view to and as the condition of] forgiveness of sins should be preached in His name to all nations, beginning from Jerusalem.

48 You are witnesses of these things.

49 And behold, I will send forth upon you what My Father has promised; but remain in the city [Jerusalem] until you are clothed with power from on high.

50 Then He conducted them out as far as Bethany, and, lifting up His hands, He invoked a blessing on them.

51 And it occurred that while He was blessing them, He parted from them and was taken up into heaven.

52 And they, worshiping Him, went back to Jerusalem with great joy;

53 And they were continually in the temple *celebrating with praises and* blessing *and* extolling God. *Amen (so be it).*

x George Ricker Berry, *Greek-English New Testament Lexicon.*

John

Author:
Apostle John

Date:
Near the close of the first century

Everyday Life Principles:
We live under a new commandment: to love one another. This is essential.

Apart from Jesus, we can do nothing.

The Holy Spirit is our Comforter, our Counselor, our Helper and our Teacher. He is also the Spirit of Truth.

While Matthew, Mark and Luke differ in several ways, they are similar in that they include many of the same teachings and parables of Jesus in sequential order. John, on the other hand, does not take such a chronological approach, but tells about Jesus in terms of themes and topics.

One of the great themes in John is love—loving God, receiving His love and loving others. In John 13:34, Jesus says: "I give you a new commandment: that you should love one another. Just as I have loved you, so you too should love one another." This is one of the most important principles of our faith and is vital to our lives as believers.

Another important theme in John is the necessity of abiding in Jesus. In John 15:5, He tells us: " . . . apart from Me [cut off from vital union with Me] you can do nothing." We must stay as close to Jesus as we possibly can. As we do, we are blessed and our lives bear much fruit.

John also gives us great insight into the ministry of the Holy Spirit (see chapters 14—16), who is our Teacher, our Comforter, our Helper, our Counselor and the Spirit of Truth.

As you read John, be reminded of God's love for you and of the necessity of staying intimately connected to Jesus. Allow the Holy Spirit to minister to you in every area of your life.

1 IN THE beginning [before all time] was the Word ([a]Christ), and the Word was with God, and the Word was God [b]Himself. [Isa. 9:6.]

2 He was present originally with God.

3 All things were made *and* came into existence through Him; and without Him was not even one thing made that has come into being.

4 In Him was Life, and the Life was the Light of men.

5 And the Light shines on in the darkness, for the darkness has never overpowered it [put it out or absorbed it or appropriated it, and is unreceptive to it].

6 There came a man sent from God, whose name was John. [Mal. 3:1.]

7 This man came to witness, that he might testify of the Light, that all men might believe in it [adhere to it, trust it, and rely upon it] through him.

8 He was not the Light himself, but came that he might bear witness regarding the Light.

9 There it was—the true Light [was then] coming into the world [the genuine, perfect, steadfast Light] that illumines every person. [Isa. 49:6.]

10 He came into the world, and though the world was made through Him, the world did not recognize Him [did not know Him].

11 He came to that which belonged to Him [to His own—His domain, creation, things, world], and they who

were His own did not receive Him *and* did not welcome Him.

12 But to as many as did receive *and* welcome Him, He gave the authority (power, privilege, right) to become the children of God, that is, to those who believe in (adhere to, trust in, and rely on) His name—[Isa. 56:5.]

13 Who owe their birth neither to [c]bloods nor to the will of the flesh [that of physical impulse] nor to the will of man [that of a natural father], but to God. [They are born of God!]

14 And the Word (Christ) became flesh (human, incarnate) and tabernacled (fixed His tent of flesh, lived awhile) among us; and we [actually] saw His glory (His honor, His majesty), such glory as an only begotten son receives from his father, full of grace (favor, loving-kindness) and truth. [Isa. 40:5.]

15 John testified about Him and cried out, This was He of Whom I said, He Who comes after me has priority over me, for He was before me. [He takes rank above me, for He existed before I did. He has advanced before me, because He is my Chief.]

16 For out of His fullness (abundance) we have all received [all had a share and we were all supplied with] one grace after another *and* spiritual blessing upon spiritual blessing *and* even favor upon favor *and* gift [heaped] upon gift.

17 For while the Law was given

speak the Word

Thank You, Jesus, that because I have received You, You have given me the authority to become a child of God, because I believe in, adhere to and rely on Your name.
ADAPTED FROM JOHN 1:12

a In John's vision (Rev. 19), he sees Christ returning as Warrior-Messiah-King, and "the title by which He is called is The Word of God . . . and Lord of lords" (Rev. 19:13, 16). **b** Charles B. Williams, *The New Testament: A Translation in the Language of the People*: "God" appears first in the Greek word order in this phrase, denoting emphasis—so "God Himself." **c** Literal translation.

through Moses, grace ([d]unearned, undeserved favor and spiritual blessing) and truth came through Jesus Christ. [Exod. 20:1.]

18 No man has ever seen God at any time; *the only [e]unique Son, or [f]the only begotten God,* Who is in the bosom [in the intimate presence] of the Father, He has declared Him [He has revealed Him and brought Him out where He can be seen; He has interpreted Him and He has made Him known]. [Prov. 8:30.]

19 And this is the testimony of John when the Jews sent priests and Levites to him from Jerusalem to ask him, Who are you?

20 He confessed (admitted the truth) and did not try to conceal it, but acknowledged, I am not the Christ!

21 They asked him, What then? Are you Elijah? And he said, I am not! Are you the Prophet? And he answered, No! [Deut. 18:15, 18; Mal. 4:5.]

22 Then they said to him, Who are you? Tell us, so that we may give an answer to those who sent us. What do you say about yourself?

23 He said, I am the voice of one crying aloud in the wilderness [the voice of one shouting in the desert], Prepare the way of the Lord [level, straighten out, the path of the Lord], as the prophet Isaiah said. [Isa. 40:3.]

24 The messengers had been sent from the Pharisees.

25 And they asked him, Why then are you baptizing if you are not the Christ, nor Elijah, nor the Prophet?

26 John answered them, I [only] baptize [g]in (with) water. Among you there stands One Whom you do not recognize *and* with Whom you are not acquainted *and* of Whom you know nothing. [Mal. 3:1.]

27 It is He Who, coming after me, is preferred before me, the string of Whose sandal I am not worthy to unloose.

28 These things occurred in Bethany (Bethabara) across the Jordan [[h]at the Jordan crossing], where John was then baptizing.

29 The next day John saw Jesus coming to him and said, Look! There is the Lamb of God, Who takes away the sin of the world! [Exod. 12:3; Isa. 53:7.]

30 This is He of Whom I said, After me comes a Man Who has priority over me [Who takes rank above me] because He was before me *and* existed before I did.

31 And I did not know Him *and* did not recognize Him [myself]; but it is in order that He should be made manifest *and* be revealed to Israel [be brought out where we can see Him] that I came baptizing [i]in (with) water.

32 John gave further evidence, saying, I have seen the Spirit descending as a dove out of heaven, and it dwelt on Him [never to depart].

33 And I did not know Him *nor* recognize Him, but He Who sent me to baptize [i]in (with) water said to me, Upon Him Whom you shall see the Spirit descend and remain, that One is He Who baptizes with the Holy Spirit.

34 And I have seen [that happen—I actually did see it] and my testimony is that this is the Son of God!

35 Again the next day John was standing with two of his disciples,

36 And he looked at Jesus as He walked along, and said, Look! There is the Lamb of God!

37 The two disciples heard him say this, and they followed Him.

38 But Jesus turned, and as He saw them following Him, He said to them,

---

d Richard Trench, *Synonyms of the New Testament.* **e** James Moulton and George Milligan, *The Vocabulary of the Greek Testament.* **f** Marvin Vincent, *Word Studies in the New Testament*: This reading is supported by "a great mass of ancient evidence." **g** The Greek can be translated "with" or "in;" also in verses 31 and 33. The KJV prefers "with," while the ASV prefers "in." **h** George M. Lamsa, *The New Testament According to the Ancient Text.* **i** See footnote on John 1:26.

dealing with prejudice

For years, I did not understand John 1:45–47. Nathanael seemed to make a negative statement when he said, "Can anything good come out of Nazareth?" Yet in the next verse Jesus seemed to compliment Nathanael saying, "Here is an Israelite indeed [a true descendent of Jacob], in whom there is no guile nor deceit nor falsehood nor duplicity!"

Then one day I saw it. Nathanael had a negative opinion of Nazareth because the prevailing sentiment of his day was that nothing good ever happened there. So when he heard that Jesus was from Nazareth, Nathanael was initially closed to the idea that Jesus was the true Messiah simply because of where He came from.

So often we are like Nathanael. We decide that a person cannot be any good because of where he lives or where he comes from. We can be so biased and opinionated, often without even realizing it. We have prejudices that have been placed in us by others through the things they have said to us. This is why we have to carefully examine our hearts to see if they are truly open.

The thing Jesus seemed to like about Nathanael was that although he seemed convinced that nothing good could come out of Nazareth, he was willing to check it out. Even though he had a strong opinion, he had an open heart. Let me encourage you to have an open heart toward everyone you meet. Think of it. If Nathanael had been unwilling to open his heart to Jesus, he would have missed the greatest blessing of his life—a great relationship with the Lord. I believe God has blessings in store for you through relationships too, so keep your heart open.

What are you looking for? [And what is it you wish?] And they answered Him, Rabbi—which translated is Teacher—where are You staying?

39 He said to them, Come and see. So they went and saw where He was staying, and they remained with Him ʲthat day. It was then about the tenth hour (about four o'clock in the afternoon).

40 One of the two who heard what John said and followed Jesus was Andrew, Simon Peter's brother.

41 He first sought out *and* found his own brother Simon and said to him, We have found (discovered) the Messiah!—which translated is the Christ (the Anointed One).

42 Andrew then led (brought) Simon to Jesus. Jesus looked at him and said, You are Simon son of John. You shall be called Cephas—which translated is Peter [Stone].

43 The next day Jesus desired *and* decided to go into Galilee; and He found Philip and said to him, Join Me as My attendant *and* follow Me.

44 Now Philip was from Bethsaida, of the same city as Andrew and Peter.

45 Philip sought *and* found Nathanael and told him, We have found (discovered) the One Moses in the Law and also the Prophets wrote about—Jesus from Nazareth, the [legal] son of Joseph!

46 Nathanael answered him, [Nazareth!] Can anything good come out of

j George M. Lamsa, *Gospel Light from the Aramaic*: In accordance with Oriental hospitality, the guests would be invited to remain that night also.

Nazareth? Philip replied, Come and see!

47 Jesus saw Nathanael coming toward Him and said concerning him, See! Here is an Israelite indeed [a true descendant of Jacob], in whom there is no guile *nor* deceit *nor* falsehood *nor* duplicity!

48 Nathanael said to Jesus, How do You know me? [How is it that You know these things about me?] Jesus answered him, Before [ever] Philip called you, when you were still under the fig tree, I saw you.

49 Nathanael answered, Teacher, You are the Son of God! You are the King of Israel!

50 Jesus replied, Because I said to you, I saw you beneath the fig tree, do you believe in *and* rely on *and* trust in Me? You shall see greater things than this!

51 Then He said to him, I assure you, most solemnly I tell you all, you shall see heaven opened, and the angels of God ascending and descending upon the Son of Man! [Gen. 28:12; Dan. 7:13.]

2 ON THE third day there was a wedding at Cana of Galilee, and the mother of Jesus was there.

2 Jesus also was invited with His disciples to the wedding.

3 And when the wine was all gone, the mother of Jesus said to Him, They have no more wine!

4 Jesus said to her, [*Dear] woman, what is that to you and to Me? [What do we have in common? Leave it to Me.] My time (hour to act) has not yet come. [Eccl. 3:1.]

5 His mother said to the servants, Whatever He says to you, do it.

6 Now there were six waterpots of stone standing there, as the Jewish custom of purification (ceremonial washing) demanded, holding twenty to thirty gallons apiece.

7 Jesus said to them, Fill the waterpots with water. So they filled them up to the brim.

8 Then He said to them, Draw some out now and take it to the manager of the feast [to the one presiding, the superintendent of the banquet]. So they took him some.

9 And when the manager tasted the water just now turned into wine, not knowing where it came from—though the servants who had drawn the water knew—he called the bridegroom

10 And said to him, Everyone else serves his best wine first, and when people have drunk freely, then he serves that which is not so good; but you have kept back the good wine until now!

11 This, the first of His signs (miracles, wonderworks), Jesus performed in Cana of Galilee, and manifested His glory [by it He displayed His greatness and His power openly], and His disciples believed in Him [adhered to, trusted in, and relied on Him]. [Deut. 5:24; Ps. 72:19.]

12 After that He went down to Capernaum with His mother and brothers and disciples, and they stayed there only a few days.

13 Now the Passover of the Jews was

putting the Word to work

Has God ever asked you to do something that did not seem to make much sense? No doubt the servants wondered why Jesus asked them to fill pots with water when it was the wine that ran out. To their credit, they obeyed—and they witnessed Jesus' first miracle. Even when you don't understand why God asks you to do something, heed Mary's advice and do whatever God tells you to do. You will be blessed because of **your obedience.**

k G. Abbott-Smith, *Manual Greek Lexicon of the New Testament*: "a term of respect and endearment."

approaching, so Jesus went up to Jerusalem.

14 There He found in the temple [¹enclosure] those who were selling oxen and sheep and doves, and the money changers sitting there [also at their stands].

15 And having made a lash (a whip) of cords, He drove them all out of the temple [¹enclosure]—both the sheep and the oxen—spilling *and* scattering the brokers' money and upsetting *and* tossing around their trays (their stands).

16 Then to those who sold the doves He said, Take these things away (out of here)! Make not My Father's house a house of merchandise (a marketplace, a sales shop)! [Ps. 93:5.]

17 And His disciples remembered that it is written [in the Holy Scriptures], Zeal (the fervor of love) for Your house will eat Me up. [I will be consumed with jealousy for the honor of Your house.] [Ps. 69:9.]

18 Then the Jews retorted, What sign can ᵐYou show us, seeing You do these things? [What sign, miracle, token, indication can You give us as evidence that You have authority and are commissioned to act in this way?]

19 Jesus answered them, Destroy (undo) this temple, and in three days I will raise it up again.

20 Then the Jews replied, It took forty-six years to build this temple (sanctuary), and will You raise it up in three days?

21 But He had spoken of the temple which was His body.

22 When therefore He had risen from the dead, His disciples remembered that He said this. And so they believed *and* trusted *and* relied on the Scripture and the word (message) Jesus had spoken. [Ps. 16:10.]

23 But when He was in Jerusalem during the Passover Feast, many believed in His name [identified themselves with His party] after seeing His signs (wonders, miracles) which He was doing.

24 But Jesus [for His part] did not trust Himself to them, because He knew all [men];

25 And He did not need anyone to bear witness concerning man [needed no evidence from anyone about men], for He Himself knew what was in human nature. [He could read men's hearts.] [I Sam. 16:7.]

3 NOW THERE was a certain man among the Pharisees named Nicodemus, a ruler (a leader, an authority) among the Jews,

2 Who came to Jesus at night and said to Him, Rabbi, we know *and* are certain that You have come from God [as] a Teacher; for no one can do these signs (these wonderworks, these miracles—and produce the proofs) that You do unless God is with him.

3 Jesus answered him, I assure you, most solemnly I tell you, that unless a person is born again (anew, from above), he cannot ever see (know, be acquainted with, and experience) the kingdom of God.

4 Nicodemus said to Him, How can a man be born when he is old? Can he enter his mother's womb again and be born?

5 Jesus answered, I assure you, most solemnly I tell you, unless a man is born of water and [ⁿeven] the Spirit, he cannot [ever] enter the kingdom of God. [Ezek. 36:25-27.]

6 What is born of [from] the flesh is flesh [of the physical is physical]; and what is born of the Spirit is spirit.

---

l Richard Trench, *Synonyms of the New Testament.*   **m** Capitalized because of what He is, the spotless Son of God, not what the speaker may have thought He was.   **n** The Greek "kai" ("and") may be rendered "even."

people aren't perfect

Having unrealistic expectations of people sets us up to be disappointed. Am I saying that we should not be expectant? Of course not! We should expect the best out of people, but at the same time we must remember they are human beings with imperfections.

When Jesus' disciples disappointed Him, He was not devastated because He already knew and fully understood human nature, as we learn in John 2:25. Jesus expected His disciples to do their best, but He knew that even their best would still be imperfect.

I have come to realize that we tend to look for the perfect spouse, perfect friend, perfect job, perfect neighborhood, perfect church, and the truth is, *it does not exist!* As long as we are in earthly bodies we will manifest imperfection. God must have known that to be true, because He gave us instructions in His Word on how to handle people who irritate us or disappoint us.

People are not perfect, and to expect them to be flawless is frustrating for everyone involved. We must learn to be generous with mercy and to sow seeds of mercy so we can reap mercy when we need it.

We all like to plan ahead for our lives and have people cooperate with us. We want situations to go exactly the way we plan, but that rarely happens. This isn't negative; it is truth. As believers, we have the power of the Holy Spirit to help us do difficult things and deal with human imperfections—not to make our lives so easy that we never need to use our faith.

I urge you to expect good things to happen in your life. I also urge you to be realistic and realize that we all have to deal with things that are unpleasant and people who are disagreeable. Your attitude in these trying situations greatly affects your enjoyment of life. You can be realistic, walk in truth and still have a positive attitude as you deal with your own imperfections and those of the people around you.

7 Marvel not [do not be surprised, astonished] at My telling you, You must all be born anew (from above).
8 The wind blows (breathes) where it wills; and though you hear its sound, yet you neither know where it comes from nor where it is going. So it is with everyone who is born of the Spirit.
9 Nicodemus answered by asking, How can all this be possible?
10 Jesus replied, Are you the teacher of Israel, and yet do not know *nor* understand these things? [Are they strange to you?]
11 I assure you, most solemnly I tell you, We speak only of what we know [we know absolutely what we are talking about]; we have actually seen what we are testifying to [we were eyewitnesses of it]. And still you do not receive our testimony [you reject and refuse our evidence—that of Myself and of all those who are born of the Spirit].
12 If I have told you of things that

happen right here on the earth and yet none of you believes Me, how can you believe (trust Me, adhere to Me, rely on Me) if I tell you of heavenly things? **13** And yet no one has ever gone up to heaven, but there is One Who has come down from heaven—the Son of Man [Himself], °*Who is (dwells, has His home) in heaven.*

14 And just as Moses lifted up the serpent in the desert [on a pole], so must [so it is necessary that] the Son of Man be lifted up [on the cross]. [Num. 21:9.]

15 In order that everyone who believes in Him [who cleaves to Him, trusts Him, and relies on Him] may °*not perish, but* have eternal life *and* [actually] live forever!

16 For God so greatly loved *and* dearly prized the world that He [even] gave up His only begotten (ᵖunique) Son, so that whoever believes in (trusts in, clings to, relies on) Him shall not perish (come to destruction, be lost) but have eternal (everlasting) life.

17 For God did not send the Son into the world in order to judge (to reject, to condemn, to pass sentence on) the world, but that the world might find salvation *and* be made safe *and* sound through Him.

18 He who believes in Him [who clings to, trusts in, relies on Him] is not judged [he who trusts in Him never comes up for judgment; for him there is no rejection, no condemnation—he incurs no damnation]; but he who does not believe (cleave to, rely on, trust in Him) is judged already [he has already been convicted and has already received his sentence] because he has not believed in *and* trusted in the name of the only begotten Son of God. [He is condemned for refusing to let his trust rest in Christ's name.]

19 The [basis of the] judgment (indictment, the test by which men are judged, the ground for the sentence) lies in this: the Light has come into the world, and people have loved the darkness rather than *and* more than the Light, for their works (deeds) were evil. [Isa. 5:20.]

20 For every wrongdoer hates (loathes, detests) the Light, and will not come out into the Light *but* shrinks from it, lest his works (his deeds, his activities, his conduct) be exposed *and* reproved.

21 But he who practices truth [who does what is right] comes out into the Light; so that his works may be plainly shown to be what they are—wrought with God [divinely prompted, done with God's help, in dependence upon Him].

22 After this, Jesus and His disciples went into the land (the countryside) of Judea, where He remained with them, and baptized.

23 But John also was baptizing at Aenon near Salim, for there was an abundance of water there, and the people kept coming and being baptized.

speak the Word

Thank You, God, for loving me so much that You gave up Your only Son, so that if I believe in Him, I will not perish, but I will have everlasting life. I know that You did not send Your Son to condemn me, but that I might find salvation and be made safe and sound through Him.
ADAPTED FROM JOHN **3:16, 17**

o Some manuscripts add this phrase.   **p** James Moulton and George Milligan, *The Vocabulary.*

24 For John had not yet been thrown into prison.

25 Therefore there arose a controversy between some of John's disciples and a Jew in regard to purification.

26 So they came to John and reported to him, Rabbi, the Man Who was with you on the other side of the Jordan [qat the Jordan crossing]—and to Whom you yourself have borne testimony—notice, here He is baptizing too, and everybody is flocking to Him!

27 John answered, A man can receive nothing [he can claim nothing, he can rtake unto himself nothing] except as it has been granted to him from heaven. [A man must be content to receive the gift which is given him from heaven; there is no other source.]

28 You yourselves are my witnesses [you personally bear me out] that I stated, I am not the Christ (the Anointed One, the Messiah), but I have [only] been sent before Him [in advance of Him, to be His appointed forerunner, His messenger, His announcer]. [Mal. 3:1.]

29 He who has the bride is the bridegroom; but the groomsman who stands by and listens to him rejoices greatly and heartily on account of the bridegroom's voice. This then is my pleasure and joy, and it is now complete. [S. of Sol. 5:1.]

30 He must increase, but I must decrease. [He must grow more prominent; I must grow less so.] [Isa. 9:7.]

31 He Who comes from above (heaven) is [far] above all [others]; he who comes from the earth belongs to the earth, and talks the language of earth [his words are from an earthly standpoint]. He Who comes from heaven is [far] above all others [far superior to all others in prominence and in excellence].

32 It is to what He has [actually] seen and heard that He bears testimony, and yet no one accepts His testimony [no one receives His evidence as true].

33 Whoever receives His testimony has set his seal of approval to this: God is true. [That man has definitely certified, acknowledged, declared once and for all, and is himself assured that it is divine truth that God cannot lie].

34 For since He Whom God has sent speaks the words of God [proclaims God's own message], God does not give Him His Spirit sparingly or by measure, but boundless is the gift God makes of His Spirit! [Deut. 18:18.]

35 The Father loves the Son and has given (entrusted, committed) everything into His hand. [Dan. 7:14.]

36 And he who believes in (has faith in, clings to, relies on) the Son has (now possesses) eternal life. But whoever disobeys (is unbelieving toward, refuses to trust in, disregards, is not subject to) the Son will never see (experience) life, but [instead] the wrath of God abides on him. [God's displeasure remains on him; His indignation hangs over him continually.] [Hab. 2:4.]

4 NOW WHEN the Lord knew (learned, became aware) that the Pharisees had been told that

speak the Word

God, I pray that You will increase and I will decrease more and more.
ADAPTED FROM JOHN 3:30

---

q George M. Lamsa, *The New Testament.*   **r** Joseph Thayer, *A Greek-English Lexicon of the New Testament.*

Jesus was winning and baptizing more disciples than John—

2 Though Jesus Himself did not baptize, but His disciples—

3 He left Judea and returned to Galilee.

4 It was necessary for Him to go through Samaria.

5 And in doing so, He arrived at a Samaritan town called Sychar, near the tract of land that Jacob gave to his son Joseph.

6 And Jacob's well was there. So Jesus, tired as He was from His journey, sat down [to rest] by the well. It was then about the sixth hour (about noon).

7 Presently, when a woman of Samaria came along to draw water, Jesus said to her, Give Me a drink—

8 For His disciples had gone off into the town to buy food—

9 The Samaritan woman said to Him, How is it that sYou, being a Jew, ask me, a Samaritan [and a] woman, for a drink?—For the Jews have nothing to do with the Samaritans—

10 Jesus answered her, If you had only known *and* had recognized God's gift and Who this is that is saying to you, Give Me a drink, you would have asked Him [instead] and He would have given you living water.

11 She said to Him, Sir, You have nothing to draw with [no drawing bucket] and the well is deep; how then can You provide living water? [Where do You get Your living water?]

12 Are You greater than *and* superior to our ancestor Jacob, who gave us this well and who used to drink from it himself, and his sons and his cattle also?

13 Jesus answered her, All who drink of this water will be thirsty again.

14 But whoever takes a drink of the water that I will give him shall never, no never, be thirsty any more. But the water that I will give him shall become a spring of water welling up (flowing, bubbling) [continually] within him unto (into, for) eternal life.

15 The woman said to Him, Sir, give me this water, so that I may never get thirsty nor have to come [continually all the way] here to draw.

16 At this, Jesus said to her, Go, call your husband and come back here.

17 The woman answered, I have no husband. Jesus said to her, You have spoken truly in saying, I have no husband.

18 For you have had five husbands, and the man you are now living with is not your husband. In this you have spoken truly.

19 The woman said to Him, Sir, I see *and* understand that You are a prophet.

20 Our forefathers worshiped on this mountain, but you [Jews] say that Jerusalem is the place where it is necessary *and* proper to worship.

21 Jesus said to her, Woman, believe Me, a time is coming when you will worship the Father neither [merely] in this mountain nor [merely] in Jerusalem.

22 You [Samaritans] do not know what you are worshiping [you worship what you do not comprehend]. We do know what we are worshiping [we worship what we have knowledge of and understand], for [after all] salvation comes from [among] the Jews.

23 A time will come, however, indeed it is already here, when the true (genuine) worshipers will worship the Father in spirit and in truth (reality); for the Father is seeking just such people as these as His worshipers.

24 God is a Spirit (a spiritual Being) and those who worship Him must

---

s Capitalized because of what He is, the spotless Son of God, not what the speaker may have thought He was.

worship *Him* in spirit and in truth (reality).

25 The woman said to Him, I know that Messiah is coming, He Who is called the Christ (the Anointed One); and when He arrives, He will tell us everything we need to know *and* make it clear to us.

26 Jesus said to her, I Who now speak with you am He.

27 Just then His disciples came and they wondered (were surprised, astonished) to find Him talking with a woman [a married woman]. However, not one of them asked Him, What are You inquiring about? *or* What do You want? or, Why do You speak with her?

28 Then the woman left her water jar and went away to the town. And she began telling the people,

29 Come, see a Man Who has told me everything that I ever did! Can this be [is not this] the Christ? [Must not this be the Messiah, the Anointed One?]

30 So the people left the town and set out to go to Him.

31 Meanwhile, the disciples urged Him saying, Rabbi, eat something.

32 But He assured them, I have food (nourishment) to eat of which you know nothing *and* have no idea.

33 So the disciples said one to another, Has someone brought Him something to eat?

34 Jesus said to them, My food (nourishment) is to do the will (pleasure) of Him Who sent Me and to accomplish *and* completely finish His work.

35 Do you not say, It is still four months until harvest time comes? Look! I tell you, raise your eyes and observe the fields *and* see how they are already white for harvesting.

36 Already the reaper is getting his wages [he who does the cutting now has his reward], for he is gathering fruit (crop) unto life eternal, so that he who does the planting and he who does the reaping may rejoice together.

37 For in this the saying holds true, One sows and another reaps.

38 I sent you to reap a crop for which you have not toiled. Other men have labored and you have stepped in to reap the results of their work.

39 Now numerous Samaritans from that town believed in *and* trusted in Him because of what the woman said when she declared *and* testified, He told me everything that I ever did.

40 So when the Samaritans arrived, they asked Him to remain with them, and He did stay there two days.

41 Then many more believed in *and* adhered to *and* relied on Him because of His personal message [what He Himself said].

42 And they told the woman, Now we no longer believe (trust, have faith) just because of what you said; for we have heard Him ourselves [personally], and we know that He truly is the Savior of the world, *the Christ*.

43 But after these two days Jesus went on from there into Galilee—

44 Although He Himself declared that a prophet has no honor in his own country.

45 However, when He came into Galilee, the Galileans also welcomed Him *and* took Him to their hearts eagerly, for they had seen everything that He did in Jerusalem during the Feast; for they too had attended the Feast.

46 So Jesus came again to Cana of Galilee, where He had turned the water into wine. And there was a certain royal official whose son was lying ill in Capernaum.

speak the Word

Help me, God, to worship You in spirit and in truth.
ADAPTED FROM JOHN 4:24

47 Having heard that Jesus had come back from Judea into Galilee, he went away to meet Him and began to beg Him to come down and cure his son, for he was lying at the point of death. **48** Then Jesus said to him, Unless you see signs and miracles happen, you [people] never will believe (trust, have faith) at all. **49** The king's officer pleaded with Him, Sir, do come down at once before my little child is dead! **50** Jesus answered him, Go in peace; your son will live! And the man put his trust in what Jesus said and started home. **51** But even as he was on the road going down, his servants met him and reported, saying, Your son lives! **52** So he asked them at what time he had begun to get better. They said, Yesterday during the seventh hour (about one o'clock in the afternoon) the fever left him. **53** Then the father knew that it was at that very hour when Jesus had said to him, Your son will live. And he and his entire household believed (adhered to, trusted in, and relied on Jesus). **54** This is the second sign (wonderwork, miracle) that Jesus performed after He had come out of Judea into Galilee.

5 LATER ON there was a Jewish festival (feast) for which Jesus went up to Jerusalem. **2** Now there is in Jerusalem a pool near the Sheep Gate. This pool in the Hebrew is called Bethesda, having five porches (alcoves, colonnades, doorways). **3** In these lay a great number of sick folk—some blind, some crippled, and some paralyzed (shriveled up)—[t]*waiting for the bubbling up of the water.*

4 *For an angel of the Lord went down at appointed seasons into the pool and moved and stirred up the water; whoever then first, after the stirring up of the water, stepped in was cured of whatever disease with which he was afflicted.* **5** There was a certain man there who had suffered with a deep-seated *and* lingering disorder for thirty-eight years. **6** When Jesus noticed him lying there [helpless], knowing that he had already been a long time in that condition, He said to him, Do you want to become well? [Are you really in earnest about getting well?] **7** The invalid answered, Sir, I have nobody when the water is moving to put me into the pool; but while I am trying to come [into it] myself, somebody else steps down ahead of me. **8** Jesus said to him, Get up! Pick up your bed (sleeping pad) and walk! **9** Instantly the man became well *and* recovered his strength and picked up his bed and walked. But that happened on the Sabbath. **10** So the Jews kept saying to the man who had been healed, It is the Sabbath, and you have no right to pick up your bed [it is not lawful]. **11** He answered them, The [u]Man Who healed me *and* gave me back my strength, He Himself said to me, Pick up your bed and walk! **12** They asked him, Who is the Man Who told you, Pick up your bed and walk? **13** Now the invalid who had been healed did not know who it was, for Jesus had quietly gone away [had passed on unnoticed], since there was a crowd in the place. **14** Afterward, when Jesus found him in the temple, He said to him, See, you are well! Stop sinning or something worse may happen to you.

---

t Many manuscripts omit the last part of verse 3 and all of verse 4.   u Capitalized because of what He is, the spotless Son of God, not what the speaker may have thought He was.

be pitiful or be powerful

Why was this man we read about in John 5:1–9 lying beside the pool for thirty-eight years? Not only was he sick in his body, he was also sick in his soul. Sicknesses of the soul are much worse, and sometimes harder to deal with than sicknesses of the body. I believe the condition of his body and soul stole his confidence and caused him to give up in a gradual, passive kind of way.

Notice that when Jesus asked the sick man if he was "in earnest" about getting well (John 5:6), he said he had no one to help him get into the pool where he could be healed. Jesus did not stand there and pity the man. Instead, He gave very specific instruction: "Get up! Pick up your bed . . . and walk!" In other words, "Don't just lie there, do something!"

Jesus knew self-pity would not deliver the man, so He did not feel sorry for him. He had *compassion* on him, and that is different from emotional *pity*. Jesus was not being harsh, hard or mean. He was trying to set the man free!

Self-pity is a major problem. I know, because I lived in self-pity for many years. It affected me, my family and the plan of God for my life. God finally told me that I could be pitiful or I could be powerful, but I could not be both. If I wanted to be powerful, I had to give up self-pity.

Being sexually abused for approximately fifteen years and growing up in a dysfunctional home left me lacking confidence and filled with shame. I wanted to have good things in my life, but I was stuck in emotional torment and despair.

Like the man in John 5, Jesus did not give me pity either. Jesus was actually very firm with me and He applied a lot of tough love, but His refusal to let me wallow in self-pity was a turning point in my life. I am not in the pit any longer. I now have a great life. If you will reject self-pity, actively look to God and do what He instructs you to do, you can have a great life too.

15 The man went away and told the Jews that it was Jesus Who had made him well.

16 For this reason the Jews began to persecute (annoy, torment) Jesus ᵛ*and sought to kill Him,* because He was doing these things on the Sabbath.

17 But Jesus answered them, My Father has worked [even] until now, [He has never ceased working; He is still working] and I, too, must be at [divine] work.

18 This made the Jews more determined than ever to kill Him [to do away with Him]; because He not only was breaking (weakening, violating) the Sabbath, but He actually was speaking of God as being [in a special sense] His own Father, making Himself equal [putting Himself on a level] with God.

19 So Jesus answered them by saying, I assure you, most solemnly I tell you, the Son is able to do nothing of Himself (of His own accord); but He is

v Some manuscripts add this phrase.

able to do only what He sees the Father doing, for whatever the Father does is what the Son does in the same way [in His turn].

life point

John 5:19 teaches us that Jesus was always obedient to the Father and showed it by refraining from doing anything He did not first see the Father do (see also John 8:28, 29). None of us are at that level yet, but it should certainly be our goal.

I believe the world will take notice if we as the church of Jesus Christ, His body here on earth, will wage war against selfishness, walk in love and do what we see the Father doing.

20 The Father dearly loves the Son and discloses to (shows) Him everything that He Himself does. And He will disclose to Him (let Him see) greater things yet than these, so that you may marvel *and* be full of wonder *and* astonishment.
21 Just as the Father raises up the dead and gives them life [makes them live on], even so the Son also gives life to whomever He wills *and* is pleased to give it.
22 Even the Father judges no one, for He has given all judgment (the last judgment and the whole business of judging) entirely into the hands of the Son,
23 So that all men may give honor (reverence, homage) to the Son just as they give honor to the Father. [In fact] whoever does not honor the Son does not honor the Father, Who has sent Him.
24 I assure you, most solemnly I tell you, the person whose ears are open to My words [who listens to My mes-

sage] and believes *and* trusts in *and* clings to *and* relies on Him Who sent Me has (possesses now) eternal life. And he does not come into judgment [does not incur sentence of judgment, will not come under condemnation], but he has already passed over out of death into life.
25 Believe Me when I assure you, most solemnly I tell you, the time is coming and is here now when the dead shall hear the voice of the Son of God and those who hear it shall live.
26 For even as the Father has life in Himself *and* is self-existent, so He has given to the Son to have life in Himself *and* be self-existent.
27 And He has given Him authority *and* granted Him power to execute (exercise, practice) judgment because He is ʷa Son of man [very man].
28 Do not be surprised *and* wonder at this, for the time is coming when all those who are in the tombs shall hear His voice,
29 And they shall come out—those who have practiced doing good [will come out] to the resurrection of [new] life, and those who have done evil will be raised for judgment [raised to meet their sentence]. [Dan. 12:2.]
30 I am able to do nothing from Myself [independently, of My own accord—but only as I am taught by God and as I get His orders]. Even as I hear, I judge [I decide as I am bidden to decide. As the voice comes to Me, so I give a decision], and My judgment is right (just, righteous), because I do not seek *or* consult My own will [I have no desire to do what is pleasing to Myself, My own aim, My own purpose] but only the will *and* pleasure of the Father Who sent Me.
31 If I alone testify in My behalf, My testimony is not valid *and* cannot be worth anything.
32 There is Another Who testifies

ʷ Marvin Vincent, *Word Studies.*

concerning Me, and I know *and* am certain that His evidence on My behalf is true and valid.

33 You yourselves have sent [an inquiry] to John and he has been a witness to the truth.

34 But I do not receive [a mere] human witness [the evidence which I accept on My behalf is not from man]; but I simply mention all these things in order that you may be saved (made and kept safe and sound).

35 John was the lamp that kept on burning and shining [to show you the way], and you were willing for a while to delight (sun) yourselves in his light.

36 But I have as My witness something greater (weightier, higher, better) than that of John; for the works that the Father has appointed Me to accomplish *and* finish, the very same works that I am now doing, are a witness *and* proof that the Father has sent Me.

37 And the Father Who sent Me has Himself testified concerning Me. Not one of you has ever given ear to His voice or seen His form (His face—what He is like). [You have always been deaf to His voice and blind to the vision of Him.]

38 And you have not His word (His thought) living in your hearts, because you do not believe *and* adhere to *and* trust in *and* rely on Him Whom He has sent. [That is why you do not keep His message living in you, because you do not believe in the Messenger Whom He has sent.]

39 You search *and* investigate *and* pore over the Scriptures diligently, because you suppose *and* trust that you have eternal life through them. And these [very Scriptures] testify about Me!

40 And still you are not willing [but refuse] to come to Me, so that you might have life.

41 I receive not glory from men [I

life point

In John 5:38 Jesus chastised some people because they were not keeping His Word alive in their hearts. They weren't trusting God and clinging to Him and His Word. Jesus said that if we really believe in Him, we will keep His Word alive in our hearts. This is accomplished by studying and meditating on it. God's Word is His thoughts and when we give His Word first place in our lives, His thoughts become our thoughts and we will experience the good plans He has for us.

crave no human honor, I look for no mortal fame],

42 But I know you and recognize *and* understand that you have not the love of God in you.

43 I have come in My Father's name *and* with His power, and you do not receive Me [your hearts are not open to Me, you give Me no welcome]; but if another comes in his own name *and* his own power *and* with no other authority but himself, you will receive him *and* give him your approval.

44 How is it possible for you to believe [how can you learn to believe], you who [are content to seek and] receive praise *and* honor *and* glory from one another, and yet do not seek the praise *and* honor *and* glory which come from Him Who alone is God?

45 Put out of your minds the thought *and* do not suppose [as some of you are supposing] that I will accuse you before the Father. There is one who accuses you—it is Moses, the very one on whom you have built your hopes [in whom you trust].

46 For if you believed *and* relied on Moses, you would believe *and* rely on Me, for he wrote about Me [personally].

47 But if you do not believe *and* trust his writings, how then will you believe *and* trust My teachings? [How shall you cleave to and rely on My words?]

6 AFTER THIS, Jesus went to the farther side of the Sea of Galilee—that is, the Sea of Tiberias.

2 And a great crowd was following Him because they had seen the signs (miracles) which He [continually] performed upon those who were sick.

3 And Jesus walked up the mountainside and sat down there with His disciples.

4 Now the Passover, the feast of the Jews, was approaching.

5 Jesus looked up then, and seeing that a vast multitude was coming toward Him, He said to Philip, Where are we to buy bread, so that all these people may eat?

6 But He said this to prove (test) him, for He well knew what He was about to do.

7 Philip answered Him, Two hundred pennies' (forty dollars) worth of bread is not enough that everyone may receive even a little.

8 Another of His disciples, Andrew, Simon Peter's brother, said to Him,

9 There is a little boy here, who has [with him] five barley loaves, and two small fish; but what are they among so many people?

10 Jesus said, Make all the people recline (sit down). Now the ground (a pasture) was covered with thick grass at the spot, so the men threw themselves down, about 5,000 in number.

11 Jesus took the loaves, and when He had given thanks, He distributed *xto* *the disciples and the disciples* to the reclining people; so also [He did] with the fish, as much as they wanted.

12 When they had all had enough, He said to His disciples, Gather up now the fragments (the broken pieces that are left over), so that nothing may be lost *and* wasted.

13 So accordingly they gathered them up, and they filled twelve [ysmall hand] baskets with fragments left over by those who had eaten from the five barley loaves.

14 When the people saw the sign (miracle) that Jesus had performed, they began saying, Surely *and* beyond a doubt this is the Prophet Who is to come into the world! [Deut. 18:15, 18; John 1:21; Acts 3:22.]

15 Then Jesus, knowing that they meant to come and seize Him that they might make Him king, withdrew again to the hillside by Himself alone.

16 When evening came, His disciples went down to the sea,

17 And they took a boat and were going across the sea to Capernaum. It was now dark, and still Jesus had not [yet] come back to them.

18 Meanwhile, the sea was getting rough *and* rising high because of a great *and* violent wind that was blowing.

19 [However] when they had rowed three or four miles, they saw Jesus walking on the sea and approaching the boat. And they were afraid (terrified).

20 But Jesus said to them, It is I; be not afraid! [I AM; stop being frightened!] [Exod. 3:14.]

21 Then they were quite willing *and* glad for Him to come into the boat. And now the boat went at once to the land they had steered toward. [And immediately they reached the shore toward which they had been slowly making their way.]

22 The next day the crowd [that still

---

x Some manuscripts add this phrase. **y** G. Abbott-Smith, *Manual Greek Lexicon*. See also footnote on Matt. 14:20.

remained] standing on the other side of the sea realized that there had been only one small boat there, and that Jesus had not gone into it with His disciples, but that His disciples had gone away by themselves.

23 But now some other boats from Tiberias had come in near the place where they ate the bread after the Lord had given thanks.

24 So the people, finding that neither Jesus nor His disciples were there, themselves got into the small boats and came to Capernaum looking for Jesus.

25 And when they found Him on the other side of the lake, they said to Him, Rabbi! When did You come here?

26 Jesus answered them, I assure you, most solemnly I tell you, you have been searching for Me, not because you saw the miracles *and* signs but because you were fed with the loaves and were filled *and* satisfied.

27 Stop toiling *and* doing *and* producing for the food that perishes *and* decomposes [in the using], but strive *and* work *and* produce rather for the [lasting] food which endures [continually] unto life eternal; the Son of Man will give (furnish) you that, for God the Father has authorized *and* certified Him *and* put His seal of endorsement upon Him.

28 They then said, What are we to do, that we may [habitually] be working the works of God? [What are we to do to carry out what God requires?]

29 Jesus replied, This is the work (service) that God asks of you: that you believe in the One Whom He has sent [that you cleave to, trust, rely on, and have faith in His Messenger].

30 Therefore they said to Him, What sign (miracle, wonderwork)

life point

God is pleased when we believe in His Son Jesus, and He is not pleased when we do not. We can do many good and benevolent works, yet if we have no faith in Jesus, God is still not pleased with us. But if we simply believe and trust in God, He is pleased.

will ᶻYou perform then, so that we may see it and believe *and* rely on *and* adhere to You? What [supernatural] work have You [to show what You can do]?

31 Our forefathers ate the manna in the wilderness; as the Scripture says, He gave them bread out of heaven to eat. [Exod. 16:15; Neh. 9:15; Ps. 78:24.]

32 Jesus then said to them, I assure you, most solemnly I tell you, Moses did not give you the Bread from heaven [what Moses gave you was not the Bread from heaven], but it is My Father Who gives you the true heavenly Bread.

33 For the Bread of God is He Who comes down out of heaven and gives life to the world.

34 Then they said to Him, Lord, give us this bread always (all the time)!

35 Jesus replied, I am the Bread of Life. He who comes to Me will never

putting the Word to work

Your body lets you know when you are hungry. Your stomach growls; you may get cranky or feel a little light-headed. Did you know your spirit can also get hungry? Just as you feed your body daily, it is necessary to daily feed on the Bread of Life by spending time with **God and in His Word.**

z Capitalized because of what He is, the spotless Son of God, not what the speaker may have thought He was.

believe to achieve

So many times I have said to the Lord, "Father, what do You want me to do? If You will just show me what to do, I will gladly do it."

I was a doer. All anybody had to do was show me what needed to be done, and I did it—and I did my best to do it right. But what frustrated and confused me was when I did something right and it still did not work. I had not yet learned that unless the Lord builds the house, "they labor in vain who build it" (Psalm 127:1).

The people in John 6:28 wanted to know what they needed to do to please God. They wanted to know what to do in order to work the works of God. What was Jesus' answer to these people? "This is the work (service) that God asks of you: that you believe in the One Whom He has sent . . ." (John 6:29).

When the Lord first revealed this passage to me, I thought He was going to show me how to finally be successful in doing His works. And in a sense He did.

He told me, "Believe."

You and I think we are supposed to be achievers, and we are. But the way we achieve is to first believe. That frees us from worry and reasoning and enables us to live victorious, blessed lives. God has works for us to do, but faith must come first and works will follow. When done in faith, works are easy and God gets the credit instead of us. Faith without works is dead, but we must be careful not to get "the cart before the horse." When we do that, we struggle and make every effort, yet we see no progress. We are called "believers," not "achievers." Our first and foremost work is always to believe!

be hungry, and he who believes in *and* cleaves to *and* trusts in *and* relies on Me will never thirst any more (at any time).

36 But [as] I told you, although you have seen Me, still you do not believe *and* trust *and* have faith.

37 All whom My Father gives (entrusts) to Me will come to Me; and the one who comes to Me I will most certainly not cast out [I will never, no never, reject one of them who comes to Me].

38 For I have come down from heaven not to do My own will *and* purpose but to do the will *and* purpose of Him Who sent Me.

39 And this is the will of Him Who sent Me, that I should not lose any of all that He has given Me, but that I should give new life *and* raise [them all] up at the last day.

40 For this is My Father's will *and* His purpose, that everyone who sees the Son and believes in *and* cleaves to *and* trusts in *and* relies on Him should have eternal life, and I will raise him up [from the dead] at the last day.

41 Now the Jews murmured *and* found fault with *and* grumbled about Jesus because He said, I am [Myself] the Bread that came down from heaven.

42 They kept asking, Is not this

Jesus, the [a]Son of Joseph, Whose father and mother we know? How then can He say, I have come down from heaven?

43 So Jesus answered them, Stop grumbling *and* saying things against Me to one another.

44 No one is able to come to Me unless the Father Who sent Me attracts *and* draws him *and* gives him the desire to come to Me, and [then] I will raise him up [from the dead] at the last day.

45 It is written in [the book of] the Prophets, And they shall all be taught of God [have Him in person for their Teacher]. Everyone who has listened to and learned from the Father comes to Me—[Isa. 54:13.]

46 Which does not imply that anyone has seen the Father [not that anyone has ever seen Him] except He [Who was with the Father] Who comes from God; He [alone] has seen the Father.

47 I assure you, most solemnly I tell you, he who believes *in Me* [who adheres to, trusts in, relies on, and has faith in Me] has (now possesses) eternal life.

48 I am the Bread of Life [that gives life—the Living Bread].

49 Your forefathers ate the manna in the wilderness, and [yet] they died.

50 [But] this is the Bread that comes down from heaven, so that [any]one may eat of it and never die.

51 I [Myself] am this Living Bread that came down from heaven. If anyone eats of this Bread, he will live forever; and also the Bread that I shall give for the life of the world is My flesh (body).

52 Then the Jews angrily contended with one another, saying, How is He able to give us His flesh to eat?

53 And Jesus said to them, I assure you, most solemnly I tell you, you can-not have any life in you unless you eat the flesh of the Son of Man and drink His blood [unless you appropriate His life and the saving merit of His blood].

54 He who feeds on My flesh and drinks My blood has (possesses now) eternal life, and I will raise him up [from the dead] on the last day.

55 For My flesh is true *and* genuine food, and My blood is true *and* genuine drink.

56 He who feeds on My flesh and drinks My blood dwells continually in Me, and I [in like manner dwell continually] in him.

57 Just as the living Father sent Me and I live by (through, because of) the Father, even so whoever continues to feed on Me [whoever takes Me for his food *and* is nourished by Me] shall [in his turn] live through *and* because of Me.

58 This is the Bread that came down from heaven. It is not like the manna which our forefathers ate, and yet died; he who takes this Bread for his food shall live forever.

59 He said these things in a synagogue while He was teaching at Capernaum.

60 When His disciples heard this, many of them said, This is a hard *and* difficult *and* strange saying (an offensive and unbearable message). Who can stand to hear it? [Who can be expected to listen to such teaching?]

61 But Jesus, knowing within Himself that His disciples were complaining *and* protesting *and* grumbling about it, said to them: Is this a stumbling block *and* an offense to you? [Does this upset and displease and shock and scandalize you?]

62 What then [will be your reaction] if you should see the Son of Man ascending to [the place] where He was before?

---

a Capitalized because of what He is, the spotless Son of God, not what the speaker may have thought He was.

63 It is the Spirit Who gives life [He is the Life-giver]; the flesh conveys no benefit whatever [there is no profit in it]. The words (truths) that I have been speaking to you are spirit and life.
64 But [still] some of you fail to believe *and* trust *and* have faith. For Jesus knew from the first who did not believe *and* had no faith and who would betray Him *and* be false to Him.
65 And He said, This is why I told you that no one can come to Me unless it is granted him [unless he is enabled to do so] by the Father.
66 After this, many of His disciples drew back (returned to their old associations) and no longer accompanied Him.
67 Jesus said to the Twelve, Will you also go away? [And do you too desire to leave Me?]
68 Simon Peter answered, Lord, to whom shall we go? You have the words (the message) of eternal life.
69 And we have learned to believe *and* trust, and [more] we have come to know [surely] that You are *the Holy One of God*, the Christ (the Anointed One), the Son of the living God.
70 Jesus answered them, Did I not choose you, the Twelve? And [yet] one of you is a devil (of the evil one and a false accuser).
71 He was speaking of Judas, the son of Simon Iscariot, for he was about to betray Him, [although] he was one of the Twelve.

7 AFTER THIS, Jesus went from place to place in Galilee, for He would not travel in Judea because the Jews were seeking to kill Him.
2 Now the Jewish Feast of Tabernacles was drawing near.
3 So His brothers said to Him, Leave here and go into Judea, so that

[b]Your disciples [there] may also see the works that You do. [This is no place for You.]
4 For no one does anything in secret when he wishes to be conspicuous *and* secure publicity. If You [must] do these things [if You must act like this], show Yourself openly *and* make Yourself known to the world!
5 For [even] His brothers did not believe in *or* adhere to *or* trust in *or* rely on Him either.
6 Whereupon Jesus said to them, My time (opportunity) has not come yet; but any time is suitable for you *and* your opportunity is ready any time [is always here].
7 The world cannot [be expected to] hate you, but it does hate Me because I denounce it for its wicked works *and* reveal that its doings are evil.
8 Go to the Feast yourselves. I am not [yet] going up to the Festival, because My time is not ripe. [My term is not yet completed; it is not time for Me to go.]
9 Having said these things to them, He stayed behind in Galilee.
10 But afterward, when His brothers had gone up to the Feast, He went up also, not publicly [not with a caravan], but by Himself quietly *and* as if He did not wish to be observed.
11 Therefore the Jews kept looking for Him at the Feast and asking, Where can He be? [Where is that Fellow?]
12 And there was among the mass of the people much whispered discussion *and* hot disputing about Him. Some were saying, He is good! [He is a good Man!] Others said, No, He misleads *and* deceives the people [gives them false ideas]!
13 But no one dared speak out boldly about Him for fear of [the leaders of] the Jews.

b Capitalized because of what He is, the spotless Son of God, not what the speaker may have thought He was.

14 When the Feast was already half over, Jesus went up into the temple [ccourt] and began to teach.

15 The Jews were astonished. They said, How is it that this Man has learning [is so versed in the sacred Scriptures and in theology] when He has never studied?

16 Jesus answered them by saying, My teaching is not My own, but His Who sent Me.

17 If any man desires to do His will (God's pleasure), he will know (have the needed illumination to recognize, and can tell for himself) whether the teaching is from God or whether I am speaking from Myself and of My own accord and on My own authority.

18 He who speaks on his own authority seeks to win honor for himself. [He whose teaching originates with himself seeks his own glory.] But He Who seeks the glory and is eager for the honor of Him Who sent Him, He is true; and there is no unrighteousness or falsehood or deception in Him.

19 Did not Moses give you the Law? And yet not one of you keeps the Law. [If that is the truth] why do you seek to kill Me [for not keeping it]?

20 The crowd answered Him, You are possessed by a demon! [You are raving!] Who seeks to kill You?

21 Jesus answered them, I did one work, and you all are astounded. [John 5:1-9.]

22 Now Moses established circumcision among you—though it did not originate with Moses but with the previous patriarchs—and you circumcise a person [even] on the Sabbath day.

23 If, to avoid breaking the Law of Moses, a person undergoes circumcision on the Sabbath day, have you any cause to be angry with (indignant with, bitter against) Me for making a man's whole body well on the Sabbath?

24 Be honest in your judgment and do not decide at a glance (superficially and by appearances); but judge fairly and righteously.

25 Then some of the Jerusalem people said, Is not this the Man they seek to kill?

26 And here He is speaking openly, and they say nothing to Him! Can it be possible that the rulers have discovered and know that this is truly the Christ?

27 No, we know where this Man comes from; when the Christ arrives, no one is to know from what place He comes.

28 Whereupon Jesus called out as He taught in the temple [cporches], Do you know Me, and do you know where I am from? I have not come on My own authority and of My own accord and as self-appointed, but the One Who sent Me is true (real, genuine, steadfast); and Him you do not know!

29 I know Him [Myself] because I come from His [very] presence, and it was He [personally] Who sent Me.

30 Therefore they were eager to arrest Him, but no one laid a hand on Him, for His hour (time) had not yet come.

31 And besides, many of the multitude believed in Him [adhered to Him, trusted in Him, relied on Him]. And they kept saying, When the Christ comes, will He do [can He be expected to do] more miracles and produce more proofs and signs than what this Man has done?

32 The Pharisees learned how the people were saying these things about Him under their breath; and the chief priests and Pharisees sent attendants (guards) to arrest Him.

33 Therefore Jesus said, For a little while I am [still] with you, and then I go back to Him Who sent Me.

34 You will look for Me, but you will

c Richard Trench, *Synonyms of the New Testament*.

not [be able to] find Me; where I am, you cannot come.

35 Then the Jews said among themselves, Where does this Man intend to go that we shall not find Him? Will He go to the Jews who are scattered in the Dispersion among the Greeks, and teach the Greeks?

36 What does this statement of His mean, You will look for Me and not be able to find Me, and, Where I am, you cannot come?

37 Now on the final and most important day of the Feast, Jesus stood, and He cried in a loud voice, If any man is thirsty, let him come to Me and drink!

38 He who believes in Me [who cleaves to *and* trusts in *and* relies on Me] as the Scripture has said, From his innermost being shall flow [continuously] springs *and* rivers of living water.

39 But He was speaking here of the Spirit, Whom those who believed (trusted, had faith) in Him were afterward to receive. For the [Holy] Spirit had not yet been given, because Jesus was not yet glorified (raised to honor).

40 Listening to those words, some of the multitude said, This is certainly *and* beyond doubt the Prophet! [Deut. 18:15, 18; John 1:21; 6:14; Acts 3:22.]

41 Others said, This is the Christ (the Messiah, Anointed One)! But some said, What? Does the Christ come out of Galilee?

42 Does not the Scripture tell us that the Christ will come from the offspring of David and from Bethlehem, the village where David lived? [Ps. 89:3, 4; Mic. 5:2.]

43 So there arose a division *and* dissension among the people concerning Him.

44 Some of them wanted to arrest Him, but no one [ventured and] laid hands on Him.

45 Meanwhile the attendants (guards) had gone back to the chief priests and Pharisees, who asked them, Why have

life point

Notice in John 7:37–39 that Jesus did not say that rivers of living water will flow *once in a while* from those who believe in Him. He said these rivers of living water will flow *continuously*. That living water is the Holy Spirit.

In this passage, Jesus talks about the outpouring of the Holy Spirit, which we have received if we have accepted Jesus as Lord and Savior—the Person and the power of the Holy Spirit in us.

The river of living water flows within you and me. It is not supposed to be stopped up, but it is to bubble up within us and flow out of us. And we can release the power of that living water in an even greater measure by receiving the fullness of the Holy Spirit. Ask Him to fill you today and every day.

you not brought Him here with you?

46 The attendants replied, Never has a man talked as this Man talks! [No mere man has ever spoken as He speaks!]

47 The Pharisees said to them, Are you also deluded *and* led astray? [Are you also swept off your feet?]

48 Has any of the authorities or of the Pharisees believed in Him?

49 As for this multitude (rabble) that does not know the Law, they are contemptible *and* doomed *and* accursed!

50 Then Nicodemus, who came to Jesus before at night and was one of them, asked,

51 Does our Law convict a man without giving him a hearing and finding out what he has done?

52 They answered him, Are you too from Galilee? Search [the Scriptures yourself], and you will see that no prophet comes (will rise to prominence) from Galilee.

53 dAnd they went [back], each to his own house.

8 BUT JESUS went to the Mount of Olives.
2   Early in the morning (at dawn), He came back into the temple [ecourt], and the people came to Him in crowds. He sat down and was teaching them,
3   When the scribes and Pharisees brought a woman who had been caught in adultery. They made her stand in the middle of the court and put the case before Him.
4   Teacher, they said, This woman has been caught in the very act of adultery.
5   Now Moses in the Law commanded us that such [women—offenders] shall be stoned to death. But what do You say [to do with her—what is Your sentence]? [Deut. 22:22-24.]
6   This they said to try (test) Him, hoping they might find a charge on which to accuse Him. But Jesus stooped down and wrote on the ground with His finger.
7   However, when they persisted with their question, He raised Himself up and said, Let him who is without sin among you be the first to throw a stone at her.
8   Then He bent down and went on writing on the ground with His finger.
9   They listened to Him, and then they began going out, conscience-stricken, one by one, from the oldest down to the last one of them, till Jesus was left alone, with the woman standing there before Him in the center of the court.
10   When Jesus raised Himself up, He said to her, Woman, where are your accusers? Has no man condemned you?
11   She answered, No one, Lord! And Jesus said, I do not condemn you either. Go on your way and from now on sin no more.
12   Once more Jesus addressed the crowd. He said, I am the Light of the world. He who follows Me will not be walking in the dark, but will have the Light which is Life.
13   Whereupon the Pharisees told Him, You are testifying on Your own behalf; Your testimony is not valid and is worthless.
14   Jesus answered, Even if I do testify on My own behalf, My testimony is true and reliable and valid, for I know where I came from and where I am going; but you do not know where I come from or where I am going.
15   You [set yourselves up to] judge according to the flesh (by what you see). [You condemn by external, human standards.] I do not [set Myself up to] judge or condemn or sentence anyone.
16   Yet even if I do judge, My judgment is true [My decision is right]; for I am not alone [in making it], but [there are two of Us] I and the Father, Who sent Me.
17   In your [own] Law it is written that the testimony (evidence) of two persons is reliable and valid. [Deut. 19:15.]
18   I am One [of the Two] bearing testimony concerning Myself; and My Father, Who sent Me, He also testifies about Me.
19   Then they said to Him, Where is this fFather of Yours? Jesus answered, You know My Father as little as you know Me. If you knew Me, you would know My Father also.

d John 7:53 to 8:11 is absent from most of the older manuscripts, and those that have it sometimes place it elsewhere. The story may well be authentic. Indeed, Christ's response of compassion and mercy is so much in keeping with His character that we accept it as authentic, and feel that to omit it would be most unfortunate. e Richard Trench, Synonyms of the New Testament. f Capitalized because of Who He is, the everlasting Father, not who the speaker may have thought He was.

finding your true identity

Our identity is established as a result of who and what we choose to identify with. If we identify with people and what they say about us, we will end up in trouble; but if we identify with Jesus and His opinion of us, we will not have an identity crisis.

Jesus knew who He was. John 8:14 tells us Jesus knew who He was because He knew where He came from and where He was going. This infuriated many of the Pharisees, the religious leaders of the day; they thought Jesus was blaspheming by claiming to be the Son of God. They were angry at His confidence in who He was. But no matter what people said about Jesus, He did not identify with it. He identified with what His heavenly Father said about Him. He identified with God!

Identification with Christ is a doctrinal foundation of the Christian faith. It's not taught as frequently and fully as it should be. Some religious organizations spend far too much time telling people what they need to do, and not enough time telling them who they are in Christ. We need to be taught to identify with Jesus, not with people.

You belong to God! Knowing that truth will give you confidence to walk in this world with your head held high. You will be able to follow your own heart and avoid adverse effects when people do not agree with you or your choices. You will have greater confidence which will enable you to do more for God.

From now on, when people say something unkind about you, respond by saying to yourself, or to them if appropriate: "I do not identify with that."

See yourself as complete in Christ.

---

20 Jesus said these things in the treasury while He was teaching in the temple [gcourt]; but no one ventured to arrest Him, because His hour had not yet come.
21 Therefore He said again to them, I am going away, and you will be looking for Me, and you will die in (under the curse of) your sin. Where I am going, it is not possible for you to come.
22 At this the Jews began to ask among themselves, Will He kill Himself? Is that why He says, Where I am going, it is not possible for you to come?

23 He said to them, You are from below; I am from above. You are of this world (of this earthly order); I am not of this world.
24 That is why I told you that you will die in (under the curse of) your sins; for if you do not believe that I am He [Whom I claim to be—if you do not adhere to, trust in, and rely on Me], you will die in your sins.
25 Then they said to Him, Who are You anyway? Jesus replied, [Why do I even speak to you!] I am exactly what I have been telling you from the first.
26 I have much to say about you and

g Richard Trench, *Synonyms of the New Testament.*

to judge *and* condemn. But He Who sent Me is true (reliable), and I tell the world [only] the things that I have heard from Him.

27 They did not perceive (know, understand) that He was speaking to them about the Father.

28 So Jesus added, When you have lifted up the Son of Man [on the cross], you will realize (know, understand) that I am He [for Whom you look] and that I do nothing of Myself (of My own accord or on My own authority), but I say [exactly] what My Father has taught Me.

29 And He Who sent Me is ever with Me; My Father has not left Me alone, for I always do what pleases Him.

30 As He said these things, many believed in Him [trusted, relied on, and adhered to Him].

31 So Jesus said to those Jews who had believed in Him, If you abide in My word [hold fast to My teachings and live in accordance with them], you are truly My disciples.

32 And you will know the Truth, and the Truth will set you free.

33 They answered Him, We are Abraham's offspring (descendants) and have never been in bondage to anybody. What do You mean by saying, You will be set free?

34 Jesus answered them, I assure you, most solemnly I tell you, Whoever commits *and* practices sin is the slave of sin.

35 Now a slave does not remain in a household permanently (forever); the son [of the house] does remain forever.

36 So if the Son liberates you [makes you free men], then you are really *and* unquestionably free.

37 [Yes] I know that you are Abra-ham's offspring; yet you plan to kill Me, because My word has no entrance (makes no progress, does not find any place) in you.

38 I tell the things which I have seen *and* learned at My Father's side, and your actions also reflect what you have heard *and* learned from your father.

39 They retorted, Abraham is our father. Jesus said, If you were [truly] Abraham's children, then you would do the works of Abraham [follow his example, do as Abraham did].

40 But now [instead] you are wanting *and* seeking to kill Me, a Man Who has told you the truth which I have heard from God. This is not the way Abraham acted.

41 You are doing the works of your [own] father. They said to Him, We are not illegitimate children *and* born out of fornication; we have one Father, even God.

42 Jesus said to them, If God were your Father, you would love Me *and* respect Me *and* welcome Me gladly, for I proceeded (came forth) from God [out of His very presence]. I did not even come on My own authority *or* of My own accord (as self-appointed); but He sent Me.

43 Why do you misunderstand what I say? It is because you are unable to hear what I am saying. [You cannot bear to listen to My message; your ears are shut to My teaching.]

44 You are of your father, the devil, and it is your will to practice the lusts *and* gratify the desires [which are characteristic] of your father. He was a murderer from the beginning and does not stand in the truth, because there is no truth in him. When he speaks a falsehood, he speaks what is natural to

speak the Word

Help me, God, to know the Truth because only the Truth sets me free!
ADAPTED FROM JOHN 8:32

him, for he is a liar [himself] and the father of lies *and* of all that is false.

45 But because I speak the truth, you do not believe Me [do not trust Me, do not rely on Me, or adhere to Me].

46 Who of you convicts Me of wrongdoing *or* finds Me guilty of sin? Then if I speak truth, why do you not believe Me [trust Me, rely on, and adhere to Me]?

47 Whoever is of God listens to God. [Those who belong to God hear the words of God.] This is the reason that you do not listen [to those words, to Me]: because you do not belong to God *and* are not of God *or* in harmony with Him.

48 The Jews answered Him, Are we not right when we say You are a Samaritan and that You have a demon [that You are under the power of an evil spirit]?

49 Jesus answered, I am not possessed by a demon. On the contrary, I honor *and* reverence My Father and you dishonor (despise, vilify, and scorn) Me.

50 However, I am not in search of honor for Myself. [I do not seek and am not aiming for My own glory.] There is One Who [looks after that; He] seeks [My glory], and He is the Judge.

51 I assure you, most solemnly I tell you, if anyone observes My teaching [lives in accordance with My message, keeps My word], he will by no means ever see *and* experience death.

52 The Jews said to Him, Now we know that You are under the power of a demon (hinsane). Abraham died, and also the prophets, yet You say, If a man keeps My word, he will never taste of death into all eternity.

53 Are You greater than our father Abraham? He died, and all the prophets died! Who do You make Yourself out to be?

54 Jesus answered, If I were to glorify Myself (magnify, praise, and honor Myself), I would have no real glory, for My glory would be nothing *and* worthless. [My honor must come to Me from My Father.] It is My Father Who glorifies Me [Who extols Me, magnifies, and praises Me], of Whom you say that He is your God.

55 Yet you do not know Him *or* recognize Him *and* are not acquainted with Him, but I know Him. If I should say that I do not know Him, I would be a liar like you. But I know Him and keep His word [obey His teachings, am faithful to His message].

56 Your forefather Abraham was extremely happy at the hope *and* prospect of seeing My day (My incarnation); and he did see it and was delighted. [Heb. 11:13.]

57 Then the Jews said to Him, You are not yet fifty years old, and have You seen Abraham?

58 Jesus replied, I assure you, most solemnly I tell you, before Abraham was born, I AM. [Exod. 3:14.]

59 So they took up stones to throw at Him, but Jesus, by mixing with the crowd, concealed Himself and went out of the temple [ienclosure].

9 AS HE passed along, He noticed a man blind from his birth.

2 His disciples asked Him, Rabbi, who sinned, this man or his parents, that he should be born blind?

3 Jesus answered, It was not that this man or his parents sinned, but he was born blind in order that the workings of God should be manifested (displayed and illustrated) in him.

4 We must work the works of Him Who sent Me *and* be busy with His business while it is daylight; night is coming on, when no man can work.

5 As long as I am in the world, I am the world's Light.

---

h Joseph Thayer, *A Greek-English Lexicon.*   **i** Richard Trench, *Synonyms of the New Testament.*

6 When He had said this, He spat on the ground and made clay (mud) with His saliva, and He spread it [as ointment] on the man's eyes.

7 And He said to him, Go, wash in the Pool of Siloam—which means Sent. So he went and washed, and came back seeing.

8 When the neighbors and those who used to know him by sight as a beggar saw him, they said, Is not this the man who used to sit and beg?

9 Some said, It is he. Others said, No, but he looks very much like him. But he said, Yes, I am the man.

10 So they said to him, How were your eyes opened?

11 He replied, The Man called Jesus made mud and smeared it on my eyes and said to me, Go to Siloam and wash. So I went and washed, and I obtained my sight!

12 They asked him, Where is He? He said, I do not know.

13 Then they conducted to the Pharisees the man who had formerly been blind.

14 Now it was on the Sabbath day that Jesus mixed the mud and opened the man's eyes.

15 So now again the Pharisees asked him how he received his sight. And he said to them, He smeared mud on my eyes, and I washed, and now I see.

16 Then some of the Pharisees said, This Man [Jesus] is not from God, because He does not observe the Sabbath. But others said, How can a man who is a sinner (a bad man) do such signs *and* miracles? So there was a difference of opinion among them.

17 Accordingly they said to the blind man again, What do you say about Him, seeing that He opened your eyes? And he said, He is [He must be] a prophet!

18 However, the Jews did not believe that he had [really] been blind and that he had received his sight until they called (summoned) the parents of the man.

19 They asked them, Is this your son, whom you reported as having been born blind? How then does he see now?

20 His parents answered, We know that this is our son, and that he was born blind.

21 But as to how he can now see, we do not know; or who has opened his eyes, we do not know. He is of age. Ask him; let him speak for himself *and* give his own account of it.

22 His parents said this because they feared [the leaders of] the Jews; for the Jews had already agreed that if anyone should acknowledge Jesus to be the Christ, he should be expelled *and* excluded from the synagogue.

23 On that account his parents said, He is of age; ask him.

24 So the second time they summoned the man who had been born blind, and said to him, Now give God the glory (praise). This ʲFellow we know is only a sinner (a wicked person).

25 Then he answered, I do not know whether He is a sinner *and* wicked or not. But one thing I do know, that whereas I was blind before, now I see.

26 So they said to him, What did He [actually] do to you? How did He open your eyes?

27 He answered, I already told you and you would not listen. Why do you want to hear it again? Can it be that you wish to become His disciples also?

28 And they stormed at him [they jeered, they sneered, they reviled him] and retorted, You are His disciple yourself, but we are the disciples of Moses.

j Capitalized because of what He is, the spotless Son of God, not what the speaker may have thought He was.

29 We know for certain that God spoke with Moses, but as for this Fellow, we know nothing about where He hails from.

30 The man replied, Well, this is astonishing! Here a Man has opened my eyes, and yet you do not know where He comes from. [That is amazing!]

31 We know that God does not listen to sinners; but if anyone is God-fearing *and* a worshiper of Him and does His will, He listens to him.

32 Since the beginning of time it has never been heard that anyone opened the eyes of a man born blind.

33 If this Man were not from God, He would not be able to do anything like this.

34 They retorted, You were wholly born in sin [from head to foot]; and do you [presume to] teach us? So they cast him out [threw him clear outside the synagogue].

35 Jesus heard that they had put him out, and meeting him He said, Do you believe in *and* adhere to the Son of Man ᵏ*or the Son of God*?

36 He answered, Who is He, Sir? Tell me, that I may believe in *and* adhere to Him.

37 Jesus said to him, You have seen Him; [in fact] He is talking to you right now.

38 He called out, Lord, I believe! [I rely on, I trust, I cleave to You!] And he worshiped Him.

39 Then Jesus said, I came into this world for judgment [as a Separator, in order that there may be ¹separation between those who believe on Me and those who reject Me], to make the sightless see and to make those who see become blind.

40 Some Pharisees who were near, hearing this remark, said to Him, Are we also blind?

41 Jesus said to them, If you were blind, you would have no sin; but because you now claim to have sight, your sin remains. [If you were blind, you would not be guilty of sin; but because you insist, We do see clearly, you are unable to escape your guilt.]

10 I ASSURE you, most solemnly I tell you, he who does not enter by the door into the sheepfold, but climbs up some other way (elsewhere, from some other quarter) is a thief and a robber.

2 But he who enters by the door is the shepherd of the sheep.

3 The watchman opens the door for this man, and the sheep listen to his voice *and* heed it; and he calls his own sheep by name and brings (leads) them out.

4 When he has brought his own sheep outside, he walks on before them, and the sheep follow him because they know his voice.

5 They will never [on any account] follow a stranger, but will run away from him because they do not know the voice of strangers *or* recognize their call.

6 Jesus used this parable (illustration) with them, but they did not understand what He was talking about.

7 So Jesus said again, I assure you, most solemnly I tell you, that I Myself am the Door ¹for the sheep.

8 All others who came [as such] before Me are thieves and robbers, but the [true] sheep did not listen to *and* obey them.

9 I am the Door; anyone who enters in through Me will be saved (will live). He will come in and he will go out [freely], and will find pasture.

10 The thief comes only in order to steal and kill and destroy. I came that they may have *and* enjoy life, and

---

k Many ancient manuscripts read "the Son of God."　　**1** Marvin Vincent, *Word Studies.*

discerning God's voice

People ask, "How can I be sure I am hearing from God?" As believers, hearing God speak to us is our right and our privilege. The Word says that we can *know* His voice and distinguish it from others; He gives us discernment to identify His voice over voices of deception. In John 10:3–5, He parallels this discernment with the instinctive nature of sheep that recognize the voice of their shepherd.

We can discern the difference between God's voice and the voice of deception if we truly know God's character, nature, and the history of how He has led others before us. We will know that what we have heard is something that is in His nature to say. We will know that what He has said does not contradict His Word, wisdom or common sense.

If we truly belong to God, He will give us discernment to know if what we are hearing is truly from Him or not. He will enable us to distinguish His voice from the deceptive spirit of error. Then we can have confidence that we are following God's direction, whether He is leading us to go forward or telling us to wait.

To hear God and avoid the spirit of error, it is important to look into God's Word and spend time with Him there. The more we study and learn the Word, the more we will let its power flow through our lives and the better we will be able to hear, discern and obey God's voice.

have it in abundance (to the full, till it ^m overflows).

11 I am the Good Shepherd. The Good Shepherd risks *and* lays down His [own] life for the sheep. [Ps. 23.]

12 But the hired servant (he who merely serves for wages) who is neither the shepherd nor the owner of the sheep, when he sees the wolf coming, deserts the flock and runs away. And the wolf chases *and* snatches them and scatters [the flock].

13 Now the hireling flees because he merely serves for wages and is not himself concerned about the sheep [cares nothing for them].

14 I am the Good Shepherd; and I know *and* recognize My own, and My own know *and* recognize Me—

15 Even as [truly as] the Father knows Me and I also know the Father—and I am giving My [very

own] life *and* laying it down on behalf of the sheep.

16 And I have other sheep [beside these] that are not of this fold. I must bring *and* ^n impel those also; and they will listen to My voice *and* heed My call, and so there will be [they will become] one flock under one Shepherd. [Ezek. 34:23.]

17 For this [reason] the Father loves Me, because I lay down My [own] life—to take it back again.

18 No one takes it away from Me. On the contrary, I lay it down voluntarily. [I put it from Myself.] I am authorized *and* have power to lay it down (to resign it) and I am authorized *and* have power to take it back again. These are the instructions (orders) which I have received [as My charge] from My Father.

19 Then a fresh division of opinion

m Alexander Souter, *Pocket Lexicon of the Greek New Testament.*   **n** G. Abbott-Smith, *Manual Greek Lexicon.*

putting the Word to work

Have you ever had anything stolen from you? Even if you replaced the article that was stolen, it was probably a trying experience. As difficult as that might have felt, however, Satan—the thief—wants to do even more damage in your life. He does not want to steal your bicycle or your stereo or even your car—he wants to rob you of the joy and peace and hope that you have found in God. But be encouraged: Jesus, your Good Shepherd, has saved you and gives you abundant life. Ask Him to restore anything Satan has robbed from you and to teach you how to walk in the abundant life He has promised you.

arose among the Jews because of His saying these things.

20 And many of them said, He has a demon and He is mad (insane—He raves, He rambles). Why do you listen to Him?

21 Others argued, These are not the thoughts *and* the language of one possessed. Can a demon-possessed person open blind eyes?

22 After this the Feast of Dedication [of the reconsecration of the temple] was taking place at Jerusalem. It was winter,

23 And Jesus was walking in Solomon's Porch in the temple area.

24 So the Jews surrounded Him and began asking Him, How long are You going to keep us in doubt *and* suspense? If You are really the Christ (the Messiah), tell us so plainly *and* openly.

25 Jesus answered them, I have told you so, yet you do not believe Me [you do not trust Me *and* rely on Me]. The very works that I do by the power of

My Father *and* in My Father's name bear witness concerning Me [they are My credentials and evidence in support of Me].

26 But you do not believe *and* trust *and* rely on Me because you do not belong to My fold [you are no sheep of Mine].

27 The sheep that are My own hear *and* are listening to My voice; and I know them, and they follow Me.

28 And I give them eternal life, and they shall never lose it *or* perish throughout the ages. [To all eternity they shall never by any means be destroyed.] And no one is able to snatch them out of My hand.

29 My Father, Who has given them to Me, is greater *and* mightier than all [else]; and no one is able to snatch [them] out of the Father's hand.

30 I and the Father are One.

31 Again the Jews ᵒbrought up stones to stone Him.

32 Jesus said to them, My Father has enabled Me to do many good deeds. [I have shown many acts of mercy in your presence.] For which of these do you mean to stone Me?

33 The Jews replied, We are not going to stone You for a good act, but for blasphemy, because You, a mere ᵖMan, make Yourself [out to be] God.

34 Jesus answered, Is it not written in your Law, I said, You are gods? [Ps. 82:6.]

35 So men are called gods [by the Law], men to whom God's message came—and the Scripture cannot be set aside *or* cancelled *or* broken *or* annulled—

36 [If that is true] do you say of the One Whom the Father consecrated *and* dedicated *and* set apart for Himself and sent into the world, You are blaspheming, because I said, I am the Son of God?

---

o Marvin Vincent, *Word Studies.* **p** Capitalized because of what He is, the spotless Son of God, not what the speaker may have thought He was.

enjoying everyday life

Satan has one goal and that is destruction. He comes only to kill, steal and destroy everything good that God has in mind for us. Jesus said He came that we might have life and enjoy our lives.

Are you enjoying life? Are you enjoying every facet of life or just what you consider to be the "fun" parts? I truly believe that through the power of the Holy Spirit we can enjoy everything. We can enjoy our work and times of waiting. We can enjoy the journey and not just the destination. Life is really all about the journey. Even when a train arrives at whatever station it is headed for, it soon leaves again for another station. We spend more time in life waiting than we do arriving. God created us to be goal-oriented. Once we reach one goal, it is not long before we find ourselves setting another one. We must learn to enjoy where we are on the way to where we are going.

One of the ways Satan steals from us is by making us think we can only enjoy certain things and not others. But the truth is that we can get a new mindset and decide to enjoy everything in life. I spend a lot of time waiting in airports. Sometimes flights are cancelled or delayed and I used to let that steal my joy. I often became very aggravated, frustrated and upset—but that did not change my circumstances; it only stole my joy and peace. I finally learned that when circumstances change, I do not have to change with them. I can refuse to allow Satan to get me upset. When Satan steals from you or aggravates you, he really does not want your goods, he wants your joy!

Making a decision to enjoy my life was an important one for me and it may be for you too. Life is wasted if we allow ourselves to be miserable all the time. Jesus said in John 14:27 that He has left us His peace and we are to stop allowing ourselves to be upset. He has given us gifts and responsibilities. We are partners with God. His part is to provide peace and joy and our part is not to let the devil steal it. Decide today to start enjoying everyday life!

37 If I am not doing the works [performing the deeds] of My Father, then do not believe Me [do not adhere to Me and trust Me and rely on Me].
38 But if I do them, even though you do not believe Me *or* have faith in Me, [at least] believe the works *and* have faith in what I do, in order that you may know and understand [clearly] that the Father is in Me, and I am in the Father [One with Him].
39 They sought again to arrest Him,

but He escaped from their hands.
40 He went back again across the Jordan to the locality where John was when he first baptized, and there He remained.
41 And many came to Him, and they kept saying, John did not perform a [single] sign *or* miracle, but everything John said about this Man was true.
42 And many [people] there became believers in Him. [They adhered to *and* trusted in *and* relied on Him.]

11

NOW A certain man named Lazarus was ill. He was of Bethany, the village where Mary and her sister Martha lived.

2 This Mary was the one who anointed the Lord with perfume and wiped His feet with her hair. It was her brother Lazarus who was [now] sick.

3 So the sisters sent to Him, saying, Lord, he whom You love [so well] is sick.

4 When Jesus received the message, He said, This sickness is not to end in death; but [on the contrary] it is to honor God *and* to promote His glory, that the Son of God may be glorified through (by) it.

5 Now Jesus loved Martha and her sister and Lazarus. [They were His dear friends, and He held them in loving esteem.]

6 Therefore [even] when He heard that Lazarus was sick, He still stayed two days longer in the same place where He was.

7 Then after that interval He said to His disciples, Let us go back again to Judea.

8 The disciples said to Him, Rabbi, the Jews only recently were intending *and* trying to stone You, and are You [thinking of] going back there again?

9 Jesus answered, Are there not twelve hours in the day? Anyone who walks about in the daytime does not stumble, because he sees [by] the light of this world.

10 But if anyone walks about in the night, he does stumble, because there is no light in him [the light is lacking to him].

11 He said these things, and then added, Our friend Lazarus is at rest *and* sleeping; but I am going there that I may awaken him out of his sleep.

12 The disciples answered, Lord, if he is sleeping, he will recover.

13 However, Jesus had spoken of his death, but they thought that He referred to falling into a refreshing *and* natural sleep.

14 So then Jesus told them plainly, Lazarus is dead,

15 And for your sake I am glad that I was not there; it will help you to believe (to trust and rely on Me). However, let us go to him.

16 Then Thomas, who was called the Twin, said to his fellow disciples, Let us go too, that we may die [be killed] along with Him.

17 So when Jesus arrived, He found that he [Lazarus] had already been in the tomb four days.

18 Bethany was near Jerusalem, only about two miles away,

19 And a considerable number of the Jews had gone out to see Martha and Mary to console them concerning their brother.

20 When Martha heard that Jesus was coming, she went to meet Him, while Mary remained sitting in the house.

21 Martha then said to Jesus, Master, if You had been here, my brother would not have died.

22 And even now I know that whatever You ask from God, He will grant it to You.

23 Jesus said to her, Your brother shall rise again.

24 Martha replied, I know that he will rise again in the resurrection at the last day.

25 Jesus said to her, I am [Myself] the Resurrection and the Life. Whoever believes in (adheres to, trusts in, and relies on) Me, although he may die, yet he shall live;

26 And whoever continues to live and believes in (has faith in, cleaves to, and relies on) Me shall never [actually] die at all. Do you believe this?

27 She said to Him, Yes, Lord, I have believed [I do believe] that You are the Christ (the Messiah, the Anointed

One), the Son of God, [even He] Who was to come into the world. [It is for Your coming that the world has waited.]

28 After she had said this, she went back and called her sister Mary, privately whispering to her, The Teacher is close at hand and is asking for you.

29 When she heard this, she sprang up quickly and went to Him.

30 Now Jesus had not yet entered the village, but was still at the same spot where Martha had met Him.

31 When the Jews who were sitting with her in the house and consoling her saw how hastily Mary had arisen and gone out, they followed her, supposing that she was going to the tomb to pour out her grief there.

32 When Mary came to the place where Jesus was and saw Him, she dropped down at His feet, saying to Him, Lord, if You had been here, my brother would not have died.

putting the Word to work

Many people are afraid of death. Are you? Martha had just buried her brother, yet she took Jesus at His word and believed that He was the Son of God and that her brother would live again. As a believer in Jesus, you do not need to fear death. As Martha discovered, you too can know that Jesus has defeated the power of death. Although your body will one day die, your spirit will live forever with God.

33 When Jesus saw her sobbing, and the Jews who came with her [also] sobbing, He was deeply moved in spirit and troubled. [He chafed in spirit and sighed and was disturbed.]

34 And He said, Where have you laid him? They said to Him, Lord, come and see.

35 Jesus wept.

36 The Jews said, See how [tenderly] He loved him!

37 But some of them said, Could not He Who opened a blind man's eyes have prevented this man from dying?

38 Now Jesus, again sighing repeatedly *and* deeply disquieted, approached the tomb. It was a cave (a hole in the rock), and a boulder lay against [the entrance to close] it.

39 Jesus said, Take away the stone. Martha, the sister of the dead man, exclaimed, But Lord, by this time he [is decaying and] throws off an offensive odor, for he has been dead four days!

40 Jesus said to her, Did I not tell you *and* qpromise you that if you would believe *and* rely on Me, you would see the glory of God?

41 So they took away the stone. And Jesus lifted up His eyes and said, Father, I thank You that You have heard Me.

42 Yes, I know You always hear *and* listen to Me, but I have said this on account of *and* for the benefit of the people standing around, so that they may believe that You did send Me [that You have made Me Your Messenger].

43 When He had said this, He shouted with a loud voice, Lazarus, come out!

44 And out walked the man who had been dead, his hands and feet wrapped in burial cloths (linen strips), and with a [burial] napkin

life point

In John 11:41 we see a good example of Jesus giving thanks to God. When you pray, I encourage you to end your prayer, as Jesus did here, by saying, "Father, I thank You that You have heard me."

q Charles B. Williams, *The New Testament: A Translation.*

bound around his face. Jesus said to them, Free him of the burial wrappings and let him go.

45 Upon seeing what Jesus had done, many of the Jews who had come with Mary believed in Him. [They trusted in Him and adhered to Him and relied on Him.]

46 But some of them went back to the Pharisees and told them what Jesus had done.

47 So the chief priests and Pharisees called a meeting of the council (the Sanhedrin) and said, What are we to do? For this Man performs many signs (evidences, miracles).

48 If we let Him alone to go on like this, everyone will believe in Him *and* adhere to Him, and the Romans will come and suppress *and* destroy *and* take away our [holy] place and our nation [ᵣour temple and city and our civil organization].

49 But one of them, Caiaphas, who was the high priest that year, declared, You know nothing at all!

50 Nor do you understand *or* reason out that it is expedient *and* better for your own welfare that one man should die on behalf of the people than that the whole nation should perish (be destroyed, ruined).

51 Now he did not say this simply of his own accord [he was not self-moved]; but being the high priest that year, he prophesied that Jesus was to die for the nation, [Isa. 53:8.]

52 And not only for the nation but also for the purpose of uniting into one body the children of God who have been scattered far and wide. [Isa. 49:6.]

53 So from that day on they took counsel *and* plotted together how they might put Him to death.

54 For that reason Jesus no longer appeared publicly among the Jews, but left there and retired to the dis-

trict that borders on the wilderness (the desert), to a village called Ephraim, and there He stayed with the disciples.

55 Now the Jewish Passover was at hand, and many from the country went up to Jerusalem in order that they might purify *and* consecrate themselves before the Passover.

56 So they kept looking for Jesus and questioned among themselves as they were standing about in the temple [ˢarea], What do you think? Will He not come to the Feast at all?

57 Now the chief priests and Pharisees had given orders that if anyone knew where He was, he should report it to them, so that they might arrest Him.

12 SO SIX days before the Passover Feast, Jesus came to Bethany, where Lazarus was, who had died and whom He had raised from the dead.

2 So they made Him a supper; and Martha served, but Lazarus was one of those at the table with Him.

3 Mary took a pound of ointment of pure liquid nard [a rare perfume] that was very expensive, and she poured it on Jesus' feet and wiped them with her hair. And the whole house was filled with the fragrance of the perfume.

4 But Judas Iscariot, the one of His disciples who was about to betray Him, said,

5 Why was this perfume not sold for 300 denarii [a year's wages for an ordinary workman] and that [money] given to the poor (the destitute)?

6 Now he did not say this because he cared for the poor but because he was a thief; and having the bag (the money box, the purse of the Twelve), he took for himself what was put into it [pilfering the collections].

---

r Marvin Vincent, *Word Studies.*   **s** Richard Trench, *Synonyms of the New Testament.*

7 But Jesus said, Let her alone. It was [intended] that she should keep it for the time of My preparation for burial. [She has kept it that she might have it for the time of My 'embalming.]

8 You always have the poor with you, but you do not always have Me.

9 Now a great crowd of the Jews heard that He was at Bethany, and they came there, not only because of Jesus but that they also might see Lazarus, whom He had raised from the dead.

10 So the chief priests planned to put Lazarus to death also,

11 Because on account of him many of the Jews were going away [were withdrawing from and leaving the Judeans] and believing in and adhering to Jesus.

12 The next day a vast crowd of those who had come to the Passover Feast heard that Jesus was coming to Jerusalem.

13 So they took branches of palm trees and went out to meet Him. And as they went, they kept shouting, Hosanna! Blessed is He and praise to Him Who comes in the name of the Lord, even the King of Israel! [Ps. 118:26.]

14 And Jesus, having found a young donkey, rode upon it, [just] as it is written in the Scriptures,

15 Do not fear, O Daughter of Zion! Look! Your King is coming, sitting on a donkey's colt! [Zech. 9:9.]

16 His disciples did not understand and could not comprehend the meaning of these things at first; but when Jesus was glorified and exalted, they remembered that these things had been written about Him and had been done to Him.

17 The group that had been with Jesus when He called Lazarus out of the tomb and raised him from among the dead kept telling it [bearing witness] to others.

18 It was for this reason that the crowd went out to meet Him, because they had heard that He had performed this sign (proof, miracle).

19 Then the Pharisees said among themselves, You see how futile your efforts are and how you accomplish nothing. See! The whole world is running after Him!

20 Now among those who went up to worship at the Feast were some Greeks.

21 These came to Philip, who was from Bethsaida in Galilee, and they made this request, Sir, we desire to see Jesus.

22 Philip came and told Andrew; then Andrew and Philip together [went] and told Jesus.

23 And Jesus answered them, The time has come for the Son of Man to be glorified and exalted.

24 I assure you, most solemnly I tell you, Unless a grain of wheat falls into the earth and dies, it remains [just one grain; it never becomes more but lives] by itself alone. But if it dies, it produces many others and yields a rich harvest.

25 Anyone who loves his life loses it, but anyone who hates his life in this world will keep it to life eternal. [Whoever has no love for, no concern for, no regard for his life here on earth, but despises it, preserves his life forever and ever.]

26 If anyone serves Me, he must continue to follow Me ["to cleave steadfastly to Me, conform wholly to My example in living and, if need be, in dying] and wherever I am, there will My servant be also. If anyone serves Me, the Father will honor him.

27 Now My soul is troubled and distressed, and what shall I say? Father, save Me from this hour [of trial and

t Marvin Vincent, *Word Studies*. u Joseph Thayer, *A Greek-English Lexicon*.

agony]? But it was for this very purpose that I have come to this hour [that I might undergo it].

28 [Rather, I will say,] Father, glorify (honor and extol) Your [own] name! Then there came a voice out of heaven saying, I have already glorified it, and I will glorify it again.

29 The crowd of bystanders heard the sound and said that it had thundered; others said, An angel has spoken to Him!

30 Jesus answered, This voice has not come for My sake, but for your sake.

31 Now the judgment (crisis) of this world is coming on [sentence is now being passed on this world]. Now the ruler (evil genius, prince) of this world shall be cast out (expelled).

32 And I, if and when I am lifted up from the earth [on the cross], will draw and attract all men [Gentiles as well as Jews] to Myself.

33 He said this to signify in what manner He would die.

34 At this the people answered Him, We have learned from the Law that the Christ is to remain forever; how then can You say, The Son of Man must be lifted up [on the cross]? Who is this Son of Man? [Ps. 110:4.]

35 So Jesus said to them, You will have the Light only a little while longer. Walk while you have the Light [keep on living by it], so that darkness may not overtake and overcome you. He who walks about in the dark does not know where he goes [he is drifting].

36 While you have the Light, believe in the Light [have faith in it, hold to it, rely on it], that you may become sons

of the Light and be filled with Light. Jesus said these things, and then He went away and hid Himself from them [was lost to their view].

37 Even though He had done so many miracles before them (right before their eyes), yet they still did not trust in Him and failed to believe in Him—

38 So that what Isaiah the prophet said was fulfilled: Lord, who has believed our report and our message? And to whom has the arm (the power) of the Lord been shown (unveiled and revealed)? [Isa. 53:1.]

39 Therefore they could not believe [they were unable to believe]. For Isaiah has also said,

40 He has blinded their eyes and hardened and benumbed their [callous, degenerated] hearts [He has made their minds dull], to keep them from seeing with their eyes and understanding with their hearts and minds and repenting and turning to Me to heal them.

41 Isaiah said this because he saw His glory and spoke of Him. [Isa. 6:9, 10.]

42 And yet [in spite of all this] many even of the leading men (the authorities and the nobles) believed and trusted in Him. But because of the Pharisees they did not confess it, for fear that [if they should acknowledge Him] they would be expelled from the synagogue;

43 For they loved the approval and the praise and the glory that come from men [instead of and] more than the glory that comes from God. [They valued their credit with men more than their credit with God.]

speak the Word

Jesus, I will serve You and continue to follow You. I will cleave steadfastly to You, conform wholly to Your example in living and, if need be, in dying. Wherever You are, I will be also.
ADAPTED FROM JOHN 12:26

44 But Jesus loudly declared, The one who believes in Me does not [only] believe in *and* trust in *and* rely on Me, but [in believing in Me he believes] in Him Who sent Me.

45 And whoever sees Me sees Him Who sent Me.

46 I have come as a Light into the world, so that whoever believes in Me [whoever cleaves to *and* trusts in *and* relies on Me] may not continue to live in darkness.

47 If anyone hears My teachings and fails to observe them [does not keep them, but disregards them], it is not I who judges him. For I have not come to judge *and* to condemn *and* to pass sentence *and* to inflict penalty on the world, but to save the world.

48 Anyone who rejects Me *and* persistently sets Me at naught, refusing to accept My teachings, has his judge [however]; for the [very] message that I have spoken will itself judge *and* convict him at the last day.

49 This is because I have never spoken on My own authority *or* of My own accord *or* as self-appointed, but the Father Who sent Me has Himself given Me orders [concerning] what to say and what to tell. [Deut. 18:18, 19.]

50 And I know that His commandment is (means) eternal life. So whatever I speak, I am saying [exactly] what My Father has told Me to say *and* in accordance with His instructions.

13 [NOW] BEFORE the Passover Feast began, Jesus knew (was fully aware) that the time had come for Him to leave this world *and* return to the Father. And as He had loved those who were His own in the world, He loved them to the last *and* [v]to the highest degree.

2 So [it was] during supper, Satan having already put the thought of betraying Jesus in the heart of Judas Iscariot, Simon's son,

3 [That] Jesus, knowing (fully aware) that the Father had put everything into His hands, and that He had come from God and was [now] returning to God,

4 Got up from supper, took off His garments, and taking a [servant's] towel, He fastened it around His waist.

5 Then He poured water into the washbasin and began to wash the disciples' feet and to wipe them with the [servant's] towel with which He was girded.

6 When He came to Simon Peter, [Peter] said to Him, Lord, are my feet to be washed by You? [Is it for You to wash my feet?]

7 Jesus said to him, You do not understand now what I am doing, but you will understand later on.

8 Peter said to Him, You shall never wash my feet! Jesus answered him, Unless I wash you, you have no part with ([w]in) Me [you have no share in companionship with Me].

9 Simon Peter said to Him, Lord, [wash] not only my feet, but my hands and my head too!

10 Jesus said to him, Anyone who has bathed needs only to wash his feet, but is clean all over. And you [My disciples] are clean, but not all of you.

11 For He knew who was going to betray Him; that was the reason He said, Not all of you are clean.

12 So when He had finished washing their feet and had put on His garments and had sat down again, He said to them, Do you understand what I have done to you?

[v] Saint John Chrysostom, cited by Joseph Thayer, *A Greek-English Lexicon.* [w] Origen (the greatest theologian of the early Greek Church); Adam Clarke, *The Holy Bible with A Commentary*; and others so interpret this passage. Notice the "in Me" emphasis in John 15, especially in verses 4-9, words spoken concerning the same subject, and on the same evening.

great people serve

Pride never kept the Lord from showing His love. John 13:3–15 tells the story of how Jesus washed the feet of His disciples in an act of servanthood to show them how very much He loved them.

In a culture where people's sandals did not protect their feet from the dirt of the roads, servants—not masters—were supposed to wash feet. But Jesus, fully knowing who He was, being the Greatest of all, became the Servant of all.

When the Lord came to Simon Peter to wash his feet, Peter resisted Him saying, "Lord, are my feet to be washed by You?" (John 13:6). Imagine for a moment how *you* would feel if Jesus told you that He wanted to wash *your* feet. You probably would feel hesitant, as Peter did, thinking that you should be the one washing the Lord's feet, instead of Him washing yours. How did Jesus respond to Peter's rash vow of never letting Jesus wash his feet? Jesus said that unless Peter let Him do this, he would have no part in Him (see John 13:7, 8).

After Jesus completed washing all of His disciples' feet, He told them they needed to follow His example as their Lord and Teacher and wash one another's feet (see John 13:14). I believe Jesus was saying that unless we are willing to serve one another, we have no true part in Him or in each other. If we love someone to the highest degree, we will be willing to serve that person.

In our relationship with Him, Jesus calls us to sacrifice our self-will. We are not to be served, but to serve. We are to be sensitive to other people's needs, even in little things. We, like Jesus, should seek to serve others rather than merely letting them serve us. When we have people in our lives who serve us in various ways, we should always treat them with the utmost respect and be good to them.

13 You call Me the Teacher (Master) and the Lord, and you are right in doing so, for that is what I am.

14 If I then, your Lord and Teacher (Master), have washed your feet, you ought [it is your duty, you are under obligation, you owe it] to wash one another's feet.

15 For I have given you this as an example, so that you should do [in your turn] what I have done to you.

16 I assure you, most solemnly I tell you, A servant is not greater than his master, and no one who is sent is superior to the one who sent him.

17 If you know these things, blessed *and* happy *and* ˣto be envied are you if you practice them [if you act accordingly and really do them].

18 I am not speaking of *and* I do not mean all of you. I know whom I have chosen; but it is that the Scripture may be fulfilled, He who eats ʸMy bread *with Me* has raised up his heel against Me. [Ps. 41:9.]

19 I tell you this now before it occurs, so that when it does take place you may be persuaded *and* believe that I am He [Who I say I am—the Christ, the Anointed One, the Messiah].

x Alexander Souter, *Pocket Lexicon*.   y Many ancient manuscripts read "with Me."

20 I assure you, most solemnly I tell you, he who receives *and* welcomes *and* takes into his heart any messenger of Mine receives Me [in just that way]; and he who receives *and* welcomes *and* takes Me into his heart receives Him Who sent Me [in that same way].

21 After Jesus had said these things, He was troubled (disturbed, agitated) in spirit and said, I assure you, most solemnly I tell you, one of you will deliver Me up [one of you will be false to Me and betray Me]!

22 The disciples kept looking at one another, puzzled as to whom He could mean.

23 One of His disciples, whom Jesus loved [whom He esteemed and delighted in], was reclining [next to Him] on Jesus' bosom.

24 So Simon Peter motioned to him to ask of whom He was speaking.

25 Then leaning back against Jesus' breast, he asked Him, Lord, who is it?

26 Jesus answered, It is the one to whom I am going to give this morsel (bit) of food after I have dipped it. So when He had dipped the morsel of bread [into the dish], He gave it to Judas, Simon Iscariot's son.

27 Then after [he had taken] the bit of food, Satan entered into *and* took possession of [Judas]. Jesus said to him, What you are going to do, do ᶻmore swiftly than you seem to intend *and* ᵃmake quick work of it.

28 But nobody reclining at the table knew why He spoke to him *or* what He meant by telling him this.

29 Some thought that, since Judas had the money box (the purse), Jesus was telling him, Buy what we need for the Festival, or that he should give something to the poor.

30 So after receiving the bit of bread, he went out immediately. And it was night.

31 When he had left, Jesus said, Now is the Son of Man glorified! [Now He has achieved His glory, His honor, His exaltation!] And God has been glorified through *and* in Him.

32 And if God is glorified through *and* in Him, God will also glorify Him in Himself, and He will glorify Him at once *and* not delay.

33 [Dear] little children, I am to be with you only a little longer. You will look for Me and, as I told the Jews, so I tell you now: you are not able to come where I am going.

34 I give you a new commandment: that you should love one another. Just as I have loved you, so you too should love one another.

35 By this shall all [men] know that you are My disciples, if you love one another [if you keep on showing love among yourselves].

36 Simon Peter said to Him, Lord, where are You going? Jesus answered, You are not able to follow Me now where I am going, but you shall follow Me afterwards.

37 Peter said to Him, Lord, why cannot I follow You now? I will lay down my life for You.

38 Jesus answered, Will you [really] lay down your life for Me? I assure

putting the Word to work

Have you ever wondered what the best way to tell someone about Jesus is? The answer is, "Love them." Live out the selfless, sacrificial love that you have received from Jesus. Extend that love to those who have not trusted Him as Lord and Savior, and your actions will speak loudly about who Jesus is and what He is all about.

z Joseph Thayer, *A Greek-English Lexicon*. **a** Charles B. Williams, *The New Testament: A Translation*.

major in love

Is love the main theme of your life? If not, you need to make a change. Often we spend time seeking things that we think are important, but they aren't important to God at all. I did that for a long time. I tried to build a worldwide ministry, tried to change myself and my husband and children, tried to prosper and succeed. I tried a lot of things, but I ignored the one thing Jesus told us was important.

Do not major in what Jesus considers to be minor. In other words, don't spend your time and effort on things that have no lasting value and don't add to the kingdom of God. We should all take a regular and honest inventory of our love walk. Do you study love? Do you purposely walk in love? Do you even really know what love is? It is certainly more than theory or speech. The Bible says love is seen in our behavior toward one another. It is by our love that the world will know we are Jesus' disciples (see John 13:35).

The world will not be impressed with anything other than seeing a consistent love walk among Christians. That will impress them because it is rarely seen and it is impossible for anyone to maintain without Jesus Christ in their lives. Talk is easy, but the world needs to see action. God is love; so when people see real love, they see God.

Love can be described quite eloquently, but I believe the real power of love is seen in how we treat one another. Are we patient, kind, humble, ready to believe the best at all times, not easily provoked or offended and ready to lay aside our rights for other people? Are we ready to quickly and frequently forgive, and to never keep records of wrongs that we have suffered? Will we endure everything without weakening and bear with the failings of the weak? The willingness to do these things is what love is all about. Love is an effort and it always costs us something. Most people today are looking for the easy road, but that is one that leads to destruction. I encourage you to take the narrow road—the one which people who are willing to treat others as they want to be treated travel.

you, most solemnly I tell you, before a rooster crows, you will deny Me [completely disown Me] three times.

14 DO NOT let your hearts be troubled (distressed, agitated). You believe in *and* adhere to *and* trust in *and* rely on God; believe in *and* adhere to *and* trust in *and* rely also on Me.

2 In My Father's house there are many dwelling places (homes). If it were not so, I would have told you; for I am going away to prepare a place for you.

3 And when (if) I go and make ready a place for you, I will come back again and will take you to Myself, that where I am you may be also.

4 And [to the place] where I am going, you know the way.

5 Thomas said to Him, Lord, we do not know where You are going, so how can we know the way?

6 Jesus said to him, I am the Way and the Truth and the Life; no one

life point

In John 14:6, Jesus said, "I am the Way." It is important for us to see that Jesus has a certain way of doing things, and if we will submit to *His* way, everything will work out. But so often we wrestle and struggle with Him, trying to get Him to do things our way. It just doesn't work. Let Jesus be the Way in your life.

---

comes to the Father except by (through) Me.

7 If you had known Me [had learned to recognize Me], you would also have known My Father. From now on, you know Him and have seen Him.

8 Philip said to Him, Lord, show us the Father [cause us to see the Father—that is all we ask]; then we shall be satisfied.

9 Jesus replied, Have I been with all of you for so long a time, and do you not recognize *and* know Me yet, Philip? Anyone who has seen Me has seen the Father. How can you say then, Show us the Father?

putting the Word to work

Have you ever been in a car with someone who doesn't know where he is going and who refuses to ask for directions? Many people think there are many ways to God, and they search for truth in different places, ignoring the directions that God gave us. However, the reality is that there is only one way to God, and that is through Jesus Christ. As you follow Jesus, Who is the Way, He will lead you in truth and you will experience fullness of life. Pray for those who do not yet know Jesus, that they too will find life and truth in Him.

10 Do you not believe that I am in the Father, and that the Father is in Me? What I am telling you I do not say on My own authority *and* of My own accord; but the Father Who lives continually in Me does the (**b***His*) works (His own miracles, deeds of power).

11 Believe Me that I am in the Father and the Father in Me; or else believe Me for the sake of the [very] works themselves. [If you cannot trust Me, at least let these works that I do in My Father's name convince you.]

12 I assure you, most solemnly I tell you, if anyone steadfastly believes in Me, he will himself be able to do the things that I do; and he will do even greater things than these, because I go to the Father.

13 And I will do [I Myself will grant] whatever you ask in My Name [as ᶜpresenting all that I AM], so that the Father may be glorified *and* extolled in (through) the Son. [Exod. 3:14.]

14 [Yes] I will grant [I Myself will do for you] whatever you shall ask in My Name [as ᶜpresenting all that I AM].

15 If you [really] love Me, you will keep (obey) My commands.

16 And I will ask the Father, and He will give you another Comforter (Counselor, Helper, Intercessor, Advocate, Strengthener, and Standby), that He may remain with you forever—

17 The Spirit of Truth, Whom the world cannot receive (welcome, take

life point

To whatever degree we love God, to that same degree we obey Him. To whatever degree we obey Him, that is the measure of our love for Him. As our love for Jesus grows, so will our obedience.

---

b Several ancient manuscripts read "His works."   **c** Hermann Cremer, *Biblico-Theological Lexicon*.

life point

Things get hard when we try to do them independently without leaning and relying on God's grace. If everything in life were easy, we wouldn't need the power of the Holy Spirit to help us.

One way the Bible refers to the Holy Spirit is our "Helper." He is in us and with us all the time to *help* us, to enable us to do what we cannot do—and, I might add, to do with ease what would be difficult without Him.

to its heart), because it does not see Him or know *and* recognize Him. But you know *and* recognize Him, for He lives with you [constantly] and will be in you.

18 I will not leave you as orphans [comfortless, desolate, bereaved, forlorn, helpless]; I will come [back] to you.

19 Just a little while now, and the world will not see Me any more, but you will see Me; because I live, you will live also.

20 At that time [when that day comes] you will know [for yourselves] that I am in My Father, and you [are] in Me, and I [am] in you.

21 The person who has My commands and keeps them is the one who [really] loves Me; and whoever [really] loves Me will be loved by My Father, and I [too] will love him and

will show (reveal, manifest) Myself to him. [I will let Myself be clearly seen by him and make Myself real to him.]

22 Judas, not Iscariot, asked Him, Lord, how is it that You will reveal Yourself [make Yourself real] to us and not to the world?

23 Jesus answered, If a person [really] loves Me, he will keep My word [obey My teaching]; and My Father will love him, and We will come to him and make Our home (abode, special dwelling place) with him.

24 Anyone who does not [really] love Me does not observe *and* obey My teaching. And the teaching which you hear *and* heed is not Mine, but [comes] from the Father Who sent Me.

25 I have told you these things while I am still with you.

26 But the Comforter (Counselor, Helper, Intercessor, Advocate, Strengthener, Standby), the Holy Spirit, Whom the Father will send in My name [in My place, to represent Me and act on My behalf], He will teach you all things. And He will cause you to recall (will remind you of, bring to your remembrance) everything I have told you.

27 Peace I leave with you; My [own] peace I now give *and* bequeath to you. Not as the world gives do I give to you. Do not let your hearts be troubled, neither let them be afraid. [Stop allowing yourselves to be agitated and disturbed; and do not permit yourselves to be fearful and intimidated and cowardly and unsettled.]

life point

John 14:17 calls the Holy Spirit the "Spirit of Truth." He works continually in and with believers to bring us into new levels of truth awareness. Entering a new level always means leaving an old one behind, but we have nothing to fear because He promises to be with us. Always.

life point

We see plainly from John 14:27 that Jesus has provided us peace, but we must appropriate it, and not allow our hearts to be troubled or afraid. We cannot just passively wait to feel peaceful. We are to pursue God's peace and refuse to live without it.

28 You heard Me tell you, I am going away and I am coming [back] to you. If you [really] loved Me, you would have been glad, because I am going to the Father; for the Father is greater *and* mightier than I am.

29 And now I have told you [this] before it occurs, so that when it does take place you may believe *and* have faith in *and* rely on Me.

30 I will not talk with you much more, for the prince (evil genius, ruler) of the world is coming. And he has no claim on Me. [He has nothing in common with Me; there is nothing in Me that belongs to him, and he has no power over Me.]

31 But [dSatan is coming and] I do as the Father has commanded Me, so that the world may know (be convinced) that I love the Father and that I do only what the Father has instructed Me to do. [I act in full agreement with His orders.] Rise, let us go away from here.

15 I AM the True Vine, and My Father is the Vine-dresser.

2 Any branch in Me that does not bear fruit [that stops bearing] He cuts away (trims off, takes away); and He cleanses *and* repeatedly prunes every branch that continues to bear fruit, to make it bear more *and* richer *and* more excellent fruit.

3 You are cleansed *and* pruned already, because of the word which I have given you [the teachings I have discussed with you].

4 Dwell in Me, and I will dwell in you. [Live in Me, and I will live in you.] Just as no branch can bear fruit of itself without abiding in (being vitally united to) the vine, neither can you bear fruit unless you abide in Me.

5 I am the Vine; you are the branches. Whoever lives in Me and I in him

putting the Word to work

Have you ever seen fruit grow apart from the vine, tree, or plant to which it was attached? Of course not! As a disciple of Jesus, the same is true for you. Unless you stay in His presence, you will not grow or bear fruit. The word, *abide* means "to dwell; to take up residence." Allow Jesus to take up residence in your life. Just as the vine is the source of nourishment and wealth for the fruit, Jesus is your source of life. Cultivate an ever-growing relationship with Him by spending time with Him in prayer, reading and studying God's Word.

bears much (abundant) fruit. However, apart from Me [cut off from vital union with Me] you can do nothing.

6 If a person does not dwell in Me, he is thrown out like a [broken-off] branch, and withers; such branches are gathered up and thrown into the fire, and they are burned.

7 If you live in Me [abide vitally united to Me] and My words remain in you *and* continue to live in your hearts, ask whatever you will, and it shall be done for you.

8 When you bear (produce) much

life point

John 15:1–8 tells us that God prunes us and cuts away things that no longer bear the kind of fruit He desires us to show. This "cutting away" is often painful and not immediately understood, but it is necessary for us to grow into the fruit-bearing believers of Jesus Christ that He wants us to be. We need to understand that God is progressive, and sometimes He needs to prune us as He leads us to higher places.

d Marvin Vincent, *Word Studies*.

"help, Lord!"

God wants us to depend entirely on Him. He wants us to lean on, trust in and rely on Him. Actually, that is part of the definition of faith. We are partners with God, and that means we both have responsibility. But we must lean on Him in order to do the things that are our part. God called me into the ministry and He anointed (enabled) and gifted me to do what I need to do, but I still have to trust Him and remember how much I need Him at all times.

Sometimes we may think that we don't need God's help with things we have done over and over again successfully. Why would we need help with something we already know we can do? It is dangerous to become self-reliant. The book of Proverbs speaks frequently of the self-confident fool. People who think they are self-sufficient and can take care of themselves are being foolish—and eventually that will be proven to everyone including themselves.

An independent attitude is part of the baby stage of Christianity. A mature Christian knows that he can do nothing of any real value apart from Jesus. Of course, we can do things, but that doesn't mean they will be done right or that we will enjoy them or that they will produce any real lasting fruit.

When the Lord says we can do nothing apart from Him, He means things will not work properly in our lives unless we invite Him into everything. His presence can eliminate much of the struggle we experience in life. It makes impossible things possible, hard things easy and frustrating things peaceful. Do not ever be afraid to say, "Help, Lord, I can't do this without You."

fruit, My Father is honored *and* glorified, and you show *and* prove yourselves to be true followers of Mine.

9 I have loved you, [just] as the Father has loved Me; abide in My love [ᵉcontinue in His love with Me].

10 If you keep My commandments [if you continue to obey My instructions], you will abide in My love *and* live on in it, just as I have obeyed My Father's commandments and live on in His love.

11 I have told you these things, that My joy *and* delight may be in you, and that your joy *and* gladness may be of full measure *and* complete *and* overflowing.

12 This is My commandment: that you love one another [just] as I have loved you.

13 No one has greater love [no one has shown stronger affection] than to lay down (give up) his own life for his friends.

14 You are My friends if you keep on doing the things which I command you to do.

15 I do not call you servants (slaves) any longer, for the servant does not know what his master is doing (working out). But I have called you My friends, because I have made known to you everything that I have heard from My Father. [I have revealed to you everything that I have learned from Him.]

e Hermann Cremer, *Biblico-Theological Lexicon*.

16 You have not chosen Me, but I have chosen you and I have appointed you [I have planted you], that you might go and bear fruit *and* keep on bearing, and that your fruit may be lasting [that it may remain, abide], so that whatever you ask the Father in My Name [as ᶠpresenting all that I AM], He may give it to you.
17 This is what I command you: that you love one another.
18 If the world hates you, know that it hated Me before it hated you.
19 If you belonged to the world, the world would treat you with affection *and* would love you as its own. But because you are not of the world [no longer one with it], but I have chosen (selected) you out of the world, the world hates (detests) you.
20 Remember that I told you, A servant is not greater than his master [is not superior to him]. If they persecuted Me, they will also persecute you; if they kept My word *and* obeyed My teachings, they will also keep *and* obey yours.
21 But they will do all this to you [inflict all this suffering on you] because of [your bearing] My name *and* on My account, for they do not know *or* understand the One Who sent Me.
22 If I had not come and spoken to them, they would not be guilty of sin [would be blameless]; but now they have no excuse for their sin.
23 Whoever hates Me also hates My Father.
24 If I had not done (accomplished) among them the works which no one else ever did, they would not be guilty

speak the Word

of sin. But [the fact is] now they have both seen [these works] and have hated both Me and My Father.
25 But [this is so] that the word written in their Law might be fulfilled, They hated Me without a cause. [Ps. 35:19; 69:4.]
26 But when the Comforter (Counselor, Helper, Advocate, Intercessor, Strengthener, Standby) comes, Whom I will send to you from the Father, the Spirit of Truth Who comes (proceeds) from the Father, He [Himself] will testify regarding Me.
27 But you also will testify *and* be My witnesses, because you have been with Me from the beginning.

16 I HAVE told you all these things, so that you should not be offended (taken unawares and falter, or be caused to stumble and fall away). [I told you to keep you from being scandalized and repelled.]
2 They will put you out of (expel you from) the synagogues; but an hour is coming when whoever kills you will think *and* claim that he has offered service to God.
3 And they will do this because they have not known the Father or Me.
4 But I have told you these things now, so that when they occur you will remember that I told you of them. I did not say these things to you from the beginning, because I was with you.
5 But now I am going to Him Who sent Me, yet none of you asks Me, Where are You going?
6 But because I have said these

f Hermann Cremer, *Biblico-Theological Lexicon.*

welcome the Holy Spirit's work

In John 16:7, 8, Jesus told the disciples that when the Holy Spirit came, He would have close fellowship with them and would convict them of sin.

The Holy Spirit guides believers into all truth (see John 16:13), and He is the agent in the process of sanctification in their lives. This is partially accomplished by His convicting work. Every time we get off track or go in a wrong direction, the Holy Spirit convicts us that our behavior or decision is wrong. This is accomplished by a "knowing" in our spirit that what we are doing is not right.

When you and I feel convicted, we should repent and change our direction. No more and no less is required or acceptable. If we are willing to cooperate with the Holy Spirit, we can move on to spiritual maturity and release all the planned blessings of God in our lives. If, however, we ignore the Holy Spirit's conviction and go our own way, we will find it very difficult. Our lives will not be blessed and as a result, they won't bear fruit.

Satan does not want us to be convicted by the Holy Spirit, nor does he even want us to understand that we are under conviction. He always has a counterfeit for all the good things that God offers—something that appears to be similar to what God offers, but which, if received, brings destruction instead of blessing.

I believe Satan's counterfeit for true godly conviction is condemnation. Condemnation always produces feelings of guilt. It makes us feel "down" in every way. When we are condemned, we feel "under" something heavy, which is where Satan wants us.

God, on the other hand, sent Jesus to set us free and to give us righteousness, peace and joy (see Romans 14:17). Our spirits should be light and carefree, not oppressed and heavy with burdens we are unable to bear. We cannot bear our sins; Jesus came to bear them. He alone is able to do so, and we must receive His ministry.

things to you, sorrow has filled your hearts [taken complete possession of them].

7 However, I am telling you nothing but the truth when I say it is profitable (good, expedient, advantageous) for you that I go away. Because if I do not go away, the Comforter (Counselor, Helper, Advocate, Intercessor, Strengthener, Standby) will not come to you [into close fellowship with you]; but if I go away, I will send Him to you [to be in close fellowship with you].

8 And when He comes, He will convict *and* convince the world *and* bring demonstration to it about sin and about righteousness (uprightness of heart and right standing with God) and about judgment:

9 About sin, because they do not believe in Me [trust in, rely on, and adhere to Me];

10 About righteousness (uprightness of heart and right standing with God), because I go to My Father, and you will see Me no longer;

11 About judgment, because the

life point

John 16:7–11 tells us that the Holy Spirit speaks to our conscience to convict us of sin and convince us of righteousness. His conviction is intended to convince us to repent, which means to turn and go in the right direction rather than the wrong one in which we are currently headed.

Learning that conviction is different from condemnation took a long time for me. Erroneously, I condemned myself each time the Holy Spirit convicted me of something in my life that was not God's will. Godly conviction is meant to lift us out of something, to help us move up higher in God's will and plan for our lives. Condemnation on the other hand presses us down and puts us under a burden of guilt.

It is healthy and normal to feel guilty when we are initially convicted of sin; but to keep the guilty feeling after we have repented of the sin is not healthy, nor is it God's will.

ruler (evil genius, prince) of this world [Satan] is judged *and* condemned *and* sentence already is passed upon him.
12 I have still many things to say to you, but you are not able to bear them *or* to take them upon you *or* to grasp them now.
13 But when He, the Spirit of Truth (the Truth-giving Spirit) comes, He will guide you into all the Truth (the whole, full Truth). For He will not speak His own message [on His own authority]; but He will tell whatever He hears [from the Father; He will give the message that has been given to Him], and He will announce *and* declare to you the things that are to come [that will happen in the future].
14 He will honor *and* glorify Me,

because He will take of (receive, draw upon) what is Mine and will reveal (declare, disclose, transmit) it to you.
15 Everything that the Father has is Mine. That is what I meant when I said that He [the Spirit] will take the things that are Mine and will reveal (declare, disclose, transmit) it to you.
16 In a little while you will no longer see Me, and again after a short while you will see Me.
17 So some of His disciples questioned among themselves, What does He mean when He tells us, In a little while you will no longer see Me, and

life point

Truth is one of the most powerful weapons a believer has against the kingdom of darkness. Truth is light, and the Bible says that the darkness has never overpowered the light, and it never will (see John 1:5).

Jesus said that truth will set us free (see John 8:32). Truth is revealed by the Spirit of Truth.

Jesus could have showed His disciples all the truth, but John 16:12, 13 reveals that He knew they were not ready for it. He told them that they needed to wait until the Holy Spirit came down from heaven to abide with them and to dwell in them (see Luke 24:49). We know that after Jesus ascended into heaven, He did indeed send the Holy Spirit (see Acts 2:1–18).

How can we have the Holy Spirit work in our lives if we do not face truth? He is called "The Spirit of Truth" (John 16:13). A major facet of His ministry to you and me is to help us face truth—to bring us to a place of truth, because only the truth will set us free.

the Spirit of Truth

In John 16:12, 13, Jesus told His disciples that He had many things to say to them that they were unable to bear. But He promised that the Holy Spirit would come and lead them into all truth and continue to teach them (see also John 14:26).

When Jesus spoke these words, He was talking to men with whom He had spent the previous three years. They were with Him day and night, yet He indicated that He had more to teach them. We might think that if Jesus were with us personally for three years, day and night, we would have learned all there is to know. I think that if I had one uninterrupted month with people, I could tell them everything I know. But Jesus said to expect more because He will always have things to teach us and something to say to us about new situations we are facing.

Jesus always knew the right thing to do because He only did what He saw His Father do. As our Lord, we can trust Him to personally lead us on the right path every day. Jesus said, "It is written in [the book of] the Prophets, And they shall all be taught of God [have Him in person for their Teacher]. Everyone who has listened to and learned from the Father comes to Me" (John 6:45).

God knew we needed help understanding His plan for us, so He sent the Holy Spirit to dwell inside every Christian. He is our Guide, our Teacher of truth, our Counselor, and our Helper. He is also our Comforter.

Jesus said it was good for us that He went away, because if He did not go, the Holy Spirit would not come to us (see John 16:7). Jesus was confined to a body just as we are and could be only at one place at a time. But the Holy Spirit can be in each of us everywhere we go, all the time, individually leading and guiding us. If we learn to *listen* to the Holy Spirit and follow His lead, we can live the abundant life God wants us to have.

again after a short while you will see Me, and, Because I go to My Father?

18 What does He mean by a little while? We do not know *or* understand what He is talking about.

19 Jesus knew that they wanted to ask Him, so He said to them, Are you wondering *and* inquiring among yourselves what I meant when I said, In a little while you will no longer see Me, and again after a short while you will see Me?

20 I assure you, most solemnly I tell you, that you shall weep and grieve, but the world will rejoice. You will be sorrowful, but your sorrow will be turned into joy.

21 A woman, when she gives birth to a child, has grief (anguish, agony) because her time has come. But when she has delivered the child, she no longer remembers her pain (trouble, anguish) because she is so glad that a man (a child, a human being) has been born into the world.

22 So for the present you are also in sorrow (in distress and depressed); but I will see you again and [then] your hearts will rejoice, and no one can take from you your joy (gladness, delight).

23 And when that time comes, you will ask nothing of Me [you will need to ask Me no questions]. I assure you, most solemnly I tell you, that My Father will grant you whatever you ask in My Name [as ᵍpresenting all that I AM]. [Exod. 3:14.]

24 Up to this time you have not asked a [single] thing in My Name [as ᵍpresenting all that I AM]; but now ask *and* keep on asking and you will receive, so that your joy (gladness, delight) may be full *and* complete.

25 I have told you these things in parables (veiled language, allegories, dark sayings); the hour is now coming when I shall no longer speak to you in figures of speech, but I shall tell you about the Father in plain words *and* openly (without reserve).

26 At that time you will ask (pray) in My Name; and I am not saying that I will ask the Father on your behalf [for it will be unnecessary].

27 For the Father Himself [tenderly] loves you because you have loved Me and have believed that I came out from the Father.

28 I came out from the Father and have come into the world; again, I am leaving the world and going to the Father.

29 His disciples said, Ah, now You are speaking plainly to us and not in parables (veiled language and figures of speech)!

30 Now we know that You are acquainted with everything and have no need to be asked questions. Because of this we believe that you [really] came from God.

31 Jesus answered them, Do you now believe? [Do you believe it at last?]

32 But take notice, the hour is coming, and it has arrived, when you will all be dispersed *and* scattered, every man to his own home, leaving Me alone. Yet I am not alone, because the Father is with Me.

33 I have told you these things, so that in Me you may have [perfect] peace *and* confidence. In the world you have tribulation *and* trials *and* distress *and* frustration; but be of good cheer [take courage; be confident, certain, undaunted]! For I have overcome the world. [I have deprived it of power to harm you and have conquered it for you.]

17 WHEN JESUS had spoken these things, He lifted up His eyes to heaven and said, Father, the hour has come. Glorify *and* exalt *and* honor *and* magnify Your Son, so that Your Son may glorify *and* extol *and* honor *and* magnify You.

2 [Just as] You have granted Him power *and* authority over all flesh (all humankind), [now glorify Him] so that He may give eternal life to all whom You have given Him.

3 And this is eternal life: [it means] to know (to perceive, recognize, become acquainted with, and understand) You, the only true *and* real God, and [likewise] to know Him, Jesus [as the] Christ (the Anointed One, the Messiah), Whom You have sent.

4 I have glorified You down here on the earth by completing the work that You gave Me to do.

5 And now, Father, glorify Me along with Yourself *and* restore Me to such majesty *and* honor in Your presence as I had with You before the world existed.

6 I have manifested Your Name [I have revealed Your very Self, Your real Self] to the people whom You have given Me out of the world. They were Yours, and You gave them to Me, and they have obeyed *and* kept Your word.

---

g Hermann Cremer, *Biblico-Theological Lexicon*.

7 Now [at last] they know *and* understand that all You have given Me belongs to You [is really and truly Yours].

8 For the [uttered] words that You gave Me I have given them; and they have received *and* accepted [them] and have come to know positively *and* in reality [to believe with absolute assurance] that I came forth from Your presence, and they have believed *and* are convinced that You did send Me.

9 I am praying for them. I am not praying (requesting) for the world, but for those You have given Me, for they belong to You.

10 All [things that are] Mine are Yours, and all [things that are] Yours belong to Me; and I am glorified in (through) them. [They have done Me honor; in them My glory is achieved.]

11 And [now] I am no more in the world, but these are [still] in the world, and I am coming to You. Holy Father, keep in Your Name [ʰin the knowledge of Yourself] those whom You have given Me, that they may be one as We [are one].

12 While I was with them, I kept *and* preserved them in Your Name [ʰin the knowledge and worship of You]. Those You have given Me I guarded *and* protected, and not one of them has perished *or* is lost except the son of perdition [Judas Iscariot—the one who is now doomed to destruction, destined to be lost], that the Scripture might be fulfilled. [Ps. 41:9; John 6:70.]

13 And now I am coming to You; I say these things while I am still in the world, so that My joy may be made full *and* complete *and* perfect in them [that they may experience My delight fulfilled in them, that My enjoyment may be perfected in their own souls, that they may have My gladness within them, filling their hearts].

14 I have given *and* delivered to them Your word (message) and the world has hated them, because they are not of the world [do not belong to the world], just as I am not of the world.

15 I do not ask that You will take them out of the world, but that You will keep *and* protect them from the evil one.

16 They are not of the world (worldly, belonging to the world), [just] as I am not of the world.

17 Sanctify them [purify, consecrate, separate them for Yourself, make them holy] by the Truth; Your Word is Truth.

18 Just as You sent Me into the world, I also have sent them into the world.

19 And so for their sake *and* on their behalf I sanctify (dedicate, consecrate) Myself, that they also may be sanctified (dedicated, consecrated, made holy) in the Truth.

20 Neither for these alone do I pray [it is not for their sake only that I make this request], but also for all those who will ever come to believe in (trust in, cling to, rely on) Me through their word *and* teaching,

21 That they all may be one, [just] as You, Father, are in Me and I in You, that they also may be one in Us, so that the world may believe *and* be convinced that You have sent Me.

speak the Word

Sanctify me, Lord. Purify, consecrate, separate me for Yourself and make me holy by Truth. Your Word is Truth.
ADAPTED FROM JOHN **17:17**

h Albert Barnes, *Notes on the New Testament.*

22 I have given to them the glory *and* honor which You have given Me, that they may be one [even] as We are one: **23** I in them and You in Me, in order that they may become one *and* perfectly united, that the world may know *and* [definitely] recognize that You sent Me and that You have loved them [even] as You have loved Me.

putting the Word to work

Is your church affiliated with any particular denomination? While denominations provide helpful structure and teaching and tools for ministry, there is not one "right" denomination that renders all the others "wrong." Throughout Scripture, followers of God are called to unity. Be committed to the unity of the Church; pray for other churches in your neighborhoods and for Christians of every denomination to be blessed and effective in ministry.

24 Father, I desire that they also whom You have entrusted to Me [as Your gift to Me] may be with Me where I am, so that they may see My glory, which You have given Me [Your love gift to Me]; for You loved Me before the foundation of the world. **25** O just *and* righteous Father, although the world has not known You *and* has failed to recognize You *and* has never acknowledged You, I have known You [continually]; and these men understand *and* know that You have sent Me. **26** I have made Your Name known to them *and* revealed Your character *and* Your very [i]Self, and I will continue to make [You] known, that the love which You have bestowed upon Me may be in them [felt in their hearts] and that I [Myself] may be in them.

18 HAVING SAID these things, Jesus went out with His disciples beyond (across) the winter torrent of the Kidron [in the ravine]. There was a garden there, which He and His disciples entered. **2** And Judas, who was betraying Him *and* delivering Him up, also knew the place, because Jesus had often retired there with His disciples. **3** So Judas, obtaining *and* taking charge of the band of soldiers and some guards (attendants) of the high priests and Pharisees, came there with lanterns and torches and weapons. **4** Then Jesus, knowing all that was about to befall Him, went out to them and said, Whom are you seeking? [Whom do you want?] **5** They answered Him, Jesus the Nazarene. Jesus said to them, I am He. Judas, who was betraying Him, was also standing with them. **6** When Jesus said to them, I am He, they went backwards (drew back, lurched backward) and fell to the ground. **7** Then again He asked them, Whom are you seeking? And they said, Jesus the Nazarene. **8** Jesus answered, I told you that I am He. So, if you want Me [if it is only I for Whom you are looking], let these men go their way. **9** Thus what He had said was fulfilled *and* verified, Of those whom You have given Me, I have not lost even one. [John 6:39; 17:12.] **10** Then Simon Peter, who had a sword, drew it and struck the high priest's servant and cut off his right ear. The servant's name was Malchus. **11** Therefore, Jesus said to Peter, Put the sword [back] into the sheath! The cup which My Father has given Me, shall I not drink it? **12** So the troops and their captain

---

[i] Joseph Thayer, *A Greek-English Lexicon.*

and the guards (attendants) of the Jews seized Jesus and bound Him,

13 And they brought Him first to Annas, for he was the father-in-law of Caiaphas, who was the high priest that year.

14 It was Caiaphas who had counseled the Jews that it was expedient *and* for their welfare that one man should die for (instead of, in behalf of) the people. [John 11:49, 50.]

15 Now Simon Peter and another disciple were following Jesus. And that disciple was known to the high priest, and so he entered along with Jesus into the court of the palace of the high priest;

16 But Peter was standing outside at the door. So the other disciple, who was known to the high priest, went out and spoke to the maid who kept the door and brought Peter inside.

17 Then the maid who was in charge at the door said to Peter, You are not also one of the disciples of this ʲMan, are you? He said, I am not!

18 Now the servants and the guards (the attendants) had made a fire of coals, for it was cold, and they were standing and warming themselves. And Peter was with them, standing and warming himself.

19 Then the high priest questioned Jesus about His disciples and about His teaching.

20 Jesus answered him, I have spoken openly to the world. I have always taught in a synagogue and in the temple [area], where the Jews [habitually] congregate (assemble); and I have spoken nothing secretly.

21 Why do you ask Me? Ask those who have heard [Me] what I said to them. See! They know what I said.

22 But when He said this, one of the attendants who stood by struck Jesus,

saying, Is that how ʲYou answer the high priest?

23 Jesus replied, If I have said anything wrong [if I have spoken abusively, if there was evil in what I said] tell what was wrong with it. But if I spoke rightly *and* properly, why do you strike Me?

24 Then Annas sent Him bound to Caiaphas the high priest.

25 But Simon Peter [still] was standing and was warming himself. They said to him, You are not also one of His disciples, are you? He denied it and said, I am not!

26 One of the high priest's servants, a relative of the man whose ear Peter cut off, said, Did I not see you in the garden with Him?

27 And again Peter denied it. And immediately a rooster crowed.

28 Then they brought Jesus from Caiaphas into the Praetorium (judgment hall, governor's palace). And it was early. They themselves did not enter the Praetorium, that they might not be defiled (become ceremonially unclean), but might be fit to eat the Passover [supper].

29 So Pilate went out to them and said, What accusation do you bring against this ʲMan?

30 They retorted, If He were not an evildoer (criminal), we would not have handed Him over to you.

31 Pilate said to them, Take Him yourselves and judge *and* sentence *and* punish Him according to your [own] law. The Jews answered, It is not lawful for us to put anyone to death.

32 This was to fulfill the word which Jesus had spoken to show (indicate, predict) by what manner of death He was to die. [John 12:32-34.]

33 So Pilate went back again into the judgment hall and called Jesus and

j Capitalized because of what He is, the spotless Son of God, not what the speaker may have thought He was.

asked Him, Are You the King of the Jews?

34 Jesus replied, Are you saying this of yourself [on your own initiative], or have others told you about Me?

35 Pilate answered, Am I a Jew? Your [own] people *and* nation and their chief priests have delivered You to me. What have You done?

36 Jesus answered, My kingdom (kingship, royal power) belongs not to this world. If My kingdom were of this world, My followers would have been fighting to keep Me from being handed over to the Jews. But as it is, My kingdom is not from here (this world); [it has no such origin or source].

37 Pilate said to Him, Then You are a King? Jesus answered, You say it! [You speak correctly!] For I am a King. [Certainly I am a King!] This is why I was born, and for this I have come into the world, to bear witness to the Truth. Everyone who is of the Truth [who is a friend of the Truth, who belongs to the Truth] hears *and* listens to My voice.

38 Pilate said to Him, What is Truth? On saying this he went out to the Jews again and told them, I find no fault in Him.

39 But it is your custom that I release one [prisoner] for you at the Passover. So shall I release for you the King of the Jews?

40 Then they all shouted back again, Not Him [not this Man], but Barabbas! Now Barabbas was a robber.

19 SO THEN Pilate took Jesus and scourged (flogged, whipped) Him.

2 And the soldiers, having twisted together a crown of thorns, put it on His head, and threw a purple cloak around Him.

3 And they kept coming to Him and

saying, Hail, King of the Jews! [Good health to you! Peace to you! Long life to you, King of the Jews!] And they struck Him with the palms of their hands. [Isa. 53:3, 5, 7.]

4 Then Pilate went out again and said to them, See, I bring Him out to you, so that you may know that I find no fault (crime, cause for accusation) in Him.

5 So Jesus came out wearing the thorny crown and purple cloak, and Pilate said to them, See, [here is] the ᵏMan!

6 When the chief priests and attendants (guards) saw Him, they cried out, Crucify Him! Crucify Him! Pilate said to them, Take Him yourselves and crucify Him, for I find no fault (crime) in Him.

7 The Jews answered him, We have a law, and according to that law He should die, because He has claimed *and* made Himself out to be the Son of God.

8 So, when Pilate heard this said, he was more alarmed *and* awestricken *and* afraid than before.

9 He went into the judgment hall again and said to Jesus, Where are You from? [To what world do You belong?] But Jesus did not answer him.

10 So Pilate said to Him, Will You not speak [even] to me? Do You not know that I have power (authority) to release You and I have power to crucify You?

11 Jesus answered, You would not have any power *or* authority whatsoever against (over) Me if it were not given you from above. For this reason the sin *and* guilt of the one who delivered Me over to you is greater.

12 Upon this, Pilate wanted (sought, was anxious) to release Him, but the Jews kept shrieking, If you release

---

k Capitalized because of what He is, the spotless Son of God, not what the speaker may have thought He was.

this Man, you are no friend of Caesar! Anybody who makes himself [out to be] a king sets himself up against Caesar [is a rebel against the emperor]!

13 Hearing this, Pilate brought Jesus out and sat down on the judgment seat at a place called the Pavement [the Mosaic Pavement, the Stone Platform]—in Hebrew, Gabbatha.

14 Now it was the day of Preparation for the Passover, and it was about the sixth hour (about twelve o'clock noon). He said to the Jews, See, [here is] your King!

15 But they shouted, Away with Him! Away with Him! Crucify Him! Pilate said to them, Crucify your King? The chief priests answered, We have no king but Caesar!

16 Then he delivered Him over to them to be crucified.

17 And they took Jesus *and* led [Him] away; so He went out, bearing His own cross, to the spot called The Place of the Skull—in Hebrew it is called Golgotha.

18 There they crucified Him, and with Him two others—one on either side and Jesus between them. [Isa. 53:12.]

19 And Pilate also wrote a title (an inscription on a placard) and put it on the cross. And the writing was: Jesus the Nazarene, the King of the Jews.

20 And many of the Jews read this title, for the place where Jesus was crucified was near the city, and it was written in Hebrew, in Latin, [and] in Greek.

21 Then the chief priests of the Jews said to Pilate, Do not write, The King of the Jews, but, He said, I am King of the Jews.

22 Pilate replied, What I have written, I have written.

23 Then the soldiers, when they had crucified Jesus, took His garments and made four parts, one share for each soldier, and also the tunic (the long shirtlike undergarment). But the tunic was seamless, woven [in one piece] from the top throughout.

24 So they said to one another, Let us not tear it, but let us cast lots to decide whose it shall be. This was to fulfill the Scripture, They parted My garments among them, and for My clothing they cast lots. So the soldiers did these things. [Ps. 22:18.]

25 But by the cross of Jesus stood His mother, His mother's sister, Mary the [wife] of Clopas, and Mary Magdalene.

26 So Jesus, seeing His mother there, and the disciple whom He loved standing near, said to His mother, [¹Dear] woman, See, [here is] your son!

27 Then He said to the disciple, See, [here is] your mother! And from that hour, the disciple took her into his own [keeping, own home].

28 After this, Jesus, knowing that all was now finished (ended), said in fulfillment of the Scripture, I thirst. [Ps. 69:21.]

29 A vessel (jar) full of sour wine (vinegar) was placed there, so they put a sponge soaked in the sour wine on [a stalk, reed of] hyssop, and held it to [His] mouth.

30 When Jesus had received the sour wine, He said, It is finished! And He bowed His head and gave up His spirit.

31 Since it was the day of Preparation, in order to prevent the bodies from hanging on the cross on the Sabbath—for that Sabbath was a very solemn *and* important one—the Jews requested Pilate to have the legs broken and the bodies taken away.

32 So the soldiers came and broke the legs of the first one, and of the other who had been crucified with Him.

---

1 G. Abbott-Smith, *Manual Greek Lexicon:* "A term of respect and endearment."

33 But when they came to Jesus and they saw that He was already dead, they did not break His legs.

34 But one of the soldiers pierced His side with a spear, and immediately blood and water came (flowed) out.

35 And he who saw it (the eyewitness) gives this evidence, and his testimony is true; and he knows that he tells the truth, that you may believe also.

36 For these things took place, that the Scripture might be fulfilled (verified, carried out), Not one of His bones shall be broken; [Exod. 12:46; Num. 9:12; Ps. 34:20.]

37 And again another Scripture says, They shall look on Him Whom they have pierced. [Zech. 12:10.]

38 And after this, Joseph of Arimathea—a disciple of Jesus, but secretly for fear of the Jews—asked Pilate to let him take away the body of Jesus. And Pilate granted him permission. So he came and took away His body.

39 And Nicodemus also, who first had come to Jesus by night, came bringing a mixture of myrrh and aloes, [weighing] about a hundred pounds.

40 So they took Jesus' body and bound it in linen cloths with the spices (aromatics), as is the Jews' customary way to prepare for burial.

41 Now there was a garden in the place where He was crucified, and in the garden a new tomb, in which no one had ever [yet] been laid.

42 So there, because of the Jewish day of Preparation [and] since the tomb was near by, they laid Jesus.

20 NOW ON the first day of the week, Mary Magdalene came to the tomb early, while it was still dark, and saw that the stone had been removed from (lifted out of the groove across the entrance of) the tomb.

2 So she ran and went to Simon Peter and the other disciple, whom Jesus [tenderly] loved, and said to them, They have taken away the Lord out of the tomb, and we do not know where they have laid Him!

3 Upon this, Peter and the other disciple came out and they went toward the tomb.

4 And they came running together, but the other disciple outran Peter and arrived at the tomb first.

5 And stooping down, he saw the linen cloths lying there, but he did not enter.

6 Then Simon Peter came up, following him, and went into the tomb and saw the linen cloths lying there;

7 But the burial napkin (kerchief) which had been around Jesus' head, was not lying with the other linen cloths, but was [still] ᵐrolled up (wrapped round and round) in a place by itself.

8 Then the other disciple, who had reached the tomb first, went in too; and he saw and was convinced *and* believed.

9 For as yet they did not know (understand) the statement of Scripture that He must rise again from the dead. [Ps. 16:10.]

10 Then the disciples went back again to their homes (lodging places).

11 But Mary remained standing outside the tomb sobbing. As she wept, she stooped down [and looked] into the tomb.

12 And she saw two angels in white sitting there, one at the head and one at the feet, where the body of Jesus had lain.

13 And they said to her, Woman, why are you sobbing? She told them, Because they have taken away my Lord, and I do not know where they have laid Him.

14 On saying this, she turned around

m Marvin Vincent, *Word Studies.*

putting the Word to work

You have probably heard the saying, "It is not what you know, but who you know that is important." As a Christian, you are most likely learning that this is true! Are you searching for something more in your life? Jesus did not ask Mary "what" she was looking for, He asked her "who" she was looking for, and that made all the difference. Knowing about Jesus is important, but it is the act of knowing Jesus, the Risen Savior, that is most important in our lives. Ask Him to help you know Him more fully.

and saw Jesus standing [there], but she did not know (recognize) that it was Jesus.
15 Jesus said to her, Woman, why are you crying [so]? For Whom are you looking? Supposing that it was the gardener, she replied, Sir, if you carried Him away from here, tell me where you have put Him and I will take Him away.
16 Jesus said to her, Mary! Turning around she said to Him in Hebrew, Rabboni!—which means Teacher or Master.
17 Jesus said to her, Do not cling to Me [do not hold Me], for I have not yet ascended to the Father. But go to My brethren and tell them, I am ascending to My Father and your Father, and to My God and your God.
18 Away came Mary Magdalene, bringing the disciples news (word) that she had seen the Lord and that He had said these things to her.
19 Then on that same first day of the week, when it was evening, though the disciples were behind closed doors for fear of the Jews, Jesus came and stood among them and said, Peace to you!
20 So saying, He showed them His

hands and His side. And when the disciples saw the Lord, they were filled with joy (delight, exultation, ecstasy, rapture).
21 Then Jesus said to them again, Peace to you! [Just] as the Father has sent Me forth, so I am sending you.
22 And having said this, He breathed on them and said to them, Receive the Holy Spirit!

putting the Word to work

As a Christian, you have been sent into the world to do the work that Jesus began. Do you ever get tired or discouraged as you do so? Ask God on a regular basis for a fresh filling of the Holy Spirit so you will be empowered to do all that He has called you to do.

23 [Now having received the Holy Spirit, and being [n]led and directed by Him] if you forgive the sins of anyone, they are forgiven; if you retain the sins of anyone, they are retained.
24 But Thomas, one of the Twelve, called the Twin, was not with them when Jesus came.
25 So the other disciples kept telling him, We have seen the Lord! But he said to them, Unless I see in His hands the marks made by the nails and put my finger into the nail prints, and put my hand into His side, I will never believe [it].
26 Eight days later His disciples were again in the house, and Thomas was with them. Jesus came, though they were behind closed doors, and stood among them and said, Peace to you!
27 Then He said to Thomas, Reach out your finger here, and see My hands; and put out your hand and place [it] in My side. Do not be faithless and incredulous, but [stop your unbelief and] believe!

n Matthew Henry, *Commentary on the Holy Bible*.

forgiveness and the Holy Spirit

I believe the number one rule in forgiving sins is to do as Jesus commanded in John 20:22 and receive the Holy Spirit, Who provides the strength and ability to forgive. None of us can do that on our own.

I believe when Jesus breathed on the disciples and they received the Holy Spirit, they were born again, at that very moment. The next thing He said to them was whatever sins they forgave were forgiven and whatever sins they retained were retained (see John 20:23).

The forgiving of sins seems to be the first power conferred upon people when they are born again. If that is so, then the forgiving of sins is our first duty as believers. But although we have the *power* to forgive sins, it is not always *easy* to forgive sins.

Whenever someone does something to me I need to forgive, I pray, "Holy Spirit, breathe on me and give me the strength to forgive this person." I do that because my emotions are screaming inside of me, "You have hurt me—and that is not fair!"

At that point I have to remember to let go and allow the God of justice to work out everything. I have to remind myself that my job is to pray; His job is to be my Vindicator. When we trust God He always makes wrong things right in due time.

When someone does something hurtful to you, go to the Lord and receive from Him the strength to place your will on the altar and say, "Lord, I forgive this person. I loose him; I let him go." Once you have done that, let it drop. Don't think or talk about it anymore.

28 Thomas answered Him, My Lord and my God!
29 Jesus said to him, Because you have seen Me, *Thomas,* do you now believe (trust, have faith)? Blessed *and* happy *and* °to be envied are those who have never seen Me and yet have believed *and* adhered to *and* trusted *and* relied on Me.
30 There are also many other signs *and* miracles which Jesus performed in the presence of the disciples which are not written in this book.
31 But these are written (recorded) in order that you may believe that Jesus is the Christ (the Anointed One), the Son of God, and that through believing *and* cleaving to *and* trusting *and* relying upon Him you may have life through (in) His name [ᵖthrough Who He is]. [Ps. 2:7, 12.]

21 AFTER THIS, Jesus let Himself be seen *and* revealed [Himself] again to the disciples, at the Sea of Tiberias. And He did it in this way:
2 There were together Simon Peter, and Thomas, called the Twin, and Nathanael from Cana of Galilee, also

o Alexander Souter, *Pocket Lexicon*.   p Hermann Cremer, *Biblico-Theological Lexicon*.

putting the Word to work

Have you ever doubted God? If you are like most Christians, you probably have, and you may have even felt guilty about doubting Him. Jesus welcomes you to bring your doubts to Him. Like Thomas, be honest with Jesus about your doubts.

He will meet you where you are if you are honest with Him. Ask Him to show you that He is Who He says He is and to help you believe that He can do what He says He can do. He will be faithful to do so, and like Thomas, your faith will increase.

the sons of Zebedee, and two others of His disciples.

3 Simon Peter said to them, I am going fishing! They said to him, And we are coming with you! So they went out and got into the boat, and throughout that night they caught nothing.

4 Morning was already breaking when Jesus came to the beach and stood there. However, the disciples did not know that it was Jesus.

5 So Jesus said to them, qBoys (children), you do not have any meat (fish), do you? [Have you caught anything to eat along with your bread?] They answered Him, No!

6 And He said to them, Cast the net on the right side of the boat and you will find [some]. So they cast the net, and now they were not able to haul it in for such a big catch (mass, quantity) of fish [was in it].

7 Then the disciple whom Jesus loved said to Peter, It is the Lord! Simon Peter, hearing him say that it was the Lord, put (girded) on his upper garment (his fisherman's coat, his outer tunic)—for he was stripped [for work]—and sprang into the sea.

8 And the other disciples came in the small boat, for they were not far from shore, only some hundred yards away, dragging the net full of fish.

9 When they got out on land (the beach), they saw a fire of coals there and fish lying on it [cooking], and bread.

10 Jesus said to them, Bring some of the fish which you have just caught.

11 So Simon Peter went aboard and hauled the net to land, full of large fish, 153 of them; and [though] there were so many of them, the net was not torn.

12 Jesus said to them, Come [and] have breakfast. But none of the disciples ventured *or* dared to ask Him, Who are You? because they [well] knew that it was the Lord.

13 Jesus came and took the bread and gave it to them, and so also [with] the fish.

14 This was now the third time that Jesus revealed Himself (appeared, was manifest) to the disciples after He had risen from the dead.

15 When they had eaten, Jesus said to Simon Peter, Simon, son of John, do you love Me more than these [others do—with reasoning, intentional, spiritual devotion, as one loves the Father]? He said to Him, Yes, Lord, You know that I love You [that I have deep, instinctive, personal affection for You, as for a close friend]. He said to him, Feed My lambs.

16 Again He said to him the second time, Simon, son of John, do you love Me [with reasoning, intentional, spiritual devotion, as one loves the Father]? He said to Him, Yes, Lord, You know that I love You [that I have a deep, instinctive, personal affection for You, as for a close friend]. He said to him, Shepherd (tend) My sheep.

17 He said to him the third time, Simon, son of John, do you love Me

q Alexander Souter, *Pocket Lexicon*.

[with a deep, instinctive, personal affection for Me, as for a close friend]? Peter was grieved (was saddened and hurt) that He should ask him the third time, Do you love Me? And he said to Him, Lord, You know everything; You know that I love You [that I have a deep, instinctive, personal affection for You, as for a close friend]. Jesus said to him, Feed My sheep.

18 I assure you, most solemnly I tell you, when you were young you girded yourself [put on your own belt or girdle] and you walked about wherever you pleased to go. But when you grow old you will stretch out your hands, and someone else will put a girdle around you and carry you where you do not wish to go.

19 He said this to indicate by what kind of death Peter would glorify God. And after this, He said to him, Follow Me!

20 But Peter turned and saw the disciple whom Jesus loved, following—the one who also had leaned back on His breast at the supper and had said, Lord, who is it that is going to betray You?

21 When Peter saw him, he said to Jesus, Lord, what about this man?

22 Jesus said to him, If I want him to stay (survive, live) until I come, what is that to you? [What concern is it of yours?] You follow Me!

life point

In John 21:18, Jesus told Peter about the hardships he would endure in order to serve and glorify Him. As soon as Jesus said these things to him, Peter turned, saw John and immediately asked Jesus what His will was for that disciple. Peter wanted to make sure that if he were going to have rough times ahead, so would John.

In response, Jesus politely told Peter to mind his own business. When you are tempted to compare yourself with others or be jealous, remember this advice!

23 So word went out among the brethren that this disciple was not going to die; yet Jesus did not say to him that he was not going to die, but, If I want him to stay (survive, live) till I come, what is that to you?

24 It is this same disciple who is bearing witness to these things and who has recorded (written) them; and we [well] know that his testimony is true.

25 And there are also many other things which Jesus did. If they should be all recorded one by one [in detail], I suppose that even the world itself could not contain (have room for) the books that would be written.

Acts

Author:
Attributed to Luke

Date:
About AD 62

Everyday Life Principles:
We desperately need the power of the Holy Spirit in our lives today, and thank God, it is readily available to us!

Christianity is not a religious activity; it is a way of life.

The Holy Spirit wants to be involved in every area of your life, every day.

The book of Acts basically picks up where the Gospels end. Before His death and resurrection, Jesus told His disciples that it was "profitable (good, expedient, advantageous)" for them that He would go away, because if He did not, the Holy Spirit would not come to them (see John 16:7). In Acts, we see that the Holy Spirit did come and we learn that He is still on earth today teaching, guiding, helping, and empowering us to do the things God calls us to do.

Acts gives us a clear and vivid picture of how the church should operate. It shows us that we need unity and the power of the Holy Spirit and that we need to constantly reach out to others and help people. In this book, we see that when the Holy Spirit is given free rein in our lives and in the church, there is tremendous growth in the kingdom of God and in our lives as individuals.

As you read Acts, I pray you will see that Christianity is so much more than going to church; it is also allowing the Holy Spirit to guide us in *all* the affairs of our lives. He came to help and empower us in *every* area of our lives, not just the parts we call "spiritual." We are not to divide our lives into secular and sacred; everything about us belongs to God and He wants to be involved in all of it.

1 IN THE former account [which I prepared], O Theophilus, I made [a continuous report] dealing with all the things which Jesus began to do and to teach [Luke 1:1-4.]

2 Until the day when He ascended, after He through the Holy Spirit had instructed *and* commanded the apostles (special messengers) whom He had chosen.

3 To them also He showed Himself alive after His passion (His suffering in the garden and on the cross) by [a series of] many convincing demonstrations [unquestionable evidences and infallible proofs], appearing to them during forty days and talking [to them] about the things of the kingdom of God.

4 And while being in their company *and* eating with them, He commanded them not to leave Jerusalem but to wait for what the Father had promised, Of which [He said] you have heard Me speak. [John 14:16, 26; 15:26.]

5 For John baptized with water, but not many days from now you shall be baptized with (ᵃplaced in, introduced into) the Holy Spirit.

6 So when they were assembled, they asked Him, Lord, is this the time when You will reestablish the kingdom *and* restore it to Israel?

7 He said to them, It is not for you to become acquainted with *and* know ᵇwhat time brings [the things and events of time and their definite periods] or fixed ᶜyears and seasons (their critical niche in time), which the Father has appointed (fixed and reserved) by His own choice *and* authority *and* personal power.

8 But you shall receive power (ability, efficiency, and might) when the Holy Spirit has come upon you, and you shall be My witnesses in Jerusalem and all Judea and Samaria

life point

Jesus told His disciples in Acts 1:4 to wait for what the Father promised them. He was referring to the *power* they would receive "when the Holy Spirit has come upon you" (Acts 1:8). Jesus was saying, "Do not try to do any mighty works until you have received that *power* from on high." The disciples knew that if they did not wait, they would not have power. They did as He instructed and waited for the coming of the Holy Spirit.

Jesus' instruction to wait was not only for His disciples then. It is a truth that applies to us today. I encourage you to "actively" wait for the promises of God by listening for what He is telling you to do instead of running ahead of God and doing something in the flesh. *Wait* for the Word of God and for His promises.

and to the ends (the very bounds) of the earth.

9 And when He had said this, even as they were looking [at Him], He was caught up, and a cloud received *and* carried Him away out of their sight.

10 And while they were gazing intently into heaven as He went, behold, two men [dressed] in white robes suddenly stood beside them,

11 Who said, Men of Galilee, why do you stand gazing into heaven? This same Jesus, Who was caught away *and* lifted up from among you into heaven, will return in [just] the same way in which you saw Him go into heaven.

12 Then [the disciples] went back to Jerusalem from the hill called Olivet, which is near Jerusalem, [only] a Sabbath day's journey (three-quarters of a mile) away.

a Kenneth Wuest, *Word Studies in the Greek New Testament.* b Joseph Thayer, *A Greek-English Lexicon of the New Testament.* c Richard Trench, *Synonyms of the New Testament.*

"you shall receive power"

We all need and want power, and Jesus promised in Acts 1:8 that "you shall receive power when the Holy Spirit has come upon you." I do not know of any person who hopes and prays for weakness and inability. God desires for us to be powerful and live and enjoy power-packed lives—lives that include victory over Satan and all of His wicked plots and schemes.

The Holy Spirit is the enabling power of God, and when He comes into our lives we become more powerful. We might even say that our power level is dependent on the level that we surrender to Him. Have you surrendered every room in your heart to the Holy Spirit? Have you invited Him into every area of your life, or do you reserve certain areas for yourself where you want no interference from anyone, not even God?

Spiritual maturity is a process. We release areas of our lives to the Lord little by little. The more we release to Him, the better our lives become. We often cling to the very things that make us miserable and yet we are afraid to let go. Trust God and know for certain that everything He asks you to do is for your good and will make your life better.

The power of the Holy Spirit enables us to be what God wants us to be. I noticed years ago that Acts 1:8 states that the people received power to "be" witnesses, not power to "do" witnessing. God wants us to become what He has in mind for us and then, out of who we are, we will begin to do what He wants us to do. "Doing" witnessing is good, but we must also "be" witnesses for Christ in our everyday lives. We can show up at church and do good deeds, but God's deepest desire for each of us is that we become like Christ in all of our thoughts, attitudes, words, and deeds.

We often make the mistake of being overly concerned about what is happening in our circumstances when our priority should be what is happening in our hearts. God is more interested in changing us than He is in changing our circumstances. Invite the Lord to have His way in you and your life, and you will experience an increase of the Holy Spirit's power.

---

13 And when they had entered [the city], they mounted [the stairs] to the upper room where they were [*d*indefinitely] staying—Peter and John and James and Andrew, Philip and Thomas, Bartholomew and Matthew; James son of Alphaeus and Simon the Zealot, and Judas [son] of James. **14** All of these with their minds in full agreement devoted themselves steadfastly to prayer, [waiting together] with the women and Mary the mother of Jesus, and with His brothers. **15** Now on one of those days Peter arose among the brethren, the whole number of whom gathered together was about a hundred and twenty. **16** Brethren, he said, it was necessary

---

d James Moulton and George Milligan, *The Vocabulary of the Greek Testament.*

wait for God

I believe the key word in Acts 1:13 is *indefinitely*. The disciples went into the Upper Room with a mind-set that said, "We are not coming out of here until God shows up." They did not go in there to wait ten minutes. They did not go in there to wait two days. They did not go in there to wait three months. No, they went in there saying, "We cannot do all that God wants us to do without His full power in our lives." Like those who entered the Upper Room to wait for the promised outpouring of the Holy Spirit, we should approach God with an attitude that says, "I am waiting on You, Lord, *indefinitely, until I receive power from on high!*"

Waiting for God indefinitely is hard for us to do. We have so much energy and zeal in our flesh that even if we ever get around to waiting, we pause only for short periods of time and then the energy of our flesh takes over again.

If God does not do something as quickly as we want Him to do it, then our bright ideas overtake us again, and we get right back in the flesh. We constantly cover the same ground. We make some progress and then we become impatient and lose it. We gain a little ground and then we lose it. We have to "gain and maintain." We must stand fast in the liberties we are given and not submit again to a yoke of bondage we have once put off (see Galatians 5:1). Even when we do not "see" something or "feel" that God is working, He is working mightily in our behalf. We inherit the promises of God through faith and patience (Hebrews 10:36).

The mind-set we need to have is this: "God, I have come to the end of myself. I have tried this, and I have tried that. I have tried everything I can possibly think of for all these years. Now it is obvious that I cannot do what needs to be done by myself. God, I need You. Only You can do it. So I am waiting on You."

Be willing to wait indefinitely for God—as long as it takes.

that the Scripture be fulfilled which the Holy Spirit foretold by the lips of David, about Judas who acted as guide to those who arrested Jesus.

17 For he was counted among us and received [by divine allotment] his portion in this ministry.

18 Now this man obtained a piece of land with the [money paid him as a] reward for his treachery *and* wickedness, and falling headlong he burst open in the middle [of his body] and all his intestines poured forth.

19 And all the residents of Jerusalem became acquainted with the facts, so that they called the piece of land in their own dialect—Akeldama, that is, Field of Blood.

20 For in the book of Psalms it is written, Let his place of residence become deserted *and* gloomy, and let there be no one to live in it; and [again], Let another take his position *or* overseership. [Ps. 69:25; 109:8.]

21 So one of the [other] men who have accompanied us [apostles] during all the time that the Lord Jesus went in and out among us,

22 From the baptism of John at the outset until the day when He was taken up from among us—one of these men must join with us and become a witness to testify to His resurrection.

23 And they accordingly proposed (nominated) two men, Joseph called Barsabbas, who was surnamed Justus, and Matthias.

24 And they prayed and said, You, Lord, Who know all hearts (ᵉtheir thoughts, passions, desires, appetites, purposes, and endeavors), indicate to us which one of these two You have chosen

25 To take the place in this ministry and receive the position of an apostle, from which Judas fell away *and* went astray to go [where he belonged] to his own [proper] place.

26 And they drew lots [between the two], and the lot fell on Matthias; and he was added to *and* counted with the eleven apostles (special messengers).

2 AND WHEN the day of Pentecost had fully come, they were all assembled together in one place,

2 When suddenly there came a sound from heaven like the rushing of a violent tempest blast, and it filled the whole house in which they were sitting.

3 And there appeared to them tongues resembling fire, which were separated *and* distributed and which settled on each one of them.

4 And they were all filled (diffused throughout their souls) with the Holy Spirit and began to speak in other (different, foreign) languages (tongues), as the Spirit ᶠkept giving them clear *and* loud expression [in each tongue in appropriate words].

5 Now there were then residing in Jerusalem Jews, devout *and* God-fearing men from every country under heaven.

6 And when this sound was heard,

the multitude came together and they were astonished *and* bewildered, because each one heard them [the apostles] speaking in his own [particular] dialect.

7 And they were beside themselves with amazement, saying, Are not all these who are talking Galileans?

8 Then how is it that we hear, each of us, in our own (particular) dialect to which we were born?

9 Parthians and Medes and Elamites and inhabitants of Mesopotamia, Judea and Cappadocia, Pontus and [the province of] Asia,

10 Phrygia and Pamphylia, Egypt and the parts of Libya about Cyrene, and the transient residents from Rome, both Jews and the proselytes [to Judaism from other religions],

11 Cretans and Arabians too—we all hear them speaking in our own native tongues [and telling of] the mighty works of God!

12 And all were beside themselves with amazement and were puzzled *and* bewildered, saying one to another, What can this mean?

13 But others made a joke of it *and* derisively said, They are simply drunk *and* full of sweet [intoxicating] wine.

14 But Peter, standing with the eleven, raised his voice and addressed them: You Jews and all you residents of Jerusalem, let this be [explained] to you so that you will know *and* understand; listen closely to what I have to say.

15 For these men are not drunk, as you imagine, for it is [only] the third hour (about 9:00 a.m.) of the day;

16 But [instead] this is [the beginning of] what was spoken through the prophet Joel:

17 And it shall come to pass in the last days, God declares, that I will pour out of My Spirit upon all mankind, and your sons and your daughters shall

e Joseph Thayer, *A Greek-English Lexicon.*   **f** Marvin Vincent, *Word Studies in the New Testament.*

prophesy [⁸telling forth the divine counsels] and your young men shall see visions (ʰdivinely granted appearances), and your old men shall dream [ʰdivinely suggested] dreams.

18 Yes, and on My menservants also and on My maidservants in those days I will pour out of My Spirit, and they shall prophesy [ᵗtelling forth the divine counsels and ʰpredicting future events pertaining especially to God's kingdom].

life point

Not only do you need God, God needs you! Do not discount yourself by thinking that God could not possibly use you. Note that in Acts 2:17, 18, God speaks of pouring out His Spirit on *all* mankind—menservants, maidservants, sons, and daughters. Joel 2:28, 29 first prophesied these words, and Peter repeats them here in Acts. This prophetic word from the Lord definitely includes you and me!

19 And I will show wonders in the sky above and signs on the earth beneath, blood and fire and smoking vapor;

20 The sun shall be turned into darkness and the moon into blood before the obvious day of the Lord comes— that great and notable *and* conspicuous and renowned [day].

21 And it shall be that whoever shall call upon the name of the Lord [ʰinvoking, adoring, and worshiping the Lord—Christ] shall be saved. [Joel 2:28-32.]

22 You men of Israel, listen to what I have to say: Jesus of Nazareth, a Man accredited *and* pointed out *and* shown forth *and* commended *and* attested to you by God by the mighty works and

[the power of performing] wonders and signs which God worked through Him [right] in your midst, as you yourselves know—

23 This Jesus, when delivered up according to the definite *and* fixed purpose *and* settled plan and foreknowledge of God, you crucified *and* put out of the way [killing Him] by the hands of lawless *and* wicked men.

24 [But] God raised Him up, liberating Him from the pangs of death, seeing that it was not possible for Him to continue to be controlled *or* retained by it.

25 For David says in regard to Him, I saw the Lord constantly before me, for He is at my right hand that I may not be shaken *or* overthrown *or* cast down [from my secure and happy state].

26 Therefore my heart rejoiced and my tongue exulted exceedingly; moreover, my flesh also will dwell in hope [will encamp, pitch its tent, and dwell in hope in anticipation of the resurrection].

27 For You will not abandon my soul, leaving it helpless in Hades (the state of departed spirits), nor let Your Holy One know decay *or* see destruction [of the body after death].

28 You have made known to me the ways of life; You will enrapture me [diffusing my soul with joy] with *and* in Your presence. [Ps. 16:8-11.]

29 Brethren, it is permitted me to tell you confidently *and* with freedom concerning the patriarch David that he both died and was buried, and his tomb is with us to this day.

30 Being however a prophet, and knowing that God had sealed to him with an oath that He would set one of his descendants on his throne, [II Sam. 7:12-16; Ps. 132:11.]

31 He, foreseeing this, spoke [by foreknowledge] of the resurrection of

---

g G. Abbott-Smith, *Manual Greek Lexicon of the New Testament.*   **h** Joseph Thayer, *A Greek-English Lexicon.*   **i** G. Abbott-Smith, *Manual Greek Lexicon.*

the power of Jesus' name

I want to share a story with you about the power of Jesus' name (see Acts 2:21). A person I know was driving through an intersection one day and his little three- or four-year-old son was in the car with him. He did not realize that the car door on the passenger side was not secured tightly, and he made a sharp turn. This happened before seat-belt laws were passed, and the child was not wearing one. The car door flew open, and the little boy rolled out of the vehicle right into the middle of traffic coming from four ways! The last thing my friend saw was a set of car wheels about to roll over his son. This car was moving at a very fast rate of speed. All my friend knew to do was cry, "JESUS!"

As soon as he could bring his car to a halt, he jumped out and ran to his son, who was perfectly all right. But the man driving the car that almost hit the child was absolutely hysterical. My friend went over to him and started trying to comfort him.

"Man, don't be upset!" he said. "My son is all right. He's okay. Don't be concerned about it. Just thank God you were able to stop!"

"You don't understand!" the man responded. "I never touched my brakes!"

This was a crisis situation. There was no time for anyone to do anything, no time to think, plan, or reason. Although there was nothing either man could do, the name of Jesus prevailed. Miracle-working power came on the scene, and the boy's life was spared.

I believe we need more confidence in the name of Jesus and less confidence in ourselves or anyone else to solve our problems.

There is power in the name of Jesus!

the Christ (the Messiah) that He was not deserted [in death] *and* left in Hades (the state of departed spirits), nor did His body know decay *or* see destruction. [Ps. 16:10.]
32 This Jesus God raised up, and of that all we [His disciples] are witnesses.
33 Being therefore lifted high by *and* to the right hand of God, and having received from the Father 'the promised [blessing which is the] Holy Spirit, He has made this outpouring which you yourselves both see and hear.
34 For David did not ascend into the

heavens; yet he himself says, The Lord said to my Lord, Sit at My right hand *and* share My throne
35 Until I make Your enemies a footstool for Your feet. [Ps. 110:1.]
36 Therefore let the whole house of Israel recognize beyond all doubt *and* acknowledge assuredly that God has made Him both Lord and Christ (the Messiah)—this Jesus Whom you crucified.
37 Now when they heard this they were stung (cut) to the heart, and they said to Peter and the rest of the

j Joseph Thayer, *A Greek-English Lexicon.*

apostles (special messengers), Brethren, what shall we do?

38 And Peter answered them, Repent (change your views and purpose to accept the will of God in your inner selves instead of rejecting it) and be baptized every one of you, in the name of Jesus Christ for the forgiveness of *and* release from your sins; and you shall receive the gift of the Holy Spirit.

39 For the promise [of the Holy Spirit] is to *and* for you and your children, and to *and* for all that are far away, [even] to *and* for as many as the Lord our God invites *and* bids to come to Himself. [Isa. 57:19; Joel 2:32.]

40 And [Peter] ᵏsolemnly *and* earnestly witnessed (testified) and admonished (exhorted) with much more continuous speaking *and* warned (reproved, advised, encouraged) them, saying, Be saved from this crooked (perverse, wicked, unjust) generation.

41 Therefore those who accepted *and* welcomed his message were baptized, and there were added that day about 3,000 souls.

42 And they steadfastly persevered, devoting themselves constantly to the instruction and fellowship of the apostles, to the breaking of bread [including the Lord's Supper] and prayers.

43 And a sense of awe (reverential fear) came upon every soul, and many wonders and signs were performed through the apostles (the special messengers).

44 And all who believed (who adhered to and trusted in and relied on Jesus Christ) were united and [together] they had everything in common;

speak the Word

putting the Word to work

Acts 2:42–47 gives us a snapshot of life for the believers in the early church. Being a part of a local church is one of the great joys and responsibilities of every believer. However, it involves more than showing up on Sunday! How do you participate in the life of your church? While you experience different levels of involvement in a church during different seasons of your life, be sure to consistently avail yourself of opportunities to fellowship, worship, serve, and receive teaching of the Word.

45 And they sold their possessions (both their landed property and their movable goods) and distributed the price among all, according as any had need.

46 And day after day they regularly assembled in the temple with united purpose, and in their homes they broke bread [including the Lord's Supper]. They partook of their food with gladness and simplicity *and* generous hearts,

47 Constantly praising God and being in favor *and* goodwill with all the people; and the Lord kept adding [to their number] daily those who were being saved [from spiritual death].

3 NOW PETER and John were going up to the temple at the hour of prayer, the ninth hour (three o'clock in the afternoon),

2 [When] a certain man crippled

Thank You, Lord, that the promise of the Holy Spirit is for me and for my children, and for all who come to You.
ADAPTED FROM ACTS 2:39

k Marvin Vincent, *Word Studies*: The preposition *dia* gives this force.

from his birth was being carried along, who was laid each day at that gate of the temple [which is] called Beautiful, so that he might beg for charitable gifts from those who entered the temple.

3   So when he saw Peter and John about to go into the temple, he asked them to give him a gift.

4   And Peter directed his gaze intently at him, and so did John, and said, Look at us!

5   And [the man] paid attention to them, expecting that he was going to get something from them.

6   But Peter said, Silver and gold (money) I do not have; but what I do have, that I give to you: in [the ʰuse of] the name of Jesus Christ of Nazareth, walk!

7   Then he took hold of the man's right hand with a firm grip and raised him up. And at once his feet and ankle bones became strong and steady,

8   And leaping forth he stood and ᵐbegan to walk, and he went into the temple with them, walking and leaping and praising God.

9   And all the people saw him walking about and praising God,

10   And they recognized him as the man who usually sat [begging] for alms at the Beautiful Gate of the temple; and they were filled with wonder and amazement (bewilderment, consternation) over what had occurred to him.

11   Now while he [still] firmly clung to Peter and John, all the people in utmost amazement ran together and

crowded around them in the covered porch (walk) called Solomon's.

12   And Peter, seeing it, answered the people, You men of Israel, why are you so surprised and wondering at this? Why do you keep staring at us, as though by our [own individual] power or [active] piety we had made this man [able] to walk?

13   The God of Abraham and of Isaac and of Jacob, the God of our forefathers, has glorified His Servant and ⁿSon Jesus [doing Him this honor], Whom you indeed delivered up and denied and rejected and disowned in the presence of Pilate, when he had determined to let Him go. [Exod. 3:6; Isa. 52:13.]

14   But you denied and rejected and disowned the Pure and Holy, the Just and Blameless One, and demanded [the pardon of] a murderer to be granted to you.

15   But you killed the very Source (the Author) of life, Whom God raised from the dead. To this we are witnesses.

16   And His name, through and by faith in His name, has made this man whom you see and recognize well and strong. [Yes] the faith which is through and by Him [Jesus] has given the man this perfect soundness [of body] before all of you.

17   And now, brethren, I know that you acted in ignorance [not aware of what you were doing], as did your rulers also.

18   Thus has God fulfilled what He foretold by the mouth of all the prophets, that His Christ (the

speak the Word

Father, help me to be like Peter and freely use the name of Jesus to bless those in need around me.

ADAPTED FROM ACTS 3:6

---

l Joseph Thayer, *A Greek-English Lexicon.*   **m** Marvin Vincent, *Word Studies.*   **n** The Greek word used here means both "Servant" and "Child" ("Son").

His presence refreshes

Acts 3:19 teaches us that "times of refreshing" come to us when we spend time in God's presence. Until we come to the place where we want God's presence more than anything else, the devil will have an edge over us. Once we see God's truth, the devil loses his advantage, and we begin making radical progress in our relationship and fellowship with God.

Most of us will try almost everything else before we finally learn that what we need is not what God can *give* us, but God *Himself*. These times often represent years of frustration and misery. But thank God, His Holy Spirit lives in us, teaches us, and reveals truth to us as we continue to study, read, and listen to the Word of God.

If you are diligent to seek God, you will know Him in a deeper, more intimate way; God will reveal Himself to you; He will be found by you (see Jeremiah 29:13, 14). When God wants to manifest Himself, He will. You do not need to get frustrated trying to find God. Just learn to wait on Him and pray, "God, reveal Yourself to me. Manifest Your presence to me."

God manifests His presence in many ways. Sometimes we cannot see Him but, as with the wind, we can see the work He does in us. If I am weary, tired, worn-out, frustrated, or bothered about something, and I become refreshed after spending time with God, then I know that the "wind" of the Lord has blown upon me.

God wants to bring a refreshing into your life, like a mighty wind. Do not be poverty-stricken in your soul when the answer is so close. If you are too busy to spend time with God, then make some adjustments to your lifestyle. Do not get burned-out, upset, weary, and stressed-out when times of refreshing are available to you.

Learn to separate yourself from the busyness of life to spend time with God the way Jesus did. I tell people, "You had better come apart and spend time with God before you fall apart." I encourage you to take those words personally and do the same!

Messiah) should undergo ill treatment *and* be afflicted *and* suffer.

19 So repent (change your mind and purpose); turn around *and* return [to God], that your sins may be erased (blotted out, wiped clean), that times of refreshing (of recovering from the effects of heat, of °reviving with fresh air) may come from the presence of the Lord;

20 And that He may send [to you] the Christ (the Messiah), Who before was designated *and* appointed for you—even Jesus,

21 Whom heaven must receive [and retain] until the time for the complete restoration of all that God spoke by the mouth of all His holy prophets for ages past [from the most ancient time in the memory of man].

22 Thus Moses said *to the forefathers,* The Lord God will raise up for you a

o Marvin Vincent, *Word Studies.*

Prophet from among your brethren as [He raised up] me; Him you shall listen to *and* understand by hearing *and* heed in all things whatever He tells you.

23 And it shall be that every soul that does not listen to *and* understand by hearing *and* heed that Prophet shall be utterly ᴾexterminated from among the people. [Deut. 18:15-19.]

24 Indeed, all the prophets from Samuel and those who came afterwards, as many as have spoken, also promised *and* foretold *and* proclaimed these days.

25 You are the descendants (sons) of the prophets and the heirs of the covenant which God made *and* gave to your forefathers, saying to Abraham, And in your Seed (Heir) shall all the families of the earth be blessed *and* benefited. [Gen. 22:18; Gal. 3:16.]

26 It was to you first that God sent His Servant *and* Son *Jesus,* when He raised Him up [ᑫprovided and gave Him for us], to bless you in turning every one of you from your wickedness *and* evil ways. [Acts 2:24; 3:22.]

4 AND WHILE they [Peter and John] were talking to the people, the high priests and the military commander of the temple and the Sadducees came upon them,

2 Being vexed *and* indignant through *and* through because they were teaching the people *and* proclaiming in [the case of] Jesus the resurrection from the dead.

3 So they laid hands on them (arrested them) and put them in prison until the following day, for it was already evening.

4 But many of those who heard the message believed (adhered to and trusted in and relied on Jesus as the Christ). And their number grew *and* came to about 5,000.

5 Then on the following day, their magistrates and elders and scribes were assembled in Jerusalem.

6 Including Annas the high priest and Caiaphas and John and Alexander and all others who belonged to the high priestly relationship.

7 And they set the men in their midst and repeatedly demanded, By what sort of power or by what kind of authority did [such people as] you do this [healing]?

8 Then Peter [because he was] filled with [and controlled by] the Holy Spirit said to them, Rulers of the people and members of the council (the Sanhedrin),

9 If we are being put on trial [here] today *and* examined concerning a good deed done to benefit a feeble (helpless) cripple, by what means this man has been restored to health,

10 Let it be known *and* understood by all of you, and by the whole house of Israel, that in the name and through the power *and* authority of Jesus Christ of Nazareth, Whom you crucified, [but] Whom God raised from the dead, in Him *and* by means of Him this man is standing here before you well *and* sound in body.

11 This [Jesus] is the Stone which was despised *and* rejected by you, the builders, but which has become the Head of the corner [the Cornerstone]. [Ps. 118:22.]

12 And there is salvation in *and* through no one else, for there is no other name under heaven given among men by *and* in which we must be saved.

13 Now when they saw the boldness *and* unfettered eloquence of Peter and John and perceived that they were unlearned *and* untrained in the

---

p Alexander Souter, *Pocket Lexicon of the Greek New Testament.*   **q** Robert Jamieson, A.R. Fausett and David Brown, *A Commentary on the Old and New Testaments.*

schools [common men with no educational advantages], they marveled; and they recognized that they had been with Jesus.

putting the Word to work

Do you ever feel inadequate sharing with other people about God because you have not received much formal Christian education or training, like Peter and John in Acts 4:13? The best schooling is what I call "the school of the Holy Spirit." Ask Him to teach you through the Word, as you spend time in prayer, and as you rely on His grace. We learn through the Word of God and our experiences in life. Experience itself is a good teacher. God's Spirit leads us through many situations and will teach us as we go through them if we are open to learning. Enroll in the school of the Holy Spirit and you will get an education that far exceeds anything you can learn in a traditional classroom.

14 And since they saw the man who had been cured standing there beside them, they could not contradict the fact *or* say anything in opposition.
15 But having ordered [the prisoners] to go aside out of the council [chamber], they conferred (debated) among themselves,
16 Saying, What are we to do with these men? For that an extraordinary miracle has been performed by (through) them is plain to all the residents of Jerusalem, and we cannot deny it.
17 But in order that it may not spread further among the people *and* the nation, let us warn *and* forbid them with a stern threat to speak any more to anyone in this name [or about this Person].
18 [So] they summoned them and

life point

In the Gospels, Jesus does miracles, but in Acts, ordinary people do miracles by the power of the Holy Spirit (see Acts 4:16). Believe that He can use you in mighty ways!

imperatively instructed them not to converse in any way *or* teach at all in *or* about the name of Jesus.
19 But Peter and John replied to them, Whether it is right in the sight of God to listen to you *and* obey you rather than God, you must decide (judge).
20 But we [ourselves] cannot help telling what we have seen and heard.
21 Then when [the rulers and council members] had further threatened them, they let them go, not seeing how they could secure a conviction against them because of the people; for everybody was praising *and* glorifying God for what had occurred.
22 For the man on whom this sign (miracle) of healing was performed was more than forty years old.
23 After they were permitted to go, [the apostles] returned to their own [company] and told all that the chief priests and elders had said to them.
24 And when they heard it, lifted their voices together with one united mind to God and said, O Sovereign Lord, You are He Who made the heaven and the earth and the sea and everything that is in them, [Exod. 20:11; Ps. 146:6.]
25 Who by the mouth of our forefather David, Your servant *and* child, said through the Holy Spirit, Why did the heathen (Gentiles) become wanton *and* insolent *and* rage, and the people imagine *and* study *and* plan vain (fruitless) things [that will not succeed]?
26 The kings of the earth took their stand in array [for attack] and the

rulers were assembled *and* combined together against the Lord and against His Anointed (Christ, the Messiah). [Ps. 2:1, 2.]

27 For in this city there actually met and plotted together against Your holy Child *and* Servant Jesus, Whom You consecrated by anointing, both Herod and Pontius Pilate with the Gentiles and peoples of Israel, [Ps. 2:1, 2.]

28 To carry out all that Your hand and Your will *and* purpose had predestined (predetermined) should occur.

29 And now, Lord, observe their threats and grant to Your bond servants [full freedom] to declare Your message fearlessly,

30 While You stretch out Your hand to cure and to perform signs *and* wonders through the authority *and* by the power of the name of Your holy Child *and* Servant Jesus.

31 And when they had prayed, the place in which they were assembled was shaken; and they were all filled with the Holy Spirit, and they continued to speak the Word of God with freedom *and* boldness *and* courage.

32 Now the company of believers was of one heart and soul, and not one of them claimed that anything which he possessed was [exclusively] his own, but everything they had was in common *and* for the use of all.

33 And with great strength *and* ability *and* power the apostles delivered their testimony to the resurrection of the Lord Jesus, and great grace (loving-kindness and favor and goodwill) rested richly upon them all.

34 Nor was there a destitute *or* needy person among them, for as many as were owners of lands or houses proceeded to sell them, and one by one they brought (gave back) the amount received from the sales

35 And laid it at the feet of the apostles (special messengers). Then distribution was made according as anyone had need.

36 Now Joseph, a Levite and native of Cyprus who was surnamed Barnabas by the apostles, which interpreted means Son of Encouragement,

37 Sold a field which belonged to him and brought the sum of money and laid it at the feet of the apostles.

5 BUT A certain man named Ananias with his wife Sapphira sold a piece of property,

2 And with his wife's knowledge *and* connivance he kept back *and* wrongfully appropriated some of the proceeds, bringing only a part and putting it at the feet of the apostles.

3 But Peter said, Ananias, why has Satan filled your heart that you should lie to *and* attempt to deceive the Holy Spirit, and should [in violation of your promise] withdraw secretly *and* appropriate to your own use part of the price from the sale of the land?

4 As long as it remained unsold, was it not still your own? And [even] after it was sold, was not [the money] at your disposal *and* under your control? Why then, is it that you have proposed *and* purposed in your heart to do this thing? [How could you have the heart to do such a deed?] You have not [simply] lied to men [playing false and showing yourself utterly deceitful] but to God.

5 Upon hearing these words,

speak the Word

God, help me live and do business in perfect integrity, never attempting to deceive Your Holy Spirit.
ADAPTED FROM ACTS 5:1–3

Ananias fell down and died. And great dread *and* terror took possession of all who heard of it.

6 And the young men arose and wrapped up [the body] and carried it out and buried it.

7 Now after an interval of about three hours his wife came in, not having learned of what had happened.

8 And Peter said to her, Tell me, did you sell the land for so much? Yes, she said, for so much.

9 Then Peter said to her, How could you two have agreed *and* conspired together to try to deceive the Spirit of the Lord? Listen! The feet of those who have buried your husband are at the door, and they will carry you out [also].

10 And instantly she fell down at his feet and died; and the young men entering found her dead, and they carried her out and buried her beside her husband.

11 And the whole church and all others who heard of these things were appalled [great awe and strange terror and dread seized them].

12 Now by the hands of the apostles (special messengers) numerous *and* startling signs *and* wonders were being performed among the people. And by common consent they all met together [at the temple] in the covered porch (walk) called Solomon's.

13 And none of those who were not of their number dared to join *and* associate with them, but the people held them in high regard *and* praised *and* made much of them.

14 More *and* more there were being added to the Lord those who believed [those who acknowledged Jesus as their Savior and devoted themselves to Him joined and gathered with them], crowds both of men and of women,

15 So that they [even] kept carrying out the sick into the streets and plac-ing them on couches and sleeping pads, [in the hope] that as Peter passed by, at least his shadow might fall on some of them.

16 And the people gathered also from the towns *and* hamlets around Jerusalem, bringing the sick and those troubled with foul spirits, and they were all cured.

17 But the high priest rose up and all who were his supporters, that is, the party of the Sadducees, and being filled with ʳjealousy *and* indignation *and* rage,

18 They seized and arrested the apostles (special messengers) and put them in the public jail.

19 But during the night an angel of the Lord opened the prison doors and, leading them out, said,

20 Go, take your stand in the temple courts and declare to the people the whole doctrine concerning this Life (the eternal life which Christ revealed).

21 And when they heard this, they accordingly went into the temple about daybreak and began to teach. Now the high priest and his supporters who were with him arrived and called together the council (Sanhedrin), even all the senate of the sons of Israel, and they sent to the prison to have [the apostles] brought.

22 But when the attendants arrived there, they failed to find them in the jail; so they came back and reported,

23 We found the prison quite safely locked up and the guards were on duty outside the doors, but when we opened [it], we found no one on the inside.

24 Now when the military leader of the temple area and the chief priests heard these facts, they were much perplexed *and* thoroughly at a loss about them, wondering into what this might grow.

r G. Abbott-Smith, *Manual Greek Lexicon*.

25 But some man came and reported to them, saying, Listen! The men whom you put in jail are standing [right here] in the temple and teaching the people!
26 Then the military leader went with the attendants and brought [the prisoners], but without violence, for they dreaded the people lest they be stoned by them.
27 So they brought them and set them before the council (Sanhedrin). And the high priest examined them by questioning,
28 Saying, We definitely commanded *and* strictly charged you not to teach in *or* about this Name; yet here you have flooded Jerusalem with your doctrine and you intend to bring this ˢMan's blood upon us.
29 Then Peter and the apostles replied, We must obey God rather than men.
30 The God of our forefathers raised up Jesus, Whom you killed by hanging Him on a tree (cross). [Deut. 21:22, 23.]
31 God exalted Him to His right hand to be Prince *and* Leader and Savior *and* Deliverer *and* Preserver, in order to grant repentance to Israel and to bestow forgiveness *and* release from sins.
32 And we are witnesses of these things, and the Holy Spirit is also, Whom God has bestowed on those who obey Him.
33 Now when they heard this, they were cut to the heart *and* infuriated and wanted to kill the disciples.
34 But a certain Pharisee in the council (Sanhedrin) named Gamaliel, a teacher of the Law, highly esteemed by all the people, standing up, ordered that the apostles be taken outside for a little while.
35 Then he addressed them [the council, saying]: Men of Israel, take

care in regard to what you propose to do concerning these men.
36 For before our time there arose Theudas, asserting himself to be a person of importance, with whom a number of men allied themselves, about 400; but he was killed and all who had listened to *and* adhered to him were scattered and brought to nothing.
37 And after this one rose up Judas the Galilean, [who led an uprising] during the time of the census, and drew away a popular following after him; he also perished and all his adherents were scattered.
38 Now in the present case let me say to you, stand off (withdraw) from these men and let them alone. For if this doctrine *or* purpose or undertaking *or* movement is of human origin, it will fail (be overthrown and come to nothing);
39 But if it is of God, you will not be able to stop *or* overthrow *or* destroy them; you might even be found fighting against God!
40 So, convinced by him, they took his advice; and summoning the apostles, they flogged them and sternly forbade them to speak in *or* about the name of Jesus, and allowed them to go.
41 So they went out from the presence of the council (Sanhedrin), rejoicing that they were being counted worthy [dignified by the indignity] to suffer shame *and* be exposed to disgrace for [the sake of] His name.
42 Yet [in spite of the threats] they never ceased for a single day, both in the temple area and at home, to teach *and* to proclaim the good news (Gospel) of Jesus [as] the Christ (the Messiah).

6 NOW ABOUT this time, when the number of the disciples was greatly increasing, complaint

---

ˢ Capitalized because of what He is, the spotless Son of God, not what the speakers may have thought He was.

was made by the Hellenists (the Greek-speaking Jews) against the [native] Hebrews because their widows were being overlooked *and* neglected in the daily ministration (distribution of relief).

2 So the Twelve [apostles] convened the multitude of the disciples and said, It is not seemly *or* desirable *or* right that we should have to give up *or* neglect [preaching] the Word of God in order to attend to serving at tables *and* superintending the distribution of food.

3 Therefore select out from among yourselves, brethren, seven men of good *and* attested character *and* repute, full of the [Holy] Spirit and wisdom, whom we may assign to look after this business *and* duty.

4 But we will continue to devote ourselves steadfastly to prayer and the ministry of the Word.

5 And the suggestion pleased the whole assembly, and they selected Stephen, a man full of faith (a strong and welcome belief that Jesus is the Messiah) and full of *and* controlled by the Holy Spirit, and Philip, and Prochorus, and Nicanor, and Timon, and Parmenas, and Nicolaus, a proselyte (convert) from Antioch.

6 These they presented to the apostles, who after prayer laid their hands on them.

7 And the message of God kept on

choose your battles

Acts 6:2–4 teaches us that it is not wise to be involved in everything that is going on around us. Instead, we should select our activities cautiously so we can remain calm, cool, and steady in life. I often refer to this as "choosing your battles carefully."

There are many things I could do at my office that I have learned to just stay out of and let another qualified person handle. Previously, I wanted to be part of everything that happened, especially the problems. I learned the hard way that I simply cannot be involved in everything; too much is going on for me to do that. I pick my battles now, and that has greatly increased my level of peace.

I firmly believe that God provides for whatever He assigns to us. He will make sure we have all the people we need to help us, but it is not their fault if we will not rely on them.

If you find yourself trying to do something and you do not have the help you need, you might need to ask yourself if you are doing the right thing. Why would God ask you to do something, then sit by and watch you be frustrated and miserable because the burden is too much? God meets all of our needs, including the people we need to work alongside us.

Acts 6:2–4 gives an example of this act of wisdom. Had the apostles not recognized their need for help, their priorities would have remained out of line and their true assignment unfulfilled. They would have ended up frustrated, and just like the people they were trying to serve, they could have lost their peace, and therefore, their power. It is quite possible that the loss of peace was what triggered their decision to ask for help. This is an excellent example for us to follow.

spreading, and the number of disciples multiplied greatly in Jerusalem; and [besides] a large number of the priests were obedient to the faith [in Jesus as the Messiah, through Whom is obtained eternal salvation in the kingdom of God].

8 Now Stephen, full of grace (divine blessing and favor) and power (strength and ability) worked great wonders and signs (miracles) among the people.

9 However, some of those who belonged to the synagogue of the Freedmen (freed Jewish slaves), as it was called, and [of the synagogues] of the Cyrenians and of the Alexandrians and of those from Cilicia and [the province of] Asia, arose [and undertook] to debate *and* dispute with Stephen.

10 But they were not able to resist the intelligence *and* the wisdom and [the inspiration of] the Spirit with which *and* by Whom he spoke.

11 So they [secretly] instigated *and* instructed men to say, We have heard this man speak, using slanderous *and* abusive *and* blasphemous language against Moses and God.

12 [Thus] they incited the people as well as the elders and the scribes, and they came upon Stephen and arrested him and took him before the council (Sanhedrin).

13 And they brought forward false witnesses who asserted, This man never stops making statements against this sacred place and the Law [of Moses];

14 For we have heard him say that this Jesus the Nazarene will tear down *and* destroy this place, and will alter the institutions *and* usages which Moses transmitted to us.

15 Then all who sat in the council (Sanhedrin), as they gazed intently at Stephen, saw that his face had the appearance of the face of an angel.

7 AND THE high priest asked [Stephen], Are these charges true?

2 And he answered, Brethren and fathers, listen to me! The God of glory appeared to our forefather Abraham when he was still in Mesopotamia, before he [went to] live in Haran, [Gen. 11:31; 15:7; Ps. 29:3.]

3 And He said to him, Leave your own country and your relatives and come into the land (region) that I will point out to you. [Gen. 12:1.]

4 So then he went forth from the land of the Chaldeans and settled in Haran. And from there, after his father died, [God] transferred him to this country in which you are now dwelling. [Gen. 11:31; 12:5; 15:7.]

5 Yet He gave him no inheritable property in it, [no] not even enough ground to set his foot on; but He promised that He would give it to Him for a ᵗpermanent possession and to his descendants after him, even though [as yet] he had no child. [Gen. 12:7; 17:8; Deut. 2:5.]

6 And this is [in effect] what God told him: That his descendants would be aliens (strangers) in a land belonging to other people, who would bring them into bondage and ill-treat them 400 years.

7 But I will judge the nation to whom they will be slaves, said God, and after that they will escape *and* come forth and worship Me in this [very] place. [Gen. 15:13, 14; Exod. 3:12.]

8 And [God] made with Abraham a covenant (an agreement to be religiously observed) ᵗof which circumcision was the seal. And under these circumstances [Abraham] became the father of Isaac and circumcised him on the eighth day; and Isaac [did so] when he became the father of Jacob, and Jacob [when each of his sons was born], the twelve patriarchs. [Gen. 17:10-14; 21:2-4; 25:26; 29:31-35; 30:1-24; 35:16-26.]

9 And the patriarchs [Jacob's sons], boiling with envy *and* hatred *and* anger, sold Joseph into slavery in Egypt; but God was with him, [Gen. 37:11, 28; 45:4.]

10 And delivered him from all his distressing afflictions and won him goodwill *and* favor and wisdom *and* understanding in the sight of Pharaoh, king of Egypt, who made him governor over Egypt and all his house. [Gen. 39:2, 3, 21; 41:40-46; Ps. 105:21.]

11 Then there came a famine over all of Egypt and Canaan, with great distress, and our forefathers could find no fodder [for the cattle] *or* vegetable sustenance [for their households]. [Gen. 41:54, 55; 42:5.]

12 But when Jacob heard that there was grain in Egypt, he sent forth our forefathers [to go there on their] first trip. [Gen. 42:2.]

13 And on their second visit Joseph revealed himself to his brothers, and the family of Joseph became known to Pharaoh *and* his origin *and* race. [Gen. 45:1-4.]

14 And Joseph sent an invitation calling to himself Jacob his father and all his kindred, seventy-five persons in all. [Gen. 45:9, 10.]

15 And Jacob went down into Egypt, where he himself died, as did [also] our forefathers; [Deut. 10:22.]

16 And their ᵘbodies [Jacob's and Joseph's] were taken back to Shechem and laid in the tomb which Abraham had purchased for a sum of [silver] money from the sons of Hamor in Shechem. [Gen. 50:13; Josh. 24:32.]

17 But as the time for the fulfillment of the promise drew near which God had made to Abraham, the [Hebrew] people increased and multiplied in Egypt,

18 Until [the time when] there arose over Egypt another *and* a different king who did not know Joseph [neither knowing his history and services nor recognizing his merits]. [Exod. 1:7, 8.]

19 He dealt treacherously with *and* defrauded our race; he abused *and* oppressed our forefathers, forcing them to expose their babies so that they might not be kept alive. [Exod. 1:7-11, 15-22.]

20 At this juncture Moses was born, and was exceedingly beautiful in God's sight. For three months he was nurtured in his father's house; [Exod. 2:2.]

21 Then when he was exposed [to perish], the daughter of Pharaoh rescued him and took him *and* reared him as her own son. [Exod. 2:5, 6, 10.]

22 So Moses was educated in all the wisdom *and* culture of the Egyptians, and he was mighty (powerful) in his speech and deeds.

23 And when he was in his fortieth year, it came into his heart to visit his kinsmen the children of Israel [ᵛto help them and to care for them].

24 And on seeing one of them being unjustly treated, he defended the oppressed man and avenged him by striking down the Egyptian *and* slaying [him].

25 He expected his brethren to understand that God was granting them deliverance by his hand [taking it for granted that they would accept him]; but they did not understand.

26 Then on the next day he ʷsuddenly appeared to some who were

---

u Stephen greatly compresses Old Testament accounts of two land purchases and two burial places (at Hebron and Shechem). See Gen. 23:17-18 and Gen. 33:19. **v** G. Abbott-Smith, *Manual Greek Lexicon.* **w** Marvin Vincent, *Word Studies.*

quarreling *and* fighting among themselves, and he urged them to make peace *and* become reconciled, saying, Men, you are brethren; why do you abuse *and* wrong one another?

27 Whereupon the man who was abusing his neighbor pushed [Moses] aside, saying, Who appointed you a ruler (umpire) and a judge over us?

28 Do you intend to slay me as you slew the Egyptian yesterday?

29 At that reply Moses sought safety by flight and he was an exile *and* an alien in the country of Midian, where he became the father of two sons. [Exod. 2:11-15, 22; 18:3, 4.]

30 And when forty years had gone by, there appeared to him in the wilderness (desert) of Mount Sinai an angel, in the flame of a burning bramblebush.

31 When Moses saw it, he was astonished *and* marveled at the sight; but when he went close to investigate, there came to him the voice of the Lord, saying,

32 I am the God of your forefathers, the God of Abraham and of Isaac and of Jacob. And Moses trembled *and* was so terrified that he did not venture to look.

33 Then the Lord said to him, Remove the sandals from your feet, for the place where you are standing is holy ground *and* worthy of veneration.

34 Because I have most assuredly seen the abuse *and* oppression of My people in Egypt and have heard their sighing *and* groaning, I have come down to rescue them. So, now come! I will send you back to Egypt [as My messenger]. [Exod. 3:1-10.]

35 It was this very Moses whom they had denied (disowned and rejected), saying, Who made you our ruler (referee) and judge? whom God sent to be a ruler and deliverer *and* redeemer, by *and* with the [protecting and helping] hand of the Angel that appeared to him in the bramblebush. [Exod. 2:14.]

36 He it was who led them forth, having worked wonders and signs in Egypt and at the Red Sea and during the forty years in the wilderness (desert). [Exod. 7:3; 14:21; Num. 14:33.]

37 It was this [very] Moses who said to the children of Israel, God will raise up for you a Prophet from among your brethren as He raised me up. [Deut. 18:15, 18.]

38 This is he who in the assembly in the wilderness (desert) was the go-between for the Angel who spoke to him on Mount Sinai and our forefathers, and he received living oracles (words that still live) to be handed down to us. [Exod. 19.]

39 [And yet] our forefathers determined not to be subject to him [refusing to listen to *or* obey him]; but thrusting him aside they rejected him, and in their hearts yearned for *and* turned back to Egypt. [Num. 14:3, 4.]

40 And they said to Aaron, Make us gods who shall [be our leaders and] go before us; as for this Moses who led us forth from the land of Egypt—we have no knowledge of what has happened to him. [Exod. 32:1, 23.]

41 And they [even] made a calf in those days, and offered sacrifice to the idol and made merry *and* exulted in the work of their [own] hands. [Exod. 32:4, 6.]

42 But God turned [away from them] and delivered them up to worship *and* serve the host (stars) of heaven, as it is written in the book of the prophets: Did you [really] offer to Me slain beasts and sacrifices for forty years in the wilderness (desert), O house of Israel? [Jer. 19:13.]

43 [No!] You took up the tent (the portable temple) of Moloch *and* carried it [with you], and the star of the god Rephan, the images which you [yourselves] made that you might worship them; and I will remove you [carrying you away into exile] beyond Babylon. [Amos 5:25-27.]

44 Our forefathers had the tent (tabernacle) of witness in the wilderness, even as He Who directed Moses to make it had ordered, according to the pattern *and* model he had seen. [Exod. 25:9-40.]

45 Our forefathers in turn brought it [this tent of witness] in [with them into the land] with Joshua when they dispossessed the nations which God drove out before the face of our forefathers. [So it remained here] until the time of David, [Deut. 32:49; Josh. 3:14-17.]

46 Who found grace (favor and spiritual blessing) in the sight of God and prayed that he might be allowed to find a dwelling place for the God of Jacob. [II Sam. 7:8-16; Ps. 132:1-5.]

47 But it was Solomon who built a house for Him. [I Kings 6.]

48 However, the Most High does not dwell in houses *and* temples made with hands; as the prophet says, [Isa. 66:1, 2.]

49 Heaven [is] My throne, and earth the footstool for My feet. What [kind of] house can you build for Me, says the Lord, or what is the place in which I can rest?

50 Was it not My hand that made all these things? [Isa. 66:1, 2.]

51 You stubborn *and* stiff-necked people, still heathen *and* uncircumcised in heart and ears, you are always ˣactively resisting the Holy Spirit. As your forefathers [were], so you [are and so you do]! [Exod. 33:3, 5; Num. 27:14; Isa. 63:10; Jer. 6:10; 9:26.]

52 Which of the prophets did your forefathers not persecute? And they slew those who proclaimed beforehand the coming of the Righteous One, Whom you now have betrayed and murdered—

life point

Have you ever wondered what an uncircumcised heart is (see Acts 7:51)? To "circumcise" is to cut off. When a person has an uncircumcised heart and something wicked comes into it, he does not cut it off. Instead, he lets the evil stay there. But a person who has a circumcised heart will immediately cut off any wrong attitude that comes into his mind and heart.

Remember, the devil is going to come at us with wrong heart attitudes at every opportunity, but taking his bait never helps us. It only hinders our growth and development. If we want to have circumcised hearts, we must immediately get rid of anger, hatred, jealousy, envy, and any other kind of wrong attitude when it first comes into our minds. If we let that wrong thing stay in our hearts, we are not being what God has called us to be. We are living our lives before Him with an uncircumcised hearts.

A victorious believer maintains a circumcised heart by saying no to anything that will keep him or her from being a person whose heart is

53 You who received the Law as it was ordained *and* set in order *and* delivered by angels, and [yet] you did not obey it!

54 Now upon hearing these things, they [the Jews] were cut to the heart *and* infuriated, and they ground their teeth against [Stephen].

55 But he, full of the Holy Spirit *and* controlled by Him, gazed into heaven and saw the glory (the splendor and majesty) of God, and Jesus standing at God's right hand;

x Marvin Vincent, *Word Studies*.

56 And he said, Look! I see the heavens opened, and the Son of man standing at God's right hand!

57 But they raised a great shout and put their hands over their ears and rushed together upon him.

58 Then they dragged him out of the city and began to stone him, and the witnesses placed their garments at the feet of a young man named Saul. [Acts 22:20.]

59 And while they were stoning Stephen, he prayed, Lord Jesus, receive *and* accept *and* welcome my spirit!

60 And falling on his knees, he cried out loudly, Lord, fix not this sin upon them [lay it not to their charge]! And when he had said this, he fell asleep [y][in death].

8 AND SAUL was [not only] consenting to [Stephen's] death [he was [z]pleased and [a]entirely approving]. On that day a great *and* severe persecution broke out against the church which was in Jerusalem; and they were all scattered throughout the regions of Judea and Samaria, except the apostles (special messengers).

2 [A party of] devout men [z]with others helped to carry out *and* bury Stephen and made great lamentation over him.

3 But Saul shamefully treated *and* laid waste the church continuously [with cruelty and violence]; and entering house after house, he dragged out men and women and committed them to prison.

4 Now those who were scattered abroad went about [through the land from place to place] preaching the glad tidings, the Word [[z]the doctrine concerning the attainment through

Christ of salvation in the kingdom of God].

5 Philip [the deacon, not the apostle] went down to the city of Samaria and proclaimed the Christ (the Messiah) to them [the people]; [Acts 6:5.]

6 And great crowds of people with one accord listened to *and* heeded what was said by Philip, as they heard him *and* watched the miracles *and* wonders which he kept performing [from time to time].

7 For foul spirits came out of many who were possessed by them, screaming *and* shouting with a loud voice, and many who were suffering from palsy or were crippled were restored to health.

8 And there was great rejoicing in that city.

9 But there was a man named Simon, who had formerly practiced magic arts in the city to the utter amazement of the Samaritan nation, claiming that he himself was an extraordinary *and* distinguished person.

10 They all paid earnest attention to him, from the least to the greatest, saying, This man is that exhibition of the power of God which is called great (intense).

11 And they were attentive *and* made much of him, because for a long time he had amazed *and* bewildered *and* dazzled them with his skill in magic arts.

12 But when they believed the good news (the Gospel) about the kingdom of God and the name of Jesus Christ (the Messiah) as Philip preached it, they were baptized, both men and women.

13 Even Simon himself believed [he adhered to, trusted in, and relied on the teaching of Philip], and after being baptized, devoted himself

y Hermann Cremer, *Biblico-Theological Lexicon of New Testament Greek*. **z** Joseph Thayer, *A Greek-English Lexicon*. **a** Alexander Souter, *Pocket Lexicon*.

constantly to him. And seeing signs *and* miracles of great power which were being performed, he was utterly amazed.

14 Now when the apostles (special messengers) at Jerusalem heard that [the country of] Samaria had accepted *and* welcomed the Word of God, they sent Peter and John to them,

15 And they came down and prayed for them that the Samaritans might receive the Holy Spirit;

16 For He had not yet fallen upon any of them, but they had only been baptized into the name of the Lord Jesus.

17 Then [the apostles] laid their hands on them one by one, and they received the Holy Spirit.

18 However, when Simon saw that the [Holy] Spirit was imparted through the laying on of the apostles' hands, he brought money *and* offered it to them,

19 Saying, Grant me also this power *and* authority, in order that anyone on whom I place my hands may receive the Holy Spirit.

20 But Peter said to him, Destruction overtake your money and you, because you imagined you could obtain the [free] gift of God with money!

21 You have neither part nor lot in this matter, for your heart is all wrong in God's sight [it is not straightforward or right or true before God]. [Ps. 78:37.]

22 So repent of this depravity *and* wickedness of yours and pray to the Lord that, if possible, this ᵇcontriving thought *and* purpose of your heart may be removed *and* disregarded *and* forgiven you.

23 For I see that you are in the gall of bitterness and in ᶜa bond forged by iniquity [to fetter souls]. [Isa. 58:6.]

24 And Simon answered, Pray for me [beseech the Lord, both of you], that nothing of what you have said may befall me!

25 Now when [the apostles] had borne their testimony and preached the message of the Lord, they went back to Jerusalem, proclaiming the glad tidings (Gospel) to many villages of the Samaritans [on the way].

26 But an angel of the Lord said to Philip, Rise and proceed southward *or* at midday on the road that runs from Jerusalem down to Gaza. This is the desert [ᵇroute].

27 So he got up and went. And behold, an Ethiopian, a eunuch of great authority under Candace the queen of the Ethiopians, who was in charge of all her treasure, had come to Jerusalem to worship.

28 And he was [now] returning, and sitting in his chariot he was reading the book of the prophet Isaiah.

29 Then the [Holy] Spirit said to Philip, Go forward and join yourself to this chariot.

30 Accordingly Philip, running up to him, heard [the man] reading the prophet Isaiah and asked, Do you really understand what you are reading?

31 And he said, How is it possible for me to do so unless someone explains it to me *and* guides me [in the right way]? And he earnestly requested Philip to come up and sit beside him.

32 Now this was the passage of

putting the Word to work

Do you always understand what you read in Scripture? Acts 8:26–31 reminds us that there is no shame in asking for help to understand; it is actually wise to do so. Always ask the Holy Spirit, your Teacher, to help you understand, and also ask God to place trusted people around you who can help you personally apply God's Word in your life.

b Marvin Vincent, *Word Studies*. c Joseph Thayer, *A Greek-English Lexicon*.

Scripture which he was reading: Like a sheep He was led to the slaughter, and as a lamb before its shearer is dumb, so He opens not His mouth.

33 In His humiliation [d]He was taken away by distressing *and* oppressive judgment *and* justice was denied Him [caused to cease]. Who can describe *or* relate in full [e]the wickedness of His contemporaries (generation)? For His life is taken from the earth *and* [f]a bloody death inflicted upon Him. [Isa. 53:7, 8.]

34 And the eunuch said to Philip, I beg of you, tell me about whom does the prophet say this, about himself or about someone else?

35 Then Philip opened his mouth, and beginning with this portion of Scripture he announced to him the glad tidings (Gospel) of Jesus *and* about Him.

36 And as they continued along on the way, they came to some water, and the eunuch exclaimed, See, [here is] water! What is to hinder my being baptized?

37 [g]*And Philip said, If you believe with all your heart [if you have [f]a conviction, full of joyful trust, that Jesus is the Messiah and accept Him as the Author of your salvation in the kingdom of God, giving Him your obedience, then] you may. And he replied, I do believe that Jesus Christ is the Son of God.*

38 And he ordered that the chariot be stopped; and both Philip and the eunuch went down into the water, and [Philip] baptized him.

39 And when they came up out of the water, the Spirit of the Lord [e]suddenly] caught away Philip; and the eunuch saw him no more, and he went on his way rejoicing.

40 But Philip was found at Azotus, and passing on he preached the good news (Gospel) to all the towns until he reached Caesarea.

9 MEANWHILE SAUL, [e]still drawing his breath hard from threatening and murderous desire against the disciples of the Lord, went to the high priest

2 And requested of him letters to the synagogues at Damascus [authorizing him], so that if he found any men or women belonging to the Way [of life as determined by faith in Jesus Christ], he might bring them bound [with chains] to Jerusalem.

3 Now as he traveled on, he came near to Damascus, and suddenly a light from heaven flashed around him,

4 And he fell to the ground. Then he heard a voice saying to him, Saul, Saul, why are you persecuting Me [harassing, troubling, and molesting Me]?

5 And Saul said, Who are You, Lord? And He said, I am Jesus, Whom you are persecuting. [h]*It is dangerous and it will turn out badly for you to keep kicking against the goad [to offer vain and perilous resistance].*

6 *Trembling and astonished he asked, Lord, what do You desire me to do? The Lord said to him,* But arise and go into the city, and you will be told what you must do.

7 The men who were accompanying him were unable to speak [for terror], hearing the voice but seeing no one.

8 Then Saul got up from the ground, but though his eyes were opened, he could see nothing; so they led him by the hand and brought him into Damascus.

9 And he was unable to see for three days, and he neither ate nor drank [anything].

10 Now there was in Damascus a disciple named Ananias. The Lord said

---

d Adam Clarke, *The Holy Bible with A Commentary.*　**e** Marvin Vincent, *Word Studies.*　**f** Joseph Thayer, *A Greek-English Lexicon.*　**g** Many manuscripts do not contain this verse.　**h** Many manuscripts do not contain this portion of verse 5 and the first part of verse 6.

to him in a vision, Ananias. And he answered, Here am I, Lord.

11 And the Lord said to him, Get up and go to the street called Straight and ask at the house of Judas for a man of Tarsus named Saul, for behold, he is praying [there].

12 And he has seen *in a vision* a man named Ananias enter and lay his hands on him so that he might regain his sight.

13 But Ananias answered, Lord, I have heard many people tell about this man, especially how much evil *and* what great suffering he has brought on Your saints at Jerusalem;

14 Now he is here and has authority from the high priests to put in chains all who call upon Your name.

15 But the Lord said to him, Go, for this man is a chosen instrument of Mine to bear My name before the Gentiles and kings and the descendants of Israel;

16 For I will make clear to him how much he will be afflicted *and* must endure *and* suffer for My name's sake.

17 So Ananias left and went into the house. And he laid his hands on Saul and said, Brother Saul, the Lord Jesus, Who appeared to you along the way by which you came here, has sent me that you may recover your sight and be filled with the Holy Spirit.

18 And instantly something like scales fell from [Saul's] eyes, and he recovered his sight. Then he arose and was baptized,

19 And after he took some food, he was strengthened. For several days [afterward] he remained with the disciples at Damascus.

20 And immediately in the synagogues he proclaimed Jesus, saying, He is the Son of God!

21 And all who heard him were amazed and said, Is not this the very man who harassed *and* overthrew *and* destroyed in Jerusalem those who called upon this Name? And he

has come here for the express purpose of arresting them *and* bringing them in chains before the chief priests.

22 But Saul increased all the more in strength, and continued to confound *and* put to confusion the Jews who lived in Damascus by comparing *and* examining evidence *and* proving that Jesus is the Christ (the Messiah).

putting the Word to work

God can use even the most unexpected people in extraordinary ways to further His kingdom purposes. Is there someone in your life who seems so far away from God that he or she will never become a believer? Be encouraged; God's transforming power changed Paul from a great persecutor of the church to one of the church's greatest advocates (see Acts 9:20–22). Pray for the unsaved people in your life, that they, like Paul, will receive salvation and live for God.

23 After considerable time had elapsed, the Jews conspired to put Saul out of the way by slaying him,

24 But [the knowledge of] their plot was made known to Saul. They were guarding the [city's] gates day and night to kill him,

25 But his disciples took him at night and let him down through the [city's] wall, lowering him in a basket *or* hamper.

26 And when he had arrived in Jerusalem, he tried to associate himself with the disciples; but they were all afraid of him, for they did not believe he really was a disciple.

27 However, Barnabas took him and brought him to the apostles, and he explained to them how along the way he had seen the Lord, Who spoke to him, and how at Damascus he had preached freely *and* confidently *and* courageously in the name of Jesus.

how Paul was filled with the Holy Spirit

Some people say that believers receive everything they will ever get or need when they accept Jesus as Savior. That may be the case with some believers, but certainly not with all. Different people have different experiences. I do not deny that some may be born again and baptized in the Holy Spirit at the same time; but others are not, and Paul was one of them (see Acts 9:17, 18).

Chapter 9 of Acts tells the story of how Paul was saved and filled with the Holy Spirit. As you probably know, Paul was formerly called Saul and had been a zealous but misguided Pharisee (see Acts 23:6). He persecuted Christians and believed that he did God a service by doing so (see Philippians 3:5, 6).

As Saul was on the way to bring believers back to Jerusalem for trial and punishment, a light from heaven shone around him, and he fell to the ground. He heard a voice say, "Saul, Saul, why are you persecuting Me?" (Acts 9:4). Trembling, Saul said, "Lord, what do You desire me to do?" (Acts 9:6). This was the moment of Saul's conversion, the time of his surrender to God. Saul called Jesus "Lord" and then offered his will to Him in surrender. God told him to arise, go into the city, and wait there for further instructions.

Saul was blinded during this experience. For three days he could not see and did not eat or drink anything. In a vision, the Lord spoke to a disciple named Ananias in Damascus and told him where he would find Saul, noting that he would be praying. At the same time, Saul had a vision and saw a man named Ananias enter and place his hands on him so he would regain his sight.

Because Ananias knew of Saul and how much evil he had brought on the saints, he was reluctant to go. But the Lord said to Ananias, "Go," and so he went. The Lord told Ananias that Saul was a chosen instrument of His to bear His name before the Gentiles and the descendants of Israel (see Acts 9:10–15).

In Acts 9:17 we see that Ananias laid his hands on Saul, calling him "Brother Saul." The fact that he called him a brother is another proof of Saul's conversion. Ananias said the Lord sent him to Saul and that he would recover his sight and be "filled with the Holy Spirit." After Saul miraculously and instantly received his sight, he arose and was baptized (see Acts 9:18).

This seems to be quite clear. Saul was converted first; then, three days later, he was filled with the Holy Spirit and baptized in water. If Saul, who became the apostle Paul, needed to be completely filled with the Holy Spirit, then I believe we need to be also. When we are born again (accept Jesus as our Savior) we receive the Holy Spirit, but we need to be completely filled with the Holy Spirit. As I said, this occurs for different people at different times. As a believer in Jesus you have the Holy Spirit, but does the Holy Spirit have you? And, if He does, how much of you does He have? It may be time for a *complete* surrender in your life. Ask God to completely fill you with His Spirit and keep you "ever filled" with the Spirit, as Ephesians 5:18 teaches.

28 So he went in and out [as one] among them at Jerusalem,
29 Preaching freely *and* confidently *and* boldly in the name of the Lord. And he spoke and discussed with *and* disputed against the Hellenists (the Grecian Jews), but they were seeking to slay him.
30 And when the brethren found it out, they brought him down to Caesarea and sent him off to Tarsus [his home town].
31 So the church throughout the whole of Judea and Galilee and Samaria had peace and was edified [growing in wisdom, virtue, and piety] and walking in the respect *and* reverential fear of the Lord and in the consolation *and* exhortation of the Holy Spirit, continued to increase *and* was multiplied.
32 Now as Peter went here and there among them all, he went down also to the saints who lived at Lydda.
33 There he found a man named Aeneas, who had been bedfast for eight years and was paralyzed.
34 And Peter said to him, Aeneas, Jesus Christ (the Messiah) [now] makes you whole. Get up and make your bed! And immediately [Aeneas] stood up.
35 Then all the inhabitants of Lydda and the plain of Sharon saw [what had happened to] him and they turned to the Lord.
36 Now there was at Joppa a disciple [a woman] named [in Aramaic] Tabitha, which [in Greek] means Dorcas. She was abounding in good deeds and acts of charity.
37 About that time she fell sick and died, and when they had cleansed her, they laid [her] in an upper room.
38 Since Lydda was near Joppa [however], the disciples, hearing that Peter was there, sent two men to him begging him, Do come to us without delay.
39 So Peter [immediately] rose and accompanied them. And when he had arrived, they took him to the upper room. All the widows stood around him, crying and displaying undershirts (tunics) and [other] garments such as Dorcas was accustomed to make while she was with them.
40 But Peter put them all out [of the room] and knelt down and prayed; then turning to the body he said, Tabitha, get up! And she opened her eyes; and when she saw Peter, she raised herself *and* sat upright.
41 And he gave her his hand and lifted her up. Then calling in God's people and the widows, he presented her to them alive.
42 And this became known throughout all Joppa, and many came to believe on the Lord [to adhere to and trust in and rely on Him as the Christ and as their Savior].
43 And Peter remained in Joppa for considerable time with a certain Simon a tanner.

10 NOW [living] at Caesarea there was a man whose name was Cornelius, a centurion (captain) of what was known as the Italian Regiment,
2 A devout man who venerated God *and* treated Him with reverential obedience, as did all his household; and he gave much alms to the people and prayed continually to God.
3 About the ninth hour (about 3:00 p.m.) of the day he saw clearly in a vision an angel of God entering and saying to him, Cornelius!
4 And he, gazing intently at him, became frightened and said, What is it, Lord? And the angel said to him, Your prayers and your [generous] gifts to the poor have come up [as a sacrifice] to God *and* have been remembered by Him.
5 And now send men to Joppa and have them call for *and* invite here a

certain Simon whose surname is Peter;

6 He is lodging with Simon a tanner, whose house is by the seaside.

7 When the angel who spoke to him had left, Cornelius called two of his servants and a God-fearing soldier from among his own personal attendants.

8 And having rehearsed everything to them, he sent them to Joppa.

9 The next day as they were still on their way and were approaching the town, Peter went up to the roof of the house to pray, about the sixth hour (noon).

10 But he became very hungry, and wanted something to eat; and while the meal was being prepared a trance came over him,

11 And he saw the sky opened and something like a great sheet lowered by the four corners, descending to the earth.

12 It contained all kinds of quadrupeds *and wild beasts* and creeping things of the earth and birds of the air.

13 And there came a voice to him, saying, Rise up, Peter, kill and eat.

14 But Peter said, No, by no means, Lord; for I have never eaten anything that is common *and* unhallowed or [ceremonially] unclean.

15 And the voice came to him again a second time, What God has cleansed *and* pronounced clean, do not you defile *and* profane by regarding *and* calling common *and* unhallowed or unclean.

16 This occurred three times; then immediately the sheet was taken up to heaven.

17 Now Peter was still inwardly perplexed *and* doubted as to what the vision which he had seen could mean, when [just then] behold the messengers that were sent by Cornelius, who had made inquiry for Simon's house,

stopped *and* stood before the gate.

18 And they called out to inquire whether Simon who was surnamed Peter was staying there.

19 And while Peter was [i]earnestly revolving the vision in his mind *and* meditating on it, the [Holy] Spirit said to him, Behold, three men are looking for you!

20 Get up and go below and accompany them without any doubt [about its legality] *or* any discrimination *or* hesitation, for I have sent them.

21 Then Peter went down to the men and said, I am the man you seek; what is the purpose of your coming?

22 And they said, Cornelius, a centurion (captain) who is just *and* upright *and* in right standing with God, being God-fearing *and* obedient and well spoken of by the whole Jewish nation, has been instructed by a holy angel to send for you to come to his house; and he [i]has received in answer [to prayer] a warning to listen to *and* act upon what you have to say.

23 So Peter invited them in to be his guests [for the night]. The next day he arose and went away with them, and some of the brethren from Joppa accompanied him.

24 And on the following day they entered Caesarea. Cornelius was waiting for *and* expecting them, and he had invited together his relatives and his intimate friends.

25 As Peter arrived, Cornelius met him, and falling down at his feet he made obeisance *and* paid worshipful reverence to him.

26 But Peter raised him up, saying, Get up; I myself am also a man.

27 And as [Peter] spoke with him, he entered the house and found a large group of persons assembled;

28 And he said to them, You yourselves are aware how it is not lawful *or* permissible for a Jew to keep

i Marvin Vincent, *Word Studies.*

company with or to visit or [even] to come near or to speak first to anyone of another nationality, but God has shown and taught me by words that I should not call any human being common or unhallowed or [ceremonially] unclean.

29 Therefore when I was sent for, I came without hesitation or objection or misgivings. So now I ask for what reason you sent for me.

30 And Cornelius said, This is now the fourth day since about this time I was observing the ninth hour (three o'clock in the afternoon) of prayer in my lodging place; [suddenly] a man stood before me in dazzling apparel,

31 And he said, Cornelius, your prayer has been heard and harkened to, and your donations to the poor have been known and ⁱpreserved before God [so that He heeds and is about to help you].

32 Send therefore to Joppa and ask for Simon who is surnamed Peter; he is staying in the house of Simon the tanner by the seaside.

33 So at once I sent for you, and you [being a Jew] have done a kind and ᵏcourteous and handsome thing in coming. Now then, we are all present in the sight of God to listen to all that you have been instructed by the Lord to say.

34 And Peter opened his mouth and said: Most certainly and thoroughly I now perceive and understand that God shows no partiality and is no respecter of persons,

35 But in every nation he who venerates and has a reverential fear for

God, treating Him with worshipful obedience and living uprightly, is acceptable to Him and ¹sure of being received and welcomed [by Him].

36 You know the contents of the message which He sent to Israel, announcing the good news (Gospel) of peace by Jesus Christ, Who is Lord of all—

37 The [same] message which was proclaimed throughout all Judea, starting from Galilee after the baptism preached by John—

38 How God anointed and consecrated Jesus of Nazareth with the [Holy] Spirit and with strength and ability and power; how He went about doing good and, ⁱin particular, curing all who were harassed and oppressed by [the power of] the devil, for God was with Him.

39 And we are [eye and ear] witnesses of everything that He did both in the land of the Jews and in Jerusalem. And [yet] they put Him out of the way (murdered Him) by hanging Him on a tree;

40 But God raised Him to life on the third day and caused Him to be manifest (to be plainly seen),

41 Not by all the people but to us who were chosen (designated) beforehand by God as witnesses, who ate and drank with Him after He arose from the dead.

42 And He charged us to preach to the people and to bear solemn testimony that He is the God-appointed and God-ordained Judge of the living and the dead.

43 To Him all the prophets testify

speak the Word

---

j Joseph Thayer, *A Greek-English Lexicon.*   k Marvin Vincent, *Word Studies.*   l *Webster's New International Dictionary* offers this phrase as a definition of "acceptable."

God has no favorites

Acts 10:34 tells us that God has no favorites and that He is impartial. If we want to love as God loves, then we must not show partiality either.

This does not mean that we cannot have special friends or that we cannot be involved more with certain people than others. It does mean that we cannot treat some people one way and other people differently. We cannot be kind to those who are good friends with us, and not care how we treat those who are of no interest or importance to us.

I know many people with whom I am not interested in having deep personal relationships, because I know that, for one reason or another, it would not be fruitful for either of us. This does not mean these people are bad; it just means a casual relationship between us is better than a close relationship.

All of us need certain things from our close friends, and not all people are able to give it to us. God has what I call "divine connections" for all of us—people who are just right for us.

God has given me several people like that in my life, and I appreciate them very much. But He has also taught me to treat all people with respect, to make them feel valued, to listen to them when they are talking to me, and not to judge them in a critical way.

Our love walk with God is readily seen by how we treat people who cannot do us any good. If we truly want to love as God loves, we will treat everyone impartially, with equal honor and respect.

(bear witness) that everyone who believes in Him [who adheres to, trusts in, and relies on Him, giving himself up to Him] receives forgiveness of sins through His name.

44 While Peter was still speaking these words, the Holy Spirit fell on all who were listening to the message.

45 And the believers from among the circumcised [the Jews] who came with Peter were surprised *and* amazed, because the free gift of the Holy Spirit had been bestowed *and* poured out largely even on the Gentiles.

46 For they heard them talking in [unknown] tongues (languages) and extolling *and* magnifying God. Then Peter asked,

47 Can anyone forbid *or* refuse water

for baptizing these people, seeing that they have received the Holy Spirit just as we have?

48 And he ordered that they be baptized in the name of Jesus Christ (the Messiah). Then they begged him to stay on there for some days.

11 NOW THE apostles (special messengers) and the brethren who were throughout Judea heard [with astonishment] that the Gentiles (heathen) also had received *and* accepted *and* welcomed the Word of God [the doctrine concerning the attainment through Christ of salvation in the kingdom of God].

2 So when Peter went up to

be filled with the Holy Spirit

The Word of God teaches that though some people received the Holy Spirit through the laying on of hands, other times the Holy Spirit was simply poured out upon people. Acts 10:44 says that while Peter preached to the people, the Holy Spirit fell on all who listened. The following verses in Acts 10 tell us that the believers who came with Peter were amazed because they witnessed how freely the gift of the Holy Spirit was poured out on the crowd as evidenced by their talking in unknown tongues.

You can ask God to fill you and baptize you in the Holy Spirit right now, right where you are, by simply praying. Here is a prayer you may want to use:

Father, in Jesus' name, I ask You to baptize me in the Holy Spirit with the evidence of speaking in tongues. Grant me boldness as You did those who were filled on the Day of Pentecost, and give me any other spiritual gifts that You desire me to have.

Now you may want to confirm your faith by saying out loud, "I believe I have received the baptism in the Holy Spirit, and I will never be the same again."

If you have prayed that prayer, wait on God quietly and believe you have received that for which you asked. If you do not believe you have received, then even if you have received, it will be to you as if you have not. You cannot act upon something you do not believe you have.

I want to stress the importance of "believing by faith" that you have received, and not making your decision based on feelings. Believe and keep believing!

Jerusalem, the circumcision party [certain Jewish Christians] found fault with him [separating themselves from him in a hostile spirit, opposing and disputing and contending with him],
3 Saying, Why did you go to uncircumcised men and [even] eat with them?
4 But Peter began [at the beginning] and narrated *and* explained to them step by step [the whole list of events]. He said:
5 I was in the town of Joppa praying, and [falling] in a trance I saw a vision of something coming down from heaven, like a huge sheet lowered by the four corners; and it descended until it came to me.
6 Gazing intently *and* closely at it, I observed in it [a variety of] four-footed animals and wild beasts and reptiles of the earth and birds of the air,
7 And I heard a voice saying to me, Get up, Peter; kill and eat.
8 But I said, No, by no means, Lord; for nothing common *or* unhallowed or [ceremonially] unclean has ever entered my mouth.
9 But the voice answered a second time from heaven, What God has cleansed *and* pronounced clean, do not you defile *and* profane by regarding *or* calling it common *or* unhallowed or unclean.
10 This occurred three times, and

then all was drawn up again into heaven.

11 And right then the three men sent to me from Caesarea arrived at the house in which we were.

12 And the [Holy] Spirit instructed me to accompany them without [the least] hesitation or misgivings or discrimination. So these six brethren accompanied me also, and we went into the man's house.

13 And he related to us how he had seen the angel in his house which stood and said to him, Send men to Joppa and bring Simon who is surnamed Peter;

14 He will give and explain to you a message by means of which you and all your household [as well] will be saved [mfrom eternal death].

15 When I began to speak, the Holy Spirit fell on them just as He did on us at the beginning. [Acts 2:1-4.]

16 Then I recalled the declaration of the Lord, how He said, John indeed baptized with water, but you shall be baptized with (nbe placed in, introduced into) the Holy Spirit.

17 If then God gave to them the same Gift [equally] as He gave to us when we believed in (adhered to, trusted in, and relied on) the Lord Jesus Christ, who was I and what power or authority had I to interfere or hinder or forbid or withstand God?

18 When they heard this, they were quieted and made no further objection. And they glorified God, saying, Then God has also granted to the Gentiles repentance ounto [real] life [after resurrection].

19 Meanwhile those who were scattered because of the persecution that arose in connection with Stephen had traveled as far away as Phoenicia and Cyprus and Antioch, without delivering the message [concerning othe

attainment through Christ of salvation in the kingdom of God] to anyone except Jews.

20 But there were some of them, men of Cyprus and Cyrene, who on returning to Antioch spoke to the Greeks also, proclaiming [to them] the good news (the Gospel) about the Lord Jesus.

21 And the presence of the Lord was with them with power, so that a great number [learned] to believe (to adhere to and trust in and rely on the Lord) and turned and surrendered themselves to Him.

22 The rumors of this came to the ears of the church (assembly) in Jerusalem, and they sent Barnabas to Antioch.

23 When he arrived and saw what grace (favor) God was bestowing upon them, he was full of joy; and he continuously exhorted (warned, urged, and encouraged) them all to cleave unto and remain faithful to and devoted to the Lord with [resolute and steady] purpose of heart.

24 For he was a good man [mgood in himself and also at once for the good and the advantage of other people], full of and controlled by the Holy

m Hermann Cremer, *Biblico-Theological Lexicon.*   **n** Kenneth Wuest, *Word Studies.*   **o** Joseph Thayer, *A Greek-English Lexicon.*

Spirit and full of faith (of his [p]belief that Jesus is the Messiah, through Whom we obtain eternal salvation). And a large company was added to the Lord.

25 [Barnabas] went on to Tarsus to hunt for Saul.

26 And when he had found him, he brought him back to Antioch. For a whole year they assembled together with *and* [q]were guests of the church and instructed a large number of people; and in Antioch the disciples were first called Christians.

27 And during these days prophets (inspired teachers and interpreters of the divine will and purpose) came down from Jerusalem to Antioch.

28 And one of them named Agabus stood up and prophesied through the [Holy] Spirit that a great *and* severe famine would come upon the whole world. And this did occur during the reign of Claudius.

29 So the disciples resolved to send relief, each according to his individual ability [in proportion as he had prospered], to the brethren who lived in Judea.

30 And so they did, sending [their contributions] to the elders by the hand of Barnabas and Saul.

12 ABOUT THAT time Herod the king stretched forth his hands to afflict *and* oppress *and* torment some who belonged to the church (assembly).

2 And he killed James the brother of John with a sword;

3 And when he saw that it was pleasing to the Jews, he proceeded further and arrested Peter also. This was during the days of Unleavened Bread [the Passover week].

4 And when he had seized [Peter], he put him in prison and delivered him to four squads of soldiers of four each to guard him, purposing after the Passover to bring him forth to the people.

5 So Peter was kept in prison, but fervent prayer for him was persistently made to God by the church (assembly).

6 The very night before Herod was about to bring him forth, Peter was sleeping between two soldiers, fastened with two chains, and sentries before the door were guarding the prison.

7 And suddenly an angel of the Lord appeared [standing beside him], and a light shone in the place where he was. And the angel gently smote Peter on the side and awakened him, saying, Get up quickly! And the chains fell off his hands.

8 And the angel said to him, Tighten your belt and bind on your sandals. And he did so. And he said to him, Wrap your outer garment around you and follow me.

9 And [Peter] went out [along] following him, and he was not conscious that what was apparently being done by the angel was real, but thought he was seeing a vision.

10 When they had passed through the first guard and the second, they came to the iron gate which leads into the city. Of its own accord [the gate] swung open, and they went out and passed on through one street; and at once the angel left him.

11 Then Peter came to himself and said, Now I really know *and* am sure that the Lord has sent His angel and delivered me from the hand of Herod and from all that the Jewish people were expecting [to do to me].

12 When he, at a glance, became aware of this [[r]comprehending all the elements of the case], he went to the

p Joseph Thayer, *A Greek-English Lexicon.* **q** Alternate translation. **r** Marvin Vincent, *Word Studies.*

house of Mary the mother of John, whose surname was Mark, where a large number were assembled together and were praying.

13 And when he knocked at the gate of the porch, a maid named Rhoda came to answer.

14 And recognizing Peter's voice, in her joy she failed to open the gate, but ran in and told the people that Peter was standing before the porch gate.

15 They said to her, You are crazy! But she persistently *and* strongly *and* confidently affirmed that it was the truth. They said, It is his angel!

16 But meanwhile Peter continued knocking, and when they opened the gate and saw him, they were amazed.

17 But motioning to them with his hand to keep quiet *and* listen, he related to them how the Lord had delivered him out of the prison. And he said, Report all this to James [the Less] and to the brethren. Then he left and went to some other place.

18 Now as soon as it was day, there was no small disturbance among the soldiers over what had become of Peter.

19 And when Herod had looked for him and could not find him, he placed the guards on trial and commanded that they should be led away [to execution]. Then [Herod] went down from Judea to Caesarea and stayed on there.

20 Now [Herod] cherished bitter animosity *and* hostility for the people of Tyre and Sidon; and [their deputies] came to him in a united body, and having made Blastus the king's chamberlain their friend, they asked for peace, because their country was nourished by *and* depended on the king's [country] for food.

21 On an appointed day Herod arrayed himself in his royal robes, took his seat upon [his] throne, and addressed an oration to them.

22 And the assembled people shouted, It is the voice of a god, and not of a man!

23 And at once an angel of the Lord smote him *and* cut him down, because he did not give God the glory (the preeminence and kingly majesty that belong to Him as the supreme Ruler); and he was eaten by worms and died.

24 But the Word of the Lord [concerning the attainment through Christ of salvation in the kingdom of God] continued to grow and spread.

25 And Barnabas and Saul came back from Jerusalem when they had completed their mission, bringing with them John whose surname was Mark. [Acts 11:28-30.]

13 NOW IN the church (assembly) at Antioch there were prophets (inspired interpreters of the will and purposes of God) and teachers: Barnabas, Symeon who was called Niger [Black], Lucius of Cyrene, Manaen a member of the court of Herod the tetrarch, and Saul.

2 While they were worshiping the Lord and fasting, the Holy Spirit said, Separate now for Me Barnabas and Saul for the work to which I have called them.

3 Then after fasting and praying, they put their hands on them and sent them away.

4 So then, being sent out by the Holy Spirit, they went down to Seleucia, and from [that port] they sailed away to Cyprus.

5 When they arrived at Salamis, they preached the Word of God [concerning the attainment through Christ of salvation in the kingdom of God] in the synagogues of the Jews. And they had John [Mark] as an attendant to assist them.

6 When they had passed through the entire island of Cyprus as far as

Paphos, they came upon a certain Jewish wizard *or* sorcerer, a false prophet named Bar-Jesus.

7 He was closely associated with the proconsul, Sergius Paulus, who was an intelligent *and* sensible man of sound understanding; he summoned to him Barnabas and Saul and sought to hear the Word of God [concerning salvation in the kingdom of God attained through Christ].

8 But Elymas ˢthe wise man—for that is the translation of his name [ᵗwhich he had given himself]— opposed them, seeking to keep the proconsul from accepting the faith.

9 But Saul, who is also called Paul, filled with *and* controlled by the Holy Spirit, looked steadily at [Elymas]

10 And said, You master in every form of deception *and* recklessness, unscrupulousness, *and* wickedness, you son of the devil, you enemy of everything that is upright *and* good, will you never stop perverting *and* making crooked the straight paths of the Lord *and* plotting against His saving purposes? [Hos. 14:9.]

11 And now, behold, the hand of the Lord is upon you, and you will be blind, [so blind that you will be] unable to see the sun for a time. Instantly there fell upon him a mist and a darkness, and he groped about seeking persons who would lead him by the hand.

12 Then the proconsul believed (became a Christian) when he saw what had occurred, for he was astonished *and* deeply touched at the teaching concerning the Lord *and* from Him.

13 Now Paul and his companions sailed from Paphos and came to Perga in Pamphylia. And John [Mark] separated himself from them and went back to Jerusalem,

14 But they [themselves] came on from Perga and arrived at Antioch in Pisidia. And on the Sabbath day they went into the synagogue there and sat down.

15 After the reading of the Law and the Prophets, the leaders [of the worship] of the synagogue sent to them saying, Brethren, if you have any word of exhortation *or* consolation *or* encouragement for the people, say it.

16 So Paul arose, and motioning with his hand said, Men of Israel and you who reverence *and* fear God, listen!

17 The God of this people Israel selected our forefathers and made this people great *and* important during their stay in the land of Egypt, and then with an uplifted arm He led them out from there. [Exod. 6:1, 6.]

18 And for about forty years ᵘ*like a fatherly nurse* He cared for them in the wilderness *and* endured their behavior. [Deut. 1:31.]

19 When He had destroyed seven nations in the land of Canaan, He gave them [the Hebrews] their land as an inheritance [distributing it to them by lot; all of which took] about 450 years. [Deut. 7:1; Josh. 14:1.]

20 After that, He gave them judges until the prophet Samuel.

21 Then they asked for a king; and God gave them Saul son of Kish, a man of the tribe of Benjamin, for forty years.

22 And when He had deposed him, He raised up David to be their king; of him He bore witness and said, I have found David son of Jesse a man after My own heart, who will do all My will *and* carry out My program fully. [I Sam. 13:14; Ps. 89:20; Isa. 44:28.]

23 Of this man's descendants God has brought to Israel a Savior [in the person of Jesus], according to His promise.

---

s G. Abbott-Smith, *Manual Greek Lexicon.* **t** Henry Alford, *The Greek New Testament, with Notes.* **u** Some ancient manuscripts so read.

24 Before His coming John had [already] preached baptism of repentance to all the people of Israel.

25 And as John was ending his course, he asked, What *or* *who* do you secretly think that I am? I am not He [the Christ. No], but note that after me One is coming, the sandals of Whose feet I am not worthy to untie!

26 Brethren, sons of the family of Abraham, and all those others among you who reverence *and* fear God, to us has been sent the message of this salvation [the salvation obtained through Jesus Christ]. [Ps. 107:20.]

27 For those who dwell in Jerusalem and their rulers, because they did not know *or* recognize Him or understand the utterances of the prophets which are read every Sabbath, have actually fulfilled these very predictions by condemning *and* sentencing [Him].

28 And although they could find no cause deserving death with which to charge Him, yet they asked Pilate to have Him executed *and* put out of the way.

29 And when they had finished *and* fulfilled everything that was written about Him, they took Him down from the tree and laid Him in a tomb.

30 But God raised Him from the dead.

31 And for many days He appeared to those who came up with Him from Galilee to Jerusalem, and they are His witnesses to the people.

32 So now we are bringing you the good news (Gospel) that what God promised to our forefathers,

33 This He has *completely fulfilled for us, their children, by raising up Jesus, as it is written in the second psalm, You are My Son; today I have begotten You [*caused You to arise, to be born; *formally shown You to

be the Messiah by the resurrection]. [Ps. 2:7.]

34 And as to His having raised Him from among the dead, now no more to return to [undergo] putrefaction *and* dissolution [of the grave], He spoke in this way, I will fulfill *and* give to you the holy and sure mercy *and* blessings [that were promised and assured] to David. [Isa. 55:3.]

35 For this reason He says also in another psalm, You will not allow Your Holy One to see corruption [to undergo putrefaction and dissolution of the grave]. [Ps. 16:10.]

36 For David, after he had served God's will *and* purpose *and* counsel in his own generation, fell asleep [*in death] and was buried among his forefathers, and he did see corruption *and* undergo putrefaction *and* dissolution [of the grave].

37 But He Whom God raised up [to life] saw no corruption [did not experience putrefaction and dissolution of the grave].

38 So let it be clearly known *and* understood by you, brethren, that through this Man forgiveness *and* removal of sins is now proclaimed to you;

39 And that through Him everyone who believes [who *acknowledges Jesus as his Savior and devotes himself to Him] is absolved (cleared and freed) from every charge from which he could not be justified *and* freed by the Law of Moses *and* given right standing with God.

40 Take care, therefore, lest there come upon you what is spoken in the prophets:

41 Look, you scoffers *and* scorners, and marvel and perish *and* vanish away; for I am doing a deed in your days, a deed which you will never have confidence in *or* believe,

v Some manuscripts so read. **w** Marvin Vincent, *Word Studies*. **x** Joseph Thayer, *A Greek-English Lexicon.* **y** Hermann Cremer, *Biblico-Theological Lexicon.*

[even] if someone [²clearly describing it in detail] declares it to you. [Hab. 1:5.]

42 As they [Paul and Barnabas] went out [of the synagogue], the people earnestly begged that these things might be told to them [further] the next Sabbath.

43 And when the congregation of the synagogue dispersed, many of the Jews and the devout converts to Judaism followed Paul and Barnabas, who talked to them and urged them to continue [to trust themselves to and to stand fast] in the grace (the unmerited favor and blessing) of God.

44 The next Sabbath almost the entire city gathered together to hear the Word of God [concerning ªthe attainment through Christ of salvation in the kingdom of God].

45 But when the Jews saw the crowds, filled with envy *and* jealousy they contradicted what was said by Paul and talked abusively [reviling and slandering him].

46 And Paul and Barnabas spoke out plainly *and* boldly, saying, It was necessary that God's message [concerning ªsalvation through Christ] should be spoken to you first. But since you thrust it from you, you pass this judgment on yourselves that you are unworthy of eternal life *and* out of your own mouth you will be judged. [Now] behold, we turn to the Gentiles (the heathen).

47 For so the Lord has charged us, saying, I have set you to be a light for the Gentiles (the heathen), that you may bring [eternal] salvation to the uttermost parts of the earth. [Isa. 49:6.]

48 And when the Gentiles heard this, they rejoiced and glorified (praised and gave thanks for) the Word of God; and as many as were destined (appointed and ordained) to eternal life believed (adhered to, trusted in, and relied on Jesus as the Christ and their Savior).

49 And so the Word of the Lord [concerning eternal salvation through Christ] scattered *and* spread throughout the whole region.

50 But the Jews stirred up the devout women of high rank and the outstanding men of the town, and instigated persecution against Paul and Barnabas and drove them out of their boundaries.

51 But [the apostles] shook off the dust from their feet against them and went to Iconium.

52 And the disciples were continually filled [throughout their souls] with joy and the Holy Spirit.

14 NOW AT Iconium [also Paul and Barnabas] went into the Jewish synagogue together and spoke with such power that a great number both of Jews and of Greeks believed (became Christians);

2 But the unbelieving Jews [who rejected their message] aroused the Gentiles and embittered their minds against the brethren.

3 So [Paul and Barnabas] stayed on there for a long time, speaking freely *and* fearlessly *and* boldly in the Lord, Who continued to bear testimony to the Word of His grace, granting signs and wonders to be performed by their hands.

4 But the residents of the town were divided, some siding with the Jews and some with the apostles.

5 When there was an attempt both on the part of the Gentiles and the Jews together with their rulers, to insult *and* abuse *and* molest [Paul and Barnabas] and to stone them,

6 They, aware of the situation, made their escape to Lystra and

---

z Marvin Vincent, *Word Studies*.   **a** Joseph Thayer, *A Greek-English Lexicon*.

Derbe, cities of Lycaonia, and the neighboring districts;

7 And there they continued to preach the glad tidings (Gospel).

8 Now at Lystra a man sat who found it impossible to use his feet, for he was a cripple from birth and had never walked.

9 He was listening to Paul as he talked, and [Paul] gazing intently at him and observing that he had faith to be healed,

10 Shouted at him, saying, Stand erect on your feet! And he leaped up and walked.

11 And the crowds, when they saw what Paul had done, lifted up their voices, shouting in the Lycaonian language, The gods have come down to us in human form!

12 They called Barnabas Zeus, and they called Paul, because he led in the discourse, Hermes [god of speech].

13 And the priest of Zeus, whose [temple] was at the entrance of the town, brought bulls and garlands to the [city's] gates and wanted to join the people in offering sacrifice.

14 But when the apostles Barnabas and Paul heard of it, they tore their clothing and dashed out among the crowd, shouting,

15 Men, why are you doing this? We also are [only] human beings, of nature like your own, and we bring you the good news (Gospel) that you should turn away from these foolish *and* vain things to the living God, Who made the heaven and the earth and the sea and everything that they contain. [Exod. 20:11; Ps. 146:6.]

16 In generations past He permitted all the nations to walk in their own ways;

17 Yet He did not neglect to leave some witness of Himself, for He did you good *and* [showed you] kindness and gave you rains from heaven and fruitful seasons, satisfying your hearts with nourishment and happiness.

18 Even in [the light of] these words they with difficulty prevented the people from offering sacrifice to them.

19 But some Jews arrived there from Antioch and Iconium; and having persuaded the people *and* won them over, they stoned Paul and [ᵇafterward] dragged him out of the town, thinking that he was dead.

20 But the disciples formed a circle about him, and he got up and went back into the town; and on the morrow he went on with Barnabas to Derbe.

21 When they had preached the good news (Gospel) to that town and made disciples of many of the people, they went back to Lystra and Iconium and Antioch,

22 Establishing *and* strengthening the souls *and* the hearts of the disciples, urging *and* warning *and* encouraging them to stand firm in the faith, and [telling them] that it is through many hardships *and* tribulations we must enter the kingdom of God.

23 And when they had appointed *and* ordained elders for them in each church with prayer and fasting, they committed them to the Lord in Whom they had come to believe [being full of joyful trust that He is the Christ, the Messiah].

24 Then they went through Pisidia and arrived at Pamphylia.

25 And when they had spoken the Word in Perga [the doctrine concerning the attainment through Christ of salvation in the kingdom of God], they went down to Attalia;

26 And from there they sailed back to Antioch, where they had [first] been commended to the grace of God for the work which they had [now] completed.

27 Arriving there, they gathered the

b Henry Alford, *The Greek New Testament.*

church together and declared all that God had accomplished with them and how He had opened to the Gentiles a door of faith [in Jesus as the Messiah, through Whom we obtain salvation in the kingdom of God].
28 And there they stayed no little time with the disciples.

15 BUT SOME men came down from Judea and were instructing the brethren, Unless you are circumcised in accordance with the Mosaic custom, you cannot be saved. [Gen. 17:9-14.]
2 And when Paul and Barnabas had no small disagreement and discussion with them, it was decided that Paul and Barnabas and some of the others of their number should go up to Jerusalem [and confer] with the apostles (special messengers) and the elders about this matter.
3 So, being ᶜfitted out *and* sent on their way by the church, they went through both Phoenicia and Samaria telling of the conversion of the Gentiles (the heathen), and they caused great rejoicing among all the brethren.
4 When they arrived in Jerusalem, they were heartily welcomed by the church and the apostles and the elders, and they told them all that God had accomplished through them.
5 But some who believed [who ᶜacknowledged Jesus as their Savior and devoted themselves to Him] belonged to the sect of the Pharisees, and they rose up and said, It is necessary to circumcise [the Gentile converts] and to

charge them to obey the Law of Moses.
6 The apostles and the elders were assembled together to look into *and* consider this matter.
7 And after there had been a long debate, Peter got up and said to them, Brethren, you know that quite a while ago God made a choice *or* selection from among you, that by my mouth the Gentiles should hear the message of the Gospel [concerning the ᶜattainment through Christ of salvation in the kingdom of God] and believe (credit and place their confidence in it).
8 And God, Who is acquainted with *and* understands the heart, bore witness to them, giving them the Holy Spirit as He also did to us;
9 And He made no difference between us and them, but cleansed their hearts by faith (ᶜby a strong and welcome conviction that Jesus is the Messiah, through Whom we obtain eternal salvation in the kingdom of God).
10 Now then, why do you try to test God by putting a yoke on the necks of the disciples, such as neither our forefathers nor we [ourselves] were able to endure?
11 But we believe that we are saved through the grace (the undeserved favor and mercy) of the Lord Jesus, just as they [are].
12 Then the whole assembly remained silent, and they listened [attentively] as Barnabas and Paul rehearsed what signs and wonders God had performed through them among the Gentiles.

speak the Word

c Joseph Thayer, *A Greek-English Lexicon.*

13 When they had finished talking, James replied, Brethren, listen to me. **14** Simeon [Peter] has rehearsed how God first visited the Gentiles, to take out of them a people [to bear and honor] His name.
15 And with this the predictions of the prophets agree, as it is written,
16 After this I will come back, and will rebuild the house of David, which has fallen; I will rebuild its [very] ruins, and I will set it up again,
17 So that the rest of men may seek the Lord, and all the Gentiles upon whom My name has been invoked,
18 Says the Lord, Who has been making these things known from the beginning of the world. [Isa. 45:21; Jer. 12:15; Amos 9:11, 12.]
19 Therefore it is my opinion that we should not put obstacles in the way of *and* annoy *and* disturb those of the Gentiles who turn to God,
20 But we should send word to them in writing to abstain from *and* avoid anything that has been polluted by being offered to idols, and all sexual impurity, and [eating meat of animals] that have been strangled, and [tasting of] blood.
21 For from ancient generations Moses has had his preachers in every town, for he is read [aloud] every Sabbath in the synagogues.
22 Then the apostles and the elders, together with the whole church, resolved to select men from among their number and send them to Antioch with Paul and Barnabas. They chose Judas called Barsabbas, and Silas, [both] leading men among the brethren, *and* sent them.
23 With [them they sent] the following letter: The brethren, both the apostles and the elders, to the brethren who are of the Gentiles in Antioch and Syria and Cilicia, greetings:
24 As we have heard that some persons from our number have disturbed you with their teaching, unsettling your minds *and* [d]throwing you into confusion, although we gave them no express orders *or* instructions [on the points in question],
25 It has been resolved by us in assembly to select men and send them [as messengers] to you with our beloved Barnabas and Paul,
26 Men who have hazarded their lives for the sake of our Lord Jesus Christ.
27 So we have sent Judas and Silas, who themselves will bring you the same message by word of mouth.
28 For it has seemed good to the Holy Spirit and to us not to lay upon you any greater burden than these indispensable requirements:
29 That you abstain from what has been sacrificed to idols and from [tasting] blood and from [eating the meat of animals] that have been strangled and from sexual impurity. If you keep yourselves from these things, you will do well. Farewell [be strong]!
30 So when [the messengers] were sent off, they went down to Antioch; and having assembled the congregation, they delivered the letter.
31 And when they read it, the people rejoiced at the consolation *and* encouragement [it brought them].
32 And Judas and Silas, who were themselves prophets (inspired interpreters of the will and purposes of God), urged *and* warned *and* consoled *and* encouraged the brethren with many words and strengthened them.
33 And after spending some time there, they were sent back by the brethren with [the greeting] peace to those who had sent them.
34 *However, Silas decided to stay on there.*
35 But Paul and Barnabas remained

d Marvin Vincent, *Word Studies*.

in Antioch and with many others also continued teaching and proclaiming the good news, the Word of the Lord [concerning the ᵉattainment through Christ of eternal salvation in God's kingdom].

36 And after some time Paul said to Barnabas, Come, let us go back and again visit *and* help *and* minister to the brethren in every town where we made known the message of the Lord, and see how they are getting along.

37 Now Barnabas wanted to take with them John called Mark [his near relative].

38 But Paul did not think it best to have along with them the one who had quit *and* deserted them in Pamphylia and had not gone on with them to the work.

39 And there followed a sharp disagreement between them, so that they separated from each other, and Barnabas took Mark with him and sailed away to Cyprus.

40 But Paul selected Silas and set out, being commended by the brethren to the grace (the favor and mercy) of the Lord.

41 And he passed through Syria and Cilicia, establishing *and* strengthening the churches.

16 AND [Paul] went down to Derbe and also to Lystra. A disciple named Timothy was there, the son of a Jewish woman who was a believer [she had become ᵉconvinced that Jesus is the Messiah and the Author of eternal salvation, and yielded obedience to Him]; but [Timothy's] father was a Greek.

2 He [Timothy] had a good reputation among the brethren at Lystra and Iconium.

3 Paul desired Timothy to go with him [ᶠas a missionary]; and he took him and circumcised him because of

the Jews that were in those places, all of whom knew that his father was a Greek.

4 As they went on their way from town to town, they delivered over [to the assemblies] for their observance the regulations decided upon by the apostles and elders who were at Jerusalem.

5 So the churches were strengthened *and* made firm in the faith, and they increased in number day after day.

6 And Paul and Silas passed through the territory of Phrygia and Galatia, having been forbidden by the Holy Spirit to proclaim the Word in [the province of] Asia.

7 And when they had come opposite Mysia, they tried to go into Bithynia, but the Spirit of Jesus did not permit them.

8 So passing by Mysia, they went down to Troas.

9 [There] a vision appeared to Paul in the night: a man from Macedonia stood pleading with him and saying, Come over to Macedonia and help us!

10 And when he had seen the vision, we [including Luke] at once endeavored to go on into Macedonia, confidently inferring that God had called us to proclaim the glad tidings (Gospel) to them.

11 Therefore, setting sail from Troas, we came in a direct course to Samothrace, and the next day went on to Neapolis.

12 And from there [we came] to Philippi, which is the chief city of the district of Macedonia and a [Roman] colony. We stayed on in this place some days;

13 And on the Sabbath day we went outside the [city's] gate to the bank of the river where we supposed there was an [accustomed] place of prayer, and we sat down and addressed the women who had assembled there.

e Joseph Thayer, *A Greek-English Lexicon.*   **f** Marvin Vincent, *Word Studies.*

open your heart

In the city of Philippi, where God directed Paul and those traveling with him, a group of women gathered together on the bank of a river for prayer (see Acts 16:12–14). Paul began speaking to these women, telling them some things they never heard before. They were accustomed to living under the Jewish Law, and Paul delivered a message of grace. One of the women named Lydia "opened her heart" to receive what Paul said (Acts 16:14).

We, like Lydia, need to open our hearts to the things of God. The reason an open heart is so important is that without it, we will not listen to new things—not strange, off-the-wall things, but different things God wants to do in our lives. It is amazing the great promises in the Bible we refuse to believe because they are not part of what we have been taught in the past. Why can't our believing be progressive? Why can't we accept that there may be a few things we do not know?

I am not saying we should be so open that we believe anything we are told or that the devil wants to dump on us, but I am saying we should avoid being so narrow-minded that we reject great, new things from God. We should not be afraid to listen to what is being said and check it out for ourselves by reading the Bible and talking to God about it to see if it is really true.

We are supposed to be single-minded, not narrow-minded. I get concerned about people who think there is only one way to do things, and it is their way. People like that are very difficult to work with. They often have so much pride they will not listen to anything that anybody tells them. In contrast, a humble believer's heart is open to the truth.

We need to have open hearts. God's Word and our hearts will affirm truth to us when we hear truth. Our minds may be closed, but our hearts must be open to God to allow Him to do new things in our everyday lives.

14 One of those who listened to us was a woman named Lydia, from the city of Thyatira, a dealer in fabrics dyed in purple. She was [already] a worshiper of God, and the Lord opened her heart to pay attention to what was said by Paul.

15 And when she was baptized along with her household, she earnestly entreated us, saying, If in your opinion I am one really convinced [that Jesus is the Messiah and the Author of salvation] *and* that I will be faithful to the Lord, come to my house and stay. And she induced us [to do it].

16 As we were on our way to the place of prayer, we were met by a slave girl who was possessed by a spirit of divination [claiming to foretell future events and to discover hidden knowledge], and she brought her owners much gain by her fortunetelling.

17 She kept following Paul and [the rest of] us, shouting loudly, These men are the servants of the Most High God! They announce to you the way of salvation!

18 And she did this for many days. Then Paul, being sorely annoyed *and* worn out, turned and said to the

spirit within her, I charge you in the name of Jesus Christ to come out of her! And it came out that very ᵍmoment.

19 But when her owners discovered that their hope of profit was gone, they caught hold of Paul and Silas and dragged them before the authorities in the forum (marketplace), [where trials are held].

20 And when they had brought them before the magistrates, they declared, These fellows are Jews and they are throwing our city into great confusion.

21 They encourage the practice of customs which it is unlawful for us Romans to accept or observe!

22 The crowd [also] joined in the attack upon them, and the rulers tore the clothes off of them and commanded that they be beaten with rods.

23 And when they had struck them with many blows, they threw them into prison, charging the jailer to keep them safely.

24 He, having received [so strict a] charge, put them into the inner prison (the dungeon) and fastened their feet in the stocks.

25 But about midnight, as Paul and Silas were praying and singing hymns of praise to God, and the [other] prisoners were listening to them,

26 Suddenly there was a great earthquake, so that the very foundations of the prison were shaken; and at once all the doors were opened and everyone's shackles were unfastened.

27 When the jailer, startled out of his sleep, saw that the prison doors were open, he drew his sword and was on the point of killing himself, because he supposed that the prisoners had escaped.

28 But Paul shouted, Do not harm yourself, for we are all here!

29 Then [the jailer] called for lights

life point

Acts 16:22–26 relates an incident in the lives of Paul and Silas and how their joy preceded and precipitated a "sudden" breakthrough.

These men of God exercised the power of joy in the midst of very difficult circumstances. Their clothes were torn off, they were beaten with rods and thrown into jail, and yet they did nothing wrong. In that depressing situation, they expressed a supernatural joy evidenced by their praying and singing. Their joy could not have been a natural response, because there was nothing in the natural to be joyful about.

As a result of seeing firsthand the supernatural joy of Paul and Silas, the jailer was saved (see Acts 16:27–34). I believe more people in the world will receive the salvation that waits for them when Christians truly begin to express the joy of their salvation.

and rushed in, and trembling *and* terrified he fell down before Paul and Silas.

30 And he brought them out [of the dungeon] and said, Men, what is it necessary for me to do that I may be saved?

31 And they answered, Believe in the Lord Jesus *Christ* [ʰgive yourself up to Him, ⁱtake yourself out of your own keeping and entrust yourself into His keeping] and you will be saved, [and this applies both to] you and your household as well.

32 And they declared the Word of the Lord [the doctrine concerning the ʰattainment through Christ of eternal salvation in the kingdom of God] to him and to all who were in his house.

g James Moulton and George Milligan, *The Vocabulary.* **h** Joseph Thayer, *A Greek-English Lexicon.* **i** Kenneth Wuest, *Word Studies.*

33 And he took them the same hour of the night and ʲbathed [them because of their bloody] wounds, and he was baptized immediately and all [the members of] his [household].

34 Then he took them up into his house and set food before them; and he ᵏleaped much for joy *and* exulted with all his family that he believed in God [accepting and joyously welcoming what He had made known through Christ].

35 But when it was day, the magistrates sent policemen, saying, Release those fellows *and* let them go.

36 And the jailer repeated the words to Paul, saying, The magistrates have sent to release you *and* let you go; now therefore come out and go in peace.

37 But Paul answered them, They have beaten us openly *and* publicly, without a trial *and* uncondemned, men who are Roman citizens, and have thrown us into prison; and do they now thrust us out secretly? No, indeed! Let them come here themselves and conduct us out!

38 The police reported this message to the magistrates, and they were frightened when they heard that the prisoners were Roman citizens;

39 So they came themselves and [striving to appease them by entreaty] apologized to them. And they brought them out and asked them to leave the city.

40 So [Paul and Silas] left the prison and went to Lydia's house; and when they had seen the brethren, they warned *and* urged *and* consoled *and* encouraged them and departed.

17 NOW AFTER [Paul and Silas] had passed through Amphipolis and Apollonia, they came to Thessalonica, where there was a synagogue of the Jews.

2 And Paul entered, as he usually did, and for three Sabbaths he reasoned *and* argued with them from the Scriptures,

3 Explaining [them] *and* [quoting passages] setting forth *and* proving that it was necessary for the Christ to suffer and to rise from the dead, and saying, This Jesus, Whom I proclaim to you, is the Christ (the Messiah).

4 And some of them [accordingly] were induced to believe and associated themselves with Paul and Silas, as did a great number of the devout Greeks and not a few of the leading women.

5 But the unbelieving Jews were aroused to jealousy, and, getting hold of some wicked men (ruffians and rascals) and loungers in the marketplace, they gathered together a mob, set the town in an uproar, and attacked the house of Jason, seeking to bring [Paul and Silas] out to the people.

6 But when they failed to find them, they dragged Jason and some of the brethren before the city authorities, crying, These men who have turned the world upside down have come here also,

7 And Jason has received them to his house *and* privately protected them! And they are all ignoring *and* acting contrary to the decrees of Caesar, [actually] asserting that there is another king, one Jesus!

8 And both the crowd and the city authorities, on hearing this, were irritated (stirred up and troubled).

9 And when they had taken security [bail] from Jason and the others, they let them go.

10 Now the brethren at once sent Paul and Silas away by night to Beroea; and when they arrived, they entered the synagogue of the Jews.

---

j Marvin Vincent, *Word Studies.* **k** Robert Young, *Analytical Concordance to the Bible.*

11 Now these [Jews] were better disposed *and* more noble than those in Thessalonica, for they were entirely ready *and* accepted *and* welcomed the message ['concerning the attainment through Christ of eternal salvation in the kingdom of God] with inclination of mind *and* eagerness, searching *and* examining the Scriptures daily to see if these things were so.

putting the Word to work

Receiving good teaching from pastors, teachers, and ministers is a blessing, but it is equally important to study Scripture for yourself (see Acts 17:10, 11). Do you regularly set aside time each day to read the Word of God? If not, ask Him to help you have a hunger to read and study His Word, and make every effort to do so daily.

12 Many of them therefore became believers, together with not a few prominent Greeks, women as well as men. **13** But when the Jews of Thessalonica learned that the Word of God ['concerning the attainment through Christ of eternal salvation in the kingdom of God] was also preached by Paul at Beroea, they came there too, disturbing *and* inciting the masses. **14** At once the brethren sent Paul off on his way to the sea, but Silas and Timothy remained behind. **15** Those who escorted Paul brought him as far as Athens; and receiving instructions for Silas and Timothy that they should come to him as soon as possible, they departed. **16** Now while Paul was awaiting them at Athens, his spirit was grieved *and* roused to anger as he saw that the city was full of idols.

17 So he reasoned *and* argued in the synagogue with the Jews and those who worshiped there, and in the marketplace [where assemblies are held] day after day with any who chanced to be there. **18** And some also of the Epicurean and Stoic philosophers encountered him *and* began to engage in discussion. And some said, What is this babbler with his scrap-heap learning trying to say? Others said, He seems to be an announcer of foreign deities—because he preached Jesus and the resurrection. **19** And they took hold of him and brought him to the ᵐAreopagus [Mars Hill meeting place], saying, May we know what this novel (unheard of and unprecedented) teaching is which you are openly declaring? **20** For you set forth some startling things, foreign *and* strange to our ears; we wish to know therefore just what these things mean— **21** For the Athenians, all of them, and the foreign residents *and* visitors among them spent all their leisure time in nothing except telling or hearing something newer than the last— **22** So Paul, standing in the center of the Areopagus [Mars Hill meeting place], said: Men of Athens, I perceive in every way [on every hand and with every turn I make] that you are most religious *or* very reverent to demons. **23** For as I passed along and carefully observed your objects of worship, I came also upon an altar with this inscription, To the unknown god. Now what you are already worshiping as unknown, this I set forth to you. **24** The God Who produced *and* formed the world and all things in it,

l Joseph Thayer, *A Greek-English Lexicon*. m Many modern interpreters note that the Areopagus may also have been a reference to the Council of the Areopagus, the supreme court of Athens, custodians of teachings that introduced new religions and foreign gods. See also Acts 17:34.

being Lord of heaven and earth, does not dwell in handmade shrines.

25 Neither is He served by human hands, as though He lacked anything, for it is He Himself Whogives life and breath and all things to all [people]. [Isa. 42:5.]

26 And He made from one [common origin, one source, one blood] all nations of men to settle on the face of the earth, having definitely determined [their] allotted periods of time and the fixed boundaries of their habitation (their settlements, lands, and abodes),

27 So that they should seek God, in the hope that they might feel after Him and find Him, although He is not far from each one of us.

28 For in Him we live and move and have our being; as even some of your [own] poets have said, For we are also His offspring.

29 Since then we are God's offspring, we ought not to suppose that Deity (the Godhead) is like gold or silver or stone, [of the nature of] a representation by human art and imagination, or anything constructed or invented.

30 Such [former] ages of ignorance God, it is true, ignored and allowed to pass unnoticed; but now He charges all people everywhere to repent ([n]to change their minds for the better and heartily to amend their ways, with abhorrence of their past sins),

31 Because He has fixed a day when He will judge the world righteously (justly) by a Man Whom He has destined and appointed for that task, and He has made this credible and given conviction and assurance and evidence to everyone by raising Him from the dead. [Ps. 9:8; 96:13; 98:9.]

32 Now when they had heard [that there had been] a resurrection from the dead, some scoffed; but others said, We will hear you again about this matter.

33 So Paul went out from among them.

34 But some men were on his side and joined him and believed (became Christians); among them were Dionysius, a judge of the Areopagus, and a woman named Damaris, and some others with them.

18 AFTER THIS [Paul] departed from Athens and went to Corinth.

2   There he met a Jew named Aquila, a native of Pontus, recently arrived from Italy with Priscilla his wife, due to the fact that Claudius had issued an edict that all the Jews were to leave Rome. And [Paul] went to see them,

3   And because he was of the same occupation, he stayed with them; and they worked [together], for they were tentmakers by trade.

4   But he discoursed and argued in the synagogue every Sabbath and won over [both] Jews and Greeks.

5   By the time Silas and Timothy arrived from Macedonia, Paul was completely engrossed with preaching, earnestly arguing and testifying to the Jews that Jesus [is] the Christ.

6   But since they kept opposing and abusing and reviling him, he shook out his clothing [against them] and said to them, Your blood be upon your [own] heads! I am innocent [of it]. From now on I will go to the Gentiles (the heathen). [Acts 13:46.]

7   He then left there and went to the house of a man named Titus Justus, who worshiped God and whose house was next door to the synagogue.

8   But Crispus, the leader of the synagogue, believed [that Jesus is the Messiah and acknowledged Him with joyful trust as Savior and Lord], together with his entire household; and many of the Corinthians who

n Joseph Thayer, *A Greek-English Lexicon.*

"in Christ"

The phrases "in Christ," "in Him," or, "in Whom" that are found in many books of the New Testament are vitally important. If we do not understand these terms, we will never have proper insight concerning our "who" and we will be frustrated as we spend our lives trying to improve our "do."

Acts 17:28 says, "For in Him we live and move and have our being." When we receive Jesus Christ as Savior, we are considered to be "in Him." What He earned and deserves, we receive by inheritance. Examining the relationship with our natural children may better help us understand this subject.

I have four children who were originally "in me." Many aspects of their appearances and personalities result from the fact that they began their lives "in me." They received my physical makeup, my nature, my temperament, and so forth. Now that they are grown, they are free to go about life "doing" things that will make me proud of them—but it must never be forgotten that they began "in me." That relationship will last forever.

Relationship with Jesus is referred to in John 3:3, 4 as being "born again." Nicodemus asked Jesus, "How can a man be born when he is old? Can he enter his mother's womb again?" Nicodemus failed to see that Jesus spoke of a spiritual birth, a birth where we are taken out of a worldly way of living and placed "into Christ" and into a new way of thinking, speaking, and acting.

We all must know who we are in Christ. That is our beginning, the place from where we begin the new life. Without a deep understanding of this truth, we will ramble around in life and even in Christianity believing the lie that our acceptance by God is based on our performance.

The truth is that our acceptance by God is based on Jesus' performance, not ours. When He died on the cross, we died with Him. When He was buried, we were buried with Him. When He was resurrected, we were resurrected with Him. That is the way God chooses to see all of us who sincerely believe in Jesus as our substitutionary sacrifice and the payment for all our sins. That is what it means to be "in Him." When we know who we are "in Him," our behavior will change and we will progressively behave more and more in ways that are Christlike.

listened [to Paul also] believed and were baptized.

9 And one night the Lord said to Paul in a vision, Have no fear, but speak and do not keep silent;

10 For I am with you, and no man shall assault you to harm you, for I have many people in this city. [Isa. 43:5; Jer. 1:8.]

11 So he settled down among them for a year and six months, teaching the Word of God [concerning the °attainment through Christ of eternal salvation in the kingdom of God].

o Joseph Thayer, *A Greek-English Lexicon.*

12 But when Gallio was proconsul of Achaia (most of Greece), the Jews unitedly made an attack upon Paul and brought him before the judge's seat,

13 Declaring, This fellow is advising *and* inducing *and* inciting people to worship God in violation of the pLaw [of Rome and of Moses].

14 But when Paul was about to open his mouth to reply, Gallio said to the Jews, If it were a matter of some misdemeanor or villainy, O Jews, I should have cause to bear with you *and* listen;

15 But since it is merely a question [of doctrine] about words and names and your own law, see to it yourselves; I decline to be a judge of such matters *and* I have no intention of trying such cases.

16 And he drove them away from the judgment seat.

17 Then they [the Greeks] all seized Sosthenes, the leader of the synagogue, and beat him right in front of the judgment seat. But Gallio paid no attention to any of this.

18 Afterward Paul remained many days longer, and then told the brethren farewell and sailed for Syria; and he was accompanied by Priscilla and Aquila. At Cenchreae he [qPaul] cut his hair, for he had made a vow.

19 Then they arrived in Ephesus, and [Paul] left the others there; but he himself entered the synagogue and discoursed *and* argued with the Jews.

20 When they asked him to remain for a longer time, he would not consent;

21 But when he was leaving them he said, I will return to you if God is willing, and he set sail from Ephesus.

22 When he landed at Caesarea, he went up and saluted the church [at Jerusalem], and then went down to Antioch.

23 After staying there some time, he left and went from place to place in an orderly journey through the territory of Galatia and Phrygia, establishing the disciples *and* imparting new strength to them.

24 Meanwhile, there was a Jew named Apollos, a native of Alexandria, who came to Ephesus. He was a cultured *and* eloquent man, well versed *and* mighty in the Scriptures.

25 He had been instructed in the way of the Lord, and burning with spiritual zeal, he spoke and taught diligently *and* accurately the things concerning Jesus, though he was acquainted only with the baptism of John.

26 He began to speak freely (fearlessly and boldly) in the synagogue; but when Priscilla and Aquila heard him, they took him with them and expounded to him the way of God more definitely *and* accurately.

27 And when [Apollos] wished to cross to Achaia (most of Greece), the brethren wrote to the disciples there, urging *and* encouraging them to accept *and* welcome him heartily. When he arrived, he proved a great help to those who through grace (God's unmerited favor and mercy) had believed (adhered to, trusted in, and relied on Christ as Lord and Savior).

28 For with great power he refuted the Jews in public [discussions], showing *and* proving by the Scriptures that Jesus is the Christ (the Messiah).

19 WHILE APOLLOS was in Corinth, Paul went through the upper inland districts and came down to Ephesus. There he found some disciples.

---

p The Jews were claiming that Paul was advocating a religion not recognized by Roman law as Judaism was.   q Some commentators (such as Marvin Vincent, *Word Studies* and Henry Alford, *The Greek New Testament*) believe Paul is the one who made the vow, while others think Aquila is meant.

2 And he asked them, Did you receive the Holy Spirit when you believed [on Jesus as the Christ]? And they said, No, we have not even heard that there is a Holy Spirit.

3 And he asked, Into what [baptism] then were you baptized? They said, Into John's baptism.

4 And Paul said, John baptized with the baptism of repentance, continually telling the people that they should believe in the One Who was to come after him, that is, in Jesus [having a conviction full of joyful trust that He is Christ, the Messiah, and being obedient to Him].

5 On hearing this they were baptized [again, this time] in the name of the Lord Jesus.

6 And as Paul laid his hands upon them, the Holy Spirit came on them; and they spoke in [foreign, unknown] tongues (languages) and prophesied.

7 There were about twelve of them in all.

8 And he went into the synagogue and for three months spoke boldly, persuading *and* arguing and pleading about the kingdom of God.

9 But when some became more and more stubborn (hardened and unbelieving), discrediting *and* reviling *and* speaking evil of the Way [of the Lord] before the congregation, he separated himself from them, taking the disciples with him, and went on holding daily discussions in the lecture room of Tyrannus *from about ten o'clock till three.*

10 This continued for two years, so that all the inhabitants of [the province of] Asia, Jews as well as Greeks, heard the Word of the Lord [concerning the ʳattainment through Christ of eternal salvation in the kingdom of God].

11 And God did unusual *and* extraor-dinary miracles by the hands of Paul,

12 So that handkerchiefs *or* towels or aprons which had touched his skin were carried away *and* put upon the sick, and their diseases left them and the evil spirits came out of them.

13 Then some of the traveling Jewish exorcists (men who adjure evil spirits) also undertook to call the name of the Lord Jesus over those who had evil spirits, saying, I solemnly implore *and* charge you by the Jesus Whom Paul preaches!

14 Seven sons of a certain Jewish chief priest named Sceva were doing this.

15 But [one] evil spirit retorted, Jesus I know, and Paul I know ˢabout, but who are you?

16 Then the man in whom the evil spirit dwelt leaped upon them, mastering ᵗtwo of them, and was so violent against them that they dashed out of that house [in fear], stripped naked and wounded.

17 This became known to all who lived in Ephesus, both Jews and Greeks, and alarm *and* terror fell upon them all; and the name of the Lord Jesus was extolled *and* magnified.

18 Many also of those who were now believers came making ᵘfull confession *and* thoroughly exposing their [former deceptive and evil] practices.

19 And many of those who had practiced curious, magical arts collected their books and [throwing them, ᵘbook after book, on the pile] burned them in the sight of everybody. When they counted the value of them, they found it amounted to 50,000 pieces of silver (ᵘabout $9,300).

20 Thus the Word of the Lord [concerning the ʳattainment through Christ of eternal salvation in the kingdom of God] grew *and* spread *and* intensified, prevailing mightily.

---

r Joseph Thayer, *A Greek-English Lexicon.* **s** A weaker verb. **t** The best texts read "both of them." **u** Marvin Vincent, *Word Studies.*

21 Now after these events Paul determined in the [Holy] Spirit that he would travel through Macedonia and Achaia (most of Greece) and go to Jerusalem, saying, After I have been there, I must visit Rome also.

22 And having sent two of his assistants, Timothy and Erastus, into Macedonia, he himself stayed on in [the province of] Asia for a while.

23 But as time went on, there arose no little disturbance concerning the Way [of the Lord].

24 For a man named Demetrius, a silversmith, who made silver shrines of [the goddess] Artemis v[Diana], brought no small income to his craftsmen.

25 These he called together, along with the workmen of similar trades, and said, Men, you are acquainted with the facts *and* understand that from this business we derive our wealth *and* livelihood.

26 Now you notice and hear that not only at Ephesus but almost all over [the province of] Asia this Paul has persuaded *and* induced people to believe his teaching and has alienated a considerable company of them, saying that gods that are made with human hands are not really gods at all.

27 Now there is danger not merely that this trade of ours may be discredited, but also that the temple of the great goddess Artemis may come into disrepute *and* count for nothing, and that her glorious magnificence may be degraded and fall into contempt—she whom all [the province of] Asia and the wide world worship.

28 As they listened to this, they were filled with rage and they continued to shout, Great is Artemis of the Ephesians!

29 Then the city was filled with confusion; and they rushed together into the amphitheater, dragging along with them Gaius and Aristarchus, Macedonians who were fellow travelers with Paul.

30 Paul wished to go in among the crowd, but the disciples would not permit him to do it.

31 Even some of the Asiarchs (political or religious officials in Asia) who were his friends also sent to him and warned him not to risk venturing into the theater.

32 Now some shouted one thing and some another, for the gathering was in a tumult and most of them did not know why they had come together.

33 Some of the crowd called upon Alexander [to speak], since the Jews had pushed *and* urged him forward. And Alexander motioned with his hand, wishing to make a defense *and* [planning] to apologize to the people.

34 But as soon as they saw him *and* recognized that he was a Jew, a shout went up from them as the voice of one man, as for about two hours they cried, Great is Artemis of the Ephesians!

35 And when the town clerk had calmed the crowd down, he said, Men of Ephesus, what man is there who does not know that the city of the Ephesians is guardian of the temple of the great Artemis and of the sacred stone [image of her] that fell from the sky?

36 Seeing then that these things cannot be denied, you ought to be quiet (keep yourselves in check) and do nothing rashly.

37 For you have brought these men here, who are [guilty of] neither temple robberies nor blasphemous speech about our goddess.

38 Now then, if Demetrius and his fellow tradesmen who are with him have a grievance against anyone, the courts are open and proconsuls are

---

v Artemis is the Greek name for the Roman goddess Diana.

[available]; let them bring charges against one another [legally].

39 But if you require anything further about this *or about other matters*, it must be decided *and* cleared up in the regular assembly.

40 For we are in danger of being called to render an account *and* of being accused of rioting because of [this commotion] today, there being no reason that we can offer to justify this disorder.

41 And when he had said these things, he dismissed the assembly.

20 AFTER THE uproar had ceased, Paul sent for the disciples and warned *and* consoled *and* urged *and* encouraged them; then he embraced them *and* told them farewell and set forth on his journey to Macedonia.

2 Then after he had gone through those districts and had warned *and* consoled *and* urged *and* encouraged the brethren with much discourse, he came to Greece.

3 Having spent three months there, when a plot was formed against him by the Jews as he was about to set sail for Syria, he resolved to go back through Macedonia.

4 He was accompanied by Sopater the son of Pyrrhus from Beroea, and by the Thessalonians Aristarchus and Secundus, and Gaius of Derbe and Timothy, and the Asians Tychicus and Trophimus.

5 These went on ahead and were waiting for us [including Luke] at Troas,

6 But we [ourselves] sailed from Philippi after the days of Unleavened Bread [the Passover week], and in five days we joined them at Troas, where we remained for seven days.

7 And on the first day of the week, when we were assembled together to break bread [ʷthe Lord's Supper], Paul discoursed with them, intending to leave the next morning; and he kept on with his message until midnight.

8 Now there were numerous lights in the upper room where we were assembled,

9 And there was a young man named Eutychus sitting in the window. He was borne down with deep sleep as Paul kept on talking still longer, and [finally] completely overcome by sleep, he fell down from the third story and was picked up dead.

10 But Paul went down and bent over him and embraced him, saying, Make no ado; his life is within him.

11 When Paul had gone back upstairs and had broken bread and eaten [with them], and after he had talked confidentially *and* communed with them for a considerable time—until daybreak [in fact]—he departed.

12 They took the youth home alive, and were not a little comforted *and* cheered *and* refreshed *and* encouraged.

13 But going on ahead to the ship, the rest of us set sail for Assos, intending to take Paul aboard there, for that was what he had directed, intending himself to go by land [on foot].

14 So when he met us at Assos, we took him aboard and sailed on to Mitylene.

15 And sailing from there, we arrived the day after at a point opposite Chios; the following day we struck across to Samos, and the next day we arrived at Miletus.

16 For Paul had determined to sail on past Ephesus, lest he might have to spend time [unnecessarily] in [the province of] Asia; for he was hastening on so that he might reach Jerusalem, if at all possible, by the day of Pentecost.

Joseph Thayer, *A Greek-English Lexicon.*

17 However, from Miletus he sent to Ephesus and summoned the elders of the church [to come to him there].

18 And when they arrived he said to them: You yourselves are well acquainted with my manner of living among you from the first day that I set foot in [the province of] Asia, and how I continued afterward,

19 Serving the Lord with all humility in tears and in the midst of adversity (affliction and trials) which befell me, due to the plots of the Jews [against me];

20 How I did not shrink from telling you anything that was for your benefit and teaching you in public meetings and from house to house,

21 But constantly *and* earnestly I bore testimony both to Jews and Greeks, urging them to turn in repentance [ˣthat is due] to God and to have faith in our Lord Jesus Christ [ˣthat is due Him].

22 And now, you see, I am going to Jerusalem, bound by the [Holy] Spirit *and* obligated *and* compelled by the [convictions of my own] spirit, not knowing what will befall me there—

23 Except that the Holy Spirit clearly *and* emphatically affirms to me in city after city that imprisonment and suffering await me.

24 But *none of these things move me;* neither do I esteem my life dear to myself, if only I may finish my course *with joy* and the ministry which I have obtained from [which was entrusted to me by] the Lord Jesus, faithfully to attest to the good news (Gospel) of God's grace (His unmerited favor, spiritual blessing, and mercy).

25 And now, observe, I perceive that all of you, among whom I have gone in and out proclaiming the kingdom, will see my face no more.

26 Therefore I testify *and* protest to you on this [our parting] day that I am

life point

Whatever your present station in life, whatever you are called to do, wherever you are called to go, enjoy the journey, so that you can do as Acts 20:24 encourages, and finish your course with joy. Do not waste one day of the precious life God has given you!

clean *and* innocent *and* not responsible for the blood of any of you.

27 For I never shrank *or* kept back *or* fell short from declaring to you the whole purpose *and* plan *and* counsel of God.

28 Take care *and* be on guard for yourselves and the whole flock over which the Holy Spirit has appointed you bishops and guardians, to shepherd (tend and feed and guide) the church of the Lord *or* ʸof God which He obtained for Himself [buying it and saving it for Himself] with His own blood.

29 I know that after I am gone, ferocious wolves will get in among you, not sparing the flock;

30 Even from among your own selves men will come to the front who, by saying perverse (distorted and corrupt) things, will endeavor to draw away the disciples after them [to their own party].

31 Therefore be always alert *and* on your guard, being mindful that for three years I never stopped night or day seriously to admonish *and* advise *and* exhort you one by one with tears.

32 And now [brethren], I commit you to God [I deposit you in His charge, entrusting you to His protection and care]. And I commend you to the Word of His grace [to the commands and counsels and promises of His unmerited favor]. It is able to build you up and to give you [your rightful]

---

x Marvin Vincent, *Word Studies*. **y** Many ancient manuscripts read "of God."

inheritance among all God's set-apart ones (those consecrated, purified, and transformed of soul).

33 I coveted no man's silver or gold or [costly] garments.

34 You yourselves know personally that these hands ministered to my own needs and those [of the persons] who were with me.

35 In everything I have pointed out to you [by example] that, by working diligently in this manner, we ought to assist the weak, being mindful of the words of the Lord Jesus, how He Himself said, It is more blessed (makes one happier and more ^zto be envied) to give than to receive.

36 Having spoken thus, he knelt down with them all and prayed.

37 And they all wept freely and threw their arms around Paul's neck and kissed him fervently *and* repeatedly,

38 Being especially distressed *and* sorrowful because he had stated that they were about to see his face no more. And they accompanied him to the ship.

21 AND WHEN we had torn ourselves away from them *and* withdrawn, we set sail and made a straight run to Cos, and on the following [day came] to Rhodes and from there to Patara.

2 There we found a ship crossing over to Phoenicia; so we went aboard and sailed away.

3 After we had sighted Cyprus, leaving it on our left we sailed on to Syria and put in at Tyre, for there the ship was to unload her cargo.

4 And having looked up the disciples there, we remained with them for seven days. Prompted by the [Holy] Spirit, they kept telling Paul not to set foot in Jerusalem.

5 But when our time there was ended, we left and proceeded on our journey; and all of them with their wives and children accompanied us on our way till we were outside the city. There we knelt down on the beach and prayed.

6 Then when we had told one another farewell, we went on board the ship, and they returned to their own homes.

7 When we had completed the voyage from Tyre, we landed at Ptolemais, where we paid our respects to the brethren and remained with them for one day.

8 On the morrow we left there and came to Caesarea; and we went into the house of Philip the evangelist, who was one of the Seven [first deacons], and stayed with him. [Acts 6:5.]

9 And he had four maiden daughters who had the gift of prophecy.

10 While we were remaining there for some time, a prophet named Agabus came down from Judea.

11 And coming to [see] us, he took Paul's belt and with it bound his own feet and hands and said, Thus says the Holy Spirit: The Jews at Jerusalem shall bind like this the man who owns this belt, and they shall deliver him into the hands of the Gentiles (heathen).

12 When we heard this, both we and the residents of that place pleaded with him not to go up to Jerusalem.

13 Then Paul replied, What do you mean by weeping and breaking my heart like this? For I hold myself in readiness not only to be arrested *and* bound *and* imprisoned at Jerusalem, but also [even] to die for the name of the Lord Jesus.

14 And when he would not yield to [our] persuading, we stopped [urging and imploring him], saying, The Lord's will be done!

15 After these days we packed our

---

z Alexander Souter, *Pocket Lexicon.*

baggage and went up to Jerusalem.
16 And some of the disciples from
Caesarea came with us, conducting us
to the house of Mnason, a man from
Cyprus, one of the disciples of long
standing, with whom we were to
lodge.

17 When we arrived in Jerusalem,
the brethren received *and* welcomed
us gladly.

18 On the next day Paul went in with
us to [see] James, and all the elders of
the church were present [also].

19 After saluting them, Paul gave a
detailed account of the things God
had done among the Gentiles through
his ministry.

20 And upon hearing it, they adored
and exalted *and* praised *and* thanked
God. And they said to [Paul], You see,
brother, how many thousands of
believers there are among the Jews,
and all of them are enthusiastic
upholders of the [Mosaic] Law.

21 Now they have been informed
about you that you continually teach
all the Jews who live among the Gentiles to turn back from *and* forsake
Moses, advising them not to circumcise their children or pay any attention to the observance of the [Mosaic]
customs.

22 What then [is best that] should be
done? A multitude will come together,
for they will surely hear that you have
arrived.

23 Therefore do just what we tell
you. With us are four men who have
taken a vow upon themselves.

24 Take these men and purify yourself along with them and pay their
expenses [for the temple offering], so
that they may have their heads
shaved. Thus everybody will know
that there is no truth in what they
have been told about you, but that you
yourself walk in observance of the
Law.

25 But with regard to the Gentiles
who have believed (adhered to, trusted in, and relied on Christ), we have
sent them a letter with our decision
that they should keep themselves free
from anything that has been sacrificed to idols and from [tasting] blood
and [eating the meat of animals]
which have been strangled and from
all impurity *and* sexual immorality.

26 Then Paul took the [four] men
with him and the following day [he
went through the rites of] purifying
himself along with them. And they
entered the temple to give notice
when the days of purification (the
ending of each vow) would be fulfilled
and the usual offering could be presented on behalf of each of them.

27 When the seven days were drawing to a close, some of the Jews from
[the province of] Asia, who had
caught sight of Paul in the temple,
incited all the rabble and laid hands
on him,

28 Shouting, Men of Israel, help!
[Help!] This is the man who is teaching everybody everywhere against the
people and the Law and this place!
Moreover, he has also [actually]
brought Greeks into the temple; he
has desecrated *and* polluted this holy
place!

29 For they had previously seen
Trophimus the Ephesian in the city
with Paul and they supposed that he
had brought the man into the temple
[into the inner court forbidden to
Gentiles].

30 Then the whole city was aroused
and thrown into confusion, and the
people rushed together; they laid
hands on Paul and dragged him outside the temple, and immediately the
gates were closed.

31 Now while they were trying to kill
him, word came to the commandant of
the regular Roman garrison that the
whole of Jerusalem was in a state of
ferment.

32 So immediately he took soldiers
and centurions and hurried down

among them; and when the people saw the commandant and the troops, they stopped beating Paul.

33 Then the commandant approached and arrested Paul and ordered that he be secured with two chains. He then inquired who he was and what he had done.

34 Some in the crowd kept shouting back one thing and others something else, and since he could not ascertain the facts because of the furor, he ordered that Paul be removed to the barracks.

35 And when [Paul] came to mount the steps, he was actually being carried by the soldiers because of the violence of the mob;

36 For the mass of the people kept following them, shouting, Away with him! [Kill him!]

37 Just as Paul was about to be taken into the barracks, he asked the commandant, May I say something to you? And the man replied, Can you speak Greek?

38 Are you not then [as I supposed] the Egyptian who not long ago stirred up a rebellion and led those 4,000 men who were cutthroats out into the wilderness (desert)?

39 Paul answered, I am a Jew, from Tarsus in Cilicia, a citizen of no insignificant or undistinguished city. I beg you, allow me to address the people.

40 And when the man had granted him permission, Paul, standing on the steps, gestured with his hand to the people; and there was a great hush. Then he spoke to them in the Hebrew dialect, saying:

22

BRETHREN AND fathers, listen to the defense which I now make in your presence.

2 And when they heard that he addressed them in the Hebrew tongue, they were all the more quiet. And he continued,

3 I am a Jew, born in Tarsus of Cilicia but reared in this city. At the feet of Gamaliel I was educated according to the strictest care in the Law of our fathers, being ardent [even a zealot] for God, as all of you are today.

4 [Yes] I harassed (troubled, molested, and persecuted) this Way [of the Lord] to the death, putting in chains and committing to prison both men and women,

5 As the high priest and whole council of elders (Sanhedrin) can testify; for from them indeed I received letters with which I was on my way to the brethren in Damascus in order to take also those [believers] who were there, and bring them in chains to Jerusalem that they might be punished.

6 But as I was on my journey and approached Damascus, about noon a great blaze of light flashed suddenly from heaven and shone about me.

7 And I fell to the ground and heard a voice saying to me, Saul, Saul, why do you persecute Me [harass and trouble and molest Me]?

8 And I replied, Who are You, Lord? And He said to me, I am Jesus the Nazarene, Whom you are persecuting.

9 Now the men who were with me saw the light, but they did not hear [[a]the sound of the uttered words of] the voice of the One Who was speaking to me [so that they could [b]understand it].

10 And I asked, What shall I do, Lord? And the Lord answered me, Get up and go into Damascus, and there it will be told you all that it is destined and appointed for you to do.

11 And since I could not see because [of the dazzlingly glorious intensity] of the brightness of that light, I was led by the hand by those who were with

---

a Joseph Thayer, *A Greek-English Lexicon.* **b** Marvin Vincent, *Word Studies.*

me, and [thus] I arrived in Damascus.

12 And one Ananias, a devout man according to the Law, well spoken of by all the Jews who resided there,

13 Came to see me, and standing by my side said to me, Brother Saul, ᶜlook up *and* receive back your sight. And in that very ᵈinstant I [recovered my sight and] looking up saw him.

14 And he said, The God of our forefathers has destined *and* appointed you to come progressively to know His will [to perceive, to recognize more strongly and clearly, and to become better and more intimately acquainted with His will], and to see the Righteous One (Jesus Christ, the Messiah), and to hear a voice from His [own] mouth *and* a message from His [own] lips;

15 For you will be His witness unto all men of everything that you have seen and heard.

16 And now, why do you delay? Rise and be baptized, and ᵉby calling upon His name, wash away your sins.

17 Then when I had come back to Jerusalem and was praying in the temple [ᶠenclosure], I fell into a trance (an ecstasy);

18 And I saw Him as He said to me, Hurry, get quickly out of Jerusalem, because they will not receive your testimony about Me.

19 And I said, Lord, they themselves well know that throughout all the synagogues I cast into prison and flogged those who believed on (adhered to and trusted in and relied on) You.

20 And when the blood of Your witness (martyr) Stephen was shed, I also was personally standing by and consenting *and* approving and guarding the garments of those who slew him.

21 And the Lord said to me, Go, for I will send you far away unto the Gentiles (nations).

22 Up to the moment that Paul made this last statement, the people listened to him; but now they raised their voices and shouted, Away with such a fellow from the earth! He is not fit to live!

23 And as they were shouting and tossing *and* waving their garments and throwing dust into the air,

24 The commandant ordered that Paul be brought into the barracks, and that he be examined by scourging in order that [the commandant] might learn why the people cried out thus against him.

25 But when they had stretched him out with the thongs (leather straps), Paul asked the centurion who was standing by, Is it legal for you to flog a man who is a Roman citizen and uncondemned [without a trial]?

26 When the centurion heard that, he went to the commandant and said to him, What are you about to do? This man is a Roman citizen!

27 So the commandant came and said to [Paul], Tell me, are you a Roman citizen? And he said, Yes [indeed]!

28 The commandant replied, I purchased this citizenship [as a capital investment] for a big price. Paul said, But I was born [Roman]!

29 Instantly those who were about to examine *and* flog him withdrew from him; and the commandant also was frightened, for he realized that [Paul] was a Roman citizen and he had put him in chains.

30 But the next day, desiring to know the real cause for which the Jews accused him, he unbound him and ordered the chief priests and all the council (Sanhedrin) to assemble; and

---

c Joseph Thayer, *A Greek-English Lexicon.*   **d** James Moulton and George Milligan, *The Vocabulary.*
e Charles B. Williams, *The New Testament: A Translation in the Language of the People*: Circumstantial participle expressing manner or means.   **f** Richard Trench, *Synonyms of the New Testament.*

he brought Paul down and placed him before them.

23 THEN PAUL, gazing earnestly at the council (Sanhedrin), said, Brethren, I have lived before God, doing my duty with a perfectly good conscience until this very day [gas a citizen, a true and loyal Jew].

2 At this the high priest Ananias ordered those who stood near him to strike him on the mouth.

3 Then Paul said to him, God is about to strike you, you whitewashed wall! Do you sit as a judge to try me in accordance with the Law, and yet in defiance of the Law you order me to be struck?

4 Those who stood near exclaimed, Do you rail at *and* insult the high priest of God?

5 And Paul said, I was not conscious, brethren, that he was a high priest; for the Scripture says, You shall not speak ill of a ruler of your people. [Exod. 22:28.]

6 But Paul, when he perceived that one part of them were Sadducees and the other part Pharisees, cried out to the council (Sanhedrin), Brethren, I am a Pharisee, a son of Pharisees; it is with regard to the hope and the resurrection of the dead that I am indicted *and* being judged.

7 So when he had said this, an angry dispute arose between the Pharisees and the Sadducees; and the whole [crowded] assemblage was divided [into two factions].

8 For the Sadducees hold that there is no resurrection, nor angel nor spirit, but the Pharisees declare openly *and* speak out freely, acknowledging [their belief in] them both.

9 Then a great uproar ensued, and some of the scribes of the Pharisees' party stood up and thoroughly fought the case, [contending fiercely] and declaring, We find nothing evil *or* wrong in this man. But if a spirit or an angel [really] spoke to him—? *Let us not fight against God!*

10 And when the strife became more and more tense *and* violent, the commandant, fearing that Paul would be torn in pieces by them, ordered the troops to go down and take him forcibly from among them and conduct him back into the barracks.

11 And [that same] following night the Lord stood beside Paul and said, Take courage, *Paul,* for as you have borne faithful witness concerning Me at Jerusalem, so you must also bear witness at Rome.

12 Now when daylight came, the Jews formed a plot and bound themselves by an oath *and* under a curse neither to eat nor drink till they had done away with Paul.

13 There were more than forty [men of them], who formed this conspiracy [swearing together this oath and curse].

14 And they went to the chief priests and elders, saying, We have strictly bound ourselves by an oath *and* under a curse not to taste any food until we have slain Paul.

15 So now you, along with the council (Sanhedrin), give notice to the commandant to bring [Paul] down to you, as if you were going to investigate his case more accurately. But we [ourselves] are ready to slay him before he comes near.

16 But the son of Paul's sister heard of their intended attack, and he went and got into the barracks and told Paul.

17 Then Paul, calling in one of the centurions, said, Take this young man to the commandant, for he has something to report to him.

g Marvin Vincent, *Word Studies.*

18 So he took him and conducted him to the commandant and said, Paul the prisoner called me to him and requested me to conduct this young man to you, for he has something to report to you.

19 The commandant took him by the hand, and going aside with him, asked privately, What is it that you have to report to me?

20 And he replied, The Jews have agreed to ask you to bring Paul down to the council (Sanhedrin) tomorrow, as if [they were] intending to examine him more exactly.

21 But do not yield to their persuasion, for more than forty of their men are lying in ambush waiting for him, having bound themselves by an oath *and* under a curse neither to eat nor drink till they have killed him; and even now they are all ready, [just] waiting for your promise.

22 So the commandant sent the youth away, charging him, Do not disclose to anyone that you have given me this information.

23 Then summoning two of the centurions, he said, Have two hundred footmen ready by the third hour of the night (about 9:00 p.m.) to go as far as Caesarea, with seventy horsemen and two hundred spearmen.

24 Also provide beasts for mounts for Paul to ride, and bring him in safety to Felix the governor.

25 And he wrote a letter having this message:

26 Claudius Lysias sends greetings to His Excellency Felix the governor.

27 This man was seized [as prisoner] by the Jews, and was about to be killed by them when I came upon them with the troops and rescued him, because I learned that he is a Roman citizen.

28 And wishing to know the exact accusation which they were making against him, I brought him down before their council (Sanhedrin),

29 [Where] I found that he was charged in regard to questions of their own law, but he was accused of nothing that would call for death or [even] for imprisonment.

30 [However] when it was pointed out to me that there would be a conspiracy against the man, I sent him to you immediately, directing his accusers also to present before you their charge against him.

31 So the soldiers, in compliance with their instructions, took Paul and conducted him during the night to Antipatris.

32 And the next day they returned to the barracks, leaving the mounted men to proceed with him.

33 When these came to Caesarea and gave the letter to the governor, they also presented Paul before him.

34 Having read the letter, he asked to what province [Paul] belonged. When he discovered that he was from Cilicia [an imperial province],

35 He said, I will hear your case [h]fully when your accusers also have come. And he ordered that an eye be kept on him in Herod's palace (the Praetorium).

24 FIVE DAYS later, the high priest Ananias came down [from Jerusalem to Caesarea] with some elders and a certain forensic advocate Tertullus [acting as spokesman and counsel]. They presented to the governor their evidence against Paul.

2 And when he was called, Tertullus began the complaint [against him] by saying: Since through you we obtain *and* enjoy much peace, and since by your foresight *and* provision wonderful reforms (amendments and improvements) are introduced *and*

---

h Marvin Vincent, *Word Studies*.

effected on behalf of this nation,
3 In every way and in every place,
most excellent Felix, we accept *and*
acknowledge this with deep appreciation *and* with all gratitude.
4 But not to hinder *or* detain you too
long, I beg you in your clemency *and*
courtesy *and* kindness to grant us a
brief *and* 'concise hearing.
5 For we have found this man a perfect pest (a real plague), an agitator
and source of disturbance to all the
Jews throughout the world, and a
ringleader of the [heretical, 'division-
producing] sect of the Nazarenes.
6 He also [even] tried to desecrate
and defile the temple, but we laid
hands on him *'and would have sentenced him by our Law,*
7 *But the commandant Lysias came
and took him from us with violence and
force,*
8 *And ordered his accusers to present themselves to you.* By examining
and cross-questioning him yourself,
you will be able to ascertain the truth
from him about all these things with
which we charge him.
9 The Jews also agreed *and* joined
in the accusation, declaring that all
these things were exactly so.
10 And when the governor had beck-
oned to Paul to speak, he answered:
Because I know that for many years
you have been a judge over this
nation, I find it easier to make my
defense *and* do it cheerfully *and* with
good courage.
11 As you can readily verify, it is not
more than twelve days since I went up
to Jerusalem to worship;
12 And neither in the temple nor in
the synagogues nor in the city did
they find me disputing with anybody
or bringing together a seditious
crowd.
13 Neither can they present argu-

ment *or* evidence to prove to you what
they now bring against me.
14 But this I confess to you, however,
that in accordance with the Way [of
the Lord], which they call a [heretical,
division-producing] sect, I worship
(serve) the God of our fathers, still
persuaded of the truth of *and* believing in *and* placing full confidence in
everything laid down in the Law [of
Moses] *or* written in the prophets;
15 Having [the same] hope in God
which these themselves hold *and* look
for, that there is to be a resurrection
both of the righteous and the unrighteous (the just and the unjust).
16 Therefore I always exercise *and*
discipline myself [mortifying my
body, deadening my carnal affections,
bodily appetites, and worldly desires,
endeavoring in all respects] to have a
clear (unshaken, blameless) conscience, void of offense toward God
and toward men.
17 Now after several years I came up
[to Jerusalem] to bring to my people
contributions of charity and offerings.
18 While I was engaged in presenting these, they found me [occupied in
the rites of purification] in the temple,
without any crowd or uproar. But
some Jews from [the province of] Asia
[were there],
19 Who ought to be here before you
and to present their charges, if they
have anything against me.
20 Or else let these men themselves
tell of what crime *or* wrongdoing they
found me guilty when I appeared
before the council (Sanhedrin),
21 Unless it be this one sentence
which I cried out as I stood among
them, In regard to the resurrection of
the dead I am indicted *and* on trial
before you this day!
22 But Felix, having a rather accurate understanding of the Way [of the

i Marvin Vincent, *Word Studies.* j Many manuscripts do not contain the remainder of verse 6, all of
verse 7, and the first part of verse 8.

Lord], put them off *and* adjourned the trial, saying, When Lysias the commandant comes down, I will determine your case more fully.

23 Then he ordered the centurion to keep [Paul] in custody, but to treat him with indulgence [giving him some liberty] and not to hinder his friends from ministering to his needs *and* serving him.

24 Some days later Felix came with his wife Drusilla, who was a Jewess; and he sent for Paul and listened to him [talk] about faith in Christ Jesus.

25 But as he continued to argue about uprightness, purity of life (the control of the passions), and the judgment to come, Felix became alarmed *and* terrified and said, Go away for the present; when I have a convenient opportunity, I will send for you.

26 At the same time he hoped to get money from Paul, for which reason he continued to send for him and was in his company *and* conversed with him often.

27 But when two years had gone by, Felix was succeeded in office by Porcius Festus; and wishing to gain favor with the Jews, Felix left Paul still a prisoner in chains.

25 NOW WHEN Festus had entered into his own province, after three days he went up from Caesarea to Jerusalem.

2 And [there] the chief priests and the principal men of the Jews laid charges before him against Paul, and they kept begging *and* urging him,

3 Asking as a favor that he would have him brought to Jerusalem; [meanwhile] they were planning an ambush to slay him on the way.

4 Festus answered that Paul was in custody in Caesarea and that he himself planned to leave for there soon.

5 So, said he, let those who are in a position of authority *and* are influential among you go down with me, and if there is anything amiss *or* criminal about the man, let them so charge him.

6 So when Festus had remained among them not more than eight or ten days, he went down to Caesarea, took his seat the next day on the judgment bench, and ordered Paul to be brought before him.

7 And when he arrived, the Jews who had come down from Jerusalem stood all around him, bringing many grave accusations against him which they were not able to prove.

8 Paul declared in [his own] defense, Neither against the Law of the Jews, nor against the temple, nor against Caesar have I offended in any way.

9 But Festus, wishing to ingratiate himself with the Jews, answered Paul, Are you willing to go up to Jerusalem and there be put on trial [[k]before the Jewish Sanhedrin] in my presence concerning these charges?

10 But Paul replied, I am standing before Caesar's judgment seat, where I ought to be tried. To the Jews I have done no wrong, as you know [k]better [than your question implies].

11 If then I am a wrongdoer *and* a criminal and have committed anything for which I deserve to die, I do not beg off *and* seek to escape death; but if there is no ground for their accusations against me, no one can give me up *and* make a present of me [[l]give me up freely] to them. I appeal to Caesar.

12 Then Festus, when he had consulted with the [[k]men who formed his] council, answered, You have appealed to Caesar; to Caesar you shall go.

13 Now after an interval of some days, Agrippa the king and Bernice arrived at Caesarea to pay their

k Marvin Vincent, *Word Studies*.   **l** G. Abbott-Smith, *Manual Greek Lexicon*.

respects to Festus [to welcome him and wish him well].

14 And while they remained there for many days, Festus acquainted the king with Paul's case, telling him, There is a man left a prisoner in chains by Felix;

15 And when I was at Jerusalem, the chief priests and the elders of the Jews informed me about him, petitioning for a judicial hearing *and* condemnation of him.

16 But I replied to them that it was not the custom of the Romans to [m]give up freely any man for punishment before the accused had met the accusers face to face and had opportunity to defend himself concerning the charge brought against him.

17 So when they came here together, I did not delay, but on the morrow took my place on the judgment seat and ordered that the man be brought before me.

18 [But] when the accusers stood up, they brought forward no accusation [in his case] of any such misconduct as I was expecting.

19 Instead they had some points of controversy with him about their own religion *or* superstition and concerning one Jesus, Who had died but Whom Paul kept asserting [over and over] to be alive.

20 And I, being puzzled to know how to make inquiries into such questions, asked whether he would be willing to go to Jerusalem and there be tried regarding them.

21 But when Paul had appealed to have his case retained for examination *and* decision by the emperor, I ordered that he be detained until I could send him to Caesar.

22 Then Agrippa said to Festus, I also desire to hear the man myself. Tomorrow, [Festus] replied, you shall hear him.

23 So the next day Agrippa and Bernice approached with great display, and they went into the audience hall accompanied by the military commandants and the prominent citizens of the city. At the order of Festus Paul was brought in.

24 Then Festus said, King Agrippa and all the men present with us, you see this man about whom the whole Jewish people came to me *and* complained, both at Jerusalem and here, insisting *and* shouting that he ought not to live any longer.

25 But I found nothing that he had done deserving of death. Still, as he himself appealed to the emperor, I determined to send him to Rome.

26 [However] I have nothing in particular *and* definite to write to my lord concerning him. So I have brought him before all of you, and especially before you, King Agrippa, so that after [further] examination has been made, I may have something to put in writing.

27 For it seems to me senseless *and* absurd to send a prisoner and not state the accusations against him.

26 THEN AGRIPPA said to Paul, You are permitted to speak on your own behalf. At that Paul stretched forth his hand and made his defense [as follows]:

2 I consider myself fortunate, King Agrippa, that it is before you that I am to make my defense today in regard to all the charges brought against me by [the] Jews,

3 [Especially] because you are so fully *and* unusually conversant with all the Jewish customs and controversies; therefore, I beg you to hear me patiently.

4 My behavior *and* manner of living from my youth up is known by all the Jews; [they are aware] that from [its]

---

m G. Abbott-Smith, *Manual Greek Lexicon.*

commencement my youth was spent among my own race in Jerusalem.

5 They have had knowledge of me for a long time, if they are willing to testify to it, that in accordance with the strictest sect of our religion I have lived as a Pharisee.

6 And now I stand here on trial [to be judged on the ground] of the hope of that promise made to our forefathers by God, [Acts 13:32, 33.]

7 Which hope [of the Messiah and the resurrection] our twelve tribes confidently expect to realize as they fervently worship [without ceasing] night and day. And for that hope, O king, I am accused by Jews *and* considered a criminal!

8 Why is it thought incredible by any of you that God raises the dead?

9 I myself indeed was [once] persuaded that it was my duty to do many things contrary to *and* in defiance of the name of Jesus of Nazareth.

10 And that is what I did in Jerusalem; I [not only] locked up many of the [faithful] saints (holy ones) in prison by virtue of authority received from the chief priests, but when they were being condemned to death, I cast my vote against them.

11 And frequently I punished them in all the synagogues to make them blaspheme; and in my bitter fury against them, I harassed (troubled, molested, persecuted) *and* pursued them even to foreign cities.

12 Thus engaged I proceeded to Damascus with the authority and orders of the chief priests,

13 When on the road at midday, O king, I saw a light from heaven surpassing the brightness of the sun, flashing about me and those who were traveling with me.

14 And when we had all fallen to the ground, I heard a voice in the Hebrew tongue saying to me, Saul, Saul, why do you continue to persecute Me [to harass and trouble and molest Me]? It is dangerous *and* turns out badly for you to keep kicking against the goads [to keep offering vain and perilous resistance].

15 And I said, Who are You, Lord? And the Lord said, I am Jesus, Whom you are persecuting.

16 But arise and stand upon your feet; for I have appeared to you for this purpose, that I might appoint you to serve as [My] minister and to bear witness both to what you have seen of Me and to that in which I will appear to you,

17 [n]Choosing you out [selecting you for Myself] *and* [o]delivering you from among this [Jewish] people and the Gentiles to whom I am sending you— [Ezek. 2:1, 3.]

18 To open their eyes that they may turn from darkness to light and from the power of Satan to God, so that they may thus receive forgiveness *and* release from their sins and a place *and* portion among those who are consecrated *and* purified by faith in Me. [Isa. 42:7, 16.]

19 Wherefore, O King Agrippa, I was not disobedient unto the heavenly vision,

20 But made known openly first of all to those at Damascus, then at Jerusalem and throughout the whole land of Judea, and also among the Gentiles, that they should repent and turn to God, and do works *and* live lives consistent with *and* worthy of their repentance.

21 Because of these things the Jews seized me in the temple [[p]enclosure] and tried to do away with me.

22 [But] to this day I have had the help which comes from God [as my [o]ally], and so I stand here testifying to

n Joseph Thayer, *A Greek-English Lexicon.*   **o** G. Abbott-Smith, *Manual Greek Lexicon.*   **p** Richard Trench, *Synonyms of the New Testament.*

small and great alike, asserting nothing beyond what the prophets and Moses declared would come to pass—
23 That the Christ (the Anointed One) must suffer and that He, by being the first to rise from the dead, would declare *and* show light both to the [Jewish] people and to the Gentiles.
24 And as he thus proceeded with his defense, Festus called out loudly, Paul, you are mad! Your great learning is driving you insane!
25 But Paul replied, I am not mad, most noble Festus, but I am uttering the straight, sound truth.
26 For the king understands about these things well enough, and [therefore] to him I speak with bold frankness *and* confidence. I am convinced that not one of these things has escaped his notice, for all this did not take place in a corner [in secret].
27 King Agrippa, do you believe the prophets? [Do you give credence to God's messengers and their words?] I perceive *and* know that you do believe.
28 Then Agrippa said to Paul, You think it a small task to make a Christian of me [just offhand to induce me with little ado and persuasion, at very short notice].
29 And Paul replied, Whether short or long, I would to God that not only you, but also all who are listening to me today, might become such as I am, except for these chains.
30 Then the king arose, and the governor and Bernice and all those who were seated with them;
31 And after they had gone out, they said to one another, This man is doing nothing deserving of death or [even] of imprisonment.
32 And Agrippa said to Festus, This man could have been set at liberty if he had not appealed to Caesar.

27 NOW WHEN it was determined that we [including Luke] should sail for Italy,

they turned Paul and some other prisoners over to a centurion of the imperial regiment named Julius.
2 And going aboard a ship from Adramyttium which was about to sail for the ports along the coast of [the province of] Asia, we put out to sea; and Aristarchus, a Macedonian from Thessalonica, accompanied us.
3 The following day we landed at Sidon, and Julius treated Paul in a loving way, with much consideration (kindness and care), permitting him to go to his friends [there] and be refreshed *and* be cared for.
4 After putting to sea from there we passed to the leeward (south side) of Cyprus [for protection], for the winds were contrary to us.
5 And when we had sailed over [the whole length] of sea which lies off Cilicia and Pamphylia, we reached Myra in Lycia.
6 There the centurion found an Alexandrian ship bound for Italy, and he transferred us to it.
7 For a number of days we made slow progress and arrived with difficulty off Cnidus; then, as the wind did not permit us to proceed, we went under the lee (shelter) of Crete off Salmone,
8 And coasting along it with difficulty, we arrived at a place called Fair Havens, near which is located the town of Lasea.
9 But as [the season was well advanced, for] much time had been lost and navigation was already dangerous, for the time for the Fast [the Day of Atonement, about the beginning of October] had already gone by, Paul warned *and* advised them,
10 Saying, Sirs, I perceive [after careful observation] that this voyage will be attended with disaster and much heavy loss, not only of the cargo and the ship but of our lives also.
11 However, the centurion paid greater attention to the pilot and to

the owner of the ship than to what Paul said.

12 And as the harbor was not well situated *and* so unsuitable to winter in, the majority favored the plan of putting to sea again from there, hoping somehow to reach Phoenice, a harbor of Crete facing southwest and northwest, and winter there.

13 So when the south wind blew softly, supposing they were gaining their object, they weighed anchor and sailed along Crete, hugging the coast.

14 But soon afterward a violent wind [of the character of a typhoon], called a northeaster, came bursting down from the island.

15 And when the ship was caught and was unable to head against the wind, we gave up and, letting her drift, were borne along.

16 We ran under the shelter of a small island called Cauda, where we managed with [much] difficulty to draw the [ship's small] boat on deck *and* secure it.

17 After hoisting it on board, they used supports with ropes to undergird *and* brace the ship; then afraid that they would be driven into the Syrtis [quicksands off the north coast of Africa], they lowered the gear (sails and ropes) and so were driven along.

18 As we were being dangerously tossed about by the violence of the storm, the next day they began to throw the freight overboard;

19 And the third day they threw out with their own hands the ship's equipment (the tackle and the furniture).

20 And when neither sun nor stars were visible for many days and no small tempest kept raging about us, all hope of our being saved was finally abandoned.

21 Then as they had eaten nothing for a long time, Paul came forward into their midst and said, Men, you should have listened to me, and should not have put to sea from Crete and brought on this disaster and harm *and* misery *and* loss.

22 But [even] now I beg you to be in good spirits *and* take heart, for there will be no loss of life among you but only of the ship.

23 For this [very] night there stood by my side an angel of the God to Whom I belong and Whom I serve *and* worship,

24 And he said, Do not be frightened, Paul! It is necessary for you to stand before Caesar; and behold, God has given you all those who are sailing with you.

25 So keep up your courage, men, for I have faith (complete confidence) in God that it will be exactly as it was told me;

26 But we shall have to be stranded on some island.

27 The fourteenth night had come and we were drifting *and* being driven about in the Adriatic Sea, when about midnight the sailors began to suspect that they were drawing near to some land.

28 So they took soundings and found twenty fathoms, and a little farther on they sounded again and found fifteen fathoms.

29 Then fearing that we might fall off [our course] onto rocks, they dropped four anchors from the stern and kept wishing for daybreak to come.

30 And as the sailors were trying to escape [secretly] from the ship and were lowering the small boat into the sea, pretending that they were going to lay out anchors from the bow,

31 Paul said to the centurion and the soldiers, Unless these men remain in the ship, you cannot be saved.

32 Then the soldiers cut away the ropes that held the small boat, and let it fall *and* drift away.

33 While they waited until it should become day, Paul entreated them all to take some food, saying, This is the fourteenth day that you have been continually in suspense *and* on the alert without food, having eaten nothing.

34 So I urge (warn, exhort, encourage, advise) you to take some food [for your safety]—it will give you strength; for not a hair is to perish from the head of any one of you.

35 Having said these words, he took bread and, giving thanks to God before them all, he broke it and began to eat.

36 Then they all became more cheerful *and* were encouraged and took food themselves.

37 All told there were 276 souls of us in the ship.

38 And after they had eaten sufficiently, [they proceeded] to lighten the ship, throwing out the wheat into the sea.

39 Now when it was day [and they saw the land], they did not recognize it, but they noticed a bay with a beach on which they [taking counsel] purposed to run the ship ashore if they possibly could.

40 So they cut the cables *and* severed the anchors and left them in the sea; at the same time unlashing the ropes that held the rudders and hoisting the foresail to the wind, they headed for the beach.

41 But striking a crosscurrent (a place open to two seas) they ran the ship aground. The prow stuck fast and remained immovable, and the stern began to break up under the violent force of the waves.

42 It was the counsel of the soldiers to kill the prisoners, lest any of them should swim to land and escape;

43 But the centurion, wishing to save Paul, prevented their carrying out their purpose. He commanded those who could swim to throw themselves overboard first and make for the shore,

44 And the rest on heavy boards or pieces of the vessel. And so it was that all escaped safely to land.

28 AFTER WE were safe on the island, we knew *and* recognized that it was called Malta.

2 And the natives showed us unusual *and* remarkable kindness, for they kindled a fire and welcomed *and* received us all, since it had begun to rain and was cold.

3 Now Paul had gathered a bundle of sticks, and he was laying them on the fire when a viper crawled out because of the heat and fastened itself on his hand.

4 When the natives saw the little animal hanging from his hand, they said to one another, Doubtless this man is a murderer, for though he has been saved from the sea, Justice [�q the goddess of avenging] has not permitted that he should live.

5 Then [Paul simply] shook off the small creature into the fire and suffered no evil effects.

6 However, they were waiting, expecting him to swell up or suddenly drop dead; but when they had watched him a long time and saw nothing fatal *or* harmful come to him, they changed their minds and kept saying over and over that he was a god.

7 In the vicinity of that place there were estates belonging to the head man of the island, named Publius, who accepted *and* welcomed *and* entertained us with hearty hospitality for three days.

8 And it happened that the father of Publius was sick in bed with recurring attacks of fever and dysentery; and Paul went to see him, and after

q Alexander Souter, *Pocket Lexicon.*

life point

Acts 28:1–5 tells the story of Paul and his traveling companions when they were shipwrecked on the island of Malta. Paul was busy gathering sticks to make a fire and dry his clothes when a poisonous snake, driven out of the flames, suddenly bit Paul's hand. The Bible says Paul simply shook it off into the fire and "suffered no evil effects" (Acts 28:5). You and I should do the same when things try to "bite" us—we too should be bold inwardly and shake it off!

Whatever may trouble you from the past, *shake it off!* God has a great future planned for you. The dreams of the future have no room for the snakebites of the past!

praying and laying his hands on him, he healed him.

9 After this had occurred, the other people on the island who had diseases also kept coming and were cured.

10 They showed us every respect *and* presented many gifts to us, honoring us with many honors; and when we sailed, they provided *and* put on [board our ship] everything we needed.

11 It was after three months' stay there that we set sail in a ship which had wintered in the island, an Alexandrian ship with the Twin Brothers [Castor and Pollux] as its figurehead.

12 We landed at Syracuse and remained there three days,

13 And from there we made a circuit [following the coast] and reached Rhegium; and one day later a south wind sprang up, and the next day we arrived at Puteoli.

14 There we found some [Christian] brethren and were entreated to stay with them for seven days. And so we came to Rome.

15 And the [Christian] brethren there, having had news of us, came as far as the Forum of Appius and the Three Taverns to meet us. When Paul saw them, he thanked God and received new courage.

16 When we arrived at Rome, *the centurion delivered the prisoners to the captain of the guard, but* Paul was permitted to live by himself with the soldier who guarded him.

17 Three days after [our arrival], he called together the leading local Jews; and when they had gathered, he said to them, Brethren, though I have done nothing against the people or against the customs of our forefathers, yet I was turned over as a prisoner from Jerusalem into the hands of the Romans.

18 After they had examined me, they were ready to release me because I was innocent of any offense deserving the death penalty.

19 But when the Jews protested, I was forced to appeal to Caesar, though it was not because I had any charge to make against my nation.

20 This is the reason therefore why I have begged to see you and to talk with you, since it is because of the Hope of Israel (the Messiah) that I am bound with this chain.

21 And they answered him, We have not received any letters about you from Judea, and none of the [Jewish] brethren coming here has reported or spoken anything evil about you.

22 But we think it fitting *and* are eager to hear from you what it is that you have in mind *and* believe *and* what your opinion is, for with regard to this sect it is known to all of us that it is everywhere denounced.

23 So when they had set a day with him, they came in large numbers to his lodging. And he fully set forth *and* explained the matter to them from morning until night, testifying to the kingdom of God and trying to persuade them concerning Jesus both from the Law of Moses and from the Prophets.

24 And some were convinced *and* believed what he said, and others did not believe.

25 And as they disagreed among themselves, they began to leave, [but not before] Paul had added one statement [more]: The Holy Spirit was right in saying through Isaiah the prophet to your forefathers:

26 Go to this people and say to them, You will indeed hear *and* hear with your ears but will not understand, and you will indeed look *and* look with your eyes but will not see [not perceive, have knowledge of or become acquainted with what you look at, at all].

27 For the heart (the understanding, the soul) of this people has grown dull (stupid, hardened, and calloused), and their ears are heavy *and* hard of hearing and they have shut tight their eyes, so that they may not perceive *and* have knowledge *and* become acquainted with their eyes and hear with their ears and understand with their souls and turn [to Me and be converted], that I may heal them. [Isa. 6:9, 10.]

28 So let it be understood by you then that [this message of] the salvation of God has been sent to the Gentiles, and they will listen [to it]! [Ps. 67:2.]

29 *rAnd when he had said these things, the Jews went away, arguing and disputing among themselves.*

30 After this Paul lived there for two entire years [at his own expense] in his own rented lodging, and he welcomed all who came to him,

31 Preaching to them the kingdom of God and teaching them about the Lord Jesus Christ with boldness *and* quite openly, and without being molested *or* hindered.

r Many manuscripts do not contain this verse.

Romans

Author:
Paul

Date:
About AD 57

Everyday Life Principles:
Separate your "who" from your "do." You may do things that God is not pleased with, but He is always pleased with who you are because you are in Christ.

We cannot do anything to earn or deserve God's love; we must receive it as a gift from Him.

Jesus has made us righteous and because of His death on the cross, we are in right relationship with God.

The book of Romans contains many vital truths that are essential to a proper understanding of Christianity. I personally feel that people who do not know and understand Romans will struggle tremendously to really comprehend what it means to have new life in Christ and will probably fail to enjoy much of the blessed life God has for His people.

I like to talk about the difference between our "who" and our "do." Though Paul did not use those terms, much of the book of Romans addresses that very issue with clarity and detail. Paul understood so well that the things we *do* are separate from *who* we are. He teaches that once we know who we are in Christ, our behavior (our "do") will change, but trying to simply change behavior will never work. He knows that transformation comes to our "do" as we understand our "who" from God's perspective.

Many of Christianity's basic truths are found in Romans: we cannot earn God's love, but we must receive it as a gift; everyone sins; sin requires death; Jesus' death paid the price for our sin; in Christ, we are made righteous; we do not have to live under guilt and condemnation; *nothing* can separate us from God's love.

As you read the book of Romans, remember the truths on which our faith is built. Remember especially that you are righteous because of Jesus (see Romans 3:26) and that nothing can ever separate you from the love of God (see Romans 8:35–39).

1 FROM PAUL, a bond servant of Jesus Christ (the Messiah) called to be an apostle, (a special messenger) set apart to [preach] the Gospel (good news) of *and* from God,

2 Which He promised in advance [long ago] through His prophets in the sacred Scriptures—

3 [The Gospel] regarding His Son, Who as to the flesh (His human nature) was descended from David,

4 And [as to His divine nature] according to the Spirit of holiness was openly [a]designated the Son of God in power [in a striking, triumphant and miraculous manner] by His resurrection from the dead, even Jesus Christ our Lord (the Messiah, the Anointed One).

5 It is through Him that we have received grace (God's unmerited favor) and [our] apostleship to promote obedience to the faith *and* make disciples for His name's sake among all the nations,

6 And this includes you, called of Jesus Christ *and* invited [as you are] to belong to Him.

7 To [you then] all God's beloved ones in Rome, called to be saints *and* designated for a consecrated life: Grace *and* spiritual blessing and peace be yours from God our Father and from the Lord Jesus Christ.

8 First, I thank my God through Jesus Christ for all of you, because [the report of] your faith is made known to all the world *and* is [a]commended everywhere.

9 For God is my witness, Whom I serve with my [whole] spirit [rendering priestly and spiritual service] in [preaching] the Gospel *and* [telling] the good news of His Son, how incessantly I always mention you when at my prayers.

10 I keep pleading that somehow by God's will I may now at last prosper *and* come to you.

11 For I am yearning to see you, that I may impart *and* share with you some spiritual gift to strengthen *and* establish you;

12 That is, that we may be mutually strengthened *and* encouraged *and* comforted by each other's faith, both yours and mine.

13 I want you to know, brethren, that many times I have planned *and* intended to come to you, though thus far I have been hindered *and* prevented, in order that I might have some fruit (some result of my labors) among you, as I have among the rest of the Gentiles.

14 Both to Greeks and to barbarians (to the cultured and to the uncultured), both to the wise and the foolish, I have an obligation to discharge *and* a duty to perform *and* a debt to pay.

15 So, for my part, I am willing *and* eagerly ready to preach the Gospel to you also who are in Rome.

16 For I am not ashamed of the Gospel (good news) *of Christ,* for it is God's power working unto salvation [for deliverance from eternal death] to everyone who believes *with* a personal trust *and* a confident surrender *and* firm reliance, to the Jew first and also to the Greek,

17 For in the Gospel a righteousness which God ascribes is revealed, both springing from faith and leading to

speak the Word

God, I declare that I am not ashamed of the Gospel of Jesus Christ, because it is Your power that works unto salvation for everyone who believes.
ADAPTED FROM ROMANS 1:16

a Marvin Vincent, *Word Studies in the New Testament.*

consistent, confident faith

Romans 1:17 teaches us that people who are just and upright "shall live by faith." Faith is confidence in God. It is important that we learn to be *consistently* confident, not *occasionally* confident. Let me give you an example to illustrate what I mean.

In ministry, I learned to remain confident in God when someone got up and walked out while I was preaching. In the beginning of my ministry, that type of occurrence brought out all of my insecurities and practically destroyed my confidence. Due to a lack of properly understanding God's Word, some of our friends and family members told me that a woman should not preach the Word of God. I also knew that some people, particularly men, had difficulty receiving the Word from a woman. This was confusing to me because I knew God called me and anointed me to preach His Word. I could not have done it otherwise, but people's rejection still affected me because I lacked confidence. I had to grow in confidence to the place where people's opinions and their acceptance or rejection did not alter my confidence level. My confidence had to be in God, not in people.

When the growth and progress of my ministry seemed painfully slow, I had to practice being consistently confident. It is easier to remain confident when we see progress, but during times of waiting the devil attacks our confidence and attempts to destroy it. We must resist him.

Romans 1:17 speaks about the whole issue of faith. It says that we shall live by faith. The King James Version of this verse says the righteousness of God is revealed "from faith to faith." In other words, we can go from faith to faith. I spent many years going from faith to doubt to unbelief and then back to faith. I lost a lot of precious time until I became consistent in my faith walk. Since then, I have tried to practice being confident in all things, with God's help.

You can have consistent and confident faith too. Ask God to help you resist the enemy's attack when he tries to rob you of that faith. Learn to go from "faith to faith" with overcoming confidence.

faith [disclosed through the way of faith that arouses to more faith]. As it is written, The man who through faith is just *and* upright shall live *and* shall live by faith. [Hab. 2:4.]

18 For God's [holy] wrath *and* indignation are revealed from heaven against all ungodliness and unrighteousness of men, who in their wickedness repress *and* hinder the truth *and* make it inoperative.

19 For that which is known about God is evident to them *and* made plain in their inner consciousness, because God [Himself] has shown it to them.

20 For ever since the creation of the world His invisible nature *and* attributes, that is, His eternal power and divinity, have been made intelligible *and* clearly discernible in *and* through the things that have been made (His handiworks). So [men] are without excuse [altogether without any defense or justification], [Ps. 19: 1-4.]

21 Because when they knew *and* recognized Him as God, they did not honor *and* glorify Him as God or give Him thanks. But instead they became futile *and* [b]godless in their thinking [with vain imaginings, foolish reasoning, and stupid speculations] and their senseless minds were darkened.

22 Claiming to be wise, they became fools [professing to be smart, they made simpletons of themselves].

23 And by them the glory and majesty *and* excellence of the immortal God were exchanged for *and* represented by images, resembling mortal man and birds and beasts and reptiles.

24 Therefore God gave them up in the lusts of their [own] hearts to sexual impurity, to the dishonoring of their bodies among themselves [abandoning them to the degrading power of sin],

25 Because they exchanged the truth of God for a lie and worshiped and served the creature rather than the Creator, Who is blessed forever! Amen (so be it). [Jer. 2:11.]

26 For this reason God gave them over *and* abandoned them to vile affections *and* degrading passions. For their women exchanged their natural function for an unnatural *and* abnormal one,

27 And the men also turned from natural relations with women and were set ablaze (burning out, consumed) with lust for one another—men committing shameful acts with men and suffering in their own [c]bodies *and* personalities the inevitable consequences *and* penalty of their wrong-doing *and* going astray, which was [their] fitting retribution.

28 And so, since they did not see fit to acknowledge God *or* approve of Him *or* consider Him worth the know-ing, God gave them over to a base *and* condemned mind to do things not proper *or* decent *but* loathsome,

29 Until they were filled (permeated and saturated) with every kind of unrighteousness, iniquity, grasping *and* covetous greed, and malice. [They were] full of envy *and* jealousy, murder, strife, deceit *and* treachery, ill will *and* cruel ways. [They were] secret backbiters *and* gossipers,

30 Slanderers, hateful to *and* hating God, full of insolence, arrogance, [and] boasting; inventors of new forms of evil, disobedient *and* undutiful to parents.

31 [They were] without understanding, conscienceless *and* faithless, heartless *and* loveless [and] merciless.

32 Though they are fully aware of God's righteous decree that those who do such things deserve to die, they not only do them themselves but approve *and* applaud others who practice them.

2 THEREFORE YOU have no excuse *or* defense *or* justification, O man, whoever you are who judges *and* condemns another. For in posing as judge *and* passing sentence on another, you condemn yourself, because you who judge are habitually practicing the very same things [that you censure and denounce].

2 [But] we know that the judgment (adverse verdict, sentence) of God falls justly *and* in accordance with truth upon those who practice such things.

3 And do you think *or* imagine, O man, when you judge *and* condemn those who practice such things and yet do them yourself, that you will escape God's judgment *and* elude His sentence *and* adverse verdict?

4 Or are you [so blind as to] trifle with *and* presume upon *and* despise

b Alexander Souter, *Pocket Lexicon of the Greek New Testament.* **c** *Webster's New International Dictionary* offers this as a definition of "selves."

life point

Romans 2:1 teaches us that the things we judge in other people are the very things we do ourselves.

The Lord once gave me a good example to help me understand this principle. I was pondering why we would do something ourselves and think it was perfectly all right, but judge someone else for doing it. He said, "Joyce, you look at yourself through rose-colored glasses, but you look at everyone else through a magnifying glass."

We make excuses for our own behavior, but when someone else behaves exactly the same way, we are often merciless. Doing unto others as we want them to do to us (see Matthew 7:12) is a good life principle to follow, one that prevents us from indulging in judgment and criticism.

Judgmental thoughts come from a negative mind—a mind that thinks about what is wrong with an individual instead of what is right.

I encourage you to learn to be positive and not negative! Others will benefit, but you will benefit more than anyone.

and underestimate the wealth of His kindness and forbearance and long-suffering patience? Are you unmindful *or* actually ignorant [of the fact] that God's kindness is intended to lead you to repent ([d]to change your mind and inner man to accept God's will)?

5 But by your callous stubbornness *and* impenitence of heart you are storing up wrath *and* indignation for yourself on the day of wrath *and* indignation, when God's righteous judgment (just doom) will be revealed.

6 For He will render to every man according to his works [justly, as his deeds deserve]: [Ps. 62:12.]

7 To those who by patient persistence in well-doing [[e]springing from piety] seek [unseen but sure] glory and honor and [[e]the eternal blessedness of] immortality, He will give eternal life.

8 But for those who are self-seeking *and* self-willed *and* disobedient to the Truth but responsive to wickedness, there will be indignation and wrath.

9 [And] there will be tribulation *and* anguish and calamity *and* constraint for every soul of man who [habitually] does evil, the Jew first and also the Greek (Gentile).

10 But glory and honor and [heart] peace shall be awarded to everyone who [habitually] does good, the Jew first and also the Greek (Gentile).

11 For God shows no partiality [[f]undue favor or unfairness; with Him one man is not different from another]. [Deut. 10:17; II Chron. 19:7.]

12 All who have sinned without the Law will also perish without [regard to] the Law, and all who have sinned under the Law will be judged *and* condemned by the Law.

13 For it is not merely hearing the

speak the Word

Thank you, God, that You show no partiality, undue favor, or unfairness. With You, one person is no different from another.
ADAPTED FROM ROMANS 2:11

---

d Alexander Souter, *Pocket Lexicon.* **e** Joseph Thayer, *A Greek-English Lexicon of the New Testament.* **f** James Moulton and George Milligan, *The Vocabulary of the Greek Testament.*

Law [read] that makes one righteous before God, but it is the doers of the Law who will be held guiltless *and* acquitted *and* justified.

14 When Gentiles who have not the [divine] Law do instinctively what the Law requires, they are a law to themselves, since they do not have the Law.

15 They show that the essential requirements of the Law are written in their hearts *and* are operating there, with which their consciences (sense of right and wrong) also bear witness; and their [moral] ᵍdecisions (their arguments of reason, their condemning or approving ʰthoughts) will accuse or perhaps defend *and* excuse [them]

16 On that day when, as my Gospel proclaims, God by Jesus Christ will judge men in regard to ʰthe things which they conceal (their hidden thoughts). [Eccl. 12:14.]

17 But if you bear the name of Jew and rely upon the Law and pride yourselves in God *and* your relationship to Him,

18 And know *and* understand His will and discerningly approve the better things *and* have a sense of what is vital, because you are instructed by the Law;

19 And if you are confident that you [yourself] are a guide to the blind, a light to those who are in darkness, and [that

20 You are] a corrector of the foolish, a teacher of the childish, having in the Law the embodiment of knowledge and truth—

21 Well then, you who teach others, do you not teach yourself? While you teach against stealing, do you steal (take what does not really belong to you)?

22 You who say not to commit adultery, do you commit adultery [are you unchaste in action or in thought]? You who abhor *and* loathe idols, do you rob temples [do you appropriate to your own use what is consecrated to God, thus robbing the sanctuary and ⁱdoing sacrilege]?

23 You who boast in the Law, do you dishonor God by breaking the Law [by stealthily infringing upon or carelessly neglecting or openly breaking it]?

24 For, as it is written, The name of God is maligned *and* blasphemed among the Gentiles because of you! [The words to this effect are from your own Scriptures.] [Isa. 52:5; Ezek. 36:20.]

25 Circumcision does indeed profit if you keep the Law; but if you habitually transgress the Law, your circumcision is made uncircumcision.

26 So if a man who is uncircumcised keeps the requirements of the Law, will not his uncircumcision be credited to him as [equivalent to] circumcision?

27 Then those who are physically uncircumcised but keep the Law will condemn you who, although you have the code in writing and have circumcision, break the Law.

28 For he is not a [real] Jew who is only one outwardly *and* publicly, nor is [true] circumcision something external and physical.

29 But he is a Jew who is one inwardly, and [true] circumcision is of the heart, a spiritual and not a literal [matter]. His praise is not from men but from God.

3 THEN WHAT advantage remains to the Jew? [How is he favored?] Or what is the value *or* benefit of circumcision?

2 Much in every way. To begin with, to the Jews were entrusted the oracles

---

g Joseph Thayer, *A Greek-English Lexicon of the New Testament.* **h** Henry Alford, *The Greek New Testament, with Notes.* **i** James Moulton and George Milligan, *The Vocabulary.*

(the brief communications, the intentions, the utterances) of God. [Ps. 147:19.]

3 What if some did not believe *and* were without faith? Does their lack of faith *and* their faithlessness nullify *and* make ineffective *and* void the faithfulness of God *and* His fidelity [to His Word]?

4 By no means! Let God be found true though every human being is false *and* a liar, as it is written, That You may be justified *and* shown to be upright in what You say, and prevail when You are judged [by sinful men]. [Ps. 51:4.]

5 But if our unrighteousness thus establishes *and* exhibits the righteousness of God, what shall we say? That God is unjust *and* wrong to inflict His wrath upon us [Jews]? I speak in a [purely] human way.

6 By no means! Otherwise, how could God judge the world?

7 But [you say] if through my falsehood God's integrity is magnified *and* advertised *and* abounds to His glory, why am I still being judged as a sinner?

8 And why should we not do evil that good may come?—as some slanderously charge us with teaching. Such [false teaching] is justly condemned by them.

9 Well then, are we [Jews] superior *and* better off than they? No, not at all. We have already charged that all men, both Jews and Greeks (Gentiles), are under sin [held down by and subject to its power and control].

10 As it is written, None is righteous, just *and* truthful *and* upright *and* conscientious, no, not one. [Ps. 14:3.]

11 No one understands [no one intelligently discerns *or* comprehends]; no one seeks out God. [Ps. 14:2.]

12 All have turned aside; together they have gone wrong *and* have become unprofitable *and* worthless; no one does right, not even one!

13 Their throat is a yawning grave; they use their tongues to deceive (to mislead and to deal treacherously). The venom of asps is beneath their lips. [Ps. 5:9; 140:3.]

14 Their mouth is full of cursing and bitterness. [Ps. 10:7.]

15 Their feet are swift to shed blood.

16 Destruction [as it dashes them to pieces] and misery mark their ways.

17 And they have no experience of the way of peace [they know nothing about peace, for a peaceful way they do not even recognize]. [Isa. 59:7, 8.]

18 There is no [reverential] fear of God before their eyes. [Ps. 36:1.]

19 Now we know that whatever the Law says, it speaks to those who are under the Law, so that [the murmurs and excuses of] every mouth may be hushed and all the world may be held accountable to God.

20 For no person will be justified (made righteous, acquitted, and

life point

Romans 3:17 describes how my life used to be. I had no experience at all with enjoying a peaceful life; I did not even know how to begin. I grew up in an atmosphere of strife, and that was all I ever knew. I had to learn an entirely new way of living.

Now I am addicted to peace. As soon as my peace disappears, I ask myself how I lost it and start looking for ways to get it back.

I believe that you will become so hungry for peace with God, peace with yourself, and peace with others that you will be willing to make whatever adjustments you need to make in order to have it. I also believe that you will begin to follow peace at all times because peace will lead you into God's perfect will for your life.

all have sinned

We sometimes fall into the trap of thinking we are the worst people on the face of the earth and that nobody does as many wrong things as we do. But Romans 3:23 says that *all* have sinned and fallen short of the glory (excellence) of God. Every man, woman, or child who was ever born, or ever will be, has a problem with sin. But the good news is that God has provided an answer to our dilemma.

Just as all have sinned, all are justified and made righteous through the redemption provided in Christ Jesus. That means that, as believers in Jesus Christ, we now have "rightness" instead of "wrongness." For much of my life I felt all wrong. I had a recording playing in my head over and over again: *What is wrong with me?*

Satan wants us to feel wrong, worthless, and like hopeless messes. He knows that without confidence we will never step out in faith to fulfill our God-ordained destinies. He knows if he can keep us in the prison of self-hatred, self-rejection, or just plain not liking ourselves that he will prevent us from making progress or ever being a threat to him and to the kingdom of darkness.

We must believe we have been made righteous in God's sight before we will behave rightly. We cannot produce the fruit of something for which no seed has been sown. Jesus Himself is the Righteous Seed sown in death and resurrected in power, so we can say along with the apostle Paul, "For our sake He made Christ [virtually] to be sin Who knew no sin, so that in and through Him we might become [endued with, viewed as being in, and examples of] the righteousness of God [what we ought to be, approved and acceptable and in right relationship with Him, by His goodness]" (II Corinthians 5:21).

judged acceptable) in His sight by observing the works prescribed by the Law. For [the real function of] the Law is to make men recognize *and* be conscious of sin [[j]not mere perception, but an acquaintance with sin which works toward repentance, faith, and holy character].

21 But now the righteousness of God has been revealed independently *and* altogether apart from the Law, although actually it is attested by the Law and the Prophets,

22 Namely, the righteousness of God which comes by believing *with* personal trust *and* confident reliance on Jesus Christ (the Messiah). [And it is meant] for all who believe. For there is no distinction,

23 Since all have sinned and are falling short of the honor *and* glory [[j]which God bestows *and* receives.

24 [All] are justified *and* made upright *and* in right standing with God, freely *and* gratuitously by His grace (His unmerited favor and mercy), through the redemption which is [provided] in Christ Jesus,

25 Whom God put forward [[k]before the eyes of all] as a mercy seat *and*

j Marvin Vincent, *Word Studies*.   **k** Johann Bengel, *Gnomon Novi Testamenti*.

propitiation by His blood [the cleansing and life-giving sacrifice of atonement and reconciliation, to be received] through faith. This was to show God's righteousness, because in His divine forbearance He had passed over *and* ignored former sins without punishment.

26 It was to demonstrate *and* prove at the present time ([1]in the now season) that He Himself is righteous and that He justifies *and* accepts as righteous him who has [true] faith in Jesus.

27 Then what becomes of [our] pride *and* [our] boasting? It is excluded (banished, ruled out entirely). On what principle? [On the principle] of doing good deeds? No, but on the principle of faith.

28 For we hold that a man is justified

life point

If we truly desire to succeed at being ourselves, we absolutely must have a thorough understanding of what justifies us and makes us right with God. This wonderful scripture, Romans 3:28, gives great news! It tells us we are justified by faith in Christ alone and not by our works (see also Ephesians 2:8, 9).

If we have real faith, we will do good works, but our dependence will not be on works. Our works will be done as acts of love for God—in obedience to Him—rather than as "works of the flesh" by which we hope to gain right standing and acceptance with Him.

speak the Word

and made upright by faith independent of *and* distinctly apart from good deeds (works of the Law). [The observance of the Law has nothing to do with justification.]

29 Or is God merely [the God] of Jews? Is He not the God of Gentiles also? Yes, of Gentiles also,

30 Since it is one and the same God Who will justify the circumcised by faith [[m]which germinated from Abraham] and the uncircumcised through their [newly acquired] faith. [For it is the same trusting faith in both cases, a firmly relying faith in Jesus Christ].

31 Do we then by [this] faith make the Law of no effect, overthrow it *or* make it a dead letter? Certainly not! On the contrary, we confirm *and* establish *and* uphold the Law.

4 [BUT] IF so, what shall we say about Abraham, our forefather humanly speaking—[what did he] find out? [How does this affect his position, and what was gained by him?]

2 For if Abraham was justified ([n]established as just by acquittal from guilt) by good works [that he did, then] he has grounds for boasting. But not before God!

3 For what does the Scripture say? Abraham believed in (trusted in) God, and it was credited to his account as righteousness (right living and right standing with God). [Gen. 15:6.]

4 Now to a laborer, his wages are not counted as a favor *or* a gift, but as an obligation (something owed to him).

Thank You, Lord, that I am justified and in right standing with You by Your grace and through the redemption You have provided for me in Jesus Christ.
ADAPTED FROM ROMANS 3:24

1 Literal translation. **m** Marvin Vincent, *Word Studies*. **n** Hermann Cremer, *Biblico-Theological Lexicon of New Testament Greek*.

5 But to one who, not working [by the Law], trusts (believes fully) in Him Who justifies the ungodly, his faith is credited to him as righteousness (the standing acceptable to God).
6 Thus David °congratulates the man *and* pronounces a blessing on him to whom God credits righteousness apart from the works he does:
7 Blessed *and* happy *and* °to be envied are those whose iniquities are forgiven and whose sins are covered up *and* completely buried.
8 Blessed *and* happy *and* °to be envied is the person of whose sin the Lord will take no account *nor* reckon it against him. [Ps. 32:1, 2.]
9 Is this blessing (happiness) then meant only for the circumcised, or also for the uncircumcised? We say that faith was credited to Abraham as righteousness.
10 How then was it credited [to him]? Was it before or after he had been circumcised? It was not after, but before he was circumcised.
11 He received the mark of circumcision as a token *or* an evidence [and] seal of the righteousness which he had by faith while he was still uncircumcised—[faith] so that he was to be made the father of all who [truly] believe, though without circumcision, and who thus have righteousness (right standing with God) imputed to them *and* credited to their account,
12 As well as [that he be made] the father of those circumcised persons who are not merely circumcised, but also walk in the way of that faith which our father Abraham had before he was circumcised.
13 For the promise to Abraham or his posterity, that he should inherit the world, did not come through [observing the commands of] the Law but through the righteousness of faith. [Gen. 17:4-6; 22:16-18.]

14 If it is the adherents of the Law who are to be the heirs, then faith is made futile *and* empty of all meaning and the promise [of God] is made void (is annulled and has no power).
15 For the Law results in [divine] wrath, but where there is no law there is no transgression [of it either].
16 Therefore, [inheriting] the promise is the outcome of faith *and* depends [entirely] on faith, in order that it might be given as an act of grace (unmerited favor), to make it stable *and* valid *and* guaranteed to all his descendants—not only to the devotees *and* adherents of the Law, but also to those who share the faith of Abraham, who is [thus] the father of us all.
17 As it is written, I have made you the father of many nations. [He was appointed our father] in the sight of God in Whom he believed, Who gives life to the dead and speaks of the nonexistent things that [He has foretold and promised] as if they [already] existed. [Gen. 17:5.]

life point

I encourage you to take a positive look at the possibilities of the future and speak of those things that are nonexistent as though they do exist (see Romans 4:17). Think and speak about your future in a positive way according to what God has placed in your heart—not according to what you have seen in the past or are seeing even now in the present. He has a great future for you. Believe it and confess it!

18 [For Abraham, human reason for] hope being gone, hoped in faith that he should become the father of many nations, as he had been promised, So [numberless] shall your descendants be. [Gen. 15:5.]

o Alexander Souter, *Pocket Lexicon.*

life point

Look beyond where you are and see with the eyes of faith, believing God for even the impossible! Romans 4:18 says that Abraham had no reason at all to hope, but he hoped in faith that God's promise to him would be fulfilled (see Genesis 15:5). A hopeful mind and attitude administer peace and joy, while fear and discouragement steal both.

It costs nothing to be positive and believe that God can change you and your life. Jump-start your blessings by saying you love your life, and be thankful in all things, no matter what the circumstances may be.

19 He did not weaken in faith when he considered the [utter] impotence of his own body, which was as good as dead because he was about a hundred years old, or [when he considered] the barrenness of Sarah's [deadened] womb. [Gen. 17:17; 18:11.]
20 No unbelief *or* distrust made him waver (doubtingly question) concerning the promise of God, but he grew strong *and* was empowered by faith as he gave praise *and* glory to God,
21 Fully satisfied *and* assured that God was able *and* mighty to keep His word *and* to do what He had promised.
22 That is why his faith was credited to him as righteousness (right standing with God).
23 But [the words], It was credited to him, were written not for his sake alone,
24 But [they were written] for our sakes too. [Righteousness, standing acceptable to God] will be granted *and* credited to us also who believe in (trust in, adhere to, and rely on) God,

Who raised Jesus our Lord from the dead,
25 Who was betrayed *and* put to death because of our misdeeds and was raised to secure our justification (our Pacquittal), [making our account balance and absolving us from all guilt before God].

5 THEREFORE, SINCE we are justified (Pacquitted, declared righteous, and given a right standing with God) through faith, let us [grasp the fact that we] have [the

life point

Romans 4:18–21 reminds us that God promised Abraham he would have an heir from his own body (see Genesis 15:1–6). Many years came and went and still there was no child as a result of Abraham and Sarah's relationship. Abraham still stood in faith, believing that what God had said would come to pass. As he stood, he was attacked with thoughts of doubt, and the spirit of unbelief pressed him to disobey God.

Disobedience in a situation like this can simply be giving up when God prompts us to press on. Disobedience is disregarding the voice of the Lord, or whatever God is speaking to us personally, not just transgressing the Ten Commandments or a specific Bible verse.

Romans 4:20 states that Abraham continued to be steadfast; he kept praising and giving glory to God. As he did so, he grew strong in faith. He felt confident that God would keep His word. Follow Abraham's example and keep your heart filled with faith and your actions filled with obedience.

p G. Abbott-Smith, *Manual Greek Lexicon of the New Testament.*

faith for fulfillment

When I am in a battle, knowing what God has promised but still experiencing attacks from doubt and unbelief, I like to meditate on Romans 4:18–21.

When God tells us something or asks us to do something, the faith to believe or do it comes with a word from God. It is ridiculous to think that God would expect us to do something without giving us the ability to believe we can do it. Satan knows how dangerous we are when our hearts are full of faith, so he attacks us with doubt and unbelief. It isn't that we do not have faith; it is just that Satan tries to destroy our faith with lies.

Let me give you an example concerning the time I received my call to the ministry. It was an ordinary morning like any other, except that I had just finished listening to my first Christian teaching tape. I was stirred in my heart and amazed that anyone could teach from one scripture for a whole hour, and that all of his teaching would be interesting. I suddenly felt an intense desire to teach God's Word well up in me. Then the voice of the Lord came to me, saying, "You will go all over the place and teach My Word, and you will have a large teaching tape ministry." I did not hear God's audible voice, but I did hear a still small voice deep inside of me.

There would have been no natural reason at all for me to believe that God actually spoke to me, or that I could or ever would do what I thought I just heard. I had many problems within myself. I did not look like "ministry material," but God chooses the weak and foolish things of the world to put the wise to shame (see I Corinthians 1:27). He looks on the heart of man and not the outward appearance (see I Samuel 16:7). If a person's inner heart is right, God can change the outside.

Although there was nothing in the natural to indicate that I should believe when the desire for a teaching ministry came over me, I was filled with faith that I could do what the Lord wanted me to do. When God calls, He gives desire, faith, and ability to do the job. But I also want to tell you that during the years I spent in training and waiting, the devil regularly attacked me with doubt and unbelief.

God places dreams and visions in the hearts of His people; they begin as little "seeds." Just as a woman has a seed planted into her womb when she becomes pregnant, so we become "pregnant," so to speak, with the things God speaks and promises. During the "pregnancy," Satan works hard to try and get us to "abort" our dreams. One of the tools he uses is doubt; another is unbelief. Both of these work against the mind.

Faith is a product of the spirit; it is a spiritual force. The enemy does not want your mind to agree with your spirit. He knows that if God places in you the faith to do something, and you get positive and start consistently believing that you can actually do it, then you will do considerable damage to his kingdom.

I encourage you to be assured in your faith that God will follow through with what He has promised you by His Word. Get His promises into your mind; think about them; speak of them; and let your faith increase.

putting the Word to work

Have you ever wondered if God can really do what He has promised? Abraham had good reason to doubt— God promised him a child even though he and his wife were far beyond child-bearing years. Yet God's Word tells us that Abraham's faith grew as he waited for the fulfillment of God's promise (see Romans 4:20). When you are tempted to doubt God's promises, ask God to give you growing faith like Abraham's, so you too will be convinced that what God promises, He will fulfill in your life.

peace of reconciliation to hold and to ᑫenjoy] peace with God through our Lord Jesus Christ (the Messiah, the Anointed One).
2 Through Him also we have [our] access (entrance, introduction) by faith into this grace (state of God's favor) in which we [firmly and safely] stand. And let us rejoice *and* exult in our hope of experiencing *and* enjoying the glory of God.
3 Moreover [let us also be full of joy now!] let us exult *and* triumph in our troubles *and* rejoice in our sufferings, knowing that pressure *and* affliction *and* hardship produce patient *and* unswerving endurance.
4 And endurance (fortitude) develops maturity of ʳcharacter (approved faith and ˢtried integrity). And character [of this sort] produces [the habit of] ᵗjoyful and confident hope of eternal salvation.
5 Such hope never disappoints *or* deludes *or* shames us, for God's love has been poured out in our hearts through the Holy Spirit Who has been given to us.

6 While we were yet in weakness [powerless to help ourselves], at the fitting time Christ died for (in behalf of) the ungodly.
7 Now it is an extraordinary thing for one to give his life even for an upright man, though perhaps for a noble *and* lovable *and* generous benefactor someone might even dare to die.
8 But God shows *and* clearly proves His [own] love for us by the fact that while we were still sinners, Christ (the Messiah, the Anointed One) died for us.

putting the Word to work

Would you give your life for someone who despised you? That is exactly what Jesus did, according to Romans 5:6–8. God loved you so much, that even before you loved Him, when you were against Him, He sent Jesus to die for you. Thank God for His awesome love today!

9 Therefore, since we are now justified (ᵘacquitted, made righteous, and brought into right relationship with God) by Christ's blood, how much more [certain is it that] we shall be saved by Him from the indignation *and* wrath of God.
10 For if while we were enemies we were reconciled to God through the death of His Son, it is much more [certain], now that we are reconciled, that we shall be saved (daily delivered from sin's dominion) through His [ᵘresurrection] life.
11 Not only so, but we also rejoice *and* exultingly glory in God [in His love and perfection] through our Lord Jesus Christ, through Whom we have now received *and* enjoy [our] reconciliation. [Jer. 9:24.]

q Literal translation: "have" or "hold," so "enjoy."   r Alexander Souter, *Pocket Lexicon*.   s Marvin Vincent, *Word Studies*.   t Joseph Thayer, *A Greek-English Lexicon*.   u G. Abbott-Smith, *Manual Greek Lexicon*.

you are loved

Romans 5:5 says that the love of God is poured out in our hearts by the Holy Spirit, Whom He gave to us. This simply means that when the Lord, in the form of the Holy Spirit, comes to dwell in our hearts through our faith in His Son, Jesus Christ, He brings love with Him, because God is love (see I John 4:8).

We all need to ask ourselves is what we are doing with the love of God that has been given freely to us. Do we reject it because we don't think we are valuable enough to be loved? Do we believe God is like other people who have rejected and hurt us? Or do we receive His love by faith, believing that He is greater than our failures and weaknesses?

What kind of relationship do you have with God, with yourself, and ultimately with others?

For a long time, I did not know that I had a relationship with myself. It was something I never thought of until God began teaching me in this area. I now realize that I spend more time with myself than with anyone else, and it is vital that I get along well with me. Of course, the same is true for you.

We all know how agonizing it is to work day after day with someone we do not get along with, but at least we do not have to take that person home with us at night. But we are with ourselves all the time, day and night. We never have one minute away from ourselves, not even one second—therefore, it is of the utmost importance that we have peace with ourselves and accept God's love into our hearts. I encourage you to receive God's love in a fresh way today.

12 Therefore, as sin came into the world through one man, and death as the result of sin, so death spread to all men, [ᵛno one being able to stop it or to escape its power] because all men sinned.

13 [To be sure] sin was in the world before ever the Law was given, but sin is not charged to men's account where there is no law [to transgress].

14 Yet death held sway from Adam to Moses [the Lawgiver], even over those who did not themselves transgress [a positive command] as Adam did. Adam was a type (prefigure) of the One Who was to come [in reverse, ᵛthe former destructive, the Latter saving]. [Gen. 5:5; 7:22; Deut. 34:5.]

15 But God's free gift is not at all to be compared to the trespass [His grace is out of all proportion to the fall of man]. For if many died through one man's falling away (his lapse, his offense), much more profusely did God's grace and the free gift [that comes] through the undeserved favor of the one Man Jesus Christ abound *and* overflow to *and* for [the benefit of] many.

16 Nor is the free gift at all to be compared to the effect of that one [man's] sin. For the sentence [following the trespass] of one [man] brought condemnation, whereas the free gift

v Joseph Thayer, *A Greek-English Lexicon.*

[following] many transgressions brings justification (ʷan act of righteousness).

17 For if because of one man's trespass (lapse, offense) death reigned through that one, much more surely will those who receive [God's] overflowing grace (unmerited favor) and the free gift of righteousness [putting them into right standing with Himself] reign as kings in life through the one Man Jesus Christ (the Messiah, the Anointed One).

18 Well then, as one man's trespass [one man's false step and falling away led] to condemnation for all men, so one Man's act of righteousness [leads] to acquittal *and* right standing with God and life for all men.

19 For just as by one man's disobedience (failing to hear, ˣheedlessness, and carelessness) the many were constituted sinners, so by one Man's obedience the many will be constituted righteous (made acceptable to God, brought into right standing with Him).

20 But then Law came in, [only] to expand *and* increase the trespass [making it more apparent and exciting opposition]. But where sin increased *and* abounded, grace (God's unmerited favor) has surpassed it *and* increased the more *and* superabounded,

21 So that, [just] as sin has reigned in death, [so] grace (His unearned and undeserved favor) might reign also through righteousness (right standing with God) which issues in eternal life through Jesus Christ (the Messiah, the Anointed One) our Lord.

6 WHAT SHALL we say [to all this]? Are we to remain in sin in order that God's grace (favor and mercy) may multiply *and* overflow?

2 Certainly not! How can we who died to sin live in it any longer?

life point

What do you believe about yourself? Do you believe you must have approval from people in order to be happy? If so, you will never be happy when anyone disapproves of you. Do you believe that you are all wrong? If you do, you will continue to produce wrong behavior. Your life will bear fruit on the outside of what you believe about yourself on the inside.

God wants us to behave correctly, so He gives us what we need in order to do that. God never requires us to do something without giving us what we need to do it. God gives us the gift of righteousness so we can become righteous in what we think, say, and do! Although we sin, God's free gift of righteousness cannot even be compared to our sin. Our sin is great, but His free gift of righteousness is greater. Our sin is swallowed up in His righteousness. Our righteousness is not found in what people think of us, it is found in Christ. Romans 5:17 says that Christ is our righteousness from God.

Let that truth sink into your heart and mind. Jesus Christ is your righteousness. You are righteous in Him, and because of that God is pleased with you.

3 Are you ignorant of the fact that all of us who have been baptized into Christ Jesus were baptized into His death?

4 We were buried therefore with Him by the baptism into death, so that just as Christ was raised from the dead by the glorious [power] of the Father, so we too might [habitually] live *and* behave in newness of life.

---

w Literal translation. **x** Marvin Vincent, *Word Studies*.

the power of obedience

Romans 5:19 teaches us that our choices to obey or not to obey not only affect us, but many other people too. We see an example of this in Scripture when the Israelites experienced the fruit of their disobedience after their exodus from Egypt. If they had promptly obeyed God, how much greater their lives would have been (see Hebrews 3:8–11)! Many of them and their children died in the wilderness because they would not submit to God's ways. Their children were affected by their decisions, and so are ours.

Recently, my oldest son said, "Mom, I have something to tell you, and I may cry, but hear me out. I have been thinking about you and Dad and the years you have put into this ministry, and all the times you chose to obey God and how it has not always been easy for you. I realize, Mom, that you and Dad have gone through things that nobody knows about, and I want you to know that this morning God made me aware that I am benefiting greatly from your obedience, and I appreciate it."

What he said meant a lot to me, and it reminded me of Romans 5:19.

Your decision to obey God affects other people, and when you decide to disobey God, that also affects others too. You may disobey God and choose to stay in the wilderness, but please keep in mind that if you now have children or ever will have children, your decisions will keep them in the wilderness with you. They may manage to get themselves out when they are grown, but I can assure you that they will pay a price for your disobedience.

Obedience is a far-reaching choice; it closes the gates of hell and opens the windows of heaven, and it has the power to affect many people. Just think of it: Because of Jesus' willingness to be obedient, countless multitudes will be brought into right standing with God.

Your life might be in better shape now if someone in your past obeyed God. If there is a cycle of disobedience in your family or among your friends, why not break it by refusing to be disobedient in your own life? Tell God you want to obey and ask Him to help you. That way, you will set yourself and your children up for great blessings!

5 For if we have become one with Him by sharing a death like His, we shall also be [one with Him in sharing] His resurrection [by a new life lived for God].
6 We know that our old (unrenewed) self was nailed to the cross with Him in order that [our] body [which is the instrument] of sin might be made ineffective *and* inactive for evil, that we might no longer be the slaves of sin.
7 For when a man dies, he is freed (loosed, delivered) from [the power of] sin [among men].
8 Now if we have died with Christ, we believe that we shall also live with Him,

9 Because we know that Christ (the Anointed One), being once raised from the dead, will never die again; death no longer has power over Him.
10 For by the death He died, He died to sin [ending His relation to it] once for all; and the life that He lives, He is living to God [in unbroken fellowship with Him].
11 Even so consider yourselves also dead to sin *and* your relation to it broken, but alive to God [living in unbroken fellowship with Him] in Christ Jesus.
12 Let not sin therefore rule as king in your mortal (short-lived, perishable) bodies, to make you yield to its cravings *and* be subject to its lusts *and* evil passions.
13 Do not continue offering or yielding your bodily members [and ^yfaculties] to sin as instruments (tools) of wickedness. But offer *and* yield yourselves to God as though you have been raised from the dead to [perpetual] life, and your bodily members [and ^yfaculties] to God, presenting them as implements of righteousness.
14 For sin shall not [any longer] exert dominion over you, since now you are not under Law [as slaves], but under grace [as subjects of God's favor and mercy].
15 What then [are we to conclude]? Shall we sin because we live not under Law but under God's favor *and* mercy? Certainly not!
16 Do you not know that if you continually surrender yourselves to anyone to do his will, you are the slaves of him whom you obey, whether that be to sin, which leads to death, or to obedience which leads to righteousness (right doing and right standing with God)?
17 But thank God, though you were once slaves of sin, you have become

putting the Word to work

Romans 6:15 says that knowing we will receive forgiveness does not mean we are free to sin! Grace is not meant to encourage sin. Rather, we are to live in obedience. Is there an area of sin in your life that you struggle with? Do not treat it casually because you know you will be forgiven, but ask God to strengthen you and to help you stop committing this sin.

obedient with all your heart to the standard of teaching in which you were instructed *and* to which you were committed.
18 And having been set free from sin, you have become the servants of righteousness (of conformity to the divine will in thought, purpose, and action).
19 I am speaking in familiar human terms because of your natural limitations. For as you yielded your bodily members [and ^yfaculties] as servants to impurity and ever increasing lawlessness, so now yield your bodily members [and ^yfaculties] once for all as servants to righteousness (right being and doing) [which leads] to sanctification.
20 For when you were slaves of sin, you were free in regard to righteousness.
21 But then what benefit (return) did you get from the things of which you are now ashamed? [None] for the end of those things is death.
22 But now since you have been set free from sin and have become the slaves of God, you have your present reward in holiness and its end is eternal life.
23 For the wages which sin pays is death, but the [bountiful] free gift of

---

y Marvin Vincent, *Word Studies*: Greek *mele*—"Physical; though some commentators interpret it to include the mental faculties as well."

putting the Word to work

What is the difference between a paycheck and a gift? You earn a paycheck, but you receive a gift. In Romans 6:23, Paul teaches that the payment, the unavoidable consequence we earned because of our sin, is death. What a relief that God offers to every individual the gift—something we cannot earn—of eternal life in Jesus Christ. If you have received this gift, thank God for His generosity and grace! If you have not yet received God's gift of eternal life, I encourage you to ask Him for it. He will gladly give it to you!

God is eternal life through (in union with) Jesus Christ our Lord.

7 DO YOU not know, brethren—for I am speaking to men who are acquainted with the Law—that legal claims have power over a person only for as long as he is alive? 2 For [instance] a married woman is bound by law to her husband as long as he lives; but if her husband dies, she is loosed *and* discharged from the law concerning her husband. 3 Accordingly, she will be held an adulteress if she unites herself to another man while her husband lives. But if her husband dies, the marriage law no longer is binding on her [she is free from that law]; and if she unites herself to another man, she is not an adulteress. 4 Likewise, my brethren, you have undergone death as to the Law through the [crucified] body of Christ, so that now you may belong to Another, to Him Who was raised from the dead in order that we may bear fruit for God. 5 When we were living in the flesh (mere physical lives), the sinful passions that were awakened *and* aroused up by [what] the Law [makes sin] were constantly operating in our natural powers (in our bodily organs, [z]in the sensitive appetites and wills of the flesh), so that we bore fruit for death. 6 But now we are discharged from the Law *and* have terminated all intercourse with it, having died to what once restrained *and* held us captive. So now we serve not under [obedience to] the old code of written regulations, but [under obedience to the promptings] of the Spirit in newness [of life]. 7 What then do we conclude? Is the Law identical with sin? Certainly not! Nevertheless, if it had not been for the Law, I should not have recognized sin *or* have known its meaning. [For instance] I would not have known about covetousness [would have had no consciousness of sin or sense of guilt] if the Law had not [repeatedly] said, You shall not covet *and* have an evil desire [for one thing and another]. [Exod. 20:17; Deut. 5:21.] 8 But sin, finding opportunity in the commandment [to express itself], got a hold on me *and* aroused *and* stimulated all kinds of forbidden desires (lust, covetousness). For without the Law sin is dead [the sense of it is inactive and a lifeless thing]. 9 Once I was alive, but quite apart from *and* unconscious of the Law. But when the commandment came, sin lived again and I died (was sentenced by the Law to death). [Ps. 73:22.] 10 And the very legal ordinance which was designed *and* intended to bring life actually proved [to mean to me] death. [Lev. 18:5.] 11 For sin, seizing the opportunity *and* getting a hold on me [by taking its incentive] from the commandment,

z Matthew Henry, *Commentary on the Holy Bible*.

enjoy your freedom

Romans 6:18 affirms that those of us who are Christians have been set free from sin. As children of God, we should experience the glorious freedom and liberty Jesus died to give us—freedom to enjoy all God has given to us through His Son.

But Satan tries to rob us of enjoying our lives. He accuses us, condemns us, and makes us feel insecure because he knows we cannot simultaneously enjoy life and have negative feelings about ourselves. Thank God, we can break out of his trap and start enjoying our blood-bought freedom and liberty.

Jesus talked about our right to be free in John 8:31, 32: "If you abide in My word . . . you are truly My disciples. And you will know the Truth, and the Truth will set you free" (see also John 8:36).

Are you enjoying spiritual freedom in Jesus or are you sacrificing your joy because you are trapped in the legalistic, rigid mind-set of believing you have to do it all? If you live an inflexible life, you will not have an enjoyable life. I know. The time came when I faced the fact that I was legalistic and rigid, and though this truth was hard on me emotionally, God used it to set me free.

Jesus came that we might have and enjoy life to the fullest, until it overflows (see John 10:10). Following a legalistic lifestyle will lead us into works—futile efforts that cause us to struggle and live in frustration. Remember, there is no bondage or burden in God. His rules (His ways for us to do things) are fulfilling and liberating. Jesus came to set us free!

Feeling guilty and condemned most of the time is not freedom. Being in mental and emotional turmoil is not freedom. Being sad and depressed is not freedom.

Have you reached the point where you are tired of trying to be in control of everything and run the world? Are you willing to give up and ask God to help you? If so, pray this prayer:

Lord, I am tired of being legalistic and complicated. I just want to have some peace and enjoy my life. So, Lord, give me the desire to do what is right in Your eyes. If You do not do what needs to be done, then it is not going to get done. I completely surrender and I place my trust in You.

I encourage you to lay aside the limitations and defeat of legalism and do your best, beginning right now, to enjoy the life of freedom God makes available to you in Jesus Christ.

newness of life

The old covenant is finished and has been replaced with a new and better covenant (see Hebrews 8:13). God's law no longer comes to us on stone tablets, but is written in our hearts. We no longer live under the Law, which *tells* us God's will; we now live under grace which enables us to *do* God's will because we want to and not merely because it is the Law. The Law ministers death, but grace ministers life.

Grace is the power of the Holy Spirit in our lives enabling us to do whatever God instructs us to do. It is by grace (God's power) through faith that we are saved and made partakers of Christ's salvation.

Romans 7:6 teaches that we are to be led by the inner promptings of the Holy Spirit. The Holy Spirit lives in us and wants us to willingly allow Him to lead, guide, and control us. When we submit to His promptings, we experience newness of life. The Law only gives us rules and regulations and we feel guilty and condemned when we do not follow them. But the Spirit gives us not only the desire to do what is right, but also the ability and a fresh zeal to do it. He enables us to serve God with enthusiasm, not out of a sense of obligation.

Learning to be led by the Holy Spirit should be one of the primary goals of every believer in Jesus Christ. Only the Holy Spirit knows the mind of God concerning our lives and our circumstances. He will reveal God's will to us and lead us into its fullness as we diligently follow His promptings.

To *prompt* means "to remind" or "to give a cue." It does not indicate force, control, or manipulation. When someone reminds us to do something we have forgotten or are in danger of forgetting, we can still choose whether or not we will act on that reminder. The Holy Spirit is a gentleman and will never force Himself or God's will. God sets before each of us life and death and encourages us to choose life so that we and our descendants may have the lives He has carefully planned for us.

I encourage you to learn all you can about how to be led by the Holy Spirit because doing so is a blessing, a privilege, and an act of obedience for Christians.

beguiled *and* entrapped *and* cheated me, and using it [as a weapon], killed me.

12 The Law therefore is holy, and [each] commandment is holy and just and good.

13 Did that which is good then prove fatal [bringing death] to me? Certainly not! It was sin, working death in me

by using this good thing [as a weapon], in order that through the commandment sin might be shown up clearly to be sin, that the extreme malignity and immeasurable sinfulness of sin might plainly appear.

14 We know that the Law is spiritual; but I am a creature of the flesh [carnal, unspiritual], having been sold

into slavery under [the control of] sin.
15 For I do not understand my own actions [I am baffled, bewildered]. I do not practice *or* accomplish what I wish, but I do the very thing that I loathe [ªwhich my moral instinct condemns].

16 Now if I do [habitually] what is contrary to my desire, [that means that] I acknowledge *and* agree that the Law is good (morally excellent) *and* that I take sides with it.

17 However, it is no longer I who do the deed, but the sin [principle] which is at home in me *and* has possession of me.

18 For I know that nothing good dwells within me, that is, in my flesh. I can will what is right, but I cannot perform it. [I have the intention and urge to do what is right, but no power to carry it out.]

19 For I fail to practice the good deeds I desire to do, but the evil deeds that I do not desire to do are what I am [ever] doing.

20 Now if I do what I do not desire to do, it is no longer I doing it [it is not myself that acts], but the sin [principle] which dwells within me [ᵇfixed and operating in my soul].

21 So I find it to be a law (rule of action of my being) that when I want to do what is right *and* good, evil is ever present with me *and* I am subject to its insistent demands.

22 For I endorse *and* delight in the Law of God in my inmost self [with my new nature]. [Ps. 1:2.]

23 But I discern in my bodily members [ᶜin the sensitive appetites and wills of the flesh] a different law (rule of action) at war against the law of my mind (my reason) and making me a prisoner to the law of sin that dwells in my bodily organs [ᶜin the sensi-

tive appetites and wills of the flesh].
24 O unhappy *and* pitiable *and* wretched man that I am! Who will release *and* deliver me from [the shackles of] this body of death?

25 O thank God! [He will!] through Jesus Christ (the Anointed One) our Lord! So then indeed I, of myself with the mind *and* heart, serve the Law of God, but with the flesh the law of sin.

8 THEREFORE, [there is] now no condemnation (no adjudging guilty of wrong) for those who are in Christ Jesus, *who live* [and] walk not after the dictates of the flesh, but after the dictates of the Spirit. [John 3:18.]

2 For the law of the Spirit of life [which is] in Christ Jesus [the law of our new being] has freed me from the law of sin and of death.

3 For God has done what the Law could not do, [its power] being weakened by the flesh [ᵈthe entire nature of man without the Holy Spirit]. Sending His own Son in the guise of sinful flesh and as an offering for sin, [God] condemned sin in the flesh [ᵇsubdued, overcame, ᵉdeprived it of its power over all who accept that sacrifice], [Lev. 7:37.]

4 So that the righteous *and* just requirement of the Law might be fully met in us who live *and* move not in the ways of the flesh but in the ways of the Spirit [our lives governed not by the standards and according to the dictates of the flesh, but controlled by the Holy Spirit].

5 For those who are according to the flesh *and* are controlled by its unholy desires set their minds on *and* ᵇpursue those things which gratify the flesh, but those who are according to the Spirit *and* are controlled by the

a Frederic Godet, cited by Marvin Vincent, *Word Studies.* **b** Joseph Thayer, *A Greek-English Lexicon.* **c** Matthew Henry, *Commentary on the Holy Bible.* **d** Philip Melanchthon, cited by Marvin Vincent, *Word Studies.* **e** Marvin Vincent, *Word Studies.*

life point

When condemnation comes against you, let me encourage you to quote Romans 8:1 as a "Word weapon." Remind Satan and yourself that you do not walk after the flesh but after the Spirit. Walking after the flesh is depending on yourself; walking after the Spirit is depending on God.

When you fail (which you will), that does not mean you are a failure. It simply means that you do not do everything right. We all have to accept the fact that we have strengths along with weaknesses. Let Christ be strong in your weaknesses; let Him be your Strength on your weak days. If you are waiting for the victory in an area and you have not seen it, rather than feeling condemned about it, be patient. Do not receive condemnation; walk in the Spirit.

desires of the Spirit set their minds on *and* ᶠseek those things which gratify the [Holy] Spirit.
6 Now the mind of the flesh [which is sense and reason without the Holy Spirit] is death [death that ᶠcomprises all the miseries arising from sin, both here and hereafter]. But the mind of the [Holy] Spirit is life and [soul] peace [both now and forever].
7 [That is] because the mind of the flesh [with its carnal thoughts and purposes] is hostile to God, for it does not submit itself to God's Law; indeed it cannot.
8 So then those who are living the life of the flesh [catering to the appetites and impulses of their carnal nature] cannot please *or* satisfy God, *or* be acceptable to Him.
9 But you are not living the life of the flesh, you are living the life of the Spirit, if the [Holy] Spirit of God [real-

ly] dwells within you [directs and controls you]. But if anyone does not possess the [Holy] Spirit of Christ, he is none of His [he does not belong to Christ, is not truly a child of God]. [Rom. 8:14.]
10 But if Christ lives in you, [then although] your [natural] body is dead by reason of sin *and* guilt, the spirit is alive because of [the] righteousness [that He imputes to you].
11 And if the Spirit of Him Who raised up Jesus from the dead dwells

life point

When the deceiver speaks to us, he cannot give peace. When we try to solve things with our own reasoning, we cannot find peace, because according to Romans 8:6, the mind of the flesh is death, but the mind of the Holy Spirit is life and peace.

Do you have to make a decision? Lay it on the "peace scale," and do not proceed if peace cannot hold its weight against the guidance you have heard. You do not have to explain to others why you do not have peace about it; sometimes you will not know why yourself. You can say simply, "It's not wise for me to do this, because I don't have peace about it."

Even when you believe God has spoken to you, you should wait to act until peace fills your soul to do what He has instructed you to do. In this way you are assured that your timing is right.

I often say, "Let emotions subside and then decide." If we wait for God's true peace, we will be obedient with faith. Peace is true confirmation that we are hearing from God.

f Joseph Thayer, *A Greek-English Lexicon.*

no condemnation in Christ

Even though Romans 8:1 teaches us that there is no condemnation for those who are in Christ, many believers still struggle greatly with guilt and condemnation. Because of our love for God we want to do what is right, yet there are times we walk in the flesh instead of in the Spirit and we make mistakes. We sin and make wrong choices. When we realize we have sinned we should quickly and thoroughly repent, being willing to turn away from the sin and do what is right with God's help. Once we have repented and asked God to forgive us, we are not to continue carrying those heavy burdens of condemnation. Jesus delivered us from both iniquity and guilt. When we repent and ask God to forgive us, He not only forgives, but He forgets and removes our sin as far as the east is from the west (see Psalm 103:12; Hebrews 10:17, 18).

Jesus died as the perfect sacrifice for sin—and no other sacrifice is or will ever be needed (see Hebrews 10:11, 12). The guilt we feel when we sin is often our way of "sacrificing" to pay for the sins we have committed. We think that somehow if we are miserable and do not allow ourselves to enjoy life that our feelings of condemnation help balance the scales of justice. That kind of thinking is wrong!

Guilt is an invisible burden that wears us out and does no good at all. It actually prevents progress and renders us incapable of proper fellowship with God because we must approach Him in faith and with boldness, not with fear and guilt.

Some people are literally addicted to guilt. They do not feel right unless they feel wrong! I was like that for many years and God taught me to use my faith to live free from guilt and condemnation. We either believe that Jesus paid for our sins in full or we believe we must add our sacrifices to His, which, of course, is incorrect.

Romans 8:1 instructs us to walk after the Spirit, and not the flesh. One of the ways we do that is by handling our sins the way the Holy Spirit tells us to, which is definitely not to repent and then feel guilty. God promises that He is faithful to forgive our sins and cleanse us from them if we will repent and admit them (see I John 1:9). God never does anything halfway. Jesus' work on the cross is finished, so start enjoying the freedom from guilt and condemnation that is available to you. Do not believe your feelings more than you believe God's Word!

in you, [then] He Who raised up Christ *Jesus* from the dead will also restore to life your mortal (short-lived, perishable) bodies through His Spirit Who dwells in you.

12 So then, brethren, we are debtors, but not to the flesh [we are not obligated to our carnal nature], to live [a life ruled by the standards set up by the dictates] of the flesh.

13 For if you live according to [the dictates of] the flesh, you will surely die. But if through the power of the [Holy] Spirit you are [habitually] putting to death (making extinct, deadening) the [evil] deeds prompted by the body, you shall [really and genuinely] live forever.

14 For all who are led by the Spirit of God are sons of God.

life point

Romans 8:6–14 helps us understand the differences between following our fleshly desires and allowing God's Spirit to lead us. Any time our flesh wants to do one thing and the Spirit of God wants us to do something else, by choosing to follow the Spirit of God we need to know that our flesh will suffer. We do not like that, but the Bible says that if we want to share Christ's glory, we have to be willing to share His suffering (see I Peter 4:13).

I like to encourage those who are just beginning to walk with God that once the fleshly appetite is no longer in control, they will get to the point where it is easier to obey God. Even if obedience is difficult they will get to the place where they actually *enjoy* doing it. If you are new to the Christian faith, be encouraged!

15 For [the Spirit which] you have now received [is] not a spirit of slavery to put you once more in bondage to fear, but you have received the Spirit of adoption [the Spirit producing sonship] in [the bliss of] which we cry, Abba (Father)! Father!
16 The Spirit Himself [thus] testifies together with our own spirit, [assuring us] that we are children of God.
17 And if we are [His] children, then we are [His] heirs also: heirs of God and fellow heirs with Christ [sharing His inheritance with Him]; only we must share His suffering if we are to share His glory.
18 [But what of that?] For I consider that the sufferings of this present time (this present life) are not worth being compared with the glory that is about to be revealed to us *and* in us *and* ᵍfor us *and* ʰconferred on us!

life point

Romans 8:15 teaches us that the Holy Spirit is the "Spirit of adoption." Here, the word *adoption* means that we have been brought into God's family even though we were previously outsiders, unrelated to Him in any way. We were sinners who served Satan, but God in His great mercy redeemed us and purchased us with the blood of His own Son. Think of yourself as a child of God: loved, accepted, and empowered by His unconditional love for you.

19 For [even the whole] creation (all nature) waits expectantly *and* longs earnestly for God's sons to be made known [waits for the revealing, the disclosing of their sonship].
20 For the creation (nature) was subjected to ʰfrailty (to futility, condemned to frustration), not because of some intentional fault on its part, but by the will of Him Who so subjected it—[yet] with the hope [Eccl. 1:2.]
21 That nature (creation) itself will be set free from its bondage to decay

putting the Word to work

Paul suffered greatly during his lifetime—shipwrecks, beatings that left him near death, abandonment of friends, imprisonment, and eventually, execution (see II Corinthians 11:23–28). Scripture teaches us that all of us face various forms of suffering in our lives (see John 16:33). How can you withstand suffering? One way is to ask God to help you have Paul's attitude of confidence that earthly sufferings cannot come close to comparing to the glory you will one day see (see Romans 8:18).

---

g Charles B. Williams, *The New Testament: A Translation in the Language of the People.* h Joseph Thayer, *A Greek-English Lexicon.*

and corruption [and gain an entrance] into the glorious freedom of God's children.

22 We know that the whole creation [of irrational creatures] has been moaning together in the pains of labor until now. [Jer. 12:4, 11.]

23 And not only the creation, but we ourselves too, who have *and* enjoy the firstfruits of the [Holy] Spirit [a foretaste of the blissful things to come] groan inwardly as we wait for the redemption of our bodies [from sensuality and the grave, which will reveal] our adoption (our manifestation as God's sons).

24 For in [this] hope we were saved. But hope [the object of] which is seen is not hope. For how can one hope for what he already sees?

25 But if we hope for what is still unseen by us, we wait for it with patience *and* composure.

26 So too the [Holy] Spirit comes to our aid *and* bears us up in our weakness; for we do not know what prayer to offer *nor* how to offer it worthily as we ought, but the Spirit Himself goes to meet our supplication *and* pleads in our behalf with unspeakable yearnings *and* groanings too deep for utterance.

27 And He Who searches the hearts of men knows what is in the mind of the [Holy] Spirit [what His intent is], because the Spirit intercedes *and* pleads [before God] in behalf of the saints according to *and* in harmony with God's will. [Ps. 139:1, 2.]

28 We are assured *and* know that [¹God being a partner in their labor] all things work together *and* are [fitting into a plan] for good to *and* for those who love God and are called according to [His] design *and* purpose.

29 For those whom He foreknew [of whom He was ʲaware and ᵏloved

life point

God did not create us for failure. We may fail at some things on our way to success, but if we trust Him, He will take even our errors and work them out for our good (see Romans 8:28). God can take our mistakes and turn them into miracles, if we continue to trust confidently in Him.

beforehand], He also destined from the beginning [foreordaining them] to be molded into the image of His Son [and share inwardly His likeness], that He might become the firstborn among many brethren.

30 And those whom He thus foreordained, He also called; and those whom He called, He also justified (acquitted, made righteous, putting them into right standing with Himself). And those whom He justified, He also glorified [raising them to a heavenly dignity and condition or state of being].

31 What then shall we say to [all] this? If God is for us, who [can be] against us? [Who can be our foe, if God is on our side?] [Ps. 118:6.]

32 He who did not withhold *or* spare [even] His own Son but gave Him up for us all, will He not also with Him freely *and* graciously give us all [other] things?

life point

God approved of you before anybody else ever got a chance to disapprove. If God approves of you and accepts you as you are, why worry about what anyone else thinks? If God is for you—and He is, according to Romans 8:31—who can effectively be against you?

---

i Some manuscripts read, "God works all things with them."   j H.A.W. Meyer, cited by Marvin Vincent, *Word Studies*.   k John Murray, *The Sovereignty of God*.

safe or obedient?

Even when we are in a place of obedience to God, we often have no natural way of knowing for sure whether we are right or wrong. We have nothing more than faith to help us take that first step. We may not be certain that what we are doing is the right thing until after we have done it and then look back to see if God's grace was there to cause our efforts to bear good fruit.

Sometimes we may be wrong. That thought seems frightening, so we think *I had better just stay here where it is safe*. But if we do that, we will soon be miserable if God truly has told us to move forward.

If our hearts are right, and we do our best when we hear from Him, God will redeem us and honor our steps of obedience. If we move in childlike trust to obey what we believe in our hearts He has told us to do, even if that decision is wrong, God will take that mistake and work it out for our good. I know this is true because Romans 8:28 says that all things work together and fit into God's plan for good for those of us who are called according to His purpose.

Many people are afraid to move because they think that if they make a mistake, God will be angry with them. But this is where trusting His character is so vital to walking in faith. People who are too afraid to obey are so miserable anyway that they cannot get any worse off by stepping out and trying to do what God is telling them to do.

I once had a ministry position at our home church. I loved it, but felt God was leading me to step out into something new. I did leave, but not because I wanted to. I left because God's anointing and power for me to be there had lifted, and I became miserable until I obeyed Him. I realized I would find peace only if I left my "safety zone" and tested what I believed He told me to do. That was the only way to find out if I was right or wrong about hearing His voice. I had to step out to find out!

I exhort you with this truth: Do not spend all your life playing it safe! Safety is very comfortable, but it may keep you from God's perfect plan for your life. Trust His Word and keep your heart willing and ready to obey. You will find throughout your life that God regularly calls us out of our comfort zones and into new places of faith and growth in Him.

33 Who shall bring any charge against God's elect [when it is] God Who justifies [that is, Who puts us in right relation to Himself? Who shall come forward and accuse or impeach those whom God has chosen? Will God, Who acquits us?]
34 Who is there to condemn [us]? Will Christ Jesus (the Messiah), Who died, or rather Who was raised from the dead, Who is at the right hand of God actually pleading *as* He intercedes for us?
35 Who shall ever separate us from Christ's love? Shall suffering *and* affliction *and* tribulation? Or calamity

God is for you

Romans 8:31 tells us clearly that God is for us. We also know that Satan is against us. The question we must ask is: are we going to agree with God or with the devil? You know the answer. Stop opposing yourself and mentally beating yourself up just because Satan is against you!

Sad to say, sometimes we discover people are also against us. Satan does not always work alone in the spiritual realm; he also works through people in the natural realm. He attacks our confidence through the things people say or do not say. He can cause us to feel unworthy or rejected because of another person's words or actions.

How important are people's opinions of us? Are we thinking for ourselves, or are we always agreeing with everyone else's opinion? If people's opinions, judgments, and attitudes toward us are sometimes inspired by the devil, then we must resist what people think and say instead of agreeing with it.

If we know God is for us, then it should not matter how we feel or what other people think of us. As the Bible says in Romans 8:31, who can be against us if God is for us? If He is on our side, then what can others do to us? Hebrews 13:6 makes a similar point: "So we take comfort and are encouraged and confidently and boldly say, The Lord is my Helper; I will not be seized with alarm [I will not fear or dread or be terrified]. What can man do to me?"

Most of us, to some extent, need to be delivered from the fear of people and from caring too much about what others think. People who always need the approval of others desperately want everyone to look at them from head to toe and say, "Perfect." When they do any kind of a job, they want everybody to look at it and say, "Perfect." In everything they do—the way they look, the things they say, every action they take—they want people to say, "Perfect."

If we try to be perfect, we will be disappointed. It will not work because you and I are imperfect human beings. Even if we could manifest perfection, some people would still not be satisfied simply because they are unhappy individuals who will not ever be content with anything until they change their own attitudes.

We need to be confident that God accepts us with our imperfections. Even though He continues to work in us to make us more Christlike, we do not have to struggle to win His approval or the approval of others. If God is for us—and He is—we do not need to fear anyone who is against us.

life point

All that Jesus asks of the Father, God answers. So whatever He prays for me, whatever He prays for you, we will receive! Jesus never stops praying for us. This means that we can relax, because Romans 8:34 promises that Jesus sits at the right hand of the Father and intercedes for us. Think of it! Jesus is praying for you.

and distress? Or persecution or hunger or destitution or peril or sword?
36 Even as it is written, For Thy sake we are put to death all the day long; we are regarded *and* counted as sheep for the slaughter. [Ps. 44:22.]
37 Yet amid all these things we are more than conquerors [1]*and* gain a surpassing victory through Him Who loved us.
38 For I am persuaded beyond doubt (am sure) that neither death nor life, nor angels nor principalities, nor things [m]impending *and* threatening nor things to come, nor powers,
39 Nor height nor depth, nor anything else in all creation will be able to

putting the Word to work

Do your circumstances ever cause you to question God's love for you? The truth is, even in the midst of the most difficult of circumstances, God's love is real and active in your life. Nothing can ever separate you from His love; nothing can ever cause Him to love you less (see Romans 8:35–39). In the midst of difficulty, cling to God's love for you, and ask Him to keep revealing His love to you.

separate us from the love of God which is in Christ Jesus our Lord.

9 I AM speaking the truth in Christ. I am not lying; my conscience [enlightened and prompted] by the Holy Spirit bearing witness with me
2 That I have bitter grief and incessant anguish in my heart.
3 For I could wish that I myself were accursed *and* cut off *and* banished from Christ for the sake of my brethren *and* instead of them, my natural kinsmen *and* my fellow countrymen. [Exod. 32:32.]
4 For they are Israelites, and to them belong God's adoption [as a nation] and the glorious Presence (Shekinah). With them were the special covenants made, to them was the Law given. To them [the temple] worship was

life point

The apostle Paul said in Romans 9:1 that he knew he was doing the right thing, not because his reasoning said it was right, but because it bore witness *in his spirit.*

The mind does aid the spirit at times. The mind and the spirit work together, but the spirit should always be honored above the mind.

If you know in your spirit that something is wrong, you should not allow reasoning to talk you into doing it. Also, if you know something is right, do not allow reasoning to talk you out of doing it. Do as Romans 9:1 instructs and allow the Holy Spirit to bear witness with you concerning whether something is right or wrong. Let your conscience always be enlightened and prompted by the Holy Spirit.

l Joseph Thayer, *A Greek-English Lexicon.* m Marvin Vincent, *Word Studies.* The literal translation is "standing in sight."

revealed and [God's own] promises announced. [Exod. 4:22; Hos. 11:1.]

5   To them belong the patriarchs, and as far as His natural descent was concerned, from them is the Christ, Who is exalted *and* supreme over all, God, blessed forever! Amen (so let it be).

6   However, it is not as though God's Word had failed [coming to nothing]. For it is not everybody who is a descendant of Jacob (Israel) who belongs to [the true] Israel.

7   And they are not all the children of Abraham because they are by blood his descendants. No, [the promise was] Your descendants will be called *and* counted through the line of Isaac [though Abraham had an older son]. [Gen. 21:9-12.]

8   That is to say, it is not the children of the body [of Abraham] who are made God's children, but it is the offspring to whom the promise applies that shall be counted [as Abraham's true] descendants.

9   For this is what the promise said, About this time [next year] will I return and Sarah shall have a son. [Gen. 18:10.]

10   And not only that, but this too: Rebecca conceived [two sons under exactly the same circumstances] by our forefather Isaac,

11   And the children were yet unborn and had so far done nothing either good or evil. Even so, in order further to carry out God's purpose of selection (election, choice), which depends not on works *or* what men can do, but on Him Who calls [them],

12   It was said to her that the elder [son] should serve the younger [son]. [Gen. 25:21-23.]

13   As it is written, Jacob have I loved, but Esau have I hated (held in ⁿrelative disregard in comparison with My feeling for Jacob). [Mal. 1:2, 3.]

14   What shall we conclude then? Is there injustice upon God's part? Certainly not!

15   For He says to Moses, I will have mercy on whom I will have mercy and I will have compassion (pity) on whom I will have compassion. [Exod. 33:19.]

16   So then [God's gift] is not a question of human will and human effort, but of God's mercy. [It depends not on one's own willingness nor on his strenuous exertion as in running a race, but on God's having mercy on him.]

17   For the Scripture says to Pharaoh, I have raised you up for this very purpose of displaying My power in [dealing with] you, so that My name may be proclaimed the whole world over.

18   So then He has mercy on whomever He wills (chooses) and He hardens (makes stubborn and unyielding the heart of) whomever He wills.

19   You will say to me, Why then does He still find fault *and* blame us [for sinning]? For who can resist *and* withstand His will?

20   But who are you, a mere man, to criticize *and* contradict *and* answer back to God? Will what is formed say to him that formed it, Why have you made me thus? [Isa. 29:16; 45:9.]

21   Has the potter no right over the clay, to make out of the same mass (lump) one vessel for beauty *and* distinction *and* honorable use, and another for menial *or* ignoble *and* dishonorable use?

22   What if God, although fully intending to show [the awfulness of] His wrath and to make known His power *and* authority, has tolerated with much patience the vessels (objects) of [His] anger which are ripe for destruction? [Prov. 16:4.]

23   And [what if] He thus purposes to make known *and* show the wealth of His glory in [dealing with] the vessels (objects) of His mercy which He has prepared beforehand for glory,

---

n G. Abbott-Smith, *Manual Greek Lexicon.*

24 Even including ourselves whom He has called, not only from among the Jews but also from among the Gentiles (heathen)?

25 Just as He says in Hosea, Those who were not My people I will call My people, and her who was not beloved [I will call] My beloved. [Hos. 2:23.]

26 And it shall be that in the very place where it was said to them, You are not My people, they shall be called sons of the living God. [Hos. 1:10.]

27 And Isaiah calls out (solemnly cries aloud) over Israel: Though the number of the sons of Israel be like the sand of the sea, only the remnant (a small part of them) will be saved [°from perdition, condemnation, judgment]!

28 For the Lord will execute His sentence upon the earth [He will conclude and close His account with men completely and without delay], rigorously cutting it short in His justice. [Isa. 10:22, 23.]

29 It is as Isaiah predicted, If the Lord of hosts had not left us a seed [from which to propagate descendants], we [Israel] would have fared like Sodom and have been made like Gomorrah. [Isa. 1:9.]

30 What shall we say then? That Gentiles who did not follow after righteousness [who did not seek salvation by right relationship to God] have attained it by faith [a righteousness imputed by God, based on and produced by faith],

31 Whereas Israel, though ever in pursuit of a law [for the securing] of righteousness (right standing with God), actually did not succeed in fulfilling the Law. [Isa. 51:1.]

32 For what reason? Because [they pursued it] not through faith, relying [instead] on the merit of their works [they did not depend on faith but on what they could do]. They have stumbled over the Stumbling Stone. [Isa. 8:14; 28:16.]

33 As it is written, Behold I am laying in Zion a Stone that will make men stumble, a Rock that will make them fall; but he who believes in Him [who adheres to, trusts in, and relies on Him] shall not be put to shame *nor* be disappointed in his expectations. [Isa. 28:16.]

10 BRETHREN, [with all] my heart's desire *and* goodwill for [Israel], I long and pray to God that they may be saved.

2 I bear them witness that they have a [certain] zeal *and* enthusiasm for God, but it is not enlightened *and* according to [correct and vital] knowledge.

3 For being ignorant of the righteousness that God ascribes [which makes one acceptable to Him in word, thought, and deed] and seeking to establish a *righteousness (a means of salvation)* of their own, they did not obey *or* submit themselves to God's righteousness.

4 For Christ is the end of the Law [the limit at which it ceases to be, for the Law leads up to Him Who is the fulfillment of its types, and in Him the purpose which it was designed to accomplish is fulfilled. That is, the purpose of the Law is fulfilled in Him] as the means of righteousness (right relationship to God) for everyone who

speak the Word

o Hermann Cremer, *Biblico-Theological Lexicon*.

trusts in *and* adheres to *and* relies on Him.

5 For Moses writes that the man who [can] practice the righteousness (perfect conformity to God's will) which is based on the Law [with all its intricate demands] shall live by it. [Lev. 18:5.]

6 But the righteousness based on faith [imputed by God and bringing right relationship with Him] says, Do not say in your heart, Who will ascend into Heaven? that is, to bring Christ down;

7 Or who will descend into the abyss? that is, to bring Christ up from the dead [as if we could be saved by our own efforts]. [Deut. 30:12, 13.]

8 But what does it say? The Word (God's message in Christ) is near you, on your lips and in your heart; that is, the Word (the message, the basis and object) of faith which we preach, [Deut. 30:14.]

9 Because if you acknowledge *and* confess with your lips that Jesus is Lord and in your heart believe (adhere to, trust in, and rely on the truth) that God raised Him from the dead, you will be saved.

10 For with the heart a person believes (adheres to, trusts in, and relies on Christ) and so is justified (declared righteous, acceptable to God), and with the mouth he confesses (declares openly and speaks out freely his faith) *and* confirms [his] salvation.

11 The Scripture says, No man who believes in Him [who adheres to, relies on, and trusts in Him] will [ever] be put to shame *or* be disappointed. [Ps. 34:22; Isa. 28:16; 49:23; Jer. 17:7.]

12 [No one] for there is no distinction between Jew and Greek. The same Lord is Lord over all [of us] and He generously bestows His riches upon all who call upon Him [in faith].

13 For everyone who calls upon the name of the Lord [invoking Him as Lord] will be saved. [Joel 2:32.]

14 But how are people to call upon Him Whom they have not believed [in Whom they have no faith, on Whom they have no reliance]? And how are they to believe in Him [adhere to, trust in, and rely upon Him] of Whom they have never heard? And how are they to hear without a preacher?

15 And how can men [be expected to] preach unless they are sent? As it is written, How beautiful are the feet of those who bring glad tidings! [How welcome is the coming of those who preach the good news of His good things!] [Isa. 52:7.]

putting the Word to work

Romans 10:14, 15 reminds us that we need to tell people about God and His love for them. Many people may have heard of God, and may even believe that He is a loving God, but they have not heard about His love for them personally. Do you remember the first person who shared with you the good news of God's love for you? Take a moment and thank God for that person and ask Him to show you someone with whom you can share the good news about His love!

16 But they have not all heeded the Gospel; for Isaiah says, Lord, who has believed (had faith in) what he has heard from us? [Isa. 53:1.]

17 So faith comes by hearing [what is told], and what is heard comes by the preaching [of the message that came from the lips] of Christ (the Messiah Himself).

18 But I ask, Have they not heard? Indeed they have; [for the Scripture says] Their voice [that of nature bearing God's message] has gone out to all the earth, and their words to the far bounds of the world. [Ps. 19:4.]

19 Again I ask, Did Israel not understand? [Did the Jews have no warning

life point

When the Word is heard, faith is imparted to believe it (see Romans 10:17). Once we have heard the Word and believe it, we should continue believing. God invites us to live from faith to faith. As believers, one of our most important jobs is to simply believe. Jesus said, "Believe and rely on Me, [and] you [will] see the glory of God" (John 11:40).

that the Gospel was to go forth to the Gentiles, to all the earth?] First, there is Moses who says, I will make you jealous of those who are not a nation; with a foolish nation I will make you angry. [Deut. 32:21.]
20 Then Isaiah is so bold as to say, I have been found by those who did not seek Me; I have shown (revealed) Myself to those who did not [consciously] ask for Me. [Isa. 65:1.]
21 But of Israel he says, All day long I have stretched out My hands to a people unyielding *and* disobedient and self-willed [to a faultfinding, contrary, and contradicting people]. [Isa. 65:2.]

11 I ASK then: Has God totally rejected *and* disowned His people? Of course not! Why, I myself am an Israelite, a descendant of Abraham, a member of the tribe of Benjamin! [I Sam. 12:22; Jer. 31:37; 33:24-26; Phil. 3:5.]
2 No, God has not rejected *and* disowned His people [whose destiny] He had marked out *and* appointed *and* foreknown from the beginning. Do you not know what the Scripture says of Elijah, how he pleads with God against Israel? [Ps. 94:14; I Kings 19.]
3 Lord, they have killed Your prophets; they have demolished Your altars, and I alone am left, and they seek my life.

4 But what is God's reply to him? I have kept for Myself seven thousand men who have not bowed the knee to Baal! [I Kings 19:18.]
5 So too at the present time there is a remnant (a small believing minority), selected (chosen) by grace (by God's unmerited favor and graciousness).
6 But if it is by grace (His unmerited favor and graciousness), it is no longer conditioned on works or anything men have done. Otherwise, grace would no longer be grace [it would be meaningless].
7 What then [shall we conclude]? Israel failed to obtain what it sought [God's favor by obedience to the Law]. Only the elect (those chosen few) obtained it, while the rest of them became callously indifferent (blinded, hardened, and made insensible to it).
8 As it is written, God gave them a spirit (an attitude) of stupor, eyes that should not see and ears that should

life point

What the apostle Paul tells us in Romans 11:6 is simply this: grace and works are diametrically opposed to one another. They cannot fellowship together or have anything to do with each other.

Stated another way, grace and works of the flesh are mutually exclusive. Where one exists, the other cannot exist.

If you and I are into our own works, then we are out of grace. If we are in grace, then we are out of works. Anytime we get into works, the grace of God ceases to operate on our behalf. God has no choice but to back off and wait until we have finished trying to handle things ourselves. Take your hands off of the situations, circumstances, and relationships that concern you—and let God's grace go to work for you!

not hear, [that has continued] down to this very day. [Deut. 29:4; Isa. 29:10.]

9 And David says, Let their table (their feasting, banqueting) become a snare and a trap, a pitfall and a [p]just retribution [[q]rebounding like a boomerang upon them]; [Ps. 69:22.]

10 Let their eyes be darkened (dimmed) so that they cannot see, and make them bend their back [stooping beneath their burden] forever. [Ps. 69:23.]

11 So I ask, Have they stumbled so as to fall [to their utter spiritual ruin, irretrievably]? By no means! But through their false step and transgression salvation [has come] to the Gentiles, so as to arouse Israel [to see and feel what they forfeited] and so to make them jealous.

12 Now if their stumbling (their lapse, their transgression) has so enriched the world [at large], and if [Israel's] failure means such riches for the Gentiles, think what an enrichment and greater advantage will follow their full reinstatement!

13 But now I am speaking to you who are Gentiles. Inasmuch then as I am an apostle to the Gentiles, I lay great stress on my ministry and magnify my office,

14 In the hope of making my fellow Jews jealous [in order to stir them up to imitate, copy, and appropriate], and thus managing to save some of them.

15 For if their rejection and exclusion from the benefits of salvation were [overruled] for the reconciliation of a world to God, what will their acceptance and admission mean? [It will be nothing short of] life from the dead!

16 Now if the first handful of dough offered as the firstfruits [Abraham and the patriarchs] is consecrated (holy), so is the whole mass [the nation of Israel]; and if the root [Abraham] is consecrated (holy), so

are the branches. [Num. 15:19-21.]

17 But if some of the branches were broken off, while you, a wild olive shoot, were grafted in among them to share the richness [of the root and sap] of the olive tree,

18 Do not boast over the branches and pride yourself at their expense. If you do boast and feel superior, remember it is not you that support the root, but the root [that supports] you.

19 You will say then, Branches were broken (pruned) off so that I might be grafted in!

20 That is true. But they were broken (pruned) off because of their unbelief (their lack of real faith), and you are established through faith [because you do believe]. So do not become proud and conceited, but rather stand in awe and be reverently afraid.

21 For if God did not spare the natural branches [because of unbelief], neither will He spare you [if you are guilty of the same offense].

22 Then note and appreciate the gracious kindness and the severity of God: severity toward those who have fallen, but God's gracious kindness to you—provided you continue in His grace and abide in His kindness; otherwise you too will be cut off (pruned away).

23 And even those others [the fallen branches, Jews], if they do not persist in [clinging to] their unbelief, will be grafted in, for God has the power to graft them in again.

24 For if you have been cut from what is by nature a wild olive tree, and against nature grafted into a cultivated olive tree, how much easier will it be to graft these natural [branches] back on [the original parent stock of] their own olive tree.

25 Lest you be self-opinionated (wise in your own conceits), I do not want you to miss this hidden truth and mystery, brethren: a hardening (insensibility)

p Marvin Vincent, Word Studies.   q Literal translation: "a return, a recompense."

has [temporarily] befallen a part of Israel [to last] until the ʳfull number of the ingathering of the Gentiles has come in,

26 And so all Israel will be saved. As it is written, The Deliverer will come from Zion, He will banish ungodliness from Jacob. [Isa. 59:20, 21.]

27 And this will be My covenant (My agreement) with them when I shall take away their sins. [Isa. 27:9; Jer. 31:33.]

28 From the point of view of the Gospel (good news), they [the Jews, at present] are enemies [of God], which is for your advantage *and* benefit. But from the point of view of God's choice (of election, of divine selection), they are still the beloved (dear to Him) for the sake of their forefathers.

29 For God's gifts and His call are irrevocable. [He never withdraws them when once they are given, and He does not change His mind about those to whom He gives His grace or to whom He sends His call.]

30 Just as you were once disobedient *and* rebellious toward God but now have obtained [His] mercy, through their disobedience,

31 So they also now are being disobedient [when you are receiving mercy], that they in turn may one day, through the mercy you are enjoying, also receive mercy [that they may share the mercy which has been shown to you—through you as messengers of the Gospel to them].

32 For God has consigned (penned up) all men to disobedience, only that He may have mercy on them all [alike].

33 Oh, the depth of the riches and wisdom and knowledge of God! How unfathomable (inscrutable, unsearchable) are His judgments (His decisions)! And how untraceable (mysterious, undiscoverable) are His ways (His methods, His paths)!

34 For who has known the mind of the Lord *and* who has understood His thoughts, or who has [ever] been His counselor? [Isa. 40:13, 14.]

life point

We need to realize that God is smarter than we are (see Romans 11:34). His plan really is better. No matter what you or I may think, God's way is better than ours.

I look back now at many of the frustrating times I went through in my life as I tried to make things happen in my timing and how I grew frustrated when none of my efforts worked and I had to wait. I realize now that I really was not ready for those things.

God knew I was not ready, but I thought I was. I spent so much of my time asking, "Why, God, why?" and "When, God, when?" I asked questions that only God had the answers to, and He had no intention of answering me.

Remember, God wants our trust, not our questions. God does not need our counsel in order to work; He needs our faith.

35 Or who has first given God anything that he might be paid back *or* that he could claim a recompense?

36 For from Him and through Him and to Him are all things. [For all things originate with Him and come from Him; all things live through Him, and all things center in and tend to consummate and to end in Him.] To Him be glory forever! Amen (so be it).

12 I APPEAL to you therefore, brethren, *and* beg of you in view of [all] the

---

r Joseph Thayer, *A Greek-English Lexicon.*

mercies of God, to make a decisive dedication of your bodies [presenting all your members and faculties] as a living sacrifice, holy (devoted, consecrated) and well pleasing to God, which is your reasonable (rational, intelligent) service *and* spiritual worship.

life point

Do you know what Paul is telling us in Romans 12:1? He says that we are to dedicate everything about ourselves to God—not just our possessions, money, time, energy, and efforts, but also our bodies, heads, hands, tongues, and even our minds, emotions, and attitudes.

We are to dedicate everything about ourselves to God as a "living sacrifice," holy, devoted, consecrated, and pleasing to Him. This is our "reasonable, (rational, intelligent) service and spiritual worship."

Often we get the impression that to totally serve and worship God means to involve our bodies and spirits, but there is more. Here Paul says that we are to serve and worship Him with our minds and emotions also. Invite God to think and speak through you. Let Him touch people through you. You can even serve God with your face by smiling and showing yourself to be friendly to other people. Allow God to use all of you. The more of yourself and your life that you release to Him, the more you will be fulfilled and experience His peace and joy.

2 Do not be conformed to this world (this age), [fashioned after and adapted to its external, superficial customs], but be transformed (changed) by the [entire] renewal of your mind [by its new ideals and its new attitude], so that you may prove [for

life point

Romans 12:2 informs us that God has a plan in mind for us. His will toward us is good and acceptable and perfect, but we must completely renew our minds before we will ever experience the good things God has planned. We renew our minds and get new attitudes and new ideals by studying God's Word. His Word is Truth (see John 17:17).

yourselves] what is the good and acceptable and perfect will of God, *even* the thing which is good and acceptable and perfect [in His sight for you].
3 For by the grace (unmerited favor of God) given to me I warn everyone among you not to estimate *and* think of himself more highly than he ought [not to have an exaggerated opinion of his own importance], but to rate his ability with sober judgment, each according to the degree of faith apportioned by God to him.
4 For as in one physical body we have many parts (organs, members) and all of these parts do not have the same function *or* use,
5 So we, numerous as we are, are one body in Christ (the Messiah) and individually we are parts one of another [mutually dependent on one another].
6 Having gifts (faculties, talents, qualities) that differ according to the grace given us, let us use them: [He whose gift is] prophecy, [let him prophesy] according to the proportion of his faith;
7 [He whose gift is] practical service, let him give himself to serving; he who teaches, to his teaching;
8 He who exhorts (encourages), to his exhortation; he who contributes, let him do it in simplicity *and* liberality; he who gives aid *and* superintends, with zeal *and* singleness of mind; he

putting the Word to work

Can you imagine a church where everyone did the same thing and had the same gifts? It would not be very exciting or effective, would it? The Word of God teaches us that there are different gifts and functions within the church, and Romans 12:4–8 reminds us that we should graciously use the gifts we have been given, united as one body in Christ. Ask God to reveal your gifts to you, and teach you how you can make your unique contribution as a member of the body of Christ.

who does acts of mercy, with genuine cheerfulness *and* joyful eagerness.
9 [Let your] love be sincere (a real thing); hate what is evil [loathe all ungodliness, turn in horror from wickedness], but hold fast to that which is good.
10 Love one another with brotherly affection [as members of one family], giving precedence *and* showing honor to one another.
11 Never lag in zeal *and* in earnest endeavor; be aglow *and* burning with the Spirit, serving the Lord.
12 Rejoice *and* exult in hope; be steadfast and patient in suffering *and*

putting the Word to work

Have you ever heard the saying, "if you talk the talk, you have to walk the walk?" As Christians we must live by the principles found in the Word of God. Romans 12:9–21 includes practical principles for living the Christian life. As you read this passage, identify areas in your life where you need to put some of these principles into practice. Be intentional about making these principles a lifestyle, and ask the Holy Spirit to help you do so. You will see for yourself how by living this way, good will overcome evil.

tribulation; be constant in prayer.
13 Contribute to the needs of God's people [sharing in the necessities of the saints]; pursue the practice of hospitality.
14 Bless those who persecute you [who are cruel in their attitude toward you]; bless and do not curse them.
15 Rejoice with those who rejoice [sharing others' joy], and weep with those who weep [sharing others' grief].
16 Live in harmony with one another; do not be haughty (snobbish, high-minded, exclusive), but readily adjust yourself to [people, things] *and* give yourselves to humble tasks. Never overestimate yourself *or* be wise in your own conceits. [Prov. 3:7.]
17 Repay no one evil for evil, but take thought for what is honest *and* proper *and* noble [aiming to be above reproach] in the sight of everyone. [Prov. 20:22.]
18 If possible, as far as it depends on you, live at peace with everyone.

life point

Some people are basically impossible to get along with, but I love Romans 12:18, which essentially says to do as much as you can to live at peace with everyone if at all possible. You cannot do *their* parts, but you must do *your* part to maintain peace with others.

I challenge you to be a maker and maintainer of peace today and every day of your life.

19 Beloved, never avenge yourselves, but leave the way open for [God's] wrath; for it is written, Vengeance is Mine, I will repay (requite), says the Lord. [Deut. 32:35.]
20 But if your enemy is hungry, feed him; if he is thirsty, give him drink; for by so doing you will heap burning coals upon his head. [Prov. 25:21, 22.]

how to stay on fire for God

Romans 12:11 instructs us to be aglow and burn with the Spirit as we serve the Lord. In order to do this, we have to stay "on fire."

How do we stay "on fire?" I have discovered that the Word of God coming out of my own mouth in the form of prayer, praise, preaching, or confession is the best way I can fan the fire. It stirs up the gift within me, keeps the fire aflame, and prevents my spirit from sinking within me. Staying thankful also keeps me enthusiastic.

The writer of Ecclesiastes tells us, "Whatever your hand finds to do, do it with all your might, for there is no work or device or knowledge or wisdom in Sheol (the place of the dead), where you are going" (Ecclesiastes 9:10). Stay active; there is no point in putting off doing things until later. That is an expression of passivity, and it is one of the greatest tools Satan uses against God's people. The more passive we are, the more our flames diminish. Procrastination and laziness are the cousins of passivity, and they usually all attack in a group. Passive people wait to be moved by an outside force before they take action. But we are to be motivated and led by the Holy Spirit within us, not by outside forces. The best way to be on guard against the spirit of passivity is to do what we need to do now, and do it with all our might.

Remember, everything we do is to be done unto the Lord and for His glory (see I Corinthians 10:31). We should do it through Him, to Him, for Him, by Him, and with Him. And we should do it willingly, with our whole hearts stirred up and on fire within us.

21 Do not let yourself be overcome by evil, but overcome (master) evil with good.

13

LET EVERY person be loyally subject to the governing (civil) authorities. For there is no authority except from God [by His permission, His sanction], and those that exist do so by God's appointment. [Prov. 8:15.]

2   Therefore he who resists *and* sets himself up against the authorities resists what God has appointed *and*

life point

Romans 12:19 encourages us not to try to get people back for what they have done to us. Leave it in God's hands.

life point

The Bible tells us that the way to defeat evil is by overcoming it with good (see Romans 12:21). But that takes effort and determination. It will not just happen; you have to decide to do it. Start where you are and God will take you where you need to end up.

arranged [in divine order]. And those who resist will bring down judgment upon themselves [receiving the penalty due them].

3   For civil authorities are not a terror to [people of] good conduct, but to [those of] bad behavior. Would you have no dread of him who is in authority? Then do what is right and

you will receive his approval *and* commendation.

4 For he is God's servant for your good. But if you do wrong, [you should dread him and] be afraid, for he does not bear *and* wear the sword for nothing. He is God's servant to execute His wrath (punishment, vengeance) on the wrongdoer.

5 Therefore one must be subject, not only to avoid God's wrath *and* escape punishment, but also as a matter of principle *and* for the sake of conscience.

6 For this same reason you pay taxes, for [the civil authorities] are official servants under God, devoting themselves to attending to this very service.

7 Render to all men their dues. [Pay] taxes to whom taxes are due, revenue to whom revenue is due, respect to whom respect is due, and honor to whom honor is due.

8 Keep out of debt *and* owe no man anything, except to love one another; for he who loves his neighbor [who practices loving others] has fulfilled the Law [relating to one's fellowmen, meeting all its requirements].

9 The commandments, You shall not commit adultery, You shall not kill, You shall not steal, You shall not covet (have an evil desire), and any other commandment, are summed up in the single command, You shall love your neighbor as [you do] yourself. [Exod. 20:13-17; Lev. 19:18.]

10 Love does no wrong to one's neighbor [it never hurts anybody]. Therefore love meets all the requirements *and* is the fulfilling of the Law.

11 Besides this you know what [a critical] hour this is, how it is high time now for you to wake up out of your sleep (rouse to reality). For salvation (final deliverance) is nearer to us now than when we first believed (adhered to, trusted in, and relied on Christ, the Messiah).

12 The night is far gone and the day is almost here. Let us then drop (fling away) the works *and* deeds of darkness and put on the [full] armor of light.

13 Let us live *and* conduct ourselves honorably *and* becomingly as in the [open light of] day, not in reveling (carousing) and drunkenness, not in immorality and debauchery (sensuality and licentiousness), not in quarreling and jealousy.

14 But clothe yourself with the Lord Jesus Christ (the Messiah), and make no provision for [indulging] the flesh [put a stop to thinking about the evil cravings of your physical nature] to [gratify its] desires (lusts).

14 AS FOR the man who is a weak believer, welcome him [into your fellowship], but not to criticize his opinions *or* pass judgment on his scruples *or* perplex him with discussions.

2 One [man's faith permits him to] believe he may eat anything, while a weaker one [limits his] eating to vegetables.

3 Let not him who eats look down on *or* despise him who abstains, and let not him who abstains criticize *and* pass judgment on him who eats; for God has accepted *and* welcomed him.

4 Who are you to pass judgment on *and* censure another's household servant? It is before his own master that he stands or falls. And he shall stand *and* be upheld, for the Master (the Lord) is mighty to support him *and* make him stand.

5 One man esteems one day as better than another, while another man esteems all days alike [sacred]. Let everyone be fully convinced (satisfied) in his own mind.

6 He who observes the day, observes it in honor of the Lord. He also who eats, eats in honor of the Lord, since he gives thanks to God; while he who

abstains, abstains in honor of the Lord and gives thanks to God.

7 None of us lives to himself [but to the Lord], and none of us dies to himself [but to the Lord, for]

8 If we live, we live to the Lord, and if we die, we die to the Lord. So then, whether we live or we die, we belong to the Lord.

9 For Christ died and lived again for this very purpose, that He might be Lord both of the dead and of the living.

10 Why do you criticize *and* pass judgment on your brother? Or you, why do you look down upon *or* despise your brother? For we shall all stand before the judgment seat of God.

11 For it is written, As I live, says the Lord, every knee shall bow to Me, and every tongue shall confess to God [acknowledge Him to His honor and to His praise]. [Isa. 45:23.]

12 And so each of us shall give an account of himself [give an answer in reference to judgment] to God.

life point

Confronting the criticism and judgment of other people becomes easier when we remember that ultimately it is before our own Master that we stand or fall. In the end, we will answer to God alone (see Romans 14:12).

13 Then let us no more criticize *and* blame *and* pass judgment on one another, but rather decide *and* endeavor never to put a stumbling block *or* an obstacle or a hindrance in the way of a brother.

14 I know and am convinced (persuaded) as one in the Lord Jesus, that nothing is [forbidden as] essentially unclean (defiled and unholy in itself). But [none the less] it is unclean (defiled and unholy) to anyone who thinks it is unclean.

15 But if your brother is being pained *or* his feelings hurt *or* if he is being injured by what you eat, [then] you are no longer walking in love. [You have ceased to be living and conducting yourself by the standard of love toward him.] Do not let what you eat hurt *or* cause the ruin of one for whom Christ died!

16 Do not therefore let what seems good to you be considered an evil thing [by someone else]. [In other words, do not give occasion for others to criticize that which is justifiable for you.]

17 [After all] the kingdom of God is not a matter of [getting the] food and drink [one likes], but instead it is righteousness (that state which makes a person acceptable to God) and [heart] peace and joy in the Holy Spirit.

18 He who serves Christ in this way is acceptable *and* pleasing to God and is approved by men.

19 So let us then definitely aim for *and* eagerly pursue what makes for harmony and for mutual upbuilding (edification and development) of one another.

20 You must not, for the sake of food, undo *and* break down and destroy the work of God! Everything is indeed [ceremonially] clean *and* pure, but it is wrong for anyone to hurt the conscience of others *or* to make them fall by what he eats.

21 The right thing is to eat no meat or drink no wine [at all], or [do anything else] if it makes your brother stumble *or* hurts his conscience *or* offends or weakens him.

22 Your personal convictions [on such matters]—exercise [them] as in God's presence, keeping them to yourself [striving only to know the truth and obey His will]. Blessed (happy, [s]to be envied) is he who has

s Alexander Souter, *Pocket Lexicon.*

no reason to judge himself for what he approves [who does not convict himself by what he chooses to do].

23 But the man who has doubts (misgivings, an uneasy conscience) about eating, and then eats [perhaps because of you], stands condemned [before God], because he is not true to his convictions *and* he does not act from faith. For whatever does not originate *and* proceed from faith is sin [whatever is done without a conviction of its approval by God is sinful].

15 WE WHO are strong [in our convictions and of robust faith] ought to bear with the failings *and* the frailties *and* the tender scruples of the weak; [we ought to help carry the doubts and qualms of others] and not to please ourselves.

2 Let each one of us make it a practice to please (make happy) his neighbor for his good *and* for his true welfare, to edify him [to strengthen him and build him up spiritually].

3 For Christ did not please Himself [gave no thought to His own interests]; but, as it is written, The reproaches *and* abuses of those who reproached *and* abused you fell on Me. [Ps. 69:9.]

4 For whatever was thus written in former days was written for our instruction, that by [our steadfast and patient] endurance and the encouragement [drawn] from the Scriptures we might hold fast to *and* cherish hope.

5 Now may the God Who gives the power of patient endurance (steadfastness) and Who supplies encouragement, grant you to live in such mutual harmony *and* such full sympathy with one another, in accord with Christ Jesus,

6 That together you may [unanimously] with united hearts *and* one voice, praise and glorify the God and

Father of our Lord Jesus Christ (the Messiah).

7 Welcome *and* receive [to your hearts] one another, then, even as Christ has welcomed *and* received you, for the glory of God.

8 For I tell you that Christ (the Messiah) became a servant *and* a minister to the circumcised (the Jews) in order to show God's truthfulness *and* honesty by confirming (verifying) the promises [given] to our fathers,

9 And [also in order] that the Gentiles (nations) might glorify God for His mercy [not covenanted] to them. As it is written, Therefore I will praise You among the Gentiles and sing praises to Your name. [Ps. 18:49.]

10 Again it is said, Rejoice (exult), O Gentiles, along with His [own] people; [Deut. 32:43.]

11 And again, Praise the Lord, all you Gentiles, and let all the peoples praise Him! [Ps. 117:1.]

12 And further Isaiah says, There shall be a 'Sprout from the Root of Jesse, He Who rises to rule over the Gentiles; in Him shall the Gentiles hope. [Isa. 11:1, 10; Rev. 5:5; 22:16.]

13 May the God of your hope so fill you with all joy and peace in believing [through the experience of your faith] that by the power of the Holy Spirit you may abound *and* be overflowing (bubbling over) with hope.

14 Personally I am satisfied about you, my brethren, that you yourselves are rich in goodness, amply filled with all [spiritual] knowledge and competent to admonish *and* counsel *and* instruct one another also.

15 Still on some points I have written to you the more boldly *and* unreservedly by way of reminder. [I have done so] because of the grace (the unmerited favor) bestowed on me by God

16 In making me a minister of Christ Jesus to the Gentiles. I act in the

t G. Abbott-Smith, *Manual Greek Lexicon.*

pleasing God, pleasing others

Wanting to please and be acceptable is a natural trait. We might even say it is godly. God wants us to be good to people and strive to accommodate them. Romans 15:2, 3 teaches us to make a practice of pleasing our neighbors. But we need to balance that.

Above all, we are to be God-pleasers, not self-pleasers or people-pleasers. If we seek and love the approval of others, we are probably people-pleasers. We usually discover in our experiences that if we do not please people, they do not approve of us; therefore, if we have an out-of-balance need for approval, we will be people-pleasers.

The apostle Paul said in Galatians that he did not seek popularity with man, yet in I Corinthians he stated that he tried to please people and accommodate himself to their opinions and desires in order that they might be saved. Let us read and compare these two scriptures:

"Now am I trying to win the favor of men, or of God? Do I seek to please men? If I were still seeking popularity with men, I should not be a bond servant of Christ (the Messiah)" (Galatians 1:10).

"Just as I myself strive to please [to accommodate myself to the opinions, desires, and interests of others, adapting myself to] all men in everything I do, not aiming at or considering my own profit and advantage, but that of the many in order that they may be saved" (I Corinthians 10:33).

When we consider these two verses, they almost seem to oppose one another; yet if we understand the heart behind them, we see that they are not contradictory.

Paul wanted to please people. He wanted to maintain good relationships with people, especially for the purpose of leading them to accept Jesus as their Savior. He also wanted to please God and fulfill the call on his life. Paul knew how to maintain balance in this area. He tried to please people, as long as pleasing them did not cause him to displease the Lord. The Bible says in Acts 5:29, "We must obey God rather than men."

Pleasing people is good, but it is not good to become people-pleasers. I define *people-pleasers* as those who try to please people even if they have to compromise their consciences to do so. People-pleasers are those who need approval so desperately that they allow others to control, manipulate, and use them. They are not led by the Holy Spirit, as God's Word instructs us to be (see Romans 8:14).

People-pleasers are fear-based individuals. They fear rejection, judgment, what people think and say, and especially anger or disapproval. God-pleasers are grace-based individuals who do not seek approval out of insecurity or fear. They strive to follow God with all their hearts, but they also seek to please and minister to others without compromise or fear of rejection.

life point

One night I felt miserable. I was just walking around my house doing what I needed to do, but I was not happy, not enjoying life.

"What is the matter with me, Lord?" I asked. "What is my problem?"

A sense of heaviness engulfed me, something that drained the joy out of me. As I wandered around the house, I began looking at a Scripture box I kept on my desk. I flipped it open to Romans 15:13 and the Holy Spirit within me instantly confirmed the truth that I saw in this verse.

I recognized immediately that a large part of my problem was simply that I was doubting instead of believing. I was doubting the call of God on my life, wondering if He would meet our financial needs, questioning my decisions and actions, etc.

I became negative instead of positive. I doubted instead of believing.

Doubt is an attitude that can easily creep up on us; that is why we must be watchful not to permit it to do so.

Doubt may certainly knock at the door of your heart. When it does, answer with a believing heart, and you will always maintain the victory. Doubt steals your joy, but believing releases it.

priestly service of the Gospel (the good news) of God, in order that the sacrificial offering of the Gentiles may be acceptable [to God], consecrated *and* made holy by the Holy Spirit.
17 In Christ Jesus, then, I have legitimate reason to glory (exult) in my work for God [in what through Christ Jesus I have accomplished concerning the things of God].
18 For [of course] I will not venture (presume) to speak thus of any work except what Christ has actually done through me [as an instrument in His hands] to win obedience from the Gentiles, by word and deed,
19 [Even as my preaching has been accompanied] with the power of signs and wonders, [and all of it] by the power of the Holy Spirit. [The result is] that starting from Jerusalem and as far round as Illyricum, I have fully preached the Gospel [faithfully executing, accomplishing, carrying out to the full the good news] of Christ (the Messiah) in its entirety.
20 Thus my ambition has been to preach the Gospel, not where Christ's name has already been known, lest I build on another man's foundation;
21 But [instead I would act on the principle] as it is written, They shall see who have never been told of Him, and they shall understand who have never heard [of Him]. [Isa. 52:15.]
22 This [ambition] is the reason why I have so frequently been hindered from coming to visit you.
23 But now since I have no further opportunity for work in these regions, and since I have longed for ᵘenough years to come to you,
24 I hope to see you in passing [through Rome] as I go [on my intended trip] to Spain, and to be aided on my journey there by you, after I have enjoyed your company for a little while.
25 For the present, however, I am going to Jerusalem to bring aid (relief) for the saints (God's people there).
26 For it has been the good pleasure of Macedonia and Achaia to make some contribution for the poor among the saints of Jerusalem.

u Marvin Vincent, *Word Studies*.

27 They were pleased to do it; and surely they are in debt to them, for if these Gentiles have come to share in their [the Jerusalem Jews'] spiritual blessings, then they ought also to be of service to them in material blessings.
28 When therefore I have completed this mission and have delivered to them [at Jerusalem] what has been raised, I shall go on by way of you to Spain.
29 And I know that when I do come to you, I shall come in the abundant blessing *of the Gospel* of Christ.
30 I appeal to you [I entreat you], brethren, for the sake of our Lord Jesus Christ and by the love [given by] the Spirit, to unite with me in earnest wrestling in prayer to God in my behalf.
31 [Pray] that I may be delivered (rescued) from the unbelievers in Judea and that my mission of relief to Jerusalem may be acceptable *and* graciously received by the saints (God's people there),
32 So that by God's will I may subsequently come to you with joy (with a happy heart) and be refreshed [by the interval of rest] in your company.
33 May [our] peace-giving God be with you all! Amen (so be it).

16 NOW I introduce *and* commend to you our sister Phoebe, a deaconess of the church at Cenchreae,
2 That you may receive her in the Lord [with a Christian welcome], as saints (God's people) ought to receive one another. And help her in whatever matter she may require assistance from you, for she has been a helper of many including myself [shielding us from suffering].

speak the Word

3 Give my greetings to Prisca and Aquila, my fellow workers in Christ Jesus,
4 Who risked their lives [endangering their very necks] for my life. To them not only I but also all the churches among the Gentiles give thanks.
5 [Remember me] also to the church [that meets] in their house. Greet my beloved Epaenetus, who was a firstfruit (first convert) to Christ in Asia.
6 Greet Mary, who has worked so hard among you.
7 Remember me to Andronicus and Junias, my tribal kinsmen and once my fellow prisoners. They are men held in high esteem among the apostles, who also were in Christ before I was.
8 Remember me to Ampliatus, my beloved in the Lord.
9 Salute Urbanus, our fellow worker in Christ, and my dear Stachys.
10 Greet Apelles, that one tried *and* approved in Christ (the Messiah). Remember me to those who belong to the household of Aristobulus.
11 Greet my tribal kinsman Herodion, and those in the Lord who belong to the household of Narcissus.
12 Salute those workers in the Lord, Tryphaena and Tryphosa. Greet my dear Persis, who has worked so hard in the Lord.
13 Remember me to Rufus, eminent in the Lord, also to his mother [who has been] a mother to me as well.
14 Greet Asyncritus, Phlegon, Hermes, Patrobas, Hermas, and the brethren who are with them.
15 Greet Philologus, Julia, Nereus and his sister, and Olympas, and all the saints who are with them.
16 Greet one another with a holy

Thank You, God, that You are a peace-giving God! I receive Your peace today.
ADAPTED FROM ROMANS 15:33

(consecrated) kiss. All the churches of Christ (the Messiah) wish to be remembered to you.

17 I appeal to you, brethren, to be on your guard concerning those who create dissensions and difficulties *and* cause divisions, in opposition to the doctrine (the teaching) which you have been taught. [I warn you to turn aside from them, to] avoid them.

18 For such persons do not serve our Lord Christ but their own appetites *and* base desires, and by ingratiating and flattering speech, they beguile the hearts of the unsuspecting *and* simpleminded [people].

19 For while your loyalty *and* obedience is known to all, so that I rejoice over you, I would have you well versed *and* wise as to what is good and innocent *and* guileless as to what is evil.

20 And the God of peace will soon crush Satan under your feet. The grace of our Lord Jesus Christ (the Messiah) be with you.

21 Timothy, my fellow worker, wishes to be remembered to you, as do Lucius and Jason and Sosipater, my tribal kinsmen.

22 I, Tertius, the writer of this letter, greet you in the Lord.

23 Gaius, who is host to me and to the whole church here, greets you. So do Erastus, the city treasurer, and our brother Quartus.

24 *The grace of our Lord Jesus Christ (the Messiah) be with you all. Amen (so be it).*

25 Now to Him Who is able to strengthen you in the faith which is in accordance with my Gospel and the preaching of (concerning) Jesus Christ (the Messiah), according to the revelation (the unveiling) of the mystery of the plan of redemption which was kept in silence *and* secret for long ages,

26 But is now disclosed and through the prophetic Scriptures is made known to all nations, according to the command of the eternal God, [to win them] to obedience to the faith,

27 To [the] only wise God be glory forevermore through Jesus Christ (the Anointed One)! Amen (so be it).

First Corinthians

Author:
Paul

Date:
About AD 55

Everyday Life Principles:
Our motives and behavior are extremely important to God.

If you want to walk in love, read I Corinthians 13 and apply its principles to your life.

Let everything you do be done in love.

First Corinthians covers a variety of subjects and is full of practical information for everyday life, but if I had to reduce the main theme to its simplest form, I would say that this book is about our motives and our behavior as believers—and both are very important to God. This letter was written by the apostle Paul and addressed to the Christians in Corinth, a wealthy city on the Mediterranean Sea, where people from various cultures and religions often converged. Their diverse backgrounds and religious experiences often caused problems in the church and created a need for Paul to write this letter.

First Corinthians deals with everything from spiritual issues such as the gifts of the Holy Spirit, the importance of unity among believers, being confident in God, and how to behave in church. It also gives us advice on practical matters, such as healthy eating and taking care of our bodies and handling money and possessions. Perhaps most important, this book gives us the Bible's most extensive and vivid definition of love and teaches us how to walk in love (see chapter 13); without it we are "a useless nobody" (I Corinthians 13:2).

As you read I Corinthians, I pray you will apply its excellent and varied teachings to your life and that you will take the great advice of I Corinthians 16:14 and, "Let everything you do be done in love."

1 PAUL, SUMMONED by the will *and* purpose of God to be an apostle (special messenger) of Christ Jesus, and our brother Sosthenes,

2 To the church (assembly) of God which is in Corinth, to those consecrated *and* purified *and* made holy in Christ Jesus, [who are] selected *and* called to be saints (God's people), together with all those who in any place call upon *and* give honor to the name of our Lord Jesus Christ, both their Lord and ours:

3 Grace (favor and spiritual blessing) be to you and [heart] peace from God our Father and the Lord Jesus Christ.

4 I thank my God at all times for you because of the grace (the favor and spiritual blessing) of God which was bestowed on you in Christ Jesus,

5 [So] that in Him in every respect you were enriched, in full power *and* readiness of speech [to speak of your faith] and complete knowledge *and* illumination [to give you full insight into its meaning].

6 In this way [our] witnessing concerning Christ (the Messiah) was so confirmed *and* established *and* made sure in you

7 That you are not [consciously] falling behind *or* lacking in any special spiritual endowment *or* Christian grace [[a]the reception of which is due to the power of divine grace operating in your souls by the Holy Spirit], while you wait *and* watch [constantly living in hope] for the coming of our Lord Jesus Christ *and* [His] being made visible to all.

8 And He will establish you to the end [keep you steadfast, give you strength, and guarantee your vindication; He will be your warrant against all accusation or indictment so that you will be] guiltless *and* irreproachable in the day of our Lord Jesus Christ (the Messiah).

9 God is faithful (reliable, trustworthy, and therefore ever true to His promise, and He can be depended on); by Him you were called into companionship *and* participation with His Son, Jesus Christ our Lord.

10 But I urge *and* entreat you, brethren, by the name of our Lord Jesus Christ, that all of you be in perfect harmony *and* full agreement in what you say, and that there be no dissensions *or* factions *or* divisions among you, but that you be perfectly united in your common understanding and in your opinions *and* judgments.

11 For it has been made clear to me, my brethren, by those of Chloe's household, that there are contentions *and* wrangling *and* factions among you.

12 What I mean is this, that each one of you [either] says, I belong to Paul, or I belong to Apollos, or I belong to Cephas (Peter), or I belong to Christ.

13 Is Christ (the Messiah) divided into parts? Was Paul crucified on behalf of you? Or were you baptized into the name of Paul?

14 I thank God that I did not baptize any of you except Crispus and Gaius,

15 Lest anyone should say that I baptized in my own name.

speak the Word

God, I declare that in You, I am not lacking in any spiritual endowment or Christian grace. Thank You for establishing me to the end and giving me strength.
ADAPTED FROM I CORINTHIANS 1:7, 8

a Joseph Thayer, *A Greek-English Lexicon of the New Testament.*

putting the Word to work

Do you ever look around and notice the competition in our society today, even among Christians? There is simply no room for rivalry in the body of Christ; we are called to be one in Him (see I Corinthians 1:10–17). Pray for and do all you can to promote unity and harmony everywhere you go.

16 [Yes] I did baptize the household of Stephanas also. More than these, I do not remember that I baptized anyone.

17 For Christ (the Messiah) sent me out not to baptize but [to evangelize by] preaching the glad tidings (the Gospel), and that not with verbal eloquence, lest the cross of Christ should be deprived of force *and* emptied of its power *and* rendered vain (fruitless, void of value, and of no effect).

18 For the story *and* message of the cross is sheer absurdity *and* folly to those who are perishing *and* on their way to perdition, but to us who are being saved it is the [manifestation of] the power of God.

19 For it is written, I will baffle *and* render useless *and* destroy the learning of the learned *and* the philosophy of the philosophers and the cleverness of the clever *and* the discernment of the discerning; I will frustrate *and* nullify [them] *and* bring [them] to nothing. [Isa. 29:14.]

20 Where is the wise man (the philosopher)? Where is the scribe (the scholar)? Where is the investigator (the logician, the debater) of this present time *and* age? Has not God shown up the nonsense *and* the folly of this world's wisdom?

21 For when the world with all its earthly wisdom failed to perceive *and* recognize *and* know God by means of its own philosophy, God in His wisdom was pleased through the foolishness of preaching [salvation, procured by Christ and to be had through Him], to save those who believed (who clung to and trusted in and relied on Him).

22 For while Jews [demandingly] ask for signs *and* miracles and Greeks pursue philosophy *and* wisdom,

23 We preach Christ (the Messiah) crucified, [preaching which] to the Jews is a scandal *and* an offensive stumbling block [that springs a snare or trap], and to the Gentiles it is absurd *and* utterly unphilosophical nonsense.

24 But to those who are called, whether Jew or Greek (Gentile), Christ [is] the Power of God and the Wisdom of God.

25 [This is] because the foolish thing [that has its source in] God is wiser than men, and the weak thing [that springs] from God is stronger than men.

26 For [simply] consider your own call, brethren; not many [of you were considered to be] wise according to human estimates *and* standards, not many influential *and* powerful, not many of high *and* noble birth.

27 [No] for God selected (deliberately chose) what in the world is foolish to put the wise to shame, and what the world calls weak to put the strong to shame.

28 And God also selected (deliberately chose) what in the world is lowborn *and* insignificant and branded *and* treated with contempt, even the things that are nothing, that He might depose *and* bring to nothing the things that are,

29 So that no mortal man should [have pretense for glorying and] boast in the presence of God.

30 But it is from Him that you have your life in Christ Jesus, Whom God made our Wisdom from God, [revealed to us a knowledge of the divine plan of salvation previously hidden, manifesting itself as] our Righteousness [thus making us upright and putting us in

life point

God works through imperfect people, or what I often call "jars of clay" or "cracked pots" (see I Corinthians 1:27–29). This means that we are all flawed, so when people look at us and see amazing things happening, they know that God must be at work because without Him, we certainly could not achieve or accomplish what we do. I believe anyone who really knows me has no difficulty realizing the work I am doing today certainly must be God at work in and through me. They give Him the glory, not me, because they see my imperfections and know my limitations. God indeed chooses the "weak and foolish" on purpose so that no human being can have pretense for glorying in His presence.

Imagine a clay pot with a lamp in it and a lid on it. Even though it may be filled with light, no one can see the light within it. Yet if the pot is cracked, the light will shine through the cracks. In this same way, God works through our imperfections. Ask Him to work through you, in spite of your imperfections. You will be amazed at what He can accomplish through you!

right standing with God], and our Consecration [making us pure and holy], and our Redemption [providing our ransom from eternal penalty for sin].
31 So then, as it is written, Let him who boasts *and* proudly rejoices *and* glories, boast *and* proudly rejoice *and* glory in the Lord. [Jer. 9:24.]

2 AS FOR myself, brethren, when I came to you, I did not come proclaiming to you the testimo-

ny *and* evidence *or* [b]*mystery and secret* of God [concerning what He has done through Christ for the salvation of men] in lofty words of eloquence or human philosophy *and* wisdom;
2 For I resolved to know nothing (to be acquainted with nothing, to make a display of the knowledge of nothing, and to be conscious of nothing) among you except Jesus Christ (the Messiah) and Him crucified.
3 And I was in ([c]passed into a state of) weakness and fear (dread) and great trembling [[c]after I had come] among you.
4 And my language and my message were not set forth in persuasive (enticing and plausible) words of wisdom, but they were in demonstration of the [Holy] Spirit and power [[d]a proof by the Spirit and power of God, operating on me and stirring in the minds of my hearers the most holy emotions and thus persuading them],
5 So that your faith might not rest in the wisdom of men (human philosophy), but in the power of God.
6 Yet when we are among the full-grown (spiritually mature Christians who are ripe in understanding), we do impart a [higher] wisdom (the knowledge of the divine plan previously

putting the Word to work

Do you sometimes hesitate to share about God because you are not sure what to say? Even Paul, a great evangelist and teacher, did not count on flowery speech or his ability to persuade people; he depended on the Holy Spirit to speak through him (see I Corinthians 2:1–5). Ask the Holy Spirit to speak through you too and believe that He will.

b Many ancient manuscripts so read. **c** Marvin Vincent, *Word Studies in the New Testament.*
d Joseph Thayer, *A Greek-English Lexicon.*

life point

First Corinthians 2:5 teaches us not to put our faith in human wisdom or philosophy, but in the power of God. Verse 11 of this same chapter says that no one discerns the thoughts of God except the Spirit of God. Since the Holy Spirit knows the secret counsel of God, it is a vital necessity for us to know how to hear what He wants to say to us. The Holy Spirit helps us realize and comprehend and appreciate the gifts of divine favor and blessing that God bestows on us. Human wisdom does not teach us this truth; it comes from the Holy Spirit, Who gives us the mind of Christ (see I Corinthians 2:12–16). Ask Him to give you the mind of Christ today.

hidden); but it is indeed not a wisdom of this present age *or* of this world nor of the leaders *and* rulers of this age, who are being brought to nothing *and* are doomed to pass away.

7 But rather what we are setting forth is a wisdom of God once hidden [from the human understanding] and now revealed to us by God—[that wisdom] which God devised *and* decreed before the ages for our glorification [to lift us into the glory of His presence].

8 None of the rulers of this age *or* world perceived *and* recognized *and* understood this, for if they had, they would never have crucified the Lord of glory.

9 But, on the contrary, as the Scripture says, What eye has not seen and ear has not heard and has not entered into the heart of man, [all that] God has prepared (made and keeps ready) for those who love Him [ewho hold Him in affectionate reverence, promptly obeying Him and gratefully recognizing the benefits He has bestowed]. [Isa. 64:4; 65:17.]

10 Yet to us God has unveiled *and* revealed them by *and* through His Spirit, for the [Holy] Spirit searches diligently, exploring *and* examining everything, even sounding the profound and bottomless things of God [the edivine counsels and things hidden and beyond man's scrutiny].

11 For what person perceives (knows and understands) what passes through a man's thoughts except the man's own spirit within him? Just so no one discerns (comes to know and comprehend) the thoughts of God except the Spirit of God.

12 Now we have not received the spirit [that belongs to] the world, but the [Holy] Spirit Who is from God, [given to us] that we might realize *and* comprehend *and* appreciate the gifts [of divine favor and blessing so freely and lavishly] bestowed on us by God.

13 And we are setting these truths forth in words not taught by human wisdom but taught by the [Holy] Spirit, combining *and* interpreting spiritual truths with spiritual language [to those who possess the Holy Spirit].

14 But the natural, nonspiritual man does not accept *or* welcome *or* admit into his heart the gifts *and* teachings

speak the Word

Thank You, God, for preparing for me things that my eyes have not seen, my ears have not heard, and my heart has not thought of—things that can only be revealed to me by Your Spirit.
ADAPTED FROM I CORINTHIANS 2:9, 10

e Joseph Thayer, *A Greek-English Lexicon.*

life point

First Corinthians 2:14 explains that natural man cannot understand spiritual things because they must be spiritually discerned. This means that spiritual things take place in the regenerated (born-again) spirit of the inner man, not in the natural mind.

I am very grateful for discernment and spiritual understanding. I appreciate the fact that you and I, as believers in Jesus Christ, filled with His Spirit, can make decisions courageously because we can trust what is in our hearts.

and revelations of the Spirit of God, for they are folly (meaningless nonsense) to him; and he is incapable of knowing them [of progressively recognizing, understanding, and becoming better acquainted with them] because they are spiritually discerned *and* estimated *and* appreciated.

15 But the spiritual man tries all things [he [f]examines, investigates, inquires into, questions, and discerns all things], yet is himself to be put on trial and judged by no one [he can read the meaning of everything, but no one can properly discern *or* appraise *or* get an insight into him].

16 For who has known *or* understood the mind (the counsels and purposes) of the Lord so as to guide *and* instruct Him *and* give Him knowledge? But we have the mind of Christ (the Messiah) *and* do hold the thoughts (feelings and purposes) of His heart. [Isa. 40:13.]

3 HOWEVER, BRETHREN, I could not talk to you as to spiritual [men], but as to nonspiritual [men of the flesh, in whom the carnal nature predominates], as to

mere infants [in the new life] in Christ [[g]unable to talk yet!]

2 I fed you with milk, not solid food, for you were not yet strong enough [to be ready for it]; but even yet you are not strong enough [to be ready for it],

3 For you are still [unspiritual, having the nature] of the flesh [under the control of ordinary impulses]. For as long as [there are] envying and jealousy *and* wrangling and factions among you, are you not unspiritual *and* of the flesh, behaving yourselves after a human standard *and* like mere (unchanged) men?

4 For when one says, I belong to Paul, and another, I belong to Apollos, are you not [proving yourselves] ordinary (unchanged) men?

5 What then is Apollos? What is Paul? Ministering servants [not heads of parties] through whom you believed, even as the Lord appointed to each his task:

6 I planted, Apollos watered, but God [all the while] was making it grow *and* [He] gave the increase.

7 So neither he who plants is anything nor he who waters, but [only] God Who makes it grow *and* become greater.

8 He who plants and he who waters are equal (one in aim, of the same importance and esteem), yet each shall receive his own reward (wages), according to his own labor.

9 For we are fellow workmen (joint promoters, laborers together) with *and*

life point

Envy and jealousy cause us to strive after things that God gives us in His timing, if it is His will that we have them. A jealous, envious heart never blesses God. We are not to envy what other people have (see I Corinthians 3:3).

f Joseph P. Lightfoot, *Notes on the Epistles of Saint Paul.*   g Literal translation: "non-speakers."

the difference between knowing and *really* knowing

The natural man does not understand the spiritual man (see I Corinthians 2:14). Some of the choices and decisions a spiritual person makes do not make sense at all to a non-spiritual person. Those who are natural or non-spiritual try to understand everything with their minds, but the spiritual person discerns things by the Spirit. He lives out of his new heart and out of the attitude that God gives him. Recently I told someone something I believed and they said, "That makes no sense at all." I responded by saying, "I know it, I believe a lot of things that do not make sense to my mind." The carnal or natural man wants to know things in his mind and with his intellect, but the spiritual man knows things by the Spirit. When he needs answers he looks to his heart, not his head.

There is a difference in "knowing" and "really knowing." Someone who has met me might say, "I know Joyce Meyer," when in reality that person does not really know very much about me at all. But, when my husband says, "I know Joyce Meyer," he really knows me thoroughly and completely. He has seen me in every kind of situation and often knows how I will respond to certain circumstances before I even have a chance to respond.

The spiritual realm is just as real to the spiritual man as the natural world is to the natural man. Just because we cannot see it does not mean that it does not exist. We depend entirely too much on what we see, feel, and understand. Satan sends lies to your mind and you can either believe what he says or you can ask yourself, "Now, what do I know in my heart about this?"

Spiritual people are hard to understand mentally. Sometimes they might even seem a bit odd to non-spiritual people. They live by discernment. They look into things with their spirit, not just their natural eyes. They live by what they know and truly feel in their spirit, not what they see or feel. Faith has nothing to do with feelings and sight—and that is exactly how the spiritual man lives. He lives by faith! He is saved by faith, justified by faith, made right with God by faith, and he walks by faith. The spiritual life is definitely misunderstood by natural, non-spiritual people, but it is a wonderful, fulfilling, exciting life.

for God; *you* are God's ʰgarden *and* vineyard *and* field under cultivation, [you are] God's building. [Isa. 61:3.]
10 According to the grace (the special endowment for my task) of God bestowed on me, like a skillful architect *and* master builder I laid [the] foundation, and now another [man] is building upon it. But let each [man] be careful how he builds upon it,
11 For no other foundation can anyone lay than that which is [already] laid, which is Jesus Christ (the Messiah, the Anointed One).
12 But if anyone builds upon the Foundation, whether it be with gold, silver, precious stones, wood, hay, straw,

h Johann Bengel, *Gnomon Novi Testamenti.*

envy prevents blessing

First Corinthians 3:3 teaches us that envy comes from fleshly impulses.

I discovered that the best way to get over envy or jealousy is to admit it. When you feel jealous or envious, be honest with God and ask Him to help you live free from it. Anything we hide has power over us, so bringing hidden things into the light not only exposes them but weakens their power over us.

I must admit, there are times when I hear about a blessing that someone receives, and I start to think, *When is that going to happen to me?* When that thought enters my mind, I immediately open my mouth and say, "I am happy for him. If God can do it for him, He can do it for me too."

If a young woman is unmarried and prays and asks God to give her a husband, she may have difficulty being truly happy for her friends when they get married.

In similar situations, instead of being unhappy or jealous or envious, we all need to learn to be happy for others and let their blessings be an encouragement to us. We can believe that what God did for them, He can do for us. If He did it once, He can do it again!

We should learn to pray for other people to be blessed. We should pray for God to do for them what we want Him to do for us. What we sow into others through our prayers, God can make happen for us.

We should bless others and not be afraid they will get ahead of us. We must not envy anyone else's appearance, possessions, education, social standing, marital status, gifts and talents, job, or anything else because that will only hinder our own blessing.

Being jealous and envious of one another is a total waste of time. We all have gifts that God gives us; they do not come from any other source. We must be content with what heaven sends us. God has a unique plan for each of our lives, and the gifts He gives us are part of that plan. We can trust Him; He knows His business. What He does for others is actually none of our business. Our business is to walk in love.

13 The work of each [one] will become [plainly, openly] known (shown for what it is); for the day [of Christ] will disclose *and* declare it, because it will be revealed with fire, and the fire will test *and* critically appraise the character *and* worth of the work each person has done.

14 If the work which any person has built on this Foundation [any product of his efforts whatever] survives [this test], he will get his reward.

15 But if any person's work is burned up [under the test], he will suffer the loss [of it all, losing his reward], though he himself will be saved, but

First Corinthians 3:9–11 teaches us about foundations. People try to build their lives on many things—money, education, job titles, possessions, and other things. However, these are all faulty foundations. Let me ask you: Who or what is the foundation of your life? Jesus Christ is the only sure foundation you can build your life upon. Ask God to help you build your life wisely upon the firm foundation of Jesus.

only as [one who has passed] through fire. [Job 23:10.]

16 Do you not discern *and* understand that you [the whole church at Corinth] are God's temple (His sanctuary), and that God's Spirit has His permanent dwelling in you [to be at home in you, ⁱcollectively as a church and also individually]?

17 If anyone ʲdoes hurt to God's temple *or* corrupts it [ⁱwith false doctrines] *or* destroys it, God will ʲdo hurt to him *and* bring him to the corruption of death *and* destroy him. For the temple of God is holy (sacred to Him) and that [temple] you [ⁱthe believing church and its individual believers] are.

life point

When we accept Christ, the Holy Spirit comes to dwell in us (see John 14:17). God chooses to move into our spirit—into the center core of our lives—where He can be closer to us than any other living thing. When God's Holy Spirit moves into our human spirit, our spirit is prepared as a dwelling place for God and is made holy because God is there (see I Corinthians 3:16, 17).

18 Let no person deceive himself. If anyone among you supposes that he is wise in this age, let him become a fool [let him discard his worldly discernment and recognize himself as dull, stupid, and foolish, without true learning and scholarship], that he may become [really] wise. [Isa. 5:21.]

19 For this world's wisdom is foolishness (absurdity and stupidity) with God, for it is written, He lays hold of the wise in their [own] craftiness; [Job 5:13.]

20 And again, The Lord knows the thoughts *and* reasonings of the [humanly] wise *and* recognizes how futile they are. [Ps. 94:11.]

21 So let no one exult proudly concerning men [boasting of having this or that man as a leader], for all things are yours,

22 Whether Paul or Apollos or Cephas (Peter), or the universe or life or death, or the immediate *and* ᵏthreatening present or the [subsequent and uncertain] future—all are yours,

23 And you are Christ's, and Christ is God's.

4 SO THEN, let us [apostles] be looked upon as ministering servants of Christ and stewards (trustees) of the mysteries (the secret purposes) of God.

2 Moreover, it is [essentially] required of stewards that a man should be found faithful [proving himself worthy of trust].

3 But [as for me personally] it matters very little to me that I should be put on trial by you [on this point], *and* that you or any other human tribunal should investigate *and* question *and* cross-question me. I do not even put myself on trial *and* judge myself.

4 I am not conscious of anything

i Matthew Henry, *Commentary on the Holy Bible.*   j *The Cambridge Bible for Schools and Colleges.*
k Marvin Vincent, *Word Studies.*

against myself, *and* I feel blameless; but I am not vindicated *and* acquitted before God on that account. It is the Lord [Himself] Who examines *and* judges me.

5 So do not make any hasty *or* premature judgments before the time when the Lord comes [again], for He will both bring to light the secret things that are [now hidden] in darkness and disclose *and* expose the [secret] aims (motives and purposes) of hearts. Then every man will receive his [due] commendation from God.

6 Now I have applied all this [about parties and factions] to myself and Apollos for your sakes, brethren, so that from what I have said of us [as illustrations], you may learn [to think of men in accordance with Scripture and] not to go beyond that which is written, that none of you may be puffed up *and* inflated with pride *and* boast in favor of one [minister and teacher] against another.

7 For who separates you from the others [as a faction leader]? [Who makes you superior and sets you apart from another, giving you the preeminence?] What have you that was not given to you? If then you received it [from someone], why do you boast as if you had not received [but had gained it by your own efforts]?

8 [¹You behave as if] you are already filled *and* think you have enough [you are full and content, feeling no need of anything more]! Already you have become rich [in spiritual gifts and graces]! [Without any counsel or instruction from us, in your conceit], you have ascended your thrones *and* come into your kingdom without including us! And would that it were true *and* that you did reign, so that we might be sharing the kingdom with you!

9 For it seems to me that God has made an exhibit of us apostles, exposing us to view last [of all, like men in a triumphal procession who are] sentenced to death [and displayed at the end of the line]. For we have become a spectacle to the world [a show in the world's amphitheater] with both men and angels [as spectators].

10 We are [looked upon as] fools on account of Christ *and* for His sake, but you are [supposedly] so amazingly wise *and* prudent in Christ! We are weak, but you are [so very] strong! You are highly esteemed, but we are in disrepute *and* contempt!

11 To this hour we have gone both hungry and thirsty; we [ᵐhabitually] wear but one undergarment [and shiver in the cold]; we are roughly knocked about and wander around homeless.

12 And we still toil unto weariness [for our living], working hard with our own hands. When men revile us [ⁿwound us with an accursed sting], we bless them. When we are persecuted, we take it patiently *and* endure it.

13 When we are slandered *and* defamed, we [try to] answer softly *and* bring comfort. We have been made and are now the rubbish *and* filth of the world [the offscouring of all things, the scum of the earth].

14 I do not write this to shame you, but to warn *and* counsel you as my beloved children.

15 After all, though you should have ten thousand teachers (guides to direct you) in Christ, yet you do not have many fathers. For I became your father in Christ Jesus through the glad tidings (the Gospel).

16 So I urge *and* implore you, be imitators of me.

17 For this very cause I sent to you

---

l Henry Alford, *The Greek New Testament, with Notes.* **m** Alexander Souter, *Pocket Lexicon of the Greek New Testament.* **n** Kenneth Wuest, *Word Studies in the Greek New Testament.*

a father's heart

Paul had a father's heart toward the believers in the church at Corinth (see I Corinthians 4:15).

A father's heart is that tender, nurturing, training, teaching, stick-to-it kind of attitude that does not give up on people just because they do not learn quickly.

A father delights in teaching his children how to walk or to play ball. He does not get angry with them because they do not master the steps the first time. He keeps working and working with them until they learn how to do it. A good father does not give up on his children. He is committed to them all of their lives.

Paul said the church is full of instructors, full of teachers, full of people who can preach a sermon and tell others what to do. But he also said there are not enough fathers in the church.

If you want to be a leader in the body of Christ, especially if you want to be a pastor, you must have the heart of a father.

Perhaps you feel unqualified to "father" someone in the spiritual life. Perhaps you did not have a father who was a good role model to you. Perhaps you do not know how to be "father-like." The truth is that we all have had less-than-perfect fathers here on earth. You need to realize that God is a good heavenly Father. He can nurture you as your loving Father, and He can show you how to treat others the same way. Ask Him to help you. He will.

Timothy, who is my beloved and trustworthy child in the Lord, who will recall to your minds my methods of proceeding *and* course of conduct *and* way of life in Christ, such as I teach everywhere in each of the churches.
18 Some of you have become conceited *and* arrogant *and* pretentious, counting on my not coming to you.
19 But I will come to you [and] shortly, if the Lord is willing, and then I will perceive *and* understand not what the talk of these puffed up *and* arrogant spirits amount to, but their force (°the moral power and excellence of soul they really possess).
20 For the kingdom of God consists of *and* is based on not talk but power (°moral power and excellence of soul).
21 Now which do you prefer? Shall I come to you with a rod of correction, or with love and in a spirit of gentleness?

speak the Word

Thank You, God, that Your kingdom is not based on talk, but on power and excellence.
ADAPTED FROM I CORINTHIANS 4:20

o Joseph Thayer, *A Greek-English Lexicon.*

5 IT IS actually reported that there is sexual immorality among you, impurity of a sort that is condemned *and* does not occur even among the heathen; for a man has [his own] father's wife. [Deut. 22:30; 27:20.]

2 And you are proud *and* arrogant! And you ought rather to mourn (bow in sorrow and in shame) until the person who has done this [shameful] thing is removed from your fellowship *and* your midst!

3 As for my attitude, though I am absent [from you] in body, I am present in spirit, and I have already decided *and* passed judgment, as if actually present,

4 In the name of the Lord Jesus *Christ,* on the man who has committed such a deed. When you and my own spirit are met together with the power of our Lord Jesus,

5 You are to deliver this man over to Satan [p]for physical discipline [to destroy carnal lusts which prompted him to incest], that [his] spirit may [yet] be saved in the day of the Lord Jesus.

6 [About the condition of your church] your boasting is not good [indeed, it is most unseemly and entirely out of place]. Do you not know that [just] a little leaven will ferment the whole lump [of dough]?

7 Purge (clean out) the old leaven that you may be fresh (new) dough, still uncontaminated [as you are], for Christ, our Passover [Lamb], has been sacrificed.

8 Therefore, let us keep the feast, not with old leaven, nor with leaven of vice *and* malice and wickedness, but with the unleavened [bread] of purity (nobility, honor) *and* sincerity and [unadulterated] truth. [Exod. 12:19; 13:7; Deut. 16:3.]

9 I wrote you in my [previous] letter not to associate [closely and habitually] with unchaste (impure) people—

10 Not [meaning of course that you must] altogether shun the immoral people of this world, or the greedy graspers and cheats *and* thieves or idolaters, since otherwise you would need to get out of the world *and* human society altogether!

11 But now I write to you not to associate with anyone who bears the name of [Christian] brother if he is known to be guilty of immorality or greed, or is an idolater [whose soul is devoted to any object that usurps the place of God], or is a person with a foul tongue [railing, abusing, reviling, slandering], or is a drunkard or a swindler *or* a robber. [No] you must not so much as eat with such a person.

12 What [business] of mine is it *and* what right have I to judge outsiders? Is it not those inside [the church] upon whom you are to pass disciplinary judgment [passing censuring sentence on them as the facts require]?

13 God alone sits in judgment on those who are outside. Drive out that wicked one from among you [expel him from your church].

6 DOES ANY of you dare, when he has a matter of complaint against another [brother], to go to law before unrighteous men [men neither upright nor right with God, laying it before them] instead of before the saints (the people of God)?

2 Do you not know that the saints (the believers) will [one day] judge *and* govern the world? And if the world [itself] is to be judged *and* ruled by you, are you unworthy *and* incompetent to try [such petty matters] of the smallest courts of justice?

3 Do you not know also that we [Christians] are to judge the [very] angels *and* pronounce opinion

---

p G. Abbott-Smith, *Manual Greek Lexicon of the New Testament.*

between right and wrong [for them]? How much more then [as to] matters pertaining to this world *and* of this life only!

4 If then you do have such cases of everyday life to decide, why do you appoint [as judges to lay them before] those who [from the standpoint] of the church count for least *and* are without standing?

5 I say this to move you to shame. Can it be that there really is not one man among you who [in action is governed by piety and integrity and] is wise *and* competent enough to decide [the private grievances, disputes, and quarrels] between members of the brotherhood,

6 But brother goes to law against brother, and that before [Gentile judges who are] unbelievers [without faith or trust in the Gospel of Christ]?

7 Why, the very fact of your having lawsuits with one another at all is a defect (a defeat, an evidence of positive moral loss for you). Why not rather let yourselves suffer wrong *and* be deprived of what is your due? Why not rather be cheated (defrauded and robbed)?

8 But [instead it is you] yourselves who wrong and defraud, and that even your own brethren [by so treating them]!

9 Do you not know that the unrighteous *and* the wrongdoers will not inherit *or* have any share in the kingdom of God? Do not be deceived (misled): neither the impure *and* immoral, nor idolaters, nor adulterers, nor those who participate in homosexuality,

10 Nor cheats (swindlers and thieves), nor greedy graspers, nor drunkards, nor foulmouthed revilers *and* slanderers, nor extortioners *and* robbers will inherit *or* have any share in the kingdom of God.

11 And such some of you were

[once]. But you were washed clean (purified by a complete atonement for sin and made free from the guilt of sin), and you were consecrated (set apart, hallowed), and you were justified [pronounced righteous, by trusting] in the name of the Lord Jesus Christ and in the [Holy] Spirit of our God.

12 Everything is permissible (allowable and lawful) for me; but not all things are helpful (good for me to do, expedient and profitable when considered with other things). Everything is lawful for me, but I will not become the slave of anything *or* be brought under its power.

life point

The apostle Paul wrote that something may be permissible for him, but at the same time it may not be helpful or profitable for him (see I Corinthians 6:12). There are many things that we *could* do, and God will not say a thing about them. We refer to this as God's "permissive will." He is not likely to give us a divine word about every single move we make, but He will always give us wisdom if we ask for it. Walk in wisdom and you will not live in regret.

13 Food [is intended] for the stomach and the stomach for food, but God will finally end [the functions of] both *and* bring them to nothing. The body is not intended for sexual immorality, but [is intended] for the Lord, and the Lord [is intended] for the body [qto save, sanctify, and raise it again].

14 And God both raised the Lord to life and will also raise us up by His power.

15 Do you not see *and* know that your bodies are members (bodily parts) of

---

q *The Cambridge Bible.* See also Rom. 8:11; I Cor. 15:35-54.

Christ (the Messiah)? Am I therefore to take the parts of Christ and make [them] parts of a prostitute? Never! Never!

16 Or do you not know *and* realize that when a man joins himself to a prostitute, he becomes one body with her? The two, it is written, shall become one flesh. [Gen. 2:24.]

17 But the person who is united to the Lord becomes one spirit with Him.

18 Shun immorality *and* all sexual looseness [flee from impurity in thought, word, or deed]. Any other sin which a man commits is one outside the body, but he who commits sexual immorality sins against his own body.

19 Do you not know that your body is the temple (the very sanctuary) of the Holy Spirit Who lives within you, Whom you have received [as a Gift] from God? You are not your own,

20 You were bought with a price [purchased with a ʳpreciousness and paid for, ʳmade His own]. So then, honor God *and* bring glory to Him in your body.

7 NOW AS to the matters of which you wrote me. It is well [and by that I mean advantageous, expedient, profitable, and wholesome] for a man not to touch a woman [to cohabit with her] *but* to remain unmarried.

2 But because of the temptation to impurity *and* to avoid immorality, let each [man] have his own wife and let each [woman] have her own husband.

3 The husband should give to his

speak the Word

wife her conjugal rights (goodwill, kindness, and what is due her as his wife), and likewise the wife to her husband.

4 For the wife does not have [exclusive] authority *and* control over her own body, but the husband [has his rights]; likewise also the husband does not have [exclusive] authority *and* control over his body, but the wife [has her rights].

5 Do not refuse *and* deprive *and* defraud each other [of your due marital rights], except perhaps by mutual consent for a time, so that you may devote yourselves unhindered to prayer. But afterwards resume marital relations, lest Satan tempt you [to sin] through your lack of restraint of sexual desire. [Exod. 19:15.]

6 But I am saying this more as a matter of permission *and* concession, not as a command *or* regulation.

7 I wish that all men were like I myself am [in this matter of

r Joseph Thayer, *A Greek-English Lexicon.*

self-control]. But each has his own special gift from God, one of this kind and one of another.

8 But to the unmarried people and to the widows, I declare that it is well (good, advantageous, expedient, and wholesome) for them to remain [single] even as I do.

9 But if they have not self-control (restraint of their passions), they should marry. For it is better to marry than to be aflame [with passion and tortured continually with ungratified desire].

10 But to the married people I give charge—not I but the Lord—that the wife is not to separate from her husband.

11 But if she does [separate from and divorce him], let her remain single or else be reconciled to her husband. And [I charge] the husband [also] that he should not put away *or* divorce his wife.

12 To the rest I declare—I, not the Lord [for Jesus did not discuss this]— that if any brother has a wife who does not believe [in Christ] and she consents to live with him, he should not leave *or* divorce her.

13 And if any woman has an unbelieving husband and he consents to live with her, she should not leave *or* divorce him.

14 For the unbelieving husband is set apart (separated, withdrawn from heathen contamination, and affiliated with the Christian people) by union with his consecrated (set-apart) wife, and the unbelieving wife is set apart *and* separated through union with her consecrated husband. Otherwise your children would be unclean (unblessed heathen, ˢoutside the Christian covenant), but as it is they are ᵗprepared for God [pure and clean].

15 But if the unbelieving partner [actually] leaves, let him do so; in such [cases the remaining] brother or sister is not morally bound. But God has called us to peace.

16 For, wife, how can you be sure of converting *and* saving your husband? Husband, how can you be sure of converting *and* saving your wife?

17 Only, let each one [seek to conduct himself and regulate his affairs so as to] lead the life which the Lord has allotted *and* imparted to him and to which God has invited *and* summoned him. This is my order in all the churches.

18 Was anyone at the time of his summons [from God] already circumcised? Let him not seek to remove the evidence of circumcision. Was anyone at the time [God] called him uncircumcised? Let him not be circumcised.

19 For circumcision is nothing *and* counts for nothing, neither does uncircumcision, but [what counts is] keeping the commandments of God.

20 Everyone should remain after God calls him in the station *or* condition of life in which the summons found him.

21 Were you a slave when you were called? Do not let that trouble you. But if you are able to gain your freedom, avail yourself of the opportunity.

22 For he who as a slave was summoned in [to union with] the Lord is a freedman of the Lord, just so he who was free when he was called is a bond servant of Christ (the Messiah).

23 You were bought with a price [purchased with a preciousness and paid for by Christ]; then do not yield yourselves up to become [in your own estimation] slaves to men [but consider yourselves slaves to Christ].

24 So, brethren, in whatever station *or* state *or* condition of life each one

---

s Robert Jamieson, A.R. Fausset and David Brown, *A Commentary on the Old and New Testaments*.
t Joseph Thayer, *A Greek-English Lexicon*.

was when he was called, there let him continue with *and* close to God.

25 Now concerning the virgins (the marriageable ᵘmaidens) I have no command of the Lord, but I give my opinion *and* advice as one who by the Lord's mercy is rendered trustworthy *and* faithful.

26 I think then, because of the impending distress [that is even now setting in], it is well (expedient, profitable, and wholesome) for a person to remain as he *or* she is.

27 Are you bound to a wife? Do not seek to be free. Are you free from a wife? Do not seek a wife.

28 But if you do marry, you do not sin [in doing so], and if a virgin marries, she does not sin [in doing so]. Yet those who marry will have physical *and* earthly troubles, and I would like to spare you that.

29 I mean, brethren, the appointed time has been ᵘwinding down *and* it has grown very short. From now on, let even those who have wives be as if they had none,

30 And those who weep *and* mourn as though they were not weeping *and* mourning, and those who rejoice as though they were not rejoicing, and those who buy as though they did not possess anything,

31 And those who deal with this world [ᵘoverusing the enjoyments of this life] as though they were not absorbed by it *and* as if they had no dealings with it. For the outward form of this world (the present world order) is passing away.

32 My desire is to have you free from all anxiety *and* distressing care. The unmarried man is anxious about the things of the Lord—how he may please the Lord;

33 But the married man is anxious about worldly matters—how he may please his wife—

34 And he is drawn in diverging directions [his interests are divided *and* he is distracted from his devotion to God]. And the unmarried woman or girl is concerned *and* anxious about the matters of the Lord, how to be wholly separated *and* set apart in body and spirit; but the married woman has her cares [centered] in earthly affairs—how she may please her husband.

35 Now I say this for your own welfare *and* profit, not to put [a halter of] restraint upon you, but to promote what is seemly *and* in good order and to secure your undistracted *and* undivided devotion to the Lord.

36 But if any man thinks that he is not acting properly toward *and* in regard to his virgin [that he is preparing disgrace for her or incurring reproach], in case she is passing the bloom of her youth and if there is need for it, let him do what to him seems right; he does not sin; let them marry.

37 But whoever is firmly established in his heart [strong in mind and purpose], not being forced by necessity but having control over his own will *and* desire, and has resolved this in his heart to keep his own virginity, he is doing well.

38 So also then, he [the father] who gives his virgin (his daughter) in marriage does well, and he [the father] who does not give [her] in marriage does better.

39 A wife is bound to her husband by law as long as he lives. If the husband dies, she is free to be married to whom she will, only [provided that he too is] in the Lord.

40 But in my opinion [a widow] is happier (more blessed and ᵛto be envied) if she does not remarry. And also I think I have the Spirit of God.

---

u Marvin Vincent, *Word Studies.* **v** Alexander Souter, *Pocket Lexicon.*

8 NOW ABOUT food offered to idols: of course we know that all of us possess knowledge [concerning these matters. Yet mere] knowledge causes people to be puffed up (to bear themselves loftily and be proud), but love (affection and goodwill and benevolence) edifies *and* builds up *and* encourages one to grow [to his full stature].

life point

In I Corinthians 8:1, Paul said that knowledge puffs up, but love builds up. If we seek to walk in real love more than we seek to know things we are much better off. Pride makes us think we do not need God. Pride always comes before destruction. Beware of pride and seek love. Love is humble, not puffed up or inflated with pride. Instead of being anxious to tell others what we know, let us strive to edify them and build them up. We do not need to try to impress other people; we need to humble ourselves and let God exalt us in His timing.

2 If anyone imagines that he has come to know *and* understand much [of divine things, without love], he does not yet perceive *and* recognize *and* understand as strongly *and* clearly, *nor* has he become as intimately acquainted with anything as he ought *or* as is necessary.

3 But if one loves God truly [*w*with affectionate reverence, prompt obedi-

ence, and grateful recognition of His blessing], he is known by God [*x*recognized as worthy of His intimacy and love, and he is owned by Him].

4 In this matter, then, of eating food offered to idols, we know that an idol is nothing (has no real existence) and that there is no God but one. [Deut. 6:4.]

5 For although there may be so-called gods, whether in heaven or on earth, as indeed there are many of them, both of gods and of lords *and* masters,

6 Yet for us there is [only] one God, the Father, Who is the Source of all things and for Whom we [have life], and one Lord, Jesus Christ, through *and* by Whom are all things and through *and* by Whom we [ourselves exist]. [Mal. 2:10.]

7 Nevertheless, not all [believers] possess this knowledge. But some, through being all their lives until now accustomed to [thinking of] idols [as real and living], still consider the food [offered to an idol] as that sacrificed to an [actual] god; and their weak consciences become defiled *and* injured if they eat [it].

8 Now food [itself] will not cause our acceptance by God *nor* commend us to Him. Eating [food offered to idols] gives us no advantage; neither do we come short *or* become any worse if we do not eat [it].

9 Only be careful that this power of choice (this permission and liberty to do as you please) which is yours, does not [somehow] become a hindrance (cause of stumbling) to the weak *or*

speak the Word

God, I declare that You are the only God. You are the Source of all things, and I am living for You. I declare that Jesus Christ is the only Lord. Through Him and by Him, all things exist, including me!
ADAPTED FROM I CORINTHIANS 8:6

---

w Joseph Thayer, *A Greek-English Lexicon.*   x Alexander Souter, *Pocket Lexicon.*

overscrupulous [giving them an impulse to sin].

10 For suppose someone sees you, a man having knowledge [of God, with an intelligent view of this subject and] reclining at table in an idol's temple, might he not be encouraged *and* emboldened [to violate his own conscientious scruples] if he is weak *and* uncertain, and eat what [to him] is for the purpose of idol worship?

11 And so by your enlightenment (your knowledge of spiritual things), this weak man is ruined (is lost and perishes)—the brother for whom Christ (the Messiah) died!

12 And when you sin against your brethren in this way, wounding *and* damaging their weak conscience, you sin against Christ.

13 Therefore, if [my eating a] food is a cause of my brother's falling *or* of hindering [his spiritual advancement], I will not eat [such] flesh forever, lest I cause my brother to be tripped up *and* fall *and* to be offended.

9 AM I not an apostle (a special messenger)? Am I not free (unrestrained and exempt from any obligation)? Have I not seen Jesus our Lord? Are you [yourselves] not [the product and proof of] my workmanship in the Lord?

2 Even if I am not considered an apostle (a special messenger) by others, at least I am one to you; for you are the seal (the certificate, the living evidence) of my apostleship in the Lord [confirming and authenticating it].

3 This is my [real ground of] defense (my vindication of myself) to those who would put me on trial *and* cross-examine me.

4 Have we not the right to our food and drink [at the expense of the churches]?

5 Have we not the right also to take along with us a Christian sister as wife, as do the other apostles and the Lord's brothers and Cephas (Peter)?

6 Or is it only Barnabas and I who have no right to refrain from doing manual labor for a livelihood [in order to go about the work of the ministry]?

7 [Consider this:] What soldier at any time serves at his own expense? Who plants a vineyard and does not eat any of the fruit of it? Who tends a flock and does not partake of the milk of the flock?

8 Do I say this only on human authority *and* as a man reasons? Does not the Law endorse the same principle?

9 For in the Law of Moses it is written, You shall not muzzle an ox when it is treading out the corn. Is it [only] for oxen that God cares? [Deut. 25:4.]

10 Or does He speak certainly *and* entirely for our sakes? [Assuredly] it is written for our sakes, because the plowman ought to plow in hope, and the thresher ought to thresh in expectation of partaking of the harvest.

11 If we have sown [the seed of] spiritual good among you, [is it too] much if we reap from your material benefits?

12 If others share in this rightful claim upon you, do not we [have a still better and greater claim]? However, we have never exercised this right, but we endure everything rather than put a hindrance in the way [of the spread] of the good news (the Gospel) of Christ.

13 Do you not know that those men who are employed in the services of the temple get their food from the temple? And that those who tend the altar share with the altar [in the offerings brought]? [Deut. 18:1.]

14 [On the same principle] the Lord directed that those who publish the good news (the Gospel) should live (get their maintenance) by the Gospel.

15 But I have not made use of any of these privileges, nor am I writing this

putting the Word to work

When you tithe, do you know how all of your offering is used? Probably not, but most likely a portion of it goes to pay the pastors and staff at your church. It is scriptural for us to give to those who take care of us spiritually (see I Corinthians 9:13, 14). That is God's will and His plan for how they should be supported, and it is one of the ways we show appreciation for what they have done for us. Always give with a cheerful heart because it glorifies God when you do.

[to suggest] that any such provision be made for me [now]. For it would be better for me to die than to have anyone make void *and* deprive me of my [ground for] glorifying [in this matter].
16 For if I [merely] preach the Gospel, that gives me no reason to boast, for I feel compelled of necessity to do it. Woe is me if I do not preach the glad tidings (the Gospel)!
17 For if I do this work of my own free will, then I have my pay (my reward); but if it is not of my own will, but is done reluctantly *and* under compulsion, I am [still] entrusted with a [sacred] trusteeship *and* commission.
18 What then is the [actual] reward that I get? Just this: that in my preaching the good news (the Gospel), I may offer it [absolutely] free of expense [to anybody], not taking advantage of my rights *and* privileges [as a preacher] of the Gospel.
19 For although I am free in every way from anyone's control, I have made myself a bond servant to everyone, so that I might gain the more [for Christ].
20 To the Jews I became as a Jew, that I might win Jews; to men under the Law, [I became] as one under the Law, though not myself being under the Law, that I might win those under the Law.

21 To those without (outside) law I became as one without law, not that I am without the law of God *and* lawless toward Him, but that I am [especially keeping] within *and* committed to the law of Christ, that I might win those who are without law.
22 To the weak (wanting in discernment) I have become weak (wanting in discernment) that I might win the weak *and* overscrupulous. I have [in short] become all things to all men, that I might by all means (at all costs and in any and every way) save some [by winning them to faith in Jesus Christ].
23 And I do this for the sake of the good news (the Gospel), in order that I may become a participator in it *and* share in its [blessings along with you].
24 Do you not know that in a race all the runners compete, but [only] one receives the prize? So run [your race] that you may lay hold [of the prize] *and* make it yours.
25 Now every athlete who goes into training conducts himself temperately *and* restricts himself in all things. They do it to win a wreath that will soon wither, but we [do it to receive a crown of eternal blessedness] that cannot wither.
26 Therefore I do not run uncertainly (without definite aim). I do not box like one beating the air *and* striking without an adversary.
27 But [like a boxer] I buffet my body [handle it roughly, discipline it by hardships] and subdue it, for fear that after proclaiming to others the Gospel *and* things pertaining to it, I myself should become unfit [not stand the test, be unapproved and rejected as a counterfeit].

10 FOR I do not want you to be ignorant, brethren, that our forefathers were all under *and* protected by the cloud [in

life point

Those of us who intend to run the race to win must conduct ourselves temperately and restrict ourselves in all things (see I Corinthians 9:24–27). We cannot expect someone else to make us do what is right. We must listen to the Holy Spirit and take action ourselves.

Paul said he buffeted his body. He means that he disciplined it because he did not want to preach to others, tell them what they should do, and then fail to do it himself. Paul was running the race to win! He knew he could not develop his potential without bringing his body, mind, and emotions under control.

Self-discipline is essential to the Christian life. Unless we discipline our minds, our mouths, and our emotions, we will live in ruin. Unless we learn to rule our tempers, we can never achieve the successes that rightfully belong to us.

which God's Presence went before them], and every one of them passed safely through the [Red] Sea, [Exod. 13:21; 14:22, 29.]
2 And each one of them [allowed himself also] to be baptized into Moses in the cloud and in the sea [they were thus brought under obligation to the Law, to Moses, and to the covenant, consecrated and set apart to the service of God];
3 And all [of them] ate the same spiritual (supernaturally given) food, [Exod. 16:4, 35.]
4 And they all drank the same spiritual (supernaturally given) drink. For they drank from a spiritual Rock which followed them [produced by the sole power of God Himself without natural

instrumentality], and the Rock was Christ. [Exod. 17:6; Num. 20:11.]
5 Nevertheless, God was not pleased with the great majority of them, for they were overthrown *and* strewn down along [the ground] in the wilderness. [Num. 14:29, 30.]
6 Now these things are examples (warnings and admonitions) for us not to desire *or* crave *or* covet *or* lust after evil *and* carnal things as they did. [Num. 11:4, 34.]
7 Do not be worshipers of false gods as some of them were, as it is written, The people sat down to eat and drink [the sacrifices offered to the golden calf at Horeb] and rose to sport (to dance and give way to jesting and hilarity). [Exod. 32:4, 6.]
8 We must not gratify evil desire *and* indulge in immorality as some of them did—and twenty-three thousand [suddenly] fell *dead* in a single day! [Num. 25:1-18.]
9 We should not tempt the Lord [try His patience, become a trial to Him, critically appraise Him, and exploit His goodness] as some of them did—and were killed by poisonous serpents; [Num. 21:5, 6.]
10 Nor discontentedly complain as some of them did—and were [y]put out of the way entirely by the destroyer (death). [Num. 16:41, 49.]
11 Now these things befell them by way of a figure [as an example and warning to us]; they were written to admonish *and* fit us for right action by good instruction, we in whose days the ages have reached their climax (their consummation and concluding period).
12 Therefore let anyone who thinks he stands [who feels sure that he has a steadfast mind and is standing firm], take heed lest he fall [into sin].
13 For no temptation (no trial regarded as enticing to sin), [no

y Joseph Thayer, *A Greek-English Lexicon.*

matter how it comes or where it leads] has overtaken you *and* laid hold on you that is not common to man [that is, no temptation or trial has come to you that is beyond human resistance and that is not ᶻadjusted and ᵃadapted and belonging to human experience, and such as man can bear]. But God is faithful [to His Word and to His compassionate nature], and He [can be trusted] not to let you be tempted *and* tried *and* assayed beyond your ability *and* strength of resistance *and* power to endure, but with the temptation He will [always] also provide the way out (the means of escape to ᵇa landing place), that you may be capable *and* strong *and* powerful to bear up under it patiently.

life point

First Corinthians 10:13 promises us that God will not allow us to be tempted beyond what we can bear, but with every temptation He will also provide the way out—the means of escape. The end result will be that we are capable and strong to patiently bear up under whatever negative circumstances we face.

14 Therefore, my dearly beloved, shun (keep clear away from, avoid by flight if need be) any sort of idolatry (of loving or venerating anything more than God).

15 I am speaking as to intelligent (sensible) men. Think over *and* make up your minds [for yourselves] about what I say. [I appeal to your reason and your discernment in these matters.]

16 The cup of blessing [of wine at the Lord's Supper] upon which we ask [God's] blessing, does it not mean [that in drinking it] we participate in *and* share a fellowship (a communion) in the blood of Christ (the Messiah)? The bread which we break, does it not mean [that in eating it] we participate in *and* share a fellowship (a communion) in the body of Christ?

17 For we [no matter how] numerous we are, are one body, because we all partake of the one Bread [the One Whom the communion bread represents].

18 Consider those [physically] people of Israel. Are not those who eat the sacrifices partners of the altar [united in their worship of the same God]? [Lev. 7:6.]

19 What do I imply then? That food offered to idols is [intrinsically changed by the fact and amounts to] anything *or* that an idol itself is a [living] thing?

20 No, I am suggesting that what the pagans sacrifice they offer [in effect] to demons (to evil spiritual powers) and not to God [at all]. I do not want you to fellowship *and* be partners with diabolical spirits [by eating at their feasts]. [Deut. 32:17.]

21 You cannot drink the Lord's cup and the demons' cup. You cannot partake of the Lord's table and the demons' table.

22 Shall we thus provoke the Lord to jealousy *and* anger *and* indignation? Are we stronger than He [that we should defy Him]? [Deut. 32:21; Eccl. 6:10; Isa. 45:9.]

23 All things are legitimate [permissible—and we are free to do anything we please], but not all things are helpful (expedient, profitable, and wholesome). All things are legitimate, but not all things are constructive [to character] *and* edifying [to spiritual life].

24 Let no one then seek his own good *and* advantage *and* profit, but [rather]

---

z Joseph Thayer, *A Greek-English Lexicon.*   **a** Henry Alford, *The Greek New Testament.*   **b** Marvin Vincent, *Word Studies.*

each one of the other [let him seek the welfare of his neighbor].

25 [As to meat offered to idols] eat anything that is sold in the meat market without raising any question *or* investigating on the grounds of conscientious scruples,

26 For the [whole] earth is the Lord's and everything that is in it. [Ps. 24:1; 50:12.]

27 In case one of the unbelievers invites you to a meal and you want to go, eat whatever is served to you without examining into its source because of conscientious scruples.

28 But if someone tells you, This has been offered in sacrifice to an idol, do not eat it, out of consideration for the person who informed you, and for conscience's sake—

29 I mean for the sake of his conscience, not yours, [do not eat it]. For why should another man's scruples apply to me *and* my liberty of action be determined by his conscience?

30 If I partake [of my food] with thankfulness, why am I accused *and* spoken evil of because of that for which I give thanks?

31 So then, whether you eat or drink, or whatever you may do, do all for the honor *and* glory of God.

32 Do not let yourselves be [hindrances by giving] an offense to the Jews or to the Greeks or to the church

life point

Real joy comes from being an empty vessel for God's use and glory, letting Him choose where He takes you, what He does with you, when He is does it— and not arguing about it. Be willing to do everything for the honor and glory of God, as I Corinthians 10:31 instructs, and you will have great contentment and joy in your life.

c Joseph Thayer, *A Greek-English Lexicon.*

of God [cdo not lead others into sin by your mode of life];

33 Just as I myself strive to please [to accommodate myself to the opinions, desires, and interests of others, adapting myself to] all men in everything I do, not aiming at *or* considering my own profit *and* advantage, but that of the many in order that they may be saved.

11 PATTERN YOURSELVES after me [follow my example], as I imitate *and* follow Christ (the Messiah).

2 I appreciate *and* commend you because you always remember me in everything and keep firm possession of the traditions (the substance of my instructions), just as I have [verbally] passed them on to you.

3 But I want you to know *and* realize that Christ is the Head of every man, the head of a woman is her husband, and the Head of Christ is God.

4 Any man who prays or prophesies (teaches, refutes, reproves, admonishes, and comforts) with his head covered dishonors his Head (Christ).

5 And any woman who [publicly] prays or prophesies (teaches, refutes, reproves, admonishes, or comforts) when she is bareheaded dishonors her head (her husband); it is the same as [if her head were] shaved.

6 For if a woman will not wear [a head] covering, then she should cut off her hair too; but if it is disgraceful for a woman to have her head shorn or shaven, let her cover [her head].

7 For a man ought not to wear anything on his head [in church], for he is the image and [reflected] glory of God [cthis function of government reflects the majesty of the divine Rule]; but woman is [the expression of] man's glory (majesty, preeminence). [Gen. 1:26.]

the spiritual in the natural

It is true that there are earthly things we must tend to on earth. We cannot be "spiritual" all the time. But, if any person has what I call a "religious spirit" about him, he will either ignore the natural things he should take care of, or he will not enjoy the earthly things he does handle. He will always rush through those mundane things, trying to get back to some spiritual activity, thinking it is only then that he can feel good about himself. He only feels approval from God when he does what he thinks are "spiritual" things.

We must learn that we can communicate with God while doing the laundry as well as on bended knee. I personally believe God prefers a person who talks to Him intermittently throughout the day to a person who sets a clock for a certain amount of time to spend with Him. The instant the time is up, he cuts off communication with God until the next day.

The Lord is ever present and always available for fellowship when we pray and study. But, in order to enjoy our entire life, we need to learn that He is willing to be involved in everything we do.

According to I Corinthians 10:31, we should do everything to the glory of God. This includes the everyday things we do in the secular realm as well as our spiritual pursuits in the spiritual realm.

8 For man was not [created] from woman, but woman from man; [Gen. 2:21-23.]
9 Neither was man created on account of or for the benefit of woman, but woman on account of and for the benefit of man. [Gen. 2:18.]
10 [d]Therefore she should [be subject to his authority and should] have a covering on her head [as a token, a symbol, of her submission to authority, [e]that she may show reverence as do] the angels [and not displease them].
11 Nevertheless, in [the plan of] the Lord and from His point of view woman is not apart from and independent of man, nor is man aloof from and independent of woman;
12 For as woman was made from man, even so man is also born of woman; and all [whether male or female go forth] from God [as their Author].
13 Consider for yourselves; is it proper and decent [according to your customs] for a woman to offer prayer to God [publicly] with her head uncovered?
14 Does not [e]the native sense of propriety (experience, common sense, reason) itself teach you that for a man to wear long hair is a dishonor [humiliating and degrading] to him,
15 But if a woman has long hair, it is her ornament and glory? For her hair is given to her for a covering.
16 Now if anyone is disposed to be argumentative and contentious about this, we hold to and recognize no other custom [in worship] than this, nor do the churches of God generally.
17 But in what I instruct [you] next I

d G.D. Kypke, cited by Adam Clarke, *The Holy Bible with A Commentary.* **e** Joseph Thayer, *A Greek-English Lexicon.*

do not commend [you], because when you meet together, it is not for the better but for the worse.

18 For in the first place, when you assemble as a congregation, I hear that there are cliques (divisions and factions) among you; and I in part believe it,

19 For doubtless there have to be factions *or* parties among you in order that they who are genuine *and* of approved fitness may become evident *and* plainly recognized among you.

20 So when you gather for your meetings, it is not the supper instituted by the Lord that you eat,

21 For in eating each one [hurries] to get his own supper first [not waiting for the poor], and one goes hungry while another gets drunk.

22 What! Do you have no houses in which to eat and drink? Or do you despise the church of God *and* mean to show contempt for it, while you humiliate those who are poor (have no homes and have brought no food)? What shall I say to you? Shall I commend you in this? No, [most certainly] I will not!

23 For I received from the Lord Himself that which I passed on to you [it was given to me personally], that the Lord Jesus on the night when He was treacherously delivered up *and* while His betrayal was in progress took bread,

24 And when He had given thanks, He broke [it] and said, *Take, eat.* This is My body, which is broken for you. Do this to call Me [affectionately] to remembrance.

25 Similarly when supper was ended, He took the cup also, saying, This cup is the new covenant [ratified and established] in My blood. Do this, as often as you drink [it], to call Me [affectionately] to remembrance.

26 For every time you eat this bread and drink this cup, you are representing *and* signifying *and* proclaiming the

putting the Word to work

What do you think about when you receive the Lord's Supper? The next time you partake of this special meal, remember that Jesus' body was broken for you and His blood was shed for you (see I Corinthians 11:23–25) and celebrate that your sins are forgiven. Rejoice that one day He will come back. Receive the healing, restoration, and strength that He purchased for you with His body and blood.

fact of the Lord's death until He comes [again].

27 So then whoever eats the bread or drinks the cup of the Lord in a way that is unworthy [of Him] will be guilty of [profaning and sinning against] the body and blood of the Lord.

28 Let a man [thoroughly] examine himself, and [only when he has done] so should he eat of the bread and drink of the cup.

29 For anyone who eats and drinks without discriminating *and* recognizing with due appreciation that [it is Christ's] body, eats and drinks a sentence (a verdict of judgment) upon himself.

30 That [careless and unworthy participation] is the reason many of you are weak and sickly, and quite enough of you have fallen into the sleep of death.

31 For if we searchingly examined ourselves [detecting our shortcomings and recognizing our own condition], we should not be judged *and* penalty decreed [by the divine judgment].

32 But when we [fall short and] are judged by the Lord, we are disciplined *and* chastened, so that we may not [finally] be condemned [to eternal punishment along] with the world.

33 So then, my brothers, when you gather together to eat [the Lord's Supper], wait for one another.

34 If anyone is hungry, let him eat at home, lest you come together to bring judgment [on yourselves]. About the other matters, I will give you directions [personally] when I come.

12 NOW ABOUT the spiritual gifts (the special endowments of supernatural energy), brethren, I do not want you to be misinformed.

2 You know that when you were heathen, you were led off after idols that could not speak [habitually] as impulse directed *and* whenever the occasion might arise.

3 Therefore I want you to understand that no one speaking under the power *and* influence of the [Holy] Spirit of God can [ever] say, Jesus be cursed! And no one can [really] say, Jesus is [my] Lord, except by *and* under the power *and* influence of the Holy Spirit.

4 Now there are distinctive varieties *and* distributions of endowments (gifts, [f]extraordinary powers distinguishing certain Christians, due to the power of divine grace operating in their souls by the Holy Spirit) and they vary, but the [Holy] Spirit remains the same.

5 And there are distinctive varieties of service *and* ministration, but it is the same Lord [Who is served].

6 And there are distinctive varieties of operation [of working to accomplish things], but it is the same God Who inspires *and* energizes them all in all.

7 But to each one is given the manifestation of the [Holy] Spirit [the evidence, the spiritual illumination of the Spirit] for good *and* profit.

8 To one is given in *and* through the [Holy] Spirit [the power to speak] a message of wisdom, and to another [the power to express] a word of

knowledge *and* understanding according to the same [Holy] Spirit;

9 To another [[g]wonder-working] faith by the same [Holy] Spirit, to another the extraordinary powers of healing by the one Spirit;

10 To another the working of miracles, to another prophetic insight ([h]the gift of interpreting the divine will and purpose); to another the ability to discern *and* distinguish between [the utterances of true] spirits [and false ones], to another various kinds of [unknown] tongues, to another the ability to interpret [such] tongues.

11 All these [gifts, achievements, abilities] are inspired *and* brought to pass by one and the same [Holy] Spirit, Who apportions to each person individually [exactly] as He chooses.

12 For just as the body is a unity and yet has many parts, and all the parts, though many, form [only] one body, so it is with Christ (the Messiah, the Anointed One).

f Joseph Thayer, *A Greek-English Lexicon.* g Marvin Vincent, *Word Studies.* h G. Abbott-Smith, *Manual Greek Lexicon.*

life point

I believe there are certain individuals to whom God gives the gift of faith (see I Corinthians 12:9) for specific occasions such as a dangerous missionary trip or a challenging situation. When this gift operates in people, they are able to comfortably believe God for something that other people would see as impossible. They have total faith for something that terrifies others.

A person operating under a gift of faith must be careful to avoid thinking that those who do not have this gift are faithless or cowards. He needs to understand that when the gift of faith operates in a person, God gives that individual an unusual portion of faith to ensure that His purpose in the earth is accomplished.

Every person is given a certain measure of faith (see Romans 12:3). We can be assured that God will always give us enough faith to receive His grace for the fulfillment of every task He gives us.

13 For by [imeans of the personal agency of] one [Holy] Spirit we were all, whether Jews or Greeks, slaves or free, baptized [and jby baptism united together] into one body, and all made to drink of one [Holy] Spirit.
14 For the body does not consist of one limb or organ but of many.
15 If the foot should say, Because I am not the hand, I do not belong to the body, would it be therefore not [a part] of the body?
16 If the ear should say, Because I am not the eye, I do not belong to the body, would it be therefore not [a part] of the body?
17 If the whole body were an eye, where [would be the sense of] hearing? If the whole body were an ear, where [would be the sense of] smell?
18 But as it is, God has placed and arranged the limbs and organs in the body, each [particular one] of them, just as He wished and saw fit and with the best adaptation.
19 But if [the whole] were all a single organ, where would the body be?
20 And now there are [certainly] many limbs and organs, but a single body.
21 And the eye is not able to say to the hand, I have no need of you, nor again the head to the feet, I have no need of you.
22 But instead, there is [absolute] necessity for the parts of the body that are considered the more weak.
23 And those [parts] of the body which we consider rather ignoble are [the very parts] which we invest with additional honor, and our unseemly parts and those unsuitable for exposure are treated with seemliness (modesty and decorum),
24 Which our more presentable parts do not require. But God has so adjusted (mingled, harmonized, and subtly proportioned the parts of) the whole body, giving the greater honor and richer endowment to the inferior parts

putting the Word to work

Do you ever feel like your spiritual gifts are not as important as someone else's? That's like saying your eyes are not as important as your ears. The truth is, every gift is necessary for the body of Christ to function as God intends (see I Corinthians 12:20–25). Recognize and celebrate the importance of each person's gifts, including your own. However, be sure not to think more highly of your gifts than of someone else's.

i Kenneth Wuest, *Word Studies*.   j Joseph Thayer, *A Greek-English Lexicon*.

the gift of discernment

I believe that the discerning of spirits mentioned as a gift of the Holy Spirit in I Corinthians 12:10 is an extremely valuable gift, and I encourage you to desire and develop it.

I also encourage you not to be limited in your understanding of what this gift is. The discerning of spirits gives people supernatural insight into the spirit realm when God allows it. It is not exclusively the discerning of evil or demon spirits, as when Paul identified the spirit of divination in a girl who told fortunes at Philippi (see Acts 16:16–18); it is also the discerning of divine spirits, as when Moses looked into the spirit realm and saw the "back" of God (see Exodus 33:18–23), or when John was in exile on the isle of Patmos and had a vision of the resurrected Jesus (see Revelation 1:9–18).

The discerning of spirits also helps us know the true nature of those we deal with, whether they are good or evil. In other words, it helps us know the motivation behind a person or the true nature of a situation. For example, someone may appear to do a good thing, yet we may feel wrong about that person inside. That is often God's way of warning us that the person's intention is evil. Satan himself uses such people to deceive Christians and demolish their godly endeavors.

I have prayed a lot for discernment in my years in ministry and I rely on it a great deal. Let me encourage you to pray for this gift as well, because it can help you as you deal with many of the people and situations in your life.

which lack [apparent importance], **25** So that there should be no division *or* discord *or* lack of adaptation [of the parts of the body to each other], but the members all alike should have a mutual interest in *and* care for one another.

26 And if one member suffers, all the parts [share] the suffering; if one member is honored, all the members [share in] the enjoyment of it.

27 Now you [collectively] are Christ's body and [individually] you are members of it, each part severally *and* distinct [each with his own place and function].

28 So God has appointed some in the church [*k*for His own use]: first apostles (special messengers); second prophets (inspired preachers and expounders); third teachers; then wonder-workers; then those with ability to heal the sick; helpers; administrators; [speakers in] different (unknown) tongues.

29 Are all apostles (special messengers)? Are all prophets (inspired interpreters of the will and purposes of God)? Are all teachers? Do all have the power of performing miracles?

30 Do all possess extraordinary powers of healing? Do all speak with tongues? Do all interpret?

31 But earnestly desire *and* zealously cultivate the greatest *and* best gifts *and* graces (the higher gifts and the choicest graces). And yet I will show you a still more excellent way [one that is better by far and the highest of them all—love].

k Marvin Vincent, *Word Studies*.

love above all

Love is the greatest thing in the world. First Corinthians 12:31 teaches us that love should be number one on our spiritual priority list. We should study love, pray about love, and develop the fruit of love by practicing loving others. We learn in Galatians 5:22, 23 that love is one of the nine fruits of the Spirit available to those in whom God's Holy Spirit lives.

God is love, so when we walk in His love we abide in Him. Because we walk in God's love by receiving and expressing it, we should not deceive ourselves into thinking we can love God while we hate other people (see I John 4:20).

We seek many things during our lifetimes, hoping to find fulfillment in them. But without love, these things fall short of the desired goal. When we put our time and energy into things that do not fulfill us, we feel frustrated.

Love is the best thing we can commit our life to. It took me about forty-five years to realize that my priorities were mixed up and that love was not the main thing in my life. It was not my first priority, but it needed to be. The commitment to learn how to walk in love has been the single best decision I have ever made as a Christian.

Love not only blesses others; it also blesses the one doing the loving. Concentrating on being a blessing to others has brought me joy. I find it exciting.

All of us need to become students of love, excelling in the most important quality of all—love.

13 IF I [can] speak in the tongues of men and [even] of angels, but have not love (that reasoning, intentional, spiritual devotion such ¹as is inspired by God's love for and in us), I am only a noisy gong or a clanging cymbal.

2 And if I have prophetic powers (ᵐthe gift of interpreting the divine will and purpose), and understand all the secret truths *and* mysteries and possess all knowledge, and if I have [sufficient] faith so that I can remove mountains, but have not love (God's love in me) I am nothing (a useless nobody).

3 Even if I dole out all that I have [to the poor in providing] food, and if I surrender my body to be burned *or* ⁿin order that I may glory, but have not love (God's love in me), I gain nothing.

4 Love endures long *and* is patient and kind; love never is envious *nor* boils over with jealousy, is not boastful *or* vainglorious, does not display itself haughtily.

5 It is not conceited (arrogant and inflated with pride); it is not rude (unmannerly) *and* does not act unbecomingly. Love (God's love in us) does not insist on its own rights *or* its own

---

l Alexander Souter, *Pocket Lexicon*. **m** G. Abbott-Smith, *Manual Greek Lexicon*. **n** Some ancient manuscripts so read.

life point

First Corinthians 13:1–3 begins a discourse on love. It tells us clearly that no matter how many gifts of the Spirit we may operate in, if we are not operating in love, all other gifts are useless. If we speak in tongues, but do not love, we just make a big noise. If we have prophetic power, and power to understand and interpret secrets and mysteries, if we have all knowledge and so much faith we can move mountains, but have not love, according to the apostle Paul, we are useless nobodies. Even if we give away all that we have to feed the poor and surrender our very lives, but do it with wrong motives and not out of love, we gain nothing.

way, *for* it is not self-seeking; it is not touchy *or* fretful *or* resentful; it takes no account of the evil done to it [it pays no attention to a suffered wrong].

6 It does not rejoice at injustice *and* unrighteousness, but rejoices when right *and* truth prevail.

7 Love bears up under anything *and* everything that comes, is ever ready to believe the best of every person, its hopes are fadeless under all circumstances, and it endures everything [without weakening].

8 Love never fails [never fades out or becomes obsolete or comes to an end]. As for prophecy (°the gift of interpreting the divine will and purpose), it will be fulfilled *and* pass away; as for tongues, they will be destroyed *and* cease; as for knowledge, it will pass away [it will lose its value and be superseded by truth].

9 For our knowledge is fragmentary (incomplete and imperfect), and our

prophecy (our teaching) is fragmentary (incomplete and imperfect).

10 But when the complete *and* perfect (total) comes, the incomplete *and* imperfect will vanish away (become antiquated, void, and superseded).

11 When I was a child, I talked like a child, I thought like a child, I reasoned like a child; now that I have become a man, I am done with childish ways *and* have put them aside.

12 For now we are looking in a mirror that gives only a dim (blurred) reflection [of reality as ᵖin a riddle or enigma], but then [when perfection comes] we shall see in reality *and* face to face! Now I know in part (imperfectly), but then I shall know *and* understand ᵖfully *and* clearly, even in the same manner as I have been ᵖfully *and* clearly known *and* understood [�q by God].

13 And so faith, hope, love abide [faith—conviction and belief respecting man's relation to God and divine things; hope—joyful and confident expectation of eternal salvation; love—true affection for God and man, growing out of God's love for and in us], these three; but the greatest of these is love.

14 EAGERLY PURSUE *and* seek to acquire [this] love [make it your aim, your great quest]; and earnestly desire *and* cultivate the spiritual endowments (gifts), especially that you may prophesy (°interpret the divine will and purpose in inspired preaching and teaching).

2 For one who speaks in an [unknown] tongue speaks not to men but to God, for no one understands *or* catches his meaning, because in the [Holy] Spirit he utters secret truths

---

o G. Abbott-Smith, *Manual Greek Lexicon.* p Marvin Vincent, *Word Studies.* q Matthew Henry, *Commentary on the Holy Bible.*

life point

Love is the greatest thing in life (see
I Corinthians 13:13), and walking in love
should be our main focus. God is love,
and He wants us to love one another
(see I John 4:11, 16). We can only truly
love others by receiving and expressing
God's love. In order to do that, we need
to understand that He loves us and
accept His love. When we do, we begin a
love walk that causes us to live in a new
way—a new way of thinking, a new way
of speaking, and a new way of acting.

Love is expressed in many different
ways, but one factor is always the same:
love gives.

I pray that you will become addicted to
walking in love and blessing people.
Give Satan a nervous breakdown—
become radical in your love walk by
joining me in praying as I often do: *Lord,
reduce me to love!*

and hidden things [not obvious to the
understanding].
3   But [on the other hand], the one
who prophesies [who ʳinterprets the
divine will and purpose in inspired
preaching and teaching] speaks to
men for their upbuilding *and* constructive spiritual progress and
encouragement and consolation.
4   He who speaks in a [strange]
tongue edifies *and* improves himself,

life point

First Corinthians 14:3 tells us that
prophecy builds people up. It does
not tear people down; rather it
constructively aids their spiritual
progress and gives them encouragement
and consolation in the process.

but he who prophesies [ʳinterpreting
the divine will and purpose and
teaching with inspiration] edifies *and*
improves the church *and* promotes
growth [in Christian wisdom, piety,
holiness, and happiness].
5   Now I wish that you might all
speak in [unknown] tongues, but
more especially [I want you] to
prophesy (to be inspired to preach
and interpret the divine will and purpose). He who prophesies [who is
inspired to preach and teach] is
greater (more useful and more important) than he who speaks in
[unknown] tongues, unless he should
interpret [what he says], so that the
church may be edified *and* receive
good [from it].
6   Now, brethren, if I come to you
speaking in [unknown] tongues, how
shall I make it to your advantage
unless I speak to you either in revelation (disclosure of God's will to man)
in knowledge or in prophecy or in
instruction?
7   If even inanimate musical instruments, such as the flute or the harp,
do not give distinct notes, how will
anyone [listening] know *or* understand what is played?
8   And if the war bugle gives an
uncertain (indistinct) call, who will
prepare for battle?
9   Just so it is with you; if you in the
[unknown] tongue speak words that
are not intelligible, how will anyone
understand what you are saying?
For you will be talking into empty
space!
10   There are, I suppose, all these
many [to us unknown] tongues in the
world [somewhere], and none is destitute of [its own power of] expression
and meaning.
11   But if I do not know the force *and*
significance of the speech (language),
I shall seem to be a foreigner to the

---

r G. Abbott-Smith, *Manual Greek Lexicon.*

the most important thing

First Corinthians 13:13 says that love is the greatest thing. Faith and hope are vitally necessary, but as important as they are, they are not more important than love. Jesus gave us one new commandment which is to love one another as He loved us. He said that this would be the way the world knows we are His disciples (see John 13:34).

Love is not theory or talk, but action. It is revealed in the way we talk to people, how we treat them, and what we do or don't do for them. Love has many very practical facets and can be seen in a variety of ways. For example, love is patient. When people are walking in love, they are longsuffering with the weaknesses and faults of others. Instead of believing the worst, love always believes the best of every person.

Love is not rude. It actually strives to have good manners and that is something we desperately need in society today. Love takes time to say "please" and "thank you." Love takes time to really listen when others are talking. It is genuinely interested in others. Love builds people up; it edifies. Love does not find fault and criticize.

One of the facets of love that I enjoy thinking about is that love covers a multitude of sins. Love does not expose people's faults. Instead it actually covers them unless, of course, something really needs to be exposed and then love handles the situation appropriately and with wisdom. So often we rush to tell every negative thing we hear or know about anybody, but real love does not behave that way. Love treats other people the way it wants to be treated. Ask yourself, "Would I want someone to spread rumors about me and be a tale-bearer, or would I want them to cover my faults and pray for me?" Of course, we know the answer, but still we often follow the flesh and do what we know we should not do.

Be hopeful at all times and walk in faith, but above all seek love and walk in it. God is love, and when we walk in love we show Him to those we come in contact with.

one who speaks [to me], and the speaker who addresses [me] will seem a foreigner to me.
12 So it is with yourselves; since you are so eager *and* ambitious to possess spiritual endowments *and* manifestations of the [Holy] Spirit, [concentrate on] striving to excel *and* to abound [in them] in ways that will build up the church.

13 Therefore, the person who speaks in an [unknown] tongue should pray [for the power] to interpret *and* explain what he says.
14 For if I pray in an [unknown] tongue, my spirit [by the sHoly Spirit within me] prays, but my mind is unproductive [it bears no fruit and helps nobody].
15 Then what am I to do? I will pray

s Marvin Vincent, *Word Studies*.

a word about personal prophecy

First Corinthians 14:1, 3, 4 help us understand prophecy and prophetic ministry. Prophecy must be in line with the Word of God, and a personal word of prophecy should confirm something that is already in your heart. It is nice when that happens, because you know that the person giving you that word did not know anything about what God was saying to you. But if somebody tells you to go to the mission field, or to Bible college, do not quit your job and go unless *you know* that God has spoken to your heart this same word. I have seen people get into horrendous messes by trying to run their lives based on what other people have told them was a "prophetic message from God."

If the prophecy does not bear witness in your heart, do not worry about it. There are a lot of well-meaning people who think they hear from God for others, but they do not. If someone prophesies to you something that is not already in your heart, then I suggest you write down the words that are spoken over you and just wait for the Lord to reveal to you whether or not the words are from Him.

If a word of prophecy is truly from God, He will make it happen in His own time. Lay aside the prophecy and wait to see if God brings it to pass. He will speak to you in other ways to confirm it, if it is really from Him.

I know of situations in which five to ten years passed before something happened to prove that a prophecy was truly from God. So even when we have clear direction from God, we need to let Him fulfill His promises without trying to manipulate their manifestation. When a promise does come to pass, the Holy Spirit will help us recall that word we received years before to let us know we are indeed walking in God's perfect plan.

If prayerful godly believers have spoken a good word over you, then opposition is one of the greatest signs that their message was truly from God. Refer back to the spoken or written message when the devil tells you that you are not called, that you are never going to do what is in your heart to do, that you are never going to prosper, or that you are never going to get a breakthrough in your situation or whatever the case may be. One of your weapons against his attacks will be the word that has been prophesied to you.

Remember, what has been said through the gift of prophecy will help you remain steadfast in faith when the devil wages war against your calling or purpose. If the prophecy is truly from God, the devil will eventually try to discourage you from believing the truth, and you will be able to stand firm in faith because you know what the Lord has said about you.

with my spirit [by the 'Holy Spirit that is within me], but I will also pray [intelligently] with my mind *and*

understanding; I will sing with my spirit [by the Holy Spirit that is within me], but I will sing [intelligently] with

t Marvin Vincent, *Word Studies*.

my mind *and* understanding also.
16 Otherwise, if you bless *and* render thanks with [your] spirit [ᵘthoroughly aroused by the Holy Spirit], how can anyone in the position of an outsider *or* he who is not gifted with [interpreting of unknown] tongues, say the Amen to your thanksgiving, since he does not know what you are saying? [I Chron. 16:36; Ps. 106:48.]
17 To be sure, you may give thanks well (nobly), but the bystander is not edified [it does him no good].
18 I thank God that I speak in [strange] tongues (languages) more than any of you *or* all of you put together;
19 Nevertheless, in public worship, I would rather say five words with my understanding *and* intelligently in order to instruct others, than ten thousand words in a [strange] tongue (language).
20 Brethren, do not be children [immature] in your thinking; continue to be babes in [matters of] evil, but in your minds be mature [men].
21 It is written in the Law, By men of strange languages *and* by the lips of foreigners will I speak to this people, and not even then will they listen to Me, says the Lord. [Isa. 28:11, 12.]
22 Thus [unknown] tongues are meant for a [supernatural] sign, not for believers but for unbelievers [on the point of believing], while prophecy (inspired preaching and teaching, interpreting the divine will and purpose) is not for unbelievers [on the point of believing] but for believers.
23 Therefore, if the whole church assembles and all of you speak in [unknown] tongues, and the ungifted *and* uninitiated or unbelievers come in, will they not say that you are demented?
24 But if all prophesy [giving inspired testimony and interpreting the divine will and purpose] and an unbeliever or untaught outsider comes in, he is told of his sin *and* reproved *and* convicted *and* convinced by all, and his defects *and* needs are examined (estimated, determined) *and* he is called to account by all,
25 The secrets of his heart are laid bare; and so, falling on [his] face, he will worship God, declaring that God is among you in very truth.
26 What then, brethren, is [the right course]? When you meet together, each one has a hymn, a teaching, a disclosure of special knowledge *or* information, an utterance in a [strange] tongue, or an interpretation of it. [But] let everything be constructive *and* edifying *and* for the good of all.
27 If some speak in a [strange] tongue, let the number be limited to two or at the most three, and each one [taking his] turn, and let one interpret *and* explain [what is said].
28 But if there is no one to do the interpreting, let each of them keep still in church and talk to himself and to God.
29 So let two or three prophets speak [those inspired to preach or teach], while the rest pay attention *and* weigh *and* discern what is said.
30 But if an inspired revelation comes to another who is sitting by, then let the first one be silent.
31 For in this way you can give testimony [prophesying and thus interpreting the divine will and purpose] one by one, so that all may be instructed and all may be stimulated *and* encouraged;
32 For the spirits of the prophets (the speakers in tongues) are under the speaker's control [and subject to being silenced as may be necessary],
33 For He [Who is the source of their prophesying] is not a God of confusion *and* disorder but of peace *and*

---

u Joseph Thayer, *A Greek-English Lexicon.*

order. As [is the practice] in all the churches of the saints (God's people),

34 The women should keep quiet in the churches, for they are not authorized to speak, but should take a secondary *and* subordinate place, just as the Law also says. [Gen. 3:16.]

35 But if there is anything they want to learn, they should ask their own husbands at home, for it is disgraceful for a woman to talk in church ['for her to usurp and exercise authority over men in the church].

36 What! Did the word of the Lord originate with you [Corinthians], or has it reached only you?

37 If anyone thinks *and* claims that he is a prophet [filled with and governed by the Holy Spirit of God and inspired to interpret the divine will and purpose in preaching or teaching] or has any other spiritual endowment, let him understand (recognize and acknowledge) that what I am writing to you is a command of the Lord.

38 But if anyone disregards *or* does not recognize ["that it is a command of the Lord], he is disregarded *and* not recognized [he is ˣone whom God knows not].

39 So [to conclude], my brethren, earnestly desire *and* set your hearts on prophesying (on being inspired to preach and teach and to interpret God's will and purpose), and do not forbid *or* hinder speaking in [unknown] tongues.

40 But all things should be done with regard to decency *and* propriety and in an orderly fashion.

15 AND NOW let me remind you [since it seems to have escaped you], brethren, of the Gospel (the glad tidings of salvation) which I proclaimed to you, which

you welcomed *and* accepted and upon which your faith rests,

2 And by which you are saved, if you hold fast *and* keep firmly what I preached to you, unless you believed at first without effect *and* all for nothing.

3 For I passed on to you first of all what I also had received, that Christ (the Messiah, the Anointed One) died for our sins in accordance with [what] the Scriptures [foretold], [Isa. 53:5-12.]

4 That He was buried, that He arose on the third day as the Scriptures foretold, [Ps. 16:9, 10.]

5 And [also] that He appeared to Cephas (Peter), then to the Twelve.

6 Then later He showed Himself to more than five hundred brethren at one time, the majority of whom are still alive, but some have fallen asleep [in death].

7 Afterward He was seen by James, then by all the apostles (the special messengers),

8 And last of all He appeared to me also, as to one prematurely *and* born dead ['no better than an unperfected fetus among living men].

9 For I am the least [worthy] of the apostles, who am not fit *or* deserving to be called an apostle, because I once wronged *and* pursued *and* molested the church of God [oppressing it with cruelty and violence].

10 But by the grace (the unmerited favor and blessing) of God I am what I am, and His grace toward me was not [found to be] for nothing (fruitless and without effect). In fact, I worked harder than all of them [the apostles], though it was not really I, but the grace (the unmerited favor and blessing) of God which was with me.

11 So, whether then it was I or they, this is what we preach and this is what you believed [what you

---

v W. Robertson Nicoll, ed., *The Expositor's Greek New Testament.* **w** Joseph Thayer, *A Greek-English Lexicon.* **x** Marvin Vincent, *Word Studies.* Some manuscripts read: "he is not known." **y** Marvin Vincent, *Word Studies.*

adhered to, trusted in, and relied on].
12 But now if Christ (the Messiah) is preached as raised from the dead, how is it that some of you say that there is no resurrection of the dead?
13 But if there is no resurrection of the dead, then Christ has not risen;
14 And if Christ has not risen, then our preaching is in vain [it amounts to nothing] and your faith is devoid of truth *and* is fruitless (without effect, empty, imaginary, and unfounded).
15 We are even discovered to be misrepresenting God, for we testified of Him that He raised Christ, Whom He did not raise in case it is true that the dead are not raised.
16 For if the dead are not raised, then Christ has not been raised;
17 And if Christ has not been raised, your faith is mere delusion [futile, fruitless], and you are still in your sins [under the control and penalty of sin];
18 And further, those who have died in [²spiritual fellowship and union with] Christ have perished (are lost)!
19 If we who are [abiding] in Christ have hope only in this life *and* that is all, then we are of all people most miserable *and* to be pitied.
20 But the fact is that Christ (the Messiah) has been raised from the dead, and He became the firstfruits of those who have fallen asleep [in death].
21 For since [it was] through a man that death [came into the world, it is] also through a Man that the resurrection of the dead [has come].
22 For just as [because of their ²union of nature] in Adam all people die, so also [by virtue of their ªunion

speak the Word

of nature] shall all in Christ be made alive.
23 But each in his own rank *and* turn: Christ (the Messiah) [is] the firstfruits, then those who are Christ's [own will be resurrected] at His coming.
24 After that comes the end (the completion), when He delivers over the kingdom to God the Father after rendering inoperative *and* abolishing every [other] rule and every authority and power.
25 For [Christ] must be King *and* reign until He has put all [His] enemies under His feet. [Ps. 110:1.]
26 The last enemy to be subdued *and* abolished is death.
27 For He [the Father] has put all things in subjection under His [Christ's] feet. But when it says, All things are put in subjection [under Him], it is evident that He [Himself] is excepted Who does the subjecting of all things to Him. [Ps. 8:6.]
28 However, when everything is subjected to Him, then the Son Himself will also subject Himself to [the Father] Who put all things under Him, so that God may be all in all [be everything to everyone, supreme, the indwelling and controlling factor of life].
29 Otherwise, what do people mean by being [themselves] baptized in behalf of the dead? If the dead are not raised at all, why are people baptized for them?
30 [For that matter], why do I live [dangerously as I do, running such risks that I am] in peril every hour?
31 [I assure you] by the pride which I

z Joseph Thayer, *A Greek-English Lexicon.* **a** Robert Jamieson, A.R. Fausset and David Brown, *A Commentary.*

have in you in [your ᵇfellowship and union with] Christ Jesus our Lord, that I die daily [I face death every day and die to self].

32 What do I gain if, merely from the human point of view, I fought with [wild] beasts at Ephesus? If the dead are not raised [at all], let us eat and drink, for tomorrow we will be dead. [Isa. 22:13.]

33 Do not be so deceived *and* misled! Evil companionships (communion, associations) corrupt *and* deprave good manners *and* morals *and* character.

putting the Word to work

First Corinthians 15:33 teaches us that "Evil company corrupts good habits." It is not realistic to think you will always be surrounded by other Christians, and God's Word teaches that you are to be light in a dark world. However, it is important to remember that you are to be a godly influence on the lives of those around you, and to stay on guard against evil influences. Be sure when you are around evil or ungodly people that you affect them and they do not infect you.

34 Awake [ᶜfrom your drunken stupor and return] to sober sense *and* your right minds, and sin no more. For some of you have not the knowledge of God [you are utterly and willfully and disgracefully ignorant, and continue to be so, lacking the sense of God's presence and all true knowledge of Him]. I say this to your shame.

35 But someone will say, How can the dead be raised? With what [kind of] body will they come forth?

36 You foolish man! Every time you plant seed, you sow something that does not come to life [germinating, springing up, and growing] unless it dies first.

37 Nor is the seed you sow then the body which it is going to have [later], but it is a naked kernel, perhaps of wheat or some of the rest of the grains.

38 But God gives to it the body that He plans *and* sees fit, and to each kind of seed a body of its own. [Gen. 1:11.]

39 For all flesh is not the same, but there is one kind for humans, another for beasts, another for birds, and another for fish.

40 There are heavenly bodies (sun, moon, and stars) and there are earthly bodies (men, animals, and plants), but the beauty *and* glory of the heavenly bodies is of one kind, while the beauty *and* glory of earthly bodies is a different kind.

41 The sun is glorious in one way, the moon is glorious in another way, and the stars are glorious in their own [distinctive] way; for one star differs from *and* surpasses another in its beauty *and* brilliance.

42 So it is with the resurrection of the dead. [The body] that is sown is perishable *and* decays, but [the body] that is resurrected is imperishable (immune to decay, immortal). [Dan. 12:3.]

43 It is sown in dishonor *and* humiliation; it is raised in honor *and* glory. It is sown in infirmity *and* weakness; it is resurrected in strength *and* endued with power.

44 It is sown a natural (physical) body; it is raised a supernatural (a spiritual) body. [As surely as] there is a physical body, there is also a spiritual body.

45 Thus it is written, The first man Adam became a living being (an individual personality); the last Adam (Christ) became a life-giving Spirit [restoring the dead to life]. [Gen. 2:7.]

46 But it is not the spiritual life which

b Joseph Thayer, *A Greek-English Lexicon.*   **c** Marvin Vincent, *Word Studies.*

different is okay

We are all different. Like the sun, the moon, and the stars (see I Corinthians 15:41), God created us to be different from one another, and He did it on purpose. Each of us meets a need, and we are all part of God's overall plan. When we struggle to be like others, not only do we lose ourselves, but we also grieve the Holy Spirit. God wants us to fit into His plan, not to feel pressured to try and fit into everyone else's plans. Different is okay; it is all right to be different.

We are all born with different temperaments, different physical features, different fingerprints, different gifts and abilities, etc. Our goal is to discover what we are supposed to be as individuals, and then succeed at that.

Romans 12 teaches us that we are to give ourselves to our gift. In other words, we are to find out what we are good at and then throw ourselves wholeheartedly into exercising our gifts.

I discovered that I enjoy doing what I am good at doing. Some people feel they are not good at anything, but that is not true. When we make an effort to do what others are good at doing, we often fail because we are not gifted for those things; but that does not mean we are good for nothing. We should look for what we are good at and function in it.

We all have limitations, and we must accept them. That is not bad; it is just a fact. It is wonderful to be free to be different, not to feel that something is wrong with us because we are different.

We should be free to love and accept one another, as well as ourselves, without feeling pressure to compare or compete. Secure people who know God loves them and has a plan for them are not threatened by the abilities of others. I encourage you to be secure enough to enjoy what other people can do and to enjoy what you can do. Say positive things about yourself instead of negative things because that will help release the gifts God has placed in you.

came first, but the physical and then the spiritual.

47 The first man [was] from out of earth, made of dust (earthly-minded); the second Man [is] *the Lord* from out of heaven. [Gen. 2:7.]

48 Now those who are made of the dust are like him who was first made of the dust (earthly-minded); and as is [the Man] from heaven, so also [are those] who are of heaven (heavenly-minded).

49 And just as we have borne the image [of the man] of dust, so shall we *and so* ^d*let us* also bear the image [of the Man] of heaven.

50 But I tell you this, brethren, flesh and blood cannot [become partakers of eternal salvation and] inherit *or* share in the kingdom of God; nor does the perishable (that which is decaying) inherit *or* share in the imperishable (the immortal).

51 Take notice! I tell you a mystery (a

d Many ancient manuscripts read "let us."

putting the Word to work

The loss of a loved one through death is very painful. Are you mourning such a loss right now? Ask God to comfort you with His presence and with the assurance that for believers in Jesus the sting of death is swallowed up by the victory of Jesus Christ and His resurrection (see I Corinthians 15:50–57). Death is not the end, because in Christ we live forever. Pray for those in your life who do not yet know Jesus that they too will believe in Him and enjoy eternal life.

secret truth, an event decreed by the hidden purpose or counsel of God). We shall not all fall asleep [in death], but we shall all be changed (transformed)

52 In a moment, in the twinkling of an eye, at the [sound of the] last trumpet call. For a trumpet will sound, and the dead [in Christ] will be raised imperishable (free and immune from decay), and we shall be changed (transformed).

53 For this perishable [part of us] must put on the imperishable [nature], and this mortal [part of us, this nature that is capable of dying] must put on immortality (freedom from death).

54 And when this perishable puts on the imperishable and this that was capable of dying puts on freedom from death, then shall be fulfilled the Scripture that says, Death is swallowed up (utterly vanquished [e]forever) in *and* unto victory. [Isa. 25:8.]

55 O death, where is your victory? O death, where is your sting? [Hos. 13:14.]

56 Now sin is the sting of death, and sin exercises its power [f][upon the soul] through [f][the abuse of] the Law.

57 But thanks be to God, Who gives us the victory [making us conquerors] through our Lord Jesus Christ.

58 Therefore, my beloved brethren, be firm (steadfast), immovable, always abounding in the work of the Lord [always being superior, excelling, doing more than enough in the service of the Lord], knowing *and* being continually aware that your labor in the Lord is not futile [it is never wasted or to no purpose].

putting the Word to work

Do you ever feel like your work for God is not making a difference? Be encouraged by I Corinthians 15:58! This verse promises that even if you cannot always see the results, your work is not in vain. Ask God to make you steadfast and to strengthen you daily for the work that He has called you to. God sees your labor for Him and He will reward you.

16 NOW CONCERNING the money contributed for [the relief of] the saints (God's people): you are to do the same as I directed the churches of Galatia to do.

2 On the first [day] of each week, let each one of you [personally] put aside something and save it up as he has prospered [in proportion to what he is given], so that no collections will need to be taken after I come.

3 And when I arrive, I will send on those whom you approve *and* authorize with credentials to carry your gift [of charity] to Jerusalem.

4 If it seems worthwhile that I should go too, they will accompany me.

5 After passing through Macedonia, I will visit you, for I intend [only] to pass through Macedonia;

6 But it may be that I will stay with you [for a while], perhaps even spend

---

e Marvin Vincent, *Word Studies*.   **f** Joseph Thayer, *A Greek-English Lexicon*.

the winter, so that you may bring me forward [on my journey] to wherever I may go.

7 For I am unwilling to see you right now [just] in passing, but I hope later to remain for some time with you, if the Lord permits.

8 I will remain in Ephesus [however] until Pentecost,

9 For a wide door of opportunity for effectual [service] has opened to me [there, a great and promising one], and [there are] many adversaries.

10 When Timothy arrives, see to it that [you put him at ease, so that] he may be fearless among you, for he is [devotedly] doing the Lord's work, just as I am.

11 So [see to it that] no one despises him *or* treats him as if he were of no account *or* slights him. But send him off [cordially, speed him on his way] in peace, that he may come to me, for I am expecting him [to come along] with the other brethren.

12 As for our brother Apollos, I have urgently encouraged him to visit you with the other brethren, but it was not at all his will *or* ᵍGod's will that he should go now. He will come when he has opportunity.

13 Be alert *and* on your guard; stand firm in your faith (ʰyour conviction respecting man's relationship to God and divine things, keeping the trust and holy fervor born of faith and a part of it). Act like men *and* be courageous; grow in strength! [Ps. 31:24.]

14 Let everything you do be done in love (true love to God and man as inspired by God's love for us).

15 Now, brethren, you know that the

household of Stephanas were the first converts *and* our firstfruits in Achaia (most of Greece), and how they have consecrated *and* devoted themselves to the service of the saints (God's people).

16 I urge you to pay all deference to such leaders *and* to enlist under them *and* be subject to them, as well as to everyone who joins *and* cooperates [with you] *and* labors earnestly.

17 I am happy because Stephanas and Fortunatus and Achaicus have come [to me], for they have made up for your absence.

18 For they gave me ⁱrespite from labor *and* rested me *and* refreshed my spirit as well as yours. Deeply appreciate *and* thoroughly know *and* fully recognize such men.

19 The churches of Asia send greetings *and* best wishes. Aquila and Prisca, together with the church [that meets] in their house, send you their hearty greetings in the Lord.

20 All the brethren wish to be remembered to you *and* wish you well. Greet one another with a holy kiss.

21 I, Paul, [add this final] greeting with my own hand.

22 If anyone does not love the Lord [does not have a friendly affection for Him and is not kindly disposed toward Him], he shall be accursed! Our Lord will come! (Maranatha!)

23 The grace (favor and spiritual blessing) of our Lord Jesus *Christ* be with you.

24 My love (that true love growing out of sincere devotion to God) be with you all in Christ Jesus. *Amen (so be it).*

speak the Word

Father, I pray that everything I do will be done in love.
ADAPTED FROM I CORINTHIANS 16:14

---

g Although "his" may refer to Apollos, the probable reference here is to "God's will." **h** Joseph Thayer, *A Greek-English Lexicon.* **i** G. Abbott-Smith, *Manual Greek Lexicon.*

Second Corinthians

Author:
Paul

Date:
About AD 55, seemingly a few months after I Corinthians

Everyday Life Principles:
In Christ, you are a new creation. Your past is finished and you are made new.

Because of Jesus, you are righteous, which means that you are in a right relationship with God.

You are an ambassador for Jesus Christ everywhere you go.

Second Corinthians is perhaps the most personal of all letters from the apostle Paul. Obviously, it is his second letter to the believers in Corinth, probably because their problems continued after his first letter. Into their situation of strife and conflict, Paul sends this letter to thank and encourage those who have been faithful to God and loyal to him, to share some personal insights and struggles and to encourage people in the church.

One of the great themes in II Corinthians is that a believer in Jesus Christ is a new creation, one who has right standing with God and is an ambassador for Him. When we receive Jesus as Savior and Lord, our pasts are completely washed away. We do not have to feel guilty about them anymore (because we are forgiven) or let past behaviors or thoughts influence us anymore. Instead, we are made new in our hearts and we are continually to renew our minds in the Word of God, which further strengthens us and grounds us in the realities of our faith.

As you read II Corinthians, I hope you will become increasingly aware that your old life has passed away and that you are a new creation in Jesus Christ. You are in right relationship with God and you are His representative to the people around you. These are extremely important aspects of your Christian faith and they will lead you to victory in your everyday life.

1 PAUL, AN apostle (a special messenger) of Christ Jesus by the will of God, and Timothy [our] brother, to the church (assembly) of God which is at Corinth, and to all the saints (the people of God) throughout Achaia (most of Greece):

2   Grace (favor and spiritual blessing) to you and [heart] peace from God our Father and the Lord Jesus Christ (the Messiah, the Anointed One).

3   Blessed be the God and Father of our Lord Jesus Christ, the Father of sympathy (pity and mercy) and the God [Who is the Source] of every comfort (consolation and encouragement),

4   Who comforts (consoles and encourages) us in every trouble (calamity and affliction), so that we may also be able to comfort (console and encourage) those who are in any kind of trouble *or* distress, with the comfort (consolation and encouragement) with which we ourselves are comforted (consoled and encouraged) by God.

5   For just as Christ's [ªown] sufferings fall to our lot ᵇ[as they overflow upon His disciples, and we share and experience them] abundantly, so through Christ comfort (consolation and encouragement) is also [shared and experienced] abundantly by us.

6   But if we are troubled (afflicted and distressed), it is for your comfort (consolation and encouragement) and [for your] salvation; and if we are comforted (consoled and encouraged), it is for your comfort (consolation and encouragement), which works [in you] when you patiently endure the same evils (misfortunes and calamities) that we also suffer *and* undergo.

7   And our hope for you [our joyful and confident expectation of good for you] is ever unwavering (assured and unshaken); for we know that just as

putting the Word to work

Times of suffering and trials are a part of everyone's life. Is this a time of suffering in your life? Ask God to surround you with His comfort and to help you experience it in tangible ways. He is able to comfort you no matter what the trial. Although it may not help much right now, know that someday you will be able to comfort someone else as God comforts you (see II Corinthians 1:3–5).

you share *and* are partners in [our] sufferings *and* calamities, you also share *and* are partners in [our] comfort (consolation and encouragement).

8   For we do not want you to be uninformed, brethren, about the affliction *and* oppressing distress which befell us in [the province of] Asia, how we were so utterly and unbearably weighed down *and* crushed that we despaired even of life [itself].

9   Indeed, we felt within ourselves that we had received the [very] sentence of death, but that was to keep us from trusting in *and* depending on ourselves instead of on God Who raises the dead.

10   [For it is He] Who rescued *and* saved us from such a perilous death, and He will still rescue *and* save us; in *and* on Him we have set our hope (our joyful and confident expectation) that He will again deliver us [from danger and destruction and ᶜdraw us to Himself],

11   While you also cooperate by your prayers for us [helping and laboring together with us]. Thus [the lips of] many persons [turned toward God will eventually] give thanks on our

---

a Marvin Vincent, *Word Studies in the New Testament.*   **b** Marvin Vincent, *Word Studies.*   **c** Joseph Thayer, *A Greek-English Lexicon of the New Testament:* Primary meaning: "to draw to one's self."

find comfort in God

Have you been disappointed, hurt, or mistreated? Have you had changes in your life or are you experiencing loss of some kind? Have you failed in some way? Are you just simply tired? What is your trouble today? Second Corinthians 1:3, 4 says that God wants to help you by comforting you when you need it.

The Holy Spirit is actually called "the Comforter" (see John 14:26). His various names describe His character. They reveal what He does and what He desires to do for believers. He is willing to do a great deal for us if we are willing to receive His help.

For many years, I regularly became angry with my husband, Dave, because he would not comfort me when I felt I needed it. I am sure he was trying, but now I realize that God would not allow Dave to give me the comfort I should have been seeking from Him. God was longing to give me that comfort by the Holy Spirit, if only I had asked!

God will allow people to do only a certain amount for us, and no more. Even those people who are extremely close to us cannot give us everything we need all the time. When we expect others to do for us what only God can do, we have our expectations in the wrong place, and we will always be disappointed.

No comfort is as good as God's. People can never give us what we really need unless God Himself uses other people to reach us, which He often does. Whether He uses another person to comfort you or He comforts you Himself by the Holy Spirit, let me remind you that He is the Comforter. Ask for and receive His comfort whenever you need it.

behalf for the grace (the blessing of deliverance) granted us at the request of the many who have prayed.

12 It is a reason for pride *and* exultation to which our conscience testifies that we have conducted ourselves in the world [generally] and especially toward you, with devout *and* pure motives and godly sincerity, not in fleshly wisdom but by the grace of God (the unmerited favor and ᵈmerciful kindness by which God, exerting His holy influence upon souls, turns them to Christ, and keeps, strengthens, and increases them in Christian virtues).

13 For we write you nothing else but simply what you can read and understand [there is no double meaning to what we say], and I hope that you will become thoroughly acquainted [with ᵈdivine things] *and* know *and* understand [them] accurately *and* well to the end,

14 [Just] as you have [already] partially known *and* understood *and* acknowledged us *and* recognized that you can [honestly] be proud of us, even as we [can be proud] of you on the day of our Lord Jesus.

15 It was with assurance of this that I wanted *and* planned to visit you first

d Joseph Thayer, *A Greek-English Lexicon of the New Testament.*

[of all], so that you might have a double favor *and* token of grace (goodwill).

16 [I wanted] to visit you on my way to Macedonia, and [then] to come again to you [on my return trip] from Macedonia and have you send me forward on my way to Judea.

17 Now because I changed my original plan, was I being unstable *and* capricious? Or what I plan, do I plan according to the flesh [like a worldly man], ready to say Yes, yes, [when it may mean] No, no?

18 As surely as God is trustworthy *and* faithful *and* means what He says, our speech *and* message to you have not been Yes [that might mean] No.

19 For the Son of God, Christ Jesus (the Messiah), Who has been preached among you by us, by myself, Silvanus, and Timothy, was not Yes and No; but in Him it is [always the divine] Yes.

20 For as many as are the promises of God, they all find their Yes [answer] in Him [Christ]. For this reason we also utter the Amen (so be it) to God through Him [in His Person and by His agency] to the glory of God.

21 But it is God Who confirms *and* makes us steadfast *and* establishes us [in joint fellowship] with you in Christ, and has consecrated *and* anointed us [[e]enduing us with the gifts of the Holy Spirit];

22 [He has also appropriated and acknowledged us as His by] putting His seal upon us and giving us His [Holy] Spirit in our hearts as the security deposit *and* guarantee [of the fulfillment of His promise].

23 But I call upon God as my soul's witness: it was to avoid hurting you that I refrained from coming to Corinth—

life point

If we pray in the Holy Spirit, we can always be assured that all things will work out for good (see Romans 8:27, 28). God is great and mighty; there is no situation that He cannot use for good as we pray and trust Him. We dare not pray the way we want to, but as we are led by the Holy Spirit. I believe Spirit-filled prayers receive a "Yes" and "Amen" from God, as we read about in II Corinthians 1:20.

24 Not that we have dominion [over you] *and* lord it over your faith, but [rather that we work with you as] fellow laborers [to promote] your joy, for in [your] faith ([f]in your strong and welcome conviction or belief that Jesus is the Messiah, through Whom we obtain eternal salvation in the kingdom of God) you stand firm.

2 BUT I definitely made up my mind not to grieve you with another painful *and* distressing visit.

2 For if I cause you pain [with merited rebuke], who is there to provide me enjoyment but the [very] one whom I have grieved *and* made sad?

3 And I wrote the same to you so that when I came, I might not be myself pained by those who are the

putting the Word to work

Do you know that all of the promises of God are for you (see II Corinthians 1:20)? As you spend time in the Word, search out the promises of God. Ask Him to show you how He has already fulfilled certain promises and to fill you with expectation that He will fulfill others.

e Brooke F. Westcott, *The Epistles of Saint John*, has a helpful insight here in his comment on I John 2:20. **f** Joseph Thayer, *A Greek-English Lexicon*.

[very] ones who ought to make me glad, for I trusted in you all *and* felt confident that my joy would be shared by all of you.

4　For I wrote you out of great sorrow and deep distress [with mental torture and anxiety] of heart, [yes, and] with many tears, not to cause you pain but in order to make you realize the overflowing love that I continue increasingly to have for you.

5　But if someone [the one among you who committed incest] has caused [all this] grief *and* pain, he has caused it not to me, but in some measure, not to put it too severely, [he has distressed] all of you.

6　For such a one this censure by the majority [which he has received is] sufficient [punishment].

7　So [instead of further rebuke, now] you should rather turn *and* [graciously] forgive and comfort *and* encourage [him], to keep him from being overwhelmed by excessive sorrow *and* despair.

8　I therefore beg you to reinstate him in your affections *and* assure him of your love for him;

9　For this was my purpose in writing you, to test your attitude *and* see if you would stand the test, whether you are obedient *and* altogether agreeable [to following my orders] in everything.

10　If you forgive anyone anything, I too forgive that one; and what I have forgiven, if I have forgiven anything, has been for your sakes in the presence [and with the approval] of Christ (the Messiah),

11　To keep Satan from getting the advantage over us; for we are not ignorant of his wiles *and* intentions.

12　Now when I arrived at Troas [to preach] the good news (the Gospel) of Christ, a door of opportunity was opened for me in the Lord,

13　Yet my spirit could not rest (relax, get relief) because I did not find my brother Titus there. So I took leave

life point

Second Corinthians 2:10, 11 teaches us that we are to forgive in order to keep Satan from gaining an advantage over us. When we forgive others, we not only do them a favor, we do ourselves an even greater favor.

The reason we do ourselves such a favor is that unforgiveness fills us with resentment and produces a root of bitterness that poisons our entire system.

Bitterness always belongs to bondage. Forgiveness releases bitter bondage.

from them *and* departed for Macedonia.

14　But thanks be to God, Who in Christ always leads us in triumph [as trophies of Christ's victory] and through us spreads *and* makes evident the fragrance of the knowledge of God everywhere,

15　For we are the sweet fragrance of Christ [which exhales] unto God, [discernible alike] among those who are being saved *and* among those who are perishing:

16　To the latter it is an aroma [wafted] from death to death [a fatal odor, the smell of doom]; to the former it is an aroma from life to life [a vital

life point

God always energizes us to do what He leads us to do. It is only when we go beyond His will to follow our own wills (or other people's desires) that we are likely to get exhausted. Second Corinthians 2:14 says that God always "leads us in triumph." His will is not for us to live defeated, weak lives; He wants us to be more than conquerors (see Romans 8:37). His will for us is strength, not weakness; victory, not defeat.

fragrance, living and fresh]. And who is qualified (fit and sufficient) for these things? [Who is able for such a ministry? We?]

17 For we are not, like so many, [like hucksters making a trade of] peddling God's Word [shortchanging and adulterating the divine message]; but like [men] of sincerity *and* the purest motive, as [commissioned and sent] by God, we speak [His message] in Christ (the Messiah), in the [very] sight *and* presence of God.

3 ARE WE starting to commend ourselves again? Or we do not, like some [false teachers], need written credentials *or* letters of recommendation to you or from you, [do we]?

2 [No] you yourselves are our letter of recommendation (our credentials), written in ᵍyour hearts, to be known (perceived, recognized) and read by everybody.

3 You show *and* make obvious that you are a letter from Christ delivered by us, not written with ink but with [the] Spirit of [the] living God, not on tablets of stone but on tablets of human hearts. [Exod. 24:12; 31:18; 32:15, 16; Jer. 31:33.]

4 Such is the reliance *and* confidence that we have through Christ toward *and* with reference to God.

5 Not that we are fit (qualified and sufficient in ability) of ourselves to form personal judgments *or* to claim *or* count anything as coming from us, but our power *and* ability *and* sufficiency are from God.

6 [It is He] Who has qualified us [making us to be fit and worthy and sufficient] as ministers *and* dispensers of a new covenant [of salvation through Christ], not [ministers] of the letter (of legally written code) but of the Spirit; for the code [of the

putting the Word to work

Many cultures today place a very high value on self-sufficiency. Do you believe that you are self-sufficient? The truth is that no one is sufficient in himself. Second Corinthians 3:5 says that our only sufficiency is from God. Whether you recognize it or not, your ability to do anything, including minister to others, comes from God alone. Thank Him that you do not have to depend on yourself, but can rely on His strength and power for everything you do!

Law] kills, but the [Holy] Spirit makes alive. [Jer. 31:31.]

7 Now if the dispensation of death engraved in letters on stone [the ministration of the Law], was inaugurated with such glory *and* splendor that the Israelites were not able to look steadily at the face of Moses because of its brilliance, [a glory] that was to fade *and* pass away, [Exod. 34:29-35.]

8 Why should not the dispensation of the Spirit [this spiritual ʰministry whose task it is to cause men to obtain and be governed by the Holy Spirit] be attended with much greater *and* more splendid glory?

9 For if the service that condemns [the ministration of doom] had glory, how infinitely more abounding in splendor *and* glory must be the service that makes righteous [the ministry that produces and fosters righteous living and right standing with God]!

10 Indeed, in view of this fact, what once had splendor [ⁱthe glory of the Law in the face of Moses] has come to have no splendor at all, because of the overwhelming glory that exceeds *and* excels it [ⁱthe glory of the Gospel in the face of Jesus Christ].

11 For if that which was but passing

g Many ancient manuscripts read "our." **h** Joseph Thayer, *A Greek-English Lexicon*. **i** Marvin Vincent, *Word Studies*.

relationship, not "religion"

I feel sometimes that "religion" is killing people. In II Corinthians 3:6, Paul said, "The code [of the Law] kills, but the [Holy] Spirit makes alive."

There are so many precious people who seek a relationship with God, and the religious community continues to tell them they need to "do" something else in order to be acceptable to Him.

Do not be offended by my use of the word "religion." I realize that it has been a popular, spiritual-sounding word for centuries. I am only trying to present a clear difference between an impersonal set of rules and regulations and a personal relationship with the living God.

Jesus talked of His personal relationship with the Father, and the religious leaders of His day persecuted Him. I am amazed when I encounter certain people who are opposed to hearing others talk about God in a personal way or about feeling empowered by God. Obviously, Satan hates a personal relationship with God and the power it makes available in the life of a believer.

In certain religious circles, if you and I were to talk about God as though we know Him, we would be judged and criticized. People would ask, "Who do you think you are?" Religion wants us to picture God as being far away—somewhere up in the sky—not approachable by anyone except the "elite" of the church. And, furthermore, they want us to believe that He can be reached only through rule keeping and good behavior.

This "religious spirit" was alive in Jesus' day, and He died to put an end to it and bring people into a close personal relationship with Himself, the Father, and the Holy Spirit. That same religious spirit still torments people to this day if they do not know the truth.

The Law was given in order to show people their need for a Savior. We try to keep it until we realize that we absolutely cannot, and then hopefully we humble ourselves and ask God to help us, which He did in the person of Jesus Christ. As you walk with God, remember to keep your relationship with Him at the center and to keep "religion" far from you.

---

and fading away came with splendor, how much more must that which remains *and* is permanent abide in glory *and* splendor!

12 Since we have such [glorious] hope (such joyful and confident expectation), we speak very freely *and* openly *and* fearlessly.

13 Nor [do we act] like Moses, who put a veil over his face so that the Israelites might not gaze upon the finish of the vanishing [splendor which had been upon it].

14 In fact, their minds were grown hard *and* calloused [they had become dull and had lost the

life point

In II Corinthians 3:13–15 we read that when the Law is read, a veil lies over the hearts and minds of the people. A veil is a separation.

As long as we read the Bible as Law, a separation will exist between God and us and it will prevent proper relationship. Even though the old covenant is now made void and done away with, if we are legalistic, we will read legalism into everything the Bible says.

Remember, a legalist is someone who is overly concerned with rulekeeping. He exalts rules above relationship. Do not be a legalist, hiding behind a veil of rules and regulations, but come to God just as you are with an open heart and unveiled face.

power of understanding]; for until this present day, when the Old Testament (the old covenant) is being read, that same veil still lies [on their hearts], not being lifted [to reveal] that in Christ it is made void *and* done away.
15 Yes, down to this [very] day whenever Moses is read, a veil lies upon their minds *and* hearts.
16 But whenever a person turns [in repentance] to the Lord, the veil is stripped off *and* taken away.
17 Now the Lord is the Spirit, and where the Spirit of the Lord is, there is liberty (emancipation from bondage, freedom). [Isa. 61:1, 2.]
18 And all of us, as with unveiled face, [because we] continued to behold [in the Word of God] as in a mirror the glory of the Lord, are constantly being transfigured into His *very own* image in ever increasing splendor *and* from one degree of glory to another; [for this comes] from the Lord [Who is] the Spirit.

4 THEREFORE, SINCE we do hold *and* engage in this ministry by the mercy of God [granting us favor, benefits, opportunities, and especially salvation], we do not get discouraged (spiritless and despondent with fear) *or* become faint with weariness and exhaustion.
2 We have renounced disgraceful ways (secret thoughts, feelings, desires and underhandedness, the methods and arts that men hide through shame); we refuse to deal craftily (to practice trickery and cunning) *or* to adulterate *or* handle dishonestly the Word of God, but we state the truth openly (clearly and candidly). And so we commend ourselves in

life point

Second Corinthians 3:17 affirms that God wants us to have liberty and not legalism. *The Amplified Bible* defines liberty as emancipation from bondage: freedom. "If the Son liberates you . . . then you are really and unquestionably free," we read in John 8:36.

You may ask, "What am I free from?" You are:

Free from the power of sin!

Free from manipulation and control!

Free from fear of what others think of you!

Free from comparing yourself with everybody else!

Free from competition with others!

Free from selfishness!

Free from legalism!

Free to be an individual!

Free to be you!

Free! Free! Free!

life point

We change gradually, little by little, or as II Corinthians 3:18 states, "from one degree of glory to another." While these changes take place, we still make mistakes, and God's forgiveness is always available to us through Jesus Christ. Receiving this forgiveness actually strengthens us and enables us to keep pressing on toward new levels of holiness and better behavior.

the sight *and* presence of God to every man's conscience.

3   But even if our Gospel (the glad tidings) also be hidden (obscured and covered up with a veil that hinders the knowledge of God), it is hidden [only] to those who are perishing *and* obscured [only] to those who are spiritually dying *and* veiled [only] to those who are lost.

4   For the god of this world has blinded the unbelievers' minds [that they should not discern the truth], preventing them from seeing the illuminating light of the Gospel of the glory of Christ (the Messiah), Who is the Image *and* Likeness of God.

5   For what we preach is not ourselves but Jesus Christ as Lord, and ourselves [merely] as your servants (slaves) for Jesus' sake.

6   For God Who said, Let light shine out of darkness, has shone in our hearts so as [to beam forth] the Light for the illumination of the knowledge of the majesty *and* glory of God [as it is manifest in the Person and is

speak the Word

revealed] in the face of *Jesus* Christ (the Messiah). [Gen. 1:3.]

7   However, we possess this precious treasure [the divine Light of the Gospel] in [frail, human] vessels of earth, that the grandeur *and* exceeding greatness of the power may be shown to be from God and not from ourselves.

8   We are hedged in (pressed) on every side [troubled and oppressed in every way], but not cramped *or* crushed; we suffer embarrassments *and* are perplexed *and* unable to find a way out, but not driven to despair;

9   We are pursued (persecuted and hard driven), but not deserted [to stand alone]; we are struck down to the ground, but never struck out *and* destroyed;

10   Always carrying about in the body the liability *and* exposure to the same putting to death that *the Lord* Jesus suffered, so that the [ʲresurrection] life of Jesus also may be shown forth by *and* in our bodies.

11   For we who live are constantly [experiencing] being handed over to death for Jesus' sake, that the [ʲresurrection] life of Jesus also may be evidenced through our flesh which is liable to death.

12   Thus death is actively at work in us, but [it is in order that ᵏour] life [may be actively at work] in you.

13   Yet we have the same spirit of faith as he had who wrote, I have believed, and therefore have I spoken. We too believe, and therefore we speak, [Ps. 116:10.]

14   Assured that He Who raised up the Lord Jesus will raise us up also

Thank You, God, for allowing me to possess the light of the Gospel in my frail, human vessel so everyone will know that the power in my life comes from You.
ADAPTED FROM II CORINTHIANS 4:7

j Marvin Vincent, *Word Studies*.   k Joseph Thayer, *A Greek-English Lexicon*.

free to be

In II Corinthians 3:18 we read that we must come "with unveiled face" in order to receive the benefit God wants us to have from the new covenant.

To me, this means that when I stop being religious and legalistic and just come to Jesus, when I lay aside all "my" works and begin to see Him, when I allow Him to remove the veil from my eyes, then He and I can enter into personal relationship that will ultimately change me into His image.

We must learn to "be" and not always feel that we must "do."

There is a big emphasis in Christian circles today on spending personal time with the Lord, and rightly so. More than anything else, we need His presence. He is the only One Who can do anything for us that will be permanent. Unfortunately, many people are frustrated by this emphasis in teaching. They want to spend time with God, but feel uncomfortable; or, they do not know what to do during these times.

Others express that they never sense God's presence. They find prayer and fellowship to be a dry experience. I believe one of the reasons this happens is that people live under the Law instead of under grace. Grace is not the freedom to sin; it is the power to live a holy life.

But grace also sees when our hearts are right toward God and even though our performance may not always be perfect, grace forgives and helps us get from where we are to where we need to be.

The Law condemns. Grace removes the condemnation and sets us free—free *from* and free *to*. Free *from* condemnation, self-hatred, self-rejection, fear of God, and many other negative traps. And free *to* serve God without pressure, free to use the life and energy we are given to behave better, rather than to fight condemnation.

When you spend time with God, do not try to be or sound "religious," just be yourself. Talk to Him and listen to hear what He will speak to your heart. Read His Word and other Christian books that will edify and help you grow as a believer in Jesus Christ. Do not make your time with Him complicated, keep it simple, and trust Him to teach you in all areas of life.

with Jesus and bring us [along] with you into His presence.
15 For all [these] things are [taking place] for your sake, so that the more grace (divine favor and spiritual blessing) extends to more and more people *and* multiplies through the many, the more thanksgiving may increase [and redound] to the glory of God.
16 Therefore we do not become discouraged (utterly spiritless, exhausted, and wearied out through fear). Though our outer man is [progressively] decaying *and* wasting away, yet our inner self is being [progressively] renewed day after day.

17 For our light, momentary affliction (this slight distress of the passing hour) is ever more and more abundantly preparing *and* producing *and* achieving for us an everlasting weight of glory [beyond all measure, excessively surpassing all comparisons and all calculations, a vast and transcendent glory and blessedness never to cease!],

18 Since we consider *and* look not to the things that are seen but to the things that are unseen; for the things that are visible are temporal (brief and fleeting), but the things that are invisible are deathless *and* everlasting.

5 FOR WE know that if the tent which is our earthly home is destroyed (dissolved), we have from God a building, a house not made with hands, eternal in the heavens.

2 Here indeed, in this [present abode, body], we sigh *and* groan inwardly, because we yearn to be clothed over [we yearn to put on our celestial body like a garment, to be fitted out] with our heavenly dwelling,

3 So that by putting it on we may not be found naked (without a body).

4 For while we are still in this tent, we groan under the burden *and* sigh

this too shall pass

When I face difficult times, I tell myself, "This can't last forever. This, too, shall pass."

You can probably look back at your life and see many difficult times you endured even though at the time you thought, *I cannot stand this for another day.* The devil probably tempted you every five minutes to believe the trial was going to last forever.

As you consider how many times you have already made it to the other side of pain, you can be confident you will make it again through Christ, Who strengthens you (see Philippians 4:13). And on the other side of trials, you will see how God turned those experiences into good for your life (see Romans 8:28).

If you have had a problem for more than six months, you probably feel as though your problem has lasted for an eternity. But our years on earth are only a little drop of nothing compared to forever.

Paul said in II Corinthians 4:17, 18 that the seasons of trials pass. It is tough when we are going through trials, but Paul learned to keep his eyes on the prize of heaven and trusted God to prepare him so that God's glory was revealed through his life.

When you are tempted to become discontented, remember: "This, too, shall pass." Your afflictions are "light and momentary" from the perspective of eternity. No matter how bad your current situation may look, God loves you. Never let go of the truth that God loves you, no matter what happens in your life. You can trust that everything will work out because of His great love for you.

putting the Word to work

Are you facing some physical challenges at this time in your life? It can be discouraging to know that your body cannot do everything it used to be able to do (see II Corinthians 5:1–8). Ask God for strength to face those physical challenges, and be encouraged, knowing that your eternal body will always be perfect and strong, and that you will live with Him forever.

deeply (weighed down, depressed, oppressed)—not that we want to put off the body (the clothing of the spirit), but rather that we would be further clothed, so that what is mortal (our dying body) may be swallowed up by life [¹after the resurrection].

5 Now He Who has fashioned us [preparing and making us fit] for this very thing is God, Who also has given us the [Holy] Spirit as a guarantee [of the fulfillment of His promise].

6 So then, we are always full of good *and* hopeful *and* confident courage; we know that while we are at home in the body, we are abroad from the home with the Lord [that is promised us].

7 For we walk by faith [we ¹regulate our lives and conduct ourselves by our conviction or belief respecting man's relationship to God and divine things, with trust and holy fervor; thus we walk] not by sight *or* appearance.

8 [Yes] we have confident *and* hopeful courage and are pleased rather to be away from home out of the body and be at home with the Lord.

9 Therefore, whether we are at home [on earth away from Him] or away from home [and with Him], we are constantly ambitious *and* strive earnestly to be pleasing to Him.

10 For we must all appear *and* be revealed as we are before the judgment seat of Christ, so that each one may receive [his pay] according to what he has done in the body, whether good or evil [considering ᵐwhat his purpose and motive have been, and what he has ¹achieved, been busy with, and given himself and his attention to accomplishing].

11 Therefore, being conscious of fearing the Lord with respect *and* reverence, we seek to win people over [to persuade them]. But ¹what sort of persons we are is plainly recognized *and* thoroughly understood by God, and I hope that it is plainly recognized *and* thoroughly understood also by your consciences (your inborn discernment).

12 We are not commending ourselves to you again, but we are providing you with an occasion *and* incentive to be [rightfully] proud of us, so that you may have a reply for those who pride themselves on surface appearances [¹on the virtues they only appear to have], although their heart is devoid of them.

13 For if we are beside ourselves [mad, as some say], it is for God *and* concerns Him; if we are in our right mind, it is for your benefit,

14 For the love of Christ controls *and* urges *and* impels us, because we are of the opinion *and* conviction that

speak the Word

Thank You, God, for giving me the Holy Spirit as a guarantee of the fulfillment of Your promise in my life.
ADAPTED FROM II CORINTHIANS 5:5

l Joseph Thayer, *A Greek-English Lexicon.*   **m** Alexander Souter, *Pocket Lexicon of the Greek New Testament.*

fickle feelings

Second Corinthians 5:7 says we walk by faith and not by sight; we do not make decisions by what we see or feel. We have to search our hearts, where faith abides, and live from there. The kingdom of God is *within* us, and we should follow those inner promptings that lead to righteousness, peace, and joy in the Holy Spirit.

Feelings can mislead us and steal our faith more than any other single influence. The problem with feelings is that they change constantly. We can feel one thousand ways about the same thing in thirty days. One minute we may feel like doing something, and the next minute we do not. Feelings also provoke us to say things that are unwise, and we talk a lot about how we feel!

Do you believe the god of your feelings or the God of the Bible? This is a question we must all ask ourselves. More than anything, people who come to me for help and counsel tell me how they feel. We should tell each other what the Word of God says, not just how we feel.

Our feelings do not convey truth to us; Satan uses them to deceive and lead us astray. Emotions are unreliable; do not believe them or trust them. Respond with your heart, where the Spirit of God abides, and always be sure that you have peace. Check with your heart, not your emotions, before making a decision. Learn to walk by faith, not by things you can see, touch, or feel.

life point

The more we love Jesus, the more we operate in self-control. It is easier for us to say no to selfish desires and yes to God, because "the love of Christ" (II Corinthians 5:14) urges us to do so.

As our love for God grows, we will not want to offend Him. We will not want to grieve the Holy Spirit. We will want to do what God wants us to do, and obedience will give us great joy in our everyday lives.

Our walks with God are progressive and we do get better and better in every way as we continue in His Word. Do not be discouraged with yourself. You may not be where you want to be, but thank God you are not where you used to be!

[if] One died for all, then all died; 15 And He died for all, so that all those who live might live no longer to *and* for themselves, but to *and* for Him Who died and was raised again for their sake.

16 Consequently, from now on we estimate *and* regard no one from a [purely] human point of view [in terms of natural standards of value]. [No] even though we once did estimate Christ from a human viewpoint *and* as a man, yet now [we have such knowledge of Him that] we know Him no longer [in terms of the flesh].

17 Therefore if any person is [ingrafted] in Christ (the Messiah) he is a new creation (a new creature altogether); the old [previous moral and spiritual condition] has passed away. Behold, the fresh *and* new has come! 18 But all things are from God, Who through *Jesus* Christ reconciled us to Himself [received us into favor,

life point

As "a new creation," you do not have to allow the old things that happened to you affect your new life in Christ. You are a new creature with a new life in Christ (see II Corinthians 5:17). You can have your mind renewed according to the Word of God. Good things will happen to you. Rejoice! It is a new day!

brought us into harmony with Himself] and gave to us the ministry of reconciliation [that by word and deed we might aim to bring others into harmony with Him].

19 It was God [personally present] in Christ, reconciling *and* restoring the world to favor with Himself, not counting up *and* holding against [men] their trespasses [but cancelling them], and committing to us the message of reconciliation (of the restoration to favor).

20 So we are Christ's ambassadors, God making His appeal as it were through us. We [as Christ's personal representatives] beg you for His sake to lay hold of the divine favor [now offered you] *and* be reconciled to God.

21 For our sake He made Christ [virtually] to be sin Who knew no sin, so

Do you know that you are Christ's ambassador (see II Corinthians 5:20)? Just as you were reconciled to God through Jesus, He now entrusts you to tell others that they, too, can be reconciled to God and have a loving, personal relationship with Him. Think of someone to whom you can be Christ's ambassador, and pray for an opportunity to share God's love with that person.

life point

According to II Corinthians 5:20 we are God's ambassadors, His personal representatives. And God makes His appeal to mankind to be saved through us as believers in Jesus Christ. This is a very big responsibility, one we should take seriously. We need to display the character of Jesus through our love for one another and through the good fruit He has produced in our lives, so that others will be drawn to Him.

that in *and* through Him we might become [[n]endued with, viewed as being in, and examples of] the righteousness of God [what we ought to be, approved and acceptable and in right relationship with Him, by His goodness].

6 LABORING TOGETHER [as God's fellow workers] with Him then, we beg of you not to receive the grace of God in vain [that [o]merciful kindness by which God exerts His holy influence on souls and turns them to Christ, keeping and strengthening them—do not receive it to no purpose].

2 For He says, In the time of favor (of an assured welcome) I have listened to *and* heeded your call, and I have helped you on the day of deliverance (the day of salvation). Behold, now is truly the time for a gracious welcome *and* acceptance [of you from God]; behold, now is the day of salvation! [Isa. 49:8.]

3 We put no obstruction in anybody's way [we give no offense in anything], so that no fault may be found *and* [our] ministry blamed *and* discredited.

4 But we commend ourselves in every way as [true] servants of God:

n Henry Alford, *The Greek New Testament, with Notes.*   **o** Joseph Thayer, *A Greek-English Lexicon.*

God's ambassadors

Do you understand from II Corinthians 5:18–20 that God wants us—and through us, everyone on earth—to be in favor with Him? Do you also understand from what we have said that the devil steals that favor through deceit and delusion? Jesus came to restore favor to God's people—and through us to everyone everywhere.

Part of our inheritance is to have and enjoy favor. Part of our ministry is to act as Christ's ambassadors by drawing others to receive God's wonderful gift of forgiveness and reconciliation and to share in His marvelous grace, His unmerited favor.

God wants to restore us to favor with Him so we can act as His ambassadors in the earth. This is how we need to look upon ourselves, as emissaries from a foreign land. The Bible says we are aliens and strangers here, that this earth is not our home, that we are merely passing through (see I Peter 2:11.) Through us God makes His appeal to others to receive His forgiveness, grace, and favor.

Now think for a moment: how are foreign ambassadors treated? Are they not treated royally? That is the way we should expect to be treated, and that is the way we should treat others to whom we are sent by the Lord for the sake of His kingdom.

The Bible tells us that not only are we ambassadors for Christ, but that we are kings and priests unto our God (see Revelation 1:6, KJV). That is why we need a different attitude toward ourselves and others. We need to act like royal ambassadors, like divine diplomats, because we are God's representatives on earth.

through great endurance, in tribulation *and* suffering, in hardships *and* privations, in sore straits *and* calamities,

5 In beatings, imprisonments, riots, labors, sleepless watching, hunger;

6 By innocence *and* purity, knowledge *and* spiritual insight, longsuffering *and* patience, kindness, in the Holy Spirit, in unfeigned love;

7 By [speaking] the word of truth, in the power of God, with the weapons of righteousness for the right hand [to attack] and for the left hand [to defend];

8 Amid honor and dishonor; in defaming *and* evil report and in praise *and* good report. [We are branded] as deceivers (impostors), and [yet vindicated as] truthful *and* honest.

9 [We are treated] as unknown *and* ignored [by the world], and [yet we are] well-known *and* recognized [by God and His people]; as dying, and yet here we are alive; as chastened by suffering and [yet] not killed;

10 As grieved *and* mourning, yet [we are] always rejoicing; as poor [ourselves, yet] bestowing riches on many; as having nothing, and [yet in reality] possessing all things.

11 Our mouth is open to you, Corinthians [we are hiding nothing, keeping nothing back], and our heart is expanded wide [for you]! [Isa. 60:5; Ezek. 33:22.]

12 There is no lack of room for you in [our hearts], but you lack room in your own affections [for us].

life point

A large number of believers are tormented by negative thinking about themselves. They think about how God must be so displeased with them because of all their weaknesses and failures.

How much time do you waste living under guilt and condemnation? Notice that I asked how much time is *wasted*, because that is exactly what that kind of thinking is—a waste of time!

Do not think about how terrible you were before you came to Christ. Instead, think about the fact that you have been made the righteousness of God in Him. Remember: thoughts turn into actions. If you ever want to behave better, you have to change your thinking first. Keep thinking about how terrible you are, and you will only act worse. Every time a negative, condemning thought comes to your mind, remind yourself that God loves you, that you have been made the righteousness of God in Christ.

You are changing for the better all the time. Every day you grow spiritually. God has a glorious plan for your life. These are the truths you must think about.

13 By way of return then, do this for me—I speak as to children—open wide your hearts also [to us].
14 Do not be unequally yoked with unbelievers [do not make mismated alliances with them or come under a different yoke with them, inconsistent with your faith]. For what partnership have right living *and* right standing with God with iniquity *and* lawlessness? Or how can light have fellowship with darkness?
15 What harmony can there be between Christ and Belial [the devil]? Or what has a believer in common with an unbeliever?

16 What agreement [can there be between] a temple of God and idols? For we are the temple of the living God; even as God said, I will dwell in *and* with *and* among them and will walk in *and* with *and* among them, and I will be their God, and they shall be My people. [Exod. 25:8; 29:45; Lev. 26:12; Jer. 31:1; Ezek. 37:27.]
17 So, come out from among [unbelievers], and separate (sever) yourselves from them, says the Lord, and touch not [any] unclean thing; then I will receive you kindly *and* treat you with favor, [Isa. 52:11.]
18 And I will be a Father to you, and you shall be My sons and daughters, says the Lord Almighty. [Isa. 43:6; Hos. 1:10.]

7 THEREFORE, SINCE these [great] promises are ours, beloved, let us cleanse ourselves from everything that contaminates *and* defiles body and spirit, and bring [our] consecration to completeness in the [reverential] fear of God.
2 Do open your hearts to us again [enlarge them to take us in]. We have wronged no one, we have betrayed *or* corrupted no one, we have cheated *or* taken advantage of no one.

putting the Word to work

Relationships are an important part of life, and close relationships that are healthy and godly can be great blessings in our lives. However, II Corinthians 6:14–18 warns against being in a close relationship with anyone who causes us to stray from God's purposes and will. Are you in any relationships that cause you to compromise your faith? Ask God to help you know how to eliminate wrong, ungodly relationships, to give you wisdom in your relationships, and to provide you with healthy, godly friendships.

right with God

Being made right with God and being acceptable to Him through Jesus Christ (see II Corinthians 5:21) is a wonderful privilege and blessing. Just think of it! We no longer have to fear or feel ashamed and condemned when we try to pray or fellowship with God. We can approach the throne of God boldly, unreservedly, and as often as we choose. God loves us and welcomes us with open arms. He loves to hear our requests and work with us to bring us into the fullness of His will for us.

Most people feel wrong about themselves, not right. Prior to accepting Jesus as Savior, we cannot do anything but feel wrong because many things about us are wrong. We say wrong things, make wrong choices, do wrong things, and behave in wrong ways toward other people. But through Christ, we are made right with God and we become acceptable to Him. We still do things that are wrong, but justice is satisfied in Jesus Christ, Who paid the debt we owed and became the final sacrifice for our sins.

We place our faith in Jesus and we give Him everything we have, everything we are, and especially everything we are not; and in exchange He gives us everything He has and is. That is the best deal anyone will find anywhere.

When I married my husband, Dave, he had a car. I did not have a car while I was single, but when we married I suddenly had a car. Everything Dave had became mine after I made a full commitment of my life to Dave. His car was not legally mine as long as we were dating, but as soon as we were married everything he had was legally mine and everything I had was his. Dave had money and I did not, so suddenly I had some money. He had a large loving family and mine was rather dysfunctional, so suddenly I had a good family too. Dave had a lot more than I did, which reminds me of my relationship with Jesus.

We have sin and Jesus has righteousness, so when we make a full commitment to Him we give Him our sin and He gives us His righteousness. Exchange your sin consciousness for a righteousness consciousness and you will start seeing wonderful changes in your life and behavior.

3 I do not say this to reproach *or* condemn [you], for I have said before that you are [nested] in our hearts, [and you will remain there] together [with us], whether we die or live.
4 I have great boldness *and* free *and* fearless confidence *and* cheerful courage toward you; my pride in you is great. I am filled [brimful] with the comfort [of it]; with all our tribulation *and* in spite of it, [I am filled with comfort] I am overflowing with joy.

speak the Word

5 For even when we arrived in Macedonia, our bodies had no ease *or* rest, but we were oppressed in every way *and* afflicted at every turn—fighting *and* contentions without, dread *and* fears within [us].

6 But God, Who comforts *and* encourages *and* refreshes *and* cheers the depressed *and* the sinking, comforted *and* encouraged *and* refreshed *and* cheered us by the arrival of Titus.

7 [Yes] and not only by his coming but also by [his account of] the comfort with which he was encouraged *and* refreshed *and* cheered as to you, while he told us of your yearning affection, of how sorry you were [for me] and how eagerly you took my part, so that I rejoiced still more.

8 For even though I did grieve you with my letter, I do not regret [it now], though I did regret it; for I see that that letter did pain you, though only for a little while;

9 Yet I am glad now, not because you were pained, but because you were pained into repentance [and so turned back to God]; for you felt a grief such as God meant you to feel, so that in nothing you might suffer loss through us *or* harm for what we did.

10 For godly grief *and* the pain God is permitted to direct, produce a repentance that leads *and* contributes to salvation *and* deliverance from evil, and it never brings regret; but worldly grief (the hopeless sorrow that is characteristic of the pagan world) is deadly [breeding and ending in death].

11 For [you can look back now and] observe what this same godly sorrow has done for you *and* has produced in you: what eagerness *and* earnest care to explain *and* clear yourselves [of all ᵖcomplicity in the condoning of incest], what indignation [at the sin], what alarm, what yearning, what zeal

[to do justice to all concerned], what readiness to mete out punishment [ᵖto the offender]! At every point you have proved yourselves cleared *and* guiltless in the matter. [I Cor. 5.]

12 So although I did write to you [as I did], it was not for the sake *and* because of the one who did [the] wrong, nor on account of the one who suffered [the] wrong, but in order that you might realize before God [that your readiness to accept our authority revealed] how zealously you do care for us.

13 Therefore we are relieved *and* comforted *and* encouraged [at the result]. And in addition to our own [personal] consolation, we were especially delighted at the joy of Titus, because you have all set his mind at rest, soothing *and* refreshing his spirit.

14 For if I had boasted to him at all concerning you, I was not disappointed *or* put to shame, but just as everything we ever said to you was true, so our boasting [about you] to Titus has proved true also.

15 And his heart goes out to you more abundantly than ever as he recalls the submission [to his guidance] that all of you had, and the reverence *and* anxiety [to meet all requirements] with which you accepted *and* welcomed him.

16 I am very happy because I now am of good courage *and* have perfect confidence in you in all things.

8 WE WANT to tell you further, brethren, about the grace (the favor and spiritual blessing) of God which has been evident in the churches of Macedonia [arousing in them the desire to give alms];

2 For in the midst of an ordeal of severe tribulation, their abundance of joy and their depth of poverty [together] have overflowed in wealth of lavish generosity on their part.

3 For, as I can bear witness, [they gave] according to their ability, yes, and beyond their ability; and [they did it] voluntarily,

4 Begging us most insistently for the favor *and* the fellowship of contributing in this ministry for [the relief and support of] the saints [in Jerusalem].

5 Nor [was this gift of theirs merely the contribution] that we expected, but first they gave themselves to the Lord and to us [as His agents] by the will of God [ᵈentirely disregarding their personal interests, they gave as much as they possibly could, having put themselves at our disposal to be directed by the will of God]—

6 So much so that we have urged Titus that as he began it, he should also complete this beneficent *and* gracious contribution among you [the church at Corinth].

7 Now as you abound *and* excel *and* are at the front in everything—in faith, in expressing yourselves, in knowledge, in all zeal, and in your love for us—[see to it that you come to the front now and] abound *and* excel in this gracious work [of almsgiving] also.

8 I give this not as an order [to dictate to you], but to prove, by [pointing out] the zeal of others, the sincerity of your [own] love also.

9 For you are becoming progressively acquainted with *and* recognizing more strongly *and* clearly the grace of our Lord Jesus Christ (His kindness, His gracious generosity, His undeserved favor and spiritual blessing), [in] that though He was [so very] rich, yet for your sakes He became [so very] poor, in order that by His poverty you might become enriched (abundantly supplied).

10 [It is then] my counsel *and* my opinion in this matter that I give [you when I say]: It is profitable *and* fitting for you [now to complete the enterprise] which more than a year ago you not only began, but were the first to wish to do anything [about contributions for the relief of the saints at Jerusalem].

11 So now finish doing it, that your [enthusiastic] readiness in desiring it may be equalled by your completion of it according to your ability *and* means.

12 For if the [eager] readiness to give is there, then it is acceptable *and* welcomed in proportion to what a person has, not according to what he does not have.

13 For it is not [intended] that other people be eased *and* relieved [of their responsibility] and you be burdened *and* suffer [unfairly],

14 But to have equality [share and share alike], your surplus over necessity at the present time going to meet their want *and* to equalize the difference created by it, so that [at some other time] their surplus in turn may be given to supply your want. Thus there may be equality,

15 As it is written, He who gathered much had nothing over, and he who gathered little did not lack. [Exod. 16:18.]

speak the Word

q Joseph Thayer, *A Greek-English Lexicon.*

16 But thanks be to God Who plant-ed the same earnest zeal *and* care for you in the heart of Titus.

17 For he not only welcomed *and* responded to our appeal, but was himself so keen in his enthusiasm *and* interest in you that he is going to you of his own accord.

18 But we are sending along with him that brother [Luke?] whose praise in the Gospel ministry [is spread] throughout all the churches;

19 And more than that, he has been appointed by the churches to travel as our companion in regard to this boun-tiful contribution which we are administering for the glory of the Lord Himself and [to show] our eager readiness [as Christians to help one another].

20 [For] we are on our guard, intend-ing that no one should find anything for which to blame us in regard to our administration of this large contribu-tion.

21 For we take thought beforehand *and* aim to be honest *and* absolutely above suspicion, not only in the sight of the Lord but also in the sight of men.

22 Moreover, along with them we are sending our brother, whom we have often put to the test and have found him zealous (devoted and earnest) in many matters, but who is now more [eagerly] earnest than ever because of [his] absolute confidence in you.

23 As for Titus, he is my colleague and shares my work in your service; and as for the [other two] brethren, they are the [special] messengers of the churches, a credit *and* glory to Christ (the Messiah).

24 Show to these men, therefore, in the sight of the churches, the reality *and* plain truth of your love (your affection, goodwill, and benevolence)

and what [good reasons] I had for boasting about *and* being proud of you.

9 NOW ABOUT the offering that is [to be made] for the saints (God's people in Jerusalem), it is quite superfluous that I should write you;

2 For I am well acquainted with your willingness (your readiness and your eagerness to promote it) and I have proudly told about you to the people of Macedonia, saying that Achaia (most of Greece) has been prepared since last year for this con-tribution; and [consequently] your enthusiasm has stimulated the major-ity of them.

3 Still, I am sending the brethren [on to you], lest our pride in you should be made an empty boast in this particular case, and so that you may be all ready, as I told them you would be;

4 Lest, if [any] Macedonians should come with me and find you unpre-pared [for this generosity], we, to say nothing of yourselves, be humiliated for our being so confident.

5 That is why I thought it necessary to urge these brethren to go to you before I do and make arrangements in advance for this bountiful, promised gift of yours, so that it may be ready, not as an extortion [wrung out of you] but as a generous *and* willing gift.

6 [Remember] this: he who sows sparingly *and* grudgingly will also reap sparingly *and* grudgingly, and he who sows generously [ʳthat blessings may come to someone] will also reap generously *and* with blessings.

7 Let each one [give] as he has made up his own mind *and* purposed in his heart, not reluctantly *or* sorrow-fully or under compulsion, for God loves (He ʳtakes pleasure in, prizes above other things, and is unwilling to abandon or to do without) a cheerful

---

r Joseph Thayer, *A Greek-English Lexicon.*

putting the Word to work

Have you ever thought about not tithing in order to save money or to use that money for something else? I think we have all been tempted to use our tithe for something else, but that is a temptation we should aggressively resist. The tithe does not even belong to us; it belongs to God. He says in Malachi 3 that if we withhold it we are robbing Him. Second Corinthians 9:6–8 is both a warning and a wonderful promise. God is a God of abundance, not scarcity. Ask Him to give you a cheerful heart as you give and to increase your faith to see abundance for every good work.

(joyous, "prompt to do it") giver [whose heart is in his giving]. [Prov. 22:9.]

8 And God is able to make all grace (every favor and ˢearthly blessing) come to you in abundance, so that you may always *and* under all circumstances *and* whatever the need ᵗbe self-sufficient [possessing enough to require no aid or support and furnished in abundance for every good work and charitable donation].

9 As it is written, He [the benevolent person] scatters abroad; He gives to the poor; His deeds of justice *and* goodness *and* kindness *and* benevolence will go on *and* endure forever! [Ps. 112:9.]

10 And [God] Who provides seed for the sower and bread for eating will also provide and multiply your

[resources for] sowing and increase the fruits of your righteousness [ˢwhich manifests itself in active goodness, kindness, and charity]. [Isa. 55:10; Hos. 10:12.]

11 Thus you will be enriched in all things *and* in every way, so that you can be generous, and [your generosity as it is] administered by us will bring forth thanksgiving to God.

12 For the service that the ministering of this fund renders does not only fully supply what is lacking to the saints (God's people), but it also overflows in many [cries of] thanksgiving to God.

13 Because at [your] standing of the test of this ministry, they will glorify God for your loyalty *and* obedience to the Gospel of Christ which you confess, as well as for your generoushearted liberality to them and to all [the other needy ones].

14 And they yearn for you while they pray for you, because of the surpassing measure of God's grace (His favor and mercy and spiritual blessing which is shown forth) in you.

15 Now thanks be to God for His Gift, [precious] beyond telling [His indescribable, inexpressible, free Gift]!

10 NOW I myself, Paul, beseech you, by the gentleness and consideration of Christ [Himself; I] who [am] lowly enough [so they say] when among you face to face, but bold (fearless and outspoken) to you when [I am] absent from you!

2 I entreat you when I do come [to

speak the Word

Thank You, God, for providing seed for the sower and for multiplying my resources for sowing and increasing the fruits of my righteousness. Thank You that I am enriched in all things and in every way so that I can be generous.
ADAPTED FROM II CORINTHIANS 9:10, 11

s Joseph Thayer, *A Greek-English Lexicon.* **t** Marvin Vincent, *Word Studies.*

the mind is the battlefield

Our thoughts get us into trouble more than anything else. This is because our thoughts are the roots of every word and deed.

In Isaiah 55:8, the Lord says, "For My thoughts are not your thoughts, neither are your ways My ways." No matter what you or I may think, God has written down His thoughts for us in His book, the Bible. We must choose to examine our thoughts in light of the Word of God, always being willing to submit our thoughts to His thoughts, knowing that His are best.

This is exactly the point made in II Corinthians 10:4, 5. Through careful strategy and cunning deceit, Satan attempts to set up "strongholds" in our minds. A stronghold is an area in which we are held in bondage due to a wrong way of thinking. Examine what is in your mind. If it does not agree with God's thoughts (the Bible), then cast down your own thoughts and think God's thoughts instead. In order to do this, you must know God's Word well enough to compare your thoughts with what is in the mind of God.

People living in the vanity of their own minds not only destroy themselves, but far too often, they bring destruction to others around them. Those who live by God's truth, on the other hand, are blessed and bring blessings to others.

The mind is the battlefield!

On the battleground of the mind you will either win or lose the war that Satan has launched against you. My heartfelt prayer is that you will cast down imaginations and every high and lofty thing that exalts itself against the knowledge of God, bringing *every* thought into captivity, into obedience to Jesus Christ so that you can live in victory, joy, and peace.

you] that I may not [be driven to such] boldness as I intend to show toward those few who suspect us of acting according to the flesh [on the low level of worldly motives and as if invested with only human powers].

3 For though we walk (live) in the flesh, we are not carrying on our warfare according to the flesh *and* using mere human weapons.

4 For the weapons of our warfare are not physical [weapons of flesh and blood], but they are mighty before God for the overthrow *and* destruction of strongholds,

5 [Inasmuch as we] refute arguments *and* theories *and* reasonings and every proud *and* lofty thing that sets itself up against the [true] knowledge of God; and we lead every thought *and* purpose away captive into the obedience of Christ (the Messiah, the Anointed One),

6 Being in readiness to punish every [insubordinate for his] disobedience, when your own submission *and* obedience [as a church] are fully secured *and* complete.

7 Look at [this obvious fact] which is before your eyes. If anyone is confident that he is Christ's, let him reflect *and* remind himself that even as he is Christ's, so too are we.

8 For even though I boast rather

freely about our power *and* authority, which the Lord gave for your upbuilding and not for demolishing you, yet I shall not be put to shame [for exceeding the truth],

9 Neither would I seem to be overawing *or* frightening you with my letters;

10 For they say, His letters are weighty *and* impressive and forceful *and* telling, but his personality *and* bodily presence are weak, and his speech *and* delivery are utterly contemptible (of no account).

11 Let such people realize that what we say by letters when we are absent, [we put] also into deeds when we are present—

12 Not that we [have the audacity to] venture to class or [even to] compare ourselves with some who exalt *and* furnish testimonials for themselves! However, when they measure themselves with themselves and compare themselves with one another, they are without understanding *and* behave unwisely.

life point

I believe one of the biggest mistakes we make is comparing ourselves with other people and our gifts with their gifts.

God is not going to help me be anyone but myself and, likewise, He will not help you be anyone but yourself. He is not calling us to compete with others, but to love and help them. We should use our gifts to enhance other people's gifts, never allowing ourselves to fall prey to the spirit of jealousy that is so prevalent in our society.

13 We, on the other hand, will not boast beyond our legitimate province *and* proper limit, but will keep within the limits [of our commission which] God has allotted us as our measuring line and which reaches *and* includes even you.

14 For we are not overstepping the limits of our province *and* stretching beyond our ability to reach, as though we reached not (had no legitimate mission) to you, for we were [the very first] to come even as far as to you with the good news (the Gospel) of Christ.

15 We do not boast therefore, beyond our proper limit, over other men's labors, but we have the hope *and* confident expectation that as your faith continues to grow, our field among you may be greatly enlarged, still within the limits of our commission,

16 So that [we may even] preach the Gospel in lands [lying] beyond you, without making a boast of work already done in another [man's] sphere of activity [before we came on the scene].

17 However, let him who boasts *and* glories boast *and* glory in the Lord. [Jer. 9:24.]

18 For [it is] not [the man] who praises *and* commends himself who is approved *and* accepted, but [it is the person] whom the Lord accredits *and* commends.

11 I WISH you would bear with me while I indulge in a little [so-called] foolishness. Do bear with me!

2 For I am [u]zealous for you with a godly eagerness *and* a divine jealousy, for I have betrothed you to one Husband, to present you as a chaste virgin to Christ. [Hos. 2:19, 20.]

3 But [now] I am fearful, lest that even as the serpent beguiled Eve by his cunning, so your minds may be corrupted *and* seduced from wholehearted *and* sincere *and* pure devotion to Christ. [Gen. 3:4.]

u G. Abbott-Smith, *Manual Greek Lexicon of the New Testament.*

4 For [you seem readily to endure it] if a man comes and preaches another Jesus than the One we preached, or if you receive a different spirit from the [Spirit] you [once] received or a different gospel from the one you [then] received *and* welcomed; you tolerate [all that] well enough!

5 Yet I consider myself as in no way inferior to these [precious] ˅extra-super [false] apostles.

6 But even if [I am] unskilled in speaking, yet [I am] not [unskilled] in knowledge [I know what I am talking about]; we have made this evident to you in all things.

7 But did I perhaps make a mistake *and* do you a wrong in debasing *and* cheapening myself so that you might be exalted *and* enriched in dignity *and* honor *and* happiness by preaching God's Gospel without expense to you?

8 Other churches I have robbed by accepting [more than their share of] support for my ministry [from them in order] to serve you.

9 And when I was with you and ran short financially, I did not burden any [of you], for what I lacked was abundantly made up by the brethren who came from Macedonia. So I kept myself from being burdensome to you in any way, and will continue to keep [myself from being so].

10 As the truth of Christ is in me, this my boast [of independence] shall not be debarred (silenced or checked) in the regions of Achaia (most of Greece).

v Frederick W. Farrar, *The Life and Work of Saint Paul.*

the beauty of simplicity

In II Corinthians 11:3, Paul warns the people not to let their minds be corrupted from "wholehearted and sincere and pure devotion to Christ." I especially like the way the King James Version renders that phrase: the "simplicity that is in Christ."

Learn to keep life as simple as possible. It is fine to have a plan for your life and for your everyday activities, but be open to following God's plan if He has another direction in which He wants you to go. We can block God's plan by following our own fleshly desires and plans without consulting Him.

God's plans for us are actually so simple that many times we miss them. We tend to look for something more complicated—something more difficult, something we think we are expected to do to please God.

Jesus told us what to do to follow God's plan: Believe! My life is an example of the magnitude of God's ability to fulfill His plan in our lives, no matter how unlikely the possibility may seem, when we simply believe.

Think about the simple, uncomplicated approach a child has to life. Something that children seem to have in common is this: They are going to enjoy themselves if at all possible. They are carefree and completely without concern. They believe what they are told. Their nature is to trust unless they have had an experience that has taught them otherwise. They are simple, and they approach life with simplicity. We need to develop this aspect of childlikeness as we relate to God and as we go about our lives.

11 And why? Because I do not love you [do not have a preference for you, wish you well, and regard your welfare]? God perceives *and* knows that I do!

12 But what I do, I will continue to do, [for I am determined to maintain this independence] in order to cut off the claim of those who would like [to find an occasion and incentive] to claim that in their boasted [mission] they work on the same terms that we do.

13 For such men are false apostles [spurious, counterfeits], deceitful workmen, masquerading as apostles (special messengers) of Christ (the Messiah).

14 And it is no wonder, for Satan himself masquerades as an angel of light;

15 So it is not surprising if his servants also masquerade as ministers of righteousness. [But] their end will correspond with their deeds.

16 I repeat then, let no one think I have lost my wits; but even if you do, then bear with a witless man, so that I too may boast a little.

17 What I say by way of this confident boasting, I say not with the Lord's authority [by inspiration] but, as it were, in pure witlessness.

18 [For] since many boast of worldly things *and* according to the flesh, I will glory (boast) also.

19 For you readily *and* gladly bear with the foolish, since you are so smart *and* wise yourselves!

20 For you endure it if a man assumes control of your souls *and* makes slaves of you, or devours [your substance, spends your money] *and* preys upon you, or deceives *and* takes advantage of you, or is arrogant *and* puts on airs, or strikes you in the face.

21 To my discredit, I must say, we have shown ourselves too weak [for you to show such tolerance of us and for us to do strong, courageous things like that to you]! But in whatever any person is bold *and* dares [to boast]—

mind you, I am speaking in this foolish (witless) way—I also am bold *and* dare [to boast].

22 They are Hebrews? So am I! They are Israelites? So am I! They are descendants of Abraham? So am I!

23 Are they [ministering] servants of Christ (the Messiah)? I am talking like one beside himself, [but] I am more, with far more extensive *and* abundant labors, with far more imprisonments, [beaten] with countless stripes, and frequently [at the point of] death.

24 Five times I received from [the hands of] the Jews forty [lashes all] but one; [Deut. 25:3.]

25 Three times I have been beaten with rods; once I was stoned. Three times I have been aboard a ship wrecked at sea; a [whole] night and a day I have spent [adrift] on the deep;

26 Many times on journeys, [exposed to] perils from rivers, perils from bandits, perils from [my own] nation, perils from the Gentiles, perils in the city, perils in the desert places, perils in the sea, perils from those posing as believers [but destitute of Christian knowledge and piety];

27 In toil and hardship, watching often [through sleepless nights], in hunger and thirst, frequently driven to fasting by want, in cold and exposure *and* lack of clothing.

28 And besides those things that are without, there is the daily [inescapable pressure] of my care *and* anxiety for all the churches!

29 Who is weak, and I do not feel [his] weakness? Who is made to stumble *and* fall *and* have his faith hurt, and I am not on fire [with sorrow or indignation]?

30 If I must boast, I will boast of the things that [show] my infirmity [of the things by which I am made weak and contemptible in the eyes of my opponents].

31 The God and Father of the Lord Jesus *Christ* knows, He Who is blessed *and* to be praised forever-more, that I do not lie.

32 In Damascus, the city governor acting under King Aretas guarded the city of Damascus [on purpose] to arrest me,

33 And I was [actually] let down in a [rope] basket *or* hamper through a window (a small door) in the wall, and I escaped through his fingers.

12 TRUE, THERE is nothing to be gained by it, but [as I am obliged] to boast, I will go on to visions and revelations of the Lord.

2 I know a man in Christ who four-teen years ago—whether in the body or out of the body I do not know, God knows—was caught up to the third heaven.

3 And I know that this man—whether in the body or away from the body I do not know, God knows—

4 Was caught up into paradise, and he heard utterances beyond the power of man to put into words, which man is not permitted to utter.

5 Of this same [man's experiences] I will boast, but of myself (personally) I will not boast, except as regards my infirmities (my weaknesses).

6 Should I desire to boast, I shall not be a witless braggart, for I shall be speaking the truth. But I abstain [from it] so that no one may form a higher estimate of me than [is justified by] what he sees in me or hears from me.

7 And to keep me from being puffed up *and* too much elated by the exceeding greatness (preeminence) of these revelations, there was given me a thorn (ᵂa splinter) in the flesh, a messenger of Satan, to rack *and* buffet *and* harass me, to keep me from being excessively exalted. [Job. 2:6.]

8 Three times I called upon the Lord *and* besought [Him] about this *and* begged that it might depart from me;

9 But He said to me, My grace (My favor and loving-kindness and mercy) is enough for you [sufficient against any danger and enables you to bear the trouble manfully]; for *My* strength *and* power are made perfect (fulfilled and completed) *and* ˣshow themselves most effective in [your] weakness. Therefore, I will all the more gladly glory in my weaknesses *and* infirmi-ties, that the strength *and* power of Christ (the Messiah) may rest (yes, may ʸpitch a tent over and dwell) upon me!

life point

Jesus told Paul that His grace is sufficient for us; that His strength and power are made perfect in our weaknesses (see II Corinthians 12:9). We become frustrated when we try to achieve by *works* a life that God not only brought into being, but designed to be received by *grace*. Grace is the power of God to meet our needs and solve our problems.

10 So for the sake of Christ, I am well pleased *and* take pleasure in infirmi-ties, insults, hardships, persecutions, perplexities *and* distresses; for when I am weak [ᶻin human strength], then am I [truly] strong (able, powerful ᶻin divine strength).

11 Now I have been [speaking like] a fool! But you forced me to it, for I ought to have been [ʸsaved the neces-sity and] commended by you. For I have not fallen short one bit *or* proved myself at all inferior to those superla-tive [false] apostles [of yours], even if I am nothing (a nobody).

---

w James Moulton and George Milligan, *The Vocabulary of the Greek Testament.*　**x** Two Greek texts so read.　**y** Marvin Vincent, *Word Studies.*　**z** Joseph Thayer, *A Greek-English Lexicon.*

life point

Weakness is not very popular. Most people do not advertise their limitations. However, in II Corinthians 12:9, Paul says that he boasts in his weaknesses. Why? Because he knows that God's strength is great in the midst of his infirmity. Is there an area in your life where you feel weak? Do not try to rely on your own strength; ask God to be strong in your weakness. When you admit your frailty, God pours out His strength. Know that His grace is more than sufficient and thank God for His power that is made perfect in your weakness.

12 Indeed, the signs that indicate a [genuine] apostle were performed among you fully *and* most patiently in miracles and wonders and mighty works.

13 For in what respect were you put to a disadvantage in comparison with the rest of the churches, unless [it was for the fact] that I myself did not burden you [with my financial support]? Pardon me [for doing you] this injustice!

14 Now for the third time I am ready to come to [visit] you. And I will not burden you [financially], for it is not your [money] that I want but you; for children are not duty bound to lay up store for their parents, but parents for their children.

15 But I will most gladly spend [myself] and be utterly spent for your souls. If I love you exceedingly, am I to be loved [by you] the less?

16 But though granting that I did not burden you [with my support, some say that] I was crafty [and that] I cheated *and* got the better of you with my trickery.

17 Did I [then] take advantage of you *or* make any money out of you through any of those [messengers] whom I sent to you?

18 [Actually] I urged Titus [to go], and I sent the brother with [him]. Did Titus overreach *or* take advantage of you [in anything]? Did he *and* I not act in the same spirit? Did we not [take the] same steps?

19 Have you been supposing [all this time] that we have been defending ourselves *and* apologizing to you? [It is] in the sight *and* the [very] presence of God [and as one] in Christ (the Messiah) that we have been speaking, dearly beloved, and all in order to build you up [spiritually].

20 For I am fearful that somehow or other I may come and find you not as I desire to find you, and that you may find me too not as you want to find me—that perhaps there may be factions (quarreling), jealousy, temper (wrath, intrigues, rivalry, divided loyalties), selfishness, whispering, gossip, arrogance (self-assertion), and disorder among you.

21 [I am fearful] that when I come again, my God may humiliate *and* humble me in your regard, and that I may have to sorrow over many of those who sinned before and have not repented of the impurity, sexual vice, and sensuality which they formerly practiced.

13 THIS IS the third time that I am coming to you. By the testimony of two or three witnesses must any charge *and* every accusing statement be sustained *and* confirmed. [Deut. 19:15.]

2 I have already warned those who sinned formerly and all the rest also, and I warn them now again while I am absent, as I did when present on my second visit, that if I come back, I will not spare [them],

3 Since you desire *and* seek [perceptible] proof of the Christ Who speaks in *and* through me. [For He] is not weak *and* feeble in dealing with you, but is a mighty power within you;

4 For though He was crucified in weakness, yet He goes on living by the power of God. And though we too are weak in Him [as He was humanly weak], yet in dealing with you [we shall show ourselves] alive *and* strong in [fellowship with] Him by the power of God.

5 Examine *and* test *and* evaluate your own selves to see whether you are holding to your faith *and* showing the proper fruits of it. Test *and* prove yourselves [ᵃnot Christ]. Do you not yourselves realize *and* know [thoroughly by an ever-increasing experience] that Jesus Christ is in you—unless you are [counterfeits] disapproved on trial *and* rejected?

6 But I hope you will recognize *and* know that we are not disapproved on trial *and* rejected.

7 But I pray to God that you may do nothing wrong, not in order that we [ᵃour teaching] may appear to be approved, but that you may continue doing right, [though] we may seem to have failed *and* be unapproved.

8 For we can do nothing against the Truth [ᵇnot serve any party or personal interest], but only for the Truth [ᶜwhich is the Gospel].

9 For we are glad when we are weak (ᵃunapproved) and you are really strong. And this we also pray for: your all-round strengthening *and* perfecting of soul.

10 So I write these things while I am absent from you, that when I come to you, I may not have to deal sharply in my use of the authority which the Lord has given me [to be employed, however] for building [you] up and not for tearing [you] down.

11 Finally, brethren, farewell (rejoice)! Be strengthened (perfected, completed, made what you ought to

life point

Second Corinthians 13:5 tells us to examine ourselves, and I wholeheartedly agree that we need to do so. We should evaluate ourselves to see if we have sin in our lives or in our hearts, and if we do, we should sincerely repent, then move on to live without that sin in our lives.

There is a great difference between examination and condemnation. Examination shows us what is wrong in our behavior so we can admit it, ask for forgiveness, and go in a new direction. Allowing the Holy Spirit to guide us in proper self-examination will deliver us and set us free. Condemnation keeps us mired in the very sin we feel condemned about. Condemnation does not deliver us; it traps us! It weakens us and saps all our spiritual strength. We give our energy toward feeling condemned rather than living righteously.

be); be encouraged *and* consoled *and* comforted; be of the same [agreeable] mind one with another; live in peace, and [then] the God of love [Who is the Source of affection, goodwill, love, and benevolence toward men] and the Author *and* Promoter of peace will be with you.

12 Greet one another with a consecrated kiss.

13 All the saints (the people of God here) salute you.

14 The grace (favor and spiritual blessing) of the Lord Jesus Christ and the love of God and the presence *and* fellowship (the communion and sharing together, and participation) in the Holy Spirit be with you all. *Amen (so be it).*

a Marvin Vincent, *Word Studies.*　**b** James C. Gray and George M. Adams, *Bible Commentary.*　**c** Joseph Thayer, *A Greek-English Lexicon.*

Galatians

Author:
Paul

Date:
Approximately AD 53–57

Everyday Life Principles:
We approach God through grace, not through the Law.

Believers are to reject legalism and embrace God's grace in every area of life.

Walk in the Spirit, not in the flesh.

In Galatians, Paul addresses and emphasizes a subject that is very important to me and should be to all believers: the grace of God. Many people tend to approach God through the Law, which simply means doing what is right and obeying the "rules" of Christianity. This is called "legalism." Galatians teaches us that we approach God through grace—which is simply God's power at work in us, causing us to want to obey Him and enabling us to do so. Legalism teaches that we obey God out of obligation; grace teaches that we obey out of love. Legalism urges us to "act right" through works of the flesh, while grace enables us to "be right" by the power of the Holy Spirit.

Throughout the short but life-changing letter of Galatians, you will find encouragement to live and walk "in the Spirit." Only as you invite the Holy Spirit into your life and ask Him to help you in every situation will you truly be able to live in a way that pleases God. Without the Holy Spirit's help and enablement, all of us are left to live as best we can in our own strength. With His help, we can relax, stop striving, and enjoy life.

As you read Galatians, I pray that God's awesome grace becomes more and more real to you and that you will be able to live in God's grace and walk in the power of the Holy Spirit for the rest of your life.

1 PAUL, AN apostle—[special messenger appointed and commissioned and sent out] not from [any body of] men nor by *or* through [a]any man, but by *and* through Jesus Christ (the Messiah) and God the Father, Who raised Him from among the dead—

---

putting the Word to work

Have you ever thought that God could not or would not use you because of your past?

No one was more likely to feel that way than the apostle Paul, who tried to destroy the early church. However, Paul received God's forgiveness and recognized that it was God who gave him his ministry and authority (see Galatians 1:1). No matter what your past, God wants to use you too.

---

2 And all the brethren who are with me, to the churches of Galatia:

3 Grace *and* spiritual blessing be to you and [soul] peace from God the Father and our Lord Jesus Christ (the Messiah),

4 Who gave (yielded) Himself up [[a]to atone] for our sins [and [a]to save and sanctify us], in order to rescue *and* deliver us from this present wicked age *and* world order, in accordance with the will *and* purpose *and* plan of our God and Father—

5 To Him [be ascribed all] the glory through all the ages of the ages *and* the eternities of the eternities! Amen (so be it).

6 I am surprised *and* astonished that you are so quickly [b]turning renegade *and* deserting Him Who invited *and* called you [a]by the grace (unmerited favor) of Christ (the Messiah) [and that you are transferring your allegiance] to a different [even an opposition] gospel.

7 Not that there is [or could be] any other [genuine Gospel], but there are [obviously] some who are troubling *and* disturbing *and* bewildering you [[a]with a different kind of teaching which they offer as a gospel] and want to pervert *and* distort the Gospel of Christ (the Messiah) [into something which it absolutely is not].

8 But even if we or an angel from heaven should preach to you a gospel contrary to *and* different from that which we preached to you, let him be accursed (anathema, devoted to destruction, doomed to eternal punishment)!

9 As we said before, so I now say again: If anyone is preaching to you a gospel different from *or* contrary to that which you received [from us], let him be accursed (anathema, devoted to destruction, doomed to eternal punishment)!

10 Now am I trying to win the favor of men, or of God? Do I seek to please men? If I were still seeking popularity with men, I should not be a bond servant of Christ (the Messiah).

11 For I want you to know, brethren, that the Gospel which was proclaimed *and* made known by me is not man's gospel [a human invention, according to or patterned after any human standard].

life point

The apostle Paul said in Galatians 1:10 that if he wanted to be popular with people, he would not be a servant of the Lord Jesus Christ. Basically, Paul says that needing people's approval in an unbalanced way can steal our destinies. We cannot always be God-pleasers and people-pleasers at the same time.

---

a Marvin Vincent, *Word Studies in the New Testament.* **b** Joseph P. Lightfoot, *Notes on the Epistles of Saint Paul.*

12 For indeed I did not receive it from man, nor was I taught it, but [it came to me] through a [direct] revelation [given] by Jesus Christ (the Messiah).

13 You have heard of my earlier career *and* former manner of life in the Jewish religion (Judaism), how I persecuted *and* abused the church of God furiously *and* extensively, and [with fanatical zeal did my best] to make havoc of it *and* destroy it.

14 And [you have heard how] I outstripped many of the men of my own generation among the people of my race in [my advancement in study and observance of the laws of] Judaism, so extremely enthusiastic *and* zealous I was for the traditions of my ancestors.

15 But when He, Who had chosen *and* set me apart [even] before I was born and had called me by His grace (His undeserved favor and blessing), saw fit *and* was pleased [Isa. 49:1; Jer. 1:5.]

16 To reveal (unveil, disclose) His Son within me so that I might proclaim Him among the Gentiles (the non-Jewish world) as the glad tidings (Gospel), immediately I did not confer with flesh and blood [did not consult or counsel with any frail human being or communicate with anyone].

17 Nor did I [even] go up to Jerusalem to those who were apostles (special messengers of Christ) before I was, but I went away *and* retired into Arabia, and afterward I came back again to Damascus.

18 Then three years later, I did go up to Jerusalem to become [personally] acquainted with Cephas (Peter), and remained with him for fifteen days.

19 But I did not see any of the other apostles (the special messengers of Christ) except James the brother of our Lord.

20 Now [note carefully what I am telling you, for it is the truth], I write this as if I were standing before the bar of God; I do not lie.

life point

Paul says in Galatians 1:15, 16 that when he was called by God to preach the Gospel to the Gentiles, he did not discuss the matter with anyone else.

Many times when we receive a message from God, we confer too much with flesh and blood. We go around looking for someone to assure us that we are doing the right thing. What we need to do is believe John 14:17, which tells us that we have the Holy Spirit, the Spirit of Truth, within us. But since we have invited the Spirit of Truth to guide us, should we always shun advice from others? No, the writer of Proverbs says, " . . . in the multitude of counselors there is safety" (Proverbs 11:14). Like many other things, this is an area in which we need balance. We can and should be open to receive advice from those who are wiser and more experienced than we are in an area, but we should not depend so much on what people say that we fail to listen to God Himself.

21 Then I went into the districts (countries, regions) of Syria and Cilicia.

22 And so far I was still unknown by sight to the churches of Christ in Judea (the country surrounding Jerusalem).

23 They were only hearing it said, He who used to persecute us is now proclaiming the very faith he once reviled *and* which he set out to ruin *and* tried with all his might to destroy.

24 And they glorified God [as the Author and Source of what had taken place] in me.

2 THEN AFTER [an interval] of fourteen years I again went up to Jerusalem. [This time I went]

how to handle God's call

Paul said that he kept the news of his calling to himself; he did not check it out with "the big guys" who were supposed to hear from God (see Galatians 1:15–19). He knew what God did with him on that road to Damascus. He knew that he was changed forever (see Acts 9:3–8). He knew that the Son of God was unveiled and disclosed on the inside of him. He knew he could never go back to the life he had lived. He knew that for the rest of his life he would preach the Gospel and remain faithful to what he heard Jesus say to him.

But Paul also had the wisdom to know people would find his calling unbelievable. So he waited on God. He did not go running around checking with the other apostles, saying, "Hey guys, I saw a light on the road and fell down, and this happened and that happened. What do you all think?" Instead, he went to Arabia, and then came back to Damascus. Three years after that, he traveled to Jerusalem to become acquainted with Peter, but did not see any of the other apostles except James.

Paul kept God's Word in his heart and let it grow and manifest on its own. Then he started doing what he was called to do. Soon others recognized that the calling on him must have been from God. What was the result? Galatians 1:24 tells us that the people glorified God as the "Author and Source" of what had taken place in Paul.

Has God given you a calling to serve Him? As you stay in His Word and wait on Him, you will see growth in your life and receptivity to the message God gives you.

with Barnabas, taking Titus along with [me] also.
2 I went because it was specially *and* divinely revealed to me that I should go, and I put before them the Gospel [declaring to them that] which I preach among the Gentiles. However, [I presented the matter] privately before those of repute, [for I wanted to make certain, by thus at first confining my communication to this private conference] that I was not running or had not run in vain [guarding against being discredited either in what I was planning to do or had already done].
3 But [all went well!] even Titus, who was with me, was not compelled [as some had anticipated] to be cir-cumcised, although he was a Greek.
4 [My precaution was] because of false brethren who had been secretly smuggled in [to the Christian brotherhood]; they had slipped in to spy on our liberty *and* the freedom which we have in Christ Jesus, that they might again bring us into bondage [under the Law of Moses].
5 To them we did not yield submission even for a moment, that the truth of the Gospel might continue to be [preserved] for you [in its purity].
6 Moreover, [no new requirements were made] by those who were reputed to be something—though what was their individual position *and* whether they really were of importance or not makes no difference to me; God is not

impressed with the positions that men hold *and* He is not partial *and* recognizes no external distinctions—those [I say] who were of repute imposed no new requirements upon me [had nothing to add to my Gospel, and from them I received no new suggestions]. [Deut. 10:17.]

7 But on the contrary, when they [really] saw that I had been entrusted [to carry] the Gospel to the uncircumcised [Gentiles, just as definitely] as Peter had been entrusted [to proclaim] the Gospel to the circumcised [Jews, they were agreeable];

8 For He Who motivated *and* fitted Peter *and* worked effectively through him for the mission to the circumcised, motivated *and* fitted me *and* worked through me also for [the mission to] the Gentiles.

9 And when they knew (perceived, recognized, understood, and acknowledged) the grace (God's unmerited favor and spiritual blessing) that had been bestowed upon me, James and Cephas (Peter) and John, who were reputed to be pillars of the Jerusalem church, gave to me and Barnabas the right hand of fellowship, with the understanding that we should go to the Gentiles and they to the circumcised (Jews).

10 They only [made one stipulation], that we were to remember the poor, which very thing I was also eager to do.

11 But when Cephas (Peter) came to Antioch, I protested *and* opposed him to his face [concerning his conduct there], for he was blameable *and* stood condemned.

12 For up to the time that certain persons came from James, he ate his meals with the Gentile [converts]; but when the men [from Jerusalem] arrived, he withdrew *and* held himself aloof from the Gentiles and [ate] separately for fear of those of the circumcision [party].

13 And the rest of the Jews along with him also concealed their true convictions *and* acted insincerely, with the result that even Barnabas was carried away by their hypocrisy (their example of insincerity and pretense).

14 But as soon as I saw that they were not straightforward *and* were not living up to the truth of the Gospel, I said to Cephas (Peter) before everybody present, If you, though born a Jew, can live [as you have been living] like a Gentile and not like a Jew, how do you dare now to urge *and* practically force the Gentiles to [comply with the ritual of Judaism and] live like Jews?

15 [I went on to say] Although we ourselves (you and I) are Jews by birth and not Gentile (heathen) sinners,

16 Yet we know that a man is justified *or* reckoned righteous *and* in right standing with God not by works of the Law, but [only] through faith *and* [absolute] reliance on *and* adherence to *and* trust in Jesus Christ (the Messiah, the Anointed One). [Therefore] even we [ourselves] have believed on Christ Jesus, in order to be justified by faith in Christ and not by works of the Law [for we cannot be justified by any observance of the ritual of the Law given by Moses], because by keeping legal rituals *and* by works no human being can ever be justified (declared righteous and put in right standing with God). [Ps. 143:2.]

17 But if, in our desire *and* endeavor to be justified in Christ [to be declared

speak the Word

righteous and put in right standing with God wholly and solely through Christ], we have shown ourselves sinners also *and* convicted of sin, does that make Christ a minister (a party and contributor) to our sin? Banish the thought! [Of course not!]

18 For if I [or any others who have taught that the observance of the Law of Moses is not essential to being justified by God should now by word or practice teach or intimate that it is essential to] build up again what I tore down, I prove myself a transgressor.

19 For I through the Law [under the operation of the curse of the Law] have [in Christ's death for me] myself died to the Law *and* all the Law's demands upon me, so that I may [henceforth] live to *and* for God.

20 I have been crucified with Christ [in Him I have shared His crucifixion]; it is no longer I who live, but Christ (the Messiah) lives in me; and the life I now live in the body I live by faith in (by adherence to and reliance on and complete trust in) the Son of God, Who loved me and gave Himself up for me.

21 [Therefore, I do not treat God's gracious gift as something of minor importance and defeat its very purpose]; I do not set aside *and* invalidate *and* frustrate *and* nullify the grace (unmerited favor) of God. For if justification (righteousness, acquittal from guilt) comes through [observing the ritual of] the Law, then Christ (the Messiah) died groundlessly *and* to no purpose *and* in vain. [His death was then wholly superfluous.]

3 O YOU poor *and* silly *and* thoughtless *and* unreflecting *and* senseless Galatians! Who has fascinated *or* bewitched *or* cast a spell over you, unto whom—right before your very eyes—Jesus Christ (the Messiah) was openly *and* graphically set forth *and* portrayed as crucified?

2 Let me ask you this one question: Did you receive the [Holy] Spirit as the result of obeying the Law *and* doing its works, or was it by hearing [the message of the Gospel] and believing [it]? [Was it from observing a law of rituals or from a message of faith?]

3 Are you so foolish *and* so senseless *and* so silly? Having begun [your new life spiritually] with the [Holy] Spirit, are you now reaching perfection [by dependence] on the flesh?

life point

In Galatians 3:2–4, Paul asked the Galatians why they were trying to reach perfection by depending upon the flesh. He urged them to remember that entirely new spiritual lives were given birth because of faith and leaning on the Holy Spirit. Therefore, he asked, why did they need to try to reach perfection any way other than the way they began?

He concluded by telling them that if they did not stop this type of legalistic behavior, everything they had suffered would be in vain and accomplish no purpose.

I don't know about you, but I have come too far and gone through too much to mess it all up now. I want to know the right way to approach God, and as far as I can see in His Word, that is through faith in what Jesus has done, not faith in what I can do.

We cannot live as victorious Christians without knowing these things. We cannot succeed without stepping out in *faith*, not in our *works*. If we believe our acceptance is based on our doing, we will always feel rejected when we fail to do the right thing. But if we see that our acceptance is based on what God has done, we will truly be free.

4　Have you suffered so many things *and* experienced so much all for nothing (to no purpose)—if it really is to no purpose *and* in vain?

5　Then does He Who supplies you with His marvelous [Holy] Spirit and works powerfully *and* miraculously among you do so on [the grounds of your doing] what the Law demands, or because of your believing in *and* adhering to *and* trusting in *and* relying on the message that you heard?

6　Thus Abraham believed in *and* adhered to *and* trusted in *and* relied on God, and it was reckoned *and* placed to his account *and* credited as righteousness (as conformity to the divine will in purpose, thought, and action). [Gen. 15:6.]

7　Know *and* understand that it is [really] the people [who live] by faith who are [the true] sons of Abraham.

8　And the Scripture, foreseeing that God would justify (declare righteous, put in right standing with Himself) the Gentiles in consequence of faith,

do your part

Before we can enjoy any real victory over sin and experience change in our behavior, we must learn that only God can change us (see Galatians 3:2–5). We cannot perfect ourselves and when we try to do so, we only become very frustrated. God has called us to perfection and has given us perfect hearts, but the working out of it is a process that takes faith, patience, and time. As we face truth, admit our faults, and place our faith in God to change us we will see results, but we must trust His timing. Things do not always happen when we think they should.

We are partners with God and we do have a part to play. Our part is to believe and obey any specific instruction God might give us; His part is to work the good thing He has placed inside of us to the outside of us where it can be seen and enjoyed by others and ourselves. When we get into "works of the flesh" (our energy trying to do God's job) we get frustrated. God Himself frustrates, opposes, and defeats us until we humble ourselves and lean entirely on Him (see I Peter 5:5). It took a long time, but I finally learned that every time I felt frustrated I had stopped trusting God and started trusting myself to accomplish whatever needed to be done at the time.

We received Christ totally by faith and that is the same way we must live our lives. We realize that we need to change and frequently become very disappointed with ourselves—even feel condemned—when we do not. We are much better off to put all the energy we use trying to change ourselves into prayer and trust God to do what needs to be done.

By faith God is working in you and you will see wonderful changes, but you must turn the project of your perfection over to Him entirely. Let God be God in your life! Instead of saying, "I'll never change," say, "God is working in me as I trust Him, and I believe I am getting better and better every day. God is strengthening me in my weaknesses and helping me overcome bad habits."

proclaimed the Gospel [foretelling the glad tidings of a Savior long beforehand] to Abraham in the promise, saying, In you shall all the nations [of the earth] be blessed. [Gen. 12:3.]

9 So then, those who are people of faith are blessed *and* made happy *and* favored by God [as partners in fellowship] with the believing *and* trusting Abraham.

10 And all who depend on the Law [who are seeking to be justified by obedience to the Law of rituals] are under a curse *and* doomed to disappointment *and* destruction, for it is written in the Scriptures, Cursed (accursed, devoted to destruction, doomed to eternal punishment) be everyone who does not continue to abide (live and remain) by all the precepts *and* commands written in the Book of the Law and to practice them. [Deut. 27:26.]

11 Now it is evident that no person is justified (declared righteous and brought into right standing with God) through the Law, for the Scripture says, The man in right standing with God [the just, the righteous] shall live by *and* out of faith *and* he who through *and* by faith is declared righteous *and* in right standing with God shall live. [Hab. 2:4.]

12 But the Law does not rest on faith [does not require faith, has nothing to do with faith], for it itself says, He who does them [the things prescribed by the Law] shall live by them [not by faith]. [Lev. 18:5.]

13 Christ purchased our freedom [redeeming us] from the curse (doom) of the Law [and its condemnation] by [Himself] becoming a curse for us, for it is written [in the Scriptures], Cursed is everyone who hangs on a tree (is crucified); [Deut. 21:23.]

14 To the end that through [their receiving] Christ Jesus, the blessing [promised] to Abraham might come upon the Gentiles, so that we through faith might [all] receive [the realization of] the promise of the [Holy] Spirit.

15 To speak in terms of human relations, brethren, [if] even a man makes a last will and testament (a merely human covenant), no one sets it aside *or* makes it void *or* adds to it when once it has been drawn up *and* signed (ratified, confirmed).

16 Now the promises (covenants, agreements) were decreed *and* made to Abraham and his Seed (his Offspring, his Heir). He [God] does not say, And to seeds (descendants, heirs), as if referring to many persons, but, And to your Seed (your Descendant, your Heir), obviously referring to one individual, Who is [none other than] Christ (the Messiah). [Gen. 13:15; 17:8.]

17 This is my argument: The Law, which began 430 years after the covenant [concerning the coming Messiah], does not *and* cannot annul the covenant previously established (ratified) by God, so as to abolish the promise *and* make it void. [Exod. 12:40.]

18 For if the inheritance [of the promise depends on observing] the Law [as these false teachers would like you to believe], it no longer [depends] on the promise; however, God gave it to Abraham [as a free gift solely] by virtue of His promise.

19 What then was the purpose of the Law? It was added [later on, after the promise, to disclose and expose to

speak the Word

life point

Galatians 3:16 refers to Jesus Christ as the "Seed." I like that, because it means that if I have a seed, I can have a harvest.

Jesus is the Seed of everything good that God desires for us to have. God plants the Seed, but it must be cultivated, nurtured, watered, and cared for. The ground in which it is planted must be kept plowed up and weed-free.

Our hearts and lives are the ground. Everything that needs to be changed or removed is not taken care of all at once. There is a great work to be done, and only the Holy Spirit knows the proper "when and how." As He deals with us about certain issues, we are to submit to Him our wills, which means submitting the flesh to the leadership of the Spirit. It is not all easy, but it is definitely worth it. Going through change is hard, but staying in bondage is even more difficult.

men their guilt] because of transgressions *and* [to make men more conscious of the sinfulness] of sin; and it was intended to be in effect until the Seed (the Descendant, the Heir) should come, to *and* concerning Whom the promise had been made. And it [the Law] was arranged *and* ordained *and* appointed through the instrumentality of angels [and was given] by the hand (in the person) of a go-between [Moses, an intermediary person between God and man].

20 Now a go-between (intermediary) has to do with *and* implies more than one party [there can be no mediator with just one person]. Yet God is [only] one Person [and He was the sole party in giving that promise to Abraham. But the Law was a contract between two, God and Israel; its validity was dependent on both].

21 Is the Law then contrary *and* opposed to the promises of God? Of course not! For if a Law had been given which could confer [spiritual] life, then righteousness *and* right standing with God would certainly have come by Law.

22 But the Scriptures [picture all mankind as sinners] shut up *and* imprisoned by sin, so that [the inheritance, blessing] which was promised through faith in Jesus Christ (the Messiah) might be given (released, delivered, and committed) to [all] those who believe [who adhere to and trust in and rely on Him].

23 Now before the faith came, we were perpetually guarded under the Law, kept in custody in preparation for the faith that was destined to be revealed (unveiled, disclosed),

24 So that the Law served c[to us Jews] as our trainer [our guardian, our guide to Christ, to lead us] until Christ [came], that we might be justified (declared righteous, put in right standing with God) by *and* through faith.

25 But now that the faith has come, we are no longer under a trainer (the guardian of our childhood).

26 For in Christ Jesus you are all sons of God through faith.

27 For as many [of you] as were baptized into Christ [into a spiritual union and communion with Christ, the Anointed One, the Messiah] have put on (clothed yourselves with) Christ.

28 There is [now no distinction] neither Jew nor Greek, there is neither slave nor free, there is not male dand female; for you are all one in Christ Jesus.

29 And if you belong to Christ [are in Him Who is Abraham's Seed], then

c Marvin Vincent, *Word Studies*.   d Literal translation.

life point

Galatians 3:28 teaches that we "are all one in Christ Jesus." But, as long as time has existed, Satan has breathed life into the poisonous practice of one race or group of people being prejudiced against another. Most wars are birthed out of prejudice and hatred. The Holocaust came from that same poison, as did slavery. Even various religious sects have hated one another and allowed the spirit of pride to fill their hearts.

Hatred has existed since the beginning of humanity. Adam's son, Cain, hated his brother Abel so much that he killed him (see Genesis 4:2–8), and it seems hatred has never stopped since then. Hating people is hard work, and it kills everything good in life.

You and I may not agree with everything another person believes or does, but we have no right to hate him because of it, and we certainly should not mistreat him.

God hates sin, but He loves every sinner. He hates stubbornness and rebellion, but still loves the person who is stubborn and rebellious. He has not told us we have to approve of everyone's beliefs, choices, and actions, but He has told us to love everyone.

putting the Word to work

Have you ever been discriminated against? It is a painful experience. There is no room for discrimination in the body of Christ; rather, we are called to unity in Christ Jesus (see Galatians 3:28). Ask God to reveal to you any prejudice that may linger in your heart or mind. Repent of it, and ask God to help you bring unity where there is division around you.

you are Abraham's offspring and [spiritual] heirs according to promise.

4 NOW WHAT I mean is that as long as the inheritor (heir) is a child and under age, he does not differ from a slave, although he is the master of all the estate;

2   But he is under guardians and administrators *or* trustees until the date fixed by his father.

3   So we [Jewish Christians] also, when we were minors, were kept like slaves under [the rules of the Hebrew ritual and subject to] the elementary teachings of a system of external observations *and* regulations.

4   But when the proper time had fully come, God sent His Son, born of a woman, born subject to [the regulations of] the Law,

5   To purchase the freedom of (to ransom, to redeem, to [e]atone for) those who were subject to the Law, that we might be adopted *and* have sonship conferred upon us [and be recognized as God's sons].

6   And because you [really] are [His] sons, God has sent the [[f]Holy] Spirit of His Son into our hearts, crying, Abba (Father)! Father!

7   Therefore, you are no longer a slave (bond servant) but a son; and if a son, then [it follows that you are] an heir [g]by the aid of God, *through Christ.*

8   But at that previous time, when you had not come to be acquainted with *and* understand *and* know the true God, you [Gentiles] were in bondage to gods who by their very nature could not be gods at all [gods that really did not exist].

e *Webster's New International Dictionary* offers this as a definition of "redeem."   f Marvin Vincent, *Word Studies.*   g Joseph Thayer, *A Greek-English Lexicon of the New Testament.*

9 Now, however, that you have come to be acquainted with *and* understand *and* know [the true] God, or rather to be understood *and* known by God, how can you turn back again to the weak and beggarly *and* worthless elementary things [ʰof all religions before Christ came], whose slaves you once more want to become?

10 You observe [particular] days and months and seasons and years!

11 I am alarmed [about you], lest I have labored among *and* over you to no purpose *and* in vain.

12 Brethren, I beg of you, become as I am [free from the bondage of Jewish ritualism and ordinances], for I also have become as you are [ⁱa Gentile]. You did me no wrong [ⁱin the days when I first came to you; do not do it now].

13 On the contrary, you know that it was on account of a bodily ailment that [I remained and] preached the Gospel to you the first time.

14 And [yet] although my physical condition was [such] a trial to you, you did not regard it with contempt, or scorn *and* loathe *and* reject me; but you received me as an angel of God, [even] as Christ Jesus [Himself]!

15 What has become of that blessed enjoyment *and* satisfaction *and* self-congratulation that once was yours [in what I taught you and in your regard for me]? For I bear you witness that you would have torn out your own eyes and have given them to me [to replace mine], if that were possible.

16 Have I then become your enemy by telling the truth to you *and* dealing sincerely with you?

17 These men [the Judaizing teachers] are zealously trying to dazzle you [paying court to you, making much of you], but their purpose is not honorable *or* worthy *or* for any good. What they want to do is to isolate you [from us who oppose them], so that they may win you over to their side *and* get you to court their favor.

18 It is always a fine thing [of course] to be zealously sought after [as you are, provided that it is] for a good purpose *and* done ʰby reason of purity of heart and life, and not just when I am present with you!

19 My little children, for whom I am again suffering birth pangs until Christ is completely *and* permanently formed (molded) within you,

20 Would that I were with you now and could coax you vocally, for I am fearful *and* perplexed about you!

21 Tell me, you who are bent on being under the Law, will you listen to what the Law [really] says?

22 For it is written that Abraham had two sons, one by the bondmaid and one by the free woman. [Gen. 16:15; 21:2, 9.]

23 But whereas the child of the slave woman was born according to the flesh *and* had an ordinary birth, the son of the free woman was born in fulfillment of the promise.

24 Now all this is an allegory; these [two women] represent two covenants. One covenant originated from Mount Sinai [where the Law was given] and bears [children destined] for slavery; this is Hagar.

speak the Word

Thank You, God, for making me Your child and sending the Holy Spirit into my heart to cry out, "Father" and to help me understand what it means to belong to You.
ADAPTED FROM GALATIANS 4:6

h Joseph Thayer, *A Greek-English Lexicon of the New Testament.* **i** Marvin Vincent, *Word Studies.*

life point

In Galatians 4:24–31, the Bible speaks about two covenants, describing two ways in which we live.

The first way we choose to live is by works of our own flesh. We take care of ourselves; we make our own plans and struggle to make things happen our way, in our timing. This describes the natural way, the "normal" way most people live. It is a way that produces every kind of misery. We struggle, get frustrated, fail, and end up weary and worn-out most of the time. We are confused and defeated, and have no peace or joy.

The second way we can live is supernaturally, by the power of God. We live by faith, trusting God to do what needs to be done in our lives. This way is described in the Bible as a new and living way (see Hebrews 10:20). This new way produces peace, joy, ease, and success.

25 Now Hagar is (stands for) Mount Sinai in Arabia and she corresponds to and belongs in the same category with the present Jerusalem, for she is in bondage together with her children.
26 But the Jerusalem above ([ʲthe Messianic kingdom of Christ) is free, and she is our mother.
27 For it is written in the Scriptures, Rejoice, O barren woman, who has not given birth to children; break forth into a joyful shout, you who are not feeling birth pangs, for the desolate woman has many more children than she who has a husband. [Isa. 54:1.]
28 But we, brethren, are children [ʲnot by physical descent, as was Ishmael, but] like Isaac, born ʲin virtue of promise.

29 Yet [just] as at that time the child [of ordinary birth] born according to the flesh despised and persecuted him [who was born remarkably] according to [the promise and the working of] the [Holy] Spirit, so it is now also. [Gen. 21:9.]
30 But what does the Scripture say? Cast out and send away the slave woman and her son, for never shall the son of the slave woman be heir and share the inheritance with the son of the free woman. [Gen. 21:10.]
31 So, brethren, we [who are born again] are not children of a slave woman [ᵏthe natural], but of the free [ᵏthe supernatural].

5 IN [this] freedom Christ has made us free [and completely liberated us]; stand fast then, and do not be hampered and held ensnared and submit again to a yoke of slavery [which you have once put off].
2 Notice, it is I, Paul, who tells you that if you receive circumcision, Christ will be of no profit (advantage, avail) to you [ˡfor if you distrust Him, you can gain nothing from Him].
3 I once more protest and testify to every man who receives circumcision that he is under obligation and bound to practice the whole of the Law and its ordinances.
4 If you seek to be justified and declared righteous and to be given a right standing with God through the Law, you are brought to nothing and so separated (severed) from Christ. You have fallen away from grace (from God's gracious favor and unmerited blessing).
5 For we, [not relying on the Law but] through the [Holy] Spirit's [help], by faith anticipate and wait for the blessing and good for which our righteousness

---

j Marvin Vincent, *Word Studies*.　k Joseph S. Exell, ed., *The Biblical Illustrator*.　l John Chrysostom, one of the Doctors of the Greek Church.

and right standing with God [our [m]conformity to His will in purpose, thought, and action, causes us] to hope.

6 For [if we are] in Christ Jesus, neither circumcision nor uncircumcision counts for anything, but only faith activated *and* energized *and* expressed *and* working through love.

7 You were running the race nobly. Who has interfered in (hindered and stopped you from) your heeding *and* following the Truth?

8 This [evil] persuasion is not from Him Who called you [Who invited you to freedom in Christ].

9 A little leaven (a slight inclination to error, or a few false teachers) leavens the whole lump [it perverts the whole conception of faith or misleads the whole church].

10 [For my part] I have confidence [toward you] in the Lord that you will take no contrary view of the matter *but* will come to think with me. But he who is unsettling you, whoever he is, will have to bear the penalty.

11 But, brethren, if I still preach circumcision [as some accuse me of doing, as necessary to salvation], why am I still suffering persecution? In that case the cross has ceased to be a stumbling block *and* is made meaningless (done away).

12 I wish those who unsettle *and* confuse you would [[n]go all the way and] cut themselves off!

13 For you, brethren, were [indeed] called to freedom; only [do not let your] freedom be an incentive to your flesh *and* an opportunity *or* excuse [for [n]selfishness], but through love you should serve one another.

speak the Word

14 For the whole Law [concerning human relationships] is [n]complied with in the one precept, You shall love your neighbor as [you do] yourself. [Lev. 19:18.]

15 But if you bite and devour one another [in partisan strife], be careful that you [and your whole fellowship] are not consumed by one another.

16 But I say, walk *and* live [habitually] in the [Holy] Spirit [responsive to *and* controlled *and* guided by the Spirit]; then you will certainly not gratify the cravings *and* desires of the flesh (of human nature without God).

17 For the desires of the flesh are opposed to the [Holy] Spirit, and the [desires of the] Spirit are opposed to the flesh (godless human nature); for these are antagonistic to each other [continually withstanding and in conflict with each other], so that you are not free *but* are prevented from doing what you desire to do.

18 But if you are guided (led) by the [Holy] Spirit, you are not subject to the Law.

19 Now the doings (practices) of the

m G. Abbott-Smith, *Manual Greek Lexicon of the New Testament.* **n** Marvin Vincent, *Word Studies.*

choose life in the Spirit

Paul said we should choose to walk and live in the Spirit, and by making that choice, we will not fulfill the lusts of the flesh that continually tempt us (see Galatians 5:16).

There are many things available to lead us—people, the devil and his demons, the flesh (our own bodies, minds, wills, emotions), and the Holy Spirit. There are many voices in the world that speak to us, often several at the same time. It is imperative that we learn to be led by the Holy Spirit, to be "responsive to and controlled and guided by the Spirit," as Galatians 5:16 says. Remember: The Holy Spirit is the One Who knows the will of God and Who is sent to dwell in each of us to aid us in being all God has designed us to be and to have all God wants us to have.

It is important for us to see that the Holy Spirit lives in each of us to help us. When we allow the Holy Spirit to lead us, He becomes involved in every decision we make—both major and minor. He leads us by peace and by wisdom, as well as by the Word of God. He speaks in a still, small voice in our hearts, or what we often call "the inward witness." Those of us who desire leading by the Holy Spirit must learn to follow the inward witness and to respond quickly.

For example, if we are engaged in a conversation and we begin feeling uncomfortable inside, that inner discomfort may be the Holy Spirit signaling that we need to turn the conversation in another direction or be quiet. If we are about to purchase something, and we feel uncomfortable inside, we should wait and discern why we are uncomfortable. Perhaps we do not need the item, or we may find it on sale somewhere else, or we may be trying to purchase it at the wrong time. Remember, we do not always have to know why; we just need to obey the Spirit's leading to find peace and contentment in our daily living.

flesh are clear (obvious): they are immorality, impurity, indecency,

20 Idolatry, sorcery, enmity, strife, jealousy, anger (ill temper), selfishness, divisions (dissensions), party spirit (factions, sects with peculiar opinions, heresies),

21 Envy, drunkenness, carousing, and the like. I warn you beforehand, just as I did previously, that those who do such things shall not inherit the kingdom of God.

22 But the fruit of the [Holy] Spirit [the work which His presence within accomplishes] is love, joy (gladness), peace, patience (an even temper, forbearance), kindness, goodness (benevolence), faithfulness,

23 Gentleness (meekness, humility), self-control (self-restraint, continence). Against such things there is no law [°that can bring a charge].

24 And those who belong to Christ Jesus (the Messiah) have crucified the flesh (the godless human nature) with its passions and appetites *and* desires.

25 If we live by the [Holy] Spirit, let

o Marvin Vincent, *Word Studies.*

life point

Galatians 5:19–23 gives us a list of sins of the flesh and a list of the fruit of the Spirit, or as *The Amplified Bible* reads in verse 22, "the work which His presence within accomplishes." I really like that way of saying it. The fruit of the Holy Spirit are qualities we see in Jesus Himself: love, joy, peace, patience, kindness, goodness, faithfulness, gentleness, and self-control. This is the goal of the Holy One living within us, to produce or accomplish this fruit in our lives—big, luscious fruit for everyone to see and admire.

Love is the everlasting fruit that will not fade away. To bear fruit we must abide in God's love—to stay alert to His love for us, to dwell in His love by loving others, and to endure testing by responding to trials with love.

---

us also walk by the Spirit. [If by the Holy Spirit ᵖwe have our life in God, let us go forward �q walking in line, our conduct controlled by the Spirit.]
26 Let us not become vainglorious *and* self-conceited, competitive *and* challenging *and* provoking *and* irritating to one another, envying *and* being jealous of one another.

6 BRETHREN, IF any person is overtaken in misconduct *or* sin of any sort, you who are spiritual [who are responsive to and controlled by the Spirit] should set him right *and* restore *and* reinstate him, without any sense of superiority *and* with all gentleness, keeping an attentive eye on yourself, lest you should be tempted also.
2 Bear (endure, carry) one anoth-

life point

Galatians 6:1–3 quickly reveals how we should respond to the weakness we observe in others. It sets forth the mental attitude we are to maintain within ourselves. We must have a "holy fear" of pride and be very careful of judging others or of being critical of them.

---

er's burdens *and* ʳtroublesome moral faults, and in this way fulfill *and* observe perfectly the law of Christ (the Messiah) *and* complete �q what is lacking [in your obedience to it].
3 For if any person thinks himself to be somebody [too important to condescend to shoulder another's load] when he is nobody [of superiority except in his own estimation], he deceives *and* deludes *and* cheats himself.
4 But let every person carefully scrutinize *and* examine *and* test his own conduct *and* his own work. He can then have the personal satisfaction *and* joy of doing something commendable [�q in itself alone] without [resorting to] boastful comparison with his neighbor.
5 For every person will have to bear

life point

Paul says in Galatians 6:2 that we must learn to get along with each other. We are going to have to learn to put up with some things we do not like. All the people around us are not going to think and speak and act the way we want them to. But forgiving them is part of what we must do as members of the body of Christ. Not everyone is going to be or do what we want, but we can forgive them and love them anyway.

---

p Adam Clarke, *The Holy Bible with A Commentary*.   **q** Marvin Vincent, *Word Studies*.   **r** Joseph Thayer, *A Greek-English Lexicon*.

true love

We can move into the blessed, exceptional type of life we truly desire through developing the character qualities of the fruit of the Spirit listed in Galatians 5:22, 23. When we as Christians know what God has available for us and are open to receiving from Him, His Spirit gives us the power we need to develop the fruit and live the type of life God wants for us.

God gives us various gifts to *use,* but He gives us the fruit of the Spirit to *develop.* When the Holy Spirit lives inside us, we have everything He has. His fruit is in us. The seed is planted. In order to use the gifts in the most powerful way that God desires, we must allow the seed of the fruit to grow up and mature in us by cultivating it. The gifts of the Spirit must be accompanied by the fruit of the Spirit to get the best results.

We can cultivate all the fruit by focusing on love, the first in the list of the nine fruit, and self-control, the last in the list. Love and self-control are like bookends that hold the others in place. All of the fruit issue from love and actually are a form of love, but they are kept in place by self-control.

If you concentrate on developing the fruit of love, you will not become impatient with people as you walk through your day. You will not be anything but kind. You will be good to people, supportive, and faithful instead of being haughty or trying to appear better than others.

If you are not motivated by love, you will find that operating in the fruit is very difficult. But even when you are motivated to express God's love as a lifestyle, there will be times (*many* times when you first begin developing the fruit) when you will not feel like being patient, kind, joyful, peaceful, or even nice at all! Those are the times that you need self-control in order to continue to respond with the fruit of the Spirit even though you do not feel like it.

If you need to develop this fruit of self-control, begin by simply making little choices throughout the day to respond with the fruit to situations you encounter. Remember, love, self-control, and all the other fruit of the Spirit grow when you allow the Holy Spirit's presence within you to accomplish His work.

(sbe equal to understanding and calmly receive) his own ['little] load s[of oppressive faults].

6 Let him who receives instruction in the Word [of God] share all good things with his teacher [contributing to his support].

7 Do not be deceived *and* deluded *and* misled; God will not allow Himself to be sneered at (scorned, disdained, or mocked ⁿby mere pretensions or professions, or by His precepts being set aside.) [He inevitably deludes himself who attempts to delude God.] For whatever a man sows, that *and* ᵛthat only is what he will reap.

8 For he who sows to his own flesh (lower nature, sensuality) will from the

s Joseph Thayer, *A Greek-English Lexicon.* **t** Diminutive (indicating small size) form of the Greek word. **u** Matthew Henry, *Commentary on the Holy Bible.* **v** Marvin Vincent, *Word Studies.*

patience, not pride

I have personally read and meditated on Galatians 6:1–3 hundreds of times. I have a natural temperament that avoids humility, so I need all the scriptural help I can get. I do want to please God, and I am willing to do things His way, no matter how difficult it is. Reading this passage reminds me that while misconduct should be confronted in a loving way, I will also have times of needing simply to bear and endure the troublesome faults that others have.

Humility allows us to be patient with the mistakes of others. As we walk in love and pray for people, God will intervene and deal with their faults. We reap what we sow: If we sow mercy, we will reap mercy when we need it.

Even though we find it difficult at times to bear with the weaknesses of others, the Word of God actually strengthens and enables us to do God's will. When you are tempted to be prideful, study and meditate on the Word, asking the Holy Spirit to do through you what you certainly cannot do by sheer willpower. Remember, pride is a sin, and it is the culprit behind broken relationships.

The signs of pride include an unwillingness to admit fault or a reluctance to take responsibility for one's actions. Pride wants to do all the talking, and none of the listening. Pride does not make peace. Pride is stubborn; it does not want to be instructed, it wants to instruct others.

Pride was Lucifer's sin; he said he would lift himself and his throne above God's! Therefore, we see that kind of pride manifest when a person esteems himself above the value of another, but God says we are all equal in His eyes. Lucifer, of course, never was equal with God, but as far as human relationships are concerned, no one person is better than another. Remember that, and you will be well on your way to avoiding pride. Do not deceive yourself into thinking pride will get you where you want to go. Rather, allow the truth of Galatians 6:1–3 to sink deep in your heart and change you from the inside out.

flesh reap decay *and* ruin *and* destruction, but he who sows to the Spirit will from the Spirit reap eternal life.

putting the Word to work

We are not meant to bear the burdens of life alone. God's Word teaches us to love one another as He loves us, and it is out of this love that we are to bear one another's burdens (see Galatians 6:2). Is there someone in your life who needs your help bearing a burden? As you seek to help that person, remember that Jesus is your Burden-Bearer, and He will help you help that person.

9 And let us not lose heart *and* grow weary *and* faint in acting nobly *and* doing right, for in due time *and* at the appointed season we shall reap, if we do not loosen *and* relax our courage *and* faint.

10 So then, as occasion *and* opportunity open up to us, let us do good [ʷmorally] to all people [not only ʷbeing useful or profitable to them, but also doing what is for their spiritual good and advantage]. Be mindful to be a blessing, especially to those of the household of faith [those who belong to God's family with you, the believers].

11 See with what large letters I am

putting the Word to work

Are you ever tempted to compare yourself to someone else? The Word of God warns against such behavior because it can lead to self-conceit (see Galatians 6:3, 4). Rather, Jesus' life and teachings are the standard against which we measure our lives. Ask God to help you honestly assess what areas in your life need improvement, and thank Him for bringing transformation to other areas of your life.

writing with my own hand. [ʷMark carefully these closing words of mine.] **12** Those who want to make a good impression *and* a fine show in the flesh would try to compel you to receive circumcision, simply so that they may escape being persecuted for allegiance to the cross of Christ (the Messiah, the Anointed One).

life point

The "due season" mentioned in Galatians 6:9 is God's season, not ours. We are often in a hurry, but God is not. He takes time to do things right; He lays a solid foundation before He attempts to build a building. We are God's building under construction. He is the Master Builder, and He knows what He is doing. We may not know what He is doing, but He does, and that will have to be good enough. We may not always know all the answers, but we can be satisfied to know the One Who knows.

God's timing seems to be His own little secret. The Bible promises us that He will never be late, but I have also discovered that He is usually not early. It seems He takes every available opportunity to develop the fruit of patience in us.

ʷ Marvin Vincent, *Word Studies*.

13 For even the circumcised [Jews] themselves do not [really] keep the Law, but they want to have you circumcised in order that they may glory in your flesh (your subjection to external rites).
14 But far be it from me to glory [in anything or anyone] except in the cross of our Lord Jesus Christ (the Messiah) through Whom the world has been crucified to me, and I to the world!
15 For neither is circumcision [now] of any importance, nor uncircumcision, but [only] a new creation [the result of a new birth and a new nature in Christ Jesus, the Messiah].
16 Peace and mercy be upon all who walk by this rule [who discipline themselves and regulate their lives by this principle], even upon the [true] Israel of God! [Ps. 125:5.]
17 From now on let no person trouble me [by ʷmaking it necessary for me to vindicate my apostolic authority and the divine truth of my Gospel], for I bear on my body the [brand] marks of the Lord Jesus [the wounds, scars, and other outward evidence of persecutions—these testify to His ownership of me]!
18 The grace (spiritual favor, blessing) of our Lord Jesus Christ (the Anointed One, the Messiah) be with your spirit, brethren. Amen (so be it).

life point

In Galatians 6:14 the apostle Paul makes clear that he did not glory in anything or anyone, because the world was crucified to him and he to the world. He kept all things—including people, places, and positions—in proper balance in his life. He was not dependent upon anyone or anything for his joy and peace and victory except the Lord. Let me encourage you to be the same way!

Ephesians

Author:
Paul

Date:
About AD 60

Everyday Life Principles:
God loves you.

You are totally accepted in Christ.

God has a great plan for your life.

Though Ephesians is literally filled with wisdom, encouragement, and great teaching about what it means to be a Christian and how the church should operate, I believe one of the most important messages in this letter is that you and I are unconditionally loved and totally accepted in Christ. Indeed, one of the key points in this book is that *God loves you* and that you can receive and enjoy that love and become increasingly rooted and grounded in it.

In addition, this book addresses the spiritual blessings that belong to us in Christ, our position of authority in Christ, the mysteries of God, the need to walk in love and in the light, the importance of unity among believers, proper order in families and relationships, how to deal with anger, and how to war against the powers and principalities in the spiritual realm.

As you spend time in Ephesians, I hope that its many rich teachings will take root in your heart and that you will apply them in your everyday life. I especially hope and pray that through this book, you experience God's love and acceptance in a deeply personal way and that you are filled with a sense of purpose as you read about how He feels about you. God has great things for you, things He ordained before the foundation of the world. Ask Him to reveal them and enable you to do them by the power of the Holy Spirit.

1 PAUL, AN apostle (special messenger) of Christ Jesus (the Messiah), by the divine will (the purpose and the choice of God) to the saints (the consecrated, set-apart ones) ᵃat Ephesus who are also faithful *and* loyal *and* steadfast in Christ Jesus:

2 May grace (God's unmerited favor) and spiritual peace [which means peace with God and harmony, unity, and undisturbedness] be yours from God our Father and from the Lord Jesus Christ.

3 May blessing (praise, laudation, and eulogy) be to the God and Father of our Lord Jesus Christ (the Messiah) Who has blessed us *in Christ* with every spiritual (given by the Holy Spirit) blessing in the heavenly realm!

4 Even as [in His love] He chose us [actually picked us out for Himself as His own] in Christ before the foundation of the world, that we should be holy (consecrated and set apart for Him) and blameless in His sight, *even* above reproach, before Him in love.

5 For He foreordained us (destined us, planned in love for us) to be adopted (revealed) as His own children through Jesus Christ, in accordance with the purpose of His will [ᵇbecause it pleased Him and was His kind intent]—

6 [So that we might be] to the praise *and* the commendation of His glorious grace (favor and mercy), which He so freely bestowed on us in the Beloved.

7 In Him we have redemption (deliverance and salvation) through His blood, the remission (forgiveness) of our offenses (shortcomings and trespasses), in accordance with the riches *and* the generosity of His gracious favor,

8 Which He lavished upon us in every kind of wisdom and understanding (practical insight and prudence),

9 Making known to us the mystery (secret) of His will (of His plan, of His purpose). [And it is this:] In accordance with His good pleasure (His merciful intention) which He had previously purposed *and* set forth in ᶜHim,

10 [He planned] for the maturity of the times *and* the climax of the ages to unify all things *and* head them up *and* consummate them in Christ, [both]

life point

Ephesians 1:4 is a wonderful scripture! In it, the Lord tells us that we are His, and He sets forth what He wants for us—that we should know we are loved, special, and valuable and that we should be holy, blameless, and above reproach in our lives.

Naturally, we should do what we can to live holy lives. But thank God, when we do make mistakes, we can be forgiven. We do not lose our God-given position of holiness, and we remain blameless and above reproach—all "in Christ."

speak the Word

Thank You, God, that You foreordained me and planned in love to adopt me as Your own child through Christ Jesus, so that I could be to the praise of Your glorious grace, which You so freely bestowed on me in Your beloved Son.
ADAPTED FROM EPHESIANS 1:5, 6

a Some manuscripts do not contain "at Ephesus." b Marvin Vincent, *Word Studies in the New Testament*. c Some commentators interpret "in Him" to mean "in Himself," while others see it as "in Christ."

you have been chosen

One of the strongest desires human beings have is to be loved, to be accepted, and to feel that they belong. We want a sense of connection and belonging to something or someone. We want to feel valuable. We cannot be guaranteed of always getting that in our dealings with people, but we can get it from God. Even though God knows everything about us—and I do mean everything—He still chooses us on purpose. According to Ephesians 1:4, He actually picked us out on purpose to be His very own and to belong to Him. I encourage you to say aloud right now, "I belong to God."

God set us apart for Himself and made provision in Jesus for us to be holy, blameless, and consecrated. We can live before Him in love without reproach. That means we do not have to feel guilty and bad about all of our weaknesses and faults. You and I are no surprise to God. He knew exactly what He was getting when He chose us. God did not choose us and then become disappointed because of our inabilities. God has hope for us, and He believes in us and is working in us to help us be all that He has in His plan for us.

I encourage you to relax in God's love. Learn to receive God's love. Think about it, thank Him for it, and watch for the manifestation of it in your daily life. God shows His love for us in many ways, but we often are unaware of it. He loves us first, so we can love Him and other people. God never expects us to give away something that He has not first given us. His love is poured into our hearts by the Holy Spirit and He wants us to live before Him in love.

Let love in and let it out. You are destined to be a channel for God to flow through, and not a reservoir that merely sits and collects things. You are special and God has a special plan for you. Get excited about that and rejoice!

things in heaven and things on the earth.

11 In Him we also were made [God's] heritage (portion) *and* we obtained an inheritance; for we had been foreordained (chosen and appointed beforehand) in accordance with His purpose, Who works out everything in agreement with the counsel *and* design of His [own] will,

12 So that we who first hoped in Christ [who first put our confidence in Him have been destined and appointed to] live for the praise of His glory!

13 In Him you also who have heard the Word of Truth, the glad tidings (Gospel) of your salvation, and have believed in *and* adhered to *and* relied on Him, were stamped with the seal of the long-promised Holy Spirit.

speak the Word

Thank You, Jesus, that in You I have redemption, deliverance, and salvation through Your blood, the remission of my offenses, in accordance with the riches of Your gracious favor, which You have lavished upon me in every kind of wisdom and understanding.
ADAPTED FROM EPHESIANS 1:7, 8

14 That [Spirit] is the guarantee of our inheritance [the firstfruits, the pledge and foretaste, the down payment on our heritage], in anticipation of its full redemption *and* our acquiring [complete] possession of it—to the praise of His glory.

15 For this reason, because I have heard of your faith in the Lord Jesus and your love toward all the saints (the people of God),

16 I do not cease to give thanks for you, making mention of you in my prayers.

17 [For I always pray to] the God of our Lord Jesus Christ, the Father of glory, that He may grant you a spirit of wisdom and revelation [of insight into mysteries and secrets] in the [deep and intimate] knowledge of Him,

18 By having the eyes of your heart flooded with light, so that you can know *and* understand the hope to which He has called you, and how rich is His glorious inheritance in the saints (His set-apart ones),

19 And [so that you can know and understand] what is the immeasurable *and* unlimited *and* surpassing greatness of His power in *and* for us who believe, as demonstrated in the working of His mighty strength,

20 Which He exerted in Christ when He raised Him from the dead and seated Him at His [own] right hand in the heavenly [places],

21 Far above all rule and authority and power and dominion and every name that is named [above every title that can be conferred], not only in this age *and* in this world, but also in the age *and* the world which are to come.

22 And He has put all things under His feet and has appointed Him the universal and supreme Head of the church [a headship exercised throughout the church], [Ps. 8:6.]

23 Which is His body, the fullness of Him Who fills all in all [for in that body lives the full measure of Him Who makes everything complete, and Who fills everything everywhere with Himself].

2 AND YOU [He made alive], when you were dead (slain) by [your] trespasses and sins

2 In which at one time you walked [habitually]. You were following the course *and* fashion of this world [were under the sway of the tendency of this present age], following the prince of the power of the air. [You were obedient to and under the control of] the [demon] spirit that still constantly works in the sons of disobedience [the careless, the rebellious, and the unbelieving, who go against the purposes of God].

3 Among these we as well as you once lived *and* conducted ourselves in the passions of our flesh [our behavior governed by our corrupt and sensual nature], obeying the impulses of the flesh and the thoughts of the mind [our cravings dictated by our senses and our dark imaginings]. We were then by nature children of [God's] wrath *and* heirs of [His] indignation, like the rest of mankind.

4 But God—so rich is He in His mercy! Because of *and* in order to satisfy the great *and* wonderful *and* intense love with which He loved us,

5 Even when we were dead (slain) by [our own] shortcomings *and* trespasses, He made us alive together in fellowship *and* in union with Christ; [He gave us the very life of Christ Himself, the same new life with which He quickened Him, for] it is by grace (His favor and mercy which you did not deserve) that you are saved (ᵈdelivered from judgment and made partakers of Christ's salvation).

---

d Joseph Thayer, *A Greek-English Lexicon of the New Testament.*

seated in heavenly places

The Bible depicts Jesus after His resurrection as seated in heavenly places at the right hand of God. Being "seated" refers to being in the rest of God. God wants each of us to enter His rest. He wants us to be relaxed, not worried or anxious, and to enjoy life while we wait for Him to make all of our enemies a footstool for our feet. Our part is to believe and rest in Him and His part is to work on our behalf.

According to Scripture, we died with Christ when He died, we were buried with Him, resurrected with Him, and we are now seated with Him in heavenly places (see Ephesians 2:6). How can we be seated with Him in heaven when we can clearly see that we are here on earth? Simply because we are spirits, we have souls, and we live in bodies. Physically, we are on earth, but simultaneously we can be spiritually seated with Him in heaven. That belief gives us the ability to enter His rest. The work of Christ is finished and we can enjoy its results. His kingdom offers righteousness, peace, and joy in the Holy Spirit (see Romans 14:17), and it is available to us right now, not just when we go to heaven. God wants us to enjoy the life that Jesus died to give us starting the moment we accept Him as our Savior and Lord.

Have you entered God's rest? Have you trusted Him entirely to do what needs to be done in you and in your life? Are you perhaps still working in the flesh trying to do what only God can do and the results are frustration and disappointment? Perhaps you just need to sit down! I do not mean physically, but spiritually. We can sit in a chair and still be worried, fearful, and anxious. God is not calling us to rest *from* our work, but *in* our work. As we go about our daily business, we can do it all while seated in Christ. He is our Refuge and our Hiding Place.

Be zealous and exert yourself and strive diligently to enter that place of rest. It is available today, so do not let it pass you by. Release all your frustrations and worries—and have a seat in Christ.

6 And He raised us up together with Him and made us sit down together [giving us ᵉjoint seating with Him] in the heavenly sphere [by virtue of our being] in Christ Jesus (the Messiah, the Anointed One).

7 He did this that He might clearly demonstrate through the ages to come the immeasurable (limitless, surpassing) riches of His free grace (His unmerited favor) in [His] kindness *and* goodness of heart toward us in Christ Jesus.

8 For it is by free grace (God's unmerited favor) that you are saved (ᶠdelivered from judgment *and* made

putting the Word to work

Can you imagine trying to earn your way into God's favor? That would be an impossible task. No amount of good works would ever be enough. Take a moment and reflect on the riches of God's grace and thank Him for His love and kindness toward you (see Ephesians 2:4–7).

e H.A.W. Meyer, *Commentary on the New Testament.*   f Joseph Thayer, *A Greek-English Lexicon.*

life point

Grace is a wonderful thing. It is God's unmerited favor by which we are saved through faith in Jesus Christ, as Paul tells us in Ephesians 2:8.

The Holy Spirit ministers grace to us from God the Father. It can be said that grace is the Holy Spirit's power flowing out from God's throne to save us; it enables us to live holy lives and to accomplish the will of God.

partakers of Christ's salvation) through [your] faith. And this [salvation] is not of yourselves [of your own doing, it came not through your own striving], but it is the gift of God;

9 Not because of works [not the fulfillment of the Law's demands], lest any man should boast. [It is not the result of what anyone can possibly do, so no one can pride himself in it or take glory to himself.]

10 For we are God's [own] handiwork (His workmanship), ᵍrecreated in Christ Jesus, [born anew] that we may do those good works which God predestined (planned beforehand) for us [taking paths which He prepared ahead of time], that we should walk in them [living the good life which He prearranged and made ready for us to live].

11 Therefore, remember that at one time you were Gentiles (heathens) in the flesh, called Uncircumcision by those who called themselves Circumcision, [itself a ʰmere mark] in the flesh made by human hands.

speak the Word

life point

Ephesians 2:10 tells us that we are God's own handiwork. He created us with His own hands. We human beings got messed up along the way, so we were re-created in Christ Jesus. We had to be born again spiritually so we could go ahead and do the good works that God preplanned for us before Satan tried to ruin us.

Just because you and I have made mistakes or have trouble in our lives, does not mean that God's plan has changed. It is still there. All we have to do is get back in it by trusting and obeying Him.

12 [Remember] that you were at that time separated (living apart) from Christ [excluded from all part in Him], utterly estranged *and* outlawed from the rights of Israel as a nation, and strangers with no share in the sacred compacts of the [Messianic] promise [with no knowledge of or right in God's agreements, His covenants]. And you had no hope (no promise); you were in the world without God.

13 But now in Christ Jesus, you who once were [so] far away, through (by, in) the blood of Christ have been brought near.

14 For He is [Himself] our peace (our bond of unity and harmony). He has made us both [Jew and Gentile] one [body], and has broken down (destroyed, abolished) the hostile dividing wall between us,

15 By abolishing in His [own crucified] flesh the enmity [caused by] the

Thank You, Jesus, for being my peace.
ADAPTED FROM EPHESIANS 2:14

g Arthur S. Way, *Way's Epistles: The Letters of St. Paul to Seven Churches and Three Friends.*
h Arthur S. Way, *The Letters of St. Paul to Seven Churches and Three Friends.*

God has a good plan

God had a good plan laid out for each one of us long before we made our appearances on this planet (see Ephesians 2:10). It is not a plan of failure, misery, poverty, sickness, disaster, and disease. God's plan is a good plan, a plan for life and health, happiness, and fulfillment. Other scriptures affirm this truth.

In Jeremiah 29:11 we read, "For I know the thoughts and plans that I have for you, says the Lord, thoughts and plans for welfare and peace and not for evil, to give you hope in your final outcome."

In John 10:10 Jesus said, "The thief comes only in order to steal and kill and destroy. I came that they may have and enjoy life, and have it in abundance (to the full, till it overflows)."

In III John 2 we read, "Beloved, I pray that you may prosper in every way and (that your body) may keep well, even as (I know) your soul keeps well and prospers."

We will benefit greatly if we say to ourselves several times a day, "God has a good plan for my life." Why should we do that? We need to be firmly convinced of that truth to keep us from being affected by our changing circumstances and emotions.

You may ask, "If God has such a wonderful plan for my life, why am I not living in it?"

I understand why you ask that question. It does seem strange that if God loves us so much and has such good plans for us, we still suffer as we sometimes do. What you must remember is that we have an enemy who is out to disrupt God's wonderful plan and to destroy the good things God has in mind for us. This happened to me. Though God had a good plan for my life, I grew up in an abusive environment because the devil came and tried to disrupt that good plan.

But there is something else, something really awesome that we need to understand about God. God does not like it when someone hurts us and tries to undermine His plan for us. He always has a plan for our healing and restoration. While He is making us lie down in green pastures to restore our souls (see Psalm 23:2), He is getting up to do something about our situation!

God is on our side and it should be a great comfort to us to know that what we cannot do for ourselves, the Lord will do for us—if we entrust ourselves to Him. Only He has the power to restore what was lost to us, whether that loss was our own fault or the fault of our enemy.

Law with its decrees and ordinances [which He annulled]; that He from the two might create in Himself one new man [one new quality of humanity out of the two], so making peace.

16 And [He designed] to reconcile to God both [Jew and Gentile, united] in a single body by means of His cross, thereby killing the mutual enmity *and* bringing the feud to an end.

17 And He came and preached the glad tidings of peace to you who were afar off and [peace] to those who were near. [Isa. 57:19.]

18 For it is through Him that we both [whether far off or near] now have an introduction (access) by one [Holy] Spirit to the Father [so that we are able to approach Him].

19 Therefore you are no longer outsiders (exiles, migrants, and aliens, excluded from the rights of citizens), but you now share citizenship with the saints (God's own people, consecrated and set apart for Himself); and you belong to God's [own] household.

20 You are built upon the foundation of the apostles and prophets with Christ Jesus Himself the chief Cornerstone.

21 In Him the whole structure is joined (bound, welded) together harmoniously, and it continues to rise (grow, increase) into a holy temple in the Lord [a sanctuary dedicated, consecrated, and sacred to the presence of the Lord].

22 In Him [and in fellowship with one another] you yourselves also are being built up [into this structure] with the rest, to form a fixed abode (dwelling place) of God in (by, through) the Spirit.

3 FOR THIS reason [[i]because I preached that you are thus built up together], I, Paul, [am] the prisoner of Jesus the Christ [i]for the sake *and* on behalf of you Gentiles—

2 Assuming that you have heard of the stewardship of God's grace (His unmerited favor) that was entrusted to me [to dispense to you] for your benefit,

3 [And] that the mystery (secret) was made known to me *and* I was allowed to comprehend it by direct revelation, as I already briefly wrote you.

4 When you read this you can understand my insight into the mystery of Christ.

5 [This mystery] was never disclosed to human beings in past generations as it has now been revealed to His holy apostles (consecrated messengers) and prophets by the [Holy] Spirit.

6 [It is this:] that the Gentiles are now to be fellow heirs [with the Jews], members of the same body and joint partakers [sharing] in the same divine promise in Christ through [their acceptance of] the glad tidings (the Gospel).

7 Of this [Gospel] I was made a minister according to the gift of God's free grace (undeserved favor) which was bestowed on me by the exercise (the working in all its effectiveness) of His power.

8 To me, though I am the very least of all the saints (God's consecrated people), this grace (favor, privilege) was granted *and* graciously entrusted: to proclaim to the Gentiles the unending (boundless, fathomless, incalculable, and exhaustless) riches of Christ [wealth which no human being could have searched out],

9 Also to enlighten all men *and* make plain to them what is the plan [regarding the Gentiles and providing for the salvation of all men] of the mystery kept hidden through the ages *and* concealed until now in [the mind of] God Who created all things *by Christ Jesus.*

10 [The purpose is] that through the church the [j]complicated, many-sided wisdom of God in all its infinite variety *and* innumerable aspects might now be made known to the angelic rulers and authorities (principalities and powers) in the heavenly sphere.

i Matthew Henry, *Commentary on the Holy Bible*: The Jews persecuted and imprisoned Paul because he was an apostle to the Gentiles and preached the Gospel to them.   **j** *Webster's New International Dictionary* offers this as a definition of "manifold" (the *King James Version's* rendering of the Greek *polupoikilos*).

11 This is in accordance with the terms of the eternal *and* timeless purpose which He has realized *and* carried into effect in [the person of] Christ Jesus our Lord,

12 In Whom, because of our faith in Him, we dare to have the boldness (courage and confidence) of free access (an unreserved approach to God with freedom and without fear).

13 So I ask you not to lose heart [not to faint or become despondent through fear] at what I am suffering in your behalf. [Rather glory in it] for it is an honor to you.

14 For this reason [kseeing the greatness of this plan by which you are built together in Christ], I bow my knees before the Father *of our Lord Jesus Christ,*

15 For Whom every family in heaven and on earth is named [that Father from Whom all fatherhood takes its title and derives its name].

16 May He grant you out of the rich treasury of His glory to be strengthened *and* reinforced with mighty power in the inner man by the [Holy] Spirit [Himself indwelling your innermost being and personality].

17 May Christ through your faith [actually] dwell (settle down, abide, make His permanent home) in your hearts! May you be rooted deep in love *and* founded securely on love,

18 That you may have the power *and* be strong to apprehend *and* grasp with all the saints [God's devoted people, the experience of that love] what

speak the Word

putting the Word to work

Do you really understand the depths of God's love for you? Paul fervently prayed that the Ephesians would understand the width and length and depth and height of God's love for them, and that they would be rooted and grounded in that boundless love. Take time to meditate on Ephesians 3:14–19. Ask God to reveal to you more and more of His love and to expand your capacity to receive this awesome love and all the fullness of God.

is the breadth and length and height and depth [of it];

19 [That you may really come] to know [practically, lthrough experience for yourselves] the love of Christ, which far surpasses lmere knowledge [without experience]; that you may be filled [through all your being] lunto all the fullness of God [may have the richest measure of the divine Presence, and mbecome a body wholly filled and flooded with God Himself]!

20 Now to Him Who, by (in consequence of) the [action of His] power that is at work within us, is able to [carry out His purpose and] do superabundantly, far over *and* above all that we [dare] ask or think [infinitely beyond our highest prayers, desires, thoughts, hopes, or dreams]—

21 To Him be glory in the church and in Christ Jesus throughout all generations forever and ever. Amen (so be it).

---

k Many manuscripts consider that Paul here resumes the thread of verse 1.   l Marvin Vincent, *Word Studies.*   m Joseph Thayer, *A Greek-English Lexicon.*

be filled!

Just imagine having your personality filled with the Holy Spirit of the living God and being a body wholly filled with God Himself (see Ephesians 3:16–19)! The apostle Paul was a person filled with the Holy Spirit; he was also a person who forsook all to follow Jesus. Any area of our lives that we hold back from God is an area where we cannot be filled with His Spirit. I encourage you to open and surrender every room in your heart to God. Your time is His; your money is His, as are your gifts and talents, your family, your career, thoughts, attitudes, and desires. He wants to be involved in every area of your life: how you dress, the friends you choose, what you do for entertainment, what you eat, and so on.

After conversion, Jesus is our Savior, but is He our Lord? Any area we claim as our own is one we have not surrendered to the lordship of Jesus Christ.

I lived a defeated life for many years simply because I was not fully surrendered. I accepted Jesus as Savior; I had enough of Jesus to stay out of hell, but I had not accepted Him as my Lord in every area of my life; I had not accepted enough of Him to walk in victory—and there is a difference.

The blessedness of being filled with the Spirit is clearly visible in the change in the people's lives after Pentecost. Peter, for example, who displayed great fear in not being willing to even admit that he knew Jesus, became a bold apostle who stood in the streets of Jerusalem and preached the gospel so fervently that three thousand souls were added to the church in one day (see Acts 2:40, 41).

Complete surrender to God brings good change into our lives. Surrendering to Him actually opens the door to the things we desire, and yet we waste our own energy trying to obtain access to them our own way. I encourage you today to surrender every area of your life to God so you may be filled to overflowing with His Spirit in every way.

life point

Ephesians 3:20 teaches us that God is able to do exceedingly abundantly above and beyond all we could dare to hope, ask, or think, according to His great power that is at work in us. It is God's power, but it is done through us, so we need to cooperate with Him. This means we need to be daring in our faith and in our prayers. I encourage you to stretch your faith into new realms beyond your "highest prayers, desires, thoughts, hopes, or dreams."

4 I THEREFORE, the prisoner for the Lord, appeal to *and* beg you to walk (lead a life) worthy of the [divine] calling to which you have been called [with behavior that is a credit to the summons to God's service,

2 Living as becomes you] with complete lowliness of mind (humility) and meekness (unselfishness, gentleness, mildness), with patience, bearing with one another *and* making allowances because you love one another.

3 Be eager *and* strive earnestly to guard *and* keep the harmony *and* oneness of [and produced by] the

believe big

In the natural, many things are impossible. But in the supernatural realm with God, nothing is impossible. God wants us to believe for great things, make big plans, and expect Him to do things so great that we are left with our mouths hanging open in awe. James 4:2 tells us we have not because we ask not! We can be bold in our asking, and Ephesians 3:20 challenges us to ask for big things.

When our desires seem overwhelmingly big and we do not see the way to accomplish them, we should remember that even though we do not know the way, we know the Waymaker!

God has a way for us to do everything He places in our hearts. He does not put dreams and visions in us to frustrate us. We must keep our confidence in God all the way through to the end, not just for a little bit and then give up when it looks as though the mountain is too big!

It is untold what people can do—even people who do not appear to be able to do anything. God does not usually call people who are capable; if He did, He would not get the glory. He frequently chooses those who, in the natural, feel as if they are in completely over their heads but who are ready to stand up on the inside and take bold steps of faith as they receive direction from God.

We usually want to wait until we "feel ready" before we step out, but if we feel ready, then we tend to lean on ourselves instead of on God.

Know your weaknesses and know God; know His strength and faithfulness. Remember that He is able to do "superabundantly, far over and above" everything you could ever dare to ask or think!

Spirit in the binding power of peace.
4 [There is] one body and one Spirit—just as there is also one hope [that belongs] to the calling you received—
5 [There is] one Lord, one faith, one baptism,
6 One God and Father of [us] all, Who is above all [Sovereign over all], pervading all and [living] in [us] all.
7 Yet grace (God's unmerited favor) was given to each of us individually [not indiscriminately, but in different ways] in proportion to the measure of Christ's [rich and bounteous] gift.
8 Therefore it is said, When He ascended on high, He led captivity captive [He led a train of [n]vanquished foes] and He bestowed gifts on men. [Ps. 68:18.]
9 [But He ascended?] Now what can this, He ascended, mean but that He had previously descended from [the heights of] heaven into [the depths], the lower parts of the earth?
10 He Who descended is the [very] same as He Who also has ascended high above all the heavens, that He

n Matthew Henry, *Commentary on the Holy Bible*: "He conquered those who had conquered us—such as sin, the devil, and death."

[His presence] might fill all things (the whole universe, from the lowest to the highest).

11 And His gifts were [varied; He Himself appointed and gave men to us] some to be apostles (special messengers), some prophets (inspired preachers and expounders), some evangelists (preachers of the Gospel, traveling missionaries), some pastors (shepherds of His flock) and teachers.
12 His intention was the perfecting *and* the full equipping of the saints (His consecrated people), [that they should do] the work of ministering toward building up Christ's body (the church),
13 [That it might develop] until we all attain oneness in the faith and in the comprehension of the [°full and accurate] knowledge of the Son of God, that [we might arrive] at really mature manhood (the completeness of personality which is nothing less than the standard height of Christ's own perfection), the measure of the stature of the fullness of the Christ *and* the completeness found in Him.
14 So then, we may no longer be children, tossed [like ships] to and fro between chance gusts of teaching *and* wavering with every changing wind of doctrine, [the prey of] the cunning *and* cleverness of ᴾunscrupulous men, [gamblers engaged] in every shifting form of trickery in inventing errors to mislead.
15 Rather, let our lives lovingly °express truth [in all things, speaking truly, dealing truly, living truly]. Enfolded in love, let us grow up in every way *and* in all things into Him Who is the Head, [even] Christ (the Messiah, the Anointed One).
16 For because of Him the whole body (the church, in all its various parts), closely joined and firmly knit together by the joints *and* ligaments

with which it is supplied, when each part [with power adapted to its need] is working properly [in all its functions], grows to full maturity, building itself up in love.
17 So this I say and solemnly testify in [the name of] the Lord [as in His presence], that you must no longer live as the heathen (the Gentiles) do in their perverseness [in the folly, vanity, and emptiness of their souls and the futility] of their minds.
18 Their °moral understanding is darkened *and* their reasoning is beclouded. [They are] alienated (estranged, self-banished) from the life of God [with no share in it; this is] because of the ignorance (the want of

life point

Ephesians 4:17–19 says that unbelievers can be so callous and hard that they are "past feeling." But the same verse says they live by their feelings in unbridled sensuality and carnality. As I meditated on what appears to be a paradox here, the Lord showed me that such people are past doing what they should be doing with their feelings.

God gives people feelings for a specific purpose and use in their walk with Him. But people who have alienated themselves from God are hardened to the place where they are beyond using their feelings for the right purpose. Satan moves them into an area where they live riotous lives, doing whatever they feel like doing.

What is the world's philosophy today? "If it feels good, do it!" You and I are not to live that way, but to make the truth of God's Word our standard and to obey it by the power of the Holy Spirit.

o Marvin Vincent, *Word Studies*.   **p** Literal translation: "dice-playing."

knowledge and perception, the willful blindness) that is qdeep-seated in them, due to their hardness of heart [to the insensitiveness of their moral nature].

19 In their spiritual apathy they have become callous *and* past feeling *and* reckless and have abandoned themselves [a prey] to unbridled sensuality, eager *and* greedy to indulge in every form of impurity [that their depraved desires may suggest and demand].

20 But you did not so learn Christ!

21 Assuming that you have really heard Him *and* been taught by Him, as [all] Truth is in Jesus [embodied and personified in Him],

22 Strip yourselves of your former nature [put off and discard your old unrenewed self] which characterized your previous manner of life and becomes corrupt through lusts *and* desires that spring from delusion;

23 And be constantly renewed in the spirit of your mind [having a fresh mental and spiritual attitude],

24 And put on the new nature (the regenerate self) created in God's image, [Godlike] in true righteousness and holiness.

25 Therefore, rejecting all falsity *and* being done now with it, let everyone express the truth with his neighbor, for we are all parts of one body *and* members one of another. [Zech. 8:16.]

life point

In Ephesians 4:23 we read that we are to be "constantly renewed" in the spirits of our minds, having "a fresh mental and spiritual attitude." Attitudes begin in the mind. Our minds are renewed by the Word of God. Reading the Word daily renews our minds and changes our attitudes. Renew your mind in the Word today!

q Marvin Vincent, *Word Studies*.

26 When angry, do not sin; do not ever let your wrath (your exasperation, your fury or indignation) last until the sun goes down.

27 Leave no [such] room *or* foothold for the devil [give no opportunity to him].

28 Let the thief steal no more, but rather let him be industrious, making an honest living with his own hands, so that he may be able to give to those in need.

29 Let no foul *or* polluting language, *nor* evil word *nor* unwholesome *or*

life point

Ephesians 4:26, 27 basically tells us to let go of our anger before bedtime. There is only one problem: What happens when we become good and angry just before bedtime? If we become angry in the morning, at least we have all day to get over it. But when we become angry close to bedtime, we have to make a quick decision about what to do with our anger.

Why is it so unwise for us to go to bed angry? I think it is because while we sleep, what we are angry about has time to take root in us. But the Word admonishes us not to leave room for the devil to gain a foothold through our anger. If we refuse to get over our anger by bedtime, we open a door for the devil and give him a foothold. Once Satan gets a foothold in our lives, he sees an opportunity to move on to a stronghold.

I encourage you today to deal with your anger quickly and decisively so the devil sees no opportunity to take advantage of the situation. No matter how you feel, you can *choose* to forgive and walk in love.

how to really change

Ephesians 4:22–24 teaches us about the connection between our thoughts and our actions. Verse 22 says we should strip ourselves of our former natures and discard our old unrenewed selves. Verse 24 continues the thought and tells us to put on the new nature created in God's image "in true righteousness and holiness."

So we see that verse 22 basically tells us to stop acting improperly, and verse 24 tells us to begin acting properly. But verse 23 is what I call "the bridge scripture." It tells us how to get from verse 22 (wrong actions) to verse 24 (right actions): "And be constantly renewed in the spirit of your mind [having a fresh mental and spiritual attitude]."

It is impossible to get from wrong behavior to right behavior without first changing our thoughts. A passive person may want to do the right thing, but he never will do so unless he purposely activates his mind and lines it up with God's Word and His will.

An example that comes to mind involves a man who once got into the prayer line at one of my seminars. He had a problem with lust. He really loved his wife and did not want their marriage to be destroyed, but his problem needed a solution or he would surely ruin his marriage.

"Joyce," he said, "I just cannot seem to stay away from other women. Will you pray for my deliverance? I have been prayed for many times, but I never seem to make any progress."

This is what the Holy Spirit prompted me to tell him, "Yes, I will pray for you, but you must be accountable for what you are allowing to show on the picture screen of your mind. You cannot visualize pornographic pictures in your thinking, or imagine yourself with these other women, if you ever want to enjoy freedom."

Like this man, others realize why they are not experiencing a breakthrough even though they want to be free: they want to change their behavior—but not their thinking. If you desire to act differently, you will have to start by thinking differently because your behavior starts with your thoughts. Wrong thoughts lead to wrong actions, but right thoughts lead to right actions!

worthless talk [ever] come out of your mouth, but only such [speech] as is good *and* beneficial to the spiritual progress of others, as is fitting to the need *and* the occasion, that it may be a blessing *and* give grace (God's favor) to those who hear it.

30 And do not grieve the Holy Spirit of God [do not offend or vex or sadden Him], by Whom you were sealed (marked, branded as God's own, secured) for the day of redemption (of final deliverance through Christ from evil and the consequences of sin).

31 Let all bitterness and indignation *and* wrath (passion, rage, bad temper) and resentment (anger, animosity) and quarreling (brawling, clamor, contention) and slander (evil-speaking, abusive or blasphemous language) be banished from you, with all malice (spite, ill will, or baseness of any kind).

32 And become useful *and* helpful *and* kind to one another, tenderhearted (compassionate, understanding,

loving-hearted), forgiving one another [readily and freely], as God in Christ forgave you.

5 THEREFORE BE imitators of God [copy Him *and* follow His example], as well-beloved children [imitate their father].

2 And walk in love, [esteeming and delighting in one another] as Christ

a tender conscience

Having a tender heart (see Ephesians 4:32) is equivalent to having a tender conscience, and tenderness of conscience is vital to being used by God.

In I Timothy 4:1, 2, Paul wrote, "But the [Holy] Spirit distinctly and expressly declares that in latter times some will turn away from the faith, giving attention to deluding and seducing spirits and doctrines that demons teach, through the hypocrisy and pretensions of liars whose consciences are seared (cauterized)."

It is dangerous to become hard-hearted and to develop a seared conscience. If we do, we cannot really tell if we are doing anything wrong or not. One way we develop tender consciences is by being quick to repent and avoid excuses when God convicts us of something.

When God shows us we did something wrong, we need to say, "You are right, Lord. I am wrong. There is no excuse, so please forgive me and help me not do it again."

It is amazing how much that will help us have tender consciences toward God. But as soon as we start trying to reason things out and make excuses for our wrongs, we start getting a little callous on our consciences. It becomes just a little bit harder for us to feel than it was the time before.

For example, if I mistreat someone and do not repent, my conscience begins to callous. The next time I do it, my conscience gets a little more callous. Soon, though I go around presenting myself as a person who loves God, He cannot use me anymore because I am mistreating people in how I talk to them and behave toward them. The worst thing is that I do not even realize I am doing it because I no longer have a tender heart and a tender conscience toward God.

We must remember that God does not care how gifted or talented we are; His primary concern is our heart attitude. If we have willing hearts, stirred-up hearts, wise hearts, perfect hearts, and tender consciences, the devil's plan for destruction is destroyed because then nothing can stop us from being used by God.

putting the Word to work

Is there someone in your life you admire so much that you try to be like that person? It is not bad to have godly role models. Ephesians 5:1, 2 tells us that our best role model is God and that we are to imitate Him. One of the best ways to do that is to walk in love. Ask God often to show you how to walk in His love, how to receive it from Him, and then how to extend it to others.

loved us and gave Himself up for us, a ʳslain offering and sacrifice to God [for you, so that it became] a sweet fragrance. [Ezek. 20:41.]

3 But immorality (sexual vice) and all impurity [ˢof lustful, rich, wasteful living] or greediness must not even be named among you, as is fitting *and* proper among saints (God's consecrated people).

4 Let there be no filthiness (obscenity, indecency) nor foolish *and* sinful (silly and corrupt) talk, nor coarse jesting, which are not fitting *or* becoming; but instead voice your thankfulness [to God].

5 For be sure of this: that no person practicing sexual vice or impurity in thought or in life, or one who is covetous [who has lustful desire for the property of others and is greedy for gain]—for he [in effect] is an idolater—has any inheritance in the kingdom of Christ and of God.

6 Let no one delude *and* deceive you with empty excuses *and* groundless arguments [for these sins], for

through these things the wrath of God comes upon the sons of rebellion *and* disobedience.

7 So do not associate *or* be sharers with them.

8 For once you were darkness, but now you are light in the Lord; walk as children of Light [lead the lives of those native-born to the Light].

9 For the fruit (the effect, the product) of the Light *or* ᵗthe Spirit [consists] in every form of kindly goodness, uprightness of heart, and trueness of life.

10 And try to learn [in your experience] what is pleasing to the Lord [let your lives be constant proofs of what is most acceptable to Him].

11 Take no part in *and* have no fellowship with the fruitless deeds *and* enterprises of darkness, but instead [let your lives be so in contrast as to] ˢexpose *and* reprove *and* convict them.

12 For it is a shame even to speak of *or* mention the things that [such people] practice in secret.

13 But when anything is exposed *and* reproved by the light, it is made visible *and* clear; and where everything is visible *and* clear there is light.

14 Therefore He says, Awake, O sleeper, and arise from the dead, and Christ shall shine (make day dawn) upon you *and* give you light. [Isa. 26:19; 60:1, 2.]

15 Look carefully then how you walk! Live purposefully *and* worthily *and* accurately, not as the unwise *and* witless, but as wise (sensible, intelligent people),

16 Making the very most of the time

speak the Word

Father, I pray that I learn what is pleasing to You and that my life is a constant proof of the things that are most acceptable to You.
ADAPTED FROM EPHESIANS 5:10

r Marvin Vincent, *Word Studies*.   **s** Joseph Thayer, *A Greek-English Lexicon*.   **t** Some ancient manuscripts so read.

[buying up each opportunity], because the days are evil.

17 Therefore do not be vague *and* thoughtless *and* foolish, but understanding *and* firmly grasping what the will of the Lord is.

putting the Word to work

Time is a very valuable commodity. Have you ever found yourself wishing there were more than twenty-four hours in a day? Ask God to teach you to live wisely (see Ephesians 5:15–17). Pay attention to the way you spend your time and make the most of every opportunity.

18 And do not get drunk with wine, for that is debauchery; but ever be filled *and* stimulated with the [Holy] Spirit. [Prov. 23:20.]

19 Speak out to one another in psalms and hymns and spiritual songs, offering praise with voices [ᵘand instruments] and making melody with all your heart to the Lord,

20 At all times and for everything giving thanks in the name of our Lord Jesus Christ to God the Father.

21 Be subject to one another out of reverence for Christ (the Messiah, the Anointed One).

22 Wives, be subject (be submissive and adapt yourselves) to your own husbands as [a service] to the Lord.

23 For the husband is head of the wife as Christ is the Head of the church, Himself the Savior of [His] body.

24 As the church is subject to Christ, so let wives also be subject in everything to their husbands.

speak the Word

life point

Ephesians 5:18–20 is such a powerful passage! How can we obey it and stay ever filled with the Holy Spirit? We can do it by speaking to ourselves (through our thoughts) or to others (through our words) in psalms and hymns and spiritual songs. We need to keep our thoughts and words full of God's Word by continuously offering praise and giving thanks to Him.

25 Husbands, love your wives, as Christ loved the church and gave Himself up for her,

26 So that He might sanctify her, having cleansed her by the washing of water with the Word,

27 That He might present the church to Himself in glorious splendor, without spot or wrinkle or any such things [that she might be holy and faultless].

28 Even so husbands should love their wives as [being in a sense] their own bodies. He who loves his own wife loves himself.

29 For no man ever hated his own flesh, but nourishes *and* carefully protects and cherishes it, as Christ does the church,

30 Because we are members (parts) of His body.

31 For this reason a man shall leave his father and his mother and shall be joined to his wife, and the two shall become one flesh. [Gen. 2:24.]

32 This mystery is very great, but I speak concerning [the relation of] Christ and the church.

33 However, let each man of you

God, I give thanks to You at all times and for everything in the name of my Lord Jesus Christ.
ADAPTED FROM EPHESIANS 5:20

u George R. Berry, *Greek-English New Testament Lexicon.*

[without exception] love his wife as [being in a sense] his very own self; and let the wife see that she respects *and* reverences her husband ['that she notices him, regards him, honors him, prefers him, venerates, and esteems him; and 'that she defers to him, praises him, and loves and admires him exceedingly]. [I Pet. 3:2.]

6 CHILDREN, OBEY your parents in the Lord [as His representatives], for this is just and right.
2   Honor (esteem and value as precious) your father and your mother— this is the first commandment with a promise—[Exod. 20:12.]
3   That all may be well with you and that you may live long on the earth.
4   Fathers, do not irritate *and* provoke your children to anger [do not exasperate them to resentment], but rear them [tenderly] in the training *and* discipline and the counsel *and* admonition of the Lord.

putting the Word to work

Some of the most rewarding and most challenging relationships can be those with family members, but Ephesians 6:1–4 helps us know how to live with our families in a godly way. If your parents are still living, how can you honor them, even as an adult? If you are a parent, how can you raise your children according to God's principles?

5   Servants (slaves), be obedient to those who are your physical masters, having respect for them and eager concern to please them, in singleness of motive *and* with all your heart, as [service] to Christ [Himself]—
6   Not in the way of eye-service [as if they were watching you] and only to please men, but as servants (slaves) of Christ, doing the will of God heartily *and* with your whole soul;
7   Rendering service readily with goodwill, as to the Lord and not to men,
8   Knowing that for whatever good anyone does, he will receive his reward from the Lord, whether he is slave or free.
9   You masters, act on the same [principle] toward them and give up threatening *and* using violent *and* abusive words, knowing that He Who is both their Master and yours is in heaven, and that there is no respect of persons (no partiality) with Him.
10 In conclusion, be strong in the Lord [be empowered through your union with Him]; draw your strength from Him [that strength which His boundless might provides].
11 Put on God's whole armor [the armor of a heavy-armed soldier which God supplies], that you may be able successfully to stand up against [all] the strategies *and* the deceits of the devil.
12 For we are not wrestling with flesh and blood [contending only with physical opponents], but against the despotisms, against the powers, against [the master spirits who are] the world rulers of this present darkness, against the spirit forces of wickedness in the heavenly (supernatural) sphere.
13 Therefore put on God's complete armor, that you may be able to resist *and* stand your ground on the evil day [of danger], and, having done all [the crisis demands], to stand [firmly in your place].
14 Stand   therefore   [hold   your ground], having tightened the belt of

life point

Ephesians 6:12 gives us insight into the spiritual war that all believers are in. Our enemies are not natural, but spiritual. We can never win our battles if we fight against the wrong source in a wrong way. We tend to think that people or circumstances are our problem, but the source of many of our troubles is Satan and his demons. We cannot fight him with carnal (natural) weapons, but only with supernatural ones that God gives us for the destruction of Satan's strongholds (see II Corinthians 10:4).

truth around your loins and having put on the breastplate of integrity *and* of moral rectitude *and* right standing with God,

putting the Word to work

Would you ever leave your house half-dressed? Of course not! However, many of us often forget to put on our spiritual clothing. Every day the forces of Satan wage war against you, and it is important to be protected! With this spiritual protection and authority, you can stand against evil forces. Learn about your spiritual armor (see Ephesians 6:10–18), and as you put your clothes on each day, also put on your armor and pick up your sword! For example, walking in peace is equivalent to putting on your shoes of peace, or walking in righteousness, is equivalent to putting on your breastplate of righteousness which protects your heart from condemnation. God supplies the armor you need to defeat all the attacks of the devil, but you must put it on!

life point

Many of us fight battles in the realm of our emotions, but as Ephesians 6:11–18 teaches, our battle is not just with our emotions, but with the spiritual forces that play on our emotions.

In the King James Version of Ephesians 6:12 we are told that we do not war with flesh and blood, but against principalities and powers, "rulers of the darkness of this world, against spiritual wickedness in high places." This means we war against strong spiritual entities.

It is important for us to see that we cannot fight darkness with darkness. I believe the best way to resist and overcome our powerful spiritual enemy is not by venting our anger and frustration in some fleshly manner. Rather, we need to put on our spiritual armor as described in Ephesians 6:13–17 and yield ourselves to the power and presence of the Holy Spirit within us as we pray (see Ephesians 6:18).

15 And having shod your feet in preparation [to face the enemy with the ʷfirm-footed stability, the promptness, and the readiness ˣproduced by the good news] of the Gospel of peace. [Isa. 52:7.]
16 Lift up over all the [covering] shield of ʷsaving faith, upon which you can quench all the flaming missiles of the wicked [one].
17 And take the helmet of salvation and the sword that the Spirit ʸwields, which is the Word of God.
18 Pray at all times (on every occasion, in every season) in the Spirit, with all [manner of] prayer and

w Marvin Vincent, *Word Studies.* **x** Joseph Thayer, *A Greek-English Lexicon.* **y** Charles B. Williams, *The New Testament: A Translation in the Language of the People*: Subjective genitive—a type of genitive of possession. Thus here the Spirit is the subject or agent of the verbal action.

entreaty. To that end keep alert and watch with strong purpose *and* perseverance, interceding in behalf of all the saints (God's consecrated people).

19 And [pray] also for me, that [freedom of] utterance may be given me, that I may open my mouth to proclaim boldly the mystery of the good news (the Gospel),

20 For which I am an ambassador in a coupling chain [in prison. Pray] that I may declare it boldly *and* courageously, as I ought to do.

21 Now that you may know how I am and what I am doing, Tychicus, the beloved brother and faithful minister in the Lord [and His service], will tell you everything.

22 I have sent him to you for this very purpose, that you may know how we are and that he may ᵞconsole *and* cheer *and* encourage *and* strengthen your hearts.

23 Peace be to the brethren, and love joined with faith, from God the Father and the Lord Jesus Christ (the Messiah, the Anointed One).

24 Grace (God's undeserved favor) be with all who love our Lord Jesus Christ with undying *and* incorruptible [love]. *Amen (so let it be).*

z Joseph Thayer, *A Greek-English Lexicon.*

Philippians

Author:
Paul

Date:
About AD 61

Everyday Life Principles:
Strength comes from the joy of the Lord.

Rejoice in all things and cultivate real joy in your life.

Joy is more than emotional happiness; it can be anything from extreme hilarity to calm delight. Practice that calm delight in every area of your life.

Philippians is full of truths and principles for living a victorious Christian life; it contains much practical advice for everyday life; and it is a book of great joy. Even though Paul wrote this book from a prison cell, undoubtedly in very bad conditions, he had real joy in his heart and he encouraged his readers to do the same. He knew that the joy of the Lord is so important because it is our strength and a source of power (see Nehemiah 8:10). He knew that the enemy always wants to steal our joy so he can sap our strength. His words are as true today as they were when he wrote them, and you and I need to develop and maintain our joy just as the Philippians did so long ago.

I define joy as "anything from extreme hilarity to calm delight, a feeling of pleasure." We all enjoy extreme hilarity from time to time, but what we want in everyday life is that calm delight—that steadfast sense of peace, pleasure, and well-being we can only find through a personal relationship with God.

Whatever you are facing as you read Philippians, let me urge you to rejoice. Even in the midst of difficulties or sadness, the joy of the Lord is available to you and it is your strength. Do learn the many practical lessons that Philippians teaches, but above all, learn to live in the strength that comes from rejoicing in God in every situation. Remember that happiness is based on what happens, but joy is a fruit of the Holy Spirit Who dwells in us as believers in Jesus Christ.

1 PAUL AND Timothy, bond servants of Christ Jesus (the Messiah), to all the saints (God's consecrated people) in Christ Jesus who are at Philippi, with the bishops (overseers) and deacons (assistants):

2 Grace (favor and blessing) to you and [heart] peace from God our Father and the Lord Jesus Christ (the Messiah).

3 I thank my God in all my remembrance of you.

4 In every prayer of mine I always make my entreaty *and* petition for you all with joy (delight).

5 [I thank my God] for your fellowship (your ªsympathetic cooperation and contributions and partnership) in advancing the good news (the Gospel) from the first day [you heard it] until now.

6 And I am convinced *and* sure of this very thing, that He Who began a good work in you will continue until the day of Jesus Christ [right up to the time of His return], developing [that good work] *and* perfecting *and* bringing it to full completion in you.

7 It is right *and* appropriate for me to have this confidence *and* feel this way about you all, because ᵇyou have me in your heart *and* I hold you in my heart as partakers *and* sharers, one *and* all with me, of grace (God's unmerited favor and spiritual blessing). [This is true] both when I am shut up in prison and when I am out in the defense and confirmation of the good news (the Gospel).

8 For God is my witness how I long

life point

Do not be discouraged with yourself just because you have not yet arrived at a place of perfection in your thoughts and behavior. God would not be angry with you if He came back today and found you just as you are, as long as He sees that you have the right attitude and are cooperating with the work He is doing in you. He knows you are a work in progress—and you will be for as long as you live (see Philippians 1:6). Enjoy where you are on the way to where you are going!

for *and* ᶜpursue you all with love, in the tender mercy of Christ Jesus [Himself]!

9 And this I pray: that your love may abound yet more and more *and* extend to its fullest development in knowledge and all keen insight [that your love may ªdisplay itself in greater depth of acquaintance and more comprehensive discernment],

10 So that you may surely learn to sense what is vital, *and* approve *and* prize what is excellent *and* of real value [recognizing the highest and the best, and distinguishing the moral differences], and that you may be untainted *and* pure and unerring *and* blameless [so that with hearts sincere and certain and unsullied, you may approach] the day of Christ [not stumbling *nor* causing others to stumble].

11 May you abound in *and* be filled

speak the Word

God, I pray that my love may abound more and more and extend to its fullest development in knowledge and all keen insight, that it may display itself in greater depth of acquaintance and more comprehensive discernment.
ADAPTED FROM PHILIPPIANS 1:9

---

a Marvin Vincent, *Word Studies in the New Testament.* **b** Alternate translation. **c** Joseph Thayer, *A Greek-English Lexicon of the New Testament.*

God will finish the work

God always finishes what He starts. He has called us unto Himself and started a good work in us, and He will finish it (see Philippians 1:6). That is a promise. Of course, we have a part to play, which is to keep believing Him and cooperating with the sanctifying work of the Holy Spirit in our lives. I know it is frustrating sometimes to feel we are in the middle of something and do not know how to go forward, but to also know that we cannot go back. We love Jesus and want to go all the way through to the finish with Him, but sometimes it becomes difficult. Jesus Himself understands that.

Jesus lived in a fleshly body while He was here on earth and He understands what it is like to be tempted. You may experience temptation to sin or even just to quit and give up, but God will strengthen you to go all the way to the finish with Him if you ask Him. Keep your eyes on the prize. It may be uncomfortable now, but you will be pleased in the end if you allow God to do whatever He wants to do in you.

So many people today start things that they never finish and that is not pleasing to God. In fact, that is not even a good representation of a person who desires to walk in integrity. It is easy to start something because all of our emotions are excited about something new. But, character is seen in what people do when their feelings are no longer supporting them and perhaps they are left alone with just God and a lot of hard work. God's character is to always finish what He starts. What about you? Before you begin anything, count the cost and make the decision that you will finish.

God has promised to finish the work He started in you. Will you make a similar commitment to Him to finish whatever He gives you to do in this life?

with the fruits of righteousness (of right standing with God and right doing) which come through Jesus Christ (the Anointed One), to the honor and praise of God [dthat His glory may be both manifested and recognized].

12 Now I want you to know *and* continue to rest assured, brethren, that what [has happened] to me [this imprisonment] has actually only served to advance *and* give a renewed impetus to the [spreading of the] good news (the Gospel).

13 So much is this a fact that throughout the whole imperial guard and to all the rest [here] my imprison-

ment has become generally known to be in Christ [that I am a prisoner in His service and for Him].

14 And [also] most of the brethren have derived fresh confidence in the

putting the Word to work

Is this a challenging time in your life? Know that God can work through you in any circumstance to further the Gospel and His purposes, just as He did for Paul in Philippians 1:12–14. Ask Him to help you see Him at work even through ways you will not expect.

d Marvin Vincent, *Word Studies in the New Testament*.

Lord because of my chains and are much more bold to speak *and* publish fearlessly the Word of God [acting with more freedom and indifference to the consequences].

15 Some, it is true, [actually] preach Christ (the Messiah) [for no better reason than] out of envy and rivalry (party spirit), but others are doing so out of a loyal spirit *and* goodwill.

16 ᵉThe latter [proclaim Christ] out of love, because they recognize *and* know that I am [providentially] put here for the defense of the good news (the Gospel).

17 ᵉBut the former preach Christ out of a party spirit, insincerely [out of no pure motive, but thinking to annoy me], supposing they are making my bondage more bitter *and* my chains more galling.

18 But what does it matter, so long as either way, whether in pretense [for personal ends] or in all honesty [for the furtherance of the Truth], Christ is being proclaimed? And in that I [now] rejoice, yes, and I shall rejoice [hereafter] also.

19 For I am well assured *and* indeed know that through your prayers and a ᶠbountiful supply of the Spirit of Jesus Christ (the Messiah) this will turn out for my preservation (for the spiritual health and ᶠwelfare of my own soul) *and* avail toward the saving work of the Gospel.

20 This is in keeping with my own eager desire *and* persistent expectation *and* hope, that I shall not disgrace myself *nor* be put to shame in anything; but that with the utmost freedom of speech *and* unfailing courage, now as always heretofore, Christ (the Messiah) will be magnified *and* get glory *and* praise in this body of mine *and* be boldly exalted in my person, whether through (by) life or through (by) death.

21 For me to live is Christ [His life in me], and to die is gain [the gain of the glory of eternity].

22 If, however, it is to be life in the flesh *and* I am to live on here, that means fruitful service for me; so I can say nothing as to my personal prefer- ence [I cannot choose],

23 But I am hard pressed between the two. My yearning desire is to depart (to be free of this world, to set forth) and be with Christ, for that is far, far better;

24 But to remain in my body is more needful *and* essential for your sake.

25 Since I am convinced of this, I know that I shall remain and stay by you all, to promote your progress and joy in believing,

26 So that in me you may have abun- dant cause for exultation *and* glorying in Christ Jesus, through my coming to you again.

27 Only be sure as citizens so to con- duct yourselves [that] your manner of life [will be] worthy of the good news (the Gospel) of Christ, so that whether I [do] come and see you or am absent, I may hear this of you: that you are standing firm in united spirit *and* pur- pose, striving side by side *and* con- tending with a single mind for the faith of the glad tidings (the Gospel).

28 And do not [for a moment] be frightened *or* intimidated in anything by your opponents *and* adversaries, for such [constancy and fearlessness] will be a clear sign (proof and seal) to them of [their impending] destruc- tion, but [a sure token and evidence] of your deliverance *and* salvation, and that from God.

29 For you have been granted [the privilege] for Christ's sake not only to believe in (adhere to, rely on, and trust in) Him, but also to suffer in His behalf.

---

e The order of verses 16 and 17 is that of the most ancient manuscripts; the *King James Version* has them reversed.   **f** Marvin Vincent, *Word Studies*.

constant and fearless

Notice the two words "constancy" and "fearlessness" in Philippians 1:28. They describe the rock-like temperament you and I should display in the face of attacks and onslaughts by our opponents and adversaries—both physical and spiritual.

When people or events come against us to destroy us, we should stand firm and confident that everything is going to work out for the best. We are not to change, but we must remain constant and let God do the changing of the circumstances.

When problems arise—and they will from time to time—we are not to assume that the Lord will intervene and take care of all our problems for us without our invitation. We are to pray and ask Him to change our circumstances. Then we are to remain constant and unchanging, which is a sign to the enemy of his impending downfall and destruction.

Do you know why our constancy and fearlessness are signs to Satan that he will fail? Because he knows that the only way he can overcome a believer is through deception and intimidation. How can he threaten someone who has no fear of him? How can he deceive someone who recognizes his lies and refuses to believe them? What good does it do him to try to stir up fear or anger or depression in someone who will not be moved by emotions but who chooses to stand firmly on the Word of God?

When the devil sees his tactics are not working, he realizes he is failing and will be utterly defeated. Stay constant and fearless and you will overcome the enemy in your life.

30 So you are engaged in the same conflict which you saw me [wage] and which you now hear to be mine [still].

2 SO BY whatever [appeal to you there is in our mutual dwelling in Christ, by whatever] strengthening *and* consoling *and* encouraging [our relationship] in Him [affords], by whatever persuasive ᵍincentive there is in love, by whatever participation in the [Holy] Spirit [we share], and by whatever depth of affection and compassionate sympathy,

2 Fill up *and* complete my joy by living in harmony *and* being of the same mind *and* one in purpose, having the same love, being in full accord and of one harmonious mind *and* intention.

3 Do nothing from factional motives [through contentiousness, strife, selfishness, or for unworthy ends] or prompted by conceit *and* empty arrogance. Instead, in the true spirit of humility (lowliness of mind) let each regard the others as better than *and* superior to himself [thinking more highly of one another than you do of yourselves].

4 Let each of you esteem *and* look upon *and* be concerned for not [merely] his own interests, but also each for the interests of others.

5 Let this same attitude *and* purpose *and* [humble] mind be in you which was in Christ Jesus: [Let Him be your example in humility:]

6 Who, although being essentially one with God *and* in the form of God

g Marvin Vincent, *Word Studies*.

life point

Inspired by the Holy Spirit, the apostle Paul tells us in Philippians 2:3, 4 how to avoid strife through the true spirit of humility by regarding others as "better than and superior" to ourselves. That is a difficult challenge because our flesh wants to shout, "But what about me?"

Yet, this passage clearly exhorts us to be of the same humble mind that Jesus displayed: to think of others as better than ourselves, to be more concerned for their interests and welfare than for our own, and to do nothing from conceit or empty arrogance. If we are obedient to this instruction, if we humble ourselves and are willing to serve others, we will live in harmony and therefore be pleasing to God.

[hpossessing the fullness of the attributes which make God God], did not ithink this equality with God was a thing to be eagerly grasped ior retained,
7 But stripped Himself [of all privileges and jrightful dignity], so as to assume the guise of a servant (slave), in that He became like men *and* was born a human being.
8 And after He had appeared in human form, He abased *and* humbled Himself [still further] and carried His obedience to the extreme of death, even the death of the cross!
9 Therefore [because He stooped so

speak the Word

life point

Jesus set the example for obedience, as we see in Philippians 2:5–8. I want to encourage you to come up to a higher level of obedience. Be quick and prompt to obey, radical and extreme in your obedience.

low] God has highly exalted Him and has kfreely bestowed on Him the name that is above every name,
10 That in (at) the name of Jesus every knee lshould (must) bow, in heaven and on earth and under the earth,
11 And every tongue [kfrankly and openly] confess *and* acknowledge that Jesus Christ is Lord, to the glory of God the Father.
12 Therefore, my dear ones, as you have always obeyed [my suggestions], so now, not only [with the enthusiasm you would show] in my presence but much more because I am absent, work out (cultivate, carry out to the goal, and fully complete) your own salvation with reverence *and* awe and trembling (self-distrust, kwith serious caution, tenderness of conscience, watchfulness against temptation, timidly shrinking from whatever might offend God and discredit the name of Christ).
13 [Not in your own strength] for it is God Who is all the while keffectually at work in you [energizing and creating in you the power and desire], both to will and to work for His good pleasure *and* satisfaction *and* mdelight.

Thank You, God, that You are effectually at work in me to will and to work for Your good pleasure, satisfaction, and delight.
ADAPTED FROM PHILIPPIANS 2:13

h B.B. Warfield, *Biblical Doctrines.* i Joseph Thayer, *A Greek-English Lexicon.* j George R. Berry, *Greek-English New Testament Lexicon.* k Marvin Vincent, *Word Studies.* l "Should" is the past tense of "shall," implying authority or compulsion. m Alexander Souter, *Pocket Lexicon of the Greek New Testament.*

14 Do all things without grumbling *and* faultfinding *and* complaining [ⁿagainst God] and ⁿquestioning *and* doubting [among yourselves],

15 That you may show yourselves to be blameless *and* guileless, innocent *and* uncontaminated, children of God without blemish (faultless, unrebukable) in the midst of a crooked *and* wicked generation [spiritually perverted and perverse], among whom you are seen as bright lights (stars or beacons shining out clearly) in the [dark] world,

putting the Word to work

Do you ever wonder if your life as a Christian makes a difference to those around you? The Bible teaches that it certainly does! In Philippians 2:14, 15, Paul says that just as stars brightly shine against the dark of night, so our lives as Christians shine like light in the spiritual darkness of the world. Ask God to help you shine brightly with His love and joy to those around you.

16 Holding out [to it] *and* offering [to all men] the Word of Life, so that in the day of Christ I may have something of which exultantly to rejoice *and* glory in that I did not run my race in vain or spend my labor to no purpose.

17 Even if [my lifeblood] must be poured out as a libation on the sacrificial offering of your faith [to God], still I am glad [to do it] and °congratulate you all on [your share in] it.

18 And you also in like manner be glad and °congratulate me on [my share in] it.

19 But I hope *and* trust in the Lord Jesus soon to send Timothy to you, so that I may also be encouraged *and* cheered by learning news of you.

20 For I have no one like him [no one of so kindred a spirit] who will be so genuinely interested in your welfare *and* devoted to your interests.

21 For the others all seek [to advance] their own interests, not those of Jesus Christ (the Messiah).

22 But Timothy's tested worth you know, how as a son with his father he has toiled with me zealously in [serving and helping to advance] the good news (the Gospel).

23 I hope therefore to send him promptly, just as soon as I know how my case is going to turn out.

24 But [really] I am confident *and* fully trusting in the Lord that shortly I myself shall come to you also.

25 However, I thought it necessary to send Epaphroditus [back] to you. [He has been] my brother and companion in labor and my fellow soldier, as well as [having come as] your special messenger (apostle) and minister to my need.

26 For he has been [homesick] longing for you all and has been distressed because you had heard that he was ill.

27 He certainly was ill [too], near to death. But God had compassion on him, and not only on him but also on me, lest I should have sorrow [over him] ⁿcoming upon sorrow.

28 So I have sent him the more willingly *and* eagerly, that you may be gladdened at seeing him again, and that I may be the less disquieted.

29 Welcome him [home] then in the Lord with all joy, and honor *and* highly appreciate men like him,

30 For it was through working for Christ that he came so near death, risking his [very] life to complete the deficiencies in your service to me [which distance prevented you yourselves from rendering].

---

n Marvin Vincent, *Word Studies*. **o** Joseph P. Lightfoot, *Saint Paul's Epistle to the Philippians* and James Moulton and George Milligan, *The Vocabulary of the Greek Testament*.

the spiritual and the natural

In Philippians 2:25–30 we find a man named Epaphroditus who was sick due to overwork in the ministry. He was emotionally distressed and homesick. He probably was away from home a long time and possibly lonely. He became so ill that he almost died. But the apostle Paul tells us God had compassion on him and spared his life. In this passage, Paul writes to the Philippians to tell them he was sending Epaphroditus home to rest and recuperate.

I find it interesting that though God healed this man, he still needed time off to rest.

This same principle is evident in the story of Jesus' raising of a young girl from death. In the eighth chapter of Luke, we read that a Jewish religious leader named Jairus approached Jesus asking Him to come to his house and heal his twelve-year-old daughter who was dying. By the time they got to Jairus' home, the girl had already died. But Jesus raised her from the dead. As soon as she got up from her bed, the first thing Jesus told her parents was to give her something to eat (see Luke 8:55).

From those two stories I received the understanding that there is a spiritual side to life and there is also a natural side, and both of them must be kept in balance. Jesus took care of the spiritual side of this young girl's life, but then He instructed her parents to tend to the natural side of her life.

God expects us to use common sense with our spirituality. I encourage you to live a balanced life, obeying both spiritual principles and natural laws. Even though Epaphroditis worked for the Lord, he still became ill because he was not taking care of himself. We cannot break God's laws of health and expect to have no adverse consequences. Remember to stay in balance because that will help you keep the devil out of your life.

3 FOR THE rest, my brethren, delight yourselves in the Lord *and* continue to rejoice that you are in Him. To keep writing to you [over and over] of the same things is not irksome to me, and it is [a precaution] for your safety.
2 Look out for those dogs [Judaizers, legalists], look out for those mis-chief-makers, look out for those who mutilate the flesh.
3 For we [Christians] are the true circumcision, who worship God in spirit *and* by the Spirit of God and exult *and* glory *and* pride ourselves in Jesus Christ, and put no confidence *or* dependence [on what we are] in the flesh *and* on outward privileges *and*

speak the Word

Lord, I delight myself in You and I will continue to rejoice because I am in You!
ADAPTED FROM PHILIPPIANS 3:1

life point

We are not to put confidence in the flesh (see Philippians 3:3)—ours or anybody else's. Where does God want our confidence to be placed? In Him alone.

God despises independence. He wants us to be totally reliant upon Him. He wants us to be as dependent upon Him as a branch is on a vine; the branch withers quickly if it is detached from the vine (see John 15:5). He wants us to lean on Him for everything in our lives and be confident in His love and provision.

physical advantages *and* external appearances—

4 Though for myself I have [at least grounds] to rely on the flesh. If any other man considers that he has *or* seems to have reason to rely on the flesh *and* his physical *and* outward advantages, I have still more!

5 Circumcised when I was eight days old, of the race of Israel, of the tribe of Benjamin, a Hebrew [and the son] of Hebrews; as to the observance of the Law I was of [the party of] the Pharisees,

6 As to my zeal, I was a persecutor of the church, and by the Law's standard of righteousness (supposed justice, uprightness, and right standing with God) I was proven to be blameless *and* no fault was found with me.

7 But whatever former things I had that might have been gains to me, I have come to consider as [Pone combined] loss for Christ's sake.

8 Yes, furthermore, I count everything as loss compared to the possession of the priceless privilege (the overwhelming preciousness, the surpassing worth, and supreme advantage) of knowing Christ Jesus my Lord *and* of progressively becoming more deeply *and* intimately acquainted with Him [of perceiving and recognizing and understanding Him more fully and clearly]. For His sake I have lost everything and consider it all to be mere rubbish (refuse, dregs), in order that I may win (gain) Christ (the Anointed One),

9 And that I may [actually] be found *and* known as in Him, not having any [self-achieved] righteousness that can be called my own, based on my obedience to the Law's demands (ritualistic uprightness and supposed right standing with God thus acquired), but possessing that [genuine righteousness] which comes through faith in Christ (the Anointed One), the [truly] right standing with God, which comes from God by [saving] faith.

10 [For my determined purpose is] that I may know Him [that I may progressively become more deeply and intimately acquainted with Him, perceiving and recognizing and understanding the wonders of His Person more strongly and more clearly], and that I may in that same way come to know the power outflowing from His resurrection [qwhich it exerts over believers], and that I may so share His sufferings as to be continually transformed [in spirit into His likeness even] to His death, [in the hope]

11 That if possible I may attain to the [rspiritual and moral] resurrection [that lifts me] out from among the dead [even while in the body].

12 Not that I have now attained [this ideal], or have already been made perfect, but I press on to lay hold of (grasp) *and* make my own, that for which Christ Jesus (the Messiah) has laid hold of me *and* made me His own.

p Marvin Vincent, *Word Studies*: His "gains" are plural, but they are all counted as one combined "loss" (singular). q Marvin Vincent, *Word Studies*. r Charles B. Williams, *The New Testament: A Translation in the Language of the People*: A spiritual, moral resurrection—not the final, physical one, which will be the climax.

take the pressure off

In Philippians 3:9 Paul says he wants to achieve one thing in life—to be found and known in Christ.

This needs to be our attitude also. We cannot always manifest perfect *behavior*, but with God's help we can keep pressing toward the goal.

Do you know why God never lets us achieve perfect behavior? If we ever did, we would derive our sense of worth from our perfection and performance rather than from His love and grace.

If you and I behaved perfectly all the time, we would think God owed us an answer to our prayers because of our obedience to all the rules and regulations. So do you know what God does? He leaves us some weaknesses so we will have to go to Him constantly to ask for His help. Our weaknesses keep us dependent on Him, whether we like it or not.

God is not going to let us work our way into a sense of peace and fulfillment. But He will allow us to work ourselves into a fit and frenzy. Why? So we realize that works of the flesh produce nothing but misery and frustration (see Romans 3:20).

If that is so, what are we supposed to do? Trust God, relax, and enjoy life. We need to learn to enjoy God more. That will not only help us, it will also take the pressure off the people around us. We need to quit demanding perfection from ourselves and everyone around us. We need to start enjoying people just as they are.

In essence Paul said he wanted to stand before God and say, "Well, here I am, Lord, and though I do not have a perfect record, I do believe in Jesus. My righteousness is in Him, not in my ability to perform." Make that your goal, too!

13 I do not consider, brethren, that I have captured *and* made it my own [yet]; but one thing I do [it is my one aspiration]: forgetting what lies behind and straining forward to what lies ahead,

putting the Word to work

Do you know your purpose in life? Paul says in Philippians 3:12 that there is a specific, unique purpose in life for which Christ took hold of you. Ask God to continue revealing to you what your unique purpose is so you can lay hold of all that God has for you!

14 I press on toward the goal to win the [supreme and heavenly] prize to which God in Christ Jesus is calling us upward.
15 So let those [of us] who are spiritually mature *and* full-grown have this mind *and* hold these convictions; and if in any respect you have a different attitude of mind, God will make that clear to you also.
16 Only let us hold true to what we have already attained *and* walk *and* order our lives by that.
17 Brethren, together follow my example and observe those who live after the pattern we have set for you.
18 For there are many, of whom I

1957

life point

The devil wants each of us to concentrate on how far we have fallen, rather than how far we have risen. Satan wants us to focus on our pasts instead of our futures and on how far we still have to go, rather than how far we have come. He wants us to think about how many times we fail, rather than how many times we succeed.

But *God* wants us to focus on our strengths and not our weaknesses, our victories and not our losses, our joys and not our problems. Philippians 3:13, 14 tells us that God wants us to press forward and respond to His upward call and forget what lies behind us. Pay attention to what you focus on and magnify the works of the Lord. Do not believe the lies of the devil.

have often told you and now tell you even with tears, who walk (live) as enemies of the cross of Christ (the Anointed One).

19 They are doomed *and* their ˢfate is eternal misery (perdition); their god is their stomach (their appetites, their sensuality) and they glory in their shame, ˢsiding with earthly things *and* being of their party.

20 But we are citizens of the state (commonwealth, homeland) which is in heaven, and from it also we ᵗearnestly *and* patiently await [the coming of] the Lord Jesus Christ (the Messiah) [as] Savior,

21 Who will ᵗtransform *and* fashion anew the body of our humiliation to conform to *and* be like the body of His glory *and* majesty, by exerting that power which enables Him even to subject everything to Himself.

4 THEREFORE, MY brethren, whom I love and yearn to see, my delight and crown (wreath of victory), thus stand firm in the Lord, my beloved.

2 I entreat *and* advise Euodia and I entreat *and* advise Syntyche to agree *and* to work in harmony in the Lord.

3 And I exhort you too, [my] genuine yokefellow, help these [two women to keep on cooperating], for they have toiled along with me in [the spreading of] the good news (the Gospel), as have Clement and the rest of my fellow workers whose names are in the Book of Life.

putting the Word to work

Have you ever thought it would be neat to be mentioned in the Bible? Imagine being known in God's Word, as Euodia and Syntyche are in Philippians 4:2, 3, for arguing! When you disagree with others, ask God to give you a gracious spirit and do all you can to resolve conflicts when they happen.

4 Rejoice in the Lord always [delight, gladden yourselves in Him]; again I say, Rejoice! [Ps. 37:4.]

5 Let all men know *and* perceive *and* recognize your unselfishness (your considerateness, your forbearing spirit). The Lord is near [He is ˢcoming soon].

6 Do not fret *or* have any anxiety about anything, but in every circumstance *and* in everything, by prayer and petition (ˢdefinite requests), with thanksgiving, continue to make your wants known to God.

7 And God's peace [shall be yours, that ˢtranquil state of a soul assured of its salvation through Christ, and so fearing nothing from God and being content with its earthly lot of whatever

s Joseph Thayer, *A Greek-English Lexicon*.   **t** Marvin Vincent, *Word Studies*.

life point

In Philippians 4:6 the apostle Paul teaches us how to solve our problems. He instructs us to pray "with thanksgiving" in every circumstance.

The Lord taught the same principle to me this way: "Joyce, why should I give you anything else, if you are not thankful for what you already have? Why should I give you something else to complain about?"

If we cannot offer our current prayer requests from the foundation of a life that is currently filled with thanksgiving, we will not get a favorable response. The Word does not instruct us to pray with complaining; it says to pray with thanksgiving.

putting the Word to work

Do you ever think about what you are thinking about? If you are not careful, your thought life can lead you into problems. It is important to think before you act, and if you concentrate on things that are true, worthy of reverence and honorable, just, pure, lovely, kind and gracious, virtuous, and excellent (see Philippians 4:8), your actions will reflect God's character and heart.

it, and the God of peace (of ᵛuntroubled, undisturbed well-being) will be with you.

10 I was made very happy in the Lord that now you have revived your interest in my welfare after so long a time; you were indeed thinking of me, but you had no opportunity to show it.

11 Not that I am implying that I was in any personal want, for I have learned how to be ᵂcontent (satisfied to the point where I am not disturbed or disquieted) in whatever state I am.

12 I know how to be abased and live humbly in straitened circumstances, and I know also how to enjoy plenty and live in abundance. I have learned in any and all circumstances the secret of facing every situation, whether well-fed or going hungry, having a sufficiency and enough to spare or going without and being in want.

13 I have strength for all things in Christ Who empowers me [I am ready for anything and equal to anything

sort that is, that peace] which transcends all understanding shall ᵘgarrison and mount guard over your hearts and minds in Christ Jesus.

8 For the rest, brethren, whatever is true, whatever is worthy of reverence and is honorable and seemly, whatever is just, whatever is pure, whatever is lovely and lovable, whatever is kind and winsome and gracious, if there is any virtue and excellence, if there is anything worthy of praise, think on and weigh and take account of these things [fix your minds on them].

9 Practice what you have learned and received and heard and seen in me, and model your way of living on

speak the Word

I declare, Lord, that I have strength for all things in Christ Who empowers me. I am ready for anything and equal to anything through Him.
ADAPTED FROM PHILIPPIANS 4:13

u William Gurnall, cited by Marvin Vincent, *Word Studies*. v Hermann Cremer, *Biblico-Theological Lexicon of New Testament Greek*. w Literal translation: "self-sufficient."

think about what you're thinking about

The Bible presents detailed instruction on what kinds of things we should think about. You can see from Philippians 4:8 that we are instructed to think on good things, things that will build us up and not tear us down.

Our thoughts certainly affect our attitudes and moods. Everything the Lord tells us is for our own good. He knows what makes us happy and what makes us miserable. When people are full of wrong thoughts, they are miserable, and I have learned from personal experience that miserable people usually end up making others miserable also.

Take a personal inventory on a regular basis and ask yourself, "What have I been thinking about?" Spend some time examining your thought life.

Thinking about what you are thinking about is very valuable because Satan usually deceives people into thinking that the source of their misery or trouble is something other than what it really is. He wants them to think they are unhappy due to what is going on around them (their circumstances), but the misery is actually due to what is going on *inside* them (their thoughts).

For many years I really believed I was unhappy because of things others were doing or not doing. I blamed my misery on my husband and my children. I thought I would be happy if they were different, if they would be more attentive to my needs, if they would help around the house more. It was first one thing and then another for years. I finally faced the truth, which was that none of these things made me unhappy if I chose to have the right attitude. My thoughts were making me miserable.

I urge you to *think about what you are thinking about*. When you change the things you allow your mind to dwell on, you are on your way to greater freedom, wholeness, and victory.

through Him Who ˣinfuses inner strength into me; I am ʸself-sufficient in Christ's sufficiency].

14 But it was right *and* commendable *and* noble of you to contribute for my needs *and* to share my difficulties with me.

15 And you Philippians yourselves well know that in the early days of the Gospel ministry, when I left Macedonia, no church (assembly) entered into partnership with me *and* opened up [a debit and credit] account in giving and receiving except you only.

16 For even in Thessalonica you sent [me contributions] for my needs, not only once but a second time.

17 Not that I seek *or* am eager for [your] gift, but I do seek *and* am eager for the fruit which increases to your credit [the harvest of blessing that is accumulating to your account].

x Marvin Vincent, *Word Studies*.   **y** Note that in Phil. 4:11, the Greek *autarkas*, translated "content," is literally "self-sufficient."

putting the Word to work

All of us have daily needs and wants. Do you realize that sometimes what you want might not be what you need? Thank God that He knows exactly what you need and He will be faithful to provide (see Philippians 4:19).

18 But I have [your full payment] and more; I have everything I need *and* am amply supplied, now that I have received from Epaphroditus the gifts you sent me. [They are the] fragrant odor of an offering *and* sacrifice which God welcomes *and* in which He delights.

19 And my God will liberally supply (²fill to the full) your every need according to His riches in glory in Christ Jesus.

20 To our God and Father be glory forever and ever (through the endless eternities of the eternities). *Amen (so be it).*

21 Remember me to every saint (every born-again believer) in Christ Jesus. The brethren (my ªassociates) who are with me greet you.

22 All the saints (God's consecrated ones here) wish to be remembered to you, especially those of Caesar's household.

23 The grace (spiritual favor and blessing) of the Lord Jesus Christ (the Anointed One) be with your spirit. *Amen (so be it).*

life point

Philippians 4:13 is frequently quoted, especially in its King James translation: "I can do all things . . . " I believe sometimes this verse is taken out of context. It does not mean that I can do anything I *want* to do, or that I can do anything someone else does. It means that I am able to do whatever God assigns me.

In this context, the apostle Paul refers to the ability to be abased or to abound and to be content either way (see Philippians 4:12). He knew that whatever state he was in, it was God's will for him at that moment, and he also knew that God would strengthen him to do what He was calling him to do. Paul believed that even unpleasant things would ultimately work out for his good (see Romans 8:28).

This understanding of Philippians 4:13 helps me a great deal in my life to deal with difficulties and remain positive, and it helps me in my ministry. It teaches me to remain within the boundaries of what the Lord has called and equipped me to do and not try to undertake things that are not within my God-given talents and abilities to accomplish. This attitude takes pressure off of me and it will do the same for you.

z Joseph Thayer, *A Greek-English Lexicon.*　**a** Alexander Souter, *Pocket Lexicon.*

Colossians

Author:
Paul

Date:
About AD 61

Everyday Life Principles:
In everything you do, keep Jesus first.

Do everything you do as though you are working for God.

Remember that you are complete and fully forgiven in Christ.

Paul's message in his letter to the Colossians is all about Jesus. In this book, Paul addresses a popular false teaching that undermined the sufficiency and lordship of Jesus Christ and was prevalent in the city of Colossae. In response, Paul wrote throughout Colossians of Jesus' power and preeminence, of His superiority over worldly thinking, legalism, and carnal Christianity. His loyalty and passion for Jesus is seen throughout this letter, and I hope that his zeal inspires you today.

Among all the great teaching in Colossians, Paul continually urges us to keep Jesus first in our lives. He exhorts us to do everything as though we are doing it for God and not for other people (see Colossians 3:23). He tells us that Christ is in us as the hope of glory (see Colossians 1:27) and reminds us that we are complete and forgiven in Him (see Colossians 2:10, 13).

As you read Colossians, my prayer for you is the same as Paul's prayer in Colossians 1:9–11: that you are filled with the knowledge of God's will, that you have spiritual discernment, that you walk in a manner worthy of the Lord, that your life bears fruit, that you grow and increase in the knowledge of God, and that you are strengthened with all power and with joy. I also pray that you see Jesus in ways you never have before and that His presence and power will increase daily in your life.

1 PAUL, AN apostle (special messenger) of Christ Jesus (the Messiah), by the will of God, and Timothy [our] brother,

2 To the saints (the consecrated people of God) and [a]believing *and* faithful brethren in Christ who are at Colossae: Grace (spiritual favor and blessing) to you and [heart] peace from God our Father.

3 We [b]continually give thanks to God the Father of our Lord Jesus Christ (the Messiah), as we are praying for you,

4 For we have heard of your faith in Christ Jesus [[c]the leaning of your entire human personality on Him in absolute trust and confidence in His power, wisdom, and goodness] and of the love which you [have and show] for all the saints (God's consecrated ones),

life point

According to Colossians 1:4, faith is the leaning of the entire human personality on God in absolute trust and confidence in His power, wisdom, and goodness.

Do you know what that says to me? It says that my faith is manifested as I lean on God totally, taking all the weight off myself and placing everything on Him, trusting in: 1) His power and ability to do *what* needs to be done, 2) His wisdom and knowledge to do it *when* it needs to be done, and 3) His goodness and love to do it the *way* it needs to be done.

5 Because of the hope [of experiencing what is] laid up ([a]reserved and waiting) for you in heaven. Of this [hope] you heard in the past in the message of the truth of the Gospel,

6 Which has come to you. Indeed, in the whole world [that Gospel] is bearing fruit *and* still is growing [d][by its own inherent power], even as it has done among yourselves ever since the day you first heard and came to know *and* understand the grace of God in truth. [You came to know the grace or undeserved favor of God in reality, deeply and clearly and thoroughly, becoming accurately and intimately acquainted with it.]

7 You so learned it from Epaphras, our beloved fellow servant. He is a faithful minister of Christ in our stead *and* as our representative *and* [e]yours.

8 Also he has informed us of your love in the [Holy] Spirit.

9 For this reason we also, from the day we heard of it, have not ceased to pray *and* make [[a]special] request for you, [asking] that you may be filled with the [a]full (deep and clear) knowledge of His will in all spiritual wisdom [[d]in comprehensive insight into the ways and purposes of God] and in understanding *and* discernment of spiritual things—

10 That you may walk (live and conduct yourselves) in a manner worthy of the Lord, fully pleasing to Him *and* [f]desiring to please Him in all things, bearing fruit in every good work and steadily growing *and* increasing in *and*

putting the Word to work

What kind of prayers do you pray for yourself and for others? Colossians 1:9–11 is an awesome prayer to pray. Ask God to fill you with the knowledge of His will in all spiritual wisdom, understanding, and discernment so you can live a life worthy of Him and bear fruit. Ask Him also to strengthen you with power and might.

a Marvin Vincent, *Word Studies in the New Testament*.   b Marvin Vincent, *Word Studies in the New Testament*: "Continually" belongs with "give thanks," not elsewhere.   c Alexander Souter, *Pocket Lexicon of the Greek New Testament*.   d Alexander Souter, *Pocket Lexicon*.   e Many ancient manuscripts read "yours."   f Joseph Thayer, *A Greek-English Lexicon of the New Testament*.

by the knowledge of God [with fuller, deeper, and clearer insight, ᵍacquaintance, and recognition].

11 [We pray] that you may be invigorated *and* strengthened with all power according to the might of His glory, [to exercise] every kind of endurance and patience (perseverance and forbearance) with joy,

life point

Paul prayed that the Colossians would endure "with joy" (Colossians 1:11). Why with joy? Joy enables us to enjoy our journey in life whether we are in adverse circumstances or not. Joy is also our strength and a weapon of spiritual warfare. Joy is a fruit of the Holy Spirit.

We will never experience the joy Jesus intended for us to have if we wait until every circumstance is perfect in our lives. No matter what we endure, we can pray for one another to experience God's joy. I encourage you to pray for and live in that joy.

12 Giving thanks to the Father, Who has qualified *and* made us fit to share the ʰportion which is the inheritance of the saints (God's holy people) in the Light.

13 [The Father] has delivered *and* ⁱdrawn us to Himself out of the control *and* the dominion of darkness and has transferred us into the kingdom of the Son ʲof His love,

speak the Word

14 In Whom we have our redemption *through His blood,* [which means] the forgiveness of our sins.

15 [Now] He is the ᵏexact likeness of the unseen God [the visible representation of the invisible]; He is the First-born of all creation.

16 For it was in Him that all things were created, in heaven and on earth, things seen and things unseen, whether thrones, dominions, rulers, or authorities; all things were created *and* exist through Him [by His service, intervention] and in *and* for Him.

17 And He Himself existed before all things, and in Him all things consist (cohere, are held together). [Prov. 8:22-31.]

18 He also is the Head of [His] body, the church; seeing He is the Beginning, the Firstborn from among the dead, so that He alone in everything *and* in every respect might occupy the chief place [stand first and be preeminent].

19 For it has pleased [the Father] that all the divine fullness (the sum total of the divine perfection, powers, and attributes) should dwell in Him ʰpermanently.

20 And God purposed that through (ⁱby the service, the intervention of) Him [the Son] all things should be completely reconciled ʰback to Himself, whether on earth or in heaven, as through Him, [the Father] made peace by means of the blood of His cross.

21 And although you at one time

g G. Abbott-Smith, *Manual Greek Lexicon of the New Testament.* **h** Marvin Vincent, *Word Studies.* **i** Joseph Thayer, *A Greek-English Lexicon.* **j** Literal translation. **k** Charles B. Williams, *The New Testament: A Translation in the Language of the People*: Strong terms—thus translated "exact likeness."

strengthened with joy

We learn a good lesson by examining the prayers of the apostle Paul. It seems to me that he never prayed for deliverance from things, but for the strength to endure them with joy and good temper. He also prayed that for the church at Colossae, as we see in Colossians 1:11.

In thirty years of ministry, I never had anyone ask me to pray for them to endure with joy, but I am frequently asked to pray for deliverance from situations. I believe we can learn a valuable lesson from Paul's prayer.

God is more interested in changing us than He is in changing our circumstances. He does not delight in watching us suffer or have a difficult time, but He does delight in our spiritual growth. If we are honest with ourselves we must admit that most of our spiritual maturity develops during the hard times in our lives, not during the easy times.

Opposition stretches us. It stretches our faith, teaches us not to trust in ourselves to solve our problems, and gives us compassion for other people who go through difficulties. The apostle James said that our trials will eventually bring out patience and that when patience is fully developed in us, we will lack nothing (see James 1:4). He even states that we should be exceedingly joyful in various trials and tribulations because of what they are working in us (see James 1:2, 3).

I want to encourage you to pray the way Paul prayed in Colossians 1:11. Ask for strength to endure with joy rather than wanting to avoid everything that is difficult and remember that anything God allows will ultimately work out for your good if you trust Him and keep on praying.

were estranged *and* alienated from Him and were of hostile attitude of mind in your wicked activities,

22 Yet now has [Christ, the Messiah] reconciled [you to God] in the body of His flesh through death, in order to present you holy and faultless and irreproachable in His [the Father's] presence.

23 [And this He will do] provided that you continue to ¹stay with *and* in the faith [in Christ], well-grounded and settled *and* steadfast, not shifting *or* moving away from the hope [which rests on and is inspired by] the glad tidings (the Gospel), which you heard and which has been preached ᵐ[as being designed for and offered without restrictions] to every person under heaven, and of which [Gospel] I, Paul, became a minister.

24 [Even] now I rejoice in ¹the midst of my sufferings on your behalf. And in my own person I am making up whatever is still lacking *and* remains to be completed [¹on our part] of Christ's afflictions, for the sake of His body, which is the church.

25 In it I became a minister in accordance with the divine ¹stewardship which was entrusted to me for you [as its object and for your benefit], to

l Marvin Vincent, *Word Studies*.   **m** Adam Clarke, *The Holy Bible with A Commentary*.

first priority

When setting our priorities, it is important to understand that Jesus is the holding power of all that is good in our lives, according to Colossians 1:17. He should always be our first priority because He holds everything together.

A couple cannot have a good marriage if Jesus is not holding it together. In fact, people have difficulty having good personal relationships with *anybody* if Jesus is not leading and influencing individuals to love each other. Our finances are usually a mess without Jesus. Our thoughts are clouded and confused without Jesus. Our emotions are out of control without Him.

Colossians 1:18 tells us that Jesus is the head of the church body; therefore, He alone, in every respect, should occupy the chief place in our lives. If Jesus is not first in our lives, then we need to rearrange our priorities. Matthew 6:33 says if we seek "first of all" the kingdom of God and His righteousness, other things will be added to our lives. The *Amplified Bible* defines this righteousness as "His way of doing and being right."

Seeking the kingdom means finding out how God wants things done; finding out how He wants us to treat people; finding out how He wants us to act in situations and circumstances; finding out what He wants us to do with our money; finding out what kind of an attitude we should have; even finding out what kind of entertainment Jesus approves of.

Our lives will not be blessed if we keep God in a little Sunday-morning box and let Him have our priority attention for only forty-five minutes once a week during a church service. As long as we are here in this world, we will have to resist becoming like the world. Life in our world can be a daily battle, but the key to victory is to remember that Jesus holds everything together and that we need to keep Him first in our lives.

make the Word of God fully known [among you]—

26 The mystery of which was hidden for ages and generations [nfrom angels and men], but is now revealed to His holy people (the saints),

27 To whom God was pleased to make known how great for the Gentiles are the riches of the glory of this mystery, which is Christ within *and* among you, the Hope of [realizing the] glory.

28 Him we preach *and* proclaim, warning *and* admonishing everyone and instructing everyone in all wisdom (ocomprehensive insight into the ways and purposes of God), that we may present every person mature (full-grown, fully initiated, complete, and perfect) in Christ (the Anointed One).

29 For this I labor [punto weariness], striving with all the psuperhuman

n Johann Bengel, *Gnomon Novi Testamenti* and Henry Alford, *The Greek New Testament.*   o Alexander Souter, *Pocket Lexicon.*   p Marvin Vincent, *Word Studies.*

the hope of glory

Colossians 1:26, 27 tells us that Christ "within and among" us is the Hope of glory. You and I can only realize and experience the glory of God in our lives because Christ is in us. He is our hope of seeing better things.

The glory of God is His manifested excellence. As the children of God, we have a blood-bought right to experience the best God has planned for us. Satan furiously fights the plan of God in each of our lives, and his primary weapon is deception. When we are deceived, we believe something that is not true. Even though it is not true, it seems true to us because that is what we believe.

Much of the time we feel defeated as we look at ourselves and our lack of ability. What we need to do is remember that Christ in us is our "Hope [of realizing] the glory." He keeps us encouraged enough to press on toward better things. We limit ourselves when we look to ourselves alone and fail to see Jesus.

In John 11:40 Jesus said to Martha, "Did I not tell you and promise you that if you would believe and rely on Me, you would see the glory of God?" The Lord has destined His church for glory. Glory is manifested excellence and goodness. He is coming back for a glorious church (see Ephesians 5:27). We can be excellent people with excellent attitudes, excellent thoughts, and excellent words. God's glory can be manifested in us and among us only if we believe it is possible.

God is looking for someone who will believe and receive. Start expecting more of His glory in your life. He is waiting to manifest His glory to you and through you!

energy which He so mightily enkindles *and* works within me.

2 FOR I want you to know how great is my solicitude for you [how severe an inward struggle I am engaged in for you] and for those [believers] at Laodicea, and for all who [ᵈlike yourselves] have never seen my face *and* known me personally.

2 [For my concern is] that their hearts may be ᑫbraced (comforted, cheered, and encouraged) as they are knit together in love, that they may come to have all the abounding wealth *and* blessings of assured conviction of understanding, and that they may become progressively ʳmore intimately acquainted with *and* may know more definitely *and* accurately *and* thoroughly that mystic secret of God, [which is] Christ (the Anointed One).

3 In Him all the treasures of [divine] wisdom (ˢcomprehensive insight into the ways and purposes of God) and [all the riches of spiritual] knowledge *and* enlightenment are stored up *and* lie hidden.

4 I say this in order that no one may mislead *and* delude you by plausible *and* persuasive *and* attractive arguments *and* beguiling speech.

5 For though I am away from you in body, yet I am with you in spirit, delighted at the sight of your [standing shoulder to shoulder in such] orderly array and the firmness *and*

q Marvin Vincent, *Word Studies.*   r Richard Trench, *Synonyms of the New Testament.*   s Alexander Souter, *Pocket Lexicon.*

life point

Glory is the manifestation of God's excellence and goodness. We all want glory, but we can only hope to experience it because of God's presence in our lives as believers in Jesus Christ. That is what Paul talks about in Colossians 1:27.

Christ must live in us; otherwise there is no hope of our ever experiencing the glory of God. We can look forward to new realms of glory on a continual basis because of His grace and favor, which He gives to those who believe. Rejoice in the Hope of glory, which is Christ in you.

the solid front *and* steadfastness of your faith in Christ [that ¹leaning of the entire human personality on Him in absolute trust and confidence in His power, wisdom, and goodness].
6 As you have therefore received Christ, [even] Jesus the Lord, [so] walk (regulate your lives and conduct yourselves) in union with *and* conformity to Him.
7 Have the roots [of your being] firmly *and* deeply planted [in Him, fixed and founded in Him], being continually built up in Him, becoming

increasingly more confirmed *and* established in the faith, just as you were taught, and abounding *and* overflowing in it with thanksgiving.
8 See to it that no one carries you off as spoil *or* makes you yourselves captive by his so-called philosophy *and* intellectualism and vain deceit (idle fancies and plain nonsense), following human tradition (men's ideas of the material rather than the spiritual world), just crude notions following the rudimentary *and* elemental teachings of the universe and disregarding [the teachings of] Christ (the Messiah).
9 For in Him the whole fullness of Deity (the Godhead) continues to dwell in bodily form [giving complete expression of the divine nature].
10 And you ᵘare in Him, made full *and* having come to fullness of life [in Christ you too are filled with the Godhead—Father, Son and Holy Spirit—and reach full spiritual stature]. And He is the Head of all rule and authority [of every angelic principality and power].
11 In Him also you were circumcised with a circumcision not made with hands, but in a [spiritual] circumcision [performed by] Christ by stripping off the body of the flesh (the whole corrupt, carnal nature with its passions and lusts).

speak the Word

Thank You, Jesus, that all the treasures of divine wisdom and insight into the ways and purposes of God are stored up and hidden in You. I ask You to reveal them to me.
ADAPTED FROM COLOSSIANS 2:3

God, I pray that the roots of my being are firmly and deeply planted in Christ, that I am continually built up in Him, becoming increasingly established in the faith.
ADAPTED FROM COLOSSIANS 2:7

t Alexander Souter, *Pocket Lexicon.*   **u** Marvin Vincent, *Word Studies.*

12 [Thus ᵛyou were circumcised when] you were buried with Him in [your] baptism, in which you were also raised with Him [ʷto a new life] through [your] faith in the working of God [ʷas displayed] when He raised Him up from the dead.

13 And you who were dead in trespasses and in the uncircumcision of your flesh (your sensuality, your sinful carnal nature), [God] brought to life together with [Christ], having [freely] forgiven us all our transgressions,

14 Having cancelled *and* blotted out *and* wiped away the handwriting of the note (bond) with its legal decrees *and* demands which was in force *and* stood against us (hostile to us). This [note with its regulations, decrees, and demands] He set aside *and* cleared ʷcompletely out of our way by nailing it to [His] cross.

15 [God] disarmed the principalities and powers that were ranged against us and made a bold display *and* public example of them, in triumphing over them in Him *and* in it [the cross].

16 Therefore let no one sit in judgment on you in matters of food and drink, or with regard to a feast day or a New Moon or a Sabbath.

17 Such [things] are only the shadow of things that are to come, *and* they have only a symbolic value. But the reality (the substance, the solid fact of what is foreshadowed, the body of it) belongs to Christ.

18 Let no one defraud you by acting as an umpire *and* declaring you unworthy *and* disqualifying you for the prize, insisting on self-abasement and worship of angels, taking his stand on visions [he claims] he has seen, vainly puffed up by his sensuous notions *and* inflated by his unspiritual thoughts *and* fleshly conceit,

19 And not holding fast to the Head, from Whom the entire body, supplied and knit together by means of its joints and ligaments, grows with a growth that is from God.

20 If then you have died with Christ to material ways of looking at things *and* have escaped from the world's crude *and* elemental notions *and* teachings of externalism, why do you live as if you still belong to the world? [Why do you submit to rules *and* regulations?—such as]

21 Do not handle [this], Do not taste [that], Do not even touch [them],

22 Referring to things all of which perish with being used. To do this is to follow human precepts and doctrines. [Isa. 29:13.]

23 Such [practices] have indeed the outward appearance [that popularly passes] for wisdom, in promoting self-imposed rigor of devotion *and* delight in self-humiliation *and* severity of discipline of the body, but they are of no value in checking the indulgence of the flesh (the lower nature). [Instead, they do not honor God but serve only to indulge the flesh.]

3 IF THEN you have been raised with Christ [to a new life, thus sharing His resurrection from the dead], aim at *and* seek the [rich,

speak the Word

Thank You, Jesus, for disarming the principalities and powers that were against me and making a bold display of them by triumphing over them at the cross.
Colossians 2:15

---

v Marvin Vincent, *Word Studies*: "The aorist tense puts the burial as contemporaneous with the circumcision." **w** Marvin Vincent, *Word Studies*.

eternal treasures] that are above, where Christ is, seated at the right hand of God. [Ps. 110:1.]

2 And set your minds *and* keep them set on what is above (the higher things), not on the things that are on the earth.

3 For [as far as this world is concerned] you have died, and your [new, real] life is hidden with Christ in God.

4 When Christ, Who is our life, appears, then you also will appear with Him in [the splendor of His] glory.

life point

If you want to live the resurrection life. that Jesus provides, then seek that new, powerful life by setting your mind and keeping it set on things above, not on things on the earth.

The apostle Paul is simply saying in Colossians 3:1, 2 that if you and I want the good life, then we must keep our minds on good things.

Many believers want the good life, but they passively sit around wishing for something good to happen. Often, they are jealous of others who live in victory and are resentful that their own lives are so difficult.

If you desire victory over your problems, if you truly want to live the resurrection life, you must have backbone and not just wishbone! You must be *determined* to have victory and refuse to settle for anything less than the best that God has for you. You must be active, not passive. Right action begins with right thinking. Do not be passive in your mind. Start today choosing right thoughts. Set your mind on the things that are above and keep it there!

5 So kill (deaden, ˣdeprive of power) the evil desire lurking in your members [those animal impulses and all that is earthly in you that is employed in sin]: sexual vice, impurity, sensual appetites, unholy desires, and all greed *and* covetousness, for that is idolatry (the deifying of self and other created things instead of God).

6 It is on account of these [very sins] that the [holy] anger of God is ever coming upon the sons of disobedience (those who are obstinately opposed to the divine will),

7 Among whom you also once walked, when you were living in *and* addicted to [such practices].

8 But now put away *and* rid yourselves [completely] of all these things: anger, rage, bad feeling toward others, curses *and* slander, and foulmouthed abuse *and* shameful utterances from your lips!

9 Do not lie to one another, for you have stripped off the old (unregenerate) self with its evil practices,

10 And have clothed yourselves with the new [spiritual self], which is [ever in the process of being] renewed *and* remolded into [fuller and more perfect ʸknowledge upon] knowledge after the image (the likeness) of Him Who created it. [Gen. 1:26.]

putting the Word to work

Think about your life before you became a Christian. How is your life different now? Most likely, Colossians 3:5–11 describes some of the changes you have made in your life. Ask God to continue to help you put off the "old self" and put on the "new self" created in His image. Be intentional about pursuing righteousness in every area of your life.

---

x Joseph Thayer, *A Greek-English Lexicon*. **y** Literal translation.

11 [In this new creation all distinctions vanish.] There [z]is no room for *and* there can be neither Greek nor Jew, circumcised nor uncircumcised, [nor difference between nations whether alien] barbarians or Scythians [[z]who are the most savage of all], nor slave or free man; but Christ is all and in all [[a]everything and everywhere, to all men, without distinction of person].

12 Clothe yourselves therefore, as God's own chosen ones (His own picked representatives), [who are] purified *and* holy and well-beloved [by God Himself, by putting on behavior marked by] tenderhearted pity *and* mercy, kind feeling, a lowly opinion of yourselves, gentle ways, [and] patience [which is tireless and long-suffering, and has the power to endure whatever comes, with good temper].

life point

I turn to Colossians 3:12 often to remind myself of what kind of behavior I should display in all situations. I remind myself that patience is not my ability to wait, but my ability to keep a good attitude while I wait. I encourage you too to exercise patience in every circumstance.

13 Be gentle *and* forbearing with one another and, if one has a difference (a grievance or complaint) against another, readily pardoning each other; even as the Lord has [freely] forgiven you, so must you also [forgive].

14 And above all these [put on] love *and* enfold yourselves with the bond of perfectness [which binds everything together completely in ideal harmony].

15 And let the peace (soul harmony which comes) from Christ rule (act as umpire continually) in your hearts [deciding and settling with finality all questions that arise in your minds, in that peaceful state] to which as [members of Christ's] one body you were also called [to live]. And be thankful (appreciative), [giving praise to God always].

16 Let the word [spoken by] Christ (the Messiah) have its home [in your hearts and minds] *and* dwell in you in [all its] richness, as you teach and admonish *and* train one another in all insight *and* intelligence *and* wisdom [in spiritual things, and as you sing] psalms and hymns and spiritual songs, making melody to God with [His] grace in your hearts.

life point

If you let the Word have its home in your heart and mind, it will give you insight and intelligence and wisdom. Let God's rich Word dwell in you (see Colossians 3:16), and you will see the difference in your life!

17 And whatever you do [no matter what it is] in word or deed, do everything in the name of the Lord Jesus *and* in [dependence upon] His Person, giving praise to God the Father through Him.

18 Wives, be subject to your husbands [subordinate and adapt yourselves to them], as is right *and* fitting *and* your proper duty in the Lord.

19 Husbands, love your wives [be affectionate and sympathetic with them] and do not be harsh *or* bitter *or* resentful toward them.

20 Children, obey your parents in everything, for this is pleasing to the Lord.

21 Fathers, do not provoke *or* irritate *or* fret your children [do not be hard on them or harass them], lest they

z Marvin Vincent, *Word Studies.*   **a** James C. Gray and George M. Adams, *Bible Commentary.*

let peace be your umpire

Colossians 3:15 instructs us to let God's peace act as an umpire in our hearts.

The umpire in a ball game decides if a player is "in" or "out." Peace is to be the umpire that decides if something in your life should be in or out.

Many people do not enjoy peace because they are out of the will of God. They follow their own will rather than God's will. They do what they feel like doing or what they think is right rather than follow God's Word and be led by peace.

Quite often something comes up that I want to do. It sounds good, feels good, and can even be good. However, if I do not have peace about it, I have learned to leave it alone. Occasionally, I am offered an opportunity for a speaking engagement that I want to take, but I do not have peace about it. I do not know why, but sometimes the peace is just not there. I have learned that if I take the opportunity anyway, I always find out later the reason I should have followed peace and declined the offer.

One engagement I remember was when I first started traveling. I received an invitation to speak at a church in Texas. I was so excited that I immediately said I would go. As my emotions calmed down, I got a gnawing feeling inside every time I thought about it. It got stronger and stronger. I plainly had no peace about going, and yet God gave me no reason for the unrest. I waited and waited. Finally, I knew I had to call them and ask for a release from the commitment. I told them I would come if they could not find a suitable replacement, but for some reason, I had no peace about going. They released me from the commitment.

A few weeks later I found out that my home church was dedicating their new building the weekend I would have been gone. I was an associate pastor in that church for quite some time, and it was very important for me to be with them on that occasion.

Why didn't the Lord just tell me what was going on? For some reason, He chose not to. His Word says to be led by peace. Many times that is all He will give you to let you know if you are in or out of His will. Later you may know why, or you may never know why.

Be led by peace. Do not buy something, especially a major purchase, if you do not have peace about it. No matter how much you want it, you will be sorry if you go against the leading of the Holy Spirit. Take time to acknowledge God in all your ways and He will direct your path (see Proverbs 3:6).

You will never enjoy a peaceful life if you disobey His leading and follow your own will. If you do obey His guidance and follow peace, you will be blessed.

become discouraged *and* sullen *and* morose *and* feel inferior *and* frustrated. [Do not break their spirit.]

22 Servants, obey in everything those who are your earthly masters, not only when their eyes are on you as pleasers of men, but in simplicity of purpose [with all your heart] because of your reverence for the Lord *and* as a sincere expression of your devotion to Him.

life point

Colossians 3:22 tells us that we are to be good, faithful, loyal, profitable, and hardworking employees. We are to do our jobs well and with a good attitude. We are not to be two-faced, showing our employers what we think they want to see and then showing something different when they are not around. We need to be real, sincere, honest, and trustworthy all the time.

I think it is sad when those of us who have jobs grumble about them when there are so many people who do not have jobs. We should be grateful for our work and thankful we are able to do it. Thank God today for the work He has given you to do!

23 Whatever may be your task, work at it heartily (from the soul), as [something done] for the Lord and not for men,

24 Knowing [with all certainty] that it is from the Lord [and not from men] that you will receive the inheritance which is your [real] reward. [The One Whom] you are actually serving [is] the Lord Christ (the Messiah).

speak the Word

25 For he who deals wrongfully will [reap the fruit of his folly and] be punished for his wrongdoing. And [with God] there is no partiality [no matter what a person's position may be, whether he is the slave or the master].

4 MASTERS, [on your part] deal with your slaves justly and fairly, knowing that also you have a Master in heaven. [Lev. 25:43, 53.]

2 Be earnest *and* unwearied *and* steadfast in your prayer [life], being [both] alert *and* intent in [your praying] with thanksgiving.

3 And at the same time pray for us also, that God may open a door to us for the Word (the Gospel), to proclaim the mystery concerning Christ (the Messiah) on account of which I am in prison;

4 That I may proclaim it fully *and* make it clear [speak boldly and unfold that mystery], as is my duty.

5 Behave yourselves wisely [living prudently and with discretion] in your relations with those of the outside world (the non-Christians), making the very most of the time *and* seizing (buying up) the opportunity.

6 Let your speech at all times be gracious (pleasant and winsome), seasoned [as it were] with salt, [so that you may never be at a loss] to know how you ought to answer anyone [who puts a question to you].

7 Tychicus will give you full information about my affairs; [he is] a much-loved brother and faithful ministering assistant and fellow servant [with us] in the Lord.

8 I have sent him to you for this very purpose, that you may know how

God, I pray that You will help me be earnest and unwearied and steadfast in my prayer life, being alert and intent in my prayers with thanksgiving.
ADAPTED FROM COLOSSIANS 4:2

putting the Word to work

Colossians 4:6 gives us good instruction about our speech. Do you always think before you speak? If not, you may experience trouble you could avoid. Very often we are not sensitive to other people when we open our mouths and say things. We might give correction at a time when a person needs edification or we may tell them something that causes them to worry at a time when they have many other situations they are dealing with. Not only do we need to use wisdom with our words, but timing is very important. We may need to discuss a matter with someone, but if we do it at the wrong time we will only create more problems. Ask God to give you wisdom to know when to speak, to whom to speak, and what to say.

we are faring and that he may comfort *and* cheer *and* encourage your hearts.
9   And with [him is] Onesimus, [our] faithful and beloved brother, who is [one] of yourselves. They will let you know everything that has taken place here [in Rome].
10 Aristarchus my fellow prisoner wishes to be remembered to you, as does Mark the relative of Barnabas. You received instructions concerning him; if he comes to you give him a [ᵇhearty] welcome.
11 And [greetings also from] Jesus, who is called Justus. These [Hebrew Christians] alone of the circumcision are among my fellow workers for [the extension of] God's kingdom, and they have proved a relief *and* a comfort to me.
12 Epaphras, who is one of yourselves, a servant of Christ Jesus, sends you greetings. [He is] always striving for you earnestly in his prayers, [pleading] that you may [as persons of ripe character and clear conviction] stand firm *and* mature [in spiritual growth], convinced *and* fully assured in ᶜeverything willed by God.
13 For I bear him testimony that he has labored hard in your behalf and for [the believers] in Laodicea and those in Hierapolis.
14 Luke the beloved physician and Demas salute you.
15 Give my greetings to the brethren at Laodicea, and to Nympha and the assembly (the church) which meets in her house.
16 And when this epistle has been read before you, [see] that it is read also in the assembly (the church) of the Laodiceans, and also [see] that you yourselves in turn read the [letter that comes to you] from Laodicea.
17 And say to Archippus, See that you discharge carefully [the duties of] the ministry *and* fulfill the stewardship which you have received in the Lord.
18 I, Paul, [add this final] greeting, writing with my own hand. Remember I am still in prison *and* in chains. May grace (God's unmerited favor and blessing) be with you! *Amen (so be it).*

b Charles B. Williams, *The New Testament: A Translation*: A very strong verb—thus translated "give him a hearty welcome."   c Marvin Vincent, *Word Studies*.

First Thessalonians

Author:
Paul

Date:
Probably AD 51

Everyday Life Principles:
As you wait for His return, honor Jesus and represent Him well in your everyday life.

When you suffer persecution, do so with courage and steadfast faith.

Take a look at the instructions in I Thessalonians 5:14–22 and incorporate them into your daily activities.

In every chapter of I Thessalonians, Paul mentions the second coming of Jesus Christ. This is a topic that has sparked interest, speculation, excitement, and controversy for years. I do not believe that trying to figure out when Jesus will return is a good use of time or energy. Instead, I believe we need to live with an awareness of His return and to conduct our everyday lives in ways that honor Him and represent Him well—treating other people as we want to be treated, keeping God first in our lives, obeying Him, and seeking to do good—while we wait.

Also in this book, Paul commends the Thessalonians' courage and steadfast faith in the midst of persecution. Their conduct serves as an example and an encouragement to us today when we are persecuted or ridiculed.

As you read I Thessalonians, I hope you will pay attention to all of the important insights in this book, especially to I Thessalonians 5:14–22, which is a wonderful list of instructions for everyday life. I want to encourage you, as Paul did the Thessalonians, to always remember that "Faithful is He Who is calling you [to Himself] and utterly trustworthy, and He will also do it [fulfill His call by hallowing and keeping you]" (I Thessalonians 5:24).

1 PAUL, SILVANUS (Silas), and Timothy, to the assembly (church) of the Thessalonians in God the Father and the Lord Jesus Christ (the Messiah): Grace (spiritual blessing and divine favor) to you and [heart] peace.

2 We are ever giving thanks to God for all of you, continually mentioning [you when engaged] in our prayers,

3 Recalling unceasingly before our God and Father your work energized by faith and service motivated by love and unwavering hope in [the return of] our Lord Jesus Christ (the Messiah). [I Thess. 1:10.]

4 [O] brethren beloved by God, we recognize *and* know that He has selected (chosen) you;

5 For our [preaching of the] glad tidings (the Gospel) came to you not only in word, but also in [its own inherent] power and in the Holy Spirit and with great conviction *and* absolute certainty [on our part]. You know what kind of men we proved [ourselves] to be among you for your good.

6 And you [set yourselves to] become imitators of us and [through us] of the Lord Himself, for you welcomed our message in [spite of] much persecution, with joy [inspired] by the Holy Spirit;

7 So that you [thus] became a pattern to all the believers (those who adhere to, trust in, and rely on Christ Jesus) in Macedonia and Achaia (most of Greece).

8 For not only has the Word concerning *and* from the Lord resounded forth from you unmistakably in Macedonia and Achaia, but everywhere the report has gone forth of your faith in God [of your ªleaning of your whole personality on Him in complete trust and confidence in His power, wisdom, and goodness]. So we [find that we] never need to tell people anything [further about it].

9 For they themselves volunteer testimony concerning us, telling what an entrance we had among you, and how you turned to God from [your] idols to serve a God Who is alive and true *and* genuine,

10 And [how you] look forward to *and* await the coming of His Son from heaven, Whom He raised from the dead—Jesus, Who personally rescues *and* delivers us out of *and* from the wrath [bringing punishment] which is coming [upon the impenitent] *and* ᵇdraws us to Himself [ᶜinvesting us with all the privileges and rewards of the new life in Christ, the Messiah].

2 FOR YOU yourselves know, brethren, that our coming among you was not useless *and* fruitless.

2 But though we had already suffered and been outrageously treated at Philippi, as you know, yet in [the strength of] our God we summoned courage to proclaim to you unfalteringly the good news (the Gospel) with earnest contention *and* much conflict *and* great opposition.

3 For our appeal [in preaching] does not [originate] from delusion *or* error or impure purpose *or* motive, nor in fraud *or* deceit.

4 But just as we have been

speak the Word

Thank You, Lord, that You love me and that You have chosen and selected me.
ADAPTED FROM I THESSALONIANS 1:4

---

a Alexander Souter, *Pocket Lexicon of the Greek New Testament.*   b Literal translation of the verb "to deliver."   c Marvin Vincent, *Word Studies in the New Testament.*

approved by God to be entrusted with the glad tidings (the Gospel), so we speak not to please men but to please God, Who tests our hearts [dexpecting them to be approved].

5 For as you well know, we never resorted either to words of flattery or to any cloak to conceal greedy motives *or* pretexts for gain, [as] God is our witness.

6 Nor did we seek to extract praise *and* honor *and* glory from men, either from you or from anyone else, though we might have asserted our authority [stood on our dignity and claimed honor] as apostles (special missionaries) of Christ (the Messiah).

7 But we behaved gently when we were among you, like a devoted mother nursing *and* cherishing her own children.

8 So, being thus tenderly *and* affectionately desirous of you, we continued to share with you not only God's good news (the Gospel) but also our own lives as well, for you had become so very dear to us.

9 For you recall our hard toil and struggles, brethren. We worked night and day [and plied our trade] in order not to be a burden to any of you [for our support] while we proclaimed the glad tidings (the Gospel) of God to you.

10 You are witnesses, [yes] and God [also], how unworldly and upright and blameless was our behavior toward you believers [who adhered to and trusted in and relied on our Lord Jesus Christ].

11 For you know how, as a father [dealing with] his children, we used to exhort each of you personally, stimulating *and* encouraging and charging you

12 To live lives worthy of God, Who calls you into His own kingdom and the glorious blessedness [einto which

true believers will enter after Christ's return].

13 And we also [especially] thank God continually for this, that when you received the message of God [which you heard] from us, you welcomed it not as the word of [mere] men, but as it truly is, the Word of God, which is effectually at work in you who believe [fexercising its superhuman power in those who adhere to and trust in and rely on it].

life point

According to I Thessalonians 2:13, God is at work in your life right this very minute, whether you know it or not. I encourage you to say every day, "God is working in me right now. He is changing me!" Speak from your mouth what the Word says, not what you feel.

14 For you, brethren, became imitators of the assemblies (churches) of God in Christ Jesus which are in Judea, for you too have suffered the same kind of treatment from your own fellow countrymen as they did [who were persecuted at the hands] of the Jews,

15 Who killed both the Lord Jesus and the prophets, and harassed *and* drove us out, and continue to make themselves hateful *and* offensive to God and to show themselves foes of all men,

16 Forbidding *and* hindering us from speaking to the Gentiles (the nations) that they may be saved. So as always they fill up [to the brim the measure of] their sins. But God's wrath has come upon them at last [completely and forever]! [Gen. 15:16.]

17 But since we were bereft of you, brethren, for a little while in person,

---

d G. Abbott-Smith, *Manual Greek Lexicon of the New Testament.*   **e** Joseph Thayer, *A Greek-English Lexicon of the New Testament.*   **f** Marvin Vincent, *Word Studies.*

[of course] not in heart, we endeavored the more eagerly and with great longing to see you face to face,

18 Because it was our will to come to you. [I mean that] I, Paul, again and again [wanted to come], but Satan hindered *and* impeded us.

19 For what is our hope or happiness or our victor's wreath of exultant triumph when we stand in the presence of our Lord Jesus at His coming? Is it not you?

20 For you are [indeed] our glory and our joy!

3 THEREFORE, WHEN [the suspense of separation and our yearning for some personal communication from you] became intolerable, we consented to being left behind alone at Athens.

2 And we sent Timothy, our brother and God's servant in [spreading] the good news (the Gospel) of Christ, to strengthen *and* establish and to exhort *and* comfort *and* encourage you in your faith,

3 That no one [of you] should be disturbed *and* beguiled *and* led astray by these afflictions *and* difficulties [to which I have referred]. For you yourselves know that this is [unavoidable in our position, and must be recognized as] our appointed lot.

4 For even when we were with you, [you know] we warned you plainly beforehand that we were to be pressed with difficulties *and* made to suffer affliction, just as to your own knowledge it has [since] happened.

5 That is the reason that, when I could bear [the suspense] no longer, I sent that I might learn [how you were standing the strain, and the endurance of] your faith, [for I was fearful] lest somehow the tempter had tempted you and our toil [among you should prove to] be fruitless *and* to no purpose.

6 But now that Timothy has just come back to us from [his visit to] you and has brought us the good news of [the steadfastness of] your faith and [the warmth of your] love, and [reported] how kindly you cherish a constant *and* affectionate remembrance of us [and that you are] longing to see us as we [are to see] you,

7 Brethren, for this reason, in [spite of all] our stress and crushing difficulties we have been filled with comfort *and* cheer about you [because of] your faith ([g]the leaning of your whole personality on God in complete trust and confidence).

8 Because now we [really] live, if you stand [firm] in the Lord.

9 For what [adequate] thanksgiving can we render to God for you for all the gladness *and* delight which we enjoy for your sakes before our God?

10 [And we] continue to pray especially *and* with most intense earnestness night and day that we may see you face to face and mend *and* make good whatever may be imperfect *and* lacking in your faith.

11 Now may our God and Father Himself and our Lord Jesus *Christ (the Messiah)* guide our steps to you.

12 And may the Lord make you to increase and excel *and* overflow in love for one another and for all people, just as we also do for you,

13 So that He may strengthen *and* confirm *and* establish your hearts faultlessly pure *and* unblamable in holiness in the sight of our God and Father, at the coming of our Lord Jesus *Christ (the Messiah)* with all His saints (the [h]holy and glorified people of God)! *Amen, (so be it)!*

4 FURTHERMORE, [h]BRETHREN, we beg and admonish you in [virtue of our union with] the Lord Jesus, that [you follow the

g Alexander Souter, *Pocket Lexicon*. **h** Marvin Vincent, *Word Studies*.

putting the Word to work

Have you ever heard the saying, "You've got to look out for number one"? This means, live for yourself, because that is what everyone else is trying to do. However, as a Christian, you are called to live a life that is pleasing to God (see I Thessalonians 4:1). Ask Him to continually show you how to live to please Him.

putting the Word to work

Do you know that God is concerned about your body as well as your soul? God commands you to abstain from sexual immorality (see I Thessalonians 4:3–6) because engaging in sexual activity outside of marriage will keep you from living a holy life. Avoid situations that may tempt you or that cause lust to rise up in you. Practice fidelity in marriage and chastity in singleness.

instructions which] you learned from us about how you ought to walk so as to please *and* gratify God, as indeed you are doing, [and] that you do so even more and more abundantly [attaining yet greater perfection in living this life].
2 For you know what charges *and* precepts we gave you [ⁱon the authority and by the inspiration of] the Lord Jesus.
3 For this is the will of God, that you should be consecrated (separated and set apart for pure and holy living): that you should abstain *and* shrink from all sexual vice,
4 That each one of you should know how to ʲpossess (control, manage) his own ᵏbody in consecration (purity, separated from things profane) and honor,

5 Not [to be used] in the passion of lust like the heathen, who are ignorant of the true God *and* have no knowledge of His will,
6 That no man transgress and overreach his brother *and* defraud him in this matter *or* defraud his brother in business. For the Lord is an avenger in all these things, as we have already warned you solemnly *and* ⁱtold you plainly.
7 For God has not called us to impurity but to consecration [to dedicate ourselves to the most thorough purity].
8 Therefore whoever disregards (sets aside and rejects this) disregards not man but God, Whose [very] Spirit [Whom] He gives to you is holy (chaste, pure).

speak the Word

Lord, I pray that You make me increase and overflow in love for my fellow believers and for all people and that You strengthen, confirm, and establish my heart faultlessly pure and blameless in holiness in Your sight.
ADAPTED FROM I THESSALONIANS 3:12, 13

Thank You, Father, that You have called me to consecration. I dedicate myself to purity in every way.
ADAPTED FROM I THESSALONIANS 4:7

i G. Abbott-Smith, *Manual Greek Lexicon.* j *The American Standard Version* and others so read.
k Some of the early versions of the Bible read "vessel" here. The reading "body" is supported by most lexicons, and by such translations as Ronald Knox, *The Holy Bible: A Translation from the Latin Vulgate*; J.B. Phillips, *New Testament in Modern English*; and Arthur S. Way, *Way's Epistles: The Letters of St. Paul to Seven Churches and Three Friends.*

9 But concerning brotherly love [for all other Christians], you have no need to have anyone write you, for you yourselves have been [personally] taught by God to love one another. **10** And indeed you already are [extending and displaying your love] to all the brethren throughout Macedonia. But we beseech *and* earnestly exhort you, brethren, that you ¹excel [in this matter] more and more,
11 To make it your ambition *and* definitely endeavor to live quietly *and* peacefully, to mind your own affairs, and to work with your hands, as we charged you,
12 So that you may bear yourselves becomingly *and* be correct *and* honorable *and* command the respect of the outside world, being dependent on nobody [self-supporting] *and* having need of nothing.
13 Now also we would not have you ignorant, brethren, about those who fall asleep [ᵐin death], that you may not grieve [for them] as the rest do who have no hope [beyond the grave].
14 For since we believe that Jesus died and rose again, even so God will also bring with Him through Jesus those who have fallen asleep [ᵐin death].
15 For this we declare to you by the Lord's [own] word, that we who are alive and remain until the coming of the Lord shall in no way precede [into His presence] *or* have any advantage at all over those who have previously fallen asleep [in Him ᵐin death].
16 For the Lord Himself will descend from heaven with a loud cry of summons, with the shout of an archangel, and with the blast of the trumpet of God. And those who have departed this life in Christ will rise first.
17 Then we, the living ones who remain [on the earth], shall simultaneously be caught up along with [the resurrected dead] in the clouds to meet the Lord in the air; and so always (through the eternity of the eternities) we shall be with the Lord!
18 Therefore comfort *and* encourage one another with these words.

5 BUT AS to the suitable times and the precise seasons *and* dates, brethren, you have no necessity for anything being written to you.
2 For you yourselves know perfectly well that the day of the [return of the] Lord will come [as unexpectedly

life point

Did you know the Bible specifically tells us in I Thessalonians 4:11 to mind our own business?

Minding our own business is a principle we need to follow, and we will discover that we enjoy life so much more when we apply it. Many times we get into things that were really none of our business to begin with, and those very things end up making us miserable.

God does not give us an anointing to handle someone else's business; He gives us anointing for our own. This is why things become so messy when we get involved where we should not. There is obviously a time to get involved and help people in need, but there is also a balance that should be honored. Ask God to help you know when to get involved in a situation and when to mind your own business!

---

1 G. Abbott-Smith, *Manual Greek Lexicon*. **m** Hermann Cremer, *Biblico-Theological Lexicon of New Testament Greek*.

and suddenly] as a thief in the night.
3 When people are saying, All is well and secure, *and,* There is peace and safety, then in a moment unforeseen destruction (ruin and death) will come upon them as suddenly as labor pains come upon a woman with child; and they shall by no means escape, for there will be no escape.
4 But you are not in [given up to the power of] darkness, brethren, for that day to overtake you by surprise like a thief.
5 For you are all sons of light and sons of the day; we do not belong either to the night or to darkness.
6 Accordingly then, let us not sleep, as the rest do, but let us keep wide awake (alert, watchful, cautious, and on our guard) and let us be sober (calm, collected, and circumspect).
7 For those who sleep, sleep at night, and those who are drunk, get drunk at night.
8 But we belong to the day; therefore, let us be sober and put on the breastplate (corslet) of faith and love and for a helmet the hope of salvation.
9 For God has not appointed us to [incur His] wrath [He did not select us to condemn us], but [that we might] obtain [His] salvation through our Lord Jesus Christ (the Messiah)
10 Who died for us so that whether we are still alive or are dead [at Christ's appearing], we might live together with Him *and* share His life.
11 Therefore encourage (admonish, exhort) one another and edify (strengthen and build up) one another, just as you are doing.
12 Now also we beseech you, brethren, get to know those who labor

speak the Word

putting the Word to work

The Bible is full of practical instructions for everyday life, and I Thessalonians 5:12–22 is an excellent list of exhortations for us. How can you apply these instructions practically in your everyday life?

among you [recognize them for what they are, acknowledge and appreciate and respect them all]—your leaders who are over you in the Lord and those who warn *and* kindly reprove *and* exhort you.
13 And hold them in very high and most affectionate esteem in [intelligent and sympathetic] appreciation of their work. Be at peace among yourselves.
14 And we earnestly beseech you, brethren, admonish (warn and seriously advise) those who are out of line [the loafers, the disorderly, and the

life point

After encouraging us to thank God in everything, the Bible says not to "quench (suppress or subdue)" the Holy Spirit (I Thessalonians 5:18, 19).

I believe one way we quench the Holy Spirit is through complaining. The truth is, we *need* the Holy Spirit to work in our lives, and the more thankful we are, the more freedom the Holy Spirit has to work in our circumstances. Our natural tendency is to complain, but it is supernatural to give thanks when we are tested and tried by life's circumstances.

Thank You, God, that You have not appointed me to wrath or condemnation, but to salvation through Jesus Christ, Who died for me so that I might live with Him and share His life.
ADAPTED FROM I THESSALONIANS 5:9, 10

pray without ceasing

The King James Version of I Thessalonians 5:17 says, "Pray without ceasing." I used to read those words and wonder, "Lord, how can I ever get to the place that I am able to pray without ceasing?" To me, the phrase, "without ceasing" meant nonstop, without ever quitting. I could not see how that was possible.

Now I have a better understanding of what Paul said. He meant that prayer should be like breathing, something we do continually but often unconsciously, without even being totally aware of it.

You and I live by breathing. Our physical lives require that we inhale and exhale, and the air we breathe sustains our bodies. In the same way, our spiritual lives are designed to be nurtured and sustained by prayer.

Religious thinking sometimes gives us the mistaken idea that if we do not keep up a certain schedule of prayer we miss the mark. We have become too "clock-oriented" concerning prayer.

The Lord gave me the following example to illustrate the way we are to pray: Just as we breathe all day long but never spend time counting our breaths, so we are to pray all day long without keeping track of our prayers.

I have never carried a clock around with me for reminding me to breathe every so many seconds. I have never come home from work at night and written in a journal how many times I breathed that day. I just breathe when I need to, continually, without even being aware that I am doing it.

That is the way we are to be about our prayers.

I do not know how many times I pray a day; I just know I pray throughout the day. I start praying when I get up in the morning, and I pray many times until I go to sleep at night. I also enjoy special "set apart" times for prayer, but I do not just pray for thirty minutes in the morning and then forget about God the rest of the day. As one intercessor said, "I never pray very long at one time, but I never go very long without praying."

Does all this mean I am always thinking about prayer and spiritual things? No, there are periods when I give myself to other things, just as we all must do. But as we grow in spiritual maturity and endeavor to deepen our prayer lives, it is important for us to realize that we can pray at all times in every season, on every occasion and in every place (see Ephesians 6:18)—just as naturally as we breathe. Let me encourage you to pray that way!

give thanks

Having a thankful heart is very important. We are to be thankful and to give thanks (see I Thessalonians 5:18). We need to express our gratitude to God and to the people He uses to help and bless us. Be thankful for small things as well as big things. I often thank God for hot water in which to take a bath. I think of all the people in the world who do not even have clean water, let alone hot water and I am reminded of how blessed I am to go to a faucet anytime I desire and get clean hot and cold water.

Voicing our thanks helps because when we do, we also remind ourselves afresh of how blessed we are. It is easy to fall into the trap of looking at what we do not have and complaining about it, but God looks for people who are thankful and give thanks in all circumstances. There is something good in everything if we will search for it.

I remember a time when I asked God to give me something I desired and He showed me that until I stopped complaining about what I already had, there was no point in His giving me anything else because I would ultimately complain about that also. Why should God give us more if we complain about what we already have? Complaining grieves and quenches the Holy Spirit.

Giving thanks in all things is God's will for us, according to I Thessalonians 5:18. If we will not submit to His will in something like being thankful and saying so, how can we expect to be led into His will for greater things? Many people want to know what God's specific will is for their lives, but they have not yet fulfilled His general will (what His Word says to all of us) for them. We see His will throughout the Bible in instructions to be thankful, to walk in love, to give, to repent of our sins, to stay peaceful, and others. As we strive to obey God in these ways, He reveals and leads us into His specific calling and will for each of us.

I encourage you to take some time every day and choose to think of all the things and people God has blessed you with and *voice* your thankfulness to Him. Also form a habit of expressing gratitude to those who help you and make your life better. This way, you can be certain that you are fulfilling the will of God.

unruly]; encourage the timid *and* fainthearted, help *and* give your support to the weak souls, [and] be very patient with everybody [always keeping your temper]. [Isa. 35:4.]
15 See that none of you repays another with evil for evil, but always aim to show kindness *and* seek to do good to one another and to everybody.
16 Be happy [in your faith] *and* rejoice *and* be glad-hearted continually (always);
17 Be unceasing in prayer [praying perseveringly];
18 Thank [God] in everything [no matter what the circumstances may be, be thankful and give thanks], for this is the will of God for you [who are] in Christ Jesus [the Revealer and Mediator of that will].

do not despise prophecy

Following the instruction in I Thessalonians 5:19 not to quench the Holy Spirit, we have an instruction not to despise prophesying (or, as *The Amplified Bible* says, not to "depreciate prophetic revelations"), in I Thessalonians 5:20.

In both the Old and New Testaments, prophets were valuable vessels for God. In the Old Testament, God spoke to His people using prophets as His mouthpieces. Wise kings listened and obeyed these prophetic words; unwise kings who refused to listen brought themselves and their kingdoms into eventual ruin. In the New Testament, we see that among the gifts God gave to the church were people who functioned as prophets (see Ephesians 4:11; I Corinthians 12:28). First Corinthians 14:3 describes the New Testament prophet as one who "interprets the divine will and purpose in inspired preaching and teaching" and who speaks to people "for their upbuilding and constructive spiritual progress and encouragement and consolation."

There are, of course, modern-day prophets gifted by God to foretell future events, but not everyone who prophesies is called to stand in the office of a prophet. First Corinthians 12:10 states that prophecy is "the gift of interpreting the divine will and purpose" of God. I believe anointed teachers of God's Word prophesy every time they teach. They interpret, or tell forth, the divine will and counsel of God.

What does the Bible mean when it says if we despise prophesying we will quench the Holy Spirit?

First, I believe it means we must love the preaching of God's Word, or we will quench the progress the Holy Spirit desires us to make. It is impossible to grow spiritually without God's Word. His Word is to the spirit what food is to the body; we must have it regularly to be healthy.

Second, I believe it means we should not have a judgmental or otherwise bad attitude toward the gift of prophecy or any of the other gifts of the Spirit. We should have respect for all the ways God chooses to work through men and women. We should cherish the gifts and honor those through whom they flow. Their gifts were given to them by the Holy Spirit for our benefit, to help us grow and mature.

19 Do not quench (suppress or subdue) the [Holy] Spirit;
20 Do not spurn the gifts *and* utterances of the prophets [do not depreciate prophetic revelations nor despise inspired instruction or exhortation or warning].

21 But test *and* prove all things [until you can recognize] what is good; [to that] hold fast.
22 Abstain from evil [shrink from it and keep aloof from it] in whatever form *or* whatever kind it may be.
23 And may the God of peace Himself

sanctify you through and through [separate you from profane things, make you pure and wholly consecrated to God]; and may your spirit and soul and body be preserved sound *and* complete [and found] blameless at the coming of our Lord Jesus Christ (the Messiah).

24 Faithful is He Who is calling you [to Himself] *and* utterly trustworthy, and He will also do it [fulfill His call by hallowing and keeping you].

25 Brethren, pray for us.

26 Greet all the brethren with a sacred kiss.

27 I solemnly charge you [in the name of] the Lord to have this letter read before all the brethren.

28 The grace (the unmerited favor and blessings) of our Lord Jesus Christ (the Messiah) be with you all. *Amen, (so be it).*

life point

Many people do not understand that we are tri-part beings: spirit, soul and body. We *are* a spirit, we *have* a soul (composed of our mind, will and emotions), and we *live in* a body. Our new birth begins in our spirit, is carried out through our soul, and is finally visible to other people through a demonstration of God's glory in our physical lives.

Many Christians make the mistake of thinking that God cares only about the spirit. But He wants us to be whole in soul and body, too. Be blessed in the knowledge that God is faithful and will sanctify you in body, soul, and spirit.

speak the Word

Lord, I declare that You are faithful and utterly trustworthy. You will fulfill Your call by hallowing and keeping me.

ADAPTED FROM I THESSALONIANS 5:24

Second Thessalonians

Author:
Paul

Date:
Probably AD 51

Everyday Life Principles:
Remember that no one knows exactly when Jesus will return. Keep a proper perspective on life as you wait.

Remember that rebellion and lawlessness are two of the characteristics of the end times. Be careful to stay submitted to the authority God has placed in your life.

Use your time wisely and spend your life doing the things you know Jesus wants you to do.

Because the people in Thessalonica did not properly understand some of the things Paul wrote to them in his first letter, he soon had to write them a second time. In this letter, he addressed the fact that some people overreacted to his comments on Jesus' return to earth. They thought the second coming of Christ was so imminent that they lost their proper perspective on life.

Like the Thessalonian believers centuries ago, you and I also wait for the return of Christ. We do not know when it will happen, but Paul's advice in this letter to them also applies to us. He tells them to watch for the signs preceding Christ's second coming: lawlessness, apostasy, rebellion against authority, counterfeit signs and wonders. He also encourages them to hold fast to their faith and to the truth of God and reminds them that "the Lord is faithful, and He will strengthen [you] and set you on a firm foundation and guard you from the evil [one]" (II Thessalonians 3:3).

Let II Thessalonians encourage you to live every day as though Jesus is coming back at any minute. Do the things you want to be found doing if He were to suddenly appear. Stay at peace; keep your joy; use your time wisely; submit to authority; love God; and love other people. Regardless of when He returns, Jesus will be pleased with these things in your life.

1 PAUL, SILVANUS (Silas), and Timothy, to the church (assembly) of the Thessalonians in God our Father and the Lord Jesus Christ (the Messiah, the Anointed One):

2 Grace (unmerited favor) be to you and [heart] peace from God the Father and the Lord Jesus Christ (the Messiah, the Anointed One).

3 We ought *and* indeed are obligated [as those in debt] to give thanks always to God for you, brethren, as is fitting, because your faith is growing exceedingly and the love of every one of you each toward the others is increasing *and* abounds.

4 And this is a cause of our mentioning you with pride among the churches (assemblies) of God for your steadfastness (your unflinching endurance and patience) and your firm faith in the midst of all the persecutions and crushing distresses *and* afflictions under which you are holding up.

5 This is positive proof of the just *and* right judgment of God to the end that you may be deemed deserving of His kingdom [a plain token of His fair verdict which designs that you should be made *and* counted worthy of the kingdom of God], for the sake of which you are also suffering.

6 [It is a fair decision] since it is a righteous thing with God to repay with distress *and* affliction those who distress *and* afflict you,

7 And to [ªrecompense] you who are so distressed *and* afflicted [by granting you] relief *and* rest along with us [your fellow sufferers] when the Lord Jesus is revealed from heaven with His mighty angels in a flame of fire,

8 To deal out retribution (chastisement and vengeance) upon those who do not know *or* perceive *or* become acquainted with God, and [upon those] who ignore *and* refuse to obey the Gospel of our Lord Jesus *Christ*.

9 Such people will pay the penalty *and* suffer the punishment of everlasting ruin (destruction and perdition) *and* eternal exclusion and banishment from the presence of the Lord and from the glory of His power,

10 When He comes to be glorified in His saints [on that day He will be made more glorious in His consecrated people], and [He will] be marveled at *and* admired [in His glory reflected] in all who have believed [who have adhered to, trusted in, and relied on Him], because our witnessing among you was confidently accepted *and* believed [and confirmed in your lives].

11 With this in view we constantly pray for you, that our God may deem *and* count you worthy of [your] calling and [His] every gracious purpose of goodness, and with power may complete in [your] every particular work of faith (faith which is that ᵇleaning of the whole human personality on God in absolute trust and confidence in His power, wisdom, and goodness).

12 Thus may the name of our Lord Jesus *Christ* be glorified *and* become more glorious through *and* in you, and may you [also be glorified] in Him

speak the Word

God, I pray that my faith grows exceedingly and that my love for others increases and abounds.
ADAPTED FROM II THESSALONIANS 1:3

---

a Robert Jamieson, A.R. Fausset and David Brown, *A Commentary on the Old and New Testaments.*
b Alexander Souter, *Pocket Lexicon of the Greek New Testament.*

putting the Word to work

Do you know that there are Christians in the world today who cannot worship freely and have been disowned by their families, imprisoned, or even killed for their faith? I encourage you to remember and pray regularly for persecuted believers around the world. Pray they will have strength to withstand the persecution they face, remain strong in their faith, and that the name of Jesus will be glorified in and through their lives (see II Thessalonians 1:11, 12).

according to the grace (favor and blessing) of our God and the Lord Jesus Christ (the Messiah, the Anointed One).

2 BUT RELATIVE to the coming of our Lord Jesus Christ (the Messiah) and our gathering together to [meet] Him, we beg you, brethren,

2 Not to allow your minds to be quickly unsettled *or* disturbed or kept excited *or* alarmed, whether it be by some [pretended] revelation of [the] Spirit or by word or by letter [alleged to be] from us, to the effect that the day of the Lord has [already] arrived *and* is here.

3 Let no one deceive *or* beguile you in any way, for that day will not come except the ᶜapostasy comes first [unless the predicted great ᶜfalling away of those who have professed to

be Christians has come], and the man of lawlessness (sin) is revealed, who is the son of doom (of perdition), [Dan. 7:25; 8:25; I Tim. 4:1.]

4 Who opposes and exalts himself so proudly *and* insolently against *and* over all that is called God or that is worshiped, [even to his actually] taking his seat in the temple of God, proclaiming that he himself is God. [Ezek. 28:2; Dan. 11:36, 37.]

5 Do you not recollect that when I was still with you, I told you these things?

6 And now you know what is restraining him [from being revealed at this time]; it is so that he may be manifested (revealed) in his own [appointed] time.

7 For the mystery of lawlessness (that hidden principle of rebellion against constituted authority) is already at work in the world, [but it is] restrained only until ᵈhe who restrains is taken out of the way.

8 And then the lawless one (the antichrist) will be revealed and the Lord Jesus will slay him with the breath of His mouth and bring him to an end by His appearing at His coming. [Isa. 11:4.]

9 The coming [of the lawless one, the antichrist] is through the activity *and* working of Satan and will be attended by great power and with all sorts of [pretended] miracles and signs *and* delusive marvels—[all of them] lying wonders—

10 And by unlimited seduction to evil

speak the Word

Father, I pray that You will count me worthy of my calling and of Your gracious purpose, and that You complete every work of faith in me so that the name of Jesus is glorified in and through me.
ADAPTED FROM II THESSALONIANS 1:11, 12

---

c A possible rendering of the Greek *apostasia* is "departure [of the church]."   d Many believe this One Who restrains the antichrist to be the Holy Spirit, Who lives in all believers and will be removed with them at Christ's coming; yet a majority thinks it refers to the Roman Empire.

and with all wicked deception for those who are perishing (going to perdition) because they did not welcome the Truth *but* refused to love it that they might be saved.

11 Therefore God sends upon them a misleading influence, a working of error *and* a strong delusion to make them believe what is false,

12 In order that all may be judged *and* condemned who did not believe in [who refused to adhere to, trust in, and rely on] the Truth, but [instead] took pleasure in unrighteousness.

13 But we, brethren beloved by the Lord, ought *and* are obligated [as those who are in debt] to give thanks always to God for you, because God chose you from the beginning ᵉ*as His firstfruits (first converts)* for salvation through the sanctifying work of the [Holy] Spirit and [your] belief in (adherence to, trust in, and reliance on) the Truth.

14 [It was] to this end that He called you through our Gospel, so that you may obtain *and* share in the glory of our Lord Jesus Christ (the Messiah).

15 So then, brethren, stand firm and hold fast to the traditions *and* instruc-

putting the Word to work

Encouragement is a powerful and valuable gift. Who do you receive encouragement from? When you need encouragement, remember that God Himself is always ready to encourage you (see II Thessalonians 2:16, 17), to bring comfort to you, and to strengthen you.

speak the Word

life point

In II Thessalonians 2:17, Paul prays that God will encourage the Thessalonians and keep them "steadfast in every good work and word." What an awesome thing it is to be good to people!

The Bible says that God anointed Jesus with the Holy Spirit and with strength, ability and power; and that He went about doing good, for God was with Him (see Acts 10:38). Jesus spent His days being good to all people. He helped and encouraged people everywhere He went.

We are anointed to bless people as Jesus did. God gives us the strength, ability, and power to do awesome works in His name. Take the advice of II Thessalonians 2:17, and strengthen your heart "in every good work and word."

tions which you were taught by us, whether by our word of mouth or by letter.

16 Now may our Lord Jesus Christ Himself and God our Father, Who loved us and gave us everlasting consolation *and* encouragement and wellfounded hope through [His] grace (unmerited favor),

17 Comfort *and* encourage your hearts and strengthen them [make them steadfast and keep them unswerving] in every good work and word.

3 FURTHERMORE, BRETHREN, do pray for us, that the Word of the Lord may speed on (spread

God, I pray that You comfort and encourage my heart and strengthen it in every good work and word.
ADAPTED FROM II THESSALONIANS 2:16, 17

e Many ancient manuscripts so read.

putting the Word to work

Do you regularly pray for your pastor and other church leaders? It is important to do so (see II Thessalonians 3:1, 2). Pray that they are wise and effective in their ministries and that the Word of God goes forth in power. Pray also for their protection and for their families.

rapidly and run its course) and be glorified (extolled) *and* triumph, even as [it has done] with you,

2   And that we may be delivered from perverse (improper, unrighteous) and wicked (actively malicious) men, for not everybody has faith *and* is held by it.

3   Yet the Lord is faithful, and He will strengthen [you] *and* set you on a firm foundation and guard you from the evil [one].

4   And we have confidence in the Lord concerning you, that you are doing and will continue to do the things which we suggest *and* with which we charge you.

5   May the Lord direct your hearts into [realizing and showing] the love of God and into the steadfastness *and*

enjoy the wait!

In II Thessalonians 3:5, Paul prays for his readers to realize that God wants to work several important character traits in them. One of these qualities is patience. I have learned that patience is not my *ability* to wait; it is how I *act* while I am waiting. I need to learn to wait with a good attitude.

Waiting is a fact of life. We are going to wait no matter what we do. We actually spend more time waiting than we do receiving. Our attitudes and actions during the wait determine whether we enjoy the trip and also help determine the length of the wait.

There is a good reason that we need to be patient. We must deal with attitudes that hinder us, such as: being jealous of others who already have what we are waiting for; regularly having our own "pity parties;" riding an emotional roller coaster; giving birth to "Ishmaels" in our own strength (see Genesis 12–16), and displaying all other kinds of bad attitudes. These ways of thinking and feeling need to be worked out of us, and they are the very reasons we need to wait! Preparation is a process that requires time—and any length of time requires a wait.

Even when we are more mature and ready for some of God's best, we may be waiting for God to deal with the other people who will be involved with us.

God's work is always intricate and multifaceted. You will be better off if you just let God work. Let God be God in your life and learn patience while He works unhealthy attitudes out of you. You will enjoy your wait so much more if you do!

do the right thing

Doing what is right occasionally or for a short while will not bring the breakthroughs we need in life. Second Thessalonians 3:13 exhorts us to continue doing the right thing. We must do it over and over and over, and when we feel ourselves becoming weary, we should go to God and wait on Him to give us fresh strength so we are enabled by His grace to press through to the completion of His will.

Doing what is right when we do not seem to be getting right results is difficult, but it must be done. When a farmer plants seed in the ground, he must keep his patient vigil over it until it finally sprouts and produces a harvest. It is a process that takes time and effort. If the farmer gives up on his garden and stops caring for it, he will miss the joy of harvest.

One of Satan's favorite things to do to us is to try to get us to give up! However, God tells us to endure, persist, continue, and finish. He teaches us to be long-suffering, patient, determined, and steadfast.

My experience has taught me that I often have to treat other people rightly for a long time before they begin to treat me the same way. I have to do the right thing with a right attitude for a long time before I start getting right results. Just as natural seed finally takes root and the beginning of a plant breaks through the ground, we also will see breakthrough if we continue to do the right thing, regardless of what others do.

People frequently give up too easily. When their feelings quit on them, they quit too. *I have learned that I can feel wrong and still choose to do what is right.* One sign of spiritual maturity is the ability to live beyond our feelings. People who are spiritually mature live by decisions made based on God's Word, not on how they feel. When we advance to this stage of growth we are well on our way to a wonderful harvest that will leave us amazed.

Let me encourage you today: Do not give up; keep on keeping on!

---

patience of Christ *and* ⁱin waiting for His return.

6 Now we charge you, brethren, in the name *and* on the authority of our Lord Jesus Christ (the Messiah) that you withdraw *and* keep away from every brother (fellow believer) who is slack in the performance of duty *and* is disorderly, living as a shirker *and*

not walking in accord with the traditions *and* instructions that you have received from us.

7 For you yourselves know how it is necessary to imitate our example, for we were not disorderly *or* shirking of duty when we were with you [we were not idle].

8 Nor did we eat anyone's bread

---

f Joseph Thayer, *A Greek-English Lexicon of the New Testament.*

without paying for it, but with toil and struggle we worked night and day, that we might not be a burden *or* impose on any of you [for our support].

9 [It was] not because we do not have a right [to such support], but [we wished] to make ourselves an example for you to follow.

10 For while we were yet with you, we gave you this rule *and* charge: If anyone will not work, neither let him eat.

11 Indeed, we hear that some among you are disorderly [that they are passing their lives in idleness, neglectful of duty], being busy with other people's affairs instead of their own and doing no work.

12 Now we charge and exhort such persons [as ^gministers in Him exhorting those] in the Lord Jesus Christ (the Messiah) that they work in quietness and earn their own food *and* other necessities.

13 And as for you, brethren, do not become weary *or* lose heart in doing right [but continue in well-doing without weakening].

14 But if anyone [in the church] refuses to obey what we say in this letter, take note of that person and do not associate with him, so that he may be ashamed.

15 Do not regard him as an enemy, but simply admonish *and* warn him as [being still] a brother.

16 Now may the Lord of peace Himself grant you His peace (the peace of His kingdom) at all times and in all

life point

The Bible instructs us in II Thessalonians 3:10–12 to work. Why is that?

I believe people are happier and experience more joy and peace in life when they use their resources and work. We all have a built-in knowledge that it is right to make progress and wrong to sit idle and watch life pass us by.

People who do nothing are often jealous of those who prosper. I encourage you not to be jealous of what others have if you are not willing to do what they did to get it.

God expects us to manage the resources He gives us and to use them wisely so they will increase. When we follow God's instruction to work, it may be hard at times, but we will reap blessings and fulfillment in life that idle people do not possess.

ways [under all circumstances and conditions, whatever comes]. The Lord [be] with you all.

17 I, Paul, write you this final greeting with my own hand. This is the mark *and* sign [that it is not a forgery] in every letter of mine. It is the way I write [my handwriting and signature].

18 The grace (spiritual blessing and favor) of our Lord Jesus Christ (the Messiah) be with you all. *Amen (so be it).*

speak the Word

Thank You, Lord, that You are faithful, and that You strengthen me, set me on a firm foundation and guard me from the evil one.
ADAPTED FROM II THESSALONIANS 3:3

Lord, I pray that You grant me Your peace at all times and under all circumstances, whatever comes.
ADAPTED FROM II THESSALONIANS 3:16

g Robert Jamieson, A.R. Fausset and David Brown, *A Commentary.*

First Timothy

Author:
Paul

Date:
Possibly AD 63–65

Everyday Life Principles:
Pray for people, especially for those in positions of authority over you.

Pursue righteousness, godliness, faith, love, steadfastness and gentleness in your everyday life.

Do not give up or be discouraged in your Christian walk, but fight the good fight of faith.

First Timothy is the first of two letters the apostle Paul wrote to a young minister, his "true son in the faith," named Timothy. This letter is relevant to all of us, but it is especially helpful to leaders and ministers because it includes instructions on how to lead God's people and how to deal with problems in the church.

In I Timothy, Paul emphasizes the importance of praying for people, especially those who are in authority. He writes, "First of all, then, I admonish and urge that petitions, prayers, intercessions and thanksgivings be offered on behalf of all men. For kings and all who are in positions of authority . . ." (I Timothy 2:1, 2). This is an instruction I take seriously, and I hope you will too. Also in I Timothy, we find the qualifications and characteristics needed in church leaders (see I Timothy 3), instruction on proper behavior in church services, insight on dealing with doctrinal error, and exhortation to honor widows, elders, and people in authority.

As you read I Timothy, I hope you will apply all of its lessons to your life. I also want to encourage you as Paul did Timothy: " . . . aim at and pursue righteousness (right standing with God and true goodness), godliness (which is the loving fear of God and being Christlike), faith, love, steadfastness (patience), and gentleness. Fight the good fight of the faith . . ." (I Timothy 6:11, 12).

1 PAUL, AN apostle (special messenger) of Christ Jesus by appointment *and* command of God our Savior and of Christ Jesus (the Messiah), our Hope,

2 To Timothy, my true son in the faith: Grace (spiritual blessing and favor), mercy, and [heart] peace [be yours] from God the Father and Christ Jesus our Lord.

3 As I urged you when I was on my way to Macedonia, stay on where you are at Ephesus in order that you may warn *and* admonish *and* charge certain individuals not to teach any different doctrine,

4 Nor to give importance to *or* occupy themselves with legends (fables, myths) and endless genealogies, which foster *and* promote useless speculations *and* questionings rather than acceptance in faith of God's administration *and* the divine training that is in faith ([a]in that leaning of the entire human personality on God in absolute trust and confidence)—

5 Whereas the object *and* purpose of our instruction *and* charge is love, which springs from a pure heart and a good (clear) conscience and sincere (unfeigned) faith.

6 But certain individuals have missed the mark on this very matter [and] have wandered away into vain arguments *and* discussions *and* purposeless talk.

7 They are ambitious to be doctors of the Law (teachers of the Mosaic ritual), but they have no understanding either of the words *and* terms they use or of the subjects about which they make [such] dogmatic assertions.

speak the Word

8 Now we recognize *and* know that the Law is good if anyone uses it lawfully [for the purpose for which it was designed],

9 Knowing *and* understanding this: that the Law is not enacted for the righteous (the upright and just, who are in right standing with God), but for the lawless and unruly, for the ungodly and sinful, for the irreverent and profane, for those who strike *and* beat *and* [even] murder fathers and strike *and* beat *and* [even] murder mothers, for manslayers,

10 [For] impure *and* immoral persons, those who abuse themselves with men, kidnapers, liars, perjurers—and whatever else is opposed to wholesome teaching *and* sound doctrine

11 As laid down by the glorious Gospel of the blessed God, with which I have been entrusted.

12 I give thanks to Him Who has granted me [the needed] strength *and* made me able [for this], Christ Jesus our Lord, because He has judged *and* counted me faithful *and* trustworthy, appointing me to [this stewardship of] the ministry.

13 Though I formerly blasphemed and persecuted and was shamefully *and* outrageously *and* aggressively insulting [to Him], nevertheless, I obtained mercy because I had acted out of ignorance in unbelief.

14 And the grace (unmerited favor and blessing) of our Lord [actually] flowed out superabundantly *and* beyond measure for me, accompanied by faith and love that are [to be realized] in Christ Jesus.

Thank You, Lord, that You give me all the strength and ability that I need in order to do what You have called me to do.
ADAPTED FROM I TIMOTHY 1:12

---

a Alexander Souter, *Pocket Lexicon of the Greek New Testament.*

15 The saying is sure *and* true and worthy of full *and* universal acceptance, that Christ Jesus (the Messiah) came into the world to save sinners, of whom I am foremost.

16 But I obtained mercy for the reason that in me, as the foremost [of sinners], Jesus Christ might show forth *and* display all His perfect long-suffering *and* patience for an example to [encourage] those who would thereafter believe on Him for [the gaining of] eternal life.

17 Now to the King of eternity, incorruptible *and* immortal, invisible, the only God, be honor and glory forever and ever (to the ages of ages). Amen (so be it).

18 This charge *and* admonition I commit in trust to you, Timothy, my son, [b]in accordance with prophetic intimations which I formerly received concerning you, so that inspired *and* aided by them you may wage the good warfare,

19 Holding fast to faith ([c]that leaning of the entire human personality on God in absolute trust and confidence) and having a good (clear) conscience. By rejecting *and* thrusting from them [their conscience], some individuals have made shipwreck of their faith.

20 Among them are Hymenaeus and Alexander, whom I have delivered to Satan in order that they may be disciplined [by punishment and learn] not to blaspheme.

2 FIRST OF all, then, I admonish *and* urge that petitions, prayers, intercessions, and thanksgivings be offered on behalf of all men,

2 For kings and all who are in positions of authority *or* high responsibility, that [outwardly] we may pass a quiet *and* undisturbed life [and inwardly] a peaceable one in all god-

life point

All disobedience is sin and is the root cause of unhappiness. Our sin and disobedience grieve the Holy Spirit, especially when we know that our behavior is going against God's commands.

There are times in our lives when we disobey God, but we do it ignorantly. The apostle Paul is an example of a person who did not know he was disobeying God before his conversion to Christ. Paul once persecuted Christians zealously and thought he was doing God a favor. He was a very religious man who sincerely believed that Christians were evil. The Lord confronted him, and Paul immediately converted to Christ and was baptized (see Acts 9:1–22). He writes in I Timothy 1:13 that he received mercy from God because he acted in ignorance and unbelief. Notice that he says God bestowed *superabundant* grace upon him, a chief sinner, and that he received God's mercy so that Jesus Christ might be seen in him as an example to those who believe (see I Timothy 1:14–16).

All of our sin, whether known or unknown, must be dealt with at the cross of Jesus Christ. We do receive great mercy when we sin unintentionally, and we stand in need of God's mercy all the time. Anyone who wishes to live a life filled with the peace and joy of God's grace needs to be obedient to God.

liness *and* reverence and seriousness in every way.

3 For such [praying] is good *and* right, and [it is] pleasing *and* acceptable to God our Savior,

4 Who wishes all men to be saved

---

b Marvin Vincent, *Word Studies in the New Testament.* **c** Alexander Souter, *Pocket Lexicon.*

life point

When the apostle Paul exhorts us in I Timothy 2:1 to make "petitions, prayers, intercessions, and thanksgivings" on behalf of all men, I believe he means we are to pray for all people everywhere. To intercede for someone is to pray for him and plead his case before the throne of God.

Jesus and the Holy Spirit are our examples; they intercede for us. Hebrews 7:25 speaks of Christ when it says: "He is always living to make petition to God and intercede with Him and intervene for them." In Romans 8:27, Paul teaches us that: ". . . the Spirit intercedes and pleads [before God] in behalf of the saints according to . . . God's will."

Intercession is one of the most important ways we carry on the ministry of Jesus Christ. Obey the instruction of I Timothy 2:1 and pray for others often. God will lead you as you pray, and blessing will be the fruit of your prayers.

and [increasingly] to perceive *and* recognize *and* discern *and* know precisely *and* correctly the [divine] Truth.
5 For there [is only] one God, and [only] one Mediator between God and men, the Man Christ Jesus,
6 Who gave Himself as a ransom for all [people, a fact that was] attested to at the right *and* proper time.
7 And of this matter I was appointed a preacher and an apostle (special messenger)—I am speaking the truth *in Christ,* I do not falsify [when I say this]—a teacher of the Gentiles in [the realm of] faith and truth.
8 I desire therefore that in every place men should pray, without anger *or* quarreling *or* resentment or doubt [in their minds], lifting up holy hands.

putting the Word to work

Have you ever complained about the government of your country? Scripture teaches that if we are to enjoy the blessing of good government, we must pray for all those in authority over us (see I Timothy 2:1, 2). Commit to pray for government officials on local, state and national levels. Be sure to include prayers of thanksgiving for their leadership, for wisdom as they govern, and prayers for the salvation of those who do not know Jesus.

9 Also [I desire] that women should adorn themselves modestly *and* appropriately and sensibly in seemly apparel, not with [elaborate] hair arrangement or gold or pearls or expensive clothing,
10 But by doing good deeds (deeds in themselves good and for the good and advantage of those contacted by them), as befits women who profess reverential fear for *and* devotion to God.
11 Let a woman learn in quietness, in entire submissiveness.
12 I allow no woman to teach or to have authority over men; she is to remain in quietness *and* keep silence [in religious assemblies].
13 For Adam was first formed, then Eve; [Gen. 2:7, 21, 22.]
14 And it was not Adam who was deceived, but [the] woman who was deceived *and* deluded and fell into transgression. [Gen. 3:1-6.]
15 Nevertheless [the sentence put upon women of pain in motherhood does not hinder their souls' salvation, and] they will be saved [eternally] if they continue in faith and love and holiness with self-control, [saved indeed] ᵈthrough the Childbearing *or* by the birth of the divine Child.

d Marvin Vincent, *Word Studies.* See also Gal. 4:4.

be found faithful

The third chapter of I Timothy gives an extensive list of character qualities people need to develop if they want to lead in the body of Christ. All of these requirements point to one overall qualification as a leader: We must be *faithful*. Just as God tested the Israelites in the wilderness, we must learn how to be faithful in the wilderness, faithful in the hard times. We must be faithful to keep on doing what is right, even when everything around us is wrong.

God works through and blesses faithful people, those who are faithful in the wilderness as well as in the Promised Land. Being faithful is being devoted, supportive and loyal. Faithful people are worthy of trust or belief; they are reliable, consistent, constant, steady, and steadfast, meaning that they will stay wherever God places them and be true to those with whom God has given them to work. There is a reward for such people.

If we want to exercise authority, we must also know how to come under authority. We must learn to be faithful and stay wherever God has placed us until He moves us. We must respect and obey those in authority over us. We must do the right thing simply because it is right, even though we may never understand why—which is a real test of our faithfulness and obedience.

If you want to be a spiritual leader, you desire a good thing. Expect to be tested in your faithfulness and obedience as God works these qualities in you so that you will develop the faithfulness necessary for a good leader to possess.

3 THE SAYING is true *and* irrefutable: If any man [eagerly] seeks the office of bishop (superintendent, overseer), he desires an excellent task (work).
2 Now a bishop (superintendent, overseer) must give no grounds for accusation *but* must be above reproach, the husband of one wife, circumspect *and* temperate *and* self-controlled; [he must be] sensible *and* well behaved *and* dignified and lead an orderly (disciplined) life; [he must be] hospitable [showing love for and being a friend to the believers, especially strangers or foreigners, and be] a capable *and* qualified teacher,
3 Not given to wine, not combative but gentle *and* considerate, not quarrelsome *but* forbearing *and* peaceable,
and not a lover of money [insatiable for wealth and ready to obtain it by questionable means].
4 He must rule his own household well, keeping his children under control, with true dignity, commanding their respect in every way *and* keeping them respectful.

life point

Paul asks a very important question in I Timothy 3:4, 5: How can a person rule the church if he does not know how to rule his own household? Paul is not talking here about dictatorial, controlling, or iron-fisted rule. The successful leader is capable of guiding, leading, and nurturing his household with godly wisdom, love, and understanding.

the well-rounded leader

First Timothy 3:2 tells us that a spiritual leader must live his life in such a way that no one has grounds to accuse him; he must be above reproach. In other words, he must behave so well that people cannot find any reason to blame him for wrongdoing.

Notice that the leader must be circumspect, temperate, self-controlled, and *sensible*. I love that! The biggest problem with many people, including some in the body of Christ, is that they are just plain goofy. They frequently do not use common sense in decision making. Sometimes it seems that when people become born again and filled with the Holy Spirit, or filled with God's power and ability to fulfill His will for their lives, some think they have to throw all common sense out the window in order to be "spiritual." Just the opposite is true. If a person is going to build a ministry, he is going to need a lot of plain old common sense. Notice also that a leader must be well behaved and dignified, leading an orderly and disciplined life.

A leader needs to be hospitable and friendly, especially to foreigners or those who are outsiders. For example, at social gatherings a good leader will go out of his way to make people outside of his circle of family and friends feel comfortable and accepted.

Finally, a leader must be a capable and qualified teacher. This involves teaching by example. People want to see Christians who live good, clean lives. They want to be able to trust someone, and it is our job to set a good example and pass along the principles of godly living to others.

5 For if a man does not know how to rule his own household, how is he to take care of the church of God?
6 He must not be a new convert, or he may [develop a beclouded and stupid state of mind] as the result of pride [be blinded by conceit, and] fall into the condemnation that the devil [once] did. [Isa. 14:12-14.]
7 Furthermore, he must have a good reputation *and* be well thought of by those outside [the church], lest he become involved in slander *and* incur reproach and fall into the devil's trap.
8 In like manner the deacons [must be] worthy of respect, not shifty *and* double-talkers *but* sincere in what

they say, not given to much wine, not greedy for base gain [craving wealth and resorting to ignoble and dishonest methods of getting it].
9 They must possess the mystic secret of the faith [Christian truth as hidden from ungodly men] with a clear conscience.
10 And let them also be tried *and* investigated *and* proved first; then, if they turn out to be above reproach, let them serve [as deacons].
11 e[The] women likewise must be worthy of respect *and* serious, not gossipers, but temperate *and* self-controlled, [thoroughly] trustworthy in all things.

e Either their wives or the deaconesses, or both.

life point

In I Timothy 3:10, Paul warns against putting people into leadership positions too quickly. Before they lead, they need to be prepared; they need to be "tried and investigated and proved."

Preparation for ministry involves going through some tests and some hard, dry places. Hard times change us. They can make us bitter or better. Hopefully they develop our character; they mature us; and they force us to look to God instead of to ourselves, to people, or to things. We have a choice to make about how we will respond to hard times. I encourage you to make choices that will help prepare you for the great future God has planned for you.

12 Let deacons be the husbands of but one wife, and let them manage [their] children and their own households well.

13 For those who perform well as deacons acquire a good standing for themselves and also gain much confidence *and* freedom *and* boldness in the faith which is [founded on and centers] in Christ Jesus.

14 Although I hope to come to you before long, I am writing these instructions to you so that,

15 If I am detained, you may know how people ought to conduct themselves in the household of God, which is the church of the living God, the pillar and stay (the prop and support) of the Truth.

16 And great *and* important *and* weighty, we confess, is the hidden truth (the mystic secret) of godliness. He [[f]God] was made visible in human flesh, justified *and* vindicated in the [Holy] Spirit, was seen by angels, preached among the nations, believed

on in the world, [and] taken up in glory.

4 BUT THE [Holy] Spirit distinctly *and* expressly declares that in latter times some will turn away from the faith, giving attention to deluding *and* seducing spirits and doctrines that demons teach,

2 Through the hypocrisy *and* pretensions of liars whose consciences are seared (cauterized),

3 Who forbid people to marry and [teach them] to abstain from [certain kinds of] foods which God created to be received with thanksgiving by those who believe *and* have [an increasingly clear] knowledge of the truth.

4 For everything God has created is good, and nothing is to be thrown away *or* refused if it is received with thanksgiving.

5 For it is hallowed *and* consecrated by the Word of God and by prayer.

6 If you lay all these instructions before the brethren, you will be a worthy steward *and* a good minister of Christ Jesus, ever nourishing your own self on the truths of the faith and of the good [Christian] instruction which you have closely followed.

7 But refuse *and* avoid irreverent

putting the Word to work

It is sad and distressing to see another Christian stray from faith in Christ. Yet I Timothy 4:1, 2 warns that before Christ comes again, there will be those who depart from the faith. Do you know anyone who questions his or her faith? Pray that these people will not fall into deception and become hardened to spiritual truth. Guard yourself against deceptive doctrine through diligent study of the Word of God.

f Some manuscripts read "God."

legends (profane and impure and godless fictions, mere grandmothers' tales) and silly myths, *and* express your disapproval of them. Train yourself toward godliness (piety), [keeping yourself spiritually fit].

8 For physical training is of some value (useful for a little), but godliness (spiritual training) is useful *and* of value in everything *and* in every way, for it holds promise for the present life and also for the life which is to come.

9 This saying is reliable *and* worthy of complete acceptance by everybody.

10 With a view to this we toil and strive, [yes and] *gsuffer reproach*, because we have [fixed our] hope on the living God, Who is the Savior (Preserver, Maintainer, Deliverer) of all men, especially of those who believe (trust in, rely on, and adhere to Him).

11 Continue to command these things and to teach them.

12 Let no one despise *or* think less of you because of your youth, but be an example (pattern) for the believers in speech, in conduct, in love, in faith, and in purity.

13 Till I come, devote yourself to [public and private] reading, to exhortation (preaching and personal appeals), and to teaching *and* instilling doctrine.

14 Do not neglect the gift which is in you, [that special inward endowment] which was directly imparted to you [by the Holy Spirit] by prophetic utterance when the elders laid their hands upon you [at your ordination].

15 Practice *and* cultivate *and* medi-

putting the Word to work

Do you remember when you turned sixteen? How about twenty-one? In many cultures, turning a particular age has special significance and such milestones often bring greater privileges and responsibilities. In the Christian life, however, your age is not as important as your conduct. No matter how young, you are called to live a life that is an example—in speech, conduct, faith, love, and purity—to other believers (see I Timothy 4:12).

tate upon these duties; throw yourself wholly into them [as your ministry], so that your progress may be evident to everybody.

16 Look well to yourself [to your own personality] and to [your] teaching; persevere in these things [hold to them], for by so doing you will save both yourself and those who hear you.

5 DO NOT sharply censure *or* rebuke an older man, but entreat *and* plead with him as [you would with] a father. Treat younger men like brothers;

2 [Treat] older women like mothers [and] younger women like sisters, in all purity.

3 [Always] treat with great consideration *and* give aid to those who are truly widowed (solitary and without support).

4 But if a widow has children or grandchildren, see to it that these are first made to understand that it is their religious duty [to defray their

speak the Word

g Some manuscripts so read.

a Christian duty

Are you helping take care of and provide for any relatives you have who are unable to take care of themselves, especially parents and grandparents? Did you know that doing so is God's will? It is our Christian duty (see I Timothy 5:4).

I was abused during my childhood and as a result, my attitude toward this biblical instruction was that I was exempt from this expectation due to how I was treated. After all, how could God expect me to take care of people who never did anything for me but hurt me? Perhaps you have been hurt by your parents and now you ignore them. This is understandable, but not acceptable. We must realize that "hurting people hurt people," and develop a merciful, forgiving attitude toward those who have hurt us. When we have truly forgiven we are willing to help those who do not deserve to be helped. We do not deserve God's help, but He helps us anyway and He expects us to do the same for others.

Although it was difficult, there came a time when I made the decision to take care of my elderly parents and I have seen God's favor and blessing as a result. We may do other "good works," or "church work," but if we ignore this duty, we are not doing what is right. If a believer fails to provide for his relatives he is worse than an unbeliever who does perform his obligation in this matter (see I Timothy 5:8).

Maybe you were not ever mistreated by your parents, but are now too busy to call them, your grandparents and your other relatives. Perhaps your schedule is too full to attend family functions. Most of our schedules are too full of things that are not even important. They are filled with things we want to do, not with things we should do. Although God wants us to be blessed and have our desires met, He first and foremost wants us to do our duty as believers in Jesus Christ. If we do not care for our own families, God is not pleased.

God's Word teaches us not to hide ourselves from the needs of our own flesh and blood (see Isaiah 58:7). The instruction is followed by a promise of blessing: "Then shall your light break forth and your healing (your restoration and the power of a new life) shall spring forth speedily ... ." (Isaiah 58:8). Blessings do follow obedience. Let me encourage you specifically to obey I Timothy 5:4–8. I believe you will experience blessings as you do.

natural obligation to those] at home, and make return to their parents *or* grandparents [for all their care by contributing to their maintenance], for this is acceptable in the sight of God.

5 Now [a woman] who is a real widow and is left entirely alone *and* desolate has fixed her hope on God and perseveres in supplications and prayers night and day,

6 Whereas she who lives in pleasure *and* self-gratification [giving herself up to luxury and self-indulgence] is dead even while she [still] lives.

7 Charge [the people] thus, so that they may be without reproach *and* blameless.

8 If anyone fails to provide for his relatives, and especially for those of his own family, he has disowned the faith [by failing to accompany it with fruits] and is worse than an unbeliever [who performs his obligation in these matters].

life point

First Timothy 5:8 tells us we have a responsibility to care for our families. We have a duty not only to care for our spouses and our children, but if we have elderly parents or grandparents, we need to provide for them as well. This is a duty we must perform whether we feel like it or not.

You may have dependent elderly parents who never really took proper care of you. They may have even abused you. Is it really your duty to take care of them now? Yes, it is. If you cannot do it for *them*, do it for *God* with a good attitude. As you do, you will demonstrate the kind of fruit that accompanies obedient faith.

9 Let no one be put on the roll of widows [who are to receive church support] who is under sixty years of age or who has been the wife of more than one man;

10 And she must have a reputation for good deeds, as one who has brought up children, who has practiced hospitality to strangers [of the brotherhood], washed the feet of the saints, helped to relieve the distressed, [and] devoted herself diligently to doing good in every way.

11 But refuse [to enroll on this list the] younger widows, for when they become restive *and* their natural desires grow strong, they withdraw themselves against Christ [and] wish to marry [again].

12 And so they incur condemnation for having set aside *and* slighted their previous pledge.

13 Moreover, as they go about from house to house, they learn to be idlers, and not only idlers, but gossips and busybodies, saying what they should not say *and* talking of things they should not mention.

14 So I would have younger [widows] marry, bear children, guide the household, [and] not give opponents of the faith occasion for slander or reproach.

15 For already some [widows] have turned aside after Satan.

16 If any believing woman *or believing man* has [relatives or persons in the household who are] widows, let him relieve them; let the church not be burdened [with them], so that it may [be free to] assist those who are truly widows (those who are all alone and are dependent).

17 Let the elders who perform the duties of their office well be considered doubly worthy of honor [and of adequate ʰfinancial support], especially those who labor faithfully in preaching and teaching.

18 For the Scripture says, You shall not muzzle an ox when it is treading out the grain, and again, The laborer is worthy of his hire. [Deut. 25:4; Luke 10:7.]

19 Listen to no accusation [presented before a judge] against an elder unless it is confirmed by the testimony of two or three witnesses. [Deut. 19:15.]

20 As for those who are guilty *and* persist in sin, rebuke *and* admonish them in the presence of all, so that the rest may be warned *and* stand in wholesome awe *and* fear.

21 I solemnly charge you in the presence of God and of Christ Jesus and of the chosen angels that you guard *and* keep [these rules] without personal

h Marvin Vincent, *Word Studies*.

prejudice *or* favor, doing nothing from partiality.

22 Do not be in a hurry in the laying on of hands [giving the sanction of the church too hastily in reinstating expelled offenders or in ordination in questionable cases], nor share *or* participate in another man's sins; keep yourself pure.

23 Drink water no longer exclusively, but use a little wine for the sake of your stomach and your frequent illnesses.

24 The sins of some men are conspicuous (openly evident to all eyes), going before them to the judgment [seat] *and* proclaiming their sentence in advance; but the sins of others appear later [following the offender to the bar of judgment and coming into view there].

25 So also, good deeds are evident *and* conspicuous, and even when they are not, they cannot remain hidden [indefinitely].

6 LET ALL who are under the yoke as bond servants esteem their own [personal] masters worthy of honor *and* fullest respect, so that the name of God and the teaching [about Him] may not be brought into disrepute *and* blasphemed.

putting the Word to work

Are you ever tempted to think that you would be more content in life if you had more money? This is certainly a common idea in our society, but I Timothy 6:6–10 warns that striving to be rich and the love of money are dangerous snares that lead to destruction, not to contentment.

Ask God to help you be content in His provision for you, knowing He knows everything you need and is faithful to provide.

2 Let those who have believing masters not be disrespectful *or* scornful [to them] on the grounds that they are brothers [in Christ]; rather, they should serve [them all the better] because those who benefit by their kindly service are believers and beloved. Teach and urge these duties.

3 But if anyone teaches otherwise and does not [i]assent to the sound *and* wholesome messages of our Lord Jesus Christ (the Messiah) and the teaching which is in agreement with godliness (piety toward God),

4 He is puffed up with pride *and* stupefied with conceit, [although he is] woefully ignorant. He has a [j]morbid fondness for controversy and disputes *and* strife about words, which result in (produce) envy *and* jealousy, quarrels *and* dissension, abuse *and* insults *and* slander, and base suspicions,

5 And protracted wrangling *and* wearing discussion *and* perpetual

life point

The kingdom of God offers great benefits. As we see in I Timothy 6:6, one benefit is the privilege of being content and satisfied even when circumstances in our lives do not suit us.

First Timothy 6:8 says that it is possible for us to be content if we just have food and clothing. Most of us have at least that, but we still have much discontentment. This verse is not saying that food and clothing are all God wants us to have. But it does say that we do not need extra things to make us happy. We are wise to be content with the basic necessities in life because we realize life does not consist of the abundance of things we possess. We may have things, but our joy and contentment cannot be in them.

i Marvin Vincent, *Word Studies.*   j Joseph Thayer, *A Greek-English Lexicon of the New Testament.*

the secret of true contentment

You may not realize it yet, but contentment is worth more than all the material possessions you can possibly accumulate in a lifetime. Nothing you have or will obtain is worth anything if you are not satisfied inside. Apostle Paul referenced this when he wrote I Timothy 6:6.

Paul also talks about finding contentment in the fourth chapter of Philippians. He says, "I have learned how to be content (satisfied to the point where I am not disturbed or disquieted) in whatever state I am. I know how to be abased and live humbly in straitened circumstances, and I know also how to enjoy plenty and live in abundance. I have learned in any and all circumstances the secret of facing every situation . . . " (Philippians 4:11, 12).

We usually do not learn contentment until we give up seeking it our own way. What usually happens is that we live discontented lives for a long time and then finally pray, "Lord, I do not want to live this way any longer. Getting this thing or having that thing is not worth it. I do not want to be miserable anymore. Just give me what You want me to have because unless You want me to have it, I do not want it. From now on I'm not going to compare myself with anyone else. I'm not going to be jealous of anyone. I'm not going to be jealous of people who receive a promotion at work. I'm not going to be envious of anyone. I do not want what anyone else has. Lord, I want only what You want me to have and I want to be content with that."

Saying to God, "Lord, I want only what You want me to have," and meaning it, is the secret to finding peace, happiness and contentment in life.

friction among men who are corrupted in mind and bereft of the truth, who imagine that godliness *or* righteousness is a ᵏsource of profit [a moneymaking business, a means of livelihood]. *From such withdraw.*
6 [And it is, indeed, a source of immense profit, for] godliness accompanied with contentment (that contentment which is a sense of ᵏinward sufficiency) is great *and* abundant gain.
7 For we brought nothing into the world, and *obviously* we cannot take anything out of the world;
8 But if we have food and clothing, with these we shall be content (satisfied).

life point

Keeping our thoughts pure and in the will of God is a lifetime battle. We must "fight the good fight of the faith," according to I Timothy 6:12.

The mind is the battlefield on which we fight. Satan wages war in the realm of our thoughts because he knows that if he controls our thoughts, he controls us and our destinies. As we live our lives and pursue our destinies, there will be times of fighting the good fight of faith, and if we win enough battles, we will win the war.

k Marvin Vincent, *Word Studies.*

fight the good fight

To be aggressive is to be a fighter. Just as the apostle Paul said he fought the good fight of faith (see also II Timothy 4:7), so he instructed his young disciple Timothy to "fight the good fight" in I Timothy 6:12. In the same way, we should fight the good fight of faith in our daily lives as we struggle against spiritual enemies in high places and in our own minds and hearts.

One part of fighting the good fight of faith is the ability to recognize our enemy. As long as we are passive, Satan will torment us. Nothing is going to change about our situation if all we do is sit and wish things were different. We have to take action. Too often we do not move against the enemy when he comes against us with discouragement, fear, doubt, or guilt. We just draw back into a corner somewhere and let him beat us up. We believe his lies when we should stand against them with the truth of God's Word.

You and I are not supposed to be punching bags for the devil; instead, we are called to be fighters and respond aggressively to his attacks.

The devil tries to trick us into fighting with others around us. But God wants us to forget all the junk that Satan stirs up within us to get us offended toward other people. Instead, He wants us to fight against the spiritual enemies who try to war over our lives and steal our peace and joy.

Take Paul's words to heart. Lay hold of the eternal life you have been called to receive and fight the good fight of faith.

9 But those who crave to be rich fall into temptation and a snare and into many foolish (useless, godless) and hurtful desires that plunge men into ruin *and* destruction and miserable perishing.
10 For the love of money is a root of all evils; it is through this craving that some have been led astray *and* have wandered from the faith and pierced themselves through with many ¹acute [mental] pangs.
11 But as for you, O man of God, flee from all these things; aim at *and* pursue righteousness (right standing with God and true goodness), godliness (which is the loving fear of God and being Christlike), faith, love, steadfastness (patience), and gentleness of heart.

12 Fight the good fight of the faith; lay hold of the eternal life to which you were summoned and [for which] you confessed the good confession [of faith] before many witnesses.
13 In the presence of God, Who preserves alive all living things, and of Christ Jesus, Who in His testimony before Pontius Pilate made the good confession, I [solemnly] charge you
14 To keep all His precepts unsullied *and* flawless, irreproachable, until the appearing of our Lord Jesus Christ (the Anointed One),
15 Which [appearing] will be shown forth in His own proper time by the blessed, only Sovereign (Ruler), the King of kings and the Lord of lords,
16 Who alone has immortality [in the sense of exemption from every kind of

1 Alexander Souter, *Pocket Lexicon*.

death] and lives in unapproachable light, Whom no man has ever seen or can see. Unto Him be honor and everlasting power *and* dominion. Amen (so be it).

17 As for the rich in this world, charge them not to be proud *and* arrogant *and* contemptuous of others, nor to set their hopes on uncertain riches, but on God, Who richly *and* ceaselessly provides us with everything for [our] enjoyment.

18 [Charge them] to do good, to be rich in good works, to be liberal *and* generous of heart, ready to share [with others],

19 In this way laying up for themselves [the riches that endure forever as] a good foundation for the future, so that they may grasp that which is life indeed.

20 O Timothy, guard *and* keep the deposit entrusted [to you]! Turn away from the irreverent babble *and* god-

putting the Word to work

If you were rich, would you be more secure in life? Worldly riches are uncertain (see I Timothy 6:17–19); true security is found in trusting God Who gives generously. If you are wealthy, you have a great responsibility to honor God with your wealth and to be a faithful steward of it, doing good works and being eager to share your resources with others.

less chatter, with the vain *and* empty *and* worldly phrases, and the subtleties *and* the contradictions in what is falsely called knowledge *and* spiritual illumination.

21 [For] by making such profession some have erred (missed the mark) as regards the faith. Grace (divine favor and blessing) be with you all! *Amen (so be it).*

speak the Word

Thank You, Lord, for richly and ceaselessly giving me everything to enjoy. Help me to do good, to be rich in good works, to be generous of heart and to share with others.
ADAPTED FROM I TIMOTHY 6:17, 18

Second Timothy

Author:
Paul

Date:
AD 66–67

Everyday Life Principles:
Hold fast to the teachings of your Christian faith, being diligent to know, honor and obey God's Word.

Be a good "first class" soldier of Christ Jesus.

Finish your race on earth having kept the faith.

Second Timothy is filled with encouragement, perhaps because the young man Timothy really needed it! Many scholars believe Paul wrote this letter shortly before his death, while he was suffering a much more harsh imprisonment than he previously endured. For that reason, this is quite a personal letter from the older Apostle to his spiritual son—like Paul's final instructions before he finished his course on earth.

We find many practical instructions for living the Christian life in II Timothy, exhortations we really need to apply to our lives today. For example, we are encouraged to boldly testify of the Lord and not be ashamed of our faith; to hold fast to the teaching of the gospel; to be diligent and hardworking; to be strong in the grace that is found in Jesus; to avoid trivial disagreements that lead to strife and to endure hardship "as a good (first class) soldier of Christ Jesus" (II Timothy 2:3); to know, honor and obey the truth of God's Word and to fulfill God's calling on our lives.

I pray that you apply the instructions and exhortations of II Timothy to your life so that when the time draws near for the end of your earthly life, you will be able to say, as Paul did: "I have fought the good (worthy, honorable, and noble) fight, I have finished the race, I have kept (firmly held) the faith" (II Timothy 4:7).

1 PAUL, AN apostle (special messenger) of Christ Jesus by the will of God, according to the promise of life that is in Christ Jesus,

2 To Timothy, [my] beloved child: Grace (favor and spiritual blessing), mercy, and [heart] peace from God the Father and Christ Jesus our Lord!

3 I thank God Whom I worship with a pure conscience, [a]in the spirit of my fathers, when without ceasing I remember you night and day in my prayers,

4 And when, as I recall your tears, I yearn to see you so that I may be filled with joy.

5 I am calling up memories of your sincere *and* unqualified faith (the [b]leaning of your entire personality on God in Christ in absolute trust and confidence in His power, wisdom, and goodness), [a faith] that first lived permanently in [the heart of] your grandmother Lois and your mother Eunice and now, I am [fully] persuaded, [dwells] in you also.

6 That is why I would remind you to stir up (rekindle the embers of, fan the flame of, and keep burning) the [gracious] gift of God, [the inner fire] that is in you by means of the laying on of my hands [[a]with those of the elders at your ordination].

7 For God did not give us a spirit of timidity (of cowardice, of craven and cringing and fawning fear), but [He has given us a spirit] of power and of love and of calm *and* well-balanced mind *and* discipline *and* self-control.

8 Do not blush *or* be ashamed then,

life point

It appears that Timothy was getting fearful, weary, and unsure of his call. His spirit was sinking, so Paul came in with a strong word to revive him. In II Timothy 1:5, Paul reminded him of his faith and how it came to him. He told him in essence, "I remember your grandmother's faith. I remember your mother's faith. I remember when I laid my hands on you and we prayed for you to receive the gifts that are in you." Then he said, "Now stir up the gift within you" (see II Timothy 1:6).

Nobody can stir up your gift, that fire within you, the way you can. Other people can stir you up, but as soon as you are alone, you can grow cold again. That is when you have to stir up yourself. Pray, worship, and praise God. Remember what He has spoken to you. Preach to yourself if you have to. Just do whatever it takes for you to stay stirred up in God!

to testify to *and* for our Lord, nor of me, a prisoner for His sake, but [[a]with me] take your share of the suffering [to which the preaching] of the Gospel [may expose you, and do it] in the power of God.

9 [For it is He] Who delivered *and* saved us and called us with a calling in itself holy *and* leading to holiness [to a life of consecration, a vocation of holiness]; [He did it] not because of

speak the Word

Father, I declare that You have not given me a spirit of fear. You have given me a spirit of power and of love and of a calm, well-balanced mind and of discipline and self-control.

ADAPTED FROM II TIMOTHY 1:7

a Marvin Vincent, *Word Studies in the New Testament*. **b** Alexander Souter, *Pocket Lexicon of the Greek New Testament*.

power, love, and discipline

Second Timothy 1:7 tells us that timidity, which is the same as fear, is not from God and that God gives us power, love, a calm and well-balanced mind, discipline, and self-control.

I am going to tell you a little secret: fear will never stop coming against us. We must learn to do what God tells us to do whether we feel fear or not. We must "do it afraid" if necessary, but that is what courage does; it feels the fear and does what it should anyway!

I always thought that as long as I felt fear, I was a coward, but I have learned differently. When God told Joshua repeatedly to fear not (see Joshua 1:9; 10:8), He let him know that fear was going to attack him, but that he must walk in obedience to what God spoke.

We are not cowards because we feel fear. We are cowards only if we let fear rule our decisions.

Fear is a spirit that produces physical and emotional symptoms. When fear attacks us, we may feel shaky and weak or find ourselves sweating. It may take everything we can muster just to speak or move. None of that means we are cowards. The Word of God does not say "sweat not, shake not, tremble not." The Word says, many times, "fear not." The way to conquer fear is to press on through it and get to the other side of it—the side of freedom, which is the side of power.

anything of merit that we have done, but because of *and* to further His own purpose and grace (unmerited favor) which was given us in Christ Jesus before the world began [eternal ages ago].

10 [It is that purpose and grace] which He now has made known *and* has fully disclosed *and* made real [to us] through the appearing of our Savior Christ Jesus, Who annulled death *and* made it of no effect and brought life and immortality (immunity from eternal death) to light through the Gospel.

11 For [the proclaiming of] this [Gospel] I was appointed a herald (preacher) and an apostle (special messenger) and a teacher *of the Gentiles.*

12 And this is why I am suffering as I do. Still I am not ashamed, for I know (perceive, have knowledge of, and am acquainted with) Him Whom I have believed (adhered to and trusted in and relied on), and I am [positively] persuaded that He is able to guard *and* keep that which has been entrusted to me *and* which 'I have committed [to Him] until that day.

13 Hold fast *and* follow the pattern of wholesome *and* sound teaching which you have heard from me, in [all] the faith and love which are [for us] in Christ Jesus.

14 Guard *and* keep [with the greatest care] the precious *and* excellently adapted [Truth] which has been entrusted [to you], by the [help of the]

a Marvin Vincent, *Word Studies in the New Testament.*   b Alexander Souter, *Pocket Lexicon of the Greek New Testament.*

c Alternate translation.

Holy Spirit Who makes His home in us.

15 You already know that all who are in Asia turned away *and* forsook me, Phygelus and Hermogenes among them.

16 May the Lord grant [His] mercy to the family of Onesiphorus, for he often showed me kindness *and* ministered to my needs [comforting and reviving and bracing me like fresh air]! He was not ashamed of my chains *and* imprisonment [for Christ's sake].

17 No, rather when he reached Rome, he searched diligently *and* eagerly for me and found me.

18 May the Lord grant to him that he may find mercy from the Lord on that [great] day! And you know how many things he did for me *and* what a help he was at Ephesus [you know better than I can tell you].

2 SO YOU, my son, be strong (strengthened inwardly) in the grace (spiritual blessing) that is [to be found only] in Christ Jesus.

2 And the [instructions] which you have heard from me along with many witnesses, transmit *and* entrust [as a deposit] to reliable *and* faithful men who will be competent *and* qualified to teach others also.

3 Take [with me] your share of the hardships *and* suffering [which you are called to endure] as a good (first-class) soldier of Christ Jesus.

4 No soldier when in service gets entangled in the enterprises of [civil-ian] life; his aim is to satisfy *and* please the one who enlisted him.

5 And if anyone enters competitive games, he is not crowned unless he competes lawfully (fairly, according to the rules laid down).

6 [It is] the hard-working farmer [who labors to produce] who must be the first partaker of the fruits.

7 Think over these things I am saying [understand them and grasp their application], for the Lord will grant you full insight *and* understanding in everything.

8 Constantly keep in mind Jesus Christ (the Messiah) [as] risen from the dead, [as the prophesied King] descended from David, according to the good news (the Gospel) that I preach. [Ps. 16:10.]

9 For that [Gospel] I am suffering affliction *and* even wearing chains like a criminal. But the Word of God is not chained *or* imprisoned!

10 Therefore I [am ready to] persevere *and* stand my ground with patience *and* endure everything for the sake of the elect [God's chosen], so that they too may obtain [the] salvation which is in Christ Jesus, with [the reward of] eternal glory.

11 The saying is sure *and* worthy of confidence: If we have died with Him, we shall also live with Him.

12 If we endure, we shall also reign with Him. If we deny *and* disown *and* reject Him, He will also deny *and* disown *and* reject us.

13 If we are faithless [do not believe

speak the Word

and are untrue to Him], He remains true (faithful to His Word and His righteous character), for He cannot deny Himself.

14 Remind [the people] of these facts and [solemnly] charge them in the presence of the Lord to avoid petty controversy over words, which does no good but upsets *and* undermines the faith of the hearers.

15 Study *and* be eager *and* do your utmost to present yourself to God approved (tested by trial), a workman who has no cause to be ashamed, correctly analyzing *and* accurately dividing [rightly handling and skillfully teaching] the Word of Truth.

16 But avoid all empty (vain, useless, idle) talk, for it will lead people into more *and* more ungodliness.

17 And their teaching [will devour; it] will eat its way like cancer *or* spread like gangrene. So it is with Hymenaeus and Philetus,

18 Who have missed the mark *and* swerved from the truth by arguing that the resurrection has already taken place. They are undermining the faith of some.

19 But the firm foundation of (laid by) God stands, sure *and* unshaken, bearing this seal (inscription): The Lord knows those who are His, and, Let everyone who names [himself by] the name of the Lord give up all iniquity *and* stand aloof from it. [Num. 16:5; Isa. 26:13.]

20 But in a great house there are not only vessels of gold and silver, but also [utensils] of wood and earthenware, and some for honorable *and* noble [use] and some for menial *and* ignoble [use].

life point

Second Timothy 2:16 instructs us to "avoid all empty (vain, useless, idle) talk." Instead, we need to learn to speak as God speaks. It is the Word of God, spoken in truth and love from our lips that will return to Him after accomplishing His will and purpose. But in order to speak that Word in truth and love, our hearts must be right before the Lord, for it is out of the abundance of the heart that the mouth speaks, for good or for evil (see Matthew 12:34).

You are bound by your words and by your declaration. You are also judged by them. That is why it is so important to place a guard upon your lips so that what issues forth from them is not only truthful, but also kind, positive, edifying, and in line with the will of God.

You can change your actions and behavior, but in order to do so you must first change your thoughts and words. To do that, you need the help of the indwelling Spirit of God. Ask Him to help you. He will!

21 So whoever cleanses himself [from what is ignoble *and* unclean, who separates himself from contact with contaminating and corrupting influences] will [then himself] be a vessel set apart *and* useful for honorable *and* noble purposes, consecrated *and* profitable to the Master, fit *and* ready for any good work.

22 Shun youthful lusts *and* flee from them, and aim at *and* pursue righteousness (all that is virtuous and

speak the Word

God, I pray that You will help me correctly analyze, accurately divide, rightly handle, and skillfully teach Your Word of Truth.
ADAPTED FROM II TIMOTHY 2:15

special people for special purposes

God's Word instructs us in II Timothy 2:20, 21 to be vessels consecrated and ready for the Master's use. These verses make clear that to be consecrated is to be set apart for a special use.

To God, we are precious treasures. According to His great plan, we are vessels He sets aside for a special purpose. God wants to show His glory through us. He wants to use us to bring others to Himself. We are His representatives, His ambassadors here on earth. God makes His appeal to the world through us (see II Corinthians 5:20).

The meaning of the word *consecrate* is very similar to to the word *dedicate;* it means to give, to offer to another, or to set aside for a purpose. If I say that a room in my house is dedicated to prayer, I mean that I want that particular room used primarily for the purpose of prayer and not for other things.

I own some dresses that I wear for fancy parties. I have set them aside in a certain place in my closet and keep them inside garment bags for protection. This makes them special; they are not used for ordinary occasions, but are set apart for special purposes. This is the way God views us; we are not meant for the world's purposes, but for God's. We are in the world, yet Jesus tells us we are not "of" the world (see John 15:19). So do not be worldly, adopting its ways and methods.

Even after we dedicate ourselves to God, we should regularly rededicate ourselves to our real purpose, as Romans 12:1 encourages: "I appeal to you therefore, brethren, and beg of you in view of [all] the mercies of God, to make a decisive dedication of your bodies [presenting all your members and faculties] as a living sacrifice, holy (devoted, consecrated) and well pleasing to God, which is your reasonable (rational, intelligent) service and spiritual worship."

It is not too much for God to ask us to dedicate every facet of our being to Him. In fact, that is actually our worship and spiritual service. Under Old Covenant law, God required animal sacrifices to atone for sin. He no longer wants dead sacrifices; He wants us offering ourselves as "living sacrifices" unto Him for His purpose and use. Consecrate yourself to God and be set apart and ready for any good work!

good, right living, conformity to the will of God in thought, word, and deed); [and aim at and pursue] faith, love, [and] peace (harmony and concord with others) in fellowship with all [Christians], who call upon the Lord out of a pure heart.

23 But refuse (shut your mind against, have nothing to do with) trifling (ill-informed, unedifying, stupid) controversies over ignorant questionings, for you know that they foster strife *and* breed quarrels.

24 And the servant of the Lord must not be quarrelsome (fighting and contending). Instead, he must be kindly to everyone *and* mild-tempered [preserving the bond of peace]; he must be a skilled *and* suitable teacher, patient *and* forbearing *and* willing to suffer wrong.

25 He must correct his opponents

avoid strife at all costs

The servant of the Lord must be a maker and maintainer of peace (see II Timothy 2:23, 24). He must not strive. Strife is bickering, arguing, heated disagreement, and an angry undercurrent. Strife is dangerous and destructive. Strife is like a deadly, contagious disease. It spreads rapidly unless it is confronted and stopped.

Strife destroys marriages, friendships, businesses, and churches. It is a tool that Satan uses to stop the will of God. Strife or contention comes only by pride (see Proverbs 13:10). The servant of the Lord must be willing to humble himself and go the extra mile to maintain peace. Paul told the Philippians they would complete his joy if they lived in harmony (see Philippians 2:2). Paul knew the power believers have if they commit to live in unity and agreement (see Matthew 18:19). We must pursue peace, crave it, and seek it with all of our heart and soul. Without peace we are without power!

Do not get involved in conversations that head toward strife. Avoid controversies over things that really do not even matter and refuse to be involved in gossip and tale bearing, which are ungodly and unnecessary. Do not spread rumors or tell other people's secrets. These things cause an angry undercurrent and they hinder or eliminate God's power and blessing. Many homes cannot prosper and be blessed because everyone is in strife. Mom and Dad bicker and argue, the siblings argue and resent one another and nobody is happy but the devil.

I want to repeat that strife is very dangerous and that as servants of the Lord we must not be part of it. It is good and pleasant when brethren dwell together in unity. Unity releases anointing (God's presence and power) and it is also where God commands the blessing to be released (see Psalm 133).

God instructed Dave and me to stay out of strife when we began our ministry. He showed us that He could not bless us and that we would not succeed if we allowed strife in our marriage, home, or ministry. We have worked diligently over the years to keep strife out of our lives. It requires willingness to constantly communicate and confront issues. Strife will not go away if it is ignored; it must be dealt with. I encourage you to ask for the Holy Spirit's help to be a person who avoids strife and restores peace everywhere you go.

with courtesy *and* gentleness, in the hope that God may grant that they will repent and come to know the Truth [that they will perceive and recognize and become accurately acquainted with and acknowledge it],

26 And that they may come to their senses [and] escape out of the snare of the devil, having been held captive

by him, [henceforth] to do His [God's] will.

3 BUT UNDERSTAND this, that in the last days will come (set in) perilous times of great stress *and* trouble [hard to deal with and hard to bear].

2 For people will be lovers of self

life point

In II Timothy 2:24 the apostle Paul teaches us that the servants of the Lord must not fight with one another. Instead, we need to be kind and good to everyone. We must be peacemakers, not troublemakers.

and [utterly] self-centered, lovers of money and aroused by an inordinate [greedy] desire for wealth, proud and arrogant and contemptuous boasters. They will be abusive (blasphemous, scoffing), disobedient to parents, ungrateful, unholy and profane.
3 [They will be] without natural [human] affection (callous and inhuman), relentless (admitting of no truce or appeasement); [they will be] slanderers (false accusers, troublemakers), intemperate and loose in morals and conduct, uncontrolled and fierce, haters of good.
4 [They will be] treacherous [betrayers], rash, [and] inflated with self-conceit. [They will be] lovers of sensual pleasures and vain amusements more than and rather than lovers of God.
5 For [although] they hold a form of piety (true religion), they deny and

life point

Just as Paul predicted long ago when he wrote II Timothy 3:1, 2, we live in an unthankful and ungrateful generation. It seems the more people have, the less they appreciate.

As believers, we are in the world, but we must strive not to be like it. The more others around us complain, the more we should express gratitude to God.

putting the Word to work

Does it seem to you that we are living in perilous times? Think of the world around you as you read II Timothy 3:1–5; you probably see evidence of many of the vices described. In times such as these, you must stand strong in the truth of God's Word and have nothing to do with people who seem religious but do not exhibit true godliness or spiritual power.

reject and are strangers to the power of it [their conduct belies the genuineness of their profession]. Avoid [all] such people [turn away from them].
6 For among them are those who worm their way into homes and captivate silly and weak-natured and spiritually dwarfed women, loaded down with [the burden of their] sins [and easily] swayed and led away by various evil desires and seductive impulses.
7 [These weak women will listen to anybody who will teach them]; they are forever inquiring and getting information, but are never able to arrive at a recognition and knowledge of the Truth.
8 Now just as [d]Jannes and Jambres were hostile to and resisted Moses, so these men also are hostile to and oppose the Truth. They have depraved and distorted minds, and are reprobate and counterfeit and to be rejected as far as the faith is concerned. [Exod. 7:11.]
9 But they will not get very far, for their rash folly will become obvious to everybody, as was that of those [magicians mentioned].
10 Now you have closely observed and diligently followed my teaching, conduct, purpose in life, faith, patience, love, steadfastness,

d Neither of these men is mentioned in the Old Testament, but according to Jewish tradition they were the Egyptian court magicians who opposed Moses.

11 Persecutions, sufferings—such as occurred to me at Antioch, at Iconium, and at Lystra, persecutions I endured, but out of them all the Lord delivered me.
12 Indeed all who delight in piety *and* are determined to live a devoted *and* godly life in Christ Jesus will meet with persecution [will be made to suffer because of their religious stand].

life point

Second Timothy 3:12 tells us that we will suffer persecution as believers. Satan brings opposition, trouble, trials, and tribulations in the hope of driving us away from God. If we intend to succeed at being victorious believers and being all God wants us to be, we must be prepared to stand strong in times of persecution.

If we will stay standing on the inside, God will take care of the outside. If we do what we can do, God will do what we cannot do.

13 But wicked men and imposters will go on from bad to worse, deceiving *and* leading astray others and being deceived *and* led astray themselves.
14 But as for you, continue to hold to the things that you have learned and of which you are convinced, knowing from whom you learned [them],
15 And how from your childhood you have had a knowledge of *and* been acquainted with the sacred Writings, which are able to instruct you *and* give you the understanding for salvation which comes through faith in Christ Jesus [through the [e]leaning of the entire human personality on God in Christ Jesus in absolute trust and confidence in His power, wisdom, and goodness].
16 Every Scripture is God-breathed (given by His inspiration) and prof-

itable for instruction, for reproof *and* conviction of sin, for correction of error *and* discipline in obedience, [and] for training in righteousness (in holy living, in conformity to God's will in thought, purpose, and action),
17 So that the man of God may be complete *and* proficient, well fitted *and* thoroughly equipped for every good work.

putting the Word to work

Though written by men, all of Scripture is divinely inspired (literally, God-breathed), and it is our authority and rule for faith and life (see II Timothy 3:16). What can you do to become a more serious student of God's Word, the Bible, so that you can be complete and equipped for every good work (see II Timothy 3:17)?

4 I CHARGE [you] in the presence of God and of Christ Jesus, Who is to judge the living and the dead, and by (in the light of) His coming and His kingdom:
2 Herald *and* preach the Word! Keep your sense of urgency [stand by, be at hand and ready], whether the opportunity seems to be favorable or unfavorable. [Whether it is convenient or inconvenient, whether it is welcome or unwelcome, you as preacher of the Word are to show people in what way their lives are wrong.] And convince them, rebuking *and* correcting, warning *and* urging *and* encouraging them, being unflagging *and* inexhaustible in patience and teaching.
3 For the time is coming when [people] will not tolerate (endure) sound *and* wholesome instruction, but, having ears itching [for something pleasing and gratifying], they will gather to themselves one teacher after another to a considerable number, chosen to

e Alexander Souter, *Pocket Lexicon*.

putting the Word to work

Have you ever waited for the "perfect time" to share your faith with someone? The truth of the matter is that there may not always be the "perfectly right" time to share, but it is important to be ready to take advantage of every opportunity that God gives to share your faith and to proclaim and teach His Word. Pray that God will help you recognize every opportunity and give you boldness to share!

satisfy their own liking *and* to foster the errors they hold,

4   And will turn aside from hearing the truth and wander off into myths *and* man-made fictions.

5   As for you, be calm *and* cool *and* steady, accept *and* suffer unflinchingly every hardship, do the work of an evangelist, fully perform all the duties of your ministry.

6   For I am already about to be sacrificed [my life is about to be poured out as a drink offering]; the time of my [spirit's] release [from the body] is at hand *and* I will soon go free.

life point

In II Timothy 4:5, Paul gives Timothy some helpful instructions on how to handle his ministry. What he says is good advice for all of us. If we are calm and steady, people know they can depend on us. God can depend on us. No one has to wonder what we might be like from one day to the next. When our unsaved friends see the calm and steady faith we have, they will be open to our testimony of the Gospel. Stability is a necessary trait in every believer's life, one that brings personal blessings and peace, which attracts others.

7   I have fought the good (worthy, honorable, and noble) fight, I have finished the race, I have kept (firmly held) the faith.

8   [As to what remains] henceforth there is laid up for me the [victor's] crown of righteousness [for being right with God and doing right], which the Lord, the righteous Judge, will award to me *and* recompense me on that [great] day—and not to me only, but also to all those who have loved *and* yearned for *and* welcomed His appearing (His return).

9   Make every effort to come to me soon.

10   For Demas has deserted me for love of this present world and has gone to Thessalonica; Crescens [has gone] to Galatia, Titus to Dalmatia.

11   Luke alone is with me. Get Mark and bring him with you, for he is very helpful to me for the ministry.

12   Tychicus I have sent to Ephesus.

13   [When] you come, bring the cloak that I left at Troas with Carpus, also the books, especially the parchments.

14   Alexander the coppersmith did me great wrongs. The Lord will pay him back for his actions.

15   Beware of him yourself, for he opposed *and* resisted our message very strongly *and* exceedingly.

16   At my first trial no one acted in my defense [as my advocate] *or* took my part *or* [even] stood with me, but all forsook me. May it not be charged against them!

17   But the Lord stood by me and strengthened me, so that through me the [Gospel] message might be fully proclaimed and all the Gentiles might hear it. So I was delivered out of the jaws of the lion.

18   [And indeed] the Lord will certainly deliver *and* ꟿdraw me to Himself from every assault of evil. He will

f Joseph Thayer, *A Greek-English Lexicon of the New Testament*: A primary meaning of the Greek *ruomai*: "draw to one's self."

the heart of a hero

Paul experienced a lot to take the Gospel to the early world. He was persecuted, beaten and thrown in prison for preaching the Good News. Many times he suffered because of opposition, as he describes in II Timothy 4:14–16.

In this passage, Paul basically says, "Alexander the coppersmith has done me great wrong, but I am not going to worry about it. I am not going to get full of bitterness and hatred. I am going to let God handle it. He will take care of it."

How much better our lives would be if we took that attitude toward so many things, if we would just cast our care on the Lord and allow Him to handle them for us.

In verse 16, Paul tells how no one came to his defense in his trial. I wonder how we would feel if we suffered everything that Paul went through to bless so many others only to end up without a single soul to stand up for us in our time of greatest need. Paul risked his very life for others, yet they were not willing to be associated with him for fear they might be punished too.

What was Paul's response to their abandonment? He prayed that their failure would not be laid to their charge. That shows us his heart.

We can go through the Bible and look at the great men and women of God, and we can quickly see why they were called heroes of the faith. It was not because they were smarter than everybody else or because they had more going for them in the natural than others. It was simply because they had great hearts. Ask God to give you the heart of a hero too.

preserve *and* bring me safe unto His heavenly kingdom. To Him be the glory forever and ever. Amen (so be it). **19** Give my greetings to Prisca and Aquila and to the household of Onesiphorus. **20** Erastus stayed on at Corinth, but Trophimus I left ill at Miletus.

21 Do hasten *and* try your best to come to me before winter. Eubulus wishes to be remembered to you, as do Pudens and Linus and Claudia and all the brethren. **22** The Lord *Jesus Christ* be with your spirit. Grace (God's favor and blessing) be with you. *Amen (so be it).*

Titus

Author:
Paul

Date:
Probably between AD 63–65

Everyday Life Principles:
Good Christian doctrine should lead to good Christian living.

Be diligent and enthusiastic about doing good works in order to demonstrate your love for Jesus.

Make sure your good works are led and empowered by the Holy Spirit.

Titus, like Timothy, was a young minister who followed Paul's leadership and received oversight of the church in Crete. This church seems unorganized and full of people who needed much instruction and correction. To help Titus, Paul wrote this letter, which addresses several subjects he also wrote about in I Timothy. In Titus, Paul emphasizes the proper structure of the church, solid doctrine and godly living, especially in the form of good works.

In fact, Paul writes in Titus 2:14 that Jesus, "gave Himself on our behalf that He might redeem us (purchase our freedom) from all iniquity and purify for Himself a people [to be peculiarly His own, people who are] eager and enthusiastic about [living a life that is good and filled with] beneficial deeds." We must remember that people know us as believers by our fruit; we reveal our love for Jesus more through what we do than through any other means.

As you read the book of Titus, I pray you will remember how important it is to be in a good church and to submit to godly spiritual leadership. I also hope you will remember to demonstrate your faith by good works and by living a holy life. Remember that good works and holiness for the sake of good works and holiness will result in legalism, but when these endeavors are led and empowered by the Holy Spirit, they will bring life to you and to others.

1 PAUL, A bond servant of God and an apostle (a special messenger) of Jesus Christ (the Messiah) to stimulate *and* promote the faith of God's chosen ones and to lead them on to accurate discernment *and* recognition of *and* acquaintance with the Truth which belongs to *and* harmonizes with *and* tends to godliness,

2 [Resting] in the hope of eternal life, [life] which the ever truthful God Who cannot deceive promised before the world *or* the ages of time began.

3 And [now] in His own appointed time He has made manifest (made known) His Word *and* revealed it as His message through the preaching entrusted to me by command of God our Savior;

4 To Titus, my true child according to a common (general) faith: Grace (favor and spiritual blessing) and [heart] peace from God the Father and *the Lord* Christ Jesus our Savior.

life point

In many of Paul's epistles, he greets his readers with a message of "grace and peace," just as he does in Titus 1:4. We cannot enjoy peace unless we understand and receive grace. Ask God to help you receive grace so that you can be at peace.

5 For this reason I left you [behind] in Crete, that you might set right what was defective *and* finish what was left undone, and that you might appoint elders *and* set them over the churches (assemblies) in every city as I directed you.

6 [These elders should be] men who are of unquestionable integrity *and* are irreproachable, the husband of [but] one wife, whose children are [well trained and are] believers, not open to the accusation of being loose in morals *and* conduct or unruly *and* disorderly.

7 For the bishop (an overseer) as God's steward must be blameless, not self-willed *or* arrogant *or* presumptuous; he must not be quick-tempered or given to drink *or* pugnacious (brawling, violent); he must not be grasping *and* greedy for filthy lucre (financial gain);

8 But he must be hospitable (loving and a friend to believers, especially to strangers and foreigners); [he must be] a lover of goodness [of good people and good things], sober-minded (sensible, discreet), upright *and* fairminded, a devout man *and* religiously correct, temperate *and* keeping himself in hand.

9 He must hold fast to the sure *and* trustworthy Word of God as he was taught it, so that he may be able both to give stimulating instruction *and* encouragement in sound (wholesome) doctrine and to refute *and* convict those who contradict *and* oppose it [showing the wayward their error].

10 For there are many disorderly *and* unruly men who are idle (vain, empty) *and* misleading talkers and self-deceivers *and* deceivers of others. [This is true] especially of those of the circumcision party [who have come over from Judaism].

11 Their mouths must be stopped, for they are mentally distressing *and* subverting whole families by teaching what they ought not to teach, for the

putting the Word to work

Having godly church leaders is so important. Paul specifically addresses the character and responsibilities of church leaders called elders in Titus 1:5–16. Do you know who the various leaders of your church are? Be sure to pray for them often, and ask God to continue to build in them the character, spiritual maturity, and abilities necessary to be wise and faithful church leaders.

purpose of getting base advantage *and* disreputable gain.

12 One of their [very] number, a prophet of their own, said, Cretans are always liars, hurtful beasts, idle *and* lazy gluttons.

13 And this account of them is [really] true. Because it is [true], rebuke them sharply [deal sternly, even severely with them], so that they may be sound in the faith *and* free from error,

14 [And may show their soundness by] ceasing to give attention to Jewish myths *and* fables or to rules [laid down] by [mere] men who reject *and* turn their backs on the Truth.

15 To the pure [in heart and conscience] all things are pure, but to the defiled *and* corrupt and unbelieving nothing is pure; their very minds and consciences are defiled *and* polluted.

16 They profess to know God [to recognize, perceive, and be acquainted with Him], but deny *and* disown *and* renounce Him by what they do; they are detestable *and* loathsome, unbelieving *and* disobedient *and* disloyal *and* rebellious, and [they are] unfit *and* worthless for good work (deed or enterprise) of any kind.

2 BUT [as for] you, teach what is fitting *and* becoming to sound (wholesome) doctrine [the character and right living that identify true Christians].

2 Urge the older men to be temperate, venerable (serious), sensible, self-controlled, and sound in the faith, in the love, and in the steadfastness *and* patience [of Christ].

3 Bid the older women similarly to be reverent *and* devout in their deportment as becomes those engaged in sacred service, not slanderers or slaves to drink. They are to give good counsel *and* be teachers of what is right *and* noble,

4 So that they will wisely train the young women to be [a]sane and sober of mind (temperate, disciplined) and to love their husbands and their children,

5 To be self-controlled, chaste, homemakers, good-natured (kindhearted), adapting *and* subordinating themselves to their husbands, that the word of God may not be exposed to reproach (blasphemed or discredited).

6 In a similar way, urge the younger men to be self-restrained *and* to behave prudently [taking life seriously].

7 And show your own self in all respects to be a pattern *and* a model of good deeds *and* works, teaching what is unadulterated, showing gravity [having the strictest regard for truth and purity of motive], with dignity *and* seriousness.

8 And let your instruction be sound *and* fit *and* wise *and* wholesome, vigorous *and* [b]irrefutable *and* above censure, so that the opponent may be put to shame, finding nothing discrediting *or* evil to say about us.

9 [Tell] bond servants to be submissive to their masters, to be pleasing *and* give satisfaction in every way. [Warn them] not to talk back *or* contradict,

10 Nor to steal by taking things of small value, but to prove themselves

speak the Word

a Marvin Vincent, *Word Studies in the New Testament*: The Greek verb here translated "train" means "to make sane or sober of mind, to moderate, to discipline."   **b** Arthur S. Way, *Way's Epistles: The Letters of St. Paul to Seven Churches and Three Friends*.

walk the talk

Paul instructed Titus to teach good sound doctrine and to teach people to live right so they might be identified as true Christians (see Titus 2:1). One of the greatest needs of the church today is credibility. The reputation of Christianity has been terribly hurt by people who tell others what to do but do not do it themselves. They are people who call themselves Christians but do not conduct their lives as Christians should; in other words, they do not "walk the talk." Those of us chosen by God to live at this point in history have an opportunity to repair the damage done by others who have gone before us. We must each choose an excellent lifestyle that displays the true attributes of Jesus Christ.

The way you live your life is very important! When you put a Christian bumper sticker on your car, wear jewelry with the cross on it or shirts with scriptures and go to church, people watch you—and they look for authenticity.

Wearing a bracelet with the letters "WWJD" became a fad at one time. The initials stood for "What would Jesus do?" Wearing a bracelet is nice, but what is inside a person should match what he or she promotes on the outside. How would you like it if you saw a grocery store sign and when you went inside you found hardware? You would be aggravated because what was advertised was not what was offered. I believe the world feels the same way about people who advertise Christianity through bumper stickers, jewelry, t-shirts, and church attendance but do not live the life they should.

The Bible is filled with instructions on how to live. It teaches us how to think, talk, and act, as well as who to associate with, and how to manage our money. It also teaches us not to be lazy or out of balance in any area. What good does it do to have a "Jesus loves you" bumper sticker on our car and then break the speed limit, refuse to wear a seat belt, and park in handicapped parking spaces when we are not handicapped? I encourage you to examine your life regularly and make sure that the way you live accurately represents what you say you believe. Be authentic!

truly loyal *and* entirely reliable *and* faithful throughout, so that in everything they may be an ornament *and* do credit to the teaching [which is] from *and* about God our Savior.

11 For the grace of God (His unmerited favor and blessing) has come forward (appeared) for the deliverance from sin *and* the eternal salvation for all mankind.

12 It has trained us to reject *and* renounce all ungodliness (irreligion) and worldly (passionate) desires, to live discreet (temperate, self-controlled),

speak the Word

Thank You, Lord, for sending Your grace to deliver me from sin and to provide eternal salvation for everyone.
ADAPTED FROM TITUS 2:11

upright, devout (spiritually whole) lives in this present world,

13 Awaiting *and* looking for the [fulfillment, the realization of our] blessed hope, even the glorious appearing of our great God and Savior Christ Jesus (the Messiah, the Anointed One),

14 Who gave Himself on our behalf that He might redeem us (purchase our freedom) from all iniquity and purify for Himself a people [to be peculiarly His own, people who are] eager *and* enthusiastic about [living a life that is good and filled with] beneficial deeds. [Deut. 14:2; Ps. 130:8; Ezek. 37:23.]

putting the Word to work

Most people are familiar with the term VIP – Very Important Person. Do you know that Jesus gave Himself for you in order to make you His own special person (see Titus 2:14)? He redeemed you from evil and made you holy (see Titus 2:14). He has also given you a desire to do good works. Ask God to show you each day the good works that He has prepared for you to do and then be eager to do them!

15 Tell [them all] these things. Urge (advise, encourage, warn) and rebuke with full authority. Let no one despise *or* disregard *or* think little of you [conduct yourself and your teaching so as to command respect].

3 REMIND PEOPLE to be submissive to [their] magistrates and authorities, to be obedient, to be prepared *and* willing to do any upright *and* honorable work,

2 To slander *or* abuse *or* speak evil of no one, to avoid being contentious, to be forbearing (yielding, gentle, and conciliatory), and to show unqualified courtesy toward everybody.

3 For we also were once thoughtless

life point

Titus 3:1 encourages us to be submissive to our authorities. If you are not in a position of leadership in your job or in your church, you need to have a healthy attitude toward the people who are. With God, the attitude of the heart is everything. We can do what our bosses tell us to do while murmuring and grumbling behind their backs, but if we do that, we are not the kind of employees the Bible tells us to be. We may seem to get away with this attitude for a while, but we will not be rewarded.

Our reward comes from obeying the specific calling God places on our lives, not from trying to be like someone else or managing to accomplish great things. God rewards those who follow an obedient lifestyle, which includes submission to authority. If we will just do what God asks us to do and be the persons He made us to be, His rewards will chase us down and flood our lives.

and senseless, obstinate *and* disobedient, deluded *and* misled; [we too were once] slaves to all sorts of cravings *and* pleasures, wasting our days in malice and jealousy *and* envy, hateful (hated, detestable) and hating one another.

4 But when the goodness and loving-kindness of God our Savior to man [as man] appeared,

5 He saved us, not because of any works of righteousness that we had done, but because of His own pity *and* mercy, by [the] cleansing [bath] of the new birth (regeneration) and renewing of the Holy Spirit,

6 Which He poured out [so] richly upon us through Jesus Christ our Savior.

7 [And He did it in order] that we

how to live the good life

In Titus 2:14, Paul writes that Jesus gave His life so that we could be people who are "eager and enthusiastic about [living a life that is good and filled with] beneficial deeds."

We are not to spend our lives moping around, depressed, discouraged, and despondent. We are not to spend so much time thinking about all of our faults that we lose our hope and enthusiasm about living a good life.

God is not honored by people who have bad attitudes toward themselves; in fact, that is downright insulting to Him. If you loved and valued a group of people so much that you were willing to suffer horribly and die for them so they could enjoy themselves and their lives, how would you feel if they refused your gift? I pray you see what I am trying to say.

Paul said that he knew he was not perfect, but he pressed on to lay hold of that for which Christ Jesus laid hold of him and made him His own (see Philippians 3:12). He was speaking of the quality of life Jesus wanted him to have. Paul knew that he did not deserve it, but for Jesus' sake he was determined to have it. Likewise, we do not deserve "the good life," but Jesus died to give it to us, so we honor Him when we receive it with eagerness and enthusiasm.

If you struggle with negative attitudes that hold you back from the good things of God in your life, I urge you to make a change today. Choose a new attitude toward yourself. Paul had to make that choice, I had to make it, and you must make it also if you want to glorify God with your life.

putting the Word to work

What country do you live in? As a Christian, you are a citizen of God's kingdom, and you are also a citizen of your earthly country. You submit to God, and you should also be obedient to civil laws and authorities (see Titus 3:1). As you respect those in authority and obey the laws of the land, you have an opportunity to demonstrate principles of the kingdom of God as you do so peaceably, in humility, without speaking evil of anyone, and ready to do every good work (see Titus 3:1, 2). You will bless others and honor God as you do so.

might be justified by His grace (by His favor, wholly undeserved), [that we might be acknowledged and counted as conformed to the divine will in purpose, thought, and action], and that we might become heirs of eternal life according to [our] hope.

8 This message is most trustworthy, and concerning these things I want you to insist steadfastly, so that those who have believed in (trusted in, relied on) God may be careful to apply themselves to honorable occupations *and* to doing good, for such things are [not only] excellent *and* right [in themselves], but [they are] good *and* profitable for the people.

9 But avoid stupid *and* foolish

prepare to prosper

God does not do anything without first being prepared, and neither will He allow us to do His work without adequate preparation.

In Titus 3:1, Paul writes, "Be prepared for and willing to do any upright and honorable work." And in II Timothy 2:15 he instructs his young disciple: "Study and be eager and do your utmost to present yourself to God approved (tested by trial), a workman who has no cause to be ashamed, correctly analyzing and accurately dividing [rightly handling and skillfully teaching] the Word of Truth."

Your preparation may mean going to Bible college or getting some other kind of formal training, or it may mean spending a few years working under someone else's authority so you know how to handle your life in the future. It could mean working at a job that you do not particularly like for a boss of whom you are not very fond. It could also mean spending some years in which your basic needs are met, but you definitely are not living in abundance because you are learning how to believe God for prosperity and how to handle it when it comes.

Many people desire to prosper, but not all want to prepare to prosper.

Preparation can take place in a lot of different settings and has many different phases. Each phase we go through in our preparation is important. There is something to be learned at every step. It is all part of our preparation. We must "graduate," so to speak, from each phase or level into the next one, and this comes after we prove ourselves on the current level. Between all of these stages of preparation, there is a lot of waiting.

Unless we learn to wait well, we will be miserable. Miserable people are usually grouchy, critical, and just generally hard to get along with. Miserable people usually make other people miserable.

Enjoy the trip! Being miserable will not make it any shorter, but it can make it longer. Realize that you are in training and becoming equipped for something great in the kingdom. Prepare to prosper.

controversies and genealogies and dissensions and wrangling about the Law, for they are unprofitable and futile.

10 [As for] a man who is factious [a heretical sectarian and cause of divisions], after admonishing him a first

speak the Word

Thank You, Lord, for saving me not because of any work of righteousness that I have done, but because of Your mercy, which you poured out so richly through Jesus Christ my Savior.
ADAPTED FROM TITUS 3:5

and second time, reject [him from your fellowship and have nothing more to do with him],

11 Well aware that such a person has utterly changed (is perverted and corrupted); he goes on sinning [though he] is convicted of guilt *and* self-condemned.

12 When I send Artemas or [perhaps] Tychicus to you, lose no time *but* make every effort to come to me at Nicopolis, for I have decided to spend the winter there.

13 Do your utmost to speed Zenas the lawyer and Apollos on their way; see that they want for (lack) nothing.

14 And let our own [people really] learn to apply themselves to good deeds (to honest labor and honorable employment), so that they may be

---

putting the Word to work

Do you know someone who argues incessantly? Not only can this be frustrating, but the Word of God warns that there is no room for division in the life of the church, and that a person who brings division is sinful (see Titus 3:9–11). Pray and work for unity in your church and in the entire body of Christ.

---

able to meet necessary demands ᶜwhenever the occasion may require and not be living idle *and* uncultivated *and* unfruitful lives.

15 All who are with me wish to be remembered to you. Greet those who love us in the faith. Grace (God's favor and blessing) be with you all. *Amen (so be it).*

---

c Marvin Vincent, *Word Studies*.

Philemon

Author:
Paul

Date:
AD 60–61

Everyday Life Principles:
There may come a time when you need to "go to bat" for fellow believers. If so, be sure to handle the matter in an orderly fashion.

If you find yourself in a tense situation involving other believers, remember that humility and genuine love never fail.

As a believer in Jesus Christ, do everything you can as the Holy Spirit leads you to bring mutual respect, unity, and reconciliation among all of the Christians in your life.

Philemon is a very short book with a very important message. From prison, Paul wrote this letter to his friend, a prominent and wealthy Christian man named Philemon. According to the customs of his time, Philemon was a slave-owner. His slave, Onesimus, escaped, went to Rome, became converted, and met Paul. When Paul realized what happened, he decided to write Philemon and encourage reconciliation and forgiveness between the two men.

Paul handled this matter very well, in an orderly fashion. Relationships among Christians are not perfect, and there are times when a third party needs to be involved. When this happens, interactions must take place in order and with the right heart attitudes.

Paul opens his letter by addressing Philemon as "dearly beloved," making sure to show respect and affection for a fellow believer. He then affirms Philemon's work and ministry before confronting Philemon with the need to take Onesimus back as his slave and receive him as a Christian brother. Throughout this letter, there is a tone of friendship and unity in Christ. Paul's humility and genuine love for both Philemon and Onesimus are evident and allow him to make a bold request for their reconciliation.

Let Paul's letter to Philemon serve as an example for handling relationships in an orderly way, and let it encourage you to handle all of your relationships properly, with a humble heart, and seek to bring love, forgiveness, and restoration everywhere you go.

1 PAUL, A prisoner [for the sake] of Christ Jesus (the Messiah), and our brother Timothy, to Philemon our dearly beloved sharer with us in our work,

2 And to Apphia our sister and Archippus our fellow soldier [in the Christian warfare], and to the church [assembly that meets] in your house:

3 Grace (spiritual blessing and favor) be to all of you and [heart] peace from God our Father and the Lord Jesus Christ (the Messiah).

4 I give thanks to my God for you always when I mention you in my prayers,

5 Because I continue to hear of your love and of your loyal faith which you have toward the Lord Jesus and [which you show] toward all the saints (God's consecrated people).

putting the Word to work

Do you thank God for the people He has placed in your life? Paul did, and we read about his prayers for Philemon in Philemon 4–6. Be sure to thank God often for the people He blesses you with and let them know you are praying for them.

6 [And I pray] that the participation in *and* sharing of your faith may produce *and* promote full recognition *and* appreciation *and* understanding *and* precise knowledge of every good [thing] that is ours in [our identification with] Christ *Jesus* [and unto His glory].

speak the Word

7 For I have derived great joy and comfort *and* encouragement from your love, because the hearts of the saints [who are your fellow Christians] have been cheered *and* refreshed through you, [my] brother.

8 Therefore, though I have abundant boldness in Christ to charge you to do what is fitting *and* required *and* your duty to do,

life point

In Philemon 8–21, Paul encourages Philemon to forgive Onesimus. Forgiveness is extending love and mercy to someone who has wronged or hurt you. It is not saying that what was done was acceptable, or that it did not matter, but it is a choice to release the person from the burden of guilt for what they have done wrong and not allow that offense to affect your relationship. Have you ever wronged someone and received forgiveness from them? If so, you know that forgiveness clears the way for reconciliation. If there is someone you need to receive forgiveness from or extend forgiveness to, do not procrastinate. Seek the restoration of your relationship through forgiveness.

9 Yet for love's sake I prefer to appeal to you just for what I am—I, Paul, an ambassador [of Christ Jesus] *and* an old man and now a prisoner for His sake also—

10 I appeal to you for my [own

Thank You, God, for giving me grace, spiritual blessing, favor, and heart peace.
ADAPTED FROM PHILEMON 3

Father, I pray that the sharing of my faith may produce full understanding and appreciation of every good thing that is mine in Christ Jesus.
ADAPTED FROM PHILEMON 6

life point

The communication of our faith is made effectual by acknowledging every good thing that is in us in *Christ Jesus* (see Philemon 6), not by acknowledging everything that is wrong with *us*.

The devil wants us to acknowledge every bad thing we see in ourselves. He is known as the "accuser of the brethren" (see Revelation 12:10), and he continually tries to redirect our focus from who we are in Christ back onto our shortcomings. He bombards us with opportunities to think negative thoughts about ourselves so we will return to the patterns of thinking most of us learned growing up and fall again into the deception that our worth is based on our performance, and that because of our faults, we are worthless.

One reason it is so important to avoid speaking negatively about ourselves is that we believe what we say more than what anybody else says. But once we truly understand who we are in Christ and see how much He did for us through shedding His blood to make us worthy, we will realize we actually insult our heavenly Father by excessively meditating on our faults, flaws, and failures.

Rather than dwell on your inadequacies, focus on every good thing that is yours through your identification with Jesus Christ.

spiritual] child, Onesimus [meaning profitable], whom I have begotten [in the faith] while a captive in these chains.

11 Once he was unprofitable to you, but now he is indeed profitable to you as well as to me.

12 I am sending him back to you in ᵃhis own person, [and it is like sending] my very heart.

13 I would have chosen to keep him with me, in order that he might minister to my needs in your stead during my imprisonment for the Gospel's sake.

14 But it has been my wish to do nothing about it without first consulting you *and* getting your consent, in order that your benevolence might not seem to be the result of compulsion *or* of pressure but might be voluntary [on your part].

15 Perhaps it was for this reason that he was separated [from you] for a while, that you might have him back as yours forever,

16 Not as a slave any longer but as [something] more than a slave, as a brother [Christian], especially dear to me but how much more to you, both in the flesh [as a servant] and in the Lord [as a fellow believer].

17 If then you consider me a partner *and* a ᵃcomrade in fellowship, welcome *and* receive him as you would [welcome and receive] me.

18 And if he has done you any wrong in any way or owes anything [to you], charge that to my account.

19 I, Paul, write it with my own hand, I promise to repay it [in full]—and that is to say nothing [of the fact] that you owe me your very self!

20 Yes, brother, let me have some profit from you in the Lord. Cheer *and* refresh my heart in Christ.

21 I write to you [perfectly] confident of your obedient compliance, knowing that you will do even more than I ask.

22 At the same time prepare a guest room [in expectation of extending your hospitality] to me, for I am hoping through your prayers to be granted [the gracious privilege of coming] to you.

a Marvin Vincent, *Word Studies in the New Testament.*

expect the best

Paul prayed and asked God to allow him to visit Philemon, and it is interesting to me that he told Philemon to prepare a room in *expectation* of his visit (see Philemon 22). How does an expectant mother behave? She prepares ahead of time for the child she is expecting but does not have yet. Are you living with expectation? Are you expecting God to do wonderful things in your life? Are you expecting favor everywhere you go? Are you expecting God to enable you to be a blessing to people any time you see a need?

We should all ask ourselves, "What am I expecting?" We might be surprised to find that we are receiving nothing because we expect nothing.

We say that we pray in faith, but part of faith is hope and active expectancy. Faith is not asking and doubting or asking and being afraid; it is not asking and worrying. Faith asks and believes that God is working, and it expects and looks forward to the answer with joy. The conversation of faith is filled with expectancy, which I like to define as, "a joy-filled looking forward to receiving a desired result." Real faith does not pray for the salvation of a wayward child and then say to a friend over lunch, "I'm so afraid my son is going to get in trouble and ruin his life." Faith says, "I'm expecting my son to change. I believe God is working in his life and I'm looking forward to the day when he and I can study God's Word together."

The phrase "wait on the Lord," is amplified to include "expect," "look for," and "hope in Him" (see Isaiah 40:31). When we read with those additional meanings, we see a better picture of the attitude that we need to have. Waiting on God is not a passive state of doing absolutely nothing. We may do nothing physically, but spiritually we are excited and enthusiastic; we expect and look for God to show up in our circumstances at any moment and we are full of hope, which is joyful and confident expectation.

Do an attitude check. Are you praying and waiting, but not waiting properly? If so, make a change and start expecting aggressively. Even confess aloud things you expect God to do. Expectancy prepares the way for God's miracle-working power!

putting the Word to work

God's Word encourages us to be hospitable (see Philemon 22). Extending hospitality is a great way to show appreciation for traveling or visiting ministers or missionaries, or to people who are lonely. In what ways can you show hospitality to visitors, newcomers, or people who need a friend?

23 Greetings to you from Epaphras, my fellow prisoner here in [the cause of] Christ Jesus (the Messiah),
24 And [from] Mark, Aristarchus, Demas, and Luke, my fellow workers.
25 The grace (blessing and favor) of the Lord Jesus Christ (the Messiah) be with your spirit. *Amen (so be it).*

Hebrews

Author:
Unknown

Date:
Before AD 70

Everyday Life Principles:
Jesus is superior to everything in heaven and on earth.

In Jesus, we have the best possible covenant and the best possible Mediator of that covenant. When we have Him, we have everything we need.

The blessings of the new covenant are made real in our lives through faith.

Simply put, the book of Hebrews is about "better things." Written to believers under pressure to turn back to their former Jewish faith or to mix Judaism with Christianity, this book emphasizes a new and better covenant that we have with God though Jesus Christ, and Jesus Himself as the Mediator of that New Covenant. Hebrews exalts Jesus' supremacy over all kinds of former things, such as prophets, angels, and God's spokesmen (Moses, Aaron, and Joshua). It clearly reveals the superiority of the new covenant over old religious places and things, such as the tabernacle, the sacrificial system, and the old covenant.

Hebrews contains a thorough description of Jesus as our Great High Priest and mankind's once-for-all perfect sacrifice for sin. It also includes and addresses the extreme importance of faith in our lives, for the new covenant is experienced through faith, and includes the "Hall of Faith" in chapter 11 and such well-known verses as: " . . . let us run with patient endurance and steady and active persistence the appointed course of the race that is set before us" (Hebrews 12:1), and, "Jesus Christ (the Messiah) is [always] the same, yesterday, today, [yes] and forever . . ." (Hebrews 13:8).

As you read the book of Hebrews, I pray that God gives you continual revelation about the New Covenant you have with Him through Jesus Christ and that you are able to receive and enjoy everything that belongs to you through that relationship.

1 IN MANY separate revelations [^aeach of which set forth a portion of the Truth] and in different ways God spoke of old to [our] forefathers in *and* by the prophets,

2 [But] in ^bthe last of these days He has spoken to us in [the person of a] Son, Whom He appointed Heir *and* lawful Owner of all things, also by *and* through Whom He created the worlds *and* the reaches of space *and* the ages of time [He made, produced, built, operated, and arranged them in order].

3 He is the sole expression of the glory of God [the Light-being, the ^cout-raying or radiance of the divine], and He is the perfect imprint *and* very image of [God's] nature, upholding *and* maintaining *and* guiding *and* propelling the universe by His mighty word of power. When He had *by offering Himself* accomplished *our* cleansing of sins *and* riddance of guilt, He sat down at the right hand of the divine Majesty on high,

4 [Taking a place and rank by which] He Himself became as much superior to angels as the glorious Name (title) which He has inherited is different from *and* more excellent than theirs.

5 For to which of the angels did [God] ever say, You are My Son, today I have begotten You [established You in an official Sonship relation, with kingly dignity]? And again, I will be to Him a Father, and He will be to Me a Son? [II Sam. 7:14; Ps. 2:7.]

6 Moreover, when He brings the firstborn Son ^dagain into the habitable world, He says, Let all the angels of God worship Him.

7 Referring to the angels He says, [God] Who makes His angels winds and His ministering servants flames of fire; [Ps. 104:4.]

8 But as to the Son, He says to Him, Your throne, O God, is forever and ever (to the ages of the ages), and the scepter of Your kingdom is a scepter of absolute righteousness (of justice and straightforwardness).

9 You have loved righteousness [You have delighted in integrity, virtue, and uprightness in purpose, thought, and action] and You have hated lawlessness (injustice and iniquity). Therefore God, [even] Your God (^eGodhead), has anointed You with the oil of exultant joy *and* gladness above *and* beyond Your companions. [Ps. 45:6, 7.]

10 And [further], You, Lord, did lay the foundation of the earth in the beginning, and the heavens are the works of Your hands.

11 They will perish, but You remain *and* continue permanently; they will all grow old *and* wear out like a garment.

12 Like a mantle [thrown about one's self] You will roll them up, and they will be changed *and* replaced by others. But You remain the same, and Your years will never end *nor* come to failure. [Ps. 102:25-27.]

13 Besides, to which of the angels has He ever said, Sit at My right hand [associated with Me in My royal dignity] till I make your enemies a stool for your feet? [Ps. 110:1.]

14 Are not the angels all ministering spirits (servants) sent out in the service [of God for the assistance] of those who are to inherit salvation?

2 SINCE ALL this is true, we ought to pay much closer attention than ever to the truths that we have heard, lest in any way we drift past [them] *and* slip away.

2 For if the message given through angels [the Law spoken by them to

a Marvin Vincent, *Word Studies in the New Testament.* **b** Henry Alford, *The Greek New Testament, with Notes.* **c** Literal translation. **d** Henry Alford, *The Greek New Testament, with Notes* and W. Robertson Nicoll, ed., *The Expositor's Greek New Testament.* **e** Arthur S. Way, *Way's Epistles: The Letters of St. Paul to Seven Churches and Three Friends.*

angels are everywhere

What a comfort to know that God provides angels to minister to and help us (see Hebrews 1:14)! Angels are everywhere even though we cannot see them. How can we increase the activity of angels in our lives? The Bible says that the angels of God are moved by the Word of God (see Psalm 103:20). This means they are not moved by complaining, grumbling, fear, worry, anxiety, or any other negative emotions that provoke negative comments. If we want angels to work in our lives, we must be careful about what we say.

Psalm 91 teaches us that God gives His angels charge over us to defend and protect us in all of our ways (of obedience and service). Angels will not help us if we disobey God or live selfish, self-centered lives. But, when we speak God's Word and walk in His will, angels are on the scene, helping us more than we can imagine.

I believe we have angels with us everywhere we go and that they keep us from harm. A friend of mine sat in a folding chair in a fishing boat on the lake. She was reading Psalm 91 and thanking God for her angels when the boat suddenly hit a wave and knocked over her chair. She hit her head on the side of the boat, but she was not really harmed. She was rather distraught by the fact she fell and hit her head, so she asked God, "Where were my angels?" God spoke to her heart and said, "You are not dead, are you?" In other words, she may have hit her head, but it could have been much, much worse had her angels not been there.

I wonder how many times our angels save our lives and we do not even know it? How often do we complain about some minor bump in life without realizing that our angels protected us from a major crisis? Let us begin to be more thankful for all the divine, supernatural help that God gives us, including the angels He sends to assist and protect us.

Moses] was authentic *and* proved sure, and every violation and disobedience received an appropriate (just and adequate) penalty,

3 How shall we escape [appropriate retribution] if we neglect *and* refuse to pay attention to such a great salvation [as is now offered to us, letting it drift past us forever]? For it was declared at first by the Lord [Himself], and it was confirmed to us *and* proved to be real *and* genuine by those who personally heard [Him speak].

4 [Besides this evidence] it was also established *and* plainly endorsed by God, Who showed His approval of it by signs and wonders and various miraculous manifestations of [His] power and by imparting the gifts of the Holy Spirit [to the believers] according to His own will.

5 For it was not to angels that God subjected the habitable world of the future, of which we are speaking.

6 It has been solemnly *and* earnestly said in a certain place, What is man that You are mindful of him, or the son of man that You graciously *and* helpfully care for *and* visit *and* look after him?

7 For some little time You have ranked him lower than *and* inferior to the angels; You have crowned him with glory and honor *and set him over the works of Your hands,* [Ps. 8:4-6.]

8 For You have put everything in subjection under his feet. Now in putting everything in subjection to man, He left nothing outside [of man's] control. But at present we do not yet see all things subjected to him [man].

9 But we are able to see Jesus, Who was ranked lower than the angels for a little while, crowned with glory and honor because of His having suffered death, in order that by the grace (unmerited favor) of God [to us sinners] He might experience death for every individual person.

10 For it was an act worthy [of God] *and* fitting [to the divine nature] that He, for Whose sake and by Whom all things have their existence, in bringing many sons into glory, should make the Pioneer of their salvation perfect [should bring to maturity the human experience necessary to be perfectly equipped for His office as High Priest] through suffering.

11 For both He Who sanctifies [making men holy] and those who are sanctified all have one [Father]. For this reason He is not ashamed to call them brethren;

12 For He says, I will declare Your [the Father's] name to My brethren; in the midst of the [worshiping] congregation I will sing hymns of praise to You. [Ps. 22:22.]

13 And again He says, My trust *and* assured reliance *and* confident hope shall be fixed in Him. And yet again, Here I am, I and the children whom God has given Me. [Isa. 8:17, 18.]

14 Since, therefore, [these His] children share in flesh and blood [in the physical nature of human beings], He [Himself] in a similar manner partook of the same [nature], that by [going through] death He might bring to nought *and* make of no effect him who had the power of death—that is, the devil—

15 And also that He might deliver *and* completely set free all those who through the [haunting] fear of death were held in bondage throughout the whole course of their lives.

16 For, as we all know, He [Christ] did not take hold of angels [[f]the fallen angels, to give them a helping and delivering hand], but He did take hold of [[f]the fallen] descendants of Abraham [to reach out to them a helping and delivering hand]. [Isa. 41:8, 9.]

17 So it is evident that it was essential that He be made like His brethren in every respect, in order that He might become a merciful (sympathetic) and faithful High Priest in the things related to God, to make atonement *and* propitiation for the people's sins.

18 For because He Himself [in His humanity] has suffered in being tempted (tested and tried), He is able [immediately] [g]to run to the cry of

speak the Word

Thank You, Jesus, that by Your death You have brought the devil to nothing and made him of no effect.
ADAPTED FROM HEBREWS 2:14

Thank You, Jesus, for immediately hearing my cry and running to my aid when I am tempted and tried.
ADAPTED FROM HEBREWS 2:18

f Matthew Henry, *Commentary on the Holy Bible*. **g** Kenneth Wuest, *Word Studies in the New Testament*.

settle down and be faithful

In Hebrews 3:1, 2, we read that during His earthly life, Jesus was faithful to the One Who appointed Him. Yet Jesus went through some silent years. After His marvelous birth and prophetic baptism, we hear nothing about Him again until age twelve, when He was found debating with the teachers in the temple. All we are told about these silent years is that " . . . the Child grew and became strong in spirit, filled with wisdom; and the grace (favor and spiritual blessing) of God was upon Him" (Luke 2:40). After that, the Bible tells us nothing about what transpired in Jesus' life except that He " . . . increased in wisdom (in broad and full understanding) and in stature and years, and in favor with God and man" (Luke 2:52).

Jesus spent thirty years in preparation for a three-year ministry, a time where He was faithful and obedient to His earthly parents as well as to His heavenly Father. It was during those silent years that He grew in strength, wisdom, and favor.

The "instant" society that we live in today is ruining people. Because everything is so instant and so easy, we think everything coming from God should be instant and easy. But godly strength, wisdom, knowledge, spiritual maturity, and character are developed in us as we go through tests and continue to do what we know is right, even when it does not feel right or does not feel good to us. If we want to grow up in God and do what He has called us to do, we have to settle down and be faithful.

(assist, relieve) those who are being tempted *and* tested *and* tried [and who therefore are being exposed to suffering].

3 SO THEN, brethren, consecrated *and* set apart for God, who share in the heavenly calling, [thoughtfully and attentively] consider Jesus, the Apostle and High Priest Whom we confessed [as ours when we embraced the Christian faith].

2 [See how] faithful He was to Him Who appointed Him [Apostle and High Priest], as Moses was also faithful in the whole house [of God]. [Num. 12:7.]

3 Yet Jesus has been considered worthy of much greater honor *and* glory than Moses, just as the builder of a house has more honor than the house [itself].

4 For [of course] every house is built *and* furnished by someone, but

the Builder of all things *and* the Furnisher [of the entire equipment of all things] is God.

5 And Moses certainly was faithful in the administration of all God's house [but it was only] as a ministering servant. [In his entire ministry he was but] a testimony to the things which were to be spoken [the revelations to be given afterward in Christ]. [Num. 12:7.]

6 But Christ (the Messiah) was faithful over His [own Father's] house as a Son [and Master of it]. And it is we who are [now members] of this house, if we hold *fast and firm to the end* our joyful *and* exultant confidence and sense of triumph in our hope [in Christ].

7 Therefore, as the Holy Spirit says: Today, if you will hear His voice,

8 Do not harden your hearts, as [happened] in the rebellion [of Israel]

the "ifs" and "buts" of biblical faith

I want to call your attention to the word "if" in Hebrews 3:6 because we often do not like to pay attention to the "ifs" and "buts" in the Bible. In scriptures like this one, we see what God will do, *if* we will do what we are supposed to do.

You and I have the awesome privilege of being members of the Father's house, if we remain firm in faith until the end. Going to the altar and praying a sinner's prayer is only the beginning of our walk with Him; we must follow through and continue in faith. We must believe in Him!

Confidence and faith are virtually synonymous; sometimes they can be interchanged without losing the context of what is being said at all. I can give a long fancy definition of faith, but let us boil it down: *faith is confidence in God*. In simple terms, faith is the act of knowing that if God says He will do something, He will do it. Even if it does not look like He is doing it right now, it will come to pass in His timing, *if* we remain confident in Him.

The only two things that can interrupt faith are: 1) the manifestation of what is believed; or 2) the manifestation of doubt and unbelief. Once we receive the manifestation of what we have believed for, we no longer need faith, so it ceases in that case. In the same way, the manifestation of doubt and unbelief—that is, receiving the lies of Satan and believing them—interrupts faith, so it ceases to exist.

Our faith must continue even when it seems that everything and everyone is against us. In Christ, we can remain standing firm on the inside because we know that our real life is within us, not in the people or circumstances outside of us.

and their provocation *and* [h]embitterment [of Me] in the day of testing in the wilderness,

9 Where your fathers tried [My patience] *and* tested [My forbearance] and [i]found I stood their test, and they saw My works for forty years.

10 And so I was provoked (displeased and sorely grieved) with that generation, and said, They always err *and* are led astray in their hearts, and they have not perceived *or* recognized My ways *and* become progressively better *and* more experimentally *and* intimately acquainted with them.

11 Accordingly, I swore in My wrath *and* indignation, They shall not enter into My rest. [Ps. 95:7-11.]

12 [Therefore beware] brethren, take care, lest there be in any one of you a wicked, unbelieving heart [which refuses to cleave to, trust in, and rely on Him], leading you to turn away *and* desert *or* stand aloof from the living God.

13 But instead warn (admonish, urge, and encourage) one another every day, as long as it is called Today, that none of you may be hardened [into settled rebellion] by the deceitfulness of sin [by the fraudulence, the stratagem, the trickery which the delusive glamor of his sin may play on him].

14 For we [j]have become fellows with Christ (the Messiah) *and* share in all

h Alexander Souter, *Pocket Lexicon of the Greek New Testament*. **i** Charles B. Williams, *The New Testament: A Translation in the Language of the People*. **j** Marvin Vincent, *Word Studies*.

life point

When we hear from God, we can choose to respond with humility and trust or harden our hearts and ignore Him. Regrettably, when people do not get what they want or when they go through trials and tests, many of them choose to harden their hearts.

This is exactly what happened to the Israelites when they made the trip through the wilderness (see Hebrews 3:7, 8). God led them into the wilderness so He could prove to them that He would do good for them and that they could trust Him (see Deuteronomy 8:2, 3). He had great things planned for them, but He tested them first to see if they were really going to believe Him. That is why He tells us not to harden our hearts as they did. He has great things planned for you too, so keep your heart soft and tender before Him.

He has for us, if only we hold our first newborn confidence *and* original assured expectation [in virtue of which we are believers] firm *and* unshaken to the end.
15 Then while it is [still] called Today, if you would hear His voice *and* when you hear it, do not harden your hearts as in the rebellion [in the desert, when the people provoked and irritated and embittered God against them]. [Ps. 95:7, 8.]
16 For who were they who heard *and* yet were rebellious *and* provoked [Him]? Was it not all those

who came out of Egypt led by Moses?
17 And with whom was He irritated *and* provoked *and* grieved for forty years? Was it not with those who sinned, whose ᵏdismembered bodies were strewn *and* left in the desert?
18 And to whom did He swear that they should not enter His rest, but to those who disobeyed [who had not listened to His word and who refused to be compliant or be persuaded]?
19 So we see that they were not able to enter [into His rest], because of their unwillingness to adhere to *and* trust in *and* rely on God [unbelief had shut them out]. [Num. 14:1-35.]

4 THEREFORE, WHILE the promise of entering His rest still holds *and* is offered [today], let us be afraid [ᵏto distrust it], lest any of you should ᵏthink he has come too late *and* has come short of [reaching] it.
2 For indeed we have had the glad tidings [Gospel of God] proclaimed to us just as truly as they [the Israelites of old did when the good news of deliverance from bondage came to them]; but the message they heard did not benefit them, because it was not mixed with faith (with ˡthe leaning of the entire personality on God in absolute trust and confidence in His power, wisdom, and goodness) by those who heard it; ᵐ*neither were they united in faith with the ones* [Joshua and Caleb] who heard (did believe).
3 For we who have believed (adhered to and trusted in and relied on God) do enter that rest, ᵏin accordance with His declaration that those [who did not believe] should not enter

speak the Word

Help me, Lord, never to harden my heart to Your voice, but to keep it soft and responsive when You speak.
ADAPTED FROM HEBREWS 3:15

---

k Marvin Vincent, *Word Studies*.   **l** Alexander Souter, *Pocket Lexicon*.   **m** Many manuscripts so read.

when He said, As I swore in My wrath, They shall not enter My rest; and this He said although [His] works had been completed *and* prepared [and waiting for all who would believe] from the foundation of the world. [Ps. 95:11.]

4 For in a certain place He has said this about the seventh day: And God

putting the Word to work

Hebrews 4:3 teaches that those who did not listen to God's Word or obey His instructions did not enter into the place of rest He offered them. So when you feel frustrated or upset, or if you lose your peace and your joy, ask yourself, "Am I believing God's Word?"

The only way we will ever be free from struggling is to believe the Word and obey whatever Jesus puts in our hearts to do. Believing God's Word delivers us from struggling so that we can rest in the promises of God.

Are you in need of God's rest? Adhere to Him, trust in Him and rely on Him and experience the rest He has prepared for you.

rested on the seventh day from all His works. [Gen. 2:2.]

5 And [they forfeited their part in it, for] in this [passage] He said, They shall not enter My rest. [Ps. 95:11.]

6 Seeing then that the promise remains over [from past times] for some to enter that rest, and that those

speak the Word

who formerly were given the good news about it *and* the opportunity, failed to appropriate it *and* did not enter because of disobedience,

7 Again He sets a definite day, [a new] Today, [and gives another opportunity of securing that rest] saying through David after so long a time in the words already quoted, Today, if you would hear His voice *and* when you hear it, do not harden your hearts. [Ps. 95:7, 8.]

8 [This mention of a rest was not a reference to their entering into Canaan.] For if Joshua had given them rest, He [God] would not speak afterward about another day.

9 So then, there is still awaiting a full *and* complete Sabbath-rest reserved for the [true] people of God;

10 For he who has once entered [God's] rest also has ceased from [the weariness and pain] of human labors, just as God rested from those labors [n]peculiarly His own. [Gen. 2:2.]

11 Let us therefore be zealous *and* exert ourselves *and* strive diligently to enter that rest [of God, to know and experience it for ourselves], that no one may fall *or* perish by the same kind of unbelief *and* disobedience [into which those in the wilderness fell].

12 For the Word that God speaks is alive and full of power [making it active, operative, energizing, and effective]; it is sharper than any two-edged sword, penetrating to the dividing line of the [o]breath of life (soul) and [the immortal] spirit, and of joints and marrow [of the deepest parts of

Thank You, God, that Your Word is alive and full of power. It is sharper than any two-edged sword; it divides soul and spirit; and it judges the thoughts and purposes of the heart.
ADAPTED FROM HEBREWS 4:12

n Marvin Vincent, *Word Studies.*   **o** Joseph Thayer, *A Greek-English Lexicon of the New Testament.*

the rest of God

Hebrews 4:3 teaches that those who believe God enter into His rest. Experiencing His rest is one way you can tell whether you are really *in* faith, or whether you are just trying to *have* faith. When you truly enter into the realm of faith, you enter into the rest of God.

Rest is freedom from excessive reasoning, struggle, fear, inner turmoil, worry, and frustration, which develop because of our working to do what only God can do. Being in God's rest is not necessarily resting from physical activity, but resting in confidence in the midst of everything that goes on in life. It is a rest of the soul where the mind, will, and emotions are at peace.

You can rest in God because you know He will take care of you and meet your needs. You do not know when or how, and you really do not care because you are enjoying the life you have right now while God works on your problem.

God wants us to live at peace and in His rest. But in order for us to do that, we need to "believe that God exists and that He is the rewarder of those who earnestly and diligently seek Him [out]" (Hebrews 11:6).

If you are worn out, I urge you to enter into God's rest. I encourage you to quit trying to control everyone and everything around you and simply allow God to do for you what only He can do.

No matter what you face, God wants to help you and give you rest.

our nature], exposing *and* sifting *and* analyzing *and* judging the very thoughts and purposes of the heart.
13 And not a creature exists that is concealed from His sight, but all things are open *and* exposed, naked *and* defenseless to the eyes of Him with Whom we have to do.
14 Inasmuch then as we have a great High Priest Who has [already] ascended *and* passed through the heavens, Jesus the Son of God, let us hold fast our confession [of faith in Him].
15 For we do not have a High Priest Who is unable to understand *and* sympathize *and* have a shared feeling with our weaknesses *and* infirmities *and* liability to the assaults of temptation, but One Who has been tempted in every

respect as we are, yet without sinning.
16 Let us then fearlessly *and* confidently *and* boldly draw near to the throne of grace (the throne of God's unmerited favor to us sinners), that we may receive mercy [for our failures] and find grace to help in good time for every need [appropriate help and well-timed help, coming just when we need it].

life point

Jesus understands our human frailty because He was tempted in every way that we are, yet without sinning (see Hebrews 4:15). How freeing it is to have our High Priest—Who is both sinless and understanding—intercede for us.

Jesus understands

Hebrews 4:15 states that Jesus experienced every emotion and suffered every feeling you and I do, but He did it without sin. Why did He not sin? Because He did not give in to His wrong feelings. He knew the Scripture in every area of life because He spent years studying it before He began His ministry.

You and I will never be able to say no to our feelings if we do not have within us a strong knowledge of God's Word. Jesus had the same feelings we do, but He never sinned by giving in to them.

When I am hurt by someone and I feel angry or upset, it is such a comfort to me to lift my face and hands and voice to the Lord and say, "Jesus, I am so glad that You understand what I am feeling right now and that You do not condemn me for feeling this way. I do not want to give vent to my emotions. Help me, Lord, to get over them. Help me to forgive those who have wronged me and not slight them, avoid them, or seek to pay them back for the harm done me."

Why not bow your head and thank the Lord for understanding you too? Pray with me: "Thank You, God, for understanding me and not condemning me. Thank You for not giving up on me. I ask for Your help, that I may become more understanding like You are."

life point

When you and I pray, we need to make sure we approach God as believers, not as beggars. Remember, according to Hebrews 4:16, we are to come boldly to God's throne: not beggarly, but boldly; not belligerently, but boldly.

Be sure to keep the balance. Stay respectful, but be bold. Approach God with confidence and recognize your need for grace. Believe that He delights in your prayers and is ready to answer any request that is in accordance with His will.

5 FOR EVERY high priest chosen from among men is appointed to act on behalf of men in things relating to God, to offer both gifts and sacrifices for sins.

2 He is able to exercise gentleness *and* forbearance toward the ignorant and erring, since he himself also is liable to moral weakness *and* physical infirmity.
3 And because of this he is obliged to offer sacrifice for his own sins, as well as for those of the people.
4 Besides, one does not appropriate for himself the honor [of being high priest], but he is called by God *and* receives it of Him, just as Aaron did.
5 So too Christ (the Messiah) did not exalt Himself to be made a high priest, but was appointed *and* exalted by Him Who said to Him, You are My Son; today I have begotten You; [Ps. 2:7.]
6 As He says also in another place, You are a Priest [appointed] forever after the order (with ᵖthe rank) of Melchizedek. [Ps. 110:4.]
7 In the days of His flesh [Jesus] offered up definite, special petitions [for that which He not only wanted

ᵖ Joseph Thayer, *A Greek-English Lexicon*.

qbut needed] and supplications with strong crying and tears to Him Who was [always] able to save Him [out] from death, and He was heard because of His reverence toward God [His godly fear, His piety, rin that He shrank from the horrors of separation from the bright presence of the Father].

8 Although He was a Son, He learned [active, special] obedience through what He suffered

9 And, [His completed experience] making Him perfectly [equipped], He became the Author and Source of eternal salvation to all those who give heed and obey Him, [Isa. 45:17.]

10 Being sdesignated and recognized and saluted by God as High Priest after the order (with tthe rank) of Melchizedek. [Ps. 110:4.]

11 Concerning this we have much to say which is hard to explain, since you have become dull in your [spiritual] hearing and sluggish [even qslothful in achieving spiritual insight].

12 For even though by this time you ought to be teaching others, you actually need someone to teach you over again the very first principles of

---

q G. Abbott-Smith, *Manual Greek Lexicon of the New Testament.* r Robert Jamieson, A.R. Fausset and David Brown, *A Commentary on the Old and New Testaments.* s Alexander Souter, *Pocket Lexicon.* t Joseph Thayer, *A Greek-English Lexicon.*

use your pain for gain

Have you ever needed a job, but every employment ad you read asked for someone with experience? You wanted a job but did not have any experience, and it frustrated you. I have been in that situation, and I remember thinking, "How can I get experience if nobody will give me a job?"

God also wants experienced help. When we go to work for God in His kingdom, He will use everything in our past. No matter how painful it was, He considers it experience. Many of us have gone through difficult things, and those things qualify us to help take someone else through them too. Hebrews 5:8, 9 tells us that even Jesus gained experience through the things He suffered.

How could I write to you right now if I had not gone through some difficult things and gained some valuable experience? How could I teach others how to forgive those who have hurt them if I had not first had the experience of forgiving those who hurt me?

I encourage you to look at your pain from a different viewpoint. A right perspective makes all the difference in your life. Take a look at how you can use your pain for someone else's gain. Can your mess become your ministry? Maybe you have gone through so much that you feel you have enough experience to be a specialist in some area. I am a specialist in overcoming shame, guilt, poor self-image, lack of confidence, fear, anger, bitterness, self-pity, etc. Let me encourage you to be positive about your past and your pain, and realize that it can all be used for good in God's kingdom.

life point

Hebrews 5:11 warns us that we will miss learning rich life principles if we do not have a listening attitude. We should not limit our hearing just to those times when we desperately need help. (Of course, we are always ready to hear from Him if we are in trouble!) God wants to speak to us on a regular basis and we need to hear Him all the time. Do not allow your hearing to become muted; rather keep your spiritual ears open to hear His voice.

God's Word. You have come to need milk, not solid food.

13 For everyone who continues to feed on milk is obviously inexperienced *and* unskilled in the doctrine of righteousness (of conformity to the divine will in purpose, thought, and action), for he is a mere infant [not able to talk yet]!

14 But solid food is for full-grown men, for those whose senses *and* mental faculties are trained by practice to discriminate *and* distinguish between what is morally good *and* noble and what is evil *and* contrary either to divine or human law.

putting the Word to work

Hebrews 5:12–14 teaches us about growing up spiritually. Do adults drink milk from baby bottles or eat only baby food? Of course not! Likewise, let me encourage you as a Christian to be diligent in studying the Bible so you will understand it and be able to apply it to your everyday life. In this way you will grow in faith and move from spiritual "milk" to spiritual "meat." How can you apply a particular truth from God's Word to your life today?

6 THEREFORE LET us go on and get past the elementary stage in the teachings *and* doctrine of Christ (the Messiah), advancing steadily toward the completeness *and* perfection that belong to spiritual maturity. Let us not again be laying the foundation of repentance *and* abandonment of dead works (dead formalism) and of the faith [by which you turned] to God,

2 With teachings about purifying, the laying on of hands, the resurrection from the dead, and eternal judgment *and* punishment. [These are all matters of which you should have been fully aware long, long ago.]

3 If indeed God permits, we will [now] proceed [to advanced teaching].

4 For it is impossible [to restore and bring again to repentance] those who have been once for all enlightened, who have consciously tasted the heavenly gift and have become sharers of the Holy Spirit,

5 And have felt how good the Word of God is and the mighty powers of the age *and* world to come,

6 If they then deviate from the faith *and* turn away from their allegiance— [it is impossible] to bring them back to repentance, for (because, while, as long as) they nail upon the cross the Son of God afresh [as far as they are concerned] and are holding [Him] up to contempt *and* shame *and* public disgrace.

7 For the soil which has drunk the rain that repeatedly falls upon it and produces vegetation useful to those for whose benefit it is cultivated partakes of a blessing from God.

8 But if [that same soil] persistently bears thorns and thistles, it is considered worthless and near to being cursed, whose end is to be burned. [Gen. 3:17, 18.]

9 Even though we speak this way, yet in your case, beloved, we are now firmly convinced of better things that are near to salvation *and* accompany it.

10 For God is not unrighteous to forget *or* overlook your labor and the love which you have shown for His name's sake in ministering to the needs of the saints (His own consecrated people), as you still do.

11 But we do [ᵘstrongly and earnestly] desire for each of you to show the same diligence *and* sincerity [all the way through] in realizing *and* enjoying the full assurance *and* development of [your] hope until the end,

life point

I encourage you to take the message of Hebrews 6:11 seriously by following through on the things you start.

It is so easy to begin something, but it takes great courage to finish! At the beginning of a new thing, we get all excited and usually have a lot of support to do it. But when our emotions wear off and all that is left is hard work and the need for extreme patience, we find out what it takes to truly succeed. Be a person who does succeed and finishes well!

12 In order that you may not grow disinterested *and* become [spiritual] sluggards, but imitators, behaving as do those who through faith (ᵛby their leaning of the entire personality on God in Christ in absolute trust and confidence in His power, wisdom, and goodness) and by practice of patient endurance *and* waiting are [now] inheriting the promises.

13 For when God made [His] promise to Abraham, He swore by Himself, since He had no one greater by whom to swear,

14 Saying, Blessing I certainly will bless you and multiplying I will multiply you. [Gen. 22:16, 17.]

15 And so it was that he [Abraham], having waited long *and* endured patiently, realized *and* obtained [in the birth of Isaac as a pledge of what was to come] what God had promised him.

16 Men indeed swear by a greater [than themselves], and with them in all disputes the oath taken for confirmation is final [ending strife].

17 Accordingly God also, in His desire to show more convincingly *and* beyond doubt to those who were to inherit the promise the unchangeableness of His purpose *and* plan, intervened (mediated) with an oath.

18 This was so that, by two unchangeable things [His promise and His oath] in which it is impossible for God ever to prove false *or* deceive us, we who have fled [to Him] for refuge might have mighty indwelling strength *and* strong encouragement to grasp *and* hold fast the hope appointed for us *and* set before [us].

19 [Now] we have this [hope] as a sure and steadfast anchor of the soul [it cannot slip and it cannot ᵘbreak down under whoever steps out upon it—a hope] that reaches ᵘfarther *and* enters into [the very certainty of the Presence] within the veil, [Lev. 16:2.]

20 Where Jesus has entered in for us [in advance], a Forerunner having become a High Priest forever after the order (with ʷthe rank) of Melchizedek. [Ps. 110:4.]

7 FOR THIS Melchizedek, king of Salem [and] priest of the Most High God, met Abraham as he returned from the slaughter of the kings and blessed him,

u Marvin Vincent, *Word Studies.* **v** Alexander Souter, *Pocket Lexicon.* **w** Joseph Thayer, *A Greek-English Lexicon.*

2 And Abraham gave to him a tenth portion of all [the spoil]. He is primarily, as his name when translated indicates, king of righteousness, and then he is also king of Salem, which means king of peace.

3 Without [record of] father or mother or ancestral line, neither with beginning of days nor ending of life, but, resembling the Son of God, he continues to be a priest without interruption *and* without successor.

4 Now observe *and* consider how great [a personage] this was to whom even Abraham the patriarch gave a tenth [the topmost or the pick of the heap] of the spoils.

5 And it is true that those descendants of Levi who are charged with the priestly office are commanded in the Law to take tithes from the people— which means, from their brethren— though these have descended from Abraham.

6 But this person who has not their Levitical ancestry received tithes from Abraham [himself] and blessed him who possessed the promises [of God].

7 Yet it is beyond all contradiction that it is the lesser person who is blessed by the greater one.

8 Furthermore, here [in the Levitical priesthood] tithes are received by men who are subject to death; while there [in the case of Melchizedek], they are received by one of whom it is testified that he lives [perpetually].

9 A person might even say that Levi [the father of the priestly tribe] himself, who received tithes (the tenth), paid tithes through Abraham,

10 For he was still in the loins of his forefather [Abraham] when Melchizedek met him [Abraham].

11 Now if perfection (a perfect fellowship between God and the worshiper) had been attainable by the Levitical priesthood—for under it the people were given the Law—why was it further necessary that there should arise another *and* different kind of Priest, one after the order of Melchizedek, rather than one appointed after the order *and* rank of Aaron?

12 For when there is a change in the priesthood, there is of necessity an alteration of the law [concerning the priesthood] as well.

13 For the One of Whom these things are said belonged [not to the priestly line but] to another tribe, no member of which has officiated at the altar.

14 For it is obvious that our Lord sprang from the tribe of Judah, and Moses mentioned nothing about priests in connection with that tribe.

15 And this becomes more plainly evident when another Priest arises Who bears the likeness of Melchizedek, [Ps. 110:4.]

16 Who has been constituted a Priest, not on the basis of a bodily legal requirement [an externally imposed command concerning His physical ancestry], but on the basis of the power of an endless *and* indestructible Life.

17 For it is witnessed of Him, You are a Priest forever after the order (with the rank) of Melchizedek. [Ps. 110:4.]

18 So a previous physical regulation *and* command is cancelled because of its weakness *and* ineffectiveness and uselessness—

19 For the Law never made anything perfect—but instead a better hope is introduced through which we [now] come close to God.

20 And it was not without the taking of an oath [that Christ was made Priest],

21 For those who formerly became priests received their office without its being confirmed by the taking of an oath by God, but this One was designated *and* addressed *and* saluted with an oath, The Lord has sworn and will not regret it *or* change His mind,

You are a Priest forever *according to the order of Melchizedek.* [Ps. 110:4.]

22 In keeping with [the oath's greater strength and force], Jesus has become the Guarantee of a better (stronger) agreement [a more excellent and more advantageous covenant].

23 [Again, the former successive line of priests] was made up of many, because they were each prevented by death from continuing [perpetually in office];

24 But He holds His priesthood unchangeably, because He lives on forever.

25 Therefore He is able also to save to the uttermost (completely, perfectly, finally, and for all time and eternity) those who come to God through Him, since He is always living to make petition to God *and* intercede with Him *and* intervene for them.

26 [Here is] the High Priest [perfectly adapted] to our needs, as was fitting—holy, blameless, unstained by sin, separated from sinners, and exalted higher than the heavens.

27 He has no day by day necessity, as [do each of these other] high priests, to offer sacrifice first of all for his own [personal] sins and then for those of the people, because He [met all the requirements] once for all when He brought Himself [as a sacrifice] which He offered up.

28 For the Law sets up men in their weakness [frail, sinful, dying human beings] as high priests, but the word of [God's] oath, which [was spoken later] after the institution of the Law, [chooses and appoints as priest One Whose appointment is complete and permanent], a Son Who has been made perfect forever. [Ps. 110:4.]

8 NOW THE main point of what we have to say is this: We have such a High Priest, One Who is seated at the right hand of the majestic [God] in heaven, [Ps. 110:1.]

2 As officiating Priest, a Minister in the holy places *and* in the true tabernacle which is erected not by man but by the Lord.

3 For every high priest is appointed to offer up gifts and sacrifices; so it is essential for this [High Priest] to have some offering to make also.

4 If then He were still living on earth, He would not be a priest at all, for there are [already priests] who offer the gifts in accordance with the Law.

5 [But these offer] service [merely] as a pattern and as a foreshadowing of [what has its true existence and reality in] the heavenly sanctuary. For when Moses was about to erect the tabernacle, he was warned by God, saying, See to it that you make it all [exactly] according to the copy (the model) which was shown to you on the mountain. [Exod. 25:40.]

6 But as it now is, He [Christ] has acquired a [priestly] ministry which is as much superior *and* more excellent [than the old] as the covenant (the agreement) of which He is the Mediator (the Arbiter, Agent) is superior *and* more excellent, [because] it is enacted *and* rests upon more important (sublimer, higher, and nobler) promises.

7 For if that first covenant had been without defect, there would have been no room for another one *or* an attempt to institute another one.

8 However, He finds fault with them [showing its inadequacy] when

speak the Word

Thank You, Jesus, that You are able to save to the uttermost and that You are always living to make petition to God and to intercede with Him for me.
ADAPTED FROM HEBREWS 7:25

He says, Behold, the days will come, says the Lord, when I will make *and* ratify a new covenant *or* agreement with the house of Israel and with the house of Judah.

9 It will not be like the covenant that I made with their forefathers on the day when I grasped them by the hand to help *and* relieve them *and* to lead them out from the land of Egypt, for they did not abide in My agreement with them, and so I withdrew My favor *and* disregarded them, says the Lord.

10 For this is the covenant that I will make with the house of Israel after those days, says the Lord: I will imprint My laws upon their minds, even upon their innermost thoughts *and* understanding, and engrave them upon their hearts; and I will be their God, and they shall be My people.

11 And it will nevermore be necessary for each one to teach his neighbor and his fellow citizen or each one his brother, saying, Know (perceive, have knowledge of, and get acquainted by experience with) the Lord, for all will know Me, from the smallest to the greatest of them.

12 For I will be merciful *and* gracious toward their sins and I will remember their deeds of unrighteousness no more. [Jer. 31:31-34.]

13 When God speaks of a new [covenant or agreement], He makes the first one obsolete (out of use). And what is obsolete (out of use and annulled because of age) is ripe for disappearance *and* to be dispensed with altogether.

9 NOW EVEN the first covenant had its own rules *and* regulations for divine worship, and it had a sanctuary [but one] of this world. [Exod. 25:10-40.]

2 For a tabernacle (tent) was erected, in the outer division *or* compartment of which were the lampstand and the table with [its loaves of] the showbread set forth. [This portion] is called the Holy Place. [Lev. 24:5, 6.]

3 But [inside] beyond the second curtain *or* veil, [there stood another] tabernacle [division] known as the Holy of Holies. [Exod. 26:31-33.]

4 It had the golden ˣaltar of incense and the ark (chest) of the covenant, covered over with wrought gold. This [ark] contained a golden jar which held the manna and the rod of Aaron that sprouted and the [two stone] slabs of the covenant [bearing the Ten Commandments]. [Exod. 16:32-34; 30:1-6; Num. 17:8-10.]

5 Above [the ark] and overshadowing the mercy seat were the representations of the cherubim [winged creatures which were the symbols] of glory. We cannot now go into detail about these things.

6 These arrangements having thus been made, the priests enter [habitually] into the outer division of the tabernacle in performance of their ritual acts of worship.

7 But into the second [division of the tabernacle] none but the high priest goes, and he only once a year, and never without taking a sacrifice of blood with him, which he offers for himself and for the errors *and*

speak the Word

x Henry Alford, *The Greek New Testament, with Notes*: Not kept permanently in the Holy of Holies, but taken in on the Day of Atonement.

sins of ignorance *and* thoughtless- ness which the people have commit- ted. [Lev. 16:15.]

8 By this the Holy Spirit points out that the way into the [true Holy of] Holies is not yet thrown open as long as the former [the outer portion of the] tabernacle remains a recognized institution *and* is still standing,

9 Seeing that that first [outer por- tion of the] tabernacle was a parable (a visible symbol or type or picture of the present age). In it gifts and sacri- fices are offered, and yet are inca- pable of perfecting the conscience *or* of cleansing *and* renewing the inner man of the worshiper.

10 For [the ceremonies] deal only with clean and unclean meats and drinks and different washings, [mere] external rules *and* regulations for the body imposed to tide the worshipers over until the time of setting things straight [of reformation, of the com- plete new order when Christ, the Messiah, shall establish the reality of what these things foreshadow—a bet- ter covenant].

11 But [that appointed time came] when Christ (the Messiah) appeared as a High Priest of the better things that have come *and* are to come. [Then] through the greater and more perfect tabernacle not made with [human] hands, that is, not a part of this material creation,

12 He went once for all into the [Holy of] Holies [of heaven], not by virtue of the blood of goats and calves [by which to make reconciliation between God and man], but His own blood, having found *and* secured a complete redemption (an everlasting release for us).

13 For if [the mere] sprinkling of unholy *and* defiled persons with blood of goats and bulls and with the ashes of a burnt heifer is sufficient for the purification of the body, [Lev. 16:6, 16; Num. 19:9, 17, 18.]

14 How much more surely shall the blood of Christ, Who [y]by virtue of [His] eternal Spirit [His own preexis- tent [z]divine personality] has offered Himself as an unblemished sacrifice to God, purify our consciences from dead works *and* lifeless observances to serve the [ever] living God?

15 [Christ, the Messiah] is therefore

life point

Notice that Jesus offered His blood by the Spirit (see Hebrews 9:14). The Spirit and the blood work together. The promised Holy Spirit could not be poured out on the Day of Pentecost until after the blood was poured out on the cross of Calvary. The blood and the Spirit still work together today. Honor the blood, and you will see the Spirit poured out in your life.

the Negotiator *and* Mediator of an [entirely] new agreement (testament, covenant), so that those who are called *and* offered it may receive the fulfillment of the promised everlast- ing inheritance—since a death has taken place which rescues *and* deliv- ers *and* redeems them from the trans- gressions committed under the [old] first agreement.

16 For where there is a [last] will *and* testament involved, the death of the one who made it must be established,

17 For a will *and* testament is valid and takes effect only at death, since it has no force *or* legal power as long as the one who made it is alive.

18 So even the [old] first covenant (God's will) was not inaugurated *and* ratified *and* put in force without the shedding of blood.

19 For when every command of the

---

y Marvin Vincent, *Word Studies.*　**z** Henry Alford, cited by Kenneth Wuest, *Word Studies.*

Law had been read out by Moses to all the people, he took the blood of slain calves and goats, together with water and scarlet wool and with a bunch of hyssop, and sprinkled both the Book (the roll of the Law and covenant) itself and all the people,

20 Saying these words: This is the blood that seals *and* ratifies the agreement (the testament, the covenant) which God commanded [me to deliver to] you. [Exod. 24:6-8.]

21 And in the same way he sprinkled with the blood both the tabernacle and all the [sacred] vessels *and* appliances used in [divine] worship.

22 [In fact] under the Law almost everything is purified by means of blood, and without the shedding of blood there is neither release from sin *and* its guilt *nor* the remission of the due *and* merited punishment for sins.

23 By such means, therefore, it was necessary for the [earthly] copies of the heavenly things to be purified, but the actual heavenly things themselves [required far] better *and* nobler sacrifices than these.

24 For Christ (the Messiah) has not entered into a sanctuary made with [human] hands, only a copy *and* pattern *and* type of the true one, but [He has entered] into heaven itself, now to appear in the [very] presence of God on our behalf.

25 Nor did He [enter into the heavenly sanctuary to] offer Himself regularly again and again, as the high priest enters the [Holy of] Holies every year with blood not his own.

26 For then would He often have had to suffer [over and over again] since the foundation of the world. But as it now is, He has once for all at the consummation *and* close of the ages appeared to put away *and* abolish sin by His sacrifice [of Himself].

27 And just as it is appointed for [all] men once to die, and after that the [certain] judgment,

28 Even so it is that Christ, having been offered to take upon Himself *and* bear as a burden the sins of many once *and* [a]once for all, will appear a second time, not to carry any burden of sin *nor* to deal with sin, but to bring to full salvation those who are [eagerly, constantly, and patiently] waiting for *and* expecting Him.

10 FOR SINCE the Law has merely a rude outline (foreshadowing) of the good things to come—instead of fully expressing those things—it can never by offering the same sacrifices continually year after year make perfect those who approach [its altars].

2 For if it were otherwise, would [these sacrifices] not have stopped being offered? Since the worshipers had [a]once for all been cleansed, they would no longer have any guilt *or* consciousness of sin.

3 But [as it is] these sacrifices annually bring a fresh remembrance of sins [to be atoned for],

4 Because the blood of bulls and goats is powerless to take sins away.

5 Hence, when He [Christ] entered into the world, He said, Sacrifices and offerings You have not desired, but instead You have made ready a body for Me [to offer];

6 In burnt offerings and sin offerings You have taken no delight.

7 Then I said, Behold, here I am, coming to do Your will, O God—[to fulfill] what is written of Me in the volume of the Book. [Ps. 40:6-8.]

8 When He said just before, You have neither desired, nor have You taken delight in sacrifices and offerings and burnt offerings and sin offerings—all of which are offered according to the Law—

---

a G. Abbott-Smith, *Manual Greek Lexicon.*

9 He then went on to say, Behold, [here] I am, coming to do Your will. Thus He does away with *and* annuls the first (former) order [as a means of expiating sin] so that He might inaugurate *and* establish the second (latter) order. [Ps. 40:6-8.]

10 And in accordance with this will [of God], we have been made holy (consecrated and sanctified) through the offering made once for all of the body of Jesus Christ (the Anointed One).

11 Furthermore, every [human] priest stands [at his altar of service] ministering daily, offering the same sacrifices over and over again, which never are able to strip [from every side of us] the sins [that envelop us] *and* take them away—

12 Whereas this One [Christ], after He had offered a single sacrifice for our sins [that shall avail] for all time, sat down at the right hand of God,

13 Then to wait until His enemies should be made a stool beneath His feet. [Ps. 110:1.]

14 For by a single offering He has forever completely cleansed *and* perfected those who are consecrated *and* made holy.

15 And also the Holy Spirit adds His testimony to us [in confirmation of this]. For having said,

16 This is the agreement (testament, covenant) that I will set up *and* conclude with them after those days, says the Lord: I will imprint My laws upon their hearts, and I will inscribe them on their minds (on their inmost thoughts and understanding),

17 He then goes on to say, And their sins and their lawbreaking I will remember no more. [Jer. 31:33, 34.]

18 Now where there is absolute remission (forgiveness and cancellation of the penalty) of these [sins and lawbreaking], there is no longer any offering made to atone for sin.

19 Therefore, brethren, since we have full freedom *and* confidence to enter into the [Holy of] Holies [by the power and virtue] in the blood of Jesus,

20 By this fresh (new) and living way which He initiated *and* dedicated *and* opened for us through the separating curtain (veil of the Holy of Holies), that is, through His flesh,

21 And since we have [such] a great *and* wonderful *and* noble Priest [Who rules] over the house of God,

22 Let us all come forward *and* draw near with true (honest and sincere) hearts in unqualified assurance *and* absolute conviction engendered by faith (by [b]that leaning of the entire human personality on God in absolute trust and confidence in His power, wisdom, and goodness), having our hearts sprinkled *and* purified from a

life point

Believing we are made right with God through our faith in Jesus Christ is a fresh, new, and living way (see Hebrews 10:20), one that gives us freedom, boldness, and confidence. Trying to follow the Law (trying to do everything right) in order to earn God's acceptance ministers death (every kind of misery) to us; but Jesus offers us His grace, which produces life.

speak the Word

Thank You, Jesus, for shedding Your blood so that I could have full freedom and confidence to enter into God's presence.
ADAPTED FROM HEBREWS 10:19

b Alexander Souter, *Pocket Lexicon*.

putting the Word to work

Have you ever wondered if you were truly welcome in God's presence? Take heart, because through His blood, Jesus made a new and living way for you to draw near to God with confidence (see Hebrews 10:20). Thank God for the joy of being in His presence!

guilty (evil) conscience and our bodies cleansed with pure water.
23 So let us seize *and* hold fast *and* retain without wavering the ^chope we cherish *and* confess *and* our acknowledgement of it, for He Who promised is reliable (sure) *and* faithful to His word.
24 And let us consider *and* give ^dattentive, continuous care to watching over one another, studying how we may stir up (stimulate and incite) to love *and* helpful deeds *and* noble activities,
25 Not forsaking *or* neglecting to assemble together [as believers], as is the habit of some people, but admonishing (warning, urging, and encouraging) one another, and all the more faithfully as you see the day approaching.

putting the Word to work

Sunday morning church services are a great opportunity for Christians to gather together. However, Hebrews 10:24, 25 encourages us to gather together often so we can encourage one another in love and in doing good deeds. How can you find ways to spend quality time with other Christians? Be intentional about including time in your schedule for gathering together with other believers. You will be encouraged!

26 For if we go on deliberately *and* willingly sinning after once acquiring the knowledge of the Truth, there is no longer any sacrifice left to atone for [our] sins [no further offering to which to look forward].
27 [There is nothing left for us then] but a kind of awful *and* fearful prospect *and* expectation of divine judgment and the fury of burning wrath *and* indignation which will consume those who put themselves in opposition [to God]. [Isa. 26:11.]
28 Any person who has violated *and* [thus] rejected *and* set at naught the Law of Moses is put to death without pity *or* mercy on the evidence of two or three witnesses. [Deut. 17:2-6.]
29 How much worse (sterner and heavier) punishment do you suppose he will be judged to deserve who has spurned *and* [thus] trampled underfoot the Son of God, and who has considered the covenant blood by which he was consecrated common *and* unhallowed, thus profaning it *and* insulting *and* outraging the [Holy] Spirit [Who imparts] grace (the unmerited favor and blessing of God)? [Exod. 24:8.]
30 For we know Him Who said, Vengeance is Mine [retribution and the meting out of full justice rest with Me]; I will repay [I will exact the compensation], *says the Lord.* And again, The Lord will judge *and* determine *and* solve *and* settle the cause *and* the cases of His people. [Deut. 32:35, 36.]
31 It is a fearful (formidable and terrible) thing to incur the divine penalties *and* be cast into the hands of the living God!
32 But be ever mindful of the days gone by in which, after you were first spiritually enlightened, you endured a great *and* painful struggle,
33 Sometimes being yourselves a gazingstock, publicly exposed to

c William Tyndale, *The Tyndale Bible*, Miles Coverdale, *The Coverdale Bible*, and others.   **d** Marvin Vincent, *Word Studies*.

insults *and* abuse and distress, and sometimes claiming fellowship *and* making common cause with others who were so treated.

34 For you did sympathize *and* suffer along with those who were imprisoned, and you bore cheerfully the plundering of your belongings *and* the confiscation of your property, in the knowledge *and* consciousness that you yourselves had a better and lasting possession.

35 Do not, therefore, fling away your fearless confidence, for it carries a great *and* glorious compensation of reward.

36 For you have need of steadfast patience *and* endurance, so that you may perform *and* fully accomplish the will of God, and thus receive *and* ^ecarry away [and enjoy to the full] what is promised.

life point

Hebrews 10:35, 36 speaks of our need for patience. Who do we need to be patient with? We need to be patient with ourselves because sometimes we are slow in learning; we need to be patient with God because He does not always move in our timing; and we need to be patient with other people. Ask God to help you. He will.

37 For still a little while (a very little while), and the Coming One will come and He will not delay.

38 But the just shall live by faith [My righteous servant shall live ^fby his conviction respecting man's relationship to God and divine things, and holy fervor born of faith and conjoined with it]; and if he draws back *and* shrinks in fear, My soul has no delight *or* pleasure in him. [Hab. 2:3, 4.]

39 But our way is not that of those who draw back to eternal misery (perdition) and are utterly destroyed, but we are of those who believe [who cleave to and trust in and rely on God through Jesus Christ, the Messiah] *and* by faith preserve the soul.

11 NOW FAITH is the assurance (the confirmation, ^gthe title deed) of the things [we] hope for, being the proof of things [we] do not see *and* the conviction of their reality [faith perceiving as real fact what is not revealed to the senses].

2 For by [faith—^ftrust and holy fervor born of faith] the men of old had divine testimony borne to them *and* obtained a good report.

3 By faith we understand that the worlds [during the successive ages] were framed (fashioned, put in order, and equipped for their intended purpose) by the word of God, so that what we see was not made out of things which are visible.

4 [Prompted, actuated] by faith Abel brought God a better and more acceptable sacrifice than Cain, because of which it was testified of him that he was righteous [that he was upright and in right standing with God], and God bore witness by accepting *and* acknowledging his gifts. And though he died, yet [through the incident] he is still speaking. [Gen. 4:3-10.]

5 Because of faith Enoch was caught up *and* transferred to heaven, so that he did not have a glimpse of death; and he was not found, because God had translated him. For even before he was taken to heaven, he received testimony [still on record] that he had pleased *and* been satisfactory to God. [Gen. 5:21-24.]

e Marvin Vincent, *Word Studies.*   **f** Joseph Thayer, *A Greek-English Lexicon.*   **g** James Moulton and George Milligan, *The Vocabulary of the Greek Testament.*

6 But without faith it is impossible to please *and* be satisfactory to Him. For whoever would come near to God must [necessarily] believe that God exists and that He is the rewarder of those who earnestly *and* diligently seek Him [out].

life point

Notice in Hebrews 11:6 that without faith you cannot please God; therefore, no matter how many "good works" you offer, God will not be pleased if they were done to earn His favor.

Whatever we do for God should be because we love Him, not because we try to get something from Him.

Hebrews 11:6 says that God is a rewarder of those who diligently seek Him. I rejoiced when I finally realized this! I know I have made many mistakes in the past, but I also know I have diligently sought the Lord with all my heart. That means that I qualify for rewards. I decided a long time ago that even though I did not deserve them, I would receive any blessings that God wanted to give me. I hope you will do the same.

7 [Prompted] by faith Noah, being forewarned by God concerning events of which as yet there was no visible sign, took heed *and* diligently *and* reverently constructed *and* prepared an ark for the deliverance of his own family. By this [his faith which relied on God] he passed judgment *and* sentence on the world's unbelief and became an heir *and* possessor of righteousness (ʰthat relation of being right into which God puts the person who has faith). [Gen. 6:13-22.]
8 [Urged on] by faith Abraham, when he was called, obeyed and went forth to

a place which he was destined to receive as an inheritance; and he went, although he did not know *or* trouble his mind about where he was to go.
9 [Prompted] by faith he dwelt as a temporary resident in the land which was designated in the promise [of God, though he was like a stranger] in a strange country, living in tents with Isaac and Jacob, fellow heirs with him of the same promise. [Gen. 12:1-8.]
10 For he was [waiting expectantly and confidently] looking forward to the city which has fixed *and* firm foundations, whose Architect *and* Builder is God.
11 Because of faith also Sarah herself received physical power to conceive a child, even when she was long past the age for it, because she considered [God] Who had given her the promise to be reliable *and* trustworthy *and* true to His word. [Gen. 17:19; 18:11-14; 21:2.]
12 So from one man, though he was physically as good as dead, there have sprung descendants whose number is as the stars of heaven and as countless as the innumerable sands on the seashore. [Gen. 15:5, 6; 22:17; 32:12.]
13 These people all died controlled *and* sustained by their faith, but not having received the tangible fulfillment of [God's] promises, only having seen it *and* greeted it from a great distance by faith, and all the while acknowledging *and* confessing that they were strangers *and* temporary residents *and* exiles upon the earth. [Gen. 23:4; Ps. 39:12.]
14 Now those people who talk as they did show plainly that they are in search of a fatherland (their own country).
15 If they had been thinking with [homesick] remembrance of that country from which they were emigrants, they would have found constant opportunity to return to it.

h Joseph Thayer, *A Greek-English Lexicon.*

16 But the truth is that they were yearning for *and* aspiring to a better *and* more desirable country, that is, a heavenly [one]. For that reason God is not ashamed to be called their God [even to be surnamed their God—the God of Abraham, Isaac, and Jacob], for He has prepared a city for them. [Exod. 3:6, 15; 4:5.]

17 By faith Abraham, when he was put to the test [while the testing of his faith was ¹still in progress], ¹had already brought Isaac for an offering; he who had gladly received *and* welcomed [God's] promises was ready to sacrifice his only son, [Gen. 22:1-10.]

18 Of whom it was said, Through Isaac shall your descendants be reckoned. [Gen. 21:12.]

19 For he reasoned that God was able to raise [him] up even from among the dead. Indeed in the sense that Isaac was figuratively dead [potentially sacrificed], he did [actually] receive him back from the dead.

20 [With eyes of] faith Isaac, looking far into the future, invoked blessings upon Jacob and Esau. [Gen. 27:27-29, 39, 40.]

21 [Prompted] by faith Jacob, when he was dying, blessed each of Joseph's sons and bowed in prayer over the top of his staff. [Gen. 48.]

22 [Actuated] by faith Joseph, when nearing the end of his life, referred to [the promise of God for] the departure of the Israelites out of Egypt and gave instructions concerning the burial of his own bones. [Gen. 50:24, 25; Exod. 13:19.]

23 [Prompted] by faith Moses, after his birth, was kept concealed for three months by his parents, because they saw how comely the child was; and they were not overawed *and* terrified by the king's decree. [Exod. 1:22; 2:2.]

24 [Aroused] by faith Moses, when he had grown to maturity *and* ʲbecome great, refused to be called the son of Pharaoh's daughter, [Exod. 2:10, 15.]

25 Because he preferred to share the oppression [suffer the hardships] *and* bear the shame of the people of God rather than to have the fleeting enjoyment of a sinful life.

26 He considered the contempt *and* abuse *and* shame [borne for] the Christ (the Messiah Who was to come) to be greater wealth than all the treasures of Egypt, for he looked forward *and* away to the reward (recompense).

27 [Motivated] by faith he left Egypt behind him, being unawed *and* undismayed by the wrath of the king; for he never flinched *but* held staunchly to his purpose *and* endured steadfastly as one who gazed on Him Who is invisible. [Exod. 2:15.]

28 By faith (simple trust and confidence in God) he instituted *and* carried out the Passover and the sprinkling of the blood [on the doorposts], so that the destroyer of the firstborn (the angel) might not touch those [of the children of Israel]. [Exod. 12:21-30.]

29 [Urged on] by faith the people crossed the Red Sea as [though] on dry land, but when the Egyptians tried to do the same thing they were swallowed up [by the sea]. [Exod. 14:21-31.]

putting the Word to work

Have you ever wondered what faith in action really looks like? Study the lives of the heroes of faith in Hebrews 11:1–40, and you can see many different ways that faith was lived out in everyday life. Remember that faith is the certain assurance of the things we hope for and the conviction of the reality of things we cannot see.

---

i Marvin Vincent, *Word Studies*.   j Literal translation.

30 Because of faith the walls of Jericho fell down after they had been encompassed for seven days [by the Israelites]. [Josh. 6:12-21.]

31 [Prompted] by faith Rahab the prostitute was not destroyed along with those who refused to believe *and* obey, because she had received the spies in peace [without enmity]. [Josh. 2:1-21; 6:22-25.]

32 And what shall I say further? For time would fail me to tell of Gideon, Barak, Samson, Jephthah, of David and Samuel and the prophets, [Judg. 4:1-5; 6:1-8, 35; 11:1-12, 15; 13:1-16; I Sam. 1-30; II Sam. 1-24; I Kings 1-2; Acts 3:24.]

33 Who by [the help of] faith subdued kingdoms, administered justice, obtained promised blessings, closed the mouths of lions, [Dan. 6.]

34 Extinguished the power of raging fire, escaped the devourings of the sword, out of frailty *and* weakness won strength *and* became stalwart, even mighty *and* resistless in battle, routing alien hosts. [Dan. 3.]

35 [Some] women received again their dead by a resurrection. Others were tortured [k]to death with clubs, refusing to accept release [offered on the terms of denying their faith], so that they might be resurrected to a better life. [I Kings 17:17-24; II Kings 4:25-37.]

36 Others had to suffer the trial of mocking and scourging and even chains and imprisonment.

37 They were stoned to death; they were lured with tempting offers [to renounce their faith]; they were sawn asunder; they were slaughtered by the sword; [while they were alive] they had to go about wrapped in the skins of sheep and goats, utterly destitute, oppressed, cruelly treated—

38 [Men] of whom the world was not worthy—roaming over the desolate places and the mountains, and [living] in caves *and* caverns and holes of the earth.

39 And all of these, though they won divine approval by [means of] their faith, did not receive the fulfillment of what was promised,

40 Because God had us in mind *and* had something better *and* greater in view for us, so that they [these heroes and heroines of faith] should not come to perfection apart from us [before we could join them].

12 THEREFORE THEN, since we are surrounded by so great a cloud of witnesses [who have borne testimony to the Truth], let us strip off *and* throw aside every encumbrance (unnecessary weight) and that sin which so readily (deftly and cleverly) clings to *and* entangles us, and let us run with patient endurance *and* steady *and* active persistence the appointed course of the race that is set before us,

2 Looking away [from all that will distract] to Jesus, Who is the Leader *and* the Source of our faith [giving the first incentive for our belief] and is also its Finisher [bringing it to maturity and perfection]. He, for the joy [of

putting the Word to work

When a runner runs in a race, his focus is not on the people in the stands or on the runners around him, but on the finish line! As a believer, your life is like a race, and as you run, it is important to keep your eyes fixed on Jesus (see Hebrews 12:1, 2). Give Him your undivided attention. Is anything distracting you from God or keeping you from making progress as you grow in faith? What do you need to do in order to focus more fully on Jesus as you run the race of your life?

---

k Marvin Vincent, *Word Studies*.

throw off excess baggage

Hebrews 12:1 tells us that if we are going to run our race, we must lay aside every weight and run the race with patience. I have heard this point summarized this way: Running our race with no hindrances means stripping for the contest.

In the days when this verse was written, the writer was drawing a parallel that was much better understood than it is today. In those days, runners conditioned their bodies for a race just as athletes do today. But at the time of the race, they stripped off their clothing, wearing only a loincloth, so that when they ran there was nothing to hinder them. They also oiled their bodies with fine oils.

In the same way, we need to be well-oiled or anointed with the Holy Spirit if we want to win our race. We also need to remove anything from our lives that hinders us as we run the race set before us.

There are many different hindrances to running a race well and developing our full potential. Too many commitments is one that keeps us from developing our potential. Letting other people control us keeps us from developing our potential. Not knowing how to say no keeps us from developing our potential. Getting overly involved in someone else's goals and vision or becoming entangled in someone else's problems instead of keeping our eyes on our own goals will also keep us from fulfilling our potential.

I find that the devil comes up with a thousand ways every week to entangle me and get me into something that will prevent me from doing what I am supposed to be doing. They all seem like emergencies, and it seems I must be the one to handle them all.

If we want do what God called us to do, we must stay focused because the world we live in is filled with distractions and entanglements. Let me encourage you to keep your focus on the Lord and be diligent to lay aside everything that might distract you or hold you back.

obtaining the prize] that was set before Him, endured the cross, despising *and* ignoring the shame, and is now seated at the right hand of the throne of God. [Ps. 110:1.]

3 Just think of Him Who endured from sinners such grievous opposition *and* bitter hostility against Himself [reckon up and consider it all in comparison with your trials], so that you may not grow weary *or* exhausted, losing heart *and* relaxing *and* fainting in your minds.

4 You have not yet struggled *and* fought agonizingly against sin, *nor* have you yet resisted *and* withstood to the point of pouring out your [own] blood.

5 And have you [completely] forgotten the divine word of appeal *and* encouragement in which you are reasoned with *and* addressed as sons? My son, do not think lightly *or* scorn to submit to the correction *and* discipline of the Lord, nor lose courage *and* give up *and* faint when you are reproved *or* corrected by Him;

6 For the Lord corrects *and*

life point

I want to encourage you to keep your eyes off of yourself and the things that distract you. Instead, focus firmly on Jesus and His power (see Hebrews 12:2). He already knows your troubles. He is ready, willing, and able to bring about the changes that need to be made in you and in your life. He will bring you to maturity and perfection, if you will just ask Him and trust Him to do so. You can count on God; He is the Source of your faith and its Finisher.

disciplines everyone whom He loves, and He punishes, even scourges, every son whom He accepts *and* welcomes to His heart *and* cherishes.
7 You must submit to *and* endure [correction] for discipline; God is dealing with you as with sons. For what son is there whom his father does not [thus] train *and* correct *and* discipline?
8 Now if you are exempt from correction *and* left without discipline in which all [of God's children] share, then you are illegitimate offspring *and* not true sons [at all]. [Prov. 3:11, 12.]
9 Moreover, we have had earthly fathers who disciplined us and we yielded [to them] *and* respected [them for training us]. Shall we not much more cheerfully submit to the Father of spirits and so [truly] live?
10 For [our earthly fathers] disciplined us for only a short period of time *and* chastised us as seemed proper *and* good to them; but He disciplines us for our certain good, that we may

become sharers in His own holiness.
11 For the time being no discipline brings joy, but seems grievous *and* painful; but afterwards it yields a peaceable fruit of righteousness to those who have been trained by it [a harvest of fruit which consists in righteousness—in conformity to God's will in purpose, thought, and action, resulting in right living and right standing with God].
12 So then, brace up *and* reinvigorate *and* set right your slackened *and* weakened *and* drooping hands and strengthen your feeble *and* palsied *and* tottering knees, [Isa. 35:3.]
13 And cut through *and* make firm *and* plain *and* smooth, straight paths

life point

Hebrews 12:6 tells us that God disciplines us because He loves us. This truth about God's correction and discipline of those He loves is verified by Jesus Himself in Revelation 3:19 when He says, "Those whom I [dearly and tenderly] love, I tell their faults and convict and convince and reprove and chasten [I discipline and instruct them]. So be enthusiastic and in earnest burning with zeal and repent [changing your mind and attitude]."

Change often requires correction, but people who do not know they are loved have a very difficult time receiving correction. Correction does you no good at all if you cannot receive it. I encourage you to receive the Lord's correction in your life as a sign of His love for you.

speak the Word

Thank You, Lord, for loving me enough to correct and discipline me. Help me receive Your correction as a reminder of Your love, Your acceptance, and the fact that You deal with me as Your beloved child.
ADAPTED FROM HEBREWS 12:6, 7

for your feet [yes, make them safe and upright and happy paths that go in the right direction], so that the lame *and* halting [limbs] may not be put out of joint, but rather may be cured.

14 Strive to live in peace with everybody and pursue that consecration *and* holiness without which no one will [ever] see the Lord.

15 Exercise foresight *and* be on the watch to look [after one another], to see that no one falls back from *and* fails to secure God's grace (His unmerited favor and spiritual blessing), in order that no root of resentment (rancor, bitterness, or hatred) shoots forth and causes trouble *and* bitter torment, and the many become contaminated *and* defiled by it—

life point

We must refuse to let bitterness take root in our hearts (see Hebrews 12:15) or allow ourselves to be offended or remain angry. This means we cannot follow our feelings; we must press past feelings and do what God asks us to do.

If you struggle in this area, I encourage you to pursue God's grace—His unmerited favor and spiritual blessing. Let His grace disintegrate the deep roots of bitterness that entangle you.

16 That no one may become guilty of sexual vice, or become a profane (godless and sacrilegious) person as Esau did, who sold his own birthright for a single meal. [Gen. 25:29-34.]

17 For you understand that later on, when he wanted [to regain title to] his inheritance of the blessing, he was rejected (disqualified and set aside), for he could find no opportunity to repair by repentance [what he had done, no chance to recall the choice he had made], although he sought for it carefully with [bitter] tears. [Gen. 27:30-40.]

18 For you have not come [as did the Israelites in the wilderness] to a [material] mountain that can be touched, [a mountain] that is ablaze with fire, and to gloom and darkness and a raging storm,

19 And to the blast of a trumpet and a voice whose words make the listeners beg that nothing more be said to them. [Exod. 19:12-22; 20:18-21; Deut. 4:11, 12; 5:22-27.]

20 For they could not bear the command that was given: If even a wild animal touches the mountain, it shall be stoned to death. [Exod. 19:12, 13.]

21 In fact, so awful *and* terrifying was the [phenomenal] sight that Moses said, I am terrified (aghast and trembling with fear). [Deut. 9:19.]

22 But rather, you have come to Mount Zion, even to the city of the living God, the heavenly Jerusalem, and to countless multitudes of angels in festal gathering,

23 And to the church (assembly) of the Firstborn who are registered [as citizens] in heaven, and to the God Who is Judge of all, and to the spirits of the righteous (the redeemed in heaven) who have been made perfect,

24 And to Jesus, the Mediator (Gobetween, Agent) of a new covenant, and to the sprinkled blood which speaks [of mercy], a better *and* nobler *and* more gracious message than the blood of Abel [which cried out for vengeance]. [Gen. 4:10.]

25 So see to it that you do not reject Him *or* refuse to listen to *and* heed Him Who is speaking [to you now]. For if they [the Israelites] did not escape when they refused to listen *and* heed Him Who warned *and* divinely instructed them [here] on earth [revealing with heavenly warnings His will], how much less shall we escape if we reject *and* turn our backs on Him Who cautions *and* admonishes [us] from heaven?

26 Then [at Mount Sinai] His voice

shook the earth, but now He has given a promise: Yet once more I will shake *and* make tremble not only the earth but also the [starry] heavens. [Hag. 2:6.]

27 Now this expression, Yet once more, indicates the final removal *and* transformation of all [that can be] shaken—that is, of that which has been created—in order that what cannot be shaken may remain *and* continue. [Ps. 102:26.]

28 Let us therefore, receiving a kingdom that is firm *and* stable *and* cannot be shaken, offer to God pleasing service *and* acceptable worship, with modesty *and* pious care and godly fear *and* awe;

29 For our God [is indeed] a consuming fire. [Deut. 4:24.]

13 LET LOVE for your fellow believers continue *and* be a fixed practice with you [never let it fail].

2 Do not forget *or* neglect *or* refuse to extend hospitality to strangers [in the brotherhood—being friendly, cordial, and gracious, sharing the comforts of your home and doing your part generously], for through it some have entertained angels without knowing it. [Gen. 18:1-8; 19:1-3.]

3 Remember those who are in prison as if you were their fellow prisoner, and those who are ill-treated, since you also are liable to bodily sufferings.

4 Let marriage be held in honor (esteemed worthy, precious, of great price, and especially dear) in all things. And thus let the marriage bed

speak the Word

be undefiled (kept undishonored); for God will judge *and* punish the unchaste [all guilty of sexual vice] and adulterous.

5 Let your [1]character *or* moral disposition be free from love of money [including greed, avarice, lust, and craving for earthly possessions] and be satisfied with your present [circumstances and with what you have]; for He [God] [1]Himself has said, I will not in any way fail you *nor* [1]give you up *nor*

life point

Have you faced times when you wondered if God would really come through and meet your needs? Hebrews 13:5 is an encouraging scripture that will greatly help you in this circumstance. In it, the Lord lets us know that we do not need to have our minds set on money or worry how we will take care of ourselves, because He will take care of these things for us. He promises never to fail us or forsake us.

It is important for us to do our part, but we must not try to do God's part. The load is too heavy to bear by ourselves, and if we are not careful, we will break under the weight of it.

Do not worry. Take this promise to heart: "Trust (lean on, rely on, and be confident) in the Lord and do good; so shall you dwell in the land and feed surely on His faithfulness, and truly you shall be fed" (Psalm 37:3). Now that is a great promise!

Father, I pray that love for my fellow believers will always continue in my heart and will be a fixed practice that will never fail in my life.
ADAPTED FROM HEBREWS 13:1

---

1 Marvin Vincent, *Word Studies.*

leave you without support. [I will] not, [m][I will] not, [I will] not in any degree leave you helpless *nor* forsake *nor* [m]let [you] down ([n]relax My hold on you)! [[o]Assuredly not!] [Josh. 1:5.]

6 So we take comfort *and* are encouraged *and* confidently *and* boldly say, The Lord is my Helper; I will not be seized with alarm [I will not fear or dread or be terrified]. What can man do to me? [Ps. 27:1;118:6.]

7 Remember your leaders *and* superiors in authority [for it was they] who brought to you the Word of God. Observe attentively *and* consider their manner of living (the outcome of their well-spent lives) and imitate their faith ([p]their conviction that God exists and is the Creator and Ruler of all things, the Provider and Bestower of eternal salvation through Christ, and their [o]leaning of the entire human personality on God in absolute trust and confidence in His power, wisdom, and goodness).

8 Jesus Christ (the Messiah) is [always] the same, yesterday, today, [yes] and forever (to the ages).

9 Do not be carried about by different *and* varied and alien teachings; for it is good for the heart to be established *and* ennobled *and* strengthened by means of grace (God's favor and spiritual blessing) and not [to be devoted to] foods [rules of diet and ritualistic meals], which bring no [spiritual] benefit *or* profit to those who observe them.

10 We have an altar from which those who serve *and* [n]worship in the tabernacle have no right to eat.

11 For when the blood of animals is brought into the sanctuary by the high priest as a sacrifice for sin, the victims' bodies are burned outside the limits of the camp. [Lev. 16:27.]

12 Therefore Jesus also suffered *and* died outside the [city's] gate in order that He might purify *and* consecrate the people through [the shedding of] His own blood *and* set them apart as holy [for God].

13 Let us then go forth [from all that would prevent us] to Him outside the camp [at Calvary], bearing the contempt *and* abuse *and* shame with Him. [Lev. 16:27.]

14 For here we have no permanent city, but we are looking for the one which is to come.

15 Through Him, therefore, let us constantly *and* at all times offer up to God a sacrifice of praise, which is the fruit of lips that thankfully acknowledge *and* confess *and* glorify His name. [Lev. 7:12; Isa. 57:19; Hos. 14:2.]

16 Do not forget *or* neglect to do kindness *and* good, to be generous *and* distribute *and* contribute to the needy [of the church [p]as embodiment and proof of fellowship], for such sacrifices are pleasing to God.

17 Obey your spiritual leaders and submit to them [continually recognizing their authority over you], for they are constantly keeping watch over your souls *and* guarding your spiritual welfare, as men who will have to render an account [of their trust]. [Do your part to] let them do this with gladness and not with sighing *and* groaning, for that would not be profitable to you [either].

18 Keep praying for us, for we are convinced that we have a good (clear)

speak the Word

Thank You, Jesus, for being the same yesterday, today, and forever!
ADAPTED FROM HEBREWS **13:8**

m Kenneth Wuest, *Word Studies*: Three negatives precede the verb. **n** Marvin Vincent, *Word Studies*. **o** Alexander Souter, *Pocket Lexicon*. **p** Joseph Thayer, *A Greek-English Lexicon*.

conscience, that we want to walk uprightly *and* live a noble life, acting honorably *and* in complete honesty in all things.

19 And I beg of you [to pray for us] the more earnestly, in order that I may be restored to you the sooner.

20 Now may the God of peace [Who is the Author and the Giver of peace], Who brought again from among the dead our Lord Jesus, that great Shepherd of the sheep, by the blood [that sealed, ratified] the everlasting agreement (covenant, testament), [Isa. 55:3; 63:11; Ezek. 37:26; Zech. 9:11.]

21 Strengthen (complete, perfect) *and* make you what you ought to be *and* equip you with everything good that you may carry out His will; [while He Himself] works in you *and* accomplishes that which is pleasing in His sight, through Jesus Christ (the Messiah); to Whom be the glory forever and ever (to the ages of the ages). Amen (so be it).

22 I call on you, brethren, to listen patiently *and* bear with this message of exhortation *and* admonition *and* encouragement, for I have written to you briefly.

23 Notice that our brother Timothy has been released [from prison]. If he comes here soon, I will see you along with him.

24 Give our greetings to all of your spiritual leaders and to all of the saints (God's consecrated believers). The Italian Christians send you their greetings [also].

25 Grace (God's favor and spiritual blessing) be with you all. *Amen (so be it).*

speak the Word

Father, I pray that You will strengthen, complete, and perfect me; that You will make me what I should be; that You will equip me with everything good to carry out Your will while You work in me and accomplish what is pleasing in Your sight.
ADAPTED FROM HEBREWS **13:20, 21**

James

Author:
James

Date:
Approximately AD 48

Everyday Life Principles:
Genuine faith produces good deeds.
Good works are the fruit of true faith.

Watch your mouth, and remember that
words are powerful.

Earnest, heartfelt prayers are effective.

The book of James emphasizes the fact that true faith in God must be accompanied by good works. Let me be quick to point out that good works do not prove a person's belief in God or relationship with Him, but having faith always leads to good works. Faith has to come first because when good works are done in faith, God always gets the glory.

In addition to his focus on unwavering faith and good works, James also provides tremendous practical advice for our everyday lives, including extensive teaching on the joy that is found in suffering and the power of the tongue. He writes about wisdom, about resisting temptation, and about prayer. He penned the familiar words: "Consider it wholly joyful, my brethren, whenever you are enveloped in or encounter trials of any sort or fall into various temptations" (James 1:2) and, " . . . the earnest (heartfelt, continued) prayer of a righteous man makes tremendous power available [dynamic in its working]" (James 5:16).

As you read the book of James, I hope it will not only stir your faith, but also inspire you to perform good works that glorify God and are motivated by your love for Him. Let it also serve as a reminder of the power of your words and of the necessity of wisdom, and as a call to earnest, heartfelt prayer that makes tremendous power available in your life.

1

JAMES, A servant of God and of the Lord Jesus Christ, to the twelve tribes scattered abroad [among the Gentiles in the dispersion]: Greetings (ªrejoice)!

2 Consider it wholly joyful, my brethren, whenever you are enveloped in *or* encounter trials of any sort *or* fall into various temptations.

3 Be assured *and* understand that the trial *and* proving of your faith bring out endurance *and* steadfastness *and* patience.

life point

James 1:2, 3 teaches us that we should rejoice in difficult situations, knowing that through them God tests our faith to bring out patience. I find that trials do eventually produce patience, but first they bring all kinds of junk to the surface such as pride, anger, rebellion, self-pity, and complaining. We need to face and deal with these ungodly traits before patience can come forth.

The Bible talks about purification, sanctification, sacrifice, and suffering. These are not popular words; nevertheless, if we are to be Christlike in character, we must sometimes go through difficult circumstances to learn His ways. I struggled with this process for a long time, but I finally realized that God was not going to do things my way. He placed people and situations in my life that caused me to want to quit this whole process, and He did not want an argument from me. He only wanted to hear, "Yes, Lord. Your will be done."

4 But let endurance *and* steadfastness *and* patience have full play *and* do a thorough work, so that you may be [people] perfectly and fully developed [with no defects], lacking in nothing.

5 If any of you is deficient in wisdom, let him ask of ªthe giving God [Who gives] to everyone liberally *and* ungrudgingly, without reproaching or faultfinding, and it will be given him.

6 Only it must be in faith that he asks with no wavering (no hesitating, no doubting). For the one who wavers (hesitates, doubts) is like the billowing surge out at sea that is blown hither *and* thither and tossed by the wind.

life point

There are two ways to handle problems—the natural way and the spiritual way. James 1:5, 6 tells how to solve your problems the spiritual way. It says if you have trouble, simply ask God what you should do. You may not receive an answer immediately, but you will find that divine wisdom (wisdom beyond your natural understanding) will begin to operate through you, helping you know what to do.

7 For truly, let not such a person imagine that he will receive anything [he asks for] from the Lord,

8 [For being as he is] a man of two minds (hesitating, dubious, irresolute), [he is] unstable *and* unreliable *and* uncertain about everything [he thinks, feels, decides].

9 Let the brother in humble circumstances glory in his elevation [as a Christian, called to the true riches and to be an heir of God],

10 And the rich [person ought to glory] in being humbled [by being shown his human frailty], because like the flower of the grass he will pass away.

11 For the sun comes up with a scorching heat and parches the grass; its flower falls off and its beauty fades

a Literal translation.

away. Even so will the rich man wither *and* die in the midst of his pursuits.
[Isa. 40:6, 7.]
12 Blessed (happy, [b]to be envied) is
the man who is patient under trial *and*
stands up under temptation, for when
he has stood the test *and* been
approved, he will receive [the victor's]
crown of life which God has promised
to those who love Him.
13 Let no one say when he is tempted, I am tempted from God; for God is
incapable of being tempted by [what
is] evil and He Himself tempts no one.
14 But every person is tempted when
he is drawn away, enticed *and* baited
by his own evil desire (lust, passions).
15 Then the evil desire, when it has
conceived, gives birth to sin, and sin,
when it is fully matured, brings forth
death.
16 Do not be misled, my beloved brethren.
17 Every good gift and every perfect
([c]free, large, full) gift is from above; it
comes down from the Father of all
[that gives] light, in [the shining of]
Whom there can be no variation [ris-
ing or setting] or shadow cast by His
turning [as in an eclipse].
18 And it was of His own [free] will
that He gave us birth [as sons] by
[His] Word of Truth, so that we
should be a kind of firstfruits of His
creatures [a sample of what He created to be consecrated to Himself].

speak the Word

putting the Word to work

James 1:12–15 teaches us about
dealing with temptation. When was the
last time you were tempted? Are you
struggling with temptation right now?
It is important to remember that
temptation—the desire to have or
to do something that you know you
should avoid—never comes from God.
Temptation comes from ungodly desires
within us, and such desires, left
unchecked, lead to sinful actions. When
you are tempted, recognize that God is
not testing you; rather, He wants to give
you strength to overcome the temptation
you are facing. Ask Him to do so.

19 Understand [this], my beloved
brethren. Let every man be quick to
hear [a ready listener], slow to speak,
slow to take offense *and* to get angry.
20 For man's anger does not promote
the righteousness God [wishes and
requires].
21 So get rid of all uncleanness and
the rampant outgrowth of wickedness, and in a humble (gentle, modest) spirit receive *and* welcome the
Word which implanted *and* rooted [in
your hearts] contains the power to
save your souls.
22 But be doers of the Word [obey the
message], and not merely listeners to

*Father, I thank You that every good and perfect gift in my life comes down from
You, and that there is never any variation with You.*
ADAPTED FROM JAMES 1:17

*Help me, Lord, be a ready listener, but slow to speak, slow to take offense, and
slow to get angry.*
ADAPTED FROM JAMES 1:19

---

b Alexander Souter, *Pocket Lexicon of the Greek New Testament.*   **c** Marvin Vincent, *Word Studies in
the New Testament.*

how to walk in the power of God

We see from James 1:21 that the Word has the power to save us from a life of sin, but only as it is received and welcomed in our hearts. When we pay wholehearted attention to God's Word, it becomes implanted and rooted in us.

If you and I are to walk in the power of God, we need to heed the advice of verse 22 to become doers of the Word and not hearers only. Otherwise we deceive ourselves by reasoning that is contrary to the truth.

It is the truth, and the truth alone, that sets us free and keeps us free. In order for it to work in our lives, and in order for us to receive God's promises from the Word, we must be responsible and obedient to the Word. We cannot try to excuse away our sins and weaknesses. Instead, we must become bondservants to God and not to our human nature or to other people or things.

The bottom line is this: God is your Helper. He is your Healer. He has a personalized plan for your life. Make sure you know what it is; then begin to walk in obedience to the truth one step at a time. Obeying the Word requires consistency and diligence. It cannot be "hit and miss." You cannot just try it to see if it works, but you must have a dedication and commitment to obey the Word whatever the outcome.

I encourage you today to keep your mind tuned in to God's Word more than anything else. Let His Word become planted deep into your heart and listen to what it tells you. Obey Him. Then you will be a doer of the Word, not just a hearer of it—and you will walk in the power of God.

it, betraying yourselves [into deception by reasoning contrary to the Truth].

23 For if anyone only listens to the Word without obeying it *and* being a doer of it, he is like a man who looks carefully at his [own] natural face in a mirror;

24 For he thoughtfully observes himself, and then goes off and promptly forgets what he was like.

25 But he who looks carefully into the faultless law, the [law] of liberty, and is faithful to it *and* perseveres in looking into it, being not a heedless listener who forgets but an active doer [who obeys], he shall be blessed in his doing (his life of obedience).

26 If anyone thinks himself to be

life point

It can be difficult to grasp the idea of the "law of liberty" because law and liberty seem to be opposites: A law says one thing, while liberty says another. I believe the law of liberty spoken of in James 1:25 refers to the freedom of self-control, because God puts a new heart in you that *wants* to obey His law of love.

With this new heart that Jesus gave you, you have the ability to be led of the Spirit, Who gives you the power and freedom to love others. Enjoy your day by allowing the Lord to love others through you.

religious (piously observant of the external duties of his faith) and does not bridle his tongue but deludes his own heart, this person's religious service is worthless (futile, barren).

life point

Our words are verbal expressions of our souls. Until our mouths are brought under control and submitted to the Lord, He cannot redeem and restore our souls—our minds, wills, and emotions.

27 External ᵈreligious worship [ᵉreligion as it is expressed in outward acts] that is pure and unblemished in the sight of God the Father is this: to visit and help and care for the orphans and widows in their affliction and need, and to keep oneself unspotted and uncontaminated from the world.

2 MY BRETHREN, pay no servile regard to people [show no prejudice, no partiality]. Do not [attempt to] hold and practice the faith of our Lord Jesus Christ [the Lord] of glory [together with snobbery]!

2 For if a person comes into your congregation whose hands are adorned with gold rings and who is wearing splendid apparel, and also a poor [man] in shabby clothes comes in,

3 And you pay special attention to the one who wears the splendid clothes and say to him, Sit here in this preferable seat! while you tell the poor [man], Stand there! or, Sit there on the floor at my feet!

4 Are you not discriminating among your own and becoming critics and judges with wrong motives?

5 Listen, my beloved brethren: Has not God chosen those who are poor in the eyes of the world to be rich in faith and in their position as believers and to inherit the kingdom which He has promised to those who love Him?

6 But you [in contrast] have insulted (humiliated, dishonored, and shown your contempt for) the poor. Is it not the rich who domineer over you? Is it not they who drag you into the law courts?

7 Is it not they who slander and blaspheme that precious name by which you are distinguished and called [the name of Christ invoked in baptism]?

8 If indeed you [really] fulfill the royal Law in accordance with the Scripture, You shall love your neighbor as [you love] yourself, you do well. [Lev. 19:18.]

9 But if you show servile regard (prejudice, favoritism) for people, you commit sin and are rebuked and convicted by the Law as violators and offenders.

10 For whosoever keeps the Law [as a] whole but stumbles and offends in one [single instance] has become guilty of [breaking] all of it.

11 For He Who said, You shall not commit adultery, also said, You shall not kill. If you do not commit adultery but do kill, you have become guilty of transgressing the [whole] Law. [Exod. 20:13, 14; Deut. 5:17, 18.]

12 So speak and so act as [people should] who are to be judged under the law of liberty [the moral instruction given by Christ, especially about love].

13 For to him who has shown no mercy the judgment [will be] merciless, but mercy [full of glad confidence] exults victoriously over judgment.

---

d Robert Jamieson, A.R. Fausset and David Brown, *A Commentary on the Old and New Testaments*: "Religion in its rise interests us about **ourselves**; in its progress, about our **fellow creatures**; in its highest stage, about the honor of **God**." e G. Abbott-Smith, *Manual Greek Lexicon of the New Testament*.

14 What is the use (profit), my brethren, for anyone to profess to have faith if he has no [good] works [to show for it]? Can [such] faith save [his soul]?

15 If a brother or sister is poorly clad and lacks food for each day,

16 And one of you says to him, Good-bye! Keep [yourself] warm and well fed, without giving him the necessities for the body, what good does that do?

17 So also faith, if it does not have works (deeds and actions of obedience to back it up), by itself is destitute of power (inoperative, dead).

18 But someone will say [to you then], You [say you] have faith, and I have [good] works. Now you show me your [alleged] faith apart from any [good] works [if you can], and I by [good] works [of obedience] will show you my faith.

19 You believe that God is one; you do well. So do the demons believe and shudder [in terror and horror such as fmake a man's hair stand on end and contract the surface of his skin]!

20 Are you willing to be shown [proof], you foolish (unproductive, spiritually deficient) fellow, that faith apart from [good] works is inactive *and* ineffective *and* worthless?

21 Was not our forefather Abraham [shown to be] justified (made acceptable to God) by [his] works when he brought to the altar as an offering his [own] son Isaac? [Gen. 22:1-14.]

22 You see that [his] faith was cooperating with his works, and [his] faith was completed *and* reached its

supreme expression [when he implemented it] by [good] works.

23 And [so] the Scripture was fulfilled that says, Abraham believed in (adhered to, trusted in, and relied on) God, and this was accounted to him as righteousness (as conformity to God's will in thought and deed), and he was called God's friend. [Gen. 15:6; II Chron. 20:7; Isa. 41:8.]

24 You see that a man is justified (pronounced righteous before God) through what he does and not alone through faith [through works of obedience as well as by what he believes].

25 So also with Rahab the harlot—was she not shown to be justified (pronounced righteous before God) by [good] deeds when she took in the scouts (spies) and sent them away by a different route? [Josh. 2:1-21.]

26 For as the human body apart from the spirit is lifeless, so faith apart from [its] works of obedience is also dead.

3 NOT MANY [of you] should become teachers (gself-constituted censors and reprovers of others), my brethren, for you know that we [teachers] will be judged by a higher standard *and* with greater severity [than other people; thus we assume the greater accountability and the more condemnation].

2 For we all often stumble *and* fall *and* offend in many things. And if anyone does not offend in speech [never says the wrong things], he is a fully developed character *and* a

speak the Word

f Marvin Vincent, *Word Studies.*   g John Calvin, cited by Robert Jamieson, A.R. Fausset and David Brown, *A Commentary.*

perfect man, able to control his whole body *and* to curb his entire nature.
3 If we set bits in the horses' mouths to make them obey us, we can turn their whole bodies about.
4 Likewise, look at the ships: though they are so great and are driven by rough winds, they are steered by a very small rudder wherever the impulse of the helmsman determines.
5 Even so the tongue is a little member, and it can boast of great things. See how much wood *or* how great a forest a tiny spark can set ablaze!
6 And the tongue is a fire. [The tongue is a] world of wickedness set among our members, contaminating *and* depraving the whole body and setting on fire the wheel of birth (the cycle of man's nature), being itself ignited by hell (Gehenna).
7 For every kind of beast and bird, of reptile and sea animal, can be tamed and has been tamed by human genius (nature).
8 But the human tongue can be tamed by no man. It is a restless (undisciplined, irreconcilable) evil, full of deadly poison.
9 With it we bless the Lord and Father, and with it we curse men who were made in God's likeness!
10 Out of the same mouth come forth blessing and cursing. These things, my brethren, ought not to be so.
11 Does a fountain send forth [simultaneously] from the same opening fresh water and bitter?
12 Can a fig tree, my brethren, bear olives, or a grapevine figs? Neither can a salt spring furnish fresh water.
13 Who is there among you who is wise and intelligent? Then let him by

speak the Word

life point

James 3:5–10 teaches us about the power of the tongue. There is power in the tongue indeed, for good or evil. We can bless ourselves or curse ourselves by the way we speak. When we bless, we speak well of; when we curse, we speak evil of. By the words of our mouths, you and I can bless our own lives and bring joy to them, or we can curse them and bring misery upon ourselves.

I encourage you to ask God to help you control your tongue. Learn to speak blessing, not cursing. Watch the joy that comes to your life as a result!

his noble living show forth his [good] works with the [unobtrusive] humility [which is the proper attribute] of true wisdom.
14 But if you have bitter jealousy (envy) and contention (rivalry, selfish ambition) in your hearts, do not pride yourselves on it and thus be in defiance of *and* false to the Truth.
15 This [superficial] wisdom is not such as comes down from above, but is earthly, unspiritual (animal), even devilish (demoniacal).
16 For wherever there is jealousy (envy) and contention (rivalry and selfish ambition), there will also be confusion (unrest, disharmony, rebellion) and all sorts of evil *and* vile practices.
17 But the wisdom from above is first of all pure (undefiled); then it is peace-loving, courteous (considerate, gentle). [It is willing to] yield to reason, full of

Thank You, Lord, that the wisdom You give is first pure and undefiled, then peace-loving and courteous. It is willing to yield to reason, full of compassion and good fruits, impartial, free from doubt, unwavering, and sincere.
ADAPTED FROM JAMES **3:17**

the power of the tongue

The Bible says a great deal about the tongue and the words of our mouths. The tongue holds the power of life and death (see Proverbs 18:21). The apostle James said that if any man can control his tongue he is "a fully developed character" and can also control his entire being (see James 3:2). The tongue is a little member of the body, but it causes tremendous problems. Relationships often end because of things that are said or not said. People lose jobs, cause strife and misunderstanding, and embarrass themselves all with that one tiny organ—the tongue.

No man can tame the tongue, so we need God's help. King David prayed that God would put a watch or a guard over his mouth (see Psalm 141:3). He also prayed that the words of his mouth and the meditation of his heart would be acceptable in God's sight (see Psalm 19:14). David knew he could not control his mouth without God's help, and neither can we.

We should avoid all harsh, hard, unjust words (see Isaiah 58:9). Jesus said we must take His yoke upon us and learn of Him because He is gentle, meek, and humble, not harsh, hard, sharp, and pressing (see Matthew 11:29, 30). A gentle tongue (with its healing power) is a tree of life, but willful contrariness in it breaks down the spirit (see Proverbs 15:4). Even the tone of our voice is important because it reveals the condition of our hearts.

We can speak words of healing or words that wound; we can edify and build up or discourage and tear down. Words are containers for power and they carry either positive or negative power. The decision is up to us! Words are seeds that we sow and they definitely bring a harvest in our lives. Those who indulge the tongue must eat the fruit of their words, whether they are for life or death (Proverbs 18:21).

One of the things we should strive to do is think before we speak. The Bible says that we are not to be rash with our mouths, but how many times do we say things and then think, "Oh, I wish I had not said that"? But then it is too late because the words are already doing their work. I recommend a thorough study of all these subjects and a sincere prayer asking for God's help to tame the tongue.

compassion and good fruits; it is wholehearted *and* straightforward, impartial *and* unfeigned (free from doubts, wavering, and insincerity).

18 And the harvest of righteousness (of conformity to God's will in thought and deed) is [the fruit of the seed] sown in peace by those who work for *and* make peace [in themselves and in others, that peace which means con-cord, agreement, and harmony between individuals, with undisturbedness, in a peaceful mind free from fears and agitating passions and moral conflicts].

4 WHAT LEADS to strife (discord and feuds) *and* how do conflicts (quarrels and fightings) originate among you? Do they not arise

from your sensual desires that are ever warring in your bodily members? **2** You are jealous *and* covet [what others have] and your desires go unfulfilled; [so] you become murderers. [To hate is to murder as far as your hearts are concerned.] You burn with envy *and* anger and are not able to obtain [the gratification, the contentment, and the happiness that you seek], so you fight and war. You do not have, because you do not ask. [I John 5:15.] **3** [Or] you do ask [God for them] and yet fail to receive, because you ask with wrong purpose and evil, selfish motives. Your intention is [when you get what you desire] to spend it in sensual pleasures. **4** You [are like] unfaithful wives [having illicit love affairs with the world and breaking your marriage vow to God]! Do you not know that being the world's friend is being God's enemy? So whoever chooses to be a friend of the world takes his stand as an enemy of God. **5** Or do you suppose that the Scripture is speaking to no purpose that says, The Spirit Whom He has caused to dwell in us yearns over us *and* He yearns for the Spirit [to be welcome] with a jealous love? [Jer. 3:14; Hos. 2:19ff.] **6** But He gives us more and more grace ([h]power of the Holy Spirit, to meet this evil tendency and all others fully). That is why He says, God sets Himself against the proud and haughty, but gives grace [continually] to the lowly (those who are humble enough to receive it). [Prov. 3:34.] **7** So be subject to God. Resist the devil [stand firm against him], and he will flee from you. **8** Come close to God and He will come close to you. [Recognize that you are] sinners, get your soiled hands clean; [realize that you have

life point

All human beings have evil tendencies, but James 4:6 teaches us that God will give us more and more grace to deal with these tendencies.

I spent much of my Christian life trying to overcome my own wrong motives and intentions. All my trying brought much frustration. I had to come to a place of humility. I needed to learn that God gives grace to the humble, not the proud (see I Peter 5:5).

We have our own ideas about what we can accomplish, but often we think more highly of ourselves than we ought. We need humble attitudes, knowing that apart from God, we can do nothing.

If you are planning your own way, trying to make things happen in the strength of your own flesh, then no doubt you are frustrated. You probably have said, "No matter what I do, nothing seems to work!" Nothing will ever work until you learn to trust in God's grace.

Relax. Let God be God. Stop being so hard on yourself. Change is a process; it comes little by little. You are on your way to perfection, so enjoy the trip.

been disloyal] wavering individuals with divided interests, and purify your hearts [of your spiritual adultery]. **9** [As you draw near to God] be deeply penitent and grieve, even weep [over your disloyalty]. Let your laughter be turned to grief and your mirth to dejection *and* heartfelt shame [for your sins]. **10** Humble yourselves [feeling very insignificant] in the presence of the Lord, and He will exalt you [He will

[h] Adam Clarke, *The Holy Bible with A Commentary*.

just ask!

I believe James is saying to us in James 4:1, 2, "You stay upset all the time because you try to get all the things you want through your own efforts. You are never going to get them that way. You are just going to end up being jealous, hating people, and having bad relationships because you want what they have."

Then James summarizes the whole situation in one sentence: "You do not have, because you do not ask" (James 4:2). Essentially, he points to how we try to get things ourselves instead of asking God for them.

You may think, "But I *have* asked God for things; He just has not given them to me."

If you ask God for something and He does not give it to you, the reason is not that He is holding out on you. It may be that it is not His will or that now is not His time. It may be that there is something better He wants to give you, but you are not yet spiritually mature enough to have it. Whatever the reason, it is never because He does not want you to be blessed.

You are God's child, and He loves you. He is a good God Who only does good things, and He wants to do for you so much more than you could possibly imagine (see Ephesians 3:20). But He loves you too much to give you something that is going to hurt you. He loves you too much to give you things that will ultimately make you more carnal or more fleshly or that may even drag you into sin because you are not yet ready to handle them.

Does a loving parent give his children the keys to the car before they are old enough to drive? Of course not, because the parent knows they may get hurt in a wreck through their inexperience. God is the same way with His children. Because He loves us, He will not give us something before we have the spiritual maturity to handle it.

Many people use manipulation and worldly ways to get things they have no business having—and those very things end up ruining them.

I have discovered that the secret of being content is to ask God for what I want and to rest in the knowledge that if it is right, He will bring it to pass at the right time. If it is not right, He will do something much better than what I asked for.

lift you up and make your lives significant].

11 [My] brethren, do not speak evil about or accuse one another. He that maligns a brother or judges his brother is maligning *and* criticizing the Law *and* judging the Law. But if you judge the Law, you are not a practicer of the Law but a censor *and* judge [of it].

12 One only is the Lawgiver *and* Judge Who is able to save and to destroy [the One Who has the absolute power of life and death]. [But you] who are you that [you presume to] pass judgment on your neighbor?

13 Come now, you who say, Today or

life point

We must remember that the devil is not going to just sit back and allow us to take new ground without putting up a fight. Any time we make progress in building the kingdom of God, our enemy is going to come against us. But James 4:7 says that he will flee if we submit to God and resist the enemy.

Many times we make the mistake of trying to use faith to get to the place where we have total freedom from trouble. What we do not realize is that the purpose of faith is not always to keep us from having trouble; it is often to carry us *through* trouble. If we never had trouble, we would never need faith.

Although we are tempted to run away from our problems, the Lord says that we are to go through them. The good news is that He promises we will never have to go through them alone. He will always be there to help us in every way. He tells us, "Fear not, for I am with you."

In our daily experience, we must learn to stand our ground and run the devil off our property and drive him out of different areas of our lives. Learning to be stable in hard times is one of the best ways to do this. Remember, the devil will oppose you, but you have the power to resist him—and he will flee!

tomorrow we will go into such *and* such a city and spend a year there and carry on our business and make money.
14 Yet you do not know [the least thing] about what may happen tomorrow. What is the nature of your life? You are [really] but a wisp of vapor (a puff of smoke, a mist) that is visible for a little while and then disappears [into thin air].

putting the Word to work

Do you like to plan excessively? Some people seem to have their lives all figured out. They map out a plan for their career, their family, their retirement years, and their financial portfolios. While it is wise to prepare and plan, the Word of God reminds us that we actually do not know what tomorrow will bring (see James 4:13–15). However, we can depend completely on God, and trust Him fully with our lives. Ask God to continue to reveal His will for your life to you—and be willing to adjust your plans accordingly.

15 You ought instead to say, If the Lord is willing, we shall live and we shall do this or that [thing].
16 But as it is, you boast [falsely] in your presumption *and* your self-conceit. All such boasting is wrong.
17 So any person who knows what is right to do but does not do it, to him it is sin.

5 COME NOW, you rich [people], weep aloud and lament over the miseries (the woes) that are surely coming upon you.
2 Your abundant wealth has rotted *and* is ruined, and your [many] garments have become moth-eaten.

putting the Word to work

Did you know that you can sin by *not* doing something? You can, according to James 4:17. Committing evil deeds is certainly sinful, but so is failing to do what you know God wants you to do. Spend time praying and reading your Bible so you can grow in your understanding of sinful practices to avoid and learn to actively engage in what is pleasing to God.

3 Your gold and silver are completely rusted through, and their rust will be testimony against you and it will devour your flesh as if it were fire. You have heaped together treasure for the last days.

4 [But] look! [Here are] the wages that you have withheld by fraud from the laborers who have reaped your fields, crying out [for vengeance]; and the cries of the harvesters have come to the ears of the Lord of hosts.

5 [Here] on earth you have abandoned yourselves to soft (prodigal) living and to [the pleasures of] self-indulgence *and* self-gratification. You have fattened your hearts in a day of slaughter.

6 You have condemned and have murdered the righteous (innocent man), [while] he offers no resistance to you.

worry-free decisions

After making a decision, stand firm. Let your "yes" be a simple yes and your "no" be a simple no.

I believe indecision and double-mindedness not only bring confusion and complication, but, as James 5:12 noted, they also cause condemnation. If we believe in our hearts that we should do something and then allow our heads to talk us out of it, we leave an open door for condemnation. We often labor over decisions when actually we just need to pray and then follow our hearts.

Start making decisions without worrying about them. Do not live in fear of being wrong. If your heart is right and you make a decision that is not in accordance with God's will, He will forgive you and get you back on course.

Once you do make a decision, do not let self-doubt torment you. Being double-minded and never deciding anything is complicated. Doubting your decisions after they are made will steal the enjoyment from everything you do.

My husband does not mind shopping with me at all, which is a blessing because most men do not enjoy shopping. He gives me a reasonable amount of time to make my choices, but if I go back and forth too many times, he wants to leave. He says, "Do something. I do not mind being here if we make progress, but just wandering around and never making any choices is a waste of time."

This does not mean it is wrong to take a certain amount of time to look things over and search for a good bargain, but if looking and searching go too far, decision-making becomes complicated. Keep it simple. Buy something and move on to the next thing.

Similarly, make decisions in life as simple as you can, whether your decisions are small ones like I just described, or big decisions that affect your future. Be prayerful and seek to obey God; then make a decision and go on without looking back.

7 So be patient, brethren, [as you wait] till the coming of the Lord. See how the farmer waits expectantly for the precious harvest from the land. [See how] he keeps up his patient [vigil] over it until it receives the early and late rains.

8 So you also must be patient. Establish your hearts [strengthen and confirm them in the final certainty], for the coming of the Lord is very near.

9 Do not complain, brethren, against one another, so that you [yourselves] may not be judged. Look! The Judge is [already] standing at the very door.

10 [As] an example of suffering and ill-treatment together with patience, brethren, take the prophets who spoke in the name of the Lord [as His messengers].

life point

Patience is not just the ability to wait; it is the ability to keep a good attitude while waiting.

James 5:7 does not say to be patient *if* you wait; it says to be patient "as you wait." Waiting is part of life. Many people do not "wait well," and yet, we actually spend more time in our lives waiting than we do receiving. Ask God to help you wait well!

11 You know how we call those blessed (happy) who were steadfast [who endured]. You have heard of the endurance of Job, and you have seen the Lord's [purpose and how He

tell the right person

James 5:16 teaches us that confessing our faults to one another aids us in the process of healing and restoration. Many times we receive a release from what is troubling us when we finally tell someone else those things that have been hidden in our lives—sometimes for years. Anything we feel we have to hide has power over us, but when things are exposed, the truth will make us free.

I caution you to use wisdom as you choose a person to confide in. Be Spirit-led. Choose someone you know you can trust—someone who is understanding and will not judge you. Do not share things with people to help yourself if those things will hurt them. For example, if your grandfather abused you forty years ago, and now your grandmother is eighty-five years old, I advise you not to tell her what happened so many years ago. That would not be wise. It might help you to release it, but it would burden her. Instead, find a trusted spiritual leader, minister or counselor.

Using wisdom and balance is so important in these matters. If you are going to share your problems with someone, let God show you who to choose as a confidant. Find a mature believer, someone who will not be burdened or harmed by what you share or use it to hurt you or make you feel worse about yourself.

We do not always need to confess every fault to someone else, but there are times when it is very helpful. I strongly encourage you to follow the biblical instruction to confess your faults to others when you need to in order for you to be healed and restored—just use wisdom as you do.

richly blessed him in the] end, inasmuch as the Lord is full of pity *and* compassion *and* tenderness and mercy. [Job 1:21, 22; 42:10; Ps. 111:4.]

12 But above all [things], my brethren, do not swear, either by heaven or by earth or by any other oath; but let your yes be [a simple] yes, and your no be [a simple] no, so that you may not sin *and* fall under condemnation.

13 Is anyone among you afflicted (ill-treated, suffering evil)? He should pray. Is anyone glad at heart? He should sing praise [to God].

14 Is anyone among you sick? He should call in the church elders (the spiritual guides). And they should pray over him, anointing him with oil in the Lord's name.

15 And the prayer [that is] of faith will save him who is sick, and the Lord will restore him; and if he has committed sins, he will be forgiven.

16 Confess to one another therefore your faults (your slips, your false steps, your offenses, your sins) and pray [also] for one another, that you may be healed *and* restored [to a spiritual tone of mind and heart]. The earnest (heartfelt, continued) prayer of a righteous man makes tremendous power available [dynamic in its working].

17 Elijah was a human being with a nature such as we have [with feelings, affections, and a constitution like ours]; and he prayed earnestly for it not to rain, and no rain fell on the earth for three years and six months. [I Kings 17:1.]

18 And [then] he prayed again and the heavens supplied rain and the land produced its crops [as usual]. [I Kings 18:42-45.]

19 [My] brethren, if anyone among you strays from the Truth *and* falls into error and another [person] brings him back [to God],

20 Let the [latter] one be sure that whoever turns a sinner from his evil course will save [that one's] soul from death and will cover a multitude of sins [iprocure the pardon of the many sins committed by the convert].

---

i Adam Clarke, *The Holy Bible with A Commentary* and many other translators.

First Peter

Author:
Peter

Date:
Early AD Sixties

Everyday Life Principles:
Remember that you always have hope in Jesus.

Live a godly life in the midst of an ungodly world.

Be patient and stay faithful in the midst of suffering.

First Peter is such an encouragement to those of us who believe because it reminds us that we always have hope in Jesus. This letter is full of practical advice for everyday living, especially in the midst of hard times, and urges us to keep the glory of our inheritance in view while we are living here on earth.

First Peter teaches us that there is such a thing as godly suffering. Some suffering is done *in* Christ and some is done *for* Him. When a believer suffers in order to do God's will, that is cause for rejoicing (see I Peter 4:13). Saying no to self and suffering in the flesh leads to the death of selfishness, and that kind of hardship yields tremendous freedom and strength.

First Peter also calls us to develop lifestyles that are holy and pleasing to the Lord. It addresses not only our behavior, but also our intentions, and causes us to examine our hearts so we can operate from pure motives. The words of this book also give us nuggets of truth to fight the spiritual war and overcome the enemy. It exhorts us to remember that everything about our lives is a witness that tells others something about God, that we are to live humble before God and that above all, we are to love one another intensely (see I Peter 4:8).

I hope this book encourages you when you go through trials and difficult times in your life and that it inspires you to develop and maintain godly attitudes and behaviors in every area of your life.

1 PETER, AN apostle (a special messenger) of Jesus Christ, [writing] to the elect exiles of the dispersion scattered (sowed) abroad in Pontus, Galatia, Cappadocia, Asia, and Bithynia,

2 Who were chosen *and* foreknown by God the Father and consecrated (sanctified, made holy) by the Spirit to be obedient to Jesus Christ (the Messiah) and to be sprinkled with [His] blood: May grace (spiritual blessing) and peace be given you in increasing abundance [that spiritual peace to be ᵃrealized in and through Christ, ᵇfreedom from fears, agitating passions, and moral conflicts].

3 Praised (honored, blessed) be the God and Father of our Lord Jesus Christ (the Messiah)! By His boundless mercy we have been born again to an ever-living hope through the resurrection of Jesus Christ from the dead,

life point

When we become born again by accepting Jesus as our Savior, we have an "ever-living hope" in our hearts, according to I Peter 1:3.

4 [Born anew] into an inheritance which is beyond the reach of change *and* decay [imperishable], unsullied and unfading, reserved in heaven for you,

5 Who are being guarded (garrisoned) by God's power through [your] faith [till you fully inherit that ᶜfinal] salvation that is ready to be revealed [for you] in the last time.

6 [You should] be exceedingly glad on this account, though now for a little while you may be distressed by trials *and* suffer temptations,

7 So that [the genuineness] of your faith may be tested, [your faith] which is infinitely more precious than the perishable gold which is tested *and* purified by fire. [This proving of your faith is intended] to redound to [your] praise and glory and honor when Jesus Christ (the Messiah, the Anointed One) is revealed.

8 Without having seen Him, you love Him; though you do not [even] now see Him, you believe in Him and exult *and* thrill with inexpressible and glorious (triumphant, heavenly) joy.

9 [At the same time] you receive the result (outcome, consummation) of your faith, the salvation of your souls.

10 The prophets, who prophesied of the grace (divine blessing) which was intended for you, searched and inquired earnestly about this salvation.

11 They sought [to find out] to whom or when this was to come which the Spirit of Christ working within them was indicating when He predicted the sufferings of Christ and the glories that should follow [them].

12 It was then disclosed to them that the services they were rendering were not meant for themselves *and* their period of time, but for you. [It is these very] things which have now already been made known plainly to you by those who preached the good news (the Gospel) to you by the [same] Holy Spirit sent from heaven. Into these things [the very] angels long to look!

13 So brace up your minds; be sober (circumspect, morally alert); set your hope wholly *and* unchangeably on the grace (divine favor) that is coming to you when Jesus Christ (the Messiah) is revealed.

14 [Live] as children of obedience [to God]; do not conform yourselves to

---

a Hermann Cremer, *Biblico-Theological Lexicon of New Testament Greek.* **b** *Webster's New International Dictionary* offers this as a definition of "peace." **c** Charles B. Williams, *The New Testament: A Translation in the Language of the People.*

the evil desires [that governed you] in your former ignorance [when you did not know the requirements of the Gospel].

15 But as the One Who called you is holy, you yourselves also be holy in all your conduct *and* manner of living.

16 For it is written, You shall be holy, for I am holy. [Lev. 11:44, 45.]

life point

God never tells us to be holy, as I Peter 1:15, 16 instructs, without giving us the help we need to make us that way. An unholy spirit can never make us holy, so God sends His Holy Spirit into our hearts to do a complete and thorough work in us.

17 And if you call upon Him as [your] Father Who judges each one impartially according to what he does, [then] you should conduct yourselves with true reverence throughout the time of your temporary residence [on the earth, whether long or short].

18 You must know (recognize) that you were redeemed (ransomed) from the useless (fruitless) way of living inherited by tradition from [your] forefathers, not with corruptible things [such as] silver and gold,

19 But [you were purchased] with the precious blood of Christ (the Messiah), like that of a [sacrificial] lamb without blemish or spot.

20 It is true that He was chosen *and* foreordained (destined and foreknown for it) before the foundation of the world, but He was brought out to public view (made manifest) in these last days (at the end of the times) for the sake of you.

21 Through Him you believe in (adhere to, rely on) God, Who raised Him up from the dead and gave Him honor *and* glory, so that your faith and hope are [centered and rest] in God.

22 Since by your obedience to the Truth *through the* [*Holy*] *Spirit* you have purified your hearts for the sincere affection of the brethren, [see that you] love one another fervently from a *pure* heart.

23 You have been regenerated (born again), not from a mortal [d]origin ([e]seed, sperm), but from one that is immortal by the *ever* living and lasting Word of God.

life point

The Holy Spirit, according to I Peter 1:22, is the One Who purifies our hearts so we can allow the sincere love of God to flow through us to others. The Holy Spirit's aim is to get us to the place where the sincere love of God flows through us, which helps us to "ever be filled with the Holy Spirit" (see Ephesians 5:18).

Walking in the love of God is the ultimate goal of Christianity, and should be the primary pursuit of our lives. We should keep our love for Jesus red-hot! We should also have a fervent love for one another (see I Peter 4:8). Jesus Himself instructed us to love one another as He loves us (see John 15:12). He said that was the new commandment He came to pronounce and that all other commandments are summed up in the exhortation to love God and to love other people (see John 13:34; Matthew 22:37–40).

When I think of what I can do for myself or how I can get others to bless me, I am filled with me. When I think of other people and how I can bless them, I find myself filled with the Holy Spirit, Who is the Spirit of love.

d Joseph Thayer, *A Greek-English Lexicon of the New Testament*. **e** G. Abbott-Smith, *Manual Greek Lexicon of the New Testament*.

24 For all flesh (mankind) is like grass, and all its glory (honor) like [the] flower of grass. The grass withers and the flower drops off,

25 But the Word of the Lord ([f]divine instruction, the Gospel) endures forever. And this Word is the good news which was preached to you. [Isa. 40:6-9.]

2 SO BE done with every trace of wickedness (depravity, malignity) and all deceit and insincerity (pretense, hypocrisy) and grudges (envy, jealousy) and slander *and* evil speaking of every kind.

2 Like newborn babies you should crave (thirst for, earnestly desire) the pure (unadulterated) spiritual milk, that by it you may be nurtured *and* grow unto [completed] salvation,

3 Since you have [already] tasted the goodness *and* kindness of the Lord. [Ps. 34:8.]

4 Come to Him [then, to that] Living Stone which men [g]tried *and* threw away, but which is chosen [and] precious in God's sight. [Ps. 118:22; Isa. 28:16.]

5 [Come] and, like living stones, be yourselves built [into] a spiritual house, for a holy (dedicated, consecrated) priesthood, to offer up [those] spiritual sacrifices [that are] acceptable *and* pleasing to God through Jesus Christ.

6 For thus it stands in Scripture: Behold, I am laying in Zion a chosen ([g]honored), precious chief Cornerstone, and he who believes in Him [who adheres to, trusts in, and relies

life point

Like "living stones" (I Peter 2:5) we are to live dedicated, consecrated lives that include spiritual sacrifices, but only the kind that are pleasing and acceptable to God. The only ones that are pleasing and acceptable to God are those done with the right motives, such as a desire to express our love for Him or a desire to honor Him and thank Him for what He has done for us.

on Him] shall never be [f]disappointed *or* put to shame. [Isa. 28:16.]

7 To you then who believe (who adhere to, trust in, and rely on Him) is the preciousness; but for those who disbelieve [it is true], The [very] Stone which the builders rejected has become the main Cornerstone, [Ps. 118:22.]

8 And, A Stone that will cause stumbling and a Rock that will give [men] offense; they stumble because they disobey *and* disbelieve [God's] Word, as those [who reject Him] were destined (appointed) to do.

9 But you are a chosen race, a royal priesthood, a dedicated nation, [God's] own [h]purchased, special people, that you may set forth the wonderful deeds *and* display the virtues and perfections of Him Who called you out of darkness into His marvelous light. [Exod. 19:5, 6.]

10 Once you were not a people [at all], but now you are God's people; once you were unpitied, but now you

speak the Word

---

f Joseph Thayer, *A Greek-English Lexicon.*   **g** Marvin Vincent, *Word Studies in the New Testament.* **h** John Wycliffe, *The Wycliffe Bible.*

are pitied *and* have received mercy. [Hos. 2:23.]

11 Beloved, I implore you as aliens and strangers *and* exiles [in this world] to abstain from the sensual urges (the evil desires, the passions of the flesh, your lower nature) that wage war against the soul.

12 Conduct yourselves properly (honorably, righteously) among the Gentiles, so that, although they may slander you as evildoers, [yet] they may by witnessing your good deeds [come to] glorify God in the day of inspection [ʲwhen God shall look upon you wanderers as a pastor or shepherd looks over his flock].

13 Be submissive to every human institution *and* authority for the sake of the Lord, whether it be to the emperor as supreme,

14 Or to governors as sent by him to bring vengeance (punishment, justice) to those who do wrong and to encourage those who do good service.

15 For it is God's will *and* intention that by doing right [your good and honest lives] should silence (muzzle, gag) the ignorant charges *and* ill-informed criticisms of foolish persons.

16 [Live] as free people, [yet] without employing your freedom as a pretext for wickedness; but [live at all times] as servants of God.

17 Show respect for all men [treat them honorably]. Love the brotherhood (the Christian fraternity of which Christ is the Head). Reverence God. Honor the emperor.

18 [You who are] household servants, be submissive to your masters with all [proper] respect, not only to those who are kind and considerate *and* reasonable, but also to those who are surly (overbearing, unjust, and crooked).

19 For one is regarded favorably (is approved, acceptable, and thankwor-thy) if, as in the sight of God, he endures the pain of unjust suffering.

20 [After all] what ʲkind of glory [is there in it] if, when you do wrong and are punished for it, you take it patiently? But if you bear patiently with suffering [which results] when you do right *and* that is undeserved, it is acceptable *and* pleasing to God.

21 For even to this were you called [it is inseparable from your vocation]. For Christ also suffered for you, leaving you [His personal] example, so that you should follow in His footsteps.

22 He was guilty of no sin, neither was deceit (guile) ever found on His lips. [Isa. 53:9.]

23 When He was reviled *and* insulted, He did not revile *or* offer insult in return; [when] He was abused *and* suffered, He made no threats [of vengeance]; but he trusted [Himself and everything] to Him Who judges fairly.

24 He personally bore our sins in His [own] body on the tree ᵏ[as on an altar and offered Himself on it], that we might die (cease to exist) to sin and live to righteousness. By His wounds you have been healed.

25 For you were going astray like [so many] sheep, but now you have come back to the Shepherd and Guardian (ʲthe Bishop) of your souls. [Isa. 53:5, 6.]

3 IN LIKE manner, you married women, be submissive to your own husbands [subordinate yourselves as being secondary to and dependent on them, and adapt yourselves to them], so that even if any do not obey the Word [of God], they may be won over not by discussion but by the [godly] lives of their wives,

2 When they observe the pure *and* modest way in which you conduct yourselves, together with your

---

i J. Rawson Lumby, cited by *Speaker's Commentary*.   **j** Literal translation.   **k** Marvin Vincent, *Word Studies*.

it's all in your attitude

Suffering is one of the most difficult things to understand in life and in Christianity. We know that God is good and we know that He sees everything and is all powerful, but why does He allow us to suffer, especially unjustly? This question has been asked by millions throughout the ages: "Why, God? Why?"

God does not delight in our suffering, but He is honored and pleased when we endure it with a good attitude (see I Peter 2:19, 20). Trust requires unanswered questions. If we knew all the answers, faith would not even be necessary.

Some people become angry at God when tragedy or extreme difficulty comes their way. This is the worst thing anyone can do because He is the only One Who can help us. One man I know endured the tragic experience of watching his only son die of cancer. Afterward, he bitterly asked God, "Where were you when my son died?" God replied, "The same place I was when Mine died."

God gave His only Son and allowed Him to go through unspeakable suffering that He did not deserve, and He did it for us. There are times when we go through things that God intends to use for our good and the good of others later in our lives.

During my childhood, I was abused for many years. I prayed and prayed, but no deliverance came. I did receive strength to endure and a determination to overcome and to someday do something great with my life. Many character traits developed in me during those years that have greatly helped me in the ministry I have today. One of them is that I truly can relate to people who have been hurt by others. I can teach from experience how important it is to forgive our enemies and help people know how to do it. Suffering can make us bitter or better; the decision is ours!

The true test of faith is how we behave during trials and tribulations, especially ones we feel are totally unfair. Peter said that fiery ordeals will come to test the quality of our faith and that we are not to be amazed and bewildered (see I Peter 4:12, 13). Instead of being concerned about *why* you suffer, just make a decision to get through it with a good attitude and you will see God work everything together for good (see Romans 8:28).

[l]reverence [for your husband; you are to feel for him all that reverence includes: to respect, defer to, revere him—to honor, esteem, appreciate, prize, and, in the human sense, to adore him, that is, to admire, praise, be devoted to, deeply love, and enjoy your husband].

3 Let not yours be the [merely] external adorning with [elaborate] [m]interweaving *and* knotting of the hair, the wearing of jewelry, or changes of clothes;
4 But let it be the inward adorning *and* beauty of the hidden person of

---

l Joseph Thayer, *A Greek-English Lexicon*.   m Joseph Thayer, *A Greek-English Lexicon*.

the hidden person of the heart

First Peter 3:4 talks about "the hidden person of the heart," which means who a person really is underneath his or her appearance. When we interact with others, we should endeavor to know who they really are, in their hearts, and not make hasty judgments against them or judge them according to their appearance. When we do not endeavor to know the "hidden man of the heart," we make a mistake in one of two ways: 1) we approve of someone because they appear to be something they are not; or 2) we disapprove of someone because of some outward appearance or action, when that individual is actually a wonderful person on the inside.

I have found that we all have our little quirks and our little odd actions, behaviors, and ways that other people do not easily understand. God Himself does not judge by appearance, and we need to follow His example (see I Samuel 16:7).

David would have never been chosen by man to be king unless God looked on the heart. Even his own family disregarded him. They did not even include him in the selection process (see I Samuel 19:1–13)! But the Lord saw David's heart, the heart of a shepherd. God saw a worshiper, someone with a heart for Him—someone who was pliable and moldable in His hand. These are the qualities He looks for in us.

I often think of the geodes—crude, ugly-looking rocks that appear hideous on the outside, but are absolutely gorgeous on the inside. Some are actually gemstones inside, but their rough, crusty exteriors are terribly unattractive.

Like the geodes, we are often rough, crusty, and crude on the outside, but God knows that He has placed such beauty within us. Just as the gold miner knows he must be patient when digging for gold, God knows He must be patient with us as the Holy Spirit continues working with us, digging in our lives, and eventually bringing out the treasures that are within us.

What we sow into the lives of other people, we will surely reap in our own. If we sow harsh, hasty judgment, we will in turn reap harsh, hasty judgment. So, when the temptation to judge or criticize is at the door, resist it. Instead, do your best to look for the best in others and see what God values about each one—the hidden man of the heart.

I also remind you to examine your own heart and be sure you have right motives and heart attitudes. Our secret thoughts and attitudes should be godly. We may hide from other people what is going on inside of us, but we cannot hide anything from God. Our outer man is our reputation with people, but the hidden man of the heart is our reputation with God. We should be much more concerned about our reputation in heaven than our reputation on earth.

the heart, with the incorruptible *and* unfading charm of a gentle and peaceful spirit, which [is not anxious or wrought up, but] is very precious in the sight of God.

5 For it was thus that the pious women of old who hoped in God were [accustomed] to beautify themselves and were submissive to their husbands [adapting themselves to them as themselves secondary and dependent upon them].

6 It was thus that Sarah obeyed Abraham [following his guidance and acknowledging his headship over her by] calling him lord (master, leader, authority). And you are now her true daughters if you do right and let nothing terrify you [not giving way to hysterical fears or letting anxieties unnerve you].

7 In the same way you married men should live considerately with [your wives], with an ⁿintelligent recognition [of the marriage relation], honoring the woman as [physically] the weaker, but [realizing that you] are joint heirs of the grace (God's unmerited favor) of life, in order that your prayers may not be hindered *and* cut off. [Otherwise you cannot pray effectively.]

8 Finally, all [of you] should be of one *and* the same mind (united in spirit), sympathizing [with one another], loving [each other] as brethren [of one household], compassionate *and* courteous (tenderhearted and humble).

9 Never return evil for evil or insult for insult (scolding, tongue-lashing, berating), but on the contrary blessing [praying for their welfare, happiness, and protection, and truly pitying and loving them]. For *know that* to this you have been called, that you may yourselves inherit a blessing [from God— that you may obtain a blessing as heirs, bringing welfare and happiness and protection].

10 For let him who wants to enjoy life and see good days [good—whether apparent or not] keep his tongue free from evil and his lips from guile (treachery, deceit).

life point

If we want to enjoy life, which is possible even when there is no apparent reason for us to enjoy life, we must keep our tongues free from evil (see I Peter 3:10). If we speak positively and keep the truth of God's Word on our lips, we will have joy even in the midst of difficulties.

11 Let him turn away from wickedness *and* shun it, and let him do right. Let him search for peace (harmony; undisturbedness from fears, agitating passions, and moral conflicts) and seek it eagerly. [Do not merely desire peaceful relations with God, with your fellowmen, and with yourself, but pursue, go after them!]

12 For the eyes of the Lord are upon the righteous (those who are upright and in right standing with God), and His ears are attentive to their prayer. But the face of the Lord is against those who practice evil [to oppose them, to frustrate, and defeat them]. [Ps. 34:12-16.]

13 Now who is there to hurt you if you are °zealous followers of that which is good?

14 But even in case you should suffer for the sake of righteousness, [you are] blessed (happy, to be envied). Do not dread *or* be afraid of their threats, nor be disturbed [by their opposition].

15 But in your hearts set Christ apart as holy [and acknowledge Him] as Lord. Always be ready to give a logical defense to anyone who asks you to

---

n Marvin Vincent, *Word Studies*.   **o** Best manuscripts read "zealous."

account for the hope that is in you, but do it courteously and respectfully. [Isa. 8:12, 13.]

16 [And see to it that] your conscience is entirely clear (ᵖunimpaired), so that, when you are falsely accused as evil-doers, those who threaten you abusively *and* revile your right behavior in Christ may come to be ashamed [of slandering your good lives].

17 For [it is] better to suffer [unjustly] for doing right, if that should be God's will, than to suffer [justly] for doing wrong.

18 For Christ [the Messiah Himself] died for sins once ᵍfor all, the Righteous for the unrighteous (the Just for the unjust, the Innocent for the guilty), that He might bring us to God. In His human body He was put to death, but He was made alive in the spirit,

19 In which He went and preached to the spirits in prison,

20 [The souls of those] who long before in the days of Noah had been disobedient, when God's patience waited during the building of the ark in which a few [people], actually eight in number, were saved through water. [Gen. 6-8.]

21 And baptism, which is a figure [of their deliverance], does now also save you [from inward questionings and fears], not by the removing of outward body filth [bathing], but by [providing you with] the answer of a good and clear conscience (inward cleanness and peace) before God [because you are demonstrating what you believe to be yours] through the resurrection of Jesus Christ.

22 [And He] has now entered into heaven and is at the right hand of God, with [all] angels and authorities and powers made subservient to Him.

4

SO, SINCE Christ suffered in the flesh ʳ*for us, for you*, arm yourselves with the same thought *and* ˢpurpose [patiently to suffer rather than fail to please God]. For whoever has suffered in the flesh [having ᵗthe mind of Christ] is done with [intentional] sin [has stopped pleasing himself and the world, and pleases God],

2 So that he can no longer spend the rest of his natural life living by [his] human appetites *and* desires, but [he lives] for what God wills.

life point

First Peter 4:1, 2 helps us know how to face suffering. "Suffering" and "sacrifice" are not always popular words among Christians, but they are biblical words. Spiritual maturity or "Christlikeness" cannot be obtained without dying to self, which simply means saying yes to God and no to our flesh when our will and God's will are in opposition.

3 For the time that is past already suffices for doing what the Gentiles like to do—living [as you have done] in shameless, insolent wantonness, in lustful desires, drunkenness, reveling, drinking bouts *and* abominable, lawless idolatries.

4 They are astonished *and* think it very queer that you do not now run hand in hand with them in the same excesses of dissipation, and they abuse [you].

5 But they will have to give an account to Him Who is ready to judge *and* pass sentence on the living and the dead.

6 For this is why the good news (the

---

p Marvin Vincent, *Word Studies*.   **q** Joseph Thayer, *A Greek-English Lexicon*.   **r** Some ancient manuscripts read "for us," while some "for you."   **s** G. Abbott-Smith, *Manual Greek Lexicon*.   **t** *The Cambridge Bible for Schools and Colleges*.

have fervent love

One of the most amazing things I have ever learned—a lesson that still thrills my soul—is that love is actually spiritual warfare. This truth makes spiritual warfare fun, because loving people is very enjoyable.

I have learned that instead of looking like I am "oppressed and under something" all the time, I can actually look happy. I have found that I can be *on* the attack instead of *under* the attack.

First Peter 4:8 teaches us to have "intense and unfailing love for one another." The King James Version translates this verse to say that we are to have "fervent love" for one another. The verb form of the Greek word that is translated *fervent* means, "to be hot, to boil." Our love walk needs to be hot, on fire, and boiling over; not tepid, cold, or barely noticeable.

I once heard someone say that even a fly is smart enough to know not to land on a hot stove. If we are hot enough with love, Satan cannot stay around us for long. We might say we will be "too hot to handle!"

Have you ever let something cook in the microwave for too long and found yourself unable to remove it from the oven because it was too hot to handle? That is the way I want to be. I want the love of God in my heart to be so red-hot that Satan dreads to see me get out of bed in the morning!

Let your love be red-hot. Let it be fervent toward God and toward other people, and as you do, you will not only live in obedience to the Word, you will also be too hot and on fire with God's love for the enemy to handle.

Gospel) was preached [[u]in their lifetime] even to the dead, that though judged in fleshly bodies as men are, they might live in the spirit as God does.

7 But the end *and* culmination of all things has now come near; keep sound minded *and* self-restrained and alert therefore for [the practice of] prayer.

8 Above all things have intense *and* unfailing love for one another, for love covers a multitude of sins [forgives and [v]disregards the offenses of others]. [Prov. 10:12.]

9 Practice hospitality to one another (those of the household of faith). [Be hospitable, be a lover of strangers, with brotherly affection for the unknown guests, the foreigners, the poor, and all others who come your way who are of Christ's body.] And [in each instance] do it ungrudgingly (cordially and graciously, without complaining but as representing Him).

10 As each of you has received a gift (a particular spiritual talent, a gracious divine endowment), employ it for one another as [befits] good trustees of God's many-sided grace [faithful stewards of the [v]extremely

---

u Most commentators interpret this preaching to be a past event, done not after these people had died, but while they were still alive.   v Joseph Thayer, *A Greek-English Lexicon.*

the Spirit of glory

First Peter 4:14 states that the Spirit of God and the Spirit of glory is resting upon us when we are reproached for the name of Christ. Just imagine: We think it is awful when people mistreat us because we are Christians, but God sees it in an entirely different light. God never expects us to suffer for Him without His help. Therefore, we can firmly believe that any time we are reproached or mistreated because of our faith in Christ, God gives us an extra measure of His Spirit to counterbalance the attack.

The Holy Spirit often acts as a shock absorber. Automobiles have shock absorbers to soften the blow of unexpected potholes in the road. The road of life is full of potholes, but God softens the blow and actually comforts us in all of our difficult times.

People who are not serving God and trusting Him to meet their needs sometimes look and act as if they are much older than they actually are. Their faces show the strain of the years they have lived without the Holy Spirit's help and protection. Their attitudes are sour, due to years of adversity. They often become bitter because they have deemed life unfair. They do not realize that their lives would be different if they had served God and leaned on His Spirit to guide and protect them.

Many times in my life I was reproached for the name of Christ, but now I know that the Spirit of glory was always upon me. Right in the middle of attack and adversity, God kept making my life better and better. He loves to take a mess and make something glorious out of it.

If you ask Him, He will take your mess and turn it into your ministry. When the Spirit of glory is upon you and within you, you can help others who face the same kinds of things God has helped you overcome. Your burden can become your blessing, and your weakness can become your weapon.

diverse powers and gifts granted to Christians by unmerited favor].

11 Whoever speaks, [let him do it as one who utters] oracles of God; whoever renders service, [let him do it] as with the strength which God furnishes [w]abundantly, so that in all things God may be glorified through Jesus Christ (the Messiah). To Him be the glory and dominion forever and ever (through endless ages). Amen (so be it).

12 Beloved, do not be amazed *and* bewildered at the fiery ordeal which is taking place to test your quality, as though something strange (unusual and alien to you and your position) were befalling you.

13 But insofar as you are sharing Christ's sufferings, rejoice, so that when His glory [full of radiance and splendor] is revealed, you may also rejoice with triumph [exultantly].

14 If you are censured *and* suffer abuse [because you bear] the name of

w Joseph Thayer, *A Greek-English Lexicon*.

Christ, blessed [are you—happy, fortunate, ˣto be envied, ʸwith life-joy, and satisfaction in God's favor and salvation, regardless of your outward condition], because the Spirit of glory, the Spirit of God, is resting upon you. *On their part He is blasphemed, but on your part He is glorified.* [Isa. 11:2.]

15 But let none of you suffer as a murderer or a thief or any sort of criminal, or as a mischief-maker (a meddler) in the affairs of others [infringing on their rights].

16 But if [one is ill-treated and suffers] as a Christian [which he is contemptuously called], let him not be ashamed, but give glory to God that he is [deemed worthy to suffer] in this name.

17 For the time [has arrived] for judgment to begin with the household of God; and if it begins with us, what will [be] the end of those who do not respect *or* believe *or* obey the good news (the Gospel) of God?

18 And if the righteous are barely saved, what will become of the godless and wicked? [Prov. 11:31.]

19 Therefore, those who are ill-treated *and* suffer in accordance with God's will must do right and commit their souls [in charge as a deposit] to the One Who created [them] and will never fail [them].

5 I WARN *and* counsel the elders among you (the pastors and spiritual guides of the church) as a fellow elder and as an eyewitness [called to testify] of the sufferings of Christ, as well as a sharer in the glory (the honor and splendor) that is to be revealed (disclosed, unfolded):

2 Tend (nurture, guard, guide, and fold) the flock of God that is [your responsibility], not by coercion *or* constraint, but willingly; not dishonorably motivated by the advantages *and* profits [belonging to the office], but eagerly *and* cheerfully;

3 Not domineering [as arrogant, dictatorial, and overbearing persons] over those in your charge, but being examples (patterns and models of Christian living) to the flock (the congregation).

4 And [then] when the Chief Shepherd is revealed, you will win the ᶻconqueror's crown of glory.

5 Likewise, you who are younger *and* of lesser rank, be subject to the elders (the ministers and spiritual guides of the church)—[giving them due respect and yielding to their counsel]. Clothe (apron) yourselves, all of you, with humility [as the garb of a servant, ᵃso that its covering

putting the Word to work

To humble yourself "under the mighty hand of God, that in due time He may exalt you" (I Peter 5:6) means to ask the Lord for what you need and then wait on Him to provide as He sees fit, knowing that His timing is always perfect. Are you humbling yourself under His hand in every situation of your life and trusting that He knows what is best for you? He has great plans for you, so I encourage you to be still, stop striving, and allow Him to show you how to cooperate with His purposes for you.

Also, be sure to cast all your cares upon the Lord (see I Peter 5:7). Do not worry about anything because staying peaceful is actually proof that you have humbled yourself and that you trust God to do what needs to be done.

---

x Alexander Souter, *Pocket Lexicon of the Greek New Testament.*   **y** Hermann Cremer, *Biblico-Theological Lexicon.*   **z** Marvin Vincent, *Word Studies*: When Paul uses the word translated "crown," he typically has the conqueror's crown in mind, using the imagery of the winner of an athletic contest (see I Cor. 9:25). Peter seems to have this same imagery in mind as a symbol of the heavenly reward.   **a** Johann Bengel, *Gnomon Novi Testamenti.*

keep your balance

Maintaining balance in all things is so important! If we do not, we open a door to Satan, who roams around hungrily seeking to devour us (see I Peter 5:8). I want to share some thoughts that will help you stay balanced in one particular area of your life—your self-image. Of course, there are many other aspects of life that need to be kept in balance as well, but I want to focus first on self-image because it is such a foundational issue.

In order to develop a balanced, healthy, God-centered self-image, incorporate the thoughts below into the way you think about yourself.

1. I know God created me, and He loves me.
2. I have faults and weaknesses, and I want to change. I believe God is working in my life. He is changing me bit-by-bit, day-by-day. While He is working on me, I can still enjoy my life and myself.
3. Everyone has faults, so I am not a failure just because I am not perfect.
4. I am going to work with God to overcome my weaknesses, but I realize that I will always have something to deal with; therefore, I will not become discouraged when God convicts me of areas of my life that need improvement.
5. I want to make people happy and have them like me, but my sense of worth is not dependent upon what others think of me. Jesus has already affirmed my value by His willingness to die for me.
6. I will not be controlled by what other people think, say or do. Even if they totally reject me, I will survive. God has promised never to reject or condemn me as long as I keep believing (see John 6:29).
7. No matter how often I fail, I will not give up because God is with me to strengthen and sustain me. He has promised never to leave me or forsake me (see Hebrews 13:5).
8. I like myself. I do not like everything I do, and I want to change—but I refuse to reject myself.
9. I am right with God through Jesus Christ.
10. God has a good plan for my life. I am going to fulfill my destiny and be all I can be for His glory. I have God-given gifts and talents, and I intend to use them to help others.
11. I am nothing, and yet I am everything! In myself I am nothing, and yet in Jesus I am everything I need to be.
12. I can do everything God calls me to do, through His Son Jesus Christ (see Philippians 4:13).

As I mentioned, there are many other areas where we should strive for balance. We should maintain the balance of work and rest, eat a balanced diet, never spend more than we earn, and enjoy people but also have solitude. Although we want to please people and have their approval we must put God and His will first in our lives at all times.

If we do not maintain balance in our lives, Satan will take advantage of the door we have opened. Check your life and if you find areas out of balance, ask God to help you make whatever adjustments are necessary.

cannot possibly be stripped from you, with freedom from pride and arrogance] toward one another. For God sets Himself against the proud (the insolent, the overbearing, the disdainful, the presumptuous, the boastful) — [and He opposes, frustrates, and defeats them], but gives grace (favor, blessing) to the humble. [Prov. 3:34.]

6 Therefore humble yourselves [demote, lower yourselves in your own estimation] under the mighty hand of God, that in due time He may exalt you,

7 Casting the ᵇwhole of your care [all your anxieties, all your worries, all your concerns, ᵇonce and for all] on Him, for He cares for you affectionately *and* cares about you ᵇwatchfully. [Ps. 55:22.]

8 Be well balanced (temperate, sober of mind), be vigilant *and* cautious at all times; for that enemy of yours, the devil, roams around like a lion roaring [ᵇin fierce hunger], seeking someone to seize upon *and* devour.

9 Withstand him; be firm in faith [against his onset—rooted, established, strong, immovable, and determined], knowing that the same (ᵇidentical) sufferings are appointed to your brotherhood (the whole body of Christians) throughout the world.

10 And after you have suffered a little while, the God of all grace [Who imparts all blessing and favor], Who has called you to His [own] eternal glory in Christ *Jesus,* will Himself complete *and* make you what you ought to be, establish *and* ground you securely, and strengthen, and settle you.

11 To Him be the dominion (power, authority, rule) forever and ever. Amen (so be it).

12 By Silvanus, a true (loyal, consistent, incorruptible) brother, as I consider him, I have written briefly to you, to counsel *and* urge *and* stimulate [you] and to declare [to you] that this is the true [account of the] grace (the undeserved favor) of God. Be steadfast *and* persevere in it.

13 She [your sister church here] in Babylon, [who is] elect (chosen) with [yourselves], sends you greetings, and [so does] my son (disciple) Mark.

14 Salute one another with a kiss of love [the symbol of mutual affection]. To all of you that are in Christ *Jesus* (the Messiah), may there be peace (ᶜevery kind of peace and blessing, especially peace with God, and ᵈfreedom from fears, agitating passions, and moral conflicts). *Amen (so be it).*

---

b Marvin Vincent, *Word Studies.* **c** Joseph Thayer, *A Greek-English Lexicon.* **d** *Webster's New International Dictionary* offers this as a definition of "peace."

Second Peter

Author:
Peter

Date:
AD 65–68

Everyday Life Principles:
Be on guard and do not be deceived.

Study and seek to know the truth.

Be a lifetime learner of the truth of God.

Second Peter was written to people who either did not know the truth of God or were not standing firm in it, so they were in danger of being deceived concerning the second coming of Jesus Christ. The Bible exhorts us in several places in the New Testament not to be deceived. We are living in a day when deception is all around us—and it will only increase as we draw nearer to Jesus' second coming. The only way to avoid being deceived is to *know* the truth for yourself. People who think they "know it all" fall into deception.

Let the book of II Peter cause you to make a fresh commitment to being a victorious Christian and a "lifetime learner," one who continually seeks and studies the truth of God's Word. Do not simply listen to other people, but be convinced for yourself. Study and read on your own; do not just take second-hand information. Stay close to the Word of God. Pray that you will not be deceived, and do whatever it takes to make sure you have accurate knowledge of the Bible. As you pursue deeper and deeper knowledge of the truth, let me encourage you with the words Peter used to close this letter: "But grow in grace (undeserved favor, spiritual strength) and recognition and knowledge and understanding of our Lord and Savior Jesus Christ (the Messiah). To Him [be] glory (honor, majesty, and splendor) both now and to the day of eternity" (II Peter 3:18).

1 SIMON PETER, a servant and apostle (special messenger) of Jesus Christ, to those who have received (obtained an equal privilege of) like precious faith with ourselves in *and* through the righteousness of our God and Savior Jesus Christ:

2 May grace (God's favor) and peace (which is [a]perfect well-being, all necessary good, all spiritual prosperity, and [b]freedom from fears and agitating passions and moral conflicts) be multiplied to you in [the full, personal, [c]precise, and correct] knowledge of God and of Jesus our Lord.

3 For His divine power has bestowed upon us all things that [are requisite and suited] to life and godliness, through the [[d]full, personal] knowledge of Him Who called us by *and* to His own glory and excellence (virtue).

4 By means of these He has bestowed on us His precious and exceedingly great promises, so that through them you may escape [by flight] from the moral decay (rottenness and corruption) that is in the world because of covetousness (lust and greed), and become sharers (partakers) of the divine nature.

5 For this very reason, [d]adding your diligence [to the divine promises],

employ every effort in [e]exercising your faith to develop virtue (excellence, resolution, Christian energy), and in [exercising] virtue [develop] knowledge (intelligence),

6 And in [exercising] knowledge [develop] self-control, and in [exercising] self-control [develop] steadfastness (patience, endurance), and in [exercising] steadfastness [develop] godliness (piety),

7 And in [exercising] godliness [develop] brotherly affection, and in [exercising] brotherly affection [develop] Christian love.

8 For as these qualities are yours and increasingly abound in you, they will keep [you] from being idle or unfruitful unto the [e]full personal]

speak the Word

a Matthew Henry, *Commentary on the Holy Bible.*   **b** *Webster's New International Dictionary* offers this as a definition of "peace."   **c** Joseph Thayer, *A Greek-English Lexicon of the New Testament.*   **d** Marvin Vincent, *Word Studies in the New Testament.*   **e** Marvin Vincent, *Word Studies.*

everything we need

According to II Peter 1:3, God's power provides everything we need to enjoy great and godly lives, but what He provides comes to us through the full, personal knowledge of Him. We cannot know God through someone else. We can know about Him through others, but to know Him for ourselves we must study His Word ourselves and spend time with Him individually.

You can be as close to God as you want to be. He is no respecter of persons and if one person can have a close, intimate relationship with Him, then so can everyone else. Why do some people seem so close to God and yet others do not? I believe it all depends on how much time we are willing to put into developing our personal relationship with Him.

Going to church does not necessarily make us close to God. Going to church is a good and right thing to do, but we need more than an hour on Sunday morning with God if we are going to learn enough to fulfill our destiny and truly enjoy life.

Second Peter 1:3 tells us that God calls us to His own glory and excellence. Wow! He wants us to have excellent lives, but He also expects us to learn how to behave excellently. Finding the strength to do so only comes as we wait on Him. They that wait upon the Lord shall change and renew their strength (see Isaiah 40:31), and spending time in God's Word teaches us right from wrong. The Bible gives many instructions about how to behave with people and in certain circumstances. It teaches us to be excellent and to go the extra mile and do whatever we do as best we can and unto the Lord.

I once heard, "If you do not read, you will be the same in five years as you are now." That is certainly true where the Bible is concerned. As we study God's Word, we are transformed into His image, from glory to glory (see II Corinthians 3:18).

Make a commitment of time to God and I believe you will see the life and power that is available to you through His promises. Be a lifetime learner. Refuse to have a second-hand relationship with God; get to know Him for yourself.

knowledge of our Lord Jesus Christ (the Messiah, the Anointed One).

9 For whoever lacks these qualities is blind, [[f]spiritually] shortsighted, [g]seeing only what is near to him, and has become oblivious [to the fact] that he was cleansed from his old sins.

10 Because of this, brethren, be all the more solicitous *and* eager to make sure (to ratify, to strengthen, to make steadfast) your calling and election; for if you do this, you will never stumble *or* fall.

11 Thus there will be richly *and* abundantly provided for you entry into the eternal kingdom of our Lord and Savior Jesus Christ.

12 So I intend always to remind you

f Marvin Vincent, *Word Studies in the New Testament.*   **g** Joseph P. Rotherham, *The Emphasized Bible.*

about these things, although indeed you know them and are firm in the truth that [you] now [hold].

13 I think it right, as long as I am in this tabernacle (tent, body), to stir you up by way of remembrance,

14 Since I know that the laying aside of this body of mine will come speedily, as our Lord Jesus Christ made clear to me.

15 Moreover, I will diligently endeavor [to see to it] that [even] after my departure (decease) you may be able at all times to call these things to mind.

16 For we were not following cleverly devised stories when we made known to you the power and coming of our Lord Jesus Christ (the Messiah), but we were eyewitnesses of His majesty (grandeur, authority of sovereign power).

17 For when He was invested with honor and glory from God the Father and a voice was borne to Him by the [splendid] Majestic Glory [in the bright cloud that overshadowed Him, saying], This is My beloved Son in Whom I am well pleased *and* delight,

18 We [actually] heard this voice borne out of heaven, for we were together with Him on the holy mountain.

19 And we have the prophetic word [made] firmer still. You will do well to pay close attention to it as to a lamp shining in a dismal (squalid and dark) place, until the day breaks through [the gloom] and the Morning Star rises (ʰcomes into being) in your hearts.

20 [Yet] first [you must] understand this, that no prophecy of Scripture is [a matter] of any personal *or* private *or* special interpretation (loosening, solving).

21 For no prophecy ever originated because some man willed it [to do so—it never came by human impulse], but men spoke from God who were borne along (moved and impelled) by the Holy Spirit.

2 BUT ALSO [in those days] there arose false prophets among the people, just as there will be false teachers among yourselves, who will subtly *and* stealthily introduce heretical doctrines (destructive heresies), even denying *and* disowning the Master Who bought them, bringing upon themselves swift destruction.

2 And many will follow their immoral ways *and* lascivious doings; because of them the true Way will be maligned *and* defamed.

3 And in their covetousness (lust, greed) they will exploit you with false (cunning) arguments. From of old the sentence [of condemnation] for them has not been idle; their destruction (eternal misery) has not been asleep.

4 For God did not [even] spare angels that sinned, but cast them into hell, delivering them to be kept there in pits of gloom till the judgment *and* their doom.

5 And He spared not the ancient world, but preserved Noah, a preacher of righteousness, with seven other persons, when He brought a flood upon the world of ungodly [people]. [Gen. 6-8; I Peter 3:20.]

6 And He condemned to ruin *and*

---

h G. Abbott-Smith, *Manual Greek Lexicon of the New Testament.*

extinction the cities of Sodom and Gomorrah, reducing them to ashes [and thus] set them forth as an example to those who would be ungodly; [Gen. 19:24.]

7 And He rescued righteous Lot, greatly worn out *and* distressed by the wanton ways of the ungodly *and* lawless—[Gen. 19:16, 29.]

8 For that just man, living [there] among them, tortured his righteous soul every day with what he saw and heard of [their] unlawful and wicked deeds—

9 Now if [all these things are true, then be sure] the Lord knows how to rescue the godly out of temptations *and* trials, and how to keep the ungodly under chastisement until the day of judgment *and* doom,

10 And particularly those who walk after the flesh and indulge in the lust of polluting passion and scorn *and* despise authority. Presumptuous [and] daring [self-willed and self-loving creatures]! They scoff at *and* revile dignitaries (glorious ones) without trembling,

11 Whereas [even] angels, though superior in might and power, do not bring a defaming charge against them before the Lord.

12 But these [people]! Like unreasoning beasts, mere creatures of instinct, born [only] to be captured and destroyed, railing at things of which they are ignorant, they shall utterly perish in their [own] corruption [in their destroying they shall surely be destroyed],

13 Being destined to receive [punishment as] the reward of [their] unrighteousness [suffering wrong as the hire for their wrongdoing]. They count it a delight to revel in the daytime [living luxuriously and delicately]. They are blots and blemishes, reveling in their ⁱdeceptions *and* carousing

life point

Second Peter 2:10 says that presumption is a treacherous trait of a person who walks after the flesh.

We must always be on guard against presumption. Presumption is behavior that is arrogant, overconfident, and unreasonably bold. Presumption causes disrespect and rebellious attitudes toward authority.

Presumptuous people talk when they should be quiet. They try to dictate direction to those from whom they should receive counsel. They give orders when they should be receiving them; and they do things without asking permission.

Presumption is a big problem and comes from a wrong heart. God does not want us to be presumptuous. He wants us to be humble. Eliminate presumption from your life and cultivate humility.

together [even] as they feast with you.

14 They have eyes full of harlotry, insatiable for sin. They beguile *and* bait *and* lure away unstable souls. Their hearts are trained in covetousness (lust, greed), [they are] children of a curse [ʲexposed to cursing]!

15 Forsaking the straight road they have gone astray; they have followed the way of Balaam [the son] of Beor, who loved the reward of wickedness. [Num. 22:5, 7.]

16 But he was rebuked for his own transgression when a dumb beast of burden spoke with human voice and checked the prophet's madness. [Num. 22:21-31.]

17 These are springs without water and mists driven along before a tempest, for whom is reserved *forever* the gloom of darkness.

---

i Some ancient manuscripts read "love feasts."   j Joseph Thayer, *A Greek-English Lexicon.*

18 For uttering loud boasts of folly, they beguile *and* lure with lustful desires of the flesh those who are barely escaping from them who are wrongdoers.

19 They promise them liberty, when they themselves are the slaves of depravity *and* defilement—for by whatever anyone is made inferior *or* worse *or* is overcome, to that [person or thing] he is enslaved.

20 For if, after they have escaped the pollutions of the world through [the full, personal] knowledge of our Lord and Savior Jesus Christ, they again become entangled in them and are overcome, their last condition is worse [for them] than the first.

21 For never to have obtained a [full, personal] knowledge of the way of righteousness would have been better for them than, having obtained [such knowledge], to turn back from the holy commandment which was [verbally] delivered to them.

22 There has befallen them the thing spoken of in the true proverb, The dog turns back to his own vomit, and, The sow is washed only to wallow again in the mire. [Prov. 26:11.]

3 BELOVED, I am now writing you this second letter. In [both of] them I have stirred up your unsullied (sincere) mind by way of remembrance,

2 That you should recall the predictions of the holy (consecrated, dedicated) prophets and the commandment of the Lord and Savior [given] through your apostles (His special messengers).

speak the Word

3 To begin with, you must know *and* understand this, that scoffers (mockers) will come in the last days with scoffing, [people who] walk after their own fleshly desires

4 And say, Where is the promise of His coming? For since the forefathers fell asleep, all things have continued exactly as they did from the beginning of creation.

5 For they willfully overlook *and* forget this [fact], that the heavens [came into] existence long ago by the word of God, and the earth also which was formed out of water and by means of water,

6 Through which the world that then [existed] was deluged with water and perished. [Gen. 1:6-8; 7:11.]

7 But by the same word the present heavens and earth have been stored up (reserved) for fire, being kept until the day of judgment and destruction of the ungodly people.

8 Nevertheless, do not let this one fact escape you, beloved, that with the Lord one day is as a thousand years and a thousand years as one day. [Ps. 90:4.]

9 The Lord does not delay *and* is not tardy *or* slow about what He promises, according to some people's conception of slowness, but He is long-suffering (extraordinarily patient) toward you, not desiring that any should perish, but that all should turn to repentance.

10 But the day of the Lord will come like a thief, and then the heavens will vanish (pass away) with a thunderous crash, and the [kmaterial] elements [of the universe] will be dissolved with fire, and the earth and the works

Father, I thank You that You do not delay and You are not tardy or slow about what You promise, but you are long-suffering and extraordinarily patient.
ADAPTED FROM II PETER 3:9

k G. Abbott-Smith, *Manual Greek Lexicon*.

"when, God, when?"

Second Peter 3:8 reminds us that God has His own sense of timing. God does not move in our timing. He is never late, but He is usually not early either. He is often the God of the midnight hour. He *sometimes* waits until the last second before He gives us what we need.

We must learn to trust God's timing. But before we can do that, we must come to the place where we are broken before Him. What I mean is that our self-will and our spirit of independence must be broken before God is free to work His will in our lives and circumstances. Before He intervenes on our behalf, He has to be sure that we are not going to take matters into our own hands and do something out of His perfect timing.

Galatians 6:9 says, "And let us not be weary in well doing: for in due season we shall reap, if we faint not" (King James Version). The interesting thing about this scripture is that it always seems to encourage people. Yet really, in this verse, God does not tell us *when* something is going to happen because "due season" is not specific. If we start checking references that have to do with timing in the Bible, we will find descriptions like: "at the appointed season, in due time, in due season."

Many times when I am waiting on God in a situation and I get discouraged about the time it is taking for Him to answer, someone gives me one of those kinds of scriptures and it encourages me. I still do not know any details because "due time" is really just the time that God knows is right, but the scripture does remind me to trust God.

David wrote a power passage in Psalm 31:14, 15: "But I trusted in, relied on, and was confident in You, O Lord; I said, You are my God. My times are in Your hands; deliver me from the hands of my foes and those who pursue me and persecute me." Like David, we must learn to put our confidence in the Lord, trusting Him to deliver us out of our circumstances—and into the next right thing—in His perfect timing.

that are upon it will be burned up. **11** Since all these things are thus [in the process of being dissolved], what kind of person ought [each of] you to be [in the meanwhile] in consecrated *and* holy behavior and devout *and* godly qualities,

12 While you wait and earnestly long for (expect and hasten) the coming of the day of God by reason of which the flaming heavens will be dissolved, and the [[m]material] elements [of the universe] will flare *and* melt with fire? [Isa. 34:4.]

13 But we look for new heavens and a new earth according to His promise, in which righteousness (uprightness, freedom from sin, and right standing with God) is to abide. [Isa. 65:17; 66:22.]

14 So, beloved, since you are expecting these things, be eager to be found by Him [at His coming] without spot or blemish and at peace [in serene

l Marvin Vincent, *Word Studies*.   **m** G. Abbott-Smith, *Manual Greek Lexicon*.

putting the Word to work

Do you ever look at all of the evil in the world and wonder why Jesus has not yet returned to earth? The promise of His coming is certain, yet II Peter 3:9 tells us that God, in His mercy and patience toward sinners, is waiting. He does not want any person to perish, but wants everyone to come to salvation through repentance and faith in Jesus. Pray for salvation for those in your life who do not yet know Jesus as Lord and Savior.

confidence, [n]free from fears and agitating passions and moral conflicts].

15 And consider that the long-suffering of our Lord [[o]His slowness in avenging wrongs and judging the world] is salvation ([o]that which is conducive to the soul's safety), even as our beloved brother Paul also wrote to you according to the spiritual insight given him,

16 Speaking of this as he does in all of his letters. There are some things in those [epistles of Paul] that are difficult to understand, which the ignorant and unstable twist *and* misconstrue to their own [o]utter destruction, just as

putting the Word to work

What measures do you take to guard your valuables? Perhaps you have an alarm system in your home; you probably lock the doors of your car and keep your money in the bank. Likewise, you should guard the truth of God's Word that you have in your heart so you are not led astray by false teaching (see II Peter 3:17). Growing in your relationship with the Lord and in His grace will help you stand firm in the truth.

[they distort and misinterpret] the rest of the Scriptures.

17 Let me warn you therefore, beloved, that knowing these things beforehand, you should be on your guard, lest you be carried away by the error of lawless *and* wicked [persons and] fall from your own [present] firm condition [your own steadfastness of mind].

18 But grow in grace (undeserved favor, spiritual strength) and [p]recognition *and* knowledge *and* understanding of our Lord and Savior Jesus Christ (the Messiah). To Him [be] glory (honor, majesty, and splendor) both now and to the day of eternity. Amen (so be it)!

life point

Once we understand grace, we must grow and learn how to receive it in every situation, as II Peter 3:18 encourages us.

We grow in grace by putting our faith in God and receiving His grace in situations that are difficult or impossible for us. Sometimes we put our faith in God, and He gives us grace for deliverance. At other times we put our faith in God, and He gives us grace to "go through." We must leave that choice to Him and know that either way we can have victory, but only by grace through faith.

If you struggle with something right now in your life, ask yourself honestly if you are putting your faith in God and that you believe His grace will meet the need. Remember, grace is unmerited favor to us sinners. It is God's power coming into our situation to do for us what we cannot do for ourselves.

n *Webster's New International Dictionary* offers this as a definition of "peace." **o** Joseph Thayer, *A Greek-English Lexicon*. **p** Hermann Cremer, *Biblico-Theological Lexicon of New Testament Greek*.

First John

Author:
John

Date:
Probably between AD 85–95

Everyday Life Principles:
God is light.

God is love.

God loves you.

The letters we call I, II, and III John were written by the same apostle John who wrote the Gospel of John and the book of Revelation. This man was a disciple of Jesus Christ; he knew Him personally and was one of three disciples with whom Jesus spent a great deal of time.

Two of I John's themes are love and light. In chapter 1, we read that God is light and that there is no darkness in Him. This is important because it enables believers to have true fellowship with God and with other believers. Just think about that: Living in the light means that we can have deep genuine friendships, honest communication, and good times with each other. When we live in God's light, nothing is hidden; we do not have to try to cover up anything. We can be real before God and before others.

We also read of God's love several times in I John. We see that God loved us long before we ever loved Him and that He loves us as His own sons and daughters (see I John 3:1). We read about His love and sacrifice in sending His Son, Jesus, to die for us, and about the total, absolute cleansing power of Jesus' blood.

I pray that I John will remind you of how much God loves you and that reading this epistle strengthens your love for others and encourages you to express that love every chance you get.

1 [WE ARE writing] about the Word of Life [[a]in] Him Who existed from the beginning, Whom we have heard, Whom we have seen with our [own] eyes, Whom we have gazed upon [for ourselves] and have touched with our [own] hands.

2 And the Life [[a]an aspect of His being] was revealed (made manifest, demonstrated), and we saw [as eyewitnesses] and are testifying to and declare to you the Life, the eternal Life [[a]in Him] Who already existed with the Father and Who [actually] was made visible (was revealed) to us [His followers].

3 What we have seen and [ourselves] heard, we are also telling you, so that you too may [a]realize *and* enjoy fellowship as partners *and* partakers with us. And [this] fellowship that we have [which is a [a]distinguishing mark of Christians] is with the Father and with His Son Jesus Christ (the Messiah).

4 And we are now writing these things to you so that our joy [in seeing you included] may be full [and [b]*your* joy may be complete].

5 And this is the message [the message of [a]promise] which we have heard from Him and now are reporting to you: God is Light, and there is no darkness in Him at all [[c]no, not in any way].

6 [So] if we say we are partakers together *and* enjoy fellowship with Him when we live *and* move *and* are walking about in darkness, we are [both] speaking falsely and do not live *and* practice the Truth [which the Gospel presents].

7 But if we [really] are living *and* walking in the Light, as He [Himself] is in the Light, we have [true, unbroken] fellowship with one another, and the blood of Jesus *Christ* His Son cleanses (removes) us from all sin *and*

life point

What happens when we turn on a light in a messy, dirty room? We see bugs scurrying away from the light, and we see clutter and dirt!

First John 1:5 says God is Light. When He gets involved in our lives, He shows us things we may prefer not to look at; things we have hidden—even from ourselves. We are frequently deceived, especially about ourselves. We do not want to deal with our faults, nor do we delight in having them exposed. We may feel condemned about them, but at least we feel they are hidden.

Anything hidden has power over us because we fear it may be found out. The best and most freeing thing we can do is face up to what God wants to expose and get beyond the fear of it (see I John 3:20; I Corinthians 4:5).

Let the light of God shine on your hidden motives and dark places. He knows about them anyway and wants to bring you to a place of freedom.

guilt [keeps us cleansed from sin in all its forms and manifestations].

8 If we say we have no sin [refusing to admit that we are sinners], we delude *and* lead ourselves astray, and the Truth [which the Gospel presents] is not in us [does not dwell in our hearts].

9 If we [freely] admit that we have sinned *and* confess our sins, He is faithful and just (true to His own nature and promises) and will forgive our sins [dismiss our lawlessness] and [continuously] cleanse us from all unrighteousness [everything not in

---

a Marvin Vincent, *Word Studies in the New Testament.*   **b** Many ancient manuscripts read "your joy."
c Literal translation.

life point

Notice in I John 1:9 that we are told if we will confess our sins to God, He will "continuously" cleanse us. I believe this is the spiritual parallel to the way our physical blood continuously cleanses our body.

Our blood works for us all the time to keep us cleansed of all poison, and the blood of Jesus works all the time, continuously cleansing us from sin in all its forms and manifestations (see I John 1:7). There is power in the shed blood of Jesus Christ! You and I are continually cleansed, not just every once in awhile, but frequently and continuously.

The Bible states that there is only one requirement on our part: we must freely admit that we have sinned and confess our sins.

Be quick to repent. Do not try to hide anything from God. He will never reject you. He knows everything anyway, but repentance releases the power of His blood on your behalf and makes it effective in your life. Confess your sins and allow the blood of Jesus to cleanse you on a regular basis.

conformity to His will in purpose, thought, and action].

10 If we say (claim) we have not sinned, we contradict His Word *and* make Him out to be false *and* a liar, and His Word is not in us [the divine message of the Gospel is not in our hearts].

2 MY LITTLE children, I write you these things so that you may not violate God's law *and* sin.

But if anyone should sin, we have an Advocate (One Who will intercede for us) with the Father—[it is] Jesus Christ [the all] righteous [upright, just, Who conforms to the Father's will in every purpose, thought, and action].

2 And He [ᵈthat same Jesus Himself] is the propitiation (the atoning sacrifice) for our sins, and not for ours alone but also for [the sins of] the whole world.

3 And this is how we may discern [ᵈdaily, by experience] that we are coming to know Him [to perceive, recognize, understand, and become better acquainted with Him]: if we keep (bear in mind, observe, practice) His teachings (precepts, commandments).

4 Whoever says, I know Him [I perceive, recognize, understand, and am acquainted with Him] but fails to keep *and* obey His commandments (teachings) is a liar, and the Truth [ᵉof the Gospel] is not in him.

5 But he who keeps (treasures) His Word [who bears in mind His precepts, who observes His message in its entirety], truly in him has the love of *and* for God been perfected (completed, reached maturity). By this we may perceive (know, recognize, and be sure) that we are in Him:

6 Whoever says he abides in Him ought [as ᵈa personal debt] to walk *and* conduct himself in the same way in which He walked *and* conducted Himself.

7 Beloved, I am writing you no new commandment, but an old commandment which you have had from the beginning; the old commandment is the message which you have heard [the ᵉdoctrine of salvation through Christ].

8 Yet I am writing you a new commandment, which is true (is realized) in Him and in you, because the

d Marvin Vincent, *Word Studies*. **e** Joseph Thayer, *A Greek-English Lexicon of the New Testament*.

darkness ([f]moral blindness) is clearing away and the true Light ([f]the revelation of God in Christ) is already shining.

9 Whoever says he is in the Light and [yet] hates his brother [Christian, [g]born-again child of God his Father] is in darkness even until now.

10 Whoever loves his brother [believer] abides (lives) in the Light, and in It *or* in him there is no occasion for stumbling *or* cause for error *or* sin.

11 But he who hates (detests, despises) his brother [[g]in Christ] is in darkness and walking (living) in the dark; he is straying *and* does not perceive *or* know where he is going, because the darkness has blinded his eyes.

12 I am writing to you, little children, because for His name's sake your sins are forgiven [pardoned through His name and on account of confessing His name].

13 I am writing to you, fathers, because you have come to know (recognize, be aware of, and understand) Him Who [has existed] from the beginning. I am writing to you, young men, because you have been victorious over the wicked [one]. I write to you, [h]boys (lads), because you have come to know (recognize and be aware) of the Father.

14 I write to you, fathers, because you have come to know (recognize, be conscious of, and understand) Him Who [has existed] from the beginning. I write to you, young men, because you are strong *and* vigorous, and the Word of God is [always] abiding in you (in your hearts), and you have been victorious over the wicked one.

15 Do not love *or* cherish the world or the things that are in the world. If anyone loves the world, love for the Father is not in him.

life point

First John 2:15 urges us not to love the things that are in the world. Instead we should love people and use things to bless them. This is hard for us to do if we love things too much! You and I must strive to keep possessions in their proper place in our lives. We must not put worldly possessions before people. We must always put people first!

16 For all that is in the world—the lust of the flesh [craving for sensual gratification] and the lust of the eyes [greedy longings of the mind] and the pride of life [assurance in one's own resources or in the stability of earthly things]—these do not come from the Father but are from the world [itself].

17 And the world passes away *and* disappears, and with it the forbidden cravings (the passionate desires, the lust) of it; but he who does the will of God and carries out His purposes in his life abides (remains) forever.

18 [h]Boys (lads), it is the last time (hour, the end of this age). And as you have heard that the antichrist [he who will oppose Christ in the guise of

putting the Word to work

Love is a central theme of I John. There are things, as a believer, however, that you are not to love. What does it mean to not love the world or the things in the world (see I John 2:15)? It does not mean that you should not enjoy the natural beauty of creation, but pursuing what the world offers—things that distract you from God and His purposes for your life—are pursuits rooted in lust and pride. Ask God to deepen your love for Him and the things of His kingdom.

f Marvin Vincent, *Word Studies*.   **g** Joseph Thayer, *A Greek-English Lexicon of the New Testament*.
h G. Abbott-Smith, *Manual Greek Lexicon of the New Testament*.

"in," but not "of"

Jesus told us to be in the world but not of the world. We can enjoy the world and the things it offers, but we must maintain balance and not get too attached to them (see I John 2:15). We are to live in the world as strangers and aliens, and remember that we are just passing through; this world is not our home. God is our home and we are on our way to live in His manifest presence for eternity.

One of the ways we can determine if things mean more to us than they should is to watch how we behave when one of our possessions is lost or damaged. It may disappoint us, but it should not devastate us. How would you act if your spouse or child broke your favorite possession? Recently, my daughter and I were thinking about years gone by and she said, "Mom, one of the things you did that really meant a lot to me was what you said when I accidentally broke your new bottle of favorite perfume. You said, 'Do not worry about it. You are more important to me than the perfume."' Now, I did not always behave so lovingly, but on this occasion I did and she remembered. I urge you not to ever make people feel that they are not as important as things.

I believe God tests us in these areas just to help us maintain right attitudes. The apostle Paul said that he learned how to be content whether he was abased or abounding (see Philippians 4:12). We may experience times of plenty and times of need, but if we remain steady and unchanging no matter what, then we know that things do not have an ungodly hold on us. God wants us to be blessed and to enjoy the best life has to offer, but He wants us to keep Him first in our lives. One man said, "I am very rich, but when I got cancer I called on God, not the first bank of the U.S."

When everything else is gone, and it will be some day, there will be God. We must keep Him in first place in our lives. We came into the world with nothing and we will leave the same way. You cannot take money and things with you when you go, so do not worship them while you are here.

Christ] is coming, even now many antichrists have arisen, which confirms our belief that it is the final (the end) time.

19 They went out from our number, but they did not [really] belong to us; for if they had been of us, they would have remained with us. But [they withdrew] that it might be plain that they all are not of us.

20 But you have been anointed by [you hold a sacred appointment from, you have been given an unction from] the Holy One, and you all know [the Truth] *or you know all things*.

21 I write to you not because you are ignorant *and* do not perceive *and* know the Truth, but because you do perceive *and* know it, and [know positively] that nothing false (no deception, no lie) is of the Truth.

22 Who is [such a] liar as he who denies that Jesus is the Christ (the Messiah)? He is the antichrist (the antagonist of Christ), who ['habitually] denies *and* refuses to acknowledge the Father and the Son.

23 No one who ['habitually] denies

i Marvin Vincent, *Word Studies*.

(disowns) the Son [j]even has the Father. *Whoever confesses (acknowledges and has) the Son has the Father also.*

24 As for you, keep in your hearts what you have heard from the beginning. If what you heard from the first dwells *and* remains in you, then you will dwell in the Son and in the Father [always].

25 And this is what He Himself has promised us—the life, the eternal [life].

26 I write this to you with reference to those who would deceive you [seduce and lead you astray].

27 But as for you, the anointing (the sacred appointment, the unction) which you received from Him abides [[k]permanently] in you; [so] then you have no need that anyone should instruct you. But just as His anointing teaches you concerning everything and is true and is no falsehood, so you must abide in (live in, never depart from) Him [being [k]rooted in Him, knit to Him], just as [His anointing] has taught you [to do].

28 And now, little children, abide (live, remain [k]permanently) in Him, so that when He is made visible, we may have *and* enjoy perfect confidence (boldness, assurance) and not be ashamed *and* shrink from Him at His coming.

29 If you know (perceive and are sure) that He [Christ] is [absolutely] righteous [conforming to the Father's will in purpose, thought, and action], you may also know (be sure) that everyone who does righteously [and is therefore in like manner conformed

speak the Word

life point

Sometimes we give more consideration to what people tell us than to what God says to us. If we pray diligently and hear from God, but then start asking everybody else what they think, we are honoring people's opinions above the Word of God. This attitude prevents us from developing a relationship where we consistently hear from God.

First John 2:27 confirms that we can trust God to instruct us without needing constant reassurance from others. But is this verse saying we do not need anybody to teach us the Word? No, because God appointed some people to teach in the body of Christ. But I John 2:27 says that if we are in Christ, we have an anointing that abides on the inside of us to guide and direct our lives. We might occasionally ask someone for their wisdom, but we do not constantly need to go to other people and ask them about decisions we need to make for our own lives.

to the divine will] is born (begotten) of Him [[l]God].

3 SEE WHAT [[j]an incredible] quality of love the Father has given (shown, bestowed on) us, that we should [be permitted to] be named *and* called *and* counted the children of God! And so we are! The reason that the world does not know

j Marvin Vincent, *Word Studies.* **k** Joseph Thayer, *A Greek-English Lexicon.* **l** Brooke F. Westcott, *The Epistles of Saint John*: When John thinks of God in relation to men, he never thinks of Him apart from Christ.

(recognize, acknowledge) us is that it does not know (recognize, acknowledge) Him.

2 Beloved, we are [even here and] now God's children; it is not yet disclosed (made clear) what we shall be [hereafter], but we know that when He comes *and* is manifested, we shall [[m]as God's children] resemble *and* be like Him, for we shall see Him [n]just as He [really] is.

3 And everyone who has this hope [resting] on Him cleanses (purifies) himself just as He is pure (chaste, undefiled, guiltless).

4 Everyone who commits (practices) sin is guilty of lawlessness; for [that is what] sin is, lawlessness (the breaking, violating of God's law by transgression or neglect—being unrestrained and unregulated by His commands and His will).

5 You know that He appeared in visible form *and* became Man to take away [upon Himself] sins, and in Him there is no sin [[n]essentially and forever].

6 No one who abides in Him [who lives and remains [n]in communion with and in obedience to Him—deliberately, knowingly, and [n]habitually] commits (practices) sin. No one who [habitually] sins has either seen *or* known Him [recognized, perceived, or understood Him, or has had an experiential acquaintance with Him].

7 [o]Boys (lads), let no one deceive *and* lead you astray. He who practices righteousness [who is upright, conforming to the divine will in purpose, thought, and action, living a consistently conscientious life] is righteous, even as He is righteous.

8 [But] he who commits sin [who practices evildoing] is of the devil [takes his character from the evil one], for the devil has sinned (violated the divine law) from the beginning. The reason the Son of God was made manifest (visible) was to undo (destroy, loosen, and dissolve) the works the devil [has done].

9 No one born (begotten) of God [deliberately, knowingly, and [n]habitually] practices sin, for God's nature abides in him [His principle of life, the divine sperm, remains permanently within him]; and he cannot practice sinning because he is born (begotten) of God.

10 By this it is made clear who take their nature from God *and* are His children and who take their nature from the devil *and* are his children: no one who does not practice righteousness [who does not conform to God's will in purpose, thought, and action]

life point

I like to teach I John 3:9 this way: I used to be a full-time sinner, and once in a while I "accidentally" did something right. But now that I have spent many years developing a deep, personal relationship with God and His Word, I concentrate on being a full-time obedient child of God. I still make mistakes, but not nearly as many as I once did. I am not where I need to be, but thank God, I am not where I used to be. There are times when I accidentally make mistakes, but it is not the desire of my heart to do wrong. I do not deliberately or knowingly commit sin. I do not habitually sin. So I do not allow those occasions to make me feel insecure. I do not do everything right, but I do know that the attitude of my heart is right. I encourage you to look at the sins and mistakes you make—and at the attitude of your heart—the same way.

---

m Robert Jamieson, A.R. Fausset and David Brown, *A Commentary on the Old and New Testaments*.
n Marvin Vincent, *Word Studies*. **o** G. Abbott-Smith, *Manual Greek Lexicon*.

putting the Word to work

According to I John 3:10, righteousness
and loving other believers are two
indicators of belonging to God. Is there
a fellow Christian in your life that you
have a hard time getting along with?
Ask God to show you practical ways
to show His love to this person, and as
you do these things, ask God to change
your heart.

is of God; neither is anyone who does
not love his brother (his fellow Pbe-
liever in Christ).

11 For this is the message (the
announcement) which you have
heard from the first, that we should
love one another,

12 [And] not be like Cain who [took
his nature and got his motivation]
from the evil one and slew his brother. And why did he slay him? Because
his deeds (activities, works) were
wicked *and* malicious and his brother's were righteous (virtuous).

13 Do not be surprised *and* wonder,
brethren, that the world detests *and*
pursues you with hatred.

14 We know that we have passed
over out of death into Life by the fact
that we love the brethren (our fellow
Christians). He who does not love
abides (remains, is Pheld and kept
continually) in [spiritual] death.

15 Anyone who hates (abominates,
detests) his brother [in Christ] is [at
heart] a murderer, and you know that
no murderer has eternal life abiding
(Ppersevering) within him.

16 By this we come to know (pro-

speak the Word

gressively to recognize, to perceive, to
understand) the [essential] love: that
He laid down His [own] life for us;
and we ought to lay [our] lives down
for [those who are our] brothers [Pin
Him].

17 But if anyone has this world's
goods (resources for sustaining life)
and sees his brother *and* Pfellow
believer in need, yet closes his heart of
compassion against him, how can the
love of God live *and* remain in him?

18 Little children, let us not love
[merely] in theory *or* in speech but in
deed and in truth (in practice and in
sincerity).

19 By this we shall come to know
(perceive, recognize, and understand)
that we are of the Truth, and can reassure (quiet, conciliate, and pacify) our
hearts in His presence,

20 Whenever our hearts in [qtor-
menting] self-accusation make us feel
guilty *and* condemn us. [For qwe are in
God's hands.] For He is above *and*
greater than our consciences (our
hearts), and He knows (perceives and
understands) everything [nothing is
hidden from Him].

putting the Word to work

First John 3:16–18 teaches us some
things about love. How do you define
love? Clearly, one aspect of love is
helping meet the needs of others. It is
important to tell people that God loves
them and that you love them; it is also
necessary to demonstrate that love
through action and good deeds,
especially toward fellow believers.

*Father, I pray that I would not love merely in theory or in speech but in deed and
truth, in practice and sincerity.*
ADAPTED FROM I JOHN **3:18**

p Joseph Thayer, *A Greek-English Lexicon.* **q** Marvin Vincent, *Word Studies.*

confidence, not condemnation

First John 3:20, 21 speaks to us about condemnation in our hearts. A condemned heart steals confidence. Anyone who wants to be a victorious Christian must learn to handle condemnation. When he sins, he needs to know how to shake it off and quickly go on because no one is perfect. He may have a perfect heart, a heart that genuinely loves and seeks to please God, but he still will not be perfect in every thought, word, and deed.

I know how condemning it is to teach others about what is right and then foul up in that very area. When we do things like that, we feel a double dose of condemnation because the devil says to us, "You of all people ought to know better." If we listen to him, he will make us feel that we are not worthy of God's love.

We must be able to shake off feelings of condemnation. If we can not, we will have no confidence before God. Without confidence, our faith will not work. And without faith, we cannot please God or receive from Him the things we need in order to do what He has called us to do.

That is why Proverbs 4:23 teaches us to guard our hearts with all diligence and reminds us that the issues of life flow out of our hearts.

God convicts us of our wrongdoing; He does not condemn us. Conviction helps us repent and be lifted out of our problems; condemnation only pushes us down and makes us feel bad about ourselves.

Romans 8:33, 34 tells us that God justifies us; He does not bring charges against us. Jesus does not condemn us. He died for us. He sits at the Father's right hand, actually pleading in intercession for us (see Romans 8:34). I have learned from this scripture that when I feel condemned, I either do it to myself or the devil does it to me. Always submit to God's conviction, but resist Satan's condemnation.

21 And, beloved, if our consciences (our hearts) do not accuse us [if they do not make us feel guilty and condemn us], we have confidence (complete assurance and boldness) before God,
22 And we receive from Him whatever we ask, because we [ʳwatchfully] obey His orders [observe His suggestions and injunctions, follow His plan for us] *and* [ʳhabitually] practice what is pleasing to Him.

23 And this is His order (His command, His injunction): that we should believe in (put our faith and trust in and adhere to and rely on) the name of His Son Jesus Christ (the Messiah), and that we should love one another, just as He has commanded us.
24 All who keep His commandments [who obey His orders and follow His plan, live and continue to live, to stay and] abide in Him, and He in them. [ˢThey let Christ be a home to them

r Marvin Vincent, *Word Studies*.   s Bede, a translator of portions of the Bible from the Latin into Old English.

and they are the home of Christ.] And by this we know *and* understand *and* have the proof that He [really] lives *and* makes His home in us: by the [Holy] Spirit Whom He has given us.

4 BELOVED, DO not put faith in every spirit, but prove (test) the spirits to discover whether they proceed from God; for many false prophets have gone forth into the world.

2 By this you may know (perceive and recognize) the Spirit of God: every spirit which acknowledges *and* confesses [the fact] that Jesus Christ (the Messiah) [actually] has become man *and* has come in the flesh is of God [has God for its source];

3 And every spirit which does not acknowledge *and* confess *that* Jesus *Christ has come in the flesh* [but would ᵗannul, destroy, ᵘsever, disunite Him] is not of God [does not proceed from Him]. This [ᵛnonconfession] is the [spirit] of the antichrist, [of] which you heard that it was coming, and now it is already in the world.

4 Little children, you are of God [you belong to Him] and have [already] defeated *and* overcome them [the agents of the antichrist], because He Who lives in you is greater (mightier) than he who is in the world.

5 They proceed from the world *and* are of the world; therefore it is out of the world [its ᵛwhole economy morally considered] that they speak, and the world listens (pays attention) to them.

6 We are [children] of God. Whoever is learning to know God [progres-

sively to perceive, recognize, and understand God by observation and experience, and to ᵛget an ever-clearer knowledge of Him] listens to us; and he who is not of God does not listen *or* pay attention to us. By this we know (recognize) the Spirit of Truth and the spirit of error.

7 Beloved, let us love one another, for love is (springs) from God; and he who loves [his fellowmen] is begotten (born) of God and is coming [progressively] to know *and* understand God [to perceive and recognize and get a better and clearer knowledge of Him].

8 He who does not love has not become acquainted with God [does not and never did know Him], for God is love.

9 In this the love of God was made manifest (displayed) where we are concerned: in that God sent His Son, the only begotten *or* ᵂunique [Son], into the world so that we might live through Him.

10 In this is love: not that we loved God, but that He loved us and sent His Son to be the propitiation (the atoning sacrifice) for our sins.

11 Beloved, if God loved us so [very

life point

The world looks for something real, something tangible. People look for love, and God is love (see I John 4:8). Because we know God, we can offer the answer to the searching hearts around us and the needs of the people we encounter in life—the God of love talked about in I John 4:8 is that answer.

speak the Word

I pray, Lord, that You would help me love other people, for love is from You.
ADAPTED FROM I JOHN 4:7

---

t An ancient reading.   u *The Latin Vulgate.*   v Marvin Vincent, *Word Studies.*   w James Moulton and George Milligan, *The Vocabulary of the Greek Testament.*

much], we also ought to love one another.

12 No man has at any time [yet] seen God. But if we love one another, God abides (lives and remains) in us and His love (that love which is essentially His) is brought to completion (to its full maturity, runs its full course, is perfected) in us!

13 By this we come to know (perceive, recognize, and understand) that we abide (live and remain) in Him and He in us: because He has given (imparted) to us of His [Holy] Spirit.

14 And [besides] we ourselves have seen (have deliberately and steadfastly contemplated) and bear witness that the Father has sent the Son [as the] Savior of the world.

15 Anyone who confesses (acknowledges, owns) that Jesus is the Son of God, God abides (lives, makes His home) in him and he [abides, lives, makes his home] in God.

16 And we know (understand, recognize, are conscious of, by observation and by experience) and believe (adhere to and put faith in and rely on) the love God cherishes for us. God is love, and he who dwells *and* continues in love dwells *and* continues in God, and God dwells *and* continues in him.

17 In this [union and communion with Him] love is brought to completion *and* attains perfection with us, that we may have confidence for the day of judgment [with assurance and boldness to face Him], because as He is, so are we in this world.

18 There is no fear in love [dread does not exist], but full-grown (complete,

enjoying God's love

The Bible says many times that God loves us. But how many of God's children still lack revelation concerning God's love? The truth is, very few of God's people really know how much He loves them. If they did, they would act differently.

Many years ago, I began studying how people can learn to receive God's love, and I realized that I was in desperate need of it myself. The Lord led me in my study to I John 4:16 and emphasized the importance of being conscious of His love. This means God's love should be something we are actively aware of. But how does one find this awareness?

I studied this subject for a long time, and I became conscious of God's love for me through thinking about His love and by confessing it aloud. I learned scriptures about the love of God, and I meditated on them and confessed them out of my mouth. I did this over and over for months, and all the time the revelation of His unconditional love for me was becoming more and more of a reality to me.

Now, His love is so real to me that even in hard times, I am comforted by the "conscious knowing" that He loves me and that I no longer have to live in fear. This can happen to you, too.

I encourage you to know and believe His love for you. Meditate on and speak about God's love that He expresses to you in His love letters—the Scriptures. Why not start with I John 4:16!

perfect) love ˣturns fear out of doors *and* expels every trace of terror! For fear ʸbrings with it the thought of punishment, and [so] he who is afraid has not reached the full maturity of love [is not yet grown into love's complete perfection].

19 We love *Him,* because He first loved us.

20 If anyone says, I love God, and hates (detests, abominates) his brother [ʸin Christ], he is a liar; for he who does not love his brother, whom he has seen, cannot love God, Whom he has not seen.

21 And this command (charge, order, injunction) we have from Him: that he who loves God shall love his brother [ʸbeliever] also.

5 EVERYONE WHO believes (adheres to, trusts, and relies on the fact) that Jesus is the Christ (the Messiah) is a born-again child of God; and everyone who loves the Father also loves the one born of Him (His offspring).

2 By this we come to know (recognize and understand) that we love the children of God: when we love God and obey His commands (orders, charges)—[when we keep His ordinances and are mindful of His precepts and His teaching].

3 For the [true] love of God is this: that we do His commands [keep His ordinances and are mindful of His precepts and teaching]. And these orders of His are not irksome (burdensome, oppressive, or grievous).

4 For whatever is born of God is victorious over the world; and this is the victory that conquers the world, even our faith.

5 Who is it that is victorious over [that conquers] the world but he who believes that Jesus is the Son of God [who adheres to, trusts in, and relies on that fact]?

6 This is He Who came by (with) water and blood [ˣHis baptism and His death], Jesus Christ (the Messiah)—not by (in) the water only, but by (in) the water and the blood. And it is the [Holy] Spirit Who bears witness, because the [Holy] Spirit is the Truth.

7 So there are three witnesses ᶻ*in heaven: the Father, the Word and the Holy Spirit, and these three are One;*

8 *and there are three witnesses on the earth:* the Spirit, the water, and the blood; and these three agree [are in unison; their testimony coincides].

9 If we accept [as we do] the testimony of men [if we are willing to take human authority], the testimony of God is greater (of stronger authority), for this is the testimony of God, even the witness which He has borne regarding His Son.

10 He who believes in the Son of God [who adheres to, trusts in, and relies on Him] has the testimony [possesses this divine attestation] within himself. He who does not believe God [in this way] has made Him out to be *and* represented Him as a liar, because he has not believed (put his faith in, adhered to, and relied on) the evidence (the testimony) that God has borne regarding His Son.

11 And this is that testimony (that

speak the Word

Thank You, Lord, that there is no fear in love, but that full-grown, complete, and perfect love turns fear out of doors.
ADAPTED FROM I JOHN 4:18

---

x Marvin Vincent, *Word Studies.*　**y** Joseph Thayer, *A Greek-English Lexicon.*　**z** The italicized section is found only in late manuscripts.

praying according to God's will

First John 5:14, 15 teaches us about prayer and God's will. The Word clearly spells out many things that are God's will for our lives. We know we can certainly ask for those things boldly without being concerned about whether or not they are within God's will.

However, when dealing with daily situations in which we are unsure of God's perfect will, we should pray that His will is done and not ours.

Many times I ask God for something in prayer, but if I do not have a specific Bible verse to back up my request, I tell the Lord, "This is what I think I want—at least, it seems to me that it would be good this way—but if I am wrong in what I am asking, Lord, please do not give it to me. Your will is what I want, not mine."

When learning to pray God's will, it is important for us to consider God's timing. We can pray for something that is the will of God, but until His timing is right in our lives we will not see the physical manifestation of our answer.

Remember: "Faith is the substance of things hoped for, the evidence of things not seen" (Hebrews 11:1, KJV). If you have the Word of God to back up your requests, stand in faith until you see the results. But remember that real faith causes us to enter the rest of God, so waiting on Him should be a pleasant experience, not one of frustration.

evidence): God gave us eternal life, and this life is in His Son.

12 He who possesses the Son has that life; he who does not possess the Son of God does not have that life.

13 I write this to you who believe in (adhere to, trust in, and rely on) the name of the Son of God [in ªthe peculiar services and blessings conferred by Him on men], so that you may know [with settled and absolute knowledge] that you [already] have life, ᵇyes, eternal life.

14 And this is the confidence (the assurance, the privilege of boldness) which we have in Him: [we are sure] that if we ask anything (make any request) according to His will (in agreement with His own plan), He listens to *and* hears us.

15 And if (since) we [positively] know that He listens to us in whatever we ask, we also know [with settled and absolute knowledge] that we have [granted us as our present possessions] the requests made of Him.

16 If anyone sees his brother [believer] committing a sin that does not

speak the Word

God, I have confidence that if I ask anything in Your name, according to Your will and in agreement with Your plan that You listen and You hear me.
ADAPTED FROM I JOHN 5:14

a Joseph Thayer, *A Greek-English Lexicon.* **b** Brooke F. Westcott, cited by *Speaker's Commentary.*

life point

When you pray, believe God hears you! This is a promise from I John 5:14, 15.

What comes to mind when you think of an idol? Often, people think of statues or figurines representing gods that other cultures worship. However, an idol is anything that you place more importance on or love more than God. It can be your career, money, sports, or a relationship. Do you have any idols in your life? Take time to evaluate your pursuits and priorities; make sure that God is your deepest love and highest priority.

[lead to] death (the extinguishing of life), he will pray and [God] will give him life [yes, He will grant life to all those whose sin is not one leading to death]. There is a sin [that leads] to death; I do not say that one should pray for that.

17 All wrongdoing is sin, and there is sin which does not [involve] death [that may be repented of and forgiven].

18 We know [absolutely] that anyone born of God does not [deliberately and knowingly] practice committing sin, but the One Who was begotten of God carefully watches over *and* protects him [Christ's divine presence within him preserves him against the evil], and the wicked one does not lay hold (get a grip) on him *or* touch [him].

19 We know [positively] that we are of God, and the whole world [around us] is under the power of the evil one.

20 And we [have seen and] know [positively] that the Son of God has [actually] come to this world and has

given us understanding *and* insight [progressively] to perceive (recognize) *and* come to know better *and* more clearly Him Who is true; and we are in Him Who is true—in His Son Jesus Christ (the Messiah). This [Man] is the true God and Life eternal.

21 Little children, keep yourselves from idols (false gods)—[from anything and everything that would occupy the place in your heart due to God, from any sort of substitute for Him that would take first place in your life]. *Amen (so let it be).*

Second John

Author:
John

Date:
Probably between AD 85–95

Everyday Life Principles:
Always remember that Jesus is God's Son in the flesh.

Do not welcome or receive false teachers.

Be a diligent student of God's Word so that you will know the truth.

Second John is addressed to "the elect (chosen) lady (Cyria) and her children." Though we do not know if this "lady" was an individual or a group of believers who collectively comprised a church, we do know that John loved this person or these people dearly.

John's reason for writing this letter was that his readers were dealing with false teachers who traveled from place to place spreading error and refused to admit that Jesus Christ ever came to earth in bodily form, in the flesh, and was both fully human and fully divine. The recipients of this letter needed strength and encouragement to persevere in their faith and know how to relate to the false teachers. John clearly told them not to receive such ministers (see II John 10) and that anyone who did welcome or receive them would be participating in the spread of false teaching.

The only way to combat false teaching is to know the truth of God's Word. Concerning that, John wrote that "the Truth . . . lives and stays on in our hearts and will be with us forever" (II John 2).

As you read II John, I hope you will remember how valuable truth is. Guard the truth that you have already, and commit to be a person who is "progressively learning to recognize and know and understand the Truth" (II John 1).

1 THE ELDERLY elder [of the church addresses this letter] to the elect (chosen) lady (Cyria) and her children, whom I truly love—and not only I but also all who are [progressively] learning to recognize *and* know *and* understand the Truth—

2 Because of the Truth which lives *and* stays on in our hearts and will be with us forever:

3 Grace (spiritual blessing), mercy, and [soul] peace will be with us, from God the Father and from Jesus Christ (the Messiah), the Father's Son, in all sincerity (truth) and love.

4 I was greatly delighted to find some of your children walking (living) in [the] Truth, just as we have been commanded by the Father [Himself].

5 And now I beg you, lady (Cyria), not as if I were issuing a new charge (injunction or command), but [simply recalling to your mind] the one we have had from the beginning, that we love one another.

6 And what this love consists in is this: that we live *and* walk in accordance with *and* guided by His commandments (His orders, ordinances, precepts, teaching). This is the commandment, as you have heard from the beginning, that you continue to walk in love [guided by it and following it].

7 For many imposters (seducers, deceivers, and false leaders) have gone out into the world, men who will not acknowledge (confess, admit) the coming of Jesus Christ (the Messiah)

putting the Word to work

Have you ever heard the saying, "if you talk the talk, you have to walk the walk?" As a Christian, it is not enough to know the truth of God's Word; we have to live it out. The Word of God is full of ways to practically apply and walk in the truth that we know. In what ways can you apply the truth that you know to your everyday life right now? Let me encourage you to study the Word diligently, and ask God to keep showing you how to walk in the truth more and more.

in bodily form. Such a one is the imposter (the seducer, the deceiver, the false leader, the antagonist of Christ) and the antichrist.

8 Look to yourselves (take care) that

putting the Word to work

In this day of e-mail, text messages, and cell phones, taking time for personal visits is not always a priority. When was the last time you had a face-to-face visit with a Christian friend? While there are many ways to communicate, there is no substitute for taking time to fellowship and to share with one another about what God is teaching you and to encourage and pray with one another. Whether sharing a meal, going for a walk, or meeting for a cup of coffee, how can you make time to experience the joy of being together with other Christians?

speak the Word

Father, I pray that I will always walk in Truth, just as You have commanded me.
ADAPTED FROM II JOHN 4

God, I pray that I would live and walk in accordance with and guided by Your commandments and that I will continue to walk in love.
ADAPTED FROM II JOHN 6

love leads to obedience

Jesus said that when we love Him, we will obey Him (see John 14:15), and the apostle John writes that love for God consists of our obedience to Him (see II John 6). I like to say that the level of our obedience to Jesus determines the level of our love for Him. I believe our love for Him and obedience to Him can grow—and they do. Everything in our relationship with God after initial salvation is a process. Do not be disappointed with yourself if you are still in the process. Jesus will not be angry when He comes to get you if you have not arrived at the mark of perfection, but He does expect to find all of us pressing on.

The commandment we should strive to obey throughout our lives is to walk in love. Our lives and behavior will change dramatically if all of our thoughts, words, and actions are guided by love. They are to be guided by our love for God, ourselves, and others. God's Word teaches us to love everyone, including ourselves. I like to say, "Do not be *in* love with yourself, but love yourself in a balanced way." If you refuse to love yourself, then you are not receiving the gift God wants to give you. We cannot deserve God's love. It comes to us unconditionally. God loves us first, and He pours His love into us so we can love Him, ourselves, and others. He does not expect us to give away anything we do not have.

Sometimes we make being a Christian very difficult and complicated. We think we must follow hundreds of rules and do multitudes of things, but Jesus said that if we simply walk in love, that is enough (see John 15:12). The reason for this is that if we concentrate on love, all the other things He asks us to do will also get done. Love motivates us to obey, pray, be kind and merciful, give, forgive, repent, and practice other aspects of our Christian faith.

Let me encourage you to study love. Read everything you can about love. Think about it, talk about it, and practice it. God is love and when love is the theme of our lives, He is the theme also.

you may not lose (throw away or destroy) all that we *and* you have labored for, but that you may [persevere until you] win *and* receive back a perfect reward [in full].

9 Anyone who runs on ahead [of God] and does not abide in the doctrine of Christ [who is not content with what He taught] does not have God; but he who continues to live in the doctrine (teaching) of Christ [does have God], he has both the Father and the Son.

10 If anyone comes to you and does not bring this doctrine [is disloyal to what Jesus Christ taught], do not receive him [do not accept him, do not welcome or admit him] into [your] house or bid him Godspeed *or* give him any encouragement.

11 For he who wishes him success [who encourages him, wishing him Godspeed] is a partaker in his evil doings.

12 I have many things to write to you, but I prefer not to do so with paper and ink; I hope to come to see you and talk with you face to face, so that our joy may be complete.

13 The children of your elect (chosen) sister wish to be remembered to you. *Amen (so be it).*

Third John

Author:
John

Date:
Probably between AD 85–95

Everyday Life Principles:
Do what you can to send missionaries and traveling ministers on their way in a manner that is worthy of God's service.

Support the spread of the Gospel every way you can.

Imitate good, not evil.

Third John is a brief letter addressed to a man named Gaius, who was most likely a pastor or leader in the early church. Where John has to warn the recipients of his second letter not to associate with false teachers, this letter provides Gaius with instructions on how to treat traveling ministers and missionaries who teach the truth. Specifically, he writes: "You will do well to forward them on their journey [and you will please do so] in a manner worthy of God's service" (III John 6).

He goes on to say that we need to "support such people [to welcome and provide for them], in order that we may be fellow workers in the Truth (the whole Gospel) and cooperate with its teachers" (III John 8).

In this letter, John also urges us not to imitate evil, but to imitate good. Those who do good, he writes, are of God, but those who do evil have no experience with Him and do not know Him in any way (see III John 11).

As you read III John, I pray for you as John did for Gaius: "that you may prosper in every way and [that your body may keep well, even as [I know] your soul prospers" (v. 2). Let these verses inspire you to participate in the work of the ministry and the sharing of the Gospel in every way you can. Do your part to support the spread of God's love and truth, just as John urged his readers to do.

1 THE ELDERLY elder [of the church addresses this letter] to the beloved (esteemed) Gaius, whom I truly love.

2 Beloved, I pray that you may prosper in every way and [that your body] may keep well, even as [I know] your soul keeps well *and* prospers.

3 In fact, I greatly rejoiced when [some of] the brethren from time to time arrived and spoke [so highly] of the sincerity *and* fidelity of your life, as indeed you do live in the Truth [the whole Gospel presents].

4 I have no greater joy than this, to hear that my [spiritual] children are living their lives in the Truth.

putting the Word to work

How can you give joy to others as you walk in truth? Walking in truth means living out the truth you read in the Word of God. Others will take note of your faithfulness and it will encourage them.

5 Beloved, it is a fine *and* faithful work that you are doing when you give any service to the [Christian] brethren, and [especially when they are] strangers.

6 They have testified before the church of your love *and* friendship. You will do well to forward them on their journey [and you will please do so] in a way worthy of God's [service].

7 For these [traveling missionaries] have gone out for the Name's sake

putting the Word to work

There are many people all around the world who work tirelessly for the sake of the Gospel. It is important to extend hospitality to such individuals as you have opportunity. Even if you cannot host such a person in your home, what can you do to support these ministries? As you do, you share in their work for God's kingdom.

(for His sake) and are accepting nothing from the Gentiles (the heathen, the non-Israelites).

8 So we ourselves ought to support such people [to welcome and provide for them], in order that we may be fellow workers in the Truth (the whole Gospel) *and* cooperate with its teachers.

9 I have written briefly to the church; but Diotrephes, who likes to take the lead among them *and* put himself first, does not acknowledge my authority *and* refuses to accept my suggestions *or* to listen to me.

10 So when I arrive, I will call attention to what he is doing, his boiling over *and* casting malicious reflections upon us with insinuating language. And not satisfied with that, he refuses to receive *and* welcome the [missionary] brethren himself, and also interferes with *and* forbids those who would welcome them, and tries to expel (excommunicate) them from the church.

speak the Word

Father, I pray that You will prosper me in every way and that my body will keep well even as my soul prospers and keeps well.
ADAPTED FROM III JOHN 2

Help me, God, to live my life in Your Truth.
ADAPTED FROM III JOHN 4

prosper with purpose

One of God's most fervent desires for us is that we prosper *in our souls*. This means He wants us to mature spiritually, to be full-grown in mind, will, and emotions. He wants us to think with the mind of Christ and according to His Word. When we are able to do this, we can separate our emotions from decisions we need to make and use our will to line up our lives with His will for us.

To the degree that we do that, He also wants us to prosper and be healthy in all areas of life (see III John 2). There has been a great deal of discussion over whether God wants His children to prosper. Some believe poverty is a virtue, while others believe that all Christians should be rich. I do not believe either one of those extremes. I believe we should concentrate on spiritual maturity and keep God first in our lives and He will gladly give us everything we need to live happy, generous, blessed, and prosperous lives. God is more concerned with how we behave than what we own.

Matthew told us to seek first God's kingdom and His righteousness (His ways of being and doing) and all these things would be added to us (see Matthew 6:33). God wants us to have things as long as things do not have us. Yes, God wants us to be very blessed and He wants us to be a blessing to other people. We are to have "prosperity with a purpose."

God told Abraham that He would bless him and make him a blessing causing him to dispense good to others (see Genesis 12:2). How can anyone be a blessing if he or she has not first been blessed? We cannot give away something we do not have. The Bible says that Abraham was extremely wealthy (see Genesis 13:2), so it is obvious to me that God has no problem with His servants' prospering in every way, including materially, as long as they can handle it properly.

The question often surfaces that "if God wants us to have prosperity, is a poor person godly?" Of course a poor person can be godly, but we do not have to worship poverty. Sick people can be godly, but that does not keep them from seeking healing. Love God with all of your heart no matter what your station is in life, but seek His best and use it for His purposes.

putting the Word to work

To imitate something is to use or follow it as a model. Whose life exhibits goodness that you can imitate? Do not imitate those who do evil, who gossip, and who seek to exert control over others. As you do good, you will demonstrate that you belong to God.

11 Beloved, do not imitate evil, but imitate good. He who does good is of God; he who does evil has not seen (discerned or experienced) God [has enjoyed no vision of Him and does not know Him at all].

12 Demetrius has warm commendation from everyone—and from the Truth itself; we add our testimony also, and you know that our testimony is true.

13 I had much [to say to you when I began] to write, but I prefer not to put it down with pen (a reed) and ink;

14 I hope to see you soon, and we will talk together face to face.

15 Peace be to you! (Good-bye!) The friends here send you greetings. Remember me to the friends there [to every one of them personally] by name.

speak the Word

God, I pray that I will not imitate evil, but that I will always do good because I know You.
ADAPTED FROM III JOHN **11**

Jude

Author:
Jude

Date:
AD 65–80

Everyday Life Principles:
Refute error and contend for the faith.

Build yourself up by spending time in God's Word and by praying in the Holy Spirit.

Trust God to keep you from slipping and to hold you firmly in place in your faith as you do your part to walk in truth.

The book of Jude warns believers against false teaching and provides a helpful list of characteristics of false teachers and erroneous teaching. False teachers are ungodly; they want to use God's grace as an opportunity for disobedience; and they deny Jesus Christ as Lord and Master (see Jude 4). They reject authority (see Jude 8) and look down on what they do not understand (see Jude 10). They are like "clouds without water" and like "trees without fruit" (Jude 12). Furthermore, they grumble and complain, allow their emotions and passions to control them, brag about themselves, and flatter people in manipulative ways so they can get what they want and cause division.

But Jude knows that false teachers will not succeed and he urges believers to "contend for the faith" (Jude 3), to fight for what they know is true. To do that, Jude instructs them to " . . . build yourselves up [founded] on your most holy faith [make progress, rise like an edifice higher and higher], praying in the Holy Spirit" and to "Guard and keep yourselves in the love of God; expect and patiently wait for the mercy of our Lord Jesus Christ (the Messiah)—which will bring you] unto life eternal" (Jude 20, 21). We must do our part, and then trust God to keep us from stumbling or slipping as He enables us to continue walking in truth.

1 JUDE, A servant of Jesus Christ (the Messiah), and brother of James, [writes this letter] to those who are called (chosen), dearly loved by God the Father *and separated (set apart)* and kept for Jesus Christ:

2 May mercy, [soul] peace, and love be multiplied to you.

3 Beloved, my whole concern was to write to you in regard to our common salvation. [But] I found it necessary *and* was impelled to write you and urgently appeal to *and* exhort [you] to contend for the faith which was once for all ªhanded down to the saints [the faith which is that sum of Christian belief which was delivered ªverbally to the holy people of God].

4 For certain men have crept in stealthily [ᵇgaining entrance secretly by a side door]. Their doom was predicted long ago, ungodly (impious, profane) persons who pervert the grace (the spiritual blessing and favor) of our God into lawlessness *and* wantonness *and* immorality, and disown *and* deny our sole Master and Lord, Jesus Christ (the Messiah, the Anointed One).

5 Now I want to remind you, though you were fully informed once for all, that though the Lord [at one time] delivered a people out of the land of Egypt, He subsequently destroyed those [of them] who did not believe [who refused to adhere to, trust in, and rely upon Him].

6 And angels who did not keep (care for, guard, and hold to) their own first place of power but abandoned their proper dwelling place—these He has reserved in custody in eternal chains (bonds) under the thick gloom of utter darkness until the judgment *and* doom of the great day.

7 [The wicked are sentenced to suffer] just as Sodom and Gomorrah and the adjacent towns—which likewise gave themselves over to impurity and indulged in unnatural vice *and* sensual perversity—are laid out [in plain sight] as an exhibit of perpetual punishment [to warn] of everlasting fire. [Gen. 19.]

8 Nevertheless in like manner, these dreamers also corrupt the body, scorn *and* reject authority *and* government, and revile *and* libel *and* scoff at [heavenly] glories (the glorious ones).

9 But when [even] the archangel Michael, contending with the devil, judicially argued (disputed) about the body of Moses, he dared not [presume to] bring an abusive condemnation against him, but [simply] said, The Lord rebuke you! [Zech. 3:2.]

10 But these men revile (scoff and sneer at) anything they do not happen to be acquainted with *and* do not understand; and whatever they do understand physically [that which they know by mere instinct], like irrational beasts—by these they corrupt themselves *and* are destroyed (perish).

11 Woe to them! For they have run riotously in the way of Cain, and have abandoned themselves for the sake of gain [it offers them, following] the error of Balaam, and have perished in rebellion [like that] of Korah! [Gen. 4:3-8; Num. 16; 22-24.]

speak the Word

God, I pray that I will always contend for my faith and my Christian beliefs, no matter what.
ADAPTED FROM JUDE 3

---

a G. Abbott-Smith, *Manual Greek Lexicon of the New Testament.*   b The use of this verb paints this kind of picture.

let God decide

What did Balaam, Korah, and Cain (see Jude 11) do that we need to beware of? All of them tried to get something that God was not giving them. Cain was jealous of Abel, who had God's approval, so he killed him. He wanted what Abel had, but was not willing to do what Abel did to get it. Abel gave an acceptable offering and Cain did not. When we do not want to give God what He asks for, we cannot resent others who do and are blessed because of it.

Baalam disobeyed God in favor of a promotion promised by an earthly king. He chose a position of earthly honor over doing God's will and became so deceived that God spoke to him through his donkey in order to get his attention.

Korah resented Moses because he wanted his position and power. The world is filled with similar people who want position and power and compromise their integrity to get it. They do things that war against their conscience and even if they get the things they thought they wanted, they are never happy with them. Korah's rebellion ended up costing him his life.

All of these men sinned against God in order to try to get something that God was not ready to give them. We can ask God for anything, but we must trust Him to give it to us if it is His will and in His timing. God has an individual plan for each of us and it is wrong to look at other people's lives and covet what they have. If we are happy for their blessings and trust God for ourselves, He will take care of us.

We must learn to wait on God and not take matters into our own hands. There is a way that seems right to man but the end of it is death (see Proverbs 16:25). Delight yourself in the Lord and He will give you the desires of your heart; commit your way to the Lord and He will bring it to pass (see Psalm 37:4, 5).

Enjoy where you are right now on the way to where you are going and do not try to get ahead of God. He has a great plan for you, and even though you may have to wait, you will be blessed in the end.

12 These are hidden reefs (elements of danger) in your love feasts, where they boldly feast sumptuously [carousing together in your midst], without scruples providing for themselves [alone]. They are clouds without water, swept along by the winds; trees, without fruit at the late autumn gathering time—twice (doubly) dead, [lifeless and] plucked up by the roots; 13 Wild waves of the sea, flinging up the foam of their own shame *and* disgrace; wandering stars, for whom the gloom of eternal darkness has been reserved forever.

14 It was of these people, moreover, that Enoch in the seventh [generation] from Adam prophesied when he said, Behold, the Lord comes with His myriads of holy ones (ten thousands of His saints) 15 To execute judgment upon all and to convict all the impious (unholy ones) of all their ungodly deeds which they have committed [in such an] ungodly [way], and of all the severe (abusive, jarring) things which ungodly sinners have spoken against Him. 16 These are inveterate murmurers (grumblers) who complain [of their lot

in life], going after their own desires [controlled by their passions]; their talk is boastful *and* arrogant, [and they claim to] admire men's persons *and* pay people flattering compliments to gain advantage.

17 But you must remember, beloved, the predictions which were made by the apostles (the special messengers) of our Lord Jesus Christ (the Messiah, the Anointed One).

18 They told you beforehand, In the last days (in the end time) there will be scoffers [who seek to gratify their own unholy desires], following after their own ungodly passions.

19 It is these who are [agitators] setting up distinctions *and* causing divisions—merely sensual [creatures, carnal, worldly-minded people], devoid of the [Holy] Spirit *and* destitute of any higher spiritual life.

20 But you, beloved, build yourselves up [founded] on your most holy faith [ᶜmake progress, rise like an edifice higher and higher], praying in the Holy Spirit;

21 Guard *and* keep yourselves in the love of God; expect *and* patiently wait for the mercy of our Lord Jesus Christ (the Messiah)—[which will bring you] unto life eternal.

22 And *refute [so as to]* convict some who dispute with you, *and* on some have mercy who waver *and* doubt.

23 [Strive to] save others, snatching [them] out of [the] fire; on others take

life point

Jude 20 instructs us to pray "in the Holy Spirit." It is the Holy Spirit of God within us Who motivates us and leads us to pray. We must learn to yield to the leading of the Spirit as soon as we sense it, not later when the moment has passed by. That is part of learning to pray without ceasing, to pray all manner of prayers at all times, wherever we may be, and whatever we may be doing (see Ephesians 6:18).

I encourage you to pray in the Holy Spirit, and as you do, you will experience the joy that comes from praying in agreement with God's will.

pity [but] with fear, loathing even the garment spotted by the flesh *and* polluted by their sensuality. [Zech. 3:2-4.]

24 Now to Him Who is able to keep you without stumbling *or* slipping *or* falling, and to present [you] unblemished (blameless and faultless) before the presence of His glory in triumphant joy *and* exultation [with unspeakable, ecstatic delight]—

25 To the one only God, our Savior through Jesus Christ our Lord, be glory (splendor), majesty, might *and* dominion, and power *and* authority, before all time and now and forever (unto all the ages of eternity). Amen (so be it).

speak the Word

Help me, God, to stay built up in my faith, to pray often in the Holy Spirit, and to keep myself in Your love.
ADAPTED FROM JUDE 20, 21

Thank You, God, that You are able to keep me from stumbling or falling, and to present me blameless and faultless before Your presence.
ADAPTED FROM JUDE 24

c Joseph Thayer, *A Greek-English Lexicon of the New Testament.*

Revelation

Author:
John

Date:
AD 70–95

Everyday Life Principles:
Remember that Jesus loves you and that you are always victorious in Him.

In Revelation, focus on what you do understand. Pray for increased understanding, but do not stumble over problematic passages.

Remember that, in the end, Jesus wins.

There are many different perspectives and interpretations of the book of Revelation, and it can be difficult to understand. In this Bible, I chose to deal with the practical aspects of this book, and I simply want to point out that Revelation reminds us that we do have an enemy, Satan; that there is a spiritual war being waged between the forces of God and the forces of the enemy; and, best of all, Jesus wins. As the struggle unfolds, there will be days of deception and the anti-Christ will arise. But, through the Holy Spirit, we can live with discernment during these times and look forward to the Second Coming of Christ. If you are a believer in Jesus Christ, you—and with everyone throughout history who has ever believed in Him as Lord and Savior—are on the winning team and can anticipate an eternity with Him.

Remember that the book of Revelation is a revelation—an unveiling, a clearer picture than we previously had—of Jesus Christ. It teaches us about Who He is and what is important to Him. It reveals His mighty power over the enemy and His great love for His bride, the church.

Revelation is the only book of the Bible that specifically promises that those who read it will be blessed (see Revelation 1:3). As you read, do not get caught up in the parts you do not understand, but focus on its undeniable truths: Jesus is the Son of God; He is worthy of all glory and honor and praise; He loves you; one day He will return to earth; and everyone who believes on Him will live forever with Him in a place where there is no more sickness or sadness. Be encouraged; stand strong in your faith, no matter what comes your way; and enjoy God's love for you every day and look forward to the day when you will live with God in eternity.

1 [THIS IS] the revelation of Jesus Christ [His unveiling of the divine mysteries]. God gave it to Him to disclose *and* make known to His bond servants certain things which must shortly *and* speedily come to pass [a]in their entirety. And He sent and communicated it through His angel (messenger) to His bond servant John,

2 Who has testified to *and* vouched for all that he saw [[a]in his visions], the word of God and the testimony of Jesus Christ.

3 Blessed (happy, [b]to be envied) is the man who reads aloud [in the assemblies] the word of this prophecy; and blessed (happy, [b]to be envied) are those who hear [it read] and who keep themselves true to the things which are written in it [heeding them and laying them to heart], for the time [for them to be fulfilled] is near.

4 John to the seven assemblies (churches) that are in Asia: May grace (God's unmerited favor) be granted to you and spiritual peace ([c]the peace of Christ's kingdom) from Him Who is and Who was and Who is to come, and from the seven Spirits [[d]the sevenfold Holy Spirit] before His throne, [Isa. 11:2.]

5 And from Jesus Christ the faithful *and* trustworthy Witness, the Firstborn of the dead [first to be brought back to life] and the Prince (Ruler) of the kings of the earth. To Him Who [e]ever loves us and has [e]once [for all]

speak the Word

life point

Revelation 1:5 affirms how much Jesus Christ loves us by shedding His own blood that we might be freed from sin. The passage communicates this strong message: *You are worth something because Jesus loves you and shed His blood for you.*

Do not allow your sense of worth to be based on the opinions or actions of others. Do not try to find your worth in how you look or what you do. Do not try to find your worth in how other people treat you. Instead, let your sense of worth come through a relationship with Jesus Christ. You are secure in Him. He loves you!

loosed *and* freed us from our sins by His own blood, [Ps. 89:27.]

6 And formed us into a kingdom (a royal race), priests to His God and Father—to Him be the glory and the power *and* the majesty and the dominion throughout the ages *and* forever and ever. Amen (so be it). [Exod. 19:6; Isa. 61:6.]

7 Behold, He is coming with the clouds, and every eye will see Him, even those who pierced Him; and all the tribes of the earth shall gaze upon Him *and* beat their breasts *and* mourn *and* lament over Him. Even so [must it be]. Amen (so be it). [Dan. 7:13; Zech. 12:10.]

Thank You, Jesus, that You are faithful and true, that You love me and have once and for all freed me from my sins by Your own blood.
ADAPTED FROM REVELATION 1:5

a Marvin Vincent, *Word Studies in the New Testament.* **b** Alexander Souter, *Pocket Lexicon of the Greek New Testament.* **c** G. Abbott-Smith, *Manual Greek Lexicon of the New Testament.* **d** Richard of St. Victor, cited by Richard Trench, *Synonyms of the New Testament.* **e** Charles B. Williams, *The New Testament: A Translation in the Language of the People*: "ever" and "once" captures the idea of ongoing and completed action contained within the Greek present and aorist (past) verb tenses used here.

8 I am the Alpha and the Omega, *the Beginning and the End,* says the Lord God, He Who is and Who was and Who is to come, the Almighty (the Ruler of all). [Isa. 9:6.]

9 I, John, your brother and companion (sharer and participator) with you in the tribulation and kingdom and patient endurance [which are] in Jesus *Christ,* was on the isle called Patmos, [banished] on account of [my witnessing to] the Word of God and the testimony (the proof, the evidence) for Jesus *Christ.*

10 I was in the Spirit [rapt in His power] on the Lord's Day, and I heard behind me a great voice like the calling of a ʾwar trumpet,

11 Saying, *I am the Alpha and the Omega, the First and the Last.* Write promptly what you see (your vision) in a book and send it to the seven churches *which are in Asia*—to Ephesus and to Smyrna and to Pergamum and to Thyatira and to Sardis and to Philadelphia and to Laodicea.

12 Then I turned to see [whose was] the voice that was speaking to me, and on turning I saw seven golden lampstands,

13 And in the midst of the lampstands [One] like a Son of Man, clothed with a robe which reached to His feet and with a girdle of gold about His breast. [Dan. 7:13; 10:5.]

14 His head and His hair were white like white wool, [as white] as snow, and His eyes [flashed] like a flame of fire. [Dan. 7:9.]

15 His feet glowed like burnished (bright) bronze as it is refined in a furnace, and His voice was like the sound of many waters. [Dan. 10:6.]

16 In His right hand He held seven stars, and from His mouth there came forth a sharp two-edged sword, and His face was like the sun shining in full power at midday. [Exod. 34:29.]

17 When I saw Him, I fell at His feet as if dead. But He laid His right hand on me and said, Do not be afraid! I am the First and the Last, [Isa. 44:6.]

18 And the Ever-living One [I am living in the eternity of the eternities]. I died, but see, I am alive forevermore; and I possess the keys of death and Hades (the realm of the dead).

19 Write therefore the things you see, what they are [and signify] and what is to take place hereafter.

20 As to the hidden meaning (the mystery) of the seven stars which you saw on My right hand and the seven lampstands of gold: the seven stars are the seven angels (messengers) of the seven assemblies (churches) and the seven lampstands are the seven churches.

2 TO THE angel (messenger) of the assembly (church) in Ephesus write: These are the words of Him Who holds the seven stars [which are the messengers of the seven churches] in His right hand, Who goes about among the seven golden lampstands [which are the seven churches]:

2 I know your industry *and* activities, laborious toil *and* trouble, and your patient endurance, and how you cannot tolerate wicked [men] and have tested *and* critically appraised those who call [themselves] apostles (special messengers of Christ) and yet are not, and have found them to be impostors *and* liars.

3 I know you are enduring patiently and are bearing up for My name's sake, and you have not fainted *or* become exhausted *or* grown weary.

4 But I have this [one charge to make] against you: that you have left (abandoned) the love that you had at first [you have deserted Me, your first love].

f Marvin Vincent, *Word Studies.*

putting the Word to work

How did you feel when you first began your relationship with God through Jesus Christ? You probably experienced a variety of feelings such as joy and peace and felt a new sense of freedom and a desire to love and to follow God with all your heart. God was probably your first love (see Revelation 2:4), but it can be easy to let other things in life—relationships, career, studies, even going to church—get in the way of passionately loving God. Spend some time in prayer inviting God to show you anything or anyone in your life that has become more important to you than He is. Ask His forgiveness and ask Him to help you make Him your first love once again.

5 Remember then from what heights you have fallen. Repent (change the inner man to meet God's will) and do the works you did previously [when first you knew the Lord], or else I will visit you and remove your lampstand from its place, unless you change your mind *and* repent.

6 Yet you have this [in your favor and to your credit]: you hate the works of the Nicolaitans [what they are doing as corrupters of the people], which I Myself also detest.

7 He who is able to hear, let him listen to *and* give heed to what the Spirit says to the assemblies (churches). To him who overcomes (is victorious), I will grant to eat [of the fruit] of the tree of life, which is in the paradise of God. [Gen. 2:9; 3:24.]

8 And to the angel (messenger) of the assembly (church) in Smyrna write: These are the words of the First

and the Last, Who died and came to life again: [Isa. 44:6.]

9 I know your affliction *and* distress *and* pressing trouble and your poverty—but you are rich! and how you are abused *and* reviled *and* slandered by those who say they are Jews and are not, but are a synagogue of Satan.

10 Fear nothing that you are about to suffer. [Dismiss your dread and your fears!] Behold, the devil is indeed about to throw some of you into prison, that you may be tested *and* proved *and* critically appraised, and for ten days you will have affliction. Be loyally faithful unto death [even if you must die for it], and I will give you the crown of life. [Rev. 3:10, 11.]

11 He who is able to hear, let him listen to *and* heed what the Spirit says to the assemblies (churches). He who overcomes (is victorious) shall in no way be injured by the second death.

12 Then to the angel (messenger) of the assembly (church) in Pergamum write: These are the words of Him Who has *and* wields the sharp two-edged sword:

13 I know where you live—a place where Satan sits enthroned. [Yet] you are clinging to *and* holding fast My name, and you did not deny My faith, even in the days of Antipas, My witness, My faithful one, who was killed (martyred) in your midst—where Satan dwells.

14 Nevertheless, I have a few things against you: you have some people there who are clinging to the teaching of Balaam, who taught Balak to set a trap *and* a stumbling block before the sons of Israel, [to entice them] to eat food that had been sacrificed to idols and to practice lewdness [giving

speak the Word

Jesus, I pray that I will never leave or abandon You, my first love.
ADAPTED FROM REVELATION 2:4

themselves up to sexual vice]. [Num. 25:1, 2; 31:16.]

15 You also have some who in a similar way are clinging to the teaching of the Nicolaitans [those corrupters of the people] *which thing I hate*.

16 Repent [then]! Or else I will come to you quickly and fight against them with the sword of My mouth.

17 He who is able to hear, let him listen to *and* heed what the Spirit says to the assemblies (churches). To him who overcomes (conquers), I will give to eat of the manna that is hidden, and I will give him a white stone with a new name engraved on the stone, which no one knows *or* understands except he who receives it. [Ps. 78:24; Isa. 62:2.]

18 And to the angel (messenger) of the assembly (church) in Thyatira write: These are the words of the Son of God, Who has eyes that flash like a flame of fire, and Whose feet glow like bright *and* burnished *and* white-hot bronze: [Dan. 10:6.]

19 I know your record *and* what you are doing, your love and faith and service and patient endurance, and that your recent works are more numerous *and* greater than your first ones.

20 But I have this against you: that you tolerate the woman Jezebel, who calls herself a prophetess [claiming to be inspired], and who is teaching and leading astray my servants *and* beguiling them into practicing sexual vice and eating food sacrificed to idols. [I Kings 16:31; II Kings 9:22, 30.]

21 I gave her time to repent, but she has no desire to repent of her immorality [symbolic of idolatry] *and* refuses to do so.

22 Take note: I will throw her on a bed [gof anguish], and those who commit adultery with her [her paramours] I will bring down to hpressing

distress *and* severe affliction, unless they turn away their minds from conduct [such as] hers *and* repent of itheir doings.

23 And I will strike her children (her proper followers) dead [thoroughly exterminating them]. And all the assemblies (churches) shall recognize *and* understand that I am He Who searches minds (the thoughts, feelings, and purposes) and the [inmost] hearts, and I will give to each of you [the reward for what you have done] as your work deserves. [Ps. 62:12; Jer. 17:10.]

24 But to the rest of you in Thyatira, who do not hold this teaching, who have not explored *and* known the depths of Satan, as they say—I tell you that I do not lay upon you any other [fresh] burden:

25 Only hold fast to what you have until I come.

26 And he who overcomes (is victorious) and who obeys My commands to the [very] end [doing the works that please Me], I will give him authority *and* power over the nations;

27 And he shall rule them with a sceptre (rod) of iron, as when earthen pots are broken in pieces, and [his power over them shall be] like that which I Myself have received from My Father; [Ps. 2:8, 9.]

28 And I will give him the Morning Star.

29 He who is able to hear, let him listen to *and* heed what the [Holy] Spirit says to the assemblies (churches).

3 AND TO the angel (messenger) of the assembly (church) in Sardis write: These are the words of Him Who has the seven Spirits of God [ithe sevenfold Holy Spirit] and the seven stars: I know your record *and* what you are doing; you are supposed

---

g Marvin Vincent, *Word Studies*. **h** Literal translation. **i** Many ancient manuscripts so read. **j** Richard of St. Victor, cited by Richard Trench, *Synonyms of the New Testament*.

to be alive, but [in reality] you are dead.

2 Rouse yourselves *and* keep awake, and strengthen *and* invigorate what remains and is on the point of dying; for I have not found a thing that you have done [any work of yours] meeting the requirements of My God *or* perfect in His sight.

3 So call to mind the lessons you received and heard; continually lay them to heart *and* obey them, and repent. In case you will not rouse yourselves *and* keep awake *and watch*, I will come upon you like a thief, and you will not know *or* suspect at what hour I will come.

4 Yet you still have a few [persons'] names in Sardis who have not soiled their clothes, and they shall walk with Me in white, because they are worthy *and* deserving.

5 Thus shall he who conquers (is victorious) be clad in white garments, and I will not erase *or* blot out his name from the Book of Life; I will acknowledge him [as Mine] *and* I will confess his name openly before My Father and before His angels. [Ps. 69:28; Dan. 12:1.]

6 He who is able to hear, let him listen to *and* heed what the [Holy] Spirit says to the assemblies (churches).

7 And to the angel (messenger) of the assembly (church) in Philadelphia write: These are the words of the Holy One, the True One, He Who has the key of David, Who opens and no one shall shut, Who shuts and no one shall open: [Isa. 22:22.]

8 I know your [record of] works *and* what you are doing. See! I have set before you a door wide open which no one is able to shut; I know that you have but little power, and yet you have kept My Word *and* guarded My message and have not renounced *or* denied My name.

9 Take note! I will make those of the synagogue of Satan who say they are Jews and are not, but lie—behold, I will make them come and bow down before your feet and learn *and* acknowledge that I have loved you. [Isa. 43:4; 49:23; 60:14.]

10 Because you have guarded *and* kept My word of patient endurance [have held fast the ᵏlesson of My patience with the ᵏexpectant endurance that I give you], I also will keep you [safe] from the hour of trial (testing) which is coming on the whole world to try those who dwell upon the earth.

11 I am coming quickly; hold fast what you have, so that no one may rob you *and* deprive you of your crown.

12 He who overcomes (is victorious), I will make him a pillar in the sanctuary of My God; he shall never be put out of it *or* go out of it, and I will write on him the name of My God and the name of the city of My God, the new Jerusalem, which descends from My God out of heaven, and My own new name. [Isa. 62:2; Ezek. 48:35.]

13 He who can hear, let him listen to *and* heed what the Spirit says to the assemblies (churches).

14 And to the angel (messenger) of the assembly (church) in Laodicea write: These are the words of the Amen, the trusty *and* faithful and true

speak the Word

God, I pray that I will keep Your Word and guard Your message and never renounce or deny Your name.
ADAPTED FROM REVELATION 3:8

k Joseph Thayer, *A Greek-English Lexicon of the New Testament*: The Greek, which we translate "of patient endurance," paints a picture of "a patient, steadfast waiting" for someone or something.

step out and find out

We all need to hear from God each day about many different issues, but there are critical times in our lives when we especially need to know we are hearing clearly from Him. God wants to speak to us, but we have to be careful that we do not develop a closed mindset about *how* He wants to speak to us.

Sometimes God speaks by opening or closing a door to something we want to do, as Revelation 3:7 suggests. My husband, Dave, and I know from experience that God can open doors of opportunity that no one can close, and He can also close doors that we simply cannot open. I pray that God will open only the doors through which He wants me to pass. I may sincerely think something is right to do, when it may be wrong; therefore, I depend on God to close doors I am trying to walk through if I am in fact making a mistake: "A man's mind plans his way, but the Lord directs his steps and makes them sure" (Proverbs 16:9).

Sometimes the only way to discover God's will is to practice what I call "stepping out and finding out." If I pray about a situation and do not feel sure about what I should do, I take a step of faith. God has shown me that trusting Him is like standing before the automatic door to a supermarket. We can stand and look at the door all day, but it will not open until we take a step forward and trigger the mechanism that opens the door.

There are times in life when we must take a step forward in order to find out— one way or the other—what we should do. Some doors will never open unless we take a step toward them. At other times we may take a step and find that God will not open the door. If we trust Him for guidance, and the door opens easily, we can trust that He is leading us to enter into the opportunity before us.

In I Corinthians 16:9 Paul states that God opened a wide door of opportunity for him and his companions. He also mentions that there were many adversaries, so we must not mistake opposition for a closed door.

Paul and his coworkers did not sit and wait for an angel to appear or a vision to be given to them while praying for direction. They took steps in the direction they felt was correct. Many times God did open the door, but there were times when He closed the door. This did not discourage them. They were not afraid of "missing God." They were men of faith and action. They also knew to back off quickly when it became evident that God was not permitting them to follow their own plan. I encourage you to be the same way. Take the steps you believe you need to take in life and see if God opens or shuts the doors.

Witness, the Origin *and* Beginning *and* Author of God's creation: [Isa. 55:4; Prov. 8:22.]

15 I know your [record of] works *and* what you are doing; you are neither cold nor hot. Would that you were cold or hot!

16 So, because you are lukewarm and neither cold nor hot, I will spew you out of My mouth!

17 For you say, I am rich; I have prospered *and* grown wealthy, and I am in need of nothing; and you do not realize *and* understand that you are

wholehearted service

God wants us to serve Him enthusiastically and wholeheartedly. He does not appreciate any half-hearted effort. Revelation 3:15, 16 warns us against being lukewarm and teaches us that being neither hot nor cold is not acceptable to God. Actually, He would prefer that we be cold toward Him rather than lukewarm. His desire is that we be red-hot, on fire, stirred up, and excited about Him, His Word, His principles, and His will for our lives.

Why would God rather someone be cold than lukewarm? It seems that lukewarm is better than nothing. I believe it is because lukewarm people are easily deceived into thinking they are doing what they should be doing when in fact they are not. They are offering sacrifices, not whole-hearted obedience. For example, they might go to church as an obligation but in reality they do not want to be there at all. However, when a person is totally cold toward God, at least they know it and can be dealt with more easily than someone who is deceived.

I once taught a message titled, "Get In, Get Out, or Get Run Over." My theory was that God is moving and we can either get on board and move with Him or remain rebellious and obstinate and get left behind. As far as I am concerned, life is not worth living at all if Jesus Christ is not the center of it. Sadly, many people waste most of their lives before they realize this is true; some never do.

God never does anything halfway and we should not either. Whatever your task may be, work at it heartily (with all your heart) as something for the Lord (see Colossians 3:23).

The first and principle commandment of God is that we love Him with our whole heart, soul, and mind. If we do that, He will be honored and we will be very fulfilled and blessed. Never lag in zeal and in earnest endeavor; be aglow and burn with the Spirit; serving the Lord (see Romans 12:11).

wretched, pitiable, poor, blind, and naked. [Hos. 12:8.]
18 Therefore I counsel you to purchase from Me gold refined *and* tested by fire, that you may be [truly] wealthy, and white clothes to clothe you and to keep the shame of your nudity from being seen, and salve to put on your eyes, that you may see.
19 Those whom I [dearly and tenderly] love, I tell their faults and convict *and* convince *and* reprove and chasten [I discipline and instruct them]. So be enthusiastic *and* in earnest *and* burn-

ing with zeal and repent [changing your mind and attitude]. [Prov. 3:12.]
20 Behold, I stand at the door and knock; if anyone hears *and* listens to

life point

Revelation 3:20 teaches us that Jesus knocks at the door of many hearts right now, but we must remember that the doorknob is on our side. He is a gentleman; He will not force His way into our lives. We must welcome Him.

putting the Word to work

Have you ever had your home broken into or known someone who has? There is a terrible sense of intrusion and violation when something like that occurs. Jesus will never enter a place in your life where He is not welcome. God wants to bring healing and wholeness to every area of your life, but He will wait for your invitation (see Revelation 3:20). Ask God to show you where you need Him to do some work in your life, and know that He is eager to bring restoration, healing, and wholeness.

and heeds My voice and opens the door, I will come in to him and will eat with him, and he [will eat] with Me.
21 He who overcomes (is victorious), I will grant him to sit beside Me on My throne, as I Myself overcame (was victorious) and sat down beside My Father on His throne.
22 He who is able to hear, let him listen to *and* heed what the [Holy] Spirit says to the assemblies (churches).

4 AFTER THIS I looked, and behold, a door standing open in heaven! And the first voice which I had heard addressing me like [the calling of] a ¹war trumpet said, Come up here, and I will show you what must take place in the future.
2 At once I came under the [Holy] Spirit's power, and behold, a throne stood in heaven, with One seated on the throne! [Ezek. 1:26.]
3 And He Who sat there appeared like [the crystalline brightness of] jasper and [the fiery] sardius, and encircling the throne there was a halo that looked like [a rainbow of] emerald. [Ezek. 1:28.]
4 Twenty-four other thrones sur-

rounded the throne, and seated on these thrones were twenty-four elders (ᵐthe members of the heavenly Sanhedrin), arrayed in white clothing, with crowns of gold upon their heads.
5 Out from the throne came flashes of lightning and rumblings and peals of thunder, and in front of the throne seven blazing torches burned, which are the seven Spirits of God [ⁿthe sevenfold Holy Spirit];

life point

Revelation 4:5 speaks of the seven Spirits of God that are before God's throne (see also Revelation 1:4; 3:1). We know there is only one Holy Spirit, but this reference to the seven-fold Holy Spirit shows us that He has various ways of manifesting and expressing Himself among us to bring fullness to our lives. Just as the Trinity is one God in three Persons, so the Holy Spirit is one Spirit with different operations or modes of expression.

6 And in front of the throne there was also what looked like a transparent glassy sea, as if of crystal. And around the throne, in the center at each side of the throne, were four living creatures (beings) who were full of eyes in front and behind [with intelligence as to what is before and at the rear of them]. [Ezek. 1:5, 18.]
7 The first living creature (being) was like a lion, the second living creature like an ox, the third living creature had the face of a man, and the fourth living creature [was] like a flying eagle. [Ezek. 1:10.]
8 And the four living creatures, individually having six wings, were full of eyes all over and within [underneath their wings]; and day and night they

---

1 Marvin Vincent, *Word Studies.* **m** George R. Berry, *Greek-English New Testament Lexicon.* **n** Richard of St. Victor, cited by Richard Trench, *Synonyms of the New Testament.*

never stop saying, Holy, holy, holy is the Lord God Almighty (Omnipotent), Who was and Who is and Who is to come. [Isa. 6:1-3.]

9 And whenever the living creatures offer glory and honor and thanksgiving to Him Who sits on the throne, Who lives forever and ever (through the eternities of the eternities), [Ps. 47:8.]

10 The twenty-four elders (°the members of the heavenly Sanhedrin) fall prostrate before Him Who is sitting on the throne, and they worship Him Who lives forever and ever; and they throw down their crowns before the throne, crying out,

11 Worthy are You, our Lord and God, to receive the glory and the honor and dominion, for You created all things; by Your will they were [brought into being] and were created. [Ps. 19:1.]

5 AND I saw lying on the ᵖopen hand of Him Who was seated on the throne a scroll (book) written within and on the back, closed *and* sealed with seven seals; [Isa. 29:11; Ezek. 2:9, 10; Dan. 12:4.]

2 And I saw a strong angel announcing in a loud voice, Who is worthy to open the scroll? And [who is entitled and deserves and is morally fit] to break its seals?

3 And no one in heaven or on earth or under the earth [in the realm of the dead, Hades] was able to open the scroll or to take a [single] look at its contents.

4 And I wept audibly *and* bitterly because no one was found fit to open the scroll or to inspect it.

speak the Word

5 Then one of the elders [°of the heavenly Sanhedrin] said to me, Stop weeping! See, the Lion of the tribe of Judah, the Root (Source) of David, has won (has overcome and conquered)! He can open the scroll and break its seven seals! [Gen. 49:9, 10; Isa. 11:1, 10; Rev. 22:16.]

6 And there between the throne and the four living creatures (beings) and among the elders [°of the heavenly Sanhedrin] I saw a Lamb standing, as though it had been slain, with seven horns and with seven eyes, which are the seven Spirits of God [�q the sevenfold Holy Spirit] Who have been sent [on duty far and wide] into all the earth. [Isa. 53:7; Zech. 3:8, 9; 4:10.]

7 He then went and took the scroll from the right hand of Him Who sat on the throne.

8 And when He had taken the scroll, the four living creatures and the twenty-four elders [°of the heavenly Sanhedrin] prostrated themselves before the Lamb. Each was holding a harp (lute or guitar), and they had golden bowls full of incense (fragrant spices and gums for burning), which are the prayers of God's people (the saints).

9 And [now] they sing a new song, saying, You are worthy to take the scroll and to break the seals that are on it, for You were slain (sacrificed), and with Your blood You purchased men unto God from every tribe and language and people and nation. [Ps. 33:3.]

10 And You have made them a kingdom (royal race) and priests to our God, and they shall reign [as kings]

Lord, I declare that You are worthy to receive glory and honor and dominion.
ADAPTED FROM REVELATION 4:11

---

o George R. Berry, *Greek-English New Testament Lexicon.* **p** Marvin Vincent, *Word Studies.* **q** Richard of St. Victor, cited by Richard Trench, *Synonyms of the New Testament.*

lion or lamb?

The characteristics of the lion are totally different from those of the lamb, yet the Lord is recognized as having both qualities in Revelation 5:5, 6.

Someone once gave me a picture of a lion and a lamb lying down together, and it reminds me that I am supposed to be a good, godly mixture of both qualities. I never had any trouble with the lion part, but I had a lot of trouble with the lamb part. When we need to communicate with someone, especially concerning confrontational issues, we should first pray for God's grace and mercy to anoint us as lion-hearted lambs. Then we should wait until we have balance in our perspective and approach.

Throughout the Gospels, Jesus seems to act in two contrasting ways. He confronts the moneychangers in the temple with lion-like intensity, overthrowing their tables and firmly demonstrating God's will to all those who watched Him. He said to them, "The Scripture says, My house shall be called a house of prayer; but you have made it a den of robbers" (Matthew 21:13). Yet in other places, we see Jesus as a lamb, standing falsely accused, without speaking one word in His own defense (Matthew 27:12–14).

What are we to learn from His communication patterns? He was a lion when He needed to be and yet always a lamb—He never sinned or failed to be excellent in speech. It is a challenge not to defend yourself when someone comes against you. It is difficult to ignore insults and shun retaliation.

Isaiah 53:7 says that Jesus "was oppressed, [yet when] He was afflicted, He was submissive and opened not His mouth; like a lamb that is led to the slaughter, and as a sheep before her shearers is dumb, so He opened not His mouth."

Sometimes I find that one of the hardest things God asks us to do is be Christ-like in our communication with others. When people are rude and tell you off, mistreat, or insult you, it is hard to look at them with godly love and just wait on God.

Thank God, He gives us the power to change and to become like Christ—a healthy person who knows when to be a lion and when to be a lamb.

over the earth! [Exod. 19:6; Isa. 61:6.] **11** Then I looked, and I heard the voices of many angels on every side of the throne and of the living creatures and the elders [ʳof the heavenly Sanhedrin], and they numbered ten thousand times ten thousand and thousands of thousands, [Dan. 7:10.] **12** Saying in a loud voice, Deserving is the Lamb, Who was sacrificed, to receive all the power and riches and wisdom and might and honor and majesty (glory, splendor) and blessing! **13** And I heard every created thing in

ʳ George R. Berry, *Greek-English New Testament Lexicon.*

heaven and on earth and under the earth [in Hades, the place of departed spirits] and on the sea and all that is in it, crying out together, To Him Who is seated on the throne and to the Lamb be ascribed the blessing and the honor and the majesty (glory, splendor) and the power (might and dominion) forever and ever (through the eternities of the eternities)! [Dan. 7:13, 14.]

14 Then the four living creatures (beings) said, Amen (so be it)! And the elders [ˢof the heavenly Sanhedrin] prostrated themselves and worshiped *Him Who lives forever and ever.*

6 THEN I saw as the Lamb broke open one of the seven seals, and as if in a voice of thunder I heard one of the four living creatures call out, Come!

2 And I looked, and saw there a white horse whose rider carried a bow. And a crown was given him, and he rode forth conquering and to conquer. [Ps. 45:4, 5; Zech. 1:8; 6:1-3.]

3 And when He broke the second seal, I heard the second living creature call out, Come!

4 And another horse came out, flaming red. And its rider was empowered to take the peace from the earth, so that men slaughtered one another; and he was given a huge sword.

5 When He broke open the third seal, I heard the third living creature call out, Come *and look*! And I saw, and behold, a black horse, and in his hand the rider had a pair of scales (a balance).

6 And I heard what seemed to be a voice from the midst of the four living creatures, saying, A quart of wheat for a denarius [a whole day's wages], and three quarts of barley for a denarius; but do not harm the oil and the wine! [II Kings 6:25.]

7 When the Lamb broke open the fourth seal, I heard the fourth living creature call out, Come!

8 So I looked, and behold, an ashy pale horse [ᵗblack and blue as if made so by bruising], and its rider's name was Death, and Hades (the realm of the dead) followed him closely. And they were given authority *and* power over a fourth part of the earth to kill with the sword and with famine and with plague (pestilence, disease) and with wild beasts of the earth. [Ezek. 5:12; Hos. 13:14.]

9 When the Lamb broke open the fifth seal, I saw at the foot of the altar the souls of those whose lives had been sacrificed for [adhering to] the Word of God and for the testimony they had borne.

10 They cried in a loud voice, O [Sovereign] Lord, holy and true, how long now before You will sit in judgment and avenge our blood upon those who dwell on the earth? [Gen. 4:10; Ps. 79:5; Zech. 1:12.]

11 Then they were each given a ᵘlong *and* flowing *and* festive white robe and told to rest *and* wait patiently a little while longer, until the number should be complete of their fellow servants and their brethren who were to be killed as they themselves had been.

12 When He [the Lamb] broke open the sixth seal, I looked, and there was a great earthquake; and the sun grew black as sackcloth of hair, [the full disc of] the moon became like blood. [Joel 2:10, 31.]

13 And the stars of the sky dropped to the earth like a fig tree shedding its unripe fruit out of season when shaken by a strong wind. [Isa. 34:4.]

14 And the ᵛsky rolled up like a scroll *and* vanished, and every mountain

---

s George R. Berry, *Greek-English New Testament Lexicon.*   t A description of the livid, ashen, discolored appearance of the dead; it symbolizes death and pestilence.   u Marvin Vincent, *Word Studies.*   v James Moulton and George Milligan, *The Vocabulary of the Greek Testament.*

and island was dislodged from its place.

15 Then the kings of the earth and their noblemen and their magnates and their military chiefs and the wealthy and the strong and [everyone, whether] slave or free hid themselves in the caves and among the rocks of the mountains, [Isa. 2:10.]

16 And they called to the mountains and the rocks, Fall on (before) us and hide us from the face of Him Who sits on the throne and from the ʷdeepseated indignation *and* wrath of the Lamb. [Isa. 2:19-21; Hos. 10:8.]

17 For the great day of His wrath (vengeance, retribution, indignation) has come, and who is able to stand before it? [Joel 2:11; Mal. 3:2.]

7 AFTER THIS I saw four angels stationed at the four corners of the earth, ʷfirmly holding back the four winds of the earth so that no wind should blow on the earth or sea or upon any tree. [Zech. 6:5.]

2 Then I saw a second angel coming up from the east (the rising of the sun) and carrying the seal of the living God. And with a loud voice he called out to the four angels who had been given authority *and* power to injure earth and sea,

3 Saying, Harm neither the earth nor the sea nor the trees, until we have sealed the bond servants of our God upon their foreheads. [Ezek. 9:4.]

4 And [then] I heard how many were sealed (marked) out of every tribe of the sons of Israel: there were 144,000.

5 Twelve thousand were sealed (marked) out of the tribe of Judah, 12,000 of the tribe of Reuben, 12,000 of the tribe of Gad,

6 Twelve thousand of the tribe of Asher, 12,000 of the tribe of Naphtali, 12,000 of the tribe of Manasseh,

7 Twelve thousand of the tribe of Simeon, 12,000 of the tribe of Levi, 12,000 of the tribe of Issachar,

8 Twelve thousand of the tribe of Zebulun, 12,000 of the tribe of Joseph, 12,000 of the tribe of Benjamin.

9 After this I looked and a vast host appeared which no one could count, [gathered out] of every nation, from all tribes and peoples and languages. These stood before the throne and before the Lamb; they were attired in white robes, with palm branches in their hands.

10 In loud voice they cried, saying, [Our] salvation is due to our God, Who is seated on the throne, and to the Lamb [to Them we owe our deliverance]!

11 And all the angels were standing round the throne and round the elders [ˣof the heavenly Sanhedrin] and the four living creatures, and they fell prostrate before the throne and worshiped God.

12 Amen! (So be it!) they cried. Blessing and glory *and* majesty *and* splendor and wisdom and thanks and honor and power and might [be

putting the Word to work

Every two years, the eyes of much of the world focus on the Summer or Winter Olympics. Have you ever watched the opening ceremonies and the Parade of Nations? With athletes from more than 175 nations parading under the banner of their nation's flag, it is quite a sight to see! Yet it pales in comparison to the multitude from every tribe, nation, people and tongue that will gather together before the throne of God (see Revelation 7:9, 10). Let me encourage you to pray regularly for the nations and people of the world, and for those who take the good news of the Gospel to them.

w Marvin Vincent, *Word Studies.* x George R. Berry, *Greek-English New Testament Lexicon.*

ascribed] to our God to the ages and ages (forever and ever, throughout the eternities of the eternities)! Amen! (So be it!)

13 Then, addressing me, one of the elders [Yof the heavenly Sanhedrin] said, Who are these [people] clothed in the long white robes? And from where have they come?

14 I replied, Sir, you know. And he said to me, These are they who have come out of the great tribulation (persecution), and have washed their robes and made them white in the blood of the Lamb. [Gen. 49:11; Dan. 12:1.]

15 For this reason they are [now] before the [very] throne of God and serve Him day and night in His sanctuary (temple); and He Who is sitting upon the throne will protect *and* spread His tabernacle over *and* shelter them with His presence.

16 They shall hunger no more, neither thirst any more; neither shall the sun smite them, nor any Yscorching heat. [Isa. 49:10; Ps. 121:6.]

17 For the Lamb Who is in the midst of the throne will be their Shepherd, and He will guide them to the springs of the waters of life; and God will wipe away every tear from their eyes. [Ps. 23:2; Isa. 25:8; Ezek. 34:23.]

8 WHEN HE [the Lamb] broke open the seventh seal, there was silence for about half an hour in heaven.

2 Then I saw the seven angels who stand before God, and to them were given seven trumpets.

3 And another angel came and stood over the altar. He had a golden censer, and he was given very much incense (fragrant spices and gums which exhale perfume when burned), that he might mingle it with the prayers of all the people of God (the saints) upon the golden altar before the throne. [Ps. 141:2.]

4 And the smoke of the incense (the perfume) arose in the presence of God, with the prayers of the people of God (the saints), from the hand of the angel.

5 So the angel took the censer and filled it with fire from the altar and cast it upon the earth. Then there followed peals of thunder *and* loud rumblings and blasts *and* noises, and flashes of lightning and an earthquake. [Lev. 16:12; Ezek. 10:2.]

6 Then the seven angels who had the seven trumpets prepared to sound them.

7 The first angel blew [his] trumpet, and there was a storm of hail and fire mingled with blood cast upon the earth. And a third part of the earth was burned up and a third of the trees was burned up and all the green grass was burned up. [Exod. 9:23-25.]

8 The second angel blew [his] trumpet, and something resembling a great mountain, blazing with fire, was hurled into the sea. [Jer. 51:25.]

9 And a third of the sea was turned to blood, a third of the living creatures in the sea perished, and a third of the ships were destroyed.

10 The third angel blew [his] trumpet, and a huge star fell from heaven, burning like a torch, and it dropped on a third of the rivers and on the springs of water—

11 And the name of the star is Wormwood. A third part of the waters was changed into wormwood, and many people died from using the water, because it had become bitter.

12 Then the fourth angel blew [his] trumpet, and a third of the sun was smitten, and a third of the moon, and a third of the stars, so that [the light of] a third of them was darkened, and a third of the daylight [itself] was withdrawn,

y George R. Berry, *Greek-English New Testament Lexicon.*

and likewise a third [of the light] of the night was kept from shining.

13 Then I [looked and I] saw a solitary eagle flying in midheaven, and as it flew I heard it crying with a loud voice, Woe, woe, woe to those who dwell on the earth, because of the rest of the trumpet blasts which the three angels are about to sound!

9 THEN THE fifth angel blew [his] trumpet, and I saw a star that had fallen from the sky to the earth; and to the angel was given the key ᶻof the shaft of the Abyss (the bottomless pit).

2 He opened the ᶻlong shaft of the Abyss (the bottomless pit), and smoke like the smoke of a huge furnace puffed out of the ᶻlong shaft, so that the sun and the atmosphere were darkened by the smoke from the long shaft. [Gen. 19:28; Exod. 19:18; Joel 2:10.]

3 Then out of the smoke locusts came forth on the earth, and such power was granted them as the power the earth's scorpions have. [Exod. 10: 12-15.]

4 They were told not to injure the herbage of the earth nor any green thing nor any tree, but only [to attack] such human beings as do not have the seal (mark) of God on their foreheads. [Ezek. 9:4.]

5 They were not permitted to kill them, but to torment (distress, vex) them for five months; and the pain caused them was like the torture of a scorpion when it stings a person.

6 And in those days people will seek death and will not find it; and they will yearn to die, but death evades and flees from them. [Job 3:21.]

7 The locusts resembled horses equipped for battle. On their heads was something like golden crowns. Their faces resembled the faces of people. [Joel 2:4.]

8 They had hair like the hair of women, and their teeth were like lions' teeth. [Joel 1:6.]

9 Their breastplates (scales) resembled breastplates made of iron, and the [whirring] noise made by their wings was like the roar of a vast number of horse-drawn chariots going at full speed into battle. [Joel 2:5.]

10 They have tails like scorpions, and they have stings, and in their tails lies their ability to hurt men for [the] five months.

11 Over them as king they have the angel of the Abyss (of the bottomless pit). In Hebrew his name is Abaddon [destruction], but in Greek he is called Apollyon [destroyer].

12 The first woe (calamity) has passed; behold, two others are yet to follow.

13 Then the sixth angel blew [his] trumpet, and from the four horns of the golden altar which stands before God I heard a solitary voice,

14 Saying to the sixth angel who had the trumpet, Liberate the four angels who are bound at the great river Euphrates.

15 So the four angels who had been in readiness for that hour in the appointed day, month, and year were liberated to destroy a third of mankind.

16 The number of their troops of cavalry was twice ten thousand times ten thousand (200,000,000); I heard what their number was.

17 And in [my] vision the horses and their riders appeared to me like this: the riders wore breastplates the color of fiery red and sapphire blue and sulphur (brimstone) yellow. The heads of the horses looked like lions' heads, and from their mouths there poured fire and smoke and sulphur (brimstone).

18 A third of mankind was killed by these three plagues—by the fire and the smoke and the sulphur

z Marvin Vincent, *Word Studies*.

(brimstone) that poured from the mouths of the horses.

19 For the power of the horses to do harm is in their mouths and also in their tails. Their tails are like serpents, for they have heads, and it is by means of them that they wound people.

20 And the rest of humanity who were not killed by these plagues even then did not repent of [the worship of] the works of their [own] hands, so as to cease paying homage to the demons and idols of gold and silver and bronze and stone and wood, which can neither see nor hear nor move. [Ps. 115:4-7; 135:15-17; Isa. 17:8.]

21 And they did not repent of their murders or their practice of magic (sorceries) or their sexual vice or their thefts.

10 THEN I saw another mighty angel coming down from heaven, robed in a cloud, with a [halo like a] rainbow over his head; his face was like the sun, and his feet (legs) were like columns of fire.

2 He had a little book (scroll) open in his hand. He set his right foot on the sea and his left foot on the land,

3 And he shouted with a loud voice like the roaring of a lion; and when he had shouted, the seven thunders gave voice *and* uttered their message in distinct words.

4 And when the seven thunders had spoken (sounded), I was going to write [it down], but I heard a voice from heaven saying, Seal up what the seven thunders have said! Do not write it down!

5 Then the [mighty] angel whom I had seen stationed on sea and land raised his right hand to heaven (the asky), [Deut. 32:40; Dan. 12:6, 7.]

6 And swore in the name of (by) Him Who lives forever and ever, Who cre-

ated the heavens (asky) and all they contain, and the earth and all that it contains, and the sea and all that it contains. [He swore] that no more time should intervene *and* there should be no more waiting *or* delay,

7 But that when the days come when the trumpet call of the seventh angel is about to be sounded, then God's mystery (His secret design, His hidden purpose), as He had announced the glad tidings to His servants the prophets, should be fulfilled (accomplished, completed). [Dan. 12:6, 7.]

8 Then the voice that I heard from heaven spoke again to me, saying, Go and take the little book (scroll) which is open on the hand of the angel who is standing on the sea and on the land.

9 So I went up to the angel and asked him to give me the little book. And he said to me, Take it and eat it. It will embitter your stomach, though in your mouth it will be as sweet as honey. [Ezek. 2:8, 9; 3:1-3.]

10 So I took the little book from the angel's hand and ate *and* swallowed it; it was as sweet as honey in my mouth, but once I had swallowed it, my stomach was embittered.

11 Then they said to me, You are to make a fresh prophecy concerning many peoples *and* races and nations and languages and kings. [Jer. 1:10.]

11 A REED [as a measuring rod] was then given to me, [shaped] like a staff, and I was told: Rise up and measure the sanctuary of God and the altar [of incense], and [number] those who worship there. [Ezek. 40:3.]

2 But leave out of your measuring the court outside the sanctuary of God; omit that, for it is given over to the Gentiles (the nations), and they will trample the holy city underfoot

---

a G. Abbott-Smith, *Manual Greek Lexicon.*

for 42 months (three and one-half years). [Isa. 63:18; Zech. 12:3.]

3 And I will grant the power of prophecy to My two witnesses for 1,260 (42 months; three and one-half years), dressed in sackcloth.

4 These [witnesses] are the two olive trees and the two lampstands which stand before the Lord of the earth. [Zech. 4:3, 11-14.]

5 And if anyone attempts to injure them, fire pours from their mouth and consumes their enemies; if anyone should attempt to harm them, thus he is doomed to be slain. [II Kings 1:10; Jer. 5:14.]

6 These [two witnesses] have power to shut up the sky, so that no rain may fall during the days of their prophesying (their bprediction of events relating to Christ's kingdom and its speedy triumph); and they also have power to turn the waters into blood and to smite and scourge the earth with all manner of plagues as often as they choose. [Exod. 7:17, 19; I Kings 17:1.]

7 But when they have finished their testimony and their evidence is all in, the beast (monster) that comes up out of the Abyss (bottomless pit) will wage war on them, and conquer them and kill them. [Dan. 7:3, 7, 21.]

8 And their dead bodies [will lie exposed] in the open street (ca public square) of the great city which is in a spiritual sense called [by the mystical and allegorical names of] Sodom and Egypt, where also their Lord was crucified. [Isa. 1:9.]

9 For three and a half days men from the races and tribes and languages and nations will gaze at their dead bodies and will not allow them to be put in a tomb.

10 And those who dwell on the earth will gloat and exult over them and rejoice exceedingly, taking their ease and sending presents [in congratulation] to one another, because these two prophets had been such a vexation and trouble and torment to all the dwellers on the earth.

11 But after three and a half days, by God's gift the breath of life again entered into them, and they rose up on their feet, and great dread and terror fell on those who watched them. [Ezek. 37:5, 10.]

12 Then [the two witnesses] heard a strong voice from heaven calling to them, Come up here! And before the very eyes of their enemies they ascended into heaven in a cloud. [II Kings 2:11.]

13 And at that [very] hour there was a tremendous earthquake and one tenth of the city was destroyed (fell); seven thousand people perished in the earthquake, and those who remained were filled with dread and terror and were awe-struck, and they glorified the God of heaven.

14 The second woe (calamity) has passed; now the third woe is speedily to come.

15 The seventh angel then blew [his] trumpet, and there were mighty voices in heaven, shouting, The dominion (kingdom, sovereignty, rule) of the world has now come into the possession and become the kingdom of our Lord and of His Christ (the Messiah), and He shall reign forever and ever (for the eternities of the eternities)! [Ps. 22:28; Dan. 7:13, 14, 27.]

16 Then the twenty-four elders [of dthe heavenly Sanhedrin], who sit on their thrones before God, prostrated themselves before Him and worshiped,

17 Exclaiming, To You we give thanks, Lord God Omnipotent, [the One] Who is and [ever] was, for assuming the high sovereignty and

b Joseph Thayer, *A Greek-English Lexicon.*   **c** Alexander Souter, *Pocket Lexicon.*   **d** George R. Berry, *Greek-English New Testament Lexicon.*

the great power that are Yours and for beginning to reign.

18 And the heathen (the nations) raged, but Your wrath (retribution, indignation) came, the time when the dead will be judged and Your servants the prophets and saints rewarded— and those who revere (fear) Your name, both low and high *and* small and great—and [the time] for destroying the corrupters of the earth. [Ps. 2:1.]

19 Then the sanctuary of God in heaven was thrown open, and the ark of His covenant was seen standing inside in His sanctuary; and there were flashes of lightning, loud rumblings (blasts, mutterings), peals of thunder, an earthquake, and a terrific hailstorm. [I Kings 8:1-6.]

12 AND A great sign (wonder)—[warning of future events of ominous significance] appeared in heaven: a woman clothed with the sun, with the moon under her feet, and with a crownlike garland (tiara) of twelve stars on her head.

2 She was pregnant and she cried out in her birth pangs, in the anguish of her delivery.

3 Then another ominous sign (wonder) was seen in heaven: Behold, a huge, fiery-red dragon, with seven heads and ten horns, and seven kingly crowns (diadems) upon his heads. [Dan. 7:7.]

4 His tail swept [across the sky] *and* dragged down a third of the stars and flung them to the earth. And the dragon stationed himself in front of the woman who was about to be delivered, so that he might devour her child as soon as she brought it forth. [Dan. 8:10.]

5 And she brought forth a male Child, One Who is destined to shepherd (rule) all the nations with an iron staff (scepter), and her Child was caught up to God and to His throne. [Ps. 2:8, 9; 110:1, 2.]

6 And the woman [herself] fled into the desert (wilderness), where she has a retreat prepared [for her] by God, in which she is to be fed *and* kept safe for 1,260 days (42 months; three and one-half years).

7 Then war broke out in heaven; Michael and his angels went forth to battle with the dragon, and the dragon and his angels fought.

8 But they were defeated, and there was no room found for them in heaven any longer.

9 And the huge dragon was cast down *and* out—that age-old serpent, who is called the Devil and Satan, he who is the seducer (deceiver) of all humanity the world over; he was forced out *and* down to the earth, and his angels were flung out along with him. [Gen. 3:1, 14, 15; Zech. 3:1.]

10 Then I heard a strong (loud) voice in heaven, saying, Now it has come— the salvation and the power and the kingdom (the dominion, the reign) of our God, and the power (the sovereignty, the authority) of His Christ (the Messiah); for the accuser of our brethren, he who keeps bringing

life point

In Revelation 12:10, Satan is called "the accuser of our brethren." He tries to make us feel guilty and condemned. When we feel unhealthy guilt and condemnation, we must remember that God does not make us feel that way. God wants us to experience His love and feel the power of His forgiveness.

Guilt depresses us and makes us feel as though we are under a heavy burden. Jesus came to lift us up, to bring good news to us that our sins are forgiven and the penalty for them removed. Resist guilt and condemnation by embracing the salvation and authority of Christ in your life.

before our God charges against them day and night, has been cast out! [Job 1:9-11.]

11 And they have overcome (conquered) him by means of the blood of the Lamb and by the utterance of their testimony, for they did not love *and* cling to life even when faced with death [holding their lives cheap till they had to die for their witnessing].

12 Therefore be glad (exult), O heavens and you that dwell in them! But woe to you, O earth and sea, for the devil has come down to you in fierce anger (fury), because he knows that he has [only] a short time [left]! [Isa. 44:23; 49:13.]

13 And when the dragon saw that he was cast down to the earth, he went in pursuit of the woman who had given birth to the male Child.

14 But the woman was supplied with the two wings of a giant eagle, so that she might fly from the presence of the serpent into the desert (wilderness), to the retreat where she is to be kept safe *and* fed for a time, and times, and half a time (three and one-half years, or 1,260 days). [Dan. 7:25; 12:7.]

15 Then out of his mouth the serpent spouted forth water like a flood after the woman, that she might be carried off with the torrent.

16 But the earth came to the rescue of the woman, and the ground opened its mouth and swallowed up the stream of water which the dragon had spouted from his mouth.

17 So then the dragon was furious (enraged) at the woman, and he went away to wage war on the remainder of her descendants—[on those] who obey God's commandments and who have the testimony of Jesus *Christ* [and adhere to it and ᵉbear witness to Him].

13 [AS] ᶠI stood on the sandy beach, I saw a beast coming up out of the sea with ten horns and seven heads. On his horns he had ten royal crowns (diadems) and blasphemous titles (names) on his heads.

2 And the beast that I saw resembled a leopard, but his feet were like those of a bear and his mouth was like that of a lion. And to him the dragon gave his [own] might *and* power and his [own] throne and great dominion.

3 And one of his heads seemed to have a deadly wound. But his death stroke was healed; and the whole earth went after the beast in amazement *and* admiration.

4 They fell down *and* paid homage to the dragon, because he had bestowed on the beast all his dominion *and* authority; they also praised *and* worshiped the beast, exclaiming, Who is a match for the beast, and, Who can make war against him?

5 And the beast was given the power of speech, uttering boastful and blasphemous words, and he was given freedom to exert his authority *and* to exercise his will during forty-two months (three and a half years). [Dan. 7:8.]

6 And he opened his mouth to speak slanders against God, blaspheming His name and His abode, [even vilifying] those who live in heaven.

7 He was further permitted to wage war on God's holy people (the saints) and to overcome them. And power was given him to extend his authority over every tribe and people and tongue and nation, [Dan. 7:21, 25.]

8 And all the inhabitants of the earth will fall down in adoration *and* pay him homage, everyone whose name has not been recorded in the Book of Life of the Lamb that was

e Charles B. Williams, *The New Testament: A Translation in the Language of the People.*   **f** Many ancient manuscripts read "he."

slain [in sacrifice] gfrom the foundation of the world.

9 If anyone is able to hear, let him listen:

10 Whoever leads into captivity will himself go into captivity; if anyone slays with the sword, with the sword must he be slain. Herein is [the call for] the patience and the faith *and* fidelity of the saints (God's people). [Jer. 15:2.]

11 Then I saw another beast rising up out of the land [itself]; he had two horns like a lamb, and he spoke (roared) like a dragon.

12 He exerts all the power *and* right of control of the former beast in his presence, and causes the earth and those who dwell upon it to exalt *and* deify the first beast, whose deadly wound was healed, *and* to worship him.

13 He performs great signs (startling miracles), even making fire fall from the sky to the earth in men's sight.

14 And because of the signs (miracles) which he is allowed to perform in the presence of the [first] beast, he deceives those who inhabit the earth, commanding them to erect a statue (an image) in the likeness of the beast who was wounded by the [small] sword and still lived. [Deut. 13:1-5.]

15 And he is permitted [also] to impart the breath of life into the beast's image, so that the statue of the beast could actually talk and cause to be put to death those who would not bow down *and* worship the image of the beast. [Dan. 3:5.]

16 Also he compels all [alike], both small and great, both the rich and the poor, both free and slave, to be marked with an inscription [hstamped] on their right hands or on their foreheads,

17 So that no one will have power to buy or sell unless he bears the stamp

(mark, inscription), [that is] the name of the beast or the number of his name.

18 Here is [room for] discernment [a call for the wisdom hof interpretation]. Let anyone who has intelligence (penetration and insight enough) calculate the number of the beast, for it is a human number [the number of a certain man]; his number is 666.

14 THEN I looked, and behold, the Lamb stood on Mount Zion, and with Him 144,000 [men] who had His name and His Father's name inscribed on their foreheads.

2 And I heard a voice from heaven like the sound of great waters and like the rumbling of mighty thunder; the voice I heard [seemed like the music] of harpists iaccompanying themselves on their harps.

3 And they sang a new song before the throne [of God] and before the four living creatures and before the elders [of jthe heavenly Sanhedrin]. No one could learn [to sing] that song except the 144,000 who had been ransomed (purchased, redeemed) from the earth.

4 These are they who have not defiled themselves by relations with women, for they are [kpure as] virgins. These are they who follow the Lamb wherever He goes. These are they who have been ransomed (purchased, redeemed) from among men as the firstfruits for God and the Lamb.

5 No lie was found to be upon their lips, for they are blameless (spotless, untainted, without blemish) *before the throne of God.*

6 Then I saw another angel flying in midair, with an eternal Gospel (good news) to tell to the inhabitants of the earth, to every race and tribe and language and people.

g Alternate translation: "recorded from the foundation of the world in the Book of Life of the Lamb that was slain [in sacrifice]." **h** Joseph Thayer, *A Greek-English Lexicon.* **i** Marvin Vincent, *Word Studies.* **j** George R. Berry, *Greek-English New Testament Lexicon.* **k** Charles B. Williams, *The New Testament: A Translation.*

7 And he cried with a mighty voice, Revere God and give Him glory (honor and praise in worship), for the hour of His judgment has arrived. Fall down before Him; pay Him homage *and* adoration *and* worship Him Who created heaven and earth, the sea and the springs (fountains) of water.

8 Then another angel, a second, followed, declaring, Fallen, fallen is Babylon the great! She who made all nations drink of the [maddening] wine of her passionate unchastity [[idolatry]. [Isa. 21:9.]

9 Then another angel, a third, followed them, saying with a mighty voice, Whoever pays homage to the beast and his statue and permits the [beast's] stamp (mark, inscription) to be put on his forehead or on his hand,

10 He too shall [have to] drink of the wine of God's indignation *and* wrath, poured undiluted into the cup of His anger; and he shall be tormented with fire and brimstone in the presence of the holy angels and in the presence of the Lamb. [Gen. 19:24.]

11 And the smoke of their torment ascends forever and ever; and they have no respite (no pause, no intermission, no rest, no peace) day or night— these who pay homage to the beast and to his image and whoever receives the stamp of his name upon him. [Isa. 34:10.]

12 Here [comes in a call for] the steadfastness of the saints [the patience, the endurance of the people of God], those who [habitually] keep God's commandments and [their] faith in Jesus.

13 Then I heard further [[perceiving the distinct words of] a voice from heaven, saying, Write this: Blessed (happy, [m]to be envied) are the dead from now on who die in the Lord! Yes, blessed (happy, [m]to be envied indeed), says the Spirit, [in] that they may rest from their labors, for their works (deeds) do follow (attend, accompany) them!

14 Again I looked, and behold, [I saw] a white cloud, and sitting on the cloud [n]One resembling a Son of Man, with a crown of gold on His head and a sharp scythe (sickle) in His hand. [Dan. 7:13.]

15 And another angel came out of the temple sanctuary, calling with a mighty voice to Him Who was sitting upon the cloud, Put in Your scythe and reap, for the hour has arrived to gather the harvest, for the earth's crop is fully ripened. [Joel 3:13.]

16 So He Who was sitting upon the cloud swung His scythe (sickle) on the earth, and the earth's crop was harvested.

17 Then another angel came out of the temple [sanctuary] in heaven, and he also carried a sharp scythe (sickle).

18 And another angel came forth from the altar, [the angel] who has authority *and* power over fire, and he called with a loud cry to him who had the sharp scythe (sickle), Put forth your scythe and reap the fruitage of the vine of the earth, for its grapes are entirely ripe.

19 So the angel swung his scythe on the earth and stripped the grapes *and* gathered the vintage from the vines of the earth and cast it into the huge winepress of God's indignation *and* wrath.

20 And [the grapes in] the winepress were trodden outside the city, and blood poured from the winepress, [reaching] as high as horses' bridles, for a distance of 1,600 stadia (about 200 miles). [Joel 3:13.]

---

l Joseph Thayer, *A Greek-English Lexicon.* m Alexander Souter, *Pocket Lexicon.* n There is no consensus of opinion concerning the figure resembling a "son of man." Thus the capitals are tentatively presented as a possible interpretation. Many commentators question whether this refers to Christ.

15 THEN I saw another wonder (sign, token, symbol) in heaven, great and marvelous [warning of events of ominous significance]: There were seven angels bringing seven plagues (afflictions, calamities), which are the last, for with them God's wrath (indignation) is completely expressed [reaches its climax and is ended]. [Lev. 26:21.]

2 Then I saw what seemed to be a glassy sea blended with fire, and those who had come off victorious from the beast and from his statue and from the number corresponding to his name were standing beside the glassy sea, with harps of God in their hands.

3 And they sang the song of Moses the servant of God and the song of the Lamb, saying, Mighty and marvelous are Your works, O Lord God the Omnipotent! Righteous (just) and true are Your ways, O Sovereign of the ages (King of the °nations)! [Exod. 15:1; Ps. 145:17.]

4 Who shall not reverence and glorify Your name, O Lord [giving You honor and praise in worship]? For You only are holy. All the nations shall come and pay homage and adoration to You, for Your just judgments (Your righteous sentences and deeds) have been made known and displayed. [Ps. 86:9, 10; Jer. 10:7.]

5 After this I looked and the sanctuary of the tent of the testimony in heaven was thrown open,

6 And there came out of the temple sanctuary the seven angels bringing the seven plagues (afflictions, calamities). They were arrayed in pure

speak the Word

gleaming linen, and around their breasts they wore golden girdles.

7 And one of the four living creatures [then] gave the seven angels seven golden bowls full of the wrath and indignation of God, Who lives forever and ever (in the eternities of the eternities).

8 And the sanctuary was filled with smoke from the glory (the radiance, the splendor) of God and from His might and power, and no one was able to go into the sanctuary until the seven plagues (afflictions, calamities) of the seven angels were ended. [I Kings 8:10; Isa. 6:4; Ezek. 44:4.]

16 THEN I heard a mighty voice from the temple sanctuary saying to the seven angels, Go and empty out on the earth the seven bowls of God's wrath and indignation. [Ps. 69:24; Isa. 66:6.]

2 So the first [angel] went and emptied his bowl on the earth, and foul and painful ulcers (sores) came on the people who were marked with the stamp of the beast and who did homage to his image. [Exod. 9:10, 11; Deut. 28:35.]

3 The second [angel] emptied his bowl into the sea, and it turned into blood like that of a corpse [thick, corrupt, ill-smelling, and disgusting], and every living thing that was in the sea perished.

4 Then the third [angel] emptied out his bowl into the rivers and the springs of water, and they turned into (became) blood. [Exod. 7:17-21.]

5 And I also heard the angel of the

Lord, I declare that Your works are mighty and marvelous, and that Your ways are righteous and true.
ADAPTED FROM REVELATION **15:3**

o Many manuscripts read "nations."

waters say, Righteous (just) are You in these Your decisions *and* judgments, You Who are and were, O Holy One!

6 Because they have poured out the blood of Your people (the saints) and the prophets, and You have given them blood to drink. Such is their due [they deserve it]! [Ps. 79:3.]

7 And [from] the altar I heard [the] cry, Yes, Lord God the Omnipotent, Your judgments (sentences, decisions) are true and just *and* righteous! [Ps. 119:137.]

8 Then the fourth [angel] emptied out his bowl upon the sun, and it was permitted to burn (scorch) humanity with [fierce, glowing] heat (fire).

9 People were severely burned (scorched) by the fiery heat, and they reviled *and* blasphemed the name of God, Who has control of these plagues, and they did not repent of their sins [felt no regret, contrition, and compunction for their waywardness, refusing to amend their ways] to give Him glory.

10 Then the fifth [angel] emptied his bowl on the throne of the beast, and his kingdom was [plunged] in darkness; and people gnawed their tongues for the torment [of their excruciating distress and severe pain] [Exod. 10:21.]

11 And blasphemed the God of heaven because of their anguish and their ulcers (sores), and they did not deplore their wicked deeds *or* repent [for what they had done].

12 Then the sixth [angel] emptied his bowl on the mighty river Euphrates, and its water was dried up to make ready a road for [the coming of] the kings of the east (from the rising sun). [Isa. 11:15, 16.]

13 And I saw three loathsome spirits like frogs, [leaping] from the mouth of the dragon and from the mouth of the beast and from the mouth of the false prophet. [Exod. 8:3; I Kings 22:21-23.]

14 For really they are the spirits of demons that perform signs (wonders, miracles). And they go forth to the rulers *and* leaders all over the world, to gather them together for war on the great day of God the Almighty.

15 Behold, I am going to come like a thief! Blessed (happy, [p]to be envied) is he who stays awake (alert) and who guards his clothes, so that he may not be naked and [have the shame of being] seen exposed!

16 And they gathered them together at the place which in Hebrew is called Armageddon. [II Kings 9:27.]

17 Then the seventh [angel] emptied out his bowl into the air, and a mighty voice came out of the sanctuary *of heaven* from the throne [of God], saying, It is done! [It is all over, it is all accomplished, it has come!] [Isa. 66:6.]

18 And there followed lightning flashes, loud rumblings, peals of thunder, and a tremendous earthquake; nothing like it has ever occurred since men dwelt on the earth, so severe *and* far-reaching was that earthquake. [Exod. 19:16; Dan. 12:1.]

19 The mighty city was broken into three parts, and the cities of the nations fell. And God kept in mind mighty Babylon, to make her drain the cup of His furious wrath *and* indignation.

20 And every island fled and no mountains could be found.

21 And great (excessively oppressive) hailstones, as heavy as a talent [between fifty and sixty pounds], of immense size, fell from the sky on the people; and men blasphemed God for the plague of the hail, so very great was [the torture] of that plague. [Exod. 9:23.]

---

p Alexander Souter, *Pocket Lexicon.*

17 ONE OF the seven angels who had the seven bowls then came and spoke to me, saying, Come with me! I will show you the doom (sentence, judgment) of the great harlot (idolatress) who is seated on many waters, [Jer. 51:13.]

2 [She] with whom the rulers of the earth have joined in prostitution (idolatry) and with the wine of whose immorality (idolatry) the inhabitants of the earth have become intoxicated. [Jer. 25:15, 16.]

3 And [the angel] bore me away [rapt] in the Spirit into a desert (wilderness), and I saw a woman seated on a scarlet beast that was all covered with blasphemous titles (names), and he had seven heads and ten horns.

4 The woman was robed in purple and scarlet and bedecked with gold, precious stones, and pearls, [and she was] holding in her hand a golden cup full of the accursed offenses and the filth of her lewdness and vice. [Jer. 51:7.]

5 And on her forehead there was inscribed a name of mystery [with a secret symbolic meaning]: Babylon the great, the mother of prostitutes (idolatresses) and of the filth and atrocities and abominations of the earth.

6 I also saw that the woman was drunk, [drunk] with the blood of the saints (God's people) and the blood of the martyrs [who witnessed] for Jesus. And when I saw her, I was utterly amazed and wondered greatly.

7 But the angel said to me, Why do you wonder? I will explain to you the [secret symbolic meaning of the] mystery of the woman, as well as of the beast having the seven heads and ten horns that carries her.

8 The beast that you saw [once] was, but [now] is no more, and he is going to come up out of the Abyss (the bottomless pit) and proceed to go to perdition. And the inhabitants of the earth whose names have not been recorded in the Book of Life from the foundation of the world will be astonished when they look at the beast, because he [once] was, but [now] is no more, and he is [yet] to come. [Dan. 7:3.]

9 This calls for a mind [to consider that is packed] with wisdom and intelligence [it is something for a particular mode of thinking and judging of thoughts, feelings, and purposes]. The seven heads are seven hills upon which the woman is sitting;

10 And they are also seven kings, five of whom have fallen, one still exists [and is reigning]; the other [the seventh] has not yet appeared, and when he does arrive, he must stay [but] a brief time.

11 And as for the beast that [once] was, but now is no more, he [himself] is an eighth ruler (king, head), but he is of the seven and belongs to them, and he goes to perdition.

12 Also the ten horns that you observed are ten rulers (kings) who have as yet received no royal dominion, but together they are to receive power and authority as rulers for a single hour, along with the beast. [Dan. 7:20-24.]

13 These have one common policy (opinion, purpose), and they deliver their power and authority to the beast.

14 They will wage war against the Lamb, and the Lamb will triumph over them; for He is Lord of lords and King of kings—and those with Him and on His side are chosen and called [elected] and loyal and faithful followers. [Dan. 2:47.]

15 And [the angel further] said to me, The waters that you observed, where the harlot is seated, are races and multitudes and nations and dialects (languages).

16 And the ten horns that you saw, they and the beast will [be the very

ones to] hate the harlot (the idolatrous woman); they will make her cheerless (bereaved, desolate), and they will strip her and eat up her flesh and utterly consume her with fire.

17 For God has put it into their hearts to carry out His own purpose by acting in harmony in surrendering their royal power *and* authority to the beast, until the prophetic words (intentions and promises) of God shall be fulfilled.

18 And the woman that you saw is herself the great city which dominates *and* controls the rulers *and* the leaders of the earth.

18 THEN I saw another angel descending from heaven, possessing great authority, and the earth was illuminated with his radiance *and* splendor.

2 And he shouted with a mighty voice, She is fallen! Mighty Babylon is fallen! She has become a resort *and* dwelling place for demons, a dungeon haunted by every loathsome spirit, an abode for every filthy and detestable bird.

3 For all nations have drunk the wine of her passionate unchastity, and the rulers *and* leaders of the earth have joined with her in committing fornication (idolatry), and the businessmen of the earth have become rich with the wealth of her excessive luxury *and* wantonness. [Jer. 25:15, 27.]

4 I then heard another voice from heaven saying, Come out from her, my people, so that you may not share in her sins, neither participate in her plagues. [Isa. 48:20; Jer. 50:8.]

5 For her iniquities (her crimes and transgressions) are piled up as high as heaven, and God has remembered her wickedness *and* [her] crimes [and calls them up for settlement]. [Jer. 51:9.]

6 Repay to her what she herself has paid [to others] and double [her doom] in accordance with what she has done. Mix a double portion for her in the cup she mixed [for others]. [Ps. 137:8.]

7 To the degree that she glorified herself and reveled in her wantonness [living deliciously and luxuriously], to that measure impose on her torment *and* anguish and tears *and* mourning. Since in her heart she boasts, I am not a widow; as a queen [on a throne] I sit, and I shall never see suffering *or* experience sorrow— [Isa. 47:8, 9.]

8 So shall her plagues (afflictions, calamities) come thick upon her in a single day, pestilence and anguish *and* sorrow and famine; and she shall be utterly consumed (burned up with fire), for mighty is the Lord God Who judges her.

9 And the rulers *and* leaders of the earth who joined her in her immorality (idolatry) and luxuriated with her will weep *and* beat their breasts and lament over her when they see the smoke of her conflagration. [Ezek. 26:16, 17.]

10 They will stand a long way off, in terror of her torment, and they will cry, Woe *and* alas, the great city, the mighty city, Babylon! In one single hour how your doom (judgment) has overtaken you!

11 And earth's businessmen will weep and grieve over her because no one buys their freight (cargo) any more. [Ezek. 27:36.]

12 Their merchandise is of gold, silver, precious stones, and pearls; of fine linen, purple, silk, and scarlet [stuffs]; all kinds of scented wood, all sorts of articles of ivory, all varieties of objects of costly woods, bronze, iron, and marble; [Ezek. 27:12, 13, 22.]

13 Of cinnamon, spices, incense, ointment *and* perfume, and frankincense, of wine and olive oil, fine flour and wheat; of cattle and sheep, horses and conveyances; and of slaves (the bodies) and souls of men!

14 The ripe fruits *and* delicacies for which your soul longed have gone from you, and all your luxuries *and* dainties, your elegance *and* splendor are lost to you, never again to be recovered *or* experienced!

15 The dealers who handled these articles, who grew wealthy through their business with her, will stand a long way off, in terror of her doom *and* torment, weeping and grieving aloud, and saying,

16 Alas, alas for the great city that was robed in fine linen, in purple and scarlet, bedecked *and* glittering with gold, with precious stones, and with pearls! [Ezek. 27:31, 36.]

17 Because in one [single] hour all the vast wealth has been destroyed (wiped out). And all ship captains *and* pilots, navigators and all who live by seafaring, the crews and all who ply their trade on the sea, stood a long way off, [Isa. 23:14; Ezek. 27:26-30.]

18 And exclaimed as they watched the smoke of her burning, What city could be compared to the great city!

19 And they threw dust on their heads as they wept and grieved, exclaiming, Woe *and* alas, for the great city, where all who had ships on the sea grew rich [through her extravagance] from her great wealth! In one single hour she has been destroyed *and* has become a desert! [Ezek. 27:30-34.]

20 Rejoice (celebrate) over her, O heaven! O saints (people of God) and apostles and prophets, because God has executed vengeance for you upon her! [Isa. 44:23; Jer. 51:48.]

21 Then a single powerful angel took up a boulder like a great millstone and flung it into the sea, crying, With such violence shall Babylon the great city be hurled down to destruction and shall never again be found. [Jer. 51:63, 64; Ezek. 26:21.]

22 And the sound of harpists and minstrels and flute players and trumpeters shall never again be heard in you, and no skilled artisan of any craft shall ever again be found in you, and the sound of the millstone shall never again be heard in you. [Isa. 24:8; Ezek. 26:13.]

23 And never again shall the light of a lamp shine in you, and the voice of bridegroom and bride shall never be heard in you again; for your businessmen were the great *and* prominent men of the earth, and by your magic spells *and* poisonous charm all nations were led astray (seduced and deluded).

24 And in her was found the blood of prophets and of saints, and of all those who have been slain (slaughtered) on earth. [Jer. 51:49.]

19 AFTER THIS I heard what sounded like a mighty shout of a great crowd in heaven, exclaiming, Hallelujah (praise the Lord)! Salvation and glory (splendor and majesty) and power (dominion and authority) [belong] to our God!

2 Because His judgments (His condemnation and punishment, His sentences of doom) are true *and* sound and just *and* upright. He has judged (convicted, pronounced sentence, and doomed) the great *and* notorious harlot (idolatress) who corrupted *and* demoralized *and* poisoned the earth with her lewdness *and* adultery (idolatry). And He has avenged (visited on her the penalty for) the blood of His servants at her hand. [Deut. 32:43.]

3 And again they shouted, Hallelujah (praise the Lord)! The smoke of her [burning] shall continue to ascend forever and ever (through the eternities of the eternities). [Isa. 34:10.]

4 Then the twenty-four elders [of qthe heavenly Sanhedrin] and the

q George R. Berry, *Greek-English New Testament Lexicon.*

four living creatures fell prostrate and worshiped [paying divine honors to] God, Who sits on the throne, saying, Amen! Hallelujah (praise the Lord)!

5 Then from the throne there came a voice, saying, Praise our God, all you servants of His, you who reverence Him, both small and great! [Ps. 115:13.]

6 After that I heard what sounded like the shout of a vast throng, like the boom of many pounding waves, and like the roar of terrific *and* mighty peals of thunder, exclaiming, Hallelujah (praise the Lord)! For now the Lord our God the Omnipotent (the All-Ruler) reigns!

7 Let us rejoice and shout for joy [exulting and triumphant]! Let us celebrate *and* ascribe to Him glory *and* honor, for the marriage of the Lamb [at last] has come, and His bride has prepared herself. [Ps. 118:24.]

8 She has been permitted to dress in fine (radiant) linen, dazzling and white—for the fine linen is (signifies, represents) the righteousness (the upright, just, and godly living, deeds, and conduct, and right standing with God) of the saints (God's holy people).

9 Then [the angel] said to me, Write this down: Blessed (happy, ʳto be envied) are those who are summoned (invited, called) to the marriage supper of the Lamb. And he said to me [further], These are the true words (the genuine and exact declarations) of God.

10 Then I fell prostrate at his feet to worship (to pay divine honors) to him, but he [restrained me] and said, Refrain! [You must not do that!] I am [only] another servant with you and your brethren who have [accepted and hold] the testimony borne by Jesus. Worship God! For the substance (essence) of the truth revealed by Jesus is the spirit of all prophecy [the vital breath, the inspiration of all inspired preaching and interpretation of the divine will and purpose, including both mine and yours].

11 After that I saw heaven opened, and behold, a white horse [appeared]! The One Who was riding it is called Faithful (Trustworthy, Loyal, Incorruptible, Steady) and True, and He passes judgment and wages war in righteousness (holiness, justice, and uprightness). [Ezek. 1:1.]

12 His eyes [blaze] like a flame of fire, and on His head are many kingly crowns (diadems); and He has a title (name) inscribed which He alone knows *or* can understand. [Dan. 10:6.]

13 He is dressed in a robe dyed by ˢdipping in blood, and the title by which He is called is The Word of God.

14 And the troops of heaven, clothed in fine linen, dazzling and clean, followed Him on white horses.

15 From His mouth goes forth a sharp sword with which He can smite (afflict, strike) the nations; and He

speak the Word

God, I worship You.
ADAPTED FROM REVELATION 19:10

Thank You, Jesus, that You are Faithful, Trustworthy, Loyal, Incorruptible, Steady, and True.
ADAPTED FROM REVELATION 19:11

r Alexander Souter, *Pocket Lexicon.*   s Some ancient manuscripts read "sprinkled with blood."

life point

Examination of Revelation 19:11–16 readily reveals that Jesus is waging war in the heavenlies (see also Revelation 19:19–21), and that the Word, the name, and the blood are present and being exalted, just as they should be in our daily lives here on earth.

will shepherd *and* control them with a staff (scepter, rod) of iron. He will tread the winepress of the fierceness of the wrath *and* indignation of God the All-Ruler (the Almighty, the Omnipotent). [Ps. 2:9.]

16 And on His garment (robe) and on His thigh He has a name (title) inscribed, KING OF KINGS AND LORD OF LORDS. [Deut. 10:17; Dan. 2:47.]

17 Then I saw a single angel stationed in the sun's ‡light, and with a mighty voice he shouted to all the birds that fly across the sky, Come, gather yourselves together for the great supper of God, [Ezek. 39:4, 17-20.]

18 That you may feast on the flesh of rulers, the flesh of generals *and* captains, the flesh of powerful *and* mighty men, the flesh of horses and their riders, and the flesh of all humanity, both free and slave, both small and great!

19 Then I saw the beast and the rulers *and* leaders of the earth with their troops mustered to go into battle *and* make war against Him Who is mounted on the horse and against His troops.

20 And the beast was seized *and* overpowered, and with him the false prophet who in his presence had worked wonders *and* performed miracles by which he led astray those who had accepted *or* permitted to be placed upon them the stamp (mark) of the beast and those who paid homage *and* gave divine honors to his statue. Both of them were hurled alive into the fiery lake that burns *and* blazes with brimstone.

21 And the rest were killed with the sword that issues from the mouth of Him Who is mounted on the horse, and all the birds fed ravenously *and* glutted themselves with their flesh.

20 THEN I saw an angel descending from heaven; he was holding the key of the Abyss (the bottomless pit) and a great chain was in his hand.

2 And he gripped *and* overpowered the dragon, that old serpent [of primeval times], who is the devil and Satan, and [securely] bound him for a thousand years.

3 Then he hurled him into the Abyss (the bottomless pit) and closed it and sealed it above him, so that he should no longer lead astray *and* deceive *and* seduce the nations until the thousand years were at an end. After that he must be liberated for a short time.

4 Then I saw thrones, and sitting on them were those to whom authority to act as judges *and* to pass sentence was entrusted. Also I saw the souls of those who had been slain with axes [beheaded] for their witnessing to Jesus and [for preaching and testifying] for the Word of God, and who had refused to pay homage to the

speak the Word

‡ Joseph Thayer, *A Greek-English Lexicon.*

beast or his statue and had not accepted his mark *or* permitted it to be stamped on their foreheads or on their hands. And they lived again and ruled with Christ (the Messiah) a thousand years. [Dan. 7:9, 22, 27.]

5 The remainder of the dead were not restored to life again until the thousand years were completed. This is the first resurrection.

6 Blessed (happy, ᵘto be envied) and holy (spiritually whole, of unimpaired innocence and proved virtue) is the person who takes part (shares) in the first resurrection! Over them the second death exerts no power *or* authority, but they shall be ministers of God and of Christ (the Messiah), and they shall rule along with Him a thousand years.

7 And when the thousand years are completed, Satan will be released from his place of confinement,

8 And he will go forth to deceive *and* seduce *and* lead astray the nations which are in the four quarters of the earth—Gog and Magog—to muster them for war; their number is like the sand of the sea. [Ezek. 38:2, 9, 15, 22.]

9 And they swarmed up over the broad plain of the earth and encircled the fortress (camp) of God's people (the saints) and the beloved city; but fire descended from heaven and consumed them. [II Kings 1:10-12; Ezek. 38:2, 22.]

10 Then the devil who had led them astray [deceiving and seducing them] was hurled into the fiery lake of burning brimstone, where the beast and false prophet were; and they will be tormented day and night forever and ever (through the ages of the ages).

11 Then I saw a great white throne and the One Who was seated upon it, from Whose presence *and* from the sight of Whose face earth and sky fled away, and no place was found for them.

12 I [also] saw the dead, great and small; they stood before the throne, and books were opened. Then another book was opened, which is [the Book] of Life. And the dead were judged (sentenced) by what they had done [ᵛtheir whole way of feeling and acting, their aims and endeavors] in accordance with what was recorded in the books.

13 And the sea delivered up the dead who were in it, death and Hades (ʷthe state of death or disembodied existence) surrendered the dead in them, and all were tried *and* their cases determined by what they had done [according to their motives, aims, and works].

14 Then death and Hades (ʷthe state of death or disembodied existence) were thrown into the lake of fire. This is the second death, the lake of fire.

15 And if anyone's [name] was not found recorded in the Book of Life, he was hurled into the lake of fire.

21 THEN I saw a new ᵛsky (heaven) and a new earth, for the former ᵛsky and the former earth had passed away (vanished), and there no longer existed any sea. [Isa. 65:17; 66:22.]

2 And I saw the holy city, the new Jerusalem, descending out of heaven from God, all arrayed like a bride beautified *and* adorned for her husband;

3 Then I heard a mighty voice from the throne *and* I perceived its distinct words, saying, See! The abode of God is with men, and He will live (encamp, tent) among them; and they shall be His people, and God shall personally be with them and be their God. [Ezek. 37:27.]

4 God will wipe away every tear from their eyes; and death shall be no more, neither shall there be anguish (sorrow and mourning) nor grief nor

---

u Alexander Souter, *Pocket Lexicon.* **v** Joseph Thayer, *A Greek-English Lexicon.* **w** James Orr et al., eds., *The International Standard Bible Encyclopedia.*

putting the Word to work

What do you imagine heaven will be like? One of the wonderful promises about heaven is that we will enjoy unbroken fellowship with God and that there will be no more death, sorrow, crying, or pain (see Revelation 21:3, 4). God Himself will wipe every tear from your eye. If you are in a difficult season of life, know that God is your very present help in trouble right now, and the day is coming when you will be troubled no more. Thank God for His promise, and receive His strength for today and His hope for tomorrow.

pain any more, for the old conditions *and* the former order of things have passed away. [Isa. 25:8; 35:10.]
5   And He Who is seated on the throne said, See! I make all things new. Also He said, Record this, for these sayings are faithful (accurate, incorruptible, and trustworthy) and true (genuine). [Isa. 43:19.]
6   And He [further] said to me, It is done! I am the Alpha and the Omega, the Beginning and the End. To the thirsty I [Myself] will give water without price from the fountain (springs) of the water of Life. [Isa. 55:1.]
7   He who is victorious shall inherit all these things, and I will be God to him and he shall be My son.
8   But as for the cowards *and* the ignoble *and* the contemptible *and* the cravenly lacking in courage *and* the cowardly submissive, and as for the unbelieving and faithless, and as for the depraved and defiled with abominations, and as for murderers and the lewd *and* adulterous and the practicers of magic arts and the idol-

speak the Word

life point

God is the Alpha and Omega, the Beginning and the End (see Revelation 21:6). Since this is the case, He is also everything in between. He knows your situation and will lead you and guide you if you trust Him to do so. Rely on your heavenly Father to give you what you need, one day at a time.

aters (those who give supreme devotion to anyone or anything other than God) and all liars (those who knowingly convey untruth by word or deed)—[all of these shall have] their part in the lake that blazes with fire and brimstone. This is the second death. [Isa. 30:33.]
9   Then one of the seven angels who had the seven bowls filled with the seven final plagues (afflictions, calamities) came and spoke to me. He said, Come with me! I will show you the bride, the Lamb's wife.
10 Then in the Spirit He conveyed me away to a vast and lofty mountain and exhibited to me the holy (hallowed, consecrated) city of Jerusalem descending out of heaven from God, [Ezek. 40:2.]
11 Clothed in God's glory [in all its splendor and radiance]. The luster of it resembled a rare *and* most precious jewel, like jasper, shining clear as crystal.
12 It had a massive and high wall with twelve [large] gates, and at the gates [there were stationed] twelve angels, and [on the gates] the names of the twelve tribes of the sons of Israel were written: [Exod. 28:21; Ezek. 48:30-35.]
13 On the east side three gates, on the north side three gates, on the south

Thank You, God, that You make all things new.
ADAPTED FROM REVELATION 21:5

side three gates, and on the west side three gates.

14 And the wall of the city had twelve foundation [stones], and on them the twelve names of the twelve apostles of the Lamb.

15 And he who spoke to me had a golden measuring reed (rod) to measure the city and its gates and its wall. [Ezek. 40:5.]

16 The city lies in a square, its length being the same as its width. And he measured the city with his reed—12,000 stadia (about 1,500 miles); its length and width and height are the same.

17 He measured its wall also—144 cubits (about 72 yards) by a man's measure [ˣof a cubit from his elbow to his third fingertip], which is [the measure] of the angel.

18 The wall was built of jasper, while the city [itself was of] pure gold, clear and transparent like glass.

19 The foundation [stones] of the wall of the city were ornamented with all of the precious stones. The first foundation [stone] was jasper, the second sapphire, the third chalcedony (or white agate), the fourth emerald, [Isa. 54:11, 12.]

20 The fifth onyx, the sixth sardius, the seventh chrysolite, the eighth beryl, the ninth topaz, the tenth chrysoprase, the eleventh jacinth, the twelfth amethyst.

21 And the twelve gates were twelve pearls, each separate gate being built of one solid pearl. And the main street (the broadway) of the city was of gold as pure *and* translucent as glass.

22 I saw no temple in the city, for the Lord God Omnipotent [Himself] and the Lamb [Himself] are its temple.

23 And the city has no need of the sun nor of the moon to give light to it, for the splendor *and* radiance (glory) of God illuminate it, and the Lamb is its lamp. [Isa. 24:23; 60:1, 19.]

24 The nations shall walk by its light and the rulers *and* leaders of the earth shall bring into it their glory.

25 And its gates shall never be closed by day, and there shall be no night there. [Isa. 60:11.]

26 They shall bring the glory (the splendor and majesty) and the honor of the nations into it.

27 But nothing that defiles *or* profanes *or* is ʸunwashed shall ever enter it, nor anyone who commits abominations (unclean, detestable, morally repugnant things) or practices falsehood, but only those whose names are recorded in the Lamb's Book of Life.

22 THEN HE showed me the river whose waters give life, sparkling like crystal, flowing out from the throne of God and of the Lamb

2 Through the middle of the broadway of the city; also, on either side of the river was the tree of life with its twelve varieties of fruit, yielding each month its fresh crop; and the leaves of the tree were for the healing *and* the restoration of the nations. [Gen. 2:9.]

3 There shall no longer exist there anything that is accursed (detestable, foul, offensive, impure, hateful, or horrible). But the throne of God and of the Lamb shall be in it, and His servants shall worship Him [pay divine honors to Him and do Him holy service]. [Zech. 14:21.]

4 They shall see His face, and His name shall be on their foreheads. [Ps. 17:15.]

5 And there shall be no more night; they have no need for lamplight or sunlight, for the Lord God will illuminate them *and* be their light, and they shall reign [as kings] forever and ever (through the eternities of the eternities).

6 And he [of the seven angels fur-

---

x Adam Clarke, *The Holy Bible with A Commentary.*   **y** Alexander Souter, *Pocket Lexicon.*

ther] said to me, These statements are reliable (worthy of confidence) and genuine (true). And the Lord, the God of the spirits of the prophets, has sent His messenger (angel) to make known *and* exhibit to His servants what must soon come to pass.

7   And behold, I am coming speedily. Blessed (happy and [z]to be envied) is he who observes *and* lays to heart *and* keeps the truths of the prophecy (the predictions, consolations, and warnings) contained in this [little] book.

8   And I, John, am he who heard and witnessed these things. And when I heard and saw them, I fell prostrate before the feet of the messenger (angel) who showed them to me, to worship him.

9   But he said to me, Refrain! [You must not do that!] I am [only] a fellow servant along with yourself and with your brethren the prophets and with those who are mindful of *and* practice [the truths contained in] the messages of this book. Worship God!

10   And he [further] told me, Do not seal up the words of the prophecy of this book *and* make no secret of them, for the time [a]when things are brought to a crisis *and* the period of their fulfillment is near.

11   He who is unrighteous (unjust, wicked), let him be unrighteous still; and he who is filthy (vile, impure), let him be filthy still; and he who is righteous (just, upright, in right standing with God), let him do right still; and he who is holy, let him be holy still. [Dan. 12:10.]

12   Behold, I am coming soon, and I shall bring My wages *and* rewards with Me, to repay *and* render to each one just what his own actions *and* his own work merit. [Isa. 40:10; Jer. 17:10.]

13   I am the Alpha and the Omega, the First and the Last (the Before all and the End of all). [Isa. 44:6; 48:12.]

14   Blessed (happy and [z]to be envied) are those who cleanse their garments, that they may have the authority *and* right to [approach] the tree of life and to enter through the gates into the city. [Gen. 2:9; 3:22, 24.]

15   [But] without are the dogs and those who practice sorceries (magic arts) and impurity [the lewd, adulterers] and the murderers and idolaters and everyone who loves and deals in falsehood (untruth, error, deception, cheating).

16   I, Jesus, have sent My messenger (angel) to you to witness *and* to give you assurance of these things for the churches (assemblies). I am the Root (the Source) and the Offspring of David, the radiant *and* brilliant Morning Star. [Isa. 11:1, 10.]

17   The [Holy] Spirit and the bride (the church, the true Christians) say, Come! And let him who is listening say, Come! And let everyone come who is thirsty [who is painfully conscious of his need [a]of those things by which the soul is refreshed, supported, and strengthened]; and whoever [earnestly] desires to do it, let him come, take, appropriate, *and* drink the water of Life without cost. [Isa. 55:1.]

18   I [personally solemnly] warn everyone who listens to the statements of the prophecy [the [a]predictions and the consolations and admonitions pertaining to them] in this book: If anyone shall add anything to them, God will add *and* lay upon him the plagues (the afflictions and the calamities) that are recorded *and* described in this book.

19   And if anyone cancels *or* takes away from the statements of the book of this prophecy [these [a]predictions relating to Christ's kingdom and its speedy triumph, together with the consolations and admonitions or warnings pertaining to them], God

---

z Alexander Souter, *Pocket Lexicon.*   **a** Joseph Thayer, *A Greek-English Lexicon.*

payday is coming

Every person, with no exceptions, will one day stand before God and give an account of his life (see Romans 14:12). I want to encourage you not to "live like there is no tomorrow," because tomorrow always comes. Jesus will come for us when we least expect it, and then it will be too late to do all the things we intended to do but never got around to. One of the spiritual laws we see throughout the Word of God is that we reap what we sow. Galatians says very emphatically that we are not to be deceived and misled, for whatever a man sows that and that *only* is what he will reap.

Salvation is a gift of God; it is given by His grace and is to be received by faith. We do not get into heaven because of our good works, but Revelation 22:12 teaches us that our works will be judged and rewarded according to what we have merited.

Our works are not even judged only by what we have done, but by the motives behind them. Works done for impure motives will be burned up. If we give money or things, but do so to be seen of men or to be admired and well thought of, then we should be sure that satisfies us because that is all the reward we will ever get.

God sees what we do in secret and we will be rewarded openly. Everything that is now done behind closed doors will one day be brought out in the open, so we should be sure that we realize nothing is really eternally hidden. The day of reckoning will come.

Some people might think, *Well, as long as I am going to heaven, that is enough*. If this is our only motive in life, then we are living selfishly. We should live for God and His glory. We should realize that we are alive for a purpose and part of that purpose is to be used by God to reconcile others to Him. We are actually created for the good works that God prepared for us ahead of time (see Ephesians 2:10). It is God's desire and will that we do good works, but we are to do them because He loves us, not to get Him to love us or to impress people.

Payday is coming! Are you ready?

will cancel *and* take away from him his share in the tree of life and in the city of holiness (purity and hallowedness), which are described *and* promised in this book.
20 He Who gives this warning *and* affirms *and* testifies to these things says, Yes (it is true). [Surely] I am com-

ing quickly (swiftly, speedily). Amen (so let it be)! Yes, come, Lord Jesus!
21 The grace (blessing and favor) of the Lord Jesus *Christ (the Messiah)* be [b]with all the saints (God's holy people, [c]those set apart for God, to be, as it were, exclusively His). Amen (so let it be)!

speak the Word

Lord Jesus, come quickly!
ADAPTED FROM REVELATION 22:20

b Some manuscripts have "be with all," while others have "be with the saints." **c** Joseph Thayer, *A Greek-English Lexicon.*

How to Receive Jesus as Your Lord and Savior

The most important relationship of your life is a personal relationship with Jesus Christ. If you would like to receive Him as your Lord and Savior, and enter into the greatest relationship you have ever known, please pray the prayer below.

Father,
You loved the world so much that You gave Your only begotten Son to die for our sins so that whoever believes in Him will not perish but have eternal life.

Your Word says we are saved by grace through faith as a gift from You. There is nothing we can do to earn salvation.

I believe and confess with my mouth that Jesus Christ is Your Son, the Savior of the world. I believe He died on the cross for me and bore all of my sins, paying the price for them.

I believe in my heart that You raised Jesus from the dead and that He is alive today.

I am a sinner and I am sorry for my sins and I ask You to forgive me. By faith I receive Jesus Christ now as my Lord and Savior. I believe that I am saved and will spend eternity with You! Thank You, Father. I am so grateful! In Jesus' name, amen.

Everyday Life Articles

Genesis 1:31 Enjoy Your Life
Genesis 2:19, 20 A Very Creative God
Genesis 2:24 Becoming One
Genesis 3:8–15 The Devil's Doom
Genesis 6:5–8 The Importance of a Right Heart
Genesis 12:1 One Step at a Time
Genesis 13:14, 15 Lift Up Your Eyes
Genesis 15:1–5 Give God Time
Genesis 16:1, 2 Don't Have an Ishmael
Genesis 17:15, 16 What's in a Name?
Genesis 32:28 Everybody Limps
Genesis 39:20–23 Receive God's Favor
Genesis 41:39, 40 From the Pit to the Palace
Genesis 50:20 Turn Your Mess into Your Message
Exodus 3:10–14 "I AM."
Exodus 12:7, 13 Apply the Blood to Your Life
Exodus 13:17, 18 When Life Gets Difficult
Exodus 16:4 Grace for Today and Every Day
Exodus 18:13–18 No One Can Do Everything
Exodus 18:23–26 Dealing with Overload
Exodus 20:7 Speak God's Name with Purpose
Exodus 25:1, 2 Check Your "Want To"
Exodus 30:10 The Blood Makes Atonement
Exodus 32:30–32 Time to Grow Up
Exodus 33:12–14 Rest in His Presence
Exodus 35:21 How to Get Stirred Up for God
Leviticus 8:1–30 Why the Ceremony?
Leviticus 11:1–43 Please God with Your Eating
Leviticus 20:6, 7 In God Alone
Leviticus 25:39–41 Release Your Grudges
Leviticus 26:4 Wait for God's Timing
Numbers 6:22–26 Aglow with God's Glory
Numbers 11:4–6 Don't Turn Back
Numbers 12:3 The Meaning of Meekness
Numbers 13:17–31 Giant-Sized Problems
Numbers 13:32, 33 Slaying the Giants in Your Land
Numbers 14:5–9 On Your Face
Numbers 21:8, 9 Look and Live
Deuteronomy 1:2, 6–8 Walk Out of Your Wilderness
Deuteronomy 8:2–6 Seek God's Presence, Not His Presents
Deuteronomy 11:18–21 Defeating Deception
Deuteronomy 17:12, 13 Presumption Kills
Deuteronomy 18:10–12 The Danger of Occult Practices
Deuteronomy 20:1–4 Gentle as a Lamb, Bold as a Lion
Deuteronomy 25:17, 18 When Weariness Attacks

Deuteronomy 28:1–14 Receiving Outrageous Blessings
Deuteronomy 30:19 Choose Life
Deuteronomy 31:6–8 God Will Go with You
Joshua 1:2 Leave the Past Behind
Joshua 1:16, 17 Passing the Faithfulness Test
Joshua 3:7 Common People, Uncommon Things
Joshua 5:2–7 Roll Away the Reproach
Joshua 15:1–4 Boundaries are a Good Thing
Joshua 24:15 "I Will Serve the Lord"
Judges 6:8–10 What about Prophecy?
Judges 6:14, 15 How to Have a Healthy Self-Image
Judges 7:1–3 The Reward of Relying on God
Judges 7:14, 15 Praise God Preemptively
Judges 16:16, 17 Resisting Temptation
Ruth 1:16, 17 Commitment over Comfort
Ruth 1:20 Better, not Bitter
I Samuel 3:1–10 How to Hear God's Voice
I Samuel 10:6 Changed by the Holy Spirit
I Samuel 15:22, 23 Obedience is Better than Sacrifice
I Samuel 15:23 Breaking the Cycle of Abuse and Rebellion
I Samuel 17:28–30 Reject Rejection
I Samuel 30:6 Encourage Yourself!
II Samuel 9:1 Looking for People to Bless
II Samuel 9:6–8 No More Dead Dogs
II Samuel 12:13 The Gift of Repentance
II Samuel 12:20–23 Beyond Grief
II Samuel 13:1–14 The Deepest Kind of Shame
II Samuel 22:33, 34 Let God be Your Strength
II Samuel 23:3 Fear God, Not People
I Kings 3:9, 10 Seek the Best
I Kings 5:12 Handling Your Relationships Wisely
I Kings 8:6–13 His Awesome Presence
I Kings 18:21 The Truth about Doubt
I Kings 18:41 Right as Rain
I Kings 18:42–45 Worship Before the Rain
I Kings 19:1–3 Keep Your Balance!
I Kings 19:4 Avoiding Burnout
I Kings 19:11, 12 Hearing God's Still, Small Voice
II Kings 2:9, 10 Double-Portion Blessings
II Kings 3:19 Flow Freely Again
II Kings 4:1–7 The First Step to Fullness
II Kings 4:7 Owe No Man Anything but Love
II Kings 22:1 Like a Child
II Kings 22:19 The Gift of a Tender Heart
I Chronicles 1:27, 28 Do Things God's Way
I Chronicles 2:2 Be Faithful and Be Blessed
I Chronicles 12:33 The Power of Focus
I Chronicles 16:7 Take a Praise Pause
I Chronicles 17:1–4 Words and Actions
I Chronicles 22:14 Give When It Hurts

I Chronicles 29:9 Be Willing to be Willing
II Chronicles 16:9 How to Have a "Perfect" Heart
II Chronicles 20:1–3 Run to the Throne
II Chronicles 20:6–11 These are Fighting Words
II Chronicles 20:12 Rest in the Storm
II Chronicles 25:1, 2 Doing the Right Thing with the Right Heart
II Chronicles 32:7, 8 God's Strong Arm
II Chronicles 32:22–31 Looking Up
Ezra 4:1-5 Grace to Overcome Opposition
Ezra 6:14, 15 The Truth about Hard Work
Ezra 8:23 Seek God Desperately
Nehemiah 4:20 God Will Fight Evil for You
Nehemiah 6:15 Finish Well
Nehemiah 8:9-12 The Joy of the Lord is Your Strength
Nehemiah 9:20 Trusting Day by Day
Esther 2:15–17 Believe for God's Favor
Esther 3:5, 6 A Better Plan
Esther 4:14 For Such a Time as This
Esther 6:1–3 God Does Not Forget
Job 4:1 Understanding Misunderstanding
Job 7:21 Passing the Frustration Test
Job 19:7–11 Faith Over Feelings
Job 23:10 Trained to Trust
Psalm 3:1–3 Hold Your Head High
Psalm 7:9 When God Tests Your Emotions
Psalm 12:1, 2 The Importance of Faithfulness
Psalm 19:1–4 Enjoy God's Handiwork
Psalm 23:1–3 God Restores and Leads
Psalm 25:12, 13 At Ease
Psalm 27:4 Seek the "One Thing"
Psalm 27:13, 14 The Land of the Living
Psalm 31:19 Everyday Christianity
Psalm 34:1 At *All* Times
Psalm 37:4, 5 Delight Yourself in God
Psalm 40:6 Pray and Obey
Psalm 42:5 How to Deal with Discouragement
Psalm 44:15 Be Free from Shame
Psalm 47:1 Express Yourself!
Psalm 57:7 Steadfast and Confident
Psalm 62:8 Stability Releases Ability
Psalm 78:7, 8 Leave Your Stubbornness Behind
Psalm 91:2 What Do You Say?
Psalm 105:17–19 Remember Joseph
Psalm 106:12–15 Be Happy
Psalm 109:22 Healed Healers
Psalm 111:1–5 Your Provider
Psalm 116:10 Confess the Word
Psalm 118:4–6 The Right Kind of Fear
Psalm 121:1, 2 Seek God First
Psalm 126:2, 3 Fill Your Mouth with Laughter

Psalm 133:1 Getting Rid of "What If"

Psalm 139:13–16 God's Good Plan

Psalm 141:3 When Your Mouth Gets You in Trouble

Psalm 143:3–10 A Biblical Prescription for Depression

Proverbs 2:1–5 Understanding People

Proverbs 3:5, 6 Why Not Ask, "Why?"

Proverbs 4:5 The Benefits of Wisdom

Proverbs 8:15, 16 A Little Common Sense Goes a Long Way

Proverbs 13:12 From Disappointment to Reappointment

Proverbs 14:10 Free from Bitterness

Proverbs 16:1 The Wise Answer of the Tongue

Proverbs 16:5 Humble People are Happy People

Proverbs 17:22 People Who Laugh, Last

Proverbs 18:14 Strengthen the Weak

Proverbs 18:21 Power in Your Mouth

Proverbs 23:7 Think As God Thinks

Proverbs 28:1 Bold as a Lion

Proverbs 29:18 The Importance of Vision

Proverbs 31:26 Kindness on Your Lips

Ecclesiastes 2:17, 18 The Secret of Fulfillment

Ecclesiastes 5:1 Stay on Track

Ecclesiastes 5:18 Enjoy Your Journey

Ecclesiastes 7:9 Be Slow to Anger

Ecclesiastes 11:4 The Pitfall of Procrastination

Song of Solomon 2:16 Fulfillment in Marriage

Song of Solomon 3:11 First a Wedding, then a Marriage

Isaiah 2:22; 3:1 When God Removes Your Props

Isaiah 6:1–9 Cleansed, then Used

Isaiah 9:6, 7 God's Government

Isaiah 14:12–15 Vote against Yourself

Isaiah 14:26, 27 A Person of Purpose

Isaiah 30:13, 14 From Brokenness to Blessing

Isaiah 30:21 This is the Way

Isaiah 40:6, 7 Magnets for His Power

Isaiah 40:31 Waiting on God

Isaiah 42:9 God Declares New Things

Isaiah 43:2 Through It All

Isaiah 53:3–6 Condemnation or Conviction?

Isaiah 54:4 Free from Shame

Isaiah 55:11 The Power of God's Word

Isaiah 58:7, 8 First Things First

Isaiah 61:1–3 Healing in Every Way

Isaiah 61:7 Double for Your Trouble

Jeremiah 1:5 Approved!

Jeremiah 1:8 You Are Chosen

Jeremiah 2:13 Make Your Work Succeed

Jeremiah 5:14 Words of Fire

Jeremiah 11:20 How to Pass Life's Tests

Jeremiah 17:9 Live Deeper

Jeremiah 29:11 God's Good Plan

Jeremiah 31:34 "I Will Remember Your Sin No More"
Jeremiah 34:15 Proclaim Liberty
Jeremiah 36:27, 28 Do It Again!
Lamentations 3:22, 23 New Every Morning
Ezekiel 11:19 The Cure for Hardheartedness
Ezekiel 16:49 The Sin of Ignoring the Needy
Ezekiel 20:40 Put God First
Ezekiel 22:30 Stand in the Gap
Ezekiel 36:26, 27 An Exchange of Hearts
Ezekiel 37:1–4 Hear the Word of the Lord
Daniel 1:8, 9 The Blessings of Wholehearted Commitment
Daniel 2:48 Refuse to Conform
Daniel 6:3 Be Excellent!
Daniel 6:10–24 Uncompromising Worship
Daniel 7:25 How to Resist Satan
Hosea 4:6 When We Know Right, We can Choose to Do Right
Hosea 14:4 God Loves You Freely
Joel 2:23 Rejoice!
Joel 2:25, 26 God of Restoration
Amos 5:15 A Healthy Kind of Anger
Obadiah 3 Who, Me?
Jonah 2:2 Never Too Late
Jonah 3:1 The God of the Second Chance
Micah 6:8 God's Requirements
Micah 7:7, 8 Outlast the Devil
Nahum 1:7 In the Day of Trouble
Habakkuk 2:2, 3 Discovering Your Vision
Habakkuk 3:17–19 The Lord Is Your Strength
Haggai 1:2–7 Consider Your Ways
Haggai 2:9 More and More Glory
Zechariah 4:6 By His Spirit
Zechariah 4:10 Small Things Lead to Big Things
Zechariah 9:12 Prisoners of Hope
Zechariah 12:1–10 The Spirit of Grace and Supplication
Malachi 3:2 The Refiner's Fire
Malachi 3:13–15 Are You Angry with God?
Malachi 3:16, 17 A Book of Remembrance
Matthew 5:8 Pure-hearted and Powerful
Matthew 6:1 Secret Goodness
Matthew 6:7, 8 Short and Simple
Matthew 6:33 First Place
Matthew 7:6 Do Not Judge
Matthew 7:7, 8 Persistent, Not Repetitious
Matthew 7:20 Known by Our Fruit
Matthew 8:13 As You Have Believed
Matthew 9:13 Treasure Mercy
Matthew 11:28–30 Lighten Your Load
Matthew 16:22 "Not Me!"
Matthew 18:21, 22 *How* Many Times?
Matthew 19:19 Love Yourself

Matthew 19:26 All Things Are Possible
Matthew 24:12, 13 Keep Love from Growing Cold
Matthew 25:14, 15 Use It or Lose It
Mark 4:26–28 When Your Breakthrough is Delayed
Mark 4:35–40 What to Do on a Sinking Boat
Mark 6:11 Shake Off Rejection
Mark 6:45–47 The Lonely Leader
Mark 8:14–17 Reasoning Robs Your Peace
Mark 8:34 The Cross We Bear
Mark 10:29, 30 When Obedience Means Sacrifice
Mark 10:46–52 Jesus Loves to Be Merciful
Mark 11:13, 14 Walk the Talk
Mark 11:22–26 What to Do with Your Mountain
Mark 14:22–24 The Meaning of Communion
Luke 2:19 When *Not* to Speak
Luke 5:4 Step Out and Find Out
Luke 5:31 Give Jesus All You Are Not
Luke 6:27, 28 Further than Forgiveness
Luke 6:44, 45 The Root of Unhealthy Attitudes
Luke 7:37 The Woman with a Past
Luke 10:1 Intimacy with Jesus
Luke 10:38–42 Take Time to Enjoy Jesus
Luke 11:9–13 Ask, Seek, Knock
Luke 12:2 Uncovering the Treasures in God's Word
Luke 16:13 The Problem with a Double Purpose
Luke 17:5, 6 How to Increase Your Faith
Luke 18:9–14 The Trap of Trusting Yourself
Luke 22:24–26 Who is the Greatest?
John 1:45–47 Dealing with Prejudice
John 2:25 People Aren't Perfect
John 5:1–9 Be Pitiful or Be Powerful
John 6:27–29 Believe to Achieve
John 8:12–14 Finding Your True Identity
John 10:3–5 Discerning God's Voice
John 10:10 Enjoying Everyday Life
John 13:3–15 Great People Serve
John 13:34, 35 Major in Love
John 15:5 "Help, Lord!"
John 16:7, 8 Welcome the Holy Spirit's Work
John 16:12, 13 The Spirit of Truth
John 20:21–23 Forgiveness and the Holy Spirit
Acts 1:8 "You Shall Receive Power"
Acts 1:13 Wait for God
Acts 2:21 The Power of Jesus' Name
Acts 3:19 His Presence Refreshes
Acts 6:2–4 Choose Your Battles
Acts 9:17, 18 How Paul was Filled with the Holy Spirit
Acts 10:34 God Has No Favorites
Acts 10:44 Be Filled with the Holy Spirit
Acts 16:12–14 Open Your Heart

Acts 17:28 "In Christ"
Romans 1:17 Consistent, Confident Faith
Romans 3:23, 24 All Have Sinned
Romans 4:18–21 Faith for Fulfillment
Romans 5:5 You are Loved
Romans 5:19 The Power of Obedience
Romans 6:18 Enjoy Your Freedom
Romans 7:6 Newness of Life
Romans 8:1 No Condemnation in Christ
Romans 8:28 Safe or Obedient?
Romans 8:31 God is For You
Romans 12:11 How to Stay on Fire for God
Romans 15:2, 3 Pleasing God, Pleasing Others
I Corinthians 2:14, 15 The Difference between Knowing and *Really* Knowing
I Corinthians 3:3 Envy Prevents Blessing
I Corinthians 4:15 A Father's Heart
I Corinthians 10:31 The Spiritual in the Natural
I Corinthians 12:10 The Gift of Discernment
I Corinthians 12:31 Love Above All
I Corinthians 13:13 The Most Important Thing
I Corinthians 14:1, 3, 4 A Word about Personal Prophecy
I Corinthians 15:41 Different is Okay
II Corinthians 1:3, 4 Find Comfort in God
II Corinthians 3:6 Relationship, Not "Religion"
II Corinthians 3:18 Free to Be
II Corinthians 4:17, 18 This Too Shall Pass
II Corinthians 5:7 Fickle Feelings
II Corinthians 5:18–20 God's Ambassadors
II Corinthians 5:21 Right with God
II Corinthians 10:4, 5 The Mind is the Battlefield
II Corinthians 11:3 The Beauty of Simplicity
Galatians 1:15–19 How to Handle God's Call
Galatians 3:2–5 Do Your Part
Galatians 5:16 Choose Life in the Spirit
Galatians 5:22, 23 True Love
Galatians 6:1–3 Patience, Not Pride
Ephesians 1:4 You Have Been Chosen
Ephesians 2:6 Seated in Heavenly Places
Ephesians 2:10 God Has a Good Plan
Ephesians 3:16–19 Be Filled!
Ephesians 3:20 Believe Big
Ephesians 4:22–24 How to Really Change
Ephesians 4:32 A Tender Conscience
Philippians 1:6 God Will Finish the Work
Philippians 1:28 Constant and Fearless
Philippians 2:25–30 The Spiritual and the Natural
Philippians 3:9 Take the Pressure Off
Philippians 4:8 Think about What You're Thinking About
Colossians 1:11 Strengthened with Joy
Colossians 1:17, 18 First Priority

Colossians 1:26, 27 The Hope of Glory
Colossians 3:15 Let Peace be Your Umpire
I Thessalonians 5:17 Pray Without Ceasing
I Thessalonians 5:18 Give Thanks
I Thessalonians 5:20 Do Not Despise Prophecy
II Thessalonians 3:5 Enjoy the Wait!
II Thessalonians 3:13 Do the Right Thing
I Timothy 3:1–12 Be Found Faithful
I Timothy 3:2 The Well-Rounded Leader
I Timothy 5:4 A Christian Duty
I Timothy 6:6 The Secret of True Contentment
I Timothy 6:12 Fight the Good Fight
II Timothy 1:7 Power, Love and Discipline
II Timothy 2:20, 21 Special People for Special Purposes
II Timothy 2:23, 24 Avoid Strife at All Costs
II Timothy 4:14–16 The Heart of a Hero
Titus 2:1 Walk the Talk
Titus 2:14 How to Live the Good Life
Titus 3:1 Prepare to Prosper
Philemon 22 Expect the Best
Hebrews 1:14 Angels are Everywhere
Hebrews 3:1, 2 Settle Down and Be Faithful
Hebrews 3:6 The "Ifs" and "Buts" of Biblical Faith
Hebrews 4:3 The Rest of God
Hebrews 4:15 Jesus Understands
Hebrews 5:8, 9 Use Your Pain for Gain
Hebrews 12:1 Throw Off Excess Baggage
James 1:21, 22 How to Walk in the Power of God
James 3:8–10 The Power of the Tongue
James 4:1, 2 Just Ask!
James 5:12 Worry-Free Decisions
James 5:16 Tell the Right Person
I Peter 2:19, 20 It's All in Your Attitude
I Peter 3:4 The Hidden Person of the Heart
I Peter 4:8 Have Fervent Love
I Peter 4:14 The Spirit of Glory
I Peter 5:8 Keep Your Balance
II Peter 1:3 Everything We Need
II Peter 3:8 "When, God, When?"
I John 2:15 "In," but Not "Of"
I John 3:20, 21 Confidence, Not Condemnation
I John 4:16 Enjoying God's Love
I John 5:14, 15 Praying According to God's Will
II John 6 Love Leads to Obedience
III John 2 Prosper with Purpose
Jude 11 Let God Decide
Revelation 3:7 Step Out and Find Out
Revelation 3:15, 16 Whole-hearted Service
Revelation 5:5, 6 Lion or Lamb?
Revelation 22:12 Payday is Coming

Life Points

Genesis 1:26, 27
Genesis 1:28
Genesis 3:1–6
Genesis 12:2
Genesis 15:1
Genesis 17:10–12
Genesis 26:18
Genesis 37:5
Genesis 39:2–5
Genesis 41:15, 16
Genesis 50:20
Exodus 3:5
Exodus 16:29, 30
Exodus 18:18–22
Exodus 28:3
Exodus 35:30–33
Leviticus 17:11
Leviticus 17:14
Leviticus 19:31
Leviticus 20:26
Leviticus 22:29
Leviticus 25:17
Leviticus 26:3
Numbers 10:35
Numbers 13:30–33
Numbers 14:1–3
Numbers 20:3–5
Numbers 21:4, 5
Deuteronomy 2:3
Deuteronomy 7:22
Deuteronomy 8:3
Deuteronomy 8:5
Deuteronomy 8:7–9
Deuteronomy 8:17
Deuteronomy 11:16, 17
Deuteronomy 11:26–28
Deuteronomy 13:4
Deuteronomy 27:10
Deuteronomy 30:2
Deuteronomy 31:6
Deuteronomy 32:4
Deuteronomy 33:27
Joshua 1:1–3
Joshua 1:8
Joshua 2:1

Joshua 3:17
Joshua 8:1
Joshua 9:12
Joshua 10:25
Joshua 10:40
Joshua 17:9
Judges 3:10
Judges 5:1–5
Judges 6:34
Judges 6:36–40
Judges 7:3
Judges 7:16–20
Ruth 1:3
Ruth 1:5
Ruth 1:21
Ruth 2:15, 16
Ruth 3:1–5
Ruth 4:15
I Samuel 2:7
I Samuel 13:1–14
I Samuel 15:22
I Samuel 16:7
I Samuel 17:33–37
I Samuel 17:48
I Samuel 18:5
I Samuel 20:14–16
I Samuel 26:7–11
II Samuel 1:11, 12
II Samuel 4:4
II Samuel 6:6, 7
II Samuel 9:3, 4
II Samuel 11:15
II Samuel 22:4
II Samuel 22:32, 33
II Samuel 24:10
I Kings 6:18–21
I Kings 8:23
I Kings 11:1
I Kings 17:9
I Kings 19:4
I Kings 19:5–8
I Kings 19:12
II Kings 20:1–6
I Chronicles 5:1
I Chronicles 10:13, 14

I Chronicles 16:25
I Chronicles 16:34
I Chronicles 17:1–4
I Chronicles 22:13
I Chronicles 22:14
I Chronicles 23:30
I Chronicles 29:6
II Chronicles 2:7
II Chronicles 5:13, 14
II Chronicles 6:19
II Chronicles 20:13–17
II Chronicles 20:22
II Chronicles 32:31
Ezra 3:3
Ezra 3:11
Nehemiah 1:4
Nehemiah 1:6, 7
Nehemiah 4:7–9
Nehemiah 5:7–10
Nehemiah 6:9
Nehemiah 6:11
Nehemiah 6:19
Nehemiah 8:5
Nehemiah 8:6
Nehemiah 8:10
Nehemiah 13:13
Nehemiah 13:19
Esther 2:22
Esther 5:2
Esther 6:7–10
Esther 8:1, 2
Esther 9:25
Esther 10:3
Job 5:22
Job 19:25
Job 22:21
Job 32:17–20
Job 37:14
Job 38:19
Job 42:7–10
Job 42:12
Psalm 1
Psalm 2:7
Psalm 8:4–6
Psalm 16:11

Psalm 17:15	Proverbs 16:2	Lamentations 3:25
Psalm 19:14	Proverbs 18:21	Ezekiel 11:19
Psalm 22:3	Proverbs 18:24	Ezekiel 25:15–17
Psalm 23:4–6	Proverbs 23:7	Ezekiel 36:26, 27
Psalm 32:9	Proverbs 23:12	Ezekiel 37:1–4
Psalm 34:7–9	Proverbs 24:10	Daniel 1:5
Psalm 37:23, 24	Proverbs 24:17, 18	Daniel 3:14
Psalm 40:1, 2	Proverbs 25:17	Daniel 3:16–18
Psalm 42:5	Proverbs 28:20	Daniel 3:24–27
Psalm 45:13	Ecclesiastes 1:14	Daniel 5:12
Psalm 46:10	Ecclesiastes 3:1	Daniel 6:10
Psalm 48:9	Ecclesiastes 5:1	Daniel 6:28
Psalm 51:6	Ecclesiastes 5:2	Daniel 7:21–25
Psalm 63:1	Ecclesiastes 5:3	Hosea 5:15
Psalm 63:4	Ecclesiastes 8:12	Hosea 6:1
Psalm 63:5, 6	Ecclesiastes 12:13	Hosea 12:6
Psalm 66:4	Song of Solomon 1:4	Joel 2:28
Psalm 77:6	Song of Solomon 2:15	Amos 3:3
Psalm 84:5–7	Song of Solomon 3:4	Amos 6:8
Psalm 91:1	Song of Solomon 4:9	Obadiah 3
Psalm 94:12–15	Song of Solomon 4:16	Obadiah 17
Psalm 100:4	Isaiah 11:3, 4	Jonah 1:1–3
Psalm 111:10	Isaiah 26:3	Jonah 4:2
Psalm 116:17	Isaiah 30:1, 2	Micah 3:8
Psalm 119:1	Isaiah 30:3–7	Nahum 1:7
Psalm 119:6	Isaiah 30:18	Habakkuk 2:3
Psalm 119:130	Isaiah 40:29	Habakkuk 2:20
Psalm 125:1, 2	Isaiah 40:31	Habakkuk 3:2
Psalm 127:1	Isaiah 41:10	Habakkuk 3:18
Psalm 143:5	Isaiah 42:16	Habakkuk 3:19
Psalm 143:5–8	Isaiah 43:18, 19	Zephaniah 3:19
Psalm 143:9–12	Isaiah 46:9, 10	Haggai 2:11–13
Psalm 144:1, 2	Isaiah 46:10	Zechariah 4:6
Proverbs 1:1–4	Isaiah 48:3	Zechariah 4:7
Proverbs 1:23	Isaiah 48:17	Zechariah 4:10
Proverbs 3:7	Isaiah 50:4	Zechariah 9:12
Proverbs 3:26	Isaiah 53:3	Zechariah 12:10
Proverbs 3:27, 28	Isaiah 55:11	Malachi 1:14
Proverbs 4:18	Isaiah 56:7	Malachi 2:5–7
Proverbs 4:23	Isaiah 58:5	Malachi 2:13–17
Proverbs 5:12	Isaiah 58:9–12	Malachi 3:6
Proverbs 8:6–9	Isaiah 61:1	Malachi 3:10–12
Proverbs 8:34–36	Isaiah 61:3	Matthew 2:1–16
Proverbs 12:25	Jeremiah 6:10	Matthew 5:4
Proverbs 13:16	Jeremiah 10:23	Matthew 5:13
Proverbs 14:30	Jeremiah 11:20	Matthew 6:2
Proverbs 15:1	Jeremiah 18:1–4	Matthew 6:5, 6
Proverbs 15:4	Jeremiah 29:11	Matthew 6:34
Proverbs 15:7	Jeremiah 29:13	Matthew 7:1, 2
Proverbs 15:13	Lamentations 3:19–24	Matthew 7:3–5

Matthew 7:13, 14

Matthew 12:33

Matthew 12:34

Matthew 12:36

Matthew 16:17, 18

Matthew 16:19

Matthew 18:18, 19

Matthew 20:16

Matthew 25:1–10

Matthew 26:41

Mark 1:10

Mark 1:35

Mark 2:6–8

Mark 3:27

Mark 4:24

Mark 4:39

Mark 5:25–29

Mark 8:31

Mark 9:23

Mark 11:22

Mark 14:43–46

Mark 15:37, 38

Mark 16:17, 18

Mark 16:20

Luke 4:1–12

Luke 5:15, 16

Luke 6:39

Luke 10:5–7

Luke 10:41, 42

Luke 11:9

Luke 12:31

Luke 18:8

Luke 18:17

Luke 18:27

Luke 19:8–10

Luke 22:1–4

John 5:19

John 5:38

John 6:28, 29

John 7:37–39

John 11:41

John 14:6

John 14:15

John 14:16

John 14:17

John 14:27

John 15:1–8

John 16:7–11

John 16:12, 13

John 21:18–22

Acts 1:4

Acts 2:17, 18

Acts 4:16

Acts 7:51

Acts 16:22–26

Acts 20:24

Acts 28:1–5

Romans 2:1

Romans 3:17

Romans 3:28

Romans 4:17

Romans 4:18

Romans 4:18–21

Romans 5:17

Romans 8:1

Romans 8:6

Romans 8:6–14

Romans 8:15

Romans 8:28

Romans 8:31

Romans 8:34

Romans 9:1

Romans 10:17

Romans 11:6

Romans 11:34

Romans 12:1

Romans 12:2

Romans 12:18

Romans 12:19

Romans 12:21

Romans 14:12

Romans 15:13

I Corinthians 1:27–29

I Corinthians 2:5

I Corinthians 2:14

I Corinthians 3:3

I Corinthians 3:16, 17

I Corinthians 6:12

I Corinthians 8:1

I Corinthians 9:24–27

I Corinthians 10:13

I Corinthians 10:31

I Corinthians 12:9

I Corinthians 13:1–3

I Corinthians 13:13

I Corinthians 14:3

II Corinthians 1:20

II Corinthians 2:10, 11

II Corinthians 2:14

II Corinthians 3:13–15

II Corinthians 3:17

II Corinthians 3:18

II Corinthians 5:14

II Corinthians 5:17

II Corinthians 5:20

II Corinthians 5:21

II Corinthians 10:12

II Corinthians 12:9

II Corinthians 13:5

Galatians 1:10

Galatians 1:15, 16

Galatians 3:2–4

Galatians 3:16

Galatians 3:28

Galatians 4:24–31

Galatians 5:19–23

Galatians 6:1–3

Galatians 6:2

Galatians 6:9

Galatians 6:14

Ephesians 1:4

Ephesians 2:8

Ephesians 2:10

Ephesians 3:20

Ephesians 4:17–19

Ephesians 4:23

Ephesians 4:26, 27

Ephesians 5:18–20

Ephesians 6:11–18

Ephesians 6:12

Philippians 1:6

Philippians 2:3, 4

Philippians 2:5–8

Philippians 3:3

Philippians 3:13, 14

Philippians 4:6

Philippians 4:13

Colossians 1:4

Colossians 1:11

Colossians 1:27

Colossians 3:1, 2

Colossians 3:12

Colossians 3:16

Colossians 3:22

I Thessalonians 2:13

I Thessalonians 4:11

I Thessalonians 5:18, 19

I Thessalonians 5:23, 24

II Thessalonians 2:17

II Thessalonians 3:10–12

I Timothy 1:13–16
I Timothy 2:1
I Timothy 3:4, 5
I Timothy 3:10
I Timothy 5:8
I Timothy 6:8
I Timothy 6:12
II Timothy 1:5–7
II Timothy 2:16
II Timothy 2:24
II Timothy 3:1, 2
II Timothy 3:12
II Timothy 4:5
Titus 1:4
Titus 3:1
Philemon 6
Philemon 8–21
Hebrews 3:7, 8
Hebrews 4:15
Hebrews 4:16

Hebrews 5:11
Hebrews 6:11
Hebrews 9:14
Hebrews 10:20
Hebrews 10:35, 36
Hebrews 11:6
Hebrews 12:2
Hebrews 12:6
Hebrews 12:15
Hebrews 13:5
James 1:2, 3
James 1:5, 6
James 1:25
James 1:26
James 3:5–10
James 4:6
James 4:7
James 5:7
I Peter 1:3
I Peter 1:15, 16

I Peter 1:22
I Peter 2:5
I Peter 3:10
I Peter 4:1, 2
II Peter 2:10
II Peter 3:18
I John 1:5
I John 1:9
I John 2:15
I John 2:27
I John 3:9
I John 4:8
I John 5:14, 15
Jude 20
Revelation 1:5
Revelation 3:20
Revelation 4:5
Revelation 12:10
Revelation 19:11–16
Revelation 21:6

Speak the Word

Genesis 1:28
Genesis 6:8
Genesis 7:5
Genesis 15:1
Genesis 17:1
Genesis 18:14
Genesis 24:40
Genesis 28:15
Genesis 32:10
Genesis 41:52
Genesis 50:20
Exodus 4:12
Exodus 6:6
Exodus 8:10
Exodus 14:13
Exodus 15:11, 13
Exodus 20:5
Exodus 20:6
Exodus 23:20
Exodus 23:30
Exodus 24:3
Exodus 31:3
Exodus 32:29
Exodus 33:15
Leviticus 1:3
Leviticus 10:3
Leviticus 10:10
Leviticus 11:45
Leviticus 18:4, 5
Leviticus 20:8
Leviticus 25:18, 19
Leviticus 26:9
Leviticus 26:12
Numbers 6:24–26
Numbers 10:29
Numbers 12:7, 8
Numbers 14:14
Numbers 16:5
Numbers 22:32
Numbers 23:19
Numbers 27:16, 17
Numbers 27:18
Deuteronomy 1:30
Deuteronomy 3:22
Deuteronomy 4:29

Deuteronomy 4:31
Deuteronomy 5:32, 33
Deuteronomy 6:3
Deuteronomy 7:6
Deuteronomy 7:9
Deuteronomy 10:12
Deuteronomy 15:8
Deuteronomy 23:5
Deuteronomy 28:1, 2
Deuteronomy 28:13
Deuteronomy 30:9
Deuteronomy 33:3
Deuteronomy 33:11
Deuteronomy 34:9
Joshua 4:24
Joshua 21:44
Joshua 22:5
Joshua 23:14
Joshua 24:15
Joshua 24:24
Judges 2:1
Judges 10:6
Judges 21:25
Ruth 2:12
I Samuel 2:1
I Samuel 2:2
I Samuel 3:10
I Samuel 3:19
I Samuel 10:6
I Samuel 12:12
I Samuel 12:24
I Samuel 13:14
I Samuel 17:47
I Samuel 18:14
II Samuel 2:6, 7
II Samuel 5:10
II Samuel 5:20
II Samuel 7:15
II Samuel 18:31
II Samuel 22:7
II Samuel 22:40
II Samuel 24:14
I Kings 2:3
I Kings 3:9
I Kings 4:29

I Kings 8:28
I Kings 8:43
I Kings 8:61
I Kings 15:5
I Kings 22:14
II Kings 6:16
II Kings 10:16
II Kings 17:8
II Kings 17:39
II Kings 18:5, 6
II Kings 19:15
II Kings 21:22
II Kings 22:19
I Chronicles 4:10
I Chronicles 12:18
I Chronicles 12:32
I Chronicles 16:8, 9
I Chronicles 16:27, 28
I Chronicles 17:23
I Chronicles 17:26
I Chronicles 28:9
I Chronicles 28:20
II Chronicles 2:5
II Chronicles 6:4
II Chronicles 6:27
II Chronicles 6:41
II Chronicles 14:11
II Chronicles 15:7
II Chronicles 16:9
II Chronicles 30:8
Ezra 5:8
Ezra 7:10
Ezra 7:23
Ezra 7:27, 28
Ezra 8:22
Nehemiah 2:8
Nehemiah 2:20
Nehemiah 4:15
Nehemiah 9:5
Nehemiah 9:20
Nehemiah 9:31
Nehemiah 13:2
Esther 2:15
Esther 4:16
Job 1:1

Job 1:22	Proverbs 1:5	Jeremiah 23:28
Job 12:10	Proverbs 2:6	Jeremiah 24:6, 7
Job 12:13	Proverbs 10:6	Jeremiah 30:17
Job 13:15	Proverbs 10:22	Jeremiah 31:3
Job 23:5	Proverbs 14:3	Jeremiah 31:13
Job 42:1	Proverbs 14:9	Jeremiah 31:17
Psalm 4:3	Proverbs 14:26	Jeremiah 31:25
Psalm 5:11	Proverbs 16:3	Jeremiah 33:14
Psalm 6:9	Proverbs 18:10	Jeremiah 42:3
Psalm 9:1, 2	Proverbs 19:21	Jeremiah 46:28
Psalm 18:2	Proverbs 20:22	Lamentations 2:19
Psalm 18:30	Proverbs 21:30, 31	Lamentations 3:32
Psalm 25:4, 5	Proverbs 30:5	Lamentations 3:41
Psalm 28:7	Ecclesiastes 2:26	Lamentations 3:57, 58
Psalm 30:5	Ecclesiastes 9:7	Ezekiel 2:2
Psalm 33:4	Song of Solomon 1:4	Ezekiel 3:10
Psalm 36:5, 6	Song of Solomon 1:16	Ezekiel 16:62
Psalm 36:9	Song of Solomon 6:3	Ezekiel 20:12
Psalm 39:7	Isaiah 2:3	Ezekiel 34:16
Psalm 40:8	Isaiah 6:3	Ezekiel 36:9
Psalm 43:3	Isaiah 6:8	Ezekiel 37:14
Psalm 50:7	Isaiah 8:10	Ezekiel 40:4
Psalm 52:9	Isaiah 9:6	Ezekiel 44:23
Psalm 54:4	Isaiah 12:2	Daniel 1:17
Psalm 55:18	Isaiah 25:1	Daniel 4:37
Psalm 55:22	Isaiah 26:4	Daniel 6:16
Psalm 59:10	Isaiah 28:29	Daniel 9:9
Psalm 60:12	Isaiah 30:15	Daniel 9:14
Psalm 62:8	Isaiah 32:17	Daniel 11:32
Psalm 66:20	Isaiah 33:6	Hosea 2:14, 15
Psalm 68:19, 20	Isaiah 38:5	Hosea 2:19, 20
Psalm 70:4	Isaiah 40:8	Hosea 6:3
Psalm 71:14	Isaiah 43:1	Hosea 10:12
Psalm 85:12, 13	Isaiah 43:25	Hosea 13:4
Psalm 86:11	Isaiah 49:16	Hosea 13:9
Psalm 89:1	Isaiah 49:23	Joel 2:13
Psalm 90:12	Isaiah 49:25	Joel 2:21
Psalm 90:17	Isaiah 52:12	Joel 3:10
Psalm 94:19	Isaiah 53:4, 5	Joel 3:16
Psalm 97:11	Isaiah 54:5	Amos 5:4
Psalm 101:2	Isaiah 54:10	Amos 5:24
Psalm 102:28	Isaiah 54:13	Jonah 2:2
Psalm 112:3	Isaiah 54:17	Jonah 2:6, 7
Psalm 119:18	Isaiah 59:19	Micah 5:5
Psalm 121:2–8	Isaiah 60:19	Micah 6:8
Psalm 130:5	Isaiah 61:10	Micah 7:7, 8
Psalm 136:12	Jeremiah 9:24	Micah 7:18
Psalm 138:8	Jeremiah 15:16	Micah 7:20
Psalm 142:7	Jeremiah 17:14	Nahum 1:3
Psalm 146:5	Jeremiah 20:11	Habakkuk 1:13

Habakkuk 2:4
Zephaniah 2:3
Zephaniah 3:5
Haggai 2:4
Haggai 2:9
Haggai 2:19
Zechariah 2:8
Zechariah 10:12
Zechariah 13:9
Malachi 1:6
Matthew 3:8
Matthew 10:16
Matthew 11:28–30
Matthew 13:23
Matthew 14:28–30
Matthew 26:7
Matthew 28:6
Mark 5:36
Mark 10:27
Mark 12:30, 31
Luke 1:37
Luke 3:22
Luke 6:36
Luke 10:39
Luke 11:10
Luke 12:22–24
Luke 22:61
John 1:12
John 3:16, 17
John 3:30
John 4:24
John 8:32
John 12:26
John 15:15
John 17:17
Acts 2:39
Acts 3:6
Acts 5:1–3
Acts 10:34
Acts 15:8
Romans 1:16
Romans 2:11
Romans 3:24
Romans 10:4
Romans 15:33
I Corinthians 1:7, 8
I Corinthians 2:9, 10

I Corinthians 4:20
I Corinthians 6:19, 20
I Corinthians 8:6
I Corinthians 15:10
I Corinthians 16:14
II Corinthians 4:7
II Corinthians 5:5
II Corinthians 6:18
II Corinthians 8:9
II Corinthians 9:10, 11
Galatians 2:16
Galatians 3:13
Galatians 4:6
Galatians 5:16
Ephesians 1:5, 6
Ephesians 1:7, 8
Ephesians 2:14
Ephesians 3:16, 17
Ephesians 5:10
Ephesians 5:20
Philippians 1:9
Philippians 2:13
Philippians 3:1
Philippians 4:13
Colossians 1:13, 14
Colossians 2:3
Colossians 2:7
Colossians 2:15
Colossians 4:2
I Thessalonians 1:4
I Thessalonians 3:12, 13
I Thessalonians 4:7
I Thessalonians 5:9, 10
I Thessalonians 5:24
II Thessalonians 1:3
II Thessalonians 1:11, 12
II Thessalonians 2:16, 17
II Thessalonians 3:3
II Thessalonians 3:16
I Timothy 1:12
I Timothy 4:6
I Timothy 6:17, 18
II Timothy 1:7
II Timothy 1:14
II Timothy 2:1
II Timothy 2:15
Titus 2:7

Titus 2:11
Titus 3:5
Philemon 3
Philemon 6
Hebrews 2:14
Hebrews 2:18
Hebrews 3:15
Hebrews 4:12
Hebrews 7:25
Hebrews 8:12
Hebrews 10:19
Hebrews 12:6, 7
Hebrews 13:1
Hebrews 13:8
Hebrews 13:20, 21
James 1:17
James 1:19
James 2:17
James 3:17
I Peter 2:9
II Peter 1:2
II Peter 1:3
II Peter 3:9
I John 3:1
I John 3:18
I John 4:7
I John 4:18
I John 5:14
II John 4
II John 6
III John 2
III John 4
III John 11
Jude 3
Jude 20, 21
Jude 24
Revelation 1:5
Revelation 2:4
Revelation 3:8
Revelation 4:11
Revelation 15:3
Revelation 19:10
Revelation 19:11
Revelation 19:16
Revelation 21:5
Revelation 22:20

Putting the Word to Work

Genesis 4:4–12
Genesis 6:12
Genesis 7:1
Genesis 19:17
Genesis 21:1–3
Genesis 27:30–32
Genesis 29:17
Genesis 34:1, 2
Exodus 1:15–17
Exodus 11:3
Exodus 17:12
Exodus 31:14
Exodus 40:36–38
Leviticus 7:11
Leviticus 11:2
Leviticus 19:16
Leviticus 19:18
Leviticus 24:16
Numbers 4:1–14
Numbers 9:8
Numbers 11:14
Deuteronomy 5:16
Deuteronomy 6:23
Deuteronomy 10:16
Deuteronomy 15:11
Joshua 3:15, 16
Joshua 6:1
Joshua 18:12
Judges 19:5
Ruth 4:10
I Samuel 1:20
I Samuel 18:3
I Samuel 18:29
I Samuel 23:2
I Samuel 30:8
II Samuel 5:12
II Samuel 6:11, 12
II Samuel 6:16–23
II Samuel 11:1
II Samuel 23:3, 4
I Kings 2:15
I Kings 3:5–10
I Kings 3:28
I Kings 6:14 — 7:51
I Kings 10:1–3

I Kings 11:1–6
I Kings 17:1–9
I Kings 17:8–16
I Kings 18:25–39
II Kings 2:2–8
II Kings 4:8–17
II Kings 4:42–44
II Kings 5:9–14
II Kings 5:20–27
II Kings 17:6–3
II Kings 18:1–7
II Kings 22:1
II Kings 22:18–20
II Kings 23:1–3
I Chronicles 3
I Chronicles 13:1
I Chronicles 16:7–36
I Chronicles 22:1–5
I Chronicles 22:6–11
I Chronicles 22:19
I Chronicles 29:2–16
I Chronicles 29:3
II Chronicles 1:9–12
II Chronicles 5:11–14
II Chronicles 6:12–15
II Chronicles 7:14
II Chronicles 9:23
II Chronicles 15:1–4
II Chronicles 20:1–4
Ezra 3:10, 11
Ezra 3:12, 13
Ezra 8:21–23
Ezra 9:1–6
Nehemiah 1:5–11
Nehemiah 3:26–31
Nehemiah 4:16, 17
Nehemiah 5:14–19
Nehemiah 9:5-15
Nehemiah 12:27–43
Esther 2:12, 13
Esther 2:15
Esther 4:14–16
Esther 5:2–5
Esther 6:6–10
Job 2:11–13

Job 9:32, 33
Job 10:12
Job 19:13–26
Job 26:7–14
Job 28:12–28
Job 29:1–25
Job 31:24, 25, 28
Job 32:7–9
Job 42:10
Psalm 8:3–5
Psalm 19:7–11
Psalm 23:4
Psalm 34:8
Psalm 42:1, 2
Psalm 61:1–4
Psalm 67:2, 3
Psalm 73:25–28
Psalm 84:10
Psalm 86:1–7
Psalm 105:5
Psalm 119:9–11
Psalm 119:105
Psalm 141:3
Psalm 150
Proverbs 11:14
Proverbs 11:25
Proverbs 22:6
Ecclesiastes 2:24
Ecclesiastes 3:17
Song of Solomon 4:7
Isaiah 11:2
Isaiah 26:3
Isaiah 40:4
Isaiah 57:15
Jeremiah 3:15
Jeremiah 34:17
Lamentations 3:40
Ezekiel 14:6
Daniel 1:8
Daniel 2:20–22
Hosea 4:6
Hosea 14:3, 4
Joel 2:12–14
Joel 2:25–27
Joel 2:28, 29

Joel 2:30–32
Joel 3:14
Amos 1:1
Amos 2:4
Amos 7:7–9
Amos 7:14, 15
Obadiah 12–14
Obadiah 19–21
Jonah 1:10–16
Jonah 2:3–10
Jonah 3:1–5
Jonah 3:5–10
Micah 4:1–4
Micah 7:7
Micah 7:18–20
Nahum 1:2–6
Nahum 1:7, 8
Nahum 1:15
Habakkuk 1:2–6
Habakkuk 2:1–3
Habakkuk 2:9, 10
Zephaniah 1:4–6
Zephaniah 1:14
Zephaniah 1:18
Zephaniah 3:17
Haggai 1:1, 2
Haggai 1:3–11
Haggai 2:3, 4
Haggai 2:15–19
Zechariah 3:3–5
Zechariah 8:16, 17
Zechariah 13:9
Malachi 1:11–14
Malachi 3:13–16
Malachi 4:2
Matthew 3:13–17
Matthew 4:1–11
Matthew 6:19–21
Matthew 6:25–34
Matthew 10:37–39
Matthew 18:15–17
Matthew 18:21–35
Matthew 28:18–20
Mark 1:16–20
Mark 2:1–4
Mark 6:30–44
Mark 9:14–27
Mark 10:35–52
Mark 11:1–11
Mark 13:32–37

Luke 1:26–34
Luke 2:52
Luke 6:43–45
Luke 6:47–49
Luke 10:29–37
Luke 11:1–4
Luke 15:1–10
Luke 17:11–19
Luke 22:39–42
Luke 23:39–43
John 2:1–11
John 6:32–35
John 10:7–10
John 11:25–27
John 13:34, 35
John 14:4–6
John 15:1–7
John 17:20–23
John 20:11–18
John 20:21, 22
John 20:24–29
Acts 2:42–47
Acts 4:13
Acts 8:26–31
Acts 9:20–22
Acts 11:19–24
Acts 17:10, 11
Romans 4:20, 21
Romans 5:6–8
Romans 6:15
Romans 6:23
Romans 8:18
Romans 8:35–39
Romans 10:14, 15
Romans 12:4–8
Romans 12:9–21
I Corinthians 1:10–17
I Corinthians 2:1–5
I Corinthians 3:9–11
I Corinthians 6:20
I Corinthians 9:13, 14
I Corinthians 11:23–25
I Corinthians 12:4–11
I Corinthians 12:20–25
I Corinthians 15:33
I Corinthians 15:50–57
I Corinthians 15:58
II Corinthians 1:3–5
II Corinthians 1:20
II Corinthians 3:5

II Corinthians 5:1–8
II Corinthians 5:18–16:1
II Corinthians 6:14–18
II Corinthians 9:6–8
Galatians 1:1
Galatians 3:28
Galatians 5:13, 14
Galatians 6:2
Galatians 6:3, 4
Ephesians 2:4–7
Ephesians 3:14–19
Ephesians 5:1, 2
Ephesians 5:15–17
Ephesians 6:1–4
Ephesians 6:10–18
Philippians 1:12–14
Philippians 2:14, 15
Philippians 3:12
Philippians 4:2, 3
Philippians 4:8
Philippians 4:19
Colossians 1:9–11
Colossians 3:5–11
Colossians 4:6
I Thessalonians 4:1
I Thessalonians 4:3–6
I Thessalonians 5:12–22
II Thessalonians 1:11, 12
II Thessalonians 2:16, 17
II Thessalonians 3:1, 2
I Timothy 2:1, 2
I Timothy 4:1, 2
I Timothy 4:12
I Timothy 6:6–10
I Timothy 6:17–19
II Timothy 3:1–5
II Timothy 3:16, 17
II Timothy 4:2
Titus 1:5–16
Titus 2:14
Titus 3:1, 2
Titus 3:9–11
Philemon 4–6
Philemon 22
Hebrews 4:3
Hebrews 5:12–14
Hebrews 10:20
Hebrews 10:24, 25
Hebrews 11:1–40
Hebrews 12:1, 2

James 1:12–15
James 4:13–15
James 4:17
I Peter 5:6, 7
II Peter 1:3, 4
II Peter 1:5–7
II Peter 3:9

II Peter 3:17
I John 2:15–17
I John 3:10
I John 3:16–18
I John 5:21
II John 4
II John 12

III John 3, 4
III John 5–8
III John 10, 11
Revelation 2:4
Revelation 3:20
Revelation 7:9, 10
Revelation 21:3, 4

The Word for Your Everyday Life

The Word of God gives us insight, advice, and direction about every area of our lives. In the following pages, you will find a list of topics, needs, or situations you may be facing right now or may face in the future. Let me encourage you to become familiar with the issues in this section so that you will know where to look to find biblical answers and encouragement for many circumstances you will likely encounter at some point. Use the scriptures in this section to strengthen your heart and align your thoughts and words (conversation) with the Word of God so you can have victory in every aspect of your life.

Anger
Psalm 37:8
Psalm 103:8
Proverbs 14:29
Proverbs 15:1
Proverbs 15:18
Proverbs 19:11
Ecclesiastes 7:9
Ephesians 4:26
Ephesians 4:31, 32
Colossians 3:8
James 1:19, 20

Anointing
Psalm 20:6
Psalm 23:5
Psalm 45:7
Psalm 92:10
Isaiah 10:27
Isaiah 61:1
Mark 6:13
2 Corinthians 1:21
I John 2:20
I John 2:27

Anxiety and Worry
Deuteronomy 31:6
Psalm 86:7
Psalm 139:23, 24
Proverbs 15:15
Matthew 6:27
Matthew 6:31, 33
Matthew 6:34
Mark 4:19
Philippians 4:6, 7
I Peter 5:7

Authority of the Believer
Matthew 12:29
Matthew 16:19
Matthew 28:18, 19
Mark 16:17, 18
Luke 10:19
Ephesians 1:17–22; 2:6
James 4:7

Compromise
Exodus 34:12
Psalm 1:1
Psalm 119:2, 3
Proverbs 25:26
Acts 23:1
I Timothy 3:9
Hebrews 11:25
I Peter 2:9

Civil Responsibility
Deuteronomy 4:7
II Chronicles 7:14
Psalm 122:6, 7
Proverbs 11:11
Proverbs 24:21
Proverbs 28:7
Jeremiah 29:7
Matthew 22:21
Romans 13:1
Romans 13:7
I Timothy 2:1–3
Titus 3:1, 2
I Peter 2:13–17

Confessions for Husbands
Joshua 24:15
Proverbs 3:3

Ecclesiastes 9:9
Mark 10:6–9
Ephesians 4:31, 32
Ephesians 5:25–28
Colossians 3:8–10
I Corinthians 13:1–8
Hebrews 13:4
James 5:16
I Peter 3:7

Confessions for Wives
Proverbs 12:4
Proverbs 19:14
Proverbs 31:10–12
Proverbs 31:26
I Corinthians 6:20
I Corinthians 7:3
I Corinthians 13:1–8
Ephesians 5:33
I Thessalonians 5:11, 15–18
I Timothy 3:11
Titus 2:4, 5
I Peter 3:1–5
I John 3:18

Confessions for Parents
Deuteronomy 6:2, 5
Deuteronomy 28:13
Deuteronomy 30:19, 20
Proverbs 14:16
Proverbs 17:6
Proverbs 31:28
Isaiah 54:13
Jeremiah 18:6
Romans 15:2
I Corinthians 15:33
II Corinthians 6:14
Galatians 5:16
Ephesians 1:17, 18
Ephesians 6:4
Philippians 2:14
Colossians 1:3, 5, 9–14
II Timothy 2:15

Confessions for Singles
Psalm 3:3, 4
Psalm 27:4
Psalm 27:14
Psalm 37:1
Psalm 37:3–5
Psalm 55:22

Psalm 91:14–16
Ecclesiastes 7:8, 9
Isaiah 43:1–3
Isaiah 61:1–3
Jeremiah 31:13
Matthew 28:20
Romans 8:25
I Peter 5:7

Confessions for Families
Deuteronomy 28:8, 11, 12
Joshua 24:15
Proverbs 24:3, 4
Acts 20:32
Ephesians 1:3
Ephesians 6:1–3
Colossians 3:13–15
I John 4:7, 11
III John 4

What the Bible Says about Confessing the Word
Joshua 1:8
Psalm 119:105
Isaiah 48:6, 7
Isaiah 55:11
Isaiah 65:16
Jeremiah 1:12
Romans 4:17
Hebrews 4:12
Mark 11:23
Hebrews 4:14
Hebrews 10:23

Confidence
Joshua 1:9
Psalm 18:29
Psalm 37:3
Psalm 57:7
Psalm 84:12
Psalm 131:1, 2
Proverbs 29:25
Isaiah 26:3
Isaiah 30:15
Micah 7:7
Philippians 1:6
Philippians 3:3
Hebrews 4:16
Hebrews 10:35

Contentment
Psalm 16:6
Psalm 17:15

Psalm 84:10
Psalm 92:4, 5
Psalm 107:8, 9
Proverbs 14:30
John 6:35
Philippians 4:10, 11
Philippians 4:19
I Timothy 6:6–8
Hebrews 13:5, 6

Control
Acts 5:29
Romans 8:9
I Corinthians 4:3, 4
II Corinthians 5:14
Galatians 1:10
Colossians 1:10
I Thessalonians 2:4

Courage
Deuteronomy 31:6
Joshua 1:9
II Chronicles 32:7, 8
Psalm 27:14
Psalm 31:24
Matthew 14:27
I Corinthians 15:58
I Corinthians 16:13
I John 5:14

Depression
Deuteronomy 31:8
Psalm 3:3
Psalm 34:15, 17
Psalm 40:1–3
Psalm 42:5
Psalm 42:6, 8, 11
Psalm 77:1, 2
Psalm 91:14–16
Isaiah 54:4
Isaiah 60:1
2 Corinthians 7:6
I Peter 5:6, 7

Determination
Isaiah 40:31
I Corinthians 2:2
Colossians 3:2
I Thessalonians 4:11, 12
I Timothy 6:11–14
I Peter 5:9

Diligence
Exodus 15:26
Deuteronomy 4:9
Psalm 119:4
Proverbs 4:23
Proverbs 8:17
Proverbs 10:4
Proverbs 12:24
Proverbs 13:4
Proverbs 21:5
Hebrews 11:6

Discouragement and Despair
Psalm 3:3
Psalm 30:11, 12
John 10:10
John 16:33
Romans 8:28
II Corinthians 1:4
II Corinthians 4:8
II Corinthians 4:16, 17
II Corinthians 12:9
Philippians 4:13

Emotions
Psalm 7:9
Psalm 30:5
Psalm 34:18
Psalm 42:5
Psalm 51:8, 12
Psalm 94:13
Psalm 147:3
Romans 8:8
Philippians 4:11
Hebrews 4:15, 16
I Peter 5:9

Encouragement and Comfort
Psalm 27:5
Psalm 31:7
Psalm 57:2, 3
Psalm 62:1, 2
Psalm 119:50
Psalm 138:7, 8
II Corinthians 1:3, 4
II Corinthians 4:17, 18
II Thessalonians 2:16, 17

Faith
Habakkuk 2:4
Matthew 17:20
Mark 11:23

Romans 3:28
Romans 5:2
Romans 10:17
Romans 14:23
Romans 15:13
I Corinthians 2:5
II Corinthians 5:7
Galatians 3:24, 25
Ephesians 3:12
Ephesians 6:16
I Timothy 6:12
Hebrews 10:22, 23
Hebrews 11:1, 3
Hebrews 11:6
James 2:17

Favor
Job 10:12
Psalm 5:12
Psalm 30:7
Psalm 89:17
Proverbs 3:4
Proverbs 11:27
Proverbs 12:2
Proverbs 14:9
Matthew 5:4
II Corinthians 12:9
II Corinthians 4:14, 15
Ephesians 2:4–7
Hebrews 4:16

Fear
Psalm 23:4
Psalm 27:1
Psalm 91:4, 5
Psalm 112:7, 8
Proverbs 29:25
Isaiah 41:10
Isaiah 54:14
Luke 12:32
II Timothy 1:7
Hebrews 13:5, 6
I Peter 3:14
I John 4:18

Forgiveness
II Chronicles 30:9
Matthew 6:14
Mark 11:25, 26
Luke 6:37
Romans 4:7, 8

Ephesians 4:32
Colossians 3:13
James 5:15
I John 1:9, 10
I John 2:12

Grace
Psalm 84:11
Acts 13:43
Romans 3:24
Romans 5:15
Romans 5:20, 21
I Corinthians 3:9–11
Ephesians 2:8
James 4:6

Guilt and Condemnation
Psalm 18:23
Psalm 51:1, 2
Psalm 51:7-9
Isaiah 53:5
Romans 3:11, 12, 21, 22
Romans 8:1, 2
Romans 8:10
Romans 8:33, 34
II Corinthians 5:21
Hebrews 1:3
Hebrews 10:22, 23
I John 3:18-20

Health and Healing
Psalm 30:2
Psalm 103:2, 3
Psalm 107:20
Psalm 118:17
Psalm 147:3
Proverbs 4:20-22
Isaiah 58:8
Jeremiah 17:14
Jeremiah 30:17
James 5:14, 15
I Peter 2:24
III John 2

Hearing from God
Deuteronomy 28:1
Psalm 40:6
Psalm 95:7, 8
Psalm 119:129, 130
Jeremiah 7:23
Matthew 7:24, 25
Matthew 13:19, 23

John 10:5
John 10:27
Romans 10:17
James 1:22–25

Help
Psalm 28:7
Psalm 34:15, 17
Psalm 50:15
Psalm 55:22
Psalm 94:17–19
Psalm 143:10, 11
Isaiah 41:13
Isaiah 50:7
Nahum 1:7
Hebrews 13:6

Holiness
Leviticus 20:7
Acts 24:16
Romans 6:22
Romans 12:1, 2
I Corinthians 6:19, 20
Ephesians 1:4
Ephesians 4:23, 24
Colossians 1:22
Hebrews 12:10
Hebrews 12:14
I Peter 1:14, 15

Hope
Psalm 33:18
Psalm 147:11
Proverbs 13:12
Lamentations 3:24–26
Romans 12:12
Romans 15:4
Romans 15:13
I Corinthians 13:10, 12, 13
I Corinthians 15:51, 52, 54
Ephesians 1:18
I Peter 1:13

Humility and Pride
Psalm 25:9
Psalm 69:32
Psalm 147:6
Proverbs 11:2
Proverbs 15:33
Proverbs 16:19
Proverbs 29:23
Micah 6:8

James 4:10
I Peter 5:6

Insecurity
Psalm 27:1
Psalm 91:1, 4
Proverbs 1:33
Proverbs 14:26
Proverbs 18:10
Isaiah 41:10
Isaiah 54:17
Romans 8:28
Romans 8:37–39
II Corinthians 12:9
Philippians 4:13
Hebrews 13:6

Integrity
Psalm 15:4
Psalm 25:21
Psalm 26:1-5
Proverbs 11:2, 3
Matthew 5:41
Acts 23:1
Acts 24:16
Romans 9:1
I Corinthians 12:31
Philippians 1:10, 11
I Timothy 1:5
I Timothy 1:19
II Peter 1:3

Laziness and Passivity
Proverbs 5:23
Proverbs 6:4, 10, 11
Proverbs 12:9
Proverbs 20:4
Proverbs 26:15, 16
Ecclesiastes 10:18
Colossians 3:1
Hebrews 6:11, 12
Hebrews 11:6
Revelation 3:15, 16

Loneliness
Genesis 28:15
I Samuel 12:22
Psalm 25:16
Psalm 27:10
Psalm 46:1
Isaiah 41:10
Matthew 28:20

John 14:18
II Corinthians 6:18
Hebrews 13:5

Patience
Psalm 37:34
Psalm 40:1
Ecclesiastes 7:8
Romans 5:3, 4
Galatians 6:9
Colossians 1:11, 12
Hebrews 6:11, 12
James 1:2–4
James 5:7, 8
Revelation 3:10

Peace
Job 22:21
Psalm 85:8, 10, 11
Proverbs 16:7
Isaiah 26:3
Isaiah 54:10
Isaiah 58:8
John 14:27
Philippians 4:7
II Thessalonians 3:16
Hebrews 12:14

Power
Isaiah 40:29
Luke 10:19
Acts 1:8
I Corinthians 15:57
II Corinthians 1:21, 22
II Corinthians 12:9
Ephesians 1:17, 19
Ephesians 3:16
II Timothy 1:7

Prayer
Job 22:27
Psalm 34:4, 15
Psalm 38:15
Psalm 145:18, 19
Proverbs 15:29
Isaiah 55:6
Matthew 7:7, 8
Matthew 18:19
Luke 18:1
John 16:24

Romans 8:26
I Thessalonians 5:17
Hebrews 4:16

Prosperity, Finances, and Giving
Deuteronomy 8:18
Deuteronomy 28:8, 11
Psalm 1:3
Psalm 34:10
Malachi 3:10
Matthew 6:3, 4
Matthew 6:19–21
Luke 6:38
Acts 10:4
Romans 13:8
II Corinthians 9:6, 7
Philippians 4:19
III John 2

Protection
Deuteronomy 33:27
Job 11:18, 19
Psalm 9:9
Psalm 32:7
Psalm 52:8, 9
Psalm 91:1, 2
Psalm 91:9–11
Proverbs 14:26
Hebrews 6:18

Receiving God's Love
Proverbs 8:17
John 3:16
John 15:9
John 16:27
Romans 5:5
I Corinthians 8:3
I Corinthians 16:14
II Corinthians 5:14, 15
Ephesians 3:17–19
Ephesians 4:15
Ephesians 5:2
I John 4:16
I John 4:19
Jude 20, 21

Rejection
Leviticus 26:11
Joshua 1:9
Isaiah 54:17

Matthew 28:20
Luke 10:10, 11
John 15:16
Romans 8:31
Romans 8:37
Ephesians 1:4–6

Relating to Husbands
I Corinthians 8:3
I Peter 3:1, 2

Seeking God
Deuteronomy 4:29
II Chronicles 7:14
II Chronicles 15:2
Psalm 27:4
Lamentations 3:25
Matthew 6:33
Matthew 7:7, 8
Luke 12:29, 31
John 5:30
Colossians 3:1
Hebrews 11:6

Self-Control
Proverbs 15:18
Proverbs 25:28
Proverbs 31:16
Ecclesiastes 5:2
Ecclesiastes 5:4
Ecclesiastes 7:9
Lamentations 3:26, 27
Luke 21:19
I Corinthians 6:12
I Corinthians 13:4, 5
Galatians 5:22, 23
Colossians 3:12-14
II Peter 1:5–7

Selfishness
Proverbs 28:27
Mark 8:34
Romans 12:10
Romans 15:2
I Corinthians 9:19
I Corinthians 10:24
I Corinthians 10:33
II Corinthians 5:15
Galatians 6:2
Philippians 2:3–7
I Timothy 5:6
I John 3:17, 18

Spiritual Warfare
Deuteronomy 28:7
Psalm 35:1-3
Romans 7:23-25
Romans 8:37
II Corinthians 10:3, 4
Ephesians 6:11
I Timothy 6:12
I Peter 2:11, 12
I Peter 5:8

Stress
Psalm 37:5
Psalm 39:6
Psalm 127:2
Isaiah 40:29
Matthew 6:25, 31, 33
Mark 4:19
Luke 12:27
Luke 21:34
I Corinthians 7:32
Philippians 1:10
Philippians 4:6
Philippians 4:8, 9
I Peter 5:7

Submission to Authority: God's and Man's
Joshua 24:24
I Samuel 15:23
Psalm 103:17, 18
Psalm 112:1
Psalm 119:44, 45
Isaiah 1:19, 20
Luke 11:28
Ephesians 6:5
James 4:7, 8
I Peter 2:18, 19
I John 3:22

Taking Care of Your Body
Exodus 23:25
Proverbs 3:7, 8
Proverbs 4:10
Proverbs 4:20–22
Proverbs 16:24
Proverbs 17:22
Proverbs 18:9
Jeremiah 30:17
I Corinthians 6:13
I Corinthians 6:19, 20

I Thessalonians 5:23
I Peter 5:8
III John 2

Temptation
Psalm 46:1
Psalm 138:3
Psalm 143:10
Proverbs 1:10, 15
Proverbs 4:14, 15
Mark 14:38
Luke 22:40
Romans 12:21
James 1:12
James 4:7

The Goodness of God
Psalm 34:8
Psalm 37:4–6
Psalm 84:11
Psalm 135:3
Psalm 145:9
Proverbs 10:22
Jeremiah 29:11
Jeremiah 33:11
Nahum 1:7
Luke 12:32
I Corinthians 2:9
Philippians 4:19

The Mind
Psalm 139:1–4
Proverbs 3:5, 6
Proverbs 21:5
Proverbs 23:7
Romans 12:2
II Corinthians 10:5
Ephesians 4:22–24
Philippians 4:8
II Timothy 1:7

The Power of Words
Psalm 19:14
Psalm 34:13
Psalm 141:3
Proverbs 10:11
Proverbs 10:31
Proverbs 13:3
Proverbs 15:1
Proverbs 15:23
Proverbs 16:23

Proverbs 18:21
Proverbs 25:11
Isaiah 50:4
Matthew 12:34–37
Ephesians 4:29
I Peter 3:10

Trust
II Samuel 22:31–33
Psalm 2:12
Psalm 18:2, 3
Psalm 20:7
Psalm 31:14, 15
Psalm 56:3, 4
Psalm 62:8
Proverbs 3:5–8
Proverbs 29:25
Isaiah 30:15
Nahum 1:7
I Timothy 4:10
Hebrews 2:13

Victory
II Samuel 8:6
I Chronicles 29:11
Psalm 149:4
Proverbs 24:6
Romans 8:37
I Corinthians 15:54, 57
II Corinthians 2:14
I John 5:1–5

Waiting on God and His Timing
Psalm 25:5
Psalm 31:14, 15
Psalm 37:7
Psalm 39:7, 8
Psalm 62:1, 2
Psalm 145:15, 16
Isaiah 30:18
Isaiah 40:31
Habakkuk 2:3

Walking in Love
Deuteronomy 10:12
John 13:34
Ephesians 4:1, 2
Ephesians 5:2
Colossians 3:12–14
I John 4:7, 8
I John 4:12
I John 4:17–19

Wisdom
Psalm 111:10
Proverbs 1:5
Proverbs 2:1–5
Proverbs 3:5–7
Proverbs 3:13–15
Proverbs 3:35
Proverbs 8:11
Proverbs 8:35
Proverbs 19:20
James 1:5

Worship
Psalm 5:7
Psalm 22:27
Psalm 25:14
Psalm 29:2
Psalm 119:38
Proverbs 3:7
Ecclesiastes 3:14
John 4:24
Romans 12:1
Philippians 3:3
Hebrews 12:28

Wisdom

Psalm 111:10
Proverbs 1:5
Proverbs 2:1–5
Proverbs 3:5–7
Proverbs 3:13–15
Proverbs 3:35
Proverbs 8:11
Proverbs 8:35
Proverbs 19:20
James 1:5

Worship

Psalm 5:7
Psalm 22:27
Psalm 25:14
Psalm 29:2
Psalm 119:38
Proverbs 3:7
Ecclesiastes 3:14
John 4:24
Romans 12:1
Philippians 3:3
Hebrews 12:28

Everyday Life Notes

I believe that God will do many things in your life as you read, study, and live according to His Word. For that reason, I wanted to provide the following pages as a place for you to write notes in this Bible. You may want to use them to record your prayer requests and answered prayers, to make a list of your favorite scriptures, to jot down understanding or revelation God gives you through His Word, or to keep some sort of diary or journal of your walk with God. Just as this Bible is a compilation of many years of life lessons and ministry experience for me, I hope you will use these pages to write about all the lessons God is teaching you and the experiences you are having with Him during ths time in your life.

—Joyce Meyer